THE OXFORD COMPANION TO

African American Literature

THE OXFORD COMPANION TO

African American Literature

EDITORS

William L. Andrews

Frances Smith Foster

Trudier Harris

FOREWORD BY

Henry Louis Gates, Jr.

New York   Oxford

OXFORD UNIVERSITY PRESS

1997

OXFORD UNIVERSITY PRESS

Oxford   New York

Athens   Auckland   Bangkok   Bogotá   Bombay   Buenos Aires
Calcutta   Cape Town   Dar es Salaam   Delhi   Florence   Hong Kong
Istanbul   Karachi   Kuala Lumpur   Madras   Madrid   Melbourne
Mexico City   Nairobi   Paris   Singapore   Taipei   Tokyo   Toronto

and associated companies in
Berlin   Ibadan

Published by Oxford University Press, Inc.,
198 Madison Avenue, New York, New York 10016–4314

Oxford is a registered trademark of Oxford University Press

Library of Congress Cataloging-in-Publication Data

The Oxford companion to African American literature / editors, William
L. Andrews, Frances Smith Foster, Trudier Harris;
foreword by Henry Louis Gates, Jr.
p.   cm.
Includes bibliographical references and index.
ISBN 0-19-506510-7
1. American literature—Afro-American authors—Encyclopedias.
2. Afro-Americans in literature—Encyclopedias.   I. Andrews,
William L., 1946– .   II. Foster, Frances Smith.   III. Harris,
Trudier.
PS153.N5096   1997
810.8'0896073—DC20   96-41565
CIP

1 3 5 7 9 8 6 4 2

Printed in the United States of America
on acid-free paper

Contents

The Oxford Companion to
African American Literature

Foreword

In 1977, when I first proposed to the editors at Oxford University Press that they publish a *Companion* to African American literature, the editors and I discussed their worries about the potential size of the readership for such a work. Perhaps a *Companion*—the first in the still nascent field of African American studies—that treated the whole of African American *culture* would be preferable to one that dealt with one discipline or subfield alone. We agreed to continue to discuss the matter, and to allow the field to develop.

Many of us who had chosen to teach African American studies found ourselves wondering about the future of a discipline that had been created largely as a result of student demands in 1968, rather than because of faculty interest in a subfield that had evolved, logically, from a larger discipline or disciplines, such as American studies from history and English, or biochemistry from those two traditional departments. Could the scholars who had claimed this field as their own transform the energy and the impulse that had created it into a raison d'être compelling enough for the American academy to make it a permanent part of a standard curriculum in any respectable faculty of arts and sciences?

To be part of a generation that institutionalized the most sophisticated scholarship concerning the history, culture, and social institutions of blacks would require the creation of foundational research tools, such as dictionaries, encyclopedias, anthologies, and compendia. These sorts of reference works establish a field by consolidating the most reliable and solid research in an easily accessible form, thereby contributing to the creation of a shared baseline of knowledge about the subject, a common culture of shared referents, a canon of common knowledge.

Only such a body of shared information can end the curse on scholars of African and African American studies: that each generation must reinvent the proverbial wheel, must, that is, reestablish even the most basic facts about the tradition before deeper interpretation and analysis can begin to occur. Basic factual data that our colleagues in American history, let's say, or in English or American literature, take for granted, often have required hours and hours of arduous archival research to uncover. We are still uncovering texts published by black novelists; periodical literature remains vastly under explored; and often basic biographical and bibliographical data about the writers and the texts in the tradition remain elusive or obscure.

The publication of *The Oxford Companion to African American Literature* within months of the appearance *The Norton Anthology of African American Literature* (1997) and the *Encyclopedia of African-American Culture and History* (1996) makes this a signal moment in the history of the discipline of African American studies. The *Companion* is of such extraordinary importance to the evolution of both the scholarship and the interpretation of African American literature, specifically, and its broader cultural context, more generally, because it documents more than two centuries of literary production, from slaves and ex-slaves to Toni Morrison's receipt in 1993 of the Nobel Prize for Literature.

And what a feast of wonders this *Companion* is! Read it like a novel. In the latter half of the 1970s, my Yale colleague John W. Blassingame, a professor of history, and I used to sit in a New Haven pizza shop, plotting the future of the Afro-American Studies Program, and, by extension, the future of African American research in our respective disciplines. We would dream of being able to turn to a single-volume reference work on the shelves in our studies, to explore such topics as the "A.M.E. Book Concern," the "Chicago Renaissance," "Funeral and Mourning Customs," "Canonization," the "Mulatto," or even "Signifying" as a practice in the black vernacular tradition. Two decades ago, the prospects for such a reference work seemed very remote indeed.

With the publication of *The Oxford Companion*, any reader can find articles on these subjects and hundreds more. Expressive cultural forms, for example, are explicated here, both their aesthetic status as "texts" and their social and historical functions. This *Companion* establishes, at last, the firmest foundation for the study of African American literature, by presenting articles on virtually every aspect of the history and development of the literature created by persons of African descent, including biographies of authors and critics; plot summaries for canonical novels; sketches of major characters; and essays on central critical concepts, periods, and the broader social, historical, and cultural contexts in which black literary production evolved.

This *Companion* is a monumental contribution to literary studies, generally, and to the study of African American literature, more specifically. I believe that its publication is one of the genuine signposts in the history of the study of African American literature, as important in its way as the anthologies *The New Negro* (1925), edited by Alain Locke, and *Negro Caravan* (1941), edited by Sterling A. Brown, Arthur P. Davis, and Ulysses Lee, or Vernon Loggins's pathbreaking study, *The Negro Author, His Development in America* (1930), were in establishing the canon. This volume is essential reading for all students and scholars of African American literature. But it is also a model of how accessible and encompassing, how lively and engaging, a great reference work can be.

Henry Louis Gates, Jr.
Cambridge, Massachusetts

Introduction

Pulitzer Prize–winning author Alice Walker once said that if she were stranded on a desert island and had only one book to read, she would be content with a copy of Zora Neale Hurston's *Their Eyes Were Watching God* (1937). Hurston's novel tells the story of an early twentieth-century black woman of the South, Janie Crawford, and the people she encounters in her lifelong quest for self-determination and fulfillment. With her third husband, a guitar-playing bluesman named Tea Cake (who is just as sweet as his name), Janie achieves her goal. Tea Cake stands beside Janie in her efforts to define freedom and responsibility and to trade materialism for the more spiritual things in life. The compelling drama through which Hurston's novel, completed in only six weeks, brings Janie, her lovers, her friends, and an entire African American community into imperishable vitality is one of the treasures of African American literature.

Walker's discovery of Hurston greatly influenced Walker's life and literary career. Like her, through the doorway opened by a novel such as *Their Eyes Were Watching God*, countless readers have discovered the ever-expanding library of African American literature, founded in the examples of Phillis Wheatley, a young enslaved poet in eighteenth-century Massachusetts, and such outspoken fugitive slaves as William and Ellen Craft and Frederick Douglass in the nineteenth century, and extending forward to figures such as dramatists May Miller and Willis Richardson, poets Countee Cullen and Langston Hughes, and novelists Nella Larsen and Richard Wright in the early twentieth century. Hurston pointed readers into the richness of the 1950s, when James Baldwin and Lorraine Hansberry gave us, respectively, Gabriel Grimes in *Go Tell It on the Mountain* (1953) and Mama Lena Younger in *A Raisin in the Sun* (1959). In contemporary times readers encounter Randall Kenan, a young North Carolina author, who tells of a sixteen-year-old boy trying to escape his homosexual tendencies by using ancient incantations that he hopes will transform him into a bird. They read Toni Morrison's evocation of a baby ghost in *Beloved* (1987) who haunts a family in Ohio, and J. California Cooper's tale of a character in *Family* (1991) whose attempted suicide leaves her in an immortal state of limbo watching over her family through hundreds of years. Whether in the realistic realms of a Hurston, Baldwin, or Hansberry, or in the fantastic worlds that Kenan, Morrison, and Cooper create, or in the many nuanced dimensions in between, African American literature enthralls readers from Maine to California, Minnesota to Florida, Spain to South Africa, Italy to Germany, Canada to Jamaica, Japan to Korea. It inspires literary journals such as *African American Review* and *Callaloo* and magazines such as *Black Books Bulletin* and *Quarterly Black Review of Books*. African American literature is regularly featured in *World Literature Today*, a journal that circulates to sixty-three countries, and it inspires international conferences around the world and on almost every continent. In its national and international reach, therefore, African American literature has attained an unprecedented level of popularity, critical attention, and scholarly inquiry. The richness of the literature and the ever-expanding worldwide focus upon it have led to the conception and publication of this *Companion.*

The Oxford Companion to African American Literature is a comprehensive reference volume devoted to the texts and the historical and cultural contexts of African American literature. Although appropriate recognition of African American writing *as* literature has been a long time coming in the United States, in the last three decades general interest in and appreciation of African American literature, its history and aesthetics, have grown considerably. Since 1970 Rita Dove, Yusef Komunyakaa, James Alan McPherson, Toni Morrison, Gloria Naylor, and Alice Walker have joined Gwendolyn Brooks and Ralph Ellison as winners of prestigious honors such as the Pulitzer Prize, the National and American Book Awards, and, in Morrison's case, the Nobel Prize for Literature. As the readership of African American writing expands and waxes increasingly multiethnic, it is rare to find a library (particularly in schools and universities) that does not collect, or a general-purpose bookstore that does not market, literary works by African Americans. In the academy, the reading and study of African American literature are no longer relegated to what was once called Black studies; African American writers play increasingly prominent roles in newly reconstituted American literature and American studies, as well as women's studies and ethnic studies, curricula. In the late twentieth century, research in African American literature and the publication of reference books, especially detailed bibliographies of both primary and secondary writing and biographical dictionaries, have given readers and students of African American literature much valuable information. It is almost as if the scholarly and publishing communities have been working overtime to make up for past neglect. Nevertheless, up to this point no one-volume text has been designed to serve the increasing variety of needs and purposes arising among the multiple readerships of African American literature. We have constructed *The Oxford Companion to African American Literature* so that it will be a reliable resource for both the introductory and the experienced reader, the student and the scholar, the seeker of particular information and the browser intent on opening up her or his intellectual horizons.

We are aware (and regret) that no reference book can be all things to all people. Certainly no one volume can encompass all that is interesting or important about African American literature. As far as this project is concerned, our priority has been to highlight the writers and the writing that have made African American literature valuable and distinctive. The concept of literature that underlies this *Companion* is based in the traditional belletristic genres, such as poetry, fiction, and drama. *The Oxford Companion to African American Literature* extensively documents each of these genres and offers substantial essays that chart the historical development of the Novel and the Short Story, various kinds of Poetry, and Theater and Drama. In these and many other articles on the genres and subgenres of African American literature, the *Companion* reflects an evolving scholarly consensus on the major innovators, the key texts, and the changing critical climates in which each of these genres grew.

Though we are aware of the dismissal of so much black American writing for so many years because it did not conform to prevailing aesthetic or critical canons, our understanding of literature is not restricted to these traditional genres. *The Oxford Companion to African American Literature* gives the same kind of sustained analysis to genres of special import and influence in African American literature, with articles on topics such as Autobiography and Biography, Folklore and Folk Literature, Slave Narratives and Blues poems, Essays and Criticism, Oratory, and Sermons and Preaching. In thinking of literary traditions and practices that deserve attention in this volume, we incorporated entries on the familiar ones, such as the Biblical Tradition, the Plantation Tradition, Humor, and Protest Literature, and on those more recent or still only partially emergent, such as Gay Literature and Lesbian Literature, Speculative Fiction, Film, Musicals, and Travel Writing. Allotting almost sixty individual essays to genres and traditions, this *Companion* offers the most diverse and extensive guide yet available to the organizing formal and thematic principles (and their historical evolution) that have constituted African American literature.

To provide readers with the essentials of African American literary history, *The Oxford Companion to African American Literature* contains a thoroughgoing overview of this topic under the title Literary History. Here a lengthy, five-part essay encapsulates the full sweep of African American writing in the United States, beginning with the colonial and early national eras and carrying forward to the present day. Essays on specific social, cultural, and artistic movements, such as the Antislavery Movement, the Harlem Renaissance, and the Black Arts Movement, help our readers understand the interrelationship between literary and cultural history in black America. Discussions of Diasporic Literature as a whole, complemented by specific treatments of African Literature, West Indian Literature, and African–Native American Literature, provide readers of this *Companion* the opportunity to consider African American literature in multiple national and international contexts. Recognizing the underappreciated roles that Journalism, Periodicals, Libraries and Research Centers, Churches, Literary Societies, Women's Clubs, and Publishing enterprises have played in the creation of literature and the dissemination of literary ideas and criticism by and about people of African descent in the United States, this *Companion* offers its readers a broadly conceived image of African American literary culture by including pieces on these alternative contexts.

Biographies of writers comprise the largest single category of articles in this volume, from little-known figures such as Mignon Anderson and Annie Burton to famous and prizewinning personages such as W. E. B. Du Bois, Maya Angelou, Ed Bullins, and Lucille Clifton. More than four hundred African American writers receive individual biographical treatment in this book, making the *Companion* the largest and most diverse compendium of African American literary biography ever published. Biographical articles vary in length, from approximately two hundred words for less prominent authors such as John Marrant or Effie Waller Smith to more than two thousand words for centrally important writers such as James Baldwin and Toni Morrison. Many factors influence the lengths of biographical articles, among them the amount of information available on a given writer's life, the editors' estimate of the extent and importance of each writer's contribution to African American literature, and the space we could allot to biographies in the *Companion* relative to the many other kinds of entries we wanted to include. In many cases, particularly in those articles pertaining to living authors, our judgment of a subject's importance and our assignment of length and scope can be only provisional. Time will play its traditional role in distinguishing the short-run popular hit from the long-run exemplary career. We also know full well that hitherto undiscovered writing by figures of the past and as yet unpublished works by contemporary men and women will surely revise current judgments. Although the academy has produced many critics and scholars whose research has enhanced our understanding of African American literature, the *Companion* reserves for separate biographical treatment only critics, such as Arnold Rampersad and bell hooks, whose work has extended beyond the academy in terms of the kinds of writing they have done and the audiences they have reached. One reason why we look forward to a second edition of this *Companion* is the opportunity it will present us to revise and expand many of the biographies in this volume to reflect the evolving course of literary history.

In addition to biographies of writers, this *Companion* includes compact biographical treatments and cultural assessments of a considerable number of persons—musicians, sports figures, political leaders, activists, and artists—whose presence in or influence on African American literature is of such a magnitude as to be noteworthy. Thus John Coltrane, Marcus Garvey, John Brown, Jackie Robinson, Harriet Beecher Stowe, and Harriet Tubman, to mention just a few figures who have achieved virtually iconic status in African American literature, are profiled in such a way as to lead the reader to literary texts significantly influenced by the person under consideration.

The Oxford Companion to African American Literature devotes more than one hundred fifty articles to descriptions and concise appraisals of texts that we as editors consider to be major works in the African American literary tradition. The largest genre of works in this category is fiction; plot outlines of more than eighty African American novels may be found in this volume. An equal number of entries is allotted to key texts of poetry, drama, autobiography, essay collections, and children's and young adult literature. More than sixty prominent literary characters, ranging from Frado in Harriet E. Wilson's *Our Nig* (1859) to Sethe Suggs in Toni Morrison's *Beloved*, also receive individual attention. Unlike actual people, who are listed alphabetically under their last names in the *Companion*, the names of these fictional characters are alphabetized according to the first letters of their names. Thus Bigger Thomas of Richard Wright's *Native Son* (1940) is listed under "B" instead of "T," and Dessa Rose, the title character of Sherley Anne Williams's 1986 novel, is listed under "D" instead of "R." Cross-references in each of these articles make it easy to find the literary work in which the character appears.

Because African American literature is peopled by a number of character types who have appeared in many different guises across the generations, this *Companion* allots entries to figures such as Aunt Jemima, Brer Rabbit, John Henry, Sambo, Stackolee, and Uncle Tom. Those occupations and professions that have furnished roles for countless African American literary characters—from Barbers and Beauticians to Domestics, Preachers and Deacons, and Prostitutes—are also examined in separate articles. Finally, figures from folklore—the Trickster, the Badman, the Devil, and many more—are considered in their own articles. Discussions of character types, occupational and professional representatives, and folkloric figures aim to identify the salient features of these types and point to specific literary texts in which these figures play notable parts.

The impress of culture on literature is not confined merely to the ways characters are identified or stories are told. Longstanding and often controversial cultural issues that have become themes and leitmotifs in African American literature—including Gender, Sexuality, Class, Identity, and the idea of Race itself—demand and receive substantial essays in this *Companion*. Key terms and idioms—Manhood, Soul, Freedom, and Slavery, for instance—have sufficient special resonance in African American literature to warrant individual entries in this volume. By including entries on customs (Conjuring, Names and Naming, Signifying), cultural expression (Blues, Dance, Dress, Music, Speech and Dialect), cultural standards and ideals (Afrocentricity, Black Nationalism, Womanism), and realms of ethnically specific experience (Blue Vein Societies, Middle Passage, Passing, Underground Railroad), this *Companion* also serves as a primer on African American cultural literacy.

HOW TO USE THIS BOOK

Embarking upon the adventure of this volume you will quickly discover that African American literature is much more than the protest tradition so frequently associated with Richard Wright and Ann Petry. Have you wondered who the detective novelist is whom President Bill Clinton identified as one of his favorite writers? Look up Walter Mosley and find out what he wrote, then go on to the cross-referenced article on Crime and Mystery Writing. Are you curious about the science fiction of MacArthur Prize–winning Octavia E. Butler and the "Dean of Science Fiction," Samuel R. Delany? They are both in this *Companion* along with articles on Speculative Fiction and Butler's celebrated novel *Kindred* (1979). In these pages the children's fiction of Arna Bontemps, Walter Dean Myers, Alice Childress, and Virginia Hamilton is discussed, as well as the courageous stories of escape and endurance epitomized in narratives such as Margaret Walker's *Jubilee* (1966) and Alex Haley's *Roots* (1976). If you elect a regional approach to the literature, you can meet Raymond Andrews, Tina McElroy Ansa, and Brenda Marie Osbey on southern soil; Elizabeth Keckley, Mary Church Terrell, Ralph Ellison, and Claude Brown in urban territory; and Al Young, Joyce Carol Thomas, and Ishmael Reed in the West. You will find many black feminist authors here, discussed individually and under such rubrics as Feminism, Womanism, and Gender. If your interests run to modernist or contemporary stylistic experimenters, key figures such as Jean Toomer, Carlene Hatcher Polite, Xam Wilson Cartiér, and Trey Ellis all have entries. If poetry is where you begin, read about Gwendolyn Brooks, Rita Dove, and Yusef Komunyakaa; then follow up with the long article on Poetry. Although they are generations apart, these poets, you will find, have one prominent thing in common—discover what it is. If drama strikes your fancy, you can look up individual playwrights, such as August Wilson (find out how many Pulitzer Prizes he has received; learn how close he is to reaching his goal of writing a play for every decade of African American life in the twentieth century). Or you can look up entries such as Drama and learn about Wilson in historical and cultural context, or examine the entry on Theater to find out where most black actors began their professional careers.

There are many ways to plunge into *The Oxford Companion to African American Literature* and come up with treasure, but perhaps you'd like to be a little more systematic in your search. If you have a name, a title, or a topic that you wish to look up in this *Companion,* you can search for it by consulting the index that appends the *Companion* or by heading directly into the text of the *Companion* itself. The index serves as a comprehensive guide to the *Companion's* subject matter. In addition to providing the page number on which every individual entry appears, the index lists other pages on which many authors, titles, or topics are discussed. For instance, the citation of Frederick Douglass in the index refers not only to the biographical article devoted to Douglass but also to the pages in a large number of other entries in which Douglass is prominently mentioned. The index also cites persons, such as Michelle Cliff, Rosa Parks, Sidney Poitier, Carl Van Vechten, and Brent Wade; titles, such as Gunnar Myrdal's *An American Dilemma* (1944) and Alice Walker's *Meridian* (1976); and events and organizations, such as the Great Depression and the Student Nonviolent Coordinating Committee (SNCC), that are substantively referred to in this *Companion* but do not receive individual entries. To discover whether a person, title, or topic is treated in *The Oxford Companion to African American Literature,* the first place to look is in the index.

Because *The Oxford Companion to African American Literature* is organized alphabetically, you can easily look up a name, title, or topic in the text itself to see if an individual entry exists for that subject. To find an author's name, look it up according to her or his last name (e.g., Chesnutt, Charles Waddell). You will find that biographies in the *Companion* include the subject's birth and death dates (if known or applicable), followed by a sentence fragment that briefly identifies her or him. Biographical entries are listed according to how an author signs his or her work, that is, as Iceberg Slim (not Beck, Robert) or Malcolm X (not Little, Malcolm). The given names of these writers and others, such as Paulette Williams or Chloe Anthony Wofford, are entered alphabetically in this *Companion* with a directive to the name (*see* Shange, Ntozake, or *see* Morrison, Toni) under which the biography of the writer is discussed.

To find a literary work in this volume, look up the first important word of its title (e.g., *House behind the Cedars, The*). The titles of entries on literary works are either italicized or put within quotation marks; unlike the titles of all other types of entries, which are capitalized, the titles of literary works appear in mixed upper- and lowercase letters. To find the name of a character in a literary work, look it up under the character's first name (e.g., Rena Walden, *not* Walden, Rena). Topics are alphabetized according to the first letter of a term (e.g., "M" for Miscegenation) or the first word in a descriptive phrase (e.g., Novel of Passing, *not* Passing, Novel of). Entries that begin with the same word are alphabetized letter-by-letter, so that *Colored American Magazine, The* precedes Color Line, and Manhood precedes *Man Who Cried I Am, The.*

The Oxford Companion to African American Literature is extensively cross-referenced to help a reader follow an initial inquiry into useful related areas. An asterisk (*) before a name, title, word, or phrase in any article in this volume indicates that a separate article has been devoted to that item in this *Companion.* Occasionally cross-references are given in parentheses within an article. At the end of many articles in this volume are additional cross-references that point the reader to further entries relevant to the reader's interests. Thus the article on Zora Neale Hurston contains many internal cross-references that point to additional articles on (1) works by Hurston, such as *Their Eyes*

Were Watching God; (2) characters in Hurston's work, such as Janie Crawford; (3) people important to Hurston, such as Langston Hughes; (4) movements Hurston participated in, such as the Harlem Renaissance; (5) topics she addressed in her writing, such as Folklore; and (6) traditions and genres she contributed to, such as Humor and the Novel. At the end of the article on Hurston, the reader is urged to *"See also"* several more entries in the *Companion* that someone interested in Hurston might find informative, namely, Conjuring, Federal Writers' Project, Nanny, Sermons and Preaching, and Tea Cake.

Bibliographies are appended to most articles in this *Companion*. The longer the article, the more titles are offered as recommendations for further reading. Titles in these bibliographies are listed chronologically to help the reader follow the development of important scholarship on a given topic. The principal purpose of these bibliographies is to direct the reader of the *Companion* to nonspecialized texts, particularly biographies and critical studies, that will open up, rather than narrow down, the reader's perspective on the topic at hand.

All the entries in *The Oxford Companion to African American Literature* are signed by their authors, who are listed, along with their institutional affiliation (if any) and the title(s) of their article(s), in the list of contributors that follows this introduction. Our basic request of each contributor, regardless of the subject or scope of her or his article, was to provide readers of this *Companion* with the most reliable, complete, and readable treatment of the topic possible, given the limits of space and the need for succinctness that a one-volume reference book demanded of us all. The interpretive emphases and critical judgments that appear in the *Companion*'s articles reflect the diverse points of view of their authors. As editors who wish neither to beat a drum nor grind an ax for or against any writer or subject in this volume, we have tried to ensure that the critical posture of *The Oxford Companion to African American Literature* is historically informed, thoughtfully researched, and fair-minded. The variety of terms available to apply to persons of African descent—Black, black, and African American, for instance—appear in this volume according to the individual tastes and purposes of the contributors. We have selected African American (deliberately unhyphenated) for the title of this volume because we believe this term to be an accurate descriptor of the intersecting ethnic and national literary traditions that form the purview of this *Companion*. We also see African American as the best alternative to the "hyphenated American" designations and politicized naming agendas of the past.

ACKNOWLEDGMENTS

The Oxford Companion to African American Literature has been an enormous collaborative undertaking from the outset. Initially conceived by Houston A. Baker, Jr., and Henry Louis Gates, Jr., the *Companion* came into the hands of William L. Andrews, Frances Smith Foster, and Trudier Harris early in the planning of the project. From the conceptual phase we have overseen the *Companion* through its design, its writing and editing, and its production—a seven-year enterprise. Coordinating an undertaking involving more than three hundred fifty contributors requires a great deal of advice, support, and encouragement. As editors of the *Companion*, we thank the Trade

Reference Department of Oxford University Press, particularly Hannah Borgeson, Margaret Hogan, Linda Halvorson Morse, Marion Osmun, and Ann Toback, for their guidance, institutional support, and steady encouragement. We are also grateful to our Advisory Board, particularly to those who not only gave us sound counsel but were also willing to author some of the more challenging essays in the volume. Most of all, however, we are indebted to the hundreds who wrote entries for this *Companion*. Ranging from independent scholars to advanced graduate students to professors in the United States and abroad, the contributors to this book have taught its editors a great deal about African American literature and about the collegiality and creativity of those working in African American literary and cultural studies. *The Oxford Companion to African American Literature* is thus a vital testimonial, first to the lasting import of the traditions it seeks to define and chart, and second to the dedication of the scholars and critics who, through collaborative efforts such as this volume, have worked to constitute African American literature as an intellectual field and academic discipline.

William L. Andrews
Frances Smith Foster
Trudier Harris

Contributors

Christina Accomando, *Lecturer in Literature, University of California, San Diego*
Attaway, William; "We Shall Overcome"

Opal Palmer Adisa, *Associate Professor of Ethnic Studies, California College of Arts and Crafts, Oakland*
davenport, doris

Sandra Carlton Alexander, *Professor of English, North Carolina Agricultural and Technical State University, Greensboro*
Identity

Elizabeth Ammons, *Harriet H. Fay Professor of American Literature, Tufts University, Medford, Massachusetts*
Cooper, Anna Julia; Voice from the South, A

Larry R. Andrews, *Dean, Honors College; Associate Professor of English, Kent State University, Ohio*
Murphy, Beatrice M.

William L. Andrews, *E. Maynard Adams Professor of English, University of North Carolina at Chapel Hill*
Amanuensis; Antislavery Movement; Autobiography, *articles on* Overview *and* Secular Autobiography; Brown, William Wells; Chesnutt, Charles Waddell; Douglass, Frederick; Elaw, Zilpha; Folks from Dixie; Foote, Julia A. J.; Fulton, David Bryant; Green, J. D.; Green, John Patterson; Johnson, William; Lyrics of Lowly Life; Majors and Minors; McGirt, James Ephraim; My Bondage and My Freedom; Narrative of the Life of Frederick Douglass; Pickens, William; Purvis, Robert; Remond, Charles Lenox; Russwurm, John Browne; Slave Narrative; Steward, Theophilus Gould; Terry, Lucy; Turner, Nat; Whipper, William; Wife of His Youth, The

Herbert Aptheker, *San Jose, California*
Insurrections

Molefi Kete Asante, *Professor of Africology, Temple University, Philadelphia, Pennsylvania*
Afrocentricity

Bertram D. Ashe, *American Studies Program, The College of William and Mary, Williamsburg, Virginia*
Mossell, Gertrude

Gary Ashwill, *Department of English, Duke University, Durham, North Carolina*
Brown, Henry "Box"; Clotel; Emigration; Lee, Spike; L'Ouverture, Toussaint; Redding, J. Saunders; Wilkins, Roger; Woodson, Carter G.

Lori Askeland, *Department of English, University of Kansas, Lawrence*
Broughton, Virginia W.; Drinking Gourd, The

Allan D. Austin, *Professor of English and African American Studies, Springfield College, Massachusetts*
Blake; Delany, Martin R.; Henry Blake

Michael Awkward, *Professor of English, University of Pennsylvania, Philadelphia*
Baker, Houston A., Jr.; Manhood

Ronald W. Bailey, *Professor of African-American Studies and History, Northeastern University, Boston, Massachusetts*
Black Studies

Marva O. Banks, *Associate Professor of English and Modern Languages, Albany State College, Georgia*
Heard, Nathan C.

Margarita Barceló, *President's Postdoctoral Fellow in Ethnic Studies, University of California, Berkeley*
Walrond, Eric

Philip Barnard, *Associate Professor of English, University of Kansas, Lawrence*
Cenelles, Les; Séjour, Victor

Deborah H. Barnes, *Assistant Professor of African American Literature, Gettysburg College, Pennsylvania*
Schomburg, Arthur A.; Tubman, Harriet

Paula C. Barnes, *Associate Professor of English, Hampton University, Virginia*
Cuffe, Paul; Smith, Effie Waller

Lindon Barrett, *Assistant Professor of English, University of California, Irvine*
Literacy

Anthony Gerard Barthelemy, *Associate Professor of English, University of Miami, Coral Gables, Florida*
Escape, The; Ward, Theodore

Katherine Clay Bassard, *Assistant Professor of English, University of California, Berkeley*
Autobiography, *article on* Spiritual Autobiography

Freda R. Beaty, *Assistant Professor of English, Stephen F. Austin State University, Nacogdoches, Texas*
Andrews, Raymond

Elizabeth Ann Beaulieu, *Department of English, Appalachian State University, Boone, North Carolina*
Tolson, Melvin B.

Herman Beavers, *Associate Professor of English, University of Pennsylvania, Philadelphia*
Autobiography of an Ex-Colored Man, The; Johnson, James Weldon; Up from Slavery; Washington, Booker T.

Juda Bennett, *Washington University, St. Louis, Missouri*
Sexuality

Joseph Benson, *Professor of English, North Carolina Agricultural and Technical State University, Greensboro*
Sister Outsider

Roger A. Berger, *Associate Professor of English and Comparative Literature, Wichita State University, Kansas*
Cleaver, Eldridge; Haley, Alex; Kunta Kinte; Roots; Soul on Ice

Germain J. Bienvenu, *Academic Center for Athletes, Louisiana State University at Baton Rouge*
Lanusse, Armand

Susan L. Blake, *Professor of English, Lafayette College, Easton, Pennsylvania*
Poinsettia Jackson

Edith Blicksilver, *Associate Professor of Literature, Georgia Institute of Technology, Atlanta*
Vroman, Mary Elizabeth

Karen R. Bloom, *Department of English, Emory University, Atlanta, Georgia*
Boyd, Melba; Lester, Julius

Mary Anne Stewart Boelcskevy, *Department of English and American Literature and Language, Harvard University, Cambridge, Massachusetts*
Hernton, Calvin C.; Waniek, Marilyn Nelson

Graeme M. Boone, *Los Angeles, California*
Blues

Brad S. Born, *Assistant Professor of English, Bethel College, North Newton, Kansas*
Allen, William G.; Banneker, Benjamin; "Heroic Slave, The"; Northup, Solomon; Shadd, Mary Ann

Melanie Boyd, *Institute for Women's Studies, Emory University, Atlanta, Georgia*
Poston, Ted

Melba Joyce Boyd, *Associate Professor of Africana Studies, Wayne State University, Detroit, Michigan*
Aunt Chloe Fleet; Iola Leroy; "Two Offers, The"

Joanne M. Braxton, *Frances and Edwin L. Cummings Professor of American Studies and English, The College of William and Mary, Williamsburg, Virginia*
Dunbar, Paul Laurence

Jonathan Brennan, *Department of Comparative Ethnic Studies, University of California, Berkeley*
African–Native American Literature

Marcela Breton, *Danbury, Connecticut*
Davis, Miles

Jacqueline Brice-Finch, *Professor of English, James Madison University, Harrisonburg, Virginia*
Seacole, Mary

Margaret Bernice Smith Bristow, *Associate Professor of English, Hampton University, Virginia*
Hamilton, Virginia; M. C. Higgins, the Great

Mary Hughes Brookhart, *Associate Professor of English, North Carolina Central University, Durham*
Allen, Samuel W.

A. Russell Brooks, *Chairman Emeritus of English, Kentucky State University, Frankfort*
CLA Journal

E. Barnsley Brown, *Department of English, University of North Carolina at Chapel Hill*
Gibson, Patricia Joann; Jones-Meadows, Karen

Phiefer L. Browne, *Assistant Professor of English, Fisk University, Nashville, Tennessee*
Austin, Doris Jean; Brown, Linda Beatrice; Golden, Marita; Marriage

Elizabeth Brown-Guillory, *Associate Professor of English, University of Houston, Texas*
Childress, Alice; Hero Ain't Nothin' but a Sandwich, A; Like One of the Family; Mildred Johnson

Dickson D. Bruce, Jr., *Professor of History, University of California, Irvine*
Corrothers, James D.; Double Consciousness; Grimké, Archibald; Grimké, Francis J.; Hawkins, Walter Everette; Literary History, *article on* Reconstruction Era; Protest Literature

Cedric Gael Bryant, *Associate Professor of American and African American Literature, Colby College, Waterville, Maine*
Criticism, *article on* Criticism from 1920 to 1964; Race

Jennifer Burton, *Harvard University, Cambridge, Massachusetts*
Atkins, Russell; Redmond, Eugene

Marilyn D. Button, *Associate Professor of English, Lincoln University, Pennsylvania*
Cornish, Samuel; Rogers, Elymas Payson

Keith E. Byerman, *Professor of English and Women's Studies, Indiana State University, Terre Haute*
Bildungsroman; Criticism, *article on* Criticism Since 1965; Epistolary Novel; Major, Clarence

Rudolph P. Byrd, *Associate Professor of American Studies, Graduate Institute of the Liberal Arts, Emory University, Atlanta, Georgia*
Cane; Toomer, Jean

John F. Callahan, *Morgan S. Odell Professor of Humanities, Lewis and Clark College, Portland, Oregon*
Lynching

Mary C. Carruth, *Instructor of English and Women's Studies, University of New Orleans, Louisiana*
Dusk of Dawn; Grimké, Angelina Weld; Ruggles, David; Smith, Amanda Berry

Sharon Carson, *Assistant Professor of English, Philosophy, and Religious Studies, University of North Dakota, Grand Forks*
Baker, Josephine; Danner, Margaret Esse; Manchild in the Promised Land; Mays, Benjamin E.; Payne, Daniel A.

Warren J. Carson, *Associate Professor of English, University of South Carolina, Spartanburg*
Brown, Cecil; Hercules, Frank

Linda M. Carter, *Assistant Professor of English, Morgan State University, Baltimore, Maryland*
Coppin, Fanny Jackson

Steven R. Carter, *Associate Professor of English, Salem State College, Massachusetts*
Collins, Kathleen; King, Woodie, Jr.; Shine, Ted; Wesley, Richard; Wolfe, George

Deborah G. Chay, *Assistant Professor of English,*
Dartmouth College, Hanover, New Hampshire
hooks, bell

Miriam M. Chirico, *Department of English, Emory*
University, Atlanta, Georgia
Young, Al

Robert Chrisman, *Editor,* The Black Scholar; *Lecturer in*
English and Afro-American Studies, University of
Michigan, Ann Arbor
Black Scholar, The

Keith Clark, *Assistant Professor of English, George Mason*
University, Fairfax, Virginia
Amen Corner, The; Another Country; Braxton, Joanne M.;
Gabriel Grimes; Giovanni's Room; Go Tell It on the
Mountain; John Grimes; Rufus Scott

Geneva Cobb-Moore, *Associate Professor of English*
and Women's Studies, University of Wisconsin–Whitewater
Diaries and Journals; Forten, Charlotte

Alisha R. Coleman, *Plainsboro, New Jersey*
Ebony; Franklin, Aretha; Herron, Carolivia

Michael Collins, *Department of English and Comparative*
Literature, Columbia University, New York
History; Plumpp, Sterling; Spellman, A. B.

Kimberly Rae Connor, *Charlottesville, Virginia*
Spirituals; Tanner, Benjamin T.

Wayne F. Cooper, *Vinalhaven, Maine*
Home to Harlem

JoAnne Cornwell, *Associate Professor of Africana Studies*
and French, San Diego State University, California
African Literature; Negritude; Pan-Africanism

Angelo Costanzo, *Professor of English, Shippensburg*
University of Pennsylvania
Equiano, Olaudah; Gronniosaw, James Albert Ukawsaw;
Marrant, John

Daryl Cumber Dance, *Professor of English, University of*
Richmond, Virginia
Moore, Opal

Rita B. Dandridge, *Professor of English, Norfolk State*
University, Norfolk, Virginia
Matheus, John F.; Meriwether, Louise; Shockley, Ann
Allen; Societies and Clubs; Southerland, Ellease

Adenike Marie Davidson, *Department of English,*
University of Maryland at College Park
Black No More; Lutie Johnson; Schuyler, George S.;
Street, The

Thadious M. Davis, *Gertrude Conaway Vanderbilt*
Professor of English, Vanderbilt University, Nashville,
Tennessee
Larsen, Nella

Emma Waters Dawson, *Professor of English; Chair,*
Department of Languages and Literature, Florida A. & M.
University, Tallahassee
Smith, William Gardner

Sharon G. Dean, *Assistant Professor of Language Arts,*
University of Cincinnati, Ohio
Potter, Eliza

Miriam DeCosta-Willis, *Professor of African American*
Studies, University of Maryland, Baltimore County
Wells-Barnett, Ida B.

James de Jongh, *Professor of English, The City College and*
Graduate School, The City University of New York
Places

Dominique-René de Lerma, *Professor of Musicology,*
Lawrence University, Appleton, Wisconsin
Opera

Carolyn C. Denard, *Associate Professor of American*
Literature, Georgia State University, Atlanta
Family

Christopher C. De Santis, *Department of English,*
University of Kansas, Lawrence
Badman; Baltimore Afro-American; Chicago Defender,
The; Journal of Negro History; Langston Hughes Review,
The; Phylon

Susanne B. Dietzel, *Program in American Studies,*
University of Minnesota at Minneapolis St. Paul
Pulp Fiction

Kim Jenice Dillon, *Department of Literature, University of*
California, San Diego
Bonner, Marita; Shearer, John; Troupe, Quincy Thomas,
Jr.

Joseph Donahue, *Assistant Professor of English, Stevens*
Institute of Technology, Hoboken, New Jersey
Cruz, Victor Hernández

Bobby Donaldson, *Department of History, Emory*
University, Atlanta, Georgia
Gayle, Addison, Jr.

C. K. Doreski, *Department of Rhetoric and Humanities,*
Boston University, Massachusetts
Cornish, Sam

David F. Dorsey, Jr., *Professor of English and*
African/African American Studies, Clark Atlanta University,
Atlanta, Georgia
Evans, Mari

Ann duCille, *Professor of American and African American*
Literature, University of California, San Diego
Work

David L. Dudley, *Assistant Professor of English, Georgia*
Southern University, Statesboro
Brown, Claude; Thomas, Piri

Gerald Early, *Merle Kling Professor of Modern Letters,*
Washington University, St. Louis, Missouri
Ali, Muhammad; Color; Crouch, Stanley; Cullen,
Countee; Essay; Johnson, Jack; Louis, Joe; Music;
Robinson, Jackie; Robinson, Sugar Ray

Paula Gallant Eckard, *Senior Lecturer in English,*
University of North Carolina at Charlotte
Aun' Peggy; Conjure Woman, The; Moody, Anne; Terrell,
Mary Church; Uncle Julius McAdoo

Gregory Eiselein, *Assistant Professor of English, Kansas*
State University, Manhattan
Garnet, Henry Highland; Langston, John Mercer; Lynch,
John R.; Nell, William C.; Walker, David

Arlene A. Elder, *Professor of English and Comparative Literature, University of Cincinnati, Ohio*
Griggs, Sutton E.; Imperium in Imperio; Quest of the Silver Fleece, The

Marilyn Elkins, *Associate Professor of English, California State University, Los Angeles*
Fences; Piano Lesson, The; Wilson, August

Joan C. Elliott, *Professor of Languages and Literature, Tennessee State University, Nashville*
Davis, Angela

Elizabeth Sanders Delwiche Engelhardt, *Institute for Women's Studies, Emory University, Atlanta, Georgia*
Johnson, Fenton; Neal, Larry; West, Cornel

Klaus Ensslen, *Associate Professor of American Literature, Amerika-Institut, University of Munich, Germany*
Bradley, David; Chaneysville Incident, The

Hazel Arnett Ervin, *Associate Professor of English, Morehouse College, Atlanta, Georgia*
Petry, Ann; Tituba of Salem Village

M. Giulia Fabi, *Department of English, University of Bologna, Italy*
Criticism, *article on* Criticism to 1920; Johnson, Amelia E.

SallyAnn H. Ferguson, *Associate Professor of English, University of North Carolina at Greensboro*
Blacker the Berry, The; Dress; Johnson, Helene; Niggerati Manor; Porter, Dorothy; Thurman, Wallace

Robert Fikes, Jr., *Librarian, San Diego State University, California*
Haskins, James; Motley, Willard

Michael W. Fitzgerald, *Associate Professor of History, St. Olaf College, Northfield, Minnesota*
Fortune, T. Thomas

Robert E. Fleming, *Professor of English, University of New Mexico, Albuquerque*
Kelley, William Melvin

Chester J. Fontenot, Jr., *Associate Professor of English, University of Illinois, Urbana*
Churches

P. Gabrielle Foreman, *Assistant Professor of English and Comparative Literary Studies, Occidental College, Los Angeles, California*
Burton, Annie Louise; Frado; Our Nig; Wilson, Harriet E.

Frances Smith Foster, *Professor of English and Women's Studies, Emory University, Atlanta, Georgia*
Biblical Tradition; Boyd, Candy; Canonization; Class; Detter, Thomas P.; Diasporic Literature; Easy Rawlins; Hansen, Joyce; Harper, Frances Ellen Watkins; Helga Crane; Kindred; Mosley, Walter; Myers, Walter Dean; Offord, Carl Ruthven; Passing (the novel); Quicksand; Rivers, Conrad Kent; Sunday School Literature

Virginia C. Fowler, *Associate Professor of English, Virginia Polytechnic Institute and State University, Blacksburg*
Giovanni, Nikki

Robert Elliot Fox, *Associate Professor of English, Southern Illinois University at Carbondale*
Brothers and Keepers; Flight to Canada; Last Days of Louisiana Red, The; Mumbo Jumbo; Papa LaBas; Philadelphia Fire; Raven Quickskill; Reed, Ishmael; Terrible Twos, The; Yellow Back Radio Broke-Down

Allison E. Francis, *Department of English and African Amercian Literature, Washington University, St. Louis, Missouri*
Sexuality

Karla Y. E. Frye, *Assistant Professor of English, University of Alabama, Tuscaloosa*
Elder, Lonne, III; Sounder

Jan Furman, *Assistant Professor of English, University of Michigan, Flint*
Albert, Octavia V. Rogers

Joanne V. Gabbin, *Professor of English, James Madison University, Harrisonburg, Virginia*
Poetry

Floyd Gaffney, *Professor Emeritus of Theatre, University of California, San Diego*
Day of Absence; Ward, Douglas Turner

Deborah Garfield, *Assistant Professor of English, University of California, Los Angeles*
Delaney, Lucy A.; Matthews, Victoria Earle

Donald B. Gibson, *Professor of English, Princeton University, New Jersey*
Bigger Thomas; Black Boy; Mary Dalton; Native Son; Uncle Tom's Children; Wright, Richard

Glenda E. Gill, *Associate Professor of Drama, Department of Humanities, Michigan Technological University, Houghton*
Millican, Arthenia J. Bates

William A. Gleason, *Assistant Professor of English, Princeton University, New Jersey*
House behind the Cedars, The; Marrow of Tradition, The; Rena Walden

Kenneth W. Goings, *Professor of History, University of Memphis, Tennessee*
Still, William; Still, William Grant

Anne E. Goldman, *Assistant Professor of English, University of Colorado, Boulder*
Cookbooks

Amy S. Gottfried, *Assistant Professor of Rhetoric, College of General Studies, Boston University, Massachusetts*
Corregidora; Eva Medina Canada; Eva's Man; Jones, Gayl; Ursa Corregidora

Sandra Y. Govan, *Associate Professor of English; Coordinator, Ronald E. McNair Postbaccalaureate Achievement Program, University of North Carolina at Charlotte*
Barnes, Steven; Bennett, Gwendolyn; Delany, Samuel R.; McKnight, Reginald; Neely, Barbara; Speculative Fiction

Maryemma Graham, *Director, Project on the History of Black Writing, Northeastern University, Boston, Massachusetts*
Novel

Elizabeth Elkin Grammer, *Assistant Professor of English, University of the South, Sewanee, Tennessee*
Collective Biography

Nathan L. Grant, *Assistant Professor of African American Studies, State University of New York at Buffalo*
Bass, Kingsley, Jr.; Bullins, Ed; Caldwell, Ben; Clara's Ole Man; Goin' a Buffalo; In New England Winter; Nugent, Richard Bruce

Herman Gray, *Associate Professor of Sociology, University of California, Santa Cruz*
Television

Michael E. Greene, *Professor of English, North Carolina Agricultural and Technical State University, Greensboro*
Cobb, Charles E., Jr.; Marvin X

Farah Jasmine Griffin, *Assistant Professor of English, University of Pennsylvania, Philadelphia*
Gordon, Taylor; Holiday, Billie; Migration; Rainey, Ma; Smith, Bessie; Waters, Ethel; West, Dorothy

Johnanna L. Grimes-Williams, *Associate Professor of English, Tennessee State University, Nashville*
Character Types; Lewis, Theophilus

John C. Gruesser, *Assistant Professor of English, Kean College of New Jersey, Union*
Bruce, John E.; Colored American Magazine, The; Travel Writing

Bernice Forrest Guillaume, *Associate Professor of History, St. Louis University, Missouri*
Bush-Banks, Olivia Ward

Sandra Gunning, *Assistant Professor of English and African American Literature, Unversity of Michigan, Ann Arbor*
Violence; Woman's Era, The

Beverly Guy-Sheftall, *Anna J. Cooper Professor of English and Women's Studies; Director, Women's Research and Resource Center, Spelman College, Atlanta, Georgia*
Sapphire

Minrose C. Gwin, *Professor of English, University of New Mexico, Albuquerque*
Drumgoold, Kate

Michelle Habell-Pallán, *Visiting Professor of Cultural Studies, Loyola Marymount University, Los Angeles, California*
Mackey, Nathaniel

Karen Isabelle Halil, *Department of English, Harvard University, Cambridge, Massachusetts*
Hoagland, Everett H., III

James C. Hall, *Assistant Professor of African-American Studies and English, University of Illinois, Chicago*
Brown, Frank London; Coltrane, John; Parker, Charlie

Stephen Gilroy Hall, *Department of History, Ohio State University, Columbus*
Williams, George Washington

Trudier Harris, *J. Carlyle Sitterson Professor of English, University of North Carolina at Chapel Hill*
Ancestors; Bad Woman; Baldwin, James; Barber; Beautician; Churchwoman; Cosmetics; Domestic;

Dumas, Henry; Entertainer; Fire Next Time, The; Folk Literature; Healing; Jeffers, Lance; Komunyakaa, Yusef; Mammy; Matriarch; Midwife; New Cultural Mulatto; Notes of a Native Son; Prostitute; Speech and Dialect; Sula Peace

Violet J. Harris, *Associate Professor of Curriculum and Instruction (Literacy), University of Illinois, Champaign*
Walter, Mildred Pitts; Wilkinson, Brenda; Yarbrough, Camille

William J. Harris, *Associate Professor of English, Pennsylvania State University, University Park*
Black Aesthetic

James V. Hatch, *Professor of Theatre, Graduate Program, The City University of New York*
Dodson, Owen; Theater

Heather Hathaway, *Assistant Professor of English, Marquette University, Milwaukee, Wisconsin*
McKay, Claude

Kathleen A. Hauke, *Instructor in English, Spelman College, Atlanta, Georgia*
Fields, Julia

Chanta M. Haywood, *Assistant Professor of African American Literature, Florida State University, Tallahassee*
A.M.E. Book Concern; Christian Recorder; Greenfield, Eloise

Elanna N. Haywood, *Takoma Park, Maryland*
Miller, E. Ethelbert

James L. Hill, *Professor of English; Dean of the School of Arts and Sciences, Albany State College, Georgia*
Foxes of Harrow, The; Woman Called Fancy, A; Yerby, Frank

Karla FC Holloway, *Professor of English; Director, African and Afro-American Studies Program, Duke University, Durham, North Carolina*
Gender

Maureen Honey, *Professor of English, University of Nebraska at Lincoln*
Johnson, Georgia Douglas

Helen R. Houston, *Professor of English, Tennessee State University, Nashville*
Franklin, J. E.; Lee, George Washington; Ottley, Roi; Richardson, Willis; This Child's Gonna Live; Wright, Sarah Elizabeth

Dolan Hubbard, *Associate Professor of English and African American Studies, University of Georgia, Athens*
Sermons and Preaching

Theodore R. Hudson, *Former Graduate Professor of English, Howard University, Washington, D.C.*
Fauset, Arthur Huff

Sheila Hassell Hughes, *Institute for Women's Studies, Emory University, Atlanta, Georgia*
Fair, Ronald L.; Murray, Pauli; River Niger, The; Walker, Joseph A.

Elwanda D. Ingram, *Professor of English, Winston-Salem State University, North Carolina*
Holman, John

Agnes Moreland Jackson, *Peter S. and Gloria Gold Professor of English and World Literature and Black Studies, Pitzer College, Claremont, California*
Religion

Cassandra Jackson, *Department of English, Emory University, Atlanta, Georgia*
Davis, Ossie

Gregory S. Jackson, *Department of English, University of California, Los Angeles*
Dunham, Katherine; Obsidian

Charles L. James, *Professor of English Literature; Coordinator of Black Studies Program, Swarthmore College, Pennsylvania*
Black Thunder; Bontemps, Arna; God Sends Sunday; Popo and Fifina; Sad-Faced Boy

Kenneth R. Janken, *Assistant Professor of Afro-American Studies, University of North Carolina at Chapel Hill*
Expatriatism

Abby Arthur Johnson, *Professorial Lecturer, Liberal Studies Program, Georgetown University, Washington, D.C.*
Periodicals, *article on* Scholarly Journals and Literary Magazines

Allen E. Johnson, *Visiting Assistant Professor of American Literature, Christian Brothers University, Memphis, Tennessee*
Straker, David Augustus

Carol S. Taylor Johnson, *Adjunct Professor of Educational and Professional Studies, West Virginia Graduate College, Charleston*
Conjuring; High John the Conqueror

Lonnell E. Johnson, *Associate Professor of English, Otterbein College, Westerville, Ohio*
Henderson, George Wylie

Ronald Maberry Johnson, *Professor of History, Georgetown University, Washington, D.C.*
Periodicals, *article on* Scholarly Journals and Literary Magazines

Ronna C. Johnson, *Lecturer in American Studies and Women's Studies, Tufts University, Medford, Massachusetts*
His Own Where; Jordan, June; Polite, Carlene Hatcher

Dianne Johnson-Feelings, *Associate Professor of English, University of South Carolina, Columbia*
Brownies' Book, The; Children's and Young Adult Literature; Tate, Eleanora

Yvonne Robinson Jones, *Associate Professor of Languages and Literature, Shelby State Community College, Memphis, Tennessee*
Censorship

Donald Franklin Joyce, *Dean of Library and Media Services, Austin Peay State University, Clarksville, Tennessee*
Publishing

Joyce A. Joyce, *Professor of English; Associate Director of the Gwendolyn Brooks Center, Chicago State University, Illinois*
Don't Cry, Scream; Madhubuti, Haki R.

John R. Keene, *Jersey City, New Jersey*
Callaloo

Arlene R. Keizer, *Department of Ethnic Studies, University of California, Berkeley*
Poetry, Religious and Didactic

Allison Kimmich, *Institute for Women's Studies and Deartment of English, Emory University, Atlanta, Georgia*
Forbes, Calvin

Debra Walker King, *Assistant Professor of English, University of Florida, Gainesville*
Brownfield Copeland; Celie; Color Purple, The; In Search of Our Mothers' Gardens; Possessing the Secret of Joy; Shug Avery; Temple of My Familiar, The; Third Life of Grange Copeland, The; Walker, Alice

Lovalerie King, *Department of English, University of North Carolina at Chapel Hill*
Cooper, J. California; De Veaux, Alexis; Funnyhouse of a Negro; Kennedy, Adrienne; Lesbian Literature; Lesbians

Keneth Kinnamon, *Ethel Pumphrey Stephens Professor of English, University of Arkansas, Fayetteville*
Anthologies

Lynda Koolish, *Associate Professor of English, San Diego State University, California*
Cuney-Hare, Maud; Miller, May

Karen Ruth Kornweibel, *University of Texas at Austin*
Brown, Lloyd; Iron City

Beverly Threatt Kulii, *Lecturer in English, North Carolina Agricultural and Technical State University, Greensboro*
Brer Rabbit; Lorde, Audre

Elon A. Kulii, *Professor of English and Folklore, North Carolina Agricultural and Technical State University, Greensboro*
Brer Rabbit; Preachers and Deacons

Vera M. Kutzinski, *Professor of English, African-American Studies and American Studies, Yale University, New Haven, Connecticut*
Wright, Jay

Lois R. Kuznets, *Professor of English and Comparative Literature, San Diego State University, California*
Harriet and the Promised Land; Lawrence, Jacob

Henry C. Lacey, *Associate Professor of English; Vice President of Academic Affairs, Dillard University, New Orleans, Louisiana*
Baraka, Amiri; Dutchman; Home: Social Essays; Preface to a Twenty-Volume Suicide Note; System of Dante's Hell, The

John Lang, *Professor of English, Emory and Henry College, Emory, Virginia*
Autobiography of Miss Jane Pittman, The; Dixon, Melvin; Gaines, Ernest J.; McCluskey, John A., Jr.

Candis LaPrade, *Assistant Professor of English, Longwood College, Farmville, Virginia*
Lee, Jarena

Jeffrey B. Leak, *Department of American Studies and African-American Literature, Graduate Institute of the Liberal Arts, Emory University, Atlanta, Georgia*
Carmichael, Stokely

A. Robert Lee, *Reader in American Literature, University of Kent at Canterbury, England*
Ai; Periodicals, *article on* Black Periodical Press; War Experience

Valerie Lee, *Associate Professor of English and Women's Studies, Ohio State University, Columbus*
Journalism; Newspaper Columns

Charles Leonard, *Department of English, Emory University, Atlanta, Georgia*
Gordone, Charles; No Place to Be Somebody

Keith D. Leonard, *Department of English and American Literature, Stanford University, California*
Harper, Michael S.

Cheryl Lester, *Associate Professor of English and American Studies, University of Kansas, Lawrence*
Letters; Paynter, John H.

Neal A. Lester, *Associate Professor of English, University of Alabama, Tuscaloosa*
Ceremonies in Dark Old Men; Hair

Emily M. Lewis, *Educational Researcher, Technology Based Learning and Research, Arizona State University, Tempe*
"I Have a Dream"; King, Martin Luther, Jr.; "Letter from Birmingham Jail"

Saundra Liggins, *Departments of English and American Studies, University of California, San Diego*
Christopher Cat; Mathis, Sharon Bell; Zeely

Kathryne V. Lindberg, *Associate Professor of American Literature; Adjunct in Africana Studies, Wayne State University, Detroit, Michigan*
Jackson, Mae; Joans, Ted; Kaufman, Bob

Françoise Lionnet, *Associate Professor of French and Comparative Literature, Northwestern University, Evanston, Illinois*
Angelou, Maya; I Know Why the Caged Bird Sings

Jonathan D. Little, *Assistant Professor of English, Alverno College, Milwaukee, Wisconsin*
Middle Passage; Miscegenation; Mulatto; Novel of Passing

Monroe H. Little, Jr., *Associate Professor of History, Indiana University, Indianapolis*
Education

Andrea M. Lockett, *Publisher, Kitchen Table: Women of Color Press, Brooklyn, New York*
Kitchen Table: Women of Color Press

Jeff Loeb, *Senior Teacher, The Pembroke Hill School, Kansas City, Missouri*
Beckham, Barry

Richard A. Long, *Atticus Haygood Professor of Interdisciplinary Studies, Emory University, Atlanta, Georgia*
Burroughs, Margaret Taylor Goss; Fuller, Hoyt; Locke, Alain; New Negro, The

Eric Lott, *Assistant Professor of English, University of Virginia, Charlottesville*
Coon; Minstrelsy; Stepin Fetchit

Mason I. Lowance, Jr., *Professor of English, University of Massachusetts–Amherst*
Antislavery Movement; Bibb, Henry

Barbara Lowe, *Graduate Instructor in English, University of Mississippi, University*
Jackson, Jesse; Steptoe, John

John Lowe, *Professor of English, Louisiana State University at Baton Rouge*
Humor; Lane, Pinkie Gordon; Osbey, Brenda Marie

Donnarae MacCann, *Visiting Assistant Professor, African American World Studies Program, University of Iowa, Iowa City*
McKissack, Patricia C.; Newsome, Effie Lee

Lucinda H. MacKethan, *Professor of English, North Carolina State University at Raleigh*
Plantation Tradition

Wanda Macon, *Assistant Professor of African American and American Literature, Jackson State University, Mississippi*
Cotillion, The; Fuller, Charles H., Jr.; Greenlee, Sam; Killens, John O.; McMillan, Terry; Soldier's Play, A; Spook Who Sat by the Door, The

Naomi Long Madgett, *Professor Emerita of English, Eastern Michigan University, Ypsilanti*
Broadside Press; Lotus Press; Randall, Dudley; White, Paulette Childress

Yolanda M. Manora, *Emory University, Atlanta, Georgia*
Jackson, Elaine

Jennifer Margulis, *Department of English, Emory University, Atlanta, Georgia*
Kincaid, Jamaica; McElroy, Colleen; Rahman, Aishah; Simmons, Herbert Alfred

Carol P. Marsh-Lockett, *Assistant Professor of English, Georgia State University, Atlanta*
Ansa, Tina McElroy; Cleage, Pearl; Womanism

Daniel J. Martin, *Department of English, University of Kansas, Lawrence*
Early, Gerald

Theodore O. Mason, Jr., *Associate Professor of English, Kenyon College, Gambier, Ohio*
Rampersad, Arnold; Robeson, Paul; Signifying

Valerie N. Matthews, *Department of English, University of North Carolina at Chapel Hill*
Goines, Donald

Claudia May, *Department of Ethnic Studies, University of California, Berkeley*
Class

Vivian M. May, *Institute for Women's Studies, Emory University, Atlanta, Georgia*
Flowers, A. R.; Thelwell, Michael

Katherine J. Mayberry, *Professor of Language and Literature, Rochester Institute of Technology, New York*
Gunn, Bill

Barbara McCaskill, *Assistant Professor of English, University of Georgia, Athens*
Hemings, Sally; Spencer, Anne

John McCluskey, Jr., *Professor and Chair of Afro-American Studies, Indiana University at Bloomington*
Fisher, Rudolph; Walls of Jericho, The

Robert E. McGlone, *Assistant Professor of History, University of Hawai'i at Manoa*
Brown, John

Sara Gallob McIntyre, *Crawford, Colorado*
Blue Vein Societies

Jacquelyn Y. McLendon, *Associate Professor of English, The College of William and Mary, Williamsburg, Virginia*
Comedy: American Style; Fauset, Jessie Redmon; There Is Confusion

Adam Meyer, *Assistant Professor of English, Fisk University, Nashville, Tennessee*
Blyden, Edward Wilmot; Jews

Mildred R. Mickle, *Department of English, University of North Carolina at Chapel Hill*
Butler, Octavia E.; Dessa Rose (the novel and the character); Rufel, Miss; Williams, Sherley Anne

Tiya Miles, *Program in American Studies, University of Minnesota at Minneapolis*
Third World Press

James A. Miller, *Professor of English and African-American Studies, University of South Carolina, Columbia*
Bennett, Hal; Communism; Forrest, Leon

Keith D. Miller, *Associate Professor of English, Arizona State University, Tempe*
"I Have a Dream"; King, Martin Luther, Jr.; "Letter from Birmingham Jail"

Keith Bernard Mitchell, *Department of Comparative Literature, University of North Carolina at Chapel Hill*
Brown Girl, Brownstones; Chosen Place, the Timeless People, The; Marshall, Paule; Selina Boyce

Marilyn Sanders Mobley, *Department of English, George Mason University, Fairfax, Virginia*
Bluest Eye, The; Milkman Dead; Morrison, Toni; Pecola Breedlove; Pilate Dead

Joycelyn K. Moody, *Assistant Professor of English, University of Washington, Seattle*
Brown, Hallie Q.; Clifton, Lucille; Elizabeth; Everett Anderson; Jackson, Mattie J.; Jackson, Rebecca Cox; Taylor, Susie King

William R. Nash, *Assistant Professor of American Literature, Middlebury College, Vermont*
Dialect Poetry; Johnson, Charles R.; Man Who Cried I Am, The; Middle Passage (the novel); Rutherford Calhoun; Williams, John A.

Dana D. Nelson, *Associate Professor of English, University of Kentucky, Lexington*
Craft, William and Ellen; Stereotypes, *article on* White Stereotypes

Charles I. Nero, *Assistant Professor of Rhetoric and Theatre, Bates College, Lewiston, Maine*
Gay Literature; Gay Men

Elaine Nichols, *Curator of African-American Culture and History, South Carolina State Museum, Columbia*
Funeral and Mourning Customs

Terri Hume Oliver, *Teaching Fellow in English, Harvard University, Cambridge, Massachusetts*
Iceberg Slim

Ted Olson, *Graduate Instructor in English, University of Mississippi, University*
Devil; Folklore; Jim Crow; John Henry; Moses

Sondra O'Neale, *Dean, College of Liberal Arts; Professor of English, Wayne State University, Detroit, Michigan*
Hammon, Jupiter

Nell Irvin Painter, *Edwards Professor of American History, Princeton University, New Jersey*
Truth, Sojourner

Sandra Pouchet Paquet, *Associate Professor of Caribbean and African American Literature; Director, Caribbean Writers Summer Institute, University of Miami, Coral Gables, Florida*
Prince, Mary; West Indian Literature

Tracy J. Patterson, *Berkeley, California*
Drugstore Cat, The; Jackson, Angela; Scott-Heron, Gil; Soul

James Robert Payne, *Professor of English, New Mexico State University, Las Cruces*
Colter, Cyrus; Cotter, Joseph Seamon, Jr.; Cotter, Joseph Seamon, Sr.

Linda M. Perkins, *Associate Professor of Educational Foundations, Hunter College, The City University of New York*
Women's Clubs

Pearlie Peters, *Assistant Professor of English, Rider University, Lawrenceville, New Jersey*
Color Line; Ebony Jr!; Masking

Bernard L. Peterson, Jr., *Professor Emeritus of English and Drama, Elizabeth City State University, North Carolina*
Drama

Joyce Pettis, *Associate Professor of English, North Carolina State University at Raleigh*
Dance

Jennifer H. Poulos, *Department of English, Emory University, Atlanta, Georgia*
Thomas, Lorenzo

Cassie Premo, *Department of Comparative Literature, Emory University, Atlanta, Georgia*
Knight, Etheridge

Arnold Rampersad, *Woodrow Wilson Professor of Literature, Princeton University, New Jersey*
Big Sea, The; Biography; Du Bois, W. E. B.; Hughes, Langston; Madam Alberta K. Johnson; Montage of a Dream Deferred; "Negro Speaks of Rivers, The"; Simple; Souls of Black Folk, The; Weary Blues, The

Gloria Thomas Randle, *Assistant Professor of English, Michigan State University, East Lansing*
Address, Forms of

Ralph Reckley, Sr., *Professor of English, Speech and the Humanities, Morgan State University, Baltimore, Maryland*
Bledsoe, Dr.; Ellison, Ralph; Invisible Man; Mary Rambo; Norton, Mr.; Ras the Destroyer; Rinehart; Shadow and Act; Todd Clifton; Trueblood

Margaret Ann Reid, *Associate Professor of English, Morgan State University, Baltimore, Maryland*
Amini, Johari; Turpin, Waters

Ann E. Reuman, *Department of English, Tufts University, Medford, Massachusetts*
Cables to Rage; Cancer Journals, The

James W. Richardson, Jr., *Atlanta, Georgia*
Derricotte, Toi; Touré, Askia M.

Marilyn Richardson, *Watertown, Massachusetts*
Stewart, Maria W.

Janet M. Roberts, *Department of American and African American Studies, University of California, San Diego*
Tarry, Ellen; Thompson, Era Bell

Beverly J. Robinson, *Associate Professor of Theater Arts and Folklore Studies, University of California, Los Angeles*
Musicals

Lawrence R. Rodgers, *Associate Professor of English, Kansas State University, Manhattan*
Downing, Henry F.; Miller, Kelly; Sport of the Gods, The; Talented Tenth, The; Webb, Frank J.

Ruby V. Rodney, *Professor of English, Winston-Salem State University, North Carolina*
Mayfield, Julian

Ramon Royal Ross, *Professor of Education Emeritus, San Diego State University, California*
Bryan, Ashley

Daniel J. Royer, *Assistant Professor of English and Composition Studies, Grand Valley State University, Allendale, Michigan*
Anglo-African Magazine, The; Southern Workman, The; Voice of the Negro, The

Ashraf H. A. Rushdy, *Associate Professor of African American Studies and English, Wesleyan University, Middletown, Connecticut*
Neo–Slave Narrative

John Saillant, *Associate, W. E. B. Du Bois Institute for Afro-American Research, Harvard University, Cambridge, Massachusetts*
Allen, Richard; Haynes, Lemuel

Kalamu ya Salaam, *New Orleans, Louisiana*
Black Arts Movement

Maggie Sale, *Assistant Professor of Women's and Gender Studies and English and Comparative Literature, Columbia University, New York*
Dove, Rita; First World; Historical Novel; Negro World; Scottsboro Boys; Temperance; Thomas and Beulah

Wilfred D. Samuels, *Associate Professor of English and Ethnic Studies; Director, African American Studies Program; Coordinator, Ethnic Studies Program, University of Utah, Salt Lake City*
Wideman, John Edgar

Scott A. Sandage, *Assistant Professor of History, Carnegie-Mellon University, Pittsburgh, Pennsylvania*
Anderson, Marian; Lincoln, Abraham

Leslie Catherine Sanders, *Associate Professor of Humanities, Atkinson College, York University, Toronto, Ontario, Canada*
Black Theatre

Mark A. Sanders, *Assistant Professor of English, Emory University, Atlanta, Georgia*
Hayden, Robert; Hill, Leslie Pinckney; Himes, Chester; "Runagate Runagate"

Elizabeth Schultz, *Professor of English; Chancellor's Club Teaching Professor, University of Kansas, Lawrence*
Parks, Gordon

Robin G. Schulze, *Assistant Professor of English, Pennsylvania State University, State College*
Braithwaite, William Stanley

Meryl F. Schwartz, *Instructor of English, Lakeland Community College, Kirkland, Ohio*
Kelley, Emma Dunham

Daniel M. Scott III, *Assistant Professor of English, Rhode Island College, Providence*
Barrax, Gerald W.; Pharr, Robert Deane

J. D. Scrimgeour, *Assistant Professor of English, DePauw University, Greencastle, Indiana*
Autobiography of Malcolm X, The; Malcolm X

John Sekora, *Professor of English; Dean, School of Graduate Studies, North Carolina Central University, Durham*
Freedom; Libraries and Research Centers; Literary History, article on Antislavery Era; Slavery

Caroline Senter, *Department of Literature, University of California, San Diego*
Van Dyke, Henry

Barry Shank, *Assistant Professor of American Studies, University of Kansas, Lawrence*
Murray, Albert

Joan R. Sherman, *Associate Professor of English, Rutgers University, New Brunswick, New Jersey*
Bell, James Madison; Campbell, James Edwin; Davis, Daniel Webster; Horton, George Moses; Reason, Charles L.; Vashon, George B.; Whitfield, James Monroe; Whitman, Albery Allson

John C. Shields, *Professor of English, Illinois State University, Normal*
Literary History, article on Colonial and Early National Eras; Poems on Various Subjects, Religious and Moral; Short Story; Smith, Venture; Wheatley, Phillis

Ann Allen Shockley, *Associate Professor of Library Science, Fisk University, Nashville, Tennessee*
Gomez, Jewelle

Jonathan Silverman, *University of Texas at Austin*
"Atlanta Exposition Address"

Janet Sims-Wood, *Assistant Chief Librarian, Reference/Reader Services Department, Moorland-Spingarn Research Center, Howard University, Washington, D.C.*
Bibliography

Amritjit Singh, *Professor of English, Rhode Island College, Providence*
Harlem Renaissance; New Negro

Deborah Ayer Sitter, *Lecturer in English, Emory University, Atlanta, Georgia*
Sanchez, Sonia; We a BaddDDD People

Joseph T. Skerrett, Jr., *Professor of English, University of Massachusetts at Amherst*
God's Trombones; "Lift Every Voice and Sing"

Jeanne R. Smith, *Lecturer in English, University of Texas at Arlington*
Trickster

Karen Patricia Smith, *Associate Professor, Graduate School of Library and Information Studies, Queens College, The City University of New York, Flushing*
Patterson, Lillie

Valerie Smith, *Professor of English, University of California, Los Angeles*
Lee, Andrea; Literary History, *article on* Late Twentieth Century

Virginia Whatley Smith, *Assistant Professor of English, University of Alabama in Birmingham*
Cain, George; Demby, William; Oliver, Diane; Peterson, Louis

Geneva Smitherman, *University Distinguished Professor of English, Michigan State University, East Lansing*
Address, Forms of

Stephen F. Soitos, *Lecturer in English, Springfield College, Massachusetts*
Crime and Mystery Writing; Micheaux, Oscar

Maia Angelique Sorrells, *College of Notre Dame, Belmont, California*
Caines, Jeannette Franklin

Jon Michael Spencer, *Tyler and Alice Haynes Professor of American Studies; Professor of Music, University of Richmond, Virginia*
Lincoln, C. Eric

Ann Folwell Stanford, *Assistant Professor, School for New Learning, De Paul University, Chicago, Illinois*
Bambara, Toni Cade; Minnie Ransom; Salt Eaters, The; Velma Henry

Sandra K. Stanley, *Associate Professor of English, California State University, Northridge*
Coleman, Wanda

Robert B. Stepto, *Professor of African American Studies, American Studies, and English, Yale University, New Haven, Connecticut*
Authentication

Albert E. Stone, *Professor Emeritus of American Studies and English, University of Iowa, Iowa City*
Confessions of Nat Turner, The

Claire Taft, *Visiting Instructor, Department of Languages and Literature, Texas A&M University, Kingsville*
Mufaro's Beautiful Daughters

Australia Tarver, *Associate Professor of English, Texas Christian University, Fort Worth*
Anderson, Mignon Holland; Branch, William Blackwell; Chase-Riboud, Barbara; Edwards, Junius; Ellis, Trey

Claudia Tate, *Professor of American and African American Literature, George Washington University, Washington, D.C.*
Contending Forces; Hopkins, Pauline E.; Hunter, Kristin; Tillman, Katherine Davis Chapman; Woman's Era

Clyde Taylor, *Fletcher Professor of Rhetoric and Debate, Tufts University, Medford, Massachusetts*
Film

Betty Taylor-Thompson, *Professor of English, Texas Southern University, Houston*
Baby Suggs; Beloved; Eva Peace; for colored girls; Hannah Peace; Jadine Childs; Jazz (the novel); Paul D; Sethe Suggs; Shadrack; Shange, Ntozake; Song of Solomon; Son Green; Sula; Tar Baby

Lorenzo Thomas, *Associate Professor of English, University of Houston–Downtown, Texas*
Blues Aesthetic; Zu-Bolton, Ahmos, II

John Edgar Tidwell, *Associate Professor of English, Miami University, Oxford, Ohio*
Brown, Sterling A.; Davis, Frank Marshall; Slim Greer

Mary Titus, *Associate Professor of English, St. Olaf College, Northfield, Minnesota*
Dunbar-Nelson, Alice Moore

Charles P. Toombs, *Associate Professor of Africana Studies, San Diego State University, California*
Henson, Josiah; Perkins, Eugene; Salaam, Kalamu ya; Thomas, Joyce Carol; Weatherly, Tom

Patricia A. Turner, *Associate Professor of African-American and African Studies and American Studies, University of California, Davis*
Sambo; Shine; Stackolee; Uncle Tom

Timothy B. Tyson, *Assistant Professor of Afro-American Studies, University of Wisconsin–Madison*
Civil Rights Movement

Siva Vaidhyanathan, *Department of American Civilization, University of Texas at Austin*
Jazz

R. Goldman Vander, *Curriculum in Comparative Literature, University of North Carolina at Chapel Hill*
Aubert, Alvin

Marsha C. Vick, *Lecturer in Afro-American Studies Curriculum, University of North Carolina at Chapel Hill*
Cartiér, Xam Wilson; Rodgers, Carolyn M.; Sanders, Dori

Wendy Wagner, *Adjunct Instructor in English, Pace University, New York*
Freedom's Journal; North Star, The; Pickaninny; Stowe, Harriet Beecher

Gayle Wald, *Assistant Professor of English, George Washington University, Washington, D.C.*
Passing; White, Walter

Robbie Jean Walker, *Professor of English; Interim Dean of the School of Liberal Arts, Auburn University at Montgomery, Alabama*
Mitchell, Loften; Williams, Samm-Art

Cheryl A. Wall, *Associate Professor of English, Rutgers University, New Brunswick, New Jersey*
Dust Tracks on a Road; Hurston, Zora Neale; Janie Crawford; Jonah's Gourd Vine; Mule Bone; Nanny; Tea Cake; Their Eyes Were Watching God

Jon Wallace, *Professor of English, Graceland College, Lamoni, Iowa*
Elbow Room; McPherson, James Alan

Kimberly Wallace Sanders, *Associate Director, Women's Research and Resource Center, Spelman College, Atlanta, Georgia*
Allen, Clarissa Minnie Thompson; Buck; Feminism; Ray, Henrietta Cordelia

Wendy W. Walters, *Instructor in Literature, University of California, San Diego*
Coffin Ed Johnson; Cotton Comes to Harlem; Grave Digger Jones; If He Hollers Let Him Go

Jerry W. Ward, Jr., *Lawrence Durgin Professor of Literature, Tougaloo College, Mississippi*
Dent, Tom; For My People; Jubilee; Walker, Margaret

Anne Bradford Warner, *Associate Professor of English, Spelman College, Atlanta, Georgia*
Keckley, Elizabeth

Kenneth W. Warren, *Associate Professor of English, University of Chicago, Illinois*
David Walker's Appeal; Gates, Henry Louis, Jr.

Nagueyalti Warren, *Assistant Dean; Adjunct Associate Professor of African American Studies, Emory University, Atlanta, Georgia*
Aunt Jemima; Fabio, Sarah Webster; Graham, Shirley; Guy, Rosa; Roll of Thunder, Hear My Cry; Taylor, Mildred D.

Kimberly Weaver, *Atlanta, Georgia*
Harris, E. Lynn

George F. Wedge, *Associate Professor Emeritus of English, University of Kansas, Lawrence*
Madgett, Naomi Long

Joe Weixlmann, *Professor of English, Indiana State University, Terre Haute*
African American Review; Wright, Charles S.

Craig H. Werner, *Professor of Afro-American Studies, University of Wisconsin–Madison*
Chicago Renaissance; Literary History, *article on* Early Twentieth Century

Dorothy Burnett Porter Wesley, *Curator Emerita, Moorland-Spingarn Research Center, Howard University, Washington, D.C., deceased*
Literary Societies

Elizabeth J. West, *Department of English, Emory University, Atlanta, Georgia*
Black Nationalism; Crummell, Alexander

Craig Howard White, *Assistant Professor of Literature and Humanities, University of Houston–Clear Lake, Texas*
Crisis, The; Federal Writers' Project; Fire!!; Messenger, The; Opportunity; Survey Graphic

William H. Wiggins, Jr., *Professor of Afro-American Studies and Folklore, Indiana University at Bloomington*
Festivals; Performances and Pageants

Margaret B. Wilkerson, *Professor of African American Studies; Director, Center for Theater Arts, University of California, Berkeley*
Beneatha Younger; Hansberry, Lorraine; Mama Lena Younger; Raisin in the Sun, A; Walter Lee Younger

Michelle J. Wilkinson, *Institute of the Liberal Arts, Emory University, Atlanta, Georgia*
Cortez, Jayne

Bettye J. Williams, *Assistant Professor of English, University of Arkansas at Pine Bluff*
Names and Naming

Derek A. Williams, *Appalachian State University, Boone, North Carolina*
Milner, Ron; Russell, Charlie L.

Kenny Jackson Williams, *Professor of English, Duke University, Durham, North Carolina*
Annie Allen; Brawley, Benjamin; Bronzeville Boys and Girls; Brooks, Gwendolyn; In the Mecca; Maud Martha; Plato, Ann; Street in Bronzeville, A

Kim D. Hester Williams, *Department of Literature, University of California, San Diego*
Graham, Lorenz

Patricia Robinson Williams, *Professor of British Romantic Literature and Linguistics, Texas Southern University, Houston*
Folks from Dixie; Garvey, Marcus; Lyrics of Lowly Life; Majors and Minors

Roland L. Williams, Jr., *Assistant Professor of American Literature, Temple University, Philadelphia, Pennsylvania*
All God's Dangers; Cobb, Ned; Hammon, Briton

Charles E. Wilson, Jr., *Associate Professor of English, Old Dominion University, Norfolk, Virginia*
Pennington, James W. C.; Roper, Moses

Kari J. Winter, *Assistant Professor of English, University of Vermont, Burlington*
Oratory; Prince, Nancy; Underground Railroad

Jean Fagan Yellin, *Distinguished Professor of English, Pace University, New York*
Incidents in the Life of a Slave Girl; Jacobs, Harriet A.

Kristine A. Yohe, *Department of English, University of North Carolina at Chapel Hill*
Kenan, Randall; Mama Day; Naylor, Gloria; Women of Brewster Place, The

Reggie Young, *Assistant Professor of English and African American Studies, Louisiana State University at Baton Rouge*
Stereotypes, *article on* Black Stereotypes

Abbreviations

AA	Associate in Arts	LLB	Legum Bachelor (Bachelor of Laws)
AB	Artium Baccalaureus (Bachelor of Arts)	LLD	Legum Doctor (Doctor of Laws)
AM	Artium Magister (Master of Arts)	LLM	Legum Master (Master of Laws)
AME	African Methodist Episcopal	MA	Master of Arts
Audelco	Audience Development Committee	MD	Medicinae Doctor (Doctor of Medicine)
b.	born		
BA	Bachelor of Arts	MEd	Master of Education
BFA	Bachelor of Fine Arts	MFA	Master of Fine Arts
BL	Bachelor of Law	MSW	Master of Social Work
BS	Bachelor of Science	NAACP	National Association for the Advancement of Colored People
c.	circa		
CA	*Contemporary Authors*	n.d.	no date
CIA	Central Intelligence Agency	no(s).	number(s)
comp(s).	compiler(s), compiled by	orig.	original
d.	died	p(p).	page(s)
DA	Doctor of Arts	PEN	International Association of Poets, Playwrights, Editors, Essayists and Novelists
DANB	*Dictionary of American Negro Biography*		
DD	Doctor of Divinity	PhD	Doctor of Philosophy
diss.	dissertation	PhG	Graduate in Pharmacy
DLB	*Dictionary of Literary Biography*	rev.	revised
ed(s).	editor(s), edited by; edition(s)	rpt.	reprint
et al.	et alia (and others)	trans.	translator, translated by
FBI	Federal Bureau of Investigation	vol(s).	volume(s)
FWP	Federal Writers' Project	WPA	Works Progress Administration
IRS	Internal Revenue Service	*WWABA*	*Who's Who among Black Americans*
JD	Juris Doctor (Doctor of Laws)		

THE OXFORD COMPANION TO
African American Literature

A

ABOLITION. *See* Antislavery Movement.

ADDRESS, FORMS OF. As general linguistic phenomena, forms of address reflect the social status of individual interlocutors as well as the relationship between them. On one level, such forms simply name a person, for example, Helen. However, because these forms are governed by deeply imbedded sociocultural rules, on another level they reveal what Brown and Gilman (1960) call "power and solidarity," for example, Helen versus Miz Helen. Given the habitual and systematic nature of language behavior, interlocutors may not always be conscious of the social nuances revealed in the forms of address they use. On the other hand, speakers can and do consciously manipulate forms of address in acts of control and subordination, as demonstrated in the exchange between a white policeman and Black psychiatrist Alvin Poussaint.

> Policeman: What's your name, boy?
> Poussaint: Dr. Poussaint. I'm a physician.
> Policeman: What's your first name, boy?
> Poussaint: Alvin.

Now a classic in the annals of the African American experience, this interaction demonstrates racial subordination not only in the policeman's use of "boy," but also in his implicit refusal to follow the naming practices of American society by which professionals are addressed—by their title and last name.

The policeman's linguistic behavior exemplifies the unequal and discriminatory practices of whites as reflected in the use and misuse of forms of address. Names and titles are fundamental in the construction of identity, but these have historically been withheld from African Americans by white American society. This linguistic phenomenon is mirrored in forms of address both imposed upon and claimed (or reclaimed) by real and fictional characters across the panorama of African American literature from slavery to the present time. The historical use of improper modes of address by white society not only reflects the lack of respect accorded African Americans; it also explains, at least in part, the singular emphasis placed upon naming and titles in the Black community. As Maya *Angelou notes in her 1969 *bildungsroman, *I Know Why the Caged Bird Sings,*

> Every person I knew had a hellish horror of being "called out of his name." It was a dangerous practice to call a Negro anything that could be loosely construed as insulting because of the centuries of their having been called niggers, jigs, dinges, blackbirds, crows, boots and spooks.

Caged Bird also records a depression-era incident in which three young white girls address Angelou's grandmother, as was customary, by her first name, "Annie," whereas the grandmother is obliged to greet the children as "Miz Helen . . . Miz Ruth . . . Miz Eloise."

Stolen names and withheld titles are but one aspect of the system that mandated complete extinction of the enslaved African's past in a social hierarchy determined solely by *race. Olaudah *Equiano's 1789 *slave narrative suggests, by its very title, the fractured *identity of Africans brought to America. *The Interesting Narrative of the Life of Olaudah Equiano, or Gustavus Vassa, the African* inscribes both the African and the "slave name": "While I was on board of this ship my captain and master named me GUSTAVUS VASSA. . . . When I refused to answer to my new name, which at first I did, it gained me many a cuff; so at length I submitted, and by it I have been known ever since." The editors of Mary *Prince's 1831 slave narrative note that the common practice of facetious misnaming was simply one of many means by which the colonists expressed their established contempt of African Americans. Prince's owners christen her "Mary, Princess of Wales," in the same mocking spirit with which Equiano's white shipmates call him Vassa, after a Scandinavian hero.

During *slavery, the only titles conferred upon Africans by the white citizenry were those based upon age. "Aunt" and "Uncle" were used generically to refer to any older Black person. Charles Waddell *Chesnutt's *The *Conjure Woman* (1899) illustrates this naming through the main narrator, *Uncle Julius McAdoo, and through other characters with whose stories Uncle Julius regales his white listeners, such as "ole *Aun' Peggy." Vestiges of this practice are observable today in the commercial marketing of products such as "Uncle Ben's" rice and "*Aunt Jemima" pancake mix.

Contrary to the racial subordination inherent in such kinship terms as "aunt" and "uncle" when used by European Americans, African Americans have historically referred to one another with such language to connote a true sense of kinship. Dr. Endesha Ida Mae Holland's celebrated signature play, *From the Mississippi Delta* (1988), relates that her mother was "A'nt Baby" to the entire family. Similarly, Maya Angelou is called "Sister" by all her relatives. In fact, it is her brother Bailey's unique rendition of Angelou's "family" name—"Mya Sister"—that ultimately gives birth to her professional name "Maya." Patriarchal and matriarchal terms are generally reserved for those community members whose age, wisdom, and resources qualify them for symbolic leadership: Mrs. Smith, widowed community activist and owner of a boardinghouse in Pauline E. *Hopkins's *Contending Forces* (1899), is affectionately called "Ma Smith" by her boarders. The prophetic but enigmatic old wise man in the drama "Kabnis" from Jean *Toomer's *Cane* (1923) is addressed simply as "Father."

A significant aspect of the sense of community within African American culture is the shared spirituality of many of its members. The sense of a collective historical experience and spiritual kinship account for the extension of the traditional Black *church terms "Brother" and "Sister"—themselves reflecting African naming practices—into the secular arena. The all-inclusive "Brethren," used, for example, by Henry Highland *Garnet in his impassioned 1843 "Address to the Slaves of the United States," acquires gender specificity in later works. "Brer Primus" and "Sis' Becky," two characters who populate Chesnutt's Conjure Woman, are so called by the other slaves on the plantation, not by their "owners." Countless later African American texts—from the poetry of Langston *Hughes and Gwendolyn *Brooks, among others, to all genres of prose (e.g., Richard *Wright's *Black Boy, 1945; The *Autobiography of Malcolm X, 1965; John Edgar *Wideman's *Brothers and Keepers, 1984; Bebe Moore Campbell's Brothers and Sisters, 1994)—mirror the continued prevalence of these forms of address in both the Black church and the broader Black speech community. James *Baldwin's 1957 short story "Sonny's Blues" illustrates, and accounts for, this usage.

> The revival was being carried on by three sisters in black, and a brother. . . . The brother was testifying. . . . The woman with the tambourine . . . was divided by very little from the woman who stood watching her. Perhaps they both knew this, which was why, when, as rarely, they addressed each other, they addressed each other as Sister.

The designations "Mr.," "Mrs.," or "Dr." were not permitted to a people legally prohibited from marrying or pursuing an education. Further, long after slavery was abolished, policy replaced law so that African Americans were still denied proper address. Angelou relates the error through which her grandmother becomes "the only Negro woman in Stamps [Ark.] referred to once as Mrs." When a Black defendant cites her for having given him refuge in her store, "Mrs. Henderson" is subpoenaed in a local court case. The white people find the apellation amusing but excuse the judge's faux pas because he was from another town. Mister T., the television personality, has said that his mother named him as she did to compel white people to call him "Mister." Possibly, a similar train of thought fed into the construction of the professional names of such musical royalty as Count Basie and Duke Ellington.

Individuals with titles always get their props within the African American community. Sociolinguistic rules of respectable address are a serious matter, taught to children early on, as Angelou explains: "The impudent child was detested by God and a shame to its parents. . . . All adults had to be addressed as Mister, Missus, Miss, Auntie, Cousin, Unk, Uncle, Bubbah, Sister, Brother and a thousand other appellations." The literature shows that, because of the importance of education, titles that denote educational and/or professional achievement are scrupulously acknowledged. Turn-of-the-century Black townspeople's respect for, and pride in, the "only colored doctor" in town extends even as far as the physician's street, which they rechristen "Doctor Street," in Toni *Morrison's *Song of Solomon (1977). The Black college president and visiting speaker of Ralph *Ellison's *Invisible Man (1952) are invariably addressed as Dr. *Bledsoe and Rev. Homer Barbee, respectively. (If a minister also possesses a PhD degree, s/he is often addressed by the dual title of "Rev. Dr.") Jody Starks is always addressed as "Mayor" in Zora Neale *Hurston's 1937 novel *Their Eyes Were Watching God; Matt Bonner's familiar yet respectful dual address, "Brother Mayor," signals his particular friendship with Jody. When *Janie Crawford marries Jody, the townspeople even call her "Mrs. Mayor Starks" by virtue of her husband's position.

From the era of slavery to the present, African American literature illuminates the importance of history, social convention, and nuance with regard to forms of address. Transcending authorial gender, genre, and generation, an explicit leitmotif underlying forms of address in the literature is the theme of reclamation. In countless acts of reappropriation—a classic response to oppression and discrimination—the African American community has historically reclaimed that which has been lost or stolen. Through such indicators as forms of address, the culture perpetually restores, and even embraces, terms and denotations that have been debased by mainstream American culture. Reflecting reality, African American literature compellingly illustrates how meaning and symbol are uniquely reconstructed to function positively and meaningfully within the linguistic and cultural realms of the African American community.

[See also Class; Names and Naming.]

• Roger William Brown and Albert Gilman, "The Pronouns of Power and Solidarity," in Style in Language, ed. Thomas Albert Sebeok, 1960, pp. 253–376. Alvin F. Poussaint, "A Negro Psychiatrist Explains the Negro Psyche," New York Times Magazine, 20 August 1967. Chinosole, "Tryin' to Get Over: Narrative Posture in Equiano's Autobiography," in The Art of Slave Narrative: Original Essays in Criticism and Theory, eds. John Sekora and Darwin T. Turner, 1982, pp. 45–54. Mary Prince, "The History of Mary Prince, a West Indian Slave," in The Classic Slave Narratives, ed. Henry Louis Gates, Jr., 1982, pp. 185–215. Geneva Smitherman, Black Talk: Words and Phrases from the Hood to the Amen Corner, 1994.

—Geneva Smitherman and Gloria Thomas Randle

ADOLESCENT LITERATURE. See Children's and Young Adult Literature.

African American Review has evolved through three distinct phases. Founded at Indiana State University by John F. Bayliss in 1967 as Negro American Literature Forum, the journal for its first six years exhibited a decidedly pedagogical focus, although subsequent editors Hannah Hedrick and W. Tasker Witham (1973–1976) placed increasing emphasis on the critical analysis of literary texts. Reorganized in the winter of 1976 by current editor Joe Weixlmann, the quarterly began appearing as Black American Literature Forum (BALF) and emphasized cutting-edge literary studies, studies in related areas of cultural production (including *theater, *film, art, and *music), and poetry. In 1983, BALF was named the official publication of the Modern Language

Association's Division on Black American Literature and Culture, a distinction the journal still holds. The quarterly's third phase, accompanied by a name change to *African American Review (AAR)* in the spring of 1992, signaled the impact of the cultural studies movement on the publication, which has more fully embraced *essays on nonliterary topics while expanding its commitment to print high-quality fiction and poetry. This mix has proved successful in helping *AAR*'s circulation grow to approximately four thousand. *BALF/AAR* has produced pioneering issues on a variety of African American writers, as well as on African American autobiography, critical theory, film, science fiction, and women's writing.

[*See also* Periodicals, *article on* Scholarly Journals and Literary Magazines.]   —Joe Weixlmann

AFRICAN LITERATURE. The term "African literature" is understood by most to refer to the written literatures of sub-Saharan (East and West) Africa. North African nations (Algeria, Tunisia, Morocco) as well as Egypt are often included under this heading as well. However, because of close historical links between sub-Saharan Africa and African American culture, we will limit our focus to this region. The first observation to be made constitutes a central irony surrounding African literatures today: their primary languages of expression are European, not African. This fact has been a consistent source of debate and, though not of primary concern here, will explain our focus on writers and movements from the two largest language groupings, English and French.

Not many would dispute the division of modern African literatures into three broad phases, taken from Guy Ossito Midiohouan's *L'idéologie dans la littérature négro-africaine* (1986). The first, from 1920 to the mid-1940s, could be characterized as a period of cultural reawakening. The second phase extends from 1945 to the early 1960s and covers the independence period for most of sub-Saharan Africa; this was a period of protest and indictment of the colonial social order. The third phase, from 1960 into the 1980s, saw the focus of African writers turn inward with the emergence of national literatures and literatures in African languages. It may be most useful to view this third phase as being open-ended and suggestive of new phases to come.

One qualification to this periodization applies— that of South Africa. This nation's political evolution took a separate path that was directly reflected in its literature. For example, though the 1960s established a new trajectory for most of the writers in the newly independent nations of sub-Saharan Africa, South Africa was barely affected at all. This is because of the apartheid system of racial segregation in place since 1948, which continued to impose limitations on black writers. During this period, while the majority of black authors had little or no access to publishing outlets, many noted white South Africans such as Alan Paton, Nadine Gordimer, Doris Lessing, Athol Fugard, Andre Brink, and J. M. Coetzee produced the bulk of South African literature. Despite the obstacles, however, certain black writers such as Es'kia

Mphahlele, Dennis Brutus, Bessie Head, Alex LaGuma, and Peter Abrahams continued to publish in exile through the worst periods of apartheid's repression. This racial dynamic makes the literature of South Africa unique and warrants separate discussion.

Ethnic nations throughout the remainder of sub-Saharan Africa are widely recognized for their extensive oral traditions that produced elaborate and complex "oratures" consisting of epics, legends, stories, fables, riddles, proverbs, and so forth. These cultures also use poetic and figurative rhetorical modes in disciplines such as law and governance that fall outside of what in the West is generally considered the creative realm. Written African literatures remain grounded in many of these traditional expressive forms of culture, and this creates an ongoing challenge for those seeking to categorize and evaluate these literatures.

A look at the forerunners of modern African literatures written in European languages reveals a surprising and unsettling array of contributors. Participants in an ill-defined European literary movement dating from around 1870 were driven by a fascination with exoticism and began focusing their attention on Africa. Early in the nineteenth century, French, English, and other writers—responding at times to outrageous travel literature—took up their pens. Many, despite never having left their own countries, authored works of "African literature." These works became very popular among other nontraveled European readers. In many ways they were replicas of popular romances of the day, with African characters as surrogates for stock character types. Thus imagined African peoples and landscapes helped form the outside world's impressions of African "reality." *Ourika*, written by Madame de Duras in 1824, though not the first of these works, is an excellent example of this early genre, where rumor readily inspired popular creative dramatization. Earlier in 1826, Madame Dard had published *The African Cottage (La Chaumière africaine ou l'histoire d'une famille française jettée sur la côte occidentale de l'Afrique à la suite du naufrage de la frégate "La Méduse")*. This work was inspired by an 1818 published report of the survivors of a shipwreck off the coast of Africa. The report drew so much popular attention that it enjoyed several republications and inspired a well-known painter to illustrate the fourth edition.

As Europe became more familiar with the outside world, its fascination with exoticism faded somewhat, making way for the next movement, referred to as "colonial literature." European writers during the period from the late 1800s into the 1920s continued to speak on behalf of Africans, though this time they used their experiences as colonials and colonial administrators as vouchsafes for the authenticity of their writings. Many hold writers of this period responsible for popularizing the most damaging stereotypes about African peoples— stereotypes that still hold sway today. *Le Roman d'un Saphi*, written in 1881 by Pierre Loti, has been attributed with setting the cornerstone for the "myth of black Africa."

Little by little, African participants in colonial administrations in Africa also began producing written works of literature in European languages. Christian moralist Felix Couchoro, infantryman in the French colonial army Bakary Diallo, and ethnographer Paul Hazoume were among their number. Though the works of these writers at times may actually have been apologies for the colonial system, they would nonetheless serve as precursors for later African literary movements. Notably, René Maran, a Martinican working as a French colonial administrator, wrote *Batoula* in 1921. Though the novel itself was rather tame, its preface clearly indicted the abuses of the colonial system and its consequences for Africans. The work thus set the tone for a literature of indictment that would be carried out by later African writers. This type of literature would predominate well into the postcolonial period.

As African literature moved from its first phase into its second, isolated reactions to the colonial structure by writers such as René Maran or the young Aimé Césaire were joined by Mongo Beti, Ferdinand Oyono, Tchicaya u'Tam'Si, Wole Soyinka, Chinua Achebe, and others as literary production in European languages began to take root. The primary factors contributing to this were the scholastic system, the publishing infrastructure, and the energetic cross-cultural milieu. By virtue of the veritable explosion of African writers onto the international literary scene, the hybrid nature of African literatures became plainly evident. Not surprisingly, early serious critiques of these literatures suffered from serious blind spots, notably the inability to account for and accurately assess the cultural hybridity of African writers. For instance, European and American critics tended not to account for African cultural conventions, while African critics tended to overvalue protest literature and discount anything resembling "art for art's sake." Along these lines, works such as *The Palm Wine Drinkard* by Amos Tutuola and *L'Enfant noir (The Dark Child)* by Camara Laye became subjects of intense debates among critics. Perhaps works like these seemed more accessible to non-Africans because they apparently fit neatly into the existing Western literary frameworks? Were they welcomed into Western canons because they were benign expressions of a nonthreatening African reality or masterful translations of complex and little understood African cultural realities?

Assuredly, African writers did not enter the international literary arena devoid of influences from their own cultures. They carried with them a whole array of aesthetic structures that drove their creative work, as well as models for the production and dissemination of written literature derived from the oral tradition. This resulted in an outlook that tended to downplay individual idiosyncracy in authorship, value the relevance of social conscience, and embrace the social function and responsibility of authorship. This outlook also accounts for the very high level of involvement by successful African writers as activists in other nonliterary arenas. Some of Africa's best-known writers are examples of this: renowned poet Léopold Sédar Senghor became president of Senegal; prolific Nigerian writer Chinua Achebe became not only an outspoken social critic but has also worked to develop the broadcast media in Nigeria; Nobel Prize–winner Wole Soyinka is also noted for his biting cultural analyses. Other writers such as Ngugi wa Thiong'o and V. Y. Mudimbe have bridged gaps between creative writing, social criticism, and even philosophy.

Early concerns about authenticity, language of expression, and the need for a literature of protest have evolved over time in light of changing political, social, and aesthetic issues. It is clear, however, that the concerns of earlier periods have not entirely disappeared. This was made evident in a series of interviews published in 1984 reflecting how writers felt about the continuing need for social activism. Results from more than eighty-three writers interviewed indicated that the overwhelming majority still rejected the notion of "art for art's sake" and expressed in some way the need for African writers to be socially or politically involved, or to inform or educate the public.

The social involvement of African writers has been well documented over the years, as has their tendency to be social critics. This involvement in the form of a critique is reflected in the language issue that continues to be important for African writers seeking to balance the need to speak in their authentic voices with needing to reach publishing outlets that are largely outside of Africa. The fact that African literatures are expressed primarily in European languages has been called a "radical anomaly." There is a strong link between literature and language that has both cultural and ideological implications. As critic Abiola Irele (*The African Experience in Literature and Ideology*, 1981) states, "We cannot feel that we are in full possession of this literature so long as it is elaborated in a language that does not belong to us in an immediate and original way." Thus the third phase of African literature reveals a persistent and growing movement toward literary expression in African languages.

Also characteristic of this third phase is the emergence of national literatures. Rather than relating exclusively through their "Africanness" many writers have chosen to articulate their specificity in terms of a national literature shaped by their own country's political and social history. Kikuyu writer Ngugi Wa Thiong'o (Kerya) is one of the best known early proponents of both the use of African languages and the shift toward national literatures. He abandoned a successful writing career in English to devote himself to the production of local literary and theatrical productions in the Kikuyu language. Three of the most prolific African nations in terms of literary production are Nigeria, Ghana, and Senegal. Writers from these nations include many of those best known to the outside world: Chinua Achebe, Cyprian Ekwensi, Flora Nwapa, Wole Soyinka; Ama Ata Aidoo, Kofi Awoonor, Ayi Kwei Armah, Efua Sutherland; Mariama Ba, Cheikh Hamidou Kane, Amadou Kourouma, Sembene Ousmane, Léopold Sédar Senghor.

Circumstances during the colonial period did not favor female participation in the educational system.

As a result there is a conspicuous lack of participation by women as published writers until the third phase in the development of African literatures. This is ironic given that within the oral tradition women are widely recognized as principal purveyors of culture through narrative forms. Flora Nwapa is the earliest widely published woman writer. Her first novel, *Efuru*, appeared in 1966. Other women soon followed, including Mariama Ba, Aminata Sow Fall, Buchi Emecheta, Micere Githae Mugo, Rebeka Njau, Werewere Liking, and Ken Bugul, and Bessie Head and Ellen Kuzwayo of South Africa. Issues facing African women writers bear a strong similarity to those faced by women elsewhere in their struggle to carve out space within male-dominated territories. While most do not readily identify themselves as feminists, there is nonetheless a consensus that an association of African women writers is needed to create more access for women writing throughout Africa.

The historical relationship between African literatures and African American literary and social movements is extremely significant though little known. The *Harlem Renaissance that took place in New York in the 1920s directly inspired the authors of the *Negritude movement abroad and helped move modern African literature into its second phase. Negritude was the single most important literary movement of the pre-independence era. It began in France and spread throughout the French-speaking African world. It called for writers to carry out the vindication of African cultures that had been silenced by European cultural hegemony. The driving force of both the Harlem Renaissance and the Negritude movement emanated from their strong poetic traditions. Claude *McKay, a Harlem Renaissance poet, has even been identified by one critic as the real inventor of Negritude by virtue of his attacks on Christianity, technology, "reason," and anything that favored or legitimated *slavery, colonization, or social inferiority. Richard *Wright, another extremely influential writer of the period, became hugely popular among Negritude writers and activists abroad. Unfortunately, few critics have pursued comparative work on African and African American writers or developed studies that track literary connections. Most work of this kind has been published outside of the United States, whether in English or even in translation. One notable example is Alain Ricard's *Théâtre et nationalisme* (1972). Published in Paris, Ricard's study compares the work and significance of Wole Soyinka and LeRoi Jones (Amiri *Baraka). There remains much more comparative work to be done.

*Pan-Africanism, launched during the early years of this century by W. E. B. *Du Bois and others, also had a tremendous though indirect impact on the development of modern African literatures. The Pan-African movement is a unique brand of African nationalism wherein the national principal as it is typically understood can actually play a minor role. It is fundamentally a political and cultural movement for the liberation of African peoples from external domination. As a liberation movement, it played well into the activist ideologies of many English-speaking African writers. On the political side, Pan-Africanism was the driving force behind Kwame Nkrumah's Ghana, the first independent modern African nation. Pan-Africanist social ideology also influenced the consciousness of many English-speaking African writers. The overwhelming consensus that writers needed to be socially responsible was linked to the tenets of this movement.

All in all, the strongest literary influences seem to have moved from America to Africa and not the other way around. Other than perhaps Chinua Achebe and Wole Soyinka, few African authors are well known within African Americanist literary and critical circles. This is due in part to university curricula that do not tend to make room for African literatures within world or comparative literature frameworks. This is unfortunate since there is a high degree of resonance between African and African American literatures.

[*See also* Afrocentricity.]

• Bernard Lecherbonnier, *Initiation à la littérature négro-africaine*, 1977. R. Chemain and A. Chemain-Degrange, *Panorama critique de la littérature congolaise contemporaine*, 1979. Leon Fanoudh-Siefer, *Le mythe du nègre et de l'Afrique noire*, 1980. Abiola Irele, *The African Experience in Literature and Ideology*, 1981. Lee Nichols, *African Writers at the Microphone*, 1984. Adeola James, *In Their Own Voices*, 1990.

—JoAnne Cornwell

AFRICAN METHODIST EPISCOPAL BOOK CONCERN. *See* A.M.E. Book Concern.

AFRICAN–NATIVE AMERICAN LITERATURE. The literatures of African–Native Americans arose from African–Native American cultural communities created by Native American and African American slaves; from runaway African American or African–Native American slaves who created maroon nations or joined Native nations (especially Seminole); from the enslavement of African Americans by members of Cherokee and other Native nations; and from interactions between free or indentured African Americans and Native Americans throughout the United States. Thus began the development of a literature that expressed both African and Native American traditions, among the earliest of which were mixed folktales and mythologies. African Americans and Native Americans borrowed from each other's folktale traditions to create a body of African-Native folktales. African-Native mythologies were also developed; a Seminole creation myth, for example, was adapted to account for the creation of both Africans and Native Americans.

Among the early African–Native American writers were Paul *Cuffe (1759–1817), Wampanoag–African American; William Apess (1798–?), Pequot–African American; and Ann *Plato (early 1800s–?), African–Native American. Cuffe's autobiographical travel narrative documents his navigations, trade, and travel to Sierra Leone and argues against the slave trade in Africans. Apess, whose writings contain his fiery analyses and indictments of European American racism, published five works, including two *autobiographies, a *sermon, political *essays, and a eulogy of King Philip. Plato published one volume of *poetry and essays. In her poem "The Natives of America," there is a conversation between Plato and her father in which he relates his grief at the European colonization that has left him "roaming" without a nation. In the "Daughter's Inquiry," Plato writes to her father to return from this "roaming" to his family. "To the First of August" celebrates emancipation in the British West Indies.

Two nineteenth-century autobiographers, Okah Tubbee (1810–?), African-Choctaw, and James Beckwourth (1798–1866), African-European-Crow, spoke their autobiographies to a collaborating editor (Tubbee to his wife/editor Laah Ceil [1817–?], Mohawk-Delaware). As in many *slave narratives, a series of letters and attestations of character are appended to Tubbee's autobiography. The autobiography is also marked by a number of dreams—confessional and spiritual—narrated in Native American, African American, and European American Christian traditions. Beckwourth narrates much of his autobiography in the form of traditional Crow coup tales. Like many African-Native autobiographers, he negotiates his racial/cultural *identity depending upon his audience and circumstances.

In the early twentieth century, the poet Joseph Seamon *Cotter, Jr. (1895–1919), African-European-Native American, published *Band of Gideon* (1918) and sonnets in the *A.M.E. Zion Quarterly Review* before dying of tuberculosis. Olivia Ward *Bush-Banks (1869–1944), African-Montauk, attended powwows and was the Montauk tribal historian; she also lived in Harlem and dedicated her first published work to her African American community. Bush-Banks published two volumes of poetry, a play, and three essays; she also wrote many unpublished poems, plays, vignettes, sketches in black dialect, and an autobiography.

Among the many contemporary African–Native American writers are Alice *Walker (b. 1944) and Clarence *Major (b. 1936). In much of her published work, Walker has developed her African-Cherokee identity. In *Meridian* (1976), *The *Color Purple* (1982), and *Living by the Word* (1988), Walker discusses both the existence of African-Cherokee culture and the reasons for its denial. She cites *Black Elk Speaks*, explores the relationship of African American to Native American culture, and discusses African-Cherokee *folklore.

Clarence Major was born into an African-Cherokee family and community in Atlanta, Georgia. Two of Major's novels, *Such Was the Season* (1987) and *Painted Turtle: Woman with Guitar* (1988), and one book of poetry, *Some Observations of a Stranger at Zuni in the Latter Part of the Century* (1989), offer a substantial discussion of African–Native American identity. *Such* focuses on an African-Cherokee family and community. *Painted Turtle* explores the struggle for cultural definition, the oscillations between insider and outsider.

In *Some Observations*, Major uses both Zuni and English languages. He also writes about a "liberal" who wants to make a film about Gatumlati, an African-Cherokee woman, until the filmmaker discovers that she was not the "pure" Cherokee on which his "Cherokee" film insists. Major, along with many other African–Native American writers, struggles with the same issues while fashioning an identity in his writing and must negotiate the fixed racial/cultural boundaries that often do not allow a Cherokee to be part African American or even an African American to be part Cherokee. Their writing is a clear articulation of the cultural negotiations that take place within an African–Native American and demands an analysis from scholar of both African American and Native American literatures.

• William Loren Katz, *Black Indians: A Hidden Heritage,* 1986. Jonathan Brennan, "Speaking Cross Boundaries: An African/Native American Autobiography," *A/B: Auto/Biography Studies* 7.2 (Fall 1992): 219–238. Jack D. Forbes, *Africans and Native Americans: The Language of Race and the Evolution of Red-Black Peoples,* 1993. Sharon Holland, "If You Know I Have a History, You Will Respect Me: A Perspective on Afro–Native American Literature," *Callaloo* 17.1 (Feb. 1994): 334–350.   —Jonathan Brennan

AFROCENTRICITY is a philosophical and theoretical perspective, as distinct from a system, whose conceptual origins are attributed to a trilogy of works by Molefi Kete Asante. These books, *Afrocentricity* (1988), *The Afrocentric Idea* (1987), and *Kemet, Afrocentricity, and Knowledge* (1990), form the essential core of the idea that literary interpretation can be based on location. In the Afrocentrist's view, location takes several forms, including psychological, cultural, economic, and social positions. One is able to interpret a text, or in the language of Afrocentricity, locate a text by identifying the elements in it that reveal the author's personal location. The marking constituents of a textual, hence, personal location are found in the attitude, direction, and language of the text. It is possible to determine location, dislocation, and relocation by examining the text for centeredness, that is, the congruence between the writer's consciousness of agency and the display of that agency according to the marking constituents.

Based largely on the empirical works of several predecessors, Afrocentricity is among the most dynamic intellectual theories presented by African scholars. Seizing the opportunity to reinterpret much of what was written by early Africans in Africa and the Americas as Afrocentric, Molefi Kete Asante launched a decisive attempt to project a method found in the essence of African agency. Afrocentricity thus became a growing intellectual idea in the 1980s as scores of African American and African scholars adopted an Afrocentric orientation to data. Afrocentricity is generally opposed to theories that "dislocate" Africans to the periphery of human thought and experience. Consequently the adherents of the Afrocentric perspective find the historical works of Cheikh Anta Diop and Pathe Diagne and the linguistic works of Theophile Obenga and Moussa Lam locatable bases for their own works. Considerable weight is given in Afrocentricity to the Senegalese historical school of thought originated by Cheikh Anta Diop who found much of his intellectual authority in the massive works of Cheikh Amadou

Bamba, the most prolific African writer of the twentieth century.

Afrocentricity is a particular perspective for analysis that argues that subject relationship to data is a critical tool for assessing location. For example, to speak of classical music, theater, or dance is usually to refer to European music, theater, or dance. This means that Europe occupies all of the intellectual and artistic seats in such a situation and leaves no room for others, according to the Afrocentric school. When a university promotes a Department of Modern Languages, the Afrocentrist objection is that "modern" is usually defined as European and entire departments with such names exist with no Asian or African languages. In these examples the relationship to data of the European subject assumes universality when in fact it is a particularism.

In the Afrocentric view the problem of location takes precedence over the topic or the data under consideration. The argument is that Africans have been moved off of social, political, philosophical, and economic terms in most discourse in the West for half a millennium. When Africans are moved from stasis by the aggrandizement of Eurocentrism, Africa becomes an object rather than a subject. Consequently it becomes necessary to examine all data from the standpoint of Africans as subjects, human agents, rather than as objects in a European frame of reference if we are to understand African literary or dramatic expression. Afrocentricity has implications for fields as different as dance, economics, architecture, social work, literature, politics, and psychology. Scholars in these fields have written extensively about the motifs of location and the constituents of decenteredness in various areas.

A contradiction between concrete history and intellectual perspective produces a kind of incongruity called decenteredness. Thus when an African American writes from the viewpoint of Europeans who came to the Americas on the *Mayflower,* or when literary critics write of Africans as "the Other," Afrocentrists claim that Africans are being peripheralized, sometimes, by Africans themselves. Consequently continental Africans who speak of Mungo Park as the discoverer of the Niger River or who accept David Livingstone's naming of *Musi wa Tunya* as Victoria Falls as their own reality are dislocated. In such situations, the Afrocentrists call for a recentering or a re-locating of Africans in an agent position.

Afrocentrists contend that human beings cannot divest themselves of culture; they are either participating in their own historical culture or that of some other group. This does not mean that one has to be a participant in only one culture. One can participate in a multiplicity of cultural locations. However, the participation is itself the truth of the matter. One cannot not participate in culture.

Implications exist, however, for general studies outside of the African studies field. Use of terms such as "World War I" when it was chiefly a European war and the "Continent" in reference to the European continent are checked by the Afrocentrists as imperialistic. Thus, the need is for such terminology to be "recentered" in a human context that allows for the intellectual space to be shared by all human and cultural agents.

Afrocentrists accept the multiplicity of cultural centers and therefore do not negate Eurocentrism except where Eurocentrism promotes itself as universal. It is considered valid for those of European backgrounds, whatever their specific culture, to use literary allusions, tropes, and figures that emerge from that cultural center.

Metaphors of location and dislocation are the principal tools of analysis as events, situations, texts, phenomena, dreams, and authors are seen as displaying various levels of centeredness. To be centered is to be located as an agent instead of as the Other. Such a critical shift in thinking means that the Afrocentric perspective provides new insights and dimensions to the understanding of literary phenomena.

Contemporary issues in Afrocentric thinking have involved the explanation of psychological misorientation and disorientation, attitudes that affect Africans who consider themselves to be Europeans or who believe that it is impossible to be simultaneously African and human. Severe forms of this attitude have been labeled extreme misorientation by some Afrocentrists. Additional issues have been the influence of a centered approach to *education, particularly as it relates to the revision of the American educational curriculum.

A growing group of Afrocentric writers at major universities in Africa, South America, Europe, and North America has established several professional associations and journals. Principal Afrocentric journals include the prestigious *Journal of Black Studies, Imhotep,* the *International Journal of African Dance,* and the *Afrocentric Scholar.*

The principal center for the Afrocentric intellectual movement is the Temple University school of scholars, frequently referred to as the Temple Circle. Among the members of this group (in addition to Molefi Kete Asante) are Kariamu Welsh, C. T. Keto, Theophile Obenga, Ama Mazama, Abu Abarry, Aisha Blackshire-Belay, Nilgun Anadolu Okur, and Terry Kershaw. The Temple Circle features a strong emphasis on ancient Egyptian texts, aesthetics, behavior, *race, *gender, ethics, and culture. Afrocentric location theory is a key component of the interpretation of texts, data, and phenomena. Other important Afrocentrists include Errol Henderson of the University of Florida, Maulana Karenga of California State University, Marimba Ani of Hunter College, Linda James Myers of Ohio State University, and Wade Nobles. Martin Bernal of Cornell University and Sandra Van Dyke of Bloomfield College have also been called Afrocentrists because of their work. However, with doctoral students from every continent engaged in the study of African phenomena from an Afrocentric perspective, Temple University remains the core of this vibrant philosophical movement.

A number of centers, institutes, and professional organizations are related to the Afrocentric philosophy. Terry Kershaw directs the Center for Advanced Afrocentric Theory at Temple University; C. Tsehloane Keto directs the Institute of African American Affairs, an Afrocentric research unit, and Kariamu

Welsh Asante directs the International Institute for African Dance Research. A professional organization, the National Afrocentric Institute, is led by Don McNeely who is also the editor of its newsletter, *MA'AT.* Numerous other agencies and organizations not affiliated with the Temple school of Afrocentricity exist and are proliferating in urban communities in Africa, Europe, North America, and South America.

[*See also* African Literature; Black Aesthetic; Criticism, *article on* Criticism since 1965; Pan-Africanism.]

• Cheikh Anta Diop, *Civilization or Barbarism*, 1990. Maulana Karenga, *Introduction to Black Studies*, 1990. Jean Clinton, *Behind the Eurocentric Veils*, 1991. Innocent C. Onyewuenyi, *The African Origin of Greek Philosophy: An Exercise in Afrocentrism*, 1993. Marimba Ani, *Yurugu: An Africa Centered Critique of European Thought and Behavior*, 1994.
—Molefi Kete Asante

AI (b. 1947), poet. Born in Tucson, Arizona, the poet AI, pseudonym of Florence Anthony, looks to a complex American multicultural ancestry—a Japanese father and a mother part black, Choctaw, and Irish. Raised also in Las Vegas and San Francisco, she majored in Japanese at the University of Arizona and immersed herself in Buddhism. Currently based in Tempe, she has received awards from the Guggenheim Foundation, the National Endowment for the Arts, and various universities; she has also been a frequent reader-performer of her work.

So eclectic, not to say peaceable, an upbringing makes a striking contrast with the kind of *poetry that has won her ongoing attention. Her particular forte has been to adapt Robert Browning's dramatic monologue to her own purposes, poems whose different voices speak of fracture, violence, revenge, sexual hunger, as if to emphasize the human disorder both beneath (and often enough at the surface of) society.

Cruelty (1973) offers a run of soliloquies dealing with, among other things, suicide, abortion, female masturbation, hanging, child-beating, and the unpredictability of desire. AI's style of poetic utterance has from the outset rarely been other than tough-edged, in the words of an early critic, "as if she made her poem(s) with a knife." Little wonder that the title poem in *Cruelty* begins with an image of a dead wildcat. In *Killing Floor* (1978), a poem like "The Kid" assumes the voice of a boy-murderer, a natural-born killer, who methodically and pathologically destroys his entire family only to emerge sweet-faced and apparently unperturbed.

Sin (1986) attempts yet more complex personae—ruminations, for the most part, of men of power, Joe McCarthy to the Kennedy brothers. In "The Testament of J. Robert Oppenheimer" the note is transcendental, millennial, that of the Manhattan Project leader eventually troubled by the possibilities of nuclear mass-destruction. In "The Good Shepherd," however, the voice, more locally but no less chillingly, belongs to the anonymous mass-murderer of Atlanta's black youth. "Saturn . . . devours its children," says the killer. *Fate: New Poems* (1991) offers a

further gallery, equally dark, a speaking dead that includes General George Custer, Mary Jo Kopechne (now the bitter, retrospective party-girl), Elvis Presley, Lenny Bruce, and President Lyndon Johnson.

AI opens her fifth collection, *Greed* (1993), with "Riot Act, April 29, 1992," a poem spoken as if by an unnamed black rioter taken into police custody in South Central Los Angeles, who ruefully construes the looting and fires in the aftermath of Rodney King's beating as "the day the wealth finally trickled down." A similar bittersweet note runs through "Self Defense." Washington, D.C.'s mayor Marion Barry, sentenced for crack possession after an FBI setup, is forced to conclude, "That is how you hold the nigger down." In "Hoover, Edgar J.," law enforcement as paranoia has its say, the meanness at once racist, homophobic, class-loaded. The diatribe ends boastingly and bullyingly: "J. Edgar Hoover rules." Other monologue-poems equally offer markers for the times—whether in the voice of Jack Ruby, or of a witness to the Marcos regime in Manila, or of a street girl contemplating Mike Tyson and the Desiree Washington rape.

As always this amounts to a slightly stylized ventriloquy, creating an effect of distance, things seen at one remove. All has not by any means been praise; critics have on occasion thought the poetry monotone, close to mannerism, too determinedly dour or black-humored. But AI is not to be denied her own kind of verse Gothic, an America, a world, seen as though through disembodied witness and nothing if not at one with her slightly maverick status in contemporary African American poetry.

• Paula Giddings, ed., *When and Where I Enter: The Impact of Black Women on Race and Sex in America*, 1984. Cheryl A. Wall, ed., *Changing Our Own Words: Essays on Criticism, Theory, and Writing by Black Women*, 1989. Sandi Russell, *Render Me My Song: African-American Women Writers from Slavery to the Present*, 1990.
—A. Robert Lee

ALBERT, OCTAVIA V. ROGERS (1824–c. 1890), biographer of former slaves, educator, and community leader. Octavia Victoria Rogers Albert is best known for her volume of collected *slave narratives, *The House of Bondage, or Charlotte Brooks and Other Slaves* (1890). The collection assembles the brief narratives (as told to Albert) of seven former slaves whose earnest testimonies, Albert believed, exposed the brutality of slaveholding in general and the hypocrisy of Christian slaveholding in particular. But more importantly, the narratives demonstrated, according to Albert, the narrators' spiritual courage and strong Christian faith.

Albert was born a slave on 12 December 1824 in Oglethorpe, Georgia, but neither *slavery nor its far-reaching effects stifled her achievements. After the Civil War, she attended Atlanta University and became a teacher, interviewer, and researcher. Asserting that the complete story of slavery had not been told, she invited former slaves into her home, taught some to read and write, sang hymns and read scriptures to others, and encouraged them all to recount their histories, which she recorded.

In her comments, which weave a sympathetic and

outraged voice throughout the narratives, Albert decries the inhumanity of slavery and continually
raises the alarm over slaveholders who professed
Christian ideals of compassion and brotherhood;
they would carry the sin of slavery upon their souls.
But as much as Albert yearned to set straight the
record of the past, she also looked with optimism toward the future of the freed people. If they saved
their earnings, bought homes, educated their children, built up character, obeyed the laws of the country, served God, and protested injustices, their status
would improve.

Albert was married to the Reverend A. E. P. Albert.
She met him in 1873 during her first teaching assignment in Montezuma, Georgia, where he was teaching at the same school. They were married the following year on 21 October 1874 and moved to
Houma, Louisiana (where Albert conducted her interviews with former slaves). In 1877, her husband
was ordained a minister in the Methodist Episcopal
Church, and in 1878, Albert, who was a member of
the African Methodist Episcopal Church, converted
to her husband's denomination. She was baptized by
her husband.

Albert's husband and their only child, Laura T. F.
Albert, published *The House of Bondage* a few
months after the author's death as a serial story in
the *Southwestern Christian Advocate*. Its popularity
encouraged publication in book form as a memorial
to the author.

• Octavia V. Rogers Albert, *The House of Bondage*, 1893; rpt.
1988. Frances Smith Foster, *Written by Herself*, 1993.

—Jan Furman

ALEXANDER, MARGARET WALKER. *See* Walker,
Margaret.

ALFRADO. *See* Frado.

ALI, MUHAMMAD (b. 1942), prizefighter. Despite
the considerable achievements of such important African American athletes as Jesse Owens, Joe *Louis,
Wilma Rudolph, Jim Brown, and Jackie *Robinson,
the young brash prizefighter from Louisville, Kentucky, may very well have eclipsed their significance.
He surely eclipsed their fame as, at the height of his
career in the early and middle 1970s, Muhammad Ali
was, without question, the most famous African
American in history and among the five most recognized faces on the planet.

Born Cassius Marcellus Clay, Jr., in 1942 (named
after both his father and the famous Kentucky abolitionist), the gregarious, handsome, and extraordinarily gifted boxer garnered world attention by winning
a gold medal in the 1960 Olympics. He further
stunned the sports world by beating the heavily
favored Sonny Liston to win the heavyweight title
in 1964, and shocked white America by announcing right after that fight that he had joined the militant, antiwhite Nation of Islam, the Black Muslims,
whose most well-known figure was the fiery orator
*Malcolm X. He also announced that he was chang-
ing his name to Muhammad Ali. When he opposed
being drafted during the Vietnam War on religious

grounds and was subsequently convicted of violating
the Selective Service Act in 1967, he was denied a license to fight anywhere in the United States. He was,
at this time, among white America, probably the
most hated black public figure since heavyweight
boxing champion Jack *Johnson. After an exile of
three and a half years, Ali returned triumphantly to
boxing in 1970, even though he lost his title to Joe
Frazier in 1971. He eventually won back his title in
1974, and after losing it once in 1978 regained it
again later that year.

Ali exercised an extraordinary influence on African American culture in the 1960s, doing much to
keep the Nation of Islam popular in the black community after the assassination of Malcolm X in 1965.
He figured in the writings of such important 1960s
black literary figures as Amiri *Baraka, Eldridge
*Cleaver, Malcolm X, and Larry *Neal, not to men-
tion numerous black journalists and poets. He came
to symbolize black *manhood and masculinity, unbowed and uncompromising, adversarial and combative, a virtually one-person definition of African
American self-determination in the middle and late
1960s. But his boyish bragging and his poetic predictions of doom for his opponents made him an important public prefigure for the performance art of rap.
Ali's *autobiography, *The Greatest: My Own Story*,
was coauthored with Richard Durham and published
in 1975. Toni *Morrison served as the book's editor.

—Gerald Early

ALLEN, CLARISSA MINNIE THOMPSON (?–?),
educator and writer. Born into a middle-class family
in Columbia, South Carolina, Clarissa Minnie
Thompson was educated at the Howard School and
South Carolina State Normal School. She began
writing *essays for the *Christian Recorder* at an early
age. Thompson subsequently wrote and published
fiction and *poetry. Her versatility aligns her with
her contemporaries Frances Ellen Watkins *Harper
and Anna Julia *Cooper.

Three chapters of her *novel *Treading the Winepress, or A Mountain of Misfortune* were published in
the *Christian Recorder* in 1885 before the editorial
staff found the novel's theme unsuitable. The novel
centers on two aristocratic African American *families, the Tremains and the De Vernes, whose lives are
marked by romantic triangles, murder, and insanity.
The plot is often sensational, but the novel is one of
the earliest attempts to address African American
elitism and racial loyalty.

All forty chapters of *Treading the Winepress* were
subsequently published by an African American paper, the *Boston Advocate*, in 1885–1886. The novel
has never been published in book form. In her later
years Thompson was very critical of her earlier approach to serious social concerns.

Thompson continued to write as she made teaching her lifelong profession and eventually served as
principal of the Poplar Grove School in Abbeville,
South Carolina. In 1886 Thompson left South Carolina to teach in Texas, where her temperance poem,
"A Glass of Wine," was published in the *Blade*. The

Dallas Enterprise published her novella *Only a Flirtation.*

Thompson was a loyal contributor to the African American press and often used the pseudonym Minnie Myrtle when submitting *letters and poetry.

• Monroe Majors, *Noted Negro Women*, 1971. Ann Allen Shockley, *Afro-American Women Writers (1746–1933)*, 1988.
—Kimberly Wallace Sanders

ALLEN, RICHARD (1760–1831), Philadelphia preacher, church founder, and social leader. Born a slave in the household of a prominent Philadelphian, Richard Allen was sold to a Delaware farmer who allowed him and his brother to work as day laborers to purchase their *freedom. In Delaware, Allen also encountered exhorters of the Methodist Society, then still affiliated with the Church of England. The antislavery position of the Methodists attracted him, while their inspiration led him to teach himself to read and write and to feel a spiritual awakening, described at the outset of his *autobiography, *The Life, Experience and Gospel Labors of the Rt. Rev. Richard Allen* (1833; rpt. 1960). His 1786 return to Philadelphia introduced him to Absalom Jones, an African American preacher some years his senior, and to African Americans who were hungry for social and religious leadership in their home city. The Methodist emphasis on inner faith and weekly meetings of the faithful nourished Allen's compatriots in times that were frequently trying. Still, at Saint George's Church, an institution African American Philadelphians had supported with their labor and donations, the lay exhorter Allen found himself and his fellow African American worshipers segregated and ultimately ousted from their seats during a service. In response, in 1787, Allen and Jones formed the Free African Society, a benevolent association that evolved into the Bethel Church. In 1799 Allen was ordained by famed Methodist bishop Francis Asbury. During the War of 1812, Allen helped organize twenty-five hundred African Americans who constructed bulwarks to safeguard Philadelphia. African Methodist Episcopal (AME) congregations multiplied until in 1816 their religious leaders established a separate denomination. Allen became the first AME bishop. As this branch of African American *religion grew under his care, he also worked as a master shoemaker, organized schools for African American children, denounced both *slavery and colonizationist schemes to expatriate African Americans, and aided the first African American newspaper, *Freedom's Journal.* To Allen fell the task of preaching execution sermons for African American Philadelphians condemned by the state.

Allen's sermons, addresses, devotional pieces, and autobiography constitute an important chapter in American writing. Charity, the first of Christian virtues, wrote Allen, should orient white Americans to the bodily and spiritual needs of African Americans, including the need for freedom. With Jones, he recounted African Americans' charitable services during the raging yellow fever of 1793—aiding the sick, caring for orphans, burying the dead—and bitterly noted that not only had whites lied about a supposed African immunity to the disease, but also scorned and insulted their African American benefactors once the epidemic ebbed. Faith and the experience of racial inequities led Allen to an African American reconstruction of Christianity premised upon the conviction that since the gospel addresses the needs of the oppressed, a gospel that serves oppressors is merely a human creation, not a divine one. The expression of this religious reconstruction in his writings and in African American institutions was the genius of Allen's life.

[*See also* Churches; Literary History, *article on* Colonial and Early National Era; Sermons and Preaching.]

• Charles H. Wesley, *Richard Allen: Apostle of Freedom*, 2d ed., 1969. Carol V. R. George, *Segregated Sabbaths: Richard Allen and the Emergence of Independent Black Churches, 1760–1840*, 1973.
—John Saillant

ALLEN, SAMUEL W. (b. 1917), poet, educator, translator, and lawyer. Born in Columbus, Ohio, Samuel Allen (also known as Paul Vesey) studied creative writing under James Weldon *Johnson at Fisk where he graduated magna cum laude in 1938. He received his JD from Harvard in 1941. Until 1968 when he formally left law for literature, he was active in both fields.

He was drafted into the U.S. Armed Services in 1942 and served as an officer, though under the constraints of the segregated system, until 1946. From 1946 to 1947 he was deputy assistant district attorney in New York City. The following year he studied humanities at the New School for Social Research. In 1948 he went to Paris on the GI Bill, and after studying French, studied at the Sorbonne. He was employed variously with the U.S. Armed Forces from 1951 to 1955, as historian, claims officer, and civilian attorney in Wiesbaden, Germany, and in France. After a brief private law practice in Brooklyn, Allen taught law at Texas Southern University from 1958 to 1960. During the Kennedy and Johnson administrations, he served in Washington, D.C., as assistant general counsel in the U.S. Information Agency from 1961 to 1964, and as chief counsel in the U.S. Community Relations Service from 1965 to 1968.

Aided by Richard *Wright in Paris, Allen first published poetry in 1949 in *Présence Africaine*. Upon leaving France to film *Native Son*, Wright asked Allen to take over his role of editing the journal's English materials. Thus Allen became acquainted with that journal's circle of writers and thinkers with whom he shared an enduring commitment to African culture. Allen's interest in francophone African poetry prompted his translating Sartre's *Orphée noir* for *Présence Africaine*. In the early 1950s, more than a decade ahead of American receptivity for such ideas, Allen tried in vain to interest American editors in the writers and ideas represented by *Présence Africaine* (Ellen Conroy Kennedy, *The Negritude Poets*, 1975; 1989). Among other works Allen published in *Présence Africaine* was the influential and frequently reprinted "Negritude and Its Relevance to the American Negro Writer" (1959), which he delivered that same year at the New York Black Writers'

Conference. Georg Dickenberger early pointed out that Allen's own *poetry reflects the dual consciousness of Africa and America and called him "the first of a new generation" ("Paul Vesey," *Black Orpheus*, Oct. 1958). In 1956 in Germany, Allen's first book of poetry appeared under the pen name Paul Vesey, the name by which many already knew his poetry. The book, *Elfenbein Zähne* (*Ivory Tusks*), consists of twenty poems that appear in both English and German and an afterword by Janheinz Jahn, one of the foremost European Africanists of his day. Many of these poems still rank among his finest. Ezekiel Mphahlele, celebrated South African novelist and critic, quotes Allen as having once said of "The Staircase," "Upon it . . . I would rest my case . . . and that of the Negro in this land" (*Voices in the Whirlwind*, 1972).

After being published mostly in Europe where he was living from 1948 to the mid-1950s, Allen's poetry was not widely known in the United States until the 1960s when his poems began appearing in anthologies by Arna *Bontemps (1963) and Langston *Hughes (1964). In 1962 he coedited, introduced, and contributed to *Pan-Africanism Reconsidered*. In 1968 his second book of poetry, *Ivory Tusks and Other Poems*, was published, though in a limited edition. Even though it shares the title and the title poem with Allen's first book, most of the poems are new.

Since 1968, except for pro bono work for many good causes, Allen's career has been entirely literary. He was Avalon Professor of Humanities from 1968 to 1970 at Tuskegee Institute and visiting professor at Wesleyan University the following year. He taught African and African American literature at Boston University from 1971 until retiring in 1981. Over a two-year period he conducted a writers' workshop on a volunteer basis at Massachusetts Correctional Institute in Norfolk. Eugene *Redmond has called Allen's 1971 essay, "The African Heritage" in *Black World*, a "brilliant and cogent" statement of black artistic expression rooted in Africa (*Drumvoices*, 1976). In 1973 Allen edited *Poems from Africa*, a collection illustrated by Romare Beardon and introduced by Allen, who also translated some of the poems. In 1975 his third book of poetry, *Paul Vesey's Ledger*, appeared as the last of Paul Breman's Heritage series. Written in the three years after Allen stopped practicing law, these poems are intense responses to the suffering, courage, and vitality of both famous and nameless African Americans. The stance is often ironic with the tone varying from elegiac to angry and prophetic. Allen has continued writing, giving readings throughout the United States and abroad, and conducting workshops. He had an NEA Creative Writing Fellowship in Poetry (1979–1980) and residence grants from the Wurlitzer Foundation in Taos and the Rockefeller Foundation Conference and Study Center in Bellagio, Italy. His poetry has been included in over two hundred anthologies, and his work has been translated into French and Italian as well as German.

Every Round and Other Poems (1987) makes available most of Allen's previously published poems as well as excellent new ones. One can trace reworkings of earlier poems and subjects as in "Nat Turner or Let Him Come." More importantly, one can experience the depth and impressive scope; the humor, the outrage, and the humanity; and the consistency of a vision rooted in his African American heritage and experience. One of the poets included in Woodie *King, Jr.'s *The Forerunners: Black Poets in America* (1975), poets whom Addison *Gayle, Jr., terms the literary godparents of those emerging in the 1960s, Samuel Allen has stayed relevant. Although Allen is known and respected among scholars, his poetry calls out for a wider audience and the extensive critical attention it has yet to receive.

• Ruth L. Brittin, "Samuel W. Allen," in *DLB*, vol. 41, *Afro-American Poets since 1955*, eds. Trudier Harris and Thadious M. Davis, 1985, pp. 8–17.

—Mary Hughes Brookhart

ALLEN, SARAH A. *See* Hopkins, Pauline E.

ALLEN, WILLIAM G. (?–?), professor and journalist. After graduating from Oneida Institute in 1844 and studying law in Boston, William Allen became Professor of the Greek and German Languages, and Rhetoric and Belles-Lettres at New York Central College, in McGrawville, joining two other professors of African American descent, Charles L. *Reason and George B. *Vashon, in what apparently was the country's first interracial college faculty. Allen briefly edited the *National Watchman* in Troy, New York, in the 1840s, contributed *letters to the *Liberator*, and wrote an *essay on Placido, the martyred Cuban poet, published in the 1853 *Autographs for Freedom*.

In April 1851, while lecturing in Fulton, New York, Allen met the daughter of his white abolitionist host, Mary King, who subsequently attended college in McGrawville, where their friendship grew romantic. On 30 January 1853, while Allen was visiting Mary at her parents' home in Fulton to discuss marriage, a mob gathered to prevent "amalgamation" in their fair city. In *The American Prejudice Against Color* (1853), his bitter, sardonic commentary on the affair, Allen attacks the "mob spirit" and "malignant character" of American prejudice that made "respectable" citizens want to tar and feather him and roll him in an empty barrel spiked with nails. The townsmen's patronizing treatment of Mary, whom they felt obliged to rescue from her errant path, also receives Allen's scornful treatment. Most pointedly, Allen attacks the hypocrisy of "Abolitionists and Christians" whose prejudice he likens to the "bondage" of southern *slavery. Narrowly escaping the lynch mob, Allen met Mary two months later in New York City, where they quietly married on 30 March. Ten days later the couple left for England, fleeing what Allen would call in his book—published later that year in London—"American Caste and skin-deep Democracy."

• Benjamin Quarles, *Black Abolitionists*, 1969. R. J. M. Blackett, *Building an Antislavery Wall*, 1983.

—Brad S. Born

All God's Dangers, which won a National Book Award in 1974, is a collaboration between an illiterate tenant farmer and a Harvard graduate student. In 1969, the student, Theodore Rosengarten, met the farmer, Ned *Cobb, while researching an Alabama sharecroppers' union. In explaining why he joined the union, the eighty-four-year-old Cobb (named Nate Shaw in *All God's Dangers* for "protection and privacy") told eight hours' worth of stories that "built upon one another so that the sequence expressed the sense of a man 'becoming.'"

Beginning his story in the late nineteenth century, Nate Shaw gives an account of his lineage that reveals "the way of life that [he] was born and raised to." He makes it apparent that his upbringing suffered from social customs gathered from "slavery time days," which turned his "daddy" and others in his family into sharecroppers with a poor sense of worth. The local culture, Shaw indicates, consisted of a racial hierarchy that placed "colored farmers" under the authority of "white landlords." His relatives and neighbors should have received *freedom from bondage at the end of the Civil War, when his father was fifteen, but "what they got wasn't what they wanted, it wasn't freedom, really." As in *slavery, they found themselves expected "to do whatever the white man directed em to do" without saying a word about "their heart's desire."

While his father resigns himself "to take what come and live for today" and thus simply manages to eke out a living, Shaw, inspired by his grandmother, looks for more out of life. He imagines that skill and diligence can help him to rise in the world "like a boy climbin a tree." By 1931, known throughout his region for his work ethic, he says, "I was doin as well as any poor colored man could do in this country." He has a wife and ten children at the time, lives in a "pretty good old house," and owns two mules as well as two cars. Undoubtedly, he seems set for continued success.

But as boys slip and fall from trees, Shaw takes a step that causes him to lose prestige and much more. One December day in 1932, after joining the Sharecroppers Union, full of pride and emboldened by the union's teachings yet virtually alone, Shaw opposes the efforts of four deputy sheriffs to confiscate a neighbor's property for the benefit of a white landlord. A violent struggle follows; it leaves Shaw wounded and under arrest. He is convicted of a felony in court and sentenced to twelve years in prison.

Shaw serves his time stoically. When he is set free, he returns to a home in disrepair. His wife dying, his children scattered, he has paid a dear price for his act of defiance. Still, he maintains his old outlook. He resumes working on the farm and looking for ways to prosper with dignity. Regardless of others' opinions, Shaw thinks that he has done good for his people by taking his stand and suffering the consequences.

All God's Dangers reflects a literary convention that emerged in the eighteenth century and continues to evolve. Works in this tradition regret that time and again American society has denied African Americans a fair chance to succeed. Looking back to the *slave narratives and forward to prominent texts such as *Up from Slavery* (1901), *Black Boy* (1945), and The *Autobiography of Malcolm X* (1965), *All God's Dangers* exemplifies African American life

stories, contending that anyone in an evenhanded society can realize honor and well-being through a commitment to ingenuity and enterprise.

[*See also* Autobiography, *article on* Secular Autobiography.]

• William Nichols, "This Old 'ism'," *The American Scholar* 44 (Spring 1975): 310–314. Albert E. Stone, "Two Recreate One," in *Autobiographical Occasions and Original Acts: Versions of American Identity from Henry Adams to Nate Shaw*, 1982, pp. 231–264.   —Roland L. Williams, Jr.

AMANUENSIS. An amanuensis represents in written form what another dictates. Throughout the history of African American *autobiography, amanuenses have played important roles in transcribing the narratives of persons who were either preliterate or not confident of their abilities to express themselves adequately in writing. Most early African American autobiographies, such as *A Narrative of the Life and Adventures of Venture A Native of Africa* (1798), got into print as a result of a collaboration between the subject of the text and an amanuensis. In general these amanuenses were whites who acknowledge in their prefaces that they not only took down what was related to them but also "arranged" or "improved" it to suit their own standards. During the first half of the nineteenth century, white abolitionists, among them the noted poet John Greenleaf Whittier, served as amanuenses for unlettered fugitive slave narrators. Frederick *Douglass considered using white assistance in creating *Narrative of the Life of Frederick Douglass* (1845) but decided that his autobiography would have greater authenticity if he wrote it himself. Most major African American autobiographers since the mid-nineteenth century followed Douglass's example and eschewed the use of an amanuensis. But The *Autobiography of Malcolm X* (1965), written by Alex *Haley, and *All God's Dangers* (1974), transcribed by Theodore Rosengarten from the oral storytelling of Ned *Cobb, testify to the continuing collaboration with amanuenses in recent African American autobiography. Sherley Anne *Williams's *Dessa Rose* (1986) offers a fictional portrayal of a combative relationship between a sinister white amanuensis and a female slave insurrectionist.

[*See also* Autobiography, *article on* Secular Autobiography; Slave Narrative.]

• Albert E. Stone, "Two Recreate One: The Act of Collaboration in Recent Black Autobiography—Ossie Guffy, Nate Shaw, Malcolm X," in *Autobiographical Occasions and Original Acts*, 1982, pp. 231–264. William L. Andrews, *To Tell a Free Story: The First Century of Afro-American Autobiography, 1760–1865*, 1986.   —William L. Andrews

A.M.E. BOOK CONCERN. Established in 1817 by Richard *Allen to publish and distribute books necessary for the mission and management of the African Methodist Episcopal Church, the A.M.E. Book Concern may be the first African American *publishing company. The Book Concern's first publications were church disciplines, ledgers, church histories, hymnals, and Sunday school materials. In 1841, the Concern initiated the *Monthly Magazine*, the first of several literary periodicals. The *Christian Recorder, begun in 1852 as a weekly newspaper, continues in an altered form to the present, thereby claiming distinction as the oldest continuous African American newspaper. Despite financial and other obstacles, the Concern took on increasingly ambitious projects and was incorporated in 1855. Operating under the concept that "books and newspapers are the educators of this century," the Book Concern established a bookstore, supervised itinerant salespeople, and expanded its publications to include autobiographies, fiction, *poetry, philosophical and political *essays, as well as theological treatises.   —Chanta M. Haywood

Amen Corner, The. James *Baldwin's *The Amen Corner* did not reach Broadway until 1965, twelve years after its completion. A morality play echoing his novel *Go Tell It on the Mountain* (1953), *The Amen Corner* has a laborious history. Although the play failed to generate professional interest, writer Owen *Dodson directed a student production at Howard University in 1955. It opened at the Ethel Barrymore Theatre a decade later on 15 April 1965 under Lloyd Richards's direction.

The drama critiques the *church's role in African Americans' lives. Center stage are Sister Margaret, the pastor of a Pentecostal church; Luke, her estranged husband; David, their son; Odessa, Margaret's sister; and church members. Described by the author as a "tyrannical matriarch," Margaret applies a harsh, Calvinistic doctrine to her family and parishioners. However, she fails to heed her opening sermon, "Set thine house in order." Instead, she journeys to Philadelphia to resuscitate a "wicked" church, ignoring threats at home: the "Elders" of her congregation raise questions about her financial and domestic matters; the jazz-playing Luke returns to make amends before dying; and David questions the righteous path that his mother imposes. We also learn that Margaret left Luke after the death of their baby, which Margaret took as a sign from God concerning her marriage to an incontrovertible "sinner." Margaret appears in limbo when Luke dies, David flees, and the church deposes her. However, she finds redemption after acknowledging her rigid Christianity: "It ain't all in the singing and the shouting. It ain't all in the reading of the Bible."

The Amen Corner reflects many of Baldwin's own religious experiences; thus, he deftly incorporates gospel *music and *sermons and preaching. Like *dramas such as T. S. Eliot's *Murder in the Cathedral* and Arthur Miller's *The Crucible*, Baldwin's play foregrounds the powerful role of *religion and problematizes "good" and "evil." One of the few African American dramas about the church, *The Amen Corner* is still widely performed.

• Therman B. O'Daniel, ed., *James Baldwin: A Critical Evaluation*, 1977. C. W. E. Bigsby, *The Second Black Renaissance: Essays in Black Literature*, 1980.   —Keith Clark

American Hunger. See Black Boy.

AMINI, JOHARI (b. 1935), poet, essayist, short story writer, and chiropractor. Johari Amini, born Jewel Christine McLawler to William and Alma (Bazel) McLawler on 13 January 1935 in Philadelphia, Pennsylvania, changed her name after her consciousness-raising by Haki R. *Madhubuti (then Don L. Lee), whom she met as a thirty-two-year-old freshman at Wilson Junior College. Johari is Swahili for "Jewel," and Amini is Swahili for "honesty and fidelity." Amini believes that the meaning of a name becomes an inherent part of the person carrying that name, and she wanted names that would reflect her personality and her values of honesty and fidelity— values that she lived by and that she wanted her writings to convey.

Amini's meeting Madhubuti was the beginning of a long literary and political association, which is demonstrated in her poetic style as well as in her social criticism. She was a staff member of the Institute of Positive Education, and she was assistant, then associate, editor of *Third World Press and *Black Books Bulletin*, institutions that Madhubuti founded. Amini's sociopolitical consciousness-raising is quite evident in her *poetry, *essays, book and movie reviews, and monographs on health. Her writings exhibit the essence of African American womanhood and the survival of African Americans. Gwendolyn *Brooks praises the poet for understanding the "rubble and mire of society" and then conveying that understanding to others (*Let's Go Somewhere*, 1970). Amini feels that her personal and professional responsibility is fulfilled when she is advising her people through her writings. This concern for her people is her reason for returning to college to become a chiropractor. For Amini, being a chiropractor as well as a writer is a necessary asset for helping African Americans.

The concerns of Amini the poet are the concerns of Amini the woman. These are expressed in a poetic essay entitled "Letter to a Blkwoman's Daughter, Written to Marcia," presumably Amini's daughter Marciana. The letter cautions the daughter about the imperative to define one's blackness, to claim and to affirm one's *identity. Doing so is a vital part of a person's survival. Amini has declared in several forums that she is an African American first, then a writer.

Amini and the 1960s poets felt compelled to affirm their blackness as they rejected America's racist society. To demonstrate their defiance and to make their protest more effective, the poets rejected the traditional themes, forms, and language of American poetry. They demanded that their voices be heard, so they used features attributed to the vernacular of African Americans—multiple negation, zero copula, the invariant "be," zero possessives, clipped verb endings, slang vocabulary, unorthodox spelling and capitalization, zero punctuation, and abbreviated words. The rhythmic cadence of the poetry was not the iambic pentameter or other such metrical patterns but free verse with words scattered randomly across the printed page. These nontraditional rhetorical strategies demanded attention in order to convey the urgent message of protest against the inequality and injustices in America. Although Amini uses these nontraditional linguistic strategies, she adamantly cautions that students be taught formal English so that they will be able to function in contemporary society. (She has taught composition and African American literature in colleges in Chicago.) While Amini does not view her linguistic strategies as a part of her political stance, she agrees that the political stance manifested in her writing is who she is; her words reflect the very essence of her being an African American woman in today's society.

Amini's poetry collections are *Images in Black* (1967), *Black Essence* (1968), *A Folk Fable* (1969), *Let's Go Somewhere* (1970), and *A Hip Tale in Earth Style* (1972). Her poems and short stories are included in many journals and anthologies. Her essays in *An African Frame of Reference* (1972) theorize that one's values predetermine one's behavior. Amini's training as a psychologist gives her added insight as to how the larger society imposes its values on African Americans to their psychological detriment. Her interest in the whole person motivated her to write *A Commonsense Approach to Eating* (1975). It is obvious in her writings that Amini's touchstone is African Americans' survival. She emphasizes that survival will come only as people know their identity, which is an absolute priority for survival. Perhaps now that she is a practicing chiropractor in Atlanta, Georgia, Amini will again spew bullet words, for her poetry and essays—even her short stories—provide insightful knowledge that African Americans need.

• Sonia Sanchez, review of *Black Essence*, *Negro Digest* 18 (Apr. 1969): 91–92. Gwendolyn Brooks, introduction to *Let's Go Somewhere*, 1970. Sarah Webster Fabio, review of *Let's Go Somewhere*, *Black World* 20 (Dec. 1970): 68, 98. Eugene Redmond, *Drumvoices: The Mission of Afro-American Poetry*, 1976. Fahamisha Patricia Brown, "Johari M. Amini," in *DLB*, vol. 41, *Afro-American Poets since 1955*, eds. Trudier Harrris and Thadious M. Davis, 1985.   —Margaret Ann Reid

ANCESTORS. A common word in general parlance, "ancestors" is a relatively newly articulated concept in African American literary creation and studies, though, like the *blues, the basic idea has been around for a long time. In "Rootedness: The Ancestor as Foundation," Toni *Morrison asserts that the presence of an ancestor figure is one of the defining characteristics of African American literature, whether that ancestor is a grandfather, as in Ralph *Ellison's *Invisible Man* (1952), or the healer, *Minnie Ransom, in Toni Cade *Bambara's The *Salt Eaters* (1980). The important point is that ancestors "are sort of timeless people whose relationships to the characters are benevolent, instructive, and protective, and they provide a certain kind of wisdom." The idea of ancestors gained momentum particularly in critical discussion of Morrison's own novels. There is frequently an individual, often female, who guides members of the younger generation in some way. Characters such as M'Dear and Aunt Jimmy in The *Bluest Eye* (1970), Ondine and Sydney in *Tar Baby* (1981), and *Baby Suggs in *Beloved* (1987) may be viewed as ancestors. So may the shadowy female images that haunt *Jadine Childs in *Tar Baby*, for she is clearly painted as a person estranged from her heritage; according to the washerwoman, Thérèse, Jadine has forgotten her "ancient properties." The concept of ancestor perhaps applies best to *Pilate Dead

in *Song of Solomon* (1977). From romantic and realistic perspectives, Pilate is a person enviously in tune with the ancestral spirit of those who have spawned her, represented by the ghost of her dead father, as well as capable of imagining what lies ahead, reflected in *Milkman Dead, who gently guides her into the unknown but embraceable possibilities of the future.

• Toni Morrison, "Rootedness: The Ancestor as Foundation," in *Black Women Writers (1950–1980): A Critical Evaluation*, ed. Mari Evans, 1984, pp. 339–345.   —Trudier Harris

ANDERSON, MARIAN (1897–1993), recitalist, opera singer, and diplomat. Marian Anderson's 1939 concert at the Lincoln Memorial, in Washington, D.C., marked the symbolic beginning of the *civil rights movement. Born to a poor family in Philadelphia, Anderson came to public attention in 1924 as the winner of a New York Philharmonic voice competition. Because the *color line impeded American bookings, the contralto studied and performed in Europe for several years. In 1935, the impresario Sol Hurok brought Anderson back for a successful New York concert. Thereafter, she toured the United States as an acclaimed soloist and sang at the White House in 1936. In 1939, the Daughters of the American Revolution (DAR) refused to allow the singer to perform at Constitution Hall, stating explicitly that their auditorium was available to "white artists only." First Lady Eleanor Roosevelt publicly resigned from the DAR in protest. African American leaders from Howard University and from the NAACP arranged for Anderson to sing instead at the Lincoln Memorial on Easter Sunday. Broadcast over national radio and attended by 75,000 people, the recital was a symbolic triumph that inspired a generation of African American activists and artists. Never a political activist, Marian Anderson nonetheless continued to overturn racial barriers. In 1955, thirty-one years after her New York debut, she became the first African American to sing a role at the Metropolitan Opera. In 1957, she toured India and Asia as a singer and cultural ambassador for the U.S. Department of State; later, President Dwight D. Eisenhower appointed her an alternate representative to the Human Rights Committee of the United Nations. Anderson performed at the inaugurations of Presidents Eisenhower and John F. Kennedy, and in 1963 she returned to the Lincoln Memorial to sing at the March on Washington for Jobs and Freedom. She received the Presidential Medal of Freedom in 1963 and gave her farewell concert in 1965.

[*See also* Music.]

• Marian Anderson, *My Lord, What a Morning: An Autobiography*, 1956; rpt. 1984. Allan Keiler, *Marian Anderson: A Singer's Journey*, forthcoming 1997.   —Scott A. Sandage

ANDERSON, MIGNON HOLLAND (b. c. 1945), short story writer, editor, and member of the Fisk University Writers Workshop conducted by John O. Killens (1966). Although there are almost no biographical sources on Mignon Holland Anderson, it is clear that as an apprentice writer during the late

1960s she received support, direction, and encouragement from John O. *Killens and his wife Grace and from Haki R. *Madhubuti. Anderson pays homage to the Killenses in her collection of short stories, *Mostly Womenfolk and a Man or Two* (1976). This collection was well advertised in *Black Books Bulletin* and published by *Third World Press, both principally edited and organized by Madhubuti. Like a number of aspiring writers in groups such as Chicago's Organization of Black American Culture (OBAC) Writers Workshop, Anderson, as a student at Fisk (1963– c. 1967), took advantage of the experience of established writers like John Killens.

After her work with the Fisk Writers Workshop, Anderson moved to New York and was employed by the *New Yorker.* By 1968 she had left the *New Yorker* to devote more time to writing. The short story that may have resulted from this period of concentration is "In the Face of Fire I Will Not Turn Back." The narrator of this story is a symbol of the evolution of African American women from Africa to America. In the fashion of a monologue or soliloquy, the narrator characterizes her ability to survive and care for her family through captivity, the *Middle Passage, *slavery, the joblessness and despair of her husband, and her struggle to do domestic work for whites while her own family suffers. Through this evolutionary description of survival, the speaker celebrates the advent of the 1960s, a new era in which African Americans reclaim their African heritage and protest their mistreatment with the promise of fire.

The evolution of black men and women provides the structure for *Mostly Womenfolk and a Man or Two.* Anderson describes the setting of this collection, the Eastern Shore of Virginia, as being inhabited first by Native Americans and then changed by European encroachment. The historical development of the Eastern Shore is paralleled in the stories by the stages of the characters' lives from birth to death. Taken together, the stories suggest that birth and death are connected in an inevitable chain characterized by the African American struggle to survive against poverty, ignorance, fear, and bigotry. The first section of stories, organized under the heading "Born," evolves from the voice of a woman describing the night she conceived to a portrait of the birth of her daughter Nora. To heighten the impact of fetal consciousness prior to birth, Anderson, in "Momma's Child," portrays an all-knowing voice describing the parents as they make love. In the sections on birth and childhood, Anderson suggests that birth occurs on several levels: physical, sexual, and spiritual. A recurring theme of the struggle to achieve spiritual awareness begins in the birth and childhood sections as characters try to arrive at a self-image free of color consciousness. All of these stages are necessary to prepare for the struggle of adulthood, which Anderson presents through the eyes of a soldier in Vietnam ("Thicket"), a mortician ("The Real Hidden Meaning of Undertaking"), and an African captured in slavery ("Grief"). Their disparate roles do not obscure Anderson's intent: to demonstrate the irony, vulnerability, and alienation in being a victim of racism. In "Thicket" and "The Real Hidden

Meaning," the characters recognize that as African Americans, they have no legal protection against white *violence. Although he is congratulated for killing a Vietnamese, the soldier will be punished according to the law for striking a fellow white soldier who endangered the lives of the entire troop. The undertaker is openly confronted with death for using legal means to protect his daughter against racist attacks at school. In the final section, Anderson shows that death is no less complex than racism. Through the characters who confront death, she blurs the line between chronological age and experience. "November" and "The Funeral" are seen from the perspective of a child who, at first, seeks comfort at the death of a friend and finally is the source of comfort as she holds on to and encourages an elderly man to cry over the death of his grandson. Throughout this collection, Anderson infuses character, language, and setting with southern folk beliefs and idioms. There is also an allegorical quality about these stories; the characters represent the life cycles with which many African Americans have struggled. In his review of this collection, George Kent cautions the reader not to rely solely on traditional views of the short story. In her edition of Kevin Dounuts's *Doomed to Die: A Lonely Walk* (1993) Anderson has continued to break new ground by appealing to children with a nonfictional work about AIDS.

[*See also* Short Story.]

• Mignon Holland Anderson, "In the Face of Fire I Will Not Turn Back," *Negro Digest* 17 (Aug. 1968): 20–23. George Kent, review of *Mostly Womenfolk and a Man or Two, Black Books Bulletin* 4.4 (Winter 1976): 52–53.

—Australia Tarver

ANDREWS, RAYMOND (1934–1991), novelist, essayist, and winner of first James Baldwin Prize. Raymond Andrews was born near Madison, Georgia, in Morgan County, the fourth of ten children born to sharecropping parents George and Viola Andrews. He helped with the farm work and absorbed the ambience of rural living that was to color his later writings. Andrews left home at fifteen and worked at a variety of jobs while beginning to write. He eventually took a position in New York City with an airline, a job that enabled him to travel extensively in the United States and Europe.

Raymond Andrews's first published piece was an article on baseball, which appeared in *Sports Illustrated* in 1975. In 1976, *Ataraxia*, a small journal edited by Phillip Lee Williams and Linda Williams, excerpted a section from the novel *Appalachee Red*, which was published in its entirety by Dial Press (1978). *Appalachee Red*, winner of the first James *Baldwin Prize, was followed by *Rosiebelle Lee Wildcat Tennesee* (1980) and *Baby Sweet's* (1983), completing the trilogy about life in the fictional Muskhogean County, Georgia. After Dial Press was closed by its parent group, Doubleday Press, Andrews's books were out of print until 1987, when they were picked up and reprinted by the Brown Thrasher imprint of the University of Georgia Press. Andrews subsequently went to Peachtree Press to publish his next two books, *The Last Radio Baby: A Memoir* (1991) and *Jessie and Jesus and Cousin Clare* (1991). Peachtree Press plans to publish *Once Upon a Time in Atlanta*, also a memoir, written about the years after Andrews left Madison and moved to Atlanta. Andrews also left manuscripts for two additional novels; their publishing future is unknown.

Andrews's unique style owes a great deal to the cadences of rural southern speech; he noted in the preface to the 1987 edition of *Appalachee Red* that his "American roots (like those of most Afro-Americans) are southern rural." He reported that his earliest favorite writers were Erskine Caldwell, William Faulkner, Sinclair Lewis, and John Steinbeck. Indeed, Andrews remarked that the character Pirate in Steinbeck's *Tortilla Flat* made him realize that the creation of a character was possible.

Andrews primarily drew from a rich lode of oral tradition that he absorbed from his family and community. There are echoes of the southern folk preacher, the streetwise *badman who inhabits bars and liquor houses, the folk wisdom of elderly black women who pass on their knowledge to the younger African American girls, and the rhythms of *jazz and *blues music. Andrews wrote from his own culture, and his broader experiences in the places outside Georgia only helped him to focus more clearly on the culture from which he sprang.

His work, like the man himself, is ribald, often obscene, but never vulgar. It is gently ironic, not confrontational, and not intended to be political. Andrews has said that he intended to include all that life includes—sadness, boredom, sex, happiness, violence, and joy—without trying to proselytize and without attempting to change the essential truth of the way life was at a particular time. In fact he took issue with writers who he felt attempted to show only the oppressor and the oppressed. While some of the characters in Andrews's books might be seen as victims, the intent is to show the humanity of all the inhabitants of a community, not to point to the degradation of one race by another.

Appalachee Red (originally titled *Red, White, and Blue*) explores the way of life of rural blacks in the fictional north Georgia county of Muskhogean, an area much resembling Morgan County, Georgia, Andrews's home. The novel spans nearly thirty years in the history of a small town and in the lives of its denizens, both black and white. The tale is at times comic, at times violent, but is always imbued with Andrews's characteristic knack for storytelling. Upon being queried about the lack of a political statement in the book, Andrews responded that he was not interested in preaching, that he was telling a story.

Andrews, himself the product of mixed marriages and relationships, recognized the conflicts and tensions that existed between races, and recognized the possibility that one race might seem to have the upper hand at certain times, but he chose to focus instead on the inherent humanity in all people, and thus on their similarities rather than their differences. Consequently, in *Appalachee Red*, as in the two other books in the Muskhogean trilogy, blacks and whites and Native Americans mingle, marry, and do business together, sometimes with felicitous results, sometimes with disastrous results.

Men and women also find their own voices through Andrews's exuberant prose; indeed, Andrews remarked that *Appalachee Red* was not about Red, but about Baby Sweet, the woman whom he saves from the clutches of an evil white policeman named Boots. Andrews further commented that *Baby Sweet's*, named for the brothel that Baby Sweet opens on the premises of her house after the mysterious departure of Red, is in fact about Lea; Lea is the product of a racially mixed relationship and has chosen to work for the brothel in order to provide services for the black men of the community.

Andrews's female characters are neither oppressors nor oppressed. They are not marginalized females, dependent only on a man's largesse. The difficulties of being a black woman involved with a white man are, in Andrews's novels, fodder for his utter delight with humanity. Many of the strongest, most memorable characters in the novels are women. The characters, both men and women, are not drawn as mere cardboard figures to be revered for their nobility or pitied for their victimization. Everyone, particularly the women, is given her own sense of power within the context of the situation.

Andrews's characters are quintessentially human —people making decisions as best they can, based on their individual conditions. These are real people, living their lives with no apologies, following the dictates of their hearts. If they from time to time appear to make bad choices, the reader must remember that they are given choices, not simply forced into situations for the purpose of a political agenda.

The Last Radio Baby, Andrews's memoir, is a charming look at the vagaries of growing up in a large, talented family with little money. Eventually the family produced artists (including Benny Andrews, who illustrated all the books for his brother), writers, architects, and poets. The successes of Raymond Andrews and his parents, brothers, and sisters point out the importance to him of community.

Andrews died tragically by his own hand on 25 November 1991. His collected letters and assorted family memorabilia are available in a special collection at Emory University, Atlanta, Georgia. Andrews's novels and memoirs are a valuable addition to the world of contemporary African American literature; they provide a fresh, apolitical look at the world of the rural South and are notable for their vivacity of language and fascinating characterization.

• Melville Herskovitz, *The Myth of the Negro Past*, 1941. Addison Gayle, Jr., ed., *Black Expression*, 1969. Ladell Payne, *Black Novelists and the Southern Literary Tradition*, 1981. Robert B. Stepto, *From Behind the Veil*, 1979. Peter Bruck and Wolfgang Karrer, *The Afro-American Novel since 1960*, 1982. Charles East, ed., *The New Writers of the South*, 1987.

—Freda R. Beaty

ANGELOU, MAYA (b. 1928), autobiographer, poet, playwright, director, producer, performance artist, educator, and winner of the Horatio Alger Award. A prolific author, with a successful career as a singer, actress, and dancer, Maya Angelou became one of

America's most famous poets when she stood before the nation to deliver her poem "On the Pulse of Morning" at President Bill Clinton's inauguration on 20 January 1993. At sixty-four years old, she was the first black woman to be asked to compose such a piece, and the second poet to be so recognized after the pairing of Robert Frost and John F. Kennedy in 1961. Born Marguerite Johnson in St. Louis, but raised in Arkansas, Angelou was a natural choice for the forty-second president and fellow Arkansan. The poem reflects a theme that is common to all of Angelou's published works, namely that human beings are more alike than different, and that a message of hope and inclusion is a most inspiring dream and ideal, something to be savored at such a moment of political change. She writes of the triumph of the human spirit over hardship and adversity. Her voice speaks of healing and reconciliation, and she is a willing symbol for the - American nation on the eve of the twenty-first century.

The great-granddaughter of a slave-born Arkansas woman, Angelou has had a rich and varied life, and her serial *autobiography intertwines in a harmonious way her individual experiences with the collective social history of African Americans. As she recounts in the first volume of her serial autobiography, *I Know Why the Caged Bird Sings (1970), Angelou spent her first three years in California. Her father, Bailey Johnson, was a navy cook and her mother, Vivian Baxter, a glamorous and dynamic woman, was a sometime nightclub performer and owner of a large rooming house in San Francisco in the 1940s. When Angelou's parents divorced in the early 1930s, her father sent her and her brother Bailey by train, with name tags on their wrists, to live with his mother, Momma Henderson, who ran the only black-owned general store in Stamps, Arkansas. Angelou writes eloquently of the customs and harsh circumstances of life in the segregated pre–civil rights South, and of the dignity and mutual support that rural blacks extended to one another during the depression. After Stamps came time in St. Louis with her mother's family, the discovery of urban greed and alienation, and her rape at age eight, a trauma that left her mute for several years. Upon her return to the South, she buried herself in the cocoon of her grandmother's store and in her imagination, and read widely. Books became her lifeline and prepared the terrain for her artistic and literary career. She moved back to California as a teenager, graduated from high school, and gave birth to her only child, Guy Johnson, himself a poet. In the 1960s, Angelou was active in the *civil rights movement in the United States and abroad, and became briefly involved with African activist Vusumzi Make. She has been married and divorced.

By the time she was in her early twenties, Angelou had worked at a variety of odd jobs, as a waitress, a cook, and a streetcar conductor, flirting briefly with prostitution and drug addiction. She then worked as a stage performer, establishing a reputation among the avant-garde of the early 1950s, and appearing in *Porgy and Bess* on a twenty-two–nation tour sponsored by the U.S. State Department in 1954–1955. She studied *dance with Martha Graham. Off-Broadway, she acted in Jean Genet's *The Blacks* in 1960. She worked as an associate editor for the *Arab Observer* in Cairo, Egypt, in 1961–1962 and as a writer for the Ghanaian *Times* and the Ghanaian Broadcasting Corporation in 1964–1966. She appeared in *Mother Courage* at the University of Ghana in 1964 and made her Broadway debut in *Look Away* in 1973. She directed her own play, *And Still I Rise*, in California in 1976. In 1977, she had a part in the *television adaptation of Alex *Haley's *Roots* and received an Emmy Award nomination for best supporting actress. She has lectured on campuses, been a guest on many talk shows, and continues to be an extremely popular speaker. She is currently the Reynolds Professor of American Studies at Wake Forest University in North Carolina.

Her autobiographical fictions include *Gather Together in My Name* (1974) and *Singin' and Swingin' and Gettin' Merry Like Christmas* (1976), which received moderate critical praise; and *The Heart of a Woman* (1981) and *All God's Children Need Traveling Shoes* (1986), which were acclaimed as important works covering exciting periods in African American and African history, the civil rights marches, and the era of decolonization. These narratives survey the difficulties and personal triumphs of a remarkable woman with a keen understanding of the power of language to affect change, and of the role of "image making" in the self-representation of groups who have been historically oppressed. In her interview with Claudia Tate, Angelou acknowledged her debt to the black women writers who were her predecessors, Frances Ellen Watkins *Harper and Zora Neale *Hurston in particular, and to her friend James *Baldwin who encouraged her to write after hearing her childhood stories. Angelou's personal experiences typify the changes that have occurred in America in the course of her lifetime. She consciously strives to be the kind of writer who brings people and traditions together and who appeals to the nobler sentiments of her readers. She is a humanist and a protean personality who has, against all odds, made her own life into the great American success story. Her works have a profound resonance with a long tradition that begins with the eighteenth- and nineteenth-century *slave narratives. Her style captures the cadences and aspirations of African American women whose strength she celebrates. She has been instrumental in helping refocus attention on black women's voices.

[*See also* Feminism.]

• Claudia Tate, *Black Women Writers at Work*, 1983, pp. 1–38. Selwyn Cudjoe, "Maya Angelou and the Autobiographical Statement," in *Black Women Writers (1950–1980): A Critical Evaluation*, ed. Mari Evans, 1984, pp. 6–24. Lynn Z. Bloom, "Maya Angelou," in *DLB*, vol. 38, *Afro-American Writers after 1955: Dramatists and Prose Writers*, eds. Thadious M. Davis and Trudier Harris, 1985, pp. 3–12. Françoise Lionnet, "Con Artists and Storytellers: Maya Angelou's Problematic Sense of Audience," in *Autobiographical Voices: Race, Gender, Self Portraiture*, 1989, pp. 130–166.

—Françoise Lionnet

Anglo-African Magazine, The. Founded in 1859 by Thomas Hamilton in New York City, the *Anglo-African Magazine* ceased as a monthly magazine in April of 1861. It continued as a weekly until 1865. A journal for and about African Americans, it was often called the "black man's *Atlantic Monthly.*" It was not strictly an abolitionist forum, for Hamilton published work on many aspects of African American life.

Hamilton's magazine contained work by the most important African American intellectuals and public figures of the day. Considered the first African American literary journal in America, its pages contained *essays, *poetry, satire, short fiction, and *biography. Contributors included Martin R. *Delany, James McCune Smith, Frederick *Douglass, and Frances Ellen Watkins *Harper. The *Anglo-African* brought together imaginative writing and essays on human rights, a tradition continued by later African American magazines in the nineteenth and twentieth centuries.

[*See also* Journalism.]

• Charles S. Johnson, "Rise of the Negro Magazine," *Journal of Negro History* 13 (Jan. 1928): 7–21. Walter C. Daniel, *Black Journals of the United States,* 1982.   —Daniel J. Royer

Annie Allen. The second book of poems by Gwendolyn *Brooks, *Annie Allen* (1949) won the Eunice Tietjens Prize offered by *Poetry Magazine* and the 1950 Pulitzer Prize for *poetry.

The collection is dominated by a long narrative poem, "The Anniad." Somewhat more complex than some of her earlier poems, "The Anniad" is an exercise in various poetic techniques, employing a diction associated more often with the epic form. The protagonist is not "heroic" in the usual sense of the term, but her ability to survive is just as "heroic" as any figure from classical literature.

The poem charts the changes in a young woman as she moves from her youthful dreams to the reality of married life in the ghetto. We see Annie Allen grow from childhood to womanhood in an atmosphere conditioned by poverty, racial discrimination, parental expectations, and unhappiness. Like Maud Martha, a later Brooks heroine, Annie Allen does not completely give in or give up. In fact, in some respects, *Annie Allen* is a mirror image of the later *Maud Martha* (1953); however, the latter is a prose narrative with poetic overtones, the former is poetry with prose overtones.

The action of "The Anniad" is simple. In order to get away from home, Annie wants to get married. There then follows a courtship, marriage, and separation because of war. When her husband returns, the marriage is weakened by Annie's expectations and his infidelity. They separate and temporarily reconcile. Eventually he deserts Annie for good.

Annie Allen is another one of Brooks's very ordinary, totally undistinguished characters. She is a product of an urban ghetto, the daughter of Andrew and Maxie Allen. Her parents are typical of those in the generation that actually believed the American dream could be realized, that people would be rewarded for hard work and goodness. Much of Annie's

early life is devoted to trying to please her mother, who insists that Annie learn to count her blessings and be grateful for what she has, rather than spend energy longing for what she does not. On one level, of course, this is a realistic approach to life; however, it also represses dreams, hopes, and aspirations. If the external Annie is a nonadventurous, passive soul, the internalization of the character reveals one with an active imagination and ever-present dreams.

The simplicity of the narrative thread belies the complexity of form and interpretation. The poem records the numerous repressive forces that operate upon Annie and, in a measure, imprison her. There are, for example, the limitations that result from interracial discrimination and those that result from a sometimes intraracial prejudice relating to skin color. Like many other such women in similar predicaments, Annie longs to escape but does not really have the courage to do so.

The other poems in the volume are also marked by experimentation and unusual imagery. They differ from Brooks's earlier poetry primarily because she shifts from the reality of locale and the exactness of the surroundings to the reality of the mind. Although set in Chicago, *Annie Allen* is not really a collection of regional poems. Moreover, the volume reveals quite clearly what were to become the dominant themes in Brooks's poetry: the roles of women in an unfriendly urban environment and the moral issues that lead to distinctions between right and wrong.

• Maria K. Mootry and Gary Smith, eds., *A Life Distilled: Gwendolyn Brooks, Her Poetry and Fiction,* 1987.

                              —Kenny Jackson Williams

Another Country. Immensely complex because of its size and scope, *Another Country* is James *Baldwin's most ambitious *novel. This novel of ideas covers myriad issues and themes, all related to the transcending power of love. Through interlocking events and episodes, *Another Country* critiques a "moral" and "democratic" America that fosters prejudice based on *race, *class, and *sexuality. The author began writing it in the mid-1950s, completing it in Istanbul; Dial Press published the novel in 1962, and it became a best-seller.

Baldwin creates characters of various racial, sexual, and social backgrounds to illustrate how personal, cultural, and national identities intersect. We first encounter *Rufus Scott, a black *jazz musician and one of the novel's many artists. He mentally and physically abuses his lover Leona, a white Southerner who goes insane. Psychically and physically debilitated by a virulent self-hatred, Rufus portends America's fate if it continues to prevent people from connecting irrespective of differences. Baldwin uses Rufus's suicide as an ironic narrative device, for he permeates the novel and illuminates the characters' wrenching attempts to come together. The phrase Rufus hears in a wailing saxophone, "Do you love me," reverberates throughout the text.

The rest of the book concerns Ida, Rufus's sister and an aspiring singer; Vivaldo, Ida's lover, Rufus's best friend, and an aspiring novelist; Eric, a white actor from the South and Rufus's erstwhile lover who has fled to France; Yves, Eric's current lover; and Cass Silenski and her novelist husband Richard, both Vivaldo's friends. Purposely resisting a discernible plot, Baldwin's postmodernist text traverses spatial, temporal, and personal boundaries: the transatlantic setting includes Greenwich Village, Harlem, Alabama, and France; time vacillates between past and present; and characters who would be labeled straight or gay, black or white, male or female, rich or poor all commingle, albeit painfully. Redemption occurs only when one exorcises his or her demons, often rooted in the aforementioned oppositions. Baldwin's characters must divest themselves of "safe" distinctions—for instance, Vivaldo must atone for failing Rufus through a sexual union with Eric, the novel's unifying figure. Especially cogent is how Baldwin resists facile categories of "good" and "bad" characters: blacks and whites can alternatively be victims and victimizers. Apropos of his religious background, Baldwin posits that only through pain, suffering, and acceptance can one enter another country —a metaphoric utopia that eliminates artificial, socially constructed distinctions. The novel ends with Ida-Vivaldo and Eric-Yves tentatively reconciling.

Another Country remains both manifesto and cultural history, a document of the turbulent 1960s. The novel created controversy both critically and popularly: Robert Bone called it "a failure on the grand scale," while citizens complained to J. Edgar Hoover about its "pornographic" content, which resulted in an FBI inquiry. But other critics such as Langston *Hughes recognized the novel's "power," the basis of which Baldwin himself elucidates: ". . . *Another Country* was harder and more challenging than anything I'd ever attempted, and I didn't cheat in it" (Fred L. Standley and Louis H. Pratt, eds., *Conversations with James Baldwin*, 1989). Indeed, Baldwin's multicultural epic disrupts and challenges American racial and sexual discourse. As its continuing popularity attests, *Another Country* assiduously explores the conundrum of the self and its potential for love.

• Robert A. Bone, *The Negro Novel in America*, 1965. Louis H. Pratt, *James Baldwin*, 1978.   —Keith Clark

ANSA, TINA McELROY (b. 1949), fiction writer, essayist, and journalist. Tina McElroy Ansa was born in Macon, Georgia, and educated at Mount DeSales, a Catholic school in Macon, and at Spelman College in Atlanta. Early in her career, she worked primarily as a journalist. She freelanced and worked for the *Atlanta Constitution* and for the *Charlotte Observer* (N.C.). She has also conducted writing workshops in Georgia at Brunswick College, Emory University, and Spelman College.

Ansa's best-known work is her fiction. She may be considered a southern writer, for her fiction clearly draws on the physical landscape, specifically the middle Georgia setting, and the mores and folkways that shape the psyche of the American South. Unlike much of southern fiction, however, her tales are devoid of the subtextual exploration of the undercurrent of dysfunction and perversion that exists in the South. That is not to say that her fictive worlds are

without dysfunction or moral conflict. Her fiction, however, confronts such problems openly in the worlds of the texts. Her *novels and short fiction reflect the positive impact of her having grown up in a middle-class family in the racially segregated South. The South portrayed in her fiction consists of a supportive, closely bonded, and self-sufficient African American community that renders itself impervious to the horrors of southern racism. More specifically, her fiction explores some of the dynamics of the African American female experience.

Ansa's two major works are her novels *Baby of the Family* (1989) and *Ugly Ways* (1993). Both make use of traditional folk beliefs and the conventions of the ghost story. Ansa's fiction avoids self-conscious polemic and the predictability of protest fiction. The soundly middle-class McPhersons of *Baby of the Family* and the Lovejoys of *Ugly Ways* enjoy affluent existences and are relatively unharassed by racism and overt, brutal sexism. The dilemmas faced by these families stem from internal family issues rather than external forces.

Upon its publication, *Baby of the Family* was named a Notable Book of the Year in 1989 and 1990 by the *New York Times Book Review*. The novel won the 1989 Georgia Authors Series Award and was cited by the American Library Association as a best book for young adults in 1990. Set in the fictive town of Mulberry, the novel depicts the coming of age of Lena McPherson who, like Ansa herself, was born in the late 1940s with a caul, an indicator, according to folk belief, that a child is endowed for life with psychic powers. Unfortunately, her mother, Nellie, discounts folk tradition and inadvertently subjects Lena to a childhood of frustration and fearful experiences. What thus becomes Lena's affliction, however, is countered by the affluence and strong emotional support of the McPherson household. Buffered by the family's love, Lena escapes being overwhelmed by her difference from her peers. Simultaneously, because of her connection to the supernatural, Lena acquires information about African American traditions and roots necessary for her spiritual coming of age. The novel, therefore, suggests that the ideal existence for African Americans is one that embraces traditional American success while respecting African American traditions.

Also set in the fictive middle-Georgia town of Mulberry, *Ugly Ways* portrays southern African American women confronting problems of life in the 1990s. Since its publication the novel has been widely reviewed and has been at the top of the African American Best Sellers/Blackboard list and on bestsellers lists compiled by the *Quarterly Black Review of Books* and the *African American Literary Review*. In the novel, Ansa subverts the image of the African American family dominated and sustained by the strong African American matriarch. In this novel, the three successful Lovejoy sisters, Betty, Emily, and Annie Ruth, who have gathered in Mulberry for the funeral of Mudear, their mother, confront the neuroses that prevent them from fully enjoying life. The barrier to their sound emotional health has been Mudear's emotional absenteeism, psychologically abusive behavior, and her refusal to care for them physically. The story is told from each sister's point of view with Mudear's recalcitrant spirit furnishing commentary and supplying her own story throughout the narrative. Situated, then, in an African American context, *Ugly Ways* is a cautionary tale that suggests the need for reasonable alternatives to the traditional roles assigned to mothers.

Ansa's work has been well received. Her works are widely read and taught and bear the hallmarks of enduring American classics.

—Carol P. Marsh-Lockett

ANTHOLOGIES. Although anthologies of African American literature have appeared mainly in the twentieth century, two earlier works deserve mention. The first was *Les *Cenelles* (1845), a collection of eighty-five poems in French by seventeen free New Orleans Creoles. Totally disengaged from issues of slavery and emancipation, these poets are squarely in the French Romantic tradition. In contrast, *Autographs for Freedom* (1853), edited by Julia Griffiths, was fully committed to the antislavery cause. Its contributors included Charles Reason, George Vashon, J. McCune Smith, John Mercer Langston, William Wells *Brown, and Frederick *Douglass, as well as white writers.

Almost all other anthologies, whether general or specialized, were published after 1920. They may be divided into the following categories: multigenre collections, *poetry, fiction, *drama, and nonfiction. Several anthologies appeared in the 1920s, few in the 1930s and 1940s, almost none in the 1950s. Beginning in the 1960s, production accelerated, and the brisk pace continues to the present.

The pioneer general anthology in the field is the work of V. F. Calverton, a white Marxist. In his introduction to *Anthology of American Negro Literature* (1929), he relates black art and literature to economic forces, especially *slavery, and disputes white racist assumptions. He had an eye for good writing and helped to bring Jean *Toomer, Langston, *Hughes, Claude *McKay, W. E. B. *Du Bois, Countee *Cullen, and others to wider notice.

During the next two decades three collections by black academicians appeared. *Readings from Negro Authors* (1931), edited by Otelia Cromwell, Lorenzo Dow Turner, and Eva G. Dykes, and Herman Dreer's *American Literature by Negro Authors* (1950) were far surpassed by *The Negro Caravan* (1941), edited by Sterling A. *Brown, Arthur P. Davis, and Ulysses Lee. No single work has had greater influence in establishing the canon of African American literature. For the first time in a general collection the early literature (except Olaudah *Equiano) is amply represented. In addition to fiction, poetry, *autobiography, and *biography, the work includes a strong selection of *folklore, two dozen *essays, and a group of speeches, pamphlets, and *letters, mostly from the nineteenth century. The apparatus of *The Negro Caravan* is fuller than prior anthologies, but what most distinguishes it is a superior literary intelligence and a closer knowledge of the field. It can still be read with profit decades after its compilation.

The same cannot be said for Sylvester C. Watkins's *Anthology of American Negro Literature* (1944), Abraham Chapman's *Black Voices* (1968), or Lindsay Patterson's *An Introduction to Black Literature in America from 1746 to the Present* (1968). As predominantly white colleges and universities suddenly manifested interest in black studies after the assassination of Dr. Martin Luther *King, Jr., publishers scrambled to meet the new demand for materials. The resulting anthologies compiled by instant experts were clearly unsatisfactory, and even the two anthologies edited by seasoned specialists, Charles T. Davis and Daniel Walden's *On Being Black: Writings by Afro-Americans from Frederick Douglass to the Present* (1970) and Darwin T. Turner's *Black American Literature: Essays, Poetry, Fiction, Drama* (1970), show signs of haste and pressure from publishers.

Several general anthologies cannot be so quickly dismissed. *Dark Symphony: Negro Literature in America* (1968), edited by James A. Emanuel and Theodore L. Gross, was begun before the rush. It is arranged by chronological sections, not by genres; the section introductions are substantial; and the bibliography is well planned and executed. More belletristic than most anthologies in the field, *Dark Symphony* states emphatically that "intrinsic artistic merit" is the criterion for inclusion, not social or historical relevance. A weakness is the paucity of women writers and the absence of Phillis *Wheatley and Zora Neale *Hurston. Nick Aaron Ford's *Black Insights: Significant Literature by Black Americans— 1760 to the Present* (1971) eschews the somewhat narrow emphasis of Emanuel and Gross, offering selections from forty-three authors arranged chronologically. Less comprehensive but more judicious is *Black Literature in America* (1971), edited by Houston A. *Baker, Jr., who argues that an anthology must "include standards that are indigenous to black american literature" as well as "existing critical standards." Baker begins with folklore, omits eighteenth-century writers, and includes only six nineteenth-century authors before moving to his ampler representation of twentieth-century works. Ruth Miller's *Blackamerican Literature 1760–Present* (1971) gives adequate representation to the earliest African American literature, but, instead of introductions to its six chronological parts, the editor provides only chronologies of historical and literary events. Barbara Dodds Stanford's *I, Too, Sing America: Black Voices in American Literature* (1971) is a small collection designed for a high-school audience.

The three best general anthologies since *The Negro Caravan* also appeared in the early 1970s: *Cavalcade: Negro American Writing from 1760 to the Present* (1971), edited by Arthur P. Davis and J. Saunders *Redding; *Black Writers of America: A Comprehensive Anthology* (1972), edited by Richard Barksdale and Keneth Kinnamon; and *Afro-American Writing: An Anthology of Prose and Poetry* (1972), edited by Richard A. Long and Eugenia Collier. *Cavalcade* is a handsome volume, attractively printed with striking art work. Literary merit, the editors assert, is the prime criterion for inclusion, but they also attempt "to cover . . . Negro life in America for the past two hundred years" and to avoid unnecessary duplication of materials in other anthologies. Cogent introductory essays precede the five sections. Though they maintain scholarly objectivity in their selections, Davis and Redding themselves lean toward the integrationist camp. By the time *The New Cavalcade* appeared in two volumes twenty years later, Redding was dead and Joyce A. Joyce joined Arthur Davis as coeditor, her nationalist aesthetic balancing the conservatism of the original editors. The term "Negro," already becoming anachronistic in 1971, was replaced in the subtitle by "African American"; the treatment of militant writers was drastically revised; and a final section—"The African American Literary Revival: The 1970s to the Present"—was added. Throughout *The New Cavalcade* headnotes have been revised and updated, and the original bibliography has almost tripled in size.

Another excellent anthology is *Black Writers of America*, which has sold more than seventy thousand copies. Barksdale and Kinnamon take issue with the criteria of some other anthologists:

> Recognizing the limitations of a narrowly esthetic approach to a body of writing of great social import, we have provided generous selections of autobiographies, essays, speeches, letters, political pamphlets, histories, journals, and folk literature as well as poems, plays, and stories. Our criteria for inclusion were both artistic and social; indeed, facile or rigid separation of the two seems to us misguided.

The six parts include eighty-five writers plus a generous sampling of *folk literature. The introductions to the several parts are much fuller than in other anthologies, as are the headnotes to individual authors. The extensive bibliographical apparatus in the author headnotes and in the nonoverlapping general bibliography of more than a thousand items has proven useful to scholars as well as students. A special feature is the designation of the following as "The Major Writers": Equiano, Wheatley, Douglass, Alexander *Crummell, Charles Waddell *Chesnutt, Paul Laurence *Dunbar, Du Bois, James Weldon *Johnson, McKay, Toomer, Hughes, Cullen, Richard *Wright, Melvin B. *Tolson, Robert *Hayden, Ralph *Ellison, Gwendolyn *Brooks, James *Baldwin, and Amiri *Baraka.

Long and Collier's *Afro-American Writing* is another good anthology, but its scope is considerably smaller than either *Black Writers of America* or *The New Cavalcade*. Similarly, the period introductions and headnotes are brief, and only minimal bibliographical aid is provided. Still, the selections are well made. Problems of literary property prevented the inclusion of Cullen and Wright.

A recent general anthology is Deirdre Mullane's *Crossing the Danger Water: Three Hundred Years of African-American Writing* (1993), which includes much nonliterary material: Clarence Thomas and Maxine Waters are included, but not Toni *Morrison or Rita *Dove. The apparatus is inadequate. Such will not be the case with two other general anthologies nearing completion in the mid-1990s. The long-awaited Norton anthology of African American

literature, with Henry Louis *Gates, Jr., and Nellie McKay as general editors and with other distinguished scholars involved, is one, and the other, to be published by Houghton-Mifflin, is edited by Patricia Liggins Hill with R. Baxter Miller, Trudier Harris, Bernard Bell, William J. Harris, and Sondra O'Neale as section editors. Each of these projects promises to take its place among the very best anthologies in the field.

A different kind of general anthology is designed not to provide a comprehensive overview of the entire tradition, but to capture or even define a particular moment. The most celebrated example is that central document of the *Harlem Renaissance, Alain *Locke's The *New Negro (1925), which included contributions by established figures while highlighting "the younger generation" to whom the volume is dedicated: Toomer, Hughes, McKay, Hurston, Arna *Bontemps, Cullen, Rudolph *Fisher, Eric *Walrond, and others. A similar book is Charles S. Johnson's *Ebony and Topaz: A Collectanea* (1927). Still too little known, this book includes some younger writers not to be found in *The New Negro*: Sterling A. Brown, Frank Horne, George S. *Schuyler, and Helene *Johnson. Many of the contributors to *The New Negro* and *Ebony and Topaz* also provided articles or poems for Nancy Cunard's huge, profusely illustrated collection *Negro* (1934), whose scope includes Africa, the West Indies, and Europe as well as the United States. In this astonishing book, one of the freest spirits of the age gathers commentary on literature, *music, art, racial struggle, and other topics from one hundred contributors.

In recent decades several collections have likewise codified distinct stages of African American literary history. Herbert Hill's *Soon, One Morning: New Writing by American Negroes, 1940–1962* (1963) exemplified the integrationist aesthetic in its essays, fiction, and poems. Only five years later the most important collection devoted to a militant, nationalist aesthetic appeared: LeRoi Jones and Larry *Neal's *Black Fire: An Anthology of Afro-American Writing* (1968), which included ten plays as well as a generous selection of essays, poetry, and short stories. Most of the contributors were born in the 1930s, 1940s, and 1950s. A similar but less impressive collection followed quickly, *Black Arts: An Anthology of Black Creations* (1969), edited by Ahmed Alhamisi and Harun Kofi Wangara. From the West Coast came the more stylistically experimental, often humorous *19 Necromancers from Now* (1970), edited by Ishmael *Reed. The white anthologist Abraham Chapman supplemented his earlier *Black Voices* with *New Black Voices: An Anthology of Contemporary Afro-American Literature* (1972), which brings a lot of writing between two covers but is somewhat perfunctory in its editorial apparatus. Perhaps the most important of all the successors to *The New Negro* is *Chant of Saints: A Gathering of Afro-American Literature, Art, and Scholarship* (1979), edited by Michael S. *Harper and Robert Stepto. Avowedly an effort to construct "the Afro-American canon in our time," it includes Sterling A. Brown (to whom the volume is dedicated), Harper himself, Robert Hayden, James Alan

*McPherson, Sherley Anne *Williams, Leon *Forrest, Ralph Ellison, Derek Walcott, Toni Morrison, John Stewart, Chinua Achebe, Ernest J. *Gaines, Gayl *Jones, Alice *Walker, and Jay *Wright among the creative writers. Conspicuously absent are writers like Amiri Baraka, Don L. Lee (Haki R. *Madhubuti), Nikki *Giovanni, Ed *Bullins, and other militants.

Other multigenre anthologies focus on longer historical periods. One of the pioneering scholars of African American literature was Benjamin Brawley of Howard University, whose *Early Negro American Writers* (1935) performed a real service in collecting twenty authors, many of them otherwise inaccessible, from the eighteenth century through the Civil War. A much fuller collection also came from Howard, *Early Negro Writing 1760–1837* (1971), edited by Dorothy *Porter. Here one may find numerous historical documents as well as more literary works. Also useful is William H. Robinson's *Early Black American Prose* (1971), which includes letters, essays and addresses, *slave narratives, short stories, and excerpts from *novels and plays.

The Harlem Renaissance has also been well served by anthologists. Michael W. Peplow and Arthur P. Davis's *The New Negro Renaissance: An Anthology* (1975) and Nathan Irvin Huggins's *Voices from the Harlem Renaissance* (1976) take thematic approaches. More recently David Levering Lewis has compiled *The Portable Harlem Renaissance Reader* (1994), the fullest and best of the three collections.

Anthologies edited by famous writers often derive importance from what they reveal about the anthologist's literary tastes. This is true of *Afro-American Literature: An Introduction* (1971), edited by Robert Hayden, David J. Burrows, and Frederick R. Lapides; Gwendolyn Brooks's *Jump Bad: A New Chicago Anthology* (1971); and *Confirmation: An Anthology of African American Women* (1983), edited by Amiri and Amina Baraka.

The last-named was not the first multigenre anthology of women's literature, an honor that goes instead to Toni Cade *Bambara's *The Black Woman: An Anthology* (1970). Others include Pat Crutchfield Exum's *Keeping the Faith: Writings by Contemporary Black American Women* (1974), Barbara Smith's *Home Girls: A Black Feminist Anthology* (1983), Rita B. Dandridge's absorbing *Black Women's Blues: A Literary Anthology, 1934–1988* (1992), and Margaret Busby's large and impressive *Daughters of Africa* (1992), which includes not only some eighty-four U.S. women writers but dozens of others from elsewhere in the Americas, from Africa, and from Europe.

Another important recent collection is regional—*Black Southern Voices: An Anthology of Fiction, Poetry, Drama, Nonfiction, and Critical Essays* (1992), edited by John O. *Killens and Jerry W. Ward, Jr. The fifty-six authors presented here make plausible the claim made by Killens in the introduction that "there is a black southern literary tradition, a voice that is special, profound, and distinct from any other in the country." Several other multigenre collections can only be listed: Charlemae Rollins's charming *Christmas Gif': An Anthology of Christmas Poems, Songs,* and Stories Written by and about Negroes (1963), Budd Schulberg's *From the Ashes: Voices from Watts* (1967), R. Baird Shuman's *A Galaxy of Black Writing* (1970), Edward Margolies's *A Native Sons Reader* (1970), Raman K. Singh and Peter Fellowes's *Black Literature in America: A Casebook* (1970), Etheridge *Knight's *Black Voices from Prison* (1970), Elena Lewis's *Who Took the Weight?: Black Voices from Norfolk Prison* (1972), Eugene *Perkins's *Poetry of Prison: Poems by Black Prisoners* (1972), William H. Robinson's *Nommo: An Anthology of Modern Black African and Black American Literature* (1972), Edward Spargo's pedagogical *Selections from the Black* (1974), Joseph Beam's *In the Life: A Black Gay Anthology* (1986), and Paula L. Woods and Felix H. Liddell's beautifully produced *I Hear a Symphony: African Americans Celebrate Love* (1994). Finally, of *Erotique Noire, Black Erotica* (1992), edited by Miriam DeCosta-Willis, Reginald Martin, and Roseann P. Bell, it can be said that only a moribund reader can fail to have her or his interest aroused.

Since the time of the *Greek Anthology*, poetry has lent itself to anthologizing more readily than other genres. *Les Cenelles* has been mentioned. In the twentieth century a very high standard was set by James Weldon Johnson in *The Book of American Negro Poetry* (1922, rev. ed. 1931), which has been more influential than any other collection in establishing the African American poetic canon. Johnson's long preface is an exposition and defense of black cultural achievement, for in his view "the final measure of the greatness of all peoples is the amount and standard of the literature and art they have produced." Thus the white majority's recognition of black cultural production becomes an avenue of racial advancement. This is a classic anthology.

At the same time a few white scholars were looking at black poetry with interest. Robert T. Kerlin's *Negro Poets and Their Poems* (1923) went through four editions, the last in 1947. It contains several poems not anthologized elsewhere as well as numerous scarce photographs of poets. According to their preface, Newman Ivey White and Walter Clinton Jackson (self-described as "Southern white men who desire the most cordial relations between the races") had their *An Anthology of Verse by American Negroes* (1924) ready for printing in 1921, before Johnson or Kerlin.

With early African American poets well represented in these anthologies, Countee Cullen decided to focus on more recent poets in *Caroling Dusk: An Anthology of Verse by Negro Poets* (1927), especially those associated with the Harlem Renaissance. In the same year another mainstay of the Renaissance, Alain Locke, issued the pamphlet *Four Negro Poets*—McKay, Toomer, Cullen, and Hughes. Appropriately, Hughes is represented by more poems than are the others.

Anthologizing slowed down considerably during the depression and war years. Beatrice M. *Murphy tried to make a virtue of her lack of selectivity in *Negro Voices* (1938) and *Ebony Rhythm* (1948), but the results are not impressive. Arna Bontemps joined Johnson and Cullen as a poet-anthologist with

Golden Slippers: An Anthology of Negro Poetry for Young Readers (1941).

Bontemps and his good friend Langston Hughes share honors with Johnson as the best and most influential anthologists of poetry. Their coedited volume, *The Poetry of the Negro* (1949), revised and expanded in 1970, is printed as poetry should be printed, with ample margins and respect for stanzaic pattern. It is one of the most readable of anthologies. Separately Bontemps compiled *American Negro Poetry* (1963) and Hughes *New Negro Poets U.S.A.* (1964), shorter collections allowing some interesting comparisons of their respective tastes. Additional comparisons became possible just three years later when another poet-anthologist, Robert Hayden, published *Kaleidoscope: Poems by American Negro Poets* (1967). Among the younger poets, Hayden includes some not appearing in Bontemps or Hughes or the 1970 Hughes and Bontemps.

The poetic explosion of the late 1960s occasioned numerous new anthologies. R. Baird Shuman's *Nine Black Poets* (1968) presents numerous poems by each of his poets and supplies a historical introduction. Of the seventy-six poets in *The New Black Poetry* (1969), edited by Clarence *Major, only thirteen were represented in earlier anthologies. In *Dices or Black Bones: Black Voices of the Seventies* (1970), Adam David Miller selects fewer poets but represents them with more than one poem each. A similar tactic is employed with more poets by Orde Coombs in *We Speak as Liberators: New Black Poets* (1970) and by Woodie *King, Jr., in *Black Spirits: A Festival of New Black Poets in America* (1972). New York, Newark, Chicago, Detroit, and San Francisco were the main centers of poetry during the 1960s and 1970s. Today the reader may sample the urgency of the time by perusing such pamphlet collections as David Henderson's *Umbra Anthology, 1967–1968* out of New York or Newark's *Anthology of the B.C.D.* (1969), dedicated to Baraka. Ishmael Reed's *19 Necromancers from Now* and Gwendolyn Brooks's *Jump Bad* represent the San Francisco and Chicago scenes. In Detroit the key figure was poet-publisher Dudley *Randall, whose anthologies *Black Poetry* (1969) and *The Black Poets* (1971) may also be consulted.

Other anthologies in these boom years included some earlier poets as well as recent voices. Darwin Turner's slim but well-selected *Black American Literature: Poetry* (1969) begins with Wheatley and ends with Don L. Lee. June *Jordan's *Soulscript: Afro-American Poetry* (1970) is especially good in its representation of women poets, some in their teens and twenties. Bernard W. Bell began his scholarly career with *Modern and Contemporary Afro-American Poetry* (1972). Lindsay Patterson's *A Rock Against the Wind: Black Love Poems* (1973) ranges over the whole gamut of emotions involved in one of the most elemental of poetic subjects. Looking back to pre-twentieth-century poetry, William H. Robinson's scholarly *Early Black American Poets* (1969) is organized by type: Orator Poets, Formalist Poets, Romantic Poets, and Dialect Poetry.

With increasing interest in writing by women in the 1970s, an anthology of African American women poets became inevitable. Nikki Giovanni's *Night Comes Softly* (1970) was a start, but the need was better met by Erlene Stetson's *Black Sister: Poetry by Black American Women, 1746–1980* (1981), a good collection with an excellent bibliography and introductory material but, regrettably, no biographical notes. "Anthology" may not be the right word for the four volumes of *Collected Black Women's Poetry* (1988), edited by Joan R. Sherman, but this important reprinting of eleven complete volumes of poetry originally published from 1867 to 1916 cannot go unmentioned. More conventionally an anthology is Sherman's excellent *African-American Poetry of the Nineteenth Century* (1992) with authoritative headnotes.

For an introduction to the poetry of our own half century, the reader can turn to *Every Shut Eye Ain't Asleep: An Anthology of Poetry by African Americans since 1945* (1994), edited by Michael Harper and Anthony Walton. It offers abundant evidence of the continuing vitality of the genre. The same can be said of the beautifully produced *In Search of Color Everywhere: A Collection of African-American Poetry* (1994), edited by E. Ethelbert *Miller with impressive illustrations and graphics by Terrance Cummings.

Other anthologies of varying degrees of utility are *Beyond the Blues: New Poems by American Negroes* (1962), edited by Rosey E. Pool; *Sixes and Sevens: An Anthology of New Negro Poetry* (1962) and *You Better Believe It: Black Verse in English from Africa, the West Indies, and the United States* (1973), both edited by Paul Breman; *I Am the Darker Brother: An Anthology of Modern Poems by Negro Americans* (1968) and *Black Out Loud: An Anthology of Modern Poems by Black Americans* (1970), both edited by Arnold Adoff; *3000 Years of Black Poetry* (1970), edited by Alan Lomax and Raoul Abdul; *Poems by Blacks* (1973, 1975) in two volumes, edited by Pinkie Gordon *Lane; *The Forerunners: Black Poets in America* (1975), edited by Woodie King, Jr.; and *Renewal: A Volume of Black Poems* (1977), edited by Houston A. Baker, Jr., and Charlotte Pierce-Baker.

Anthologies of fiction are less numerous. The first, misleadingly titled *Best Short Stories by Afro-American Writers* (1950), edited by Nick Aaron Ford and H. L. Faggett, may be safely disregarded. The second and third anthologies are both excellent: John Henrik Clarke's *American Negro Short Stories* (1966, rev. ed. 1993) and Langston Hughes's *The Best Short Stories by Negro Writers* (1967). The next two collections were designed as textbooks. Darwin T. Turner's *Black American Literature: Fiction* (1969) has a concise introduction, good headnotes, and a bibliography, but includes only fourteen stories. Charles L. James's *From the Roots: Short Stories by Black Americans* (1970) is fuller, with twenty-seven stories in five chronological sections. Arnold Adoff has twenty stories in his *Brothers and Sisters: Modern Stories by Black Americans* (1970). A more sharply focused collection is John Henrik Clarke's *Harlem* (1970), collecting twenty stories from that major cultural center.

Anthology production shifted into high gear in the early 1970s. After James, Adoff, and Clarke in 1970, seven collections emphasizing recent fiction appeared in the next five years: Donald B. Gibson and Carol Anselment's *Black and White: Stories of American Life* (1971), Martin Mirer's *Modern Black Stories* (1971), Toni Cade Bambara's *Tales and Stories for Black Folks* (1971), Orde Coombs's *What We Must See: Young Black Story Tellers* (1971), Woodie King's *Black Short Story Anthology* (1972), Sonia *Sanchez's *We Be Word Sorcerers: 25 Stories by Black Americans* (1973), and Quandra Prettyman Stadler's *Out of Our Lives: A Selection of Contemporary Black Fiction* (1975).

Most of the stories in anthologies such as these were by male writers, but now this imbalance has been corrected, thanks especially to the work of Mary Helen Washington. Her *Black-Eyed Susans: Classic Stories by and about Black Women* (1975) proved to be an excellent introduction. It was followed in 1980 by *Midnight Birds: Stories by Contemporary Black Women Writers*. Both were reissued in a single volume in 1989. Two more Washington anthologies are similarly helpful and readable: *Invented Lives: Narratives of Black Women, 1860–1960* (1987) and *Memory of Kin: Stories about Family by Black Writers* (1991), the latter including works by men as well as women. Elizabeth Ammons performs a real service by reprinting in *Short Fiction by Black Women, 1900–1920* (1991) forty-six stories from *Colored American Magazine* and the *Crisis. From there the reader can proceed to *The Sleeper Wakes: Harlem Renaissance Stories by Women* (1993), edited by Marcy Knopf, an impressive collection of twenty-seven stories by fourteen writers.

Although most anthologies of fiction are confined to short stories and excerpts from novels, a few gather longer works. Here the pioneer is Ronald T. Takaki, whose *Violence in the Black Imagination: Essays and Documents* (1972, rev. ed. 1993) combines the texts of Douglass's "The *Heroic Slave," Martin R. *Delany's *Blake, and Brown's *Clotel with a substantial essay on each and a bibliographical essay. By coincidence, in 1990 Henry Louis Gates, Jr., and William L. Andrews brought out collections with the same title: *Three Classic African-American Novels*. Gates reprints *Clotel*, *Iola Leroy*, and *The *Marrow of Tradition*. Andrews includes "The Heroic Slave," *Clotel*, and *Our Nig. In a subsequent companion volume, *The African-American Novel in the Age of Reaction* (1992), Andrews collects *Iola Leroy*, *The Marrow of Tradition*, and *The *Sport of the Gods*.

With the appearance in recent years of three important collections, twentieth-century short fiction is also well served. William Andrews's *Classic Fiction of the Harlem Renaissance* (1994) complements his nineteenth-century collections with four short stories by Toomer, two by Hurston, one each by Fisher and Hughes, an excerpt from *Infants of the Spring*, and *Home to Harlem* and *Quicksand* in their entirety. The general introduction and the introductions to each author are well done. Terry *McMillan's *Breaking Ice: An Anthology of Contemporary African-American Fiction* (1990) contains fifty-seven stories by as many writers. Clarence Major's *Calling the Wind: Twentieth Century African-American Short Stories*

(1993) begins with Chesnutt and Dunbar and comes down to McMillan's 1991 story "Quitting on the Rebound." *Breaking Ice* and *Calling the Wind* attest to the expansive vigor of the recent work in fiction.

Drama is represented by fewer anthologies than poetry or fiction. The three earliest—and for a long time the only ones—were Alain Locke and Montgomery Gregory's *Plays of Negro Life* (1927), Willis *Richardson's *Plays and Pageants from the Life of the Negro* (1930, reissued with a long introduction by Christine R. Gray in 1993), and Richardson and May *Miller's *Negro History in Thirteen Plays* (1935).

More than three decades passed before the next drama anthology appeared, William Couch's *New Black Playwrights* (1968). This collection brings together six plays by five dramatists, two of whom, Adrienne *Kennedy and Ed Bullins, were beginning major careers. Bullins himself at the time was preparing the important Black Theater issue of *Drama Review* (Summer 1968) and *New Plays from the Black Theatre* (1969). Later he brought out *The New Lafayette Theatre Presents* (1974). Turning away from protest to a white audience, Bullins and his colleagues committed themselves to a black consciousness and a black theater dedicated to what he called "the *dialectic of change* and the *dialectic of experience*." In *Three Negro Plays* (1969) the English critic C. W. E. Bigsby gathers standard works of the African American repertoire: Hughes's *Mulatto*, Jones's *The Slave*, and Lorraine *Hansberry's *The Sign in Sidney Brustein's Window*. More academic in tone and purpose are William Brasmer and Dominick Consolo's *Black Drama: An Anthology* (1970), William R. Reardon and Thomas D. Pauley's *The Black Teacher and the Dramatic Arts: A Dialogue, Bibliography, and Anthology* (1970), William Adams, Peter Conn, and Barry Slepian's *Afro-American Literature: Drama* (1970), Darwin Turner's *Black Drama in America: An Anthology* (1971), and Clinton F. Oliver and Stephanie Sills's *Contemporary Black Drama* (1971). In *Black Theater* (1971) Lindsay Patterson adds only a brief subjective introduction to the dozen plays he selects. The earliest is Bontemps and Cullen's *St. Louis Woman*, not easily available elsewhere. A unique collection also appeared in the early 1970s, *Black Scenes* (1971), edited by Alice *Childress. The title is literal: only scenes are presented from fifteen plays. Of considerable theoretical importance is the prefatory material by Oliver Jackson and Paul Carter Harrison to the latter's *Kuntu Drama: Plays of the African Continuum* (1974). The dramatists chosen to represent "modally conceived plays/events utilizing our native traditions" and involving the audience in a ritual of spiritual power are Toomer, Aimé Césaire, Baraka, Adrienne Kennedy, Lenox Brown, Clay Goss, and Harrison himself.

The best and most comprehensive anthologies of African American drama, however, are Woodie King and Ron *Milner's *Black Drama Anthology* (1973) and James Hatch and Ted *Shine's *Black Theatre, U.S.A.: Forty-five Plays by Black Americans, 1847–1974* (1974). Only one play—Loften *Mitchell's *Star of the Morning*—appears in both anthologies. King and Milner's twenty-three plays are all from the 1950s and after with the exception of Langston Hughes's brief *Mother and Child*. The apparatus in *Black Drama Anthology* is minimal but the selections are excellent. In *Black Theatre, U.S.A.* one will find numerous plays not previously published as well as familiar works, all presented in a full historical context to illustrate not only "the evolution of black dramaturgy in America," but also "what black playwrights think and feel about themselves, their people, and their country." The editorial apparatus is examplary in its scholarship.

Production of drama anthologies slowed down after the mid-1970s. In 1981 Eileen Joyce Ostrow published *Center Stage: An Anthology of 21 Contemporary Black-American Plays*, almost half of them from California. More recently Sylvia Kamerman put together for a juvenile audience *Plays of Black Americans* (1987), Errol Hill collected seven plays about *Black Heroes* (1989), and veteran anthologist Woodie King, Jr., assembled fifteen one-act plays in *New Plays for the Black Theatre* (1989). William Blackwell *Branch's *Black Thunder: An Anthology of Contemporary African American Drama* (1992) is a selection of nine plays produced from 1975 to 1980. As the subtitle indicates, Paul Carter Harrison's *Totem Voices: Plays from the Black World Repertory* (1989) includes African and Caribbean as well as American works. A similar anthology is William B. Branch's *Crosswinds: An Anthology of Black Dramatists in the Diaspora* (1993). Going backward in time rather than outward to Africa and the West Indies, *The Roots of African American Drama: An Anthology of Early Plays, 1856–1939* (1990), edited by Leo Hamalian and James Hatch, contains some previously unpublished work.

Women playwrights have been receiving close attention in recent years. The first collection was Margaret B. Wilkerson's *9 Plays by Black Women* (1986), with a thoughtful introduction, good headnotes, and a brief bibliography. *Black Female Playwrights* (1989), edited by Kathy A. Perkins, contains nineteen plays by women writing before midcentury. Equally valuable is Elizabeth Brown-Guillory's *Wines in the Wilderness: Plays by African American Women from the Harlem Renaissance to the Present* (1990). The apparatus is outstanding. For a vivid introduction to contemporary black women's theater, one has Sydné Mahone's *Moon Marked and Touched by Sun: Plays by African American Women* (1994). Although no woman playwright has yet reached the level of Morrison in fiction or Dove in poetry, talent is abundant and the future is promising.

Coverage of nonfiction will be restricted here to collections of autobiographical writing and literary prose. In the nineteenth century, of course, oratory was considered to be an important literary genre, and the black oratorical tradition has continued to the present. An excellent collection is Carter G. *Woodson's *Negro Orators and Their Orations* (1925). Here one can listen to the protest against slavery, the congressional speeches of Reconstruction politicians, speeches on race relations, and much more. Another collection of speeches is in Arthur L. Smith's *Rhetoric of Black Revolution* (1969).

The first twentieth-century anthology of any kind was D. W. Culp's misleadingly titled *Twentieth Century Negro Literature* (1902). "One Hundred of America's Greatest Negroes," as they are designated on the title page, contribute as many essays on various important racial issues at the turn of the century. Four decades later Bucklin Moon's *Primer for White Folks* (1945) attempted to confront white racism with the truth as expressed in mainly short selections by numerous writers, black and white. More forceful are John A. *Williams's *The Angry Black* (1962) and *Beyond the Angry Black* (1966; rpt. 1969). Darwin Turner and Jean Bright edited *Images of the Negro in America* (1965). Turner also edited *Black American Literature: Essays* (1969). Fifteen essayists are included beginning with William Wells Brown and ending with Eldridge *Cleaver. An ampler selection is Gladys J. Curry's *Viewpoints from Black America* (1970), "designed primarily as a reader for writers." Although some short stories are included in *Amistad 1* (1970) and *Amistad 2* (1971), both edited by John A. Williams and Charles F. Harris, their lively contents are mainly essays, mostly concerned with the contemporary scene. Another key book of the early 1970s is Addison *Gayle, Jr.'s influential *The Black Aesthetic* (1971). This collection of essays included not only current movers and shakers but such forerunners as Du Bois, J. A. Rogers, Hughes, Locke, and Wright. Gayle also edited *Bondage, Freedom, and Beyond: The Prose of Black Americans* (1971). Two other essay collections from these years are Arnold Adoff's *Black on Black* (1968) and Douglas A. Hughes's *From a Black Perspective: Contemporary Black Essays* (1970). More sharply focused is Marita *Golden's recent *Wild Women Don't Wear No Blues: Black Women Writers on Love, Men, and Sex* (1993), a provocative and highly readable collection of fifteen uninhibited essays. Angelyn Mitchell's *Within the Circle: An Anthology of African American Literary Criticism from the Harlem Renaissance to the Present* (1994), the first collection of its kind, will be indispensable to scholars.

The standard against which other anthologies of the African American essay must be measured, however, is the two-volume *Speech and Power: The African-American Essay and Its Cultural Content, from Polemics to Pulpit* (1992; rpt. 1993), edited by Gerald *Early, himself a master essayist. In its more than nine hundred pages, the reader will find over a hundred essays by all the major writers of the twentieth century and many lesser lights. As Early explains in the introduction, racial consciousness is the common denominator of black essays, but there is an immense variety of approach and position, a fact demonstrated by the inclusiveness of the collection.

Autobiographical writing has always been important in the African American tradition. Indeed, the slave narrative was the most important genre until the latter part of the nineteenth century. Since most of these narratives are short, they can be readily anthologized. Three such anthologies appeared in a single year, 1969: *Great Slave Narratives*, edited by Arna Bontemps; *Puttin' on Ole Massa*, edited by Gilbert Osofsky; and *Five Slave Narratives*, edited by William Loren Katz. Happily, of the eleven narratives included in these collections, only two appear twice. The introductions by Bontemps and Osofsky are both helpful; Katz's is much less so. A different tack is taken by Julius *Lester in *To Be a Slave* (1968), which alternates excerpts from narratives with the editor's explanatory comments. In *Black Slave Narratives* (1970) John Bayliss also collects brief excerpts—snippets, really—from twenty narratives. Better is Abraham Chapman's *Steal Away: Stories of the Runaway Slaves* (1971), which contains excerpts from five works recalling the African homeland and ten focusing on slave life and escape from it, as well as Douglass's "The Heroic Slave" in its entirety. The best of the books using this method is *Black Men in Chains: Narratives by Escaped Slaves* (1972), edited by Charles H. Nichols. Selections from sixteen of the most important narratives are presented along with a knowledgeable introduction and informative headnotes.

Most collections of autobiographies neglected women writers of the genre until the late 1980s. In *Sisters of the Spirit* (1986), William L. Andrews presents the spiritual narratives of Jarena *Lee, Zilpha *Elaw, and Julia A. J. *Foote. The important Schomburg Library of Nineteenth-Century Black Women Writers includes three relevant anthologies, all appearing in 1988. In *Six Women's Slave Narratives* Andrews presents Mary *Prince, "Old Elizabeth," Mattie J. *Jackson, Lucy Delaney, Kate *Drumgoold, and Annie Louise *Burton. Anthony G. Barthelemy's *Collected Black Women's Narratives* includes works by Nancy *Prince, Louisa Picquet, Bethany Veney, and Susie King *Taylor. Complementing these mainly secular narratives are those contained in Sue E. Houchins's *Spiritual Narratives* of Maria W. *Stewart, Jarena Lee, Julia Foote, and Virginia W. *Broughton.

Especially noteworthy are two collections edited by Henry Louis Gates, Jr.: *The Classic Slave Narratives* (1987) and *Bearing Witness* (1991). The former is the best, least expensive, and most easily available work of its kind. *Bearing Witness*, like Early's *Speech and Power*, is a collection of twentieth-century writing. Gates collects here what he calls "autobiographical statements" from twenty-eight authors exemplifying the dual motives of self-definition and racial witness that the editor in his brilliant introduction shows to be characteristic of the genre.

It is clear that anthologies have increased exponentially since the lean years before the 1960s. More will be forthcoming, as anthologists continue to track developments in the African American literary tradition.
　　　　　　　　　　　　　　　　　—Keneth Kinnamon

ANTISLAVERY MOVEMENT. The antislavery movement refers to those who opposed the enslavement of human beings, especially during the period when the U.S. government officially sanctioned *slavery (1776–1863). The antislavery philosophy must be distinguished from the abolitionist movement in the United States, which formally commenced with the publication of William Lloyd Garrison's *Liberator* in the spring of 1831. The abolitionists were a loosely organized biracial group, both in England and the United States, who demanded the abolition of slavery. The most uncompromising abolitionists took unpopular and often confrontational stands against slavery as it was widely practiced in the United States. More than a few abolitionists took significant physical risks and exposed their homes and families to retaliation. Antislavery philosophy was embraced by theologians, especially in the North, who argued a "monogenetic" theory of evolution of mankind, that is, that all human beings were derived from a single created original, Adam and Eve, and that differences are cultural and ethnic but not essential. Opposing this view was that of the "polygeneticists," who believed that the human race was evolved from several original creations and that the contemporary differences in ethnic and racial composition were the result of an intentional separation of the races at the time of creation. Proslavery advocates like Josiah Nott, who published *Types of Mankind, or Ethnological Researches* in 1843, were vigorously opposed by antislavery thinkers such as Alexander McLeod, William Lloyd Garrison, and Wendell Phillips.

The most prominent vehicle for this confrontation was the abolitionist newspaper and the sermonic tract, combined with the powerful rhetoric of the speaker's platform. Wendell Phillips was particularly well regarded as a prominent abolitionist speaker, and he and Garrison became the leading white spokesmen in the antebellum United States for the antislavery cause. They were joined by the former slave Frederick *Douglass, who not only spoke widely and eloquently of his personal experiences of the "peculiar institution" but also wrote an internationally disseminated *slave narrative in 1845, *Narrative of the Life of Frederick Douglass, An American Slave*. Women abolitionists were also influential. *Incidents in the Life of a Slave Girl* (1861) by Harriet A. *Jacobs drew attention to the plight of women under the harsh treatment of the chattel system. Harriet Beecher *Stowe's protest novel *Uncle Tom's Cabin* was published in 1852, translated into twenty languages, and sold more than three million copies worldwide. Stowe's book did much to advance the cause of antislavery, though ironically it was a fictional account of the slave system, based on less well-known sources such as T. D. Weld's *American Slavery As It Is: The Testimony of a Thousand Witnesses* (1839)—a compilation of documents relating to slavery and the slave trade. The most noted abolitionist organization was the American Anti-Slavery Society, founded in 1833 and dominated by Garrison. Such societies were responsible for publishing numerous tracts, pamphlets, slave narratives, and *periodicals opposing slavery. Most of the leading African American writers of the mid-nineteenth century, including Douglass, Jacobs, and William Wells *Brown, broke into print under the auspices of the antislavery movement.

Not all abolitionists were writers and speakers. John *Brown, well known for his raid on the federal arsenal at Harpers Ferry, Virginia, not only vigorously opposed slavery in speech; he also vowed to end it through whatever means necessary, including *violence. The Harpers Ferry raid gave Brown a reputation for violent opposition to the institution and the admiration of some more pacific antislavery advocates such as Henry David Thoreau, who wrote the eloquent "A Plea for Captain John Brown" in 1859, in the few weeks between his arrest after Harpers Ferry and his hanging on 2 December. During the Civil War the soldiers of the Federal Army, marching to "John Brown's Body Lies A'Mouldering in the Grave," celebrated the Harpers Ferry attack as the high point of the antislavery movement. But Brown's heroic antislavery militancy had its wellspring in African American activist writers such as David *Walker, author of *David Walker's Appeal (1829), and Henry Highland *Garnet, whose powerful call to slave revolt, "An Address to the Slaves of the United States of America," was published in 1848 in tandem with Walker's *Appeal. The financing of this most radical of all black antislavery publishing efforts was provided by John Brown.

[See also Literary History; Oratory; Publishing.]

• James M. McPherson, The Struggle for Equality, 1964. William H. Pease and Jane H. Pease, eds., The Antislavery Argument, 1965. Benjamin Quarles, Black Abolitionists, 1969. James Brewer Stewart, Holy Warriors, 1976.

—William L. Andrews and Mason I. Lowance, Jr.

ATKINS, RUSSELL (b. 1926), poet, composer, theorist, editor, and leading innovator in experimental artistic movements of the 1940s through the 1970s. Born 25 February 1926 in Cleveland, Ohio, Russell Atkins began studying piano at age seven with his mother. From childhood, he exhibited talent in painting, drawing, *music, and writing. By age thirteen he had won several *poetry contests. Atkins published his first poem in 1944 in his high school yearbook. With the support of prominent literary figures, Atkins published his poetry in journals and newspapers, including Experiment (1947–1951) and the New York Times (1951).

Atkins continued his studies of music, performance, and the visual arts through Cleveland College, Cleveland Music School Settlement, Cleveland Institute of Music, Karamu Theatre, and Cleveland School of Art. Musical training is a key to Atkins's poetic style since musical structures are central in his writing.

In 1950 Atkins cofounded what is probably the oldest black-owned literary magazine, Free Lance, a publication of avant-garde writing that contributed to the development of New American poetry. He created a style of concrete poetry in which visual presentation of words on the page predominates. He experimented stylistically with the extreme use of the apostrophe, embedding of words within words, and use of continuous words. In the mid-1950s he began utilizing an abstract technique he called "phenomenalism," which juxtaposed unfamiliar and familiar elements. Atkins advocated using the imagination "to exploit range, to create a body of effect, event, colors, characteristics, moods, verbal stresses pushed to a maximum." He did not try to make his work comprehensible to casual readers but strove for dense complexity of meaning.

Atkins experimented with "poems in play forms," publishing two plays in 1954, The Abortionist and The Corpse. Like his poetry, his plays radically challenged conventions of both form and content.

In its 1955–1956 issue, Free Lance published Atkins's influential article, "A Psychovisual Perspective for 'Musical' Composition." Using Gestalt theory of pattern formation, Atkins argues for the brain and not the ear as the focus of composition.

In 1960 Atkins published his first collection of poetry, A Podium Presentation. Subsequent volumes include Phenomena (1961), Objects (1963), Objects 2 (1964), Heretofore (1968), The Nail, to Be Set to Music (1970), Maleficium (1971), Here in The (1976), and Whichever (1978).

• Eugene Redmond, Drumvoices: The Mission of Afro-American Poetry, A Critical History, 1976. Ronald Henry High, "Russell Atkins," in DLB, vol. 41, Afro-American Poets since 1955, eds. Trudier Harris and Thadious M. Davis, 1985, pp. 24–32.
—Jennifer Burton

"Atlanta Compromise Speech." See "Atlanta Exposition Address."

"Atlanta Exposition Address." The turning point of Booker T. *Washington's tenure as African American leader was his address to the Cotton States and International Exposition at Atlanta in 1895. Before the address, referred to as "The Atlanta Compromise Address" or "The Atlanta Exposition Address," Washington was the head of the Tuskegee Institute in Atlanta; afterward, he was the acknowledged leader of the African American people.

Washington's address essentially ratified the status quo in southern race relations, which had been on a decline since Reconstruction. In the speech he called for African Americans to work for their salvation through economic advancement, and for southern whites to help them on this path. "To those of my race who depend on bettering their condition in a foreign land, or who underestimate the importance of cultivating friendly relations with the Southern white man who is their next neighbor, I would say cast down your bucket where you are, cast it down in making friends, in every manly way, of the people of all races by whom we are surrounded." He also downplayed the quest for civil equality in the South, reassuring his white audience: "In all things that are purely social we can be as separate as the fingers, yet one as the hand in all things essential to mutual progress." Economic advancement was more important to African Americans in the South than civil rights, Washington maintained. Once black people had made a success in the world of *work, they could expect ultimately to be respected by whites as fellow citizens.

The African American response to the "Atlanta Exposition Address" was initially supportive. But in The *Souls of Black Folk (1903) W. E. B. *Du Bois took exception to what he saw as Washington's abandonment of the historic obligation of African American leadership to demand fair play and justice for their people. Washington's doctrine "has tended to make the whites, North and South, shift the burden of the

Negro problem to the Negro's shoulders and stand aside as critical and rather pessimistic spectators; when in fact the burden belongs to the nation." Growing opposition to the ideas articulated in the "Atlanta Exposition Address" led to the founding of the NAACP in 1909.

To his supporters, Washington was making the best of limited oportunities for African Americans in the South. To his detractors, Washington was abetting the continuous subjugation of African Americans by letting whites believe that African Americans were content to wait for the rights guaranteed by the Constitution. As the twentieth century progressed, Du Bois's view prevailed, but for a period of twenty years and more, the views espoused by Washington in the Atlanta Exposition speech generally received widespread approval from African Americans and whites alike.

[See also Oratory.]

• August Meier, *Negro Thought in America, 1880–1915*, 1963. Emma Lou Thornbrough, ed., *Booker T. Washington*, 1969.

—Jonathan Silverman

ATTAWAY, WILLIAM (1911–1986), novelist, composer, and scriptwriter. William Attaway was born 19 November 1911, in Greenville, Mississippi, to Florence Parry Attaway, a teacher, and William Alexander Attaway, a physician and founder of the National Negro Insurance Association. When he was five, his family moved to Chicago, taking part in the Great Migration that he later chronicled as a novelist. The family moved to protect the children from the corrosive racial attitudes of the South.

Attaway's early interest in literature was sparked by Langston *Hughes's *poetry and by his sister who encouraged him to write for her theater groups. He attended the University of Illinois until his father's death, when Attaway left school and traveled west. He lived as a vagabond for two years, working a variety of jobs and writing. In 1933 he returned to Chicago and resumed his schooling, graduating in 1936. Attaway's play *Carnival* (1935) was produced at the University of Illinois, and in 1936 his short story, "The Tale of the Blackamoor," was published in *Challenge*.

Attaway was involved with the *Federal Writers' Project in 1935 and befriended Richard *Wright, whom he once invited to speak to the university literary society. Attaway reported that as Wright read "Big Boy Leaves Home," an unflinching look at the racism and violence that forces one young African American to leave the South, audience members fled, finally leaving only Wright and himself in the room. Attaway understood that the issues he would address in his own fiction might disturb readers, but the event did not dissuade him from providing blunt depictions of racism and struggle.

After graduation, Attaway lived in New York City and held several jobs including labor organizer. While working as an actor, Attaway completed his first *novel, written in the tradition of naturalist and proletarian novels of the period. *Let Me Breathe Thunder* (1939) follows two young white migrant farmworkers, Step and Ed, who travel by rail in the

west at the end of the depression. They befriend a nine-year-old Mexican youth, Hi Boy, whose optimism serves as a contrast to Step's cynicism. While many critics emphasized Attaway's focus on whites, some noted the marginalized status of those characters and the strength of the novel's African American characters.

Blood on the Forge (1941), called by critic Robert Bone the most perceptive novel about the Great Migration, centers on three African American half brothers who escape a lynch mob in 1919 and leave Kentucky for the steel mills of Pennsylvania. Like other literature of the migration, this novel questions the notion of the North as the promised land. While the brothers escape the violence of the South, they soon encounter the violence of northern industrial capitalism. The three are ultimately devastated: Big Mat is killed, Chinatown blinded, and Melody spiritually injured. Many critics compared the novel to Wright's *Native Son*, especially linking Big Mat with Wright's *Bigger Thomas. Attaway's use of language that expresses a sense of the folk idiom has been compared to Zora Neale *Hurston's use of African American oral tradition. Ralph *Ellison praised the book's examination of transition and conflict but critiqued its omission of characters not destroyed by the transition north, saying that Attaway understood the destruction of folk culture but missed its regeneration in other forms.

While well received by critics, Attaway's books sold poorly, and he wrote no more novels. Although he published the short story "Death of a Rag Doll" in 1947, he turned his creative focus to composing and arranging *music (he was especially interested in West Indian music and collaborated with his friend Harry Belafonte). He published two music-oriented books: *Calypso Song Book* (1957) and *Hear America Singing* (1967). Attaway also explored other media, writing scripts for radio, *television, and *film. In 1966, he wrote the script for *One Hundred Years of Laughter*, a television special on African American *humor. He wrote a screenplay adaptation of *The Man*, Irving Wallace's novel about the first African American president. Attaway's version, foregrounding racial conflict and emphasizing African American voices, was ultimately rejected by the producers.

Attaway had some involvement in the *civil rights movement, including the 1965 voting rights march to Selma, Alabama. He lived in Barbados for eleven years, with his wife and two children. His last years were spent in California, where he worked on the script for *The Atlanta Child Murders* (1985). He died in Los Angeles in 1986.

As one of the first African American novelists to focus on the subject, Attaway is primarily known for his contribution to the literature of the Great Migration. He vividly portrayed the causes and often devastating consequences of that exodus. While refusing to sentimentalize, he wrote with compassion and rich detail about working-class characters of different races and their various, usually tragic, struggles.

[See also Emigration; Migration.]

• Ralph Ellison, "Transition," *Negro Quarterly* 1 (Spring 1942): 87–92. Edward Margolies, "Migration: William

Attaway and *Blood on the Forge*," in *Native Sons: A Critical Study of Twentieth-Century Negro American Authors*, 1968, pp. 47–64. Richard Yarborough, afterword in *Blood on the Forge*, 1941; rpt. 1987. Samuel Garren, "'He Had passion': William Attaway's Screenplay Drafts of Irving Wallace's *The Man*," *CLA Journal* 37 (Mar. 1994): 245–260.

—Christina Accomando

AUBERT, ALVIN (b. 1930), poet, educator, editor, short story writer, and dramatist. Born 12 March 1930 in Lutcher, Louisiana, Alvin Bernard Aubert's presence in African American literature is marked by his creative, editorial, and scholarly contributions to the discipline. As a poet his works often reflect upon childhood and adolescence in Louisiana, and through these observations comment on the ubiquitous states of human existence. As the founding editor of *Obsidian*, he has provided a journal with a nurturing environment for the publication of African American literature and theoretical discourse.

Aubert earned a bachelor's degree in English literature with a minor in French from Southern University in Baton Rouge in 1959. As an undergraduate he was encouraged by Blyden Jackson, chair of the English department, to consider graduate studies and a career in teaching. He received a Woodrow Wilson Fellowship for graduate studies to the University of Michigan at Ann Arbor where he completed a master's degree in English literature the following year.

His first teaching position was in the English department at Southern where he coordinated and taught one of the first courses on African American literature offered by the university. Citing his own lack of knowledge as a student, he sought to increase others' awareness of African American literature by reading texts from the *Harlem Renaissance to the present. Additional graduate work at the University of Illinois, on sixteenth- and seventeenth-century authors Shakespeare and Milton, illuminated the importance of allusions and their ability to enrich a particular text by referring to myths, the Bible, and earlier literatures. Applying these studies on language to African American literature, he began to recognize the means through which expressive language was capable of eloquently describing everyday activities. Aubert's career continued with his teaching African American literature and creative writing at both the State University of New York in Fredonia (1970–1979) and later at Wayne State University (1979–1992). He founded *Obsidian: Black Literature in Review* in 1975, which functioned as a catalyst for aspiring writers to publish. He remained the journal's editor until it ceased publication in 1982. In 1986 the journal was reissued as *Obsidian II* and is published under the auspices of the English department at North Carolina State University.

Considering the African American poet's relationship to the community, Aubert has at times debated the poet's success or failure in effectively communicating to others. Given the inconclusive nature of the dilemma, he resigned himself to a philosophy that the reader should be educated in language. This "education" was not formal but rather an individual's sensitivity to language and its unlimited potential for conveying and re-creating experiences and sentiments. Aubert rejected notions of artistic compromise and regarded the poet as belonging and committed to *poetry.

It was this type of sensibility that provoked criticism from colleagues who often regarded his works as dispassionate and allusive. While others writing during the 1960s and 1970s produced politically and socially charged poems reflecting the times, his poetry remained centered on personal experiences. Therefore his writing contrasted with that of others by reminding readers that, when closely viewed, individual members of the African American community celebrated unique experiences.

Since 1966, Aubert's poetry has been included in numerous journals and *anthologies. Over the years his poetry has experienced an evolution of themes and self-awareness. His first collection, *Against the Blues* (1972), primarily focused on childhood in Louisiana while *Feeling Through* (1975), experimenting with techniques, reflected on military experiences, knowledge of African American writings, and adolescence. With *South Louisiana: New and Selected Poems* (1985), he again referenced African American art and literature although the overall collection reflected a diverse range of experiences. This collection along with *If Winter Come: Collected Poems 1967–1992* (1994) included several previously published poems and new poems suggesting Aubert's arrival at a crossroads in life. *If Winter Come* ranges from childhood experiences ("My Dog Ringo/The Dolphin") and relationships ("Woman in Me"), to African Americans ("Like Miles Said," "James *Baldwin, 1924–1987") and the poet's work ("Here Now"). His last collection, *Harlem Wrestler* (1995), incorporates these familiar themes and continues with reflections on national holidays ("Dear Columbus/11-11-93," "MLK Day 1992"), retirement ("Legacies"), self-awareness ("And No Harm's Done to the Tree"), and maturing romance ("Lovely Lady").

Besides poetry, Aubert's creative works have included *short stories and plays. His fiction has appeared in literary journals and an anthology. His first play, *Home from Harlem* (1986), was an adaptation of Paul Laurence *Dunbar's *The *Sport of the Gods*. In the mid-1990s Aubert was revising his second play and writing a first *novel. Maintaining his tradition, both stories are set in Louisiana.

• James Schokoff, "Aubert's Poems Have Depth," *Buffalo Courier Express*, 8 June 1973, 22. Herbert Woodward Martin, "Alvin Aubert: *South Louisiana: New and Selected Poems*," *Black American Literature Forum* 21.3 (Fall 1987): 343–348. Jerry W. Ward, Jr., "Alvin Aubert: Literature, History, Ethnicity," *Xavier Review* 7.2 (1987): 1–12. Tom Dent, "Alvin Aubert: *South Louisiana: New and Selected Poems*," *Black American Literature Forum* 22.1 (Spring 1988): 127–129.

—R. Goldman Vander

AUN' PEGGY, a powerful conjure woman whose magic and spells lie at the heart of *Uncle Julius McAdoo's tales in *The *Conjure Woman* (1899) by Charles Waddell *Chesnutt. Aun' Peggy's abilities, deeply rooted in African American folk knowledge and traditions, add mystery, strength, and purpose to

Uncle Julius's stories. Feared and respected by white and black, Aun' Peggy lives as a free woman outside of Patesville (Fayetteville, N.C.). She is a shrewd, independent businesswoman who insists on payment for her services. Working with roots, snakeskins, and "yuther conjuh-fixins," she gives people rheumatism and fits, causes them to waste away, and turns them into animals. Only Uncle Jube (in "The Gray Wolf's Ha'nt") is a more powerful conjurer. Aun' Peggy's spells or "goophers" are used for a variety of purposes, often to resist white control. In "Sis' Becky's Pickaninny" she reunites a slave mother and child by turning the child into a bird. In "Mars Jeems's Nightmare" she turns a cruel plantation owner into a slave so that he might experience firsthand the difficult lives his slaves lead. Some of Aun' Peggy's *conjuring is not for the benefit of the African American community. In "The Goophered Grapevine" she casts a deadly spell for Mars Dugal to keep slaves away from his scuppernongs. Thus, Aun' Peggy is a complex character whose power and presence are pivotal in *The Conjure Woman*. She also serves as a literary foremother to such modern-day conjure women as those depicted in Gloria *Naylor's *Mama Day* (1988).

• Sylvia Render, introduction to *The Short Fiction of Charles W. Chesnutt*, 1974. William L. Andrews, *The Literary Career of Charles Chesnutt*, 1980.   —Paula Gallant Eckard

AUNT CHLOE FLEET is the unifying character for six poems in Frances Ellen Watkins *Harper's *Sketches of Southern Life* (1872): "Aunt Chloe," "The Deliverance," "Aunt Chloe's Politics," "Learning to Read," "Church Building," and "The Reunion." This poetry emulates the *slave narrative, a literary form that characterized much of the literature written by and about African Americans during the nineteenth century. It is distinctive because Harper invented a dialect technique that used aural association and syntax rather than phonetics to create an authentic black voice. This innovation is seen in literature by African American writers of subsequent generations, a technique that effectively captures the dialect without reducing folk characters to *stereotypes or caricatures.

Aunt Chloe's voice represents the agony of all slave women when the slave mistress sells Aunt Chloe's children in order to defray a debt. The dramatic style of the narrative also includes other characters who warn and console Chloe, demonstrating the strength of the slave community as a social and political network. The work's broader setting is the Civil War and Reconstruction, and the poems reflect the perspective of the black woman as Aunt Chloe interprets those events and struggles for *freedom, *literacy, and self-determination.

The theme of the poetry is a spiritual message that conveys a deep belief in Jesus as the spirit of salvation, rebirth, and justice. Aunt Chloe's voice exhibits wit, tenacity, and strong political views. Recited before black and white audiences, and sometimes before exclusively black female audiences, the book was widely circulated as Harper traveled and promoted black liberation and women's rights throughout the country.

[*See also* Feminism.]

• Frances Smith Foster, ed., *A Brighter Coming Day: A Frances Ellen Watkins Harper Reader*, 1990. Melba Joyce Boyd, *Discarded Legacy: Politics and Poetics in the Life of Frances E. W. Harper 1825–1911*, 1994.

—Melba Joyce Boyd

AUNT JEMIMA, trademark, stereotype, cultural icon to many whites, and racist caricature to many African Americans. For Chris Rutt and Charles Underwood, Aunt Jemima was the perfect symbol for their experiment with the first packaged pancake mix. These white entrepreneurs attended a vaudeville show in 1889, featuring black-faced comedians in a New Orleans–style cakewalk tune entitled "Aunt Jemima." Emblazoned on the posters announcing the act grinned the familiar image of *mammy. Rutt appropriated the name and image, for who could better sell processed foods to American housewives than mammy, ready to save them from kitchen drudgery? Barbara Christian's *Black Women Novelists* (1980) analyzes how Jemima kept particular images about white women intact. African American writers used the *stereotype subversively, as described by Trudier Harris in *From Mammies to Militants* (1982).

Jemima, the offshoot of irascible mammy, was sweet, jolly, even-tempered, and polite. Jemima, Hebrew for "dove," was Job's youngest daughter, symbolizing innocence, gentleness, and peace. But the name belies its meaning. The caricature connotes not naïveté but stupidity, not peace but docility. Jemima was an obese, darkly pigmented, broad-bosomed, handkerchief-headed, gingham-dressed, elderly servant content in her subjugation.

African American resentment regarding Aunt Jemima stemmed not from a rejection of the maternal or domestic image she presented, but from unabashed attempts to create, with this single image, a monolithic African American woman and market her to the world. By 1900, more than 200,000 Jemima dolls, 150,000 Jemima cookie jars, and numerous memorabilia in the form of black-faced buttons and toothpick holders had been sold.

R. T. Davis brought to life the caricature when he purchased the trademark in 1890. He found a three hundred pound model in the person of Nancy Green, a former slave born in Kentucky, who possessed perfectly even white teeth, a stark contrast to her dark complexion. Green signed a lifetime contract with Aunt Jemima. The highlight of her career was her 1893 appearance at the Chicago World's Fair where her pancake-flipping antics and tales of *slavery concretized a negative stereotype of African American women. Ironically, the controversial image transformed her life to one of affluence. Green died a celebrity, lauded as the Pancake Queen.

Anna Robinson promoted Jemima's image from 1933 to 1950, and Edith Wilson, a show personality, transformed her to modern, with a stylish hairdo and pearl earrings. This version adorns the pancake box today, but for many African Americans the light brown skin and updated clothes do little to repair the disfigured image of the past.

• Purd Wright, "The Life of Aunt Jemima, The Most Famous Colored Woman in the World," in *Brands, Trademarks and Good Will: The Story of the Quaker Oats Company*, ed. Arthur F. Marquette, 1967, pp. 137–158. Nagueyalti Warren, "From Uncle Tom to Cliff Huxtable, Aunt Jemima to Aunt Nell: Images of Blacks in Film and the Television Industry," in *Images of Blacks in American Culture*, ed. Jessie Carney Smith, 1988, pp. 51–117.
                                            —Nagueyalti Warren

AUSTIN, DORIS JEAN (c. 1949–1994), novelist and essayist. Doris Jean Austin is the author of one novel, *After the Fall* (1987), and a frequent contributor to such periodicals as *Essence* and the *New York Times Book Review*. In *Essence*, she has published articles such as "The Men in My Life," "Fighting Off the Fears," and "Holistic Healing: Mind: Taming the Demons" (all 1992).

Austin was born in Mobile, Alabama, where she lived until she was six, when her family moved to Jersey City, New Jersey. That city serves as the locale for her fictional creation. She has been a MacDowell Colony fellow and a recipient of the DeWitt Wallace/Reader's Digest Award for Literary Excellence. That recognition came with the publication of *After the Fall*.

Episodic in structure, *After the Fall* takes place over a twenty-three year period, from 1939 to 1962. It presents a self-contained African American world little impacted by the turbulent historical events of the period, although they are mentioned from time to time, and little impacted by white racism. It presents a rich and varied African American world in the middle-class community of Astor Place, the working-class community of Kearney Avenue, the school, the neighborhood bar, and the *church.

Growing up in a three-generational household, Austin experienced firsthand the value of strong kinship ties. The novel reflects that. Beginning on the day that heroine Elzina James begins menstruation, the novel is an extended coming-of-age story. Elzina must resolve allegiances to Rosalie Tompkins, the puritanical and strong-willed grandmother who raised her, and her husband Jesse, whom her grandmother despises because of his lower-class background.

The novel is one of the narratives in African American literature that dramatizes the class conflicts and disparate value systems found within the African American community. Rosalie Tompkins, whose life revolves around the church and raising her granddaughter, has only two wishes before she dies: to return to the red clay of her native, beloved Alabama and to see Elzina enrolled at Tuskegee Institute. Her wishes are thwarted when Elzina, at fifteen, loses her virginity to the high-school heartthrob Jesse, of the free-spirited, hard-partying James clan, marries him, and has a son, Charles. The young couple resides in Rosalie's house and the grandmother-granddaughter relationship remains unchanged by Elzina's marriage and presumed adult status. Jesse chafes under Rosalie's thinly veiled contempt for him and resentment over the thwarted plans for her granddaughter.

His unemployment and Elzina's refusal to ask her grandmother for money for him to finance a gas station exacerbate the tensions in the marriage. At the height of a quarrel Jesse tells Elzina: "'We ain't got no business married. . . . At least I know my black ass ain't got no business married to no *Tompkins*! I ain't nothing but a po' ol' field nigger, that's me!'" Jesse becomes an accomplice in an armed robbery and receives a harsh sentence. Although Rosalie dies midway through the novel, she lives on in the values instilled in her granddaughter, whose life revolves around being a model single mother and the proprietor of a well-run, profitable boardinghouse.

Truselle James, Elzina's mother-in-law, the matriarch of the James clan, provides a contrast to Rosalie. Whereas Rosalie's house is like "a musty old museum," Truselle's house, the headquarters of her large extended family, is permeated by the smell of barbecue and the laughter of her grandchildren. The sexlessness of Rosalie, suggested by her long, flat breasts (which remind Elzina of soft, empty leather purses) contrasts with the fecundity of Truselle, who, as a kind of earth mother, has ten children by an assortment of men. The large-hearted Truselle nurtures the troubled members, not only of her own family, but also Orelia Jeter, the mother of Jesse's illegitimate daughter, and even Elzina following her complete nervous collapse brought about by her husband's tragic death from a freak hunting accident. The novel ends on a note of female intergenerational harmony. Just as Truselle as surrogate mother has been instrumental to Elzina's recovery, a recovered Elzina assumes a healing role of surrogate motherhood to Jesse's illegitimate, orphaned daughter.

Well-known African American critic Robert G. O'Meally reviewed the novel in the *New York Times* and praised, above all else, Austin's "courageous confrontation of character"; he deemed it "most impressive." While Austin was not prolific, she certainly struck a note in African American literary creativity and popular magazine writing that warrants further study.

• Blyden Jackson, *A History of Afro-American Literature*, 1989. Valerie Smith, *African American Writers*, 1991. Frank N. Magill, *Masterpieces of African-American Literature*, 1992.
                                            —Phiefer L. Browne

AUTHENTICATION. The authenticity of *slave narratives has always been an issue for scholars, especially for historians. Since the 1970s, literary scholars have been additionally involved in studying the strategies within narratives that are employed to confirm, or at least suggest, the authenticity of those narratives. Central to this study is the awareness that these strategies function to confirm not only the veracity of the narrative but also the real-life existence of the slave narrator. Investigating how all these matters are managed in a narrative has come to be called the study of authentication in the narratives.

A typical slave narrative includes many documents—prefaces, letters, guarantees, testimonies, appendices, and so forth—that serve to confirm that the story is true and that the narrator is a real person, not a fiction. Much can be learned about the slave narrator's *literacy and new relations with his or her guarantors (of both races) by studying how the documents are marshaled and distributed within the text. In general, the more the documents are woven into and thus subsumed by the narrative the more it seems likely that the narrator has taken control of the narrative and is relatively self-assured in life as well. Frederick *Douglass's narratives and posture in life illustrate this point.

Authentication and the related matter of authorial control are concerns for the study of any narrative in which strategies are mounted in anticipation of doubts of its veracity. This particular way of examining slave narratives has thus provided new ways of reading, for example, modern *autobiographies and memoirs. However, it is in the study of slave narratives, and all other narratives in which the narrator must overcome the racialized doubts of majority-group readers, that the study of authentication becomes a vital and essential activity.

• Robert B. Stepto, *From Behind the Veil: A Study of AfroAmerican Narrative*, 2d ed., 1991.

—Robert B. Stepto

AUTOBIOGRAPHY. *This entry consists of three articles that illustrate the basic features of African American autobiography. The* Overview *outlines the history and central characteristics of the genre of autobiography. The subsequent discussions—*Secular Autobiography *and* Spiritual Autobiography—*define the two major traditions of first-person writing in African American literature and comment on the most noteworthy texts in both traditions.*

OVERVIEW

Autobiography holds a position of priority, if not pre-eminence, among the narrative traditions of black America. From its origins in narratives of enslavement and accounts of religious conversion, African American autobiography has testified since the late eighteenth century to the commitment of people of color to realize the promise of their American birthright and to articulate their achievements as individuals and as persons of African descent. Perhaps more than any other form of literary discourse, autobiography has been chosen by African Americans to articulate ideals of selfhood integral to an African American sense of *identity, both individual and communal. At the same time that autobiography has helped African Americans bear witness to an evolving tradition of liberated and empowered individuality, autobiography has also provided a forum for addressing the sociopolitical as well as cultural obstacles that impede the liberation and empowerment of African Americans in the United States.

The most influential early African American autobiographies, the narratives of fugitive slaves, were sponsored by nineteenth-century abolitionists out of a conviction that first-person accounts of those victimized by and yet triumphant over *slavery would mobilize white readers more profoundly than any other kind of antislavery discourse. In the process of revealing the truth about the institution of slavery, fugitive slave narrators such as Frederick *Douglass and Harriet A. *Jacobs established a heroic precedent in African American literature for men and women of the word whose mode of personal storytelling demonstrated their *freedom. After emancipation in 1865, African Americans, led by Booker T. *Washington, clung to autobiography as a means of celebrating their triumphs both during and after slavery and affirming their dedication to the American middle-class ideals of industry, property ownership, and upward mobility. Generations of struggle against segregation capped by the rigors of the depression era infused into African American autobiography in the modern era a degree of skepticism and irony unheard of in the form since the antislavery era. Nevertheless, major early twentieth-century autobiographers such as W. E. B. *Du Bois, Zora Neale *Hurston, and Richard *Wright maintained the potential of autobiography to represent graphically the social problems endemic to the American *color line and to speak compellingly and personally to white readers about racial prejudice, ignorance, and fear.

Since World War II, autobiography in the hands of persons as different as *Malcolm X, Ned *Cobb, Audre *Lorde, and Itabari Njeri has taken on an increasingly diverse agenda as African Americans explore denominators additional to *race—among them *sexuality, *religion, *class, and *family—to assist in the task of full self-definition. Some of the most skilled writers in contemporary black America, among them Maya *Angelou, John Edgar *Wideman, and Samuel R. *Delany, have produced prizewinning autobiographies in recent decades, confirming the continuing literary vitality of African American first-person narrative in American multiethnic society.

[See also Neo–Slave Narrative; Slave Narrative.]

• Rebecca Chalmers Barton, *Witnesses for Freedom*, 1948. Stephen Butterfield, *Black Autobiography in America*, 1974. Russell C. Brignano, *Black Americans in Autobiography*, 1984. William L. Andrews, *To Tell a Free Story: The First Century of Afro-American Autobiography, 1760–1865*, 1986. Joanne M. Braxton, *Black Women Writing Autobiography*, 1989. William L. Andrews, ed., *African American Autobiography: A Collection of Critical Essays*, 1993.

—William L. Andrews

SECULAR AUTOBIOGRAPHY

The originators of African American autobiography in the late eighteenth century did not recognize easy or sharp distinctions between the spiritual and secular realms. The Africans who were brought to the Americas in slave ships viewed Man, Nature, and God as distinct but inseparable aspects of what Lawrence Levine in *Black Culture and Black Consciousness* (1977) has characterized as "a sacred whole." Although the first African American autobiography, *A Narrative of the Uncommon Sufferings and Surprizing Deliverance of Briton Hammon, a Negro Man* (1760), directs its primary focus on the physical perils of Briton *Hammon's grueling thirteen-year sojourn at sea away from his Boston master, the narrative concludes on a distinctly religious note, praising God for delivering Hammon as the Lord did King David of the Old Testament. Most early African American autobiographies are more explicitly pious than Hammon's, interweaving secular elements of experience, such as African childhood, enslavement in the Americas, captivity by American Indians, emancipation, and struggles to succeed and prosper in *freedom, into narratives that attend seriously to spiritual issues, particularly conversion to Christianity and the pursuit of a godly life.

The most widely read and influential early African American autobiography, the two-volume *Interesting Narrative of the Life of Olaudah Equiano, or Gustavus Vassa, the African* (1789), is written from as worldly a point of view as can be found in the first century of African American personal narrative. Yet when Olaudah *Equiano analyzes the most systemic problem of the Western social order, chattel *slavery, he adopts the religious posture and moral language of a biblical prophet: "O, ye nominal Christians! might not an African ask you—Learned you this from your God, who says unto you, Do unto all men as you would men should do unto you?" Although African American autobiography has long been considered remarkable for its persistent engagement with transpersonal social, economic, and political issues, one cannot discuss the secular tradition in African American first-person narrative without predicating the social consciousness of this form on the social conscience that it absorbed from its rootedness in the spirit of African American Christianity.

As a form of discourse African American autobiography can best be understood in terms of the three constituent elements of the word itself—*autos* (self), *bios* (life), and *graphe* (writing). Undoubtedly the window that autobiography opens onto African American life, especially aspects of that life that have made black experience distinctive, has been crucial to the success of the genre with the popular reader in the United States and abroad. From the southern plantation of the nineteenth century to the inner-city ghetto of the twentieth, most widely read African American autobiographers can credit a significant degree of their success to their willingness to reveal (sometimes voyeuristically) dimensions of African American life that are little known or superficially appreciated by the majority culture. Still, no one should discount the social import of the African American autobiographer's concern with claiming a psychological as well as an experiential distinctiveness for him- or herself. In the United States, whose founding Constitution established the legal definition of a slave as but three-fifths of a person, to claim and articulate an independent selfhood has traditionally been among the boldest and most controversial gestures initiated by African Americans in and through autobiography. A key manifestation of *autos* since the beginning of the African American autobiographical enterprise has been the struggle to attain the autonomy of authorship, the right to express oneself independent of the direction or approval of white sponsors and editors. For this reason, the subtitle "Written by Himself" on the cover of a fugitive *slave narrative in the first half of the nineteenth century bore considerable political as well as literary import. Increasingly in the twentieth century, the act of writing, the representation of selfhood through a personalized storytelling style, has become the sign of the African American autobiographer's assertion of independence of mind and individuality of vision. The realization that selfhood is itself constituted by language, along with a poststructuralist wariness of granting any text—especially autobiography—the authority of an unmediated representation of a life or a self, have contributed to the insistence in the 1980s and 1990s on a careful study of the styles and rhetoric adopted by (or subtly required of) autobiographers of color since the inception of the genre in North America. After decades of being read more as documentary evidence of something else—the conditions of slavery, the sociology of *race, the experience of the ghetto—than as a monument to the self-expressive traditions that shaped it into a meaningful entity in and of itself, African American autobiography has finally arrived on the literary scene, ready to reward examination by a multitude of disciplines.

Although autobiography is by definition a self-oriented form of writing and thus open to the charge of egoism, African American autobiographers have traditionally felt an obligation to speak for and to people of color, rather than just on behalf of self alone. Harriet A. *Jacobs, author of *Incidents in the Life of a Slave Girl* (1861), prefaced her narrative by announcing, "I have not written my experiences in order to attract attention to myself. . . . But I do earnestly desire to arouse the women of the North to a realizing sense of the condition of two millions of women at the South, still in bondage, suffering what I suffered." A little more than a century later Claude *Brown began *Manchild in the Promised Land* (1965) by stating, "I want to talk about the first Northern urban generation of Negroes. . . . This is a story of their searching, their dreams, their sorrows, their small and futile rebellions, and their endless battle to establish their own place in America's greatest metropolis—and in America itself." By emphasizing one's representativeness and offering oneself as a spokesperson, many African American autobiographers have made communal identification, rather than an individualistic *identity, a valorizing theme of their writing. From Frederick *Douglass through Ida B. *Wells-Barnett and *Malcolm X, African American autobiographers have understood that by identifying their individual ambitions with the aspirations of the people of black America, the ideals of freedom, human dignity, and personal expressiveness could be mutually advanced.

During its first century of existence, from 1760 to 1865, African American autobiography was dominated by the first-person narratives of former slaves. The best-known slave narratives were authored by fugitives who used their personal histories to illustrate in carefully documented detail the horrors of America's "peculiar institution." As autobiographies the most effective slave narratives focus as much on the individuality of the slave as on the institution of slavery, placing special attention on how slaves prepared themselves to resist and escape their oppression. Classics of the slave narrative genre, in particular the *Narrative of the Life of Frederick Douglass, an American Slave* (1845), William Wells

*Brown's *Narrative of William W. Brown, a Fugitive Slave* (1847), and Jacobs's *Incidents in the Life of a Slave Girl*, center on the former slave's intellectual, psychological, and spiritual rite of passage from bondage in the South to relative freedom in the North. In addition to their denunciation of slavery, the most notable pre–Civil War African American autobiographies, in particular Douglass's *My Bondage and My Freedom* (1855) and *Incidents*, indict the North for its pervasive practice of segregation, thus dispelling the myth of the "free states" in a manner calculated to force white America as a whole to face up to the national sin of racism.

Advertised in the abolitionist press and sold at antislavery meetings and in churches throughout the English-speaking world, at least a dozen of the more than seventy slave narratives published in book or pamphlet form during the pre-emancipation era went through multiple editions. A few, such as the narratives of Equiano and Douglass, sold in the tens of thousands and were translated into several European languages. The first two African American works of long fiction, Douglass's "The *Heroic Slave" (1853) and Brown's *Clotel, or The President's Daughter* (1853), were designed by their authors, themselves former slave narrators, to complement and develop through the art of fiction the image of heroic African American male and female selfhood introduced into American literature by the slave narrative. Ever since the mid-nineteenth century, the history of African American narrative has been informed by a call-and-response relationship between autobiography and its successor, the *novel.

From the end of the Civil War to the onset of the Great Depression, the ex-slave narrative remained the preponderant subgenre of African American autobiography, comprising slightly more than one-half of the ninety autobiographies published by African Americans between 1865 and 1930. The author of the post–Civil War slave narrative, however, was no longer the rebel-fugitive whose ascent to freedom in the North had been extolled in the antebellum slave narrative. The large majority of postbellum ex-slave autobiographers made no secret of the fact that they had endured, rather than escaped, slavery. Refusing to accept the popular American *stereotype of the incompetent, dependent freedman, ex-slave narrators of the late nineteenth century, both male and female, took pride in having done their *work well, in having maintained and often reunited their *families, and in having secured the respect of whites and blacks through their diligence, reliability, hard work, and sobriety. Avowedly middle class in their values and their goals, the postbellum slave narrator instances a pragmatic view of life that finds its epitome in Booker T. *Washington's *Up from Slavery* (1901).

In *Up from Slavery*, Washington likens slavery to a "school" from which he and his people graduated not by *violence but by dutifulness, industry, and a forgiving, progressive attitude toward the future. The founder of the most famous industrial school of his time, Tuskegee Institute in Alabama, Washington wrote his autobiography in part to show the great benefit that such institutional training could be to African Americans making the transition from slavery to freedom. The best-selling African American autobiography of the early twentieth century, *Up from Slavery* combined the classic formula of the individual American success story with a shrewd though oblique and politic plea for racial solidarity through affiliation with African American–controlled institutions.

As African Americans learned the bitter lessons of the post-Reconstruction era, which saw cradle-to-grave segregation presiding over the South by the turn of the century, autobiographers focused less on the individual's quest for personal power and more on the realization of communal power and prestige in African American institutions, particularly the school and the *church. Educators, headed by Washington and his many protégés who wrote autobiographies, and ministers, whose influential memoirs range from Bishop Daniel A. *Payne's *Recollections of Seventy Years* (1888) to Bishop Alexander Walters's *My Life and Work* (1917), argued that African American survival, not to mention fulfillment, depended largely on building institutional bulwarks against the divide-and-conquer strategy of American white supremacy. By sublimating his personal desires and ambitions in larger frameworks, the institutional man of African American autobiography asked the world to judge him primarily according to his "usefulness," his ability to work within the existing socioeconomic order to accomplish good for his people.

Although the *New Negro era of the 1920s was a time of comparatively few noteworthy autobiographies, William *Pickens and Ida B. Wells-Barnett, both of them southern born, middle class, and dedicated to civil rights activism, made signal contributions to African American autobiography. Unwilling to conform to the literary etiquette of institutional men like Washington, Pickens chronicles his evolution from conservative to militant in *Bursting Bonds* (1923). Ridiculing the "usable" Negroes who allowed themselves to become the instruments of white and black power brokers in the South, Pickens concluded his autobiography with his move to New York City in 1920, where he sought a different identity as a new kind of leader in the fledgling NAACP. Wells-Barnett's posthumously published *Crusade for Justice* (1970) tells an equally compelling story of its author's dauntless commitment to a life of agitation and protest on behalf of African Americans. The pioneering efforts of Pickens and Wells-Barnett in the 1920s and James Weldon *Johnson's *Along This Way* in 1933 helped to reorient African American autobiography to its roots in the slave narrative ideal of the African American leader as articulate hero who uses words as weapons in the fight for individual and communal freedom.

The decade and a half after the New Negro Renaissance saw the publication of several important autobiographies by literary figures such as Claude *McKay (*A Long Way from Home*, 1937), W. E. B. *Du Bois (*Dusk of Dawn*, 1940), Langston *Hughes (*The *Big Sea*, 1940), Zora Neale *Hurston (*Dust Tracks on a Road*, 1942), and Richard *Wright (*Black Boy,

1945). The unprecedented emphasis in these texts on the search for an authentic selfhood, predicated on the writers' skepticism about the repressiveness of institutions and epitomized in their heightened sensitivity to literary style as self-presentation, marks a turning point in the history of African American autobiography. Instead of portraying themselves as representative men and women in the traditional, nineteenth-century way of conceiving African American selfhood in autobiography, the likes of Hurston, Hughes, McKay, and Wright argue that they were sufficiently different that they could appeal to nothing more valid than the example of their own individuality as a standard for judging what they said about themselves and about African American experience in general.

In *Dust Tracks on a Road*, Hurston describes herself as having felt impelled from her earliest school days to undertake an "inside search" that often placed her at odds with outside authorities, both black and white. Acknowledging a "feeling of difference from my fellow men" that both inhibited and inspired her growing up, Hurston's iconoclasm, particularly on matters of race, has annoyed and perplexed many reviewers and critics of *Dust Tracks* who do not take into account Hurston's desire to break out of the model (what she called the "statue") that prescribed how African American women were to represent themselves. *Black Boy*, a Book-of-the-Month Club selection, became the most widely read and discussed African American autobiography for at least twenty years after its publication, primarily because of its grim portrayal of a southern black youth's evolution into the quintessentially alienated modernist writer dedicated to speaking the truth for no one but himself.

Wright's insistence on the autobiographer's foremost responsibility to absolute authenticity of self-expression, regardless of its acceptability or usefulness to blacks or whites, stands as twentieth-century African American autobiography's most extreme reaction against the circumspect, self-effacing preoccupation with sincerity and constructiveness that were the hallmark of the rhetoric of nineteenth-century institutional men such as Booker T. Washington. In *Invisible Man* (1952), the most celebrated African American novel of the twentieth century, Ralph *Ellison created a Southerner in search of self and community in the North whose choice of autobiographical discourse enabled Ellison to dramatize an African American everyman's attempt to reconcile a Wrightian desire for personal authenticity with a more traditional sense of obligation to play a socially responsible role.

Wright's successors in autobiography, particularly the self-styled "revolutionaries" of the 1960s, endorsed his notion of personal authenticity but wrote as though such authenticity could be achieved only by identifying with the oppressed masses of black America and then "telling it like it is" to white America on their behalf. The exemplar of this mode of testimony was *The *Autobiography of Malcolm X* (1965), which turned a streetcorner organizer for a splinter group of black separatists into a cultural hero for young, disaffected middle-class whites and their black counterparts in search of a standard-bearer for a new racial consciousness. Malcolm's successors in autobiography, among them Anne *Moody (*Coming of Age in Mississippi*, 1968), H. Rap Brown (*Die, Nigger Die!*, 1969), and Angela *Davis (*Angela Davis: An Autobiography*, 1974), produced a chorus of denunciations of American racism and hypocrisy unmatched since the era of the fugitive slave narrative.

The appearance in 1970 of Maya *Angelou's *I Know Why the Caged Bird Sings* signaled one of the most remarkable developments in recent African American autobiography—the unprecedented outpouring of personal, sometimes very intimate, narratives by black women. Although women had been longtime contributors to such bedrock African American traditions as the conversion narrative, recent women's personal texts, inspired by Angelou's serial autobiography of the 1970s and 1980s, Audre *Lorde's reflections on the evolution of her sexuality in *Zami: A New Spelling of My Name* (1982), and Itabari Njeri's bittersweet evocation of her family in *Every Good-Bye Ain't Gone* (1990), have re-envisioned the ideas of the spirit and salvation, discovering them anew in the secular experience of black female artists and activists. Meanwhile the search for a communal means of expressing contemporary African American identity and its roots in hitherto unrecorded *history continues in texts such as the 1974 National Book Award winner *All God's Dangers*, the oral history of Ned *Cobb, an Alabama folk hero; *Brothers and Keepers* (1984), the dialogue of John Edgar *Wideman, acclaimed novelist, and his brother Robert, convicted felon; and *Tight Spaces* (American Book Award, 1987–1988), the collaborative effort of three Detroit women, Kesho Scott, Cherry Muhanji, and Egyirba High, to plumb the significance of their shared experience. Through such re-invigorations of traditional forms and themes, autobiography continues to bear profound witness to its cultural heritage and to its ongoing responsibility to represent the individual and communal voices of African Americans.

[*See also* Antislavery Movement.]

• Rebecca Chalmers Barton, *Witnesses for Freedom*, 1948. Stephen Butterfield, *Black Autobiography in America*, 1974. Sidonie Smith, *Where I'm Bound: Patterns of Slavery and Freedom in Black American Autobiography*, 1974. Russell C. Brignano, *Black Americans in Autobiography*, 1984. William L. Andrews, *To Tell a Free Story: The First Century of Afro-American Autobiography, 1760–1865*, 1986. Joanne M. Braxton, *Black Women Writing Autobiography*, 1989. William L. Andrews and Nellie Y. McKay, eds., *Twentieth-Century African-American Autobiography*, 1990. *Black American Literature Forum* 24 (1990): 195–415. David L. Dudley, *My Father's Shadow: Intergenerational Conflict in African American Men's Autobiography*, 1991. William L. Andrews, ed., *African American Autobiography: A Collection of Critical Essays*, 1993.
—William L. Andrews

SPIRITUAL AUTOBIOGRAPHY

African American spiritual autobiography has its origins in the late eighteenth century, the period of greatest activity in the transatlantic African slave trade. Four factors contributed to the development of this literary genre: (1) a rise in the number of conversions of African Americans to Christianity following the evangelistic efforts of Methodists and Baptists; (2) the appearance in the northern states of gradual emancipation laws after the American Revolution, which rapidly increased the free African American population in the North; (3) an increase in *literacy and educational opportunities in the North for some African Americans; and (4) the rise of African American *churches and denominations, culminating in the formation of the African Methodist Episcopal (AME) church, the first African American denomination in the United States.

Texts surviving from the first sixty years of African American spiritual autobiography (1770–1830) are closely related to, and in many cases barely distinguishable from, African American autobiography as a whole. Representative texts of this originary phase of the genre include James Albert Ukawsaw *Gronniosaw, A Narrative of the Most Remarkable Particulars in the Life of James Albert Ukawsaw Gronniosaw, an African Prince (1770); John *Marrant, A Narrative of the Lord's Wonderful Dealings with John Marrant (1790); George White, A Brief Account of the Life, Experiences, Travels, and Gospel Labours of George White, an African: Written by Himself, and Revised by a Friend (1810); and John Jea, The Life, History, and Unparalleled Sufferings of John Jea, the African Preacher (c. 1811).

To some extent, almost all African American autobiographies of this period make some reference to salvation, Christian conversion, and deliverance. Thus, important early texts, like Briton *Hammon's Narrative of the Uncommon Sufferings, and Surprizing Deliverance of Briton Hammon, a Negro Man (1760) and Olaudah *Equiano's Interesting Narrative of the Life of Olaudah Equiano, or Gustavus Vassa, the African. Written by Himself (1789), have strong elements of spiritual autobiography. In addition, texts considered representative of this early phase of the genre often comprise a combination of several literary genres as the spiritual journey of the writer is embedded within *travel writing (e.g., James Albert Ukawsaw Gronniosaw), captivity narrative (e.g., John Marrant), or *slave narrative (e.g., John Jea).

The classic form of spiritual autobiography emerges in the work of George White as he chronicles not only an inward spiritual journey, but his journey through the institution of the Methodist church, at this time an all-white (as well as all-male) hierarchy. White's quest for the right to preach from the great Western text of the Christian Bible sets the tone for the development of African American spiritual autobiography as simultaneously a recording of the individual soul's search for God and representative of a people's challenge to institutions of power and authority that threaten to limit African Americans' claims to humanity and *freedom.

This dual purpose—inner journey and outward struggle—is most evident in the texts that form the second period in the development of African American spiritual autobiography. It is no accident that this era, roughly the two decades of the 1830s and the 1840s, coincides with the evangelistic fervor of the Second Great Awakening in America. African Americans comprised a large segment of the revivals and camp meetings that swept through the country at this time. During this period, many of the finest examples of the genre were published.

Richard *Allen, one of the founders and the first bishop of the AME church, published his Life, Experience and Gospel Labors of the Rt. Rev. Richard Allen in Philadelphia in 1833. Following on the example of George White's autobiography over two decades earlier, Allen's spiritual autobiography is both an individual testimony—the journey of the individual soul from sinner to saint, and the individual person from slave to free—and a story of collective struggle. Allen not only tells his own story, but recounts the bold breaking away of African American worshippers from St. George's Methodist Episcopal Church in Philadelphia after they encountered racism there. Allen and others went on to form first the Free Africa Society in 1789, then the congregation of Bethel AME Church (referred to as Mother Bethel) in Philadelphia. Difficulties with the Methodist Episcopal denomination, again on racial grounds, resulted in the organization and incorporation of the AME denomination in 1816, with Allen as its first bishop. It is no surprise that the focal point of Allen's autobiography is not only the challenge to the traditional Methodist Episcopal institution, but the building of another institution, the AME church. Thus key scenes in the autobiography involve putting the spade in the ground to begin digging the foundation of Mother Bethel, the signing of legal papers and documents of incorporation, and the like.

Perhaps the defining characteristic of this important period of spiritual autobiography is the emergence of texts written by African American women. In many ways the rise in popularity of the slave narrative during the 1830s and 1840s made it the preferred vehicle for the autobiographical expression of African American males. The emergence of African American women's prose narratives found its earliest expression in spiritual autobiography. Jarena *Lee's Life and Religious Experience of Jarena Lee, a Coloured Lady, Giving an Account of Her Call to Preach the Gospel. . . . Written by Herself (1836) followed the example of her predecessor and mentor Richard Allen in detailing an intense inner struggle within the context of a battle with institutionalized *religion. In Lee's case, however, the institutional context is not the racism of a white Methodist Episcopal church, but the sexism within the AME hierarchy, which prohibited women from preaching from a pulpit and "taking a text," preaching from the Bible. The climax of her autobiography is a scene in which Lee boldly interrupts an African American male minister and preaches her own sermon, a deed that, rather than resulting in her having to leave the church, caused Richard Allen himself to acknowledge publicly the validity of her call to preach.

Even when women did receive limited recognition of their abilities for church leadership, they faced numerous obstacles in ministry. Zilpha *Elaw, a contemporary of Lee's with whom she shared at least one pulpit, published her autobiography, *Memoirs of the Life, Religious Experience, Ministerial Travels and Labours of Mrs. Zilpha Elaw, an American Female of Color. . . . Written by Herself,* in 1846. Like Lee, Elaw experienced private and public assaults on her ministry. What distinguishes Elaw's text, however, is her broader focus on her travels to England to preach for her denomination, the Methodist Episcopal church, which involves her in issues of nationality as well as *gender, *race, and *class differences. Lee's second expanded edition, *Religious Experience and Journal of Mrs. Jarena Lee, Giving an Account of Her Call to Preach the Gospel* (1849) marks the end of this productive period.

During the quarter century from 1850 to 1875, the genre continued to be dominated by African American women. Two texts published in 1850 are particularly noteworthy. The first is Nancy *Prince's *Narrative of the Life and Travels of Mrs. Nancy Prince,* which, harkening back to the spiritual narratives of the first period, is a blend of travel literature, *essay, and spiritual autobiography. The second is Sojourner *Truth's *Narrative of Sojourner Truth,* which chronicles the life of one of the nation's leading abolitionists and women's rights activists. In contrast to Truth's fame, an almost anonymous writer known simply as "*Elizabeth" published a short narrative entitled *Memoir of Old Elizabeth, a Coloured Woman* in 1863 at the age of ninety-seven, adding her voice to the texts by itinerant ministers like Jarena Lee and Zilpha Elaw. Published in 1854, Daniel Peterson's *The Looking Glass: Being a True Report and Narrative of the Life, Travels and Labors of the Rev. Daniel H. Peterson, a Colored Clergyman* both looks back to the tradition of African American clergy autobiographies like those by George White and Richard Allen and looks ahead to the postbellum period and the rise in African American ministerial autobiography.

The popularity of African American spiritual autobiography declined in the half-century after Reconstruction (1875–1925). In this period, African American churches became even more institutionalized and hierarchical, losing many of the distinctive features of New World African worship that they had enjoyed during the antebellum period. Thus, many of the spiritual narratives began to be published under the auspices of the churches with fewer narrators operating with the "free agency" that Richard Allen or Jarena Lee enjoyed. As more or less "official" documents of religious institutions, these autobiographies are often more didactic than the earlier texts. A refreshing exception is Julia A. J. *Foote's *A Brand Plucked from the Fire: An Autobiographical Sketch* (1879), which continued the involvement of African American women writers in the holiness tradition, using spiritual experience as a challenge to the increasing institutionalization of the churches. Toward the turn of the century, Amanda Berry *Smith's lengthy *Autobiography: The Story of the Lord's Dealings with Mrs. Amanda Smith the Colored Evangelist* (1892) continued the tradition of depicting the spiritual journey in concert with travel narrative.

The most important development after Reconstruction was the rise of the ministerial autobiography as African American churches and denominations became more entrenched in patriarchal structure. Daniel A. *Payne's *Recollections of Seventy Years* (1888) is representative as it chronicles the parallel development of both man and institution.

Currently, the genre of African American spiritual autobiography is primarily relegated to popular forms, for example, Paule *Murray's *Proud Shoes* (1956), which tells of her struggle to become the first African American woman Episcopal priest, or Rosa Parks's recent *Quiet Strength: The Faith, the Hope, and the Heart of a Woman Who Changed a Nation* (1994). Similarly, the theme of religious conversion continues to be a key element in autobiographies, such as in The *Autobiography of Malcolm X. While religion and spirituality remain important topics in African American literature, the genre of spiritual autobiography clearly reached its heyday in the nineteenth century. The issues of freedom, human dignity, and the quest for the divine, however, remain timeless themes in the literary tradition.

[See also Preachers and Deacons; Sermons and Preaching.]

• William L. Andrews, ed., *Sisters of the Spirit: Three Black Women's Autobiographies of the Nineteenth Century,* 1986. William L. Andrews, *To Tell a Free Story: The First Century of Afro-American Autobiography,* 1986. Sue E. Houchins, introduction to *Spiritual Narratives,* 1988. Joanne M. Braxton, *Black Women Writing Autobiography: A Tradition Within a Tradition,* 1989.   —Katherine Clay Bassard

Autobiography of an Ex-Colored Man, The.

Originally published anonymously in 1912, James Weldon *Johnson's *novel *The Autobiography of an Ex-Colored Man* advances the narrative of the "tragic *mulatto" who passes for white beyond the constraints imposed by the form as it was practiced in nineteenth-century American literature. Though in some ways conforming to the conventional *novel of passing in suggesting that a mixed racial heritage makes a person incapable of functioning in either the black or the white world, Johnson's novel turns this notion on its head by invoking *double consciousness, as his narrator makes clear:

> It is this, too, which makes the colored people of this country, in reality, a mystery to the whites. It is a difficult thing for a white man to learn what a colored man really thinks; because, generally, with the latter an additional and different light must be brought to bear on what he thinks. . . . This gives to every colored man, in proportion to his intellectuality, a sort of dual personality. . . .

As this passage demonstrates, Johnson's novel is the first to give voice in fictional form to "the Veil," W. E. B. *Du Bois's construction of African American racial consciousness.

The novel's plot deals with the product of a clandestine love affair between a white Southerner and a fair-skinned African American woman. Compelled to relocate to the North, the unnamed narrator of the story is reared in a small town in Connecticut, where he displays a prodigious talent as a pianist. Learning from his teacher that he is not white, he decides to attend Atlanta University, a black school in the South. But after his funds are stolen, he takes a job in a cigar factory, where he mingles with blacks of different classes and hues while gaining exposure to African American culture. When the factory closes, the narrator moves to New York City and joins a bohemian world in which he works as a ragtime piano player. Attachment to a white patron enables the narrator to make a tour of Europe, where he decides to devote his talent to the development of vernacular African American *music into classical musical forms. Returning to the roots of African American musical traditions in the South, the narrator is so shocked by a *lynching that he rejects his new vocation and spurns identification with "a people that could with impunity be treated worse than animals." Cutting himself off from his cultural heritage, he returns to New York to pass for white, become a successful businessman, and marry and raise a family on the white side of the *color line. Only at the end of the novel does he acknowledge the tragedy of having sold what he calls his "birthright" for "a mess of pottage."

Though reviewers hailed the novel as a sociological study, especially after Johnson acknowledged his authorship in 1927, the greater importance of the book lies in its rejection of didacticism and overt propaganda in favor of a psychological realism that revealed the complex conflicting negotiations informing an African American's quest for *identity as an artist, a person of color, and a modern American male.

• Robert B. Stepto, *From Behind the Veil: A Study of Afro-American Narrative*, 1979. Bernard W. Bell, *The Afro-American Novel and Its Tradition*, 1987.   —Herman Beavers

Autobiography of Malcolm X, The.
Published posthumously, *The Autobiography of Malcolm X* (1965) was written with the assistance of Alex *Haley, and, in all published editions, is accompanied by a long epilogue of Haley's that offers his perspective on *Malcolm X and the making of the work. Extremely well received by both whites and African Americans, the work helped give voice to the emerging Black Power movement, offered a spectacular example of dedication and accomplishment, and presented an indictment of racism in the United States. The *Autobiography* covers Malcolm's life from his childhood in East Lansing, Michigan, through his time as a street hustler, prison inmate, Nation of Islam minister, and, finally, his last year as an independent Muslim minister and black nationalist.

As is common with the genre, especially for African Americans, the *Autobiography* is at once a sociological document and an assertion of individuality. Malcolm X vacillates between presenting his life as representative and as exemplary. His account of his criminal past, in which he sold drugs and prostituted women, displays the degrading effects of racism upon African Americans. His account of his transformation in prison, in which he read extensively and

adopted the Nation of Islam's strict moral code, presents a story of remarkable dedication and will.

Like much of the literature of the turbulent 1960s, the text also contains the rhetoric of protest. By utilizing personal experience to argue for a major restructuring of American society, the work echoes a mode of African American literature descended from the *slave narratives. The later chapters blend accounts of Malcolm's years as a minister with excerpts from his speeches condemning white America. As the text concentrates less on the incidents of Malcolm's life, the drama focuses on the development of Malcolm's philosophy from the strict "all whites are devils" beliefs of the Nation of Islam to a less rigid, more humanist approach to *race.

Because Malcolm's life changed rapidly as he composed the *Autobiography*, and because he was assassinated before he read and revised the final draft that Haley had sent him, the book, like the life, seems incomplete. The *Autobiography* captures a mind in flux. Opinions contradict each other in the text, especially those on the Nation, the organization that he credits with saving his life, but that he split from rancorously while he was fashioning his life story. Such contradictions generally enhance the text, for they present an attractive protean self, one willing to learn and change when confronted with new knowledge. The extraordinary blend of so many autobiographical modes, and so many "Malcolms," deeply enriches both the text and its subject.

Through its immediate and enduring popularity, the *Autobiography* is primarily responsible for what biographer Peter Goldman calls the "beatification" of Malcolm X, making him an icon for black pride, achievement, and protest. Without his life story, Malcolm X might have been forgotten. The *Autobiography* guarantees his permanence on the American cultural landscape and arguably stands as the most stunning accomplishment of a remarkable life.

[See also Autobiography; Black Nationalism.]

• Peter Goldman, *The Death and Life of Malcolm X*, 2d ed., 1979. David Gallen, *Malcolm X as They Knew Him*, 1992.
          —J. D. Scrimgeour

Autobiography of Miss Jane Pittman, The
(1971). Widely praised as Ernest J. *Gaines's best book, this *historical novel builds upon fugitive *slave narratives as well as the oral tradition. The first-person narrator, some 110 years old, is one of the most memorable characters in all African American fiction. Set in rural Louisiana, the novel is divided into four parts—The War Years, Reconstruction, The Plantation, and The Quarters—that progress from the 1860s to the 1960s. It is the immediacy and authenticity of Miss Jane's voice, the book's greatest literary achievement, that enable the author to unify the text's panoramic sweep and its highly episodic structure. Jane is both an effectively realized individual and a representative figure, a spokesperson for the African American experience from *slavery times to the era of the *civil rights movement. Gaines's "Introduction" presents her story as the outcome of a series of interviews by the novel's ostensible editor not only with Jane but with other members of her

community, and Gaines thereby stresses both the centrality of the oral tradition in African American culture and the interdependence of the individual and the group. The popular oral history methodology of the time of the novel's composition recognized that people like Miss Jane had been excluded from traditional histories. Gaines thus perceived his book as filling a void in the historical record, as embodying what he termed "folk autobiography."

The opening chapter, in which Jane abandons her slave name, Ticey, and refuses—despite a beating—to relinquish her new name, testifies to Gaines's concern with *identity, a major theme in African American literature generally and in the *autobiography as a genre. This episode also demonstrates qualities in Jane's character that persist throughout the book, helping to establish her heroic stature: determination, personal integrity, self-assertion, endurance. Much of the novel focuses on the violence with which such attempts at African American self-determination are met by whites: the massacre of the newly emancipated slaves in book 1; the assassination of Ned (whom Jane adopts after his mother is killed in the massacre) in book 2; and the murder of Jimmy Aaron, a civil rights worker, at the end of book 4, an act that fails, however, to prevent Jane from joining the protest march with which the novel closes. The deaths of Ned and Jimmy highlight the book's pervasive religious elements, for both characters are depicted as Christlike figures, men whose blood is shed to redeem their people. In book 3, significantly, Gaines portrays the white Tee Bob in similar terms when Tee Bob commits suicide because southern mores preclude his marrying a Creole. Gaines thus reveals the destructive consequences of racism for the entire South, indeed for all of American society. Written in the years immediately following the civil rights era, Miss Jane's narrative, more than any other single book, helped Americans understand the personal experiences and emotions, as well as the historical events, that had produced the revolution in U.S. race relations during the 1960s.

• Keith E. Byerman, *Fingering the Jagged Grain: Tradition and Form in Recent Black Fiction*, 1985. John F. Callahan, *In the African-American Grain: The Pursuit of Voice in Twentieth-Century Black Fiction*, 1988.   —John Lang

B

BABY SUGGS. Baby Suggs Holy is the mother-in-law of *Sethe Suggs, the protagonist of Toni *Morrison's *Beloved* (1987). The *novel begins with Sethe's escape to Baby Suggs, who lives in Ohio. Halle, Sethe's husband and Baby Suggs's son, has succeeded in buying his mother's *freedom by working extra on Sundays. Baby Suggs becomes a holy figure and preaches self-love to her people in an open area near her home. Sethe arrives mutilated, bruised, and worn out, and Baby Suggs tenderly ministers to her daughter-in-law and her baby, healing Sethe's body.

After Sethe's arrival, Stamp Paid (the ferryman who brings the former slaves to Ohio) brings them huge buckets of blackberries, and the women decide to have a feast and share the pies with the other colored people in the area. The people, however, resent their generosity and feel that Baby Suggs is showing off; therefore, they fail to warn them of the arrival of schoolteacher, Sethe's owner, who plans to return Sethe and her children to *slavery. When Sethe sees schoolteacher, she kills Beloved rather than see her returned to slavery. This incident causes the complete disillusionment of Baby Suggs, and she no longer preaches. She takes to the "keeping room" where she contemplates colors until the end of her life.

Baby Suggs's experiences as a female slave included the loss of most of her children and the additional responsibility of servicing her masters sexually. In rendering the story of the life and death of Baby Suggs, Morrison reminds the reader that Baby Suggs's life has been destroyed by slavery even though she attained physical freedom.

• Brian Finney, "Temporal Defamiliarization in Toni Morrison's *Beloved*," *Obsidian II* 18 (Spring 1990): 59–77. Wilfred D. Samuels and Clenora Hudson-Weems, *Toni Morrison*, 1990. Trudier Harris, *Fiction and Folklore: The Novels of Toni Morrison*, 1991. Kristin Boudreau, "Pain and the Unmaking of Self in Toni Morrison's *Beloved*," *Contemporary Literature* 36.3 (Fall 1995): 447–465. Danielle Taylor-Guthrie, "Who Are the Beloved? Old and New Testaments, Old and New Communities of Faith," *Religion and Literature* 27.1 (Spring 1995): 119–129.

—Betty Taylor-Thompson

BADMAN. Folklorists generally agree that the badman figure in African American *folklore emerged during the years following Reconstruction and gained wide recognition, especially in the Deep South, during the last decade of the nineteenth century. Often based on the experiences of real men such as Morris Slater, an Alabama turpentine worker who killed a policeman and escaped arrest by jumping a freight train, badman was characterized in toasts, songs, and ballads by his propensity for gambling, *violence, and other acts of lawlessness; by his strength and virility; and, according to many folklorists, by his purely self-interested antagonism toward both the dominant white social order and the oppressed African American community. Of the many badmen who became legendary in African American folklore, *Stackolee, John Hardy, and Railroad Bill (a figure based on the exploits of Morris Slater) are perhaps the most widely recognized.

Early studies of African American folk heroes tended to consider the badman and the "bad nigger"—a character type whose violence and destruction were actuated without regard for African American communal values—as synonymous. These conceptions of badman emphasized his amorality and his profound rage and rebellion against organized society, and suggested that the character type provided no model of behavior for emulation by African Americans. More recent studies argue that badman and the "bad nigger" are each distinct character types, the former offering a model of behavior for African Americans attempting to survive and, indeed thrive, in a postbellum social order that was still based on the racial subjugation of one group of people by another.

Similarly, there has been some disagreement among folklorists over the reasons for the proliferation of badmen in African American folklore. One theory suggests that the badman is a reflection of the anger and despair that gripped the African American community following emancipation, a figure whose sense of hopelessness results in acts of fury rather than attempts toward social change. Another point of view suggests that the badman's propensity for violence represents an outlet for repressed male *sexuality, perhaps stemming from fears of castration by lynch mobs. A third study argues that badman represents a response to the political, social, and economic oppression of African Americans by whites following Reconstruction. This theory suggests that African Americans combined traits of the *trickster and the *conjuring figures from *slavery to create the badman, a figure whose acts of lawlessness, particularly gambling, secured some of the benefits that the white social order systematically denied African Americans. Among figures in African American literature whose behavior and outlook on life owe something to the badman are *Bigger Thomas in Richard *Wright's *Native Son* (1940) and, before his conversion to the Nation of Islam, *Malcolm X in *The *Autobiography of Malcolm X* (1965).

• Lawrence W. Levine, *Black Culture and Black Consciousness: Afro-American Folk Thought from Slavery to Freedom*, 1977. John W. Roberts, *From Trickster to Badman: The Black Folk Hero in Slavery and Freedom*, 1989.

—Christopher C. De Santis

BAD WOMAN. African American female characters are usually created within an "ark of safety" in fictional works; that ark can be marriage, the church, a grandmother, or a religious-minded community. Women in the literature who fall outside that safety and indeed may be judged to be a threat to safety become bad women. It is important to note, however, that a judgment of "bad" is heavily dependent upon perspective. In keeping with the flexibility characteristic of African American culture, it is seldom for inherent reasons of evil that women are thought to be bad; however, sexuality and morality figure prominently. For various reasons, then, characters such as Esther in James *Baldwin's *Go Tell It on the Mountain (1953), *Sula Peace in Toni *Morrison's *Sula (1974), *Jadine Childs in Morrison's *Tar Baby (1981), and *Sethe Suggs in Morrison's *Beloved (1987) would be considered bad women. From *Gabriel Grimes's point of view, it is Esther and her robust sexuality that have caused him to fall from the lofty position of preacher. People in the Bottom make Sula into a witch because they do not approve of her life, and they deem her bad for reputedly sleeping with white men. Jadine is bad for *Son Green because she tempts him to abandon his folk roots. And perhaps Sethe forgets morality when she kills Beloved. The same could apply to *Dessa Rose when she kills white men in the fight for freedom from slavery in Sherley Anne *Williams's *Dessa Rose (1986). From a different perspective, Charles R. *Johnson's Faith Cross (Faith and the Good Thing, 1974) might be considered a bad woman because of her easy sexual habits; the same might be true of *Shug Avery in Alice *Walker's The *Color Purple (1982) or of Etta Mae Johnson in Gloria *Naylor's The *Women of Brewster Place (1982). Andrea *Lee's title character in Sarah Phillips (1984) and Terry *McMillan's Mama (1987) are also unlike the usual portraits of church-going, respectable black women; they live as they please, and Mama advises her daughters on everything from alcohol to men. More recently, Jamaica *Kincaid's Lucy (Lucy, 1991) highlights the sexually promiscuous while Carolivia *Herron's Johnnie in Thereafter Johnnie (1991) aggressively pursues her father for the requiting of an incestuous relationship. Such women mark a different path for development of African American female characters, one that allows for additional complexity in conceptualization.

Another strand of badness is that reflected in Nikki *Giovanni's "Ego Tripping" (1975), where the narrator asserts that she can fly "like a bird in the sky." Maya *Angelou picks up this braggadocio in poems such as "Phenomenal Woman" and "And Still I Rise" (1978). Generally, though, for clearer definitions of badness, we return to characters like Gayl *Jones's *Eva Medina Canada in *Eva's Man (1976), who not only kills her lover but bites off his penis. And to Ruby in Gloria Naylor's *Mama Day (1988), whose insane jealousy causes her to try to kill Cocoa, using spells comparable to those of Margaret *Walker's "Molly Means" (1942). Unguided by morality or an obligation to community, these women set themselves beyond any traditional forms of safety and become accountable only to themselves.

[See also Prostitute.]

—Trudier Harris

BAKER, HOUSTON A., JR. (b. 1943), critic, poet, editor, and president of the Modern Language Association (1992). In an October 1985 Pennsylvania Gazette profile, Houston A. Baker, Jr., speaks of his intellectual journey from graduate studies in late-Victorian literature to the then relatively uncharted field of African American literature as "a great awakening and a conversion experience rolled into one." Baker's *blues journey home has resulted in the field's richest, most consistently probing body of work, and has established him as one of a handful of preeminent scholars of American literature to have emerged in the wake of the *civil rights movement struggles of the 1960s.

Born in Louisville, Kentucky, Baker matriculated at Howard University, where he was elected to Phi Beta Kappa, and then earned a PhD in English at the University of California at Los Angeles in 1968. After brief stints at Yale University, the site of his conversion, and the University of Virginia, Baker moved to the University of Pennsylvania in 1974, where he has been, since 1982, a chaired professor in the humanities and, since 1986, director of the Center for the Study of Black Literature and Culture.

In his first book, Long Black Song (1972), which examines the resonances of folkloric tropes and images in the works of such figures as Frederick *Douglass, W. E. B. *Du Bois, and Richard *Wright, Baker pursues issues that have dominated his work. Baker's critical project constitutes a search for strategies that help expose the richness, sophistication, and distinctiveness of African American expressivity. Moving from New Critical analyses in Singers of Daybreak (1974); to formulations of an African American "anthropology of art" in The Journey Back (1980); to the poststructuralist interrogations of history, generational differences between African American critics, and literary form in his most influential study, Blues, Ideology, and Afro-American Literature (1984); to encounters with women's texts, *feminism, and phenomenology in Workings of the Spirit (1991), Baker has sought to identify the constitutive sounds and meanings of blackness. In Afro-American Poetics (1988), he argues that "only by paying special attention to the sociology, psychology, and entrancing sounding of *race does a critic of Afro-American culture arrive at an inclusive perspective."

For Baker, an informed interdisciplinarity yields an acute understanding of the complexities of the act of African American cultural production. In The Journey Back (1980), Baker concludes that *Narrative of the Life of Frederick Douglass reflects not "the authentic voice of black American slavery" or of blackness more generally, but, rather, "the voice of a self transformed" by Douglass's engagement with "the linguistic codes, literary conventions, and audience expectations of a literate population." Sounding blackness, then, means self-consciously rendering how an articulation of an African American cultural inheritance is influenced by a variety of discursive and historical contexts. His sophisticated analyses of cultural production have been highly influential, and have placed Baker at the center of American academic debates in the 1980s and

1990s about such important topics as race, culture, and *class.

[*See also* Criticism, *article on* Criticism since 1965.]

• Michael Berube, "Power Surge: Houston Baker's Vernacular Spectacular," *Voice Literary Supplement* 109 (Oct. 1992): 15–17. Houston A. Baker, Jr., *Black Studies, Rap, and the Academy*, 1993.

—Michael Awkward

BAKER, JOSEPHINE (1906–1975), dancer, theater performer, writer, and civil rights activist. Although she spent most of her adult life living in France and touring the world, Josephine Baker was born in St. Louis, Missouri. After a difficult childhood, she left home at thirteen, starting her *dance career with a vaudeville troupe called the Dixie Steppers. In the early 1920s, she worked in African American *theater productions in New York such as *Shuffle Along* and *Chocolate Dandies*. In 1925 Baker left for Paris to begin her long international career with companies like Revue Nègre, Folies Bergères, and, later, the Ziegfeld Follies.

As her career evolved, Baker increasingly focused on political concerns. During World War II Baker toured North Africa while providing information to French and British intelligence. Later she used her considerable fame to advance civil rights issues during her frequent visits to the United States. In 1951 the NAACP honored her political work by declaring an official Baker Day in Harlem. Baker is also remembered for her advocacy of racial reconciliation: she adopted children of varied races and nationalities and worked throughout her life to promote racial and national cooperation.

Baker's *autobiography *Josephine* (1976; trans. to English in 1977), posthumously compiled and coauthored by her estranged husband Jo Bouillon, consists of sections authored by Baker herself intermixed with commentary by Bouillon, numerous friends, professional associates, and several of her adult children. The result is a book at moments autobiographical, but strongly biographical. Her life story is essentially framed by Bouillon's editing, leaving inevitable questions as to the narrative structure that may have emerged in an autobiography completed by Baker herself. Four other volumes, all written in French, also carry some autobiographical interest because of Baker's collaborative involvement: *Les Mémoires de Joséphine Baker* (1927) and *Voyages et aventures de Joséphine Baker* (1931), both authored by Marcel Sauvage; *Joséphine Baker: Une Vie de toutes les coueurs* (1935), by André Rivollet; and *La Guerre secrète de Joséphine Baker* (1948), by Jacques Abtey. Baker also helped plan a *novel dealing with racial themes, which was eventually authored by Giuseppe (Pepito) Abatino and Félix del la Camara, entitled *Mon Sang dans tes veines* (*My Blood in Your Veins*, 1931).

• Phyllis Rose, *Jazz Cleopatra: Josephine Baker in Her Time*, 1989.

—Sharon Carson

BALDWIN, JAMES (1924–1987), novelist, essayist, playwright, scriptwriter, director, poet, filmmaker, college professor, lecturer, and expatriate. Easily recognized as one of the leading African American authors, James Baldwin has contributed to a variety of genres in American literary creativity. He has especially used *novels and *essays to focus on his favorite themes: the failure of the promise of American democracy, questions of racial and sexual *identity, the failures of the Christian church, difficult family relationships, and the political and social worlds that shaped the American "Negro" and then despised him for that shaping. Frequently employing a third person plural voice in his essays, Baldwin exhorts the exploiters and the exploited to save the country from its own destructive tendencies. An activist who put his body on the line with his politics, Baldwin was intimidatingly articulate in "telling it like it is" in interviews as well as on paper. A small man whose voice was one of the largest America had ever heard, Baldwin was intent upon pricking the consciences of all Americans in an era—particularly the 1960s—when a liberal climate was especially receptive to that pricking. Pushed slightly into the literary background with the wide publishing of works by African American women writers and the scholarly focus on their works after 1980, Baldwin published fewer book-length works but never lost sight of his ultimate objectives: to write well and to be a good man.

James Arthur Baldwin was born in Harlem, New York, on 2 August 1924. His mother, Emma Berdis Jones, gave birth to James while she was single. When Baldwin was a toddler, Jones married David Baldwin, an itinerant preacher from Louisiana, who would prove to be the bane of young Jimmy's existence. Not only did his stepfather assert that James was ugly and bore the mark of the devil, but he refused to recognize James's native intelligence or his sanctioning by white teachers. This painful autobiographical material would provide the substance of Baldwin's first novel, *Go Tell It on the Mountain* (1953). *John Grimes, the protagonist in that novel, is a precocious child applauded by white teachers and principals, but whose father cannot abide the fact that this "imposter," this illegitimate son, is infinitely more obedient and "holy" than his legitimate son. John also wrestles with homosexual leanings, which the young Baldwin, by contrast, was able to resolve fairly early in life—he had homosexual as well as heterosexual relationships. Homosexuality would serve as the theme for Baldwin's second novel, *Giovanni's Room* (1956), in which a white American slumming in Paris becomes sexually involved with a young Italian. David, the American, contemplates his sexual identity and its negative consequences on the evening that Giovanni, convicted for killing an older man who wanted sexual favors from him, is executed for that crime.

Baldwin grew up as the caretaker for his eight younger siblings. As he cradled babies in his arms, he read avidly, borrowing initially from the two Harlem public libraries and later from the Forty-second Street New York Public Library. One of the works that would prove significant for his later critical development was Harriet Beecher *Stowe's *Uncle Tom's Cabin* (1852). Baldwin asserts that he had read the book so many times by the fifth grade that his mother moved it to a shelf beyond his diminutive reach. Later, Baldwin would criticize the novel for its dependence upon the *protest literature tradition. The young Jimmy's writing talent was also discovered early, and his teachers requested special assignments from him on several occasions. At Frederick Douglass Junior High School (P.S. 139), he edited the school newspaper, the *Douglass Pilot*, to which he contributed a short story and several editorials and sketches. Baldwin had the privilege of studying with *Harlem Renaissance poet Countee *Cullen, who not only taught but served as adviser to the literary club.

The best that can be said of Baldwin's teenage years is that they were uneasy. As he recounts in The *Fire Next Time (1962), he found himself the target of the police as well as unscrupulous neighbors. Their physical and potential sexual exploitation of him led him to embrace the *church at the age of fourteen when he encountered a black woman evangelist, Mother Horn, who asked "Whose little boy are you?" The question so evoked a sense of belonging in Baldwin that he simply replied, "Why, yours," and joined her church. From that time until he was seventeen, Baldwin was a "young minister" in the Pentecostal Church. Heavy doses of Bible reading and abstinence from even simple pleasures like going to the movies led Baldwin to believe he had made a mistake. Church folks were trying to keep him out of the theater, he asserted later, when all along he had been performing in one. The implication that performance was an important (and problematic) feature of church membership would surface in several of Baldwin's works, including especially his play The *Amen Corner (1955).

At De Witt Clinton High School, Baldwin published "The Woman at the Well," "Mississippi Legend," and "Incident in London," all stories reflecting a religious influence, in the school newspaper, the *Magpie*. He also served—with Richard Avedon, with whom he would later collaborate on *Nothing Personal*—as editor in chief of the newspaper. Upon graduation in 1942, he worked briefly on the construction of a railroad depot in New Jersey, a job from which Baldwin was repeatedly fired. A couple of years later, in 1944, he moved to Greenwich Village, where he began exploring his writing potential more seriously. It was here that he began a novel he first called "Crying Holy," then "In My Father's House," before it would be published as *Go Tell It on the Mountain*. Acquaintance with Richard *Wright led to Wright recommending Baldwin for a Eugene Saxton Fellowship, which he received in 1945. A book review in the *Nation* in 1946 officially launched Baldwin's professional career.

After repeated disastrous racial and personal encounters, Baldwin was convinced that he should leave the country for his own sanity. He bought a one-way ticket to France and sailed on 11 November 1948, shortly after he received a Rosenwald Fellowship. Before his departure, he also terminated wedding plans and threw the engagement rings into the Hudson River. That was the last occasion on which Baldwin seriously considered a heterosexual liaison. His intimate relationships would become decidedly

homosexual, although his preference was for bisexuality in his partners.

France might have provided the psychological space that Baldwin needed, but it was not without its racial tensions. Baldwin was acutely aware of the plight of Algerians in France, and he was aware of how white Americans acted toward him and other black Americans on their visits abroad. In *Notes of a Native Son (1955) he commented on the difficulties presented when "black" (Africans) met "brown" (African Americans) on foreign soil. Tensions were also created when he inadvertently received a bed sheet from a helpful friend who did not mention he had taken it from the hotel at which he resided. Arrested and left to stumble around a jail cell without his shoe strings or belt, Baldwin compared the systemic control of black lives in Paris with that of blacks in America. He concluded that his adopted country was no less racist than his native one. Yet Baldwin would remain in France—except for sojourns in other European locales, in Africa, and periodic returns to the United States for *civil rights movement activism (1957, 1960), lecturing, and teaching engagements—until his death in 1987. During returns to the United States in the 1950s and early 1960s, Baldwin marched or conversed with civil rights activists such as Martin Luther *King, Jr., Stokely *Carmichael, and *Malcolm X, and he joined Lorraine *Hansberry and others in an infamous meeting with Attorney General Robert Kennedy in 1963.

His early years in Paris enabled Baldwin to interact with such luminaries as Richard Wright, although their relationship would be strained later. It was in part because Baldwin moved to France that black artist Beauford Delaney moved there. He held a special role as a father figure to Baldwin, but his increasing delusions and onset of insanity in later years caused Baldwin much distress before Delaney was finally institutionalized. From France, however, Baldwin continued his creative output, producing essays and plays in addition to novels. Along with *Go Tell It on the Mountain, Notes of a Native Son* and *Giovanni's Room* made Baldwin's first decade out of the country a particularly creative period.

Baldwin also spent time in Switzerland. Indeed, he completed *Go Tell It on the Mountain* in the Swiss village home of Lucien Happersberger, who by 1952 had become Baldwin's primary intimate partner. Another stint out of Paris took Baldwin to Istanbul in the 1960s. Biographer David Leeming, who worked as secretary to Baldwin during the period in Istanbul, paints Baldwin during these years as an indefatigable party-goer, with an almost infinite capacity to consume liquor and to get himself into compromising sexual situations. He describes Baldwin as suicidal on many occasions, with well-meaning friends intervening just in the nick of time to prevent some disastrous consequence. Yet for all his personal and psychological lapses, Baldwin remained strikingly productive, with novels, essays, and other creative works pouring from his typewriter.

Out of New York and America physically, but never spiritually or imaginatively, Baldwin returned to his home territory to complete several creative works. *Another Country (1962) uses New York, Paris, and Alabama as settings for a variety of characters trying to resolve issues of sexual and racial identities. Tell Me How Long the Train's Been Gone (1968), If Beale Street Could Talk (1974), and Just above My Head (1979) all take Baldwin symbolically and physically back to New York, as characters encounter blatant racism, destructively insensitive police and legal systems, and systemic as well as individual obstacles to personal fulfillment.

In the early 1980s, Baldwin traveled to Atlanta, Georgia, to interview persons intimately affected by the Atlanta child murders that took place in 1980 and 1981. He produced his penultimate collection of essays, The Evidence of Things Not Seen (1985), about those murders. Not as powerful in conception or execution as his earlier collections of essays, the volume nonetheless reveals a Baldwin eternally committed to racial justice in a country that professes to be democratic and that has sufficient resources for each citizen to reap the fruits of that designation. Baldwin's final collection of essays, The Price of the Ticket (1985), includes previously published as well as new material.

The late 1970s to mid-1980s found Baldwin constantly on planes between Paris and New York, as he accepted various lecturing and teaching commitments in the United States, including an arrangement as a spring semester visiting professor at the University of Massachusetts at Amherst. He also accepted teaching appointments at Bowling Green State University and the University of California at Berkeley. As his career moved to a new level, Baldwin easily met the challenges until his very body failed him. He died of cancer in Saint-Paul-de-Vence shortly after midnight on 1 December 1987.

[See also Drama; Expatriatism; Gay Literature.]

• Fern Marja Eckman, The Furious Passage of James Baldwin, 1966. Stanley Macebuh, James Baldwin: A Critical Study, 1973. W. J. Weatherby, Squaring Off: Mailer vs. Baldwin, 1977. Louis H. Pratt, James Baldwin, 1978. Carolyn Wedin Sylvander, James Baldwin, 1980. John W. Roberts, "James Baldwin," in DLB, vol. 33, Afro-American Fiction Writers after 1955, eds. Thadious M. Davis and Trudier Harris, 1984, pp. 3–16. Trudier Harris, Black Women in the Fiction of James Baldwin, 1985. Horace A. Porter, Stealing the Fire: The Art and Protest of James Baldwin, 1989. Fred L. Standley and Louis H. Pratt, Conversations with James Baldwin, 1989. Quincy Troupe, ed., James Baldwin: The Legacy 1989. Randall Kenan, James Baldwin: American Writer, 1994. David Leeming, James Baldwin: A Biography, 1994. Trudier Harris, New Essays on Baldwin's Go Tell It on the Mountain, 1996.
—Trudier Harris

Baltimore Afro-American.

The second oldest African American newspaper, published continuously from its inception in 1892 to the present, the Baltimore Afro-American, founded by the Rev. William M. Alexander, gained national prominence through a unique blend of regional *church and society news, a focus on events in Africa, sensational headlines that drew attention to racial outrages in the United States, and editorials that achieved a careful balance between indignation and moderation.

The Afro-American has a distinguished history of contributions to the advancement of the African American community, some of the most visible being its campaign against the Southern Railroad for the use of *Jim Crow cars, its initiation of lawsuits against the Maryland Art Institute and the University of Maryland Law School for segregationist admissions policies, and its fight for equalization of public school teacher's salaries in Maryland. In 1969, the Afro-American was formally recognized for this record of service when it became the first African American publication to receive the American Society of Journalism School Administrator's annual award.

Among the Afro-American's most notable contributors were Langston *Hughes, J. Saunders *Redding, Samuel H. Lacy, and William Worthy. Hughes served as a foreign correspondent to the newspaper during the Spanish Civil War, and produced many *essays that reflected his love of the common people and his abhorrence of fascism. Redding's literary-critical reviews, Lacy's indignant articles against segregation in professional baseball, and Worthy's distinguished career as a foreign correspondent further enhanced the Afro-American's status as one of the most influential representatives of the African American press.

[See also Journalism; Periodicals, article on Black Periodical Press.]

• Roland Edgar Wolseley, The Black Press, U.S.A., 2d ed., 1990.
—Christopher C. De Santis

BAMBARA, TONI CADE

BAMBARA, TONI CADE (1939–1995), novelist, short fiction writer, essayist, filmmaker, lecturer, and educator. Well known for her collections of *short stories and her *novel, The *Salt Eaters (1980), Toni Cade Bambara always insisted that social commitment is inseparable from the production of art. Bambara's early years as a social worker and commitment as a community organizer influenced her work from its earliest beginnings.

Born Toni Cade in 1939 in New York City to Helen Brent Henderson Cade, she and her brother, Walter, grew up in New York, New Jersey, and the South. Bambara's mother, whom she credited as one of her major influences, gave her room to think, dream, and write for herself. Other influences were rooted in the urban environment in which Bambara grew up. She noted especially visiting the Apollo Theater with her father; listening to the music of the 1940s and 1950s; and hearing the trade unionists, Pan-Africanists, Rastas, and others from the Speaker's Corner with her mother. She also cited her editor and friend, Toni *Morrison, as an important influence. Writing as Toni Cade between 1959 and 1970, she changed her name to Bambara when she discovered it as a signature in a sketchbook found in a trunk of her grandmother's things. She had one daughter, Karma.

Bambara's first short story, "Sweet Town," was published in Vendome Magazine in 1959, the same year she graduated with a BA in theater arts from Queens College and won the John Golden Award for Fiction, as well as the Pauper Press Award in Journalism from the Long Island Star. From 1959 to 1961,

Bambara worked as a family and youth caseworker at the New York Department of Welfare and embarked on an MA in American literature from City College of New York. In 1960, her second published short story, "Mississippi Ham Rider," appeared in the *Massachusetts Review*.

In 1961, Bambara worked for a year as Director of Recreation in the psychiatric division of Metro Hospital in New York City. From 1962 to 1965, she worked as Program Director of the Colony Settlement House. Completing her MA in 1965, Bambara taught in City College's SEEK (Search for Education, Elevation, Knowledge) program for four years, working with its black *theater group as well as with publications sponsored by SEEK (*Obsidian*, *Onyx*, and the *Paper*). During these years, Bambara's short stories and articles began appearing in such magazines and journals as *Essence*, *Redbook*, *Negro Digest*, *Prairie Schooner*, the *New York Times*, the *Washington Post*, *Phylon*, *Ms.*, *Black World*, and the *Liberator*.

Bambara taught as a writer in residence at Spelman College (1978–1979), the Neighborhood Arts Center (1975–1979), and Stephens College (1976). She also became the founding member of the Southern Collective of African American Writers, as well as working with the Pomoja Writers Guild and several other organizations. Joining the faculty of Livingston College (at Rutgers University) as an assistant professor in 1969, Bambara was active in black student organizations and arts groups for five years, winning a service award from Livingston's black community before leaving in 1974. In 1975, Bambara became a visiting professor in Afro-American Studies at Emory University and in 1977, at Atlanta University where she was also an instructor in the School of Social Work until 1979.

Bambara refused to separate the struggle for civil rights from a commitment to women's struggle for *freedom. In 1970, she published *The Black Woman*, an *anthology that made connections between civil rights and the women's movement and included fiction, nonfiction, and *poetry by well-known writers such as Nikki *Giovanni, Alice *Walker, Paule *Marshall, and Bambara herself, as well as work by her students from the SEEK program. An important book, it was the first to highlight, as issues of justice, African American women's lives. Like much 1970s feminist criticism, it focused on images of women and the connection of those images to women's oppression, but the book was singular because it was firmly rooted in the diverse experience of black women, both celebrating that experience and critiquing popular *stereotypes.

A second edited anthology appeared in 1971, *Tales and Stories for Black Folks*. Bambara had meant the book for an audience of high school and college students, but it proved to have broader appeal. The book included a section with stories by Langston *Hughes, Ernest J. *Gaines, Pearl Crayton, Alice Walker, and, as before, the work of students.

Bambara's most famous collection of short stories (most of them written between 1950 and 1970), *Gorilla, My Love*, was published in 1972 and has been reprinted many times. The book contains fifteen sto-

ries and "A Sort of Preface" that humorously disclaims any biographical content in the narratives. Set in the rural South as well as the North, most of the stories look at relationships. A major theme centers on the way black women could (and must) participate in supporting and nurturing each other, and healing each other's inner wounds. The book was enthusiastically reviewed as an example of portraits of black life that focused on black love and created memorable characters.

In 1973, Bambara visited Cuba where she met with women's organizations and women workers and was inspired to think further about the connection between writing and social activism, as well as about possibilities for women in the United States. Another important event was her visit to Vietnam in 1975 as a guest of the Women's Union, a visit that moved her more deeply into community organizing.

Influenced by her foreign travel, Bambara's second collection was named after one of its short stories set in southeast Asia. The stories in *The Sea Birds Are Still Alive* (1977) stress the need for people to pull together and organize, as well as to keep their spiritual connections, themes that became increasingly important to Bambara's writing. Reviewers were mixed in their assessment of the collection.

In 1978, Bambara began work on her first novel, *The Salt Eaters*, published in 1980. A novel that one critic has noted is sometimes left unfinished because of its complexity, *The Salt Eaters* focuses on the relationships among such issues as social activism, individual mental and physical health, community well-being, and personal and collective history, as well as the many roots and branches of a spirituality necessary to hold together what Bambara considers to be the primarily dissipated and fractured energies of 1970s social change movements. As with most of her writing, Bambara tends to avoid linear plot, structuring her work in what one critic characterizes as concentric circles. With a dizzying array of characters and settings, the novel employs nearly seamless shifts of time and place to trace the journey of the main character, *Velma Henry—and in fact her entire community—toward *healing and wholeness. The novel, considered by its editors at Random House as somewhat experimental, was well received for the most part, but some reviewers criticized the fast pace and numerous characters. Accolades were given for the rich and idiomatic language and Bambara's fine ear for dialogue, as well as for the import and complexity of the story's message. The novel was issued in paperback in 1981, published in 1982 in the United Kingdom, and reprinted by Vintage in 1992. *The Salt Eaters* won the American Book Award and the Langston Hughes Society Award in 1981, as well as awards from Medallion (1986) and the Zora Neale *Hurston Society (1986). In 1981, Bambara received a National Endowment for the Arts Literature Grant.

In *essays and interviews, Bambara maintained that underlying all of her writing is the concern that the best traditions of her people be nurtured and called forth to build a strong interior life that is always at the service of social change. With almost missionary fervor, Bambara sought, in her writing and other work, to articulate ways the political, artistic, and metaphysical join together.

Bambara served as general editor for the African American Life Series of Wayne State University Press and judge for the National Book Awards (fiction), as well as sitting on numerous advisory boards from *film to literature to community organizations. She was honored with citations of merit from Detroit (1989) and Atlanta (1989), as well as numerous arts and service awards. Her essays and stories have been widely anthologized and reprinted, both in the United States and abroad in Swedish, Dutch, German, Japanese, Norwegian, French, and Spanish presses.

Returning to her original interest in the performing arts in the 1980s, Bambara spent time in filmmaking. In 1986, she worked as writer and narrator for Louis Massiah's *The Bombing of Osage Avenue*, for which she won the Best Documentary Academy Award, the American Book Award, and awards from the Pennsylvania Association of Broadcasters and Black Hall of Fame. She narrated, performed, edited, and wrote for documentary films such as the United Hands Community Land Trust's *More than Property*, Frances Negron's series on Puerto Rico, Nadine Patterson's documentary on Anna Russell Jones, John Akumfrah's *Seven Songs of Malcolm*, and documentaries on John *Coltrane and Cecil B. Moore. Bambara was the coordinating writer for Massiah's film, *W. E. B. Du Bois—A Biography in Four Voices*. Her last novel, tentatively titled *Ground Cover*, will be published posthumously in 1997.

Widely anthologized, Bambara's is one of the earliest voices in contemporary African American literature to call intentionally into tension the questions of *race and *gender. Bambara's work yields fresh significance as scholars apply different methodologies and theoretical lenses to the work, and as general readers continue simply to enjoy it.

[See also Feminism.]

• Beverly Guy-Sheftall, "Commitment: Toni Cade Bambara Speaks," in *Sturdy Black Bridges: Visions of Black Women in Literature*, eds. Roseann P. Bell, Bettye J. Parker, and Beverly Guy-Sheftall, 1979, pp. 230–249. Nancy D. Hargrove, "Youth in Toni Cade Bambara's *Gorilla, My Love*," *The Southern Quarterly* 22.1 (1983): 81–99. Eleanor W. Traylor, "Music as Theme: The Jazz Mode in the Works of Toni Cade Bambara," in *Black Women Writers (1950–1980)*, ed. Mari Evans, 1984, pp. 58–70. Alice Deck, "Toni Cade Bambara," in *DLB*, vol. 38, *Afro-American Writers after 1955: Dramatists and Prose Writers*, eds. Thadious M. Davis and Trudier Harris, 1985, pp. 12–22. Keith Byerman, "Healing Arts: Folklore and the Female Self in Toni Cade Bambara's *The Salt Eaters*," *Postscript* (1988): 37–43. Elliott Butler-Evans, *Race, Gender, and Desire: Narrative Strategies in the Fiction of Toni Cade Bambara, Toni Morrison, and Alice Walker*, 1989. Martha M. Vertreace, "A Bibliography of Writings about Toni Cade Bambara," in *American Women Writing Fiction: Memory, Identity, Family, Space*, ed. Mickey Pearlman, 1989, pp. 168–171. Lois F. Lyles, "Time, Motion, Sound and Fury in *The Sea Birds Are Still Alive*," *CLA Journal* 36:2 (1992): 134–144.

—Ann Folwell Stanford

BANNEKER, BENJAMIN (1731–1806), farmer, mathematician, astronomer, and writer. Benjamin Banneker was born 9 November 1731 in Baltimore County, Maryland, the first child of free African American parents Mary Banneker and Robert, a former slave whose freedom she had purchased and who took her surname upon marriage. Growing up on their tobacco farm, Benjamin received little formal schooling, learning to read and write from his grandmother and attending for several seasons an interracial school where he first developed his lifelong interest in mathematics. Following his parents' deaths and three sisters' departures from home, Banneker remained on the farm, working the crops and cultivating his intellect in relative seclusion.

In 1771, he befriended George Ellicott, a Quaker neighbor whose family had developed a large complex of mills on the adjoining property. With astronomical texts and instruments borrowed from Ellicott, he trained himself to calculate ephemerides, tables establishing the positioning of the sun, moon, and stars for each day of the year. When in 1791 George's cousin Andrew was appointed by President George Washington to conduct the survey of the new Federal Territory (today's District of Columbia), he selected Banneker as his field assistant. After this surveying Banneker returned home to complete an ephemeris for 1792, which failed to find a publisher. Banneker then sought George Ellicott's assistance. Through abolitionist contacts the Ellicotts soon had the material placed with three prospective printers, who were still reviewing it when in August 1791 Banneker sent a manuscript copy of his ephemeris with an accompanying letter to Thomas Jefferson, entreating him to dispel prejudice and exhorting him to fulfill the ideology of the American Revolution and his own Declaration of Independence by granting liberty and unalienable rights to people "of my complexion." While the significance of Banneker's letter and Jefferson's noncommittal response is clear, less evident is Banneker's motivation for writing. Silvio A. Bedini, author of the only full-length biography, *The Life of Benjamin Banneker* (1972), finds Banneker's manifesto uncharacteristic of his quiet temperament, suggesting that he wrote it—perhaps with the encouragement of abolitionist publishers—to draw a response from Jefferson that could in turn be printed to boost the almanac's distribution and extend its message, which indeed occurred.

Published yearly from 1792 through 1797, the Banneker almanacs were widely distributed, appearing in at least twenty-nine separate editions. Featuring Banneker's astronomical tables, the almanacs also included short verse, *essays, proverbs, and general practical information selected by the printer, as was customary with the genre. While not responsible for the literary materials in his almanacs, he did become interested in writing during this period and composed short "Dream" narratives as well as verse. Having retired in 1792 from active farming, he spent his remaining years recording in his journal various observations of nature, mathematical puzzles, as well as yearly ephemerides, even after the almanacs' publication ceased. He died at age seventy-five on 9 October 1806. Although his scientific achievements are especially noteworthy, Banneker's correspondence with Jefferson and his success in the popular almanac genre make him an important contributor to early African American literature.

[*See also* Antislavery Movement; Letters.]

• Silvio A. Bedini, "Banneker, Benjamin," in *DANB*, eds. Rayford W. Logan and Michael R. Winston, 1982, pp. 22–25. Sidney Kaplan and Emma Nogrady Kaplan, "Benjamin Banneker," in *The Black Presence in the Era of the American Revolution*, rev. ed., 1989, pp. 132–151.

—Brad S. Born

BARAKA, AMIRI (b. 1934), poet, playwright, essayist, activist, lecturer, novelist, editor, anthologist, and director. One of the most influential and prolific African American writers of the twentieth century, Amiri Baraka first came to the attention of readers and critics as LeRoi Jones. He was born Everett LeRoy Jones on 7 October 1934 in Newark, New Jersey. His solidly middle-class upbringing figures prominently in his creative work and must be considered one of the major distinguishing features in any comparative treatment of Baraka and other seminal African American literary artists. The son of postal employee Coyt LeRoy Jones and social worker Anna Lois (Russ) Jones, Baraka articulates the angst of the African American middle class with unsurpassed effect in works from every phase of his artistic development. This concern is most apparent in such relatively early works as the Beat-inspired *Preface to a Twenty-Volume Suicide Note* (1961), the theatrical triumph *Dutchman* (1964), the barometric *essays collected in *Home: Social Essays* (1966), and The *System of Dante's Hell* (1965), Baraka's only attempt at the *novel. Although completed at a relatively early point in the artist's development, these works evidence the writer's protracted struggle with the issues of racial *identity and artistic responsibility, the two concerns that have remained his most dominant themes over the years.

Baraka attended the public schools of Newark, New Jersey, Rutgers University, and Howard University. On leaving Howard University, he enlisted in the U.S. Air Force. Upon his discharge, he settled in New York City, studied comparative literature at Columbia University, and began to cultivate strong relationships with a number of avant garde artists on the Lower East Side of New York City. In association with his first wife, Hettie (Cohen) Jones, whom he married in 1958, Baraka edited the journal *Yugen*, which was dedicated to the publication of works by struggling East Village writers. Around this time, he also served as coeditor of *Floating Bear*, an underground literary newsletter. Moreover, he and Diane di Prima cofounded the American Theater for Poets in 1961. This experimental dramatic troupe, too, was primarily concerned with presenting the works of lesser-known local writers.

Generally recognized as a "mover and shaker" on the Lower East Side art scene, Baraka quickly earned the respect of artists of all mediums, particularly the writers of the so-called Beatnik movement. His emergence as a personality and leader among this group is reflected in a 1964 feature article entitled "King of the East Village," which appeared in the *New York Herald Tribune*. His stature was further enhanced

with the publication of his first collection of poems, *Preface to a Twenty-Volume Suicide Note*, and two early dramatic works, *The Baptism* and *The Toilet* (both jointly published in 1967, but performed in 1964 and 1961, respectively).

Although it appeared well past the zenith of the Beat movement, *Preface* is most representative of the literature produced by the more characteristic Beat writers. Reflecting scorn for convention, pretence, and materialism, the poems share also the brooding, self-deprecating tone of these artists. While the two plays of this period are strikingly different in mode of presentation—*The Baptism*, a highly experimental, absurdist effort, and *The Toilet*, a markedly naturalistic work—they too evidence notable Beat tendencies. In both plays, homosexual characters figure prominently as symbols of openness and tolerance, direly needed qualities in the convention-bound, excessively prohibitive straight world.

Despite the clarity of Baraka's Beat-inspired criticism of society, however, the works from this period of the writer's development reflect, paradoxically, a growing unease with the very culture from which they emerge. This is most profoundly felt in the works of *Preface*, which posit a poignant dissatisfaction with the essentially apolitical protestations of the Beats. These poems are most notable in their expressions of concern with the poetic process and with questions of audience and artistic engagement. The author's employment of the racial theme in a number of the poems is indicative of his attempts to effect a reconciliation of his art with his emerging political activism. Examination of Baraka's essays from this period, works that later found their way into *Home: Social Essays*, reveals the depth of his thought on these issues at the time.

The various essays of *Home: Social Essays*, originally published in a number of liberal and leftist journals, present a record of Baraka's artistic transformation from black Beat poet to "Father of the *Black Arts movement." Becoming increasingly involved in political and artistic pursuits that took him beyond the confines of the Lower East Side, he shows in these essays an intense disaffection for liberalism, the gradualism of the *civil rights movement, all manifestations of cultural shame, and assimilationist behavior by African Americans.

Despite his growing attraction to direct political action and racial concerns (as evidenced in his membership in such Harlem-based groups as the militant "On Guard for Freedom Committee" in 1961), Baraka was still very much involved with the Beat coterie during the writing of many of the aforementioned essays. His poems continued to appear in publications edited and supported by this group. Moreover, his first published fictional efforts appeared during this period in these same journals. Of particular significance was the appearance of *The System of Dante's Hell* (1965), Baraka's only novel. The author's final triumph, however, as denizen of the Lower East Side, was the explosive *drama *Dutchman* (1964). Along with the poems of *The Dead Lecturer* (1964), these works reflect the tremendous psychological tension experienced by the artist during this phase of his development. Informed by an increasingly African American frame of reference, they represent, to a great extent, the artist's attempts to rationalize his new posture.

The poems of *The Dead Lecturer* represent Baraka's farewell to the closed, apolitical circle of Beat peers. Marked by an ever-increasing preoccupation with racial concerns, these lyrics evince the artist's crystallization of his commitment to revolutionary action and his disavowal of what he perceives to be the apolitical decadence of former compatriots. In withering attacks on his "friends," the poet shows impatience with the life of reflection and dead-end intellectualism. Manifesting his sense of guilt for not being more actively involved in the rapidly expanding black liberation movement, he frequently invokes the prodigal theme in the poems of *The Dead Lecturer* and the essays of *Home*.

The poems and essays of these early works are also characterized by Baraka's commitment to the articulation of a *Black Aesthetic. Poems such as "Black Dada Nihilismus," "Crow Jane," and "Rhythm and Blues 1 (for Robert Williams in Exile)" must be viewed as the lyrical equivalents to such essays as "LeRoi Jones Talking," "A Dark Bag," and "The Revolutionary Theater."

The dramatic works *Dutchman* and *The Slave* (1964) should be seen as highly representative of this transitional period in Baraka's artistic development. Poets and marginal men, the heroes of both works give voice to many of the sentiments expressed in the *poetry and prose of this period. Both Clay of *Dutchman* and Walker Vessels of *The Slave* are shown wrestling with the demons of self-denial that Baraka himself was attempting to eradicate between the years 1961 and 1965. C. W. E. Bigsby offers, in *The Second Black Renaissance: Essays in Black Literature* (1980), some of the most perceptive critical commentary available on these two works. Writing of *Dutchman*, he notes, "[It] remains one of the best plays ever written by a black author and one of the most impressive works of recent American *theater. . . . At its heart is a consideration of the artistic process, a debate over the legitimacy of sublimating social anguish into aesthetic form." In his treatment of *The Slave*, he refers to the drama as "a personal act of exorcism," a description that could serve as well in discussion of most of the works of this phase of Baraka's artistic and personal development.

Baraka's espousal of a thoroughly political, race-conscious art was given dramatic emphasis by the continued shifting of his base of activities from the Lower East Side to Harlem. His involvement with the Black Arts Repertory Theater/School, located in Harlem, provided him with a base and a vehicle to test the aesthetic theories of the emerging cultural nationalist. Formally opened in early 1965, the Black Arts Repertory Theater/School was of critical importance in the development of the Black Arts movement of the later 1960s and early 1970s. Describing its programmatic thrust and strict adherence to the ideas put forth by Baraka, Larry *Neal noted, "the

Black Arts Theater took its programs into the streets of Harlem. For three months, the theater presented plays, concerts, and poetry readings to the people of the community. Plays that shattered the illusions of the American body politic, and awakened Black people to the meaning of their lives" ("The Black Arts Movement," *Drama Review*, Summer 1968). Although short-lived, the Black Arts Repertory Theater/ School's influence was widespread. Groups fashioned in its image sprang up throughout the country, and Baraka, its chief architect, was generally recognized as a seminal influence and leader.

Following the demise of the Black Arts Repertory Theater/School, Baraka returned to his hometown of Newark, New Jersey, to continue the work begun in Harlem. In doing so, he established Spirit House and its troupe of actors, called the Spirit House Movers. He also exercised his political acumen by organizing and leading the Black Community Development and Defense Organization, which proved to be an effective force in advancing the cause of Newark's African American community.

It was during this period that the writer changed his name. Having become a proponent of the Kawaida faith, a hybridization of orthodox Islam and traditional African practices, he became Ameer Baraka ("blessed Prince"). Taking on the role of priest in his growing commune, he added the title Imamu ("spiritual Leader") and changed "Ameer" to "Amiri," with no change in its regal connotation. He later dropped the title Imamu.

The poems, plays, and essays of the committed cultural nationalist are characterized by a markedly hortatory or didactic manner. Directed to an African American audience, they were intended to "raise the consciousness" of a divided and debased people. Baraka exerted tremendous influence on a generation of young African American writers during this period. Haki *Madhubuti (formerly Don L. Lee), Nikki *Giovanni, and Sonia *Sanchez are only a few of the younger writers who attracted the attention of readers and listeners as disciples of Baraka.

The poems of *Black Magic: Collected Poetry, 1961–1967* (1969), *It's Nation Time* (1970), and *In Our Terribleness* (1970) are typical of the verse produced by cultural nationalist, poet/priest Baraka. *Black Magic* contains a number of poems that reflect the self-accusatory, brooding tone of the Beat and post-Beat periods. However, the latter works more frequently evidence the assured exhortations of the committed revolutionary. Moreover, these efforts are marked by an increase in the use of the language of the streets and black oral modes. In poems such as "Black Art," Baraka also continues the formulation of prescriptive artistic manifestos begun in the essays of *Home*. Like the play, the poem must be put to revolutionary use.

The dramatic works produced in this phase of Baraka's development show an extremely conscious employment of what is, perhaps, best described as the allegorical-didactic technique of medieval drama. Such an approach was logical for the playwright desirous of reaching, and teaching, a largely unlettered audience, hence, such plays as *Experimental Death Unit #1*, *Madheart*, and *Great Goodness of Life*, all published in *Four Black Revolutionary Plays* (1969). It should be noted, however, that Baraka, the avant garde dramatist, is also in evidence here. In addition to the stylized devices of medieval drama, the plays abound with expressionistic techniques. Moreover, Baraka produces what is arguably his most innovative and challenging drama, *Slave Ship: An Historical Pageant* (1967), a moving example of "environmental" or "living" theater, during this phase of his development.

During the early 1970s, Baraka played key roles in the organization of such major African American political conferences as the Pan African Congress of African Peoples in Atlanta (1972) and the National Black Political Convention in Gary, Indiana (1974). Around this same time, he made another dramatic ideological shift by announcing his formal adoption of a Marxist-Leninist perspective. Rejecting a narrowly prescribed cultural nationalism, he notes, in one of his earliest statements from this period ("The Congress of Afrikan People: A Position Paper," *Black Scholar*, Jan./Feb. 1975), "Nationalism is backward when it says we cannot utilize the revolutionary experience of the world . . . the theories and experience of men like Marx, Engels, Lenin, Stalin, Mao Tse-Tung . . . Fidel Castro . . . to utilize all this revolutionary experience and revolutionary theory, by integrating it with the concrete practice of the black liberation movement." With publication of such work as *Hard Facts* (1975), *Poetry for the Advanced* (1979), and *Daggers and Javelins* (1984), Baraka has continued his efforts to reconcile the more positive or useful aspects of cultural nationalism with the scientific accuracy of Marxism. As with his earlier works, the critical reception has been mixed.

Amiri Baraka's example is in many ways emblematic of the collective experience of African Americans since the momentous decade of the 1960s. His spiritual and artistic journey reflects, in microcosm and, to be sure, in the extreme, the movement from doubt to self-assurance, from self-contempt to self-acceptance. Moreover, in his more recent disavowal of the confining dictums of cultural nationalism, we see a suggestion of the larger African American community's movement toward greater openness to diversity and cross-cultural collaboration. Baraka's greatest contribution, however, lies in his tremendous influence on the direction of post-1960s African American writing. In encouraging a generation of writers to use, confidently and unapologetically, their own rich African American cultural heritage as well as experimental modes of presentation, he proved himself a key facilitator in the maturation of a good number of innovative young artists. By freeing these aspiring writers from all vestiges of cultural shame and the lock-step realistic/naturalistic mode, he contributed immeasurably to African American literature specifically and American literature in general.

[See also Class; Communism; Literary History, *article on* Late Twentieth Century.]

• Donald B. Gibson, ed., *Modern Black Poets: A Collection of Critical Essays*, 1973. Theodore Hudson, *From LeRoi Jones to Amiri Baraka: The Literary Works*, 1973. Kimberly Benston, *Baraka: The Renegade and the Mask*, 1976. Werner Sollors, *Amiri Baraka/LeRoi Jones: The Quest for a "Populist Modernism,"* 1978. Lloyd Brown, *Amiri Baraka*, 1980. William C. Fisher, "Amiri Baraka," in *American Writers*, supplement 2, part 1, ed. A. Walton Litz, 1981, pp. 29–63. Henry C. Lacey, *To Raise, Destroy, and Create: The Poetry, Drama, and Fiction of Imamu Amiri Baraka (LeRoi Jones)*, 1981. William J. Harris, *The Poetry and Poetics of Amiri Baraka: The Jazz Aesthetic*, 1985. Robert Elliot Fox, *Conscientious Sorcerers: The Black Post Modernist Fiction of LeRoi Jones/Amiri Baraka, Ishmael Reed, and Samuel R. Delany*, 1987.   —Henry C. Lacey

BARBER. Barbers hold one of the most respected occupations in African American literature, and their shops are sites for microcosmic reflections of the larger world in which African Americans live. While some barbers merely provide local color in the literature, others have offered jobs to young men at crucial points in their lives, or they have played key roles in the development of a number of characters. Equally important, barbers serve as arbiters of the political, social, and personal commentary that characterizes their establishments. Since barbershops are integral to black communities as gathering places, sources for information about everything from grooming to sex, and sites on which manhood can be challenged or affirmed, barbers have a secular status for black men comparable to *preachers and deacons in the sacred realm. Barbershops are a talkers' haven, and barbers preside, usually cheerfully, over the proceedings. In Barry *Beckham's *My Main Mother* (1969), Mitchell recognizes how much his neighborhood barbershop is a part of a tradition, and he learns from the men in the barbershop. Toni *Morrison allows her male characters to learn about and comment upon Emmett Till's murder in a barbershop in *Song of Solomon* (1977), and Charlie L. *Russell, in his play *Five on the Black Hand Side* (1950), selects a barbershop as the site upon which black women decide to protest women's exclusion from this male world as well as their general treatment by men. Most of the action in Lonne *Elder III's *Ceremonies in Dark Old Men* (1965) takes place in a barbershop, with Mr. Parker and his son Theo serving as the sometimes barbers. In this standard setting, black men play checkers, debate, reminisce, and scheme about business dealings. The setting highlights the significance of this space in historical communities as well as the function it serves in bolstering or debunking dreams. The place and prevailing male attitudes also illustrate, as they do in Russell's play, rather negative feelings toward black women. Theo, his brother Bobby, and their father all live off the meager earnings of Adele, their sister and daughter, and from whom they expect no less than total sacrifice of her life for them. Elder and the other writers join William *Demby, Ronald Williams, Richard *Wright, and many other authors in focusing on barbers and barbershops in their works. While few barbers play primary roles in literary works, they nonetheless play essential ones. Their presence and their establishments provide the cultural texturing for black male life-spaces even as they enhance African American communities.

[*See also* Hair.]

• Trudier Harris, "The Barbershop in Black Literature," *Black American Literature Forum* 13.3 (Fall 1979): 112–118.

—Trudier Harris

BARNES, STEVEN (b. 1952), novelist, short story writer, television script writer, screenplay writer, lecturer, creative consultant, and martial arts authority. A Los Angeles native and later resident of Vancouver, Washington, Steven Emory Barnes is the third African American author after 1960 to have chosen science fiction and fantasy writing as his primary profession. Barnes established himself through the 1980s as a determined and disciplined writer, one who had followed a cherished childhood dream to become a commercially successful professional writer.

The youngest child of Emory F. Barnes and Eva Mae (Reeves) Barnes, Steven Barnes grew up in Los Angeles. He attended Los Angeles High, Los Angeles City College, and Pepperdine University, Malibu, California (1978–1980). At Pepperdine he majored in communication arts but withdrew from school before completing a degree, frustrated because he thought no one on the faculty could teach him about building a career as a professional writer. It was not until Barnes made contact with established science fiction writer Ray Bradbury, who sent the novice writer two encouraging letters after reading some of his stories, and with film director, producer, and scriptwriter John Landis, who also encouraged him, that Barnes began to feel he could be successful. Recognizing that more guidance from working writers could help him learn his craft, in 1979 Barnes sought out well-established science fiction author Larry Niven at the Burbank Science Fiction and Fantasy Club and began a literary apprenticeship with him.

From the early 1980s to the mid-1990s the mentoring arrangement between Niven and Barnes proved very productive, resulting in five coauthored novels. As a team the two wrote the progressively linked *Dream Park* novels, a combination of action-suspense and thriller–science fiction set in a near-future, highly technological, Disneyesque theme park. *Dream Park* (1981), *The Barsoom Project* (1989), and *The California Voodoo Game* (1991) comprise the trilogy. Barnes and Niven also collaborated on *The Descent of Anansi* (1982) and *Achilles' Choice* (1991). In 1987 and in 1995, Barnes joined forces with both Niven and Jerry Pournelle to produce *The Legacy of Heorot* (1987) and *Beowulf's Children* (1995).

Working independently, Barnes wrote *The Kundalini Equation* (1986), a novel based upon East Indian myths, and three other books featuring the larger-than-life martial arts expert and zero-gravity "nullboxer" Aubry Knight. Knight became Barnes's black mythic champion, his response to a childhood diet of comic books and fantasy tales without positive images of African Americans performing heroic acts. While young, Barnes began creating his own dark-hued imitation Conan stories to help establish a

context for his life. Believing myths are vitally important to all cultures, he went on to fashion the heroic Aubry Knight, who represents an outgrowth of Barnes's understanding of the popular, and profitable, fantastic hero. Giving more flesh to the type, Barnes drew Aubry as a man capable of growth; his Knight must learn what it is to become human, to become a man and not just a fighter. The shattered, vicious, and seemingly dystopian universe Knight inhabits reflects Barnes's fascination with anger and violence, his insight into what he deemed as "the dark side" of human nature or the "dark side of the force." Yet after Aubry Knight has been through hell and back in *Streetlethal* (1983) and *Gorgon Child* (1989), when he reappears in *FireDance* (1993) the world has become more stable, and he has evolved to become a more balanced, mature man. Growth, balance, the unity of mind, body, and spirit, the sometimes thin line between feeling and action—these are all undercurrents in Barnes's independent novels.

Between 1981 and 1996, Barnes published thirteen *novels, including a five-part graphic novel called *Fusion* for Eclipse Comics (1987). Although he has not written many, his *short stories have been well received. "The Locusts," the first collaboration between Nivens and Barnes, appeared in *Analog* (June 1979) and was nominated for a Hugo, one of two prestigious awards given in science fiction. His stories have been included in Roger Zelazny's *Warriors of Mist and Dream* (1995) anthology and Robert Adam's two *Horseclans* anthologies (1987 and 1988); he has also been published in *Isaac Asimov's Science Fiction Magazine*. In addition, Barnes occasionally writes for television, adapting stories or composing scripts for popular programs such as *The Twilight Zone*, *Real Ghostbusters*, *Baywatch*, and *The Outer Limits*. Barnes has also written several essays for martial arts publications and served as a columnist for *Black Belt Magazine* from 1986 to 1989.

Maintaining that he has no interest in writing either the traditional realistic American novel or the "great American black novel," Steven Barnes declared that his interest has been and remains fantasy fiction. "I once tried to stop writing for two years, just to see if there was something else I could do with myself . . . and there wasn't. I couldn't stop writing. Science fiction gives me the widest areas to play in." The three most important aspects of Steven Barnes's life are creating the science fiction and suspense tales that allow him to develop his own mythos, the martial arts, and his family and friends.

[*See also* Speculative Fiction.]

• "Barnes, Stephen Emory," in *CA*, vol. 105, 1982, p. 50. Francis Hamit, "The Self-Evolution of Steven Barnes," *Players* 14.9 (Feb. 1988): 36–40.

—Sandra Y. Govan

BARRAX, GERALD W. (b. 1933), poet and educator. Bridging the poetic radicalism and experimentalism of the 1960s to the lyrical and confessional modes of the 1980s, the *poetry of Gerald William Barrax draws on the life of the poet as well as the state of African American experience for its intimate power. Whether relating the details of his life with wife and children or questioning the roles of African American leaders, Barrax's poetry continually invokes anxieties concerning responsibility and participation in contemporary American life.

Born in Attala, Alabama, on 21 June 1933, Barrax spent his early years in the rural South. Once his family moved to Pittsburgh in 1944, Barrax completed his primary and secondary education, worked in the post office, and completed a bachelor's degree at Duquesne University. Upon receipt of a master's degree in English from the University of Pittsburgh in 1969, Barrax moved to North Carolina, where he studied and joined the faculty of North Carolina State University in Raleigh. During this period Barrax lived some of the material that has become crucial concerns of his poetry: the experience of family, of work, of race and racism, and of transcendence. This transcendence—through social participation, through home and family, through an inquisition of doubt and faith—is the most characteristic element of his work.

One can discern three distinct periods within Barrax's work: the first, a period defined loosely by an encounter with existentialism, the *Black Arts movement, and experiment with form; the second by the exploration of a distinctly personal, anecdotal, confessional poetic voice; and the third by an elaboration of this confessional tone into a sustained lyricism that addresses both personal and collective anxieties.

Divided into three sections ("Forecast," "Drought," and "Another Kind of Rain"), Barrax's first collection of poetry, *Another Kind of Rain* (1970), describes the search for and the attainment of renewal. One of the text's dominant themes is the father-son relationship, a relationship that has particular resonance in the poet's life (Barrax is separated from his first wife and three sons) and, more generally, in African American experience at large. In poems such as "Efficiency Apartment," "First Carolina Rain," and "Earthlog: Final Entry" the poet explores the disconnection and the painful and joyous connection that persists between himself and his sons. Technically, the poems range from confessional lyrics to free verse poems filled with "street talk" and typographical dynamism. *Another Kind of Rain* also establishes Barrax's wide-ranging eclecticism (alluding variously to Homer, William Shakespeare, Alfred, Lord Tennyson, William Butler Yeats, T. S. Eliot, e. e. cummings) that, paired with his intimate tone and confessional subjects, results in an eclectic and allusive document of the persistence of universal themes in contemporary experience.

The unproblematic perspective of the "I" in *Another Kind of Rain* becomes the poet's subject in Barrax's second collection, *An Audience of One* (1980). An exploration of the subjectivity of the poet who moves from one marriage into another, from one family to another, *An Audience of One* plays out a poetic dialogue between objectivity (the preponderant image of the camera in "The Only Way My Dumb Flesh Knows") and subjective possibilities that a new family and new beginnings bring ("I Travel with Her," "Shani"). It is a pivotal work in its movement from poetic duality in his early poems (they were either personal or public, intimate or political) to a fulfillment of the public within the personal, the political within the intimate detail of everyday life. *The Deaths of Animals and Lesser Gods* (1984) extends this renovation of self, family, and community through faith. The transcendent possibilities of belief and of the belief in belief become Barrax's central subject. He asserts the need for certainty, peace, and clarity, which far from separating humanity from the divine actually brings it closer to participation in others and ourselves: "God is love as long as one of us lives."

Barrax's *Leaning Against the Sun* (1992) consolidates the impulses of his decades-long process. After two wives and five children, Barrax celebrates the renewing ritual of domestic tranquility and the identity-building value of attempting to understand God, man, and community. Formally, Barrax returns in some of these poems ("Epigraphs," "Cello Poem") to rhyme and meter. Alluding to his poetic antecedents (Walt Whitman, Denise Levertov, Emily Dickinson), Barrax's meditations on freedom, faith, and manhood gain a rhythmic, musical depth. Transcendence is found in simple tasks and simple moments treasured simply.

Ultimately, Gerald W. Barrax's work offers a vein of allusion, eclecticism, and inclusiveness to the tradition of African American poetry. An eclectic nexus of tendencies and themes in African American poetry, Barrax's poetry enacts the contradictory and complex discourses motivating the tradition-bound and tradition-breaking impulses of contemporary African American poetry.

• Lorenzo Thomas, review of *The Deaths of Animals and Lesser Gods, Black American Literature Forum* 19 (Fall 1985): 132–133. Lenard D. Moore, "On Hearing Gerald W. Barrax," *Black American Literature Forum* 21 (Fall 1987): 241–242. Dennis Sampson, review of *Leaning Against the Sun, Hudson Review* 45 (Winter 1993): 670–671. Lenard D. Moore, review of *Leaning Against the Sun, African American Review* 28 (Summer 1994): 311–315.   —Daniel M. Scott III

"Bars Fight." *See* Terry, Lucy.

BASS, KINGSLEY, JR., is the pseudonym of Black Theater movement playwright Ed *Bullins for the publication of *We Righteous Bombers* in the anthology *New Plays from the Black Theatre* (1969) and the play's production at the New Lafayette Theatre in Harlem in May of 1969.

New Plays from the Black Theatre lists Kingsley B. Bass, Jr., as "a 24-year-old Black man murdered by Detroit police during the uprising," but in a panel discussion of *We Righteous Bombers* at the New Lafayette Theatre (11 May 1969), playwright *Marvin X reported that Bullins in fact wrote the play and used the pseudonym "to suggest the type of play that a brother killed in the Detroit Revolution would have written." Bass, who never existed, seemed able to achieve for himself a fine, if ironic, honor: a small notice by Larry *Neal printed below prefatory notes to the panel discussion (which also contributed to the confusion over the play's authorship) announced

Bass's winning the Harriet Webster Updike Award for literary excellence.

We Righteous Bombers is modeled almost strictly after Albert Camus's *Les Justes* (1946; trans., *The Just Assassins*, 1958). Both plays ask whether the decision to commit murder to end the suffering of humanity is an enterprise that can ultimately be legitimated. *Bombers*, however, whose racialized conflict is more deeply visceral and whose concomitant intensity of hatred and fear is further enhanced by elements of expressionistic *theater (Bullins constructs time achronologically and uses *music and still projections throughout the play), seems even more horrific a presentation of this question than its predecessor. Additionally, the proximity of the play to present-day America and its racial dilemmas lends significantly to the consternation of its audience. Jack B. Moore's suggestion that the play reveals "the realities of hate and fear and desire that the everyday life of black and white behavior only masks" invites speculation of Bullins's motivation to use a pseudonym: the authorial *masking and the confusion surrounding it become a metaphor for the play's ability to unmask society and render the apocalypse beneath.

The post-production panel discussion itself produced an array of reactions regarding the importance of the play as a revolutionary work—specifically, its accurate depiction of revolutionary spirit and its psychological impact on a public in search of bold revolutionary characterizations of African Americans. Robert Macbeth, director of the New Lafayette, defended *Bombers* and expected that new plays would naturally evolve from its questions and flaws. Dissenting were Askia M. *Touré and Ernie Mkalimoto, who stated that the only proper image of the African American revolutionary, that of keeper of myth and *folklore and designer of a new world *history, was cheapened by characterizations of weakness among the play's revolutionaries. Larry Neal and Amiri *Baraka (LeRoi Jones) philosophized that there is a reciprocity between art and activism. Baraka, in his final appeal to the audience, made the claim for a clarity of statement over the "mysticism of art," suggesting that without clarity, such mysticism can plainly deceive, overwhelming artist and audience in more ways than one can ever know.

• Larry Neal, "Lafayette Theatre Reaction to *Bombers*," *Black Theatre* 4 (1969): 16–25. Larry Neal, "Toward a Relevant Black Theatre," *Black Theatre* (1969): 14–15. Jack B. Moore, "The (In)humanity of Assassination: Plays by Albert Camus and Kingsley B. Bass, Jr.," *MELUS* 8.3 (Fall 1981): 45–56.
—Nathan L. Grant

BAUMFREE, ISABELLA. *See* Truth, Sojourner.

BEAUTICIAN. Comparable to *barbers in the roles they play in African American communities, beauticians represent yet another respectable occupation for black women. Although many black women in the literature are full-time beauticians, others frequently use the job as a secondary source of income. In shops of their own, or working out of their homes, beauticians play an important role in young black female characters coming into their own as women. A

first trip to a beauty parlor becomes a ritual of initiation into womanhood over which the beautician presides. If the young visitor is too young to be pronounced "woman," the first trip at least signifies a new departure in *hair care. These points of initiation occur with *Selina Boyce in Paule *Marshall's *Brown Girl, Brownstones* (1959), as well as with Lena McPherson in Tina McElroy *Ansa's *Baby of the Family* (1989). Miss Thompson, the beautician in Marshall's novel, understands the particular traumas that the young Selina is undergoing—perhaps better than her mother; she therefore takes special care in "fixing" (the usual verb for getting hair done) a grown-up hairdo for Selina. When Lena's unruly hair leads to an extended discussion about what will happen when she goes swimming, her mother turns her over to a beautician, who braids Lena's hair into about two hundred segments, or so it seems to family observers. Epitomizing the idea of "water as enemy" to black straightened—or processed—hair, Ansa captures what has historically been a problem for black women.

The literature consistently reflects historical features of black hair and attempts to manage it. The prototypical twentieth-century beautician, business woman Madam C. J. Walker, enabled black women to move from tightly curled, or "kinky," hair in the first decade of the twentieth century by inventing the straightening comb that led to the perennial clash with water. In his autobiographical *Colored People* (1994), Henry Louis *Gates, Jr., recounts how his mother would straighten the hair of her friends in her kitchen in West Virginia, and how the "kitchen," that especially kinky part of the hair at the nape of the neck, was the test site for judging when a new "do" was necessary. By commenting on the kitchen as the place where hairdressing occurred, Gates recognizes a long-standing historical pattern for business as well as a social gathering site for black women. Many autobiographers have joined Gates in noting—somewhat nostalgically—the smell of hair that characterized the process of straightening.

Gwendolyn *Brooks, in her only novel, *Maud Martha* (1953), provides the beauty shop setting as well as the social climate that necessitated its growth and development. A white saleswoman comments offhandedly to beautician Sonia Johnson that she has been working "like a nigger to make a few pennies," even as she is trying to sell her products to black women. Her standards for work and beauty obviously exclude black women. Yet it is precisely to enhance their beauty that black women visit such shops, as is vividly illustrated in Brooks's poem "at the hairdresser's" (1945), where a black woman with naturally short hair wants the beautician to increase her romantic competitiveness by giving her longer hair, an "upsweep. . . . With humpteen baby curls." Toni *Morrison's Hagar in *Song of Solomon* (1977) bases *Milkman Dead's rejection of her on her infrequent trips to beauty parlors. Her climactic trip finds a beautician, Marcelline, ready to serve her—without an appointment—rather than reap the wrath of this potentially wild woman.

Beauticians, therefore, have the power in their hands to create beauty, as Morrison's Violet does in *Jazz* (1992). Their appearance in the literature reflects their historical counterparts. They are masters of a skill, indeed an art, to which the larger society pays little notice but which is crucial to *identity and sanity in literary works.   —Trudier Harris

BECK, ROBERT. *See* Iceberg Slim.

BECKHAM, BARRY (b. 1944), novelist and publisher. Barry Beckham began his first *novel, *My Main Mother* (1969), while he was a senior at Brown University, completing it while living in New York City. He returned to Brown in 1970 as a visiting lecturer in English and, after being appointed to a professorship, remained there for seventeen years, several as director of the graduate creative writing program. In 1972, his second novel, *Runner Mack*, was nominated for the National Book Award, and his play *Garvey Lives!* was produced in Providence. In 1974, he was commissioned to write a *biography of New York playground basketball legend Earl Manigault. The book was published in 1981 as a "novelized biography," *Double Dunk*. In 1987, Beckham moved to Washington, D.C., teaching at Hampton University for two years. Partly because of difficulties with publishers over another of his projects, *The Black Student's Guide to Colleges* (1982), he has since dedicated himself to "developing a major black-oriented book company," Beckham House Publishers. At present, Beckham is working on his *autobiography, a novel responding to his perceived "need for a description of a passionate black love relationship," and a collaborative autobiography with Jackie Robinson's daughter Sharon.

My Main Mother has a rural setting based on one of Beckham's childhood homes, Woodbury, New Jersey, where his was the only black family in the area. The novel depicts a distraught and highly fragmented narrator who, while sitting in a junked car awaiting the arrival of the police, tells in one night (Scheherazade-like) how and why he killed his mother, whose vain self-indulgence had led her to abandon him by running away with a man to New York to become a singer. While representations of alienating family life suggest the lineage of Richard *Wright, the novel also reflects a gothic tradition that Beckham attributes to the influence of both his writing teacher, novelist John Hawkes, and Franz Kafka.

Runner Mack, Beckham's most accomplished work, is the story of naive Henry Adams, who moves from Mississippi to a northern city dreaming of playing professional baseball, only to be frustrated in his ambitions, first by having to go to work in a factory and later by being drafted into the army. While fighting in the fraudulently conceived "Alaska War," a veiled satire of Vietnam, Henry meets Black Power advocate Runner Mack (based on a New York acquaintance of Beckham's), becomes a revolutionary himself, and eventually participates in an abortive attempt to bomb the White House. The novel's structure is a pastiche of the classic African American as-

cent narrative, each event representing an aspect of white exploitation of African Americans from *slavery to the present, notably through professional sports, military service, and the *migration north to work in industry. The factory scenes suggest the surreal, hallucinatory Liberty Paint episode in Ralph *Ellison's *Invisible Man* (1952), while the broad characterizations and conscious employment of African American *slave narrative and autobiographical traditions prefigure Ishmael *Reed's *Flight to Canada* (1976).

[*See also* Publishing; War Experience.]

• Joe Weixlmann, "The Dream Turned 'Daymare': Barry Beckham's *Runner Mack*," *MELUS* 8.4 (Winter 1981): 93–103. Wiley Lee Umphlett, "The Black Man as Fictional Athlete: *Runner Mack*, the Sporting Myth, and the Failure of the American Dream," *Modern Fiction Studies* 33.1 (Spring 1987): 73–83.   —Jeff Loeb

BELL, JAMES MADISON (1826–1902), poet. The "Bard of the Maumee," Ohio's first native African American poet, was born in Gallipolis where he spent his first sixteen years. From 1842 to 1853, Bell worked as a plasterer in Cincinnati and there married Louisiana Sanderlin with whom he had several children. He plied the plasterer's trade in Canada West, Ontario (1854–1860); there he became a friend of John *Brown's, raised funds for Brown's 1859 raid, and later dedicated *The Day and the War* to "The Hero, Saint and Martyr of Harpers Ferry." For the next thirty years, until he settled in Toledo in 1890, Bell pursued the trades of plasterer and poet-lecturer in San Francisco (1860–1865) and many other cities north and south. He championed abolitionism and black educational and legal rights, served as a prominent lay worker for the African Methodist Episcopal (AME) Church, and briefly worked in Republican Party politics. In 1901, at the insistence of Bishop Benjamin Arnett, Bell published his life's *poetry in *Poetical Works*.

Bell specialized in long verse-orations (each of 750 to 950 lines) that recounted the history of *slavery, the Civil War, emancipation, and Reconstruction: *A Poem* (1862); *A Poem Entitled the Day and the War* (1864); *An Anniversary Poem Entitled the Progress of Liberty* (1866); and *A Poem Entitled the Triumph of Liberty* (1870). These poems require the spirited dramatic recitals Bell offered on his tours, where, William Wells *Brown observed, his "soul-stirring appeals" inspired "enthusiasm of admiration" in his listeners. On the printed page the orations' abstractions, clichés, and monotonously regular iambic tetrameter and rhymes smother both emotional force and intellectual conviction. Occasionally specific references to historical persons and events or variations in stanza length add distinctiveness to Bell's poetic declamations on liberty and racial justice. Collected with the long poems in *Poetical Works* are a dozen conventional shorter poems, most on racial themes, and a daring, vigorous satire of President Andrew Johnson, "Modern Moses, or 'My Policy' Man" (c. 1867). In every age, writes Bell, "an assassin's blow" has raised to power someone "Whose acts unseemly and unwise, / Have caused the people to despise / And curse the hours of his reign, / And brand him with the mark of Cain." Worse than Cain is Johnson, "My liege of graceless dignity," our Judas, Satan's minion, a false *Moses. Exposing Johnson's political treacheries, dissipations, and vulgarities in 377 lines, Bell combines shrewd *humor and irony, concrete topicality, and uninhibited personal emotion for his most inventive and readable work. As poet and public speaker, Bell was one of the nineteenth century's most dedicated propagandists for African American *freedom and civil rights.

[*See also* Protest Literature.]

• Benjamin W. Arnett, "Biographical Sketch," in *Poetical Works*, by James Madison Bell, 1901, pp. 3–14. Joan R. Sherman, *Invisible Poets: Afro-Americans of the Nineteenth Century*, 2d ed., 1989.   —Joan R. Sherman

Beloved. Toni *Morrison's fifth novel, *Beloved* (1987), won a Pulitzer Prize in 1988 and is an accurate portrayal of the black slave woman's experience. Beginning in pre–Civil War Kentucky, *Beloved* is the story of *Sethe Suggs and her family. Nineteen years old and pregnant with her fourth child, Sethe wants nothing more than to free her family from slavery. The Suggses had been owned by Mr. Garner, a "humane slave master," but when he dies his brother schoolteacher comes to run the plantation. The Suggses escape but schoolteacher finds them in Ohio, and when Sethe sees him approaching she tries to kill her children—to prevent their return to *slavery—but only succeeds in killing her young daughter, Beloved. Realizing Sethe's intentions, schoolteacher leaves and Sethe serves a short jail sentence, nursing her newly born daughter, Denver. She then supports her family as a cook.

Beloved returns to haunt her mother's house. As a baby ghost she turns over tables and makes fingerprints in cakes, ultimately driving her two brothers away. When *Paul D, a former slave from the same plantation, arrives at Sethe's house, he vanquishes the baby ghost by yelling and striking at the air, but she eventually returns as a twenty-year-old spirit in human form with a demanding infantile personality. Because of Sethe's guilt and the "rememory" of tortured slavery, Beloved is able to take over Sethe's mind, body, and heart, following her everywhere, questioning her endlessly, and causing Sethe's mental and physical deterioration. Beloved in turn grows fat to the point of appearing pregnant. Denver, who has isolated herself since she learned that her mother killed Beloved, decides that she must take action when Sethe quits her job and becomes increasingly unable to resist Beloved's outrageous demands for attention and food. Their resources depleted, Denver symbolically steps off her porch to ask the neighbors for help. They initially respond by mysteriously providing food, and later, when they hear tales of Beloved beating Sethe, they descend upon Sethe's house to perform a rite of exorcism. Humming, singing, and praying, they force Beloved to flee. Morrison hints that Beloved's human form disintegrates. *Freedom from the ghost does not bring immediate health for Sethe, although it and the act of seeking assistance serve to reincorporate Denver into the community. Sethe languishes in an effort to will herself to death until Paul D returns to inspire her with a budding desire to live.

Morrison based the novel on the story of Margaret Garner, a slave who in circumstances similar to Sethe's killed one child and tried to kill her three others. The novel is important for depicting the concern slave mothers had for their children and their determination to win freedom for themselves and their offspring. It was critically acclaimed for its poetic language, intricate plot, and understanding portrayal of the forces that would cause Sethe to kill her child. *Beloved* acknowledges the horror of slavery and portrays the horrendous treatment and torturous memories of the slaves' past while documenting the effect of this history on future generations of African Americans.

[*See also* Neo–Slave Narrative.]

• Brian Finney, "Temporal Defamiliarization in Toni Morrison's *Beloved*," *Obsidian II* 18 (Spring 1990): 59–77. Trudier Harris, *Fiction and Folklore: The Novels of Toni Morrison*, 1991. Sunny Falling-rain, "A Literary Patchwork Crazy Quilt: Toni Morrison's *Beloved*," *Uncoverings* 15 (1994): 110–140. Deborah Guth, "'Wonder What God Had in Mind': *Beloved's* Dialogue with Christianity," *Journal of Narrative Technique* 24.2 (Spring 1994): 83–97. Caroline Rody, "Toni Morrison's *Beloved*: History, 'Rememory,' and a Clamor for a Kiss," *American Literary History* 7.1 (Spring 1995): 92–119.
                    —Betty Taylor-Thompson

BENEATHA YOUNGER, a character in the 1959 play A *Raisin in the Sun*, is a mild parody of the author of the play, Lorraine *Hansberry at age twenty, and has no precedent on the American stage. The daughter of *Mama Lena Younger and the sister of *Walter Lee Younger, Beneatha represents the young women of the so-called silent generation of the 1950s on the verge of new and unprecedented *freedom. Refusing to labor under typical racial and *gender roles, she dares to "seek her *identity" or "express" herself by studying guitar, learning horseback riding, and engaging in other activities considered frivolous in a traditional, black, working-class household. Her knowledge of America's rich history and revolutionary present challenge the Tarzan myths of the period. By rejecting a rich, middle-class suitor, she questions prevailing expectations that women should be satisfied as housewives or sex objects. In the original script, Beneatha chooses to wear her hair natural—in an Afro, the first ever on the American stage; however, the material was cut from the first production and later restored in 1987. Beneatha anticipates the next generation of African American women intellectuals.

Beneatha evokes critical character traits of the play's main characters, Lena and Walter Lee. Her atheistic views reveal the complex authoritarian and traditional values held by her mother. Beneatha's plans to study medicine elicit her brother's sexist comment that she should be satisfied with nursing. In the last act, Beneatha's disavowal of her brother's demeaning plans rouses Mama to deliver the most eloquent speech in the play as she reminds Beneatha that her brother deserves her love especially when he is suffering the most. Beneatha remains an unusually provocative depiction of the independent African American woman.

• Doris E. Abramson, *Negro Playwrights in the American Theatre, 1925–1959*, 1969, pp. 165–266. Amiri Baraka, "A Raisin in the Sun's Enduring Passion," in *A Raisin in the Sun and The Sign in Sidney Brustein's Window*, ed. Robert Nemiroff, 1987, pp. 9–20.   —Margaret B. Wilkerson

BENNETT, GWENDOLYN (1902–1981), poet, short-story writer, artist, illustrator, journalist, teacher, and participant in the Harlem Renaissance. Although she never collected her published *poetry into a volume nor produced a collection of *short stories, Gwendolyn Bennett was recognized as a versatile artist and significant figure in the *Harlem Renaissance.

Torn between her ambition to work as a graphic artist and her desire to become a proficient writer using the medium of either poetry or prose, Bennett maintained the profile of an arts activist in New York City's African American arts community for over twenty years. However, the five-year period spanning 1923 to 1928 proved to be the most productive for her as a creative writer. It was within this brief span that James Weldon *Johnson recognized Bennett as a lyric poet of some power.

Born in Giddings, Texas, Bennett led a nomadic childhood before her father, Joshua Robbin Bennett, finally settled his family into comfortable surroundings in Brooklyn, New York. Bennett completed her secondary education at Girls' High, where she had been active in both the literary society and the school's art program. Graduating in 1921, Bennett came of age just as the Harlem Renaissance was beginning to flower. Attempting to remain loyal to both of her dreams, Bennett began college classes at Columbia University in the Department of Fine Arts but she subsequently transferred to and graduated from Pratt Institute in 1924. While studying painting and graphic design at Pratt, Bennett also began seeking artistic outlets in the two major journals accepting work from African American artists—the NAACP's the *Crisis and the Urban League's *Opportunity.

Bennett's banner years were 1923 to 1925. The *Crisis* carried a cover she illustrated and her poem "Heritage" was published by *Opportunity* in 1923. In 1924 her commemorative poem "To Usward" was chosen as the dedication poem to honor the publication of a Jessie Redmon *Fauset novel at the showcase Civic Club dinner for Harlem's writers sponsored by Charles S. Johnson of the Urban League. Both "Heritage," with its allusions to "lithe Negro girls" dancing around "heathen fires," and "To Usward," which celebrated the spirit of youth on the march, anticipated and invoked African and African American images, motifs, themes, or cultural icons that became central to much of the literature of the Harlem Renaissance.

In this same period Bennett began a warm, supportive, and sustained association with a cadre of younger writers and artists known in Harlem circles. Belonging to this group were Langston *Hughes, Countee *Cullen, Eric *Walrond, Helene *Johnson,

Wallace *Thurman, Richard Bruce *Nugent, Aaron and Alta Douglass, Rudolph *Fisher, and later the irrepressible Zora Neale *Hurston. These young artists supported and encouraged each other and were, in turn, encouraged to pursue their aspirations by older, more established scholars and writers such as Charles S. Johnson, Alain *Locke, W. E. B. *Du Bois, Jessie Fauset, and James Weldon Johnson. In a 1979 interview Bennett noted that it was "fun to be alive and to be part of this. . . ." There was, she observed, "nothing like this particular life in which you saw the same group of people over and over again. You were always glad to see them. You always had an exciting time when you were with them."

The supportive energy Bennett drew from her contact with her peers helped sustain her whether she was in Harlem or not. She kept her connections alive when she went to teach art at Howard University in 1924. She also maintained contact while studying art in Paris from 1925 to 1926. From France she wrote to Hughes and Cullen giving them the news; each wrote back, giving her news of the opportunities available to Negro artists and urging her to write for publication. Returning to Harlem in 1926, Bennett joined with Hughes, Thurman, Nugent, and a few others to form the editorial board of *Fire!!*, a quarterly journal created to serve the younger African American artists. Bennett's "Wedding Day" first appeared in *Fire!!*. Despite her return to Howard (1927–1928), Bennett relied upon her network contacts as news sources to inform her "Ebony Flute," a literary chit-chat and arts news column which she produced for *Opportunity* for almost two years.

The Great Depression of the 1930s effectively altered the arts landscape through which Gwendolyn Bennett moved. The new era's change of tone caused a shift in her own artistic sensibility from exuberant and often whimsical personal poetry toward the cause of public advocacy for the arts and artists in the community.

•James Weldon Johnson, ed., *The Book of American Negro Poetry*, 1922; enlarged, 1931. Gloria Hull, "Black Women Poets from Wheatley to Walker," *Negro American Literature Forum* 9 (Fall 1975): 91–96. Walter C. Daniel and Sandra Y. Govan, "Gwendolyn Bennett," in *DLB*, vol. 51, *Afro-American Writers from the Harlem Renaissance to 1940*, ed. Trudier Harris, 1987, pp. 3–10.   —Sandra Y. Govan

BENNETT, HAL (b. 1930), novelist and short fiction writer. Born in Buckingham, Virginia, on 21 April 1930, George Harold Bennett was raised and educated in Newark, New Jersey. He sold his first *short story when he was fifteen, became a feature writer for the Newark *Herald News* at the age of sixteen, and edited his high school yearbook. During the Korean War he served a tour of duty in the U.S. Air Force, where he wrote for the Public Information Division and edited a newsletter for U.S. airmen. After his discharge, he continued to pursue his career as a writer, serving as fiction editor for several African American newspapers between 1953 and 1955 and attempting to launch his own newspaper in Westbury, Long Island. After that venture failed, he moved to Mexico, where he attended Mexico City College and became a fellow of the Centro Mexicano de Escritores. During this period he completed most of his first *novel, *A Wilderness of Vines*, a manuscript that won him a fiction fellowship from the Bread Loaf Writer's Conference in 1966. Several years later, in 1970, Bennett was selected most promising writer of the year by *Playboy* magazine for his short story "Dotson Gerber Resurrected." He received the PEN/Faulkner Award in 1973.

Between 1966 and 1976, Hal Bennett published five novels; his collection of short fiction, *Insanity Runs in Our Family*, was published in 1977. Bennett's experiences in both Buckingham, Virginia, and Newark, New Jersey, provide the backdrop for his fictional settings of Burnside, Virginia, and Cousinville, New Jersey—the terrain between which many of his characters shuttle back and forth, vainly seeking a salvation that somehow always manages to elude them. Somewhat like William Faulkner's Yoknapatawpha County, Bennett's Burnside and Cousinville are self-contained fictional universes. His novels and short stories are linked by characters who restlessly move north and south—often reappearing in other novels and stories—and by recurring themes and preoccupations. In a broad sense, Bennett's novels recount the saga of African Americans who—like other dreamers, seekers, and outcasts—seek a new life through *migration from the South to the North, from the country to the city. In Bennett's case, however, this story is filtered through an iconoclastic, satiric, and absurdist sensibility.

Set in 1939, *A Wilderness of Vines* (1966) introduces the racial pathology of the pre–World War II black community of Burnside, Virginia, a community in which the worship of hierarchies based on color has become elevated to the status of a religion. It also introduces Bennett's recurring stylistic and thematic concerns: his inversion of traditional Christian symbols and images; his preoccupation with sex, salvation, and insanity; his perspective on the corrosive legacy of America's racial history. In many respects, the community of Burnside emerges as a corruption of the garden of Eden—and as a microcosm of the American insanity forged by centuries of racism and sexual hypocrisy. The novel concludes with an act of brutal *violence and the exodus north of the key characters, followed by prostitutes, the insane, the downhearted, and the defeated. Bennett's subsequent novels explore the lives and experiences of those characters who have participated in the exodus. *The Black Wine* (1968) spans the years between 1953 and 1960 and is concerned with the lives and fates of those who traveled north to Cousinville. Like *A Wilderness of Vines*, *The Black Wine* concludes on a note of explosive violence and with ambiguous proclamations of faith. *Lord of Dark Places* (1970) introduces the character of Joe Market, an outrageous, southern-born, black phallic hero, and offers a sustained and profane assault on the racial and sexual mythologies that have haunted American life. The novel begins in 1951 in Burnside and ends in June 1968, shortly after the assassination of Robert Kennedy, with Joe's execution in New Jersey. *Wait until the Evening* (1974) begins in 1944 and ends in

1970, with the central character, Kevin Brittain, plotting the murder of his father in Burnside. *Seventh Heaven* (1976)—the sardonic title conferred upon a seedy housing project in Cousinville—begins in the wake of the urban riots of the 1960s and ends with the Watergate scandal. Like so many of Bennett's characters, Bill Kelsey travels from the South to the North only to be engulfed in the larger madness of American life. Taken together, Bennett's novels constitute an extended saga of post–World War II African American life and a disturbing and satirical vision of the underside of American society.

Bennett's irreverence, iconoclasm, and gift for satire are reminiscent of George S. *Schuyler and Wallace *Thurman, and his sense of the absurd parallels that of Chester *Himes. His novels and his short fiction offer a highly idiosyncratic and often outrageous vision of the possibilities of American life.

• Ronald Walcott, "The Novels of Hal Bennett," part 1, *Black World* 23.8 (June 1974): 36–48, 89–97. Ronald Walcott, "The Novels of Hal Bennett," part 2, *Black World* 23.9 (July 1974): 78–96. Bernard W. Bell, *The Afro-American Novel and Its Tradition*, 1987, pp. 324–329.
—James A. Miller

BIBB, HENRY (1815–1854), fugitive slave narrator and journalist. Henry Bibb is best known through his *Narrative of the Life and Adventures of Henry Bibb, An American Slave*, which was first published by Bibb himself in 1849. While Frederick *Douglass gained credibility through his assertion of authorship and by way of the introductions composed for his narrative by William Lloyd Garrison and Wendell Phillips, Bibb enjoyed no such reception and was forced to subvene the publication of his own story. The narrative is rich in detail, including an account of Bibb's use of "*conjuring" to avoid punishment for running away, and the use of "charms" to court his slave wife. Bibb also gives eloquent testimony to the conditions and the culture of *slavery in Kentucky and the South. John Blassingame describes it as "one of the most reliable of the slave *autobiographies," and it firmly established Bibb, together with Douglass and Josiah *Henson, as one of the leading antebellum slave narrators.

Bibb was born on 10 May 1815, one of seven children. His mother was a resourceful woman named Mildred Jackson, and his father was Kentucky state senator James Bibb. He was owned by Willard Gatewood on whose plantation he served an early life of misery. His siblings were sold away to other plantations, and in his frustration and anger he attempted escape and suffered horrible punishments. He was sold to six different owners, ultimately escaping to Detroit where he became active in the *antislavery movement and abolitionist lecture circuit. Outraged by the passage of the Compromise of 1850 and its Fugitive Slave Act, Bibb is said to have remarked, "If there is no alternative but to go back to slavery, or to die contending for liberty, then death is far preferable," a clear echo of Patrick Henry. As he was an escaped slave, he emigrated to Canada, an action appropriated by Harriet Beecher *Stowe in the character of George Harris, who rejects America for

Canada. In Canada Bibb became a journalist and founded Canada's first Black abolitionist newspaper, *The Voice of the Fugitive*. Bibb devoted much of the decade preceding the Civil War to activities supporting the removal of American slaves to Canada, collaborating with the *Underground Railroad. He viewed Canada as a safety zone for escaped Negroes and purchased a two thousand–acre tract of land near Windsor, Ontario, to become a center for Negro culture. He organized the North American Convention of Colored People, a group that opposed the colonization of African Americans back to Africa. He died young, at age thirty-nine, in 1854. His *Narrative* provides a superb picture of life on the plantation even as it censures slavery as inhuman oppression.

[*See also* Periodicals, *article on* Black Periodical Press; Slave Narrative.]

• Roger W. Hite, "Voice of a Fugitive: Henry Bibb and Antebellum Black Separatism," *Journal of Black Studies* 4.3 (Mar. 1974): 269–284. John Blassingame, *The Slave Community: Plantation Life in the Antebellum South*, 1979. Charles Davis and Henry Louis Gates, Jr., *The Slave's Narrative*, 1985. William L. Andrews, *To Tell a Free Story: The First Century of Afro-American Autobiography*, 1986.

—Mason I. Lowance, Jr.

BIBLICAL TRADITION. The Bible, particularly the King James Version, may be the most pervasive and significant influence in the creation and development of African American literature. It is important as tool and text, object and inspiration, subject and symbol.

The Bible is a tool because it is the book from which most slaves and many free African Americans learned to read, in part because it was the most ubiquitous book in the country and in part because missionaries and ministers believed along with their converts and the merely curious that knowledge of the Bible was fundamental to Protestantism. Thus, many who otherwise might have opposed or ignored African American interest in *literacy and literature found themselves initiating, encouraging, and even teaching and publishing. *Slave narratives, personal journals, and other first person accounts are replete with references to the Bible as primer or as manifestation of a miraculous literacy. As Toni *Morrison shows in *Song of Solomon* (1977) with the naming of *Pilate Dead, for a long time it was common practice that a newborn infant's name be known by opening a Bible and allowing one's finger to land upon the chosen word. In literature, as in life, the Bible also serves as a repository for family history in which births, deaths, marriages, and important papers are kept. Ownership of a Bible is often depicted as an indication of social status and the abilities to quote its verses, to retell its stories, to apply its themes, and to interpret its intentions give personal prestige and, often, political power.

The Bible's importance as tool or symbol is not limited to those writers who practice or describe any of the myriad theologies and rituals derived from the Judeo-Christian heritage. In Adrienne *Kennedy's "A Rat's Mass" (1966), Sister Rat and Brother Rat, like characters in many other texts, swear vows of se-

crecy upon the Bible. Ishmael *Reed acknowledges the Bible's historical significance in *Mumbo Jumbo* (1972) when "The Text" becomes the object of *Papa LaBas's quest. In many texts the Bible serves as talisman or is the source of cures, curses, spells, and divinations. In *Mules and Men* (1935), Zora Neale *Hurston reports that "the Bible is the greatest conjure book in the world. Moses is honored as the greatest conjurer." Hurston also wrote that part of her initiation ceremony into voodoo required her to read the third chapter of Job.

Biblical themes and stories are often retold in African American folk tales and creation myths. As Virginia *Hamilton notes, stories such as "Malindy and Little Devil" come "directly from Sunday-school teachings." Tales such as "Woman and Man Started Even" elaborate upon the Garden of Eden myth to demonstrate that God intended gender equality and that the perversion of this harmony came from men and the devil.

The center of the biblical tradition, however, is occupied by those who write to proclaim the Bible's efficacy or to demonstrate its powerful influence in African American culture. Many Christians generally understood the Bible to allow, encourage, or even demand that they break the silences dictated by class, gender, race, and other social conventions and become preachers, prophets, teachers, leaders, and writers. Many took literally passages such as "Write the vision; make it plain on tablets" (Habakkuk 2:2) and the several psalms that command believers to "Sing unto the Lord a new song." Sermons and *spirituals, conversion narratives and political tracts often cite biblical injunctions for their authority and for their authorial impulses. Jarena *Lee begins her *Religious Experience and Journal* (1849) with the passage "And it shall come to pass . . . that I will pour out my Spirit upon all flesh; and your sons, and your *daughters* shall prophecy" (emphasis hers). Nat *Turner testified that verses such as "he that knoweth his Master's will, and doeth it not . . ." were among the signs that convinced him that "the great day of Judgment was at hand" and he was obligated to carry it out. His identification with the messianic characters was so complete that when questioned as to his feelings concerning his impending execution, he answered "Was not Christ crucified?" While Turner's was one of the extreme examples of messianic identification, versions of this are represented in texts by Alexander *Crummell, David *Walker, Maria W. *Stewart, Frances Gaudet, Marcus *Garvey, Pauli *Murray, Martin Luther *King, Jr., and numerous others.

The earliest extant published literature by African Americans was inspired by Christian theology, structured after biblical models, and punctuated with biblical references and quotes. Briton *Hammon's *A Narrative of the Uncommon Sufferings, and Surprizing Deliverance* (1760) is an autobiographical account of trials and sufferings encountered during a fourteen-year journey that began in Boston on Christmas Day, 1747. Comparing himself to David saved from the lion and the bear, Hammon wrote to "show how great things the Lord hath done for me" and to urge his readers to "praise the Lord for His Goodness." Jupiter *Hammon, a Long Island slave, perhaps coincidentally, composed "An Evening Thought, Salvation by Christ, with Penitential Cries" on 25 December 1760. In it Jupiter Hammon asserts that every human is a slave to sin unless that person repents, exercises Christian faith, and "accept[s] the Word." The earliest known volume published by an African American is Phillis *Wheatley's *Poems on Various Subjects, Religious and Moral (1773). Many of Wheatley's poems are addressed to or written about ministers and practicing Christians. She is adamant and audacious in admonishing students at Cambridge to behave and in reminding "Christians" that "Negroes, black as Cain, / May be refin'd, and join th' angelic train" (emphasis hers).

Generally, before the twentieth century, African American writers used the Bible as authority, as a source for subjects and themes, and as a model for diction and narrative technique. During the twentieth century, the biblical tradition became more complicated as the Bible and the rituals, beliefs, and communities it engendered are used in multiple ways. In *I Know Why the Caged Bird Sings (1970), Maya *Angelou depicts the humiliation and psychological crucifixion of a young child who forgets her speech during an Easter program. She offers a humorous but provocative scene wherein a sister overcome with the Word attacks the preacher. And the very sanctity of the Word itself is explored in a scene wherein Mama strikes her daughter for saying "By the way."

Ann Allen *Shockley's Say Jesus and Come to Me (1982) represents another manifestation of the Bible, the *church, and the impact of words and actions. Myrtle Black is an evangelist who interprets the Bible to empower her to challenge social mores. She preaches and lives Luke 4:18, which says "The Spirit of the Lord has anointed me to preach good news to the poor. He has sent me to proclaim release to the captives and recovering sight to the blind, to set at liberty those who are oppressed." Thus, her lesbian affair with Travis Lee, her civil rights work with the Student Government Association, and her investigation of the murder of two prostitutes are all part of her healing ministry.

Many scholars agree with Theophus H. Smith's statement that African Americans generally have tended to adapt the Bible to themselves and "to 'read' their historical and contemporary experience into the texts of biblical narratives in the terms provided by its coded, figural universe." Spirituals and gospels such as "Oh Mary, Don't You Weep," "Were You There?" "Walking in Jerusalem Just Like John," "Sweet Canaan," and "I Stood on the Banks of the Jordan" are obvious examples. Antebellum slave narrators generally plotted their narratives to progress from innocence to the knowledge of evil and from emotional bondage to spiritual freedom. The protagonist is born into an Eden of innocence, expelled into a wilderness of tribulations, sustained by providential aid, and rewarded by entry into the promised land.

The biblical typology and allusions adopted in antebellum slave narratives—the South as Egypt, the Ohio River as the Red Sea, the North as the promised land, and so forth—continue in twentieth-century texts as Claude *Brown's *Manchild in the Promised Land (1965) suggests. Biblical geography and allusions such as Sterling A. *Brown's "Slim in Hell," James *Baldwin's The *Fire Next Time (1963), and Amiri *Baraka's The *System of Dante's Hell (1965) illustrate another variation.

African American narrators relate conversion experiences that seem modeled after the New Testament account of the transformation of Saul into Paul. A few, such as John *Marrant in A Narrative of the Lord's Wonderful Dealings (1785), are virtually identical. On his way to harass Christians, Saul was struck to the ground, blinded, convinced of his sins, initiated into Christology by Ananias, and reborn as a theologian named Paul. To be sure, John Marrant's original hostility was less extreme than Saul's. Saul set out to slaughter the disciples and arrest their followers. Marrant's goal was simply to disrupt the revival meeting by blowing his trumpet during the sermon; however, as Marrant writes, "I was struck to the ground, and lay both speechless and senseless." Convinced of his sinfulness, Marrant repented and with the help of a colonial Ananias, was reborn as an evangelist whose published narrative of his experiences were part of his ministry.

In his deliberate plans to disrupt, or prevent, a worship service, John Marrant was an exception. Most simply acknowledge that they were ignorant of, or individually failed to follow, biblical precepts. Their conversion narratives, though, are essentially the same. Suddenly and often literally "struck to the ground," they are convinced of their transgressions. They repent, struggle to obtain signs of forgiveness, and are mentored into proper behavior. Finally, convinced they have been sanctified, or at least given a second chance, they create a new identity and write to promulgate their experiences as models for others.

Works such as Jarena Lee's Life and Religious Experience (1836), Thomas W. Henry's From Slavery to Salvation (1872), and Julia A. J. *Foote's A Brand Plucked from the Fire (1879) exemplify the nineteenth-century spiritual narrative tradition; however, conversion is significant in other genres such as Zilpha *Elaw's Memoirs (1846), Rebecca Cox *Jackson's journals, and the multitude of oral testimonies recorded in collections such as God Struck Me Dead. Works such as Gloria Wade-Gayles's Pushed Back to Strength (1993), Andrew Young's A Way Out of No Way (1994), and Albert Raboteau's A Fire in the Bones (1995) are contemporary examples in the same tradition. And novels such as Morrison's Song of Solomon and Paule *Marshall's Praisesong for the Widow (1983), while more subtle, also narrate conversion experiences similar to Saul/Paul's in the book of Acts.

One of the premier examples of a twentieth-century conversion is James Baldwin's *Go Tell It on the Mountain (1953). Not only does the plot center around *John Grimes's Seventh-Day experience in the Temple of the Fire Baptized, but the novel incorporates conversion accounts of Gabriel, Elizabeth, Florence, and others. John is struck down and convicted of sins, repents, and experiences the first signs of redemption, but he does not complete the traditional process. Baldwin's story ends with Gabriel standing between John and the door to their home. Looking up at his father, who is a minister and a major obstacle to John's salvation, he acknowledges the difficulties he has yet to face. Baldwin's convert can only affirm that "I'm ready. . . . I'm on my way." In the ambiguity of this ending, Baldwin is like other twentieth-century writers who write about Protestant conversion experiences with the traditional pattern but question, or at least fail to affirm, the possibility of sanctification or even the probability of being safe or saved.

Some such as Chester *Himes use the conversion pattern for *humor. In "Mama's Missionary Money" Lemuel steals money from his mother's purse and spends it on movies, food, and other sinful pleasures. His conversion comes when he is confronted by his father and struck to the ground by his mother's switch. He quickly repents of his sin, announces his conversion, and saves himself from further punishment. Others such as Nella *Larsen present conversions as illusionary and ultimately more harmful than good. In *Quicksand* (1928), *Helga Crane's experience at the altar leads her to renounce her former life, marry the Reverend Mr. Pleasant Green, and attempt to witness to the women of her rural southern congregation. However, Helga is ineffectual, her resolve fades, and the conversion experience appears to have been merely another in a series of flights from personal responsibility and reality.

From Phillis Wheatley's "Goliath of Gath" and "Isaiah LXIII. 1–85" to the present, African American literature abounds in retold, revised, and critiqued Bible stories. Frances Ellen Watkins *Harper's "Vashti," "Ruth and Naomi," and "The Syrophenican Woman" are representative of well-known stories subtly revised to reflect African American imperatives. Individuals, particularly those identified with Africa, who were treated as outcasts or persecuted "for righteousness' sake" or who risked their personal safety for the good of someone else, populate and inspire African American literature in a variety of ways. Simon of Cyrene, Hagar, *Moses, Joseph, Job, Daniel, Esther, David, the Good Samaritan, and Jesus frequently appear in African American texts. Two, Moses and Jesus, are part of the very woof and weave of the biblical tradition in African American literature. Moses is most often depicted as a Hebrew freedom fighter and God's emissary. From renaming heroes as was done with Harriet *Tubman to identifying oneself as a leader who "may not get to the Promised Land" with his people but who has "been to the mountain top" and knows the eventual outcome of their struggles as in Martin Luther King, Jr.'s *oratory, to rewriting the entire Exodus story as did Frances Ellen Watkins Harper in Moses, A Story of the Nile (1868) and Zora Neale Hurston in Moses, Man of the Mountain (1939), African American writers have freely appropriated this figure. He is often conflated with Jesus of Nazareth as a messiah. Characters such as Henry Holland in *Blake (1859), Gabriel Prosser in *Black Thunder (1936), Tucker Caliban in A Different Drummer (1962), and Dan Freeman in The *Spook Who Sat by the Door (1969) are examples.

Identification of Jesus Christ as a model and a martyr takes many forms in African American literary history, but none is so telling or explicit as the character and theme known as the Black Christ. Grounded in Afro-Christian theology, the Black Christ emerged not merely from a need to visualize a deity in whose image Black people were made. Nor was it simply because some believed that a person born in Bethlehem and described as having hair like lamb's wool would probably not be white. The Black Christ is also popular because he represents liberation. He (rarely she) is a person whose faith and courage enabled his martyrdom and consequent salvation for African Americans. He is an outcast who manifests love but is not afraid to defy evil, who suffers and is crucified for insisting upon what is right and just, but who proves impossible to destroy because love and the freedom it engenders can triumph even over death. The Black Christ is not a passive or ethereal person but one who lives as directed by the Holy Spirit, challenges perversions of God's natural harmonies, and in so doing shows the way to a better life. The Black Christ is then the epitome of the messianic impulse—the individual whose spiritual purity infuses the secular actions and in so doing saves both the person and the community. Countee *Cullen's epic poem "The Black Christ" is an archetypal example. Narrated by the surviving brother whose faith and determination have been affected by what he has witnessed, the poem tells of the life, death, and resurrection of Jim, a young Black man of the South. Jim did not accept the religion of his mother because it would not confront the discrimination and violence of the "Christless rood" worshipped by the dominant society. Jim early evidenced his "imperial blood" because he lived by love in harmony with nature. One spring, Jim met a fellow "worshiper," a white woman who also rejected traditional barriers of "rank and caste." They spoke a "common tongue" of beauty and love. But a white man interrupted their communion and blasphemous words "bound and gagged" the young woman's "spirit." Jim kills him. Jim is then pursued and crucified by an angry mob. However, like Christ, a resurrected Jim appears to his mother and brother to provide assurance that truth triumphs over perversion, freedom over bondage, and, therefore, life over death.

The King James Version of the Bible more than any other influenced African American literary style. Sometimes the author acknowledges a direct influence as does Maria Stewart who writes, "I have borrowed much of my language from the holy Bible. During the years of childhood and youth, it was the book that I most studied." At other times, the influence comes from the stories repeated in sermons infused with lengthy quotes, vivid imagery, and dramatic allusions. It is shown in the solemn intonations of William *Whipper who in "An Address on Non-Resistance to Offensive Aggression" (1837) asks "Is it possible that any christian man or woman, that will flog and maltreat their fellow beings, can be in *earnest,* when they ask their heavenly Father to 'forgive their trespass as they forgive others?'" and also in the whimsy of Paul Laurence *Dunbar's speaker in "Ante-Bellum Sermon" (c. 1896) who proclaims "I'm talkin' 'bout ouah freedom / In a Bibleistic way." A "Bibleistic way" includes liberal use of metaphors, parables, and aphorisms. It splices dialogue and poetry. It repeats, revises, rephrases, and repeats again. It rolls in the rhetoric of W. E. B. *Du Bois's *The *Souls of Black Folk* (1903) and shimmers in the meditations of Howard Thurman's *For the Inward Journey* (1984). Artists such as James Weldon *Johnson in *God's Trombones* (1927) imitate its imagery and rhymes.

So pervasive is the biblical tradition in African American literature that it is easier to go through the eye of a needle than to fairly assess or appreciate the literary tradition when one is ignorant of the Bible and the rituals and rhetoric derived from it.

[*See also* Churches; Religion; Sermons and Preaching; Sunday School Literature.]

• Benjamin E. Mays, *The Negro's God as Reflected in His Literature,* 1938. Janet Duitsman Cornelius, *When I Can Read My Title Clear: Literacy, Slavery, and Religion in the Antebellum South,* 1991. Wilson Jeremiah Moses, *Black Messiahs and Uncle Toms,* 1993. Sandra A. O'Neale, *Jupiter Hammon and the Biblical Beginnings of African-American Literature,* 1993. Kelly Brown Douglas, *The Black Christ,* 1994. Dolan Hubbard, *The Sermon and the African American Literary Tradition,* 1994. Theophus H. Smith, *Conjuring Culture: Biblical Formations of Black America,*1994.

—Frances Smith Foster

BIBLIOGRAPHY. In her 1982 book, *Early Black Bibliographies,* Betty Gubert notes that "bibliography is the foundation of scholarship."

This article is a broad overview of African American bibliographies relating to the field of literature. Excluded are journal articles, chapters in books, and most theses and dissertations. It is a chronological listing of major and less-well-known book-length bibliographies in such areas as *poetry and fiction, and on several topics including *children's and young adult literature, Black *drama, and *anthologies. It begins with the 1945 publication of Dorothy *Porter's *North American Negro Poets: A Bibliographical Checklist of Their Writings, 1760–1944,* which updates Arthur A. *Schomburg's 1916 checklist of American Negro poetry.

Bibliographies of African American literature were extremely scarce until the late 1960s. In 1968 Barbara Dodds published *Negro Literature for High School Students,* a 157-page list of junior *novels and *biographies to help English teachers. John Swisher and Jill Archer published a joint bibliography in 1969 on *Black American Literature and Black American Folklore* for the Indiana University series entitled Focus: Black America. Also published in 1969 was Pat Ryan's *Black Writing in the U.S.A.: A Bibliographic Guide.*

The 1970s brought a proliferation of published bibliographies on African American literature. In 1970 Darwin T. Turner's *Afro-American Writers,* a bib-

liography of primary and secondary sources, was published. In 1971 a bibliography on poetry was published by Frank Deodene and William P. French. Their book, *Black American Poetry since 1944: A Preliminary Checklist,* cites first editions from 1944 through 1971. Charles Rowell's 1972 doctoral dissertation, *Afro-American Literary Bibliographies: An Annotated List of Bibliographical Guides for the Study of Afro-American Literature, Folklore and Related Areas,* is still used today as an excellent source for bibliographic references. In the area of poetry, in 1974 Dorothy Chapman published her *Index to Black Poetry* with author, title, and first line listings. Over 1,600 authors are chronicled as part of the African-American Materials Project in Geraldine Matthews' 1975 bibliography, *Black American Writers, 1773–1949: A Bibliography and Union List.* Two major publications came out in 1976. Some 1,500 plays and 530 Black playwrights are profiled in Esther Arata and Nicholas Rotoli's *Black American Playwrights, 1800 to the Present: A Bibliography.* And as part of a course on African American *oratory at Dartmouth College, Robert Glen published *Black Rhetoric: A Guide to Afro-American Communication,* which lists bibliographies, anthologies, books, *essays, and speeches by African American writers. Three reference sources of note were published in 1977: Curtis Ellison and E. W. Metcalf's *Charles W. Chesnutt: A Reference Guide* includes writings by and about Charles Waddell *Chesnutt between 1887 and 1975. In an effort to help producers locate plays and to help scholars who seek historical data, James V. Hatch and Omanii Abdullah listed over 2,700 plays by 900 playwrights in their book, *Black Playwrights, 1823–1977: An Annotated Bibliography.* Helen Houston's *The Afro-American Novel, 1965–1975: A Descriptive Bibliography of Primary and Secondary Material* presents literature from a sociological rather than literary approach, providing a descriptive listing with critical analysis of works published since 1964. Several bibliographies came out in 1978, including Esther Arata's *More Black American Playwrights: A Bibliography,* which updates her 1976 book and lists some 490 playwrights. Continuing their bibliographies on individual authors, Curtis Ellison and E. W. Metcalf published *William Wells *Brown and Martin R. *Delany: A Reference Guide.* Adding to the list of bibliographies on fiction, Carol Fairbanks and Eugene Engeldinger published *Black American Fiction: A Bibliography,* which includes *novels, *short stories, book reviews, biography, and *criticism. Robert Fleming compiled *James Weldon *Johnson and Arna Wendell *Bontemps: A Reference Guide,* which lists books about the authors dating from 1905 to 1976. M. Thomas Inge, Maurice Duke, and Jackson Bryer published a two-volume set in the series *Black American Writers, Bibliographical Essays.* Volume 1 covers the beginning through the *Harlem Renaissance and Langston *Hughes. Volume 2 covers Richard *Wright, Ralph *Ellison, James *Baldwin, and Amiri *Baraka. Langston Hughes was again the subject of bibliographic research in 1979 when R. Baxter Miller published *Langston Hughes and Gwendolyn *Brooks: A Reference Guide.* Three other reference sources of note published in 1979 are Edward Margolies and David Bakish's *Afro-American Fiction, 1853–1976: A Guide to Information Sources*, which lists novels, anthologies, bibliographies, and citations on individual novelists. This was part of Gale Research Company's American Literature, English Literature, and World Literatures in English Information Guide Series. Jessamine Kallenbach's *Index to Black American Literary Anthologies* was sponsored by the Center of Educational Resources at Eastern Michigan University. Charles Peavy added to the Gale Research Company's American Studies Information Guide Series with *Afro-American Literature and Culture since World War II: A Guide to Information Sources*. Much of the literature in this book reflects the cultural revolution of this time and differs dramatically from the protest, assimilationist, or integrationist literature of earlier periods.

The 1980s showed a dynamic increase of publications in the field of literature. G. K. Hall published two individual bibliographies in 1980. They were *Samuel R. *Delany: A Primary and Secondary Bibliography, 1962–1979* by Michael W. Peplow and Robert Bravard and *James Baldwin: A Reference Guide* by Fred and Nancy Standley. In 1981 there were two major additions to the field. Richard Newman published *Black Index: Afro-Americana in Selected *Periodicals, 1907–1949*, part of Garland Publishing's Critical Studies on Black Life and Culture, and William Robinson published *Phillis *Wheatley: A Bio-Bibliography* which also gives a good analysis of her works. Both Garland Publishing and G. K. Hall published two volumes each in 1982 on African American literature. They include Charles Davis and Michel Fabre's *Richard Wright: A Primary Bibliography*, which made extensive use of the Richard Wright Archive at Yale. Betty Gubert's *Early Black Bibliographies, 1863–1918* brings together nineteen rare and out-of-print bibliographies. The *Harlem Renaissance was a significant period for Black writers, which Margaret Perry documented in *The Harlem Renaissance: An Annotated Bibliography and Commentary*. This work includes editorials, *letters, commentaries on social and cultural milieus, *films, and other media from 1919 to 1980. Elizabeth and Thomas Settle published a chronological listing entitled *Ishmael *Reed: A Primary and Secondary Bibliography*. In order to provide hard-to-locate biographical information on 1,900 Blacks, Dorothy Campbell published an *Index to Black American Writers in Collective Biographies* in 1983. Richard Newman published two bibliographies in 1984. They were *Black Access: A Bibliography of Afro-American Bibliographies*, which was done not only to be a comprehensive listing but also to show the gaps that need to be filled. Newman's other work that year was *Lemuel *Haynes: A Bio-Bibliography*, which shows his primary and secondary works and where they can be found. Russell Brignano's *Black Americans in *Autobiography*, an annotated listing of first-person narratives written after 1865, also appeared in 1984. Two fairly obscure bibliographies were published in 1985. Mary Hopkins published *Black American Poetry: A Selected Bibliography* for the Clinton-Essex-Franklin Library

System in New York, and Edward Clark published *Black Writers in New England*. These authors are in the Collection of Afro-American Literature as part of Suffolk University and the Museum of Afro American History in Boston. In 1986 Preston Yancy's *The Afro American Short Story: A Comprehensive, Annotated Index with Selected Commentaries* was published, while 1987 marked the publication of three bibliographies on Ann Allen *Shockley, Toni *Morrison, and Zora Neale *Hurston. Rita B. Dandridge published *Ann Allen Shockley: An Annotated Primary and Secondary Bibliography*, David Middleton published *Toni Morrison: An Annotated Bibliography*, and Adele S. Newson published her dissertation, *Zora Neale Hurston: A Reference Guide*. Four significant bibliographies came out in 1988. Marie Foster published *Southern Black Creative Writers, 1829–1953: Biobibliographies*. A *Richard Wright Bibliography: Fifty Years of Criticism and Commentary, 1933–1982* was published by Keneth Kinnamon. Louis and Darnell Pratt published a descriptive bibliography entitled *Alice Malsenior *Walker, An Annotated Bibliography, 1968–1986*, which explores her social and literary philosophies. In an effort to cover a generally neglected area, Barbara Rollock published *Black Authors and Illustrators of Children's Books: A Biographical Directory*, which includes 115 sketches. The 1980s end with the publication of three bibliographies on African American women. Erma Banks and Keith Byerman published *Alice Walker: An Annotated Bibliography, 1968–1986*, which lists primary and secondary sources, periodical articles, and interviews with Walker. Ronda Glikin published *Black American Women in Literature: A Bibliography 1976 through 1987* and updates information on more than 300 women, while Craig Werner published *Black American Women Novelists: An Annotated Bibliography*, which provides a historical overview of these women.

In 1992 Michel Fabre, Robert Skinner, and Lester Sullivan published *Chester *Himes: An Annotated Primary and Secondary Bibliography*. Perhaps 1993 was the most dramatic for publishing, especially on women. Hazel Ervin published *Ann *Petry: A Bio-Bibliography* about one of the living legends of our time, while Casper LeRoy Jordan published *A Bibliographical Guide to African American Women Writers*, which documents the works of about 900 writers. In 1994 Matthew Bruccoli and Judith Baughman added to the Essential Bibliography of American Fiction Series by publishing *Modern African Writers*.

[*See also* Libraries and Research Centers.]

—Janet Sims-Wood

BIGGER THOMAS, the chief character of Richard *Wright's 1940 best-selling novel *Native Son*, is unlike any protagonist ever to have appeared in African American literature. Before Bigger Thomas, black heroes and heroines were generally virtuous, polite, upright, intelligent, sensitive, and knowledgeable. Bigger Thomas is crude, barely literate, unclean, untrustworthy, and a murderer. But Wright emphasizes that Bigger's character is in part the result of a crippling environment. Bigger seems driven by a fear of whites that was the legacy of *slavery. Every act he performs has its roots in dread. He fights his friend Gus to conceal his own fear of robbing a white man. He inadvertently suffocates *Mary Dalton because he is terrified of being discovered in a white woman's bedroom. He incinerates Mary because he fears white accusations of rape and murder. He brutally murders Bessie because he fears capture. The ending of the novel finds him having rid himself of fear of whites by discovering through self-examination something of his own *identity, by accepting who he is in all its terribleness: "What I killed for I am. . . . Tell Mister. . . . Tell Jan hello. . . ." The conclusion of the novel finds Bigger arriving at a personal and psychological resolution of his situation, not a political or social one.

—Donald B. Gibson

Big Sea, The. Langston *Hughes's first volume of *autobiography (1940) covers the years of his life from his birth in 1902 to the spring of 1931. Fundamentally episodic, *The Big Sea* is a succession of brief chapters, written in deceptively simple prose, that recount various adventures through which Hughes had passed during his formative years in Kansas, Illinois, and Ohio; his extended stays with his father in Mexico; his unhappy year at Columbia University; his discovery of Harlem and his visit to Africa and Europe; a year among the black bourgeoisie in Washington, D.C.; and, at great length, his experiences, good and bad, as a star of the *Harlem Renaissance.

The book opens with Hughes's decision in 1923, as he set sail as a messboy on a freighter to Africa, to throw overboard all of the many books he had brought on board. It ends with the collapse of his relationship with the wealthy patron who had pampered then dumped him under baffling, hurtful circumstances in 1930. Both episodes were deeply significant. The first had to do with his intimate search for literary and racial *identity; the second transformed him into a radical. Yet both are related with such a constant appeal to *humor that they epitomize the spirit of the book, which appears to reflect the same triumph of laughter and art over adverse circumstances that marks the African American art form most admired by Hughes: the *blues.

Central to the structure of the book is Hughes's depiction of his father. Cold and materialistic, his father disliked not only *poetry but other black Americans, who seemed to him passive and unreliable. In response, Hughes casually, sometimes humorously, inscribed a portrait of his father as almost satanic, a figure who tempts his son with wealth if he would betray blacks and poetry. Thus Hughes quietly underscores what he wishes to be seen as the bedrock of his integrity: his twinned devotions to African Americans, on the one hand, and to writing, on the other.

Although Hughes points out that most black Harlemites had no idea a renaissance was going on, much of the book is devoted to the Harlem Renaissance. This section remains the most detailed firsthand account of the era in existence. Another feature of the book is its silence about Hughes's radicalism. Written as World War II was gathering force and as Hughes began to shift toward the political center, the book avoids almost all references to Hughes's leftist ties. Indeed, the story ends precisely when the avoidance of such references would have been almost impossible.

Although Hughes had high hopes for the book, its reception was disappointing, especially compared to that of Richard Wright's *Native Son the same year. Many reviewers saw the charm of the book without recognizing its depth; Ralph *Ellison, for one, questioned the appropriateness of its tone to a black American's autobiography. However, it is admired both for its extended commentary on the Harlem Renaissance and as a self-portrait by one of the most beloved and deceptively complex of African American artists.

• Arnold Rampersad, *The Life of Langston Hughes*, vol. 1, *1902–1941: I, Too, Sing America*, 1986.

—Arnold Rampersad

BILDUNGSROMAN. The African American "novel of development," as the bildungsroman is often called, is closely related to the strong tradition of black *autobiography, running from the *slave narratives to *Malcolm X and Maya *Angelou. What these forms share is the presentation of a black self that must emerge in the context of a dominant society that denies the validity of black *identity. Thus, if the bildungsroman is defined in its classical terms as a narrative of the spiritual, psychological, and social development of a young person to a point of integration into society and culture, its relationship to African American fiction is highly problematic.

With these qualifications, African American variations on the bildungsroman can be identified. These emphasize a critique of the larger society through calls for reform, validation of African American culture as an alternative, escape, ambiguity about the protagonist's achievement, or failed integration.

The reform mode emphasizes the individual's emerging understanding of the wrongs that exist in the world; he or she then discovers the inner strength to resist and the political means of doing so. W. E. B. *Du Bois, in The *Quest of the Silver Fleece (1911) and *Dark Princess* (1928), has his young men and women resist through socialist utopian gestures, while Alice *Walker, in The *Third Life of Grange Copeland (1970) and *Meridian* (1976), emphasizes the importance of civil rights activity in the moral development of her young women. Works such as Albert *Murray's *Train Whistle Guitar* (1974), Al *Young's *Snakes* (1970), and Leon *Forrest's Forest County trilogy (1973–1983) focus on the young hero's incorporation of African American folk and other expressive traditions as a way to develop a self resilient enough to withstand the problems of living in a racist society. The escape tradition grows out of the slave narratives, which indicated the necessity of moving outside an environment that denied the validity of the black self. In The *Autobiography of an Ex-Colored Man (1912), James Weldon *Johnson's protagonist responds to oppression by choosing to live as a white man. In *Invisible Man (1952), Ralph *Ellison's narrator ends the *novel underground telling the story of his experiences. Two works that can be considered almost classic versions of the bildungsroman end in deep ambiguity about their protagonists. In Toni *Morrison's *Song of Solomon* (1977), *Milkman Dead, after a quest for personal and cultural meaning, leaps to what appears his death in a gesture that might also be his salvation. James *Baldwin's *Go Tell It on the Mountain* (1953) has its central character undergo a religious conversion that seems to exacerbate rather than resolve the conflicts he has experienced in the novel. Total failure can also be an outcome of this struggle. In Morrison's *The *Bluest Eye* (1970) and Gayl *Jones's *Eva's Man* (1976), the key female characters are driven insane by their social educations and experiences.

African American cultural expression has historically shown an impulse toward improvisation and *signifying on conventional forms. Given the conditions of black life in American society, it is not surprising that variations on the traditional bildungsroman are needed to show the development of the African American self.

• Robert B. Stepto, *From Behind the Veil: A Study of Afro-American Narrative*, 1979. Randolph P. Shaffner, *The Apprenticeship Novel: A Study of the "Bildungsroman" as a Regulative Type in Western Literature*, 1983. Bernard W. Bell, *The Afro-American Novel and Its Tradition*, 1987. Valerie Smith, *Self-Discovery and Authority in Afro-American Narrative*, 1987. Susan Ashley Gohlman, *Starting Over: The Task of the Protagonist in the Contemporary Bildungsroman*, 1990. James Hardin, ed., *Reflections and Action: Essays on the Bildungsroman*, 1991.   —Keith E. Byerman

BIOGRAPHY, a word derived from the Greek words for "life" and "writing," has been a significant part of literary production in Western culture. Among African Americans, for a variety of reasons, its place historically has been less prominent and in some ways even controversial. Nevertheless, the genre is of increasing importance, and the publishing of full-length biographies of writers and other leading figures has become a growing feature of African American literature in recent years.

Biography is intimately related as a field to *autobiography, which arguably has been the central literary form in African American culture from the *slave narratives to our own time. For two centuries, however, biography has been a poor relation of black autobiography. Biography typically involves academic training in historical methods, a sustained effort at research, and the *freedom to reflect on and write the life story in question. With these demands, it has attracted and held far fewer writers than the fields of autobiography, *poetry, or fiction, for example. The vigorous recent growth of black biography has coincided, not surprisingly, with the widespread acceptance in the national academic community, and especially in research-oriented universities, of African American literature and *history as challenging fields of study.

Certain distinctions are frequently made within the field of biography. One common term is "intellectual biography," in which the emphasis may be on the ideas of an individual and not on his or her writings. Another is "literary biography," which is commonly applied to works that focus on writers. Yet another is "definitive biography," offered as the ultimate accolade to the biographer. These terms may point unwittingly to the instability of standards and values in the field. "Intellectual biography" is virtually a contradiction in terms, since biography should be about the full life. "Literary biography" often implies that the study in question includes much literary *criticism, which may or may not be helpful to narrative integrity, and is sometimes so much padding. The term "definitive" often obscures two factors: that few scholars are ever in a proper position to make such a judgment, which requires a detailed knowledge of the life in question and must take into consideration the sources available to the biographer, and that it is impossible to "define" a life, especially one lived a long time ago.

Accordingly, many observers have inveighed against biography as a form. These hostile critics include the psychologist Sigmund Freud, who insisted that biographical truth was impossible to achieve and that biography should be avoided (although he was a biographer himself), and the novelist F. Scott Fitzgerald, who called biography an art but also "the falsest of the arts." Various modern writers have resisted biographers and urged their families and friends to do the same; in one way or another, T. S. Eliot, W. H. Auden, and J. D. Salinger have taken this position. Such individuals may wish to be remembered by their art, not their full lives, or may fear the biographer's ability to unearth and emphasize unsavory facts. Although few African American writers have taken a similar public position, their biographers may be under special pressures to avoid offering information or opinion that might diminish the reputation of the writer in question.

The earliest efforts in African American biography typically involved not a sustained effort on a single figure but collected biographical essays about prominent blacks. Such efforts, based perhaps on the classical model of Plutarch's *Lives*, which was influential in America, may have started with *The Black Man: His Antecedents, His Genius, and His Achievements* (1863) by the black abolitionist and writer William Wells *Brown. In 1887 came William J. Simmons's *Men of Mark: Eminent, Progressive and Rising*, and in 1893, *Noted Negro Women, Their Triumphs and Activities*, by Monroe A. Majors. In his landmark volume *The *Souls of Black Folk* (1903), W. E. B. *Du Bois included the chapter "Of Alexander *Crummell," a brief biography of a black clergyman described as a paragon of virtue and spirituality. In 1914, John W. Cromwell published *The Negro in American History: Men and Women Eminent in the Evolution of the American of African Descent*, and 1937 saw the literature professor Benjamin *Brawley's *Negro Builders and Heroes*.

In this vein, an outstanding effort of more recent years has been the *Dictionary of American Negro Biography*, edited by Rayford W. Logan and Michael R. Winston (1982). This volume sought to rectify the relative neglect of African Americans in the otherwise authoritative *Dictionary of American Biography*. In the 1990s, Darlene Clark Hine has also expertly edited several volumes on the lives of African

American women, notably the two-volume *Black Women in America* (1993).

Full-length biographies of African American literary figures were once rare. Perhaps the earliest was Lida Keck Wiggins's *The Life and Works of Paul Laurence *Dunbar* (1907). Her book remained typical in two ways. Fundamentally uncritical, it showed no effort to restrain her admiration of Dunbar. In addition, Wiggins was white. Observers who question the ability of whites to understand and interpret black writing often have even more profound reservations about the ability of whites to understand and represent a black life. Nevertheless, the vast majority of biographies of blacks have been written by whites. Even a figure as important to *Afrocentricity as *Malcolm X falls into this category. It might be argued, however, that writing a biography entails several ideal requirements, of which similarity of "*race," or of *gender, between writer and subject is but one category. Ultimately, diligence despite setbacks in gathering archival material, intelligence and insight in interpreting this material, a basic devotion to the biographical subject, and flexibility of style as a writer may be more important than race or gender in a biographer.

The 1970s marked a turning point in the history of African American biography, just as it marked a new level of accomplishment in African American literary criticism. A landmark publication was the French scholar Michel Fabre's *The Unfinished Quest of Richard *Wright* (1973), which applied rigorous scholarly standards to the project. Perhaps the most important single text to the new movement, however, was Robert Hemenway's biography *Zora Neale *Hurston: A Literary Biography* (1977). Although Hemenway suggested in his foreword that this book should have been written by a black and a woman, it was immediately accepted and admired, and contributed mightily to the rise to prominence of Hurston. The work was deeply sympathetic to its specific and general subjects but also sophisticated in its approaches.

Later came a succession of biographies that have either enjoyed or deserved critical and even popular praise. (Wright himself inspired other biographies, by Constance Webb and Addison *Gayle.) The field saw accomplished studies such as Wayne Cooper's *Claude *McKay: Rebel Sojourner in the *Harlem Renaissance* (1987), a comprehensive study of the life despite its subtitle; Arnold *Rampersad's two-volume *The Life of Langston *Hughes* (1986–1988); *The Lives of Jean *Toomer: A Hunger for Wholeness* (1987), by Cynthia Earl Kerman and Richard Eldridge; David Leeming's *James *Baldwin* (1994); and Thadious Davis's *Nella *Larsen: Novelist of the Harlem Renaissance* (1994). Other works of similar interest include Robert M. Farnsworth's *Melvin B. *Tolson: Plain Talk and Poetic Prophecy, 1898–1966* (1984) and Elsonore Van Notten's *Wallace *Thurman's Harlem Renaissance* (1994), which was written as a doctoral dissertation in Holland.

All of these biographers have been either scholars of English or freelance writers. However, the greatest public honors in the field have gone to academic historians. The most acclaimed have been Louis Harlan, with his two-volume *Booker T. *Washington* (1972 and 1983); William McFeely, author of *Frederick *Douglass* (1991); and David Levering Lewis, whose *W. E. B. Du Bois: The Biography of a Race, 1868–1919* (the first of two projected volumes) swept the most prestigious prizes in biography and history after it appeared in 1993. Among other outstanding biographies of African Americans of some relevance to the study of literature are David Garrow's *Bearing the Cross: Martin Luther *King, Jr., and the Southern Christian Leadership Conference* (1986) and Martin Duberman's *Paul *Robeson* (1989).

Despite the undoubted success of various writers in the area of biography, much work remains to be done. Students of African American literature have long awaited full-length biographies of figures such as Harriet A. *Jacobs, Arna *Bontemps, Alain *Locke, Countee *Cullen, and Jessie Redmon *Fauset. A modern study of Paul Laurence Dunbar, for example, is certainly overdue. James Weldon *Johnson has been chronicled well as a political figure by the historian Eugene Levy in *James Weldon Johnson: Black Leader, Black Voice* (1973), but also deserves a biography that emphasizes his considerable achievement as a poet, novelist, and lyricist.

The major problem standing in the way of these and other biographies is the relative unavailability of archives of *letters and other manuscripts that would facilitate the writing of biographies. This situation is not unrelated to the beleaguered social and economic conditions under which blacks have been made to live in the United States. In the absence of such material, the biographer must search patiently and also remember to avoid the pitfalls of overspeculation in the absence of hard evidence. The main archival sources for African American biography are at *libraries and research centers such as the Schomburg Collection of the New York Public Library, the James Weldon Johnson Collection at the Beinecke Rare Book and Manuscript Library at Yale University, the Moorland-Spingarn Collection at Howard University, and various smaller collections at Atlanta University and elsewhere.

In the future, all biographers will face the problem of the diminishing importance of letters as a means of communication, in favor primarily of the telephone. This will place additional emphasis on the use of interviews and other oral material. Despite the significance and usefulness of oral-history collections, the general trustworthiness of many interviews is open to question. Nevertheless, biography is potentially such an important part of African American literary culture and heritage that its writers will be obliged to continue to compose the life stories that enable generations of readers to have a richer, more human understanding of the personal context that is the source of all literary production.

[*See also* Collective Biography.]

• Robert Hemenway, *Zora Neale Hurston*, 1977. Marc Pachter, ed., *Telling Lives*, 1981. Arnold Rampersad, "Biography, Autobiography, and Afro-American Culture," *Yale Review* 73 (Autumn 1983): 1–16. Arnold Rampersad, *The Life of Langston Hughes, Vol. 1, 1902–1941: I, Too, Sing America*,

1986. David Levering Lewis, *W. E. B. Du Bois: The Biography of a Race, 1868–1919*, 1993. Thadious Davis, *Nella Larsen: Novelist of the Harlem Renaissance*, 1994.

—Arnold Rampersad

BLACK AESTHETIC. Although the term *Black Aesthetic* originated in the 1960s, since at least the early part of the nineteenth century African Americans have formulated racial aesthetics, that is, general artistic rules based on ethnic concerns and preoccupations. However, the Black Aesthetic of the 1960s was a distinctive and highly self-conscious formulation of a racial aesthetic and is the main focus of this article. To fully appreciate both its uniqueness and continuity with earlier and later racial aesthetics we need to trace the history of black racial aesthetics in the United States since roughly the 1820s. This approach helps us correct certain misconceptions about the singularity of the 1960s Black Aesthetic and helps us see its impact on later ethnic aesthetics.

Early African American Writers. African American written literature began with the desires to achieve *freedom and to define the racial self. In 1827 in *Freedom's Journal*, the first black newspaper, the editors argue, "We wish to plead our own cause. Too long have others spoken for us." These journalists felt that whites had misrepresented their case too often and had shown the *race in too negative a light. In the *North Star*, his antislavery newspaper started in 1847 and addressed to Negroes first and white abolitionists second, Frederick *Douglass contends that "he who has *endured the cruel pangs of *Slavery* is the man to *advocate Liberty*. . . . In the grand struggle for liberty and equality now waging, it is meet, right and essential that there should arise in our ranks authors . . . for it is in these capacities that the most permanent good be rendered to our cause." Pauline E. *Hopkins echoes these sentiments but applies them to creative writing. In *Contending Forces* (1900) she argues that fiction is an excellent medium for preserving the religious, political, and social customs of the African American and that nobody is better suited to "faithfully portray the inmost thoughts and feelings of the Negro" than the Negro himself. This first ethnic aesthetic posited that it was essential for African Americans to speak for themselves. There is no formal aspect to it, though; the authors unreflectively accepted standard white English and Euro-American forms without questioning them. At this point there is no desire to find an authentic black voice in the folk. In fact, the radical black abolitionist David *Walker, who also wrote primarily for black audiences, in *David Walker's Appeal* (1829) instructs black students to learn standard English and makes no reference to the oral folk or African traditions. Yet in The *Souls of Black Folk* (1903) the historian, sociologist, and author W. E. B. *Du Bois explores black expression in the *spirituals, finding them a unique African American expression and the only original American art form. In essence, Du Bois discovered the folk and their artistic achievement.

The historian Herbert Aptheker states that William H. Ferris made one of the earliest explicit calls for a racially conscious African American litera-ture. In his work *The African Abroad* (1913), he contends, "The civilization of a people is reflected in its literature. . . . It is the expression, in artistic form, of the deep-seated thought and feelings, dreams and longings of the race." Ferris felt that through literature black people would gain a sense of their ethnic selves. The historian Wilson Moses states that for Sutton E. *Griggs, another black author who wrote for black audiences, the purpose of literature was "to serve the masses of black people . . . provide a basis for racial unity and . . . to create channels of legitimate leadership." In *Life's Demands, or According to Law* (1916), Griggs observes that literature is "the method of embalming" the memories of those who have served the race. Ferris, Hopkins, and Griggs all felt that the function of African American literature was to provide a permanent record of the characteristics of the people.

The Harlem Renaissance. The racial aesthetic of the *Harlem Renaissance focused on the folk. Although *folklore was utilized before the Harlem Renaissance by such writers as Paul Laurence *Dunbar and Charles Waddell *Chesnutt, the renaissance writers of the 1920s used folk material more extensively and used such forms as *spirituals, *blues, ballads, and folk *sermons and preaching as models for their own writings. In *The Book of Negro Poetry* (1992), poet James Weldon *Johnson calls for a form that will express the Negro's spirit, ". . . a form expressing the imagery, the idioms, the peculiar turns of thought, and the distinctive *humor and pathos . . . of the Negro." We see that the desire to capture the spirit of the folk is a recurrent theme of African American *criticism. He also asserts that the conventions of Negro *dialect poetry make it a poor instrument for sincere black expression. In the *Crisis (July 1926) W. E. B. Du Bois argues for "A Negro Theatre." Du Bois's fundamental Afrocentric principles sound a great deal like those of the black aesthetic of the 1960s. He insists that the plays must be "written by Negro authors who understand from birth and continual association just what it means to be a Negro today" and furthermore the subject matter must be black life. The *theater must be primarily for blacks and the plays must be performed in black neighborhoods since Du Bois feels that the main function of black theater is to interpret black life for black people. Moreover Du Bois argues we have been judged too long by the white world and we must judge our own work by African American standards. That is, Du Bois was challenging white standards in the 1920s. In fact, as early as *The Souls of Black Folk* he is painfully conscious of the fact that white people sneeringly set the standards for black intellectual and artistic excellence.

The most militant poem of the 1920s was Claude *McKay's "If I Must Die" (first published 1919), in which the poet contends if blacks must die in battle let them die gloriously like men fighting back and not like passive ignoble beasts. Ironically, this militant and racial poem is written in the "enemy's" white form: not only is it a Shakespearean sonnet but it unself-consciously employs nineteenth-century English poetic diction. This question of form and style would also be relevant to the militant *poetry of the 1960s. Langston *Hughes in his famous manifesto, "The Negro Artist and the Racial Mountain" (1926), asserts that the middle-class black artist has been cut off from authentic working-class culture and can only become a great artist by embracing black working-class culture and overcoming the desire to be white. The black artist must find the beauty of black culture and himself. Like other writers of the renaissance, Hughes celebrated the black urban proletariat instead of the rural black folk, that is, celebrated the hordes of black folk who came north to Harlem.

Alain *Locke, the editor of the groundbreaking anthology The *New Negro (1925) and the philosopher of the Harlem Renaissance, felt that the main objective of Negro art is the "portrayal of Negro folk-life true in both letter and spirit to the idiom of the folk's own way of feeling and thinking." Once again we see the critic's desire for literature to record the folk, in keeping with the general affirmation during the 1920s of folk culture, the culture created by the black masses. Racial aesthetics are usually based on the idea of an authentic folk culture. That is, southern folk culture serves as a link to Africa, the homeland. Therefore, the folk culture is the source of an authentic and distinctive black self. Conversely, from at least Langston Hughes to Amiri *Baraka the black middle class has been associated with false values, the desire to be white and therefore inauthentic. Locke also maintains: "We ought and must have a school of Negro art, a local and a racially representative tradition." He insists that black art must seek out new styles and its characteristic idioms draw on the forms and values of Africa. Like other artists and intellectuals of the 1920s Locke's racial aesthetic insists on Africa as a source of African American art and civilization.

1930s Writers. Like many major white writers of the 1930s, many major black writers turned to Marxism. In "Blueprint for Negro Writing" (1937), the acclaimed novelist Richard *Wright argued for a black literature based on the black folk tradition but unlike the writers of the Harlem Renaissance he did not want his art limited to the indigenous folk culture. He wanted to place the black struggle within the context of the global struggle of "minority people everywhere" and to borrow from any tradition that led to the liberation of his people. He wanted to draw on the oral tradition, the "unwritten and unrecognized" culture of the black masses. Moreover, by fusing folk with Marxist values, both traditions embodying the struggle for freedom, the writer would create a tradition that would call for revolutionary action. Wright envisioned the writer as an agent of social change. In the 1930s Langston Hughes was also calling for the revolt of the masses, both white and black, in such works as "Good Morning, Revolution" (1932) and "Goodbye, Christ" (1932). Even though Hughes's revolutionary poetry was radical internationalist, it always spoke from a black perspective.

Middle Period Writers. Sterling A. *Brown and Margaret *Walker both affirmed the folk tradition. Racializing the poet Carl Sandburg's "strong men," from his classic poem by the same name (1931), Brown envisions the black masses gaining collective strength through American adversity: this black force, this black will cannot be derailed by any form of white American injustice. Unlike the main figures of the renaissance he did not write of the northern folk but returned to the theme of the southern folk. He also revived the popularity of black *dialect poetry, insisting that "Dialect, or the speech of the people, is capable of expressing whatever the people are." Brown's aesthetic is a racial one dedicated to the faithful depiction of the people in their own language. In her famous poem "*For My People" (1942), Margaret Walker says, "Let the martial songs be written. . . ." Walker presents the black will as being even more militant than Brown. She calls for the black masses to take power. Since her poetry anticipates the militancy, spirit, and style of the poetry of the 1960s, the black aesthetician Addison *Gayle, Jr., quotes her for the main epigraph for his classic anthology, The Black Aesthetic (1971). It is not surprising that in 1976 she wrote "Some Aspects of the Black Aesthetic," a sympathetic essay on the Black Aesthetic. Like Hughes and Brown, Walker celebrates the black masses and sees poetry as a weapon. These writers contributed to the racial aesthetic of celebrating the folk tradition and extended the styles and forms of the Harlem Renaissance.

Post–World War II Writers. In the 1940s and 1950s African American writers turned their backs on racial art. The involvement of blacks in the Second World War, reversal of federal policy on segregation, the integration of the military, and federal laws challenging segregation made African Americans more optimistic about American democracy. In the *anthology The Negro Caravan (1941), typical of the time, the editors declare, "The Negro writes in the forms evolved in English and American literature" and therefore there is no distinctive African American literature, only American literature. In the early 1960s Lorraine *Hansberry insisted that her play, A *Raisin in the Sun (1959), was not a Negro *drama, but one about people who happened to be Negro and moreover that she was not a Negro playwright but a writer "who happened to be a Negro." This statement also epitomizes the period in its integrationist and universalist mood, which de-emphasizes cultural difference. In particular, the black 1960s were responding to this integrationist period. The critic Houston A. Baker, Jr., describes the underlying artistic principle of the time as "the poetics of integration."

The Black Arts Movement. With the *Black Arts movement of the 1960s, the name and specific concept of the "Black Aesthetic" developed. The key theorists of the Black Aesthetic were Amiri Baraka (then LeRoi Jones), Larry *Neal, Addison Gayle, Hoyt *Fuller, and Maulana Ron Karenga. Fuller defined it nicely when he said that the "Black aesthetic [is] a system of isolating and evaluating the artistic works of black people which reflect the special character and imperatives of black experience." In Black Fire (1968), a classic Black Nationalist anthology of the time coedited by Neal and Baraka, Neal declared that the "artist and the political activist are one."

Continuing the tradition of the 1920s and 1930s, black art is seen as a political weapon. In the poem "Black Art" (1966), Baraka argues that poems are useful only if they are weapons that will create a new black world and destroy the white one. Unlike the McKay poem and like the Margaret Walker poem the poet is fighting to win; the poem is written in a language highly influenced by the black vernacular, that is, in a language of the people instead of "the white enemy," standard English.

Like the racial art of earlier periods, the audience is envisioned as the black masses but the black masses this time are envisioned as "the brother[s] on the street," the urban black working class, and even the lumpenproletariat. Karenga insists that "Black Art like everything else in the Black community, must respond positively to the reality of revolution" and "Black Art must be functional, collective, and committed." In *The Black Aesthetic* (1971), in trying to differentiate between generations of African American writers, Gayle mistakenly observes that "black artists of the past" wrote for whites but correctly observes that "today's black artist . . . speak[s] to his brothers."

The Black Aestheticians attacked the idea of universal art. Critic George Hall asserts that even though the themes and symbols of the Black Aesthetic were present in the Harlem Renaissance, what was different about the 1960s was that blacks had evolved their own standards. To a degree this might be true, but Du Bois in the 1920s was struggling toward African American, not white, standards and Locke called for the use of African forms. The poet Dudley *Randall amusingly attacks the universalist aesthetic in his poem "Black Poet, White Critic," where the white critic advises the black writer to write about something universal, a white unicorn. They felt what white critics meant by universal was white art, art that conformed to white standards, to what Gayle calls "the white aesthetic."

In his classic Black Aesthetic essay, "the legacy of *malcolm x, and the coming of the black nation" (1966), Baraka argues, continuing Du Bois's argument for black judgment, that "The Black artist . . . is desperately needed to change the images his people identify with, by asserting Black feeling, Black mind, Black judgement." Furthermore, the black artist must teach the black masses to harden their hearts toward the whites. In "Black Art," Baraka declares no love poems can be written until the world is transformed into a more human place. In "The True Import of Present Dialogue" (1968), the poet Nikki *Giovanni chillingly asks, "Nigger / Can you kill" a white man? Like other militant poets of the period, such as Haki R. *Madhubuti (Don L. Lee), Baraka, and Sonia *Sanchez, in her poetry Giovanni was trying to incite the black masses to revolt. This was the time of the summer riots or uprisings of African Americans in Watts (1965), Detroit (1967), Newark (1967), and other cities—a time when blacks showed their discontent with the American dream by mass disorderliness, looting, and destruction of property. Many African American artists and intellectuals saw the uprisings as the first stage of an impending black revolution that they wanted to advance.

The New Breed. In the 1970s Ishmael *Reed, Al *Young, Cecil *Brown, Quincy Thomas *Troupe, Jr., and others rebelled against the Black Aesthetic; this New Breed found the Black Aesthetic too prescriptive and narrowly political. But they did not want to return to a universalist aesthetic. Like the Black Aesthetic writers, they felt that the universalist aesthetic was simply a white aesthetic by another name. In his novel *Mumbo Jumbo* (1972), Reed brilliantly attacks the Western cultural "snow job" that inflates the importance of its art and civilization at the expense of all other civilizations. The New Breed aesthetic was grounded in African American folk culture. Like the Harlem Renaissance writers and the writers of the Middle Period, these artists' values and forms derived from the folk culture. Unlike the Black Aestheticians, they felt the battleground was not the street but the mind. They wanted to dethrone the Western mind from the seat of intellectual power and prestige. In "O. O. Blues," Al Young parodies Black Aesthetic art, claiming it is not revolutionary but simply titillation for white liberals, that is, entertainment to scare them like horror movies but having no impact in the real world of white institutions. Moreover, the New Breed expanded the definition of ethnic aesthetic by claiming not only that blacks but that all cultures deserve to be celebrated. In their magazine, the *Yardbird Reader*, they celebrated American diversity by publishing writers of various backgrounds, including Native American, Asian American, Hispanic, and others. They redefined American literature to include all Americans, not only male Anglo-Saxons.

The Neo–Black Aesthetic. In the 1980s and 1990s a new literary generation appeared who had been influenced by both the Black Aesthetic of the 1960s and the New Breed folk aesthetic of the 1970s. However, these writers rejected the earlier universalist monochromatic aesthetic. They self-consciously saw themselves writing out of African American tradition and black experience. In *Callaloo*, in his essay "The New Black Aesthetic" (1987), the young novelist Trey *Ellis coined the term "the New Black Aesthetic" and declared this group of young writers to be "*new cultural mulattoes," drawing on both white and black culture. Even though the new writers were grounded in the black experience they felt comfortable borrowing ideas from white culture. However, they would never give up their black heritage for white culture. The popular novelist Terry *McMillan claims that the new black writers are not writing for white people and simplifies the black past by assuming that all the old black writers were guilty of that sin. She and others are apolitical even though they affirm a racial aesthetic. They look on the political art of the 1960s as mere propaganda. In the December 1986 *Voice Literary Supplement* Greg Tate, the most intellectual of the new writers, argues in "Cult-Nats Meet Freaky-Deke" for the importance of the Black Aesthetic—he argues that Black Aesthetic writers taught the younger writers the profound genius of African American culture, in fact, convinced the young writers that black culture was more profound and beautiful than anything produced by the white world—however, he also sees its limitations, its sexism, anti-Semitism, and romantic view of Africa.

There have been a number of racial aesthetics formulated by African Americans since the 1820s. Certain historical moments, such as the early twentieth century, the 1920s, and the 1960s, were more responsive to their articulation than others. The Black Aesthetic of the 1960s was in many ways similar to earlier black racial aesthetics, with its emphasis on the black experience, the masses, and Africa, but it was also different from them with its self-conscious and exhaustive theorizing—that is, it often spelled out ideas that had been implicit or partial in earlier generations' formulations—and its radical desire for total disassociation from Western thought. Furthermore the 1960s aesthetic seems to have a continuing impact that has at least momentarily if not permanently made it impossible for any African American writer to disassociate himself or herself from African American culture. No post–Black Aesthetic writer would say that he or she happened to be black as Lorraine Hansberry did in the early 1960s—now ethnicity is at the core of African American literature.

[*See also* Afrocentricity; Black Nationalism; Identity; Race.]

• Eugene B. Redmond, *Drumvoices: The Mission of Afro-American Poetry,* 1976. Herbert Aptheker, ed., *A Documentary History of the Negro People in the United States, 1910–1932,* vol. 3, 1977. Abby A. Johnson, *Propaganda and Aesthetics: The Literary Politics of Afro-American Magazines in the Twentieth Century,* 1979. Rebecca T. Cureau, "Toward an Aesthetic of Black Folk Expression," in *Alain Locke, Reflections on a Modern Renaissance Man,* ed. Russell Linnemann, 1982, pp. 77–90. George Hall, "Alain Locke and the Honest Propaganda of Truth and Beauty," in *Alain Locke, Reflections on a Modern Renaissance Man,* ed. Russell Linnemann, 1982, pp. 91–99. Reginald Martin, *Ishmael Reed and the New Black Aesthetic Critics,* 1988. Wilson Moses, *The Wings of Ethiopia: Studies in African-American Life and Letters,* 1990. David Lionel Smith, "The Black Arts Movement and Its Critics," *American Literacy History* 3 (Spring 1991): 93–110.

—William J. Harris

Black American Literature Forum. *See* African American Review.

BLACK ARTS MOVEMENT. Both inherently and overtly political in content, the Black Arts movement was the only American literary movement to advance "social engagement" as a sine qua non of its aesthetic. The movement broke from the immediate past of protest and petition (civil rights) literature and dashed forward toward an alternative that initially seemed unthinkable and unobtainable: Black Power.

In a 1968 essay, "The Black Arts Movement," Larry *Neal proclaimed Black Arts the "aesthetic and spiritual sister of the Black Power concept." As a political phrase, Black Power had earlier been used by Richard *Wright to describe the mid-1950s emergence of independent African nations. The 1960s' use of the term originated in 1966 with Student Nonviolent Coordinating Committee civil rights workers

Stokely *Carmichael and Willie Ricks. Quickly adopted in the North, Black Power was associated with a militant advocacy of armed self-defense, separation from "racist American domination," and pride in and assertion of the goodness and beauty of Blackness.

Although often criticized as sexist, homophobic, and racially exclusive (i.e., reverse racist), Black Arts was much broader than any of its limitations. Ishmael *Reed, who is considered neither a movement apologist nor advocate ("I wasn't invited to participate because I was considered an integrationist"), notes in a 1995 interview,

I think what Black Arts did was inspire a whole lot of Black people to write. Moreover, there would be no multiculturalism movement without Black Arts. Latinos, Asian Americans, and others all say they began writing as a result of the example of the 1960s. Blacks gave the example that you don't have to assimilate. You could do your own thing, get into your own background, your own history, your own tradition and your own culture. I think the challenge is for cultural sovereignty and Black Arts struck a blow for that.

History and Context. The Black Arts movement, usually referred to as a "sixties" movement, coalesced in 1965 and broke apart around 1975/1976. In March 1965 following the 21 February assassination of *Malcolm X, LeRoi Jones (Amiri *Baraka) moved from Manhattan's Lower East Side (he had already moved away from Greenwich Village) uptown to Harlem, an exodus considered the symbolic birth of the Black Arts movement. Jones was a highly visible publisher (*Yugen* and *Floating Bear* magazines, Totem Press), a celebrated poet (*Preface to a Twenty-Volume Suicide Note,* 1961, and *The Dead Lecturer,* 1964), a major music critic (*Blues People,* 1963), and an Obie Award–winning playwright (*Dutchman,* 1964) who, up until that fateful split, had functioned in an integrated world. Other than James *Baldwin, who at that time had been closely associated with the *civil rights movement, Jones was the most respected and most widely published Black writer of his generation.

While Jones's 1965 move uptown to found the Black Arts Repertory Theatre/School (BARTS) is the formal beginning (it was Jones who came up with the name "Black Arts"), Black Arts, as a literary movement, had its roots in groups such as the Umbra Workshop. Umbra (1962) was a collective of young Black writers based in Manhattan's Lower East Side; major members were writers Steve Cannon, Tom *Dent, Al Haynes, David Henderson, Calvin C. *Hernton, Joe Johnson, Norman Pritchard, Lenox Raphael, Ishmael Reed, Lorenzo *Thomas, James Thompson, Askia M. *Touré (Roland Snellings; also a visual artist), Brenda Walcott, and musician-writer Archie Shepp. Touré, a major shaper of "cultural nationalism," directly influenced Jones. Along with Umbra writer Charles Patterson and Charles's brother, William Patterson, Touré joined Jones, Steve Young, and others at BARTS.

Umbra, which produced *Umbra Magazine,* was the first post–civil rights Black literary group to make an impact as radical in the sense of establishing their own voice distinct from, and sometimes at odds with, the prevailing white literary establishment. The attempt to merge a Black-oriented activist thrust with a primarily artistic orientation produced a classic split in Umbra between those who wanted to be activists and those who thought of themselves as primarily writers, though to some extent all members shared both views. Black writers have always had to face the issue of whether their work was primarily political or aesthetic. Moreover, Umbra itself had evolved out of similar circumstances: In 1960 a Black nationalist literary organization, On Guard for Freedom, had been founded on the Lower East Side by Calvin Hicks. Its members included Nannie and Walter Bowe, Harold Cruse (who was then working on *Crisis of the Negro Intellectual,* 1967), Tom Dent, Rosa *Guy, Joe Johnson, LeRoi Jones, and Sarah *Wright, among others. On Guard was active in a famous protest at the United Nations of the American-sponsored Bay of Pigs Cuban invasion and was active in support of the Congolese liberation leader Patrice Lumumba. From On Guard, Dent, Johnson, and Walcott along with Hernton, Henderson, and Touré established Umbra.

Another formation of Black writers at that time was the Harlem Writers Guild, led by John O. *Killens, which included Maya *Angelou, Jean Carey Bond, Rosa Guy, and Sarah Wright among others. But the Harlem Writers Guild focused on prose, primarily fiction, which did not have the mass appeal of *poetry performed in the dynamic vernacular of the time. Poems could be built around anthems, chants, and political slogans, and thereby used in organizing work, which was not generally the case with *novels and short stories. Moreover, the poets could and did publish themselves, whereas greater resources were needed to publish fiction. That Umbra was primarily poetry- and performance-oriented established a significant and classic characteristic of the movement's aesthetics.

When Umbra split up, some members, led by Askia Touré and Al Haynes, moved to Harlem in late 1964 and formed the nationalist-oriented "Uptown Writers Movement," which included poets Yusef Rahman, Keorapetse "Willie" Kgositsile from South Africa, and Larry Neal. Accompanied by young "New Music" musicians, they performed poetry all over Harlem. Members of this group joined LeRoi Jones in founding BARTS.

Jones's move to Harlem was short-lived. In December 1965 he returned to his home, Newark (N.J.), and left BARTS in serious disarray. BARTS failed but the Black Arts center concept was irrepressible mainly because the Black Arts movement was so closely aligned with the then-burgeoning Black Power movement.

The mid- to late 1960s was a period of intense revolutionary ferment. Beginning in 1964, rebellions in Harlem and Rochester, New York, initiated four years of long hot summers. Watts, Detroit, Newark, Cleveland, and many other cities went up in flames, culminating in nationwide explosions of resentment and anger following Martin Luther *King, Jr.'s April 1968 assassination.

In his seminal 1965 poem "Black Art," which quickly became the major poetic manifesto of the Black Arts literary movement, Jones declaimed "we want poems that kill." He was not simply speaking metaphorically. During that period armed self-defense and slogans such as "Arm yourself or harm yourself" established a social climate that promoted confrontation with the white power structure, especially the police (e.g., "Off the pigs"). Indeed, Amiri Baraka (Jones changed his name in 1967) had been arrested and convicted (later overturned on appeal) on a gun possession charge during the 1967 Newark rebellion. Additionally, armed struggle was widely viewed as not only a legitimate, but often as the only effective means of liberation. Black Arts' dynamism, impact, and effectiveness are a direct result of its partisan nature and advocacy of artistic and political *freedom "by any means necessary." America had never experienced such a militant artistic movement.

Nathan Hare, the author of *The Black Anglo-Saxons* (1965), was the founder of 1960s *Black Studies. Expelled from Howard University, Hare moved to San Francisco State University where the battle to establish a Black Studies department was waged during a five-month strike during the 1968–1969 school year. As with the establishment of Black Arts, which included a range of forces, there was broad activity in the Bay Area around Black Studies, including efforts led by poet and professor Sarah Webster *Fabio at Merrit College.

The initial thrust of Black Arts ideological development came from the Revolutionary Action Movement (RAM), a national organization with a strong presence in New York City. Both Touré and Neal were members of RAM. After RAM, the major ideological force shaping the Black Arts movement was the US (as opposed to "them") organization led by Maulana Karenga. Also ideologically important was Elijah Muhammad's Chicago-based Nation of Islam.

These three formations provided both style and ideological direction for Black Arts artists, including those who were not members of these or any other political organization. Although the Black Arts movement is often considered a New York–based movement, two of its three major forces were located outside New York City.

As the movement matured, the two major locations of Black Arts' ideological leadership, particularly for literary work, were California's Bay Area because of the *Journal of Black Poetry* and the *Black Scholar,* and the Chicago–Detroit axis because of *Negro Digest/Black World* and *Third World Press in Chicago, and *Broadside Press and Naomi Long *Madgett's *Lotus Press in Detroit. The only major Black Arts literary publications to come out of New York were the short-lived (six issues between 1969 and 1972) *Black Theatre* magazine published by the New Lafayette Theatre and *Black Dialogue,* which had actually started in San Francisco (1964–1968) and relocated to New York (1969–1972).

In 1967 LeRoi Jones visited Karenga in Los Angeles and became an advocate of Karenga's philosophy of Kawaida. Kawaida, which produced the "Nguzo Saba" (seven principles), Kwanzaa, and an emphasis on African names, was a multifaceted, categorized activist philosophy. Jones also met Bobby Seale and Eldridge *Cleaver and worked with a number of the founding members of the Black Panthers. Additionally, Askia Touré was a visiting professor at San Francisco State and was to become a leading (and long-lasting) poet as well as, arguably, the most influential poet-professor in the Black Arts movement. Playwright Ed *Bullins and poet *Marvin X had established Black Arts West, and Dingane Joe Goncalves had founded the *Journal of Black Poetry* (1966). This grouping of Ed Bullins, Dingane Joe Goncalves, LeRoi Jones, Sonia *Sanchez, Askia M. Touré, and Marvin X became a major nucleus of Black Arts leadership.

Theory and Practice. The two hallmarks of Black Arts activity were the development of Black theater groups and Black poetry performances and journals, and both had close ties to community organizations and issues. Black theaters served as the focus of poetry, *dance, and *music performances in addition to formal and ritual *drama. Black theaters were also venues for community meetings, lectures, study groups, and *film screenings. The summer of 1968 issue of *Drama Review*, a special on Black theater edited by Ed Bullins, literally became a Black Arts textbook that featured essays and plays by most of the major movers: Larry Neal, Ben *Caldwell, LeRoi Jones, Jimmy Garrett, John O'Neal, Sonia Sanchez, Marvin X, Ron *Milner, Woodie *King, Jr., Bill *Gunn, Ed Bullins, and Adam David Miller. Black Arts theater proudly emphasized its activist roots and orientations in distinct, and often antagonistic, contradiction to traditional theaters, both Black and white, which were either commercial or strictly artistic in focus.

By 1970 Black Arts theaters and cultural centers were active throughout America. The New Lafayette Theatre (Bob Macbeth, executive director, and Ed Bullins, writer in residence) and Barbara Ann Teer's National Black Theatre led the way in New York. Baraka's Spirit House Movers held forth in Newark and traveled up and down the East Coast. The Organization of Black American Culture (OBAC) and Val Grey Ward's Kuumba Theatre Company were leading forces in Chicago, from where emerged a host of writers, artists, and musicians including the OBAC visual artist collective whose "Wall of Respect" inspired the national community-based public murals movement and led to the formation of Afri-Cobra (the African Commune of Bad, Revolutionary Artists). There was David Rambeau's Concept East and Ron Milner and Woodie King's Black Arts Midwest, both based in Detroit. Ron Milner became the Black Arts movement's most enduring playwright and Woodie King became its leading theater impresario when he moved to New York City. In Los Angeles there was the Ebony Showcase, Inner City Repertory Company, and the Performing Arts Society of Los Angeles (PALSA) led by Vantile Whitfield. In San Francisco was the aforementioned Black Arts West. BLKARTSOUTH (led by Tom Dent and Kalamu ya *Salaam) was an outgrowth of the Free Southern Theatre in New Orleans and was instrumental in en-

couraging Black theater development across the south from the Theatre of Afro Arts in Miami, Florida, to Sudan Arts Southwest in Houston, Texas, through an organization called the Southern Black Cultural Alliance. In addition to formal Black theater repertory companies in numerous other cities, there were literally hundreds of Black Arts community and campus theater groups.

A major reason for the widespread dissemination and adoption of Black Arts was the development of nationally distributed magazines that printed manifestos and critiques in addition to offering publishing opportunities for a proliferation of young writers. Whether establishment or independent, Black or white, most literary publications rejected Black Arts writers. The movement's first literary expressions in the early 1960s came through two New York–based, nationally distributed magazines, *Freedomways* and *Liberator*. *Freedomways*, "a journal of the Freedom Movement," backed by leftists, was receptive to young Black writers. The more important magazine was Dan Watts's *Liberator*, which openly aligned itself with both domestic and international revolutionary movements. Many of the early writings of critical Black Arts voices are found in *Liberator*. Neither of these were primarily literary journals.

The first major Black Arts literary publication was the California-based *Black Dialogue* (1964), edited by Arthur A. Sheridan, Abdul Karim, Edward Spriggs, Aubrey Labrie, and Marvin Jackmon (Marvin X). *Black Dialogue* was paralleled by *Soulbook* (1964), edited by Mamadou Lumumba (Kenn Freeman) and Bobb Hamilton. Oakland-based *Soulbook* was mainly political but included poetry in a section ironically titled "Reject Notes."

Dingane Joe Goncalves became *Black Dialogue*'s poetry editor and, as more and more poetry poured in, he conceived of starting the *Journal of Black Poetry*. Founded in San Francisco, the first issue was a small magazine with mimeographed pages and a lithographed cover. Up through the summer of 1975, the *Journal* published nineteen issues and grew to over one hundred pages. Publishing a broad range of more than five hundred poets, its editorial policy was eclectic. Special issues were given to guest editors who included Ahmed Alhamisi, Don L. Lee (Haki R. *Madhubuti), Clarence *Major, Larry Neal, Dudley *Randall, Ed Spriggs, and Askia Touré. In addition to African Americans, African, Caribbean, Asian, and other international revolutionary poets were presented.

Founded in 1969 by Nathan Hare and Robert Chrisman, the *Black Scholar*, "the first journal of black studies and research in this country," was theoretically critical. Major African-disasporan and African theorists were represented in its pages. In a 1995 interview Chrisman attributed much of what exists today to the groundwork laid by the Black Arts movement:

> If we had not had a Black Arts movement in the sixties we certainly wouldn't have had national Black literary figures like Henry Louis *Gates, Jr., Alice *Walker, or Toni

*Morrison because much more so than the Harlem Renaissance, in which Black artists were always on the leash of white patrons and publishing houses, the Black Arts movement did it for itself. What you had was Black people going out nationally, in mass, saying that we are an independent Black people and this is what we produce.

For the publication of Black Arts creative literature, no magazine was more important than the Chicago-based Johnson publication *Negro Digest/Black World*. Johnson published America's most popular Black magazines, *Jet* and *Ebony*. Hoyt *Fuller, who became the editor in 1961, was a Black intellectual with near-encyclopedic knowledge of Black literature and seemingly inexhaustible contacts. Because *Negro Digest*, a monthly, ninety-eight-page journal, was a Johnson publication, it was sold on newsstands nationwide. Originally patterned on *Reader's Digest*, *Negro Digest* changed its name to *Black World* in 1970, indicative of Fuller's view that the magazine ought to be a voice for Black people everywhere. The name change also reflected the widespread rejection of "Negro" and the adoption of "Black" as the designation of choice for people of African descent and to indicate identification with both the diaspora and Africa. The legitimation of "Black" and "African" is another enduring legacy of the Black Arts movement.

Negro Digest/Black World published both a high volume and an impressive range of poetry, fiction, criticism, drama, reviews, reportage, and theoretical articles. A consistent highlight was Fuller's perceptive column Perspectives ("Notes on books, writers, artists and the arts") which informed readers of new publications, upcoming cultural events and conferences, and also provided succinct coverage of major literary developments. Fuller produced annual poetry, drama, and fiction issues, sponsored literary contests, and gave out literary awards. Fuller published a variety of viewpoints but always insisted on editorial excellence and thus made *Negro Digest/Black World* a first-rate literary publication. Johnson decided to cease publication of *Black World* in April 1976, allegedly in response to a threatened withdrawal of advertisement from all of Johnson's publications because of pro-Palestinian/anti-Zionist articles in *Black World*.

The two major Black Arts presses were poet Dudley Randall's Broadside Press in Detroit and Haki Madhubuti's Third World Press in Chicago. From a literary standpoint, Broadside Press, which concentrated almost exclusively on poetry, was by far the more important. Founded in 1965, Broadside published more than four hundred poets in more than one hundred books or recordings and was singularly responsible for presenting older Black poets (Gwendolyn *Brooks, Sterling A. *Brown, and Margaret *Walker) to a new audience and introducing emerging poets (Nikki *Giovanni, Etheridge *Knight, Don L. Lee/Haki Madhubuti, and Sonia Sanchez) who would go on to become major voices for the movement. In 1976, strapped by economic restrictions and with a severely overworked and overwhelmed three-person staff, Broadside Press went

into serious decline. Although it functions mainly on its back catalog, Broadside Press is still alive.

While a number of poets (e.g., Amiri Baraka, Nikki Giovanni, Haki Madhubuti, and Sonia Sanchez), playwrights (e.g., Ed Bullins and Ron Milner), and spoken-word artists (e.g., the Last Poets and Gil *Scott-Heron, both of whom were extremely popular and influential although often overlooked by literary critics) are indelibly associated with the Black Arts movement, rather than focusing on their individual work, one gets a much stronger and much more accurate impression of the movement by reading seven *anthologies focusing on the 1960s and the 1970s.

Black Fire (1968), edited by Baraka and Neal, is a massive collection of essays, poetry, fiction, and drama featuring the first wave of Black Arts writers and thinkers. Because of its impressive breadth, *Black Fire* stands as a definitive movement anthology.

For Malcolm X, Poems on the Life and the Death of Malcolm X (1969), edited by Dudley Randall and Margaret Taylor Goss *Burroughs, demonstrates the political thrust of the movement and the specific influence of Malcolm X. There is no comparable anthology in American poetry that focuses on a political figure as poetic inspiration.

The Black Woman (1970), edited by Toni Cade *Bambara, is the first major Black feminist anthology and features work by Jean Bond, Nikki Giovanni, Abbey Lincoln, Audre *Lorde, Paule *Marshall, Gwen Patton, Pat Robinson, Alice Walker, Shirley Williams, and others.

Edited by Addison *Gayle, Jr., *The Black Aesthetic* (1971) is significant because it both articulates and contextualizes Black Arts theory. The work of writers such as Alain *Locke, W. E. B. *Du Bois, Langston *Hughes, and J. A. Rogers showcases the movement's roots in an earlier era. Divided into sections on theory, music, fiction, poetry, and drama, Gayle's seminal anthology features a broad array of writers who are regarded as the chief Black Arts theorists-practitioners.

Stephen Henderson's *Understanding the New Black Poetry* (1972) is important not only because of the poets included but also because of Henderson's insightful and unparalleled sixty-seven page overview. This is the movement's most thorough exposition of a Black poetic aesthetic. Insights and lines of thought now taken for granted were first articulated in a critical and formal context by Stephen Henderson, who proposed a totally innovative reading of Black poetics.

New Black Voices (1972), edited by Abraham Chapman, is significant because its focus is specifically on the emerging voices in addition to new work by established voices who were active in the Black Arts movement. Unlike most anthologies, which overlook the South, *New Black Voices* is geographically representative and includes lively pro and con articles side by side debating aesthetic and political theory.

The seventh book, Eugene *Redmond's *Drumvoices, The Mission of Afro-American Poetry: A Critical History* (1976), is a surprisingly thorough survey that has been unjustly neglected. Although some of his opinions are controversial (note that in the movement controversy was normal), Redmond's era by era and city by city cataloging of literary collectives as well as individual writers offers an invaluable service in detailing the movement's national scope.

The Movement's Breakup. The decline of the Black Arts movement began in 1974 when the Black Power movement was disrupted and co-opted. Black political organizations were hounded, disrupted, and defeated by repressive government measures, such as Cointelpro and IRS probes. Black Studies activist leadership was gutted and replaced by academicians and trained administrators who were unreceptive, if not outright opposed, to the movement's political orientation.

Key internal events in the disruption were the split between nationalists and Marxists in the African Liberation Support Committee (May 1974), the Sixth Pan African Congress in Tanzania where race-based struggle was repudiated/denounced by most of the strongest forces in Africa (Aug. 1974), and Baraka's national organization, the Congress of Afrikan People (CAP), officially changing from a "Pan Afrikan Nationalist" to a "Marxist Leninist" organization (Oct. 1974).

As the movement reeled from the combination of external and internal disruption, commercialization and capitalist co-option delivered the coup de grace. President Richard Nixon's strategy of pushing Black capitalism as a response to Black Power epitomized mainstream co-option. As major film, record, book, and magazine publishers identified the most salable artists, the Black Arts movement's already fragile independent economic base was totally undermined.

In an overwhelmingly successful effort to capitalize on the upsurge of interest in the feminist movement, establishment presses focused particular attention on the work of Black women writers. Although issues of sexism had been widely and hotly debated within movement publications and organizations, the initiative passed from Black Arts back to the establishment. Emblematic of the establishment overtaking (some would argue "co-opting") Black Arts activity is Ntozake *Shange's *for colored girls, which in 1976 ended up on Broadway produced by Joseph Papp even though it had been workshopped at Woodie King's New Federal Theatre of the Henry Street Settlement on the Lower East Side. Black Arts was not able to match the economic and publicity offers tendered by establishment concerns.

Corporate America (both the commercial sector and the academic sector) once again selected and propagated one or two handpicked Black writers. During the height of Black Arts activity, each community had a coterie of writers and there were publishing outlets for hundreds, but once the mainstream regained control, Black artists were tokenized. Although Black Arts activity continued into the early 1980s, by 1976, the year of what Gil Scott-Heron called the "Buy-Centennial," the movement was without any sustainable and effective political or economic bases in an economically strapped Black community. An additional complicating factor was the economic recession, resulting from the oil crisis,

which the Black community experienced as a depression. Simultaneously, philanthropic foundations only funded non-threatening, "arts oriented" groups. Neither the Black Arts nor the Black Power movements ever recovered.

The Legacy. In addition to advocating political engagement and independent publishing, the Black Arts movement was innovative in its use of language. Speech (particularly, but not exclusively, Black English), music, and performance were major elements of Black Arts literature. Black Arts aesthetics emphasized orality, which includes the ritual use of call and response both within the body of the work itself as well as between artist and audience. This same orientation is apparent in rap music and 1990s "performance poetry" (e.g., Nuyorican Poets and poetry slams).

While right-wing trends attempt to push America's cultural clock back to the 1950s, Black Arts continues to evidence resiliency in the Black community and among other marginalized sectors. When people encounter the Black Arts movement, they are delighted and inspired by the most audacious, prolific, and socially engaged literary movement in America's history.

[See also Afrocentricity; Black Nationalism; Criticism, articles on Criticism from 1920 to 1964 and Criticism since 1965; Double Consciousness; Journalism; Literary History, article on Late Twentieth Century; Periodicals, article on Scholarly Journals and Literary Magazines.]

• Frank Kofsky, Black Nationalism and the Revolution in Music, 1970. George Kent, Blackness and the Adventure of Western Culture, 1972. Abby A. Johnson and Ronald Maberry Johnson, Propaganda and Aesthetics: The Literary Politics of Afro-American Magazines in the Twentieth Century, 1979. Carolyn Fowler, Black Arts and Black Aesthetics: A Bibliography, 1981. Gladstone L. Yearwood, Black Cinema Aesthetics, 1982. Mari Evans, ed., Black Women Writers 1950–1980, 1984.

—Kalamu ya Salaam

Black Boy. Richard *Wright's 1945 *autobiography Black Boy covers his life from four years of age to the moment of his departure from the South (Memphis, Tennessee, where he had earlier migrated from Mississippi) to the North (Chicago) at nineteen. Its subject and title place it in the tradition of African American autobiography, beginning with the nineteenth-century *slave narrative, a genre in which the autobiographer describes the particularities of his own life in order to speak of the situation and condition of the race in general. While presenting the details of one life, Black Boy is intended to reveal the horrors, cruelties, and privations undergone by the masses of African Americans living in the South (and in the United States as a whole) during the first decades of the twentieth century.

Originally Wright's Black Boy was the first section of a much longer work titled American Hunger and divided into two parts: "Southern Night," detailing Wright's early life in the South, and "The Horror and the Glory," treating his life in Chicago and describing racism northern style. After Harper & Brothers received the manuscript from Wright, they submitted it to the Book-of-the-Month Club for consideration as a monthly selection. The club agreed to accept it on condition that its first section alone, later titled by Wright *Black Boy*, be published. The complete text of the second section of *American Hunger* was first published in 1977 by Harper & Row. The entire work, composed of both sections, as Wright originally wrote it, was published for the first time in 1992 by the Library of America.

One of the primary themes of Wright's autobiographical narrative involves the influence of racism on the personal interrelations not only among the individuals of the oppressed group but within the *family itself. The first episode of the narrative, in which Wright at four years of age innocently burns down the family home, has no racial implications per se, but the response of his mother does. As punishment Wright is so severely beaten with a tree limb that he lapses into semi-consciousness and requires the attention of a physician. The mother's response is in direct correlation to the family's economic circumstance. They are poor because they are black, and the harshness of his punishment reflects the degree of the family's economic loss. On another occasion, when Wright is badly cut behind the ear by a broken bottle in a fight between black and white boys, his mother, instead of extending the comfort and sympathy ordinarily expected of a parent toward a wounded child, beats him to warn him of the dangers of fighting whites.

Black Boy's historical significance lies in its recapitulation of the thrust of black autobiography in its use of the form as a means of righting social wrong. Other African American writers have used literature to perform this function, but none before Wright had been as outspoken. In episode after episode Wright describes through his own experience of racial repression that undergone by millions of his brothers and sisters. At the same time, he relates the story of his own growth.

[*See also* Identity; Migration.]

• Michel Fabre, *The Unfinished Quest of Richard Wright*, 1973.   —Donald B. Gibson

Blacker the Berry, The. Wallace *Thurman's first *novel, *The Blacker the Berry: A Novel of Negro Life* (1929) takes its title from an old folk saying, "the blacker the berry, the sweeter the juice." It is an autobiographical satire whose neurotic, dark-skinned protagonist, Emma Lou Morgan, internalizes biases against dark-complexioned people after a midwestern upbringing by colorstruck relatives mimicking racist societal values. Like Thurman, Emma Lou goes to the University of Southern California and then to Harlem. Unlike Thurman, who was primarily drawn to the artistic renaissance blooming there, Emma Lou hopes Harlem will enable her to escape finally the harsh intraracial prejudice that is exacerbated by her sex and egocentrism.

Among the mundane settings of Harlem tenement buildings, employment agencies, public dance halls, rent parties, cabarets, and movie houses, Emma Lou has numerous opportunities to overcome her obsession with color and class consciousness. She is, indeed, discriminated against by both blacks and whites, but not to the degree that she believes. In a crowded one-room apartment filled with liquor-gorging intellectuals resembling Langston *Hughes (Tony Crews), Zora Neale *Hurston (Cora Thurston), and Richard Bruce *Nugent (Paul), Truman (Thurman himself) explains intraracial discrimination by examining the parasitic nature of humankind. He argues that "people have to feel superior to something . . . [other than] domestic animals or steel machines. . . . It is much more pleasing to pick some individual or group . . . on the same plane." Thus, he suggests that *mulattoes who ostracize darker-skinned African Americans merely follow a hierarchy of discrimination set by materially powerful white people. Truman's anatomy of racism, however, is ignored by Emma Lou.

The Blacker the Berry received reviews that, while mixed, praised Thurman for his ironic depiction of original settings, characters, and themes then considered off limits for African American literary examination. Many others also criticized him for emphasizing the seamier side of Harlem life. But Thurman was never pleased with *Blacker*, and his caricature of the female protagonist shows why. Emma Lou behaves unlike traditional African American females who tend to revise rather than accept the values of both African American and white men. After she is repeatedly degraded by light-skinned Alva, Emma Lou's spiritual liberation begins only when she acknowledges the Thurmanian and Emersonian ideal that salvation rests with the individual, first expressed by white Campbell Kitchen (Carl Van Vechten). In other words, Thurman becomes trapped in the alien body of Emma Lou and does not have the creative imagination to break her racial fixation by summoning up a female perspective. Instead, Emma Lou trades an obsession with skin color for one that is viewed by a patriarchal society as being even more perverse. When she catches Alva embracing the homosexual Bobbie, Emma Lou finally gathers the strength to leave him. Herein lies an example of the dominant literary problem exhibited by the *Harlem Renaissance old guard and avant garde alike. Their art is consumed by the paradox in creating liberated African American male and female voices while mouthing the ethics of the American patriarchy.

• Hugh Gloster, *Negro Voices in American Fiction*, 1948. Bernard W. Bell, *The Afro-American Novel and Its Traditions*, 1987.   —SallyAnn H. Ferguson

BLACK NATIONALISM grew out of the American enslavement of Africans who, after being abducted and brought to America, found that despite their disparate kinship lines, *race unified them on American soil. Black nationalism in America has sought to unify a people without the benefits of a land base—it lacks a physical space for its nation. Although many black nationalists have called for land base plans, for example back to Africa movements and territorial separatist movements within the United States, black nationalism has in great part founded its tenets on common experience rather than a common tie to a geographic region. The *Middle Passage brought Africans from numerous tribal groups; upon arrival in America, families and tribal kin were soon separated. As *slavery grew into an American institution, generations of blacks emerged with few of the cultural links to Africa that their ancestors had known. Blacks in America represented a new people, a people isolated from their long tribal and familial ties in a land that marked them by their skin color. Race and slavery, then, significantly influenced the development of African Americans. Whether slaves or free, blacks found that their hue meant an instant association with slavery and degradation.

Out of this shared experience of oppression, blacks in America became a nation within a nation—a people in, but excluded from, the dominant culture. W. E. B. *Du Bois identified this phenomenon as the "twoness" of the African American *identity. In his 1903 collection of *essays and *short stories, *The *Souls of Black Folk*, Du Bois explains the peculiarity of being both black and American: "One ever feels his twoness—an American, a Negro; two souls, two thoughts, two unreconciled strivings; two warring ideals in one dark body, whose dogged strength alone keeps it from being torn asunder." Du Bois describes the tenuous experience of African Americans—an experience dating back to at least the Revolutionary War. Because blacks fought and died for the American cause in this war, many had hoped that cries for liberty and *freedom would ring for the elimination of America's own injustice.

As America turned a deaf ear to cries from its darker inhabitants, blacks who had the means began self-help organizations for their downtrodden fellows. In the late eighteenth century, black businessmen like Paul *Cuffe and James Forten gave money and time for the aid of less fortunate African Americans. For varied reasons, free blacks like Cuffe and Forten considered their own destinies tied to the overwhelming majority of blacks in bondage. For blacks in America, freedom did not necessarily precipitate assimilation into American culture; on the contrary, it could often mean alienation as well as social and economic deprivation. The isolation that African Americans experienced fostered their unified efforts on a number of fronts; by the middle of the nineteenth century blacks had formed political coalitions, social organizations, *churches, and relief societies. On all fronts the central theme was invariably racial uplift. Blacks denounced the prevailing degenerative *stereotypes that had become woven into the fabric of American thought, and African American leaders found the printed word useful in this mission. Literature proved a powerful tool in this struggle, as it provided a medium for blacks to organize and unite their efforts, as well as to explore and formulate theories of selfhood. From the antebellum period to the present day, black writers have used these theories to varying degrees, magnifying them during times of increased racial tensions, and retracting them when blacks seem to experience periods of high achievement.

Throughout the African presence in America, black nationalism has prevailed as a theory of self-identification. Although its meaning has not remained unchanged, black nationalism in its broadest sense means the collective effort of blacks to secure social, political, and economic rights. Black nationalism presupposes that in America, African ancestry unifies blacks, who must work together as a group to overcome the ill effects of their common experience of oppression. Beyond this rather simple creed the picture of black nationalism becomes hazy, as different leaders and groups have offered varied plans of action for black mobilization. This lack of consensus dates back to the pre–Civil War era when black leaders disagreed and often oscillated on the question of separatism and emigrationism. Frederick *Douglass, who in his abolitionist years argued that blacks should stay in America to secure their freedom, found himself in opposition to black nationalists Martin R. *Delany, Alexander *Crummell, and Henry Highland *Garnet. In a speech entitled "An Address to the Slaves of the United States," delivered before the 1843 National Negro Convention in Buffalo, New York, Garnet illustrated the racial bond that had become the unifying thread of black nationalism. More than half a century before Du Bois spoke of the "twoness" of the African American, Garnet demonstrated his understanding of this dilemma. Though a free man, Garnet dedicated much energy and time to abolitionism, and in this address he made plain his view that black Americans are one people united by their common deprivation of ties to home and family, and their search for a humane existence in the nation that had devalued their ancestral legacies and denied them full membership in its society. Garnet would take his concept of cultural nationalism to encourage blacks to work together as a unified people, and ultimately promoted the idea that blacks should leave America and create their own government on African soil.

Cries for self-help would be repeated often by black leaders, especially those who held to the conviction that blacks constituted a family, a race of people whose destiny was inextricably interdependent. In both his ante- and postbellum writings, Alexander Crummell repeatedly called for blacks to unite their efforts for their own good. As evidenced in his 1855 celebration address on the occasion of Liberia's national independence, Crummell's own form of black nationalism consisted of a combination of biblical prophesy and civilizationism: "The race, in the aggregate, is to go forward and upward. This is the destiny which God has incorporated in the very elements of our moral being" (*Future of Africa*). Decades later and back on American soil, Crummell still extolled the essential virtues and the divine destiny of the black race. He would lead the way for the nationalist propaganda of future generations; in particular, Du Bois and Bishop Henry McNeal Turner would identify him as influential in their racial philosophies. But nationalism in the eyes of these men varied. Whereas Crummell maintained an anchoring in Christian doctrine, Du Bois, as he matured, depended less on biblical prophesy for his form of nationalism. Crummell eventually abandoned his ambitions for a black national base on the African continent, but Du Bois in his later years became disenchanted with America and directed his hopes toward Africa. Henry McNeal Turner first embraced the idea of African emigrationism after hearing a speech by Crummell, and he would remain convinced that the future of African Americans lay in their return to Africa. Turner's many addresses on the question of black *emigration and the special destiny of blacks are included in the 1971 collection of his works, *The Writings and Speeches of Henry McNeal Turner.* After the disappointment of America's failed post-war Reconstruction, Turner believed that blacks would never find justice and social equality in America. Blacks had to return to their homeland, to Africa, where they could establish their own government, their own nation, and engage in self-rule and self-determination. Turner argued that blacks were a nation of people whose homeland was Africa. Their plight in America had paved the way for their Christianization; now that the conversion of blacks was achieved, it was time for their return to their homeland.

The writings of Crummell, Du Bois, and Turner illustrate the diverse foundations of black nationalism—in particular separatism, millennialism, assimilationism, and cultural nationalism. These nationalistic views would find a place in African American literature. Black writers—self-proclaimed nationalists and not so evident nationalists—of both fiction and nonfiction developed narratives around these issues. In both African American fiction and nonfiction, scholars have often credited nineteenth-century black author and abolitionist Martin R. Delany with being one of America's earliest and most celebrated black nationalists. Delany's writings address a number of perspectives of black nationalism. While he committed his efforts to the Civil War and Reconstruction, Delany advocated emigration during the prewar period. He promoted the idea that blacks needed a geographic base, not Africa in particular, but a land base from which they could resurrect themselves as a unified people. His 1852 text, *The Condition, Elevation, Emigration and Destiny of the Colored People of the United States, Politically Considered,* covers in detail his emigrationist philosophy. In *Principia of Ethnology: The Origin of Races and Color* (1879), Delany suggests that race serves as the nationalistic thread that unites black Americans; he proclaims the uniqueness of blacks as a race and credits them with having made significant contributions to humanity. Delany gave his nationalistic vision literary form in his 1859 novel, *Blake, or The Huts of America.* Probably the first black nationalist novel, *Blake* promotes the ideas of racial essentialism, black freedom representing the fulfillment of divine prophesy, and the future separate and self-ruling state of the black race.

Sutton E. *Griggs at the turn of the century would surpass Delany as the black nationalist novelist. Griggs's five novels wrestle with the question of African Americans' place in American society where they constantly face the duality of existence. Although each of these novels demonstrates characteristics of his black nationalist outlook, two in particular, *Imperium in Imperio* (1899) and *The Hindered Hand* (1905), provide in-depth looks at some of the prevailing issues and conflicts in black nationalist doctrine. Both novels address one of the most pressing ideological disputes among black nationalists: should blacks separate themselves physically from the dominant white culture and establish an autonomous government or can they remain physically and idealistically American while simultaneously maintaining a cultural identity? Griggs offers the reader a dubious answer; neither novel unwaveringly affirms either argument. In both *The Hindered Hand* and *Imperium,* Griggs created protagonists who struggle with their love for race and country, and the seeming irreconcilable coexistence of both. In *The Hindered Hand,* Ensall Ellwood desires to be both American and black, and abandons his dream of assimilation into American society only after his experiences lead him to believe that America will never extend her promises of liberty and freedom to her black citizens. Similarly, in *Imperium,* the black conspirators choose separation only after concluding that the dream of black assimilation into American society is futile. Here, too, Griggs presents two opposing faces of black nationalism—Bernard Belgrave, the impatient militant who, disenchanted with America, encourages his fellow conspirators to move hastily in their plan to separate from the United States; and Belton Piedmont, the more meditative leader. Although Piedmont holds fast to the conviction that the common experience of blacks in America has bound them and shaped them into a group—a nation within a nation—he also remains unwilling to abandon his hopes that white America will accept its darker citizens and guarantee them the rights of the Constitution.

Griggs wrote more than twenty years after the end of Reconstruction; the future that had looked so bright at the close of the Civil War had been eclipsed by what historian Rayford Logan called the period of America's lowest race relations—the nadir. By the turn of the century, all blacks, even that small class of wealthy and educated ones, began to question whether white America would ever cease alienating blacks and marking them as the subordinate other. Griggs, along with a number of African American writers, responded to the alienation and discrimination that had become the spirit of the day in turn-of-the-century America. Like Griggs, these writers addressed the controversies among black nationalists and they illustrated the varied and sometimes contradictory philosophical positions that black nationalism might take. In her novel *Contending Forces* (1900), Pauline *Hopkins allows her characters to explore blackness. She clearly argues that blackness is not simply skin color or common ancestry. Several characters in this novel ponder the question of what constitutes a black person in a nation where most blacks are, to some degree, a product of racial mixing. The heroic characters in this novel show that the unifying force, the peculiar circumstance that makes blacks in America a nation, is their common legacy of slavery and oppression. Jesse Montfort, for instance, the son of a white man and a dark-skinned white woman, could have passed for white, but casts his lot instead with the African American community that raised him. After his parents' deaths, Jesse escapes slavery and travels to a Massachusetts town where he settles into a black community. His shared experiences with blacks outweighs his overwhelming physical appearance of whiteness, and he chooses to live as a black man. In addition to her allusions to cultural nationalism, Hopkins presents two characters who represent the assimilationist/separatist debate. In "Will Smith's Defense of His Race," Hopkins has Will respond to popular ideas on the collective goals of the black race. Will argues that blacks in America should not return to Africa, for the chance that they might return to a savage existence would be great. Will promotes the education of blacks and urges them to unite to sway public opinion in the same manner that abolitionists had done before emancipation. Through Will, Harper promotes the idea of cultural nationalism and assimilationism.

Frances Ellen Watkins *Harper's *Iola Leroy* (1892) also demonstrates the growing tide of cultural black nationalism at the turn of the century. Though a black woman, Iola, like many turn-of-the-century black protagonists, has white features: her complexion is white, and she has blue eyes and long hair. But Iola has lived as a slave, although only for a brief interval, and the experience has caused her to align herself unhesitatingly with blacks. She turns down an offer of marriage by a white suitor and assures him that someday blacks will prove themselves a superior people to whites. Harper uses *Iola* to present her own racial sentiments—to assert the essential goodness, bravery, and loyalty of blacks—and to affirm her assimilationist vision. Blacks will become a great nation, a great people, but they will find success only through the fusion of their own ethnic strengths with the referential social rhetoric of the dominant culture.

The writings and legends of Booker T. *Washington and W. E. B. Du Bois represent the most well-known black nationalist debates. Both men understood that the shared legacy of oppression among blacks constituted their cultural bond, but they would ultimately disagree on the primary methods for racial uplift. In his 1901 *autobiography, *Up from Slavery*, Washington used the story of his own life to promote his plan for race progress. Contrary to Du Bois, Washington determined that African American progress could occur only if blacks learned to accommodate whites in the South. He recommended that blacks not agitate for political and social equality, but instead accept their exclusion from mainstream America and work to build themselves up within their own world. In Du Bois's 1903 collected works, *The Souls of Black Folk*, and in his novels *Dark Princess* (1928) and *The *Quest of the Silver Fleece* (1911), he responded to Washington's accommodationist doctrine. Du Bois insisted that blacks need to agitate, to outwardly demand their rights as citizens and human beings. He often employed the doctrine of black essentialism to suggest that blacks were a distinct and separate people within American society. At times he promoted the mythical assertion

that God had preordained the rise of the black race. But whether divinely ordained or the result of common oppression, America's black nation had sprouted from the seeds of American slavery and discrimination.

The *Harlem Renaissance ushered in more assertive and more militant black nationalists. Writers like Langston *Hughes, Claude *McKay, and Zora Neale *Hurston exemplify the shift from the turn-of-the-century black nationalism, which often promoted a racial uplift founded on white constructions of civilization. During the Harlem Renaissance, black writers constructed their models of community by looking back to African civilizations and to the African American culture that had blossomed throughout the United States. Countee *Cullen's poem "Heritage" demonstrates the awakened vision of African American writers as they began to reconsider Africa and its relationship to their existence. "Heritage" suggests that perhaps blacks lost something native and valuable when they substituted Jesus Christ for their own heathen gods. Though none matched Sutton Griggs's preoccupation with a mass black movement, these writers emphasized a departure from the Victorian and genteel traditions. Instead they began to celebrate and acknowledge what they considered the cultural peculiarities of African American life—peculiarities that an earlier generation had considered primal and uncivilized. These writers confirmed the notion of cultural black nationalism, that though black Americans have diverse ancestral ties, they have developed into a nation of people in the United States. This culture is celebrated in the literature of the Harlem Renaissance. In *novels like Claude McKay's *Home to Harlem* (1928) and Zora Neale Hurston's *Their Eyes Were Watching God* (1937), the authors created protagonists who either have tasted white life or have had the opportunity to forsake their black roots for a lifestyle more imitative of white society. In both cases—*Janie Crawford in *Their Eyes Were Watching God* and Jake in *Home to Harlem*—the protagonists show no yearning for acceptance by white America; instead, they elect to live in the black community where they find happiness in spite of the lingering shadow of America's racism.

In *Not Without Laughter* (1930), Langston Hughes affirms the existence of a nurturing, wholesome black community whose identity and values are less vested in the white middle-class ideals to which turn-of-the-century black writers ascribed. The black community in Hughes's novel shows little regard for how whites see them; they are a community of people guided and driven by their own values. His female protagonist, Harriet, best exemplifies this. After working as a prostitute and a singer in a number of questionable places, Harriet finds fame and wealth. But neither the narrator nor Harriet gives much reflection on her sordid past. Like so many blacks in America, Harriet has responded to her limited world of opportunities. She has carved a fruitful existence out of her impoverished beginnings, and with her financial assistance Harriet intends to see that her young nephew, Sandy, will be able to help the black race. While Hughes does not offer the overt nationalist plot evident in Griggs's novels, his message is nevertheless distinctly similar: blacks in America are bound by their common legacy of oppression and will improve their lives by working as a unified people. In *Not Without Laughter,* Sandy exemplifies the model black male who seeks to improve himself in order to contribute to the advancement of the race.

Hughes and McKay also alluded to cultural black nationalism in their *poetry; however, McKay's "If We Must Die" reveals his more militant Garveyite leaning. McKay, a follower of the black nationalist Marcus *Garvey, preferred the Garvey philosophy of territorial separation of blacks from white America. Though most Harlem Renaissance writers extolled the virtues of being black, unlike Garvey they would not recommend that blacks totally sever ties with America. The dream of black assimilation into American society was still very much alive.

The Great Depression and World War II quelled the nationalistic voices of the Harlem Renaissance. World War II renewed hopes of assimilation for black Americans. The fight against the racist Nazi regime compelled African Americans to put aside their thoughts of separatism and their memories of America's exclusionary policies. But the end of the Second World War brought no more promise of the American dream than the end of World War I. By the 1960s, broken dreams had exploded into a new black militant front, and black writers spearheaded the campaign of aggressive agitation. The 1960s introduced louder and more diverse black groups. Black nationalism was once again central to discussions of racial uplift. *Malcolm X, Martin Luther *King, Jr., Elijah Muhammed, Amiri *Baraka, and Stokely *Carmichael were among the more well-known black voices proclaiming their vision of racial progress. Baraka's avant-garde militant poetry exemplifies the black nationalist poetry of this era. In the poetry of writers like Baraka, Nikki *Giovanni, Sonia *Sanchez, Mari *Evans, and Don L. Lee, cries for racial equality become more demanding. Black literary voices are no longer asking for their rights—they are demanding them, and proclaiming loudly their humanity and worth as a people. These artists celebrate blackness but not without apprehension, for they recognize that black cultural nationalism must somehow find its place in the prevailing white culture.

This cultural confrontation—the affirmation of an African American culture within the dominant American culture—also proved central in the writings of acclaimed novelists James *Baldwin, Richard *Wright, and Ralph *Ellison. Their novels show that African Americans exist in a distinct and separate world from that of white America, and in keeping with the militant fervor of the day, they demonstrated in their fiction the possible outcome for American society should it continue to demoralize its black population. These novelists continued the black nationalist ideology that insists on the interdependence of blacks in America, and though not separatists themselves, they explored the implications of black separatism. Though part of the most militant era of black activism in America, these three leading black novelists could not confirm the most rigid black nationalist doctrine. They readily proclaimed a black cultural nationalism, but they saw the African American's past and future as intricately woven seams in the fiber of American society. This black militant literature would argue once again that the overwhelming dilemma of black Americans is to maintain those cultural values that keep them a unified force while simultaneously seeking a significant place in American culture. Although the separatist form of nationalism appears and reappears with fluctuations in race relations, cultural nationalism has remained since its birth in the early years of African American history, and has consistently found expression through voices in African American literature.

[*See also* Black Aesthetic; Identity; Miscegenation; Pan-Africanism; Protest Literature.]

• Alexander Crummell, *The Future of Africa,* 1862. Alexander Crummell, *Africa and America,* 1891. W. E. B. Du Bois, *The Souls of Black Folk,* 1903. E. U. Essien-Udom, *Black Nationalism: A Search for an Identity in America,* 1962. John A. Bracey, Jr., August Meier, and Elliott Rudwick, eds., *Black Nationalism in America,* 1970. Peter R. Ullman, *Martin R. Delany: The Beginnings of Black Nationalism,* 1971. Floyd J. Miller, *The Search for a Black Nationality: Black Emigration and Colonization 1787–1863,* 1975. Wilson Jeremiah Moses, *Golden Age of Black Nationalism 1850–1925,* 1978. Wilson Jeremiah Moses, *Black Messiahs and Uncle Toms,* 1982. Wilson Jeremiah Moses, *The Wings of Ethiopia: Studies in African-American Life and Letters,* 1990.

—Elizabeth J. West

Black No More. George *Schuyler's first *novel, originally published in 1931 by the Macaulay Company and reissued in 1989 by Northeastern University Press, *Black No More* is generally considered the first full-length satire by an African American. In *Black No More,* Schuyler fictionalizes the political ideas that he was best known for: outrage at the notion that *race makes difference and at America's social stratification based on race. While society searched for a solution to the "race problem," Schuyler, in this anti-utopian novel, uses satire and science fiction to reveal that race was not the problem.

His satire is aimed specifically at myths of racial purity and white supremacy and presents ways in which the perpetuation of racism serves economic purposes. Greed is the primary motivation of his characters. He caricatures organizations such as the NAACP, the KKK, and the Urban League, presenting their leaders as hustlers in different shades.

In the preface, Schuyler dedicates *Black No More* to all of the "pure Caucasians" of the world, setting up any such readers for a shock. We are then introduced to Max Disher, a brown *trickster, and his sidekick, Bunny Brown, and the racist environment in which they live. Max is rejected by a racist white woman, Helen, who is entertained by black cabaret performers but is repulsed at the idea of dancing with a black man. This rejection sends Max to Dr. Crookman, inventor of Black-No-More, Inc., where all traces of blackness are removed and Max becomes Matt. The rest of the novel traces Max's adventures as a Caucasian: he marries the same Helen that previously rejected him, and with Bunny, infiltrates the major racist organization of the country, extorts millions of dollars, and finally flees to Europe. The reader is also privy to the effects of the runaway success of Black-No-More, Inc., on American society. As the black population is changed to white, black race leaders are put out of the "leadership" business; as America loses its cheap black labor, an increasingly violent labor situation erupts; and lying-in hospitals are created to secretly change newborns to white. In an attempt to decipher a "proper" race hierarchy, scientists discover that over half of the Caucasian population has "tainted" blood, including those who most advocated racial purity. Just as America goes wild with frenzy, Dr. Crookman brings order by revealing that the "newly" white are actually two to three shades lighter than the "real" Caucasians. Suddenly white is no longer right and everyone panics while sales increase for skin-darkening lotions. "Normality" is returned at the end of the novel with black being beautiful. Schuyler makes clear that there are advantages to possessing white skin in a society that worships this, but human nature does not change purely because of skin color.

—Adenike Marie Davidson

BLACK POWER MOVEMENT. *See* Black Arts Movement.

Black Scholar, The. The *Black Scholar, Journal of Black Studies and Research*, was founded in 1969 by Robert Chrisman, Nathan Hare, and Allan Ross. Chrisman continues as editor in chief and publisher, Robert L. Allen as senior editor. The *Black Scholar's* contributing and advisory editors have included authors James *Baldwin, Melba *Boyd, Conyus, Jayne *Cortez, Pinkie Gordon *Lane, John O. *Killens, Audre *Lorde, Michael S. *Harper, Haki R. *Madhubuti, Nancy Morejon, Andrew Salkey, Sonia *Sanchez, David L. Smith, Hortense J. Spillers, and Michael *Thelwell.

In those issues focused on literature, the *Black Scholar* emphasizes original work over *criticism and publishes new authors, although it reviews books regularly. Besides the editors, authors and critics published include Maya *Angelou, Amiri *Baraka, Toni Cade *Bambara, Gwendolyn *Brooks, Cecil *Brown, Ed *Bullins, Rita *Dove, Henry *Dumas, Mari *Evans, Ernest J. *Gaines, Lance *Jeffers, Gayl *Jones, Woodie *King, Jr., Etheridge *Knight, George Lamming, Clarence *Major, Adam D. Miller, Larry *Neal, Eugene *Redmond, Ishmael *Reed, Charles Rowell, Ntozake *Shange, Quincy Thomas *Troupe, Jr., Darwin G. Turner, Alice *Walker, Margaret *Walker, John A. *Williams, and Sherley Anne *Williams. Among Latin American and African writers published are Chinua Achebe, Miguel Barnet, Dennis Brutus, Lisandro Chavez, Nicolas Guillen, Keorapetse Kgostisile, and Ngugi wa Thiongo. The Black Scholar Press publishes volumes on an irregular basis. Poetry titles include *I've Been a Woman,* by Sonia Sanchez (1978); *Children of Empire,* by Robert Chrisman (1981); *In the Hills Where Her Dreams Live,* by Andrew Salkey (1981); *Where the Island Sleeps Like a Wing,* by Nancy Morejon (1985); *A Tree Beyond*

Telling, by Kenneth McClane (1983); and *Cowboy Amok* (1987) and *Civil Rites* (1996), by D. L. Crockett-Smith. The *Black Scholar* issued six to ten numbers per year through 1989, but became a quarterly in 1990. The *Black Scholar* is published in Oakland, California, by the Black World Foundation, an independent, nonprofit corporation.

[*See also* Periodicals, *article on* Scholarly Journals and Literary Magazines.]   —Robert Chrisman

BLACK STUDIES. Broadly speaking, according to Abdul Alkalimat and associates' *Introduction to Afro-American Studies* (1986), Black Studies can be defined as "an academic field which combines general intellectual history, academic scholarship in the social sciences and the humanities, and a radical movement for fundamental educational reform." This discipline, as we know it, resulted from the Black Power movement of the 1960s. As Black citizens pushed U.S. society to address their exclusion from mainstream America, the number of Black college students increased sharply and programs were developed to serve their needs. Black Studies emerged in response to Black students' demand for a "relevant" *education.

Introduction to Afro-American Studies has also popularized a history of Black Studies in four stages of development: innovation, experimentation, crisis, and consolidation/professionalization. It is imperative to understand that the first stage—"Social Innovation"—began in the period of intense social turmoil that characterized the United States in the late 1960s. This led to experimentation, in which hundreds of colleges and universities evolved new models for administration, curriculum, pedagogy, research, and community service. With declining interest in race relations and a downturn in the U.S. economy that forced cutbacks in higher education in the 1980s, Black Studies programs were unfortunately among those considered expendable, and a period of crisis emerged. Intent on maintaining an institutionalized presence in higher education, many Black Studies practitioners have been developing professional standards to consolidate the field during the 1990s. But the main promise and the continuing challenge of Black Studies is not to be found in its administrative consolidation, but in the intellectual gauntlet it laid before higher education. St. Clair Drake supplied a pithy summary of this central intellectual and academic mission in a 1969 address to Brooklyn College:

> The very use of the term Black Studies is by implication an indictment of American and Western European scholarship. It makes the bold assertion that what we have heretofore called "objective" intellectual activities were actually white studies in perspective and content; and that corrective bias, a shift in emphasis, is needed, even if something called "truth" is set as a goal. To use a technical sociological term, the present body of knowledge has an ideological element in it, and a counter-ideology is needed. Black Studies supply that counter-ideology.

The historical roots of Black Studies extend much further back than the 1960s. Harry Greene's *Holders* of *Doctorates Among American Negroes* (1946), which lists all doctorates between 1876 and 1943, shows a large number of dissertations focused on the Black experience: 56 percent of the seventy-seven in the social sciences, 67 percent of seventy-one in education, 21 percent of forty-three in language and literature, and 15 percent of twenty-six in psychology and philosophy. Most of these early Black scholars were located in historically Black colleges and universities, or HBCUs, as they came to be called. The historical importance of such colleges and universities in the study of the Black experience and the development of a solid foundation for the new discipline has been underestimated by most contemporary Black Studies scholars and almost completely ignored by others. Black colleges were the sites upon which evolved other precursors of the modern Black Studies movement. Several notable professional organizations emerged as Black scholars sought to counter the racism that prevented them from being full participants in the academic mainstream. Among the notable examples were the Association for the Study of Negro Life and History, founded by historian Carter G. *Woodson in 1915; the Southern Association of Dramatic and Speech Arts, founded in 1936 by Randoph Edwards at Dillard University, initially formed as the Negro Intercollegiate Dramatic Association in 1930; and the Association of Teachers of English in Negro Colleges, founded by Hugh Gloster at LeMoyne College in 1937 and known as the College Language Association since 1941.

HBCUs were and are hosts to several major journals as well. Among the oldest are the *Journal of Negro History* (1916), *Phylon* (founded at Atlanta University by W. E. B. *Du Bois in 1940), and the *CLA Journal* (led by Therman O'Daniel at Morgan State in 1957). A survey, published in the Howard University–based *Journal of Negro Education*, reported that scholars based at historically Black institutions continue to play the leading role in the editorial direction and in the publications of articles in Black Studies–related journals. A popular magazine that cannot be ignored in any complete history of Black Studies is *Negro Digest*, edited by Hoyt Fuller between 1942 and 1970. Conferences sponsored by professional organizations and by community-based institutions are undervalued in the important role they have played in Black Studies, a fact that reflects the failure to publish proceedings.

In the 1990s, Black Studies programs exist on many campuses and in many diverse forms. Estimates by the National Council of Black Studies and others indicate that hundreds of campuses offer majors and minors in Black Studies and that few campuses in the United States do not offer at least one course in this subject area. However, attempts by budget-cutting college administrators to dismantle or merge Black Studies departments and programs are increasing. But the impact and practice of Black Studies are much more pervasive than any quantitative survey of Black Studies departments can measure.

One significant feature of Black Studies that was well ahead of similar trends in other disciplines has been its interdisciplinary (or multidisciplinary or cross-disciplinary) nature. This was formalized in a report on national curriculum standards adopted by the National Council for Black Studies in 1989. For majors and minors in Black Studies, the proposed standard argued for introductory and advanced courses in three disciplinary groupings: historical studies, cultural studies, and social and behavioral studies. In addition, the proposal called for a broad introductory course that would familiarize students with core knowledge from each of the three groupings and a senior "capstone" seminar that would allow reflection and synthesis of the knowledge gained and an assessment of the usefulness of this knowledge for future professional and personal endeavors.

Black Studies also emphasized studying the Black experience as a way to help transform social conditions facing Black people and the broader society. While other disciplines valued knowledge for its own sake and emphasized "objectivity," Black Studies adopted this more utilitarian view of the knowledge it was to produce. This general relationship was captured in a motto developed by Alkalimat and Bailey and adopted by the National Council for Black Studies: "Academic Excellence and Social Responsibility."

For years, the National Council for Black Studies has been the leading organization in the field. However, much of the dynamism that characterized this group's early years subsided as younger scholars with an interest in Black Studies gravitated toward the "mainstream" professional organizations in their fields. Other Black organizations that helped shape the field are the African Heritage Studies Association, the National Council of Black Political Scientists, the National Association of Black School Educators, and SCASI—the Southern Conference on Afro-American Studies, Inc.

Literature and literary studies have always been key in the study of the Black experience. Literature, especially with increasing *literacy rates and educational levels, has historically been an accessible and more enduring vehicle for self-expression among Black people. Writings have been left that can be appropriated and studied by succeeding generations of scholars. In "The Black Academic and Southern Literature" Blyden Jackson reminds us that many of the influential teachers and scholars of literature, particularly in the South, have also been writers: Melvin B. *Tolson, J. Saunders *Redding, Sterling A. *Brown, Margaret *Walker, and M. Carl Holman. Many of their students emerged as writers, thus extending the impact of these university-based educators.

Moreover, the major historical periods of the Black experience—from Africa to the slave trade, from *slavery through the emancipation period to rural life, and through *migration to the period of urban life—have provided both the substantive content and the shaping influences for African American literature since the 1700s. The major literary movements among African Americans—the *Harlem Renaissance or New Negro movement, the depression era/WPA movement, and the *Black Arts movement—continue to serve as key topics in any comprehensive study of the Black experience, including major themes, cultural artists, and issues of aesthetics and cultural production.

The *CLA Journal (founded 1957), a journal of literary scholars in Black Studies, illustrates important points about the contours of Black Studies scholarship. During the journal's first decade more than half of its articles were "racially oriented," according to Blyden Jackson. In its second decade, the ratio increased to three racially oriented articles for every one that was not, and seventeen special issues of the journal between 1969 and 1976 dealt with some aspect of Black Studies. These trends, which could be more thoroughly examined, illustrate that Black Studies has historically endeavored to provide the intellectual and academic space for Black people to "tell their own story," and at the same time to facilitate a rewriting and reconceptualization of all of American and world history and society.

In *Propaganda and Aesthetics* (1979), Abby Arthur Johnson and Ronald M. Johnson point to another key source of literature's impact on Black Studies: the literary materials contained in African-American magazines in the twentieth century. These publications include the *Crisis, *Opportunity, the *Messenger, *Fire!!, Challenge, Negro Quarterly, Negro Story, *Phylon, Harlem Quarterly, and others. "More than mere magazines, . . . [they] have provided black writers with an outlet for their work and have thereby participated in the shaping of Black literature and culture. At the same time they have recorded basic concerns of each period and become historical documents in their own right."

Given the importance of literature in Black Studies, it should not be surprising that literary studies is the source of the most innovative "archaeology" efforts to recover lost or fugitive material. The two most notable are the Afro-American *Novel Project, later renamed the History of Black Writing Project, under the direction of Maryemma Graham at Northeastern University in Boston, and the Black Periodical Literature Project based at Harvard University under the direction of Henry Louis Gates, Jr.

However the history of the field of Black Studies is summed up, its future will inevitably be shaped by and will shape both the theorizing and the practice related to the dynamics of race relations over the next few decades. There are deteriorating conditions of physical survival faced by the masses of Black people. There is the persisting and even growing reality of racism—both in ideology and in physical attacks; the struggle on the ideological front that has always provided Black Studies with its credibility will thus continue to be a dynamic one. There are also fundamental shifts in the international arena that affect the lives of people in Africa and in the Caribbean and throughout the African diaspora, where the struggle for both political and economic democratization is raging. Many of the ideological debates in Black Studies will be judged, ultimately, in terms of their contribution to present-day struggles for freedom, democracy, and development. Finally, there are stirrings reminiscent of the civil rights era, most dramatically illustrated in the October 1995 Million Man

March and the 1996 Stand for Children Rally, both in Washington, D.C. Thus, the conditions facing Black people, and the ideological and political differences within the Black community and among other potential allies of the Black freedom struggle, are such that Black Studies will be expected to contribute to an intellectual foundation for forging greater unity. Fueled by increasing attacks on affirmative action, a deepening social crisis, and increased community-based activism, student interest in Black Studies is likely to increase. For Black Studies to remain a positive and forward-moving force in higher education and in the broader society, its commitment both to academic excellence and to social responsibility must be strengthened.

• Floyd B. Barbour, ed., *The Black Power Revolt: A Collection of Essays*, 1968. Armstead Robinson et al., *Black Studies in the University: A Symposium*, 1969. John W. Blassingame, *New Perspectives in Black Studies*, 1973. Nick Aaron Ford, *Black Studies: Threat or Challenge*, 1973. Molefi Kete Asante, *Afrocentricity*, 1980. Johnella E. Butler, *Black Studies: Pedagogy and Revolution*, 1981. Maulana Karenga, *Introduction to Black Studies*, 1982. Gerald McWorter and Ronald Bailey, "Black Studies Curriculum Development in the 1980s: Its Patterns and History," *Black Scholar* 15.2 and 15.6 (Mar.–Apr. and Nov.–Dec. 1984). Abdul Alkalimat, *Paradigms in Black Studies*, 1993.
—Ronald W. Bailey

Black Theatre. A journal published intermittently by the New Lafayette Theatre in Harlem, *Black Theatre* served the entire Black Theater movement as a forum where its emerging philosophy and techniques were proclaimed and fiercely debated. Its editor, and the theater's playwright in residence, Ed *Bullins, was one of the period's most talented and prolific dramatists; *Black Theatre*'s staff and contributors included such pivotal figures in the *Black Arts movement as Amiri *Baraka, Larry *Neal, Askia M. *Touré, Sonia *Sanchez, Woodie *King, Jr., Ben *Caldwell, Maulana Ron Karenga, and New Lafayette Theatre director Robert Macbeth. Each of the issues (simply numbered one through six and published between 1968 and 1972) reported on black *theater activity around the United States; the final two issues included reports from Jamaica and Nigeria. All included *poetry and dramatic scripts; several contained transcripts of symposia on critical debates related to black theater, some of which were sponsored by the New Lafayette. Striking illustrations, woodcuts, and etchings adorned each issue. Upon the collapse of the New Lafayette Theatre, the journal ceased, yet *Black Theatre* remains an invaluable source of black theater history.

[See also Drama; Periodicals, *article on* Scholarly Journals and Literary Magazines.]
—Leslie Catherine Sanders

Black Thunder. Arna Bontemps's novel *Black Thunder: Gabriel's Revolt: Virginia 1800* was published in 1936. This conflation of *history and imagination is based on an actual slave rebellion reported in contemporary newspapers and recorded in the *Calendar of Virginia State Papers* (vol. 9, 1890). The chronicle begins in the great house of old Moseley Sheppard whose dependence on old Ben Woodfolk, his faithful house servant, has developed over the years into veiled companionship. Old Bundy, Ben's work-worn counterpart, once a fieldhand on the neighboring plantation but now reduced to scavenging throughout the neighborhood, intrudes on Ben's peace to beg for rum and surreptitiously to invite him to join the slave Gabriel's scheme for *insurrection. It is old Bundy's misfortune to be observed with his jug of rum by Thomas Prosser, his merciless master, who uses the excuse to beat him to death.

Bundy's murder adds fresh resolve to Gabriel's plans and subverts the comfort of reluctant individuals like old Ben. Indeed, Gabriel had chosen the occasion of Bundy's funeral to elaborate his strategy to amass some eleven hundred men and one woman to take the city of Richmond in their first step toward *freedom. The remarkable funeral seems to emerge from a collective preliterate tradition whose origins are African and whose inspiration to freedom arises from the natural world. Under these conditions, old Ben swears allegiance to the conspiracy in the presence of the principal plotters, at first with apprehension and then with deep trepidation.

Gabriel, the strapping six-foot two-inch coachman for Thomas Prosser, had earned the respect of slaves and "free" blacks throughout Henrico County, Virginia, about a year earlier by winning a titan's battle with Ditcher, the brutal driver of slaves from another plantation. Gabriel wins fealty for his resoluteness and a generosity of spirit, which appeals to persons as diverse as Mingo, the literate freeman, and the tempestuous Juba, Gabriel's woman; he finds personal inspiration in the proclamation of General Toussaint *L'Ouverture, the Haitian liberator, who still lived, and in biblical text read aloud by Mingo.

At the appointed hour of insurrection, a relentless, unprecedented downpour transforms Henrico County into a flood plain; Gabriel's insurgents find it impossible to execute their grand design and are forced to pull back in favor of a more propitious time. The delay, however, is sufficient to uncover the treachery of Pharoah, who immediately snatches the opportunity to turn informant. Out of loyalty to Moseley Sheppard, old Ben confesses his role and names leaders.

Across the nation amazement accompanies alarm, for it is inconceivable that illiterate chattel are capable of conceiving such a scheme on their own. Every literate white person who is not native to the region is suspect, as Scotsman John Callender, friend of Thomas Jefferson, rudely learns. Frenchman M. Creuzot, printer, is particularly imperiled and flees north for his safety. Before long all the major figures in the conspiracy, including Gabriel, are captured and hung. Pharoah, meanwhile, literally loses his mind, but perfidious old Ben endures, however uneasily.

Richard *Wright generously noted in his 1936 review that Black Thunder broke new ground in African American fiction by addressing concerns not previously touched upon in African American novels. Most critics readily concur that given its myriad voices and many points of view, the controlling idea of the novel is its universal determination toward freedom, a principle that warrants their generous attention to its political purpose. Others, however, noting its contribution to the vernacular tradition, cite meaningful distinctions between *literacy and orality as racial and cultural markers.

[See also Historical Novel; Slavery.]

• Mary Kemp Davis, "From Death Unto Life: The Rhetorical Function of Funeral Rites in Arna Bontemps' Black Thunder," Journal of Ritual Studies 1 (Jan. 1987): 85–101. Daniel Reagan, "Voices of Silence: The Representation of Orality in Arna Bontemps' Black Thunder," Studies in American Fiction 19 (Spring 1991): 71–83. Arnold Rampersad, introduction to the 1992 ed., and Arna Bontemps, introduction to the 1968 ed., Black Thunder: Gabriel's Revolt: Virginia 1800, 1992.
—Charles L. James

Black World. See First World.

BLACUS, HENRICO. See Henry Blake.

Blake. Martin R. *Delany's Blake, or the Huts of America: A Tale of the Mississippi Valley, the Southern United States, and Cuba is an awkward, brave, and complex *novel. Twenty-six chapters from a promised eighty appeared in the *Anglo-African Magazine (Jan.–July 1859); and, after revisions, the complete tale appeared in the Weekly Anglo-African Newspaper (New York City, Nov. 1861–June 1862). Installments appeared on the front pages; the American Baptist said Blake was "beautifully written"; both Anglo-African introductions encouraged blacks to read it. In part, however, because issues including the last six chapters have been lost, today Blake's realistic portrayal of white carelessness and oppression of black people across the African diaspora is more impressive than its romantic dream of deliverance.

Out of print until 1970 and still lacking an unmodernized critical edition, Blake has received complaints about its untrained author's shortcomings: awkward, complex plots and sentences, lack of narrative bridges, inadequate descriptions of action, and a too often passively observant hero. Others have enthusiastically praised Blake's informative range of midcentury sociopolitical conditions, characters, attitudes, and boldly black-nationalist, Pan-African perspective. Fewer have recognized its fifty black-originated or adopted songs and poems, or its varied vernaculars and *folklore pointed out in Delany's footnotes and in conversations that are Blake's major story-telling vehicle.

Its plot is complicated. Part 1's first chapter introduces international characters involved in the illegal slave trade. On a Mississippi plantation the novel's unadulterated black hero, Henry (who uses several surnames), finds his slave wife has been sold away to Cuba. He complains about false Christians, confronts his master, and considers running away, but decides instead to organize a slave rebellion conspiracy. He travels through twelve southern states and Indian Territory creating cadres of comrades—male and female—ready to strike upon his signal. He returns to lead his son and wife's parents north to Canada. Part 1 ends with Henry going to New York City and thence to Cuba.

In Part 2, the hero, who now calls himself *Henry Blake, organizes Cuba, rescues his wife, enlists the *mulatto elite, works on a slave ship to and from Africa, attempts to turn Africans against the trade, returns to Cuba, and arranges sales of the cargo to coconspirators in his antiwhite revolution.

Blake enlarges Emerson's call for an American epic (1842) and answers African American calls for literature by their own (1844–1854) as it touches all shores known to African Americans. Negatively, *Blake* borrows the doomed tones of Byronic romances and his own *Condition of the Colored People* (1852) and revives two historical heroes dead long before 1850 (Blake from Haiti's General Charles Belair, and Plácido [Gabriel Valdés] from Cuba). Positively, its hero bravely struggles before rescuing his wife as in the *Odyssey*; he is like a *Moses and a looked-for savior from the Bible and black folklore, while occasional footnotes ground hopeful scenes in Delany's personal experiences.

Blake's black hero and its emphasis admit no white abolitionists or *underground railroad agents, revising tales of light-skinned heroes and white allies in *slave narratives and by contemporary mulatto storytellers Frederick *Douglass, William Wells *Brown, George B. *Vashon, and Frank J. *Webb. Its *Afrocentricity counters Euro-centered tales of slave rebels by such whites as Edgar Allan Poe, Richard Hildreth, Harriet Beecher *Stowe, Herman Melville, and J. B. Jones.

[*See also* Black Nationalism; Diasporic Literature; Insurrections; Pan-Africanism.]

• Martin R. Delany, *Blake, or the Huts of America*, ed. Floyd J. Miller, 1970. Kristin Herzog, *Women, Ethnics and Exotics: Images of Power in Mid-Nineteenth Century American Fiction*, 1983. Bernard W. Bell, *The Afro-American Novel and Its Tradition*, 1987. Paul Gilroy, *The Black Atlantic: Modernity and Double Consciousness*, 1993. Eric J. Sundquist, *To Wake the Nations: Race in the Making of American Literature*, 1993.

—Allan D. Austin

BLEDSOE, DR. Dr. Bledsoe, the president of the college from which Ralph *Ellison's narrator is expelled in *Invisible Man* (1952), is pivotal to the *novel's structure, for it is Bledsoe who ejects the narrator out of his idyllic setting into the harsh world of reality. It is also Bledsoe who gives the narrator the false sense of security in the letters of recommendation, intended literally to keep the narrator running. In addition to his structural function in the novel, Bledsoe represents the type of leadership that Ellison believed to be detrimental to the development of Blacks. Ellison maintains in *Shadow and Act* (1964) that when he started writing *Invisible Man* he was displeased with the leadership in the Black community: "It seemed to me that [Black leaders] acknowledged no final responsibility to the Negro community for their acts and implicit in their roles were constant acts of betrayal. This made for a sad, chronic division between their values and the values of those they were supposed to represent." Bledsoe typifies the negative qualities of Black leadership. He is a dishonest, Machiavellian schemer. Not only does he have the narrator and the physician at the Golden Day shipped out of his area because they threaten his stability, but he also informs the narrator that he has "played the nigger" to acquire the power and the prestige of his position. He affirms: ". . . I'll have every Negro in the county hanging on a tree limb by morning if it means staying where I am." Such ruthlessness makes Bledsoe a threat to the stability of the community, for it is obvious that he is willing to sacrifice that community in order to maintain power.

It seems too that Bledsoe has alienated himself from the people he serves. In discussing the narrator's punishment with Mr. *Norton, he says to the trustee, "You can't be soft with these people. We mustn't pamper them." The Blacks he serves have become "these people," not "my people," and his use of "we" clearly indicates that he associates himself not with Blacks but with the white power structure. Bledsoe is only concerned with his personal interests. Through his character, Ellison seems to attack much of what is negative in Black leadership.

—Ralph Reckley, Sr.

BLUES. The blues is arguably the most influential art form of the twentieth century. Born as a genre of improvisatory secular song among African Americans of the rural South, it has played a decisive role since World War I in American *music, literature, and other art forms. It draws on central features of African American style, including testifying; call and response; improvisation; blue notes; intensity of expression; and vital, embodied rhythms. This is true to such an extent that the blues has been considered, like the *spiritual, as reaching inward to the very core of African American life. At the same time, with its flexibility of style, simplicity of means, and expressive power, it has reached outward to touch generations of Americans of every background. For these reasons the blues is also a common theme, and a common thread, running through twentieth-century African American literature. With its elements of suffering, survival, and social communication, it has stood for many writers as a powerful symbol, or proof, of the flourishing of African American *identity in an oppressive environment. It has also been seen, increasingly, as an agent of African American cultural autonomy.

The precise origins of the blues, deeply embedded in oral culture of the prerecorded era, are mysterious. Some elements ultimately derive from African and European sources; more immediately, the blues is indebted to earlier African American musical genres, including *spirituals and work songs. But as a specific form and genre, the blues is distinctive. Secular in subject matter, it is a confessional, lyrical song, cast in a unique poetic and musical form, and usually treating the subjects of love and sex. Judging by extant documentation, it first appears in the 1890s, sung and played by self-taught musicians in simple taverns or on street corners. The principal catalyst for its emergence at that time may have been the maturing of African Americans born after the Civil War, a generation surrounded by the paradox of new freedom and mobility on the one hand, and increasingly harsh exploitation and marginalization on the other. Just so, the blues seem uncannily to distill the theme of self-determination, set in a context of social adversity and expressed through the universal currency of intimate personal relationships.

The earliest published blues, however, are not folk blues, but rather the popular versions of African American cornetist and bandleader W. C. Handy (1873–1958), "Father of the Blues." By his own account, Handy had heard the blues in the black camps and taverns of Mississippi in 1903: he found them strange, monotonous, dissonant, but packed with commercial potential. His "St. Louis Blues" (1914), perhaps the most famous of all blues, was published as sheet music, as were many of his compositions. Handy's reaction to folk blues—that it was intriguing, but also marginal and in need of "polishing" to be acceptable—reflects the attitude of leading African American writers of the period, including W. E. B. *Du Bois (1868–1963) and James Weldon *Johnson (1871–1938), who called for the raising of African American art up from its folk roots and into an American mainstream permeated by European American values. The blues, from this perspective, was held to be secondary to the spiritual in significance, if not dismissible altogether. The spiritual, embodying dignity, tradition, profound religiosity, and a certain autonomy of black culture, could also serve to represent an ideal of harmonious existence within the larger white society, which had embraced it in its tamer, "parlor" form. The blues could not be accommodated to any such model: commonly described as "weird" in sound, arising from marginal elements even in black society, and opposed, within that society, to the strictures of a proper, church-going life, it seemed altogether volatile, Dionysian, and profane. The two genres drew on common musical and expressive roots, influenced each other, and were often performed by the same musicians, but they were precisely opposed: Saturday night, as the dictum goes, versus Sunday morning.

The form of blues Handy popularized is by far the most common blues form and is often called "standard" or "twelve-bar" blues. It is also called "classic" or "city" blues, when sung in the styles of vaudeville and early *jazz. Its stanzaic form is in three verses, of which the first two are identical or slightly varied, producing an *aab* structure (rhyme scheme: *aaa*). Each verse is set to four bars of music, with a fixed harmonic progression; as sung, the verse is of such a length as to last for a little over two bars, leaving roughly two bars that act as an accompanimental response or respite. Together, the three statements make a total of twelve bars for the entire stanza. The number of stanzas is not predetermined, but depends on the song, or on the performer's improvised choice. Close variants of the standard form, including refrain blues, and also the sixteen-, eight-, and thirty-two-bar blues, differ in the relative length of their musical and poetic phrases, but retain the same underlying chord progression (I IV I V I).

In 1917 the blues burst onto the national scene again from a new musical angle and via a fresh medium: the first recordings of New Orleans jazz, made by the white Original Dixieland Jazz Band (ODJB). Entirely instrumental, their "Livery Stable Blues" follows the standard blues form, but is faster, more raucous, and abounds in African American traits that could not have been easily represented in sheet music, including blue notes, animal cries, improvised syncopation, and spontaneous polyphony. The highlighting of blues by the ODJB reflects its essential role in jazz; it also shows that the blues could be a form of dance music and of improvisatory instrumental music. Distinctly audible in the ODJB and other early jazz recordings are the most commonly named melodic feature of the blues, its "blue notes." These are places in the melodic spectrum—falling, in scalar terms, between the major and minor third, between the perfect and flatted fifth, and between the major and minor seventh—where pitch is not absolutely fixed, but may land at different points or slide around. A great deal of the expressivity characteristic of blues melody depends upon the inflection of these notes, which allow the singing voice to wail, moan, or approximate spoken inflection without losing any of its musicality. The fact that blue notes are so closely related to African American speech inflections and are found in such a broad range of African American music, including *sermons and preaching, spirituals, songs, and instrumental music of all kinds, indicates how integral the blues is to African American music and expression.

By 1920 the growing migration of African Americans out of the South had created a vast market for commercialized black music. That year, the runaway success of the first recording of sung blues ("Crazy Blues," by Mamie Smith) opened the eyes of the thoroughly white-dominated record industry and led to the first large-scale recording of black performers. By 1923 a new marketing category, "race records," was established for the African American public. The relatively abstract and fluid media of recordings and radio also allowed African American music to reach into other communities, and soon blues and jazz, performed by African Americans, gained tremendous influence on popular musical styles around the country. This was the period of the most pronounced blues craze, which reached its peak in the mid-1920s, when Bessie *Smith (1894–1937, the "Empress of the Blues") made many of her best recordings. In 1926, prompted once again by an unexpected enthusiasm from black audiences, recording companies began to concentrate on a less polished kind of blues that is known today as "folk," "rural," or "downhome" blues. More revelatory of the earliest vocal blues styles, folk blues contrasted with vaudeville blues in its greater irregularity of form, its more shouted, crying, or slurred style of delivery, and its consistently simple accompaniments (most often a guitar, less often a piano). It was also dominated by male singers. Tradition, seconded by scholarship, differentiates between regional styles of southern folk blues, including the Texas, Delta (Mississippi), and (eastern) Piedmont styles. Among the leading proponents of early folk blues were Blind Lemon Jefferson (from Texas; 1897–1929) and Charley Patton (from Mississippi; 1887–1934).

Younger writers active in the 1920s, the period of

the *Harlem Renaissance, embraced the blues. Zora Neale *Hurston, Sterling A. *Brown, and Langston *Hughes, in particular, found it to be essential to African American folk culture; all three collected it and used its images, language, and rhythms in their writings. Hughes's poem "The Weary Blues" (1924), providing the title for his first anthology of poems, stands as a landmark in this development. Filtering the blues through a heightened literary language, he proclaims it as central to, and inalienable from, a distinct and elemental African American identity.

The Great Depression marked a significant turning point in American cultural life. In the cities, large dance halls proliferated; new, sophisticated dance steps such as the Lindy Hop emerged; and the urbane jazz style called "swing," featuring large, virtuosic, and tightly knit big bands fronted by debonair showmen, swept the country. Blues was an essential element in swing jazz, but rougher blues styles, played in jook joints and Saturday night parties, also continued to flourish. This bifurcation of stylistic directions, between smooth sophistication and rough intensity, had important consequences. By the later 1940s, the cutting edge of swing had yielded a new jazz style of unprecedented virtuosity called bebop, while the ongoing dance-hall styles of blues had produced a new niche in the recording market, called rhythm and blues. From this point, the history of jazz, while still drawing strongly on the blues, would continue in the direction of an intellectually challenging, but commercially marginal, listener's music, while rhythm and blues, sold to a national audience and imitated by white performers in the mid-1950s, would engender the unprecedented market phenomenon of rock 'n' roll. As a distinct genre, the blues also held its own, but became increasingly urbanized. The careers of Muddy Waters (McKinley Morganfield, 1915–1983) and B. B. ("Blues Boy") King (b. 1925) are emblematic in this respect. First recorded on a rural Mississippi plantation in 1941, Waters moved north to Chicago's South Side, where he added electrical amplification and a strong beat to traditional Mississippi style. His hard, impassioned sound had a profound influence on later developments in rock music. By contrast, B. B. King, the most famous postwar blues musician, went in the opposite direction with a sweeter guitar sound, rich with bent notes, responding to a crying vocal style with jazz-influenced, string- or horn-band accompaniment. King rejected the more explicit sexual and violent elements common in traditional and Chicago-style blues lyrics in favor of a cleaner image more compatible with the popular mainstream.

The multiple functions of blues-related music, heard more than ever in everyday life, are eloquently reflected in postwar African American writings. Blues features prominently in the work of writers such as James *Baldwin and Ralph *Ellison, both as subject and context (e.g., Baldwin's "Sonny's Blues") and as a medium through which many subjects and feelings may be projected (e.g., the treatment of jazz in the prologue to Ellison's *Invisible Man, 1952). Woven through a discourse by, for, and about African Americans, it offers the key to a popular identity that,

still oppressed by the evils of a divided society, is more forcefully resistant to them and, at times, simply immune to them.

Since the 1950s, the blues continues to provide a profound impetus to every major innovation in African American music, including those of free jazz, soul, funk, fusion, gospel, rap, and hip-hop. Meanwhile, among African American writers, the blues has been promoted, more than ever, as an essential source of African American identity. From the time of the *civil rights movement, writers such as Amiri *Baraka and Larry *Neal have tied the blues to an agenda of radical self-determination in which European American culture is sharply criticized or rejected so that of African Americans can flourish on its own terms. Grounded in a traditional oral culture leading directly back to Africa, tracing a path of suffering and survival through American history, the blues is also seen as leading forward to free jazz, a revolutionary, avant-garde music that challenges the cultural and economic politics of the mainstream. Female writers such as Alice *Walker, Gayl *Jones, and Toni *Morrison, meanwhile, have presented the blues as a more intimate, but no less fundamental grounding force, one with the capacity to advance the struggles of women in a harsh social environment prevailing within, and not just around, African American communities. Focusing on the transformative power of blues singing, stories such as Jones's *Corregidora (1975) and Walker's The *Color Purple (1982) evoke the original, existential function of the blues, as part of a living African American folk history of survival and revelation.

Finally, certain writers and critics, including Albert *Murray and Houston A. *Baker, Jr., have interpreted the blues as an expressive force in the broadest sense; "the script," as Baker has written, "in which African American cultural discourse is inscribed." If so, then while such expressive forms as funk, tagging, rap, and basketball have recently displaced blues music as an aesthetic focus in black communities, the blues can retain its full relevance as an underlying force, independent of any necessary single form or genre of its own. Whether or not one takes such a broad view, it remains true that no other source-identity, excepting the related traditions of testifying and *signifying, can challenge the blues in its importance to African American expressive culture.

Interest in historical blues has grown steadily, among artists and writers alike, to the extent that retrospection has become a major aspect of recent blues-influenced music, just as it is elsewhere in late-twentieth-century culture. With its musical and expressive capabilities, its fundamental position in African American life, and its own rich history, the blues seems certain to continue projecting an abiding identity in the face of a changeable American world.

[See also Blues Aesthetic; Musicals.]

• Amiri Baraka, Blues People, 1964. William Christopher Handy, Father of the Blues: An Autobiography by W. C. Handy, ed. Arna Bontemps, 1941; rpt. 1970. Albert Murray, Stomping the Blues, 1976. Lawrence L. Levine, Black Culture and

Black Consciousness, 1977. Jeff Todd Titon, *Early Downhome Blues: A Musical and Cultural Analysis*, 1977. David Evans, *Big Road Blues: Tradition and Creativity in the Folk Blues*, 1982. Houston Baker, *Blues, Ideology, and Afro-American Literature: A Vernacular Theory*, 1984. Steven Tracy, *Langston Hughes and the Blues*, 1988. Paul Oliver, *Blues Fell This Morning: Meaning in the Blues*, 2d ed., 1990. Charles Keil, *Urban Blues*, 2d ed., 1991.   —Graeme M. Boone

BLUES AESTHETIC. In 1897, addressing the American Negro Academy, W. E. B. *Du Bois stated that African American people were "a nation stored with wonderful possibilities of culture" that could be realized not by imitating Europeans but by pursuing and preserving their own "stalwart originality." Thirty years later, in an article in the *Crisis titled "Criteria of Negro Art," Du Bois explained that "until the art of the black folk compels recognition they will not be rated as human." Howard University philosophy professor Alain *Locke took the term "folk" quite literally, arguing in numerous articles and in his *anthology The *New Negro (1925) that the artistic expression of untutored African Americans contained the vital ingredients that would enable educated composers and writers to create a great *music and literature that would elevate the world's estimation of the intellectual capabilities of African people.

In many ways, African American intellectuals and artists have continued attempting to identify precisely the elements of culture referred to in Du Bois's early paper, and one avenue of investigation has resulted in the development of what may be called the blues aesthetic.

The influence of the *blues, a vital folk music, on African American art and literature can be seen in two quite important areas: (1) the blues as a formal structure of music and verse or as a formal compositional method that emphasizes a stock repertoire of traditional verses and themes organized according to a style of improvisation that allows the artist to select themes from the repertoire that are appropriate to any specific occasion and (2) the blues as ethos, meaning a specific historically grounded philosophical perspective or worldview that is derived from the African American experience in the early twentieth century.

Writers who experimented with blues form include Langston *Hughes, Sterling A. *Brown, Melvin B. *Tolson, and Sterling *Plumpp. Others such as Allen Ginsberg, Joel Oppenheimer, and poets of the Beat movement also experimented with the form. Critics and writers who have explored the blues as ethos include Richard *Wright, Ralph *Ellison, Albert *Murray, Houston A. *Baker, Jr., Gayl *Jones, Craig Werner, and Henry Louis *Gates, Jr. The work of Sterling Stuckey, Amiri *Baraka (LeRoi Jones), and Stephen Henderson is particularly important in the attempt to articulate and define the blues ethos.

The blues represents a commentary specific to the singer's community—often very specific indeed and highly personal, even though, as with much lyric *poetry, not necessarily autobiographical. Generally, the singer employs a persona that allows listeners to recognize their own experiences and moods in the lyrical narrative. Texas folklorist John A. Lomax made an early attempt to define the subject matter of the blues in a 1917 article in *The Nation* entitled "Self-Pity in Negro Folk-Songs." This well-intentioned but condescending *essay presents a wide range of song lyrics collected by Lomax or by Howard Odum and notes that "a prevailing mood is one of introspection." By the 1920s, however, the folk blues had achieved great popularity due to phonograph recordings, and blues forms had been adapted by commercialized popular and vaudeville entertainers ranging from Ma *Rainey and Bessie *Smith to Hollywood's Mae West.

"The Blues," wrote poet Sterling A. Brown in 1930, "have deservedly come into their own, and, unfortunately for the lover of folk art, into something more than their own." In the first published study to seriously consider the blues lyric as a style of poetry, Brown carefully distinguished authentic folk expression from the "clever approximations" of the popular entertainment industry. In an attempt to correct misinterpretations such as Lomax's, Brown noted that blues lyrics were so numerous and diverse "that any preconception might be proved about Negro folk life, as well as its opposite." He thought that the songs provided historical commentary on the *migration of rural African Americans to the cities, but Brown was most interested in the poetic view of life expressed in blues lyrics. In a formulation that parallels the poetic theories of the imagists and the new poetry movement that began just before World War I, Brown found the formal poetic style of the blues lyric most powerful "in substituting *the thing seen* for the bookish dressing up and sentimentalizing" found in conventional poetry. In much the same way that William Carlos Williams and others sought to replace nineteenth-century poetic diction with an American vernacular speech rhythm, Brown saw the blues as an authentic folk poetry that could be profitably studied by sophisticated African American writers.

Brown and Langston Hughes were the first African American poets to adapt the blues form for literary use. The blues stanza is essentially a rhymed couplet with the first line repeated and a caesura in each line. Langston Hughes defined it as "one long line repeated, and a third line to rhyme with the first two. Sometimes the second line in repetition is slightly changed and sometimes, but very seldom, it is omitted." Hughes's blues poems of the 1920s adhered to this strict pattern and also reproduced the characteristically unadorned everyday vernacular of ordinary speech. A poem such as "The Weary Blues," however, suggests the more elaborate verse and chorus structure of popular songs and allows the poet to combine blues verses and a commentary on them in the same poem. In this way, Hughes also suggests the antiphonal effect of a sung lyric and instrumental accompaniment. Stephen C. Tracy's *Langston Hughes and the Blues* (1988) offers a thorough critical evaluation of the poet's experiments with the blues as both form and theme.

By the 1960s, poets—particularly those connected with the *Black Arts movement—were interested in defining their style as a "national literature" distinct from American poetry per se. In addition to a large body of poetry, this interest led to a number of theoretical works. Critics such as Stephen Henderson were the first to apply an appropriate evaluative method to poetry that self-consciously adapted folk and popular art forms and attempted to replace standard English with African American vernacular in both vocabulary and metrical cadence. Henderson pointed out in *Understanding the New Black Poetry: Black Speech and Black Music as Poetic References* (1973) and many subsequent articles that, in addition to using music and folklore as subject matter and sources of literary allusion, African American poets tended to follow the blues and *jazz tradition by considering the written text of a poem as a "score" to be interpreted and improvised upon in oral recitation or "performance." For many such poets direct study of the blues influenced their approach.

In *Blues People: Negro Music in White America* (1963), poet Amiri Baraka presents the blues as a folk form that could only be created by English-speaking Africans in the United States. The "classic blues" of the 1920s is clearly a popular entertainment form derived from the earlier, as he terms it, primitive blues. In either case, to the extent that the blues is firmly rooted in the community of the former slaves and expresses that community's own values, it also functions as the authentic voice of a social class. In the 1940s, he wrote, "Rhythm & Blues was still an exclusive music. It was performed almost exclusively for, and had to satisfy, a Negro audience." The blues and its modernized expression in rhythm and blues were "a music that was hated by the middle-class Negro and not even understood by the white man." Though that contention is debatable, it emphasizes Baraka's interest in exploring and adapting a cultural form that, from his point of view, remained untainted by a frustrated racial "*double consciousness."

Bernard W. Bell's *The Folk Roots of Contemporary Afro-American Poetry* (1974) is an important text that originally appeared in the journal *Black World* and influenced many of the poets involved in the Black Arts movement. Bell traced literary interest in folk art to the German philosopher Johann Gottfried von Herder (1744–1803) who saw folk songs as the base of a national literature. Bell examines the different approaches African American poets such as Langston Hughes, James Weldon *Johnson, and Sonia *Sanchez employed to reflect the folk music heritage and also shows how a sophisticated popular songwriter such as Curtis Mayfield adapted the same folk sources to produce a popular rhythm and blues art form that in its turn influenced the poets of the 1960s and 1970s.

Houston A. Baker, Jr., offers the blues as "an interpretive metaphor" in *Blues, Ideology, and Afro-American Literature: A Vernacular Theory* (1984), suggesting that such a metaphor allows readers to more fully appreciate writers such as Frederick *Douglass, Zora Neale *Hurston, Richard Wright, Ralph Ellison, Paul Laurence *Dunbar, Amiri Baraka, and Toni *Morrison. Baker's theory suggests that blues songs can be viewed as random performances of traditional "travelling verses" and improvisational instrumental accompaniment resulting in "a nonlinear, freely associative, nonsequential meditation" that may be analogous to the way a novelist such as Ellison draws upon a wide selection of folk and literary allusions in creating the complex pattern of *Invisible Man* (1952). Baker's argument is similarly complex but his logical basis is clearly stated. As a critic, Baker's purpose is to identify the distinctive and specific elements of African American literature and culture, and he finds—as does Baraka in *Blues People*—blues to be an indigenous African American form of verbal art rooted in the material conditions of *slavery and the postslavery period. For Baker, this product of African American culture can also serve as a guide for understanding the process of cultural development. "Afro-American culture," he writes, "is a complex, reflexive enterprise which finds its proper figuration in blues conceived as a matrix."

Albert Murray in his *novel *Train Whistle Guitar* (1974) and numerous essays—including *The Hero and the Blues* (1973) and *Stomping the Blues* (1976)—has offered eloquent discussions of the blues ethos. Murray proposes "the Blues idiom style" that, according to critic W. Lawrence Hogue, depends upon a use of stream-of-consciousness narrative technique that reproduces the call-and-response or theme and variations structure of blues and *jazz music. Several critics have also noted a similar approach to narrative structure in the novels of Toni Morrison.

Richard Wright's *White Man, Listen!* (1957) drew a polemical distinction between "narcissistic" and assimilationist writing by Black authors and the body of African American folk expression that Wright termed "the Forms of Things Unknown . . . strangely positive manifestations of expression" that might supply the material for novels and poems that would accurately reflect the experiences of Black Americans. Ralph Ellison certainly utilizes such folkore in the complex patterning of his *Invisible Man*. What Houston A. Baker, Jr., called "the experiencing of experience" in the blues lyric and performance style is memorably defined in Ellison's *Shadow and Act* (1965) as "an impulse to keep the painful details and episodes of a brutal experience alive in one's aching consciousness, to finger the jagged grain, and to transcend it." Ellison stated, unequivocally and often, that this aspect of the blues ethos should be understood as the philosophical underpinning of his own work.

Critic Craig Werner proposes a triad of "Blues impulse," "Jazz impulse," and "Gospel impulse" as historical foundational elements of African American music and literature and identifies aspects of the blues as both form and ethos in the works of writers such as novelist Leon *Forrest. Similar in effect to the choral singing of the African American *church or the cathartic lyrical narratives of the blues singer, Werner's three "impulses" in their literary form offer readers "communal affirmation of individual experience."

Critical examination of the blues as both form and ethos has continued. In 1989 art historian Richard J. Powell curated an exhibition entitled *The Blues Aesthetic: Black Culture and Modernism*, which, once again drawing upon Alain Locke's ideas, affirmed the development of the blues "from music to cultural ethos" and demonstrated the relevance of folk visual art in the evolution of sophisticated African American painting and sculpture. The contribution of the writers who had earlier attempted to articulate this blues aesthetic was also noted, as was their influence on the visual artists. Recent critics such as Gayl *Jones, Berndt Ostendorf, and Eleanor W. Traylor continue to explore the use of the blues ethos in contemporary African American fiction since the 1950s. For several critics, however, Ralph Ellison's *Invisible Man* remains the most accomplished example of a literary work that expresses the blues aesthetic.

[*See also* Criticism; Folk Literature; Folklore; Speech and Dialect.]

• LeRoi Jones, *Blues People: Negro Music in White America*, 1963. Bernard W. Bell, *The Folk Roots of Contemporary Afro-American Poetry*, 1974. Albert Murray, *Stomping the Blues*, 1976. Houston A. Baker, Jr., *Afro-American Poetics: Revisions of Harlem and the Black Aesthetic*, 1988. Stephen C. Tracy, *Langston Hughes and the Blues*, 1988. Richard J. Powell, *The Blues Aesthetic: Black Culture and Modernism*, 1989. Craig Hansen Werner, *Playing the Changes: From Afro-modernism to the Jazz Impulse*, 1994.   —Lorenzo Thomas

Bluest Eye, The. The first *novel by Nobel Laureate Toni *Morrison, *The Bluest Eye* was published in 1970 and was heralded for its sensitive treatment of African American female *identity. It is the tragic story of a young African American girl, *Pecola Breedlove, whose loneliness and desire for love and attention is manifested in her desire to have blue eyes. The novel opens with an epigraph from a Dick and Jane primer that presents an ideal family with a house, mother, father, children, cat, dog, and friend. The story that shapes the novel is narrated through the eyes and voice of Claudia McTeer, whose narrative shifts the reader's attention to a very different world from that of the primer. Before she commits the taboo of telling the community the secret of Pecola's demise, however, she connects her own childhood desire to dismember white dolls, and her transference of that hatred to white girls, with her desire to understand why white girls were loved and African American girls were not.

Claudia then proceeds to tell not only a story of Pecola's painful childhood with an indifferent mother and an alcoholic father, and the trauma of rape by her father that results in her pregnancy and plunge into insanity, but also the story of the community's role in Pecola's tragic fate. The novel both deconstructs the image of the white community as the site of normalcy and perfection and illustrates the realities of life in a poverty-stricken African American community whose socioeconomic status is complicated by the politics of race, especially internalized racism. Pecola's mother, Pauline Breedlove, works as a *domestic and escapes from her own feelings of ugliness and low self-worth in the home of her white employer. Pauline's education about female beauty comes from her avid moviegoing but ends abruptly when she loses a tooth and convinces herself she will never look like Jean Harlow. She turns to the *church

and *religion out of resignation to her feelings of unattractiveness and contempt for her husband, Cholly. Her contempt for Cholly colors her relationship with Pecola as well. In one pivotal scene, when Pecola comes to visit her at work and accidentally spills a freshly baked blueberry pie on the floor, Pauline humiliates Pecola by slapping and scolding her while consoling the daughter of her white employer. Cholly Breedlove's attempt to construct an acceptable image of himself as a black man is complicated by memories of a racial incident that alters his ability to love his wife and daughter in appropriate ways. His drunkenness, routine fights with Pauline, and incestuous relationship with Pecola form the context out of which Pecola's own self-loathing develops. The story unravels the community's propensity to scapegoat Pecola, to measure its identity by devaluing and eventually destroying her humanity, to engage in intraracial politics by valuing the skin color and *hair texture of some African American girls but not others, and to be seduced by fraudulent characters like Soaphead Church, the bootleg preacher who, out of sympathy, tricks Pecola into thinking he has given her blue eyes.

Published in the midst of the period of pride in blackness associated with the late 1960s and early 1970s, *The Bluest Eye* ultimately calls into question the aesthetics of beauty that, in the words of the novel, "originated in envy, thrived in insecurity, and ended in disillusion." Moreover, though Morrison's first novel was surpassed in critical recognition by the acclaim given to her later novels, it nevertheless marked the beginning of what would be the most significant period of literary production of books by African American women about African American female identity.

[*See also* Bildungsroman; Mulatto; Passing; Race.]

• Michael Awkward, *Inspiriting Influences: Tradition, Revision, and Afro-American Women's Novels*, 1989. Trudier Harris, *Fiction and Folklore: The Novels of Toni Morrison*, 1991.
                    —Marilyn Sanders Mobley

BLUE VEIN SOCIETIES were elite *mulatto cliques whose primary criterion for membership was skin light enough for the blue veins to show underneath. In African American literature, they often exemplified the part that color played in determining *class and status. In Wallace *Thurman's *The Blacker the Berry* (1929), the blue vein society is a paradigm of intraracial prejudice. His heroine, the dark-skinned offspring of blue veiners, is rejected by her mother and grandmother and driven to extreme color consciousness by the prejudice directed against her dark skin. In Sutton E. *Griggs's *Overshadowed* (1901), the blue vein society figures as an illustration of the false values that accompany class consciousness. In the novel, a blue vein society ostracizes the heroine because in choosing to work she contradicts the genteel values of the light-skinned middle class. Charles Waddell *Chesnutt, himself reputedly a member of one of these societies, is also included in the number of authors who represent blue vein societies in their works. In his short stories "The *Wife of His Youth" (1899) and "A Matter of Principle" (1899), he explores the conflicting values of the elite societies.

• Judith Berzon, *Neither White nor Black: The Mulatto Character in American Fiction*, 1978. Joel Williamson, *New People*, 1980.
—Sara Gallob McIntyre

BLYDEN, EDWARD WILMOT (1832–1912), essayist, journalist, educator, statesman, and politician. Little remembered today, Edward Wilmot Blyden was the most important African thinker of the nineteenth century, leading one of the most varied careers of any Black man in that era. Born in Saint Thomas, Blyden came to America in 1850 to attend Rutgers Theological College but was rejected because of his *race. He subsequently emigrated to Liberia, grew enamored of African life, and became a staunch supporter of his new homeland. Feeling called upon to undermine misconceptions about "the dark continent" and to encourage Blacks throughout the diaspora to repatriate, Blyden spent the remainder of his life serving this cause in several capacities. As a journalist, Blyden edited the *Liberia Herald* and founded and edited the *Negro* and the *West African Reporter*, two of the first Pan-African journals. As an educator, he served as principal of Alexander High School, Monrovia; Liberia's educational commissioner to Britain and America; professor of classics at, and president of, Liberia College; and director of Mohammedan education in Sierra Leone. As a politician, Blyden was variously Liberian secretary of state, government agent to the interior in Sierra Leone, Liberian ambassador to the Court of Saint James, Liberian minister of interior, unsuccessful candidate for Liberia's presidency, agent of native affairs in Lagos, and Liberian minister plenipotentiary and envoy extraordinary to London and Paris.

Despite these impressive credentials, Blyden remains most significant for his intellectual achievements, writing voluminously on a wide variety of topics. His most famous volume, *Christianity, Islam and the Negro Race* (1887), expounded his belief that the effects of Christianity had been largely detrimental to Africans, while the effects of Islam had been largely salutary. Blyden believed in the popular notion that each race had its own qualities, an idea usually invoked to the disparagement of Africans but which he saw instead as a way of extolling the virtues of "the African personality." One of the first and strongest believers in African nationalism, Blyden felt that the political dominance the European-minded coastal Liberians were then enjoying would eventually, and rightfully, give way to a form of government created by the true, uncorrupted Africans of the interior. Blyden also championed *Pan-Africanism, believing that the whole continent needed to work together to protect itself from being divided up by the European powers.

Whether writing as historian (*The Negro in Ancient History*, 1869; *West Africa before Europe*, 1905), pedagogue (*The West African University*, 1872), traveler (*From West Africa to Palestine*, 1873), or sociologist (*African Life and Customs*, 1908), Blyden was always insightful. He invariably emphasized the achievements and potential of Africans and their descendants, to which end he became his own best example. Although not always liked—witness his defeat in the Liberian presidential race and his near-lynching in 1871, both of which he blamed on "traitorous" *mulattoes—Blyden was always admired for his intellect. His influence, whether acknowledged or not, can be seen in such later figures as Marcus *Garvey, Aimé Césaire, Léopold Senghor, Kwame Nkrumah, George Padmore, *Malcolm X, and Amiri *Baraka.

[*See also* African Literature.]

• Hollis R. Lynch, *Edward Wilmot Blyden: Pan-Negro Patriot*, 1967. Richard West, *Back to Africa*, 1970.

—Adam Meyer

BONNER, MARITA (1899–1971), essayist, playwright, and short fiction writer. Born 16 June 1899 in Boston, Marita Bonner graduated from Radcliffe in 1922 and taught high school in West Virginia and Washington, D.C. She married William Almy Occomy in 1930. While living in Washington, she was a member of the "S" Street Salon, a group of writers who met usually at the home of Georgia Douglas *Johnson. Encouraged and influenced by writers such as Johnson, May *Miller, Langston *Hughes, Jean *Toomer, Alain *Locke, Countee *Cullen, and other major figures of the *Harlem Renaissance, Occomy began to publish works that embodied her concern for the deplorable conditions facing African American men and women living in an America characterized by racial, *class, and *gender inequities.

Occomy published two *essays that Elizabeth Brown-Guillory describes as those "that captured the spirit of the Black Renaissance." "On Being Young—A Woman—and Colored," which won first place in the *Crisis* literary contest of 1925, elucidates the particular situation of African American women whose worth in American mainstream society is doubly devalued and describes segregation's practice of forcing African Americans from diverse backgrounds together—"in a bundle"—as embroilment "in the seaweed of a Black Ghetto." "The Young Blood Hungers" (1928) is militant and apocalyptic in tone as it warns of ensuing *violence resulting from poor race relations. The concerns raised in these essays persist in her plays and *short stories.

Occomy published three plays. *The Pot Maker: A Play to Be Read* (1927) is an exploration of infidelity. *The Purple Flower* (1928) promotes a revolutionary response to racism, which Margaret Wilkerson describes as "perhaps the most provocative play" written by an African American woman prior to 1950. *Exit, an Illusion: A One-Act Play* (1929) examines the complications of mixed ancestry. Experimental in structure, featuring second-person narration and plot development reliant on a central metaphor, these plays assert moral dilemmas that challenge the characters to prove their worth. Apparently written to be read, the plays were not produced in Occomy's lifetime.

Published mostly in *Opportunity* and the *Crisis*, Occomy's short stories encompass a diverse range of subjects and themes. Class differentiation among African Americans is explored in her first published short story, "The Hands" (1925), and "The Prison-Bound" (1926) addresses issues of class and gender, and notions of "beauty." "Nothing New" (1926) is her first published story of life in Chicago's Black Belt, a setting that predominates her later work, and communicates the tensions and entanglements of racial intermixture. "Drab Rambles" (1927) illustrates how both a female and a male protagonist deal with gender-specific confrontations in their respective struggles against economic hardship and racism.

After 1930, Frye Street—a fictitious "ethnic intersection" where African American residents must coexist with Chinese, Russian, and various other European immigrants—dominates the majority of Occomy's stories. Appearing mostly in *Opportunity*, many of the stories were published in separate parts. Notable works include the trilogy "The Triple Triad on Black Notes" (1933) and the two-part story "Tin Can" (1934), which won the 1933 literary prize. The various stories thematize issues of colorism, marital betrayal, family strife, and poverty. "A Sealed Pod" (1936), an unflattering image of peas not touching despite their closeness, metaphorizes Frye Street while it chronicles the murder of a young woman by her lover. Three stories published in 1939, "The Makin's," "The Whipping," and "Hongry Fire," differently depict the corrosive effects of the urban environment on children. "Patch Quilt" (1940), set in the rural South, resists the contemporary tendency to romanticize the southern small town, portraying the environment as confining rather than pastoral. Occomy's last published short story, "One True Love" (1941), again illustrates the double bind of the African American woman's position described in "On Being Young—A Woman—and Colored."

Marita Bonner Occomy died in 1971 from injuries sustained in a fire in her Chicago apartment. Publishing for only sixteen years, her literary contribution to African American literature is significant. Her characterization of urban environments as destructive and corrupting prefigures, even perhaps influenced, Richard *Wright's portrayal of the urban in *Native Son* (1940). Her ability to traverse genres and treat a myriad of themes demonstrates not only the versatility of her talents but also the diversity of African American culture and experience during the interwar era.

• Diane Isaacs, "Bonner, Marita/Marita Odetta," in *The Harlem Renaissance: A Historical Dictionary for the Era*, ed. Bruce Kellner, 1984, p. 45. Margaret Wilkerson, introduction to *Nine Plays by Black Women*, 1986. Joyce Flynn, introduction to *Frye Street and Environs: The Collected Works of Marita Bonner*, eds. Joyce Flynn and Joyce Occomy Stricklin, 1987. Joyce Flynn, "Marita Bonner Occomy," in *DLB*, vol. 51, *Afro-American Writers from the Harlem Renaissance to 1949*, ed. Trudier Harris, 1987, pp. 222–228. Nellie McKay, "What Were They Saying? Black Women Playwrights of the Harlem Renaissance," in *The Harlem Renaissance Re-Examined*, ed. Victor Kramer, 1987, pp. 129–147. Elizabeth Brown-Guillory, ed., *Wines in the Wilderness: Plays by African American Women from the Harlem Renaissance to the Present*, 1990.

—Kim Jenice Dillon

BONTEMPS, ARNA (1902–1973), novelist, poet, and librarian. Born in Alexandria, Louisiana, the first child of a Roman Catholic bricklayer and a Methodist schoolteacher, Arna Wendell Bontemps grew up in California and graduated from Pacific Union College. After college he accepted a teaching position in Harlem at the height of the *Harlem Renaissance, and in 1926 and 1927 won first prizes on three separate occasions in contests with other "*New Negro" poets. The same years marked his marriage to Alberta Johnson and the start of a family of six children.

Bontemps's first effort at a *novel (*Chariot in the Cloud*, 1929), a *bildungsroman set in southern California, never found a publisher, but by mid-1931, as his teaching position in New York City ended, Harcourt accepted *God Sends Sunday* (1931), his novel about the rise and notoriety of Little Augie. This tiny black jockey of the 1890s, whose period of great luck went sour, was inspired by Bontemps's favorite uncle, Buddy.

While teaching at Oakwood Junior College, Bontemps began the first of several collaborations with Langston *Hughes, *Popo and Fifina: Children of Haiti* (1932), a colorful travel book for juveniles that portrays two black children who migrate with their parents from an inland farm to a busy fishing village. The success of this new genre encouraged him to make juvenile fiction an ongoing part of his repertoire.

Residence in the Deep South proved fruitful for his career, for in quick succession he published his best-known short story, "A Summer Tragedy" (1932), the compelling narrative of a simple yet dignified couple worn weary by a lifetime of sharecropping on a southern plantation; wrote a dozen other tales of the South that were compiled years later under the title *The Old South* (1973); completed yet another profitable juvenile book, *You Can't Pet a Possum* (1934), for its time a charming rural Alabama story about an eight-year-old named Shine Boy and his yellow hound, Butch; initiated contact with composer and musician W. C. Handy to ghostwrite Handy's *autobiography; and, in a visit to Fisk University in Nashville, "discovered" its rich and seemingly forgotten repository of narratives by former slaves.

Late in 1932 Bontemps started writing *Black Thunder: Gabriel's Revolt: Virginia 1800* (1936), his singular and inspired representation of an actual slave *insurrection that failed because of weather and treachery. This work establishes the concept of *freedom as the principal motif of his ensuing works and evokes questions regarding differences between writing and orality as racial and cultural markers. But because he was forced out of Oakwood at the end of the 1934 school year, the novel was completed in the cramped space of his father's California home, where the family had retreated.

Ironic relief arrived a year later from the Adventists in the form of a principalship at their Shiloh Academy on Chicago's battered South Side. The venture was bright with promise because the city and the university had attracted a young and savvy coterie of social radicals including Richard *Wright, Margaret *Walker, and Jack Conroy. Favorable critical reception of *Black Thunder* assured Bontemps's celebrity among the group, and his application to the Julian Rosenwald Fund to research and write a third novel met with success. In *Sad-Faced Boy (1937), he relates the travels to Harlem of three quaint Alabama boys who in time nostalgically discover the charm of their own birthplace. In 1938 he secured an appointment as editorial supervisor to the *Federal Writers' Project of the Illinois WPA. He sailed for the Caribbean in the fall of 1938 and put the finishing touches on Drums at Dusk (1939), his historical portrayal of the celebrated eighteenth-century black revolution on the island of Santo Domingo.

With great relief he completed Father of the Blues (1941), the "autobiography" commissioned by the ever-testy W. C. Handy; he edited his first compilation, Golden Slippers: An *Anthology of Negro *Poetry for Young Readers (1941); he then published a humorous American tall tale for children coauthored with his WPA colleague Jack Conroy titled The Fast Sooner Hound (1942); he was awarded two additional Rosenwald grants to pursue a degree and to write a book on "the Negro in Illinois"; and in 1943 he completed a master's degree in library science at the University of Chicago, clearing the way to his appointment as librarian at Fisk University.

In 1946 the controversial *musical based on his first novel reached Broadway as St. Louis Woman for a short but successful run. Arguably his most distinguished work of the decade was The Story of the Negro (1948), a race *history since Egyptian civilization that won him the Jane Addams Children's Book Award for 1956. Then, with Langston Hughes, he edited The Poetry of the Negro (1949), a comprehensive collection of poems by blacks and tributary poems by nonblacks.

An assortment of histories and *biographies, largely written with youths in mind, emerged from Fisk throughout the 1950s and the succeeding civil rights years. Bontemps and Hughes's collaboration produced two anthologies during this period, The Book of Negro Folklore (1959) and American Negro Poetry (1963).

After Hughes's death in 1967, Bontemps compiled Hold Fast to Dreams (1969), a montage of poems by black and white writers. But compilations of a more personal sort rounded off his long career. They include The Harlem Renaissance Remembered (1972), featuring an introductory reflection by Bontemps and twelve critical *essays on literary figures from the era; Personals (1963), a collection of his own poems reissued in 1973 as a third edition with a prefatory personal history; and The Old South: "A Summer Tragedy" and Other Stories of the Thirties (1973), which opens with the personal essay "Why I Returned," places most of his short fiction under a single cover.

Retirement from Fisk in 1966 brought recognition in the form of two honorary degrees and distinguished professorial appointments at the University of Illinois (Chicago Circle), Yale University, and back at Fisk as writer in residence. Following his death in 1973, early estimates of his career from Sterling A. *Brown and Aaron Douglas noted that he deserves to be known much better than he has been. Aptly, the Yale appointment included the title of Curator of the James Weldon Johnson Collection at the Beinecke Library, for prevalent views have come to regard him as a chronicler and keeper of black cultural heritage. It is worth noting that the vast and unique body of extant correspondence with his friend Langston Hughes is housed in this archive. Bontemps's most distinctive works are ringing affirmations of the human passion for freedom and the desire for social justice inherent in us all. Arnold *Rampersad called him the conscience of his era and it could be fairly added that his tendency to fuse history and imagination represents his personal legacy to a collective memory.

[See also Children's and Young Adult Literature; Historical Novel.]

• Charles H. Nichols, ed., Arna Bontemps–Langston Hughes Letters, 1925–1967, 1988. Kirkland C. Jones, Renaissance Man from Louisiana: A Biography of Arna Wendell Bontemps, 1992. Eric J. Sundquist, The Hammers of Creation: Folk Culture in Modern African-American Fiction, 1992. Charles L. James, "Arna W. Bontemps' Creole Heritage," Syracuse University Library Associates Courier 30 (1995): 91–115.

—Charles L. James

BOYD, CANDY (b. 1946), born Marguerite Dawson, educator, activist, and novelist. Educating people about their positive potential has long been Candy Boyd's priority. As a high school student, she tried to stop blockbusting in her native Chicago by convincing three of her friends, an African American, a Jew, and a Protestant, to join her in personal visits to more than two hundred white families. She withdrew from college to work as an organizer for the Southern Christian Leadership Conference. When she finally earned her bachelor's degree from Northeastern Illinois State University, she became, in her own words, a "militant teacher." She worked with Operation PUSH, organized neighborhood beautification projects, and used her Saturdays to take students on excursions to parks, theaters, and other neighborhoods.

When Boyd moved to Berkeley, California, and began teaching in a more diversely multicultural setting, her frustration with literary *stereotypes and negative depictions of African Americans was exacerbated by her discovery that Asians, Latinos, and many Euro-Americans suffered similar literary treatment. She decided to write books for children that were honest, interesting, and inspiring. Though she had earned a PhD in education from the University of California and had been teaching for several years, Boyd prepared for this task by taking courses in writing for children and by reading every children's book in the Berkeley Public Library.

Named Professor of the Year at St. Mary's College in 1992, Candy Boyd is renowned for training teachers and creating organizations that encourage and develop reading among young people. In her books, schools are sites for learning and developing responsibility outside the family. Her characters encounter bullies, liars, and other misdirected classmates and teachers. They also build relationships with adults and children who inspire and guide them.

Candy Boyd's books explore complex and perplexing questions about the world and the emotions engendered as youngsters experience it. Her plots generally focus upon family relations complicated by external forces. In *Charlie Pippin* (1987), Charlie's father's experiences in Vietnam hinder family communication. In *Circle of Gold* (1984), the death of Mattie Benson's father requires her mother to work two jobs to support the family. Death and grieving nearly defeat twelve-year-old Toni Douglas in Boyd's second book, *Breadsticks and Blessing Places* (1985; republished as *Forever Friends* in 1986). Toni Douglas wants to please her family by being accepted into King Academy but her frustration with math, her need to babysit her brother, and her desire to socialize with her friends were already interfering when her friend Susan is killed in an automobile accident. First rejected by publishers because of its "relentless" focus on death, *Breadsticks and Blessing Places* was later selected for the Children's Book of the Year List.

Boyd's characters are not merely survivors; they are intriguingly typical, basically competent young people who have (or who create) supportive families and friends to help them face crises and move toward more hopeful futures. The protagonists are generally from working- or middle-class homes and their dilemmas are realistic. Joey Davis in *Chevrolet Saturdays* (1993) was the best science student in his fourth grade class whose testing for the gifted classes was postponed because of budget cuts. Mrs. Hamlin, his fifth grade teacher, however, is an inexperienced and unhappy individual without particular interest or competence in science and with a decided preference for those already certified as high achievers. Misinterpreting Joey's preoccupation with his mother's remarriage and his father's pending move to Chicago as evidence of low intelligence, Mrs. Hamlin recommends Joey be placed in a class for slow learners. Unlike admission to the gifted classes, this transfer threatens to occur without further ado. When his stepfather takes a strong part in challenging the teacher's recommendation, when Joey learns to balance his afterschool job at the neighborhood pharmacy with more positive classroom behavior, and when he atones for the family dog's injury by judiciously nursing him back to health, things begin to work out.

Candy Boyd's novels have received awards from the Children's Book Council, the American Library Association, and the International Reading Association. *Circle of Gold* was designated a Coretta Scott King Honor Book. Like Walter Dean *Myers, Sharon Bell *Mathis, Mildred D. *Taylor, John *Steptoe, and other contemporary African American writers, Boyd's emphasis upon positive development and the strengths of the African American communities does not ignore or downplay the problems and challenges of racism and prejudice. Instead she uses lively, realistic, and compelling characters to illustrate the message that "you make it. It's going to be hard and tough and it's not fair . . . but you make it."

• Barbara Rollock, *Black Authors and Illustrators of Children's Books*, 1988. Sonia Benson, "Candy Dawson Boyd," in *CA*, vol. 138, ed. Donna Dendorf, 1993, pp. 52–55. Sonia Benson, "Candy Dawson Boyd," in *Something about the Author*, vol. 72, ed. Diane Telgen, 1993, pp. 14–19.

—Frances Smith Foster

BOYD, MELBA (b. 1950), poet, educator, editor, essayist, and biographer. Melba Joyce Boyd was born on 2 April 1950 to John Percy Boyd and Dorothy Winn, since divorced, in Detroit, Michigan. She is married with two children. Boyd received her BA in English from Wayne State University in 1971 and an MA in English from the same institution in 1972. She served as a teacher at Cass Technical High School (1972–1973), an instructor at Wayne County Community College (1972–1982), and assistant editor of the *Broadside* (1972–1977; 1980–1982). In 1979, Boyd received her doctorate in English from the University of Michigan at Ann Arbor. She taught at the University of Iowa (1982–1988) and Ohio State University (1988–1989) before becoming the director of Afro-American Studies at the University of Michigan at Flint in 1989. She is currently on the faculty at Wayne State University. Among other awards, she received a Faculty Research Grant from the University of Michigan in 1990 and was Senior Fulbright Lecturer in Germany (1982–1983).

Boyd began publishing *poetry after graduating from college. Her earliest work appeared in *The Broadside Annual* and African American periodicals such as the *Black Scholar* and *First World*, and explored the intersection of personal and African American political experience. In 1978 Boyd's first volume of poetry, *Cat Eyes and Dead Wood*, was published with accompanying illustrations by Michele G. Russell. Later volumes, such as *thirteen frozen flamingoes* (1988) and *Song for Maya* (1989), also incorporate illustrations. After 1983 Boyd drew on her German experience to write poetry. *Song for Maya* and *thirteen frozen flamingoes* are both published by German presses. The former is written in both German and English, with English on one side of the page and German on the other, while the latter includes occasional German phrases. Boyd has been anthologized in two collections of African American literature, *Black Sister: Poetry by Black American Women, 1746–1980* (1981) and *Sturdy Black Bridges: Visions of Black Women in Literature* (1979). The poet's essay on her poem *Song for Maya*, an exploration of the difficulties being multiracial poses for individuals and for American society, appears in *Missions in Conflict: Essays on U.S.–Mexican Relations and Chicano Culture*, edited by Renate von Bardeleben (1986). Her *biography of Frances Ellen Watkins *Harper, *Discarded Legacy: Politics and Poetics in the Life of Frances E. W. Harper*, was published by Wayne State University Press in 1994.

Stylistically, Boyd's poetry has remained consistent. Her earliest published work, such as "silver lace (for herb)" (1978), introduces her characteristic short, powerful lines, concern with individual words, and manipulation of punctuation to create form and meaning. Boyd uses the language and imagery of contemporary culture, creating startling, Sextonesque phrases such as "cultural insurancemen," and often evokes female *sexuality through sensory moments. Less frequently she draws on musical patterns and rhyme: "save the bones/for willie jones," for example, or the sibilance of "bussstop." While still concerned with the personal and political issues of *race, *class, and *gender, Boyd's work has gradually become less dependent on the poet's individual experience to communicate meaning and more concerned with others' experience.

• Theresa Gunnels Rush, Carol Fairbanks Myers, and Esther Spring Arata, *Black American Writers Past and Present: A Biographical and Bibliographical Dictionary*, vol. 1, 1975. "Melba Joyce Boyd" in *WWABA*, ed. Shirelle Phelps, 1994, pp. 142–143.   —Karen R. Bloom

BRADLEY, DAVID (b. 1950), author and professor of creative writing. Born and raised in Bedford, Pennsylvania, David Bradley's horizon was shaped by a rural world near the soft-coal region of western Pennsylvania and by his father, a church historian and eloquent preacher, who frequently took his son on trips to the South. After high school Bradley was named Benjamin Franklin National Achievement and Presidential Scholar. In 1972, he graduated summa cum laude from the University of Pennsylvania and was awarded a Thouron Scholarship for the University of London, where he received his MA in 1974, and established a lasting interest in nineteenth-century American *history, resulting in the writing of four versions of his second *novel when he returned to America.

In 1975, with the publication of his first novel, *South Street*, Bradley showed a keen interest in depicting everyday life and in the use of vernacular language. The book is centered on a black bar, a black church, and a hotel lobby on Philadelphia's South Street. In an ironic black urban version of the Western genre, Bradley has the black poet Adlai Stevenson Brown temporarily live and work amidst the unstable conditions of the black ghetto. Brown functions as a catalyst for the fantasies of hustlers, drinkers, whores, and preachers, whose sexual and material power games, articulated in vividly idiomatic speech and couched in ebullient or caustic *humor, add up to a virtuoso dramatization of a vibrant, though depressed, city milieu.

Bradley's second novel, *The *Chaneysville Incident* (1981), won the PEN/Faulkner Award in 1982 and was quickly recognized as a major text of African American fiction. Its protagonist, John Washington, a history professor in Philadelphia, in the process of exploring his family and group history finds himself confronted with his father's dying friend Old Jack (an embodiment of the black oral tradition); with the life plans of his father Moses and his ancestor C. K. Washington (who both tried to exert covert influence on the white power structure); and with his white girl friend, Judith, a psychologist, who eventually helps John to make meaningful a partially buried and fragmented history through an imaginative complementation of the data from several incidents near Chaneysville, especially the voluntary suicide of a group of fugitive slaves when threatened with reenslavement.

After shorter spells as an editor and a professor of English, David Bradley settled at Temple University in Philadelphia as professor of creative writing in 1977. He has published a variety of *essays, book reviews, and interviews in prestigious periodicals, magazines, and newspapers treating topics such as black *education and literature, the exemplary lives and self-concepts of black athletes, and the status and reception of *Malcolm X. Bradley worked on a Malcolm X *film script for Warner Brothers between 1984 and 1988 but gave up hope when faced with the systematic evisceration of Malcolm's figure by Hollywood.

Some rumors about Bradley's working on a detective novel notwithstanding, the author in a 1992 interview claimed to be at work on a nonfiction book about the founding documents and the continuing tradition of racism in America.

[*See also* Historical Novel.]

• Valerie Smith, "David Bradley," in *DLB*, vol. 33, *Afro-American Fiction Writers after 1955*, eds. Thadious M. Davis and Trudier Harris, 1983, pp. 28–32. David Bradley, "The Business of Writing: An Interview with David Bradley," interview by Susan L. Blake and James A. Miller, *Callaloo* 7 (1984): 19–39. Michael G. Cooke, *Afro-American Literature in the Twentieth Century*, 1984. David Bradley, "An Interview with David Bradley," interview by Kay Bonetti, *Missouri Review* 15 (1992): 69–88.   —Klaus Ensslen

BRAGG, LINDA BROWN. *See* Brown, Linda Beatrice.

BRAITHWAITE, WILLIAM STANLEY (1878–1962), poet, editor, publisher, anthologist, and influential critic who strived to reanimate and draw attention to American verse in the early twentieth century. Born and raised in Boston, William Stanley Braithwaite began life in a prosperous, cultured home but, on the death of his father, was forced to quit school at the age of twelve to help support his family. Lacking formal instruction, Braithwaite rigorously educated himself. He eventually found work as a typesetter in a Boston printing firm. Setting poems by John Keats and William Wordsworth, Braithwaite developed a love of lyric *poetry that inspired his own writing. He began to publish poems and reviews in the Boston *Journal* and *Transcript* and eventually produced his first book of poetry, *Lyrics of Life and Love*, in 1904, followed by *The House of Falling Leaves* (1908). In 1906, Braithwaite started his critical career in earnest with a regular feature in the Boston *Transcript*. From the pages of the *Transcript* and other prestigious newspapers and journals, Braithwaite championed Robert Frost, Edwin Arlington Robinson, and Amy Lowell, and brought serious critical attention to the works of African American poets such as Paul Laurence *Dunbar, James Weldon *Johnson, Georgia Douglas *Johnson, Countee *Cullen, who dedicated *Caroling Dusk: An Anthology of Verse by Negro Poets* (1927) to Braithwaite, and Claude *McKay, whose poem "The Harlem Dancer" remained a favorite of Braithwaite's throughout his career. In 1912, Braithwaite, sensing the American public's increasing appetite for verse, set out to produce a Boston-based magazine of American poetry entitled *Poetry Journal*. After his effort proved ill-fated, primarily because of the almost concurrent appearance of Harriet Monroe's *Poetry: A Magazine of Verse*, Braithwaite turned his attention in 1913 to his *Anthology of Magazine Verse*, an annual collection, inclusion in which soon became a coveted mark of poetic success. Harriet Monroe herself dubbed Braithwaite "Sir Oracle" in grudging reference to his power to determine literary careers.

Throughout his years compiling the *Anthology*, Braithwaite remained committed to the notion that verse should be an expression of spiritual truth and eternal beauty beyond what he conceived of as the limits of merely political or racial concerns. Consistently wary of poetry that he considered polemical or didactic, Braithwaite favored traditional, formal, lyric voices in African American verse over harsher cries, and remained suspicious of African American *dialect poetry, like Dunbar's, that, despite its power, he saw as perpetuating the image of the African American as uneducated and poetically unsophisticated. Despite his muted and somewhat romantic editorial preferences, Braithwaite introduced the general poetry-reading public to a wide range of African American voices they might otherwise never have heard.

After weathering the depression with his wife and seven children, Braithwaite accepted a teaching position in 1935 at Atlanta University, where he spent the next ten years as a professor of creative literature. In 1946, he moved to Harlem and spent the remainder of his career compiling his *Selected Poems* (1948) and writing a book on the Brontës before his death in 1962.

[*See also* Anthologies.]

• Phillip Butcher, "William Stanley Braithwaite's Southern Exposure: Rescue and Revelation," *Southern Literary Journal* 3.2 (1971): 49–61. Phillip Butcher, ed., *The William Stanley Braithwaite Reader*, 1972. Kenny J. Williams, "An Invisible Partnership and an Unlikely Relationship: William Stanley Braithwaite and Harriet Monroe," *Callaloo* 10.3 (Summer 1987): 516–550.   —Robin G. Schulze

BRANCH, WILLIAM BLACKWELL (b. 1927), playwright, educator, media writer-producer, critic, entrepreneur, editor, and prominent dramatist in the 1950s. In his *drama *anthology, *Crosswinds* (1993), William Branch admits that his interest in *theater developed from childhood when he observed his father in the pulpit and participated in backyard dramatic activities. Born in New Haven, Connecticut, Branch grew up in New York, North Carolina, and Washington, D.C., where his father was assigned by the Methodist Church. After receiving a BS in speech from Northwestern University (1949), Branch presented his first play, *A Medal for Willie* (1951), at Club Baron (Harlem). The cast included Julian *Mayfield and Eli Wallach. Written while in the army, Branch's second play, *In Splendid Error*, was staged at the Greenwich Mews Theatre (New York) from October 1954 to January 1955. Branch continued his educa-

tion, receiving an MFA in dramatic arts at Columbia University (1958). He had further training at Columbia in *film production (1958–1959) and was a Yale fellow in screenwriting (1965–1966). His career has been diverse. He has written extensively for radio, *television, and the film industry; owns William Branch Associates (a media consulting and production firm established in 1973); and is a professor of theater at Cornell.

The themes of Branch's best-known plays, *A Medal for Willie*, *In Splendid Error*, and *Baccalaureate* (1975), focus on conflicts between an African American's personal values and those of the larger society; on African American and white American historical figures and events; on family relationships; and on the determination of the African American to fight racial bigotry for collective progress. In *Medal*, whites in a small southern town are more interested in the attention given by the Pentagon to memorialize Willie than in the African American community that he represents. Willie's mother publicly rejects the medal, a symbolic protest against honoring a man whose needs were ignored while he lived. In his anthology *Black Drama in America* (1971), Darwin Turner notes that *Medal* anticipates veterans' forceful demands for change at home. *In Splendid Error* highlights the dialogue of historical figures Frederick *Douglass and John *Brown. Douglass is left to ponder his refusal to join Brown at Harpers Ferry. In Doris Abramson's *Negro Playwrights in the American Theatre, 1925–1959* (1969), Branch's view is that these characters reflect current opposing views on how revolutionary movements can be achieved. The implication of *Baccalaureate* is that African Americans who choose to educate themselves may improve the race, but at personal and spiritual sacrifice. Complex issues of *gender, sex, *class, and *family relationships are introduced in this play. Branch's interest in African themes is reflected in his stage adaptation of South African writer Peter Abraham's *A Wreath for Udomo*, which depicts the dilemmas of an African prime minister in his recently liberated state. Branch's works demonstrate the growth of African American dramatists during the 1950s and their entry into the commercial world.

• Loften Mitchell, *Black Drama: The Story of the American Negro in the American Theatre*, 1967. "William Blackwell Branch," in *Black American Writers Past and Present*, eds. Theressa Rush, Carol Myers, and Esther Arata, vol. 1, 1975, pp. 91–92.   —Australia Tarver

BRAWLEY, BENJAMIN (1882–1939), educator, historian, and critic. As was customary for many black intellectuals during his day, Benjamin Brawley received two college degrees—one from a black institution and one from a predominantly white school. As a graduate of Morehouse College in Atlanta, he was very much influenced by the city's black elite and notion of a "*talented tenth." As a graduate of the University of Chicago, he placed a great deal of emphasis upon the life of the mind. After receiving an MA degree from Harvard University, Brawley spent the remainder of his life as a college teacher, historian, and literary critic. Positions at Shaw University and Morehouse College ultimately led to his appointment at Howard University, where he served as the head of the English department.

Brawley was a prolific writer. His *essays appeared in the leading journals of his day, and such books as *A Social History of the American Negro* (1921), *Early Negro American Writers* (1935), *Paul Laurence Dunbar: Poet of His People* (1936), and *The Negro Genius* (1937) as well as the many editions of *The Negro in Literature and Art in the United States* give a sense of both the range and the limitations of his scholarship.

Brawley's literary *criticism has created tensions within some black communities. Just before his death, he was subjected to a great deal of censure for being too bourgeois. Among some of the younger critics, "Brawleyism" came to signify a type of genteel spirit in life and scholarship that some members of the *Harlem Renaissance found objectionable. He, however, found them to be offensive because he thought the renaissance writers emphasized the underclass too much. As a result he took the writers of the Harlem Renaissance to task because he felt they stressed the unusual and the exotic. In his opinion their association with the latter represented "one of the most brazen examples of salesmanship in the United States." He was intent upon defining African American life in terms of its success stories, its heroes, and its similarities to the dominant American culture.

As a critic Brawley searched for a means to relate African American literature to mainstream American and British literature. Yet he found much that was objectionable in modern literature. Like William Stanley *Braithwaite, whose work he admired, Brawley thought free verse lacked meaning and significance because it did not have an identifiable traditional form. He also felt that verse should not generally deal with overt protest. This stance excluded a great deal of the *poetry of the Harlem Renaissance. However, it must be said in Brawley's defense that he exhibited impeccable taste in writing and was an excellent stylist. Even though later scholarship has revealed material unavailable to him when he was writing, his studies of African American literature remain perceptive and comprehensive.

• Saunders Redding, "Benjamin Griffith Brawley," in *DANB*, eds. Rayford W. Logan and Michael R. Winston, 1982, pp. 60–61. Steven J. Leslie, "Benjamin Brawley," in *Encyclopedia of African American Culture and History*, eds. Jack Saltzman, David Lionel Smith, and Cornel West, 1996, pp. 427–428.

—Kenny Jackson Williams

BRAXTON, JOANNE M. (b. 1950), poet and critic. A distinguished writer and teacher, Joanne M. Braxton has published important *poetry and *criticism while maintaining the significance of historical and communal ties.

Joanne Margaret Braxton was born in Lakeland, Maryland, on 25 May 1950 to Mary Ellen Weems Braxton and Harry McHenry Braxton, Sr. The second of four children, she graduated from Northwestern Senior High School in Hyattsville, Maryland. Brax-

ton found her poetic voice as an undergraduate at Sarah Lawrence College; after graduating, she entered Yale University, where she earned her PhD in American Studies in 1984. Braxton wrote her dissertation on black women's *autobiography under the tutelage of scholars Charles Davis and John Blassingame.

Braxton has enjoyed a fruitful publishing career. *Sometimes I Think of Maryland* (1977), a volume of poetry, reflects the centrality of folkloric and familial traditions; Gwendolyn *Brooks hailed it for its economy, courage, and genuine expression of youthful energy. Braxton's critical study, *Black Women Writing Autobiography: A Tradition within a Tradition* (1989), is a pioneering contribution to African American feminist scholarship, presenting trenchant analyses of historical and contemporary figures such as Harriet A. *Jacobs and Maya *Angelou. In addition, Braxton is the editor of *Wild Women in the Whirlwind: Afra-American Culture and the Contemporary Literary Renaissance* (with Andree Nicola McLaughlin, 1990) and *The Collected Poetry of Paul Laurence *Dunbar* (1993). Braxton has also been a Danforth Fellow, a Roothbert Fellow, a Mellon Fellow, an American Council of Learned Societies Fellow, and a member of the Michigan Society of Fellows.

A devoted teacher as well as writer, Braxton has taught at Yale and the University of Michigan. A member of the English and American Studies departments at the College of William and Mary since 1980, she has held the Frances L. and Edwin L. Cummings chair since 1989. A renowned professor, Braxton earned the prestigious "Outstanding Virginia Faculty Award" in 1992. Braxton views herself as a cultural critic and literary historian and encourages students to participate in "reclamation," unearthing stories that have not been told. As she states in the introduction to *Wild Women*, "the current flowering of Black women's writing must be viewed as part of a cultural continuum and an evolving consciousness, a consciousness that will continue to evolve and unfold."

An exemplary scholar and teacher, Braxton has been praised widely and has worked to find her own critical voice and to empower her students so that they might find theirs. Joanne Braxton continues her scholarly and artistic pursuits, researching slave *music and preparing another edition of poetry.

[*See also* Feminism.]

• Edward T. Washington, "Joanne M. Braxton," in *DLB*, vol. 41, *Afro-American Poets since 1955*, eds. Trudier Harris and Thadious M. Davis, 1985, pp. 42–47. Hilary Holladay, "Joanne Braxton Named Outstanding Professor," *William and Mary Alumni Gazette* 60.2 (Sept. 1992): 9.

—Keith Clark

BRENT, LINDA. *See* Jacobs, Harriet A.

BRER RABBIT is the archetypal hero-*trickster character from African American oral literature. While Brer Rabbit got much exposure in Joel Chandler Harris's *Uncle Remus: His Songs and His Sayings* (1881), folklorists and literature scholars are well aware of the rich cycle of tales that circulate around this tricky and cunning figure. These tales thrived especially during the pre- and post-slave era up until the mid-1900s. Resembling the two major tricksters of Africa (Anansi, the Ashanti spider, and Ijapa, the Yoruba turtle), "Buh" Rabbit has always seemed to be the most helpless and most afraid of all the animals in the kingdom.

Brer Rabbit is constantly at odds with the likes of Brer Bear, Brer Wolf, and Sly Brer Fox. This trio, singularly or collectively, attempts to humiliate, outsmart, and sometimes even kill Brer Rabbit. In contrast, Brer Rabbit tries to nullify the plans of his stronger archenemies by using his superior intelligence and his quick thinking. He usually gets the better of the bigger and stronger animals.

Since the Brer Rabbit cycle of tales flourished during the time of *slavery and almost always involved the weak in a neverending contest with the strong, scholars view these tales as slave expressions of subversive sentiments against the institution of slavery. It was much too dangerous for slaves to reveal to slave owners the harsh realities and cruelties of slavery. But slaves could vent some of their frustrations and hostilities against their masters by participating in the performance of the Brer Rabbit tales.

As time progressed, criticism of slavery became less indirect in Brer Rabbit literature. African American oral literature gave birth to the "John and Ole Boss Tales." In this group of tales, John (sometimes known as George, Sam, Jack, Efan, or Rastus) now becomes the human analogue to Brer Rabbit. John is always in conflict with Ole Master ("Massa" or "Marse") and, like Brer Rabbit, attempts to outwit Ole Boss. Most stories show John winning over the master, but there are a sizable number of tales where "Whitey" outsmarts John.

Although the Brer Rabbit tradition and the John and Ole Boss cycle of tales are not as strong as they once were, it does seem that the "Bad Nigger" oral tales became the substitute for these earlier stories. As long as there is an environment of disparity in America, the underclass will need Brer Rabbit tales to help cope with or mask its displeasure with the inequities of the system.

[See also Folk Literature; Folklore.]

• Joel Chandler Harris, Uncle Remus: His Songs and His Sayings, 1881. Roger D. Abrahams, ed., Afro-American Folktales: Stories from Black Traditions in the New World, 1985.

—Elon A. Kulii and Beverly Threatt Kulii

BROADSIDE PRESS was founded by Dudley *Randall in Detroit in 1965 to protect by publication one of his own poems that had been set to music and recorded. Not intending further involvement, he nevertheless became a pioneer in *publishing African American *poetry through a series of broadsides, chapbooks, full-length collections, and recordings that included the work of more than two hundred poets. A critical series was also introduced. Many Broadside publications appealed to a wide audience of young readers through easily accessible poems that expressed their own frustration and rage, especially during the *Black Arts movement.

Early poets whose reputations are now well established include Sonia *Sanchez, Haki R. *Madhubuti

(Don L. Lee), and Nikki *Giovanni, as well as the late Audre *Lorde and Etheridge *Knight. Veteran poets Gwendolyn *Brooks and Sterling A. *Brown also published with Broadside.

The press experienced a period of virtual inactivity when its founder suffered a lengthy illness, rallied under temporary ownership by the Alexander *Crummell Center, and again went into decline.

In 1985 Don and Hilda Vest assumed ownership of Broadside Press and restructured it on a nonprofit basis. Under their leadership seven new titles by local poets, including an *anthology, have been published. In addition, many of the early publications have been made available again as "Broadside classics." The goal of the Vests is to develop and encourage new poets through public readings and workshops and to implement literature and arts programs in the community.

—Naomi Long Madgett

Bronzeville Boys and Girls. Often overlooked in analyses of the career of Gwendolyn *Brooks are her works for children. As a result of her own childhood filled with books, she is committed not only to the importance of reading for young people but also to the notion that there must be some material for them. Bronzeville Boys and Girls (1956) is the first in a series of works designed specifically for younger readers. The thirty-four poems in the collection are simple and extremely brief. Most of them rely heavily on the traditional rhyme scheme of abcb often coupled with very short lines. As a result the poetic voice seems to suggest not only poems for a child but poems in the voice of a child. When she turns to *poetry for children, there is a strain of romantic idealism as she suggests the beauty of uncrowded nature.

Like the earlier A Street in Bronzeville (1945), this collection is also set in Chicago, but it could take place in any crowded urban area, and the characters who are black Chicagoans could be of any race or ethnic group. Race and locale are less important than the fact that the young characters are in the process of self-discovery. Some poems express happiness as does the opening poem "Maxie and Birdie," which records two youngsters having a "tiny tea-party" with "pink cakes." Others are sad as they recount the experiences of children like Lyle, who looks at a tree lovingly because the tree can stay where it is whereas Lyle has "waved good-bye to seven homes." There is Otto who did not get the Christmas present he wanted but is mature enough to hide his feelings from his father. Then there is the contemplative Rudolph, who "is tired of the city" and who explains overcrowding by observing "these buildings are too close to me." These are just a few of the children who populate Bronzeville Boys and Girls.

The sense of belonging and a feeling for one's neighborhood inform the poems in this collection. Rather than viewing impoverished or deteriorating surroundings with loathing, Brooks suggests that one can find the beauty in family and home no matter how unpleasant a locale may be.

[See also Children's and Young Adult Literature.]

• Maria K. Mootry and Gary Smith, eds., *A Life Distilled: Gwendolyn Brooks, Her Poetry and Fiction*, 1987.

—Kenny Jackson Williams

BROOKS, GWENDOLYN (b. 1917), poet, novelist, and children's writer. Although she was born on 7 June 1917 in Topeka, Kansas—the first child of David and Keziah Brooks—Gwendolyn Brooks is "a Chicagoan." The family moved to Chicago shortly after her birth, and despite her extensive travels and periods in some of the major universities of the country, she has remained associated with the city's South Side. What her strong family unit lacked in material wealth was made bearable by the wealth of human capital that resulted from warm interpersonal relationships. When she writes about families that—despite their daily adversities—are not dysfunctional, Gwendolyn Brooks writes from an intimate knowledge reinforced by her own life.

Brooks attended Hyde Park High School, the leading white high school in the city, but transferred to the all-black Wendell Phillips, then to the integrated Englewood High School. In 1936 she graduated from Wilson Junior College. These four schools gave her a perspective on racial dynamics in the city that continues to influence her work.

Her profound interest in *poetry informed much of her early life. "Eventide," her first poem, was published in *American Childhood Magazine* in 1930. A few years later she met James Weldon *Johnson and Langston *Hughes, who urged her to read modern poetry—especially the work of Ezra Pound, T. S. Eliot, and e. e. cummings—and who emphasized the need to write as much and as frequently as she possibly could. By 1934 Brooks had become an adjunct member of the staff of the *Chicago Defender* and had published almost one hundred of her poems in a weekly poetry column.

In 1938 she married Henry Blakely and moved to a kitchenette apartment on Chicago's South Side. Between the birth of her first child, Henry, Jr., in 1940 and the birth of Nora in 1951, she became associated with the group of writers involved in Harriet Monroe's still-extant *Poetry: A Magazine of Verse*. From this group she received further encouragement, and by 1943 she had won the Midwestern Writer's Conference Poetry Award.

In 1945 her first book of poetry, *A *Street in Bronzeville* (published by Harper and Row), brought her instant critical acclaim. She was selected one of *Mademoiselle* magazine's "Ten Young Women of the Year," she won her first Guggenheim Fellowship, and she became a fellow of the American Academy of Arts and Letters. Her second book of poems, *Annie Allen* (1949), won *Poetry* magazine's Eunice Tietjens Prize. In 1950 Gwendolyn Brooks became the first African American to win a Pulitzer Prize. From that time to the present, she has been the recipient of a number of awards, fellowships, and honorary degrees usually designated as Doctor of Humane Letters.

President John Kennedy invited her to read at a Library of Congress poetry festival in 1962. In 1985 she was appointed poetry consultant to the Library of Congress. Just as receiving a Pulitzer Prize for poetry marked a milestone in her career, so also did her selection by the National Endowment for the Humanities as the 1994 Jefferson Lecturer, the highest award in the humanities given by the federal government.

Her first teaching job was a poetry workshop at Columbia College (Chicago) in 1963. She went on to teach creative writing at a number of institutions including Northeastern Illinois University, Elmhurst College, Columbia University, Clay College of New York, and the University of Wisconsin.

A turning point in her career came in 1967 when she attended the Fisk University Second Black Writers' Conference and decided to become more involved in the *Black Arts movement. She became one of the most visible articulators of "the *black aesthetic." Her "awakening" led to a shift away from a major publishing house to smaller black ones. While some critics found an angrier tone in her work, elements of protest had always been present in her writing and her awareness of social issues did not result in diatribes at the expense of her clear commitment to aesthetic principles. Consequently, becoming the leader of one phase of the Black Arts movement in Chicago did not drastically alter her poetry, but there were some subtle changes that become more noticeable when one examines her total canon to date.

The ambiguity of her role as a black poet can be illustrated by her participation in two events in Chicago. In 1967 Brooks, who wrote the commemorative ode for the "Chicago Picasso," attended the unveiling ceremony along with social and business dignitaries. The poem was well received even though such lines as "Art hurts. Art urges voyages . . ." made some uncomfortable. Less than two weeks later there was the dedication of the mural known as "The Wall of Respect" at 43rd and Langley streets, in the heart of the black neighborhood. The social and business elites of Chicago were not present, but for this event Gwendolyn Brooks wrote "The Wall." In a measure these two poems illustrate the dichotomy of a divided city, but they also exemplify Brooks's ability both to bridge those divisions and to utilize nonstrident protest.

Gwendolyn Brooks has been a prolific writer. In addition to individual poems, *essays, and reviews that have appeared in numerous publications, she has issued a number of books in rapid succession, including *Maud Martha* (1953), *Bronzeville Boys and Girls* (1956), and *In the Mecca* (1968). Her poetry moves from traditional forms including ballads, sonnets, variations of the Chaucerian and Spenserian stanzas as well as the rhythm of the *blues to the most unrestricted free verse. In short, the popular forms of English poetry appear in her work; yet there is a strong sense of experimentation as she juxtaposes lyric, narrative, and dramatic poetic forms. In her lyrics there is an affirmation of life that rises above the stench of urban kitchenette buildings. In her narrative poetry the stories are simple but usually transcend the restrictions of place; in her dramatic poetry, the characters are often memorable not because of any heroism on their part but merely because they are trying to survive from day to day.

Brooks's poetry is marked by some unforgettable characters who are drawn from the underclass of the nation's black neighborhoods. Like many urban writers, Brooks has recorded the impact of city life. But unlike the most committed naturalists, she does not hold the city completely responsible for what happens to people. The city is simply an existing force with which people must cope.

While they are generally insignificant in the great urban universe, her characters gain importance—at least to themselves—in their tiny worlds, whether it be Annie Allen trying on a hat in a milliner's shop or DeWitt Williams "on his way to Lincoln Cemetery" or Satin-Legs Smith trying to decide what outlandish outfit to wear on Sundays. Just as there is not a strong naturalistic sense of victimization, neither are there great plans for an unpromised future nor is there some great divine spirit that will rescue them. Brooks is content to describe a moment in the lives of very ordinary people whose only goal is to exist from day to day and perhaps have a nice funeral when they die. Sometimes these ordinary people seem to have a control that is out of keeping with their own insignificance.

Although her poetic voice is objective, there is a strong sense that she—as an observer—is never far from her action. On one level, of course, Brooks is a protest poet; yet her protest evolves through suggestion rather than through a bludgeon. She sets forth the facts without embellishment or interpretation, but the simplicity of the facts makes it impossible for readers to come away unconvinced—despite whatever discomfort they may feel—whether she is writing about suburban ladies who go into the ghetto to give occasional aid or a black mother who has had an abortion.

Trying to determine clear lines of influence from the work of earlier writers to later ones is always a risky business; however, knowing some identifiable poetic traditions can aid in understanding the work of Gwendolyn Brooks. On one level there is the English metaphysical tradition perhaps best exemplified by John Donne. From nineteenth-century American poetry one can detect elements of Walt Whitman, Emily Dickinson, and Paul Laurence *Dunbar. From twentieth-century American poetry there are many strains, most notably the compact style of T. S. Eliot, the frequent use of the lower-case for titles in the manner of e. e. cummings, and the racial consciousness of the *Harlem Renaissance, especially as found in the work of Countee *Cullen and Langston Hughes; but, of perhaps greater importance, she seems to be a direct descendant of the urban commitment and attitude of the "Chicago School" of writing. For Brooks, setting goes beyond the Midwest with a focus on Chicago and concentrates on a small neglected corner of the city. Consequently, in the final analysis, she is not a carbon copy of any of the Chicago writers.

She was appointed poet laureate of Illinois in 1968 and has been perhaps more active than many laureates. She has done much to bring poetry to the people through accessibility and public readings. In fact, she is one of our most visible American poets. Not only is she extremely active in the poetry workshop movement, but her classes and contests for young people are attempts to help inner-city children see "the poetry" in their lives. She has taught audiences that poetry is not some formal activity closed to all but the most perceptive. Rather, it is an art form within the reach and understanding of everybody—including the lowliest among us.

[See also Protest Literature.]

• Gwendolyn Brooks, Report from Part One, 1972. Maria K. Mootry and Gary Smith, eds., A Life Distilled: Gwendolyn Brooks, Her Poetry and Fiction, 1987. George E. Kent, A Life of Gwendolyn Brooks, 1990.

—Kenny Jackson Williams

Brothers and Keepers (1984) is one of John Edgar *Wideman's two major works of nonfiction; the other is Fatheralong (1994). Of Wideman's numerous books, it is Brothers and Keepers for which he is probably best known to the general reading public. Described by Wideman as a personal *essay about his younger brother Robby and himself, it deals with the first of two tragic events in the author's life: Robby's imprisonment for his involvement in a crime, which Wideman previously had given fictional treatment in his *novel Hiding Place (1981). (The second tragedy, the conviction and imprisonment for murder of Wideman's youngest son, is dealt with somewhat obliquely in Wideman's novel *Philadelphia Fire, 1990, and in "Father Stories," the final piece in Fatheralong.)

One question Wideman wrestles with in the book—and that the reader must wrestle with also—is how can two brothers raised in the same environment (the black neighborhood of Homewood in Pittsburgh, Pennsylvania, locale of the majority of Wideman's fiction) end up having such radically different lives: one a Rhodes Scholar, college professor, and acclaimed author, the other a drug addict with dreams of being a big-time dealer who now is serving a life sentence? This stark polarity—the middle-class professional versus the "gangsta"—is something Wideman attempts to explore and deconstruct in his narrative. It isn't that he fails to recognize that he and his brother are different; rather, since they shared the same family upbringing, the important thing for Wideman is, given the similarities between Robby and himself, what has created the gulf between them? For all his brotherly concern, Wideman cannot absolve Robby from responsibility for the choices he and many other young black men like him have made, yet he is eloquent in evoking the forces in our society that have conspired to distort and limit those choices.

Reviewers as divergent as Christopher Lehmann-Haupt and Ishmael *Reed have found the book's undoubted strengths to be the gripping quality of the story it tells and the skillful interplay between the two quite distinct voices of Wideman and his younger brother.

Wideman has reiterated in several interviews that all of his books are about family—its intricacies, agonies, and strengths. And the troubles and triumphs of a particular family—Wideman's own, rendered in fact and in fiction—are clearly related to the problems and promises of that extended family called the community, the nation. In a time of much rhetorical obeisance to "family values," a book like *Brothers and Keepers* reminds us that the stresses of the nuclear family and those of the national family are mutually interlocked, and that being your brother's keeper in the traditional sense may be one way to avoid his being "caged" by keepers of quite another sort.

Brothers and Keepers is part of the long tradition of tale-telling, self-discovery, and social arraignment that constitutes African American *autobiography. Like Nathan McCall's *Makes Me Wanna Holler* (1994) and Brent Staples's *Parallel Time* (1994), Wideman's book continues the story of flight begun in the *slave narratives into a present still tormented by the unresolved legacies of "*race," where even those black Americans who can be said to have "made it" nevertheless see themselves as fugitives.

—Robert Elliot Fox

BROUGHTON, VIRGINIA W. (18?–1934), educator, leader and organizer of African American Baptist women, missionary, and feminist theologian. Author of both a spiritual autobiography, *Twenty Year's Experience of a Missionary* (1907), and a work of feminist theology, *Women's Work, as Gleaned from the Women of the Bible, and Bible Women of Modern Times* (1904), Virginia W. Broughton also wrote for *periodicals connected with the black Baptist church. Born before the Civil War to self-emancipated parents, Broughton attended a private school and was a member of Fisk University's first graduating class in 1875. After graduation she began teaching in the Memphis public school system and rapidly advanced to head teacher despite challenging sexist and racist promotion practices.

Broughton taught for twelve years before completely devoting her time to the missionary work on which her autobiography focuses. She began her work during her first attendance at a missionary meeting for women only at the invitation of Joanna Moore, a white missionary with the American Baptist Home Mission Society and founder of the Fireside Schools, where Broughton worked for several years. At that meeting they organized the first Bible Band in Memphis, which rapidly grew and spread under Broughton's leadership. In 1888 Broughton was asked to organize a district association of Bible Bands to help fund the black Baptist "Bible and Normal Institute," where Broughton taught during the 1890s. An official missionary as of 1892, Broughton traveled throughout the state and to various southern cities, often finding herself in places where few African American men had ever preached, let alone women of any race. Broughton was instrumental in organizing a separate convention for African American women, and in 1900 the Women's Convention, Auxiliary of the National Baptist Convention, USA, elected her recording secretary, a position she held for several years.

Broughton's works are not widely known today, but her autobiography, which concludes with out-lines of biblically based arguments supporting women's spiritual work, fits into the tradition of women's spiritual writings that dates from the Middle Ages. *Twenty Year's Experience as a Missionary*, moreover, offers an important contribution to the tradition of African American women's spiritual writings that begins with Phillis *Wheatley and continues in the spiritual narratives of other preaching women such as Jarena *Lee, Maria W. *Stewart, Julia A. J. *Foote, Zilpha *Elaw, and Amanda Berry *Smith. The businesslike tone of her autobiography, written entirely in the third person and heavily laced with commercial metaphors, particularly emphasizes that these women were career women as well as intensely spiritual beings.

[*See also* Autobiography, *article on* Spiritual Autobiography; Feminism.]

• Sue E. Houchins, introduction to *Spiritual Narratives*, 1988. Evelyn Brooks Higginbotham, *Righteous Discontent: The Women's Movement in the Black Baptist Church, 1880–1920*, 1993.

—Lori Askeland

BROWN, CECIL (b. 1943), novelist and short story and script writer. Cecil Brown has not been a prolific writer; indeed, the bulk of his literary reputation rests on his first *novel, *The Life and Loves of Mr. Jiveass Nigger*, published in 1969. Yet to dismiss Brown as a minor writer based on the lack of prolificacy is to diminish the tremendous impact that his starkly ironic and penetratingly satiric narrative voice has made on the development of contemporary African American letters. Brown's influence has grown tremendously in the quarter century since his literary debut, and the discomfiting hilarity that is his trademark is now far more the rule than the exception in African American literature, particularly among African American male writers.

Cecil Brown was born 3 July 1943 in Bolton, North Carolina, in the southeastern section of the state, to tobacco sharecropper parents. He began his college education at North Carolina A & T State University in Greensboro but later transferred to Columbia University, where he was awarded a BA in English in 1966. He earned an MA degree from the University of Chicago in 1967 before embarking upon the dual career of writer and teacher at the collegiate level. He later earned a PhD in *folklore from the University of California at Berkeley.

After a few short articles placed in reputable journals like the *Kenyon Review* and *Negro Digest*, Brown's *The Life and Loves of Mr. Jiveass Nigger* appeared in 1969 to mixed, though often exuberant, reviews. Most critics point to the novel's central character, George Washington, as the archetypal figure of the prodigal son who wanders far from home (to Copenhagen in this case), wastes himself in riotous living, meets with adversity and misfortune, and resolves to return home where things are infinitely better than he had earlier supposed. Brown infuses new life into a predictable plot with an insistence on the importance of myth and storytelling, and with a narrative voice that bridges Ralph *Ellison's comic elegance of the 1940s and 1950s with the comic bawdiness and perverseness of writers like Ishmael *Reed, Clarence *Major, Charles R. *Johnson, and Percival Everett of subsequent decades.

Brown continued the development of both theme and technique in subsequent works, most notably in a *short story, "The Time Is Now" (1981), in his second novel, *Days Without Weather* (1982), and in his *autobiography, *Coming Up Down Home* (1993). Here the homecoming of the prodigal son is more in the spiritual sense of recognizing, embracing, and understanding one's roots. The tone is customarily comic and sardonic.

Dating back to the early years of his career, Cecil Brown has been involved in writing screenplays and stage plays, including some work with the comic actor Richard Pryor. These endeavors, while sustaining him between publishing projects, also demonstrate Brown's appreciation of the comic aspects of African American life and his knowledge that within the comedy one also finds irony, complexity, beauty, and strength.

• Jean M. Bright, "Cecil Brown," in *DLB*, vol. 33, *Afro-American Fiction Writers after 1955*, eds. Trudier Harris and Thadious M. Davis, 1984, pp. 32–35. Randall Kenan, *"Coming Up Down Home*: A Memoir of Southern Childhood," *New York Times Book Review*, 22 Aug. 1993, 13.

—Warren J. Carson

BROWN, CLAUDE (b. 1937), autobiographer, writer, and social commentator. Claude Brown was born in New York City on 23 February 1937 to Henry Lee and Ossie Brock Brown, South Carolinians who had come north in 1935 looking for economic opportunities unavailable in the South. Growing up in Harlem involved Claude Brown in crime and *violence early in his life. By the time he was ten, he had joined the stealing division of a notorious street gang and had a history of truancy and expulsion from school. At eleven, Brown was sent to the Wiltwyck school for delinquent boys, where he came under the supervision of Dr. Ernest Papanek, whose positive influence in his life Brown would later acknowledge.

Back on the streets after two years at Wiltwyck, at age thirteen Brown was shot during an attempted robbery. A year later, he was sent to the Warwick school for boys, where he completed three terms before his final release in July 1953. From this point on, Brown gradually freed himself from the destructive street life of the Harlem ghetto. He began high school when he was sixteen and graduated in 1957. During these years, Brown held various odd jobs in New York and played *jazz in Greenwich Village.

Claude Brown continued his education at Howard University, finishing a degree in government and business in 1965, the same year that Macmillan published his *autobiography, *Manchild in the Promised Land*. The work originated from a piece Brown had written for *Dissent* magazine. Encouraged to expand the work into a full-length narrative, Brown produced a 1,537-page manuscript that became, after extensive editing, a hugely successful best-seller. Critics praised the vivid realism of *Manchild* and favorably compared Brown to James *Baldwin, Ralph

*Ellison, and Richard *Wright. Like them, Brown was hailed as a powerful, relentless chronicler of the brutal reality of African American life in northern urban cities. Additionally, *Manchild in the Promised Land* was held up as an American success story, the narrative of one who beat the odds of his childhood and saved his own life.

The publication of his autobiography made Claude Brown a new authoritative voice in the African American community. He published a second book, *The Children of Ham*, in 1976. Much less well received than *Manchild*, this book records the stories of thirteen Harlem residents, focusing on their struggles against poverty, crime, and drugs.

Brown has largely dropped from public view since the publication of his books, but his work reveals his continuing concern for the problems facing people in the inner city. For example, his 1987 documentary "Manchild Revisited: A Commentary by Claude Brown" addresses urban crime. In it, Brown supports capital punishment; voluntarism in black neighborhoods to fight crime; more prosecutors, judges, and prisons; and the decriminalization of drugs. Although nothing Brown has done since publishing *Manchild in the Promised Land* has created the sensation that book did, Brown remains a thoughtful, sometimes controversial commentator on African American social issues.

[*See also* Identity; Manhood.]

• "Brown, Claude," in *CA*, vols. 73–76, ed. Frances Carol Locher, 1978, pp. 88–189.

—David L. Dudley

BROWN, FRANK LONDON (1927–1962), novelist, activist, and important figure among Chicago-based urban realists. Born in Kansas City, Frank London Brown moved to Chicago at age twelve. Educated at Roosevelt University and the University of Chicago, Brown worked numerous jobs to support his literary ambitions. Most significant of these was his work as an organizer and program officer for the United Packinghouse Workers of America and other labor unions. Brown was profoundly impacted by the musical culture of African American Chicago, most significantly *jazz, but also gospel and *blues. A devotee of bebop, Brown published a seminal interview with Thelonious Monk in *Downbeat* and pioneered in the reading of fiction to jazz accompaniment. Many critics have also noted the importance of a trip Brown made as a journalist to cover the Emmett Till murder case. At the time of his death, he was an accomplished writer on the Chicago scene and a regular contributor to *Negro Digest* and various literary magazines. He was also a candidate for a PhD from the University of Chicago's Committee on Social Thought and was director of the Union Research Center.

His reputation is largely based upon his 1959 *novel, *Trumbull Park*, an account of the struggles facing African American families attempting to integrate a Chicago housing development. However, his short fiction and especially his 1969 posthumous novel, *The Myth Maker*, deserve greater attention.

Trumbull Park was typical of social realist fiction in the style of Theodore Dreiser and Upton Sinclair, while *The Myth Maker* demonstrates an interest in Fyodor Dostoyevsky and the existentialist novel. Both texts are clearly influenced by the work of Richard *Wright. Their great accomplishment is the detailed description of the "everyday" of urban African American experience, excellent attention to vernacular *speech and dialect, and a philosophically sophisticated account of the rise of despair in the ghetto and the continuing deprecatory impact of institutionalized racism. Both novels are occasionally limited by deficient character and plot development. *Trumbull Park* has received a moderate amount of critical attention and *The Myth Maker* none. Brown's occasional *short stories also reveal attention to language and a strong commitment to realism as a mode of expression and investigation. His most popular story, "McDougal" (Abraham Chapman, *Black Voices*, 1968) is noteworthy for its sympathetic treatment of a white trumpet player attempting to succeed as a jazz musician within the very environment of Chicago's 58th Street that Brown had long chronicled.

In addition to the accomplishment of his two novels, Brown's reputation should also be enhanced by his exploration of the possibility of an artistic life irreducibly connected to a life of social action. His participation in leftist political activity and countercultural artistic movements at the height of McCarthyism and the Cold War is suggestive of a courageous intellect. His succumbing to leukemia in March of 1962 just prior to the dawning of the *Black Arts movement in Chicago is one of the major tragedies of contemporary African American literature.

•Sterling Stuckey, "Frank London Brown—A Remembrance," in *Black Voices*, ed. Abraham Chapman, 1968, pp. 669–676. Maryemma Graham, "Bearing Witness in Black Chicago: A View of Selected Fiction by Richard Wright, Frank London Brown, and Ronald Fair," *CLA Journal* 33 (March 1990): 280–297.   —James C. Hall

BROWN, HALLIE Q. (c. 1847–1949), elocutionist, educator, suffragist, civil rights activist, and biographer. Hallie Quinn Brown was born to former slaves in Pittsburgh, Pennsylvania; her parents' abolitionism fostered in her a lifelong commitment to human rights advocacy. Early educated in Ontario, Canada, where her family resided from 1864 to 1870, Brown earned a bachelor's degree at Ohio's Wilberforce University in 1873. At Wilberforce, she heard Susan B. Anthony speak on women's suffrage, and immediately incorporated women's rights into her impassioned activism. She graduated from Chautauqua Lecture School in 1886 and received honorary advanced degrees from both Chautauqua (1890) and Wilberforce (1936).

In 1873, Brown migrated south to instruct exslaves in South Carolina and Mississippi. During the next fifty years, her educational service included dean of Allen University in Columbia, South Carolina; dean of women during Booker T. *Washington's administration at Tuskegee Institute; and professor of elocution at Wilberforce. An illustrious orator, Brown also traveled throughout Europe intermittently between 1894 and 1910, addressing international conventions of women's temperance and missionary societies. Her leadership of the Ohio Federation of Colored Women's Clubs from 1905 to 1912 yielded the formation of affiliate clubs in other cities, and eventually of the National Association of Colored Women, over which she presided from 1920 to 1924.

Brown's more than seven publications include *Homespun Heroines and Other Women of Distinction* (1926), an elegantly illustrated compilation of sixty *biographies of distinguished African American women born between the mid-1700s and 1875. Exemplars of domesticity, morality, and industry, these subjects, and their twenty-eight biographers, epitomize African American women's definitive contributions to American society and economy.

[See also Collective Biography; Oratory.]

• Randall K. Burkett, ed., introduction to *Homespun Heroines and Other Women of Distinction*, 1988.
                                                —Joycelyn K. Moody

BROWN, HENRY "BOX" (1815–?), fugitive slave, antislavery lecturer, and author of the *Narrative of the Life of Henry "Box" Brown, Written by Himself* (1851). The earlier *Narrative of Henry Box Brown, Who Escaped from Slavery Enclosed in a Box 3 Feet Long and 2 Wide* (1849) was not written by Henry Brown himself, but by a white abolitionist, Charles Stearns, who compiled the book from a statement by Brown.

Henry Brown, born into *slavery outside Richmond, Virginia, decided to escape after his wife and children were sold. His nickname comes from the unusual method he chose: while praying for guidance, the idea came to him to ship himself to *freedom in a box. With the help of white friends, he executed the plan and was shipped by Adams Express from Richmond to Philadelphia, where an abolitionist society received him. Brown spent much of the twenty-seven-hour trip in agony, the box upended and Brown turned on his head. After his escape, Brown lectured against slavery, touring the northern states and, after passage of the Fugitive Slave Act (1850), removing to England for several years. The date and place of his death are unknown.

Brown's *Narrative*, using familiar themes of antislavery rhetoric, condemns slavery's "withering touch" on slaves and masters alike, especially its destructive effects on morality (especially sexual), religion, and the family. As in many *slave narratives, Brown sees his achievement of *freedom as a kind of rebirth, a "resurrection from the grave of slavery." After passing through the dangerous, painful purgatory of confinement in the box, he emerges a free man among equals: "I had risen as it were from the dead." The circumstances of Brown's escape intensify this resurrection imagery to a degree unusual in slave literature, underscoring the crucial role of Christianity in Brown's experience.

[See also Antislavery Movement.]

• "Henry 'Box' Brown," in *Black Men in Chains: Narratives by Escaped Slaves*, ed. Charles H. Nichols, 1972, pp. 177–199.
                                                —Gary Ashwill

BROWN, JOHN (1800–1859), also known as Osawatomie Brown, white abolitionist and leader of the Harpers Ferry raid. African American essayists, historians, novelists, playwrights, and poets have found in John Brown both a symbol of sacrifice and a touchstone of commitment to the cause of black *freedom. A devoutly religious radical abolitionist descended from six generations of Connecticut farmers, John Brown organized and led the 16–18 October 1859 raid on Harpers Ferry, Virginia (now West Virginia), that ended in seventeen deaths and his own capture and execution on 2 December. His failed attempt to destroy American *slavery by force and his eloquent courtroom defense of the rights of slaves made him a hero to African Americans. Frederick *Douglass said of his friend: "I could live for the slave, but he could die for him." W. E. B. *Du Bois's 1909 *biography of Brown was an avowed "tribute to the [white] man who of all Americans has perhaps come nearest to touching the souls of black folk."

For some African American writers Brown transcends race and time. In 1974 Lerone Bennett, Jr., claimed that Brown was "of no color . . . of no race or age" and that his example helped African Americans understand the "limitations and possibilities" of their own lives. In Michael S. *Harper's 1972 poetic eulogy, "History as Cap'n Brown," Brown cries, "Come to the crusade . . . not Negroes, *brothers*." At the height of the Black Power movement, when radicals dismissed Abraham *Lincoln as a reluctant emancipator and white supremacist, they used Brown as an archetype of self-sacrifice against which white liberals might be judged. "If you are for me and my problems," *Malcolm X said in 1965, "then you have to be willing to do as old John Brown did."

Other African American writers celebrate John Brown as a clarion call echoing through the "long black song" of their people's quest for freedom. To promote pride in black heroes, William Blackwell *Branch wrote the play *In Splendid Error* (1953) to justify Frederick Douglass's decision not to go with Brown to Harpers Ferry. Yet Branch honors Brown's passion even as he constructs a heroic Douglass whose "cold wisdom" and sense of duty to his people instruct him not to die with Brown. In the 1960s, as Stephen Butterfield has written, alienated young African American radicals sought to kindle the "sacred fire" of John Brown's memory without permitting it to "burn the black out of their souls."

Through the years, African American writers have seen Brown variously as a symbol of humanity and brotherhood, a martyr to the cause of emancipation, a voice for forcible resistance, a prophet of racial strife, God's instrument to ignite a war to end slavery, and a sign of white America's eventual redemption.

[*See also* Antislavery Movement.]

• W. E. Burghardt Du Bois, *John Brown*, 1909; rpt. 1962. Benjamin Quarles, ed., *Blacks on John Brown*, 1972. Daniel C. Littlefield, "Blacks, John Brown, and a Theory of Manhood," in *His Soul Goes Marching On*, ed. Paul Finkelman, 1995.   —Robert E. McGlone

BROWN, LINDA BEATRICE (b. 1939), poet, novelist, and professor. Linda Beatrice Brown was a rising young poet of the 1960s and 1970s whose mentor was the poet Gwendolyn *Brooks. She has one published volume of *poetry, *A Love Song to Black Men* (1974). In 1984 she published a novel, *Rainbow Roun Mah Shoulder* (under the name Linda Brown Bragg). This work is in the tradition of Zora Neale *Hurston's *Their Eyes Were Watching God* (1937) in its southern African American heroine, skillful use of southern African American speech patterns, and depiction of the interrelatedness of God, nature, and the supernatural in the African American folk community. Some of her first poems appeared in the well-known anthology edited by Rosey Pool entitled *Beyond the Blues* (1960), and her work later appeared in publishing outlets such as the *Black Scholar*, *Encore*, *Ebony*, and *Writer's Choice*.

Brown was born in Akron, Ohio, on 14 March 1939 to Raymond and Edith Player Brown. She attended college at the historic all-black, all-female Bennett College in Greensboro, North Carolina, where she had opportunities to hear poetry readings by Langston *Hughes and Sterling A. *Brown. While a junior in college she published her first poem, "Precocious Curiosity," in *Beyond the Blues*; she earned her bachelors degree in 1961. She furthered her education by obtaining a masters degree in 1962 from Case Western Reserve University, where she was a Woodrow Wilson Teaching Fellow. That was also the year she married Harold Bragg. She spent the next two years on a teaching fellowship at Kent State University. Her son Christopher was born in 1967 and her daughter Willa in 1969. For sixteen years (1970–1986), Brown taught at the University of North Carolina at Greensboro. She also earned a PhD from Union Graduate School in Cincinnati, Ohio, in 1980.

Brown recognizes a variety of influences on her poetry. The English Romantics, the focus of her graduate studies, were an influence on her early poetry. She says later influences were Robert Frost because of his "simplicity, his use of conversational feeling, and his quiet serenity"; Brooks because of "her clean use of language, her unconventional metaphor"; and Haki R. *Madhubuti (Don L. Lee) because of his "rhythmic quality."

A Brown poem may have a conversational or musical rhythm. A line of speech ringing in her head may be the inspiration for a poem with natural, conversational rhythm. A background saturated with *music (she took voice lessons for several years) accounts for the musical rhythm of some of her poetry. Her poem "High on Sounds," for instance, has the rhythm of African American music.

Brown writes primarily for an African American audience, and some facet of the African American experience is usually the inspiration for or subject of her poetry. She views her poetry as an instrument for African American survival. She feels the African American poet has the responsibility to make political statements but should also have the freedom to write on any subject. Brown feels no conflict between being political as well as artistic in her poetry.

Like other African American female writers, Brown often writes about the African American male-female relationship. In "Don't Honey Me," she asserts that the African American female has traditionally been independent because of the African American male's preoccupation with survival. In "The Race" the relay race is a metaphor for the African American woman running interference for the survival of African Americans.

Brown depicts the strength of the African American woman in *Rainbow Roun Mah Shoulder* (1984; she returned to using the name Brown when the *novel was reissued in 1989). This episodic novel, which takes place from 1915 to 1954, mainly in North Carolina, traces the life and loves of Rebecca Florice. As a young woman Florice leaves her husband and home in New Orleans to obey an inner calling to become a spiritual healer. Florice is a multifaceted character who becomes a pillar of strength to those around her, healing them physically with prayer and a laying on of hands. But she is plagued by tragic relationships with men. When a married minister breaks off an affair of several years' duration with her, she tries to commit suicide. What sustains her are her vocation and her long-term friendship to Ronnie, her goddaughter. The novel ends with Florice's death, but her spirit lives on in Ronnie, the inheritor of her spiritual gifts. A recurring metaphor of butterflies and moths suggests Florice's transformation into a deeply spiritual person and her inner beauty and strength. The National Endowment for the Arts selected the novel "as one of a few titles to represent new American writing in international book exhibits."

Brown's 1994 novel, *Crossing Over Jordan* (published under the name Linda Beatrice Brown), traces the lives of four generations of African American women from the post–Civil War era to the mid-twenty-first century. From Georgia McCloud, born a slave, to her great-granddaughter, Hermine, we see the lonely lives of African American women marred by abuse and sustained by *religion. The greater part of the novel shows the mellowing of the mother-daughter relationship in the growing mutual respect of Georgia's granddaughter Story and Story's daughter Hermine, who becomes involved in the tumultuous recent past.

Brown, married to artist Vandorn Hinnant, resides in Greensboro, North Carolina. She is on the faculty at Guilford College, where she teaches African American literature and creative writing.

• Linda Beatrice Brown, interview by Virginia W. Smith and Brian J. Benson, *CLA Journal* 20.1 (Sept. 1976): 75–87. Mary Brookhart, "Linda Beatrice Brown," *Black Women in America*, vol. 1, ed. Darlene Clark Hine, 1993, pp. 179–180.

—Phiefer L. Browne

BROWN, LLOYD (b. 1913), novelist, short fiction writer, journalist, and editor of *New Masses* and *Masses and Mainstream*. Lloyd Louis Brown grew up in an African American home for the elderly. His *short story "God's Chosen People" (1948) is based on this experience. Brown had little formal education beyond elementary school; he was self-taught. In 1929, Brown joined the Young Communist Youth League.

A trade union organizer for many years, Brown

was incarcerated for seven months in 1941 on conspiracy charges. His prison experience and friendship with the inmate Willie Jones became the basis for his *novel *Iron City* (1951), which exposes the Jim Crow nature of the prison system and suggests *communism as the answer to the American racial question.

The stories "Jericho, USA" (1946) and "Battle in Canaan" (1947), which center on African American troops being trained for World War II, depict Jim Crow in the army and, like his other fiction, are rich with the folk traditions of Brown's people. Brown spent three and a half years in the army air force during the war.

Brown was an editor of the communist journals *New Masses* and *Masses and Mainstream* (1946–1954), to which he contributed short stories, editorials, articles, and book reviews. He often reviewed works by African American writers. He always reviewed on political grounds, criticizing anticommunist ideas and negative characteristics of African Americans. In his editorials and articles Brown discusses many subjects: racism, civil rights, white chauvinism, censorship, McCarthyism, and the Smith Act.

Perhaps Brown's most important *essay is "Which Way for the Negro Writer?" (1951). Brown contradicts his contemporaries who argue for universality and distance from African American subject matter, by asserting that African American writers need to work toward their own people and move with them to universality. He denies that there is a contradiction between universal themes and African American subject matter or forms, claiming that the problem with African American literature is that it has not been close enough to the African American people and culture.

Brown wrote an unpublished novel, *Year of Jubilee*, a chapter of which appeared in *Masses and Mainstream* in 1953 as "Cousin Oscar," but did not publish the novel because literary critics advised against it.

In 1953, for personal not philosophical reasons, Lloyd Brown left the Communist party. He worked for many years with Paul *Robeson, collaborating on Robeson's *Freedom* articles and *autobiography *Here I Stand*. Unlike many other African American authors, Brown never denounced communism or the party; he wrote a procommunist novel at a time when many African American authors were becoming disenchanted with the Communist party. Despite the racism and anticommunism that Brown so clearly depicts in his work, he was still able to express the dignity of his people and their culture, and his hope. Although his ideas were disseminated widely in the communist journals, his work is largely ignored today.

[*See also* Journalism; Protest Literature.]

• Jabari Onaje Simama, "Black Writers Experience Communism," PhD diss., Emory University, 1978.

—Karen Ruth Kornweibel

BROWN, STERLING A. (1901–1989), poet, critic, and anthologist. Sterling Allen Brown was born on

1 May 1901 into what some have called the "smug" or even "affected" respectability of Washington's African American middle class. He grew up in the Washington world of racial segregation, which engendered a contradiction between full citizenship and marginalized existence. The son of a distinguished pastor and theologian, Brown graduated with honors from the prestigious Dunbar High School in 1918. That fall, he entered Williams College on a scholarship set aside for minority students. By the time he left in 1922, he had performed spectacularly: election to Phi Beta Kappa in his junior year, the Graves Prize for his *essay "The Comic Spirit in Shakespeare and Molière," the only student awarded "Final Honors" in English, and cum laude graduation with an AB degree.

At Harvard University from 1922 to 1923, Brown took an MA degree in English. In retrospect, he always talked about his fortuitous discovery of Louis Untermeyer's *Modern American Poetry* (1921). This *anthology, more than any other single work he read, radically altered his view of art by introducing him to the New American Poetry of Edwin Arlington Robinson, Robert Frost, Carl Sandburg, Vachel Lindsay, and other experimenters in melding vernacular language, democratic values, and "the extraordinary in ordinary life." When he left, however, he left knowing what the illustrator of *Southern Road* (1932) would later observe about him: "Harvard only gave you the way to *put it down,* not how to feel about things."

The sensitivity to the philosophical and poetic potential in African American folk life, lore, and language was developed in Brown during a series of teaching assignments in Negro colleges, including Virginia Seminary and College (1923–1926), Lincoln University in Missouri (1926–1928), and Fisk University (1928–1929). In each of these locations, he set about absorbing the cultural and aesthetic influences that would define the folk-based metaphysic of his art. On numerous "*folklore collecting trips" into "jook-joints," barbershops, and isolated farms, Brown absorbed the wit and wisdom of Mrs. Bibby, Calvin "Big Boy" Davis, *Slim Greer, and many more actual persons who are refashioned into the many memorable folk characters of his *poetry.

The poetry collected into *Southern Road* challenges James Weldon *Johnson's dictum that the poetic and philosophical range of Black *speech and dialect is limited to pathos and *humor. Although the minstrel and *plantation traditions had heavily burdened African American speech with the yoke of racial *stereotypes, Brown, along with Langston *Hughes and Zora Neale *Hurston, admirably demonstrated the aesthetic potential of that speech when it is centered in careful study of the folk themselves. Brown came to this conclusion, as he said in a 1942 speech, when he discovered the way folklore became a lens through which to view African American vernacular language. Taking the approach of a creative writer to folklore, he said: "I was first attracted by certain qualities that I thought the speech of the people had, and I wanted to get for my own writing a flavor, a color, a pungency of speech. Then later, I came to something more important—I wanted to get

an understanding of people, to acquire an accuracy in the portrayal of their lives."

Brown found support for his vision of "folk" in the work of Benjamin A. Botkin, whose term "folk-say" suggested a profound shift in folklore studies that Brown knew and approved of. Folklore, as Botkin pointed out, was something more than collecting, verifying, indexing, and annotating sources; it was people talking, doing, and describing themselves. To underscore this new emphasis, Botkin published a series of regional miscellanies under the name *Folk-Say* beginning in 1929. Brown contributed eighteen poems and two essays to editions two through four of *Folk-Say*.

The success of Brown's "theory" of folklore is revealed in its implementation. Brown's poetry received its motivation from a need to reveal the humanity that lies below the surface racial stereotypes only skim. There he found qualities erased by racial stereotype: "tonic shrewdness, the ability to take it, and the double-edged humor built up of irony and shrewd observation." Structurally, he made use of, as he said, "the clipped line, the *blues form, and the refrain poem." Those folk forms were complemented by his astute experiments with traditional forms, such as the sonnet, villanelle, and ballad. Brown's frequent allusions to Black folk heroes such as *John Henry, *Stackolee, and Casey Jones also raised ordinary experience to mythic proportions.

Recently, literary historians have acknowledged the persistence of Brown's folk-based aesthetic in his critical and editorial work, too. But despite its coherence, his approach has received little study. Beginning in 1931–1932, when he returned to Harvard for doctoral study, Brown focused his critical writing on examinations of representational issues. The result was "Plays of the Irish Character: A Study in Reinterpretation" (an unpublished 1932 course thesis), "Negro Character as Seen by White Authors," *The Negro in American Fiction* (1937), and *Negro Poetry and Drama* (1937). The connecting link in Brown's editorial and research work for the *Federal Writers' Project, the Carnegie-Myrdal Study, and *The Negro Caravan* (1941), the most comprehensive literary anthology of Black writing of its time, is also his folk-based aesthetic. Collectively, this work points to Brown's need to demonstrate the diversity as well as the complexity of African American life. Against the conclusion of Gunnar Myrdal's *An American Dilemma* (1944) that Black life was a "distorted development, or a pathological condition, of the general American condition," Brown presented evidence that African American folk humor functioned as a strategy for exerting control in an often hostile world. Or when the specious argument was made accusing African Americans of having contributed very little to American literature, Brown, with coeditors Arthur P. Davis and Ulysses Lee, presented *The Negro Caravan* as irrefutable proof of Black literary achievement.

Brown also attempted to correct the myopic lens used to view African Americans by writing a number of prose sketches that were to be collected and published as "A Negro Looks at the South." These pieces included "Out of Their Mouths," "Words on a Bus," "The Muted South," and several more. The shared reference to speech tells us much about Brown's view of language as a vehicle for determining cultural authenticity. That Brown admits to viewing these pieces as poems reveals more about his aesthetic, too. Each dialogue or conversation was a unit of speech and thus needed, as he said, "counterpoint, cadence, rhyming, timing, etc. for impact and truth." Therefore, if cuts had to be made, whole units of dialogue should be cut, not cuts within the unit.

The careful reconsideration of Black speech as a viable medium of artistic expression became for Brown the predominant means for reclaiming the humanity of African Americans. This pursuit, of course, had social implications. Brown and others shared the view that "art is a handmaiden to social policy." Although a staunch believer in the promises of the Constitution, Brown was aware that such provisions as the infamous "three-fifths compromise" began a lengthy list of stumbling blocks to achieving life, liberty, and the pursuit of happiness. The American dream meant for Brown the addition of two-fifths more, making a whole number. The root word in "integration" is "integer," which means "whole or complete." As literary historians and cultural critics reexamine the value of the vernacular in their respective pursuits, Brown's daring efforts to make Black folk speech claim a rightful place for him and his people will be properly acknowledged.

[See also Criticism, article on Criticism from 1920 to 1964.]

• Sterling A. Brown, "A Son's Return: 'Oh, Didn't He Ramble,'" in Chant of Saints: A Gathering of Afro-American Literature, Art, and Scholarship, eds. Michael S. Harper and Robert B. Stepto, 1979, pp. 3–22. Robert G. O'Meally, "An Annotated Bibliography of the Works of Sterling A. Brown," in The Collected Poems of Sterling A. Brown, ed. Michael S. Harper, 1980. Kimberly W. Benston, "Sterling Brown's After-Song," Callaloo 14, 15; 5.1, 5.2 (1982): 33–42. Joanne V. Gabbin, Sterling A. Brown: Building the Black Aesthetic Tradition, 1985. Robert B. Stepto, "Sterling A. Brown: Outsider in the Harlem Renaissance?" in The Harlem Renaissance: Revaluations, eds. Amritjit Singh et al., 1989, pp. 73–81. Mark A. Sanders, "Distilled Metaphysics: The Dynamics of Voice and Vision in the Poetry of Sterling A. Brown," PhD diss., Brown University, 1992. John Edgar Tidwell, "Recasting Negro Life History: Sterling A. Brown and the Federal Writers' Project," Langston Hughes Review 12.2 (Summer/Winter 1995): 77–82. John Edgar Tidwell, "'The Summer of '46': Sterling A. Brown among the Minnesotans," Black Heartland 1.1 (1996): 27–41.
—John Edgar Tidwell

BROWN, WILLIAM WELLS (1814–1884), antislavery lecturer, slave narrator, novelist, dramatist, and historian. William Wells Brown is generally regarded as the first African American to achieve distinction as a writer of belles lettres. A famous antislavery lecturer and fugitive slave narrator in the 1840s, Brown turned to a variety of genres, including *poetry, fiction, *travel writing, and *history, to help him dramatize his case against *slavery while promoting sympathetic and heroic images of African Americans in both the United States and England.

William Wells Brown was born sometime in 1814 on a plantation near Lexington, Kentucky, the son of a white man and a slave woman. Light-complexioned and quick-witted, Brown spent his first twenty years mainly in St. Louis, Missouri, and its vicinity, working as a house servant, a fieldhand, a tavernkeeper's assistant, a printer's helper, an assistant in a medical office, and finally a handyman for James Walker, a Missouri slave trader with whom Brown claimed to have made three trips on the Mississippi River between St. Louis and the New Orleans slave market. Before he escaped from slavery on New Year's Day, 1834, this unusually well-traveled slave had seen and experienced slavery from almost every perspective, an education that he would put to good use throughout his literary career.

After seizing his *freedom, Brown (who received his middle and last name from an Ohio Quaker who helped him get to Canada) worked for nine years as a steamboatman on Lake Erie and a conductor for the *Underground Railroad in Buffalo, New York. In 1843, the fugitive slave became a lecturing agent for the Western New York Anti-Slavery Society. Moving to Boston in 1847, he wrote the first and still the most famous version of his *autobiography, Narrative of William W. Brown, a Fugitive Slave, Written by Himself, which went through four American and five British editions before 1850, earning its author international fame. Brown's Narrative was exceeded in popularity and sales only by the *Narrative of the Life of Frederick Douglass, an American Slave, which appeared in 1845. In 1849, Brown went abroad to attend an international peace conference in Paris and to lend his voice to the antislavery crusade in England. In addition to his demanding speaking schedule, he found time to try his hand at a new form of first-person narrative, which he entitled Three Years in Europe, or Places I Have Seen and People I Have Met (1852). This was the first travel book authored by an African American; it was favorably received by the British press in general as well as by the American antislavery press. A year later *Clotel, or The President's Daughter, generally regarded as the first full-length African American *novel, was published.

After returning to the United States in 1854, Brown continued his pioneering literary work, publishing The *Escape, or A Leap for Freedom (1858), the first *drama by an African American. During the 1860s he brought out three more versions of Clotel: Miralda, or The Beautiful Quadroon (1860–1861), Clotelle: A Tale of the Southern States (1864), and Clotelle, or The Colored Heroine (1867). Brown also wrote two volumes of African American history in the 1860s, The Black Man: His Antecedents, His Genius, and His Achievements (1863) and The Negro in the American Rebellion (1867). The latter is the first military history of the African American in the United States. Brown's final autobiography, My Southern Home, or The South and Its People (1880), returned again to the scene of his years in slavery, not to retrace his own steps from bondage to freedom but rather to characterize from an intimate perspective the power struggles between blacks and whites in the South both before and after the Civil War. William Wells Brown died in Chelsea, Massachusetts, on 6 November 1884.

In the modest, understated plain style of Brown's autobiographies, it is often the ordinary, the representative, and the nonheroic—even the antiheroic—that come to the fore. Brown's willingness to focus on these aspects of his experience reveals a striking brand of realism in his first-person writing. Like many of his African American literary contemporaries during the 1850s, Brown felt obliged to create characters that epitomized the ideals of aspiring men and women of color in order to educate an American readership that saw mostly the defamation of African American character in newspapers, magazines, and books. Thus the real and the ideal maintain an uncertain balance in Brown's writing. Nevertheless the tension between them and the problematic ways Brown tried to resolve them tell us much about the conflicting aesthetic and ideological agendas underlying early African American literature.

[See also Antislavery Movement; Slave Narrative.]

• William Edward Farrison, William Wells Brown, 1969. Sidonie Smith, Where I'm Bound: Patterns of Slavery and Freedom in Black American Autobiography, 1974. William L. Andrews, To Tell a Free Story: The First Century of Afro-American Autobiography, 1760–1865, 1986. Blyden Jackson, A History of Afro-American Literature, vol. 1, The Long Beginning, 1746–1895, 1989.   —William L. Andrews

BROWNFIELD COPELAND. The brownish autumn color of a dying Georgia cotton field was the inspiration for Brownfield Copeland's naming. This character, presented in Alice *Walker's *novel The *Third Life of Grange Copeland (1970), is the son of Grange and Margaret Copeland. His life, like his name, symbolizes the decay, death, and *violence that often trails behind human resignation to hopelessness.

When Brownfield is fifteen, his father abandons him and his mother commits suicide. The young boy sets out on a journey that leads him to a life of sex and irresponsibility in the juke joint world of his father's lover, Josie, and her daughter, Lorene. After years of scandalous living, Brownfield meets and marries Mem, Josie's niece. Their relationship is a good one, at first. But because of Brownfield's inability to break out of an agricultural system that supports the virtual enslavement of tenant farmers, their relationship sours. Brownfield grows enraged and brutal toward his wife and eventually kills her. Unlike his father, who acknowledges his wrongs and attempts to make amends, Brownfield refuses to accept responsibility for anything he does and pays for that refusal with his life.

Brownfield is a vindictive, cruel, and abusive man. There is no doubt that he is a poor representation of African American *manhood. But contrary to the negative criticism the novel has received, Walker's artistic treatment of this character is revealing. Without overstating her argument, Walker presents the condition of a soul entrapped by racism and self-defeat that is both horrifying and painfully realistic.

—Debra Walker King

Brown Girl, Brownstones. Paule *Marshall's first *novel, Brown Girl, Brownstones, published in 1953, is considered a first in many respects in the development of the African American novel. It is one of few novels up until that time written by an African American author that thoughtfully and accurately concerns itself with the interior life of a young African American female protagonist. It is also one of the first African American novels to accurately portray the complexities of African American mother-daughter relationships, and it portends the kinds of feminist writing that contemporary African American women writers would come to produce.

The novel is a *bildungsroman, that is, a novel of development. It is perhaps the first in which a young African American girl and her coming-of-age take center stage. It is also one of the first to deal with cross-cultural conflict of two different groups of people of African descent. The protagonist, *Selina Boyce, is the daughter of first-generation Barbadian immigrant parents, Deighton and Silla, who have come to America in search of the ever elusive American dream. In the novel, Silla Boyce represents the new breed of West Indian immigrants, hell-bent to conquer America, "this man country." She is determined to acquire her piece of the American dream and initially works as a cleaning woman for the uptown whites so that one day she, too, will be able to own property, or "buy house" as she and her other West Indian neighbors refer to it. Her husband, Deighton, on the other hand, has his heart and mind set on eventually returning to Barbados once they have acquired enough money. Selina, as a young girl, is torn between two worlds: that of her mother, who is strong, determined, and mean enough to do anything short of murder to own property, and that of her father, who simply does not have the fortitude to be successful and who dreams of returning to Barbados.

The possibility for Deighton's return home presents itself in the novel when a deceased sister wills him a small piece of property in Barbados. Silla is determined to stay in America, for she feels that there is nothing in Barbados for her or her family. She is obsessed with owning a brownstone and goes so far as to forge Deighton's signature on legal documents so that she can get the money for the property she covets. She does so, but at a very high price. Deighton, overwhelmed and mournful of his lost dreams, spends all of the money in one frivolous spree to spite his wife. He is subsequently deported, turned in by Silla as being an illegal alien. Fraught with despair, he dies within a few miles of the coast of Barbados, though it is ambiguous whether he is pushed off the ship or commits suicide. This leaves Silla alone with her newly acquired brownstone as well as her guilt, and Selina with the task of coming to terms with strong, ambivalent feelings toward her mother and her own West Indian American heritage.

[See also West Indian Literature.]

• Trudier Harris, "No Outlet for the Blues: Silla Boyce's Plight in Brown Girl, Brownstones," Callaloo 17–19 (1983): 57–67. Vanessa D. Dickerson, "The Property of Being in Paule Marshall's Brown Girl, Brownstones," Obsidian II 6 (1991): 1–13.   —Keith Bernard Mitchell

Brownies' Book, The. From January 1920 through December 1921, W. E. B. *Du Bois and Augustus Granville Dill published the *Brownies' Book*, a young people's magazine dedicated especially to African American children from six to sixteen years of age. Although this was an independent publishing effort, the magazine functioned as the youth counterpart to the *Crisis*, NAACP's magazine. Novelist Jessie Redmon *Fauset served as the associate editor and contributed regularly. (Other frequent contributors were Langston *Hughes and Nella *Larsen.) At a cost of fifteen cents a copy or one dollar and fifty cents per year, its circulation was approximately five thousand per month.

Among the objectives of the *Brownies' Book* were "to make colored children realize that being 'colored' is a normal, beautiful thing" and "to make them familiar with the history and achievements of the Negro race" (*Crisis*, Oct. 1919). With only one exception, all of the drawings in the magazine were by black artists. Depicting black children from various classes and geographical regions, the magazine spoke powerfully to the social, psychological, spiritual, intellectual, and aesthetic needs and sensibilities of a range of people. To a large degree, its publication marks the genesis of what is now called African American children's literature.

[*See also* Children's and Young Adult Literature; Periodicals, *article on* Black Periodical Press.]

• Violet Harris, "The Brownies' Book: Challenge to the Selective Tradition in Children's Literature," PhD diss., University of Georgia, 1986. Dianne Johnson, *Telling Tales: The Pedagogy and Promise of African American Literature for Youth*, 1990.

—Dianne Johnson-Feelings

BRUCE, JOHN E. (1856–1924), columnist, editor, essayist, historian, novelist, and orator. Born a slave in Maryland, John Edward Bruce grew up in Washington, D.C. Developing an interest in *journalism, he worked as a general helper in the office of the Washington correspondent for the *New York Times* in 1874. By the time Bruce was twenty he was writing for newspapers, using the pen name "Rising Sun," and in 1879 he started his own paper, the *Argus*, in Washington, D.C. In 1884 Bruce began writing under the name "Bruce Grit" in the *Cleveland Gazette* and the *New York Age*, eventually becoming one of the most widely read and influential African American journalists of his era. In his writings and speeches, Bruce decried mixed-race marriages, denounced Euro-American imperialism, aggressively promoted race pride and solidarity, championed self-help, and advocated the study of black *history to combat the anti-Negro rhetoric of the post-Reconstruction period.

Bruce served as a conduit linking people of African descent separated by age and geography. A prolific letter writer and a member of several African American organizations, including the Prince Hall Masons, the American Negro Academy, and the Negro Society for Historical Research, which he founded with Arthur A. *Schomburg in 1911, Bruce knew key nineteenth-century figures such as Alexan-

der *Crummell and Edward Wilmot *Blyden, met and corresponded with Africans who had studied in or visited the United States, and wrote for African periodicals and Duse Mohammed Ali's London-based *African Times and Orient Review*. He was one of Marcus *Garvey's most important contacts when the Jamaican first came to America in 1916, introducing him to prominent people in New York, including W. E. B. *Du Bois. Bruce held the title of Duke of Uganda in the Universal Negro Improvement Association (UNIA), wrote a weekly column for Garvey's *Negro World* beginning in 1918, became an important liaison between the UNIA and African organizations, and was given a hero's funeral at Harlem's Liberty Hall in a ceremony attended by more than five thousand people, at which Garvey spoke.

Ralph L. Crowder has suggested that Bruce represents a significant nationalist force in African American society at the turn of the century that was independent of the movements associated with Du Bois and Booker T. *Washington. Crowder attributes Bruce's obscurity today to his refusal to court white recognition or approval. Bruce wrote *Biographical Sketches of Eminent Negro Men and Women in Europe and the United States* (1910) and *The Awakening of Hezekiah Jones* (1916), a *novel about the political astuteness of African Americans that has received almost no critical attention, as well as several pamphlets about African American history and politics. He also wrote an early detective novel containing scenes set in Africa entitled *The Black Sleuth*, which appeared serially from 1907 to 1909 (John E. Bruce Papers, Schomburg Center for Research in Black Culture, New York). Nearly fifty years after Bruce's death, some of his newspaper pieces and speeches were published in *The Selected Writings of John Edward Bruce* (1971), which helped to generate some short-lived critical interest in the author.

[*See also* Black Nationalism; Collective Biography; Letters; Protest Literature.]

• Peter Gilbert, "The Life and Thought of John Edward Bruce," in *The Selected Writings of John Edward Bruce: Militant Black Nationalist*, ed. Peter Gilbert, 1971, pp. 1–9. Ralph L. Crowder, "John Edward Bruce: Pioneer Black Nationalist," *Afro-Americans in New York Life and History* 2 (July 1978): 47–66. Ernest Kaiser, "Bruce, John Edward (Bruce Grit)," in *DANB*, eds. Rayford W. Logan and Michael R. Winston, 1982, pp. 76–77.

—John C. Gruesser

BRYAN, ASHLEY (b. 1923), teacher, painter, illustrator, writer, and storyteller. Ashley Bryan's parents migrated to New York City from Antigua. Bryan showed an early talent for drawing, and with family encouragement he put together his first book when he was five years old. He earned degrees from Cooper Union Art School and Columbia University and is professor emeritus of art at Dartmouth College, where for many years he taught painting and drawing. Bryan has received numerous honors, including most recently the University of Southern Mississippi's twenty-seventh Annual Silver Medallion Award for Contributions to Children's Literature.

Bryan's work is rooted in African American

culture, particularly *spirituals, folk tales, and early-twentieth-century *poetry. In public performances he always reads aloud from the works of poets such as Langston *Hughes and Paul Laurence *Dunbar before sharing his own work, insisting that only in the oral mode does one hear the real "voice" of the artist.

His interest in "voice" began at Cooper Union, when Bryan first began illustrating African tales as they had been written down by anthropologists and missionaries in the 1800s. These tellings were, as he puts it, "Dull . . . bald . . . skeletal versions of the original stories." Later, he began fleshing out these brief summaries with the intent of imparting, in written form, the "implied voice" of the original teller of the tale. The result is stories so alive with images and sounds that they demand to be read aloud.

Bryan has also found a rich source of materials in African American spirituals, which he sees as unique in the song literature of the world and as perhaps America's most distinctive contribution to world *music. In Climbing Jacob's Ladder (1991) nine great figures from the Old Testament—Noah, Abraham, Jacob, *Moses, Joshua, David, Ezekiel, Daniel, and Jonah—are strikingly illustrated in brilliant colors. What a Morning (1987) tells the Christmas story using five spirituals and vivid paintings.

In his work as an illustrator, Bryan uses a variety of media and techniques, ranging from linoleum block prints to brush-and-ink sketches to full-color paintings, with a palette varying from the earthy ochres and blacks and reds of The Ox of the Wonderful Horns (1971) and Beat the Story Drum, Pum-Pum (1980) to the sun-drenched, exuberant Caribbean hues of Climbing Jacob's Ladder. A sunny, ebullient sense of light and joy pervades Bryan's work, whether written, spoken, or painted.

While usually considered children's books, Bryan's creations clearly cross lines of age and culture. "Art is like an explosion," he says, "opening up the world. As an artist, what I'm trying to do is to get down on paper something of that culture I come from which other people can absorb. I want the people who read these stories to feel something of the excitement of the adventure; to get them to appreciate these ancient stories in a living way, as part of their lives."

• Sharron L. McElmeel, Book People, a Multicultural Album, 1992, pp. 9–19. "Bryan, Ashley" in Something about the Author, vol. 72, ed. Diane Telgen, 1993, pp. 26–29.

—Ramon Royal Ross

BUCK. The African American buck is one of various fictitious props evoking the mythic traditional southern plantation. The buck is typically a field worker whose body is most often described in animalistic terms. His strength is usually compared to that of a horse and his reliability to that of a mule. These animalistic traits are used to justify his lack of humanity. The emphasis on his body makes him sexually threatening; he is typically known as a breeder on slave plantations.

An intermediary type, the buck is the literary descendant of the "noble savage" and the literary forerunner of the "black brute." The positive qualities of the noble savage—size, strength, and agility—are exaggerated until they become grotesque and reveal the slave's subhuman nature. The noble savage is fairly innocuous, but the black brute is primarily characterized as a rapist. The buck is therefore a transitional character, a slave more likely to become a militant rebel than remain a contented retainer. This character is standard in the antiblack Reconstruction fiction of Thomas Nelson Page. In Page's Red Rock (1898) the buck Moses is characterized as more creature than man, with a protruding lower jaw, blue gums, low forehead, and rolling eyes.

African American authors confronted the image with ironic variations on this type. Frederick *Douglass's "The *Heroic Slave" (1853) and Charles Waddell *Chesnutt's The *Marrow of Tradition (1901) are two examples. Douglass's hero, Madison Washington, has all of the positive qualities assigned to a buck; he is tall and strong with a lion's strength. Yet Washington is not a caricature but a complex and humane character who is also gentle, intelligent, articulate, and brave. Josh Green from Marrow is depicted as a black giant whose size and courage enable Chesnutt to transform this buck from a rebellious troublemaker into a fiercely militant leader.

[See also Character Types; Stereotypes, article on Black Stereotypes.]

• Sterling A. Brown, "Negro Characters as Seen by White Authors," Journal of Negro Education 2 (Apr. 1933): 179–203.

—Kimberly Wallace Sanders

BULLINS, ED (b. 1935), born Edward Artie, African American playwright and pioneering artist of the Black Theater movement of the 1960s and 1970s. In the typical Ed Bullins play, characters move through a gritty existence toward little that can be called self-realization or existential triumph. Indeed, these traditional outcomes have little to do with the world Bullins conceives, which is a world created by the "natural"—not naturalistic, as Bullins cautions—style of his *drama.

Much of the tension and energy of Bullins's plays comes from his memory of the tough North Philadelphia neighborhood where he was raised. As a youth he developed an early association with street life, whose bootleg whiskey, gang *violence, and sudden deaths—Bullins himself was nearly fatally stabbed but miraculously recovered—have strong reverberations in much of his work. In 1952 Bullins dropped out of high school to join the navy; this experience also commands attention in his plays, as recurrent characters Cliff Dawson and his half-brother Steve Benson are former navy men.

Bullins moved to Los Angeles in 1958 after having returned from the navy to a still dangerous Philadelphia. "I went to Los Angeles because it was the farthest I could go," he says. At Los Angeles City College Bullins took courses and began writing in 1961; he also founded a campus literary magazine, the Citadel. Restlessness, however, caused him to travel around the country to learn more about how African Americans lived. He returned to California in 1964, this time to San Francisco, and there he began writing plays. The one-act play *How Do You Do?* was his first, and Bullins's own pleasure with it convinced him to remain with *theater. But because many critics thought his work obscene, he could not find a producer. He staged his own plays in almost any available space, and finally his small company took their talents to coffeehouses and pubs in the San Francisco area.

The plays of LeRoi Jones (later Amiri *Baraka), notably *Dutchman* and *The Slave*, perhaps saved a despairing Bullins from giving up playwriting entirely. Jones's plays, using elements of Absurdist theater to portray the irony of African American life, greatly influenced Bullins and also fueled a revolutionary spirit among other African American artists in the San Francisco area. Bullins joined them to form Black Arts West, a militant cultural and political organization; he later became the cultural director of the Black House Theater in nearby Oakland. Among the participants in Black House were Bobby Seale, Eldridge *Cleaver, and Huey Newton—three actors who, as revolutionaries, would shortly enter the national consciousness as leaders of the Black Panther Party, of which Bullins became minister of culture.

Bullins's commitment to art over ideology was in early evidence when the Black House experienced a schism between members who wanted to use theater for revolutionary propaganda and those who saw theater's potential for cultural change. While writing agitprop plays to satisfy the revolutionary wing, he also developed his own theatrical ventures but soon found that the radicalized cultural atmosphere of the African American West Coast would not support his efforts. Bullins left Black House in 1967, was thus unconnected to any production support, and was preparing to leave the United States. Robert Macbeth, who directed the New Lafayette Theatre in Harlem, had read a copy of Bullins's *Goin' a Buffalo* (1968), a circumstance that forestalled Bullins's departure. Upon deciding to produce Bullins's *In the Wine Time*, Macbeth brought Bullins to New York to aid in the running of the theater, whose reputation thereafter was founded principally on Bullins's own work.

Bullins's most ambitious dramaturgical project has been his Twentieth-Century Cycle, a proposed series of twenty plays on the African American experience that deals not with race relations but primarily with the everyday lives of African Americans. Though both *Clara's Ole Man* (1965) and *Goin' a Buffalo* are considered noncycle plays, they nevertheless exhibit the characteristic of detailed African American life to be found in the five plays common to the Cycle; additionally, Bullins's intimation about the placement of *Goin' a Buffalo* in a 1972 *New York Times* interview with Clayton Riley suggests its later admission to this group, which canonically lists *In the Wine Time* (1968), *In New England Winter* (1971), *The Duplex* (1970), *The Fabulous Miss Marie* (1971), and *Home Boy* (1976).

The "natural" style of Bullins's plays is evident in his choice of having his characters reveal themselves to one another and to the audience, but disclosing only what they wish. Bullins never imposes his own view upon the action, an approach apparently consistent with the demands of a *Black Aesthetic, the code for an African American naturalism and heightening of sensibility. *Music is a very important part of a Bullins play, particularly the Cycle plays; the popular *jazz and rhythm-and-blues recordings of the time in which the plays are set ensure a fidelity to everyday African American life not found in more stylized productions. The music that is part of *In the Wine Time*, for example, comes from a radio, which has its own role written into the script; art here imitates life or, perhaps more accurately, merges with it.

The idea of naturalness also informs one of his most expressive contributions to drama. In the *essay "A Short Statement on Street Theatre," Bullins prescribes the "short, sharp, incisive" play that "subliminally broadcasts blackness"; to masses of African Americans, the immediacy of the skit or short political farce is designed to convey great communicative power. "Each individual in the crowd," writes Bullins, "should have his sense of reality confronted, his consciousness assaulted." Similarly, the stage plays, as portrayals of African American life startling in their immediacy, seek to challenge the audience with elements of violence, alcoholism, and infidelity—components of a determinism that is finally a species of naturalism. It represents not only life as Bullins knew it but also depicts the psychosocial anger of African American culture, a culture in opposition to prevailing Euro-American mores and structures of power.

Though by 1977 Bullins had written more than fifty plays, his efforts to be staged on Broadway were forever to be thwarted. His closest and most heroic attempt was *The Taking of Miss Janie* (1975), whose story of an interracial relationship that culminates in a rape explores the conflict between blackness and white liberalism. It won the prestigious New York Drama Critics Circle Award and was called the best American play of the year. Other awards include three Obie awards for outstanding drama, one National Endowment for the Arts grant, four Rockefeller Playwright grants, the distinguished Vernon Rice Award (for *Clara's Ole Man*), and a Creative Artists Public Service Program award. In 1972 Bullins headed the playwright's workshop at the New York Shakespeare Festival, and when the New Lafayette was in danger of closing in 1973, Bullins became a playwright in residence at the American Place Theater.

Bullins's notable attempts in other genres include a collection of his early *short stories, *The Hungered One* (1971), and a *novel, *The Reluctant Rapist* (1973), in which the character Steve Benson, a veteran of several Bullins plays and widely regarded as Bullins's alter ego, embodies the twin senses of disillusionment and bewilderment that mark so many of the plays. As guest editor of a special African American theater issue of *Drama Review* (Summer 1968), Bullins featured not only his own work but also that of Jones, Ben *Caldwell, Ron *Milner, and others; Larry *Neal's "The Black Aesthetic," the land-mark essay of the period, also appeared in this number.

Known in both theatrical and political circles for the incisive race consciousness with which he fashioned his work, Bullins made news in 1977 by having collaborated with white composer Mildred Kayden on the musicals *Storyville* and *Sepia Star*. This did not, however, lead to a departure from established philosophy. The tragic accidental death of his son Edward, Jr., in 1978 led to Bullins's return to the West Coast and the establishment of the Bullins Memorial Theatre, whose *Black Theatre Newsletter* not only featured news of productions of plays by other prominent African American playwrights but also listed some forty-four Bullins plays available for production.

Despite an apparent reluctance to acknowledge the influence of playwrights other than Baraka earlier in his career, Bullins later confessed to a broader eclecticism; he sees the dramaturgy of Eugene O'Neill and Samuel Beckett as having been additional significant influences and also notes that African American novelist Chester *Himes and Iranian poet Idris Shah have had their own profound effect on his work. These writers lend elements of suspense and lyrical renditions of the absurd to later plays by Bullins, notably *A Teacup Full of Roses* (1989) and *Dr. Geechee and the Blood Junkies* (1991), both antidrug plays. *Salaam, Huey Newton, Salaam* (1990), a play on the life of the celebrated Black Panther activist, was published in the collection *Best Short Plays of 1990*. After a tempestuous thirty-year odyssey through art, culture, and politics that began on the West Coast, Bullins seemed to have come full circle; with playwright Jonal Woodward, he headed the Bullins/Woodward Theater Workshop in San Francisco, which stages plays, teaches playwriting seminars, and holds theater workshops. By September 1995, however, Bullins left the workshop to accept a professorship in theater at Northeastern University. *Boy x Man* (1995), the latest addition to the Twentieth-Century Cycle, was staged in October 1995 in Greensboro, North Carolina.

The complex themes of revolution that characterized the African American stage of the 1960s and 1970s are easily measured and shaped by the work of Bullins; the efficacy of the rueful defiance he brought to this stage is reflected in his complete domination of Off-Broadway theater for more than a decade. Bullins's natural style and codification of the period's African American dramaturgical techniques are a historical and logical development of the techniques of the Free Southern Theater, which sought to use drama as a means of organizing African Americans in the South. The rawness of the Bullins plays, however, makes them seem to some to be a leap through tradition. If the critical response to the plays appears uneven—if their perceived greatness is mixed with an interpretation of African American anger deemed to be antiwhite by some, and even anti-American by others—then the debate, which Bullins's work perforce extends, as to the synergy of art and a consciousness of *insurrection and its possible consequences must continue.

[*See also* Black Arts Movement.]

• Ed Bullins, ed., *Drama Review* 12 (1967–1968). Ed Bullins, interviewed by Marvin X, *New Plays from the Black Theater*, ed. Ed Bullins, 1969. Ed Bullins, introduction to *The Theme Is Blackness*, 1972. Clayton Riley, "Bullins: 'It's Not the Play I Wrote,'" *New York Times*, 19 Mar. 1972, 1. Jervis Anderson, "Profiles—Dramatist," *New Yorker*, 16 June 1973, 40–79. Richard Scharine, "Ed Bullins Was Steve Benson (But Who Is He Now?)," *Black American Literature Forum* 13 (Fall 1979): 103–109. Genevieve Fabre, *Drumbeats, Masks and Metaphor*, 1983. John L. DiGaetani, *In Search of a Postmodern Theater*, 1991.   —Nathan L. Grant

BURIAL CUSTOMS. *See* Funeral and Mourning Customs.

BURROUGHS, MARGARET TAYLOR GOSS (b. 1917), poet, visual artist, educator, and arts organizer. Margaret Burroughs was born in St. Rose, Louisiana, near New Orleans, but was brought at the age of five by her parents, Alexander and Octavia Pierre Taylor, to Chicago where she grew up, was educated, and where her distinctive career has unfolded. She attended the public schools of Chicago, including the Chicago Teacher's College. In 1946, she received a BA in education and in 1948, an MA in education from the Art Institute of Chicago. From 1940 to 1968 she was a teacher in the Chicago public schools and subsequently a professor of humanities at Kennedy-King College in Chicago (1969–1979).

Burroughs has a national reputation as a visual artist and as an arts organizer. Her long exhibition record as a painter and printmaker began in 1949 and has included exhibitions throughout the United States and abroad. A retrospective of her work was held in Chicago in 1984. As an organizer she has been associated with the founding and conduct of a number of arts organizations. It was her founding in 1961 of the DuSable Museum of African-American History, however, that placed her among the outstanding institution builders of her generation. She served as a director of the museum until her appointment as a Commissioner of the Chicago Park District in 1985.

Burroughs has also had a commitment to progressive politics, as exemplified by her contributions to such publications as *Freedomways*, founded by, among others, W. E. B. *Du Bois and Paul *Robeson, both of whom were special heroes to her. She has felt a special affinity to the Mexican muralists and both studied and collaborated with artists in Mexico.

Burroughs began her writing career by doing articles and reviews for the Associated Negro Press, founded and directed by Claude Barnett. Her work as an educator led her into writing for children. Her works in this category include *Jasper, the Drummin' Boy* (1947) and the *anthology *Did You Feed My Cow?* (1956), both of which underwent subsequent editions.

Burroughs has made a distinctive contribution as a poet and as an editor of poets. The bulk of her poems are published in the volumes *What Shall I Tell My Children Who Are Black?* (1968) and *Africa, My Africa* (1970). Her most notable work as an editor was her collaboration with Dudley *Randall in the production of the commemorative volume *For Malcolm* (1967). The forty-three poets represented include established poets such as Gwendolyn *Brooks, Margaret *Walker, and Robert *Hayden; as well as a younger group associated with the *Black Arts movement, such as Sonia *Sanchez, Amiri *Baraka, Larry *Neal, and Mari *Evans. Burroughs's own poem on *Malcolm X was also included. In this poem, "Brother Freedom," Burroughs places Malcolm in a pantheon with Toussaint *L'Ouverture, Joseph Cinque, Nat *Turner, and other heroes of black consciousness. Burroughs also contributed to the rediscovery of the poet Frank Marshall *Davis by editing *Jazz Interlude* (1987).

Burroughs's own poems exult in African and African American culture, taking imagery primarily from the urban milieu of Chicago in which she has spent her life. Her connection to Africa has been solidified by annual trips to the continent beginning in the late 1960s and continuing into the 1990s. As an early and often lonely pioneer of black consciousness, Burroughs welcomed in her *poetry the apparent explosion in the ranks of those subscribing to her vision, particularly among the young. Her welcome, however, was tempered by a critical stance informed by her own progressive politics. In the poem "Only in This Way," for example, she downplays "wayout hairdos" in favor of blacks "knowing and accepting" themselves.

The influence of Margaret Burroughs has been felt in a variety of organizations with which she has been associated, as well as by those who have participated in programs of the DuSable Museum. As an essayist, poet, and writer for children, her literary endeavors have interfaced directly with other aspects of her creative and social agendas.

[See also Children's and Young Adult Literature.]

• Eugene Feldman, *The Birth and the Building of the DuSable Museum*, 1981.
—Richard A. Long

BURTON, ANNIE LOUISE (1860–?), autobiographer. *Slave narratives are usually recognized and treated as an antebellum genre. Yet a significant group of ex-slaves who were children at the close of the Civil War also published their *autobiographies. Annie Burton is one of the few such authors who, instead of dictating her story to someone else, wrote her own narrative. For some readers, Burton's *Memories of Childhood's Slavery Days* (1909) may seem to be a disjointed and nostalgic tale of what she calls the "Great Sunny South." She breaks the narrative into eight sections: two autobiographical sketches, "a vision," a piece she authored for her graduating *essay, a radically progressive essay by the black minister Dr. P. Thomas Stanford entitled "The Race Question in America," her own short "historical composition," and her "favorite poems" and "favorite hymns." The first section is a wistful sketch of her

childhood in Clayton, Alabama, which then transforms into a chronicle of her economic life as an adult. She calls the second, in which she describes her mother, who ran away before the war and then came back to claim her children, a sequel; both are primarily accounts of travel, work, worth, and compensation.

Burton's pining memories of plantation days seem to align her prose with Thomas Nelson Page's revisionist "happy darky" novels, while her representation of her later economic ventures invokes the revisionist rehistoricizing of white *violence offered by Booker T. *Washington. Yet Burton uses nostalgia as a cover and then disrupts the expectations her readers might have. While she seems to echo both the postbellum revision of *slavery and Washington's vision of "industrial education" and economics, by including Stanford's piece, she challenges Washington's paradigmatic postbellum narrative *Up from Slavery* (1901). Like Harriet E. *Wilson, for example, Annie Burton evokes the idealized plantation mansion in order to critique her place in the hierarchy it symbolizes.

• William L. Andrews, "The Representation of Slavery and the Rise of Afro-American Literary Realism (1865–1920)," in *Slavery and the Literary Imagination*, eds. Deborah McDowell and Arnold Rampersad, 1989, pp. 62–80.
—P. Gabrielle Foreman

BUSH-BANKS, OLIVIA WARD (1869–1944), poet, playwright, short fiction writer, essayist, journalist, lecturer, and educator. Olivia Ward Bush-Banks was born in Sag Harbor, Long Island, New York, was raised in Providence, Rhode Island, and Boston, Massachusetts, and lived in Chicago and New York City. Bush-Banks's life and works reflect her consciously cultivated African American and Native American (Montauk and Poosepatuck [Unkechaug Nation]) heritage. Her earliest collection, *Original Poems* (1899), contains protests against discrimination as well as lyrics reminiscent of Alexander Pope and the "Fireside school" of John Greenleaf Whittier and Henry Wadsworth Longfellow. Bush-Banks's second *poetry collection, *Driftwood* (1914), ends with a soliloquy foreshadowing her use of free verse in later years. Posthumously published works like "Shadows: Dedicated to Miss Marian *Anderson" and "To [Richmond] Barthe . . ." show the influence of *Negritude on Bush-Banks during the 1920s and 1930s.

Bush-Banks discussed her parents' Native American heritage in a 1914 autobiographical *essay. Prior to 1916 she served as the Montauk tribal historian and her poem "On the Long Island Indian" appeared in the tribe's *Annual Report* (1916). Bush-Banks regularly attended the "June Meeting," an Algonquian ancestral memorial held at the Poosepatuck and Shinnecock Indian reservations on Long Island. Her religious lyric "Morning on Shinnecock" (1899) reflects these visits.

Bush-Banks's most notable contribution to African American literature is "Aunt Viney's Sketches," six of which are extant of an original twelve. These vignettes feature a female African American dialect character as a wry commentator on depression-era Harlem life. Completed in the late 1930s, Bush-Banks's "Aunt Viney's Sketches" recall Frances Ellen Watkins *Harper's *Aunt Chloe Fleet poems in 1872 and anticipate Langston *Hughes's "*Simple" stories of the 1940s and 1950s.

[See also African–Native American Literature.]

• Bernice F. Guillaume, comp., *The Collected Works of Olivia Ward Bush-Banks*, 1991. "Bush-Banks, Olivia Ward," in *The Pen Is Ours*, comps. Jean Fagin Yellin and Cynthia D. Bond, 1991, pp. 32–34.   —Bernice Forrest Guillaume

BUTLER, OCTAVIA E. (b. 1947), short fiction writer, novelist, and science fiction writer. Hugo and Nebula award–winning author, and a MacArthur Fellow, Octavia E. Butler was born on 22 June 1947 in Pasadena, California. Butler has helped to enrich the ever-expanding genre of *speculative fiction by adding to it a previously excluded experience: the African American female's. She makes a way out of no way by drawing on her experiences growing up in one of America's most culturally diverse states. In struggling against the odds of racism and sexism, breaking into and publishing prolifically in America and abroad in the predominantly white and male dominated science fiction genre, Butler has made a substantial contribution to African American culture and literature.

Butler's emphasis on *slavery and its cultural implications (the mixing of races and cultures) predominates from her science fiction to her critically acclaimed and only mainstream *novel to date, *Kindred* (1979). In viewing her works we see that all of her characters try to free themselves from some system of bondage. This leitmotif of bondage situates her firmly in the African American literary tradition, which is infused with the racial memories of slavery. However, Butler not only appropriates slavery, she attempts to move beyond it.

In her first work, *Patternmaster* (1976), she devises a plot based on genetic evolution and vassalage, and this provides the framework for each successive novel. Several subthemes from *slavery, like survival of the fittest, patterns of control and organization, sexual propagation or biological order, and allusions to African traditions, develop. In *Patternmaster* these subthemes situate themselves in a tier of societies based on the refinement, or lack thereof, of telepathic ability, and this pattern develops through an intricate process of breeding to evolve to a state of linked minds governed by the strongest telepath. With this pattern of mental prowess, Butler inadvertently suggests how it is ironic that the human mind can evolve and unify, and yet still rely on a slave system to maintain order.

In *Mind of My Mind* (1977) the slave state is shown in its protagonist, Mary, who breaks free of the bonds of poverty and racial oppression to establish the pattern of minds that will culminate in *Patternmaster*. *Survivor* (1978) picks up the strain of race stratification and enslavement by outlining an African Asian girl's experiences dealing with humans, fighting addiction to an alien drink, "meklah," and

joining the alien Garkohns, a race of furry aliens whose planet humans have colonized in an attempt to escape the Clayark invasion on earth. Butler published the *historical novel *Kindred* next, and its subject matter positions it chronologically into a segment of *Wild Seed* (1980), because it explores the maintenance of the slave plantation. The encounters with systems of bondage in both works also illuminate the ethical issues of propagation, biological order, and cultural and racial interbreeding that are associated with slavery, by having their protagonists decide just how much they are willing to do to survive and make sure that their future generation succeeds.

Wild Seed continues the motif of slavery and propagation by going to the ancestral African beginning of the pattern and relating how it was conceived and instigated by Doro, a Nubian ogbanje (a spirit who cannot die and who manifests itself by continually being born into bodies that die). Butler plays with a societal order based not on race, but on a genetic capacity for telepathic power. The protagonist, a female African shapeshifter called Anyanwu, makes the *Middle Passage and works to undercut Doro's need to kill. By the appropriation of the Middle Passage, an ogbanje, and an African shapeshifter and healer, Butler recreates her former works' tension, which comes from having to decide how to free oneself from racial-biological or mental-telepathic slavery. Either, she suggests, is a slave state of mind that will destroy.

The next wave of fiction develops a paradigm of biological enslavement due to alien intervention and drug addiction. In *Clay's Ark* (1984); the Xenogenesis Trilogy, *Dawn* (1987), *Adulthood Rites* (1988), and *Imago* (1989); and *The Parable of the Sower* (1993), the slave state is also located in the biological realm. These stories focus on humans who, through alien integration or drug abuse, are reprogrammed along a biological drive to reproduce or destroy at all costs. The price becomes cultural deconstruction and genetic mutation into something beyond human. However, what is interesting about the trilogy is how societal structure is determined not just by genetic mutation but also by the need to interact with one's environment on mutually beneficial terms that help both survive. *The Parable of the Sower* moves to economic and spiritual enslavement caused by drug addiction. In this story Butler creates a multicultural society or family united by acceptance of a spiritual worldview of change, "earthseed," to combat the spiritual deterioration and cultural chaos hinted at in *Clay's Ark*.

Like her novels, the pattern of slavery and multicultural generation resulting from a slave state derives from Butler's earlier *short stories: "Crossover" (1971), "Near of Kin" (1979), and "The Evening and the Morning and the Night" (1987). Two, "Speech Sounds" (1983) and "Bloodchild" (1984), won Hugo Awards. The tie between Butler's short stories and her fiction comes from her daring to explore taboo and untouched material, for in them she travels the realms of incest, chemical poisoning and the genetic mutations that result, and the tension of bonds between men and women. And she did this well before it became fashionable to do so. Butler's works, whether viewed as science fiction or not, develop the slave state to arrive at an evolution of the mind.

• Veronica Mixon, "Futurist Woman: Octavia Butler," *Essence*, Apr. 1979, 12, 15. Frances Smith Foster, "Octavia Butler's Black Female Future Fiction," *Extrapolation* 23.1 (1982): 37–48. Sandra Y. Govan, "Connections, Links, and Extended Networks: Patterns in Octavia Butler's Science Fiction," *Black American Literature Forum* 18.2 (Spring 1984): 82–87. Ruth Salvaggio, "Octavia Butler and the Black Science-Fiction Heroine," *Black American Literature Forum* 18.2 (Spring 1984): 78–81. Joe Weixlmann, "An Octavia E. Butler Bibliography," *Black American Literature Forum* 18.2 (Spring 1984): 88–89. Thelma J. Shinn, "The Wise Witches: Black Women Mentors in the Fiction of Octavia E. Butler," in *Conjuring: Black Women, Fiction, and Literary Tradition*, eds. Marjorie Pryse and Hortense J. Spillers, 1985, pp. 203–215. Octavia E. Butler, "*Black Scholar* Interview with Octavia Butler: Black Women and the Science Fiction Genre," interview by Frances M. Beal, *Black Scholar* 17.2 (Mar.–Apr. 1986): 14–18. Sandra Y. Govan, "Homage to Tradition: Octavia Butler Renovates the Historical Novel," *MELUS* 13.1–2 (Spring–Summer 1986): 79–96. Octavia E. Butler, "An Interview with Octavia E. Butler," interview by Randall Kenan, *Callaloo* 14.2 (1991): 495–504.   —Mildred R. Mickle

C

Cables to Rage, published in London in 1970 by Paul Breman Limited, was the second volume of *poetry written by African American poet, essayist, and activist Audre *Lorde. While this collection was only republished once (1972) under the same title, more than two-thirds of the pieces in the early volume were later selected for inclusion in *Chosen Poems: Old and New* (1982) and *Undersong: Chosen Poems Old and New, Revised* (1992).

Although Lorde's poetry was published in several British and European *anthologies as well as in African American literary magazines during the 1960s, it was not until she received a grant from the National Endowment for the Arts in 1968 that she was able to devote herself full-time to her writing. Her experience as a poet in residence at Tougaloo College in Mississippi (her first trip to the Deep South, her first workshop situation with young African American students, her first time away from her children) and the circumstances that followed her stay there (Martin Luther *King, Jr.'s assassination, Robert Kennedy's death, a close friend's accident) made her see the shortness of life and the necessity for immediate action. The pieces in her second volume of poetry reflect this urgency and the function, for Lorde, of art to protest if not change destructive social patterns.

Rooted in her anger at the racism and sexism that have marked the history of the United States, the poems in *Cables to Rage* introduced themes that carried through much of Lorde's work: *violence, hunger, cloaks of lies, dishonest silences, struggle for voice, faith in the capacity to love, growth through dreams, desperate hope and defiance amid dying and loss, and painful birthing. Recurrent in these poems are images of shedding and of fiery renewal: obsolete or false coverings (snakeskin, cocoon, weeds, dead poems) must be stripped and discarded so that the new can grow. While many African American poets of her time focused on *black nationalism and urban realism, Lorde placed relationships amid global concerns and gave voice to what many had rejected, hidden, or ignored. "Martha," for instance, Lorde's first overtly lesbian poem to be published and the longest piece in the volume, was strategically centered in *Cables to Rage*. A writer who saw herself in relational dialogue with the rest of the world, Lorde explained that her work owed much to her ancestors, to the love and support of women, and to African and African American artists, and she insisted in her poetry and prose that without community, coalition across differences, and freedom from all oppression, there is no true liberation at all.

[*See also* Feminism; Lesbian Literature; Protest Literature.]

• Claudia Tate, ed., *Black Women Writers at Work*, 1983, pp. 100–116. Audre Lorde, "My Words Will Be There," in *Black Women Writers, 1950–1980*, ed. Mari Evans, 1984, pp. 261–268.
                                                    —Ann E. Reuman

CAIN, GEORGE (b. 1943), novelist. Little information exists about George Cain other than from his autobiographical novel *Blueschild Baby*. He speaks through his alter ego, and in effect, Cain utilizes the trope of the doppleganger or "double" popularized by German writers and by African American historian W. E. B. *Du Bois in his theory of *double consciousness.

Born during October or November 1943, Cain grew up in Harlem and showed academic promise as an adolescent. He entered Iona College (New Rochelle, N.Y.) on a basketball scholarship but left to travel in California, Mexico, and Texas. Upon returning to New York in 1966, Cain started *Blueschild Baby* and spent four years completing the project. In the interim, he married and moved to Bedford Stuyvesant in Brooklyn with his wife, Jo Lynne, and daughter, Nataya, to whom he dedicates the work.

Blueschild Baby is a *blues refrain of suffering delineating the hero's addiction to heroin. Originally published in 1970, its popularity resurged in the mid-1990s because of recognition by African American scholars of Cain's prescient message. Drug addiction still ravages the African American community, though its cause is crack cocaine. The reader is introduced on the first page of the novel to the hero, Georgie Cain, in the throes of withdrawal—alternate dreamfulness and wakefulness, a runny nose, and a queasy stomach that signal he needs a fix. Georgie the parolee shows fear of the police because a drug infraction would return him to prison for another two years.

Blueschild Baby, however, is also an autobiographical novel of emancipation similar to the *slave narrative, but the white master this time is "horse," the street name for heroin. In its progression from Georgie's enslavement to freedom from drugs, the novel incorporates archetypal devices attendant to quests—the hero's journey to salvation, his death-rebirth experience, and his redemption by triumphing over evil. The work also parallels *Native Son* with its viewpoint limited to the hero's perspective as he struggles against naturalistic forces threatening to expose or kill him during Georgie's drug adventures on the streets of Harlem, Brooklyn, or New Jersey.

Temporal shifts reflect Georgie's sane or disoriented thinking according to his drug intake. Past and present oscillate as do Georgie's physical or psychological movements when he returns to his Harlem childhood, New Jersey home, or private school experiences. Black Harlem would seem to be the archetypal site that had fostered Georgie's drug problem, but that is the ironic twist to Georgie's journey to self-knowledge. He actually begins to use drugs recreationally while attending Brey Academy, a white private school where he is one of two African American students. Hashish relieves the pressures of feeling economically displaced or scholastically and athletically mandated to be a basketball hero. Hard drugs inevitably become Georgie's coping device to handle these racial adjustments. At the end, a black woman, Nandy, is Georgie's salvation. *Blueschild Baby* is a gripping narrative of emancipation from drugs.

• Houston A. Baker, Jr., "From the Inferno to the American Dream: George Cain's *Blueschild Baby*," in *Singers of Daybreak*, 1974, pp. 81–89. Edith Blicksilver, "George Cain" in *DLB*, vol. 33, *Afro-American Fiction Writers after 1955*, eds. Thadious M. Davis and Trudier Harris, 1984, pp. 41–43. Gerald Early, foreword to *Blueschild Baby*, 1987.

—Virginia Whatley Smith

CAINES, JEANNETTE FRANKLIN (b. 1937), writer. The works of Jeannette Franklin Caines are generally concerned with parent-child communication and other social and political issues. Jeannette Caines often presents these topics in the voice of a child. *Abby* (1973) explores the dynamics of adoption and the complex issues surrounding the expansion of the *family, while her second book, *Daddy* (1977), deals with divorce and the necessity of maintaining healthy relationships between the child and both parents. *Chilly Stomach* (1986) concerns the difficulties of defining and confronting sexual abuse. Often Caines's books end without a resolution to the problem. This encourages thought and discussion and facilitates effective communication and problem solving between parents and children.

Caines was born in New York in 1937 and has dedicated much of her life to improving the quality of *children's and young adult literature. In addition to receiving the National Black Child Development Institute's Certificate of Merit and Appreciation, she has been a member of the Coalition of One Hundred Black Women, the Council for Adoptable Children, and the Negro Business and Professional Women of Nassau County. Her academic concentration in psychology and child development and her professional and entrepreneurial success lend her credibility and effectiveness as an author of children's literature.

• Barbara T. Rollock, "Caines, Jeannette Franklin," in *Black Authors and Illustrators of Children's Books*, 1988, p. 22. "Caines, Jeannette Franklin," in *Authors of Books for Young People*, eds. Martha E. Ward et al., 1990, p. 105.

—Maia Angelique Sorrells

CALDWELL, BEN (b. 1937), dramatist of the Black Arts movement of the 1960s, known particularly for the sardonic style he employed in examining the lives of African Americans. Born in Harlem, Ben Caldwell had an early engagement with the arts. Having come of age in the 1960s, he was one of many sensitive and creative young African Americans to have been influenced by the work of Amiri *Baraka (then LeRoi Jones), who read Caldwell's plays and encouraged him.

During 1965 and 1966 Caldwell lived in Newark, New Jersey, with Baraka and several other artists; he refers to this time as his "Newark Period," in which he wrote *Hypnotism* (1969) and his most critically acclaimed work, *The Militant Preacher* (1967), which later appeared in *A Black Quartet: Four New Plays* under the title *Prayer Meeting, or The First Militant Minister* (produced, 1969; published, 1970). The remaining plays are by other outstanding Black Arts playwrights: Baraka, Ron *Milner, and Ed *Bullins.

Caldwell's plays uniquely satirize not only the racism and the naïveté of whites, but also those African Americans who seek either to emulate whites, be unduly materialistic, or anchor themselves to *stereotypes. Some of these works also employ revolutionary rhetoric common to the period, but as Stanley *Crouch suggests, Caldwell's movement to agitprop from a deftly crafted concatenation of satirical moments renders the whole formulaic, clinical, and trite.

Many of his works are very short one-act plays; four of these, appearing in a special issue of *Drama Review* (vol. 12, 1967–1968), occupy only eleven pages. Caldwell's great power, however, is his ability to communicate racial issues with both mordancy and a superb economy of dramaturgy. The revolutionary spirit compromised through materialism is the theme of *Riot Sale, or Dollar Psyche Fake Out*, as a weapon that shoots currency makes rioting African Americans stop to gather the money and run to nearby stores; *Top Secret, or A Few Million after B.C.* focuses on a secret meeting between the President and select members of his cabinet to discover a method of imposing birth control on African Americans. The method: convincing African Americans, many of whom wish to emulate whites anyway, that having more than two children is uncivilized.

One of his more mature efforts in this vein is *The King of Soul, or The Devil and Otis Redding* (1969), in which the theme of materialism is further complicated by both the history of the exploitation of talented entertainers such as Redding and by the inclusion of Redding and the Faustian bargain he makes —though never understands. This kind of pithy acidity helped earn Caldwell a Guggenheim Fellowship in 1970.

After 1970, Caldwell wrote *essays and *poetry in addition to *drama. As late as 1982, the Henry Street Settlement's New Federal Theater had staged *The World of Ben Caldwell*, a series of sketches that attempted to reveal the absurdity of the American dream. In one of these comic sketches, actor Morgan Freeman portrayed risqué stand-up comedian Richard Pryor; actors Reginald VelJohnson and Garrett Morris alternated portrayals of actor-comedian Bill Cosby. Mel Gussow, reporting in the *New York Times*, wrote that Caldwell showed such deftness and caustic cleverness in these sketches that he might well consider writing material for Pryor.

Since 1968 Caldwell has run the Third World Cultural Center in New York's South Bronx, where plays, poetry readings, and various other artistic activities are staged. By the early 1980s, Caldwell's interests had turned increasingly to the visual arts; in 1983 in New York's Kenkeleba Gallery he participated in an exhibit that connected the media of painting and *jazz with such artists as Camille Billops, Norman Lewis, Faith Ringgold, and Romare Bearden. In 1991, however, a fire swept through his Harlem apartment, destroying more than forty years' worth of manuscripts, paintings, and memorabilia. Undaunted, Caldwell is returning to writing the acerbically witty monologues and sketches that won him notoriety in the late 1970s and early 1980s; his most frequent writing of these has been for African American humorist and political activist Dick Gregory.

Though his particular brand of satire is far less in evidence in today's African American *theater, Caldwell's central themes represent his unalloyed gift to this period of revolutionary drama. The short skit or one-act play whose most compact and devastating message with respect to the spirit of African American revolution was the exposure of African American self-hatred and self-deception is a gift considered by some to have been given with the left hand. But while some may decry it as antirevolutionary, it appears nevertheless to have an important and inexorable progressive aspect: while enumerating the evils of the adversary, it courts reflection on the foibles of the insurgent.

[See also Black Arts Movement.]

• Charles D. Peavy, "Satire and Contemporary Black Drama," Satire Newsletter 7 (Fall 1969): 40–49. Ronald V. Ladwing, "The Black Comedy of Ben Caldwell," Players 51.3 (1976): 88–91. Stanley Crouch, "Satireprop," Village Voice, 27 Apr. 1982, 104. Mel Gussow, "Federal Office 'World of Ben Caldwell,'" New York Times, 10 April 1982, 13.
                                           —Nathan L. Grant

Callaloo. A literary journal of African American and African (and African diaspora) arts and letters, Callaloo first appeared in 1976 at Southern University in Baton Rouge, Louisiana, as a "Black South Journal," to ensure publication of original creative and scholarly work by the black southern writing community that emerged during the 1960s and early 1970s. Despite its initially parochial emphasis, Callaloo's editorial scope rapidly expanded to include an even broader range of creative and scholarly writing, as well as visual art, from throughout Africa and the African diaspora. Early examples of this breadth included selections of original Afro-Brazilian *poetry, *African literature, and *West Indian literature. In 1977, Callaloo's editor, Charles H. Rowell, moved the journal to the University of Kentucky, where it stayed for nine years before settling at the University of Virginia in 1986, at which time it established a publishing relationship with the Johns Hopkins University Press.

Indicative of Callaloo's vision of the interrelation of black writing across the diaspora, the journal has devoted whole issues and special sections to the work of internationally renowned African and Caribbean writers, such as Léopold Sédar Senghor, Chinua Achebe, Aimé Césaire, and Nicholás Guillén; American writers, such as Toni *Morrison, Jay *Wright, Alice *Walker, Ernest J. *Gaines, Paule *Marshall, and Audre *Lorde; and major younger writers, such as Rita *Dove, Caryl Phillips, and Yusef *Komunyakaa. Throughout its history, Callaloo's literary scholarship has mirrored the most recent critical and theoretical models, including the New Historicism and cultural studies, and the journal has kept pace with the various currents and innovations in contemporary American poetry, fiction, and *drama.

In the 1990s, Callaloo has presented double issues on Haitian arts and letters, which won first prize from the Council of Editors of Learned Journals in 1992; as well as numbers and special sections on Francophone and Anglophone women's writing, Native American literatures, and Puerto Rican women's writing; and writers such as Wilson Harris, Ralph *Ellison, and Maryse Condé.

[See also Diasporic Literature; Periodicals, article on Scholarly Journals and Literary Magazines.]
                                           —John R. Keene

CAMPBELL, JAMES EDWIN (1867–1895), journalist and poet. The son of Lethia (Stark) and James Campbell was born in Pomeroy, Ohio, and graduated from Pomeroy High School in 1884. He taught school in Ohio and participated in Republican politics there. In West Virginia (1890–1894) Campbell served as principal of Langston School (Point Pleasant) and of the newly opened Collegiate Institute (Charleston), an agricultural and mechanical arts school for African American youths. He married Mary Champ, a teacher, in 1891. Moving to Chicago, Campbell joined the staff of the Times-Herald and contributed articles and poems to several periodicals. His promising career was tragically cut short when he died of pneumonia in Pomeroy at age twenty-eight.

Campbell published two *poetry collections: Driftings and Gleanings (1887) and Echoes from the Cabin and Elsewhere (1895); the latter contains what some have judged to be the finest group of dialect poems of the nineteenth century. Campbell's peers and leading critics during and after his lifetime praised his poems in the Gullah dialect for their originality; hard realism; aptness of phrasing, rhymes, and rhythms; and truth to the spirit, philosophy, and *humor of antebellum plantation folk. Jean Wagner (Black Poets of the United States, 1973) notes that Campbell's "racial consciousness," "satirical spirit," and religious skepticism foreshadow the poetry of the *Harlem Renaissance.

Campbell captures "the joy and pathos" of cabin life without lapsing into *minstrelsy or surrendering race pride. He varies verse forms, moods, and speech patterns to suit individualized subjects, and leavens pungent satire with sympathetic appreciation for folkways. A few poems emulate traditional animal fables, such as "Ol' Doc' Hyar," in which wily Doctor Hare loses a patient but not his fee: "'Not wut fokses does, but fur wut dee know / Does de folkses git paid'—an' Hyar larfed low." Other dialect lyrics include work songs, lullabies, or vivid portrayals of activities such as horse trading, good eating, backsliding from *church, and superstitions. In standard English, Campbell's poems celebrate wine, women, song, and the beauties of nature; his "The Pariah's Love" (300 lines) recounts an interracial love affair. These serious, metrically varied verses are aesthetically superior to most of the century's African American poetry, but his *dialect poetry dedicated to "the Negro of the old regime" remains his most notable work.

[*See also* Speech and Dialect.]

• Carter G. Woodson, "James Edwin Campbell, a Forgotten Man of Letters," *Negro History Bulletin* 2 (Nov. 1938): 11. Frank R. Levstick, "James Edwin Campbell," in *DANB*, eds. Rayford W. Logan and Michael R. Winston, 1982, pp. 32–36. Joan R. Sherman, *Invisible Poets: Afro-Americans of the Nineteenth Century,* 2d ed., 1989.   —Joan R. Sherman

Cancer Journals, The. *The Cancer Journals,* published in 1980 by Spinsters Ink, was the first major prose work of African American poet and essayist Audre *Lorde as well as one of the first books to make visible the viewpoint of a lesbian of color. In this collection, Lorde challenged traditional Western notions of illness and advocated women's ability, responsibility, and right to make decisions about their health.

A three-part piece developed from journal entries and *essays written between 1977 and 1979, *The Cancer Journals* chronicles Lorde's experiences with her mastectomy and its aftermath. The first section of the book, "The Transformation of Silence into Language and Action," is a short address that was delivered by Lorde on a lesbians and literature panel of the Modern Language Association in 1977, soon after she had recovered from surgery that discovered a benign breast tumor. The second chapter, subtitled "A Black Lesbian Feminist Experience," frankly describes the emotions experienced by one without role models through the course of diagnosis, surgery, and recovery. Central to this section is Lorde's recognition of her fierce desire to survive, to be a warrior rather than a victim, and her acknowledgment of the network of women whose love sustained her. The last chapter, entitled "Breast Cancer: Power vs. Prosthesis," traces the development of Lorde's decision not to wear a prosthesis, a cosmetic device that she felt placed profit and denial of difference over health and well-being.

In each of the sections of the book, Lorde sought the strength that could be found at the core of her experience of cancer. Balancing her "wants" with her "haves," she used this crisis to change patterns in her life. Rather than ignoring pain and fear, she acknowledged, examined, and used them to better understand mortality as a source of power. This tendency to face and metabolize pain Lorde saw as a particularly African characteristic. Death, she realized, had to be integrated with her life, loving, and work; consciousness of limitations and shared mourning of her loss increased her appreciation of living. Underlining the possibilities of self-healing, specifically the need to love her altered body, Lorde further stressed the importance of accepting difference as a resource rather than perceiving it as a threat. Perhaps most crucially, Lorde realized through the experience of cancer the necessity of visibility and voice. Seeing silence as a tool for separation and powerlessness, she understood the important function of her writing not only to free herself of the burden of the experience but also to share her experiences so that others might learn. Survival, she wrote, is only part of the task; the other part is teaching.

In 1981, *The Cancer Journals* won the American Library Association Gay Caucus Book of the Year Award. In 1982, Lorde published *Zami: A New Spelling of My Name,* a "biomythography" that she claimed was a "lifeline" through her cancer experience. Six years after her mastectomy, Lorde was diagnosed with liver cancer, the meaning of which she explored in the title essay of *A Burst of Light* (1988). That *The Cancer Journals, Zami,* and *A Burst of Light,* the three works that perhaps most directly reveal Lorde's deeply felt vulnerabilities and affirmations, were all published by small feminist presses and neglected by mainstream publishing firms attests to the work still to be done. Before she died, Lorde in an African naming ceremony took the name Gambda Adisa, meaning Warrior: She Who Makes Her Meaning Known.

[*See also* Feminism; Lesbian Literature.]

• Claudia Tate, ed., *Black Women Writers at Work,* 1983. Audre Lorde, "My Words Will Be There," in *Black Women Writers, 1950–1980,* ed. Mari Evans, 1984, pp. 261–268.
                    —Ann E. Reuman

Cane. A classic of the *New Negro movement or *Harlem Renaissance, Jean *Toomer's *Cane* (1923) captures the spirit of experimentalism at the core of American modernism. A seminal work of sketches, *poetry, and *drama, *Cane*'s ancestry is as complex as that of its author who was physically white but racially mixed and who defined himself not as an African American but as an American. Hybridity and innovation are the defining features of the artist as well as the classic he produced. *Cane* bears the influence of Gertrude Stein's *Three Lives* (1909), James Weldon *Johnson's *The *Autobiography of an Ex-Colored Man* (1912), Sherwood Anderson's *Winesburg, Ohio* (1919), and *slave narratives. It exercised a shaping influence upon the poetry of Langston *Hughes and Sterling A. *Brown, and Zora Neale *Hurston's *Their Eyes Were Watching God* (1937).

Conceived in Sparta, Georgia, where, during the summer of 1921 Toomer was acting principal of the Sparta Agricultural and Industrial Institute, *Cane* is a record of Toomer's discovery of his southern heritage, an homage to a folk culture that he believed was doomed to extinction because of the *migration of African Americans from the South to the North, and a meditation upon the forces that he believed accounted for the spiritual fragmentation of the modern era. Published in 1923 by Horace Liveright, several of the sketches and poems of *Cane* had first appeared in the *Crisis, Double Dealer, Liberator, Modern Review, Broom,* and *Little Review.* When he submitted the manuscript to Liveright, Toomer had only written the sketches, poems, and drama that comprise the first and third sections, and which are set in the fictional community of Sempter, Georgia. Impressed by the poetic treatment of African American folklife but desirous of a lengthier manuscript, Liveright suggested that Toomer enlarge the work. Subsequently, the stories and poems that have

Chicago and Washington, D.C., as their setting were added to what is now the middle section of *Cane*.

Although praised by reviewers, *Cane* sold less than five hundred copies when it was first published. Many readers were unprepared for the daring treatment of black *sexuality, *miscegenation, and *slavery. The ambiguous nature of *Cane's* form also alienated many readers. The lyricism, the calculated mixture of poetry and prose, the experimental narrative strategies, and shifting point of view defy conventional definitions of the novel. These elements remain the basis for an ongoing scholarly debate regarding *Cane's* formal identity.

While scholars are divided on questions of genre and meaning, there is widespread agreement regarding *Cane's* central place in the African American literary tradition. Retrieved from obscurity in 1969 with the publication of a new edition, *Cane's* influence is clearly discernible in the writings of such contemporary African American writers as Ernest J. *Gaines, Alice *Walker, Michael S. *Harper, Charles R. *Johnson, and Gloria *Naylor. These and other writers admire *Cane* for the challenge it poses to conventional definitions of the novel, its nuanced representation of African American history and culture, and its deeply philosophical approach to questions of *identity.

• Nellie Y. McKay, *Jean Toomer, Artist: A Study of His Literary Life and Work, 1894–1936*, 1984. Rudolph P. Byrd, *Jean Toomer's Years with Gurdjieff: Portrait of an Artist, 1923–1936*, 1990.   —Rudolph P. Byrd

CANONIZATION. "Canon," a term apparently derived from the Greek *kanon*, which meant a measuring rod or rule, until recently had been limited to discussions of ecclesiastical concerns or even more specifically to the books of the Bible that were officially recognized as "genuine and inspired." During the late 1960s, the argument began to prevail that literary "classics" held a similar status. Likening the identification and exaltation of particular writers to religious canonization, some readers pointed out that the writers and works dominating the "Great Books" list were white men of European descent with aesthetics and arguments that were essentially the same. Critics appropriated the word "canon" to emphasize the subjectivities, ideologies, or acts of faith that blessed some works and banished others. Debate over who and what determines "the best thoughts of the best minds" has become so fierce that it is sometimes dubbed the "canon wars."

Few scholars question the notion of canon as a synonym for a "Great Books" list. Canonization is also generally accepted as a relevant metaphor for the process of compiling such a list. Many scholars agree that canonization is a continuing if not contested process influenced by a variety of factors, including when a work is published and by whom, who wrote it, how representative it is, who reviewed it, and who champions it. They disagree, however, over whether canons are necessary or inevitable and if so, what criteria and which judges should prevail.

The *civil rights movement and subsequent cultural events sparked current literary contests by focusing upon apparent relationships between the canon in English and the considerable uniformities of *race, *gender, and *class among the canonical authors. When publishers such as Negro Universities Press, Third World Press, Arte Publico Press, and the Feminist Press began to reprint neglected or lost literature by white women and people of color, it became easier for readers to compare the contributions of other groups and to campaign for revised or alternative canons. As a result, many previously ignored or undervalued works are now collected in anthologies. Literary genres such as the *slave narrative and *corrido* and sensibilities such as the *blues aesthetic and sentimentalism are more appreciated. Writers such as Harriet Beecher *Stowe, Maxine Hong Kingston, N. Scott Momaday, and Tomás Rivera appear on college syllabi. Schoolchildren sometimes find Virginia *Hamilton, Walter Dean *Myers, Lucille *Clifton, and Tom Feelings on classroom bookshelves.

Attention to African American writing has changed the curricula of many schools and universities, the holdings of libraries, and the inventories of bookstores. African American writers such as Ralph *Ellison, Toni *Morrison, and Rita *Dove are now sometimes taught as "American writers." Reviewers and critics have found it expedient, if not elevating, to include at least a token representation of African American literary contributions in their discussions. African American writers have now been awarded Nobel, Newbery, Pulitzer, National Book, and other major prizes and awards. Some, therefore, argue that the American literary canon has become more inclusive.

There is evidence that an African American literary canon was forming as early as the eighteenth century when Jupiter *Hammon's poem "An Address to Miss Phillis Wheatley, Ethiopian Poetess" both named Wheatley as a celebrated African American writer and articulated standards by which such writers were judged. During the nineteenth century, African American *periodicals such as the *Christian Recorder* and the *A. M. E. Church Review* published lists of African American classics. The rise of *Black Studies established a canon that favored men who wrote *poetry, plays, and polemic *essays that espoused *black aesthetics or social protest issues. Among those canonized as "major writers" were Langston *Hughes, Countee *Cullen, Richard *Wright, James *Baldwin, and Amiri *Baraka. The emergence of feminist theory and women's studies added writers such as Zora Neale *Hurston, Maya *Angelou, Alice *Walker, and Audre *Lorde.

Literary canons result from a number of conscious and coincidental efforts. Central to the development of the African American literary canon have been the findings of large, high-profile recovery enterprises such as Henry Louis *Gates, Jr.'s Black Periodical Literature Project based at Harvard University and Maryemma Graham's Project on the History of Black Literature at Northeastern University. The titles in such series as the Schomburg Library of Nineteenth Century Black Women Writers and the American Negro: His History and Literature were determined in part by the accessibility of private collections and copyright permissions for microfilming and reprinting. Inclusion in *anthologies such as *The Norton Anthology of Afro-American Literature* and reference books such as *The Oxford Companion to African American Literature* and *Masterpieces of African American Literature* plays a large role. The rediscovery work of individual scholars, including William L. Andrews, Frances Smith Foster, Henry Louis Gates, Jr., and Jean Fagan Yellin, has installed writers such as Frederick *Douglass, Frances Ellen Watkins *Harper, Harriet E. *Wilson, and Harriet A. *Jacobs in several canons. Professional conferences and periodicals devoted to African American literature and the development of caucuses and divisions within established organizations such as the Modern Language Association and the American Studies Association provide the visibility and impetus for publication of scholarship and criticism that are the infrastructure for literary canons. Such work and the theoretical and methodological processes that serve it create and revise African American and other canons by making particular authors more accessible to readers and scholars and by promoting interpretations and evaluations that define and celebrate them.

[*See also* Criticism; Literary History.]

• Paul Lauter, *Canons and Contexts*, 1991. Henry Louis Gates, Jr., *Loose Canons*, 1992. Stephen Greenblatt and Giles Gunn, eds., *Redrawing the Boundaries*, 1992.

—Frances Smith Foster

CARIBBEAN LITERATURE. *See* West Indian Literature.

CARMICHAEL, STOKELY (b. 1941), civil rights leader and figure in the black nationalist movement of the 1960s. When Richard *Allen and others founded the African Methodist Episcopal Church in the early nineteenth century, a movement of resistance and protest was begun whose declaration of black humanity remains with us today. It is within this rich tradition that Stokely Carmichael obtained a place in American history. Born in Port-of-Spain, Trinidad, Carmichael came of age in the late 1960s while a student at Howard University, where he received the baccalaureate degree in 1964. In the tradition of student protests that characterized the 1960s, he assumed leadership positions in various organizations, joining the Congress of Racial Equality (CORE) and later becoming head of the Student Nonviolent Coordinating Committee (SNCC).

Shortly after becoming the Head of SNCC, Carmichael made famous the phrase "Black Power." In *Stokely Speaks* (1965), Carmichael asserts that "Black Power means that all people who are black should come together, organize themselves and form a power base to fight for their liberation. That's Black Power." Realizing that civil rights legislation was not necessarily morally transformative and that integration in many instances resulted in black assimilation to white norms and values, Carmichael rendered a powerful and annoying political voice, suggesting that much of the civil rights legislation amounted to an illusion of inclusion, because political inclusion is rendered powerless without economic power. At the heart of Carmichael's analysis was a Marxist critique of American democracy and capitalism. While Carmichael may have been somewhat reductive in offering socialism as the exclusive panacea to America's ills, his observations concerning the exclusionary and racist tenets of the American democratic experiment serve as a recurrent theme in African American fiction and *poetry, especially in works by those writers who began their careers as novelists and poets in the late 1960s and 1970s.

His exhortations on black pride and beauty are thematically treated in Toni *Morrison's first novel, *The *Bluest Eye* (1970), in which *Pecola Breedlove, a young black girl with kinky hair, engages in a process of self-hatred because the world in which she finds herself only values girls and women who have blue eyes and straight hair. Having articulated the various frustrations confronted by black men, Carmichael's observations inform Alice *Walker's *The *Third Life of Grange Copeland* (1970), in which Grange Copeland confronts the sense of despair and triumph that characterize the African American experience. Moreover, Carmichael's militant politics pervade the poetry of Nikki *Giovanni.

Adopting the first and last names of his African mentors, presidents Kwame Nkrumah of Ghana and Ahmed Sekou Ture of Guinea, Carmichael calls himself Kwame Ture. Since 1968, he has been living in the West African country of Guinea, devoting himself to liberation movements worldwide. With college students as his primary audience, Ture continues to offer social critique rooted in the spirit of *black nationalism and rhetoric of protest.

[*See also* Civil Rights Movement.]

• Stokely Carmichael, *Stokely Speaks*, 1965. John H. Bracey, Jr., ed., *Black Nationalism in America*, 1970.

—Jeffrey B. Leak

CARTIÉR, XAM WILSON (b. 1949), novelist. Xam Wilson Cartiér, the Missouri-born author, pianist, artist, and dancer, moved to San Francisco in young adulthood to pursue her artistic gifts. Having gained recognition in the early 1980s as the author of successful *television scripts and stage *dramas, she published her first novel, *Be-Bop, Re-Bop*, in 1987. The story of an unnamed African American woman who is searching for *identity, this first-person narrative also provides a broad view of the African American experience—its highs and lows, its past and present, its male and female perspectives, and its rural and urban environments. The narrator, who has been greatly influenced by her father and his love of *jazz, reflects on her father's experiences in the 1930s and 1940s, examines her own youth in the 1950s, and recalls her relationships with her mother and her former husband. Cartiér demonstrates the power of the bebop style of jazz to help the narrator alleviate her hardships, recall personal and collective ancestral roots, and improvise her actions and reactions as she begins to overcome her sense of alienation and construct a new life with her young daughter.

With a similar emphasis on the power and emotion of jazz, Cartiér's second novel, *Muse-Echo Blues* (1991), follows the fantasies of Kat, a 1990s African

American pianist who has composer's block. While coping with this difficulty and others involving relationships with men, Kat muses about the jazz scene of the 1930s and 1940s. She finds herself transported into the lives of two foresisters: Kitty, who loved a drug-addicted saxophone player named Chicago; and Lena, a jazz singer who had abandoned her son, this same Chicago, years before. Kat finds strength and artistic inspiration in the sorrowful but affirming legacy of these African American women who teach her to transform their jazz sensibility into the creation of her own music.

Like other African American postmodern novelists, Cartiér exposes the perversity of American racism while illuminating and affirming both the *speech and dialect and the *music that many African Americans use to express reality. She thematizes language and the telling of one's own story by using jazz-influenced African American speech as an aesthetic device to unite collective memory and recollections with current realities. She incorporates African American music in the storytelling process and the content of her fiction, which produces the kind of tension that exists between the music-making and statement in the polyrhythmic creations of jazz musicians. Both novels manifest characteristics akin to the Jazz Aesthetic: musical rhythm and "scat" syntax in the speech patterns, the feel of improvisation in the italicized fantasies and the temporal variations on the major themes, and spontaneity in the witty, riff-like comments on narrative events. Cartiér's successful fusion of jazz language and rhythms with narrative is a major innovation in the African American novel, comparable to those of Langston *Hughes, Bob *Kaufman, and other creators of African American jazz poetry.

• Valerie Smith, "Dancing to Daddy's Favorite Jam," *New York Times*, 13 December 1987, 7:12. Rayfield Allen Waller, "'Sheets of Sound': A Woman's Bop Prosody," *Black American Literature Forum* 24.4 (Winter 1990): 791–802.

—Marsha C. Vick

CELIE is the protagonist of Alice *Walker's *novel *The *Color Purple* (1982). Her story is a testimony against death and dying—not the death of the corporal being, but one more intensely painful than that. Celie's battle is against a spiritual death that begins with her silent acceptance of abuse and disrespect. At fourteen, she is raped by a man she believes to be her natural father. Later, she is beaten by her husband, who also brings his lover to live in their home. Celie is so oppressed by the men in her life that by the time she matures, only a remnant of her spirit, enshrined within the *letters she writes, remains.

Some readers find Celie's story incomprehensible. They simply cannot fathom how an African American woman could live as passively as Celie does. The reason for the character's docility is easy to explain: it is all she knows. She is so conditioned by abuse that she even advises Harpo, her stepson, to abuse his wife, Sofia.

Celie's salvation is found within the refuge of female love and support. There she gains confidence and self-respect. Her most notable female influence is her husband's lover, *Shug Avery, a woman who nurses Celie's dying spirit and transforms it. Shug becomes Celie's lover, teaching her the beauty of her own body, the wonders of true love, and the value of a positive self-image. Empowered by this new knowledge, Celie breaks through the chains of male domination to celebrate the beauty, the power, and the joy that has always been hers to claim.

• Linda Abbandoonato, "Rewriting the Heroine's Story in *The Color Purple*," in *Alice Walker: Critical Perspectives Past and Present*, eds. Henry Louis Gates and K. A. Appiah, 1988, pp. 296–308. Daniel W. Ross, "Celie in the Looking Glass: The Desire for Selfhood in *The Color Purple*," *Modern Fiction Studies* 34.1 (1988): 69–84.   —Debra Walker King

Cenelles, Les. *Les Cenelles*, published in 1845 in New Orleans, was the first *anthology of *poetry by Americans of color. The title's use of the word *"cenelles,"* meaning holly or hawthorne berries, suggests that the volume contains the collected fruit of the Creole community that produced it. Edited by poet and educator Armand *Lanusse (1812–1867), the collection features the work of seventeen New Orleans poets who, like Lanusse, were well-to-do "free people of color" *(gens de couleur libres)*, a group with a unique cultural life distinct from that of whites on the one hand and slaves on the other. Contributors range from prosperous merchants such as cigar maker Nicol Riquet and mason Auguste Populus to such locally well-known figures as Lanusse, who worked to found black educational institutions; Joanni Questy, a widely read journalist for the militant newspaper *La tribune de la Nouvelle Orléans*; and Victor *Séjour, whose highly successful playwriting career in Paris made him antebellum Louisiana's most distinguished writer.

Lanusse explains in the introduction that the collection is intended to defend his community and race, preserving for future readers its high level of cultural-educational achievement. Culture serves here as a means of refuting and struggling against rationales for a racially divided society.

In content and form, the eighty-four poems in *Les Cenelles* are modeled on French romanticism. They are self-consciously elegant, conventional poetic statements (conventionality here is an index of sophistication) ranging from the facetious to the elegiac and tragic. Principle themes are love, both disappointed and fulfilled; disillusionment and the contemplation of death (five poems concern suicide); and the vicissitudes and dignity of the poetic vocation. Considering its general emphasis on disappointment and disillusionment, the collection is not, as some commentators suggest, primarily a group of light, sentimental love poems. Love in romantic poetry is a surrogate for higher aspirations that for this racially defined community remain frustrated and unfulfilled. When love appears in positive terms, it is cultural refinement and elevation rather than simple passion that is being affirmed.

Les Cenelles reflects the Creole community's experience of imposed limitations and thwarted ambitions in antebellum America. It also manifests the community's deep cultural orientation toward

France. Faced with separatism and eager to develop an elite cultural space of their own, Lanusse and his cocontributors look to Parisian models in order to celebrate one aspect of their heritage and to contest another. Both thematically and in its linguistic and cultural distance from the rest of antebellum culture, this first anthology of African American poetry bespeaks its authors' social alienation as well as their attempts to overcome it through culture.

• Edward Maceo Coleman, ed., *Creole Voices*, 1945 (contains rpt. of *Les Cenelles*). Rodolphe Lucien Desdunes, *Nos Hommes et Notre Histoire*, 1911; republished as *Our People and Our History*, tr. Dorothea Olga McCants, 1973.

—Philip Barnard

CENSORSHIP involving African American literature had its beginning during *slavery. Though learning to read and write was denied the slave and considered an illegal act, blacks—and some helpful whites—ignored the law. It is certainly not surprising then to find in Cathy N. Davidson's *Revolution and the Word: The Rise of the Novel in America* (1986) that even though laws existed, they were not obeyed. Therefore, any evidence of a slave's *literacy existed as an infraction and testimony of dissent; it was proof of intellectual aggression, as well as achievement. Moreover, since African American history is, primarily, grounded in a history of enslavement and the struggles for liberation, one can certainly deduce that the literature will reflect this historical experience.

A protest strand in the tradition of African American literature has throughout the years generated controversy among mainstream readers and critics. The negative criticism is often recalled to illustrate the boundaries and double standard that writers have inherited, as in the comment critic Louis Simpson made about the *poetry of Gwendolyn *Brooks. In the October 1963 *New York Herald Tribune Book Week*, Simpson questioned the quality of a literature that only rendered the African American experience. Simpson's criticism reminded African American writers of not only the double standard that their works were at the mercy of, since white writers generally write about themselves, but also the racist attitudes of some critics who often influence a mainstream reading community. Simpson's view also reflects the standards of a Western, male-centered literary canon, historically existing as a measuring device for any text; however, such standards determine the literary merit of an African American text in particular because of the subjugated and marginal status of African Americans in the United States. If a people's very being is denigrated and questioned, then anything that they produce, in this case writing, has the potential for the same treatment.

African American writers have been under the close scrutiny of not only mainstream critics and readers but also the readership of their own community. The sociocultural and political milieu in the United States created a context that was unavoidable for such writers, with the *slave narrative setting a precedent for the reception of the works. Since the narrative was not only used as a tool for voicing the liberation struggles of the narrators but also those of black people still in slavery, it instilled certain expectations in an African American readership—a nationalist spirit, representing the struggles and aspirations of a community. This communal bonding, along with a mainstream readership and the literary standards of a dominant culture, assisted in forming a rubric under which African American literature developed and was held up for censure. Thus, for the African American writer, censorship has involved several factors: monitoring by a mainstream and African American readership and evaluation by mainstream literary criteria.

In Phillis *Wheatley's poem "On Being Brought from Africa to America" (1773), the line "Remember, Christians, Negros, black as Cain, May be refined and join th' angelic train" is often interpreted in a religious context; however, the poem could metaphorically suggest something else (John Shields, ed., *The Collected Works of Phillis Wheatley*, 1988). The introductory "remember" could be viewed as an admonishment, reminding white colonialists not only of the spiritual capabilities of Wheatley's people but also of their intellectual potential—that conversion to Christianity can also carry with it a "refinement"—a conversion to the positive aspects of American culture. Thus, joining the "angelic train," or acculturation, could also suggest that whatever the dominant culture deems as whiteness and goodness, the enslaved African was certainly capable of imitating, even mastering, for Wheatley herself was proof of such transformation because she was reared in a Eurocentric environment. Since Wheatley's poetry had its neoclassical, religious qualities, it posed no threat to whites. However, she had to prove her authorship before it could be published. This enslaved woman's literacy was too uniquely impressive for whites to accept without question.

Having to garner acceptance from whites is clear from examining the prefaces, forewords, and introductions in colonial and early-nineteenth-century literature. Censorship in these works manifests itself in the close scrutiny under which writings were produced. In order for their literacy not to be perceived as a threat to whites, blacks not only had to assume a subservient posture, they had to have a mediator, a Caucasian, speak on their behalf. The dedication to Olaudah *Equiano's *The Interesting Narrative of the Life of Olaudah Equiano, or Gustavus Vassa, the African* (1789), not only contains the purpose of the *Narrative*, "to exite in your august assemblies a sense of compassion from the miseries which the Slave-Trade has entailed on my unfortunate countrymen," but also a more cautionary voice that realizes that such brazenness or, in the author's own terms, boldness, creates risks, "I trust that *such a man*, pleading in *such a cause*, will be acquitted of boldness and presumption" (Henry Louis Gates, Jr., ed., *The Classic Slave Narratives*, 1987). The *Narrative* is a consequence of disobedience and a product that Equiano must be apologetic for because it challenges and contradicts the dominant, orthodox view—that slaves cannot and should not produce any work of literary merit. The narrator is also very much aware of the necessity of exhibiting subservience in order to avoid being perceived as a transgressor. In addition, he must assert that the *Narrative* is without literary merit. Such disclaiming in the introductory parts of earlier eighteenth-century and nineteenth-century texts reveals a self-imposed censoring in response to anticipated reception. This self-consciousness had to occur prior to as well as during the process of composing.

In Georges Bataille's *Evil and Literature* (1973), the author speaks of writing as a transgressive act. This concept is an appropriate one for viewing the slave narrative, which is perhaps the most obvious genre to foster a transgressive posture. However, writing as a rebellious act was already ensconced in early America, with Thomas Paine's essay "Common Sense" (1776), followed by the incendiary essay of African American David *Walker entitled *David Walker's Appeal* (1829). As Richard *Wright spoke of writer and critic H. L. Mencken in Wright's modern version of the slave narrative, the autobiographical *Black Boy* (1945), "This man was fighting, fighting with words . . . perhaps I could use them as a weapon." The narrators of slave narratives were similarly compelled. Moreover, the management of the slave narrative by an outsider, including editing and shaping such discourse for publication or speaking, could be considered as a subsequent stage of censoring, as such narratives were primarily typeset and read by whites. Regardless of the humanitarianism of the editor, the writer as client (like Frederick *Douglass, the slave, to William Lloyd Garrison, the abolitionist) was under the auspices of white control: a white printing press and a primarily white readership.

In the preface of Frederick Douglass's *Narrative of the Life of Frederick Douglass, an American Slave* (1845), Douglass's abolitionist comrade, Garrison, voices the risk the writer encumbers in telling his story. Wendell Phillips views the *Narrative* as Douglass's signature and capable of provoking retaliation, placing Douglass in a situation comparable to that of the signers of the Declaration of Independence, itself a revolutionary and endangering document. Also, a reading of Douglass's narrative will reveal a litany of transgressions only a fugitive slave could make against a slaveholding community: he fights and defeats the meanest slave breaker, Covey; he clandestinely teaches the other slaves to read; he escapes and is recaptured; he unabashedly expresses his desire for *freedom and respect; and, most important, he reveals the religious hypocrisy of slavery in a self-proclaimed Christian state. Perhaps it was Douglass's ingenious literary talent that mesmerized his readers at the time, for certainly he was subject to physical attack, and the *Narrative* could have been banned.

In contrast to Douglass, Harriet A. *Jacobs's *Incidents in the Life of a Slave Girl* (1861) had to be published under the pseudonym Linda Brent. This narrative fills the feminist void in the slave narrative canon and is cited as pleading the case of the sexually exploited, enslaved African American female. And because of the narrative's emphasis, it presents a strong-willed voice under the threat and vengeance of a male oppressor. Jacobs's editor, Lydia Maria Child, adamantly proclaims the former's authorship and her own role as editor. However, Child's anticipation of doubt among readers is evidenced when she informs them that she "had no reason for changing her [Jacobs's] lively and dramatic way of telling her own story."

Moreover, Jacobs's narrative becomes dialectical because it not only exposes sexual exploitation but also the accessibility of the African American slave woman, who, because of her usually forced sexual relations with white males, inadvertently becomes a blamed victim. Even Jacobs's grandmother in *Incidents* questions the narrator's character when she consciously chooses to bear children by a white male. The relationship between enslaved females and white male slave owners carried with it a shroud of suspicion, even enigma, regarding the sexuality of African American females. And because of this cultural phenomenon, the portrayal of the African American female's *sexuality in literature becomes significant. In W. E. B. *Du Bois's 1924 review of Jean *Toomer's *Cane* (1923) in the *Crisis*, he suggests that a preconception is brought to the text regarding the characterization of African American females. Because of the sexual context in which enslaved females are portrayed in early American literature, for example, as bearers of mulatto children as a result of rape and sexual exploitation, Du Bois felt that Toomer's portraiture of African American women in *Cane* would "emancipate the colored world from the convention of sex" (quoted in *Selections from the Crisis*, ed. Herbert Aptheker, 1983). And Du Bois recognizes the sensitivity of African American readers regarding this tabooed subject with his further comment, "There are his [Toomer's] women, painted with a frankness that is going to make his black readers shrink and criticize; and yet they are done with a certain splendid, careless truth."

Harriet E. Adams *Wilson's *Our Nig* (1859), considered one of the earliest African American novels, includes a preface that anticipates censorship. There are two assumptions that Wilson makes: disapproval from supporters of slavery and condemnation from her own people for exhibiting literacy, uncommon among them. Thus, her request for impunity from both audiences is quintessential to easing her mental state. The final plea in Wilson's preface is for her people to support her endeavor, "[to] rally around me [as] a faithful band of supporters and defenders" (William L. Andrews, ed., *Three Classic African American Novels*, 1990). Even though she wished to avoid punishment from whites, Wilson's ultimate aim was to not alienate her own people. It is this type of communal bonding that influences the writing process, and though Wilson is writing fiction, her technique reflects the same strategies used in slave narratives. Wilson's cautionary voice augments that of her predecessors by propagandizing the struggle for liberation, demonstrating literacy, and laying the foundation for more strident voices that would ensue.

Two voices that created the most obvious cases of censorship aimed at African American writers are those of David Walker and Ida B. *Wells-Barnett, the journalist who spoke out against lynching. Wells-Barnett's journalistic courage provoked the most vehement criticism and death threats, but a precedent involving *violence directed toward an African American writer had been set even earlier with Walker's *Appeal*. The pamphlet presented the most scathing indictment against slavery and criticized American whites, causing them to seek revenge. Richard K. Barksdale's and Keneth Kinnamon's *Black Writers of America* (1973) relates the serious punitive measures that ensued: threats of death for slaves caught with Walker's pamphlet and legislation reminding whites of the illegality of teaching slaves. David Walker's mysterious death, allegedly from poisoning, and Wells-Barnett's forced flight from Memphis certainly attest to the seriousness of the African American writer's position in America's literary history.

In the twentieth century, the controversy regarding the use of dialect arose especially involving Paul Laurence *Dunbar (1872–1906), more noted for his poems written in dialect than those in Standard English; it continued to plague other African American writers in the early twentieth century. When Dunbar published his collection of poetry, *Lyrics of Lowly Life* (1896), the introduction by writer and critic William Dean Howells became the kiss of death because it praised the dialect pieces more than the others; Dunbar wanted all of his works to be accepted and appreciated by mainstream and African American audiences. But Dunbar realized his creative dilemma and metaphorically expressed it in his poem, "The Poet": "But ah, the world, it turned to praise / A jingle in a broken tongue."

Howells's comments praising Dunbar's dialect poems and contrasting them with those in Standard English confirmed the views of some white Americans that romanticized and happy characters, speaking in dialect, were acceptable; perhaps the gaiety helped to ease the guilt of whites, but it also possibly further denigrated freed persons in post–Civil War America. Since African Americans were no longer legally enslaved, the resistance to their assimilation into a mainstream American culture and economy made the minstrel *stereotype expedient.

James Weldon *Johnson (1871–1938), lyricist, poet, and critic, was among a community of artists who accepted the mission to eradicate harmful African American images. Johnson was cognizant of the cultural significance of dialect, but he was also aware of its limitations. He recognized dialect as a natural language variation in black folk culture but considered it at variance with African Americans' attempts to be socialized into mainstream American life. In *The Book of American Negro Poetry* (1922), Johnson presents his claim that dialect is incapable of capturing the varied aspects and psychology of the African American's life, and even he had to use a feigned white (passing *mulatto) to attract both white and African American readers with his novel, *The *Autobiography of an Ex-Colored Man* (1912). Johnson, along with his *Harlem Renaissance contemporaries, was facing a new awakening in African American literary history; they were cognizant of the sociopolitical landscape of the African American community. Wars, *lynchings, disenfranchisement, Jim Crow laws, and more education prepared African Americans to fight injustice and to be intolerant of a stereotyped image of themselves.

Alain *Locke's *The *New Negro* (1925) presented an examination of this metamorphosis in African American literature. Locke signaled the new beginning that was being so dramatically enacted by the writers of the Harlem Renaissance, most often dated from around 1918 to approximately 1930. It was a flowering of African American arts, producing writers who were proud of their African roots, disgruntled with America's racism and Jim Crow laws, and receptive to the financial support and encouragement of a white patronage. Though the Renaissance canon was male-dominated with Langston *Hughes, Jean Toomer, Claude *McKay, and Countee *Cullen, female writers like Zora Neale *Hurston, Jessie Redmon *Fauset, and Nella *Larsen were also among this community of writers. Perhaps it is the case of Hurston that clearly illustrates the sexist milieu in which African American female writers produced. Thus, gender was another operative in the censoring process, another indication that suppression of the African American female voice is only a microcosm of the macrocosmic American patriarchal literary tradition. Hurston's literary career was influenced by several factors: the standards and criteria emanating from an African American and white male–dominated canon; the expectations of black readers; and an emerging Black Aesthetic, born of an established African American literary tradition. Claude McKay's poem "If We Must Die" (1919) solidified the protest stance of African American writing, and though Hurston had received awards and accolades for her writings, the publication of *Their Eyes Were Watching God* in 1937 was inconsequential. The novel's folkloric emphasis and uniquely assertive female protagonist, *Janie Crawford, did not allow Hurston to reach parity with her male literary counterparts. Richard Wright caustically criticized the novel and maintained that it was not the (W)right voice that America needed to hear from an African American writer.

Though Wright and Hughes were able to sustain careers as writers, their endangerment as such reached fruition when they were tracked by the State Department and FBI because of their leftist views. Addison *Gayle, Jr.'s *Richard Wright: Ordeal of a Native Son* (1980) examines documents from agencies in the United States and Europe, especially France and England. Gayle's research on Wright uncovered a series of memos that revealed surveillance from such agencies as the United States Information Service, the Foreign Service, and the Department of State, as well as the tactics of the FBI's J. Edgar Hoover and staff. Hoover deduced that Wright's ultimate intention was to simply write about what he termed "the Negro problem"; however, Hoover was unaware of an irony: Wright intended to expose white America as "the Negro problem." Langston Hughes's subpoena by the House Un-American Activities Committee in 1953 placed him in the same company with the avowed Marxist writer, Wright. In addition, Wright's membership in the Communist Party represented the black intellectual's odyssey in attempting to find a philosophical base not only for creative endeavors but also for solving the problems of the people. Though Wright severed his ties with the party, it was not soon enough, for he, along with Hughes and Ralph *Ellison, suffered when African American writers, with their philosophical associations, were viewed as exceeding their prescribed boundaries.

Hughes's philosophy of art, expressed in his *essay "The Negro Artist and the Racial Mountain" (*Nation*, June 1926), addresses the problematic and censorious path of the African American writer. His anecdotal account of the young African American writer who espouses, "I want to be a poet—not a Negro poet" illustrates the idealism of not just a younger generation but the dilemma of a preceding one. Though in 1926 Hughes himself was a young writer, he felt he had found a philosophical niche for creative expression, writing "We younger Negro artists who create now intend to express our individual dark-skinned selves without fear or shame." But the ending thought of the essay, "If white people are pleased, we are glad. If they are not, it doesn't matter. If colored people are pleased, we are glad. If they are not, their displeasure doesn't matter either," gave Hughes a false sense of autonomy. He finally realized that displeasure does matter when, in 1953, he was questioned by Senator Joseph McCarthy's Senate Committee. Apparently this experience caused Hughes to acquiesce, but ironically resulted in his own criticism of the overt protestations of 1960s African American poets.

Hughes's criticism of his literary colleagues raises an issue that writer and critic bell *hooks addresses in her essay "Censorship from Left and Right" (*Outlaw Culture: Resisting Representation*, 1994). According to hooks, even though the right of free speech exists, too often there is a clandestine censoring among academics and writers when it comes to critiquing each other; they fear being labeled as disloyal or divisive. As a result, the critic contemplates or chooses silence for fear of being alienated or severely castigated by the African American academic and literary community. James *Baldwin's essay "Everybody's Protest Novel" (1949), in its criticism of Richard Wright's *Native Son* (1940), was viewed by some, and especially Wright, as an act of betrayal. This incident with Baldwin and Wright implicates the following issues: the right of African American writers to differ with and critique each other without being castigated and the argument that protestation deemphasizes literary artistry—an issue that pervades hermeneutics in African American and American literary criticism. We have inherited the differing philosophies of Booker T. *Washington and W. E. B. Du Bois and have not finally accepted or rejected either. However, we are also aware of the dissent they caused, especially among their own people, for taking a position and standing by it. The politics of the writer always factors into the writing process, either motivating overt protestation or obscuring it.

Baldwin, however, had to deal with his homosexuality, which he eventually avowed, and some of his novels sent shocks through a traditionally homophobic African American readership. His innocuous *Giovanni's Room* (1956) was an attempt to achieve autonomy and avoid a racial diatribe. But Baldwin's essays in *Nobody Knows My Name* (1961) reevaluate Wright's fiction and cause him to recant his views; he eventually perceived a universal quality in *Native Son*, as well as Wright's other fiction. America's race problem to Baldwin was no longer an ideologue's illusion; it was a reality that had to be sincerely addressed, which he candidly did in *The *Fire Next Time* (1963).

The relationship that African Americans had with each other often brought about some provocative and insightful views. The role and the politics of the African American writer became crucial points of controversy among critics and writers during the turbulent and fecund 1960s, an era politically charged with the *civil rights movement and anti-war demonstrations. This social and political upheaval, along with the fiery rhetoric of 1960s poetry, mobilized a community of people, revolutionized their thinking, and set the stage for a cultural nationalist rejuvenation among African Americans in the United States. The academy was affected, ushering in what were initially called *black studies programs, as well as women's and feminist studies. The African American writer, as in the Harlem Renaissance, was in vogue. In addition, the feminist movement and the founding of a feminist press helped female writers; the atmosphere was ripe for the emergence of the African American female writer. However, such attention raised the question among some male writers of whether female writers and characters were extolled at the expense of their male counterparts, but the often alleged African American male–female relational conflicts precluded the pervasiveness of such criticism.

Alice *Walker's *short story collection *In Love and Trouble* (1973) presented to readers an obvious sympathetic rendering of African American feminine consciousness. The characterization of females in canonized literature was, of course, being assessed by the women's movement of the dominant culture. Also, the tradition of the African American female writer was emphasized and rediscovered, with Walker's *In Search of Our Mothers' Gardens* (1983) presenting this tradition in juxtaposition with a male-centered literary canon being revised. Walker also coined the term *womanism, focusing on race and class, which African American female scholars found useful. Hurston's *Their Eyes Were Watching God* was resurrected as a feminist text, and critical texts created what has come to be a substantive body of feminist and womanist scholarship that examines and evaluates women writers and writings about women.

Nevertheless, the lesbian overtones of Alice Walker's *The *Color Purple* (1982) presented another aspect of African American life that had not been focused on in fiction. Readers of African American literature had been accustomed to male homosexuality through the novels of Baldwin, but the African American lesbian was basically still closeted until the poetry of Audre *Lorde and the fiction of Gloria *Naylor's *Women of Brewster Place* (1989) surfaced. The subject of male homosexuality was difficult enough, but female homosexuality was certainly a tabooed subject, even though it had a graceful debut in a primarily heterosexually oriented narrative. The so-called radical feminists had an agenda, and they would not be silenced. Moreover, *Home Girls: A Black Feminist Anthology* (1983), edited by Barbara Smith, proclaimed that all aspects of African American sexuality, especially that of women, should be represented in literature regardless of African American cultural traditions.

The enormous amount of popular literature creates another censorious debate regarding the criteria brought to a text to determine its merit in a revised literary canon that is still basically grounded in tradition. Terry *McMillan's *Disappearing Acts* (1989) and *Waiting to Exhale* (1992) present unadulterated accounts of the sexual relationships between males and females that had generally not been portrayed in African American fiction. Moreover, McMillan's novels have captured a large, receptive readership, especially among African American females. Nevertheless, even though the parameters for African American writers have widened, other issues arise, whether it involves their acceptance or rejection by the academy or factions in the community (school districts, libraries, and city councils) for allegedly espousing hate like some rap artists do. The testimony of bell hooks regarding the banning of her book *(Black Looks)* in Canada for being considered as hate literature is an exemplary case regarding the latter. Nevertheless, regardless of the writings of African Americans, their art has had as much of a struggle for acceptance as the very struggles they have portrayed. They have endured a vigorously challenging past and present in trying to be accepted by audiences, both African American and white. Thus, the double consciousness theory of W. E. B. Du Bois has just as much relevance in a literary context as in a sociocultural one. With hundreds of years of enslavement haunting a people, and the problems of racism and sexism having the potential to be activated at any time, African American writing will continue to be provocative and open for censure. Regardless, perhaps one of the best legacies Langston Hughes left African American writers is "displeasure doesn't matter."

[*See also* Afrocentricity; Black Aesthetic; Black Nationalism; Gay Literature; Lesbian Literature; Protest Literature; Speech and Dialect.]

• Lida Keck Wiggins, *The Life and Works of Paul Laurence Dunbar,* 1907. Louis Simpson, "Don't Take a Poem by the Horns," *New York Herald Tribune Book Week,* 27 October 1963, 6, 25. Richard K. Barksdale and Keneth Kinnamon, eds., *Black Writers of America: A Comprehensive Anthology,* 1972. Georges Bataille, *Literature and Evil,* 1973. W. E. B. Du Bois and Alain Locke, "The Younger Literary Movement," in *Selections from the* Crisis, ed. Herbert Aptheker, 1983, pp. 372–373. Cathy N. Davidson, *Revolution and the Word: The Rise of the Novel in America,* 1986. Henry Louis Gates, Jr., ed., *The Classic Slave Narratives,* 1987. John Shields, ed., *The Collected Works of Phillis Wheatley,* 1988. William L. Andrews, ed., *Three Classic African American Novels,* 1990. Richard Wright, *Black Boy,* 1993. bell hooks, "Censorship from Left and Right," in *Outlaw Culture: Resisting Representation,* 1994, pp. 63–72.   —Yvonne Robinson Jones

CEREMONIES. *See* Festivals; Performances and Pageants.

Ceremonies in Dark Old Men.

Lonne *Elder III's *Ceremonies in Dark Old Men* (1969) is a dramatization of rituals—of survival, of friendship, of deception and manipulation, of self-deception, of black male friendship, of shifting intrafamilial allegiances, and of black *manhood. As Elder presents the ineffectual lives of a Harlem family entrapped by rituals of economic and spiritual dependence, he urges African Americans and African American communities to become aware of and to break free of "ceremonies" that assuredly lead to personal loss and tragedy. Echoing Douglas Turner *Ward's warning to black Americans whose "happiness" and survival are predicated upon white America's relationship to black America in *Happy Ending* (1966), *Ceremonies* challenges the myth that the social, political, and economic plight of black America rests in white people's hands. Through layers of ritual, Elder demonstrates the futility, corruption, and internal disruptions that result from efforts to undermine a capitalist system that seeks to determine and define African Americans' worth and selfhood.

That the play is specifically concerned with black male rituals is at the heart of Elder's barbershop setting, where two old men claim a territorial space that removes them temporarily from a world that has deemed them powerless and insignificant. The checkerboard ritual reaffirms not only their friendship, manifested in playful dares and insults, but it also symbolizes the lack of control Russell Parker especially feels in a world where he is for whatever reasons unable to find satisfactory employment options. In the hours that Parker's daughter Adele is away working to support the family, Parker can reign supreme despite the fact that the barbershop is not providing an income for him and he is subsequently forced to rely on Adele for his survival. Parker and his friend Jenkins's efforts to manipulate and deceive each other in this game represent the larger game of the "business" deal Parker reluctantly becomes part of despite his initial misgivings.

While Jenkins and Parker are content to hide their activities from Adele, Parker's sons, Theodore and Bobby, are convinced that the only way to assume their black manhood is to become economically empowered "by any means necessary." That they end up profiting from stealing, scheming, bootlegging, and hiding from the law, capitalizing on racism, and compromising their moral values becomes problematic only when parental roles are reversed and breakdowns occur in familial and personal trust. No longer are honesty and fairness acceptable as each participant in this game becomes trapped by personal greed and selfishness. With Bobby's death and with internal trusts violated, rituals of deception and self-deception become an initiation rite for

Adele and Theodore. That Parker is still trapped in the fantasies of his own alleged past manhood when others' efforts were devoted to making his life more pleasant renders the play's ending all the more tragic as he is unable or unwilling to accept the reality of his younger son's "business-related" death.

Unsurprisingly, the play's chauvinistic presentation of black women is characteristic of many "revolutionary" plays of the 1960s wherein black manhood is synonymous with race consciousness. As a champion of political and social awareness, Elder, like Amiri *Baraka, Ben *Caldwell, Ron *Milner, and Ed *Bullins, relegates black women to positions of relative insignificance. Indeed, the younger black males adopt the attitudinal and behavioral rituals of the older men who see women as objects for their own personal satisfaction. Parker truly believes that his deceased wife enjoyed working herself to death to make him happy. Even Adele is directionless when she is unable to fill her nurturing role for the males in her family. Only through *violence, alleged sexual prowess, and economic autonomy can black males in this play validate themselves in a world that makes them otherwise powerless.

Ceremonies is Elder's challenge to black Americans to free themselves of the psychological chains that bind and limit their possibilities for attaining fulfilled selfhood personally and collectively. Only through an abandonment of selfish ideals, Elder demonstrates, can an African American community become whole and autonomous.

• Lance Jeffers, "Bullins, Baraka, and Elder: The Dawn of Grandeur in Black Drama," *CLA Journal* 16 (Sept. 1972): 32–48. Chester J. Fontenot, "Mythic Patterns in *River Niger* and *Ceremonies in Dark Old Men*," *MELUS* 7 (Spring 1980): 41–49.
—Neal A. Lester

Chaneysville Incident, The. In David *Bradley's *The Chaneysville Incident* (1981), the protagonist John Washington, professor of history in Philadelphia, when called to the deathbed of Jack Crawley, his father's closest friend, finds himself involuntarily plunged into confronting his family and group *history. Nearby Chaneysville, a station of the preemancipation *Underground Railroad for fugitive slaves in western Pennsylvania, becomes the symbolic stage. John's personal ambivalence and distrust toward white America have increasingly led to emotional paralysis and sardonic detachment, affecting both his scholarship and his love for Judith, a white psychologist. Jack Crawley's stories rekindle John's interest in the life, death, and legacy of his father Moses (especially the library spiked with clues for reconstructing black history). John learns about his father's covert control of local white politicians (via a "moonshine" dossier), and about a concrete Chaneysville incident where Moses (with Jack's help) prevented the *lynching of their friend Josh White and afterward eliminated the gangleaders. John uncovers a subversive black counterhistory in the plan of his forebear C. K. Washington to undermine the South's economy by leading as many slaves as possible to freedom. According to local legend, C. K. and thirteen slaves committed collective suicide at Chaneys-

ville. (Bradley's mother discovered their unmarked graves in 1969.)

John's efforts to understand this first Chaneysville incident (ritually emulated by his father's suicide at the slaves' gravesite) remain abortive despite intensive research and an impressive card catalog. When Judith (descendant of Virginia slaveholders) joins John and questions his motives, the factual gaps of the Chaneysville riddle can be imaginatively bridged to restore a suppressed and fragmented history. The slaves, C. K., and his wife chose death to avoid being recaptured, and a white miller respectfully buried them. John and Judith repeat the act of mutual empathy, and by ritually burning the card catalog at the end reopen the emotional and cultural space for their relationship.

History and storytelling (or fictionalization) are seen as converging or germane enterprises in Bradley's *novel (recalling new historiographic theory as initiated by Hayden White). His text dramatizes an impressive array of documented and invented history, of vernacular and formal discourse (bridging oral and literary conventions). It combines modes of white mainstream narrative (the self-reflexive Jamesian narrator John, Faulknerian rhetoric and ritualizations of landscape and hunting, essayistic digressions) with specifically African American forms of narrative: the dialogical use of voices; African cultural concepts (death as a continuum of the living and their ancestors, embodied in the voices in the wind heard by John, and in suicide as going home); the creative resumption and reinvention of the earlier *slave narrative; and novels by Ishmael *Reed, Charles R. *Johnson, and Toni *Morrison. Without slurring over the antagonistic nature in America of unjust white power versus black marginalization and resistance, the novel proffers a utopian outlook for a possible convergence of black and white self-concepts via a therapeutic acceptance of the other's past and perspective. Bradley's novel is an eloquent example in a growing number of narrative texts by African American authors engaged in an intensive reassessment and reappropriation of their historical past.

• Martin J. Gliserman, "David Bradley's *The Chaneysville Incident*: The Belly of the Text," *American Imago* 43.2 (1986): 97–120. Klaus Ensslen; "Fictionalizing History: David Bradley's *The Chaneysville Incident*," *Callaloo* 11.2 (1988): 280–296. Klaus Ensslen, "The Renaissance of the Slave Narrative in Recent Critical and Fictional Discourse," in *Slavery in the Americas*, ed. W. Binder, 1993, pp. 601–626. Matthew Wilson, "The African-American Historian: David Bradley's *The Chaneysville Incident*," *African American Review* 20.1 (1995): 97–107.
—Klaus Ensslen

CHARACTER TYPES in African American literature are as varied as in any other literature. In fact, there are more that appear across genres and recur through the major periods of African American literary history than can be covered in this article. African American character types may be individual representations or they may represent particular segments or groups within the culture. Many are very similar to those that appear in other literary traditions; however, the specific depictions including nuances of personality and motivation, the activities, and the contexts of their activities generally differentiate those in the African American literary tradition.

The tragic *mulatto is one of the earliest individual character types to appear in African American literature. Generally the tragic mulatto is physically indistinguishable from whites and often grows up believing that she or he is white. Yet there is an African ancestry, sometimes identified as "a drop of African blood," and upon having such heritage revealed this character is identified as black and treated accordingly. These mulatto characters are "tragic" because their racial identification results in personality disintegration and even death. The figure appears, for example, in William Wells *Brown's *Clotel, or The President's Daughter* (1853), the earliest known novel to be published by an African American author. In this work, the heroine, being identified as black, not only cannot marry her white lover but is later enslaved and eventually commits suicide. Charles Waddell *Chesnutt's *short story "The Sheriff's Children" (1899) focuses on the son of a white sheriff; here, the son's demise is directly attributable to the conflicts he experiences because of his mixed heritage. In the 1920s Langston *Hughes returns to this character type in the short poem "Cross" (1926) in which the speaker articulates his internal conflicts as he wonders where he belongs since he is neither black nor white.

The *trickster is another early recognizable individual character type. Having its analogues in the oral tradition, specifically the tales of *Brer Rabbit and the John and Marster cycle, the trickster is typically in a weaker position than the adversary but triumphs through guile and manipulation or by donning a mask of helplessness, ignorance, superstition, or innocence. Charles Chesnutt's *Uncle Julius McAdoo in The *Conjure Woman* (1899) is an early literary example. Uncle Julius's manipulative tales have the ostensible purpose of engendering sympathy within his audience, in this case the northern landowner and his wife, in order to achieve some objective beneficial to himself. Uncle Julius operates purely from self-interest, and although he is often devious, he is not evil. His stories have the added significance of allowing Chesnutt the opportunity to reveal the dehumanizing effects of slavery within a frame structure. Later writers have expanded the possibilities of this type by exploring the ambiguities inherent in the figure and sometimes exposing a more sinister side. The shifting shape of Ralph *Ellison's *Rinehart in *Invisible Man* (1952), for instance, reveals to the protagonist the unlimited possibilities and freedom that reality offers, that is, until he realizes that the trickster's power to manipulate reality raises ethical questions about Rinehart's existence and about his relationship to the community. It can be quite disconcerting when, through a series of disguises, an individual can be both numbers runner and preacher. In The Bloodworth Orphans (1977), Leon *Forrest depicts W. W. W. Ford, another trickster who possesses a degree of malevolence, for the falseness that is at the core of his being leads to the disillusionment and lostness of several of the characters, possibly including the protagonist.

*Preachers and deacons also recur in African American literature. In fact, Paul Laurence *Dunbar's poem "An Antebellum Sermon" (The Collected Poems, 1913) shows what happens when an author blends a preacher with the trickster as the speaker in this work utters sentiments, seemingly by accident, that he knows will not be acceptable to the white master. On the other hand, the celebratory *God's Trombones: Seven Negro Sermons in Verse (1927) by James Weldon *Johnson shows why this figure holds such possibilities for writers, for these sermon-poems convey some of the preacher's powerful ability to create vivid images and to explore the ranges of his voice, which is his instrument. Reverend Homer Barbee's voice in Invisible Man enables him to re-create the past and invoke the myth of the Founder so vividly that the audience is entranced for the moment, or in the sentiments of the protagonist, blinded by the experience. As presented in James *Baldwin's The *Amen Corner (1955), the preacher, in this case a female character, retains the power of the preacher's presence, although she is engaged in a battle between the spiritual and the physical self.

Another character type that made its appearance early in the literature is the musician. James Weldon Johnson's "O Black and Unknown Bards" expresses appreciation for the anonymous creators/singers of the *spirituals. However, musicians of every style have captured the imagination of African American writers. Other poets who have utilized this figure include Robert *Hayden ("Homage to the Empress of the Blues," 1966) and Sterling A. *Brown ("Ma Rainey," 1932). Typically the musician is a representative of cultural values that have sustained a people as well as a figure who provides the community with avenues that lead to overcoming limiting circumstances. In fiction, for example, Ellison's allusions to Louis Armstrong in Invisible Man present lessons to the hero regarding identity and transcendence over external definitions through improvisation. Another powerful example of this type is Luzana Cholly in Albert *Murray's Train Whistle Guitar (1974). In this work the character functions as a role model for Scooter, the protagonist, because of his personal tastes and his way of living, both of which are defined by improvisation and instrumentation. It is significant that Zora Neale *Hurston decided to add a musical dimension to *Tea Cake in *Their Eyes Were Watching God (1937), for this facet of his character as a repository of cultural values other than those of the village reinforces his importance to *Janie Crawford's journey toward self-definition.

Tea Cake, in fact, illustrates how a writer may merge types in creating a multifaceted individual, for his role as a vagabond is also significant within the narrative and illustrates another recurring type within African American literature. As the label suggests, the vagabond is a wanderer, one without connections, detached from the expectations or values of a specific community. The lifestyle of the vagabond is one of constant movement, *freedom, and liberation. It is Tea Cake's wanderlust that takes Janie, Hurston's protagonist, to the Muck to be exposed to a lifestyle that is completely antithetical to the life and mores of the village. The vagabond seems to be closer to elemental life, a life unfettered by the false overlay of society. Claude *McKay's Jake in *Home to Harlem (1928) is another example of this character type.

From vagabond to *badman or outlaw is not such a gigantic leap, and the latter appears throughout African American literary history. Having its analogues in oral tradition heroes such as *Stackolee and Railroad Bill, these are figures of great courage, challenging forces lawful and unlawful, completely unafraid. These are individuals who do not avoid confrontation and who sometimes appear to be supernatural in their power. Cholly, the representative man in Murray's Train Whistle Guitar, is even more meaningful to the main character's maturation because he has survived and transcended the penitentiary experience. Another example from this novel is Stagolee Dupas (fils), a musician whose confrontation with Sheriff Timberlake echoes the experience of the legendary Stackolee. Usually, the badmen are male characters, but there are female characters whose lifestyles and personalities echo that toughness, assertiveness, and unrestrained freedom that are the measures of their male counterparts. *Sula Peace, the title character in Toni *Morrison's *novel (1974), is a vivid example of the *bad woman. Sula's total disregard for the mores of the Bottom—her involvement in the death of Chicken Little, her pursuit of her best friend's husband—make her a law unto herself. She does not consider herself to be answerable to the expectations of the community, and as a result, she becomes a threat to the bonds that hold that community together.

Related to the outlaw figure is the brute for whom the violent response seems to be the only form of communication; at least he seems to lack the ability to articulate in any other form the frustrations that he experiences. Richard *Wright's *Bigger Thomas in *Native Son (1940) fits this mold as he strikes out blindly at the forces that he does not understand and over which he has no control.

One character who has been much maligned is the mother figure or *matriarch, who in her stereotypical guise is generally depicted as the all-powerful destroyer of the African American male psyche. A more balanced view, however, recognizes the strength of this type while not overlooking her capacity to love and nurture her children and to function as a repository of enduring values and wisdom. One of the most vivid portrayals of the matriarch is Lena Younger in Lorraine *Hansberry's A *Raisin in the Sun (1959). Lena stands at the center of the family and of this drama, determined to steer her children in the direction of her dream of escaping urban poverty. Her son, *Walter Lee Younger, has other ideas about realizing that dream, and, fortunately, Lena realizes that she must relinquish some of the control in the family in order for him to reach self-actualization. There are other maternal voices, representative of this type, including the speaker in Langston Hughes's "Mother to Son" (1926), who advises her son not be overcome by the inevitable obstacles that he will meet. There is

also the mother in Gwendolyn *Brooks's sonnet series "The Womanhood" (1949), who ruminates on her dreams for her children and her concerns about preparing them for the world. The speaker in Brooks's "The Mother" section from A *Street in Bronzeville (1945) sadly reflects upon the difficult choices that she has had to make in her struggle to exist. The depiction of the strong, caring, nurturing individual, who sometimes does not know how to vocalize her love, is vividly portrayed in Ernest J. *Gaines's "The Sky Is Gray," from his collection of short stories, Bloodline (1968).

While the traditional image of the mother is that of a strong, nurturing human being, a more ambiguous representative of this type appears in Toni Morrison's *Sula in the character of *Eva Peace. According to town legend, Eva, Sula's grandmother, had thrown herself under a train to collect the insurance money, thus enabling her to care for her two children. While Eva is capable of such incredible sacrifice, she is also capable of unbelievable destruction. When her son, Plum, succumbs to drug addiction, she descends the stairs to his room, in all her magnificence, and burns him alive. An act that baffles through its apparent malevolence is for her an act that frees Plum from his own destruction. Muhdear in Tina McElroy *Ansa's Ugly Ways (1993) is by no means as imposing as Eva Peace, yet she too falls outside of the nurturing role that may be traditionally ascribed to the mother figure.

Related to these matriarchal figures, who are biologically related to other characters, are the surrogate mothers who in many instances serve as moral guides or vessels of cultural values. *Mary Rambo in Ellison's Invisible Man falls into this category. Aunty Breedy in Forrest's There Is a Tree More Ancient Than Eden (1973) is there to comfort and motivate Nathan as he struggles toward redemption. Toni Morrison uses this type for great effect in *Song of Solomon (1977) as *Pilate Dead leads the protagonist, *Milkman Dead, back to and through the family's and the group's history to his self-realization.

Not all moral guides are female, however. In Ernest Gaines's "Three Men" (1963), Mumford Bazille serves this function for Proctor Lewis, the main character, who in turn provides the same guidance for a newly arrived inmate. Like Murray's Luzana Cholly, neither of these characters is cast in the conservative mold of a moral guide who has been the epitome of virtue in the community, at least not in the usual sense. These are men who have lived rough lives and may continue to do so, yet they feel a sense of responsibility to present the young with an alternative path away from the destructive one on which they are headed.

Guides may also appear in the literature as freedom fighters or rebels, both historical and fictional. These are individuals whose political and social consciousness has awakened; thus they serve as inspiration for others. In "Runagate Runagate," Robert Hayden, for instance, commemorates Harriet *Tubman and nameless others who followed her. Following his assassination, *Malcolm X became the focus of many writers, including Robert Hayden ("El-Hajj Malik El-

Shabazz," 1970) and Haki R. *Madhubuti ("Malcolm Spoke / Who Listened," 1971). Gwendolyn Brooks has added her poetic voice to these expressions celebrating freedom fighters/rebels in her poems "Medgar Evers" (1968) and "Malcolm" (1968). Fictionalized characters like Aunt Sue in Richard Wright's "Bright and Morning Star" (1936) fit in this category. Here Wright has created a character who, contrary to appearances, assumes a revolutionary stance against the political and social forces gathered to destroy her and her son, although she is killed in the process. In a similar vein, there is Brooks's "The Ballad of Rudolph Reed" (1960), which commemorates a character coming to political and social awareness as he realizes that there are those who believe that he and his family should not be inheritors of the American dream.

Seekers/questers are those seeking to emerge from their old identities in order to create a new self. Such characters are both male and female and may experience some alienation between themselves and the group/community. In order to discover who they are, they may embark on literal or figurative journeys. There are, of course, many examples of this type, including the protagonist in *Invisible Man*, Janie Crawford in *Their Eyes Were Watching God*, Milkman in *Song of Solomon*, and *Celie in Alice *Walker's *The *Color Purple* (1982).

Other character types in African American literature represent not individual personalities but rather certain segments of the group. There are, for instance, characters who may be referred to as Everyman/Everywoman figures, for they reflect the everyday experience of the group. The southern rural experience is manifested in characters and spokespersons in several poems by Sterling Brown, for example, Joe Meek in "The Ballad of Joe Meek" (1932), whose beating by a southern policeman transforms him into militant Joe who no longer turns the other cheek. Brown's Old Lem expresses the experience of those whose lot is circumscribed by individuals who wield social and political power. The urban counterpart to these rural spokespersons is Langston Hughes's, Jesse B. Semple ("*Simple"), who expresses not only the frustrations born out of urban reality, but also the wisdom gained from that experience as well. *Madam Alberta K. Johnson, also created by Hughes, is Simple's female counterpart.

Just as there are character types that reflect the common experience, an experience that one might associate with lower socioeconomic reality, there are others that reflect the bourgeois experience, those who have achieved a measure of material success but who may also feel a certain degree of dissatisfaction. Several of the characters in Cyrus *Colter's short stories, for instance, Elijah in "The Beach Umbrella" (1970) and Anita and Dave Hill in "Black for Dinner" (*The Amoralists & Other Tales*, 1988) fit into this category.

While the aforementioned character types are those that appear primarily in the "classics," there are others that appear in the popular genre that are worthy of note. For instance, the detective story is a genre to which such writers as Rudolph *Fisher,

Chester *Himes, and, most recently, Walter *Mosley and Eleanor Taylor Bland have made contributions. *Coffin Ed Johnson and *Grave Digger Jones are the police detectives in *A Rage in Harlem* (1957) by Chester Himes. As their names suggest, they are not averse to using what appears to be gratuitous violence as they move about Harlem. Mosley's *Easy Rawlins (*Devil in a Blue Dress*, 1990, and others) encounters violence in the streets of Los Angeles; however, he appears to be more cerebral than Himes's characters. Yet both authors have created very distinctive individuals within this category.

The character types represented in this survey are not intended to be exhaustive, but they do indicate the categories of characters that have caught the imagination of various writers across the decades of African American literature.

[See also Aunt Jemima; Barber; Beautician; Buck; Churchwoman; Coon; Devil; Domestic; Entertainer; Gay Men; High John the Conqueror; Jews; Jim Crow; John Henry; Lesbians; Mammy; Midwife; New Cultural Mulatto; Pickaninny; Prostitute; Sambo; Sapphire; Shine; Stereotypes; Uncle Tom.]

• Seymour Gross and John Edward Hardy, *Images of the Negro in American Literature*, 1966. Sterling Brown, "A Century of Negro Portraiture in American Literature," in *Black Voices*, ed. Abraham Chapman, 1968, pp. 564–589. Trudier Harris, *Black Women in the Fiction of James Baldwin*, 1985. John Roberts, *From Trickster to Badman: The Black Folk Hero in Slavery and Freedom*, 1989.

—Johanna L. Grimes-Williams

CHASE-RIBOUD, BARBARA (b. 1936), sculptor, poet, novelist, essayist, and literary and visual pluralist. As a visual artist and writer Barbara Dewayne Chase-Riboud (D'ashnash Tosi) blends African worlds with European, Asian, and Muslim worlds. Embracing differences is central to her idea of coupling or combining opposites. Chase-Riboud was born in Philadelphia to parents who encouraged her talents in the arts. With their support, her interest in the visual arts grew. She received a BFA from Temple University (1957). In the same year she was awarded a John Hay Whitney Fellowship to study art in Rome. Returning to the United States, Chase-Riboud completed an MFA at Yale (1960). From 1957 to 1977 Chase-Riboud exhibited widely in Europe, the Middle East, Africa, and the United States. Although she is not an expatriate, Chase-Riboud lives with her second husband, Sergio Tosi, in Paris and Rome.

Her world travels with her first husband (photojournalist Marc Riboud) during the 1960s inspired Chase-Riboud's initial efforts as a writer. *From Memphis to Peking* (1974) is her collection of *poetry based on the motif of traveling spiritually, physically, and sensually to Egypt (Memphis) and the People's Republic of China, where she was the first woman visitor since the 1949 revolution. With her publication of *Sally Hemings* (1979) and *Echo of Lions* (1989), Chase-Riboud can be included in the African American *neo–slave narrative tradition, which extends from Margaret *Walker's *Jubilee* (1966) to J. California *Cooper's *Family* (1991). Although Chase-Riboud is not the first African American novelist to treat the alleged Jefferson-Sally *Hemings affair (see William Wells *Brown, *Clotel, 1853), her novel reignited the controversy over the authenticity of the relationship. At the heart of Sally Hemings is the interrelationship among love, politics, and *slavery. Chase-Riboud suggests that Jefferson's abandonment of antislavery sentiments is due to his relationship with Hemings, his wife's half sister, whom he keeps in bondage because setting her free would mean she would have to leave Virginia. Valide: A Novel of the Harem (1986) depicts slavery in the Ottoman Empire during the late eighteenth century. Chase-Riboud uncovers the little known world of the harem through the protagonist, a Martinican woman who is captured and sold to Sultan Abdulhamid I. The woman rises through the ranks of the harem to become valide when her son becomes sultan. Although still a slave, as valide, she holds the highest position for women in the empire. The novel portrays harem women as living lives of boredom and self-indulgence, engaging in murder or manipulation in the competition to be chosen by the sultan. Portrait of a Nude Woman As Cleopatra (1987), Chase-Riboud's second collection of poems, connects her visual and literary talents. Observing a Rembrandt sketch with the same title, Chase-Riboud was inspired to write a narrative dialogue between Mark Antony and Cleopatra framed by Plutarch's story. In Echo of Lions (1989) Chase-Riboud presents the story of Joseph Cinque and fifty-three men who, as slave captives, murder most of the slave ship's crew and attempt to sail back to Africa. The Africans land off the coast of Long Island and are jailed but John Quincy Adams successfully defends them.

In all of her literary works, Chase-Riboud gives a voice to those silenced by history. Pursuing this theme, she achieves a synthesis of human experience, bringing the past and present, the African and European worlds together.

• Charity Simmons, "Thomas Jefferson: Intimate History, Public Debate," Chicago Tribune, 3 July 1979, 2, 4. Theresa Leininger, "Barbara Chase-Riboud," in Notable Black American Women, ed. Jessie Carney Smith, 1992, pp. 177–181.

—Australia Tarver

CHESNUTT, CHARLES WADDELL (1858–1932), short story writer and novelist. Charles W. Chesnutt was the most influential African American writer of fiction during the late nineteenth and early twentieth centuries. From 1899 to 1905, during which time he published two collections of *short stories and three *novels, Chesnutt skillfully enlisted the white-controlled *publishing industry in the service of his social message. More successfully than any of his predecessors in African American fiction, Chesnutt gained a hearing from a significant portion of the national reading audience that was both engaged and disturbed by his analyses and indictments of racism.

Born in Cleveland, Ohio, in 1858, the son of free African American émigrés from the South, Charles Chesnutt grew up in Fayetteville, North Carolina, during the turbulent Reconstruction era. By his late teens he had distinguished himself sufficiently as a teacher to be appointed assistant principal of the lo-

cal normal school for persons of color. But his marriage in 1878 and his impatience with the restrictions of his life in the South fueled his ambitions to find better opportunities in the North where he might pursue a literary career. In 1884, Chesnutt moved to Cleveland, where he settled his family, passed the Ohio state bar, and launched a business career as a legal stenographer.

In August 1887, the Atlantic Monthly printed Chesnutt's "The Goophered Grapevine," his first important work of fiction. Set in North Carolina and featuring an ex-slave raconteur who spins wonderful tales about antebellum southern life, "The Goophered Grapevine" was singular in its presentation of the lore of "conjuration," African American hoodoo beliefs and practices, to a white reading public largely ignorant of black folk culture. In this story, Chesnutt also introduced a new kind of African American storytelling protagonist, *Uncle Julius McAdoo, who shrewdly adapts his recollections of the past to secure his economic advantage in the present, sometimes at the expense of his white employer. In March 1899, The *Conjure Woman, a collection of "conjure stories" based on the model established in "The Goophered Grapevine," made its debut under the prestigious imprint of Boston's Houghton Mifflin publishing house. The most memorable stories in the collection, such as "The Goophered Grapevine" and "Po' Sandy," portray *slavery as a crucible that placed black people under almost unbearable psychological pressures, eliciting from them tenacity of purpose, firmness of character, and imaginative ingenuity in order to preserve themselves, their families, and their community.

In the fall of 1899, Houghton Mifflin published a second Chesnutt short story collection, The *Wife of His Youth and Other Stories of the Color Line. The majority of the stories in The Wife of His Youth explore the moral conflicts and psychological strains experienced by those who lived closest to the *color line in Chesnutt's day, namely, mixed-race persons like himself. After reading The Wife of His Youth, some critics, like the noted white novelist William Dean Howells, wrote admiringly about Chesnutt's realistic portrayals of life along the color line. But other reviewers were put off by his unapologetic inquiries into topics considered too delicate or volatile for short fiction, such as segregation, mob *violence, *miscegenation, and white racism.

Around the same time, Chesnutt closed his prosperous court-reporting business in Cleveland to pursue his lifelong dream—a career as a full-time author. In the next six years he published three novels of purpose, The *House Behind the Cedars (1900), The *Marrow of Tradition (1901), and The Colonel's Dream (1905), which surveyed racial problems in the postwar South and tested out a number of possible social, economic, and political solutions. The House Behind the Cedars, a *novel of passing, was generally well received, and The Marrow of Tradition was reviewed extensively throughout the country as a disturbing but timely study of a contemporary southern town in the throes of a white supremacist revolution. Yet by the time Chesnutt began writing The Colonel's

Dream, the story of a failed attempt to revive a southern town blighted by exploitation and racism, the author knew that his brand of fiction would not sell well enough to sustain his experimental literary career. Although he continued writing and speaking on various social and political issues after *The Colonel's Dream* was published, Chesnutt produced only a handful of short stories in the last twenty-five years of his life. Among African American readers, however, admiration for his achievement never waned. In 1928, the NAACP awarded him its Spingarn Medal for his "pioneer work as a literary artist depicting the life and struggles of Americans of Negro descent, and for his long and useful career as scholar, worker, and freeman of one of America's greatest cities."

In 1931 in "Post-Bellum—Pre-Harlem," an *essay in literary *autobiography, Chesnutt accepted the fact that writing fashions had passed him by, but he took pride in pointing out how far African American literature and the attitude of the white literary world toward it had come since the days when he first broke into print. Although he was too modest to do so, Chesnutt might have claimed an important role in preparing the American public for the advent of the *New Negro author of the 1920s. In a basic sense, the new movement followed his precedent in unmasking the false poses and images of its era in order to refocus attention on the real racial issues facing America. Today, historians of African American writing point out that Charles Chesnutt deserves credit for almost singlehandedly inaugurating a truly African American literary tradition in the short story. He was the first writer to make the broad range of African American experience his artistic province and to consider practically every issue and problem endemic to the American color line worthy of literary attention. Because he developed literary modes appropriate to his materials, Chesnutt also left to his successors a rich formal legacy that underlies major trends in twentieth-century black fiction, from the ironies of James Weldon *Johnson's classic African American fiction of manners to the magical realism of Charles R. *Johnson's contemporary *neo–slave narratives.

[*See also* Aun' Peggy; Conjuring; Folk Literature; Protest Literature; Rena Walden.]

• Helen M. Chesnutt, *Charles Waddell Chesnutt: Pioneer of the Color Line,* 1952. Sylvia Lyons Render, ed., *The Short Fiction of Charles W. Chesnutt,* 1974. Frances Richardson Keller, *An American Crusade: The Life of Charles Waddell Chesnutt,* 1978. William L. Andrews, *The Literary Career of Charles W. Chesnutt,* 1980. Richard H. Brodhead, ed., *The Journals of Charles W. Chesnutt,* 1993. Eric J. Sundquist, *To Wake the Nations: Race in the Making of American Literature,* 1993.
                                          —William L. Andrews

Chicago Defender, The. Founded in 1905 by Robert S. Abbott, a Hampton Institute graduate influenced by the journalistic and oratorical successes of Frederick *Douglass, Ida B. *Wells-Barnett, and Booker T. *Washington, the *Chicago Defender* boldly encroached on a relatively crowded market: the *Broad Ax,* the Illinois *Idea,* and the *Conservator* were, at the time, already established as representatives of the Chicago African American press. Nevertheless,

the balance struck by Abbott between reports of progress within the African American community on one hand, and sensational headlines documenting *lynchings and other crimes against African Americans on the other, resulted in the *Defender's* gradual prominence both locally and nationally. Its banner proudly boasted "World's Greatest Weekly," and Abbott's paper soon established itself as an influential voice for African Americans in the Midwest, the West, and the deep South.

The *Defender's* moment of greatest influence came with Abbott's "The Great Northern Drive" campaign of 1917, in which he urged African Americans living in the southern states to migrate to the North. Poor living standards in the South, combined with Abbott's sensational headlines, testimonials from African Americans who had made the journey north, and more practical listings of job opportunities and train schedules did much to sustain the Great *Migration, and the *Defender,* in the early part of the century. Later additions of regular columnists such as Langston *Hughes, Walter *White, and S. I. Hayakawa further increased the *Defender's* prominence. It was in its pages that one of African American literature's most memorable fictional characters, Hughes's Jesse B. Semple ("*Simple"), was born.

[*See also* Journalism; Periodicals, *article on* Black Periodical Press.]

• Roi Ottley, *The Lonely Warrior: The Life and Times of Robert S. Abbott,* 1955. Roland Edgar Wolseley, *The Black Press, U.S.A.,* 2d ed., 1990.
                                      —Christopher C. De Santis

CHICAGO RENAISSANCE. Sometimes referred to as the "Black Chicago Renaissance," the explosion of cultural activity in Chicago between the mid-1930s and the early 1950s has assumed an important position in African American literary history. Described by Robert Bone ("Richard Wright and the Chicago Renaissance," *Callaloo,* Summer 1986), the idea of a Chicago Renaissance in African American letters has gradually supplanted definitions emphasizing "proletarian writing," "*protest literature," or "the School of Richard *Wright." Important both for the art created by participants in the renaissance and for the continuing influence of the period's sociological vocabulary, the Chicago Renaissance is often treated as a cultural movement, the import of which rivals that of the *Harlem Renaissance or the *Black Arts movement.

Like the Harlem Renaissance, the Chicago Renaissance established connections between African American artists and intellectuals from throughout the United States. Originating in the "Great *Migration" of blacks from the rural South to the urban North, the Chicago Renaissance was based in the "black belt" on the South Side where laborers fleeing the brutalities of *lynching and sharecropping settled in search of the economic opportunities provided by the factories and stockyards. As Wright's introduction to Horace Cayton and St. Clair Drake's sociological classic *Black Metropolis* (1945) makes clear, however, for most black migrants the harsh reality of Chicago belied the utopian images propagated by Robert Abbott's *Chicago Defender*, which was widely read in black communities throughout the nation.

Nonetheless, the rapidly expanding black community provided an ideal setting for the development of new forms of expression, particularly in literature and *music. Chicago had been home to several significant black writers prior to the renaissance, among them poet Fenton *Johnson; *short story writer Marita *Bonner, who moved to Chicago from New York in 1930; and novelist Nella *Larsen, whose *Quicksand* (1928) focused on conditions in her native city. Supported intellectually by various literary organizations and financially by the *Federal Writers' Project and the fellowship program of the Julius Rosenwald Fund, African American writers began to produce a wide range of work during the mid-1930s. The most visible and influential of the new generation of writers, Richard Wright set *Lawd Today* (written 1935, published 1963) and *Native Son* (1940) in Chicago. Arna *Bontemps's *Black Thunder* (1936), William *Attaway's *Blood on the Forge* (1941), and Willard *Motley's *Knock on Any Door* (1947) are among the other major works of fiction of the period. Chicago Renaissance poets, many of whom participated in socialite Inez Cunningham Stark's workshops at the South Side Community Art Center, included Margaret *Walker, Margaret Esse *Danner, Frank Marshall *Davis, and Gwendolyn *Brooks, who won the workshop's first contest. The Chicago unit of the Federal Theatre Project supported work by numerous black playwrights including Theodore *Ward, whose *Big White Fog* (1938) is the best known of the dramatic works of the period. Autobiographical works written during or about the renaissance include Wright's *Black Boy* (1945) and *American Hunger* (written 1940s, published 1973), Cayton's *Long Old Road* (1970), Katherine *Dunham's *A Touch of Innocence* (1959), Era Bell *Thompson's *American Daughter* (1946), and Gwendolyn Brooks's *Report from Part One* (1972).

Based in Chicago, the Rosenwald Fund played a role similar to that of individual patrons during the Harlem Renaissance, providing fellowships both to Chicago-based writers and to national figures including Claude *McKay, Zora Neale *Hurston, W. E. B. *Du Bois, James Weldon *Johnson, Sterling A. *Brown, and Langston *Hughes, a frequent visitor to Chicago who published many of his *Simple stories in his *Defender* column. In addition to the Rosenwald Fund, both inter- and intraracial organizations supported the development of renaissance writing. The South Side Writers Group, organized in 1936, brought together Wright, Davis, Ward, Bontemps, Fern Gayden, and Walker, whose *For My People* (1942) was the most important collection of renaissance *poetry prior to Brooks's A *Street in Bronzeville* (1945). Meanwhile the John Reed Clubs, sponsored by the Communist Party of the United States, and the Illinois branch of the Federal Writers' Project, helped establish contacts between black writers and white contemporaries including Nelson Algren and Saul Bellow. Publication outlets for aspiring writers included *Negro Story*, published out of the South Side home of Alice Browning; *Negro Digest*, an important outlet for black fiction; and Dorothy *West's *Challenge* (1934–1937), which announced the emergence of "a young Chicago group" that provided the focus for *New Challenge* (1937). Coedited by Wright and Marian Minus, *New Challenge* served as the national announcement of the Chicago Renaissance, publishing four poems by Walker alongside Wright's influential "Blueprint for Negro Writing," the primary aesthetic manifesto of the era.

Complementing this flurry of literary activity, important new styles of African American music were being crafted by southern-born performers who had come to Chicago as part of the Great Migration. Chicago-based musicians such as Mahalia Jackson, Big Mama Thornton, Muddy Waters, and Howlin' Wolf played crucial roles in the transformation of southern musical styles into the forms of gospel and *blues music, which in turn metamorphosed into *soul and rock-and-roll.

Perhaps the most broadly influential aspect of the renaissance, however, derived from the University of Chicago, where the department of sociology, supported by black alumni including Charles S. Johnson and E. Franklin Frazier, encouraged the academic study of racial tensions. Despite the significant contributions of the Chicago sociologists to the progressive political activities culminating in the *Brown v. Board of Education* Supreme Court decision, their work exerted a problematic impact on African American cultural history. Reenforced by the public response to *Native Son* as a "protest" novel presenting black Chicago as a "problem," sociological approaches to cultural activity allowed white readers to underestimate the individuality and complexity of African American expression. To a disturbing extent, the sociological premises traceable to the renaissance continue to distort discussions of African American culture, reducing complex works of art to "representative" expressions of social unrest. Ironically, some of the artists most affected by such simplification include younger Chicagoans with inclusive sensibilities, among them playwright Lorraine *Hansberry, novelist Leon *Forrest, and composer/performers Richard Muhal Abrams and Anthony Braxton. Focusing on the Chicago Renaissance rather than Wright encourages a broader and deeper understanding of African American cultural production from the 1930s to the 1950s and beyond.

[See also Literary History, *article on* Early Twentieth Century.]

• Michel Fabre, *The Unfinished Quest of Richard Wright*, 1973. Abby Arthur Johnson and Ronald Maberry Johnson, *Propaganda and Aesthetics: The Literary Politics of Afro-American Magazines in the Twentieth Century*, 1979. Trudier Harris, ed., *DLB*, vol. 76, *Afro-American Writers, 1940–1955*, 1988. Margaret Walker, *Richard Wright: Daemonic Genius*, 1988. George Kent, *A Life of Gwendolyn Brooks*, 1990. Craig Werner, "Leon Forrest, the AACM and the Legacy of the Chicago Renaissance," *The Black Scholar* 23.3–4 (Summer/Fall 1993): 10–23.
—Craig H. Werner

CHILDREN'S AND YOUNG ADULT LITERATURE. The American Library Association makes formal distinctions between children's literature and young adult literature as distinct categories, although they overlap. Literature for children commonly refers to illustrated books designed to be read aloud to non-readers and those with text suitable for elementary school children. Literature for young adults includes books designed for readers from approximately ten through eighteen years old and deals largely, but not exclusively, with coming-of-age and *identity issues. These categories are not always strict. Preadolescents often enjoy young adult titles and adults often enjoy illustrated texts. For example, Tom Feelings's *Soul Looks Back in Wonder* (1993), winner of the Coretta Scott King Award, is a picture book for teenagers. Artist James Ransome has illustrated James Weldon *Johnson's folk sermon *poetry collection *God's Trombones* (orig. 1927) in picture book form (1994). And in 1993, Jerry Pinkney illustrated Zora Neale *Hurston's *Harlem Renaissance classic *novel *Their Eyes Were Watching God* (1937), signaling the publisher's interest in expanding the market to include younger readers. Moreover, many artists write and/or illustrate in both categories. Joyce Carol *Thomas is one example. Her *Brown Honey in Broomwheat Tea* (1994), suitable for all ages, is an illustrated collection of her poetry, while *Marked by Fire* (1982), winner of the American Book Award for a first novel, is for older readers. Certainly, there is a long tradition of teenagers being introduced to adult "classics" while still in high school. But since the genre of African American young adult literature began to develop in the 1970s, American educators have not always done a good job of integrating it into existing curricula. This is changing as critics and educators acknowledge that much young adult literature is itself classic and sophisticated enough for readers of all ages. A prime example is Mildred D. *Taylor's *Roll of Thunder, Hear My Cry* (1976), winner of the Newbery Medal, the highest honor in the world of American literature for young adults. This and the other books in her series that chronicles a land-owning African American family and their community in depression-era Mississippi should be considered indispensable reading.

Publishing companies tend to group children's literature and young adult literature into a single "children's literature" category. And despite the official distinction recognized by the American Library Association, in practice, "children's librarians" oversee both genres. The same situation exists in terms of scholarly work in the field. The major journals, which include *Children's Literature Association Quarterly* and *Children's Literature*, cover literature written for both children and young adults.

The histories of African American children's literature and young adult literature are so intertwined as to be almost inseparable. The creators of African American children's and young adult literature have all been engaged in the same battles with the publishing industry and other structures in this society to see that their art has the opportunity to flourish. African American children's and young adult literatures both have developed out of a respect for the power of literature to communicate with, inspire, and educate African American and other young people of every age. Those who have devoted their careers to their creation have a gift for speaking with and to the young without condescending to them and without underestimating their capacities for reflection or for appreciating beauty and honesty.

As with African American literature as a whole, the history of African American children's and young adult literature is still being discovered, still being written, and still being contested. Another primary issue in the definition of African American children's literature is the significance of race for writer, reader, and character. The term "African American literature" usually refers to the ethnic *identity of the authors. The term "children's literature" refers to the audience. When the two terms are combined into "African American children's literature" the parameters of this third category are unclear. Over time not only have white authors been accepted as the creators of literature about or for African American young people but they have been encouraged to fill this role. Thus, literature with African American characters, whether aimed at a white, African American, or mixed audience, has been routinely categorized as African American. African American children's literature, for the purposes of this essay, however, is defined as literature created by African American authors and illustrators. Often, their intended audience is African American young people in particular. But on the whole, the literature exists for the enjoyment, education, and edification of any and all readers.

Historically, the temptation of most critics writing in the field has been to dwell on the literature with African American characters written by white American writers, whether aimed at an audience of African or European American youngsters, as if the author's racial or cultural experiences were neutral. More recently, more critics have begun to recognize that it is important to examine the *stereotypes of black people appearing in popular literature largely because the development of African American children's literature is in part a response to that literature. A notable example is the prolonged debate that took place during the early 1980s in response to Margot Zemach's *Jake and Honeybunch Go to Heaven* (1982). Zemach's version of an African American folktale portrays a man and his mule being killed by a train and entering a heaven presided over by an African American god dressed like Uncle Sam and inhabited by angels eating barbeque. The jubilant Jake behaves like a "flying fool." Zemach's stated purposes were to write a book for African American children that preserved their *folklore and with which they could identify visually. Instead, what she produced was a book that was eventually banned or stored in closed reserves in many children's libraries because many believed it perpetuated stereotypical images of African American people.

Of course, there are numerous examples of racist or stereotypical imaging from the late nineteenth and early twentieth centuries. For instance, the preeminent American magazine for young people was *St. Nicholas* (1873–1945), in the pages of which it was not uncommon to read such verses as "ten little niggers went out to dine, one choked his little self, and then there were nine." W. E. B. *Du Bois, Augustus Granville Dill, and Jessie Redmon *Fauset, publishers and editors of the *Brownies' Book, an early African American children's periodical, were almost certainly familiar with this publication and others when they decided to create their own. Likewise, there are more and more critics engaged in the process of reconstructing and discussing the history and significance of African American children's literature on its own terms.

The Brownies' Book was not the first publication for African American young people. Mrs. Amelia E. *Johnson founded an eight-page monthly magazine entitled the Joy in 1887. In 1889 she wrote Clarence and Corinne, or God's Way and in 1894 The Hazeley Family, both books for young readers but with apparently European American protagonists. As critic Hortense Spillers suggests in her introduction to the Schomburg Library edition, the books are "packaged in the wrappings of ethnic neutrality." This book was published by the white-administered American Baptist Publication Society. The Black-administered National Baptist Publishing Board began publishing Sunday School materials for African American youth in 1896. It wouldn't be at all surprising if future researchers and critics were to discover other materials from this era and from the arena of church presses.

But at this juncture, in addition to Johnson's work, only a few other early pieces have been identified. One of these is Paul Laurence *Dunbar's collection of *dialect poetry entitled Little Brown Baby (1895). There is some question about whether this book was designed by Dunbar for children or whether an editor had the idea to collect in one volume some of his poems that were suitable for children. Yet another early volume is entitled An Alphabet for Negro Children by Leila A. Pendleton. Though no date of publication is given, it is mentioned in the authors' notes in a volume entitled The Upward Path. Silas X. Floyd's Floyd's Flowers, or Duty and Beauty for Colored Children was published in 1905. With various titles, this volume was printed in at least three editions through 1925.

Like Floyd's Flowers, The Upward Path was an *anthology of poetry, *essays, *short stories, folklore, biographical sketches, and drawings by prominent African American writers, educators, and other personalities of the time. It was compiled by Myron T. Pritchard, principal of the Everett School in Boston, and Mary White Ovington, Caucasian author and one of the founders of the NAACP. All of the illustrations were done by Laura Wheeler. The writers whose work is represented include Paul Laurence Dunbar, Angelina Weld *Grimké, Azalia Hackley, Ruth Anna Fisher, Augusta Bird, Jessie Fauset, and W. E. B. Du Bois.

For a variety of reasons, the substantive development of African American children's and young adult literature began about 1920, the publication date of the Brownies' Book. For its time, it was quite a progressive magazine, even Pan-African in its philosophy. Dill, Du Bois, and Fauset were concerned about

the negative images of African Americans both in fiction and in school materials. They wanted the children of their community to know that people of African descent had made significant contributions to world civilizations. Further, they consistently stressed the standards of beauty and aesthetic quality of people of African descent. With very few exceptions, the graphics in the Brownies' Book were by African American artists, a policy that the editors saw as their contribution to the development of "modern Negro art." Du Bois, Dill, and Fauset advocated race pride, responsibility to the collective group, social uplift, and education.

The Brownies' Book, not unlike the volume The Upward Path, was problematic in certain ways. Foremost among them was the manifestation of class tensions. For example, there was the occasional short story in which the writer privileged long hair and fair skin. Other contradictions were apparent in the attitudes of various writers toward Africa and understandings about the terms "civilization" and "culture." But to the credit of the editors, they allotted space to different perspectives and opinions. And to the credit of the young readers, parents, and other interested adults, much debate went on in letters and other submissions.

Unlike the Brownies' Book, which welcomed discussion of difficult issues both in the United States and around the world, *Ebony Jr! (1973–1985), published by the Johnson Publishing Company in Chicago, emphasized positive representations of African Americans. Contributors were asked not to submit materials that dealt with topics such as death, violence, or religion. Despite this weakness, Ebony Jr! made a definite contribution to literature for African American children. It was an arena in which children could regularly read poetry and stories written by African American writers, strengthen their own verbal skills through using the exercises provided, and see visual images of African Americans. Just as the Brownies' Book was a place for younger writers such as the teenage Langston *Hughes to get published, Ebony Jr! encouraged young writers through their regular writing contests.

The Brownies' Book and Ebony Jr! are part of a tradition of African American children's and young adult literature, defined in broad terms to include periodical literature, anthologies, poetry, novels, historical fiction, picture books, and *biography. In particular, they are part of a tradition of independent African American *publishing. In addition to the Brownies' Book, Du Bois & Dill Publishing Company also published a collection of biographies written by E. Haynes entitled Unsung Heroes (1921) and J. Henderson's A Child's Story of Dunbar (1921). Noted scholar Carter G. *Woodson later formed Associated Publishers, which published both literature and school texts. Associated Publishers' titles are many, including J. Shackleford's The Child's Story of the Negro (1938) and Woodson's own African Heroes and Heroines (1939). Associated Publishers, located in Washington, D.C., remains active in the 1990s.

During the early years, Arna *Bontemps and Langston Hughes were the only African American writers for children with consistent access to the mainstream publishing industry. Hughes's *The Dream Keeper*, a collection of poetry suitable for children, was published in 1932 and again in 1962. The 1994 edition, which includes seven additional poems, substitutes artist Brian Pinkney's scratchboard illustrations for the original drawings by Helen Sewell. Bontemps and Hughes's joint effort, a short novel entitled *Popo and Fifina* (1932), was first published in 1932 also. It too appears in a new edition (1993) as part of Oxford University Press's Iona and Peter Opie Library of Children's Literature. Bontemps had a long career in children's books. His *Lonesome Boy* (1955) was republished in 1988 by Beacon Press. Other important titles of Bontemps's include *Sad-Faced Boy* (1937), the first "Harlem story" for children; *We Have Tomorrow* (1945), a collection of biographies; and *The Story of the Negro* (1948). His extensive 1941 poetry anthology, *Golden Slippers*, is a classic.

For the most part, in the dominant European American publishing world the status of literature about African Americans remained insignificant from the 1930s through the 1950s, though there were fledgling efforts at change beginning in the 1940s. During this period some publishers decided to use photographs of African Americans in an effort to reduce the amount of controversy generated by offensive and stereotypical illustration. The industry would later do things such as simply color white characters brown instead of enlisting the talents of African American writers and illustrators. But no matter the form of the visual part of the books of the 1930s through the 1950s, with a few exceptions—such as *Popo and Fifina*, Ann *Petry's animal story The *Drugstore Cat* (1949, 1988) and Gwendolyn *Brooks's poetry collection *Bronzeville Boys and Girls* (1956)—the texts were based largely upon the premise that racial integration is one of the ultimate goals and ideals of American society.

To a great extent, this kind of literature was targeted to white audiences, with the implied or sometimes blatant message that people should be colorblind, that all people are the same underneath the skin. Likewise, this category of literature said to African American youth that "white" is ideal and to be aspired to. It almost invariably suggested that the overriding majority of white people are "good" and that if "the Negro" allied with them, the "bad" elements could be overcome. Thus, most of the children's literature of the 1940s and 1950s that included African American characters at all was paternalistic toward them and completely ignored the existence of institutionalized racism. There are countless books that tell the stories of "Negroes" who, because of hard work and good faith, achieve their goals of being the first African American student at a particular school, to hold a particular job, or the like. These books are written in a manner that deemphasizes the social impact of racism and stresses the virtues of personal responsibility regardless of social or political context.

Jesse *Jackson is the most notable African American writer for young adults during the 1940s to participate in this kind of "integrationist" literature. His *Call Me Charley* (1945) confronts the racial bigotry ingrained in this society through the character of a twelve-year-old boy who learns that because of his race he is not welcome to use public facilities. Lorenz *Graham, W. E. B. Du Bois's brother-in-law, examined similar themes in his series that includes *South Town* (1958), *North Town* (1965), *Whose Town* (1969), and *Return to South Town* (1976). But as James A. Miller points out ("Black Images in American Children's Literature" in *Masterworks of Children's Literature*, 1986), *Return to South Town* might indicate Graham's feeling that integration may not have been, or is not, the answer to the issues he was attempting to address in *South Town* almost twenty years earlier. The value of this work, however, is that it is not about African American people as objects but as individuals who have names and fully realized characterizations. It is written for African American and white audiences, rooted in the author's stance as an African American male.

In the 1960s and 1970s Lorenz Graham also wrote books in pidgin English, of which *I, Momolu* (1966) and *Song of the Boat* (1975) are two. Set in West Africa, these books are important because they represent the interest in the African diaspora that African American writers and illustrators of children's books have had throughout the history of this genre—an interest that is related to but separate from the stories that deal with American race relations. Another important example of this interest in "African heritage" is Muriel and Tom Feelings' *Moja Means One: Swahili Counting Book* (1971). For this book, Tom became the first African American illustrator whose work was designated as a Caldecott Honor Book, one of the highest honors in the world of American children's literature. Illustration team Leo and Diane Dillon went on to win the Caldecott Medal two years in a row for *Why Mosquitoes Buzz in People's Ears* (1976), an African folktale, and *Ashanti to Zulu* (1977), an alphabet book based on African ethnic groups. John *Steptoe's *Mufaro's Beautiful Daughters* (1988), another folktale set in Africa, is also a Caldecott Honor Book.

Generally, all of these books are nonthreatening to the European American publishing establishment. They are set outside the United States and so do not deal with issues such as *slavery or American apartheid. When set in African societies, they generally avoid problematic issues. However, this is not always the case with African American children's literature.

Believing that African American children's literature would probably never be recognized for its full beauty, artistry, and range by mainstream organizations, some African American members of the American Library Association, including Glyndon Greer and Mabel McKissick, rallied for the creation of the Coretta Scott King Award. Established in 1970, this award recognizes outstanding contributions to children's literature by African American writers and illustrators. It has been the mechanism through which many African American artists have gained not only recognition by professionals in the field but widespread visibility by a larger public.

This gain, like all gains in the history of African American children's literature, was hard-won. Basically, except for Bontemps and the few others mentioned above, the literature was invisible until the change of political climate that accompanied the *civil rights and "black is beautiful" movements. One of the most important stimulants to the publishing of African American literature, largely as a response to political agitation, was the federal government's commitment to provide funding to school districts to purchase books created by African Americans. Finally, the mainstream publishing industry felt an economic, if not philosophical, impetus to encourage artists from this community. In the late 1960s the Council on Interracial Books for Children began holding contests to help identify young artists, and more important, to encourage artists to consider careers in children's literature. The HarperCollins Center for Multicultural Children's Books, established in the 1990s, carries on the work of the council by matching established writers and illustrators from various American cultures—largely African American—with those who are new to children's books. A program with similar goals is sponsored by the Center for Multicultural Literature at the University of Wisconsin. Out of one of their contests came Michael Bryant's impressive first book, *Our People* (1994), illustrated by Angela Shelf Medaris.

The winner of the Council on Interracial Books for Children's first contest in 1968 was Kristin *Hunter, whose *The Soul Brothers and Sister Lou* (1969) sold more than a million copies. Walter Dean *Myers is arguably the most important writer to get his start during this time period. Since his first novel for young adults, *Fast Sam, Cool Clyde and Stuff* (1975)—named an American Library Association Notable Book—he has gone on to produce scores of books, both fiction and nonfiction, for all age groups. Among the many awards they have garnered are the Coretta Scott King Award for *Motown and Didi* and a Newbery Honor Award for *Scorpions*. The recipient of a 1994 American Library Association special lifetime achievement award, Myers is known especially for his stories about Harlem and its residents. *Fallen Angels* (1989), for example, is about the Vietnam War experiences of a teenage soldier from Harlem who begins to make connections between his life circumstances and those of other people of color throughout the world. *Fallen Angels* won the Coretta Scott King Award and was named both an American Library Association Best Book for Young Adults and a Notable Children's Trade Book in the Social Studies.

Harlem is the setting of many books of the period spanning the late 1960s through the early 1980s. Louise *Meriwether's *Daddy Was a Numbers Runner* (1970) is a poignant, realistic story of life in the urban north. Sharon Bell *Mathis's *Listen for the Fig Tree* (1973) falls into the same category, but in addition to exploring urban African American life, the book has as its central character a blind girl. Such stories help expand the concepts of African American humanity replete with a whole host of experiences, not all of which are race related. In Mathis's story,

Muffin incorporates into her worldview values she has learned from Black Muslims, from Christianity, and from the precepts of the Kwanzaa celebration.

June *Jordan's *His Own Where* (1971) is a riveting love story of urban teens. As they discover the meaning of a romantic, caring relationship, young Buddy wrestles with his father's hospitalization and impending death and Angela copes with her parents' protectiveness. Its distinctiveness rests, however, not in its subject matter but in its experimental language. Often referred to as the first children's book written in Black English, *His Own Where* was in the vanguard of literature that helped to expand representations of African American people. The prolific Lucille *Clifton, Pulitzer Prize–nominated poet, accomplished the same thing with her picture book texts. She used Black English when it fit a character and standard English when it fit another character and language from any- and everywhere along the English language continuum as appropriate.

Clifton's *Everett Anderson series is especially effective in chronicling the sometimes simple, sometimes complex growing up process of an African American boy and his family, including his estranged father, his mother, the man who is to become his stepfather, and his half sister. These titles include *Some of the Days of Everett Anderson* (1970) and the book in which the young child deals with his father's death, *Everett Anderson's Goodbye* (1983). One of Rosa *Guy's young adult series set in New York City consists of *The Friends* (1973), *Ruby* (1976), and *Edith Jackson* (1978), three novels that explore the coming-of-age of female characters. The main characters in *The Friends* are a West Indian family trying to make a good life for themselves. Part of the importance of the book is that it explores what happens when Africans from different parts of the diaspora actually come into contact with one another, what happens to the ideas of sisterhood and brotherhood, what the "American dream" means to different people. *Ruby* was boldly innovative in exploring the lesbian relationship of two black teenagers. Guy was an innovator too with her Imamu Jones mysteries, which include *The Disappearance* (1979), *New Guys around the Block* (1983), and *And I Heard a Bird Sing* (1987). These two series and her recent examinations of middle-class African American life in books such as *The Music of Summer* (1992) all help to expand readers' notions about the range of material that is available to African American writers.

The prolific, talented, award-winning Virginia *Hamilton is another author who has written in many genres. *The Magical Adventures of Pretty Pearl* (1983) is a mix of legend, history, and mythology in which Pretty Pearl, a god-child from Africa, comes via a slave ship to America with her brother, John de Conquer. *The People Could Fly* (1985) is a folklore collection. *Justice and Her Brothers* (1978) and its sequels are science fiction. She has written biographies of both W. E. B. Du Bois and Paul *Robeson as well as *Anthony Burns: The Defeat and Triumph of a Fugitive Slave* (1988), advertised as a historical reconstruction. Her realistic fiction is original and thought provoking. *M. C. Higgins, the Great* (1974) was honored by several awards, including the Boston Globe–Horn Book Award and the Newbery Medal. But in some ways, the most "important" of Hamilton's books is *The House of Dies Drear* (1974). It is based upon the experiences of the fictional family of an African American history professor after they move into a house that was once a part of the *Underground Railroad. Its significance lies in the way that it brings alive the subject of history—recovering it, rewriting it, and reconceptualizing it.

Historical (re)visioning has been a major preoccupation of writers of African American children's and young adult literature throughout its existence. Today, this concern has resulted in several significant patterns. First, there are a large number of books set during slavery. Preeminent among these is Julius *Lester's *To Be a Slave* (1968), illustrated by Tom Feelings. Lester revised certain *slave narratives, modernized punctuation and dialect spellings, and constructed them as a collection divided into useful sections, including "The Auction Block," "Resistance to Slavery," and "After Emancipation." He provides context throughout and includes an extensive bibliography. Designated as a Newbery Honor Book, the volume is still used extensively in high schools. Equally exciting is his 1981 *This Strange New Feeling*, ingeniously conceptualized as a collection of love stories set during slavery—quite a hook to gain the interest of teenagers.

Joyce *Hansen's *Which Way Freedom?* (1986) and its sequel, *Out from This Place* (1988), explore slavery and Reconstruction in an all African American community in South Carolina. Hansen's *The Captive* (1994), in contrast, is set first in West Africa and then in Puritan New England. There the fictional main character's story becomes intertwined with that of Paul *Cuffe, the historical figure remembered for building ships for the purpose of returning former slaves to Africa.

Several picture books deal with slavery on a level that is appropriate for readers of picture books. Writer-illustrator Dolores Johnson does this with *Now Let Me Fly* (1993). Its one shortcoming is, perhaps, that it is somewhat simplistic in depicting African complicity in the slave trade. To Johnson's credit, her story includes the role of Native American communities in providing refuge for escaped slaves. Perhaps the most well known picture book about slavery is Jacob *Lawrence's *Harriet and the Promised Land* (1968, 1993). Bold, strong, and ugly, as slavery is ugly, it is the story of Harriet *Tubman and her mission to deliver numbers of her people out of slavery.

Harriet not only belongs to the literature of slavery but it is also part of a tendency in African American children's literature to concentrate on biography. This is partly because of the sentiment, early expressed by Du Bois, that "the Negro has had little chance to be great, heroic, or beautiful" (*Brownies' Book*, 1920). Biography helps to demonstrate that all of these qualities belong to African people in the United States and elsewhere, a message expressed consistently in both picture books and young adult novels. Some examples of the former are illustrator

Will Clay's *The Real McCoy* (1993), about the inventor Elijah McCoy, and Andrea Davis Pinkney and Brian Pinkney's *Alvin Ailey* (1993).

James *Haskins is the foremost writer of biography for young people. He has written dozens of life stories, ranging from *James Van Der Zee: The Picture-Takin' Man* (1979) to *The Magic Johnson Story* (1980) to *Barbara Jordan* (1977). He has also written the stories of American and African American cultural institutions. These include *Street Gangs: Yesterday and Today* (1977), *The Statue of Liberty: America's Proud Lady* (1986), *The Cotton Club* (1977), and *Black Theater in America* (1982).

Patricia C. *McKissack, another outstanding biographer, is also an accomplished writer of fiction. *Mirandy and Brother Wind* (1988), illustrated by Jerry Pinkney, is a favorite of book lovers. McKissack's biographies include the stories of Michael Jackson, Frederick *Douglass, Paul Laurence Dunbar, and Mary McLeod Bethune. Along with her husband, Frederick McKissack, she has coauthored, among other titles, *Taking a Stand against Racism and Racial Discrimination* (1990) and *A Long Hard Journey: The Story of the Pullman Porter* (1989). Biography can give young people the misleading impression that African American history consists simply of the contributions of successful individuals to society. Biographies by McKissack and Haskins place the lives of individuals into larger social, cultural, and economic contexts.

Yet another tradition within African American children's literature consists of visual artists, artist-writers, and writers thought of as "adult artists" contributing to the development of children's literature. The visual artists include Elton Fax, Ernest Crichlow, E. Simms Campbell, and Romare Bearden. Newer artists now entering the field include Synthia St. James, Brenda Joysmith, Jonathan Green, and Kathleen Atkins Wilson, who won the 1991 Coretta Scott King Award for David A. Anderson's *The Origin of Life on Earth*. Faith Ringgold, known primarily as a quilt artist, is now translating that art into titles such as *Tar Beach* (1991) and *Dinner at Aunt Connie's House* (1993). Illustrator Jan Spivey Gilchrist made her debut as an author-artist with *Indigo and Moonlight Gold* (1993).

In addition to Langston Hughes and Gwendolyn Brooks, other recognizable "adult" writers have contributed to children's literature. Ann Petry wrote several picture book texts, and her *Tituba of Salem Village* (1964) and *Harriet Tubman* (1955) remain revealing and important. John O. *Killens's *Great Gittin' Up Morning: The Story of Denmark Vesey* (1972) is a powerful story of that slave revolt leader. James *Baldwin's *Little Man, Little Man* (1976) was publicized as a children's book for adults that is also an adult book for children. Novelist and playwright Alice *Childress's riveting stories of teenage life in the urban north, *A *Hero Ain't Nothin' But a Sandwich* (1973) and *Rainbow Jordan* (1981), are two landmark African American young adult novels.

A few have reshaped previously written pieces for children. Sherley Anne *Williams, for example, teamed with veteran illustrator Carole Byard to produce the lyrical, matter-of-fact, powerful *Working Cotton* (1992) based on poetry from *The Peacock Poems* (1975). Alice *Walker's first of two picture books, *To Hell with Dying* (1988), was based upon an earlier short story. Nikki *Giovanni has packaged several collections of poetry for children, most notably *Spin a Soft Black Song* (1985). Her 1994 story, *Knoxville, Tennessee*, is beautiful in its simplicity. Simple and spare in a different way is Maya *Angelou's 1994 children's book, *Life Doesn't Frighten Me at All*, an interpretation of the accompanying paintings by Jean-Michel Basquiat.

Eloise *Greenfield is the foremost contemporary poet for young people. *Honey, I Love* (1978) and *Daydreamers* (1981), illustrated by Tom Feelings, are both classics. Acknowledging the fact that the form of the picture book is a true collaborative effort, Greenfield has very strong feelings, not shared by all African American writers, about who illustrates her books. She demonstrates her political and artistic ideals by having it written into her contracts that only African American artists can illustrate her words.

A full discussion of African American picture artists belongs elsewhere. But the artists who are now part of this tradition do deserve acknowledgement here. They include Jerry Pinkney, Leo Dillon, Ashley Bryan, Tom Feelings, John Steptoe, Pat Cummings, Carole Byard, Donald Crews, James Ransome, John Ward, Floyd Cooper, Will Clay, Jan Spivey Gilchrist, and Cheryl Hanna. George Ford, most recently illustrating several titles for Just Us Books Company, was the winner of one of the earliest (1974) Coretta Scott King awards for illustrating Sharon Bell Mathis's *Ray Charles*.

Jerry Pinkney is one of the most celebrated American children's books illustrators. He is known especially for his method of posing models, sometimes dressed in period costumes, and then working from photographs of them. In contrast to Pinkney, Tom Feelings is celebrated for his on-the-spot drawings of nonmodels and for his black-and-white work, which demonstrates that young people appreciate more than primary colors. He is both writer and illustrator of *Tommy Traveler in the World of Black History* (1991), drawn from a comic strip done for the *New York Age* newspaper in the 1960s. He is also the illustrator of what could be called adult picture books.

The illustration legacy established by these pioneers continues with artists such as Brian Pinkney, the son of Jerry Pinkney, and Javaka Steptoe, the son of John Steptoe, who are carrying on family traditions as well. Too, Brian Pinkney and Andrea Davis Pinkney have collaborated successfully on several picture book projects as have Jerry Pinkney and Gloria Jean Pinkney. The relationship between illustrations and texts is symbiotic. Visual artists help readers see the words in specific contexts.

In addition to treating the sometimes complex feelings of young people seriously, Candy *Boyd's work is notable for its school settings and emphasis on the value of education. If there are such categories as boys' books and girls' books, Boyd works equally well in each. *Chevrolet Saturdays* (1993) is an exam-

ple of the former; *Breadsticks and Blessing Places* (1985) is an example of the latter. Eleanora *Tate's stories, which include *The Secret of Gumbo Grove* (1987) and *Thank You, Dr. Martin Luther King, Jr.* (1989), appeal to both young men and women. However, Tate suggests specifically that the value of her work rests in building the self-esteem of African American girls as they experience "rites of passage." Her *Just an Overnight Guest* (1980) was made into a movie by Phoenix Films. Brenda Wilkinson's *Ludell* (1975) and its sequels comprise an excellent contemporary love story series. Mildred Pitts *Walter writes for every age group. Part of the significance of her work rests too in the diversity of African American experiences it depicts. These range from *Justin and the Best Biscuits in the World* (1986), which invokes the legacy of African American cowboys, and *Trouble's Child* (1985), set in the Louisiana bayou. Patricia McKissack, Alice Childress, Kristin Hunter, Nikki Grimes, Alexis *De Veaux, and Camille *Yarbrough have also helped to shape this field.

Among several outstanding anthologies that are an important part of the literature are Dorothy Strickland's *Listen Children: An Anthology of Black Literature* (1982), which includes short selections of fiction, poetry, and drama; Joyce Carol *Thomas's multiethnic *A Gathering of Flowers: Stories about Being Young in America* (1990), short stories representing various American ethnic groups; Tom Feelings's *Soul Looks Back in Wonder* (1993), for which writers ranging from Margaret *Walker to Lucille Clifton to Haki R. *Madhubuti wrote poetry; and Tonya Bolden's *Rites of Passage: Stories about Growing Up by Black Writers from around the World* (1994), representative of the entire African disapora.

Among the newer writers whose work deserves attention are Vaunda Micheaux Nelson, Johnniece Marshall Wilson, Kay Brown, Valerie Wilson Wesley, Rita Williams-Garcia, Irene Smalls, Jacqueline Woodson, Belinda Rochelle, and Gloria Pinkney. Dolores Johnson is both a writer and an illustrator. Elizabeth Fitzgerald Howard's stories of middle-class African Americans are particularly compelling. Connie Porter is the author of *Meet Addy* (1993) and its sequels, the first stories of an African American character in the Pleasant Company's the American Girls Collection. Elizabeth Fitzgerald Howard's *Aunt Flossie's Hats (and Crab Cakes Later)* (1991), for example, describes an aunt who shares with her nieces a story connected with each hat she owns. Angela Johnson's children's books, among them *Do Like Kyla* (1990) and *When I Am Old with You* (1990), are simple, fluid, and moving. Set in the western United States, and with a grandmother figure who has grown dreadlocks, Johnson's first book for young adults, *Toning the Sweep* (1993) is sophisticated and revealing.

At this point in the history of African American children's and young adult literature, when children's literature in general is a thriving industry, more and more African Americans are the interpreters of their own stories. Walter Dean *Myers, in particular, is at the height of his influence in the industry. His 18 Pine St. series, initiated in 1992 with *Sort of Sisters*, is created by Myers, but ghostwritten by Stacie Johnson. This project is the first of its kind for an African American. Another development is the U.S. publishing and distribution of the work of an increasing number of Afro-Caribbean, Afro-British, and Afro-Canadian children's authors. They include the prolific James Berry, Lynn Joseph, Marlene Nourbese Philip, and Merle Hodge.

Of the approximately five thousand children's books published each year, African American writers and illustrators are responsible for less than 4 percent of these titles. Some writers and scholars are fearful that if the multicultural movement fades, as did the "black is beautiful" movement, the scenario will worsen. Already many mainstream publishers arrogantly interpret multiculturalism to mean that those of European ancestry now have additional license to continue telling the stories of peoples of color. One response has been the expansion of the tradition of African American independent publishers to include children's literature in their programs. Johnson Publications published several illustrated books in the late 1960s. Haki Madhubuti's *Third World Press is part of the same tradition. More recently, Kassahun Checole's Africa World Press has as one of its priorities the development of Afrocentric children's books. David Anderson's award-winning *The Origin of Life on Earth* (1991) was published by Sights Productions. African American Family Press has published *Psalm Twenty-Three* (1993), beautifully illustrated by Tim Ladwig. Wade and Cheryl Hudson's Just Us Books and Glen Thompson's Black Butterfly Press/Readers & Writers are leaders in this endeavor. Behind the scenes are agents such as Marie Brown who use their experience in every aspect of publishing to now serve the interests of African American writers, illustrators, and publishers of children's and young adult literature. In addition, a growing number of scholars and critics are turning their attention to this literature. Much of their effort, to this point, has gone toward simply reconstructing its history. As this task continues, however, scholars are beginning to ask why, for example, women are the primary writers of children's literature. Is this considered women's work? As African American female writers of children's literature, they are triply marginalized.

Increasingly, scholars are not only celebrating the genre's existence but examining it carefully, looking at feminist issues, class issues, language usage, and its place in the larger realm of African American literature as a whole. Even in this modern world of computer literacy, children still master basic literacy through books. Thus, children's literature must be acknowledged as a potentially powerful tool for transmitting not just innocent stories but interpretation of histories and ideologies. African American literature for children and young adults deserves the attention of young people, parents, teachers, librarians, and scholars, for with the exception of books for beginning readers, good children's literature is simply good literature. With our interest, constructive analysis, and celebration, it will continue to be an important part of a living African American literary tradition.

[*See also* Bildungsroman; Diasporic Literature; Pan-Africanism; Periodicals, *article on* Black Periodical Press.]

• Donnarae MacCann and Gloria Woodard, eds., *The Black American in Books for Children: Readings in Racism,* 1972. Dorothy Broderick, *Image of the Black in Children's Fiction,* 1973. Bob Dixon, *Catching Them Young: Sex, Race and Class in Children's Fiction,* 1977. Rudine Sims, *Shadow and Substance: Afro-American Experience in Contemporary Children's Fiction,* 1982. James Miller, "Black Images in American Children's Literature," in *Masterworks of Children's Literature,* ed. Jonathan Cott, 1986. Barbara Rollock, *Black Authors and Illustrators of Children's Books: A Biographical Dictionary,* 1988. Dianne Johnson, *Telling Tales: The Pedagogy and Promise of African American Literature for Youth,* 1990. Osayimwense Osa, ed., *Journal of African Children's and Youth Literature* 3 (1991–1992), special issue on "African American Children's Literature." Violet Harris, ed., *Teaching Multicultural Literature,* 1992. Theresa Perry and James W. Fraser, eds., *Freedom's Plow: Teaching in the Multicultural Classroom,* 1993. Hazel Rochman, *against Borders: Promoting Books for a Multicultural World,* 1993. Karen Patricia Smith, ed., *African American Voices,* 1995.

—Dianne Johnson-Feelings

CHILDRESS, ALICE (1916–1994), actress, director, playwright, novelist, columnist, essayist, lecturer, and theater consultant. Alice Childress established herself as a cultural critic and champion for the masses of poor people in America. Her writings reflect her commitment to the underclass whose lives are often portrayed inaccurately in American literature. Her works explore the debilitating effects of racism, sexism, and classism on people of color as they struggle daily to maintain their dignity. She portrays African Americans who triumph largely because of familial and community support. Childress's works censure American government for its exploitation of the poor in the name of capitalism. Her writings clearly speak against a government that would rather support African Americans as charity cases than allow them to succeed or fail on their own. Her integrity as a writer is evidenced by her refusal to recreate versions of long-held negative *stereotypes of African Americans, even though this has cost her financial security.

Alice Childress was born on 12 October 1916 in Charleston, South Carolina. At the tender age of five, she boarded a train bound for Harlem where she grew up under the nurturing hand of her grandmother, Eliza Campbell. Her grandmother's yen for the arts motivated her to expose Childress to museums, libraries, art galleries, theaters, and concert halls. Childress credits her grandmother for teaching her the art of storytelling. Her grandmother also made a point of exposing Childress to Wednesday night testimonials at Salem Church in Harlem. At these testimonials poor people told of their troubles, which Childress stored up for future writing.

Childress attended Public School 81, The Julia Ward Howe Junior High School, and then Wadleigh High School for three years, before dropping out when both her grandmother and mother died in the late 1930s. A voracious reader with a curious intellect, Childress discovered the public library as a child and read two or more books a day. Always very independent and capable, Childress held down a host of jobs during the 1940s to support herself and her daughter Jean, an only child from her first marriage. She worked as an assistant machinist, photo retoucher, domestic worker, salesperson, and insurance agent, all jobs that kept her in close proximity to working-class people like those characterized in her works. Her characters in fiction and *drama included domestic workers, washerwomen, seamstresses, and the unemployed, as well as dancers, artists, and teachers.

Childress married professional musician and music instructor Nathan Woodard on 17 July 1957. A reticent and very private person, Childress disclosed little about her life after 1957, except that her only child died on Mother's Day in 1990. Childress resided in Long Island, New York with Woodard at the time of her death on 14 August 1994. She was at work on her memoirs and a sixth novel.

Childress began her writing career in the early 1940s shortly after she chose acting as a career. In 1943 Childress began an eleven-year association with the American Negro Theater (ANT), an organization that served as a home for countless African American playwrights, actors, and producers, such as Sidney Poitier, Ossie *Davis, Ruby Dee, and Frank Silvera. Childress involved herself in every aspect of the *theater as was the tradition upheld by anyone connected with ANT. Childress is recognized as one of the founders of ANT, which institutionalized theater in the African American community. As a result of her commitment to ANT, in the 1950s Childress was instrumental in getting advanced, guaranteed pay for union Off-Broadway contracts in New York.

Childress's first play, *Florence* (1949), was prompted by a challenge from longtime friend Sidney Poitier who insisted that a strong play could not be written overnight. Poitier lost his bet because *Florence*, written overnight, is a well-crafted play that levels an indictment against presumptuous whites who think they know more about African Americans than African Americans know about themselves. *Florence* is also about the need for African Americans to reject stereotyped roles. On another level, *Florence* pays tribute to African American parents who encourage their children to reach their fullest potential by any means necessary. Her first play reveals Childress's superb skill at characterization, dialogue, and conflict.

Following the ANT production of *Florence*, Childress went on to write a host of plays and children's books, including *Just a Little Simple* (1950), *Gold through the Trees* (1952), *Trouble in Mind* (1955), *Wedding Band: A Love/Hate Story in Black and White* (1966), *The World on a Hill* (1968), *String* (1969), *The Freedom Drum*, retitled *Young Martin Luther King* (1969), *Wine in the Wilderness* (1969), *Mojo: A Black Love Story* (1970), *When the Rattlesnake Sounds* (1975), *Let's Hear It for the Queen* (1976), *Sea Island Song*, retitled *Gullah* (1984), and *Moms* (1987). Alice Childress's plays incorporate the liturgy of the African American *church, traditional *music,

African mythology, *folklore, and fantasy. She has experimented by writing sociopolitical, romantic, biographical, historical, and feminist plays.

Childress's *Trouble in Mind* garnered for her the Obie Award for the best Off-Broadway play of the 1954–1955 season. When the media praised her for being the first African American woman to win this award, Childress insisted that she would feel proud when she was the one hundredth poor woman of color to be recognized for her talent. She felt that to be the "first" only pointed out that African Americans have been denied opportunities. *Trouble in Mind* attacks the stereotyping of African Americans. *Wedding Band*, which was broadcast nationally on ABC television but which was banned from an Atlanta, Georgia, theater in 1966, explores the explosiveness of interracial love in a Jim Crow South Carolina. *Wine in the Wilderness*, perhaps Childress's best-known play, was presented on National Educational Television (NET) in 1969. The play pokes fun at bourgeois affectation. Childress levels an indictment against middle-class African Americans who scream brotherhood, togetherness, and Black Power, but who have no love or empathy for poor, uneducated, and unrefined African Americans. Tommorrow Marie, the heroine, teaches these vapid bourgeois the ugliness of their own superciliousness. Childress's *Sea Island Song* (1979) was commissioned by the South Carolina Arts Commission, which officially designated the time of the play's run as Alice Childress Week in Columbia and Charleston.

Childress's writings have garnered for her several awards, including writer in residence at the MacDowell Colony; featured author on a BBC panel discussion on "The Negro in the American Theater"; winner of a Rockefeller grant administered through the New Dramatists and an award from the John Golden Fund for Playwrights; and a Harvard appointment to the Radcliffe Institute for Independent Study (now Mary Ingraham Bunting Institute) from which she received a graduate medal.

While Alice Childress was principally a playwright, she was also a skilled novelist. Her first novel, *Like One of the Family: Conversations from a Domestic's Life* (1956), demonstrates Childress's quick wit as the heroine, a *domestic, teaches her white employers to see their own inhumanity. A *Hero Ain't Nothin' But a Sandwich* (1973) was made into a movie with Childress as author of the screenplay. This novel explores the necessity of African Americans' taking responsibility for nurturing their young sons. *A Short Walk* (1979) provides historical and cultural insights into the African American experience from the *Harlem Renaissance to the *civil rights movement of the 1960s. *Rainbow Jordan* (1981) explores the ramifications of growing up Black and female under the guidance of a host of women from the community. While her mother abandons her, Rainbow's surrogate mothers nurture and usher her into adulthood. Childress's most recent novel, *Those Other People* (1989), addresses issues of homophobia, racism, sexism, and classism. Childress's incisive language and skillfull manipulation of multiple narrators place her with writers such as

William Faulkner and Ernest J. *Gaines. Her novels, like her plays, portray poor people who struggle to survive in a capitalist America. She incorporates African American history in her novels to instruct young African Americans about the heroic lives that have paved a way for them to succeed.

Possessing great discipline, power, substance, wit, and integrity, Alice Childress stands out as a writer who was always a step ahead of her contemporaries. She deliberately chose not to write about what was in vogue, but instead wrote about controversial and delicate matters and had the audacity to reject a Broadway option because the producer wanted her to distort her vision of African Americans. Alice Childress's brilliance, her intense and microscopic penetration into life, and her deft handling of language match such great twentieth-century dramatists as Anton Chekhov, August Strindberg, Jean Anouilh, Sean O'Casey, Noel Coward, Tennessee Williams, Wole Soyinka, and Sholem Aleichem, a playwright that Childress singled out as one of her favorite writers. Peopling her works with characters who are challenging, innovative, and multidimensional, Childress became a frontrunner in the development of African American theater and a novelist of significant merit. Alice Childress's major contribution to African American life and culture was her balanced portrayal of Black men and women working together to heal their wounds and survive whole in a fragmented world. The men and women in her works do not give up on each other; often the strong and spirited women reach out to save their men from disaster. Childress passionately created dignified images of African Americans, particularly America's dispossessed and disinherited.

[See also Mildred Johnson.]

• Alice Childress, "Knowing the Human Condition," in Black American Literature and Humanism, ed. R. Baxter Miller, 1981, pp. 8–11. Trudier Harris, "Alice Childress," in DLB, vol. 38, Afro-American Writers after 1955: Dramatists and Prose Writers, eds. Thadious Davis and Trudier Harris, 1985, pp. 66–79. Elizabeth Brown-Guillory, "Alice Childress: A Pioneering Spirit," SAGE 4 (Spring 1987): 104–109. Elizabeth Brown-Guillory, Their Place on the Stage: Black Women Playwrights in America, 1988. Elizabeth Brown-Guillory, ed., Wines in the Wilderness: Plays by African American Women from the Harlem Renaissance to the Present, 1990. Drama Criticism, vol. 4, ed. Lawrence Trudeau, 1992, pp. 64–94.

—Elizabeth Brown-Guillory

Chosen Place, the Timeless People, The. Paule

*Marshall's second novel, The Chosen Place, the Timeless People (1969) is thematically the culmination of almost all her concerns as a novelist. Written on the cusp of both the feminist and Pan-African movements, it concerns itself not only with personal as well as public revolution in terms of both revolt and coming full circle to self-actualization, but also ageism, Western hegemony, and nuclear proliferation. According to Marshall, it is her best-loved novel, and this is due in large part to the stunning delineation of the heroine, Merle Kimbona.

The novel concerns itself with Bourne Island, a tiny imaginary landscape set in the Caribbean. It is an island replete with contradictions that become part of a special development project instigated by the American-based Philadelphia Research Institute and carried out by one of its numerous divisions, the Center for Applied Social Research, in the hopes that it will bring this "backward" island into the twentieth century. Almost ironically, the island itself is nearly equally divided geographically. Half of it, Bournehills, wallows in poverty, while the other half, New Bristol, has taken advantage of corrupt modernization schemes and equally corrupt politics to bring itself into the modern era. It is the hope of these twentieth-century missionaries to bring profound political, social, and economic change to the island.

The protagonist of the novel, Merle Kimbona, is the link between these two disparate worlds, the past and the future. She is known and loved by both those who call for progress and those who fear for the destruction of a particular culture that progress will more than likely obliterate. Merle is the thematic conduit through which these two opposing forces might eventually come together in the poverty stricken Bournehills. In fact, Merle is described in the novel as somehow being Bournehills itself. She represents a division that is not only a part of her own personal history but also the history of the island itself.

The Chosen Place, the Timeless People is perhaps Marshall's most political novel. In the narrative she weaves mini history lessons in the hopes that she as a writer might initiate a kind of healing in the psychological rift borne by blacks of the diaspora that has been brought about by the broken and divided history of African peoples located throughout the world. The heroic, ancestral figure of Cuffee Ned, the larger-than-life leader of a slave revolt, is one of the historical figures that Merle, as well as Paule Marshall as author, feels will help the people of Bourne Island, and black people in general, to reconstitute their historically and psychologically fragmented sense of self. She feels that by following his spiritual lead, there is nothing that can prevent the people, the "li'l fella," from rising out of the muck and mire of political, social, economic, and historical oppression. To accomplish this, the people, like Merle herself, must come to terms with their fragmented past before they will be able to forge a viable future.

• Joseph T. Skerrett, Jr., "Paule Marshall and the Crisis of the Middle Years: The Chosen Place, the Timeless People," in Callaloo 17–19 (1983): 69–73. Hortense J. Spillers, "Chosen Place, Timeless People: Some Figurations on the New World," in Conjuring: Black Women, Fiction, and Literary Tradition, 1985, pp. 151–175.

—Keith Bernard Mitchell

Christian Recorder. The Christian Recorder Pub-

lished by the African Methodist Episcopal Church in the United States, for the Dissemination of Religion, Morality, Literature, and Science was first issued on 1 July 1852. Evolved from the Christian Herald, which itself was the 1848 reincarnation of political activist and writer Martin R. *Delany's The Mystery, as its complete title reveals, the weekly paper was intended to provide a forum and leadership for the African American community and to demonstrate African

American capabilities as the *church became more than just a place of worship.

As the "official organ" of the AME Church, the *Recorder* printed official church business and transactions, such as notes and minutes from district and general church conferences, as well as finance and committee reports. It also contained obituaries, *autobiographies, *biographies, *poetry, *short stories, serialized *novels, and *essays dealing with religious and sociopolitical topics that ranged from raising children and the negative impact of high-fashion attire to the unconstitutionality of *slavery, the significance of *education to African Americans, and debates on international affairs.

Its publication was sometimes erratic and finances were always a source of worry, but many nineteenth-century intellectuals and activists contributed to the *Recorder*. Some frequent contributors were Frances Ellen Watkins *Harper, Morris Brown, Daniel A. *Payne, Fanny Jackson *Coppin, Benjamin T. *Tanner, and Josephine Heard. Published in Philadelphia, the *Recorder* was nationally distributed before the Civil War and is generally recognized as the oldest continuously published African American newspaper.

[See also Journalism; Periodicals, *article on* Black Periodical Press.] —Chanta M. Haywood

CHRISTOPHER CAT (?–?), a cat, coauthor of two children's books with Countee *Cullen, and a poet of the *Harlem Renaissance. Christopher, colored white and orange, was named after his father. One of a litter of three, Christopher Cat claimed a distinguished heritage—his father was a direct descendant of the Christopher Cat who sailed on Noah's Ark.

Christopher Cat's first book, a collection of poems entitled *The Lost Zoo* (1940), came about after a discussion with his friend and master—or as Christopher called him, Human Being—Countee Cullen. Cullen, who liked to frequent the zoo, had gloated to Christopher about its wonders. Christopher, being the stubborn cat that he was, was not impressed with Cullen's account of the monkeys and lions and asked if Cullen had seen animals such as a Squilililigee, a Wakeupworld, or a Lapalake. Of course Cullen could not admit to ever seeing any of these animals before, and Christopher Cat proceeded to tell him why that was the case, by relating the story from the Christopher Cat who had been on Noah's Ark about the animals who did not get on, even though they had received an invitation. What resulted from this discussion was Countee Cullen's—with Christopher Cat's permission—*The Lost Zoo*. Christopher Cat's payment for contributing to *The Lost Zoo* was small, either by cat or human standards. Countee Cullen rewarded him with an extra supply of catnip, milk, and liver. Christopher Cat, unsatisfied, demanded credit for his work by being named coauthor of the book. Countee Cullen, never able to refute Christopher's arguments, agreed.

Christopher Cat's second book, *My Lives and How I Lost Them* (1942), originated from another discussion with Countee Cullen. It is common knowledge now that cats have nine lives, but at the time, Countee Cullen was unwilling to believe such an idea and considered Christopher to be six and a quarter years old, for that was as long as Christopher had been with Cullen. When pressed further by Christopher, a very persistent cat, Cullen responded that Christopher was "one life" old, since Cullen believed that cats, like individuals, had only one life. Christopher quickly corrected Cullen by saying that he was in the middle of his ninth life, then gave an account of each and every one of his other eight lives. Countee Cullen was willing to write Christopher's story down so that other humans would be convinced of what Cullen had just learned—that cats do indeed have nine lives.

The last account of Christopher's life was in *My Lives and How I Lost Them*, where Christopher detailed spending his ninth and final life under the very protective care of his playmate Mitzi, a Royal Persian, and his Human Being, Countee Cullen.

—Saundra Liggins

CHURCHES. Many scholars have considered how the independent African American Protestant churches helped give voice to writers of African descent in America. In 1938, Benjamin E. *Mays published *The Negro's God As Reflected in His Literature*, which opened scholarly inquiry into the ways that African Americans' belief in a personal deity who is on the side of the oppressed provides some of the essential themes, images, characters, and plots for their creative writings. Literary critics and biblical scholars such as Henry K. Mitchell, Hortense Spillers, and Dolan Hubbard have followed Mays's lead by discussing the influence of the African American sermonic form on the language and structure of the creative writings of people of African descent in this country. Others have discussed ways that African American churches published and disseminated creative writings. For example, the African Methodist Episcopal (AME) Church created a publishing company in the early 1800s. The involvement of independent African American churches in the production and distribution of texts written by African Americans was widespread in many communities throughout this country during the *Harlem Renaissance. And the *Black Arts movement was nurtured by a cooperative relationship between African American institutions (such as the church), the Black Power movement, and African American writers working together to demystify the institutional structures that generate racism and inequality. Dudley *Randall's *Broadside Press, for example, was housed temporarily in the basement of the Alexander Crummell Memorial Episcopal Church.

The language generated by this movement provided the mechanism to "deconstruct" the institutional structures that have and continue to oppress African Americans. One of the primary sources of this literature was the language of liberation and empowerment embedded in the African American Christian tradition. This language evolved as a response to the attempts of white "pretenders to Christianity," to paraphrase David *Walker in his *Appeal* (1830), to negate the personhood of people of African descent by claiming they were not the result of a creative, divine act of God, but rather were the result of evolutionary chance and sin. Since these religious racists saw people of African descent as the embodiment of God's displeasure, they empowered themselves to alter their relationship with their slaves from that of person to person to that of person to object or possession. The Bible was used selectively to emphasize the inferiority and inhumanity of slaves, an objective made easier with the prohibition against slaves learning or anyone teaching them to read and write. And so the very act of writing by African Americans argues against the wholesale negation of the race as a people fit for little more than serving as "hewers of wood and drawers of water."

The early writings of people of African descent indicate that they were attempting both to emphasize the humanity of their people and to criticize the Europeanized concept of the African as a subhuman species cursed by God. Writing in the collective voice of millions of West Africans who were kidnapped from their villages, transported in the filthy hulls of slave ships, and sold into *slavery, Olaudah *Equiano in his Interesting Narrative (1789) argues against the commonly held conception that Africans were heathens with no culture. He insists on the civility and orderliness of his African tribe, the Ibo, of the country now known as Nigeria. Equiano not only compares the culture of his tribe to that of the Jews, but he also offers a critique of the language of "abuse and reproach" of "more civilized people." He refers to the language of the slave system that cast people of African descent as nonbeings, as "niggers." Throughout the narrative, Equiano insists upon the integrity of his traditional African culture and offers a critique of religious slaveholders as people who are caught in a contradiction: They espouse faith in God and adherence to the principles that Jesus taught while, at the same time, they have created and maintained a system of oppression that is, in its very nature, ungodly, inhumane, and opposed to Christian principles. He offers a direct challenge to Europeanized Christianity when he writes,

> Are there not causes enough to which the apparent inferiority of an African may be ascribed without limiting the goodness of God, and supposing he forebore to stamp understanding on certainly his own image, because "carved in ebony." Might it not naturally be ascribed to their situation? . . . Let the polished and haughty European recollect that his ancestors were once like the Africans, uncivilized, and even barbarous. . . .

Equiano's narrative was widely read; its publication during the eighteenth century corresponds to the birth of a number of independent African American denominations: the African Baptist Church, the AME Church, and the AME Zion Church. Equiano's tendencies to compare his culture to that of Jews, to question the civility of Europeans, and to insist upon the brotherhood of all people are consistent with the doctrines espoused by the aforementioned church denominations.

The language of empowerment that characterizes African American religious expressions was widespread during the nineteenth century. Rev. Lemuel B. *Haynes published a sermon titled "Universal Salvation—A Very Ancient Doctrine" (1875) in which he presented the devil as an enemy of mankind in search of salvation from God. In David Walker's Appeal, the author points out the perversion of the Christian faith by its white professors. He says that "white Christians of America who hold us in slavery (or, more properly speaking, pretenders to Christianity) treat us more cruel and barbarous than any heathen nation did any people whom it had subjugated. . . ." Walker's salvific language suggests judgment on the false pretenders to Christianity—"looking for the Millennial day." The language of impending judgment found its way into a number of subsequent writings by African Americans following Walker. Nat *Turner, in The *Confessions of Nat Turner (1831), defends his violent acts against slaveholders by maintaining that he was "ordained for some great purpose in the hands of the Almighty" by the "Spirit that spoke to the prophet in former days. . . ." Turner clearly was affected by the language of Walker's Appeal in that he compares himself to the Old Testament prophet Elijah who killed the prophets of the false god Baal in rendering Jehovah's, the true God's, judgment. On the other hand, William *Whipper, a free African American who was closely affiliated with the AME Church, became an important leader in the Moral Reform Society. In "An Address on Non-Resistance to Offensive Aggression," published in 1837, Whipper argued for the high moral standing of nonviolence as a response to oppression, a vantage point that establishes a foundation within the African American religious tradition upon which twentieth-century African American leaders, such as the Rev. Dr. Martin Luther *King, Jr., built.

The language of impending judgment led not only to insurrections but to damning critiques of slavery. In 1845 Frederick *Douglass, who became closely affiliated with the AME Church, published his seminal *Narrative of the Life of Frederick Douglass, an American Slave. He argued against the inhumanity of a slave system that made slaves out of men and women, and against those who professed Christianity while holding slaves. In the narratives of Solomon *Northup and Henry Bibb, each criticizes slaveholders' attempts to corrupt Christianity into a religious doctrine that supports slavery. In a letter to Charles B. Dunbar in 1861, Alexander *Crummell, an African American Episcopal priest, complained against the attempts of the American government to rid itself of slavery not by declaring slavery unconstitutional, immoral, and unchristian, but by sending slaves back to Africa through the colonization society. Likewise, Theodore S. Wright, a nineteenth-century Presbyterian minister, wrote the satirical "Prayer of a Colonizationist" (1840).

In 1843 Henry Highland *Garnet, a Presbyterian minister, delivered "An Address to the Slaves of the United States of America" at the National Negro Convention in Buffalo, New York. He argued that

Christianity was at fault for allowing unrepentant slaveholders to make "the bleeding captive plead his innocence," while they worshiped someone "who stood weeping at the cross."

This language of empowerment found its way into creative writing by African Americans by the middle of the nineteenth century. In 1853 James *Whitfield published a poem, "America," that offers a scathing critique of racial discrimination that was being perpetrated by those who professed to be Christians: "Here Christian writes in bondage still, / Beneath his brother Christian's rod, / And pastor's trample down at will, / The image of the living God." In 1896 Paul Laurence *Dunbar, who found a hospitable audience for his poetry in the congregations of independent African American churches, published *Lyrics of Lowly Life, a collection of poetry that contained the often-quoted poem, "We Wear the Mask." Although a critique of Christianity is not central to this poem, Dunbar presents the predicament of African Americans struggling against the repressive era of hostile legislation. Dunbar writes, "We smile, but O great Christ, our cries / To thee from tortured souls arise."

The publication of Booker T. *Washington's *Up from Slavery (1901) solidified the African Americans' appropriation of the language of empowerment that was born in the critique of white Christian involvement in the slave institution. Washington, who initially thought of entering the Baptist ministry through enrolling in a seminary, established Tuskegee Institute and within it a Bible college to train African American ministers. In his *autobiography, Washington argues, among other things, that adherence to traditional Christian values—a high moral fiber, industriousness, dedication, industrial education, and self-discipline—was the primary factor behind his personal success and his institution's success in training African American leaders. In a number of speeches made before the national assemblies of two independent African American denominations—the AME Church and the National Baptist Convention—Washington insisted that the church lacked an emphasis on "old time religion," which he defined as traditional American values that had contributed to the success of American immigrants in gaining economic and political stability in this country. In 1903 W. E. B. *Du Bois published The *Souls of Black Folk, a text that does not explicitly claim the language of the African American Christian tradition but nonetheless appropriates the language of empowerment drawn from this religious movement. In this text Du Bois, who was initially a member of the Congregational Church, interweaves Christian language and symbolism with "the sorrow songs," which he defined as the utterances of a people who were faced with hopelessness and therefore gained their collective voices through singing to God about their plight.

The influence of the African American Protestant church can also be seen in literature produced during the Harlem Renaissance. Mule Bone (1931), a play coauthored by Langston *Hughes and Zora Neale *Hurston, uses stock characters from the African American religious community to embody the conflict in an all-Black town over two characters who were once friends but have become antagonists as the result of their affections for a young lady. The townspeople support either character on the basis of their religious affiliation: half of the town belongs to the AME Church while the other half embraces the Baptist Church. This split embodies the conflict between these two denominations for national African American leadership that occurred during the play's era. Another major writer during this period, James Weldon *Johnson, published a collection of sermons in verse, *God's Trombones (1927), that appropriates slaves' belief in a personal God intimately involved in human affairs who was on the side of the oppressed. Countee *Cullen, the son of a Methodist minister, utilized the language of the African American religious tradition in many of his writings, most notably in the poems "Heritage" (1925), "The Black Christ" (1929), and "Yet Do I Marvel" (1925). While Cullen finds value in Christianity, in "Heritage" he wishes that "He I served were black." Claude *McKay likewise challenged the appropriateness of Christianity for people of African descent in a number of poems, most notably "St. Isaac's Church" and "Petrograd." Langston Hughes, the prolific writer widely known for his *jazz and *blues *poetry, also wrote within the language of this tradition in a number of poems, such as "Christ in Alabama," and his first novel, Not without Laughter (1930). In this work Hughes embodies the language of the African American religious and secular traditions by presenting characters—Aunt Hagar and Jimboy—who are representative of the conflict that is present within the African American community between the independent African American churches and secular institutions that at the time of the novel's publication were on the rise. Zora Neale Hurston, unlike her counterparts, saw the African American church movement not solely as a Christian movement, but as an eclectic one that embraced Africanized Christianity and hoodoo. In her first novel, *Their Eyes Were Watching God (1937), Hurston juxtaposes the language of orthodox Christianity—mouthed by *Nanny, the heroine's grandmother—with the language of the African American tradition that embraces Africanized Christianity and the jazz-blues tradition. Jean *Toomer's *Cane (1923) appropriates the language of the independent African American religious movement as the narrator judges the "sins" of his people against themselves and their heritage by leaving the land of their ancestors—the South—in favor of the materialistic promises of the northern cities. And Rudolph *Fisher, in "City of Refuge," creates King Solomon Gillis, who uses the language of the African American religious tradition to gain an advantage in secular life.

The contemporary influence of the independent African American Protestant church can be traced back not only to the response of slaves to their plight and of freemen to the empty promises of America, but can also be seen in the radical critique of Christianity that was offered both by Richard *Wright and by the Black Power movement. *Bigger Thomas, the protagonist in Wright's *Native Son* (1940), offers a damning critique of Christianity in rejecting his mother's Protestant work ethic and by disposing of the cross that the African American minister gives him during a visit to his jail cell. Wright skillfully appropriates the language of the African American religious tradition to empower Bigger as an antihero, one who creates by destruction, who kills, has symbolically killed before, and who finds that "killing makes me live." Ralph *Ellison, in *Invisible Man* (1952), uses this language to empower the protagonist when he is in New York. For example, when the protagonist begins to eat again and experiences a moment that awakens him by bringing together the disparate elements that have torn at his being, he cries out, "I YAM WHAT I AM." This statement merges the African American religious tradition— God's statement declaring his identity to Moses on Mount Sinai by telling him "I Am What I Am"—with the yam that symbolizes the African American southern tradition. Melvin B. *Tolson, who wrote *Harlem Gallery: Book 1, The Curator* (1965) with the intent of winning a place for himself and the African American literary tradition within academic institutions, juxtaposes the language of the Judeo-Christian world with that of the African American one. And James *Baldwin, in *Go Tell It on the Mountain* (1953), creates a salvific narrative in which John, the protagonist, is "saved," both socially and spiritually, yet fails to win his father's affections.

During the Black Power movement the relationship of Christianity to people of African descent came under intense critical scrutiny from a number of sources. The Nation of Islam, under the leadership of Elijah Muhammad as espoused by *Malcolm X, offered a powerful, sustained critique of Christianity as the religion of the oppressor that had "messed up the minds of African Americans." In a powerful diatribe against Euro-American Christianity, the Nation of Islam offered its version of Islam as the corrective to the misrepresentation of Christianity that had taken hold of the minds, spirits, and souls of people of African descent in America. Following this lead, the leaders of the Black Power movement, most notably Stokely *Carmichael, challenged the African American churches to become more involved in the liberation of their people. These critiques, along with a recasting of theology by religious scholars and theologians—such as James Cone and Gayraud Wilmore—to empower African Americans led to the development of Black Theology.

These challenges were expressed in the literature of the Black Arts movement. A plethora of young writers offered their art as both a political weapon and as the means of awakening the dormant, sleeping potential of the African American churches. Nikki *Giovanni, Haki R. *Madhubuti, Etheridge *Knight, and others wrote poems that attempted to initiate critical discussions of the role of the African American church and religion in the lives of oppressed people. Ralph Ellison's short story "And Hickman Arrives" (1956) cast an African American minister, Rev. Hickman, as the protagonist. James

*Baldwin's play *The *Amen Corner* (1968) centered on a minister who loses his congregation's respect through the disclosure of marital infidelity. Gwendolyn *Brooks wrote many poems that utilized the structure of the African American sermonic form and the language of this tradition. Amiri *Baraka merges the orthodox Christian tradition with African American religious expression in his novel *The *System of Dante's Hell* (1965), in which a New Jersey inner city is presented as Hell, complete with cantos that reflect the sins of the people against themselves and their culture. In *The *Autobiography of Malcolm X* (1964) Alex *Haley appropriates the language of salvation to describe the transformation of Malcolm Little, the antihero, into the personality known as Malcolm X.

Late-twentieth-century African American writers draw from the long history of this language in their texts. In most of Toni *Morrison's novels, the language of the African American religious tradition is central to the development of characters and plots. In *Sula* (1974), for example, *Sula Peace embodies the community's preoccupation with superstition, impending doom, and economic impotence. Sula becomes the archetype of the demonic, a witch in the eyes of the community, because they have misappropriated the language of the African American religious tradition. In *Beloved* (1988) the apparition that haunts an entire community becomes the collective guilt of the people for their failure to embrace their heritage. Much like Toni Morrison, Gloria *Naylor uses this language to offer a critique of middle-class aspirations in *Linden Hills* (1985), an African American middle-class community depicted as a group of individuals who have sold their souls for the opportunity simply to say that they live near the Needed family, the founders of the community who are presented as the demonic. And Alice *Walker in *The *Color Purple* (1982) creates *Celie, whose prayers to God in the first section of the text are finally replaced with letters to her sister who is in Africa. Celie's failure to employ the African American prayer tradition—which forms a partnership between the individual who prays and the God who answers by empowering the individual to seek a remedy to his or her own situation—leads to despair. It is only when Celie abandons the prayer tradition in which she expects God to solve her problems with her husband and "maleness," and embraces the secular gospel of the blues tradition that she finds salvation through Shug and reunites with her sister.

The African American independent church movement has had considerable impact on the development of African American literature. It has not only provided authors with publishing outlets and hospitable audiences, but it has also offered a powerful linguistic discourse allowing writers to critique both the institutional structures in America that generate racism and inequality, and the inability of African American people to appropriate this tradition in its purest form. While not all writers of African descent in America draw on this linguistic tradition, it is prevalent enough in a significant number of major texts to suggest that these writers consciously signify on what, for them, is an important part of their heritage. And while many of these authors have rejected the African American churches for a number of reasons, they have found that the language generated by its sustained critique of Euro-American Christianity has value.

[See also A.M.E. Book Concern; Biblical Tradition; Religion; Sermons and Preaching; Sunday School Literature.]

• Carter G. Woodson, The History of the Negro Church, 1921. C. Eric Lincoln, The Black Muslims in America, 1961. LeRoi Jones and Larry Neal, eds., Black Fire, 1968. Albert B. Cleage, Jr., The Black Messiah, 1969. James H. Cone, A Black Theology of Liberation, 1970. Gayraud S. Wilmore, Black Religion and Black Radicalism, 1973. J. F. Maxwell, Slavery and the Catholic Church, 1975. Albert J. Raboteau, Slave Religion, 1978. Gayraud S. Wilmore and James Cone, eds., Black Theology: A Documentary History, 1966–1979, 1979. Mildred A. Hill-Lubin, "African Religion: That Invisible Institution in African and African-American Literature," in Interdisciplinary Dimensions of African Literature, eds. Kofi Anyidoho et al., 1985, pp. 197–210. Milton C. Sernett, ed., Afro-American Religious History: A Documentary Witness, 1985. C. Eric Lincoln, The Black Church in the African-American Experience, 1990. Dwight N. Hopkins and George Cummings, eds., Cut Loose Your Stammering Tongue: Black Theology in the Slave Narratives, 1991. Kimberly Rae Connor, Conversions and Visions in the Writings of Afro-American Women, 1992.

—Chester J. Fontenot, Jr.

CHURCHWOMAN. Churchwomen are the standard-bearers for *religion and religious behavior in African American fictional communities. By being solidly grounded in the *church (usually fundamentalist), religion, and God, they determine who else should be, under what circumstances, and when. These characters are most notable in the works of James *Baldwin, where they pressure young men to become saved (*Go Tell It on the Mountain, 1953, and "The Outing," 1951) and abandon their husbands and children for the church (The *Amen Corner, 1955); they contrast sharply with the Baldwin women who are out of the "ark of safety," such as Esther in Go Tell, Ida Scott in *Another Country (1962), and the older Julia Miller in Just above My Head (1979). Other writers present strong black women, often in the matriarchal role, who find their strength in the church and God and who believe it is their duty to manage the lives of their offspring, such as Aunt Hagar Williams in Langston *Hughes's Not without Laughter (1930) and *Mama Lena Younger in Lorraine *Hansberry's A *Raisin in the Sun (1959). Both *Celie (in Alice *Walker's The *Color Purple, 1982) and Avey Johnson (in Paule *Marshall's Praisesong for the Widow, 1983) feel the sting of churchwomen's judgment; Celie is ostracized within her congregation, and Aunt Cuney is cast out of hers. On the other hand, Mattie Michael in Gloria *Naylor's The *Women of Brewster Place (1982) uses her strength gained from the church to become a great source of comfort to women around her. While the church has certainly served historically as a source of strength for black women, as well as within the literature, it is with a mixture of appreciation and accusation that many black writers treat characters grounded in that institution. While these characters

may have good intentions, they can just as easily stunt the growth of people around them as facilitate it.

• Jacquelyn Grant, "Black Women and the Church," in But Some of Us Are Brave, eds. Gloria T. Hull, Patricia Bell Scott, and Barbara Smith, 1982, pp. 141–152. Cheryl Townsend Gilkes, "The Role of Women in the Sanctified Church," Journal of Religious Thought (Spring/Summer, 1986): 24–41.

—Trudier Harris

CIVIL RIGHTS MOVEMENT. Rooted in centuries-old traditions of resistance and self-expression, the modern African American freedom movement began in the all-black political mobilizations during World War II, surged in the local struggles and national campaigns from 1960 to 1965, and culminated in the cultural triumphs and political tragedies of Black Power. This renewed quest for liberation became known as "the civil rights movement," even though its objectives went beyond mere citizenship rights.

Supported by decades of NAACP litigation, black activism during the war opened thirty years of dramatic effort and significant success. Beginning with the Montgomery bus boycott of 1955–1956, aggressive nonviolent direct action campaigns—alongside the threatening alternative posed by urban uprisings—brought about the Civil Rights Act of 1964 and the Voting Rights Act of 1965. More important, the black self-affirmation fueled by the movement repudiated the crippling legacy of white supremacy. In a larger sense, the African American freedom movement inspired citizens around the world to a broader sense of democratic possibility.

African Americans saw World War II as an opportunity and moved to seize it, agreeing with black author Chester *Himes that "Now is the Time! Here is the Place!" Compelled to oppose the contorted racial ideologies of the Axis nations, the NAACP's Roy Wilkins observed in 1944, "white Americans were jockeyed into declaring against [racial supremacy] theories." Langston *Hughes, whose writings would reflect the movement's evolution into the 1960s, conceded to white Americans that Adolph Hitler was evil, but speculated that the dictator "took lessons from the ku klux klan." Confronting the U.S. government with these contradictions, labor leader A. Philip Randolph organized the all-black March on Washington Movement (MOWM), threatening to bring thousands of protesters to Washington, D.C., in 1941. To avert the march, President Franklin Roosevelt issued Executive Order 8802, banning racial discrimination in defense industries.

While African Americans contributed to the war effort, homefront black activism persisted. NAACP organizers like Ella Baker expanded its membership rolls by nine hundred percent during the war. Inspired by the MOWM, James Farmer, Bayard Rustin, and an interracial group of pacifists founded the Congress of Racial Equality (CORE) in 1942 to promote Gandhian nonviolence. Students at Howard University held sit-ins at restaurants in Washington, D.C., holding signs that read "We die together— why can't we eat together?" In 1944 E. D. Nixon, a labor leader in Montgomery, Alabama, led 750 black citizens to the courthouse to demand the right to vote. Later that year in *Smith v. Allwright*, the Supreme Court ruled the "white primary" unconstitutional, a victory that NAACP legal counsel Thurgood Marshall later regarded as more important than *Brown v. Board of Education.*

Wartime racial violence underlined what sociologist Gunnar Myrdal's 1942 classic, *An American Dilemma*, identified as the nation's central problem: the distance between the rhetoric of democracy and the reality of racism. Researchers at Fisk University recorded 242 racial battles in forty-seven cities in 1943 alone. On 20 June, a riot in Detroit left thirty-four dead and hundreds injured. Less than two months later, six African Americans were killed, hundreds injured, and an estimated five million dollars worth of property destroyed during an upheaval in Harlem. These events influenced such literary works as Ann *Petry's "In Darkness and Confusion" (1945) and Ralph *Ellison's *Invisible Man* (1952).

Black self-assertion and white terrorism swept both South and North in the wake of the war. Between 1 May 1944 and 20 July 1946, forty-six black families in Chicago lost their homes to racial bombings. This is the same city in which Lorraine *Hansberry's characters would test segregation laws in *A *Raisin in the Sun* (1959). In January 1946, one hundred veterans marched in Birmingham to demand the right to vote, but local police under Eugene "Bull" Connor killed five black veterans during the first six weeks of the year. On 25 July state police and local citizens in Monroe, Georgia, murdered two black couples; the *Atlanta Constitution* published a letter of protest by seventeen-year-old Martin Luther *King, Jr. "Up until George went in the army," a leader of the Monroe lynch mob explained, "he was a good nigger. But when he came out, they thought they were as good as any white people."

Along with repressive violence, the rise of postwar domestic anticommunism, which framed civil rights activism as communist-inspired, hobbled the incipient movement. Nevertheless, campaigns in numerous southern cities presaged later movement strategies. In 1947 CORE sponsored the Journey of Reconciliation, a test of segregated interstate bus transportation that the organization would repeat in its 1961 "Freedom Rides." In Baton Rouge in 1953, black citizens organized a bus boycott that served as a model for Montgomery. Faced with intransigent white terrorism, some activists pondered guerilla resistance. The 1955 lynching of fourteen-year-old Emmett Till, a black boy accused of flirting with a white woman in Mississippi—and the acquittal of his confessed killers—did nothing to diminish that prospect. Till's murder inspired much black writing, notably James *Baldwin's *Blues for Mr. Charlie* (1964) and Gwendolyn *Brooks's "The Last Quatrain of the Ballad of Emmett Till" (1960); it also serves a key function in Toni *Morrison's *Song of Solomon* (1977).

On 17 May 1954 the U.S. Supreme Court issued its historic *Brown v. Board of Education* decree that "in the field of public education the doctrine of 'separate but equal' has no place." The U.S. Attorney General wrote in support of the decision that racial discrimination "furnishes grist for the Communist propaganda mills" and "raises doubt even among friendly nations as to the intensity of our devotion to the democratic faith." The unanimous decision appeared an unequivocal statement of national law. "Once that happened," Bayard Rustin explained, "it was very easy for that militancy which had been building up to express itself in the Montgomery Bus Boycott of 1955–1956."

On 1 December 1955 police in Montgomery, Alabama, arrested Rosa Parks for defying segregation statutes aboard a local bus. Respected in the black community, Parks worked for the local NAACP and the Brotherhood of Sleeping Car Porters (BSCP) under E. D. Nixon. Her defiance of the segregation laws was almost routine. "My resistance to being mistreated on the buses and anywhere else was just a regular thing with me and not just that day," Parks explained.

E. D. Nixon, who had been president of both the state and local NAACP and the BSCP, persuaded Parks that her arrest could spark a movement. When the president of the Women's Political Council (WPC), Jo Ann Robinson, heard of the arrest, the WPC stenciled thousands of leaflets calling for a bus boycott. The organizers selected a young minister named Martin Luther King, Jr., to head the campaign.

At the initial mass meeting, King delivered a speech that unveiled not only an extraordinary voice but an expansive vision for the movement. "The only weapon that we have in our hands this evening is the weapon of protest," he declared, articulating the movement in Christian love and American citizenship. "If we were incarcerated behind the iron curtains of a Communistic nation we couldn't do this," he stated. "But the great glory of American democracy is the right to protest for right." Having embraced the rhetoric of American democracy, King reminded listeners that black citizens could undermine as well as affirm America's leadership in the world. God was not merely the God of love, he proclaimed, but "also the God that standeth before the nations and says, 'Be still and know that I am God—and if you don't obey Me I'm gonna break the backbone of your power—and cast you out of the arms of your international and national relationships.'" This reference to the Cold War underlined the threat that black protest could pose to America's international aims. "Not only are we using the tools of persuasion," King warned, "but we've got to use the tools of coercion."

Black citizens walked and shared rides to keep the buses empty. Unable to exact any compromise from the city government, they expanded the original goal of better treatment to demand an end to segregation on the buses. Under the influence of Bayard Rustin and Glenn Smiley, King adopted the philosophy of nonviolent direct action. He did not mistake nonviolence for passivity: "A mass movement exercising nonviolence," King wrote, "is an object lesson in power under discipline."

Black Montgomery overcame external coercion and internal division to achieve solidarity in support of the boycott. Money poured in from across the country as journalists riveted the world's attention on Montgomery. After 381 days, the U.S. Supreme Court ruled Alabama's bus segregation statutes unconstitutional. The movement had seized a crucial success and affirmed a promising strategy: nonviolent direct action. The triumph in Montgomery—and organizing by Ella Baker and Bayard Rustin—gave birth to the Southern Christian Leadership Conference (SCLC) in 1957. SCLC gave King a vehicle for communicating his vision to an international audience, even when SCLC was only marginally connected to local struggles. Ella Baker said it best: "The movement made Martin rather than Martin making the movement."

"It is becoming clear," King foresaw in 1957, "that the Negro is in for a season of suffering." In the wake of *Brown* and Montgomery, white Southerners responded with widespread terrorism and with economic reprisals that made it almost impossible for civil rights advocates to keep a job in the South. Mob *violence over school desegregation in Little Rock, Arkansas, forced President Eisenhower to send troops in 1957, a crisis that prompted Gwendolyn Brooks to write "The Chicago Defender Sends a Man to Little Rock." Federal intervention fanned segregationists to white-hot ferocity. The Southern Regional Council reported 530 instances of violent racial attacks from 1955 to 1959. Many activists armed themselves; in Monroe, North Carolina, a local NAACP president named Robert F. Williams organized black veterans into a militia that repelled the Ku Klux Klan with gunfire. Racial conflicts in the segregated South saturate the works of Alice *Walker, Ernest J. *Gaines, and Richard *Wright, among others.

On 1 February 1960 four black college students sat down at a segregated lunch counter in Greensboro, North Carolina, launching a sit-in movement that within weeks had spread to fifty-four cities in nine states. Ella Baker, acting director of SCLC, convened students in Raleigh, North Carolina, to found the Student Nonviolent Coordinating Committee (SNCC), which spearheaded an aggressive, student-led phase of the movement. Student organizers appear in Walker's "Everyday Use" as well as in Ted *Shine's *Contribution* (1969). Alice Walker worked in voter registration activity in Mississippi. In 1961, when mob violence stopped the Freedom Rides launched by CORE to challenge interstate bus segregation, SNCC activists continued the rides. Inspired by the sit-ins, a young Harlem-born and Harvard-educated mathematician named Bob Moses went to the Mississippi Delta for SNCC, where he met Amzie Moore, who had been working for racial justice there since 1946. Moore recruited Moses to his vision of a voting rights campaign in the Delta that SNCC helped launch. Bold and uncompromising, SNCC's vision of "the beloved community" meshed with southern, rural black traditions to leave a legacy of grassroots democracy.

SCLC, by contrast, used local communities as a stage for national mobilizations that dramatized the justice of black demands for civil rights and the barbarity of the southern social order. Televised images of peaceful protestors facing police dogs, fire hoses, and white mobs fueled SCLC's strategy of using local campaigns to achieve national reforms. King, whose style permitted him to address a range of audiences, became the leading voice of the movement.

In Albany, Georgia, in 1962, King met his first serious setback. SNCC activists had organized black citizens into the Albany Movement. Dr. William Anderson, president of the coalition, invited King into Albany, an offer that SCLC accepted without sufficient forethought. Police Chief Laurie Pritchett stymied King's crusade with a nonviolent strategy of his own; by studying King's methods and training his officers to refrain from violence, Pritchett prevented the news coverage that SCLC needed.

The subsequent campaign in Birmingham would prove that SCLC had learned the lessons of Albany. Haven to the South's most violent Ku Klux Klan chapter, Birmingham was probably the most segregated city in the country. Dozens of unsolved bombings and police killings had terrorized the black community since World War II. Yet King foresaw that "the vulnerability of Birmingham at the cash register would provide the leverage to gain a breakthrough in the toughest city in the South."

Wyatt Tee Walker, who planned the crusade, said that before Birmingham "we had been trying to win the hearts of white Southerners, and that was a mistake, a misjudgement. We realized that you have to hit them in the pocket." Birmingham offered the perfect adversary in Public Safety Commissioner Eugene "Bull" Connor, who provided dramatic brutality for an international audience. SCLC's goal was to create a political morality play so compelling that the Kennedy administration would be forced to intervene: "The key to everything," King observed, "is federal commitment."

The movement initially found it hard to recruit supporters, with black citizens reluctant and Birmingham police restrained. Slapped with an injunction to cease the demonstrations, King decided to go to jail himself. During his confinement, King penned *"Letter from Birmingham Jail," an eloquent critique of "the white moderate who is more devoted to 'order' than to justice" and a work included in many composition and literature courses.

The breakthrough came when SCLC's James Bevel organized thousands of black school children to march in Birmingham. Police used school buses to arrest hundreds of children who poured into the streets each day. Lacking jail space, "Bull" Connor used dogs and firehoses to disperse the crowds. Images of vicious dogs and police brutality emblazoned front pages and television screens around the world. As in Montgomery, King grasped the international implications of SCLC's strategy. The nation was "battling for the minds and the hearts of men in Asia and Africa," he said, "and they aren't gonna respect the United States of America if she deprives men and women of the basic rights of life because of the color of their skin."

President Kennedy lobbied Birmingham's white business community to reach an agreement. On 10 May local white business leaders consented to desegregate public facilities, but the details of the accord mattered less than the symbolic triumph. Kennedy pledged to preserve this mediated halt to "a spectacle which was seriously damaging the reputation of both Birmingham and the country."

The next day, however, bombs exploded at King's headquarters and at his brother's home. Violent uprisings followed, as poor blacks who had little commitment to nonviolence ravaged nine blocks of Birmingham. Rocks and bottles rained on Alabama state troopers who attacked black citizens in the streets. The violence threatened to mar SCLC's victory but also helped cement White House support for civil rights. President Kennedy feared that black Southerners might become "uncontrollable" if reforms were not negotiated. It was one of the enduring ironies of the civil rights movement that the threat of violence was so critical to the success of nonviolence.

Across the South, the triumph in Birmingham inspired similar campaigns; in a ten-week period, at least 758 racial demonstrations in 186 cities sparked 14,733 arrests. Eager to compete with SCLC, the national NAACP pressed Medgar Evers to launch demonstrations in Jackson, Mississippi. On 11 June President Kennedy made a historic address on national television, describing civil rights as "a moral issue" and endorsing federal civil rights legislation. Later that night, a member of the White Citizen's Council assassinated Medgar Evers.

Tragedy and triumph marked the summer of 1963. As A. Philip Randolph sought to fulfill his vision of a march on the capitol for jobs, King convinced him to shift the focus to civil rights. Joining with leaders from SCLC, SNCC, the Urban League, and the NAACP, Randolph chose Bayard Rustin as march organizer. Kennedy endorsed the march, hoping to gain support for the pending civil rights bill. On 28 August about 250,000 rallied in the most memorable mass demonstration in American history. King's "I Have a Dream" oration would endure as a historical emblem of nonviolent direct action. Prominent in the crowd was writer James Baldwin, widely regarded as a black spokesperson, especially since the 1962 publication of his influential work, The *Fire Next Time. *Malcolm X's denunciation of the event as the "farce on Washington" and sharp differences over the censorship of a speech by SNCC's John Lewis would later seem to foreshadow the fragmentation of the movement. But against the lengthening shadow of political violence and racial division—the dynamite murder of four black children at the 16th Street Baptist Church in Birmingham two weeks later and the assassination of President Kennedy on November 22—the march gleamed as the apex of interracial liberalism. Toni Morrison used the bombing of the church as part of the rationale for her characters forming a black vigilante group in Song of Solomon.

King's eloquent evocation of the "dream" of racial equality elicited broad admiration but caused the Federal Bureau of Investigation to mark him as "the most dangerous Negro of the future in this nation from the standpoint of communism, the Negro and national security." The FBI's campaign of surveillance and harassment sought to "expose King as an immoral opportunist" who was "exploiting the racial situation for personal gain." The cabal included attempts to blackmail King into suicide, but in the long run did more to discredit the FBI than King.

In the summer of 1964, SNCC and its allies brought about 650 mostly white college students into the state to press black voter registration. The "Freedom Summer" crusade seemed "a strange combination of children headed for summer camp and soldiers going off to war," one wrote to her parents. Project leaders expected violence. "If there were gonna take some deaths to do it," Dave Dennis explained, "the death of a white college student would bring more attention to what was going on." The project was only days old when the Ku Klux Klan and the Neshoba County Sheriff's Department murdered two white volunteers and one black Mississippian. The killings turned the eyes of the world toward Mississippi, giving the movement crucial visibility. Freedom Summer was the most violent since Reconstruction: 35 shootings; 35 churches and 30 homes bombed or burned; at least six murders.

Though voter registration was the stated goal of Freedom Summer, volunteers undertook a range of community projects. They staffed Freedom Schools that underlined the importance of black culture and history. They helped organize the Mississippi Freedom Democratic Party (MFDP), which challenged the legitimacy of Mississippi's all-white delegation at the Democratic National Convention in Atlantic City. The failure of the Democratic Party to support the MFDP widened the growing fissure between the black freedom movement and its less-committed white allies.

The Civil Rights Act of 1964 and the Voting Rights Act of 1965, along with the Brown decision, represent the central legal achievements of the freedom movement. Responding to the SCLC's 1965 mobilization in Selma, Alabama, which paralleled the Birmingham campaign, President Lyndon Johnson addressed the nation on 15 March, explaining that the Selma protests "must be our cause, too. Because it is not just Negroes, but really all of us who must overcome the crippling legacy of bigotry and injustice. And," he declared, adding the prestige of the presidency to the freedom chorus that echoed through the streets of the South, "we shall overcome."

By the time that mainstream white liberals could say "we shall overcome," youthful black insurgents had begun to sneer that the lyrics should be changed to "We Shall Overrun." On 5 June 1966, James Meredith had begun a solo "March against Fear" across Mississippi; a sniper ambushed him the next day. King, Stokely Carmichael of SNCC, Floyd McKissick of CORE, Roy Wilkins of NAACP, and Whitney Young of the National Urban League met near Meredith's Memphis hospital room to plan the continuation of his march. Differences over tactics and strategy, however, reflected the fragmentation of the movement.

The three-week trek across Mississippi registered thousands of new black voters, but the media focused on tensions between SNCC and SCLC. SCLC's chants of "Freedom Now!" competed with SNCC's new call for "Black Power!" While its meaning remained ambiguous, "Black Power" took on connotations of separatism, alienation, and violence. Vice President Hubert Humphrey spoke for many liberals when he said, "racism is racism—and there is no room in America for racism of any color." Roy Wilkins called Black Power "the reverse of Mississippi, a reverse Hitler, and a reverse Ku Klux Klan." King termed the slogan "an unfortunate choice of words" but called attention to its roots in traditions of racial pride, economic uplift, and cultural self-affirmation. King conceded Stokely *Carmichael's point that other ethnic groups in America had risen through group solidarity, but pointed out that such groups had acquired clout without chants of Irish or Jewish Power: "Somehow, we managed to get just the slogan," King said.

The most famous icons of Black Power were the Black Panthers. Founded in Oakland in 1966 by Huey Newton and Bobby Seale, the Black Panther Party modeled their views after Robert F. Williams, Malcolm X, Franz Fanon, and Mao Tse-tung. Wearing their uniform of black leather jackets and black berets, Panthers carried weapons into the California State Legislature in 1967, setting off national press coverage that, though decidedly negative, attracted thousands to Panther chapters that spread across the urban United States. Many who did not join adopted the Panthers' political posture and rhetorical style.

What began as a slogan became almost a new movement, ambiguous in its precise meaning, contradictory in its political consequences, but liberating in its cultural implications. The cultural wing of Black Power, often called the *Black Arts movement, gave rise to vital, community-based cultural movements. Among those who combined radical politics and literary creativity were Amiri *Baraka and Ed *Bullins, minister of culture of the Black Panthers. Despite—and sometimes because of—this cultural energy, the activism that had given the movement its major victories dissolved into black separatism and white backlash. Many SNCC activists, long scornful of SCLC for confusing speechmaking with movement building, abandoned grassroots organizing in favor of militant rhetoric and charismatic leadership. Fiery orators like Stokely Carmichael and H. "Rap" Brown, fashioning their speech after the fallen Malcolm X, declared black independence while relying upon white-dominated media for their prominence. Crying "Power to the People," black firebrands often lost touch with black communities.

The fissure between mainstream liberalism and the black freedom movement became a chasm in the late 1960s. Many white liberals, long uneasy with black self-assertion, found in "Black Power" an easy escape into apathy or opposition. Others, near-paralyzed by guilt, found it impossible to oppose even the most ludicrous demands from African American spokespersons, even those without followers. But the central political reality among white Americans in the late 1960s was illuminated by the presidential bids of Alabama's racebaiting Governor George Wallace. Wallace's 1964 and 1968 campaigns pointed toward a race-based abandonment of the Democratic Party among white Southerners and located broad, resentful white constituencies in the suburbs of the North, Upper Midwest and mid-Atlantic states. Civil rights and Black Power, along with upheavals fed by the anti–Vietnam War and women's liberation movements and the counterculture, enabled Richard Nixon to use Wallace's wedge tactics to fashion a racially driven transformation in American politics. Voting rolls showed more new white Southerners registered than black ones during the 1960s, most of whom quickly followed Strom Thurmond into the Republican Party. After the assassination of Martin Luther King, Jr., on 4 April 1968, the fractured freedom movement disintegrated amid street violence, government repression, apocalyptic fantasies, and bitter disillusionment. King's death would inspire numerous creative works, including a poem by Nikki *Giovanni.

When "Black Power" had emerged as a slogan in 1966, it was seen as a repudiation of nonviolence and of "the civil rights movement" itself. In truth, the shift from "civil rights" to "Black Power" reflected rhythms of emphasis that had existed in African American politics for centuries. Virtually every element of "Black Power" was already present in the small towns of the South where the civil rights movement was born in the 1950s. From the start, independent political action, black cultural pride, and what Robert Williams called "armed self-reliance" operated both in tension and in tandem with legal efforts and nonviolent protest. The change from "civil rights" to "Black Power" was a costly abandonment of the organizing traditions that had created the movement in favor of "militant" rhetorical traditions and a new cultural energy. To its credit, the Black Power phase of the movement made a lasting and significant cultural and psychological impact in the lives of African Americans.

Resistance to white supremacy and affirmation of black identity endures, even in a time when many white Americans find unity in opposing the movement's legacy. Not only does the movement continue to press for African American advancement, it has inspired similar movements among women, Native Americans, gay and lesbian citizens, and other victims of discrimination. Reaction against the revolutionary achievements of the civil rights movement may define American political possibility well into the twenty-first century. But the largely unheralded black and white citizens whose hands painstakingly stitched the quilt of legal equality have forever enlarged the meaning of democracy.

[See also Afrocentricity; Black Aesthetic; Black Nationalism; Pan-Africanism.]

• Richard Kluger, Simple Justice, 1976. William H. Chafe, Civilities and Civil Rights: Greensboro, North Carolina and the Black Struggle for Freedom, 1980. Clayborne Carson, In Struggle: SNCC and the Black Awakening of the 1960s, 1981. Aldon Morris, Origins of the Civil Rights Movement: Black Communities Organizing for Change, 1984. David Garrow, Bearing the Cross: Martin Luther King, Jr., and the Southern Christian Leadership Conference, 1986. Adam Fairclough, To Redeem the Soul of America: The Southern Christian Leadership Conference and Martin Luther King, Jr., 1987. Taylor Branch, Parting the Waters: America in the King Years 1954–63, 1988. Armstead Robinson and Patricia Sullivan, eds., *New Directions in Civil Rights Studies*, 1991. William L. Van Deburg, *New Day in Babylon: The Black Power Movement and American Culture, 1965–75*, 1992. David S. Cecelski, *Along Freedom Road: Hyde County, North Carolina and the Fate of Black Schools in the South*, 1994. John Dittmer, *Local People: The Struggle for Civil Rights in Mississippi*, 1994. John Egerton, *Speak Now against the Day: The Generation before the Civil Rights Movement in the South*, 1994. Dan T. Carter, *The Politics of Rage: George Wallace, the Origins of the New Conservatism, and the Transformation of American Politics*, 1995. Charles Payne, *I Got the Light of Freedom: The Organizing Tradition and the Mississippi Freedom Struggle*, 1995. Patricia Sullivan, *Days of Hope: Race and Democracy in the New Deal*, 1996. Timothy B. Tyson, *Radio Free Dixie: Robert F. Williams and the Roots of Black Power*, forthcoming.

—Timothy B. Tyson

CLA Journal. The *CLA Journal*, official organ of the College Language Association, evolved from the *News-Bulletin* (1928–1941) when the organization was the Association of Teachers of English in Negro Colleges, and later when "Language" was substituted for "English" in its official name (1941–1949). In 1949 it further broadened its scope and took on its present name, the College Language Association. The *News-Bulletin* became the *CLA-Bulletin* in 1949, and it was succeeded by the *CLA Journal* in 1957. It carried two issues for the first volume, three each from the second to the ninth, and four from the tenth volume in 1966 to the present, with issues coming from the press in September, December, March, and June.

The *Journal* has never had an official institutional sponsor, but institutions in which the only three editors in its history have served as professors have provided office space, reductions in teaching load, and part-time secretarial service: Morgan State College (later University) to Therman B. O'Daniel, founder and first editor (1957–1978); Morehouse College to Edward A. Jones (1978–1979) and Cason L. Hill (1979–).

The association's bulletins and publications have from its earliest years reflected a special concern with race-related aspects of language and literature. Whatever the subject, in both the English and foreign language areas, however, the outlook and intention have generally been in accordance with the best requirements of scholarship in the field. But the ethnic concern prevails. This was particularly evident during the Black consciousness upsurge of the 1960s and 1970s, when in one ten-year period the number of articles on ethnic-related subjects increased from sixty-three to three hundred. After the 1970s, on the other hand, the number of articles about white authors by whites and African Americans has risen noticeably. Even so, the intellectual and psychological direction of the *Journal* remains ethnic but not ethnocentric.

• A. Russell Brooks, "The *CLA Journal* as a Mirror of Changing Ethnic and Academic Perspectives," *CLA Journal* 26.3 (Mar. 1983): 265–276. Therman B. O'Daniel, *A Twenty-five-Year Author-Title Cumulative Index to the CLA Journal*, 1985.

—A. Russell Brooks

Clara's Ole Man. Perhaps the best-known play of Ed *Bullins's Twentieth-Century Cycle, *Clara's Ole Man* was first performed at San Francisco's Firehouse Repertory Theater in August 1965. Set in mid-1950s South Philadelphia, it features Clara, an attractive eighteen-year-old girl; Big Girl, her abrasive, domineering lesbian lover; Baby Girl, Big Girl's retarded teenage sister; and Jack, a young man who self-consciously affects middle-class speech and behavior.

Big Girl's love of cheap drink, her abuse of Clara, and her ridicule of Jack's pretensions reflect her outspokenness, which is her way of releasing her anger and frustration at being overweight and unattractive. The need to release is her reason for having taught Baby Girl to curse, for holding in the frustration of everyday life can only mean a risk of sanity. Big Girl also cares for her invalid Aunt Toohey (who remains offstage); Toohey's daily visits from her alcoholic friend Miss Famie, which mean hours of drinking for both, only compound Big Girl's intolerance and cynicism.

Baby Girl believes she sees a cat having kittens in the yard outside. Her delusion is a metaphor for the difficult pregnancy and stillbirth Clara endured before she was taken in by Big Girl; one clue to this interpretive possibility is Clara's opening description as "feline." The imagined cats also signify the recessed status of Clara's character, made so by the boisterousness and prepossessiveness of Big Girl. Clara's relative weakness is again captured by the stage description that she "smiles—rather, blushes—often."

Clara's character seems to match Jack's in this regard, for he too seems to be engaged in attempts to escape his past. His deliberate grandiloquence masks the self that is slowly revealed by his increasing drunkenness; the three toughs who arrive later remember him as a member of a now-defunct gang. As his patrician speech falters, he is reviled by the gang members for his Ivy League dress and overall *class disloyalty. When he goes too far in presuming the possibility of a heterosexual relationship with Clara, Big Girl, ever protective of her domain, orders his beating by the gangsters.

W. D. E. Andrews concurs with the idea of the cat as symbolic lack but recalls a similar element in the story of the dog in Edward Albee's *The Zoo Story* or that of the imaginary son in *Who's Afraid of Virginia Woolf?* In most discussions of the play, the idea of a representative heroism in Big Girl is a significant issue in a play without heroes; the spirit of the triumphant seems grounded in the play's liminal awarenesses and critiques of class stratification. Lance *Jeffers finds more order in the world of Bullins's characters than in that portrayed in Thomas Mann's stories, wherein "the middle class has lost its life principle"; Andrews states also that Big Girl, though brutal, is vital and, as such, forms a sharp, even victorious contrast with Jack's false presentation of self—"the bad effect of white culture."

• Lance Jeffers, "Bullins, Baraka, and Elder: The Dawn of Grandeur in Black Drama," *CLA Journal* 16 (1972–1973): 32–48. W. D. E. Andrews, "Theater of Black Reality: The Blues Drama of Ed Bullins," *Southwest Review* (Spring 1980): 178–190.

—Nathan L. Grant

CLARK, AL C. *See* Goines, Donald.

CLASS is generally understood as a social stratum in which individuals have similar economic, political, and cultural positions. In the United States it is an amorphous and contradictory concept. Although the nation's founding documents imply a classless society in which "all men are created equal" and all have "certain unalienable rights," the authors of the Declaration of Independence and the United States Constitution deliberately omitted women and most people of color. Subsequent laws and social practices not only used *race and *gender to relegate certain members of society to subservient positions but also tended to privilege property holders over others. On the other hand, the American dream assumes class exists but promises that one can, with hard work and determination, rise to the upper stratum of American society. Yet, for African Americans especially, this has not been the case. Given the particular legacies of *slavery and racism in the United States, traditional indexes of class, wealth, education, and access to power, while operative to an extent, are not as viable in the African American class system. In African American society, factors that include occupation, physical appearance, clothing, language, recreational activities, neighborhood, and church affiliation are significant in determining one's social class. In the nineteenth century, occupations such as catering, carpentry, and dressmaking connoted a higher social status in the black communities than in the white ones. Later, working for the post office or as a railway porter gave as much prestige as being a teacher, nurse, or social worker. Entertainers, athletes, and others of impressive wealth or popularity are not necessarily accepted among the upper echelons of African American society, for along with vestiges of color consciousness and family origin, African Americans of the elite and middle classes still consider *education, decorum, race pride, and community service as significant class indicators. It is that combination of education, service, and economic independence that has made doctors, ministers, professors, and morticians prominent members of the African American elite. Like William Wells *Brown, James W. C. *Pennington, and others, many former slaves earned, or borrowed, the PhD and the MD within a few years of gaining their freedom.

The *talented tenth, a concept identified with W. E. B. *Du Bois and other members of the early twentieth-century black intelligentsia, was a guiding principle that prompted the founding of antebellum *literary societies such as Boston's Afric American Female Intelligence Society in 1832 and Baltimore's Watkins Academy for Negro Youth in the 1840s. The idea behind the talented tenth was that only 10 percent of the African American population had the immediate capabilities to participate in U.S. society on an equal basis and therefore that group was responsible for the progress and protection of the other 90 percent. "Lifting as We Climb," the motto of the National Association of Colored Women (founded in 1896), may well explain the heavy involvement of African American *churches and clubs, sororities and fraternities, lodges and family groups in social service projects, educational scholarships, and youth activities to this day.

In African American literature, class has been indicated in various ways. During the eighteenth and nineteenth centuries, distinctions were made between those born in Africa and those born in the New World, between slave and free, between Christian and pagan, between rural and urban, between literate and illiterate, as well as between those of property and those without. Because a small but significant number of white fathers tended to favor the children black women bore them with educations, easier or more skilled jobs, and even *freedom and property, class was often signified by skin color, and words such as "*mulatto," "octoroon," "blue vein," "blue gummed," and "undiluted African" conveyed class distinctions as well. Class distinctions based upon occupation are evident in terms such as "house servant" and "field hand." Social distance is inherent in words such as "hincty," "saddity," or "dicty" that are generally used as hostile or disapproving terms for those whose language, *dress, or other elements of behavior seem to indicate an attitude of superiority. Toni *Morrison's The *Bluest Eye (1970) provides an excellent example of class differences played out in a small Ohio town.

*Slave narratives affirm the acts of agency initiated by slaves who were determined to rise above the lowest rung of the class hierarchical order. Their escapes from the southern "house of bondage" to the "promised land" of the North augmented the existing geographical definition of class that bestows more prestige upon those who inhabit certain states and cities. By using the slave narrative as a political tool for change, nineteenth-century African American writers affiliated with the *antislavery movement reorganized the patronage of more powerful individuals to facilitate the elimination of the slave class. The slave narrators themselves were versions of the African American dream. These former slaves had achieved freedom and generally lived in the northern United States, Canada, or England, all *places of higher status generally than the rural South, the western frontier, and even the Caribbean islands. Often the narrators were literate, employed Christians whose social prominence was further enhanced by the publication of their stories. Other writers, such as George Moses *Horton, William Grimes, and Harriet E. *Wilson published and marketed their stories, poems, and other literary creations to directly change the social and economic conditions of themselves and their loved ones.

The published literature by African Americans before the Civil War, whether by slaves, former slaves, or free-born African Americans, was essentially the production of privileged individuals. But as Frederick *Douglass and others have testified, the "sorrow songs," work songs, *spirituals, and animal and *trickster tales had originated and thrived among the working classes. The literary creations of the masses were neither recorded nor respected with any consistency until the arrival of northern missionaries, teachers, and others during the Civil War and immediately after. Then began the first collections of stories, songs, and other speech acts of those lower-class individuals, especially in the rural South, who were generally referred to as the "folk." The subject matter, language, and other formal structures of African American *folklore provide insight into the experiences, attitudes, and aspirations of the majority of slaves and former slaves who comprise the category of "folk." Frances Ellen Watkins *Harper was one of the earliest African American writers to create positive literary representations of the lives and language of the folk and uneducated classes. *Sketches of Southern Life* (1868) uses dialect and the strong, commonsense perspective of *Aunt Chloe Fleet, a denizen of the Reconstruction South, to reveal the heroic contributions and community consciousness of laboring classes. Paul Laurence *Dunbar's *dialect poetry interprets the southern rural experiences from the perspective of a northern urban African American artist.

Another index of class segments within African American culture comes from the titles of nineteenth- and early twentieth-century black *periodicals. The *Pacific Appeal*, the *Southern Workman*, the *Iowa Colored Woman*, *L'Album Littéraire*, the *Woman's Era*, *Student's Repository*, *Musical Messenger*, *Colored Teacher*, *Negro Agriculturist*, *Journal of the National Medical Association*, *Freeman*, and *National Domestic* are but a few that indicate not only that the class structure was varied and complex but that these divisions were large enough to warrant their own publications. In the African American press and, less commonly, in mainstream periodicals, Mary Ann *Shadd, Thomas P. *Detter, Ida B. *Wells-Barnett, and other journalists wrote editorials, exposés, sketches, and other materials that demonstrate the diverse and amorphous class system within nineteenth-century African America.

Works such as Emma Dunham *Kelley's *Megda* (1891) and *Four Girls at Cottage City* (1898), Alice Moore *Dunbar-Nelson's *Violets and Other Tales* (1895), Sutton E. *Griggs's *Imperium in Imperio* (1899), Booker T. *Washington's *Up from Slavery* (1901), W. E. B. Du Bois's *The *Souls of Black Folk* (1903), and James Weldon *Johnson's *The *Autobiography of an Ex-Colored Man* (1912) focus upon economic and social mobility while offering perceptive and specific information about those who summered in resort towns; lived on the bayous and levees of Louisiana; used their college educations to foment revolutions, to found education dynasties, or to document cultural contributions; or worked in Florida cigar factories before joining the bohemian life in New York City or *passing as members of the white middle class.

The *Harlem Renaissance clearly documents a thriving class system. Claude *McKay's *Home to Harlem* (1928) features Jake, who works as ship's stoker, Ray, a Haitian American intellectual, and Felice, a "too nice to be mean" *prostitute. In Wallace *Thurman's *The *Blacker the Berry* (1929) Emma Lou Morgan is a dark-skinned native of Idaho who attended college in Southern California before moving to Harlem where she became involved with Alva, a fair-skinned, heavy-drinking ladies' man. Angela

Murray in Jessie Redmon *Fauset's *Plum Bun* (1929) is from a Philadelphia working-class background and becomes a successful artist who negotiates between Greenwich Village and Harlem. *Not without Laughter* (1930) by Langston *Hughes is a story of a working-class African American boy who grows up in a small Kansas town. In Zora Neale *Hurston's *Their Eyes Were Watching God* (1937), the life stories of *Janie Crawford and her grandmother recount the movements from slavery to *domestic service to farming, shopkeeping, migrant labor, and others levels of society.

For those African American writers who are critical of the economic and social infrastructures of America, an appreciation of class formation is often modulated by race. In the poem "Strong Men," Sterling A. *Brown records the exploitation of migrant labor when he compares the brutal workload endured by slaves to the male-dominated work gangs that built railroads throughout the vast landscape of America. Claude McKay's poem "Harlem Shadows" (1920) describes the world of poverty that African Americans suffered when settling in Harlem, New York. In her poem "From the Talking Back of Miss Valentine James # One" (1976), June *Jordan gives voice to women who juggle responsibilities of managing the home with their outside work commitments. Plays such as Mary Burrill's *They That Sit in Darkness* (1919), Myrtle Smith Livingston's *For Unborn Children* (1926), Langston Hughes's *Don't You Want to Be Free?* (1937), and Theodore *Ward's *Big White Fog* (1938) tell of the harsh economic conditions and inadequate medical, housing, and educational resources available to working-class urban communities.

Richard *Wright's *Native Son* (1940) shadows the experiences of protagonist *Bigger Thomas, who strives to make sense of his urban existence. Faced with long-term unemployment, and as the eldest son, Bigger struggles to make sense of providing for his family. Wright's depiction of the family, residing in a cramped tenement housing project, is a dismal one. In the opening scene a rat is trapped in the small one-bedroom apartment shared by Bigger, his mother, his sister, and his younger brother. Unable to escape from its dingy location, the rat is cornered and subsequently killed by Bigger. Within this plotline an allegory of class formation in America unfolds, for the rat symbolizes the extent to which the Thomas family is caught within a rigid class and racialized system perpetuated by low-paid menial work and underfunded welfare and educational services.

In *The *Street* (1946), Ann *Petry's *Lutie Johnson struggles to escape the black urban ghetto of New York and attain a better life for herself and her son. As a domestic worker and sometime waitress, the beautiful Lutie resists the sexual advances of her landlord, rejects attempts by pimps to seduce her into a world of prostitution, and refuses the propositions of other suitors who desire to make her their concubine.

Lorraine *Hansberry's prize-winning Broadway play *A *Raisin in the Sun* (1959) offers an alternative to Wright's version of the Chicago working-class family. Though the featured family resides in a tenement not significantly different from that of Bigger Thomas's family, *Walter Lee Younger is a chauffeur who wants to own his own business, *Beneatha Younger is a premed student, and Ruth and *Mama Lena Younger both work as domestic servants. They too find their lives stifled by poverty and the cramped uncomfortable apartment they struggle to maintain, but by using the insurance money from Walter Younger, Sr.'s death, the Youngers are able to move out of the ghetto—to a racially hostile, all-white suburb.

Two other authors whose portrayal of class in African American society are highly significant are Ralph *Ellison and Chester *Himes. Himes introduces Robert Jones, a Los Angeles shipyard worker, in *If He Hollers Let Him Go (1945). Jones is an educated idealist who becomes consumed by his passion to move from being a "token black" employee to one whose skin color is irrelevant. Himes also contributes to our understanding of class in the African American communities with his series on black Harlem detectives *Coffin Ed Johnson and *Grave Digger Jones. Ellison's National Book Award winner, *Invisible Man (1952), charts the invisibility of African Americans, both in the South and in the North, who are defined as a mass group but whose subjective experiences are erased from the American imagination.

Late twentieth-century African American works charting upward economic and social mobility include Ishmael *Reed's *Flight to Canada (1976), John Edgar *Wideman's Sent for You Yesterday (1983), Ntozake *Shange's Betsey Brown (1985), Gloria *Naylor's Linden Hills (1985), Lorene Cary's Black Ice (1991), Thulani Davis's 1959 (1992), Dennis A. Williams's Crossover (1992), Brent Staples's Parallel Time (1994), and Terry *McMillan's How Stella Got Her Groove Back (1996).

By examining the intersections between class, race, and gender, such writers critique notions that establish the working-class and middle- and upper-class African Americans as monolithic groups. Some debunk myths that darker-skinned blacks faced the brunt of racial prejudice as their light-skinned heroines confront racial discrimination and, like their working-class counterparts, are allowed limited entry into job sectors outside service-oriented positions.

African American writers have also made connections between class formation and the nuances of Christianity. As early as the eighteenth century African American Christians proclaimed that spiritual renewal would complement slaves' bids to realize emancipation. On 24 June 1797 Prince Hall urged fellow Masons of his African lodge to follow God first. The autobiographical writings of preachers such as Jarena *Lee's The Life and Religious Experience of Jarena Lee, A Colored Lady (1836), Zilpha *Elaw's Memoirs of the Life, Religious Experience, Ministerial Travels and Labours of Mrs. Zilpha Elaw (1846), Nancy *Prince's A Narrative of the Life and Travels of Mrs. Nancy Prince (1850), and Richard *Allen's The Life, Experience and Gospel Labors of the

Rt. Rev. Richard Allen (1880) used the Bible as an authoritative text to condemn the various forms of discrimination combated by African Americans. Toward the beginning of the twentieth century a slew of African American denominations rose out of the mass demographical shifts of the black population. Distinctions between the churched and the unchurched mirrored class categories that were prevalent within some African American communities. High church reflected those denominations that emerged out of mainstream Christian orders. As C. Eric Lincoln and Lawrence H. Mamiya point out in The Black Church in the African American Experience (1990), the economic disparity within the three primary offshoots of the Black Methodist Church—the African Methodist Episcopal (AME) Church, Christian Methodist Episcopal Church, and the AME Zion churches—was substantial. For example, in their survey of 2,150 Methodist churches, Lincoln and Mamiya discovered only one storefront church that was affiliated with these Methodist organizations. In *Go Tell It on the Mountain (1953), James *Baldwin locates storefront churches as a prominent fixture of poor African American communities. Financially strapped parishioners could not afford to build more elaborate premises.

The issue of whether the creation of an existential community can act as a buffer against racial prejudice and the hierarchical nature of class formation is expounded upon in Octavia E. *Butler's science fiction novels such as Patternmaster (1976). African American activists, writers, spiritual leaders, and political thinkers have long grappled with the question of how African Americans should define and realize freedom and how if at all economic mobility and class formation should factor into the equation of African Americans' quest for freedom.

By the time he completed *Dusk of Dawn: An Essay Toward an Autobiography of a Race Concept (1940), Du Bois was influenced by the writings of left-wing theorists such as Marx and Lenin. Challenged by the works of leaders of the African diaspora and encouraged by the activism of members affiliated with southern and northern branches of the Communist Party of America (CPUSA), Du Bois asserted that an alliance between members of the working class and the transformation of the capitalist infrastructures and superstructures of America were essential if any substantial improvement in the civil liberties of all American citizens was to be attained. In varying degrees Richard Wright's *Uncle Tom's Children (1938), William *Attaway's Blood on the Forge (1941), Lloyd *Brown's *Iron City (1951), Charles Denby's Indignant Heart: A Black Worker's Journal (1978), and the reportage writings of CPUSA members such as Ben Davis, William Patterson, and Claudia Jones draw upon left theoretical praxes to illuminate their understanding of racial, class, and gender formation(s). One must be reminded that relations between African American writers and the CPUSA were not without their problems. In his essay "I Tried to Be a Communist," Richard Wright accused the CPUSA of forcing writers to adhere to dogmatic guidelines that complemented the party's agendas and theoretical positions; Wright considered such practices restrictive and stifling to the creative process.

The connections between class, gender, and *sexuality are prevalent in several literary contributions by African American writers. The questions of sexuality and class formation refute one-dimensional characterizations of black communities as homogeneous and also complicate class designations. The works of James Baldwin, including *Giovanni's Room (1956) and *Another Country (1962), Audre *Lorde's The Erotic As Power (1978) and Zami: A New Spelling of My Name (1982), Larry Duplechan's Blackbird (1986), Melvin *Dixon's Vanishing Rooms (1991), and June Jordan's Haruko/Love Poetry: New and Selected Love Poems (1993) expose underlying significances of the alliance between the Protestant ethic and class mobility. Within this strain of Protestant ideology multiple identities of race, gender, and sexuality are reduced, nullified, and ultimately submerged into a monolithic framework that promotes conformity to heterosexuality, patriarchy, and Anglo-Europeanism. The aforementioned writers identify the Protestant ethic and the puritanical mores that legitimate strict sexual codes of behavior as contributing to the further marginalization of African American gay, lesbian, and bisexual men and women, regardless of their class affiliations.

Surveying the instances and nuances of class formulations in African American literature, it is clear that a plethora of interpretations and perspectives exist. During periods such as the abolitionist and *Civil Rights movements, class distinctions were often downplayed. Sometimes, as during the *Black Arts movement, the middle class was villainized, ghetto life was celebrated, and conscious efforts to form a homogeneous African American community defined as *black nationalism were the order of the day. Recently it seems the pendulum has swung the other way and the small but evident group of what Trey *Ellis calls "cultural mulattos" claims a significant part of African American literary attention. Even the most cursory survey reveals, however, that class in African American culture is intricately related to race, gender, and creed, and it is that intricate and evolving relationship that has occupied and continues to inform the pens of some of our most distinguished writers.

[See also Blue Vein Societies; Communism; Literacy; Religion.]

• W. E. B. Du Bois, The Philadelphia Negro, 1899. E. Franklin Frazier, Black Bourgeoisie, 1957. Leon Litwack, Been in the Storm So Long: The Aftermath of Slavery, 1979. Angela Y. Davis, Women Race and Class, 1983. Manning Marable, How Capitalism Undeveloped Black America, 1983. Mark Naison, Communists in Harlem during the Depression, 1983. Jacqueline Jones, Labor of Love, Labor of Sorrow: Black Women, Work and the Family from Slavery to the Present, 1985. Ellis Cose, The Rage of a Privileged Class, 1993. Barbara Foley, Radical Representations: Politics and Form in U.S. Proletarian Fiction, 1929–1941, 1993. Bettye Collier-Thomas and James Turner, "Race, Class and Color: The African American Discourse on Identity," Journal of American Ethnic History 14.1 (Fall 1994): 5–31. bell hooks, Killing Rage Ending Racism, 1995.
—Frances Smith Foster and Claudia May

CLAY, CASSIUS MARCELLUS, JR. See Ali, Muhammad.

CLEAGE, PEARL (b. 1948), poet, playwright, prose writer, performance artist, and editor of Catalyst magazine. Pearl Cleage was born in Detroit, Michigan, and was educated at Howard University, Spelman College, and Atlanta University. Early in her life her family encouraged an African American view of the world. Her father, Jaramogi Abebe Azaman (Albert Cleage), founded and developed Black Christian Nationalism. She also came under the direct influence of the political and intellectual ferment of the 1960s and 1970s.

Cleage's writing is highly polemical. A strong political spirit and commitment to the liberation of African Americans, particularly African American women, infuse her work. While she ultimately advocates the healthy solidarity of the African American community, she also broaches the taboo topics of sexism and *violence against women in the African American community. She refuses to subordinate discussions of *gender to *race and sometimes makes the link between the two. Her writings, therefore, both invite political discussion and inspire literary analysis.

Her first books, We Don't Need No Music (1971), The Brass Bed and Other Stories (1990), and Mad at Miles: The Blackwoman's Guide to Truth (1991), have received little or no critical attention. However, Deals with the Devil and Other Reasons to Riot (1993) has received substantially more public attention and popular acclaim. While this work blends personal experience and observation with a celebration of the African American female perspective and experience, the greatest confluence of Cleage's craft and vision is found in her *dramas. These works advocate the necessity of African American women empowering themselves as individuals, surmounting the differences of *class, personal experience, and philosophy, and forming supportive networks as models of survival for the African American community.

Cleage's plays are frequently performed and are beginning to appear in print. Hospice (1983) earned five Audelco Recognition Awards for achievement Off Broadway. This one-act play portrays an exchange between Alice Anderson, a forty-seven-year-old cancer patient, and her thirty-year-old daughter, Jenny, who is about to give birth. In keeping with the theme of the need for strong relationships between women, the play explores the complicated mother-daughter relationship and mandates healing where ruptures exist. Chain (1992) and Late Bus to Mecca (1992) similarly explore the condition of African American women. In Chain Cleage depicts the impact of drugs on the African American community through the story of Rosa Jackson, a sixteen-year-old addict whose empowerment is sabotaged by her drug-addicted boyfriend and the desperation of her parents. Late Bus to Mecca dramatizes the value of African American sisterhood. The play depicts an encounter between Ava Gardner Johnson and a nameless African American woman who is too physically and psychologically battered to speak. Although a *prostitute, the resourceful and self-assured Ava is able to offer love and support to another African American woman and affirm the viability of her own philosophy. *Flyin' West* (1994) portrays black participation in frontier development resulting from the 1860 Homestead Act and dramatizes intraracial and gender dynamics in that experience.

Cleage's art is womanist in spirit and effort. Her work stands as a testament to the union of artistic vision, political and cultural sensibility, and analytic intellect.   —Carol P. Marsh-Lockett

CLEAVER, ELDRIDGE (b. 1935), essayist, sociocultural theorist, and minister. Born in Wabbaseka, Arkansas, Leroy Eldridge Cleaver moved west to Los Angeles in 1946, where his family lived in an impoverished African American/Chicano neighborhood. In 1953 and 1957 Cleaver was convicted for narcotics possession and assault and spent almost thirteen years in the California penitentiary system. While in prison he affiliated with the Black Muslims and became an ardent follower of *Malcolm X.

After his 1966 parole Cleaver worked for *Ramparts* magazine and met several radical and countercultural activists, among them Huey Newton and Bobby Seale, cofounders of the Oakland-based Black Panther Party, of which he soon became the minister of information. On 6 April 1968 Cleaver was wounded and arrested after a violent encounter between the Black Panthers and the Oakland police.

In February 1968 Cleaver published *Soul on Ice*, an enormously popular and influential collection of *essays and *letters on American culture, *race and *gender relations, and his own prison life. *Soul on Ice* gained Cleaver instant national recognition as the potential intellectual and political heir to Malcolm X. During 1968 Cleaver became involved in several political controversies, including an invitation to lecture at the University of California at Berkeley and his own legal struggle to remain free. Ordered back to prison, Cleaver fled the country on 27 November 1968 and spent the next seven years in Cuba, Algeria, and France. He continued to publish radical essays in *Black Panther, Ramparts,* and the *Black Scholar.*

During his exile he became increasingly disenchanted with the Third World and authoritarian communism and returned in 1975 as a political conservative to prison in the United States and total rejection by his former associates. He also began a religious odyssey that took him through evangelical Christianity to the Mormon Church, some of which is chronicled in *Soul on Fire* (1978), a conversion *autobiography.

• Robert Scheer, ed., *Eldridge Cleaver: Post-Prison Writings and Speeches,* 1969. Kathleen Rout, *Eldridge Cleaver,* 1991.
                                               —Roger A. Berger

CLIFTON, LUCILLE (b. 1936), poet, juvenile fiction writer, autobiographer, and educator. Lucille Sayles Clifton was born in Depew, New York, to Samuel L. and Thelma Moore Sayles. Her father worked for the New York steel mills; her mother was a launderer, homemaker, and avocational poet. Although neither parent was formally educated, they provided their large family with an appreciation and an abundance of books, especially those by African Americans. At age sixteen, Lucille entered college early, matriculating as a drama major at Howard University in Washington, D.C. Her Howard associates included such intellectuals as Sterling A. *Brown, A. B. *Spellman, Chloe Wofford (now Toni *Morrison), who later edited her writings for Random House, and Fred Clifton, whom she married in 1958.

After transferring to Fredonia State Teachers College in 1955, Clifton worked as an actor and began to cultivate in *poetry the minimalist characteristics that would become her professional signature. Like other prominent *Black Aesthetic poets consciously breaking with Eurocentric conventions, including Sonia *Sanchez and her Howard colleague, LeRoi Jones (Amiri *Baraka), Clifton developed such stylistic features as concise, untitled free verse lyrics of mostly iambic trimeter lines, occasional slant rhymes, anaphora and other forms of repetition, puns and allusions, lowercase letters, sparse punctuation, and a lean lexicon of rudimentary but evocative words.

Poet Robert *Hayden entered her poems into competition for the 1969 YW-YMHA Poetry Center Discovery Award. She won the award and with it the publication of her first volume of poems, *Good Times.* Frequently inspired by her own family, especially her six young children, Clifton's early poems are celebrations of African American ancestry, heritage, and culture. Her early publications praise African Americans for their historic resistance to oppression and their survival of economic and political racism. Acclaimed by the *New York Times* as one of the best books of 1969, *Good Times* launched Clifton's prolific writing career.

In 1970 Clifton published two picture verse books for children, *The Black BC's* and *Some of the Days of Everett Anderson.* *Everett Anderson, a small boy living in the inner city, became the protagonist of eight of the fourteen works of juvenile fiction she published between 1970 and 1984. One in this series, *Everett Anderson's Goodbye,* received the Coretta Scott King Award in 1984. Another of her children's books, *Sonora Beautiful* (1981), represents a thematic departure for Clifton in that it features a white girl as the main character. Like her poetry, Clifton's short fiction extols the human capacity for love, rejuvenation, and transcendence over weakness and malevolence even as it exposes the myth of the American dream.

Clifton's prose maintains a familial and cultural tradition of storytelling. Adapting a genealogy prepared by her father, *Generations: A Memoir* (1976) constitutes a matrilineal *neo–slave narrative; it traces the Sale/Sayles family from its Dahomeian ancestor who became known as Caroline Sale Donald (1823–1910) after her abduction in 1830 from West Africa to New Orleans, Louisiana. Most of the biographical sketches in *Generations* are written from a first-person perspective in which various family members are represented as narrating their own stories. In them, Clifton further honors African

American oral and oratorical traditions with her use of black vernacular.

In 1987 Clifton reprinted her complete published poems in *Good Woman: Poems and a Memoir,* which, in addition to *Generations,* contains *Good Times, Good News about the Earth* (1972), *An Ordinary Woman* (1974), and *Two-Headed Woman* (1980), a Pulitzer Prize nominee and winner of the Juniper Prize. The themes of these exceptional poems reflect both Clifton's ethnic pride and her *womanist principles, and integrate her race and gender consciousness. Casting her persona as at once plain and extraordinary, Clifton challenges pejorative Western myths that define women and people of color as predatory and malevolent or vulnerable and impotent. Her poems attest to her political sagacity and her lyrical mysticism. Poem sequences throughout her works espouse Clifton's belief in divine grace by revising the characterization of such biblical figures as the Old Testament prophets, Jesus, and the Virgin Mary, and in *An Ordinary Woman* she shows herself in conflict and consort with Kali, the Hindu goddess of war and creativity.

Good Woman also narrates a personal and collective history as it addresses the poet's enduring process of self-discovery as poet, woman, mother, daughter, sibling, spouse, and friend. Some of its most complex and effective poems mourn Thelma Sayles's epilepsy, mental illness, and premature death when Clifton was twenty-three. A persistent witness to America's failed promises to former slaves, Native Americans, and other victims of its tyranny, Clifton is nonetheless witty and sanguine as she probes the impact of history on the present. She testifies to the pain of oppression manifested in her parents' tormented marriage, in racism that undermines progressive movements for social change, in disregard for the planet Earth as a living and sentient being.

In 1987 Clifton published *Next: New Poems,* most of which are constructed as "sorrow songs" or requiems. Some lament personal losses—the deaths by disease of the poet's mother at age forty-four on 13 February 1959; of her husband at age forty-nine on 10 November 1984; and of a Barbadian friend, "Joanne C.," who died at age twenty-one on 30 November 1982. Other poems grieve for political figures or tragedies, including an elegy sequence for the American Indian chief, Crazy Horse, and a trilogy mourning the massacres at Gettysburg, Nagasaki, and Jonestown. The persona also testifies to the crime and tragedy of child molestation, a theme developed in poem sequences featuring the mythical African shape-shifter in both *Next* and *The Book of Light* (1993). In the tradition of Langston *Hughes, Gwendolyn *Brooks, and Etheridge *Knight, Clifton's heroic meditations in *The Book of Light* offer pithy and grievous contemplations of diverse epistemological and metaphysical questions.

Clifton served as Poet Laureate of Maryland from 1979 to 1982. Her achievements also include fellowships and honorary degrees from Fisk University, George Washington University, Trinity College, and other institutions; two grants from the National Endowment for the Arts; and an Emmy Award from the American Academy of Television Arts and Sciences. Clifton is Distinguished Professor of Humanities at St. Mary's College in Maryland and has a position at Columbia University from 1995 to 1999.

[*See also* Children's and Young Adult Literature.]

• Audrey T. McCluskey, "Tell the Good News," in *Black Women Writers,* ed. Mari Evans, 1984, pp. 139–149. Andrea Benton Rushing, "Lucille Clifton: A Changing Voice for Changing Times," in *Coming to Light: American Women Poets in the Twentieth Century,* eds. Diane Wood Middlebrook and Marilyn Yalom, 1985, pp. 214–222. Lucille Clifton, *Quilting,* 1991. Shirley M. Jordan, ed., *Broken Silences: Interviews with Black and White Women Writers,* 1993.

—Joycelyn K. Moody

Clotel. The first known full-length African American *novel, *Clotel,* by William Wells *Brown, was originally published in London as *Clotel, or The President's Daughter: A Narrative of Slave Life in the United States* (1853). It first appeared in the United States as *Miralda, or The Beautiful Quadroon: A Romance of American Slavery Founded on Fact* (serialized in the *Weekly Anglo-African* during the winter of 1860–1861), then in book form, substantially revised, as *Clotelle: A Tale of the Southern States* (1864) and *Clotelle, or The Colored Heroine: A Tale of the Southern States* (1867).

Based on persistent rumors about Thomas Jefferson's relations with a slave mistress, *Clotel* begins with the auction of Jefferson's mistress (Currer) and her two daughters by Jefferson (Clotel and Althesa). Currer and Althesa both die in the course of the narrative, Althesa in particularly tragic circumstances: she has married her owner and raised two daughters as free white women. When she and her husband die, their daughters are sold into *slavery by their father's creditors.

Clotel's owner in Virginia falls in love with her, fathers a child by her, and, despite vague promises of marriage, sells her. She escapes from a slave dealer and returns to Virginia disguised as a white man to free her daughter, Mary, still a house slave. Unfortunately, Clotel returns in the midst of Nat *Turner's *insurrection (1831). The unusually vigilant authorities detect her imposture, seize her, and transfer her to prison in Washington, D.C. When Clotel bolts from her captors, they pursue and trap her on a bridge over the Potomac, and she leaps to her death in the river. Mary ultimately escapes to England, where she marries George Green, another fugitive and a veteran of Turner's rebellion.

Clotel, like other examples of early African American fiction, retains some features of *slave narratives. Brown, himself a fugitive slave, bases many of the novel's details, anecdotes, and characters on incidents and figures in his own life. Like slave narratives, the novel emphasizes its basis in fact in order to buttress its authority as an indictment of slavery. *Clotel,* however, outstrips most slave narratives in its use of a variety of genres and voices, from anecdotes, vignettes of slave life, newspaper accounts, and *folklore to songs, poems, and abolitionist rhetoric.

Clotel also bears a strong resemblance to white abolitionist fiction, especially its predecessor, Harriet

Beecher *Stowe's *Uncle Tom's Cabin* (1852), though Brown's ironic tone sets it somewhat apart from such works. Like Stowe's Little Eva, *Clotel's* Georgiana Peck is a virtuous white woman responsible, just before her own tragic death, for freeing the slaves on her father's plantation. The novel follows abolitionist propaganda in emphasizing slavery's destruction of the family and its corrosive effect on sexual mores, black and white, and contains an important development of the "tragic *mulatto" theme. Most daringly, *Clotel* attacks not only the hypocrisy of slaveowning and slavery-condoning Christians but also the similar hypocrisy of such republican icons as Jefferson, suggesting that the existence of slavery fatally compromised the very ideals of the republic.

[*See also* Antislavery Movement.]

• Robert A. Bone, *The Negro Novel in America*, rev. ed. 1965. William E. Farrison, *William Wells Brown: Author and Reformer*, 1969. Bernard W. Bell, *The Afro-American Novel and Its Tradition*, 1987. William L. Andrews, "The Novelization of Voice in Early African American Narrative," *PMLA* 105.1 (Jan. 1990): 23–34.   —Gary Ashwill

CLOTHES. *See* Dress.

CLUBS. *See* Societies and Clubs.

COBB, CHARLES E., JR. (b. 1943), poet, essayist, and journalist. Charles E. Cobb, Jr., was born in Washington, D.C., in 1943. The son of a Methodist minister, he lived in several eastern states before enrolling in the African American program at Howard University in 1961. He left in 1962 to work for five years with the Student Nonviolent Coordinating Committee (SNCC) in several southern states, and was involved in the tense struggle for voting rights in Mississippi.

Cobb's first volume of poetry, *In the Furrows of the World* (1967), illustrated with his own photographs, grew out of his civil rights work and his 1967 visit to Vietnam. The poems were written in lyrical free verse with little capitalization or punctuation, and expressed concern, anger, and hope. Some of the poems, like "Nation," spoke with quiet eloquence of a time when African Americans would have a proud sense of self and nationhood.

After his SNCC years, Cobb worked with the Center for Black Education in Washington from 1968 to 1969, and then served on the board of directors of Drum and Spear Press from 1969 to 1974. In 1969 he also made an extended visit to Tanzania, where he came to recognize the need for an intensive examination of the link between African Americans and their African heritage. Cobb published another volume of poetry, *Everywhere Is Yours*, in 1971. The eight poems in that volume continued the theme of hope in the face of oppression. One particularly moving poem in the volume, "Koyekwisa Ya Libala," was an account of an African wedding and included several passages of wisdom from the ancient priest, incorporated into the marriage chant. In another poem, "To Vietnam," Cobb implied a parallel between Vietnamese nationalism and the fight against American racism. Cobb also discussed his African experience in *African Note-book: Views on Returning Home* in 1971. He advocated an intensive examination of the link between African Americans and their African heritage, but he also advised against the American tendency to romanticize Africa because of ignorance. His concern with the lesson Africa could teach was also reflected in another poem, "Nation No. 3," from *Everywhere Is Yours*, where he spoke of standing "son to Mother Africa" and claiming all its experience as his own.

Cobb's more recent work as an essayist and journalist has reflected his interest in social, environmental, and political issues. He served as foreign affairs reporter for the Public Broadcasting System from 1976 to 1979, and wrote and produced numerous documentaries from 1979 to 1985. He also wrote freelance articles for several journals, and joined the staff of *National Geographic* in 1985. His credits for *National Geographic* include articles on such places as Grenada, Zimbabwe, and the Outer Banks of North Carolina. Although Cobb has turned his focus away from poetry, his writing has matured, and the vitality and concern with people, their rights and possibilities, that energized his earliest work has continued.

• James Forman, *The Making of Black Revolutionaries*, 1972, pp. 297–299. Charles E. Cobb, Jr., interview by Howell Raines, *My Soul Is Rested*, 1977, pp. 244–248. Clara Williams, "Charles E. Cobb, Jr.," in *DLB*, vol. 41, *Afro-American Poets since 1955*, eds. Trudier Harris and Thadious M. Davis, 1985, pp. 60–64. "Cobb, Charles E., Jr.," in *CA*, vol. 142, ed. James G. Lesniak, 1994, pp. 77–78.
                    —Michael E. Greene

COBB, NED (1885–1973), autobiographer. Born in Alabama, Ned Cobb was a tenant farmer and social activist who spent twelve years in a penitentiary for staging a protest that turned violent. Though an illiterate man, Cobb had a talent for storytelling that enabled him in his eighties to relate the story of his life to Theodore Rosengarten, a Harvard graduate student, who recorded the older man's account and eventually had it published under the title *All God's Dangers: The Life of Nate Shaw* (1974). The book contains a long, episodic narrative that portrays Shaw (Cobb's pseudonym) as a thoughtful and industrious person whose prison sentence resulted from a clear refusal to tolerate social inequality.

In *All God's Dangers*, Shaw appears in contrast to his father, Hayes Shaw, a former slave turned sharecropper, who has grown accustomed to "take what come and live for today." While Nate Shaw observes that the social order confines "poor colored farmers" to an outrageous second-class citizenship and thereby strips them of ambition, from his youth he plans on "climbin up in the world like a boy climbin a tree." By learning as much as he can about farming his crop and diligently applying the knowledge that he gains, Shaw manages to make a decent enough living to raise ten children in "a pretty good old house." His fortune changes, however, beginning in December 1932, when he takes a stand for equality by defying four deputy sheriffs sent to seize a neighbor's property in order to compensate a white landlord. A bloody confrontation lands Shaw in jail for over a decade and decimates his family.

All God's Dangers compares favorably to *slave narratives written by Olaudah *Equiano, Frederick *Douglass, and Harriet A. *Jacobs, all of whom represent learning as a source of *freedom. Shaw's personal narrative belongs to an "as-told-to" tradition of African American *autobiographies transcribed by an *amanuensis, which includes The *Confessions of Nat Turner (1831) as well as The *Autobiography of Malcolm X (1965). Since Shaw lived from the Reconstruction era of the late nineteenth century through the *civil rights movement of the mid-twentieth, his story serves as a valuable chronicle of the manner in which African Americans in rural communities struggled for equality during the period of legal segregation in the United States.

—Roland L. Williams, Jr.

COFFIN ED JOHNSON makes up half of Chester *Himes's two-man African American detective team. Coffin Ed and his partner *Grave Digger Jones almost always act in tandem, and rarely is one seen without the other throughout Himes's nine-book series of detective novels. Like his partner, Coffin Ed is a middle-class workingman who lives in Astoria, Long Island. Each day he and Grave Digger drive together to Harlem, their regular beat as detectives. Leaving behind their stable, yet rarely mentioned, family lives with wives and children, they step daily into the chaotic pandemonium of Himes's Harlem.

*Violence is a relentless part of the two detectives' jobs, indeed of the whole urban environment as created by Himes. Coffin Ed, in fact, suffers a brutal brush with the daily violence of his job: in For Love of Imabelle (1957), Himes's first Harlem crime novel, a villain throws acid in Coffin Ed's face. This vicious attack scars the detective both physically and emotionally for the rest of the series. Coffin Ed's acid-scarred face is often described in grotesque and frightening terms and comes to represent the potential terror he himself could unleash. As a result of this incident, Ed is known to be very quick to the trigger and subject to extremely violent rages when interrogating suspected criminals. This is one of the few characteristics that distinguishes him from his partner, Grave Digger. Grave Digger often acts as the restraining voice or hand when Ed seems close to the edge of excessive force.

• Robert E. Skinner, Two Guns from Harlem: The Detective Fiction of Chester Himes, 1989.   —Wendy W. Walters

COLEMAN, WANDA (b. 1946), poet, short fiction writer, and performer. Identifying herself as an "L. A. poet," Wanda Coleman not only grew up in Los Angeles, California, but also uses that city as her primary urban setting for the raw, imagistically graphic, and politically charged *poetry and *short stories that she writes. Desiring to "rehumanize the dehumanized," Coleman focuses upon the lives of the "down and out"; thus she populates her texts with working-class individuals struggling against daily indignities and social outcasts struggling simply to survive. The primary voice represented in her poems is that of the African American woman whose head is bloodied but unbowed, who is just as tough as the harsh city in which she lives.

Born Wanda Evans in Watts to George and Lewana Evans, Coleman found herself drawn to poetry as a young child, and, encouraged by her parents to write, she published several poems by the time she was fifteen. During the 1960s, she became a political activist and, influenced by Ron Karenga's Afrocentric "US" movement, wrote, as she put it, "for the cause." Later, resisting the rhetoric of political movements, Coleman conceived of her cultural role as that of the artist, not of the political activist or social scientist who felt compelled to be "Wanda the Explainer." Nevertheless, significantly shaped by the *civil rights movement, she continued to write of the disenfranchised and dispossessed, and the themes of racism, sexism, poverty, and marginalization would continue to permeate her work.

Although she resists being defined by any one tradition, Coleman acknowledges that her writing has been influenced by the *blues tradition and the *music of the African American church as well as the prosody of such poets as Ezra Pound, Edgar Allan Poe, and Charles Olson. Moreover, attesting to the hybrid influences of a multicultural Los Angeles, Coleman's work has also been affected by a wide range of cultural images and sounds—from the visceral works of Los Angeles poets such as Charles Bukowski, to the Latino/a influence of the Southwest, to the rhythmic sounds of Black English vernacular. Despite the demands of her life—raising three children, often juggling more than one job—Coleman has found the time to write and perform her works. Since the late 1970s, Coleman has had eight books published: Art in the Court of the Blue Fag (1977), Mad Dog Black Lady (1979), Imagoes (1983), A War of Eyes and Other Stories (1988), Dicksboro Hotel and Other Travels (1989), African Sleeping Sickness: Stories and Poems (1990), Heavy Daughter Blues: Poems and Stories (1991), and Hand Dance (1993).

Although Coleman has gotten some recognition for her work—an Emmy for her writing (1976), a National Endowment for the Arts grant (1981–1982), a Guggenheim Fellowship for poetry (1984)—national fame still eludes her. Distinguishing herself from other African American writers from the South and the East, Coleman sees herself as a distinctly West Coast writer. Despite her ambivalent relationship with Los Angeles, she remains dedicated to depicting the varied lives in the city, giving voice to the dispossessed, making visible the invisible, putting a human face onto anonymous statistics.

• Tony Magistrale, "Doing Battle with the Wolf: A Critical Introduction to Wanda Coleman's Poetry," Black American Literature Forum 23 (Fall 1989): 539–554. Wanda Coleman, "Sweet Mama Wanda Tells Fortunes: An Interview with Wanda Coleman," interview by Tony Magistrale and Patricia Ferreira, Black American Literature Forum 24 (Fall 1990): 491–507. Kathleen K. O'Mara, "Wanda Coleman, in DLB, vol. 130, American Short Story Writers since World War II, ed. Patrick Meanor, 1993, pp. 82–88.   —Sandra K. Stanley

COLLECTIVE BIOGRAPHY refers to books, by one hand or many, that gather brief biographical sketches of notable people. The genre arose in classical antiquity (e.g., Plutarch's *Lives of the Noble Grecians and Romans*) and has flourished virtually ever since. In their modern incarnations, most collective *biographies take their inspiration from Thomas Carlyle's teaching that history is shaped by the lives of great individuals. Because the genre lends itself to popular rather than scholarly uses, collective biographies have usually aimed for inspirational effects, presenting exemplary lives for the admiration of common readers, particularly young ones.

Nineteenth-century America produced hundreds of collective biographies celebrating the achievements of the young nation. But these books normally excluded African Americans, or at best mentioned only a few prominent figures—usually Phillis *Wheatley, Frederick *Douglass, and Sojourner *Truth. A few collective biographies of African Americans were published by white abolitionists: Abigail Field Mott, for example, wrote *Biographical Sketches and Interesting Anecdotes of Persons of Color* (1825), and Lydia Maria Child wrote *The Freedman's Book* (1865; rpt. 1968), both of which, like nearly all the titles mentioned in this entry, can be found in the comprehensive microfiche collection *Black Biographical Dictionaries* (1987).

Beginning in 1855, however, when William C. *Nell produced *The Colored Patriots of the American Revolution* (rpt. 1968), African Americans began collecting the biographies of their own heroes and heroines. William Wells *Brown wrote *The Black Man: His Antecedents, His Genius, and His Achievements* in 1863 (rpt. 1969) and *The Rising Son, or The Antecedents and Advancement of the Colored Race* in 1874 (rpt. 1969), the latter of which, like many African American collective biographies, combines a general narrative of racial progress with biographical sketches of successful individuals to illustrate that progress. William J. Simmons issued *Men of Mark* in 1887 (rpt. 1970); shortly thereafter W. H. Quick and Charles Alexander published *Negro Stars in All Ages of the World* (1890) and *One Hundred Distinguished Leaders* (1899), respectively.

Though some women were included in Brown's *The Rising Son*, these early works typically describe the accomplishments of men. At the turn of the century, however, when middle-class African American women were making their own mark in local and national clubs, entering the literary marketplace in numbers, and leading the race's social uplift efforts, collective biographies devoted exclusively to the achievements of African American women began to be published. The most prominent were Monroe Majors's *Noted Negro Women* (1893; rpt. 1971), L. A. Scruggs's *Women of Distinction* (1893), Gertrude *Mossell's *The Work of the Afro-American Woman* (1894; rpt. 1988), Benjamin *Brawley's *Women of Achievement* (1919), and Hallie Q. *Brown's *Homespun Heroines* (1926; rpt. 1988). Indeed, the turn of the century saw the development of a remarkable subspecialization within the genre of African American collective biography. Hundreds of volumes

whose emphases were geographical (e.g., George F. Bragg's *Men of Maryland*, 1925), sectarian (Susie Shorter's *The Heroines of African Methodism*, 1891), vocational (Susan M. Steward's *Women in Medicine*, 1915), or some combination thereof (Revels Adams's *Cyclopedia of African Methodism in Mississippi*, 1902) were published throughout the period and continue to appear today.

While almost every collective biography published in the nineteenth and twentieth centuries takes as one of its chief aims the inspiration of the youth of the race, the twentieth century witnessed the birth of collective biographies written solely for children: see, for example, *Unsung Heroines* by Elizabeth Haynes (1921), *Stories of Black Folk for Little Folk* by Bessie Landrum (1923), and *For Freedom* by Arthur Huff *Fauset (1927). The tradition persists today: a visit to any large bookstore will reveal a sizable death of recently published works, from James *Haskins's *One More River to Cross* (1992) to the Chelsea House series *Profiles of Great Black Americans* (1994). Many collective biographies, by white and African American authors, were designed specifically as school textbooks to promote self-esteem among African American children and improve race relations by educating their white contemporaries: among the most interesting are YMCA executive Ralph Bullock's *In Spite of Handicaps* (1927), Carter G. *Woodson's *Negro Makers of History* (1928), and *The Upward Climb: A Course in Negro Achievement* (1927) by the Secretary of Literature of the Methodist Episcopal Church, South, Sara Estelle Haskin.

The genre has changed in some respects since 1855; mainly these changes have to do with the genre's sense of audience. The earliest specimens, and those written during the first great flowering of the form, the late-nineteeth-century "nadir" of African American *history, are obviously written as much for white readers as for black ones: they aim not only to inspire African Americans but to defend them against racist assumptions about their intellectual and moral inferiority. Later books—such as those written during the genre's second flowering, roughly 1965 to the present—seem to envisage a substantial African American readership and adopt a tone more celebratory than defensive.

But the continuities across time are pronounced. Most nineteenth-century collective biographies, aiming to impress a white readership, wholeheartedly adopt the values of middle-class culture: African Americans, they protest, are as successful, genteel, and Christain as other middle-class Americans; they are "self-made" men (rising sons) and useful, motherly women (homespun heroines). But modern specimens of the genre are equally enthusiastic in their endorsement of middle-class virtues, particularly those of competitive excellence and high achievement. In *Black Light: The African American Hero* (1993), for example, the radical activist Angela *Davis keeps company with such figures as "Magic" Johnson and Oprah Winfrey, the common denominator being simply their shared achievement of fame. Books like Mary Campbell Mossell-Griffin's *Afro-American Men and Women Who Count* (1915) and

Columbus Salley's *The Black 100: A Ranking of the Most Influential African-Americans, Past and Present* (1993) make their commitment to competitive individualism even more explicit. In fact, such a commitment seems inherent in the form; by emphasizing the role of the individual in his or her elevation, collective biographies—though acknowledging the barriers to African American achievement—almost inevitably encode a politics of self-reliance and an economics of bootstrap capitalism. As William J. Simmons asked his readers in 1887, "If the persons herein mentioned could rise to the exalted stations which they have and do now hold, what is there to prevent any young man or woman from achieving greatness?"

[*See also* Children's and Young Adult Literature.]

• Randall K. Burkett et al., eds., *Black Biographical Dictionaries: 1790–1950*, 1987.

—Elizabeth Elkin Grammer

College Language Association Journal. *See* CLA Journal.

COLLINS, KATHLEEN (1941–1988), playwright, scriptwriter, filmmaker, director, novelist, short story writer, and educator. Born Kathleen Conwell in Jersey City, she was the daughter of Frank and Loretta Conwell. Her father, who had worked as a mortician, became the principal of a high school now named after him and the first black New Jersey state legislator. In 1963, after receiving her BA in philosophy and religion from Skidmore College, Collins worked on black southern voter registration for the Student Nonviolent Coordinating Committee. In 1966 she earned an MA in French literature and cinema through the Middlebury program at Paris's Sorbonne. Joining the editorial and production staff at a New York City Public Broadcasting Service station, Collins worked as a *film editor and began writing stories. In 1974, soon after ending her marriage to Douglas Collins, she became a professor of film history and screenwriting at the City College of New York. Adapting Henry H. Roth's fiction for the screen in *The Cruz Brothers and Mrs. Malloy* (1980), Collins became the first African American woman to write, direct, and produce a full-length feature film. Her film won first prize at the Sinking Creek Film Festival.

Collins's second feature, *Losing Ground* (1982), directed, coproduced, and based on an original screenplay by her, won Portugal's Figueroa de Foz Film Festival and garnered international acclaim. (Her screenplay, which differs in some significant ways from the film, is included in *Screenplays of the African American Experience*, 1991, edited by Phyllis Rauch Klotman.) A philosophical comedy that probes painful and deadly serious experiences, *Losing Ground* begins with a discussion of existentialism's roots in the futile attempt to explain away the chaos of war and ends with a symbolic act of violence that provides a release from order. It centers on a philosophy professor's efforts to escape the confinements of academic living, marriage to an abstract painter who denies her respect and private

space, and her own cold and orderly mind by moving from the analytical study of ecstasy to the experience itself.

While making films, Collins produced equally remarkable *drama. *In the Midnight Hour* (1981) portrayed a black middle-class family at the outset of the *civil rights movement. *The Brothers* (1982) was named one of the twelve outstanding plays of the season by the Theatre Communications Group and published in Margaret B. Wilkerson's *Nine Plays by Black Women* (1986). It delineates the impact of racism and sexism on a black middle-class family from 1948 to 1968 as articulated by six intelligent, witty, and strikingly different women. The brothers themselves, though never seen, are vibrant presences through the women's remarks and mimicry.

In 1983 Collins reencountered Alfred Prettyman whom she had known twenty years earlier and four years later they were married. One week after their marriage, she learned that she had cancer. At the time of her death, she had completed a new screenplay, *Conversations with Julie*, her sixth stage play, *Waiting for Jane*, and a final draft of her *novel, *Lollie: A Suburban Tale*. As more of her work appears, her already fine reputation as filmmaker and playwright will surely rise and be further enhanced by a new reputation in fiction.

• Note: Much of the published information on Kathleen Collins is unreliable, particularly because another writer has the same name and several sources have blended information about the two writers.
Bernard L. Peterson, Jr., "Kathleen Collins," in *Contemporary Black American Playwrights and Their Plays*, 1988, pp. 116–118. Phyllis Rauch Klotman, "Kathleen Collins: Biographical Sketch," in *Screenplays of the African American Experience*, 1991, p. 123. Seret Scott, "Kathleen Conwell Collins Prettyman," in *The Encyclopedia of African American Culture and History*, forthcoming.

—Steven R. Carter

COLONIZATION. *See* Emigration.

Color. Harper and Brothers published *Color*, Countee *Cullen's first volume of verse, in 1925. At the time it was considered a signal event in the *New Negro Renaissance as Cullen, who was well known because most of these poems had been published previously in impressive literary magazines, was so highly regarded by both blacks and whites. Critics received the book more enthusiastically than any subsequent Cullen work. At twenty-two, Cullen seemed a major literary star in the making, a full-blown lyric poet of considerable power and possibilities, more skilled in versification, more educated, and more fully developed as a poetic talent than any of his contemporaries and certainly any of his predecessors. Although ambivalent about seeing himself as a racial poet, about one-third of *Color* deals with African American themes and some of these works—"Heritage," "Incident," "Yet Do I Marvel," and "The Shroud of Color"—are among the most famous and best-remembered poems not only of Cullen's entire canon but also of African American *poetry as a genre. Clearly several of these racial poems established Cullen's main themes of alienation from the white

West, quest for a theological purpose for black suffering, a hatred of segregation and racism, which played upon pity and irony, and the conflict between a Christian present and a pagan past. Most of the poems employ the forms of the sonnet, rhymed couplets, and ballad stanzas, and most were composed while Cullen was an undergraduate at New York University.

• Darwin Turner, *In a Minor Chord: Three Afro-American Writers and Their Search for Identity,* 1971. Alan Shucard, *Countee Cullen,* 1984. Gerald Early, ed., *My Soul's High Song: The Collected Writings of Countee Cullen, Voice of the Harlem Renaissance,* 1991.   —Gerald Early

Colored American Magazine, The.

Colored American Magazine, The. The most widely distributed African American journal before 1910, the *Colored American Magazine* first appeared in May 1900. Featuring articles on a wide variety of subjects of interest to African Americans, this monthly was founded by Walter W. Wallace in Boston and edited for most of the first four years of its existence by Pauline E. *Hopkins. Elizabeth Ammons (*Short Fiction by Black Women, 1900–1920,* 1991) and Abby and Ronald Johnson (*Propaganda and Aesthetics: The Literary Politics of African-American Magazines in the Twentieth Century,* 1991) have acknowledged the key role that Hopkins and the *Colored American Magazine* played at the start of the century in encouraging, *publishing, and promoting literary works by African American writers. The author of a significant percentage of the fiction and nonfiction that appeared within the pages of the magazine, Hopkins regarded herself as a race historian. She strove to create an audience for her revisionist race *history, frequently invoking New England's abolitionist past in the hopes of reviving the spirit of protest during an era characterized by *violence and disenfranchisement campaigns against African Americans. Amidst advertisements for Frederick *Douglass watches and products reputed to lighten skin color and straighten hair, Hopkins pursued a politically charged cultural agenda that challenged the accommodationist policies of the influential Booker T. *Washington. Hopkins paid the price for her unconciliatory editorial policies in 1904 when Washington's ally Fred Moore bought the *Colored American Magazine,* moved its offices to New York, and fired her. The journal reached a peak readership estimated at fifteen thousand in 1905; it ceased publication in November 1909.

[*See also* Journalism; Periodicals, *article on* Black Periodical Press.]

• Penelope L. Bullock, *The Afro-American Periodical Press, 1838–1909,* 1981. Brian Joseph Benson, "Colored American," in *Black Journals of the United States,* ed. Walter C. Daniel, 1982, pp. 123–130.   —John C. Gruesser

COLOR LINE.

COLOR LINE. The color line is a means of measuring an individual's identity and social sense of being strictly by skin pigmentation or racial origin. Of crucial significance is the term's dual interracial and intraracial definitions as Blacks interact with whites and with members of their own race. On the interracial level, the color line connotes institutionalized racism and prejudices that were originated to segregate, oppress, and instill in Blacks a sense of inferiority to the dominant race. The color dividing line of American racism identifies the superior race as white and right, while the second-class race is recognized as dark inferiors whose burden of blackness is to experience the humiliating effects of *Jim Crow and a double-conscious identity. Appropriately, then, W. E. B. *Du Bois stated in 1903 that "the problem of the twentieth century is the problem of the color line."

In the intraracial context, the color line refers to the self-imposed color prejudices and subsequent class divisions that exist within the Black race and between Blacks of various skin hues. The lighter the skin, supposedly, the closer kinship to whiteness and perfection to "pass," as is illustrated in the intraracial writings of Charles Waddell *Chesnutt, Nella *Larsen, Jessie Redmon *Fauset, Wallace *Thurman, Ralph *Ellison, and Toni *Morrison, who explore the dynamics of being light-skinned and color struck. Color line prejudice within and outside the race affects social and psychological wholeness.

[*See also* Double Consciousness; Passing (the term).]   —Pearlie Peters

Color Purple, The.

Color Purple, The. *The Color Purple* (1982) is Alice *Walker's most magnificent and controversial literary achievement. The *novel outraged African American male critics as well as a few female critics who argued that Walker's story did not reveal an accurate picture of African American life. One California mother was so insulted by the novel's content that she attempted to ban it from public school libraries. Others claimed that the novel was flawed because it defined a woman's *identity in relationship to her sexual experiences. Even the language of the novel's protagonist has been found lacking. Regardless of its initial reception, accolades for Walker's piercing story of an abused, African American woman have included the Pulitzer Prize (1983), the National Book Award (1983), and an Academy Award nomination. It has attracted the appreciation of the masses and ignited passions within both popular culture and academic thought.

The Color Purple is the first African American, woman-authored, *epistolary novel. It embodies Walker's womanist views without being reduced to a mere platform for ideological rhetoric. In this novel, Walker's writing reveals the transformative power of female bonding and female love. It offers frank portrayals of bisexual, *lesbian, and heterosexual relationships amidst situations that penetrate the core of female spiritual and emotional development.

The novel opens with a demand for silence that leaves a fourteen-year-old girl named *Celie with no way to express her pain and confusion except in the *letters she writes to God. Celie is raped repeatedly by her stepfather, Alphonso, and has two children by him—children he gives away without her consent. Later, she is forced into a loveless marriage, leaving her sister Nettie alone with Alphonso. Nettie escapes his sexual advances by moving in with Celie and her husband, Mr. Albert ———. This arrangement is no better than the previous one and Nettie is again forced to leave. She ultimately ends up in Africa where she writes to Celie of her experiences.

For Celie, marriage is nothing more than a shift within the quicksands of abuse and male domination. Albert beats her because she is not *Shug Avery, the woman he loves but does not have the courage to marry. Surprisingly, Celie and Shug develop an intimate relationship. More than anyone, Shug's influential presence and acceptance give Celie the strength she needs to redefine herself, take charge of her life, and leave Albert. Shug and Celie move to Memphis where Celie begins a career designing and selling unisex pants. After her stepfather's death, she returns to her family home. Nettie also returns with Celie's two children. The novel ends with a reconciliation of Celie and Albert's friendship.

Both *The Color Purple* and the subsequent *film directed by Steven Spielberg (1985) have opened the minds of millions to the plight of African American women in crisis. If knowledge and personal insight is empowering, then *The Color Purple* offers those who acknowledge its truths a wealth of strength. And for women like Celie, it is a starting point for change and healing.

[*See also* Sexuality; Womanism.]

• Calvin C. Hernton, "Who's Afraid of Alice Walker," in *The Sexual Mountain and Black Women Writers: Adventures in Sex, Literature and Real Life*, 1987, pp. 1–36. Henry Louis Gates, Jr., "Color Me Zora: Alice Walker's (Re) Writing of the Speakerly Text," in *The Signifying Monkey*, 1988, pp. 239–258.   —Debra Walker King

COLTER, CYRUS (b. 1910), novelist, lawyer, U.S. Army captain, and professor. After careers in government service, law, the army, and academia, Cyrus Colter began writing at fifty. Colter placed his first *short story, "A Chance Meeting," in *Threshold* in 1960. He went on to place stories in such little magazines as *New Letters, Chicago Review*, and *Prairie Schooner*. Fourteen of his stories are collected in his first book, *The Beach Umbrella* (1970). In 1990 Colter published a second collection of short fiction, *The Amoralists and Other Tales*.

Colter's first *novel, *The Rivers of Eros* (1972) relates the efforts of Clotilda Pilgrim to raise her grandchildren to lives of respectability. When Clotilda discovers that her sixteen-year-old granddaughter is involved with a married man, the grandmother becomes obsessed with the idea that the girl is repeating her grandmother's own youthful mistakes. Clotilda eventually kills the girl in order to stop what she perceives as a pattern of transgression. Other memorable characters include Clotilda's roomer Ambrose Hammer, who is researching a "History of the Negro Race," and the granddaughter's lover, who in contrast with the hopeful Hammer, is cynical about the prospects of blacks in America. *Rivers* is significant for its portrayal of a range of black society, as well as for its representation of *place, its Chicago setting.

The Hippodrome (1973), a more experimental novel, opens with Jackson Yeager, a writer on Christian topics, in flight, carrying his wife's head in a bag.

She had been involved with a white man, who was left mutilated by Yeager. Yeager finds refuge with Bea, who runs the Hippodrome, where blacks perform a sexual theater for whites. Yeager is required to perform yet cannot bring himself to do so. He flees and is joined by Darlene, who has also escaped from the Hippodrome, which Yeager comes to think of as perhaps a fantasy. Critics noting Yeager's sense of being subject to chance, of discrepancies between appearance and reality, and his feelings of the absurdity of life suggest the novel's existentialist French connection.

With *Night Studies* (1980) Colter returned to what some have regarded as his own realist-naturalist ground. In the first book of this four-part work, we are introduced to the three main characters: John Calvin Knight, leader of the Black Peoples Congress; Griselda Graves, a seemingly white young woman unaware of her black racial heritage, who appears irresistibly drawn to the Black Peoples Congress political organization; and Mary Dee Adkins, a young black woman of wealthy background. When she learns that marriage to her white lover is not a possibility because of his family's opposition, Mary Dee, too, plunges into the black political movement.

Following an assassination attempt, John Knight is hospitalized. Under medication and through semiconscious reveries Knight envisions scenes of the *Middle Passage, *slavery, and Reconstruction. This panorama of African American *history comprises Book Two. Following a climactic scene at the end of Book Three, in which Knight vainly attempts to promulgate his moderate position at an unruly meeting of the Black Peoples Congress, Book Four concludes with Knight's retreat from political activity to solitary study—"night studies"—of black history. Critics have acknowledged Colter's effective presentation of a wide range of black and white voices in *Night Studies*, as well as the novel's compelling suggestion of the influence of the African American past on present America.

In his complexly structured narrative of *A Chocolate Soldier* (1988) Colter continues his exploration of black social history through the central character, Rollo "Cager" Lee. A questionably reliable theological student manqué narrates this work, in contrast with an anonymous third-person narrator used in Colter's previous novels. As Reginald Gibbons has noted, in reformulating in *A Chocolate Soldier* the question "Why *were* we slaves?"—the essential question that haunted Knight in *Night Studies*—Colter raises issues of black history as well as issues about the novel itself.

In his late work *City of Light* (1993) Colter presents Paul Kessey, a fair-skinned, wealthy Princeton graduate who founds in Paris the Coterie, a group whose aim is to establish an African homeland for disaffected blacks of the diaspora. In addition to important political and class themes, *City of Night* is noteworthy for its psychological study of Kessey, who has obsessively focused his love on two unattainable women, his dead mother and his mistress, who is happily married to someone else. Overall, Colter's life and work exemplify the worth of growth, experiment, and change.

• Robert M. Farnsworth, "Conversation with Cyrus Colter," *New Letters* 39 (Spring 1973): 16–39. John O'Brien, *Interviews with Black Writers*, 1973, pp. 17–33. Robert M. Bender, "The Fiction of Cyrus Colter," *New Letters* 48 (Fall 1981): 92–103. Helen R. Houston, "Cyrus Colter," in *DLB*, vol. 33, *Afro-American Fiction Writers After 1955*, eds. Thadious M. Davis and Trudier Harris, 1984, pp. 48–52. Gilton Gregory Cross et al., "Fought for It and Paid Taxes Too: Four Interviews with Cyrus Colter," *Callaloo* 14 (Fall 1991): 855–897. Reginald Gibbons, "Colter's Novelistic Contradictions," *Callaloo* 14 (Fall 1991): 898–905.

—James Robert Payne

COLTRANE, JOHN (1926–1967), saxophonist, composer, and iconic figure. John Coltrane's immersion in modern *jazz took place in bands led by Eddie Vinson, Dizzy Gillespie, and Johnny Hodges. In 1955 he joined the Miles *Davis quintet and was soon identified as one of the most talented tenor saxophonists of the era. The story of Coltrane becoming a major African American cultural icon really began, however, in 1957. In that year he underwent a spiritual "conversion" concomitant with his overcoming a drug addiction. A brief but salient collaboration with Thelonius Monk followed and Coltrane was on his way to becoming one of the major innovators in jazz. Associated with the radical improvisatory style called "Free Jazz" (or pejoratively "anti-jazz"), Coltrane's own contribution was sometimes referred to as "sheets of sound," a lightning fast style of improvisation, with great attention given to melodic freedom. His mid-1960s recordings were increasingly complex and dense, often reflecting an interest in Eastern and African music, and were marked by radical experimentation in instrumentation. Coltrane died at age forty of a liver ailment.

Coltrane had a major impact on literary artists who came of age in the 1960s. Kimberly Benston has suggested that the "Coltrane poem" exists as a distinct genre within contemporary African American literature. Coltrane's premature death has generated a most compelling body of elegies. There is no question that at some level many artists were affected by his creativity and genius, but the evidence suggests that Coltrane's spirituality as much as his musicianship created disciples. Coltrane's monumental 1964 work *A Love Supreme* became a kind of musical scripture to many poets, novelists, and playwrights. His commitment to experimentation, his cross-cultural interests, in addition to his search for a life contrary to the sterility of the mainstream, made Coltrane a hero to a generation whose hopes were nurtured by the energy of the *Black Arts movement.
[*See also* Music.]

• Art Lange and Nathaniel Mackey, *Moment's Notice: Jazz in Poetry and Prose*, 1993. Eric Nisenson, *Ascension: John Coltrane and His Quest*, 1993. —James C. Hall

Comedy: American Style, Jessie Redmon *Fauset's last *novel (1933), challenges and revises "tragic *mulatto" and "*passing" fiction wherein characters born of mixed parentage are plagued with fears and unattainable desires aroused by their mixed blood. If they are able to pass for white, they are unable to lead normal lives because they fear that telltale markings of "blood" will reveal their secret. Many of Fauset's characters are only phenotypically mulatto—both parents are "black"—thus subverting conventional use of the mulatto, of passing, and, indeed, the blood theory.

The protagonist of *Comedy: American Style*, Olivia Blanchard, is obsessed with skin color. Influenced early by the racist notions of a white school teacher and by her own mother's admitted *class consciousness and habits of passing, light-skinned Olivia has internalized the ideology of white superiority and grows into a cold, selfish, manipulative woman whose goal is to marry a light-skinned man. She eventually marries Christopher Cary, not because she loves him, but because he is fair enough to give her "white" children through whom, the text says, she could "obtain her heart's desire." Similarly misguided by a well-meaning mother, young Christopher marries Olivia because he sees in her the coldness he has been taught marks a "good woman." After the birth of their children—Teresa, Christopher, Jr., and Oliver—he watches passively as Olivia nearly destroys their entire family and, indeed, completely destroys their only "dark" child, Oliver. At the end of the novel, it is Christopher, Jr., and his wife, Phebe, with their devotion to family and race pride, who attempt to rebuild everything Olivia has destroyed.

Fauset's detractors have generally misread Olivia's color-mania and other values as signs of Fauset's own attitudes, thereby misinterpreting the significance of her extensive descriptions of household furnishings, her emphasis on various characters' physical attributes, and her emphasis on origins. Carolyn Wedin Sylvander, Fauset's biographer, and a few other scholars counter misreadings by exploring Fauset's "deliberate" use of rhetorical strategies, such as satire to critique bourgeois society. Olivia Blanchard Cary is not exemplary in any positive sense, despite her money, polished manners, and white skin. The portraiture of Olivia is in fact the most scathing indictment of a black mother written by a black woman up to this time.

The irony of the title *Comedy: American Style* may be read, in part, as an articulation of Fauset's belief in the comic incongruities of human existence. Further, that the novel is structurally built on the elements of a play shows Fauset's continued experimentation with form, something she shares with other *Harlem Renaissance writers. Also like them, she addresses a wide range of social and racial issues, which scholars have begun to explore in an attempt to reevaluate the significance of Jessie Fauset's contribution to the complex cultural movement of 1920s Harlem.

• Carolyn Wedin Sylvander, *Jessie Redmon Fauset, Black American Writer*, 1981. Jacquelyn Y. McLendon, *The Politics of Color in the Fiction of Jessie Fauset and Nella Larsen*, 1995. —Jacquelyn Y. McLendon

COMMUNISM. The term "Communism" refers specifically to the politics and ideas associated with the Third International of the Communist Party, organized by the Soviet Union in 1919, but in a broader sense the term has also come to encompass rival currents to the Communist Party, and within Marxist thought, as well: socialists, Trotskyists, and unaffiliated Marxists, among others. Within this context, the relationships between African American writers and Communism span several decades, from the years immediately following World War I to the 1950s, and vary considerably—depending, among other factors, upon the writers' backgrounds, their social and literary networks, and the nature and duration of their commitment to Marxist politics.

Beginning with the poet Claude *McKay, who in 1919 enthusiastically embraced the ideals of the Russian Revolution from the vantage point of his position as a staff member of Max Eastman's radical magazine the *Liberator*, many African American writers and intellectuals responded to the appeal of Communism during the next several decades. In addition to the *Liberator*, other radical magazines during the 1920s opened their pages to black writers and to discussions of African American art and culture, most notably Mike Gold's *New Masses* and V. F. Calverton's *Modern Quarterly*. An independent Marxist, Calverton turned *Modern Quarterly* into a forum for African American writers in the late 1920s, routinely featuring articles by Alain *Locke, W. E. B. *Du Bois, E. Franklin Frazier, and George S. *Schuyler. With the outset of the Great Depression, the Communist Party–organized John Reed Clubs offered yet another outlet for aspiring writers and artists.

Claude McKay traveled to the Soviet Union in 1922 to see firsthand the Soviet experiment. He attended the Fourth Congress of the Third Communist International in Moscow, sat on the same platform with Comintern chairman Zinoviev, and discussed racial conditions in the United States with Leon Trotsky. When he returned to the United States in 1934, however, after a twelve-year absence, he was bitterly disillusioned with the Communist Party. McKay's disillusionment had no impact upon those writers who saw in the rhetoric and programs of the Communist Party a radical alternative to the bleak conditions facing the black community during the Great Depression—most notably the two most well-known African American writers of the 1930s: Langston *Hughes and Richard *Wright. During this period the poet Hughes moved very far to the left, closely associating with the New York John Reed Club and *New Masses* magazine and freely lending his name to a number of causes supported by the Communist Party. Although Hughes never joined the Communist Party, and in fact spent a great deal of his subsequent life denying that he did, he embraced its rhetoric in his poetry and public statements. Richard Wright joined the Chicago John Reed Club in 1932 and took membership in the Communist Party shortly afterward, a relationship he maintained until 1944. During the mid-1930s in Chicago, Wright was a central figure in the South Side Writers Group, a group that included the playwright Theodore *Ward, the poet and novelist Margaret *Walker, and the poet Frank Marshall *Davis, among others. According to

Margaret Walker, this group collectively developed the ideas Wright later published as "Blueprint for Negro Writing," an early attempt to reconcile the claims of Marxism and black nationalism. Wright also served as associate editor of Dorothy *West's magazine *New Challenge*, playing a critical role in pushing the editorial policy of the magazine toward the left before its demise in 1937.

During the period of the Communist Party's greatest influence in American public life and the black community, the 1930s to the eve of World War II, the imprint of its ideas could be seen in all genres of African American writing: in Melvin B. *Tolson's newspaper column, "Caviar and Cabbage," as well as in his poetry, which began to appear in V. F. Calverton's *Modern Monthly* and *Modern Quarterly* in the late 1930s; in Frank Marshall Davis's two collections of poetry, *Black Man's Verse* (1935) and *I Am the American Negro* (1937); in Arna *Bontemps's 1936 novel *Black Thunder*; in Theodore Ward's 1938 play *Big White Fog*; and in Richard Wright's first collection of short stories, *Uncle Tom's Children* (1938), and, of course, his best-selling 1940 novel *Native Son*. The imprint of Marxist ideas can also be seen in the poetry and criticism of Sterling A. *Brown, in Robert *Hayden's first collection of poetry, *Heartshape in the Dust* (1940), in Margaret Walker's *For My People* (1942), and in William *Attaway's novels *Let Me Breathe Thunder* (1939) and *Blood on the Forge* (1941). In *theater, the pioneering efforts of Langston Hughes's Suitcase Theater provided the prototype for peoples' theaters in black communities in other parts of the country. It was also an important antecedent to the Rose McClendon Players, the American Negro Theatre, and the Negro Playwrights Company—efforts which, in turn, helped to shape the outlook and careers of Alice *Childress, Ossie *Davis, Ruby Dee, and Lorraine *Hansberry, among others.

By the 1950s a dramatic shift in the political climate of the United States, the outlook of the Communist Party, the political culture of the left, and the sensibilities of a new generation of African American writers signaled a corresponding shift in the tenor and direction of African American writing. Although Lloyd *Brown's 1951 novel *Iron City* located itself squarely within a tradition of African American Marxist values, the dominant mood was expressed most fully by Ralph *Ellison's *Invisible Man* (1952) and Richard Wright's *The Outsider* (1953)—two novels that, in symbolic and literal terms, called into question the ideology and rhetoric of Communism.

Although the dominant narrative about the relationships between African American writers and Communism has been constructed as a cautionary tale of seduction and betrayal, recent scholarship points to a wider range of political involvement by African American writers than is sometimes assumed, and a more complex and varied range of responses to Marxist ideology and politics. Although most African American writers did not join the Communist Party, many of them were attracted by its programs and rhetoric, appropriating what they found useful in their pursuit of an imaginative vision of American life. From the late 1920s through the 1950s, the Communist Party occupied the center of a vital political culture, one that clearly left its imprint upon successive generations of African American writers.

• Wilson Record, *The Negro and the Communist Party*, 1951; rpt. 1971. Harold Cruse, *The Crisis of the Negro Intellectual*, 1967; rpt. 1984. Mark Naison, *Communists in Harlem during the Depression*, 1984. Barbara Foley, *Radical Representations: Politics and Form in U.S. Proletarian Fiction*, 1929–1941, 1993. Alan M. Wald, *Writing from the Left: New Essays on Radical Culture and Politics*, 1994. Earl Ofari Hutchinson, *Blacks and Reds: Race and Class in Conflict 1919–1990*, 1995.
—James A. Miller

Confessions of Nat Turner, The.

Page for page, no antebellum *slave narrative had a swifter impact on the American public than *The Confessions of Nat Turner* (1831). Published by its Virginian author, a white lawyer and slaveholder named Thomas R. Gray, and printed by Lucas & Deaver, Baltimore, the book followed quickly upon the capture and execution, 5 November 1831, of Nat *Turner. Quickly copyrighted, as many as forty or fifty thousand copies were printed. Public curiosity and horror at news of the bloodiest of nineteenth-century American slave revolts led Gray to compile *The Confessions* speedily and successfully. Historians and critics allege that the book has become a rarity, although many university and some public libraries possess copies. A second edition appeared in 1881 and many reprints followed in this century, especially during the 1960s after the publication of William Styron's controversial novel *The Confessions of Nat Turner* (1967).

Part dictation, part paraphrase of Turner, and part editorial commentary by Gray, the narrative must be read with caution. Nevertheless, Gray is a prime source of information and ideology associated with Nat Turner's life and the revolt and one white Southerner's immediate response. Gray's horrified condemnation of the slave's messianic attack upon *slavery is mixed with mystery and finally with awe. Turner's reported words encourage these responses. The prophet role adopted by Turner and enthusiastically embraced by northern abolitionists and later by African Americans and their allies, emerges in passages of succinct power such as the following: "Ques. Do you not find yourself mistaken now? Ans. Was not Christ crucified." Another is Gray's summary:

> He is a complete fanatic, or plays his part most admirably. The calm, deliberate composure with which he spoke of his late deeds and intentions, the expression of his fiend-like face when excited by enthusiasm, still bearing the stains of the blood of helpless innocence about him; clothed with rags and covered with chains; yet daring to raise his manacled hands to heaven, with a spirit soaring above the attributes of man; I looked on him and my blood curdled in my veins.

In the 1830s, these passages played persuasively upon diverse readers' imaginations disturbed also by historic events: in the North, the spread of the *antislavery movement, the appearance of William Lloyd Garrison's *Liberator*, John Browne *Russwurm's *Freedom's Journal*, and David *Walker's *Appeal*. In Virginia and across the South, as the slave population grew, Nat Turner helped provoke a historic debate on abolition in the Virginia legislature (1831–1832) and the strengthening of Black Codes, and reawakened anxious memories of the conspiracies of Gabriel Prosser (1800) and Denmark Vesey (1822). American authors have long been inspired by *The Confessions*, notably Harriet Beecher *Stowe, Arna *Bontemps, Robert *Hayden, Herbert Aptheker, Daniel Panger, Vincent Harding, and Sherley Anne *Williams.

[See also Autobiography; Insurrections; Violence.]

• Herbert Aptheker, *Nat Turner's Slave Rebellion*, 1966. Albert E. Stone, *The Return of Nat Turner*, 1992.
—Albert E. Stone

Conjure Woman, The.

A collection of seven *short stories by Charles Waddell *Chesnutt published in 1899, *The Conjure Woman* focuses on plantation and slave life in eastern North Carolina. Written in the local color tradition, the work reveals Chesnutt's mastery of the dialect story and the *plantation tradition popular in the late nineteeth century. Unlike the fiction of such white writers as Thomas Nelson Page and Joel Chandler Harris, Chesnutt's stories do not sentimentalize plantation life in the Old South. Instead, *The Conjure Woman* reveals the destructive and dehumanizing force of *slavery.

Set in Patesville (Fayetteville), North Carolina, the stories contain both a frame narrator and a folk narrator. John, a midwestern businessman transplanted to the South, takes up grape cultivation as a living and hires *Uncle Julius McAdoo, an aged ex-slave, as his coachman. John's narration provides the outer framework for the stories, while Uncle Julius's tales about slave life, *conjuring, and superstitions create a complex inner structure.

As a newcomer to the South, John's favorable descriptions of the countryside, the agricultural potential of the area, and the pleasing manners and customs of its people render an idyllic portrait of the New South. In certain respects, *The Conjure Woman* can be viewed as part of the reconciliation movement in southern literature that developed after the Civil War to appeal to both northern and southern readers. Uncle Julius enhances this conciliatory effort to a small degree, as one of his purposes is to instruct John, his wife Annie, and the reader about southern life and culture. On the surface, he seems simple and naive, but he successfully uses his wily storytelling gifts to outwit his employer. Moreover, the stories Julius tells subtly undercut the wholesome picture of the New South that John describes in his frame narration.

A masterful *trickster, Julius tells stories that reveal the inglorious past of the plantation South. His stories center on the conjuring activities of *Aun' Peggy, a freewoman who earns her living through working spells and magic. In most of the stories, Julius describes the plight of slaves whose only real defense against the inhumanity of slavery lies in Aun' Peggy's conjure spells. In "Mars Jeems Nightmare," she turns a plantation owner into a slave, and he learns firsthand of his overseer's cruelty. In "Po' Sandy," "Sis Becky's Pickaninny," and "Hot Foot Hannibal," slaves turn to Aun' Peggy's magic to help keep their loved ones close, sometimes to no avail. In "The Goophered Grapevine" Aun' Peggy's conjuring serves less sympathetic purposes when she casts a spell on Mars Dugal's grapevines to keep the slaves from stealing the scuppernongs. Henry, an aged slave, falls victim to her conjuring and finds that his life mysteriously and tragically parallels the growing process of the vines.

In "The Conjurer's Revenge" and "The Gray Wolf's Ha'nt," Uncle Julius shifts the focus from Aun' Peggy to free black conjure *men*, whose spells are used for spite and revenge against plantation slaves. In "The Conjurer's Revenge" a slave is transformed into a mule for stealing from the conjurer, while in "The Gray Wolf's Ha'nt" another slave suffers a conjurer's evil and vengeful retaliation for the death of the conjurer's son.

While stories in *The Conjure Woman* do not tackle the social and racial problems explored in Chesnutt's *The *Wife of His Youth and Other Stories of the Color Line* (1899), Uncle Julius's tales are emotionally moving and contain deeply troubling messages about slavery. Most important, they reveal the essential humanity of slave characters with great empathy and understanding.

• William L. Andrews, *The Literary Career of Charles W. Chesnutt*, 1980. Eric J. Sundquist, "Charles Chesnutt's Cakewalk," in *To Wake the Nations*, 1993, pp. 271–454.

—Paula Gallant Eckard

CONJURING, a complex system of magic referred to by a variety of terms, including "roots," "goopher," "gris-gris," "hands," "hoodoo," "mojo," "juju," and (in the Caribbean) "obeah." This folk system is a syncretistic blend of Christianity and African Old World religions. It developed when enslaved Africans in the New World transformed their respective native religious practices and beliefs to combat the enslavers' systematic suppression of African institutional religions and cultural symbols. The oppressive *slavery system in the United States openly denounced the legitimacy of African religious practices and, for the most part, discouraged any public manifestation of African religious expressions. Powerful native *religions, religious leaders, and customs were viewed as a threat to the establishment and an affront to a "civilized," Christian world. Consequently the brutal enslavement process and other New World conditions imposed on African Americans prevented a reconstitution of indigenous African forms, but rather religious elements and ritualistic practices merged in a new environment absent of the respected Old World temple and its legitimacy.

Conjuring as practiced in African American communities in North and South America and the Caribbean emerged as a tradition deeply rooted in African religious views about magic, the universe, the spirit world, and the nature of existence. It is based upon the assumption that events of the material world are not accidental but rather determined by an invisible world inhabited by spirits and forces. These spirits presumably may be influenced for good or evil. It is believed that, under certain conditions, phenomena of this unseen world may cause sudden death or disrupt one's physical, social, psychological, and/or financial well-being. Illness, disease, and misfortune are the direct result of an human agent's ill will or malevolent actions toward a victim. Similar medico-religious folk systems include *curanderismo* in some Latino communities and shamanism in Native American communities.

The conjurer functions as an intermediary between the material and the spirit worlds. She is expected to provide a diagnosis, identify the source of the problem, cast a spell upon a selected victim through the use of charms and/or poison for the purpose of avenging the malignant deeds of an enemy, provide counteractants to remove a spell that has been placed maliciously upon a victim, provide a protective "hand" or charm for a client to help him control antagonistic circumstances, give advice in the management of daily affairs, and predict future events. Conjurers assist in matters related to health, love, and social, economic, and personal empowerment.

The materials used in conjuring vary among root doctors (a term used interchangeably with conjurers) and are dependent upon their availability in particular geographic regions. In large urban areas rootworking paraphernalia, including candles, incense burners, oils, roots, powders, rabbits' feet, and crosses may be openly displayed in various shop windows such as that in front of Prophet David's office in Ann *Petry's *The *Street* (1946). During the slavery era root workers were more likely to obtain their materials through less commercial means given the availability of medicinal herbs and wildlife before extensive land development and urban migration. The most frequently used conjuring materials are roots such as *High John the Conqueror and asafetida; whiskey; reptiles; goopher dust (dirt from a grave); ashes from the fireplace; black cats' bones and rabbits' feet; human body elements of a victim such as urine, strands of hair from the pubic area and armpits, fingernails, and pieces of skin; personal effects of a victim such as underclothes, socks, and menstrual cloth; and red flannel for shielding charms.

Conjuring as a medico-religious folk system has maintained an unorthodox status in this Christian Eurocentric society that came to valorize the scientific biomedical model of Western medicine. The illegitimate position in which rootworking has been placed by powerful institutions such as the medical and religious establishments largely affects how the tradition functions in a community in terms of the credibility of those associated with the tradition, the compatibility of the tradition with competing frameworks, and the accessibility of specialists providing services.

Root workers must be met with approval by some level of the community to practice. Some may keep an affiliation with organized religion and claim to be a minister, counselor, or teacher. This connection may enhance the compatibility component of the tradition with Christianity and make it appear less threatening. Others may choose to disassociate themselves from Christian sects, like the priests in Oyotunjui Village or the "African Village," located a few miles south of Sheldon, South Carolina. The villagers identify themselves as Yoruba and have made a conscious effort to subscribe to beliefs and practices derived from West African models. Ultimately, it is the reputation (personal and "professional") conjurers establish that determines whether they can remain a viable resource (though certainly not without controversy) in the community. Most clients learn about the "legitimate" (those sanctioned by members in the community but not necessarily the establishment) and the fraudulent conjurers through word of mouth. Those with perceived success rates will be recommended highly in very discreet ways.

In considering the origins of the conjuring tradition, Olaudah *Equiano's eighteenth-century slave narrative entitled *The Life of Olaudah Equiano, or Gustavus Vassa, the African* (1789) is a telling example of how religion, medicine, and magic were interconnected in his native land of Benin (a part of Nigeria), where the priests were the healers, soothsayers, and magicians. These medical specialists, known as wise men and *ah-affoe-way*, were held in high regard by the society and, according to Equiano, were quite capable of healing wounds, expelling poisons, and determining maligned behavior, including jealousy, theft, and poisoning. Equally revealing in this narrative is the problematic relationship the enslaved Christian narrator maintains in regard to his African origins. On the one hand, he fondly recalls a rich culture from which he was brutally taken away. On the other hand, he embraces the prejudices of his enslavers by referring to Africans as "uncivilized" beings inferior to Europeans. Such ambivalence is manifested in other texts, including *Narrative of the Life of Frederick Douglass* (1845) where Frederick *Douglass embraces some level of belief in conjuring by taking the root that Sandy offers him as a protection against Edward Covey's brutality. William Wells *Brown, in *My Southern Home* (1880), talks about the reality of Dinkie's conjuring ability and the fear that it induced in blacks and whites on the Poplar Farm. Both narrators denounce this power as the "devil's work."

Zora Neale *Hurston's pioneering works, *Mules and Men* (1935) and *Tell My Horse* (1938), were the first extensive studies to examine conjuring on its own terms. Challenging the Western biases of her audience, Hurston points out similarities between Christianity and conjuring. She reminds her audience that some of the greatest conjurers have come from the Bible. The idea of the Bible as conjuring book is taken seriously in her 1939 novel *Moses, Man of the Mountain* where she fuses the Old Testament Moses with the *Moses of black *folklore. She traces his development as a magician and rebel leader of the Hebrew people.

Hurston's fieldwork on voodoo took her to New Orleans, Jamaica, and Haiti. Remarkably, she exposes the underground world of the conjurer, revealing the specifics of clandestine rituals. Indeed her

participation in a death ritual to kill "the enemy" of a conjurer's client is controversial, particularly when the enemy dies.

The conjuring motif operates on significant levels in African American culture and, by extension, the literary canon. Its repeated presence in the literature bespeaks the fascination that folk and literary artists have maintained toward this tradition. The transformative power of words combined with symbolic acts is at the heart of the "magic" of conjuring. The notion that words can heal, maim, or kill is an ancient one and indeed appealing to the literary imagination. Tales of love and the possibility of its manipulation through conjuration, rebellion against an unjust system, and revenge against perceived enemies are some dominant themes.

In the literature, love as an overpowering emotion between a male and female is depicted as leading to temporary fullfillment for both partners. While the community may sanction what seemingly is the "ideal union," this relationship invariably will be challenged by one of questionable character who, for selfish reasons, wants the relationship terminated. The personal vulnerabilities of either character will become intensified once the potential lover seeks the help of a conjurer to destroy the "ideal union" by casting a spell on the unsuspecting victim. When the roots begin to work, the conjured victim will go against societal norms and abandon his loving partner for the arms of the malevolent character. Formulaic actions of this sort are evident in such texts as Paul Laurence *Dunbar's "The Conjuring Contest" (1899) and Hurston's *Jonah's Gourd Vine* (1934). Harmony in the community is disrupted while the ill-matched pair are passionately involved. Balance is restored when another conjurer provides a counteractant to break the spell, or some other force causes the victim to regain his sanity. In *Jonah's Gourd Vine*, the powerful memory of John Pearson's dead wife, Lucy, frees him from the spell of the undesirable Hattie Tyson.

The theme of rebellion for the purpose of individual and/or group liberation has been at the forefront of African American struggles. The literature contains numerous examples of characters using conjuration to protect individual autonomy and to aid in group liberation. Gullah Jack, a conjurer, and the most valuable player in the historical Denmark Vesey conspiracy, convinced those who joined the slave rebellion that they would have immunity from danger and threatened the recalcitrants with the wrath of the gods. In Arna *Bontemps's novel *Black Thunder* (1936), old Catfish Primus makes a "fighting hand" for all the young men joining Gabriel Prosser's massive slave insurrection in Richmond, Virginia. Similarly, in Charles Waddell *Chesnutt's "The Conjurer's Revenge" (from *The *Conjure Woman*, 1899), Primus defies the rules restricting movement imposed upon the slaves while whites pretend to be unaware of his goings and comings.

Ideally, conjurers are believed to possess the power to withstand death and to alter their appearance, character, or circumstances, or those of their clients. *Pilate Dead in Toni *Morrison's *Song of

Solomon (1977) physically alters her appearance to prevent her nephew Milkman and his friend Guitar from being incarcerated by a system that historically has been unjust to black males. The folktale "The People Who Could Fly" is the ultimate conjuration story given that a metamorphosis supposedly occurs allowing a group of New World African slaves to be physically transported, through supernatural means, back to their native land.

The theme of retribution against a perceived enemy invariably involves a confrontation between two powers. The confrontation may be direct, resulting in extreme transformations. Chesnutt's "The Gray Wolf's Hant" (1899) is an appropriate example here. Uncle Jube, a veteran conjurer, turns Dan into a wolf and causes him to kill his wife after Dan accidentally kills Jube's ill-intentioned son. The confrontation may be subtle and indirect initially yet may escalate into violent acts. For instance, in Gloria *Naylor's *Mama Day* (1988), Miss Miranda, an old midwife who devotes her energies to healing and health preservation, reluctantly uses her roots to inflict harm upon Ruby after learning that Ruby has "fixed" Cocoa (Miranda's grandniece), causing her to become deathly ill. In anger, Miss Miranda sprinkles powder around Ruby's house while hitting it with her cane. Ruby's house is later struck by lightning and is completely destroyed.

The conjurer as visionary is noted by a series of terms such as "two headed," "two-faced," "long-headed," and "double-sighted." The source of these unique powers is indicated in specific ways. He may have been born the seventh son (Willie Dixon, "Seventh Son," 1953) or with an extra layer of skin over the eyes (Tina McElroy *Ansa, *Baby of the Family*, 1989). She may have acquired her knowledge by serving as an apprentice under a master conjurer (Morrison, *Song of Solomon*).

The unique visionary powers of the conjurer place him in a marginal position in relation to the community. This "outsidedness" is manifested in very significant terms, namely the otherworldly place the conjurer inhabits and the marks of distinction associated with the healer. In rural agrarian communities the conjurer often lives in a dilapidated hut, off the main path somewhere near the edge of the forest and the edge of the community. For example, Wumba, the obeah man in Claude *McKay's *Banana Bottom* (1933), lives in a cave concealed by a broad cashew tree and guarded by a growling dog trained to announce arrivals. Elias in Octavia Winbush's "Conjure Man" (1938) lives close to the cypress swamp in a cabin with a roof made of tar paper and slate. Symbolically, this residence exists on a somewhat magical plane uninhabited by civilization. Clients entering this domain do so discreetly, often late at night to avoid being discovered by folk in the everyday world.

In urban environments such as that depicted in Rudolph *Fisher's *The Conjure Man Dies* (1932), the conjurer in Harlem utilizes the icons of professionalism by practicing in an office with a desk and assistant. The turban that he wears and the white velvet drapes behind which he works, however, make him appear somewhat exotic. Like the root doctors

in the rural environments, he only sees clients at night.

The physical descriptions of root doctors often are in pejorative terms, for example, wrinkled, dirty, and ugly. Another category of descriptions that challenges this depiction may be noted. The conjurer as spiritual guide and teacher is evident in Roger Mais's *Brother Man* (1954), Alice *Walker's "The Revenge of Hannah Kemhuff," Morrison's *Song of Solomon*, and Naylor's *Mama Day*. Most often their powers are used to bring about harmony in the community and hope to a dying world.

[*See also* Folk Literature; Healing.]

• Richard M. Dorson, ed., *American Negro Folktales*, 1967. Harry M. Hyatt, *Hoodoo, Conjuration, Witchcraft, Rootwork*, 2 vols., 1970. Alan Dundes, ed., *Mother Wit from the Laughing Barrel*, 1981. John Roberts, *From Trickster to Badman*, 1989.

—Carol S. Taylor Johnson

Contending Forces. The first of four *novels written by Pauline E. *Hopkins, *Contending Forces: A Romance Illustrative of Negro Life North and South* was published by the Colored Co-operative Publishing Company of Boston in 1900. The novel is Hopkins's manifesto on the value of fiction to social activism in black America at the turn of the century. By relying on the stock devices of sentimental melodrama, the novel refutes *stereotypes about degraded *mulattoes and licentious black women, celebrates the *work ethic among upwardly mobile African Americans of the post-Reconstruction period, and provides a historically accurate depiction of the racist oppression that they endured. Like Frances Ellen Watkins *Harper's *Iola Leroy* (1892), *Contending Forces* recalls a tragic antebellum story as the basis of another about emancipatory optimism.

In 1780 Charles Montfort moves his family from Bermuda to North Carolina to operate a cotton plantation. Almost immediately a rival planter, Anson Pollock, suspects that Montfort's beautiful wife, Grace, is partly black. He murders Montfort, claims Grace as his concubine, and makes slaves out of her sons, Charles and Jesse. Grace commits suicide to escape Pollock. He sells Charles to an Englishman, who frees him and takes him to England. Jesse eventually escapes to New England, where he becomes a progenitor of the Smith family—the widow Ma Smith and her children, Will and Dora—of the novel's main plot.

The postbellum story is set in Boston. Will is a Harvard philosophy student (reminiscent of W. E. B. *Du Bois), and Dora assists her mother in running a comfortable boarding house. Two tenants, Sappho Clark, a beautiful white mulatta with a secret southern past, and John Langley, who is engaged to Dora, share the Smith household. Will falls in love with Sappho and asks her to marry him, but John blackmails her in an attempt to make her his mistress. She abandons Will in order to escape John. In a letter left for Will, Sappho reveals John's immoral intentions and her past suffering as a victim of interracial rape. Will shares this information with Dora who breaks her engagement with John. Frustrated by his unsuccessful attempt to find Sappho, Will goes abroad to pursue his studies. Dora eventually marries Dr. Arthur Lewis, the head of a Louisiana industrial school for Negroes, while John dies seeking his fortune in mining for gold. Will returns to the United States and marries Sappho.

Early scholars of African American literature regarded the writings of Hopkins and her black female contemporaries as unworthy of literary merit. This critical viewpoint prevailed until the 1980s when scholars reclaimed the artistic complexity and political interventionary agendas of Hopkins's writings. The novel unites racial activism and woman-centered concerns as well as redefines a virtuous black womanhood on the bases of the moral integrity of female character and the nobility of her labor rather than on the legacy of sexual violation or the elitism of *class privilege.

• Hazel V. Carby, *Reconstructing Womanhood: The Emergence of the Afro-American Woman Novelist*, 1987. Richard Yarborough, introduction to *Contending Forces*, 1988. Claudia Tate, *Domestic Allegories of Black Political Desire*, 1992.

—Claudia Tate

COOKBOOKS. Generally we do not perceive cookbooks as literature, let alone as the opening for autobiographical musing, cultural critique, or political commentary. But even a glance at the titles of a small sampling of culinary narratives by contemporary African Americans—LeRoi Jones/Amiri *Baraka's 1962 *essay on "Soul Food," VertaMae Smart-Grosvenor's *Vibration Cooking, or The Travel Notes of a Geechee Girl* (1970), or Norma Jean and Carole Darden's 1978 cookbook *Spoonbread and Strawberry Wine: Recipes and Reminiscences of a Family*—ensures that we pay close attention to the equations such authors make between the presentation of a recipe and the articulation of personal and collective *history. Across two centuries and several continents, the edible provides more than material nourishment. It also reconstructs a cultural heritage, grounds familial reminiscence, and authorizes personal narrative. In the hands of African American writers, the cookbook becomes a vehicle with which to sustain a sense of culture. Like retelling a story, reproducing a recipe requires the engagement of a community, the act of passing down a recipe from generation to generation providing an apt metaphor for the transfer of knowledge and the establishment of links between self, family, and nation.

Cooking as a metaphor for the reproduction of culture has a long history in African American narrative. In his essay on nineteenth-century cookbooks, "House and Home in the Victorian South: The Cookbook As Guide" (*In Joy and in Sorrow: Women, Family, and Marriage in the Victorian South*, ed. Carol Bleser, 1991), Alan Grubb cites a white text, Mary Stuart Smith's *The Virginia Cookery Book* (1885), for its recirculation of the *mammy figure in the person of an old cook who produces rolls of miraculous quality without a recipe. When a white visitor inquires how she might reproduce them, the cook is apparently unable to account for their appearance, other than to answer that she "dar'n't make 'em no different." Considered against Nell Kane's recollec-

tions in *Between Women*, Judith Rollins's 1985 study of African American *domestic workers and their white employers, the cook's "puzzlement" looks more studied than accidental, her vacant inability to reproduce her recipe the result of a highly conscious effort to retain control over her cooking artistry. Though it is a full century removed from the antics catalogued in *The Virginia Cookery Book*, Nell Kane's own insistence on keeping her recipe and serving ideas in the family by scripting them in a book she intends to pass on to her children dignifies a mundane labor by acknowledging its potential as an expressive art.

Like Kane's recollections, contemporary African American cookbooks call attention to the larger cultural contest that underlies, for instance, the exchange of—or struggle over—a recipe. Books like Helen Mendes's *African Heritage Cookbook*, Edna Lewis's *The Ebony Cookbook*, and Smart-Grosvenor's own *Vibration Cooking* were published within the *Black Arts movement of the mid to late 1960s, a context that took for granted the need to develop a separatist aesthetic and in which the development of an explicitly political art was not so much censured as it was mandated. Smart-Grosvenor's homage to African American cooking and Jessica B. Harris's later Afrocentric guide, *Iron Pots and Wooden Spoons: Africa's Gifts to New World Cooking* (1989) are authorized by a well-established critical apparatus, a movement that has critiqued Martin Luther *King, Jr.'s advocacy of civil rights as too closely connected to leftists of the white middle class, a movement that has watched the Black Panthers on national television and listened to *Malcolm X in the streets, a movement that by the late 1960s had produced literary *anthologies with names like *Black Fire* (eds. Larry *Neal and LeRoi Jones, 1968) and volumes of poetry like Don L. Lee's 1968 *Black Pride* and 1969 *Think Black*.

The immediate precursor to Smart-Grosvenor's *Vibration Cooking* is unarguably Amiri Baraka's essay "Soul Food" published in the 1962 collection *Home: Social Essays*. Replaying Ralph *Ellison's own debt to Proustian memory, where the fragrance of roasting sweet potatoes recalls the narrator of *Invisible Man* to himself and all of black southern history, Baraka's sweet potato pies invite personal reminiscence and afford an opportunity for the author to critique what he sees as the pretensions of the African American middle class. Thematically Smart-Grosvenor's own riff on greens owes much to Baraka's, but its tone and form recall a distinguished series of feminine autobiographical precursors: Harriet E. *Wilson's 1859 *Our Nig* and Harriet A. *Jacobs's 1861 *Incidents in the Life of a Slave Girl*. But it is Zora Neale *Hurston—as anthropologist and autobiographer in her 1942 memoir *Dust Tracks on a Road*—that *Vibration Cooking's* complicated, jokey self-situating most closely duplicates. Like James *Baldwin's characterizations of the *blues in the 1962 *The *Fire Next Time* as "tart and ironic, authoritative and double-edged," Smart-Grosvenor's own assessments are self-conscious and street smart. Recipes affirm black pride as they critique the poverty of white culture. While African American tradition is celebrated through culinary custom, Anglo American culture is denounced through its edibles as a contradiction in terms. The implicit contrast between such cultural poverty and the richness of African American life is drawn over and over again, the white cultural repast demonstrated as scant at best: show without substance, containing little real nourishment, let alone flavor.

Although it was published eight years following *Vibration Cooking*, the Darden sisters' 1978 *Spoonbread and Strawberry Wine* seems a half-century distant, determinedly nostalgic and relentlessly backward-glancing. The familial "seat" we see described in the opening pages of their recollections may advance their grandfather to the status of unofficial town ruler, but if the Dardens are intent on providing their own middle-class status with a historical precedent, they are equally interested in providing ignorant readers with lessons in nineteenth-century American history more generally. Recalling bourgeois African American life as it is played out in the town of Wilson through the middle and late 1870s allows the Dardens to retrace the shift from the promise of Reconstruction through the terror of the Ku Klux Klan that follows. In the context of this oppression, Charles Henry Darden signifies black resistance. Coding their narrative as a rereading of the nineteenth-century work of racial uplift and Washingtonian self-reliance, these cookbook writers recall the small heroisms of a middle class too often scorned or ignored by contemporary African American political and literary figures.

Jessica Harris's more recent *Iron Pots and Wooden Spoons* (1989) returns to the language of the Black Arts movement, her book acting as a coda to Smart-Grosvenor's *Vibration Cooking*. Harris provides her book with a format that emphasizes the similarities between food preparation across three continents in order to create a community that gains its authority not from a sense of its rootedness but from the very experience of dislocation. As the historical focal point for this culinary narrative, the Atlantic slave trade provides Harris with a way to acknowledge history, not in order to bemoan the fate of the scattered survivors but rather to recuperate a notion of agency on behalf of her self and her people. Likewise, her recollections of her mother's cooking implicitly attest to the relationships between cooking, culture, and colonialism. Describing the care and labor with which family dinners are prepared every night, the writer pays tribute to her mother's artistry and acknowledges the repressive social context within which she worked. Trained as a dietician, she is discouraged from food service work and so exercises her culinary skills at home.

If they exploit very different languages with which to evoke food traditions, writers such as the Dardens and Jessica Harris, among others, help to establish a literary context rich in historical resonance, political association, and cultural permanence. For ethnic writers generally and African American women writers specifically, the very domestic and commonplace quality of cooking makes it an attractive forum for describing culture. For such authors, presenting a family recipe and representing its circulation within a community of readers provides a metaphor that is culturally resonant in its evocation of the relation between the labor of the individual and her conscious efforts to reproduce familial and community traditions and values. The reproduction of dishes like okra gumbo and pig's feet thus works to maintain cultural specificity in the face of assimilative pressures attempting constantly to amalgamate cultures for the benefit of the "melting pot" or "national interests."

[*See also* Autobiography.]

• Susan Leonardi, "Recipes for Reading: Summer Pasta, Lobster à la Riseholme, and Key Lime Pie," *PMLA* 3 (May 1989): 340–347. Anne Goldman, "Same Boat, Different Stops": Re-collecting Culture in Black Culinary Autobiography," in *Take My Word: Autobiographical Innovations of Ethnic American Working Women*, 1996. Rafia Zafar, "Cooking up a Past: *Vibration Cooking* and *Spoonbread and Strawberry Wine*," *Ethnic Voices*, vol. 2, ed. Claudine Raynaud, special issue of *GRAAT* 13 (1996).

—Anne E. Goldman

COON. A perennial racial *stereotype and slur of uncertain derivation, the term "coon" referred in the early nineteenth century to a white rural person or, conversely, a sharpster. Its connotation was of slickness and opportunism, but not wholly, if at all, racially inflected. Even after the 1820s emergence of a popular blackface minstrel character, the urban "dandy" black Zip Coon, racial application of the epithet was quite varied. Only in the last two decades of the nineteenth century, due in no small part to the minstrel show and other stereotypes that identified blacks with racoons and racoon hunting, did the term coon come into common racist parlance as shorthand for absurdly elevated blacks, or blacks generally. The word's heyday came in the 1880s and 1890s, when the blackface minstrel show transmuted into the black *musical stage form known as the coon show. Featuring a wide array of black stage stars, chief among them Bert Williams and George Walker, the coon show was a mine of problematic racial representations, from razor-toting hustlers and gamblers to chicken-thieving loafers. Famous productions in this vein included Will Marion Cook and Paul Laurence *Dunbar's *Clorindy, or Origins of the Cakewalk* (1898), Cook's *In Dahomey* (1903), and Bob Cole's *A Trip to Coontown* (1898); coon songs such as Ernest Hogan's "All Coons Look Alike to Me," Cook and Dunbar's "Who Dat Say Chicken in Dis Crowd?," and Williams and Walker's "Two Real Coons" secured the popularity of such fare. Despite all appearances, coon shows were a crucially important, if obviously highly circumscribed, arena of black performance and self-portrayal, and their appeal among black audiences as well as white allowed real talents like Bert Williams to work against the types he was forced to inhabit. African American writers have often looked askance at the coon show—Paul Laurence Dunbar's *novel *The *Sport of the Gods* (1902) asserts the corrupt values of northern urban African Americans through their love of the coon show, while Wallace *Thurman's *The *Blacker the Berry* (1929) depicts a quasi–coon show stage performance as the quintessence of African American color conscious-ness. Yet *Harlem Renaissance writer Jessie Redmon *Fauset struck a note echoed by many later writers when she celebrated Bert Williams in a 1922 issue of the *Crisis as an embodiment of African American comic pathos.

[See also Minstrelsy; Theater.]

• Sam Dennison, Scandalize My Name: Black Imagery in American Popular Music, 1982. David R. Roediger, The Wages of Whiteness: Race and the Making of the American Working Class, 1991.   —Eric Lott

COOPER, ANNA JULIA (1858–1964), educator, scholar, writer, feminist, and activist. Anna Julia Haywood Cooper was born in Raleigh, North Car-olina, the daughter of a slave, Hannah Stanley Hay-wood, and her white master, George Washington Haywood, with whom neither she nor her mother maintained any ties. At age nine she received a schol-arship to attend the St. Augustine's Normal School and Collegiate Institute for newly freed slaves, and in 1877 she married an instructor at the school, a Ba-hamian-born Greek teacher named George Cooper. Left a widow in 1879, she never remarried. She en-rolled in 1881 at Oberlin College, where educator and activist Mary Church (later *Terrell) also studied, and elected to take the "Gentleman's Course," rather than the program designed for women. She received her bachelor's degree in 1884, and after teaching for a year at Wilberforce University and then returning briefly to teach at St. Augustine's, she went back to Oberlin to earn her master's degree in mathematics in 1887.

Cooper was recruited that same year to teach math and science and later Latin at the Washington Colored High School in Washington, D.C., also known as the M Street School and, later, the Paul Laurence Dunbar High School. In 1902 she became the principal of this elite public school, which during its history educated many African American leaders. In 1906, however, she was forced to resign in what was known as the "M Street School Controversy"; Cooper was attacked for lax disciplinary policies and for including among the boarders in her house a male teacher, John Love, to whom she was known to be close, although the exact character of their rela-tionship remains unclear. In the opinion of current scholars, Cooper was dismissed because of the racism and sexism of white critics, who, among other things, objected to her refusal to embrace vocational training for all African American youth. She moved to Lincoln University in Jefferson City, Missouri, where she taught until a new superintendent in 1910 recalled her to the M Street School. While she was in Missouri, Cooper declined a marriage proposal from Love.

Although she worked full-time, in the 1910s Cooper studied for her PhD at Columbia University and in the summers at the Sorbonne. She wrote her dissertation on French attitudes toward *slavery and was awarded the doctorate from the University of Paris in 1925 at the age of sixty-seven, making her, according to current knowledge, the fourth African American woman to receive the PhD. She continued

to teach following her retirement from the M Street School in 1930, serving from 1930 to 1940 as presi-dent of Frelinghuysen University, a night school for working people. When necessary, she held classes in her home at 201 T Street NW, and she stayed on as the registrar of this institution until 1950.

Committed to the struggle for both *race and *gender equality, Cooper was an active, vocal partici-pant in the *Woman's Era at the turn of the century. She helped found the Colored Women's League of Washington, D.C., in 1892. She was one of a very small number of African American women asked to speak at the World's Congress of Representative Women at the Chicago World's Fair in 1893, an event she and others criticized for its racism. She was one of the few women invited to talk at the first Pan-African Conference in London in 1900, organized by, among others, W. E. B. *Du Bois. She participated in the founding of the Colored Women's YWCA in 1905 and established the first chapter of the Camp Fire Girls in 1912. Also during these years of full-time em-ployment and active feminist and racial organiza-tional work, Cooper adopted and raised a relative's five orphaned grandchildren.

Anna Julia Cooper's most famous writing is her only booklength work, the major feminist text, A *Voice from the South (1892). Cooper's book mingles and manipulates Victorian ideologies of true woman-hood and turn-of-the-century racial uplift rhetoric to advocate racial justice and equal rights for African American women. Cooper also wrote Legislative Measures Concerning Slavery in the United States (1942) and Equality of Races and the Democratic Movement (1945), and she is the editor of the two-volume Life and Writings of the Grimké Family (1951).

Committed throughout her life to an activist belief in the power of *education to change lives individu-ally and collectively, Cooper is today grouped with other well-known social and political leaders at the turn of the century, such as W. E. B. Du Bois, Ida B. *Wells-Barnett, Mary Church Terrell, and Fannie Barrier Williams. She died in her sleep in Washing-ton, D.C., on 27 February 1964.

[See also Feminism.]

• Hazel Carby, Reconstructing Womanhood: The Emergence of the Afro-American Woman Novelist, 1987. Mary Helen Washington, introduction to A Voice from the South, 1988. David W. H. Pellow, "Anna 'Annie' J. Cooper," in Notable Black American Women, ed. Jessie Carney Smith, 1992, pp. 218–224. Debra Calhoun and Glenda Elizabeth, "Anna J. Cooper," in African American Women: A Biographical Diction-ary, ed. Dorothy C. Salem, 1993, pp. 124–126.
                                        —Elizabeth Ammons

COOPER, J. CALIFORNIA (b.19?), short fiction writer, playwright, and novelist. Joan California Cooper's birthdate is conspicuously absent from available written material about her life and work. She was born in Berkeley, California, to Maxine Rosemary and Joseph C. Cooper, and she has a daughter, Paris Williams.

Cooper's success as a writer must be attributed solely to natural gifts. She began composing plays and performing them before family and friends when she was a very young child. Indeed, the first glimpse by the public-at-large of Cooper's work was through her plays; she had written at least seventeen by the mid-1990s, including: *Everytime It Rains; System, Suckers, and Success; How Now; The Unintended; The Mother; Ahhh; Strangers;* and *Loners. Strangers* earned the 1978 Black Playwright of the Year award and was performed at the San Francisco Palace of Fine Arts. *Loners,* anthologized in Eileen Ostrow's *Center Stage* (1981), is the story of Cool, a somewhat egotistical man of thirty-seven who realizes too late that his inability to commit to the shy but strong Emma results in his own loneliness. Emma tires of Cool's callous neglect and decides to marry someone who is not so self-centered that he fails to notice her quiet strength. Cooper's plays have been performed before live audiences, as well as on radio and public television. She is a prolific writer, who, like Emily Dickinson, took up writing to satisfy a private, personal need; much of her early work was long hidden from public view until her plays began to receive attention.

Cooper is better known for her short stories, whose narrators witness and relate tale after tale with a folksy, homespun wisdom in conversation with the reading audience that brings to mind the relationship between Alice *Childress's urban domestic workers, *Mildred Johnson and Marge, in *Like One of the Family* (1956). Cooper has published five short story collections: *A Piece of Mine* (1984); *Homemade Love* (1986), which won the 1989 American Book Award; *Some Soul to Keep* (1987); *The Matter Is Life* (1991); and *Some Love, Some Pain, Sometime* (1995).

Like Alice *Walker, whose company published Cooper's first collection of short stories, Cooper acts in spiritual communion with certain characters who relate their experiences; as medium, Cooper retells the stories in writing. Her primary characters are usually women who have been victimized in some way by the men in their lives. Cooper's profound messages come packaged in what appear to be simple and straightforward stories; this method is reminiscent of one often employed by Frances Ellen Watkins *Harper. Her writing shares Harper's didacticism, but Cooper's reliance on the Ten Commandments for many of her themes is not as conducive to invoking Christian piety. One story from the collection *A Piece of Mine,* entitled "One Hundred Dollars and Nothing!," retells the rise and fall of a boastful but unenterprising man who marries a well-to-do, enterprising woman named Mary. The husband, Charles, feels he has done the nappy-headed, bow-legged Mary a favor by marrying her, and he is fond of telling Mary that, with one hundred dollars and nothing, he could outperform her anyday. Mary endures years of abuse by Charles, and she eventually dies; but, prior to her death, she is able to set into motion events that will leave Charles with one hundred dollars and nothing more. She punishes Charles from the grave. The female protagonists in *A Piece of Mine,* survive, through spiritual (and often physical) transcendence, all manner of abuse and neglect. They emerge with a greater realization of their inner strength, self-actualized.

Homemade Love consists of thirteen short stories about girls who, despite warning and example, fall into the same traps as their parents. "Without Love" is the story of the parallel lives of two friends. Totsy, neglected by her alcohol-abusing mother, is sexually active at eleven and becomes an unwed teenage mother. Her friend Geneva narrates the story of Totsy's early reliance on sex without love and the impact such an attitude has on Totsy's inability to mature and become self-actualized. Geneva, by contrast, combines sex with love and marriage, works hard to achieve a middle-class lifestyle, and grows old and content with her husband by her side as her best friend. Totsy is finally forced by the circumstances of old age and declining health to rely on the son she has never nurtured. *Homemade Love* simply suggests that homemade love is what nurtures the mind, body, and soul.

Cooper has also written two novels, *Family* (1991) and *In Search of Satisfaction* (1994). *Family* is narrated by Clora, the freed spirit of an enslaved woman who committed suicide. Clora follows the experiences of and watches over her favorite child, Always. Because the narrator exists in spirit only, she is superomniscient, able to enter into and disclose other characters' states of mind. *In Search of Satisfaction* echoes the simple message heard in much of Cooper's other work: happiness comes from within. In a note to that novel, Cooper uses the analogy of the three little pigs to make the point that each of us is responsible for laying the proper foundation for our own personal satisfaction.

The American Library Association's Literary Lion Award (1988) and the James Baldwin Writing Award (1988) are only two of the many prizes presented to Cooper for her writing. Cooper is a person who carefully guards those matters that she considers private. She resides in rural Texas.

• J. California Cooper, interview by Lynn Gray, *FM Five* (Nov.–Dec. 1985): 1, 12. Alice Walker, "J. California Cooper," in *Contemporary Literary Criticism,* vol. 56, ed. Roger Matuz, 1989, pp. 69–72. Barbara J. Marshall, "Kitchen Table Talk: J. California Cooper's Use of Nommo—Female Bonding and Transcendence," in *Language and Literature in the African American Imagination,* 1992, pp. 91–102. Rebecca Carroll, "J. California Cooper," in *I Know What the Red Clay Looks Like,* ed. Carol Alisha Blackshire-Belay, 1994, pp. 63–80. Kristine A. Yohe, "J. California Cooper," in *The Oxford Companion to Women's Writing in the United States,* eds. Cathy N. Davidson and Linda Wagner-Martin, 1995, p. 218.

—Lovalerie King

COPPIN, FANNY JACKSON (1837–1913), educator, missionary, newspaper contributor, and autobiographer. Born into *slavery in Washington, D.C., Fanny Muriel Jackson Coppin resided there until her aunt purchased her *freedom. In 1850, she moved to New Bedford, Massachusetts, and worked as a *domestic. One year later, Coppin moved to Newport, Rhode Island, in search of better educational opportunities. Her refusal to allow *race and/or *gender to defer her dreams resulted in Coppin's enrolling at Oberlin College in 1860. She achieved distinction for her talents as a public speaker and class poet, and she established an evening class for free African Americans.

After graduating in 1865, Coppin was appointed principal of the Female Department of the Institute for Colored Youth in Philadelphia prior to becoming principal of the entire school during an era when few women, especially African American, were principals of coed high schools with male faculty. She refused to resign when she married the Reverend Levi Coppin in 1881; however, illness forced her to retire in 1902. Later that year Coppin was able to accompany her husband to Capetown, South Africa, where they served as missionaries for two years. Illness forced Coppin to spend her remaining years in confinement at her Philadelphia home.

Having previously written children's stories and a column for the *Christian Recorder, Coppin began her *Reminiscences of School Life and Hints on Teaching*. Upon her death, her former student William C. Bolivar completed the *autobiography's section on the Institute for Colored Youth. It was published in 1913. *Reminiscences* represents one of the earliest autobiographies, if not the first, to be published by an African American female with a college degree. *Reminiscences* begins as a *slave narrative, documenting Coppin's desire to gain an *education, and ends as a teaching manual, heralding her desire to educate others.

• Linda M. Perkins, *Fanny Jackson Coppin and the Institute for Colored Youth, 1865–1902*, 1987.

—Linda M. Carter

CORNISH, SAM (b. 1935), poet, essayist, editor of children's literature, photographer, educator, and figure in the Black Arts movement. Born into urban poverty in Baltimore, Maryland, on 22 December 1935, Samuel James Cornish was the youngest of the two sons of Herman and Sarah Cornish. From his older brother Herman he learned early the lessons of the street, which he later would incorporate into a street-tough observancy in his *poetry.

Cornish served in the U.S. Army Medical Corps (1958–1960), then returned to Baltimore, where he published two poetry collections—*In This Corner: Sam Cornish and Verses* (1961) and *People Beneath the Window* (1964). While working at the Enoch Pratt Free Library, he became part of Baltimore's political and literary underground, self-publishing a sixteen-page pamphlet entitled *Generations and Other Poems* (1964). A subsequent edition of *Generations* (1966) appeared when Cornish was editing *Chicory*, a literary magazine by children and young adults in the Community Action Target Area of Baltimore. Lucian W. Dixon and Cornish edited a selection from the magazine entitled *Chicory: Young Voices from the Black Ghetto* (1969). In 1968 Cornish won the Humanities Institute of Coppin State College Poetry Prize for his "influence on the Coppin poets" and a grant from the National Endowment for the Arts. Soon poets as diverse as Maxine Kumin, Clarence *Major, and Eugene *Redmond would acknowledge Cornish's significance.

By 1970 Cornish was represented in the LeRoi Jones (Amiri *Baraka) and Larry *Neal *anthology *Black Fire* (1968) as well as in the Clarence Major collection *New Black Poetry* (1969). He reconsidered his early poems of black historicized kinship, restructuring them into the Beacon Press's *Generations* (1971). After a brief stay in Boston, Cornish returned to Baltimore to work in secondary school and college writing programs. While there, Cornish published *Sometimes* (1973) with Cambridge's Pym-Randall Press. Teaching poetry in the schools led to several children's books: *Your Hand in Mine* (1970), *Grandmother's Pictures* (1974), and *My Daddy's People* (1976).

Returning to Boston in the mid-1970s, Cornish worked with the Educational Development Corporation and attended Goddard College in Vermont. He appeared in a host of new anthologies, from George Plimpton and Peter Ardery's *American Literary Anthology* (1970) and Harry Smith's *Smith Poets* (1971), to Ted Wilentz and Tom Weatherly's *Natural Process* (1972) and Arnold Adoff's *One Hundred Years of Black Poetry* (1972). *Sam's World* (1978) continued the historical and genealogical project of *Generations*.

Since the 1980s Cornish has divided his time between bookselling and teaching creative writing and literature at Emerson College in Boston. *Songs of Jubilee: New and Selected Poems, 1969–1983* (1986) recasts earlier work into sequences of a historical and biographical nature. His autobiographical narrative, *1935: A Memoir* (1990), blends poetry and prose into a montage of twentieth-century history. The poems of *Folks Like Me* (1993) offer political and cultural portraits of African Americans from the depression to the early 1960s. Current projects include the next volume of his *autobiography, *1955*, and a critical study of Langston *Hughes.

• Jon Woodson, "Sam Cornish," in *DLB*, vol. 41, *Afro-American Poets since 1955*, eds. Trudier Harris and Thadious M. Davis, 1985, pp. 64–69. C. K. Doreski, "Kinship and History in Sam Cornish's *Generations*," *Contemporary Literature* 33 (Winter 1992): 665–687.

—C. K. Doreski

CORNISH, SAMUEL (1795–1858), evangelist, educator, social activist, journalist, and editor of America's first African American newspaper. Samuel E. Cornish's many antebellum social, religious, and political involvements aimed at ameliorating the condition of African Americans in the United States. Born in Sussex County, Delaware, Cornish was ordained in the New York Presbytery as an evangelist (1822) and served various churches intermittently until 1847. During his thirty-year public career, he was associated with over eighteen organizations for racial uplift, including four New York City newspapers: *Freedom's Journal, the *Rights of All, the *Weekly Advocate, and the *Colored American. In March 1827 he started *Freedom's Journal*, the first African American newspaper, to counter racist propaganda and provide a forum of communication among African Americans. After about six months Cornish left the journal in the hands of his coeditor, John Browne *Russwurm, but resumed editorial responsibilities in March 1828 when Russwurm emigrated to Liberia, changing the paper's name in May 1829 to the *Rights of All*. Cornish's editorial policy, which continued until the paper's death on 29 October 1829, reflects his dislike of the colonization movement.

Cornish is credited with editing the *Weekly*

Advocate from January 1837 until 4 March 1837, when its name was changed to the *Colored American*. He continued as editor until 18 April 1838, advocating nonpartisan responsible journalism and optimism regarding the future of African Americans. Cornish's other involvements included the African Free Schools, the Negro Convention movement, the American Anti-Slavery Society, and the American Missionary Society.

Cornish's life was saddened by the death of his wife Jane Livingston in 1844, the emigration of his son William to Liberia, the death of his oldest daughter, Sarah, in 1846, and the mental derangement of his daughter Jane in 1851. Cornish nevertheless remained active in public life until his death in 1858.

[*See also* Journalism; Periodicals, *article on* Black Periodical Press.]

• I. Garland Penn, *The Afro-American Press and Its Editors*, 1891; rpt. 1969. Frankie Hutton, *The Early Black Press in America, 1827–1860*, 1993. —Marilyn D. Button

Corregidora. In 1975, while still a graduate student at Brown University, Gayl *Jones published *Corregidora*, her first *novel. A work that combines stark, deliberately raw language with poetry and dreamlike lyricism, it is narrated by *Ursa Corregidora, a Kentucky *blues singer who weaves her own story of thwarted desire and artistic strivings with that of her family. As Brazilian slaves and *prostitutes, her great-grandmother and grandmother are repeatedly raped by their master, Old Corregidora, who fathers Ursa's grandmother as well as her mother, until Great Gram commits an undisclosed act of *violence that makes him murderously obsessed with her. She flees to Kentucky, returning only to retrieve her now pregnant daughter. Like her mother, Ursa has heard this story since birth and has been frequently instructed to raise a child who will in turn bear witness to Corregidora's atrocities; thus does Great Gram try to empower her family, changing her daughters' *identity from chattel to bearers of vengeance. But when Ursa is pregnant, her jealous husband (Mutt Thomas) pushes her down a flight of stairs and she loses the baby. Her injuries require a hysterectomy, and Ursa's resulting distress at being unable to "make generations" also affects her capacity for sexual pleasure.

After turning away from Cat Lawson, a friend whose lesbianism disconcerts her, Ursa marries again, only to have the marriage end when her husband accuses her of frigidity. Alternately yearning for and despising Mutt, a man marked by his own family scars of *slavery and possessiveness, Ursa spends the next twenty years singing and writing songs, and grappling with her family's fraught histories of sexual desire and violent abuse. Mutt's reappearance catalyzes an uneasy reunion for Ursa, merging undercurrents of violence with the possibility of healing. Performing fellatio, Ursa finally realizes what Great Gram did to Corregidora (she bit his penis just before orgasm), and thus recognizes the victim's own capacity for violence. Ursa also recognizes the combination of pain and pleasure, power and vulnerability,

that constitutes what Jones has called "the blues relationship" between men and women. In acknowledging her own blues relationship with Mutt, Ursa sees how desire survives, however maimed and thwarted, even after a history of abuse. Yet the novel's ambiguous close finds Ursa still searching for a song and identity of her own to replace the angry refrain of vengeance her mothers have taught her.

Critical perspectives about *Corregidora* focus on its use of African American oral traditions: the frequent call-and-response pattern of Jones's dialogue, the spiraling refrains of the blues, the improvisations of *jazz, the echoes of black dialects, the emphasis on performance as part of black *folklore. Additionally, Jones's depiction of a female African American singer relates to themes in contemporary black women's writing about the search for a voice and the defiance of a rigid, imposed, and usually sexual identity. Perhaps equally important, *Corregidora*'s portrayal of the complexities between mothers and daughters meshes with Jones's treatment of the double-edged sword of memory for African Americans, who need to remember their history without being imprisoned by it.

• Keith Byerman, *Fingering the Jagged Grain: Tradition and Form in Recent Black Fiction*, 1985. Missy Dehn Kubitschek, *Claiming the Heritage: African-American Women Novelists and History*, 1991. Sally Robinson, *Engendering the Subject: Gender and Self-Representation in Contemporary Women's Fiction*, 1991. —Amy S. Gottfried

CORROTHERS, JAMES D. (1869–1917), writer and minister. Born in Michigan, James D. Corrothers was raised in the predominantly white community of South Haven by his paternal grandfather, a man of Cherokee and Scotch-Irish ancestry. He moved to Muskegon at age fourteen, supporting himself and his grandfather. Shortly thereafter he moved to Indiana, then to Springfield, Ohio, working as a laborer. There, in his teens, he began his literary career, publishing a poem, "The Deserted School House," in the local newspaper.

Corrothers's literary career received a boost when, at eighteen, he relocated to Chicago. Working in a white barber shop, he met journalist-reformer Henry Demarest Lloyd and showed him some poems. Lloyd arranged for their publication in the Chicago *Tribune*, getting Corrothers a custodial job in the *Tribune* offices. Corrothers was soon asked to do an article on Chicago's African American elite. He was chagrined when the story appeared, rewritten by a white reporter in a way that stereotyped its subjects; he was equally chagrined when the paper's editor refused to pay him for his efforts.

Corrothers returned to day labor and even did some boxing, but remained dedicated to writing. In 1890 he appeared before Thomas Fortune's National Afro-American League, reading his poem "The Psalm of the Race," a work protesting American discrimination but predicting a brighter future.

Beginning in 1890, Corrothers furthered his education. An aunt in Chicago helped him enter Northwestern University, where, with additional support from Lloyd and temperance activist Frances Willard, he studied from 1890 to 1893. He also spent a brief period at Bennett College, in North Carolina.

Leaving Northwestern, Corrothers did freelance reporting for Chicago dailies. Influenced by humorist Finley Peter Dunne, Hoosier poet James Whitcomb Riley, and dialect poet Paul Laurence *Dunbar, he also began writing *dialect poetry and sketches for the Chicago *Journal*, focusing on working-class African American urban life. These pieces brought him his first popularity; nevertheless, within a year, aware that racism limited his opportunities in journalism, he entered the African Methodist Episcopal (AME) ministry, subsequently taking posts in Bath, New York, and in Red Bank and Hackensack, New Jersey. Forced by scandal from the AME Church in 1902, he soon reentered the field as a Baptist. In the last two years of his life, he became a Presbyterian, pastoring a church in Westchester, Pennsylvania.

Corrothers's ministerial career did not exclude further literary work. He continued to find success in dialect. His sentimental "'Way in de Woods, an' Nobody Dar" appeared in one of America's leading magazines, *Century*, in 1899, quickly followed there by other dialect pieces. He also collected and published his newspaper sketches in book form as *The Black Cat Club* (1902).

The Black Cat Club was, and has remained, Corrothers's most noted work, its urban setting marking him as an innovator within the dialect tradition. Corrothers also integrated authentic folk materials into his sketches, although his "dialect" came more from literary than from folk sources. The book's real strength was its satire, including a thinly veiled attack on Booker T. *Washington and even on the uncritical vogue for dialect within African American letters. Corrothers was ambivalent about dialect and later said he regretted having written the book; he was no less ambivalent about the African American working classes, whose lives the book portrayed. Still, along with his earlier work, *The Black Cat Club* gave him a national audience, one he continued to cultivate through such poems as the self-reflective "Me 'N' Dunbar" (1903) and "An Awful Problem Solved" (1903), which turned the form toward protest.

Corrothers also worked increasingly in standard English, writing sentimental pieces and protest verse. Among the more important was "The Snapping of the Bow" (1901), condemning racism but expressing the belief that, ultimately, "the race might rise." Toward the end of his career, reflecting a less sanguine perspective, Corrothers wrote "At the Closed Gate of Justice" (1913), protesting the apparently intractable character of American racial injustice.

Also toward the end of his career, Corrothers returned to prose. Most notable was a two-part story, "A Man They Didn't Know" (1913–1914), predicting a war pitting the United States against dark-skinned Japanese and Mexican enemies, one in which he portrayed African American loyalty as an uncertain but crucial factor. He also published his *autobiography, *In Spite of the Handicap* (1916),

seeking to justify his career and his views of American racial problems.

Corrothers was one of the most widely published African American writers of the late nineteenth and early twentieth centuries. As a result, he did much to bring visibility to African American letters.

[*See also* Journalism; Protest Literature; Speech and Dialect.]

• Kevin K. Gaines, *Uplifting the Race: Black Leadership, Politics, and Culture in the Twentieth Century*, 1966. Richard Yarborough, "James D. Corrothers," in *DLB*, vol. 50, *Afro-American Writers before the Harlem Renaissance*, ed. Trudier Harris, 1986, pp. 52–62. Dickson D. Bruce, Jr., *Black American Writing from the Nadir: The Evolution of a Literary Tradition, 1877–1915*, 1989. Dickson D. Bruce, Jr., "James Corrothers Reads a Book; or, The Lives of Sandy Jenkins," *African American Review* 26 (Winter 1992): 665–673. Kevin Gaines, "Assimilationist Minstrelsy As Racial Uplift Ideology: James D. Corrothers's Literary Quest for Black Leadership," *American Quarterly* 45 (Sept. 1993): 341–369.
—Dickson D. Bruce, Jr.

CORTEZ, JAYNE (b. 1936), literary and performance poet, significant figure in the development of jazz-poetry readings and recordings, director, and publisher. Jayne Cortez's significance as an African American poet resonates beyond the printed page. The immense reputation Cortez has garnered worldwide comes from her performances combining live *music, especially *jazz, with powerfully spoken *poetry. The strength of her *performance, however, does not detract from her achievement as a literary figure. For example, Cortez received the Before Columbus Foundation American Book Award for excellence in literature in 1980 and the New York Foundation for the Arts award for poetry in 1987. In addition, Cortez was twice honored with a National Endowment of the Arts fellowship. Cortez's commitment to African American artistic expression is many faceted and consistent. She has been heralded for meshing surrealist images with raw, jarring descriptive detail. Her tone is serious and sometimes sarcastic but always full of pleasure and pain and politics. Among others, she cites Langston *Hughes, Aimé Césaire, Léon Damas, Nicolás Guillén, and Sterling A. *Brown as literary inspirations for her work.

Born in Fort Huachuca, Arizona, on 10 May 1936, Jayne Cortez resides in New York City. In 1954 Cortez married jazz musician Ornette Coleman and gave birth to their son, Denardo, in 1956. Cortez studied *drama in Los Angeles and cofounded the Watts Repertory Theatre Company in 1964, where she remained artistic director until 1970. This was her formal initiation into the world of performance: directing, acting, and reciting poetry to live audiences. By 1972 Cortez had moved to New York City and published two volumes of poetry—*Pisstained Stairs and the Monkey Man's Wares* (1969) and *Festivals and Funerals* (1971)—before founding her own publishing company, Bola Press. ("Bola" is a Yoruba word meaning successful.) From 1977 to 1983 Cortez was a writer in residence and a literature professor at Livingston College of Rutgers University.

Cortez's first volume, *Pisstained Stairs and the Monkey Man's Wares*, focuses mainly on music and the musician's significance to the black community. Love and the *blues, drugs and the drudgery of ghetto life abound in this work. The much cited "How Long Has Trane Been Gone" is an example of the elegiac style of poetics popular in Cortez's work. The move toward political poetics surfaces in the title poem of Cortez's second volume, *Festivals and Funerals*. This collection confirms Cortez's desire to integrate African and American cultural signs into her poetry. Still, the need to actively pledge her allegiances does not deny Cortez a moment to self-reflect as in "I Would Like to Be Serene," where she reminds us that the geographies of the heart map a politics of love.

New York and Nigeria, Satchmo and Orisha coexist in Cortez's third volume of poetry, *Scarifications* (1973). The poems are full of the gritty and raw word concoctions that began in *Pisstained Stairs*, but they are more irreverent and less imitable. As the title suggests, *Scarifications* is littered with scabs and bumps, blood and tears, spit and sweat. Thus, the body and the city intersect with traditional and modern African emblems to create a surreal sensory extravaganza.

In *Mouth on Paper* (1977) Cortez stresses the significance of reading aloud by writing poems that come alive upon vocalization. The power of chanting becomes resoundingly obvious in this volume where repetition and rhythm birth orality and musicality. The title, *Mouth on Paper*, best describes Cortez's aesthetic expectations. In *Firespitter* (1982), Cortez continues the balancing act between the art on the page and art of the stage. The politics of *gender are also significant in *Firespitter* as two of its most noted poems deal with *violence against women: "If the Drum Is a Woman" and "Rape." These pieces exemplify not only Cortez's ability to do praise songs for our artists and political leaders but also her strength at depicting the unknown and unsung survivors of racial and sexual oppression. The uncompromising tone of these poems makes clear Cortez's position: the war against women must be fought and won. It was also in 1982 that Cortez published *There It Is*, her third album of poetry.

In 1984 Cortez published *Coagulations: New and Selected Poems*. One of the new poems, "Everything Is Wonderful," epitomizes Cortez's brand of sarcasm by enumerating exceptions to the title pronouncement. This poem and many others have been reprinted in *anthologies and journals worldwide. Cortez's latest volume is entitled *Poetic Magnetic* (1991); recent collections featuring her work include *The Jazz Poetry Anthology* (1991) and *Every Shut Eye Ain't Asleep: An Anthology of Poetry by African Americans since 1945* (1994), edited by Yusef *Komunyakaa and Michael S. *Harper, respectively.

In addition to publishing the majority of her books through Bola Press, Cortez has used the company for her sound recordings. After her first recording, *Celebrations and Solitudes* (1975), Bola Press issued all other accompanied readings: *Unsubmissive Blues* (1980), *There It Is* (1982), and *Maintain Control* (1986). [Her son Denardo Coleman and the band "The Firespitters" are the regular musicians on these recordings, and Ornette Coleman was a guest artist on *Maintain Control*.] Cortez's latest recording is *Everywhere Drums*.

Jayne Cortez's involvement in the *Black Arts movement and her successful development of a jazz-poetry mediating between the likes of Amiri *Baraka and The Last Poets has earned her a definitive place in the African American literary tradition. Furthermore, her surrealist aesthetics and womanist ideology make Cortez's work acutely unique in its attempt to liberate black voices through artistic activism. Moving from the period of the Black Arts jazz-poetry of the 1960s and 1970s into the current cultural renaissance of music and letters in the 1980s and 1990s, Jayne Cortez's life suggests the performance art of a womanist-warrior-poet.

• D. H. Melhem, *Heroism in the New Black Poetry: Introductions and Interviews*, 1990.
—Michelle J. Wilkinson

COSMETICS. Even when African Americans did not have access to commercially produced products, they enhanced their beauty by the ways in which they styled their *hair and wore their clothing, as well as by the mixtures of oils, herbs, and other ingredients that they used in baths and hair preparations. They proved particularly adept at using the natural products they found in the woods, meadows, and gardens as well as products from various food animals, such as oil from cows. After slavery, it was easier for most to pay attention to bodily appearance, and cosmetics assumed a greater importance. Such attention could signal membership in a particular class or organization, or a certain educational background. Hairstyles and makeup sometimes signaled particular political or religious attitudes; for example, in the 1960s Afros and lack of makeup became signs of varying degrees of militancy among young blacks, but throughout history *churchwomen have generally downplayed the use of cosmetics.

William Wells *Brown provides one of the earliest accounts of white American awareness that enslaved persons should look a certain way if they were to be perceived to be salable and healthy. Brown recounts having responsibility for preparing enslaved persons for market by applying dye to their hair to cover up any gray strands and oil to their faces and limbs to make them appear supple and firmer than they were. While the primary purpose was certainly not aesthetic, blacks were undoubtedly aware of the possibilities inherent in improving their appearance. Brown depicts in *Clotel* (1853) how a black butler applies butter to his hair to effect an appearance. The quality of the effect is perhaps less important than the signaling of concern with appearance.

Black women invented various mixtures for grooming their hair. In the absence of beauty parlors and *beauticians available to assist them, they did what they could to prevent breakage and to deal with insect problems. Indeed, the problem with lice served as one of the inspirations to Madam C. J. Walker (1876–1919) in the development of her million-dollar hair-care business at the turn of the twentieth century. Not only did she develop and sell hair-care products to black women, but she assisted them in setting up beauty shops, learning the trade, and improving their opportunities to make money.

Facial care naturally accompanied hair care, and though black women were not dramatic pioneers in this area, they were again resourceful in the methods they used. For example, initially certain "folk" cosmetics such as henna for hair color, Vaseline for moisturizing, and yeast and oatmeal for facials were available. Later black women used the products invented and sold by others. Often those products did not take into account the varying colors of black women's skins, or even blackness at all; frequently black women found themselves forcing their faces into shades and colors that were clearly designed for white women. It would be well into the mid-twentieth century before companies such as Fashion Fair, a line of cosmetics designed specifically for black women, emerged, and even later before popular nonblack companies, such as Mary Kay and Estée Lauder, created powder shades and lip colors appropriate to darker skins. In the 1990s, many companies have recognized the spending power of black women and have incorporated their needs into their product lines.

Such awareness was not available in the early decades of the twentieth century, and if it had been, it is clear that not all black women would have been drawn to such developments. Issues of color and *double consciousness dominated many black women's perceptions of themselves. At a time when darker skins were not universally appreciated, some black women tried to lighten their skins. The many concerns with color during the *Harlem Renaissance highlight this trend in the literature. Zora Neale *Hurston's Color Struck (1925) makes the issue of the preference for light skin clear, and Wallace *Thurman's The *Blacker the Berry (1929) illustrates vividly the negative attitudes that could be conveyed to a woman of darker skin and the pathetic and desperate actions she takes to try to alleviate her situation. Emma Lou's attitude toward her darker skin allows her to be used by a light-skinned man of questionable morals. She even takes care of the mentally handicapped child he has fathered by another woman. Her self-esteem is so low that she willingly allows herself to be trampled on, all because she is dark. She imagines acquiring "an efficient bleaching agent, a magic cream that would remove this unwelcome black mask from her face." She eats arsenic wafers and uses a peroxide solution in the vain hope of lightening her skin. Her entire cosmetic routine underscores her self-hatred:

> Before putting on her dress she stood in front of her mirror for over an hour, fixing her face, drenching it with a peroxide solution, plastering it with a mudpack, massaging it with a bleaching ointment, and then, as a final touch, using much vanishing cream and powder. She even ate an arsenic wafer. The only visible effect of all this on her complexion was to give it an ugly purple tinge, but Emma Lou was certain that it made her skin less dark.

Connotations of color and what the society prefers—even blacks—have consistently guided black women in their use of cosmetics and other beauty preparations. Gwendolyn *Brooks's *Maud Martha (1953) suffers because of her dark skin, as does little Mabbie in Brooks's "The Ballad of Chocolate Mabbie." No amount of cosmetics could change the intra- or interracial prejudices toward such women.

In the 1960s, however, when black became beautiful, the need for cosmetics was minimized among a large portion of the population. Natural skin, sans makeup, was as much of a political statement as Afros were. Clean-faced women were all the rage in the society as well as in the literature. That trend continued after the 1960s as well, though Ntozake *Shange's character passion flower in *for colored girls (1977) deliberately uses her makeup and body to enhance her sexual power by seducing a succession of men. For other characters in the literature, however, colored touches of beauty could be indicated in other places on the body, such as polished fingernails or toenails. Indeed, the recognition that she polishes her toenails is one of the things that reconciles Kiswana Browne to her mother in Gloria *Naylor's The *Women of Brewster Place (1982). Women with secure self-esteem, so this logic went, did not need facial markers/paintings of that esteem.

One of the most striking wars over the use of makeup occurs in Toni *Morrison's *Song of Solomon (1977), where Hagar, in pursuit of her cousin *Milkman Dead, undergoes a cosmetically transforming ritual that leads to her death. Afraid that Milkman is more attracted to women of lighter hue and better breeding, Hagar mistakenly locates the sense of his displeasure with her in herself and goes on a quest to remake herself to suit him. Her journey is a microcosm of what *Pecola Breedlove undergoes in The *Bluest Eye (1970) in being judged—and judging herself—by standards of beauty to which she cannot adhere. Hagar buys underwear and other clothing, along with a plethora of perfumes and lipsticks, and she forces the local beautician to do her hair—even though the shop is technically closed for the day. Hagar's efforts, sadly, only lead to her being caught in a rainstorm, catching pneumonia, and dying. Her desperation nonetheless reflects the situation of black women who have found their definitions of beauty outside rather than within themselves.

In African American life and literature, therefore, the use of cosmetics has been a sign of the social positioning of black women, a statement about skin color preferences, and an indication of political beliefs. In the nineteenth century, for example, "ladies" did not "paint" themselves because of the connotations attached to such use of makeup. Religious preferences might dictate that others could wear powder but not lipstick, or perfume but not mascara. Rejection of the use of cosmetics at various historical moments has signaled a transcendence of the forces that would define black women, as in the political statements of the 1960s. However, its contemporary popularity would suggest that problems inherent in the use of cosmetics have not been totally resolved in life or in literature.

• Caroline Lee Hentz, "The Fatal Cosmetic," *Godey's Lady's Book* 18 (June 1839): 265–273. Madam C. J. Walker, *Textbook of the Madam C. J. Walker Schools of Beauty*, 1928. E. Franklin Frazier, *Black Bourgeoisie*, 1957. Naomi Wolf, *The Beauty Myth*, 1991.
                                                   —Trudier Harris

Cotillion, The. *The Cotillion, or One Good Bull Is Half the Herd* (1971), represents John O. *Killens's presentation of assimilation, classism, and self-hatred set in the 1970s. The book explores African American family traditions and the political and social ramifications that influence these customs.

In *The Cotillion*, Killens steps into a community of African Americans and explores their dark sides. This satirical novel attacks the classism and assimilation that dominated many African American communities. Killens's character Lumumba represents that breed of African Americans who attempt to redefine themselves by separating themselves from their Eurocentric standards. In contrast to Lumumba's ideology, there exists a community of women that symbolizes the vise-grip Eurocentricism has on the African American.

Although most criticism of *The Cotillion* dealt with the theme of *Afrocentricity versus Eurocentricity, the text also has a strong commentary on African American adolescence. Yoruba is coming of age and experiencing an *identity crisis concerning her blackness and sexuality: to be an African queen for her new love, Lumumba, or a girl with "bourgeois inconsistencies." She is a product of middle-class blacks who place higher value on how society perceives the adolescent from this upwardly mobile environment than on self-worth. Killens allows Yoruba's sexual awareness to become a part of her maturation as a woman and an individual. Killens demonstrates the impact of socialization on the sexual attitudes of middle-class blacks. He further implies that societal expectations and myths about African American women cause adolescents to think that only whores enjoy sex. As with Yoruba, most adolescents have been taught to fear sexual desires that involve sexual intercourse. Killens also asserts through Yoruba that coming of age for many adolescents is synonymous with becoming aware of their sexual identities which is in direct conflict with the views and values of their hypocritical communities.

Killens explores the impact of socialization on sexual attitudes of middle-class blacks. Societal expectations and myths about African American women cause Yoruba's mother in the text to think that only whores enjoy sex. He creates a character who society considers bourgeois and sexually repressed but who does not conform to such expectations. Creating such characters as Lumumba and Yoruba reaffirms Killens's goal of writing literature that revolves around social protest and cultural affirmation.

Killens creates a subplot in the text that further demonstrates his satirical examination of the inner workings of so-called middle-class African Americans. Through Yoruba and Lumumba, the reader must examine the conventions of Mrs. Youngblood,

whose blood is "old" and sterile because she has accepted the conventions of white America as her own. Through these characters, Killens allows readers to examine the mirroring of characters with conventions and vice-versa. Killens gives readers Yoruba, who confronts the repressive beliefs brought on by racism and classism and accepts the love and affection of her male counterpart, as a model.

• Wanda C. Macon, "Adolescent Characters' Sexual Behavior in Selected Fiction of Six Twentieth Century African American Authors," PhD diss., Ohio State University, 1992, pp. 59–65 and 101–110.
                                                   —Wanda Macon

COTTER, JOSEPH SEAMON, JR. (1895–1919), poet, journalist, and forerunner of the African American cultural renaissance of the 1920s. Born in Louisville, Kentucky, son of the poet Joseph Seamon *Cotter, Sr., Joseph Seamon Cotter, Jr., in his brief life established himself as an accomplished and innovative voice amid the lively post–World War I American *poetry scene. Avoiding the dialect poetic style of his father and of the family friend Paul Laurence *Dunbar, the younger Cotter experimented widely with modern free verse and traditional forms before his untimely death from tuberculosis at age twenty-three. Cotter's best-known work is his collection *The Band of Gideon* (1918), which was followed by the sonnet series "Out of the Shadows" (1920) and "Poems" (1921), the latter two published posthumously in the *A.M.E. Zion Quarterly Review*.

After graduation from Louisville Central High School in 1911, Cotter enrolled at Fisk University, where he worked on the *Fisk Herald*, a monthly published by the university *literary societies. Apart from his precociously early reading in the family library, the work on the *Fisk Herald* represents the earliest documented sign of Cotter's literary predilections. During his second year at Fisk, Cotter had to return home to Louisville due to the onset of tuberculosis.

Upon his return home, Cotter accepted a position as an editor and writer for the Louisville newspaper the *Leader*, and he began to establish his brief yet brilliant career as poet. Grief over his sister's death inspired the early tribute "To Florence"; it remains one of his most moving poems. Precluded from military service in World War I because of his deteriorating physical condition but stimulated by his own interest and by the war service of a close friend, Cotter produced a number of poems, including "Sonnet to Negro Soldiers" and "O, Little David, Play on Your Harp," which place him among the best Great War poets.

Other notable poems of the *Gideon* collection include the title poem, which recalls the style of the traditional southern black *preacher and seems to encode protest regarding the treatment of black World War I veterans. Among the best modernist free verse pieces are "The Mulatto to His Critics" and the provocative "Is It Because I Am Black," which dramatically interrogates those who would dismiss or patronize the African American narrator.

Outstanding among the poems appearing in the final *A.M.E. Zion* series is "Rain Music," which anticipates the rhythm, theme, and style of works of Langston *Hughes and other *Harlem Renaissance poetic innovators. Also first published in the *Zion Quarterly* and, until recently, overlooked is Cotter's impressive nineteen-sonnet sequence "Out of the Shadows," which concludes with a moving evocation of a child dreamt of to fulfill the love celebrated in the sonnets. Cotter's posthumous publications also include the one-act World War I play "On the Fields of France," which appeared in the *Crisis* in 1920. With his lively experimentation in free verse and traditional forms, his use of natural idiom, his sense of the brilliant potential of African American verbal expression, Joseph Seamon Cotter, Jr., clearly prefigures the 1920s African American cultural renaissance.

• Eugene B. Redmond, *Drumvoices: The Mission of Afro-American Poetry*, 1976, pp. 155–169. James Robert Payne, "Joseph Seamon Cotter, Jr.: Toward a Reconsideration," in *Joseph Seamon Cotter, Jr.: Complete Poems*, ed. James Robert Payne, 1990, pp. 1–22.   —James Robert Payne

COTTER, JOSEPH SEAMON, SR. (1861–1949), poet, fictionist, educator, and community leader. Born near Bardstown, Kentucky, Joseph Seamon Cotter had to leave school at age eight to work at a variety of jobs because of family financial exigencies. Cotter had been a precocious child, learning to read at the age of three from a mother who had the gifts, as Cotter wrote later, of "a poet, storyteller, a maker of plays." When Cotter was twenty-two the prominent Louisville educator William T. Peyton encouraged the promising young man to return to school. After some remediation and two night school sessions, Cotter was able to begin his teaching career. His first Louisville position was at the Western Colored School, where he began in 1889. He went on to a career of more than fifty years as teacher and administrator with the Louisville public schools. In 1891 Cotter married his fellow educator Maria F. Cox, with whom he had three children, including the important poet in his own right Joseph Seamon *Cotter, Jr.

Although known in his own time as a prominent educator and African American civic leader, as well as for his prolific authorship in varied genres, today Cotter is remembered primarily for his *poetry. In his first collection, *A Rhyming* (1895), we see the young Cotter experimenting with varied poetic forms, including the traditional ballad and the Italian sonnet. Cotter's second book, *Links of Friendship* (1898), is another eclectic collection in varied forms that includes a poem on "The Negro's Loyalty" during the Spanish American War, a loyalty unswerving despite "the mob that puts me to the rack." The clear reference to lynchers who ravaged black America in Cotter's day belies the poet's reputation for silence about such painful American issues. A dialect piece in *Links* resulted from a visit by Paul Laurence *Dunbar to the Cotter family in 1894. The visit instigated several poetic exchanges between Dunbar and Cotter.

Cotter went on to publish three more collections of poetry, including the *Collected Poems of Joseph S. Cotter, Sr.* (1938) and the *Sequel to "The Pied Piper of*

Hamelin" and Other Poems (1939), whose title poem, a response to Robert Browning's poem "The Pied Piper," is regarded as among Cotter's finest. Overall, as A. Russell Brooks has noted, *Sequel* may well be Cotter's most successful book.

Cotter's blank verse four-act play *Caleb, the Degenerate* (1903), which reflects views of Booker T. *Washington, is essentially closet drama, mainly of historical interest, as is the case with his other plays. Cotter's *short story collection *Negro Tales* (1912) has received little attention; several of the stories may merit reappraisal. His pamphlet on the *Twenty-fifth Anniversary of the Founding of Colored Parkland or "Little Africa"* (1934) recalls Cotter's leadership in the formation of the Parkland African American community of Louisville in 1891. Cotter's final work, the miscellany *Negroes and Others at Work and Play* (1947), appeared two years before his death. Overall, it may be said that Joseph Seamon Cotter, Sr., provided a sustaining voice during one of the most difficult eras of African American history, and he was a man who backed his words with action in building the African American community.

[*See also* Drama.]

• Ann Allen Shockley, "Joseph S. Cotter, Sr.: Biographical Sketch of a Black Louisville Bard," *CLA Journal* 18 (Mar. 1975): 327–340. A. Russell Brooks, "Joseph Seamon Cotter, Sr.," in *DLB*, vol. 50, *Afro-American Writers before the Harlem Renaissance*, eds. Trudier Harris and Thadious M. Davis, 1986, pp. 62–70.   —James Robert Payne

Cotton Comes to Harlem, Chester *Himes's sixth detective *novel in a series of nine, all written after the author had left the United States for France, was first published in French by Plon under the title *Retour en Afrique* (1964) and later in the United States by G.P. Putnam's Sons as *Cotton Comes to Harlem* (1965). Considered by many critics to be Himes's best detective novel, *Cotton Comes to Harlem* was also produced as a Hollywood *film by Samuel Goldwyn, Jr., in 1970, directed by Ossie *Davis.

The book opens with a scene of a rally in Harlem conducted by Reverend Deke O'Malley, ex-con and leader of a phony back to Africa movement. While in the process of amassing $87,000 from eighty-seven Harlem families, O'Malley's own operation is robbed by white gunmen. As in all of Himes's detective novels, images of pandemonium and absurd *violence are vividly, and often comically, described. Himes's two detectives, *Coffin Ed Johnson and *Grave Digger Jones, pursue the missing $87,000, which winds up hidden in a bale of cotton. The thief, a white Southerner named Colonel Robert L. Calhoun, is promoting his own crooked repatriation scheme of sorts, a back-to-the-Southland crusade whereby urban African Americans would "return" to the South as paid agricultural laborers.

When Coffin Ed and Grave Digger finally apprehend Calhoun, they demand that he give them $87,000 from his own bank account to repay the eighty-seven Harlem families their hard-earned money. In the final comic irony of the novel, the original $87,000 turns up in the hands of junkman Uncle Bud, who uses it to move to Africa and buy five hundred cattle to exchange for one hundred wives, setting himself up as a latter-day Solomon. The comical juxtaposition of Calhoun's absurd back-to-the-Southland movement and O'Malley's corrupt back to Africa movement represents Himes's satirical commentary on repatriation in the modern era.

• Gilbert H. Muller, *Chester Himes*, 1989. Robert E. Skinner, *Two Guns from Harlem: The Detective Fiction of Chester Himes*, 1989.
—Wendy W. Walters

CRAFT, WILLIAM (c. 1826–1900) and **ELLEN** (1826–1891), escaped slaves, antislavery activists, and educators. William Craft authored *Running a Thousand Miles for Freedom* (1860), which chronicled his escape with his wife Ellen from Georgia to Boston in 1848, and their subsequent move to London after the passage of the Fugitive Slave Act (1850).

The Crafts were heralded for the brazen method of their escape. The fair-skinned Ellen disguised herself as an invalid white *man*, and William posed as "his" servant. They simply, and quite publicly, rode the train from Macon, Georgia, to Philadelphia, where they revealed themselves to a local abolitionist.

As Blyden Jackson has observed (*History of Afro-American Literature*, 1989), the Craft story was convincing and therefore useful for abolitionism. The narrative focuses mainly on the journey from Georgia to Philadelphia, and then from Boston to London, cultivating dramatic tension from its unsensational narrative style. Craft expertly presents memorable characters (such as the white gentleman who befriends the disguised Ellen and vouches for "his" ownership of William, allowing them to continue their journey) and memorable scenes (such as innkeepers realizing too late that they had mistakenly assumed Ellen was "white" when they let her a room). The narrative focus on tricking unsuspecting whites cultivates what William L. Andrews (*To Tell a Free Story*, 1986) describes as "interstitiality," as the Crafts "temporarily confuse the lines separating sexual, racial and social classification."

Ellen's triple play on *race, *gender, and *class *passing has engaged recent critical interest. In its advertisement of successful passing, the Craft narrative initiates a tradition of literary explorations of passing, such as James Weldon *Johnson's *The *Autobiography of an Ex-Colored Man* (1912), Nella *Larsen's *Passing* (1929), and George S. *Schuyler's *Black No More* (1931). William Craft's narrative is also significant, as Valerie Smith notes (*Self-Discovery and Authority in Afro-American Narrative*, 1987), because unlike most *slave narratives by men, it presents the escape as a joint endeavor.

[*See also* Antislavery Movement.]

• Dorothy Sterling, *Black Foremothers*, 1979. Mary Ellen Doyle, "Slave Narratives As Rhetorical Art," in *The Art of the Slave Narrative*, eds. John Sekora and Darwin Turner, 1982, pp. 83–95. R. J. M. Blackett, *Beating against the Barriers*, 1986. Barbara McCaskill, "A Stamp on the Envelope Upside Down Means Love," in *Multicultural Literature and Literacies: Making Space for Difference*, eds. Suzanne Miller and Barbara McCaskill, 1993, pp. 77–102.
—Dana D. Nelson

CRIME AND MYSTERY WRITING. The tradition of African American crime and mystery writing extends from the beginning of the twentieth century to the present day. African American mystery writers consciously transformed and signified on Euro-Americentric detective formulas to present issues of *race, *class, and *gender. Black writers created a new type of mystery fiction by using black detective personas, celebrating black vernaculars such as *music and language, and using hoodoo as an affirmative aspect of black culture.

In the late eighteenth and early nineteenth century, African Americans were generally not published by white-owned and -edited magazines and newspapers. Alternative black-owned publications were formed such as the *Colored American* out of Washington, the *Colored American Magazine* from Boston, and *McGirt's Magazine* based in Philadelphia. From the beginning these *periodicals were popular culture compendiums of *poetry, fiction, and *essays whose writers showed a fascination with sensational mystery and crime story formats.

Among the pioneers was Pauline E. *Hopkins, whose serialized *Hagar's Daughter* (1901–1902) introduces Venus Johnson, a black female detective. A *novel about *passing in the Civil War South, *Hagar's Daughter* uses black vernaculars such as language, music, and hoodoo and signifies upon masking and disguises. Venus's positive relationship with her mother and grandmother in the novel generally enlarge the capacities of the detective novel genre while establishing the bedrock of the black detective tradition. Venus's status as a *domestic and her use of her blackness to help solve a murder and kidnap case indicate important tropes of black detection enlarged upon in future black detective novels.

Hopkins's contemporary John E. *Bruce further enhanced the tradition with the Afrocentric worldview of the *Black Sleuth* (1908–1909), a novel that features an African-born detective who brings a black nationalist perspective on American society to the detective genre. By having strong African characters with a positive sense of family and community, Bruce created a recognizable and admirable African past for African Americans. Bruce successfully extended African American *identity beyond the confines of America and in the process showed ways in which blacks could use the detective persona to illustrate the inherent intelligence, nobility, and pride of the black race. His emphasis on the positive aspects of black identity coupled with a militant attitude toward black self-expression, dignity, and survival brought a new awareness of *black nationalism to the detective novel. Bruce followed Hopkins's lead in having a detective character use his blackness as well as disguise to solve the case.

George S. *Schuyler, author of the satirical novel *Black Empire*, first published from periodical editions in 1991, also wrote six crime and mystery short stories for the *Philadelphia Courier* during the years 1933–1939. While these stories have black characters and feature black detectives, they did little to contribute to the black detective tradition. The stories are unimaginative and formulaic and often depict

Africans as brutal and savage while describing African American cultural expressions such as hoodoo ceremonies as rigmarole and grotesque.

Rudolph *Fisher's *The Conjure Man Dies* (1932) was the first black detective novel with all black characters set in Harlem. His variation on the classical format of an amateur detective helping the police and shows elements of the modern police procedural in its use of forensic evidence. Fisher laces his novel with references to black vernaculars and urban rituals, initiating the use of a "blackground" in detective texts that introduces the reader to varied aspects of African American culture while structurally adhering to the detective story formula. However, Fisher's main achievement was his clever demonstration of how hoodoo elements might be used in a novel to reinforce black pride in important Afrocentric areas. Fisher deserves his reputation as a primary black detective writer who introduced *Harlem Renaissance themes to black detective fiction.

Chester *Himes proved to be the most prolific black writer in crime and mystery fiction. With the posthumous publication of *Plan B* (1993), Himes is responsible for ten detective novels: *For Love of Imabelle* (1957), *The Crazy Kill* (1959), *Real Cool Killers* (1959), *All Shot Up* (1960), *The Big Gold Dream* (1960), *Cotton Comes to Harlem* (1965), *The Heat's On* (1966), *Run, Man, Run* (1966), and *Blind Man with a Pistol* (1969). Himes restructures the traditional hardboiled detective narrative by introducing a simultaneous time frame while creating a mythical landscape of Harlem that is both satirical and absurd. His creation of the hardboiled detectives *Coffin Ed Johnson and *Grave Digger Jones provided a vehicle for Himes's exploration of race, class, and social conditions in the black community of Harlem. Himes worked a consistent African American viewpoint and blackground into his novels. Himes refuses to fossilize the characterizations of his detectives or formularize his detective plots. The progression of his novels from *For Love of Imabelle* to *Plan B* presents an overview of African American social and political conditions in Harlem. Perhaps his most important discovery was that *violence, usually used for dramatic effect in hardboiled detective fiction, might be applied to African American political ends.

Himes proved to be a valuable predecessor for Ishmael *Reed's reinterpretation of the detective novel. Reed acknowledges that Himes showed him the way to use the detective format for African American themes. But Reed went farther than Himes in his experimental use of the form. Reed almost abolishes the classical and hardboiled variety of the detective novel, retaining only the useful structural and iconic portions of detective fiction for his satirical novels *Mumbo Jumbo* (1972) and *The *Last Days of Louisiana Red* (1974). Reed's interest in social satire and historical revisionism displaces the traditional detective format, leaving only the armature of the detective formula on which he hangs the most sophisticated exploration of African American themes in black detective fiction to date. Reed uses the detective formula to present his neohoodoo worldview as an affirmative recreation of African American identity. As the head of a private detective agency, the Neo-Hoodoo Kathedral, *Papa LaBas represents the double-conscious *trickster detective who uses his neohoodoo powers to confront white attempts to destroy the black race. Reed confirms the importance of black vernaculars such as hoodoo to the healthy creation of a black culture and positively reinterprets African history.

Where Reed almost abolishes the detective formula through his alteration of traditional detective tropes, Clarence *Major effectively continues the transformation. In *Reflex and Bone Structure* (1975) Major retains only the barest minimum of detective allusions in his novel while forging new connections between the reader and the text. *Reflex and Bone Structure* challenges conventional notions of time and *history while continuing postmodern experimentation as an antidetective novel. Major uses the detective format to write a novel about perception and language while criticizing the novelistic conventions of characterization, plot, and predictable motivation. Utilizing his background in modern art and his interest in the poetics of prose, Major's complex postmodern novel infuses African American sensibilities in a black detective novel that questions the nature of reality and the function of the written word.

A number of African American writers have written juvenile mystery novels with black characters. John Shearer's Encyclopedia Brown series is one example. Virginia *Hamilton has many books with mystery themes including *The House of Dies Drear* (1968) and *The Mystery of Drear House* (1987). Walter Dean *Myers writes juvenile novels with crime themes such as *Scorpions* (1988) and *Somewhere in the Darkness* (1992).

The 1990s saw a revival of interest in the detective novel by black female writers. These women-centered novels express important developments in black feminist thought while continuing to develop black detective tropes. Some of these authors and novels are: Dolores Komo, *Clio Browne Private Investigator* (1988); Barbara Neely, *Blanche on the Lam* (1992) and *Blanche among the Talented Tenth* (1994); Eleanor Taylor Bland's *Dead Time* (1992) and *Slow Burn* (1993); Nikki Baker's *In the Game* (1991), *The Lavender House Murders* (1992), and *The Long Goodbyes* (1993); and Yolanda A. Joe's *Falling Leaves of Ivy* (1992), a contemporary crime novel that takes place in an eastern university setting.

Dolores Komo introduces Clio Browne as the first professional female black detective. She has inherited her agency from her father, the first black private investigator in St. Louis. Clio Browne is an independent black women with an older child who has a close relationship with her mother. The novel contrasts the socioeconomic worlds of a rich white family and working class blacks. Barbara Neely's book features Blanche White as a black woman who functions as a detective while working as a servant for a white southern family. Blanche refuses to marry and have children but cares for her nephew and niece after her sister dies. In her second book Neely has Blanche investigate a murder in an exclusive black resort showing how skin color and class consciousness affects the black community. Eleanor Taylor Bland's two mystery novels combine the police procedural with a fresh look at contemporary African American themes in an urban setting. Bland's black female police officer named Marti MacAlister works with a white male detective in and around Chicago. Nikki Baker's books feature a *lesbian detective named Virginia Kelley involved in a series of murder mysteries in the gay community.

The work of Clifford Mason's *The Case of Ashanti Gold* (1985) and Gar Anthony Haywood's *Fear of the Dark* (1988) show advancements by black male authors in the use of mystery and crime themes. Walter *Mosley provides an interesting example of how the black detective tradition has developed in the last quarter of the twentieth century. His four novels *Devil in a Blue Dress* (1990), *A Red Death* (1991), *White Butterfly* (1992), and *Black Betty* (1994) feature the detective *Easy Rawlins and take place predominately in the Watts area of Los Angeles. Each novel takes place in a specific year—1948, 1953, 1958, and 1961—depicting the changing historical and cultural milieu and, at the same time, showing a progression in Easy Rawlins's self-development. Easy Rawlins is a veteran of World War II who is part of the black southern *migration to the West Coast. He becomes a detective because his blackness allows him entry into areas of society that whites cannot access. Easy is an amateur detective who turns semiprofessional as the books progress. His first-person narration harkens back to the heyday of hardboiled detective fiction, yet his character retains important elements of the black detective tradition. His personal life and connection to the black community are integral to the progression of the plot. Easy's struggle for identity through social and political associations in the black community becomes an important theme of the novels. Mosley effectively comments on the flux of black American life without sacrificing important tropes of the detective tradition. Mosley's descriptions of the bars and clubs of Watts are reminiscent of Himes's Harlem interiors, while they concentrate the reader's attention on specific aspects of black vernacular culture. Mosley's cast of black characters and a growing, sophisticated perception of black consciousness cleverly reinterpret black crime and mystery themes.

Black detective writers have learned from each other and kept alive the tropes of black detection by experimenting with the detective persona and infusing their texts with black vernaculars. African American crime and mystery writers also enlarge the capacities of the detective novel by emphasizing community values of family and shared black identity. In the postmodern period black female authors have found the detective novel to be an important vehicle for expressing black feminist viewpoints. African American crime and mystery fiction acknowledges the continuous regeneration of the African American presence in U.S. culture by celebrating black consciousness and black cultural expressions.

• William Van Deburg, *Slavery and Race in American Popular Culture*, 1984. Gilbert H. Muller, "The Greatest Show on Earth: The Detective Fiction," in *Chester Himes*, 1989. Robert E. Skinner, *Two Guns from Harlem: The Detective Fiction of Chester Himes*, 1989. Frankie Y. Bailey, *Out of the Woodpile: Black Characters in Crime and Detective Fiction*, 1991. Stephen F. Soitos, *The Blues Detective: African American Detective Fiction*, 1995.
—Stephen F. Soitos

Crisis, The. The monthly magazine of the NAACP, the *Crisis* was founded by W. E. B. *Du Bois, who wrote in his 1968 *Autobiography*, "Most of the young writers who began what was called the renaissance of Negro literature in the 20's saw their first publication in *The Crisis* magazine." Subtitled *A Record of the Darker Races*, *Crisis* regularly featured anti-lynching reports, news of Pan-African congresses, baby and graduation pictures, and John Henry Adams's piquant cartoons. From an initial run of one thousand in 1910, circulation had soared by 1918 to one hundred thousand. Early issues featured *poetry, reviews, tributes, translations, and *short stories by Charles Waddell *Chesnutt and James Weldon *Johnson. After Jessie Redmon *Fauset became literary editor, a new generation of African American writers appeared: in 1921 Langston *Hughes published his first poem, "The *Negro Speaks of Rivers," along with early works by Countee *Cullen, Jean *Toomer, Gwendolyn *Bennett, and Anne *Spencer, as well as cover art by Aaron Douglas. Following *Opportunity's successful literary competitions, *Crisis* in 1926 began the Amy Spingarn Contest in Literature and Art and published works by the winners, including Arna *Bontemps and Rudolph *Fisher. By then, however, Du Bois had begun to regret the earthiness of *New Negro literature, Fauset had resigned, and renaissance writers found new outlets. Circulation fell and Du Bois, often at odds with NAACP policy, resigned the editorship in 1934 after a quarter century of polemic. With a circulation of more than three hundred thousand, the *Crisis* continues as the organ of the NAACP and as a general magazine of African American culture and politics.

[See also Journalism; Periodicals, *article on* Black Periodical Press.]

• George P. Cunningham, "W. E. B. Du Bois," in *African American Writers*, ed. Valerie Smith et al., 1991, pp. 71–86.
—Craig Howard White

CRITICISM. *This entry consists of three essays that provide historical overviews of African American critical and scholarly studies. They are:*

Criticism to 1920
Criticism from 1920 to 1964
Criticism since 1965

Each essay focuses on books, essays, articles, and reviews written by African Americans about African American literary topics. The essays also pay some attention to the roles of the African American media and other African American organizations in asserting and nurturing literary standards.

CRITICISM TO 1920

The intellectual origins of African American literary criticism can be located in the dual determination to affirm the role of African Americans as interpreters of their own situation and to refute dominant racist ideologies of black inferiority by documenting the artistic gifts of African American writers.

This determination found important outlets in the many biographical dictionaries that, starting from the 1790s, proliferated in the nineteenth century (the first written by an African American was Ann *Plato's 1841 *Essays: Including Biographies and Miscellaneous Pieces, in Prose and Poetry*), as well as in the early impulse to publish newspapers that also commented on literary events and figures. *Freedom's Journal*, the first known African American newspaper, was founded in 1827 (four years before William Lloyd Garrison's abolitionist *Liberator*). The opening editorial declared: "We wish to plead our own cause. Too long have others spoken for us. Too long has the publick been deceived by misrepresentations. . . ."

Before the Civil War, critical discussions of African American literature were strongly influenced by the larger political debates on *slavery, as well as by the emphasis on the connection between *literacy, humanity, and *freedom that was characteristic of Enlightenment thought. As a result, abolitionist reviewers of such early African American texts as Phillis *Wheatley's 1773 *Poems on Various Subjects, Religious and Moral* stressed the significance of the very existence of a creative work of literature by a slave.

African American writing in the antebellum period was dominated by the *antislavery movement as well, but the African American press was also active in promoting occasional literary criticism by reviewing books, publicizing cultural activities, printing *poetry (e.g., Frances Ellen Watkins *Harper's poems in the *Christian Recorder* and *Frederick Douglass's Paper*) or serializing *novels (e.g., Martin R. *Delany's *Blake* in the *Weekly Anglo-African*), and intervening in larger cultural debates about the literary representation of African Americans. An important case in point was the critical controversy surrounding the 1852 publication of Harriet Beecher *Stowe's *Uncle Tom's Cabin*, a novel that was widely discussed in *Frederick Douglass's Paper* by such African American intellectuals as William G. *Allen and Martin R. Delany.

More covert but significant instances of African American literary criticism can also be found in the early writers' own reflections upon their motivations for writing. In this sense, the conventionally modest addresses to the reader that open many *slave narratives constitute important critical statements, whereby the authors underscored not only the documentary value but also the literariness of their texts (e.g., Henry *Bibb's 1849 *Narrative* and Harriet A. *Jacobs's 1861 *Incidents in the Life of a Slave Girl*).

More systematic efforts to give shape to the African American literary tradition date back at least to the 1840s. According to critic Henry Louis *Gates, Jr., two of the earliest literary critical books are Armand *Lanusse's 1845 *Les *Cenelles*, an *anthology

of poems in French by Creole African American writers, and William G. Allen's 1849 *Wheatley, Banneker, and Horton*. Both of these texts include critical commentary that reveals the authors' budding conviction that African American literature possesses distinctive features. Their main critical purpose, however, was to undermine dominant discourses on the intellectual inferiority of African Americans by providing vindicating examples of their mastery of literary forms.

A more influential text, which went through four printings in two years, is William Wells *Brown's *The Black Man, His Antecedents, His Genius, and His Achievements* (1863). Brown explicitly argues the existence of a cultural "genius" peculiar to African Americans, which he defines as rooted both in their American past of resistance to racial oppression and in African culture (in this respect he builds on the more radically Afrocentric discourses of his contemporaries Alexander *Crummell and Martin Delany). In this text, which straddles the boundary between *biography and criticism, Brown articulates an African American literary tradition that includes such authors as Martin Delany, Frederick *Douglass, Phillis Wheatley, Frances Harper, Charlotte *Forten, and himself.

The post–Civil War years, and especially the post-Reconstruction period, witnessed a renaissance of literary activity and the rise to national fame of such African American poets and novelists as Paul Laurence *Dunbar and Charles Waddell *Chesnutt. Famous white intellectuals such as W. D. Howells and G. W. Cable promoted African American literature (e.g., Howells's 1896 review of Dunbar's *Lyrics of Lowly Life* in *Harper's Weekly*), and African American authors found more opportunities to publish in mainstream magazines (e.g., *Century* and *Atlantic*) and through large publishing houses. More important, this literary renaissance was characterized by debates about the distinctiveness of African American literature and the role of the African American artist, which laid the foundations for twentieth-century African American criticism.

In a historical context dominated by the institutionalization of segregation and the increasing virulence of racial *violence, the middle-class ideology of "uplift" (which would later be influenced by Booker T. *Washington's rise to power) gave new impetus and new meaning to the earlier belief that racism could be fought through literature. The conviction of the existence of a distinctively African American "race literature" found scholarly expression in the outpouring of critical works that not only documented the neglected literary production of African American writers but also argued for their right to self-representation.

As in the pre–Civil War period, literary critical statements are to be found in the addresses to the reader and in the appendixes that accompany many literary works published in the late 1800s (e.g., Frances Harper's 1892 *Iola Leroy*, Sutton E. *Griggs's 1899 *Imperium in Imperio*, and Pauline E. *Hopkins's 1900 *Contending Forces*). These years also witnessed the proliferation of important African American encyclopedic volumes that included writers (e.g., I. Garland Penn's 1891 *The Afro-American Press and Its Editors* and Monroe A. Majors's 1893 *Noted Negro Women, Their Triumphs and Activities*), the publication of African American literary *bibliographies (e.g., Daniel Murray's 1900 "Bibliography of Negro Literature" in the *A.M.E. Church Review*), and the growth of *periodicals of more sophisticated literary quality. The *A.M.E. Church Review*, for instance, serialized several African American novels, printed poetry and reviews regularly, and became a forum for literary critical debates (e.g., the Reverend H. Edward Bryant's 1885 "Our Duties, Responsibilities: Negro Literature"; Frances Harper's 1885 "A Factor in Human Progress"; Josephine T. Washington's 1889 "The Province of Poetry"; and Gertrude *Mossell's 1898 "Life and Literature"). The widespread belief in the power of art to promote racial equality was reflected also in the growth and the activities of *literary societies (e.g., the well-known Washington, D.C., Bethel Literary and Historical Association, of which Anna Julia *Cooper was a member) and in the organization of writers' conferences, such as the one that took place in 1892 in Wilmington, North Carolina.

The proliferation of African American *women's clubs during and after the 1890s resulted in the 1894 founding of the first African American women's newspaper (the Boston *Woman's Era*) and in the organization of conferences that also addressed the role of literature in racial uplift (e.g., the 1895 National Conference of Colored Women, where Victoria Earle *Matthews gave the address "Value of Race Literature"). At the national level, women's clubs had a strong impact on the outpouring of literature written by African American women, as well as on the literary critical debates of this period. On the one hand, women participated actively, with such texts as Anna Julia Cooper's 1892 *A *Voice from the South* and Gertrude B. Mossell's 1894 *The Work of the Afro-American Woman*, in contemporary discussions on the social usefulness of art and on the African American's greater ability to be the true artistic interpreter of his/her own experience. On the other hand, women's *temperance activism and the "lifting as we climb" mission of the National Association of Colored Women influenced the criteria of "decorum" and genteel representation that dominated late-nineteenth-century African American literature.

As a literary critic Cooper was, to quote scholar Mary Helen Washington, "uncompromising in her denunciation of white control over the black image," and she critiqued such established authors as Howells, Cable, and Joel Chandler Harris. Mossell is particularly interesting for her deliberate attempt to articulate a tradition of African American female literary criticism to counter the predominance of male voices that characterizes such previous canon-making projects as Brown's *The Black Man*. Mossell devotes two chapters specifically to African American literature. In the first, she traces the historical development of African American writing (inserting it as a distinct but integral part of American literature),

expands the criteria for female inclusion in the African American canon, and addresses the role of art and criticism in the struggle for racial equality. In the second chapter, Mossell focuses specifically on African American women's poetry, documenting and articulating a female literary tradition that she uses to challenge contemporary pseudobiological discourses on the "natural" inferiority of African Americans.

At the turn into the twentieth century, important African American journals were founded that had a pronounced literary focus and were informed by the belief in an independent African American literature (e.g., the *Colored American Magazine*, 1900–1909, and *Voice of the Negro*, 1904–1907). *Colored American Magazine* was "distinctly devoted . . . to the development of Afro-American art and literature." During the years (1900–1904) when Pauline Hopkins was on the editorial staff, the magazine printed book reviews, biographies of African American artists and intellectuals (including Hopkins's own series "Famous Men of the Negro Race" and "Famous Women of the Negro Race"), and a variety of original literature by African Americans.

These journals attracted other talented African American intellectuals of the period, including William Stanley *Braithwaite. Prominent as a poet at the turn of the century, he was also a journalist, critic, and anthologist of British and American poetry. As a critic of African American literature, he edited the "Book Reviews" column in the *Colored American Magazine*, published a wide variety of *essays, and wrote introductions for several volumes, including poet Georgia Douglas *Johnson's 1918 *The Heart of a Woman*.

The increasingly outspoken belief in the value and the uniqueness of African American literature culminated in the 1903 publication of W. E. B. *Du Bois's *The *Souls of Black Folk*. Building on earlier arguments regarding the distinctiveness of African American culture, Du Bois located the source of such distinctiveness in the blending of African and American cultural forms and especially in the African American folk heritage, which he considered less influenced by white culture.

As creative author, nonfiction writer, and editor of the influential *Crisis* magazine, Du Bois had a most profound and long-lived impact on twentieth-century African American literary scholarship. His emphasis on the syncretic nature and the folk roots of African American culture provided later critics with principles of criticism not only to articulate an independent African American literary tradition but also to evaluate autonomously the aesthetic value of African American texts. Du Bois's 1913 essay "The Negro in Literature and Art," however, betrays the masculinist bias of his canon-making emphasis on the folk. As he sketches the development of African American literature, he mentions dozens of male writers and only four women.

Benjamin *Brawley's critical production exemplifies the impact of Du Bois's theories of cultural distinctiveness on early twentieth-century literary scholarship. In his 1915 essay "The Negro Genius" as well as in his 1918 book *The Negro in Literature and Art* (which went through several expanded editions), Brawley focused on identifying the properties that make African American culture distinctive. His critical work is permeated by an interest in the impact of *folklore and folk *music on individual African American writers, as well as by a preference for literary works influenced by folklore. Such preference became a characteristic feature of male-authored African American literary scholarship in the twentieth century, and it often provided a rationale for the critical neglect of female writers in general and of nineteenth-century novels of the *color line in particular.

A pervasive pride in African American culture also informs the early critical work of cultural figures who remained prominent in the 1920s, such as Arthur A. *Schomburg (author of the 1916 *A Bibliographical Checklist of American Negro Poetry*) and James Weldon *Johnson, who prophesied the coming of great American poets of African descent in a 1915 New York *Age* column. In that same year, Frank Lincoln Mather edited the first volume of *Who's Who of the Colored Race.*

Although often overshadowed by the greater attention devoted to contemporary male intellectuals, during the first two decades of the twentieth century African American women were very active as writers and scholars. Alice Moore *Dunbar-Nelson, for instance, edited two important anthologies: *Masterpieces of Negro Eloquence: The Best Speeches Delivered by the Negro from the Days of Slavery to the Present Time* (1914), which included the speeches of several female activists, and *The Dunbar Speaker and Entertainer: Containing the Best Prose and Poetic Selections by and about the Negro Race* (1920), which aimed to foster race pride in young people. Women's pre–*Harlem Renaissance cultural activism resulted also in the 1919 founding of *Woman's Voice*, a monthly magazine that responded to the need for a medium "By Woman–Of Woman–For Woman."

Clearly, the intellectual ferment most often associated with the 1920s had deep roots in the preceding decades. A quarter of a century before Alain *Locke, novelist Sutton Griggs had prophesied the birth of a "new Negro" in *Imperium in Imperio*, and as early as 1901 Braithwaite had announced "the commencement of a 'Negroid' renaissance" from the pages of the *Colored American Magazine.*

[*See also* Canonization.]

• Darwin T. Turner, "Afro-American Literary Critics: An Introduction," in *The Black Aesthetic*, ed. Addison Gayle, Jr., 1971, pp. 57–74. Abby Arthur Johnson and Ronald Maberry Johnson, *Propaganda and Aesthetics: The Literary Politics of African-American Magazines in the Twentieth Century*, 1979. William L. Andrews, *To Tell a Free Story: The First Century of Afro-American Autobiography, 1760–1865*, 1986. Ann Allen Shockley, *Afro-American Women Writers, 1746–1933: An Anthology and Critical Guide*, 1988. Mary Helen Washington, introduction to *A Voice from the South*, by Anna Julia Cooper, 1988. Dickson D. Bruce, Jr., *Black American Writing from the Nadir: The Evolution of a Literary Tradition, 1877–1915*, 1989. Henry Louis Gates, Jr., "Canon-Formation, Literary History, and the Afro-American Tradition: From the Seen to the Told," in *Afro-American Literary Study in the 1990s*, eds. Houston A. Baker, Jr., and Patricia Redmond, 1989, pp. 14–39. Claudia Tate, *Domestic Allegories of Political Desire: The Black Heroine's Text at the Turn of the Century*, 1992. Frances Smith Foster, *Written by Herself: Literary Production by African American Women, 1746–1892*, 1993.

—M. Giulia Fabi

CRITICISM FROM 1920 TO 1964

African American literary criticism in the modern period, from 1920 to 1964, is shaped by a confluence of cultural and historical factors including the first and second world wars; the experimentation with folkloric and vernacular narrative forms; the accreditation of African American folk traditions within the academy; the efforts to define a *Black Aesthetic; the influences of politically rooted ideologies, for example social Darwinism and Marxism, on successive generations of young black artists; and the double-edged consequences of integration and the *civil rights movement. During the 1920s and 1930s, African American criticism was a dialogue centered on issues of representation and the search for what W. E. B. *Du Bois called "Criteria of Negro Art." The artist's "duty," Du Bois maintained, was the "creation" and "preservation" of beauty. The "tools" the artist uses to accomplish this end are "truth" and "goodness," by which Du Bois meant "justice, honor, and right." The artist's duty implies a moral imperative that art be both a source of personal development and a medium for social change.

The practice of African American literary criticism at this time, as Du Bois's formulations suggest, synthesized the classical aesthetics of pure art, that is art as a transcendent ideal, aesthetically "good" in itself and moving toward universal truths, on the one hand, and the utilitarian function of art as propaganda—an artistic "tool" with which to dismantle social injustice—on the other. This progressive view of art and culture was an article of faith for writers who were, in other respects, sometimes politically and philosophically very divergent, including William Stanley *Braithwaite, Sterling A. *Brown, Langston *Hughes, Alain *Locke, and Zora Neale *Hurston. The literary criticism that these writers practiced did not exist in a vacuum but was influenced by the post–World War I progressive movement in America. This was a political crusade that advocated labor and social reform and a heightened sensitivity to ethical and moral issues brought about, in part, by the mass culture impact of psychoanalysis, the rise of cultural anthropology, and the unprecedented cultural hybridization created by migratory movements beginning in the early 1900s.

Locke's seminal introductory *essay to the 1925 *anthology of black writing, *The *New Negro*, stressed an esprit de corps that he noted as the difference between the old bond that united American Negroes on the basis of a "common condition" rather than a new one based on a "common consciousness." For Locke, the great migratory waves of black people flooding into northern, industrial cities were only partly a product of new jobs created by various war industries coupled with increasing restrictions on foreign immigration. Far more important was a new collective commitment among black people to seize opportunity. For Locke, Du Bois, James Weldon *Johnson, and many other chroniclers of black America during the early modernist period, the rapid cultural changes occurring throughout the 1920s were the result of, in Locke's words, "a new vision of opportunity, of social and economic *freedom, of a spirit to seize, even in the face of an extortionate and heavy toll, a chance for the improvement of conditions. With each successive wave of it, the movement of the Negro becomes more and more a mass movement toward the larger more democratic chance— . . . a deliberate flight not only from countryside to city, but from medieval American to modern."

The rhetoric, if not always the reality, of this "new consciousness" was also abundantly evident among a generation of young black writers in the 1920s, especially Langston Hughes, Zora Neale Hurston, Sterling Brown, Claude *McKay, and Wallace *Thurman, and a "second wave" of writers during the 1930s and 1940s—Richard *Wright, Ralph *Ellison, Ann *Petry, James *Baldwin, and Chester *Himes—who saw themselves, more or less, as a revolutionary avant garde. Accordingly, these writers were critical of the politics of American middle-class accommodation in literature and its concomitant facile assimilation of Western literary traditions, which often focused on marginalizing African American culture and demonizing the "Negro." Langston Hughes's essay "The Negro Artist and the Racial Mountain" (1926) spoke in strident tones that belied his generation's dependence on white patronage of black art. Nevertheless, Hughes's call to young African Americans to fearlessly and proudly create expressions of their "individual dark-skinned selves" is one of many "manifestos" exhorting black artists to create out of their own vast cultural, that is, "racial," heritage. Hughes's essay—like Locke's "The New Negro," Richard Wright's "Blueprint for Negro Writing" (1937), Ralph Ellison's "Twentieth-Century Fiction and the Black Mask of Humanity" (1953), or Arthur P. Davis's "Integration and Race Literature" (1956)—helps define an evolving aesthetic that moves black culture from the periphery to the center of literary discourse about issues of African American, national, and global concern.

Hughes's "racial mountain" is a trope for black America's commodification of white culture and the racial erasure that results from the "urge within the race toward whiteness, the desire to pour racial individuality into the mold of American standardization, and to be as little Negro and as much American as possible." The dichotomy Hughes uses throughout the essay between "American standardization" (white, mass culture) and "Negro art and culture" presumes separable and value-laden racial differences between white and black people. The period was not without skeptics, such as Pittsburgh Courier columnist George S. *Schuyler, who dismissed contentions about racially inflected differences as "hokum." Nonetheless, the considerable effort given to defining a "criteria," "aesthetic," or "blueprint" for black literature in the modernist period was predicated on the belief that "Negro character and life" are certainly culturally, and seemingly racially, different

from other American experiences. Consequently, African American literary criticism in the early part of this period is, in part, a polemic about representation, a series of questions and responses to Negro literary portraiture (from the antebellum through the modern period) in fiction by both white and black writers.

The consensus—from William S. Braithwaite ("The Negro in American Literature") and Sterling Brown (The Negro in American Fiction and Negro Poetry and Drama) to Ralph Ellison ("Twentieth-Century Fiction and the Black Mask of Humanity")—was that twentieth-century white writers, with deplorably few exceptions, had failed, as Ralph Ellison noted, to depict African American characters with "the full, complex ambiguity" or the full complement of "good and evil," "instinct and intellect," and "passion and spirituality," that humans possess and great literature projects. The group found consensus as well in the ultimate responsibility that black writers bore for defining African American humanity for themselves. By the 1940s, emphasis on Negro portraiture in American literature, which had been exploited during the era of progressive social and political reform associated with the *Harlem Renaissance, was being pushed to a wider spectrum of overlapping concerns and issues. Chief among these was a Marxist-oriented consciousness that stressed *class struggle and economic communalism instead of the "*talented tenth" individualism of the Harlem Renaissance era.

By contrast, the depression-era 1930s and the postwar 1940s gave rise to a new humanism and collectivism that was evident in the *poetry, fiction, and cultural criticism of black writers. Their work transformed the "Negro" and blackness into symbolic sites in which an undeniably American, but emphatically universal, psychosexual drama was played out about fear, redemption, hatred, guilt, revenge, *race, class, and *gender. Richard Wright's *Native Son (1940), Chester Himes's *If He Hollers Let Him Go (1945), and Ann Petry's The *Street (1946) form a tradition within the larger American naturalistic movement earlier exemplified by Frank Norris, Stephen Crane, and Theodore Dreiser. Like most naturalistic fiction during this period, black writers documented the economic determinism that condemned successive generations of blacks to poverty and hopelessness; failed public institutions—*churches, schools, federally regulated social relief programs, the justice system; and the disintegration of the nuclear *family that was, perhaps, the most recognizable imprimatur of the modern malaise. However, race had been largely omitted from the broader naturalist movement's social commentary. By adding race to the formula, Wright, Himes, and Petry broadened the critique of modernism. Petry's *novel The Street went farther still by adding black womanhood to the female-centered novels in the genre, such as Dreiser's Sister Carrie and Crane's Maggie: A Girl of the Streets, which had elided the issue. Petry revises the male-dominated protest fiction in the 1940s by making *Lutie Johnson, her main character, a sexually experienced but emphatically moral person, and by stressing the socially constructive and interactive relationships among race, class, and gender.

The social protest that marked the 1940s was especially evident in the poetry of a second wave of defiant young black writers, including Gwendolyn *Brooks (A *Street in Bronzeville, 1945), Margaret *Walker (*For My People, 1942), Robert *Hayden (Heart-Shape in the Dust, 1940), and Melvin *Tolson (Rendezvous with America, 1944). In an important essay, "New Poets" (in Angelyn Mitchell's From within the Circle, 1950), assessing the impact of these writers, Margaret Walker argues that despite a resurgence of patriotism and general prosperity engendered by World War II, African American poetry during this period reflects "either a note of social protest or a growing concern with the terrible reality of war." This poetry often cut against the grain of popular sentiment about a war fought to preserve democracy in places far from America by exploiting brutally ironic and violent tropes to politicize human rights violations, such as *lynchings, a feudal sharecropping system, and substandard *education, at home. Mainstream *publishing houses, journals, and magazines were as reluctant to print poetry that was sometimes labelled "subversive" as they had been during the 1920s and 1930s. Fortunately, black-owned newspapers, journals, and *periodicals provided a forum for this new generation of black artists. In 1940, W. E. B. Du Bois founded *Phylon, an African American journal focused on issues of race and culture, and late in 1942, John H. Johnson began to publish the Negro Digest, which stood, without qualification, for "the winning of the war and the integration of all citizens into the democratic process." These and other publications built on a resilient tradition of African American *journalism that extends back to the founding of the *Chicago Defender in 1900, Monroe Trotter's Boston Guardian in 1901, and the *Crisis magazine (1910), which Du Bois edited.

The critical exchange between Ralph Ellison and Irving Howe in the New Leader in December 1963 and February 1964 marks the beginning of the end of the protest aesthetic. Howe's essay, "Black Boys and Native Sons," which had appeared in his magazine, Dissent, was a retrospective commentary on the 1940s—the high-water mark of *protest literature in America—and a paean to Richard Wright, the era's preeminent protest writer. Howe's assessment of black literature elevates Wright to the top of what Langston Hughes a generation earlier had called the "racial mountain"; it also implicates Ellison in James Baldwin's much-publicized rejection, in "Everybody's Protest Novel," of Wright and the protest tradition in American fiction. Howe cast Baldwin and Ellison in the role of ingrates, "black boys" oedipally driven to displace Wright, their literary father and an authentic "native son." Ellison's strong objections throughout the second section of his rebuttal essay, "The World and the Jug," are to the idea of the "Negro" as a "sterile category," and to the Negro artist as a frozen metaphor responsive only to "pain and ferocity," which, in Howe's view, provides the animus for protest fiction. For Ellison, the aesthetics that shape the writer's work and upon which it should be judged are a product of craft and technique, the human condition rather than the racial or cultural specificity of a certain group. "Protest is there," Ellison asserts, "not because I was helpless before my racial condition, but because I put it there."

Ellison's views represent a humanistic, ethically centered tradition that rejected the racially based criteria for literature of the past, as well as the new "Black Aesthetic" arising out of the *Black Arts movement. Forged by Larry *Neal, Hoyt Fuller, LeRoi Jones (Amiri *Baraka), and many others, this new aesthetic recalled an earlier generation's defiant commitment to an indigenous "Negro" art form. The 1960s movement in black arts, however, was repetition with a difference—a difference that made the political nature of all art an article of faith, and transformed race, that is, the Negro as subject, into a movement that linked black culture and art in America to black political and artistic expression throughout the diaspora. These mid-1960s developments in African American literary criticism and art were not alien to Ellison, whose critical views and artistic sensibility were shaped by modernists like T. S. Eliot, Ernest Hemingway, and Fyodor Dostoevsky. Nor are these developments foreign to writers like Baldwin, whose fiction and provocative social commentary (e.g., The *Fire Next Time) chronicles—but also helps to shape—African American consciousness through the 1960s civil rights era, the Black Arts movement, and beyond. That Ellison's first collection of essays, *Shadow and Act, in 1964, which included "Twentieth-Century Fiction and the Black Mask of Humanity" and "The World and the Jug," appears a mere four years before Larry Neal's "The Black Arts Movement" and Hoyt W. Fuller's "Towards a Black Aesthetic" is a testament to the rich diversity of African American literary criticism in the modernist period, 1920 to 1964.

Finally, this is an era that begins with the search for "criteria" for "Negro art" and ends with a "movement" toward a Black Aesthetic. These terms imply both the dialectical, progressive nature of African American literary criticism and, simultaneously, signify the circularity and wholeness that is also its essence. It is a period that echoes the rebellious Harlem Renaissance poets in the poetry of the 1960s Black Arts movement; that creates an audience that is, ultimately, both white and black; that transforms a narrow debate about racial representation into a dialogue etched in the politics of race, class, and gender; and that makes the black writer/critic's voice an inevitable part of the dialogue about American culture.

[See also Character Types; Periodicals, article on Scholarly Journals and Literary Magazines.]

• Sterling Brown, The Negro in American Fiction, 1937. Ralph Ellison, Shadow and Act, 1964. Langston Hughes, "The Negro Artist and the Racial Mountain," in Voices from the Harlem Renaissance, ed. Nathan Irvin Huggins, 1976, pp. 305–309. Arthur P. Davis, From the Dark Tower: Afro-American Writers 1900–1960, 1981. David Levering Lewis, When Harlem Was in Vogue, 1981. James Baldwin, The Price of the Ticket: Collected Non-fiction 1948–1985, 1985. Alain Locke,

The New Negro, 1925; rpt. with an introduction by Arnold Rampersad, 1992. Angelyn Mitchell, Within the Circle, 1994.

—Cedric Gael Bryant

CRITICISM SINCE 1965

African American literary criticism since 1965 has been marked by considerable conflict. In itself, this is not a new phenomenon; moreover, the terms of the controversy are often similar to those of earlier struggles. As they have been in the past, the antagonists on one side are those who see the practice and study of literature primarily in social and political terms; those on the other side focus on particular aesthetic issues such as form, style, and theme, with the added contemporary concerns for figurative language, discursive practices, and intertextuality. It is important to note that many critics have been working either across this critical divide or have chosen different sites altogether for their investigations. Nonetheless, given the intensity of the more celebrated encounters, the metaphor of battle remains appropriate.

Much of the energy of late-twentieth-century criticism has been drawn from and given over to theory. While considerable comment has been made concerning Houston A. *Baker, Jr., Henry Louis *Gates, Jr., and their poststructuralist colleagues, recent critical practice began in the theorizing of the *Black Aesthetic movement. This group, including Amiri *Baraka, Larry *Neal, and Maulana Ron Karenga, reacted against the "integrationist poetics" of the 1950s and early 1960s by applying the principles of a politics based in *black nationalism to literature. They attacked the work of James *Baldwin and Ralph *Ellison, the dominant writers of the time, as being too concerned with meeting Western aesthetic standards and with receiving the approval of white audiences and critics. These black nationalist critics rejected the idea that literature was to be judged by a universal aesthetic and not by its political content or its author's racial *identity.

Neal, Baraka, and others insisted that all literature has a social function and that the so-called universal aesthetics were oppressive and racist. Karenga argued in "Black Cultural Nationalism" (1968) that African artistic principles included functionality, collectivity, and commitment and that true black art needed to reflect these characteristics rather than those of the Western tradition. The purpose of the black artist was to be the enhancement of black life, not individual expression. Specifically, this meant contributing to "the revolution" by encouraging black pride and by making clear the nature of the race's enemies. The role of the black critic was to evaluate the extent to which the artist satisfied these ideological requirements. Sometimes the roles of critic and artist coincided. The journal Black World and the *anthologies Black Fire (eds. Baraka and Neal, 1971) and The Black Aesthetic (ed. Addison *Gayle, Jr., 1971) were major outlets for both.

Larry Neal defined the need for a distinct black mythology and symbolism that would make possible a literature separate from that of a decadent white culture and that would speak to a black audience. A principle resource for such a literature would be black *music, which he argued had managed to develop largely independently of Western society. Stephen Henderson, in Understanding the New Black Poetry (1972), undertook to spell out the characteristics of an authentically black *poetry in terms of the language, music, and cultural history of black America. Such writing, Henderson argued, would also interact with its audience; the artist needed to both speak and listen to readers, who were primarily defined as the urban underclass. The Western notion of the eternal artistic object was displaced by the work that is temporary and functional; in fact, the standard of beauty becomes its functionality rather than some abstract perfection. Literary works were expected to be "used up"; because they contributed to revolution, they necessarily would be put aside once they had served their purpose.

One problem with this approach, as Darwin Turner suggested as early as 1971, was that theory preceded literary practice. A significant body of contemporary black literature was being produced that did not fit the principles. Many works were not urban, polemical, and consistently positive in their black characterizations. Another difficulty was the changing perspectives of the theorists themselves. While some, such as Gayle and Karenga, remained consistent, both Baraka and Neal shifted their views. Baraka moved to a Marxist position, from which he viewed cultural nationalism as reactionary, and Neal came to argue for the value of using Western means to express African American concerns.

By the late 1970s a new approach was being shaped by the scholars who were themselves the academic products of the gains made through the *civil rights movement and the black nationalist movement. The methods they chose to use were those current within Western theory: structuralism, rhetorical analysis, and intertextuality, among others. The practitioners of this mode came to be called Reconstructionists after the Modern Language Association publication of Afro-American Literature: The Reconstruction of Instruction (1978), edited by Dexter Fisher and Robert Stepto. Unlike the Black Aesthetics critics, the "Reconstructionists" read African American writing in formal and literary-historical rather than political terms. For example, Henry Louis Gates examines binary oppositions in the first chapter of Frederick *Douglass's *Narrative of the Life of Frederick Douglass (1845) and Robert O'Meally considers the formal significance of *folklore in Ralph Ellison. Stepto, in From behind the Veil (1979), argues that the major tradition in African American narrative is an intertextual one in which each generation defines its literary task in terms of earlier writers and in terms of what he calls the "pregeneric myth" of *literacy and *freedom.

Gates became a leading practitioner of what Houston Baker calls the "semiotic" approach. In Figures in Black (1984), and the edited collections Black Literature and Literary Theory (1985) and "Race," Writing, and Difference (1986), Gates and others have asserted the importance of figurative language and of revoicings within black literary and expressive traditions. "*Race" itself, the crucial term for the Black

Aestheticists, is understood as a trope. The impulse in such interpretations is to exclude "extraliterary" factors such as politics and social conditions.

Not surprisingly, this stance stirred controversy. In 1981 Houston Baker, who himself had been associated with the Black Aesthetic, questioned the position of Stepto and Gates in an article in *Black American Literature Forum*. His attack, however, was based not on the earlier theory (which he labels "romantic Marxism") but on an African American "anthropology of art." The problem with Gates, said Baker, is that he claimed that literature could be understood as a system of signs independent of social institutions. But since language itself is a social institution, the issue is not whether literature expresses a particular ideology, but rather whether it can be generated and understood outside of history, society, and culture.

Gates and Baker moved closer together as each developed his ideas in terms of poststructuralist theories. Gates found in the figure of the signifying monkey a cultural image for rhetorical practices of indirection and irony. Thus, while remaining concerned with sign systems, he sought their sources in black tradition. Baker, in *Blues, Ideology and Afro-American Literature* (1984), *Modernism and the Harlem Renaissance* (1987), and *Afro-American Poetics* (1988), spelled out a position that links symbolic anthropology, sociolinguistics, social constructivism, and other elements that emphasize discursive practices in the study of literature. African American writing in this view becomes part of a complex of "texts" that includes folklore, *religion, social and political institutions, music and other arts, and *history. For critics such as Gates and Baker, literary study must not be defined either as the study of an isolated text or as an articulation of ideology but as the apprehension of a complex nexus within which the text is situated.

This emphasis on discourse provoked intense criticism. Joyce Ann Joyce, for example, contended that African American poststructuralists ignored the racial conditions that produce literature and thereby refused the traditional responsibility of the black critic to aid the artist in developing the full possibilities of African American expression and in guiding readers to an appreciation of what is most authentic in the writing.

A different debate has accompanied the emergence of black women's writing and the critical methods to interpret it. The dynamics of race and *gender created questions of whether either feminist approaches, used in the examination of nonblack women writers, or those of black criticism, used in the past mainly for the discussion of male writers, would be sufficient for writers who fit neither exclusive category. The early work of Barbara Smith and Barbara Christian, both through theoretical discussions and analyses of specific writers, established the need to articulate a distinct method. The experiences narrated, the characters created, and the traditions called upon by the writing itself demonstrated the inadequacy of other perspectives. A view that Alice *Walker named *womanism and that others designated black *feminism sought to bring together a variety of insights specific to the subject.

What proved essential was examination of voice and silence, of imagery of the black female body, and of motifs and image patterns involving distinct traditions, such as quilting and *conjuring. Also central was a sense of *family and literary traditions, as again suggested by Walker and developed especially in the work of Deborah McDowell. Other critics used the methods of poststructuralism and Marxism to help explain both the conditions of literary production and the particular themes and structures created by African American women writers. Hazel Carby and Susan Willis, for example, pursued Marxist approaches that address the roles of material conditions and commodification in shaping literary production. Others such as Hortense Spillers and Claudia Tate have adapted the insights of feminism to the situations of black women writers. Mary Helen Washington, Nellie McKay, and Frances Smith Foster are among those who helped define African American female literary traditions. Mae Henderson, Missy Dehn Kubitschek, Claudia Tate, Ann duCille, William L. Andrews, and Trudier Harris have examined aspects of these traditions. Karla Holloway, Gay Wilentz, Carol Boyce Davies, and Molara Ogundipe-Leslie have extended that tradition back and across to the influence of African women writers and cultures.

One development in women's writing that has influenced all of African American criticism is the expansion of the canon. This has occurred as known writers are critically reevaluated, which was the case with Zora Neale *Hurston; as the authenticity of texts is established, as was the case with the literary-historical detective work done by Jean Yellin on *Incidents in the Life of a Slave Girl* (1861); or as lost works are recovered, as Henry Louis Gates did with *Our Nig* and Frances Smith Foster did with the three novels by Frances Ellen Watkins *Harper. Another level of recovery is represented by the Schomburg Library of Nineteenth-Century Black Women Writers, the Black Periodical Literature Project, the Project on the History of Black Writing, and other large literary recovery efforts. They make sense of a literary tradition much fuller and more continuous than previously thought. On a lesser scale, a number of publishers have been engaged in bringing out new or reprint editions. Virago, Beacon Press, and Northeastern University Press, among others, have made available, usually in trade paperback, works by both men and women that had gone out of print.

This recovery process has raised questions about the African American canon. On the one hand, efforts have been undertaken to establish a canon through the production of anthologies, new editions, and critical commentary. This has been done not only within the field, but also through inclusion in American literature anthologies and college and university course offerings. On the other hand, the very notion of *canonization is being challenged. This debate has been more explicit and theoretical in traditionally dominant literatures, but it is implicit in the expansion of the genres and forms of works receiving critical analysis. The Schomburg series alone includes *poetry, *novels, magazine fiction,*biography and *autobiography, journals, and social commentary. Oral traditions, such as *sermons and preaching, toasts, folktales, and political speeches are being subjected to the same kinds of examination as more conventional literary expression. In the field of autobiography, William L. Andrews, in *To Tell a Free Story* (1986), and Joanne Braxton, in *Black Women Writing Autobiography* (1989), have described in detail the ways life stories have shaped and reshaped themselves since the slave narratives. Arnold *Rampersad has set a standard for the field with his biography of Langston *Hughes. Michael Dyson and bell *hooks apply the methods of cultural criticism to the "texts" of black *film, representations of the black body, and contemporary music. A wide range of reference works, including *bibliographies, literary histories, biographical dictionaries, and indexes, has also been produced recently.

Recent criticism is a vast expansion of both the subject matter and the methods of critical practice. The racial history of the nation, especially as it is manifested in literary study, produced a critical tradition that was in the past often defensive about the value of African American writing. That tradition is still influential in some of the recent debates over the ideologies of critical practice. But increasingly, scholars in the field have confidently applied whatever means seem appropriate and expended less effort on validating the worthiness of black writing as a subject of academic study. In this sense, African American criticism has achieved a sophisticated maturity.

• Mary Helen Washington, *Black-Eyed Susans: Classic Stories by and about Black Women*, 1975. Barbara Christian, *Black Women Novelists: The Development of a Tradition, 1892–1976*, 1980. Houston A. Baker, Jr., "Generational Shifts and the Recent Criticism of Afro-American Literature," *Black American Literature Forum* 15 (Spring 1981): 3–21. Joe Weixlmann and Chester J. Fontenot, eds., *Black American Prose Theory*, 1984. Sigmund Ro, "'Desecrators' and 'Necromancers': Black American Writers and Critics in the Nineteen-Sixties and the Third World Perspective," *Callaloo* 8 (Fall 1985): 563–576. Bernard W. Bell, *The Afro-American Novel and Its Tradition*, 1987. Theodore O. Mason, "Between the Populist and the Scientist: Ideology and Power in Recent Afro-American Literary Criticism, or 'The Dozens' As Scholarship," *Callaloo* 11 (Summer 1988): 606–615. Houston Baker and Patricia Redmond, eds., *Afro-American Literary Study in the 1990s*, 1989. JoAnne Cornwell-Giles, "Afro-American Criticism and Western Consciousness: The Politics of Knowing," *Black American Literature Forum* 24 (Spring 1990): 85–98. Henry Louis Gates, Jr., "African American Criticism," in *Redrawing the Boundaries: The Transformation of English and American Literary Studies*, eds. Stephen Greenblatt and Giles Gunn, 1992, pp. 303–319. bell hooks, *Black Looks: Race and Representation*, 1992. Michael Eric Dyson, *Reflecting Black: African-American Cultural Criticism*, 1993.
—Keith E. Byerman

CROUCH, STANLEY (b. 1945), jazz and cultural critic. Stanley Crouch was born in Los Angeles. His father was a heroin addict and his mother a hard-working *domestic who taught him to read before he entered school. Although Crouch attended both East Los Angeles Junior College and Southwest Junior College, he never earned a degree. In effect, he is an autodidact and his work reflects the strengths and weaknesses of the untrained intellectual. During the 1960s, Crouch became enamored of *black nationalism and the *theater. He was well known in black nationalist circles and was an actor, director, and playwright. He also was a drummer leading his own *jazz combo during these days, recording an album with Impulse Records called *Ain't No Ambulances for No Niggahs Tonight*. In the 1970s, Crouch, deeply influenced by the works of Ralph *Ellison and Albert *Murray, began to distance himself from the black nationalists. In 1975 he moved to New York and began to write for the *Village Voice*, an association that ended in 1988 when he punched out another *Voice* writer in an argument over rap music. Many of his *Voice* pieces were collected in his first book, *Notes of a Hanging Judge*, published in 1990. Crouch has subsequently won both the Whiting Writer's Prize and the MacArthur Fellowship. In 1996 he was finishing a long-awaited *biography of jazz saxophonist Charlie *Parker, as well as a *novel entitled "First Snow in Kokomo." Acerbic and withering in his critical attacks, Crouch is often characterized as a conservative or even a race traitor. He is placed with black thinkers critical of the *civil rights movement in *Challenging the Civil Rights Establishment: Profiles of a New Black Vanguard* (1993) by Joseph G. Conti and Brad Stetson. Crouch sees himself in the tradition of Ellison and Murray, understanding black American life as rich and complex, not necessarily warped by white racism and completely disconnected from an African past. Moreover, he sees himself in the tradition of an H. L. Mencken or George S. *Schuyler as a satiric denouncer of all forms of cant, quackery, and nonsense.
—Gerald Early

CRUMMELL, ALEXANDER (1819–1898), scholar, educator, lecturer, essayist, and Episcopal minister. Born in New York City to Charity and Boston Crummell, Alexander grew up in a family that placed great emphasis on *freedom, independence, and *education. Although his parents had not experienced the privilege of a formal education, they placed Alexander in the Mulberry Street School and hired additional private tutors for him. When Crummell decided to enter the priesthood, he applied for entry into the theological seminary of the Episcopal Church. According to Crummell's own account in his 1894 retirement address, "Shades and Lights," the admissions board denied his application because its policy was to exclude blacks from positions in the church hierarchy. Crummell was then forced to study privately with sympathetic clergy. These early studies shaped the stoic and methodical style that remained evident throughout his long career as writer and orator. Although he was ordained an Episcopal priest in 1844, it was not until 1847 that Crummell's dream of a formal education became reality. While in England raising funds for his New York mission, the Church of the Messiah, Crummell found English philanthropists who offered financial assistance for his education at Queen's College. When he received his AB degree in theology in 1853, Crummell found himself among a small number of formally accredited black scholars. It was not until after emancipation that African Americans entered into academia in significant numbers.

His studies completed, Crummell sailed for Liberia, where he spent nearly twenty years as missionary, educator, and statesman. After returning to the United States in 1873, he assumed the rectorship of St. Mary's Episcopal Church in Washington, D.C. Leaders such as Crummell now turned their attention to the question of how blacks would improve their lot in the hostile post-Reconstruction environment. As a public speaker and writer Crummell countered charges of black racial inferiority. In 1897, three years after his retirement from the ministry, Crummell spearheaded the establishment of the American Negro Academy, the first African American scholarly society in the United States. By the time of his death in 1898 Crummell had become the august statesman among black scholars and professionals. In his 1914 publication, *The Negro in American History*, black activist John Cromwell remembered Crummell as "easily the ripest literary scholar, the writer of the most graceful and faultless English and the most brilliant conversationalist the race has produced in this country."

As a writer Crummell was best known for his occasional sermons and his sociopolitical tracts. Traces of Crummell's activism are evident as early as 1840, when he participated in the New York Negro Convention Movement focusing on voting rights for blacks. While active as a young man in the *antislavery movement and local political campaigns, Crummell's first collection of sermons and *essays, *The Future of Africa* was not published until 1862 during his Liberian residency. In his early years Crummell had renounced the idea of the removal of African Americans to Africa but altered his position during his stay in England. As a resident of Liberia, Crummell envisioned its future as an autonomous black nation. Consequently, Crummell campaigned actively for the colonization movement. *The Future of Africa* can be viewed as Crummell's treatise on what would later be called *black nationalism. In this collection of ten essays Crummell traced the progress of Liberia, often echoing the nationalist propaganda of colonial American writers. Not unlike Cotton Mather's vision of America as a fulfillment of biblical prophecy, Crummell foresaw in Liberia the fulfillment of God's prophecy for the civilization of blacks. Just as Benjamin Franklin had encouraged industrious and hardworking men to seek their fortunes in America, Crummell in his essay "The Relations and Duties of Free Colored Men in America to Africa" recommended that those black men seeking their fortunes in Africa should be men with "high souls and lofty resolves," "men of force and energy," and most importantly, men with "strong moral proclivities." In "The Negro Race Not under a Curse," Crummell denounced the popular theological notion that blacks had been doomed by God's curse upon the descendants of Ham. In "Hope for

Africa," he spoke of the "divine providence," which he deemed the promise of the "regeneration of Africa and her children."

In 1882 Crummell published *The Greatness of Christ*—a collection of sermons more religious in scope and ruminative in style than his earlier more political tract, *The Future of Africa*. With a vision akin to that of the transcendentalists and romantics, Crummell merged his logical rhetorical style with his spiritual vision. In his sermon "Joseph," Crummell examined man's metaphysical relationship with nature and God, suggesting that "the natural is the sign and symbol of the spiritual; for all things go by doubles in God's system." Similarly, in the sermon "The Greatness of Christ," he drew parallels between occurrences in nature and those in human development. Unfailingly, Crummell guided his contemplations of the abstract back to real-world considerations. In "Joseph," Crummell juxtaposed the condition of the biblical Joseph and that of African Americans. In "The Destined Superiority of the Negro" he constructed a biblical typology that served as political rhetoric. In Crummell's estimation African Americans were a prototype of the emancipated Hebrews who eventually emerged out of Egypt stronger than the nation that had dominated them.

In his 1891 treatise, *Africa and America*, Crummell returned to more immediate and worldly themes. These essays and addresses illustrate the pressing concerns of African Americans in post-Reconstruction America—the abuse of black women in the South at the hands of the white male ruling class, the prevailing presence of racial discrimination in the postwar era, and the problem of labor and education for the emancipated African Americans (verifying the existence of a discourse among black leaders long before the Booker T. *Washington–W. E. B. *Du Bois debate on classical versus industrial education for blacks).

Collectively, the writings of Alexander Crummell not only reveal the political, social, and spiritual concerns of a nineteenth-century African American but they also represent part of the framework from which modern-day African American political rhetoric has developed. Crummell's practice of countering racism and discrimination through the application of historical and scientific information would be adopted by turn-of-the-century African American scholars who followed his example of turning scholarship into a weapon for political and social activism.

[*See also* Emigration; Religion; Sermons and Preaching.]

• Alfred A. Moss, Jr., *The American Negro Academy*, 1981. Wilson Jeremiah Moses, *Black Messiahs and Uncle Tom*, 1982. Alfred A. Moss, Jr., "Alexander Crummell: Black Nationalist and Apostle of Western Civilization," in *Black Leaders of the Nineteenth Century*, eds. Leon Litwack and August Meier, 1988, pp. 237–251. Wilson Jeremiah Moses, *Alexander Crummell: A Study of Civilization and Discontent*, 1989. J. R. Oldfield, *Alexander Crummell and the Creation of an African-American Church in Liberia*, 1990.

—Elizabeth J. West

CRUZ, VICTOR HERNÁNDEZ (b. 1949), poet. Born in Puerto Rico, Victor Hernández Cruz came to the United States with his immediate family in the early 1950s. New York City offered a vivid contrast to the secluded, rural village life his family had known. "Even the sky was cement," he wrote in "Snaps of Immigration." Beginning with his precocious debut at age nineteen with the volume *Snaps* (1968), Cruz has detailed the cultural dislocation and street life around him, sounding themes and rhythms that catch the world at a glance but also partake in the poet's quest for a *poetry and a poetics fully resonant with the richness and complexity of Puerto Rican life. Three distinct ethnic traditions—Spanish, Amerindian, and African—contribute to the culture that Cruz inherits and that he is driven to preserve and transform. Each of his volumes expands upon the sharply observed and cleanly rendered notational poetics of the first volume. The poet incorporates the larger history of *migration, mixing fables, surrealism, chants, prose poems, and *essays to show the analytical and expressive contributions writing can make in the context of Puerto Rican cultural struggle. The 1989 volume of selected and new poems, *Rhythm, Content and Flavor*, published by Arte Público Press, documents his deepening interest in two subjects that touch deeply on matters of *identity: *music and the occult. As his work makes use of these sources, Cruz utilizes a longer, more resonantly ecstatic line. His masterful collection *Red Beans*, published in 1991, contains much of his finest work to date, as well as autobiographical and cultural meditations of considerable interest. In "The Bolero of the Red Translation," Cruz offers a narrative of poetic initiation, finding in the cultic practice of displaced Puerto Rican families a ground for poetic practice that weaves diverse traditions into a single song:

> Into our living room the practitioners of espiritismo gathered. With candles and prayers they penetrated screens in the space and contacted the voices of the dead, their hands went into whirls, their bodies danced. Catholic saints stood next to Indian heads. Africans came through the open wires, old Muhammadans hung with turbans from the ceiling. . . . Poetry came to me and whispered, it came from its immense heaven where it has eternally kept vigil over the tongues of men.

Along with such poets as Jay *Wright, Cam Brathwaite, and Nathaniel *Mackey, Cruz has developed a poetics for the New World. His trope for poetic innovation is "salsa," a term that in its double meaning, as spice and as musical form, holds in balance many of poetry's oldest and most vital divisions, body and soul, mortal and god. Cruz creates new dramas out of these old divisions as he works to honor a specific community and tell its story but also, as the increasingly visionary strain of his work suggests, to call a new order into being, to sing the migration of possibility from dream to fact.

• Frances Aparicio, "Salsa, Maracas, Baile: Latin Popular Music in the Poetry of Victor Hernández Cruz," *Melus* 16.1 (Spring 1989–1990): 43–58.   —Joseph Donahue

CUFFE, PAUL (1759–1817), seaman, businessman, and African colonizer. Born 17 January 1759 on Cuttyhunk Island, Massachusetts, the seventh of ten children of African-born Coffe and Ruth Slocum, a Wampanoag Indian, Paul Cuffe is one of the pioneers of *black nationalism and self-determination. Civil rights fighter, property owner, and supporter of public *education, Cuffe began a family-owned farming, shipping, and milling enterprise. In 1783 he married Alice Pequit; they had seven children. Cuffe built and owned six ships and with an all-black crew traded along the Atlantic coast and in the West Indies and Sierra Leone. His first trip to Africa was to encourage trade, not to civilize Christians as is commonly believed. When the *Traveller* sailed for Sierra Leone on 27 December 1810, Cuffe's "Memoirs of an African Captain" had already appeared in newspapers in England and America. In 1812 his "Brief Account of the Settlement and Present Situation of the Colony of Sierra Leone in Africa" was published. It and his captain's log (journal of 1811–1812) are important for their nineteenth-century depictions of the colony. Cuffe prescribed self-determination for "the civilization of Africa"; he believed that Africans, if allowed, would traffic in goods rather than slaves. To demonstrate this he sailed *Traveller* to Liverpool, a center of slave activity, in the summer of 1811 with a cargo produced by free African labor. On the *Traveller's* second voyage to Sierra Leone in 1815, Cuffe transported thirty-eight passengers in what is identified as "the first black-initiated *emigration movement" from the United States to Africa. Upon his return to America in 1816 (his wife would not emigrate), Cuffe supported the American Colonization Society. The wealthy seaman, businessman, and colonizer died 7 September 1817. His carefully recorded journal and "Brief Account" provide valuable insights into an early Pan-African consciousness as well as the early history of African American emigration to Africa.

[*See also* Diaries and Journals; Pan-Africanism.]

• Sheldon Harris, *Paul Cuffe: Black America and the African Return*, 1972. Lamont D. Thomas, *Rise to Be a People: A Biography of Paul Cuffe*, 1986.   —Paula C. Barnes

CULLEN, COUNTEE (1903–1946), poet, anthologist, novelist, translator, children's writer, and playwright. Countee Cullen is something of a mysterious figure. He was born 30 March 1903, but it has been difficult for scholars to place exactly where he was born, with whom he spent the very earliest years of his childhood, and where he spent them. New York City and Baltimore have been given as birthplaces. Cullen himself, on his college transcript at New York University, lists Louisville, Kentucky, as his place of birth. A few years later, when he had achieved considerable literary fame during the era known as the New Negro or *Harlem Renaissance, he was to assert that his birthplace was New York City, which he continued to claim for the rest of his life. Cullen's second wife, Ida, and some of his closest friends, including Langston *Hughes and Harold Jackman, said that Cullen was born in Louisville. As James Weldon

*Johnson wrote of Cullen in *The Book of American Negro Poetry* (rev. ed., 1931): "There is not much to say about these earlier years of Cullen—unless he himself should say it." And Cullen—revealing a temperament that was not exactly secretive but private, less a matter of modesty than a tendency toward being encoded and tactful—never in his life said anything more clarifying.

Sometime before 1918, Cullen was adopted by the Reverend Frederick A. and Carolyn Belle (Mitchell) Cullen. It is impossible to state with certainty how old Cullen was when he was adopted or how long he knew the Cullens before he was adopted. Apparently he went by the name of Countee Porter until 1918. By 1921 he became Countee P. Cullen and eventually just Countee Cullen. According to Harold Jackman, Cullen's adoption was never "official." That is to say it was never consummated through proper state-agency channels. Indeed, it is difficult to know if Cullen was ever legally an orphan at any stage in his childhood.

Frederick Cullen was a pioneer black activist minister. He established his Salem Methodist Episcopal Church in a storefront mission upon his arrival in New York City in 1902, and in 1924 moved the Church to the site of a former white church in Harlem where he could boast of a membership of more than twenty-five hundred. Countee Cullen himself stated in *Caroling Dusk* (1927) that he was "reared in the conservative atmosphere of a Methodist parsonage," and it is clear that his foster father was a particularly strong influence. The two men were very close, often traveling abroad together. But as Cullen evidences a decided unease in his *poetry over his strong and conservative Christian training and the attraction of his pagan inclinations, his feelings about his father may have been somewhat ambivalent. On the one hand, Frederick Cullen was a puritanical Christian patriarch, and Cullen was never remotely that in his life. On the other hand, it has been suggested that Frederick Cullen was also something of an effeminate man. (He was dressed in girl's clothing by his poverty-stricken mother well beyond the acceptable boyhood age for such transvestism.) That Cullen was homosexual or of a decidedly ambiguous sexual nature may also be attributable to his foster father's contrary influence as both fire-breathing Christian and latent homosexual.

Cullen was an outstanding student at DeWitt Clinton High School (1918–1921). He edited the school's newspaper, assisted in editing the literary magazine, *Magpie*, and began to write poetry that achieved notice. While in high school Cullen won his first contest, a citywide competition, with the poem "I Have a Rendezvous with Life," a nonracial poem inspired by Alan Seeger's "I Have a Rendezvous with Death." At New York University (1921–1925), he wrote most of the poems for his first three volumes: *Color* (1925), *Copper Sun* (1927), and *The Ballad of the Brown Girl* (1927). If any event signaled the coming of the Harlem Renaissance, it was the precocious success of this rather shy black boy who, more than any other black literary figure of his generation, was being touted and bred to become a major crossover

literary figure. Here was a black man with considerable academic training who could, in effect, write "white" verse—ballads, sonnets, quatrains, and the like—much in the manner of Keats and the British Romantics, (albeit, on more than one occasion, tinged with racial concerns) with genuine skill and compelling power. He was certainly not the first Negro to attempt to write such verse but he was first to do so with such extensive education and with such a complete understanding of himself as a poet. Only two other black American poets before Cullen could be taken so seriously as self-consciously considered and proficient poets: Phillis *Wheatley and Paul Laurence *Dunbar. If the aim of the Harlem Renaissance was, in part, the reinvention of the native-born Negro as a being who can be assimilated while decidedly retaining something called "a racial self-consciousness," then Cullen fit the bill. If "I Have a Rendezvous with Life" was the opening salvo in the making of Cullen's literary reputation, then the 1924 publication of "Shroud of Color" in H. L. Mencken's *American Mercury* confirmed the advent of the black boy wonder as one of the most exciting American poets on the scene. After graduating Phi Beta Kappa from NYU, Cullen earned a master's degree in English and French from Harvard (1925–1927). Between high school and his graduation from Harvard, Cullen was the most popular black poet and virtually the most popular black literary figure in America. One of Cullen's poems and his popular column in *Opportunity inspired A'Leila Walker—heiress of Madame C. J. Walker's hair-care products fortune and owner of a salon where the black and white literati gathered in the late 1920s—to name her salon "The Dark Tower."

Cullen won more major literary prizes than any other black writer of the 1920s: first prize in the Witter Bynner Poetry contest in 1925, *Poetry* magazine's John Reed Memorial Prize, the Amy Spingarn Award of the *Crisis* magazine, second prize in *Opportunity* magazine's first poetry contest, and second prize in the poetry contest of *Palms*. In addition, he was the second black to win a Guggenheim Fellowship.

Cullen was also at the center of one of the major social events of the Harlem Renaissance: On 9 April 1928 he married Yolande Du Bois, only child of W. E. B. *Du Bois, in one of the most lavish weddings in black New York history. This wedding was to symbolize the union of the grand black intellectual patriarch and the new breed of younger Negroes who were responsible for much of the excitement of the Renaissance. It was an apt meshing of personalities as Cullen and Du Bois were both conservative by nature and ardent traditionalists. That the marriage turned out so disastrously and ended so quickly (they divorced in 1930) probably adversely affected Cullen, who remarried in 1940. In 1929, Cullen published *The Black Christ and Other Poems* to less than his accustomed glowing reviews. He was bitterly disappointed that *The Black Christ*, his longest and in many respects most complicated poem, was considered by most critics and reviewers to be his weakest and least distinguished.

From the 1930s until his death, Cullen wrote a

great deal less, partly hampered by his job as a French teacher at Frederick Douglass Junior High. (His most famous student was James *Baldwin.) But he wrote noteworthy, even significant work in a number of genres. His *novel One Way to Heaven, published in 1934, rates as one of the better black satires and is one of the three important fictional retrospectives of the Harlem Renaissance, the others being Wallace *Thurman's Infants of the Spring and George S. *Schuyler's *Black No More. Cullen's The Medea is the first major translation of a classical work by a twentieth-century black American writer. Cullen's contributions to *children's literature, The Lost Zoo and *Christopher Cat, are among the more clever and engaging books of children's verse, written at a time when there was not much published in this area by black writers. He also completed perhaps some of his best, certainly some of his more darkly complex, sonnets. He was also working on a musical with Arna *Bontemps called St. Louis Woman (based on Bontemps's novel God Sends Sunday) at the time of his death from high blood pressure and uremic poisoning on 9 January 1946.

For many years after his death, Cullen's reputation was eclipsed by that of other Harlem Renaissance writers, particularly Langston Hughes and Zora Neale *Hurston, and his work had gone out of print. In the last few years, however, there has been a resurgence of interest in Cullen's life and work and his writings are being reissued.

• Blanche E. Ferguson, Countee Cullen and the Negro Renaissance, 1966. Margaret Perry, A Bio-Bibliography of Countee P. Cullen, 1903–1946, 1966. Arna Bontemps, ed., The Harlem Renaissance Remembered, 1972. Arthur P. Davis, From the Dark Tower: Afro-American Writers, 1900 to 1960, 1974. Alan R. Shucard, Countee Cullen, 1984. Gerald Early, ed., My Soul's High Song: The Collected Writings of Countee Cullen, Voice of the Harlem Renaissance, 1991.

—Gerald Early

CUNEY-HARE, MAUD (1874–1936), concert pianist, music lecturer, folklorist, and historian. Maud Cuney-Hare is remembered for her literary accomplishments as a gifted playwright, biographer, and music columnist for the *Crisis. Born in Galveston, Texas, on 16 February 1874, to teacher and soprano Adelina Dowdie and Norris Wright Cuney, an important Texas political figure who was the (defeated) Republican candidate for the 1875 Galveston mayoral race, Maud Cuney-Hare was educated in Texas and became musical director at the Deaf, Dumb and Blind Institute in Austin, Texas. She held other church and college teaching positions before returning to Boston and devoting her life to performance, scholarship, and literary pursuits. She championed the 24 May 1917 Cambridge, Massachusetts, restaging of Angelina Weld *Grimké's Rachel (1916), which, according to critic Robert Fehrenbach was "the first time a play written by an Afro-American that dealt with the real problems facing American Blacks in contemporary, white, racist society was performed by entirely Black companies." The *biography she wrote about her father, Norris Wright Cuney: Tribune of the Black People (1913), suggests that he was

instrumental in encouraging self-respect, courage, and resistance in his daughter, themes that emerge in her play, Antar of Araby. The biography reveals that while she was a student at the New England Conservatory of Music in Boston, the executive committee of the conservatory wrote Norris Cuney a letter, asking that he find another place for his daughter to live, explaining, "We have a large number of pupils who are affected by race prejudices, and the Home must be conducted so as to insure the comfort and satisfaction of the largest number possible." Not only was her father's response heated and unequivocal but the incident galvanized students at nearby Harvard as well; W. E. B. *Du Bois (at one time engaged to Maud Cuney, before her marriage to William Hare in 1906) has written of how he was one of a group of Harvard students who "rushed to her defense when the New England Conservatory of Music tried to 'Jim Crow' her in the dormitory." Cuney-Hare edited an *anthology of nature poems, The Message of the Trees: An Anthology of Leaves and Branches (1918). A collector of folk songs and *dances, she traveled to Cuba, the Virgin Islands, Haiti, Puerto Rico, and Mexico documenting the African sources for much European and world music, among these, the Moorish origins of the Spanish fandango in Spain and the Afro-Cuban sources of the Haitian Méringüe. "History and Song in the Virgin Islands," a 1993 *essay she wrote for the Crisis, includes a riveting account of the 1848 slave *insurrection of Saint Croix, when more than five thousand slaves "stormed the fort and demanded freedom," later burning the town down. Cuney-Hare documents the song "Queen Mary," named for "an intrepid woman slave [who] was the Joan of Arc of the rebellion." Her play Antar of Araby (1929) borrows from foreign legend to recount a story of a man, enslaved by his own father, whose dark skin and inferior social status are impediments to the fulfillment of his talents, his happiness, and his marriage to the woman he loves. Clearly influenced by Shakespeare's diction and themes, the *drama pivots on Prince Shedad's belated recognition of Antar's worth. King Zoheir eventually blesses Antar with the words, "God protect thee, thou black in face and fair in deeds." In warrior service to the king, Antar discovers the royal lineage of his own mother, thus entitling him by rank to compete for his beloved Abla, the Arab chieftain's daughter; the power of the play, however, lies in the fact that his new social status is of little concern to Abla, who declares her unwavering love for Antar while he is still a slave. Maud Cuney-Hare died of cancer 13 February 1936, one month after the publication of her last major work, Negro Musicians and Their Music. The study notes African sources for African American music, with a particularly interesting section on *spirituals as hymns of consolation and coded means of communication; it includes a carefully researched appendix of African musical instruments. Maud Cuney-Hare has left an important legacy; she was instrumental in establishing and documenting a musical and theatrical arts movement in Black America.

—Lynda Koolish

D

DANCE. *Music and dance were vital components of all significant events in West African culture, according to Olaudah *Equiano's *The Interesting Narrative of the Life of Olaudah Equiano or Gustavus Vassa* (1789). When Africans became enslaved in North America, dance proved to be an irrepressible retention. Among the literature that acknowledges this heritage are two poems by Countee *Cullen, from the collection *Color* (1925). In "Heritage" the rhythm of rain arouses ancient memories of African dance, and in "A Song of Praise," a woman's walk recalls the nobility of African movement.

Dance figures prominently in all genres of African American literature, which confirms its appeal and persistence. Perhaps it appears so frequently as metaphor because the image of dance elicits easily identifiable motion. "[H]is words dancing on the edge of anger" (Melvin *Dixon, *Vanishing Rooms*, 1991) or they "train-danced on into the City" (Toni *Morrison, *Jazz*, 1992) are representative examples. The literal use of dance as activity is also striking. For example, in Ann *Petry's *The *Street* (1996), *Lutie Johnson and her husband spend two or three evenings in Harlem "drinking beer in someone's living room and dancing to a radio" before their separation. Among the various functions of dance in African American literature, one finds it as culture-based recreation, as a medium for creative assertion, as a unifying force in political action, and as a connector of culture and ritual throughout the African diaspora.

*Slave narratives, fiction, and *poetry illustrate the inspiritingly distractive qualities of dance amid oppression and frustration. In his *Narrative* (1845) Frederick *Douglass analyzes the politics of Christmas holidays for slaves in which recreational dance played a major role. The free time was a way for owners to protect against slave *insurrection, he observes, and it also served as psychological release from the hardships of *slavery. Harriet A. *Jacobs, like Douglass, realizes that these days of frivolity for slaves served another purpose. In *Incidents in the Life of a Slave Girl* (1861), based on Jacobs's experience in Edenton, North Carolina, families faced possible separation during the hiring days that loomed after Christmas. A seasonal activity she terms "johnkannaus" was probably a distraction from worry. Jacobs's description is valuable because it links ceremony and dance to a cultural continuum. According to John W. Nunley and Judith Bettelheim, Jonkonnu (the term has several spellings) combines European pre-Lenten festivals with traditional African masquerades and is usually celebrated around Christmas and New Year's holidays (*Caribbean Festival Arts*, 1988). Jacobs observes that it included costuming, parading, and dancing, although she specifies that it was undertaken by the lower class of slaves. Two men wear bright colored stripes with cowbells on their backs and horns on their head, twelve beat on a makeshift drum, called a gumbo box, and others dance to its rhythms, as they sing songs composed especially for this occasion. The parade of masqueraders, musicians, and dancers visits neighboring homes of whites where they collect a penny or rum (saved for later).

The slave fiddler Solomon *Northup includes dance terminology in *Twelve Years a Slave* (1858). Perhaps his role as a musician not only heightened his observation of dancing but also motivated him to value it differently. In rural Louisiana Northup observed one Christmas dance that became a contest among males competing for a slave woman's affection. They continued "tearing down" through several "sets" until exhausted, but the woman outdanced them all. If the fiddler tired, slaves created their own music through "patting," beating rhythmically on their bodies while simultaneously keeping time with their feet and singing.

In Paul Laurence *Dunbar's poem "The Party," slave dancing was performed in a circle and "jigs, cotillions, reels, and break downs, cordrills, an' a waltz er two" animated the assembly (Arna *Bontemps, *American Negro Poetry*, 1974). In Frances Ellen Watkins *Harper's *novel *Iola Leroy* (1893), Iola receives an invitation that might be for "a hop or a german," both recreational activities. The cotillion of Dunbar's poem is interchangeable, in fact, with the german, commonly used as a generic name for quadrilles, and particularly applied to a dance consisting of an elaborate series of steps and figures, called specifically the German cotillon. The presence of these terms in early literature confirms the availability of and knowledge about various dance forms popular among slaves and freed populations.

Charles Waddell *Chesnutt's *The *Marrow of Tradition* (1901) includes a scene that features the cakewalk. According to Katrina Hazzard Gordon, the dance, created by slaves, retained its popularity past World War I (*Jookin*, 1990). In Wilmington, North Carolina, in the latter 1890s, the grand hoax that a young white character perpetrates by masquerading as his elder black servant Sandy (wearing his clothes and blackface) and winning the cakewalk competition suggests the appeal of African American dance to the white population. Moreover, Chesnutt uses the dance to focus attention on easily accepted but counterfeit images fostered in the African American community through *minstrelsy. His cakewalk episode pioneers social critique through dance. The episode also concerns dance as an irreligious activity, based on the philosophy practiced at Sandy's church. References to dance as sin occur with some frequency in African American literature. See, for example, Countee Cullen's "She of the Dancing Feet Sings" in *Color*, where the persona fears that her love of dance will be sinful in the perfection of heaven, and the dictum against raising one's heel in the Ring Shout in Paule *Marshall's *Praisesong for the Widow* (1983).

During the post–World War I era in urban culture, particularly Harlem, dance as a recreational diversion escalated. Langston *Hughes's *autobiography, *The *Big Sea* (1940), cites living quarters ranging from the magnificent apartment of Alelia Walker to minuscule Harlem flats that were transformed into havens for singing and dancing. Probably this background inspired Hughes's *short story "The Blues I'm Playing," where musician Oceola Jones plays piano for dance parties in Harlem to the dismay of her art-for-art's-sake white patron (William L. Andrews, *Classic Fiction of the Harlem Renaissance*, 1994).

Toni Morrison's *Jazz* depicts the Harlem house party and its music and dance. Sixteen-year-old Dorcas sneaks out to an apartment where fast dancing precedes a dimmed room ready for slow, close movement. At one such party, Joe Trace, Dorcas's rejected lover, shoots and kills her as she possessively slow-dances with her new lover. Morrison applies the popularly used but disparaging adjective "low-down" for *blues songs and their slow dances. According to one character, the lyrics are low-down because they refer to anatomy below the waist, and the dances they compel are nasty. Although the character thinks that disorder is their consequence, she admits, paradoxically, that they enable her self-control.

Cabarets functioned as a grandiose and public version of house party activities in 1920s urban settings. Their music and dance not only attracted white spectators but brought together blacks of varying social classes. Nella *Larsen's *Quicksand* (1928) and Claude *McKay's *Home to Harlem* (1929) perhaps contain the most representative dance club scenes. Since *Helga Crane in *Quicksand* is offered as a model of black female social propriety, the club scene is an infrequent event in her lifestyle. Nevertheless, she gets caught up in a fast-paced dance performed to wild music punctuated by tom-tom drums. References to the jungle and Helga's rejection of any further rhythmic seduction confirm her awareness of and self-distancing from primitivism (a belief that originated outside the black community that black people wore only a veneer of civilized behavior and that certain stimuli such as drums and dancing would unleash particular African behaviors).

Conversely, Jake Brown, in *Home to Harlem*, revels in the night life, spending time in numerous cabarets and house parties where dancing is inseparable from other entertainment. McKay recreates the thick club atmosphere of blues performers and *jazz musicians, and always, the dancing. Unlike Larsen, who eschews primitivism, McKay unapologetically integrates the concept into his text. For his dancers, self-control is left at the cabaret entrance. They are spurred into rhythmic frenzy by music that spins their very souls. He makes dancing essential to psychological well-being, and in its description, he uses poetic language to elicit an atmosphere where dancing enables characters briefly to forget the harsh racial and economic realities of their lives as *domestics, busboys, *prostitutes, and sailors.

The artistry of performed dance replaces the concern with cabarets in Paule Marshall's *Brown Girl, Brownstones* (1959), where dance is used in the service of self-metamorphosis. In this coming-of-age novel, *Selina Boyce, as member of her college's dance troupe, performs her interpretation of the birth-life-death cycle. Her success momentarily imbues her with self-confidence and erases barriers between herself and the white troupe members. With malice aforethought, however, one dancer's mother rebuilds those barriers and demolishes the consequences of Selina's success. Her wounding words recategorize the girl as merely a black West Indian, like the woman's maid. Although the liberating effect of dance is short-lived, the entire episode is transformative. Through it, Selina experiences the onus of being woman and black in America.

The artistry of performed dance almost entirely informs Melvin Dixon's *Vanishing Rooms*, where it exists as metaphor and structure. Its prose is a dance composition. Dance is used as metaphor to suggest the relationship between characters and their lives. The protagonists Jesse Durand and Ruella McPhee are dancers and dance is the medium through which they survive and approach self-integration. It becomes their arena for expressing spiritual kinship and their source for individual expression during an improvised performance in class to Warning Cuney's "No Images." Ultimately, Jesse choreographs a piece that allows him to clarify his emotions concerning his dead homosexual lover. Similarly, dancing enables Ruella's liberation from Jesse and from her feelings of responsibility for her brother. In almost every instance of dance in the literature cited here, even beneath its recreational uses, it enables survival.

Music and dance are also transforming in the service of political resistance. Amiri *Baraka cleverly addresses this function in the story "The Screamers" in a fusion of music, dance, and revolt. First, however, male and female bodies fuse in the execution of suggestively named dances such as "The Grind," "The Rub," and "The Slow Drag." A horn style called the honk embraces a range of emotions lived with by the young dancers. The lead horn player and his band, all sounding this note, set off the dancers. They descend the stage, still playing, and join the crowd. In one line, strutting and moving, they advance into the club lobby, rhythmically descend the steps, and disruptively tumble into the center of the street and Sunday night traffic. It is a supreme moment of ecstasy in which everyone experiences a perfect expression of community. "It would be the form of the sweetest revolution, to hucklebuck into the fallen capitol, and let the oppressors lindy hop out," the narrator says. Rightly or wrongly, the dancing assembly, perceived to be riotous, is dispersed by billy club–bearing police officers (John Henrik Clarke, *American Negro Short Stories*, 1966).

In Paule Marshall's *Praisesong for the Widow* dance is ritual and confirmation of cultural continuity in the African diaspora. A young Avey Johnson learns about the Ring Shout in South Carolina, but an elder Avey dances it on the Caribbean island of Carriacou. There, the circular dance acknowledges a ritual of remembrance in tribute to the islanders' ancestors and is accompanied by drums. The movement becomes a danced plea begging foregiveness for transgressions. Through the dance, the black American widow is symbolically reunited with other descendents of the African diaspora. According to Lynne Fauley Emery, the Ring Shout kept the quality of African sacred dance alive, particularly in Georgia and South Carolina (*Black Dance*, 1992). Its formation in the Caribbean thus forms a cultural bridge between descendents of Africans there and those in the United States.

Dance is essential in African American literature as it is in African American culture. It functions as an artistic medium for individual expression and creation in literature as in culture. Because it is a phenomenon whose forms continue to be created, it never seems jaded but retains its capacity to vitalize and to sustain. Therefore, the metaphorical applications of dance in literature are infinite, and its literal applications are extensive. Thus African American literature is immeasurably enriched by the inclusion of dance as recreation, as unifying agent in political causes, as a means for individual creativity, or as symbolic of diaspora connections, linking West Africa with its New World progeny.

[*See also* Pan-Africanism; Performances and Pageants.]

• Lynne Fauley Emery, *Black Dance in the United States from 1619 to Today*, 2d. rev. ed., 1988. Judith Lynne Hanna, *Dance, Sex, and Gender: Signs of Identity, Dominance, Defiance, and Desire*, 1988. Brenda Dixon, "Black Dance and Dancers and the White Public: A Prolegomenon to Problems of Definition," *Black American Literature Forum* 24.1 (Spring 1990): 117–123. Jane C. Desmond, "Embodying Difference: Issues in Dance and Cultural Studies," *Cultural Critique* 26 (Winter 1993–1994): 33–63. Joseph M. Murphy, *Working the Spirit: Ceremonies of the African Diaspora*, 1994.

—Joyce Pettis

DANNER, MARGARET ESSE (1915–1984), poet and community activist. Born in Pryorsburg, Kentucky, Margaret Esse Danner spent her later youth in Chicago, where she also attended college at Loyola University and Northwestern University. Although she had been writing in the 1940s, and in 1945 had received an award at the poetry workshop of the Midwestern Writers Conference, her work began to receive widespread attention in the early 1950s, when she was awarded the John Hay Whitney Fellowship for "Far From Africa: Four Poems." This work was published in *Poetry* magazine in 1951, and Danner went on to become the first African American to work as an editor for the same magazine in 1956. She was poet in residence at Wayne State University in 1961 and later at Virginia Union State University. In the early 1960s Danner joined other activists in Detroit to start Boone House for the Arts. She made a long-anticipated trip to Africa in 1966, where she presented her work at the World Exposition of Negro Arts in Dakar, Senegal. During the 1970s, Danner worked as poet in residence at LeMoyne-Owen College in Memphis, Tennessee. In 1973 she and many other noted African American women poets read their work at the Phillis Wheatley Poetry Festival. Danner worked collaboratively with Dudley *Randall to publish *Poem Counterpoem* (1966). Danner's other published collections are *To Flower* (1962); *Impressions of African Art Forms* (1968, including poems originally published in the 1950s); *Iron Lace* (1968); *The Down of a Thistle: Selected Poems, Prose Poems, and Songs* (1976).

When Danner wrote a short preface to her *poetry for Addison *Gayle, Jr.'s interpretive anthology *The Forerunners: Black Poets in America* (1975), she placed her work in the long historical trajectory of African experience and influence: "I have lived long enough to see black poets applying a degree of honesty that augurs well for the salvation of the individuality of one's artistic endeavor." In her black contemporaries Danner found "the same aesthetic excellence that created the Benin Bronze and the Pyramids is still active today. . . . As for my poetry: I believe that my dharma is to prove that the Force for Good takes precedence over the force for evil in mankind. To the extent that my poetry adheres to this purpose it will endure."

Gayle, an important spokesman for the *Black Aesthetic, considered Danner a key transitional, or "bridge," writer in African American literature, claiming her as one representative example of post-renaissance (e.g., Harlem; Chicago) African American artists who were shifting away from literature of "reaction" or "service." Instead Gayle and other Black Aesthetic critics saw in Danner an emerging Africa-based voice of "Blackness," citing especially her extensive use of complex metaphor, imagery, and symbolism based in African *history and aesthetic tradition. Gayle called Danner a "literary godparent" to later, more nationalistic and/or Afrocentric poets. Interestingly, and in some contrast to this assessment, her work is listed among the "lyric" (as opposed to "social") poets in other treatments of African American literary history.

Danner's work is not only notable for its creative appropriation of African and Caribbean experience (e.g., "And through the Caribbean Sea"), but also for its pervasive, often ironic, inclusion of political metaphor. She uses, for example, metaphoric images of "prison" in her work to emphasize the artistic containment of African American writers/artists by the aesthetic expectations of white culture. Her poetry also expresses moments of ironic critique of Black Nationalist racial politics (e.g., "The Rhetoric of Langston Hughes," or "A Grandson in Hoticeberg") but balances this critique with intricately developed metaphoric, often "essentialist," celebrations of African history and Pan-African *identity. Poems here often emphasize the displacement that occurs in translating African tradition to Western culture (e.g., "Etta Moten's Attic," and "Dance of the Abakweta"). Much of her work also directly confronts white racism, along with what she suggests is the spirit-defying political aesthetic of Western literary tradition (e.g., "Garnishing the Aviary," "The Visit of the Professor of Aesthetics," and "Best Loved of Africa").

In Danner's 1966 poetic dialogue with Dudley Randall (*Poem Counterpoem*), the complexity of artistic, political, and spiritual content in her work is very much evident. She was at that time a Baha'i, and in one poetic response to Randall's poem "Ballad of Birmingham," she writes, in "Passive Resistance," of the deep challenge of nonviolent political postures, suggesting in the possible irony of her work that the tactic may be spiritually and morally suspect. This is just one example of the way much of her work is situated within the political and aesthetic debates of the 1960s yet speaks to issues of continued importance.

• Addison Gayle, Jr., ed., *The Black Aesthetic*, 1971. Don L. Lee, "Toward a Definition: Black Poetry of the Sixties (After Leroi Jones)," in *The Black Aesthetic*, ed. Addison Gayle, Jr., 1971, pp. 222–233. Dudley Randall, *The Black Poets*, 1971.

—Sharon Carson

DAVENPORT, DORIS (b. 1949), performance poet, writer, educator, and Georgia Council for the Arts/Individual Artist Award recipient. Born in Gainesville, Georgia, doris davenport was the oldest of seven children of working-class parents. The *poetry davenport writes is honest, unapologetic, satirical, and almost always woman-centered. Refusing to be restricted by a singular definition, davenport embraces multiple identities and refers to herself as an Appalachian, southern, African American, lesbian-feminist, two-headed woman, daughter of Chango and Oya (gods from the west African Yoruba pantheon religion). As davenport says, "Poetry has a function like air; it is necessary."

Exposing ills inherent in our society and ridiculing contradictions is davenport's agenda, the thread that runs through her poetry. Influenced primarily by the African American communities in northeast Georgia, davenport counts as her literary mentors Zora Neale *Hurston, Langston *Hughes, Toni *Morrison, and Nikki *Giovanni. Her first two poetry collections, *it's like this* (1980) and *eat thunder & drink rain* (1983) are very personal and mostly explore relationships.

In *it's like this*, davenport establishes her feminist focus in the poem "Vision I: Genesis for Wimmin of Color." She examines the U.S. social-racial landscape that attempts to obliterate African American women. As an insurgent poet, davenport makes readers see that which is often overlooked. She knows African American "wimmin's" reality is much more than the popular stereotype.

In *eat thunder & drink rain*, no one is exempt from davenport's critical eye. The poems have as themes love and breaking up, as in "I despise mushy sentimental lovesick *lesbian poetry worse than I do backgammon but (for SM)," to "all the way live," and "Isa Said," which are reminiscent of Langston Hughes's *blues poems. Many of the poems explore lesbian relationships, but even here davenport challenges the fallacies, as in "Dogmatic Dykes." This poem deftly engages lesbians who don traditional patriarchal roles. As with other poems, davenport doesn't merely condemn, she asks questions, such as "when will the real wimmin / appear?" forcing accusers and readers to move ahead.

An iconoclastic visionary, doris davenport celebrates the oral tradition. Her words leap off the page and caress or grate the reader's ear. Her use of African American vernacular recalls Ntozake *Shange's

poetry, but hers is a friendlier voice, southern, slow-paced, intimate. This quality is most striking in "Miz Anna—On Death" from *Voodoo Chile* (1991).

Her work recalls Audre *Lorde, the African American lesbian poet. Although Lorde's cerebral, interior style differs from davenport's, they share a philosophical outlook: the intersection of personal and political voices. The poem "interlude" from davenport's latest volume aptly encapsulates her poetic intent and situates her firmly among the griots of our time. This succinct poem has an urgent tone that engages readers in dialogue. Her poetic is clearly informed by call and response, a motif still evident in African American *churches, *theater, and *music traditions.

Voodoo Chile and *Chango's Daughter*, an *autobiography in progress, connect davenport to her African religious roots, which have been distorted in this society. Similar to the revolutionary stance of the 1960s, when African Americans claimed the word "black" to identify themselves and reinvested it with positive attributes, davenport restores African American ethos to a place of honor by claiming voodoo and Chango.

A critic and scholar, davenport has a PhD in literature from the University of Southern California (1985), an MA in English from the State University of New York, Buffalo (1971), and a BA in English from Paine College, Augusta, Georgia (1969). She has taught at several colleges, including the University of North Carolina at Charlotte, the University of Oklahoma, and Bowling Green State. She has reviewed many literary texts and has written numerous articles on pedagogy, African American "wimmin" poetry, and lesbian themes. Her poems have been published in several journals, including *Azalea, Matrix, Feminary, *Callaloo, Black American Literature Forum*, and *Catalyst*.

As of mid-1996, doris davenport resides in Sautee, Georgia, where she is a freelance writer and performance poet very much in demand.

—Opal Palmer Adisa

David Walker's Appeal. First published in pamphlet form in Boston, Massachusetts, in September of 1829, *David Walker's Appeal*, the full title of which is *David Walker's Appeal. In Four Articles; Together with a Preamble to the Coloured Citizens of the World, but in Particular, and Very Expressly, to Those of the United States of America*, was a bold attack on American *slavery. The initial printing may have totaled only a few hundred copies, but before its author's death in 1830, the pamphlet had gone through three editions and had been circulated not only among abolitionists in the North but among blacks in the South as well. The *Appeal* coupled an unsparing critique of the United States's hypocrisy in sanctioning chattel slavery with an incendiary call to blacks, both slave and free, to resist slavery, actively and, if need be, violently.

Owing to the fact that his mother was a free woman, David *Walker (1785–1830), was born legally free in Wilmington, North Carolina. After traveling extensively through the South as a young man, during which time he confirmed to himself the pervasive misery of blacks under slavery, Walker came to

Boston, where he established a clothing store in 1827 and became active in abolitionist circles, working as the Boston agent for the New York abolitionist weeklies, *Freedom's Journal* and *Rights of All*. Walker's experience in the South, his involvement with abolitionism, and his considerable reading contributed to his authoring of his *Appeal*.

The *Appeal* consists of a preamble and four articles. In each of the articles Walker argued that the "wretchedness" of black populations is a "consequence," respectively, of: slavery in the United States, which he charged, was more degrading than any form of slavery the world had seen; ignorance, or the denial of *education to blacks; *religion, specifically the teachings and actions of Christian preachers; and colonization, in particular the arguments by Henry Clay in favor of removing blacks from the United States. A scathing jeremiad in its tone, the *Appeal* repeatedly warned whites of the retribution to come should they persist in the enslavement and degradation of blacks. At the same time, it chastised blacks for their complicity in their own bondage via a willingness to content themselves with meager material satisfaction and smatterings of learning. Throughout, Walker crafted his critique with an eye to refuting claims of innate black inferiority, taking on directly Thomas Jefferson's *Notes on the State of Virginia* (1787). The *Appeal* also took the nation to task by contrasting the words of the Declaration of Independence with whites' treatment of enslaved African Americans.

Although the *Appeal* was widely denounced, Walker's efforts at broad distribution through the mails and clandestine couriers successfully placed his pamphlet in southern cities in Georgia, Virginia, Louisiana, and North Carolina. In many of these states, response to the pamphlet between 1829 and 1831 took the form of legislation that outlawed the teaching of slaves to read and write, prohibited the public assembly of free blacks, and criminalized the dissemination of antislavery materials. Although scholars have not been able to link the *Appeal* conclusively to the Nat *Turner *insurrection of 1831, its prominence in radical abolitionism is unquestionable. Among black abolitionists the *Appeal* remained influential. In 1848, the *Appeal* was republished with Henry Highland *Garnet's *An Address to the Slaves of the United States*.

[*See also* Antislavery Movement.]

• Herbert Aptheker, *"One Continual Cry": David Walker's Appeal to the Colored Citizens of the World (1829–1830), Its Setting and Its Meaning*, 1965. Vincent Harding, *There Is a River: The Black Struggle for Freedom in America*, 1981. Wilson Jeremiah Moses, *Black Messiahs and Uncle Toms: Social and Literary Manipulations of a Religious Myth*, 1982. James Turner, introduction to *David Walker's Appeal*, 1993.

—Kenneth W. Warren

DAVIS, ANGELA (b. 1944), social activist, revolutionary, philosopher, and educator. Known initially for her political activities and Marxist philosophy, Angela Yvonne Davis is a strong supporter of human and civil rights of all people, especially women. Born in Birmingham, Alabama, on 26 January 1944 to politically active parents, Angela Davis lived in a segregated community, studied in segregated schools, witnessed parades by the Ku Klux Klan, and became aware of poverty through her classmates. Against this backdrop Davis began to sow the seeds of her future militancy. From her mother she learned that the system could be protested. While attending high school in New York she was introduced to socialist ideology and joined a Marxist-Leninist group. While in college she spent her junior year at the Sorbonne in Paris, where during conversations with students from Algiers she became aware of the international struggles of oppressed people. After returning home, Davis was influenced by the teachings of the Marxist philosopher Herbert Marcuse when she studied at Brandeis University. Throughout the 1960s she joined protest groups and participated in radical politics. In time she became a militant revolutionary and an avowed Communist. She also became an active militant in the civil rights and women's liberation movements. Arrested for her political activities, she landed on the FBI's most wanted criminal list but later was acquitted of all charges. After the protest movement of the 1960s, she took up teaching and writing to denounce the inequalities of the caste system in the United States. While teaching at San Francisco State in California she developed courses in *Black Studies that emphasized the role of poverty in the black community and its devastating effect on the development and growth of black youth.

Davis's contributions to American literature emerged from her lectures in the classroom and around the country. Using a historical approach, Davis wrote numerous *essays on political and judicial reform, the rights of women, sexism, violence against women, the rights of prisoners, and mental health patients. Her book *If They Come in the Morning* (1971) and the best-selling *Angela Davis: An *Autobiography* (1974) provide insight into her life and ideas. In *Women, Race, and Class* (1982) and *Women, Culture, and Politics* (1988) she leaves the reader with an understanding of the economic, racial, and class situations in which women must struggle. She has written extensively about the sociology of poverty. She interpreted black *music in her book *Ma Rainey, Bessie Smith, and Billie Holiday: Black Women's Music* and evaluated the forces in American culture in yet another, *Shaping of Social Consciousness*. She considers racism, sexism, and poverty the most destructive forces in American society.

Davis's insight into women's concerns parallels the artistic creations of the black woman writer. Davis takes an active role in fighting poverty, prejudice, racism, sexism, and class consciousness, while her literary counterparts develop meaningful *novels, *short stories, plays, and poems on these issues. Davis describes the victimization of the black *domestic worker since her arrival in the United States during *slavery. Her counterparts in black literature depict the powerlessness and helplessness of the woman worker. Davis interprets the woman's place in industrial capitalism historically and attacks the collusion of traditions and practices that work against women. Her polemics also expose the reader constantly to the dilemma of the black woman's acceptance of self-hatred and need for self-liberation and self-acceptance.

Davis contributes to an analysis of the sexual *violence against the black woman in the United States in a chapter on rape in her book *Women, Race, and Class*. Davis, from a historical perspective, lists a litany of cruel actions of the male against the female. To be sure, Davis is concerned about the myth of the black rapist and exposes the consequences of this myth.

Speaking for women's rights on all levels, Davis advocated the right to privacy, the right to make personal decisions, the right to be in any location at any time, the right to do what one desires, the right to one's own natural appearance and weight, and the right to birth control and to control one's reproductive system. Davis and Gwendolyn *Brooks's thoughts on the right to an abortion converge as the reader listens to Brooks's poem "The Mother" and reads Davis's chapter on "Racism, Birth Control, and Reproductive Rights" in *Women, Race, and Class*.

[See also Communism; Feminism.]

• Paula Giddings, *When and Where I Enter: The Impact of Black Women on Race and Sex in America*, 1984. Joan C. Elliott, "Angela Davis," in *Notable Black American Women*, ed. Jessie Carney Smith, 1992, pp. 250–253.

—Joan C. Elliott

DAVIS, DANIEL WEBSTER (1862–1913), poet, essayist, and historian. Born in Caroline County, Virginia, to slaves Charlotte Ann (Christian) and John Davis, Daniel Webster Davis moved to Richmond after the Civil War. Davis graduated from Richmond High and Normal School (1878) and two years later began a long teaching career in Virginia, West Virginia, and the Carolinas. He married Elizabeth Eloise Smith (1893)—they had three children—while attending Lynchburg Baptist Seminary. Ordained in 1896, Davis served as pastor of the Second Baptist Church in South Richmond until his death. For more than three decades, Davis championed race betterment in the *church, in schools, on the lecture circuit throughout the United States and Canada, and in Richmond's economic, social, and literary organizations. He published two prose works, *The Life and Public Services of Rev. Wm. Washington Browne* (1910) and, with Giles B. Jackson, *The Industrial History of the Negro Race of the United States* (1908), and two volumes of *poetry, *Idle Moments* (1895) and *'Weh Down Souf* (1897).

Davis's prose, lectures, and poetry all aim to instruct and entertain. Poems in standard English, about one-third of his output, are generally sentimental or moralistic in tone. His livelier *dialect poetry describes church-going, holiday celebrations, good eating, superstitions, and recreations "way down South." The best of these blend lilting melodies, mocking *humor, and colorful details. Davis inserted such poems into his lectures as exempla of evil habits bequeathed to the race by *slavery. Thus he criticized the faults of his race, blamed white society as their source, and demanded racial justice and equal opportunities, while he exhorted African Americans to overcome the past through Christian idealism, *education, wealth, and race pride. Davis's legacy is the rich store of his writings and the example of his rise from slavery to leadership of Richmond's African American community.

• Lottie D. Harrison, "Daniel Webster Davis," *Negro History Bulletin* 18 (Dec. 1954): 55–57. Joan R. Sherman, *Invisible Poets: Afro-Americans of the Nineteenth Century*, 2d ed., 1989.

—Joan R. Sherman

DAVIS, FRANK MARSHALL (1905–1987), poet, journalist, and autobiographer. During the depression and World War II, Frank Marshall Davis was arguably one of the most distinctive poetic voices confronting W. E. B *Du Bois's profound metaphor of African American *double consciousness. Complementing a career that produced four collections of *poetry was one as a foremost journalist, from 1930 to 1955. Through the "objective" view of a newspaperman and the "subjective" vision of a poet, Davis struggled valiantly to harmonize Du Bois's dilemma of the *color line.

Frank Marshall Davis was born on 31 December 1905 in Arkansas City, Kansas, ". . . a yawn town fifty miles south of Wichita, five miles north of Oklahoma, and east and west of nowhere worth remembering" (*Livin' the Blues*). His mention of interracial schools suggested a harmonious small-town life; the reality, however, barely concealed deeper racial tensions. Housing, jobs, movie theaters, and all facets of life were tacitly divided by the color line. Retrospectively, he describes his life in "Ark City" as suspended uncertainly in limbo, between the worlds of Euro- and African Americans.

At Kansas State College, Davis nurtured his twin passions of *journalism and poetry from 1923 to 1926 and again from 1929 to 1930. His successful careers as newsman and poet rendered unimportant the fact that he never received a baccalaureate degree. For over thirty years he served as editor, managing editor, executive editor, feature writer, editorial writer, correspondent, sports reporter, *theater and *music critic, contributing editor, and fiction writer for the Chicago *Evening Bulletin*, Chicago *Whip*, Gary (Ind.) *American*, Atlanta *World*, Chicago *Star*, the Associated Negro Press, *Negro Digest*, and the Honolulu *Record*. In a rather difficult period for publishing African American poetry, he brought out *Black Man's Verse* (1935), *I Am the American Negro* (1937), *Through Sepia Eyes* (1938), and *47th Street: Poems* (1948). These two modes of self-expression effectively placed him in a unique position to observe African American cultural development and to advocate social change.

Davis's various news writings generally challenged such persistent lies as the position that African Americans had no cultural past and therefore had contributed very little to American cultural development. In this case, Davis made "Rating the Records" and "Things Theatrical," two of his weekly features for the Associated Negro Press, collectively imply a composite history of African American music. The social consequences of this strategy were enormous. The columns demonstrated West African roots of

African American music; provided, in their promotion of racially integrated bands, a model for American society to aspire to; and demonstrated African Americans' contributions to American cultural distinctiveness.

Davis found poetry to be a complementary mode of self-expression. Esteemed critics like Harriet Monroe, Stephen Vincent Benét, Alain *Locke, and Sterling A. *Brown perceived much to celebrate in Davis's poetry. In *Black Man's Verse* (1935), they saw "authentic inspiration," technical innovation, wonderfully realistic portraiture, and vivid images. Davis's verse is characterized by robust statements of urban themes, a fierce social consciousness, a strong declamatory voice, and an almost rabid race pride. Technically, he found free verse to be the best form to "contain" his thought since, like *jazz and improvisation, it represented a rebellion against conventional or standardized forms of poetry. Davis's poem "Lynching," for instance, offers "stage" directions for performing the poem to the accompaniment of orchestral music. But the experiment with music, mood, and language did not consistently win critical approval. Other Davis poems sometimes invited disagreement about whether they achieved epic sweep or simple *oratory.

By moving to Hawaii in 1948, Davis removed himself from the vortex of civil rights and labor activity on the mainland. The larger significance of his relocation was that it took him away from his best chance for a sustained literary career. In 1973 Davis rose from the depths of historical anonymity when Dudley *Randall, Stephen Henderson, and Margaret Taylor Goss *Burroughs brought him to the attention of the younger, Black Arts poets. From that time until his death in 1987, Davis enjoyed a brief celebrity. His older poems were reprinted; he also wrote, in addition to new poems, three autobiographical narratives, including *Livin' the Blues* (1992), "That Incredible Waikiki Jungle," and *Sex Rebel: Black* (1968).

The recovery of Davis's life and work has profound significance for redrawing traditional boundaries of African American literary history and cultural criticism. Guided by Alain Locke's designation of "newer Negro," Davis assists us in extending the usual geographical site and era for the so-called *Harlem Renaissance. At the same time, his discovery by the 1960s *Black Arts movement causes us to reconsider the conflicted relationship of younger writers to their literary ancestors. Finally, as we seek to understand more fully the age of the depression and World War II, cultural critics will find Davis's wide-ranging news writing to be indispensable.

• W. E. B. Du Bois, *The Souls of Black Folk*, 1903. Alain Locke, "Deep River: Deeper Sea: Retrospective Review of the Literature of the Negro for 1935," *Opportunity* 14 (1936): 6–10. Harriet Monroe, review of *Black Man's Verse, Poetry: A Magazine of Verse*, 48.5 (1936): 293–295. Jean Wagner, *Black Poets of the United States*, 1973. Frank Marshall Davis, "Mystery Man: An Interview with Frank Marshall Davis," interview by Dudley Randall, *Black World* 23.3 (1974): 37–48. Frank Marshall Davis, *Livin' the Blues: Memoirs of a Black Journalist and Poet*, ed. John Edgar Tidwell, 1992. Langston Hughes, "Chicago's South Side Comes Alive," review of *47th Street: Poems*, Associated Negro Press News Release, 18 Aug. 1948, 4–5; rpt. in *Black Moods: Selected Writings by Frank Marshall Davis*, ed. John Edgar Tidwell, forthcoming.
—John Edgar Tidwell

DAVIS, MILES (1926–1991), *jazz trumpeter and bandleader. Miles Davis's musical legacy is a haunting muted tone on ballads, the selection of complementary sidemen, and a visionary genius that placed him at the forefront of jazz's epochal stages including bop, cool, hard bop, third stream, and fusion. His accomplishments include the groundbreaking nonet sessions known as the *Birth of the Cool* (1949); the modal *Kind of Blue* (1959); the collaborations with arranger Gil Evans in *Porgy and Bess* (1958) and *Sketches of Spain* (1960); and the use of electronic instrumentation and improvisation on the best-selling *Bitches Brew* (1969). Davis also scored the Louis Malle film *Ascenseur Pour L'Echafaud* (1957).

Davis's arresting trumpet style, lyrical and elliptical, and his complicated public persona made him a living legend. His good looks and sartorial elegance, his taste for Ferraris and beautiful women, his boxing avocation, and his abhorrence of nostalgia and sentimentality projected a quintessentially hip image. The sobriquet "Prince of Darkness" identified the contradictory aspects of his personality, an exquisite musical sensibility and a brooding, volatile temperament. Davis fascinated and repelled by a mixture of hauteur, mystery, and aloofness. He turned his back on audiences and failed to introduce sidemen. This refusal to ingratiate himself to a largely white public was a pointed criticism of African American entertainers who mugged and clowned and made Davis an early representative of *black nationalism. In 1959 Davis was beaten by a white policeman enraged at seeing him with a white woman. The incident received international attention and became emblematic of American racism. That same year Davis was interviewed by Alex *Haley for *Playboy*, inaugurating the magazine's famous feature, and confirming Davis as an outspoken critic of racism. Davis's persistent ability to refashion himself fired the public imagination and made him a compelling figure throughout his forty-year career.

[*See also* Music.]

• Jack Chambers, *Milestones: The Music and Times of Miles Davis*, 1989. Miles Davis with Quincy Troupe, *Miles: The Autobiography*, 1989.
—Marcela Breton

DAVIS, OSSIE (b. 1917), playwright, actor, film director, and author of young adult fiction. Born in Cogsdell, Georgia, Ossie Davis grew up in nearby Waycross. He studied at Howard University for three years, then traveled to New York to pursue a career in the *theater. With the encouragement of Alain *Locke, Davis obtained a position with the Rose McClendon Players of Harlem, while writing in his spare time. The following year, he joined the U.S. Army, serving in the Medical Corps and in Special Services. While stationed in Liberia, he wrote and produced *Goldbrickers of 1944*, a musical variety show. Discharged in 1945, Davis returned to New York and gained the lead role in the play *Jeb*, which propelled his stage career. Also starring in the play was Davis's future wife, Ruby Dee, with whom he would continue to costar in plays and later in *film. Among Davis's stage, film, and television credits are *The Joe Louis Story* (1953), *The Fugitive* (1966), *Do the Right Thing* (1989), and *Kings on the Hill* (1993). Davis is recognized as a political activist dedicated to the *civil rights movement, and he acted as master of ceremonies for the March on Washington (1963).

Davis is best known as the creator of *Purlie Victorious* (1961), a three-act comedy which was later adapted as the feature film, *Gone Are the Days* (1963), and as the musical *Purlie* (1970). This satirical depiction of traditional southern racial relations tells the story of a black preacher who successfully vies to procure five hundred dollars from a white plantation owner to contribute to initiating an integrated church in a black community. Its mordant yet humorous representations of southern life make it clear that the issues of the play expand beyond the borders of its fictional setting, Cocthipee County. The play probes the racism of the Jim Crow South and the nation, and also explores issues of African American unity, pride, leadership, and community power. Among Davis's other plays are *Alice in Wonder* (1952), later expanded into *The Big Deal* (1953), which is stirred by political aggression against militant blacks during the McCarthy era and tells the story of a black television performer who is caught between his personal beliefs and the loss of his career when he is asked to testify against his brother-in-law; *Montgomery Footprints* (1956), which focuses on the civil rights movement; *Curtain Call* (1963), based on the life of black Shakespearean actor, Ira Aldridge; *Escape to Freedom* (1978); a children's play derived from the childhood of Frederick *Douglass; *Langston Hughes: A Play* (1982); which tells the story of the poet and playwright; and *Bingo* (1985); a musical based on William Brashler's book *Bingo Long's Traveling All Stars and Motor Kings* (1985), about a black baseball team in the 1930s. Other plays by Davis include *The Mayor of Harlem* (1949), *Point Blank* (1949), *Clay's Rebellion* (1951), *What Can You Say, Mississippi?* (1955), *Alexis Is Fallen* (1974), and *They Seek a City* (1974).

Davis is also the author of several screenplays such as *Cotton Comes to Harlem* (1969), coauthored with Arnold Perl and directed by Davis, which is based on the novel of the same title by Chester *Himes; *Black Girl* (1972), also coscripted and directed by Davis; *Count Down at Kusini* (1976), about a liberation movement in a fictional African country; and *Teacher, Teacher* (1963), a television film in which Davis also starred, winning an Emmy Award for his performance.

Davis's first *novel, *Just Like Martin* (1992), intended for young adult audiences, focuses on the height of the civil rights movement as seen through the eyes of a young black boy living in Alabama.

Davis has used the stage not only as a center of entertainment but also as a space for political and social critique and as a historical commemorative rich with the struggles of the African American community. His children's works also follow in this tradition and chronicle important moments in the history of African Americans with an instructional aim in mind.

• Lewis Funke, *The Curtain Rises: The Story of Ossie Davis*, 1971. Bernard L. Peterson, Jr., "Davis, Ossie," in *Contemporary Black American Playwrights and Their Plays: A Biographical Directory and Dramatic Index*, 1988, pp. 130–133.

—Cassandra Jackson

Day of Absence. Douglas Turner *Ward's *Day of Absence* (1965) is set in any small town in the Deep South. The action begins on a quiet street where Clem and Luke, two country crackers, are seated on a sparse stage talking, when they suddenly realize that something is wrong. It finally occurs to them that none of the town's black people have been seen since the previous evening. When this fact becomes general knowledge, the establishment comes to the brink of chaos. Without its black labor force, the town is paralyzed because of its dependence on this sector of the community.

The only blacks who can be found are lying in the hospital—in comas. In a final effort to retrieve the missing black population, Mayor Henry R. E. Lee makes a personal appeal on television. He begs and pleads and threatens black absentees. When no immediate response is forthcoming, a white mob confronts him and bedlam races through the entire community.

The final scene opens with Clem and Luke in their favorite spots the following morning when Rastus, a slow-moving, servile type enters upon the stage. When questioned concerning his whereabouts on "yestiddy," he appears not to remember. Ward offers no definitive answer.

Despite the serious message about the underlying economic importance and potential power of black people to this country, *Day of Absence* invites an audience to share in the experiences of these white townspeople through the devices of storytelling and slapstick dialogue. The text is interwoven with seemingly unrelated and fragmented actions, which move from farcical *humor through sociopolitical propaganda to melodramatic insights that dramatize the subtext of what would be possible if black people just disappeared for one day.

The play received mixed reviews from the New York critics. Martin Gottfried of *Women's Wear Daily* summarily dismissed the play as "childish, dull and silly." On the other hand, Howard Taubman, drama critic, for the *New York Times*, felt that "the most serious trouble with *Day of Absence* is Mr. Ward's failure to sustain a strong dramatic line. He is full of invention . . . and his satirical thrusts often find their mark despite the loose structure of the piece." There was criticism by some blacks who felt that Ward should have chosen another comic form for propaganda rather than drawing what they considered to be a negative image of black *stereotypes. In spite of this mixed criticism, *Day of Absence* ran for 504 performances, and Ward was honored with two Obie awards—one for his performance as mayor and one for writing the play.

A crucial component in the development of the African American *theater during the 1960s was the necessity to cultivate sympathetic audiences who could share African American experiences from *slavery through the civil rights era and beyond. Ward chose to accomplish this through the biting edge of humor. The external elements of colloquial and topical language, together with movement and gesture of farcical expansion, are funny to the core; yet just below the surface one can experience vicariously the hurt, suffering, and humiliation associated with this form and style of *drama.

• Fred Beauford, "The Negro Ensemble Company: Five Years against the Wall," *Black Creation* 3 (Winter 1972): 16–18. Trudier Harris, *From Mammies to Militants: Domestics in Black American Literature*, 1982, pp. 143–154.
—Floyd Gaffney

DELANEY, LUCY A. (c. 1830–c. 1890s), ex-slave, writer, and political and religious leader. Born to slaves, Lucy Delaney cherished her St. Louis childhood. Like Frederick *Douglass and Harriet A. *Jacobs, however, she soon witnessed the breach between its "joyful *freedom" and *slavery's later realities. When owner Major Taylor Berry, who had arranged for the family's emancipation, was killed in a duel, and his widow died, the family remained enslaved. With Lucy's father sold South, mother Polly fiercely urged her two daughters' escape. While Nancy fled to Canada and Polly to Chicago, the latter returned to bondage to protect Lucy. Polly successfully petitioned the St. Louis courts for her own liberation, and later for Lucy's in 1844. Visiting Nancy in Toronto, Lucy wed Frederick Turner, soon to be killed in a steamboat explosion; her second marriage to Zachariah Delaney in St. Louis endured at least forty-two years. When their four children died young, Delaney tempered her mourning with a liberationist's salvo: they "were born free and died free!" Lucy finally located her father outside Vicksburg, Mississippi.

Delaney's *autobiography, *From the Darkness Cometh the Light* (c. 1891), concentrates less on the escape, *literacy, and achievement of freedom that punctuate earlier *slave narratives than on the liberating feats of slave-motherhood. Delaney joins the celebrants of African American maternalism—Jacobs, Sojourner *Truth, Annie Louise *Burton, Toni *Morrison, and others. Written to "invoke [my mother's] spirit," it commences with Polly Crocket's "free" birth and her kidnapping into slavery. Despite her "commonplace virtues," Polly releases motherhood from its ties to "pure womanhood['s] fragility, realigning nurture with liberation. Hardly feminine genuflection, Polly's triumph in male-dominated courts is matched by her daughter's refusal to be whipped. *Darkness* culminates in Delaney's perpetuating her dead mother's legacy of freedom in her election to numerous civic posts, including the presidency of the "Female Union"—the first society for African American women—and of the Daughters of Zion.

• William L. Andrews, introduction to *From the Darkness Cometh the Light or Struggles for Freedom* (c. 1891), in *Six Women's Slave Narratives*, 1988, pp. 9–64. Rosalie Murphy Baum, "Delaney, Lucy A.," in *African American Women: A Biographical Dictionary*, ed. Dorothy Salem, 1993, pp. 150–151.
—Deborah Garfield

DELANY, MARTIN R. (1812–1885), political activist, early Afrocentric ideologue, explorer, lecturer, newspaper editor and correspondent, U.S. Army major, and author of several tracts and a novel. Martin Robison Delany's haphazard education began clandestinely before his family's escape from slave-state Virginia in 1822. By 1832, in Pittsburgh, Delany, always proudly black and Africa-respecting, had joined the local African Education, Antislavery, Temperance, Philanthropic, Moral Reform, and Young Men's Bible societies. Further, he cofounded the Theban *Literary Society—named after the Egyptian city.

By 1836 he began studying medicine, insisting upon civil rights, and preaching professional training for African Americans rather than barbering or manual labor suggestive of servant or second-class status. When black suffrage was rescinded in Pennsylvania in 1838, Delany, alone, passed through slave territory to then independent Texas to test its potential as a home for free blacks (1839–1840), his first adventure in *emigration and exploration. Disappointed, but with scenes and dialogues he would use later in *Blake*, his only novel, he returned to Pittsburgh.

In 1843 Delany married (eventually there were seven children named after American and foreign blacks he admired) and launched the *Mystery*, a weekly newspaper that promoted civil rights, provoked blacks and whites by its challenges to old-fashioned understandings of *race, and defended black writing and called for more.

When Frederick *Douglass began his own newspaper in December 1847, he asked Delany to join him. For eighteen months Delany worked for the *North Star* traveling, lecturing, and providing informative letters and editorials. By the summer of 1849 Delany's writing began to include apocalyptic undercurrents in prose and verse about the sins of whites and an imminent revolution in the religious and political thinking of blacks in the United States and Cuba. These black-nationalist, Pan-African thoughts reappeared in *Blake*.

Following the imposition of the Fugitive Slave Act (1850), Delany considered emigration to Canada, studied medicine at Harvard, practiced in Pittsburgh, taught school, was denied a patent because he was not recognized as a citizen, and published his first book: *The Condition, Elevation, Emigration, and Destiny of the Colored People of the United States, Politically Considered* (1852)—a prickly, unsentimental, and independent portrayal of African American conditions, with praise of productive blacks, criticism of disappointing white allies, and an argument for the need to seek another country.

In 1853 Delany wrote a defense of black Freemasonry and three letters criticizing Harriet Beecher *Stowe's *Uncle Tom's Cabin* for its treatment of pureblacks, its colonizationist conclusion, its slave languages, and for the author's having thought she could tell the story of his people. He may have felt some chagrin at not having published his novel first.

In 1854 Delany organized a National Emigration Convention and gave a black nationalist address arguing that almost anyplace was better than the United States. He moved to Canada in 1856, met with John *Brown in 1858, and he wrote. In 1859 the new black-owned and edited *Anglo-African Magazine published four short pieces and part of Blake. The Anglo-African pushed it, moving installments to its front page, but few printed responses have been found.

In May 1859 Delany visited Africa, again seeking a land where his people might become part of the ruling element. In 1861, after seven weeks in Liberia, seven months in Nigeria, and an equal time in Great Britain seeking help for his African emigration plans, Delany returned to Canada. His Official Report of the Niger Valley Exploring Party offered corroboration that, as he wrote, "I have outgrown, long since, the boundaries of North America." From November 1861 through May 1862, Blake appeared in the Weekly Anglo-African newspaper. Ten footnotes reflecting Delany's African adventures were appended. Again, few contemporary responses are known; one reader promised a dramatization.

The remainder of Delany's literary life is closely tied to his political responses to America's Civil War and Reconstruction failures. In 1863 and 1864 he recruited troops; in February 1865 he became a major in the U.S. Army. From 1865 through July 1868 he was a Freedman's Bureau officer; then he was in and out of several positions between lectures, politicking, and job-seeking in South Carolina, where hopes for black advances rose and fell: in the Bureau of Agriculture (1870); in real estate (1871); in a customs office (1872–1873); in political campaigning (1874); in a newspaper editor's chair (1875); as a trial justice and would-be Liberian emigrationist (1875–1879); and, back North, an occasional lecturer (1880–1883) and a private Central American trade agent (1884).

Delany wrote newspaper articles, *letters, and pamphlets on capital, land, labor, citizenship, and home ownership, but his two most interesting *essays were attempts to assert the once and future contributions of black people to the world. In "The International Policy of the World towards the African Race" (1867), he argued that Europeans had suppressed the facts about the historical precedence of black philosophy, *religion, and civilization. In his Origin of Races and Color (1879, 1880) Delany cited the Bible and classical writers in defense of his race and then offered original speculations on relations between Ethiopian bloodlines, religion, and civilization. A voice crying in the wilderness then, his theme has been taken up again today.

Delany may have written much more, but on the night President Lincoln was shot in April 1865, his stored papers were lost in a fire at Wilberforce University. Though hit with numerous bitter disappointments, only an occasional victory, and much neglect, one young man called the elderly Delany in 1882 the "blackest, jolliest, and most brilliant Negro I have ever seen or known." One eulogist even recalled Delany's "romance" (Blake) in 1885.

An energetic, unpolished lecturer and writer, Delany's unguided literary steps were clumsy. But his persistent interest in all things black, positive and negative, past and present, far and near, repay critical attention. Further, Blake's affinities of tone, attitude, characterization, and speech with Sutton E. *Griggs's *Imperium in Imperio (1899), W. E. B. *Du Bois's Dark Princess (1928), Zora Neale *Hurston's Moses, Man of the Mountain (1939), and Arna *Bontemps's *Black Thunder (1936), without any known direct influence, signal the existence of an African American literary river.

[See also Afrocentricity.]

• Frank A. Rollin, Life and Public Services of Martin R. Delany, 1868; rpt. 1883. Howard H. Bell, Search for a Place: Black Separatism and Africa, 1860, 1969. Dorothy Sterling, The Making of an Afro-American: Martin Robison Delany 1812–1885, 1971. Victor Ullman, Martin R. Delany: The Beginnings of Black Nationalism, 1971. Floyd J. Miller, The Search for a Black Nationality: Black Colonization and Emigration, 1787–1863, 1975. Nell Irvin Painter, "Martin R. Delany: Elitism and Black Nationalism," in Black Leaders of the Nineteenth Century, eds. Leon Litwack and August Meier, 1988, pp. 148–171.
—Allan D. Austin

DELANY, SAMUEL R. (b. 1942), novelist, short story writer, poet, critic, editor, essayist, educator, director, former folk singer, lecturer, script writer for comic books, and winner of the Hugo and Nebula awards for science fiction, the Pilgrim Award for excellence in science fiction criticism (1985), and the Bill Whitehead Memorial Award for Lifetime Excellence in Gay and Lesbian Literature (1993). Has written criticism using the aliases K. Leslie Steiner and S. L. Kermit.

Samuel R. Delany was the first highly visible and extraordinarily successful African American author to adopt the "marginal" subgenre of science fiction and make it his special province, both as a creator and a critic. A Harlem native, "Chip" Delany was the only son of Samuel R. Delany, Sr., and Margaret Carey Boyd Delany, owners of Levy and Delany, a Harlem funeral parlor. His background provided the gifted young Delany with rich and varied experiences despite strained relations with his father, problems at school largely caused by an undiagnosed dyslexia, various experiments with sexuality, and psychiatric counseling sessions. At home he studied both the violin and the guitar; he read a variety of books including classical mythology, the works of diverse African American authors, and science fiction and fantasy stories. His summers were spent in racially integrated upstate New York youth camps, and he kept a journal from childhood. From 1947 to 1956, Delany attended Manhattan's private and progressive Dalton Elementary school, where he interacted with white upper-class children and adopted the "liberal-Jewish world view," to which, as he noted in a 1986 Science Fiction and Criticism interview, he still subscribes. In 1956 he enrolled in the public Bronx High School of Science (BHSS), where he excelled in math and science. At BHSS he met Jewish poet and child prodigy

Marilyn Hacker; they married in 1961, separated in 1975, and divorced in 1980. In 1960, and from 1962 to 1963, he attended New York's City College. Delany's recollections of the pleasures, stresses, textures, and tensions of his childhood were metaphorically summarized for authors Michael Peplow and Robert Bravard (*Samuel R. Delany: A Primary and Secondary Bibliography, 1962–1979*, 1980) as "a virtually ballistic trip through a socio-psychological barrier of astonishingly restrained violence."

Called variously a child prodigy, a boy wonder, and the wunderkind of science fiction, Delany began to write when he was quite young. As a child, he had been introduced to the genre by parents, campmates, schoolmates, or friends discussing Jules Verne, Ray Bradbury, and Robert Heinlein tales. Subsequently, he came to appreciate the works of Theodore Sturgeon, Alfred Bester, and Arthur C. Clarke. As a pre-teen he had penned sword-and-sorcery fantasies in his journals; as an adolescent he wrote several unpublished novels; and at nineteen, he published his first novel, *The Jewels of Aptor* (1962).

Since his debut as a published writer Delany has written eighteen novels; three short story collections, *Driftglass*, *Distant Stars*, and *Driftglass/Starshards*; and two memoirs, including the extended autobiographical essay *Heavenly Breakfast* (1979), focused largely on his experiences in a San Francisco commune in 1967–1968, and *The Motion of Light in Water* (1988), a fuller autobiographical statement treating his life in New York and his development as an artist and writer from 1957 to 1965. In addition, he produced five collections of critical essays focused on science fiction, and in 1994, published *Silent Interviews*, a collection of written interviews that had appeared in a variety of journals; the subtitle, *On Language, Race, Sex, Science Fiction and Some Comics*, indicates the breadth of Delany's interests as a fiction writer, essayist, and critic.

Delany's early novels, from *Jewels* and his *The Fall of the Towers* trilogy (1963–1965), through *The Ballad of Beta-2* (1965), *Babel 17* (1966), and *The Einstein Intersection* (1967, originally to be called *A Fabulous, Formless Darkness*) to *Nova* (1968) can be characterized as "space opera." That is, while creating his original tales in far more "literary language" than was typical, and weaving into his plots heroic artists/outcasts as protagonists who were frequently black and/or female, the stories also adopted many of the conventions associated with formulaic science fiction. The settings were exotic, the action occurred in the distant future, and the accent fell on technology: spaceships, computers, aliens, intergalactic battle. His later novels, beginning with *The Tides of Lust* (1973, also published as *Equinox*), *Dhalgren* (1975), *Triton* (1976), and *Stars in My Pocket Like Grains of Sand* (1984), were more complex, more challenging, more anthropologically grounded with a more sophisticated narrative structure, a more theoretical underpinning, and a much greater allusive poetic density. Yet from his early science fiction to that of his later period, the essential topography of Delany's tales remained consistent. Issues of *race, *gender, *freedom, desire, language, mythology, *sexuality,

semiotics, signs, *slavery, psychology, and power persisted in his fictions. Also at issue in virtually all of his stories is his fascination with both literary and linguistic theory and historical linguistics.

The 1980s saw Delany devote most of his energy to the even more marginal form connected to science fiction called fantasy fiction or sword and sorcery. The *Return to Neveryon* series (1979–1987) consists of four volumes—*Tales of Neveryon* (1979), *Neveryona: Or the Tale of Signs and Cities* (1983), *Flight from Neveryon* (1985), and *The Bridge of Lost Desire* (1987)—interconnected "prehistorical" tales. As densely allusive and metaphorically postmodern as his later science fiction novels, the tales tell the stories of developments in a prehistoric empire with a preindustrial society. As central to each tale as the issues previously cited are Delany's depictions of political intrigue and the movement of a society from a barter to a cash economy. Already stylistically sophisticated, the intricacies of the Neveryon series are further complicated by Delany's deft blending of fiction and fact through the appended fictive critical voices of S. L. Kermit and K. Leslie Stein. Additionally, "The Tale of Plagues and Carnivals," in *Flight from Neveryon*, juxtaposes against the plot line entries from Delany's journals regarding the spread of AIDS in New York City.

Almost from the inception of his career Delany has been considered by various reviewers to be one of the most "artistic," "accomplished," "interesting," "gifted," "intelligent," "challenging," and "literate" writers in science fiction. Although often erroneously associated with science fiction's mid-1960s New Wave group, a primarily English phenomenon whose authors published in the journal *New Worlds*, and whose stories were largely set in the near future, Delany has insisted that he belongs more appropriately to its American counterpart, that group of writers associated with Harlan Ellison and the series of *Dangerous Visions* (1967) anthologies he edited.

In "Toto, We're Back," a 1986 interview first published in the *Cottonwood Review* and subsequently reprinted in *Silent Interviews*, Delany addressed the issue of labeling and marginality he has confronted as an African American writer of science fiction. "The constant and insistent experience I have had as a black man, as a gay man, as a science fiction writer in racist, sexist, homophobic America, with its carefully maintained tradition of high art and low, colors and contours every sentence I write." Delany's bold insistence on his multiple identities helped create for science fiction a broader audience and helped to generate additional African American contributors to the field.

[See also Speculative Fiction.]

• George Slusser, *The Delany Intersection: Samuel R. Delany Considered As a Writer of Semi-Precious Words*, 1977. Samuel R. Delany, *The Jewel-Hinged Jaw: Notes on the Language of Science Fiction*, 1978. Peter S. Alterman, "Samuel R. Delany," in *DLB*, vol. 8, *Twentieth-Century American Science Fiction Writers*, eds. David Cowart and Thomas L. Wymer, 1981, pp. 119–128. E. F. Bleiler, ed., *Science Fiction Writers: Critical Studies of the Major Authors from the Early Nineteenth Century to the Present Day*, 1982. Jane Branham Weedman, *Samuel R. Delany*, 1982. Sandra Y. Govan, "Samuel R.

Delany," in *DLB*, vol. 33, *Afro-American Fiction Writers after 1955*, eds. Thadious M. Davis and Trudier Harris, 1984, pp. 52–59. Robert Elliot Fox, *Conscientious Sorcerers: The Black Postmodernist Fiction of LeRoi Jones/Amiri Baraka, Ishmael Reed, and Samuel R. Delany*, 1987. Samuel R. Delany, "Black to the Future: Interviews with Samuel R. Delany, Greg Tate, and Tricia Rose," interview by Mark Derry, *South Atlantic Quarterly* 92.4 (Fall 1993): 775–778.

—Sandra Y. Govan

DEMBY, WILLIAM (b. 1922), journalist, actor, film adapter, and expatriate novelist. W. E. B. *Du Bois argued in *The *Souls of Black Folk* (1903) that African Americans possessed a unique "*double consciousness" because of their "twin rooted" heritage of being both African and American. For William Demby, this dichotomy of racial and national oppositions became an asset rather than a handicap. Born 25 December 1922 in Pittsburgh, Pennsylvania, Demby spent his formative years in a middle-class, multiethnic neighborhood where its three African American families resided harmoniously with first-generation immigrants. Individualism prevailed concomitantly with nationalism so that people felt proudly ethnic, but still American, recalls Demby. He never felt divided because of nationalistic practices of discriminating against blacks.

Demby's parents, however, experienced the color problem that Du Bois predicted would be facing the twentieth century. William Demby and Gertrude Hendricks had been aspiring architectural and medical students to Philadelphia's colleges, but were denied entrance. They lived during the race riots and *lynchings of blacks punctuating America after World War I. When they married in this period and moved from Mead to Pittsburgh where William and his siblings were born, the senior Demby redirected his goals. He first worked in a munitions factory and then joined Hopewell Natural Gas Company as a file clerk, which enabled him to support his family comfortably.

Pittsburgh's diverse community inspired young William's fledgling creative impulses to blend the real and fantastic like Romantic writers. Ghosts of Indians seemed to dwell in the woods near the thirteen-year-old's home. Ordinary transaction sheets that he processed as an after-school file clerk at Hopewell Gas Company seemed filled with Romantic characters. By the time Demby completed high school with friends and classmates who were ethnically Irish, Polish, or Italian; religiously Catholic or Protestant; or politically Socialist, Republican, or Democratic, he had become conscious of both ethnic pride and ethnic hate. His father owned one of the few radios in the neighborhood, and Demby heard the fearsome messages of fascist dictators Adolf Hitler and Benito Mussolini and the awesome prizefight between Joe *Louis and Max Schmeling in 1936 that diminished notions of Aryan superiority. This multiplicity of cultures sparked exciting musings, recalls Demby, practically forcing him to become a writer.

Demby's family's move south after his graduation from Langley High School in 1941 greatly influenced his worldview. The predominantly black world of Clarksburg, West Virginia, enthralled Demby. A socialist, writer, and *jazz musician in high school, he further pursued these musical and philosophical interests at West Virginia State College. Demby took writing classes from poet-novelist Margaret *Walker and pursued his first love, jazz, to the extent that it became academically detrimental. With World War II in progress, Demby frequently skipped classes to play at the Cotton Club in South Carolina. His absenteeisms eventually compelled Demby to join the army in 1942 and he spent the bulk of his two-year tour in Italy. Following his discharge, Demby earned a BA in liberal arts in 1944 at Fisk University, Nashville, Tennessee.

Europe, nonetheless, beckoned Demby to return. When he migrated to Italy in 1947, Demby began a fifty-year, self-imposed exile that was broken only by periodic trips to America for temporary employment or vacations. He initially went to Rome to study painting because jazz had begun to change from swing to bebop. Demby quickly became involved with Rome's artists, including Roberto Rossellini for whom he adapted two *films. His present-day position of film adapter of Italian films into English stems from this early period.

Affiliating with Rome's artistic members eventually inspired Demby to become a writer. But unlike expatriate Richard *Wright, Demby never felt compelled to avow allegiance to any movement or political group. Instead, Demby incorporated the dualistic symbolism of his bicultural heritage as a structuring trope in his writings where fact and fiction collide or merge. A prominent feature of Demby's three *novels, for instance, is his integration of his alter ego or fictional writer persona in his works. In *Beetlecreek* (1950), Demby's first novel, he posits a fictional community reminiscent of Clarksburg, West Virginia. Primarily about a rite-of-passage experience of a black Pittsburgh youth and his meeting with an elderly, reclusive, white male resident of Beetlecreek, the story employs the motifs of simultaneity and destiny that cause the paths of Johnny Johnson and Bill Trapp to intersect in tragedy. This bleak, naturalistic novel earned Demby international acclaim and representation by Mondodavi, one of Italy's prestigious publishing houses.

With *The Catacombs* (1965) and *Love Story Black* (1978), Demby's alter ego is less camouflaged in the characterizations of William Demby and Professor Edwards, the respective fictional writers of each work. A motto of the real Demby is that "The novel to be born will be written." *The Catacombs* is about the act of writing over a two-year period at which time the writer's kernel idea literally is born and becomes self-controlling. Doris, the persona Demby invents, assumes an autonomous life in the real world surrounding the Roman catacombs. *Love Story Black* repeats the fact and fantasy dualism when Edwards becomes involved in the fantasies of an eighty-year-old virgin, ex-vaudeville performer while writing her life story.

In the 1950s and 1960s, Demby also produced a series of journalistic tracts—"The Geisha Girls of

Ponto-cho," "They Surely Can't Stop Us Now," "A Walk in Tuscany," and "Blueblood Cats of Rome"—whose subjects reflect Demby's global consciousness. His belief in individualism among diverse groups at a global level is evident by his interracial marriage to Italian poet-writer Lucia Drudia with whom he shares an "artistic marriage." Their son, James, is an Italian composer. As of 1996, Demby is awaiting the birth of his next novel about Tillman, a cook from his old army outfit. To William Demby the author, the real world and the fantastic have no boundaries.

[See also Emigration.]

• Edward Margolies, "The Expatriate As Novelist: William Demby," in Native Sons: A Critical Study of Twentieth-Century Black American Authors, 1968, pp. 173–189. Robert Bone, "William Demby's Dance of Life," Tri-Quarterly 15 (Spring 1969): 127–141. Robert Bone, introduction to The Catacombs, 1965; rpt. 1969. John O'Brien, ed., Interviews with Black Writers, 1973, pp. 34–53. Roger Whitlow, Black American Literature: A Critical History, 1973, pp. 122–125. Margaret Perry, "William Demby," in DLB, vol. 33, Afro-American Fiction Writers after 1955, eds. Thadious M. Davis and Trudier Harris, 1984, pp. 59–64.

—Virginia Whatley Smith

DENT, TOM (b. 1932), poet, essayist, oral historian, dramatist, cultural activist, and noted figure in the Black Arts movement. Thomas Covington Dent, who prefers to be known as Tom Dent, was born on 20 March 1932 in New Orleans, Louisiana, the son of Dr. Albert Dent, president of Dillard University, and Jessie Covington Dent, a concert pianist. During his formative years in New Orleans, Dent wrestled with the sense of African American *identity and the sense of *place that seems to be the legacy of southern writers. Thus, it is not surprising that issues of political and cultural history are so germinal in his mature works.

After completing his early education in New Orleans, Dent earned his BA in political science from Morehouse College in 1952. Some of his earliest writing appeared in the campus newspaper, the Maroon Tiger, for which he served as editor during his senior year. After doing graduate work at Syracuse University, he served in the U.S. Army (1957–1959) and then moved to New York, where he worked for the New York Age, a black weekly, and for the NAACP Legal Defense Fund. He became a member of On Guard for Freedom, a cultural nationalist group. In 1962 he moved to the Lower East Side and founded the Umbra Workshop with Calvin C. *Hernton and David Henderson. This group chose Dent to be the editor of its poetry journal Umbra, which lasted for two issues (1963 and 1964) before the group dissolved.

What might be considered the first phase of Dent's literary career is marked by his concern with escaping from the restrictions of his black middle-class origins and acquiring a clear understanding of the issues of liberation, *black nationalism, and cultural identity that occupied African American intellectuals in the late 1950s and early 1960s. It was Dent's idea that Umbra should be a collective of writers and artists who were exploring craft and discovering

their voices and visions. It was within the group, as Dent revealed in an essay ("Lower East Side," African American Review, Winter 1993), that he discovered more respect for diversity and possibilities for rendering his vision of what history might mean. However much Dent profited from his discussions with such writers as Hernton, Henderson, Lorenzo *Thomas, Ishmael *Reed, Askia M. *Touré, and Norman Pritchard, his deepest concerns were focused on how the African American imagination fuses politics, aesthetics, and history. In 1964 some of his earliest poems appeared in the *anthologies New Negro Poets, U.S.A. and Schwartzer Orpheus.

Dent returned to New Orleans in 1965, convinced of his need to rediscover his southern past and of his ability to use the insights and ideas he had gained in New York. He began working for Free Southern Theater (FST) as an associate director, a position that initiated an intense period of writing, civil rights activity, and work in building cultural groups. In 1967 Dent wrote his most famous play, Ritual Murder, one of the most eloquent examinations of black-on-black crime in African American theater. Aware of the need to help young writers develop a cultural base in New Orleans, Dent served as director of the FST Writers' Workshop or BLKARTSOUTH (1968–1973), becoming the mentor of Kalamu ya *Salaam and other writers whose work appeared in New Black Voices (1972). He saw this group and the Congo Square Writers Union, which he founded in 1973, as outgrowths of his Umbra experiences. While he continued to write reviews and articles for such magazines as Freedomways, Southern Exposure, and Black World, Dent also cofounded the journals Nkombo (1969) and *Callaloo (1975). His first book of poems Magnolia Street was published in 1976. By the time his second poetry volume Blue Lights and River Songs (1982) appeared, Dent was very deeply involved in the work of the Southern Black Cultural Alliance (founded in 1974), a federation of community theater groups, had begun to tape oral histories about *jazz in New Orleans and with key figures in the *civil rights movement, and had begun work on an *autobiography with Andrew Young. In the early 1990s Dent worked as executive director of the New Orleans Jazz and Heritage Foundation before he resigned to work on Southern Journey, an oral history of the civil rights movement and the contemporary South.

Dent is quite representative of African American writers who despite the quality of their work seem best known for their influence on other writers and their contributions in building cultural institutions. Once his work is given critical attention, the value of the unity he has sought between literature and history may be valorized.

• Tom Dent, Gilbert Moses, and Richard Schechner, eds., The Free Southern Theater by the Free Southern Theater, 1969. Lorenzo Thomas, "The Shadow World: New York's Umbra Workshop and Origins of the Black Arts Movement," Callaloo 4 (1978): 53–76. Lorenzo Thomas, "Tom Dent," in DLB, vol. 38, African American Writers after 1955: Dramatists and Prose Writers, eds. Thadious M. Davis and Trudier

Harris, 1985, pp. 86–92. Michel Oren, "The Umbra Poets' Workshop, 1962–1965: Some Socio-Literary Puzzles," in *Studies in Black American Literature*, vol. 2, eds. Joe Weixlmann and Chester J. Fontenot, 1986, pp. 177–223. Jerry W. Ward, Jr., "Thomas C. Dent: A Preliminary Bibliography," *Obsidian II* 4 (Winter 1989): 103–112. Kim Lacy Rogers, *Righteous Lives: Narratives of the New Orleans Civil Rights Movement*, 1993.
                                              —Jerry W. Ward, Jr.

DERRICOTTE, TOI (b. 1941), poet and educator. In Toi Derricotte's poetry, the taboo, the restricted, and the repressed figure prominently; they are often the catalysts that prompt her to write, to confess the painful. Often stylistically compared to so-called confessional poets like Sylvia Plath and Anne Sexton, Derricotte, in opting for candor over decorum, wants her "work to be a wedge into the world, as what is real and not what people want to hear." This self-dubbed "white-appearing Black person," reared as a Catholic in a black, working-class Detroit community, complicates the myth of monolithic blackness with poems that speak into consciousness obscure, unconventional black bodies. And in an academy whose poststructuralist theories often either depersonalize bodies with esoteric discourse or overemphasize them with hyperbolic identity politics, Toi Derricotte's poems brave the charged, murky depths of much current poetry, stamping the language with her own complex, quirky vision—a vision both concrete and abstract, both quotidian and phantasmagoric.

Toi Derricotte was born on 12 April 1941, the daughter of Antonia Baquet, a Creole from Louisiana, and Benjamin Sweeney Webster, a Kentucky native, and later half-sister to Benjamin, Jr. At around ten or eleven years old, Derricotte began a secret journal that included, among other things, the disintegration of her parents' marriage and the death of her grandmother on whom she was very emotionally dependent. During her years at Detroit's Girls Catholic Central, Derricotte recounts a religious education that she felt was steeped in images of death and punishment, a Catholicism that, according to the poet, morbidly paraded "the crucifixion, saints, martyrs in the Old Testament and the prayers of the Mass." Coupled with these images were Derricotte's surreal reminiscences of childhood visits to her paternal grandparents' home, the bottom part of which served as a funeral parlor where bodies were prepared for viewing. Often she would stay overnight at her grandparents', where, unafraid, she would "pray over the bodies . . . especially . . . disturbed when young people died, children, babies."

Her first attempt at sharing her poems with others came when, at fifteen, she visited a cousin, a medical school student who was then taking an embryology class. Encouraged by a trip they took to the Chicago Museum to see fetuses and embryos at various stages of development, Derricotte, who was careful not to show her poems to her parents who never "even *alluded* to babies before birth . . . [or] talked to [her] about sex," anxiously showed them to this cousin who pronounced them "sick, morbid." Faced with this unexpected rebuff, Derricotte remembers being faced with several choices: "I could have said something is wrong with me and stopped writing, or I could have continued to write, but written about the things I knew would be acceptable, or I could go back underground." For Derricotte, the choice was obvious: rather than risk ostracism for openly writing about the forbidden, she opted "to go back underground."

In 1959 Derricotte graduated from Girls Catholic Central and enrolled that autumn in Wayne State University as a special education major. In 1962, her junior year at Wayne State, she gave birth to a son in a home for unwed mothers. This act of rebellion was but a presage of things to come, as Derricotte, after graduating in 1965, left Detroit for the East Coast. Her move to New York City in 1967 was a momentous one, for it was here among white, mostly female intellectuals that Derricotte's poetic voice resurfaced. Unlike the African American poets of the *Black Arts movement, many of whom heeded Amiri *Baraka's call for an artistic expression that was decidedly black nationalist, proletarian, and accessible, Derricotte wrote, instead, deeply personal, troubling, often difficult poems that talked more of black families haunted by gender oppression and familial strife than of Black Power and racial solidarity.

Having "paid her dues" as a student in numerous workshops where she endured the canon's litany of dead and near-dead white male poets like Matthew Arnold, Ezra Pound, T. S. Eliot, and Robert Lowell, often as the only black student, Derricotte first published in a "major" magazine, the *New York Quarterly*, in the fall of 1972. Her literary reputation and publications flourished, culminating in her first book, *The Empress of the Death House*, published in 1978 by Lotus Press. Derricotte's second book, *Natural Birth*, was published in 1983 by The Crossing Press. Her third book, *Captivity*, first published in 1989 by University of Pittsburgh Press, has enjoyed second (1991) and third (1993) printings. In 1996, Norton Publishing Company accepted for publication Derricotte's *The Black Notebooks*, a book she began in 1974 when her family became one of the first black families to move into Upper Montclair, New Jersey.

• Calvin C. Hernton, "Black Women Poets: The Oral Tradition," in *The Sexual Mountain and Black Women Writers*, 1987, pp. 119–155. Charles H. Rowell, "Beyond Our Lives: An Interview with Toi Derricotte," *Callaloo* 14.3 (Summer 1991): 654–664.
                                              —James W. Richardson, Jr.

Dessa Rose. Sherley Anne *Williams's *Dessa Rose* (1986) is a *historical novel that fits into the *neo–slave narrative tradition. In other words it tries to revise the eighteenth- and nineteenth-century *slave narratives that were written as a part of the *antislavery movement, in part by adding an African American woman's narrative as a valid representation of *slavery. This *novel consists of three primary sections that are framed by a prologue and an epilogue. In the three larger sections, Williams provides differing viewpoints on *Dessa Rose herself. She begins with "The Darky," which presents a white male's, Adam Nehemiah's, perceptions of the protagonist as he attempts to record the story of her rebellion on a slave coffle. Perhaps this section alludes to William Styron's flawed historical fiction *The Confessions of Nat Turner* (1967). The next section, "The Wench," incorporates Dessa's interactions with a white mistress and circumstantial abolitionist, Miss *Rufel, and consequently deconstructs their roles as slave and mistress. Lastly, "The Negress" provides Dessa's viewpoint on her experiences meeting Miss Rufel and the runaway slaves in their impromptu Underground Railroad. In this section the characters engage in a mock minstrel show that travels through the South and ironically enough sells the troupe into slavery to economically liberate these former slaves. *Dessa Rose* seeks not only to reconstruct the Black woman's voice, which has been traditionally silenced, but it also attempts to create a possible and positive fiction of a slave who successfully leads a rebellion and who has truly escaped slavery.

The central critical issues surrounding *Dessa Rose* are those of the creation of text and of *history. Creation adopts several meanings, because critics view it as the function of revising the historical text of the slave narrative, the function of the mother who creates the text of/for the child, the re-creation of a slave rebellion, and the modeling of two female slave rebels: Dessa, a black slave, and Rufel, a white woman, who is equally enslaved to her role as mistress. Williams revises Styron's *The Confessions of Nat Turner*, a neo–slave narrative that has received much criticism for what many felt to be an inaccurate portrayal of Nat Turner. The issues of the mother's role and of reconstructing the slave narrative to include the female rebel slave's story address feminist theory in that they revise what woman is and state that Dessa as slave and Rufel as mistress are more than roles assigned by society. Williams, then, creates her own rebellion both by deconstructing the roles of female slave and white mistress, by having these two become friends and work together in a minstrel parody of the slave auction to gain economic freedom, and by formally revising the slave narrative genre of the past as well as William Styron's neo–slave narrative on Nat *Turner.

• Mary Kemp Davis, "Everybody Knows Her Name: The Recovery of the Past in Sherley Anne Williams's *Dessa Rose*," *Callaloo* 40.1 (1989): 544–558. Mae G. Henderson, "(W)riting *The Work* and Working the Rites," *Black American Literature Forum* 23.4 (Winter 1989): 631–660. Anne E. Goldman, "'I Made the Ink': (Literary) Production and Reproduction in *Dessa Rose* and *Beloved*," *Feminist Studies* 16.2 (Summer 1990): 313–330. Marta E. Sanchez, "The Estrangement Effect in Sherley Anne Williams' *Dessa Rose*," *Genders* 15 (Winter 1992): 21–36.   —Mildred R. Mickle

DESSA ROSE. As the protagonist and narrator of Sherley Anne *Williams's critically acclaimed *neo–slave narrative and *historical novel, *Dessa Rose* (1986), Dessa revises the trope of the "slave woman." In her interactions with Nemi, a white male *amanuensis who attempts to record her life story, and Miss *Rufel, a white mistress of a half-finished plantation, she controls the narrative by giving them limited information on herself and by serving as omniscient narrator of the entire novel. Her control of the narra-

tive best refutes the notion of slave woman, because although she is physically constrained by jail and the aftereffects of childbirth, she stresses that what matters most is that she owns her own mind. Unlike Nemi and Miss Rufel, Dessa has few misconceptions about the world she inhabits.

In refuting the concept of slave woman, Dessa fulfills her most important function: she stands as a heroine and a positive and possible fiction. Dessa speaks in and offers the perspective of a successful African American female insurrectionist to the literary realm, where traditionally African American women have been silenced. Yet what marks her most is that this former slave woman character narrates her story to her children and ensures that it is passed down. Dessa's acquired *literacy represents the act of making history and, as such, contributes to the ever-growing body of African American texts.

• Mary Kemp Davis, "Everybody Knows Her Name: The Recovery of the Past in Sherley Anne Williams's *Dessa Rose*," *Callaloo* 40.1 (1989): 544–558.   —Mildred R. Mickle

DETECTIVE FICTION. *See* Crime and Mystery Writing.

DETTER, THOMAS P. (c. 1826–?), journalist, short story writer, minister, and politician. While details of Thomas Detter's early life are sketchy, it appears he was born in Maryland and educated in Washington, D.C., public schools. According to his father's will, he was to have been apprenticed as a shoemaker until his twenty-first birthday. Detter emigrated to San Francisco, California, in 1852, one of many African Americans lured by the economic prospects of gold and silver mining and the greater freedom of the western frontier. He quickly established himself as a community leader, becoming the Sacramento County delegate to the first Colored Citizens of the State of California Convention; serving on the State Executive Committee of that and other civil rights organizations; and campaigning in California, Nevada, Washington, and the Idaho Territory for public education, voting rights, and the admission of testimony by African Americans in court cases. Along with poet James Monroe *Whitfield, Detter was one of the first African Americans to serve on a jury in Nevada. By 1864, Thomas Detter was known as "one of the old wheelhorses" of the western civil rights movement.

In 1871, when he published *Nellie Brown, or The Jealous Wife with Other Sketches*, Thomas Detter was about forty years old and living in the isolated frontier settlement of Elko, Nevada. Detter was not, however, an unknown writer; his reputation as a correspondent for the *San Francisco Elevator* and the *Pacific Appeal* had been established for more than a decade. Detter wrote commentaries on national and local social and political issues. He was an outspoken abolitionist and a fervent supporter of Reconstruction. His *newspaper columns often included eulogies for local community leaders and writers, as well as for national figures such as Charles Sumner and Jeremiah B. Sanderson. Perhaps his most unusual contributions were the *essays he published about the status and prospects of new gold or silver mines and his descriptions of towns that cropped up in response to the expansion of railroads. Detter traveled extensively throughout the Pacific Northwest, living in various mining camps and frontier settlements, plying his trade as a barber, selling his patented cough syrups and hair restoratives, and writing articles designed to encourage African Americans to relocate to these newly established towns and territories. His newspaper reports generally focused on the grand natural beauty and the economic opportunities of the expanding territories while emphasizing the abundant rewards that African Americans of courage, persistence, and optimism could achieve.

Detter's only known separately published volume, *Nellie Brown, or The Jealous Wife with Other Sketches*, includes fiction and essays set in antebellum Virginia and Maryland, Louisiana and Cuba, Idaho and California. Published in San Francisco and distributed throughout the western United States, *Nellie Brown* is among our earliest examples of the African American literary tradition on the western frontier. The title story, "Nellie Brown, or The Jealous Wife" is a novella about the misadventures that occur when greed inspires gossip and emotions overcome logic. It is one of the early examples of "divorce fiction" that was developing in nineteenth-century American literature and as such represents a singular innovation in the African American literary tradition. "The Octoroon Slave of Cuba" is an unusual alternative to the tragic *mulatto themes of such works as William Wells *Brown's *Clotel and Frank J. *Webb's The Garies and Their Friends. "Uncle Joe" is an adaptation of the African American *trickster tale that resembles the later work of Charles Waddell *Chesnutt. Detter's essays are candidly opinionated but insightful and useful. Whether he was evaluating the impact of the "Central Pacific Railroad," predicting the future prospects of "Idaho City," or relating the painful folly of racial discrimination during "My Trip to Baltimore," Detter wrote to inspire and to inform his readers. Like his contemporaries Frances Ellen Watkins *Harper, Frederick *Douglass, Martin R. *Delany, and others, Thomas Detter was an activist writer, an innovator in African American fiction, and a pioneer of the African American press.

• Elmer E. Rusco, *"Good Time Coming?" Black Nevadans in the Nineteenth Century*, 1975. Frances Smith Foster, introduction to *Nellie Brown, or The Jealous Wife with Other Sketches*, 1996.

—Frances Smith Foster

DE VEAUX, ALEXIS (b. 1948), poet, playwright, novelist, short fiction writer, editor, lecturer, performer, educator, activist, and prize-winning essayist and author of children's stories. Born 24 September 1948 in New York City to Richard Hill and Mae De Veaux, Alexis De Veaux received a BA from Empire State College in 1976. She earned both an MA (1989) and a PhD (1992) at the State University of New York at Buffalo.

An internationally recognized author, De Veaux has published her work in English, Spanish, Japanese, Serbo-Croatian, and Dutch. She has lectured and performed across the United States, as well as abroad in Kenya (1985 NGO Forum, Nairobi), Holland (Melkweg International Women's Festival, Amsterdam), Cuba (UNEAC Writers Union, Havana), and Japan (Tokyo Joshi Women's University, Tokyo; Black Studies Association, Osaka). Her published works include six books (*Na-Ni*, 1973; *Spirits in the Street*, 1973; *Don't Explain: A Song of Billie Holiday*, 1980; *Blue Heat: Poems and Drawings*, 1985; *An Enchanted Hair Tale*, 1987; and *The Woolu Hat*, 1995) and five *short stories ("Remember Him A Outlaw," 1972; "The Riddles of Egypt Brownstone," 1980, rpt. 1990; "All Shut Eyes Ain't Closed, All Goodbyes Ain't Gone," 1983; "Adventures of the Dread Sisters," 1991; and "The Ethical Vegetarian," 1995). In addition De Veaux has published dozens of articles and essays on various subjects, including "Jayne Cortez, Revolutionary Mouth on Paper" (*Essence*, 1978) and "SisterLove" (*Afrekete: An Anthology of Black Lesbian Writing*, 1995). One of her plays, "The Tapestry" (1986), is included in the *anthology *Nine Plays by Black Women Playwrights*. Others have been produced Off-Broadway and in regional theaters across the country, and one play, "Circles" (1972), was produced at KCET-TV, California (1976).

New York City is the setting for a number of De Veaux's works, but the cultural mood is an amalgam of African rhythm and everyday Western urban drama. Readers experience her stories through a lens induced by the author's lived experience as an urban African American woman. The *novel *Spirits in the Street* is a young Harlemite insider's poetic reminiscence expressing a range of emotions from outrage over Vietnam- and Nixon-era events to a joyous embracing of that part of the self which is of African origin. Centered on Harlem's 114th Street, the novel recalls school desegregation, police brutality, outrage over the incarceration of Angela *Davis, and city streets filled with peddlers, hookers, and hustlers. *Na-Ni*, De Veaux's award-winning, illustrated children's story, presents a child's eye view of evil forces at work within the African American community and is set within the block of 133rd Street between Lenox and Seventh avenues. *Don't Explain* is a straightforward if somewhat unusual biography of singer Billie *Holiday. Lady Day's Harlem-centered life comes packaged like a jazzy *blues love song expressing the singer's passions, frustrations, pain, and joy as if experienced firsthand by its author.

An artist-activist, De Veaux's life exemplifies a progression from a concern with the development of a positive personal identity to the expression of a global vision of peaceful coexistence and freedom from the tyranny of oppression in its various manifestations. Her activism is a practical application of the theories embodied in her creative and expository writing and is demonstrative of a life that extends far beyond the confines of the welfare years of her own youth echoed in *Na-Ni*. De Veaux's involvement in projects like "Motherlands: From Manhattan to Managua to Africa, Hand to Hand," a video documentary (1986), underscores her commitment to assume a part of the responsibility for healing a worldwide human community suffering from centuries of cultural conflict.

The author is the recipient of numerous awards, including the Art Books for Children Award (Brooklyn Museum, 1974 and 1975), Coretta Scott King Awards (1981 and 1988), a National Endowment for the Arts Fellowship (1981), a Creative Artists Public Service Grant (New York, 1981), Unity in Media Awards (1982 and 1983), the Fannie Lou Hamer Award for Excellence in the Arts (1984), a PBS research and script development grant (PBS 1989), and the Lorraine Hansberry Award for Excellence in African American Children's Literature (1991).

De Veaux served as contributing editor and editor at large for *Essence* from 1978 to 1990. She was a co-founder of the Flamboyant Ladies Theater Company (1977–1984) and the founder of the Gap Tooth Girlfriends Writing Workshop (1980–1984). She has served as master artist for the New Haven, Connecticut, board of education (1974–1975), and she has taught writing and women's studies at several colleges and universities. De Veaux is an assistant professor of women's studies in the Department of American Studies at the State University of New York at Buffalo.

[*See also* Lesbian Literature.]

• Claudia Tate, "Alexis De Veaux," in *Black Women Writers at Work*, ed. Claudia Tate, 1983, pp. 49–59. Priscilla R. Ramsey, "Alexis De Veaux," in *DLB*, vol. 38, *Afro-American Writers after 1955: Dramatists and Prose Writers*, eds. Thadious M. Davis and Trudier Harris, 1985, pp. 92–97. Jewelle L. Gomez, "Alexis De Veaux," in *Contemporary Lesbian Writers of the United States: A Bio-bibliographical Critical Sourcebook*, eds. Sandra Pollack and Denise D. Knight, 1993, pp. 174–180.

—Lovalerie King

DEVIL. The Devil emerged as a folk character in African American culture during the days of *slavery. According to Jon Michael Spencer (*Blues and Evil*, 1993), slaveholders, whose European consciousness was steeped in Devil-lore, attempted to threaten slaves into compliance by showing them pictures of the Devil and by telling them that the Devil would subjugate transgressors. As African Americans assimilated Christianity into their traditional African religious belief system (which contained elements of voodoo and hoodoo), they accepted the Devil as a concrete figure embodying the essence of evil (otherwise, evil would have remained an elusive abstraction) and believed that the Devil could take the form of a wide range of creatures (human, rabbit, toad, goat, black cat).

Some African Americans thought that God had cast the Devil and his band of rebellious angels out of heaven for misbehaving; others felt that the Devil left of his own vengeful volition. However he got to hell, the Devil lured human souls from God and tortured them in hell's flames (though he occasionally helped God by accommodating overflow from heaven). Although these beliefs echoed the puritanical Anglo American interpretation of Satan, the African American conception of the Devil was unique in that African Americans attributed to the Devil qualities borrowed from traditional African American folk characters like the *trickster and the *badman;

therefore, in addition to being evil and cruel, the African American Devil was clever and defiant. According to Lawrence W. Levine (*Black Culture and Black Consciousness*, 1977) the Devil was also portrayed as semicomic, even bumbling—as if a thinly veiled commentary on the white man. Thus, traditional African American *folklore texts (especially *sermons and preaching, folk tales, *spirituals, and *blues songs) often depicted the Devil as a mighty but flawed figure who would ultimately be bested by the superior moral, spiritual, emotional, and physical strength and the keener intuition of African Americans.

• Newbell Niles Puckett, *Folk Beliefs of the Southern Negro*, 1926. Zora Neale Hurston, *Mules and Men*, 1935. Melville Herskovits, *The Myth of the Negro Past*, 1941.

—Ted Olson

DIALECT. *See* Dialect Poetry; Speech and Dialect.

DIALECT POETRY is commonly defined as a style that flourished from the 1890s through World War I; its chief characteristics are usually identified as a sentimentalization of antebellum southern culture, a regularized phonetic orthography designed to reflect common conceptions about African American vernacular speech, and an accommodationist viewpoint designed to gain acceptance with a white readership.

This generalized definition identifies the major contours of the dialect form; hopefully, it also indicates the controversial nature of the topic and the extent of the scholarly debate that the form has sparked virtually since its inception. For decades after its popularity waned, dialect poetry signified for many critics all that was negative in the tradition—indeed, for a time the term came to symbolize the difficulties inherent in the process of making art in a racially divided society. This view, prominent in our understanding of the tradition of African American literary scholarship through the commentary of critics such as James Weldon *Johnson, is gradually changing as scholars continue to revisit and reexamine the dialect poets and their works. A more recent understanding of the socioeconomic and political-historical context in which much of the work appeared has afforded scholars the opportunity to both reassess the significance of the original dialect poets and to consider expanding the definition of the form to include other writers whose work attempts some representation of African American vernacular speech. This definition, which grew to prominence particularly in the late 1960s and early 1970s, culminating perhaps in Stephen Henderson's *Understanding the New Black Poetry* (1973), stresses connections between the early poets and successors such as Langston *Hughes, Sterling A. *Brown, and Haki R. *Madhubuti, among others, who adapt the rhythms and modalities of vernacular expression to effectively present and preserve certain unique aspects of African American cultural life. This debate on the nature of the form continues to provide the impetus for much new and useful scholarship on the original dialect poets and their verse.

Regardless of their views on what became of the dialect tradition, most scholars agree on the major influences at work in the development of the tradition: nineteenth-century *minstrelsy, the literature of the *plantation tradition, and the work of non-southern white dialect writers throughout the nineteenth century. The broad outlines of the minstrel tradition have been traced and do not bear repeating here; the pertinent aspects of the form that apply in the dialect writings include the representation of vernacular speech and the emphasis on the African American as a figure of entertainment, primarily. In addition, the minstrel tradition gives rise to some of the excessive sentimentalism often associated with dialect writing. One of the most popular aspects of the minstrel show was the "coon song," often the most useful vehicle for the communication of stereotypes. The lyrics of these songs might well be said to be forerunners of the dialect tradition, especially given the similarity between these song lyrics—with their emphasis on rhyme and regularized meter—and poetry. Further proof for that assertion lies in the fact that James Weldon Johnson, who would ultimately call for the eradication of dialect usage from African American verse, wrote minstrelsy-influenced songs in dialect around the turn of the century and published several of his song lyrics as poems, beginning in 1900 with the publication of the text of "Sence You Went Away" in *Century* magazine.

The influence of the minstrel tradition on dialect poetry is similar to that of the plantation tradition, though one might well argue that the literary nature of the latter makes its influence even more profound. Generally cited as beginning with the antebellum writings of southern white writers such as John Pendleton Kennedy and William Gilmore Simms, and continuing in the work of writers such as Joel Chandler Harris, Irwin Russell, and Thomas Nelson Page, the plantation tradition took as its main purpose the valorization and (postbellum) preservation of an idealized version of southern American culture. In addition to glorifying the concepts of southern white gentlemen's honor and southern white women's purity and sentimentalizing the region, the tradition perpetuated a powerful set of stereotypes about African Americans, including the idea that African Americans thrived under and preferred the state of enslavement, the notion that African Americans were lazy, ignorant, and addicted to physical pleasures, and the conviction that African Americans were a comic people whose wishes need not be addressed seriously. As in the minstrel show, these ideas are conveyed through a combination of actions and characterizations that include the bowdlerization of English into a form intended to represent the slaves' uneducated speech. Also as in the minstrel tradition, the result was not an accurate representation of African American vernacular expression but a politically charged creation designed to reinforce popular perceptions of the race.

Arguably, the language used by many African American dialect poets resembled the plantation tradition's vernacular more closely than the "real" speech of the folk masses; with the notable exception

of James Edwin *Campbell, whom J. Saunders *Redding sees as coming the closest to actually reproducing actual speech patterns (*To Make a Poet Black*), scholars tend to associate most dialect poets' diction in the realm of this "literary" dialect instead of connecting them to "real" life.

While the plantation tradition certainly had an effect on the creation of African American poets' literary dialect, there were other trends in dialect poetry by white authors that seem significant as well. Apart from the southern writers of the plantation tradition, nineteenth-century American white writers of the local color tradition were publishing literary versions of other regional dialects. Bret Harte's southwestern dialect, made famous in his "Truthful James" poems of the 1870s, and James Whitcomb Riley's "Hoosier" poems are but two examples; scholars often list Riley as a particularly strong influence on Paul Laurence *Dunbar's dialect verse and see specific analogues between the language created by the two poets.

Beyond Riley's link to Dunbar, the influence of the white dialect poets outside the plantation tradition apparently has not been extensively traced. Nevertheless, established evidence supports the assertion that the African American writers working in dialect in the late nineteenth and early twentieth centuries were following the developments of a long-standing tradition that extended far beyond the regional boundaries often attributed to it. Recognizing the dialect verse of African Americans in this era as part of that continuum lends credence to the argument that theirs is one point in the evolution of a form that has transmogrified into the urban vernacular poetry of the present age. Whether or not one accepts that characterization, however, there is indeed evidence that the dialect work of post-Reconstruction African Americans is more than an isolated phenomenon.

While the recognition of influences for the form is generally agreed upon, there is some controversy over the point of origin for the vernacular verse of the post-Reconstruction era—the difficulty lies largely in the definition of dialect. Scholars agree that dialect poetry was common in the 1890s; however, they tend to question nearly any vernacular-oriented product appearing before that cutoff. At issue primarily is Frances Ellen Watkins *Harper's series of vernacular poems appearing in *Sketches of Southern Life* (1872). The series of poems, narrated by a wise old ex-slave named *Aunt Chloe Fleet, describe the events of the Reconstruction era in a consistent, colloquial speech loosely based on African American vernacular idioms. While scholars recognize the importance of these poems and the poet's innovations, few agree on whether Harper is of the dialect tradition or merely its predecessor. Those who exclude her from the tradition, including J. Saunders Redding and Joan R. Sherman (*Invisible Poets*) do so primarily because they see her language as too far removed from "actual" southern African American folk speech.

Regardless of whether one cites her as a forerunner or the first published African American dialect poet, however, the connections between the "Aunt Chloe" poems and later poets' works are unmistakable. Harper's Chloe embodies the virtues of piety and fidelity that will come to be hallmarks of the stock figures in the African American dialect tradition; furthermore, Chloe represents the history of *slavery without offering detailed accounts of its atrocities, another tendency prevalent in later dialect work.

In addition to these similarities, however, Harper's Aunt Chloe also presents something that some scholars contend is hardly ever present in dialect verse: a strong, personal voice of protest. Invaluable for their historical orientation and their recounting of Reconstruction era events, the poems distinguish themselves through their presentation of a strong, probably controversial, opinion on these issues. In poems like "The Deliverance" and "Aunt Chloe's Politics," Aunt Chloe recounts, respectively, the various responses of slave and master to the news of the Civil War and her outrage over attempts of politicians to buy the vote, particularly in the Reconstruction era. This image of empowerment is a significant predecessor for later poets, particularly those who, according to Dickson Bruce (*Black American Writing from the Nadir*), find a way in the post-Dunbar era to adapt the dialect form to more direct statements of protest.

Between Harper's *Sketches* and William Dean Howells's well-known praise of Dunbar's *Lyrics of Lowly Life* (1896), few poets produced dialect poetry in great quantities. As Dickson Bruce notes, the emphasis in this era generally leaned more toward proving the gentility and refinement of the African American race to whites; the more formal types of Victorian poetry were generally better suited to that undertaking. Nevertheless, poets who wrote primarily in standard English, like Albery Allson *Whitman, did produce a few dialect pieces; furthermore, Daniel Webster *Davis, a noted public speaker in his day, composed dialect verse conveying the traditional nostalgic view of antebellum society for didactic use in his speeches. Emphasizing the wickedness and weakness put upon the African American race by slavery through his comic dialect portrayals of slavery times, Davis urged the reformation of the race. As Joan R. Sherman notes (*Invisible Poets*), the spoken context of Davis's poetry is only now really becoming clear, permitting the revision of an earlier accepted portrayal of him as a spineless accommodationist.

Davis and Whitman both made significant marks on the African American poetic tradition; neither, however, holds the place of importance scholars assign to James Edwin Campbell, another Ohioan whose close friendship with Paul Laurence Dunbar leads some scholars to speculate on the poets' mutual influence on creative processes. Campbell's *Drifting and Gleanings* (1887), hailed by Sherman as the best collection of dialect poems of that era, predates Dunbar's *Oak and Ivy* (1893); Campbell's *Echoes from the Cabin and Elsewhere* (1895) also precedes the publication of Dunbar's *Lyrics of Lowly Life*. While none of these poets produced work as enduring as Dunbar's, one must recognize that the tradition was established before he published his first books of poetry, *Oak and Ivy* (1893) and *Majors and Minors* (1895).

The emphasis on establishing the context for the publication of Dunbar's early works arises from the general conception that, in some sense, the dialect poetry form began with him. Arguably, Howells's famous notice of Dunbar's dialect verse did more to advance the form than any other single event; Bruce notes that, as a result of Dunbar's fame, in the decade between the publication of *Lyrics of Lowly Life* and Dunbar's death (1906), virtually every African American poet publishing made some attempt at dialect verse. Always best known for his dialect work, Dunbar has come for some scholars to represent the inherent flaw in the tradition: using the racist preconceptions of the plantation tradition as a vehicle for gaining a larger white audience, Dunbar very successfully built a trap from which he never completely escaped, as Bernard Bell notes (*The Folk Roots of Contemporary Afro-American Poetry*). Critics have long noted that Dunbar's standard English poetry, especially "The Poet" and his famous "We Wear the Mask," can be read as examples of the poet's frustration with the form and its limitations. While such a view is perhaps convincing, it overlooks much of significance in Dunbar's dialect verses themselves.

Dunbar's critics accuse him of operating totally within the boundaries of the plantation tradition, playing accommodationist and sentimentalizing slavery with no regard for its horrific realities. Certainly some of Dunbar's poems, especially those written after he had achieved fame, adapt the conventions of the white plantation writers' works; however, even then Dunbar's accommodationism is not so extreme as some believe. In spite of these claims, one must recognize, as J. Saunders Redding and other critics have, that Dunbar's work possesses a skill and felicity that much of the plantation literature and the work of many of his African American contemporaries lacks. George Kent notes Dunbar's ability to create a world within his poems (*A Dark and Sudden Beauty*), and William H. Robinson (*Early Black American Poets*) and Dickson Bruce note that Dunbar often saw beyond the surface caricatures, creating strongly political verses.

Like much of the literature of the plantation tradition and much of other dialect poetry, Dunbar's verses sentimentalize the antebellum era, extol the virtues of patience and piety, celebrate the "natural" musical gifts of African Americans, catalog the culinary delights of the folk community, and gently mock the pretensions to gentility affected by the African Americans portrayed in his verse. Poems such as "When Malindy Sings" and "The Party" have been treated at length as examples of Dunbar's assimilation into the plantation tradition. Some critics have also noted the elements of protest in poems such as "An Antebellum Sermon," which directly addresses the issue of slaves' protest against their oppression and hints at the deception practiced on whites by the slave community. Since his death, Dunbar's reputation has passed through various stages: first hero, then accommodationist villain, and now painfully and completely human. What previous scholars have not noted, and what John Keeling argues convincingly ("Paul Dunbar and the Mask of Dialect") is the presence of several layers of protest contained within even the "happiest" of the plantation-style Dunbar poems. Keeling's argument indicates the extent to which scholars are rehabilitating Dunbar's reputation in light of new understanding about the writings' context.

The context must be considered in any assessment of both Dunbar and the entire dialect poetry movement. Dickson Bruce's *Black American Writing from the Nadir* makes the point that the 1890s saw the rise of a particularly virulent strain of racism and oppression in America, a tendency that necessitated the use of subtle means of protest in the African American community. Many of the poets writing in this era sought a readership beyond the publications owned and operated by African Americans; to a certain extent, success depended upon the acknowledgment of and adherence to the standards established by white society. In that way, all of Dunbar's contemporaries can be cited for the same failings critics attribute to his work; such a reading, however, limits our understanding of both the form and its context. Dunbar and his contemporaries—Campbell, Davis, James Ephraim *McGirt, Charles Douglas Clem, Aaron Belford Thompson, Priscilla Jane Thompson, and others—sought a balance between the need for a large readership and the desire to preserve racial integrity. Any judgment of that effort is better made with information about the racial climate in which the poets were making this choice.

One should also note the growing tendency in the early twentieth century, culminating in the decade after Dunbar's death, to use dialect poetry for more direct protest, whether by commenting more clearly on the cruelties of antebellum life, as Elliott Blaine Henderson did, or bringing elements of the folk tradition more clearly into the verse—as Charles Roundtree Shoeman did with his use of hoodoo. This stronger, more positive approach to dialect verse, providing a sense of balance to the generally negative view of the form, has often been overlooked by contemporary scholars.

Most likely, that rejection arises as the culmination of a critical strain showing the influence of James Weldon Johnson, whose remarks about dialect poetry in the introduction to *The Book of American Negro Poetry* (1922) include the famous assertion that the form has only "two stops—pathos and humor." Johnson was, ironically, a friend of Dunbar's. Johnson made his living for a time writing songs for the stage, and he was particularly adept at the dialect song. His experience with the form, and the need to conform to white ideology in order to succeed, is perhaps partially the basis of his rejection of a form he had once embraced. Regardless, one could see him as a leader in the trend that took African American poetry away from the assimilationist trappings of the dialect poets toward the more acceptable African American artistic individualism of the *Harlem Renaissance.

In the renaissance and beyond, however, one finds poets whose debt to the folk and vernacular traditions is so great that one is tempted to place them in the line of descendants of the dialect writers. Scholars tend to separate "folk speech" from dialect on grounds of authenticity and emotional expressiveness; while such a distinction is useful ideologically, it does a disservice to the accomplishments of poets such as Dunbar, James D. *Corrothers, and all the other dialect poets who saw the value of the folk culture and took steps to elevate it to the level of high art. Whether or not their attempts were ideologically pure, their innovations remain the starting point for the folk-speech oriented poetry of Langston Hughes and Sterling A. Brown and an important touchstone for a consideration of the politically charged urban vernacular poetry of the 1960s. The dialect poetry tradition's existence in a negative and dangerous context limits the extent of its innovation, perhaps, but Dunbar and the others, like their many successors, stand in the face of an overpowering white society, daring to use a voice and speech that differs markedly from what the majority will accept and affirm.

[*See also* Speech and Dialect.]

• J. Saunders Redding, *To Make a Poet Black*, 1939. William H. Robinson, *Early Black American Poets*, 1969. Stephen Henderson, *Understanding the New Black Poetry: Black Speech and Black Music As Poetic References*, 1973. Houston A. Baker, Jr., *Singers at Daybreak: Studies in Black American Literature*, 1974. Bernard Bell, *The Folk Roots of Contemporary Afro-American Poetry*, 1974. Peter Revell, *Paul Laurence Dunbar*, 1979. Henry Louis Gates, Jr., *Figures in Black: Words, Signs, and the "Racial" Self*, 1987. Dickson D. Bruce, Jr., *Black American Writing from the Nadir: The Evolution of a Literary Tradition 1877–1915*, 1989. Joan R. Sherman, *Invisible Poets: Afro-American Writing in the Nineteenth Century*, 2d ed., 1989. John Keeling, "Paul Dunbar and the Mask of Dialect," *Southern Literary Journal* 25 (Spring 1993): 24–38.
—William R. Nash

DIARIES AND JOURNALS. African American journal literature began, so far as we know, in 1822 with the *travel writing of Betsey Stockton, a missionary who sailed around Cape Horn and to the Hawaiian Islands, maintaining a travel log of her cruise experiences and descriptions of native social customs and ceremonies, published in the *Christian Advocate* in 1824 and 1825. Another important antebellum diarist, Rebecca Cox *Jackson , was a mystic, visionary, and Shaker Eldress who founded a black Shaker community in Philadelphia in 1851. *Gifts of Power: The Writings of Rebecca Jackson, Black Visionary, Shaker Eldress* (1981) is an edited compilation of her journal notes from 1830 to 1864. Illiterate, Jackson was supernaturally transformed, she writes, as she began to read the Bible extemporaneously, acquiring *literacy and empowerment after becoming frustrated with a literate brother who wrote *letters for her but "put in more than I told thee." In the South, William *Johnson, a free Negro, barber, and prosperous landowner and slaveholder in Mississippi, began a diary in 1835. *William Johnson's Natchez: The Antebellum Diary of a Free Negro* (1993) provides a local color description of old Natchez, family quarrels, marriages, births, and deaths. Like Rebecca Cox Jackson, Jarena *Lee was a preacher with little formal education, but she was "called" to preach by a voice that "seemed to say 'Preach the Gospel; I will put words in your mouth.'" Her spiritual *autobiography,

The Religious Experience and Journal of Jarena Lee (1849), was written from her ministerial journals.

The formally educated and upper-middle-class Charlotte *Forten leads a second group of diarists who wrote primarily during the Civil War and Reconstruction. *The Journals of Charlotte Forten Grimké* (1988) consists of five diaries that the author began at age sixteen in 1854 and concluded at age fifty-four in 1892. Since her journal writing spanned a period of thirty-eight years, Charlotte Forten reveals multiple images of herself. But she emerges most clearly as a champion of human rights. Diary three is the most important of the five journals, for it is here that Forten travels to South Carolina to teach contraband slaves, nurse Union soldiers, and record the reading of the Emancipation Proclamation to the historically disenfranchised.

Charles Waddell *Chesnutt, the first African American author to publish a *short story in the *Atlantic Monthly* (1887), was also a self-revealing diarist. *The Journals of Charles W. Chesnutt* (1993) includes three short works in a single book: "First Journal 1874–1875"; "Second Journal 1877–1881"; and "Third Journal 1881–1882." In all three journals Chesnutt describes aspects of southern life during Reconstruction. Chesnutt captures the opportunities and promises of the period, but also the hard economic reality for many farmers' children. The Chesnutt diaries reveal his own thwarted ambitions because of racism, and his literary aspirations and desire to succeed despite the obstacles.

Keeping diaries in this period, too, Charles Benson, George A. Maston, Charles Bennett Fisher, and Henry Turner reveal a variety of African American experiences during the Civil War. Benson's "The Travels and Tribulations of Charles Benson, Steward on the *Glide*," 1862–1880, extracted in *Essex Institute Historical Collections* (1984), is a narrative of his excursions to Zanzibar and his duties aboard ship. A midwestern teacher, barber, and Methodist minister, Maston reports on his teaching and preaching activities, Republican politics, the trial of a white man accused of killing a black man, and his optimism—"the Negro is irrepressible and bound to come to the top"—in "The Diaries and Writings of George A. Maston, Black Citizen of Lincoln, Nebraska," January–June 1883, in *Nebraska History* (1971). The *Diary of Charles B. Fisher* (1983), 1862–1864, is a travel log of Fisher's stewardship aboard the *Kearsarge* and narrative descriptions of foreign populations that he encountered on travels to England, France, the West Indies, the Canary Islands, and Spain. And, the first African American army chaplain of the First Regiment of United States Colored Troops, 1864, Turner gives an account of living quarters aboard the *Hermon Livingston*, storms at sea, and coastal battles during the Civil War. "Rocked in the Cradle of Consternation," December 1864, is excerpted in *American Heritage* (1980).

At the turn of the century and into the mid-1950s, diary writing continues to be dominated by African American men: a novelist, a navy supervisor, and an executive in the White House. These positions signify the advancement of the race, but the men's writings also reveal the crucial marker that race had become during this *Jim Crow era. Novelist Willard *Motley's *The Diaries of Willard Motley* (1979), 1926–1943, gives an overview of his racially mixed Chicago neighborhood, the Great Depression, and the odd jobs the writer held while struggling as a writer. Paul Nelson Harris's *Base Company* (1963), 1943–1945, is a World War II diary of the author's experiences with whites and black as a leader of a segregated "colored unit." Navy man Paul Nelson Harris describes life aboard the *California*. Although all military branches were under the law of Jim Crow and African American soldiers were segregated at home and abroad, the Navy restricted black men to the most menial of services. Harris had to face the low morale of his colored unit and the men's unwillingness to take orders from him.

The White House diarist Everett Frederic Morrow describes continuing racial strife and the nascent *civil rights movement during the Eisenhower administration. Morrow was the first African American to hold an executive position in the White House. As President Dwight D. Eisenhower's minority advisor, Morrow was a pioneer. The full weight of his status is clearly revealed in the diary *Black Man in the White House* (1963), 1955–1960. When Everett Frederic Morrow joined the Richard Nixon presidential campaign staff, he drafted a letter for the candidate to send to the mayor of Atlanta in support of the jailed Martin Luther King, Jr. Nixon and his staff ignored the draft and King; but Nixon's opponent, John F. Kennedy, called King's wife, and his brother, Robert F. Kennedy, contacted Atlanta officials, persuading them to release King. "This act won the election," Morrow writes on 10 November 1960, as John F. Kennedy won the black vote and barely defeated Vice President Nixon.

Peace and war abroad and chaos at home are the unifying themes of personal narratives from the 1960s. In *Where To, Black Man?* (1967), 1963–1964, Ed Smith, a teacher in Ghana under the auspices of a program of President Kennedy's vision, describes American and Ghanaian student interaction, tribal traditions, cultural and social life, and activities in Accra, Ghana's capital. Smith reflects, too, on his *identity as an African American in Africa. *GI Diary* (1968), 1965–1967, presents the Vietnam War experiences of David Parks, his services as a radio operator, his reflections on the war, and his pain in describing the human waste, the wounded and dead. In New York, James Haskins's *Diary of a Harlem School Teacher* (1969), September 1968–June 1969, cites the chaos, the poverty and *violence of students, and the friction between black and white teachers at P.S. 92. *Members of the Class Will Keep Daily Journals: The Barnard College Journals of Tobi Gillian Sanders and Joan Frances Bennett* (1968), was written, as the title suggests, by two college students on assignment. A native of South Carolina, Joan Frances Bennett's journal notes contain the radical introspectiveness of Charlotte Forten's diaries. And like Charlotte Forten, whom she follows as the fifth African American female diarist to be noted in diary research, Joan Frances Bennett responds to the issue of racial oppression: "4 April '68 Martin Luther King, the 'King,' was killed tonight. After the first shock, what did I think? . . . 'To a man of spirit it is more painful to be oppressed like a weakling than in the consciousness of strength and common hopes to meet a death that comes unfelt.' Well done, Martin Luther, well done."

With the emergence of women's liberation in the 1960s and 1970s, feminists such as Audre *Lorde deconstructed and demystified the socially constructed identity of women under patriarchy. Contemporary African American journal writers are led by the late poet Audre Lorde, as African American diary writing becomes gender-specific after her, allowing women to indulge themselves freely in diary discourse without fear of reprimand. A triple social pariah, African American, female, and *lesbian, Audre Lorde confronts the nightmare of illness first with diffidence but subsequently with a feminist's candor and power. *The Cancer Journals* (1980) is a record of her breast cancer detection in 1977, radical mastectomy in 1978, and her ongoing psychological recovery (she died of cancer in 1992). When the one-breasted Audre Lorde is advised to undergo a cosmetic silicon implant for life-enhancing purposes, she relates the symbolism of the proposal to the patriarchal denial of women's real lives. This denial "encourages a woman to focus her energies upon the mastectomy as a cosmetic occurrence, to the exclusion of other factors in a constellation that could include her own death." Audre Lorde's insistence on the truth of women's existence, with an honest passion for life, has influenced a new generation of African American diarists.

The recent publication of *Life Notes: Personal Writings by Contemporary Black Women* (1994), an *anthology edited by Patricia Bell-Scott and dedicated to Audre Lorde and Arvin Scott, consists of more than forty mininarratives of well-known and unknown, mature and youthful females. Among the contributors are writer Alice *Walker, poet Rita *Dove, scholars Barbara Smith and Deborah McDowell, and editor-scholar Patricia Bell-Scott. A particularly poignant vignette is presented by Elaine Shelly, whose journal writing "reaffirms the collage of colors that comprise my life" and a "new color was added to my life in 1989 by multiple sclerosis." Elaine Shelly, a lesbian, contemplates her illness and her outsider's status, and reclaims her humanity, writing notes to herself (just as Audre Lorde did for several years) even as she traces the trajectory of the disease to her immobility and to the ambiguity of the future. *Life Notes* addresses modernity, its problems and its challenges, and the long road traveled by African Americans and especially African American women, free to engage in the act of total self-disclosure in diary literature.

African American journals identify various stages of African American *history. Singularly and collectively, these writings are primary sources for the historian's research as the boundary between the genres of diary (which lacks closure) and *biography and *autobiography (which have a coherent core) are blurred.

• Margo Culley, ed., *One Day at a Time*, 1985. Leonore Hoffman and Margo Culley, eds., *Women's Personal Narratives:*

Essays in Criticism and Pedagogy, 1985. Laura Arksey, Nancy Pries, and Marcia Reed, eds., *American Diaries: An Annotated Bibliography of Published American Diaries and Journals*, 2 vols., 1987. Rebecca Hogan, "Engendered Autobiographies: The Diary As a Feminine Form," *Prose Studies* 14 (Sept. 1991): 95–107.

—Geneva Cobb-Moore

DIASPORIC LITERATURE, in its broadest sense, is any literature, written or oral, of a dispersed people. Although the word "diaspora" was once commonly reserved for reference to Jews scattered outside Palestine after the Babylonian captivity, the term has come to refer to any people driven off, removed, or exiled from their home who nevertheless maintain elements of their native culture while residing within a dominant culture. Writers have used the concept of an African diaspora, if not the term itself, for centuries. As various Pan-African, black nationalist, and Afrocentric political and intellectual movements have waxed and waned and as specific historical and social events have precipitated various flights or quests, the connotations and the popularity of "diaspora" as a term for people of African descent have also changed. According to Harry A. Reed, an editor of *Studies in the African Diaspora*, the term was popular at the 1965 International Congress of African Historians in Tanzania but its use "mushroomed" during the 1980s and 1990s when "diaspora" was used in the titles of more than two dozen African American history books. In general, the concept of the African diaspora emphasizes what is shared, historically and culturally, among African-descended peoples worldwide, but the application of this term is not uncontested.

Perhaps the most consistent connection of "diaspora" with people of African descent has been its connection with *slavery and suffering. Some, such as nineteenth-century Caribbean scholar Edward W. Blyden, use the term to emphasize the commonality between the Hebrews, "God's ancient people," who experienced much of their servitude and suffering on the African continent, and African people of other faiths whose dispersions were also marked by enslavement and oppression. Others focus more upon the experience of exportation and exile as it resulted from the Atlantic slave trade. The Atlantic slave trade, which began as early as the fifteenth century and reached its height between 1650 and 1850, compelled the migration of at least twelve million people from Africa to the Americas, England, and parts of Europe, and thereby produced the largest mass movement of peoples in the world up to that time. As a consequence of the African diaspora about one-third of all people of African descent live outside Africa. However, given the series of invasions, colonizations, tribal persecutions, and national partitionings within Africa, the concept of an African diaspora also includes many who never left the continent. In its broadest sense, then, when applied to the African diaspora, "diasporic literature" is any literature, written or oral, produced by African people who have experienced physical or mental dispersion. Such a definition, particularly when applied to literature of the African diaspora, is controversial.

Some define diasporic literature as focusing upon one's African heritage or upon ethnic or racial experiences and issues such as slavery, *race, colonization, or the *color line. Others argue that any literature created by an exiled or emigrated individual may be considered diasporic in part because speech patterns, word choices, aesthetic patterns, and other cultural influences are never completely obliterated. Scholar and critic Antonio Olliz Boyd, for example, argues that for those of African heritage, in particular, the "consanguineal affiliation with an oppressed group" is "an unalterable circumstance" that governs an individual's psyche and therefore any artistic creation. Some perceive a tone of alienation or loss in diasporic literature. Richard L. Jackson notes that regardless of the presence of "black language" or "black themes," a persistent identifier of diasporic literature is that writers of African ancestry "never seem to be at one or at home racially" within the societies in which they now live.

Since the Atlantic slave trade was a cataclysmic factor in the African diaspora, themes of slavery and *freedom, racial discrimination and segregation are prevalent in literature of the African diaspora. However, both the voluntary and forced scattering of Africans began long before the Atlantic slave trade and continue to this day; thus, concerns such as bondage and freedom, self-representation and *stereotypes occupy even those writers for whom slavery and colonization, racial segregation and ghettoization are events of history, metaphors, or philosophical and political interpretive stances. And *migration and immigration, exile and *expatriatism, *family and home are standard concerns in diasporic literature. Whether one requires obvious or specific references to the legacies of slavery and racism or assumes that regardless of subject matter a certain diasporic style and structure will identify the literature of this category, it is clear that even within the smaller geographic area defined by the Atlantic slave trade there are multiple possibilities for artistic creation and appreciation. This essay focuses upon the literature of the African diaspora created by the Atlantic slave trade in North and South America and parts of Europe. Even within this arbitrary limitation exists an astonishing variety of themes, languages, and literary forms. The African American section of the African diaspora includes literature by African Americans who migrated from the New England colonies to Nova Scotia, nineteenth-century settlers who moved to San Francisco and the Northwest territories, and fugitive slaves who fled to Canada and Europe, Central and South America, the Caribbean, and other portions of the globe. It includes those who left the United States to live as refugees in Europe or as exiles in Africa. Diasporic literature comes from Virgin Islanders who moved to Puerto Rico and Jamaicans who established communities in New York City, San Diego, and Atlanta. It is written, sung, and told in languages that include Portuguese, Spanish, French, Xhosa, Kiswahili, Arabic, Creole, English, and many English dialects.

The genres that comprise diasporic literature are varied and changing. *Travel writing by people of African descent forms an important part of African American diasporic literature. In the eighteenth century, narratives by Briton *Hammon and John *Marrant demonstrated two kinds of colonial literary productions. A Narrative of the Uncommon Sufferings, and Surprizing Deliverance of Briton Hammon, a Negro Man, published in 1760 in Boston, summarizes Hammon's thirteen years as a sailor residing in or visiting the Caribbean, Europe, and the Near East. Hammon's narrative resembles American Indian captivity and spiritual narratives but is distinguished by his status as an enslaved African displaced from and seeking a return to a place he could call "home." In A Narrative of the Lord's Wonderful Dealings with John Marrant, a Black, (Now gone to preach the Gospel in Nova Scotia) (1785), John Marrant chronicles his moves from New York to Saint Augustine to Georgia to Charlestown while still a child. While much of this movement resulted from attempts to find work and a safe community, Marrant does not dwell upon this displacement. His narrative focuses upon his experiences as a missionary, which brought him to live among Indians in North America and took him to England and, as the title indicates, to Nova Scotia. Other early narratives that demonstrate the wide-ranging movement of African Americans are Nancy *Prince's A Narrative of the Life and Travels of Mrs. Nancy Prince (1850), William Wells *Brown's The American Fugitive in Europe (1855), and Amanda Berry *Smith's An Autobiography: The Story of the Lord's Dealings with Mrs. Amanda Smith, the Colored Evangelist; Containing an Account of . . . Her Travels in America, England, Ireland, Scotland, India and Africa, as an Independent Missionary (1893).

Since the path of the Atlantic slave trade was the dispersion route for most African Americans prior to abolition, the experiences of enslaved Africans in North America, the Caribbean, and parts of Europe constitute a large part of early diasporic literature. Slaves told stories and published *autobiographies, created songs and *poetry, and acted out in rituals, ceremonies, and other *dramas their lives, histories, and aspirations. Scholars and researchers have discovered many ways in which the literatures have maintained commonalities despite many specific differences. For example, certain animal *trickster tales of West African tribes reappeared in Jamaica with Anansi the spider as the protagonist and in the southern United States featuring *Brer Rabbit.

*Slave narratives, the autobiographical accounts of life in slavery and attempts to gain freedom, are some of the most prominent examples of diasporic literature. Apparently, the greatest number of these narratives originated in the United States. Their emphasis upon fugitives who fled the slave South to the free North is a defining characteristic in this genre. Arna *Bontemps and others have determined that the slave narrative is the first truly original genre created in the United States and that it therefore deserves recognition as the first manifestation of a literature that is actually "American." However, the narrative generally heralded as the eighteenth-century classic does not fit this pattern and was written by an African slave who spent very little time in the United States. First published in England in 1789, *The Interesting Narrative of Olaudah *Equiano, or Gustavus Vassa, the African* begins with Equiano's kidnapping in Africa; describes his experiences as a slave in Europe, the Caribbean, and the United States; lists his several attempts to gain freedom; details his years as a sailor who lived in or visited Central America, Italy, Turkey, and the Arctic; and ends with him living as a free man in London while attempting to combine capitalism and Christianity as a missionary and merchant in Sierra Leone. Other examples of transnational influences within the slave narrative genre are *The History of Mary *Prince, a West Indian Slave . . . to which is added the Narrative of Asa-Asa, a Captured African* (1831) and Juan Francisco Manzano's *Poems by a Slave in the Island of Cuba, . . . with the History of the Early Life . . .* (1840).

Slavery, the fugitive slave narratives, and slave revolts continue to inform much diasporic literature. Several modern writers including Arna Bontemps, Alejo Carpentier, and Barbara *Chase-Riboud have used slave revolts as subject matter. Among the contemporary meditations upon slavery in the diaspora are Ishmael *Reed's *Flight to Canada* (1976), Maryse Condé's *Moi, Tituba, sorciere . . . noire de Salem* (1986), Sherley Anne *Williams's *Dessa Rose* (1986), Caryl Phillips's *Cambridge* (1991), and Michelle Cliff's *Free Enterprise* (1993). Alex *Haley with *Roots* (1976), Toni *Morrison with *Song of Solomon* (1977), and Manuel Zapata Olivella with *Changó, el gran putas* (1985) are among those who have created sagas of African American slaves and their descendants that cover multiple generations and dispersions to several geographical areas. Barbara Chase-Riboud's *Valide* (1986) provides an interesting variation with its examination of harem slavery of African women. Virginia *Hamilton's *Zeely* (1967) and *The Magical Adventures of Pretty Pearl* (1983) are examples of literature written for children that feature African deities, African American slaves, and other diasporic elements.

Colonization or repatriation has long been an issue in diasporic literature. In the nineteenth century, when some believed the answer to slavery and racism within the United States was to remove Africans and their descendants to Africa or other sites of the diaspora, responses and manifestos such as Peter Williams's "A Discourse . . . for the Benefit of the Coloured Community of Wilberforce in Upper Canada" (1830), "Emigration to Mexico by a Colored Female of Philadelphia" (1832), and Alexander *Crummell's "The Relations and Duties of Free Colored Men in America to Africa" (1861) were common. David *Walker's *Appeal in Four Articles; Together with a Preamble, to the Coloured Citizens of the World . . .* (1829) demonstrates that as early as 1829 some U.S. Americans clearly understood themselves to be remnants of a larger community and recognized slavery as an international concern. But in the first half of the twentieth century several movements converged to produce more consciously diasporic literature. One of the most well known proponents of reunification of the dispersed peoples was Marcus *Garvey, a Jamaican who lived in Central America

and England before establishing in 1914 the Universal Negro Improvement Association (UNIA), an international organization of at least two million members with headquarters in Harlem, New York. Among that organization's projects were *Negro World*, a newspaper, and the Black Star Line, a shipping enterprise owned and operated by blacks.

Garvey's presence and publications were a distinctive part of the period generally known as the *New Negro movement or the *Harlem Renaissance. Many writers and editors of that era had international ties and influence. Authors such as Eric *Walrond and Claude *McKay were born in the Caribbean and traveled extensively. Langston *Hughes, though born in Joplin, Missouri, came to Harlem from his father's home in Mexico. Hughes was particularly important as an influence upon and mentor of diasporic writers from Cuba, Mexico, Colombia, and other parts of the globe. The Harlem Renaissance brought together writers from many locations who actively sought to understand what it meant to be black in the United States and other parts of the world. Countee *Cullen's poems "Heritage" and "Incident" and Langston Hughes's "The *Negro Speaks of Rivers" are examples of meditations upon the question "What is Africa to Me?" Claude McKay's *Home to Harlem* (1928) and *Banana Bottom* (1933), Jean *Toomer's *Cane* (1923) and *Blue Meridian* (1936), Wallace *Thurman's The *Blacker the Berry* (1929), Jessie Redmon *Fauset's *Plum Bun* (1929), and Nella *Larsen's *Quicksand* (1928) are but a few of the works that explore the meanings of migrations and community among African Americans.

The influence of the Harlem Renaissance was not confined to the United States and the English-speaking Caribbean, however. Poets such as Cuba's Nicolás Guillén acknowledge the influence of the Harlem Renaissance upon their work. In Mexico, the periodical *Palms* devoted an entire issue to translations of Harlem Renaissance writers. *Negritude developed more within the French language tradition and included Léopold Sédar Senghor of Senegal, Aimé Césaire of Martinique, and Léon Damas of French Guyana, all writers who published literature in French from what they hoped would be a distinctly African aesthetic and philosophical perspective. *Pan-Africanism, a similar movement more focused upon English-speaking politics and literatures, was fostered by W. E. B. *Du Bois. And works such as C. L. R. James's *Black Jacobins* (1938) have influence far beyond Trinidad and Tobago. While not generally recognized as part of the Pan-Africanist movement, poets such as Robert *Hayden, with "Middle Passage" and "A Ballad of Remembrance," and Melvin B. *Tolson, with *Libretto for the Republic of Liberia* (1953) and *Harlem Galley* (1966), also sought to recreate and understand the diasporic world.

Within the United States, diasporic literature explores the various migrations of black people, in groups or individually, who were seeking or establishing places where they could live and express the totality of their African American heritage as they moved from South to North, from East to West, from the country to the cities and suburbs, and vice versa.

Particularly in the twentieth century, the literature demonstrates concern with dispersions of African Americans within American nations and territories and within the African American communities of the United States. Paule *Marshall's *Brown Girl, Brownstones* (1959) explores the economic and social developments among Barbadians who settled in Brooklyn during the 1950s. Rosa *Guy's *Ruby* (1973) focuses upon a friendship between Phyllisia Cathy, from a "sunlit West Indies island," and Edith Jackson, a Harlem "ragamuffin." Carlos Guillermo Wilson's *Chombo* (1981) begins with a quote from Marcus Garvey and weaves the history and myths of Panama, Africa, and the West Indies in an account of black Panamanian descendants of English-speaking Afro-Caribbeans. Manuel Zapata Olivella's *He visto la noche* (1953) is autobiographical fiction about Afro-Colombians who move to the United States. Subtitled *Las raíces de la furia negra* (The Roots of Black Rage), the chapters range from "Jim Crow in Hollywood" to "Black Chicago." In "Worshipper of Father Divine," Olivella's description of how Langston Hughes helped him socially and professionally offers additional insight into the creation and promulgation of diasporic literature.

Other diasporic writing that explores the various successes and obstacles to African American community within and without North America include Samuel Selvon's *The Lonely Londoners* (1956), a story about Trinidadians who migrate to England; Austin Clarke's *When He Was Young and Used to Wear Silks* (1971), fiction about Barbadians in Ontario, Canada; and Marlene Noubese Phillips's *Harriet's Daughters* (1988), a novel in which a Canadian teenager who watches the *Cosby Show* on television and who plays the "Underground Railway Game" for fun, tries to emulate Harriet *Tubman by helping her best friend Zulma escape from Canada and return to her grandmother in Tobago. Nigerian writer Buchi Emecheta presents an interesting departure in African American diasporic literature with *The Family* (1990), a story of a Jamaican woman who deliberately chooses a Yoruba name for the daughter she bears in London. Andrea *Lee's *Russian Journal* (1981), her personal account of life in Russia as an African American graduate student, was nominated for a National Book Award, and her novel *Sarah Phillips* (1984) tells of a Harvard-trained African American woman who wanders Europe while trying to reconcile the disparate elements of her African American identity. Yelena Khanga in *Soul to Soul: The Story of a Black Russian American Family, 1865–1992* (1992) pursues her family's roots by traveling to the United States and visiting land in Yazoo County, Mississippi, that had belonged to her grandfather. Another 1992 publication that illustrates the expanding areas of the African American diaspora is *Showing Our Colors: Afro-German Women Speak Out*, an anthology for which African American Audre *Lorde wrote the introduction.

Another version of diasporic literature treats the return of African Americans to Africa and the contemporary pilgrimages of Africans to the United States. Richard *Wright's odyssey to Ghana served to alienate him even more from Africa, as the text of *Black Power* (1954) demonstrates. Maya *Angelou joined a "colony" of African Americans living in Ghana in 1962 and writes of her experiences in *All God's Children Need Traveling Shoes* (1986). Reginald *McKnight's *I Get on the Bus* (1990) narrates the quest of Evan Norris, a middle-class African American peace corps volunteer from the United States who seeks out a Senegalese marabou for spiritual enlightenment. Alice Princess Siwundhla's journey that she describes in *Alice Princess: An Autobiography* (1965) began in Lake Malawi, went to the Luwazi Mission School, and from there to Nairobi, Khartoum, Rome, London, and Los Angeles. Her U.S.-born daughter currently anchors a national news show. *Kaffir Boy: The True Story of a Black Youth's Coming of Age in Apartheid South Africa* (1986) tells of Marc Mathabane's escape from South Africa via a tennis scholarship and his new life in the United States. A blurb on the book jacket announces this autobiography as being in the tradition of Richard Wright's *Native Son*.

The genres of diasporic literature are many and evolving. Mike Phillips, a Guyanese, writes crime fiction set in England while Njami Simon, a Senegalese, set his mystery in Paris, but both claim the influence of Ohio-born Chester *Himes, who lived in permanent exile in Europe. The plot of Simon's novel, originally published in France as *Cercueil & Cie* (1985) and translated in 1987 as *Coffin & Co.*, revolves around the efforts of two Harlem detectives who have been impersonating Himes's fictional characters to prevent the distribution of the English translation of Himes's final novel about *Grave Digger Jones and *Coffin Ed Johnson, which had been published in French. Charles R. Saunders and Octavia E. *Butler create *speculative fiction with mythic African heroes.

The multiple influences and complex interweavings of diasporic literature continue. Oyekan Owomoyela edited *A History of Twentieth-Century African Literatures* (1993), which explores the multiplicity of diasporic influences upon writers on the African continent. Osayimwense Osa, a professor at Clark Atlanta University and editor of the *Journal of African Children's and Youth Literature* found the special issue devoted to African American children's literature so popular that he published it through the African World Press as a separate book in 1995. The University of Virginia–based journal *Callaloo recently devoted an issue to Afro-Brazilian literature and one to Wilson Harris of Guyana. Scholar Amadou Bissiri uses the interpretations of Yoruba tradition from Nigerian Nobel Prize–winning author Wole Soyinka to understand *The Piano Lesson*, a play by Pulitzer Prize–winning dramatist August *Wilson. In 1995, Atlanta, Georgia, hosted the three writers from the African diaspora who have won the Nobel Prize for Literature: Derek Walcott, Toni Morrison, and Soyinka, in a conference that included U.S. poet laureate and African American Rita *Dove, and Nobel laureates from Mexico, Poland, Japan, France, and Russia. Not only was it the largest gathering of Nobel laureates in years, but it signaled the globalization of literature from the African diaspora.

[*See also* African Literature; West Indian Literature.]

• Albert H. Berrian and Richard A. Long, eds., *Negritude*, 1967. *Blacks in Hispanic Literature: Critical Essays*, ed. Miriam Decosta, 1977. Richard L. Jackson, *Black Writers in Latin America*, 1979. Edouard Glissant, *Caribbean Discourse*, 1989. Lilyan Kesleloot, *Black Writers in French*, 1991. Paul Gilroy, *The Black Atlantic: Modernism and Double Consciousness*, 1993. Tejumola Olaniyan, *Scars of Conquest, Masks of Resistance: The Inventions of Cultural Identities in African, African-American, and Caribbean Drama*, 1995. Charles Rowell, *Ancestral House: The Black Short Story in America and Europe*, 1995.   —Frances Smith Foster

DIXON, MELVIN (1950–1992), novelist, poet, educator, scholar, and translator. Born in Connecticut, Melvin Dixon earned his BA at Wesleyan University (1971) and his MA and PhD at Brown University (1973, 1975). His first book, *Change of Territory* (1983), a collection of free-verse poems, reflects his interest in his family's southern roots and his experiences—including a visit to Africa—while he was living in Paris in the mid-1970s. For Dixon, a change of territory affords new perspectives and new or enlarged identities, themes mirrored in the book's four-part structure. The opening poem, "Hungry Travel," focuses on his parents' departure for Connecticut from North Carolina's Blue Ridge Mountains. Other poems expand the poet's concept of kin to include literary influences such as Jean *Toomer, Richard *Wright, Zora Neale *Hurston, Ralph *Ellison, and Robert *Hayden. The long poem "Bobo Baoulé," which comprises part 3, emphasizes racial ancestry as it recounts the enslavement of a young African, then leaps forward in time to one of his descendants, who has returned to Africa with the Peace Corps. The book's closing poem, "Hemispheres," with its imagery of roundness, also highlights this pattern of departure and return, in this case the poet's homecoming—though the poem anticipates further travel as well, ongoing journeys of external and internal exploration.

Dixon's first *novel, *Trouble the Water* (1989), winner of the Nilon Award for Excellence in Minority Fiction, also employs the journey motif as it examines the burden of the past that haunts its protagonist, Jordan Henry, who returns to his childhood home. Set primarily in rural North Carolina along the Pee Dee River, the book traces Jordan's efforts to free himself from his grandmother's expectation—which led him to flee to the North at age thirteen—that he will avenge his seventeen-year-old mother's death in childbirth by killing his father. Dixon's complex interweaving of past and present, his skillful handling of a varied cast of characters that includes the Haitian conjure woman Mam'Zilie, his poetic evocation of the forces of nature, and his powerful use of water as an archetypal symbol—all make this first novel far more than yet another example of the southern gothic tradition. Although the climactic confrontation between Jordan and his father is somewhat contrived and the resolution of the conflict occurs too quickly and easily, Dixon effectively addresses moral issues that transcend the particulars of Jordan Henry's life.

Dixon's second novel, *Vanishing Rooms* (1991), is set in New York City's Greenwich Village. The book has frequently been compared to James *Baldwin's *Giovanni's Room* (1956), for not only do both books deal with homosexuality but Dixon has acknowledged the profound influence Baldwin's writing had on his own. Unlike Baldwin, however, Dixon focuses on an interracial gay relationship, one shattered in the opening chapter by the brutal murder of his African American protagonist's white lover. Dixon's use of three first-person narrators—Jesse, the protagonist, a dancer; Ruella, another member of the dance company and the person to whom Jesse turns when Metro is killed; and fifteen-year-old Lonny, one of the four white teenagers responsible for the murder—demonstrates Dixon's mastery of style, tone, characterization, and narrative technique. This use of multiple narrators is also meant to suggest, Dixon has noted, the social and political dimensions of racism and homophobia, problems that cannot be solved on an individual basis. Among Dixon's major achievements here is his sensitive portrait of Lonny, who unexpectedly evokes the reader's sympathy and understanding despite the violence he has helped to provoke. While Jesse must confront the racism that undermined his relationship with Metro, Lonny comes to recognize that he himself might easily have been the victim of his friends' savagery. The novel's graphic scenes of sexual violence, including Metro's murder and the gang rape of the imprisoned Lonny, are deeply disturbing, but they testify to the horrifying consequences of racism and homophobia. In Dixon's highly imagistic prose the voices of people like Jesse and Lonny are heard for almost the first time in American literature.

In addition to his *poetry and fiction, Dixon published a volume of literary criticism, *Ride Out the Wilderness: Geography and Identity in Afro-American Literature* (1987). He also translated from French both Geneviève Fabre's *Drumbeats, Masks, and Metaphor: Contemporary Afro-American Theatre* (1983) and *The Collected Poetry* of Léopold Sédar Senghor (1991), whose work Dixon came to admire during his year in Senegal as a Fulbright lecturer (1985–1986). Dixon's promising career was cut short by his death from AIDS. The final section of his posthumous collection of poems, *Love's Instruments* (1995), speaks powerfully about the effects of the AIDS epidemic on his generation.

[*See also* Criticism, *article on* Criticism since 1965; Gay Literature; Sexuality.]

• Wilfrid R. Koponen, "Melvin Dixon," in *Contemporary Gay American Novelists*, ed. Emmanuel S. Nelson, 1993, pp. 110–115.   —John Lang

DODSON, OWEN (1914–1983), poet, novelist, and playwright. For the major portion of his life, fate favored Owen Vincent Dodson. Born the ninth child of a poor Brooklyn family, he attended excellent schools: Bates College in Lewiston, Maine, for his BA

(1932–1936) and the Yale School of Drama, where he earned his MFA in playwriting (1936–1939). He taught *theater and literature in the best African American universities—Atlanta, Hampton, and Howard—and won major writing grants: General Education Board (1937); Rosenwald Fellowship (1943); Guggenheim Fellowship (1953); Rockefeller (1968). In recognition of his contribution to the theater, President Lyndon Johnson invited Dodson to the White House for celebration of Shakespeare's quadricentennial birthday.

In August of 1946, he saw the publication of his first volume of *poetry, *Powerful Long Ladder,* which established his national reputation. M. L. Rosenthal wrote in the *New York Herald Tribune Weekly Book Review,* "The positive achievements of *Powerful Long Ladder* are its vividness, its solid strength in picturing pain and disgust without losing the joy of life which marks the best artist. . . ." Several poems in the volume have become standards. Dodson's use of metaphor and conceit, which sometimes jarred readers, nonetheless added "to our stock of available reality."

Poetry remained the seminal source for his first full-length *drama, *Divine Comedy* (1938), a tale concerning the charismatic preacher Father Divine. Recipient of the Maxwell Anderson Verse Award (1942), the play became the first quality verse drama by an African American. His second verse play, *Garden of Time* (1939), reinterpreted the Medea story. Twenty-seven of his thirty-seven plays and *operas have been produced—two at the Kennedy Center.

In February 1951 Farrar, Straus and Giroux released *Boy at the Window,* Dodson's first and best *novel. The *Washington Post* critic caught the novel's essence, "Eloquent Writing: Child's Eye View of the Adult World." The autobiographical story concerned a sensitive nine-year-old growing up in a working-class neighborhood of Brooklyn in the 1920s. The heart of the novel is the death of his beloved mother, a death the boy feels he should have been able to prevent by his religious conversion. The prose, rich in imagery and metaphor, captures the intimate thoughts and voice of a child: the language is clearly the style of a poet.

In 1952 Dodson received a Guggenheim Fellowship to write a sequel, *Come Home Early, Child,* which did not find a publisher until 1977. Breaking into two sections, the latter half surrealistic, the novel may be seen as a harbinger of later surreal scenes in the novels of Ishmael *Reed, Clarence *Major, and Toni *Morrison.

It was not until his retirement from the theater department at Howard University that he was able to return to poetry, publishing in *The Harlem Book of the Dead* (1978). Camille Billops, a visual artist, had contracted the Harlem photographer James Van Der Zee to issue a series of his funeral photographs. Dodson agreed to write poems as captions for the photos.

He considered *The Confession Stone: Song Cycle* (1970) a series of monologues spoken by the Holy Family concerning the life of Jesus, to be his masterpiece. The simplicity of the language portrays the humanity of the Holy Family. His final collection of poems, "Life on the Streets," has never been published;

however, in May of 1982 the New York Public Theatre staged the work as poetry in performance.

Except for an authorized *biography, *Sorrow Is the Only Faithful One* (1993), very little critical study has been written about Dodson's poetry or plays. The reasons for this neglect are complex: First, he was an academic, and the prejudice of "those who can, do; those who can't, teach" obscured Dodson's creative reputation. Second, he was master of several crafts: theater, narrative, and poetry, making him difficult to label in a culture where image and label are vital for reputation. Third, although Dodson was in touch with his time, the time was not in touch with him. He was too young to be included in the illustrious *Harlem Renaissance and too much of a humanist to please the publishers of the angry, militant black writers in the 1960s. Finally, racism did take its toll: considered a "black writer," he had to find his publication almost solely within that designation.

• Owen Dodson, interview by John O'Brien, in *Interviews with Black Writers,* 1973, pp. 54–61. Bernard L. Peterson, Jr., "The Legendary Owen Dodson," *Crisis* 86 (Nov. 1979): 373–378. James Hatch, Douglas A. M. Ward, and Joe Weixlmann, "The Rungs of a Powerful Long Ladder: An Owen Dodson Bibliography," *Black American Literature Forum* 14 (Summer 1980): 60–68. James V. Hatch, *Sorrow Is the Only Faithful One: The Life of Owen Dodson,* 1993.

—James V. Hatch

DOMESTIC. Domestics are prominent on the landscape of African American literature, an understandable visibility since domestic labor has been the primary work available to black women for most of their history in America. The word "domestics," frequently used interchangeably with the word "maids," may refer to women who are live-in or part-time maids, cooks, nurses, or general house cleaners; "day workers" is another phrase used to describe women who do not live in with their employers. Such women usually left their own families—even small children—in the early hours of the morning to ride the bus, be picked up, or walk to their places of employment. Many times, instead of being paid for their labor, they would receive hand-me-down clothing, leftover food ("service pans"), or cast-off furniture and appliances as compensation. In the absence of union-controlled work, the women had little recourse to complaints about being cheated. They were expected to sacrifice their families and their health for the upkeep of white women's houses, and they frequently found themselves in the awkward position of serving as confidant to their white female employers. They were also occasionally the object of sexual abuse by the husbands of the white women who had hired them.

Beginning with characters who were descendants of the plantation *mammy, such as Mammy Jane in Charles Waddell *Chesnutt's *The *Marrow of Tradition* (1901), black writers have used maids in a variety of guises. Characters such as *Lutie Johnson in Ann *Petry's *The *Street* (1946) and the grandmother in Kristin *Hunter's *God Bless the Child* (1964) illustrate how domestics internalize the values of the white families for whom they work, values that are destructive to their own families. William Melvin *Kelley depicts a maid talking back to her employers in *dem* (1967), while Douglas Turner *Ward has his two domestics in *Happy Ending* (1966) make an art of appropriating goods from their white boss. Writers also portray domestics who move from verbal confrontation to more violent rejections of their status and their employers; indeed, Ed *Bullins's Mamie Lee King in *The Gentleman Caller* (1969) and Ted *Shine's Mrs. Grace Love in *Contribution* (1969) both kill their white employers, thereby reflecting how the militant movement of the 1960s affected the portrait of maids. However, writers depict domestics more frequently with humor than with violence, and Alice *Childress's *Mildred Johnson in *Like One of the Family . . . Conversations from a Domestic's Life* (1956) serves as the classic example. While Mildred certainly gets her employers to change their minds about a number of issues, including race relations, she does so with a basic respect for human beings. She has become the prototype for the domestic who effects transformation without alienating—at least not overly much—her employers. The prevalence of domestic workers in African American literature and their treatment by additional writers as diverse as Richard *Wright ("Man of All Work," 1969), Mari *Evans ("The 7:25 Trolley" and "When in Rome," 1970), and Lorenz *Graham (*South Town*, 1958) reveal the extent to which history has influenced creativity and the extent to which black writers are committed to making art out of the everyday circumstances of black people's lives.

• David M. Katzman, *Seven Days a Week: Women and Domestic Service in Industrializing America*, 1978. Trudier Harris, *From Mammies to Militants: Domestics in Black American Literature*, 1982. 　　　　　　　　　—Trudier Harris

DOMINI, RAY. *See* Lorde, Audre.

Don't Cry, Scream. Published in 1969 by Haki R. *Madhubuti's *Third World Press, *Don't Cry, Scream* is his third collection of *poetry and begins with an introduction by Gwendolyn *Brooks. Brooks addresses the most important contribution that Madhubuti makes to African American literary history: Madhubuti's poetry demonstrates his intense goal of enlightening Black people about the psychological, economical, political, and historical forces that stifle their well-being.

David Lloren's thorough profile of Haki Madhubuti, which appeared in the March 1969 issue of *Ebony*, followed the publication of *Don't Cry, Scream* and was a major influence in bringing Madhubuti's work to the attention of a wide audience. Haki Madhubuti begins this third collection of poetry with a preface entitled "Black Poetics / for the many to come." His spelling of "blackpoetry" and "blackpeople" as one word suggests that Blackness and humanity are inseparable or inextricable. For him, then, as a Black writer, the Blackness of his poetry is an inextricable aspect of his subject matter and of the ways in which he shapes his ideas. The first poem in the

collection, entitled "Gwendolyn Brooks," poetically captures the exchange of knowledge that took place when he and some of the other poets from OBAC (Organization of Black American Culture) met Brooks and ends with the idea of how the stereotyping of Gwendolyn Brooks as a "negro poet" completely fails to capture her greatness. In two related poems, "History of the Poet As a Whore (to all negro poets who deal in whi-te paronomasia)" and "a poem for negro intellectuals (if there bes such a thing)," he refers to Black poets who shun their commitment to the Black community as paper prostitutes and describes the "blk/man" and "blk/woman" actions needed to change the lives of "a people deathliving / in / abstract realities."

Like the "negro intellectual" and the poet as whore, the Black man described in what perhaps remains one of Madhubuti's most well known poems, "But He Was Cool or: he even stopped for green lights," is Black in appearance or form but has no substance or commitment. The strength of Madhubuti's dedication to Blackness in *Don't Cry, Scream* lies in his use of Black *music as poetic reference, in his use of revolutionary *jazz musicians as cultural heroes ("Don't Cry, Scream" and "blackmusic / a / beginning"), and in the poems that explore the evil associated with the assassinations of Dr. Martin Luther *King, Jr., and *Malcolm X ("Assassination" and "Malcolm Spoke / who listened?"). The most sustained poem in the collection, "Nigerian Unity / or little niggers killing little niggers (for brothers Christopher Okigbo & Wole Soyinka)," examines how the West's fight for gold in Africa and its commodification of Blackness underlay the Biafran Civil War in which the Yoruba fought the Igbo. Both Nigerian writers, Christopher Okigbo was an Igbo who joined the seceded Biafrans and was killed early in the war, and Wole Soyinka, a Yoruba who was opposed to the war, was arrested and jailed for the duration of the war for allegedly collaborating with the rebel Igbos. In this poem Madhubuti makes the connection between the commodification of Blacks in Africa and in the West and suggests how this commodification causes Blacks to fight each other.

The poems entitled "Black Sketches" and "blackwoman" capture the essence of Madhubuti's style, which separated him and his peers of the late 1960s from the mainstream tradition in white poetry. These concise sketches, because they are so short, highlight the use of slashes to emphasize rhythm, nonacademic or nonstandard English, and Black street language, including the dozens and *signifying, that characterize much of the poetry of the young Black writers of the 1960s. To date literary criticism has not yielded substantial analyses of Madhubuti, who has published seven collections of poetry in addition to *Don't Cry, Scream*.

• Paula Giddings, "From a Black Perspective: The Poetry of Don L. Lee," in *Amistad 2*, eds. John A. Williams and Charles Harris, 1971, pp. 299–318. Catherine Daniels Hurst, "Haki R. Madhubuti (Don L. Lee)," in *DLB*, vol. 41, *Afro-American Poets since 1955*, eds. Trudier Harris and Thadious M. Davis, 1985, pp. 222–232. 　　　　　　　　—Joyce A. Joyce

DOUBLE CONSCIOUSNESS. The concept of double consciousness, describing tensions and divisions in an African American identity, was first advanced by W. E. B. *Du Bois in his 1897 essay, "The Strivings of the Negro People," and, more influentially, in his 1903 book, The *Souls of Black Folk. Drawing on earlier uses of the term in American Romanticism and in medicine, where it referred to the problem of "split personality," Du Bois used "double consciousness" to describe central issues in the development of an African American self.

As Du Bois used the term, double consciousness referred to at least three different matters. One had to do with problems of self-definition resulting from living within a society pervaded by *stereotypes, negative images that all African Americans had to confront. A second involved the exclusion of African Americans from mainstream American institutions, creating a way of life that was both "American" and "not-American." The third focused on internal conflicts in the individual between what was distinctly "African," which Du Bois identified as an innate and powerful spirituality, and what was "American."

The idea of double consciousness, in all three senses, has had a continuing impact on African American literature, centering on the issue of *identity, while framing ways in which writers have explored the dynamics of inclusion and exclusion created by American racism and have sought to evoke a distinctive, meaningful African American world. It was to become particularly important when, redefined in terms of early twentieth-century concepts of "culture," it provided a foundation for such explorations of African American tradition as that formulated during the *Harlem Renaissance.

Since the late 1960s, with the reemergence of cultural models for race relations, double consciousness has provided the central paradigm for understanding not only African American but other minority literatures within a framework of cultural conflicts and differences.

• Werner Sollors, *Beyond Ethnicity: Consent and Descent in American Literature*, 1986. Arnold Rampersad, *The Art and Imagination of W. E. B. Du Bois*, 1990.

—Dickson D. Bruce, Jr.

DOUGLASS, FREDERICK (1818–1895), orator, journalist, editor, and autobiographer. Frederick Douglass, author of the most influential African American text of his era, rose through the ranks of the *antislavery movement in the 1840s and 1850s to become the most electrifying speaker and commanding writer produced by black America in the nineteenth century. From the outbreak of the Civil War until his death, Douglass was generally recognized as the premier African American leader and spokesman for his people. Douglass's writing was devoted primarily to the creation of a heroic image of himself that would inspire in African Americans the belief that color need not be a permanent bar to their achievement of the American dream, while reminding whites of their obligation as Americans to support free and equal access to that dream for Americans of all races.

The man who became internationally famous as Frederick Douglass was born on Maryland's Eastern Shore in February 1818, the son of Harriet Bailey, a slave, and an unknown white man. Although he recalls witnessing as a child the bloody whipping of his Aunt Hester by his master, Douglass says in his *autobiographies that his early experience of *slavery was characterized less by overt cruelty than by deprivations of food, clothing, and emotional contact with his mother and grandmother. Sent to Baltimore in 1826 by his master's son-in-law, Thomas Auld, Frederick spent five years as a servant in the home of Thomas Auld's brother, Hugh. At first, Hugh's wife Sophia treated the slave boy with unusual kindness, giving reading lessons to Frederick until her husband forbade them. Rather than accept Hugh Auld's dictates, Frederick took his first rebellious steps toward *freedom by teaching himself to read and write.

In 1833 a quarrel between the Auld brothers brought Frederick back to his home in Saint Michaels, Maryland. Tensions between the recalcitrant black youth and his owner convinced Thomas Auld to hire Frederick out as a farm worker under the supervision of Edward Covey, a local slave breaker. After six months of unstinting labor, merciless whippings, and repeated humiliations, the desperate sixteen-year-old slave fought back, resisting one of Covey's attempted beatings and intimidating his tormentor sufficiently to prevent future attacks. Douglass's dramatic account of his struggle with Covey would become the heroic turning point of his future autobiographies and one of the most celebrated scenes in all of antebellum African American literature.

In the spring of 1836, after a failed attempt to escape from slavery, Frederick was sent back to Baltimore to learn the caulking trade. With the aid of his future spouse, Anna Murray, and masquerading as a free black merchant sailor, he boarded a northbound train out of Baltimore on 3 September 1838 and arrived in New York City the next day. Before a month had passed Frederick and Anna were reunited, married, and living in New Bedford, Connecticut, as Mr. and Mrs. Frederick Douglass, the new last name recommended by a friend in New Bedford's thriving African American community. Less than three years later Douglass joined the radical Garrisonian wing of the abolitionist movement as a full-time lecturer.

After years of honing his rhetorical skills on the antislavery platform, Douglass put his life's story into print in 1845. The result, *Narrative of the Life of Frederick Douglass, an American Slave, Written by Himself, sold more than thirty thousand copies in the first five years of its existence. After a triumphal twenty-one-month lecture tour in England, Ireland, and Scotland, Douglass returned to the United States in the spring of 1847, resolved, against the advice of many of his Garrisonian associates, to launch his own newspaper, the *North Star. Authoring most of the articles and editorials himself, Douglass kept the *North Star* and its successors, *Frederick*

Douglass's Paper and *Frederick Douglass's Monthly,* in print from 1847 to 1863. One of the literary highlights of the newspaper was a novella, "The *Heroic Slave," which Douglass wrote in March 1853. Based on an actual slave mutiny, "The Heroic Slave" is regarded as the first work of long fiction in African American literature.

A rupture of the close relationship between Douglass and Garrison occasioned a period of reflection and reassessment that culminated in Douglass's second autobiography, *My Bondage and My Freedom* (1855). Although he had befriended and advised John *Brown in the late 1850s, Douglass declined Brown's invitation to participate in the Harpers Ferry raid but was forced to flee his Rochester, New York, home for Canada in October 1859 after he was publicly linked to Brown. Applauding the election of Abraham *Lincoln and welcoming the Civil War as a final means of ending slavery, Douglass lobbied the new president in favor of African American recruitment for the Union Army. When the war ended, Douglass pleaded with President Andrew Johnson for a national voting rights act that would give African Americans the franchise in all the states. Douglass's loyalty to the Republican Party, whose candidates he supported throughout his later years, won him appointment to the highest political offices that any African American from the North had ever won: federal marshal and recorder of deeds for the District of Columbia, president of the Freedman's Bureau Bank, consul to Haiti, and chargé d'affaires for the Dominican Republic.

The income Douglass earned from these positions, coupled with the fees he received for his popular lectures, most notably one entitled "Self-Made Men," and his investments in real estate, allowed Douglass and his family to live in comfort in Uniontown, just outside Washington, D.C., during the last two decades of his life. His final memoir, *Life and Times of Frederick Douglass,* first published in 1881 and expanded in 1892, did not excite the admiration of reviewers or sell widely, as had his first two autobiographies. But the *Life and Times* maintained Douglass's conviction that his had been a "life of victory, if not complete, at least assured." *Life and Times* shows Douglass dedicated to the ideal of building a racially integrated America in which skin color would cease to determine an individual's social value and economic options. In the last months of his life Douglass decried the increasing incidence of *lynching in the South and disputed the notion that by disenfranchising the African American man a more peaceful social climate would prevail throughout the nation. Yet Douglass never forsook his long-standing belief that the U.S. Constitution, if strictly and equally enforced, remained the best safeguard for African American civil and human rights.

In the history of African American literature, Douglass's importance and influence are virtually immeasurable. His *Narrative* and *My Bondage and My Freedom* gave the world the most compelling and sophisticated renditions of an African American selfhood seen in literature up to that time. Douglass's artistry invested this model of selfhood with a moral and political authority that subsequent aspirants to the role of African American culture hero—from the conservative Booker T. *Washington to the radical W. E. B. *Du Bois—would seek to appropriate for their own autobiographical self-portraits. In twentieth-century African American literature, from Paul Laurence *Dunbar's brooding poetic tribute "Douglass" (1903) to the idealistic characterization of Ned Douglass in Ernest J. *Gaines's novel, *The *Autobiography of Miss Jane Pittman* (1971), the criterion for an African American male heroism that uses words as a weapon in the struggle for self- and communal liberation remains the example set by Frederick Douglass.

[*See also* Oratory; Slave Narrative.]

• Benjamin Quarles, *Frederick Douglass,* 1948. Philip S. Foner, ed., *The Life and Writings of Frederick Douglass,* 1950–1975. John W. Blassingame, ed., *The Frederick Douglass Papers,* 1979– . Dickson J. Preston, *Young Frederick Douglass,* 1980. Waldo E. Martin, *The Mind of Frederick Douglass,* 1984. William L. Andrews, *To Tell a Free Story: The First Century of Afro-American Autobiography, 1760–1865,* 1986. William S. McFeely, *Frederick Douglass,* 1990. Eric Sundquist, ed., *Frederick Douglass: New Literary and Historical Essays,* 1990. William L. Andrews, ed., *Critical Essays on Frederick Douglass,* 1991.
—William L. Andrews

DOVE, RITA (b. 1952), poet, novelist, short story writer, dramatist, essayist, educator, and U.S. poet laureate. Highly prolific and greatly appreciated poet Rita Dove was born on 28 August 1952 in Akron, Ohio, the daughter of Elvira Dove and Ray Dove, a chemist. She attended Miami University in Ohio, graduating summa cum laude in 1973. A Fulbright scholarship sent her during 1974–1975 to the University of Tübingen in West Germany. She received an MFA in creative writing from the Iowa Writers Workshop at the University of Iowa in 1977. In Iowa she met her German husband, Fred Viebahn, a novelist with whom she has one child, a daughter named Aviva. That year she published the first of three chapbooks, *Ten Poems.* The following year she received the first of two literary awards from the National Endowment for the Arts (she received the second in 1989), and in 1980 at age twenty-seven she published both her second chapbook, *The Only Dark Spot in the Sky,* and her first book of poetry with a major press, *The Yellow House on the Corner* (1980).

Coming of age a decade after the peak of the *Black Arts movement, Dove writes poetry remarkably different from that of the previous generation, which was loose and improvisational in style, with urgent and inspired lyrics. Indeed, Dove has been called the most disciplined and technically accomplished poet since Gwendolyn *Brooks. Although her poems often focus on African American people, past and present, she finds many things of interest in them, not just their circumstances as racial subjects. She also extends her vision to include people of many backgrounds in order to investigate the complexities of perspective. In *The Yellow House on the Corner,* for example, she tells the story of how one enslaved woman thwarts the escape of a group of slaves when she helps the driver regain his horse. Rather than polarizing their positions, as the previous generation would have done, she illustrates their connection in the woman's recognition that she may be related to the driver. Her recognition and its result well represent one of the most profound horrors of *slavery.

In 1981 Dove joined the faculty at the Arizona State University, Tempe. In 1982 she spent a year as a writer in residence at the Tuskegee Institute, publishing her third and final chapbook, *Mandolin* (1982). Her next volume, *Museum* (1983), was (as every subsequent volume would be) published by a major publishing house. Two years later she tried her hand at short stories, publishing the collection *Fifth Sunday* (1985). During her tenure at Arizona State Dove participated in the national literary scene in innumerable ways: as a literary advisory panel member of the National Endowment for the Arts (1984–1986); as the chair of the poetry grants panel for the National Endowment for the Arts in 1985; and on the board of directors of the Associate Writing Programs (1985–1988), including serving as their president in 1986–1987. In 1987 she also began her long association as associate editor and commissioner, respectively, of two central institutions of African American culture, *Callaloo, a journal of criticism and the arts known for publishing contemporary poetry, and the Schomberg Center for Research in Black Culture. Her literary efforts were recognized with many honors, including a fellowship from the Guggenheim Foundation (1983–1984) and the Lavan Younger Poets Award from the Academy of American Poets (1986). Her work during this period culminated in *Thomas and Beulah* (1986), for which she won the 1987 Pulitzer Prize for poetry.

Loosely based on the lives of Dove's maternal grandparents, *Thomas and Beulah* is divided into two sequences, the first about Thomas and the second about Beulah. Although its subjects live together for decades, the poem sequences reveal lives that barely intersect, with the two more often moving in their own directions. More personal than Dove's previous work, this volume illustrates her ability to bring vitality and insight to the ordinary and everyday.

In 1988 Dove had a Bellagio residency sponsored by the Rockefeller Foundation, but she spent most of the year as a Mellon fellow at the National Humanities Center in North Carolina. That year and the year following she received honorary doctorates from Miami University and Knox College respectively. In 1989 she published another volume of poems, *Grace Notes,* and accepted a faculty position at the University of Virginia, where she spent the next three years at the Center for Advanced Studies. In 1993 the University of Virginia promoted her to an endowed chair as the Commonwealth Professor of English. While writing she also remained active in national poetry competitions. In 1991 alone, she served as a judge for the Walt Whitman Award of the Academy of American Poets; the Pulitzer Prize in poetry; the National Book Award poetry panel; and the Literary Lion of the New York Public Library. That same year she also was inducted into the Ohio Women's Hall of Fame. Not content to stick to poetry, Dove extended her writing talents, publishing her first novel, *Through*

the *Ivory Tower* (1992), and her first play, *The Darker Face of the Earth* (1994).

Through the Ivory Tower traces the life of a talented young African American woman, Virginia King, who becomes an artist in residence at a primary school in the town where she grew up—Akron, Ohio. Alternating between present moments and flashbacks, the story links Virginia's current life to powerful, sometimes painful recollections of her girlhood. The novel presents a series of shorter stories that through accretion build a sense of the richness of this woman's life and her connections not only to the friends and family around her, but to place, culture, and region.

1993 was a particularly big year for Rita Dove. Her list of accomplishments and awards extended even further, again illustrating her appeal to both African Americans and all Americans more generally. She published another volume of poetry, *Selected Poems,* received the Great American Artist Award from the NAACP, and became the youngest and first African American poet laureate. Dove read at the White House and spoke at the two-hundredth-anniversary celebration of the U.S. Capitol. Accolades in 1994 include the Renaissance Forum Award for Leadership in the Literary Arts from the Folger Shakespeare Library; the Golden Plate Award from the American Academy of Achievement; the Carl Sandburg Award from the International Platform Association; and additional honorary doctorates from Tuskegee; University of Miami; Washington University; Case Western University; University of Akron; and in 1995 from Arizona State University; Boston College; and Dartmouth College. Her most recent publications include another volume of poems, *Mother's Love* (1995), and her first collection of essays, *The Poet's World* (1995).

• Robert McDowell, "The Assembling Vision of Rita Dove," *Callaloo* 9.1 (Winter 1986): 61–70. Arnold Rampersad, "The Poems of Rita Dove," *Callaloo* 9.1 (Winter 1986): 52–60. Ekaterini Georgoudaki, "Rita Dove: Crossing Boundaries," *Callaloo* 14.2 (Spring 1991): 419–433. Susan M. Trosky, ed., *CA,* New Revision Series, vol. 42, 1994, pp. 127–128. Helen Vendler, "Rita Dove: Identity Markers," *Callaloo* 17.2 (Summer 1994): 381–398. Shirelle Phelps, ed., *Who's Who among African-Americans,* 1996, p. 420.   —Maggie Sale

DOWNING, HENRY F. (1846–1928), sailor, novelist, playwright, and historian. Born in New York City into a family of successful free African Americans who ran an oyster business, Henry Downing was the nephew of the esteemed politician George Thomas Downing. Henry Downing served two terms in the U.S. Navy (1864–1865 and 1872–1875). Following the Civil War, he traveled around the world, a journey punctuated by a three-year residence in Liberia, where his cousin Hilary Johnson later served as president (1884–1892). After returning to New York, he became politically active in the Democratic Party. For his strong support, President Cleveland appointed Downing consul to Loanda, Angola, a West African colony of Portugal, where he served less than a year before resigning in 1888. After returning to New York for several years, he emigrated to London in 1895, where he remained for twenty-two years. There he began a productive, if undistinguished, career as a writer. With at least six unpublished plays already written, he had five plays published (and likely performed) in 1913 alone. Melodramatic fare expressing minimal interest in race issues, these include *The Arabian Lioness, or The Sacred Jar*; *Human Nature, or The Traduced Wife*; *Lord Eldred's Other Daughter*; *The Shuttlecock, or Israel in Russia*; and *Placing Paul's Play*, coauthored with his second wife, Margarita Doyle. The reception of these plays remains unknown. Shortly before leaving London for New York, he published a *novel, *The American Cavalryman: A Liberian Romance* (1917), whose plot follows a relationship founded on mistaken racial *identity in order to glorify the possibilities of American blacks settling in Liberia. His final *drama, *The Racial Tangle* (1920), which also centered on race-based romantic intrigue, was made into the silent *film *Thirty Years Later* (1928) by Oscar *Micheaux. Downing's last works were *Liberia and Her People* (1925) and *A Short History of Liberia* (n.d.), both of which were philosophically compatible with Marcus *Garvey's back to Africa movement.

• Clarence G. Contee, Sr., "Downing, Henry F[rancis]," in *DANB*, eds. Rayford W. Logan and Michael R. Winston, 1982, pp. 188–189. Bernard Bell, *The Afro-American Novel and Its Tradition*, 1987, p. 78. Bernard L. Peterson, Jr., "Downing, Henry F. (Francis)," in *Early Black American Playwrights and Dramatic Writers: A Biographic Directory and Catalog of Plays, Films, and Broadcasting Scripts*, 1990, pp. 62–63. —Lawrence R. Rodgers

DRAMA. The development of the African American dramatist has been painfully slow. Almost a century elapsed between the emergence of the earliest playwrights before the Civil War and the beginning of their growth as serious artists. As in many other aspects of American culture, the twin factors of *slavery and lack of opportunity hindered the full participation of African Americans in the *theater, and effectively delayed the development of a significant body of African American drama.

The First Dramatist—A Native of the West Indies. The first recorded dramatist of African descent in America was a Mr. Brown (whose first name, unknown, has been conjectured to be either William or James). He was a retired ship's steward, born in the West Indies, whose play, *The Drama of King Shotaway*, was presented in 1823 by the African Company, a thriving theatrical group founded by Brown in 1816, at the African Grove Theatre located in the lower Manhattan district of New York City. The play concerned the *insurrection of the Black Caribs (or Black Caribbean Indians) on the island of Saint Vincent in the West Indies in the 1790s, which had been actually witnessed by Mr. Brown. The Black Caribs were descendants of African slaves who had escaped from other islands and settled on Saint Vincent's, where they had intermarried with the Yellow Caribs (the original Caribbean Indians), and taken on the customs, manners, and names of the early French settlers who had preceded the British. When the English came into possession of the island, they tried to oust the Caribs in order that English settlers could establish profitable sugar plantations on the island.

But the Caribs, led by their paramount chief, Joseph Chatoyer (anglicized as "Shotaway" in Brown's play) fiercely resisted the British troops for twenty years by guerrilla warfare, until their leader, thought to be invincible, was killed, and the Caribs were forced to flee to other islands. Soon after Brown's play was presented in the summer of 1823, the African Grove Theatre was closed by police, ostensibly for disturbance of the peace and violation of several city ordinances.

The First Indigenous African American Dramatist. The first truly native dramatist was William Wells *Brown, who was also the first African American novelist and one of the earliest historians. Brown, who was born a slave, escaped from bondage and fled to the North, where he educated himself and became an ardent antislavery crusader, lecturer, and writer. Among his writings were two plays: *Experience, or How to Give a Northern Man a Backbone* (1856), about a northern white preacher who had originally condoned slavery, but who learns to condemn it after he himself is sold into slavery; and *The *Escape, or A Leap for Freedom* (1857), about the thrilling escape from slavery of a newly married couple whose master planned to separate them in order to possess the beautiful young wife. Although Brown's plays were never produced, he thrilled his audiences when he read them aloud at antislavery meetings and lyceums.

Other Nineteenth-Century Writers. Since the minstrel show dominated the stage from the 1840s to the 1890s, it should be noted that within this genre African Americans were able to make many orginal dramatic contributions in the form of skits and sketches that incorporated relevant aspects of their culture within these shows. (Unfortunately these have not been preserved.) Similarly, many young talented writers, from the 1890s to the 1920s, who realized that they could not earn a living writing serious dramas, turned their talents to the development of musical shows that greatly departed from the minstrel tradition. Beginning around 1880, some efforts at serious drama can be discerned, although these were somewhat isolated and sporadic.

Pauline E. *Hopkins contributed a historical *musical, *Peculiar Sam, or The Underground Railroad* (1879), first produced in Boston in 1880 by the Hopkins Colored Troubadours. John Patterson Sampson, an African Methodist Episcopal (AME) churchman, lecturer, and author, wrote *The Disappointed Bridge, or Love at First Sight* (published 1883). William Edgar Easton, a Massachusetts-born playwright who could trace his family history back to the Revolutionary War, wrote the first of his two plays on Haitian history, *Dessalines* (1893), about the revolutionary general who helped to achieve Haiti's independence and who became the country's first king; it was produced at the Haitian pavilion of the Chicago World's Fair. His second play, *Christophe* (1911), dealt with the overthrow of Dessalines.

Paul Laurence *Dunbar, the first major African American poet, also wrote serious dramas, including two plays written for his friend, the noted actor and dramatic reader Richard B. Harrison: *Robert Herrick*

(c. 1899), a three-act comedy of manners about the English poet, and *Winter Roses* (1899), a one-act play about a loney widower, grown old, who reunites with his first love of many years before. Dunbar also wrote vaudeville sketches and contributed librettos and lyrics to several musical stage works.

Early Twentieth-Century Efforts. A few amateur playwrights and pageant writers emerged during the first two decades of the twentieth century. Most of these wrote propaganda or black history plays. Joseph Seamon *Cotter, Sr., a poet, author, and educator, published his first play, *Caleb, the Degenerate* (1903), which dramatized the industrial education and work philosophy of Booker T. *Washington. W. E. B. *Du Bois, the eminent sociologist and editor, wrote and produced *The Star of Ethiopia* (1913), a successful effort at pageantry, which dramatized the gifts that Africa had given to the world.

The plays of several African American women playwrights were also produced or published around World War I. Katherine Davis Chapman *Tillman published *Fifty Years of Freedom, or From Cabin to Congress* (1910), in celebration of the fiftieth anniversary of the Emancipation Proclamation. The NAACP Drama Committee sponsored the groundbreaking production of *Rachel* (1917), one of the earliest plays utilizing propaganda to protest racial violence and prejudice, written by Angelina Weld *Grimké. Alice Moore *Dunbar-Nelson, the widow of Paul Laurence Dunbar, published *Mine Eyes Have Seen* (1918), a patriotic play extolling the loyalty of African Americans during the war. Mary Burrill, a Washington, D.C., schoolteacher, published two plays in periodicals: *Aftermath* (1919), the tragedy of a returning African American soldier, and *They That Sit in Darkness* (also 1919), a birth control propaganda play.

Willis *Richardson and Randolph Edmonds were among the most prolific dramatists of the decade. Richardson, a civil service clerk, wrote more than forty plays (mainly one-acts), including *The Chip Woman's Fortune* (1923), the first serious play by an African American writer to be produced on Broadway. It concerned the attempt by a young man, heavily in debt, to rob an old woman of her life's savings. Richardson was also a pioneer anthologist, whose two collections, *Plays and Pageants from the Life of the Negro (1930)* and *Negro History in Thirteen Plays* (1935), made accessible many plays by playwrights of the 1920s and 1930s, including his own. Among his best-known plays were *Mortgaged* (1924), *Compromise* (1925), and *The Broken Banjo* (1925). Randolph Edmonds, an academic playwright, wrote at least fifty plays (mostly one-acts), beginning in the 1920s, many of which were published in his three collections: *Shades and Shadows* (1930), *Six Plays for a Negro Theatre* (1934), and *The Land of Cotton and Other Plays* (1942). He is best known for his later plays, *Bad Man* (1932), *Breeders* (1934), *Nat Turner* (1934), and *Earth and Stars* (1946). Edmonds, who headed drama departments at three colleges, also established important intercollegiate drama associations in the South and Southeast to encourage the writing and production of plays for the academic theater.

Several other playwrights had Broadway productions during the 1920s. Garland Anderson, a former California bellhop and moralistic philosopher, was the first to have a full-length play produced there. His *Appearances* (1925) was a courtroom melodrama in which a morally upright bellhop is tried and exonerated of the charge of raping a white woman. Frank Wilson, a stage and film actor, was represented on Broadway by *Meek Mose* (1928), about the loss of confidence in a community leader when he gives in to white demands to sell a valuable tract of land occupied and owned by members of the African American community, forcing them to move to a new site. He is vindicated when oil is discovered on the new property. Wallace *Thurman, a novelist and editor, saw his play *Harlem* (1929), coauthored with white writer William J. Rapp, produced on Broadway. It was a serious play that showed both the exotic and the sordid sides of Harlem life, including prostitution, drugs, rackets, and murder.

Several playwrights were winners of literary awards sponsored by the *Crisis and *Opportunity magazines, official organs of the NAACP and the National Urban League, respectively. Georgia Douglas *Johnson, Eulalie Spence, and John F. *Matheus won these and other prizes. Johnson, a poet, playwright, and leading member of the Washington, D.C., literati, is best known for two one-act plays: *Blue Blood* (1926), about the discovery by a newly married couple that they are children of the same white father, and *Plumes* (1927), in which a poor mother chooses to use her meager savings to provide a grand funeral for her daughter rather than to spend it on an operation that may save her life. Eulalie Spence, a Brooklyn, New York, high school teacher, wrote several prizewinning plays of domestic life, including *Undertow* (1927), about a triangular relationship between a husband, wife, and another woman, and *The Fool's Errand* (1927), about an unmarried woman mistakenly presumed to be pregnant by a group of church busybodies, which won the Samuel French Prize of two hundred dollars in the National Little Theatre Tournament of 1927. Most of her plays were produced by the Krigwa Players (Crisis Guild of Writers and Artists), sponsored by W. E. B. Du Bois and the *Crisis* magazine. Dr. John Frederick Matheus, a West Virginia State College language professor and playwright, is best known for his *'Cruitor* (1926), in which a couple of young southern tenant farmworkers are lured to an uncertain life in the North to work in a wartime munitions factory. Matheus also wrote *Ti-Yette* (1930), a tragedy of *mulatto life, in which a brother kills his own sister to prevent her from marrying a white man, and *Ouanga* (1941), a play about the Haitian emperor Dessalines, which was turned into an *opera, with *music composed by Clarence Cameron White.

Depression Years and WPA Federal Theatre. Despite the curtailment of theatrical activities in the professional theater during the Great Depression, more African American playwrights emerged during the 1930s than in any previous decade, largely through the activities of the WPA Federal Theatre Project (FTP).

Even before the FTP was put into place, however, four playwrights had their plays produced on Broadway between 1930 and 1936. *Louisiana* (1933) by J. Augustus Smith dealt with the conflict between Christianity and voodoo worship, a theme also treated in *Run, Little Chillun!* (1933), a musical drama by choir director Hall Johnson. *Legal Murder* (1934) by Dennis Donoghue was a dramatization of the infamous *Scottsboro boys case, in which nine African American youths, accused of raping two white girls, were tried, convicted, and sentenced to death. Langston *Hughes, the most important dramatist to emerge during the 1930s, reached Broadway with his play *Mulatto* (1935), on the subject of miscegenation. Other plays by Hughes produced during this decade include *Little Ham* (1935), *The Emperor of Haiti* (1935), and *Don't You Want to Be Free?* (1937), which traced the history of African Americans from slavery to the play's own time and had a record run of 135 performances in Harlem.

Undoubtedly the FTP was the greatest stimulus to the development of African American drama during the 1930s. Minority units were established in some two dozen cities throughout the country, many of which had resident playwrights. The most productive of these were in New York, Chicago, Seattle, and Newark.

The New York Negro Unit produced several plays by African Americans, including Frank Wilson's *Walk Together Children* (1936), a social drama of the conflict between two black labor groups—one brought from the South by whites, and the other an unemployed upstate New York group; *Conjur Man Dies* (1936), a mystery-melodrama dealing with occultism and superstition among Harlemites, adapted by Countee *Cullen and Arna *Bontemps from the novel by Rudolph *Fisher; and two plays by J. Augustus Smith: *Turpentine* (1936), a social drama exposing deplorable conditions in southern labor camps, and *Just Ten Days* (1937), depicting the drastic efforts of an impoverished family to avoid being evicted.

The Chicago Negro Unit, headed by playwright Shirley *Graham (Du Bois), produced *Big White Fog* (1938) by Theodore *Ward, portraying the frustrations, disillusionment, and eventual destruction of a Chicago family who had migrated from the South to escape poverty, prejudice, and injustice.

The Seattle Negro Unit's resident playwright was Theodore Browne, whose four plays produced by this unit were an African American version of *Lysistrata* (1936), adapted from the comedy of Aristophanes, and three original plays (all 1937): *Go Down Moses*, about Harriet *Tubman; *Natural Man*, a dramatization of the *John Henry myth; and *Swing, Gates, Swing*, a musical revue.

One of the most popular plays of the FTP was the New Jersey Unit's production of *The Trial of Dr. Beck*, a courtroom melodrama by Hughes Allison about color prejudices within the African American middle class. It ran on Broadway for four weeks.

Several new academic playwrights of the 1930s had received special training in playwriting at schools of drama where their first plays were written and produced. Arthur Clifton Lamb (later on the faculty of Morgan College, Baltimore) was awarded the Henry Steiner Memorial Prize in Playwriting while an undergraduate student at Grinnell College for his *Shades of Cottonlips* (1931), an expressionistic drama about the playwright's attempt to escape from the traditional minstrel *stereotypes by which he is haunted; and the Sergel Prize in Regional Playwriting, while pursuing MA studies at the State University of Iowa, for his *God's Great Acres* (1939), a labor drama dealing with the effects of farm machinery on sharecroppers. He later had his *Roughshod up the Mountain* (1953) produced at the State University of Iowa as part of his PhD studies in playwriting.

Thomas D. Pawley (for many years head of the Department of Speech and Theatre at Lincoln University, Missouri) had two plays produced as a part of his MA thesis at the University of Iowa: *Jedgement Day* (1938), a folk comedy about an errant husband who dreams of his horrendous punishment in the deepest pit of hell, and *Smokey*, a melodrama about the murder of a white plantation owner by a mild-mannered farmhand. He later had his *Crispus Attucks* (1947) produced at Iowa as a part of his PhD studies.

Owen *Dodson (for many years on the faculty of Howard University) wrote and had his best-known plays produced at Yale University while an MFA student at the School of Drama. His *Divine Comedy* (1938) dealt with the influence of the religious cult leader *Father Divine*; and his *Garden of Time* (1938) transformed the Jason-Medea story into a tragedy of interracial love relevant to the racial situation in America.

Shirley Graham (Du Bois), later director of the Chicago Negro Unit of the FTP, also had several of her plays first produced while a student at Yale University, including *Dust to Earth* (1938), a labor tragedy of the West Viriginia coal mines; *It's Morning* (1940), about a mother who kills her daughter to prevent her from being sold into slavery; and *Track Thirteen* (1940), about the superstitions of railroad porters.

Broadway and Harlem Playwrights during World War II. Although playwriting activities were substantially curbed during the 1940s and many scheduled productions were cancelled after Pearl Harbor, a few playwrights emerged during this difficult decade.

Richard *Wright's stage version of his landmark novel *Native Son (adapted with white playwright Paul Green) was produced on Broadway by Orson Welles and John Houseman in 1941. Langston Hughes had a number of his pieces in support of the war effort produced, as well as some of his more important works, including *Troubled Island* (an opera, 1949). Arna Bontemps and Countee Cullen collaborated on the musical *St. Louis Woman* (1946), adapted from Bontemps's novel, about the triangular romantic involvement of a horse jockey with a saloon keeper and a woman of easy virtue in St. Louis during the 1890s.

Abram Hill, founder and resident playwright of the American Negro Theatre (ANT), a thriving Harlem group, had several of his plays produced by ANT during the 1940s. His most popular play was *On

Striver's Row (1940), a comedy of social striving among middle-class residents of a prestigious section of upper Harlem. *Anna Lucasta*, adapted by Hill and "doctored" by white director Harry Wagstaff Gribble from the play by Philip Yordan, was first produced by ANT, then transferred to Broadway where it ran for 957 performances, becoming the longest-running play with an African American cast up to that time, bringing many of its stars into the professional theater, *film, and *television.

Theodore Ward's *Big White Fog* was revived in New York by the Negro Playwrights Company, a short-lived group that he helped to organize; and his *Our Lan'*, one of the critically acclaimed plays of the 1940s, was produced on Broadway by the Theatre Guild in 1947 and received the prestigious Theatre Guild Award. It concerned the brutal killing by federal troops of a group of freed slaves, who refused to vacate some land off the coast of Georgia where they had settled after emancipation.

Emergence of the Professional Dramatist. The post–World War II decade was a period of growth and progress, during which the African American dramatist came of age professionally. The plays of this period were more mature in technique, theme, and character than any that had been hitherto produced and presented more realistic portrayals of the interracial relationships within the larger community. The problems of integration and desegregation, domestic problems, and the concerns of African Americans both of the past and present were explored.

Langston Hughes, always in the forefront, opened the decade with the Broadway production of his opera *The Barrier* (1950), based on his earlier play *Mulatto*, depicting the tragic conflict between a white plantation owner and his son by his black housekeeper, which results in the deaths of both father and son. Louis Peterson, a professional actor, came to Broadway with his first play, *Take a Giant Step* (a Burns Mantle "Best Play" of 1953), dealing with the identity crisis of an alienated youth who had grown up in a white neighborhood and must now find relationships within the African American community. *Mrs. Patterson* (1954), cowritten by Charles Sebree and white playwright Greer Johnson, starred Eartha Kitt as a poor, adolescent southern black girl who dreams of becoming a rich white lady like Mrs. Patterson.

Other important plays by African Americans were showcased at the experimental Greenwich Mews Theatre, Off-Off Broadway, including William Blackwell *Branch's *In Splendid Error* (1954), Alice *Childress's Obie Award–winning *Trouble in Mind* (1955), and Loften *Mitchell's *A Land beyond the River* (1957).

Three portraits of African American urban life in New York's Harlem and Chicago's South Side were given premiere productions and explored problems of the church, the community, and the family. *The *Amen Corner* (1955) by James *Baldwin dramatized the crisis of a woman preacher of a Harlem storefront church, whose congregation and church elders begin to question her spiritual leadership. Langston

Hughes again reached Broadway with the intimate portrait of a colorful Harlem character named Jesse B. Semple (*Simple), in his musical comedy *Simply Heavenly* (1957).

The most successful play of the decade, and the first by an African American woman playwright on Broadway, was *A *Raisin in the Sun* (1959) by Lorraine *Hansberry. It presented the most realistic exploration of African American domestic life up to its time and revolved around the clash of dreams among members of a South Side Chicago family when they receive a large insurance settlement after the death of the father. The play provided theatergoers with new insights into the concerns of African Americans and dealt with such themes as the structure of the *family; *identity, power and pride, and the significance of the African heritage; the frustration or castration of the African American male; and the problems of integration versus separation. In addition, it was the first serious Broadway play to be directed by an African American, Lloyd Richards, and the first to receive the New York Drama Critics Award. It had a long run of 530 performances on Broadway.

Several new plays also received productions in Harlem, under the auspices of the Harlem Council on the Theatre and the Committee for the Negro in the Arts. Among these were Alice Childress's *Florence* (1950); William Branch's *A Medal for Willie* (1951); Gertrude Jeannette's *A Bolt from the Blue* (1950) and *This Way Forward* (1951); Ossie *Davis's *Alice in Wonder* (1952); and Julian *Mayfield's *The Other Foot* (1950) and *A World Full of Men* (1952).

Just before Black Theater—Non-polemic Playwrights of the 1960s. During the early to mid-1960s, many of the trends of the 1950s were still in effect. The problems of interracial relations continued to be explored, and civil rights was a dominant theme, although these subjects were treated in a congenial, symbolic, and nonthreatening way.

Ossie Davis's amicable satire of traditional white-created stereotypes, *Purlie Victorious* (1961), used laughter as a weapon against racial prejudice. Langston Hughes offered several joyful song-plays, a genre that he apparently originated and perfected. His Christmas song-play *Black Nativity* (1961) was widely performed and presented even at the Vatican; and his *Jerico-Jim Crow* (1963), tracing the history of segregation in gospel form, was produced Off-Broadway with the backing of three civil rights organizations. His *Tambourines to Glory* (1963) and *Prodigal Son* (1965) were also successfully produced.

C. Bernard Jackson and white playwright James V. Hatch presented their Off-Broadway satire of the "sit-in" movement, *Fly Blackbird* (1962), which won the Obie Award. In this musical, students debated such issues as violence versus nonviolence as effective ways of securing civil rights. Loften Mitchell and Irving Burgie dealt with important questions of racism, nationalism, and colonialism in their island musical of Barbados, *Ballad for Bimshire* (1963), which was backed Off-Broadway mainly by black investors.

Adrienne *Kennedy, an avant-garde playwright influenced by Edward Albee, achieved artistic success with her surrealistic portrayal of the psychological problems of a young girl of racially mixed parentage as she tries to cope with her identity in *Funnyhouse of a Negro* (1963), which won both a Stanley Award and an Obie Award. Vinnette Carroll, with the help of Micki Grant and members of the Urban Arts Corps, also treated the subject of coping with identity in their rousing musical, *Don't Bother Me, I Can't Cope* (1970), which effectively used the rhythms of gospel, soul, and other African American music, and played for 1,065 performances on Broadway, earning numerous awards. Earlier in the decade, Carroll had produced several other gospel musicals under the influence of Langston Hughes, whose *Black Nativity* she had directed.

Douglas Turner *Ward, later artistic director of the Negro Ensemble Company, won both a Drama Desk Award and an Obie Award for his two satirical one-act comedies, *Day of Absence* (1965), a reverse minstrel show in whiteface, in which residents of a small southern town discover that all the blacks have disappeared bringing about economic chaos by their absence, and *Happy Ending* (1965), in which two domestics, who have been enjoying a comfortable living sponging off their unsuspecting white employers, now face the possibility that their purloined "perks" may be cut off because their bosses are threatening to get a divorce. They were produced Off-Broadway on a double bill for 504 performances, establishing a record for a bill of one-act plays.

Lonne *Elder III, later an important screenwriter, had his most successful stage play, *Ceremonies in Dark Old Men* (1965), produced Off-Broadway, for 320 performances, after its initial showcase by the Negro Ensemble Company. Set in a barbershop owned by an old-time vaudevillian who operates a whiskey still in the back, it concerned the disintegration of an African American family after the death of the mother, caused by the inability of the father and his sons to face up to responsibility. It won both the Drama Desk and the Outer Critics Circle awards and was nominated for a Pulitzer Prize.

Alice Childress's *Wedding Band* (1956), about an interracial relationship between an African American woman and a white man in South Carolina, was given its first professional production at the University of Michigan, with Ruby Dee as the woman. It was later produced Off-Broadway by the New York Shakespeare Festival in 1972, where it had a successful run.

Lorraine Hansberry's *The Sign in Sidney Brustein's Window* (1964), the story of a white, Jewish, Greenwich Village intellectual, his wife, and their circle of bohemian friends, was produced Off-Broadway for 101 performances, closing on the day of Hansberry's untimely death from cancer at age thirty-four. Her subsequent plays, *To Be Young, Gifted, and Black* (1971) and the musical *Raisin* (1972), were adapted from her writings and plays by her husband and literary executor, Robert Nemiroff, who produced them posthumously, with great success, effectively keeping Hansberry's literary legacy alive.

Pioneers of the Black Theater Movement. Beginning in 1964, and continuing to the mid-1970s, a Black Theater movement, growing out of the civil rights struggle, began to flower, creating great excitement in African American drama and theater, as a new wave of black critics began to articulate the need for more positive images in plays by black playwrights and to advocate the use of drama as a weapon in the Black Power struggle. The plays that emerged under this movement were more openly militant, controversial, and shocking than ever before, and often advocated *violence, confrontation, and revolution as a means of solving racial problems.

The spokesman and high priest of the movement was Amiri *Baraka, a talented and aggressive essayist, poet, and playwright, who began his career as LeRoi Jones. He founded and directed the short-lived Black Arts Repertory Theatre and School in Harlem during the mid-1960s, and later founded and directed Spirit House, a Newark, New Jersey, community arts center and home of the Spirit House Movers, a repertory group that he also directed. His plays, mainly one-acts, which helped to define the direction of the movement, consistently used violence, allegory, and myth to symbolize race relations in the United States. His most important plays include *Dutchman* (winner of an Obie Award, 1964), about the seduction and murder of a young African American man by a sexy white blond aboard a subway train; *The Slave* (1964), in which a "black militant" tries to exorcise all that is white in his past by murdering his white wife and their children; and *The Toilet* (1964), a shocking metaphor of race relations, in which a white homosexual is brutally beaten by a gang of black youths in a school restroom because he sent a love letter to their leader.

Second only to Baraka in influence was Ed *Bullins, who had been one of the leaders of the *Black Arts movement on the West Coast during the 1950s and was founder of Black Arts/West, an experimental theater group in San Francisco patterned after Baraka's Black Arts Repertory Theatre. Bullins became resident playwright of the New Lafayette Theatre in 1957, and afterward of the American Place Theater, where many of his later plays were produced. His dramatic technique, later refined, was at first characterized less by violence than by a "street theater" or "agitprop" style of realism that was very influential. His first three one-act plays, produced Off-Broadway on a triple bill, were: *Clara's Ole Man* (1965), a study of the shocking realities of black ghetto life, in which Clara's "ole man" turns out to be a very "butch" *lesbian; *The Electronic Nigger* (1968), a biting satire of the type of so-called establishment Negro, whose thinking is programmed by whites; and *A Son, Come Home* (1968), about the deteriorating relationship between a son and his mother after a long separation. Bullins published several volumes of one-act plays and short skits before abandoning this form in favor of full-length plays of black life, many included in his projected Twentieth-Century Cycle. His most critically acclaimed full-length plays include *The Fabulous Miss Marie* (1971), winner of an Obie Award, and *The Taking of Miss Janie* (1975), winner of a Drama Critics Circle Award.

Largely under the influence of Baraka and Bullins, a growing number of transient black theater groups sprang up in almost every major city, spawning some of the most talented of the younger playwrights of the new movement. Ben *Caldwell (a product of Baraka's Spirit House) wrote such revolutionary skits as *The Job* (1966), calling for revolt against government unemployment-opportunity projects used as devices to control blacks, and *Prayer Meeting, or The First Militant Minister* (1967), in which an "Uncle Tom" preacher is converted to a "black militant" by a thief pretending to be the voice of God. Ron *Milner (from the Concept East Theatre in Detroit) wrote *The Monster* (1968), depicting a confrontation between some black students and the dean of the college, depicted as a "professional Negro," and *Who's Got His Own* (1965), which explored the problems of black manhood within a racist society. Jimmy Garrett (from Black Arts/West in San Francisco) wrote one of the most violent of the new agitprop dramas of the movement, *And We Own the Night* (1967), in which a black militant, dying of wounds received in a race war, kills his own mother, whom he considers an enemy of the revolution.

A number of more durable theatrical organizations also emerged from the Black Theater movement, from which new playwrights were developed or had their works showcased by these organizations. The most prominent of these were in New York, and the majority in Harlem.

The New York groups included the Negro Ensemble Company, which had Douglas Turner Ward as its artistic director and resident playwright; the New Lafayette Theatre, headed by Robert Macbeth, with Ed Bullins as resident playwright; the New Heritage Theatre, founded by Roger Furman, artistic director and resident playwright; the Afro-American Total Theatre, founded and directed by Hazel Bryant, also resident playwright; the National Black Theatre, founded and directed by Barbara Ann Teer, who developed and taught a black art standard that became the group's trademark; the Urban Arts Corps, directed by Vinnette Carroll, with Micki Grant as resident playwright; the Frank Silvera Writers Workshop, headed by playwright Garland Lee Thompson; and the organizations of the Black Theatre Alliance, headed by Hazel Bryant, Roger Furman, Delano Stewart (of the Bed Stuy Theatre), and Ernie McClintock (of the Afro-American Studio for Acting and Speech).

Outside of New York were such groups as the Free Southern Theatre, based first in Mississippi, then in New Orleans, headed by Gilbert Moses, John O'Neal, and Tom *Dent, all resident playwrights; the D.C. Black Repertory Theatre in Washington, D.C., founded by actor Robert Hooks; the Performing Arts Society in Los Angeles, directed by playwright Vantile Whitfield (Motojicho); and the Inner City Cultural Center in Los Angeles, with C. Bernard Jackson as artistic director and resident playwright.

Prizewinning Playwrights of the Late 1900s. Beginning in the 1950s, and increasingly with each successive decade, African American playwrights were recipients of many of the most prestigious playwriting awards with which the American theater honors its best and brightest talents. Several of these recipients have already been named, including Lorraine Hansberry, Alice Childress, Amiri Baraka, and Ed Bullins. Additional prizewinners of the 1970s, 1980s, and 1990s include the following:

Charles *Gordone was the first African American winner of the Pulitzer Prize for drama for *No Place to Be Somebody* (1970), the study of a black hustler, poet, and bar owner who desperately struggles to find his own "place" and his own identity. J. E. Gaines received a Drama Desk Award for *Don't Let It Go to Your Head* (1970), about an American prisoner of war who returns home to find that his wife has been unfaithful, and an Obie Award for *What If It Had Turned up Heads* (1971), the portrait of a group of drunks who frequent the establishment of a basement wine seller. Philip Hayes Dean received a Drama Desk Award and a Dramatists Guild Award for *The Sty of the Blind Pig* (1971), in which a blind street singer exercises a disturbing influence on an aging unmarried woman who is dominated by her mother. J. E. *Franklin received a Drama Desk Award for *Black Girl* (1971), about a troubled teenager who struggles to break away from her family in order to become a dancer. Melvin Van Peebles won a Drama Desk Award, two Tony nominations, and a Grammy Award (best score) for *Ain't Supposed to Die a Natural Death* (1971), his sensational portrait of impoverished black street life. Richard Wesley won a Drama Desk Award for his political drama *The Black Terror* (1971), in which the chief executioner of a Black Panther–style organization begins to doubt the justification of his killing other blacks. Paul Carter Harrison won an Obie Award for *The Great McDaddy* (1974), about the odyssey of the son of a wealthy, deceased West Indian bootlegger in search of the secret formula (now lost) of a palm wine that was the basis of his father's successful business. Leslie Lee won an Obie Award and a John Gassner Medallion for *The First Breeze of Summer* (1975), reflecting on three generations of a middle-class African American family and the sacrifices and heartaches that the grandmother had to make to bring them thus far. Steve Carter won the Outer Critics Circle Award for his *Eden* (1976), a Romeo-and-Juliet type love story of a West Indian girl and southern African American youth whose families are in open conflict. Joseph A. *Walker received a Drama Desk Award, a Tony, and an Obie Award for *The *River Niger* (1976), exploring the relationships among three generations of a Harlem family and focusing on the frustrations of the father, whose problems spring from his inability to be a real man in American society. Ntozake *Shange won the Outer Critics Circle Award and an Obie Award for her choreopoem *for colored girls who have considered suicide/when the rainbow is enuf* (1976), exploring the many facets of an African American woman's psyche. Loften Mitchell received a Best Broadway Musical Tony nomination for his *Bubbling Brown Sugar* (1976), a musical history of African American entertainment, which was also named London's Best Musical of the Year. Samm-Art *Williams received a Tony nomination for *Home

(1979), about a prodigal son from North Carolina who tries to seek his fortune in the North, where he becomes involved in drugs and prostitution and is finally forced to return home and rebuild his life. Charles H. *Fuller, Jr., won the Pulitzer Prize, the New York Drama Critics Circle Award, and the Outer Critics Circle Award for A *Soldier's Play (1981), a military drama in which an African American army captain is sent to a segregated camp to investigate a murder within a climate of racial hostility and mistrust; earlier he received an Obie Award for Zooman and the Sign (1980), the portrait of a teenage African American hoodlum, who successfully terrorizes a whole neighborhood, until a courageous father, whose daughter he has accidentally killed, persuades the community to help him bring the killer to justice. George *Wolfe (who later became director of the New York Shakespeare Festival) won a Dramatists Guild Award for The Colored Museum (1986), a lampoon of the African American experience in the form of a series of exhibits that come alive to reveal the stereotypes and myths of black culture, and a Tony nomination for best book and direction for his Jelly's Last Jam (1992). And, finally, August *Wilson, premier African American dramatist of the 1980s and 1990s, won the Drama Critics Circle Award for his Ma Rainey's Black Bottom (1982), a revealing look at the life and times of the great blues singer; a Pulitzer Prize for *Fences (1987), which explored the conflict between generations of an African American family, also winning a Tony Award, a Drama Critics Circle Award, an Outer Critics Circle Award, and a Drama Desk Award; and a second Pulitzer Prize, as well as nearly every other major theatrical award, for The *Piano Lesson (1990), which traced the history of a family of African Americans from slavery to the Great Depression, through the dominant symbol of its past—an upright piano that has been in the family for generations, on which are carved many of the tragic experiences through which the family has suffered.

A review of the best American plays of the late twentieth century reveals that contemporary African American playwrights are well represented and have begun to receive much of the recognition that they have long deserved as significant contributors to the literature of the American theatrical stage. African American drama has finally become a vital and accepted part of America's rich and multicultural literary heritage.

[See also Minstrelsy; Performances and Pageants.]

• Loften Mitchell, Black Drama: The Story of the American Negro in the Theatre, 1967. Doris E. Abramson, Negro Playwrights in the American Theatre, 1925–1959, 1969. Clinton F. Oliver and Stephanie Sills, eds., Contemporary Black Drama, 1971. Garff B. Wilson, Three Hundred Years of American Drama and Theatre, 1973. James V. Hatch, ed., and Ted Shine, consultant, Black Theatre, U.S.A.: Forty-Five Plays by Black Americans, 1847–1974, 1974. Errol Hill, The Theatre of Black Americans, 2 vols., 1980. Thadious M. Davis and Trudier Harris, eds., DLB, vol. 38, Afro-American Writers after 1955: Dramatists and Prose Writers, 1985. Mance Williams, Black Threatre in the 1960s and 1970s, 1985. Bernard L. Peterson, Jr., Contemporary Black American Playwrights and Dramatic Writers, 1988. Bernard L. Peterson, Jr., Early Black American Playwrights and Dramatic Writers, 1990. Leo Hamalian and James V. Hatch, eds., The Roots of African American Drama, 1991. Bernard L. Peterson, Jr., A Century of Musicals in Black and White, 1993.
—Bernard L. Peterson, Jr.

DRESS. Clothes and dress can variously enhance, hide, or reveal personal and group *identity. For nearly four centuries, the garments depicted in the writings of African Americans often symbolize the ambivalent relationship that has always existed between this racial group and a nation obsessed with imposing on them an endless variety of physical and spiritual assaults. Antebellum poems, *essays, and folktales are rife with accounts of these complex and continuing conflicts. *Slave narratives, in particular, use such motifs as nakedness and dressmaking to show how bondspeople plotted escape routes while appearing to accommodate the *slavery regime. In the early postbellum writings, clothes or the lack thereof exemplify inequality in and uncertainty about a country that was then establishing de facto slavery with *Jim Crow laws and other techniques. More specifically, the symbolism in these works warned of growing divisions within the African American *family and community. By the *Harlem Renaissance, writers sought to create a uniquely African American aesthetic at a time when race riots and *lynchings ruled the day. Their clothing imagery reflects this cultural schizophrenia and provides a useful way of evaluating their literary efforts. In the *Black Arts movement writings of the 1960s and after, dashikis and Afro hairdos mirror a growing shift in African American thinking and aesthetics. That move is away from integrationist perspectives toward a belief in spiritual rejuvenation achieved through identification with the African motherland. More recently, the clothes and dress of characters exhibit the irony of both a second-class citizenship within an intransigently racist land and the liberation of an alien, African-based self.

The depiction of nudity in slave narratives underscores the utterly defenseless position of the slaves because it is usually followed by their being bound, strung up, and whipped. In the *Narrative of the Life of Frederick Douglass, an American Slave, Written by Himself (1845), the author illustrates this condition quite graphically. Sent to the vicious slavebreaker Edward Covey because his owner, Thomas Auld, finds him disdainful, Douglass is repeatedly ordered to disrobe after a minor infraction, but does not move "to strip myself." Consequently, Covey fiercely rushes at him, tears off his clothes, and lashes and cuts him savagely. Douglass continues to receive these beatings until he engages Covey in a fistfight and wins. Significantly, Douglass develops an ironic view of his personal liberation, linking it more to a "*manhood" achieved with the same sort of *violence that his captors inflict upon him than to a brave act of self-defense. In so doing, he reveals an accommodation to a culture where undressing and being beaten signal a loss of manhood, and violent conquest means getting it back. The brutality required in both situations emphasizes that he and his enslavers are all spiritually imprisoned to one degree or another.

Similarly, in *Behind the Scenes, or Thirty Years a Slave, and Four Years in the White House* (1868), Elizabeth *Keckley seeks self-validation from the Garlands, her former St. Louis captors, who lent her out as a seamstress and for whom she earned enough money to feed their household of seventeen for nearly three years. When Keckley later remembers that her hard work brought them a good living, her "lips curled with a bitter sneer." After she buys her *freedom and heads for Washington, D.C., her reputation for making the most beautiful clothes in town gains her a prestigious customer, Mary Todd Lincoln, wife of the president. She now has the perfect platform from which to thumb her nose at the Old South. Nonetheless, the chapter entitled "Old Friends," where she visits the relatives of her former owners, presents the most peculiar message in the narrative. Keckley sentimentally describes two Garlands dying in her arms and claims that she could not have loved Nannie Garland more "had she been the sister of my unfortunate boy," whom Keckley never fully loves because he was the result of her being raped as a slave. The chapter also indicates Keckley's sincere joy about visiting the home of what amounts to her only living family, the heirs of white slaveholders. With the end of slavery, perhaps, Keckley seeks reconciliation with the old slave South, but she clearly gains some satisfaction from being the victim whose success eclipses that of her former owners. She knows her impact on the entire community, observing that "My association with Mrs, Lincoln, and my attachment for the Garlands, whose slave I had once been, clothed me with romantic interest." Her clothing image conjoins her celebrity and romantic feelings about home and family, which together liberate her economically and emotionally. In this way, she foreshadows fictional characters like Alice *Walker's *Celie in The *Color Purple (1982), whose pants-making business generates a similar sense of accomplishment after the violence of childhood rape and, later, wife-battering.

Around the turn of the century, African American writings begin to reflect a growing tension between husbands and wives that rarely occurs in the earlier works. The incipient *migration of southern African Americans to northern cities, which would become a flood during the Harlem Renaissance, provides the setting for this literature. While trying to escape southern joblessness, poverty, and violence, many become like Jim and Mandy Mason, the couple in Paul Laurence *Dunbar's *short story "Jimsella" (*Folks from Dixie, 1898). The two constantly bicker, and Jim commits adultery and neglects their daughter, Jimsella. Dunbar examines the marital strife encountered by this pair because they are poorly educated, poorly housed, and unqualified for most available jobs. He frames the story around an argument about the wife's appearance. When Jim asks Mandy why she does not fix herself up like other people, he makes a comparison between her and the other African American women on the streets of Harlem who dress more gayly and look smarter. When she

asks why he does not provide the money she needs to dress this way, she reveals her adherence to societal *gender roles that require wives to stay home and become mothers while their husbands support them. Both husband and wife are preoccupied with the appearances of home and family, mindlessly imitating the marriage pattern of mainstream America without considering the traditional ways African Americans have survived economically and psychologically despite institutionalized American racism. Although Mandy finds a way to support herself through pregnancy and the birth of Jimsella—after Jim leaves for a more attractively dressed woman—she never takes the most logical step to find a job that would help pay their bills and, maybe, buy herself some attractive clothes. While Jim eventually returns to the family, he does so because he learns that Jimsella looks like and is named after him. Nevertheless, Mandy's shoddy attire signals the lingering tension in their home since it remains a reminder of her husband's limited earning power, which he equates with a loss of manhood only temporarily propped up through the biological achievement of producing a daughter.

The Harlem Renaissance writers declared that they would write freely and frankly without accommodating to white America. They would portray unashamedly and realistically the whole African American experience in all its varied facets. But many failed at this goal because of doubt about their talents, self-hatred, and group contempt. As renaissance authors sought to depict the truth and beauty of African American life, their works more often than not continued to use white culture as the measure of its value. In *Infants of the Spring* (1932), Wallace *Thurman writes the only renaissance *novel devoted to examining the impact of this practice on the art. His satire becomes especially pointed in his portrayal of the clothes and dress of Paul Arbian, a talented painter (modeled after Richard Bruce *Nugent) who lives communally with other artists in a rented house nicknamed *Niggerati Manor.

Thurman describes Paul as very tall with wiry, untrained *hair. He habitually dispenses with any necktie, socks, or underwear, and the few clothes he does wear are musty and disheveled. His fashions and campy manner imitate the unkempt, outlandish, and sexually provocative style of the rebellious avant garde from Greenwich Village, to which he eventually absconds. While living at Niggerati Manor, however, Paul mostly struts around proclaiming his genius and mouthing praise for a long list of Eurocentric artists and intellectuals such as Oscar Wilde, Baudelaire, and Picasso. Indeed, this cataloging is a prominent motif in many Harlem Renaissance writings and exposes insecure authors who needed to pay homage to white artistic achievement in order to legitimize their own. Paul too uses cataloging to divert attention away from the fact that, like all the other residents of Niggerati Manor, he produces no art. When asked to show his work, he launches an ad hominem attack against his inquisitor. Unlike Frederick Douglass who fights to keep his clothes on lest he lose his personal dignity, Paul purposely takes them off in order to appear talented and, ironically, to reinforce *stereotypes about the inability of African Americans to master imaginative art. When he eventually puts on an exotic crimson mandarin robe and wraps his head in a batik scarf, the color and fabric of the costume signal his suicide by slashing his wrists in a bathtub. His outfit also sustains the theme of self-hatred and artistic stagnation. Paul becomes a "colorful, inanimate corpse in a crimson streaked tub," and his water-sensitive, vegetable-dyed batik turban fades as surely as his breathing and the print of the water-logged "great novel" he was leaving for posterity.

When *Malcom X expounded on ideas about African American pride, he laid down some basic philosophical principles for the Black Arts movement writers of the 1960s and 1970s. His emphasis on the need for African Americans to alter their self-perceptions inspired changing attitudes about integration into a society that remains pathologically fearful of people of color. By criticizing traditional Euro-American conceptions of Africa and race, he sought to encourage African Americans to find beauty in their own physical and creative selves. *The *Autobiography of Malcolm X* (1965), as told to Alex *Haley, uses clothing to map Malcolm's gradual coming of age. His 1940s zoot suits and conked hair interpret a youthful innocence and naïveté, a time when he was unaware of the degree to which whites regarded his black face with contempt. Shedding this fashion indicates a developing racial consciousness that leads him away from the criminal and undisciplined behavior also associated with this apparel. At his maturity, Malcolm X wears the conservative suit and bow-tie of the nationalistic Black Muslims, who reverse the traditional parasitic relationship between American racial groups so that African American self-esteem comes at the expense of white folks.

The physical looks and garments of the central characters in Alice Walker's short story "Everyday Use" (*In Love and Trouble*, 1967) also exemplify their apparently heartfelt racial pride. Newly renamed Wangero and adorned in huge earrings, bracelets, Afro hairdo, a long, flowing, loud African dress, and accompanied by a dashiki-clad boyfriend, Dee Johnson practically models her liberated self. Walker contrasts Dee's costume with her mother's flannel nightgowns and overalls that show the older woman's recognition of the realities of farm life. She also drapes the thin body of Dee's sister, shy Maggie, in a mismatched pink skirt and red blouse. The tale reaches a dramatic climax when Mrs. Johnson does the unthinkable and gives her daughter Maggie quilts that Wangero coveted, ostensibly because the younger Maggie sincerely values the family and racial heritage they symbolize.

The clothing and the quilts, however, evoke the romanticism of the ambivalent Elizabeth Keckley and reveal Walker's own mixed feelings about African American social and *class consciousness. The narrator/mother clearly shows a preference for the educated and successful Dee over pitiful Maggie, whom she compares to a lame dog and describes as a fire-scarred, snuff-dipping milquetoast who is planning to marry mossy-toothed John Thomas. Although Mrs. Johnson dislikes Dee's egocentrism and snobbery, she is proud of her academic and economic achievements and, moreover, offers Maggie the quilts because she feels sorry for her. Walker's portrait of Dee enables her to criticize those successful African Americans who owe their livelihood to an American mainstream that allows them to embrace African American cultural values only when white people declare them to be in vogue. And Dee will, indeed, dress up in matched suits and shoes when being "black" is no longer stylish. Importantly, her portrayal of Maggie and her mother allows Walker to insinuate that only poor, uneducated, unfashionable, and disfigured African Americans can embrace all aspects of their racial selves. Even so, many classes of African Americans who are disillusioned by the failures of integration and confident about their own racial identities will not return to a traditional American uniform. Apparently, Walker does not acknowledge this latter group because she imagines the African American heritage and future as sentimentally as she does Mrs. Johnson and Maggie.

There are no full-length critical studies and very few scholarly essays on the use of clothes and dress in African American literature. The essayists who have considered the subject find nudity, the clothing profession, particular garments, makeup, and adornments emblems of a complex historical struggle that African Americans have engaged in both with the country and themselves. To a greater or lesser degree throughout the years, the United States has had a duplicitous relationship with its darker-skinned citizens. By restricting their opportunities for advancement, this country has at once dared African Americans to participate in as well as reject aspects of American life. Not surprisingly, both the repulsion and the attraction of this challenge have drawn an ambivalent response from writers that persists to this day.

• Mary Jane Lupton, "Clothes and Closure in Three Novels by Black Women," *Black American Literature Forum* 20 (Winter 1986): 409–421. M. Teresa Tavormina, "Dressing the Spirit: Clothworking and Language in *The Color Purple*," *Journal of Narrative Technique* 16 (Fall 1986): 220–230. Barbara M. Starke and Lillian O. Holloman, eds., *African American Dress and Adornment: A Cultural Perspective*, 1990.

—SallyAnn H. Ferguson

DRINKING GOURD, THE. An African American name for the Big Dipper constellation, which enslaved African Americans used to direct their escapes north. The *spiritual "Follow the Drinking Gourd" relates to the activities of Peg Leg Joe, a conductor on the *Underground Railroad. Masquerading as a transient worker on southern plantations, Joe repeatedly sang this song, which encoded for his enslaved coworkers both a map to the Ohio River and a schedule for the next opportunity to meet "the old man . . . a-waitin'" for to carry you to *freedom." In 1959 Lorraine *Hansberry integrated the words and music of this spiritual into her unproduced filmscript *The Drinking Gourd*.

—Lori Askeland

Drugstore Cat, The. *The Drugstore Cat* (1949, rpt. 1988) is Ann *Petry's first published work of children's literature. It was followed by *Harriet Tubman: Conductor of the Underground Railroad* (1955), *Tituba of Salem Village* (1964), and *The Legends of the Saints* (1970). In Clara Jackson's *Twentieth Century Children's Writers*, Petry explains, "Because I was born black and female I write about survivors, (especially when I write for children)."

The Drugstore Cat was first printed in a time when few works of *children's and young adult literature by African American writers were published. While the human characters are white, the story is typical of African American stories for children in that it contains a message to guide young people in their development as individuals and members of society.

Buzzy is a fat, gray kitten with a temper as short as his Manx tail. The story opens with his mother preparing him for his new home. He is to live in a drugstore with Mr. and Miss James, brother and sister pharmacists. Buzzy's mother explains that he will enjoy his new world, but he will have no one to speak with as human beings don't understand the language of cats. Her last words to him are a warning to watch his manners so he won't be sent back to her as a disappointment.

Buzzy immediately runs into difficulty. He is lonely, with no one to speak to, and often loses his temper. When he scratches a drugstore customer, the Jameses decide they must send him back to his mother as soon as his paw, injured on an adventure, heals. Buzzy resolves to learn to control his temper so he will not be sent home in shame. He is successful and soon likes living at the drugstore with his new friends. Buzzy has one last show of temper and it saves the store from burglars. The grateful Jameses decide they must keep him. The story helps young readers learn the rewards of working to improve a difficult situation.

• "Ann Lane Petry," in *Selected Black American Authors*, comp. James Page, 1977, pp. 216–217. Sandra Carlton Alexander, "Ann Petry," in *DLB*, vol. 76, *Afro-American Writers, 1940–1955*, ed. Trudier Harris, 1988, pp. 140–147. "Ann (Lane) Petry," in *Black Writers: A Selection of Sketches from Contemporary Authors*, ed. Linda Metzger, 1989, pp. 454–455.   —Tracy J. Patterson

DRUMGOOLD, KATE (c. 1858–?), author of nineteenth-century slave narrative–inspirational autobiography. A young child living near Petersburg, Virginia, when the Civil War began, Kate Drumgoold believed her life story, as recounted in her *autobiography, A Slave Girl's Story* (1898), to be inspirational evidence of God's special attentiveness to her race. Formerly available only in a rare original edition, *A Slave Girl's Story* has been reprinted as part of the Schomburg Library of Nineteenth-Century Black Women Writers in *Six Women's Slave Narratives* (1988), with an introduction by William L. Andrews. In contrast to earlier *slave narratives describing extreme personal suffering, Drumgoold's account of her own brief experience as a very young slave pays tribute to female slave owners who served as caretakers. Drumgoold's story of her mother's experience, however, reveals the inhumanity of a system that denied and divided *families and the courage of African American women who fought to keep families together under seemingly impossible conditions. The mother of eighteen living children, one of whom was only six weeks old at the time of their separation, Drumgoold's mother was sold and sent to Georgia at the beginning of the war for money to allow her master to pay a surrogate to fight in the Confederate army. At the end of the Civil War, Drumgoold writes, her mother returned to claim her children, determinedly going from house to house demanding their return, though several of their former owners hid them and told her they were dead. In 1865 Drumgoold's mother moved her reunited family to Brooklyn, New York.

The remainder of Drumgoold's narrative describes her own religious commitment and determination to get an *education and become a teacher, goals she eventually achieved. Despite her recurrent ill health and financial hardship, *A Slave Girl's Story* consistently strikes a tone of optimism and social mission that places Drumgoold's autobiography within an important tradition of instructional and inspirational narrative in African American literary history.

• Minrose C. Gwin, *Black and White Women of the Old South: The Peculiar Sisterhood in American Literature*, 1985. Hazel V. Carby, *Reconstructing Womanhood: The Emergence of the Afro-American Woman Novelist*, 1987.

—Minrose C. Gwin

DU BOIS, SHIRLEY GRAHAM. *See* Graham, Shirley.

DU BOIS, W. E. B. (1868–1963), essayist, novelist, journalist, critic, and perhaps the preeminent African American scholar-intellectual. William Edward Burghardt Du Bois was born in Great Barrington, Massachusetts, in 1868. He was born into a small community of blacks who had settled in the region since at least the Revolutionary War, in which an ancestor had fought. His mother, Mary Sylvina Burghardt, married a restless young visitor to the region, Alfred Du Bois, who disappeared soon after the birth of his son. Du Bois grew up a thorough New Englander, as he recalled, a member of the Congregational Church and a star student in the local schools, where he was encouraged to excel.

In 1885 he left Great Barrington for Nashville, Tennessee, to enter Fisk University. The racism of the South appalled him: "No one but a Negro going into the South without previous experience of color caste can have any conception of its barbarism." Nevertheless he enjoyed life at Fisk, from which he was graduated in 1888. He then enrolled at Harvard, where he completed another bachelor's degree in 1890 before going on to graduate school there in *history.

At Harvard his professors included William James, George Santayana, and the historian A. B. Hart. He then spent two years at the University of Berlin studying history and sociology and coming close to earning a second doctorate. Du Bois enjoyed his stay in Europe, which greatly expanded his notions about the possibilities of culture and civilization. Then, in 1894, he dropped back, as he himself put it, into "nigger-hating America."

Despite his education, most jobs were closed to him. In the next few years Du Bois taught unhappily at black Wilberforce University in Ohio, carried out a complex project in empirical sociology in a black section of Philadelphia for the University of Pennsylvania, and then, in 1897, settled in to teach economics, history, and sociology at Atlanta University.

His doctoral thesis, *The Suppression of the African Slave-Trade to the United States 1638–1870*, was published in 1896 as the first volume of the Harvard Historical Studies, to be followed in 1899 by his acclaimed study in empirical sociology, *The Philadelphia Negro*. However, in 1903, as Du Bois became more disenchanted with race relations in the South and increasingly saw social science as relatively powerless to change social conditions, he moved away from strict scholarship to publish a landmark collection of prose pieces, *The *Souls of Black Folk*.

This volume, which expressly attacked Booker T. *Washington, the most powerful black American of the age, brought Du Bois to controversial prominence among blacks. Brilliantly written and extraordinarily rich and complex as a portrait of black life, it also became a sort of Bible for younger black intellectuals and artists in America.

Du Bois's growing dissatisfaction with scholarship in general led him while at Atlanta to ventures in *journalism as editor of two magazines, the *Moon* and the *Horizon*, between 1905 and 1909. He also published a *biography, *John Brown* (1909), about the martyr of Harpers Ferry, that underscored his growing interest in radical action. Finally, in 1910, he gave up his professorship in Atlanta to move to New York as director of publicity of the new NAACP and as founder and editor of its magazine, the *Crisis*.

Du Bois quickly made the journal a trumpet against all forms of racism, as well as a reliable vehicle for writers young and old. Aiming consciously to stimulate artistic activity among younger blacks, he wrote of a coming renaissance. In 1911 he himself published a *novel, *The *Quest of the Silver Fleece*, about blacks and cotton in the South, that suggested the influence of Frank Norris. In 1915, reflecting a deepening knowledge of Africa, came *The Negro*, his Pan-Africanist account of the history of blacks in Africa and around the world. In 1920 he published his second collection of fugitive pieces, this time including some verse, *Darkwater: Voices from within the Veil*. This volume showed him starkly alienated and embittered, especially as compared to the self-portrait in *The Souls of Black Folk*, with which the new volume invited comparison.

Between 1919 and 1926, Jessie Redmon *Fauset served as literary editor of the *Crisis* and helped to attract early work by Countee *Cullen, Langston *Hughes, and other young writers of the *Harlem Renaissance. In 1926, however, in a *Crisis* symposium called "The Negro in Art," Du Bois attacked many of the younger writers for failing to recognize their political responsibilities. "All art is propaganda," he insisted, in a reversal of an earlier position, "and ever must be, despite the wailing of the purists." To illustrate his point, he contributed a novel, *Dark Princess* (1928), about a black American man, the beautiful Indian princess with whom he falls in love, and a plot among representatives of the darker nations of the world to rid themselves forever of white domination.

In 1934, with the *Crisis* circulation greatly reduced and the renaissance exhausted by the Great Depression, Du Bois resigned from the NAACP after years of tension with other leaders. He returned to Atlanta University to teach there. The next year he published *Black Reconstruction in America*, a massive treatise built largely on secondary material, about the post–Civil War period in the South. The work was highly colored by Du Bois's renewed interest in Marxism, to which he had been drawn earlier, and by his sometimes overwhelming dramatic sense. In 1940 his *autobiography *Dusk of Dawn: An Essay Toward an Autobiography of a Race Concept* explored the relationship between his life and the evolution of theories of *race in America and elsewhere.

In 1944 Du Bois rejoined the NAACP in New York as director of special research. Before long, however, he was again in conflict with the Association leaders over his growing interest in *Communism and what he saw as their conservatism. In 1948 the Association fired him, this time for good. He joined forces with Paul *Robeson and others in the Council of African Affairs, an anticolonialist organization, but also associated himself openly with other elements of the international Left. In 1950 he ran unsuccessfully for the U.S. Senate on the Labor Party ticket. In 1951 he was indicted by a grand jury and arrested for operating as the unregistered agent of a foreign power because of his involvement with a group called the Peace Information Center, of which he was chairman. After the trial judge threw out the case, Du Bois wrote about his experiences in *In Battle for Peace: The Story of My Eighty-Third Birthday* (1952).

In the 1950s he consolidated his links to Communism. He was prominent in the outcry against the execution of the Rosenbergs and took part in their funeral service. The government retaliated by seizing his passport and holding it for several years. Still Du Bois continued to write. In his last years he published *The Black Flame*, a trilogy of novels: *The Ordeal of Mansart* (1957), *Mansart Builds a School* (1959), and *Worlds of Color* (1961). These novels offered an encyclopedic account of modern African American and world history seen from a radical perspective, mainly through the experiences of a stalwart though intellectually mediocre African American educator, Manuel Mansart. The trilogy was ignored by virtually all American critics and reviewers, black or white.

In 1959, after much travel following the restoration of his passport, he emigrated to Ghana. He did so at the invitation of its president, Kwame Nkrumah, to begin work on an *Encyclopedia Africana* in which Du Bois had taken an almost lifelong interest. At the same time, he publicly applied for membership in the U.S. Communist Party. In Africa, he renounced his U.S. citizenship and became a citizen of Ghana. He died in Accra in August 1963.

Merely as the author of five novels and enough poems for a slender volume, Du Bois deserves a place in African American literary history. However, his impact on black literature went well beyond his efforts as a poet or writer of fiction. *The Souls of Black Folk* revolutionized African American self-perception by locating the black personality and character in the context of history, sociology, *religion, *music, and art as it had never been located before. Du Bois's concept of *double consciousness and his image of black Americans as living behind a veil in America, which he developed in harmony with astute critical analyses of history and sociology, opened up the representational world for black artists responding to the crisis in which African Americans have been forced to live.

His many brilliant *essays, backed by a rare command of black history and social complexity, were a resource on which generations of black intellectuals and artists drew. The grand tribute given Du Bois by Arthur Spingarn of the NAACP when Du Bois resigned from the organization in 1934 is hardly off the mark: "He created, what never existed before, a Negro intelligentsia, and many who have never read a word of his writings are his spiritual disciples and descendants."

[*See also* Graham, Shirley; Pan-Africanism.]

• Francis L. Broderick *W. E. B. Du Bois: Negro Leader in a Time of Crisis*, 1959. Elliott Rudwick, *W. E. B. Du Bois: Propagandist of the Negro Protest*, 1968. Shirley Graham Du Bois, *His Day Is Marching On: A Memoir of W. E. B. Du Bois*, 1971. Herbert Aptheker, ed., *Annotated Bibliography of the Published Writings of W. E. B. Du Bois*, 1973. William L. Andrews, ed., *Critical Essays on W. E. B. Du Bois*, 1985. Herbert Aptheker, ed., *The Complete Published Works of W. E. B. Du Bois*, 35 vols., 1973–1985. Nathan I. Huggins, ed. *W. E. B. Du Bois: Writings*, 1990. Arnold Rampersad, *The Art and Imagination of W. E. B. Du Bois*, 1990. David Levering Lewis, *W. E. B. Du Bois: Biography of a Race, 1868–1919*, 1993.

—Arnold Rampersad

DUMAS, HENRY (1934–1968) poet, short fiction writer, and mythologizer. The literary legacy of Henry Dumas is one that has been kept alive almost single-handedly by fellow poet Eugene *Redmond. Dumas inspires interest not only for his unique vision of black people in the diaspora, but because of the tragedy of his own life. Mistakenly shot down by a New York City Transit policeman on 23 May 1968, when he was a mere thirty-three, his life is emblematic of the precarious position of black men in America and the painful situation of a talented young man dying so young. Observers can only speculate, sadly, about what he might have accomplished if he had somehow escaped the fate assigned to him. In many ways Dumas has become a cultural icon in African American literary circles.

Henry Dumas was born on 20 July 1934 in Sweet Home, Arkansas, where he spent his early years and was saturated with the religious and folk traditions of that soil. He claimed Moms Mabley and gospel music as particular influences upon him. At the age of ten, he was taken to Harlem, where he attended public schools and graduated from Commerce High School in 1953. He enrolled in City College that year but left to join the air force. Stationed at Lackland Air Force Base in San Antonio, Texas, he maintained his interest in religion by teaching Sunday school while there. Dumas also spent a year on the Arabian Peninsula, where he developed an interest in the Arabic language, mythology, and culture.

Dumas married Loretta Ponton on 24 September 1955, while he was still in the military. He fathered two sons before he came to his untimely death. The first son, David, was born in 1958, after Dumas had completed his tour of duty and enrolled at Rutgers University. His second son, Michael, was born in 1962, three years before Dumas terminated his part-time attendance at Rutgers; he did not complete his degree. Though he had compelling duties as a husband, father, and IBM worker (1963–1964), Dumas was nonetheless active in civil rights and humanitarian activities, including transporting food and clothing to protesters living in Mississippi and Tennessee.

In 1967 Dumas went to Southern Illinois University as a teacher, counselor, and director of language workshops in its Experiment in Higher Education program. It was here that he met Eugene Redmond, a fellow teacher in that program. Over the course of the ten months Dumas lived in East St. Louis, he and Redmond forged the collaborative relationship that would prove so fruitful to Dumas's posthumous career. He and Redmond read their poetry at common gatherings; Redmond especially remembers Dumas reading "Our King Is Dead," his elegy for Martin Luther *King, Jr. Dumas also frequented the offices of the *East St. Louis Monitor*, which Redmond edited and which featured an obituary on Dumas on 6 June 1968.

Dumas's first collection of short fiction is entitled *"Arks of Bones" and Other Stories* (edited by Redmond in 1974), which includes nine stories and in which his largely mythic vision of African American existence is apparent. In "Ark of Bones," for example, Dumas depicts an ark that lands in a river in Arkansas, to which a young African American boy, Headeye, is called to assume his priestly role on the ship. The ship contains bones, bones of black people who died in the *Middle Passage or who have otherwise lost their lives in a repressive, racist world. The only living inhabitants on the ark are the eternal caretakers of the bones; Headeye has been selected to become one of these and is initiated into the role he must play. Like *Velma Henry in Toni Cade *Bambara's *The *Salt Eaters* or the general pattern in which African Americans, especially preachers, are chosen by forces beyond this world for duties in this world, Headeye finally accepts the fact that he hears voices that other people do not hear, that he has one foot in the realm of the empirical and one foot in the realm of the extranatural. Instances of otherworldly phenomena permeating the natural environment also occur in other stories in the collection.

Redmond's commitment to making Dumas's work readily available to scholarly communities continued in the publication of *Goodbye, Sweetwater* (1988) and *Knees of a Natural Man: The Selected Poetry of Henry*

Dumas (1989). The first volume contains eight of the stories that first appeared in *"Ark of Bones,"* along with excerpts from Dumas's unfinished novel, *Jonoah and the Green Stone* (1976), stories from *Rope of Wind* (1979), and three selections from "Goodbye Sweetwater." One of the stories in the final section is "Rain God," which develops the African American folk belief that, when it is raining and the sun is shining, the devil is beating his wife. Three young black boys literally witness this phenomenon as they are on their way home one rainy-sunny day. The second volume contains previously published as well as unpublished poems, including several poems with the title "Kef" and an accompanying number, and "Saba," with the same pattern. Some of the poems in *Knees* had appeared in *Play Ebony: Play Ivory* (1974), a collection of Dumas's poetry, which Redmond edited singly in 1974 and which he had coedited in 1970. Dumas's poetry is inspired by African American music, particularly blues and jazz (he studied with Sun Ra), and he develops themes consistent with the *Black Aesthetic of the 1960s. His poetry also focuses, in keeping with his fiction, on themes of nature and the natural world.

Readers coming to Dumas's works are most struck by his extraordinary vision, his unusual ways of looking at the world, at the experiences of African Americans, and at the intersections of natural and supernatural phenomena. Redmond had done yeoman work in encouraging interest in Dumas's fictional and poetic creations. It remains to be seen whether the planted seeds will indeed sprout into a critical industry.

• Eugene B. Redmond, introduction to *"Ark of Bones" and Other Stories*, 1974. Carolyn A. Mitchell, "Henry Dumas," in *DLB*, vol. 41, *Afro-American Poets since 1955*, eds. Trudier Harris and Thadious M. Davis, 1985, pp. 89–99. Eugene B. Redmond, "The Ancient and Recent Voices within Henry Dumas," introduction to *Goodbye Sweetwater*, 1988. Eugene B. Redmond, "Poet Henry Dumas: Distance Runner, Stabilizer, Distiller," introduction to *Knees of a Natural Man: The Selected Poetry of Henry Dumas*, 1989.

—Trudier Harris

DUNBAR, PAUL LAURENCE (1872–1906), poet, fiction writer, essayist, songwriter, linguistic innovator, and prophet. Paul Laurence Dunbar published in such mainstream journals as *Century*, *Lipincott's Monthly*, the *Atlantic Monthly*, and the *Saturday Evening Post*. A gifted poet and a precursor to the *Harlem Renaissance, Dunbar was read by both blacks and whites in turn-of-the-century America.

Dunbar, the son of two former slaves, was born in Dayton, Ohio, and attended the public schools of that city. He was taught to read by his mother, Matilda Murphy Dunbar, and he absorbed her homespun wisdom as well as the stories told to him by his father, Joshua Dunbar, who had escaped from enslavement in Kentucky and served in the Massachusetts 55th Regiment during the Civil War. Thus, while Paul Laurence Dunbar himself was never enslaved, he was one of the last of a generation to have ongoing contact with those who had been. Dunbar was steeped in the oral tradition during his formative years and he

would go on to become a powerful interpreter of the African American folk experience in literature and song; he would also champion the cause of civil rights and higher education for African Americans in *essays and *poetry that were militant by the standards of his day.

During his years at Dayton's Central High, Dunbar was the school's only student of color, but it was his scholarly performance that distinguished him. He served as editor in chief of the school paper, president of the literary society, and class poet. His poetry grew more sophisticated with his repeated readings of John Keats, William Wordsworth, Samuel Taylor Coleridge, and Robert Burns; later he would add American poets John Greenleaf Whittier, Henry Wadsworth Longfellow, and James Whitcomb Riley to his list of favorites as he searched ardently for his own poetic voice. But it was his reading of Irwin Russell and other writers in the *plantation tradition that led him into difficulty as he searched for an authentic poetic diction that would incorporate the voices of his parents and the stories they told.

After graduating from high school in 1891, racial discrimination forced Dunbar to accept a job as an elevator operator in a Dayton hotel. He wrote on the job during slack hours. He became well known as the "elevator boy poet" after James Newton Mathews invited him to read his poetry at the annual meeting of the Western Association of Writers, held in Dayton in 1892.

In 1893 Dunbar published his first volume of poetry, *Oak and Ivy*, on the press of the Church of the Brethren. That same year he also attended the World's Columbian Exposition, where he sold copies of his book and gained the patronage of Frederick *Douglass and other influential African Americans.

In 1895 Dunbar initiated a correspondence with Alice Ruth Moore, a fair-skinned black Creole teacher and writer originally from New Orleans. Three years later he married Alice in secret and over the objections of her friends and family. During the years of their marriage, Dunbar began to suffer from tuberculosis and the alcohol prescribed for it. The Dunbars separated permanently in 1902 but remained friends, and Alice continued to be known as "the widow of Paul Laurence Dunbar" even after her 1916 marriage to publisher Robert J. Nelson. The Dunbars had no children.

Dunbar published eleven volumes of poetry including *Oak and Ivy* (1893), *Majors and Minors* (1895), *Lyrics of Lowly Life* (1896), *Lyrics of the Hearthside* (1899), *Poems of Cabin and Field* (1899), *Candle-Lightin' Time* (1901), *Lyrics of Love and Laughter* (1903), *When Malindy Sings* (1903), *Li'l Gal* (1904), *Howdy, Honey, Howdy* (1905), and *Lyrics of Sunshine and Shadow* (1905). Dunbar's so-called *Complete Poems* were published posthumously in 1913. The most complete edition of Dunbar's poetry, *The Collected Poetry of Paul Laurence Dunbar*, containing a selection of sixty poems not published in 1913, did not appear until 1994. Dunbar's published fiction includes *The Uncalled* (1898), *Folks from Dixie* (1898), *The Strength of Gideon and Other Stories* (1900), *The Fanatics* (1901), and *The*

Sport of the Gods (1902), but he remains best known for his poetry.

Much of the controversy surrounding Paul Laurence Dunbar concerns his *dialect poetry, wherein some scholars, such as the late Charles T. Davis, felt that Dunbar showed the greatest glimmers of genius. Sterling A. *Brown, writing in *Negro Poetry and Drama* in 1937, asserted that Dunbar was the first American poet to "handle Negro folk life with any degree of fullness" but he also found Dunbar guilty of cruelly "misreading" black *history. This points to the basic flaw in Paul Laurence Dunbar's attempts to represent authentic African American folk language in verse. He was not able to transcend completely the racist plantation tradition made popular by Joel Chandler Harris, Thomas Nelson Page, Irwin Russell, and other white writers who made use of African American folk materials and who showed the "old time Negro" as if he were satisfied serving the master on the antebellum plantation.

While Dunbar sought an appropriate literary form for the representation of African American vernacular expression, he was also deeply ambivalent about his undertaking in this area. He recognized that many of his experiments yielded imperfect results and he was concerned that prominent white critics such as William Dean Howells praised his work for the wrong reasons, setting a tone that other Dunbar critics would follow for years as they virtually ignored his standard English verse and his published experiments with Irish, German, and Western regional dialects.

Some African American critics saw a concession to racism evident in Dunbar's black dialect poetry, and while it is unlikely that any perceived concession was intentional, it can certainly be argued that dialect poems like "Parted" and "Corn Song" were more derivative of the plantation school than they were original productions of African American genius. Yet, during his lifetime, Dunbar's work was praised by Frederick Douglass, Booker T. *Washington, and W. E. B. *Du Bois, among others.

Negative treatment of Dunbar's poetry by black critics including scholar-poet James Weldon *Johnson did not surface fully until the *New Negro movement of the 1920s. On the other hand, poets Countee *Cullen and Langston *Hughes publicly admired and emulated Dunbar. A considered reading of poems like "We Wear the Mask," "When Malindy Sings," "Frederick Douglass," "The Colored Soldiers," or "The Haunted Oak" affirms Dunbar's loyalty to the black race and his pride in its achievements, as well as his righteous anger over racial injustice.

In the second half of the twentieth century Paul Laurence Dunbar was rediscovered. In 1972 centenary conferences marking the hundredth anniversary of Dunbar's birth were held at the University of Dayton and the University of California at Irvine, with prominent black poets and writers in attendance. At the Irvine conference, poet Nikki *Giovanni suggested that Dunbar's "message is clear and available . . . if we invest in Dunbar the integrity we hope others will give us."

A new edition of Dunbar's poems subsequently put long out-of-print Dunbar poems back on the classroom shelf, making it possible for teachers to acquaint a new generation of poets and scholars with Dunbar's work.

[*See also* Dunbar-Nelson, Alice Moore; Novel; Short Story.]

• Addison Gayle, Jr., *Oak and Ivy: A Biography of Paul Laurence Dunbar*, 1971. Jay Martin, ed., *A Singer in the Dawn: Reinterpretations of Paul Laurence Dunbar*, 1975. Jay Martin and Gossie Hudson, eds., *Paul Laurence Dunbar Reader*, 1975. Peter Revell, *Paul Laurence Dunbar*, 1979. Joanne M. Braxton, ed., *The Collected Poetry of Paul Laurence Dunbar*, 1993.
—Joanne M. Braxton

DUNBAR-NELSON, ALICE MOORE (1875–1935), short fiction writer, poet, diarist, journalist, and public speaker. Born in New Orleans, of mixed African American, Native American, and European American background, Alice Moore graduated from Straight College with a teaching degree in 1892. She published her first book, *Violets and Other Tales*, in 1895, a multigenre collection, including *short stories, *poetry, and *essays. The volume anticipates much of Dunbar-Nelson's later work, reflecting her interest in a range of literary forms, attraction to romantic themes and language, attention to *class differences, and ambivalence about women's roles. Notable, too, is a characteristic absence of racial designation, perhaps a consequence of Dunbar-Nelson's complex and occasionally conflicting attitudes toward the intersecting lines of *class and color shaping her Creole heritage.

After a courtship begun in correspondence, Moore married the poet Paul Laurence *Dunbar in 1898. The marriage, complicated by Dunbar's extensive travel and poor health, ended in 1902, and Dunbar-Nelson resumed her teaching career. Although she twice married, finding happiness with her third husband, journalist Robert Nelson, she retained the Dunbar name.

In 1899, Dunbar-Nelson published her finest literary work, *The Goodness of St. Rocque and Other Stories*. The collection of short fiction richly reflects New Orleans Creole culture, connecting Dunbar-Nelson to the late-nineteenth-century local color tradition. These stories are complicated by recurring imagery of disguise and entrapment that often suggests meanings masked by the romantic narrative. It is notable that in later short fiction uncollected or unpublished in her lifetime Dunbar-Nelson far more explicitly confronted questions of *gender and *race. Much of this later work is included in the three-volume *Works of Alice Dunbar-Nelson* (1988) edited by Gloria T. Hull.

Although fiction was Dunbar-Nelson's best medium, during the *Harlem Renaissance period she was known primarily as a poet. Traditional in form, her poetry treats primarily romantic themes with elevated, poetic language. Between 1917 and 1928, her poems appeared in the *Crisis and *Opportunity, and were included in several *anthologies, notably James Weldon *Johnson's *Book of American Negro Poetry* (1931).

In 1921 and from 1926 to 1931, Alice Dunbar-Nelson kept a personal diary. Edited by Gloria T. Hull, *Give Us Each Day: The Diary of Alice Dunbar-Nelson* (1984) details Dunbar-Nelson's professional labors, travels, friendships, and recurring financial difficulties and refers to her *lesbian relationships.

In addition to her work as an educator, Alice Dunbar-Nelson brought her skills and energy as speaker, writer, and organizer to movements for social change. She was active in the Women's Club movement, worked for suffrage, helped found the Industrial School for Colored Girls in Delaware, and in 1922 was a leader in the fight for passage of the Dyer Anti-Lynching Bill. Her work as a public speaker and interest in *oratory provided the foundation for two edited volumes, *Masterpieces of Negro Eloquence* (1914) and *The Dunbar Speaker and Entertainer* (1920). Toward the end of her career, Dunbar-Nelson turned from teaching to *journalism and public speaking. From 1926 to 1930, she wrote regular *newspaper columns in which she forthrightly commented on issues her fiction addressed only indirectly. From 1928 to 1931 she did extensive public speaking as executive secretary of the American Friends Inter-Racial Peace Committee.

Alice Dunbar-Nelson remains significant for the range of her written work, the complex, muted voice of her short fiction, and the rare, invaluable record her diary provides of the public and private life of an early twentieth-century African American woman writer.

[*See also* Diaries and Journals.]

• Gloria T. Hull, *Color, Sex, and Poetry: Three Women Writers of the Harlem Renaissance*, 1987. Violet Harrington Bryan, "Race and Gender in the Early Works of Alice Dunbar-Nelson," in *Louisiana Women Writers: New Essays and a Comprehensive Bibliography*, 1992, pp. 121–138.

—Mary Titus

DUNHAM, KATHERINE (b. 1909 or 1910), choreographer, dancer, anthropologist, and writer. Characterized for much of her professional life as a woman with a double *identity, as Broadway's grande dame of American *dance and as a pioneering dance anthropologist of world renown, Katherine Dunham has influenced generations with her wide array of talent. Born in Glen Ellyn, Illinois, she attended the University of Chicago, where she studied anthropology and first began to pursue the study of dance with professional aspirations. During the Great Depression Dunham opened a series of dance schools, all of which closed prematurely for financial reasons but not before they earned Dunham the attention and company of such noted individuals as Arna *Bontemps, Langston *Hughes, Horace Mann, Sterling North, Charles Sebree, and Charles White. As the recipient of a 1935 Julius Rosenwald Foundation Fellowship for the study of anthropology and dance traditions in the Caribbean, Dunham united her work in anthropology with her innovations in modern dance. She used her anthropological fieldwork to synthesize and transform indigenous Caribbean dance movements into theatrical dance forms; this study, subsequently backed by a Rockefeller Foundation Fellowship, culminated in a master's degree in anthropology from the University of Chicago and a doctoral degree in anthropology from Northwestern University.

In 1944 Dunham founded the Katherine Dunham School of Dance in New York, which immediately became the cradle of African American dance until it closed in 1955. Renowned for her technique and the ethnological studies on which she based her performance choreography, her company was the first all-Black dance company to tour the world in the late 1940s and early 1950s.

Dunham's versatility as a performance artist and dancer brought her fame on the Broadway stage and in such *films as *The Emperor Jones* (1939), the *musical *Cabin in the Sky* (1940), *Carnival of Rhythm* (1942), and *Stormy Weather* (1943). Although Katherine Dunham continued to appear in films throughout the 1940s, her chosen medium was the concert stage, upon which she would make social, artistic, and intellectual statements. As a performer she was vividly flamboyant, popularly remembered for her sudden bursts of energy to produce acrobatic executions. But Dunham's work was not purely aesthetic; she used her creative output to contest the social injustices of her time. During the 1930s and 1940s, she used choreography and dramatic presentation to protest *Jim Crow practices in transportation, education, and public accommodations. In 1951 she created *Southland*, a dramatic ballet inspired by the murder of Emmet Till, to depict and condemn southern *lynching and all such practices of race hatred.

In 1972, Dunham directed *Treemonisha*, a ragtime *opera by Scott Joplin, at the Wolf Trap Farm for the Performing Arts in Virginia.

Dunham has authored numerous scholarly articles, magazine *essays, and several books, including *Journey to Accompong* (1946), an account of her experiences as an anthropologist among the Marrons, a people living in isolated mountain regions of Jamaica; *A Touch of Innocence* (1959), a third-person *autobiography of her childhood; *Island Possessed* (1969); *Kassamance, a Fantasy* (1974); and *Dances of Haiti* (1983), the authoritative study on the subject. Katherine Dunham's legacy has been made public by her 1992 donation of a substantial portion of her costume collection, paintings, African and Caribbean folk and contemporary art, her vast collection of musical instruments from around the world, and her papers and films to the Missouri Historical Society in St. Louis.

[*See also* Theater.]

• Ruth Beckford, *Katherine Dunham*, 1979. Darlene Donloe, *Katherine Dunham*, 1993. Constance Valis Hill, "Katherine Dunham's *Southland*: Protest in the Face of Repression," *Dance Research Journal* 26.2 (Fall 1994): 1–10.

—Gregory S. Jackson

Dusk of Dawn. Published in 1940, *Dusk of Dawn: An Essay Toward an Autobiography of a Race Concept* is the second of four works by W. E. B. Du Bois that are considered autobiographical. A generic mix of *autobiography and sociological commentary, *Dusk of Dawn* seeks to reclaim the social and historical identities of early twentieth-century African Americans rather than to narrate and create the life of a singular self. As Du Bois cautions in his preface, *Dusk of Dawn* is "the autobiography of a concept of *race," and not "mere autobiography." That is, Du Bois subordinates his personal chronicle to the collective sociopolitical goal of exposing America's history of racism.

Comprising nine chapters, the work may be divided into three sections. The first four chapters relate personal data about the author. Like other African American life-writers, Du Bois shapes the story of his growing *manhood around his attainment of education. He chronicles his life from his New England childhood in Great Barrington, Massachusetts, to his attendance at Fisk University where he embraced his African American *identity, to his graduation from Harvard University, and, finally, to his study and travel in Germany. Marking the transition between Du Bois's personal autobiography and his sociological analysis is his explanation of his ideological disagreements with his literary and historical forefather Booker T. *Washington, whose promotion of the industrial *education of African Americans and of white patronage differed from Du Bois's vision of the "*Talented Tenth" of African Americans who would become the leaders of their own community. The second section of *Dusk of Dawn* treats the history of the concept of race in America and its effect on both African Americans and whites. Du Bois presents race as a social construct and not as a biological certainty. Refuting the scientific definition of race, he suggests that what unifies nonwhites is not a common genetics but the social heritage of *slavery and discrimination. The last section of *Dusk of Dawn,* consisting of the book's last two chapters, recollects public and controversial moments in the author's life, such as his founding of the *Crisis and his resignation from the NAACP, and includes his commentary on current national and international trends.

Dusk of Dawn illuminates Du Bois's stance on key political issues: he promotes voluntary self-segregation as an advancement for African Americans; he clarifies that although he accepts Marx's economic analysis of society, he is not a communist; and he sees the rise of Hitler as symptomatic of the racism entrenched in Western civilization. Although *Dusk of Dawn* may be placed within the autobiographical tradition established by such writers as Booker T. Washington and James Weldon *Johnson and by the nineteenth-century slave narrators, it departs from its predecessors in its surrender of personal history to sociopolitical analysis. It portrays Du Bois as a man in search of community in a world, an American, and an African American culture based on divisions caused primarily by racial or *class differences.

• Arnold Rampersad, *The Art and Imagination of W. E. B. Du Bois,* 1976. W. E. B. Du Bois, *Dusk of Dawn,* 1940; rpt 1984. William L. Andrews, ed., *Critical Essays on W. E. B. Du Bois,* 1985. Anthony Appiah, "The Uncompleted Argument: Du Bois and the Illusion of Race," in *"Race," Writing, and Difference,* ed. Henry Louis Gates, Jr., 1986, pp. 21–37.

—Mary C. Carruth

Dust Tracks on a Road. Zora Neale *Hurston's 1942 memoir is a book she did not want to write, and many of her admirers have wished she had not written it. Its factual information is often unreliable, its politics are contradictory, and it barely discusses Hurston's literary career, which is ostensibly the reason she wrote it. From the beginning it defies readers' expectations of *autobiography. Only in the third chapter does Hurston begin the story of her own life, and she introduces it with a warning: "This is all hear-say. Maybe some of the details of my birth as told me might be a little inaccurate, but it is pretty well established that I really did get born." Hurston, who regularly took ten years off her age, had reason to practice this deception, but *Dust Tracks* is less than forthcoming about many facts of her life.

The book won the 1942 Anisfield-Wolf Book Award, sponsored by *Saturday Review* magazine, for its contribution to race relations. The prize says more about the state of race relations than about the clarity of Hurston's views. Some of the contradictions are deliberate, as in the chapter "My People, My People," a riff on the paradoxes of race in America. But other contradictions in the book derived from the publisher's last-minute insistence on extensive revisions, notably the deletion of the chapter "Seeing the World As It Is," which included an extended critique of U.S. imperialism in Asia. After the United States entered World War II, editors deemed Hurston's foreign policy views unpatriotic. Without these opinions, the book's politics seemed reactionary to many readers. Editors insisted on other changes as well. Some of the *folklore Hurston recorded was too sexually explicit, and some of her personal opinions libelous. *Dust Tracks* was by far Hurston's most heavily edited book, and few of the changes were for the better.

And yet, passages in *Dust Tracks* are as engaging as any Hurston wrote. Recollections of her childhood are vividly evoked: Hurston chronicles adventures with her imaginary playmate; the "lying sessions" on Joe Clarke's Eatonville store porch, where "God, *Devil, *Brer Rabbit, Brer Fox, Sis Cat . . . and all the wood folk walked and talked like natural men"; and the death of her mother. Equally vibrant are the descriptions of her field work, particularly her friendship with Big Sweet, a woman she met in a sawmill camp in Polk County, Florida, who became her protector and guide, and her interviews with Cudjo Lewis, reputed to be the sole survivor of the last known slave ship to dock on U.S. shores. In other chapters she describes the drama of revival meetings, recounts her friendships with novelist Fannie Hurst and singer-actress Ethel Waters, and offers guarded reflections on romantic love.

Recent editions restore the deleted sections of *Dust Tracks,* although it is impossible to reconstruct from surviving manuscripts the exact text Hurston intended. *Dust Tracks* may be best appreciated as a "lying session," which invites readers to listen to Hurston improvise on various topics.

• Nellie McKay, "Race, Gender, and Cultural Context in Zora Neale Hurston's *Dust Tracks on a Road,*" in *Life/Lines:*

Theorizing Women's Autobiography, eds. Bella Brodzki and Celeste Schenck, 1988, pp. 175–188. Claudine Raynaud, "'Rubbing a Paragraph with a Soft Cloth?' Muted Voices and Editorial Constraints in *Dust Tracks on a Road*," in *De/Colonizing the Subject: the Politics of Gender in Women's Autobiography*, eds. Sidonie Smith and Julia Watson, 1992, pp. 34–64.
—Cheryl A. Wall

Dutchman. Amiri *Baraka's (Le Roi Jones's) most widely known dramatic work, *Dutchman* was first presented at the Cherry Lane Theater in New York City in March 1964. This explosive examination of race relations in America, easily the most talked about play of the year, brought its writer the *Village Voice's* Obie Award in recognition of the play being the most outstanding Off-Broadway production of the year. This highly controversial play was given *film treatment in 1967.

Because of its lean, parable-like quality, *Dutchman* has frequently been compared to the work of Edward Albee, perhaps the leading American dramatist of the period. Several critics have emphasized the similarities between *Dutchman* and Albee's *The Zoo Story* in particular. A masterful example of the writer's handling of fundamental dramatic conventions, *Dutchman* moves, like the train of its setting, with powerful bursts of energy and periodic lulls. Marked by a number of dramatic reversals and rapidly accelerating tension, this play is also characterized by an effective synthesis of realistic and naturalistic tendencies, as well as the suggestion of such mythical influences as the Flying Dutchman, Adam and Eve, and Lilith.

Dutchman must be seen as a highly provocative theatrical handling of the thematic concerns treated in the poems of *The Dead Lecturer* (1964), the volume of guilt-ridden, self-conscious lyrics produced toward the close of Baraka's Beat period. Evidencing the strong influence of Howard University sociologist E. Franklin Frazier, author of *Black Bourgeoisie* (1957), *Dutchman* is a sharply focused indictment of those African Americans who desire to assimilate into mainstream American society. In doing so, these individuals deny all vestiges of the racial past and make every effort to distance themselves from the reality of black existence in America. Given symbolic treatment in the character Clay, such individuals seek validation in the acceptance of white America, as symbolized by the character Lula. As his name implies, Clay is the black American who allows himself to be molded into the image of white, middle-class society. His tragic end, however, at the hands of Lula, evidences the suicidal nature of his longings.

An equally important focal point of *Dutchman* is that of the proper orientation of the black artist, a matter of preeminent concern in the *poetry of *The Dead Lecturer* and various *essays written by Baraka during this period. In search of a legitimate and thoroughly engaged black art, Baraka frequently derides what he perceives as the derivative and evasive creative efforts of black writers, himself included. In "The Myth of a Negro Literature," for example, he urges the black writer to write unapologetically, from "the point of view of the black man in this country: as its victim and its chronicler." Referring to himself as the "great would-be poet" of "some kind of bastard literature," Clay places himself clearly in the rear guard of the movement toward a black sociopolitical consciousness as well as artistic authenticity.

Despite the numerous works that followed *Dutchman*, it remains Baraka's best-known and most critically acclaimed effort. Unequaled in its taut handling of the most pervasive and persistent of national issues, *Dutchman* secured Baraka's reputation as an important American dramatist.

• C. W. E. Bigsby, "Black Drama: The Public Voice," in *The Second Black Renaissance: Essays in Black Literature*, 1980.
—Henry C. Lacey

E

EARLY, GERALD (b. 1952), essayist, cultural critic, editor, educator, and poet. Born in Philadelphia, Gerald Early earned degrees from University of Pennsylvania (BA 1974) and Cornell University (MA 1980, PhD 1982). He is the Merle Kling Professor of Modern Letters and the director of African and Afro-American Studies at Washington University in St. Louis. His first *essay collection, *Tuxedo Junction: Essays on American Culture* (1989), treats cultural topics such as politics, Miss America, boxing, and *jazz. The relevance of popular culture for Early comes from its connection to the marginalized in American society and from the enormous creative involvement of African Americans in it. Through popular culture, musicians, sports figures, and writers have at once asserted and subverted the language and symbolism of mainstream culture. Early notes how the appropriation of white discourse cast two of his literary forebears, Frederick *Douglass and Zora Neale *Hurston, into the double role of criticizing dominant culture while inevitably being part of it. The contrast between Early's youth in a working-class, mainly African American neighborhood and his adult life among many middle-class whites informs his concern with *double consciousness and *identity. He organizes a larger exploration of the double role of African Americans in his editing of *Lure and Loathing: Essays on Race, Identity, and the Ambivalence of Assimilation* (1993).

In editing the two-volume collection *Speech and Power: The African-American Essay and Its Cultural Content from Polemics to Pulpit* (1992–1993), Early asserts that one cannot adequately appreciate African American literature without an ample understanding of the essay in the hands of the African American. He also notes the impact of H. L. Mencken's essays on African American writers, including Richard *Wright and Langston *Hughes. Although conscious of the general influence of the African American autobiographical tradition (especially the work of Douglass) and the sermonic tradition found in James *Baldwin and Martin Luther *King, Jr., Early himself wanted to write essays after reading Amiri *Baraka's *Home: Social Essays* (1966).

In *The Culture of Bruising: Essays on Prizefighting, Literature, and Modern American Culture* (1994), as in *Tuxedo Junction*, he writes less about baseball, boxing, or *music and more about the surrounding symbols, personalities, and narratives from which he then draws meaning or provokes thought. As an essayist, he sets himself apart from rigidly academic criticism and theory and relies on a variety of unconventional references including personal experience, which he uses to verify or enrich his observations about cultural issues. The final essays of *The Culture of Bruising* turn more toward the personal, and he continues this autobiographical work in *Daughters: On Family and Fatherhood* (1995), where stories from his life illuminate familiar concerns such as *class divisions within race, racial prejudice, and assimilation

In addition to the works mentioned above, Early has edited *My Soul's High Song: The Collected Writings of Countee *Cullen, Voice of the Harlem Renaissance* (1991) and has published *One Nation under a Groove: Motown and American Culture* (1995) and *How the War in the Streets Is Won: Poems on the Quest of Love and Faith* (1995). His work has appeared in the annual anthology *Best American Essays*, and he received the National Book Critics Circle Award in 1994 for *The Culture of Bruising*.

—Daniel J. Martin

EASY RAWLINS. Ezekiel (Easy) Rawlins, the protagonist in Walter *Mosley's detective novels, was a World War II veteran who had earned a high school diploma in night school, migrated to South Central Los Angeles, and was "threatenin' on some college" when he lost his job at Champion Aircraft. Needing to make the mortgage payment on his home, he accepted a job searching for a missing blond. Several deaths later, Easy had solved the mystery, gained ten thousand dollars, rescued a sexually abused Mexican boy, and begun a career as a private investigator.

Unlike *Grave Digger Jones, *Coffin Ed Johnson, Aaron Gunner, Mari MacAllister, Joe Cinque, Tamara Hayle, and other African American crime fighters, Easy Rawlins is not an errant police officer struggling to maintain order in the midst of chaos. Rawlins is an ordinary working man with many loyal friends and a good reputation in his community. His forays into detective work, however, are generally marked by a certain amateurism that earns him bruises and beatings and fails to win him any permanent allies in the precincts. During the first four novels, Easy marries, divorces, and adopts two children, making him if not the only, at least one of a few, private investigators whose family life is integral to the plots. Rawlins's sidekick is his best friend, Raymond Alexander or "Mouse," a five-foot-six-inch psychotic whose readiness to kill Easy for an imagined slight is only slightly offset by his willingness to die to save Easy's life.

—Frances Smith Foster

Ebony has been in high demand since its first appearance on newsstands in November 1945. Its readership has grown from twenty-five thousand to over nine million. Its creator, John H. Johnson, envisioned a full-sized picture magazine for African Americans similar to *Time*. The original goal of the magazine was to reflect the "happier," positive aspects of African American lifestyles and everyday achievements throughout the United States. *Ebony* has helped African Americans gain respect for themselves and their heritage by acknowledging the contributions of

African Americans to the development of American culture at a time when the white media either ignored African Americans or only printed articles connecting them to poverty and crime.

Ebony is more than a monthly periodical; it is an African American institution. The mini-conglomerate, Johnson Publications, also publishes *Jet, Ebony Man, *Ebony Jr!*, and several books under its book division. *Ebony's* sister magazine, *Negro Digest*, was published from 1942 until 1951. Over the years *Ebony* has increased its number of text pieces and expanded its social and historical articles. It continues to highlight the achievements of African Americans in various fields, including entertainment, *religion, business, and the arts.

[*See also* Journalism; Periodicals, *article on* Black Periodical Press.]

—Alisha R. Coleman

Ebony Jr!. From May 1973 until it ceased publication in October 1985, *Ebony Jr!* functioned as a major children's literary magazine designed to educate, entertain, and instill positive self-awareness and cultural pride in African American children from ages six to twelve. Founded by John H. Johnson, editor and publisher of adult periodicals such as **Ebony, Black World*, and *Jet, Ebony Jr!* aimed to enrich and expand the reading and comprehension skills of its readers through stories, feature articles, games, and related linguistic activities that presented reading, writing and other learning experiences as both educational and enjoyable. Published monthly, except for two bimonthly summer issues, the colorfully illustrated periodical encouraged children to participate in its Annual Creative Writing Contest and offered adults a user's guide. During the Black-and-proud era, *Ebony Jr!* held the distinction of being the only African American children's educational and entertainment periodical of its type. It was a dominant and pivotal force most essential to the artistic development and mass circulation of African American juvenile literature that would not have otherwise been totally accessible to Black children and adults.

[*See also* Children's and Young Adult Literature; Journalism.]

• John H. Johnson, "Why *Ebony Jr!*," *Ebony Jr!*, May 1973, 4. R. Gordon Kelly, *Children's Periodicals of the United States*, 1984.

—Pearlie Peters

EDUCATION. The education of African Americans in the United States may be divided into four historical periods: (1) the period preceding the Civil War, (2) the period from the Civil War to 1895, (3) the period from 1895 to 1954, and (4) the period since 1954. Each of these periods reflects the changing legal and extralegal status of African Americans at various times in the history of the United States. It is a complex narrative of hope and disappointment, success and failure, black self-help and white philanthropy. It is the story of a people who had a significant intellectual influence on the society that became their home, even as that society had a marked influence on them.

The millions of Africans who were forcibly brought to what would become the United States came from well-developed traditional societies. As such, they brought a wealth of agricultural, scientific, technological, and humanistic knowledge with them that enabled their European captors to tame a vast wilderness in the New World. Their knowledge not only provided the basis for the nation's early economic growth, but also had a significant influence on the development of a distinctive American culture in language, the visual and performing arts, architecture, and *religion.

Many traditional institutions, such as the *family, which Africans used to transmit knowledge between the generations, were either disrupted or destroyed by the slave trade and *slavery however. An additional impediment to the formal education of Africans in the United States was the existence of racial discrimination in law as well as custom.

It was within this restricted social environment, which largely determined the extent and type of education they could receive, that the first period of formal education for African Americans began. The earliest efforts by whites to provide schooling for Africans were undertaken by the Anglican Church's Society for the Propagation of the Gospel in the late seventeenth century. Its pioneering work was soon copied by other white religious denominations. The manifest goal of such schooling was to Christianize Africans, but in the process it also taught them the rudiments of *literacy. Exact figures are unavailable, but it is estimated that by 1776 several hundred Africans were receiving some formal instruction throughout the colonies.

After the revolution, which disrupted schooling throughout the colonies, efforts to provide formal education for African Americans resumed. Despite continued opposition by many whites to teaching African Americans, they attended white-supported as well as African American *church-affiliated and independent schools in all of the former thirteen colonies as well as the new states of Ohio, Indiana, Kentucky, Tennessee, and Louisiana. These schools ranged from the New York Manumission Society's African Free School (1790) to the free African American Resolute Beneficial Society's George Bell School (1818) in Washington, D.C.

Among the singular educational institutions founded between 1790 and 1861 was the Philadelphia Institute for Colored Youth (ICY), which opened its doors in 1837. A day school was added between 1850 and 1852 and Charles L. *Reason became its first principal. Under the leadership of Reason and later Fannie Jackson *Coppin, who was appointed principal in 1869, the institute successfully prepared advanced students for the professions of teaching and the ministry. In 1884, the ICY added an industrial department that remained in existence until 1902. The institute was later reorganized and moved to Cheyney, Pennsylvania, where emphasis was placed again on teacher training. Following its relocation the ICY underwent several name changes: the Cheyney Training School for Teachers (1914); Cheyney State Normal School (1920); Cheyney State Teachers College (1951); and Cheyney State College (1959). Today, Cheyney State is considered the oldest institution of higher education for African Americans in the United States. At least two other institutions for the higher education of African Americans—Lincoln University in Pennsylvania (1854) and Wilberforce University in Ohio (1856)—also trace their beginnings to the pre–Civil War period.

The education of antebellum African Americans was not limited to schools in the United States, however. Some African Americans, such as Benjamin *Banneker, Phillis *Wheatley, and Frederick *Douglass, were largely self-educated, while Francis L. Cardoza, James McCune Smith, and Robert B. Elliott obtained part or all of their education abroad. African American churches, such as Israel Church in Washington, D.C., established *libraries for their congregations and educational societies to help young African American males prepare for the ministry. John Browne *Russwurm and Samuel *Cornish established *Freedom's Journal—the first African American newspaper published in the United States. The purpose of these and other African American–controlled publications was to inform their readers about issues of vital importance to the race, such as slavery and abolitionism. Between 1828 and 1846, free African American communities in Boston, New Bedford, New York City, Albany, Buffalo, Troy, Poughkeepsie, Schenectady, Rochester, Providence, Hartford, Philadelphia, Pittsburgh, Newark, Baltimore, Washington, Cincinnati, Columbus, and Detroit also established *literary societies to spread knowledge among their people and teach them to make better use of their leisure time.

It was not until the second historical period of African American education that formal schooling first became available to the majority of African Americans. The federal government's short-lived Freedmen's Bureau, together with northern missionaries and the newly emancipated freedpeople, established the first system of public schools in the southern United States. Immediately after the Civil War white as well as African American church and missionary groups initiated steps to establish institutions of higher education for African Americans in the South. Passage of the Second Morrill Land Grant College Act in 1890 led to the founding of publicly supported colleges for African Americans, such as Alcorn State and North Carolina A.&T., throughout the South. Hundreds of these public and private colleges and universities were founded between 1865 and 1903.

Although the majority of African American colleges and universities established after the Civil War were coeducational, five of them were either founded as or became women's colleges. These were Barber Scotia (1867), Bennett (1873), Houston-Tillotson (1877), Spelman (1881), and Hartshorn (1884). Founded as a coeducational school, Bennett became a women's college in 1926 under the auspices of the Women's Home Missionary Society of the Methodist Episcopal Church. Bennett is also notable for appointing the first African American—the Reverend Charles N. Gradison—president of a white missionary organization–supported school. In 1955, Bennett scored another educational first by appointing Willa

Player president—the first African American female to head a college for African American women.

Founded as a preparatory school in Sedalia, North Carolina, by Charlotte Hawkins Brown in 1901, Palmer Memorial Institute trained many young African Americans for successful careers. As its chief administrator, teacher, and fund-raiser, Brown expanded the school in later years. She also enjoyed modest success as an author, publishing a book of etiquette, The Correct Thing to Do, to Say, and to Wear (1941), as well as articles and *short stories, the most famous of which was entitled "Mammy: An Appeal to the Heart of the South" (1919). Brown served as president of Palmer until 1952 and continued to serve on its board of directors and as director of finances until 1955. Ten years after her death in 1961, financial difficulties forced the school to close its doors.

Although the industrial education idea was first tried at schools such as Atlanta University and Tougaloo College, it was Hampton Institute (1868), under the leadership of Samuel C. Armstrong, that attempted to make such training the centerpiece of student instruction. Booker T. *Washington—Hampton's most famous graduate as well as the founder and first principal of the Tuskegee Institute (1881)—promoted industrial training as the method of instruction best suited for African Americans, contributing to his famous rift with W. E. B. *Du Bois.

During the last decade of the nineteenth century, racial segregation hardened into an impenetrable system of caste that restricted the social, economic, and political opportunities of African Americans. The Supreme Court's Plessy v. Ferguson (1896) and Cummins v. County Board of Education (1899) decisions merely provided legal support for a system of racial inequality that was reflected in school curricula, per-pupil expenditures, and teachers' salaries. Ironically, however, the same period when separate and unequal was the law of the land might also be considered a golden age in the history of African American education.

Between 1895 and 1954, African Americans initiated a host of efforts to promote their educational progress. The first major African American learned society—the American Negro Academy (ANA)—was founded in 1897 by a group of distinguished African American intellectuals for the promotion of letters, science, and art among the race. Until its demise in 1928, the ANA claimed as members some of the most distinguished intellectuals of its time, including Alexander *Crummell, Francis J. *Grimké, William S. Scarborough, John Hope, William H. Crogman, John W. Cromwell, and James Weldon *Johnson.

The ANA was the progenitor of at least two additional organizations devoted to African American scholarship. In 1911, the Negro Society for Historical Research, which included the notable African American bibliophile and ANA member Arthur A. *Schomburg, was founded in New York state. Four years later Carter G. *Woodson, another ANA member, was the driving force behind the founding of the Association for the Study of Negro Life and History (ASNLH). Under the leadership of Woodson, the ASNLH not only held annual conventions but also promoted the celebration of Negro History Week in the nation's schools. In addition, the organization published *The Negro History Bulletin* for teachers and others interested in disseminating information about the achievements of people of African descent, as well as the *Journal of Negro History* for the publication of scholarly research. The organization's associated publishers group provided an important outlet for books by notable African American scholars, such as Charles H. Wesley and Lorenzo P. Greene, who were usually denied access to white university and commercial presses. In 1942 John H. Johnson founded *Negro Digest* (renamed *Black World* in 1970), which became another important *publishing outlet for African American writers and scholars.

African American secondary education also flowered during this period in many U.S. cities. In Washington, D.C., for example, the M Street High School—the first institution of its kind in the United States—educated a number of important persons, such as the noted civil rights attorney Charles Hamilton Houston. African American high schools in other cities, such as Crispus Attucks in Indianapolis, Charles Sumner in St. Louis, and Booker T. Washington in Atlanta, provided exemplary secondary education for many African American youths.

African American institutions of higher education underwent a significant maturation during this period. Some of these institutions as well as their faculty and graduates are especially noteworthy for their contribution to the development of African American arts and letters. Founded in 1865, Fisk University was the alma mater of W. E. B. Du Bois, who was not only a prolific writer in his own right but, as editor of the NAACP's *Crisis, published the prose and *poetry of young African American authors such as Countee *Cullen, Langston *Hughes, and Zora Neale *Hurston. Two additional African American authors whose lives are associated with Fisk are Frank *Yerby and Nikki *Giovanni.

Established in 1868, Howard University counted many distinguished African American intellectuals among its faculty during the third period of African American education. Howard could claim, for example, the Rhodes Scholar and philosopher Alain *Locke, whose interpretive *anthology The *New Negro (1925) is considered the definitive presentation of the artistic and social goals of the *New Negro movement. Benjamin *Brawley authored The Negro Genius (1937)—one of the earliest studies of the achievements of African Americans in literature and the fine arts. Howard's faculty also included Sterling A. *Brown and Margaret Just Butcher, whose respective monographs, *The Negro in American Fiction* (1938) and *The Negro in American Culture* (1956), chronicle the African American contribution to American literature. Brown's best-known work, *The Negro Caravan* (1941), edited in collaboration with Arthur Davis and Ulysses Lee, is still considered one of the best anthologies of African American literature ever written.

Founded in 1867, Morehouse College can count among its distinguished graduates Benjamin Brawley and the Reverend Martin Luther *King, Jr., who wrote *Stride Toward Freedom* (1958), *Why We Can't Wait* (1964), and *Where Do We Go from Here?* (1967) before his tragic death in 1968. Best known for his rousing *oratory, King's famous *"I Have a Dream" speech at the 1963 March on Washington is not only considered one of the world's great speeches, but is also frequently compared with Abraham *Lincoln's "Gettysburg Address."

The students and faculty of other African American colleges and universities also contributed to the growth of African American literature and literary *criticism. Hampton Institute professor J. Saunders *Redding's To Make a Poet Black (1939) surveyed African American literature. Ralph *Ellison attended Tuskegee Institute for three years before embarking on a literary career. Although best known for his novel *Invisible Man (1952), which won the National Book Award, Ellison also published two collections of *essays—*Shadow and Act (1964) and Going to the Territory (1986).

The Supreme Court's momentous *Brown v. Board of Education* decision in 1954 heralded the beginning of the fourth period of African American education. This decision altered the basic philosophy upon which the development of education among African Americans, particularly in the South, had long been based. Consequently, the racially segregated system of education for African Americans was thrown into confusion and had to be reoriented to the new legal principle of equality within racial desegregation. Consequently, the period since 1954 with regard to African American education may be characterized as one of transition.

The agonizingly slow pace of desegregation at all levels of education following *Brown*, along with a resurgence of black nationalistic sentiment, sparked two significant developments in African American education during the late 1960s. Chief among these was the demand for *Black Studies, which resulted in the creation of several hundred departments and programs of this type in the nation's colleges and universities. The 1960s and early 1970s also saw the founding of many independent African American–owned publishing houses, such as the Johnson Publishing Company, Drum and Spear Press, the Afro-American Publishing Company, *Broadside Press, Black Liberation Publishers, Black Dialogue Press, Emerson Hall Publishers, *Third World Press, *Lotus Press, Black Scholar Press, and Yardbird Press. Although some of these publishers, such as the *Journal of Black Poetry* press, were short-lived, they served as an important outlet for established African American writers such as Gwendolyn *Brooks, as well as emerging talents ranging from Don L. Lee (Haki R. *Madhubuti) and Julius Thompson to Sonia *Sanchez and Nikki Giovanni.

Today African American education confronts innumerable problems. Although more African Americans now attend traditionally white schools, colleges, and universities, education for the majority of them remains as separate and unequal as it was before the *Brown* decision. White suburban flight and shrinking inner-city tax bases have caused the financial collapse of public education in many inner cities, where the majority of African Americans live. Some black colleges and universities face crushing debts that threaten their survival. At the same time, the retention and graduation rates for African American college students, which have improved in recent years, still remain below those of whites. The percentages of African Americans receiving graduate degrees in the 1990s in the arts and humanities generally, as well as in specific disciplines such as African American studies and English, also remain pitifully small. Reductions in financial aid to students at all levels of higher education, as well as conservative attacks against affirmative action, only exacerbate the aforementioned problems. These are all matters of serious concern that African American education must address as it prepares to enter the twenty-first century.

[See also Black Studies; Societies and Clubs.]

• Carter G. Woodson, *The Education of the Negro Prior to 1861*, 1915. Dwight Oliver Wendell Holmes, *The Evolution of the Negro College*, 1934. Dorothy B. Porter, "The Organized Educational Activities of Negro Literary Societies, 1828–1846," *Journal of Negro Education* 5 (Oct. 1936): 555–576. Rayford W. Logan, *Howard University: The First Hundred Years, 1867–1967*, 1969. Frank Bowles and Frank A. DeCosta, *Between Two Worlds: A Profile of Negro Higher Education*, 1971. Martin E. Dann, ed., *The Black Press in America, 1827–1890*, 1971. James M. McPherson, *The Abolitionist Legacy: From Reconstruction to the NAACP*, 1975. Linda Perkins, *Fannie Jackson Coppin and the Institute for Colored Youth*, 1978. Alfred A. Moss, *The American Negro Academy*, 1981. Fannie Jackson-Coppin, *Reminiscences of School Life, and Hints on Teaching*, 1913; rpt. 1987. James D. Anderson, *The Education of Blacks in the South, 1860–1935*, 1988. Abu Abarry, "The African American Legacy in American Literature," *Journal of Black Studies* 20 (June 1990): 379–398.

—Monroe H. Little, Jr.

EDWARDS, JUNIUS (b. 1929), novelist and short story writer. Junius Edwards's presentation of the soldier in his *novel If We Must Die* (1961) and *short stories "Liars Don't Qualify" (1961) and "Duel with the Clock" (1967) is a part of an African American continuum from Frank *Yerby and John O. *Killens to George Davis and John A. *Williams. Like these writers, Edwards's works depict the impact of racial, psychological, and personal problems on the African American soldier. In "Duel with the Clock" a soldier seeks escape from army duty through drugs. In "Liars Don't Qualify" Edwards confronts the hypocrisy of the town that denies returning soldiers the same freedoms they had fought to preserve. This story is also the foundation for *If We Must Die*, a novel of multifaceted irony. Its simplicity of language and character does not belie the dehumanization of African Americans; the entrenched dominance of the southern white power structure during the 1950s; and the *violence that affects the life of any African American perceived as a threat to this structure. The self-esteem of the main character, a returning Korean War veteran, is contrasted with the white voter registrar, who refuses to allow the veteran to register on the grounds that he lied about being a member of the Army Reserve. The veteran is later beaten and threatened with castration. Because Edwards was born in Alexandria, Louisiana, and in his twenties

during the Korean War, his novel may have resulted from observation or experience. He studied in Chicago and at the University of Oslo and won the *Writer's Digest* Short Story Contest (1958) and a Eugene Saxton Fellowship (1959). He continues to publish in such *anthologies as *Calling the Wind* (1993), which Clarence *Major edited.

[See also War Experience.]   —Australia Tarver

ELAW, ZILPHA (c. 1790–?), preacher and spiritual autobiographer. Zilpha Elaw was born around 1790 to free parents who brought her up in the vicinity of Philadelphia, Pennsylvania. In her midteens, while working as a domestic servant, she began to have religious visions. She was converted to Christianity and joined a Methodist society in an outlying region of Philadelphia in 1808. Two years later she married Joseph Elaw, a fuller, and moved with him to Burlington, New Jersey, where their daughter was born in 1812.

During a camp meeting in 1819, Zilpha Elaw became convinced that she had been called to preach the gospel. Her *Memoirs* state that the ministers of the Methodist Society of Burlington endorsed her aspirations and that she enjoyed initial success in her local ministry despite her husband's opposition. In 1823, Joseph Elaw died, forcing his widow to find employment as a *domestic. A few years thereafter Elaw opened a school for African American children in Burlington but closed it two years later because of a growing uneasiness about having neglected her ministry. In the spring of 1828, Elaw undertook a solitary preaching mission to the slaveholding states of Maryland and Virginia. Returning home in 1830, she labored as an itinerant self-supported *preacher in the Middle Atlantic and northeastern states for the next decade. In the summer of 1840, Elaw went to England, where she preached for five years and wrote *Memoirs of the Life, Religious Experience, and Ministerial Travels and Labours of Mrs. Zilpha Elaw, an American Female of Colour*, a 172-page spiritual autobiography and ministerial narrative published in London in 1845. Although the end of Elaw's *Memoirs* suggests that she planned soon to return to the United States, nothing is known about her after 1845. Elaw's *Memoirs* testify vividly to her dauntless independence, her boldly visionary sense of mission, and her radical spiritual individualism.

[See also Autobiography, *article on* Spiritual Autobiography; Feminism; Religion.]

• William L. Andrews, ed., *Sisters of the Spirit: Three Black Women's Autobiographies of the Nineteenth Century*, 1986. Joanne M. Braxton, *Black Women Writing Autobiography*, 1989.

—William L. Andrews

Elbow Room. James Alan *McPherson's 1977 collection of twelve *short stories, *Elbow Room*, won the Pulitzer Prize for literature in 1978. In his second collection of short stories, McPherson explores the search for, or in some cases the resistance to, psychological elbow room in twentieth-century America. For Virginia Valentine of "Elbow Room," the ideal is "a self as big as the world." For others, like the intrusive narrator of the same story, the goal is to discover fresh dimensions of stories and of selfhood. For still others, like the narrator of "Story of a Scar," the point is to resist growth and human intimacy.

McPherson's handling of the latter narrator illustrates what critics have widely praised as one of his greatest achievements: the ability to universalize the experience of African Americans. The narrator of "Story of a Scar" is black, but his need to translate a scarred woman's story into self-confirming terms and thus remain ignorant of his own inadequacies is a human, not a racial trait. The same point may be made of Virginia's desire to broaden her sense of self. She confronts racism at every turn, but her ideal transcends color.

Critics have also admired McPherson's objectivity and craft. Whether they be black or white, cruel or kind, McPherson's characters are multidimensional and emphatically alive, especially in their speech, for *Elbow Room* is rich with compelling voices that ring in the ear long after the reading is over. McPherson's narrative voice is equally engaging. Like a poet, he is as interested in modulating a sentence as he is in telling a tale. As a consequence, his stories convey a satisfying sense of order and narrative control even though many of them describe suffering and struggle.

Two secondary themes in *Elbow Room* are the power of storytelling (for good and ill) and language. Both themes are central in "The Story of a Dead Man" and "Elbow Room." Each is told by a first-person narrator whose conflicts with other characters, and whose dubious assessment of them, is of primary interest.

So is their language. In "The Story of a Dead Man," for example, a law-abiding narrator uses the vocabulary of the white, educated middle class to resist the appeal (to him as well as to others) of a jive-talking and probably criminal cousin. By pitting his polished vocabulary and syntax against his cousin's crude and occasionally obscene vernacular, the narrator protects himself against self-discovery.

Although critics are not unanimous on the issue, most find an optimism in *Elbow Room* that distinguishes it from the bleakness of McPherson's first book, *Hue and Cry* (1969). In addition to claiming that McPherson is mainly concerned with black, not universal, issues, William Domnarski believes that misery and despair prevail in *Elbow Room* as they did in *Hue and Cry* ("The Voices of Misery and Despair," *Arizona Quarterly*, 1986). Edith Blicksilver and Jon Wallace argue otherwise, seeing in *Elbow Room* evidence of McPherson's belief in the possibility of justice, openness, and change.

• Edith Blicksilver, "The Image of Women in Selected Stories by James Alan McPherson," *CLA Journal* 22.4 (1979): 390–401. Jon Wallace, *The Politics of Style in Fiction by Berger, McGuane and McPherson*, 1992.

—Jon Wallace

ELDER, LONNE, III (1931–1996), dramatist and screenwriter. As an artist, Lonne Elder III expressed a commitment to conveying the "truth" about African American life in his works. Toward that end,

Elder drew much of his material from his own life's experiences. His most celebrated *drama, *Ceremonies in Dark Old Men,* is the playwright's attempt to reflect the reality of black experience in the twentieth century. Similarly, Elder's screenplays *Sounder* and *Melinda* are infused with the writer's commitment to realistic, humanistic portrayals of African Americans. Elder, who worked as a political activist, actor, waiter, dock worker, and card dealer, brought that diversity and political commitment to his work as an artist.

Elder was born in Americus, Georgia, in 1931, but moved as an infant with his family to New Jersey. After the death of his father and, soon afterward, his mother, Elder was taken in by an aunt and uncle in Jersey City, New Jersey, where he remained until completing high school. As an adolescent and teenager Elder followed his uncle, who was a numbers runner, through their neighborhood in Jersey City, collecting betting slips. Upon graduating from high school, Elder attended New Jersey State Teachers College, quitting before completing the second semester. He was soon drafted into the army and stationed at Fort Campbell, Kentucky. It was during this time that Elder, who had held an avid interest in reading and writing since he was a child, came into contact with one of his most influential mentors, scholar and poet Robert *Hayden, who was a professor at nearby Fisk University in Nashville, Tennessee. Hayden encouraged Elder's writing and urged him to read as much as possible, giving close attention to form. Elder referred to his time with Hayden as providing a more valuable education than college. Upon leaving the army in 1953, Elder moved to Harlem to pursue his writing career in earnest. He performed a number of odd jobs, including acting, in order to support his writing, and became active with the Harlem Writer's Guild, where his writing was further encouraged by John O. *Killens. For three years during this period (1953–1956), Elder shared an apartment with dramatist Douglas Turner *Ward. This relationship strongly influenced Elder's decision to focus his energies on writing for the theater. During the late 1950s, Elder continued to learn the crafts of writing, acting, and producing for the stage and worked in summer stock and with a mobile acting company. In 1959, at the request of the playwright, Elder made his acting debut as Bobo in Lorraine *Hansberry's A *Raisin in the Sun* at the Ethel Barrymore Theatre in New York City.

Elder's first play, *A Hysterical Turtle in a Rabbit's Race*, which remains unpublished, was written in 1961. The play reveals his concern with the forthright, realistic portrayal of the black *family and contains themes that would emerge in Elder's later works, particularly the celebrated *Ceremonies*.

Between 1963 and 1969, Elder spent his time writing and producing plays, with the earliest version of *Ceremonies* read and staged at Wagner College, New York, in 1965. This powerful work garnered numerous grants and fellowships for the playwright, who then studied drama and filmmaking at Yale University from 1965 to 1967. In 1967 Elder was commissioned by the New York City Mobilization for Youth to write a play. That work, *Charades on East Fourth Street*, was performed at Expo '67 in Montréal, Canada. From 1967 to 1969 he worked as a scriptwriter for the ABC series *N.Y.P.D.* and with the Negro Ensemble Company as coordinator of the directors/playwrights' unit, and acted in Ward's *Day of Absence*. Ward played the main character, Russell B. Parker, in *Ceremonies* when it was produced at the St. Mark's Playhouse by the Negro Ensemble Company in 1969. Later that year, the play moved to the Pocket Theatre. In 1975 Elder adapted the play for television for ABC.

The works he wrote for both stage and screen reflect Elder's fusion of the lessons of his experience with a commitment to the activist role of the artist. His adaptation in 1972 of the children's book *Sounder* into a screenplay that resulted in a critically acclaimed family *film is a testament to this creative vision. Of that production, Elder said that he wanted to create a film that marked a departure from the blaxploitation films of the 1970s. Ironically, just such a film, written by Elder, was released just prior to *Sounder* to mostly negative reviews. Despite its blaxploitation tendencies and Elder's ultimate disappointment in its overall message, that film, *Melinda*, also shows his concern with reflecting realistic, truthful aspects of African American lives. Elder attempted to convey the many struggles imposed on the lives of African Americans and the equally diverse ways in which they respond to and overcome adversity. His works portray the survival techniques African Americans employ in response to various forms of oppression. Although he analyzed the larger actions of the "oppressors" and emphasized the importance of including the "oppressor's" point of view, Elder revealed the effects of those actions on a microcosmic level, in the personal lives and communities of his African American characters. Hence, as in *Ceremonies*, Elder relied on the rituals and traditions of African Americans to transmit larger ideas that reflect the complexity of their lives and communities. As with *Sounder*, Elder infused the play with subtle and overt challenges to the notion that African Americans must succumb to the pressures of living in a racist, sexist society. Instead, Elder suggested, they must determine from within their daily lives the values by which to live and survive intact.

Elder also wrote scripts for the series *McCloud* (1970–1971) and the movies *The Terrible Veil* (1963) and *A Woman Called Moses* (1978), all for NBC. Other screenplays include *Part Two, Sounder* (1976) for ABC and the adaptation of *Bustin' Loose* in 1981 for Universal Pictures.

Just as the imprint of studying, association with, and tutelage of several African American writers and actors can be seen in Elder's work, so his vision as a dramatist and screenwriter influenced the works of a younger generation of dramatists, screenwriters, and contemporary filmmakers, particularly John Singleton and Spike *Lee.

• Liz Gant, "An Interview with Lonne Elder III," *Black World* 22 (Apr. 1973): 38–48. Rochelle Reed, "Lonne Elder III on *Sounder*," *Dialogue on Film* 2 (May 1973): 2–12. Wilsonia E. D. Cherry, "Lonne Elder III," in *DLB*, vol. 38, *Afro-American*

Writers after 1955, eds. Thadious M. Davis and Trudier Harris, 1985, pp. 97–103. "Lonne Elder III," in *Black Literature Criticism*, vol. 1, ed. James P. Draper, 1992, pp. 661–671.

—Karla Y. E. Frye

EL-HAJJ MALIK EL-SHABAZZ. *See* Malcolm X.

ELIZABETH (1766–1866), evangelist, educator, and autobiographer. Elizabeth was born a slave in Maryland to pious, literate Methodist parents. She early experienced divine revelations that continued throughout her life. At age eleven, she was sold away from her family but demonstrated extraordinary courage when she defiantly deserted the plantation to visit her mother. By age thirteen, she had already been called to preach the gospel. She continually evaded this appeal over the next thirty years, partly from fear of the burden of divine ordination, partly in obedience to the counsel of pastors. In 1808, however, Elizabeth preached her first sermon to a small gathering of African American women. This zealous meeting marked the advent of her itinerant evangelism, which was loosely affiliated with the African Methodist Episcopal Church. At about age eighty, she migrated to Michigan, where she established an orphanage. She retired to Pennsylvania, where she dictated her narrative to an unidentified person in 1863. It was republished by Quakers in 1889.

As spiritual *autobiography and *slave narrative, the *Memoir of Old Elizabeth* is significant for its record of a holy woman's interaction with the established church of nineteenth-century America. Although black and white clergy of the Second Great Awakening condoned women's religious exhortation, traditional ministers contended that God did not authorize women to preach. Consequently, without benefit of spouse and child, *formal education, clerical sanction, wealth, or race privilege, Elizabeth experienced great resistance to her ministry. Her autobiography passionately delineates the many challenges she faced because of her intrepid breach of standard social and religious roles for women. The *Memoir of Old Elizabeth* disproves the notion that nineteenth-century African American women were demoralized and servile by asserting the validity of the evangelist's dissension from church patriarchy, her abolitionism in slave states, and her contention that, though poor, black, and female, she is beloved of God.

[*See also* Churches; Feminism.]

• Jean M. Humez, "'My Spirit Eye': Some Functions of Spiritual and Visionary Experience in the Lives of Five Black Women Preachers, 1810–1880," in *Women and the Structure of Society: Selected Research from the Fifth Berkshire Conference on the History of Women*, eds. Barbara J. Harris and JoAnn K. McNamara, 1984, pp. 129–143. William L. Andrews, ed., *Six Women's Slave Narratives*, 1988.

—Joycelyn K. Moody

ELLIS, TREY (b. 1962), novelist, journalist, essayist, and proponent of the New Black Aesthetic. Trey Ellis's *novels, *Platitudes* (1988) and *Home Repairs* (1993), are testimonials to a declaration of artistic independence from earlier generations of African

American writers from the *Harlem Renaissance to the *Black Arts movement. As part of a generation of youth of middle-class parents, Ellis feels that the artistic traditions that he sees as having identified African Americans in the past—themes involving southern poverty, *slavery, rural isolation and deprivation, and militant or radical responses to racism—can be fused with our materialistic and technological culture and should be parodied and satirized. Ellis sees his own development as exemplary, being a part of both the African American and white worlds. In fact he labels himself and others like him as cultural hybrids, being influenced by numerous aspects of African American and Western values.

Ellis was born to parents who were college professors. He attended private high schools in New Haven, Connecticut, before graduating from Phillips Academy, in Andover, Massachusetts. He completed a BA in creative writing at Stanford and has traveled to Italy and Africa. Ellis lives in California.

Both of Ellis's novels have autobiographical strains. The central male characters come from middle-class families, have attended Ivy League schools, and are often the only African Americans in class or in social gatherings. Both characters are urbane easterners who fit very well into the diverse, fast-paced lifestyle of New York. When Ellis wrote *Platitudes* he was working as a translator in Italy, but his talent for recall of the physical and cultural qualities of New York City is remarkable. *Platitudes* is a story about a writer's appeal for help in developing his story about a middle-class youth; it is answered by an established female writer who writes her own version of the story set in the South, in her eyes, a more "valid" reflection of the African American experience. The parody of both writers' versions of the story and of the attention given to female writers like Alice *Walker points to the "platitudes" of Ellis's novel. Ellis's New Black Aesthetic is provocative but ignores some issues for critics such as Martin Favor, Eric Lott, and Tera Hunter. Ellis's call for cultural fluidity and improvisation to inspire and agitate the reader is not as successful in *Home Repairs*. Written in the form of a diary, the novel presents the development of a youth from age sixteen to his early thirties. The diary of the protagonist becomes a tool for emotional release and self-education. Like *Platitudes*, *Home Repairs* is filled with the images of popular culture: songs, brand names, films. However, images of Hugh Heffner and his playboy world seem to overtake the novel. The protagonist's journey to *manhood becomes a one-dimensional preoccupation with sex, sexual fantasies, and conquests. The value of Ellis's new aesthetic is that he represents the next generation of writers to whom audiences look for direction. So far, *Platitudes* exemplifies this new direction best.

[See also New Cultural Mulatto.]

• "Trey Ellis" in *Contemporary Literary Criticism*, vol. 55, ed. Roger Matuz, 1988, pp. 50–54. Trey Ellis, "The New Black Aesthetic," *Callaloo* 12 (Winter 1989): 233–243. Tera Hunter, "'It's a Man's Man's Man's World': Specters of the Old Re-Newed in Afro-American Culture and Criticism," *Callaloo* 12 (Winter 1989): 247–249. Eric Lott, "Response to Trey Ellis's 'The New Black Aesthetic,'" *Callaloo* 12 (Winter 1989): 244–246. Martin Favor, "Ain't Nothin' Like the Real Thing, Baby," *Callaloo* 16 (Summer 1993): 694–705.

—Australia Tarver

ELLISON, RALPH (1914–1994), sculptor, amateur photographer, electrician, collegiate actor, huntsman, editor, essayist, short story writer, and novelist. Ralph Ellison is recognized nationally and internationally as one of America's most prominent literary personalities. Best known as a novelist, he was also a scholar who taught at many of America's most prestigious colleges and universities and a literary and social critic who prodded America to recognize the humanity of its minorities. And like Nick Aaron Ford, Alain *Locke, Hugh M. Gloster, and other Black scholar-critics before him, he was not afraid to chide Black literary artists for not living up to their creative potential. An Uncle Tom to some, a literary father figure to others, Ralph Ellison has secured his niche in the canon of African American and American letters.

Named after another literary giant, Ralph Waldo Emerson, Ralph Waldo Ellison was born in Oklahoma City, Oklahoma, on 1 March 1914. His father, Lewis Alfred Ellison, originally from Abbeyville, South Carolina, was a soldier who had served in Cuba, the Philippine Islands, and China before marrying Ida Millsap of White Oak, Georgia, and migrating to Oklahoma, where he became a construction worker and later a small-scale entrepreneur. Ralph Ellison's great-grandparents were slaves, but Ellison insists that they were strong Black people who, during Reconstruction, held their own against southern whites.

An upwardly mobile couple, Lewis and Ida moved to Oklahoma because it was still considered the American frontier, and the Ellisons felt that it would provide better opportunities than the South for self-realization. Still, Oklahoma was not free of prejudice and racism, and Ellison's childhood was, to some extent, circumscribed, but not overly repressive. His father died when he was three years old, so his mother worked as a *domestic, a custodian, and sometimes as a cook to support her two sons, Ralph and Herbert.

Growing up in the Southwest did not destroy Ellison's self-image or his will to dream. Desiring to break free of the restrictions of *race, Ellison and his childhood friends decided to be Renaissance men, a concept that seems to have acted as a grounding force throughout his life. His activities in high school, his various interests in college—*music, literature, sculpture, *theater—and his vocation and various avocations as an adult indicate that the concept helped him realize his full potential.

Ellison was educated in a segregated school system in Oklahoma, graduating from Douglas High School in 1931. He excelled in music at Douglas High, but like W. E. B. *Du Bois of Great Barrington, Massachusetts, who was given a scholarship to attend Fisk University because the good people of Massachusetts did not want him to integrate their school system, Ellison was given a scholarship to attend Tuskegee Institute (in Alabama) so he would not attend a white college or university in Oklahoma. He was not financially able to attend Tuskegee immediately upon graduation, however, and he matriculated in 1933, after hitching a ride to Alabama on a freight train.

In *Going to the Territory* (1986), his second book of *essays, Ellison describes the South as restrictive because of "the signs and symbols that marked the dividing lines of segregation." He insists, too, that a great deal of his education at Tuskegee was away "from the use of the imagination, away from the attitudes of aggression and courage. . . . There were things you didn't do because the world outside was not about to accommodate you." Ellison was also baffled by the political alliances Tuskegee made with whites, especially the school's relationship with Dr. Robert E. Park, a professor at the University of Chicago's School of Sociology. Ellison observed that it was with the help of Dr. Park, whom many considered the power behind Booker T. *Washington, that Tuskegee gained a national reputation. Yet this same sociologist along with Ernest Burgess wrote *Introduction to the Science of Sociology* (1924), a textbook often used at Tuskegee, in which he disparages the Black man's intellect by affirming that "the Negro is by natural disposition neither an intellectual nor an idealist. . . . He is primarily an artist, loving life for its own sake. His *metier* is expression rather than action. He is, so to speak, the lady among the races."

Despite his misgivings, Ellison found Tuskegee to be a progressive institution. There he met Morteza Sprague, the head of the English department and to whom he later dedicated his first book of essays, *Shadow and Act* (1964). Ellison went to Tuskegee to study music because William L. Dawson, an accomplished composer and choir director, headed the department. True to his Renaissance man ideal, Ellison studied sculpting under the direction of Eva Hamlin, an art instructor who was later responsible for his meeting and studying with August Savage, a Black sculptor in New York.

Though Ellison made no serious formal attempt to study literature at Tuskegee, it was while working in the library there that he began to explore literature, examining T. S. Eliot's *The Waste Land* (1922). Ellison found the poem intriguing because, as he explains in *Shadow and Act*, he was able to relate his musical experience to it: "Somehow its rhythms were often closer to those of *jazz than were those of the Negro poets." It was the fascination with the poem's musicality that really got Ellison interested in writing. As he confesses in *Going to the Territory*, "Somehow in my uninstructed reading of Eliot and Pound, I had recognized a relationship between modern poetry and jazz music. . . . Indeed, such reading and wondering prepared me not simply to meet [Richard] Wright but to seek him out."

In 1936, at the end of his junior year, Ellison left Tuskegee to find summer employment in New York, hoping to earn enough money to return to his studies in the fall. Though he did not earn enough to get back to Tuskegee, he met Arna *Bontemps and Langston *Hughes, and they helped him to meet Richard *Wright, who first encouraged him to write. At the time, Wright was the editor of the *New Challenge*, and for the first issue he persuaded Ellison to review Waters *Turpin's *These Low Grounds*. Ellison then wrote a *short story, "Hymie Bull," for the magazine, and his writing career was begun.

The summer Ellison came to New York, the Great Depression had sapped America's economic and industrial growth. The *Harlem Renaissance, which depended heavily on white philanthropy for its existence, ran out of steam with the crash of 1929, because many of its patrons were not able to continue their financial support of the movement. Fortunately, the New York *Federal Writers' Project was established by the WPA, and Ellison and other writers were able to continue their careers. It was during this time that he worked in the Black community gathering and recording folk material that became an integral aspect of *Invisible Man* (1952).

Ellison's early writings reflect Richard Wright's creative imagination, but as Ellison continued to hone his craft, his writings demonstrated "the richness and complexity" of his own vision. Mark Busby maintains that Ellison's style was unique because of the way he combined such diverse elements as realism, surrealism, *folklore, and myth in *Invisible Man*. Ellison has written short stories, but he is most recognized for this novel, *Shadow and Act*, *Going to the Territory*, and several sections of an unpublished novel. *Invisible Man* is the story of the nameless narrator, a Black man who learns to assert himself. *Shadow and Act* has been described as autobiographical, but it only reveals the young Ellison, the Ellison who, to a great extent, is still under the influence of Wright's vision and feels it necessary to defend himself. *Going to the Territory* reveals a mature Ellison— the literary statesman, the ambassador of good will between the races, the philosopher who believes not so much in the integration of the races as he does in a culturally pluralistic society.

Ellison died on 16 April 1994, leaving unpublished his second novel, which he had begun around 1958. A fire at his summer home in Plainsfield, Massachusetts, destroyed much of the manuscript, forcing him to reconstruct much of what he had already done. At least eight excerpts of the novel have been published, and Ellison appeared on public television and on college campuses reading sections of the work and assuring his audience that the novel was forthcoming. James Alan *McPherson, writing in *Speaking for You* (ed. Kimberly W. Benston, 1987), says of this unpublished work that, though Ellison had written more than enough material for a novel, he was "worried about how the work [would] hold up as a total structure." McPherson maintains that Ellison achieved a unique style, one that combined elements from *minstrelsy and the preaching of Black Baptist ministers, yet had the timing of Count Basie. And of the author's intent McPherson affirms, "Ellison was trying to solve the central problem of American literature. He was trying to find forms invested with enough familiarity to reinvent a much broader and much more diverse world for those who take their provisional identities from groups." In early 1996 it was announced that Ellison had also left behind six unpublished short stories, all probably predating *Invisible Man.* Two were immediately printed in the *New Yorker* (Apr. 29/May 6 issue), and all six were scheduled to be published by Random House in late 1996, together with his previously published stories.

An author's standing in a literary tradition rests on how well he or she perceives that tradition and how much he or she contributes to or changes it. Ellison insists that he was following the great writers of the world and claims as his literary ancestors such giants as T. S. Eliot, Henry James, Ernest Hemingway, Mark Twain, Herman Melville, Fyodor Dostoevsky, and William Faulkner. And since his greatest work, *Invisible Man,* is episodic, he could have added to his literary ancestors Miguel de Cervantes, Alain-Rene Lesage, Thomas Nash, Daniel Defoe, and Henry Fielding. In his use of African American folk material he was following Charles Waddell *Chesnutt and Zora Neale *Hurston. Though Ellison does not claim Richard Wright as a literary ancestor, he did embrace Wright's vision of naturalistic determinism; however, Ellison found that Wright's vision was too narrow to represent the Black experience in America. He believed that Wright's writing, in many instances, only perpetuated in the larger community stereotypical images that the Black writer should attempt to deflate. In *Shadow and Act,* Ellison maintained that too many books written by Black authors were aimed at a white audience, the danger in this being that Black writers then tended to limit themselves to their audience's assumptions about what Black people were like or should be like. Because of this dynamic, the Black writer is reduced to pleading the humanity of his own race, which Ellison saw as the equivalent of questioning whether Blacks were fully human, an indulgence in a false issue that Blacks could ill afford. Believing that a naturalistic/deterministic mode could not define the Black experience, Ellison created a style that embraces the strength, the courage, the endurance, and the promise as well as the uniqueness of the Black experience in America.

In breaking away from the traditional literary path of Black writers, Ellison became a liberator, freeing Black literature from American literary colonialism and bringing it to national and international independence. Ellison's liberating spirit is evident in such writers as McPherson, Ernest J. *Gaines, Leon *Forrest, and Clarence *Major, and in the surrealism of Ishmael *Reed, the folk tradition of Toni *Morrison, the historical tradition exhibited by Gloria *Naylor, and the spirituality of Toni Cade *Bambara. These writers have developed alternative modes of expression or, as Ellison would say, they have realized new literary possibilities. They write not only about the Black experience in America but also about the American experience. While writing in the tradition of the great writers, Ellison blazed a literary trail for younger writers to follow. His innovative style was probably the first step in helping Black writers to break the literary constraints of the sociological tradition in African American letters. And, according to Mark Busby, Ellison has also had a "profound effect" on mainstream writers.

Ralph Ellison, more so than any other Black writer, brought change to the African American (and also to the American) literary canon because he refused to accept prescribed formulas for depicting the Black American. He brought a fierce reality to his vision that neither Blacks nor Caucasians were quite ready to accept. But his truth was/is so eminent, so palpable that neither race could deny it. Ellison will be remembered in literature and in life for making Blacks visible in a society where they had been invisible.

[*See also* Bledsoe, Dr.; Mary Rambo; Norton, Mr.; Ras the Destroyer; Rinehart; Todd Clifton; Trueblood.]

• Robert A. Bone, *The Negro Novel in America,* rev. ed., 1965. Therman B. O'Daniel, "The Image of Man As Protrayed by Ralph Ellison," *CLA Journal* 10 (June 1967): 277–284. Addison Gayle, Jr., ed., *The Black Aesthetic,* 1972. John Hersey, ed., *Ralph Ellison: A Collection of Critical Essays,* 1974. Robert G. O'Meally, *The Craft of Ralph Ellison,* 1980. John F. Callahan, "Chaos, Complexity, and Possibility: The Historical Frequencies of Ralph Waldo Ellison," in *Speaking for You: The Vision of Ralph Ellison,* ed. Kimberly W. Benston, 1987, pp. 125–143. James Alan McPherson, "Invisible Man," in *Speaking for You: The Vision of Ralph Ellison,* ed. Kimberly W. Benston, 1987, pp. 15–29. Jack Bishop, *Ralph Ellison,* 1988. Kerry McSweeney, *Invisible Man: Race and Identity,* 1988. Alan Nadel, *Invisible Critics: Ralph Ellison and the American Canon,* 1988. Mark Busby, *Ralph Ellison,* 1991. Ralph Ellison, *The Collected Essays of Ralph Ellison,* ed. John F. Callahan, 1995.   —Ralph Reckley, Sr.

EL MUHAJIR. *See* Marvin X.

EMIGRATION. The uprooting, transformative experiences of the *Middle Passage, escape from *slavery, and the Great *Migration make mobility a crucial theme in understanding and dramatizing both black captivity and liberation. Combined variously with Christian missionary impulses, separatist and black nationalist ideas, and *Pan-Africanism, these experiences have supplied an enduring power to the idea of African American emigration from the United States. First conceived as a means of Christianizing and "civilizing" the peoples of Africa, the idea of emigration has been fueled by fears that African Americans can never achieve the fullest expression of their racial and human *identity in a white-dominated society, and by desires to escape racial oppression in the United States. Political schemes and literary fantasies have advocated or imagined emigration to Africa as well as establishment of an independent black nation in western Canada, the American West, South and Central America, and the West Indies.

African Americans expressed interest in emigration as early as 1773, when four Massachusetts blacks indicated in a petition to a member of the state assembly their hope of settling in Africa. The 1780s saw the emergence of African American societies in Newport, Providence, Boston, and Philadelphia that served as focal points for emigrationist plans. On 4 January 1787, the abolitionist and masonic organizer Prince Hall joined seventy-five African Americans of Boston in a petition to the state general court, asking for assistance in establishing a colony in Africa. The petition contends that African Americans can never be happy in the white-dominated United States, and that the African climate would be "much more natural [and] agreeable." The primary purpose of emigration, however, would be to enlighten and civilize Africans.

Not all African Americans were primarily interested in serving as missionaries in Africa. In 1774, Phillis *Wheatley refused to accompany a Christian mission to West Africa, arguing that she would look "like a Barbarian" to the Africans, and that she did not know the language of the mission's proposed location. The narratives of James Albert Ukawsaw *Gronniosaw (1774) and Olaudah *Equiano (1789) emphasize their desire to emigrate to England, solely because of the personal *freedom they hope to find there. Paul *Cuffe, an African American ship captain and author of "A Brief Account of the Settlement and Present Situation of the Colony of Sierra Leone" (1812), combined a desire to redeem Africans with an interest in commerce, asking Congress for permission to trade with the British colony of former slaves in Sierra Leone. Toward the end of his life, Cuffe developed a view of emigration as a solution to the problem of slavery. He believed that colonization of American blacks in Africa would hamper the slave trade, and give southern slaveholders a place to deport slaves, which would avert the potentially tragic and bloody slave revolt Cuffe feared.

In 1816, a group including Henry Clay and Andrew Jackson founded an organization that became known as the American Colonization Society (ACS). The ACS initiated the settlement of Liberia on the West African coast. African American leaders who had supported Cuffe's efforts, such as James Forten and Richard *Allen, strongly opposed the ACS. David *Walker in his 1829 Appeal, Allen in his "Letter on Colonization" (1827), and Samuel *Cornish in the pages of the first African American newspaper, *Freedom's Journal, severely criticized the colonization movement, contending that it bolstered the cause of slavery by removing the free black population, and that Liberia was a puppet state controlled by the ACS.

Significantly, many of these same writers enthusiastically supported emigration to the independent black republic of Haiti, a movement that gained popularity in the 1820s. An 1824–1825 effort by the Haitian government to entice American blacks to their country failed: thousands went, but most returned, disillusioned by economic conditions and cultural and linguistic differences. This failure, combined with the paternalism, racism, and proslavery motivations so evident in the ACS's plans, served to kill off most African American interest in emigration over the next two decades.

The passage of the Fugitive Slave Act of 1850 reinvigorated emigrationist impulses. Canada, as the destination of many fugitives, became the focus of much emigrationist attention. Several African Americans who emigrated or escaped to Canada wrote in favor of their adopted country as a haven for American blacks, including Henry *Bibb, author of a narrative of his own escape and editor of the newspaper Voice of the Fugitive, and Mary Ann *Shadd, author of the pamphlets Hints to the Colored People of the North (1849) and Notes of Canada West (1852), both of which encourage fugitives to come to Canada. William Wells *Brown's play, The *Escape, or A Leap for Freedom (1858), concerns the escape of three slaves to Canada, and Joshua McCarter Simpson's poem, "Away to Canada" (1852), expresses the attractions of Canada to the tune of "O Susanna!"

Frederick *Douglass led the opposition to emigration, believing that such schemes were impractical and only distracted from the complex problems of ending slavery and coexisting in equality with whites. Yet on the eve of the Civil War Douglass editorialized seriously in Frederick Douglass's Monthly about the prospect of resettlement in the West Indies. Henry Highland *Garnet, James Theodore Holly, Samuel Ringgold Ward, and James Monroe *Whitfield were among the most articulate exponents of emigration during this period. Whitfield's 1853 collection, America and Other Poems, eloquently expresses his alienation from the United States.

Martin R. *Delany is the most important nineteenth-century literary figure associated with emigration. His 1852 study, The Condition, Elevation, Emigration, and Destiny of the Colored People of the United States, advocates economic self-sufficiency for African Americans, and despairs of the likelihood of blacks ever achieving genuine citizenship in the United States. Believing that Africans are racially superior because, unlike whites, they can adapt to any climate, Delany turned to Central or South America, especially Nicaragua and New Granada, as a potential home for African Americans. The hero of Delany's *novel, *Blake, or The Huts of America (printed serially 1859, 1861–1862), escapes from slavery and travels through the South, encouraging and organizing a general *insurrection, then leads a black revolution in Cuba. Although the novel does not explicitly promote mass emigration, Cuba is seen as a more likely stage for a successful slave revolt than America.

Despite continued skepticism, "Liberia fever" would never completely disappear in the nineteenth century, stimulated by the writings of two Liberian colonists, Edward Wilmot *Blyden and Alexander *Crummell, forerunners of Pan-Africanism. Blyden defended Liberia from Delany's attacks, crediting Cuffe and not the ACS for its founding, and opposed Delany's scheme for colonization in Central and South America, believing that American blacks had no right to the land and that indigenous peoples would oppose their presence.

The post-Reconstruction age of reaction in the South sparked renewed interest among the African American population in going elsewhere, to Liberia or to the American West, despite Frederick Douglass's continued opposition. The Exoduster movement of the 1870s culminated in the 1879–1880 exodus of thousands of African Americans from Mississippi and Louisiana to Kansas, dramatized by John Willis Menard's poem, "Good-Bye! Off for Kansas" (1879). A more recent depiction of black migration to the West can be found in Pearl *Cleage's play, *Flyin' West* (1992), about life in the all-black town of Nicodemus, Kansas.

While projects for large-scale emigration, exemplified by AME bishop Henry McNeal Turner's so-called African Dream, continued to attract support into the next century, fiction began to treat emigration as an individual response to the contradictions and pressures of being black in America. Oscar *Micheaux's protagonists in *The Conquest: The Story of a Negro Pioneer* (1913) and *The Homesteader* (1917; the basis of Micheaux's first *film in 1919) seek refuge as homesteaders in South Dakota, though they fail to escape the long arm of racism. *American Cavalryman* (1917) by Henry F. *Downing, a former U.S. consul to Angola, describes Liberia as a stage for the fullest realization of black identity. An extreme form of African American alienation can be found in Sutton E. *Griggs's *Overshadowed* (1901), whose protagonist rejects both Africa and America as white-dominated, and declares himself a "citizen of the ocean."

Marcus *Garvey's back to Africa movement, the first great mass movement of African Americans, had no real literary equivalent. As the integrationist *civil rights movement took shape under the leadership of the NAACP, the idea of emigration gradually lost political favor, although on the cultural front Pan-Africanists like W. E. B. *Du Bois clung to nationalist ideals that eventually flowered in *Negritude. Arna *Bontemps's 1927 *short story, "The Return," envisions only a metaphorical return to Africa. In Nella *Larsen's novel *Passing* (1927), the theme of emigration serves to highlight Irene Redfield's difficulty in accepting her black identity and fascination with "*passing" as white. Ralph *Ellison's *Invisible Man* (1952), insisting on the Americanness of African Americans, contains in its portrayal of *Ras the Destroyer an explicit rejection of Marcus Garvey and emigration. Other modern novels, such as William Gardner *Smith's *The Stone Face* (1963) and Clarence *Major's *NO* (1973), depict their protagonists' experiences in other countries as no more than preparation for returning to the United States.

The theme of emigration, however, does reappear in other modern novels, as part of a rebirth of interest in African American *history. In William Melvin *Kelley's *A Different Drummer* (1962), Tucker Caliban renounces all connections with his family's history as slaves, and triggers a mass exodus of African Americans from his southern state. By contrast, Paule *Marshall's *Praisesong for the Widow* (1983) and Toni *Morrison's *Song of Solomon* (1977) emphasize the recovery of history in drawing on the folktale of the "flying Africans," using magical realism and fantasy to reclaim one of the oldest examples of the emigrationist impulse in African American culture.

[*See also* Black Nationalism; Expatriatism.]

• James Redkey, *Black Exodus: Black Nationalist and Back-to-Africa Movements, 1890–1910*, 1969. Floyd J. Miller, *The Search for a Black Nationality: Black Emigration and Colonization 1787–1863*, 1975. Neil Irvin Painter, *Exodusters*, 1977. Wilson Moses, *The Golden Age of Black Nationalism, 1850–1925*, 1978. Sterling Stuckey, *Slave Culture*, 1987. V. P. Franklin, *Black Self-Determination: A Cultural History of African-American Resistance*, 2d ed., 1992.
—Gary Ashwill

ENTERTAINER. Reflecting the culture from which they derive their characters, African American writers have drawn upon several types of entertainers to texture their works. These range from a popular fascination with musicians to depictions of aspiring actors. The landscape of works set in *slavery is almost always peopled with singers, banjo players, or both. Frederick *Douglass comments on singers of *spirituals in his narrative (1845), and there are stock scenes in later works, such as Maya *Angelou's *I Know Why the Caged Bird Sings* (1970) and James *Baldwin's *Just above My Head* (1979), of performances of spirituals; Baldwin also focuses on Arthur Montana, an internationally acclaimed gospel singer, in that novel. William Wells *Brown, ever attentive to the nuances of African American culture, includes banjo players in *Clotel* (1853). In the 1920s, Willis *Richardson's play, *The Broken Banjo*, focused on what happens to a young man who loses his favorite instrument. Shortly before this play, James Weldon *Johnson had featured a classical virtuoso in the unnamed narrator of his *Autobiography of an Ex-Colored Man* (1912); the narrator makes the mistake of wanting to "classisize" traditional African American songs but is forced to give up that somewhat wrongheaded inclination when he sells his birthright "for a mess of pottage."

*Jazz and *blues musicians such as Harriet Williams in Langston *Hughes's *Not without Laughter* (1930), *Rufus and Ida Scott (Baldwin, *Another Country*, 1962), Sonny (Baldwin, "Sonny's Blues," 1957), *Ursa Corregidora (Gayl *Jones, *Corregidora*, 1975), and *Shug Avery (Alice *Walker, *The *Color Purple*, 1982) exist in worlds where music is as much salvation as it is entertainment. Their lives as performers enable most of these characters to deal with the difficult problems of their fictional existences, for the *music, as well illustrated in Hughes's "The *Weary Blues" (1926), provides cathartic release from everyday problems.

A variety of other entertainers also people the literature. Claude *McKay uses a dancer in "Harlem Dancer" (1922) to comment on the prostitution of African American art and talent during the *Harlem Renaissance. The dancer, in the manner of Tina Turner's "Private Dancer," exposes her body and her skills before a nearly drooling audience that takes pleasure from her talent without really caring about her. In *Through the Ivory Gate* (1992), Rita *Dove features a black woman, Virginia, who is a member of "Puppets & People" as well as a cello player, which makes for an unusual combination of entertainers in African American literature. Traditional actors also appear in the literature. Baldwin's Leo Proudhammer (*Tell Me How Long the Train's Been Gone*, 1968) is a noteworthy example. More recently, Horace Cross is hopelessly infatuated with an actor in Randall *Kenan's *A Visitation of Spirits* (1989).

African American writers have also created a number of works in homage to historical entertainers. These include Sterling A. *Brown's "Ma *Rainey" (1932), Robert *Hayden's "Homage to the Empress of the Blues" (for Bessie *Smith, 1962), and Nikki *Giovanni's appreciation for Aretha *Franklin in "Poem for Aretha" (1970). Indeed, these entertainers, among others, have become icons in the culture, touchstones for success who serve as inspiration for the fictional audiences as well as for the writers. Inclusion of such figures is another way for African American writers to texture their works with the culture of which they are a part.

• Donald Bogle, *Toms, Coons, Mulattoes, Mammies and Bucks*, 1973. Joseph Boskin, *Sambo: The Rise and Demise of an American Jester*, 1986.   —Trudier Harris

EPISTOLARY NOVEL. The epistolary novel, a form using letters as the principal means of narration, has not been a common genre within African American literature, just as it has not been prominent in American writing generally. Much of black American fiction deals with an oral culture and also focuses more often on action than on the reflection inherent in the epistolary tradition. The only text that relies entirely on the letter-writing form is Alice *Walker's *The *Color Purple* (1982). Walker fictionally justifies it as the means by which *Celie can tell her story of abuse and victimization and still present the reality of the silenced woman. Her "letters to God" reveal the emotional and physical effects of domestic *violence and recovery by presenting them as part of everyday experience. The writing also becomes a means of generating a history of suffering in the face of denial by the victimizers. In addition, the *letters from Celie's sister provide Walker with the opportunity to describe colonial Africa without relying on narrative exposition. The epistolary form here provides the recreation of the history of the oppressed from the inside.

Other texts have developed variations on the genre. Alice Moore *Dunbar-Nelson wrote a *novel around 1899 in the form of a diary. *The Confessions of a Lazy Woman* was the reflections of a woman who did nothing but comment on the stupidities of her neighbors. It was accepted for publication but was never brought into print.

More recently Sherley Anne *Williams has used a journal format as part of the structure of *Dessa Rose* (1986). *Signifying on the "authenticating documents" of whites used to validate *slave narratives and on William Styron's *The Confessions of Nat Turner* (1987), Williams uses the device to expose the racist underpinnings of "objective" white descriptions of black personality and behavior. In a manner similar to Toni *Morrison's use of lists in *Beloved* (1987), Williams suggests the power of language to control and oppress through naming and defining those not permitted to speak or write for themselves. Through not only characterization and speculation, but also the rendering of black *speech and dialect,

Adam Nehemiah dehumanizes Dessa even as he attempts to "understand" her.

Trey *Ellis uses an exchange of letters as a postmodern device in *Platitudes* (1988). An experimental writer invites suggestions on improving his latest, blatantly sexist novel. A radical feminist writes to castigate him and to offer her own version of the story. The correspondence becomes a plotline of the coming together of opposites in this metafiction.

[*See also* Diaries and Journals.]

• Godfrey Frank Singer, *The Epistolary Novel: Its Origin, Development, Decline, and Residuary Influence*, 1963. Natasha Wurzbach, ed., *The Novel in Letters: Epistolary Fiction in the Early English Novel, 1678–1740*, 1969. Janet Gurkin Altman, *Epistolarity: Approaches to a Form*, 1982. Bernard W. Bell, *The Afro-American Novel and Its Tradition*, 1987. Gloria T. Hull, *Color, Sex, and Poetry: Three Women Writers of the Harlem Renaissance*, 1987. Gay Wilentz, *Binding Cultures: Black Women Writers in Africa and the Diaspora*, 1992.

—Keith E. Byerman

EQUIANO, OLAUDAH (1745–1797), slave and spiritual autobiographer, creator of the slave narrative genre, and abolitionist leader. Olaudah Equiano (later also known as Gustavus Vassa) was eleven years of age when he was kidnapped in the African country that is now known as Nigeria. As he was taken to the slave ship on the coast, he witnessed the corrupting influences of European intrusions upon the African societies. Sent to Barbados and then to Virginia, he escaped a sentence to plantation *slavery when he was purchased by a British captain who changed the youth's name to Gustavus Vassa and placed him in service aboard ship. Equiano spent the next ten years of his captivity on several vessels engaged in commerce and sometimes in naval warfare.

After his daily slave duties, the industrious and thrifty Equiano worked at various private enterprises that eventually enabled him to save enough funds to purchase himself out of bondage. On 10 July 1766, he became a freeman, but continued working aboard ships. In the ensuing years, Equiano traveled to many countries in Europe, the Middle East, the Caribbean, and North, Central, and South America. He even journeyed on a scientific expedition to the Arctic regions.

When he served as a young slave on various ships, Equiano formed close relationships with the sailors, who taught him how to read and introduced him to Christianity. They fired up a lifelong desire for learning that he especially pursued whenever he visited friends in England. The religious spark ignited by the sailors led in later years to a lengthy and intense spiritual conversion experience, after which Equiano chose the Methodist faith. Eventually he settled in England, where in 1792 Equiano married the Englishwoman Susanna Cullen; they had two daughters.

In the 1780s, when the British Parliament debated whether to end the slave trade, Equiano became an active participant in the *antislavery movement. In order to sway the minds of those involved in the controversy, he undertook the writing of a two-volume *autobiography describing his life of bondage and *freedom and giving his eyewitness account of the sufferings and injustices endured by thousands of enslaved men and women. The result was *The Interesting Narrative of the Life of Olaudah Equiano, or Gustavus Vassa, the African,* which appeared in England in 1789, and in 1791 in the United States. From 1789 to 1794 the *Narrative* ran through eight editions in Great Britain. Translations were made into Dutch in 1790, German in 1792, and Russian in 1794. Nineteen editions were produced in the United States and Europe by the mid-nineteenth century.

In his lengthy account, Equiano mixes his personal remembrances of African societies, slave experiences, and a freeman's life in the West with the facts and ideas he derived from his wide range of reading in works of *history, geography, *religion, politics, and commerce. He is at his best when re-creating the opposing feelings of awe and fear that grip him when he comes into contact with both the marvels and terrors of the Western world. A vital part of Equiano's narrative is the winning of his freedom. He becomes a new man as he is reborn into a society where he now can operate on a free plane of existence. His physical and spiritual liberations enable him to complete himself as a person who can assume new and commanding roles in life. These roles include his taking charge of a vessel during a storm at sea, serving as a parson when required, and even acting as an overseer of slaves. In his mature years, the proudest roles are those of abolitionist leader and autobiographer. Thus readers of the *Interesting Narrative* come to see Equiano as an intelligent, clever, and complex man.

Equiano's *slave narrative displays one of the first attempts by an African writer to enter the literary world of Western culture. Equiano followed the spiritual autobiographical tradition of St. Augustine and John Bunyan, but added to it a new dimension consisting of social protest. His new type of personal story influenced how black narrative literature was written throughout the antislavery era. Thus Equiano's autobiography became the prototype of the slave narratives that appeared after his great work. Looking over the whole range of African American literature, one can see the structure and elements of the slave narrative genre in such important works as Frederick *Douglass's *Narrative of the Life of Frederick Douglass* (1845), Harriet Beecher *Stowe's *Uncle Tom's Cabin* (1852), Harriet A. *Jacobs's *Incidents in the Life of a Slave Girl* (1861), Richard *Wright's *Black Boy* (1945), Ralph *Ellison's *Invisible Man* (1952), and Toni *Morrison's *Beloved* (1987).

• William L. Andrews, *To Tell a Free Story: The First Century of Afro-American Autobiography, 1760–1865,* 1986. Angelo Costanzo, *Surprizing Narrative: Olaudah Equiano and the Beginnings of Black Autobiography,* 1987. Keith A. Sandiford, *Measuring the Moment: Strategies of Protest in Eighteenth-Century Afro-English Writing,* 1988. Paul Edwards, introduction to *The Life of Olaudah Equiano,* 1989.

—Angelo Costanzo

Escape, The. Although erroneously thought to be the first play written by an African American, William Wells *Brown's closet *drama *The Escape, or A Leap for Freedom* was the first dramatic work by an African American to be published. Issued as an octavo pamphlet of fifty-two pages by Robert F. Wallcut of Boston in 1858, the publication of *The Escape* attests to its popularity and confirms the play's value as antislavery propaganda. Brown claims in the author's preface to have written the play for his "own amusement and not with the remotest thought that it would ever be seen by the public eye." However after his friends arranged for him to read it "before a Literary Society," public readings soon followed with great success. Encomiums published in the 1858 octavo suggest that at least some viewed the work not only as propaganda but also as serious drama. Typical of the praise lavished on the play is the excerpt from the *Auburn* (N.Y.) *Daily Advertiser* quoted in the octavo: "MR. BROWN'S Drama is, in itself, a masterly refutation of all apologies for *slavery, and abounds in wit, satire, philosophy, argument and facts, all ingeniously interwoven into one of the most interesting dramatic compositions of modern times." In addition to the acclaim provided by the publisher, positive notice of *The Escape* also appears in William Lloyd Garrison's the *Liberator* (10 Sept. 1858; 8 Oct. 1858) and the *National Anti-Slavery Standard* (25 Dec. 1858).

Less than riveting as drama, *The Escape* has real value as antislavery propaganda and genuine potential to stir an audience when read by an orator of even moderate skill. Its flowery and elevated diction, however, deny the characters speech that approximates dialogue between real people. Although much of the play's soaring rhetoric sounds stilted and false, "the main features in the Drama are true," Brown affirms, and his audience no doubt concurred.

The Escape dramatizes the struggle of Melinda and her husband to reach *freedom in Canada. A comely *mulatto woman, Melinda endures the unremitting sexual harassment of her master, Dr. Gaines. Prefiguring Dr. Flint in Harriet A. *Jacobs' 1861 *Incidents in the Life of a Slave Girl,* Gaines torments Melinda even as he promises privileges, money, and freedom if she would abandon her husband and enter into a liaison with her master. In addition to the abuse of Dr. Gaines, Melinda suffers the harsh and jealous maltreatment of her mistress, Mrs. Gaines. After predictable trials and tribulations the slave couple finally escape to freedom in Canada.

Readers familiar with Brown's 1853 novel *Clotel* will recognize themes common to the novel and the play, most notably the sexual abuse of black women in slavery, the development of a class of phenotypically white women to use as sex slaves, the systematic and intentional intellectual degradation and deprivation of slaves, and the accompanying pathologies that deform the personality of the slave and slave holder. Yet, even as it focuses on these themes, *The Escape* celebrates the love of a couple willing to endure any hardship to remain true to each other.

• William Edward Farrison, *William Wells Brown: Author and Reformer,* 1969.   —Anthony Gerard Barthelemy

ESSAY. The essay is usually the most neglected genre of black literary endeavor. This is probably a reflection of the status of the essay in both the literary marketplace and in the academy. Essay writing generally is seen as a fugitive art, occasional pieces of momentary interest by writers whose main artistic preoccupations are with other "major" forms: *novels, *drama, *poetry, or book-length nonfiction treatises. This view is particularly unfortunate as African Americans have made considerable use of the essay as both a confessional and polemical device and such writing constitutes an important portion of their literary tradition. Indeed, some African Americans arguably have done their best and most significant writing in this mode. For instance, among the most influential books written by black writers during the 1960s were The *Fire Next Time (1963) by James *Baldwin, *Home: Social Essays (1966) by LeRoi Jones (Amiri *Baraka), and *Soul on Ice (1968) by Eldridge *Cleaver; all of them essay collections. Current writers such as Henry Louis *Gates, Jr., Michael Eric Dyson, June *Jordan, bell *hooks, Cornel *West, Stanley *Crouch, and Glen Loury make extensive use of this form; among their most important works have been collections of essays. That we find today more black intellectuals and blacks associated with the academy making use of this literary form is striking.

The essay as both confession and polemic has been popular for the black writer because, unlike most other writers in the United States, he or she sees his or her condition in almost exclusively political terms and, moreover, sees the vocation of writing as both a reflection and a result of this political condition. This is why black writers have produced few examples of belles-lettres essays. The essay is where one confesses, one argues, one teaches, one pleads, one exhorts in tones that may vary from the straightforward to the ironic, from the religious to the scientific. It is not an occasion simply to write beautifully crafted prose, although there have been several black essayists who have done that in the process of achieving something else.

James Baldwin is the most readily identified black essayist. Some of his individual essays have become among the most famous examples of the art form in the twentieth century, and many feel that he was perhaps the best American essayist of the post–World War II era. But several other black writers have produced highly esteemed volumes of essays, including Ralph *Ellison, whose *Shadow and Act (1964) and Going to the Territory (1986) have had considerable impact on African American intellectuals and on the study of African American literature; Richard *Wright, whose White Man; Listen (1957), is among the more important works on the meaning of colonialism; and Alice *Walker, whose *In Search of Our Mothers' Gardens (1983) is probably among the richest displays of a black feminist art ever constructed. But as in virtually every other aspect of African American literary life, it is W. E. B. *Du Bois who might be called the father of the modern African American essay. His collection, The *Souls of Black Folk (1903), remains the most powerful example of how deftly, and with great artistic aplomb, the African American writer can use the essay as both polemic and confession.

[See also Literary History.]

• Arthur P. Davis, et. al., The Negro Caravan, 1941. Herbert Hill, Anger and Beyond: The Negro Writer in the United States, 1966. Addison Gayle, Black Expression: Essays by and about Black Americans in the Creative Arts, 1969. Darwin Turner, Black American Literature Essays, 1969. Gerald Early, Speech and Power: The African-American Essay and Its Cultural Content from Polemics to Pulpit, 2 vols., 1992–1993.

—Gerald Early

EVA MEDINA CANADA narrates Gayl *Jones's *Eva's Man (1976). Simultaneously drawn to and repelled by men, she has experienced a series of abusive sexual encounters from an early age, beginning with her unwilling submission to a little boy's probing with a dirty Popsicle stick. Her mother's lover tries to molest her, her cousin tries to seduce her, and she briefly marries an older man who virtually imprisons her out of jealousy. Believing the stories of her mother's friend, Miss Billie, who maintains that women cannot control their own bodies and men cannot control their responses to women, Eva is generally fatalistic and passive, but she does stab a man who grabs her. This eruption of long-suppressed *violence foreshadows the crime that culminates in her madness: poisoning then orally castrating her lover.

Eva is identified with three mythical women whose hold on men proves fatal: Medusa, Eve (in Eva's case, the forbidden fruit of knowledge and power is the penis), and a local figure called the Queen Bee. While the Queen Bee believes her love to be deadly for any man and eventually commits suicide to spare her lover, Eva enacts her own version of the Queen Bee's story. Locked in a prison asylum, refusing to explain her motives to anyone—including the reader—Eva weaves her increasingly disjointed narrative out of interrogations, visions, and memories. Through her, Jones dramatizes a woman trapped by the pernicious *stereotypes of black women's *sexuality.

• Keith Byerman, Fingering the Jagged Grain: Tradition and Form in Recent Black Fiction, 1985. Sally Robinson, Engendering the Subject: Gender and Self-Representation in Contemporary Women's Fiction, 1991.

—Amy S. Gottfried

EVANS, MARI, poet, dramatist, short fiction writer, children's writer, editor, essayist, and lecturer. Since the 1960s, Mari Evans has produced a body of works unique for its personal sensitivity, political tenor, and precisely crafted diction and structures. Although principally known for her *poetry, Mari Evans's *dramas have had repeated productions over the years, and her children's books have been noted as models for unobtrusively premising a constructive, nurturing worldview. Her essays and lectures are marked by explicit political commitment, cogent logic, and quiet fervor.

Evans was born in Toledo, Ohio, in 1923. Her father proved to be a tremendous early influence upon her, and she recounts in an autobiographic essay, "My Father's Passage" (1984), how he saved her first story. She had written it while in the fourth grade, and it had appeared in the school paper. Her father not only saved it, but noted with pride his daughter's achievement. "My Father's Passage" is also important because Evans emphasizes her perception of writing as a craft, a professional occupation.

Evans attended public schools in Toledo as well as the University of Toledo. Although she studied fashion design, she did not pursue it as a career option. Her attention turned instead to poetry, almost unintentionally she asserts. Fortuitously she began her professional writing career as an assistant editor in a manufacturing firm where precision and discipline are imperative. Even in her first, intensely personal volume *Where Is All the Music?* (1968), this discipline is evident. These are poems celebrating all aspects of personal love affairs, from love at first sight to the endurance that masters disappointment and loneliness. Also evident is a hallmark of Evans's style: dispassionate language conveying profoundly moving fact and feeling.

Having received a Woodrow Wilson grant in 1968, Evans began the first of what would become a series of appointments in American universities in 1969. She was an instructor at Indiana University at Purdue, where she taught courses in African American literature and served as writer in residence. In 1970 she published *I Am a Black Woman* (incorporating most of the poems from *Music*), a more complex collection divided into titled sections that gradually expand focus to embrace the whole African American community. The first two sections concern romantic love. The next two treat victims of society's injustices and indifference, especially children. The final and longest section, "A Black Oneness, A Black Strength" draws the most overtly political inferences from this exploration of love. The effect of the poems is cumulative; although each poem is a complete, self-sufficient entity, it is enriched by its position among the others. The success of the poetry in 1970 was matched by Evans receiving an award for the most distinguished book of poetry by an Indiana writer.

Between 1970 and 1978 Evans was assistant professor and writer in residence at Indiana University, Bloomington, where she continued to write and publish, and to be recognized for her achievements. She received an honorary degree from Marion College in 1975, and she resided for a time at the MacDowell Colony. She had a visiting assistant professor appointment at Purdue University between 1978 and 1980, the same year she also had an appointment at Washington University in St. Louis, and she has visited at Cornell, SUNY Albany, and Spelman College.

In 1981 she published *Nightstar 1973–1978*, which is also arranged in titled sections that progress from the personal to the communal and political. These poems employ more experimental techniques: more complex exploitation of typography (capitalization, indentations, length of phrase or line); more expansive use of rhetorical figures such as anaphora, reiteration, direct exhortation to the reader (using "we," not "you"); a greater diversity of speakers and portraiture; careful use of African American idiom in

ways that foster the reader's respect for and identification with the speaker. Throughout, *Nightstar* reveals rather than claims heroism and grandeur as well as the simple joys of African American life.

Evans has combined teaching, writing, and publishing with many other activities. She directed *The Black Experience*, a television program in Indianapolis, between 1968 and 1973. She has consulted for agencies such as the National Endowment for the Arts (1969–1970), as well as for the Indiana Arts Commission (1976–1977). She is a popular and much-sought lecturer, and she has made repeated appearances at the National Black Writers Festival held biannually at Medgar Evers College.

A Dark and Splendid Mass (1992) represents a new development in Evans's poetic style. The only poems of romantic love celebrate the decisive rejection of perfidious lovers. All the poems are short paeans to the indomitable courage of ordinary suffering people. With a variety of personae, situations, locales, abuse, or deprivations, the poems convincingly convey the emotive perspective of the victim-survivor or hero. The book ends with poems of hard-nosed faith and hope.

Black Women Writers 1950–1980, A Critical Evaluation (1983), edited by Evans, is a unique anthology treating fifteen writers. For each there is an autobiographical statement of artistic intent, two essays of different critical perspectives, and a "bio-selected bibliography." The text holds a wide spectrum of African American critical approaches to very diverse authors.

The kind of professional service that Evans provided by becoming an anthologist is matched by her commitment to community service. She is active in movements for prison reform and against capital punishment, especially in some specific egregious cases. She works with local community organizations and with theater groups. She has a demanding lecture schedule. These activities express in action an implication that pervades her writing: that self-fulfillment for the African American must include identification with the deprived, the oppressed, and efforts to enhance the health and strength of the community.

This emphasis on a wholesome perspective on the African American community is seen in Evans's books for children, *I Look at Me* (1973), *JD* (1973), *Singing Black* (1976), and *Jim Flying High* (1979). Text and illustrations are carefully integrated to reinforce this impression. Unfamiliar words are introduced in self-explanatory contexts, and the stories encourage the reader to exult in selfhood and community.

Among her dramas, *Rivers of My Song* (first performed in 1977), *Portrait of a Man* and *Boochie* (both 1979), and *Eyes* (1979), an adaptation of Zora Neale *Hurston's *Their Eyes Were Watching God*, have all received several productions in various American cities. The first is ritualistic theater combining *music, dancers, and actors using both poetry and prose. The form is an excellent example of traditional African American theatrical productions. *Portrait of a Man* uses a divided stage. On one side we see episodes in the experience of a courageous and industrious young African American man, an experience that includes several instances of the perfidy of white Americans. Interspersed among these episodes, on the other side of the stage, we see a querulous old man confronting an impatient, offensive nurse. The two men are, of course, one, and through various allusions, the man's reliance on African American values and culture is demonstrated.

Boochie is mainly a monologue of an old woman preparing dinner for her son, Boochie, a paragon of success, duty, and affection. With deft control of revelations and peripety, the audience is led to recognize very specific consequences of social forces such as welfare, addictions, and unemployment. The drama hangs on an extremely shocking climactic event and our understanding of its causes. As in each of the other plays, vivid characterization, precisely realistic detail, and a strong but assailed African American community provide the basis for the clear political implications of the plot.

Perhaps the genius of Mari Evans centers on her succinct, specific portrayals of the human spirit, and her moral premise that evil is both personal and institutional and must be fought in all its spheres.

• David Dorsey, "The Art of Mari Evans," in *Black Women Writers 1950–1980*, ed. Mari Evans, 1983, pp. 170–189. Solomon Edwards, "Affirmation in the Works of Mari Evans," in *Black Women Writers, 1950–1980*, ed. Mari Evans, 1983, pp. 190–200. Wallace R. Peppers, "Mari Evans," in *DLB*, vol. 41, *Afro-American Poets since 1955*, eds. Trudier Harris and Thadious M. Davis, 1985, pp. 117–123.

—David F. Dorsey, Jr.

EVA PEACE is the protagonist's grandmother in Toni *Morrison's novel *Sula* (1974). Her distinction is due to the claim that she purposely allowed her leg to be cut off by a train so that she could gain the pension that would provide financial support for her children. Desertion by her husband leaves Eva destitute and desperate, and after the loss of her leg, she retreats to her upstairs bedroom and directs the lives of her children, strays, and boarders. Eva is also a mythic character who is unchaste and unwilling to submit to anyone or any God, in opposition to her Christian namesake.

Although Eva is characterized in the narrative as enthralled by "manlove," she demonstrates a contemptuous attitude toward men in her naming. She sets fire to her son Ralph, whom she called Plum, when he returns from war with a heroin addiction and attempts to "crawl back into her womb." She takes in an alcoholic white man and calls him Tar Baby and three homeless boys and calls them all Dewey. After Eva burns her son, she is unable to save her second daughter, *Hannah Peace (Sula's mother), from burning to death.

The community apparently tolerates Eva's idiosyncrasies, but she is challenged and defeated by her equally strong-willed granddaughter, *Sula Peace, who puts her in an old folks' home. Eva, however, gets the last word in the novel, pointing out after Sula's death the similarity between Sula and her former best friend Nel in spite of their deceptive surface differences. Morrison quickly dispatches the assumption that Eva will fall into the traditional "*mammy" role, for Eva is a willful, arrogant, independent woman whose strength is based on her sustained hatred for the unfaithful father of her three children.

• Barbara Christian, *Black Feminist Criticism*, 1985. Wilfred D. Samuels and Clenora Hudson-Weems, *Toni Morrison*, 1990. Trudier Harris, *Fiction and Folklore: The Novels of Toni Morrison*, 1991. Rachel Lee, "Missing Peace in Toni Morrison's *Sula* and *Beloved*," *African American Review* 28.4 (Winter 1994): 571–583.   —Betty Taylor-Thompson

Eva's Man. Like her first *novel, *Corregidora* (1975), Gayl *Jones's *Eva's Man* (1976) continues to explore African American women's sexual victimization. The novel's pivotal scene is *Eva Medina Canada's murder and mutilation of her lover. Eva spends a number of days in Davis Carter's apartment, waiting for her menstrual period to end so that they can make love. Jones creates a vaguely repellent, ambivalent feeling of imprisonment and passivity: although he leaves the door open, Davis wants Eva to remain in the apartment, and although Eva seems to feel trapped, she never steps outside the door. With neither remorse nor explanation, Eva murders Davis, bites off his penis, and then calls the police. The book begins with this violent act, moves back to Eva's childhood and adolescence, and ends with her obstinate silence in a prison's psychiatric ward.

Eva's increasingly erratic, first-person narrative shifts from one scene to another, repeating lines of dialogue in different contexts, mingling memory, dream, and fantasy in a story that explores an African American woman's formation of her *identity in a culture that devalues her *race and her sex. Unlike *Ursa Corregidora, Eva has both a father and mother present throughout her childhood. But she, too, experiences a good deal of sexual abuse, both actual and threatened, in her encounters with men who assume that she is sexually willing. Brought up to believe that women cannot control their own bodies, Eva continually alternates her silent passivity with unexpected moments of *violence. When a man follows her into an alley, trying to pay her for sex, she says nothing to dissuade him but then suddenly stabs him with a pocketknife. The older man she marries is psychotically jealous, yet she stays with him for two years. When Davis tries to dominate her, refusing even to let her comb her hair, Eva seems undisturbed by his behavior, even as she secrets away the rat poison that will kill him. She offers no motive for her action, and at one point warns an interrogator not to explain her. While *Corregidora*'s depiction of lesbianism is uneasy at best, *Eva's Man* closes with Eva's being brought to orgasm by her cellmate Elvira—a moment whose simple immediacy might constitute the novel's sole note of redemptive possibility.

Discussions of this book generally focus on Eva's coping with the stereotypical objectifications of black women, especially those that characterize them as faithless or as sexually insatiable. While several critics see Eva's behavior as a rebellion against the racist, sexist structures that posit black women as whores, others argue that Jones refuses to let Eva be so easily explained, even as the character alternately submits to and defies the social system that defines her so rigidly. Also important is the novel's adaptation of African American *folklore, especially the communal voice that Eva hears while growing up (that of her mother's friend, Miss Billie), which teaches her about ancestral duties and the fatal power of women's sexuality. Finally, although unreliable, Eva's narrative is truly hers, unlike the rote memorizations of incest and abuse that nearly imprison the protagonist of Jones's first novel.

[See also Lesbians; Sexuality.]

• Keith Byerman, "Black Vortex: The Gothic Structure of Eva's Man," MELUS 7.4 (Winter 1980): 93–101. Melvin Dixon, "Singing a Deep Song: Language As Evidence in the Novels of Gayl Jones," in Black Women Writers (1950–1980), ed. Mari Evans, 1984, pp. 236–248. Gloria Wade-Gayles, No Crystal Stair: Visions of Race and Sex in Black Women's Fiction, 1984. Keith Byerman, Fingering the Jagged Grain: Tradition and Form in Recent Black Fiction, 1985. Sally Robinson, Engendering the Subject: Gender and Self-Representation in Contemporary Women's Fiction, 1991.

—Amy S. Gottfried

EVERETT ANDERSON is the six-year-old protagonist of seven children's verse books by Lucille *Clifton, published between 1970 and 1983. Each story-poem is illustrated by pen-and-ink drawings or sepia watercolors that realistically represent the characters' Negroid physicality. In each narrative, Clifton reiterates major themes of her own poetry and of the 1960s *Black Arts movement: familial and self-love, ethnic pride, African American masculinity, resistance to racism, the inner city as home, the power of self-referentiality, and the subversion of Euro-American conventions. Moreover, Clifton at once demonstrates allegiance to second-wave *feminism and debunks myths of oppressive African American matriarchy through her characterization of Everett's mother as a loving and conscientious single parent–wage earner. In Everett Anderson's Nine Month Long (1978), Clifton uses Everett's mother's second marriage and subsequent pregnancy to illustrate parental sensitivity to a son's anxiety about displacement as well as to reveal African Americans' reverence for self-definition. Clifton also explores children's responses to multiculturalism, gender equality, and bilingualism by introducing Everett to Maria, a girl-next-door who beats him at sports and whose Spanish-speaking mother prepares Mexican food. Clifton portrays Everett as a conventional child: he attends school; exults in natural wonders, including his own brown body; sometimes misbehaves; often grieves his dead father. Yet she also insinuates the particular impact of his ethnicity on his experience: the Andersons' tenement apartment functions simultaneously as a site of lessons in self-assertion, charity, security, discipline, and patriotism and as a site of lessons in economic and political injustice and the exclusivity of the mythic American dream.

• Dianne Johnson, Telling Tales: The Pedagogy and Promise of African American Literature for Youth, 1990.

—Joycelyn K. Moody

EXPATRIATISM. During the twentieth century, and especially between 1919 and 1960, the idea (and in some cases, the practice) of expatriatism provided a powerful creative stimulant to African American intellectuals. Most did not remain permanently abroad; rather expatriation was a breather. Though there was some talk about settling in Brazil and Canada and some African Americans did leave for the Soviet Union, France was the most popular destination for self-exile, and a small but vibrant African American community sprouted in Paris in the early years after World War I. Its founders and early leading voices were African American war veterans like Rayford Logan and William Stuart Nelson (respectively, a future distinguished historian and a theologian and spiritual mentor to Martin Luther *King, Jr.), who suffered bitterly under the military's Jim Crow regime. The welcome accorded to them by the French population and France's putative reputation for racial tolerance and humane treatment of its colonial subjects encouraged them to remain abroad. These were political exiles, as they devoted much of their time to the cause of *Pan-Africanism. Their numbers were augmented in the 1920s and 1930s and again in the post–World War II years. Entertainers and authors such as Josephine *Baker and Will Marion Cook, and Gwendolyn *Bennett, Langston *Hughes, Claude *McKay, and Richard *Wright were eager to regain a psychic equilibrium that American racism had robbed and to expend their creative energies in milieus that accorded them the proper respect.

From its beginnings in the aftermath of World War I, the African American community in Paris interacted with other parts of the African diaspora. Most likely this was due to the efforts of W. E. B. *Du Bois, whose article "The African Roots of War" (1915) and other writings had argued that Europe's appetite for African colonies was the principal cause of the conflict and that the only defense against future carnage was the unity of black people the world over to remove themselves from colonial competition. African Americans joined with francophone blacks and blacks from Britain's African and West Indian colonies to form the Pan-African Association, whose program included eventual self-government for Africa and full citizenship rights for African Americans.

The central theme of the expatriate literature during the flood tide of post–World War I Pan-Africanism, roughly from 1919 to 1924, focused on the Europeans' exceptional treatment of African Americans and Westernized Africans in contrast to the *violence and inequality inherent in America's racial system. The *Crisis, the journal of the NAACP, edited by Du Bois, recounted the history of the African American soldier in the war; documented the racism of the U.S. military; recorded the honored and appreciated service of France's Senegalese troops; and reported on France's openness to participation in national life by such black figures as Senegal's Blaise Diagne and Guadeloupe's Sosthène Mortenal, the military commander who organized the defense of Paris. *Opportunity, the Urban League's monthly and an important publication for the

*Harlem Renaissance, frequently carried articles supporting France's colonial policy and praising the existence of a putative cultural pluralism—see, for example, Alain *Locke's "Black Watch on the Rhine" (Jan. 1924); in the late 1920s, both Gwendolyn Bennett's and Countee *Cullen's *Opportunity* columns regularly discussed the racial egalitarianism enjoyed by the African American residents of Paris, as did the *Chicago Defender* and other African American newspapers.

Yet the tone of most of the articles—in the case of the *Defender*, these were written both by the expatriates themselves and African Americans making the grand tour—was not emigrationist, as was the case with Marcus *Garvey's Universal Negro Improvement Association. Rather, the aim of the literature showing the favorable position of blacks in France was to present an alternative to Jim Crow and to illustrate how far African Americans might advance under a system of enlightened race relations. (Interestingly, African American expatriates and observers of European race relations displayed a severe *class bias when they substituted a small, Westernized black elite for the entire black population on French soil. The overwhelming majority of blacks in France were African war veterans and they suffered intractable economic, social, and political problems; these blacks remained practically invisible in African American literature.)

While organized Pan-Africanism in Europe went into decline after 1924, the composition of the expatriate community shifted increasingly to entertainers, especially those involved with jazz and the African American musical *theater. In the United States Josephine Baker was considered simply a "Negro dancer," which meant that her opportunities were limited; when she arrived in Paris in 1924, however, her performance was considered high art and she enjoyed wide celebrity. Several shows, including *Blackbirds of 1929*, which was the first one to arrive in Paris with a full complement of performers, met wide critical acclaim and drew a large following among both black and white French.

Europe greeted *jazz enthusiastically, subjecting it to serious criticism in the popular press by such leading cultural figures as Jean Cocteau, who hailed it as the art form that would lead Europe out of cultural stagnation and decline. Though some of the entertainers catered mainly to white clientele—the dancer and club owner Bricktop hosted parties for wealthy white Americans and Britons on holiday, and taught the Prince of Wales to dance the Charleston—quite a few of them interacted with others from the African diaspora: *La Revue du Monde Noir/Review of the Black World*, a bilingual journal of cultural criticism in the early 1930s, noted the reciprocal influence of African American and Martinican music and dance. Further, the salons of the French black elite were meeting places for the diaspora, too. René Maran, the Martinican author of the Goncourt Prize–winning *Batouala*, and Paulette Nardal, another prominent Antillian, often hosted Mercer Cook (a Romance languages scholar and future ambassador

to Senegal) and Langston Hughes, allowing them to meet with such *Negritude personalities as Léopold Senghor, Louis Achille, and Léon Damas.

While the influence of the *New Negro on francophone black literature has been extensively discussed by Mercer Cook and Michel Fabre, the impact of France on the New Negro is harder to detect, though certainly present. Langston Hughes's "Negro Dancers" and "To a Negro Jazz Band in a Parisian Cabaret" were poems inspired by Le Grand Duc, the club where he worked as a dishwasher. Many of the works that use Europe as a backdrop concern themselves with the search for place. Countee Cullen, who frequently summered in Paris, penned several poems in praise of France or drawing upon Gallic imagery—see, for example, his sonnet "To France" in *Opportunity* (Aug. 1932); France is welcoming and appreciative in ways that his own homeland is not.

Gwendolyn Bennett drew upon her first-hand knowledge of Paris's geography for her *short story "The Wedding," which appeared in *Fire!!* in 1926. It chronicles the Parisian life of Paul Watson, an African American boxer. Away from America, Watson is able, with some difficulty, to exorcise his hatred of white Americans. He falls in love with an impoverished white American woman and plans to marry her, but she backs out at the last minute. Jim Crow reaches across the Atlantic, and one is left to wonder where Watson's place is. Chester *Himes's *novel *A Case of Rape* (originally published in 1963 in France as *Une affaire de viol*) revolves around the black expatriate community in Paris and is partly autobiographical. The story of four African American men accused and tried in a French court for the rape and murder of a white American woman, the novel examines the crippling effects of racism, even in a country supposedly as free of prejudice as France.

Even when works of fiction and *poetry did not utilize European scenery, the Continental experience was still important to the production of these genres of African American literature. Walter *White wrote *Rope and Faggot* (1929) during his Guggenheim year in the South of France, and Jessie Redmon *Fauset wrote *Plum Bun* (1929) while in Paris; neither reflected on their experiences abroad. Here, Europe provided a writing environment free from the United States's racial stresses. Even after he quit America for good in 1947, Richard Wright drew principally upon African American life and race relations in the United States for his fiction; though he was an organic part of the exile community, he did not write about it. He also actively associated with French and other European thinkers and functioned self-consciously in his new residence as both a spokesperson for Afro-America and as a Western intellectual.

A notable exception to the invisibility of France in the fiction of African Americans is Claude McKay's *Banjo* (1929). Set in the port city of Marseilles among the Senegalese dock workers, *Banjo* is the story of the adventures of Ray, an itinerant African American. It was an attempt, much maligned by distinguished African Americans such as Du Bois, to elaborate an aesthetic of the African diaspora New Negro that promoted a sensuality and primitiveness that was the antithesis of Western civilization. Among its principal themes is a critical analysis of French racial attitudes and treatment of blacks; his portrayal of ordinary blacks, police brutality, and the racism of the French population was an important corrective to the dominant themes in African American letters of Gallic tolerance. *Banjo* was an important predecessor of Negritude; as students in Paris, Senghor and Aimé Césaire, two of that literary movement's founders, translated, circulated, and memorized entire parts of that novel, especially portions dealing with the West's contempt for African civilizations.

France and the expatriate experience appear most frequently in *autobiography and the nonfiction prose of African American expatriates. After recounting his trip through West Africa, which provoked volatile and contradictory emotions, Langston Hughes in *The *Big Sea* (1940) relates his immersion in the black expatriate jazz club milieu and notes that he received an extended introduction to African art and culture in Paris from Alain Locke and Paul Guillaume; in this first trip overseas, Hughes became acutely aware of the international dimensions of the African diaspora and the relations between it and the entire West and Africa. Claude McKay's articles in *Crisis* and Countee Cullen's in both *Crisis* and *Opportunity* depict an expatriate community insulated from the racism of white America and in ample contact with the black world in Paris. But in his *A Long Way from Home* (1937), McKay pokes fun at the middle-class African Americans vacationing in Europe, for their smugness and for their lack of reflection on the conditions of the masses back home. In several of his essays collected in *Notes of a Native Son* (1955), James *Baldwin was comforted by the refuge that Paris provided him as an American; but that was because he was a stranger there, and, reflecting on the treatment of Africans in Paris, he drew analogies between European and American race prejudice.

An important theme in the genre of autobiographical reflections is the Soviet Union and socialism as a haven for black people. Hughes, in his *I Wonder as I Wander* (1956), and McKay each wrote favorably of the potential of Soviet socialism to eradicate racial discrimination. Their views were part of a current in black thought in the 1930s that advocated radical change in America as the way toward racial equality.

Countee Cullen perhaps hinted at the reason foreign settings figured so seldomly in the work of African American writers. They were, he wrote in his *Opportunity* column, "The Dark Tower," Americans at heart and looked to Europe only for a brief respite before returning to the business of changing American reality. Richard Wright explained the meager presence of the expatriate experience in his and his fellow expatriates' fiction in "I Choose Exile," an unpublished essay that Michel Fabre discusses and quotes extensively in his *The World of Richard Wright* (1985). Wright states that by the time he, or any writer, turned twenty, he had stored the experiences —American experiences—upon which he drew for his fiction. Europe gave him relief from racism, as it did for Hughes and Gwendolyn Bennett before him and James Baldwin after him, but exile was primarily a perch from which to examine his native land, and his interest was in things American, not foreign.

[*See also* Journalism; Places.]

• Rayford W. Logan, "The Confessions of an Unwilling Nordic," in *The Negro Caravan*, ed. Sterling Brown, 1941, pp. 1043–1050. Mercer Cook, "Some Literary Contacts: African, West Indian, Afro-American," in *The Black Writer in Africa and the Americas*, ed. L. W. Brown, 1973, pp. 119–140. Kenneth R. Manning, *Black Apollo of Science: The Life of Ernest Everett Just*, 1983. Michel Fabre, *From Harlem to Paris*, 1991. Christopher Sawyer-Lauçanno, *The Continual Pilgrimage: American Writers in Paris, 1944–1960*, 1992. Kenneth Robert Janken, *Rayford W. Logan and the Dilemma of the African-American Intellectual*, esp. chap. 2, 1993. Jean-Claude Baker and Chris Chase, *Josephine: The Hungry Heart*, 1994.

—Kenneth R. Janken

F

FABIO, SARAH WEBSTER (1928–1979), poet, educator, and leading figure and pioneer in the Black Studies and Black Arts movements. Born in Nashville, Tennessee, on 20 January 1928, Sarah Webster Fabio was the precocious daughter of Thomas Webster and Mayme Louise Storey Webster. Fabio graduated from Nashville's Pearl High School in 1943. At age fifteen, she entered Spelman College in Atlanta, Georgia; however, she did not graduate. Returning instead to Nashville, she graduated from Fisk University in 1946, and married Cyril Fabio, a young dental student at Meharry Medical College.

After her husband completed his degree he joined the military and they were sent to Florida, where her first son was born in 1947. Another son was born in 1948, and a daughter in 1949. Despite the strictures of being a military wife frequently forced to move and mothering small children, Fabio, on one of their moves back to Nashville, enrolled in graduate school. Before she could complete her degree, the family was stationed in Germany. Two other children were born in 1955 and 1956. In 1957, the family settled in Palo Alto, California, where her husband opened a dental practice.

The mothering of five children delayed Fabio's education until 1963, when she enrolled in San Francisco State College. She earned her degree in 1965, on the day that her oldest son graduated from high school, and she landed a job teaching at Merritt College in Oakland, a seed-bed for the Black Power movement west. Bobby Seale and Huey Newton of the Black Panther Party, as well as Malauna Ron Karenga of the U.S. Organization, were students at Merritt. These were exciting times for Fabio, who had been writing since high school and had studied *poetry under Arna *Bontemps at Fisk. Fabio defined black poetry as works containing themes drawn from and saturated with language, images, and rhythms of the African American experience.

Fabio's training (a master's degree in language arts, creative writing with an emphasis on poetry) enabled her to combine Western metaphor with black realism. Grounding her work in the oral tradition and performing her poetry to *jazz accompaniments, Fabio reached a wide and diverse audience. In 1966, she performed at the First World Festival of Negro Art in Dakar, Senegal. Returning home, she lectured at the California College of Arts and Crafts and the University of California at Berkeley, where she worked to create their *Black Studies department.

Fabio's first collection of poetry, *Saga of a Black Man* (1968), was followed by *A Mirror, a Soul* (1969). In 1972, she recorded two albums on Folkways Records. Doubleday published *Black Talk: Shield and Sword* (1973). Other books include *Dark Debut: Three Black Women Coming* (1966), *Return of Margaret Walker* (1966), *Double Dozens: An Anthology of Poets from Sterling Brown to Kali* (1966), and *No Crystal Stair: A Socio-Drama of the History of Black Women in the U.S.A.* (1967).

Fabio's poetry reflects the *Black Arts movement with its trendy emphasis on the *Black Aesthetic, yet is classic in its subtle blending of non-Western and Western literary metaphors. Fabio skillfully handles both traditions.

In 1972, Fabio divorced her husband and accepted a faculty position at Oberlin College in Ohio, where she remained until 1974. In 1976, while teaching and pursuing graduate work at the University of Wisconsin, she was diagnosed with colon cancer. Fabio spent her last two years in California with her oldest daughter. She died 7 November 1979.

Fabio's most impressive collection of poetry is the seven-volume series, *Rainbow Signs* (1973). The rainbow symbolized for her a sign of hope following the storms of protest during the turbulent 1960s. "The Hurt of It All" voices the poet's farewell, saying "that's all she wrote."

• Stephen Henderson, ed., *Understanding the New Black Poetry*, 1973. James A. Page, comp., *Selected Black American Authors: An Illustrated Bio-Bibliography*, 1977, pp. 81–82. Nagueyalti Warren, *Notable Black American Women*, vol. 1, ed. Jessie Smith, 1992, pp. 332–333.

—Nagueyalti Warren

FAIR, RONALD L. (b. 1932), novelist, short story writer, and poet. Born in Chicago in 1932, Ronald L. Fair began writing as a teenager. After graduating from public school in Chicago, Fair spent three years in the U.S. Navy (1950–1953) before attending a Chicago stenotype school for two years. While supporting himself as a court reporter and stenographer for the next decade (1955–1966), he produced his first two *novels. After then working briefly as an encyclopedia writer, Fair taught for a few years—at Columbia College (1967–1968), Northwestern University (1968), and Wesleyan University (1969–1970). Fair moved to Finland in 1971 and has lived in Europe since that time. He is divorced and has three children.

Ronald Fair's first novel, *Many Thousand Gone: An American Fable* (1965), both fantastic tale and "protest novel," is a satiric re-vision of the South, where, in the mythical Jacobs County, slaves were never freed after the Civil War. Exploring the twin themes of the sexual exploitation of women and the *lynching of men from the African American community, the novel concludes with a messianic-like hope rooted in racial purity and revolutionary resistance.

In *Hog Butcher* (1966), the author's critique of racism and hypocrisy turns to the North. Set in Chicago's South Side ghetto, and drawing on Fair's experience as a court reporter, the novel centers on the police shooting of a young African American sports hero-to-be and the trial and cover-up that ensue.

Fair's third major work of fiction, *World of Nothing*

(1970), is a pair of novellas. *Jerome,* his most experimental piece, revisits the fantasy genre to explore religious hypocrisy. The second novella, *World of Nothing,* consists of a series of bittersweet episodic sketches related by an anonymous first-person narrator.

We Can't Breathe, published in 1972, after Fair had departed for Europe, is about growing up in 1930s Chicago and is his most autobiographical and documentary work. Versions of the prologue have been frequently anthologized, as have other Fair short stories.

Fair's fiction has generally met with mixed reviews. While he has received praise for his naturalistic accounts in particular, critics have accused his works, variously, of stereotype, weak dialogue, cliché, and a lack of aesthetic unity. Despite the lukewarm critical response, *Hog Butcher* was eventually made into a feature film and reissued as a mass-market paperback, *Cornbread, Earl, and Me* in 1975. Fair also received an award for *World of Nothing* from the National Endowment of Letters in 1971 and a Best Book Award from the American Library Association for *We Can't Breathe* in 1972.

During his self-imposed exile, which began during the decline of the *Black Arts movement in America, Fair has continued to explore the settings and themes of his earlier work but primarily through *poetry. In addition to contributing to various periodicals, he has published two volumes of poetry: *Excerpts* (London, 1975) and *Rufus* (Germany, 1977; United States, 1980). Fair also received an award from the National Endowment for the Arts in 1974 and a Guggenheim Fellowship in 1975.

Ronald L. Fair's most significant contribution to African American literature has perhaps been the versatility and inventive synthesis of forms with which he has explored communal themes, human types, and the workings and abuses of power.

• "Ronald L. Fair," in *New Black Voices,* ed. Abraham Chapman, 1972, p. 106. —Sheila Hassell Hughes

FAMILY. Family has been a recurring theme in African American literature since its beginning. During *slavery and immediately after emancipation, family survival and family loyalty—and, by extension, race survival and loyalty—were important thematic elements in African American literature. Historically, the intrusions on the sanctity of the family—breakups caused by sales of family members during slavery and the distress caused by rape or concubinage—threatened the very existence of African American families. Thus the attempt to find and protect members of the slave family or to reject White intrusions on the family bloodline pervades the focus of much of nineteenth-century African American literature.

In William Wells *Brown's *Clotel* (1853), the focus is upon the difficulty of nurturing family connections in a slave system that allowed, as a matter of course, uncommitted fathering by the White men on the one hand and hampered mothering by the whimsical sale of the mother and her children on the other. Harriet

A. *Jacobs's *Incidents in the Life of a Slave Girl* (1861) also focuses on a mother-centered family struggling to stay together. Linda Brent is willing to risk punishment and endure the discomfort of staying for years in a room barely large enough to stand in so that she can be near her children and protect them. In *Iola Leroy* (1892) by Frances Ellen Watkins *Harper, the protagonist, although able to pass for White, willingly accepts her Black familial connection. She suffers the forced servitude caused by her Black family connection, and later, after the Civil War, she seeks to find and unite other Black family members scattered by slavery. In an ironic twist of the mother-child separations in nineteenth-century African American literature, Harriet E. *Wilson's *Our Nig* (1859) portrays a protagonist who suffers because of the rejection of her mother. In most cases Black mothers in nineteenth-century African American literature are separated against their will from their children. In *Our Nig,* *Frado is the daughter of a White mother and a Black father. After Frado's father dies, her mother abandons the child. While Frado's plight is different from many *mulatto protagonists in nineteenth-century literature, the absence of the mother-child bond in *Our Nig* emphasizes how crucial that bond was for a sense of family connection and how even under the worst of circumstances family provided a source of strength for the protagonists.

The crisis that mixed parentage put upon Black family survival and individual *identity was prevalent in much of the literature of the nineteenth century, but not always. The *poetry of Paul Laurence *Dunbar in the late 1890s represents one example of the familial love and cohesiveness that many nineteenth-century writers affirmed. Dunbar's "Little Brown Baby," where the Black father lovingly holds his baby and affirms his love and hope for his child, is one example. Other Dunbar poems such as "Negro Love Song" and "In the Morning" tell of loving family relationships and courtship rituals that were a major source of strength for Black families. Whether demonstrating loyalty and the struggle for family survival under the worst of circumstances or lyrically rejoicing in the love and everyday rituals of Black family life, the literary works of the nineteenth century reflect, as the findings of sociologists like Herbert Gutman and Andrew Billingsley point out, that Black family life was exceedingly important and that familial ties were strong and were fiercely protected during and after slavery.

In *passing literature of the early twentieth century, where the mulatto protagonist accepts, publicly at least, a White familial definition of self, the issue of family and family connection remains a significant theme. Protagonists who passed generally felt a great sense of guilt for betraying "black family" connections. Yet, when they were revealed as not "pure" White or when they had to silently endure the racism of the White family they publicly embraced, the Black familial connections became the buffer and the balm for characters who tried to pass. Again and again in the literature, African American writers focus on the tragedy and intrigue of the implications of divided family loyalties and bloodlines, and they invariably affirm—often with pangs of regret or open redemptive returns by their characters—the primacy of Black family connections. From Charles Waddell *Chesnutt's The *House Behind the Cedars (1900) to James Weldon *Johnson's The *Autobiography of an Ex-Colored Man (1912), to the passing *novels of Nella *Larsen and Jessie Redmon *Fauset in the 1920s, these works affirm spiritually and emotionally the strength and sustenance of the Black family. The protagonist's lament at the end of Johnson's novel exemplifies the feelings of those who passed: "I have taken the lesser part; I have sold my soul for a mess of pottage."

With the exception of poems such as "Heritage" by Countee *Cullen that probed African blood connections, and of works that celebrated the love strength of families seeking to make it against social and economic odds such as Langston *Hughes's "Mother to Son," the trend toward self-identity and self-fulfillment established by passing literature continued in the 1920s and 1930s and became a central focus in African American literature through the 1950s.

More and more the struggle for self-identity, for a kind of American individualism, began to characterize the literature. Family life was certainly present in the literature during this period, but its maintenance and the protagonists' loyalty to family were not the primary focus. During the 1920s in works such as Jean *Toomer's *Cane (1923) and Wallace *Thurman's Infants of the Spring (1932) and continuing into the next decades with Zora Neale *Hurston's *Their Eyes Were Watching God (1937), Richard *Wright's *Native Son (1940), Ann *Petry's The *Street (1946), and Ralph *Ellison's *Invisible Man (1952), the family was less of a foregrounded thematic subject and more of a backdrop for a burgeoning self-awareness on the part of the major protagonists.

Jean Toomer's Cane focused on the individual life stories of women and suggested a separate, existential longing among them that was not necessarily rooted in a connection to family. Wallace Thurman's The *Blacker the Berry (1929) and Infants of the Spring and Claude *McKay's *Home to Harlem (1928) all show protagonists searching for self-realization or self-affirmation and reacting more to the larger systemic issues of *race and *class that affect their individual identities. Iola Leroy, Frances Ellen Watkins Harper's protagonist in her 1892 novel of the same name, wants to show loyalty to family; *Janie Crawford, in Their Eyes Were Watching God, wants to show loyalty to self. She rejects the ways of her grandmother, leaves her husband, and does not have children.

In the 1940s and 1950s in novels like Native Son, The Street, and Invisible Man, family, while present, is not the central focus but it is a springboard for self-expression, a place to leave in order not to be caught in the web of poverty or traditional values. Or, family is the larger victim of a spiral of political and economic racism that affects, first, the life of the individual and, second, by implication, the life of the family. *Bigger Thomas is so tightly woven into the victimization of the socioeconomic system that oppresses him, he does not build a family and, essentially, re-

jects the family bond of his mother and sister. Family is the enduring bond in Bigger's life, but neither he nor Wright gives it high value. Wright focuses here on what happens to one man and how his life implicates the larger dilemma of the race. The goal of *Lutie Johnson is to be a self-made "American success" and buy a comfortable home for herself and her son. The story becomes, like Native Son, a demonstration of the destruction of that dream and how both Lutie and her son become pawns to the larger systemic forces of race, class, and *gender that prevent both of them from realizing their dreams. In the end, Lutie is willing to leave her son in order to escape the tangle of victimization that she falls into. In Ralph Ellison's Invisible Man, the protagonist's quest brings about a singular, albeit representative, realization and not one that directly affects the survival or the wholesomeness of a particular family life. There is a noticeable lack of the enabling family bonds or blood connections explicit in nineteenth-century African American literature and implicit in the early works of the twentieth century in this later literature. Toni *Morrison, commenting on this lack of family focus in the literature of the 1940s and 1950s, says that in these works there is the absence of the "*ancestor."

In works of the 1940s and 1950s where family ties are sustaining and central, there is often a desire on the part of these protagonists to get away from family—to redefine themselves in terms beyond those of the immediate family. *John Grimes in James *Baldwin's *Go Tell It on the Mountain (1953), Maud Martha in Gwendolyn *Brooks's *Maud Martha (1953), and *Selina Boyce in Paule *Marshall's *Brown Girl, Brownstones (1959) are all members of strong family units, but they are searching for or affirming a definition of self outside of it. Lorraine *Hansberry's A *Raisin in the Sun (1959) presents a protagonist who ultimately chooses the primacy of the family, but *Walter Lee Younger also wants to make it on his own, to do something outside the dictates of family. He comes to see, however, in a way that would foreshadow the importance of family in postintegration literature, that loyalty to family is of central importance.

The vocal race pride and the rapid changes in African American life brought on by the Civil Rights Act and the subsequent dismantling of segregation that characterized the 1960s became, by the 1970s, an increasing reevaluation of what had been the cultural losses to Blacks as a result of both the popular, strident rhetoric of the 1960s and its rush toward what had been the long-sought goal of integration. In the retrospective moment of the 1970s, something seemed to have been amiss. Integration had brought greater economic, social, and educational opportunities but it had also significantly changed the insularity and protection of core community values and ways of life.

Chief among the sustaining values of African American life was the family. The intent then was not just to show how the family was challenged or how it survived, as earlier works had done, but to show family as a means of keeping African American cultural ways and history intact. The family was not about belonging so much as it was about maintaining a vehicle for transmitting group history. It was not its existence anymore that was the issue but its function. Central in that revisioning of the role of the family in literature was the role of the family elder or the *ancestor. Margaret *Walker's *Jubilee (1966), a historical novel beginning in *slavery and based on Walker's family history, had been a precursor. So too was Ernest J. *Gaines's The *Autobiography of Miss Jane Pittman (1971). Both texts shifted the focus back to the valued role of the family elder and the larger role of the family in maintaining cultural history. These works changed the theme from that of family victimization to family agency.

This new focus on family was both affirmed and given celebrated interest by the publication of Alex *Haley's *Roots in 1976. Haley's work sold over 1.5 million copies and set off an unprecedented interest in family and genealogy. Toni *Morrison's *Song of Solomon (1977) followed Haley's historical novel and placed family history in a larger mythical but similarly empowering context. Much like Haley's work in its referencing of a single remnant that becomes the clue to family history—Haley's "Kamby Bolongo" is akin to *Pilate Dead's "Song of Solomon"—the work created a heightened interest in storytelling and in family history, and the value they served for the contemporary generation. Morrison's work, like Gaines's and Haley's, also set forth the valued role of the elder or ancestor. It celebrated the transmissive role of the family elders. Pilate Dead takes on that symbolic role in Song of Solomon as Miss Jane had done in Miss Jane Pittman, and through these family ancestors the path for family connection and self-agency is revealed.

Song of Solomon was followed by such works as John Edgar *Wideman's Damballah (1981), David *Bradley's The *Chaneysville Incident (1981), and Paule *Marshall's Praisesong for the Widow (1983), all stories where the ancestor—the oldest family member—is the key to one family's history and, by implication, to the ethnic cultural integrity of the group. In *poetry, Michael S. *Harper's Images of Kin (1977) and Rita *Dove's *Thomas and Beulah (1987) affirmed the role of family in cultural maintenance, and its history, memories, and values became important metaphors in their works. In *drama, August *Wilson's Joe Turner's Come and Gone (1988) and The *Piano Lesson (1990) spoke to the symbolic role of the family and its potential for empowerment and self-agency in contemporary life.

In the literature of the 1970s and 1980s there was also a willingness on the part of African American writers to criticize the Black family. At the forefront was Alice *Walker. Walker certainly valued Black family life, as evidenced in *short story, *essay, and poetry collections like In Love and Trouble (1973), Revolutionary Petunias (1973), and *In Search of Our Mother's Gardens (1983), but Walker, like a growing number of Black women writers of this period, was also willing to point out the Black family's weaknesses. In The *Third Life of Grange Copeland (1970), Walker offers a scathing analysis of how children and wives become the immediate in-house victims of

racism that is outwardly directed toward Black men. Walker also critiques thwarted family growth in The *Color Purple (1982). Like Grange in The Third Life of Grange Copeland, the major male character in The Color Purple, Mister, experiences at least a beginning transformation. Most importantly, however, in The Color Purple, Walker points out the possibility of Black women becoming self-empowering and being able to transform their own lives without the aid of men.

In her first novel, The *Bluest Eye (1970), Morrison, too, was willing to criticize a Black family for its acceptance of a racist color hierarchy. The Breedlove family is complicit in this novel with the racist hierarchy of the larger community and thus participates in the destruction of the self-worth of their youngest family member, *Pecola Breedlove. In The *Women of Brewster Place (1982), Gloria *Naylor exposes weaknesses in Black family relationships including child abuse, homophobia, classism, and neglect. These writers do not see these weaknesses as totally disabling, for they all create within the same Black communities that they criticize enabling "extended" Black families that try to rescue or redeem the victims. Such writers expose family weaknesses—wife and child abuse, in-group rivals, and color consciousness—not to ultimately diminish the quality of African American life but instead to offer a warning regarding the dangers of such behavior to both the individual and the group and to call for a corrective. Many of these writers were criticized for their sometimes negative portrayals of the Black family in their literature, but they were ultimately healthy confrontations because they provided a language and symbolic narratives through which to talk about and view these issues.

Contemporary nonfiction prose has complemented the renewed historical interest in Black family life that existed in fiction. Memoirs and *autobiographies that recount the importance of Black family life and values as keys to individual success and personal contentment in contemporary society have gained a large readership in recent years. Popular works in the 1990s such as Once Upon a Time When We Were Colored (1989) by Clifton Taulbert, The Measure of Our Success (1992) by Marian Wright Elderman, Having Our Say (1993) by Sarah and Elizabeth Delaney, Pushed Back to Strength (1993) by Gloria Wade Gayles, and Colored People (1994) by Henry Louis *Gates, Jr., all tell moving personal stories of Black family history and the importance of its nurturance in the individual lives of its authors and, by implication, the thousands of Blacks who grew up like them. Though often of meager material means, the Black families in these works are celebrated for their rich resources of character, love, thrift, and charity and as examples of how a contemporary world that seems to have lost its center can be enabled from the small, manageable nucleus of the family.

From Clotel to The Piano Lesson, from Our Nig to Song of Solomon to the growing body of contemporary nonfiction, there has been an abiding concern for family in African American literature. Whether it has been to probe the emotional ramifications of mixed blood connections and allegiances, or to explore the need of individuals to break away from familial confines, or to celebrate the family's mythical and metaphorical meanings for African American survival, or, finally, to try to loosen it from its oppressive restrictions, family has continued to be the pivot point from which African American writers have sought to recreate, analyze, and interpret the major thematic currents of African American life in literature.

• Martha Hersey Brown, "Images of Black Women: Family Roles in Harlem Renaissance Literature," PhD diss., Carnegie-Mellon University, 1976. Toni Morrison, "Rootedness: The Ancestor as Foundation," in *Black Women Writers (1950–1980)*, ed. Mari Evans, 1984, pp. 339–345. Mildred Hill-Lubin, "The Grandmother in African and African-American Literature: A Survivor of the African Extended Family," in *Ngambika: Studies of Women in African Literature*, ed. Carole Boyce Davis, 1986, pp. 257–270. Ralph Reckley, Sr., "John A. Williams's *Sissie*: A Study of the Black Male and His Family," *MAWA Review* 5.1 (June 1990): 15–19. Frances Smith Foster, "Parents and Children in Autobiography by Southern Afro-American Writers," in *Home Ground: Southern Autobiography*, ed. Bill J. Berry, 1991, pp. 98–109. Andrew Billingsley, *Climbing Jacob's Ladder: The Enduring Legacy of African-American Families*, 1992. Claudia Tate, *Domestic Allegories of Political Desire: The Black Heroine's Text at the Turn of the Century*, 1992. Karen Smith, *A Chronicle of Family Honor: Balancing Rage and Triumph in the Novels of Mildred D. Taylor*, 1994. Lee Alfred Wright, *Identity, Family, and Folklore in African American Literature*, 1995.

—Carolyn C. Denard

FANTASY. *See* Speculative Fiction.

FAUSET, ARTHUR HUFF (1899–1983), public school teacher and principal, anthropologist, businessman, and author. From childhood, Arthur Huff Fauset's formal education was in Philadelphia, culminating in a PhD at the University of Pennsylvania. Himself a member of a prominent "old line" family that included his sister Jessie Redmon *Fauset, he was married to Crystal Byrd Fauset, who was the first African American woman elected to the Pennsylvania legislature. Arthur Fauset authored several nonfiction books, a number of articles and *essays, and, mainly for the *Crisis and *Opportunity, several *short stories. Though he was not a major writer, among his friends and associates were important literary figures of the *Harlem Renaissance and beyond. In addition to cultural and professional activities, Fauset engaged in civic and race betterment undertakings.

A fellow in the American Anthropological Association, such interest is reflected in his *Folk Lore of Nova Scotia* (1931), collected under the auspices of the American Folklore Society. His *Black Gods of the Metropolis: Negro Religious Cults of the Urban North* (1970), originally his 1942 doctoral dissertation, is a study of five Negro religious "cults" in Philadelphia. Earlier Fauset published *For Freedom* (1935) and *Sojourner Truth, God's Faithful Pilgrim* (1938; rpt. 1973). The former is a survey of notable Negroes in American history, including lesser-known persons such as Madame Sisseretta Jones (Black Patti) and Barsilai [sic] Lew as well as better-known ones such as Benjamin *Banneker, Frederick *Douglass, and Paul Laurence *Dunbar. Its preface suggests his educator background, announcing that the history "is told in the spirit of young folk"; its epilogue advises, "there are many stories that could be told about oftimes unheard of Negroes who are doing marvelous things. . . . Won't you look around and see?" In 1969 Fauset coauthored *America: Red, Black, Yellow* with Nellie Rathbone Bright, a former elementary school principal. Aimed at juvenile readers, this book emphasizes the contributions of minority groups to the discovery and evolution of the nation.

• "Fauset, Arthur Huff," in *Black American Writers Past and Present*, eds. Theresa Rush et al., vol. 1, 1975, p. 285. "Fauset, Arthur Huff," in *CA*, ed. Christine Nasso, 1st rev. ed., vols. 25–28, 1977, p. 231. —Theodore R. Hudson

FAUSET, JESSIE REDMON (1882–1961), editor, teacher, and writer. The *Harlem Renaissance—jazzy, funky, soulful; a time when "Negroes" were "in vogue," when white people descended on Harlem's cabarets to amuse themselves, and when interracial soirees were frequent. One of its leading figures, Langston *Hughes, remembers that Jessie Fauset provided a different social atmosphere in the midst of all that funk, *jazz, and soul. At her parties guests would discuss literature, read *poetry aloud, and converse in French. She did not want "sightseers" in her home; therefore, only very distinguished white people were invited to her gatherings, and then only seldomly. Hughes also reports that Fauset used her position as literary editor of the *Crisis (1919–1926) to feature his talents and those of other young black artists including Countee *Cullen, Claude *McKay, and Jean *Toomer. For this effort, Hughes dubbed her literary "midwife" of the "Negro" Renaissance.

Fauset's considerable accomplishments go far beyond her having hosted social gatherings and nurtured fledgling writers. In keeping with her desire to teach black children pride in their heritage and to encourage their creativity, she cofounded and edited a monthly children's magazine, the *Brownies' Book (1920–1921). This magazine featured historical biographies of notable black people such as Denmark Vesey and Sojourner *Truth, articles about Africa, current events, games, riddles, and *music. Fauset also wrote poetry, numerous *essays, and short fiction, which appeared in various periodicals—the *Brownies' Book* and the *Crisis* among them—as well as in *anthologies such as Countee Cullen's *Caroling Dusk* (1927) and Alain *Locke's The *New Negro (1925). The most prolific novelist during the period, Fauset wrote four *novels that were published over a nine-year span: *There Is Confusion* (1924), *Plum Bun* (1929), *The Chinaberry Tree* (1931), and *Comedy: American Style* (1933).

While the broad range of Fauset's productivity is essential to an understanding of her aesthetics, the novels provide an interesting and significant focus. The content of her first, *There Is Confusion*, was inspired by the publication of T. S. Stribling's *Birthright* (1922). Like so many stereotypical accounts of the "tragic *mulatto," Stribling's account depicts a protagonist who is the victim of persistent longing and unattainable desires aroused by his mixed blood. Fauset believed she could tell a more convincing story of black life. Light-skinned, educated blacks, some of whom "pass" for white, are always central figures in her novels, where they not only represent an existing group of black people but also best fulfill Fauset's aim to politicize issues of color, *class, and *gender. She revises conventional literary forms and themes by using the figure of the mulatto as metaphor to explore *identity and difference as they concern blacks generally and black women, specifically. In challenging the myths of mulatto fiction by precursory white writers, in particular, Fauset reveals the fundamentally political nature of her novels.

Until recently, critics have missed the political and subversive aspects of her work. Their misreadings of the novels and of narrative intent stem largely from their using her personal life, real or imagined, to explain her plots and her reasons for creating characters in direct opposition to the kinds of black characters white publishers demanded at that time. The worst of these critiques uses Fauset's marital status and age as reasons for alleged limitations of imagination and creativity—that is, she was unmarried until age forty-seven and "already" thirty-eight by the time she moved to New York and began working at the *Crisis*. She has also been labeled "prim and proper" and criticized for writing so-called "genteel" novels about people too much like herself.

Yet the bare facts of Fauset's background do not support this kind of criticism of her work. On 27 April 1882 she was born in Camden County, New Jersey, not in Philadelphia as has so often been cited. She was the youngest of seven children born to Redmon Fauset, an African Methodist Episcopal minister, and Annie Seamon Fauset. After her mother's death, her father married a widow with three children and together they had three more. Far from "prosperous," the family was "dreadfully poor," according to Arthur Huff *Fauset, her half brother and a noted anthropologist.

Indeed, Fauset's early successes are attributable to her intelligence and talent, not to any privilege of birth. She attended Girls' High in Philadelphia, a school noted for high academic achievers. Having been denied admission to Bryn Mawr because of her race, she attended Cornell University and graduated Phi Beta Kappa in 1905. She taught full-time from 1905 to 1919 in Washington, D.C.'s public schools, while earning a master's degree from the University of Pennsylvania (1919). She also studied for six months at the Sorbonne during 1925–1926. After her stint at the *Crisis*, Fauset taught French at DeWitt Clinton High School (1927–1944), and her final teaching position was a brief visiting professorship at Hampton Institute (12 September 1949 to 31 January 1950).

During the period after her last book was published and between teaching jobs, Fauset traveled and lectured, wrote poetry, and contented herself with the duties of "housewife" but published very little. She and her husband, Herbert Harris, an insurance broker, lived in Montclair, New Jersey, until his death in 1958. Fauset then moved to Philadelphia and lived with her stepbrother Earl Huff until her own death on 30 April 1961. Carolyn Wedin Sylvander's book *Jessie Redmon Fauset: Black American Writer* (1981), the most comprehensive study of Fauset's life and writings to date, includes this kind of detailed information, as well as close readings of the novels. Thorough and insightful, Sylvander's book notes and discusses discrepancies, corrects biographical misinformation, dispels many myths about the author and her work, and challenges other critics to take up the task of deeper explications of all of Fauset's writings, but especially the novels.

Fauset once said that she liked to tell a "good story." She insisted, despite the demands of the day, that black middle-class society could be interesting and dramatic. Although her work has been caught in the crossfire of the *Black Aesthetic debate then and now, current scholars are beginning to give her the attention and recognition she so richly deserves.

• Abbey A. Johnson, "Literary Midwife: Jessie Redmon Fauset and the Harlem Renaissance," *Phylon* 34 (June 1978): 153. Carolyn Wedin Sylvander, *Jessie Redmon Fauset, Black American Writer*, 1981. Deborah E. McDowell, "The Neglected Dimension of Jessie Redmon Fauset," in *Conjuring*, eds. Marjorie Pryse and Hortense Spillers, 1985. Ann Allen Shockley, *Afro-American Women Writers, 1746–1933: An Anthology and Critical Guide*, 1988. Ann duCille, *The Coupling Convention: Sex, Text, and Tradition in Black Women's Fiction*, 1993. Thadious Davis, introduction to *Afro-American Women Writers, 1910–1940*, ed. Henry Louis Gates, Jr., 1995. Jacquelyn Y. McLendon, *The Politics of Color in the Fiction of Jessie Fauset and Nella Larsen*, 1995.

—Jacquelyn Y. McLendon

FEDERAL WRITERS' PROJECT (FWP), a depression-era New Deal program that employed a number of African American writers and collected significant black *folklore and *autobiography. When President Franklin Roosevelt's Works Progress Administration (WPA) began hiring out-of-work writers to develop a *Guide to America* series, the "Black Cabinet" or "Brain Trust" of John Davis, William Hastie, and Robert Weaver pressed WPA director Harold Ickes for an Office of Negro Affairs to promote both equal employment of African American writers and *black studies. Black representation in the FWP's workforce remained token—only 106 of 4,500 workers in 1937—and inconsistent, with some southern states refusing black applications in order not to spend money for "separate facilities." Yet Virginia, Louisiana, and Florida (as well as New York and Illinois) had active black units, and through the project several African American writers of stature earned necessary income at critical phases of their careers. Richard *Wright, quitting his post office job to write copy for the project in Chicago and New York, found time to write *Native Son* (1940); Zora Neale *Hurston finished three *novels while doing field work in Florida; and young Ralph *Ellison in research on trials and folklore discovered what he called the "density" of black experience. The project also employed Claude *McKay, Margaret *Walker, Willard *Motley, and Frank *Yerby.

Beyond his limited success at influencing FWP personnel decisions, Negro Affairs director Sterling

A. *Brown was able to intercept biased material intended for the *Guide* series and to instigate important new field studies of black subjects. In Chicago, Katherine *Dunham surveyed cults, including the Nation of Islam, and Arna *Bontemps supervised *The Cavalcade of the American Negro* in conjunction with the city's 1940 Diamond Jubliee. The Georgia project's *Drums and Shadows: Survival Studies among the Georgia Coastal Negroes* (1940) sought cultural parallels between Africa and the Sea Islands. Similar studies remained fragmentary or unpublished when Congress ended support in 1939, although the writers' project survived on the state level until 1943 and some data resurfaced in later texts.

Two African American collections distinguish the project's overall work. *The Negro in Virginia* (1940), a treasury of folklore and *history supervised by Roscoe Lewis, won praise from *The Saturday Review* as "one of the most valuable contributions yet made to the American negro's history." The project's greatest monument is the Slave Narrative Collection, interviews and testimonies from more than two thousand of one hundred thousand former slaves living in the 1930s. Charles S. Johnson had initiated such research at Fisk University in 1929, and his student Lawrence Reddick launched a pilot program for the Federal Emergency Relief Administration in 1934. Two years later, white folklore editor John Lomax, on loan from the Library of Congress, designed a standard questionnaire for the American Guide Manual. Brown, along with Lomax's successor Benjamin Botkin, later refined this questionnaire, which was used in seventeen states by dozens of FWP workers. From ten thousand pages of manuscript, Botkin excerpted *Lay My Burden Down: A Folk History of Slavery* (1945), remarking that the ex-slaves' stories possess "an essential truth and humanity that surpasses as it supplements history and literature."

[See also Slave Narrative.]

• Norman Yetman, "The Background of the American Slave Collection," *American Quarterly* 19 (Fall 1967): 534–553. Monty Noam Penkower, *The Federal Writers' Project: A Study in Government Patronage of the Arts*, 1977.

—Craig Howard White

FEMINISM. Black feminism, which sociologist Patricia Hill Collins defines as a self-conscious process of struggle propelling women and men toward a more harmonic vision of community, is integral to the legacy of struggle against racism, sexism, and other forms of oppression evident in African American literature from the early nineteenth century to present times. Black feminist criticism, a further development of this tradition, more specifically intends to supply both the analytical and the pragmatic means to understand and dismantle *gender- and *race-related oppression.

There are several noteworthy anthologies of feminist literature, such as *The Black Woman* (1970), *Sisterfire* (1994), *This Bridge Called My Back* (1981), *Home Girls* (1983), and *Conditions: Five, the Black Women's Issue* (1979), that illuminate the importance of feminist themes in literature. African American feminist literary critics include bell *hooks, Barbara

Christian, Hortense Spillers, Tricia Rose, and Joyce Ann Joyce.

The interrelated and interdependent themes that advance female agency are apparent in nineteenth-century literature, when female personas become speaking subjects, thereby challenging the objectification of women and rejecting an imposed victim status. Objectification and victimization are central, for example, in the autobiographical works of former slaves Harriet A. *Jacobs, Harriet E. *Wilson, and Sojourner *Truth. We see a more direct example of the significance of voice in Maria W. *Stewart's speeches, perhaps the first examples of African American female public oration in support of women's rights. *Poetry and prose such as Frances Ellen Watkins *Harper's "Double Standard" and Ann *Plato's "Advice to Young Ladies" directly express feminist ideas.

In the late nineteenth century Anna Julia *Cooper wrote *A *Voice from the South* (1892), an eloquent narrative about the unmined potential of African women as contributors to American progress. In his career as an abolitionist, Frederick *Douglass often wrote and spoke on behalf of female slaves. Later he championed the women's suffrage movement. Other men who also wrote passionately about the degradation of African American womanhood under a racist patriarchy include W. E. B. *Du Bois and Alexander *Crummell.

The female voice in *slave narratives and nineteenth-century *essays developed into a female protagonist who defined herself independently of men and moved toward journeys of self-discovery and personal autonomy. Explorations on this theme appear in the short prose and *novels of the early nineteenth to mid-twentieth centuries. Jessie Redmon *Fauset's novella *The Sleeper Wakes* is a cautious investigation of how one woman's psychological transformation enables her to criticize the very standards of beauty from which she once benefited. Zora Neale *Hurston's well-known novel *Their Eyes Were Watching God* (1937) chronicles *Janie Crawford's physical travels as they facilitate her emotional and psychological growth towards autonomy and self-possession.

Feminist authors have consistently demanded that the African American literary canon reflect a complete range of women's experiences. This range is evident in works such as Ann *Petry's *The *Street* (1946), Paule *Marshall's *Praisesong for the Widow* (1983), Gwendolyn *Brooks's *Maud Martha* (1953), and Alice *Walker's *Meridian* (1976). The women at the center of the action in these novels draw strength from their various identities and experiences as African American women.

The focus on women's strength is also investigated in poetry by such writers as Rita *Dove, June *Jordan, Sonia *Sanchez, Lucille *Clifton, and Maya *Angelou. For example, Angelou's poem "Phenomenal Woman" celebrates women's unique strength. Audre *Lorde's poetry and her unique work *Zami* (1982) offer full explorations of women relying on inner strength to combat oppression in order to heal themselves. In *Zami*, Lorde also examines the emerging identity of a *lesbian searching for a supportive community.

The appreciation for women's space, women's relationships with other women, and women's supportive communities is a feminist theme explored in Gloria *Naylor's The *Women of Brewster Place (1982). These narratives show women's cooperative efforts encouraging and advancing female agency with various levels of success. Naylor's novel *Mama Day (1988) and Toni Cade *Bambara's The *Salt Eaters (1980) focus on spiritual and metaphysical power attained from women drawing on female ancestral connections. Nearly all of Alice Walker's work illuminates the significance of feminism as a means to attack sexism among African Americans. Ntozake *Shange's play *for colored girls who have considered suicide / when the rainbow is enuf (1977) became a platform for discussion about destructive communication between African American men and women. Walker's classic work *In Search of Our Mothers' Gardens (1983) honors feminism as a historic survival tactic. Her novel The *Color Purple (1982) became a vehicle for a larger debate on the silence surrounding sexual abuse and homophobia. These works conclude with tributes to the indomitable spirit of African American women.

The emphasis on women's relationships demands greater sensitivity for the place of *lesbian relationships in literature such as The Color Purple, Ann Allen *Shockley's novels Loving Her (1974) and Say Jesus and Come to Me (1982), and Audre Lorde's Zami. These authors, along with other accomplished lesbian poets and authors including Becky Birtha, Cheryl Clarke, Pat Parker, June Jordan, and Michelle Cliff insist that lesbian themes are an integral and historic aspect of African American life. Scholars and artists such as Barbara Smith and Ann Allen Shockley have documented African American lesbian characterization in American literature.

The commitment to include the broad spectrum of female sexuality relates to two final themes of feminism. One theme encourages a critique of prescribed roles for men and women. For example, in Their Eyes Were Watching God, Janie's independent spirit tests the social constraints of expected behavior for women. In The Color Purple, *Celie's growth is linked to her making and wearing trousers for herself and for other women. The second explores how those roles reinforce the sexual repression of women, as seen in Alice Walker's *Possessing the Secret of Joy (1992).

Feminism has not always been embraced or encouraged by African American authors, and there are many anti-feminist themes present in the literature. It will no doubt continue to be central to the lively debate about gender and African American culture.

[See also Lesbian Literature; Literary Societies; Womanism; Women's Clubs.]

• Patricia Bell Scott, All the Women Are White, All the Blacks Are Men, but Some of Us Are Brave: Black Women's Studies, 1982. Barbara Smith, Home Girls: A Black Feminist Anthology, 1983. Patricia Hill Collins, Black Feminist Thought, 1990. Darlene Clark Hine, Black Women in America: An Historical Encyclopedia, 1993, p. 418. Beverly Guy-Sheftall, Words of Fire: An Anthology of African-American Feminist Thought, 1995.
—Kimberly Wallace Sanders

Fences. The third play by an African American playwright to be awarded the Pulitzer Prize, August *Wilson's most widely known work won the award in 1987. In addition, it received the New York Drama Critics Circle Award and a Tony Award for best play. Wilson developed the play over more than five years and through, as Joan Fishman discusses ("Developing His Song: August Wilson's Fences," in August Wilson: A Casebook, 1994), more than five drafts. First read at New Dramatists in New York in 1982, the play was developed at the Eugene O'Neill Theater in the summer of 1983, produced at the Yale Repertory Theater in 1985, and taken on the road through productions in Chicago, Seattle, and San Francisco. It opened on Broadway at the 46th Street Theater on 26 March 1987. The cast featured James Earl Jones as Troy and Mary Alice as Rose.

The play centers on Troy Maxson and his family who are posed at the dawn of the *civil rights movement in 1959. An ex-con and a former player in the Negro Baseball League who feels racism crippled his athletic career, Troy now works as a garbage man. Convinced that his son Cory, a talented football player who has been promised a college scholarship, will only encounter similar racism, Troy prevents Cory from accepting the scholarship. Perhaps as a further repercussion of his experience of racism, Troy is unfaithful to his wife Rose and, when his girlfriend dies in childbirth, asks for Rose's help in rearing the child. Rose accepts Raynell, the child, but refuses to have any further conjugal relationship with Troy. After Troy's death, Raynell, Cory, and Rose acknowledge their love for this flawed man through the healing ritual of song.

Wilson wrote the play partly in response to conventional critics who had attacked Ma Rainey's Black Bottom (1984) for its unconventional structure: he wanted to demonstrate that he could write a unified play that centered around a major character. But more importantly, he wanted to elucidate the indignities that African Americans suffered but hid from their children. As Fishman points out, the character of Troy seems loosely based upon Wilson's stepfather, David Bedford, who had also experienced disappointment in *sports, a prison stay, a "new life" with Wilson's mother, and an early death. Brent Staples's review for the New York Times suggested that the play presents the life of many other African Americans as well.

The play's conventional husband-wife and father-son conflicts are subservient to its discussion of racism. It illuminates the inherent inequity in America's treatment of African American males and the ways in which this racism becomes internalized and invades the most private of societal units—the family. The title offers the central metaphor for the play, reflecting the dual nature of those structures that people design for their protection but that also become their prisons.

A critical and commercial success, Fences broke the record for nonmusical plays when it grossed eleven million dollars in one year. Howard Kissel and Michael Feingold praised Wilson's poetic ability; Clive Barnes called it the strongest American writing since that of Tennessee Williams. The play is generally considered to stand alongside the work of Henry Miller for its insightful portrayal of the problematics of the American dream.

[See Piano Lesson, The; Theater.]

—Marilyn Elkins

FESTIVALS. African American writers have always incorporated the colorful rituals and culturally centered themes of their people's traditional annual and occasional festivals in their literature.

Emancipation celebration rituals and themes can be identified in the various genres of African American literature. Perhaps this is true because one of their fifteen or so *freedom celebrations—whose historical origins began on 22 September 1862 when President Abraham Lincoln issued his preliminary proclamation and ended in 1865 with the signing of the Thirteenth Amendment—were celebrated wherever African Americans lived when *slavery was abolished in America. The date that President Lincoln issued the Emancipation Proclamation, 1 January 1863, which was originally celebrated in Massachusetts and other New England states, is now widely celebrated throughout the South, Midwest, and East. Union army victories triggered such celebrations as 8 August in Kentucky and Tennessee and 28 May along the Georgia and Alabama banks of the Chattahoochee River. In his *autobiography, *Up from Slavery (1901), Booker T. *Washington recalled a Union officer arriving to read the Emancipation Proclamation.

General Gordon Granger made the most culturally significant of these readings. Accompanied by a regiment of Union army soldiers, General Granger landed at Galveston, Texas, on 19 June 1865 and read General Order Number 3 declaring freedom of all the slaves in Texas. General Gordon's reading left in its wake a series of regional emancipation celebrations in Texas, Louisiana, Arkansas, and Oklahoma called Juneteenth. The Juneteenth speaker always addressed the themes of a longing for Africa, the horrors of slavery, and the joyous hope of *freedom.

Juneteenth has played a prominent role in the writing of African American writers who grew up celebrating this southwestern freedom day. J. Mason Brewer, who was born in Texas, published a collection of celebration stories under the title "Juneteenth" in Tone the Bell Easy (1932). Ralph *Ellison, an Oklahoma native, published a section of his second novel entitled "Juneteenth" in the Quarterly Review of Literature (1965). Wayne French, a California playwright with Juneteenth cultural roots, produced a play entitled Juneteenth at the Los Angeles Cultural Center in 1983. And Maya Angelou recalled the Juneteenth picnics that she attended while growing up in Stamps, Arkansas, in her autobiography, *I Know Why the Caged Bird Sings (1969).

African American writers continue to make literary use of the themes expressed by Emancipation Day speakers. The theme of Africa appears earliest, perhaps, in Phillis *Wheatley's poem "On Being Brought from Africa to America" (1773). Countee *Cullen's "Heritage" and Langston *Hughes's "Afro-American Fragment" are representative of later poets' treatments of this theme. *Kunta Kinte, the central character in Alex *Haley's *Roots (1976), is driven by a desire to return to Africa. Reverend Deke O'Malley, a fictional representation of Marcus *Garvey in Chester *Himes's *Cotton Comes to Harlem (1964), is the leader of a back to Africa organization. *Celie and Nettie, the long-separated sisters in Alice *Walker's The *Color Purple (1982), are reunited in Africa.

*Slavery is another Emancipation Day speech theme that has been developed by a wide range of African Americans writers. George Moses *Horton's "Slavery" in The Hope of Liberty (1829), Frances Ellen Watkins *Harper's "The Slave Auction" and "The Slave Mother" in Poems on Miscellaneous Subjects (1854), and Robert *Hayden's "Middle Passage" (1968) are poems devoted to this oratorical theme. Frank *Yerby's The *Foxes of Harrow (1946), Margaret *Walker's *Jubilee (1966), and Charles R. *Johnson's *Middle Passage (1990) are *novels that explore the painful theme of slavery.

Revivals and baptisms are religious festivals that also appear in African American literature. Anne *Moody's Coming of Age in Mississippi (1992) and Angelou's Caged Bird provide autobiographical accounts of these two religious festivals. James *Baldwin's *Go Tell It on the Mountain (1953), Owen *Dodson's The Boy at the Window (1951), and Countee Cullen's One Way to Heaven (1932) contain fictional accounts of these religious festivals. Cullen's novel opens with a sinner successfully eluding his crap-shooting creditors by running down the church aisle just as the revivalist was making his call for converts.

Traditional courtship and marriage festivals also appear in African American literature. In Mules and Men (1935), folklorist Zora Neale *Hurston describes a "toe party" courting ritual in which women line up behind a sheet with only their feet exposed; the men select their dates from this line of feet. John O. *Killens's novel The *Cotillion (1971) satirizes the courting rituals of the African American middle class. Alex Haley's novel Roots describes the slave marriage ritual of jumping the broomstick. Dorothy *West's novel The Wedding (1995) explores the social, historical, and cultural implications of an African American middle-class wedding on Martha's Vineyard during the 1950s.

Lastly, African American writers have made great use of weekly Saturday night and occasional sporting festivals in their writings. A wide range of African American literature is based on the hungover African American reveler's answer to the judge's query as to why every Monday morning found him standing before the bar making bail: "Your Honor, if you was black just one Saturday night, you'd never want to be white again." Literary renditions of this reveler's statement can be found in James Weldon *Johnson's novel The *Autobiography of an Ex-Colored Man (1912), Ernest J. *Gaines's *short story collection Bloodline (1968), Sonia *Sanchez's short story "After

Saturday Night Comes Sunday" (1971), and Richard *Wright's novel *Lawd, Today* (1963).

Each knockout scored by Joe *Louis from 1935 to 1949 was marked with parades and parties throughout all of America's African American neighborhoods. Richard Wright composed a *blues-structured poem, "King Joe Blues" (1941), which described the euphoria of these celebrations. *Malcolm X's *Autobiography of Malcolm X* (1964), Angelou's *Caged Bird*, and Quincy Thomas *Troupe, Jr.'s *Miles: The Biography of Miles Davis* (1989) give first-person accounts of these celebrations. Ernest Gaines's *The *Autobiography of Miss Jane Pittman* (1971) and *A Lesson Before Dying* (1993), and Xam Wilson *Cartiér's *Be-Bop, Re-Bop* (1987) are African American novels that mention these celebrations. Cartiér devotes a chapter to describing the wild celebrations that took place in St. Louis's African American community after Louis won the World Heavyweight Championship in 1937 by knocking out the reigning champion, James Braddock, in eight rounds and after Louis's successful defense of his title in 1938 with a first-round knockout of former World Heavyweight Champion Max Schmeling.

[*See also* Marriage.]

• William H. Wiggins, Jr., "'Lift Every Voice': A Study of Afro-American Emancipation Celebrations," in *Discovering Afro-America*, eds. Roger D. Abrahams and John F. Szwed, 1975, pp. 46–57. "Broomsticks and Orange Blossoms," in Eugene D. Genovese, *Roll, Jordon, Roll: The World the Slaves Made*, 1976, pp. 475–481. William H. Wiggins, Jr., "January 1: The Afro-American's 'Day of Days,'" in *Prospects: An Annual of American Cultural Studies*, vol. 4, ed. Jack Saltzman, 1979, pp. 331–353. Trudier Harris, *Exorcising Blackness: Historical and Literary Lynching and Burning Rituals*, 1984. William H. Wiggins, Jr., *O Freedom!: Afro-American Emancipation Celebrations*, 1987. William H. Wiggins, Jr., "From Galveston to Washington: Charting Juneteenth's Freedom Trail," in *Jubilation!: African American Celebrations in the Southeast*, eds. William H. Wiggins, Jr., and Douglas DeNatale, 1993, pp. 61–67.
—William H. Wiggins, Jr.

FETCHIT, STEPIN. *See* Stepin Fetchit.

FICTION. *See* Novel; Short Story.

FIELDS, JULIA (b. 1938), poet, short fiction writer, teacher, and dramatist. Growing up on an Alabama farm, Julia Fields imbibed a love of nature, words, and the cadences of biblical language from both parents and a commitment to craftsmanship from her preacher-carpenter father. By age twelve she had already memorized verses from the Bible and poems of Lewis Carroll, William Wordsworth, Robert Burns, William Shakespeare, and even Henry VanDyke. She recited their lines to herself as she knelt over her garden plot. She mused that poets, such as Wordsworth on Toussaint *L'Ouverture, were writing about blacks "before we did."

In seventh grade, her teacher recognized Fields's talent when she assigned the writing of an original poem. The summer she was sixteen, watching the changing colors of the sky while bringing in the cattle for milking, Fields was inspired to write "The Horizon," her first poem to be published (in *Scholastic* magazine). Fields attended the Presbyterian Knoxville College in Tennessee on scholarship. Dr. Rosey Pool, a concentration camp survivor who had known Anne Frank, visited the school. After hearing some of Fields's poems, she included several in her collection *Beyond the Blues* (1962).

Fields earned her master's degree at Breadloaf and Middlebury College in 1961. She taught in Alabama, then went to the University of Edinburgh in 1963. She was happy in Burns's country because she knew his poems by heart. At Rosey Pool's flat in London she met Langston *Hughes who introduced her to South African writer Richard Rive, who remembered her as statuesque and as a striking beauty (*Writing Black*, 1981). Fields had taught Rive's story "The Bench" to children in Alabama to calm them during times when white racists were driving by shooting. South Africa's apartheid struck a resonant chord with Americans living in the segregated South.

Influences on Fields were tall, elegant Washington poet Georgia Douglas *Johnson, who reminded her of her great aunt Sally, and Robert *Hayden, whose natural elegance also impressed her and whom she admired for giving readings and trying to get to the heart of *poetry despite his poor eyesight and all the criticism against him at one time. She has regretted that *mulatto poets such as Sterling A. *Brown and Jean *Toomer wrote so little about living pale, for that would have helped mulatto children.

Feeling split between teaching and writing poetry, Fields searched for insights. She spent two years in the Library of Congress reading John Ruskin, for example. She says that thousands of poems have come to her over the years. One night poems would not let her sleep and she got up twenty-five times to write them down.

Starting with a commonplace subject, Fields strikes out for something of beauty, such as her poem "Vigil" with its turns on Lorraine *Hansberry and *Macbeth*. A relative commented to Fields on a lady who was a *prostitute but got up every Sunday morning to take the neighborhood children to church. Fields considered that anecdote a modern-day Jesus and Mary Magdalene story. She believes that all great cultures have had this particular group of women: the "hopeless young and gifted whores."

Fields interspersed tramping and dancing, words from Greek culture, and the sacred and the profane in "Loose Feet, Skin Tight, and a Place to Dance." She treats with compassionate humor people who change name or religion for ethnic reasons as in "Sin" and "Alabama Suite," but she says that culture cannot be built on invective. Her "Mary" alludes to women in classical history; it reflects dismay that a man will walk farther for sex—("s-x")—than for justice or *freedom. "Love Poem," written in an era of swingers, was provoked by Fields's ruminating on what had happened to the love of God.

Her themes are the human condition, God's creation, war, women's survival methods, exploitation, and artists known and unknown. A private person, Fields has lived the roles of wife and mother—her two daughters are now grown—but she deflects questions about herself to her work. In teaching inner-city students she calls on her creativity in order to elicit a recognition that real life is reflected in poetry. For that reason, she contends, poetry should be incorporated into every academic discipline: it gives color to *history.

Kenneth Rexroth claimed that Fields represented the arrival of *Negritude in America, and she has been praised by such critics as Clarence *Major and Eugene *Redmond. Fields's collection *Slow Coins* (1981) contains gold mined from common life.

• Kenneth Rexroth, "New American Poets," *Harper's*, June 1965, 65–71. Clarence Major, *The Dark and Feeling: Black American Writers and Their Work*, 1974. Mercedese Broussard, "Blake's Bard," review of *A Summoning, A Shining*, by Julia Fields, *Callaloo* 1 (Dec. 1976): 60–62. Eugene B. Redmond, *Drumvoices: The Mission of Afro-American Poetry*, 1976. Richard Rive, *Writing Black*, 1981. Mary Williams Burger, "Julia Fields," in *DLB*, vol. 41, *Afro-American Poets since 1955*, eds. Trudier Harris and Thadious M. Davis, 1985, pp. 123–131.

—Kathleen A. Hauke

FILM. "Black cinema has not reached the level of accomplishment of a Richard *Wright or a Zora Neale *Hurston," said Spike *Lee at a 1992 conference at Yale. But when cinema was invented a century ago, literature routinely denigrated African Americans. The development of successful African American writers helped check the negative picture of Blacks in American literature by outwriting the racist competition. The same curvature of development may be divined from a century of cinema. But the consequences of this evolution in the politics of visual representation might be even heavier.

From fiction to film, turn-of-the-century Black representation slipped from frying pan to fire. The advance of motion over print, illusions of immediate experience over words on a page, of larger-than-life images in a darkened theatrical setting over the bright solitude of a library seemed to make the deformation of African American personality more graphic, incisive, and infectious than ever before. And the transitions from rudimentary to sophisticated style and technology in cinema's first half-century took place against an arrested primitivism in the portrayal of people of color.

Landmarks of American narrative known for their innovations or historical success have often revolved around African Americans. In films, *The Birth of a Nation* (1915) made *history as the first national blockbuster and as a compendium of technical breakthroughs. But D. W. Griffith's racist epic—really a monument of cinema fascism—is also memorable for the organized protest it provoked from the NAACP and Black activists such as W. E. B. *Du Bois and Monroe Trotter as well as liberal White allies such as Jane Addams in possibly the most concerted resistance to media denigration in U.S. history. The first sound film, *The Jazz Singer* (1927), featured Al Jolson as a blackface minstrel performer. *Gone with the Wind* (1938) made history as a Technicolor historical epic. Disney's *Song of the South* (1946) is credited with important innovations in Technicolor and the mixing of human and cartoon characters (a technique later developed in *Who Framed Roger Rabbit*,

1988, where Black *identity functioned as a subtle subtext). But the originality of these films never extended to humanized Black depiction.

Mainstream American movies have, instead, lagged in humanist significance behind films made by African Americans. Black cinema, meaning films made under African American control or for the primary interest of African Americans as "authenticating audience," first arose in search of digestible, alternative entertainment for Black audiences under the name of "race movies." The myth that Black Americans got serious about producing alternate movie images only after being provoked by *The Birth of a Nation* must be dissolved. The first Black produced-directed film, *The Railroad Porter*, was made by William Foster in Chicago in 1910, five years before Griffith's spectacle of bigotry. Chicago, with "the Stroll," a bustling entertainment district catering to African Americans, was an apt location for this experiment. Foster, a stage manager for Williams and Walker, the celebrated vaudeville team, translated the highly developed stage presence of Black entertainers to the screen. In the process he must have made some innovations, for he has been credited with inventing the madcap slapstick style made famous by the Keystone Kops.

Foster's early efforts (he made at least ten short films) were followed by a succession of venturesome pioneers hoping to fulfill the hunger of Black Americans for ennobling, or at least satisfying, self-images. Peter Jones of Chicago, the first known Black documentary filmmaker, made several nonfictional films between 1910 and 1915 validating Black progress, such as the contributions of Black soldiers to the U.S. military. A major departure came from the Lincoln Motion Picture Company, formed by Noble Johnson and associates on the balcony of a Central Avenue drugstore in Los Angeles in 1916. Lincoln presented what had never been seen before, African Americans as featured players in *serious* film dramas, as opposed to comedies, which remain the preferred genre for Blackness in majority cinema. This group initiated the "genteel *negritude" that came to dominate silent race movies. The tone is hinted at in the title of their first production, *The Realization of a Negro's Ambition* (1916). Lincoln also developed an embryonic distribution system (since distributors refused films about Blacks that were not inferiorized). In an apartheid society, race movie makers had the advantage of a captive, segregated audience.

Noble Johnson's career offers a parable on Black presence in U.S. cinema. After he started making race movies, Johnson was given an ultimatum by Universal Pictures, where he was a featured player performing such "multicultural" roles as Arab, Italian, Native American, and other ethnicities. Universal saw Johnson's double career in effect as competing against himself and, more important, against them. Either he give up his new career, where he was the starring performer in his own independent Black films made in the interest of Black social development, or surrender his place as a prolific contract player in major studio productions. Prophetically, perhaps, Johnson ended his race movie career, which spelled the end of Lincoln Pictures. This is one of the earliest indications that Hollywood took notice of independent Black films as competition.

Before Noble Johnson left the scene, he invited Oscar *Micheaux into the business by seeking the rights to his novel *The Homesteader* (1917). The deal broke down when Micheaux pushed himself as director. This was the entrance into movies of the most singular, controversial, and prolific auteur in Black cinema. As a teenaged Pullman porter traveling out of Chicago, Micheaux had scouted territory in the Great Plains to fulfill his dream of becoming a big-time farmer. When his vision of a ranch empire collapsed, he turned his experience to profit through novel-writing, beginning with the autobiographical *The Conquest* (1913).

As a novelist Micheaux is a light populist romancer but hardly a contributor to literary art. He published and sold his novels from door to door to White farmers in the Midwest and Black workers in the South. His entrepreneurial chutzpah became legendary when he turned to filmmaking. Micheaux's films stand out for their consistent reference to racial themes. A devoted admirer of Booker T. *Washington and his conservative, self-help ideology, Micheaux nevertheless drew the sharpest portrait of racism (and a graphic lynching scene) of its time in the stirring and historically crucial *Within Our Gates* (1920), which can be convincingly viewed as a recoding of *The Birth of a Nation*.

More than 150 Black-oriented independent film companies were formed from 1910 to 1950, managing to produce about 500 films of which only a few survive. Among a dozen or so surviving Micheaux films, *Body and Soul* (1924) stands out for its intelligent use of flashbacks and the intercutting between two roles played by Paul *Robeson as a corrupt preacher and his brother, an upstanding citizen. Altogether Micheaux wrote—sometimes adapting from his novels—produced, directed, and distributed forty films. A few notable silent films made by other companies also survive, such as the experimental thriller *Eleven PM* (1928) by Richard Maurice and *Scar of Shame* (1927), produced by the Colored Players of Philadelphia, which also produced *Ten Nights in a Barroom* (1926), with the only surviving film work of celebrated Black actor Charles Gilpin.

Micheaux alone among Black independents survived the costly transition to sound films. But he soon ran into new competition from a novel style of Black independent film. Ralph Cooper directed and starred in the gangster melodrama *Dark Manhattan* (1937), departing from moral uplift and imitating Hollywood styles, genres, and manners, with higher production values in the bargain. With greater involvement from White producers on the margins of Hollywood, the "race" in race movies began to evaporate, while the films became gangster and nightclub extensions of the world evoked in Apollo Theatre stage revues. Spencer Williams managed to overcome these clichés in several films combining show biz, literary, and sometimes religious sentiments, most notably *Blood of Jesus* (1941).

World War II shut down the race movie industry by curtailing the use of film stock and by scrambling the national sociology. The growing competition from Hollywood (*Cabin in the Sky, Stormy Weather*) and later from television helped turn race movies into an early example of Black institutions lost through racial integration. The shift of Black audience allegiance from flawed but self-determined cinema to more polished but hollow Hollywood fare has been a recurrent feature of the Black film scene from 1937 on. One Hollywood producer responded to an appeal for the particular interests of Black moviegoers by saying "Let 'em go to John Wayne like everybody else."

Black image making has evolved through several incarnations, each episode reflecting major historical configurations such as segregation or the civil rights era, as well as changing conditions of production and reception. Over the decades, frail symptoms have been greedily scanned for signs of a higher symbolic status on the screen, portended in a succession of "new waves" and bright futures, only to be revised as values changed and expectations rose. Sterling A. *Brown and Alain *Locke admired Hollywood's *Hallelujah* (1929), though later viewers do not always notice its sometimes keenly observant portrayal of folk manners. Black Renaissance intellectuals as a whole disapproved of Micheaux's films for their lack of polish; still, some of them celebrated the film version of *The Emperor Jones* (1932) for pioneering a tragic dignity in a leading Black character. The late 1940s and early 1950s, during which cultural identities were shifting, left Black cinema in one of its more barren periods where few choices remained but to "go to John Wayne."

At the same time, the "classical cinema" of Hollywood, its fabled Golden Age, was coming to an end. During this period, the imagery of Black people remained classical in the sense of never changing in its bizarre, incongruent antics. Among the overlooked causes of the decline of classical cinema was the upgrading of Black representation, sparked by the brotherhood propaganda of World War II. The "Negro interest" movies of 1949–1951, including such films as *Pinky, Home of the Brave*, and *Lost Boundaries*, for all their transparent condescending liberalism, helped to modify the Hollywood screen in terms of ethnicity and race.

With more controlling input from Black artists, several midcentury films hinted at productive cultural life after race movies. Playwright Carlton Moss wrote and without credit directed *The Negro Soldier* (1943), an idealized Defense Department documentary of the Black community facing war against fascism. The movie version of *Native Son* (1951), too quickly dismissed for its clumsy acting, as scripted by Richard Wright still carries a political charge, and Wright's enactment of *Bigger Thomas remains engrossing. William Alexander produced a few films in this period that went beyond the nightclub-musical-gangster formulas and looked to a more subtle, sociologically informed realism. *Souls of Sin* (1949) shares some of the urban desperation of Wright's fiction, and in its lead character, Dollar Bill, suggests the naturalistic Actors Studio "method" that would revolutionize screen performance.

But during the doldrums period for Black independent films, roughly from 1955 to 1965, Black audiences had an option other than John Wayne in Sidney Poitier. It has become fashionable to view Poitier's screen persona in these years where he became a major star as Uncle Tomish. This characterization is sometimes made in the next breath after commentators applaud the *Sambo performances of *Stepin Fetchit for the something extra he brought to demeaning caricatures. Poitier's roles were likewise dominated by the racial ethos of the times, mostly a liberal paternalism, but he also brought a more modern, crisply less servile sensibility to these roles than most of the performers who preceded him.

Two films directed by Whites that stand as transitions between the Poitier racial goodwill movies and those to come are Michael Roemer's Nothing but a Man (1964) and Anthony Harvey's British production of LeRoi Jones's (Amiri *Baraka's) play *Dutchman (1966). Nothing but a Man succeeds culturally where the Poitier films disappoint, by being willing to enter the Black community as more than a negative space from which to escape in order to service the needs of White characters or narratives. One symptom of this openness to the weight of African American lives is the focus on a Black couple, fighting to make a family in a hostile, segregated southern environment. Nothing but a Man remains readable today as an adult, literate reflection on southern Black social experience on the verge of the thrust toward Black empowerment. The film version of Dutchman continues to hold intensity as a faithful translation of Jones's explosive theater manifesto.

After these early chapters in the making of Black cinema, conditioned by the predicaments of legalized apartheid, two simultaneous episodes came out of the civil rights–Black Power period. The race relations films of Poitier prepared audiences for the first Hollywood films by Black directors—Gordon *Parks's The Learning Tree (1969) and Melvin Van Peebles's Watermelon Man (1970). But even earlier, the self-taught Madeline Anderson's short documentary Integration Report #1 (1964) signaled the rebirth of Black independent cinema. From the mid-1960s on, the major streams of filmmaking under African American direction came to reflect these two orientations.

For a brief moment, with the appearance of Melvin Van Peebles's Sweet Sweetback's Baaaaad Ass Song (1970), both currents seemed powerfully present in one film. Van Peebles's sensational film was funded under the pretense of being a porn movie. The Black exploitation movies that followed in its wake also recall porn movies in their cheap production values, minimalist acting, reliance on sociological clichés, refusal of complexity, and narratives that stagger from one poorly motivated scene to another, moving toward a climactic moment of violent physical or verbal confrontation where in a porn film there would be sex.

But Sweetback was also stylistically original, organizing episodic scenes around pivotal themes of Black historical experience rather than closely knit narrative plot points, making use of oppositional screen symbolism, heavily ideological populist verbal and visual rhetoric, and experimental camera work. Sweetback was very much a highly individualized, even auteur film that could motivate young independents in film school even while its unprecedented profits, from "four-walling" distribution (directly renting a theater) excited the opportunists of "Black Hollywood."

As the commercial offshoot of Sweetback's success, Blaxploitation was typical of Hollywood's treatment of serious issues, making grand, synthetic displays of social consciousness while funneling the narrative into the most conventional, formulaic ruts. Shaft (1971) and Superfly (1972) delivered moviegoing pleasures equal to those of "White" Hollywood movies while heavily sampling Black street style. But most of these films were grade B or lower. Years later, these films sometimes enjoy a vogue as nostalgic camp. And in their overblown, carnivalesque-corny theatrics, their exhibition of Blackness as street-corner bravado, they sometimes managed a sympathetic parody of cultural affirmation.

The rise of Black Hollywood also made possible several films that broke through the low ceiling on Blaxplo intelligence, while using its commercial vogue as leverage and cover. This description applies to a masterpiece such as playwright and actor Bill *Gunn's Ganja and Hess (1973) and to the engaging comedy on cultural identity Five on the Blackhand Side (1973), the almost credible music biz drama Sparkle (1976), the convincing exploration of Black women's experiences in Black Girl (1972), the serious-minded melodrama about antiracist revolution The *Spook Who Sat by the Door (1973), and the depiction of a captivating ensemble of young Black teenagers facing life and danger in Cooley High (1975). But when Hollywood discovered in the mid-1970s that it could rake in the Black audience's money by offering them the current version of John Wayne— such as Charles Bronson or Clint Eastwood—and stopped making Black exploitation movies altogether, opportunities for these more imaginative, less formulaic films disappeared with them.

The rise of Black-directed documentary films formed one front of resistance to the mendacity of Blaxploitation. Black Journal arose in 1968 as a television magazine on PBS devoted to the affairs of the Black community. Under the leadership of Bill Greaves, an experienced, principled documentarian, Black Journal became the incubating center for a generation of young Black independents such as Madeline Anderson, St. Claire Bourne, Stan Lathan, Kent Garret, Tony Batten, Lou Potter, and Horace Jenkins, among others. The show often featured short films by these directors among its news items and served as a laboratory for new ideas about Black film grammar.

"The L.A. Rebellion" formed another important concentration of Black independent innovation. This movement among filmmakers who studied together at UCLA in the late 1960s and 1970s aided the development of Charles Burnett, Haile Gerima, Larry Clark, theoretician Tshome Gabriel, Ben Caldwell, Julie Dash, Billy Woodberry, Alile Sharon Larkin, and Zeinabu Davis. These university-trained directors were passionately opposed to Black Hollywood movies and focused on fictional and feature films in rivalry with Hollywood's example. Inspired by the new Black African cinema, Cuban and Third World films, and independent and art films from around the world, these filmmakers, together with their independent contemporaries, assembled the freshest, most uncorrupted body of Black representation orchestrated in the nation's history. Their work continues to provide a measure of cultural maturity on the screen, whether in or outside of Hollywood.

Of these filmmakers, Haile Gerima has been the most prolific and diverse in working toward a self-identified Black film culture and is known for the explosive energy of his film style. Gerima's films include *Child of Resistance* (1973), *Harvest: Three Thousand* (1976), *Bush Mama* (1976), *Ashes and Embers* (1982), and *Sankofa* (1993). Gerima took a page from Micheaux and Van Peebles by four-walling a distribution network for *Sankofa* with great success after traditional distributors turned down this wrenching reexamination of *slavery. Gerima also organized a vital distribution company for independents, Mepheduh Film Co., and as a professor at Howard University he has trained several talented younger film professionals.

Perhaps the most identifying feature of Charles Burnett's films has been the sensitivity he brings to the binds and confusions of the South Central Los Angeles community where he developed. With this setting *Killer of Sheep* (1977) has become an independent film classic and a winner of a Golden Bear award at the Berlin Film Festival. *To Sleep with Anger* (1990), a family drama produced in Hollywood, is reminiscent of the culturally articulate plays of August *Wilson. Burnett also wrote and directed *The Glass Shield* (1995).

Daughters of the Dust (1991) by Julie Dash is the first feature film directed by an African American woman to be distributed theatrically. (Black women have, however, played crucial roles in the development of Black cinema from the beginning—including the screenplay for the first Black-produced film in 1910—a history that has yet to be written.) Following a family and community of Sea Islanders at the moment when their deeply rooted African spiritual world is about to break up, *Daughters* floods the screen with beautiful reasons for the retention of ancestral values. With this film, the uncertainty whether Black cinema would ever attain the resonance of the finest African American literature has been ended.

In other venues, Black independent film work of equal importance managed to get made against the extraordinary obstacles facing independents. Kathy Collins (*Losing Ground*, 1982) trained at the Sorbonne and taught at CUNY; Charles Lane (*A Place in Time*, 1988, remade as *Sidewalk Stories*, 1989) is a product of New York City schools and universities; Woodie *King, Jr., best known as a New York theater producer and director, has made a succession of films reflecting the momentous 1960s, including *A Torture of Mothers* (1980); and Warrington Hudlin (*Street Corner Stories*, 1978, producer, *Houseparty*, 1990) trained at Yale. Hudlin also organized the influential Black Film-makers Foundation. And the most potently revisionary recent work has come from Spike Lee, trained at New York University.

She's Gotta Have It, Lee's 1986 breakthrough film, like *Sweetback*, has been influential in competing arenas, both the commercial Hollywood scene and the world of intellectual art cinema. Perhaps more significant, Lee's work has propelled the powerful coming together of both strands. With *She's Gotta Have It*'s box-office popularity coming at the same time as Robert Townsend's *Hollywood Shuffle* (1987), Hollywood once again rediscovered the Black audience. The "new wave" of the late 1980s and the 1990s has been diverse and diffuse in its significance. Confounding predictions, university-trained youngsters have produced populist blockbusters such as John Singleton's *Boyz N the Hood* (1991) or the Hughes brothers' *Menace II Society* (1993). At the same time, artists whose main development came outside of universities have delivered some of the more reflective and literate of the new wave films, such as *One False Move* (1992), a *noir* with a message, directed by actor Carl Franklin, and *Chameleon Street* (1989), the brilliant identity fable directed by actor Wendell Harris.

Lee's own films have each broken new ground and exhibited vitalities hitherto unsuspected of the American screen, including the subversion of the hypnotic, utopian musical genre in *School Daze* (1988), the breakdown of national race hatred in *Do the Right Thing* (1989), and the magnum bio-epic *Malcolm X* (1992). Lee's excursion from Black independent cinema to Hollywood big-budget productions has carried with it the commitment to antiracist resistance in incisive, penetrating spectacles. The armature of cinema technology that was originally most fluent as a weapon of racism is now more often used in the other direction.

The new wave of films coming out of Hollywood has generally been a disappointment when viewed beside the richness of African American literature. This disappointment rises most visibly vis-à-vis teen-targeted productions such as the *Houseparty* sequels, the broad racial self-caricature of Keenan Ivory Wayans's productions, the sensationalism of Black gang-banging—all of which are accurately identified as exhumations of the money lust of Blaxploitation.

But these Blackness titillations have been less dominant than generally assumed, financially or culturally. And as in the Blaxplo episode of the 1970s, several films of humanist value continue to slip through the cracks. *Just Another Girl on the IRT* (1993) by Leslie Harris diversified the "hood" movie premise with a rare immersion into the hip lifestyle of a Black teenaged girl coming of age among the hairy excitements of the inner city. Darnell Martin's *I Like It Like That* (1994) also captured the urban explosiveness of Spike Lee and his followers in a

Bronx-based film about a young Puerto Rican woman taking charge of her risk-filled life. Ayoka Chenzira's sweet women's family tale *Alma's Rainbow* (1993) deserved better distribution than it got. And in a brief period of 1994–1995 several exciting social consciousness films appeared, such as *Drop Squad*, a social-political satire, and *Tales from the Hood*, an even wilder social satire, both with production assistance from Spike Lee. John Singleton's *Higher Learning* and Charles Burnett's *The Glass Shield* brought polish and drama to edgy issues of national, racial, and public policy. Mario Van Peebles's *Panther* made a telling re-creation of the birth of the Black Panther Party from a script by his father Melvin Van Peebles.

The development of Black cinema has surely fallen short of the needs and expectations of the Afrogentsia. It has not, for instance, placed a check on the misrepresentation of Black people in mass media or shaped an alternative to their miseducation through media and educational institutions. But by other measures, the nearly one hundred years of effort show impressive gains. Though seldom calibrated in assessments of this sort, the multiplication of Black representations and of other people of color in guises beyond depressing stereotypes has steadily altered the equation that humanity on the screen means White humanity. A measure of heightened cine-cultural consciousness is the growing understanding that "Black cinema" must mean filmmaking dominated by the prepositions *by, about,* and/or *for.*

Moreover, Black cinema in recent years has generally been more persistently and intelligently *about* something than the run-of-the-mill Hollywood movie—with the mill grinding with increasing dim-wittedness—though perhaps only occasionally up to its most distinguished level. After a century of Black screen imagery, dissatisfaction reflects a heavier moral responsibility placed on Black cinema than is expected of Hollywood generally—a weight of expectations made possible by consolidated cinema achievements. Meanwhile, a repertory of historically memorable, captivating, and intellectually energizing films is slowly amassing. A history of Black Americans as reflected in cinema is acquiring density, as well as a fascinating history of Blacks *in* cinema that is more than a litany of abuse and shame.

[*See also* Aunt Jemima; Coon; Drama; Mammy; Minstrelsy; Musicals; Sapphire; Television.]

• Thomas Cripps, *Slow Fade to Black,* 1977. Henry T. Sampson, *Blacks in Black and White,* 1977. Clyde Taylor, "Decolonizing the Image: New U.S. Black Cinema," in *Jumpcut: Hollywood, Politics and Counter-Cinema,* ed. Peter Stevens, 1985. Donald Bogle, *Blacks in American Film and Television,* 1989. *Black American Literature Forum,* "Black Film Issue," 25.2 (Summer 1991). *Wide Angle,* special issue on Black cinema, 13.3–4 (July–Oct. 1991). Pearl Bowser and Bestor Cram, codirectors, *Midnight Ramble: The Life and Legacy of Oscar Micheaux* (documentary film), 1993. Manthia Diawara, ed., *Black American Cinema,* 1993. Ed Guerrero, *Framing Blackness,* 1993. James Snead, *White Screens/ Black Images,* 1994. Clyde Taylor, *Breaking the Aesthetic Contract,* forthcoming 1997.   —Clyde Taylor

Fire!!, a 1926 journal featuring literature and art of the *Harlem Renaissance's second generation.

Langston *Hughes asked Wallace *Thurman to edit the planned quarterly, with which Hughes intended to "*epater* [amaze] *le bourgeois*" and Thurman hoped to "satisfy pagan thirst for beauty unadorned." The journal's subtitle—"Devoted to Younger Negro Artists"—also announced its departure from the social commentary of established contemporary journals such as the *Crisis, *Opportunity,* and the *Messenger.* Its single issue featured a cover drawing by Aaron Douglas and woodcuts by Richard Bruce; a play and a story by Zora Neale *Hurston; poems by Hughes, Countee *Cullen, and Arna *Bontemps; stories by Gwendolyn *Bennett and Bruce; and a rare defense, by Thurman, of Carl Van Vechten's *Nigger Heaven.* The venture suffered from poor financing (managed by John P. Davis), but this neither paid for the expensive paper and type upon which Thurman insisted the journal be printed, nor compensated for Richard Bruce *Nugent's inept distribution, the older black press's dismissive reviews, and white critics' disregard. Finally, most copies of *Fire!!* burned in an apartment-house blaze. Two years later, Thurman founded the more moderate *Harlem: A Forum for Negro Life,* but it too failed after its premier issue.

[*See also* Journalism.]

• Langston Hughes, *The Big Sea,* 1940. Carol Lynn DeKane, "Wallace Thurman," in *Black Writers: A Selection of Sketches from Contemporary Authors,* ed. Linda Metzger, 1989.
                                     —Craig Howard White

Fire Next Time, The. James *Baldwin's well-received 1963 volume *The Fire Next Time* consists of two *essays. The first, "My Dungeon Shook: Letter to My Nephew on the One Hundredth Anniversary of the Emancipation," was written on the occasion of the fourteenth birthday of Baldwin's nephew James, who was named after him. The second essay, "Down at the Cross: Letter from a Region in My Mind," recounts Baldwin's experiences growing up in New York, including his unpleasant encounters with the police, his attraction to and rejection of Christianity, his awareness of sexual pitfalls in Harlem, and his later encounter with the Honorable Elijah Muhammad. Filling in the backdrop for these specific comments is Baldwin's ever-spirited indictment of an America in which inequities between the races continue to define people's futures. Recognizing that politics are endemic to life, Baldwin uses the volume for his own political commentary, and that commentary serves to underscore the thoroughly engaging personal and social incidents he relates.

The two essays naturally set up a contrast between past and present, between the sometimes sordid adventures of the older James and the possible revisionist future for the younger James. As powerful expressions from Baldwin at his height as an essayist, the book was a best-seller as well as a popular teaching tool in the 1960s. The much shorter "My Dungeon Shook" takes the form of a letter Baldwin addresses to James. In it, he provides family history and indictments of America for the racism that has pervaded that family history. He indicates that James must remain free of racial prejudice himself, however, in order to be clear-sighted in the fight against racists, for they are themselves frequently "innocent" and "well-meaning." He enlists his nephew's aid in making America "what America must become," that is, receptive to all of its native sons and daughters, allowing the black ones the same opportunities as the white ones.

Baldwin's eloquence continues in the second, much longer essay. "Down at the Cross" is a recounting, first of all, of the perils that Baldwin himself has survived. As survivor, he can serve as example to the young James. Beginning when he himself was fourteen, Baldwin recounts his attraction to the church as a source of possible safety from the evils and fear of the society, as well as his competition with his father, incidents that would form the basis for his first, autobiographical novel, *Go Tell It on the Mountain* (1953). After a short term as a young minister, and extensive commentary on the failures of Christianity, Baldwin leaves the church. He then recounts meeting Elijah Muhammad twenty years later and being saddened that he could not be convinced that Muhammad's way was significantly different from Christianity in its possibilities for failure. He then discusses the position of black people in America and asserts that the country can never be a nation until it solves its color problem. If it does not, he predicts destructive consequences in the image of "the fire next time."

• Therman B. O'Daniel, *James Baldwin: A Critical Evaluation*, 1977.
—Trudier Harris

First World. Published inconsistently between 1977 and 1983 by the First World Foundation of Atlanta, Georgia, *First World* identified itself as a forum for diverse interpretations of the multifaceted Black experience. Edited by Hoyt *Fuller and Carole A. Parks, and sporting an impressive list of editorial advisors from a cross section of the national Black community, *First World* featured *journalism, scholarly articles, fiction, and *poetry by such well-known writers as John Henrik Clarke, Mari *Evans, Chester *Himes, June *Jordan, and Sterling Stuckey. It addressed both national and international issues, such as environmentalism, the legacy of desegregation, and apartheid in South Africa, as well as cultural and literary *criticism, such as a study of Paul *Robeson by five different writers. Although its *publishing history was brief, readers' enthusiastic greeting of *First World*, which replaced the smaller and less polished *Black World*, indicated the tremendous need for such an intellectual journal published by and for Black people.

[*See also* Periodicals.]

• Review, *Black Book Bulletin* 4 (Winter 1976): 85. Ernst J. Wilson, review of *First World*, *Black Scholar* 8.1 (Mar. 1977): 53.
—Maggie Sale

FISHER, RUDOLPH (1897–1934), novelist, short story writer, and leading figure of the Harlem Renaissance. In his short stories and two published novels Rudolph Fisher was concerned with the development of an urban community with few models to guide it. This was a community that, jazzlike, had to improvise against the history of the rural South and creeping disillusionment with the urban North.

Rudolph John Chauncey Fisher was born 9 May 1897 in Washington, D.C., to the Reverend John W. and Glendora Williamson Fisher. Fisher was the youngest of three children, with an older brother, Joseph, and an older sister, Pearl. In 1903 the family moved to New York, but by 1905 they had resettled in Providence, Rhode Island. Rudolph Fisher attended public schools in Providence and graduated from Classical High School with high honors. By the end of senior year, his interest in both literature and science was established. This was evident throughout his undergraduate career at Brown University (1915–1919). He was elected to Phi Beta Kappa and other honorary societies; he won prizes for performances in his German classes, for public speaking, and for his work in rhetoric and English composition. During his senior year he was elected a commencement-day speaker, and using as his subject the emancipation of science, Fisher attempted to argue for the compatibility of science and religion. In two stories published late in his career, "John Archer's Nose" and "The Conjure Man Dies," he would dramatize if not their compatibility, at least their resigned coexistence. Fisher received an MA in biology at Brown in 1920 and entered Howard Medical School that fall. By the time he finished medical school, Fisher had started at least four *short stories, all of which would eventually be published. His first and still one of his most popular, "The City of Refuge," was submitted to *Atlantic Monthly* during the spring of his senior year; it was published the following year. Fisher graduated with highest honors from medical school in 1924, interned for a year at Freedman's Hospital, and won a research fellowship, which supported him from September 1925 to October 1927. In 1926 his lengthy story "High Yaller" won the Amy Spingarn Prize for fiction. In just a few short years, Rudolph Fisher had distinguished himself in the study of medicine and in the writing of short fiction.

While his fiction writing continued steadily, Fisher set up practice as a roentgenologist, working at various New York City hospitals before moving into private practice at his home in Jamaica, Long Island. He was among the few who practiced in the new field of X-ray technology and among the very few African Americans who practiced the specialty between 1920 and 1940.

By 1924 Fisher had met Jane Ryder, a lively and intelligent grade-school teacher in Washington. They married within a year and a half of meeting, and by 1926 a son, Hugh, was born. Fisher promptly and jokingly nicknamed him "the *New Negro," the popular term that characterized the pride and assertiveness of many during this period.

Music was always vitally important to Rudolph Fisher and his work. By 1919 he had met and befriended Paul *Robeson, then a student at Rutgers. With Paul singing and Rudolph playing the piano and arranging, they toured the East Coast, hoping to raise money for tuition. Later, while a research fellow, Fisher helped shape some of the skits for a musical revue that was to star Robeson. An avid fan of *jazz, "Bud" Fisher, with his wife and friends, often visited Harlem cabarets, speakeasies, and nightclubs. His observations on racially integrated audiences in Harlem and the rage for jazz are wryly presented in his essay "The Caucasian Storms Harlem." In his fiction he was always sensitive to the use of music as more than backdrop or narcotic. He experimented with interesting ways to make the music an essential ingredient in the story. There are fine examples of this in "Common Meter" and "Miss Cynthie" and in the long masquerade ball scene in The *Walls of Jericho (1928).

In March, October, and December 1934, Fisher underwent surgeries for a stomach disorder. He died on 26 December 1934 at Edgecombe Sanitarium in New York City. A first lieutenant in the reserve medical corps of the 369th Infantry, Fisher was buried three days later with members of the detachment in attendance.

Fisher's bright, open comic sense encouraged the development of a Black literary voice that did not avoid the ambiguities and contradictions within the urban community. Whether applied to the specific genre of the mystery story or to literary fiction, his accounts of a group attempting to achieve community were perceptive and helped to deeply enrich as well as suggest fresh directions for a literature entering its modern period.

[See also Harlem Renaissance.]

• Arthur Davis, From the Dark Tower: Afro-American Writers (1900–1960), 1974. Robert Bone, Down Home: A History of Afro-American Short Fiction from Its Beginnings to the End of the Harlem Renaissance, 1975. Bruce Kellner, Harlem Renaissance: A Historical Dictionary for the Era, 1987. John McCluskey, Jr., City of Refuge: Collected Stories of Rudolph Fisher, 1987.   —John McCluskey, Jr.

Flight to Canada (1976), Ishmael *Reed's fifth *novel, extends his permutation of literary forms such as the Western and the mystery to the foundational genre of African American letters, the *slave narrative. In it, Reed turns his historical revisionism, formerly directed at the Crusades, the Old West, and the *Harlem Renaissance, to the antebellum South and the Civil War.

The two main protagonists of Flight to Canada are Uncle Robin, a house slave who alters his master's will, leaving the plantation to himself, and *Raven Quickskill, a runaway slave whose poem "Flight to Canada" is simultaneously the impetus for his escape and the means for tracking him down—suggesting both the power and the risk of writing. Both of these characters—like the central figures in Reed's previous books—are *tricksters. They represent different generations (the old folks and the young "blood") with different strategies for surviving and "getting over." Uncle Robin, a "radical" alternative to Harriet Beecher *Stowe's *Uncle Tom, prefers to turn things his way rather than turn the other cheek; moreover, he stays "home" and works to undermine the slaveocracy from within, instead of "flying" north. Raven does fly (by jumbo jet!), but in the end, the promise

of Canada proves illusory, and the novel concludes with his return to the plantation. Among other things, Reed implies that freedom is something we have to create, not simply seek.

Reed's use of anachronism (Lincoln's assassination, for example, takes place on television) is a strategy he has employed before, allowing him to challenge the neat, linear ordering of events that characterizes both our writing of *history and our sense of time, of "progress." It also enables him to bring the past into the present in ways that notify us we haven't gone as far as we might think in redressing old problems, in resolving persistent contradictions in the American experiment. Thus, Reed's take-off on the slave narrative is not just another example of his ongoing effort, begun in his first novel, The Freelance Pallbearers, to play with, and assert the play in, the texts of the African American tradition. Published in the year of the American bicentennial, this story of a runaway slave serves as a reminder that, two hundred years after the establishment of the nation, there still is something "fugitive" about black writing and the experience it articulates.

As has been the case with the majority of Reed's novels, some commentators have persisted in employing a laugh meter to evaluate his work—that is, assessing the degree to which Reed is funny or not. Still, with the exception of *Mumbo Jumbo, Flight to Canada is Reed's most critically acclaimed work of fiction. Henry Louis *Gates, Jr., in his *essay on Reed in the Dictionary of Literary Biography (vol. 33, 1984), considers Flight to Canada to be a major work, while Edmund White, reviewing the novel for the Nation (18 September 1976), went so far as to call it "the best work of black fiction since *Invisible Man."

• Hortense Spillers, "Changing the Letter: The Yokes, the Jokes of Discourse, or, Mrs. Stowe, Mr. Reed," in Slavery and the Literary Imagination, eds. Deborah E. McDowell and Arnold Rampersad, 1989, pp. 25–61. Ashraf H. A. Rushdy, "Ishmael Reed's Neo-HooDoo Slave Narrative," Narrative 2.2 (May 1994): 112–139.   —Robert Elliot Fox

FLOWERS, A. R. (b. 1951), novelist, essayist, and cultural activist. A native Memphian, Arthur Flowers's writing integrates regional African American culture, including *blues music, hoodoo spirituality, Delta dialect, and oral traditions. His delving into the local, linguistically and culturally, is evocative of Zora Neale *Hurston (who makes a cameo appearance in his first novel), Langston *Hughes, and Ishmael *Reed. Moreover, attending John O. *Killens's (founder of the Harlem Writer's Guild) writing workshop at Columbia University over a span of thirteen years has clearly influenced Flowers. Killens believed that art is a form of propaganda and that it can have decolonizing uses. The workshop inspired Flowers to cofound (with others, including Doris Jean *Austin and B. J. Ashanti) and to act as executive director of the New Renaissance Writer's Guild in New York. Flowers also founded a literary workshop in Memphis called the Griot Shop.

Flowers's writings can be placed in a historical continuum of activism: for him, writing is political because it is a powerful factor in shaping values and behavior. His novels and workshops therefore provide an arena for reconceptualizing African American *identity; they are linked to notions of the social responsibility of the artist as an ideological orchestrator. It is in this vein that Flowers describes himself as a literary hoodoo man and as a literary blues man.

His first novel, *De Mojo Blues* (1985), describes the physical and emotional journeys of three dishonorably discharged Vietnam veterans. Each character chooses a different path in his quest to redefine both masculinity and power: Mike attends law school and becomes active in business and politics; Willie D. works as a community activist in New York; and Tucept HighJohn apprentices hoodoo in Memphis in order to learn how to influence the mental and spiritual energies in others. Flowers's prose and dialect evoke the authenticity of place and character of the Black Power era. He captures a part of the African American community in a moment of transition and restructuring, and his use of arhythmic bluesy prose allows the reader to view both the characters and the culture from within.

Another Good Loving Blues (1993) captures another period of transition—the Great Migration—and, again, Flowers emphasizes creative survival in the face of change. Narrated by a griot named Flowers, the novel focuses on Melvira Dupree (a conjure woman) and Lucas Bodeen (a blues man). It is part love story, part fable (Flowers integrates oral traditions of parable, folktale, and toasts), and part quest for artistic authenticity. The subtext reveals many of the difficulties facing African Americans during this period of increased racial tension and violence. Flowers's prose again evokes blues music and the region.

Flowers identifies with his characters because his writing is based in his lived experiences (in Vietnam and as a blues musician, for example). Most importantly, however, in both his novels and his writing workshops, Flowers directly links participation in and knowledge of African American cultural heritage to racial consciousness.   —Vivian M. May

FOLK LITERATURE describes the imaginative achievements of oral performers in creating and passing down African American *folklore by word of mouth; it also refers to the *novels, *short stories, plays, poems, and other fictional forms in which established creative writers draw upon settings, patterns, themes, and characters from the oral traditions in the imagining of their fictional worlds. At a glance, literature and folklore might be thought to be incompatible as creative endeavors, especially since folk traditions are usually oral and anonymous while literature is written and has clearly defined creators. However, the collective imaginations of Africans enslaved in the New World and those freed to carry on their traditions reveal a striking tendency to metaphor, simile, turns of phrases, and expressions that would define the more recognizably created literary forms. Consideration of such creativity reveals that oral forms can be as "literary" as those formal expressions for which such characteristics are gener-

ally taken for granted. Since the phrase "folk literature" can be used to refer to more than one creative effort, perhaps an appropriate approach would be to establish clarifications through subdivisions within the discussion.

Literary Qualities of Folkloristic Compositions. Generally deprived of access to *literacy and the ease of written forms, African Americans passed on orally a body of lore that researchers began formally collecting in the 1890s. As early as the 1850s, however, novelist William Wells *Brown noted the propensity to rhyme among enslaved persons he encountered. He included in *Clotel, or The President's Daughter* (1853) the following quatrain: "The big bee flies high, / The little bee make the honey; / The black folks makes the cotton / And the white folks gets the money." While such a rhyme might not stack up to the formal characteristics of Elizabethan or neoclassical *poetry, it nonetheless illustrates the creative side of the folk imagination. It illustrates further the source from which much folk creativity would find its inspiration: the world of nature.

Another source for early folk creativity was the Bible. From *spirituals to *blues, enslaved and newly freed Africans derived their metaphors, similes, and analogies from biblical circumstances and characters. In spirituals and other songs in the nineteenth century, *slavery was hell and Canada was Canaan. Harriet *Tubman was the *Moses sent on God's mission of rescue as she led hundreds of enslaved blacks to free soil: "When Israel was in Egypt Land / Let my people go / Oppressed so hard they could not stand / Let my people go." Verbal creations reflected ongoing ties between Jews and African Americans, with Egypt being the American South and its horror of slavery. In the sacred as well as the secular realm, however, biblical ties proved inspiring for folk creativity. Getting religion or being converted was being "slain in the spirit" in the manner of Paul on the Damascus road. New converts had to "testify" or give "witness" to their experiences in the manner of many biblical revelations.

In the secular realm, blues musicians were especially known for the poetry of their artistic creations, and scholars have recognized their contributions to literature. Metaphor is prominent in blues lyrics, and the double entendres of sexual innuendoes are infamous: "Let me be your coffee grinder / I sure can grind that coffee good." Or, "another mule kicking in my stall." Or, "Come on and peel my potatoes." In "The Blues as Folk Poetry" (1958), Sterling A. *Brown argues convincingly for the creativity of that particular folk form. Brown gives special attention to the natural world and its attendant tragedies such as floods—from which bluespeople derive their inspiration—and pays additional attention to the images they have developed; such images are "highly compressed, concrete, imaginative, original," as in "My man's got a heart lak a rock cast in de sea," or they employ "the comic hyperbole," as in "You got a handful of gimme, a mouthful of much obliged." Writing at an early point in the scholarly focus on African American folk culture, Brown urged further study of the poetic qualities of the blues, an appeal to which later scholars such as Samuel Charters responded.

Similar literary arguments could be made of the folk poetry known as "toasts." Described as long narrative poems of rhyming couplets that feature alternating action and dialogue, these poems are especially popular among African American males, and they have been collected extensively from black male prison populations. Toasts feature characters of strength and will in the animal and human worlds and include such popular poems as "Shine and the Titanic," "The Signifying Monkey," "Stagolee," and "The Great McDaddy." The first two toasts pit the less powerful against more powerful forces, whereas the second two feature bad men who defy law and community to get whatever they want; sexual prowess plays a large role in these toasts. Comedians such as Rudy Ray Moore commercialized the form in albums considered a bit too off-color for mainstream music stores. Pigmeat Markham recited verses fairly close to the toast tradition in many of his comic routines of the 1940s, and it would not be a stretch of influence to find echoes of the form in the lyrics of contemporary rap artists. Toasts adhere to a regular rhythm and meter, usually following a pattern of four stressed syllables as the dominant memory aid: "Down in the Jungle near a dried up creek / The Signifying Monkey hadn't slept for a week." They feature active verbs to capture the dramatic encounters between clashing forces, and they highlight the violent conflict.

Settings in which such poems are recited emphasize their function in African American culture. While they are certainly forms of entertainment, they are also useful in establishing reputations. Men who recite such rhymes with flair earn reputations as "men of words," a distinction that would gain respect for them not only among the predominantly male audiences but among women as well. Reputations as good talkers carry sexual advantages as well as public approval, for it would be generally assumed that men so gifted would have an advantage in getting to know women. Solid verbal skills would also place these men in company with the better verbal artists among disc jockeys. It is that tradition of oral skill that also informed Muhammad *Ali's face-offs with his various opponents and that has now become commonplace among television wrestlers.

Verbal skills and creative dexterity also inform the dozens, a more intensely competitive form than the toast. Most popular among adolescent males, the dozens are a rhyming game in which one opponent tries to best the other by reciting traditional insults or by creating spur-of-the-moment insults directed at the other opponent's relatives, particularly his mother. Usually surrounded by an audience of boys who urge on the conflict by applauding insults and "oohing" and "aahing" over put-downs, the opponents must master the trick of quick retort and increasing insult without resorting to fisticuffs. The game is a test of keeping one's cool as well as a test of on-the-spot creative skills. Girls can also play the dozens, as can adults of both genders, but the game becomes more serious in implications for adults.

Even with young boys, it may lead to fights if one opponent is not quick enough in his comebacks to reap appreciation from the audience and thereby feels beleaguered verbally and in terms of reputation. A game might begin innocently enough, with a "clean" dozens phrase such as "I saw yo mama at a bar last night," with the retort being something like "Don't talk about my mama." From this exchange, the game quickly accelerates to the "dirty" dozens, where poetry takes over, and may include such rhymes as: "Yo mama don't wear no drawers / I seen her when she took 'em off / She washed 'em in alcohol / And hung 'em out in the hall" (Richard *Wright includes a version of this in one of his short stories, "Big Boy Leaves Home," 1938) or "I saw your mother flying through the air / I hit her on the ass with a rotten pear." Rhythm and near rhyme strive for the poetic effect, and it is a conscious striving on the part of the players in the game.

Other folk forms also share literary qualities. Tall tales, which are usually very short, share with the blues and toasts the emphasis upon original or striking images. "Yo mama so short she can sit on a sheet of paper and swing her legs" or "Ah seen it so hot till two cakes of ice left the ice house and went down the street and fainted." Folktales, the largest unit of any folk recital (whether epics, legends, or myths), share with literary creation a focus on character and conflict. Numerous are the tales of *Brer Rabbit, the less powerful foe, being pitted against larger adversaries; he is ever trying to get the best of Brer Fox or Brer Wolf in the conflict of good versus evil, or at least morality versus amorality. Brer Rabbit allows for heroic identification with a particular character and occasionally serves, so many scholars argue, as a metaphor for the expressions of enslaved and newly freed Africans against the powerful whites with whom they could not openly contend.

This trait of indirection in Brer Rabbit identifies him as the quintessential *trickster, who has become perhaps the most heroic folk figure in African American culture. Tricksters, however, can be animal or human. Brer Rabbit therefore shares the stage with a slave named John. A cycle of tales developed about his exploits with "Old Master"—his bids for freedom, his claims to be a fortune teller, his staging of various contests in which his skills enable him to earn a lot of money for his master or to acquire his own freedom. Zora Neale *Hurston also argues that *High John the Conqueror should fit into this category with John, for High John not only succeeded in encouraging many enslaved blacks to fly back to Africa but he gave the spirit of laughter to those who remained. Hurston is alone in asserting that High John is a trickster instead of the conjuring root usually identified by that name, but she nonetheless articulates the heroic or at least indirectly confrontational spirit of identification for blacks that characterized the trickster figure in African American culture.

Folklore in Literature. In their consciously created literary works, African American writers from their first publications in America have exhibited close ties to the oral culture. They have consciously adapted various oral forms for inclusion in their literary creations, or they have, as William Wells Brown did in recording folk rhymes, simply lifted items of folklore from the culture and included them in their works. Scholars studying the use of folklore in literature have concluded that such materials can be used in a variety of ways—to define character, to enhance theme, to develop plot, to give a sense of setting and locale. Used in this manner, folk materials in the literature serve a purpose, but they do not control the overall text; they are still recognizable items of traditional materials used in a one-time or recurring way to suggest something about the text under consideration.

Frederick *Douglass, for example, could comment on black folk songs in the narrative of his life, but those songs were limited to a particular point of observation in his text; the more involved story centered upon his escape from slavery to *freedom. Paul Laurence *Dunbar documented musical traditions and various folk forms throughout his poetry, novels, and stories, thereby giving a sense of the life enslaved and newly freed blacks lived. Charles Waddell *Chesnutt drew upon the conjuring and superstitious traditions in creating his characters and world view in The *Conjure Woman (1899). Spirituals and sermons served as the basis for James Weldon *Johnson's creative inspiration in *God's Trombones (1927) as he consciously sought to document African American traditions he believed to be diminishing if not fading altogether.

Writers during the *Harlem Renaissance deliberately turned to folk forms and folkways as a means of establishing their aesthetic position. Jean *Toomer included a number of songs in *Cane (1923), and he was also intent upon reflecting the actual folk speech of the black people among whom he had taught in Sparta, Georgia, as preparation for his representation in Cane. Langston *Hughes, however, was the Renaissance writer usually believed to be most appreciative of the folk and folk forms. His 1926 volume, The *Weary Blues, draws upon the blues form in the creation of several blues-like poems, which can be seen in the refrain of the title poem. Hughes also blurred the line between folk and literature even more by creating lyrics that imitated exactly the dominant three-line pattern of the blues stanza, with its a a b construction.

In the 1930s, Richard Wright incorporated the dozens and song traditions into his works. *Uncle Tom's Children (1938) also includes some of the traditional forms of prayers in African American communities that Johnson used at the beginning of God's Trombones. Wright would incorporate a few spirituals in *Native Son (1940). It is especially noteworthy that Wright would be drawn to the folk culture, for he had little patience with Zora Neale Hurston's use of it in her works. The few items he does incorporate perhaps illustrate the almost irresistible appeal folk materials held for black writers.

In many instances, such as with use of the trickster figure, the folk origin of items in literature is immediately recognizable. Ralph *Ellison would use the trickster figure in a variety of guises in *Invisible Man (1952), a novel in which folk forms abound.

The unnamed narrator tries to play the trickster role when he attempts to retaliate against the Brotherhood for abandoning Harlem, but he is unable to play the role effectively. Ellison also allows other blacks (Dr. *Bledsoe, Brother Wrestrum) and whites (Brother Jack) to play trickster roles. Traditional folk forms that also appear in the text include spirituals, blues lyrics, dozens rhymes, soul food, and tall tales. Ellison uses these forms to illustrate the richness of the culture from which the narrator tries to divorce himself and to which he will make an effort to return near the end of the novel.

Ellison is also one of the writers who adopts the motif of flying Africans into his work. This oral story asserts that a certain tribe of Africans had the ability—if they were enslaved and brought to the new world—to utter magic words and fly back to Africa. Another version of the story maintains that the magic words enabled any African to return who had not drunk water in the New World. And yet another version maintains that the magic words would allow almost anyone—not just those from a special tribe—to fly back to Africa. In the literature, the tale can be symbolic, as in Ellison's "Flying Home" (1944), or revised, as in Paule *Marshall's Praisesong for the Widow (1983). In Marshall's novel, the belief is that the Africans walked from Charleston, South Carolina, back across the water to their homeland. For Toni *Morrison, in *Song of Solomon (1977), the story reflects a literal search for the flying African ancestor whom *Milkman Dead unearths on his journey to the South. Folklorist Julius *Lester included a tale of flying Africans in his collection, Black Folktales (1969), and Virginia *Hamilton, more frequently known for her children's books, has a collection entitled The People Could Fly: American Black Folktales (1985), which was published with an accompanying tape recording and a poster. The flying African motif remains a powerful iconic touchstone in African American literature.

More contemporary African American writers continue the tradition of the incorporation of African American folk forms into their novels. These include Toni Cade *Bambara in The *Salt Eaters (1980), Morrison in almost all of her works, Gloria *Naylor in *Mama Day (1988), and Tina McElroy *Ansa in Baby of the Family (1989). They all illustrate the vibrancy of African American folk culture and the continuing appeal it holds for creative writers.

Folk Literature. Writers in the tradition of folk literature create characters, patterns, and themes that evoke oral forms; they generally saturate their texts with a sense of historical folk reality. Inspired by research conducted by Guy B. Johnson, Howard Odum, and their associates at the Institute for Research in the Social Sciences (IRSS) at the University of North Carolina at Chapel Hill in the 1920s, many Euro-American writers sought to create "authentic" folk plays and novels; more frequently, however, these works were based on white *stereotypes and misconceptions of African American people, their communities, and their folkways. Marc Connelly's The Green Pastures (1930), featuring a black preacher, "De Lawd," singing black folks, and fish fries in heaven, would fit into this category. So too would Dubose Heyward's *Porgy* (1927), about blacks in the Gullah-speaking area of South Carolina who seem to spend most of their time fighting each other, having picnics, or singing spirituals. The white public's demand that stories about blacks be entertaining seems to have been the primary criteria for composition of the play. Julia Peterkin, slightly more sensitive in her creation of black characters in the Gullah area of South Carolina, nevertheless adhered to the stereotypes of physically superior and sexually uninhibited blacks in works such as *Black April* (1927) and *Scarlett Sister Mary* (1928). The first work features a black man of striking physical proportions, though the novel ends in tragedy. The second work, which won the Pulitzer Prize, features Sister Mary, who has nine children, eight of whom are illegitimate and most of whom have different fathers.

The African American folk novel, on the other hand, is usually identified with the 1930s and 1940s and specifically with Zora Neale Hurston, Waters *Turpin, and George Wylie *Henderson. The prevailing notion of the folk during this period was that they were rural, fairly illiterate, usually fundamentalist, superstitious, and generally outside the influence of more civilizing—and hierarchically "superior"—cultural forms. Their "low" culture might have included wonderful folk expressions, colorful uses of language, traditions such as quilting and hog-killing, and quaint ways of interacting with each other, but it was from a romantic distance that more "cultured" observers would view them.

Hurston uses setting, language, themes, folk forms, and characters (folk preacher) to reflect oral traditions in *Jonah's Gourd Vine* (1934). She also lifted prayers, rhymes, and parts of sermons from materials she had collected in African American communities. From the first page of the text, therefore, readers have a sense of being in a folk world, where the aura approximates historical counterparts. There is an authenticity in the interactions of the characters and the language they use, a credibility that ties Hurston to the forms and the people about which she wrote in several *essays and about whom she created several fictional works.

In *Their Eyes Were Watching God* (1937), Hurston focused on a fictional community comparable to her hometown of Eatonville, Florida. With self-determining black people who carry on a rich oral tradition, Hurston found a setting for *Janie Crawford, her heroine of the tale. The location of the town, the types of its characters, the stories they tell, the songs they sing, the epic battles they fight against nature all become the stuff of which folk legends are made. The orality of the narrative voice Hurston achieves is one of the primary features of the novel's folk quality, a feature that Henry Louis *Gates, Jr., focuses on in his discussion of the novel in *The Signifying Monkey*.

Turpin, contemporary with but not as well known as Hurston, set his characters in rural southern worlds that evoke historical counterparts. In novels such as *These Low Grounds* (1937) and *O Canaan!* (1939), he created characters comparable to those of Hurston and Henderson. *These Low Grounds* is set,

initially, on the eastern shore of Maryland, where a family descended from slavery tries to carve out a more optimistic future. *O Canaan!*, similar to the later sections of *These Low Grounds*, focuses on blacks who migrate from southern rural to northern urban areas. Critic Burney Hollis has asserted that Turpin's characters in *These Low Grounds* are "epic, legendary figures" while those in *O Canaan!* "are of biblical and mythical stature," and the novel "is a black odyssey with a hero whose fighting spirit is equal to that of Ulysses." These folk analogies for character development indicate again the extent to which Turpin is concerned with grounding his characters in the black folk worlds from which he draws his inspiration.

In *Ollie Miss* (1935) and *Jule* (1946), Henderson joined other black writers in the creative emphasis on primarily rural settings (Alabama), characters of little education but resilient spirit, and a saturated sense of black oral traditions. Ollie Miss, like Scarlett Sister Mary, is equally independent, but she is also a physically strong young woman who believes in working her own way through the world. She is in love with and finally pregnant by Jule, the primary character of Henderson's second novel. While a violent incident occurs near the end of the novel, Henderson's primary emphasis is upon a basic goodness in the characters. *Jule* returns to the young Jule growing up in Alabama and eventually leaving for New York. Guided by the same Uncle Alex who hires Ollie Miss, he learns the folkways of the culture in which he grows up. Although he eventually migrates to Harlem because of a clash with local whites, he does not forsake the southern folk world in which he has grown to *manhood.

Folk literature in all its guises implies an integral tie between African American oral culture and the imaginative efforts expended to create lasting works about that culture, whether those works are verbal or written. The folk culture, as Ralph Ellison pointed out in *Shadow and Act* (1964), reflected the willingness of African Americans to define their own reality instead of allowing others to define it for them. In early rhymes, songs, and tales, Africans enslaved in America provided their own analyses of the inequities in their existence and that of the people who claimed to own them. They presented their own conception of God and heaven even as their masters asserted that they should only be aware of the biblical verse about obeying them. Descendants of these enslaved people, both verbal word masters and literary geniuses, continued to trust their sense of reality by fostering the blues and spiritual traditions, by enshrining characters such as the trickster in the literature, and by positing the themes of self-help and self-determination that the folk culture taught. In all their achievements, they have made "folk literature" a lasting concept on the tongue as well as on the page.

[*See also* Blues Aesthetic; Musicals; Oratory; Sermons and Preaching; Shine; Signifying; Stackolee.]

• Sterling A. Brown, "The Blues as Folk Poetry," in *The Book of Negro Folklore,* eds. Langston Hughes and Arna Bontemps, 1958. Roger Abrahams, *Deep Down in the Jungle: Negro Narrative Folklore from the Streets of Philadelphia,* 1970.

Samuel Charters, *The Poetry of the Blues*, 1970. Bruce Jackson, *Get Your Ass in the Water and Swim Like Me: Narrative Poetry from Black Oral Tradition*, 1974. Dennis Wepman, Ronald B. Newman, and Murray B. Binderman, comps., *The Life: The Lore and Folk Poetry of the Black Hustler*, 1976. Daryl Cumber Dance, *Shuckin' and Jivin': Folklore from Contemporary Black Americans*, 1978. Burney Hollis, "Waters Edward Turpin," in *DLB*, vol. 51, *Afro-American Writers from the Harlem Renaissance to 1940*, ed. Trudier Harris, 1987, pp. 289–295. Henry Louis Gates, Jr., *The Signifying Monkey*, 1988. Trudier Harris, *Fiction and Folklore: The Novels of Toni Morrison*, 1991.   —Trudier Harris

FOLKLORE. In his important study of African American folktales, *Negro Folktales in Michigan* (1956), folklorist Richard Dorson pointed out that African Americans in the South had drawn upon oral and written traditions from West Africa, the West Indies, Europe, and white America and had added new material from their own surroundings to create a complex and unique folk tradition. Still, for many years, racism and xenophobia coerced white scholars into constructing a myth that portrayed African Americans as having been thwarted by an allegedly deficient cultural background. Because these scholars studied the British and Anglo-American influences on African American culture and ignored African and Caribbean contributions, African American culture was widely depicted as being essentially derivative. In *The Myth of the Negro Past* (1941), Melville J. Herskovits called this "the myth of the Negro past" and asserted that it was "one of the principal supports of race prejudice in this country." Attacking this myth, Herskovits systematically surveyed the African cultural survivals ("Africanisms") in African American life. This study, which identified a significant number of Africanisms in African American culture, illustrated that despite being oppressed and marginalized by white society, African American culture is anything but a pale reflection of Anglo-American culture.

Herskovits's study was one of several landmark works written between the world wars—others include Newbell N. Puckett's *Folk Beliefs of the Southern Negro* (1926), Carter G. *Woodson's *The African Background Outlined* (1936), and W. E. B. *Du Bois's *Black Folk: Then and Now* (1939)—that began the process of uncovering the complex cultural background of African Americans. These studies not only clarified the African and Caribbean influences on the development of traditional African American culture, they also advanced general understanding, among both whites and African Americans, regarding the considerable extent to which African American folk culture has influenced mainstream American culture. Woodson concluded that of all the influences contributing to what we think of as uniquely American culture, African American imagination had contributed the most vital and productive elements via myths and folklore originally from Africa.

In his 1993 study *The Unpredictable Past* Lawrence W. Levine condemned historians' long marginalization of the powerful African American imagination. This imagination, observed Levine, often found expression through the African American oral tradition. In spite of vast documentation of that tradition in songs, stories, verbal games, and sermons—all of which provided proof of great articulateness among African Americans—historians have ignored this record, resulting in a depiction of African Americans as inarticulate.

Studying African American folklore is essential for understanding African American culture in general and African American literature in specific. As Houston A. *Baker, Jr., wrote in *Long Black Song* (1972), "the significance of black folklore is perhaps greater than that of any other lore in a discussion of the literary tradition of the race from which it originated. Even the most recent black American writer is closer to the earliest folk expression of his culture than are the recent writers of most other groups; the contemporary black author is but three hundred odd years removed, a bare modicum of time to the folklorist."

Indeed, many of the greatest works in African American literature reveal the lasting significance of African American folklore. The African American folk experience, for example, was the subject of much of Paul Laurence *Dunbar's *poetry, while Charles Waddell *Chesnutt's *short story collection *The *Conjure Woman* (1899) concerned voodoo, black magic, and superstition. Several authors associated with the *Harlem Renaissance were profoundly interested in traditional African American folk culture, including Jean *Toomer, whose *Cane* (1923) juxtaposed the life-affirming ritualism of rural southern folklife with the alienation and materialism of urban life in the North; Langston *Hughes, whose poetry collection *The *Weary Blues* (1926) reworked *blues forms and updated the *blues aesthetic; James Weldon *Johnson, whose *God's Trombones* (1927) echoed the language and speech patterns of folk sermons; and Zora Neale *Hurston, whose oeuvre includes *Mules and Men* (1935), a nonfiction study of African American folklore from Florida and Louisiana. Later authors who incorporated aspects of African American folklore into their work include Richard *Wright, whose *Native Son* (1940) featured a modern literary treatment of the traditional African American *badman figure; James *Baldwin, whose *Go Tell It on the Mountain* (1952) reflected its author's extensive knowledge of traditional African American religious lore; Ralph *Ellison, whose *Invisible Man* (1952) reinterpreted a wide range of African American folklore; LeRoi Jones (Amiri *Baraka), whose fascination with traditional African American music inspired poems and produced scholarly studies such as *Blues People* (1963); and Ernest J. *Gaines, whose *The *Autobiography of Miss Jane Pittman* (1971) echoed the nineteenth-century *slave narrative tradition.

For the purpose of analysis, traditional African American culture can be divided into three main categories: customary (behavioral) folklore, material (physical) folklore, and oral (verbal) folklore. African American customary folklore includes, among other traditional rituals and activities, a number of behavioral expressions of religious belief (the verbal components of such expressions are part of the oral tradition). Herskovits asserted that many aspects of

African American folk belief can be traced back to African sources, including the conviction that, in the realm of the supernatural, there is no dichotomy between good and evil, both being attributes of the same powers. Also African were some of the magical rituals of the slaves. When African American magicians attempted to conjure up the spirits of dead ancestors, they sometimes used "goopher"—grave dirt. This term was derived from a Kikongo verb *kufwa*, which meant "to die." According to a Kongo tradition, earth from a person's grave was considered to be at one with that person's spirit.

Another Africanism was the emphasis on revelation among African American folk medicine practitioners in their quest for useful plant remedies. In order to manufacture and administer folk remedies, medicine practitioners, who generally were women, collected roots, leaves, herbs, and barks, and made teas. These women became medicine practitioners either by apprenticeship or by being called to practice medicine. Some practitioners claimed that in times of crisis they heard a voice informing them about medicines that would help people.

Another group of specialized healers consisted of men who practiced with magic. Generally, men became magicians by inheritance—they might be the sons of magician fathers, which obligated them to accept their inherited powers or face misfortune or illness. A man could also become a magician voluntarily, such as if he was his father's seventh son (assuming that the father and his mate had not produced a girl). Charles Joyner ("Black Folklore," in *Encyclopedia of Southern Culture*, 1989) describes the role of the magician in traditional African American society: "With the aid of mojo hands, goopher dust, John the Conqueror root, and other substances held to be magical, [magicians] . . . protect[ed] one from misfortune and cast spells upon one's enemies."

Several types of African American folk belief involved the occult: hoodoo, a magical charm practiced by a relatively small number of people, mostly by men; signs, a more popular magical belief practiced largely by women (hoodoo was more exclusive and complex than signs, which involved reading natural phenomena in an attempt to identify future developments); and voodoo, which developed principally in Louisiana because of that region's confluence of French, Catholic, and Haitian influences. In annual ceremonies featuring elaborate decorations (with altars surrounded by hundreds of lighted candles), the cult of voodoo invoked, among other deities, Legba, a *trickster of West African and Haitian origination. Initiation into the voodoo cult involved rites of passage (seclusion, fasting, special wardrobes, dancing and possession, animal sacrifices) that closely paralleled various religious rites practiced in West Africa and Haiti. One figure associated with voodoo was Marie Laveau, whose legendary initiation into the cult involved being coaxed to join the New Orleans cult by a rattlesnake. The African American fascination with snakes can be traced back to Africa, where the serpent was an important supernatural being. For instance, in Dahomey, two rainbow-serpents (named Aido Hwedo and Damballa Hwedo) were be-

lieved to have been present at the creation of the world; similar myths concerning serpent spirits were found in Haiti.

Another Africanism was the African American belief in *haints* (ghosts). According to African tradition, haints were spirits at one stage of their being. Haints could be beneficent, such as the spirits of loved ones returning from the dead to help, protect, and counsel the living. Haints could also be evil, like the spirits of masters who returned to renew their abuse of slaves. To protect themselves from such evil spirits, slaves practiced various rituals, including putting heavy rocks on top of their masters' coffins to keep them weighted down, placing a Bible by a door to prevent spirits from entering the house, and chanting magical charms to keep evil spirits away. Slaves believed that they were not safe from their masters even in death, so they asked to be buried as far as possible from their masters.

As the slaves became Christianized, African American religious services began to combine traditional African/Caribbean and Judeo-Christian elements. One manifestation of this fusion of religious traditions was the ring shout, a religious dance in which dancers shuffled in a counterclockwise direction. Levine explained that the ring shout served to transform the dancers into participants in historic actions, so that they experienced themselves as being among Joshua's army as it marched around Jericho's walls or as being with Moses as he led the Hebrews out of Egypt. In the preemancipation South, the ring shout was acceptable as a substitute for secular dancing (and like secular dancing this sacred ritual not only lasted into the night but also encouraged ecstatic participation); thus ring shouts served religious, social, and personal needs. After the Civil War ring shouts increasingly came under the scrutiny of African American ministers, who judged them to be uncivilized if not anti-Christian.

A secular African American dance originating during the days of *slavery was the cakewalk, which was a stylized caricature of the Anglo-American waltz. By 1895 the *dance had become a mass cultural phenomenon and was appearing in Broadway productions. Soon the cakewalk was being incorporated into the high-culture *musical compositions of Claude Debussy, John Philip Sousa, and Igor Stravinsky.

One example of African American material culture is the banjo. Slaves brought from Africa a prototype version of the banjo, and until the 1830s they were the only group to play the instrument. However, by the 1840s white audiences had been widely exposed to the banjo through its use in minstrel shows, a new form of popular entertainment. At minstrel shows, white musicians in blackface (minstrels) imitated African American musicians by singing ersatz African American folk songs. Far from traditional (they were written commercially for the minstrel shows), minstrel songs romanticized the lives of plantation slaves. Anchoring their singing with banjo accompaniment, and also performing instrumental numbers on the banjo, white minstrel performers borrowed the African American style of down-stroking across the banjo strings and utilized the fifth (thumb) string of slave banjos. Minstrel performers popularized the banjo among white audiences to such an extent that, in the twentieth century, the banjo was almost exclusively played by white musicians, in the subgenre of country music known as bluegrass and in the urban folk music revival. Virtually the only African Americans still dedicated to mastering the instrument were New Orleans *jazz musicians, who continued to play the four-stringed (tenor) version of the banjo in the traditional Dixieland style.

African Americans have long displayed a great ability to construct a variety of traditional material objects. From Africa slaves brought traditional skills —especially ironworking, woodworking, and building with earth and stone—that plantation owners exploited in the New World; thus, plantation households were full of tools, furniture, quilts, pottery, and jewelry made by slaves. Similarly, plantation houses soon featured such traditional African architectural designs as central fireplaces, steeply sloping hip roofs, wide porches with overhanging roofs, and the use of moss and earth in walls.

Another important example of African American material culture is the shotgun house. First built in New Orleans in the early nineteenth century by people of color (most of whom were political refugees from Haiti), the shotgun house combined African, Caribbean, and French architectural concepts. Small and rectangular—one room wide by three rooms deep, with doors at each end, and the gable end toward the street—the shotgun house is one of the more common house designs found in the South today, utilized by whites as well as African Americans. When a young boy growing up in Tupelo, Mississippi, Elvis Presley lived in a shotgun house.

Over time, African Americans developed distinctive foodways. They accomplished this by combining foodstuffs introduced from Africa (such as yams, okra, black-eyed peas, and sorghum), European tastes, recipes involving African techniques of cooking and spicing, and New World foodstuffs and food preparation techniques. This fusion of African and American culinary traditions led to the emergence of distinctively African American dishes such as gumbo and barbecue. A moniker often applied to African American cooking is "soul food."

The most renowned aspects of the African American oral tradition are folktales and folk *music. Historically, African Americans have told a wide assortment of folktales, from tales of the sacred and the supernatural (creation legends, ghost stories, folk sermons, testimonials, and preacher tales) to secular tales (morality tales, trickster tales, and jokes). Generally speaking, these various folktales were told concisely and directly, permitting both storyteller and listener to easily process a tale's content. Although all these types of folktales have held importance to particular African Americans at particular times, both rural and urban African Americans have consistently favored two types of tales: trickster tales and jokes.

The trickster figure long held a crucial if ambivalent role in African American oral tradition. Borrow-

ing selectively from the trickster traditions of Africa (where tricksters took on either human, divine, or animal form), African Americans particularly valued tales involving animal trickster figures. Fearing reprisal if they freely conveyed their own human grievances, slaves told tales that employed animal characters in substitution for human characters; the animals represented specific human actions and generalized patterns of human behavior. According to Lawrence Levine, "The primary trickster figures of animal tales were weak, relatively powerless creatures who attain[ed] their ends through the application of native wit and guile rather than power or authority." The ultimate goal of the trickster was to subvert the corrupt and divisive moral conventions and the established order that originally enforced those morals. The best-known African American trickster figure was *Brer Rabbit, who embodied idealized human qualities valued by socially restrained African Americans. With didactic as well as narrative dimensions, the Brer Rabbit tales offered slaves both positive and negative examples of human behavior, which ultimately helped the slaves better understand their world.

A set of related nonanimal trickster tales, told in the years after the Civil War, concerned the ambivalent relationship of a fictional slave named John and his "ol' Marster." In these stories John struggles to overcome his subservient position in racist plantation society by subverting (generally covertly, but sometimes overtly) the stereotypes thrust on him by the white "Marster."

African American jokes often took the form of competitive verbal games that tested an individual's verbal dexterity. In these games players leveled "sounds" (direct insults) or "*signifying" (indirect insults) against an opponent, who could then respond in kind. "Woofing," signifying, and sounding were various names for a game in which a player humorously teased his opponent. "The Dozens" referred to a game in which a player creatively teased his opponent's mother. The loser of these strictly structured verbal contests was the person who allowed his response to veer from the ritualized impersonal insult expected of all players into mere personal insult.

Another type of folktale was the toast, a dramatic traditional narrative performed in rhymed couplets. Most frequently found in cities and prisons, the toast was commonly multiepisodic, chronicling the deeds of such antiheroic figures as badmen, pimps, and street people. A toast often presented a main character confronting a series of situations in which he needed to demonstrate his abilities through words and actions. Seldom did this loosely structured African American narrative present a dramatic climax as in many Western narratives, so the performer of the toast could add and subtract situations at will. Some well-known toasts included *The Signifying Monkey*, *Stackolee, and *The Freaks Ball*. By mastering the toast, one of the most complex forms within the African American oral tradition, the teller gained power and prestige within the African American community.

A little understood form of traditional African American verbal communication is jive. Historically, when they jived African Americans were engaging in playful conversations utilizing strongly African American vernacular speech. An exclusive mode of communication, jive was generally indecipherable to whites.

African Americans have introduced a number of words into the English language, many of which have clear African origins, such as "jazz," "boogie," "gumbo," "cooter," "okra," and "goober." Also from African sources are two familiar expressions, the affirmative phrase "uh-huh" and the negative phrase "unh-uh."

In folktales and story-songs (narrative African American songs are often referred to as blues ballads) African Americans boasted about a host of heroes and anti-heroes, both real and mythical. In addition to the aforementioned traditional stories about human and animal tricksters (like John and Brer Rabbit), African American folktales and story-songs tell of mythical figures (such as the Devil and *Moses), of human heroes (like *John Henry, Jack Johnson, and Joe *Louis), and of notorious badmen (like John Hardy, Staggerlee, and Railroad Bill).

Traditional African American music first emerged on preemancipation plantations where slaves played traditional instrumental music at dances and sang field hollers, work songs, and *spirituals. Interestingly, spirituals were not only sung during worship services; they were often sung during work because of their power to uplift. In the world of the spirituals, affirmation outweighed sorrow, confidence outweighed despair. Through singing spirituals slaves reinforced positive beliefs (such as transcendence, ultimate justice, and personal worth) and rejected negative beliefs (such as feelings of depravity and unworthiness). African American spirituals attained worldwide popularity not long after emancipation when the Fisk [University] Jubilee Singers successfully toured the United States and Europe in the 1870s, singing somewhat mannered renditions of traditional African American spirituals.

By the 1890s these early forms of African American musical expression were influencing the development of a new folk music that came to be known as the blues. Emerging as a highly localized music in the rural areas and small towns of the Deep South, particularly on large plantations and at the sites of heavy industry, the blues eventually revolutionized American music. Blues lyrics, which evoked the African American experience of social alienation in an era of restrictive *Jim Crow laws, set a new standard for lyrical creativity and directness, while the music of the blues introduced new possibilities for improvisation and individual expression.

A crossbreeding of African American and white musical traditions, *jazz first emerged as a distinctive musical form in the late nineteenth century. The primary place of the music's origination was New Orleans, though musicians in other locales—from the Mississippi Delta to St. Louis and Kansas City to New York and Washington, D.C.—also played a role in its evolution. New Orleans, however, with its unique mix of classes, races, and ethnic groups, offered the combination of musical and cultural influences that led to the music's initial development. Pioneer jazz musicians in late-nineteenth-century New Orleans—people like legendary cornet player Buddy Bolden—could listen to and learn from African American, Creole, and Cajun folk music, brass marching bands, Caribbean music, African American and Anglo-American religious music, and popular parlor music. The word "jazz," which in the African American vernacular originally referred to sexual intercourse, described well the sensuality of this new style of music. African Americans influential in the early evolution of jazz included Scott Joplin of Sedalia, Missouri, whose sophisticated ragtime composition "Maple Leaf Rag" set the groundwork for the future success of jazz by selling a million copies in sheet music form in 1899; Jelly Roll Morton, the formally trained Creole pianist and bandleader from New Orleans who in the early decades of the twentieth century helped to popularize the new music by touring extensively across the United States; and W. C. Handy in Memphis, whose blues-inspired jazz compositions helped to legitimize both blues and jazz. By the 1920s jazz had become so popular—among whites as well as African Americans—that the decade was nicknamed the Jazz Age.

Other twentieth-century musical styles first emerged in African American environments, only to find a wider reception among mainstream audiences. Unlike nineteenth-century spirituals, which were a folk phenomenon, modern African American gospel music was commercial from the beginning, in that popular gospel music songwriters—who united religious texts with secular musical forms borrowed from blues and ragtime—earned considerable royalties by formally publishing their work. One of the earliest and greatest gospel songwriters was Thomas A. Dorsey, a 1920s-era blues musician who from the 1930s onward dedicated himself entirely to gospel music. He wrote more than five hundred gospel songs, including such classics as "There Will Be Peace in the Valley" and "Precious Lord, Take My Hand" (both of which have been widely recorded by both African American and white musicians). By World War II Dorsey was promoting the careers of Mahalia Jackson and Sallie Martin, two singers who helped widen gospel music's popularity through live performances and commercial records. Jackson later gained even greater exposure for gospel music by appearing on television and at political and civil rights events. Several African American gospel groups, such as the Swan Silvertones and the Dixie Hummingbirds, also became popular with diverse audiences.

Solo and group gospel singing influenced two later African American musical developments: rhythm and blues and soul. Although many performers of these related musical styles (such as James Brown, Sam Cooke, Otis Redding, and Aretha *Franklin) rejected the didactic spiritual messages of gospel music (in order to obtain crossover popularity) and instead sang secular songs about love's travails and about social issues, rhythm and blues and soul performances nonetheless retained many of the musical qualities of gospel music, including the individuality and sincerity of the singer's persona, vocal emotionalism, and vocal interaction between the lead singer and the background singers (often termed "call and response"). Pioneer African American rock 'n' roll musicians likewise felt the overpowering presence of gospel music. Little Richard, for instance, abandoned his rock 'n' roll career midstream to preach the gospel.

One recent African American musical style, rap, is an urban version of an African American verbal tradition dating back to the preemancipation era. Historically a "rap" was a partly spoken, partly sung poetic statement, characterized by rhymed couplets, verbal wit, and rhythmic brilliancy. Like other secular crafters of language, "rappers" have long been both respected and feared within African American society—respected for their powerful verbal gifts and feared for their extraordinary insights into human experience.

A 1972 observation by Houston A. *Baker, Jr., still holds true today: There is an urgent need for more insightful scholarship in the field of African American culture, since the art of African American folk culture is still used by white America to reinforce its stereotypes and, at times, to justify victimization of African Americans. As Baker noted in 1972, America has rarely bothered to take an honest look at its African American citizens.

[See also Folk Literature; Funeral and Mourning Customs; High John the Conqueror; Minstrelsy; Preachers and Deacons; Sermons and Preaching; Uncle Tom.]

• Zora Neale Hurston, Mules and Men, 1935. Roger D. Abrahams, Deep Down in the Jungle: Negro Narrative Folklore from the Streets of Philadelphia, 1964. Peter Wood, Black Majority, 1974. Lawrence W. Levine, Black Culture and Black Consciousness: Afro-American Folk Thought from Slavery to Freedom, 1977. Roger Abrahams and John Szwed, After Africa, 1983. H. Nigel Thomas, From Folklore to Fiction: A Study of Folk Heroes and Rituals in the Black American Novel, 1988. Charles Joyner, Down by the Riverside: A South Carolina Slave Community, 1989. Charles Reagan Wilson and William Ferris, eds., Encyclopedia of Southern Culture, 1989. Joseph E. Holloway, ed., Africanisms in American Culture, 1990. Roger D. Abrahams, Singing the Master: The Emergence of African American Culture in the Plantation South, 1992. Alan Lomax, The Land Where the Blues Began, 1993.

—Ted Olson

FOLK NOVEL. See Folk Literature.

Folks from Dixie.

The first collection of *short stories written by Paul Laurence *Dunbar, Folks from Dixie (1898) is also considered the first volume of short stories by an African American to be published in the United States. Most of the twelve stories in Folks from Dixie had been published previously in popular magazines; the volume sold well and was reprinted in England in 1899. Setting the tone for the short fiction that Dunbar collected in three subsequent volumes, the stories in Folks from Dixie celebrate the simple pleasures of "down-home" living for African Americans, who find fulfillment in their own communities apart from and seemingly unmindful of the world of whites. Only a comparative few of Dunbar's stories offer candid assessments of social problems occasioned by *race.

Five stories in Folks from Dixie are set in the antebellum era and portray slaves according to the myths of the *plantation tradition. "The Colonel's Awakening" and "The Intervention of Peter," for instance, represent the loyalty of slaves and ex-slaves to whites in ways that substitute sentimentality for thoughtful reflection on the relationships of whites and blacks in the South. In "The Trial Sermon on Bull-Skin" Dunbar employs stock characters from the plantation tradition but also offers insight into the folkways and superstitions of a rural southern black community as it seeks a pastor.

More noteworthy in Folks from Dixie are Dunbar's studies of the social and economic realities of life for ordinary African Americans at the turn of the century. "Aunt Mandy's Investment" warns that African American self-help and solidarity can be betrayed as much by misplaced trust in black shysters as by dependence on white patrons. "At Shaft Eleven" speaks frankly about labor strife in a coal-mining town and focuses on a heroic African American foreman, although some critics have felt that Sam Bowles's loyalty to white bosses is troublingly similar to that displayed by ex-slaves to their former masters in plantation fiction. "Jimsella" anticipates Dunbar's The *Sport of the Gods (1902) in describing the plight of a working-class African American couple who have migrated from the South to New York in the hope of finding better opportunities. "The Ordeal at Mt. Hope" offers a distinct critique of racial discrimination, demythologizes *slavery, and explores the social and political philosophies of Booker T. *Washington and W. E. B. *Du Bois. Typically, however, the difficulties that African Americans face in Dunbar's short stories arise from their own self-deceptions and misplaced priorities, not from deeper causes, such as white racism, that would require a profounder analysis of social and economic forces.

• Arlene A. Elder, The "Hindered Hand": Cultural Implications of Early African-American Fiction, 1978. Robert A. Bone, Down Home: Origins of the Afro-American Short Story, 1988.

—William L. Andrews and Patricia Robinson Williams

FOOTE, JULIA A. J. (1823–1900), preacher and spiritual autobiographer. Julia A. J. Foote was born in Schenectady, New York, the daughter of former slaves firmly committed to Methodism and *education. Although the only formal education she received came between the ages of ten and twelve, Julia devoted herself to Bible study as a teenager. At fifteen she was converted to Christianity and joined a church in Albany, New York. In 1841, she married George Foote, a sailor, and moved with him to Boston, where she engaged in considerable informal evangelistic work under the auspices of the African Methodist Episcopal (AME) Zion *church. In Boston, Julia Foote became convinced that she had been called to preach. When her husband could not dissuade her from this course, he drifted out of her life. Julia's minister staunchly opposed the increasing agitation among women in his congregation to let her share his pulpit. In response she set out on an independent preaching career that took her throughout upstate New York and, by 1850, to Ohio and Michigan. She settled in Cleveland, Ohio, during the 1850s and 1860s but resumed her ministry in the 1870s as part of the Holiness revivals that swept the Midwest in that decade. In 1879, Foote published her 124-page *autobiography, A Brand Plucked from the Fire, in Cleveland, reprinting it in 1886. During the last decade of her life Foote became the first woman to be ordained a deacon and the second to be ordained an elder in the AME Zion church. Although her autobiography attacks racism and other social abuses, the subordination of women, especially in the spiritual realm, and her desire to inspire faith in her Christian sisters endow her life story with its distinctive voice and intensity.

[See also Feminism; Religion.]

• William L. Andrews, ed., Sisters of the Spirit: Three Black Women's Autobiographies of the Nineteenth Century, 1986. Sue E. Houchins, ed., Spiritual Narratives, 1988.

—William L. Andrews

FORBES, CALVIN (b.1945), poet, lecturer, and educator. Calvin Forbes was born the seventh of eight children in Newark, New Jersey, to Jacob and Mary Short Forbes. He was the first of the six boys in his family to graduate from high school, and he attended Rutgers University briefly before entering the New School for Social Research in New York City. There Forbes studied with poet José García Villa, who taught him the fundamentals of writing.

Forbes continued to educate himself through travel, and he was on the move frequently throughout the 1960s. He traveled widely in Europe and hitchhiked from coast to coast in America with only a suitcase, a sleeping bag, and a portable typewriter as his baggage. Forbes also lived in Hawaii for a short time; his stay there was instrumental to his writing the poems for his first volume, Blue Monday (1974). Observing Hawaii's Asian American culture, Forbes began to think of his own African American heritage as a culture that belonged to him, and as an element that belonged in his writing.

Not surprisingly, then, many poems in Blue Monday are autobiographical in their nature. "The Middle Life," for example, reflects Forbes's background in the church, and "For My Mother" tells the story of his parents' courtship and their *migration from Greenville, North Carolina, to the North. In addition to drawing on family stories and memories in his writing, Forbes also culls stories and phrases from African American oral tradition and frequently employs colloquial and idiomatic language in his *poetry. Further, Forbes puts his love for *blues music to work in Blue Monday, threading the mood and wry philosophy that underpin blues lyrics throughout his poems.

Critics have praised Forbes's first book for its metaphoric complexity, noting that he successfully employs synecdoche to make individual images represent the whole of the poem, like the poets John Donne and Gwendolyn *Brooks—writers whose work he admires. Detractors, on the other hand, have argued that elements of blues singing work against

Forbes when he tries to incorporate them into poetry: they suggest that blues music allows for a shifting of imagery and an emotional distance that sometimes weaken his work. The critics agree, however, that Blue Monday represents an innovative attempt to find an original poetic voice.

Forbes's second book, From the Book of Shine, was published in 1979 as a limited edition text (the book was also published in 1980 by Razorback Press in Wales as a limited edition). He creates a number of poems based on an African American folk character named *Shine about whom he heard stories as a young boy; Forbes expands on the folk story by giving Shine a female counterpart, Glow, and poems like "Blind Date with a Voice" and "A Post Card from Colorado" plot the development of their relationship. Here Forbes's work shows the influence of writers such as Sterling A. *Brown; like Brown, Forbes uses the African American folk hero to create poems filled with irony and subtle *humor. However, in contrast with Brown's work, throughout the volume humor gives way to a strong sense of despair about living in a racist society.

Forbes's career as a writer is paralleled by a distinguished career as an educator. He taught African American literature at Emerson College in Boston from 1969 to 1973, then left to become an assistant professor at Tufts University in Medford, Massachusetts, for a year. He subsequently took a leave of absence and traveled to Denmark, France, and England as a Fulbright scholar. In 1975, Forbes returned to Tufts and continued to teach there until 1977, when he again departed to finish an MFA at Brown University in Providence, Rhode Island. Forbes accepted a position at Howard University in Washington, D.C., in 1978. He won a National Endowment for the Arts fellowship in 1982 and moved to Jamaica, where he worked on an unpublished *novel and lectured at the University of the West Indies in Kingston. After returning to teach at Howard and other neighboring colleges and universities, Forbes moved to Chicago. He currently teaches literature and writing at the School of the Art Institute of Chicago.

Forbes has not produced a large body of work. However, he aspires, like the British poet Philip Larkin—another of his favorite writers—to concentrate on the quality of his writing rather than the quantity. His poetry continues to be anthologized, and even without further publications Forbes maintains an important position in the African American literary tradition.

• David Huddle, "Book Reviews," Georgia Review 28 (Fall 1974): 535–540. Joseph Parisi, "Personae, Personalities," Poetry 126 (July 1975): 219–241. Robert A. Coles, "Calvin Forbes," in DLB, vol. 41, Afro-American Poets since 1955, eds. Trudier Harris and Thadious M. Davis, 1985, pp. 131–134. Calvin Forbes, "Calvin Forbes," in Contemporary Authors Autobiography Series, ed. Joyce Nakamura, vol. 16, 1992, pp. 105–120.

—Allison Kimmich

for colored girls. Ntozake *Shange's for colored girls who have considered suicide / when the rainbow is enuf is a feminist *drama with unique origins. Called a choreopoem by its author, the twenty-poem drama tells the stories of the joy, pain, suffering, abuse, strength, and resilience of African American women. Its seven female characters dress in colors representing the rainbow plus brown. Each speaks individual poems and is intermittently aided and joined by other characters in collective poems, producing a choral effect. This comes directly from the work's beginning: In various cafés, bars, and *poetry houses in California and New York, Shange performed and presented the poems that eventually became a dramatic unit. It was first performed in December 1974 at a women's bar outside Berkeley, California.

*Music, dancing, and lighting are used with creative significance in *for colored girls*, with the characters often singing and dancing together to satisfy their collective need for female support. There are no props, scenery, or furniture, so lighting is used to emphasize or isolate particular characters as needed. Throughout the performance, women move in and out of the spotlight and on and off the stage. These dramatic techniques place the burden of interpretation on the actresses, who must assume different narrative personas, and require the audience members to use their imaginations.

The author notes in her stage directions that the characters live outside of large metropolitan areas in the United States, stressing their isolation from mainstream society; the "ladies" have no names for they represent all oppressed women of color. The colors of their dresses represent various degrees of emotion, with the brighter ones symbolizing vivaciousness and youth and the cooler colors designating frustration and despair. The lady in red, the most vibrant color, interprets the most violent, forceful, and memorable poem, dramatizing the plight of African American women with two significant personas. In "one," near the beginning of the drama, she portrays a lively and glittering seductress who turns into a "regular" colored woman who cries herself to sleep in the early hours of the morning. In "of no assistance," she rails against a lover who failed to assist her in maintaining a loving relationship, angrily disposing of him and sending him away with a heated explanation of her reason for remaining in the heretofore unsatisfying relationship. The lady in red's most violent and heartbreaking poem is "a nite with beau willie brown," in which she tells a horrible story of physical and emotional violence perpetuated by a demented black man against his girlfriend and children; it ends in the children's murder when he throws them from a fifth-story window. Contrastingly, the lady in brown, the only color not associated with the rainbow, interprets poems on more serious and meditative subjects that represent earthly concerns and history, such as "Toussaint," concerning the leader of the Haitian Revolution. In "pyramid," three characters join before and after a disastrous relationship with the same man who betrayed them all and endangered their friendship; however, the poem ends with the women again turning to each other for support and consolation. Shange demonstrates and defines the assertiveness that oppressed women of color must possess in order to fulfill themselves. Her characters begin as fragmented voices but end as supported ones as their isolation diminishes through the support and consolation they give one another.

The work is one of the most critically acclaimed of all African American dramas. It has been produced countless times, in high schools and colleges as well as on commercial stages. It is taught in American literature courses and has been incorporated into masters theses and doctoral dissertations. The work has also influenced younger writers such as Elizabeth Alexander, who draws upon Shange's work in her play *Diva Studies* (1996). Shange is thus an influencing and influential playwright.

• Jeffrey Elliott, "Ntozake: Genesis of a Choreopoem," *Negro History Bulletin* 41 (Jan. 1978): 797–800. Carolyn Mitchell, "'A Laying on of Hands': Transcending the City in Ntozake Shange's *for colored girls . . . ,*" in *Women Writers and the City: Essays in Feminist Literary Criticism*, ed. Susan Merrill Squier, 1984, pp. 230–248. Claudia Tate, *Black Women Writers at Work*, 1984. Elizabeth Brown-Guillory, "Ntozake Shange," in *DLB*, vol. 38, *Afro-American Writers after 1955: Dramatists and Prose Writers*, eds. Thadious M. Davis and Trudier Harris, 1985, pp. 240–250. Betty Taylor-Thompson, "Female Support and Bonding in *for colored girls . . . ,*" *Griot* 12.1 (Spring 1993): 46–51. Neal A. Lester, *Ntozake Shange: A Critical Study of the Plays*, 1995.

—Betty Taylor-Thompson

FOREMOTHER. *See* Literary History.

For Love of Imabelle. *See* Cotton Comes to Harlem.

For My People. Although Margaret Walker has published three volumes of *poetry since the 1970s—*Prophets for a New Day* (1970), *October Journey* (1973), and *This Is My Century* (1989)—her reputation as one of the most accomplished African American poets of the twentieth century was established with the 1942 publication by Yale University Press of her first book of poems, *For My People*. As the winner of the Yale University Series of Younger Poets Award, Walker became the first black woman to be so honored. That the book belongs to the category of first black American achievements is less significant than the craft and historical consciousness that give the poems enduring value and secure their special place in the literary history of African American poetry and in the cultural narrative of African American people.

For My People, particularly its title poem, can be read as a successful fulfillment of the yearning expressed in the early poem "I Want to Write" (1934). It is also, within the evolution of African American poetry, a model of how the individual locates herself in foundational orality and the tradition of formal verse, blending folk speech and fluid lyricism, biblical typology, and the disciplined genres of ballad and sonnet with the freer forms of modernist sensibility to construct a collection that is governed by the logic of response to a people's special history. Also very important for literary study is Walker's heeding of James Weldon *Johnson's call for a poetry that judiciously represented the souls and gifts of black folk, as well as her building on the antecedents of *Harlem Renaissance poetry to create works that at once demonstrate mastery of language and the revolutionary vision of the 1930s. Less overtly political than contemporaneous work by Langston *Hughes, for example, such poems as "We Have Been Believers," "Since 1619," and "Delta" illustrate Walker's unyielding commitment to the themes of liberation and social justice. Stephen Vincent Benét was perceptive in noting in his preface to For My People that the poet's voice was living, passionate, and replete with "lasting music."

"For My People," which had been published in Poetry in 1937 and in the landmark anthology The Negro Caravan (1941), and the twenty-five other poems in the book are divided into three sections that focus on the South as place of origin and lineage, on the tragicomic existentialism of folk characters, and the redemptive qualities of belief. As critics such as Eugenia Collier, Eleanor Traylor, and R. Baxter Miller have asserted, the distinguishing features of this volume are Walker's historical and prophetic vision, deft handling of symbols and biblical rhetoric, and use of myth and lore.

For My People endures as a poetic model of the signal emphasis in African American literature on matters of history, and it is the use of history that links Walker's poetic vision with those of her contemporaries Gwendolyn *Brooks, Robert *Hayden, and Melvin B. *Tolson. The iconic status "For My People" has achieved in African American cultural life serves as one warrant for continuing study of this book. Margaret Walker's lyric and narrative poems resonate with the deep structures of African American philosophy and humanism as they imaginatively look forward to the future of her people.

• Richard K. Barksdale, "Margaret Walker: Folk Orature and Historical Prophecy," in Black American Poets between Worlds, 1940–1960, ed. R. Baxter Miller, 1986, pp. 105–117. R. Baxter Miller, "The 'Etched Flame' of Margaret Walker: Biblical and Literary Re-Creation in Southern History," in Black Southern Voices, eds. John Oliver Killens and Jerry W. Ward, Jr., 1992, pp. 591–604.   —Jerry W. Ward, Jr.

FORREST, LEON (b. 1937), novelist. Leon Forrest was born in Chicago, Illinois, on 8 January 1937. An only child, he grew up in the largely segregated South Side in a family whose heritage was shaped by his mother's New Orleans, Creole, and Catholic origins and his father's Mississippi Protestant roots. This dual religious heritage is an important influence in his fiction. He attended Wendell Phillips School in his neighborhood, then became one of the few black students to attend Hyde Park High School during the years 1951–1955. He attended Wilson Junior College (1955–1956), Roosevelt University (1957–1958), and the University of Chicago (1959–1960), and served in Germany in the U.S. Army. After his term in the service, Forrest returned to Chicago determined to pursue a career as a writer. He resumed taking courses at the University of Chicago and supported himself for a while by working in a bar and liquor store managed by his mother and stepfather—the setting that inspired many of the scenes in Divine Days (1992). In the mid-1960s, while working on his first *novel, Forrest became a journalist, working initially for a

neighborhood newspaper, the Woodlawn Observer, and later for Muhammed Speaks, the newspaper of the Nation of Islam. He was promoted to associate editor of Muhammed Speaks in 1969 and managing editor in 1972. In 1973, Forrest's first novel, There Is a Tree More Ancient than Eden, was edited by Toni *Morrison and published by Random House with an introduction by Ralph *Ellison. Forrest received high praise and was immediately hailed as a major talent. Shortly after the novel's publication, he was appointed to the faculty of Northwestern University, where he is professor and chair of African American Studies.

A highly experimental and symbolically dense novel, There Is a Tree More Ancient than Eden introduces the fictional universe of Forest County, a world strikingly similar in its texture to Cook County, Illinois, where Chicago is located. Forrest shares with William Faulkner an intense concern with geographical settings, with history and culture as they unfold through family chronicles, and with the burden of personal and historical consciousness. His novels are linked by their shared location, by interlocking family genealogies, and by their exploration of the experiences and developing consciousness of Nathaniel Witherspoon, who grows to maturity over the course of Forrest's first three novels.

There Is a Tree More Ancient than Eden is a highly lyrical novel that explores the multiple layers of Nathaniel Witherspoon's consciousness in the context of his mother's death during the early 1950s. In The Bloodworth Orphans (1977), Forrest creates a crowded canvas of characters, all of whom are connected by their orphanhood and their sometimes destructive quests for father images. In this novel, Nathaniel often functions as an auditor and observer of the nightmarish saga of the black descendants of the southern white Bloodworth family, a collector of the memories, stories, and legends he hears. Similarly, Two Wings to Veil My Face (1984) begins with Nathaniel, now twenty-one, being called to the bedside of his grandmother Sweetie Reed. The stories she tells him—about her life and her slave father's—trigger a multilayered journey through time and space, history and myth. Divine Days, an epic novel of over one thousand pages, signals a shift in direction from Forrest's earlier novels. Set during one specific week in 1966, Divine Days revolves around a turning point in the life of Forrest's protagonist, Joubert Antoine Jones. Like so many of Forrest's characters, Joubert is an orphan; like Leon Forrest, he has returned to Forest County after a stint in the U.S. Army and aspires to be a writer. Like all of Forrest's novels, however, Divine Days gives free rein to his formidable creative gifts.

If Leon Forrest is concerned with the themes of historical and cultural disruption, with orphanhood as a metaphor for the African American—and human—condition, he is equally concerned with the quest for redemption. Like Ralph Ellison, whom he clearly claims as an important literary ancestor, Forrest sees African American oral traditions as rich repositories of ritual and value, sources of meaning in the face of suffering and tragedy. Storytelling, *music, *religion, and a highly developed comic sense are inextricably woven into the fabric of his fiction. A major stylistic innovator, Forrest also claims his place among other major twentieth-century literary modernists. Although his restless experimentation and complex, allusive style often prove difficult on first reading, his novels possess a complexity and depth that reward the demands he makes upon his readers.

• Keith E. Byerman, *Fingering the Jagged Grain: Tradition and Form in Recent Black Fiction*, 1985, pp. 238–255. John G. Cawelti, introduction to *The Bloodworth Orphans*, 1987. John G. Cawelti, "Earthly Thoughts on *Divine Days*," *Callaloo* 16.2 (Spring 1993): 431–447. Danille Taylor-Guthrie, "Sermons, Testifying, and Prayers: Looking Beneath the Wings in Leon Forrest's *Two Wings to Veil My Face*," *Callaloo* 16.2 (Spring 1993): 419–430. Kenneth W. Warren, "Thinking Beyond Catastrophe: Leon Forrest's *There Is a Tree More Ancient than Eden*," *Callaloo* 16.2 (Spring 1993): 409–418.

—James A. Miller

FORTEN, CHARLOTTE (1838–1914), diarist. As an African American diarist in antebellum and postbellum America, Charlotte Forten was a privileged individual by birth and endowment. Born 17 August 1838 in Philadelphia, Forten was a toddler when her famous grandfather died. James Forten, Sr., who had been a powder-boy during the American Revolution and a former student of Anthony Benezet, the Quaker abolitionist, was an ingenious man who amassed a fortune by inventing and patenting a practical sailing device. Because of his brilliant mind and rebellious spirit, he was a leading abolitionist among free Negroes in Philadelphia. Robert Forten, his son and Charlotte's father, an antislavery lecturer, hired private tutors to instruct his daughter at home before she moved to Salem, Massachusetts, in protest of Philadelphia's strictly segregated schools. Her aunts, Margaretta, Sarah, and Harriet, were active socially and politically in the women's rights and *antislavery movements. Harriet Forten, Charlotte's favorite aunt, was married to Robert *Purvis, an original signer of the American Anti-Slavery Society charter and later the president of that organization.

A product of this environment of revolutionary fervor and commitment, Charlotte Forten was immersed in the spirited politics of renewal. Her own sufferings, however, personalized her involvement in the campaign to end *slavery and racism. She may well have been an aristocratic member of the Forten clan, but her status was no protection from the discrimination that she experienced as a person of color connected irremediably to a subjugated group of people. Her journals reveal her anguish and pain as she and her friends were barred from ice cream parlors in Philadelphia and museums in Boston. Indeed, even her white classmates from the "liberal" Higginson Grammar School were capable of ostracizing her at their convenience. She confides to her diary, "I have met girls in the schoolroom—they have been thoroughly kind and cordial to me—perhaps the next day met them in the street—they feared to recognize me; these I can but regard now with scorn and contempt." Charlotte Forten was a victim of a psy-

chic conflict of *identity: she was both a blue blood and a member of an oppressed minority at the mercy of a racialized society and its racist whims.

Forten's diaries were written over a period of thirty-eight years from 1854 to 1892, time enough for her and her society to change. The journals capture these changes. There are five diaries, and each one permits Charlotte Forten to develop a new image of herself. The first diary is written from 24 May 1854 to 31 December 1856, when Charlotte Forten is a brooding teenager attending antislavery rallies in Boston, Framingham, and Salem. Written from 1 January 1857 to 27 January 1858, diary 2 mirrors the transformation of Charlotte Forten, a young adult, into an abolitionist snob. After receiving a caller who had failed to embrace the doctrine of radical abolitionism, she writes of him, "intelligent on some subjects—ignorant of true [radical] anti-slavery. I soon wearied of him." Journal 3 is the core of the diaries, for it is here that a twenty-four-year-old Charlotte Forten (upon John Greenleaf Whittier's advice) applies for a commission to travel like a soldier to South Carolina as a New England schoolmarm to teach contraband slaves and nurse Union soldiers during the Civil War. This diary covers five years, 28 January 1858 to 14 February 1863. Two of the most important events recorded here are her involvement in the Port Royal Social Experiment and her eyewitness account of the official reading of Abraham *Lincoln's Emancipation Proclamation statement to South Carolina slaves and black soldiers. Charlotte Forten left Philadelphia for the Sea Islands on 22 October 1862; excluding a two-month northern vacation, she stayed on the coast for approximately seventeen months. She taught at the Penn School, under the supervision of its founder, Laura Towne, and her assistant Ellen Murray, both New Englanders.

Forten travelled to nearby Beaufort, South Carolina, to meet Harriet *Tubman. When former slave Harriet Tubman describes her adventures in assisting fugitive slaves, the diarist writes, "My own eyes were full as I listened to her." Harriet Tubman has been called the *Moses of her people for leading, single-handedly, approximately three hundred men, women, and children to *freedom in Canada and the North. When "Moses" and the "soldier" Charlotte Forten come face to face, a symbolic union takes place: the old world of slavery and "ordinary" heroism and the new world of independence and acknowledgment that Americans of African descent, regardless of their place in society, have a shared racial heritage of oppression that makes differences of birth and *education of secondary importance in a racialized country.

In diary 4, written from 15 February 1863 to 15 May 1864, Charlotte Forten has settled into her role as nurse to contraband slaves and Union soldiers, at first relishing her relations with the all-black Fifty-Fourth Regiment (she is called the "Daughter of the Regiment") and its leader, Robert Shaw. But her happiness is turned to grief upon their defeat at Fort Wagner.

The last journal, November 1885 to July 1892, was written approximately twenty-one years after diary 4.

Although she had been married to the Princeton-educated minister Francis J. *Grimké (the *mulatto nephew of white feminists-abolitionists Angelina and Sarah Grimké) for seven years, Charlotte Forten gives no details about the marriage. Her diaries were written in secrecy, but she must have been aware of their public historical importance and apparently refused disclosure of her intimate relations. In diary 3 she asks, "What name shall I give to thee, oh *ami inconnu*? It will be safer to give merely an initial—A. And so, dear A." By giving the journal an initial rather than a full name, Charlotte Forten shows her consciousness of an implied audience and her desire to keep some privacy.

She is wistful and pleased as she reviews past events. Having lost an infant daughter, Theodora, she does not wallow in self-pity and merely cites the age the child would have been had she lived—six years old. On Christmas Day 1885, she recalls dining with the aging Frederick *Douglass one year earlier in Washington, D.C., at his "beautiful home." She takes delight in the "Normal School," managed by Booker T. *Washington, and in the emergence of "colored people of the better class." The old missionary spirit, however, is still evident, as she expresses regrets about the impending move again to Washington, D.C., from Florida, in 1889, because the latter "is a good field for missionary work."

Her last entry is dated July 1892; she is in Massachusetts, having left Washington because of its "intense heat" and her constant illnesses. During the last twenty-two years of her life, Charlotte Forten was silent, dying in 1914. But her journals supersede the status of "mere diaries." For Charlotte Forten captured the zeitgeist of the Civil War epoch, which she helped to transform into something noble and meaningful for all Americans.

[*See also* Diaries and Journals.]

• Charlotte Forten, *The Journals of Charlotte Forten*, ed. Ray Allen Billington, 1953. Esther M. Douty, *Forten the Sailmaker*, 1968. Eric Foner, *Reconstruction*, 1988. Charlotte Forten Grimké, *The Journals of Charlotte Forten Grimké*, ed. Brenda Stevenson, 1988.   —Geneva Cobb-Moore

FORTUNE, T. THOMAS (1856–1928), African American journalist and editor. Born a slave in Marianna, Florida, T. Thomas Fortune was the son of a prominent Republican politician during Reconstruction, which enabled him to hold various patronage positions during his adolescence. He studied at Howard University, leaving after a year to pursue a career in *journalism. He arrived in New York City in the early 1880s, writing for various black and white publications, most notably as the editor of the *Globe*. He established himself as a militant, prodding African Americans to abandon their unquestioned loyalty to the party of Lincoln. His near-endorsement of Grover Cleveland for president in 1884 led to management conflicts and the demise of the *Globe*, though the paper reemerged first as the *Freeman* and then the *Age*. Under his proprietorship, the *Age* would become the leading black paper of the era, and he would become the "most noted man in Afro-American journalism." As one contemporary observed, "he never writes unless he makes someone wince."

Fortune's enthusiasm for the Democrats soon waned, while his 1884 book, *Black and White: Land, Labor and Politics in the South*, cemented his reputation as a civil rights militant. In a typical vein, Fortune vowed, "let us agitate! *Agitate! AGITATE!* until the protest shall awake the nation from its indifference." He was widely condemned in the white press as a firebrand. In the early 1890s, Fortune also established the Afro-American League, an ideological precursor to the NAACP, that lapsed into inactivity after a few years.

Growing prominence brought few financial rewards for Fortune, which may have contributed to his support of Booker T. *Washington after 1895. Fortune defended Washington while distancing himself from his accommodationist approach, thus lending Washington useful journalistic cover from an established militant. Fortune also acted as his ghostwriter, and Washington's subsidies to the *Age* and personal loans became essential to Fortune's financial survival. Increasing criticism of Washington from fellow radicals like W. E. B. *Du Bois and Monroe Trotter placed Fortune in an uncomfortable position. After the turn of the century, the relationship with Washington became strained, both personally and politically, and Fortune denounced Washington's support for President Theodore Roosevelt's actions after the Brownsville affair in 1906. Marital discord and alcoholism culminated in a mental breakdown in the following year, whereupon Fortune lost control of the *Age* to Washington allies.

Fortune spent the next decade destitute and depressed, writing occasional columns for the *Age* and editing several short-lived newspapers. In 1923, Fortune assumed the position of editor of the *Negro World*, vacated by Marcus *Garvey upon his imprisonment. Though he had opposed back to Africa notions and apparently never joined Garvey's Universal Negro Improvement Association, Fortune praised the "dramatic element" in Garvey's message and his skill in securing the support of the masses. He also defended Garvey against government charges of stock fraud, and he generally shared Garvey's resentment against Du Bois and the NAACP leadership. Fortune's reputation as a journalist had recovered somewhat by the time of his death.

[*See also* Newspaper Columns; Periodicals, *article on* Black Periodical Press.]

• Emma Lou Thornbrough, *T. Thomas Fortune: Militant Journalist*, 1972.   —Michael W. Fitzgerald

Foxes of Harrow, The. Set in the antebellum South between 1825 and 1865, *The Foxes of Harrow* (1946) is a historical romance that chronicles the adventures of Stephen Fox, an Irish immigrant who rises from poverty to wealth in New Orleans society. The novel, which was written by Frank *Yerby, opens with Fox being thrown off a steamboat on the Mississippi River and ends with the destruction of his plantation, Harrow. Between 1825 and 1865, however, he wins recognition among aristocrats by amassing a fortune from gambling and selling cotton and marrying into a prominent family. An outcast in an alien culture, Fox lives on the margins, neither accepting nor adhering to its beliefs and traditions.

Unlike many protagonists in antebellum southern fiction, Fox is not magnanimous. He comes from a disreputable background, holds nonsouthern views, and succeeds by less than admirable means. Thus, while The Foxes of Harrow compares favorably to such historical romances as Gone with the Wind (1935) and Anthony Adverse (1933), it is in actuality a throwback to the picaresque tradition. Yerby's skillful adaptation and manipulation of the picaresque genre create a vehicle for him both to write entertaining fiction and debunk southern myths.

With the publication of The Foxes of Harrow, his first *novel, Yerby made an abrupt transition from protest to popular fiction. Sales of the novel skyrocketed, magazines reprinted condensed versions of it, Twentieth Century Fox purchased the screen rights, and by the end of 1946, it had sold more than one million copies. Yerby would subsequently produce an impressive list of best-sellers, but in many ways, The Foxes of Harrow remains his most defining novel. It catapulted him to national recognition as a writer, it established the commercially successful formula for all of his succeeding novels, and it charted a course for him to gain distinction as the first African American to become a millionaire writing fiction.

• Ann Bontemps, "From Lad of Ireland to Bayou Grandee," Chicago Sun Book Week, 10 Feb. 1946, 1. Alice Hackett, "New Novelists of 1946," Saturday Review of Literature 30 (15 Feb. 1947): 11–13.

—James L. Hill

FRADO. By the time Harriet *Wilson wrote *Our Nig (1859) and introduced Frado to the fictional world, many mulattas, with "glossy ringlets" and "creamy" skin, had graced the pages of American fiction. Frado joined William Wells *Brown's Clotel and Harriet Beecher *Stowe's Eliza Harris, anticipated Frances Ellen Watkins *Harper's *Iola Leroy, Nella *Larsen's *Helga Crane, and Zora Neale *Hurston's *Janie Crawford, and initiated a pattern in African American women's writing that wasn't challenged until Ann *Petry's brown-skinned *Lutie Johnson emerged in 1946. Yet Wilson creates an isolated rather than an alienated mulatta character. Moreover, unlike the vast majority of such characters, Frado's mother is white, and maternal abandonment rather than paternal legitimation is at issue. Indeed, through Frado's eyes, we see the most scathing critique of white mothers offered by an African American woman writer in the nineteenth century.

Abandoned when she is six, Frado is forced to work in New Hampshire as a virtual slave for the Bellmont family, who call her "our nig." Although Mrs. Bellmont's brutal treatment cannot break the spunky girl's spirit, it does ruin her health. When Frado leaves, the abuse she has endured has taken its toll and the eighteen year old can no longer work. After an unsuccessful *marriage, she writes Our Nig to raise money to support herself and her son. We now know that Wilson's son died five months after the

*novel's publication. While Wilson's tale seems tragic, she successfully creates a spirited, if abused, protagonist who struggles with her captors, her *identity as an isolated black child, and her readers' expectations.

[See also Mulatto.]

• Henry Louis Gates, Jr., ed., introduction to Our Nig, 1994.

—P. Gabrielle Foreman

FRANKLIN, ARETHA (b. 1942), gospel, jazz, pop, and rhythm and blues singer. Aretha Franklin was born in Memphis, Tennessee, and grew up in Detroit, Michigan. Her father, Rev. Clarence LaVaugh Franklin, was a gospel singer. Aretha was raised by him and a household of housekeepers and family friends including Clara Ward, James Cleveland, and Mahalia Jackson. She began singing in her father's church choir at the age of twelve. She recorded her first album, Songs of Faith, when she was fourteen years old. At an early age she was labeled a "young genius" because of the strength and unique quality of her voice. In 1960, Franklin moved to New York City to pursue a career as a rhythm-and-blues singer. Although she refuses to discuss intimate details of her personal life, her *music itself is autobiographical. Songs like "Respect," "Think," and "Try a Little Tenderness" reveal the pain and frustration she has experienced in her life. (She recorded "Respect" after separating from her first, abusive husband, Ted White.) Today Franklin is one of the most celebrated singers in American music. She has won at least fifteen Grammy Awards, including the 1993–1994 Grammy Lifetime Achievement Award. In 1985, the state of Michigan declared her voice a "natural resource" in honor of her twenty-fifth year in the music business. In 1987, she became the first woman to be inducted into the Rock and Roll Hall of Fame. The "Queen of Soul" has been compared to other great *blues singers like Dinah Washington, Bessie *Smith, and Billie *Holiday. Blues singers maintain an iconic importance in African American *poetry, *drama, and fictive narrative. In African American literature they often figure as sensual women who utilize music as a liberating tool to communicate pain, suffering, desire, *sexuality, and joy in an environment that normally represses female expression. Nikki *Giovanni's "Poem for Aretha," for example, is included in Re: Creation (1970), a book of poetry that advocates African American women's need for self-empowerment and self-sustenance in a spiritually destructive world. Part of "Poem for Aretha" refers to the way "we [society] eat up artists like there's going to be a famine." Writers like Giovanni are inspired by Franklin's signature voice and strive to project their own distinctive voices in their work.

• Mark Brego, Aretha Franklin, the Queen of Soul, 1989. Virginia C. Fowler, Nikki Giovanni, 1992.

—Alisha R. Coleman

FRANKLIN, J. E. (b. 1937), writer, playwright, and educator. Jennie Elizabeth Franklin was born in Houston, Texas; she began writing her impressions as a child and received a BA from the University of Texas. She was a primary school teacher in the Freedom School in Carthage, Mississippi (1964); served as a youth director at the Neighborhood House in Buffalo, New York (1964–1965); worked as an analyst in the U.S. Office of Economic Opportunity in New York City (1967–1968); and was a lecturer in education at the Herbert H. Lehman College of the City University of New York (1969–1975).

In 1964, while working with CORE in Mississippi, she engaged in an effort designed to interest students in reading. Her techniques led to her playwriting career and her first full-length play, *A First Step to Freedom* (1964), which was performed in Harmony, Mississippi, at Sharon Waite Community Center. Other produced plays include *Prodigal Daughter*, a street theater project performed at Lincoln Center and on a Bronx street corner; *The In-Crowd* (1965), performed at the Montreal Expo in 1967; *Mau Mau Room*, performed by the Negro Ensemble Company Workshop; *Two Flowers*, produced at the New Feminist Theatre; and *The Prodigal Sister*, produced at Theatre de Lys (1976). The last was a *musical, with book and lyrics by Franklin and music by Micki Grant, about an unwed mother-to-be who leaves home to escape parental displeasure; this was her second major New York production.

However, it was the play *Black Girl* (1971) that earned her acclaim and a following; it later became a movie with Ossie *Davis as director and Franklin as screenwriter. Initially, the play was produced by Woodie *King, Jr., at the New Federal Theatre and later moved to the Theatre de Lys. It ran for an entire season, and each performance opened to a full and enthusiastic house. It is the story of Billie Jean, the baby of the family, who is a high school dropout with talent and the desire to become a ballet dancer, and of her family's attempt to thwart her advancement. It is a deceptively simple play that addresses intraracial oppression, family dynamics, choices, and becoming.

In addition to her produced plays, Franklin has many unpublished and unproduced works. She has contributed articles to periodicals and written a book entitled *Black Girl, from Genesis to Revelations* (1977), which details the writing of the play, her confrontation with the theater world, and the pains and promises of converting the play into a television production and later a film.

Franklin's talent has been rewarded with the Media Women Award (1971); the New York Drama Desk Most Promising Playwright Award (1971); the Institute for the Arts and Humanities Dramatic Award from Howard University (1974); the Better Boys Foundation Playwrighting Award (1978); the Ajabei Children's Theater Annual Award (1978); the National Endowment for the Arts Creative Writing Fellowship (1979); and the Rockefeller Grant (1980). In her works, she is realistic, presents multifaceted African American life from a female perspective, and demonstrates her belief that the theater should educate, be socially aware, and present feelings and options to the viewers.

• Fred Beauford, "A Conversation with *Black Girl's* J. E. Franklin," *Black Creation* 3 (Fall 1971): 38–40. Carole A. Parks, "J. E. Franklin, Playwright," *Black World* 21 (Apr. 1972): 49–50.   —Helen R. Houston

FRATERNITIES. *See* Societies and Clubs.

Frederick Douglass's Paper. *See* Douglass, Frederick; North Star, The.

FREEDOM. "While we slaves talked of freedom, our masters talked of ale," Frederick *Douglass once recalled. From the freedom songs of 1840–1860 to the freedom songs of 1950–1970, from **Freedom's Journal*, the earliest black newspaper, founded in 1827, to *The Freedom Principle*, a study of black *music published in 1990, African American writers have been unofficial spokespersons for personal liberty in America. They explored what they could not take for granted, what they often could not excercise.

*Slavery was for many a searing classroom. "The name and nature of freedom were on everyone's lips," in the antebellum years, according to Samuel Ringgold Ward. Direct heirs of the Enlightenment, the transatlantic Romantic movement, and the American, French, and Haitian revolutions, black abolitionists translated the collective calls of earlier generations of Americans for religious and national liberty into creative doctrines of personal freedom—doctrines echoed in civil and human rights thinking for more than a century.

Few issues have been debated longer or with more agility in the western hemisphere than slavery. That fact alone guaranteed that all abolitionist leaders would become, to some degree, philosophers of liberty. Volatile subordinate issues like *migration and colonization insured that their thinking could not rest upon a few generalizations but must develop and refine itself. Political addresses and *slave narratives in particular in abolitionist writing offer a complex demand for inner and external freedom decades before emancipation. Debate remained strong after emancipation because the gulf was enormous between plantation owners and free-labor former bondsmen, sustaining a level of economic argument as elaborate as the earlier political one had been.

Because most earlier African American literature is southern writing, a sense of freedom frequently enfolded a sense of *place. As the movement west had grown mythic in significance for white writers, so the movement north—the Great Migration—became symbolic of a search for new freedom. While the gold rush and homestead movements had spurred migration west, so the Jim Crow laws and other colorphobic trends like the Hayes-Tilden agreement of 1876, which ended federal protection of blacks in the South, and the growth of the Ku Klux Klan provided the impetus north and gave the promise of self-creation—the hope that additional freedom might prove not merely incremental but genuinely transforming.

Douglass is to these early discussions of freedom as Freud is to psychology—not the last word but the first. The earliest of his *autobiographies, the

Narrative of the Life of Frederick Douglass of 1845, concerns itself with what he called public freedom—the basic political and economic rights of free citizens. But the later two, in 1855 and 1881, were directed equally toward the private rights of a creative, independent individual. Against Alexander *Crummell, he argued that colonization was more problem than solution. Against the abolitionists who wished to keep him discussing solely his life as a slave, he pointedly named his second book *My Bondage and My Freedom* (1855), giving his life as freedman equal prominence. Against the malice of the Fugitive Slave Act, he argued for an end to pacifism. Against William Lloyd Garrison, he argued for freedom *to be* and *to do*, as well as from oppression. Against Lincoln, he argued for the right of black men to fight slavery directly, as soldiers. Against the Exodusters (black laborers who sought to move west following the Hayes-Tilden agreement), he argued they belonged as much in their homelands of Georgia or Alabama as in the unfamiliar prairies of Kansas. Against the Republican Party, he argued for the right of blacks to form their own institutions. When he was a widower, he argued against his own children for the right to marry the white woman he loved.

In each case he was arguing for a deeper conception of freedom than contemporary debate permitted, for the opportunity to create one's fate where one was, without moving to some perhaps nonexistent Eden. Perpetual vigilance is the price of freedom, he said; such vigilance would not only preserve black freedom but also sharpen the collective skills of the race. From Douglass, more than any other single figure, later generations learned that to understand freedom, one must comprehend its denials. From direct experience, Douglass knew that even the most prominent of black writers could not take common liberties for granted. Emancipation was one thing, genuine freedom—of heart as well as body—something quite different.

Charlotte *Forten's *Journal* reveals how free blacks expressed their concern with local political issues. Free or not, other contemporary women writers emphasized economic and family issues. Harriet A. *Jacobs makes clear in *Incidents in the Life of a Slave Girl* (1861) that all other opportunities are secondary to her ability to earn a living for herself and to reunite her family. Although her vehicle is fictional, Harriet E. *Wilson makes a similar plea in *Our Nig* (1859). This Dickensian narrative recounts the racial and economic misery endured by a free *mulatto woman who is an indentured servant in the antebellum North. Wilson openly states that her motive for publishing the *novel is to raise enough money to be reunited with her seven-year-old son, then seriously ill. Her hope was thwarted, for the son died of a fever in a county poorhouse six months after publication.

The poorhouse remained a warning to Elizabeth *Keckley, for whom authorship and the opportunities it provided were a passage into the economic mainstream. *Behind the Scenes, or Thirty Years a Slave, and Four Years in the White House* (1868) is a rags-to-riches story of Keckley's work as a seamstress, particularly for Mary Todd Lincoln, to whom she became close. Keckley argued that the end of slavery must mean new opportunities for newly released energy and creativity. For this unusual slave narrative, she was rewarded with a contract from a large commercial publisher, one of the first to an African American writer. Although she was a harbinger, Keckley's fate resembled that of the ex-colored man in James Weldon *Johnson's novel, for she died alone in the Home for Destitute Women and Children, an institution she helped to found in Washington, D.C.

Booker T. *Washington's conception of freedom resembles Douglass's in one respect. His call to "cast down your bucket where you are" echoes the latter's pleas to black people to stay and assume dominion over the ancestral lands, the lands on which they had worked so arduously. But Douglass considered freedom to be political and collective. Washington speaks of it as economic and individual. Washington used his freedom radically—to rewrite *history and his own part in it. He was willing to revise the story of slavery in order to give black people a larger part in the present. Freedom entailed the power or opportunity to transcend facts and chronicles. In *The Future of the American Negro* (1899) and *Up from Slavery* (1901), freedom is the authority to re-create himself and to transform what he touches into his own image. In his biography of Douglass (1906), quite different from the earlier one by Charles Waddell *Chesnutt (1899), Washington rewrites his subject's life in part that Douglass might appear a precursor, a John the Baptist, to Washington himself. In the opening of the work he said that Douglass's life "falls almost wholly within the period of revolution and liberation. That period is now closed. We are at present in the period of construction and readjustment."

Of the value of economic freedom, Chesnutt, too, was convinced. "I want fame; I want money; I want to raise my children in a different rank of life from what I spring from," he wrote in his journal in 1881. Probably the most accomplished African American writer of fiction during the nineteenth century, Chesnutt was compelled to move north and to stretch the bounds of black opportunity to achieve his goals. He did so with moral authority, for like Jean *Toomer, Walter *White, and James Weldon Johnson, he was free to choose and define his *race. Between 1899 and 1905 Chesnutt published two notable collections of *short stories and three novels that deliver an uncompromising view of American racism and reached a large part of the American reading audience. During that relatively short period he greatly widened the choices of black writers through two narrative techniques that would be commonly used thereafter.

The first was to redirect dialect stories of the *plantation tradition so that they were more critical of the mean, narrow world of the slaveholders. In the best dialect stories of The *Conjure Woman (1899)—"The Goophered Grapevine," "Po' Sandy," and "Dave's Neckliss"—Chesnutt reveals slavery to have been an almost unbearable threat to the mental and physical lives of black people. In The *Wife of His Youth (1899), The *House Behind the Cedars (1900),

The *Marrow of Tradition (1901), and The Colonel's Dream (1905), the author developed a form of irony—some critics refer to it as double entendre—that explored the circumscribed lives of middle-class light-skinned African Americans like himself, while introducing them to whites who knew little about those W. E. B. *Du Bois characterized as the *talented tenth.

After 1905, the promise of inclusion into a white literary orbit faded for Chesnutt, regardless of his achievements. For his contemporary Paul Laurence *Dunbar, that promise was always ambiguous. In his novel The *Sport of the Gods (1902) Dunbar reveals the deceptions of northern greed and southern paternalism. There is no more honey and silver above the Mason-Dixon line, Dunbar says, than there is sweet harmony below. The Hamiltons of the novel, faithful *domestics for many years, are betrayed as much by unscrupulous northern capitalists as by unscrupulous southern gentry. In the final scene, they return to their fates in the South, knowing "they were powerless against some Will infinitely stronger than their own." If the North represents the best hope for black people, Dunbar says, then hope is as scarce as wealth.

The North as promised land of opportunity had been a cultural symbol long before the *Harlem Renaissance. Many did see it as a new Eden, hardly flawless but more hopeful than the peonage of the Old South. Arna *Bontemps's "A Summer Tragedy" and Richard *Wright's *Uncle Tom's Children (1937) and *Black Boy (1945) offer somewhat later versions of that view. Migration north was a significant theme for major writers such as Du Bois, in his *essays and novels, and James Weldon Johnson. The *Autobiography of an Ex-Colored Man (1912) rejects any easy identification of the North with genuine opportunity. With Dunbar, Johnson said that many people, expecting better, turned to the bullet, the bottle, or the Bible when faced with the searing experiences of the North. Yet by the 1920s, "the North," "Harlem," and "New York" had grown into potent symbols. The literary treatment of a representative black American's migration northward converged with his or her search for *identity, the creative and spiritual sources of blackness.

The Harlem Renaissance was a significant bridge in part because Harlem was itself so remarkable a gateway. In "Harlem Is Nowhere" (1953), Ralph *Ellison recalled that black Americans were caught "in a vast process of change that has swept them from slavery to the condition of industrial man in a space of time so telescoped" that they could "step from feudalism into the vortex of industrialism simply by moving across the Mason-Dixon line." The results were formidable. In Harlem "the grandchildren of those who possessed no written literature examine their lives through the eyes of Freud and Marx, Kierkegaard and Kafka, Malraux and Sartre."

In this new Harlem, writers and artists were asking for intellectual and aesthetic freedoms unknown to previous ages. As white artists looked to Harlem for inspiration, so Harlem stretched itself to accommodate new ideas and new talents. Younger writers

asked for the right to protest or to philosophize, to be serious race men and women or to ignore race altogether. To be a member of the talented tenth certainly brought responsibilities, they said, but it also conferred indispensable options—options they fully intended to exercise. Langston Hughes captured this heady mix of ancestral obligations and newfound privileges in his essay "The Negro Artist and the Racial Mountain" of 1926. As the historically minded Arthur A. *Schomburg put it in the opening to his famous "The Negro Digs Up His Past" (1925), "The American Negro must remake his past in order to make his future." For the many efforts of the age in scholarship and preservation, Schomburg served as midwife and benefactor.

The most important proponent of this new artistic freedom, however, was Alain *Locke, and its most vivid statement his *anthology The *New Negro (1925). Uniting young and established literary figures, he sought to exhibit "a significant and satisfying new phase in group development."

> The Younger Generation comes, bringing its gifts. They are the first fruits of the Negro Renaissance.... What stirs inarticulately in the masses is already vocal upon the lips of the talented few, and the future listens, however the present may shut its ears. Here we have Negro youth, with arresting visions and vibrant prophecies; forecasting in the mirror of art what we must see and recognize in the streets of reality tomorrow, foretelling in new notes and accents the maturing speech of full racial utterance.

In such new accents came a series of eloquent manifestos, calls to white audiences and publishers to loosen their artistic shackles. In "The Dilemma of the Negro Author" (1928), James Weldon Johnson castigates the *stereotypes a white audience expects. In a series of astute essays, Sterling A. *Brown describes the evasions and stereotypes that white authors provide. Two shorter essays are "Our Literary Audience" (1930) and "The Negro Author and His Publisher" (1941); valuable longer ones are Negro Poetry and The Negro in American Fiction (both 1937). A revealing interchange on the need for wider, subtler scope for black writers occurs between Wright and Hurston when she reviews Uncle Tom's Children (Saturday Review, 1937) and he comments upon *Their Eyes Were Watching God (New Masses, 1938). Wright's call for an effective form of social consciousness appears in "Blueprint for Negro Writing" (1937). Hurston takes up one of Brown's themes in "What White Publishers Won't Print" (1950).

This mythic promise of new freedoms clothed the interpretation of African American life for a long line of writers. Whether as dream or as nightmare, the North is integral to Toomer's *Cane (1923); Nella *Larsen's *Quicksand (1928); Wright's *Native Son (1940), The Outsider (1953), and Savage Holiday (1954); William *Attaway's Blood on the Forge (1941); Ann *Petry's The *Street (1946); Frank London *Brown's Trumbull Park (1959) and "Singing Dinah's Song"; Chester *Himes's dozen or so Harlem novels; LeRoi Jones/Amiri *Baraka's The *System of Dante's Hell (1965); John A. *Williams's The *Man Who Cried I Am (1967); Ernest J. *Gaines's The *Autobiography *of Miss Jane Pittman* (1971) and "A Long Day in November"; and John Edgar *Wideman's *The Lynchers* (1973).

From the 1950s onward, the *civil rights movement raised an octave higher the call for social freedom. Ellison's *Invisible Man* (1952) is one of the premier works in the language because, among other reasons, it is a virtual handbook of the trends described here. From abolition through the depression and World War II, it captures the African American quest for freedom through time, place, psychology, and philosophy, tracing the currents of the twentieth century as Douglass had done for the nineteenth. In its acuity, it not only reports paths toward freedom but also creates them. As the Invisible Man's path ends in Harlem, so it begins for *John Grimes in one of the most successful fictions of the period, James *Baldwin's *Go Tell It on the Mountain* (1953).

During the 1960s, writing about freedom in all genres underwent a seismic change whose aftereffects continue to be felt. In at least three areas—cultural liberation, cultural studies, and women's liberation—writers sought to fulfill or recover aspirations suspended since the Harlem Renaissance. To many, cultural freedom assumed the right to pursue new personal and literary identities. As LeRoi Jones evolved into Amiri Baraka, he transformed himself from a minor Beat poet and *music critic into a major spokesperson for an equally evolving black culture. He produced *Dutchman* and three other important plays in 1964, then sought to form self-contained black cultural institutions. *Black Fire,* the anthology of new writing he edited with Larry *Neal in 1968, became instrument and inscription of the new spirit in literature, as his essay of 1969, "Nationalism Vs. PimpArt," did in *criticism. As publishers responded to that new spirit, a fresh cycle of protest writings appeared, including the prison writing of George Jackson and Eldridge *Cleaver and expositions of Black Power by Stokely *Carmichael and H. Rap Brown. Capturing such facets of the age was the second volume of autobiography by Chester Himes, *My Life of Absurdity* (1976).

For other authors a changed climate meant not so much militancy as opportunity. Lonne *Elder III, representing a new generation of writers, sought the chance to move from acting with a new institution, the Negro Ensemble Company, to writing for that company, then moving to *television and *film as writer and producer. For James Alan *McPherson the changing climate meant the chance to publish cycles of short stories such as *Hue and Cry* (1969) and *Elbow Room* (1977) that are for the most part quiet, polished tales of ordinary life. For Himes and others it meant the chance to publish tales of mystery and detection. For some—such as Margaret *Walker in historical fiction and Octavia E. *Butler in *speculative fiction—it meant the chance to enter new fields. In autobiography, new authors and new angles of vision were possible, the latter well represented by Horace Cayton's use of psychoanalysis in *Long Old Road* (1965) and Wideman's extraordinary chronicle of his brother and himself, *Brothers and Keepers* (1984). In fiction, writers such as Ismael *Reed and Charles R.

*Johnson seized the chance to treat lightly or in burlesque topics previously reserved for weighty seriousness. Equally significant for the future, new opportunities meant a sizable increase in the number of authors writing for children and adolescents.

As figures such as Baraka sought to forge new connections between culture and community, others sought bridges between the creative and academic worlds. Some fifty journals were founded between 1960 and 1976, notably *Callaloo, *Black Scholar, *African American Review, Black Review, *Black Theatre, Black Academy Review, Black Orpheus,* and the *Journal of Black Poetry.* Begun in 1961, the aptly titled *Freedomways* was the third and last journal founded by W. E. B. Du Bois. A transition of symbolic importance occurred during spring 1970 when Hoyt *Fuller altered the title of his journal from *Negro Digest* to *Black World.*

Women writers and critics who had been in the vanguard since Douglass's age had often subordinated themselves and *gender issues for the sake of a collective cause. Since the early 1980s, however, that willingness has diminished. Doyenne of the movement, Gwendolyn *Brooks, called upon women to grasp for themselves the newfound freedoms they sought for their children. Women critics have redefined the canon, recovered important writers, identified techniques heretofore unnoticed, raised theoretical issues previously ignored, and in general returned questions of freedom to their roots. A charter for the current wave of criticism was *In Search of Our Mothers' Gardens* (1983), by poet and novelist Alice *Walker, which speaks to sisters of the spirit of a dimension of freedom beyond the material, a dimension that "womanist" writers regularly reach while others do not. Cultivating the freedom Walker seeks were Margaret Walker, Sherley Anne *Williams, Louise *Meriwether, Gloria *Naylor, Alice *Childress, Rosa *Guy, Ntozake *Shange, Toni Cade *Bambara, Terry *McMillan, and Tina McElroy *Ansa. The most compelling examples were Walker herself and Toni *Morrison, each of whose novels is a momentous exploration of a major issue in women's lives. In five novels—*The *Third Life of Grange Copeland* (1970), *Meridian* (1976), *The *Color Purple* (1982), *The *Temple of My Familiar* (1989), and *Possessing the Secret of Joy* (1992)—Walker has related stories as painful as those told by Harriet A. Jacobs and Harriet Wilson, even to the extreme of brutality and mutilation. "I am preoccupied with the spiritual survival . . . of my people," she has said. "But beyond that, I am committed to exploring the oppressions, the insanities, the loyalties, and the triumphs of black women."

Each of Morrison's six novels likewise treats a major event, period, or aspect of African American history in a monumental way. Beginning with *The *Bluest Eye* (1970) and *Sula* (1973), Morrison sought a different narrative technique with each new project—shifting length, narrators, time schemes, and points of view. Most ambitious of her works in the 1970s is *Song of Solomon* (1977), a meditation upon the ways ordinary people, particularly women, deal with uncertainty and ambivalence. Following *Tar Baby* (1981), she completed two prodigious works: *Beloved* (1987), the most accomplished latter-day example of the slave narrative, and *Jazz* (1992), an evocative study of the effects of the Great Migration. For her characters, as for Douglass's fugitives, freedom may be a learned, indefinable thing, but it is also "to be felt in the bones and tasted on the tongue." To her might be applied Robert *Hayden's words on Douglass—like him she has created freedom with "the lives grown of her life, the lives fleshing her dream of the beautiful, needful thing."

• William L. Andrews, *The Literary Career of Charles W. Chesnutt*, 1980. J. Lee Greene, "Southern Black Literature of the Nineteenth and Twentieth Centuries," in *The Encyclopedia of Southern Culture*, eds. Charles R. Wilson and William Ferris, 1989. Orlando Patterson, *Freedom*, 1991. Melissa Walker, *Down from the Mountaintop: Black Women's Novels in the Wake of the Civil Rights Movement, 1966–1989*, 1991. Angelyn Mitchell, ed., *Within the Circle: African American Literary Criticism from the Harlem Renaissance to the Present*, 1994. John Sekora, *Frederick Douglass*, 1996.

—John Sekora

Freedom's Journal. Initially published in New York City on 16 March 1827, *Freedom's Journal* was the first African American newspaper in the United States. Owned and edited by Samuel *Cornish and John Browne *Russwurm, it was published for two years before folding in 1829.

The introduction of *Freedom's Journal* marked the first time African Americans had a voice in the active periodical press of the early nineteenth century. The primary mission of *Freedom's Journal* was to counteract negative portrayals of African Americans that had appeared in the New York City newspapers. "Our vices and our degradation are ever arrayed against us," noted the editors in the newspaper's first editorial, "but our virtues are passed unnoticed." Not only would the newspaper note and publicize these virtues, but its very existence would testify to the presence of a literate and socially concerned community of free African Americans in the North, a community that understood the political significance and value of having a public voice: "We wish to plead our own cause. Too long have others spoken for us."

Freedom's Journal contained an eclectic mix of news, features, literary pieces, and social announcements. In addition to advocating the abolition of *slavery, *Freedom's Journal* also opposed discrimination against free African Americans in the North. The editors saw *Freedom's Journal* as a means of both fostering communication among African Americans in different states, as well as promoting a proto–Pan Africanist cultural pride in the accomplishments of people of African descent in the United States and across the world.

[See also Journalism; Periodicals, *article on* Black Periodical Press.]

• Martin E. Dann, *The Black Press 1827–1890: The Quest for National Identity*, 1971.   —Wendy Wagner

FULLER, CHARLES H., JR. (b. 1939), playwright, writer of fiction, and essayist. As a playwright, Charles H. Fuller, Jr., is one of America's innovative and provocative voices. He was born on 5 March 1939 in Philadelphia, Pennsylvania, son of Charles H. and Lillian Anderson Fuller. Because of his father's occupation as a printer, Fuller developed early on a love of reading and writing, particularly when Fuller's father asked him to proofread some of his work. Parental influence combined with a love of life's expression through art has inspired Fuller to greatness as a dramatist. Fuller's life as a child was filled with exposure to different personalities and lifestyles because of the constant stream of foster children coming through his Philadelphia home. His initial infatuation with *drama occurred after seeing a play at a Yiddish theater. Fuller's contributions range from cofounding and -directing the Afro-American Arts Theatre in Philadelphia, and writing and directing "Black Experience" on WIP Radio in Philadelphia, to writing Pulitzer Prize–winning plays. Although the literary world recognizes Fuller as a great playwright, his literary career began with *poetry, *short stories, and *essays. *Theater came after he realized that his short stories were filled with dialogue. From creating skits, he moved into writing one-act plays and finally into creating full-length dramas.

His realistic treatment of his subject matter and his humanistic approach to many of society's atrocities makes his a sensitive but forceful voice in the African American literary community. For instance, Fuller's *The Village: A Party*, produced at Princeton's McCarter Theatre (1968), focuses on a community of racially mixed couples who, through murder, attempt to maintain their peaceful, protective society. In this play, Fuller examines integration and implies that it often magnifies racial tension.

Another work, *The Brownsville Raid*, produced in New York City at the Negro Ensemble Company in December 1976, was based on a true occurrence of 1906. This play is another depiction of racism and injustice in America, stemming from the paradoxical existence of black soldiers in a white man's army. Fuller's four-year experience in the U.S. Army in Japan and Korea created the images of military life revealed in many of his works, including this one and especially in the Pulitzer Prize–winning A *Soldier's Play*.

Fuller's *Zooman and the Sign* was also produced in New York City at the Negro Ensemble Company, in November 1979. It won Fuller an Obie and proved to many critics Fuller's talent as a playwright. As in *A Soldier's Play*, *Zooman* opens with a death that becomes the center from which all the action evolves. Many critics considered Fuller's attempts to handle the complexity of such themes ambitious.

Not allowing critics to determine his genius, Fuller next wrote *A Soldier's Play* (1984), a dramatic presentation of institutional racism and self-hatred set in the 1940s that explores the psychological effects of oppression on African Americans. The setting of the play is in 1944 during World War II on an Army base in Fort Neal, Louisiana. The tragic hero, Sergeant Vernon C. Waters, takes upon himself the role of savior of all African Americans in a racist society.

This highly acclaimed commentary on the ills and trials of military life for African Americans is built on a foundation of intricate characterizations and tone. The character of Captain Richard Davenport, an investigating officer, discloses to the audience each enlisted man's story through a series of interviews. Fuller often allows one character to tell another's story. At a time when camaraderie among men is essential, Fuller creates dichotomies: Waters and his enlisted men form one, and later Davenport creates another in his leadership role.

Fuller, only the second black playwright to win a Pulitzer Prize for drama, has had an impact on the subjects discussed in theater, and his work is increasingly appreciated by audiences who cross traditional cultural boundaries.

• Walter Kerr, "A Fine Work from a Forceful Playwright," *New York Times*, 6 December 1981, 3:1. "Charles Fuller," in *CA: New Revision Series*, eds. Linda Metzger et al., 1990, pp. 206–208.
—Wanda Macon

FULLER, HOYT (1923–1981), editor, critic, and leading figure of the Black Arts movement. Born in Atlanta but reared in Detroit where he graduated from Wayne State University, Hoyt Fuller embarked on a career in *journalism and editing. He held positions with the *Michigan Chronicle*, the *Detroit Tribune*, and *Collier's Encyclopedia*, among others. Increasingly frustrated by American racism, he went abroad in 1957, living in France and in Spain; later, attracted by the anticolonial stance of Sekou Toure of Guinea, he travelled in Africa, an experience evoked in his only book, a collection of *essays, *Return to Africa* (1971). Fuller returned to the United States in 1960.

Fuller had worked briefly as an associate editor at the monthly *Ebony* in 1954 before going abroad, and when *Ebony* publisher John Johnson decided to revive the periodical *Negro Digest* in 1961, he offered Fuller the job of editing it. Fuller accepted the position but rejected the digest format, instead casting the revived periodical as a journal of creative expression and opinion. In the course of a few years, *Negro Digest* became the leading forum of the emerging *Black Arts movement. In 1970, the periodical was renamed *Black World* to more accurately reflect its scope, which extended to Africa and the African diaspora.

Negro Digest/Black World (ND/BW) reflected Fuller's concerns with politics, social action, the spiritual and economic health of the black world, as well as with a wide range of artistic expression. The monthly journal was, however, open to a variety of opinions, in spite of its nationalist editorial position. By 1970, a typical issue contained approximately eight articles, a couple of short stories, poems from several bards, and a section called "Perspectives," which was a roundup of cultural information prepared by Fuller. A short reflective essay by Fuller frequently occupied the back cover. These were occasionally replicated, as was the piece "When Is a Black Man Not an African?" In April, the "Annual Theatre Issue" appeared, eagerly awaited by a large component of the readership. In 1976, *ND/BW* was abruptly terminated by the publisher, occasioning widespread protest in the black arts community. Fuller left Chicago, reestablishing himself in Atlanta, and busying

himself with the creation of a successor journal, *First World*. Though several issues appeared, beginning in 1977, the journal was not fated to be a success.

One of Fuller's most notable activities in the 1960s had been the creation in Chicago of OBAC (Organization of Black American Culture), which functioned primarily as a writers' collective. OBAC participants included Haki R. *Madhubuti (Don L. Lee), Carolyn M. *Rodgers, Nikki *Giovanni, and Angela *Jackson. Directly influenced by OBAC was the visual arts collective AFRICOBRA, coordinated by Jeff Donaldson, a longtime associate of Fuller.

Fuller also taught creative writing and African American literature part-time at a number of colleges and universities. Over time these included Columbia College, Chicago; Northwestern University; Indiana University; Cornell University; and Metropolitan Community College, Atlanta.

Fuller attended and reported extensively on the First World Festival of Negro Arts and Culture held in Dakar in 1966, under the patronage of the President of Senegal, Léopold Sédar Senghor. In 1971, Fuller attended the Colloquium on *Negritude in Dakar at which Senghor announced a forthcoming second festival to be held in Nigeria. Fuller convened a North American assembly in Chicago to prepare for participation in this second festival, FESTAC, which was finally held in 1977. He was also active in a series of New World Festivals of the African diaspora, initiated in 1978.

Fuller's impact was strong and incisive throughout the development and expansion of a number of interrelated movements of the 1960s and 1970s: black consciousness, Black Arts, and the *Black Aesthetic. Black consciousness was directed to and concerned with the entire African American community and had to do with the affirmation of *identity and the sense of self-worth; its slogans included "Black Pride" and "Black Is Beautiful." The Black Arts movement proposed the participation of artists of all categories in letters, music, and theater in the exemplification of the experience and values of African and African American life. The Black Aesthetic embodied a program for critics that would guide their judgment of art works and performance. The major document of this movement, *The Black Aesthetic* (1971), edited by Addison *Gayle, Jr., was heavily dependent on Fuller and authors associated with *ND/BW*, such as Carolyn Fowler, who later prepared an important bibliography of the movement.

Fuller focused increasingly on what he perceived as the wider contexts of African American life and was harsh in his criticism of whites and blacks alike. In his 1972 pamphlet for the Institute of the Positive Education, "The Turning of the Wheel," he declared,

Whites maintain . . . that Blacks are strangers here, that they are not fully admitted to the human family, and Blacks are tolerated in this land as long as their energies are directed—"responsibly"—toward the eventual achievement of citizenship, the evolution of their humanity. And Blacks, understanding the terms of their toleration, accede—quietly or raucously, the accession is complete—translating their rage and shame into rhetoric.

While many found Fuller unduly strident, and while a later generation of critics and writers turned to a more nuanced, if not more benign, assessment of the American reality, Fuller's voice was a widely heralded one. His literary and cultural interactions were vast, comprising in the last two decades of his life a broad and extensive network of prominent African Americans. In addition to persons already mentioned, one notes among a numerous roster such eminent writers as James *Baldwin, Gwendolyn *Brooks, and Sterling A. *Brown; critic/scholars such as George Kent, Stephen Henderson, and Houston A. *Baker, Jr.; and theater personalities such as Woodie *King, Jr., Abera Brown, and Val Gray Ward.

Hoyt Fuller's papers are deposited at the Woodruff Library of the Atlanta University Center.

[*See also* Journalism; Periodicals, *article on* Black Periodical Press.]

• Dudley Randall, ed., *Homage to Hoyt Fuller*, 1984.

—Richard A. Long

FULTON, DAVID BRYANT (c. 1863–1941), journalist and fiction writer. David Bryant Fulton was born in Fayetteville, North Carolina, and grew up in Wilmington, North Carolina, where he attended school. In 1887, he moved to New York, finding employment as a porter with the Pullman Palace Car Company. With his wife, Virginia Moore, Fulton settled in Brooklyn, New York, and later worked for Sears, Roebuck; the Brooklyn YMCA; and a music publisher. In 1895, he founded the Society of Sons of North Carolina, a social and benevolent organization in Brooklyn. He was also a member of the Prince Hall Masonic Lodge of Brooklyn and an active contributor to the Yonkers-based Negro Society for Historical Research.

Fulton began his writing career as a correspondent to the Wilmington *Record*, an African American newspaper whose editor solicited Fulton's observations about his travels as a Pullman porter. In 1892, Fulton published a selection of these articles in a pamphlet entitled *Recollections of a Sleeping Car Porter*, in which he used his pen name "Jack Thorne" for the first time. Fulton's second book, also self-published, was a loosely constructed *novel, *Hanover, or The Persecution of the Lowly* (1900), a blend of fact and fiction designed to set the record straight about the causes and outcome of the infamous Wilmington Massacre of 1898.

Between 1903 and 1906, Fulton, writing under his pen name, became popular and respected in the Brooklyn African American community as a vigorous journalistic defender of his people. Most of the pieces in his *Eagle Clippings* (1907) show Jack Thorne attacking racial slander in books and periodicals and criticizing political and social developments that he judged hostile to African Americans. After 1907, Fulton gave his attention to a variety of literary projects. Except for a handful of *short stories published in magazines and in *Eagle Clippings*, the fiction Fulton wrote did not find its way into print. A 1913 poem, "De Coonah Man" (*African Times and Orient Review*,

Dec. 1913) relates in dialect verse the poet's memories of the John Cooner (or John Canoe) African American Christmas customs in North Carolina. "Mother of Mine; Ode to the Negro Woman" was commissioned to be read at the annual convention of the New York Colored Women's Club in 1923. Fulton's 1912 pamphlet *Plea for Social Justice for the Negro Woman* was praised by African American women's groups for its denunciation of both African American concubinage in the antebellum South and the persistence of prostitution for white patrons in the contemporary North.

Fulton stated his racial views in "Race Unification; How It May Be Accomplished" (*African Times and Orient Review*, Dec. 1913). In this *essay he rejected the amalgamation of blacks with whites as a solution to the *race problem, favoring instead a knowledge of "race history," "race achievement," and "race literature" as the stimulus necessary to "race pride" and advancement. Though not original, Fulton's espousal of race consciousness and solidarity testifies to the vitality of nationalistic thinking among African Americans in New York before Marcus *Garvey. With his associates in the Negro Society for Historical Research, John E. *Bruce and Arthur A. *Schomburg, Fulton worked to exemplify and foster a combative, community-oriented intellectual activism among African American writers in the urban North of the early twentieth century.

[*See also* Journalism; Societies and Clubs.]

• David Bryant Fulton, *Hanover*, 1969. Dickson D. Bruce, *Black American Writing from the Nadir*, 1989.

—William L. Andrews

FUNERAL AND MOURNING CUSTOMS. African American funeral and mourning customs are a synthesis of African and Christian cultures, but it is the African heritage that makes these traditions unique. One of the best examples is the practice of decorating graves, brought to America by the enslaved Bakongo people of West Africa. They believed that once a person died, it was important to assist the spirit in its journey to the watery world of the afterlife. Graves were decorated with objects that were associated with water, that belonged to or were last used by a deceased person, and sometimes with food. Placing these items on the grave helped to satisfy the spirit and prevented it from wandering or remaining in the world of the living.

Some important examples of African American funeral and mourning customs and beliefs include: that death is a transformation rather than an extinction of life; that a person's passing is a time to mourn and to celebrate; that if a person has lived a morally righteous life he will return from the afterlife to the physical world, and the cycle repeats itself; that the spirits of the dead are very powerful and continue to affect the living as good and evil forces; that passing a child over and sometimes under the coffin will protect the child from harm by the spirit; that inanimate and animate things have a spirit; that a person has a body, a soul, and a spirit, and it is important to keep the soul with the body, so the mouth is sometimes tied to keep the soul from escaping; that since the afterlife was historically believed to be a world of darkness, night burials were appropriate; that a deceased person's funeral might be preached weeks or even months after the burial; that to prevent them from doing any harm, spirits must be assisted in their journey to the spirit world; that to further protect themselves from harm, the living can confuse spirits with words, actions, colors, asymmetrical patterns, charms, and asymmetrical arrangements of graves; that proper burials (unrestrained mourning by loved ones, the presence of family members and the community, and proper attire worn at the funeral) demonstrate respect for the deceased person and the family; and that oftentimes there are signs, warnings, and omens that precede a pending death.

Excluding the *Harlem Renaissance era, funeral and mourning customs are relatively absent from the African American literary tradition from the colonial period up to the mid-1960s. When they are present, it is usually as part of secondary or tertiary events, and they are seldom given adequate description. The reader is told that a funeral and/or a burial occurred, but few if any details about the ceremony are furnished. Since these rituals are treated as ancillary to the main story, the specific nature of the customs is often obscured. After the mid-1960s there is a profound change in this pattern. Black writers began to actively explore funeral and mourning customs as essential to or as the major theme of their stories, *novels, and poems.

Early African American writers expressed little or no interest in writing about funeral and mourning customs. Their themes typically followed those of their white contemporaries: the treachery of the Native Americans, the providence of God, and the survival of a perilous journey.

Neither Lucy *Terry, recognized as the first African American writer, nor Jupiter *Hammon, John *Marrant, or Phillis *Wheatley, the most celebrated and best-educated of the four, attempted to explore African American culture per se. Even though Wheatley wrote and published a number of elegies, the religious emphasis was Methodist, and the mode of expression was neoclassicism.

After the Revolutionary War black writers focused on *slavery and the degradation of African Americans. This genre of *protest literature reached its height around 1830 but continued through the late nineteenth century, when discrimination, segregation, and violence threatened the rights of freed slaves. *Slave narratives, forming a genre that was popular between 1830 and 1860, were written to demonstrate the evils of slavery and to solicit financial as well as moral support for the abolition of slavery. In many ways the writings were designed to prove to whites that African Americans were like whites—civilized and removed from their African roots. The writings from this period offer numerous contributions on death and the pain of death but very little on the associated rituals.

It is not until the turn of the century that we see a shift, albeit a slight one. Before 1890 there were relatively few African American writers and none who attempted to make a living writing. Between 1890 and

1920, James Weldon *Johnson, Charles Waddell *Chesnutt, W. E. B. *Du Bois, and Paul Laurence *Dunbar were the most prolific. Except for Dunbar's, the bulk of their writings concentrated on important social, economic, and political issues, such as racism, employment, housing, civil rights, and the color caste system within the black community.

James Weldon Johnson's sermonic poems graphically document black folk-preaching themes, including funerary traditions. In "Go Down Death: A Funeral Sermon" (1955) Johnson comforts the mourners by noting that Caroline has simply gone home to rest in the bosom of Jesus. In other poems he describes heaven as a place where wants and suffering are nonexistent and where family, friends, and loved ones are reunited. In heaven life is a grand occasion, with trumpets, bells, chariots, robes, crowns, wings, and great *spirituals. Johnson's poem is more than a metaphor for the rest and the comfort of the departed. It symbolizes what is for many African Americans an accepted fact: that at the moment of death, the deceased is *immediately* transported to heaven and to a grand occasion where saints meet their personal friend—Jesus. This African American concept of life after death is in contrast with the Christian belief that a person's eternal fate is determined on Judgment Day.

Similarly, Paul Laurence Dunbar echoes another African American theme in "A Death Song." He pleads with his listener to bury him "beneath the willers [willows] in the grass and neigh [near] to water, Fur [for] . . . de las' long res' gwine to soothe my sperrit ef I's laying among de tings I's allus [always] knowed." Natural forms such as trees, grass, and water are associated with home and with the journey to the afterlife. To be buried near them would assure that one reaches the afterlife.

In "Death of the First Born" Dunbar mentions sitting with a body through the night. Known as a "settin' up," this mourning tradition was the equivalent of today's wake. It occurred the night before the burial. During this time family, friends, and the community gathered to remember the deceased, to pray, to sing, and to watch the body so that animals would not bother it. People often laughed as much as they cried. They sometimes told jokes or amusing stories about the dearly departed. This was not meant as disrespect but was another way to balance the loss with a celebration of the person's life. Dunbar alludes to this phenomenon in the poem "Puting the Baby Away" when he notes "you wouldn't t'ought wid all de folks, Dats roun hyeah mixin teahs an' jokes de Lawd w'd had de time to see dis chile an' tek him way from me."

By 1915 Blacks had begun to migrate in record numbers from small rural southern communities to large northern cities. In search of a new life of economic, social, and political *freedom, they no longer accepted social conventions that assigned them a lesser place based on *race and *class. They yearned to be more urbane and quickly discarded their folk traditions, such as having the "settin' up" or the wake in the home and decorating graves. The intellectual purveyors of African American culture sought to interpret this change in the sensibilities and experiences of everyday Blacks. Between 1920 and 1929, Harlem was the center of this new literary movement. In many ways Black writers of the Harlem Renaissance consciously and unconsciously preserved the folk traditions as Blacks exchanged them for more sophisticated ones.

Zora Neale *Hurston, one of the most important writers of the Harlem Renaissance, captured the rich legacy of African American folk customs, especially funerary traditions. In her own story, *Dust Tracks on a Road: Autobiography* (1942), she recounts her frustration and anguish when she could not fulfill her mother's deathbed wish. Hurston did not want the family to turn her bed toward the east (to insure an easy rising on Judgment Day), to cover the mirrors, or to remove her pillow when she died. Hurston's other writings, *Their Eyes Were Watching God* (1937), *Mules and Men* (1935), and *Sanctified Church* (1981), explain and honor African American folk traditions as no other writer has done. Her documentation and redistribution of these folk traditions has significantly contributed to the current body of literature on funerary traditions and related beliefs about ghosts, hoodoo, and conjuring.

Another writer of the Harlem Renaissance and a contemporary of Hurston is Countee *Cullen. Cullen's "A Brown Girl Dead" (1925) offers a clue to one aspect of this sacred tradition. In the poem he demonstrates how vital a proper funeral is for an African American mother who has lost her daughter. Dire circumstances force the mother to exchange one cherished object for another. The mother sells her wedding ring to buy her daughter a white dress for burial.

The thirty-year period after the Harlem Renaissance seems to represent a stagnation in Black literature that examines the rites and rituals associated with death. Although more authors explored the subject of death, the eternal rites of passage garnered less attention. Perhaps because this is another period in which Blacks are attempting to conform and be accepted, there is less emphasis on what makes them unique and different.

Arna *Bontemps's *Black Thunder* (1936) is an exception, with several references to funerary traditions. In the novel, slaves gather at the bedside of the dying Bundy. They begin to moan, chant, and pray. This ritual is primarily for the comfort of the dying, not the living. It "helps them cross over," easing the transition from this world to the afterlife. Bundy's burial, which was held at night, is replete with African traditions, and the author explicitly identifies them as such: "They were burying old Bundy in the low field by the swamp (The Negro remembered Africa in 1800) . . . a jug of rum at his feet. They roasted a hog and put it on his grave. . . ." One mourner states that Bundy's spirit has separated from the body and was observing the burial.

The period after 1965 is one of cultural paradox for African Americans. It is a time for integration and shifting toward mainstream culture, as well as a time for rediscovering African roots and cultural pride. Ironically, as African Americans shed their cultural past, Black writers (as they have previously done) are preserving that past through the written word. Between 1965 and 1975 there was a proliferation of Black writers, and many of them dealt with death in both its stark realism and its ritualistic celebration. Two bibliographical references for African American literature written between 1965 and 1975 listed approximately sixty entries that specifically identified death or funerals in the title and as part of the contents. Many of those individual works included details about specific beliefs and practices related to African American funeral and mourning customs.

The period between 1965 and 1975 witnessed a major social upheaval in America. Many taboos and social restraints were cast aside in search of greater freedom and openness. This occurred with regard to death and the process of letting go of the deceased person as an active part of the living world. During this period African American writers began to actively pursue a comprehensive examination of death and ritual in African American culture.

Contemporary writers are continuing this legacy by treating funeral and mourning customs as primary themes that can be used to engage the reader in the investigation of a significant, albeit painful, dimension of the human experience. Some customs, such as passing children over coffins and decorating graves, are experiencing a revival among African Americans and will probably be reflected in future literary themes.

An example of a writer who is focusing on this rite of passage in a bold new way is Angela Johnson in her novel *Toning the Sweep* (1994). When a family member dies, a vital component in the final phase of the grieving process is striking, or toning, the plow blade. This healing ritual is similar to the European custom of tolling a bell to inform the community of a death. In addition to acknowledging a person's passing, toning the sweep frees the person's spirit from the world of the living. In the novel, the failure to observe this ritual for the grandfather has far-reaching consequences that leave the grandmother, the daughter, and the granddaughter emotionally stuck in the distant past. It is not until the granddaughter resurrects the custom on behalf of the grandfather that all members of the family are wholly free to live their lives.

Funeral and mourning customs are no longer lesser themes relegated to a mere mention. Neither are they considered forbidden and inappropriate for the public. By treating funeral and mourning customs as major themes, contemporary African American writers provide a better framework for understanding death and its meaning in our lives.

[See also Churches; Sermons and Preaching.]

• James Weldon Johnson, *God's Trombones: Seven Negro Sermons in Verse*, 1927. Robert A. Bone, *The Negro Novel in America*, 1965. Ruth Bass, "The Little Man," in *Mother Wit from the Laughing Barrel*, ed. Alan Dundes, 1973, pp. 388–396. Blyden Jackson, *A History of Afro-American Literature: The Long Beginning, 1746–1895*, 1989. Elaine Nichols, *The Last Miles of the Way: African-American Homegoing Traditions, 1890–Present*, 1989. Dean D. Shackelford, "The Poetry of Countee Cullen," in *Masterpieces of African-American*

Literature, ed. Frank N. Magill, 1992, pp. 382–386. Janic Hart and Elsa B. Brown, comps., "Black Women in the United States: A Chronology," in *Black Women in America: An Historical Encyclopedia*, vol. 2, ed. Darlene Clark Hine, 1993.

—Elaine Nichols

Funnyhouse of a Negro. A one-act play written by Adrienne *Kennedy in 1960, *Funnyhouse of a Negro* was first produced professionally at New York City's East End Theatre beginning 14 January 1964. The director was Michael Kahn and Billie Allen played the lead role of Sarah. The other roles were played by Ellen Holly, Cynthia Belgrave, Gus Williams, Norman Bush, Ruth Volner, Leslie Rivers, and Leonard Frey. The play closed after thirty-four performances, but went on to win the Village Voice Obie for most distinguished play of 1964. It has since been produced professionally in a number of other cities including Boston (1965), London (1968), and in Paris (1968) as *Drôle de baraque.*

Funnyhouse was published in 1969 by Samuel French and has been included in the following *anthologies: *Black Drama: An Anthology* (1970), *The Best Short Plays of 1970, Contemporary Black Drama: From "A Raisin in the Sun" to "No Place to Be Somebody"* (1971), and *Adrienne Kennedy in One Act* (1988).

Kennedy submitted *Funnyhouse* as a writing sample along with her 1962 application for admission to Edward Albee's workshop, where the play was first performed at the Circle in the Square Theatre. Best defined at the time as experimental *theater, the play exudes the surrealistic qualities of a nightmare. Its protagonist is described as a young, light-skinned Negro woman named Sarah. Sarah enters the play with a bloodied, featureless face; her head is missing hair, which she carries in her hand. She is described as someone who is simultaneously young and ancient. A rope tied in a hangman's noose drapes her neck. She delivers a repetitive monologue describing her various ethnic selves, recounting her educational background, her lineage, and her desire to become an "even more pallid Negro"; she includes a denunciation of her blackness, pronouncing that black is, and has always been, evil.

Sarah is in the final phase of a state of acute schizophrenia brought on by a history of various physical and emotional abuses and, in a larger conception, colonization. Four personas coexist in her mind: Patrice Lumumba, Jesus, Queen Victoria, and the Duchess of Hapsburg. Patrice Lumumba represents the African aspect of Sarah's multiethnic and multicultural heritage. The other three personas are antagonistic toward the African presence who is charged in several mad monologues with the rape of Sarah's white-looking mother. They are informed by an irrational logic that all ensuing problems have emanated from that signal event. Blackness has infected and tainted Sarah's existence.

In her opening monologue, Negro-Sarah asserts that there is no logical relationship among her selves, no theme, and this assertion about the play was generally echoed by some early critics who panned *Funnyhouse* for being too abstract. A funnyhouse is a place of grotesque distortions, and Kennedy's play is rife with metaphor, surreal visual imagery, and allegorical complexity. Still, the relationship among madness, irrationality, discrimination, and oppression is clearly implicated. The creation of a schizophrenic character embodying ethnic and cultural diversity allows Kennedy to engage in simultaneous discourses on racial, sexual, and political matters. Early criticisms of her work as incoherent and flawed may reflect more upon a lack of preparedness by individual critics than upon Kennedy's abilities.

Although Kennedy wrote the play in 1960, the historical context for its first professional production places it in the middle of a most violent decade in United States history, a time when the country was being forced to come to terms with its African American presence. Thematically, *Funnyhouse* takes up several issues that have since become the topics of study and discussion in academic and other settings. Social justice, the psychosocial consequences of integration, gender issues like the trauma associated with the systematic rape of African American women under *slavery, colonization in a postcolonial era, and various forms of oppression are all explored to varying degrees.

Multicultural conflict is played out within Sarah as a unit divided against itself. European and Christian personas in Sarah's mind can only define the African persona as something undesirable and lacking value; but when they follow the African into the jungle to bludgeon him to death, they also obliterate themselves. Sarah's suicide is commented upon offhandedly and callously at the end of the play by her white, Jewish boyfriend and her white landlady. These two characters serve also as the grotesque and bobbing figures typically located at the door to the funnyhouse. The contrast between their indifferent treatment of Sarah's suicide and what has been revealed only moments before as the horribly tormented quality of her existence is only one among many disturbing effects carefully created by the playwright.

Early reviews of *Funnyhouse* are contained in the *New York Times* and *Newsday* (15 January 1964), *New Yorker* (25 January 1964), *Boston Globe* (12 March 1965), *Le Monde* (19 March 1968), and *Figaro Littéraire* (25 March 1968). The play was produced as part of Kennedy's September 1995 through May 1996 residence at the Signature Theatre at the Joseph Papp Public Theatre in New York.

• Susan E. Meigs, "No Place but the Funnyhouse: The Struggle for Identity in Three Adrienne Kennedy Plays," in *Modern American Drama: The Female Canon*, ed. Jane Schlueter, 1990, pp. 172–183. Werner Sollors, "Owls and Rats in the American Funnyhouse: Adrienne Kennedy's Drama," *American Literature* (Sept. 1991): 507–532. Robert Scanlan, "Surrealism as Mimesis: A Director's Guide to Adrienne Kennedy's *Funnyhouse of a Negro*," in *Intersecting Boundaries: The Theatre of Adrienne Kennedy*, eds. Paul K. Bryant-Jackson and Lois More Overbeck, 1992, pp. 93–109.

—Lovalerie King

G

GABRIEL GRIMES. One of African American literature's most famous antagonists, Gabriel Grimes of James *Baldwin's *Go Tell It on the Mountain (1953) remains one of the author's most compelling characters. Modeled after Baldwin's own stepfather, Gabriel futilely attempts to exorcise demons from his reckless southern past.

The novel's opening section introduces Gabriel as a frustrated deacon in a Harlem Pentecostal church. Obsessed with control, he clashes with his entire family, especially with his stepson, John. Meanwhile, Gabriel embraces his and Elizabeth's son, Roy, who attacks Gabriel for slapping Elizabeth. Though Gabriel sees Roy as his hallowed son, the wayward youth is merely a replica of young Gabriel.

"Gabriel's Prayer," the second section in part 2 of the novel, presents his past via flashback. Gabriel spent his youth drinking and whoring, though his mother attempted to reform him. He ostensibly repents, and Baldwin cleverly alludes to the Judgment Day in portraying his conversion. Although he attempts to expiate his sins by becoming a minister and marrying the barren Deborah, Gabriel quickly falls: his affair with Esther, a maid in the home of a white family for whom Gabriel also works, produces a son, Royal. Gabriel repudiates both lover and son and moves to Harlem after Deborah's death. Again, he vows to do penance by marrying Elizabeth and accepting her illegitimate son. Instead Gabriel continues to use *religion to denigrate others and minimize his own transgressions.

Sin and guilt haunt Gabriel throughout his life. Reminiscent of Abraham and David, he can never claim the heir he so fervently desires: Royal dies violently, Roy continues his profligate legacy, and John reciprocates his hatred. The redoubtable Reverend Grimes remains one of American literature's most memorable ministers, a descendent of Nathaniel Hawthorne's Reverend Dimmesdale and Ralph *Ellison's Homer Barbee.

[*See also* John Grimes.]

• Michel Fabre, "Fathers and Sons in James Baldwin's *Go Tell It on the Mountain*," in *James Baldwin: A Collection of Critical Essays*, ed. Keneth Kinnamon, 1974, pp. 120–138. Trudier Harris, *Black Women in the Fiction of James Baldwin*, 1985.
—Keith Clark

GAINES, ERNEST J. (b. 1933), novelist, short story writer, and teacher. Ernest J. Gaines is among the most widely read and highly respected contemporary authors of African American fiction. Born on a Louisiana plantation, where, at age eight, he worked in the fields cutting sugarcane for fifty cents a day, he experienced the racism of the Deep South firsthand. He was largely raised by a handicapped aunt, whose courage and determination are reflected in the many strong-willed women who appear in his books. At age fifteen Gaines moved to California, joining his mother and stepfather there, because his Louisiana parish had no high school for African Americans. Homesick, he unsuccessfully sought books about the kinds of people he knew in "the quarters." His reading led him to French, Russian, and Anglo-Irish authors who dealt with rural life, and to the novels of William Faulkner, a major literary influence. But the most important influence on his work seems to have been the "porch talk," the oral folk culture in which he was raised.

All of Gaines's fiction is set in Louisiana, with its unique mixture of white, African American, Creole, and Cajun cultures. The conflicts among these groups are central to his books. Like Faulkner's Yoknapatawpha County, Gaines's rural St. Raphael Parish, with its principal town of Bayonne, gives his fiction a unifying setting and reinforces his characteristic social realism. That realism is intensified by his extensive use of the speaking voice and by his remarkable ear for the subtle variations in Louisiana dialects. Finding a voice, achieving the power of speech, is both one of Gaines's major themes and one of his most effective artistic devices. The impressive range of first-person narrators he has created is among his finest achievements, one that reflects his profoundly democratic commitment to human dignity. That commitment permeates Gaines's fiction and suggests another of his central themes: the quest for *identity in a society scarred by racism.

Catherine Carmier (1964) and *Of Love and Dust* (1967), his first two *novels, are stories of thwarted love that focus on the destructive barriers dividing white from African American and African American from Creole. The male protagonist of *Catherine Carmier*, Jackson Bradley, having fled Louisiana, returns from California and rekindles his earlier love for Catherine, a Creole. Her father, both victim and practitioner of racism, opposes their relationship. Though Catherine loves Jackson, she cannot leave her father, knowing the hostility he faces from the Cajuns who covet his land. Among the most striking features of this book is the brooding silence that afflicts Jackson, who apparently finds much of his past literally unspeakable. This motif of self-imposed silence, of unarticulated anguish, reappears in other of Gaines's novels and is made all the more prominent by his customary emphasis on the speaking voice.

While *Catherine Carmier* is told from a third-person point of view, *Of Love and Dust* employs the first-person narration that has become Gaines's hallmark. This novel's narrator is not, however, the book's protagonist. Instead, Jim Kelly tells the story of Marcus Payne, a young African American convicted of murder who is released to the custody of Marshall Herbert, whose Cajun overseer, Sidney Bonbon, aims to break Marcus's spirit. To gain revenge, Marcus initiates an affair with Bonbon's wife, herself neglected by Bonbon in favor of his African American mistress.

When Marcus and Louise unexpectedly fall in love, their relationship violates the South's gravest taboo and precipitates Marcus's death. By juxtaposing these two biracial love affairs, Gaines emphasizes the destructiveness of the South's racial codes not only for African Americans but for whites themselves (as he also does in his portrait of Tee Bob in The *Autobiography of Miss Jane Pittman). The novel's events alter the narrator's—and the reader's—initial assessment of Marcus, who gradually assumes heroic stature by opposing the "fate" decreed by racism.

With the publication of Bloodline (1968), a collection of five diverse first-person narratives, and The Autobiography of Miss Jane Pittman (1971), his best-known novel, Gaines earned the wide readership and critical acclaim that have attended the remainder of his career. While he has sometimes been criticized for not embracing the tradition of social *protest literature represented by Richard *Wright's fiction, these two books—and indeed Gaines's total canon—make his political commitments clear. Implicit throughout are a critique of racism and an insistence upon the need for social change. Firmly rooted in the folk culture of the African American community and the oral traditions by which that community has sustained itself, Gaines typically portrays ordinary people whom he endows with heroic potential. His characters achieve dignity despite attempts to oppress them, and they affirm not only themselves as individuals but also the value of family and community, the importance of responsibilities to others.

Like most southern writers, Gaines has a strong sense of history and of the past's continuing impact on the present. Nowhere is that historical sense more evident than in The Autobiography of Miss Jane Pittman, for the novel's 110-year-old narrator has lived from *slavery into the civil rights struggle of the 1960s. Miss Jane's story is both personal and communal, a "folk *autobiography," as Gaines terms it. The qualities she exhibits—pride, resourcefulness, love, honor, and endurance—are those Gaines celebrates throughout his work. Miss Jane is his most memorable character, a tribute to the aunt who raised him. More than any other single book, this novel helped white Americans understand the personal emotions and the historical events that had produced the civil rights revolution.

Gaines's subsequent novel, In My Father's House (1978), proved far less successful. His only book, other than his first, to use third-person narration, is also his only book set primarily in a town rather than in the countryside. Both A Gathering of Old Men (1983) and A Lesson Before Dying (1993), in contrast, reveal an author at the height of his powers. The former, drawing on the popular genre of the detective novel, is particularly effective in creating a sense of community through the fifteen different narrators it employs. The speaking voice dominates this novel, recording both the region's long history of racial injustice and the recognizable improvement in *race relations during the 1970s. Gaines's old men, in accepting responsibility for the murder of Beau Boutan, affirm not only their capacity to speak but their ability to act. As in other works, so here Gaines augments his plot's dramatic power by limiting the main action to a single day's events. Yet the memories voiced by the community enable the reader to experience the past as well, with all its brutal injustice. Racism persists, of course, but in this novel Gaines ameliorates the African American/Cajun rivalry by having Beau's brother, Gil, refuse to participate in the family's traditional vigilante vengeance. At the same time, Gaines underscores the repressive nature of the past by noting that it took Charlie Biggs, who killed Beau in self-defense, fifty years to assert his manhood.

Whereas In My Father's House and A Gathering of Old Men are set in the 1970s, A Lesson Before Dying is set in 1948, the year the fifteen-year-old Gaines moved to California. Yet this novel clearly functions not only to remind readers of the maltreatment of African Americans in the pre–civil rights South but also to highlight the continuing effects of institutionalized racism. Gaines's predominant theme, the quest for human dignity, recurs in this book when the first-person narrator, Grant Wiggins, a teacher, is compelled by his aunt to aid her best friend's godson, who is awaiting execution for a crime he neither planned nor committed. Jefferson's attorney has attempted to save his client by equating Jefferson's mental development with that of a hog. When Jefferson's godmother pleads with Grant to teach her godson his human identity, Grant grudgingly agrees. Despite Jefferson's initial resistance, he ultimately succeeds, as the journal Jefferson produces testifies, a journal that also attests to America's deplorable failure to provide equal educational opportunities to African Americans—in the present as well as in 1948. Gaines's choice of Jefferson's name serves to suggest the ongoing betrayal of democratic political ideals that racism represents.

Throughout his career, Gaines has sought to make his fiction widely accessible. The clarity and directness of his prose, the array of engaging characters he depicts, and the effective use he makes of the speaking voice all reflect this commitment, as do the *humor and compassion that mark his novels. Gaines's books give voice to individuals long silenced by racial oppression. Like Ralph *Ellison's *Invisible Man (1952), they also articulate fundamental human values that transcend racial differences. His best novels and *short stories are likely to remain among the enduring contributions not just to African American but to world literature.

• Jerry H. Bryant, "Ernest J. Gaines: Change, Growth, and History," Southern Review 10 (Fall 1974): 851–864. Charles H. Rowell, ed., Callaloo 3 (May 1978), special Gaines issue. Jack Hicks, In the Singer's Temple, 1981. Frank W. Shelton, "In My Father's House: Ernest Gaines after Jane Pittman," Southern Review 17 (Spring 1981): 340–345. Keith E. Byerman, Fingering the Jagged Grain: Tradition and Form in Recent Black Fiction, 1985. Charles H. Rowell, "The Quarters: Ernest Gaines and the Sense of Place," Southern Review 21 (Summer 1985): 733–750. John F. Callahan, In the Afro-American Grain: The Pursuit of Voice in Twentieth-Century Black Fiction, 1988. Marcia Gaudet and Carl Wooton, Porch Talk with Ernest Gaines: Conversations on the Writer's Craft, 1990. Valerie Melissa Babb, Ernest Gaines, 1991.

—John Lang

GARNET, HENRY HIGHLAND (1815–1882), orator, minister, and abolitionist. An antislavery radical, Henry Highland Garnet is best known for "An Address to the Slaves of the United States of America" (1843), a speech delivered in Buffalo at the National Convention of Colored Citizens. In the "Address" and later texts, he advocated active resistance to *slavery, urging slaves to take *freedom for themselves. Deeply influenced by *David Walker's Appeal (1829), Garnet argued that slaves had a moral obligation to resist slavery, using *violence when necessary.

Garnet's thinking emerged from an activist-nationalist tradition within African American culture passed on to him by his family. In 1815, he was born into an enslaved family living on a Maryland plantation. His father, the son of a Mandingo leader, took enormous pride in his family's heritage. When Garnet was nine, they escaped to New York City. In 1829, while he was at sea serving as a cabin boy, slave catchers pursued his family, apprehending his sister and forcing the rest to scatter. The event had a profound impact on Garnet, who thereafter began carrying a large knife.

After studying with Theodore Wright, an eminent African American Presbyterian minister and abolitionist, and attending the New York African Free School, Garnet continued his schooling and further established his abolitionist ties by attending the Noyes Academy (an interracial school in Canaan, New Hampshire) and the Oneida Institute, where he graduated in 1840. During the 1840s Garnet developed a busy career as a minister and antislavery activist, editing and writing for newspapers, lecturing, working in the convention movement, and campaigning for the Liberty Party. In 1848, he published The Past and Present Condition, and the Destiny, of the Colored Race, elaborating his ideas on abolition and *emigration.

Following his departure in 1850 for antislavery lecturing in Great Britain and Germany and missionary work in Jamaica, Garnet's ideas about slave resistance, violence, and emigration gained growing acceptance among abolitionists, influencing militants like John *Brown. Garnet returned in 1855 to pastor Shiloh Presbyterian Church in New York City, succeeding his former mentor, Theodore Wright. During the Civil War, he pastored the Fifteenth Street Presbyterian Church in Washington, D.C., and recruited African Americans for the Union Army. In 1865, he became the first African American to deliver a sermon before the U.S. House of Representatives.

After the war, Garnet campaigned for civil rights, championed Cuban independence, and developed his always keen interest in Africa and the West Indies. In 1881, he accepted an appointment as Minister Resident and Consul General to Liberia, where he died the following year.

[See also Antislavery Movement.]

• Joel Schor, Henry Highland Garnet: A Voice of Black Radicalism in the Nineteenth Century, 1977. Sterling Stuckey, "A Last Stern Struggle: Henry Highland Garnet and Liberation Theory," in Black Leaders of the Nineteenth Century, eds. Leon Litwack and August Meier, 1988, pp. 129–147. Martin B.

Pasternak, Rise Now and Fly to Arms: The Life of Henry Highland Garnet, 1995. —Gregory Eiselein

GARVEY, MARCUS (1887–1940), social activist and journalist. As a major figure of the *Harlem Renaissance, Marcus Garvey was in the vanguard of the new awakening among African Americans. Although his philosophy was at odds with other leading figures of the era, such as W. E. B. *Du Bois, his influence could not be abated. Promoting his ideals in the art of *oratory and through his newspapers, first *Negro World and later the Blackman, Garvey has influenced almost every generation of African American writers since.

Images depicting the destructive element in racial prejudice, one of the cornerstones of Garvey's ideology, were initially seen when major fiction writers of the Harlem Renaissance, such as Nella *Larsen, grappled with the infirmities of "color" prejudice. In Larsen's so-called *passing novels, *Quicksand (1928) and *Passing (1929), *mulattoes move into the white world to escape personal oppression and limited opportunity. As is typical in Garveyism, this social mobility leads to self-hate and racial ambivalence.

Richard *Wright and his school of fiction writers was the next group to depict the struggle of African Americans against social and political forces. Richard Wright's *Bigger Thomas in *Native Son (1940), for example, is an "Everyman" motif for social, political, and cultural disenfranchisement of African Americans. Bigger acquires self-pride and faces his troubles through the aid of two white males, both unlikely cohorts, and becomes the folk hero often created through the use of Garveyism.

The next generation of writers displaying Garveyism might be termed the precursors of the *Black Arts movement. Extending James *Baldwin's protest themes in Nobody Knows My Name (1960) and *The Fire Next Time (1963), the aggressive poets of the sixties, such as Amiri *Baraka (LeRoi Jones), decry the destructive environment of the northern ghetto and portray Garvey's contempt for such dehumanizing existence. Beyond the 1960s, an aesthetic perspective that embraces the racial loyalty and pride found in Garveyism is seen in works such as Toni *Morrison's *The Bluest Eye (1970). Thus, the influence of the Garvey social and political movement continues.

[See also Black Nationalism.]

• Tony Martin, Literary Garveyism: Garvey, Black Arts and the Harlem Renaissance, 1983. James de Jongh, Vicious Modernism: Black Harlem and the Literary Imagination, 1990.
—Patricia Robinson Williams

GATES, HENRY LOUIS, JR. (b. 1950), scholar, critic, essayist, editor, professor, and chair of Afro-American studies at Harvard University. Arguably the most influential black literary scholar of the 1980s, Henry Louis Gates, Jr., who earned his PhD at Cambridge University, has been the recipient of a MacArthur Prize Fellowship and the American Book Award. In his early textual scholarship, Gates achieved prominence by establishing Harriet E. *Wilson's *Our Nig, or Sketches from the Life of a Free

Black (1859) as the first *novel published in the United States by an African American. At the same time, Gates, along with such other scholars as Robert Stepto and Dexter Fisher, who together coedited *Afro-American Literature: The Reconstruction of Instruction* (1979), were laying the groundwork for a critical approach to African American literature that sought to focus on its literariness, breaking with, as Gates argued, the social realist preoccupation of critics of previous generations.

Central to Gates's establishment of this intended break was, first, an exploration of what the advent of structuralist and poststructuralist critical theory portended for the study of African American literature, and second, an attention to the way that the formal and rhetorical features of black-authored texts could enable the positing of a distinctly black literary tradition. As an editor Gates addressed the first half of his agenda, bringing together a host of scholars in *Black Literature and Literary Theory* (1984) and *"Race," Writing, and Difference* (1986), which was first published as a special issue of the journal *Critical Inquiry*. These *essays sought to demonstrate the applicability of literary theory to a responsible reading of black-authored texts and to reconcile a commitment to a black racial difference with an awareness that *race exists as a social construction rather than a biological fact. In his own work of the period, *Figures in Black: Words, Signs and the "Racial" Self* (1987) and *The Signifying Monkey: A Theory of Afro-American Literary Criticism* (1988), Gates continued his effort to define the distinctly black rhetorical tropes and figures in literary texts. *The Signifying Monkey* argued for continuities between African—specifically Yoruban—vernacular and folk traditions, and African American vernacular *speech. These continuities, Gates claimed, were to be found in the practice of "signifyin(g)" (self-reflexive linguistic play in everyday language) and in folk tales about the *signifying monkey.

Gates's work has not been without its critics. Some readers have discerned a strain of racial essentialism in his putatively social constructionist stance. Others have charged his work with being apolitical or neoconservative in orientation. Even so, Gates's larger editorial projects may be his most enduring contribution to African American literary study. He helped focus attention on the work of Nobel Prize–winner Wole Soyinka, and through serving as general editor for the Schomburg Library of Nineteenth-Century Black Women Writers, has made readily available crucial texts for scholars and general readers in the field. He is also general editor of the *Norton Anthology of African American Literature*.

Gates's publications have extended beyond his specialty in literary criticism. His 1994 memoir, *Colored People*, chronicles fondly and humorously what it was like growing up in segregation-era Mineral County, West Virginia. His writings for the *New Republic*, the *New Yorker*, and the *New York Times* have ranged widely over cultural and political issues.

[*See also* Criticism, *article on* Criticism since 1965; Literary History, *article on* Late Twentieth Century.]

• Theodore O. Mason, Jr., "Between the Populist and the Scientist: Ideology and Power in Recent Afro-American Literary Criticism; or, 'The Dozens' as Scholarship," *Callaloo* 11 (Summer 1988): 606–615. Kwame Anthony Appiah, "The Conservation of 'Race,'" *Black American Literary Forum* 23 (1989): 37–60. Diana Fuss, "'Race' Under Erasure? Poststructuralist Afro-American Literary Theory," in *Essentially Speaking: Feminism, Nature and Difference*, 1989, pp. 73–96.
—Kenneth W. Warren

GAYLE, ADDISON, JR. (1932–1991), literary critic, educator, lecturer, essayist, and biographer. One of the chief advocates of the *Black Aesthetic, Addison Gayle, Jr., was born in Newport News, Virginia, on 2 June 1932. Inspired by the growing example of Richard *Wright, young Gayle became a fastidious reader and hoped that a writing career would enable him to overcome the strictures of poverty and racism. By the time he graduated from high school in 1950, Gayle had completed a three-hundred-page *novel.

Unable to attend college or secure profitable employment, Gayle joined the air force. During his short stint, he wrote copious drafts of his novel, *short stories, and *poetry and submitted them for publication. After an honorable discharge and several rejection letters from publishers, Gayle reluctantly returned to Virginia.

In 1960, Gayle enrolled in the City College of New York and received his BA in 1965. The following year he earned an MA in English from the University of California, Los Angeles. He taught at City College, where he participated in the SEEK (Search for Education, Elevation, and Knowledge) program and worked to increase the enrollment of African American and Latino students and to diversify the school's curriculum.

A frequent contributor to Hoyt *Fuller's journal *Black World*, Gayle edited *Black Expression: Essays By and About Black Americans in the Creative Arts* (1969), an *anthology of critical writings on African American folk culture, poetry, *drama, and fiction. His subsequent publication, *The Black Situation* (1970), contains a collection of personal *essays that chronicle his intellectual development and emerging political militancy in the wake of the *civil rights movement and the Black Power struggle.

Gayle's best-known work, *The Black Aesthetic* (1971), is a compilation of essays written by prominent African American writers and leading Black Aesthetic theorists. In both the introduction and an essay entitled "Cultural Strangulation: Black Literature and the White Aesthetic," Gayle championed cultural nationalism and argued that the central aim of the African American artist was to address and improve social and political conditions. Gayle continued his advocacy of the Black Aesthetic tradition in *Way of a New World* (1975), a literary history of the African American novel, and his three biographies: *Oak and Ivy: A Biography of Paul Laurence *Dunbar* (1971), *Claude *McKay: The Black Poet at War* (1972), and *Richard Wright: Ordeal of a Native Son* (1980). Gayle's autobiography, *Wayward Child: A Personal Odyssey* (1977), offers a frank and sobering account of his life, which painfully details the exacting price of his indefatigable pursuit of literary excellence.

Gayle also distinguished himself as a professor of English at the City University of New York's Bernard M. Baruch College, where he taught until his death in October 1991. A passionate teacher and writer, Addison Gayle remained a strong supporter of the Black Aesthetic movement and continued to affirm a fundamental link between artistic creativity and the social and political advancement of African Americans.

• Donna Olendorf, "Addison Gayle, Jr.," in *CA*, vol. 13, ed. Linda Metzger, 1984, pp. 207–208. Eleanor Blau, "Addison Gayle, Jr., Literary Critic, Is Dead at 59," *New York Times*, 5 Oct. 1991, 10.   —Bobby Donaldson

GAY LITERATURE. Gay writing was an important element of the *Harlem Renaissance. Gay and bisexual men—such as Alain *Locke, Countee *Cullen, Wallace *Thurman, Richard Bruce *Nugent, Langston *Hughes, and Claude *McKay—were vital presences in this literary movement. Locke, a professor of philosophy, mentored some of these men and published their work in his landmark *anthology *The *New Negro (1925), including Nugent's *short story "Sadji," the earliest known gay text by an African American. A year later Thurman's *Fire!! (1926)—a magazine whose explicit purpose was to shock the black reading public—appeared. According to folklore, Thurman and Nugent tossed a coin to choose as a subject either homosexuality or prostitution. Thurman got prostitution and produced the story "Cordelia, the Crude," while Nugent contributed the semiautobiographical "Smoke, Lillies, and Jade," the most explicit homoerotic text of the Renaissance. In 1932 Thurman published *Infants of the Spring*, which included several gay characters. Decades later the black gay British film director Isaac Julien used several texts by these writers in his controversial film *Looking for Langston* (1989), an exploration of homosexuality in the Harlem Renaissance.

Most Harlem Renaissance writers were not as explicit about homosexuality as Nugent or Thurman were. Instead, homosexuality is often referred to in code. Those readers familiar with homosexual coding might detect it in poems such as "Young Sailor" or "I Loved My Friend" by Langston Hughes and others might conjecture homosexuality in the recurring pagan imagery in Cullen's poems. However, it is often difficult to detect homosexual coding because the settings in which gay life occurred in the 1920s no longer exist. For instance, the now extinct bachelor subcultures that provide the setting for McKay's *Home to Harlem (1928) were sites for gay life in the 1920s and 1930s. Analyses of this *novel and others by McKay have yet to consider the full significance of the homoerotic settings in which they take place.

Gay writing was even more concealed after the Harlem Renaissance ended. The economy collapsed bringing on the Great Depression, the second world war raged, and, after the war ended, the persecution of homosexuals increased. During the Cold War, in particular, the FBI targeted homosexuals as enemies of the state and many were imprisoned, fired from jobs, or forced to hide their identities. Nevertheless, during this period Langston Hughes denounced the persecution of gays and lesbians in his poem "Cafe 3 A.M.," which first appeared in the 1951 collection *Montage of a Dream Deferred*. Hughes's 1963 *Something in Common and Other Stories* also contained "Blessed Assurance," his first short story with gay characters. During this post-war period Owen *Dodson, a professor at Howard University, published plays, *poetry, and the semiautobiographical novel *Boy at the Window* (1951).

James *Baldwin's emergence in the 1950s as a leading writer was a watershed event for black gay writing. Shortly after emigrating to Paris, he wrote a defense of homosexuality, "The Preservation of Innocence" and published it in *Zero* (1949), a little-known Moroccan journal. He explored adolescent homosexual yearnings in the short story "Outing" and in *Go Tell It on the Mountain* (1953). In his next novel Baldwin took a strange course for an African American writer, and particularly for one well-known as a critic of American racism. In *Giovanni's Room (1956) all the major characters were white, the setting was in Europe, and the plot concerned a bisexual love triangle. *Giovanni's Room* created controversy, but it earned Baldwin a major place in the gay literary tradition. He would explore gay and bisexual themes in future novels *Another Country (1962), *Tell Me How Long the Train's Been Gone* (1968), and *Just above My Head* (1979).

Since Baldwin, black gay writing has increased significantly. The reasons for this increase are that the gay and lesbian rights movement has had some important successes: the creation of gay publishing houses, the growth of gay-owned independent bookstores, and—in the 1980s—the discovery of a reading public, not exclusively African American, interested in black gay writing. These reasons bear on two seminal works published in the 1980s. Although ideologically dissimilar, Michael J. Smith's *Black Men/White Men: A Gay Anthology* (1983) and Joseph Beam's *In the Life: A Black Gay Anthology* (1986) were published by small gay presses. The fact that both were anthologies is significant. Contributors such as Essex Hemphill, Larry Duplechan, and Melvin *Dixon who would later publish with mainstream houses gained attention in these pioneering anthologies.

The black gay anthology is also informative about how black gay writing gets published. Much of the published black gay writing comes out of grassroots community organizing. Importantly, that has enabled the establishment of a variety of black gay-owned publishing concerns. The New York City–based Other Countries writing collective released two critically praised anthologies, *Other Countries Journal: Black Gay Voices* (1988) and the award-winning *Sojourner: Black Gay Voices in the Age of AIDS* (1993). The poet and playwright Assotto Saint founded his own Galiens Press and published his poetry *Stations* (1989), the elegiac *Wishing for Wings* (1995), and also the work of others in *The Road Before Us: One Hundred Gay Black Poets* (1991) and *Here to Dare: Ten Gay*

Black Poets (1992). The arrival of the personal computer and widespread use of desktop publishing also increased the proliferation of black gay writing such as "fanzines" and periodicals. A notable instance of a desktop publishing venture that attracted national attention is E. Lynne *Harris's first novel, *Invisible Life* (1991), which a major press reprinted in 1994.

Despite incalculable losses due to the AIDS pandemic, black gay writing is in a healthy state. The writing exists in a variety of genres, notably poetry, short fiction, *autobiography, *essay, and the novel, and publishers seem eager to release works by black gay writers. Small (white) gay-owned presses such as Alyson Publications in Boston, for instance, released Essex Hemphill's anthology *Brother to Brother: New Writings by Black Gay Men* (1991) and novels by Steven Corbin (*Fragments That Remain*, 1993; *A Hundred Days from Now*, 1994), Larry Duplechan (*Captain Swing*, 1993), James Earl Hardy (*B Boy Blues*, 1994), and Canaan Parker (*The Color of Trees*, 1992). Still, within the last decade both mainstream and university presses published an astonishing array of black gay literature: Don Belton (*Almost Midnight*, 1986), Cyrus Cassells (*Soul Make a Path Through Shouting*, 1995), Steven Corbin (*No Easy Place to Be*, 1989), Samuel R. *Delaney (*The Motion of Light in Water*, 1988; *The Mad Man*, 1994; *Atlantis*, 1995), Melvin Dixon (*Trouble the Water*, 1989; *Vanishing Rooms*, 1991), Larry Duplechan (*Blackbird*, 1986; *Tangled Up in Blue*, 1989), E. Lynn Harris (*Just as I Am*, 1994), Gordon Heath (*Deep Are the Roots: Memoirs of a Black Expatriate*, 1992), Essex Hemphill (*Ceremonies*, 1992), Bill T. Jones (*Last Night on Earth*, 1995), Randall *Kenan (*A Visitation of Spirits*, 1989; *Let the Dead Bury the Dead*, 1992), and George C. *Wolfe (*The Colored Museum*, 1987).

[*See also* Gay Men; Gender; Lesbian Literature; Lesbians; Sexuality.]

• Faith Berry, *Langston Hughes: Before and Beyond Harlem*, 1983. Gerald Early, introduction to *My Soul's High Song: The Collected Writings of Countee Cullen; Voice of the Harlem Renaissance*, 1991. Emmanuel Nelson, "Critical Deviance: Homophobia and the Reception of James Baldwin's Fiction," *Journal of American Culture* 14 (Fall 1991): 91–96. James V. Hatch, *Sorrow Is the Only Faithful One: The Life of Owen Dodson*, 1993. George Chauncey, *Gay New York: Gender, Urban Culture, and the Making of the Gay Male World, 1890–1940*, 1994.
—Charles I. Nero

GAY MEN. The image of gay men in black writing is complicated by homophobic values in society that make homosexuality unspeakable and gays invisible. Contributors to black gay anthologies such as *In the Life* (1986) and *Brother to Brother: New Writings by Black Gay Men* (1991) both challenge and document homophobic images of gays in black literature, social theory, and popular culture. In the most virulent homophobic works gays are effeminate, sarcastic males who lead meaningless lives; they disrupt families, are misogynists, and are marginal to black communities and institutions. Sometimes such works also offer homophobic explanations for the origins of homosexuality among black men. They argue erroneously that homosexuality originates in decadent European

cultures, to which black men are then exposed, or that it is an unfortunate condition caused by racial oppression, such as imprisonment or psychological obstacles created by whites to prevent black males from becoming men.

Fortunately, in black writing gays are not always figures for debased or wasted masculinity. Writers associated with the *Harlem Renaissance sometimes depicted homosexuality as an exhilarating component of human nature. Writings by black gays since the 1950s debunk homophobic images by ending the silence about homosexuality and presenting a variety of gay experiences. For instance, James *Baldwin made men's sexuality a central issue in American literature through his depictions of homosexual lovers and bisexual men; although he did not always avoid the old *stereotypes, he nevertheless presented complex characters in a positive light. Since the 1980s black gay writers have been presenting gays in a variety of literary genres and media. Images of gay life involve AIDS, racism, interracial and intraracial love and sex, *feminism and sexism, activism, the negotiating of *identity in the American mainstream, coming out, the Christian church, bisexuality, and a marked preoccupation with the well-being of black families and communities.

[*See also* Gay Literature; Lesbian Literature; Lesbians.]

• Joseph F. Beam, ed., *In the Life: A Black Gay Anthology*, 1986. Essex Hemphill, ed., *Brother to Brother: New Writings by Black Gay Men*, 1991.
—Charles I. Nero

GENDER. It is important to understand gender as different from *sexuality. Sexuality concerns physical and biological differences that distinguish males from females. Cultures construct differences in gender. These social constructions attach themselves to behaviors, expectations, roles, representations, and sometimes to values and beliefs that are specific to either men or women. Gendered differences—those that society associates with men and women—have no necessary biological component. Instead of biology, socially agreed upon and constructed conduct, and the meanings cultures assign to that conduct, constitute the area of gendered difference.

Labels of "essentialism" can attach themselves to arguments that gender and sex have an inherent relationship. However, a cultural essentialist, who is interested in issues of gender, may argue that a historical relationship exists between gender, a culture's experience, and its public *identity and representation that is so pervasive and so intimate that it seems nearly inherent.

The study of gender in African American literature considers the way in which the texts of black writers have distinctive and unique expressions in men and women writers. Critical and theoretical studies may explore the consequences of gendered identity upon the structure, theme, or style of African American texts. The historical development of these textual markers of gender across the tradition of the literature may also be a focus. Cultural essentialism has some place in such studies because African American literature has a racial identity. Discussions of gender and racial identity provoke vigorous argument because socially constructed differences are a matter of debate and discrimination and because essentialism of any design holds a pejorative context among many theorists.

In the 1960s and 1970s, the insistent surge of the *civil rights movement and *Black Power movement into the political fabric of life in the United States made the issue of *race and its political and social stratifications the signal cultural issue for these decades. Dramatic political activity within the women's movement during the same era eventually matched the intensity of the critical attention to race. Contention surrounds the attention garnered by each agenda. Many identify white women as the women's movement's targeted beneficiaries. In an often competitive play for power and visibility, white women arguably shadowed and dominated the movement for racial equity and authority. Notably, contemporary reflections on the civil rights and Black Power movements launch equally critical challenges to the masculinist authority of these organizations.

Among the most significant and prolific in establishing the cultural text of gendered studies has been bell *hooks in her penetrating analyses of culture and gender. In *Ain't I a Woman* (1981) hooks established the parameters of the debate asserting that conversations about black people "tend to be on black men; and when women are talked about the focus tends to be on *white* women." Hooks returned to this forceful declaration of the frames of the eventual debate in *Feminist Theory from Margin to Center* (1984), a conversation about radical social and political change that obligated a confrontation with intersecting dynamics of gender constructions and cultural identity. Her work vigorously engages the complicated spheres of power within the domains of race, *class, and feminist thought and in many ways is a disciplinary standard and touchstone for contemporary cultural studies.

Given the national political conversations and confrontations of the latter half of the twentieth century, where the rights of those on the margin—women and people of color—have determined a national discourse, it would have been difficult to emerge from this era without the coalescence of these dual issues of race and gender. Consequently, the activity of the women's rights, civil rights, and Black Power movements anticipate the eventual turn to a critical focus on black women.

As social and political scientists looked critically at the activity of the women's rights and Black Power movements, literary critics and theorists turned their attention to the intersection of race and gender in the literary tradition of the United States. Prior to this historical moment, the study of the African American tradition largely concerned the history and development of its cultural presence and identity within the American literary tradition. In other words, "difference"—as a critical category—focused on the difference of race. Initially, literature's critical studies focused on determining the ways that race and gender

revealed significant differences in the writing of African American women.

Even though critical studies did not directly address gender construction in African American literatures prior to the twentieth century, it would be a mistake to assume that these cultural representations were not an expressed concern in the individual works of creative writers and scholars. Frederick *Douglass, for example, certainly made it clear that he understood the differences of gender in his narrative and in "The *Heroic Slave" (1853). Contemporary scholars have noted the rigidity in men's and women's identities in his *autobiography and the troubled associations these rigid constructions enured. Similarly, women writers such as Harriet E. *Wilson, Julia A. J. *Foote, and Frances Ellen Watkins *Harper made the difficulties of women's gender a focus in their works and underscored how it often constrained their struggles for equity and respect. In other words, although an intertextual collaboration of gender issues was neither the means nor the focus of scholarly critique prior to the mid-twentieth century, individual writers certainly made it clear that gender identities were part and parcel of the struggle for equity in African American cultures.

Issues of "*manhood" and the challenges that U.S. culture presented to black males are evident in the literature of William Wells *Brown, Martin R. *Delany, W. E. B. *Du Bois, Charles Waddell *Chesnutt, and James Weldon *Johnson. Ralph *Ellison, Richard *Wright, and Claude *Brown made men's and boy's lives a thematic focus in their works prior to the theorizing of gender constructions that characterizes the turn of the century and the end of the millennium. Similarly, dilemmas of "womanhood" clearly complicate the fiction and prose by Jarena *Lee, Harriet A. *Jacobs, Ida B. *Wells-Barnett, and Sojourner *Truth as well as Jessie Redmon *Fauset, Nella *Larsen, Zora Neale *Hurston, Lorraine *Hansberry, and Gwendolyn *Brooks. All of these writers' works, and a host of others, create the body of literatures that is the focus of contemporary critical studies of gender.

Although, as noted, these first critical studies focused on black *feminism, the end of the millennium finds a parallel interest in representations of a black masculinist presence in the arts, literature, and popular cultures of the United States emerging as a sustained and coherent critical project.

Since the 1970s and through the early 1990s, the popularity of women's writing and issues of feminist theory have been at the fore of gendered studies in literature. However, because feminist politics did not initially demonstrate concern for issues of race and culture, it was necessary for literary study to address this absence as it focused on black women writers.

In the preface to *In Search of Our Mothers' Gardens: Womanist Prose* (1983) Alice *Walker argues for a "feminist of color"—a "womanist" for whom culture and gender are both essential. Although this was likely not her intent, Walker's term "womanist" underscores the tension between the feminist agendas of a woman's movement that was initially inattentive to cultural difference and to black women's issues. It has encountered contestation and some debate. In *Talking Back* (1989), bell hooks argues that "*womanism*" does not engage the dynamics of radical and transformative political struggle and change. Others argue that its separatist agenda underscores potentially divisive problematics of race in gender studies. In this latter sense, womanism has a clearly historical evolution as it calls for attention to the discrete cultural issues of the tradition that do not only implicate gendered differences. In some ways, it may even be considered as a response to Barbara Smith's 1977 argument in what is widely held to be the generative *essay for critical attention to women writers in the African American literary tradition.

In that 1977 essay, "Toward a Black Feminist Criticism," Barbara Smith writes that the "politics of sex *as well as* the politics of race and class are crucially interlocking factors in the works of Black women writers" (emphasis added). Smith's essay provoked great controversy in the emergent studies of black feminism. Her arguments concerning a black woman's language and cultural experience that were evidence of "an identifiable literary tradition" seemed problematically essentialist to many readers. What is a black woman's language? How does language indicate a gender and a culture? Do all black women writers "inherently" (i.e., biologically) use this language? These difficult questions raised within the essay's thesis were not, however, its most debatable aspect. More bothersome to some was Smith's insistence on bringing a black female lesbian voice into the discourse of black feminism. Smith's thesis concerned both gender and sex, and for each of these differences the issue of culture was critical. At this point in the developing field of black feminist literary studies, the complications and controversies inherent to the intersecting relationships of culture, sexuality, and gender were riveted to its disciplinary identity. Of these issues, culture and gender have received the most sustained academic study.

A pivotal *anthology for the development of and attention to black feminist criticism preceded Smith's essay. Toni Cade *Bambara's *The Black Woman* (1970) gathered prose and *poetry of black women writers of the era and forced a focused consideration of their presence in American arts and letters. Bambara's work lay the ground for the 1982 publication edited by Gloria Hull, Patricia Bell-Scott, and Barbara Smith—*All the Women Are White, All the Blacks Are Men, But Some of Us Are Brave*. This text would fix a disciplinary home-place for black women's studies in the academy.

Both the archival projects of critics and theorists' figurative constructions of a poetics of women's writing find distinctions that are apparent and consistent in the voice, structure, and language of African American women writers' texts. Issues of language have a discrete configuration in black women writers according to the work of several theorists, including Mae Henderson's "Speaking in Tongues: Dialogics, Dialectics, and the Black Women Writer's Literary Tradition" (in *Changing Our Own Words*, ed. Cheryl *Wall, 1989), Houston A. *Baker, Jr.'s *Workings of the Spirit: The Poetics of Afro-American Women's Writing*

(1991), and Karla Holloway's *Moorings and Metaphors: Figures of Culture and Gender in Black Women's Writing* (1992). Hazel Carby's *Reconstructing Womanhood: The Emergence of the Afro-American Woman Novelist* (1987) reconstructs the cultural history "of the forms in which black women intellectuals made political [and] literary interventions" in their social domains. Roseann Bell, Mari *Evans, Gloria Wade-Gayles, Barbara Christian, Joanne Braxton and Andree McLauglin, Henry Louis *Gates, Jr., and Cheryl Wall explore generational continuities of thesis, character, and language as well as complex intersections of these issues in the literature of nineteenth- and twentieth-century women writers in rich and provocative critical essays. Finally, the 1988 publication of *The Schomburg Library of Nineteenth-Century Black Women Writers*—a project of massive archival documentation and recovery—places back into print heretofore lost volumes of African American women writers. The Schomburg Library collection stands as testament to the scholarly interest in African American women's writing and to the significant and perceptive initiative of Bambara's *The Black Woman*.

As in the developmental history of black feminism, the intersection of race and gender in U.S. sociopolitical discourse is also the likely impetus for the late-twentieth-century focus on black male writers. A critically significant moment in this encounter was the 1994 New York City exhibition at the Whitney Museum of American Art—*Black Male: Representations of Masculinity in Contemporary American Art*. The Whitney exhibit honed in upon this discourse as it indicated, through its collective and eclectic sweep, the newly pervasive subjectivity of the black male. *Black Male*, the exhibit catalog, brings together what seem to be disparate aesthetic commentaries regarding black male representations—from visual art, *film, *music, literature, and popular culture. The collage-like structure of both the exhibit and the catalog make it apparent that the "invention" of the black man, in public cultures and in private literary/artistic cultures, is a force that dramatically patterns the history and progress of America's racial and sexual stereotype of black masculinity (*see also* Stereotypes, *article on* Black Stereotypes).

To some degree, the sustained interest in black women's writing has been a provocative agent in the recently focused attention on black male writers. In a gendered critique that represented vigorously negative assessments of their work, some black male writers and critics launched bitterly aimed diatribes against black women writers and the attention, celebrity, and publishing opportunities lavishly available to them. Ishmael *Reed, Charles R. *Johnson, David *Bradley, and Stanley *Crouch have been among the most vocal. These writers and critics present what they identify as the selective politics of corporate publishing decisions. Their contentions? First, that black feminist politics have made the contemporary works of black male writers, especially in the 1970s and 1980s, less visible and therefore less important than the work of black women writers; and second, that black women writers' celebrity is constructed by a parallel denigration of black males within the characterizations of their texts. Much of this debate began with the publication of Alice Walker's *The *Color Purple* (1982)—a text in which her black male characters were read, by an American public, as being representative of an abusive black masculine ethos.

However, of more significance than the factional and fracturing disputes about publishing and celebrity are the issues that emerge once expressions of black male cultures come under critical and theoretical scrutiny. Critical interest in individual male writers' characterizations, themes, and issues has not been absent from literary studies of the tradition. Although Edward Margolies's 1968 *Native Sons* critically studies sixteen twentieth-century "Negro American Authors," all of whom are male, his is not a gendered study. The male collective of Margolies's anthology of essays expresses selective bias rather than critical methodology. There is a similar absence of intertextual gendered study in Charles Johnson's 1988 *Being and Race: Black Writing since 1970*. Following an impressive and widely ranging discussion on the philosophy of being and its expressive impact on race, fiction, and novelistic form, *Being and Race* has two sections: "The Men" and "The Women." However, despite the promise of these categorical dividers, Johnson's project does not develop an intertextual conversation concerning thematic exchange or stylistic patterns that are consistent in black men's literature nor does it concern the collective effects of gendered issues in black male writing.

A gendered critique of the literary and intellectual history of African American writing would address lingering issues and questions about the male writers of various eras in the tradition and the male-identified gender associations within those literary periods. Hazel Carby's study accomplishes such a perspective for women novelists. However, critical studies have yet to address, in a sustained manner, questions that concern male writers and their works. In what ways does gender identify the earliest writing of enslaved Africans in America? Why is *protest literature male identified? What differences and critical perspectives do gendered studies of the *Black Arts movement reveal? Does the writing from the era known as *Black Aesthetics contradict the sexism of the Black Power movement or does it reify those stereotypes?

In the 1990s, interest in the study of gendered intertextualities that focus exclusively on representations of males seems to bear some relationship to a contemporary swell in autobiographical writings by contemporary African American men. This literature, creatively expressed in a variety of personal narrative forms (autobiography, biography, memoir, and reflection), forces a sustained attention to the shared experiences of black male bodies in the United States and to the visceral qualities and exchangeable expressions of those experiences in writers from the beginnings of the tradition to the present. Within this frame, early writers such as Martin Delany and Frederick Douglass, turn-of-the-century authors such as Charles Chesnutt and James Weldon Johnson, the protest literature of Richard Wright and Ralph Ellison, the public courage and challenge recorded in *The *Autobiography of Malcolm X* (1965) as well as the quietly courageous, yet fiercely intimate passion of John Edgar *Wideman's *Fatheralong: A Meditation on Fathers and Sons, Race and Society* (1994) benefit from the discrete attention of a gendered critique. Considering the rich history of critical and theoretical work about gender and women's writing in the tradition, it is probable that the developing scholarly attention to the intersections of culture and masculinity in African American literature will follow a similar trajectory as it defines and theorizes along the lines of gender.

Representing Black Men (eds. Marcellus Blount and George Cunningham, 1995) indicates this developing trajectory. It argues that the social sciences have defined African American men as "absences" and therefore chooses to explore "constructions of African American masculinities as presences" in theories of the culture and its literature. Certainly the 1995 publication of *Brotherman: The Odyssey of Black Men in America* (eds. Herb Boyd and Robert Allen), a hefty anthology of black men's writing, echoes back a quarter of a century and recalls Bambara's 1970 publication, *The Black Woman*. The publication of *Brotherman* augurs an era when the intellectual history of the literature of African American writers, fully attentive to the cultural critique of gendered representations, comes full circle.

[*See also* Gay Literature; Lesbian Literature.]

• Roseann P. Bell et al., eds., *Sturdy Black Bridges: Visions of Black Women in Literature*, 1979. Barbara Christian, *Black Women Novelists: The Development of a Tradition*, 1980. Mari Evans, ed., *Black Women Writers, 1950–1980: The Development of a Tradition*, 1984. Gloria Wade-Gayles, *No Crystal Stair*, 1984. Joann Braxton and Andree McLaughlin, eds., *Wild Women in the Whirlwind: Afra-American Culture and the Contemporary Literary Renaissance*, 1989. Cheryl Wall, ed., *Changing Our Own Words: Essays on Criticism, Theory, and Writing by Black Women*, 1989. Henry L. Gates, Jr., ed., *Reading Black, Reading Feminist*, 1990. France Smith Foster, *Written by Herself: Literary Production by African American Women, 1746–1892*, 1993. Thelma Golden, ed., *Black Male: Representations of Masculinity in Contemporary American Art*, 1994.
—Karla FC Holloway

GIBSON, PATRICIA JOANN (b. ?), playwright, teacher, and lecturer. P. J. Gibson has demonstrated her talent in writing ranging from poems and *short stories to public service announcements and media publications. However, she is best known for her plays, three of which have been anthologized.

Gibson was born in Pittsburgh, Pennsylvania, and grew up in Trenton, New Jersey. While in her early teens, she studied under J. P. Miller (*The Days of Wine and Roses*, 1973). In the early 1970s, she earned a BA in *drama, *religion, and English from Keuka College in New York. She was then awarded a Shubert Fellowship to study playwriting at Brandeis University in Massachusetts, where she completed her MFA in 1975. Aside from J. P. Miller, Gibson's mentors include Don Peterson (*Does a Tiger Wear a Necktie?*, 1969) and Israel Horovitz (*Indian Wants the Bronx*, 1968).

Although Gibson has had several mentors, Lorraine *Hansberry is one of her primary influences. In fact, in the late 1960s, after seeing a play based on Hansberry's life and writing, *To Be Young, Gifted and Black* (1969), Gibson was inspired to start writing plays. Since that time, she has written twenty-six, a number of which have been produced in various countries. She is quite prolific and explains that "If I live to be 150, I still won't have enough time to write about all the black women inside of me" (Margaret B. Wilkerson, *Nine Plays by Black Women*, 1986).

Gibson's commitment to creating substantial roles for African American women is evident in her first play, *The Black Woman*, which debuted in a one-act version in 1971 and was later produced in a three-act version in 1972. The play consists of a chronological sequence of monologues spoken by twenty African American women characters who live during different periods of history.

The Black Woman was followed by *Void Passage* and *Konvergence*, two one-acts produced as companion pieces in 1973 by Players Company of Trenton, New Jersey. *Void Passage* focuses on the conflicts of two women who have been labeled "strong Black women" while *Konvergence*, published in Woodie *King, Jr.'s New Plays for the Black Theatre* (1989), depicts the turbulent reunion of a married couple after a year's separation. This upwardly mobile couple struggles with whether or not to assimilate into middle-class society and "become another chocolate-covered android of the system," yet another statistic of the vacuous, materialistic American dream.

The failure of the American dream returns as a theme in *Miss Ann Don't Cry No More* (1980), the play that earned an NEA grant for Gibson. In this, Gibson reveals the failed dreams of the inhabitants of an apartment house and again presents the challenges and struggles urban America presents to African Americans. *Miss Ann* was first performed as a reading at the Frank Silvera Writer's Workshop in 1977 and later mounted as a full production at the Frederick Douglass Creative Arts Center in 1980.

The next year, the Arts Center also staged a reading of one of Gibson's most compelling plays, *Brown Silk and Magenta Sunsets*. Later published in Margaret Wilkerson's *Nine Plays by Black Women* (1986), this play details the tragic results of obsessive love. The plot revolves around Lena Larson Salvinoli, the attractive and affluent widow of an Italian man she did not love. As a teenager Lena was fascinated by a much older musician who lived in the same apartment building and she desperately tries to recover the passionate intensity of this first and only true love. Her obsession for him led to his death and the death of their daughter, and finally leads to Lena's own suicide in the play.

Death also figures prominently in *Long Time since Yesterday*, Gibson's play about the reunion of a group of middle-aged women after the suicide of one of their college girlfriends. Published in *Black Thunder: An Anthology of Contemporary African American Drama* (William Branch, 1992), the play ran twice at the New Federal Theatre in 1985 and won five Au-

delco awards, including those for the best dramatic production and playwright of the year. Thematically, the play reveals "that strange closeness women have with women" as well as the delicate boundaries between friendship and romantic love.

Gibson has taught as an assistant professor of English at the John Jay College of Criminal Justice in New York City, where she earned a teaching award in 1987. Two stories and one poem of hers have appeared in *Erotique Noire/Black Erotica* (Miriam Decosta-Willis et al., 1992). She is currently writing a novel entitled *Neidyana* as well as a collection of *short stories.

• Bernard L. Peterson, Jr., "Gibson, P. J.," in *Contemporary Black American Playwrights and Their Plays*, 1988, pp. 189–193. Margaret B. Wilkerson, "Music as Metaphor: New Plays of Black Women," in *Making a Spectacle: Feminist Essays on Contemporary Women's Theatre*, ed. Lynda Hart, 1989, pp. 61–75. Donna Olendorf, "Gibson, P. J.," in *CA*, vol. 142, 1994, pp. 146–147.
                                                                —E. Barnsley Brown

GIOVANNI, NIKKI (b. 1943), poet, essayist, lecturer, and educator. Born Yolande Cornelia Giovanni, Jr., on 7 June in Knoxville, Tennessee, to Jones and Yolande Giovanni, Nikki Giovanni became one of the most prominent young poets to emerge from the *Black Arts movement of the late 1960s and early 1970s. Her initial achievement of national recognition grew out of the militant, revolutionary poems included in her first two volumes, *Black Feeling, Black Talk* (1968) and *Black Judgement* (1969); this early success became the foundation for a sustained career as an important, often controversial, writer, the recipient of numerous honors and awards, including ten honorary doctorates.

Although she grew up in Cincinnati, Ohio, Giovanni was profoundly influenced by and has consciously identified with the values and traditions of the South. She spent many summer vacations with her maternal grandparents in Knoxville and lived with them during her high school years (1957–1960). Her grandmother, Emma Louvenia Watson, helped shape Giovanni's belief in the power of the individual and her commitment to serving others, values important in both her *poetry and her conception of herself as a writer. Like Langston *Hughes, Giovanni has identified herself throughout her career as a "poet of the people," and she has consistently addressed ordinary people, rather than literary scholars or critics, in her poetry and *essays.

At age seventeen, Giovanni entered Fisk University as an early entrant but was dismissed at the end of her first semester because, as she states in *Gemini* (1971), her "attitudes did not fit those of a Fisk woman." She returned to Fisk four years later and graduated magna cum laude in February 1967 with a degree in history. While she was a student, she participated in the Fisk Writing Workshops directed by John O. *Killens and reinstituted the campus chapter of the Student Nonviolent Coordinating Committee. She briefly pursued graduate study, first in social work at the University of Pennsylvania (1967–1968) and then in fine arts at Columbia University (1969). By 1970, she had given birth to a son (Thomas

Watson Giovanni), combined and published with William Morrow her first two volumes (originally self-published) under the title *Black Feeling, Black Talk/Black Judgement*, and distributed through *Broadside Press a third volume, *Re: Creation* (1970). Some of the poems in these early volumes gained even wider recognition when, in 1971, she recorded them in juxtaposition to gospel music on the award-winning album *Truth Is on Its Way*. Although Giovanni was not the first of her generation to combine poetry and *music, her album enjoyed an unprecedented success. Along with the hundreds of readings and lectures she gave during the early 1970s on college campuses and in *churches and civic centers throughout the country, *Truth* helped establish her as an oral poet whose work was intimately connected to its performance.

Many of the poems that led to Giovanni's identification as an angry, militant poet appear in *Black Feeling, Black Talk/Black Judgement*, including such well-known poems as "The True Import of Present Dialogue, Black vs. Negro" and "The Great Pax Whitie." These poems are matched, however, by short lyric poems that explore more private concerns or celebrate personal and familial relationships, such as the well-known poems "Knoxville, Tennessee" and "Nikki Rosa." This division between political and revolutionary themes, on the one hand, and more personal themes, on the other, continues, in different permutations, throughout Giovanni's later volumes of poetry and prose. The anger at injustices perpetrated by the forces of racism that is expressed in "And the word was death to all niggers" ("The Great Pax Whitie") continues to be counterpointed by the celebration of African American people so eloquently captured in the famous line from "Nikki Rosa," "Black love is black wealth."

Perhaps because Giovanni eventually abandoned the rhetoric of militancy, and perhaps because she insisted on her own independence and autonomy, her critics and reviewers voiced increasing disapproval of her poetry. Margaret B. McDowell, analyzing reviews of Giovanni's work between 1969 and 1974, has shown that "critics have allowed personal and political attitudes not merely to affect their judgment but to dominate it." In fact, although the poems in *Re: Creation* and the pivotal *My House* (1972) do not employ the kind of explosive language characteristic of *Black Feeling, Black Talk/Black Judgement*, many of them do concern themselves with subjects that today are recognized as socially and politically significant. As an African American woman and single mother, Giovanni confronts in these volumes questions concerning female *identity and female autonomy. She rejects the male constructions of female identity that have led to the double oppression of African American women and asserts instead the right and the necessity for African American women to shape their own identities. Included in *Re: Creation*, for example, is the now classic "Ego Tripping"; through a sustained use of hyperbole, the poem celebrates the African American woman as the creator of the universe and all the treasures within it. The concluding lines of the poem reveal why Giovanni's work has had

an empowering effect on the lives of many young African American women: "I am so perfect so divine so ethereal so surreal / I cannot be comprehended / except by my permission / I mean . . . I . . . can fly / like a bird in the sky."

The poems in *My House* similarly offer a series of statements about Giovanni's conception of herself as an African American woman and as a poet. The volume opens with "Legacies," which acknowledges the importance of one's past and one's ancestors in the creation of identity, and concludes with "My House," which uses the house as a symbol of the female poet and the domestic activities within the house as figures to express the authority and power of the poet. The poem insists—as do others in the volume—on the poet's right to decide the meaning of "revolution," her right to decide the appropriate subject matter of her poetry, and, ultimately, her right to create her own identity.

My House is divided into two sections, "The Rooms Inside" and "The Rooms Outside"; the first group charts the poet's individual, personal growth, while the second provides the social, historical, and cultural contexts in which that self has been shaped. In "The Rooms Outside," for example, three short poems about the poet's visits to Africa explore the ambivalent relationship of African Americans to Africa. "Africa I" sounds the keynote of the volume as well as of Giovanni's work in general. The question facing the speaker is whether to trust her own vision of Africa or to allow that vision to be "corrected" by others apparently more knowledgeable: "but my grandmother stood up / from her rocker just then / and said you call it / like you see it / john brown and i are with you." These lines might almost function as Giovanni's credo in their insistence that the writer, supported and empowered by her ancestors, must trust the authority of her own vision.

In her subsequent volumes of adult poetry—*The Women and the Men* (1975), *Cotton Candy on a Rainy Day* (1978), and *Those Who Ride the Night Winds* (1983)—Giovanni continues to write both introspective poems and poems addressing social and political issues. Also apparent in all her poetry, from *Re: Creation* onward, is the influence of music—the *blues, rhythm and blues, and *jazz—on her poetic forms and figures. Students can now more readily trace the development of Giovanni's poetic career in the recent collection of her poetry, *The Selected Poems of Nikki Giovanni* (1996), which brings together some 150 poems. The alternation between personal and social concerns is also evident in *Gemini*, a collection of autobiographical essays, some written in a private voice remembering the personal past, and others written in a public voice responding to larger social issues. This duality continues in Giovanni's essay collections, *Sacred Cows . . . And Other Edibles* (1988) and *Racism 101* (1994). In the latter volume, Giovanni alternately fuses and juxtaposes these two voices, often with brilliant results.

Giovanni's early success led to two important "conversations" with other writers: *A Dialogue: James Baldwin and Nikki Giovanni* (1972) and *A Poetic Equation: Conversations Between Nikki Giovanni and*

Margaret Walker (1974). Giovanni has also written several volumes of poetry for children: *Spin a Soft Black Song* (1971), *Ego Tripping and Other Poems for Young Readers* (1973), and *Vacation Time* (1979). Several of her poems have been published as illustrated children's books: *Knoxville, Tennessee*, illustrated by Larry Johnson (1994), *The Genie in the Jar*, illustrated by Chris Raschka (1996), and *The Sun Is So Quiet*, illustrated by Ashley *Bryan (1996). Giovanni's poems for children are characterized by a playfulness with language and rhythms that appeals to children of all ages; in their re-creation of the sounds and smells and sights of childhood, many of these poems clearly have appeal to both children and adults. Her commentary on Harlem Renaissance poets in the anthology *Shimmy Shimmy Like My Sister Kate* (1996) is similarly of interest to both young and mature readers.

While the guardians of literary history have often been puzzled by the sometimes dizzying contradictions posed by Giovanni's poetry and prose, ordinary people—the people for whom she states she has always written—continue to keep her works in print, continue to fill the auditoriums in which she reads and lectures. Her place in literary history is undisputed because her voice speaks to and for people—about their joys and their sorrows, the forces arrayed against them and the strengths they bring as resistance—in tones and language they can understand.

• Suzanne Juhasz, *Naked and Fiery Forms: Modern American Poetry by Women, A New Tradition*, 1976. Eugene B. Redmond, *Drumvoices: The Mission of Afro-American Poetry*, 1976. Anna T. Robinson, *Nikki Giovanni: From Revolution to Revelation*, 1979. Claudia Tate, *Black Women Writers at Work*, 1983. William J. Harris, "Sweet Soft Essence of Possibility: The Poetry of Nikki Giovanni," in *Black Women Writers 1950–1980*, ed. Mari Evans, 1984, pp. 218–228. Margaret B. McDowell, "Groundwork for a More Comprehensive Criticism of Nikki Giovanni," in *Belief vs. Theory in Black American Literary Criticism*, eds. Joe Weixlmann and Chester J. Fontenot, *Studies in Black American Literature*, vol. 2, 1986, pp. 135–160. Martha Cook, "Nikki Giovanni: Place and Sense of Place in Her Poetry," in *Southern Women Writers: The New Generation*, ed. Tonette Bond Inge, 1990, pp. 279–300. Virginia C. Fowler, *Nikki Giovanni*, 1992.
—Virginia C. Fowler

Giovanni's Room. A groundbreaking *novel for its exploration of homosexuality, James *Baldwin's *Giovanni's Room* (1956) holds a unique place in the American and African American literary traditions. Baldwin published it against the advice of Alfred Knopf, who published his acclaimed debut novel, *Go Tell It on the Mountain* (1953); editors warned Baldwin that he would jeopardize his potential as a "Negro" author by writing a book about white male sexual and cultural *identity. However, the determined Baldwin found a British publisher, Mark Joseph, and Dial Press eventually published *Giovanni's Room* in America.

The first-person narrative centers around David, a white American attempting to "find himself" in France. The novel opens in the present with David recalling his internecine upbringing and an adolescent homosexual encounter. In Paris awaiting the return of his girlfriend and possible fiancée, Hella, David

engages in a torrid affair with Giovanni, an Italian bartender. Giovanni loves him unashamedly, and they live together for two months; however, David transforms Giovanni's room into a symbol of their "dirty" relationship. Upon Hella's return from Spain, David abruptly leaves the destitute Giovanni, who has been fired by bar owner Guillaume, a "disgusting old fairy." David's desertion psychologically destroys Giovanni, who enters a sexually and economically predatory gay underworld. Giovanni eventually murders Guillaume, who reneges on a promise to rehire him in exchange for sex; he is later caught and sentenced to death.

Meanwhile, David, despondent over his mistreatment of Giovanni and the truth about his homosexuality, attempts to rejuvenate himself via marriage. But upon discovering him and a sailor in a gay bar, Hella vows to return to America, wishing "I'd never left it." The novel's closing tableau replicates its opening: David ponders Giovanni's impending execution and his complicity in his erstwhile lover's demise.

Giovanni's Room fuses the personal, the actual, and the fictional: Baldwin exorcises demons surrounding his own sexual identity while simultaneously capturing the subterranean milieu he encountered in Paris during the late 1940s and early 1950s; he bases the murder plot on an actual crime involving the killing of an older man who purportedly propositioned a younger one; and he weaves a Jamesian tale of expatriate Americans fleeing their "complex fate" in search of their "true" selves. The novel received favorable reviews, many critics applauding Baldwin's restrained yet powerful handling of a "controversial" subject. Ultimately, the book is more than a study of sexual identity, as Baldwin himself posited: "It is not so much about homosexuality, it is what happens if you are so afraid that you finally cannot love anybody." *Giovanni's Room* maintains a seminal place in American, African American, and gay and lesbian literary studies.

[*See also* Gay Literature.]

• Georges-Michel Sarotte, *Like a Brother, Like a Lover: Male Homosexuality in the American Novel and Theatre from Herman Melville to James Baldwin*, trans. Richard Miller, 1978. Horace A. Porter, *Stealing the Fire: The Art and Protest of James Baldwin*, 1989.
—Keith Clark

God Sends Sunday. A *novel by Arna *Bontemps, *God Sends Sunday* was published in 1931. According to local legend, Little Augie, born with a caul over his face, is blessed with the double gifts of luck and clairvoyance, but the notion is small solace for the timid, frail, undersized youngster who firmly believes his destiny lies in wandering until he exhausts his luck and meets his destruction.

When Little Augie attains *manhood and becomes a full-fledged jockey, success transforms him into a swaggering, cigar-smoking gallant with a relish for *mulatto women, only to find himself in hopeless rivalry with Mr. Woody for voluptuous Florence Dessau. First Augie turns to drinking whiskey and singing the *blues, then he departs for St. Louis in search of a substitute for Florence and finds Della Green, a "fancy woman" on the infamous Targee

Street. They thrive famously until Augie kills his impulsive competitor Biglow Brown who had challenged Augie's courage.

Some thirty years later, withered with age, wearing a frayed Prince Albert outfit, Little Augie wends his way to Mudtown, a black country neighborhood in southern California and new home of his sister Leah and her teenaged grandchild, Terry. His battered traveling bag, a bottle of whiskey, and his old accordion represent the complete remains of his character. Soon Augie is reanimated by handling Leah's livestock—especially her worn out old racehorse—and dares to dream of new beginnings. His schemes, however, are disturbed by menacing signs and dark forebodings. When Little Augie gravely wounds a man in a fight, once again he must move on, and he is last seen making his way to Mexico.

This novel was praised for its poetic style and challenged for its racy content, but Hugh Gloster perceived it as setting a new trend in African American fiction because of its abandonment of Harlem for its background. Countee *Cullen joined Bontemps in a dramatization of the story that subsequently became the controversial yet successful 1946 Broadway musical entitled *St. Louis Woman*.

—Charles L. James

God's Trombones. James Weldon *Johnson's major contribution to the *Harlem Renaissance explosion of black American writing was his book of poems, *God's Trombones: Seven Negro Sermons in Verse*, published in 1927. For almost ten years Johnson worked on these folk sermons in verse whenever the demands of NAACP work relented enough to make writing possible. "The Creation" was published in 1918, and two others were published in magazines during the mid-1920s. In this work he followed the principles he had developed in writing the long preface to *The Book of American Negro Poetry*:

> What the colored poet in the United States needs to do is something like what Synge did for the Irish; he needs to find a form that will express the racial spirit by symbols from within rather than symbols from without, such as the mere mutilation of English spelling and pronunciation. . . . He needs a form that is freer and larger than dialect . . . a form expressing the imagery, the idioms, the peculiar terms of thought and distinctive humor and pathos, too, of the Negro. (Quoted in Johnson's introduction to *God's Trombones*)

The completed book presents seven sermons—"The Creation," "The Prodigal Son," "Go Down Death—A Funeral Sermon," "Noah Built the Ark," "The Crucifixion," "Let My People Go," and "The Judgment Day"—preceded by an opening poem, "Listen, Lord—A Prayer." While the book as a whole does not have a narrative structure, as the sermons stand independent of one another, the sermons as poems bring together the narrative element of the stories from the Bible on which they are each based, the narrative/dramatic moment of the sermon, and the lyric quality of the folk preacher's language.

God's Trombones is a radical departure from the beaten pathway for Johnson the aesthetic conservative. While remaining connected to the late Romantic dramatic monologue form that Paul Laurence *Dunbar and other black American poets had long favored, Johnson here admits the free verse tradition of Walt Whitman to mingle with the rhetorical imagery and verbal excitement of the folk preacher. Not forced to represent speech rhythms with mechanical metrics or distracting rhymes, Johnson is able to focus attention on the metaphoric and ironic creativity of the African American oral tradition. His preacher connects a world of Bible-based ideas to the congregation/reader's mundane reality.

Johnson is remarkably successful in creating a poetic equivalent of the language of what he calls in the introduction "the old time Negro preacher." In "The Creation," the first and most famous of these poems, he creates that old-time preacher's voice as a mixture of vibrant folk idiom, King James version grandeur, and apt metaphor. Thus God makes man of the clay from the riverbed while kneeling "like a *mammy bending over her baby." The rather abstract and distant creator of the Bible text is humanized by the preacher's narrative details and poetic touches.

The imagery and rhetoric of the poems draw upon the traditions of sacred song as well as sermons. In "Let My People Go" Johnson echoes his favorite *spiritual, while at the same time addressing both black readers and white.

Commonly accepted as James Weldon Johnson's highest achievement in *poetry, *God's Trombones* demonstrated in art the dignity and power of African American folk culture. With its illustrations by Aaron Douglas, the collection has enjoyed continuous popularity among scholars and general readers alike.

[*See also* Biblical Tradition; Churches; Dialect Poetry; Folklore; Oratory; Preachers and Deacons; Sermons and Preaching.]

• Jean Wagner, *Black Poets of the United States*, 1973.

—Joseph T. Skerrett, Jr.

Goin' a Buffalo. One of the Black consciousness plays of Ed *Bullins's *Twentieth-Century Cycle*, *Goin' a Buffalo* first appeared as a staged reading at the American Place Theater in June of 1968.

The play features the tough, streetwise Curt and his nubile wife Pandora, who sells her body to bring Curt money; Curt's friend Rich; Mamma Too Tight, a young white woman who is wholly dependent upon her pimp, Shaky; and Art, a quiet, seemingly naive sort who, after having saved Curt in a prison fight, is befriended by him. Though some of these decide to leave the hostility of Los Angeles, it is Curt who decides on Buffalo as an actual destination, hoping that he and Pandora can start a legitimate business there. As the play proceeds, however, this goal dissolves in a mixture of *violence, manipulation, and deception.

Leitmotifs of prison, money, drugs, and sex expose the gritty urban life and fragmented individual lives of the characters. Money for a sexuality based in violence (e.g., the play's manifold sexual connotations based on "Pandora's 'box'") is the governing equation in a world without love. The play moves through a long middle sequence in a neighborhood nightclub where Pandora sings; there, the Bullinsian element of violence controls every interaction between characters, the cast by now having been augmented by unpaid, disgruntled musicians who are both white and African American. This sequence ends in a bloody brawl as Deeny, the club's disreputable manager, arrives to announce that the show is closing and that no one will be paid. Though the issue of racial tension is obvious in a play about African Americans at odds with poverty and with the criminal justice system, Bullins as playwright interestingly adds greater dramaturgical possibilities by writing stage directions that allow Deeny, the Bouncer, and a customer to be cast as whites—possibilities through which, Bullins writes, "there might be added tensions."

The game of chess is also a metaphor; it opens the play as Curt customarily beats Rich. Art, too, prevails at chess but also deftly manipulates the feelings, fears, and aspirations of these desperate characters, especially Mamma and Pandora. Through his machinations, the city of Buffalo itself becomes the object of the endgame in the play's surprise ending.

The scenes in Curt's apartment and in the nightclub are enclosed spaces from which the stricken African American spirit must emerge; Buffalo represents the unrealizable wide-open space of *freedom. Robert Tener finds that these spatial boxes are themselves placed within the larger "box" of the American metropolis, which is itself a construction of whiteness that engulfs these characters. Geneva Smitherman sees instead a conscious self-awareness in these and other Bullins characters, one in which their humanity sometimes leads to heroism. This divergence of views is almost certainly due to the fact that Bullins, rather than determining a moral perspective in presenting the lives of his characters, instead allows their movement in and through their particular milieu, thus revealing his execution of naturalistic technique.

• Geneva Smitherman, "Everybody Wants to Know Why I Sing the Blues," *Black World* 23 (Apr. 1974): 4–13. Robert L. Tener, "Pandora's Box: A Study of Ed Bullins' Dramas," *CLA Journal* 18 (1974–1975): 533–544.   —Nathan L. Grant

GOINES, DONALD (1937–1974), novelist. Donald Goines spent his writing career exploring the underbelly of black urban life in what his publisher dubbed "black experience *novels." He wrote and published sixteen novels in the span of his five-year career and is still touted by his publisher as "America's best-selling black author."

Born 15 December 1937 in Detroit to parents who owned their own dry-cleaning business, and a product of Catholic elementary school, Goines spent his formative years outside the world he treats in his novels. This began to change during his midteens, however, when he falsified his age to join the U.S. Air Force, served in Japan during the Korean War, and returned to Detroit a heroin addict at the age of seventeen.

After leaving the air force, Goines's range of experiences provided the background for his novels. At various times he was a pimp, professional gambler, car thief, armed robber, and bootlegger. These illegal activities landed him in jail several times, which proved to be productive: Goines was heroin-free only while in prison and focused on his literary talents there as well. During a term in Jackson State Prison in 1965, Goines wrote his first novels, which were Westerns. After being discouraged from writing in this genre and being inspired by *Iceberg Slim's *Trick Baby*, Goines began to write in earnest and produced the first of his ghetto novels during another prison term at Jackson in 1969. After a fellow inmate gave the work his approval and suggested Goines submit it to Slim's publisher, Goines sent *Whoreson, The Story of a Ghetto Pimp* to Holloway House and the manuscript was accepted. *Whoreson* (1972) is Goines's most autobiographical novel and the only one written in the first person. He uses his own experiences as a pimp and multifaceted hustler to paint a vivid portrait of a ghetto pimp and the types of street characters who surround him.

His second novel, but the first to be published, is *Dopefiend: The Story of a Black Junkie* (1971). In this Goines explains the power dynamics between dealer and junkie and illustrates how a perverted, cowardly, black drug dealer in a dilapidated ghetto house can exert his influence across socioeconomic boundaries over anyone who becomes addicted to heroin. Goines emphasizes that no heroin user can emerge from the experience unscathed.

He lived his own lesson. After leaving prison with an advance from his publisher in 1970, Goines resumed his life as a heroin addict. He did continue writing, however, and his next novel, *Black Gangster,* appeared in 1972. This novel tells the story of a gang leader named Prince who uses his organization, the Freedom Now Liberation Movement, as a front for illegal activity. Although Prince's ability to mobilize his community is admirable, Goines illustrates how the positive efforts of the black community are often stunted by the American system that continually proves individual capitalistic gain the only insurance for survival, while it blocks the path that leads to legitimate economic success.

Goines's next significant novel (which follows *Street Players,* 1973) is *White Man's Justice, Black Man's Grief* (1973), framed by Goines's "An Angry Preface," which exposes the racial and economic inequities in the bail-bond system and urges politicians to make changes. The story that follows personalizes the issue and demonstrates how this type of discrimination targets mostly poor black men who become hopelessly tangled in the "justice" system once they have entered it.

Goines's next novel, *Black Girl Lost* (1973), is his most sustained treatment of the black ghetto experience from a woman's perspective. It is also the last novel Goines published before Holloway House requested that he use a pseudonym. The next nine novels, *Cry Revenge!, Eldorado Red, Swamp Man, Never Die Alone, Daddy Cool, Crime Partners, Death List, Kenyatta's Escape* (all published in 1974), and *Kenyatta's Last Hit* (1975), were published under his friend Al C. Clark's name. In these novels, Goines continues to write what critic Greg Goode calls "ghetto realism" without the kind of glamorization one might expect in the era of "blacksploitation."

The last four of these novels comprise a series that features the militant leader Kenyatta. In these novels Kenyatta's army of revolutionaries mounts a campaign to kill white policemen and remove drugs and prostitution from the black ghetto. As the series progresses, Kenyatta comes closer to his goal but is ultimately killed as he is about to assassinate a Los Angeles drug kingpin.

Goines's last novel, *Inner City Hoodlum*, was published posthumously in 1975 after he and his common-law wife, Shirley Sailor, were shot and killed in their Detroit home. Goines's novels have never been out of print and have been embraced by the hip-hop generation of the 1990s.

• Eddie Stone, *Donald Writes No More: A Biography of Donald Goines*, 1974. Greg Goode, "Donald Goines," in *DLB*, vol. 38, *Afro-American Fiction Writers after 1995*, eds. Thadious M. Davis and Trudier Harris, 1984, pp. 96–100. Greg Goode, "From *Dopefiend* to *Kenyatta's Last Hit*: The Angry Black Crime Novels of Donald Goines," *MELUS* 2 (Fall 1984): 41–48.
—Valerie N. Matthews

GOLDEN, MARITA (b. 1950), novelist, poet, and educator. Marita Golden's works, especially her fiction, present some of the problems faced by contemporary African American women. They also capture the turbulent but exhilarating milieu of the civil rights era with its challenges and opportunities for commitment.

Her first work, *Migrations of the Heart* (1983), was a well-received memoir begun when she was just twenty-nine. It recounts, for example, her involvement in the black consciousness movement while attending American University as a scholarship student from Washington's inner city. It also describes her life as an expatriate in Lagos, Nigeria, where she lived in the mid-1970s, and the failure of her marriage to the Nigerian architect with whom she had fallen in love as a student at the Columbia School of Journalism.

Her first *novel, A Woman's Place (1986), chronicles a fifteen-year period in the lives of three African American women, Faith, Crystal, and Serena, who meet and become lifelong friends at an elite Boston college during the 1970s. After dropping out of college as a casualty of its new open admissions policy and suffering the death of a child, Faith becomes the wife of an orthodox Muslim nearly twenty years her senior. This relationship deteriorates as her husband becomes increasingly jealous and possessive. Crystal, who becomes a professional poet, enters into a rocky marriage with a white documentary filmmaker. This marriage to a white man alienates her from her father and brother. Serena makes her way as a women's rights advocate in a newly independent African nation. The novel employs multiple narrators, including not only the three major characters but also their husbands, children, and parents.

Golden's second novel, *Long Distance Life* (1989), chronicles the lives of four generations of an upwardly mobile African American family in Golden's home town of Washington, D.C. The story takes place against the background of the Great *Migration, the Marcus *Gravey movement, Washington, D.C., history, and the *civil rights movement. It begins with the relocation of the matriarch of the family, Naomi, from her North Carolina farm to Washington to better her prospects. The inspiration for this character was Golden's own mother, Beatrice Lee Reid, who left the poverty of Greensboro, North Carolina, for Washington, D.C., in the late 1920s. Golden says, "It's not conscious, but I find that the women in my work find themselves negotiating the tension between personal and political choices and are compelled to leave home to further their self-definition" (*Essence*, Nov. 1989). Forty years after Naomi leaves the South, her daughter Esther returns there to work in the civil rights movement. One of Esther's sons becomes a physician and the other a drug dealer whose murder is drug-related. The novel employs a third-person narrative interspersed with Naomi's first-person reflections on her life and those of her loved ones. It ends with an eighty-year-old Naomi reflecting that in spite of such tragedies as her grandson's untimely death, she has lived a rewarding, full life and wouldn't have changed any of it.

Golden's third novel, *And Do Remember Me* (1992), traces the lives of two African American women, Jessie and Macon. Jessie escapes from a dysfunctional family in Mississippi, where she is a victim of father-daughter incest, into the civil rights movement. She forms a close friendship with the civil rights activist Macon, the only person with whom she can unburden herself about her incestuous past. Jessie becomes addicted to alcohol, but with the help of an activist-playwright lover, she finds recovery and success in a professional acting career. Macon becomes a professor at a predominantly white college, where she tries to help African American students cope with campus racism. This work is suitable for both adults and young adults.

Golden has edited and introduced a collection of *essays, *Wild Women Don't Wear No Blues: Black Women Writers on Love, Men, and Sex* (1993). In her introduction she asserts that if, according to W. E. B. *Du Bois, racism is the basic problem of the twentieth century, sex, as revealed in the ongoing abortion controversy and the worldwide AIDS epidemic, may be the "defining metaphor" for the twenty-first.

Saving Our Sons: Raising Black Children in a Turbulent World (1994) is Golden's personal account of raising her son Michael in a crime-ridden neighborhood in Washington, D.C. This work shows how it takes not only parents but a support network of friends, relatives, and teachers for the African American male child to make a successful passage to *manhood.

Golden's novels are in the tradition of contemporary African American women's fiction in her heroines' quests for self-definition and fulfillment. Also like characters in such works as *Waiting to Exhale* (1992) by Terri *McMillan, *The *Color Purple* (1982) by Alice *Walker, and *The *Women of Brewster Place* (1982) by Gloria *Naylor, they find strength and sustenance in the female relationship.

• Thulani Davis, "Don't Worry, Be Buppie: Black Novelists Head for the Mainstream," *Village Voice Literary Supplement*, May 1990, 26–29. Sharon Malinowski, ed., *Black Writers*, 2d ed., 1994. Mary Grimley Mason, *American Women Writers*, vol. 5, supplement, ed. Carol Hurd Green, 1994. Susan M. Trotsky, ed., *CA*, vol. 42, 1994.   —Phiefer L. Browne

GOMEZ, JEWELLE (b. 1948), poet, novelist, short story writer, essayist, teacher, and political activist. Jewelle Gomez contributes to the growing genre of *gay literature and *lesbian literature by African Americans. Born in Boston, daughter of John ("Duke") Gomes, a bartender of Portuguese descent, and Delores Minor LeClair, a nurse, she lived on welfare with her Native American great-grandmother, Gracias Archelina Sportsman Morandus, until the age of twenty-two.

After receiving her BA from Northeastern University in 1971 and her MS from Columbia University School of Journalism in 1973, she worked as a *television production assistant in Boston and New York and as a stage manager for Off-Broadway plays from 1971 to 1981. She was director of the Literature Program for the New York State Council on the Arts from 1989 to 1993 and taught creative writing and women's studies.

Upon hearing the revolutionary *poetry of Nikki *Giovanni and Audre *Lorde and seeing Ntozake *Shange's play *for colored girls, she was inspired "to write about women's lives" and "the women she had known." She self-published two books of poetry, *The Lipstick Papers* (1980) and *Flamingoes and Bears* (1987), that extolled love and *sexuality. *The Gilda Stories* (1991), a first *novel, introduces through fantasy/science fiction the first black lesbian vampire. The book won two Lambda Literary Awards for Lesbian Fiction and Lesbian Science Fiction/Fantasy in 1991. This was her third award for fiction, following the Beard's Fund (1985) and Barbara Deming (1990) awards.

Gomez's *essays, *Forty-three Septembers* (1993), reflect on family members, childhood, self-discovery as a lesbian, and social and feminist issues. Despite her productivity and recognition as a literary critic, Gomez wavers on the outer edge of the writing mainstream because of her unconventional gay and lesbian subjects. To her, the nontraditional themes in her works contribute "to support the idea that African American is not simply one way of being."

• Lisa L. Nelson, "An Interview with Jewelle Gomez," *Poets & Writers* 21 (July–Aug. 1993): 34–45. Michael Bronski, "Jewelle Gomez," in *Gay and Lesbian Literature*, ed. Sharon Malinowski, 1994, pp. 163–164.

—Ann Allen Shockley

GORDON, TAYLOR (1893–1971), singer and author. Emanuel Taylor Gordon was born in White Sulphur Springs, Montana, a member of the only black family in that western settlement. He left home in 1910 and spent the next fifteen years on the road working as a Pullman porter and as the driver and valet of John Ringling of Ringling Brothers Circus. Arriving in New York in 1925, Gordon met Rosamond Johnson, whose arrangements of Negro *spirituals Gordon

learned to sing with such success that he attracted the attention of Carl Van Vechten, a white promoter of the *Harlem Renaissance. Through his friendship with Van Vechten, Gordon was able to publish his *autobiography, *Born to Be*, in 1929. With a foreword by Van Vechten and illustrations by the celebrated Miguel Covarrubias, and edited by Muriel Draper, another white admirer from the New York elite, *Born to Be* became a notable document of the Harlem Renaissance.

Draper portrays Gordon in her editorial preface as an uninhibited natural genius "unfettered by literary self-consciousness" and "free from racial self-consciousness." Gordon's free-wheeling narrative concentrates on the hedonistic side of his life; his goals seem summed up in the title of the last chapter of his autobiography, "All the Milk and Honey I Can Get." Gordon's sexual candor is unusual among African American autobiographers of his time. His depictions of Harlem nightlife, including house rent parties, drag queens at the Savoy, and black exotic dancers, provide a useful guide to the more flamboyant features of the New Negro Renaissance.

Taylor Gordon pursued an acting career, appearing in plays such as *Shoot the Works* and *The Gay Divorcee* and the *film *The Emperor Jones*. In 1935 he completed a novel, *Daonda*, which was never published. Following World War II, Gordon suffered numerous bouts with mental illness. His autobiography, reissued in 1975 and 1995, remains a valuable portrait of an African American working-class individualist, the kind of hero celebrated by Langston *Hughes and Claude *McKay.

—Farah Jasmine Griffin

GORDONE, CHARLES (1925–1995), playwright, actor, director, screenwriter, lecturer, and Pulitzer Prize recipient. When Charles Gordone became the first African American to receive a Pulitzer Prize for *drama in 1970 for *No Place to Be Somebody* (1969), *New York Times* drama critic Walter Kerr described him as "the most astonishing new American playwright since Edward Albee." The NAACP's *Crisis remarked that "Charles Gordone has definitely arrived." Although *No Place* was by far Gordone's most successful project, it marked the middle of an extensive career, spanning well over forty years, in writing, acting, directing, and teaching.

Gordone, born in Cleveland, Ohio, on 12 October 1925, grew up in Elkhart, Indiana. Excelling in academics and athletics, he still struggled to gain acceptance in a predominantly white section of town where he lived and among African Americans in the town who questioned his racial allegiance. Though his diverse racial heritage excited an early preoccupation with *identity that extended throughout his life and works, Gordone later, on numerous occasions, boasted of being "part Indian, part French, part Irish, and part nigger." Following a semester of study at UCLA and some time in the air force, Gordone studied *music at Los Angeles City College and subsequently received a degree in drama from California State University at Los Angeles in 1952.

After graduation Gordone moved to New York City to pursue acting and soon joined a Broadway production of Moss Hart's *Climate of Eden*, portraying the racially mixed character, Logan—a role he later revisited in 1961. In the 1950s and 1960s, while working in local theaters and managing Vantage, his own theater in Queens, Gordone directed several plays and continued a stage acting career. With few acting jobs available to African Americans, Gordone began writing out of necessity and, between performance engagements, worked as a waiter at Johnny Romero's, a Greenwich Village bar that later served as the framework for *No Place*. In 1961 Gordone performed in Jean Genet's *The Blacks* and shared the stage with a cast including Maya *Angelou, Godfrey Cambridge, James Earl Jones, and Cecily Tyson. He later cited this six-year experience as a cornerstone in his personal and artistic development. At another notable juncture in his acting career, Gordone, in an all–African American cast of John Steinbeck's *Of Mice and Men*, received an Obie Award for Best Performance in 1964.

Although he continued to distinguish himself as an actor and director, Gordone increased his political involvement off the stage. During the convulsant climate of the 1960s, Gordone served as chairman of the Committee for the Employment of Negro Performers, established in 1962 by the Congress of Racial Equality (CORE). A year later, he worked as the production manager for *The Negro in America*, a documentary funded by the United States Information Agency, and he accepted an appointment by President Lyndon Johnson to the Presidential Commission on Civil Disorders in 1968.

With the release of his first play *No Place* shortly thereafter, Gordone, like his contemporaries in the *Black Arts movement, converged political activism and artistic production. Between 1970 and 1977, Gordone directed national tours of *No Place* and, despite the accolades the play received, claimed the success of the play interrupted his creative momentum. However, Gordone continued to work against racial injustice and social disparity in the late 1970s as an instructor in the Cell Block Theatre Program, an effort to rehabilitate inmates in the New Jersey state prison system. As cofounder, along with Susan Kouyomijian, and director in residence of American Stage (1982–1985) in Berkeley, California, Gordone continued to challenge racial and cultural conceptions of the American theater and broadened the acting opportunities of African Americans, Latinos, and Asians by casting them in traditionally white roles.

In 1987 Gordone accepted a position as a distinguished lecturer at Texas A & M University, where he taught English and theater until his death in November 1995. In his later years Gordone remained active on stage as a playwright, director, and screenwriter. Through his work, Gordone probed the complexity of racial and cultural identity. Attempting to forge an inclusive American identity and to offer a poignant analysis of the place of African Americans in American society, Gordone emphasized the contiguity of human experience while underscoring the importance of an acknowledgment of racial and cultural

difference. Works to his credit include *No Place to Be Somebody* (1969), *Gordone Is a Mutha* (1970), *Baba Chops* (1975), *The Last Chord* (1976), *Anabiosis* (1979), and two incomplete works, "Roan Brown and Cherry" and "Ghost Riders."

• Warren Marr, "Black Pulitzer Awardees," *Crisis* 77 (May 1970): 186–188. Jean Ross, "Charles Gordone," in *DLB*, vol. 7, *Twentieth Century American Dramatists*, ed. John MacNicholas, 1987, pp. 227–231. Charles Gordone, "An Interview with Charles Gordone," interview by Susan Harris Smith, *Studies in American Drama, 1945–Present*, vol. 3, eds. Philip C. Kolin and Colby H. Kullman, 1988, pp. 122–132. Bernard L. Peterson, Jr., *Contemporary Black American Playwrights*, 1988.   —Charles Leonard

Go Tell It on the Mountain (1953) remains James *Baldwin's most critically acclaimed *novel. Its working titles—"In My Father's House" and "Crying Holy"—reflect its central concerns, as Baldwin himself explains: the novel "was about my relationship to my father and to the *church, which is the same thing really. It was an attempt to exorcise something, to find out what happened to my father, what happened to all of us" (*Conversations with James Baldwin*). Lyrically autobiographical, the book represents Baldwin's wrenching attempt to reconcile *religion, *family, and *sexuality. Ten years in the making, Baldwin finished the first draft in 1952 in Switzerland. Upon revision, Knopf published the novel in May 1953.

The tripartite novel innovatively tells the story of the Harlem-based Grimes family. Told from *John Grimes's perspective, "The Seventh Day" establishes his social and familial marginalization; the section opens with the plaintive boy wondering who will remember his fourteenth birthday. Based on the young Baldwin, John is berated constantly for his "ugliness," unmanliness, and intellect. We also witness the family's domestic strife: *Gabriel Grimes, John's stepfather, dominates his wife Elizabeth, John, and his siblings. The Pentecostal church provides the battlefield on which John wrestles with his hatred of Gabriel, his nascent homosexuality, and his estrangement.

Part 2, "The Prayers of the Saints," consists of flashbacks involving John's aunt, father, and mother. "Florence's Prayer" conveys how the uncaring mother prefers her son, Gabriel, to her daughter, Florence. Rejecting a constricting southern ethos, Florence flees to Harlem and marries Frank, a hard-drinking *blues singer; subsequently, she repudiates him for rejecting her middle-class American values. Ill and alone, Florence ultimately seeks refuge in the church while thwarting Gabriel's mistreatment of his family. "Gabriel's Prayer" exposes the minister's profligate past. Attempting to expiate for his sins and to attain power, he outwardly embraces the Lord and the barren Deborah, who was raped by white men. However, Gabriel engages Esther in an adulterous liaison, only to deny his own culpability by rejecting their son. "Elizabeth's Prayer" concludes the middle section, revealing how her life parallels John's. Reared by a "religious" aunt whom she despises, Elizabeth finds solace with Richard, one of Baldwin's archetypal sensitive, angry young men. After Richard's suicide, Elizabeth bears John and seeks atonement by marrying God's messenger, Gabriel.

Part 3, "The Threshing-Floor," recounts the Herculean struggle for John's soul. During a series of surrealistic visions, John hears voices summoning him to the Lord. However, his conversion is spurious: like Gabriel, he uses religion to reinvent himself and to control others. John metaphorically "kills" Gabriel and replaces him with God. However, John's transformation brings little relief from the squalid Harlem life that mocks him mercilessly. John's hope rests in his budding love for Brother Elisha, an older adolescent who conducts his spiritual pilgrimage.

In this resplendent text Baldwin synthesizes a black American family's struggles and innovative modernist techniques. His African American and Anglo-American influences are myriad: the cadences of black *sermons and preaching and *spirituals; the Joycean adolescent experience in which a boy must negotiate religion and the attendant sexual guilt; biblical stories such as Abraham's quest for an heir; and the Jamesian psychological novel that utilizes a free indirect narrative device. *Go Tell It on the Mountain* maintains a seminal place in Baldwin's oeuvre, with critic Bernard Bell calling it Baldwin's "most carefully wrought novel."

[See also Gay Literature; Preachers and Deacons.]

• Louis Pratt, *James Baldwin*, 1978. Horace A. Porter, *Stealing the Fire: The Art and Protest of James Baldwin*, 1989. Fred L. Standley and Louis H. Pratt, eds., *Conversations with James Baldwin*, 1989.   —Keith Clark

GRAHAM, LORENZ (1902–1989), novelist, short story writer, folklorist, educator, lecturer, and award-winning children's and young adult's author. Lorenz Bell Graham was born on 27 January 1902 in New Orleans, Louisiana, to Elizabeth Etta Bell Graham and David Andrew Graham, an African Methodist Episcopal (AME) minister whose duties led the family to various parts of the country. After attending and completing high school in Seattle, Graham pursued undergraduate study at the University of Washington in 1921; the University of California, Los Angeles from 1923 to 1924; and Virginia Union University in Richmond, Virginia, from 1934 to 1936, where he received his bachelor's degree.

One of the consequential events of Graham's life came when he interrupted his college studies at UCLA in 1924 in order to travel to Liberia, West Africa. The decision was initiated by a bishop of the AME Church who had established a school in Liberia and whom Graham had heard make a plea for the help of trained young people. He soon thereafter volunteered and was accepted to go to Liberia and teach, which he did from 1924 to 1928 at Monrovia College. While in Liberia, Graham met Ruth Morris, another missionary-teacher, and they were married on 20 August 1929. Before his exposure to Africa as a teacher and missionary, Graham was unfamiliar with African culture and admittedly held many misperceptions about what he would find. Shortly after his arrival, he began to see the uninformed and false nature of his views and came to the realization that the people of Africa were very much like the people in other lands.

As a result, Graham's tenure in West Africa provided a solid foundation for the kind of writing that he was to pursue upon his return to the United States. Graham often stated that his teaching experience in Africa gave him new insight on human diversity. He also became keenly aware of the "gap" in representations of Africans, and consequently of African Americans, in literature. He was increasingly convinced that writing could promote understanding and more truthful images of people of African descent, both in Africa and the United States. These experiences became the impetus and subject matter for much of his writing.

Graham's first major work, *How God Fix Jonah* (1946), recounts twenty-one stories of the Bible as told in West African idiom. Graham's use of biblical stories provided a way for him to encourage greater understanding of the African people and their common link with the American reader, both child and adult. Graham followed *How God Fix Jonah* with other African tales, namely *Tales of Momolu* (1946) and *I, Momolu* (1966), which observe the protagonist, Momolu, as he is initiated into *manhood and experiences events that mark his maturation process. Through these stories, the reader comes to know Momolu's family and the importance of the entire tribe to his development.

Graham's most acclaimed work is his *South Town* series, a succession of novels for young adults. In *South Town* (1958), Graham follows the Williams family through the various trials and obstacles that racism presents in their lives. *South Town* is followed by three installments: *North Town* (1965), *Whose Town* (1969), and *Return to South Town* (1976). The series focuses attention on David Williams as he and his family seek fairness of treatment and better opportunities in America. Graham stated that he was trying to establish with young people the idea that in every person is potential, and there is a need for struggle and courage and movement toward definite goals. Graham also parallels many of his characters' plights with those of his own lived experiences with racism and discrimination.

Included in his varied written work is a historical biography of John *Brown entitled *John Brown: A Cry for Freedom* (1980) and four novelettes for and about juveniles published in 1972. Graham received numerous awards for his work, including the Follett Award in 1958, the Child Study Association of America Award in 1959, and the Association for Study of Negro Life and History Award in 1959.

Graham's writing has a distinguished and substantial place in the history and production of multicultural literature for children and adolescents, as well as within the production of African American literature. Through his honest and moving portrayals of both African and African American life, Graham has contributed to the representation of these communities as self-determinant and courageous actors in the struggle for civil rights, human dignity, and the recognition and respect of human diversity.

[See also African Literature.]

• Lee Bennett Hopkins, *More Books by More People*, 1974. Rudine Sims, *Shadow and Substance: Afro-American Experience in Contemporary Children's Fiction*, 1982. Charles Irby, "A Melus Interview: Lorenz Bell Graham—Living with Literary History," *Melus* 12.2 (1985): 75–86. "Lorenz B. Graham," in *Children's Library Review*, ed. Gerard J. Senick, vol. 10, 1986, pp. 101–112. Ora Williams, "Lorenz Graham" in *DLB*, vol. 76, *Afro-American Writers, 1940–1955*, ed. Trudier Harris, 1988, pp. 57–66.   —Kim D. Hester Williams

GRAHAM, SHIRLEY (1896–1977), author, political activist, musical director, composer, and multitalented recipient of the National Academy of Arts and Letters Award for contributions to American literature. Shirley Lola Graham, the only daughter of Etta Bell Graham and Reverend David A. Graham, was born on 11 November 1896 in Indianapolis, Indiana, the oldest of five children. Free-spirited, talented, and ambitious, Graham resisted the shackles of *race and *gender. She divorced her first husband, worked to support two sons, and established a career for herself at a time when women had only recently gained the right to vote.

In 1926, Graham studied *music and French at the Sorbonne. Although her tenure there predates the *Negritude movement, her musical training was enriched by interaction with African and Afro-Caribbean students in Paris. In 1931, she enrolled with advanced standing as a sophomore at Oberlin College in Ohio. Her statement of intent there, recorded in the college's archives, made clear her goals of doing "constructive work with Negro music" and research in Africa.

Graham's breakthrough in musical *theater came when she turned her one-act play, *Tom-Tom*, into an opera. Billed as *Tom-Tom: An Epic of Music and the Negro* with an all-black cast, the widely publicized opera opened in June 1932 at Cleveland Stadium. It received mixed reviews, though most were positive. While not the first "all-Negro" opera some sources reported, it was the first produced by an African American woman.

Completing a bachelor's degree in 1934, and a master's in music history and fine arts at Oberlin in June 1935, Graham worked with the Federal Theater Project directing, designing sets, and composing musical scores that included the theme songs for John Brownwell's *Mississippi Rainbow* (1936) and Theodore *Ward's *Big White Fog* (1937). In 1938, a Rosenwald Fund grant financed two years of study at the Yale School of Drama, where she composed the music for Owen *Dodson's *Garden of Time* and then turned to writing plays. Her works include a musical entitled *Deep Rivers* (1939); *It's Morning* (1940), a one-act tragedy about a mother who contemplates infanticide; *I Gotta Home* (1940), a one-act drama; *Track Thirteen* (1940), a comedy for radio and her only published play; *Elijah's Raven* (1941), a three-act comedy; and *Dust to Earth* (1941), a three-act tragedy.

Graham's inability to make the plays commercially successful Broadway shows frustrated her, as a letter to W. E. B. *Du Bois (25 Apr. 1940) indicates, "If I had no responsibility other than myself I'd feel perfectly safe to strike out into the professional world and take what comes." Her positions became increasingly political. As director of the YWCA-USO at Fort Huachuca, Arizona, her politics against racism caused her dismissal. She went on to become NAACP field secretary in New York.

In 1951, Shirley Graham married Du Bois and moved to Ghana with him in 1961. While some biographers note that in Du Bois's shadow her work suffered or that her creative aspirations were submerged to his causes, closer observation reveals his causes were hers. She merely switched genres, using language instead of music. Her intent changed little from that articulated in 1931—to do research in Africa and to bring the achievements of African Americans to the attention of the world. The critical *biographies she wrote accomplish this goal.

Graham authored the following works: *Dr. George Washington Carver, Scientist* (1944), a biography for young readers; *Paul *Robeson: Citizen of the World* (1946), also for young readers; *There Once Was a Slave* (1947), the Messner Prize–winning historical novel on the life of Frederick *Douglass; *Your Most Humble Servant* (1949), the Anisfield-Wolf Prize–winning biography of Benjamin *Banneker; *The Story of Phillis *Wheatley* (1949); *The Story of Pocahantas* (1953); *Jean Baptiste Pointe duSable: Founder of Chicago* (1953); *Booker T. *Washington: Educator of Hand, Head, and Heart* (1955); *His Day Is Marching On* (1971), a memoir of W. E. B. Du Bois; *Gamal Abdel Nasser, Son of the Nile* (1972); *Zulu Heart* (1974), a novel set in South Africa; *Julius K. Nyerere: Teacher of Africa* (1975); and *A Pictorial History of W. E. B. Du Bois* (1976). Her most important political essays include "Egypt Is Africa," "The Struggle in Lesotho," and "The Liberation of Africa: Power, Peace and Justice," all published in the *Black Scholar* (May, Sept., and Nov. 1970). She also was founding editor of *Freedomways*.

Shirley Graham Du Bois died 27 March 1977 in Beijing, China, where she was undergoing treatment for cancer. Her music, plays, meticulously researched biographies for young people, her one novel unique in its portrayal of South African whites, and the political essays seasoned with firsthand experiences secure her place in African American arts and letters.

[*See also* Federal Writers' Project.]

• Herbert Aptheker, ed., *The Correspondence of W. E. B. Du Bois*, 2 vols., 1976. Kathy Perkins, "The Unknown Career of Shirley Graham," *Freedomways* 25 (1985): 6–18.

—Nagueyalti Warren

GRAVE DIGGER JONES is the constant partner of *Coffin Ed Johnson in the detective novels of Chester *Himes. Though the two African American detectives are very much alike, Grave Digger is often the more philosophical of the two, and he frequently acts as spokesperson for the pair. It is Grave Digger who offers most of Himes's commentary on U.S. racism and on the plight of urban African Americans living in poverty-stricken ghettos. Though Grave Digger is usually portrayed as the more rational of the two detectives, he can be brutal in his investigative tactics.

His gun, a custom-made long-barreled nickel-plated .38, is feared by all Harlemites inhabiting Himes's novels. Paradoxically, Coffin Ed and Grave Digger have hero/legend status among the citizens of their beat even though they work for a white-dominated police force and therefore are seen by many as upholding a white power structure that oppresses African Americans.

Grave Digger's comments throughout the novels show that the two detectives are keenly aware of the racial politics of police work in urban America. In several of the books, the arch criminal is a white man who is not a member of the Harlem community but who has entered the neighborhood to exploit its citizens. In such cases Grave Digger and Coffin Ed's ultimate aim is to restore order and protect the Harlem community from further invasion by the white police force. It is this double-edged nature of their characters, at once protectors and violent enforcers, that makes them complex literary creations.

• Gilbert H. Muller, *Chester Himes*, 1989. Robert E. Skinner, *Two Guns from Harlem: The Detective Fiction of Chester Himes*, 1989.   —Wendy W. Walters

GREAT MIGRATION. *See* Migration; Emigration.

GREEN, J. D. (1813–?), slave narrator. Jacob D. Green was born a slave in Queen Anne's County, Maryland, and during his boyhood served as a house servant on a large plantation owned by Judge Charles Earle. When he was twelve years old his mother was sold; he never saw her again. He began thinking of escape while a teenager but did not attempt it because religious teachings convinced him that running away from his master would be a sinful act. When his wife was sold away from him in 1839, however, Green made the first of three escape attempts, the last of which took him from Kentucky to Toronto, Canada, in 1848 and soon thereafter to England. Working as an antislavery lecturer, Green published his forty-three page *Narrative of the Life of J. D. Green, a Runaway Slave* in England in 1864. According to its title page, eight thousand copies of Green's *Narrative* were printed. The *Narrative* is notable for its depiction of Green as a wily and unapologetic slave *trickster who exploits whites and blacks alike to achieve his ends. Green's unsentimental, rough-and-tumble portrayal of life on the plantation is one of several distinctively unconventional features of his *Narrative*.

[*See also* Slave Narrative.]

• William L. Andrews, *To Tell a Free Story: The First Century of Afro-American Autobiography, 1760–1865*, 1986.
                              —William L. Andrews

GREEN, JOHN PATTERSON (1845–1940), essayist and autobiographer. John Patterson Green was born in Newbern, North Carolina, the son of free persons of color who left the state in 1857 to settle in Cleveland, Ohio. Green's formal education was spotty, but between odd jobs in his youth he studied on his own. In 1866, he had five of his school compositions printed under the title *Essays on Miscellaneous Sub-*jects by a Self-Educated Colored Youth, which he advertised and sold in an attempt to earn money. After graduating from Cleveland High School the same year, Green enrolled in law school, completing his degree in 1870. He returned to the South, was admitted to the South Carolina bar, and became active in Reconstruction politics. His perspective on this turbulent era is recorded in *Recollections of the Inhabitants, Localities, Superstitions, and Ku Klux Outrages of the Carolinas*, which Green published in 1880, seven years after his return to Ohio to pursue a successful legal and political career. *Recollections* interweaves Green's progressive, though not vindictive, Republican political views with local color commentary by a self-described "carpet-bagger." Establishing a successful criminal law practice in Cleveland, Green was twice elected to the Ohio State House of Representatives and, in 1892, to the State Senate. A respected stump speaker for several Republican presidential candidates, Green wrote numerous political articles for the Afro-American News Syndicate during the late nineteenth century. In 1920, he published his memoirs, *Fact Stranger than Fiction*, in which he celebrated his successes; articulated a moderate, middle-class position with regard to racial advancement; and reminisced admiringly about his relationships to a number of prominent men, including John D. Rockefeller and President William McKinley.

[*See also* Autobiography, *article on* Spiritual Autobiography; Journalism.]

• Russell H. Davis, *Black Americans in Cleveland*, 1972. Kenneth L. Kusmer, *A Ghetto Takes Shape: Black Cleveland, 1930–1970*, 1976.   —William L. Andrews

GREENFIELD, ELOISE (b. 1929), author of prize-winning children's books. Eloise Greenfield was born 17 May 1929, the second oldest of five children, in Parmele, North Carolina, during the early days of the Great Depression. Though money was scarce, Greenfield has fond memories of how family and neighbors made her childhood enjoyable. Influenced by her personal childhood memories and experiences, by observations, and by other stories she has read and heard about, Greenfield has created lively, humorous, rhythmic books and stories that are deeply rooted in reality. Her stories are for children ranging in age from prekindergarten to junior high school. One of her books, *Honey I Love* (1978), which is a collection of love poems, crosses age groups and is enjoyed by kindergartners, teens, and adults. In her stories, Greenfield tries to create what she describes as "word madness," or that feeling of excitement that one gets when reading (interview by Jean Ross in *Contemporary Authors*, 1987). To attain this "word madness" Greenfield explains that she tries to "choose and order words that children will celebrate." She wants children to "celebrate" such issues as family solidarity, relationships, Black heritage, and the joys and turmoils of everyday life.

Familial and platonic relationships are central themes in Greenfield's works. Several stories revolve around her idea that there is no monolithic, typical *family and that friendships are crucial to a child's growth and development. Presenting stories with families that are extended, that have single or both parents, and that have experienced divorce and sometimes death, several of Greenfield's works depict families coping with bad and good aspects of life. For example, in *Sister* (1974) a young girl copes with the death of a parent, and through the help of other family members, she attains the strength she needs to survive this ordeal. *Daddy and I* (1991) highlights the relationship between father and son and how they enjoy each other's company playing basketball and doing the laundry together. *Me and Nessie* (1975) is about best friends who want to play with each other all the time. *Big Friend, Little Friend* (1991) is the story of a child learning from an older friend who then teaches what he has learned to one of his younger friends.

Equally important to Greenfield is the significance of Black history and heritage to Black children. She has created books that provide true and positive portrayals of Black historical figures, heritage, and experiences. Greenfield feels that such portrayals instill in young Black readers a sense of self awareness and confidence that is threatened by superficial, stereotypical, and empty depictions of Blacks in *television. Some positive images that Greenfield feels "children needed to meet" are seen in her accessible autobiographies of Rosa Parks, Paul *Robeson, and Mary McLeod Bethune.

Greenfield wants her stories to provide "emotional sustenance" for children readers. Her stories tap into those emotions that are created by everyday experiences of playing, death, accidents, and divorce. Her stories help children better understand their emotions as legitimate and common. For instance, in *She Come Bringing Me That Little Baby Girl* (1974), Kevin must cope with feelings of envy and jealousy brought about by having to share his parents' love and attention with his new baby sister. *Alesia* (1981) is one of Greenfield's most poignant and touching stories. It speaks to the courage and strength of a young girl handicapped by a tragic childhood accident. Based on a true story, it shows Alesia's commendable determination to lead a normal life as an adolescent. A collection of poems, *Night on Neighborhood Street* (1991), deals with everyday life issues of young black children in urban communities. *Night on Neighborhood Street* depicts children playing with and missing their friends, confronting and avoiding drug dealers, attending church, entertaining parents, and participating in other typical everyday activities.

Greenfield has received several awards for her works, including the Carter G. Woodson Book Award; the Coretta Scott King Award; the American Library Association notable book citation; and the National Black Child Development Institute Award.

Greenfield's books add to the body of African American literature in several genres (*poetry, *biography, semiautobiography, and *novels) that provide insight into the life, history, and everyday experiences of Blacks and Black children. Her works instill in Black children a sense of self-confidence and awareness and an appreciation of Black art and writing.

• "Greenfield, Eloise," in *Something about the Author*, vol. 19, ed. Anne Commire, 1980, p. 43. Eloise Greenfield, interview by Jean Ross, in *Contemporary Authors: New Revision Series*, vol. 19, ed. Linda Metzger, 1987, pp. 215–218.
—Chanta M. Haywood

GREENLEE, SAM (b. 1930), poet, fiction writer, novelist, essayist, screenwriter, producer, director, actor, and teacher. Sam Greenlee has employed the Black literary tradition to produce such masterpieces as *The *Spook Who Sat by the Door* (1969) and *Baghdad Blues* (1976). Greenlee was born on 13 July 1930 in the heart of Chicago, Illinois. As a young man he attended the University of Wisconsin, where he received his BS in 1952. Greenlee further studied at the University of Chicago (1954–1957) and the University of Thessaloniki, Greece (1963–1964). His career started as a United States Information Agency Foreign Service Officer in Iraq, Pakistan, Indonesia, and Greece. His military service included time in the U.S. Army Infantry from 1952 to 1954. Greenlee received the *London Sunday Times* book of the year award in 1969 for *The Spook Who Sat by the Door*, and the Meritorious Service Award from the United States Information Agency. He currently resides in Chicago, Illinois.

In *The Spook Who Sat by the Door*, Greenlee presents a satirical *novel that criticizes the racist atmosphere of the United States by examining the life of a fictitious black CIA agent, Dan Freeman. It is evident that Greenlee creates his images from his experience in the military and United States Information Agency.

References to Freeman as a "spook" in both the title and the novel possess a sense of duality or *double consciousness: spook is used as a racial insult directed toward Blacks, in addition to being a slang term for spies. Greenlee uses this duality to establish a connection between Freeman's character and the African American experience during the turbulent 1960s, which parallels Greenlee's service time. With this multifaceted character, Greenlee begins to examine the mask that has been worn by African Americans for generations to hide their true feelings.

Greenlee is also known for such works as *Blues for an African Princess* (1971), a collection of poems. His novel *Baghdad Blues* (1976) and *Ammunition: Poetry and Other Raps* (1975) both deal with African Americans' pain, anger, and fear, particularly that of those who are caught up in the racism and oppression of government agencies.

Greenlee's contributions to the literary tradition in African American literature have caused his readers to examine closely the racial awareness or unawareness within agencies and institutions that are designed to serve all Americans. His presentation of African Americans' duality and paradoxical existence in a racist society is still providing scholars with text to investigate the themes of racism. Greenlee is masterful in his presentation of characters and community; his work is saturated with the African American literary tradition.

• Walter Burrell, "Rappin' with Sam Greenlee," *Black World* 20.9 (1971): 42–47. Catherine Starks, *Black Portraiture in American Fiction*, 1971.   —Wanda Macon

GRIGGS, SUTTON E. (1872–1933), novelist, essayist, biographer, publisher, Baptist minister, and pastor. Born in Chatfield, Texas, on 19 June 1872, the son of Reverend Allen R. Griggs, a pioneer Baptist preacher in Texas, Sutton Elbert Griggs attended public schools in Dallas, graduated from Bishop College in Marshall, Texas, and trained for the ministry at the Richmond Theological Seminary. While he held pastorates in Virginia and Tennessee he produced the thirty-three books (including five *novels) urging African American pride and self-help that garnered him widespread renown among African American readers. Because he established the Orion Publishing Company in Nashville, Tennessee, which promoted the sale of his books from 1908 until 1911, his works were probably more widely circulated among African Americans than the works of contemporaries Charles Waddell *Chesnutt and Paul Laurence *Dunbar. During the height of his creative production, both his writings and sermons militantly protested injustices and espoused the rights of his people. By 1920, however, when Griggs moved to Memphis and took up the pastorate of the Tabernacle Baptist Church, he had begun to temper his earlier fiery rhetoric and insistence upon African American self-determination and to emphasize instead interracial trust. In this spirit of cooperation, Griggs worked during World War I as a speaker in black communities in support of the purchase of Liberty Bonds. Increasingly during the last decade of his life, he devoted his energies to the *church. He served as president of the American Baptist Theological Seminary from 8 April 1925 to 1 October 1926, resigning to accept his father's former pastorate in Texas, where he died in Houston on 3 January 1933.

Griggs's novels reflect the aesthetic dilemmas of his predecessors in their attempts to sound an authentic African American voice through the strategies of nineteenth-century popular fiction; his novels also set the stage for twentieth-century political analyses and symbolic interpretations of *slavery and neoslavery experiences. Like earlier fictional representatives of their *race in African American literature, Griggs's heroes and heroines are counterstereotypes designed to refute racist images of African Americans in the public mind. All are extremely handsome or beautiful, cultured, talented, intellectual, virtuous, politically aware, and most are committed to either subversive or overt revolutionary action. Despite the complicated love entanglements of his novels, Griggs's focus is not on romance or adventure, but on the political realities and theories that his characters express. His fiction's primary function is to embody conflicting political possibilities for the "*New Negro" of the turn of the century and to highlight the consequences of *miscegenation, especially for African American women.

Griggs's first novel, *Imperium in Imperio* (1899), is a visionary, political work positing the establishment of a national, secret organization of revolutionary African Americans demanding either a complete redress of grievances or the formation of a separate state for their people. While sympathetic with this frustration and desire for autonomy, Griggs warns against self-serving political leaders whose quest for personal power guarantees the failure of the community's efforts. The Imperium and a selfless leader, Belton Piedmont, are both sacrificed by just such a demagogue, the *mulatto Bernard Belgrade. The personal destruction also intrudes into the domestic sphere; accepting racist, "scientific" theories of the time, Viola Martin, in love with Bernard, commits suicide rather than weaken the African American blood line by marrying a mulatto. In his second novel, *Overshadowed* (1901), Griggs lowers his sights from utopian plans for racial organization and nationhood to focus upon the destructive conflicts within the emerging African American middle class. His tone is satiric, ridiculing in particular the group's insecurity, which causes it to sacrifice its own members, like the hard-working Erma Wysong, on the altar of white social standards. This novel is Griggs's most pessimistic and Astral Herndon the most pitiful of his protagonists. Astral is merely representative of the personal frustrations of the new generation, with none of the necessary energy and perception to save either his people or himself. While also reflecting liberal rather than radical values, Dorlan Warthell in *Unfettered* (1902) is a clear contrast to the demoralized Astral. He severs his ties with the Republican party over the issue of imperialism, but when convinced by the expansionist-minded Morlene that America's presence in the Philippines will lead to cultural uplift for the Filipinos, he accepts the decisions of the national administration. Choosing to work with the African American masses, he rejects the opportunity to travel to Africa as the long-sought descendant of an African prince and, at Morlene's urging, develops "Dorlan's Plan" for ethnic cooperation based upon his people's economic self-determination. *The Hindered Hand* (1905) focuses on Ensal Ellwood who, like Dorlan, publishes a self-help essay offering practical methods of African American betterment. The novel also involves its heroine, Tiara Marlow, in an incredibly convoluted plot designed to demonstrate the fallacy Griggs saw in the schemes of the time to use light skin color to infiltrate the white power structure. Ensal reflects the ambivalence present in many turn-of-the-century African Americans who vacillated between feeling connected with, even dependent upon, Africa and, on the other hand, judging themselves superior to it. Baug Peppers of *Pointing the Way* (1908) is Griggs's final development of his New Negro. The young lawyer attempts to ensure aid for African American success by urging support of liberal, white southern politicians also desirous of such cooperation. Professionally more successful than any of Griggs's other leaders, Peppers appears before the Supreme Court to argue for African American voting rights. Although the outcome of this case is ignored by Griggs at the book's end in favor of a focus on romantic intrigue between Peppers and the victimized Eina, the work's final political view appears optimistic. Griggs's new professional has moved from Belton Piedmont in *Imperium in Imperio*, who is killed by his own people for his "treasonous" refusal to participate in a violent attack on the government, to Baug Peppers who is so honored by his fellows in *Pointing the Way* that he is allowed to represent their case for full citizenship before the country's highest court.

Like the characters he portrays, Sutton Griggs is a transitional figure. His allegiance to the modes of sentimental fiction and flashes of Emersonian optimism and trust in ethnic cooperation blunt the edge of his protest and dim his utopian vision. Nevertheless, his promotion of political activism and self-determination clearly establish Griggs, like Martin *Delany, as a middle-class forerunner to the revolutionary artists of the 1960s.

[*See also* Black Nationalism; Insurrections; Publishing; Protest Literature.]

• Ruth Marie Powell, *Lights and Shadows, The Story of the American Baptist Theological Seminary, 1924–64,* 1964. Arlene A. Elder, *The "Hindered Hand": Cultural Implications of Early African American Fiction,* 1978. Wilson J. Moses, "Literary Garveyism: The Novels of Reverend Sutton E. Griggs," *Phylon* 40.3 (Fall 1979): 203–216. James Kinney, *Amalgamation!: Race, Sex, and Rhetoric in the Nineteenth-Century American Novel,* 1985. Steven C. Tracy, "Saving the Day: The Recordings of the Reverend Sutton E. Griggs," *Phylon* 47.2 (1986): 159–166.   —Arlene A. Elder

GRIMKÉ, ANGELINA WELD (1880–1958), poet, playwright, essayist, and short fiction writer of the Harlem Renaissance. Although Angelina Weld Grimké's writings appeared in many leading publications of the *Harlem Renaissance, such as Alain *Locke's The *New Negro* (1925), Countee *Cullen's *Caroling Dusk* (1927), and Charles S. Johnson's *Ebony and Topaz* (1927), she was not a highly visible member of the literary movement, perhaps because of her retiring personality. The product of a biracial marriage, Grimké grew up in the progressive, aristocratic society of old Boston. Named for her white great-aunt, Angelina Grimké Weld, the famous abolitionist and advocate of women's rights, young Angelina was reared by her devoted but demanding father, Archibald *Grimké, the son of Charleston aristocrat Henry Grimké, and his slave, Nancy Weston. Angelina's white mother, Sarah Stanley Grimké, separated from her father in Angelina's early childhood, presumably because of mental and physical illness. Angelina's family background informed the style and content of her literary works. Her father's high standards impelled her to aspire toward the "*talented tenth" and to create *poetry that was polished and formal. Her heritage of social activism influenced her to use her fiction and *drama as propagandist tools. The absence of her mother during her early childhood accounts for her interest in motherhood in much of her drama and fiction.

Angelina's initial writings and publications occurred in verse, with poems appearing in the early 1900s in such *periodicals as the *Colored American Magazine,* the *Boston Transcript,* and the *Pilot.* Turning from poetry and fiction to drama, she produced her most prominent work, *Rachel,* a sentimental so-

cial protest play performed in Washington, D.C., in 1916 and then published in 1920. Depicting the effects of *lynching on an African American *family and the sadness of having children in a racist society, this drama was the first by an African American playwright to be performed by African American actors for a white public. Although some critics praised it for its dramaturgical skills, others faulted its sentimentality, a feature that was less pronounced in Grimké's second and last, but unpublished, drama, "Mara," which explored similar themes. Considered the least impressive of her works, her *short stories also probed the subject of racial injustice, notably in "The Closing Door," a tale of lynching and infanticide published in *The Birth Control Review* of 1919. Grimké is best known for her poetry, whose hallmark is its brevity, well-wrought images, and pensive moods. Its themes range from the loss of love, especially that of a woman, to tributes to famous people, to the contemplation of nature, to philosophical and racial issues. Grimké's love sonnets, addressed to women from the perspectives of white male personae, have led feminist scholars to reclaim her as a lesbian poet. Unfortunately, much of her work has been ignored, partly because she was eclipsed, as a woman, by the male literati of the Harlem Renaissance.

• Gloria T. Hull, *Color, Sex, and Poetry: Three Women Writers of the Harlem Renaissance,* 1987. Helene Keyssar, "Rites and Responsibilities: The Drama of Black American Women," in *Feminine Focus: The New Women Playwrights,* ed. Enoch Brater, 1989. Carolivia Herron, ed., *Selected Works of Angelina Weld Grimké,* 1991.   —Mary C. Carruth

GRIMKÉ, ARCHIBALD (1849–1930), scholar, essayist, and activist. Born a slave in Charleston, South Carolina, Archibald Henry Grimké was the nephew of white abolitionists Sarah Grimké and Angelina Grimké Weld, brother of Francis J. *Grimké, and father of the poet Angelina Weld *Grimké. Grimké was educated at Lincoln University in Pennsylvania and Harvard Law School, from which he graduated in 1874.

Grimké's literary career began in 1884, when he became editor of the Boston *Hub,* a Republican newspaper. In 1886, he resigned his editorship, having switched to the Democratic party, but continued to speak and write, focusing on African American rights, women's suffrage, and tariff reform. After serving as consul to the Dominican Republic from 1894 to 1898, he engaged almost exclusively in racial and intellectual activism. He was president of the influential American Negro Academy from 1903 to 1919. He became a major figure in the turn-of-the-century debates over Booker T. *Washington's policies, opposing Washington's views but seeking a middle ground between the factions those views had created within the African American leadership. After 1913, he devoted himself to the NAACP, receiving the NAACP's Spingarn Medal in 1919.

As a writer, Grimké was influenced by the abolitionist tradition. Author of major *biographies of William Lloyd Garrison (1891) and Charles Sumner (1892), Grimké found in the careers of both a role he coveted for himself. He published widely throughout his lifetime and did much to set the terms for debate within the African American community, as well as in the challenge to American racism. His efforts were especially important in the development of an economic interpretation of racial discrimination, and in the identification of bases for racism in a white calculus of sexual gains and losses. Through his efforts, Grimké helped to mold both the organizational and intellectual frameworks for African American thought in the twentieth century.

• Dickson D. Bruce, Jr., *Archibald Grimké: Portrait of a Black Independent*, 1993.   —Dickson D. Bruce, Jr.

GRIMKÉ, CHARLOTTE FORTEN. *See* Forten, Charlotte.

GRIMKÉ, FRANCIS J. (1850–1937), theologian and minister. Frances James Grimké was born a slave in Charleston, South Carolina, younger brother of Archibald *Grimké and nephew of white abolitionists Sarah Grimké and Angelina Grimké Weld. Educated at Lincoln University in Pennsylvania and at Princeton Theological Seminary, he became minister of the elite Fifteenth Street Presbyterian Church in Washington, D.C., upon his graduation in 1878. In that same year, he married the writer and former abolitionist Charlotte *Forten. Excepting a period from 1885 to 1889, when he pastored a *church in Jacksonville, Florida, he held the Washington post until his retirement in 1928.

Grimké combined pastoral duties with scholarship as a leading figure in the turn-of-the-century fight against racial injustice. Influenced by the Calvinist tradition to which he was exposed at Princeton, Grimké was noted for the intellectual rigor of his thought and his conservative approach to *religion. Stressing the absolute sovereignty of God, and a view of Christian discipline that admitted little deviation, he formulated a prophetic condemnation of American racial discrimination. An uncompromising integrationist, he opposed both white supremacy and separatist tendencies within African American thought.

But Grimké's greatest influence derived from his role as an intellectual. His home was always a salon for the Washington African American intellectual elite. He was also a major figure in such organizations as Washington's Bethel Literary and Historical Association, a center for discussion and debate in the late nineteenth and early twentieth centuries, and a founder and active participant in the American Negro Academy, the foremost African American scholarly body before World War I. Helping to give a militant edge to both organizations, Grimké also aided in the creation of networks that encouraged the formation of an African American intellectual community during the period. Such efforts did much to organize African American intellectual life through the *Harlem Renaissance and beyond.

• Carter G. Woodson, ed., *The Works of Francis James Grimké*, 4 vols., 1942. Henry Justin Ferry, "Francis James Grimké: Portrait of a Black Puritan," PhD diss., Yale University, 1970.   —Dickson D. Bruce, Jr.

GRIT, BRUCE. *See* Bruce, John E.

GRONNIOSAW, JAMES ALBERT UKAWSAW (c. 1710–?), spiritual and slave autobiographer. *A Narrative of the Most Remarkable Particulars in the Life of James Albert Ukawsaw Gronniosaw, An African Prince* appeared in London in 1770, related by a former slave from America in need of financial support for his family. In the work, Gronniosaw mentions how the Puritan spiritual writers John Bunyan and Richard Baxter influenced him. Thus, he tells his life story in accordance with the spiritual autobiography's traditional pattern of sin, conversion, and subsequent rebirth.

The narrative deals with Gronniosaw's remembrance of Africa, where he was kidnapped and sold into *slavery. Transported to Barbados, he was resold to a young gentleman in New York and later to a minister who taught him about Christianity. A schoolmaster generously offered instructional services to the young slave, who gained *freedom when his master died. Gronniosaw then worked aboard various ships until he settled in England. There he married "white Betty" and, some years later, took his family to live in a religious community. However, their lives were marred by poverty and misfortune due in large part to racial discrimination and prejudice.

A popular work that ran through many editions, Gronniosaw's narrative was known by other ex-slave writers. By using the spiritual autobiographical form to relate his life experience, he no doubt influenced the pattern of slave writing that emerged in England and America. Gronniosaw is mentioned by Olaudah *Equiano in his 1789 two-volume autobiography, which became the model for the *slave narrative genre that developed in the nineteenth century during the abolitionist era.

[*See also* Autobiography, *article on* Spiritual Autobiography.]

• Henry Louis Gates, Jr., "James Gronniosaw and the Trope of the Talking Book," *Southern Review* 22 (April 1986): 252–272. Angelo Costanzo, *Surprizing Narrative: Olaudah Equiano and the Beginnings of Black Autobiography*, 1987.
                          —Angelo Costanzo

GUNN, BILL (1934–1989), playwright, novelist, screenplay writer, and actor. Bill Gunn's literary and dramatic talents found expression in a number of provocative, if obscure, *novels, plays, and *films. William Harrison Gunn was born to a middle-class African American family in Philadelphia, where he attended integrated public schools. His mother, Louise Alexander Gunn, was an actress who formed and ran her own theater group; his father, William Harrison Gunn (also Bill Gunn), was an unpublished poet, musician, and comedian.

After a stint in the navy, Gunn moved to New York City to become an actor. While moderately successful in the 1950s and 1960s as a Broadway and Off-Broadway performer, Gunn turned to writing plays in the late 1950s. His first play, *Marcus in the High Grass*, was produced in Westport, Connecticut, in 1958. Although *Marcus* was not directly concerned with racial issues, the characters were written as

African American; nevertheless, the production management of the play elected to cast the play with white actors. This fact is worth noting because from 1958 on, Gunn's literary work—both plays and novels—steadily developed a racial consciousness. Indeed, his writing gave him an opportunity to ponder the implications of racial *identity for one's art and one's understanding of self.

Gunn's first novel, *All the Rest Have Died* (1964), was his first work to raise these issues explicitly, although the issue of racial identity remains secondary to the broader themes of personal development and self-discovery. Influenced by French existentialist novelists like Camus and Sartre, *All the Rest Have Died* records the experiences of a young African American actor, Barney Gifford, seeking his future in New York City. Barney spends most of the novel unwittingly living life for and through a dead cousin (light-skinned and blond) who had similarly come to New York to act but was killed in a freak accident. With the help of some erratic artist friends, Barney comes to recognize his failure to live for himself and to know himself. As would become typical of Gunn's career, this novel received far less critical attention than did his plays.

In later works, Gunn's increasing interest in racial issues focused on the role of the African American artist. In his plays *Johannas* (1968) and *Black Picture Show* (1975), for which Gunn won the Audelco Award for best playwright, as well as in his last novel, *Rhinestone Sharecropping*, the African American artist is depicted as being at odds with the greed, racism, and commercialism of the white world. For the African American man, artistic talent is both a blessing and a curse: while offering escape from poverty and obscurity, its integrity is inevitably challenged and exploited by a crass white world. The influence of contemporary African American writers is felt most strongly in *Rhinestone Sharecropping*, which closes with an embittered and exploited screenplay writer quoting James *Baldwin: "When you finish crying, then what you gonna do? Get up. Get up."

• Noel Schraufnagel, *From Apology to Protest: The Black American Novel*, 1973, pp. 123–135. Ilona Leki, "Bill Gunn," in *DLB*, vol. 38, *Afro-American Writers after 1955: Dramatists and Prose Writers*, eds. Thadious M. Davis and Trudier Harris, 1985, pp. 109–114.   —Katherine J. Mayberry

GUY, ROSA (b. 1925), internationally acclaimed writer of adult and young people's fiction centering on the African diaspora and cofounder of the Harlem Writers Guild. Rosa Cuthbert Guy is of dual heritage—born in Trinidad, she grew up in Harlem, where events in her own life shaped her creative outlook, forming her unforgettable themes and characters. Rosa and her sister Ameze were left with relatives when their parents Audrey and Henry Cuthbert emigrated to the United States in 1927. The girls joined their parents in 1932, and briefly the family was united; however, in 1933, Rosa's mother became ill and the children were sent to Brooklyn to live with a cousin. The cousin was a Garveyite whose politics of *black nationalism profoundly affected young

Rosa. In 1934, Rosa's mother died and she and her sister returned to Harlem to live with their father who remarried. The girls lived briefly with a stepmother until 1937, when their father then died.

Poised on the threshold of adolescence, then orphaned in New York, Guy's experiences breathe life into her works for young people. Guy's maturation process, made difficult by her outsider status in the African American community because she was West Indian, produced a vision that scrutinized both worlds. Following their father's death, Rosa and her sister lived in an orphanage. At age fourteen, Guy left school to work in a brassiere factory in the garment district.

In 1941, Rosa met and married Warner Guy. She was sixteen. While her husband served in World War II, Guy continued to work in the factory but sought creative ways to express herself. A coworker introduced Guy to the American Negro Theater (ANT). ANT, established in 1940, proved a launching pad for such actors as Sidney Poitier and Ruby Dee. Guy did not perform in any of the theater productions but studied acting there. In 1942, she gave birth to Warner, her only child.

When the war ended, Guy moved with her husband and son to Connecticut. Five years later her marriage dissolved and she returned to New York and resumed her factory job. Again she sought the artistic community, but the thriving theater group had vanished. Another organization, the Committee for the Negro in the Arts, had replaced it. The committee's purpose was to eliminate racial *stereotypes in the arts. Interaction with this group resulted in Guy writing and performing in her first play, *Venetian Blinds* (1954), a successful one-act play produced Off-Broadway at the Tropical Theater.

The committee enabled Guy to meet many artists, some of them writers, including John O. *Killens. Killens and she shared similar aims, wanting to project an authentic black voice in their works. Guy's artistic orientation predates the *Black Arts movement and probably owes a debt to the Garvey movement. In 1951, Guy and Killens formed a workshop that became the Harlem Writers Guild. With such participants as Paule *Marshall, Audre *Lorde, Douglas Turner *Ward, and Maya *Angelou, the workshop achieved fame long before Guy ever published her first work. Between 1951 and 1970, more than half of all successful African American writers were associated with the workshop.

The workshop and Killens provided the encouragement Guy needed to perfect her craft. In spite of her limited schooling, working, and single-parenting, Guy had no choice but to write. Although she never directly said so, her works seem to indicate that she was, in fact, writing to save her life—or more specifically, writing herself into being. She states that writing "was a driving force in that orphan, out there on the streets . . . who needed something through which to express herself, through which to become a full-bodied person" (Jerrie Norris, *Presenting Rosa Guy*, 1988).

Guy's first published works consist of two *short stories of which there are no surviving copies. "The

Carnival," reflecting her West Indian heritage, and another her New York experience, were published in a Trinidadian newspaper by C. L. R. James, who in 1960 was editor. *Bird at My Window* (1966), Guy's first *novel, received mixed reviews. J. Saunders *Redding's now famous remark was the most negative criticism, claiming that "preoccupation with repossessing a heritage had led to distortion of values and reality . . . making heroes out of heels" (*Crisis,* Apr. 1966). Guy's protagonist, Wade Williams, like her former husband who was murdered, was destroyed by poverty and racism. She dedicated the novel to *Malcolm X, calling him "pure gold salvaged from the gutter of the ghettos."

The assassinations of Malcolm X and Martin Luther *King, Jr., prompted Guy to embrace another genre. She wanted to know how *violence affected young people and traveled South for the first time in her life to interview her subjects. *Children of Longing* (1970), a collection of *essays, resulted from her investigations. However, the work upon which Guy's reputation as a writer is based is her trilogy for young adults: *The Friends* (1973); *Ruby* (1976); and *Edith Jackson* (1978). The trilogy gives new meaning to the *bildungsroman tradition, including *race, *gender, culture, and *class previously missing from this genre.

Guy's other books include *The Disappearance* (1979), the first in a series about young detective Imamu Jones; *Mirror of Her Own* (1981), which focuses on white characters and received mixed reviews; *Mother Crocodile* (1981), an adaptation of an African fable for younger readers; *New Guys Around the Block* (1983), the second Imamu Jones book; *A Measure of Time* (1983), an adult novel that reached number one on the best-seller list in England; *Paris, Peewee, and Big Dog* (1984), another highly praised novel; *My Love, My Love, or The Peasant Girl* (1985), a novel based on "Little Mermaid"; *And I Heard a Bird Sing* (1987), the third in the Imamu Jones trilogy; *The Ups and Downs of Carl Davis III* (1989); *Billy the Great Child* (1991); *The Music of Summer* (1992); and *Caribbean Carnival: Songs of the West Indies* (1992), a collection of songs for children.

Guy's approach to her audience, adults as well as young readers, is sincere and honest. She says "a novel . . . is an emotional history of a people in time and place" ("Young Adult Books," *Horn Book Magazine,* 1985). Her works expose her own emotional history as the young West Indian woman, dislocated and marginalized, often longing for love and acceptance. We see also Guy's understanding of the African American urban experience. Utilizing her particular emotional history, loneliness, and pain she speaks to readers over chasms of generations and cultures about the experiences of life.

• J. Saunders Redding, review of *Bird at My Window, Crisis* 103.3 (Apr. 1966): 225–227. Jerrie Norris, *Presenting Rosa Guy,* 1988.

—Nagueyalti Warren

H

HAIR. In her 1985 HBO special, comedian Whoopi Goldberg, assuming the persona of a six-year-old black girl, drapes a white shirt around her head and pretends the shirt is her "long luxurious blonde hair." Ashamed of her own short, thick Nubian dreadlocks, the young girl complains: "it don't blow in the wind, it don't cas-sca-sca-dade down my back, and when I put that bouncin' and behavin' stuff on it, it didn't even listen." Such a routine cuts at the heart of Americans' Eurocentric and allegedly definitive images of ideal female beauty. And popular culture of the past—such as minstrel and coon songs like Gussie Davis's "When They Straighten All the Colored People's Hair" (1894), Stephen Foster's "Uncle Ned" (1900), Raymond Egan's "Mammy's Little Coal Black Rose" (1916), and Sidney D. Mitchell's "Mammy's Chocolate Soldier" (1918)—and the present—1990s television commercials like Pro-Line's "Just for Me," Dark & Lovely's "Excelle," and Luster's "PCJ Pretty-N-Silky," and magazine advertisements like TCB's "Bone Straight," "Good Hair," and Revlon's "Creme of Nature," and any number of Black Entertainment Television music videos—continues to reflect tensions between the hair ideal as white, the undesirable as black. Indeed hair has become one of the most prominent traits in helping to define *identity in racial terms—its length, texture, alleged manageability, and care. To those African Americans who subscribe to this Eurocentric hair ideal, "good hair" is smooth, silky, long, straight, fine, bouncy, shiny, capable of being "let down," wind-tossed, flung, of having fingers run through it with ease, and "cas-sca-sca-dading" down the back, traits commonly associated with whites' hair. The opposite of this ideal—"bad hair" (not connected with the temporary circumstances of a "bad hair" day)—is short, tightly matted, coarse, nappy, kinky, curly, steel wooly, and dull, traits associated with blacks' hair. While many African Americans—old and young alike—know all too well this deeply ingrained desire to have and to celebrate "good hair," black feminist theorist and activist bell *hooks admits that "no one says so. No one says your hair is so nice, so beautiful because it is like white folks' hair. We pretend that the standards we measure our beauty by are our own invention— that it is questions of time and money that lead us to make distinctions between good hair and bad hair" ("Black Is a Woman's Color," 1989). Both hooks ("Straightening Our Hair," 1992) and Alice *Walker ("Oppressed Hair Puts a Ceiling on the Brain," 1988) move this discussion beyond the level of black female coming-of-age and community ritual.

Mabel Lincoln, in a personal testimonial concerning the legacy of *slavery, admits in John L. Gwaltney's *Drylongso: A Self-Portrait of Black America* (1980), "Too many black folks are fools about color and hair. That is probably the most mixed-up thing in this world." Certainly, intraracist ideals of "good" and "bad" hair are rooted in African Americans' slave past. With forced *miscegenation rampant on slave plantations, not only did blacks' skin tones become more variable, hence connecting lighter skin with a white ideal and darker tones with an undesirable element, but differences in hair textures occurred as well. Willie Morrow's docudrama "Four-Hundred Years Without a Comb: The Inferior Seed" (1989) and Naomi Sims's *All about Hair Care for the Black Woman* (1982) explain that slave women's alleged ease at grooming masters' and mistresses' children's hair often led to internalized feelings of inferiority about the texture and alleged manageability of their own hair; such feelings of inferiority were sometimes overt in their rejection of their own children's hair and in their wearing of kerchiefs to shield their perceived aesthetically displeasing hair from white superiors. And since light-complected slaves closer to masters' and mistresses' skin color generally had "good hair" that was closer to whites', these slaves were the "privileged" house slaves; darker-skinned slaves with "bad hair" remained in the fields—hence the beginnings of a caste hierarchy that created intraracism. Slaves not born with "good hair" often turned to chemicals like axle grease and lye to make their hair temporarily straight, slick, and subsequently longer. In their minds, they came as close as they could to this perceived hair ideal. Once legally emancipated, some African Americans remained enslaved by a beauty ideal associated with hair. Madame C. J. Walker's phenomenally popular invention of the straightening comb (1907) and the subsequent creation of chemical relaxers were avenues for achieving one aspect of the American ideal.

Continual exposure to beauty ideals regarding hair occurs early in black children's experiences. The impact on black females particularly is effectively addressed in works by Maya *Angelou, Toni *Morrison, Zora Neale *Hurston, and Lorraine *Hansberry, among others.

Young Marguerite in Maya Angelou's *I Know Why the Caged Bird Sings* (1970) offers testimony of a personal conflict between a white beauty ideal and her perceived black ugliness. She reconciles this tension through fantasizing about hair that is "long and blond."

*Pecola Breedlove in Toni Morrison's *The *Bluest Eye* (1970) prays desperately for the bluest eyes because "all the world had agreed that a blue-eyed, yellow-haired, pink-skinned doll was what every girl treasured," and she extrapolates these values to her own person. Attacking these perceived beauty ideals, Morrison demonstrates the psychological and social self-destruction of a community trapped in W. E. B. *Du Bois's realm of *double consciousness (*The *Souls of Black Folk*, 1903). In *Their Eyes Were Watching God* (1937), to the men around *Janie Crawford, herself a *mulatto, it is her hair—hair that "swings down her back to her waist and unravels in the wind"—that largely defines her sexuality and sensuality.

Hair is again an issue for the young college-educated black female in Lorraine Hansberry's A *Raisin in the Sun* (1959). *Beneatha Younger is convinced by her Nigerian suitor that her straightened hair contradicts her alleged new-found connection with her African roots. When Beneatha cuts her processed hair, she is ridiculed by Ruth, Walter, and George who represent in this instance cultural assimilation, particularly as related to black women's hair options. Hairstyle and dress do not necessarily signify automatic celebration of African heritage and culture any more than processed hair necessarily signifies cultural assimilation or physical mutilation (*The *Autobiography of Malcolm X*, 1964).

This caste system among blacks is never more revealing than in the discussion of "good hair" and "bad hair" in Spike *Lee's *film *School Daze* (1988), which features the musical number "Straight and Nappy: Good and Bad Hair," performed by light-complected Wannabees with hair weaves and extensions, bleached blond hair coloring, and blue contacts, and darker-skinned Jigaboos with tight locks and short cropped Afros.

This "hair issue" as it relates specifically to black female identity is explored at length by black feminist dramatists Adrienne *Kennedy and Ntozake *Shange, who both use hair as a central metaphor in positing racial and feminist statements. In *Funnyhouse of a Negro* (1964), Kennedy uses accelerated female balding to represent a black female's racial and ancestral self-hatred that leads to her own self-destruction.

Ntozake Shange's *spell #7: geechee jibara quik magic trance manual for technologically stressed third world people* (1979) offers two segments that connect hair with black female beauty. Challenging the myth that black people's hair is "too nappy to be beautiful," a black female actor imagines herself the black counterpart to Rapunzel. Accompanying her monologue with fastidious hairbrushing motions, the actor concludes that a life controlled by hairbrushing, head tossing, and hair flinging is one void of meaning and possibilities for full selfhood. The image of Rapunzel recurs in a second fantasy exercise about white females. In "being a white girl for a day," another actor explains, "today i'm gonna be a white girl . . . the first thing a white girl does in the morning is fling her hair."

While head hair continues to be a social differential and a manifestation of social ideals, some of these alleged hair ideals are consciously exploded through redefinition, comedy, and direct inversion. Some black writers, Richard *Wright for instance, use the image of black hair as "wooly" as a term of identification within black communities. When he writes of the playful battle that turns bloody in his autobiographical *essay, "The Ethics of Living Jim Crow" (*Uncle Tom's Children*, 1938), he uses "wooly" as a term of endearment instead of an antithesis of a silky hair ideal.

Comedy is also used by African Americans to at-

tack ideals directly associated with hair. For instance, Fox Network's *In Living Color* regularly satirizes African Americans' attraction to wet, drippy, Jheri curls. Roseann P. Bell, in her *short story "The Three-Token Stradivarius" (*Black Erotica*, 1992), writes of a middle-aged black female sexually attracted to a younger black man but amusingly distracted by this man's "scary" Jheri curl. The woman asks the man about his curl: "I want you to tell me why a good-looking twenty-nine-year old fine specimen like you is wearing that greasy shit in your head." *In Living Color* also regularly includes skits of a decidedly unattractive black woman, Wanda, played by a male, who, in addition to her other exaggerated physical features—lips and backside—wears a blond disheveled wig. And rhythm and blues group Bobby Jimmy and the Critters' "Hair or Weave?" (Priority Records, 1990) parodies black women's alleged obsession with long hair weaves that they try to pass off as their own "natural" hair.

Some public figures who identify themselves and whom others recognize and accept as racially political and social activists such as comedian Whoopi Goldberg, singer-actor Patti LaBelle, actor-director Debbie Allen, and rapper Sistah Souljah intentionally challenge public perceptions with their daringness to wear long, flowing, straight wigs to contradict the white faces that usually accompany this hair. Sister Souljah's straight shoulder-length ponytail is attached to her short curly hair. Even model Naomi Campbell's thigh-length straight hair inverts this racial ideal. Comedian Sinbad, singers Donna Summer and Mary J. Blige, poet Nikki *Giovanni, and actor Jada Pickett have been blond for short periods, and black feminist poet-playwright Ntozake Shange has had shoulder-length braids with blond tips. Clearly this subversiveness is not based on "celebrity" or "noncelebrity" status but rather on individuals' motives and publicly acknowledged attitudes toward that hairstyle and the politics of hair. Such creative moves explode the boundaries of an alleged monolithic Eurocentric beauty ideal. Drag supermodel Ru-Paul celebrates the diversity and sociology of blacks' hairstyles in her music video "Back to My Roots" (1993) and often performs in big, bleached blond wigs. Even basketball star Dennis Rodman has been blond for some time.

The centrality of head hair consciously and subconsciously has long been documented in African American culture. Hairstyles, textures, and lengths signal complex ideologies and aesthetics—ascribed, manipulated, and absorbed—that continue to contribute to both racial and gender oppression. Ntozake Shange's epigram to her poetry collection *nappy edges* (1972) affirms a richness of African Americans' hair, a richness that redefines, legitimizes, and celebrates African American experience and identity: "the roots of your hair / what turns back when we sweat, run, make love, dance, get afraid, get happy: the tell-tale sign of living." Celebrating black identity in one of its rawest forms, Shange reveals here the reality that no matter how straight blacks' hair can become, the ever-growing roots are a constant reminder of that black person's truer physiological and even psychological identity. Gwendolyn *Brooks in her poem "To Those of My Sisters Who Have Kept Their Naturals (Never to Look a Hot Comb in the Teeth)" echoes Shange's celebration of black folks' natural hair order: "Your hair is Celebration in the world!"

To suggest that those with straightened or chemically processed hair are falsely aware of their racial or cultural identity does not acknowledge the complexity of this issue. While some consciously subvert racially biased beauty ideals associated with hair, ultimately an individual's motives can only be determined by that individual, if realized at all. Certainly an important element in hairstyles and hairstyling involving colors and textures and other options involves personal choice or preference, perhaps nothing more and nothing less. Acknowledging individual choice does not, however, prevent social, cultural, and political debates regarding our responses to others' hairstyles and textures. And the return to straightening and relaxing after the Afro—an alleged symbol of *black nationalism and racial awareness after 1965—does not necessarily reveal self-hatred or false consciousness. Whether blacks, particularly women, are changing their hair textures as "fashion" or as part of black women's rituals of sociability and community, the hair issue is alive and well in African American communities. Despite progressive moves consciously toward *Afrocentricity in styles and attitudes toward hair—its styling, its textures, and even its colorings—head hair remains a controversially heated and often publicly neglected or deliberately shunned dimension of the complex nuances and textures of African American identity and behavior.

[See also Beautician; Class; Talented Tenth, The.]

• Ayoka Chenzira, Hairpiece: A Film for Nappy-Headed People, Women Make Movies, 1985. "Intra-Racism," The Oprah Winfrey Show, Transcript #W172 (12 May 1987): 1–11. George C. Wolfe, "The Hairpiece," in The Colored Museum, 1987, pp. 19–23. Alice Walker, "Oppressed Hair Puts a Ceiling on the Brain," Ms., June 1988, 52–53. Audre Lorde, "Is Your Hair Still Political?," Essence, Sept. 1990, 40. Paulette M. Caldwell, "A Hair Piece: Perspectives on the Intersection of Race and Gender," Duke Law Journal, 1991, 365–396. bell hooks, "Straightening Our Hair," in Reading Culture: Contexts for Critical Reading and Writing, eds. Diana George and John Trimbur, 1992, pp. 290–299. Kathy Russell et al., "Hair: The Straight and Nappy of It All," in The Color Complex: The Politics of Skin Color among African Americans, 1992, pp. 81–93. Marcia Ann Gillespie, "Mirror, Mirror," Essence, Jan. 1993, 73–74, 96. Kim Green, "The Pain of Living the Lye," Essence, June 1993, 38. Paulette M. Caldwell, "A Hair Piece," in Life Notes: Personal Writings by Contemporary Black Women, ed. Patricia Bell-Scott, 1994, pp. 142–147. Henry Louis Gates, Jr., "In the Kitchen," New Yorker, 18 Apr. 1994, 82–85. Veronica Chambers, "Blond Like Me," New York Magazine, 25 June 1995, 49.   —Neal A. Lester

HALEY, ALEX (1921–1992), journalist and novelist. Born on 11 August 1921 in Ithaca, New York, Alexander Murray Palmer Haley grew up in Henning, Tennessee, the first of three sons to Simon Henry Haley, a professor of agriculture, and Bertha George Palmer, a schoolteacher. In 1937, he attended Hawthorne College in Mississippi, and then transferred to Elizabeth City State Teachers College in North Carolina, which he attended for two years. He enlisted in the U.S. Coast Guard in 1939 and completed a twenty-year tour of duty, first as a messboy, and then, in 1950, as Chief Journalist. He married three times, fathering three children. During the 1940s, Haley began writing short anecdotal sketches about the coast guard, some of which he published in Coronet magazine. In the 1950s, he continued to publish short, mostly biographical pieces in Coronet, as well as in Readers Digest, Atlantic, and Harper's. He retired from the coast guard in 1959 to become a freelance writer.

In the early 1960s, he continued to publish short articles, among them an exposé of Elijah Muhammad and the Nation of Islam for the Saturday Evening Post. At the same time, he began a series of interviews for Playboy magazine, including ones with Miles *Davis, *Malcolm X, Martin Luther *King, Jr., Cassius Clay (later Muhammad *Ali), Jim Brown, and Quincy Jones. His interview with Malcolm X led to their collaboration on The *Autobiography of Malcolm X (1965). Haley's probing questions of Malcolm X and editorial skills helped shape what has undoubtedly become the most influential twentieth-century African American *autobiography.

Almost immediately after his work on the Autobiography, Haley initiated research into his own family's genealogy, eventually discovering his maternal great-great-great-great-grandfather, *Kunta Kinte, who, he claims, was captured in West Africa in 1767 and transported to and enslaved in Virginia. Haley incorporated this narrative in *Roots (1976), a Pulitzer Prize–winning, seven-generation family chronicle that ends with Haley's own life and research. The publication of Roots, along with two enormously popular televised versions of it—Roots in 1977 and Roots: The Next Generations in 1979—made Haley an international celebrity and lecturer. An estimated 80 to 130 million viewers watched the last episode of Roots, generating greater interest in the *novel and prompting thousands of Americans to investigate their own family genealogies. The novel and the *television series also provoked a national discussion about the history and legacy of racism and *slavery.

In the 1980s, Haley continued to publish short pieces, although most of his creative energy was directed into television productions. He also wrote A Different Kind of Christmas (1988), a historical novella about the political transformation of a slaveower's son into an abolitonist. When Haley died on 21 February 1992 he left several unfinished manuscripts, one of which, Alex Haley's Queen (1993), was completed by David Stevens.

Haley's ultimate historical impact has been perhaps more cultural than literary. Roots was criticized for its historical inaccuracy and lack of originality. Nonetheless, it undeniably sparked a popular interest and pride in African American history and in the African ancestry of African Americans.

[See also Historical Novel; Journalism.]

• Alfred Balk and Alex Haley, "Black Merchants of Hate," Saturday Evening Post 236 (26 Jan. 1963): 68–73. Alex Haley, "My Furthest-Back Person—'The African,'" New York Times Magazine, 16 July 1972, 12–16. Alex Haley, "In Search of 'The

African,'" *American History Illustrated* 8 (Feb. 1974): 21–26. Alex Haley, "There Are Days When I Wish It Hadn't Happened," *Playboy*, March 1979, 115+. Murray Fisher, ed., *Alex Haley: The Playboy Interviews*, 1993.

—Roger A. Berger

HAMILTON, VIRGINIA (b. 1936), writer for children and young adults, first African American to win Newbery Medal (1974), and first American to win Hans Christian Andersen Medal (1992). Since the 1970s, the number of children's books featuring African American characters has declined; however, the continuous publication of Virginia Esther Perry Hamilton's provocative works reminds the public that artistic integrity in African American–authored *children's and young adult literature has not been relinquished. Hamilton maintains this integrity by uniting politics and art and by continuing to capture the universal in the particulars and complexities of the African American experience. Hamilton, who has published more than thirty books, generally satisfies her goal "to find a certain form and content to express black literature as American literature and perpetuate a pedigree of American black literature for the young," as stated by Violet Harris (*Black Women in America*).

Within this pedigree, Hamilton has published African American children's fiction in more genres than any other writer. She remains the only African American who has written science fiction/fantasy featuring African American children, in the *Justice* trilogy. This pedigree also includes contemporary realistic fiction most recently seen in *Plain City* (1993), historical fiction such as *Cousins* (1989), folk tales, fantasy, *slave narratives like *Many Thousands Gone* (1993), mysteries such as *House of Dies Drear* (1973), and biographies that include Hugo Black, Paul *Robeson, W. E. B. *Du Bois, and Anthony Burns.

Hamilton's work captures unconventional themes and multitextured characterizations in African American children's literature, addressing such issues as the environment in *M. C. Higgins, the Great* (1974) and *Drylongso* (1992). Her use of unconventional stream of consciousness and language in *Arilla Sun Down* (1976) is also noteworthy. Perhaps most important, though, is Hamilton's string of "firsts": the first young adult novel to feature a black–Native American family; the first modern urban African American *trickster, in the *Jahdu* books (1969, 1973, 1980); the first modern African American myth of ancestral origins for African American children as seen in *The Magical Adventures of Pretty Pearl* (1984), as well as superbly revisioning African American folk heroes such as *John Henry and *High John the Conqueror; the first to create a young adult novel featuring the ties between African Americans and Caribbeans, in *Junius Over Far* (1985); the first African American children's novel based on slave history, *The House of Dies Drear* (1970); the first to capture the theme of homelessness in African American children's novels, in *The Planet of Junior* (1974); and the first author to examine the theme of interracial (black/white) dating among teenagers, in *A White Romance* (1987). For all of this, Hamilton has received

an unprecedented number of awards: the Newbery Medal, several Newbery Honor awards, three Globe–Horn Book Awards, the Regina Medal, the Edgar Allen Poe Award, and honorary doctorates. She was also the first children's author to receive the prestigious MacArthur Prize Fellowship. Since the 1980s, Kent State University has had an annual conference named after her.

Born in Yellow Spring, Ohio, 12 March 1936, the fifth and youngest child of Kenneth James and Ette Belle, Hamilton still lives on land her family purchased in the 1850s after her great-great-grandmother escaped with her son from slavery in Virginia. Coming from a family of storytellers, Virginia knew she wanted to be a writer. At age nine she wrote her first novel, entitled *The Novel*, which was her juvenile collection of gossip. She later lost it and once commented that psychologically her writing may be an attempt to gain back her "lost novel."

As a child she freely explored the surrounding rural area of Glen Helen, which served as a model for the setting of several of her books. She remembers as a child a strange big house that served as a model for the abolitionist house in *The House of Dies Drear*. Although she did not encounter overt racism as a child, she was aware that after her father earned a degree in business, he dressed impeccably in a suit and tie, went to the bank to apply for a job as a teller, and was instead handed a mop and bucket.

Virginia Hamilton enrolled in Antioch College with a five-year scholarship. There Hamilton wrote short stories that she remembers being asked to revise for their unusual plots and characterizations. Her first novel, *Zeely, nominated for the Newbery Medal in 1968, was begun at Antioch. She later attended Ohio State University (1957–1958) and the New School for Social Research. At the latter she took a writing course taught by Hiriam Hayden, founder of Atheneum Publishers, who unsuccessfully encouraged publishers to print her first adult novel, *Mayo*.

She worked in New York for fifteen years at various jobs including bookkeeping and singing, and married Arnold Adoff, a poet and anthologist, on 19 March 1960. *The Planet of Junior Brown* and the *Jahdu* books, whose settings are Harlem, reflect her New York experiences.

Returning to Yellow Spring with her husband, son, and daughter, Hamilton bought land from her mother and built a home. She was later to say home was freedom and internment—dominant binary oppositions in her fiction that was early influenced by Edgar Allen Poe, William Faulkner, Zora Neale *Hurston, and Carson McCullers.

Of the thirty or more books she has written, Hamilton considers *The Magical Adventures of Pretty Pearl* her magnum opus. It connects well with African American literary tradition in its superb development of African American *folklore. With *Pretty Pearl*, Hamilton pioneered the demonstration of African mythological influences on African American mythology to young readers. Like Alice *Walker, Paule *Marshall, and Toni *Morrison, Hamilton too has planted her folk roots, soared her mythic wings, and elevated rituals of storytelling in a way to provoke a child's or young adult's imagination.

Critics have criticized yet applauded Hamilton for her divergence from the conventional, her complexities in language, characters, and narrative style.

Hamilton resides in Yellow Spring, Ohio. Manuscripts of her work can be found at Kent State and the Kerlan collection of the University of Minnesota.

• Ann Commire, ed., "Virginia Hamilton," in *Something about the Author*, 1989, pp. 19–21. Margaret Bristow, "The Analysis of Myth in Selected Novels of Virginia Hamilton," PhD diss., University of Virginia, 1990. Darlene Hines, ed., *Black Women in America*, 1993. Nina Mikkelson, *Virginia Hamilton, A Critical Biography*, 1994.

—Margaret Bernice Smith Bristow

HAMMON, BRITON (?–?), autobiographer. *The Narrative of the Uncommon Sufferings and Surprising Deliverance of Briton Hammon, a Negro Man* (1760), which recounts almost thirteen years of Hammon's adventures at sea, contains all that is known about Briton Hammon. Covering a mere fourteen pages, Hammon's account opens with a humble introduction expressing the hope that the reader will overlook any flaws in the text, since the author's "Capacities and Condition of Life are very low." It turns into a tale of amazing events that occur after Hammon obtains permission from his master, General Winslow, to leave Marshfield, Massachusetts, to go to sea. On Christmas day 1747, he sails from Plymouth on a sloop bound for Jamaica; in due course, he arrives safely on the island. Returning from it, however, his vessel catches on a reef off the coast of Florida. Hostile natives attack the ship and kill everyone on board save Hammon; they hold him captive until Spaniards help him to escape. His release brings little relief because his rescuers subject Hammon to a Cuban prison. Eventually, he breaks free once again, takes passage on other ships, and at last lands in England, where, after getting a job on a boat to Boston, he gladly finds that one of its passengers is his old master. Hammon ends his story with an expression of gratitude to "Providence" for delivering him from trying times.

Hammon's *Narrative* was printed in Boston in 1760. It is generally recognized as the first African American *autobiography, although Hammon's authorship of the text is uncertain. The *Narrative* is also generally regarded as the first American *slave narrative.

• Dorothy Porter, ed., *Early Negro Writing 1760–1837*, 1971. Blyden Jackson, *A History of Afro-American Literature, volume I, 1746–1895*, 1989.   —Roland L. Williams, Jr.

HAMMON, JUPITER (1711–c. 1806), poet, essayist, preacher, and the first published African American writer. Jupiter Hammon gave birth to formal African American literature with the publication of *An Evening Thought, Salvation, by Christ, with Penitential Cries* (1760). Hammon was born on 17 October 1711 at the Lloyd plantation in Oyster Bay, Long Island, New York. He was almost fifty years old when he published his first poem, "Salvation Comes by Christ Alone," on 25 December 1760.

Hammon was a slave to the wealthy Lloyd family. It is evident that he received some education, and he was entrusted with the family's local savings and worked as a clerk in their business. There is no record of his having a wife or child.

By the time he was eighty, Hammon had published at least three other poems—"An Address to Miss Phillis Wheatly [sic], Ethiopian Poetess," "A Poem for Children with Thoughts of Death," and "A Dialogue Entitled the Kind Master and the Dutiful Servant"—and three sermon *essays—*A Winter Piece: Being a Serious Exhortation, with a Call to the Unconverted; A Short Contemplation on the Death of Jesus;* and *An Evening's Improvement, Showing, the Necessity of Beholding the Lamb of God.* He wrote several other works that have not yet been found, including a poem celebrating the visit of Prince William Henry to Oyster Bay and *An Essay on the Ten Virgins,* advertised in the Connecticut *Courant* in December of 1779.

Hammon's first poem declares that Christ offers redemption to "everyone" of "every nation" of "all the world." He calls his fellow slaves "Africans by nation" or "Ethiopians," and refers to his brethren as "ancient," uplifting them with a sense of a *history older than that of their British masters.

Hammon died around the year 1806. Born before the *antislavery movement had gained momentum, he did not have the opportunities afforded to Phillis *Wheatley or Olaudah *Equiano, but he left them a legacy of survival, subtle protest, and living witness.

[*See also* Poetry.]

• Jupiter Hammon, *America's First Negro Poet: The Complete Works of Jupiter Hammon of Long Island*, 1970. Sondra O'Neale, *Jupiter Hammon and the Biblical Beginnings of African-American Literature*, 1993.

—Sondra O'Neale

HANNAH PEACE is *Eva Peace's second daughter and is the mother of the eponymous protagonist in Toni *Morrison's *novel *Sula* (1974). Described as a lovely woman who is widowed young and has no intention of marrying again, it is suggested that she inherited from her mother the love of maleness or "manlove," and that she desires and requires touching everyday. Still, Hannah is careful about whom she *sleeps* with, because "sleeping with someone implied for her a measure of trust and definite commitment." Thus, she is "a daylight lover" for whom sex is an ordinary, pleasurable part of life.

*Sula Peace, her daughter, hears Hannah say that she loves her but does not like her and so watches with interest and curiosity as her mother burns to death because of a shift of the wind. One-legged Eva jumps out of a window in an unsuccessful attempt to save her. Years before, Hannah had asked Eva why she had burned Plum, Hannah's drug-dependent younger brother, to death and if Eva had ever loved her children. Now, ironically, Eva shows her love by trying to save Hannah from the same element that she used to destroy her son. On the day prior to Hannah's burning, Sula had acted unusually crazy, distracting Eva and Hannah from seriously contemplating their dreams—which foreshadowed death according to the dream books. Hannah's personality and lifestyle had impressed her young daughter, and the two fiery deaths that Sula witnesses ultimately scorch all the women in the novel.

Like her mother and her daughter, Hannah defied stereotypes, and she cannot be quietly assigned the role of seductress; rather, Hannah has a natural sensuality and remains independent although she would make love to practically any man.

• Barbara Christian, *Black Feminist Criticism*, 1985. Wilfred D. Samuels and Clenora Hudson-Weems, *Toni Morrison*, 1990. Trudier Harris, *Fiction and Folklore: The Novels of Toni Morrison*, 1991.
—Betty Taylor-Thompson

HANSBERRY, LORRAINE (1930–1965), playwright, essayist, poet, and leading literary figure in the civil rights movement. Lorraine Vivian Hansberry was twenty-eight years old when her first play, A *Raisin in the Sun*, opened on Broadway to instant success. Capturing the spirit of the *civil rights movement, this play won the 1959 New York Drama Critics Circle Award and made Hansberry the first black, youngest person, and fifth woman to win that prize. A *Raisin in the Sun*, the first play by an African American woman produced on Broadway, has become a classic of the American *theater and has enjoyed numerous professional revivals.

The roots of Hansberry's artistic vision and activism are in Chicago. Born into a family of substantial means, Hansberry was the youngest of four children—Carl, Jr., Perry, and Mamie. Her father, Carl Augustus Hansberry, Sr., was from Gloucester, Mississippi, moved to Chicago after attending Alcorn College, and became known as the "kitchenette king" after subdividing large homes vacated by whites moving to the suburbs and selling these small apartments or kitchenettes to African American migrants from the South. Hansberry's mother, Nannie Perry, a schoolteacher and, later, ward committeewoman, was from Tennessee. At the time of Lorraine's birth, she had become an influential society matron who hosted major cultural and literary figures such as Paul *Robeson, Langston *Hughes, and Joe *Louis. Although Lorraine and her siblings enjoyed privileges unknown to their working-class schoolmates, the parents infused their children with racial pride and civic responsibility. They founded the Hansberry Foundation, an organization designed to inform African Americans of their civil rights, and encouraged their children to challenge the exclusionary policies of local restaurants and stores.

Carl and Nannie Hansberry challenged restrictive real estate covenants by moving into an all-white neighborhood. A mob of whites gathered in front of the house and threw a brick through the front window, narrowly missing eight-year-old Lorraine and forcing the family to move out. Her father won a narrow victory over restrictive covenants from the Supreme Court, but the decision failed to set precedent on this issue.

Hansberry attended public schools: Betsy Ross Elementary and Englewood High School, where she encountered the children of the working class whose independence and courage she came to admire.

Their struggle would become the subject of her first major play. Departing from the family tradition of attending black colleges, Hansberry enrolled at the University of Wisconsin at Madison, a predominantly white university, to study journalism, but was equally attracted to the visual arts. She integrated an all-white women's dormitory and became active in the campus chapter of the Young Progressive Association, a national left-wing student organization, serving as its president during her sophomore year. After seeing a moving performance of Sean O'Casey's *Juno and the Paycock*, she decided to become a writer and to capture the authentic voice of the African American working class.

Hansberry left Wisconsin after two years and moved to New York City in 1950. She took a job with *Freedom*, a newspaper founded by Paul Robeson whose passport had been revoked by the U.S. State Department. She soon became associate editor, working closely with Louis Burnham, who became her mentor. In 1952, she replaced Robeson at a controversial, international peace conference in Montevideo, Uruguay, and subsequently spoke at public rallies and meetings, often critiquing U.S. policy. Hansberry's association with *Freedom* placed her in the midst of Harlem's rich cultural, artistic, and political life. She read avidly and widely in African American history and culture, politics, philosophy, and the arts, and was especially influenced by the works of W. E. B. *Du Bois, Frederick *Douglass, William Shakespeare, and Langston Hughes.

While participating in a demonstration at New York University, she met Robert Barron Nemiroff, son of progressive Russian Jewish immigrants, and after a short courtship, married him on 20 June 1953. Having earned his Masters degree four months earlier at New York University, he had begun writing a book on Theodore Dreiser, his thesis topic. The young couple moved to Greenwich Village and Hansberry began to write extensively about the people and lifestyles that she observed around her. She was already an experienced writer and editor, having published articles, *essays, and *poetry in *Freedom*, *New Challenge*, and other leftist magazines.

After leaving *Freedom* in 1953 to concentrate on her writing, Hansberry worked various odd jobs including tagger in the garment industry, typist, program director at Camp Unity (an interracial summer camp), recreation leader for the physically disabled, and teacher at the Marxist-oriented Jefferson School for Social Science. When her husband cowrote "Cindy Oh Cindy" (1956), a ballad that became an instant hit, the revenue freed Hansberry to devote her full energies to a play about a struggling, working-class black family, like the families who rented her father's properties on Chicago's South Side—A *Raisin in the Sun*.

A *Raisin in the Sun* depicts the frustrations of a black family whose dreams of economic progress have been thwarted. After a pre-Broadway tour, it opened at the Ethel Barrymore Theatre in New York City on 11 March 1959 to instant critical and popular success. In 1961, it was produced as a film with most of the original cast and won a special award at the

Cannes Film Festival. During this period, Hansberry was much in demand as a public speaker. She articulated her belief that art is social and that black writers must address all issues of humankind. As the civil rights movement intensified, she helped to organize fund-raising activities in support of organizations such as the Student Nonviolent Coordinating Committee (SNCC), called for the abolition of the House Un-American Activities Committee, and declared that President John F. Kennedy had endangered world peace during the Cuban Missile Crisis.

During the last four years of her life, Hansberry worked hard on several plays. *The Sign in Sidney Brustein's Window* was produced on Broadway in 1964, but critics were less receptive to this play that challenged the ennui of Greenwich Village intellectuals. During its short run, Hansberry battled pancreatic cancer, diagnosed in 1963. She died on 12 January 1965, the same night that her play closed.

Hansberry left a number of finished and unfinished writings that indicate the breadth of her social and artistic vision. Robert Nemiroff, whom she had divorced in 1964 but designated as her literary executor, adapted some of her writings for the stage under the title *To Be Young, Gifted and Black*, a show that became the longest-running drama of the 1968–1969 Off-Broadway season and toured colleges and communities in the United States during 1970 and 1971. He also edited and published an *anthology of her work (reissued in 1994) that included *Les Blancs*, a play about liberation movements; *The Drinking Gourd*, a *television play commissioned by NBC but shelved as too controversial to produce; and *What Use Are Flowers?*, a fantasy on the consequences of nuclear holocaust. Among her other writings were a musical adaptation of Oliver LaFarge's *Laughing Boy*; an adaptation of The *Marrow of Tradition* by Charles Waddell *Chesnutt; a screenplay based on Jacques Romain's novel about Haiti, *Masters of the Dew*; and a critical commentary on Simone de Beauvoir's *The Second Sex*, a book that had significant impact on Hansberry's thinking. Until 1991 when he died, Robert Nemiroff devoted his life to editing, promoting, and producing Hansberry's works on stage and television.

Hansberry's *A Raisin in the Sun* is a classic of the American theater, frequently produced and an inspiration for young writers and artists. In recent years, a feminist revisioning of her plays and some of her unpublished writings affirm her politically progressive views, her sophistication about gender issues, and her sensitivity to homosexuality and opposition to homophobia. As more of her work is made accessible, the full extent of Hansberry's vision and contribution to American letters will be revealed.

[*See also* Beneatha Younger; Mama Lena Younger; Walter Lee Younger.]

• *To Be Young, Gifted and Black: Lorraine Hansberry in Her Own Words*, adapted by Robert Nemiroff, 1969. *Freedomways*, special issue, "Lorraine Hansberry: Art of Thunder, Vision of Light" 19.4 (1979). Ernest Kaiser and Robert Nemiroff, "A Lorraine Hansberry Bibliography," *Freedomways* 19.4 (1979): 285–304. Lorraine Hansberry, "All the Dark and Beautiful Warriors," *Village Voice*, 16 Aug. 1983, 11–19. Stephen R. Carter, "Lorraine Hansberry," in *DLB*, vol. 38, *Afro-American Writers after 1955: Dramatists and Prose Writers*, eds. Thadious M. Davis and Trudier Harris, 1985, pp. 120–134. Stephen R. Carter, *Hansberry's Drama: Commitment amid Complexity*, 1991. Herb Boyd, "Lorraine Hansberry," in *Encyclopedia of the American Left*, eds. Mari Jo Buhle, Paul Buhle, and Dan Georgakas, 1992, pp. 288–289. Margaret B. Wilkerson, "Lorraine Hansberry," in *Black Women in America: An Historical Encyclopedia*, ed. Darlene Clark Hine, 1993, pp. 524–529. Lorraine Hansberry, *The Collected Last Plays: Les Blancs, The Drinking Gourd, What Use Are Flowers?*, ed. Robert Nemiroff, 1994.

—Margaret B. Wilkerson

HANSEN, JOYCE (b. 1942), novelist and educator. Joyce Hansen's interest in writing was influenced by her mother, who had wanted to become a journalist, and her father, whose photography and storytelling fueled her appreciation of the beauty in the lives of ordinary people. After graduating from Pace University with a bachelor's degree in English, New York native Joyce Hansen became a teacher at a school for adolescents with learning disabilities. Confronted with the evidence that even poor readers would complete books that were interesting to them; believing that literature was a way of helping young people have hope, develop responsibility, and understand their environments; and knowing that positive stories of everyday heroism, of those who lived in less than ideal environments but who grew up healthy and whole in loving families and communities, particularly those who were black and Hispanic, were few and far between, Hansen decided to write stories for middle school students such as those she taught. Membership in the Harlem Writers Guild supplemented her careful reading of other writers and conscientious attempts to find her own artistic voice. Using her own life experiences and names, stories, and perspectives from her family, friends, and students, Hansen began to publish *novels that reviewers praised for their convincing characters, authentic language, realistic settings, and optimism tempered with common sense. In *The Gift-Giver* (1980), Amir, a foster child, living in the same crime-ridden Bronx neighborhood as Doris, the underachieving daughter of overprotective parents, gives Doris greater understanding of the importance of friendship, of seeing "into" things in order to understand one's world, and of self reliance. In the sequel, *Yellow Bird and Me* (1982), Doris passes on Amir's lessons when she discovers that Yellow Bird plays class clown in an effort to mask his learning disability. While these and other sociopolitical themes inform her writing, Hansen's books are not didactic. Hansen fleshes out the elements that she believes are intrinsic to the African American experience—the importance of family, self-esteem, determination, and optimism—through characters, dialogue, and settings that are well drawn and credible. When Marcus, the protagonist of *Home Boy* (1982), stabs another student, scenes of his fearful flight are juxtaposed against scenes of his earlier life in St. Cruz, the destruction of the American dream for his emigrant family, and reconciliation with his father as he turns his son in to the police. Marcus, the social delinquent, is also Marcus the troubled and loved son, friend, and neighbor whose own will to reform is supported by members of his community.

In 1986, Hansen began publishing young adult novels about *slavery and the Civil War in an attempt to make history come alive for her students. *Which Way Freedom?* (1986) and its sequel *Out from This Place* (1988) give detailed descriptions of slave life in the Gullah area of South Carolina during the Civil War for Obi, Easter, and Jason, three youngsters who come to love and depend upon one another when sold to the same owner. They provide examples of strength, courage, and resilience that can inspire and teach contemporary readers; however, the characters are not larger than life and do not always behave in stereotypical heroic fashion. Obi, for example, knows that Easter and Jason would slow him down so he plans to escape without them. Contrary to many depictions, the Union soldiers do not welcome the fugitive slaves but often return them to their slave owners or force them to do menial and backbreaking work without pay. The novels aptly illustrate why escape plans were fraught with failure and why some slaves chose to remain in bondage. Hansen's interest in the Civil War period led to nonfiction with the publication of *Between Two Fires: Black Soldiers in the Civil War* (1994). In *The Captive* (1994), she turns to the problematic concepts of African participation in the slave trade and Puritans who owned slaves. Combining actual historical figures, such as Paul *Cuffe, with imagined individuals, such as Kofi, the captured African prince, and Timothy, a white indentured servant, Hansen offers an unusual but valid adventure story about African civilization and American slavery. Joyce Hansen believes that writers have the enormous responsibility of arresting ignorance, of providing insight and perspective, and of entertaining. Her work is praised for its powerful use of language to those ends.

• Donnarae MacCann, "Joyce Hansen," in *Twentieth Century Children's Writers,* ed. Tracy Chevalier, 1989, pp. 424–425. "Joyce Hansen," in *Children's Literature Review* 21 (1990): 149–152. "Joyce Hansen," in *Major Authors and Illustrators for Children and Young Adults,* eds. Laurie Collier and Joyce Nakamura, vol. 3, 1993, pp. 1055–1058.

—Frances Smith Foster

HARLEM RENAISSANCE. Known also as the Negro Renaissance or the *New Negro movement, the Harlem Renaissance refers generally to the artistic and sociocultural awakening among African Americans in the 1920s and the early 1930s. Some scholars and critics, including Sterling A. *Brown, have questioned both the term "Harlem" and the term "renaissance" to describe this phenomenon. Some of the major contributors, such as Georgia Douglas *Johnson, did not live in Harlem. Many of the issues identified with this period had been prefigured in works by Frederick *Douglass, Frances Ellen Watkins *Harper, Charles Waddell *Chesnutt, James Weldon *Johnson, and W. E. B. *Du Bois. Indeed, the concerns of Harlem Renaissance artists, philosophers, and community leaders with the peculiar racial situation in

the United States and their exploration of their emotional and historical links with Africa and the American South continue to this day. The dates of the movement are also debatable. While one may regard 1923 to 1929 as the peak years of the movement, it is possible to see the renaissance years as extending from 1910 (the founding of the NAACP and its forum, the *Crisis), 1914 (the year World War I started), or 1917 (the year Claude *McKay published his poem "Harlem Dancer"), to 1937, when Zora Neale *Hurston published *Their Eyes Were Watching God.* There is a general consensus that the publication of Richard *Wright's *Native Son* in 1940 heralded a new phase of harsh realism in African American writing.

But Harlem is symbolically appropriate to new changes in African American life and art in the 1920s. Unlike many other African American communities, Harlem had developed from a white, upper-middle-class suburb, not from the continued decline of an already poor white area. It had grown from 14,000 blacks in 1914 to 175,000 by 1925 and more than 200,000 by the beginning of the depression. The interaction of blacks from all parts of the United States, West Indies, and even Africa led to the growth of a highly race-conscious sophisticated community—something unprecedented in American history. Black writers, painters, and actors from all over the country experienced the magnetic pull of Harlem as the new cultural capital of black America. "In Harlem," wrote Alain *Locke, "Negro life is seizing upon its first chances for group expression and self-determination." It was, Locke continued, "the greatest Negro city in the world."

Harlem was also the center of several new civil rights organizations, such as the NAACP, the National Urban League, and the all-black Brotherhood of Sleeping Car Porters and Maids organized by A. Philip Randolph, and perhaps most importantly, Marcus *Garvey's Universal Negro Improvement Association. The essence of Garvey's message was that the most positive future for blacks lay in Africa, not America. Through his celebration of blackness, Garvey gained millions of followers among the demoralized African American masses in urban ghettos all over the country, for through Garveyism they found a much needed outlet for race pride and self-assertion.

In many ways, the New Negro movement was the educated, middle-class African American's response to the same changes that magnetically drew the masses to Garvey's ideas and programs. The Harlem Renaissance was a logical extension in the areas of art, *music, and literature of the New Negro's racial, cultural, and political thinking. The needs of this new self-expression in literature were served by many black journals, such as the *Crisis,* *Opportunity, and the *Messenger,* as well as by other leading journals such as the *Nation, Modern Quarterly, New Republic,* *Survey Graphic,* and *Saturday Review.* The first stage of the literary aspect of the Harlem Renaissance culminated in the December 1925 publication by Albert and Boni of *The *New Negro.* The *anthology had already sold 42,000 copies in its earlier incarnation as the March 1925 special issue on Harlem of the *Survey Graphic* magazine, a record unsurpassed by the *Survey* until World War II.

The younger writers of the Harlem Renaissance received mentoring and support from many individuals both white and black, including Du Bois, James Weldon Johnson, Carl Van Vechten, V. F. Calverton, Walter *White, and Jessie Redmon *Fauset, who, as the literary editor of the *Crisis*, modulated and broadened Du Bois's genteel and propagandistic goals in literature. The individual most identified with the Harlem Renaissance is Howard University philosophy professor Alain Locke. Not only did Locke edit *The New Negro* but he was instrumental in propounding the concept of a Negro renaissance, in negotiating the publishing contracts for and generally performing as "midwife" to aspiring writers and artists. Another figure of special influence was the sociologist Charles S. Johnson, who later became the first black president of Fisk University. As the first editor of *Opportunity*, Johnson stressed the need for African Americans to advantageously understand and absorb this change from rural South to urban North, and he aimed his magazine "to stimulate and encourage creative literary effort among Negroes . . . to encourage the reading of literature both by Negro authors and about Negro life . . . to bring these writers into contact with the general world of letters . . . to stimulate and foster a type of writing by Negroes which shakes itself free of deliberate propaganda and protest." In 1927, Johnson edited *Ebony and Topaz*, in many ways a companion volume to Locke's *The New Negro*. The third person most often associated with literary production of this movement is Carl Van Vechten. While the fad of primitivism cannot be blamed entirely on Van Vechten or on the other whites who wrote about the Negro in the 1920s, it is reasonable to suggest that the success of Van Vechten's *Nigger Heaven* (1926) made many black writers keenly aware of the commercial possibilities of the primitivistic formula, and made it more difficult for many Harlem Renaissance writers to develop their artistic potential individually or as a group with significant shared goals. The unusual success of *Nigger Heaven* and later of McKay's *Home to Harlem* (1928) clearly indicated an eagerness for works exalting the exotic, the sensual, and the primitive. Thus, black writers who were willing to render the exotic aspects of African American experience had little trouble finding sponsors and publishers.

No serious study exists yet of the Harlem Renaissance's influence on later African American writing. Since the late 1970s, Zora Neale Hurston has come to receive wide recognition for her feminist consciousness. Sharing an interest in issues of class and color with male writers such as McKay, Hughes, Jean *Toomer, and Rudolph *Fisher, women writers such as Hurston, Jessie Fauset, Nella *Larsen, Dorothy *West, Marita *Bonner, and Gwendolyn *Bennett each in her own way explored female lives and the politics of gender. Women writers of the renaissance have become for Alice *Walker and many others a source of inspiration in their own careers. Jean

Toomer appears to have been read and admired by most African American writers since the 1920s. Langston Hughes continued to support and influence the careers of many black writers until his death in 1967. The renaissance can certainly be credited for initiating discussions on many artistic and cultural concerns of African Americans that have caused heated controversy since the 1960s. Important among these are the treatment of black themes and characters by white writers and the aesthetic criteria by which to appreciate and evaluate black writing.

Later African American writers have probably learned more from the Harlem Renaissance's failings than from its achievements, but as early as the late 1920s black authors in the West Indies and Africa received positive inspiration from the spirit and individual works of the New Negro movement. Leopold Sedar Senghor of Senegal and Aimé Césaire of Martinique had read renaissance poetry and fiction in translation, and under its influence, these two poets developed their variant concepts of *Negritude. The South African writer Peter Abrahams has written in his *autobiography, *Tell Freedom* (1954), about how, as a teenager at the Bantu Men's Social Center in Johannesburg, he discovered the renaissance writers Claude McKay, Langston Hughes, Georgia Douglas Johnson, Countee *Cullen, and W. E. B. Du Bois and how they gave him both hope for a future as well as a faith in "color nationalism."

Many Harlem Renaissance writers who led active lives past the 1920s talked and wrote about the period, but Wallace *Thurman provided the only detailed contemporary account of the movement. A thinly veiled satire on the major figures of the renaissance, *Infants of the Spring* (1932) presents mediocre artists lost in a web of frivolity and recalcitrance without purpose or privacy, unable to achieve anything worthwhile. Although we are likely to reject Thurman's cripplingly self-conscious judgment on individual writers, including himself, *Infants of the Spring* represents a coming-of-age of the Harlem Renaissance literati. It demonstrates the ability of the movement to evaluate and possibly modify its direction. By the mid-1930s, exotic and genteel novels about black life were no longer popular with publishers and were attacked by a new breed of black writers and critics.

If Thurman's assessment is harsh and lopsided, it is equally unfair to evaluate the Harlem Renaissance by the hindsight judgments of Langston Hughes and Claude McKay, or the aesthetic criteria of Du Bois and Benjamin *Brawley, or the theoretical constructs and reviews of Alain Locke, who was charged with malicious misreading of their work by women writers such as Jessie Fauset. Intense intellectual and artistic activity created fruitful controversy over basic issues relating to art and its appreciation. The racial matrix of artistic expression received serious critical attention, and some of the latter-day concepts—such as *Black Aesthetic—were prefigured in discussions among Harlem Renaissance artists. This is an important legacy, even though the attitudes of most renaissance writers in these matters were characterized by ambivalence and tension, and many individual artists failed to resolve their conflicting impulses about race and art, while others found only tentative solutions.

[*See also* Chicago Renaissance; Places.]

• Langston Hughes, *The Big Sea*, 1940. Nathan Huggins, *Harlem Renaissance*, 1971. Arna Bontemps, ed., *The Harlem Renaissance Remembered*, 1972. Robert Bone, "The Harlem Renaissance: A Reappraisal," in *Down Home: Origins of the Afro-American Short Story*, 1975. Margaret Perry, ed., *The Harlem Renaissance: An Annotated Bibliography and Commentary*, 1982. Bruce Kellner, ed., *The Harlem Renaissance: A Historical Dictionary of the Era*, 1984. Gloria Hull, *Color, Sex and Poetry: Three Women Writers of the Harlem Renaissance*, 1987. David Levering Lewis, *When Harlem Was in Vogue*, 1987. Amritjit Singh et al., *The Harlem Renaissance: Revaluations*, 1989. John E. Bassett, ed., *Harlem in Review: Critical Reactions to Black American Writers, 1917–1939*, 1992. Wallace Thurman, *Infants of the Spring*, 1932; rpt. 1992. Cheryl A. Wall, *Women of the Harlem Renaissance*, 1995. Amritjit Singh, *The Novels of the Harlem Renaissance*, 1976; rev. 1996.

—Amritjit Singh

HARPER, FRANCES ELLEN WATKINS (1825–1911), novelist, poet, essayist, journalist, orator, and activist. Born free in the slave state of Maryland, Frances Ellen Watkins was orphaned at an early age. She attended the William Watkins Academy for Negro Youth in Baltimore, an institution noted for rigorous training in a classical curriculum of languages, biblical studies, and elocution, and for developing professional and religious leaders of unusual personal integrity and political activity. Harper was an exemplary alumna. At age twenty-five, she moved to Columbus, Ohio, to become the first woman professor at the newly formed Union Seminary (later Wilberforce University). Exiled from Maryland by state laws that prohibited entry of free blacks into the state and frustrated by the increasing power of slaveholders, in 1853 Harper moved to Philadelphia where she lived at an *Underground Railroad station and devoted her life and literature to abolition and other social reform movements. Her literary production at that time included poems and *essays such as "The Dying Christian," "Ethiopia," "Eliza Harris," "Christianity," and "Women's Rights." Reportedly, she published a book, *Forest Leaves*, but no known copies have survived.

In 1854, Watkins accepted a position with the Maine Anti-Slavery Society thereby becoming one of the first professional woman orators in the United States. Traveling throughout New England, southern Canada, and the western states of Michigan and Ohio, Watkins earned accolades for highly articulate and "fiery" speeches that were "marked by dignity and composure" and delivered "without the slightest violation of good taste." Her presentations often included recitations of original *poetry and this, combined with regular publication in abolitionist periodicals, earned her a national reputation. Consequently, when she combined her poetry and essays into the 1854 volume *Poems on Miscellaneous Subjects*, it merited dual publication in Boston and Philadelphia. By 1871, this book was in its twentieth edition. Though modern anthologists favor its antislavery po-

ems such as "The Slave Mother—A Tale of Ohio," "The Slave Auction," and "Ethiopia," the volume was, as its title indicates, "on Miscellaneous Subjects," including religion, heroism, women's rights, African American history, and temperance. In an 1859 letter, Watkins outlined the philosophy that informed her writing throughout her sixty-eight-year professional career: "The nearer we ally ourselves to the wants and woes of humanity in the spirit of Christ," she wrote, "the closer we get to the great heart of God; the nearer we stand by the beating of the pulse of universal love."

While she earnestly tried to "teach men and women to love noble deeds by setting them to the music, of fitly spoken words," Watkins understood that universal love realized through devotion to humanity required courage and sometimes decidedly aggressive behavior. In 1858, she protested the segregated streetcars of Philadelphia by staging a personal sit-in and in 1859, when John *Brown's raid on Harpers Ferry failed, she solicited aid for the captured revolutionaries and moved in with Mary Brown until after her husband's execution.

During the antebellum period, Frances Ellen Watkins regularly contributed to national and international abolitionist journals such as the *Provincial Freeman*, the *Liberator*, the *National AntiSlavery Standard*, and *Frederick Douglass's Monthly*. At the same time, she was active among the African American literati, publishing poems, letters, and essays regularly in African American periodicals such as the *Christian Recorder, the *Repository of Religion and Literature and of Science and Art*, the *Aliened American*, and the *Weekly Anglo African*. Along with Martin R. *Delany, Frederick *Douglass, William C. *Nell, Mary Shadd Cary, and Sarah M. Douglass, Frances Ellen Watkins is listed as an editor and contributor to what is considered the earliest African American literary journal, the *Anglo-African Magazine*. It was there that in 1859 she published what is generally considered the first *short story by an African American, "The *Two Offers."

After marrying Fenton Harper in 1860, the duties of wife, mother, and homemaker slowed but did not stop her social and literary activity. During the Civil War, Frances Harper's lectures and writings carried such titles as "To the Cleveland Union Savers," "Lincoln's Proclamation," and "The Mission of War." She was one of the first to go South to aid the freed slaves. Her husband died in 1864 and within months, Frances Harper was again on the lecture circuit. Between 1865 and 1870, she traveled in every southern state except Texas and Arkansas, lecturing to white, black, and integrated audiences on topics such as "The Claims of the Negro" and "The Work Before Us"; teaching the former slaves reading, writing, home management, and politics; and writing letters back to northern newspapers urging their moral and physical support for the Reconstruction of the United States.

Her newspaper contributions made her "the journalistic mother" of emerging writers such as Ida B. *Wells-Barnett, for whom she was a model and a mentor. Harper's influence was not confined to the postbellum era however. Her columns, "Fancy Etchings" and "Fancy Sketches," with their ongoing conversations between Jenny and Aunt Jane about economic, artistic, and social issues prefigure Olivia Ward *Bush-Banks's Aunt Viney and Langston *Hughes's *Simple series in the mid-twentieth century.

Harper's southern travels furnished material for more than *newspaper columns that mirrored and guided African American culture of the Reconstruction era, however. Harper had a particular gift for combining social issues, Afro-Protestant theology, and literary innovations. Using the biblical *Moses as a model, for example, Harper represented postbellum United States as a modern biblical narrative in her third book, a dramatic epic called *Moses, a Story of the Nile* (1868), and in her serialized *novel *Minnie's Sacrifice* (1867–1868). In 1870, she published *Sketches of Southern Life*, a collection of poems that introduced the wit and wisdom of *Aunt Chloe Fleet and helped shape the emerging interests in literary realism and local color by incorporating African American dialect, folk characters, and cultural experiences.

Frances Harper, like William Wells *Brown and others, was a strong supporter of the temperance movement. Serialized in the *Christian Recorder*, her 1867 novel, *Sowing and Reaping: A Temperance Story*, was one of many stories, poems, and essays that she contributed to this crusade. Joining words and deeds, Frances Harper worked tirelessly in this effort and became one of the first African American women to hold national office in the Women's Christian Temperance Union.

During her career, Frances Harper published several other books, including the novel *Trial and Triumph* (1888) and three 1895 poetry collections: *Atlanta Offering, Martyr of Alabama and Other Poems*, and *Poems*. But, it is for *Iola Leroy* (1892) that she is best known. Harper wrote this tale of *slavery, the Civil War, and Reconstruction both in opposition to the inaccurate but increasingly popular plantation school novelists such as Thomas Nelson Page and in answer to the need for more books that would inspire and instruct African American students. *Iola Leroy*, a culmination of the themes and techniques that guided Harper's long career, focuses upon issues of *race, *gender, and *class. Its characters represent the diversity of African American culture and heroic expression. Iola, Dr. Gresham, Robert Johnson, Aunt Linda, Dr. Latimer, Harry, Lucy, Marie, and the others are based, in part, upon actual people and many of their experiences are reincarnations and versions of those who appeared in earlier Harper poems, essays, and stories. As William *Still predicted in his introduction to the first edition, *Iola Leroy* met "with warm congratulations from a goodly number" of readers. Today it is considered a "classic" among African American novels.

Frances Ellen Watkins Harper was a prolific and popular writer who published in practically every genre. She appreciated beauty, she experimented with form and technique, and she enjoyed the accolades of a successful writing career. She believed, however, that literature was to be used to represent, to reprimand, and to revise the lives and aspirations of readers. She was a pragmatic, courageous, and lyrical writer whose major goal was to "make the songs for the people." Frances Harper died on 20 February 1911.

• Maryemma Graham, ed., *The Complete Poems of Frances E. W. Harper*, 1988. Frances Smith Foster, ed., *A Brighter Coming Day: A Frances Ellen Watkins Harper Reader*, 1990. Melba Joyce Boyd, *Discarded Legacy: Politics and Poetics in the Life of Frances E. W. Harper, 1825–1911*, 1994. Frances Smith Foster, ed., *Minnie's Sacrifice, Sowing and Reaping, Trial and Triumph: Three Rediscovered Novels by Frances E. W. Harper*, 1994.
—Frances Smith Foster

HARPER, MICHAEL S. (b. 1938), poet, scholar, teacher, and critic. Michael S. Harper was born in Brooklyn, New York, to Walter Warren Harper, a postal worker, and Katherine Johnson Harper, a medical stenographer. Harper recalls his family's move in 1951 to a predominantly white Los Angeles neighborhood grappling with racial tension as a traumatic enough experience to "make" him a poet. Also, his family had an extensive record collection that profoundly affected Harper's *poetry. Encouraged to pursue medicine, Harper became only a marginal student after an asthma condition kept him from participating in a junior high gym class, which earned him a failing grade and kept him off the honor roll. At Dorsey High School in Los Angeles, Harper was placed on the vocational track, a situation his father had to "straighten out" so that his son could be on track toward a medical career. During high school, Harper avoided preparing to become a doctor, and he even got significant encouragement from a college zoology professor who told him that black people could not get into medical school. During his high school years Harper wrote a few poems, but he had not yet considered writing as an option for a career.

In 1955, he enrolled at Los Angeles City College, and then Los Angeles State College, which he attended until 1961, during which time he was also employed as a postal worker. He says that his life began here. Many of his coworkers were educated black men like Harper's father who had bumped against the glass ceiling of advancement in the American workplace. Their experiences, which they shared freely, and his own experience of segregated housing at the Iowa Writer's Workshop formed the foundation of Harper's assessment of America as a schizophrenic society. Nonetheless, Harper credits his years at Los Angeles State, where he read John Keats's letters and Ralph *Ellison's *Invisible Man*, for preparing him for the Iowa Writer's Workshop, which he began in 1961. After a year there, Harper taught at various schools, including Pasadena City College (1962), Contra Costa College (1964–1968), and California State College (now University, 1968–1969).

The only black student in both his poetry and fiction classes at Iowa, Harper encountered painter Oliver Lee Jackson, who would influence Harper's thinking. Moreover, he lived in segregated housing, which runs counter to the democratic principles of this nation and best illustrates what Harper calls the schizophrenia of this society. This idea encompasses more than the politics and legacy of racial segregation; it is involved in the very English we speak and the logic we follow. Such binary oppositions as white and black, hot and cold, set the language against itself through a mode of thinking that separates and opposes, contrary to what Harper sees as a holistic universe where humanity is a reflection of the universe, and the universe is a reflection of humanity. This philosophy serves as a basis for the themes, aesthetics, and strategies of his poetry, which include *music, kinship, *history, and mythology.

For Harper, history and mythology are similar in that neither is fully constituted or contained by its written or commonly understood versions. Such mythologies as white supremacy, and the marred history it engenders, too rigidly encase humanity in static categories. Manipulating old European and American myths and creating new ones illustrates a goal and technique Harper uses throughout his poetry, beginning with his first volume, Dear John Dear Coltrane (1970). In the volume, John *Coltrane, who Harper knew, is both the man and his *jazz, the talented and tragic musician, and his wholistic worldview and redemptive music. With an understanding of black music similar to W. E. B. *Du Bois's in his description of the African American "sorrow songs," Harper includes the music of poetry as similar affirmation of the importance of articulating suffering to gain from it and survive it. Here, as in Harper's later volumes, musical rhythm replaces traditional metrics in the poetry without sacrificing craft. Coltrane becomes a link between the personal and historical, pain and its expression, suffering and love. To extend these themes, Harper devotes a section of the volume to poems about his own kin, thematically and literally personalizing history so that family ties become continuities of humanity as they link the individual with both a personal and collective history. This opening and overlapping of historical and personal possibility, in the context of Harper's interest in music, seems to provide a handle on Harper's difficult and abstract concept of musical and poetic modality.

In his subsequent volumes, Harper built upon and expanded his philosophy and repertoire of themes and strategies. In 1971, History Is Your Own Heartbeat garnered Harper the Poetry Award of the Black Academy of Arts and Letters. Instead of famous musicians, the volume focuses on Harper's family to explore similar issues as Harper's previous volume. Next, Song: I Want a Witness (1972) uses black *religion as a subtext for its meditations on black history, while, in the second section, the volume dialogues with William Faulkner's short story "The Bear," adding an element of literary history to Harper's thematics. From this volume also comes the limited edition Photographs: Negatives: History as Apple Tree (1972). Nightmare Begins Responsibility, a volume published in 1975, is another variation on the poet's philosophy of kinship, history, the wholistic universe, and an individual's responsibility to all of these. In many ways, it serves as the sequel to both Song: I

Want a Witness and Debridement (1973), and is considered Harper's richest volume. In it, Harper uses poems to address kinship in a jazz-*blues idiom; to consider the death of his friend Ralph Albert Dickey; to affirm responsible action, like Jackie *Robinson's, in the face of a racist nightmare; and to establish the poet's literary, personal, and historical ties to other African American literary and historical figures. Images of Kin (1977) earned Harper the Melville-Cane Award and a nomination for the 1978 National Book Award. Three other volumes, Rhode Island: Eight Poems (1981), Healing Song for the Inner Ear (1985), and a limited edition entitled Songlines: Mosaics (1991) have since been published.

By the mid 1970s, Harper's reputation as a poet, scholar, and teacher was firmly established. Among many other awards, such as the National Institute of Arts and Letters Creative Writing Award (1972), a Guggenheim fellowship (1976), and a National Endowment for the Arts grant (1977), Harper received an American specialist grant in 1977, with which he traveled to Ghana, South Africa, Zaire, Senegal, Gambia, Botswana, Zambia, and Tanzania. In several published interviews, Harper affirms the influence this trip had on his thinking and writing. Among Harper's former students are Gayl *Jones, Melvin *Dixon, and Anthony Walton. As a scholar, Harper has made several contributions, including a collaboration with Robert Stepto entitled Chant of Saints: A Gathering of Afro-American Literature, Art, and Scholarship, an edition of Sterling A. *Brown's poetry, a limited edition of Robert *Hayden's American Journal, and Every Shut Eye Ain't Sleep, an *anthology of African American poetry since 1945. Harper, poet laureate of the state of Rhode Island, is currently a professor at Brown University, where he teaches literature and creative writing.

• John O'Brien, "Michael Harper," in Interviews with Black Writers, 1973, pp. 95–107. Edwin Fussell, "Double-Conscious Poet in the Veil," Parnassus 4 (Fall/Winter 1975): 5–28. Robert B. Stepto, "Michael S. Harper, Poet as Kinsman: The Family Sequences," Massachusetts Review 17 (Autumn 1976): 477–502. Robert B. Stepto, "After Modernism, After Hibernation: Michael Harper, Robert Hayden and Jay Wright," in Chant of Saints: A Gathering of Afro-American Literature, Art, and Scholarship, eds. Michael S. Harper et al., 1979, pp. 470–486. Michael S. Harper, "My Poetic Technique and the Humanization of the American Audience," in Black American Literature and Humanism, ed. R. Baxter Miller, 1981, pp. 27–31. Gunter H. Lenz, "Black Poetry and Black Music: History and Tradition: Michael Harper and John Coltrane," in History and Tradition in Afro-American Culture, 1984, pp. 277–319. Joseph Brown, "Their Long Scars Touch Ours: A Reflection on the Poetry of Michael Harper," Callaloo 9.1 (1986): 209–220. "Michael S. Harper: American Poet," Callaloo 13.4 (Fall 1990): 749–829.

—Keith D. Leonard

Harriet and the Promised Land (1968) is the only picture book both written and illustrated by painter Jacob *Lawrence. In sparse verse, the book, dedicated to "the courageous women" of America, tells the story of Harriet *Tubman, born a slave in Maryland in 1822, who escaped but returned many times to lead some three hundred others to freedom.

This picture book, with its minimalist text and seemingly primitivist colorful pictures influenced by African art, is sophisticated in both storytelling and illustration. The text realistically emphasizes the harsh slave existence yet is permeated by Tubman's apparent faith that she, like *Moses, was to lead her people out of *slavery to the promised land. The allusion to Moses is explicit in the text, but the pictures, which begin with birth of baby Harriet in a shack open to the light of a prominent star, allude to Jesus Christ also. This allusion is likewise apparent in another picture in which a white man—one of the "good people" who has helped on the way—is depicted bathing Tubman's feet.

Early reaction to this book was mixed, especially as to the suitability of its artistry for children. It won the Brooklyn Art Books Children's Citation, but also some disapproval from the African American community. One picture that shows Harriet scrubbing a floor looked stereotypical to some. Yet others found Harriet's expressionistically distorted hand in this picture to be a vehicle for conveying real pain and suffering. Illustrations and texts in children's picture books have become more experimental since the 1960s; Lawrence's book, therefore, might be considered as having appeared before its time artistically, although its religiously inspired message was in accord with an important period in the African American *civil rights movement.

• Dianne Johnson, *Telling Tales: The Pedagogy and Promise of African American Literature for Youth*, 1990.

—Lois R. Kuznets

HARRIS, E. LYNN (b. 1955), novelist. Developing a Black male homosexual canon empowers E. Lynn Harris to testify to his experiences and spark conversation on an often taboo topic. Growing up in Little Rock, Arkansas, during the integrationist period, Harris discovered that interracial interaction could be natural and easy but it also made him realize that Little Rock represented a minute part of the world. His desire to broaden his narrow perspective caused him to dream; through frequent trips to the Little Rock public library, he developed an active imagination that spurred his quest to move beyond Little Rock.

Harris was born in Flint, Michigan, the oldest of four children (he has three sisters). Raised by a single mother, he was taken to Little Rock at the age of three and attended the Little Rock public schools. His interest in writing emerged in the ninth grade when, despite bad grades, he was picked for the newspaper staff. It was the first time that he had to write something and when his first effort was accepted, he was stunned but inspired.

Harris pursued his education and exploration of the intellect as he escaped from Little Rock. He graduated with honors and a BA in journalism from the University of Arkansas at Fayetteville in 1977. He then attended Southern Methodist's Cox School of Business part-time and was recruited by IBM as a computer salesman. In 1990, however, Harris decided to become a professional writer even though the only writing connection he had had since ninth

grade was working on the college yearbook, where he preferred managing to editing. So he moved from Washington, D.C., to Atlanta to try to focus more on writing. James *Baldwin's *Go Tell It on the Mountain* (1953) and Maya *Angelou's *I Know Why the Caged Bird Sings* (1969) mesmerized Harris and inspired him to write. He was particularly impressed with Baldwin's role in the creation of the much-needed Black gay male canon. He also admires the works of Tina McElroy *Ansa, Bebe Moore Campbell, and Terry *McMillan, but his main developmental influence was his mother, not his literary mentors.

His mother does not mirror any of the characters in his books, but she instilled in Harris a preference for goodness, decency, and self-love that shines through his literature. Not only is he recreating the images of Black males and *gay males in literature, but Harris refuses to disrespect or devalue Black women in his novels. Through the influence of his mother and his sisters, as well as his extended family, Harris refuses to conceive of Black women as failures or victims. He witnessed his mother leaving an abusive marriage with four children and providing her children with love and opportunity. Harris is also proud of the fact that his late grandmother, a *domestic, represented the "seed" to forty-four grandchildren who have never been in jail or on drugs and who range in occupation from professional writers to lawyers.

The needs to be honest to and to testify to his own story through literature remain Harris's primary concerns. His writing represents complete honesty about Black male sexuality for heterosexual and homosexual men. He regards these men as complex and more fearful of showing their feelings than other groups. He does not classify Black male sexuality as an issue because men want to be sensitive and honest with their feelings but they do not know how. He works through these issues in his two published novels.

Invisible Life (1991) functions as Harris's continuation of the Black gay male canon. Playing on the theme of invisibility in Ralph *Ellison, Harris presents the coming-of-age story of Raymond, who defies the invisible ties of sexuality by growing to accept and embrace his own sexual preference. Harris is careful to avoid stereotyping his characters based on the media's interpretation of gay men; instead, he presents a male who is realistic and timeless. The text focuses mainly on Raymond and his journey, while Harris's second novel, *Just as I Am* (1994), explores several interpersonal relationships. Harris continues to testify with honesty and conviction by broadening the representation of homosexuality and AIDS in Black communities. The second novel represents a complex journey of all its characters who face realistic and timeless dilemmas in a world that is quickly changing. In some respects, *Just as I Am* acts as a sequel to *Invisible Life*, as Raymond remains the central character who bridges the lives of characters who journey past their sexual orientation to self-acceptance. Harris's latest novel, *And This Too Shall Pass* (1996), testifies in the same spirit as his previous novels and completes a trilogy dedicated to strengthening the gay literary canon.

Harris is currently working on his memoirs, which he stopped writing in 1992 when his literary career took off. The process of recording these memories has been extremely painful but has enabled him to dispel his own myths. Also, through public speaking, he provides support to younger black gay males confronting their own sexuality.

Ellison's *Invisible Man* remains a model for Harris as he explores the invisibility of Black men and their often secret lives. Similar to Ellison's, Harris's texts travel in a circular motion where the beginning is in the end; he writes the beginning last to ensure this circular movement. He also draws upon W. E. B. *Du Bois's concept of *double consciousness to represent the realistic fear of Black men to reveal and live their gay lifestyles. For his daring representations, many Black men identify with Harris and his characters and find reinforcement in their efforts to escape the pain of denial. Harris continues to assist in the creation of the African American gay literary canon by self-healing and telling the truth. His testimony inspires others to tell their stories and leave their personal worlds of denial.

—Kimberly Weaver

HASKINS, JAMES (b. 1941), author of nonfiction books for juveniles and adults, biographer, educator, critic, editor, and educational consultant. Born into a large family in a racially segregated middle-class section of Demopolis, Alabama, where he was not allowed to visit the town's public library, James S. Haskins was deeply affected by the swirl of events related to the mid-century *civil rights movement. He received his bachelor's degree in history at Alabama State College, but limited career opportunities in the South in the early 1960s led him to seek employment in New York City. Two years of selling newspaper advertisements and working as a Wall Street stockbroker brought him to the realization that he was better suited for a career in education and thus he applied for a position in the New York City public school system. After teaching music at several locations, he found a job teaching a special education class at P.S. 92. Obsessed with the plight of his inner-city pupils, he was glad to discuss their problems with anyone who would listen, including a social worker who encouraged him to write his thoughts and experiences in a diary. This resulted in the publication of his first book, *Diary of a Harlem Schoolteacher* (1969), which was widely acclaimed. This initial success attracted the attention of major publishers who approached him to write books for children and adolescents.

An admitted need to reconcile social disparities and a desire to interpret events to young people and to motivate them to read and be influenced by accomplished individuals—particularly deprived youth whom he felt had far too few role models to read about—led him to author more than one hundred books on a diverse array of topics. Written for a general audience of juveniles, his titles include *The War and the Protest: Viet Nam* (1971), *Religions* (1973), *Jobs in Business and Office* (1974), *The Consumer Movement* (1975), *Your Rights, Past and Present: A Guide for Young People* (1975), *Teen-age Alcoholism* (1976), *The Long Struggle: The Story of American Labor* (1976), *Who Are the Handicapped* (1978), *Gambling—Who Really Wins* (1978), *Werewolves* (1981), and *The New Americans: Cuban Boat People* (1982).

Haskins launched his college teaching career in 1970 and continued lecturing on psychology, *folklore, *children's and young adult literature, and urban education at schools in New York and Indiana before landing a full-time professorship in the English department at the University of Florida at Gainesville in 1977. That same year he authored *The Cotton Club*, a pictorial and social history of the notorious Harlem night club, that seven years later was transformed into a motion picture of the same name directed by Francis Ford Coppola.

Among his books intended for adults or college-level readers are *The Psychology of Black Language* (1973) with Dr. Hugh Butts; *Black Manifesto for Education* (1973), which he edited; *Snow Sculpture and Ice Carving* (1974); *Scott Joplin: The Man Who Made Ragtime* (1978); *Voodoo and Hoodoo: Their Tradition and Craft as Revealed by Actual Practitioners* (1978); *Richard Pryor, A Man and His Madness* (1984); and *Mabel Mercer: A Life* (1988). He has contributed numerous critical *essays and reviews to periodicals. Still, he is best known for his *biographies, tailored for elementary and high school students. Most of these recount the triumphs of well-known contemporary African Americans, with whom many young people readily identify. The long list of persons he has profiled (often using the pen name Jim Haskins) include Colin Powell, Barbara Jordon, Thurgood Marshall, Sugar Ray Leonard, Magic Johnson, Diana Ross, Katherine *Dunham, Guion Bluford, Andrew Young, Bill Cosby, Kareem Adbul-Jabbar, Shirley Chisholm, Lena Horne, and Rosa *Parks. Biographies of prominent individuals who are not African American include Indira and Rajiv Gandhi, Shirley Temple Black, Corazón Aquino, Winnie Mandela, and Christopher Columbus.

One of the country's most prolific authors of nonfiction for children and young adults, he has demonstrated unusual versatility in both his selection of subject matter and in gearing his material and writing to interest readers of varying levels of maturity. Critics have noted his careful research, objectivity, and a lucid and understated but straightforward writing style. Haskins has garnered a host of awards and citations, among them the Coretta Scott King Award for *The Story of Stevie Wonder* (1976), the Carter G. *Woodson Book Award of the National Council for the Social Studies for *Black Music in America: A History Through Its People* (1987), and an American Library Association Best Book for Young Adults for *The Sixties Reader* (1988).

• Jim Haskins, "The Humanistic Black Heritage of Alabama," in *Clearings in the Thicket: An Alabama Humanistic Reader,* ed. Jerry Elijah Brown, 1985, pp. 63–69. Jim Haskins, "The Triumph of the Spirit in Nonfiction for Black Children," in *Triumphs of the Spirit in Children's Literature,* ed. Richard Rotert, 1986, pp. 88–96. "Jim Haskins," in

Something about the Author Autobiography Series, vol. 4, ed. Adele Sarkissian, 1987, pp. 197–209. "Jim Haskins," in *CA*, eds. Hal May and Deborah A. Straub, 1989, pp. 186–188.

—Robert Fikes, Jr.

HAWKINS, WALTER EVERETTE (1883–?), poet.

The son of ex-slaves, and brother of the eminent African American leader John R. Hawkins, Walter Everette Hawkins was born in Warrenton, North Carolina, and educated at Kittrell College. As a young man, he moved to Washington, where he worked as a clerk in the post office, and later settled in Brooklyn, New York.

As a poet, Hawkins helped bring about the transition between the genteel tradition of the latter nineteenth century and the militancy and *Pan-Africanism of the *Harlem Renaissance. His first volume, *Chords and Discords* (1909), was an amalgam of sentimentality and racial protest, formally conservative but with an interjection of militant language unusual for its time. Entering into the continuing debates over Booker T. *Washington's policies, Hawkins's protest *poetry from this period was vociferously anti-Washingtonian, at one point condemning Washington as a "traitor," who had "sold his race to shame."

By about 1912, Hawkins had become attracted to ideals of African American distinctiveness. Working with African American leaders who would later encourage the efforts of Marcus *Garvey, Hawkins also began to write poems, published in the Pan-Africanist *African Times and Orient Review* of London, evoking an almost mystical African American identity and heritage. This was a direction he continued to pursue through the 1920s, even as he increasingly broke with the formal conservatism that had dominated his earlier works.

Hawkins was to achieve greater prominence through an association between 1917 and 1919 with the *Messenger*, the African American socialist magazine edited by A. Philip Randolph and Chandler Owen. Described as "the Messenger Poet," Hawkins published several of his earlier works in the journal—on one occasion attracting the attention of the U.S. Department of Justice for an antilynching piece—along with such new poems as "Credo," recounting a conversion to agnosticism and political radicalism. In 1920, he also published a revised edition of *Chords and Discords*. Although many of his earlier sentimental pieces reappeared in that edition, a class-oriented radicalism dominated the new works he included. In addition, and over the next several years, Hawkins republished work that had earlier appeared in the *African Times*, chiefly in the NAACP's *Crisis*.

Hawkins continued writing into the 1930s. One late poem, a radical manifesto, appeared in Nancy Cunard's left-oriented *Negro Anthology* (1934). Hawkins's own final volume, *Petals from the Poppies* (1936), came out following his move to Brooklyn. It was filled with radical ideas, as Hawkins openly celebrated a tie between art and propaganda. Although he included some sentimental verse, the directions he had begun with his *Messenger* poetry became more prominent; he even rewrote two of his earlier celebrations of African American consciousness to orient them less toward Pan-Africanism and more toward a focus on worker solidarity.

Petals from the Poppies marked the end of Hawkins's poetic career. His work continued, however, to receive some attention from such writers associated with the Harlem Renaissance as Sterling A. *Brown, his role acknowledged in creating new directions for African American letters.

• Robert T. Kerlin, *Negro Poets and Their Poems*, 1935. Sterling A. Brown, *Negro Poetry and Drama*, 1937.

—Dickson D. Bruce, Jr.

HAYDEN, ROBERT (1913–1980), poet.

Robert Hayden looms as one of the most technically gifted and conceptually expansive poets in American and African American letters. Attending to the specificities of *race and culture, Hayden's *poetry takes up the sobering concerns of African American social and political plight; yet his poetry posits race as a means through which one contemplates the expansive possibilities of language, and the transformational power of art. An award-winning poet of voice, symbol, and lyricism, Hayden's poetry celebrates human essence.

Born to a struggling couple, Ruth and Asa Sheffey (they separated soon after his birth), Hayden was taken in by a foster family, Sue Ellen Westerfield and William Hayden, and grew up in a Detroit ghetto nicknamed "Paradise Valley." The Haydens' perpetually contentious marriage, coupled with Ruth Sheffey's competition for young Hayden's affections, made for a traumatic childhood. Witnessing fights and suffering beatings, Hayden lived in a house fraught with "chronic angers" whose effects would stay with the poet throughout his adulthood. His childhood traumas resulted in debilitating bouts of depression which he later called "my dark nights of the soul." Because he was nearsighted and slight of stature, he was often ostracized by his peer group. As a response both to his household and peers, Hayden read voraciously, developing both ear and eye for transformative qualities in literature. He attended Detroit City College (Wayne State University), and left in 1936 to work for the *Federal Writers' Project, where he researched black history and folk culture. As this work proved enriching for Ralph *Ellison, Richard *Wright, Margaret *Walker, and many other black writers, Hayden's research provided him with essential material and reading skills that would fuel much of his artistry. So too, his work in the theater at Detroit City College and later at the University of Michigan, helped to develop his sense of dramatic voicing, evident in the polyvocality of "Middle Passage," one of his best-known works.

After leaving the Federal Writers' Project in 1938, marrying Erma Morris in 1940, and publishing his first volume, *Heart-Shape in the Dust* (1940), Hayden enrolled at the University of Michigan in 1941. In pursuit of a master's degree, Hayden studied under W. H. Auden, who directed Hayden's attention to issues of poetic form, technique, and artistic discipline. After finishing his degree in 1942, then teaching several years at Michigan, Hayden went to Fisk University in 1946, where he remained for twenty-three years, returning to Michigan in 1969 to complete his teaching career.

Hayden's poetry reflects dramatic growth from imitation to a fully realized and independent artistic vision. *Heart-Shape in the Dust,* largely apprenticeship work, takes many of its cues from *Harlem Renaissance poetry, particularly that of Langston *Hughes and Countee *Cullen. Though largely derivative in concept and style, its attention to social criticism and its use of racially and culturally specific materials would mark much of Hayden's ensuing work. In 1942 Hayden assembled a second collection (it remains unpublished as such, but many of the poems appear in *Selected Poems,* 1966), "The Black Spear," using much of the material unearthed during his work for the Federal Writers' Project. Responding to Stephen Vincent Benét's invitation in *John Brown's Body* (1928) for a black writer to pen the seminal "black epic," Hayden explores the complexities of an African American presence in American history. Revealing Hayden's technical development, the collection effectively uses dramatic voices, juxtaposition, irony, and montage for heightened poetic effect.

Hayden's third collection, *The Lion and the Archer* (1948), launches the career of a mature, self-possessed artist. *The Lion and the Archer, Figures of Time: Poems* (1955), *A Ballad of Remembrance* (1962), *Selected Poems* (1966), *Words in the Mourning Time* (1970), *Night-Blooming Cereus* (1972), *Angle of Ascent* (1975), *American Journal* (1978 and 1982), and *Collected Poems* (1985) establish Hayden as a major influence in American poetry, effectively bridging modernist and postmodernist eras.

An artist passionately committed to the discipline and craft of poetry, Hayden's symbolic density emerges from his manipulation of technical detail. Much of his poetry is highly economical, relying upon compression, understatement, juxtaposition, and montage, which often create highly textured and nuanced irony. Poems such as "Snow," "Approximations," "The Diver," "The Night-Blooming Cereus," and "For a Young Artist" demonstrate the pressure Hayden applies to specific words or concise phrases in order to release a range of suggestions and symbolic possibilities.

Hayden's command of technique makes possible his innovations both within and against the symbolist tradition. Hayden's thematic movement from racial or experiential specificity to fundamental commonalities relies heavily upon a symbolic system. The sordid and oppressive nature of black political life (often represented through the slave trade or the Vietnam War) finds synthesis and resolution in the symbolic realm. Thus Cinquez in "Middle Passage," or the cereus in "Night-Blooming Cereus," or Bahauallah in "Words in the Mourning Time" offer spiritual emancipation and renewal in a realm over and above the physical and limited. Here Hayden's faith as a Baha'i is central as it reinforced his belief in "transcendent humanity," a spiritual or psychic

unity of mankind capable of overcoming divisiveness.

Michael S. *Harper refers to Hayden's poetry as "a real testament to craft, to vision, to complexity and historical consciousness, and to love and transcendence." Readers find Hayden's poetry sustaining and compelling largely because of its struggle with epistemology and language; its celebration of African American oral tradition; its engagement of history; and finally its aesthetics and form. With emotional intensity achieved through technical mastery, Hayden's poetry renders a world fraught with anguish, yet one gesturing toward liberating possibility.

• Michael S. Harper, "Remembering Robert Hayden," *Michigan Quarterly Review* 21 (Winter 1982): 182–186. Fred M. Fetrow, *Robert Hayden,* 1984. Pontheolla T. Williams, *Robert Hayden: A Critical Analysis of His Poetry,* 1987. Norma R. Jones, "Robert Hayden," in *DLB,* vol. 76, *Afro-American Writers, 1940–1955,* eds. Trudier Harris and Thadious M. Davis, 1988, pp. 75–88.   —Mark A. Sanders

HAYNES, LEMUEL (1753–1833), theologian, essayist, and preacher. Social prejudice against his father's "unmingled African extraction" led Lemuel Haynes's white mother to place her unnamed infant with a Connecticut family. Maturing as an indentured servant in the home of pious Massachusetts Calvinists, Haynes joined the Minute Men upon his release from servitude in 1774 and then the Continental Army, serving briefly in the march to Fort Ticonderoga in 1776. "Liberty Further Extended" (c. 1776) began his protests against *slavery and oppression. Trading farmwork for tutorials, he studied New Divinity theology, was ordained in 1785, and accepted a pulpit in a Rutland, Vermont, Congregational church in 1788. He became an inspiring revivalist, renowned defender of orthodoxy, and scourge of liberal *religion. Affiliated with the Federalist Party, he criticized the Republicans' policy in the War of 1812, a criticism that cost him his Rutland pulpit in 1818. A last look at slavery appears in *Mystery Developed* (1820), a narrative of innocent captives unjustly held.

Haynes's critique of slavery and oppression flowed from his religion and his patriotic service. He argued that disinterested benevolence, the social ethic of American Calvinism, must cross racial lines. He insisted that liberty and natural rights, the elements of Revolutionary republicanism, should be extended to African Americans. He noted first the hypocrisy of the slaveholding and slave-trading colonies protesting British oppression, then that of the United States in the War of 1812 protesting British impressment of white mariners while slaves existed in many states. He skillfully articulated the premise of nearly all African American writing from 1760 to 1820—*sermons and preaching, *essays, poems, and the records of benevolent organizations and *churches—that Christianity and Revolutionary republicanism demand opposition to slavery and oppression. Haynes is remembered as an African American pioneer who was among the first to be ordained and to publish.

• Timothy Mather Cooley, *Sketches of the Life and Character of Rev. Lemuel Haynes, A.M.* 1837; rpt. 1969. Richard

Newman, ed. *Black Preacher to White America: The Collected Writings of Lemuel Haynes, 1774–1833*, 1990.

—John Saillant

HEALING in African American history and culture takes a two-pronged approach. There is healing located in the folk culture, that is, healing that occurs in direct response to persons having had "spells" put upon them by conjurers. The process of healing involves removing the spell and restoring the person to physical and mental health. In the second manifestation of healing, the process occurs in response to some natural illness, or to a physical counterpart of a psychological problem, or directly to a psychological problem. When writers represent healing processes in the literature, they draw upon these particular patterns.

Healing in African American literature perhaps occurs against the grain, for seldom are black characters perceived to be in need of healing. Indeed, *stereotypes of black men and women present them as hard-headed, tough-bodied, not easily injured. This physical durability presumably has an attendant psychological quality, and seldom in the literature are characters portrayed who go insane, suffer neuroses of one kind or another, or are minimally unable to function in a racist society. Perhaps one of the prevailing self-imposed stereotypes African American writers have been guilty of adhering to is making their characters almost too healthy, almost too little in need of mental and physical nurturing. Of course there are striking exceptions to this dominant pattern.

Some of the earlier instances of healing in response to conjuration occur in Charles Waddell *Chesnutt's The *Conjure Woman* (1899). In several instances in the volume, conjuration serves to transform an infirm state to a healthy one. For example, when Sis Becky in "Sis Becky's Pickaninny" believes that she is dying of conjuration, *Aun' Peggy heals her by revealing that she has been the source of the conjure in effecting the scheme to get Sis Becky reunited with the child from whom she has been sold away. And there is the healing process that goes on throughout the volume, without conjuration, in which *Uncle Julius McAdoo, the primary storyteller, inspires Annie to feel better on several occasions simply through his verbal art. As many later narratives will depict a laying on of hands as the natural mechanism for healing, Uncle Julius presents a laying on of words, a meeting of the minds that encourages Annie to health.

In the realm of placing spells and the attendant healing from conjuration, Zora Neale *Hurston's *Mules and Men* (1935) provides prime examples. Relating instances of people in New Orleans ordering the placing or removal of spells, Hurston takes readers into the world of conjuration and its ever-present ability to hurt as well as to heal. Margaret *Walker's Molly Means learns that casting a spell on a new young bride only leads to the bride being healed of that mishap and the spell being turned back on Molly herself. (Walker's Vyry Brown, in *Jubilee* [1996], however, uses roots and herbs for purposes of heal-

ing.) Toni *Morrison's M'Dear, the conjure woman in *The *Bluest Eye* (1970), has more of a reputation for healing than for hurting in that text. "She was a competent midwife and decisive diagnostician. . . . In any illness that could not be handled by ordinary means —known cures, intuition, or endurance—the word was always, 'Fetch M'Dear.'" Although her attempt to save Aunt Jimmy ultimately fails, she is nonetheless viewed on the healthier side of conjuring activities. Like Aun' Peggy, M'Dear's reputation depends as much upon verbal communal testimony to her abilities as upon the abilities themselves.

One of the most extensive healings from conjuration takes place in Gloria *Naylor's *Mama Day* (1988). Ruby, a jealous conjure woman who believes that Mama Day's niece Cocoa is after her husband, Junior, places a spell on Cocoa; it is designed so that Cocoa will literally be eaten alive by worms Ruby plants in her body. Mama Day's task is to uncover the spell and attempt a cure. The cure becomes particularly involved because it is necessary for George, Cocoa's nonbelieving husband, to participate in it. In the absence of belief, he pursues his own path to helping Cocoa, which leads to his own demise. Cocoa lives as much because of what Mama Day has been able to do to cure her as what George has failed to do. Her phsycial healing is the beginning of a long psychological recovery that literally takes years, during which Mama Day remains her spiritual guide and mentor, and George becomes her confidant, for he achieves immortality for his part in healing Cocoa of Ruby's spell.

Healers throughout African American history have held a certain status within their communities, and the literature reflects that in the reputations of Aun' Peggy, M'Dear, and Mama Day. Women who were known to cure nosebleeds by having bleeding persons insert a dime (or some other silver coin) under their tongues while the women prayed over them are but one manifestation of the phenomenon. There were also those persons, usually women, who prescribed the whiskey toddies for ailments, or who gave their children liberal doses of castor oil or other medications. Minus extranatural power, these healers nonetheless were held in esteem in their communities.

In the literature, healings from less malevolently produced illnesses than the one to which Cocoa is subjected enable characters to commune with each other, to transcend psychologically debilitating states. In Naylor's *The *Women of Brewster Place* (1982), for example, Ciel, one of the seven featured women, must overcome an abortion and the electrocution of her young daughter and find some reason to be in the world. She is converted from a desire for death to a will to live by Mattie Michael, the central figure in the text. Mattie lays hands on Ciel by literally picking her up, rocking her in her arms, giving her a cleansing bath, and coaxing her into crying out the grief of her mother loss.

This motif of the laying on of hands in the healing process occurred earlier in Ntozake *Shange's *for colored girls who have considered suicide / when the rainbow is enuf* (1977). When Bo Willie Brown drops the two children he has fathered by Crystal from a fifth-story window to their deaths, the other women in the play gather around Crystal in a laying on of hands that stroke the grief of mother loss from her and encourage her to see something beyond the tragedy of black women's lives. Crystal and the other women relate their tales of use and abuse in what may be called a ritual of healing, a ritual of laying on of mental as well as physical hands. Through serving the roles of midwives to new lives for each other, the women highlight the need as well as the ability to heal.

That need is highlighted as well in Toni Cade *Bambara's The *Salt Eaters (1980), another novel that may be viewed as an extended ritual of healing. The novel begins with a question: "Are you sure, sweetheart, that you want to be well?" It is directed to *Velma Henry, a young black woman who has slit her wrists and placed her head in a gas oven, and who is now at an infirmary where *Minnie Ransom, a famed local healer, is trying to coax her back into a desire to live. Minnie achieves her purpose by laying hands on Velma and by encouraging Velma to get rid of the internal blockages to healing. Recognizing that Velma's physical wounds are but the manifestations of deep psychological disturbances, Minnie strives to get Velma to see that the mind and the body must not only be in harmony with each other, but with the very forces of the universe. That is also the tactic that Morrison's *Baby Suggs takes in *Beloved (1987), in encouraging her friends, relatives, and neighbors to see that the physical and psychological pains of *slavery can be transcended and that they can become whole human beings again.

Alice *Walker's *Possessing the Secret of Joy (1992) makes clear as well the intersections between physical pain and the psychological pain resulting from physicality. The story of Tashi, a woman undergoing psychotherapy as a result of having suffered genital mutilation, the novel brings sharply into focus the need for women to understand and work with women in the healing process. Castration, the counterpart to what Walker depicts, seldom leaves its victims alive long enough to need healing, so overcoming that mutilation has not become a part of the literature.

Sexual violence centering upon rape is another violation that is seldom healed in the literature. Lorraine, the lesbian who is gang-raped in Naylor's The Women of Brewster Place, goes insane, beyond the reach of healing. So too does *Pecola Breedlove in Morrison's The Bluest Eye. In both instances, the potential for healing fails because there is no community of women to lay on hands; the women in Brewster Place reject Lorraine for her lesbianism, and it is too late to overcome that rejection when her tragedy occurs. Pecola is at times close to being a latchkey kid because so few adults pay sufficient attention to her; any potential to save her is thus nullified before it can be formulated and/or realized.

The body in pain. The mind in pain. The mind in pain because the body is in pain. These manifestations of the need for healing occur throughout African American literature and overwrite the stereotype of black characters being almost invincible. As a recent instance makes clear, even the character who appears healthy at times can be in need of healing. That is the case with Grant Wiggins in Ernest J. *Gaines's A Lesson Before Dying (1993). Grant believes that he has been coerced into easing the psychological pain of Jefferson, a minimally educable black man who is destined for the electric chair, but he finds out that Jefferson heals him of the pain of being a powerless black male in 1940s plantation Louisiana. His mind is as wounded as Velma Henry's or Tashi's, and Jefferson lays hands upon it as effectively as Minnie Ransom reaches Velma. Touching the body and the mind in pain, Gaines and these others writers assert, has been through the ages and remains an essential component of African American communal survival.

[See also Conjuring; Folk Literature; Folklore.]

• Trudier Harris, "From Exile to Asylum: Religion and Community in the Writings of Contemporary Black Women," in Women's Writing in Exile, ed. Mary Lynn Broe and Angela Ingram, 1989, pp. 151–169. Trudier Harris, "'This Disease Called Strength': Some Observations on the Compensating Construction of Black Female Character," Literature and Medicine 14:1 (Spring 1995): 109–126.

—Trudier Harris

HEARD, NATHAN C. (b. 1936), novelist, lecturer, musician, educator, television host, and actor. Born in Newark, New Jersey, on 7 November 1936, to Nathan E. and Gladys Pruitt Heard (a *blues singer), Nathan Cliff Heard was reared by his mother and maternal grandmother in Newark's inner city; he dropped out of school at fifteen, drifted into a life of crime, and spent the next seventeen years (1951–1968) in and out of New Jersey State Prison at Trenton where he served time for armed robbery.

While in prison Heard distinguished himself as a talented and award-winning athlete. It was not until fellow prisoner Harold Carrington introduced him to the masters—Langston *Hughes, Samuel Beckett, James *Baldwin, Jean Genet, Amiri *Baraka, and others—that Heard began to write, at first about *music and African history. In 1963, encouraged by his fellow inmates, he wrote the manuscript for To Reach a Dream. Although the *novel did not sell, Heard continued to write and read books on writing. In 1968, he succeeded in publishing Howard Street shortly before his release from prison.

Heard is important in African American literature because of his unique ability to imbue his writing with a keen perception of his particular worlds. He infuses his fiction (especially his characters) with his own sense of the pain and hardship of the ghetto and the prison. For Heard, they are significant landscapes. Against these backgrounds, he created his fiction, one that illuminates the brutal realities, the hardships, and despair of these worlds he knew well. Heard's characters are denizens of one or both of these places. Howard Street (1968) is a gripping portrait of hustlers, pimps, *prostitutes, and other "streeters," and their lives in the ghetto. Just as

Heard exposes the horrors of the urban wasteland, he reveals the brutal, violent experiences of the prison system. Heard's *House of Slammers* (1983) is a graphic exposé of prison life, important because it offers a wider canvas than most prison fiction. In this novel, Heard shows the raw, violent life in the American penal system, especially for the nonwhites who constitute the majority of America's prison population. H. Bruce Franklin, in his book *Prison Literature in America* (1989), tells us that *"House of Slammers* is the most important novel yet published about the American prison."

Richard Yarborough, in an article in the *Dictionary of Literary Biography* (1984), describes Heard as an urban realist. In fact, Heard can be regarded as a "latter-day Richard *Wright." For, like Wright, Heard exploits with unusual skill the harsh, mean realities of the black urban experience in America, drawing sharp, biting portraits of the ghetto and prison life he knows firsthand. His writing is unquestionably an authentic representation of black street life, especially his mastery of ghetto vernacular. Heard's literary reputation rests on his novels—*Howard Street, To Reach a Dream* (1972), *A Cold Fire Burning* (1974), *When Shadows Fall* (1977), and *House of Slammers*—and articles, which include "Boodie the Player" (in *We Be Word Sorcerers: Twenty-five Stories by Black Americans*, ed. Sonia Sanchez, 1973). In 1996 he was completing another novel, "A Time of Desperation."

In addition to writing, Heard taught creative writing at Fresno State College (now California State University, Fresno) from 1969 to 1970 and was an assistant professor of English at Livingstone College (Rutgers University) from 1970 to 1972. He won the Author's Award from the New Jersey Association of Teachers of English in 1969 and from Newark College of Engineering in 1973, and the Most Distinguished Teacher Award of Fresno State College.

• Noel Schraufnagel, *From Apology to Protest*, 1973. Richard Yarborough, "Nathan C. Heard," in *DLB*, vol. 33, *Afro-American Fiction Writers after 1955*, eds. Thadious M. Davis and Trudier Harris, 1984, pp. 110–115. Linda Metzger, Sr., ed. *Black Writers: A Selection of Sketches from Contemporary Authors*, 1985. Bruce H. Franklin, *Prison Literature in American: Victim as Criminal and Artist*, 3d rev. ed., 1989.

—Marva O. Banks

HELGA CRANE is the protagonist of Nella *Larsen's 1928 *novel *Quicksand*. An intelligent, sensual, beautiful, searching, and ambitious woman, Helga's quest for security and satisfaction takes her between black society and white society, between the folk and elite cultures of the rural South, the urban North, and even Copenhagen, Denmark. Many have noted the autobiographical similarities between Crane and Larsen. Both are mixed-race women reared by their white mothers from whom they became estranged and who moved (with ambivalence) into black communities. Helga teaches at Naxos, a school modeled after Tuskegee—where Larsen briefly taught. Though biographers have found no supporting evidence, Nella Larsen claimed to have lived in Copenhagen, where Helga spends two years during her search for self-knowledge. And both Nella Larsen and Helga Crane have been noted as daring representatives of modern African American middle-class women. W. E. B. *Du Bois, for example, wrote that Helga was "typical" of the *New Negro woman "on whom the shadow of 'race' sits negligibly and Life is always first."

Contemporary critics recognize Helga Crane as an innovative case study especially open to psychoanalytic interpretations. Some see Crane's quest to be a search for happiness, peace of mind, social status, sexual fulfillment, and racial *identity. Others see her as the "marginal black woman of the middle class" and as the embodiment of Du Bois's "*double consciousness" that even the "New Negroes" could not reconcile.
—Frances Smith Foster

HEMINGS, SALLY (1773–1835), enduring icon in America's imagination since abolition and Thomas Jefferson's alleged lover for thirty-eight years. Sally Hemings was emancipated in 1828, and her mystique subjected her to legend of the magnitude that posthumously hounds Elvis Presley. Hemings sightings proliferated in antislavery periodicals, and she was fictionalized in fugitive slave William Wells *Brown's *novel *Clotel, or The President's Daughter* (1853).

Hemings was half sister to Jefferson's wife, Martha, born to Martha's father, John Wayles, and Betty, a half-white slave. An inheritance from Wayles, the quadroon Hemings was house slave at Monticello. Published documentation of the Hemings-Jefferson affair began with a 1 September 1802 exposé by James Thomson Callender in Richmond's *Recorder*.

Biographers who dispute the relationship, including Dumas Malone and Virginius Dabney, oppose historian Fawn Brodie and novelist Barbara *Chase-Riboud (*Sally Hemings*, 1979), who authenticate it. Virtually dismissed have been oral histories of descendants of Thomas Woodson, Hemings's oldest child; testimony recalled from Hemings herself; African Methodist Episcopal records; and ex-slaves' stories. This forces a confrontation on the relevance and reliability of oral traditions. The dispute emblematizes the diminished value and half-hearted evaluation of dictated, collective, and nonsecular sources in African American literature.

As did two of her children, Hemings could have passed as white. Yet names that the public imposed upon her—"Black Sal," "Dusky Sally," "African Venus"—denoted darkness exclusively, and they denigrated mulattas who threatened white racial purity. In retaliation, abolitionists such as William Wells Brown manipulated Hemings to debunk the rhetoric of unadulterated whiteness and to argue that the Republic only masqueraded as egalitarian. Hemings inspired a satirical song, "Jefferson's Daughter," in Brown's *Antislavery Harp* (1848) and a symbolic, sympathetic reference in *Iola Leroy* (1892), Frances Ellen Watkins *Harper's Reconstruction romance. Her figure asserts the hypocrisy of Jefferson's libertarian politics.

• Minnie Shumate Woodson, "Researching to Document the Oral History of the Thomas Woodson Family: Dismantling the Sable Curtain," *Journal of the Afro-American Historical and Genealogical Society* 6 (Spring 1985): 3–12. Paul Finkelman, "Thomas Jefferson and Antislavery: The Myth Goes On," *Virginia Magazine of History and Biography* 102 (Apr. 1994): 193–228. —Barbara McCaskill

HENDERSON, GEORGE WYLIE (b. 1904), novelist. Born in Warrior's Stand, Alabama, George Wylie Henderson served a printer's apprenticeship at Tuskegee before moving to New York City and eventually writing for the *Daily News* and other publications.

Henderson's acclaimed work *Ollie Miss*, a 1935 *novel of rural southern folklife, centers on an attractive eighteen-year-old, hardworking, female farmhand who accepts the consequences for her own decisions and pursues a romantic relationship with Jule, another worker. Following a nearly fatal attack by Jule's jealous lover, Ollie Miss recovers and learns she is pregnant with Jule's child yet rejects his offer to stay with her. The novel closes with Ollie Miss, serenely pregnant with hope of a new future, working her own plot of land.

Published in 1946, *Jule*, sequel to *Ollie Miss*, focuses on the illegitimate son named for his father. Young Jule moves from Hannon, Alabama, where he attacks a white man for making advances toward Bertha Mae, his teenage girlfriend, and escapes to New York where he encounters numerous characters, black and white. In learning to survive, Jule moves from innocent to experienced and becomes a printer's apprentice and even a member of the printers' union. The novel ends with Jule's return to Alabama for his mother's funeral; he plans to marry Bertha Mae and return to New York.

Ollie Miss was applauded for its authentic portrayal of rural black life through setting and characterization. Though Henderson introduced racial and social protest in *Jule*, the less favorably reviewed sequel was sharply criticized for its thin character development.

Although Henderson published no novels after *Jule*, he remains significant because his works span the end of the *Harlem Renaissance and the beginning of the social *protest literature of the 1940s and 1950s.

• Emmanuel S. Nelson, "George Wylie Henderson," in *DLB*, vol. 51, *Afro-American Writers from the Harlem Renaissance to 1940*, ed. Trudier Harris, 1987, pp. 96–100. Lonnell E. Johnson, "The Defiant Black Heroine: *Ollie Miss* and Janie Mae—Two Portraits from the '30s," *Zora Neale Hurston Forum* 4.2 (Spring 1990): 41–46. —Lonnell E. Johnson

HENRY BLACUS. *See* Henry Blake.

HENRY BLAKE. The pure-black hero of Martin R. *Delany's epic *novel, *Blake, or The Huts of America* (1859, 1861–1862), is late in assuming his titular name. Born Henrico Blacus in Cuba, he had gone to sea as a young man, had been compelled to work first in the Atlantic slave trade and later as a semifree man in Natchez, Mississippi, where—as *Blake* begins—he calls himself Harry or Henry Holland.

When his wife, a slave, is sold away to Cuba, he rapidly evolves into an anti–*Uncle Tom character—and something more than the familiar fugitive slave. Renaming himself Gilbert Hopewell, he becomes an Odyssean observer and schemer, Mosaic-Christian Gospel reviser and advisor, and Romantic-Victorian revolutionary. He boldly races through North America from Texas to Canada to New York to Cuba, promotes black unity and self-reliance in conspirators awaiting his signal for a coordinated strike against white oppressors, notes sociopolitical conditions and attitudes within and between the races, and respectfully takes in folk songs and sayings.

He returns to his island home, rescues his wife from a wicked suitor, finally identifies himself as Henry Blake, signs on to a slaveship to Africa and back, recruits the cargo for his revolutionary army, and organizes supporters. In such travels to so many corners of the African American world, Black becomes the first Afrocentric, Pan-African, revolutionary ideologue and hero in world literature. The final outcome of his scheming, however, remains unknown because of the loss of the story's last six chapters. —Allan D. Austin

HENSON, JOSIAH (1789–1883), slave narrator, Methodist preacher, educator, activist in the Underground Railroad, and prototype for the title character in Harriet Beecher *Stowe's *Uncle Tom's Cabin* (1852). Josiah Henson was born a slave in Charles County, Maryland on 15 June 1789. The details of his life are recorded in *The Life of Josiah Henson, Formerly a Slave, Now an Inhabitant of Canada, as Narrated by Himself* (1849). As a very young child Henson states that he was largely unaware that his life was in any way remarkable. It was not until the death of his master, Dr. McPherson, and the sale of his mother and siblings that the real horrors and anxieties of slave life impressed him. After his family is sold, he recalls earlier times when his mother was sexually assaulted and his father was mutilated. In spite of the cruel treatment his mother received at the hands of so-called Christians, she taught him a sense of *religion. In 1828, Henson became a preacher in the Methodist Episcopal Church. In 1830, finally convinced that his present master, Isaac Riley, was a beast, he escaped with his wife and four children, reaching Canada on 28 October. After his escape, Henson helped over a hundred slaves escape from Kentucky to Canada.

Henson's life story was first recorded in his 1849 *slave narrative, which received little public attention. Harriet Beecher Stowe, however, appreciated Henson's story and made reference to him in her *Key to Uncle Tom's Cabin*. She wrote the introduction to the enlarged 1858 text, *Truth Stranger than Fiction: Father Henson's Story of His Own Life*. Two other versions of Henson's life story appeared in 1876 and 1878; each of these texts was quite popular because Henson was known as Stowe's inspiration for her *Uncle Tom character. Henson died in Dresden, Ontario, Canada on 5 May 1883.

• Sister Mary Ellen Doyle, "Josiah Henson's Narrative: Before and After," *Black American Literature Forum* 8 (Spring 1975): 176–182.   —Charles P. Toombs

HERCULES, FRANK (b. 1917), novelist and nonfiction writer. Frank Hercules may best be termed a minor writer in the canon of African American literature. Three book-length works of fiction and several sociological works constitute his literary production, despite the fact that he has been a career writer for nearly half a century. Despite a limited output, however, the themes addressed by Hercules in his various works have earned him a place of relative importance in the African American literary field.

Hercules was born on 12 February 1917 in Trinidad, the son of an educator and activist father who was subsequently exiled from the island for his activism. Hercules studied law in London in the late 1930s and emigrated to America in the 1940s. He became an American citizen in 1959.

Although he began writing in 1942, Hercules's first novel did not appear until 1961. *Where the Hummingbird Flies* is largely a folk novel, set in Hercules's native Trinidad, that attempts a psychological probing of the effects of colonization on both colonizer and subject. The novel was a successful first novel and earned several distinctions for Hercules including the Fletcher Pratt Memorial Fellowship of the Breadloaf Writers' Conference.

Hercules's next novel, *I Want a Black Doll*, appeared in 1967 to less than enthusiastic readers in the United States, although it was relatively successful in England and Europe. Its theme, interracial marriage, and its timing during an explosive period in American life perhaps combined to prevent a positive reception of the novel in this country. Hercules's last work of fiction, *On Leaving Paradise*, published in 1980, is a picaresque novel in the tradition of *Candide*. Its central character, Johnny de Paria, is forced to leave his homeland of Trinidad for a world where his values are constantly tested as he struggles to make sense out of conflict. In the novel, Hercules demonstrates once again his keen understanding of the West Indian setting and the colonial experience.

All of the other works Hercules has published to date have been sociological in nature, beginning with several about Harlem. These *essays, "An Aspect of the Negro Renaissance" (1942), "The Decline and Fall of Sugar Hill" (1965), and "To Live in Harlem" (1977), demonstrate not only the author's keen insight into societal issues, but equally important, his fondness for the area even as he laments its decline. Hercules's major work of nonfiction appeared in 1972. *American Society and Black Revolution*, as its title suggests, explores the struggles of African Americans in an essentially racist society. These struggles, according to Hercules, are often compounded by the ineptitude of black leadership and black Americans' own inability to come to terms with the real issues of *freedom. The work is powerful in its treatment of the opposing forces of American racism and black revolutionary change, and is useful beyond measure for assessing the development of the struggle of African Americans.

Frank Hercules has not been a prolific or popular writer. His works, both fiction and nonfiction prose, however, display an artistry and insight that few can match and for which he is best remembered.

• Carol P. Marsh, "Frank Hercules," in *DLB*, vol. 33, *Afro-American Fiction Writers after 1955*, eds. Thadious M. Davis and Trudier Harris, 1984, pp. 115–119. "Frank Hercules," in *Black Writers: A Selection of Sketches from Contemporary Authors*, ed. Linda Metzger, 1989, p. 270.
                    —Warren J. Carson

HERNTON, CALVIN C. (b. 1934), poet, novelist, essayist, and educator. Born 28 April in Chattanooga, Tennessee, to Magnolia Jackson, Calvin Coolidge Hernton came of age as a writer in the late 1960s and early 1970s. His *poetry, *novels, and *essays reflect not only his education in the social sciences (a BA from Talladega College, 1954, and an MA in sociology from Fisk, 1956) but the issues predominant at that time as well. Hernton worked as a social worker in New York (1960–1961) and cofounded *Umbra* magazine in 1963. Hernton studied under R. D. Laing from 1965 to 1969 as a research fellow at the London Institute of Phenomenological Studies. He began his teaching career as an instructor in history and sociology in South Carolina (Benedict College, 1957–1958), Florida (Edward Waters College, 1958–1959), at the University of Alabama (1959–1960), and at Louisiana's Southern University (1960–1961). From 1970 to 1972, he was writer in residence at Oberlin College, where since 1973 he has been tenured as professor of *Black Studies and creative writing.

Hernton's major nonfiction works are *Sex and Racism in America* (1965) and *White Papers for White Americans* (1966). In *Sex and Racism* he argues that the complex intertwining of sex and racism begun during *slavery persists. According to Hernton, this phenomenon originated with the white male's choices: to elevate the white female beyond sexual desire and to seek the black female for sex, in reaction to his puritan discomfort about sex; and in guilt over his actions, to view the black male as desiring the white female. Hernton explains that this sexual "involvement [is] so immaculate and yet so perverse, so ethereal and yet so concrete, that all race relations tend to be, however subtly, *sexual* relations." In *White Papers*, a collection of personal essays exploring sociological issues, "Grammar of the Negro Revolution" stands as an early analysis of the nonrevolutionary middle-class aims of the *civil rights movement: "The Negro is not yet willing to run the risk of a total assault on the culture, to find that many of the things for which he has fought, and is fighting, will no longer be available, within the socioeconomic and political framework that now characterizes this nation." Written before the development of feminist theory, Hernton's analyses in these two essays presage the critique African American feminists would make in the 1970s of the unracialized, middle-class biases of the feminist "revolution."

The theme of the sexual nature of racism can be found in most of Hernton's work. His novel *Scarecrow* (1974) explores the fatal psychosexual problems of voyagers on board the *Castel Felice* to Europe; and in the free-verse poems of *Medicine Man* (1976), individuals contend with a variety of physical, social, and emotional entrapments in an unloving world. Hernton's poetry as well as his essays on James *Baldwin have been anthologized; his most recent critical work includes *The Sexual Mountain and Black Women Writers* (1987) and "The Poetic Consciousness of Langston *Hughes: From Affirmation to Revolution" (*Langston Hughes Review*, Spring 1993). Hernton's early and acute analyses of the complexities of the history of race relations in America and his insistence on the constructed nature of those relations place him as a significant contributor to African American theory.

—Mary Anne Stewart Boelcskevy

Hero Ain't Nothin' but a Sandwich, A. Alice *Childress's *A Hero Ain't Nothin' but a Sandwich* (1973) is a *novel that explores the debilitating effects of drugs on a youngster, Benjie Johnson, his family, and his community. A product of the urban ghetto, Benjie is seduced into taking and selling heroin by neighborhood ne'er-do-wells. The issues of *identity and the quest for wholeness that surround Benjie's use of drugs are significant in light of the fact that the novel is set immediately following the *civil rights movement of the 1960s, when fragmentation and alienation characterized the period. Childress portrays Benjie as a strong-willed, iconoclastic teenager who believes he has to prove something to the world while simultaneously depicting him as a hurting, confused, overwhelmed, sensitive, and intellectually curious youth who craves love and security.

Childress writes Benjie as an anesthetized youth who is having trouble coping with the fact that his biological father abandoned him and that his mother has found a surrogate father for him in Butler Craig. While Benjie's mother and grandmother do their best to nurture him, it is the men in the novel who have the greatest influence on him. His teachers, Nigeria Greene and Bernard Cohen, try to put Benjie on the right track, but it is only when Butler Craig risks his life for Benjie that he begins to want to beat his drug addiction. Butler Craig proves to be the real hero, not the celebrities that the social worker offers Benjie in her attempt to give him hope. When Butler Craig sees Benjie hanging from the ledge and has to decide whether to put himself at risk to save an arrogant stepchild, he chooses to reach out to Benjie. While the novel ends with Butler Craig waiting for Benjie to show up for a counseling session, the point is well made that Benjie does not stand a chance at surviving without someone like Butler Craig, a strong African American male figure, reminding him daily that he is loved and that he can triumph.

A Hero Ain't Nothin' but a Sandwich illustrates the pervasiveness of drug use not only in urban ghettoes but in society in general. Childress argues that the world has become a place where youngsters and adults rely heavily upon opiates to feel good about themselves. On another level, Childress boldly suggests that women can sometimes be powerless in saving their sons. She certainly implies that women

alone cannot teach their sons how to become men. She forthrightly suggests that African American men must take responsibility for their youth and try to shelter them from destructive forces. Childress urges African American men to call for nation time, a coming together of black men and women to help preserve their community and build strong self-esteem in their children.

A Hero Ain't Nothin but a Sandwich gave high visibility to Childress as a skilled author of adolescent fiction. For the first time in her writing career, she was able to reach the masses in a way that she had not been able to do with her Off-Broadway and community theater–produced plays. Childress's novel is a milestone because, unlike many of her female contemporaries, she creates a loving, sensitive, generous African American man, Butler Craig, taking responsibility for his family. Childress uniquely captures the beauty and pain of being African American, and she does so by showing that men as well as women are needed to keep the family viable.

• Ed Bullins, review of *A Hero Ain't Nothin' but a Sandwich*, *New York Times Book Review*, 4 Nov. 1973, 36–40. Elizabeth Brown-Guillory, "A Hero Ain't Nothin' but a Sandwich," in *Masterpieces of African-American Literature*, ed. Frank N. Magill, 1992, pp. 193–196.

—Elizabeth Brown-Guillory

"Heroic Slave, The." "The Heroic Slave," a novella by Frederick *Douglass, was published in March 1853 and is now recognized as the first work of African American long fiction. Amplifying the history of Madison Washington, leader of the successful 1841 *Creole* slave ship mutiny, Douglass creates for him a fuller chronicle and voice to articulate his motives and champion his actions. The story opens by insisting that despite his slave origins, Washington deserves a place of honor alongside the American Revolutionary hero evoked by his name. Douglass then introduces him through a soliloquy overheard by a white Ohioan, Listwell, who becomes an abolitionist upon hearing the unseen orator's yearning for *freedom. When years later the distinctively African-featured, intellectually keen, physically intimidating yet kind-spirited Washington escapes from Virginia, Listwell assists him in reaching Canada. Listwell next meets Washington years later in Virginia, where Washington, recaptured while attempting to free his wife, is bound for the New Orleans slave market aboard the *Creole*. In the climactic mutiny, narrated by the ship's surviving first mate, Washington displays both militancy and mercy, resolutely initiating *violence that leaves two dead but temperately preventing further bloodshed. Coupling the slaves' uprising with a contemporaneous squall, Douglass employs popular romantic sea imagery with his earlier American Revolutionary discourse to fashion a powerful statement about slaves' natural right to freedom. Studied for its rhetorical design, its relationship to Douglass's autobiographical writing, its development of a fictive voice, its gendered conception of ideal *manhood, and its endorsement of violent revolt, the tale attests to the complex motives behind early African American fiction.

[*See also* Insurrections; Novel; Slavery.]

• Richard Yarborough, "Race, Violence, and Manhood: The Masculine Ideal in Frederick Douglass's 'The Heroic Slave,'" in *Frederick Douglass: New Literary and Historical Essays*, ed. Eric J. Sundquist, 1990, pp. 166–188. Eric Sundquist, *To Wake the Nations: Race in the Making of American Literature*, 1993, pp. 115–124.   —Brad S. Born

HERRON, CAROLIVIA (b. 1947), educator, novelist, and short fiction writer. Carolivia Herron was born in Washington, D.C. She earned her BA in English literature from Eastern Baptist College, an MA in English from Villanova University, and another MA in comparative literature and creative writing and her PhD in comparative literature and literary theory from the University of Pennsylvania. Herron has taught at Harvard University (1986–1990) and at Mount Holyoke College (1990–1992). In 1985, she won a Fulbright Post-Doctoral Research award, and a Folger Shakespeare Library Post-Doctoral Research award in 1989. She edited the *Selected Works of Angelina Weld *Grimké* (1991) as part of the Schomburg Library series on nineteenth-century African American women writers. Her short story, "That Place," was published in **Callaloo* in 1987.

Herron's first and only *novel to date, *Thereafter Johnnie* (1991), took eighteen years to complete. Taking place in Washington, D.C., the novel is set against an apocalyptic race war in the year 2000 and chronicles the decline of the black middle-class family. The protagonist, Johnnie, is a product of an incestuous relationship between her mother/sister and her father/grandfather. The novel breaks down the taboos and barriers against openly discussing incest and sexual abuse. Herron herself alleges that she was sexually abused by a male relative when she was three years old. Herron's lyrical style has been compared to Toni *Morrison's. The stream of consciousness technique is reminiscent of James Joyce. Herron has also been compared to Alice *Walker, Gloria *Naylor, and Ralph *Ellison. *Thereafter Johnnie* gained its most critical acclaim for its mythic style. Herron is currently working on a three-volume study of the African American epic tradition.

• Farai Chideya, "Two Tales of the Apocalypse," *Newsweek*, 15 July 1991, 53. Andrea Stuart, "Memory and Prophecy," *New Statesman and Society* 5 (5 June 1992): 40–41.
                                              —Alisha R. Coleman

HIGH JOHN THE CONQUEROR, a folk term most often associated with conjuring powers and designated by variable names including "High John de Conker," "Low John de Conker," "John the Conqueror root," and "High John." This term may refer to a plant, or a plant-derived substance, that is believed to have conjuring capabilities. It also is said to be a *trickster figure in African American culture.

According to folk belief, High John as a "root medicine" will protect a subject against evil spirits and control potentially conflicting situations including love relationships, gambling, litigation, employment, and financial matters. It is most often associated with success, happiness, and improving one's fortune. This product may be dug directly from the woods or purchased from conjurers and used in a variety of forms, including a nonprocessed root, diced, liquid, or powder state.

The notion of High John as a traditional folk hero is somewhat speculative given that none of the collections of tales includes any reference to a figure by that specific name. Zora Neale *Hurston appears to be the first to claim that the trickster in the cycles of John and Marster tales is High John. In these tales, John, a cunning slave, may assume the posture of a rogue, naive rascal, or fool when he encounters an oppressive master who reminds him of his limited possibilities on the plantation. John may outsmart his dumbwitted boss, or he may be the unwilling recipient of a misapplied plan. Hurston eloquently valorizes the slave voice through this association. High John is a symbol of the slaves' indomitable spirit, which Hurston argues began in Africa but assumed a more physical form in the New World through High John who metaphorically becomes the ultimate conjure maker.

It is unclear how widespread the usage of this term is. The identification of High John as a root medicine is dependent upon locale and the expertise of the conjurers. They do not all agree on which particular plant or plant-derived substance "High John" is. There is little documentation to support the claim that High John as a trickster figure is derived from the African American oral tradition. None of the collected tales about John, a trickster figure in *slavery and *freedom, refers to this hero as "High John." Much more research needs to be conducted on this topic to determine more clearly its application in African American culture.

[*See also* Conjuring; Folklore.]

• Zora Neale Hurston, "High John De Conquer," *American Mercury* 57 (1943): 450–458. Harry Hyatt, *Hoodoo, Conjuration, Witchcraft, and Rootwork*, vol. 1, 1970, pp. 455–457 and 593–595.   —Carol S. Taylor Johnson

HILL, LESLIE PINCKNEY (1880–1960), educator and poet. Reflecting the fundamental goals of the *New Negro movement, Leslie Pinckney Hill devoted his professional life to the pursuit of "freedom, justice, and fundamental equality," in short, full citizenship for the African American. After receiving his elementary education in the town of his birth, Lynchburg, Virginia, and his secondary education in East Orange, New Jersey, Hill attended Harvard University, where he earned his BA (1903) and MA (1904) degrees, and began to pursue politics through education. In 1904 Hill began his career in education at Tuskegee Institute, teaching English and education under Booker T. *Washington. He was subsequently appointed principal at the Manassas Industrial Institute in Manassas, Virginia, from 1907 to 1913. In 1913 Hill began his thirty-eight-year administration of the Institute for Colored Youth, which, through his leadership, became Cheyney Training School for Teachers (1914), State Normal School (1920), and Cheyney State Teachers College (1951).

Though Hill emphasizes education as the key to racial progress, his *essay "What the Negro Wants and How to Get It: The Inward Power of the Masses" articulates the philosophy that informs his educational models and artistic works. That "the human family is one" for Hill summarizes his vision of universal brotherhood, a vision that ultimately negates racial difference in celebration of transcendent commonalities.

Hill's two artistic publications, *The Wings of Oppression* (1921), a collection of sixty-nine poems in standard verse, and *Toussaint L'Ouverture: A Dramatic History* (1928), a dramatic portrait in verse, reveal his didactic leanings and his commitment to universalities. His collection reviews racial, political, and deeply personal themes, all pointing toward the perpetual resilience of the human spirit. Likewise, Hill's *drama celebrates Toussaint *L'Ouverture's heroism and that of black Haitians, while lamenting L'Ouverture's tragic betrayal and demise. Although little known, Hill's works and career effectively illustrate the unequivocal *New Negro claim to full participation in American political, social, and intellectual life.

• Milton M. James, "Leslie Pinckney Hill," *Negro History Bulletin* 24 (Mar. 1937): 135–137. Patsy B. Perry, "Leslie Pinckney Hill," in *DLB*, vol. 51, *Afro-American Writers from the Harlem Renaissance to 1940*, ed. Trudier Harris, 1987, pp. 101–105.   —Mark A. Sanders

HIMES, CHESTER (1909–1984), novelist. A prolific writer whose career spans fifty years, Chester Himes is best known for his naturalist and detective fiction. A gambler, hustler, burglar, ex-convict, and expatriate, Himes's catholic experiences and peripatetic life provided him abundant material for fiction that portrays the near existential "absurdity" of blackness in America. Focusing on *violence—physical, political, and psychic—as a ubiquitous dynamic in American culture, Himes's fiction ponders the often futile struggle to resist a relentlessly hostile environment.

Born into a struggling middle-class family in Jefferson City, Missouri, Himes's childhood, and that of his two older brothers, Edward and Joseph, was marked by the chronic tensions between his parents and the perpetual disruptions that occurred due to the family's frequent relocation. Himes describes his father, Joseph Sandy Himes, as a dark-skinned man plagued by the internalized stigma of his blackness. Conversely, Himes saw his mother, Estelle Bomar, fair-skinned, as a woman who privileged her white heritage and aspired toward genteel refinement. Exacerbating their differences, Joseph, Sr., worked and taught machinery at several industrial schools across the South, placing Estelle Bomar in contact with rural and poorly educated black communities. After Joseph, Jr.'s accidental blinding in 1923, the family moved several times in search of medical treatment, ending up in Cleveland, Ohio, where the family finally broke up. This break up, in the middle of Himes's adolescence, coupled with a debilitating back injury (for which he was forced to wear an embarrassing brace for several years), left Himes withdrawn and profoundly alienated.

Himes enrolled at Ohio State University in the fall of 1926 to study medicine, but because of his sense of anger and alienation spent his opening quarter exploring Columbus's night life and underworld. After withdrawing from school and returning to Cleveland to live with his father, Himes committed a series of crimes resulting in a 1928 conviction for armed robbery. Facing twenty years of hard labor, Himes entered prison at age nineteen and began his writing career there. His first *short stories, "Crazy in the Stir" and "To What Red Hell," portray the hardships of prison life and reveal his preoccupation with the capricious nature of black life. The arbitrariness of persecution coupled with the severely limited means of recourse available to his black protagonists would mark Himes's early naturalist fiction.

Upon parole in 1936 Himes attempted to make a living as a writer. His career divides roughly into three phases, each emphasizing different dimensions of the fundamental predicament of black selfhood in the midst of ubiquitous racism. From 1945 to 1955, the first phase of his career, he published five naturalist novels, all largely autobiographical: *If He Hollers Let Him Go* (1945), *Lonely Crusade* (1947), *The Third Generation* (1947), *Cast the First Stone* (1952), and *The Primitive* (1955). His first two novels render a fatalistic vision of black masculinity, as the respective protagonists, Bob Jones and Lee Gordon, struggle to resist the overdetermination of their racist environments. Ralph Reckly interprets these novels as demonstrating "that the black male who does not subjugate his will to the mainstream cannot survive in America." *Cast the First Stone* reconfigures a totalizing environment in terms of prison. Drawing heavily from his own experiences, Himes presents his white protagonist, Jim Monroe, in a constant state of peril as he attempts to survive interpersonal and institutional brutality. Although Monroe is white, Himes remains focused upon the tenuous proposition of autonomous selfhood.

Completing the first phase of his career, Himes reenvisions the trauma of his childhood family life in *The Third Generation*, and examines the complexities of interracial sexual attraction in *The Primitive*. *The Third Generation* explores the ways in which adults act out their imbided racial self-hatred, and the ways in which they transmit their neuroses to their children. *The Primitive* uses a murderous interracial relationship in order to portray the overdetermination of racial *stereotypes. That Jesse Robinson, a black male, can see Kriss Cummings, a white female, only as the icon of white virtue, and that Kriss can see Jesse only in terms of primitivist sexuality predetermines a profoundly destructive relationship. Here, as with most of the early fictions, the overarching cultural conceptions of race relegate Himes's characters to severely circumscribed social and psychological spaces. Invariably violence and destruction result.

Following Richard *Wright's example, in 1953 Himes left the United States for France, becoming an expatriate in pursuit of wider personal freedoms and greater publishing opportunities. Both *If He Hollers Let Him Go* and *Lonely Crusade* had already garnered a substantial readership in France, initiating a trend that would outlast Himes's life. Upon the suggestion of an editor, Himes began writing detective fiction, originally to make quick money. From 1957 to 1969, the second phase of his career, he wrote perhaps his most famous novels, eight detective novels set in Harlem: *For Love of Imabelle* (1957), *The Real Cool Killers* (1959), *The Crazy Kill* (1959), *The Big Gold Dream* (1960), *All Shot Up* (1960), **Cotton Comes to Harlem* (1965), *The Heat's On* (1966), and *Blind Man with a Pistol* (1969). Featuring the duo *Grave Digger Jones and *Coffin Ed Johnson, Himes adopts standard detective fiction formula, but uses it to posit black violence as a response to oppressive conditions. Jones and Johnson, like most heroes of the genre, are entrusted with the protection and maintenance of the community. But the means by which they solve crimes, right wrongs, and bring criminals to justice suggest an agency and independence wholly negated in Himes's earlier fiction. The duo uses violence according to their own sense of propriety, and mete out justice in ways often independent of conventional, legal, or judicial practices.

Attesting to the popularity of Himes's detective fiction, *The Heat's On (Come Back Charleston Blue)* and *Cotton Comes to Harlem* were made into movies, and many of the novels remain in print.

During the same period Himes wrote two novels that deviate from the trend: *Pinktoes* (1961) and *Run Man Run* (1966). *Pinktoes* satirizes interracial sexual attraction, presenting self-absorbed characters acting upon their sexual desires for the racial "other." *Run Man Run*, though still detective fiction, does not feature the standard heroes or celebrate their abilities, but ponders the threat of unbridled police brutality. Jimmy Johnson, a poor black student, witnesses the second of two murders perpetrated by a black detective, Matt Walker. Attempting to cover up his crime, Walker stalks Johnson and eventually kills him. Although Walker's crimes are discovered by a fellow detective, Sergeant Brock, Brock protects Johnson out of a warped sense of familial and professional loyalty.

By the beginning of the 1970s, Himes embarked upon the final phase of his career. Along with a volume of collected works—*Black on Black: Baby Sister and Selected Writings* (1973)—and several short novels, Himes published an *autobiography in two volumes: *The Quality of Hurt* (1972) and *My Life of Absurdity* (1976). Both volumes propose a life profoundly marked by cultural and institutional racism. Himes's autobiographical hero acts and reacts according to the political and psychic violence that surrounds him, only momentarily claiming for himself a tenuous sense of peace and stability. Read as a final statement responding to both his life and art, Himes's autobiography reiterates his central concern for the random, near chaotic nature of African American life in Western culture. Several critics have commented on the compelling tension between near futility and the individual's defiant responses to such daunting environments found in Himes's work. Just short of naturalism's totalization, Himes's fiction perpetually explores the efficacy of black male agency.

[*See also* Crime and Mystery Writing; Expatriatism.]

• Stephen F. Milliken, *Chester Himes: A Critical Appraisal,* 1976. Ralph Reckley, "Chester Himes," in *DLB,* vol. 76, *Afro-American Writers, 1940–1955,* eds. Trudier Harris and Thadious M. Davis, 1988, pp. 89–103.

—Mark A. Sanders

His Own Where. The first novel of poet and essayist June *Jordan, *His Own Where* (1971) made the *New York Times* List of the Most Outstanding Books of 1971 for young adults and the American Library Association List of Best Books; it was also nominated for the National Book Award.

His Own Where is the love story of sixteen-year-old Buddy Rivers and fourteen-year-old Angela Figeroa, two African American adolescents struggling with parental abandonment and *violence, an intimidating urban environment, and social institutions indifferent to human need. The young characters define their own world and establish their own values, which are often at variance with society's and their parents' demands. Their story's unsparing depiction of society's slow extinction of youthful hopes and dreams warns about the effects of prejudice and sexism, and champions *freedom over constriction, sensuality over puritanism, living for others over living for success. Narrated from Buddy's perspective, it is told in flashbacks and dream sequences in an African American spoken English whose rhythms poeticize Buddy's often heroic conflicts with his environment to change situations he finds physically or emotionally confining. At school he agitates for free sex, contraceptives, coeducational classes in anatomy, and dancing and *music in the lunchroom; he helps Angela escape her abusive parents as well as an oppressive girls' home. Refusing to be trapped by the hopelessness of indifferent and cruel environmental elements, Buddy takes Angela to a deserted cemetery toolshed, determined to make a new life for them, which includes the prospect of a baby; he seeks "His own where, own place for loving made for making love."

His Own Where makes central June Jordan's interests in architecture and urban design and her commitment to African American English. The novel shows that space and language, vital means by which environment is shaped, bear directly on personal development and community health. Buddy's work on the house he and his father have renovated and on the toolshed he and Angela inhabit suggest that urban redesign should be enlisted to create environmental conditions that can foster African American life. The novel's poetic stream of consciousness style closes the gap between words and experience, with the result of a striking verbal immediacy that realizes the integrity of African American English as well as its energy and creativity. This reflects Jordan's educational and artistic goals to defend and preserve the language while luxuriating in its lyricism, rhythm, and poetic idiom.

His Own Where is an exemplary work from the "second renaissance" of African American culture of the 1960s and 1970s. Blending elements of fantasy and realism, the novel suggests a reconceptualization of realism from the perspective of poetic vision; its dreamlike quality and impressionistic style evoke the grittiness of urban life and the energy of being young and African American. In its emphasis on activist urban redesign and its pride in African American English, *His Own Where* is a novel of political protest that fits in a tradition of works by Alice *Walker, Toni *Morrison, and other socially conscious African American novelists of the 1970s.

[*See also* Children's and Young Adult Literature.]

• Sarah Webster Fabio, review of *His Own Where*, *New York Times Book Review*, 7 November 1971, 6, 34. June Jordan, "White English/Black English: The Politics of Translation (1972)," in *Civil Wars*, 1981, pp. 59–73. Peter B. Erikson, "June Jordan," in *DLB*, vol. 38, *Afro-American Writers after 1955: Dramatists and Prose Writers*, eds. Thadious M. Davis and Trudier Harris, 1985, pp. 146–162.

—Ronna C. Johnson

HISTORICAL NOVEL. Traditionally the historical *novel genre centers on the lives of famous historical figures and employs historical research. The historical novel in African American literature invokes and reworks this traditional model, founded by Sir Walter Scott and extended by many European and European American writers, by focusing on the lives of everyday, often enslaved people, whose lives had not been recorded because they had not been deemed worthy by writers of *history. These novels thereby challenge, either implicitly or explicitly, European American methods of record keeping, of evaluating who and what are important, and of making history.

*Slavery in the United States denied an enabling memory of life in Africa, its thriving communities, its complex cultures, its various religious traditions, its ancient histories of trading, manufacturing, and nomadic societies. This attempt at cultural erasure, through the forced acquisition of English and European-based Christianity, the outlawing of drums, and relentless *work schedules, was a principal strategy employed by slaveholders for rendering docile their workforce. The fundamental dependency of the U.S. economy in its early years on the creativity and ingenuity of enslaved people, for example, is not generally known. Given this, history for African American people, like *literacy, has never been simply an intellectual exercise. History has been a contested terrain in which European Americans have had more authority to define what is worthy of recognition, what may be considered of historical significance, and what versions or aspects of the past are important to keep alive in the present as a way of understanding who and what we are today.

Although in African American letters the historical novel came of age after 1970, African American literature from its inception has been concerned with history-making. From its earliest extant text, Frederick *Douglass's "The *Heroic Slave" (1853), this fictional tradition has challenged official versions of history with new versions based upon the perspectives of enslaved and free African American people. Douglass's fictional *biography of slave rebel leader Madison Washington explicitly supplemented factual fragments with the writer's imagination and his knowledge as a former slave. Such storytelling as the basis

of historical memory is now recognized as a narrative hallmark of African American writers. Most of the novels published prior to the *Harlem Renaissance open in the antebellum South, recounting the lives of enslaved characters whose descendants will be the novels' chief protagonists. The explicit linking of free descendant to enslaved ancestor illustrates another historical assertion of this tradition: current conditions cannot be understood apart from the past struggles that brought them into being.

Two novels written between the Harlem Renaissance and 1970 also link historical events to imagination, and present to past. Arna *Bontemps's *Black Thunder* (1936) dramatizes the story of Gabriel Prosser's unsuccessful slave rebellion of 1800. Bontemps's desire to understand the worldwide depression of the 1930s led him to seek out in history examples of resistance to oppressive conditions. He drew upon the testimony of former slaves, gathered by the Works Projects Administration (WPA), which did not contain much specific information about Prosser's rebellion but did furnish him with knowledge of the perspective of those enslaved. Bontemps questioned current histories of slavery by using sources not yet recognized as valid by historians to ground his evocation of an enslaved past. Similarly, Margaret *Walker's *Jubilee* (1966), based on such unofficial sources as oral traditions of song, recipes, and storytelling, re-created the life history of Walker's great-grandmother. Walker used and then imaginatively extended the information available to her from within her own community to create an epic of one woman's struggle to keep together her *family in the harsh conditions of the antebellum and post-Reconstruction South.

The two decades after 1970 witnessed the publication of more than ten major historical novels. This burst of activity may be attributed to interest in the historical legacies and the perspectives of African American peoples generated by the *civil rights, Black Power, and black feminist movements. Such perspectives characterize the historical novels of the last twenty-five years, otherwise quite diverse in their styles, forms, tones, and purposes. These historical novels tend to represent two time periods, the antebellum South and the early twentieth century. Although the parents of many recent writers came of age in the segregated South and post-*migration North, they often hid from their children the degrading conditions of their early years in an attempt to begin their lives anew. It is not surprising that one priority for the following generation, as evidenced by Alice *Walker's The *Third Life of Grange Copeland* (1970) and The *Color Purple* (1982), and Toni *Morrison's *Sula* (1973) and *Song of Solomon* (1977), was to renovate in fiction this recently suppressed past.

Recent historical novels are set during the time of slavery, typically in the antebellum South. Because more than fifty *slave narratives—stories of flight from slavery by those enslaved—were published during the fifteen years before the Civil War, writers have used extensively this "firsthand" information. But also influential were developments in the historiography of slavery, which grew out of political and cultural movements for social justice of the 1950s and 1960s. John Blassingame's *The Slave Community* (1972) was the first major history text to be written from the perspectives of those enslaved. Using the antebellum slave narratives as his major source of information, Blassingame dramatically shifted the terms of historical representation, which had previously been derived from documents left by slaveholders and abolitionists. Numerous historians extended Blassingame's initial challenge to traditional historiography, developing an increasingly complex and varied body of literature.

Fiction writers benefited from and contributed to this process, simultaneously relying upon and modifying developments in historiography. For example, Ernest J. *Gaines's The *Autobiography of Miss Jane Pittman* (1971), Alex *Haley's *Roots* (1976), Ishmael *Reed's *Flight to Canada* (1976), Octavia E. *Butler's *Kindred* (1979), David *Bradley's The *Chaneysville Incident* (1982), Sherley Anne *Williams's *Dessa Rose* (1986), Toni Morrison's *Beloved* (1987), Barbara *Chase-Riboud's Echo of Lions* (1989), and Charles R. *Johnson's *Middle Passage* (1990) all bring to the fore the process of creating African American history. Even the most conventional in narrative form, such as *Roots, The Autobiography of Miss Jane Pittman*, and *Echo of Lions*, incorporate reflections on this process. For example, the protagonist of Gaines's novel is interviewed late in her life, much like the narrators of the WPA testimonies; Haley recounts his own ten-year search for his ancestral family in Gambia, West Africa; while Chase-Riboud includes a discussion of her sources. Butler's *Kindred* dramatically connects past to present by having Dana, a writer of the 1970s, literally pulled back into the past of a white male slaveholding ancestor, where she experiences the contradictions of life under slavery. *The Chaneysville Incident* explicitly examines history's creation by presenting an academically trained historian confronting and retelling the silenced story of the rebellion and massacre of his hometown's enslaved residents.

Other novels complicate or question history-making through experiments in narrative form. Reed's *Flight to Canada* questions the entire project of writing history by collapsing the distance between past and present, anachronistically inserting air-flight and television into his rendition of an antebellum slave narrative. *Dessa Rose, Beloved,* and *Middle Passage* reject the omniscient narrator and linear form of traditional history writing. *Dessa Rose literally speaks herself into being over the course of the text, moving from being written about in a proslavery writer's journal to sharing a third-person narrative with a white woman, to eventually telling her own story as a first-person narrator. *Beloved* presents multiple, sometimes contradictory, versions of what happened through repetitive and circular call-and-response patterns that structure the narrative form and implicate the teller in the story she or he tells. *Middle Passage* is told through journal entries, thereby authorizing the story and perspective of the free black man who writes them.

Contemporary writers, especially women, also have turned to exploring the individual psyches of their protagonists, making their perspectives as complex, individuated, and heterogeneous as possible. These efforts challenge monolithic and homogenizing official representations of enslaved and free African American people. *Beloved*, for example, considers one woman's dramatic resistance to slavery—infanticide of her own daughter—in terms of the psychic cost to her, her family, and her community. *Dessa Rose* examines internal limits created by life in slavery, and optimistically connects the maturation of the protagonist to her increasing mental *freedom. Virginia *Hamilton's *Anthony Burns* (1988) explores the inner life of a man as he undergoes a trial that leads to his return to slavery under the Fugitive Slave Act.

Most recently, African American historical novels have spread into new geographical areas, such as Caryl Phillips's story of the Caribbean, *Cambridge* (1992), and into new historical periods, as in Alice Walker's The *Temple of My Familiar* (1989) and Toni Morrison's *Jazz* (1992).

[*See also* Insurrections; Literary History; Neo–slave Narrative; Places.]

• Bernard W. Bell, *The Afro-American Novel and Its Tradition,* 1987. William L. Andrews, "The Novelization of Voice in Early African American Narrative," *PMLA* 105 (Jan. 1990): 23–34. Barbara Christian, "'Somebody Forgot to Tell Somebody Something': African-American Women's Historical Novels," in *Wild Women in the Whirlwind: Afra-American Culture and the Contemporary Literary Renaissance,* eds. Joanne M. Braxton and Andrée Nicola McLaughlin, 1990, pp. 326–343. Missy Dehn Kubitschek, *Claiming the Heritage: African-American Women Novelists and History,* 1991. Genevieve Fabre and Robert O'Meally, eds., *History and Memory in African-American Culture,* 1994.

—Maggie Sale

HISTORY. Peoples are created and destroyed by historiography, others' or their own. John Hope Franklin, one of the founders of contemporary African American historical narrative, divides into four generations the attempt by African Americans to negate enslaving historiographies. The effort began in 1883, when the lawyer and Civil War veteran George Washington *Williams published his two-volume *History of the Negro Race in America from 1619 to 1880: Negroes as Slaves, as Soldiers, and as Citizens.* In 1909, Booker T. *Washington, the wily accommodationist, published *The Story of the Negro: The Rise of the Race from Slavery,* in which he argued for the right of African Americans to join in the American dream of perpetual progress but did not categorically condemn the practices (including *lynching) that made it difficult for them to do so. Among trained historians, the African American response to the destruction of its humanity in post–Civil War histories began with W. E. B. *Du Bois, who published the classic *The Suppression of the African Slave Trade to America* in 1895. In 1910, the year of the founding of the NAACP, whose *Crisis* magazine Du Bois edited, Du Bois published the revisionist *essay "Reconstruction and Its Benefits" in the *Journal of the American Historical Association.*

Neither that essay nor Du Bois's use of the *Crisis* to decry widespread lynchings of African Americans, many of which were offshoots of mainstream historiography, created a ripple in contemporary American accounts. Scholars, fiction writers, journalists, and others continued to grind out tales of African American depravity during the Reconstruction that reached their apotheosis in D. W. Griffith's 1915 Ku Klux Klan–endorsing film, *Birth of a Nation*.

The often polemical tone of Du Bois's 1935 masterpiece *Black Reconstruction in America 1860–1880* is a measure of the near total historiographical isolation in which he was writing. In his concluding chapter on the "Propaganda of History," Du Bois states that when writers gathered evidence about Reconstruction, "the chief witness . . . the emancipated slave himself, has been almost barred from court." Bringing this forbidden witness into the courtroom—and thereby changing the dimensions of justice itself—has been the task of all four of John Hope Franklin's generations of historians.

In the second generation, during the winter of 1916, Carter G. *Woodson began the institutionalization of African American history as an academic discipline by founding the Association for the Study of Negro Life and the *Journal of Negro History*. He outlined his purposes in his 1933 volume *The Mis-Education of the Negro*. He noted that textbooks used to educate African Americans taught them that they were "unable to subject passion to reason," yet failed to inform them of African achievements, such as the invention of ironworking. Woodson argued that knowledge of "real" history would free African Americans from mental bondage, inspire them to demand social equality, and "upset the oppressor in America and [the colonizer in] Africa."

The first eruption of "real history" that mainstream scholars found impossible to ignore came in 1944, when Gunnar Myrdal published *An American Dilemma*, a one thousand-page examination of America's deviations from its national "creed" of inclusion and opportunity. Myrdal, a Swede, was recruited for his presumed disinterestedness. He drew many of his insights and paradigms from the specially prepared studies of sociologists E. Franklin Frazier and Charles S. Johnson, and political scientist Ralph Bunche—all African Americans who made profound independent contributions to American historiography.

Frazier's works on the trials of the African American *family in *slavery and *freedom, and on the self-delusions of the African American middle class, combined with the work of successors such as Kenneth Clark, helped launch a historiography of psychic damage, even "pathology," threatening African Americans in the wake of centuries of oppression. This occurred in spite of each man's documentation of the diversity of African American responses to hostile social environments. More recent works have countered the pathology model by emphasizing African American resilience and creativity under crushing conditions, and by insisting on a sociologically "holistic" approach to complex but often-denigrated structures such as the African American family. Johnson was responsible for recorded interviews with former slaves that were useful in countering the pathology model. Bunche, by helping shape the United Nations almost from its inception, helped globalize the transcendent elements of the American creed, and helped create the forum to which W. E. B. Du Bois took the grievances of the African American community in 1947.

The suggestion of the Myrdal study, that African American history is a—perhaps *the*—key to the American dilemma of high ideals contradicted is at the center of the work of the third generation to which Franklin himself belongs. With the meticulous scholarship and careful objectivity exemplified by Franklin's magisterial *From Slavery to Freedom* (1947), this generation did much to expand the sphere of acknowledgment of African American influence to include a crucial audience: American academics.

Benjamin Quarles, a member of this third generation and author of such groundbreaking works as *The Negro in the American Revolution* (1961), argues in his 1977 essay "Black History's Diversified Clientele" that historiography varies with the audience. He divided the audience into "the Black rank and file, the Black revolutionary nationalists, the Black academicians, and the white world." The question of audience raised for him the question of methodology and historiographical tone—whether the African American historian should adopt the posture of a social scientist analyzing data and presenting it dispassionately, or whether history should be used as a tool for social action, with the historian's "citizen role" free to "overshadow his [or her] professional role."

The questions Quarles found himself posing, of course, were raised by the very effectiveness of African American historiographical thought, which over the years has been developed not only by trained historians, but also by lawyers, clergy/prophets, philosophers, artists, sociologists, and institutions such as the NAACP. Indeed, an extreme acceleration in the encroachment of "citizen" upon professional roles toward the end of the third generation was sparked by public historiography: the NAACP's carefully plotted courtroom victories against segregation; Martin Luther *King, Jr.'s nonviolent defeats of the violent enforcers of segregation in southern cities; and the exhortations of nationalists, Pan-Africanists, and others, who, like *Malcolm X or the Black Panther Party in the early 1970s, refused to rule out the use of revolutionary violence.

The cumulative impact of these planned initiatives—and unplanned ones like the Watts riots setting a kind of crown of fire on the African American demand for what Hegel calls "recognition"—was to bring American history to a boil, and to place African American concerns at the center of the nation's agenda. As historians were glued to their TV sets with the rest of America, or, especially in the case of a number of fourth generation scholars, participating in the *civil rights movement the televisions showed, African American historiography and African American studies inevitably moved to the center of the academic agenda. Quarles's meditation on audiences is part of the effort of Franklin's third generation to come to terms with the new developments and the demands for "relevance" coming from fourth generation scholars. Between the mid-1960s and mid-1970s, there was an outpouring of academic responses to the public historiography of the 1960s.

At this time there appeared studies of slavery; of the urbanization of African Americans during the two world wars; and of the folk historiography of the slaves, who created America's musical tradition and who reinterpreted Christianity so as to transform themselves into Israelites in Pharaoh's land and to establish a common moral language that allowed their descendants to communicate with their oppressors from a position of strength. It is this common moral language from which George Washington Williams draws when he opens his *History of the Negro Race* with a discourse on the unity of humankind implied by the existence of "but one nationality" before the destruction of Babel. Martin Luther King uses it in his historiographical defense of nonviolent direct action in *Why We Can't Wait* (1963). Both men articulate the internationalist position that is one of the poles of African American historiography. The other, espoused when faith in a common language is lost, is the nationalism articulated perhaps most influentially by Marcus *Garvey in the 1920s.

The academic publications were a measure not only of new interest in African Americans but also of an intensification of the wars of historiography that Williams, Woodson, and Du Bois had fought. In 1967, writing in the wake of the riots that began in 1963 to flash like signals from one American city to another, Stokely *Carmichael and Charles V. Hamilton published *Black Power: The Politics of Liberation in America.* (The term "Black Power" appears to have been coined by Richard *Wright as the title for his 1954 book on his journeys in the newborn states of Africa.) Carmichael and Hamilton described a fork in the road of American history and offered their book as a final alternative to "prolonged destructive guerrilla warfare." Declaring the American political and educational system bankrupted by "institutional racism," the authors called for "entirely new and substantially different forms of expression."

Historian Harold Cruse's *The Crisis of the Negro Intellectual*, published in the same year as *Black Power*, warned African American intellectuals of the futility of purely political or economic attempts at emancipation. Dismissing the Black Power theorists as a historically shortsighted throwback to 1920s Garveyism, Cruse argued that they were in full flight from those conceptual advances made by Malcolm X at the end of his life that were symbolized by Malcolm X's plan to take African American grievances to the United Nations. Cruse insisted that American culture—which is to say, American thought—had to be revolutionized before African American emancipation could be achieved.

Despite criticisms such as Cruse's, the Black Power movement had profound effects on fourth generation historians such as Mary Frances Berry, Sterling Stuckey, and Vincent Harding. In his 1970 essay "Beyond Chaos" (John A. Williams and Charles

F. Harris, eds., *Amistad 1*), Harding divided African American historians into essentially two generations—those who wrote "Negro History" and those who wrote "Black History." Writers of Negro history—such as Quarles—had so committed themselves to "objective truth" that they failed to question "the basic values of America," or the promise that blacks would one day be recognized as equals within the matrix of those values.

Some third generation historians, without disowning American values, were also profoundly affected by the 1960s upheavals. Nathan I. Huggins, who had shied away from African American history for fear of professional repercussions, was inspired to shift his focus to this subject area. His *Harlem Renaissance* (1965), however, used the 1920s "renaissance" to underline the paradoxical *Americanness* of African American nationalism. In an oblique comment on 1960s nationalism, Huggins, in a section on the "legacy to our time" of the *Harlem Renaissance, noted that "race promotion" at once creates a sense of *identity and enforces provincialism.

Among the fourth generation historians who gave thought to this paradox were John Blassingame, who edited the 1971 volume *New Perspectives on Black Studies* as a guide to academics seeking to come to terms with the new reality on their campuses. In "The Role of the Historian," his own contribution to the volume, Blassingame offered counterarguments to those of his more strictly nationalist contemporaries. The idea broached by some that only African Americans should teach African American history, for instance, threatened the freedom of African American scholars to teach anything else, according to Blassingame, who warned also against following in the wake of white supremacist historiography and "distorting history to prove a point."

For Blassingame the facts of history were indictment enough of America's white supremacist impulses, and he was sufficiently committed to those facts to accuse Stanley Elkins, author of the widely influential *Slavery: A Problem in American Institutional and Intellectual Life* (1959), of "criminal libel against history" for portraying African Americans as being psychologically destroyed by slavery. Blassingame's *The Slave Community* (1972) presents slave psychology as rich and resilient. *Long Memory: The Black Experience in America* (1982), his and Mary Frances Berry's overview of African American history, argues again for African American inventiveness and resiliency while condemning American attempts to crush it. Other fourth generation scholars, such as Nell Irvin Painter in her *Exodusters: Black Migration to Kansas after Reconstruction* (1977), published studies of the making of "history from below," by the genius of the masses rather than their leaders. Vincent Harding's biblically inflected *There Is a River* (1981) breaks with the canons of past scholarship by opening its re-creation of enslavement and emancipation with a choral voice—the third-person plural pronoun of the Declaration of Independence.

By this time, the public African American historiography of the 1960s had subsided and, indeed, begun to be reversed by the so-called "Reagan revolution," a major exercise in counterhistoriography that changed the political climate in America even as the increasing legitimacy and diversity of African American studies changed the climate in academia. The rise of African American feminist historiography, inspired in part by the American feminist movement, which was itself sparked by the civil rights struggle, and by *Black Nationalism, was perhaps the major new development in 1980s African American studies. It can be symbolized by the transition of philosopher Angela *Davis, who had gained international prominence as an African American radical in the 1960s, to feminist theorist. In *Women, Race and Class* (1981), Davis argues that American *feminism originated in the nineteenth-century abolitionist movement, and that feminism's "fighting spirit" derives from Sojourner *Truth's "Ain't I a Woman?" speech, but that racism among some white feminists is also as old as the abolitionist movement.

In establishing African American feminist historiography in the academy, professional historians such as Darlene Clark Hine have pointed to the lack of attention given to the role of black women in the slave families portrayed in the works of Blassingame, Herbert Gutman, and other scholars. "Lifting the Veil, Shattering the Silence: Black Women's History in Slavery and Freedom" is Hine's contribution to *The State of Afro-American History: Past, Present, and Future* (1986), the assessment of the field she edited. She argues there that African American history cannot be understood without "detailed examination" of the educational, health care, and recreational institutions created by African American women. Hine has helped to spur that detailed examination as the editor of such volumes as *Black Women in America: An Historical Encyclopedia* (1993) and, with Wilma King and Linda Reed, "We Specialize in the Wholly Impossible": A Reader in Black Women's History* (1995).

The feminists have inevitably raised the issue of sexism within the black community and, with it, the question of whether racial solidarity takes precedence over the assertion of women's rights. Hine and others assume the complementarity of *gender, racial, and other concerns. Nevertheless, a certain dialectical competition among historiographies exists. In an essay on "The Black Studies Movement" that appeared in *Hinesight* (1994), Hine defines the main contemporary camps of historiographers as Afrocentrists (such as Molefi Asante), traditionalists (such as Blassingame), and feminists such as herself. Recent attempts to dismantle federal affirmative action programs have underlined the historiographical importance of a group Hine does not mention—the so-called black conservatives, the most prominent of whom are Thomas Sowell and his intellectual protégé, Supreme Court Justice Clarence Thomas.

The conflict between the positions of nationalism (epitomized by Asante's insistence, in *Afrocentricity*, 1989, on the Egypt-centered integrity of African culture in all diaspora populations, and on Afrocentric thought as that which is in the best interests of *Afrocentricity) and internationalism (epitomized by Sowell in his *Race and Culture: A World View*, 1994; Orlando Patterson in *Freedom, Volume I: Freedom in the Making of Western Culture*, 1991; and Harding in his *Hope and History*, 1991) has rarely seemed more unresolved. Taking an international perspective but targeting such projects as the Afrocentric one, Sowell warns of "the social costs of exaggerated identity" and argues that history is driven by the diffusion and intermingling, not the uniqueness, of cultures. Arguing that diffusion proceeds because some cultural practices are more efficient or otherwise superior to others, Sowell decries the social engineering (such as via affirmative action) of equality. He insists that "equal respect" be earned. Writing from within the economic tradition of dispassionate analysis, Sowell insists that history be used to test "current theories and assumptions" about the causes of the present, not primarily as a means of altering the present.

By contrast, Harding and other contemporary thinkers, such as Mary Frances Berry, Hine, Cornel *West, Geneviéve Fabre, and Robert O'Meally, view history as an active participant in the present, in as much as memory anchors it in each human brain. Such thinkers proceed on the assumption that those who do not create historiography—which, as Blassingame shows, need not be inaccurate—are at risk of being destroyed by it. Certainly African American history offers ample support for such a position.

Harding in *Hope and History* goes further, arguing that the climax of African American history in the civil rights struggle offers ample support for not only an African American but a human renaissance. The global diffusion of Martin Luther King's nonviolent direct action campaign and the culture it represented—the African American culture of emancipation—was brought home to Harding by the "overwhelming shock of recognition" caused by the sight of Chinese students seeking freedom in Tiananmen Square, East Europeans fighting to unseat repressive regimes, and South Africans ending apartheid brandishing banners or singing the words or the tune of the civil rights era anthem *"We Shall Overcome." Patterson, in *Freedom*, speaking with the voice of nothing less than Western culture ("our civilization"), makes an argument that partly explains why African Americans could create an "expansion of democracy" in which the planet participated. Patterson argues that the West's core value—freedom—was the creation of slaves and women and of the social dread of enslavement and oppression. The gift of African American historiography is its ability to sublate, in Hegelian fashion, oppression in the "moments" of emancipation that are the core of freedom. Harding and Cornel West, in books such as *Race Matters* (1994), argue for the return of that common, prophesying moral language that the assassination of Martin Luther King, Jr., helped to shatter and that Ralph Bunche, working to raise a historiographical pyramid that any pharaoh would envy, helped make a permanent possibility in the form of the flawed but still unbroken United Nations.

[See also Diasporic Literature; Historical Novel; Literary History; Pan-Africanism; Race; Woman's Era; Womanism.]

• E. Franklin Frazier, *Black Bourgeoisie: The Rise of a New Middle Class in the United States*, 1962. Lorraine A. Williams, ed., *Africa and the Afro-American Experience: Eight Essays*, 1977. Orlando Patterson, *Slavery and Social Death: A Comparative Survey*, 1982. August Meier and Elliott Rudwick, *Black History and the Historical Profession 1915–1980*, 1986. Benjamin Quarles, *The Negro in the Making of America*, 1987. John Hope Franklin, *Race and History: Selected Essays 1938–1988*, 1989. Andrew Billingsley, *Climbing Jacob's Ladder: The Enduring Legacy of African American Families*, 1992. Mary Frances Berry, *Black Resistance/White Law: A History of Constitutional Racism in America*, 1971; rpt. 1994. Geneviéve Fabre and Robert O'Meally, eds., *History and Memory in African American Culture*, 1994.

—Michael Collins

HISTORY OF THE DISCIPLINE. *See* Black Studies; Canonization; Criticism; Literary History.

HOAGLAND, EVERETT H., III (b. 1942), poet and educator. Everett Hoagland III has published three collections of *poetry—Ten Poems: A Collection* in 1968; *Black Velvet* in 1970; and *Scrimshaw* in 1976— and has served as a teacher and administrator in public schools and universities.

Hoagland was born on 18 December 1942 in Philadelphia, Pennsylvania. He received his bachelor's degree from Lincoln University in Philadelphia, where he was the recipient of the Silvera Award for Creative Writing. After graduating in 1964, he took a position as an English teacher at Harding Junior High School in Philadelphia. In 1967 he left teaching and returned to his alma mater to serve as the assistant director of admissions until 1969. It was in 1968 that he published his first collection of poetry, *Ten Poems*, and was named one of the Outstanding Young Men of America. In 1969 he moved to California to serve as an instructor, as a poet in residence, and as an administrator at the Black Studies Center of Claremont College. While in California he also taught at various other institutions such as the Chino Institution for Men, Mount San Antonio College, and Claremont College's summer Upward Bound program.

After the publication of his best-known collection, *Black Velvet* (1970), Hoagland entered the Creative Writing Program at Brown University as a university fellow and received his master's degree in 1973. While not overtly political, *Black Velvet* reveals its indebtedness to the *Black Arts movement through its expression of African American culture as a way to reinvent *race and foster cultural pride. His poetry in this collection is not only experimental and inventive, but it blends language with musical form through sound, image, and rhythm.

In 1972 Hoagland served as humanities instructor in the preenrollment program at Swarthmore College and one year later accepted a position as professor of English at Southeastern Massachusetts University. In 1975 he was awarded a Creative Artists Fellowship from the Massachusetts Arts and Humanities Foundation and went on to publish his next collection of poetry, *Scrimshaw*, in 1976. This collection demonstrates a thematic continuity with Hoagland's previous work but also reveals the poet's changing stylistic concerns. In *Scrimshaw* his poetry

is more conventional and less reliant on linguistic experiments and has been called "sober" and even "pessimistic"; its focus is primarily upon the historical and present-day conditions of African American people.

From 1979 to 1982 Hoagland was a weekly columnist for the *New Bedford Standard-Times*. He is also a contributing editor to the *American Poetry Review*. He was awarded a Gwendolyn *Brooks Award for fiction by *Black World* magazine in 1974; he was the recipient of fellowships from the National Endowment for the Humanities in 1984 and the Artists Foundation Statewide Poetry Competition in 1986. While his work has not received much critical attention, his poetry continues to be included in numerous *anthologies such as *The New Black Poetry*, edited by Clarence *Major; *The Black Poets*, edited by Dudley *Randall; and *A Broadside Treasury*, edited by Gwendolyn Brooks. Hoagland is the father of four children and a member of the Baha'i faith.

• Don L. Lee, *Black Poets of the 1960s*, 1971, p. 2. Linda E. Scott, "Everett H. Hoagland III," in *DLB*, vol. 41, *Afro-American Poets since 1955*, eds. Trudier Harris and Thadious M. Davis, 1985, pp. 171–176.   —Karen Isabelle Halil

HOLIDAY, BILLIE (1915–1959), jazz singer and lyricist. Like many *jazz musicians, Billie Holiday ("Lady Day") began her career in brothels and after-hours clubs. After an apprenticeship at late-night jam sessions, she became one of the most significant figures in the history of jazz. Since her death she has become an American icon, perhaps better known for the stories surrounding her drug addiction and her personal life than for her artistry.

Her *autobiography, *Lady Sings the Blues* (1956), coauthored with William Dufty, has become a classic African American autobiography. The text is one of the first to contribute to the myth of Holiday as the tortured but talented jazz and pop singer. The myth is elaborated on the pages of the autobiographies of some of the twentieth century's most significant African Americans including *Malcolm X's *The *Autobiography of Malcolm X* (1965), Lena Horne's *Lena* (1965), and Maya *Angelou's *The Heart of a Woman* (1981). In these texts Holiday alternates from a hip but generous big sister to a vulgar, mean-spirited, aging woman; however, in all of them she is portrayed as a highly talented, sensitive musician who is the victim of America's racism and the sexism of black and white men.

The most exquisite evocations of Holiday appear in *poetry. Alexis *De Vaux's narrative poem, "Don't Explain: A Song of Billie Holiday" (1980); "The Day Lady Died" (1959), by white American poet Frank O'Hara; and "Sometimes You Look Like Lady Day" (1973), by Filipino American poet Jessica Tarahata Hagedorn, all immortalize Holiday in her breathtaking beauty and artistry.

Holiday is the subject of numerous *biographies. The most significant include *The Many Faces of Lady Day* (1991), by literary critic Robert O'Meally, and Donald Clarke's *Wishing on the Moon: The Life and Times of Billie Holiday* (1994). O'Meally seeks to turn attention away from the various myths of Holiday's personal life and instead to focus on her development and achievement as an extraordinary jazz artist. In so doing, he moves Holiday beyond her status as victim and situates her in the space of her agency—her *music. Clarke's is the most extensive and well researched of the Holiday biographies to date and includes a chapter on her emergence as an American icon.

[See also Blues; Entertainer.]

—Farah Jasmine Griffin

HOLMAN, JOHN (b. 1951), short story writer, essayist, and educator. John William Holman, an associate professor of English at Georgia State University in Atlanta, was born in Durham, North Carolina. He received his BA in English from the University of North Carolina at Chapel Hill in 1973, his MA in English from North Carolina Central University in Durham in 1977, and his PhD in English and creative writing from the University of Southern Mississippi in 1983.

He has published one book, *Squabble and Other Stories* (1990), a collection of eleven *short stories that originally appeared in such journals and magazines as the *New Yorker, Crescent Review,* and *Mississippi Review.* These stories are about African Americans in the New South who do not quite fit into mainstream society. Holman's own phrase, "distant weirdness" taken from his short story "Swoosh," published in the fall 1992 issue of *Appalachee Quarterly,* accurately describes his stories and characters, seemingly ordinary yet surreal people whose dialogue and whose lives do not seem to connect. They have strange—though perfectly suited—names like Grim, Cola, and Joyless.

The major character in "Squabble," Aaron, is a retrenched geography professor who gets a job tending bar at a dive called the Bellaire in his neohick hometown. The star attraction at the bar is Dog, a man with half a face. There is the story of Todd in "Pimp," who is an ex-pimp, bouncer, and bodyguard who once faked his own hanging as a Halloween joke. When he returns home for a visit, he thanks his neighborhood friend for writing him while he was away and explains to her that he did not respond because he "didn't know how to talk like [he] still lived here." In "The Story of Art History," two people dance around on red lingerie that has been thrown on the floor. Monroe, who is getting married in "Monroe's Wedding," asks Thompson, his boss of three weeks, to be his best man: "It's you or some joker I can bribe."

Holman has a deft ear for dialogue. He exercises economy in his use of words, with his predominantly short sentences. He writes in the style of Frederick Barthelme, under whom he studied at Southern Mississippi, and Raymond Carver. He uses rich, colorful, vivid, and very descriptive language. In the story "I and I," drug dealers making a stop in a small Mississippi town stay in an unfurnished house where "Every room is a different color—carpets purple, pink, blue, green. Matching drapes shaped like suffocation hang in the windows. They have funeral parlor folds, garish colors of Dracula lips."

In 1991 Holman received the Whiting Writer's Award, a prestigious annual literary prize given to ten American writers of promise. His next book will be a series of interlinking short stories. If they are anything like those in *Squabble,* these stories will firmly establish Holman as a noteworthy writer of short fiction.

• John William Holman, "Scuff," *Alabama Literary Quarterly* 6.1 (Fall/Winter 1992): 41–48. John William Holman, "Immaterial," *Forum* 27.2 (Fall/Winter 1993): 22–27.

—Elwanda D. Ingram

Home: Social Essays. The entries of Amiri *Baraka's *Home: Social Essays* (1966) chronicle the writer's rapidly emerging nationalistic posture. Including a number of *essays that were originally published in such journals as *Evergreen Review, Liberator, Kulchur, Cavalier,* the *Nation, Poetry,* the *Saturday Review,* the *New York Sunday Herald Tribune,* and *Midstream,* this collection is also representative of the collective consciousness of much of the African American populace of the period. Written in the wake of the global liberation struggles of Africans, African Americans, and people of color in general, these essays reflect a growing impatience with the gradualism of the American *civil rights movement, a contempt for liberalism, a passion for moral engagement, and a fervent embracing of African American *history and culture.

As with much of Baraka's work, there is little middle ground in appraisal of these essays. William Harris notes in the introduction to *The LeRoi Jones/Amiri Baraka Reader* (1991) that *Home* is "an important book of essays written at its author's fullest powers." A reviewer from *Newsweek* (May 1966), on the other hand, notes in an examination of *Home* that "[Baraka] writes and harangues himself out of the company of civilized men; and forfeits all claim to serious attention."

In "Cuba Libra," the longest essay in *Home,* all of the aforementioned themes are apparent. An accounting of a visit to Castro's newly liberated Cuba, this essay reflects strongly the writer's growing dissatisfaction with the "art-for-art's sake" posture of the Beats. In recounting the dialogue between himself and the more engaged Latin American poets also visiting Cuba, the writer reveals the roots of his politically charged later verse. Although this experience predates the writer's avowal of *communism by a good number of years, the idealism that made his ideological conversion possible was abundantly present at the time of this visit.

In a number of these essays, Baraka delves deeply into the roots of African American folkways. Mixing a good bit of *humor with the more tragic elements of the collective experience of his people, he celebrates those things that have become emblematic of the African American weltanschauung and style ("Soul Food," "City of Harlem," and "Expressive Language").

Much of *Home* reflects Baraka's impassioned struggle with the idea of a *Black Aesthetic. "The Myth of a 'Negro Literature,'" "A Dark Bag," "LeRoi Jones Talking," and "The Revolutionary Theater" are all fundamentally concerned with the African

American writer's finding his or her authentic, morally engaged voice. The first of these essays, originally presented as an address to the American Society for African Culture in March 1962, is most notable for its castigation of most African American writing in terms of its derivative and apologetic nature. While attacking the literature, however, he exalts the bona fide artistry of African American *music. Referring to *jazz and *blues as the only "consistent exhibitors of 'Negritude' in formal American culture," Baraka evidences embryonic patterns of thought that would appear fully developed in his monumental *Blues People* (1963). The essays referred to here, especially the hortatory "The Revolutionary Theater," served as touchstones for the many young writers who would ally themselves with the *Black Arts movement of the late 1960s.

The remaining essays evidence Baraka's progression from the posture of the cultural nationalist to that of literal black nationalist. In "American Reference: Black Male," "Blackhope," and "The Legacy of Malcolm X," each increasingly apocalyptic, hyperbolic, and darker, we observe Baraka's rationalization for the African American's separation from a dying Western culture.

[See also Black Nationalism.]

• James B. Gwynne, ed., *Amiri Baraka: The Kaleidoscopic Torch*, 1985.   —Henry C. Lacey

Home to Harlem, a picaresque novel by Claude *McKay, appeared in 1928, at the height of the *Harlem Renaissance. Its unabashed celebration of Harlem lower-class life generated great controversy among black critics and reformers, some of whom believed McKay was catering to stereotyped portrayals of blacks. The controversy helped propel *Home to Harlem* onto New York's best-seller lists, the first novel by a black to achieve such popularity.

Home to Harlem is the story of Jake Brown, McKay's natural man, whose primitive virtues and folk wisdom sustain him in the unnatural industrial world of the urban northeast. McKay's vision of an essentially healthy rural black folk struggling to stay afloat in a hostile sea of urban capitalism owed much to his own rural Jamaican background and to his interest in the works of D. H. Lawrence. McKay had also been strongly influenced by African and other "primitive" folk arts, as well as the revivals of peasant and folk themes in Jewish, Russian, and Irish literatures.

In *Home to Harlem*, Jake Brown deserts the American Army in wartime France. After the war, he returns to Harlem and works as an assistant cook on the Pennsylvania railroad. He befriends Ray, a Haitian waiter on his dining car. Ray's formal education and literary aspirations provide a contrast to the highly intense but limited activities of Jake and the other characters, almost all of whom are single working people. There are no families or children in *Home to Harlem*.

McKay's often lyrical descriptions of lower-class Harlem and its types are discordantly offset by a strong autobiographical element in *Home to Harlem* that depicts a harsher, more brutal world of loneliness, labor exploitation, *violence, and frustration. For example, Ray, McKay's fictional alter-ego, thinks of segregated Harlem as a congested "pig-pen," no fit place in which to marry or to start a family. The cumulative evidence of *Home to Harlem*, with its contradictory mixture of primitivism, *autobiography, and social realism set within a picaresque mode, suggests that the enormous disorder and despair found in today's "underclass" has a history that goes back decades further than critics often suggest.

Home to Harlem was the first of four volumes (*Banjo*, 1929; *Gingertown*, 1932; and *Banana Bottom*, 1933) in which McKay progressively defined the nature of the modern world, the position of blacks in it, and his own wanderings as an expatriate poet and writer. In all his fiction, rural black folk culture stands upon its own foundations, in some sense independent of and in opposition to an urbanized, industrialized, mechanistic, and denatured Western civilization. Few African American works have aroused more unease among black middle-class reformers and critics than *Home to Harlem*. The literary primitivism of the 1920s, of which McKay was a part, largely expired with the decade, and his novels were little read in succeeding years. But the relevance of the various issues raised in *Home to Harlem* and McKay's other fictional works remain pertinent.

• James R. Giles, *Claude McKay*, 1976. Wayne F. Cooper, *Claude McKay: Rebel Sojourner in the Harlem Renaissance, a Biography*, 1987.   —Wayne F. Cooper

HOOKS, BELL (b. 1955), writer, teacher, and cultural critic. With her first two books, *Ain't I a Woman: Black Women and Feminism* (1981) and *Feminist Theory: From Margin to Center* (1984), bell hooks (born Gloria Watkins) joined a generation of black feminists whose political perspective was explicitly forged in a consciousness of their marginality to the Black Power, *civil rights movement, and feminist movement of the 1960s. Unlike some of her contemporaries, hooks did not feel that black women's double oppression warranted advocating a separate black feminist agenda, but instead saw black women's special historical situation as relevant both for a feminist movement that had stumbled over its implicit *class and *race biases, and for a black liberation movement that remained committed to the patriarchal values of the racist society it denounced. Challenging feminist and antiracist movements to become accountable for the lives and experiences of black women, hooks envisioned black *feminism as a catalyst for transforming the historically antagonistic relationship between the two political groups.

Since the publication of her first two books, bell hooks has increasingly centered her reflections on feminism and the politics of race in the areas of popular culture and pedagogy. In *Talking Back: Thinking Feminist, Thinking Black* (1989), *Yearning: Race, Gender and Cultural Politics* (1990), *Black Looks: Race and Representation* (1992), *Outlaw Culture: Resisting Representations* (1994), *Teaching to Transgress: Education as the Practice of Freedom* (1994), and *Art on*

My Mind (1995), hooks explores questions concerning black style and commodity culture, the pedagogical implications of multicultural classrooms, and the development of African American artists and of critical methods proper to their work.

The writing of bell hooks is characterized by a concern with the ethics of criticism. In many of her *essays, hooks frankly interrogates her own position as a black woman from a working-class background writing and teaching within a professional academic context. In *Breaking Bread: Insurgent Black Intellectual Life* (1991), she addresses this issue through a dialogue with her coauthor, Cornel *West. She complicates West's well-known formulation of the dilemma of the black intellectual by noting some of the ways in which an intellectual *identity is uniquely problematic for black women. As an example hooks cites her long struggle to claim the time and space necessary to think and write when those around her regarded her need for privacy as a selfish withdrawal from the community. The format of *Breaking Bread*, which consists of interviews and paired essays, is exemplary of hooks's political strategy as a writer and a teacher. By representing her work in dialogue with the work of other black intellectuals (including filmmaker Isaac Julien and British cultural critic Paul Gilroy), by writing short anecdotal essays rather than conventional academic papers or books, and by publishing in a variety of popular and scholarly journals, from *Artforum* and *Essence* to *Black American Literature Forum* and *Zeta*, hooks appeals to a popular and a professionalized readership to become responsible members of a common intellectual community.

[*See also* Criticism, *article on* Criticism since 1965; Womanism.]

• bell hooks, "Black Woman Artist Becoming," in *Life Notes: Personal Writings by Contemporary Black Women*, ed. Patricia Bell-Scott, 1994, pp. 151–159.   —Deborah G. Chay

HOPKINS, PAULINE E. (1859–1930), editor, novelist, and leading proponent of activist black journalism during the post-Reconstruction era. Pauline Elizabeth Hopkins was born to William A. Hopkins, a veteran of the Civil War, and Sarah A. Allen in Portland, Maine, in 1859. The family moved to Boston when Hopkins was an infant. She graduated from the renowned Boston's Girls' High School and shortly thereafter pursued stenography for a livelihood. In 1892 she worked for Henry Parkman and Alpheus Sanford, prominent Boston-area Republicans, and in 1895 she was appointed stenographer in the Bureau of Statistics for the Massachusetts Decennial Census. When she died in 1930, she was working as a stenographer for the Massachusetts Institute of Technology.

Although Hopkins wrote *essays, *poetry, and musical *dramas before she was twenty, she did not try her hand at fiction until 1900, probably because there were few African American outlets for this genre until the advent of the *Colored American Magazine*. The Boston-based *Colored American* was founded by Walter Wallace, Jesse W. Watkins, Harper S. Fortune, and Walter Alexander Johnson, who also established the Colored Co-operative Publishing Company. An editorial statement, appearing in the inaugural issue (May 1900), expressed the magazine's intentions to strengthen the bonds of "brotherhood" among "the colored people of the United States" and to demonstrate "their ability and tastes, in fiction, poetry, and art, as well as in the arena of historical, social, and economic literature." This issue also published Hopkins's *short story "The Mystery Within Us," and the Co-op issued her protest *novel *Contending Forces* in 1900 (the subtitle is *A Romance Illustrative of Negro Life North and South*).

Hopkins became one of the most frequent contributors to the magazine during its formative years, often writing under her mother's name—Sarah A. Allen. Over the next four years she published three serial novels—*Hagar's Daughter: A Story of Southern Caste Prejudice, Winona: A Tale of Negro Life in the South and Southwest,* and *Of One Blood, or The Hidden Self*—seven short stories, two series of biographical articles on famous black men and women, numerous editorials, and social and political commentaries. Hoping that fiction could reawaken the political zeal of the abolitionist period, she used her fiction to persuade her readers to protest the encroachment of *Jim Crow racism and restrictive *gender prescriptions.

By 1902 Hopkins was an editor of the magazine, although her name did not appear on the masthead until 1903. As Hazel Carby explains (introduction to *The Magazine Novels of Pauline Hopkins*, 1988), Hopkins's editorial influence has been vastly underestimated, undoubtedly because of her sex. As a woman operating in what was assumed to be a male professional arena, Hopkins's influence extended well beyond the female sphere. Even though she routinely masked her editorial authority, many of her male colleagues resented her position. Nevertheless the breadth of her interests in literature, *history, *journalism, and domestic and international politics, all in the service of Du Boisian–styled racial uplift, characterized the magazine until 1904.

In 1904, Booker T. *Washington gained control of the *Colored American*. During the summer of 1904, Fred R. Moore, the new owner and general manager, moved the Co-op and the magazine to New York. Moore's editorial in the November 1904 issue emphatically endorsed Washington as "the greatest living Negro," proclaimed him as the leader of the race, and embraced his position of racial conciliation.

Contention between the political positions of Moore and Hopkins led to her disassociation from the magazine sometime in 1904, and she was forced to seek other outlets for her political journalism. In 1905 she became a regular contributor to the *Voice of the Negro*, edited by J. Max Barber and T. Thomas *Fortune, and began a series of articles entitled "The Dark Races of the Twentieth Century." Here she vigorously refuted the presumption of Anglo-Saxon superiority, challenged the binary system of racial classification, and argued that the crises of the twentieth century would be the "Negro Problem" and the conflict between "Capital and Labor." In 1905 Hopkins launched her own *publishing company—

P. E. Hopkins and Co.—with the publication of *A Primer of Facts Pertaining to the Early Greatness of the African Race*. In this project she focused on recovering the record of plundered African civilizations. In the last line of the *Primer*, Hopkins directs her attention to Africans in the United States, exhorting "NEVER GIVE UP THE BALLOT." Hopkins attempted another publishing venture with the launching of the *New Era* magazine in 1915. She saw this publication as a medium for agitating for equal rights, presenting the history of racial progress, and promoting black literature and arts. This serial was basically a duplication of the format and concerns of the early *Colored American*. Unfortunately the magazine failed after two issues.

Hopkins's publication record was as impressive as that of Paul Laurence *Dunbar, Charles Waddell *Chesnutt, or Sutton E. *Griggs. As an editor she was as influential as Barber and Fortune of the *Voice of the Negro* and W. E. B. *Du Bois of the *Moon* and the *Horizon*. Like these men and long before Richard *Wright claimed the printed word as a weapon, Hopkins clearly understood the political power of narrative. By intersecting the "rags to riches" stories of her age with African American culture, and the popular genres of the romance, the Western, and detective fiction with racial protest, Hopkins hoped to intervene in the racist discourses of the early twentieth century. And yet, until the 1980s, this most prolific black woman was routinely disregarded by literary scholars. Gender politics effaced the record of her commitment to make fiction and journalism a part of the reformist dialogues about *race, gender, and *class. Although gender politics problematized female participation in the intellectual discourse of the post-Reconstruction era, Hopkins (like Anna Julia *Cooper, Ida B. *Wells-Barnett, Gertrude *Mossell, and Victoria Earle *Matthews, to mention but a few) nevertheless offered forceful and impassioned opposition to the prevalent imperial discourses of the inferiority of people of color.

[*See also* Protest Literature.]

• Abby Arthur Johnson and Ronald Maberry Johnson, *Propaganda and Aesthetics: The Literary Politics of Afro-American Magazines in the Twentieth Century*, 1979. Hazel V. Carby, *Reconstructing Womanhood*, 1987. Hazel V. Carby, introduction to *The Magazine Novels of Pauline Hopkins*, 1988. Richard Yarborough, introduction to *Contending Forces*, 1988. Claudia Tate, *Domestic Allegories of Political Desire: The Black Heroine's Text at the Turn of the Century*, 1992.

—Claudia Tate

HORTON, GEORGE MOSES (c. 1797–c. 1883), poet. The "Colored Bard of North Carolina" was the only man to publish volumes of *poetry while in bondage and the first African American to publish any book in the South. Born on the tobacco farm of William Horton in Northampton County, North Carolina, George Moses Horton moved with his master to Chatham and worked as a "cow-boy" and farm laborer throughout his teens. During these years he taught himself to read—he could not write until 1832—and began composing verses and hymns in his head. From about 1817, Horton took weekly Sabbath walks of eight miles to the Chapel Hill campus of the University of North Carolina to sell fruit, soon winning the students' admiration by composing love lyrics and acrostics to order. He sold a dozen poems a week, dictating them to the collegians, who furthered their bard's education by giving him books of poetry, geography, *history, and *oratory. As Horton's fame as a poet spread through Chapel Hill in the 1820s, the novelist Caroline Lee Hentz transcribed his verses for his first volume, *The Hope of Liberty, Containing a Number of Poetical Pieces* (1829). In the next few years many notables, including Hentz, the university president, and the governor of North Carolina, launched several campaigns to purchase Horton's *freedom, but all appeals failed. Earning over three dollars a week in the early 1830s from sales of his love lyrics, Horton arranged to hire his time from his master to become a full-time poet, handyman, hotel waiter, and servant to the university students and staff. He married a slave of Franklin Snipes and fathered two children.

For over thirty years until emancipation, Horton was a daily fixture at the university, prodigiously writing poetry, seeking publication, and futilely appealing for his freedom. His poems appeared in antislavery periodicals as well as in a second collection, *The Poetical Works* (1845); in 1859 at Chapel Hill, he delivered an oration, "The Stream of Liberty and Science." When Union troops occupied Raleigh in April 1865, Horton found a patron in William H. S. Banks, a young captain with whom he traveled in North Carolina, composing dozens of new poems that commemorated northern and southern leaders, events of camp life, dying and homesick soldiers, as well as a substantial batch of verses on love, *slavery, *religion, and the art of poetry. Banks selected ninety of these poems (plus forty-four from *Poetical Works*) for Horton's third and final volume, *Naked Genius* (1865). In 1866, Horton traveled to Philadelphia, where he probably resided for the seventeen years until his death.

Horton's three collections contain over 150 poems, many of which show remarkable skill with meter and rhyme, firm control over content, sensitivity to language, and a tender, though sometimes cynical, appreciation of what life, and thus poetry, is all about. Horton's verse before 1865 is his best, enlivened by a joyous sense of life that originates in his enthusiasm for nature and for his muse. Although many made-to-order acrostics and love verses are formulaic, a few like "Lines to My ——" and "Early Affection" share merits of rhythmic repetition, melodious phrasing, and elegantly simple language. Several neatly crafted religious verses, including "The Gad-Fly," "On the Truth of the Savior," and "Pride in Heaven" reveal Horton's undogmatic, humanistic piety, often combined with love of poetry and nature, as in "Praise of Creation." He excels in evoking rural sights and sounds of the seasons, as in "On Summer": "The bee begins her ceaseless hum." The scene swells with noisy birds and insects, "sportive children," overheated farm animals, and bountiful fruit trees and fields. Horton also wrote a few deeply felt antislavery poems, such as "Liberty and Slavery."

Other uniquely personalized appeals for manumission include "The Slave's Complaint" and "On Hearing of the Intention of a Gentleman to Purchase the Poet's Freedom," where the poet identifies his physical liberty with the creation of poetry. Outstanding, too, are four earthy folk verses (1845), lively with colloquial detail and wry humor, such as "Troubled with the Itch and Rubbing with Sulphur." Most of Horton's verse after *Hope of Liberty* has more historical than aesthetic value; nevertheless, his lifelong struggles for *literacy, freedom, and the art of poetry make his achievements as "Poet Horton" extraordinary.

• George Moses Horton, "Life," in *Poetical Works*, 1829, pp. iii–xx. Collier Cobb, "An American Man of Letters," *The University [of North Carolina] Magazine*, n.s., 27 (Oct. 1909): 3–10. Richard Walser, *The Black Poet*, 1966. Merle A. Richmond, *Bid the Vassal Soar: Interpretive Essays on the Life and Poetry of Phillis Wheatley and George Moses Horton*, 1974, pp. 81–209. Joan R. Sherman, *Invisible Poets: Afro-Americans of the Nineteenth Century*, 2d ed., 1989.

—Joan R. Sherman

House behind the Cedars, The. This powerful exploration of *passing is both Charles Waddell *Chesnutt's first *novel and the first African American novel published by a major American press. Originally titled "Rena Walden," Chesnutt's text went through more than a decade of revision before appearing serially in *Self-Culture Magazine*, beginning in August 1900, then in book form, from Houghton Mifflin, in October of that year. Despite modest sales, *The House behind the Cedars* gained the widest readership of any African American novel up to 1900. From 1921 to 1922, after falling out of print, it was reserialized in the *Chicago Defender*.

The novel tells the story of John and *Rena Walden, the mixed-blood children of a white Southerner and his antebellum *mulatto mistress. John—who has passed successfully for ten years—returns home to coax Rena into the white world. Eager to experience the social and economic opportunities denied African Americans after the war, Rena follows John to South Carolina, where (as the strikingly beautiful "Rowena Warwick") she quickly wins the affection of aristocrat George Tryon. Convincing herself that Tryon cares nothing for her past, and anxious to protect her brother's position, Rena decides not to reveal her secret. But to little avail: Tryon accidentally discovers Rena's "true" *identity and repudiates her; Rena collapses in shock and takes seriously ill. Deciding during her convalescence to devote herself to African American uplift, Rena accepts a position as a rural schoolteacher, only to find herself besieged by both a mulatto school official and her former fiancé. One night as Rena walks home she finds each man stalking her. Fleeing in terror, she is soon lost in the woods, where she is later found unconscious. Upon waking she becomes delirious; within days she is dead.

Though in certain ways similar to conventional "tragic mulatto" fiction—particularly in its staging of Rena's demise—Chesnutt's novel refuses to portray either sibling as a stereotypically degenerate, self-loathing mulatto. Nor does it criticize their decisions to pass; indeed, Chesnutt's sympathetic depiction of the factors that compel the Waldens across the *color line breaks new ground. Certainly John is an original figure: an African American who not only considered his passing justifiable but who married a white Southerner. Early reviewers, focusing on Rena's tale, generally admired the novel's restraint, although some were uncomfortable with its seeming approval of *miscegenation, and still others interpreted its stock ending as evidence that Chesnutt favored segregation. Later critics, while often faulting the novel's sentimentality and plot contrivances, have praised Chesnutt's indictment of racial barriers. By showing Tryon's tragically belated determination to love Rena regardless of her race, moreover, Chesnutt demonstrates the pain that racism causes both African Americans and whites.

One character whose representation has divided recent critics is Frank Fowler, the dark-skinned neighbor who loves Rena from a distance. While some have seen Frank's subservient devotions as a nod to more conventional fictions, others have read his complacent acceptance of inferiority as a sign of Chesnutt's inability to escape what may have been his own color prejudices.

[See also Blue Vein Societies; Double Consciousness; Novel of Passing; Protest Literature.]

• William L. Andrews, *The Literary Career of Charles W. Chesnutt*, 1980. Dickson D. Bruce, Jr., *Black American Writing from the Nadir: The Evolution of a Literary Tradition, 1877–1915*, 1989.

—William A. Gleason

HUGHES, LANGSTON (1902–1967), poet, novelist, essayist, playwright, autobiographer, and writer of children's books. Born in 1902 in Joplin, Missouri, Langston Hughes grew up mainly in Lawrence, Kansas, but also lived in Illinois, Ohio, and Mexico.

By the time Hughes enrolled at Columbia University in New York, he had already launched his literary career with his poem "The *Negro Speaks of Rivers" in the *Crisis, edited by W. E. B. *Du Bois. He had also committed himself both to writing and to writing mainly about African Americans.

Hughes's sense of dedication was instilled in him most of all by his maternal grandmother, Mary Langston, whose first husband had died at Harpers Ferry as a member of John *Brown's band, and whose second husband (Hughes's grandfather) had also been a militant abolitionist. Another important family figure was John Mercer Langston, a brother of Hughes's grandfather who was one of the best-known black Americans of the nineteenth century. At the same time, Hughes struggled with a sense of desolation fostered by parental neglect. He himself recalled being driven early by his loneliness "to books, and the wonderful world in books."

Leaving Columbia in 1922, Hughes spent the next three years in a succession of menial jobs. But he also traveled abroad. He worked on a freighter down the west coast of Africa and lived for several months in Paris before returning to the United States late in 1924. By this time, he was well known in African American literary circles as a gifted young poet.

His major early influences were Walt Whitman

and Carl Sandburg, as well as the black poets Paul Laurence *Dunbar, a master of both dialect and standard verse, and Claude *McKay, a radical socialist who also wrote accomplished lyric *poetry. However, Sandburg, who Hughes later called "my guiding star," was decisive in leading him toward free verse and a radically democratic modernist aesthetic.

His devotion to black *music led him to novel fusions of *jazz and *blues with traditional verse in his first two books, The *Weary Blues (1926) and Fine Clothes to the Jew (1927). His emphasis on lower-class black life, especially in the latter, led to harsh attacks on him in the black press. With these books, however, he established himself as a major force of the *Harlem Renaissance. In 1926, in the Nation, he provided the movement with a manifesto when he skillfully argued the need for both race pride and artistic independence in his most memorable *essay, "The Negro Artist and the Racial Mountain."

By this time, Hughes had enrolled at the historically black Lincoln University in Pennsylvania, from which he would graduate in 1929. In 1927 he began one of the most important relationships of his life, with his patron Mrs. Charlotte Mason, or "Godmother," who generously supported him for two years. She supervised the writing of his first *novel, Not Without Laughter (1930), about a sensitive, black midwestern boy and his struggling *family. However, their relationship collapsed about the time the novel appeared, and Hughes sank into a period of intense personal unhappiness and disillusionment.

One result was his firm turn to the far left in politics. During a year (1932–1933) spent in the Soviet Union, he wrote his most radical verse. A year in Carmel, California, led to a collection of *short stories, The Ways of White Folks (1934). This volume is marked by pessimism about race relations, as well as a sardonic realism.

After his play Mulatto, on the twinned themes of *miscegenation and parental rejection, opened on Broadway in 1935, Hughes wrote other plays, including comedies such as Little Ham (1936) and a historical *drama, Emperor of Haiti (1936). Most of these plays were only moderate successes. In 1937 he spent several months in Europe, including a long stay in besieged Madrid. In 1938 he returned home to found the Harlem Suitcase Theater, which staged his agitprop drama Don't You Want to Be Free? The play, employing several of his poems, vigorously blended *black nationalism, the blues, and socialist exhortation. The same year, a socialist organization published a pamphlet of his radical verse, "A New Song."

With World War II, Hughes moved more to the center politically. His first volume of *autobiography, The *Big Sea (1940), written in an episodic, lightly comic manner, made virtually no mention of his leftist sympathies. In his book of verse Shakespeare in Harlem (1942) he once again sang the blues. On the other hand, this collection, as well as another, his Jim Crow's Last Stand (1943), strongly attacked racial segregation.

Perhaps his finest literary achievement during the war came in the course of writing a weekly column in the *Chicago Defender that began in 1942 and lasted

twenty years. The highlight of the column was an offbeat Harlem character called Jesse B. Semple, or *Simple, and his exchanges with a staid narrator in a neighborhood bar, where Simple commented on a variety of matters but mainly about race and racism. Simple became Hughes's most celebrated and beloved fictional creation, and the subject of five collections edited by Hughes, starting in 1950 with Simple Speaks His Mind.

After the war, two books of verse, Fields of Wonder (1947) and One-Way Ticket (1949), added little to his fame. However, in *Montage of a Dream Deferred (1951) he broke new ground with verse accented by the discordant nature of the new bebop jazz that reflected a growing desperation in the black urban communities of the North. At the same time, Hughes's career was vexed by constant harassment by right-wing forces about his ties to the Left. In vain he protested that he had never been a Communist and had severed all such links. In 1953 he suffered a public humiliation at the hands of Senator Joseph McCarthy, who forced him to appear in Washington, D.C., and testify officially about his politics. Hughes denied that he had ever been a party member but conceded that some of his radical verse had been illadvised.

Hughes's career hardly suffered from this episode. Within a short time McCarthy himself was discredited and Hughes was free to write at length about his year in the Soviet Union in I Wonder as I Wander (1956), his much-admired second volume of autobiography. He became prosperous, although he always had to work hard for his measure of prosperity and sometimes called himself, with good cause, a "literary sharecropper."

In the 1950s he constantly looked to the *musical stage for success, as he sought to repeat his major coup of the 1940s, when Kurt Weill and Elmer Rice had chosen him as the lyricist for their Street Scene (1947). This production was hailed as a breakthrough in the development of American *opera; for Hughes, the apparently endless cycle of poverty into which he had been locked came to an end. He bought a home in Harlem.

The Simple books inspired a musical show, Simply Heavenly (1957), that met with some success. However, Hughes's Tambourines to Glory (1963), a gospel musical play satirizing corruption in a black storefront church, failed badly, with some critics accusing him of creating caricatures of black life. Nevertheless, his love of gospel music led to other acclaimed stage efforts, usually mixing words, music, and *dance in an atmosphere of improvisation. Notable here were the Christmas show Black Nativity (1961) and, inspired by the *civil rights movement, Jericho–Jim Crow (1964).

For Hughes, writing for children was important. Starting with the successful *Popo and Fifina (1932), a tale set in Haiti and written with Arna *Bontemps, he eventually published a dozen children's books, on subjects such as jazz, Africa, and the West Indies. Proud of his versatility, he also wrote a commissioned history of the NAACP and the text of a much praised pictorial history of black America. His text in *The Sweet Flypaper of Life* (1955), where he explicated photographs of Harlem by Roy DeCarava, was judged masterful by reviewers, and confirmed Hughes's reputation for an unrivaled command of the nuances of black urban culture.

The 1960s saw Hughes as productive as ever. In 1962 his ambitious booklength poem *Ask Your Mama*, dense with allusions to black culture and music, appeared. However, the reviews were dismissive. Hughes's work was not as universally acclaimed as before in the black community. Although he was hailed in 1966 as a historic artistic figure at the First World Festival of Negro Arts in Dakar, Senegal, he also found himself increasingly rejected by young black militants at home as the civil rights movement lurched toward Black Power. His last book was the volume of verse, posthumously published, *The Panther and the Lash* (1967), mainly about civil rights. He died in May that year in New York City.

In many ways Hughes always remained loyal to the principles he had laid down for the younger black writers in 1926. His art was firmly rooted in race pride and race feeling even as he cherished his freedom as an artist. He was both nationalist and cosmopolitan. As a radical democrat, he believed that art should be accessible to as many people as possible. He could sometimes be bitter, but his art is generally suffused by a keen sense of the ideal and by a profound love of humanity, especially black Americans. He was perhaps the most original of African American poets and, in the breadth and variety of his work, assuredly the most representative of African American writers.

[*See also* Hurston, Zora Neale; Madam Alberta K. Johnson; Mulatto; Mule Bone.]

• Arnold Rampersad, *The Life of Langston Hughes*, 2 vols., 1986–1988. Langston Hughes, *Collected Poems*, 1994.

—Arnold Rampersad

HUMOR has always played a key role in African American culture. One of the sustaining resources enslaved Africans brought to the New World was a richly figured mode of discourse, brimming with exuberant, often subversive humor. The harsh realities of *slavery by no means effaced it, but did temper it into a new kind of spiritual and cultural tool.

Humor was interlaced into everyday talk, song, and verbal dueling, but had a special role in narrative. Any discussion of African American literary humor must therefore include oral versions, for the two forms have continually constituted inseparable parts of a larger whole. Enslaved Africans, for instance, were masters of oral narrative. They retold traditional stories, but refigured them with North American animals, focusing more on the animals' "mother wit" than any presumed link with gods; as many skeptical slave tales indicated, "de Lawd" was not that helpful when "de Massa" elected to play God himself.

Parody, a key element in African humor, found an American form too; slaves brought their masters and mistresses down to their level by mocking virtually every pronouncement they made. If slaves could use a white preacher's text to do so, so much the better,

especially sermons that included biblical texts on obedience. Many folk rhymes were created in this mode. A takeoff on the Lord's Prayer read "'Our Fadder, Which are in Heaben!'— / White man owe me leben and pay me seben. / 'D'y Kingdom come! D'y Will be done!'— / An' if I hadn't tuck dat, I wouldn't git none" (Thomas Washington Talley, *Negro Folk Rhymes, Wise and Otherwise*, 1968). White hymns were parodied as well. "Reign, Master Jesus Reign" could thus become "Oh rain! Oh rain! Oh rain, 'good' Mosser! / Rain, Mosser, rain! Rain hard! / Rain flour an' lard an' a big hog head / Down in my back yard" (Talley). Thus the masters' blasphemous appropriations of godlike powers were noted and mocked.

Subterfuge was imperative for protection; consequently, many of the animal fables concluded with a wily small animal (often a rabbit) causing the violent and painful death of larger animals, who represented the slaveowners. Eventually these small, sly animals found human form, in the shape and *signifying comic voice of the crafty servant John, who could outwit Ole Massa and Big Missy, or the devil himself.

John, too, however, gets tricked on occasion, as is the case with his African predecessors, the Signifying Monkey and Anancy the Spider, and their American counterpart, *Brer Rabbit. As such, the tales can double back on themselves as a caution. John's foibles, and theirs, must be seen as part of the self-reflexive aspect of African American humor, which was a perhaps inevitable result of the coded nature of the humor slaves crafted to use in the presence of whites. But self-reflexive humor also exists *within* the race, which Langston *Hughes labeled "Jokes Negroes Tell on Themselves." It may be found in a classic joke about how African Americans came to be black. The Lord calls everybody to come wash in the River of Life. One group loiters along the way, dallying and playing, taking their own good time. When they get to the river, the other folks have used up the water and emerged from it whiter than snow. The latecomers only find mud, which they scooped up in the palms of their hands, exhausting even the mud. So, the joke goes, not a thing about "negroes" is light but the palms of their hands and the soles of their feet. That's what comes of always being late.

The joke mocks both blackness and "colored people time" ("CPT"), and closely resembles the self-reflexive jokes told by *Jews among themselves. As Langston Hughes noted, such humor stems from frustration; the fact that people laugh at such tales really represents a desperate humor, a syndrome white people often cannot understand. Humor theorists today call such in-group techniques "corrective comedy." Yet another example of it is found in African American proverbs, which offer a fine example of indirect humor; because of their ambiguity and multivalent constitution, they function as "crooked sticks" that are used to "lick" home a point of comic correction, particularly in child-rearing practices, both in Africa and the United States.

Not all problems proved susceptible to solution, however, and during the *Harlem Renaissance, Jessie Redmon *Fauset declared that the remarkable thing about African American humor was the way in which it found its origins in the woes and problems that beset the race. A person experiencing great sorrow might indulge in an orgy of laughter; similarly, an oppressed and driven people indulge in compensating laughter and spontaneous fun, a kind of self-generated psychic salvation.

It should not be supposed that African American humor always comes off as heroic, creative, and exuberant. Like that of all other cultures, it can be cruel, stereotypical, sexist, and exploitive. Jokes exist within the culture that ridicule other members of the diaspora, such as West Indians; others disparage women, particularly "black black" women. Some jokes poke fun at "down-home" or uneducated brothers and sisters; others put down members of other ethnic groups. Black minstrels, for instance, offered comic and derogatory impersonations of Indians. The Irish and Jews were similar targets. In cities, today as in the past, one finds Italians, Mexicans, American Indians, and Chinese being needled by African American quipsters, and this company has lately expanded to include Asian merchants, particularly Koreans.

During the terrible decades before and after the turn of the century (the "nadir" of African American experience in America), High John tales gave way to images of heroic *badmen, such as *Stackolee, Railroad Bill, and John Hardy. All the figures in the continuum, however, developed out of oppression.

Not surprisingly, these heroic comic wordsmiths really "talk that talk," a highly esteemed skill among both men and women. The exaggerated, obscene boasting of the "Great McDaddy" offers a typical male example: "I've got a tombstone disposition, graveyard mind. I know I'm a bad motherfucker, that's why I don't mind dying."

The "toast" constitutes the genre setting par excellence for the "bad nigger" tradition and has African antecedents. That continent's poets sometimes became known for their self-praise ("boasts"), which in many ways were mini-autobiographies. The African American version, the "toast" (a long narrative poem), receives braggadocio performances on the street, in bars, or in poolrooms; the toaster seeks both audience involvement and approval.

The shift from animal fables and High John stories to toasts and Stackolee or McDaddy tales was a major event in African American culture, and was accompanied by an increase in verbal practices such as signifying, sounding, the dozens, woofing, bookooing, loud-talking, and marking. All of these eventually found their way into American literature, although sometimes in diluted, censored form. Humor in all these forms, not just in jokes, forms a metacategory of indirection all its own that deserves detailed analysis.

The nineteenth century's appetite for "Negro" folktales and folk humor proved insatiable, especially after the Civil War, when new cultural modes were sought to deal with white psychological fears caused by emancipation. But these needs were satisfied by white writers, performers, and artists. Collections of "Negro Humor," *plantation tradition *short stories and *novels, and above all, the minstrel show and popular stage productions solidified the image of the "comic darkie."

These *stereotypes began in Europe, in English plays such as George Colman's Inkle and Yarico (1787), which, although somewhat sympathetic to the slave's plight, presented grinning, singing, dialect-talking "darkies" to the public. American imitations soon appeared. Then, in the early 1820s, Thomas D. (Jim Crow) Rice, a white performer, observed an old enslaved man singing and dancing in Louisville and created a black-face act around the song "Jump Jim Crow." Rice's amazing success quickly spawned imitations, ritualized such songs and acts, and encouraged the collection of comic "Negro Stories." A collector could be an abolitionist or a southern planter; a reader could be a western miner or a Boston matron. As late as the 1950s *anthologies of racist jokes were still being written, bought, laughed over, and accepted as accurate renditions of African American humor, under titles such as Chocolate Drops from the South (1932). We should exercise caution, however, in dismissing the comic anthologies, for many of them (sometimes inadvertently) contained subversive humor and genuine contributions by African Americans, in addition to the racist material.

What was this stereotype generally like? Paradoxically, it provided doubled images, damning the African American no matter what approach was taken. To choose but one example, he was often said to be lazy; on other occasions, however, he was dumb enough to "work like a nigger." Similarly doubled labels include stupid but crafty, humble but scheming, cowardly but reckless, innocent but lascivious. The most basic all-purpose comic stereotype, however, sketched in the caricature of a slow, childish, lascivious, always happy, full of rhythm lover of chicken and watermelon who just loved to cut the buck and the wing to keep the white folks happy.

American minstrel shows, growing out of an elaboration of Rice's act, kept this image alive, with white actors in burnt-cork makeup. These entertainments complemented down-home-on-the-plantation stereotypes with a new one depicting the gaudy African dandy of New York's Broadway, "Jim Dandy." These "types" were anything but simple, and had little basis in African American culture. The rough, plain-talking, "country" *Jim Crow figure was plainly an avatar of white culture's backwoods and riverboat characters, and of "Brother Jonathan"/"Uncle Sam" figures. "Jim Dandy," by contrast, effeminate, urban, and fast-talking, was Yankee Doodle's parallel, and in comic opposition to Jim Crow, provided a smiling mask for the deep struggle between America's pastoral romanticism and onrushing urban industrialization. In another avatar he became "Zip Coon," a crafty urbanite who frequently preyed on greenhorns come to the city from "down home."

*Minstrelsy is often dismissed as a vile phenomenon of American popular culture, but its longlasting popularity was partly due to its constantly evolving nature, its ambiguities, and its comic invitation into the world of the ethnic other. Although the shows certainly stereotyped African Americans, they also created characters that spoke to white yearnings for freedom and irresponsibility, an alternative approach to life that Africans have always mirrored for whites. Indeed, such portrayals by African Americans, Jews, or Italians of their own stereotypes on stage could please members of those ethnic groups too, for both the actor and the audience would pride themselves on being above the "type" presented.

Finally, minstrelsy also included "straight" love songs for both sexes, and handsome leading men became "matinee idols"; serious themes such as poverty, *family, and *race were dealt with under the mask of shrewd folk proverbs, riddles, and idiom, so the shows went beyond both humor and stereotype at times. Over the years, the humor gained in subtlety, and the standard sets featuring cotton patches, cabins, and riverboats gave way to fancy society parties and Broadway pleasure palaces. Minstrelsy gave African American performers a chance to break into the entertainment circuit, and provided early careers for stars of later eras, such as Ernest Hogan (ragtime and musical comedy composer); Bert Williams, the musical comedy star; W. C. Handy, the bluesman; Dewey "Pigmeat" Markham, the comedian; and the *blues queens, Ma *Rainey and Bessie *Smith. In virtually every case, the artist in question found ways to work around the stereotype and to insert truly authentic African American comic forms.

Minstrelsy's legacy had an even greater "fogging" effect in the *theater and in popular *music. The gifted comedians Bert Williams and George Walker not only wore burnt cork in their early days; when they and other African American artists began acting in musical comedies (the first was A Trip to Coontown in 1898), they were singing lyrics that suggested an inseparable foursome was a watermelon, a razor, a chicken, and a coon. During the "coon song" craze of the 1890s, urban figures were spotlighted, especially their vicious way with a razor. Before judging these early performers and writers too harshly, we should remember Paul Laurence *Dunbar's assertion that the grinning entertainer's mask often hid deep sorrow, as well as the fact that such subterfuge facilitated survival.

African American humor did not loom large on the national literary horizon until the invention of mass printing and increased magazine and newspaper circulation. African American comic writers had to correct both racist stories and images in popular American magazines like Puck and Judge that had taken their cue from minstrelsy. African American and other ethnic communities set up their own newspapers to counter negative images, to bolster group confidence and *identity, and to achieve the paradoxical and somewhat opposed goals of assisting readers in the "Americanization" process, while ministering to their nostalgia for vanishing folkways, be they from the American South or the south of Europe.

The twentieth century brought phonograph records, then radio and cinema to the people, and all three forms continued and developed racial stereotypes, as in Al Jolson's blackface songs, Amos 'n'

Andy, and the various *mammies, *pickaninnies, and *Stepin Fetchits that Hollywood cranked out. One of the major results of the new technology for African Americans was the national dissemination of the blues, the great musical tradition that had evolved out of the field songs, the *church, and *spirituals. The music struck a responsive chord in white Americans, and forced an awareness of the suggestive, coded lyrics. The blues contained a lot of pain, but sweetened by wry, sometimes raunchy humor, especially in the suggestive lyrics of the blues queens. Like griots, blues artists provide laughter and entertainment, and frequently offer devastating signification on people and events. Although blues are popularly conceived to be laments of victims, they are at the same time yearning for, and expressions of, *freedom, and of the intent to expand freedom. Travel figures in many of the lyrics. It makes sense, therefore, that many of the songs, however tragic in content, get expressed humorously and playfully, for the style liberates the content.

Blues performers traveled on Rabbit Foot Minstrel Tours and "TOBY" circuit, a kind of traveling vaudeville that also featured comedians, like the duo Butterbeans and Susie, and there was constant interchange.

Further transformations of African American humor came with the printed word. Complementing the realms of orally transmitted humor and popular culture's forms of comedy, a literary synthesis of the ersatz images of African Americans and their actual cultural traditions began when Joel Chandler Harris published his Uncle Remus tales for an age already infected by stereotypical African American supporting characters in "high" white culture narratives by writers such as James Fenimore Cooper, William Gilmore Simms, Edgar Allan Poe, John Pendleton Kennedy, and Harriet Beecher *Stowe. Seen as such, the "inside tales" offered a corrective, albeit in a convoluted way, for the coded nature of African American mythology is constantly at play in the Brer Rabbit tales. Harris tirelessly collected and edited these and other classic African American animal tales from the 1870s to his death in 1905. But his racist frame story, wherein a desexualized old man tells the stories to his mistress's little blond son, caters to stereotype, and has always led unwary readers to reductive and simply wrong readings of the tales themselves; their charming surface images and boisterous humor mask core narratives of terror, trickery, and *violence, and a different, crueler, and more ironic level of laughter. At the turn of the century, Charles Waddell *Chesnutt would try to counter the image of Uncle Remus by writing a new form of plantation tradition fiction featuring credible and admirable African American characters; his *Uncle Julius McAdoo in The *Conjure Woman (1899) entertains the white folks with tales that are often superficially funny, but always subversive. The African American characters speak in dialect, but the narrative under this cloak is moving and powerful; a careful reader will soon see a devastating and sorrow-filled portrait of slave life. By contrast, in the Uncle Julius frame stories, comic reversal turns the tables on the masters time and time again.

Chesnutt wrote other stories and a number of *novels, and their serious themes are sometimes carried by, but more often counterpointed with, African American humor. In both Harris and Chesnutt, humor works in tandem with the magical, a pairing that would reemerge in the postmodern work of Ishmael *Reed and Toni *Morrison years later.

Despite his works' appeal, however, Chesnutt's books were outsold by those of white contemporaries like Thomas Nelson Page, who brought the art of depicting the "oldtime darkey" to its most genteel peak, in semicomic stories such as "Marse Chan" and "Meh' Lady." Outright racist writers such as Thomas Dixon, in books like *The Leopard's Spots* (1902) and *The Clansman* (1905), villified emancipated slaves as rapist apes, or presented them as buffoons. Popular magazines and newspapers added to these images; even the *New York Times* depicted African American men as "Brutes" or "*Sambos," replete with all the vicious stereotypes.

Sadly, even fine African American poets, such as Paul Laurence Dunbar, felt they had to cater to this tradition, and set most of their dialect-driven poems on bucolic plantations. Many of these poems nevertheless work quite well and offer a sly folk humor that often explodes the ersatz pastoralism.

Because of its catholic usage, the issue of dialect proved a particularly knotty problem for all these writers and continues to provoke divergent reactions today. Henry D. Spaulding, compiling his *Encyclopedia of Black Folklore and Humor*, wrestled with the problem and finally decided that dialect, at least as recorded and used by African American writers, needed no apology and, in fact, was one of the creative triumphs of the race. Conversely, others have eschewed dialect as a vehicle used most frequently to debase the race. It has indeed appeared in bogus representations, but also in African American literature itself, and in narratives by white writers who were mostly sympathetic with African American culture, such as Sherwood Anderson, Dubose Heyward, and Julia Peterkin.

The exchange between popular culture and print literature was never so marked as in the 1920s, the first heyday of African American comedians. New Broadway shows featured comic duos, such as Flournoy Miller and Aubrey Lyles of 1921's trail-blazing hit comedy *Shuffle Along*. This musical, set during an election in an African American southern town, in many ways prefigured Zora Neale *Hurston's rural Florida settings, but with minstrel touches. Characters spoke in malapropisms and were heavily involved in petty fraud. Unfortunately, this racist mode of depiction was part of the show's legacy as well, for audiences and producers wanted more of the same throughout the 1920s. A musical like *Put and Take* (1921), which tried to provide more sophistication with a northern locale, was critically damned. Other *Shuffle Along* wannabees followed: nine *musicals written by and starring African Americans opened on Broadway from 1921 to 1924. *Runnin' Wild* (1923) featured Miller and Lyles's comedy skits, praised because they were spontaneous and supposedly unstudied. The shows continued to trouble many African Americans, however, because the humor still depended in part on minstrel traditions; false images had once again taken America by storm, and not just on stage. *Amos 'n' Andy* was the most popular radio show in the 1920s and 1930s and combined new breakthrough representations of African Americans (eventually leading to the television version), alongside negative and stereotypical portrayals.

Not surprisingly, the first great age of African American humor writing also came during the 1920s, especially, but not only, in Harlem. In addition to the above events, ragtime, the blues, gospel, and *jazz began to percolate in the great cities of the North as the Great *Migration began. One of the most important results was the extraordinary concentration of talent that began to cluster "up in Harlem" after World War I. The stage had been set by the older generation of scholars and "race-men," like W. E. B. *Du Bois, James Weldon *Johnson, and others, who founded periodicals that subsequently published many of the "*New Negroes." Johnson himself had a fine sense of humor, as passages from his *autobiography and his short masterwork, *The *Autobiography of an Ex-Colored Man* (1912), reveal.

But it was the younger generation that turned up the steam. In his short fiction, Richard Bruce *Nugent coupled his sly humor with a strong dose of decadence, while Wallace *Thurman tempered his wicked wit with more than a little bile; his roman à clef, *Infants of the Spring* (1930), featured the bohemian tenants of "*Niggerati Manor." Using real-life models, Thurman skewered everybody in the literary movement, including himself. His bitter indictment of color prejudice within the race, *The *Blacker the Berry* (1929), avoids the pathetic via its dark and biting humor.

Rudolph *Fisher's inventive stories and novels bubbled with a far more joyous energy. He offers a wonderfully entertaining panorama of Harlem, while weaving a beguiling story, in *The *Walls of Jericho* (1928). His detective novel, *The Conjure Man Dies* (1932), makes equally good use of comic conventions of urban folk culture, taking the reader through virtually every level of Harlem society. Similarly, Claude *McKay created wonderful comedy in his even more encyclopedic *Home to Harlem* (1928), while more refined and ironic humor found its way into Nella *Larsen's slim novels and Jesse Fauset's novelistic explorations of the rising middle class. The wickedest writer of all was George S. *Schuyler, whose brilliant satire, *Black No More* (1931), tells the story of Dr. Crookman's discovery and exploitation of a process that makes African Americans white. *Slaves Today* (also 1931) unleashed Schuyler's treatment on Liberia, with less impressive results. Throughout his work, however, Schuyler used comic scorn to skewer the very idea of race itself.

Poets, too, used rollicking humor, especially Langston Hughes and Sterling A. *Brown, whose

Southern Road (1932) contributed the hilarious but evocative character of *Slim Greer to American literary lore. Neither Hughes nor Brown lived "down-home," but followed Zora Neale Hurston's lead in writing much of their best work out of the folk culture and its creative humor.

Hurston and Hughes, her longtime pal, were two of the funniest writers in American history, and when they got together things started cooking. Hurston's award-winning *short stories and plays sometimes signified wickedly on the con artists and the conned in Harlem, but more often created poignant social comedy from the materials of southern African American culture. She later published two groundbreaking collections of *folklore and hoodoo materials, *Mules and Men* (1935) and *Tell My Horse* (1938), and most importantly, four comic novels that set a very high standard: *Jonah's Gourd Vine* (1934), *Their Eyes Were Watching God* (1937), *Moses, Man of the Mountain* (1939), and *Seraph on the Suwanee* (1948). In her complex interweaving of folklore, ritual, traditional narrative, and virtually every type of African American comic expression, Hurston, perhaps more so than any other African American writer, revealed the subversive possibilities of one of the world's richest comic arsenals, while simultaneously charting fascinating stories that have proven especially instructive for American women.

Langston Hughes, who jump-started his lifelong study of African American humor at Hurston's side in the South, proved equally tireless in his attempt to render the glories of a great comic tradition. His plays (especially *Little Ham*, 1935), many of his stories and poems, and particularly his many hilarious sketches starring Jesse B. Semple (*Simple), a folksy Harlem raconteur, transfix, entertain, and instruct the reader about the various issues that faced the race and the nation during Hughes's long and extraordinary career. Hughes's many anthologies—including one of African American humor—have been of great use and pleasure.

The *Harlem Renaissance exerted a lasting influence on subsequent developments in African American humor, so one might well ask, why was so much humorous literature created "uptown" in the 1920s? Humor and joking are part of change, and change was the order of the day in Harlem; people coming, people going, customs changing, all pointed to the development of what was called the "New Negro." This demanded a change as well in literary expression, especially since the people, as usual, were ahead of the artists in coining new idioms, words, and rituals. Wisely, W. E. B. Du Bois advised those who would hear truly boisterous humor to go to Guinea, "Black Bottom," "Niggertown," or Harlem.

Humorous writing of all types became largely eclipsed in America as the shadow of the Depression fell in widening circles. Then the explosion of Richard *Wright on the literary scene coincided with the watershed of World War II, which occasioned a new debate on the role of African Americans in America. Wright's grimly naturalistic novels tore away the veil that had obscured African American suffering and anger. However, even Wright could create sly comedy,

as in his "Man of All Work" (1961), where a man desperate for employment cross-dresses to secure domestic employment. Wright also created existential/surrealist humor in "The Man Who Lived Underground" (1945), a tale modeled on Dostoyevsky but larded with bizarre wit. Wright's relentless exposure of the absurdities of racism, be it in Chicago or Mississippi, set the stage for another innovator, Ralph *Ellison, whose *Invisible Man* (1952), arguably the greatest novel by an African American, takes the readers across the spectrum of modern African American experience, North and South. Its existentialist philosophy finds a counterpoint in Ellison's exuberant and creative use of African American comic conventions. Not accidentally, Ellison was a major theorist of African American humor, and in many ways anticipated postmodern forms of comedy.

Gradually writers became more daring in their materials. Alice *Childress masterfully deconstructed saccharine but racist versions of the maid/mistress syndrome in her *Like One of the Family* (1956), which wryly considers the plight of the African American woman. During the early 1960s, the dramatic events of the *civil rights movement had seemed to dictate a sternly serious demeanor for the race's writers, but the rapid transformations of the period created an ideal climate for boisterous, innovative humor, which included Dick Gregory's in-your-face autobiography *Nigger* (1964), Charles S. *Wright's wild neopassing novel *The Wig* (1966), and Cecil *Brown's *The Loves and Lives of Mr. Jiveass Nigger* (1969). *Iceberg Slim's hilarious, often horrifying humor, expressed in works with in-your-face titles such as *Pimp* (1967), took readers inside the seamy side of ghetto life, yes, but also demonstrated the creativity and raw energy of outlaw culture. The era also produced the pyrotechnic comic turns of the "*Black Aesthetic" poets, the work of ur-feminist/womanists, and black nationalists. Poets of the time such as Nikki *Giovanni, LeRoi Jones (Amiri *Baraka), Jay *Wright, and Don L. Lee (Haki R. *Madhubuti) found inspiration from politics and ideology, but many were simultaneously influenced by the improvisations of newly popular jazz, and mingled their barbed witticisms with lyrical twists and turns.

Also during the 1960s, Chester *Himes's reputation began to grow as the creator of brilliantly patterned and often hilarious detective novels, such as *Cotton Comes to Harlem* (1964). His work in turn set standards for contemporary writers such as Walter *Mosley, who similarly mixes sleuths and sly humor.

This period saw the rise of nationally popular African American comedians, who often starred on *television and in movies. Moms Mabley, Redd Foxx, Flip Wilson, Bill Cosby, above all Richard Pryor, and later Eddie Murphy and Whoopi Goldberg, among others, all had a say in the direction of African American comic conventions, and made an impact on literary humor.

Like these comedians, contemporary writers mirror actual life, and they still find comic material in the country as well as the city. Alice *Walker spices many of her Georgia parables with womanist humor, as in "Really, *Doesn't* Crime Pay?" (1973), while

Ernest J. *Gaines employs a wry, understated humor in his tales of Louisiana (especially in comic dialogue), even when the major thrust of the story seems foreboding. Similarly, Toni Morrison concentrates on monumentally tragic themes, but often pushes her narrative (à la Ellison) into situations so absurd that they evoke laughter as well as tears. We find this technique in the creations of Gloria *Naylor, Ntozake *Shange, and Gayl *Jones as well.

Ishmael Reed's growing corpus of overtly comic works constitutes one of the richest veins of contemporary humor. Constantly experimenting (often ahead of others) with various voices and styles, Reed weaves a comic pastiche out of African American life that provides, as his predecessor Chesnutt did in the 1890s, a devastating critique of fin-de-siècle social madness. Works such as *Yellow Back Radio Broke-Down (1969) and *Mumbo Jumbo (1971) set the standard for what has become a jive version of postmodernist parody and *trickster techniques, one that has been adopted by other African American and ethnic writers, such as Charles R. *Johnson, Gerald Vizenor, Frank Chin, Jessica Hagedorn, and Maxine Hong Kingston.

Many other writers in the canon—particularly recent additions—could be featured here if space permitted. The continuing innovation and vitality of African American writers, along with the complex interchange they continue to foster with popular culture, suggest we may see even more dazzling displays of wit in the decades to come, as humor continues to find a way to change the joke and slip the yoke.

[See also Coon; Dialect Poetry; High John the Conqueror; Oratory.]

• Roger Abrahams, Deep Down in the Jungle, 1964. William Schechter, The History of Negro Humor in America, 1970. Claudia Mitchell-Kernan, "Signifying and Marking," in Directions in Social Linguistics, eds. John J. Gumperz and Dell Hymes, 1972, pp. 161–179. Alan Dundes, ed., Mother Wit from the Laughing Barrel, 1973. Lawrence Levine, Black Culture and Black Consciousness, 1977. William D. Piersen, "Puttin' Down Ole Massa: African Satire in the New World," in African Folklore in the New World, ed. Daniel J. Crowley, 1977, pp. 20–34. Geneva Smitherman, Talkin' and Testifyin', 1977. Daryl Dance, Shuckin' and Jivin', 1978. Charles H. Nichols, "Comic Modes in Black America," in Comic Relief, ed. Sarah Blancher Cohen, 1978, pp. 105–126. John W. Roberts, From Trickster to Badman, 1989. John Lowe, Jump at the Sun: Zora Neale Hurston's Cosmic Comedy, 1994. Mel Watkins, On the Real Side, 1994.   —John Lowe

HUNTER, KRISTIN (b. 1931), novelist, short story writer, and journalist. Kristin Hunter was born on 12 September 1931 to George Lorenzo and Mabel Eggleston, two schoolteachers, who planned for their only child to pursue a teaching career. However, she wanted to be a writer. After completing the BS in education from the University of Pennsylvania in 1951, Hunter taught third grade for less than a year before resigning to pursue a writing career. Currently, she lectures in the English department at the University of Pennsylvania.

Before Hunter defined herself as a novelist, she commanded notice as a screenwriter and playwright. In 1955 Hunter won first place in a national contest sponsored by CBS for her *television documentary, "Minority of One," about the integration of an all-black Catholic school in Camden, New Jersey. In 1965 her play The Double Edge was produced in Philadelphia.

Hunter's first *novel, God Bless the Child, published in 1964, won the Philadelphia Athenaeum Award. The novel recalls the tragic story of Rosie Fleming, an ambitious young woman who struggles to climb the ladder of success and to redeem what she believes is her inferior dark skin by rescuing her octoroon grandmother and her light brown mother from ghetto life. Rosie's invincible spirit cannot overcome the exploitation of those who capitalize on the dreams of young black women. She literally works herself to death to achieve false symbols of success.

The Landlord, published in 1966, continued Hunter's exploration of ghetto life. Whereas God Bless the Child is a tragedy, The Landlord is a comic novel of social optimism. The story is about the neurotic Elgar Enders, a wealthy white man who purchases an apartment building in a black ghetto and subsequently attempts to reform the tenants. His success is at best modest. What is more important is the effect on him of the tenants, who form a surrogate *family for the emotionally vulnerable Enders. The novel's critics were put off by such idealism. Indeed, as Sondra O'Neale explains (DLB, vol. 33, 1984) the 1970 United Artists movie version of the novel repudiated the novel's social optimism for a more jaded version of ghetto realism. The movie transformed Enders into a ruthless individualist.

In the late 1960s Hunter turned to a younger audience. She published Boss Cat in 1971 for juvenile readers and a series of novels for young adults: The Soul Brothers and Sister Lou (1968); The Pool Table War and Uncle Daniel and the Racoon (both 1972); and Lou in the Limelight (1981). Guests in the Promised Land, a collection of *short stories for young adults, appeared in 1973. Guests earned her the 1973 Chicago Tribune Book World Prize for juvenile literature. These works define urban black communities as sites for possible success rather than as containers for social dysfunction. For example, Louetta (Lou) Hawkins in the "Lou" series sings herself out of the ghetto. Hunter's young audience appreciated the spirited optimism of Soul Brothers and Sister Lou and made it Hunter's most popular book. It sold over a million copies and won the Children's Prize of the Council on Interracial Books in 1968.

Hunter's last two adult novels—The Survivors (1975) and Lakestown Rebellion (1978)—continue to draw on her resolute social optimism. Both novels feature protagonists who are mature black women. Each speaks her mind, demands respect, and insists that black people be responsible for their own fates. Lena Rich of The Survivors is a middle-aged dressmaker who abandons a life of hard-won self-sufficiency to become the surrogate mother of B.J., a thirteen-year-old streetwise boy. Lakestown Rebellion's Bella Lakes's rejection of her husband Abe's desire to make her into "a mock-up of some painted white doll" incites the novel's political rebellion. She insists that the residents of the small black town of

Lakestown reassert their pride in their black identities and resist the plans of the corrupt representatives of the state planning commission to build a highway that will destroy the town.

Throughout her career and long before the majority of contemporary readers had been conditioned to appreciate black women writers or their black female protagonists, Hunter wrote about black women who rely on their own convictions and fortitude to survive and sometimes prosper. Her novels depend on the comic conventions of satire, parody, caricature, and somewhat implausible plots to depict optimistic portraits of inner-city black people. Because these works reject the pathology generally associated with inner-city black people (see Hunter's article on *stereotypes in movies and on television, "Why Buckwheat Was Shot," MELUS, Fall 1984) and because juvenile fiction preserves this viewpoint to its advantage more so than adult fiction, Hunter is better known and more applauded as an author of *children's and young adult literature.

• Trudier Harris, From Mammies to Militants: Domestics in Black American Literature, 1982. Claudia Tate, Black Women Writers at Work, 1983. Sondra O'Neale, "Kristin Hunter," in DLB, vol. 33, Afro-American Fiction Writers after 1955, eds. Thadious M. Davis and Trudier Harris, 1984, pp. 119–124.

—Claudia Tate

HURSTON, ZORA NEALE (1891–1960), novelist anthropologist, folklorist, and genius of the South. In February 1927, Zora Neale Hurston left New York City aboard a southbound train. Her destination was Eatonville, Florida, her hometown, where she began collecting folktales, *spirituals, sermons, work songs, *blues, and children's games. To Hurston this frequently disparaged *folklore was priceless; it constituted the "arts of the people before they find out that there is any such thing as art." At a time when the Great Migration, the movement that brought blacks by the hundreds of thousands from the rural South to the urban North, seemed a sign of racial progress, as did the *poetry and fiction of the burgeoning *Harlem Renaissance, Hurston moved against the tide. Crisscrossing Florida, Alabama, and Louisiana, Hurston spent the next six years documenting the art of "the Negro farthest down," who, she contended, had made the greatest contribution to American culture.

Her years in the field culminated with the 1935 publication of Mules and Men, the first volume of black American folklore published by an African American. A self-styled "literary anthropologist," Hurston blurs the boundaries of literature and ethnography in her writing. She employed fictional techniques to shape the narrative of Mules and Men. Her theories about language and culture, which she summarized in a 1934 article, "Characteristics of Negro Expression," inspired the technical innovations of her fiction. Her effort was not merely to interpolate folk sayings in her *novels; it was to write fiction according to the aesthetic principles that undergirded oral culture. Consequently, Hurston strove to re-create the sense of *drama and "will to adorn" she admired in the oral culture and to create a literary language informed by the poetry as well as the perspective of rural black Southerners.

This she did in four novels: *Jonah's Gourd Vine (1934), *Their Eyes Were Watching God (1937), Moses, Man of the Mountain (1939), and Seraph on the Suwanee (1948); a second volume of ethnography based on field work in Jamaica and Haiti, Tell My Horse (1938); a memoir, *Dust Tracks on a Road (1942); and more than fifty published *short stories, *essays, and plays. No black woman writer had been as prolific. But unstinting devotion to her artistic vision and iconoclastic political views exacted a price. Despite the excellent quality of her writing, none of Hurston's books were in print when she died on 28 January 1960.

Even without her frequent embellishments, Hurston's life was as dramatic as any story she wrote. Born 7 January 1891 in Notasulga, Alabama, a small hamlet near Tuskegee, Zora was the fifth of eight children of John and Lucy Ann Potts Hurston. The family resettled in Eatonville, the first incorporated black community in America, where John served three terms as mayor. Lucy, a former country schoolteacher, encouraged her children to "jump at de sun." A bright pupil, Zora loved fanciful play and the "lies" (stories) adults told on the porch of Joe Clarke's store. But the idyll of her childhood ended with Lucy's death in 1904. Sent to school in Jacksonville, no longer "Eatonville's Zora," she "became a little colored girl."

During the next few years Hurston did domestic work as she lived with relatives in neighboring Sanford and in Memphis; she then joined a Gilbert and Sullivan troupe as a lady's maid. Leaving the troupe in Baltimore, she enrolled in the high school division of what is now Morgan State University in September 1917. The following fall she registered at Howard University in Washington, D.C. Working as a waitress and manicurist, she attended Howard intermittently from 1918 to 1924. An English major, Hurston joined the campus literary club; her first published story, "John Redding Goes to Sea," evoked her memories of Eatonville. Off campus, Hurston attended poet Georgia Douglas *Johnson's literary salon. Two of her poems appeared in *Negro World, the official newspaper of Marcus *Garvey's Universal Negro Improvement Association. After *Opportunity published the story "Drenched in Light" in December 1924, Hurston decided to ply her luck in New York.

Her luck held. Alain *Locke selected her short story "Spunk" for the landmark anthology The *New Negro (1925). Attending the Opportunity awards dinner in May 1925, she took two second-place prizes and met poets Langston *Hughes and Countee *Cullen and novelists Fannie Hurst, Annie Nathan Meyer, and Carl Van Vechten. Hurst employed her as secretary, then chauffeur, and Meyer secured her a scholarship to Barnard College in September 1926. Hurston was thirty-five years old; everyone she met in New York believed she was at least ten years younger. The only black student at Barnard, Hurston studied anthropology with Franz Boas, who pioneered the discipline in the United States. Although she continued to write, and joined Hughes and other young artists to plan the first and only issue of *Fire!!*, Hurston determined to pursue a career as a social scientist. With Boas's assistance, she obtained a research fellowship from the Association for the Study of Negro Life and History (ASNLH) and made her journey south.

Her introduction to *Mules and Men* proclaims: "I was glad when somebody told me, 'You may go and collect Negro folklore.'" But gaining the wherewithal to pursue the mission was complicated. Hurston needed more consistent funding than the ASNLH could provide. She needed a patron. Charlotte (Mrs. R. Osgood) Mason had bloodlines and bank accounts traceable to the founding of the Republic. Indians of the Southwest had been Mason's enthusiasm before Harlem's black artists caught her fancy. In December 1927 she contracted Hurston to compile and collect the "music, poetry, folk-lore, literature, hoodoo, conjure, manifestations of art and kindred subjects relating to and existing among the North American Negroes." If the list reflected Hurston's sensibility, the clause asserting that the material collected would *belong* to Mason was alien both to Hurston's assertive spirit and her understanding that folklore cannot be owned. Yet, in return for a two-hundred-dollar monthly stipend, Hurston agreed not to share the fruits of her research without Mason's permission.

Hurston signed on in lumber camps in Florida, apprenticed herself to hoodoo doctors in New Orleans, and learned Bahamian dances on a research trip to Nassau. Gaining people's confidence could be difficult. In one turpentine camp the workers thought she was a government agent until she alleviated their suspicions by pretending she was a bootlegger's girlfriend on the lam. To learn work songs, she had to sing them. To understand hoodoo curses and cures, she had to undergo harrowing initiation rituals, which she described in *Mules and Men*. Hurston's dedication contributed to the failure of a short-lived marriage to Herbert Sheen, a physician and Howard classmate, in 1927.

After compiling the lore, Hurston's challenge was to find an appropriate mode for its presentation. Although she wrote scholarly articles, notably the hundred-page "Hoodoo in America," published in the *Journal of American Folklore* in 1931, she believed black folklore was too vital to collect dust on library shelves. Instead she was convinced the lore could form the basis for "the real Negro theatre." *Mule Bone*, written in collaboration with Hughes, is the best known of her theatrical ventures, but it was never performed in their lifetimes. More successful were the folklore concerts Hurston produced, beginning in 1932, after she left Mason's payroll. Dramatizations of a day in a railroad camp, the concerts presented work songs, folktales, and other expressions in context, as part of a lived culture. The concerts helped Hurston devise a format for *Mules and Men*. By placing folklore texts in context and demonstrating the process of their creation, Hurston anticipated what is now common practice among ethnographers. She was years ahead of her time.

Some of Hurston's field work saw print first in *Jonah's Gourd Vine*. Based in part on her parents'

lives, the novel told the story of a preacher-poet, who defines himself through his art; its centerpiece is a sermon Hurston transcribed from her field notes. Her research had revealed how women were denied access to the pulpit and the store porch, the privileged site of storytelling, and consequently denied the commensurate possibility of self-definition. Throughout her writing, she revised and adapted vernacular forms to give voice to women.

In Hurston's finest novel, *Their Eyes Were Watching God*, the protagonist *Janie Crawford must reject the racist and sexist definitions society would impose on her. As her knowledge of her culture deepens, she gains the wisdom and strength to claim her voice and her self. Many vibrant voices speak through the novel; some seek to silence Janie, while others inspire her. Hurston writes the oral culture brilliantly. "Words walking without masters" is an apt metaphor for both the novel's folk speech and its singular prose.

Their Eyes was written while Hurston was in Haiti conducting ethnographic research on a Guggenheim Fellowship. The account of her field work, *Tell My Horse* (1938), is notable for its investigation of African survivals, such as "The Nine Night" in Jamaica and vodun rituals in Haiti. Songs appended to the volume were perhaps the first published transcriptions of Haitian Creole.

When she returned to the United States, Hurston worked for the Works Progress Administration (WPA), drafting sections on folklore for a proposed volume on "The Florida Negro." In time stolen from the job, she wrote the novel *Moses, Man of the Mountain* (1939). Here she explored the myth of *Moses, as recorded in the Bible and in the oral traditions of Africa, and as appropriated by American slaves. Although written in a comic mode, *Moses* was an allegorical *history of black Americans and a serious meditation on liberation and leadership. As Hurston realized, her reach in *Moses* exceeded her grasp. In another disappointment, her 1939 marriage to Albert Price, a twenty-three-year-old WPA employee, lasted only months.

Hurston had been a highly productive writer—*Dust Tracks* was her sixth book in eight years—but the quantity and quality of her work began to wane. Although her byline appeared frequently in the 1940s in such mainstream journals as *American Mercury* and the *Saturday Evening Post*, few pieces captured the verve and flair of her earlier writing. When she essayed political analysis, she wrapped sophisticated critique in the glove of folk *humor. Folk humor was passé after Richard *Wright's searing 1940 novel *Native Son* transformed the black literary landscape. Social realism and political protest were the black writers' mandate. Critics missed the protest implicit in Hurston's art: by rejecting the definitions of themselves the dominant society attempted to impose and by preserving, adapting, and creating their own cultural practices, Hurston asserted, African Americans waged a heroic struggle of resistance.

Her last novel, *Seraph on the Suwanee*, a turgid melodrama of white Floridian life, did little for Hurston's literary reputation. Worse, just as the novel was published, Hurston's personal life was shattered by scandal. She was falsely accused of molesting a ten-year-old boy. Devastated both by the charges and the scurrilous press coverage, Hurston presented her passport as evidence that she was in Honduras on an ethnographic expedition when the alleged crime occurred. The case was dismissed in March 1949.

By 1950 Hurston was working as a maid in Miami. Seeking to recover happier times, she moved to Eau Gallie, Florida, where she had written *Mules and Men*. What she wrote now, a novel fictionalizing the life of entrepreneur Madame C. J. Walker and a biography of Herod the Great, was unpublishable. Hurston's political views grew more reactionary. Long a critic of civil rights organizations, she concluded that their struggle for integration was predicated on a belief in black inferiority. She wrote the editor of the Orlando *Sentinel* condemning the 1954 Supreme Court decision in *Brown v. Board of Education*, which declared segregation unconstitutional. The sensation the letter caused marked Hurston's last public notice. Forgotten and penniless, she died in a Fort Pierce, Florida, welfare home.

Hurston's rediscovery is among the most dramatic chapters in African American literary history. It was inspired first by writers and critics such as Alice *Walker, who went "in search of our mothers' gardens." For many black women writers, Hurston is a foremother. Critics investigating the impact of oral forms on African American literature find a theoretical foundation as well as a wealth of material in Hurston's writings. Readers respond to the laugh-out-loud humor, the poetry, and the pleasure of her texts.

[*See also* Conjuring; Federal Writers' Project; Nanny; Sermons and Preaching; Tea Cake.]

• Robert Hemenway, *Zora Neale Hurston: A Literary Biography*, 1977. Alice Walker, ed., *I Love Myself: A Zora Neale Hurston Reader*, 1979. Karla F. C. Holloway, *The Character of the Word: The Texts of Zora Neale Hurston*, 1987. Mary Helen Washington, *Invented Lives: Narratives of Black Women 1860–1960*, 1987. Michael Awkward, ed., *New Essays on Their Eyes Were Watching God*, 1990. Henry Louis Gates, Jr., and Anthony Appiah, eds., *Zora Neale Hurston: Critical Perspectives Past and Present*, 1993. John Lowe, *Jump at the Sun: Zora Neale Hurston's Cosmic Comedy*, 1994. Cheryl A. Wall, *Women of the Harlem Renaissance*, 1995.

—Cheryl A. Wall

I

ICEBERG SLIM (1918–1992), novelist, autobiographer, essayist, and most prominent author of the street genre, which emerged in the 1960s. Born in Chicago, Iceberg Slim (the street and later pen name of Robert Beck) spent the happiest years of his childhood in Rockford, Illinois, where he lived between 1924 and 1928 with his mother and stepfather. Abandoned by her husband, Slim's mother had supported her infant son in a variety of jobs, including door-to-door hairdressing. Slim's stepfather, a kind and loving man, lifted his new family to economic security until Slim's mother left him for a violent gambler. For the three and a half years that they lived together, Slim hated the new man in his mother's life and resented her betrayal of his stepfather. In his book of *essays and vignettes, The Naked Soul of Iceberg Slim (1971), he asserts his belief that the drive to become a pimp derives from a disturbed mother-son relationship: "I am convinced that most pimps require the secretly buried fuel of Mother hatred to stoke their fiery vendetta of cruelty and merciless exploitation against whores primarily and ultimately all women." The name Iceberg Slim reflects his ability to be emotionally frigid and physically brutal to the women who worked as *prostitutes for him.

Although Slim's adolescence was strongly influenced by his involvement with street hustlers, his superior intelligence allowed him to graduate from high school at fifteen and to win an alumni scholarship to Tuskegee Institute. Interestingly, he attended Tuskegee in the mid-1930s, the same time that Ralph *Ellison studied there, although they were not acquainted. After two years at college Slim was expelled for selling bootleg whiskey to other students. Back in Chicago by the time he was seventeen, he began his career by convincing his girlfriend to prostitute herself. The twenty-five years that followed were spent either pimping, taking drugs, or serving time in jail.

After his return to straight life, Iceberg Slim married, fathered four children, and began writing the books that assured his reputation as the most-read practitioner of the African American street *novel. Between 1967 and 1977, Slim authored seven books including his *autobiography, Pimp: The Story of My Life (1967). One novel, Trick Baby (1967), chronicles the adventures of a light-skinned African American who chooses not to pass. This story was subsequently made into a movie and released by Universal Studios. Of all his fiction, Mama Black Widow (1969), a sensitive portrayal of a tortured, cross-dressing, gay male, is considered his most masterful book. Slim's works are marked by their deep criticism of the American justice system, devotion to the politics of the Black Panthers, very frank language, and a combination of *violence and *sexuality. These books as well as Airtight Willie and Me (1979), The Long White Con (1977), and Death Wish (1976) have gained popularity on college campuses. Between 1985 and 1995, his books were translated into both German and French. The works of Iceberg Slim have their greatest readership in prisons where they are admired for their recognition of the plight of the criminal.

• Paul Carter Harrison, The Drama of Nommo, 1972, p. 164. William Henry Robinson, comp., Nommo: An Anthology of Modern Black African and Black American Literature, 1972, p. 475. D. B. Graham, "'Negative Glamour': The Pimp Hero in the Fiction of Iceberg Slim," Obsidian 1.2 (1975): 5–17.
—Terri Hume Oliver

IDENTITY. As a concept, identity can be defined as the search for self and its relationship to social contexts and realities. The problems of biological, psychological, cultural, and social self-definition have been treated thematically in various forms of African American literature.

Because African Americans widely accepted early on that they were sociohistoric products, not bound to each other exclusively by racial and biological commonalities, but molded instead by the consequences of *slavery, emancipation, and betrayal, it is not surprising that writers of all races have long recognized the inexhaustible literary potential of African American self-examination and self-exploration. In fact, the subtle, confusing, and often contradictory interplay of *race and identity in the African American psyche has helped to shape distinctive features of the African American literary legacy, and issues of self-actualization, social legitimation, inclusion, and exclusion are at the literal or symbolic core of some significant African American works of the nineteenth and twentieth centuries.

The difficulty of maintaining a separate social, psychological, and cultural presence in the face of attempts by the white world order to define and control African American existence and image surfaced early in literary expression. Themes of self-awareness and self-definition appear in the first conscious form of African American literature—the *slave narrative. According to Arna *Bontemps in his classic work Great Slave Narratives (1969), the recorded memoirs of former slaves became a fitting artistic backdrop against which writers began to forge and construct a self-image that they could find satisfying and ennobling.

In the text of the slave narrative, identity is often regarded as a function of *place. For these early African American men and women of letters, there was a clear and inextricable relationship between the environment into which fate had placed them and their own definition of and sense of self. Invariably, the slave narratives communicate the idea that the pre–Civil War South, with its cruelty, ignorance, and callousness, destabilized human identity, but that there existed a place, in the literal sense, that could alter the definition of humanity by restoring individual dignity and personal self-worth.

Frederick *Douglass writes in the *Narrative of the Life of Frederick Douglass (1845):

> On the one hand, there stood slavery, a stern reality, glaring frightfully upon us—its robes already crimsoned with the blood of millions, and even now feasting greedily upon our own flesh. On the other hand, away back in the dim distance, under the flickering light of the north star, behind some craggy hill or snow-covered mountain stood a doubtful freedom—half-frozen—beckoning us to come and share her hospitality.

In his *Narrative* and in the two subsequent accounts of his life, *My Bondage and My Freedom (1855) and The Life and Times of Frederick Douglass (1881), literal relocation comes to represent the initial step on the road to selfhood. Identity as a function of place is the central theme in numerous slave narratives including A Narrative of the Adventures and Escape of Moses Roper from American Slavery (1837), A Narrative of the Sufferings of Lewis Milton and Clark (1846), A Narrative of the Life of William W. Brown a Fugitive (1848), A Narrative of Henry B. Brown Who Escaped from Slavery in a Box (1848), The Fugitive Bledsmith Made by Himself of Events in the History of James W. C. Pennington (1849), The Life of Josiah Henson (1949), and Narrative of the Life and Adventures of Henry Bibb an American Slave (1849).

The relationship of color to identity has been a frequent subject for numerous African American writers. In the late 1800s, the tortured seeds of *miscegenation, variously labeled as *mulattoes, quadroons, octoroons, and Creoles, made their appearance in African American fiction. In these early literary works, characters of mixed racial origin wrestle with the problems of divided loyalties, with painful allegiances to both races, and with troubling uncertainties about their rightful place in either the black or the white world.

*Passing for white, a social charade made possible by a lightness of pigmentation that rendered an individual's darker ethnic origins undetectable, figures heavily into the writings of several early novelists, beginning with the first widely distributed African American *novel, *Clotel, or The President's Daughter (1853), by William Wells *Brown. Brown's novel, with its oblique reference to the alleged miscegenous relationship that existed between President Thomas Jefferson and his slave woman Sally *Hemings, proved a timely examination of one of the most probing issues facing a newly emancipated people grappling with defining themselves in the post–Civil War South.

Charles Waddell *Chesnutt chronicles the frustrations and inner turmoil that littered the path to selfhood for a host of characters teetering on the *color line, too white to function in black society and barred from the white world by the fraction of black blood that defined them socially, politically, and economically by standards they vehemently opposed. In his collection of *short stories, The *Wife of His Youth (1889), Chesnutt focuses on the issue of color as it relates to identity and on the growth of the pigmentocracy, a socially elite *class among African Americans whose claims to superiority hinged on their fair complexions and hereditary links to white society.

Chesnutt's novel The *House Behind the Cedars (1900) tells the story of *Rena Walden's efforts to hide from her white lover the secret of her racial past. The dilemma of the tragic mulatto finds its clearest expression in the thoughts of Molly Walden, as she ponders the fate of a son who has crossed the color line and a daughter who is intent upon following him:

> The one thing she desired above all others was her daughter's happiness. Her own life had not been governed by the highest standards, but about her love for her beautiful daughter there was no taint of selfishness. The life her son had described had been to her always the ideal but unattainable life. . . . It had been conquered by her son. It beckoned to her daughter. The comparison of this free and noble life with the sordid existence of those around her broke down the last barrier of opposition.

In this novel, Chesnutt brings into sharp focus the issues of color consciousness and color snobbery, often satirizing the shallowness of character and the lack of intellectual depth that characterized uneducated African Americans of mixed racial derivation.

James Weldon *Johnson's The *Autobiography of an Ex-Colored Man (1912) was the first literary work by an African American to deal primarily with "passing." The novel focuses on the misfortunes of a fair-skinned African American man whose way is made more difficult by his frequently mistaken identity. Johnson's novel comments on the often frustrating efforts of African Americans to achieve a positive identity by adapting features of the dominant culture through assimilation. In the final analysis, the novel's protagonist acknowledges that while assimilationism creates new images of self and thus challenges the power relationship between blacks and whites, it ultimately fails to help African Americans achieve the kind of human integration and self-continuity essential for their psychological survival and stability.

No writer has more clearly described the forces frustrating African Americans in their stride toward self-awareness and wholeness than W. E. B. *Du Bois. At the very center of the African American consciousness, Du Bois wrote in his classic The *Souls of Black Folk (1903), lies a tension, a doubleness, a set of competing impulses for which there is no clear resolution:

> It is this peculiar sensation, this *double-consciousness, this sense of always looking at oneself through the eyes of others, of measuring one's soul by the tape of a world that looks on in amused contempt and pity. One even feels his twoness,—an American, a Negro; two souls, two thoughts, two unreconciled strivings, two warring ideals in one dark body, whose dogged strength alone keeps it from being torn asunder. The history of the American Negro is the history of this strife,—this longing to attain self-conscious *manhood, to merge his double self into a better and truer self.

Du Bois was not the first writer of African American descent to explore the theme of dual consciousness. As early as 1896, Paul Laurence *Dunbar had written: "We wear the mask that grins and lies" as a metaphor for conflicting identities. But, unlike Dunbar who saw the African American's act of constructing self to fit context as essential to human adaption and socioeconomic survival, Du Bois treats the quality as a spiritual and psychological paradox. For Du Bois, the desire to "satisfy two unreconcilable ideals" frustrates the process of identity building for African Americans and prevents them from emerging as whole and unified human beings.

The *New Negro writers of the *Harlem Renaissance approached the issue of identity with ambivalence. Critics have speculated that much of that ambivalence may have resulted from writers' preoccupations with their own racial backgrounds; many of them were middle-class products of mixed ancestry. Huel Perkins, for example, finds the Harlem Renaissance writers to be as "tortured as they were talented." Poet Countee *Cullen responds ambivalently to questions of racial and ethnic identity in his poems "Yet Do I Marvel" and "From the Dark Tower." Jean *Toomer, himself a fair-skinned man of mixed racial parentage, spent his life grappling with conflicting feelings about race. His hunger for wholeness and his deep-seated desire to identify with his black ancestry gave rise to the creative tensions about identity and heritage that produced *Cane (1923), a movingly lyrical collection of poems, plays, and sketches that catapulted him to fame and identified him as one of the most gifted prose stylists of the 1920s. It is perhaps Toomer's confrontation with his fate that enabled him to write so poignantly of the fragmented lives of the racially mixed Esther and Karintha in the lyrical sketches of the same name. Except for the publication of *Cane*, Toomer mostly evaded the issue of racial identity, devoting himself instead to mysticism and *religion for the remainder of his life.

Langston *Hughes, in contrast, was never ambivalent about his heritage. Despite his fair skin, straight hair, and mixed blood, Hughes seems to have reconciled the warring factions of his consciousness. His works suggest that Hughes saw African America's identity not so much as biologically based, but symbolically transformed by its rich and vibrant culture, a culture he celebrated and exalted in his novel *Not without Laughter* (1930), his humorous *essays (particularly the tales of *Simple), and his race-conscious *poetry. From his first poem, "The *Negro Speaks of Rivers," to his poetic volumes The *Weary Blues (1926) and Fine Clothes to the Jew (1927), Hughes's works are rich with details of black life, black *music, and black *folklore. He sets aside issues of class and color, affirming instead culture as the major property that identifies African American group existence and provides it with a sense of worthiness.

Like Langston Hughes, Zora Neale *Hurston leans heavily toward identity as grounded in culturally and socially constructed beliefs and values. *Janie Crawford, the protagonist in *Their Eyes Were Watching God* (1937), finds racial and personal essentialism only when she reconnects with the language and culture of the agrarian African American past.

Identity as a function of reconnection with a past place and time finds expression in numerous poems and prose pieces of the 1920s. Marcus *Garvey's back to Africa movement sparked a renewed interest in the return to a collective ancestral and racial past as the path to self-definition. Countee Cullen in his most widely anthologized poem, "Heritage," asks "What Is Africa to Me?" while Claude *McKay's poetic volume Songs of Jamaica (1912) and Eric *Walrond's short story collection Tropic Death (1926) hark back to the exotic and earthy qualities of Caribbean life and culture.

With the collapse of the Garvey movement and the promises of the Great Migration unfulfilled, the seemingly fractured relationship between identity and a past place and time became a dichotomy embodying the impossibility of achieving self-definition within the context of American society. African America's disillusionment with its failure to construct a self, embedded with and informed by layers of the past, finds its clearest expression in Rudolph *Fisher's short story "City of Refuge."

A similar disillusionment finds expression in works by Harlem Renaissance women writers who explore color and class as complications in the search for identity. Resurrecting the theme of assimilationism, Jessie Redmon *Fauset produced novels in which heroines pursue happiness and social upward mobility through acceptance of white world values and standards of beauty. Her works *There Is Confusion (1924), Plum Bun (1929), The Chinaberry Tree (1931), and *Comedy: American Style (1933) depict the tragic situations of African American women who make too much of the white world and thus can never escape its influence, an act that subverts attempts to come to terms with the centers of self and impedes the identity-building process.

Unlike Fauset, Nella *Larsen, one of the most gifted Harlem Renaissance prose stylists, focuses on the psychological rather than the social consequences of viewing identity as a function of color. In her novels *Quicksand (1928) and *Passing (1929), Larsen achieves breadth and scope in her art by positioning the mulatto's personal struggle for selfhood both within the framework of the African American's search for self-affirmation and within the tradition of humankind.

The protagonist in Wallace *Thurman's The *Blacker the Berry (1929) is as troubled by the obvious presence of dark pigmentation as Larsen and Fauset's heroines are about their mixed ancestry. The novel deals with the problems of a dark-skinned girl among her own lighter-skinned people and the extent to which racial self-hatred subverts the act of community building and sabotages from within the development of a wholesome group identity.

In his novel *Invisible Man (1952), Ralph *Ellison presents a more in-depth literary study of the African American self-in-context than any ever attempted by an African American writer, and he likewise promotes a broader view of identity. Ellison introduces a narrator/protagonist who recognizes his identity at the beginning of the novel as an identity of invisibility. For Ellison, such invisibility has its roots in white Americans' refusal to recognize the worth and value of African Americans, a refusal that has historically manifested itself as racial subjugation, exploitation, and dehumanization. An added ironic dimension of this social and psychological phenomenon is that the narrator has been invisible even to himself.

The long road to self-discovery, from blindness to vision, from private pain to public affirmation, forms the basis of the novel, which depicts in concrete detail the series of dehumanizing and disillusioning experiences from which the narrator's psychic state has evolved. In his efforts to achieve identity, the narrator makes numerous discoveries about the nature of society, about himself, and more significantly about the importance of invisibility.

Having emerged occasionally from the underground by the end of the novel, Ellison's main character is freed from symbolic blindness and recognizes that while invisibility represents dispossession and degradation on the one hand, it also evokes endless possibilities for self-creation and self-integration on the other. For Ellison such an integration is made possible through an understanding of cultural ties and a sense of appreciation for the rich tradition of African American culture, its folklore, its *music, and its language.

To the extent that self-awareness is informed and sustained by opposing forces, Ellison also suggests in his novel that invisibility has been productive for African Americans. While exposing, on the one hand, the limitations of the fragile base of domination and authority on which white America rests, invisibility, on the other hand, also opens the door to self-definition through continuous self-creation for African Americans. For Ellison, self-creationism expands the spiritual and artistic horizon for African Americans, giving free rein to endless shapings and new opportunities for being and, in the process, affirming their potential for coping with life. Recognizing these infinite possibilities and realizing that no fixed role of identity need exist is the most liberating concept of all.

The path to selfhood took a radical left turn in African American literature in the 1960s. The abrupt shift in the literary direction can be traced to the emergence of a new type of leadership in the society at large. Advocating revolutionary action and self-defense as the means to true self-definition and self-determination for African Americans, powerful agents for social change such as *Malcolm X, Stokely *Carmichael, Ron Karenga, and Huey P. Newton hailed the dawn of a new and dynamic ideal for African Americans, an ideal achievable only through repudiation of all aspects of American society that militated against a positive self-image.

Under the influence of Amiri *Baraka, writers of the *Black Arts movement heeded the call of the new leadership and sought to reflect in their literary works the rise of this revolutionary consciousness and militant spirit. Baraka, widely regarded as the father of the *Black Aesthetic, urged a shift to an attitudinal construct for achieving selfhood.

In the classic work *Black Literature in America* (1971), Houston A. *Baker, Jr., writes that the shift to an attitudinal construct for achieving self-definition manifested itself primarily in the poetry and *drama of the period and made its appearance as themes of reassessment, rejection, and revival.

Reassessment for these writers of the new left included both an intense scrutiny of the mediated reality, values, and standards of the contemporary social order and a reexamination of its impact on the identification process for African Americans. Furthermore, the literary works of the period suggest a rejection of any products, values, and standards that militated against a wholesome self-definition. And finally, the new writers of the 1960s promoted a revival of interest in and commitment to the African American folk heritage and the African past.

The impulse toward reconstructing the self by adopting new standards of pride, militancy, and intense African Americanism found expression in the works of the New Black Poets such as Nikki *Giovanni, Audre *Lorde, Clarence *Major, Carolyn M. *Rodgers, Sonia *Sanchez, Haki R. *Madhubuti, Etheridge *Knight, and Michael S. *Harper, as well as among the New Black Revolutionary Playwrights such as Charles *Gordone, Ed *Bullins, Lonne *Elder III, Jimmy Garett, and Amiri Baraka.

In the works of major female writers of the 1970s and 1980s, the search for identity is complicated by issues of race, class, and gender. In the novels and short stories of Toni *Morrison, Gloria *Naylor, Alice *Walker, and Paule *Marshall, there is evidence of identity-building through a new ethnogenesis that subverts the Western, male code of literary expression and system of values.

Toni Morrison's novels depict characters who seek identity by examining dialectical approaches to the chaos and challenge that African Americans experience in a manipulative white world: *Pecola Breedlove and Claudia McTeer in *The *Bluest Eye* (1970), Nel Wright and *Sula Peace in *Sula* (1973), Macon Dead and *Milkman Dead in *Song of Solomon* (1977), and *Son Green and *Jadine Childs in *Tar Baby* (1981). Morrison's characters who emerge triumphant in the quest for meaning in their lives, Claudia, Nel, Son, and Milkman, derive their wholeness from rejecting the falsity and materialism of the white culture and embracing instead the spiritualism and humanism inherent in the African American past. For Morrison, the core of black identity is mined not by new myths but by rediscovering old ones.

The female characters in Alice Walker's novels find selfhood in the rejection of blatantly antisexist, antiracial, and often anti-Christian and colonialist values that dehumanize, control, and destroy their lives. Walker's prose works in total comment on the necessity of disavowing the contemporary social definition of women as property, mothers, and subordinates while inviting them instead to recreate themselves in the images that will assure their psychological well-being. Her characters overcome all forces that would proscribe their existence by bonding with the community of women, as *Celie does in *The *Color Purple* (1982), by converting action into artifact as Meridian does in *Meridian* (1976), and by repossessing their own bodies, souls, and spirits as Ruth Copeland shows the promise of doing in The **Third Life of Grange Copeland* (1970).

The new African American women, these writers suggest, are those who can re-create themselves based on a knowledge and understanding of the lives of maternal ancestors like *Mama Day and *Pilate Dead.

These touchstones of identity building, who appear in works by writers who dominate the late-twentieth-century African American literary scene, are individuals who insist, as do the writers who create them, that the qualities of self-definition are those grounded in cultural, communal, and ancestral truths.

[*See also* Black Nationalism; Character Types; Gender; Names and Naming; Stereotypes; Womanism.]

• Twentieth Century Views, *The Theater of Black Americans: Roots and Rituals/The Images Makers*, vols. 1 and 2, ed. Errol Hill, 1980. Werner Sollors, *Beyond Ethnicity: Consent and Descent in American Culture*, 1986. Cheryl A. Wall, "Passing for What? Aspects of Identity in Nella Larsen's Novels," *Black American Literature Forum* 20 (Spring/Summer 1986): 97–111. Glover Jonathan, *The Philosophy and Psychology of Personal Identity*, 1988. Alan Nadel, "'Reading the Body': Alice Walker's *Meridian* and the Archeology of Self," *Modern Fiction Studies* 34 (Spring 1988): 55–68. Eugeen E. Roosens, *Creating Ethnicity: The Process of Ethnogenesis*, 1989. Eric S. Knowles and Mark E. Sibicky, "Contributions and Diversities in the Stream of Selves: Metaphorical Resolution of William James' One-in-Many Selves Paradox," *Personality and Social Psychology* 16 (1990): 676–687. Thomas K. Fitzgerald, *Metaphors of Identity*, 1993. Henry Louis Gates, Jr., *Race, Writing and Difference*, 1993. Dwight McBride, "Speaking the Unspeakable: On Toni Morrison," *Modern Fiction Studies* 39 (Fall/Winter 1993): 755–776. Susan Meisenhelder, "The Whole Picture in Gloria Naylor's *Mama Day*," *African American Review* 27 (Fall 1993): 405–410. Tang Soo Ping, "Ralph Ellison and K. S. Maniam: Ethnicity in America and Malaysia, Two Kinds of Invisibility," *MELUS* 18 (Winter 1993/94): 81–97.   —Sandra Carlton Alexander

If He Hollers Let Him Go

If He Hollers Let Him Go (1945) is Chester *Himes's first published *novel. Set in Los Angeles during World War II, the novel is narrated in the first person by its African American protagonist, Bob Jones. Himes based details of his novel on his own experiences working in shipyards in both Oakland and Los Angeles in the 1940s. Written in a style many critics find similar to 1930s and 1940s American hard-boiled or tough-guy fiction, the book chronicles five working days in Bob's life, framed by a vision of urban Los Angeles. Other critics see the novel as more closely aligned with a tradition of protest novels, and notably, as being a literary descendant of Richard *Wright's **Native Son* (1940) and Ann *Petry's The **Street* (1946).

Bob Jones is an intellectual who continually reflects on the ways his options and his actions are circumscribed by the overall systemic *violence of American racism. The reader also sees a graphic picture of 1940s Los Angeles, a city fraught with racial conflict as a result of the large influx of white Southerners and African American workers coming to labor in the defense industries. Though Bob is a lead-

man in the Atlas Shipyard, supervising a crew of African American workers, his actual authority is ineffective since white leadmen refuse to assist him by loaning their white workers to him for job projects.

One such white worker is Madge Perkins. After Madge calls Bob a nigger he returns the insult and is immediately demoted, while she goes unpunished. Through Bob's interactions with and thoughts about Madge, the novel exposes the complex intersections of *race and sexual attraction as Bob at once despises and desires Madge.

When Bob accidentally encounters Madge in a small deserted bunkroom, his impulse is to flee, but he hesitates a bit too long. Madge locks the door and screams "rape," thereby inciting the furor of the white workers. Bob escapes *lynching but is sentenced by a judge to enlist in the armed forces. Himes points out the irony in U.S. soldiers, many of them African American, being sent abroad to fight fascism in Europe while racial oppression flourishes at home.

Counterposed to Madge's uncouth nature is Bob's girlfriend, Alice Harrison, a social worker and the daughter of one of the wealthiest African American men in Los Angeles. She has no sympathy for Bob's feelings of racial oppression and encourages Bob to stop struggling against white people and instead carve out an upper-middle-class domestic niche within the bounds of societal discrimination. This type of compromise is precisely what Bob cannot do. Himes's critique of such compromises is visible in his portrayal of Alice's father as corrupt and venal.

Bob Jones is represented as an everyman who desires nothing more and nothing less than equal participation in the democratic ideals he was taught as a boy in school. For Himes, Bob's naive belief in the promise of such ideals creates his angst as an adult living in a racist culture.

• Gilbert H. Muller, *Chester Himes*, 1989. Michel Fabre, Robert E. Skinner, and Lester Sullivan, *Chester Himes: An Annotated Primary and Secondary Bibliography*, 1992.
                                               —Wendy W. Walters

"I Have a Dream."

"I Have a Dream." From the steps of the Lincoln Memorial, Martin Luther *King, Jr., delivered "I Have a Dream" to over two hundred thousand people on 28 August 1963. Watching on *television, millions heard all or part of King's speech, which served as the climax of the March on Washington, the largest rally of the *civil rights movement.

Tepid about racial equality for over two years, President Kennedy proposed major civil rights legislation after King's Birmingham crusade in spring 1963. Many viewed the 1963 March as a rally to support that legislation—an interpretation that several speakers at the March encouraged even though labor leader A. Philip Randolph and activist Bayard Rustin had begun organizing the event in 1962.

When supporters rallied at the Lincoln Memorial, they heard singers and a series of measured and unexceptional addresses by Roy Wilkins, director of the NAACP, Whitney Young, head of the Urban League, Walter Reuther, president of the United Auto Workers, and others. Although the Kennedy administration applied intense pressure to make John Lewis, leader of the Student Nonviolent Coordinating Committee, sound more moderate, he delivered a scorching oration that castigated both major political parties.

Marian *Anderson and Mahalia Jackson appeared separately to revive the wilting crowd with *spirituals and set the stage for the last speech of the day.

In seventeen minutes, King called for racial equality by presenting an inventory of religious and nationalistic themes. He opened by sketching an American nightmare. One hundred years after emancipation, he announced, "the Negro is still sadly crippled by the manacles of segregation." Attacking institutionalized racism, he contended that Thomas Jefferson, Abraham *Lincoln, and the American government had failed African Americans by issuing a check for *freedom marked "insufficient funds." Melding patriotic and religious authorities, King invoked the Declaration of Independence, the Gettysburg Address, ancient Hebrew prophets, and Christianity to argue that racial injustice was un-American and unacceptable. He championed militant nonviolence—or "soul force"—as the route between moderation and extremism.

King dedicated the second half of "I Have a Dream" to a vision of what America could become: a land of equality and peace. In his climactic "Let Freedom Ring" litany, he projected a future in which Isaiah's vision of exalted valleys, which he cited earlier, is realized in a racially harmonious America. He concluded by reciting the lyrics of "America" ("My country 'tis of thee") that Marian Anderson had sung at the memorial during her celebrated Easter concert in 1939. He borrowed and refined the entire "Let Freedom Ring" peroration from a speech by Archibald Carey, an African American pastor from Chicago.

Throughout "I Have a Dream" King and his listeners engaged in a call-and-response interaction common in African American Baptist *churches. (He later stated that he extended "I Have a Dream" because of the warm response of his audience.) His rolling cadences and parallelisms also reflected African American pulpit traditions.

King concluded by prophesying a future in which everyone would sing the spiritual: "Free at last! Free at last! Thank God Almighty, we're free at last!" The crowd roared its approval.

More moderate than King's orations in 1967 and 1968, "I Have a Dream" is the most beloved speech of his career and the most famous American oration of the twentieth century.

[See also Oratory; Preachers and Deacons; Sermons and Preaching.]

• Archibald Carey, "Address to the Republican National Convention," 1952, in Rhetoric of Revolt, ed. Roy Hill, 1964, pp. 149–154. Martin Luther King, Jr., "I Have a Dream," 1963, in A Testament of Hope: The Essential Writings of Martin Luther King, Jr., ed. James Washington, 1986, pp. 217–220.

—Keith D. Miller and Emily M. Lewis

I Know Why the Caged Bird Sings. The bestselling first volume of Maya *Angelou's serial *autobiography inaugurated a new era of African American women's writing. Published in 1970, I Know Why the Caged Bird Sings contains many of the themes that would become central to feminist theory and practice in the 1980s. Taken from the first verse of Paul Laurence *Dunbar's poem "Sympathy," the title articulates the woman writer's empowering recognition of her ability to sing her own song despite the cultural odds against her. "If growing up is painful for the Southern Black girl, being aware of her displacement is the rust on the razor that threatens the throat," Angelou writes. "It is an unnecessary insult."

Set mostly in Stamps, Arkansas, I Know Why the Caged Bird Sings traces the events in the lives of Marguerite Johnson and her brother, Bailey, who are raised by their grandmother, Momma Henderson, the owner of a general store, and their crippled Uncle Willie. Angelou paints a vast historical fresco of life in the segregated South and in the cities of St. Louis and San Francisco during the 1930s and early 1940s. Part autobiography, part fictional picaresque narrative, part social *history and commentary, this story confers an exemplary quality to the experiences of the narrator whose childhood is spent shuttling back and forth between rural and urban America. She undergoes the loss of innocence characteristic of the protagonist of picaresque tales. In St. Louis, she is raped at the age of eight by her mother's boyfriend, and having denounced him, blames herself for his murder. She loses the ability to speak until her return to Stamps, where a friend, Mrs. Flowers, inspires her to rediscover the beauty of the "human voice." Later she moves to California, and after graduating from high school at the age of seventeen, she gives birth to a son. The book begins and ends with intense physical experiences that teach the narrator that she can trust her body, that it is a source of power and knowledge rather than the liability that her racist and sexist society dictates.

George E. Kent has shown that there are two main areas of African American life that give depth to the narrative. The grandmother represents the religious influence and the gospel tradition, and the mother, "the blues-street" tradition, the fast life. Both elements of the black vernacular inform the development of the story, and show the protagonist's complex relationship to the conflicting yet complementary influences that shape her life story. A third element consists in the vast intertextual network of literary allusions and references that Angelou uses. Her narrator is an avid reader who is as familiar with Shakespeare and Molière, Defoe, Brontë, and Dickens as with Dunbar, Langston *Hughes, and Frederick *Douglass. She situates her storytelling within a specifically literary context, and develops a double-voiced message, directed toward both a white audience and the black community. This strategy is characteristic of the genre of the *slave narrative. Angelou builds upon and transforms the major tropes that define the tradition of African American letters, and she does so, as Sidonie A. Smith has argued, with a keen sense of style, as well as a rich use of poetic idioms and idiosyncratic vocabulary.

[See also Address, Forms of.]

• Sidonie A. Smith, "The Song of a Caged Bird: Maya Angelou's Quest after Self-Acceptance," *Southern Humanities Review* 7 (Fall 1973): 365–375. George E. Kent, "Maya Angelou's *I Know Why the Caged Bird Sings* and Black Autobiographical Tradition," *Kansas Quarterly* 7 (Summer 1975): 72–78. Françoise Lionnet, "Con Artists and Storytellers: Maya Angelou's Problematic Sense of Audience," in *Autobiographical Voices: Race, Gender, Self-Portraiture*, 1989, pp. 130–166.   —Françoise Lionnet

Imperium in Imperio.

Sutton E. *Griggs's first *novel, *Imperium in Imperio* (1899), is a visionary work positing the establishment of an underground organization of educated and militant African Americans bent on either an elimination of injustice in America or the establishment of an autonomous state. Functioning in the same manner as the U.S. government, the Imperium's program, however, is revolutionary, not reactionary. Its leaders organize a highly disciplined army, determined to publicize their grievances to the world. Throughout the novel, Griggs warns against demagogues who would sacrifice the African American cause for political gain. The Imperium is in the hands of such a leader, the pampered *mulatto, Bernard Belgrade, who enters politics primarily out of personal ambition. Belton Piedmont, on the other hand, modeled upon Booker T. *Washington, rejects Bernard's plot for all-out war both because he recognizes the futility of a military attempt but, also, because he believes some whites are enlightened and wish to help. Belton counters Bernard's declaration of war with a more conservative proposal. Whites need to be educated about the new African American militancy, he asserts. If after four years, however, a positive change has not occurred, Belton urges a radical solution—the Imperium's takeover of Texas and establishment of a separate government prepared to fight off invasions from foreign powers, notably the United States. Bernard immediately declares Belton a traitor to the Imperium and orders his execution. As the book ends, the organization is about to be crushed and Belton to be killed by one of his own ethnic kinsmen in a raw power play for political control. The hope for unity and progress seems, therefore, farther away than ever because of African Americans' own blindness in allowing hatred of whites to dupe them into following a self-serving, untrustworthy leader.

Despite his acute awareness of America's failures, Sutton Griggs condemns both African American and white failure to fulfill the country's professed ideals. He depicts his people's severe economic dilemma as a warning to the nation of the presence of bitterness in a growing number of frustrated, young African Americans whose energy either could explode into a suicidal attack upon the racist system or could be channeled into constructive methods of helping their people. *Imperium in Imperio* is the earliest of Griggs's five political statements in fictional form intended to arouse his readers' awareness of the vastly different directions in which turn-of-the-century African Americans might move.

[See also Black Nationalism.]

• Hugh M. Gloster. "The Negro in American Fiction: Sutton E. Griggs, Novelist of the New Negro," *Phylon* 4.4 (1943):

335–345. Addison Gayle, Jr., *The Way of the New World: The Black Novel in America*, 1976.   —Arlene A. Elder

Incidents in the Life of a Slave Girl.

Harriet A. *Jacobs's *slave narrative *Incidents in the Life of a Slave Girl: Written by Herself* is a first-person account of Jacobs's pseudonymous narrator "Linda Brent." Her story is extremely carefully shaped, and although it changes names and omits dates and places, Jacobs's "Linda" transforms the slave narrative by including not only elements of the male-authored narrative but also elements of the captivity narrative and of domestic fiction. Focusing on the forbidden topic of a woman's sexual history in *slavery, Linda presents herself as both a "fallen woman" and as a "heroic mother." In doing so she advances a fundamental critique of the nineteenth-century ideology of true womanhood that fostered all such race and gender *stereotypes.

Jacobs's Linda writes that although born a slave in the South, she enjoyed a happy childhood with her family until, when she was six, her mother died. Taken in by her mistress, she was taught to read and sew. In adolescence she was moved into the nearby home of the lecherous Dr. Flint, who subjected her to unrelenting sexual harassment. She reveals her sexual involvement with a white neighbor—which she characterizes as a desperate attempt to avoid Flint—and records the birth of her two children. Explaining that Flint's threat to make them plantation slaves prompted her decision to run away in hopes that the children's father would buy and free them, she describes her seven years hiding in town in the space above her grandmother's storeroom. Finally escaping to the North, she writes that she was reunited with her children and met the abolitionists. She ends her book by reporting that when kidnappers followed her to New York and continued to threaten her and her children, Linda's New York employer bought her *freedom.

Harriet Jacobs spelled out the conception, composition, and publication of *Incidents* in *letters she wrote to her abolitionist feminist friend, the Quaker Amy Post, between 1853 and 1860. Her first idea was to convince Harriet Beecher *Stowe to become her *amanuensis. When this failed, she determined to write her story herself. She began in secret and finished a half-dozen years later. Carrying letters of introduction from Boston abolitionists to their British colleagues, she sailed to England to find a publisher. Unsuccessful, she returned home, where, with the help of the African American activist-writer William C. *Nell, she met the white abolitionist author Lydia Maria Child, who agreed to act as her editor and agent. In 1860 Child began editing the manuscript, arranged for financial support from abolitionists, and signed a contract with a Boston publisher. When the firm went bankrupt, Jacobs brought out the book herself in January 1861. *Incidents* was advertised and reviewed in the African American press and in reform publications in the North and in Britain. In 1862, retitled *The Deeper Wrong: Incidents in the Life of a Slave Girl: Written by Herself*, it was published in London by William Tweedie.

Although Jacobs's name was openly connected with the book from the first, its title page names only Child as editor. Perhaps because of this, throughout much of the twentieth century both the authorship and the genre of *Incidents* were disputed. Since the appearance of the Harvard edition in 1987, however, *Incidents* has been hailed as the most comprehensive antebellum *autobiography by an African American woman.

[*See also* Feminism; Gender; Sexuality.]

• Hazel Carby, *Reconstructing Womanhood: The Emergence of the Afro-American Woman Novelist*, 1987. Harriet Jacobs, *Incidents in the Life of a Slave Girl*, ed. Jean Fagan Yellin, 1987.
—Jean Fagan Yellin

In New England Winter.

In the play *In New England Winter*, the second of Ed *Bullins's Twentieth Century Cycle, Cliff Dawson returns from *In the Wine Time*. Here, he is older and more subdued; though still stung by a failed marriage, he seeks to shore up ties with his estranged half-brother Steve, who caused the divorce. It is Steve's character, however, that occupies much of the play's emotional energy; his meticulousness in plotting a robbery that he, Cliff, and two cohorts are about to commit, is entirely directed toward obtaining "traveling money" for a return to New England in winter and for Liz, the woman he had long ago left there.

The play's seven sections are divided more or less evenly between a present of 1960, in which the four men are planning the robbery, and flashbacks to 1955, when Liz, Steve, and their alcoholic friends while away the time in New England. Liz, recovering from a severe breakdown, articulates a daydream about the love that she and Steve share and the children it will produce, but her fears that Steve's AWOL status from the navy may suddenly mean their separation suggest a relapse. Additionally, a drunken misunderstanding that finds Steve sleeping innocently in the arms of Liz's sister Carrie causes Liz's fears to become reality as Oscar, Carrie's angered husband, threatens to kill Steve, and Crook, another drinking partner who has been waiting for an opportunity to steal Liz, betrays Steve to the authorities.

Though Steve manages to escape, his efforts in 1960 to get back to Liz are hampered by an oppressive summer heat, the difficulty of planning the robbery, and the differences between himself and Cliff. Principally at issue is Steve's affair with Cliff's wife Lou and the child they produced while Cliff was in jail for murder; one of the cohorts, Bummie, knew of the liaison. But Cliff's prior knowledge of this is a measure of Cliff's magnanimity unknown to Steve, who kills Bummie before he can be betrayed. The brothers reconcile, and Steve resumes his plan to return to New England, but the audience's poignant understanding is that a confused and frightened Liz, after Steve's departure in 1955, had already succumbed to the charms of the serpentine Crook.

Warren R. True notes that because the play's tension seems to emanate entirely from Steve, Cliff, and the two cohorts, Steve's stabbing of Bummie does not appear to be a logical climax. That the tautness among these four grows steadily throughout the play, however, renders the crisis static and unobtrusive, and in this light the play's structure invites comparison to Chekhovian dramaturgy. Genevieve Fabre, however, finds that the folkloric aspects of Bullins's earlier plays are not in evidence here. The symbolism of snow seems gratuitous, and the simple episodic construction forces the play to depend on Bullins's preceding plays for its vigor. Additionally (and unlike Chekhov), this play, like the rest of Bullins's *dramas, depends not on tragedy but rather on melodrama, an element that appears often in African American *theater.

• Warren R. True, "Ed Bullins, Anton Chekov, and the 'Drama of Mood,'" *CLA Journal* 20.4 (June 1977): 521–532. Genevieve Fabre, *Drumbeats, Masks and Metaphor*, 1983.
—Nathan L. Grant

In Search of Our Mothers' Gardens

(1983) brings together a collection of *essays, articles, reviews, and commentaries written by Alice *Walker between 1966 and 1982. The collection defines and expresses a womanist worldview with all of the love, respect, spiritual commitment, and demands for change that the term "womanist" implies. *In Search of Our Mothers' Gardens* offers hope, healing, and wholeness to a world that often forgets that these things are possible. At the same time, the book highlights a historical past that includes many of the pioneers who forged the road of female creative expression and *freedom.

The opening essay comments upon the importance of role models. Citing the example of Vincent Van Gogh's suicide, Walker states that the absence of role models can be fatal. For an artist, Walker claims, finding role models is essential to appreciating one's own creative abilities and developing a vision for living. Throughout the book she suggests an array of models—many silent and unheralded (mothers whose gardens or hand-crafted quilts were their art) and many long-standing favorites. Walker discusses with fondness and admiration the works of Flannery O'Conner, Jean *Toomer, Langston *Hughes, and, of course, Zora Neale *Hurston. Without a doubt Hurston emerges as "queen bee." In a moving article titled "Looking for Zora," Walker describes her 1973 journey to find and mark the grave of her ancestral mentor. In a second essay, "Zora Neale Hurston: A Cautionary Tale and a Partisan View," she argues the importance of recovering and remembering Hurston as a major American writer, anthropologist, and folklorist.

Walker's major concern in each essay is for wholeness and continuity, not only for African American women but for all people. Because of this concern, the collection of nonfiction is simultaneously inspiring and difficult, even painful, to read. *In Search of Our Mothers' Gardens* discusses several subjects important to positive change in our present society (from nuclear weapons and anti-Semitism to child bearing). Almost every essay, however, is accented with Walker's memories of her life—so much so that the book often reads like a memoir. One of the most powerful of these memories is presented in the final essay, "Beauty: When the Other Dancer Is the Self."

In prose that reads like *poetry, Walker shares the story of how an accident that disfigured her right eye and left it blind affected both her self-confidence and her inner vision.

In Search of Our Mothers' Gardens speaks to every woman and offers a concept for achieving wisdom, hope, and change called *womanism. During the years since the book's publication, womanism has become a way of life for many women (and men). Womanist theories and commentaries appear in many areas of academia and popular culture, including *film, education, theology, and literature. Distinguishing between womanism and *feminism, however, has often been a subject of debate. In Walker's own words: "Womanist is to feminist as purple to lavender." The intensity and sensitive inclusiveness of the essays in *In Search of Our Mothers' Gardens* exemplify and expand Walker's comparison.

• Alma S. Freeman, "Zora Neale Hurston and Alice Walker: A Spiritual Kinship," *SAGE* 2 (Spring 1985): 37–40. Dorothy G. Grimes, "'Womanist Prose' and the Quest for Community in American Culture," *Journal of American Culture* 15.2 (Summer 1992): 19–24. —Debra Walker King

INSURRECTIONS. *Slavery existed in what is now the United States from the mid-seventeenth century until 1865. Slaves constituted a significant proportion of the population throughout the South and in some areas of the North—especially New York until about 1800. African American resistance ranged from denying allegations of their inherent and immutable inferiority to active physical resistance.

Collective resistance took two forms. One was the so-called maroon phenomenon. Although some literature (including the dictionary) asserts this existed only in the West Indies and Brazil, maroons—that is, slaves escaping to and living in communities of runaways—formed encampments in the swamps and/or mountains of the southern states. Since maroons encouraged other slaves to flee, they were a serious threat to slavery's stability and at times major military expeditions were mounted in an effort to destroy them.

The highest form of resistance was insurrection or rebellion. Here a group of slaves conspired to armed assault upon the forces of "law and order." Often the rebellions were acts of desperation, having no manifest goal except vengeance and the assertion of personhood. At times, however, such uprisings were efforts to achieve *freedom by reaching some impregnable location, or by actually overthrowing the existing social order.

Though more rare, the goal of overthrowing the existing social order seems to have been present in early eighteenth-century uprisings in South Carolina and in the early nineteenth-century efforts associated with the slave Gabriel in Virginia and with Denmark Vesey in South Carolina.

Uprisings aboard slave-trading ships were fairly frequent. For example, in 1839 rebel slaves aboard the *Creole* achieved freedom by reaching the British West Indies. An even more famous uprising of slaves was upon the foreign-owned ship, the *Amistad*. Here, after prolonged litigation in which

John Quincy Adams played a decisive role, the Africans were liberated.

The slave South seems never to have been quite free of slave uprisings and conspiracies. There do appear, however, periods of relative calm and others of widespread expression of this form of mass discontent. The latter periods were induced, apparently, by exciting surrounding events, such as the Haitian revolutionary developments, or the Jeffersonian emphasis upon "democracy," or the congressional debates revolving around questions of slavery's expansion as in the 1820s and the so-called Missouri Compromise.

Late in the 1820s, with accumulating signs of slave unrest, the federal forts in Louisiana, North Carolina, and Virginia were reinforced. The culmination of this period of unrest was the uprising led by Nat *Turner in Virginia in 1831. It was suppressed with the utmost brutality—the commanding officer of the repressing troops urged the display to cease, else, he said, it might appear to justify the uprising.

White people occasionally participated in or openly sympathized with the slave uprisings. The former was true in the case of Joseph Wood in Louisiana, who was executed in 1812, and George Boxley in Virginia who escaped in 1816. In the Vesey effort of 1822, four white men were jailed for sympathizing with the rebels; in the Turner uprising, one family of white people was deliberately left unharmed as its head had sympathized with the slaves' condition. There were other instances of this phenomenon. Several white people also participated at great risk, sometimes suffering unto death, in the efforts of slaves to flee.

The 1820s witnessed many slave conspiracies, and the appearance of intensified antislavery agitation by free Black people. This was illustrated by the appearance in 1827 of the first Black newspaper, *Freedom's Journal*, and, especially, of David *Walker's *Appeal* (1829), a passionate plea for slavery's end. From then on, the slaveowners had no moment of rest. The existence of collective slave unrest—alleged or real—broke through all efforts at concealment by the owners.

This reality influenced the abolitionist movement, which moved away from Garrison's pacifism. By 1850 that movement, in its majority, had accepted the propriety of physical resistance by the slaves. This culminated in the effort led by John *Brown and his Black and white comrades. While the Republican Party officially disavowed any sympathy with that effort, the fact is that Brown was immortalized as freedom's martyr. This was true not only of Henry David Thoreau in Massachusetts and Victor-Marie Hugo in France, but of thousands of Americans, Black and white.

During the Civil War itself, all forms of slave resistance multiplied. Uprisings of slaves occurred during the war from Mississippi to Virginia. Scores of thousands fled, almost two hundred thousand fought in Lincoln's army, some twenty-five thousand in his navy, and two hundred and fifty thousand served the nation's armed forces in other capacities. Lincoln twice declared that the Black people's contributions were essential to the Union victory. The Thirteenth

Amendment formally terminated slavery, its passage made possible by Black activity and Black-white unity.

With slavery's end, full freedom did not come, of course. Struggle has enhanced the status of the African American people, but since discrimination and oppression still exist, resistance, including forcible uprisings—mistakenly labeled riots—recur. The latter have lit up the skies of cities in decade after decade, as in Harlem in 1935, in Detroit in 1943, in dozens of cities after the murder of Martin Luther King, Jr., in 1968, and on into the final years of the twentieth century, as in Los Angeles in 1992.

Resistance has always marked oppression's existence. So it has been in the history of the African American people. And so it will be till the oppression ceases.

[*See also* Autobiography of Miss Jane Pittman, The; Black Thunder; Confessions of Nat Turner, The; Dessa Rose; Protest Literature.]

• Thomas P. Slaughter, *Bloody Dawn: The Christiana Riot and Racial Violence in the Antebellum North*, 1991. Junius P. Rodriguez, Jr., "Ripe for Revolt: Louisiana and the Tradition of Slave Insurrection," PhD diss., Auburn University, 1992. Herbert Aptheker, *American Negro Slave Revolts*, 50th anniversary edition, 1993, pp. 375–412. Douglas R. Egerton, *Gabriel's Rebellion: The Virginia Slave Conspiracies of 1800 and 1802*, 1993. Winthrop D. Jordan, *Tumult and Silence at Second Creek: The Inquiry into a Civil War Slave Conspiracy*, 1993.

—Herbert Aptheker

In the Mecca. It is perhaps ironic that *In the Mecca* (1968), Gwendolyn *Brooks's first overt attack on Chicago, appeared in the same year that she was appointed poet laureate of Illinois. The Mecca was one of the earliest examples in the United States of a multifamily dwelling for the wealthy. Located a few blocks from Prairie Avenue (the city's original "gold coast"), no luxury was spared in its construction. During the World's Columbian Exposition of 1893 it was a tourist attraction. Enclosed courtways served as entrances to the elaborate apartments of the few elite families who lived in the much-visited Mecca, but in time the neighborhood changed and the Mecca fell into disrepair. Before it was finally torn down, all that remained was an unbelievably squalid tenement where thousands actually lived, and it became a symbol for a failure in urban living patterns. Furthermore, the building was a symbol for much that was wrong in the city.

Linguistically, *In the Mecca* juxtaposes standard English with the vernacular and the language of the streets. This collection of primarily free verse poems is dominated by the long title poem, "In the Mecca," which begins with biblical overtones: "Now the way of the Mecca was on this wise." On one level, the narrative poem is relatively simple. Mrs. Sallie, after a hard day as a *domestic worker, comes home and finds one of her children missing. She begins to search for Pepita only to eventually discover that the child has been murdered by a fellow resident. Mrs. Sallie's life is filled with unpleasantness, and her discovery is just one more adversity that she must face.

Mrs. Sallie's search for Pepita is a framework by which Brooks is able to recount the stories of some of the fragmented lives in an overcrowded building in a city that does not particularly care about what happens to the dispossessed. Many of her characters recognize their predicament but are powerless to do little more than lash out at each other. Brooks captures the pervasive misery of the place and implicitly contrasts what is with what was, demonstrating that *class and *race do make a difference.

Following the title poem are other predominantly free verse selections that appear under the heading "After the Mecca." They include not only the ode to Chicago's famous outdoor Picasso sculpture but also the dedicatory poem to the Wall of Respect, a wall painted with likenesses of role models and heroes of various persuasions. Of special interest in this section is the three-part poem entitled "The Blackstone Rangers" concerning the Blackstone P. Nation, a ghetto gang. The group is so highly organized that simply its name creates terror in those who hear it; yet, this is a gang whose "country is a Nation on no map." In the final analysis, black on black crime is explained as a result of the futility that often accompanies the barrenness of urban life.

• Maria K. Mootry and Gary Smith, eds., *A Life Distilled: Gwendolyn Brooks, Her Poetry and Fiction*, 1987.

—Kenny Jackson Williams

Invisible Man has been an auspicious *novel since its publication. During the summer of 1945 while Ralph *Ellison was working on a war novel, he was forcefully drawn to type the first sentence of his now famous novel: "I am an invisible man." He then stopped writing his war novel and began *Invisible Man*. The novel took seven years to complete, and during that period two of its sections were published—the battle royal episode in 1947 in the English magazine *Horizon*, and the prologue in *Partisan Review* shortly before the novel's publication. When the novel came out in 1952, it received mostly positive reviews. However, Communists attacked it as being affected and pretentious, written to please "the white supremacy," and John O. *Killens called it "a vicious distortion of Negro life." Scholars such as Robert Bone and Richard Barksdale later praised the novel as embodying the American ideal. However, Irving Howe, who had earlier praised the work, attacked it so keenly in 1963 that Ellison felt it necessary to defend himself. Howe's argument was that the novel did not reflect the experiences of the Black American as did Richard *Wright's *Native Son* (1940), and Ellison responded by asking that his novel be judged as art: "If it fails, it fails aesthetically, not because I did or did not fight some ideological battle." Addison *Gayle, Jr., in *The Black Aesthetic* (1971) argues that the novel is of the assimilationist tradition and that such a tradition "belongs to the period of the dinosaur and the mastodon."

The novel centers on the activities of the title character, a nameless Black male who in his junior year at a southern Black college is expelled for taking a white trustee, Mr. *Norton, into a squalid settlement near the college. The narrator is an idealist who believes that if he cooperates and acquiesces to the demands of others he could become a race leader like the college's president, Dr. *Bledsoe. As he experiences a series of initiation rites that bring him closer to understanding himself and his environment, he realizes that unless he acts out of his own convictions he will become a voiceless, invisible tool in the hands of others. The first rite occurs just before he enters college, in the battle royal episode, from which he learns little about the real world. The second occurs with his expulsion and going north. Though Bledsoe and a veteran from the Golden Day explain to him that he should not be so gullible, the narrator has to be ritualized into the worlds of work (the factory) and politics (the Brotherhood) before he realizes that he alone is responsible for his self-definition. After his final initiation he realizes that "I was material, a natural resource to be used . . . except now I recognize my invisibility."

Because of its use of symbols and metaphors, its adherence to the folk tradition, and its allusion to *jazz and *blues idioms, Invisible Man transcends what Ellison refers to as the "hard-boiled novel." Ellison maintains that in writing Invisible Man, his models were Ernest Hemingway, T. S. Eliot, Fyodor Dostoevsky, Mark Twain, and William Faulkner, and that he did not imitate Richard Wright and other Black authors because they were too "ideological." But whatever Ellison owes to his white literary "ancestors," he owes just as much, if not more, to his Black experiences. When, for example, the narrator hides underground to write his memoirs, Ellison might have had Dostoevsky in mind, but, as many critics have pointed out, he was following the tradition of the *slave narrative—that of Frederick *Douglass, Olaudah *Equiano, and Harriet A. *Jacobs. Many of the narrator's dilemmas have their origin in what W. E. B. *Du Bois calls the *double consciousness that plagues all African Americans. Ellison admits that he relied heavily on the Black folk tradition in writing the novel.

In a 1955 interview Ellison was asked whether his novel would be remembered in twenty years. He responded: "I doubt it. It's not an important novel. I failed of eloquence and many of the immediate issues are rapidly fading away." Perhaps he was being modest, for Invisible Man has maintained its popularity and is now billed as an American classic.

[See also Mary Rambo; Ras the Destroyer; Rinehart; Todd Clifton; Trueblood.]

• Ralph Ellison, Shadow and Act, 1964. Archie D. Anders, "Odysseus in Black: An Analysis of the Structure of Invisible Man," College Language Association Journal 13 (Mar. 1970): 217–228. Ronald Gottesman, ed., Merrill Studes in Invisible Man, 1971. Joseph F. Trimmer, ed., A Casebook on Ralph Ellison's Invisible Man, 1972. John M. Reilly, ed., Twentieth Century Interpretations of Invisible Man: A Collection of Critical Essays, 1974. Robert O'Meally, ed., New Essays on Invisible Man, 1988.   —Ralph Reckley, Sr.

Iola Leroy, or Shadows Uplifted by Frances Ellen Watkins *Harper was first published in 1892. Until recently it was considered the first *novel by an African American woman published in the United States. Since the novel appeared in the 1890s, a time when black women's organizations surfaced throughout the country, it was widely read because it addressed pressing social and political issues affecting the Black American community; in particular, *lynching, race consciousness, suffrage, women's rights, and *temperance are presented as key themes.

Iola Leroy was published during the latter years of Harper's prolific career as a poet, essayist, and *short story and prose author. Her earlier novels, Minnie's Sacrifice (1869), Sowing and Reaping: A Temperance Story (1876–1887), and Trial and Triumph (1888–1889), appeared in serialized form in the *Christian Recorder, a periodical published by the African Methodist Episcopal Church. Harper's novels were designed for political and religious advocacy, and were especially concerned about racial *identity and commitment to social change.

The main character, Iola Leroy, embodies race, gender, and class contradictions in American society when she realizes she is black, is enslaved, and loses her status as a wealthy white woman. But unlike the tragic *mulattoes of nineteenth-century literature, Iola does not become a victim. She transcends the oppressive dynamics of historical circumstances. After she is freed from *slavery, she becomes a teacher, writer, and activist for the black race and for women's rights.

The setting of the novel begins during the Civil War and extends into Reconstruction. In the broader sense the novel is the *slave narrative of Iola, and other slave narratives incorporated as prayer meetings, provide settings for other slaves to voice their perspectives and opinions about their experiences and reality. The war activities of the enslaved and runaways refute the prevailing myth that blacks did not fight for their freedom, and critical debates about Ku Klux Klan *lynchings as well as the existence of racial discrimination in the North further demonstrate the dangers and difficulties blacks faced during Reconstruction.

In form, this novel is considerably dependent upon the interplay of dialogue to advance its thematic complexity, a format that is typical of nineteenth-century prose. At the same time, the work further demonstrates Harper's talent for capturing and contextualizing voice. Harper combines the politicized slave narrative with the episodic romanticism of the Victorian utopian novel to produce a unique prose style. Oftentimes Harper intersperses descriptions of historical settings with didactic political commentary, which disrupts the creative flow of the plot. Such commentary characterized proletarian literature of the times and is seen in Harper's earlier poetry and prose. The interjection of political analysis diffuses any tendency on the part of the audience to idealize the characters and draws direct associations between the story and historical circumstances.

The novel is firmly grounded in *history. Harper uses the surnames of famous and important black cultural, political, and historical figures for her characters. In particular, the first name of the protagonist is the nom de plume of Ida B. *Wells-Barnett, a well-known black woman radical of the 1890s. The purpose of the novel is multifaceted, and the disruption affected by the author's stylistic techniques accomplishes her objectives. Throughout the novel, the characters confront, engage, and dispel illusions in order to free their minds and to determine and renew a liberated vision.

[*See also* Miscegenation; Passing; Woman's Era.]

• Hazel V. Carby, "On the Threshold of Women's Era: Lynching, Empire, and Sexuality in Black Feminist Theory," *Critical Inquiry* 12 (Autumn 1985): 262–277. Melba Joyce Boyd, *Discarded Legacy: Politics and Poetics in the Life of Frances E. W. Harper 1825–1911*, 1994.   —Melba Joyce Boyd

Iron City, a realist *novel by Lloyd *Brown, was published in 1951 and reprinted with a critical introduction in 1994. *Iron City* is based on Brown's experiences in Pittsburgh's Allegheny County Jail in 1941. In the novel, Paul Harper, Henry Faulcon, and Isaac L. (Zach) Zachary, three African American communist political prisoners, lead a campaign to free Lonnie James, a framed African American youth on death row. As Alan Wald points out in his critical introduction to the 1994 edition, *Iron City* is possibly the first African American prison novel, and probably the first novel to depict the activities of political prisoners in the United States.

In addition to the fight to save Lonnie James, both the inner world of the characters, and the "outside" world—an ironic term to use when talking of a prison novel—are strikingly portrayed. The action of *Iron City* may be confined to the jail, but through the telling of the life stories and testimonies of the three main characters, the novel is able to move from criticizing the racism and injustice in one American institution to a critique of the American capitalist system as a whole. Through the novel's use of autobiographical, biographical, and historical materials, the novel offers a critique of racist, oppressive capitalist America and offers *communism as the answer to the American racial question.

Brown's novel was written in response to the tendency for African American writers of the 1940s and 1950s to create dark and negative portrayals of their people in such works as Richard *Wright's *Native Son* (1940). *Iron City* was a conscious attempt to introduce positive working-class African American protagonists into African American literature.

• Alan Wald, foreword to *Iron City*, 1994.

—Karen Ruth Kornweibel.

J

JACKMON, MARVIN E. *See* Marvin X.

JACKSON, ANGELA (b. 1951), poet, dramatist, and fiction writer. Angela Jackson was born in Greenville, Mississippi. Her family moved to Chicago, Illinois, while she was a child. The impact of the two locations is evident in her *poetry, which evinces southern and midwestern language influences. While at Northwestern University, Jackson emerged as a poet during the *Black Arts movement. One of the talented participants in the writer's workshop of Chicago's Organization of Black American Culture (OBAC), Jackson produces work reflective of the Black Arts movement and OBAC's aesthetic thrust. OBAC was one of the many organizations that successfully promoted art for an African American audience that was representational and functional in form and was a major influence on Jackson's style and philosophy. She entered the writer's workshop in 1970 and participated with founding members Haki R. *Madhubuti (Don L. Lee), Carolyn M. *Rodgers, and Johari *Amini (Jewel Lattimore). In 1976 she succeeded Hoyt *Fuller as coordinator. The organization's and the artists' objectives were production of high-quality literature reflecting the black experience, definition of standards by which such literature was to be judged, and development of black critics qualified to evaluate black literature accordingly while conscious of the dynamics of Western literary standards.

Jackson's creative style is distinctive yet representative of the OBAC school. Her work is not necessarily polemical but states the need for a strong African American community. Jackson has written on various aspects of the African American experience: northern and southern black life, African heritage, cultural connectivity and integration, and the wideranging experience of love. *Voodoo/Love Magic* (1974) is a collection of poems that explore *family, love as a powerful force, and African American *identity. She has written in African American vernacular in a creative and authentic manner, with an emphasis on rhythm and sound, particularly inflection, and metaphor to convey layered meaning. This style was honed in work that followed. *The Greenville Club* (1977), collected in *Four Black Poets*, presented multiple voiced perspectives of black urban community life. *Solo in the Boxcar* (1985) is composed of the voices of residents of an apartment building.

In the late 1970s and the 1980s Jackson turned to fiction, publishing the *short stories "Dreamer" (1977) and "Witch Doctor" (1977) and a piece from a *novel in progress, *Treemont Stone* (1984). In this period she adapted her poetry for the stage in *Witness!* (Chicago Showcase Theater, 1978), *Shango Diaspora: An African-American Myth of Womanhood and Love* (Chicago, Parkway Community House Theatre, 1980), and *When the Wind Blows* (Chicago, 1984).

Jackson is the recipient of many literary prizes and fellowships. Her work has taken her from Chicago, where her works were included in the Dial-a-Poem and Poetry-on-the-Buses campaigns and she participated in the Poets in the Schools program to Lagos, Nigeria, as an elected representative of the United States at the second World Festival of Black and African Arts and Culture (FESTAC) in 1977. In 1984 Jackson was appointed chair of the board of directors for the Coordinating Council of Literary Magazines, and in 1985 she became a writer in residence at Stephens College in Columbia, Missouri. Her most recent publications are *Cowboy Amok* (1992) and *Dark Legs and Silk Kisses: The Beatitudes of the Spinners* (1993), a full-length collection of poems that focus on the spider as a symbol of African American womanhood.

• D. L. Smith, "Angela Jackson," in *DLB*, vol. 41, *Afro-American Poets since 1955*, eds. Trudier Harris and Thadious M. Davis, 1985, pp. 176–183. Review of *Dark Legs and Silk Kisses: The Beatitudes of the Spinners, Publishers Weekly*, 20 Sept. 1993, 68.
—Tracy J. Patterson

JACKSON, ELAINE (b. 1943), playwright and educator. Elaine Jackson emerged as a playwright in the 1970s, a socially and politically dynamic moment in the nation's history and a renascence decade for black *theater. Beginning with her early play *Toe Jam* (1971) and continuing through her later plays of the 1970s and 1980s, Jackson presents a sometimes dark but inevitably celebratory vision of women in the process of confronting their lives and reenvisioning them. She, along with other black female dramatists of the period, working within the unique cultural climate created by the Black Power movement and the women's movement, helped to forge a vitally important theatrical space in which the lives of women of color found not only a stage presence but an authentic voice.

Born in Detroit to Essie and Charlie Jackson, the playwright began her theatrical career as an actress. After attending Wayne State University, where she majored in speech and education, Jackson moved to California to pursue her acting career. She performed in more than forty plays in Michigan, California, and New York (Off-Broadway).

In 1972, while Jackson was still working as an actress on the West Coast, two of her former theater colleagues from Detroit, Woodie *King, Jr., and Ron *Milner, published *Toe Jam* in the *Black Drama Anthology*, a seminal collection of works by twenty-two black dramatists, including Langston *Hughes and Amiri *Baraka. Jackson followed with *Cockfight* (1976), *Paper Dolls* (1979), and *Birth Rites* (1987). Her work has met with both public applause and critical recognition. She was the recipient of the Rockefeller Award for Playwriting for 1978–1979 and the Langston Hughes Playwriting Award in 1979. In

1983, she received a National Endowment for the Arts Award for playwriting. An educator since the late 1970s, Jackson served as playwright in residence at Lake Forest College in 1990 and at her alma mater, Wayne State University, in 1991. She lives with her husband, William Sparrow, and son, Dylan, in New York, where she teaches high school theater and playwriting. Currently collaborating with composer-lyricist Martin Weich on a musical version of her play *Birth Rites*, she is also working on a new play entitled *Puberty Rites*.

Jackson started writing plays as a means of creating acting roles for herself but eventually turned to writing as her primary means of expression. Often her female characters undergo a similar shift in artistic endeavor. *Toe Jam* and *Paper Dolls* both present female protagonists who, acutely aware of themselves as actors in self-negating, socially scripted *dramas, become writers in an attempt to create new roles and new life stories for themselves. In Jackson's two other works, the female characters contemplate life's critical turning points; in *Cockfight*, a couple faces the dissolution of their marriage, while in *Birth Rites* several expectant mothers anxiously await the births of their babies. Whether dealing with endings and beginnings or redefining the spaces in between, Jackson's work further opened the stage door for black playwrights and helped to set a standard in mainstream theater for richly textured portrayals of black characters and their stories.

• *Paper Dolls*, in *Nine Plays by Black Women*, ed. Margaret B. Wilkerson, 1986, pp. 347–423. Bernard L. Peterson, Jr., "Jackson, Elaine," in *Contemporary Black American Playwrights and Their Plays: A Biographical Directory and Dramatic Index*, 1988, p. 266.   —Yolanda M. Manora

JACKSON, JESSE (1908–1983), children's book author, journalist, and lecturer. Born 1 January 1908 in Columbus, Ohio, Jesse Jackson attended local schools and completed three years at Ohio State University's School of Journalism (1927–1929) before dropping out to work on the *Ohio State Press*. Jackson experienced a wide variety of jobs, including stints as an Olympic hopeful in boxing, a boxer in a carnival, a soda-jerk in Atlantic City, a juvenile probation officer, an employee of the National Bureau of Economic Research (1951–1968), and a lecturer at Appalachian State University (from 1974).

While working as a juvenile probation officer, Jackson realized the need for books that would interest nonreaders, as well as address the social issues facing African American teenagers. Jackson was assigned the case of three fourteen- to sixteen-year-old African American youths who had been sentenced to life terms in the Ohio State Penitentiary for robbing a restaurant and killing the owner for five dollars. While investigating their case, Jackson discovered that the boys had dropped out of school because they were too embarrassed to tell their teachers that they could not read. *Call Me Charley*, Jackson's first and most popular *novel, was published in 1945 as a result of his perception of a lack of appropriate reading material for African American youths. In the novel, Jackson addresses the problems faced by one African

American teenager, Charles Moss, and his attempts to be accepted by his white classmates after he and his parents move to an all-white suburb. *Call Me Charley* predated the *Brown* v. *Board of Education* Supreme Court decision by nine years and focused on the need for people of different races to get to know each other as individuals in order to eliminate *stereotypes. Many of Jackson's other books addressed the issue of relations between African American and white youths as well. Jackson wrote two sequels to *Call Me Charley*, *Anchor Man* (1947) and *Charley Starts from Scratch* (1958), as well as other works of fiction, *Room for Randy* (1957), *Tessie* (1968), and *Tessie Keeps Her Cool* (1970). Jackson also wrote several biographies for children, including two about Stonewall Jackson, *The Sickest Don't Always Die the Quickest* (1971) and *The Fourteenth Cadillac* (1972). Jackson received the National Council for Social Studies Carter G. *Woodson Award twice, in 1973 for *Black in America: A Fight for Freedom* (1971) and in 1975 for *Make a Joyful Noise unto the Lord: The Life of Mahalia Jackson, Queen of Gospel Singers* (1974). Jackson's novels and biographies paved the way for more explicit writing about race relations in *children's and young adult literature and gave African American writers an audience that had, in large measure, previously been denied them. Jackson died on 14 April 1983 in Boone, North Carolina.

• Ruby J. Lanier, "Profiles: Call Me Jesse Jackson," *Language Arts* 54.3 (Mar. 1977): 331–339. "Jackson, Jesse" in *Something about the Author*, vol. 29, ed. Anne Commire, 1982, pp. 111–114.   —Barbara Lowe

JACKSON, MAE (b. 1946), poet and activist educator. Mae Jackson was born in Earl, Arkansas, and lives and teaches middle school in Brooklyn, New York. From 1966 to 1971 she was a member of the Student Nonviolent Coordinating Committee, and she graduated from the New School of Social Research in New York City. A 1970 winner of the Conrad Kent *Rivers Memorial Award for her *poetry, through the 1970s and into the 1980s she contributed significantly to poetry journals inspired by the *Black Arts movement, including *Black Creation*, *Black Scholar*, *Essence*, *Journal of Black Poetry*, and *Negro Digest*. Her poems also appeared in the *anthologies *The Poetry of Black America* (1973, ed. Arnold Adoff) and *Black Spirits* (1972, ed. Woodie *King). Her book, *Can I Poet with You*, published by Black Dialogue in 1969, was reprinted by Dudley *Randall's *Broadside Press of Detroit in 1972. Her work, if somewhat obscurely published, invaluably draws a full picture of women's involvement in the revolutionary spirit and intellectual production of Black Power arts and activism.

The title, program, and content of *Can I Poet with You* reverse Amiri *Baraka's history of *jazz in "Swing from Verb to Noun" by insisting on the verbal and active, rather than the nominal and author-centered thrust of Black Power and revolutionary Black Art. Jackson turns "poet" from noun to verb as she lays down an agenda that returns poetry to its source beyond the common interests of poets to the community that will, she hopes, make and grow with the revolution against economic and racial oppression. "For Some Poets" asks the titular question of the book to a circle of poets, including "roi" (LeRoi Jones/Amiri Baraka) and "nikki" (Nikki *Giovanni), with whom Jackson would "poet for a little taste." Throughout the collection, she is activist and celebrant, critic and singer, feminist and race poet. In poems addressed to commercial artists like Aretha *Franklin, James Brown, and Nina Simone, Jackson charts the organic relationship of Black Arts to a community that can draw together to resist and redirect *violence. *Music and words, *blues and the manifest rage that turns victimage into victories on the page and on the stage of history ring in her short conversational lyrics. Power, Jackson repeats, comes from the people to revolutionize or rather to undo "americanism," a word she deliberately signifies upon. Her poems apply the Stokely *Carmichael quotation, "Every Negro is a potential black man," also the epigraph of "Note from a Field Nigger (Found on a Dog's Collar)." For example, "There Was a Time (for James Brown)" bespeaks the historical and rhetorical correction offered stars by the community as it describes how Brown's music became revolutionary after "some people / got him organized." Her work is not limited to *identity politics. Rather, wielded in differential concert by men and women, it makes but one weapon in a struggle requiring solidarity and individual engagement. Thus, the poem "Pledge of Alligence [sic]" states that along with "one of the twenty-two million overseas-African[s]" she will use words as revolutionary weapons.

Her poetics of direct address does not blink at sexism or color caste in Afrocentrist thought and other aspects of the Black Arts scene; accommodation and assimilation are her main targets. "Play House" turns feminist irony on the Black Arts king-princess scenario by insisting on female choice in constructing "my black self" in balanced response with other black women, "when they believe in Black Men." In her introduction to the Broadside Press edition, Nikki Giovanni, friend and mentor, sees Jackson, along with Carolyn M. *Rodgers and Jewel *Lattimore, as a woman, then twenty-three, whose life and work are about proving "that there is no difference between the warrior, the poet, and the people." Jackson's work is of historical importance to defining "Negro Intellectuals" "Black Genius" (her poem titles); current African American and other potential artists and activists can reactivate the criticism she voiced.

• Mae Jackson, Can I Poet with You, 1972. Broadside Authors and Artists: An Illustrated Biography Directory, ed. Leaonead Pack Bailey, 1974.   —Kathryne V. Lindberg

JACKSON, MATTIE J. (c. 1843–?), autobiographer. Mattie Jane Jackson was born in St. Louis to Westly and Ellen Jackson, married slaves living on different plantations. When she was scarcely twenty, she dictated The Story of Mattie J. Jackson; it describes African American resistance to *slavery and enumerates the efforts of individual members of her family to flee bondage in the years preceding the Civil War. Although her father and later her stepfather escaped while Mattie was still a child, her mother did not free herself until 1865, after seven escape attempts and more than forty-three years of servitude. Mattie achieved *freedom in 1864.

Written by Dr. L. S. Thompson, the second wife of Mattie's mother's second husband, The Story of Mattie J. Jackson (published in 1866) portrays slavery's violent rupture of American families. In addition to her escaped spouses, Ellen loses two infant children. She is separated from a third partner for more than two years when, on the eve of their wedding, southern soldiers masquerading as Unionists abduct her and her children. Jackson exposes the deleterious effects of slavery on whites by vividly recounting the murder of a slaveholder by his sadistic Rebel neighbors.

Jackson embodies slave women's extraordinary self-assertion and their intolerance of inequity. As an adolescent, she enacted her most impassioned protests against slave-beating: twice she indicted her master before the Union Army adjutant, signifying her personal integrity and reverence for justice. Written to earn funding for her formal *education, The Story of Mattie J. Jackson effectively demonstrates the intelligence and maturity of its young subject.

[See also Slave Narrative.]

• William L. Andrews, ed., Six Women's Slave Narratives, 1988.   —Joycelyn K. Moody

JACKSON, REBECCA COX (1795–1871), evangelist, Shaker eldress, and autobiographer. Rebecca Cox was born in Horntown, Pennsylvania. The deaths of her parents by 1808 necessitated her early independence. By age thirty-five, she had married Samuel S. Jackson; they resided with her older brother, the Reverend Joseph Cox, an African Methodist Episcopal (AME) Church elder. Besides keeping house for the men and her widower brother's four small children, she worked as a seamstress. In July 1830, Jackson underwent a spiritual awakening. Within a year, her sanctification at a neighborhood revival propelled her squarely into the Holiness movement.

Between 1831 and 1833, Jackson's extraordinary religious conviction, manifest in such ascetic practices as fasting and weeping, further impaired her health (already hampered by epilepsy), but empowered her with gifts of prophecy, revelation, *healing, and *literacy. Once literate, she began recording her evangelical experiences and later transformed them into spiritual autobiography. Her charismatic leadership of Christian love feasts and women's praying bands evolved into a controversial ministry as she apprehensively conceded to the call to preach in November 1833. She continued her evangelism despite the objection of AME clergy who decried women's preaching. Jackson's own abstemiousness led her to repudiate the *church's sanction of married sexual intercourse.

On 1 January 1836 Jackson foresaw her pilgrimage among New York Shakers (the United Society of Believers in Christ's Second Appearing), adumbrating her excommunication from the AME Church for heresy in 1837. Her demand for a public interdenominational trial of her case was denied and effected her estrangement from her *family. Drawn to the Shakers' celibacy and their feminist recognition of a dual-gendered divinity, Jackson traveled with another African American Shaker, Rebecca Perot. Although they experimented in the 1850s with séance spiritualism, in 1857 the two formed a predominantly African American female Shaker community at Philadelphia, over which Jackson served as Shaker eldress from 1859 until her death in 1871. Jackson's autobiographical writing was collected by Jean McMahon Humez and published in 1981.

[*See also* Autobiography, *article on* Spiritual Autobiography; Religion.]

• Jean McMahon Humez, ed., *Gifts of Power: The Writings of Rebecca Jackson, Black Visionary, Shaker Eldress*, 1981. Diane Sasson, "Life as Vision: The Autobiography of Mother Rebecca Jackson," in *The Shaker Spiritual Narrative*, ed. Sarah D. Sasson, 1983.
—Joycelyn K. Moody

JACOBS, HARRIET A. (c. 1813–1897), slave narrator, fugitive slave, and reformer. Harriet Ann Jacobs's major literary contribution is her *slave narrative *Incidents in the Life of a Slave Girl* (1861), the most comprehensive antebellum *autobiography by an African American woman. *Incidents* is the first-person account of Jacobs's pseudonymous narrator "Linda Brent," who presents a remarkably accurate, although highly selective, story of her life. Breaking taboos to present her sexual history in *slavery, Jacobs wrote a woman-centered slave narrative that, emphasizing *family relationships and incorporating the forms of the domestic *novel, reshaped the genre to encompass female experience.

About 1813, Harriet Jacobs was born into slavery in Edenton, North Carolina, to Delilah and a skilled house carpenter probably named Elijah, apparently the son of Henry Jacobs, a white farmer. Her brother John was born two years later.

In *Incidents*, Jacobs writes of the happy family life she enjoyed until the death of her mother. Then at age six she was taken into the home of her mistress, who taught her to read and to sew. At adolescence sent into the home of Dr. James Norcom, whom she characterizes as the licentious "Dr. Flint," she was subjected to unrelenting sexual harrassment. Jacobs's "Linda" confesses that to prevent "Flint" from forcing her into concubinage, at sixteen she established a liaison with a young white neighbor. This alliance produced two children, Joseph (born c. 1829) and Louisa Matilda (c. 1833–1913). Jacobs describes her master's renewed threat of concubinage, her fear that he will make her children plantation slaves, and her decision to run away in hopes that, in her absence, he will sell the children and that their father will buy and free them. She chronicles her 1835 runaway and her seven years in hiding in a tiny attic crawlspace in the home of her grandmother, a freedwoman.

Jacobs recounts her 1842 escape to New York, her reunion with her children in the North, and her 1849 move to Rochester, where she joined her activist brother, a member of Frederick *Douglass's circle. There Amy Post, a feminist Quaker, urged her to write her life. Returning to New York City after passage of the 1850 Fugitive Slave Act, she became the target of kidnappers. Although determined not to comply with slavery by allowing herself to be bought, in 1853 she was purchased from the Norcoms by her employer, Cornelia Grinnell Willis. Like other slave narratives, her book ends with *freedom.

From 1853 to 1861 Jacobs recorded the conception, composition, and publication of *Incidents* in a series of *letters to her friend Amy Post. This correspondence reveals that after an unsuccessful effort to enlist Harriet Beecher *Stowe as her *amanuensis, she wrote her life herself. She could not find a publisher, however, until in 1860 the African American author William C. *Nell introduced her to the white abolitionist writer L. Maria Child, who agreed to act as her agent and her editor. Early in 1861, Jacobs published *Incidents* pseudonymously with only Child's name on the title page as editor.

Jacobs's name was initially connected with her book, although later, before the 1987 appearance of the Harvard University Press edition, both its authorship and its autobiographical status were disputed. When the Civil War began, she used her newfound celebrity among abolitionists to establish a public career. Joining Elizabeth *Keckley, Sojourner *Truth, and others aiding the "contraband," black refugees crowding behind the lines of the Union Army, Jacobs returned South. From 1863 to 1865, supported by Quakers and reformers, she and her daughter supplied emergency relief and established the Jacobs Free School in occupied Alexandria, Virginia. In 1866 the mother-daughter team continued their efforts in Savannah.

Throughout these years, Harriet and Louisa Jacobs were known to reformers through their reports on their work in the northern press. In 1864 Jacobs was named to the executive committee of the feminist Women's Loyal National League. Two years later Louisa lectured for the radical American Equal Rights Association. In 1868 mother and daughter went to England, where *Incidents* had been published in 1862, to raise money for Savannah's black community. Although successful, back home they were confronted with the increasing antiblack *violence in the South, and mother and daughter retreated to Cambridge, Massachusetts.

By 1877 they had moved to Washington, D.C., where, in her declining years, Jacobs continued her mission among the freed people. In 1896 she was confined to a wheelchair when her daughter apparently attended the organizing meetings of the National Association of Colored Women held in Washington, D.C. Harriet Jacobs died in Washington on 7 March 1897.

• Jean Fagan Yellin, "Written by Herself: Harriet Jacobs's Slave Narrative," *American Literature* 53 (1981): 479–486. William L. Andrews, *To Tell a Free Story: The First Century of Afro-American Autobiography*, 1986. Hazel V. Carby, *Reconstructing Womanhood: The Emergence of the Afro-American Woman Novelist*, 1987. Jean Fagan Yellin, introduction to *Incidents in the Life of a Slave Girl: Written by Herself*, 1987. Joanne M. Braxton, *Black Women Writing Autobiography*, 1989. Frances Smith Foster, *Written by Herself: Literary Production by African American Women, 1746–1892*, 1993.
—Jean Fagan Yellin

JADINE CHILDS. In Toni *Morrison's *Tar Baby* (1981), Jadine Childs is the orphaned niece of Ondine and Sydney, black servants in the wealthy white household of Margaret and Valerian Street. The Streets provided for Jadine's formal education, but she received little cultural or parental nurturing. Called the "Copper Venus" by the fashion world, Jadine works as a model in Paris. She has become completely Europeanized and is engaged to a white Frenchman. She sees herself as an independent, successful, professional woman who happens to be black but has no appreciation of her black cultural heritage. That her state of *identity is confused, however, becomes apparent during her visit to the Streets by her confrontation with *Son Green—a black man hiding on the Streets' property—and an unknown African woman in a yellow dress.

Jadine and Son's relationship is doomed to failure because they represent worlds, ideals, and values that cannot be reconciled. Jadine, in fact, feels more comfortable with the Streets than with the black Floridians she visits with Son, and she is frightened by the vision of the African woman, for she represents authentic African culture and heritage and makes Jadine feel lonely and inauthentic. Jadine's expressed goal is to not belong to anyone but herself; nevertheless she is shaped by the culture of the Streets' household. Morrison paints Jadine as a woman who has forgotten her "ancient properties," that is, her ties to African American heritage and specifically to a community of black women made up of people like her Aunt Ondine. By returning to Paris and to a man she does not love, Jadine effectively opts for materialism rather than heritage. This makes it clear that she is unsentimental in choosing all that the American dream has to offer and leaving her people and culture behind. While her *mulatto status does not make her a new character in the literature, her conscious, deliberate rejection of black people does.

• Barbara Christian, *Black Feminist Criticism*, 1985. Craig Werner, "The Briar Patch as Modernist Myth: Morrison, Bartes and *Tar Baby* As-Is," in *Critical Essays on Toni Morrison*, ed. Nellie Y. McKay, 1988, pp. 150–167. Wilfred D. Samuels and Clenora Hudson Weems, *Toni Morrison*, 1990. Trudier Harris, *Fiction and Folklore: The Novels of Toni Morrison*, 1991. —Betty Taylor-Thompson

JANIE CRAWFORD. The protagonist of Zora Neale *Hurston's novel *Their Eyes Were Watching God* (1937), Janie Crawford is sixteen years old when, lying beneath a pear tree, she experiences a sexual and spiritual awakening. Before she can contemplate its meaning, her grandmother *Nanny forces her to follow the "text" she has saved for her life. For twenty years, Janie lives someone else's dream.

She marries Logan Killicks, an older man who owns a sixty-acre farm. Disillusioned when she finds that marriage does not compel love, Janie leaves Logan for a citified, stylishly dressed stranger. Joe Starks takes Janie to Eatonville, Florida, where she becomes storekeeper, postmaster, and mayor; Janie becomes his ornament. Denied the right to speak in public or even to listen to the "lying sessions" where the wit and wisdom of the culture are performed, Janie claims her voice slowly. In a dramatic confrontation, she talks back to Joe. After Joe's death, she resolves to follow her dream to journey to the horizon in search of people. She meets and marries *Tea Cake, a traveling bluesman. Living in a migrant workers camp, she works alongside Tea Cake and learns to tell stories herself. As he saves Janie during a hurricane, Tea Cake is bitten by a rabid dog. Subsequently, Janie kills him in self-defense.

Critics disagree about whether Janie becomes an articulate heroine. The novel does not record her testimony when she goes to trial for murdering her husband. But after her acquittal, Janie returns to Eatonville and tells her tale to her "kissin'-friend." —Cheryl A. Wall

JAZZ. Since the birth of jazz in the first two decades of the twentieth century, writers have incorporated jazz styles in their work in an effort to capture the mood, energy, and soul of the *music and those who love it. The challenge of rendering the improvisational unpredictability, lively *humor, visceral pathos, deep spiritualism, and soft blue moods of various forms of jazz has attracted the most gifted of writers. In turn, the cultural depth and lively themes of jazz have enriched the *poetry, prose fiction, and *autobiography that define the major and minor chords of African American culture.

But just as important as its presence in literature is the relationship between the cultural projects of jazz and African American literature. To counter the assumptions of sociologist Gunnar Myrdal (*American Dilemma*, 1944), literary critic Irving Howe, and other influential thinkers that African American culture had no distinct characteristics—that it was simply a reaction to oppression and influence from dominant white culture—many African American writers have cited jazz as an example of a distinct and brilliant art form with a clear African heritage.

The aspects of the music Americans have grown to call jazz that most often find literary expression include improvisation, syncopated rhythm, lyrics with such *blues-influenced devices as call and response, repetition, and, most importantly, the practice of *signifying: thoughtful revision and repetition of another's work.

Poetry most clearly exemplifies these devices. No poet of the jazz age was as keenly aware of the debts that African American artists owe their predecessors as Sterling A. *Brown. In the poem "Mose" from his 1932 collection of poems, *Southern Road*, Brown honors musicians who thoughtfully pay homage to artists of previous generations. Brown was not only keenly aware of the value of respectful signifying in all forms of artistic expression, he was also concerned with the status and role of the African American musician, who was drawing quite a bit of money into the clubs each night, yet taking home very little of it. Brown criticized this phenomenon in his poem "Cabaret," in which he compared the musicians to slaves, toiling for favors from their white masters who were not willing to respect them. Yet Brown's musicians retain their self-respect by playing furiously and skillfully. Just as during *slavery, music in "Cabaret" serves as a forum for rebellion, reflection, and release.

Langston *Hughes, the master of adapting blues styles to a flat piece of paper, also painted a picture of a 1920s Harlem jazz cabaret scene in his poem "Jazzonia," from his collection The *Weary Blues (1926). Hughes, unlike Brown, chose not to attack the social hypocrisy in the cabaret scene, but to focus on the aural and visual event itself. Hughes employed blues-like repetition, variation, and syncopated rhythm to capture the essence of the music.

Amiri *Baraka, formerly known as LeRoi Jones, employs jazz devices and his own loud, postmodern style to erase the line between poetry and prose. For example, in his *short story "The Screamers" (1963), Baraka fuses syncopated sounds, sights, and speech to paint a powerful yet humorous picture of an urban jazz scene. The climax of the story, when the musicians lead their charged fans into the streets, is more than musical: it is political. The fury of jazz becomes a weapon for the oppressed in Baraka's hands.

In contrast to Baraka's political portrait of the jazz experience, James *Baldwin portrays the most personal passion of jazz—the pain musicians release through the music and the price they pay for confronting it—in his story "Sonny's Blues" (1957). Sonny's older brother, a school teacher, narrates the story of Sonny's youthful escape from the hard life of Harlem, first through jazz, then through drugs. As the brothers come to terms with their mutual pain and discuss how they cope, Sonny invites his brother to a club to hear him play piano. In a stirring rendering of jazz into prose, Baldwin connects the reader to the musical experience, just as the elder brother connects to Sonny.

While a passion for jazz can unite people, a disagreement over its artistic value can divide. In his story "The Blues I'm Playing" (1934), Langston Hughes explores the relationship between patron and artist. Set in Manhattan in the late 1920s, the story follows a pianist named Oceola Jones from Harlem rent parties and church meetings to Paris salons, where her classical training is funded by a wealthy white widow. Perturbed when Oceola decides to marry a young doctor and play jazz, the patron pleads for her to stay married to her art. Oceola cannot understand how one might disengage life from art, and rebels against her patron by playing jazz at her last private recital.

James Weldon *Johnson also explored both the patron-artist relationship and the artistic value of jazz in his short *novel The *Autobiography of an Ex-Colored Man (1912). The character confronts his ethnic *identity through an encounter with ragtime in a club in New York. The classically trained pianist quickly learns ragtime techniques and displays his newfound art in Europe, where the musicians are fascinated with the new rhythms and accord it the respect that would take decades to emerge in the United States.

Getting inside an artist's head has always been a great challenge for writers. Ann *Petry takes the reader into the thoughts of drummer Kid Jones in her story "Solo on the Drums" (1947). Around the time of the birth of bebop, Jones backs an ensemble in a small Manhattan club. As Jones plays, both accompanying and soloing, he lets his mind wander to the most joyous and painful moments of his life, and almost unconsciously produces the underpinnings of a brilliant jazz performance.

The presence of jazz has been a unifying characteristic in the African American literary tradition for half a century—largely thanks to the writings of Ralph *Ellison. Ellison opens *Invisible Man (1952) with his narrator listening to Louis Armstrong wail "What Did I Do to Be So Black and Blue?" (1929). The novel can be read as an attempt to answer Armstrong's question. Because so much post–World War II literature has reflected Ellison's influence, so much later literature has tried to answer that same question. Following the tradition, Toni *Morrison answers that question in her story of a tragic love triangle set in Harlem in the 1920s, *Jazz (1993). In the novel, the hot new music becomes a symbol of youth and sensuality that both inspires and destroys its characters.

Assuming Ellison's project of declaring jazz the finest expression of American genius, and mocking the majority culture's dismissal of it, Ishmael *Reed orchestrated a comic detective story called *Mumbo Jumbo (1972). In this bebop-paced novel, the character *Papa LaBas traces the widespread effort to suppress expression of "Jes Grew," the African and African American musical and lyrical tradition. Although set in the 1920s, the influence of Charlie *Parker looms large in Reed's narrative. Like Parker, who retold old musical stories with higher peaks, lower troughs, and at higher speed than any of his influences, Reed takes the African American literary tradition on a zigzag journey through Harlem and the twentieth century.

One of the richest veins of the African American literary tradition is *autobiography, and the jazz autobiography stands as a unique contribution to American culture and history. Louis Armstrong, America's first pop music idol, initiated the autobiographical tradition among jazz masters with Satchmo: My Life in New Orleans (1954). The book uses a light conversational tone to tell the story of an ambitious boy growing into a successful man by valuing mentors—from his mother to bandleader King Oliver—and by adhering to a strong code of behavior. In the tradition of American success manuals like The Autobiography of Benjamin Franklin, Armstrong set the autobiographical themes that other musicians would soon improvise on.

Perhaps the most enlightening jazz autobiography is by clarinet player Sidney Bechet, who opens the book Treat It Gentle (1960) with a five-page description of the meaning and power of jazz. Expatriate diva Nina Simone's autobiography I Put a Spell on You (1991) relates the difficulty an African American performer has trying to earn respect in the United States and explains why she prefers to live and perform in Europe, a decision hundreds of jazz musicians have made as well. Charles Mingus wrote the most literary—and therefore least trustworthy—of jazz autobiographies called *Beneath the Underdog* (1971). It stands as the most remarkable achievement in the fusion of modern experimental fiction and autobiography.

Jazz, through its literary expressions, has contributed to a thirst for African American expressive culture throughout the twentieth century. Whether that thirst was expressed as a vulgar fascination for primitivism or as informed respect, jazz literature is central to a full understanding of how much American culture owes to its great composers of African descent.

• Amiri Baraka (LeRoi Jones), *Blues People*, 1963. Ralph Ellison, *Shadow and Act*, 1964. Arnold Rampersad, *The Life of Langston Hughes*, 2 vols., 1986–1988. Houston A. Baker, Jr., *Modernism and the Harlem Renaissance*, 1987. Henry Louis Gates, Jr., *The Signifying Monkey: A Theory of Afro-American Literary Criticism*, 1988. Larry Neal, ed., *Visions of a Liberated Future: Black Arts Movement Writings*, 1989. Kathy J. Ogren, *The Jazz Revolution: Twenties America and the Meaning of Jazz*, 1989. Marcela Breton, ed., *Hot and Cool: Jazz Short Stories*, 1990. Gayl Jones, *Liberating Voices: Oral Tradition in African American Literature*, 1991.

—Siva Vaidhyanathan

Jazz. Toni *Morrison's sixth *novel, *Jazz* (1992) takes place in 1926, when the *Harlem Renaissance was at its peak, a special time of success and attention for African American artists in all genres, including literature, art, and *music, especially *jazz. Its story line was inspired by an event that Morrison learned about in *The Harlem Book of the Dead* (1978), in which Camille Billops records the story behind James Van Der Zee's photograph of a young woman's corpse; she was shot yet refused to identify her assailant before she died.

The novel is a multifaceted narrative evolving from the early-twentieth century *migration to New York of a seemingly uncomplicated southern couple. They appear to join the hundreds of thousands of black people who left rural areas for urban areas, the South for the North, between 1890 and 1930; that migration led in part to the Harlem Renaissance. Violet and Joe Trace are thus expecting to improve their economic condition just as other migrants so hoped. The unexpected stresses of the city, however, complicate their lives.

At the beginning of the novel, Morrison relates that the over-fifty-year-old Joe, in a morose and jealous state, had murdered a seventeen-year-old girl, Dorcas, with whom he was having an affair; she had finally turned her attention to a younger man. The narrative ties in to *The Harlem Book of the Dead* because Dorcas, lying shot by Joe, refuses to allow those surrounding her to call for an ambulance until Joe has disappeared; by then, she is too near death to be revived. Violet disrupts the funeral and has to be wrestled to the floor when she attempts to attack Dorcas's corpse with a knife. She thus becomes known as "Violent" Trace. The novel then focuses on Violet and Joe's past and their continuing fascination with the dead girl as well as upon their own reconciliation. During this healing process, Violet develops relationships with Dorcas's aunt and Dorcas's best friend.

Jazz is narrated by an alternately objective, omniscient, and confused voice that reveals the consciousnesses and personal histories of the characters and their historic setting, and also gives the novel its improvisatory, jazzlike feel. During 1992, *Jazz* achieved best-seller status along with Morrison's nonfiction critical work *Playing in the Dark*. While most critics responded favorably to the novel, others complained of its structure and narrative technique, and many were simply puzzled by what Morrison was trying to accomplish. Initial detractors, however, seem now to be more appreciative of the novel.

• Henry Louis Gates, Jr., and K. A. Appiah, eds., *Toni Morrison: Critical Perspectives Past and Present*, 1993. Paula Gallant Eckard, "The Interplay of Music, Language, and Narrative in Toni Morrison's *Jazz*," *CLA Journal* 28.1 (Sept. 1994): 11–19. Sarah Aguiar Appleton, "'Everywhere and Nowhere': Beloved's 'Wild' Legacy in Toni Morrison's *Jazz*," *Notes on Contemporary Literature* 25.4 (Sept. 1995): 11–12.

—Betty Taylor-Thompson

JEFFERS, LANCE (1919–1985), poet, short fiction writer, and novelist. Lance Jeffers might accurately be described as a black nationalist without a movement. While he spanned the decades identified with the *Black Aesthetic and writers of the 1960s, he was not included in the circles of those most associated with those militant times (though *Broadside Press, which published many writers of the 1960s, did publish a couple of his volumes). Yet Jeffers's political stances as a poet are culturally nationalistic and informed by a consistent appreciation of the beauty and possibilities in black people. Though a few critics have paid attention to his work, he is among many less well-known African American writers whose works have not been incorporated into the mainstream of critical commentary on African American or American literature. In addition to singly published volumes, however, his works have appeared in *anthologies such as *The Best Short Stories of 1948*, *Burning Spear*, *A Galaxy of Black Writing*, *New Black Voices*, and *Black Fire*, as well as in journals such as *Phylon*, *Quarto*, and the *Tamarack Review*.

Lance Jeffers was born in Fremont, Nebraska, on 28 November 1919 to Henry Nelson and Dorothy May Flippin; he was their only child. His grandfather, Dr. George Albert Flippin, raised him in Stromburg, Nebraska, from the time Lance was one year old; it was this relative who inspired *Grandsire*, one of Jeffers's volumes of *poetry. Lance lived in Nebraska until his grandfather died in 1929. These years turned out to be the most formative of his career, and his grandfather proved to be perhaps the strongest influence on his life, but Lance was in essence separated from large numbers of black people. Reclaiming ties to African heritage and African peoples would occupy Jeffers for the rest of his life. At the age of ten, Lance moved to San Francisco to join his mother and stepfather, Forrest Jeffers, who was a janitor in a building whose tenants were white. Thus Jeffers did not immediately encounter many more black people than he had living with his grandfather and his white wife in Nebraska. Forrest Jeffers encouraged Lance to seek out other blacks, and he taught Jeffers the value of endurance under racially difficult circumstances.

Lance attended three high schools before graduating in 1938, then a succession of colleges before he joined the army in 1942 and served in Europe. When he left the military in 1946, he married Camille Jones, a social worker he had met in England, and, over the next few years, completed his undergraduate (cum laude) and master's work at Columbia University. Jeffers divorced Camille and married Trellie James in 1959; he had a son with Camille and three daughters with Trellie.

Like many practicing African American writers, Jeffers did not support himself exclusively through his writing. He taught at colleges and universities throughout the country, beginning in 1951 and including California State College at Long Beach and North Carolina State University in Raleigh, where he joined the faculty in 1974 and was still there at the time of his death on 19 July 1985. Trellie Jeffers continues her career as a college professor.

Jeffers's published volumes of poetry include *My Blackness Is the Beauty of This Land* (1970), *When I Know the Power of My Black Hand* (1974), *O Africa, Where I Baked My Bread* (1977), and *Grandsire* (1979). He dedicated three of the volumes to his wife Trellie, about whom he has written more than twenty poems, including the entire second section of *Grandsire*, and who served as a touchstone and constant source of inspiration to Jeffers. Other poems focus on racism, the beauty of blackness, the power of human beings to endure oppression, ancestry and homeland, topical issues such as the Vietnam War and the *civil rights movement, and global issues such as the Holocaust. *Witherspoon* (1983) is Jeffers's one and only novelistic venture. It is the story of a black minister who, during a racial crisis, learns the value of revolution.

A few critics have appreciated Jeffers's mastery of language and metaphor, his exquisite attention to the possibilities of linguistic expression, and his aggressive pride in blackness, but more expansive and sustained scholarly studies of his works have yet to appear.

• Lance Jeffers, "A Black Poet's Vision: An Interview with Lance Jeffers," interview by Doris Laryea, *CLA Journal* 26 (June 1983): 422–433. David Dorsey, "Lance Jeffers," in *DLB*, vol. 41, *Afro-American Poets since 1955*, eds. Trudier Harris and Thadious M. Davis, 1985, pp. 183–190.

—Trudier Harris

JEMIMA. *See* Aunt Jemima.

JEWS. Relations between African Americans and Jews have always been touchy, for there are equally great forces pulling them simultaneously together and apart. On the one hand, both groups have histories of being victimized and would therefore seem to be likely allies (and have indeed frequently been). On the other hand, each group views the other as a potential enemy, allowing Black anti-Semitism and Jewish racism to flourish. Individual African Americans have demonstrated a range of attitudes toward Jews, which result in corresponding depictions of Jews in African American literature.

Many African American writers stress the two groups' "basic unity of experience," to use Ralph *Ellison's words. In Richard *Wright's *Native Son* (1940), for example, a Jewish lawyer asserts that African Americans are not the only oppressed minority; he himself has received anti-Semitic mail. Zora Neale *Hurston's *Moses: Man of the Mountain* (1939) retells the life of the slave revolt leader as an allegorical denunciation of both Nazi Germany and racist America. This Biblical connection also appears in Trey *Ellis's "Guess Who's Coming to Seder?" (1989), where African Americans and Jews are unified through singing "Go Down, Moses." By showing the parallels between the two groups, such texts encourage stronger relations between them.

Other texts, however, emphasize conflicts between African Americans and Jews. Jewish figures here are loathsome, and their encounters with African Americans result in divisiveness rather than unity. A Jewish teacher in Paule *Marshall's "Brooklyn" (1961), for instance, tries to take sexual advantage of his vulnerable African American pupil. An odious Jewish butcher in Louise *Meriwether's *Daddy Was a Numbers Runner* (1971) gives a young girl an extra soup bone, but only after he molests her. This sense of Jewish exploitation, usually presented in financial terms, appears in some virulently anti-Semitic literature, including several of Amiri *Baraka's and Nikki *Giovanni's poems and some of James *Baldwin's *essays.

Such negative portrayals of Jews do appear in African American literature, but infrequently, as the majority of African American creative writers stress cooperation among people from the two heritages. Jewish characters in these works are laudable figures, dedicated to causes that will better conditions for all people. A list of such positive characters would include Saul Amron, an anthropologist in Marshall's *The *Chosen Place, the Timeless People* (1969); Lynne Rabinowitz, a civil rights activist in Alice *Walker's *Meridian* (1976); Abe Rosenberg, a labor union organizer in Chester *Himes's *Lonely Crusade* (1947); and Itzhak Hod, an Israeli commando who retaliates against racially motivated murderers in John A. *Williams's *Sons of Darkness, Sons of Light* (1969). Many other texts, such as George *Cain's *Blueschild Baby* (1970) and Carl Ruthven *Offord's *The White Face* (1943), begin with antagonisms but eventually give way to feelings of community. The conclusions of these books both demonstrate the importance of achieving an African American–Jewish alliance and point the way toward such an occurrence.

Additional African American writers who have presented Jewish characters are Hal *Bennett, Lorraine *Hansberry, John O. *Killens, Andrea *Lee, Willard *Motley, Gloria *Naylor, Ann *Petry, Ishmael *Reed, Henry *Van Dyke, and John Edgar *Wideman.

• Louis Harap, "Special Black-Jewish Literary Relations," in *Dramatic Encounters*, 1987.

—Adam Meyer

JIM CROW. The term "Jim Crow" dates back at least to 1828 when white blackface performer Thomas D. Rice witnessed the song-and-dance routine of a

Louisville slave owned by a Mr. Crow. Rice recast this slave's routine into a blackface act called "Jump Jim Crow." Featuring dancing as well as lyrics imitative of African American vernacular speech set to a well-known British melody, "Jump Jim Crow" was an immediate success throughout the United States and Great Britain. According to Robert C. Toll, Rice's choreography, which borrowed heavily from African American dancing, distinguished "Jump Jim Crow" from previous blackface routines and probably accounted for his act's great popularity. Thus, "Jump Jim Crow" was an early example of the exploitation of African American culture by Anglo American popular entertainers.

"Jim Crow" was first used as an adjective in the late 1830s. According to C. Vann Woodward, this occurred in the North, when northern transportation companies began to require African Americans to sit in "Jim Crow" sections. Although *slavery had been largely abolished in northern states by 1830, northern lawmakers and mainstream politicians before the Civil War continued to restrict the role of African Americans in northern society.

The first laws officially labelled "Jim Crow" emerged in the South around the turn of the century. After the Civil War southern states immediately tried to pass laws to limit the inroads that African Americans might make into southern white society; the northern presence in the South during Reconstruction, though, controlled the segregationist tendencies of southern whites. Thus, with the northern agents of Reconstruction present in the South, African Americans now freed from slavery gained certain advantages and rights. After Reconstruction ended in 1877, however, social relationships between African American and white Southerners worsened. White supremacists, who were generally from a lower-class background, increasingly attempted to subjugate African Americans illegally (a record number of *lynchings were committed in the 1880s), and many whites began to press for stronger and more all-encompassing segregation laws through which to separate African Americans from whites. By the 1890s southern states were instituting stronger segregation laws, a situation the U.S. Supreme Court further encouraged when it upheld the legality of "separate-but-equal" segregation in its *Plessy v. Ferguson* ruling of 1896. After that decision, official "Jim Crow" laws proliferated in southern states. For more than half a century, these laws were employed in the South to enforce segregation on trains, streetcars, steamboats, and busses; in schools, boarding houses, hospitals, and neighborhoods; at workplaces and recreation areas; and within organizations (unions, for instance). Numerous authors have depicted the African American struggle to overcome the crippling effects of segregation in the South; perhaps the most compelling literary treatment of this predicament is in Richard *Wright's work—especially in "The Ethics of Living Jim Crow" (1937) and *Uncle Tom's Children* (1938). Legal "Jim Crow" segregation in the South ended with the hard-earned victories of the *civil rights movement.

[See also Minstrelsy; Musicals; Race; Stereotypes.]

• C. Vann Woodard, *The Strange Career of Jim Crow,* 1955. Robert C. Toll, *Blacking Up: The Minstrel Show in Nineteenth-Century America,* 1974. Charles Reagan Wilson, "Jim Crow," in *Encyclopedia of Southern Culture,* eds. Charles Reagan Wilson and William Ferris, 1989, pp. 213–214. Eric Lott, *Love and Theft: Blackface Minstrelsy and the American Working Class,* 1993.   —Ted Olson

JOANS, TED (b. 1928), poet, multimedia performer, musician, painter, surrealist, traveling storyteller, Beat writer, and Black Nationalist Manifesto writer. Ted Joans was born in Cairo, Illinois, on 4 July 1928, to African American entertainers working on Mississippi riverboats. He says that by the age of thirteen, he had learned to play the trumpet as well as the crowd and otherwise to fend for himself after his father's death in the Detroit Riot of 1943. Upon earning a bachelor's degree in painting at Indiana University (1951), he headed for New York, where his studio/apartment soon became a famous salon and party site. With other New York bohemians, he attended the New School for Social Research, but the extracurricular activities of Greenwich Village and, increasingly, of Harlem's *Black Arts movement, were his preferred teaching and learning venues. After marrying and fathering four children (three of them sons, bio-blurbs remind, with heroic African surnames), he departed conventional life entirely, in order, experientially and textually, to break and reformulate habits of *music, art, sex, and politics. His friends and cohorts included Bob *Kaufman, the then LeRoi Jones (Amiri *Baraka), Jack Kerouac, John *Coltrane, Stokely *Carmichael, and Allen Ginsberg; the last, according to Joans, turned him from painting to performing his *jazz, Beat, and revolutionary *poetry at clubs, public readings, and as a "Rent-a-Beatnik" jazzman before well-paying private art consumers.

Joans met and exchanged words, ideas, and influence with many key political thinkers and creative artists in and beyond the United States. His poems, performances, and legendary conversations reflect, by turns, serious, respectful, satirical, and playfully challenging engagement with André Breton ("Nadja Rendevous," "Flying Piranha," named for Breton's parrot), Langston *Hughes ("Passed on Blues: Homage to a Poet"), *Malcolm X ("The Ace of Spades"), Kwame Nkrumah ("PAN AFRICA"), and Frantz Fanon (indirectly, in "Proposition for a Black Power Manifesto"). Typical is his poetic address to Andy Warhol, whose simultaneous exploitation and exposure of popular culture's obsessive yet repressed sexuality Joans improvised into a kind of jazz chant and/or typographically experimental text, in "Pubik Pak." Refusing equally the roles of victim, respectable bourgeois, nationalist, and traditional activist, Joans's work variously assaults assimilationism and guilty white liberalism; "Mau Mau Message to Liberals," "God Blame America," and "For the Viet Congo" are representative. In erotic, angry, dramatic, and often bitterly ironic short poems, he adopts and explodes from within various limiting personae imposed upon black men, especially African Americans. In this regard, "Let's Play Something" is programmatic, while "The Underground Bitch" bears comparison with *Baraka/Jones's *Dutchman.* While he is everywhere complex, ironic, thought-provoking, and deliberately surreal, his recurrent themes of the "virgin-whore" dichotomy and mythic Mother-Africa do not endear him to empirical feminists or mainstream postcolonialists. Nevertheless, his contributions to poetic style and his critiques of *identity politics ensure continued relevance.

For his Beat period texts in context, see *The Beat Scene,* ed. Elias Wilentz (1960) and *City Lights Journal #1* (1963), which includes "Afrique Accidentale," his first poem written from Timbuctu, predicting the full range of his continuing surrealist, Marxist, French, and African commitments. In addition to being collected or translated in France, England, Italy, Germany, and South America, Joans's short political and memorial lyrics have also been anthologized by and with African American poets, including Langston Hughes and Arna *Bontemps (*The Poetry of the Negro, 1746–1970,* 1970), Gwendolyn *Brooks (*A Broadside Treasury,* 1971), and Dudley *Randall and Margaret Taylor Goss *Burroughs (*For Malcolm,* 1973, with bio-bibliography). Sonia *Sanchez published his story "A Few Fact Filled Fiction of African Reality" (*We Be Word Sorcerers,* 1973). Major poetry, prose-poems, manifestoes, and collages in English are published or reprinted by Marion Boyars, Ltd., *A Black Manifesto in Jazz Poetry and Prose* (London, 1971); *Black Pow-Wow: Jazz Poems* (London, 1973); *Afrodisia: New Poems* (London, 1976); and, with Joyce Mansour, for Bola Press, *Flying Piranha* (1978). For years he has promised and continues to live, revise, and add to "Spadework: The Autobiography of a Hipster" (sequel to the 1961 *All of Ted Joans and No More*), "I, Black Surrealist," and a *novel "Niggers from Outer Space." Splitting residence between Paris and Timbuctu, he remains part of a casual and underground, though current and international poetry scene. Relatively neglected by critics, if not by fellow poets, the few academic essays about him show a surprising range.

• Skip [Henry Louis] Gates [Jr.], "Ted Joans: Tri-Continental Poet," *Transition* (Ghana) 48 (Spring 1975): 4–12. Michel Fabre, "Ted Joans: The Surrealist Griot," in *From Harlem to Paris: Black American Writers in France,* 1992, pp. 309–323.

—Kathryne V. Lindberg

JOHN GRIMES is a central character in James *Baldwin's autobiographical first novel, *Go Tell It on the Mountain* (1953). Modeled after Baldwin himself, John is castigated for being different—intellectually, physically, and sexually. Moreover, John must negotiate a treacherous Harlem terrain where religion becomes a bulwark against the "evils" of the external world.

Part 1, "The Seventh Day," privileges John's perspective. The action commences on his fourteenth birthday, as the plaintive youth contemplates what he considers his smallness, "ugliness," and precociousness. John's stepfather, Reverend *Gabriel Grimes, is especially abusive, blaming him for all of the family's ills; their battle royal is the novel's central conflict. Baldwin skillfully integrates psychosexual

tension into this section. John's sexual thoughts are particularly vexing, as he feels guilt for masturbating and having sexual dreams about his mother and father. However, he finds an alternative to his bleak reality in Brother Elisha, an older adolescent at his family's *church who mentors him.

The novel's final section, "The Threshing-Floor," marks John's religious conversion. Baldwin weaves biblical imagery deftly into this surrealistic episode, as John undergoes a trial by fire for his soul. Though ostensibly God's voice wins, John's conversion is equivocal: He clearly appropriates Gabriel's conception of God as a weapon. John accepts Christianity only to counter his stepfather's cruelty; *religion holds no intrinsic value, and John's spiritual rebirth brings little solace. Reminiscent of such sensitive young *bildungsroman characters as Stephen Daedelus and Invisible Man, John finds his culture asphyxiating, and his tenuous position at the novel's conclusion makes him one of African American literature's most tragic adolescents.

[See also Churches; Preachers and Deacons; Sermons and Preaching.]

• Michel Fabre, "Fathers and Sons in James Baldwin's *Go Tell It on the Mountain,*" in *James Baldwin: A Collection of Critical Essays,* ed. Keneth Kinnamon, 1974, pp. 120–138. Horace A. Porter, *Stealing the Fire: The Art and Protest of James Baldwin,* 1989.

—Keith Clark

JOHN HENRY. The African American blues-ballad *John Henry* is arguably both the best-known and the greatest traditional American folk song. Its storyline is famous: When a railroad company brings in a steam drill to speed the construction of a tunnel, an African American laborer named John Henry, standing up for his rights as a worker and a human being, challenges the machine to a duel; displaying almost superhuman strength, John Henry wins the contest. In the 1920s two scholars, Guy Johnson and Louis Chappell, determined the song was based on an actual incident that probably occurred between 1870 and 1872 at the Big Bend Tunnel on the Chesapeake and Ohio Railroad in southeastern West Virginia; however, Johnson and Chappell could not trace the exact *identity of "John Henry." Regardless, John Henry has endured into the twentieth century as a folk character and popular icon among both African Americans and whites; over the years his legend has intrigued everyone from railroad workers to union organizers to artists. According to Brett Williams (*John Henry, A Bio-Bibliography,* 1983), the most influential rendering of the legend by a white author is Roark Bradford's popular *novel *John Henry* (1931), which Bradford later (1939) recast as a short-lived Broadway *musical starring Paul *Robeson as John Henry. The most acclaimed interpretation by an African American author is John O. *Killens's novel *A Man Ain't Nothin' but a Man* (1975). Keith Byerman (*Fingering the Jagged Grain,* 1985) identifies John Henry as a prototype for fictional characters like Doc Craft in James Alan *McPherson's *short story "A Solo Song: For Doc," Raoul Carmier in Ernest J. *Gaines's novel *Catherine Carmier* (1964), and Joe Pittman in Gaines's novel *The *Autobiography of

Miss Jane Pittman (1971). Several African American authors, including Margaret *Walker, Sterling A. *Brown, and Melvin B. *Tolson, have written poems that respond to the John Henry legend.

[*See also* Character Types; Folklore.]

• Guy B. Johnson, *John Henry: Tracking Down a Negro Legend*, 1929. Louis Chappell, *John Henry: A Folk-Lore Study*, 1933.
—Ted Olson

JOHNSON, AMELIA E. (1858–1922), novelist, short fiction writer, poet, and editor, who wrote under the name of "Mrs. A. E. Johnson." Born in Toronto, Canada, of parents who were natives of Maryland, Amelia Etta Hall Johnson was educated in Montreal. In 1874 she moved to Boston, where in 1877 she married Reverend Harvey Johnson of the Union Baptist Church. They had a daughter and two sons.

Interested in young people and in encouraging African American women's writing, in 1887 Johnson started an eight-page monthly, *Joy*. She contributed poems, *short stories, and articles to various *periodicals, but her reputation as a writer rests mainly on her three *novels. With the publication of *Clarence and Corinne, or God's Way* (1890), she became the first African American and the first woman to write Sunday school fiction for the American Baptist Publication Society of Philadelphia, one of the largest *publishing houses of the time.

Like other turn-of-the-century African American writers, including Emma Dunham *Kelley and Paul Laurence *Dunbar, Johnson does not explicitly mention the racial background of the characters in her novels. Nevertheless, contemporary African American reviewers praised her for writing "from affection for the race, and loyalty to it." In her racially indeterminate fiction, poverty, alcoholism, and family *violence are discussed as societal, rather than racially specific, problems.

Clarence and Corinne opens on a scene of urban poverty. After their mother's death and their father's abandonment, Corinne is exploited as a *domestic servant by her guardian, while Clarence is falsely accused of theft. Eventually all turns out well, as the siblings acquire *educations, become financially secure, and marry two childhood friends. Christian teachings dominate the novel: love for one's neighbor and faith in Divine Providence, in "God's way," are proposed as remedies for contemporary social problems.

In *The Hazeley Family* (1894), Johnson emphasizes the Christian value and social usefulness of women's "home-work." She narrates how the self-reliant, spirited performance of her household duties enables Flora Hazeley, the protagonist, to overcome despondency, reunify her family, and become an agent of moral uplift in her community. Also Johnson's last novel, *Martina Meriden, or What Is My Motive?* (1901), focuses on the importance of having a Christian outlook on life, but it is more repetitive and less readable than her previous ones.

After being out of print for almost a century, Johnson has now begun to attract serious critical attention. While all of her novels end happily, they reveal complex underlying tensions between religious orthodoxy, domestic idealism, and a concern for the limited societal opportunities available to African American women. Flora Hazeley's successful evangelical mission, for instance, ultimately leaves her in the volunteer ranks of Sunday school teachers, while her brother's religious call receives societal sanctioning in his profession as a minister. Johnson's often veiled feminist themes offer interesting insight into the literary strategies of indirect argumentation that are characteristic of much of nineteenth-century African American women's literature.

[*See also* Sunday School Literature.]

• Barbara Christian, introduction to *The Hazeley Family*, 1988. Ann Allen Shockley, *Afro-American Women Writers, 1746–1933*, 1988. Hortense J. Spillers, introduction to *Clarence and Corinne, or God's Way*, 1988. Claudia Tate, *Domestic Allegories of Political Desire: The Black Heroine's Text at the Turn of the Century*, 1992. M. Giulia Fabi, "Taming the Amazon? The Price of Survival in Turn-of-the-Century African American Women's Fiction," in *The Insular Dream: Obsession and Resistance*, ed. Kristiaan Versluys, 1995, pp. 228–241.
—M. Giulia Fabi

JOHNSON, CHARLES R. (b. 1948), novelist, essayist, critic, philosopher, illustrator, screenwriter, and playwright. Born in Evanston, Illinois, Charles Richard Johnson first manifested his creativity in the graphic arts, which he parlayed into a job as an editorial cartoonist and then into two collections of drawings—*Black Humor* (1970) and *Half-Past Nation Time* (1972)—and a drawing program on PBS (*Charley's Pad*, 1971) before finishing his undergraduate degree at Southern Illinois University at Carbondale. Having found success with visual art, Johnson turned to fiction, writing six apprentice *novels that remain unpublished and that he describes in *Being and Race* (1988) as influenced by James *Baldwin and John A. *Williams. In 1973, while doing graduate work in philosophy at Southern Illinois University Johnson studied with John Gardner, author of numerous innovative novels and influential critical books. Drawing on African American folktales, his interest in philosophy and Buddhism, and the insights he gained from Gardner, Johnson published *Faith and the Good Thing* in 1974. An intriguing amalgamation of folk wisdom and philosophical inquiry, *Faith* defines the broad parameters of Johnson's aesthetic system and has been compared to *Invisible Man* (1952), an appropriate equation given Johnson's publicly professed admiration for Ralph *Ellison.

Johnson did course work at SUNY–Stony Brook for a PhD in philosophy; he also wrote screenplays for PBS, including the story of the oldest living African American cowboy, *Charlie Smith and the Fritter Tree* (1978), and a program on Booker T. *Washington (*Booker*, 1984). He and his family relocated to Seattle, where he teaches creative writing at the University of Washington. Other publications include the novels *Oxherding Tale* (1982) and *Middle Passage* (1990 National Book Award); a collection of stories, *The Sorcerer's Apprentice* (1986); and a book of criticism, *Being and Race: Black Writing since 1970*

(1988). He continues to write in a variety of media, completing a screenplay for the *film version of *Middle Passage* in 1993.

Johnson's second and third novels, as well as the short stories, manifest developments in his philosophical-aesthetic system. Both *Oxherding Tale* and *Middle Passage* explore nineteenth-century America from a perspective both resolutely historical and endowed with insights from contemporary philosophy. Both books fuse traditional genres and established texts—*Oxherding Tale* is a *slave narrative clearly drawing on Frederick *Douglass's *Narrative*, while *Middle Passage* is a sea story with obvious Melvillian overtones—with a philosophical system founded primarily in phenomenology. Andrew Hawkins, the protagonist of *Oxherding Tale*, and *Rutherford Calhoun, the narrator of *Middle Passage*, are African American males seeking liberation from physical and/or emotional bondage. Each highly educated, they recount self-exploration and adventures that challenge readers to expand their understanding by destroying all preconceptions they may have about the nature and definition of *freedom. The philosophical experimentation Johnson carries out in these novels is bolstered by the stories in *The Sorcerer's Apprentice*, a series of examinations and applications of a variety of philosophies, and by the theoretical chapters in his critical work, *Being and Race*, which outline a program for fiction writing, ostensibly for his use in critiquing other writers, that can be read as a clear statement of his own aesthetic goals and principles.

In his experimentation with concepts of factuality and chronology, Johnson shows the influence of John A. Williams, whose *The *Man Who Cried I Am* Johnson acknowledges as an important early inspiration. His philosophical inquiries show the influence of a series of American writers, including but not limited to Herman Melville, Edgar Allen Poe, Douglass, John Gardner, and Ellison. Furthermore, the revisions of history in his work, as well as his own statements, link him with other important contemporary writers such as Ishmael *Reed.

Johnson's contributions to contemporary African American fiction include a heightened awareness of the links between philosophy and fiction; a further development of the postmodernist sensibilities of history and chronology; and the creation of one of the most compelling and interesting contemporary philosophical-fictional tropes, the Allmuseri, his utterly unique tribe of African sorcerers who appear in several stories and in his second and third novels. Through them Johnson most effectively articulates his innovative approaches to time, history, language, and truth as constructs that bear examination; they represent the full embodiment of his ideology and challenge readers' belief systems, providing an opportunity for the reader to experience the intellectual growth the narrators do through contact with the tribesmen.

Gaining recognition for his radical and significant innovations, Johnson stands as a major contemporary writer, offering a fascinating outlook on African American history, fiction, and philosophy that will greatly influence future generations.

• Charles Richard Johnson, *Being and Race: Black Writing since 1970*, 1988. William Gleason, "The Liberation of Perception: Charles Johnson's *Oxherding Tale*," *Black American Literature Forum* 25 (Winter 1991): 706–728. Jennifer Hayward, "Something to Serve: Constructs of the Feminine in Charles Johnson's *Oxherding Tale*," *Black American Literature Forum* 25 (Winter 1991): 689–703. Jonathan Little, "Charles Johnson's Revolutionary *Oxherding Tale*," *Studies in American Fiction* 19 (Autumn 1991): 141–152. Ashraf H. A. Rushdy, "The Phenomenology of the Allmuseri: Charles Johnson and the Subject of the Narrative of Slavery," *African American Review* 26 (Sept. 1992): 373–394. Jonathan Little, "An Interview with Charles Johnson," *Contemporary Literature* 34 (Summer 1993): 159–181.

—William R. Nash

JOHNSON, FENTON (1888–1958), poet, essayist, author of short stories, editor, and educator, who created works that foreshadowed the Harlem Renaissance. Fenton Johnson's first *poetry appeared in 1913, and his last was written in the 1930s. He was a midwestern poet, influenced by that region and by the city of Chicago.

Fenton Johnson was born on 7 May 1888 in Chicago. His parents were Elijah and Jesse (Taylor) Johnson; Elijah, a railroad porter, was one of the wealthiest African Americans in Chicago. Johnson described himself as "having scribbled since the age of nine" but originally planned to join the clergy. He attended public school in Chicago and then enrolled at the University of Chicago. Johnson also attended Northwestern University and Columbia University's journalism school. He taught briefly at the State University at Louisville, a private, black Baptist-owned school in Kentucky. After his marriage to Cecilia Rhone, Johnson spent his artistic years primarily in Chicago and New York City.

Johnson produced three books of poetry, *A Little Dreaming* (1913), *Visions of the Dark* (1915), and *Songs of the Soil* (1916). All three books, which received some favorable critical notice, were directly subsidized by the author himself. In the first collection, Johnson uses a lyrical, "Victorian" style reminiscent of Paul Laurence *Dunbar. By the third collection, Johnson is experimenting with *dialect poetry in both traditional and personal idioms. Regardless of style, this early poetry provides glimpses of the despairing tone that is so memorable in his later works.

Fenton Johnson did not limit himself to poetry; he published a collection of short stories, *Tales of Darkest America* (1920), and a book of *essays, *For the Highest Good* (1920). He founded and edited literary magazines, and was also a playwright. By the age of nineteen, he says, his plays had been "produced on the stage of the old Pekin Theatre, Chicago." His playwrighting continued through 1925 at least, when "The Cabaret Girl" was performed at the Shadow Theatre in Chicago. This title is the only record of Johnson's plays; no scripts are extant.

Fenton Johnson continued producing poetry for *anthologies and journals until the 1930s. Critics have judged this later work as among Johnson's best. He increasingly used free verse forms and explored his own urban experiences. Influenced in later years by Carl Sandburg and other midwestern authors, Johnson wrote of the despair and fatalism that was part of his African American experience. Johnson's final literary collection of around forty poems, posthumously published, was created during the Works Project Association's "Negro in Illinois" program. After the 1930s, the only connection Johnson retained to the artistic community in which he was previously so active was a correspondence with Arna *Bontemps. Johnson died in 1958, at the age of seventy.

Although often judged as a minor poet who merely prefigured the *Harlem Renaissance, Fenton Johnson always exhibited a keen racial consciousness. His best work goes beyond foreshadowing to consistently give voice to a largely silent strain of despair and realism among American and African American culture.

• Countee Cullen, ed., *Caroling Dusk: An Anthology of Verse by Negro Poets,* 1927; rpt. 1955. James P. Draper, ed., *Black Literary Criticism of the Most Significant Works of Black Authors over the Past 200 Years,* vol. 2, 1992.

—Elizabeth Sanders Delwiche Engelhardt

JOHNSON, GEORGIA DOUGLAS (1880–1966), poet of the Harlem Renaissance. Born in Atlanta, Georgia, Georgia Douglas Johnson made her way to Washington, D.C., where she lived for over fifty years at 1461 S Street NW, site of one of the greatest literary salons of the *Harlem Renaissance. Johnson was the most famous woman poet of that literary movement, publishing four volumes of *poetry: *The Heart of a Woman* (1918), *Bronze* (1922), *An Autumn Love Cycle* (1928), and *Share My World* (1962).

Johnson's life illustrates the difficulties faced by African American women writers in the first half of the century. A graduate of Atlanta University (1896), where she met her husband, Henry Lincoln Johnson, Georgia Douglas Johnson did not publish her first poem until 1916, when she was thirty-six, and she remained geographically removed from the major literary circles of her day, which were in Harlem, due to her marriage to a Washington lawyer and civil employee. Her husband, moreover, expected her to look after the home and assume primary responsibility for the upbringing of two sons. When he died in 1925, Georgia Douglas Johnson was forty-five years old with two teenagers to support. Holding a series of temporary jobs between 1924 and 1934 as a substitute public school teacher and a file clerk for the Civil Service, she ultimately found a position with the Commissioner of Immigration for the Department of Labor, where hours were long and pay low. Johnson had to create her own supportive environment by establishing the Saturday night open houses that she hosted weekly soon after her husband's death and that included Langston *Hughes, Jean *Toomer, Anne *Spencer, Alain *Locke, Jessie Redmon *Fauset, and others. Although it was hard for her to write, she was able to follow through on her successes with her first two volumes of poetry by completing a third volume in 1928 that is arguably her best. *An Autumn Love Cycle* confirmed Johnson as the first African American woman poet to garner

national attention since Frances Ellen Watkins *Harper. Johnson traveled extensively in the late 1920s, giving lectures and readings, meeting Carl Sandburg in Chicago and Charles Waddell *Chesnutt in Cleveland while receiving awards from various organizations, including her alma mater, Atlanta University. She was able to send her sons to Howard University, where they studied law and medicine, while maintaining a demanding work and travel schedule.

Through the pioneering work of Gloria Hull, we now know that Johnson wrote a substantial number of plays during the 1920s, including *Plumes,* which won first prize in a contest run by *Opportunity* in 1927, and *Blue Blood,* performed by the Krigwa Players in New York City during the fall of 1926 and published the following year. Twenty-eight dramas are listed in the "Catalogue of Writings" that Johnson compiled in 1962–1963, but only a handful have been recovered. She also listed a book-length manuscript about her literary salon, a collection of short stories, and a novel, which were lost as well. Of thirty-one short stories listed in her catalog, only three have been located, under the pseudonym of Paul Tremaine (two of these were published in Dorothy *West's journal *Challenge* in 1936 and 1937). Probably much of this material was thrown away by workers clearing out Johnson's house when she died in 1966.

Georgia Douglas Johnson's prolific writing career also included a weekly *newspaper column, "Homely Philosophy," that was syndicated by twenty publications from 1926 to 1932; a collaboration with composer Lillian Evanti in the late 1940s that made use of Johnson's earlier *music training at Oberlin Conservatory and the Cleveland College of Music; and an international correspondence club that she organized and ran from 1930 to 1965. Her writing was seriously curtailed by the loss of her Department of Labor job in 1934. She then sought any work she could get, including temporary jobs in a clerical pool, while vainly applying for arts fellowships. As late as the 1960s, Johnson was still applying for fellowships that never materialized. Able to survive by living with her lawyer son, Henry Lincoln, Jr., and his wife, Johnson never lost her enthusiasm for the arts nor her generosity to needy artists who came her way. She called her home "Half-Way House" to represent her willingness to provide shelter to those in need, including, at one point, Zora Neale *Hurston. The rose-covered walk at 1461 S Street, created by Johnson fifty years ago, still stands in testimony to the many African American artists she welcomed and to the love poetry for which she is best known. Struggling without the material support that would have helped bring more of her work to light and battling racist *stereotypes that fed lynch mobs and race riots in the formative years of her life, Georgia Douglas Johnson left a legacy of indomitable pride and creative courage that has only begun to be understood.

• Erlene Stetson, ed., *Black Sister: Poetry by Black American Women, 1746–1980,* 1981. Gloria T. Hull, *Color, Sex, and Poetry: Three Women Writers of the Harlem Renaissance,* 1987. Ann Allen Shockley, ed., *Afro-American Women Writers, 1746–1933,* 1988. Maureen Honey, ed., *Shadowed Dreams: Women's Poetry of the Harlem Renaissance,* 1989. Elizabeth

Brown-Guillory, ed., *Wines in the Wilderness: Plays by African American Women from the Harlem Renaissance to the Present,* 1990. Lorraine Elena Roses and Ruth Elizabeth Randolph, eds., *Harlem, Renaissance and Beyond: Literary Biographies of 100 Black Women Writers, 1900–1945,* 1990.

—Maureen Honey

JOHNSON, HELENE

JOHNSON, HELENE (1906–1995), poet of the late Harlem Renaissance. When Helene Johnson and her cousin, novelist Dorothy *West, moved from their native Boston to Harlem in 1926, Johnson demonstrated particular promise with competent lyrics extolling romance and nature, and with fresh themes of racial self-respect that prefigured the *Black Arts movement writings of the 1960s and 1970s. But Helene Johnson never fulfilled early expectations, probably because her *poetry replicates to a greater degree than most the aesthetic confusion that beset *Harlem Renaissance literature generally.

Johnson's lifetime output amounts to a little over two dozen uncollected poems, appearing mostly in periodicals such as *Opportunity,* the *Messenger,* the *Saturday Evening Quill,* and *Vanity Fair.* Poems such as "Remember Not" and "Invocation" evoke romantic images of nature and death. For example, Johnson portrays the life cycle as returning to mother earth enclosed in a rain-drenched wooden casket, its polished wood and the cadaver becoming equals through the leveling process of death, as both gradually return to a more primordial state of nature in an unmowed plot overrun, "[r]iotous, rampant, wild and free." Such sentimentalism at once reveals Johnson's mastery of outdated poetic forms and her alienation from the aesthetic spirit of those Harlem Renaissance artists who tried to focus concretely and candidly on African American experience.

Johnson tries to deal with distinctively African American material in "Poem," which, while hailed at the time for its bold racial theme, reveals an ambiguous emotional connection to everyday African Americans. Contrary to the claim of Margaret Perry (*Silence to the Drums: A Survey of the Literature of the Harlem Renaissance,* 1976) that Johnson's work lacks artificial expression, Johnson here creates a contrived and idealized "jazz prince," whose tilted head and "patent-leathered feet" show him to be completely at ease with his racial heritage. Nonetheless, his demeanor also evinces the stereotypical image of flashily dressed African Americans often held by white and black racists. She reinforces this hackneyed portrait by evoking African tom-toms. The primitivism and racial condescension expose the conflicted nature of Harlem Renaissance writers, whose middle-class upbringings and poetic visions apparently limited their abilities to capture the lives of the African American masses. Furthermore, Johnson's poetry all too often displays the self-rejection characteristic of many Harlem Renaissance writings. Thus, Johnson's proud African American prince does not wear his hair natural but so greased down that it "shines in the spotlight." By the end of the poem, Johnson's professed joy in race has turned sarcastic with the speaker mocking the admired "boy."

• Raymond R. Patterson, "Helene Johnson," in *DLB,* vol. 51, *Afro-American Writers from the Harlem Renaissance to 1940,* ed. Trudier Harris, 1987, pp. 164–167. T. J. Bryan, "Helene Johnson," in *Notable Black American Women,* ed. Jessie Carney Smith, 1992, pp. 587–591.

—SallyAnn H. Ferguson

JOHNSON, JACK

JOHNSON, JACK (1878–1946), prizefighter. Despite the tissue of untruths that fill *In the Ring—and Out,* Jack Johnson's 1927 *autobiography, there is little doubt that even here he remained unyieldingly the auteur of his own mythology, that is, on the one indisputably true claim he made about the book. He wrote the book himself, without a ghost-writer. He is one of only, at best, a handful of star athletes who can say that.

Born in Galveston, Texas, on 31 March 1878, Johnson was the most charismatic and the most notorious African American figure in the American popular culture of his day.

He became the first black heavyweight champion in 1908. Johnson's fight against great white hope, Jim Jeffries, in July 1910, was the most discussed sporting event in American history at the time. Johnson easily won the fight but race riots broke out all over the country afterward. In Cuba in 1915, he lost the title to Jess Willard, a fight Johnson always claimed he threw.

There are few individuals in African American history who figured more prominently in black intellectual thinking and black *folklore than Johnson. He was discussed in pieces by Booker T. *Washington, W. E. B. *Du Bois, Reverdy Ransom, and others at the turn of the century. James Weldon *Johnson knew him well and talked of him at length in *Along This Way* (1933) and *Black Manhattan* (1930). Writers such as Richard *Wright and Ralph *Ellison used him symbolically in their fiction. Without question, for a time, until the coming of Joe *Louis and World War II, Johnson dominated the thinking of some blacks when they considered a certain type of black rebellion or black masculinity. Indeed, his impact has been such that his name comes up whenever a famous black male is mentioned or connected to scandal or conspicuously displays a sexual preference for white women. Johnson died in Raleigh, North Carolina, in 1946 from injuries sustained in a car accident.

—Gerald Early

JOHNSON, JAMES WELDON

JOHNSON, JAMES WELDON (1871–1938), songwriter, poet, novelist, journalist, critic, and autobiographer. James Weldon Johnson, much like his contemporary W. E. B. *Du Bois, was a man who bridged several historical and literary trends. Born in 1871, during the optimism of the Reconstruction period, in Jacksonville, Florida, Johnson was imbued with an eclectic set of talents. Over the course of his sixty-seven years, Johnson was the first African American admitted to the Florida bar since the end of Reconstruction; the cocomposer (with his brother John Rosamond) of *"Lift Every Voice and Sing," the song that would later become known as the Negro National Anthem; field secretary in the

NAACP; journalist; publisher; diplomat; educator; translator; librettist; anthologist; and English professor; in addition to being a well-known poet and novelist and one of the prime movers of the *Harlem Renaissance.

As the first son of James Johnson and the former Helen Louise Dillet, James Weldon inherited his forebears' combination of industrious energy and public-mindedness, as demonstrated by his maternal grandfather's long life in public service in the Bahamas, where he served in the House of Assembly for thirty years. James, Sr., spent many years as the headwaiter of the St. James Hotel in Jacksonville, Florida, where he had moved the family after his sponge fishing and dray businesses were ruined by a hurricane that hit the Bahamas in 1866. James, Jr., was born and educated in Jacksonville, first by his mother, who taught for many years in the public schools, and later by James C. Walter, the well-educated but stern principal of the Stanton School. Graduating at the age of sixteen, Johnson enrolled in Atlanta University, from which he graduated in 1894. After graduation, Johnson, though only twenty-three, returned to the Stanton School to become its principal.

In 1895, Johnson founded the *Daily American*, a newspaper devoted to reporting on issues pertinent to the black community. Though the paper only lasted a year (with Johnson doing most of the work himself for eight of those months) before it succumbed to financial hardship, it addressed racial injustice and, in keeping with Johnson's upbringing, asserted a self-help philosophy that echoed Booker T. *Washington. Of the demise of the paper he wrote in his *autobiography, *Along This Way*, "The failure of the *Daily American* was my first taste of defeat in public life. . . ." However the effort was not a total failure, for both Washington and his main rival, W. E. B. Du Bois, became aware of Johnson through his journalistic efforts, leading to opportunities in later years.

Turning to the study of law, Johnson studied with a young, white lawyer named Thomas A. Ledwith. But despite the fact that he built up a successful law practice in Jacksonville, Johnson soon tired of the law (his practice had been conducted concurrently with his duties as principal of the Stanton School). When his brother returned to Jacksonville after graduating from the New England Conservatory of Music in 1897, James's poems provided the lyrics for Rosamond's early songs. By the end of the decade, both brothers were in New York, providing compositions to Broadway *musicals. There they met Bob Cole, whom Johnson described as a man of such immense talent that he could "write a play, stage it, and play a part."

The brothers split their time between Jacksonville and New York for a number of years before settling in New York for good. However, their greatest composition, the one for which they are best known, was written for a Stanton School celebration of *Lincoln's birthday. "Lift Every Voice and Sing" was a song that, as Johnson put it, the brothers let pass "out of [their] minds," after it had been published.

But the song's importance grew from the students, who remembered it and taught it to other students throughout the South, until some twenty years later it was adopted by the NAACP as the "Negro National Hymn."

It was this kind of creativity under duress, coupled with his connections in the political sphere, that characterized Johnson's life as an artist and activist. Indeed, between the years 1914 and 1931, his desire to explore the limits of both worlds led him to seek a more thorough synthesis of his public and artistic sensibilities. The study of literature, which Johnson began around 1904 under the tutelage of the critic and novelist Brander Matthews, who was then teaching at Columbia University, caused Johnson to withdraw from the Cole/Johnson partnership to pursue a life as a writer. However, this creative impulse coincided with his decision in 1906 to serve as United States consul to Venezuela, a post that Washington's political connections with the Roosevelt administration helped to secure.

During the three years he held this post, Johnson completed his only *novel, The *Autobiography of an Ex-Colored Man*, which he published anonymously in 1912. Though many read the novel as a sociological document, its true value lies in the manner in which it recasts the "tragic *mulatto" story within the context of Du Bois's metaphor of the veil. The novel sparked renewed interest when Johnson announced in 1927 that he had authored the book as fiction. Indeed, so great was the public propensity to equate the novel's hero with Johnson himself that Johnson felt obliged to write his autobiography, which appeared in 1933 under the title *Along This Way*.

He had, by this time, established himself as an important figure in the Harlem Renaissance. From his post as field secretary of the NAACP, Johnson was a witness to the changes taking place in the artistic sphere. As a prominent voice in the literary debates of the day, Johnson undertook the task of editing The Book of American Negro Poetry (1922), The Book of American Negro Spirituals (1925), The Second Book of American Negro Spirituals (1926), and writing his survey of African American cultural contributions to the New York artistic scene in Black Manhattan (1930). His own career as a poet reached its culmination in *God's Trombones, Seven Negro Sermons in Verse*, published in 1927. Though not noted for playing the role of polemicist, through each of these literary enterprises Johnson worked to refute biased commentary from white critics while prodding African American writers toward a more ambitious vision of literary endeavor. It was Johnson's great hope that the contributions of younger writers would do for African Americans, "what [John Millington] Synge did for the Irish," namely utilizing folk materials to "express the racial spirit [of African Americans] from within, rather than [through] symbols from without. . . ." Hence Johnson's attempt to discredit Negro dialect, a literary convention characterized by misspellings and malapropisms, which in Johnson's view was capable of conveying only pathos or *humor. Though writers like Zora Neale *Hurston and Sterling A. *Brown would challenge this viewpoint, Johnson's point must be understood within the context of his life as a public figure.

With the arrival of the 1930s, Johnson had seen the NAACP's membership rolls and political influence increase, though the latter failed to produce tangible legislative and social reform in Washington. Retiring to a life as Professor of Creative Literature and Writing at Fisk University, Johnson lectured widely on the topics of racial advancement and civil rights, while completing *Negro Americans, What Now?* (1934), a book that argued for the merits of racial integration and cooperation, and his last major verse collection, *Saint Peter Relates an Incident: Selected Poems* (1934). Though he died in a tragic automobile accident while vacationing in Maine in June of 1938, Johnson continues to be remembered for his unflappable integrity and his devotion to human service.

• James Weldon Johnson, *Along This Way*, 1933; rpt. 1968. Eugene Levy, *James Weldon Johnson*, 1973. Robert E. Fleming, ed., *James Weldon Johnson and Arna Bontemps: A Reference Guide*, 1978. Carolyn Wedin Sylvander, "Johnson, James Weldon," in *Encyclopedia of World Literature in the Twentieth Century*, vol. 2, ed. Leonard S. Klein, 1982, pp. 517–518. Robert E. Fleming, *James Weldon Johnson*, 1987. Joseph T. Skerritt, "James Weldon Johnson," in *African American Writers*, eds. Lea Baechler, A. Walton Litz, and Valerie Smith, 1991, pp. 219–233.   —Herman Beavers

JOHNSON, WILLIAM (1809–1851), diarist. William Johnson's thirteen-volume, sixteen-year journal of life in Natchez, Mississippi, is the lengthiest and most detailed personal narrative authored by an African American during the antebellum era in the United States. Out of ordinary account books in which he tallied the daily expenditures and income of his early business ventures, Johnson's diary evolved into an extraordinary record of social, economic, and political life in his hometown of Natchez, Mississippi, as seen through the eyes of a free man of color.

Johnson was born a slave in Natchez, the son of his white master, William Johnson, and his slave, Amy. Johnson's father manumitted him in 1820. He was soon apprenticed to his free brother-in-law, Natchez barbershop proprietor James Miller. At the age of twenty-one, Johnson purchased Miller's barbershop, the first step in the young businessman's rise in the 1830s to a position of affluence as a property-holder, moneylender, land speculator, and slave-owner in the town of his birth. In 1835, Johnson married, completed a three-story brick home for his new family, and began on 12 October the diary he was to keep until the day of his death in 1851, the victim of a shooting over a land-boundary dispute.

In his diary Johnson writes most of the time as a self-appointed unofficial local historian. But on the occasions when he speaks of his own situation he provides a unique personal perspective on what it was like to negotiate daily the social margins of a slaveholding society.

[See also Diaries and Journals; Slavery; Miscegenation.]

• Edwin Adams Davis and William Ransom Hogan, *The Barber of Natchez*, 1954. William Ransom Hogan and Edwin Adams Davis, eds., *William Johnson's Natchez: The Ante-Bellum Diary of a Free Negro*, 1993.

—William L. Andrews

Jonah's Gourd Vine. When publisher Bertram Lippincott read Zora Neale *Hurston's *short story "The Gilded Six-Bits" in *Story* magazine in August 1933, he wrote to inquire whether she was working on a *novel. She was, and by early October she sent him the manuscript of *Jonah's Gourd Vine*. It was published the following May. Loosely based on the lives of Hurston's parents, *Jonah* tells the story of Lucy and John Pearson's courtship and marriage, John's swift rise to prominence as a Baptist preacher, his equally swift fall, Lucy's strength and perseverance, and the family's ultimate dissolution. All this takes place against a background of social and technological change occurring in the South at the turn of the century. These changes are subordinate to the cultural traditions that remain intact: the sermons, work songs, courtship rituals, aphorisms, children's rhymes, and hoodoo beliefs and practices. In the foreground are the experiences of Lucy and John.

In their hometown of Notasulga, Alabama, Lucy is a daughter of a well-to-do farmer, while John's family lives "over-the-creek." She excels in the classroom, while he has mastered the arts of the vernacular culture. After marrying Lucy, John decides to move the family to Florida, where his preaching wins him respect and status. But John's philandering costs him that respect and he almost loses his pastorate, until Lucy advises him how to win it back. He does, but resentful of her help, he soon is caught in the same sin. After Lucy dies, he remarries quickly and unwisely. The novel ends when John, married a third time, is killed when his car is hit by a train, the image the novel associates with him.

As Hurston confided to fellow writer James Weldon *Johnson, her protagonist represents the love of eloquence and beauty that she believed was pervasive among African Americans. But John was to represent more: in the pulpit "he becomes the voice of the spirit." As is true throughout Hurston's fiction, the spirit invoked in the novel fuses Christian theology and African belief, imaged here as the drum. Yet the novel never adequately explores the reasons John, the gifted preacher-poet, repeatedly contravenes the dictates of the spirit and misreads his own metaphors.

Lucy is also unable to achieve an *identity between word and deed, even though she possesses the insight that her husband lacks. In a passage echoed in the maternal deathbed scene in Hurston's *autobiography, *Dust Tracks on a Road* (1942), Lucy Pearson warns her daughter, "Don't you love nobody better'n you do yo'self. Do you'll be dying befo' yo' time is out." Loving John too much, Lucy has acquiesced in her own suppression. At her death, she remains on the threshold of self-discovery.

Jonah brims with the lore Hurston had spent six intensive years collecting. Some critics argue that the folk materials overwhelm the narrative. But others assert that *Jonah* is an experimental novel that dramatizes Hurston's theories of African American culture, particularly its African retentions and the primacy of spirituality.

[*See also* Folklore; Preachers and Deacons; Sermons and Preaching; Speech and Dialect.]

—Cheryl A. Wall

JONES, GAYL (b. 1949), novelist, poet, playwright, professor, and literary critic. Born in Lexington, Kentucky, a state that surfaces in much of her work, Gayl Jones has forged an eclectic career, marked by periods of silence, and since the early 1980s, a withdrawal from public existence. Jones began merging academic and creative pursuits early in her life; she was writing stories while in second grade and, as an undergraduate at Connecticut College in 1971, received the college's award for best original poem in 1969 and 1970. Her story "The Roundhouse" also won the Frances Steloff Award for Fiction in 1970. By 1975 she had earned an MA and a DA in creative writing at Brown University and had published *Corregidora*, her first novel. (Her editor for *Corregidora* and *Eva's Man*, the novel that followed it in 1976, was Toni *Morrison, then at Random House.) While still a graduate student Jones also published the play *Chile Woman* (1974) and *The Ancestor: A Street Play*. From Brown, Jones went on to become an assistant professor of English and Afro-American and African Studies at the University of Michigan. In 1975 she received the Howard Foundation Award, followed first by a National Endowment for the Arts Fellowship in 1976, and then by a fellowship from the Michigan Society of Fellows for the years 1977 to 1979.

An associate professor when she left Michigan in the early 1980s, Jones has since kept her life exceedingly private. Her reclusiveness is perhaps best illustrated, if not explained, by her once stating that she most wanted to resemble those writers who, like J. D. Salinger, are known solely by their work, not their personal lives.

For Jones that work has taken a diverse array of forms: two plays, two novels, a collection of short fiction, three books of *poetry, and, in 1991, a scholarly work examining the intersections between African American oral traditions and African American fiction—intersections for which her own fiction is noted as well. In various interviews Jones has emphasized the role of listening in her formation as a writer. The person to whom she listened first, and most closely, was her mother, herself a fiction writer. Lucille Jones would read to her children the stories she wrote for them. Additionally, because Gayl and her brother were never banished from the room when adults were talking, they grew up hearing the stories of older generations, an experience that probably catalyzed Jones's interest in exploring histories in her own fiction. The stories she listened to intrigued her with their form as well as their content, the myriad dialects, shifts, and cadences of African American voices. In fact, perhaps the single strongest element in Jones's work is its evocation of human speech; she has said that she had to hear something before she could write it.

Not surprisingly, Jones has been influenced by a wide-ranging group of artists whose voices she felt were true, including Alice *Walker, Ernest J. *Gaines, Geoffrey Chaucer, James Joyce, Michael S. *Harper, Miguel de Cervantes, Ernest Hemingway, Carlos Fuentes, Gabriel García Márquez, and Zora Neale *Hurston (although Jones has argued that Hurston's anthropological perspective distanced her from her created dialogue). And, since much of her work sings as well as speaks, musicians like Ma *Rainey, Billie *Holiday, and Ella Fitzgerald are also important to Jones.

The kind of language that stems from the call-and-response of black sermons, the improvisational motifs of *jazz, and the repetitions of the *blues structures Jones's early play *Chile Woman*, and is particularly evident in the form and "ritualistic" dialogue of *Corregidora*. Composed of bluesy refrains, lyrical monologues, and fantastic dream sequences, *Corregidora*'s form shares much with that of *Eva's Man*. Both works also display Jones's preoccupation with the manifold dimensions of language through their deliberate echoes of African American dialects and colloquialisms. To a lesser extent, *Corregidora*'s combined emphasis on family history and the virulence of racial and sexual persecution recurs in Jones's second novel. Yet it is *Corregidora* that best depicts what Jones has called the "blues relationship" between men and women: a relationship that, like the blues, encompasses both good and bad, both tenderness and *violence. Moreover, the blues' acknowledgment of simultaneous opposites helps to define Jones's authorial stance. While she recognizes the importance of political strategies for writers, Jones refuses to allow her work to be hemmed in by a political agenda. In locating the cultural and historical influences at work in the lives she depicts, Jones avoids pigeonholing her characters into politically correct categories—particularly characters that function merely as uplifting African American role models. In fact, some readers have criticized her insistence on creating literature that does not conform to positive images of black women and men (see especially her interview with Claudia Tate in Tate's *Black Women Writers at Work*, 1983).

Jones's fiction often uses violence to illustrate the interconnectedness of public events and personal lives, portraying, for example, the twentieth-century repercussions of *slavery in the Americas for black families. Perhaps most notably, her work graphically probes the harsh fusing of racism and sexism, documenting the ways in which sex can be used to degrade and brutalize primarily women (but also men) in *Corregidora*, *Eva's Man*, and the short-story collection *White Rat* (1977; rpt. 1991). In depicting sexual relationships under the double rubric of power and coercion, both heterosexual and lesbian, Jones gives some of the most unflinching renderings of sex and desire in contemporary fiction, descriptions made all the more striking by her deliberately stark, colloquial language. Yet it could be argued that several of *White Rat*'s stories make up the broadest arena for Jones's writing about sexual relations. In "The Women," a young girl tersely recalls her mother's series of lesbian relationships as she discovers her own hetero-sexuality, yet the story closes on a troubling note as the choice she makes seems half-forced upon her. In-explicable and often degrading sexual passions struc-ture "Jevata," while "Persona" deals with a female professor's silenced desire for other women. *White Rat* also gives evidence of Jones's experimentation in forms of the vernacular, ranging from the earthy prose of the title story's narrator to the rich, interior realm of madness in "Version Two," to the deliberate spare opacity of "Your Poems Have Little Color in Them"—a story that examines an artist's difficulties with both speaking and not speaking, and with story-telling. Since, according to Jones, this last is the only piece in the collection that touches on *autobiogra-phy, it may reveal some motive for the fact that, with *White Rat*, Jones stopped publishing fiction.

Most likely as a result of her mother's strong in-fluence on her, as well as that of her grandmother, playwright Amanda Wilson, Jones has also worked powerful treatments of the relationships between daughters, mothers, grandmothers, and great-grand-mothers into her fiction, especially in terms of shared histories, issues of speech and victimization, and ac-countability for the future. Interestingly, *Corregidora*'s theme of establishing those "generations" who will keep alive a familial history has a parallel in the au-thor's personal life. Jones recalls her mother's asking about her own responsibility for making generations, a responsibility that Jones has said she regards with a combined sense of guilt and ambivalence.

Jones's *poetry has been published in several liter-ary magazines, but also in three separate works: *Song for Anninho* (1981), *The Hermit Woman* (1983), and *Xarque and Other Poems* (1985). Some poems echo African American musical traditions, particu-larly pieces like "Deep Song," a "blues poem" that Jones wrote while listening to the Billie Holiday song of the same name. The Brazilian slave histories that underpin *Corregidora* take center stage in *Song for Anninho*, a prose poem about a love story between two escaped slaves in seventeenth-century Brazil. Like her fiction, much of her poetry is told from the first-person viewpoint, and is concerned with the complexities of love between men and women.

Jones's most recent book, *Liberating Voices: Oral Tradition in African American Literature* (1991), takes her fictional concerns into the realm of literary criti-cism and analysis. Her text examines the influence of dialect, *folklore, blues, and *spirituals in the po-etry of Harper, Paul Laurence *Dunbar, Langston *Hughes, and Sherley Anne *Williams; and also in authors like Hurston, Jean *Toomer, Ann *Petry, Ralph *Ellison, and Toni Morrison. The diversity of Jones's influences echoes in her critical focus, which finds in her selected authors a combination of Euro-pean and American literary traditions and African and African American oral forms.

Like Alice Walker, Jones has been criticized for what some readers see as a recurrent indictment against black men, particularly in her two novels' bleak portraits of abusive husbands and lovers. Yet such criticism is countered by a recognition of those characters' own troubled legacies of racial injustices,

as well as by *White Rat*, which offers several complex renderings of basically good-hearted men. Perhaps a more accurate appraisal of Jones's treatment of African American men—and women—would en-compass her resolute account of the ways in which racism and sexism build upon each other, victimizing both sexes. Certainly, her stern gaze makes for grim reading. Yet that grimness is inextricable from the other qualities of Jones's work: vivid delineation of the physical details of sexual desire, and a deliberate implementation of black oral forms stemming from communal speech patterns, folklore, sermons, jazz, and the blues. Together, these qualities place Jones's writing firmly within that literature that melds the substance and the form of African American cultural history.

[*See also* Eva Medina Canada; Ursa Corregidora.]

• Gayl Jones, "Gayl Jones: An Interview," interview by Michael S. Harper, *Massachusetts Review* 18.4 (Winter 1977): 692–715. Gayl Jones, "Gayl Jones Takes a Look at Corregi-dora—An Interview," interview by Roseann P. Bell, *Sturdy Black Bridges: Visions of Black Women in Literature*, eds. Roseann P. Bell et al., 1979, pp. 282–287. Valerie Gray Lee, "The Use of Folktalk in Novels by Black Women Writers," *CLA Journal* 23 (Mar. 1980): 266–272. Trudier Harris, "A Spiritual Journey: Gayl Jones's *Song for Anninho*," *Callaloo* 5.3 (Oct. 1982): 105–111. Gayl Jones, "An Interview with Gayl Jones," interview by Charles H. Rowell, *Callaloo* 5.3 (Oct. 1982): 32–53. Gayl Jones, "About My Work," in *Black Women Writers (1950–1980)*, ed. Mari Evans, 1984, pp. 233–235. Jerry W. Ward, Jr., "Escape From Trublem: The Fic-tion of Gayl Jones," in *Black Women Writers (1950–1980)*, ed. Mari Evans, 1984, pp. 249–257. Mae G. Henderson, fore-word to *White Rat*, 1977; rpt. 1991.

—Amy S. Gottfried

JONES, LeROI. *See* Baraka, Amiri.

JONES-MEADOWS, KAREN (b.1953), playwright, television and film script writer, producer, actress, and educator. Karen Jones-Meadows was born in Queens, New York, and grew up in the Bronx. As a child, she knew she would become an actress and a writer and therefore appointed herself as the spokesperson for her extended family.

After seeing the Negro Ensemble Company's pro-duction of *The River Niger* (Joseph A. *Walker, 1973) during her college years, she determined to become involved in that particular *theater and began to write plays. *Henrietta*, the first play she marketed for production and the second play she had ever written, was produced Off-Broadway by the Negro Ensemble Company in 1985. The play is one of ten chosen by Woodie *King, Jr., to be included in a forthcoming *anthology featuring recent plays produced by the ten major African American theaters in the United States.

By the mid-1990s, *Henrietta* was Jones-Meadows's most-produced play because, as she explains, it is "delicately poignant." The play chronicles the growing relationship between Henrietta, a lovable Harlem bag lady, and Sheleeah, a young upwardly mobile accountant. It is representative of Jones-Meadows's work in its spicy, realistic dialogue and strong lead character. Jones-Meadows's emphasis on the maternal relationship that develops between Henrietta and Sheleeah also situates the play within a tradition of contemporary African American women's writing in which matrifocal relationships are frequently and powerfully represented.

Jones-Meadows's next play to be produced was *Tapman* (1988), and it garnered six Audelco Award nominations. Like *Henrietta*, the play features a strong lead character, an aging *blues musician who must confront the end of his career, his alcoholism, and a tense family situation. Indeed, *Tapman's* life as well as his music are characterized by the blues.

Tapman was followed by *Major Changes* (1989), which won the fourth annual Cornerstone Competition sponsored by the Penumbra Theatre Company of St. Paul, Minnesota. Once again, this play highlights the life of one main character, Major Anderson, a man who killed his best friend. Like Jones-Meadows's other plays, *Major Changes* has freedom of self-expression and the need for spiritual transformation as themes.

The recurring theme of spirituality is perhaps most evident in *Crystals* (1994), which incorporates a multiethnic, multiracial cast and shifts in time to convey a global vision. Jones-Meadows illustrates that the quest for *freedom, which is so much a part of American and African American culture, is a universal human desire.

Other plays by Jones-Meadows include *Mystery Cycle Plays* (1989), *In the Name of the Woman* (1993), *Harriet's Return!* (1994), and two plays for young adults, *Private Conversations* (1991–1992) and *Everybody's Secret* (1994). Jones-Meadows has also written and produced several scripts for *television and *film. She has a BS in early childhood education from Wheelock College in Boston and has worked as a teacher, health educator, and arts administrator. She has also been a visiting professor at Davidson College in North Carolina, and leads ongoing writing and acting workshops for adults and youths.

- Floyd Eugene Eddleman, "Karen Jones-Meadows," in *American Drama Criticism: Supplement III to the Second Edition*, 1992, pp. 154–155. Christy Gavin, "Jones-Meadows, Karen," in *American Women Playwrights, 1964–1989: A Research Guide and Annotated Bibliography*, 1993, pp. 246–247.
—E. Barnsley Brown

JORDAN, JUNE (b. 1936), poet, novelist, essayist, playwright, educator, activist, biographer, and anthologist. In addition to her distinguished career as a college professor, June Jordan is a well-known, prolific writer of *poetry, *children's and young adult literature, and *essays. She has earned critical praise and popular recognition for her exceptional literary skill and her social and political acumen. Having come of age as a writer and cultural commentator during the "second renaissance" of African American arts in the 1960s and 1970s, Jordan is among the significant artists of this cultural revival and of the rise of black consciousness in the 1960s.

Born in Harlem, New York, on 9 July 1936, June Jordan is the only child of Granville Ivanhoe Jordan and Mildred Maud (Fisher) Jordan, who came to the United States from Jamaica. Jordan grew up in the Bedford-Stuyvesant section of Brooklyn, but as a teenager she commuted to Midwood High School, where she was the only African American student. After one year at Midwood, her parents transferred her to the Northfield School for Girls in Massachusetts (later joined with Mount Hermon), a preparatory school which she found to be even less hospitable to the development of her African American *identity.

After graduating from high school in 1953, Jordan entered Barnard College in New York City. There she met Michael Meyer, a white Columbia University student, whom she married in 1955. Jordan accompanied Meyer later that year to the University of Chicago, where he engaged in graduate study in anthropology, and she also enrolled in the university. She returned to Barnard in 1956 before finally leaving in February 1957. In 1958 the couple's only child, Christopher David Meyer, was born. Prior to the couple's divorce in 1965, Jordan had assumed full responsibility for their son, accepting a position in 1963 as an assistant to the producer for Shirley Clarke's film about Harlem, *The Cool World*.

Jordan established her writing career with the publication in the 1960s of stories and poems (under the name June Meyer) in periodicals including *Esquire*, the *Nation*, *Evergreen Review*, *Partisan Review*, *Black World*, *Black Creation*, *Essence*, the *Village Voice*, the *New York Times*, and the *New York Times Magazine*. Her writing came to national attention in 1969, when Crowell published her first book of poetry, *Who Look at Me*, a collection of works that depict interracial relations and African American experiences of self-definition in a white-dominated society. In 1970 Jordan edited *Soulscript: Afro-American Poetry*, a collection of poetry by young adults aged twelve to eighteen and by well-known poets of the 1960s. Jordan has published nineteen works to date, consisting of poetry, books for children and young adults, and collections of essays, articles, and lectures. These works include *The Voice of the Children*, a reader edited with Terri Bush (1970); *Some Changes* (poems, 1971); *His Own Where* (young adult novel, 1971); *Dry Victories* (juvenile and young adult, 1972); *Fannie Lou Hamer* (biography, 1972); *New Days: Poems of Exile and Return* (1973); *New Life: New Room* (juvenile, 1975); *Things That I Do in the Dark: Selected Poetry* (1977); *Okay Now* (1977); *Passion: New Poems, 1977–1980* (1980); *Civil Wars* (essays, articles, and lectures, 1981); *Kimako's Story* (juvenile, 1981); *Living Room: New Poems, 1980–1984* (1985); *On Call: New Political Essays, 1981–1985* (1985); *High Tide—Marea Alta* (1987); *Naming Our Destiny: New and Selected Poems* (1989); *Technical Difficulties: African-American Notes on the State of the Union* (essays, articles, and lectures, 1992). Jordan is also the author of several plays, including *In the Spirit of Sojourner Truth*, produced in New York at the Public Theater (May 1979), and *For the Arrow That Flies by Day*, a staged reading produced in New York at the Shakespeare Festival (Apr. 1981). In addition, Jordan composed the lyrics and wrote the libretto for *Bang Bang Uber Alles* in 1985.

In 1966 Jordan began her academic career as an

instructor of English and literature at the City University of New York. In 1968 she moved to Connecticut College in New London, where she taught English and directed the Search for Education, Elevation and Knowledge (SEEK) program. From 1968 to 1974 Jordan was an instructor of English at Sarah Lawrence College in Bronxville, New York. She was a visiting professor of English and Afro-American studies at Yale University from 1974 to 1975 and later in 1975 became an assistant professor of English at the City College of New York. In 1976 Jordan took a faculty position at the State University of New York at Stony Brook, and in 1982 was promoted to tenured full professor. Since 1989 Jordan has been professor of Afro-American studies and women's studies at the University of California, Berkeley.

Themes of power and empowerment, nurturance and pride, survival and advancement for both the community and its members characterize Jordan's African American literary vision across the several genres in which she writes, from her earliest writings to her last. Her work is antiracist, feminist, and avowedly political; it powerfully and skillfully explores African American experience and advocates self-determination and activism for community advancement, as well as for ameliorating interracial relations and those between the sexes. Jordan's writing for and with African American children and young adults attests to the poet's conviction of the healing empowerment of language and self-expression; moreover, her children's books expand the genre by taking on the harsh social realities they face. The award-winning *His Own Where*, a novel for young adults, is distinguished by its use of African American spoken English and its focus on urban redesign to create environmental conditions that can foster African American life. The emphasis on urban planning derives from Jordan's project to collaborate with E. Buckminster Fuller on the architectural redesign of Harlem; *His Own Where* fulfills in fiction what could not be realized in environmental planning.

Jordan is perhaps best known for her poetry and essays. Her verse has been praised for uniquely and effectively uniting in poetic form the personal everyday struggles and political oppressions of African Americans while at the same time masterfully creating art that conveys bitterness and rage at intolerance with a fine irony. She is recognized for her expert craftsmanship, a patterning of sound, rhythm, and image that interweaves disparate emotions and voices in a poetry that is never less than political and never lessened by its politics. Her poetic vision infuses all that she writes, and Jordan's explicitly political essays, especially those collected in *Civil Wars* and *Technical Difficulties*, advocate change through a personal, autobiographical focus and a clear uncompromising voice. Jordan is a witness for her community but also an intellectual with a vision for its future that embraces a feminism inclusive of men and focused on the nurturance of children and freedom of sexual orientation. In her oft-quoted essay "A New Politics of Sexuality" (*Technical Difficulties*, 1992), Jordan draws an analogy between bisexuality and "interracial or multiracial identity," insisting on the complexities of human existence and individuals' "total, always-changing social and political circumstance." Jordan's political, social, and personal artistic vision is comprehensive, humane, and charged with conviction; her poetry and essays are expansive expressions of her wide-ranging aesthetic and human concerns.

Jordan has received many grants, prizes, and fellowships for her writing, including a Rockefeller grant for creative writing in 1969 and the Prix de Rome in Environmental Design in 1970. She was granted a Yaddo fellowship in 1979, a fellowship in poetry from the National Endowment for the Arts in 1982, and a fellowship award in poetry from the New York Foundation for the Arts in 1985. *The Voice of Children* received a Nancy Bloch Award in 1971, and in the same year, *His Own Where* was selected by the *New York Times* for its List of Most Outstanding Books and was nominated for a National Book Award. Jordan is an executive board member of the American Writers Congress, a board member of the Center for Constitutional Rights and the Nicaraguan Culture Alliance, and a member of PEN. She is also a regular political columnist for *Progressive* magazine.

Jordan has been a significant voice in several traditions of African American art and culture. Her socially conscious literary expressions advance contemporary trends also practiced by Alice *Walker and Toni *Morrison; Toni Cade *Bambara has compared Jordan's achievements to W. E. B. *Du Bois's *Dusk of Dawn: An Essay Toward an Autobiography of a Race Concept* (1940). Jordan's talk-poems and her use of spoken African American English in both fiction and poetry indicate her participation in an oral tradition of African American literature exemplified by Nikki *Giovanni and Amiri *Baraka. Her feminist vision, part of her political enterprise, has been influential in the development of an antiracist, antihomophobic U.S. feminism. The political advocacy of her poetry, decidedly activist and aesthetically black, aligns her with Eldridge *Cleaver and *Malcolm X, although she brings to the radical militancy of 1960s African American thought an anger ultimately seasoned by faith, optimism, and vision.

• Toni Cade Bambara, "Chosen Weapons," review of *Civil Wars*, *Ms.*, Apr. 1981, 40–42. Alexis De Veaux, "Creating Soul Food: June Jordan," *Essence*, Apr. 1981, 82, 138–150. Sara Miles, "This Wheel's on Fire," in *Woman Poet: The East*, eds. Elaine Dallman et al., 1982, pp. 87–89. Peter B. Erickson, "June Jordan," in *DLB*, vol. 38, *Afro-American Writers after 1955: Dramatists and Prose Writers*, eds. Thadious M. Davis and Trudier Harris, 1985, pp. 146–162. June Jordan, "An Interview with June Jordan," interview by Joy Harjo, *High Plains Literary Review* 3.2 (Fall 1988): 60–76. Peter Erickson, "Putting Her Life on the Line: The Poetry of June Jordan," *Hurricane Alice: A Feminist Quarterly* 7.1–2 (Winter–Spring 1990): 4–5.
—Ronna C. Johnson

JOURNALISM. The African American press, referred to in the nineteenth century as the Negro press, provided an avenue for the self-definition of African Americans, counteracting racism and fostering a sense of racial pride at a time when society had constructed Negroes as intellectually and morally inferior. The very title of the first black newspaper, *Freedom's Journal*, started by Samuel *Cornish and John Browne *Russwurm in 1827, testifies to the relationship between journalism and black political activism. Along with the black *church, the Negro press operated as a primary institution in the community; its editors were "race men and women," agitating against the immorality of *slavery. During Reconstruction, they committed themselves to social and political uplift and the establishment of a national *identity for the Negro.

Given the crusade for sociopolitical uplift, journalism was not primarily a money-making venture. It was instead a necessary platform for social change, a way to rescue the race from *stereotypes. Accordingly, nineteenth-century black writers used the press to voice a rhetoric of opposition. In their hands, the pen became the sword to revolutionize society.

Frederick *Douglass (1818–1895) was one such writer. Reading the *Liberator*, an abolitionist paper published by William Lloyd Garrison, had a strong influence on Douglass. Throughout his life he remained committed to journalistic writing. Considered a necessary inclusion in any newspaper venture, Douglass assisted in the editing of several papers and in 1847 established his own weekly, the *North Star*, as a platform for antislavery activity. In his lifetime, Douglass was owner of a number of newspapers—small weeklies that did not enjoy long lives because of the fate of black publications within the dynamics of the market economy in the nineteenth century.

Narrative of the Life of Frederick Douglass, an American Slave, Written by Himself (1845) functioned polemically as an antislavery tract. Douglass revised his *autobiography over and over again as a way of writing himself into *history and thereby validating his right to *freedom and *manhood. His *essays, appearing in news articles or as part of his editorial columns, were to function in the same capacity. The emphasis continued to be on the portrayal of the slave as a person—a rational, thinking, and suffering being.

Similar to the way the *Liberator* had a profound effect on Douglass's life, the *Evening Star* influenced the life of Ida B. *Wells-Barnett. Wells-Barnett became editor of this weekly newspaper, and it is here that she came to the attention of the publisher of *Living Way*. Using the pen name "Iola," she created her own homespun rhetoric and wrote syndicated columns, engaging in the full range of journalistic activities not commonly accorded to women. Her written and verbal campaign against *lynching extended into the early 1900s. As crusaders for justice, Douglass and Wells-Barnett were known for their eloquence.

Martin R. *Delany (1812–1884) was another prominent figure in nineteenth-century journalism whose didactic position extended from polemical journalistic pieces into creative writing. Assistant editor to the *North Star* and later editor to his own newspaper, the *Mystery*, Delany was better known as an essayist than as a creative writer. His establishment of a weekly literary journal, the *Anglo-African Magazine* (1859), speaks to his conscious commitment to the establishment of a black literary aesthetic. It was here that he published portions of his novel, *Blake, or The Huts of America, A Tale of the Mississippi Valley, the Southern United States and Cuba*. The magazine provided a forum for the exposition of black literary talent such as poet Frances Ellen Watkins *Harper (1825–1911).

The abolition of slavery created some difficulty in accessing the *publishing market. The antislavery society no longer functioned in such a supporting role. It was now left to the black press to assist in the publication of literary material, a task they were quite willing to do as a way of creating a strong multitalented black society. Literary journals flourished in the Reconstruction period and even very small newspapers devoted space to the promotion of the arts.

The importance of essays as an integral part of black journalism had been established by Frederick Douglass. William Wells *Brown (1813–1884), a notable nineteenth-century writer who until his displacement by Harriet E. *Wilson held the place as the first African American novelist, also established a reputation for himself in the black press. His escape to England brought him to the attention of white British dailies, and he began writing his slavery experiences in London newspapers such as *Daily News*, the *Morning Advertiser*, and the *Leader*. Additionally, he wrote a travelogue of his journeys in England for the *Anti-Slavery Advocate*. When he went on the lecture circuit in Great Britain and Europe, many of his speeches were reprinted in American newspapers, including the *Liberator*. While in Europe, Brown sent letters to Frederick Douglass's newspapers detailing his experiences and observations. Among his letters were critiques of the British literary tradition, foreshadowing his own transition from journalist to author.

Brown's first novel, *Clotel, or The President's Daughter: A Narrative of a Slave's Life in the United States* (1853), was published in London. Later, an altered version of *Clotel* was written for the *Anglo-African Magazine*. Entitled "Miralda, or The Beautiful Quadroon; A Romance of American Slavery Founded on Fact," this novel came out in sixteen first-page installments between December 1860 and March 1861. Brown's contribution to the Negro press through essays, letters, and serialized novels provided detailed commentary on an era when Negroes were still trying to claim their place in the New World. His efforts, like those of Douglass and Delany, were to provide a friendlier context for the literary and journalistic efforts of people such as Frances Harper. Poet, novelist, and lecturer/activist, Harper was one of the prominent literary figures of the nineteenth century whose success the Negro press helped initiate. She came to prominence publishing her *poetry and writing articles for the *Christian Recorder*, a monthly church magazine issued by the African Methodist Episcopal (AME) Church. In this period of Reconstruction, the church perceived the press as another pulpit, an extension of its own ministry in providing the necessary moral and social directive for an emergent black society. The arts were seen as a means of achieving this mission. The AME Church also established a periodical called *The Repository of Religion* and *Literature and of Arts and Science* whose focus was on book reviews, *music, and the natural sciences. Occasionally Harper did lecture tours, and the major newspapers of the day printed her essays.

By the end of the nineteenth century, the relationship between journalism and literature had become more entrenched. Through newspapers, periodicals, journals, and literary magazines (the divisions were not distinct), writers had a voice outside of their poetry, fiction, and *drama. When they did produce creative manuscripts, placing them in journalistic forums provided a captive readership. Some magazines were created precisely to provide additional publishing opportunities for authors. James Ephraim *McGirt, founder and major contributor to *McGirt's Magazine*, published his own short stories and poems in his magazine. More importantly, the magazine published works by Frances Harper and Paul Laurence *Dunbar (1872–1906), America's first nationally known black poet. *Lippincott's Magazine* also published Dunbar's work. Another turn-of-the-century novelist and playwright, Pauline E *Hopkins (1859–1930) cofounded and edited the *Colored American Magazine*, where she serialized her work. This tightly interwoven relationship between journalism and creative writing continued in a more pronounced way in the 1920s.

During the 1920s, the *Harlem Renaissance era, most of the major fiction writers and poets were known for their journalistic writings. Indeed, many of them—Langston *Hughes (1902–1967), George S. *Schuyler (1895–1977), Georgia Douglas *Johnson (1860–1966), Gwendolyn *Bennett (1902–1981), Alice Moore *Dunbar-Nelson (1875–1935), and Countee *Cullen (1903–1946)—wrote newspaper or magazine columns that marketed their creative as well as expository writings. Creative writers registered their anxiety with defining a black twentieth-century aesthetic and engaged in debates in the press over this issue and other sociopolitical problems. Both journalism and literature reflected a circulating sense of flux as writers recorded the energy and fervor of the *New Negro movement.

The problems of limited *literacy and poor subscription that had plagued the black press in the previous century had been partially solved in large urban cities such as New York, Pittsburgh, and Chicago. Widespread *migration to the industrialized North meant that writers were able to cater to a larger black readership. While this did not preclude dependence on white advertisers and patrons, it did mean some degree of autonomy for these papers. The black press had come into its own.

New players entered the journalistic field. The National Urban League created *Opportunity: A Journal of Negro Life* (1912–1947); the NAACP created the *Crisis: A Record of the Darker Race* (1910); the United Negro Improvement Association (UNIA) published the *Negro World: A Newspaper Devoted Solely to the Interest of the Negro* (1918–1933). As organs of particular interest groups, these publications promoted literature and the arts as instruments for social change.

The *Chicago Defender* (1905) was the first black newspaper to enjoy national readership. Characterized by a radical inflammatory style, this weekly paper enjoyed a circulation of 200,000 by 1920. Further, its insistence on migration from the southern states as a way out of daily discrimination and continued acts of *lynching made it a visible player in effecting social change. Langston Hughes's columns in the *Chicago Defender* led to the creation of his popular character, Jesse B. Semple (known as *Simple). The Simple columns, begun as general commentary by Harlem's poet laureate, became an everyman's odyssey of the black urban experience.

Once called the "world's greatest weekly," the *Chicago Defender* was later displaced in popularity by the *Pittsburgh Courier* (1910), a weekly paper addressing social problems of urban Negroes. The feature stories, sports news, editorials, and columns of the *Pittsburgh Courier* became very popular, despite an often politically conservative stance. George Schuyler, then writing and editing the *Messenger: A Journal of Scientific Radicalism* (1917–1928), was an important addition as a columnist and essayist for the *Courier*. The *Messenger* publicized itself as a radical New York–based black periodical. In it, Schuyler wrote a column called "Shafts and Darts." There was also a section for critiques and reviews of current theatrical performances and book reviews. Its literature section published the poetry of Claude *McKay (1889–1948) and Langston Hughes.

Schuyler's essays in both the *Messenger* and the *Pittsburgh Courier* contributed to the growing debate on the contribution of the Negro to white America. His comments often took the form of an acerbic dismissal of the African American racial and literary heritage. Schuyler's pro-assimilation sentiment provoked an essay, "The Negro Art Hokum," which drew a rebuttal from Langston Hughes entitled "The Negro Artist and the Racial Mountain." Both essays, published in *Nation* (16 June 1926), became part of the defining discourse on the role of the Negro in all aspects of American life, especially cultural America.

Not only did Schuyler gain national prominence as a journalist, but he also achieved recognition as a novelist. His first work, *Black No More* (1931), satirized major black and white public figures. He based his second novel, *Slaves Today* (1932), on his research of slavery in Liberia, publishing his findings in the New York–based paper the *Evening Post*, for which he was a special correspondent. His autobiography, *Black and Conservative* (1966), provides insight into Schuyler's philosophical stance on the Negro aesthetic.

Author Wallace *Thurman also made a significant contribution to journalism during this period. He became editor of the literary magazine *Fire!!* (1926), where he contributed a review of Carl Van Vechten's highly controversial *Nigger Heaven* (1926) and a *short story entitled "Cordelia the Crude." A group of black writers intent on signaling the wealth of current literary material published *Fire!!* The loftiness of their intention, as embodied in its subtitle, *A Quarterly Devoted to the Younger Negro Artists*, did not preclude its bankruptcy after the first issue. The militancy of its rhetoric and the inclusion of Van Vechten as a patron did not help to garner support among the black intelligentsia upon whom it depended for subscriptions. In spite of its impressive editorial panel of the leading writers of the day—Langston Hughes, Zora Neale *Hurston, Gwendolyn Bennett, and the painter and illustrator Aaron Douglas, *Fire!!*'s sales remained dismally low, and ironically it was a fire that destroyed the warehouse where the magazine was stored. After its first issue, *Fire!!* was bankrupt.

Three years after the demise of *Fire!!*, Thurman published a play, *Harlem* (1929), and the novel *The *Blacker the Berry* (1929), an early work in a long list of texts that would satirize Anglo beauty standards. In 1932, Thurman captured the successes and failures of the Harlem Renaissance in his roman à clef, *Infants of the Spring*. Thus, the literary foundations that *Fire!!* laid were to remain intact, for *Fire!!* was in many ways a response to the issues between art and propaganda that were polarizing the writers. The controversy in *Fire!!* sparked by Van Vechten's novel, *Nigger Heaven*, provided the occasion for this ongoing debate on the responsibility of the artist and his or her representation of the Negro in literature. *Nigger Heaven* provoked a scathing review from W. E. B. *Du Bois in *Crisis* for its stereotypical presentation of the Negro as the sensual suppressed savage. Yet the commercial success of *Nigger Heaven* helped illustrate the marketing potential of the black writer's world, and this new attention by white publishers created more opportunities for aspiring black writers to secure publication.

Under the direction of W. E. B. Du Bois, the *Crisis* afforded young writers, critics, and essayists a publication outlet. In it, poets Countee Cullen, Claude McKay, and Langston Hughes wrote articles and published their poems. *Crisis* also sponsored an annual literary contest and ran a column on literary criticism, "The Browsing Reader," for which Du Bois was responsible. However, its insistence that literature serve a social and political function meant that *Crisis* was sympathetic only to literature that ascribed to its philosophy. Initially, *Crisis* accepted a broad range of literary works, but by 1926 there was a definite privileging of works that portrayed the Negro in a favorable light. The editor gained more control over who received the *Crisis* literature prize and the rules and regulations were changed to state that works address issues of race where formerly it only required that the writer be black. Du Bois's own novels, *The *Souls of Black Folks* (1903) and *Dark Princess* (1928), confirm the social and educational thrust of literature. As a self-identified arbiter of Negro culture, *Crisis* became didactic, in contrast to *Opportunity*, the journal published by the National Urban League, whose agenda was to improve social conditions in urban centers. Concerned with social and economic relationships between blacks and whites, *Opportunity* managed to avoid overt political issues. This journal had a strong literary flavor and both Countee Cullen and Gwendolyn Bennett worked as its literary critics.

Sterling A *Brown (1901–1989), a prominent folk poet and teacher, became *Opportunity*'s literary editor in the 1930s. Brown reviewed new books in his column, "The Literary Scene," and wrote critical essays on literature. Alain *Locke (1886–1954) also wrote reviews of contemporary literature. *Opportunity*, like *Crisis*, held literary contests. In 1925, Langston Hughes won *Opportunity*'s first contest, with Zora Neale Hurston and Countee Cullen as runners-up. *Opportunity*'s prevailing philosophy seemed to have been that art would effect a sense of racial identity, which would allow all to live in harmony as equals.

Negro World, a black weekly newspaper established by Marcus *Garvey, also devoted space to the coverage of the arts. Its agenda in promoting black literature was similar to that of *Crisis*. Writers such as Zora Neale Hurston came to literary prominence here. The contributors to *Negro World* were major figures in the world of black journalism, including T. Thomas *Fortune and Eric *Walrond. While some registered skepticism about Garvey's vision of repatriation to Africa, there were many who shared the dream and viewed the journalistic effort as a means of effecting and affecting social change. Literature was functional, more than art for art's sake. *Negro World* also contained sections in French and Spanish, so as to cater to a readership outside of the United States.

Another valuable contributor both to journalism and to the development of literature was James Weldon *Johnson (1871–1938). Writer of *The *Autobiography of an Ex-Colored Man* (1912), Johnson was also editorial writer for the *New York Age*. Secretary to the NAACP from 1920 to 1930, he had lifelong commitment to issues of race and remained convinced of the arts as an accurate barometer to measure a nation's success.

In more recent times, James *Baldwin (1924–1987) functioned as novelist/journalist. In addition to writing several novels, Baldwin published some of his major essays in magazines. "Stranger in the Village" appeared in *Harper's Magazine* in 1953 and *The *Fire Next Time* (1963) was an adaptation of his essays that appeared in journals.

The boundaries of journalistic writing when practiced by African American novelists and poets were fluid. Historically, the black press had always been a powerful vehicle, not simply for newsgathering but also for articulating and defining an African American agenda for literary, social, and political change. During the late twentieth century, other media have provided the writers with additional forums, authors have more access to publishing houses, and a black literary aesthetic is no longer in its infancy. Not having to prove their humanity, the writers are freer to polish their craft. Accordingly, many African American writers have won literature's top prizes, including National Book awards; Pulitzer prizes in poetry, drama, and fiction; and the Nobel Prize.

Fewer creative writers are using the newspapers and periodicals as a primary voice in ways characteristic of the Harlem Renaissance writers. Although there are many African American literary journals publishing original works by African American writers and black writers globally, the writings of the authors in these literary magazines tend to be creative rather than the fusion of creative/journalistic writings of the nineteenth- and early-twentieth-century writers.

With an emphasis on *Black Aesthetic practices and social criticism, African American writers grounded their journalism in their lives and art. In turn, journalism provided the place where many of the writers became public figures. This symbiotic relationship between journalism and literature as practiced by African American writers strengthened both. Each has helped in the generic development of the other.

[See also Literary Societies; Newspaper Columns; Periodicals.]

• Irving Garland Penn, *The Afro-American Press and Its Editors,* 1891. Frederick G. Detweiler, *The Negro Press in the United States,* 1922. Bruce Kellner, ed., *The Harlem Renaissance: A Historical Dictionary for an Era,* 1984. Cary D. Wintz, *Black Culture and the Harlem Renaissance,* 1988.

—Valerie Lee

Journal of Negro History. One of the first periodicals devoted exclusively to scholarly research on African Americans and the black diaspora, the *Journal of Negro History* served in its early years as an important outlet for revisionist studies of *slavery, the Civil War, and Reconstruction. Later issues focused increasingly on the *history of African Americans after 1877, many of which balanced historiographical research with literary scholarship.

Founded by Carter G. *Woodson in 1916 as the official organ of the Association for the Study of Negro Life and History, the *Journal of Negro History* has maintained a considerable influence on the field of historiography during its nearly eighty years of publication. Woodson, a scholar trained at the University of Chicago, Harvard, and the Sorbonne, envisioned a journal that would be, in his words, the "first systematic effort of the Negro to treat the records of the race scientifically," and his thirty-four years as general editor witnessed consistently high editorial standards and a publication that became well-respected both in the United States and abroad. After his death in 1950, Woodson was succeeded as editor of the journal by Rayford W. Logan (1950–1951), William M. Brewer (1952–1970), W. Augustus Low (1970–1974), Lorraine A. Williams (1974–1976), and Alton Hornsby, Jr. (1976).

[See also Journalism; Periodicals.]

—Christopher C. De Santis

JOURNALS. See Periodicals.

Jubilee was written as Margaret *Walker's PhD dissertation at the University of Iowa. As she typed the final lines of the story of her maternal great-grandmother, Margaret Duggans Ware Brown (on 9 Apr. 1965), Walker brought to conclusion the creative task of transforming the oral history passed on by her grandmother into a sweeping *novel of southern life before and immediately after the Civil War. *Jubilee* won the Houghton Mifflin Literary Fellowship and was published in September 1966.

The novel is divided into three major sections, representing the antebellum years, the Civil War period, and Reconstruction as witnessed by the central character, Vyry. Born a slave on a Georgia plantation, she eventually finds a peace she cannot vocalize and hope for a future in the red-clay hills of Alabama. Orphaned by the death of her mother and nurtured by the women of the slave community, Vyry suffers for being her owner's daughter and must use wit and intelligence to survive the wrath of Salina Dutton, who despises Vyry's resemblance to her own daughter, Lillian. Vyry's strengths are tested when her husband, Randall Ware, escapes to the North; refusing to abandon her two children for the promise of *freedom, she remained on the plantation during the Civil War, a model of sanity and generosity as the chaos of war brings irreversi-ble change. The interdependence of slave and slaveowner and the suffering both must endure are foils for Vyry's heroism. Assuming that Ware is dead, Vyry marries Innis Brown and seeks to begin a new life with him in Alabama at the war's end. Life is marked by the poverty, sickness, and persecution of the postwar South, and Vyry must make a hard choice when Ware reappears.

The compassion of *Jubilee* challenged *stereotypes about African American historical fiction. Published just as the focus on civil rights was shifting to Black Power and nationalism, its initial critical reception was decidedly mixed. Opinions ranged from Guy Davenport's biting conclusion in the *National Review* that the novel ironically swallowed the myth of a romantic South that never existed to Abraham Chapman's remarks in *Saturday Review* that the novel was faithful to the facts of slave life. Neither facts that might have cast light on the textual tensions, the pull between verifiable data and the author's re-creation of family history, nor the insights of feminist critique about the novel's complexity were available to early commentators. The facts would not be available until Walker published *How I Wrote Jubilee* (1972), thus enabling a more reasoned assessment of the novel within the tradition of African American historical fiction.

Since the 1970s, many critics acknowledge, as does Bernard Bell in *The Afro-American Novel and Its Tradition* (1987), that *Jubilee* is an innovative *neo–slave narrative, remarkable for its use of *folklore, knowledge of black culture, abundance of carefully researched historical detail, and the prism of woman's vision. Seen now as the precursor of such works as *Dessa Rose* (1986) and *Beloved* (1987), *Jubilee* inspires deeper studies of what it might tell us about the interrelations of memory and literary imagination in the history of African American literature and culture.

[See also Slave Narrative; Slavery.]

• Barbara Christian, *Black Women Novelists,* 1980. Eleanor Traylor, "Music as Theme: The Blues Mode in the Works of Margaret Walker," in *Black Women Writers (1950–1980),* ed. Mari Evans, 1984, pp. 511–525. Minrose C. Gwin, *Black and White Women of the Old South,* 1985. Melissa Walker, *Down from the Mountain Top: Black Women's Novels in the Wake of the Civil Rights Movement, 1966–1989,* 1991.

—Jerry W. Ward, Jr.

K

KAUFMAN, BOB (1925–1986), poet, prose poet, jazz performance artist, satirist, manifesto writer, and legendary figure in the Beat movement. Bob Kaufman successfully promoted both anonymity and myths of his racial *identity and class origins. While romanticized biographies ascribe to him such epithets as griot, shaman, saint, and prophet of Caribbean, African, Native American, Catholic, and/or Jewish traditions, respectively, Kaufman was most likely the tenth of thirteen children of an African American and part Jewish father and a schoolteacher mother from an old New Orleans African American Catholic family. After an orderly childhood that probably included a secondary education, he joined the merchant marine and became active in the radical Seafarer's Union. An itinerant drifter and self-taught poet (but for a brief stint at the New School for Social Research and among the Black Arts and Beat literati of New York), he identified with the lives and cryptically quoted the works of poet-heroes such as Herman Melville, Walt Whitman, Arthur Rimbaud, Guillaume Apollinaire, Federico García Lorca, Hart Crane, Gertrude Stein, Langston *Hughes, Frantz Fanon, Aimé Césaire, and Nicholas Guillén, as well as improvisational artists and *jazz musicians, including Charlie *Parker, after whom he named his only son. In individual poems he is, variously, an experimental stylist in the Whitman tradition ("The American Sun"), a French surrealist and existentialist ("Camus: I Want to Know"), a jazz poet after Langston Hughes, and in dialogue with bebop and the *Black Arts movement ("African Dream," "Walking Parker Home").

Still "minor," compared to his white bohemian contemporaries, as editor of *Beatitude*, a San Francisco literary magazine, Kaufman is credited by some with coining "Beat" and exemplifying its voluntarily desolate lifestyle. He enjoyed an underground existence as a "poets' poet" (in Amiri *Baraka's poem "Meditation on Bob Kaufman," *Sulfur*, Fall 1991) and as a legendary performer in the much memorialized street scenes of San Francisco's North Beach and New York's Greenwich Village during the late 1950s through the late 1970s. Kaufman is best known for short lyric poems in African American (Langston Hughes, ed., *The New Negro Poetry*, 1964, being the first) and avant-garde *anthologies (*New Directions in Prose and Poetry*, #17, 1967, covering *poetry and prose; *The Portable Beat Reader*, 1992). Works originally published by City Lights Bookstore of San Francisco are collected in two New Directions publications, *Solitudes Crowded with Loneliness* (1965) and *The Ancient Rain: Poems 1956–1978* (1981). Three early broadsides, *Abomunist Manifesto* (1959), *Second April* (1959), and *Does the Secret Mind Whisper?* (1960) extend his eclectic aesthetics into prose fiction and programmatic prose poetry. *The Golden Sardine* (1967) was translated and influential in France (as *William Burroughs, Claude Pelieu, Bob Kaufman*, Paris, 1967). The latter, along with South American and other translations, have earned Kaufman a wider reputation abroad than among mainstream critics in the United States.

Rather than address electoral, protest, or even literary politics in traditional ways, his elusive and allusive writings as well as his tragicomic life sustain a critique of the subtle rules and terrible punishments that, as he knew them, enforce American bourgeois values of race, class, sexuality, and rationality. Answering McCarthyism, Beat, and Black Arts manifestos with Dadaist anarchism and surrealist irrationalism, "Abomunism" (his contraction of, among other things, comm*unism*, *a*tom bom*b*, *Bo*b Kaufman, and *abom*ination), is serious in its "black humor." From the late 1960s onward, through stretches of withdrawal and suffering the ill effects of political blacklisting and harassment, alcohol, drugs, electroshock treatments, and imprisonment, Kaufman recorded both with *humor and pathos the pain of society's victims. While no booklength study has yet been devoted to Kaufman, several recent *essays affirm his deceptively broad intellectual interests and the ambiguous power of individual acts of cultural resistance in the continuing struggles of oppressed peoples.

• Barbara Christian, "Whatever Happened to Bob Kaufman?" *Black World* 21 (Sept. 1972): 20–29. Maria Damon, "'Unmeaning Jargon' / Uncanonized Beatitude: Bob Kaufman, Poet," *South Atlantic Quarterly* 87.4 (Fall 1988): 701–741. Kathryne V. Lindberg, "Bob Kaufman, Sir Real," *Talisman* 11 (Fall 1993): 167–182. Gerald Nicosian, ed., *Cranial Guitar: Selected Poems by Bob Kaufman*, 1996.

—Kathryne V. Lindberg

KECKLEY, ELIZABETH (c. 1818–1907), seamstress, activist, and author. Elizabeth Keckley became a center of public controversy with the 1868 publication of *Behind the Scenes, or Thirty Years a Slave and Four Years in the White House.*

Born a slave in Dinwiddie Court House, Virginia, Keckley became such an accomplished seamstress that she was able to purchase her own *freedom and her son's. After manumission she moved from St. Louis to establish herself in Washington, D.C., in 1860, becoming modiste first to the wife of Mississippi Senator Jefferson Davis and finally to Mary Todd Lincoln during Abraham *Lincoln's first term. Two-thirds of *Behind the Scenes* concerns Keckley's life with the Lincolns and the difficult period following the president's assassination, especially Mary Lincoln's desperate attempt to raise money through what became known as the "Old Clothes Scandal." A misplaced trust in her editor, James Redpath, and the sensationalist marketing of Carleton and Company culminated in a furor, the as-advertised "literary thunderbolt." Because of revelations about Mary

Lincoln and the inclusion of her personal letters, Robert Lincoln pressured the publisher to remove Keckley's book from sale and terminated all relations with Keckley. After serving as Director of Domestic Arts at Wilberforce University, Keckley retired to Washington, D.C.

While antebellum *slave narratives treat *slavery as an unadulterated evil and slaveowners as devilish, Keckley's and other post–Civil War narratives emphasize slavery as a school for instruction in self-reliance and hard work. Keckley's success, along with an awareness of the South brought low, allows her reconciling visit with the Garlands, her former owners. Although her sexual exploitation in slavery recalls that of her contemporary Harriet A. *Jacobs, Keckley refuses to make black female *sexuality an issue in *Behind the Scenes*, preferring instead to stress her achievement as a successful career woman in freedom.

• John E. Washington, *They Knew Lincoln*, 1942. Frances Smith Foster, *Written by Herself: Literary Production by African American Women, 1746–1892*, 1993.

—Anne Bradford Warner

KELLEY, EMMA DUNHAM (?–?), novelist. Little is known about the life of Emma Dunham Kelley. She wrote two *novels, *Megda* (1891) and *Four Girls at Cottage City* (1895). Kelley used the pseudonym "Forget-Me-Not" for her first novel, publishing the second under the name Emma Dunham Kelley-Hawkins, thus indicating marriage. It is probable that Kelley lived in New England, where she may have been a schoolteacher or attended school: both novels were published and set in New England, and in the preface to *Four Girls* the author acknowledges that much of the text is based on actual people, places, and events. The dedications to Kelley's novels express a sense of debt to a widowed mother who struggled to provide for her daughter and to an aunt whom she calls a "second mother."

Both of Kelley's texts are didactic novels in the tradition of the female Christian *bildungsroman, a genre that was sufficiently popular in the 1890s for *Megda* to warrant a second printing. In their rejection of social protest and their avoidance of the subject of *race, Kelley's novels are exceptional among the work of African American women publishing in the 1890s. Rather, they are typical of writing by white women in the "girl's fiction" subgenre of the sentimental novel, a category notable for its emphasis on socializing young women into the dominant social order. Yet while Kelley's texts urge acceptance of the status quo and earthly suffering as God's will, their emphasis on personal salvation may have been based in the widespread view that moral reformation of individuals was the necessary precondition for progressive social change.

Each of Kelley's novels features a group of girls whom readers follow from a carefree late adolescence through a process of Christian conversion and concomitant acceptance of the responsibilities of adult womanhood, as defined by late-nineteenth-century evangelical Protestantism. Each text features a particularly spirited, ambitious, and talented heroine who initially resists the Christian path but who in the end claims Jesus as her savior and finds her reward in a traditional *marriage and the inner peace that immediately follows upon her conversion.

There is disagreement regarding the precise racial identification of Kelley's characters. The confusion is compounded by the iconography of *Megda*, in which fair skin is almost invariably correlated with virtue, the exception being one very poor, devout young woman described as having skin significantly darker than that of her wealthier peers. Even here, coloring may be an indicator of *class status rather than racial difference. The uncertainty regarding the race of Kelley's characters is indicative of the subtle tension her novels reveal on matters of race and *gender. Though atypical among African American treatments of these topics, Kelley's texts display numerous marks of strain that suggest the uncomfortable position occupied by middle-class African American women of the period. Their female-centered Christian ethos, while rejecting social protest, anticipates the feminist spirituality found in much late-twentieth-century African American women's writing.

• Molly Hite, introduction to *Megda*, 1988. Deborah McDowell, introduction to *Four Girls at Cottage City*, 1989.

—Meryl F. Schwartz

KELLEY, WILLIAM MELVIN (b. 1937), novelist, short fiction writer, and educator. Born in New York, William Melvin Kelley attended Fieldston School and Harvard University. He has taught literature and writing at the New School for Social Research, the State University of New York at Geneseo, and the University of Paris, Nanterre.

From the beginning of his career in 1962, William Melvin Kelley has employed his distinctive form of black comedy to examine the absurdities surrounding American racial attitudes. His first *novel showed the influence of William Faulkner by creating a microcosm in a mythical southern state; his last pays tribute to James Joyce's stylistic innovations. Like Faulkner's, his works are connected by a cast of common characters.

In *A Different Drummer* (1962), multiple narrators tell the intertwined histories of the Willson and Caliban families. Tucker Caliban is the descendant of a giant African king who died rather than face *slavery under General Dewey Willson, leaving his infant son to become "First Caliban," slave, and later servant to Willson, governor of his home state. Moved by an unarticulated instinct, Tucker destroys his small farm, kills his livestock, and leaves the state for the North, emancipating not only himself, his wife Bethrah, and his unborn child but the surviving members of the Willson line, who are freed from their heritage as former slaveholders. Tucker's instinctive action is contrasted not only with his ancestor's ineffective physical rebellion but with the intellectual fight against racism waged by "Black Jesuit" leader Bennett Bradshaw, a northern civil rights advocate. Tucker and his family are followed by all the African Americans in the state, which becomes the only state to have an all-white population.

Dancers on the Shore (1964) is a collection of stories that connect *A Different Drummer* with Kelley's later work. The first story, "The Only Man on Liberty Street," features the illegitimate daughter of General Dewey Willson. In the last story, Wallace Bedlow, a character similar to singer Hudie (Leadbelly) Ledbetter, is one of the refugees inspired by Tucker Caliban. In "Cry for Me," Bedlow travels to New York City, where he forms a special bond with his nephew Carlyle, a prominent character in *dem* (1967) and *Dunfords Travels Everywheres* (1970). Wallace Bedlow plays his distinctive *music in the coffeehouses of Greenwich Village and dies during a triumphant concert at Carnegie Hall. Several stories—including "A Visit to Grandmother," "Saint Paul and the Monkeys," and "Christmas with the Great Man"—introduce the Dunford family.

Kelley's second novel, *A Drop of Patience* (1965), is the life story of blind saxophone player Ludlow Washington. Ludlow begins his career in a southern juke joint, moves to New York where he backs up a famous *blues singer, Inez Cunningham, then joins a traveling band that allows him the freedom to pursue his own groundbreaking style of *jazz. Based loosely on Charlie *Parker, Ludlow is conquered not by drugs but by his destructive relationship with a white woman. *A Drop of Patience* is tied to *A Different Drummer* by Bethra Washington, Ludlow's daughter, who becomes the wife of Tucker Caliban.

The narrator of *dem* is Mitchell Pierce, whose wife, Tam, surprises him by bearing fraternal twins, one white and one black. Guided by Carlyle Bedlow and Calvin Johnson, Pierce explores Harlem, looking for his wife's African American lover, whom he has seen once when the man was dating his maid. After visiting Harlem's nightclubs and several rent parties, Mitchell realizes that Calvin (Coolidge) Johnson is the same man he met in his own kitchen, where he was introduced to him under the man's nickname, "Cooley."

If *dem* is often surrealistic, *Dunfords Travels Everywheres* completely abandons reality. Chig Dunford lives in a foreign country where apartheid is rigorously enforced, not on a racial basis but depending on which color scheme—blue or yellow—each individual has chosen for the day. Returning to the United States by ocean liner, Dunford finds the boiler room of the ship filled with chained Africans being transported to America. Parallel to Chig's story are convoluted tales of Carlyle Bedlow's seduction of his dentist's wife and Bedlow's attempt to save a friend who has sold his soul to the devil. The novel is a mixture of straightforward narrative and language reminiscent of *Finnegan's Wake*.

Early in his career, Kelley distanced himself from racial questions, decrying "symbols or ideas disguised as people" (preface, *Dancers on the Shore*), but during the eight-year span of his career—years of turmoil for the nation—he became increasingly involved in political commentary.

• Roger Rosenblatt, *Black Fiction*, 1974, pp. 142–151. Donald M. Weyl, "The Vision of Man in the Novels of William Melvin Kelley," *Critique* 15.3 (1974): 15–33. Jill Weyant, "The Kelley Saga: Violence in America," *CLA Journal* 19 (1975): 210–220. Howard Faulkner, "The Uses of Tradition: William Melvin Kelley's *A Different Drummer*," *Modern Fiction Studies* 21 (1975–1976): 535–542. Addison Gayle, *The Way of the New World: The Black Novel in America*, 1976, pp. 367–376.

—Robert E. Fleming

KENAN, RANDALL (b. 1963), novelist, short story writer, playwright, editor, and educator. Randall Kenan was born in New York City but moved shortly thereafter to rural North Carolina. Growing up in Chinquapin, Kenan received his BA in English and creative writing with a minor in physics from the University of North Carolina at Chapel Hill in 1985. He also studied at Oxford University during the summer of 1984.

Kenan then became an editor at Knopf and began advancing in the publishing profession. In 1989 his writing career gained momentum with the publication of his first *novel, *A Visitation of Spirits*. He became a lecturer at Sarah Lawrence College in 1989, and later at Columbia University, and was a visiting professor at Duke University in 1994 and at the University of North Carolina at Chapel Hill in 1995. Kenan's many honors include nomination for the National Book Critics Circle Award, a 1995 Guggenheim Fellowship, and a 1995 Sherwood Anderson Award.

Published by Grove Press, *A Visitation of Spirits* received impressive accolades for a first novel: the dust jacket includes endorsements by Gloria *Naylor and Adrienne *Kennedy. Set in rural Tims Creek, North Carolina—a community clearly modeled after Chinquapin—the novel is divided into five sections, all of which concentrate on the Cross family, specifically sixteen-year-old Horace Cross and his older cousin, the Reverend Jimmy Greene. The focus of *A Visitation of Spirits* is on Horace and his slide into insanity and suicide. Horace's realization that he is homosexual causes him to believe that he is damned and that he can only escape by transforming himself into a red-tailed hawk. When Horace's sorcery fails to achieve this transformation, his despair is so great that he cannot return to reality. Instead, on a terrifying night filled with demons, the deranged and naked Horace revisits sites of earlier significance in his life but finds no redemption. While confronting his cousin Jimmy, Horace shoots himself in the head with his grandfather's shotgun.

Kenan's *Let the Dead Bury Their Dead* (1992) is a collection of *short stories that are also based in Tims Creek. A widely ranging group of twelve tales, the work includes some characters from his earlier work, such as Jimmy Greene, who is the "author" of the title story, a pseudoscholarly *history of the town. The first selection humorously portrays a clairvoyant five-year-old, a possessed tractor, and a talking hog. Other stories depict such wildly varied topics as an elderly woman learning that her dead grandson was gay and that his lover was white, and a middle-aged lawyer who is obsessed with his incestuous relationship with his half sister. Throughout, the only apparent link among these stories is Tims Creek.

In 1994 Kenan published a biography, *James Baldwin*, which is in the Lives of Notable Gay Men and Lesbians series, edited by Martin Duberman. In

1996, Kenan was working on a travel book, "Walking on Water: A Journey into African America," detailing his explorations of black culture throughout the United States and Canada. He was also writing another Tims Creek novel, tentatively called "The Fire and the Baptism" and a play, "The Meek Shall Inherit the Earth." In addition to his longer works, Kenan has published several short stories (in periodicals and *anthologies), as well as reviews, interviews, and articles on topics ranging from John Edgar *Wideman to hip-hop *music. As a promising young writer who openly addresses homosexuality, Kenan's impact on African American literature is significant. While his use of the supernatural is reminiscent of Toni *Morrison, an early inspiration for him, Randall Kenan's journeys through the rural South are uniquely his own.

• Robert McRuer, "Randall Kenan," in *Contemporary Gay American Novelists: A Bio-Bibliographical Critical Sourcebook*, ed. Emmanuel S. Nelson, 1993, pp. 232–236. Randall Kenan, interview by Susan Ketchin, in *The Christ-Haunted Landscape: Faith and Doubt in Southern Fiction*, by Susan Ketchin, 1994, pp. 277–302.   —Kristine A. Yohe

KENNEDY, ADRIENNE (b. 1931), author, lecturer, and prizewinning playwright. Born Adrienne Lita Hawkins on 13 September 1931 to Cornell Wallace and Etta (Haugabook) Hawkins in Pittsburgh, Pennsylvania, Kennedy grew up in Cleveland, Ohio, and attended Cleveland Public Schools. The future playwright entered Ohio State University in 1949, earning a BA in education in 1953. She also studied at Columbia University (1954–1956), the Theatre Wing of the New School for Social Research, Circle in the Square Theatre School, and Edward Albee's Theatre Workshop in New York City. On 15 May 1953 Kennedy married Joseph C. Kennedy and they have two sons, Joseph C. and Adam. The couple divorced in 1966.

Kennedy was a founding member of the Women's Theatre Council in 1971, a member of the board of directors of PEN (1976–1977), and International Theatre Institute representative in Budapest in 1978. Her numerous awards include a Village Voice Obie for *Funnyhouse of a Negro* in 1964, a Guggenheim Fellowship in 1967, several Rockefeller grants (1967–1969, 1974, 1976), a National Endowment for the Arts grant in 1973, a CBS Fellowship at the School of Drama in 1973, a Creative Artists public service grant in 1974, a Yale Fellowship (1974–1975), a Stanley Award, a New England Theatre Conference grant, and an American Book Award in 1990. In July 1995, she was named playwright in residence for the September 1995 through May 1996 season with the Signature Theater Company in New York. Two of her predecessors for this honor, Horton Foote and Edward Albee, have been awarded the Pulitzer Prize for their respective seasons.

A writer whose work continues to exemplify complexity and independent vision, Kennedy now claims authorship of some thirteen published plays, five unpublished plays, several autobiographical works of nonfiction, a *short story, and a novella. Her first published work was the short story "Because of the King of France," published under the pseudonym Adrienne Cornell in *Black Orpheus: A Journal of African and Afro-American Literature* (1963). Her first professionally produced play was *Funnyhouse* in 1964. *A Lesson in Dead Language* (published in *Collision Course*, 1968) was produced along with *Funnyhouse* in London on 28 April 1968. *A Lesson* features a classroom setting where the teacher is dressed from the waist up as a white dog. Her pupils (or pupil, depending on the production), all adolescent girls, wear white costumes with red stains signifying sexual maturation; the play deals with the accompanying trauma of the bloody rite of passage. *A Rat's Mass*, in which humans regress to the status of rats, was named one of the best plays of the season for 1966. Written in 1963, it was first produced in April 1966 by Theatre Company in Boston, and later in Rome (21 June 1966) and Turin (28 October 1966). It is anthologized in *New Black Playwrights* (1968).

At a time when other African American playwrights were making profound assertions of black pride in their works, and a sort of nationalist movement in African American *theater was afoot, Kennedy created African American female protagonists in *Funnyhouse* and *The Owl Answers* (first produced at the White Barn Theatre, Westport, Connecticut, in 1965) who were clearly confounded by their multiethnic origins. Before the advent of postmodernist drama, Kennedy's plays featured nonlinear narratives, dramatic and surrealistic imagery, split characters who existed in dreamlike states, fragmented formats, and unconventional plots. Her routine use of poetic and bouyant language, pregnant with multiple levels of meaning, makes Kennedy a deliberate master of the verbal metaphor. She combines elements of expressionism with a verbal fluidity to evoke a series of profound and provocative effects. Critics of Kennedy's work must be attuned to a variety of critical approaches and traditions to accurately assess her value to the theatrical community.

In her autobiographical memoir, *People Who Led to My Plays* (1987), Kennedy discloses an aspect of her life that may help to explain her independent vision. Her maternal grandfather was a rich white peach farmer with whom Kennedy interacted during visits to her parents' hometown of Montezuma, Georgia. From her Morehouse-educated father, the playwright learned that whites in Montezuma were of mostly British heritage. In the preface to *Deadly Triplets: A Theatre Mystery and Journal* (1990), Kennedy points out that her work in *Funnyhouse* and *The Owl Answers* was as "filled with English imagery— Queen Victoria, Chaucer, William the Conquerer—as it was filled with African images—Patrice Lumumba, savannahs, frangipani trees." Kennedy's acknowledgment of, and involvement with, combined African and British aspects of her heritage helps to account for multicultural themes in her plays. She admits to a fascination with England's legendary queens; literary influences on her personal and professional development actually include a plethora of works by authors from around the world. Her 1987 memoir tracks some of the people and images that affected her development as an author. For example, an entry under the heading "Tennessee Williams" includes the pronouncement that the summer evening she saw *The Glass Menagerie* was "when the idea of being a writer and seeing my own family onstage caught fire in my mind." Under "Wagner" she writes that his music "expressed a wild intensity that I felt growing inside me, but that I could not explain or comprehend." There are entries entitled "Checkhov, Dante, Virgil and the Bible," "Langston *Hughes," and "William Faulkner"; and under "James *Baldwin," she writes: "He sharpened my entire vision of America." Such a personal and professional engagement with the worldwide human community may be a contributing factor to the enduring quality of her work as well as her lengthy tenure as a respected writer and lecturer.

Much of Kennedy's work is taken from real-life experiences. She wrote unpublished autobiographical fiction while studying creative writing at Columbia, and an early autobiographical play, *Pale Blue Flowers* (1955), was also written there. *Deadly Triplets* consists of a mystery in novella form and a journal based on Kennedy's experiences in London from 1966 to 1969. She used a sniper incident described in Vietnam War news accounts to write *An Evening with Dead Essex*, a play first produced at New York's American Place Theatre Workshop (directed by Gaby Rodgers) in 1973. The play was also produced at the Yale Repertory Company in 1974 and published in *Theatre* (1978). *Diary of Lights*, produced in 1987 and described as a musical without songs, depicts the youthful idealism of a young black married couple living on the Upper West Side of New York City. Kennedy calls on her early fascination with Hollywood films in *A Movie Star Has to Star in Black and White* (*Wordplay 3*, 1984; *Norton Anthology of American Literature*, 1989) to examine fractured family relationships while looking at the fantasy lives of movie stars in her films (Bette Davis in "Now, Voyager," Marlon Brando in "Viva Zapata," and Montgomery Clift in "A Place in the Sun"). *A Movie Star* was first produced in New York in 1976 by Public Theatre Workshop; Ntozake *Shange directed a production at the University of Houston in 1985. *Sleep Deprivation Chamber* (1991) is based on Kennedy's own quest for justice following the beating of her son Adam by corrupt police. *The Ohio State Murders*, first produced in 1992 and included in the Kennedy volume entitled *The Alexander Plays* (1992), features protagonist Suzanne Alexander reliving and reinventing some troubling incidents from Kennedy's own days as a student at Ohio State. The other three of the Alexander plays are *She Talks to Beethoven* (first produced in 1989), *The Film Club* (a monologue), and *The Dramatic Circle* (a dramatization of *The Film Club*). *She Talks to Beethoven* is also published individually in *Plays in One Act* (1991) and *Antaeus* (Spring 1991).

A number of Kennedy's plays were commissioned. Herbert Blau and Jules Irving commissioned *A Beast's Story* for Lincoln Center, though the first production of the play was with *The Owl Answers* under the title *Cities in Belzique* (published by Samuel French in 1969). The play underscores the relationship between humans and beasts by highlighting the inhumane tendencies of humankind; it is anthologized in *Kuntu Drama: Plays of the African Continuum* (1974). Controversy surrounded the writing of *The Lennon Play: In His Own Write*, a project for which Kennedy was hired, but whose authorship she eventually shared with John Lennon and Victor Spinetti. Real and fictionalized accounts of her experiences while writing this play are contained in *Deadly Triplets*. The play was first produced in 1967 as "Act I Scene 3," opening as *The Lennon Play: In His Own Write* on 18 June 1968 at the National Theater, London. It was published in *Best Short Plays of the World Theatre* in 1968 and 1973. *Sun: A Poem for *Malcolm X Inspired by His Murder* was commissioned by the Royal Court Theatre in 1968 and published in *Scripts* (1971) and *Spontaneous Combustion* (1972). Productions were in London August 1969 and in 1970 by La Mama Experimental Theatre Club in New York City. *Boats* was commissioned for "An Omnibus of Short Works," and performed in Los Angeles on 12 October 1969. Other commissioned plays include *Black Children's Day* (Brown University, 1980); *A Lancashire Lad* (Empire State Youth Theater Institute, 1980), based on the childhood of Charles Chaplin; and *Orestes* and *Electra* (the Juilliard School, 1980), adaptations from the Euripides plays. *Orestes and Electra* are published in *Adrienne Kennedy in One Act* (1988). Kennedy mentions an additional commissioned play, *The Life of Robert Johnson*, on page three of her 1987 memoir.

Over the years, Kennedy has spent a good amount of time in classroom settings. She has taught and/or lectured at Yale (1972–1974), Princeton (1977), Brown University (1979–1980), University of California, Berkeley (1986), and Harvard (1990–1991). She published "Letter to My Students" in *Kenyon Review* in 1993.

• *Interviews with Contemporary Women Playwrights*, eds. Kathleen Betsko and Rachel Koenig, 1987. Adrienne Kennedy, interview by Elin Diamond, *Studies in American Drama 1945–Present*, eds. Philip C. Kolin et al., 1989, pp. 143–157. Jane Schlueter, "No Place but the Funnyhouse: The Struggle for Identity in Three Adrienne Kennedy Plays," in *Modern American Drama: The Female Canon*, ed. Susan E. Meigs, 1990, pp. 172–183. *Intersecting Boundaries: The Theatre of Adrienne Kennedy*, eds. Paul K. Bryant-Jackson and Lois More Overbeck, 1992. Linda Kintz, *The Subject's Tragedy: Political Poetics, Feminist Theory, and Drama*, 1992.

—Lovalerie King

KERMIT, S. L. *See* Delany, Samuel R.

KILLENS, JOHN O. (1916–1987), novelist, university professor, essayist, screenwriter, and editor. John O. Killens was born 14 January 1916 in Macon, Georgia, the son of Charles Myles, Sr., and Willie Lee (Coleman) Killens. He married Grace Ward Jones and was the father of two children: Jon Charles and Barbara Ellen Rivera. Killens's childhood and life experiences destined him to become a vital voice in African American literature. As a child he listened attentively to his great-grandmother tell outlandish and outrageous tales. He also read extensively. Killens's educational experiences included attending Edward Waters College, Morris-Brown

College, Atlanta University, Howard University, Robert Law School, Columbia University, and New York University. After struggling with law school at night and working during the day, Killens emerged as a writer. His first draft of *Youngblood* was shared over a storefront in Harlem with seven other young African Americans who had dreams of becoming writers. They later formed the Harlem Writers Guild, which came to be known and respected by the African American literary world. Killens died of cancer 27 October 1987 in Brooklyn, New York. His contributions to the African American literary tradition began with his integrational approach and became a voice of blackness later with characters like Yoruba and Lumumba in *The *Cotillion*. Killens's concern with racism, classism, assimilation, and hypocrisy is evident in the body of literature he produced.

As in many protest *novels of the time, Killens attacks the institution of racism, oppressive economics, and other injustices in *Youngblood*. The novel was published in 1954, a time when the social and civil unrest of a country dominated print media. Although laws were being passed to end segregation, the South refused to accept this change, and Killens captures this struggle in the southern black family who is fighting for survival during these turbulent times. For those readers who possess some romantic view of the South, *Youngblood* exposes the cruel realities of African Americans who tried to remain tied to their southern roots and not flee to the North for better days. The novel, set in Crossroads, Georgia, explores the lives of four characters who collectively fight against the oppressive educational, social, and economic injustices of a *Jim Crow existence.

Killens's voice rang loud and clear on the civil ills of America as demonstrated in his novel, '*Sippi* (1967), which addresses the struggles African Americans experienced during the 1960s. William H. Wiggins, Jr., in the *Dictionary of Literary Biography* states that the title originates from a "civil rights protest joke" in which a black man informs his white landlord that he will no longer include mister or miss when addressing others, including the state of Mississippi: "It's just plain Sippi from now on!" In the novel, Killens's realistic approach to many intimidating acts, such as bombings and shootings, divided critics. His response to this polarized group was that he wrote the book because he had to tell the story, not because he thought someone would respond as he had to his great-grandmother's stories.

In *The Cotillion, or One Good Bull Is Half the Herd* (1971), Killens moves away from his social protest novel and steps into a community of African Americans to explore its dark sides. This satirical novel attacks the classism and assimilation that dominated many African American communities. Killens's Lumumba represents that breed of African Americans who attempt to redefine themselves by separating themselves from their Eurocentric standards. In contrast to Lumumba's ideology, there exists a community of women who symbolize the vise-grip Eurocentrism has on the African American. Although most criticism of *The Cotillion* dealt with the theme of

*Afrocentricity versus Eurocentricity, the text also has a strong commentary on African American adolescence.

Killens's name will forever ring simultaneously with the bells of *freedom. Most of his works, including his nonfiction pieces, are commentaries on social protest and blacks embracing their blackness. His significance to the literary tradition remains twofold, to provide a silenced community with a voice and to produce a history from which a definition of self can evolve.

• Horst Ihde, "Black Writer's Burden: Remarks on John Oliver Killens," *Zeitschrift fur Anglistik and Amerikanistic* 16 (Jan. 1968): 117–137. William H. Wiggins, Jr., "The Structure and Dynamics of Folklore in the Novel Form: The Case of John O. Killens," *Keystone Folklore Quarterly* 17 (1972): 92–118. Burney J. Hollis, *Swords upon This Hill: Preserving the Literary Tradition of Black Colleges and Universities*, 1984. William H. Wiggins, Jr., "John Oliver Killens," in *DLB*, vol. 33, *Afro-American Fiction Writers after 1955*, eds. Thadious M. Davis and Trudier Harris, 1984, pp. 144–152.

—Wanda Macon

KINCAID, JAMAICA (b. 1949), short story writer, essayist, and novelist. A leading West Indian writer, Jamaica Kincaid (born Elaine Potter Richardson) left her birthplace, the nine-by-twelve-mile island of Antigua, just after her sixteenth birthday and came to the United States. Although much of her writing concerns itself with the West Indies, Kincaid did not return to the island where she was born until nineteen years after she left. Kincaid has received a good deal of attention and critical acclaim despite the modest body of work to her name: a slim book of *short stories (*At the Bottom of the River*, 1983), two short *novels (*Annie John*, 1985; *Lucy*, 1990), a longer novel (*The Autobiography of My Mother*, 1996), a nonfiction *essay about Antigua (*A Small Place*, 1988), and short sketches, short stories, and columns published in the *New Yorker* and elsewhere. Kincaid was editor of *Best American Essays 1995*.

Kincaid began her career as a writer through an exposure to the New York literary scene in the 1970s. Her growing acquaintance with contemporary writers led then *New Yorker* editor William Shawn to ask Kincaid to write a piece for "Talk of the Town." Her pithy, lyrical style was so successful that she became a regular contributor to the magazine. Her first book, *At the Bottom of the River* (1983), included seven stories originally published in the *New Yorker* and touched on themes that would be echoed in her later fiction: mother-daughter relationships, the social constraints felt by a young girl coming of age, a sense of listlessness and dissatisfaction despite surroundings of great beauty, sexual fluidity, questions of *identity, and the merging of real and imaginary worlds.

Annie John (1985), Kincaid's next work of fiction, has alternately been called a book of short stories and a novel. An episodic *bildungsroman, *Annie John* follows the path of an angry and alienated, yet exceptionally bright, ten-year-old girl as she matures.

Stifled yet exhilarated by her small life on Antigua, in love with yet furious at her mother, Annie John suffers acutely from growing pains. Her changing body is awkward to her, she is debilitated by an inexplicable illness that makes her behavior border on madness, and although imbued with a sense of her own superiority, Annie John puzzles as much over her place in the world as she does over the question of what world it is that she inhabits. The book ends with Annie John at seventeen when, not yet freed from her parents' domination but on her way off the island, she embarks on a new life in England.

Kincaid's next novel, *Lucy* (1990), centers around a character whose anger and bitterness (her name is short for Lucifer) bear a great similarity to that of Annie John. Critics have remarked that *Lucy* can be read as a continuation of *Annie John*, although the protagonists have different names. Lucy has traveled a long way from her island home (this time the island is not specified) and come to work as an au pair for a blond and smiling, yet deeply divided, white family in the United States. At nineteen, Lucy is already savvy and seemingly imperturbable. Although she rides an elevator for the first time, eats food taken from a refrigerator for the first time (her island home did not have one, and Kincaid herself grew up without electricity), Lucy is a sophisticated and often embittered young woman. Much is familiar in this new world: she recognizes, for example, her father's love of other women (with whom he had children) in the affair her employer has with his wife's best friend.

The Autobiography of My Mother (1996) is the story of a motherless child, Xuela Claudette Richardson. She negotiates her way through a sensual and desperately lonely world on the island of Dominica, suspecting that her father cherishes his bundle of dirty laundry more than he cares for her. Claiming to embody both her mother and the children she decides not to have, Xuela struggles to construct a self out of the bleak, black wind of her mother's absence.

Best known for her fiction, Kincaid has also written a nonfiction, polemical essay about Antigua. When the piece was rejected by the changing guard at the *New Yorker* (they dismissed it as too angry), Kincaid published *A Small Place* (1988) as a slim book. The essay explores Antigua's shameful past, the island's postcolonial legacy, its dilapidated buildings and astounding beauty, and the corruption and abuse of power by present-day politicians. Kincaid wrote it after a visit back to Antigua and a fresh look at her birthplace through the eyes of an adult.

Kincaid and her husband, composer and college professor Allen Shawn, live in Burlington, Vermont, with their two children, Annie and Harold.

[*See also* West Indian Literature.]

• Daryl Cumber Dance, ed., *Fifty Caribbean Writers: A Bio-Bibliographical Critical Sourcebook*, 1986. Selwyn R. Cudjoe, ed., *Caribbean Women Writers*, 1990. Moira Ferguson, *Gender Relations from Mary Wollstonecraft to Jamaica Kincaid: East Caribbean Connections*, 1993. Diane Simmons, *Jamaica Kincaid*, 1994.
—Jennifer Margulis

Kindred. Octavia E. *Butler's fourth *novel, *Kindred* (1979), is a meditation on the impact of public education, popular media, and family lore upon our conceptions of shared legacies, future prospects, and present positions. Variously classified as realistic science fiction, grim fantasy, *neo–slave narrative, and initiation novel, the book evades genre labeling. Using the fantastic convention of time travel to move Dana on repeated trips from twentieth-century southern California to antebellum Maryland, Butler narrates the coming of age of an African American woman during the social revolutions of the 1970s, explores the grim realities and legacies of antebellum *slavery, and speculates upon future possibilities for human equality.

On her twenty-sixth birthday, Dana is abruptly and involuntarily transported to a Maryland riverbank in order to save a drowning child, Rufus, who will grow up to be a slaveowner and the father of Dana's grandmother, Hagar. Dana makes several trips between the centuries for she is jerked into the nineteenth century every time Rufus believes he is dying and Rufus's temper and lack of discipline often place him in mortal danger. She is returned to the twentieth century when she believes her own life is ending. During her travels into the past, Dana comes to understand slavery as a psychological as well as a physical danger, and she also learns how inadequate the average twentieth-century education is for knowing one's historical past or for surviving without technological aid. As she lives and becomes friends with other slaves, Dana develops a new understanding of heroism and perfidy, of human potential and human limitations. Dana betrays her great-grandmother Alice in order to save Alice's life. With her great-grandfather Rufus, she insists upon mutual respect despite or because of the differences that society affords to *race, *gender, and condition of servitude.

Butler's juxtapositioning of life in nineteenth- and twentieth-century America deliberately suggests complicated comparisons. For example, Dana, a black unpublished writer, is married to Kevin, a white recently published writer, who she met when they were both working for a temporary labor pool nicknamed the "slave market." Though she loves her husband, Dana recognizes disturbing similarities between their relationship and those of the antebellum period, while Kevin comes to regard Rufus as his rival for Dana's attention and affection.

Kindred was written, Butler says, during the black consciousness period of the early 1970s as her attempt to understand her own *identity and the experiences that had shaped her ancestors. It was influenced also by her discovery of *slave narratives by writers such as Frederick *Douglass. Though the antebellum slave past marked a distinct subject and era change for Octavia Butler, *Kindred* does continue the explorations of individual heroism, human relations, and social patterns that mark her other writings.

With *Kindred* Octavia Butler was among the first of recent writers, including Virginia *Hamilton, Belinda Hurmance, Charles R. *Johnson, and Ishmael

*Reed, to employ techniques of *speculative fiction and fantasy in meditations on slavery and the human condition.

• Jewelle Gomez, "Black Women Heroes: Here's Reality, Where's the Fiction?," *The Black Scholar* 17.2 (Mar./Apr. 1986): 8–18. Robert Crossley, introduction to *Kindred,* 1988.

—Frances Smith Foster

KING, MARTIN LUTHER, JR. (1929–1968), orator, political strategist, essayist, and leader during the 1950s and 1960s *civil rights movement. Martin Luther King, Jr., was born in Atlanta, Georgia, on 15 January 1929, the child of Rev. Martin Luther King, Sr., and Alberta Williams King. Alberta King's father, Rev. A. D. Williams, helped found the Atlanta chapter of the NAACP and pastored Ebenezer Baptist Church, which King, Sr., commanded after Williams's death. Both preachers rocked the Ebenezer walls with their thunderous folk sermons while Alberta King played the organ and organized the choir. King, Jr., grew up immersed in the doctrine of Christian love and in the *music and *oratory of African American Baptist worship.

In 1948 King, Jr., earned a bachelor's degree from Morehouse College, where he heard Benjamin *Mays, his father's friend and president of the college, preach during chapel services. Electing to become a minister, King studied at Crozer Theological Seminary and at Boston University, where he received a PhD in theology in 1955.

Early in 1954 King assumed his first pulpit at Dexter Avenue Baptist Church of Montgomery, Alabama. When Rosa Parks was arrested in December 1955 for refusing to give up her bus seat to a white man, JoAnn Robinson and the Women's Political Council initiated a bus boycott. As leader of the boycott organization, King gave his initial civil rights address to an overflow crowd at Holt Street Baptist Church, inspiring his audience to continue the boycott. By the time the protest ended a year later, he emerged as a national figure in the struggle for racial equality. Appearing in 1958, his book about the boycott, *Stride toward Freedom,* articulated the politics of nonviolence.

In 1956 King began an oratorical marathon that lasted over twelve years, attacking segregation in approximately two thousand speeches and sermons as he hopscotched the nation.

In 1963, orchestrating a major civil rights campaign in Birmingham, he answered critics with his famous *essay "*Letter from Birmingham Jail." His demonstrations served as morality plays in which nonviolent demonstrators met police who used fire hoses, German shepherds, tear gas, or billy clubs to preserve white supremacy. Such brutality shocked millions watching on television. In 1963 he delivered "*I Have a Dream," the climactic speech of a massive March on Washington, the most important American civil rights rally to date. Sometimes helped by ghostwriters, he also wrote many essays and five books, including *Strength to Love* (1963), a collection of sermons.

He consistently advocated nonviolence in the quest for racial equality and peace—an approach drastically different from that of *Malcolm X, a more radical leader whose refusal to eschew *violence made King seem more reasonable to whites.

For years scholars attributed King's ideas to his exposure to Euro-American philosophers and theologians, whom he studied in graduate school. Recently, however, a group of researchers led by James Cone has challenged this view, arguing that King's theology and oratory sprang mainly from his boyhood training at Ebenezer Church.

Many of King's sermons echo earlier texts by African American pastor Howard Thurman and by such white Protestant ministers as Harry Emerson Fosdick, Robert McCracken, J. Wallace Hamilton, and George Buttrick. Borrowing sermons was common practice not only for King, but for many other preachers, black and white.

King buttressed arguments with literary quotations. He repeated and elaborated riveting phrases that often incorporated lyrics from patriotic songs and hymns. Enjoying interaction with audiences, he mastered the traditional call and response of African American pastors. His crescendoing baritone voice, rolling cadences, and anticipatory pauses mesmerized not only African American Christians accustomed to such electric delivery, but also millions of others.

Late in his career, King attempted not only to achieve civil rights, but also to stop the Vietnam War and to eliminate American poverty. Facing threats upon his life, he journeyed to a garbage workers' strike in Memphis, Tennessee, to deliver "I've Been to the Mountaintop." He recalled the Exodus and other epochal events in Western history, claiming a similar importance for the present struggle. The mayor of Memphis was a "pharaoh," and his slaves, the garbage workers, could achieve justice only through unity. At the end King dramatically compared himself to *Moses, who, standing atop a mountain, could glimpse the Promised Land. Amid shouts from enraptured listeners, he assured, "I may not get there with you;" but "we as a people will get to the Promised Land."

The next day King died when shot by a hidden gunman.

Like King, James Farmer, Medgar Evers, John Lewis, Fannie Lou Hamer, Diane Nash, and dozens of others volunteered for jail duty, choreographed dramatic confrontations, and risked their lives. King distinguished himself through his language. Simultaneously perfecting and politicizing a robust black pulpit, King translated the traditional African American demand for equality into an idiom that many whites finally tried to understand.

[*See also* Churches; Civil Rights Movement; Preachers and Deacons; Protest Literature; Sermons and Preaching.]

• Harry Emerson Fosdick, *Hope of the World,* 1933. David Garrow, *Bearing the Cross: Martin Luther King, Jr., and the Southern Christian Leadership Conference,* 1986. Martin Luther King, Jr., *A Testament of Hope: The Essential Writings of Martin Luther King, Jr.,* 1986. James Cone, *Martin and Malcolm and America,* 1991. Keith D. Miller, *Voice of Deliverance:*

The Language of Martin Luther King, Jr., and Its Sources, 1992.   —Keith D. Miller *and* Emily M. Lewis

KING, WOODIE, JR. (b. 1937), essayist, short-story writer, anthologist, dramatist, scriptwriter for film and television, producer, director, actor, and contributor to the *Black Arts movement. Born in Mobile, Alabama, Woodie King, Jr., moved to Detroit with his parents, Woodie and Ruby King, when he was five. From 1955 to 1968 to help out his family, which was supported by his mother's housework, King worked as a model for church fans and calendars. He attended Michigan's Will-O-Way School of the Theatre on scholarship from 1958 to 1962, studying every element of the *theater while immersing himself in black literature. In 1959, he married casting agent Willie Mae Washington with whom he would have three children. From 1959 to 1962, King wrote *drama criticism for the *Detroit Tribune.*

Both at Will-O-Way and at Wayne State University and the Detroit School of Arts and Crafts, where he did postgraduate study in theater, King lamented the lack of acting opportunities for blacks and, with Ron *Milner, cofounded the Concept-East Theatre. As its manager and director from 1960 to 1963, King staged plays by white and black playwrights, including Milner's, eventually exchanging the middle class for a neighborhood audience to the enlivenment of the productions.

Negro Digest published his first story, "Ghetto," in August 1962 and his second, "Beautiful Light and Black Our Dreams," in 1963. The latter, republished in Langston *Hughes's *The Best Short Stories by Negro Writers* (1967), explores the poetically expressed thoughts of a black man and his lover and is notably sympathetic toward the woman who has been disillusioned by too many black hustlers yet longs to color her romantic dreams black.

A year after his 1964 move to New York, King won a John Hays Whitney Fellowship to study directing and theater administration and became Cultural Arts Director of Mobilization for Youth. In 1966, King adapted Langston Hughes's *poetry for the stage in *The *Weary Blues,* later adapting Hughes's stories in *Simple's Blues.*

After producing in 1969 *Black Quartet,* four one-act plays by Black Arts movement dramatists (including Ron Milner), King founded the New Federal Theatre in 1970. Serving as showcase and inspiration for new black plays, the New Federal Theatre also welcomed works by other ethnic writers.

In the 1970s, King edited several landmark *anthologies, including *Black Drama Anthology* (coedited with Ron Milner), *Black Short Story Anthology* (containing his story "The Game"), and *Black Poets and Prophets: The Theory, Practice and Esthetics of the Pan-Africanist Revolution* (coedited with Earl Anthony).

King has also produced, directed, and written several films, including *The Long Night* (based on Julian *Mayfield's 1975 novel) and *The Black Theatre Movement: "A Raisin in the Sun" to the Present,* and scripted teleplays for "Sanford and Son." A collection of his *essays on *Black Theater: Present Condition* was published in 1981.

A multitalented man, King has greatly aided the development of contemporary black theater, both through his writings and encouragement of black dramatists widely varied in political and social viewpoints, and black literature through his short stories and anthologies.

• Stephen M. Vallilo, "Woodie King, Jr.," in *DLB,* vol. 38, *Afro-American Writers after 1955: Dramatists and Prose Writers,* eds. Thadious M. Davis and Trudier Harris, 1985, pp. 170–174. Bernard L. Peterson, Jr., "Woodie King, Jr.," in *Contemporary Black American Playwrights and Their Plays,* 1988, pp. 294–297.   —Steven R. Carter

KITCHEN TABLE: WOMEN OF COLOR PRESS was established in 1981 by writer/activist Barbara Smith and poet Audre *Lorde. Founded as both a literary/cultural and political activist organization, it is devoted to *publishing writings by women of color of all racial/cultural heritages, nationalities, classes, and sexual orientations.

As of mid-1995, Kitchen Table had published fifteen award-winning titles, including the groundbreaking *anthologies *This Bridge Called My Back: Writings by Radical Women of Color* and *Home Girls: A Black Feminist Anthology.* It publishes the grassroots Freedom Organizing Pamphlet series, which includes such titles as Barbara Omolade's *It's a Family Affair: The Real Lives of Black Single Mothers; I Am Your Sister: Black Women Organizing Across Sexualities* by Audre Lorde; and *Violence Against Women and the Ongoing Challenge to Racism* by Angela Y. *Davis.

Prior to the founding of Kitchen Table, the words of women of color were rarely published by mainstream or "feminist" book publishers, which are primarily dominated by and responsive to European American concerns and viewpoints. Although others have since begun to publish such writers, Kitchen Table remains a critical resource for multiply disenfranchised women. As one of the few significant means of communication in the world to be controlled by women of color, Kitchen Table's goal is to be a revolutionary tool for empowering society's most dispossessed members. It is a vehicle for shaping ideology that serves as a foundation for making practical social and political change.

[*See also* Feminism; Journalism; Lesbian Literature; Periodicals.]   —Andrea M. Lockett

KNIGHT, ETHERIDGE (1931–1991), poet. In the life and work of Etheridge Knight, the theme of prisons imposed from without (*slavery, racism, poverty, incarceration) and prisons from within (addiction, repetition of painful patterns) are countered with the theme of *freedom. His poems of suffering and survival, trial and tribute, loss and love testify to the fact that we are never completely imprisoned. Knight's poetry expresses our freedom of consciousness and attests to our capacity for connection to others.

Knight was born on 19 April 1931 in Corinth, Mississippi; he was one of seven children. After having dropped out of school in the eighth grade, he joined the army in 1947, saw active duty in Korea, where he suffered a shrapnel wound, and was discharged in 1957. Throughout this time he developed an addiction to drugs and alcohol that caused him to turn to crime to support his habit. While wandering around the United States after his discharge, Knight was arrested for robbery in 1960 and served his sentence in the Indiana State Prison, where by chance Gwendolyn *Brooks visited him and encouraged his writing. He started writing regularly, supported by members of the *Black Arts movement such as Sonia *Sanchez and Dudley *Randall, whose *Broadside Press published Knight's *Poems from Prison* in 1968, also the year of his release from prison and his marriage to Sanchez.

Poems from Prison attests to the freedom of consciousness that persists in spite of prison. "He Sees Through Stone" portrays a strong, older man in prison whose vision—ability to think, imagine, and dream—survives even behind the stone walls. "The Idea of Ancestry," one of Knight's most critically acclaimed pieces, is a cry of yearning for the freedom to be with his family and to have one of his own.

Black Voices from Prison (1970) is an *anthology of writings by men in prison that includes all of Knight's earlier poems and "A WASP Woman Visits a Black Junkie in Prison." In this poem, two people, initially separated by their differences, find common ground when he asks if she has children. The encounter leaves the man touched and softened by the woman, as are many of Knight's male speakers.

The early 1970s were productive years during which Knight gained popularity and recognition across the United States. From 1969 to 1972 Knight held positions at the University of Pittsburgh, the University of Hartford, and Lincoln University. He gave numerous *poetry readings and led Free People's Poetry Workshops, which were open to anyone. He received a National Endowment for the Arts grant in 1972 and a Guggenheim Fellowship in 1974. Still, during this time his marriage to Sanchez ended, and battling his addiction, he periodically admitted himself to veterans hospitals for treatment.

The culmination of these first years out of prison was *Belly Song and Other Poems* (1973). Now married to Mary Ann McAnally, with whom he had two children, Knight produced a volume that features some of his finest work, including many hauntingly beautiful love poems and "Belly Song," the poem that gives the volume its name. In this poem the speaker sings of love: all the emotion, pain, memory, and passion of living, which is located in the belly. Belly love comes from the sharing of memories, the common experience of survival.

In December 1978, Knight had a son with his third wife, Charlene Blackburn. Knight's next work, *Born of a Woman* (1980), presents women as healing, life-giving sources to whom men turn in desire and identification. In "The Stretching of the Belly," written for his wife, the woman's stretch marks are contrasted with the male speaker's scars: hers are marks of growth and life; his are scars from war, violence, and slavery. The volume ends with "Con/tin/u/way/shun Blues," a poem that moves from the "I" to the "we" by

means of *blues rhythms, attesting to the unifying and strengthening power of the blues tradition, which allows us to "keep on keeping on."

The Essential Etheridge Knight (1986) is divided into five sections, which correspond to his five volumes of poetry. Balanced between poems of prison and freedom, the volume attests to the power of each. Freedom's power is forcefully articulated in "Circling the Daughter," for his daughter, Tandi, upon her fourteenth year. The speaker urges his daughter to remember her goodness, signified by her birth, belly, and newly round body, and reminds her to look within for the freedom to counteract the outside world of limit. In 1991, Knight died at age fifty-nine from lung cancer, yet through his poetry, he continues to testify to the power of freedom, and human capacity to envision it even while in prison.

• Patricia Liggins Hill, "'The Violent Space': The Function of the New Black Aesthetic in Etheridge Knight's Prison Poetry," *Black American Literature Forum* 14.3 (Fall 1980): 115–121. Craig Werner, "The Poet, the Poem, the People: Etheridge Knight's Aesthetic," *Obsidian* 7.2–3 (Summer and Winter 1981): 7–17. Etheridge Knight, "A *MELUS* Interview: Etheridge Knight," interview by Steven C. Tracy, *MELUS* 12.2 (Summer 1985): 7–23.   —Cassie Premo

KOMUNYAKAA, YUSEF (b. 1947), poet. Few African American writers have won national or international literary prizes, and if fortunate enough to do so, they automatically garner extraordinary attention. That was the case with Gwendolyn *Brooks winning the Pulitzer Prize in *poetry in 1950, with August *Wilson winning two Pulitzer Prizes in *drama (1987, 1990), with Toni *Morrison winning the Nobel Prize in literature in 1993, and with Yusef Komunyakaa winning the Pulitzer Prize for poetry in 1994. Although his poetry had appeared at regular intervals in journals such as *Callaloo, Komunyakaa remained relatively unknown—in spite of having published eight volumes—before the award. The distinguishing award now places him in a small and unique group of African American writers; it has also elevated his reputation and spurred critical and teaching interest in his poetry.

Komunyakaa was born in Bogalusa, Louisiana, on 29 April 1947, the oldest of five children. His family name, he says, derives from his grandfather, who was probably a stowaway on a ship from Trinidad to the U.S. coast, who arrived wearing a boy's shoe and a girl's shoe, a scene Komunyakaa would depict in "Mismatched Shoes" in the collection *Magic City*. His father, a carpenter, created strained family relationships by being abusive and indulging in extramarital affairs that caused his mother great grief. The poet would portray some of his complicated relationship with his father in various poems. His mother early exposed him to books by buying a set of encyclopedias for him. When he was sixteen, he discovered James *Baldwin's collection of *essays, *Nobody Knows My Name*, and credits that volume with inspiring him to write.

In 1968 Komunyakaa began his military duty in Vietnam. As an information specialist, he edited a military newspaper, the *Southern Cross*. He also won a bronze star. After Vietnam he enrolled at the University of Colorado, where he obtained his bachelor's degree. It was in Colorado, in 1973, that he began writing poetry. He did graduate work at the University of California at Irvine, after also having been in the graduate program at Colorado State University. He taught briefly at various universities before moving to New Orleans, where, while teaching at the University of New Orleans, he married Mandy Sayer, an Australian novelist and short fiction writer, in 1985. It was during this period, fourteen years after the experience, that he began composing poems about Vietnam, which would lead to the publication of *Dien Cai Dau* (1988). The violence he encountered in Vietnam and the pain of returning home are recurring themes in the poetry, as is the casual violence in American society, such as young boys hunting rabbits, birds, and other game. Komunyakaa has come to question this so-called pragmatic violence.

His volumes also include *Dedications and Other Darkhorses* (1977), *Lost in the Bonewheel Factory* (1979), *Copacetic* (1984), *I Apologize for the Eyes in My Head* (1986), *Toys in the Field* (1987), *February in Sydney* (1989), *Magic City* (1992), and *Neon Vernacular* (1994), the Wesleyan University Press Pulitzer Prize–winning volume. Komunyakaa's focus centers upon autobiographical details of his life, including his childhood and his tour of duty in Vietnam. He is particularly interested in connecting the abstract to the concrete as a way of drawing readers into his poems. Indeed, he has expressed an occasional wish to be a painter, in order to capture the images that arise in his head and which he tries to capture poetically. His poetry is also undergirded—in form and subject matter—with *music, especially *blues and *jazz. Trips to Australia inform his volume on Sydney.

Komunyakaa was recognized in some literary circles for the quality of his poetry before he won the Pulitzer Prize. He has won two Creative Writing Fellowships from the National Endowment for the Arts (1981, 1987) as well as the San Francisco Poetry Center Award (1986), and in 1989–1990 he held the Lilly Professorship of Poetry at Indiana University in Bloomington, where he had been on the faculty since 1985. With continued interest in his poetry, including inclusion in the forthcoming *Norton Anthology of Southern Literature*, additional scholarly emphasis upon Komunyakaa's poetry is practically assured.

• Yusef Komunyakaa, "'Lines of Tempered Steel': An Interview with Yusef Komunyakaa," interview by Vincente F. Gotera, *Callaloo* 13.2 (Spring 1990): 215–229. Bruce Weber, "A Poet's Values," *New York Times*, 2 May 1994, B1+. Jennifer Richter, "Review of *Magic City*," *Callaloo* 17:2 (Summer 1994): 650–652.   —Trudier Harris

KRANIDAS, KATHLEEN. *See* Collins, Kathleen.

KUNTA KINTE. A major character in Alex *Haley's *Roots* (1976), Kunta Kinte was, according to Haley, his maternal great-great-great-grandfather, discovered after extensive genealogical research and several journeys to Gambia.

The first son to Omoro and Binta, Kunta Kinte, a Mandinka, is born around 1750 in Juffure along the Gambia River. After a mostly idyllic youth in which he is schooled in Islam and initiated into the Mandinka ways, Kunta Kinte is captured in 1767 and shipped to the United States. Arriving in Annapolis, he is sold to John Waller and renamed Toby. As punishment for three escapes, his foot is amputated. He is then sold to William Waller, becoming Waller's gardener and driver. His initial disgust with the other slaves eventually turns to admiration for their ability to mask their true feelings and to resist the cruel demands of the slaveowners. Kunta Kinte grudgingly accepts his condition and marries Bell, a domestic slave, with whom he has a daughter named Kizzy. Kunta Kinte teaches Kizzy African words and culture, a legacy handed down through the generations until Haley hears them as a child from relatives. The reader last sees Kunta Kinte grieving for his daughter after she is sold for helping her lover escape.

In the *novel, Kunta Kinte is depicted in heroic fashion, intelligent, resourceful, introspective, and courageous, a Mandinka warrior who never abandons his Islamic faith. He is meant to symbolize both the tragedy of American *slavery and the heroism of those who endured it.   —Roger A. Berger

L

LANE, PINKIE GORDON (b. 1923), poet. The first African American to be named Louisiana's poet laureate, the unmistakably southern writer Pinkie Gordon Lane was raised in Philadelphia, where she was born in 1923, the only child of William and Inez Gordon. The death of her father led to five years of work in a sewing factory; she subsequently left for Atlanta, where she earned her BA at Spelman College, and married Ulysses Lane. After teaching high school from 1949 to 1954, she earned an MA from Atlanta University. The Lanes subsequently moved to Baton Rouge, where Pinkie soon developed a lyrical, soaring, poetic gift that took much of its ambiance from her new surroundings.

The *poetry in her first collection, *Wind Thoughts*, bespoke a mature imagination, as it was published when she was forty-nine, shortly after her husband's early death. It offers ample display of a unique voice, but also demonstrates her admiration for the *Black Aesthetic of that time in her inscriptions from LeRoi Jones, Gwendolyn *Brooks, and Sonia *Sanchez, and in poems directly addressed to fellow black poets. On the other hand, while earning the first PhD degree ever granted to a black woman by Louisiana State University, she acquired an equally important classical sense, which produced an unusually formal tone quite different from those of the *Black Arts movement poets, along with references to John Milton, John Keats, William Butler Yeats, and e. e. cummings. Her later poems range even further for antecedents; the title poem of *The Mystic Female* cites Lao Tzu. Lane claims the most important influences on her work have been Gwendolyn Brooks, for inspiration, and Anne Sexton, for style.

Lane studs poems with unexpected, arresting images, but also with reassuring visions of nature, sometimes deceptively simple as in "Roasting Grasshoppers," or ominously foreboding as in "Opossum." Her musings about quotidian details can yield sudden insight, as in "On Being Head of the English Department," a cynical yet loving appraisal of duty; so can poems based on shocking incidents, such as "Sexual Privacy of Women on Welfare" or "Flight," which transmogrifies the discovery of a newborn baby in an airplane's toilet. The moods of love and its torments inform many poems, and white-hot heat flares in "Three Love Poems" and "St. Valentine's Eve Poem." But Lane is mainly an autobiographical poet, so her most successful works pay tribute to friends and family members who are mourned and remembered, even for sour moods and evil deeds, as in "Children," and in what may be her most powerful work, "Poems to My Father." She makes art out of the agony of her husband's fatal illness in "Songs to the Dialysis Machine," while the complex fate of her mother emerges in "Prose Poem: Portrait."

More often than not, her poems offer solitary meditations on quiet interstices of existence; the persona may be listening to the furnace crackle on a winter's evening, as in "Breathing," or reacting to music, as in several poems devoted to her drummer son, Gordon. She feels she runs against the grain with reflective poems and suggests in "A Quiet Poem" that African Americans are expected to write from anger.

Still, Lane's artistry frequently proceeds from pain. Although she can conjure love, she eschews cheap romanticism and often prefers harsh images connected by poetic integuments, as in "Bill," her portrait of a saxophone-playing heroin addict. Lane's subtle renditions of oppression can lie in her omissions as well. Her memories of childhood evoke bittersweet creations that also indict an uncaring society, as in "Rain Ditch," where children frolic in filthy water, unable (although the poem never says so) to swim in whites-only pools.

Lane's books of poetry include *Wind Thoughts* (1972); *The Mystic Female* (1978); *I Never Scream* (1985); and *Girl at the Window* (1991). She has won numerous prizes and awards, has lectured nationally and in Africa, and has been nominated for the Pulitzer Prize. She edited *Discourses on Poetry* and *Poems by Blacks*, volume 3. For years Lane was chair of the English Department at Southern University, and she recently completed a visiting professorship at Bridgewater College.

• Marilyn B. Craig, "Pinkie Gordon Lane," in *DLB*, vol. 41, *Afro-American Poets since 1955*, eds. Trudier Harris and Thadious M. Davis, 1985, pp. 212–216. Violet Harrington Bryan, "Evocations of Place and Culture in the Works of Four Contemporary Black Louisiana Writers: Brenda Osbey, Sybil Kein, Elizabeth Brown-Guillory, and Pinkie Gordon Lane," *Louisiana Literature* 4.2 (1987): 49–60.

—John Lowe

LANGSTON, JOHN MERCER (1829–1897), autobiographer, orator, lawyer, abolitionist, politician and public official, and educator. In his third-person *autobiography, *From the Virginia Plantation to the National Capitol* (1894), John Mercer Langston recounts his career as one of the most influential African American leaders of the nineteenth century. Born in Virginia and educated at Oberlin, Langston became in 1854 the first African American admitted to the Ohio bar and in 1855 the first elected to public office in the United States (town clerk of Brownhelm, Ohio). Throughout the 1850s he worked within antislavery and civil rights movements, advocating a nationalist, pro-*emigration position before becoming a Republican party activist. Heading recruitment of African American soldiers in the West during the Civil War, he rose to national prominence after the war as the president of the National Equal Rights League (a forerunner of the NAACP), an educational inspector for the Freedmen's Bureau, and a Republican party organizer. In 1868, he accepted a professorship at Howard University, where he founded its law school, and eventually became vice president and acting president of the university. In 1871, President Ulysses S. Grant appointed him to the Board of Health for Washington, D.C. In 1877, President Rutherford B. Hayes made him U.S. minister to Haiti. After eight years in Haiti, Langston returned to Virginia and accepted the presidency of the state college for African Americans in Petersburg, Virginia, Normal and Collegiate Institute. Langston crowned his public career in 1890 by serving as the first African American from Virginia in the U.S. House of Representatives.

Like his grandnephew Langston *Hughes, he combined a hope-filled vision of a more just society with insistent opposition to white supremacy. Although readers have found his autobiography unimaginative and self-serving, his speeches—collected in *Freedom and Citizenship* (1883)—remain highly regarded for their compelling and controlled rhetoric and their blending of evangelical, democratic, and African American oratorical traditions.

• William Cheek and Aimee Lee Cheek, "John Mercer Langston: Principle and Politics," in *Black Leaders of the Nineteenth Century*, eds. Leon Litwack and August Meier, 1988, pp. 103–126. William Cheek and Aimee Lee Cheek, *John Mercer Langston and the Fight for Black Freedom, 1829–1865*, 1989.   —Gregory Eiselein

Langston Hughes Review, The. As the official publication of the Langston *Hughes Society, an organization founded in 1981 by Therman B. O'Daniel, George H. Bass, and other prominent scholars of African American literature to bring together individuals committed to furthering Hughes's reputation, the *Langston Hughes Review* has published original scholarship on Hughes, his literary *ancestors, and other artists influenced by his prolific work in multiple genres. Since its inaugural issue in 1982, the *Review*—first edited by O'Daniel and Bass and published under the auspices of the African American Studies Program at Brown University and now edited by Dolan Hubbard and published by the University of Georgia—has sought to preserve Hughes's position as one of the most representative artists in the history of African American literature. In addition to literary-critical studies, the *Langston Hughes Review* also includes reprints of *poetry and *essays by Hughes, book reviews, original tributes to Hughes by contemporary poets and scholars, and notes concerning the professional activities of Langston Hughes Society members.

[*See also* Journalism; Literary Societies; Periodicals; Publishing.]   —Christopher C. De Santis

LANUSSE, ARMAND (1812–1867), New Orleans poet, educator, and editor of *Les Cenelles* (1845). Armand Lanusse was born in New Orleans in 1812 and died there in 1867. Literary historians differ on whether he received his *education in New Orleans or Paris. He helped found the New Orleans Catholic School for Indigent Orphans of Color in 1848 and served as principal from 1852 until his death.

Lanusse used his position as a free *Créole de couleur* to promote nonwhites in antebellum New Orleans through education and literary activity. Along with other Euro-African Louisianians, he contributed to *Album littérarie, journal des jeunes gens, amateurs de littérature* (*Literary Album, Journal of Young People, Lovers of Literature*, 1843) and to *Les *Cenelles* (1845), a volume of *poetry by Creoles of color, which Lanusse also edited.

Ironically, Lanusse served in the Confederate army and initially opposed Union occupation of New Orleans. The increased oppression of blacks in postbellum years led him to despair of racial equality ever becoming a reality in the United States and drew him closer to less privileged blacks.

Heavily influenced by French romanticism, Lanusse's poetry in *Les Cenelles* highlights love, death, and both the pleasures and the general oppressiveness of life. While in his personal and professional life Lanusse championed black civil rights, his poetry, like most of the *Les Cenelles* poems, does not protest racial discrimination. However, Lanusse's social and religious concerns do manifest themselves in poems treating the morality of Creole women of color. Through the comedy of "Epigram" and the serious warning of "To Elora," for example, Lanusse exposes the spiritual, emotional, and ethical predicaments of *plaçage*, a custom whereby Creole girls of color gained protection and material comfort but sacrificed virtue in becoming white men's mistresses.

As educator, poet, and editor, Lanusse played a leading role in encouraging the educational, vocational, and literary activity of nonwhites and championed their civil rights as well.

[*See also* Anthologies.]

• Régine Latortue and Gleason R. W. Adams, eds. and trans., *Les Cenelles: A Collection of Poems by Creole Writers of the Early Nineteenth Century*, 1979.
          —Germain J. Bienvenu

LARSEN, NELLA (1891–1964), novelist and participant in the Harlem Renaissance. At the end of the 1920s, Nella Larsen emerged as a premiere novelist of the *New Negro movement. In rapid succession, she produced *Quicksand* (1928) and *Passing* (1929), both published by the respected New York firm, Alfred A. Knopf. Before the appearance of her novels, Larsen was an active, though minor, presence in the literary and social life of the *Harlem Renaissance. She had published little: two brief accounts of children's games (*The *Brownies' Book*, 1920); a book review of *Certain People of Importance* by Kathleen Norris (*The *Messenger*, 1923), and two pseudonymous stories, "The Wrong Man" and "Freedom" (*Young's Realistic Stories Magazine*, 1926). Her success as a novelist had not been foreshadowed by any of her earlier publications. Her life experiences, however, had provided her with rich materials for a modern fictionist.

Born Nellie Walker in Chicago and reared in a visibly white, Danish immigrant family, Larsen was a lonely child whose dark skin separated her from both parents and a sibling. In preparation for a life within an African American world, she entered the Fisk University Normal High School in Nashville. After a year (1907–1908), she left without a diploma. She trained instead at the Lincoln Hospital School of Nursing in New York City (1912–1915) and worked initially for her alma mater, and briefly for Tuskegee Institute's Andrew Memorial Hospital as head nurse, and subsequently for New York City's Board of Health.

In 1919 Nella Larsen married a research physicist, Dr. Elmer S. Imes. With her marriage Larsen moved from the working class and obscurity to visibility within an upwardly mobile, African American middle class, conscious not only of position, but also of possibility. This social world hastened her disillusionment with nursing. She found employment at the 135th Street branch of the New York Public Library, a job that introduced her to the emerging coterie of writers in Harlem and enabled her to enter the Library School of the New York Public Library in 1922. This was the same year that Larsen and two of the emerging Harlem writers, Walter *White and Jessie Redmon *Fauset, agreed to write novels depicting the complex realities of African American life.

Quicksand and *Passing*, Larsen's only published novels, immediately earned her a considerable reputation and prominence as a writer of powerful explorations of female psychology and modern consciousness. *Quicksand* follows the exploits of an educated mixed-race woman, *Helga Crane, as she seeks self-definition, social recognition, and sexual expression. Her movement through evocative contemporary settings in the rural South and urban North, as well as in cosmopolitan Denmark, signals her determined effort to attain a space within which all parts of her identity can coexist. The episodic construction serves to inflect Helga's psychological and emotional states and to illustrate the multiple subjective spaces disallowed in marking identity only within rigid categories. Helga fails in her quest for control over her own *identity and body; her failure is represented in terms of reproduction as a part of a psychic and physical quagmire, threatening to erase a woman's autonomy and agency.

Passing, Larsen's second novel, positions two light-skinned women as antagonists and psychological doubles in a drama of racial *passing, *class and social mobility, and female desire. Irene Redfield demands safety and security in contained, self-sacrificing race and gender roles; Clare Kendry functions in a self-seeking, risk-filled existence on the edge of danger and duplicity. Although Clare's racial passing is one of the novel's concerns, Irene's obsessive desires, represented through her perspective as the central consciousness, expose a range of intense emotions all cloaked by her persistent concerns for social respectability and material comfort.

Both *Passing* and *Quicksand* illustrate Larsen's nuanced modernity. Recent attention to *Passing* has emphasized Larsen's use of passing as a device for encoding the complexities of human personality, for veiling women's homoerotic desires, and for subverting simplistic notions of female self-actualization. Similarly, recent criticism of *Quicksand* has focused on the dialogics of *race and *gender and the social production of gender, *sexuality, and race. Like Jessie Fauset, to whom she is frequently compared,

Larsen emphasizes female sexuality as a component of women's identity, but she also challenges the implication that the domestic sphere can satisfy a woman's quest for satisfaction and completion. More pessimistic than Fauset or earlier women novelists, such as Frances Ellen Watkins *Harper, about the work of uplift as an expression of the racialized female's role in society, Larsen concludes her novels with an irreparable breakdown of illusions about emancipatory strategies or possible futures for women.

Larsen received the Harmon Foundation's bronze medal for achievement in literature in 1929 and a Guggenheim Fellowship in creative writing in 1930. However, that same year, she was accused in *Forum* magazine of plagiarizing "Sanctuary" (1930), the only short story published under her own name. She spent her fellowship year in Spain and France researching a novel on racial freedom and writing a novel about her husband's infidelity. Her literary promise, however, did not achieve a full maturity. She was shattered by the reversal of her material condition: a difficult, highly publicized divorce (1933); an inability to publish her third novel and other announced writing projects; a failure of a partnership to produce collaborative novels; and a perceived loss of status in her return to nursing. Larsen stopped writing in the late 1930s. By 1941, when her former husband died, she had severed her connections with her one-time associates among New York's black and white artists. She worked as a nurse in New York City hospitals until March 1964 when she was found dead. Nearly forgotten as a novelist until the recovery of her fiction in the 1970s, Larsen has been returned to prominence as a major novelist, whose expansively complex representations of gender and race resist reductive readings.

• Deborah E. McDowell, introduction to *Quicksand and Passing by Nella Larsen*, 1986. Mary Helen Washington, "Nella Larsen," in *Invented Lives: Narratives of Black Women, 1860–1960*, 1987. Ann Allen Shockley, "Nella Marian Larsen Imes," in *Afro-American Women Writers, 1746–1933*, 1988. Thadious M. Davis, *Nella Larsen, Novelist of the Harlem Renaissance*, 1994. Cheryl A. Wall, *The Women of the Harlem Renaissance*, 1995.
—Thadious M. Davis

Last Days of Louisiana Red, The. *The Last Days of Louisiana Red* (1974) is Ishmael *Reed's fourth novel. Set primarily in northern California in the early 1970s, it deals with the efforts of *Papa LaBas, the hoodoo detective first introduced in Reed's previous novel, *Mumbo Jumbo* (1972), to combat the insidious influence of Louisiana Red, symbolizing forces of discord, especially within the black community, that keep people at one another's throats. It is a stress plague and therefore an antidote to Jes Grew, the epidemic of "boogie fever" depicted in *Mumbo Jumbo*. Other important characters are Ed Yellings, owner of Solid Gumbo Works, who has found a cure for cancer and is murdered by Louisiana Red in order to prevent him from finding a cure for heroin addiction; Ed's son Street, a thug who wraps himself in the mantle of Black Power; Street's sister Minnie, leader of the Moochers, a gang of opportunists posing as radicals; and two personae "borrowed" from Greek drama: chorus, a "characterless character" who bears a striking resemblance to Cab Calloway, and his perennial antagonist, Antigone (Minnie the Moocher's prototype), who constantly seeks to upstage if not silence him. Antigone, whose name means "born against," represents unmitigated energies of opposition in the community—a somewhat ironic target, given that Reed himself has been accused of being excessively "anti"—and she also stands for a too intense *womanism that, in Reed's view, unduly victimizes men.

Once again, Reed offers us a divergent interpretation of a classic, for in Sophocles' famous play, Antigone represents a morally superior position to the authoritarianism of Creon, who found it repugnant that a woman should get the better of a man. Reed also puts a negative spin on a canonical work of African American literature, Richard *Wright's *Native Son (1940), making the surly, loutish Street Yellings a 1970s version of *Bigger Thomas, and having a white character named Max become possessed by the spirit of Bigger, who then causes him to kill. In this novel, Reed seems to be exposing the bad side of the Business (the workings of neohoodoo) that goes under the name of Louisiana Red (the heckler in the audience, too much red pepper in the gumbo, Frankie looking for Johnny with her .44).

Gerald Duff, in his essay on Reed in the *Dictionary of Literary Biography* (vol. 2), notes that in *The Last Days of Louisiana Red*, Papa LaBas—who often serves as Reed's spokesman—takes a "stringently patriarchal" position with regard to women, which, interestingly, resembles that of the black militants Reed is satirizing, and which they claimed to be sanctioned by traditional African values. This novel, indeed, is one piece of evidence cited by those wishing to indict Reed for misogynistic tendencies.

Houston A. *Baker, Jr., who praised *Mumbo Jumbo* as an exemplary work of black consciousness, condemned Reed for his putdown of cultural nationalists in *The Last Days of Louisiana Red*, implying that he was destroying black American culture with his unrestrained satire. This typifies the antithetical nature of Reed's enterprise, which has as its only consistency a refusal to recognize any sacred cows.

[See also Black Aesthetic; Conjuring; Folklore.]

• Lorenzo Thomas, "Two Crowns of Thoth: A Study of Ishmael Reed's *The Last Days of Louisiana Red*," *Obsidian* 2.3 (1976): 5–25. —Robert Elliot Fox

LATTIMORE, JEWEL. *See* Amini, Johari.

LAWRENCE, JACOB (b. 1917), painter, professor of painting, and illustrator-author of *Harriet and the Promised Land*. The child of migrants from the South, Jacob Lawrence received most of his schooling in New York City. His artistic talent was recognized in an afterschool program in 1932, and he began studing with Charles H. Alston at the Harlem Art Workshop and Henry Bannarn in WPA art classes. In 1937, he won a scholarship to the American Artists School.

His early colorful tempera work was considered primitivist in style and social realist in subject matter. His developing tendency toward distortion resembled expressionism and abstractionism. Also influenced by muralists, Lawrence adopted the practice of assembling paintings in captioned narrative series about African American leaders—Toussaint *L'Overture (1937–1938), Frederick *Douglass (1938–1939), Harriet *Tubman (1939–1940), and John *Brown (1942)—displayed first in a one-man show at the Harlem YMCA. Winner of a Rosenwald Fund Scholarship in 1940, he began a *migration series depicting the movement from South to North. It was exhibited at a downtown gallery—his first show out of Harlem—on 7 December 1941, Pearl Harbor Day. Earlier the same year he had married Gwendolyn Knight, a painter.

Returning to civilian life after serving in the U.S. Coast Guard (1943–1945), Lawrence continued to depict African American subjects (often in theme series: Performance, 1951; Struggle, 1955; Civil Rights, 1962; and Nigeria, 1964). These works received recognition from the art world at large in shows at major museums, including an African and South American traveling exhibit (1989–1990). He won a Guggenheim Fellowship in 1946, a National Institute of Arts and Letters Award in 1953, and a Presidents for Art Award in 1990. He also taught at Black Mountain College (1947), the Pratt Institute (1956–1971), and the University of Washington, Seattle (1971–1983).

Best known as a painter of African American history and contemporary life, Lawrence won the Brooklyn Art Books Children's Citation for his picture book, *Harriet and the Promised Land* (1968). Although based on his Harriet Tubman series of 1939, this work was also artistically influenced by his African trip, as well as the expressionism and abstractionism of his later style.

• Milton W. Brown, *Jacob Lawrence*, 1974. Ellen Hawkins Wheat, *Jacob Lawrence, American Painter*, 1986.

—Lois R. Kuznets

LEE, ANDREA (b. 1953), fiction writer and journalist. Andrea Lee was born in Philadelphia in 1953 and graduated from Harvard University. Her first book, *Russian Journal* (1981), is based upon her experiences in Russia during 1978–1979 and received a National Book Award nomination, as well as the 1984 Jean Stein Award from the American Academy and Institute of Arts and Letters. Currently a staff writer for the *New Yorker*, Lee lives in Europe with her husband.

Andrea Lee is best known for her 1984 novel, *Sarah Phillips*, composed of stories that were first published in the *New Yorker*. Each is a vignette taken from the life of the title character, the daughter of a prosperous Baptist minister and schoolteacher mother. Set in the 1960s and early 1970s, *Sarah Phillips* comments on contemporary discourses around *race, *class, and *gender and problematizes the meanings of resistance in the postintegration era.

Critic Mary Helen Washington compares *Sarah Phillips* to works such as William Wells *Brown's *Clotel (1853), Frances Ellen Watkins *Harper's *Iola

Leroy (1892), James Weldon *Johnson's The *Autobiography of an Ex-Colored Man (1912), and Nella *Larsen's *Quicksand (1928), books in which privileged black characters seek to escape the trials and responsibilities that attach to their racial identities. Sarah Phillips also invites comparison with the growing number of novels and autobiographies set in the period after court-ordered desegregation: Jake Lamar's Bourgeois Blues (1991), Trey *Ellis's Platitudes (1988), Lorene Cary's Black Ice (1991), Itabari Njeri's Every Good-bye Ain't Gone (1990), Darryl Pinckney's High Cotton (1992), Stephen L. Carter's Reflections of an Affirmative Action Baby (1991), Connie Porter's All-Bright Court (1991), and Jill Nelson's Volunteer Slavery (1993). These later works explore the covert forms of racism that emerged during the eras of integration and affirmative action, the various responses these social changes produced, and the complex interconnections among constructions of race and class.

Lee's characters are complexly drawn, her descriptions nuanced, her sensibility both haunting and ironic. Yet neither Russian Journal nor Sarah Phillips is an especially popular work. This is perhaps the case because both books resist generally unspoken constructions of black women's lives. Some readers dismiss her work, considering it insufficiently assertive of a politics of resistance. However, to the extent that both works refuse to conform to conventions of representing "blackness" and "black womanhood," they raise challenging questions for the reader about what we mean when we use those terms. Sarah Phillips prompts fruitful consideration of the ways in which social and economic class position shape the meaning of racial *identity.

—Valerie Smith

LEE, DON L. See Madhubuti, Haki R.

LEE, GEORGE WASHINGTON (1894–1976), orator, insurance executive, civic worker, and leader among African American Republicans. George Washington Lee was born in Indianola, Mississippi, to sharecroppers, but this did not prohibit his gaining a higher education. He held various jobs including bellhop and pursued a degree at Alcorn Agricultural and Mechanical College. In 1917, he was selected from Tennessee to attend the first African American commissioned officers training camp. Thus, he entered World War I as one of only a few African American officers. In 1919, after a tour of duty in France and an honorable discharge, he returned to Memphis and became an insurance agent, then director of the Atlanta Life Insurance Company and its Memphis manager, and later a senior vice president of the company. Simultaneously, as an active community leader, he promoted various activities to support youth, provide food for the poor, and support the country's military efforts, and he was grand commissioner of education for the Improved Benevolent and Protective Order of Elks and the World. Additionally, he was one of the leading African American Republicans of Tennessee, known as a shrewd strategist. Lee was a delegate to every Republican national convention from 1940 to 1960. At the 1952 convention, he used his oratorical skills to make a seconding speech for the nomination of Senator Robert Taft of Ohio. He was the second African American to have his portrait displayed in the Tennessee Capitol at Nashville. Throughout his life, he reflected his race pride, his belief that African Americans must be independent and develop and emphasize their gifts. This was evidenced in his writing in publications such as Negro Digest, Southern Messenger, *Opportunity, and Memphis World. He wrote three books in which he sought to preserve a way of life, a variety of characters, a time, and a place.

His first novel, Beale Street, Where the Blues Began (1934), with a foreword by W. C. Handy, was a Book-of-the-Month Club alternate selection. It shows the positive and the negative, the two worlds of Beale Street, the struggles of W. C. Handy, the history of the *blues, and Robert R. Church, Sr.'s efforts to make Beale Street a commercial center. Included are a variety of the street's characters. Lee's second book, River George (1937), is the story of Aaron George, a character introduced in Beale Street, who after a time in college returns to the plantation and his sharecropping family and is moved by the exploitation of his race. There follows the story of his fight for justice and racial uplift. Lee's final book, Beale Street Sundown (1942), is a collection of short stories in which he presents Beale Street lifestyles and personalities. Throughout his career, he demonstrated a love for the South and for African American people, and a belief that America is not a melting pot but a place where all races can coexist and make their own particular contributions. He preached racial uplift, war against unjust treatment, and unity.

• "George W. Lee, Dies, Led Black Republicans, " Washington Star, 2 August 1976, B-4. Edward D. Clark, "George Washington Lee," in DLB, vol. 51 Afro-American Writers from the Harlem Renaissance to 1940, ed. Trudier Harris 1987, pp. 192–195.

—Helen R. Houston

LEE, JARENA (1783–?), itinerant preacher and autobiographer. Born free in Cape May, New Jersey, on 11 February 1783, Jarena Lee became both the first African American woman to write an extended account of her own life and the first African American woman whose right to preach received official acknowledgment from *church authorities. Her *autobiography, The Life and Religious Experience of Jarena Lee (1836), begins with a few brief references to her family, whom she left at the age of seven to work as a maid, and then quickly focuses on the steps she took to attain Christian salvation. Three sections follow this account of her spiritual awakening and clearly demonstrate her belief in female equality. The second section, titled "My Call to Preach the Gospel," describes the call to preach she received around the year 1807. She sought permission to answer this call from the Reverend Richard *Allen, head of the African Methodist Episcopal Church, who upheld the church's ban against women preachers. The third section of her autobiography, "My Marriage," tells of her union with Joseph Lee, the pastor of a church outside Philadelphia, whom she married in 1811. In about 1818, Joseph Lee died, leaving her with two small children to support. While married, Jarena Lee did not pursue her call to preach, though her autobiography intimates her frustration with the subordinate role of wife. The last section of her work, "The Subject of My Call to Preach Renewed," recounts the final steps she took toward becoming a preacher. Eight years after she first approached Bishop Allen with her request to preach, Lee asked for—and received—his permission to hold prayer meetings in her home and "of exhorting as I found liberty." Soon after acquiring these limited privileges, Lee unexpectedly found herself the last-minute replacement for the minister who had been scheduled to preach. Allen, who happened to be among those who heard her spontaneous sermon, acknowledged her right to preach, enabling her to embark on a career as a traveling minister. Lee wrote another, longer version of her autobiography, *Religious Experience and Journal of Mrs. Jarena Lee* (1849), the last record we have of her life. Lee's autobiographical writings offer invaluable insight into one woman's efforts to overcome the limitations imposed on her by a racist and sexist culture and show the significance of the church to African American literature.

[*See also* Autobiography, *article on* Spiritual Autobiography.]

• Jarena Lee, *The Life and Religious Experience of Jarena Lee*, 1836; rpt. in *Sisters of the Spirit: Three Black Women's Autobiographies of the Nineteenth Century*, ed. William L. Andrews, 1986. Nellie Y. McKay, "Nineteenth-Century Black Women's Spiritual Autobiographies," in *Interpreting Women's Lives*, ed. The Personal Narratives Group, 1989.

—Candis LaPrade

LEE, SPIKE (b. 1957), film director, writer, and actor. Shelton Jackson "Spike" Lee grew up in Brooklyn and earned degrees at Morehouse College (1979) and New York University (1983) before embarking on a career as perhaps the most celebrated and accomplished African American filmmaker. Aside from his major *films, Lee has also made music videos (for such artists as Miles *Davis, Anita Baker, and Public Enemy), and *television commercials; he produced, for example, campaign advertisements for Jesse Jackson's 1988 presidential bid. An actor as well as a director, Lee has become a major, outspoken public and political figure. Much of his work is politically inflected, provocative, and often controversial, and treats issues of *identity and community that resonate throughout African American literature.

Several of Lee's films deal with questions and dilemmas surrounding African American identity, *gender, and *class. His first full-length release, *She's Gotta Have It* (1986), about an African American woman and her three very different lovers, earned him the *Prix de Jeunesse* at the Cannes Film Festival. The film features innovative narrative techniques and begins Lee's exploration of the possibilities of African American male identity. His second film, *School Daze* (1988), a *musical set in an all-black college, explores questions of color and class lines, as well as sexism, within the African American community. In *Mo' Better Blues* (1990), a *jazz musician

must choose between two women, and ultimately between his music and fatherhood. *Jungle Fever* (1991) addresses interracial romance and drug addiction and their effects on the black communities. *Clockers* (1995) challenges "gangsta" stereotypes, complicating received narratives of African American poverty and *violence.

Lee may be best known for his more broadly political films, *Do the Right Thing* (1989) and *Malcolm X* (1992). The first, a dramatization of complex racial tensions and conflicts in Brooklyn, focuses on the efficacy (and risks) of violence as a response to racism or oppression. Lee situates the film's point of view between the proactive *black nationalism of *Malcolm X and the nonviolent philosophy of Martin Luther *King, Jr., quoting from both at the film's end, choosing neither (or both). In his epic treatment of Malcolm X's life, based on Alex *Haley's *The *Autobiography of Malcolm X* (1965), Lee traces Malcolm's political trajectory, including his pilgrimage to Mecca and his split with the Nation of Islam, and presents Malcolm X's legacy as a living symbol of African American struggle. The film, however, raised controversy about what some, including Amiri *Baraka, considered the commercialization of Malcolm's image.

Lee often appears in his own films and commercials (though sometimes as minor characters). The resultant blurring of Lee's public persona with his fictional characters makes him appear more personally implicated in his films than many directors and recalls the similarly ambiguous positioning of the author/narrator in many African American *novels, beginning with William Wells *Brown's *Clotel* (1853). In fact, two of his films—*School Daze* and 1994's *Crooklyn*, an episodic, nostalgic portrayal of Lee's Brooklyn childhood—have autobiographical origins. Lee's work thus evokes both the importance of *autobiography as well as the tension between the personal and the political in African American literature.

• Spike Lee, *Spike Lee's Gotta Have It: Inside Guerrilla Filmmaking*, 1987. Terry McMillan et al., *Five for Five: The Films of Spike Lee*, 1991. Gwen Sparks, "Shelton Jackson 'Spike' Lee," in *African American Encyclopedia*, ed. Michael Williams, 1993, pp. 952–955.

—Gary Ashwill

LESBIAN LITERATURE. The appearance of *Afrekete: An Anthology of Black Lesbian Writing* in 1995 was a precedent-setting event that for many signaled public acceptance of lesbian literature as part of the African American literary tradition. But many scholars and writers labored diligently to prepare the way to *Afrekete*—by identifying writers, articulating criticisms, and otherwise serving to chronicle the existence of this diverse and long-standing facet of African American literary heritage. Though many focus primarily on lesbian themes, issues, and characters, writers such as Alice *Walker, Michelle Cliff, and Alexis *De Veaux write about a range of human issues that are connected to, but not necessarily and primarily concerned with, the assertion of a strong lesbian identity. Other authors such as Gloria *Naylor and Rosa *Guy, who are not lesbian-identified, include lesbian characters and themes in their works. Finally, some lesbian authors have managed to maintain very private lesbian identities that are only revealed by the efforts of diligent literary sleuths.

Gloria T. Hull is one such sleuth, having documented the existence of lesbian relationships among early twentieth-century African American women writers. Hull's work as editor of Alice Moore *Dunbar-Nelson's diary, her essay entitled "'Under the Days': The Buried Life and Poetry of Angelina Weld *Grimké" (Home Girls, 1983), and her 1987 monograph Color, Sex and Poetry: Three Women Writers of the Harlem Renaissance identify Grimké and Dunbar-Nelson as literary foremothers of the lesbian tradition. She provides information that suggests Dunbar-Nelson's lesbian affairs with journalist Fay Jackson Robinson and artist Helen Ricks London. A number of Grimké's unpublished poems ("If," "To Her of the Cruel Lips," "Rosalie," and "My Shrine") express lesbian desire and reveal that the poet's stifled artistry was, according to Hull, related to her status as African American, woman, and lesbian. Hull's scholarship assists in better understanding what it meant to be an African American lesbian poet in the early twentieth century. In the manner articulated by Alice Walker in *In Search of Our Mothers' Gardens (1984), her efforts also help to fulfill a need of contemporary African American lesbian writers for models.

Post-1950s sociopolitical movements resulted in a resurgence of literature by African Americans, especially African American women, but works featuring openly lesbian themes and characters were not readily forthcoming. Even Toni Cade *Bambara's landmark anthology, The Black Woman (1970), while asserting an African American feminist politics, was silent on the issue of African American lesbian identity. A few items by lesbian writers began to appear in the 1970s, such as Audre *Lorde's "Martha," which featured an openly lesbian subject, and Anita Cornwell's essays in the Ladder and Dyke. These efforts, along with the appearance of Ann Allen *Shockley's novel Loving Her in 1974, helped to nourish the soil in which both movement and tradition would later flourish.

Shockley's work on two fronts added dimension and substance to the work of establishing this tradition. Loving Her may be the first published novel with an African American lesbian as the primary character. In a theme often echoed in later lesbian fiction, as well as in personal narratives like Audre Lorde's 1982 biomythography Zami: A New Spelling of My Name, Loving Her depicts the journey of a young woman into self-discovery. The novel, which has been compared to white novelist Marguerite Radclyffe Hall's pioneering lesbian novel, The Well of Loneliness (1928), presents an African American woman who chooses to leave an oppressive and abuse-ridden heterosexual marriage for a relationship with a white woman who offers both economic and emotional security. Shockley's collection of short stories, The Black and White of It (1980), and her 1982 novel, Say Jesus and Come to Me, continue her

discourse on interracial relationships and lesbian experiences, addressing issues similar to those raised in Pat Parker's Movement in Black (1978). Movement is Parker's poetic response to the demands of oppressive and abusive relationships, racism within the feminist community, and her own family's adverse reaction to Parker's white female lover. Others in the tradition who address interracial issues in their writing include Cornwell (Black Lesbian in White America, 1983) and Becky Birtha in her short story collections For Nights Like This One: Stories of Loving Women (1983) and Lovers' Choice (1987).

Shockley has also served as chronicler for the emerging tradition. Her 1979 essay, "The Black Lesbian in American Literature: An Overview," introduces several other lesbian writers—SDiane Bogus, Pat Suncircle, Stephanie Byrd, Terri Clark, Lea Hopkins, Sapphire—and asserts that the preferred mode of expression among lesbian writers is poetry. De Veaux (Blue Heat, 1985), Julie Blackwomon Carter ("Revolutionary Blues," 1981), doris *davenport (it's like this, 1980; eat thunder and drink rain, 1982 and 1983; Voodoo Chile Slight Return, 1991), Bogus (I'm Off to See the Goddam Wizard, Alright!, 1971; Her Poems: An Anniversaric Chronology, 1979; For the Love of Men: Shikata Gai Nai, 1990), Jewelle Gomez (The Lipstick Papers, 1980; Flamingoes and Bears, 1987), and Cheryl Clarke (Narratives: Poems in the Tradition of Black Women, 1982; Living as a Lesbian, 1986; Humid Pitch, 1989) are only a few representative African American lesbian poets and their works. Shockley's 1979 essay also provides the names of several periodical sources, including Azalea, Dyke, GPN News, and Christopher Street. Ache: The Bay Area's Journal for Black Lesbians, Gay Black Female, off our backs, Black/out: the Magazine of the National Coalition of Black Lesbians and Gays, Outweek, Womyn's Words, and Conditions are other periodicals that have served as primary venues for lesbian expression.

Although not all lesbians identify themselves as feminists, and not all feminists identify themselves as lesbians, the survival and development of the lesbian tradition in African American literature is linked to an accompanying feminist movement. In "Toward a Black Feminist Criticism," Barbara Smith stressed the importance of a strong activist movement to undergird the development of a literary tradition and underscored the connection between the movement and the development of a body of criticism that would, in turn, validate the literature. A special issue of Conditions, entitled Conditions, Five: The Black Women's Issue (Autumn 1979), coedited by Smith and Lorraine Bethel, featured the work of lesbians, feminists, and writers who identified as both. The works in that issue were, subsequently, included in Smith's 1983 anthology Home Girls, a one-of-a-kind sourcebook for information about the tradition, which features fiction, poetry, and essays. In the introduction to the text, Smith responds to myths about African American women with "home truths." Her work has been integral to the project of preparing a foundation that is conducive to the growth of a viable lesbian tradition in African American literature.

Other writer-scholars, such as Alice Walker, extend and expand Smith's call for critics and a body of criticism sensitive to the way language is used in African American women's texts. Cheryl Clarke's observations in "Living the Texts Out: Lesbians and the Uses of Black Women's Traditions" (1993) are helpful as well in understanding that indeed sociopolitical movement and literature are mutually reinforcing. Along with her three collections of poetry, Clarke's essays are evidence of her commitment to the parallel movement. She, along with Parker, Walker, Smith, De Veaux, Lorde, Gomez, Cliff, Bogus, and Carter have established records of national and international activism. Works like Walker's *Possessing the Secret of Joy* (1992) and June *Jordan's essays in *Technical Difficulties: African-American Notes on the State of the Union* (1992) address the abuse of women's bodies on an international scale and the need for a bisexual politics of sexuality, respectively.

Writers in this tradition engage a variety of genres and subgenres. In addition to novels, essays, short stories, and poetry, Alexis De Veaux has written a number of plays. Michelle Cliff has to her credit two autobiographical novels, a collection of poetry and prose, and a short story collection. Gomez's novel, *The Gilda Stories* (1991), Clarke's poetry, *Living as a Lesbian* (1986), and Michelle Parkerson's short story, "odds and ends" (*Waiting Rooms*, 1983), feature futuristic or fantasy settings with themes of revolution and survival. Audre Lorde, named poet laureate of New York in 1991, created her own subgenre by naming *Zami* a biomythography.

In the introduction to *Afrekete*, Catherine E. McKinley speaks of the need to insure an African American lesbian presence in the current "proliferation in mainstream publishing of lesbian and gay texts." She notes that all the writers represented in the volume "have committed themselves to the work of writing Black lesbians into history and the imagination and challenging the body of African-American, in particular, and American letters as a whole." The establishment of literary/activist foremothers, the chronicling of contributors and their works, the articulation of a criticism, and the existence of a parallel sociopolitical movement have all proven essential to providing a firm foundation for this vibrant and emerging tradition. These writers are a diverse group of women whose work adds richness to the texture of American literature.

[See also Gay Literature; Gay Men; Lesbians; Sexuality.]

• Cherrie Moraga and Gloria Anzaldúa, eds., *This Bridge Called My Back: Writings by Radical Women of Color*, 1981. J. R. Roberts, *Black Lesbians: An Annotated Bibliography*, 1981. Gloria T. Hull, Patricia Bell Scott, and Barbara Smith, *All the Women Are White, All the Blacks Are Men, But Some of Us Are Brave: Black Women's Studies*, 1982. Joanne M. Braxton and Andree Nicola McLaughlin, ed., *Wild Women in the Whirlwind: Afra-American Culture and the Contemporary Literary Renaissance*, 1990. Bonnie Zimmerman, *The Safe Sea of Women: Lesbian Fiction 1969–1989*, 1990. Lillian Faderman, *Odd Girls and Twilight Lovers: A History of Lesbian Life in Twentieth-Century America*, 1991. Marita Golden, *Wild Women Don't Wear No Blues*, 1993. Sandra Pollack and Denise D. Knight, eds., *Contemporary Lesbian Writers of the United States: A Bio-bibliographical Critical Sourcebook*, 1993. Carole Boyce Davies, *Black Women, Writing and Identity: Migrations of the Subject*, 1994. Deborah K. McDowell, *The Changing Same: Black Women's Literature, Criticism, and Theory*, 1995. Claude J. Summers, ed., *The Gay and Lesbian Literary Heritage*, 1995. —Lovalerie King

LESBIANS. The development of substantive, sensitive portrayals of African American lesbian characters in American literature has been plagued by the perpetuation of an ideology of African American women that is heavily influenced by long-term attacks on their moral and sexual character. Acknowledgement of lesbian sexuality and identity, from which the inference of deviant sexual behavior is often drawn, was especially taboo.

Thus Nella *Larsen, Angelina Weld *Grimké, Alice Moore *Dunbar-Nelson, and others were precluded by convention from depicting positive and openly lesbian characters in their writing and the earliest openly lesbian African American characters in American literature were narrowly and stereotypically drawn by white and/or male authors. Ann Allen *Shockley demonstrates that even African American women writers in the 1970s often drew one-dimensional lesbian characters, some of whom include Johnnie Mae and Beatrice in Maya *Angelou's *Gather Together in My Name* (1974), Jeffy in Gayl *Jones's *Corregidora* (1975), and the passive, "feminine" title character and her aggressive, "masculine" lover Daphne in Rosa *Guy's *Ruby* (1976).

Three of the most popularly celebrated African American lesbian characters in American literature are *Celie and *Shug Avery in Alice *Walker's *The *Color Purple* (1982) and Audre *Lorde's Zami. Walker's treatment of lesbian sexuality between Shug and Celie renders their physical lovemaking not only natural and spiritual, but also freeing, for Walker does not advocate an either/or definition of human sexuality. Lorde's matrilineal approach in *Zami: A New Spelling of My Name* (1982) discloses a strong female-oriented identification that begins with several childhood memories of her relationship with her mother and ends with the lover named Afrekete.

New Age African American lesbian characters include a vampire who is determined to survive the aftermath of slavery, a futuristic revolutionary always on the move to avoid capture by state troopers or the torture of being forced to imbibe Western classics and Norton anthologies, and two amazon warrior/lovers named Sephra and Loz, who must battle intergalactic enemies who turn out to be clones.

Catherine E. McKinley notes in her introduction to the precedent-setting *Afrekete: An Anthology of Black Lesbian Writing* (1995) that one of the objectives in compiling the anthology was to demonstrate the variety and diversity of African American lesbian experience. The characters presented in *Afrekete* by established and newly published writers alike reflect a stern adherence to that objective.

[See also Gender; Lesbian Literature; Sexuality.]

• SDiane Bogus, "The 'Queen B' Figure in Black Literature," in *Lesbian Texts and Contexts: Radical Revisions*, eds. Karla Jay and Joanne Glasgow, 1990, pp. 275–290. Allan A. Cuseo,

Homosexual Characters in YA Novels: A Literary Analysis, 1969–1982, 1992, pp. 222–225, 262–269. Sandra Pollack and Denise D. Knight, eds., *Contemporary Lesbian Writers of the United States: A Bio-bibliographical Critical Sourcebook,* 1993. Claude J. Summers, ed., *The Gay and Lesbian Literary Heritage,* 1995.

—Lovalerie King

LESTER, JULIUS (b. 1939), activist, essayist, journalist, radio broadcaster, folklorist, writer, historian, poet, and professor. Julius Lester was born on 27 January 1939 in St. Louis, Missouri, the son of Woodie Daniel Lester and Julia B. Smith Lester. He received his BA from Fisk University in 1960, with a semester at San Diego State College, and an MA from the University of Massachusetts at Amherst in 1971, where he is currently a professor. He is married to his second wife and has four children. Lester has won the Newbery Honor Award (1969) and the Massachusetts State Professor of the Year Award (1986), and was a finalist for the National Book Award (1972) and the National Jewish Book Award (1988). Lester converted to Judaism in 1982.

Julius Lester's literary career has spanned a broad variety of political events and literary genres. Lester began his career as an activist with the Student Nonviolent Coordinating Committee (SNCC), traveling to Mississippi, Cuba (with Stokely *Carmichael), North Vietnam, and Korea. In 1963 Lester coauthored *We Shall Overcome! Songs of the Southern Freedom Movement* with Guy Carawan, Candie Carawan, Ethel Raim, and Joseph Byrd. His first solo work, *Look Out, Whitey! Black Power's Gon' Get Your Mama,* was published in 1968 and followed in the same year by *To Be a Slave.* In 1969 Lester's collection of essays and articles about revolutionary movements in the United States, entitled *Revolutionary Notes,* was published and, in the same year, *Black Folktales* and *Search for a New Land.* In 1970 Lester divorced his first wife and left activism. He continued his prolific output with *The Seventh Son: The Thought &. Writings of W. E. B. Du Bois* (1971), *The Long Journey Home: Stories from Black History* and *Two Love Stories* (1972), and a book of *poetry, *Who I Am* (1974), followed in 1976 by his first *autobiography, *All Is Well.* In 1982 he began another series of books with *This Strange New Feeling* and continuing with *Do Lord Remember Me* (1984), *The Tales of Uncle Remus* (1987), *More Tales of Uncle Remus* (1988), *Lovesong,* his second autobiography (1988), *How Many Spots Does a Leopard Have?* (1989), *Falling Pieces of the Broken Sky* (1990), and *Further Tales of Uncle Remus* (1990). Four books followed in 1994: *The Last Tales of Uncle Remus, And All Our Wounds Forgiven, John Henry,* and *The Man Who Knew Too Much.*

Lester's work is characterized by his interest in education and change. His participation in academia and literature is marked by a concern both with African American culture and the need to break down the institutionalization of education and information that led him to activism in the 1960s and early 1970s. From the beginning of his career, however, Lester's work has been controversial. In the 1970s, he refused to endorse the Black Panther Party or Stokely Carmichael, consistently writing articles

that editorial boards were reluctant to publish. Lester's most recent work is still controversial. His essays, courses, and speeches celebrating Judaism and Jews have raised angry responses from some African Americans, who accuse Lester of being a self-hating African American. Lester's most recent collection of *essays, *Falling Pieces of the Broken Sky* (1990), continues to explore the intersections of *race, *religion, and education, addressing issues of personal identity and group identity, the role of spirituality in life, and the nature of formal and informal education and reeducation.

• "Julius Lester," in *Who's Who among African Americans,* 9th ed., Shirelle Phelps, 1994, p. 927.

—Karen R. Bloom

"LETTER FROM BIRMINGHAM JAIL." In spring 1963, after a failed campaign in Albany, Georgia, Martin Luther *King, Jr., and his Southern Christian Leadership Conference organized a major nonviolent crusade in Birmingham, Alabama. King, Fred Shuttlesworth, Wyatt Walker, and other organizers dispatched hundreds of protestors, including young children, across Birmingham. Recalcitrant city officials ordered police to unleash snarling dogs on the demonstrators and sent firefighters to wash them down the streets with fire hoses. Millions of Americans were horrified when they witnessed these events on *television. Hundreds of marchers were arrested, and on Easter Sunday King himself was jailed.

Early in the campaign eight clergy in Birmingham published a statement in the *Birmingham Post Herald* that called for racial harmony and an end to demonstrations, which the clergy deemed "unwise," "untimely," and "extreme." While critical of the role played by "outsiders," they addressed their declaration to the "white and Negro citizenry" of Birmingham, not to King himself, whom they never mentioned by name.

Relieved of his unrelenting schedule, the jailed King used his solitude to respond to the clergy's assertions. Writing a twenty-page *letter/essay that was broadly disseminated, he offers what is easily his most lucid analysis of segregation and his most sophisticated defense of his own tactics. He contends that the city's brutal treatment of agitators represents the less dramatic, daily humiliations imposed by racism. Living in jail, he implicitly claims, symbolizes living under segregation.

Although King apparently carried no reading materials into his jail cell, he remembered his earlier orations and reworked several familiar passages and metaphors into "Letter from Birmingham Jail," including material he originally borrowed from unacknowledged sources.

King folds these materials into a careful, complex argument that begins by defending his presence in Birmingham against the charge that he is an "outsider." Explicitly comparing himself to the apostle Paul, who traveled widely to spread the gospel, King claims that, as a Christian minister, his job is to attack injustice wherever it appears. Then, as Malinda Snow explains, he insinuates into his text numerous

Pauline allusions, which he reinforces by his simple presence in jail, where Paul also stayed.

As Richard Fulkerson observes, in "Letter" King adopts, with some modification, an ancient Greco-Roman oratorical pattern of introduction followed by proposition, division, confirmation, refutation, and peroration. Like certain classical orators, he persuades through thoughtful digressions; he adjusts classical form by shoving most of his argument into his refutation. Using what Fulkerson calls "multipremise refutation," he expresses an initial disappointment at having his efforts deemed extreme, then layers that expression within a powerful defense of a certain species of extremism. To buttress this contention, he telescopes time and space by writing about Jesus, Paul, Amos, Martin Luther, Abraham *Lincoln, and other "creative extremists" as though they shared his jail cell with him. Such leapfrogging of chronology and geography is a typical maneuver of African American folk preachers, including those King heard as a child.

For King, interlacing all these elements meant creating one of the most widely read and genuinely persuasive American *essays of this century. The eight clergy never attempted to answer it.

[See also Civil Rights Movement; Oratory; Sermons and Preaching.]

• Richard Fulkerson, "The Public Letter As a Rhetorical Form: Structure, Logic, and Style in King's 'Letter from Birmingham Jail,'" Quarterly Journal of Speech 65 (1979): 121–136. Malinda Snow, "Martin Luther King's 'Letter from Birmingham Jail' As Pauline Epistle," Quarterly Journal of Speech 71 (1985): 318–334. Martin Luther King, Jr., "Letter from Birmingham Jail," 1963, in A Testament of Hope: The Essential Writings of Martin Luther King, Jr., ed. James Washington, 1986, pp. 289–302.

—Keith D. Miller and Emily M. Lewis

LETTERS cast sharp and often heartrending light on every period of African American *history. Falling into two principal categories—public and private—African American letters offer an expansive view of the developing historical consciousness of a disenfranchised people.

At one end of the spectrum one finds, for example, rhetorically astute letters like those Frederick *Douglass wrote to his former master, Thomas Auld, and published in the Liberator in 1848. Knowing that a personal appeal was likely to fall on deaf ears, Douglass wrote an open letter to Auld passionately contrasting *freedom to *slavery while pleading for the emancipation of his siblings and grandmother, who were still in bondage to Auld. Douglass's letter sought not simply to expose the inhumanity of Auld, but also, by making an appeal to sentiment, to persuade his readers of the cruelty and injustice of slavery.

Private letters, at the other end of the spectrum, from nineteenth-century fugitives and twentieth-century migrants, which generally offer and seek news, assistance, or affection, represent less rhetorically complex testimonies to the ordeals and uncertainties of African American life, and to the sentiments ordinary people were able to muster in order to endure them. From the broadly to the narrowly

conceived, from the sophisticated to the naive, African American letters serve to correct the one-sided record of American historical experience and to portray the complexities of African American *double consciousness. The diverse range of perspectives and sentiments represented in letters also cautions us against universalizing African American historical experience.

Founded in 1915, Carter G. *Woodson's Association for the Study of Negro Life and History established an archive of letters, which the *Journal of Negro History occasionally published. Woodson's pioneering edition of letters, primarily by free African Americans, The Mind of the Negro as Reflected in Letters Written During the Crisis 1800–1860 (1926), established the importance of letters to the project of institutionalizing the study of African American history and life. Woodson disproved the persistent argument that African Americans left no written record of their experiences during the period of slavery; encouraged the subsequent discovery and publication of letters by and to African Americans; and fueled the debate over the authenticity of African American documents and testimonials, from *slave narratives to *diaries and journals, letters, and interviews. By the late 1970s, however, as John Blassingame pointed out in his valuable introduction to Slave Testimony: Two Centuries of Letters, Speeches, Interviews, and Autobiographies (1977), few historians—apart from Woodson, Ulrich Phillips, Clement Eaton, Eugene Genovese, John Spencer Bassett, and Robert Starobin—had made use of such letters.

Prefacing The Mind of the Negro with a brief selection of letters from the colonial era, written by Jupiter *Hammon, Phillis *Wheatley, and Benjamin *Banneker, Woodson offered Banneker's eloquent letter of protest to Thomas Jefferson, rather than Hammon's and Wheatley's letters counseling Christian forbearance, as a banner of the "mind" represented in the letters published in his volume. Woodson's distinction between letters meant for publication, usually focused on the politics of *race, and letters written to *family, friends, and other associates, usually concerned with the details of personal life, remains useful as a way of organizing the tradition of African American letters.

In The Mind of the Negro, the open letter of protest is represented by letters written to antislavery workers and agencies, generally by more highly educated and often prominent free African Americans in the North, but also by fugitive slaves active in the abolition movement. Featured within this early tradition are William Wells *Brown, Frederick Douglass, James Forten, Charlotte *Forten, William C. *Nell, Nathaniel Paul, Robert *Purvis, David *Ruggles, and John Browne *Russwurm.

Dorothy Sterling's We Are Your Sisters: Black Women in the Nineteenth Century (1984) serves as a corrective to the male-dominated canon of nineteenth-century letters established by Woodson. It includes personal as well as public letters by and to African American women, along with excerpts from newspaper articles, interviews, diaries, and so on. One document in this collection describes, for example, an open letter written on behalf of a committee of five hundred working women of New Orleans to Representative Benjamin Butler of Massachusetts, former military governor of New Orleans, denouncing President Rutherford B. Hayes for abandoning Reconstruction and announcing their intention, having formed an *emigration society, to migrate from the South en masse. Among the open letters from prominent women is a letter from Harriet A. *Jacobs, published in the *Liberator* in 1862, which describes her efforts to assist the African American refugees steadily streaming into the District of Columbia during the Civil War, coming to some forty thousand by the war's conclusion.

Typically published in the African American press, the open letter has continued to serve public figures, soldiers, and outspoken or desperate citizens as a means of protest. Open letters from soldiers have been particularly effective organs of political protest, articulating the contradictions sharply felt by African Americans in wartime. Notable letters by prominent figures include Kelly *Miller's "As to the Leopard's Spots: An Open Letter to Thomas Dixon, Jr." (1905) protesting the racial ideology of Dixon's novel; James *Baldwin's *The *Fire Next Time* (1963) reprinting "My Dungeon Shook: Letter to My Nephew on the One Hundredth Anniversary of the Emancipation" and "Down at the Cross: Letter from a Region in My Mind," which was originally published in the *New Yorker*; and Martin Luther *King, Jr.'s *"Letter from Birmingham Jail" justifying his political actions and explaining the purposes and strategies of a nonviolent campaign to a group of Alabama clergymen who had condemned him. Baldwin's brilliant and impassioned "Down at the Cross" offers a striking example of the African American letter as bearer of a rich prophetic tradition, concluding with a plea we must reiterate today, calling for an end to the "racial nightmare." "If we do not now dare everything," he wrote, "the fulfillment of that prophecy re-created from the Bible in song by a slave is upon us: God gave Noah the rainbow sign, No more water, the fire next time!"

One rarely encounters such rhetoric in letters not meant for publication, that is, in letters written by ordinary people, either to public and private agencies or to family, friends, and others. In *The Mind of the Negro*, the letters to the American Colonization Society, primarily from free African Americans in the South, anticipate letters inquiring about the prospects of resettlement from the period of Reconstruction through the Great *Migration. For the period of Reconstruction, Dorothy Sterling's *The Trouble They Seen: Black People Tell the Story of Reconstruction* (1976) offers a generous sampling of private letters to the Freedmen's Bureau, as well as open letters of protest concerning the hardships and bitter disappointments of the period. Emmett Scott's "Letters of Negro Migrants of 1916–1918" and "Additional Letters of Negro Migrants of 1916–1918," letters of prospective migrants requesting information and assistance from the *Chicago Defender*, which appeared in the *Journal of Negro History* (July and October 1919), are the only letters published from the period of the Great Migration. Widely dispersed in private

and public papers, such as those of the NAACP, the Departments of Justice and Agriculture, and so on, other private letters to agencies concern such topics as racial terrorism, inequality, discrimination, and political protest. These letters reveal not only a history of struggle against subordination and injustice, but also the discourses and sentiments, such as Christian faith and prophesy, *Pan-Africanism, and social democracy, that have structured and sustained this struggle.

In addition to private letters written to agencies are personal letters written to family, friends, and others. In this category, Woodson foregrounded letters by lower-class African Americans, many of them fugitives, that reflected upon newfound freedoms as well as the pain and uncertainty of dislocation and resettlement. Subsequently, Robert Starobin, John Blassingame, Randall Miller, and Bell Wiley published many more letters by slaves and former slaves, predominantly privileged house servants or foremen. Beyond the period of slavery, however, little personal correspondence—apart from that of some highly distinguished figures, such as Frederick Douglass, Booker T. *Washington, and W. E. B. *Du Bois—has made its way into print. Therefore, Charles H. Nichols's *Arna Bontemps–Langston Hughes: Letters, 1925–67* (1980), the correspondence of two distinguished figures during a period of enormous transition, stands as a unique and valuable contribution.

Alice *Walker's *epistolary novel *The *Color Purple* (1982) is virtually alone in having suggested the particular significance of personal letters, given the upheaval that has marked African American historical experience, to the sustaining traditions of African American family and communal life. Similarly, Bob Teague's open letters to his son, *Letters to a Black Boy* (1968) and *The Flip Side of Soul: Letters to My Son* (1989), have made singular use of the powerful African American tradition of the open letter of protest. The publication of Mary Stella Simpson's *Sister Stella's Babies: Days in the Practice of a Nurse-Midwife* (1978) serves to remind us that letters—both public and private—offer us access to areas of experience and expressions of sentiment neglected by historical record. From the skillful political weapon of the half-articulate plea, letters reveal sociohistorical conditions, historical consciousness, and, not least of all, the cultural and *signifying practices of the diverse range of African Americans who negotiated and protested centuries of injustice while sustaining throughout family, community, and spirit. As a source for cultural analysis, African American letters, particularly by women and of the twentieth century, remain largely untapped.

[See also Baltimore Afro-American; Libraries and Research Centers; Literacy; Newspaper Columns; Periodicals, *article on* Black Periodical Press; Protest Literature.]

• Willard B. Gatewood, Jr., ed., *"Smoked Yankees" and the Struggle for Empire: Letters from Negro Soldiers, 1898–1902*, 1971. Robert Starobin, *Blacks in Bondage: Letters of American Slaves*, 1974. Randall M. Miller, ed., *"Dear Master": Letters of a Slave Family*, 1978. Bell J. Wiley, ed., *Slaves No More: Letters from Liberia, 1833–1869*, 1980. Philip McGuire, ed., *Taps for a Jim Crow Army: Letters from Black Soldiers in World War II*, 1983. Virginia Matzke Adams, ed., *On the Altar of Freedom: A Black Soldier's Civil War Letters from the Front*, James Henry Gooding, 1991. Juanita Chenault Carman, comp., *86 Letters to the Persian Gulf War (12 Letters Received, 5 Letters "Returned to Sender")*, 1991.

—Cheryl Lester

LEWIS, THEOPHILUS (1891–1974), drama critic for the *Messenger* during the Harlem Renaissance. Theophilus Lewis was born in Baltimore, Maryland, in 1891, attended public schools, and moved to New York City. He became a manual laborer and later a postal worker, a position that he retained until his retirement. It provided his livelihood during the *Harlem Renaissance when he wrote the theater reviews in the *Messenger,* since he received no remuneration for his writing.

Lewis's theater columns, which appeared from 1923 to 1927, chronicled primarily African American stage productions presented in different venues from Harlem to Broadway at a critical stage in African American history. They also championed development of an African American little theater movement. In referring to such groups as the Ethiopian Art Theater, the Tri-Arts Club, the Krigwa Players (founded by W. E. B. *Du Bois), and the Aldridge Players, Lewis reveals his understanding of their importance to the evolution of African American theater and drama. In a 1926 column, for example, he declined to evaluate three plays presented by the Aldridge Players by strict critical standards, arguing that little theater groups afforded necessary opportunities for African American actors to perfect their craft. Lewis's indulgence did not mean that he was overly tolerant; rather that he was not interested in the craft of acting simply for its own sake. He claimed for the actor a central role in raising the standards of the usual fare available on the African American stage.

Lewis advocated the development of a national African American theater that would be clearly distinct from the American theater in materials and audience. This concern, also expressed in later columns written for *Catholic World*, aligned Theophilus Lewis with other intellectuals of the 1920s who called for the creation of a viable African American literary and artistic tradition based on the folk experience, and it anticipated some of the writers of the 1960s who called for the creation of art based on a *Black Aesthetic.

Lewis felt that a national theater that would address itself exclusively to an African American audience would assist in the development of the African American playwright, who, according to Lewis, was at the apprentice stage and needed the closeness to familiar material and a sympathetic audience in order to write legitimate drama. Lewis considered drama to be a higher form of expression than comedy, a form that pervaded the African American theater at that time. Lewis also argued against the prevalence of *stereotypes, whether present in the works of African American or white playwrights. While he enjoyed the antics of the chorus lines that appeared in the musical revues of the period, he criticized the intraracial bias evident by the light-hued ladies who comprised most of these productions. Lewis's insight and his ability to address important issues are seen particularly in his recurring discussions of the connection between the evolution of the African American theater and the economic level of its desired target audience.

Lewis's most significant contribution was his theater reviews and commentary, but he did write in other forms. He coauthored a satirical column, "Shafts and Darts," with George S. *Schuyler, reviewed books, wrote commentary on general topics, and authored a few short stories. One of these stories, "Seven Years for Rachel," which was serialized in 1923, exhibits Lewis's attempts to put some of his own pronouncements into practice. The story, subtitled "a dramatic story of Negro life," focuses on a love triangle involving Sam Jones, Rachel, and Amelia. It includes elements of African American folk culture that evoke setting and character in a story in which the primary themes are guilt and remorse.

After the Harlem Renaissance, Lewis published only occasionally. "The Frustrations of Negro Art," written in 1942, addresses the connection between the economic stability of the audience and the growth of African American art and warns of the deleterious effects when an artist must write for alien audiences with preconceived images.

Although he came to his avocation an untrained observer, Lewis was a dedicated and influential figure. His columns exhibited an enthusiasm for African American theater, and for his role as critical and moral guide.

[*See also* Criticism; *article on* Criticism from 1920 to 1964; Newspaper Columns.]

• Theodore Kornweibel, Jr., "Theophilus Lewis and the Theater of the Harlem Renaissance," in *The Harlem Renaissance Remembered*, ed. Arna Bontemps, 1972, pp. 171–189. "Theophilus Lewis," in *CA*, eds. Hal May and Susan M. Trosky, 1989, p. 292.   —Johanna L. Grimes-Williams

LIBRARIES AND RESEARCH CENTERS. In 1940, when Jacob *Lawrence decided to paint the sixty panels of his *Migration series, the *New Yorker* possessed several qualifications for the project—and one major disadvantage. He had never been farther south than upstate New Jersey. So he did what countless writers and scholars—such as W. E. B.*Du Bois, Vernon Loggins, James Weldon *Johnson, Alain *Locke, and Nancy Cunard—had done before him. He visited what is now the Schomburg Center for Research in Black Culture and, through its rich collection of clippings and photographs, filled in his knowledge of the rural South.

By the end of the twentieth century, Lawrence's good fortune could be equaled by scholars in most parts of the United States. This article will survey briefly the extent of research collections, outline their history, and describe their major examples. The West is represented by collections of African American material at UCLA and of southern African sources at Stanford. The Midwest holds the

Herskovits Library of African Studies at Northwestern, while nearby in Chicago are the Cooperative Africana Microform Project at the Center for Research Libraries and, important for students of Richard *Wright, the Vivian C. Harsh and Carter G. *Woodson Collections of the Chicago Public Library system. The Detroit Public Library has comparable holdings in its Burton and E. Azalia Hackley Collections. Oberlin College and the University of Kansas are representative of institutions holding antislavery material.

As the oldest regions, the Northeast and South of course have the largest holdings. The Boston Public Library possesses the invaluable antislavery papers of major abolitionists. Yale holds the James Weldon Johnson Memorial Collection, rich in material of the *Harlem Renaissance, including papers of Johnson, Du Bois, Countee *Cullen, Zora Neale *Hurston, Langston *Hughes, Claude *McKay, Jean *Toomer, and Richard Wright. Philadelphia houses several, including the Charles Blockson Collection at Temple University. Especially strong in *theater history, the Hatch-Billops Collection is but one of several important repositories in New York City. The District of Columbia holds not only the Library of Congress and National Archives but also the Moorland-Spingarn Collection at Howard University and such specialized holdings as that of the Association for the Study of Afro-American Life and History (ASALH). More specialized collections, present throughout the region, have grown in significance as study has advanced and are represented by the papers and manuscripts of John A. *Williams, deposited by the novelist at his alma mater, Syracuse University, and the gift of books and papers to Lincoln University in Pennsylvania by one of its former students, Langston Hughes.

Collections in the South are anchored in university libraries. At Duke Univeristy, the Southern Historical Collection of the University of North Carolina, and the Manuscript Division of the University of Virginia are housed plantation records, proslavery and antislavery antebellum publications, descriptions of the *Underground Railroad, agricultural production records for cotton and tobacco, and descriptions of the day-to-day life of slaves. While the Amistad Research Collection in New Orleans, the Woodruff Library of the Atlanta University Center, and the collection of Fisk University are outstanding national collections, almost every one of the more than one hundred historically black colleges in the region has an archival record of some consequence. Tuskegee, for instance, has the papers of Monroe Work, George Washington Carver, and a portion of those of Booker T. *Washington. Hampton University has a large antislavery collection and uncommon Native American holdings. Already possessing a large archive, Texas Southern University has acquired the papers of Barbara Jordan. North Carolina Central University has the W. Edward Farrison Collection of the literature of *slavery. Records of several African American branches of the Episcopal Church and their missionaries are housed at St. Augustine's College. All of the major collections and many of the smaller ones have printed catalogs and guides to their holdings and are connected for scholarly use to computer networks.

Like Arthur A. *Schomburg, many early black collectors explained their interest in books by way of admiration and emulation of Frederick *Douglass. Douglass advocated both *freedom through *literacy and a love of books for themselves, keeping a large, oft-used library in each of his homes, most proudly in Rochester and Cedar Hill. While his prestige may have spurred some libraries, Douglass was hardly the first collector. Early in the abolition era, on 20 March 1828, a group of free men in Philadelphia formed a Reading Room Society, the earliest recorded instance, loaning books for no longer than one week and circulating copies of Samuel *Cornish's *Freedom's Journal and Lundy's Genius of Universal Emancipation. The Philadelphia Library Company of Colored Persons was established 1 January 1833 and within five years possessed six hundred volumes. Free blacks in several large cities in the Northeast were stimulated by the activity in Philadelphia, where by 1841 at least eight *literary societies had been established.

The first black book collector, in all likelihood, was David *Ruggles (1810–1849), whose work helps to clarify the role of books and literacy during much of the century. In the several locations of his Reading Room, the most famous being the corner of Lispenard and Church streets in New York City, Ruggles maintained a circulating library of antislavery and anticolonization publications available to readers at less than twenty-five cents a month. His design was eminently practical, for the Reading Room was the headquarters too of the Vigilance Committee, a group working to usher fugitive slaves north and then protect them while in the city. Rescuing slaves, defending free blacks, and contesting racist opponents were his primary order of business. For these portentous goals, he found books and newspapers most effective allies. And the Reading Room rescued enlightened ideas, defended black rights, and contested racist ideologies. If Douglass inspired later figures, he had himself been inspired by Ruggles, who was his first contact and protector after his escape and who then served as witness to his marriage with Anna Murray, a ceremony that may have taken place in the Reading Room.

With Ruggles's utilitarian goals established by abolitionist reading societies in large northern cities, the opportunity was present by midcentury for several variations. Hence Philadelphia had not only its antislavery literary societies but also the earliest black bibliophiles in Robert Mara Adger and William Carl Bolivar. As traced by Elinor Des Verney Sinnette, most early book lovers were free males or sons of freed slaves living on the East Coast. While white bibliophiles of the age often regarded books as a hobby or diversion, their black counterparts were socially committed opponents of prejudice and injustice. Their passion for justice kindled a desire to collect and broadcast historical material; many became lay historians, journalists, publishers, and public defenders of black life. In 1854, once more in Philadelphia, thirty-seven such committed men incorporated themselves into the Benjamin *Banneker Literary Institute in order to deliver papers on aspects of black life and to debate issues of racial import. Both Adger and Bolivar were influenced by the Banneker Institute.

Born free in Charleston and brought at age six to Philadelphia, Adger (1837–1910) worked there as businessman and political spokesman the rest of his life. He was a founding member of the Afro-American Historical Society (1897) and the initial president of the American Negro Historical Society. Emphasizing abolitionist publications, he gathered a full range of material from autograph *letters, manuscripts, prints, and engravings to rare books and periodicals. His procedures for collecting were widely copied, as was his insistence that a genuine collection produce a printed catalog. Proud to have been born and educated in the city, Bolivar (1849–1914) eventually amassed a library four times larger than Adger's and was significant for pressing bibliographic interests upon the American Negro Academy and the Negro Society for Historical Research. He meanwhile became patron, friend, and frequent correspondent of a younger collector from New York, whose interests and activities came to define the role of the black bibliophile in the twentieth century, and whose library came to be the foundation of the foremost collection.

As the single most significant collector of books on the history of blacks in the United States, Latin America, and Spain, Arthur Alfonso Schomburg (1874–1938) was an inveterate foe of what he called "our false history." Reading a book by the egregious white American historian H. H. Bancroft, he made an outraged notation: "Where are our Negro historians, our defenders who have let Bancroft commit such a dastardly crime against the Negro race?" Setting the historical record straight would soon become his reason for being. "History must restore what slavery took away," he wrote, "for it is the social damage of slavery that the present generation must repair and offset."

He was one of the founders of the Negro Society for Historical Research and president of the American Negro Academy, seeking to have the latter organization coordinate bibliographic information nationally for libraries and collectors. Justly celebrated for gathering material on all sides of questions such as colonization, he hoped that future scholars might find a single repository, that their journeys toward knowledge might be swifter and simpler than his own. Among his many writings is the famous *essay "The Negro Digs up His Past," for the *Survey Graphic special issue on Harlem in 1925, later reprinted in Locke's The *New Negro.

In 1925 the New York Public Library established a Division of Negro Literature, History and Prints at the 135th Street Branch in Harlem. The following year the Carnegie Corporation purchased Schomburg's library and deposited it at the branch. The collection had grown to well over 10,000 volumes by the time of his death in 1938, when the whole was renamed the Schomburg Collection. Since then it has remained what he intended—a civic and cultural

agency for the entire community, sponsoring lectures and theatrical productions as well as research and reference activities. Attracting some of the most prominent lay and professional librarians in the nation, it was named a national resource in 1972 by the National Endowment for the Humanities, transferred to the Research Libraries division of the library system, and renamed the Schomburg Center for Research in Black Culture. Shortly thereafter it moved a short distance to a new, much larger building. It holds material in all formats concerning black people throughout the world: 85,000 books, 450 separate groups of manuscripts, 300,000 photographs, and 30,000 microforms. While continuing to be the library of first resort for many scholars, it has become widely known to a new generation for publishing the works of nineteenth-century women writers and for copying in microform its extraordinary file of clippings under 10,000 subject headings.

Two of Schomburg's associates were responsible for establishing a major library of African American affairs at Howard University. In 1914 Dean Kelly *Miller persuaded Dr. Jesse Moorland (1863–1940) to contribute his collection of 6,000 volumes (in addition to manuscripts, engravings, portraits, newspaper clippings, and curios), all dealing with black American history. A neighbor of Schomburg in Brooklyn who belonged to most of the same literary organizations, Moorland was a theologian and Howard graduate (1891) and trustee (1907–1940). To form a fully national collection, second in depth only to the Schomburg, his library was later complemented by that of Arthur Spingarn to form the Moorland-Spingarn Research Center.

"The other Arthur," as Spingarn (1878–1971) was called, was an officer and attorney for the NAACP for more than fifty years, working closely with his brother, Joel Elias Spingarn, and Du Bois. Especially strong in Cuban, Haitian, and Brazilian writers in rare editions, Spingarn's library of more than 5,000 volumes came to Howard University in 1946 and was overseen by yet another legendary figure, Dorothy *Porter, librarian of the collection from 1930 until 1973. (She had gained her initial experience working three summers for Schomburg on 135th Street.) In the late 1980s the library division numbered 150,000 volumes, while the manuscript division gathered manuscripts, *music, oral history, prints, and photographs. Among the papers housed are those of Locke, E. Franklin Frazier, Charles C. Diggs, Paul *Robeson, Vernon Jordan, Benjamin E. *Mays, George B. Murphy, Jr., Alpha Kappa Alpha, the Congressional Black Caucus, and the Ancient Order of the Mystic Shrine. The Glenn Carrington Collection of Music numbers 4,000 compositions.

One other figure from the District of Columbia should be mentioned for his importance in initiating black collections in the Library of Congress. Daniel Alexander Payne Murray (1852–1925) was a cousin of William Bolivar and friend of Schomburg who collected black material for the nation's library for fifty-two years. Among other achievements, he is a reminder that the great black collections produced not only the first black libraries but also the earliest black librarians. As testament to Murray's energy, the Library's African holdings are currently among the best in the world.

Like Howard, Atlanta University benefited from Schomburg and his bookish friends. It had hosted annual conferences from the late nineteenth century on, many chaired by Du Bois, and became a focus for research on black subjects in the 1940s. The original archival holdings included the historical records of the six institutions within the Atlanta Center, much on early black *education in the South, and the sources for the important Atlanta University Publication Series. In 1942, Harold Jackman (c. 1900–1960), the New York bibliophile and patron of several Harlem Renaissance artists, began to transfer his large collection of contemporary material to the library. Later named the Countee Cullen Memorial Collection in honor of the poet, the collection included inscribed and first editions, drafts and manuscripts, letters, poems, plays, printer's proofs, theater bills and programs, concert and other music programs, newspaper and magazine reviews, advertisements and critical notices, sheet music, Jackman's own personal journals of the 1920s, and a vast number of photographs by Carl Van Vechten. Jackman continued to contribute; so too did Hughes, Van Vechten, Owen *Dodson, Dorothy Peterson, and Cullen's estate.

This contemporary material was supplemented in 1945 by purchase of one of the best and largest private libraries in the nation, the more than 10,000 volumes of Henry Proctor Slaughter (1871–1958). Slaughter held two law degrees from Howard, edited a masonic magazine with Schomburg, and during most of his long life specialized in books on slavery, abolition, the Civil War, and Abraham *Lincoln. In later years he widened his prospect, purchasing rare French and Haitian items; the works of Dumas, Pushkin, and René Maran; complete sets of early poets; histories of black secret societies; full runs of periodicals; and several paintings by Robert Duncanson. He gathered also a unique file of 100,000 newspaper clippings.

With the Cullen-Jackman and Slaughter holdings in place, the library began to attract many donations, for example, the manuscripts of James *Baldwin and the personal papers and library of Hoyt *Fuller, and became the third-largest repository of African American material in the United States. Since 1982 it has been part of the Special Collections of the Robert W. Woodruff Library. To the earlier Trevor Arnett holdings have been added the University Archives, with unique material on women's groups, civil rights and social welfare organizations, the Southern Regional Council, and the records of the seven component seminaries of the Interdenominational Theological Center, especially strong on the history of African Americans in the Methodist Church.

Two collections born in the 1960s reveal more recent versions of the Schomburg spirit. Associated with Dillard University, the Amistad Research Center in New Orleans has created in a single generation one of the largest manuscript collections in America, measuring 3,500 linear feet of original material. It was conceived by historian Clifton H. Johnson, who saw that the papers of one major abolition group, the American Missionary Association, had never been gathered and that once collected would serve as magnet for others. Today it houses the papers of the association, the American Home Missionary Society, the Race Relations Department of the Anti-Defamation League, the Catholic Committee of the South, the National Association of Human Rights Workers, and other organizations concerned with African Americans, Native Americans, and immigrant groups. Among individuals, it holds the private papers of Mary McLeod Bethune, Alexander P. Tureaud, George Ruffin, and James H. Robinson.

The Hatch-Billops Collection in New York City had a similar beginning when in 1968 James Hatch and Camille Billops, professors at the City College of New York, realized how little had been gathered concerning the black arts. With the aid of a consistently helpful federal agency, the National Endowment for the Humanities, they began to conduct oral histories with black artists in art, *film, *dance, *drama, music, literature, and related fields. Billops began to photograph the work of black artists in exhibits and private collections; Hatch gathered black plays and theater programs. Today the theater collection of published items is one of the most complete anywhere. Housed in a Manhattan loft, it contains more than 1,000 oral history tapes, 10,000 slides, 4,000 books, hundreds of posters, programs, photographs, exhibit catalogs, and rare and scarce periodicals. It holds the drafts and scripts of several playwrights and the unpublished plays of such writers as Theodore *Ward, Owen Dodson, and Lonne *Elder III.

[See also Criticism; Periodicals.]

• Jessie Carney Smith, Black Academic Libraries and Research Collections: An Historical Survey, 1977. Wendy Ball and Tony Martin, eds., Rare Afro-Americana: A Reconstruction of the Adger Library, 1981. Alfred J. Moss, Jr., American Negro Academy: Voice of the Talented Tenth, 1981. Elinor Des Verney Sinnette, Arthur Alfonso Schomburg: Black Bibliophile and Collector, 1989. Elinor Des Verney Sinnette, W. Paul Coates, and Thomas C. Battle, eds., Black Bibliophiles and Collectors: Preservers of Black History, 1990.

—John Sekora

"Lift Every Voice and Sing." Although there is, of course, no executive or legislature to so designate it, "Lift Every Voice and Sing" is frequently referred to as the "Negro National Anthem." It was written in 1900 by James Weldon *Johnson and his brother J. [John] Rosamond Johnson for a celebration of Abraham *Lincoln's birthday in Jacksonville, Florida, their hometown. James, who contributed the lyrics, records in his *autobiography Along This Way (1933) that he and Rosamond taught the song to a chorus of five hundred schoolchildren who, after the event "kept singing the song; some of them went off to other schools and kept singing it; some of them became schoolteachers and taught it to their pupils. Within twenty years the song was being sung in schools and *churches and on special occasions throughout the South and in some other parts of the country." After the NAACP unofficially adopted "Lift Every Voice and Sing" as its own anthem, the song appeared in new, more politically charged contexts as well as in school assemblies and church meetings.

Johnson's poem, which he tells us he wrote in "a poet's ecstasy" followed by "that sense . . . which makes artistic creation the most complete of all human experiences," is both a good fit to Rosamond's *music and a rhetorically effective post-Romantic lyric. The poem's sentiments are entirely spiritual, locating the sources of strength in the connection to God. Though an agnostic himself, Johnson valorizes the people's religious faith and posits communal hope for the future as founded upon it.

The conservative sentiments of "Lift Every Voice and Sing" are one reason it receded in popularity somewhat during the *civil rights movement. In recent years, the song has again become a fixture of African American social events, now as the historically validated anthem of the new cultural nationalism. As cultural icon, it has been explored in an enormously popular recording by Melba Moore in 1990 and in a text with the music, illustrated by Elizabeth Catlett (1993).

• James Weldon Johnson, *Along This Way*, 1933; rpt. 1968. James Weldon Johnson, *Lift Every Voice and Sing*, 1993.

—Joseph T. Skerrett, Jr.

Like One of the Family.

Like One of the Family. Alice *Childress's *Like One of the Family . . . Conversations from a Domestic's Life* (1956) is a collection of sixty-two short conversations that originally appeared in Paul *Robeson's newspaper *Freedom* under the title "Conversations from Life" and were continued in the *Baltimore Afro-American* as "Here's Mildred." The novel's heroine, *Mildred Johnson, recounts for her friend Marge the daily battles she has with her white employers who either treat her like she is invisible or who try to overwork and underpay her for her services as a maid. Childress's novel uniquely celebrates the lives of countless African American women who raised families while working as *domestics. Unlike the docile, self-effacing, one-dimensional domestics often found in American literature, Mildred is assertive, intellectually superior, quick-witted, and dignified. Mildred questions authority, confronts her white employers, attacks stereotypes, and challenges the abuse of Black domestics. Childress creates a world in which a poor, Black female takes it upon herself to enlighten her employers about race, class, and gender biases.

Conversations such as "Like One of the Family," "The Pocket Book Game," and "The Health Card" illustrate Childress's skillful manipulation of her heroine. In "Like One of the Family," Mildred corrects her employer who makes the mistake of boasting that Mildred is like one of the family. Mildred reminds her that she eats in the kitchen while her employer's family eats in the dining room. She tells her that if she were to drop dead, she would be replaced within a heartbeat. Mildred also reminds her that after she has worked herself into a sweat, she does not appreciate the low wages. Mildred uses this opportunity, while she has the employer at a point of vulnerability,

to ask for a raise. In "The Pocket Book Game," the white employer holds on tightly to her purse as if she is afraid Mildred will steal from her. Mildred turns the tables when she comes running back into the house and snatches her own pocketbook. She reassures her employer that if she paid anyone as little as she did, she would hold on to her purse, too. Childress demonstrates in "The Health Card" the disruptiveness of stereotypes. When Mildred's employer asks for her health records, Mildred in turn requests health cards from each member of the white family. Mildred's humor serves to expose the rampant racism of the 1950s.

Childress's novel makes a serious contribution to African American literature because of the storytelling forms that she makes use of in the conversations. While the use of an omniscient narrator would have earned for Childress the label of didactic or propagandistic, the use of a character who speaks her own mind allows the audience to view racial tensions of the 1950s from the point of view of an impassioned character who relates her own personal experiences. In a sense, Mildred is held accountable for what she says to her white employers, and Childress as author maintains some degree of distance from the experiences.

Like One of the Family, with Mildred at its center, is unique in that it celebrates the experiences of African American women domestics. Childress gives voice to women who on bended knees improved the conditions of their families.

• Trudier Harris, "'I Wish I Was a Poet': The Character As Artist in Alice Childress's *Like One of the Family*," in *Black American Literature Forum* 14 (Spring 1980): pp. 24–30.

—Elizabeth Brown-Guillory

LINCOLN, ABRAHAM (1809–1865), sixteenth president of the United States. Abraham Lincoln is an ambiguous figure in *history and literature, with much disagreement centered on his beliefs and actions regarding African Americans. Lincoln hated *slavery but equivocated in public statements about racial equality. He considered his 1863 Emancipation Proclamation the most historic act of his presidency, but many critics interpret the order freeing Southern slaves during the Civil War as a military measure, not a humanitarian one. In a famous 1862 letter to the editor Horace Greeley, Lincoln explained that his "*official* duty" in the war was to "save the Union" but added that this stance signaled "no modification of my oft-expressed *personal* wish that all men every where could be free." Near the war's end, Lincoln vetoed a congressional bill to codify emancipation and insisted instead that the permanent end of slavery be written into the Constitution as the Thirteenth Amendment.

Assassination elevated Lincoln to national martyrdom, but his dual incarnations as "Savior of the Union" and "Great Emancipator" have coexisted uneasily. Thomas Dixon's 1905 novel *The Clansman* (filmed as D. W. Griffith's *Birth of a Nation*) portrayed Lincoln as an eager racist. Despite numerous tributes like Langston *Hughes's poem "Lincoln Monument" (1927) and William E. Lilly's *Set My*

People Free (1932), many African American writers have expressed ambivalence. Frederick *Douglass knew Lincoln and believed him to be utterly without prejudice but in an 1876 speech declared Lincoln "pre-eminently the white man's President." In 1922 W. E. B. *Du Bois provoked angry letters from readers of the *Crisis* magazine with a critical paragraph calling Lincoln "a big, inconsistent, brave man." Many civil rights leaders effectively used Lincoln as a political symbol, but criticisms continued from *Malcolm X, Julius *Lester, and more recently from Vincent Harding in *There Is a River* (1982). Lincoln remains a compelling presence, but the icon has proved even more ambiguous than the man.

[*See also* Freedom.]

• Arthur Zilversmit, ed., *Lincoln on Black and White: A Documentary History*, 1971. Stephen B. Oates, *Abraham Lincoln: The Man behind the Myths*, 1984.

—Scott A. Sandage

LINCOLN, C. ERIC (b. 1924), religion scholar, professor, and poet. C. Eric Lincoln was born in Athens, Alabama, and was educated at LeMoyne College, Fisk University, the University of Chicago, and Boston University. At Chicago he completed his divinity training, and at Boston University his doctorate in religion. During the course of his forty years in the academy, Lincoln has held professorships at Clark College, Portland State College, Union Theological Seminary, Fisk University, and Duke University, where he is professor emeritus of religion.

Lincoln is widely known as "the dean of black religious scholars," his expertise being the sociology of the black *church. Indeed, the history and character of the black church is a question whose answer has been evolving in Lincoln's writings over a period of three decades. W. E. B. *Du Bois, Carter G. *Woodson, Charles H. Wesley, E. Franklin Frazier, and Benjamin E. *Mays also wrote on the black church, but none of these earlier scholars sustained a lifetime of research on the subject or wrote on the institution with such depth, breadth, and clarity.

One of the core themes found throughout Lincoln's writings is that the black church is the sole institution that spans the history of black America, giving birth to the black community as a cultural, social, and political entity, and that any attempt to understand or interpret contemporary African American culture must therefore begin with the black church. This core theme gave impetus to his ten-year study with Lawrence Mamiya, *The Black Church in the African American Experience* (1990). In this work is revealed the acuity of vision with which Lincoln crafted a new understanding of the foundation of African American culture, and one can readily see how Lincoln's earlier scholarship paved the way for much of what is presently occurring in the various areas of contemporary African American religious scholarship, from black theology to African American biblical exegesis.

Closely related to Lincoln's work on the black church are his writings on the history and character of the *race problem in America. In this regard, Du Bois, Woodson, and Frazier are among his most rec-

ognized predecessors, with John Hope Franklin among his contemporaries. Lincoln's epoch of race writing commenced with the landmark *The Black Muslims in America* (1961) and coalesced in *Race, Religion, and the Continuing American Dilemma* (1984) and *Coming through the Fire: Surviving Race and Place in America* (1996). His literary writings—his award-winning novel, *The Avenue, Clayton City* (1988), and his *anthology of *poetry, *This Road since Freedom* (1990)—also address the problem of race.

Lincoln's novel comprises a collage of separate yet interrelated tales about pre–World War II black life in a southern rural community. Lincoln captures the joys of black folk life in Clayton City as well as the sorrows brought on by the inflictions of southern whites. While Lincoln's anthology of poetry also captures some of rural black life prior to World War II, and several of the poems are dated in the mid-1940s, most of the poems reflect Lincoln's attempt to interpret urban life subsequent to 1950, including his efforts to understand the forces that led to the assassinations of Martin Luther *King, Jr., and *Malcolm X.

In addition to his writings on race and the black church, Lincoln covers a broad range of other topics that today fall under the category of cultural criticism. He has written on the plight of the black colleges, the status of African American studies at white universities, affirmative action, religious cults, the American family, the crisis of the black male, and much more. His overall thought is a valuable asset to the endeavors of younger scholars researching on the black experience, for the insights he had as many as thirty years ago are still insightful.

• Henry J. Young, ed., *Major Black Religious Leaders since 1940*, 1979. Mary R. Sawyer, *Black Ecumenism: Implementing the Demands of Justice*, 1994.

—Jon Michael Spencer

LITERACY is an important issue in the African American literary tradition, because it has been a central concept in modern Western thinking in determining who is considered most fully human and who is not. By the eighteenth century there was a common belief that literacy was of paramount value to any community and bore great benefits in terms of self-worth, socioeconomic worth, social mobility, access to information and knowledge, and even rationality, morality, and orderliness. There were three key episodes in the ascendancy of literacy in Europe and its colonies. First was the invention of mechanical book production in Mainz, Germany, in 1447. Next was the Protestant Reformation of the sixteenth century, which brought the first sweeping campaigns for popular education. Finally, two centuries later, there was the high cultural movement known as the Enlightenment. The major texts of the Enlightenment appeared between 1720 and 1800, and signaled a period of intellectual activity primarily in England, France, and Germany among social theorists, philosophers, men of letters, and scientists who undertook an ambitious survey of the material world, human understanding, nations and national characters, religion, civil obligation and organization, as well as what is understood as the cultured arts. These figures included Edmund Burke, David Hume, Immanuel Kant, Jean-Jacques Rousseau, and Voltaire. In short, although it by no means initiated the assumptions about literacy that remain current and powerful to this day, the Enlightenment, or "age of reason," played a very important role in naturalizing and spreading these assumptions.

This period coincided with the height of European involvement in the African slave trade and the ensuring of the profitability of "New World" colonies through *slavery. A preeminent justification for the enslavement of Africans and African Americans was a belief in their inferior status. Moreover, one of the most important signs of the status of Africans and African Americans as lesser human beings was that they did not organize their societies around the exchange of an alphabetic script—that is, they were illiterate by European standards. Accordingly such literary critics as Henry Louis *Gates, Jr., and Ronald A.T. Judy point out that one important means by which some Africans and African Americans could claim full status as human beings was through the demonstration of their skills in literacy. Gates writes, for instance, that given this state of affairs "it is obvious that the creation of formal literature could be no mean matter in the life of the slave, since sheer literacy was the very commodity that separated animal from human being, slave from citizen, object from subject" (1987). That is, literacy acquires in relation to African American life and culture the status of an important mark of citizenship within the human family. The emergence of African American texts and traditions of letters thus marks signal accomplishments, because they seem to provide the most manifest and least ephemeral representations of full participation in the life of the mind.

In the context of the North American colonies that would become the United States, such texts began to appear early in the eighteenth century. By the 1770s and 1780s there were several significant and fairly well-known slave narratives in both Britain and North America, such as those of James Albert Ukawsaw *Gronniosaw (1770), Ottobah Cugoano (1787), and Olaudah *Equiano (1789). Indeed, given the importance attached to literacy in the West, the issue often emerges in the texts of displaced Africans as a subject or theme of the narratives themselves. One way these narrators gauge their assimilation into Western society is by their eventual understanding or mastery of literacy. There are somewhat stock scenes in which the narrators report their curiosity or astonishment at seeing someone read. At first they can only fathom that the reader and text are engaged in a conversation to which they are not privy but, as they grow familiar with the concept of reading, this familiarity in and of itself marks an important rite of passage into a society that remains in many ways threatening or hostile.

For the very same reasons, explicit concerns with the notion of literacy can be a contextual issue as well as a textual one for African American writing. The case of poet Phillis *Wheatley provides an early and telling example. Wheatley, who was brought from Africa to Massachusetts as a very young child in 1761, proved to be a prodigy who mastered spoken and written English very quickly and who had published a volume of poetry by 1773. As early as 1770, Wheatley's fame as a poet had spread through the American colonies; however, the publication of her *Poems on Various Subjects, Religious and Moral (1773) seems to have transformed the novelty of a literate enslaved African making claims of linguistic and artistic competence into a crisis. In the volume Wheatley's poems are prefaced by the testimony of eighteen well-respected citizens of Boston that as strange as it seemed, Wheatley was a literate African slave. In other words, the figure of an established black writer proved that the gulf between the capacities of Africans and their descendents and Europeans and their descendants was not as great as imagined. For Thomas Jefferson, for example, Wheatley's achievement proved so threatening to his fantasy of racial dispensations that he denounced the poems in his Notes on the State of Virginia (1785) as the worst sort of doggerel and as no sign therefore, of individual or racial capacity.

This skeptical response to African American literacy became even more pronounced after the 1830s with the increasing popularity and political significance of *slave narratives, the most popular genre of African American writing. The 1830s were a watershed decade in the debate concerning U.S. slavery, a debate in which slave narratives came to play a considerable part. The 1830s witnessed the beginning of the publication of the Liberator, William Lloyd Garrison's uncompromising abolitionist newspaper, the formation of the American Anti-Slavery Society and the New England Anti-Slavery Society, the narrow defeat of emancipation in Virginia, legislated emancipation in the British Caribbean, as well as Nat *Turner's slave rebellion in southwest Virginia. The year 1836 marked the inauguration of the "classic" slave narrative, an explicitly political document in the form of an ostensible *autobiography aiming to expose and denounce the U.S. slave regime and its supporters. Rather than relaying the unusual adventures of unusual members of Western society, these narratives aimed at providing first-hand accounts of the horrors and atrocity of enslavement.

The literacy of the writers of these documents became, then, a heavily scrutinized matter speaking both to the veracity of the events recorded and to the authenticity of the narrators' claims to be escaped slaves. Not all slave narratives were actually written by ex-slave narrators themselves. Some were reported to amanuenses, while the writing of others was supervised or revised by white editors. However, the eloquence of the narratives, indeed, the very literacy of ex-slaves writing independently of amanuenses and editors made some people question their veracity and authenticity and assert that the slave narratives were too well written to be the independent work of slaves.

Literacy itself remains an important theme in the narratives. Considerations or acquisition of literacy often constituted central episodes in the narrators' struggles for freedom. Many ex-slave narrators emphasized the importance of their learning to read and write in facilitating their escapes. Some also acknowledged how becoming literate allowed them to better estimate the extent of their disenfranchised positions. Thus either learning to read and write or overcoming the obstacles of illiteracy usually formed one of the climactic points of the narratives. Rather than acknowledging the narrator's growing resemblance to Western subjectivity, as was the case with eighteenth-century slave narratives, the concern with literacy reflected critical moments of subversion or transgression in the later narratives.

The preeminence of this concern with literacy in the "classic" slave narrative reflects widespread social and civic concerns with the conjunction of issues of literacy and *race. It is important to keep in mind the highly nuanced history of antebellum policies and attitudes—both legal and extralegal—toward African American literacy. The work of historian Janet Duitsman Cornelius proves valuable on this point. In her study *When I Can Read My Title Clear: Literacy, Slavery, and Religion in the Antebellum South* (1991), Cornelius demonstrates that legal sanctions restricting slave literacy were not as widespread as generally believed (even by slaves themselves). Cornelius complicates the historical issue still further in several ways. She reviews actions taken by Southerners, whether or not in accordance with legal policies, to restrict African American literacy—" the most common widely known penalty for learning to read and write was amputation"; Cornelius equally notes the efforts of considerable segments of southern society to promote literacy among African Americans (as exemplified most dramatically by the efforts of prominent South Carolina slaveholder Richard Fuller). A further noteworthy dimension of this complex history concerns equivocal policies and actions of American tract societies, like the American Bible Society, in their concerted efforts to preserve the Union while still placing "repeated emphasis on the value of reading for all people." Beyond these contingencies, it is important to recognize that underlying the less than straightforward history of social and legal barriers to African American literacy is the powerful fact that "literacy, especially the ability to write, signified an establishment of the African's human identity to the European world." Spanning the gulf between illiteracy and literacy amounts to becoming fully human—which is the same as the least racialized.

In no other period or genre of African American literature was a preoccupation with literacy so pronounced. Concerns for literacy did not altogether disappear but after 1865 they are most often subsumed under a general concern for education. A brief historical account of African American struggles for education is provided by John E. Fleming et al. in *The Lengthening Shadow of Slavery* (1976), a struggle no longer limited in African American literature to close rehearsals of the circumstances and dangers of learning to read and write, but one that celebrates the achievement of formal education and literacy production. In the *Harlem Renaissance, which be-

gan shortly after the turn of the century, the presiding concerns are those of the redefinition of self and community allowed by modernity, mass culture, and burgeoning urban spaces. For some writers, *jazz, *blues, and other forms of African American *music supplanted the cultural dynamics and meaning of literacy as points of preoccupation. Indeed, African American musical production, *folklore, and nightlife came to be valued as alternative forms of cultural codification and transmission as powerful as the dominant community's valuation of literacy. The works of Langston *Hughes, Zora Neale *Hurston, and Claude *McKay, for example, operate very much in this way. Other writers of the renaissance did not participate in depicting these aspects of African American life. W. E. B. *Du Bois and Jessie Redmon *Fauset, for example, concerned themselves with depicting a black middle class well trained both in terms of education and citizenry. Literacy, then, was of significance only insofar as it underwrote a normative social and civic condition. It was no longer presented as the mark itself of such a struggle.

Perhaps such works as Richard *Wright's *Black Boy* (1945), in which a facility with written language enables the protagonist's ultimate escape from his circumstances, and Ralph *Ellison's *Invisible Man* (1952), in which such a facility engenders the plot and the journey of the protagonist, are exceptions to the rule because of their open interest with the power of literacy for African Americans. Nevertheless, whether or not a patent concern, literacy has proven to be one of the fundamental concepts informing the status and vision of African Americans both within their own communities and dominant communities. According to the cultural logic of the West, literacy provides the most manifest formalization of the life of the mind, so that to exist outside the condition of literacy is seemingly to be immured in a less meaningful and valued bodily existence having little or nothing to do with the life of the mind and its representation. Conversely, to enter into literacy is to gain important skills for extending oneself beyond the limited condition and geography of the body. Literacy, then, forms a symbolic boundary between the most and the less fully human with which race is often conflated. To cross, subvert, or prove one's cognizance of this boundary forms one of the rudimentary dramas of African American literature, most especially in the era of the classic slave narrative.

• John E. Fleming, *The Lengthening Shadow of Slavery: A Historical Justification for Affirmative Action for Blacks in Higher Education*, 1976. Robert Pattison, *On Literacy*, 1982. Henry Louis Gates, Jr., "Literary Theory and the Black Tradition," in *Figures in Black*, 1987, pp. 3–58. Harvey J. Graff, *The Legacies of Literacy: Continuities and Contradictions in Western Culture and Society*, 1987. Henry Louis Gates, Jr., "The Trope of the Talking Book," in *The Signifying Monkey: A Theory of African-American Literary Criticism*, 1988, pp. 127–169. Marion Wilson Starling, *The Slave Narrative*, 1988. W. Ross Winterowd, *The Culture and Politics of Literacy*, 1989. Janet Duitsman Cornelius, *When I Can Read My Title Clear: Literacy, Slavery, and Religion in the Antebellum South*, 1991. Ronald A. T. Judy, "Writing Culture in the Negro: Grammatology of Civil Society and Slavery," in *(Dis)Forming* the American Canon: African-Arabic Slave Narratives and the Vernacular, 1993, pp. 63–98. Lindon Barrett, "African American Slave Narratives: Literacy, the Body, Authority," American Literary History 73 (Fall 1995): 415–442.

—Lindon Barrett

LITERARY HISTORY. *This entry consists of a five-part discussion of African American literary history from its beginnings to the present. The individual essays deal with the following time periods:*

Colonial and Early National Eras
Antislavery Era
Reconstruction Era
Early Twentieth Century
Late Twentieth Century

These discussions outline major developments in literary genres, cultural values, and the social contexts in which African American literature has evolved. Many of the notable contributors to African American literature are mentioned here. The reader should view these discussions as introductory. The extensive cross-references within and appended to these five articles will lead to more detailed information about the genres, themes, writers, and texts that highlight African American literary history.

COLONIAL AND EARLY NATIONAL ERAS

The writings of the colonial and national eras disclose virtually all the central concerns of African American literature's later periods. Lucy *Terry, Phillis *Wheatley, Jupiter *Hammon, and George Moses *Horton in *poetry, Briton *Hammon, John *Marrant, Olaudah *Equiano, Venture *Smith (Broteer), and Solomon Bayley in the *slave narrative, Jupiter Hammon and Prince Hall in the homiletic address, Johnson Green and John Joyce in confessional narratives, John Browne *Russwurm and an anonymous woman writer in the journalistic *essay, and Phillis Wheatley and Benjamin *Banneker in the literary epistle all carry on discourse about *freedom for themselves and for their African American brothers and sisters, about equal rights with a perhaps surprising generosity toward all races, and about *education, particularly for those African Americans denied the benefits of the fruits of knowledge.

Strongly motivating the drive toward literary production during the formative eras of African American literature was the conviction on the part of figures such as Wheatley, Russwurm, and Banneker that success in a variety of belletristic and practical genres of writing would give the lie to those whites who claimed, with Thomas Jefferson, that the absence of a literature worthy of the name by African Americans provided ample justification for the enslavement of black people.

African American poets composed lyrics, hymns, odes, epyllia (short epics), pastorals, elegies, and pastoral elegies. The poet who wrote in all of these genres was Phillis Wheatley, whose life, work, and example virtually dominate African American literary history until the middle of the nineteenth century. She was not, however, the first African American either to write or to publish. Lucy Terry's "Bars Fight"

(written in 1746 but not published until 1855), a ballad commemorating a skirmish between Massachusetts colonists and American Indians, represents the first known writing in English by an African American.

Such poets as Jupiter Hammon and Phillis Wheatley excelled in the subgenre of the hymn. Hammon's "An Evening Thought: Salvation by Christ, with Penitential Cries," the first poem published by an African American, appeared in 1760, on or after 25 December, and is composed in common hymn stanza. This apparently innocuous poem contains two arresting, subversive moments. Calling Jesus "thy captive Slave," Hammon suggests that the central and most acceptable focus of the Christian son of God is Hammon and his African American brothers and sisters, not their white oppressors. The phrase, "To set the Sinner free," especially when read within the context of "thy captive Slave," constructs a subversive "freeing" of Hammon and his fellow slaves. Sondra O'Neale, among others, has recently pointed out the antislavery subtext within "A Dialogue, Entitled, The Kind Master and Dutiful Servant" (1783). After the Master condescendingly commands his Servant to "follow me, / According to thy place," essentially telling him to "follow me" as God, the Servant describes the times as those "of great distress," an oblique reference not to the Revolution, whose fighting ended in 1782, but, according to O'Neale, to the condition of *slavery. Finally the Servant rather boldly calls upon the Christian God "To relieve distresses here." Of course, if the "great distress" is slavery, it follows that God has been called upon to give ease to the abominable institution.

The three poems Wheatley labels hymns all depart considerably from the hymn stanza adopted by Hammon. The companion poems "An Hymn to the Morning" and "An Hymn to the Evening" are actually lyrics to nature. They are composed in stanzas of iambic pentameter couplets and offer wholly classical paeans to Aurora and the principle of eventide, each filled with close observation of nature related in largely pastoral rhetoric. The entire Hymn to "Humanity," perhaps more closely resembling an ode, represents an intricate structure indicating the sophisticated mind of a first-rate experimentalist.

Wheatley demonstrates her skills in several other subgenres of poetry. So pervasive is her pastoralism (references to such elements of Vergil's *Eclogues* as shepherds piping "beneath the myrtle shade," where one may discover contemplation's "sacred spring") that the reader may trace a pastoral strain of subversion, especially in her 1773 *Poems*. The poems "To Maecenas" (which introduces the volume), "On Recollection," "On Imagination," "Ode to Neptune," and "A Farewell to America," all odes, Wheatley composed between March 1772 and August 1773; among her very best poems, on the surface they appear to be harmless little ditties treating conventional topics. When Wheatley speaks in "To Maecenas," however, of snatching the laurel or prize of poetic maturity from the "honour'd" heads of her white patrons (or purchasers of her *Poems*) "while you indulgent smile upon the deed," she has seized the moment to proclaim to the world her confidence in her own achievement, despite the fact of her "less happy" circumstance of writing under the yoke of slavery.

In addition to authoring *Poems on Various Subjects, Religious and Moral* (1773), the first book by an African American on any subject, Wheatley enjoyed, however briefly, a career of great distinction, which brought her international fame, prompting Voltaire to write that she was the author of "very good English verse." The poetry of George Moses Horton, though not as accomplished as that of Wheatley, was produced after the United States Constitution's ratification of slavery as a legal institution. Horton's protest against his enslaved state was, consequently, much more daring, passionate, and direct.

Writing more than forty years after Wheatley's death, Horton speaks his protest against slavery in such titles as "Slavery," "The Slave's Complaint," "On Hearing of the Intention of a Gentleman to Purchase the Poet's Freedom," and "On Liberty and Slavery." This last poem appeared in Horton's first collection, *The Hope of Liberty* (1829), and contains the affective stanza: "Say unto foul oppression, Cease: / Ye tyrants rage no more, / And let the joyful trump of peace, / Now bid the vassel soar." In "Slavery," Horton describes a particularly grim moment: "Is it because my skin is black, / That thou should'st be so dull and slack, / And scorn to set me free? / Then let me hasten to the grave. . . ." Significantly this stanza's pattern of a tetrameter couplet followed by four lines of alternating iambic trimeter and iambic tetrameter rhyming *cddc* calls up Wheatley's stanzaic pattern used in the "Humanity" hymn. Horton adopts this stanzaic pattern on several more occasions, and such phrases as "the pensive muse," "the sylvan shade," and the "peaceful grove" whence one may "Survey the flowery plume" resonate with Wheatley's pastoral. When we observe further that in 1838 and again in 1849 Horton's poems were printed in the same volumes with poems by Wheatley (on the latter occasion with *letters by Banneker), then we can conclude that Horton's acquaintance with Wheatley was more than casual; as well, we can better learn the veracity of Henry Louis *Gates, Jr.'s pronouncement that Wheatley was "the progenitor of the black literary tradition."

Wheatley's influence may also be traced within the development of the slave narrative, perhaps most strikingly in her woodcut portrait used as a frontispiece to her 1773 *Poems*. Olaudah Equiano, for example, prefaces his 1789 *Interesting Narrative* with his portrait in which he, similar to Wheatley, is holding a book; in this case that book is a Bible. While Wheatley sits musing before a desk on which her hand rests atop a page with her writing visible, a book also rests on this surface in full view. African American women writers of slave narratives and other genres, such as Jarena *Lee, Annie Louise *Burton, Sara Allen (wife of Richard *Allen), L. A. J. Moorer, and others are posed throughout the nineteenth century in varying degrees of likeness to Wheatley, but all have a book in their hand or placed near them. In any event, the point in each case appears to be to make a concrete declaration that African Americans can become just as literate as whites and are, therefore, not likely candidates for slavery.

Equiano makes clear the quest for learning and the difficulty involved in acquiring it in his *Interesting Narrative*, wherein he sets up the trope of the talking book. Having observed his master and others moving their lips and reading out loud when examining a book (a common practice before this century), he, not yet literate, concluded that they were "talking" to the book, appearing to be carrying on a conversation with it. This mysterious circumstance lost its mystery the moment Equiano became literate. The naïveté evident in this episode points directly to Equiano's dual narrator. That is, when telling the events of his early childhood and adolescence, Equiano assumes a naive, childlike persona, but he quickly and often abruptly shifts this persona to that of an experienced, disenchanted adult who has suffered the severe disadvantages of slavery, the exposure of which constitutes the primary commitment of the entire genre of the slave narrative or *autobiography. The author of *Interesting Narrative* is particularly poignant in his descriptions of the horrid Middle Passage and of slave beatings, as are the authors of many slave autobiographies. Equiano's *Narrative* enjoyed an immense, international popularity, appearing in Dutch, German, and Russian translations, all published before the end of the eighteenth century.

While not as popular as Equiano's *Narrative*, Briton Hammon's *A Narrative of the Uncommon Sufferings, and Surprizing Deliverance of Briton Hammon, A Negro Man—Servant to General Winslow* enjoys the distinction of being the first published writing by an African American. This first attempt at African Amercian autobiography displays many affinities to later examples of the genre. Apparently written by himself, this tract does not contain the caption "Written by Himself," though it does have the identifying phrase "A Negro Man" and a brief paragraph giving a synopsis of the narrative's action followed by the white Boston printers' names, Green and Russell, all on the title page and serving as a sort of testimony of *authentication. Although Hammon says he will "only relate matters of fact as they occur to my mind," he does at several points note that it was "kind Providence" that released him from the clutches of hostile Native Americans or that "the Providence of God" delivered him from confinement in a dungeon. His assertion that he "return'd to my own native land [the American Colonies] to show how great things the Lord hath done for me" aligns his text with such later spiritual slave autobiographies as those by Solomon Bayley, Richard Allen, and Jarena Lee. It should not go without observing that in his *A Narrative of Some Remarkable Incidents in the Life of Solomon Bayley, Formerly a Slave . . . Written by Himself* (2d ed. 1825), the author repeatedly speaks of his "great distress," "my distress," and "the bitterness of distress," echoing J. Hammon's "time of great distress" and J. Hammon's plea that God "relieve distresses here," strengthening the identification of the word "distress" as a code word for the institution of slavery.

A Narrative of the Lord's Wonderful Dealings with John Marrant, A Black (1785) bears obvious parallels in its title to B. Hammon's *Narrative,* although Marrant's *Narrative* was not written by himself but by a white *amanuensis named W. Aldridge. Scattered throughout, such phrases as "his kind providence" and "had a feeling concern for the salvation of my countrymen" clearly fall in line with B. Hammon's stated reason for relating his *Narrative.* Venture Smith's *A Narrative of the Life, and Adventures of Venture, A Native of Africa* (1798) seems self-consciously to be attempting to distance itself from such relations as those of B. Hammon and John Marrant. Although illiterate like Marrant and thus requiring an amanuensis, Smith clearly wants to be known as an African, his displacement notwithstanding. The pride he feels for his native Africa is also self-evident in the detail he gives of his birthplace, Dukandra in Guinea, his fond memories of his mother and father, and of his family's vicissitudes there before he was captured into slavery at the age of eight.

The oral nature of these last two autobiographies by Marrant and Smith points to the homiletic address, products of African American*oratory. Perhaps no other genre of African American letters displays a greater affinity with the old traditions of Africa, for with its familiar call-and-response praxis between minister and congregation, this genre most closely duplicates the tribal call and response so prevalent in Africa. While many of these homiletic addresses were delivered by ministers, not all were. For example, the poet Jupiter Hammon presented "An Address to the Negroes in the State of New York" in 1786, which was printed in 1787; it is likely that this delivery was not Hammon's only one. As Hammon made his New York "Address" before a combined audience of whites and African Americans, the temper of this address is somewhat self-conscious in comparison to the later addresses by African American ministers to exclusively African American audiences. After the post-Revolutionary organization of African American congregations, the subject matter of the oratory of such ministers as Prince Hall and Absalom Jones concentratedly focused upon the horrors and injustices of slavery, upon securing equal rights for all Americans, regardless of color, and upon the necessity of education.

Prince Hall, organizer of African American Masonry and early abolitionist, makes reference in "A Charge Delivered to the Brethren of the African Lodge" (25 June 1792) to "our late Reverend Brother *John Marrant.*" Amid a catalog of exemplary ancients, Hall shows familiarity with such church fathers as Tertullian, Cyprian, and even Fulgentius, an early Christian commentator on Vergil's *Aeneid.* Encouraging "love and benevolence to all the whole family of mankind," Hall devoted much time and effort during his career to the setting up of educational facilities for African American youth. In "A Thanksgiving Sermon . . . On Account of the Abolition of the African Slave Trade," delivered on 1 January 1808, the date that the United States Congress effected the

end of transatlantic traffic in slaves, Absalom Jones, abolitionist and first African American priest of the Protestant Episcopal church, celebrates the theme of deliverance throughout the history of the world.

The artistry of homiletic oratory is noticeably absent from confessional narratives. Johnson Green's "Life and Confession" (1786) was related to an amanuensis and is remarkable because it was printed as a broadside by Isaiah Thomas, one of America's most famous printers and author of the first history of printing in the American colonies and early republic. The recorder of John Joyce's "Confession" is particularly noteworthy because his name was Richard Allen, founder of the Free African Society and the African Methodist Episcopal church, and an abolitionist. Allen appears to have consciously used the event of Joyce's execution for the murder of a white woman on 14 March 1808 as an occasion to teach African Americans a lesson in morality. Prefacing a description of the trial, the judge's rendering of the sentence, and Joyce's confession is Allen's own "Address to the Public, and People of Colour." The urgency of Allen's admonition to young males, though perhaps a bit stale for today's youth, bespeaks compassion: "The midnight revel, the polluted couch, thy diseased body, and thy affrighted conscience, testify against thee. Perhaps thy Mother's heart is already broken!" If directed toward young African Americans, Allen's exhortation is especially poignant, for his effort here is to assure survival.

Survival with dignity is assuredly a major concern of journalistic essayists writing during the early republic. John B. Russwurm, a graduate of Bowdoin College who, along with Samuel *Cornish, founded *Freedom's Journal* in 1827, declares in the editorial of 16 March opening the *Journal's* first issue: "We wish to plead our own course. Too long have others spoken for us. Too long has the publick been deceived by misrepresentations, in things which concern us dearly." In a passage that bears close ties to Richard Allen's "Address to . . . People of Colour," Russwurm continues: "there are others who make it their business to enlarge upon the least trifle, which tends to the discredit of any person of colour." These ill-meaning white folks "pronounce anathemas and denounce our whole body for the misconduct of this guilty one." Russwurm takes great pains to state that one of the central concerns of the *Journal* will be to advance the cause of education among African Americans, for "It is surely time," according to the editor, "that we should awake from this lethargy of years, and make a concentrated effort for the education of our youth." Another central concern of the *Journal* is the "civil rights of a people" which are "of the greatest value," and, so he continues, "it shall ever be our duty to vindicate our brethen, when oppressed."

In an anonymous contribution, a woman writer offered to *Freedom's Journal* an editorial enlisting the public to support women's rights (10 Aug. 1827). Asserting that the "diffusion of knowledge has destroyed" the notion that woman's only office is "to darn a stocking and cook a pudding well . . . men of the present age, allow, that we have minds that are capable and deserving of culture." This progressive author further maintains that it is the duty of "all mothers" to instruct their daughters "to devote their leisure time to reading books, whence they [will] derive valuable information, which [can] never be taken from them." The graceful style, both of Russwurm and the anonymous woman author, doubtless served as models to other writers of the journalistic essay.

Phillis Wheatley cultivated the literary epistle in her proposal for a second volume of poetry, never published, which lists thirteen letters of her authorship to be included, these addressed to such notables as the Earl of Dartmouth, Benjamin Rush, and the Countess of Huntingdon. In her letter of 11 February 1774 to the Native American minister Samson Occom, Wheatley speaks of "the glorious Dispensation of civil and religious Liberty" that "are so inseparately united, that there is little or no Enjoyment of one without the other." With pointed irony toward white American agitators for independence from England she goes on: "How well the Cry for Liberty, and the reverse Disposition for the Exercise of oppressive Power over others agree—I humbly think it does not require the Penetration of a Philosopher to determine."

No examination of the literary epistle in early African American literature can omit Benjamin Banneker's letter to Thomas Jefferson, perhaps the most famous letter by an early African American. Written on 19 August 1791 and published in a pamphlet in 1792, Banneker's letter combined a moral and political protest against slavery aimed at the quintessential representative of America's paradoxical adherence to freedom and human bondage, the slaveholding author of the Declaration of Independence. In his *Notes on the State of Virginia* (1787), Jefferson speculated that blacks lacked analytic intelligence and literary imagination, two qualities basic to any race's claim to civilization, in Jefferson's view. In response Banneker sent Jefferson a copy of *Benjamin Banneker's Almanac* (1792), which contained a completely calculated ephemeris, demonstrating the signal accomplishment of this self-taught African American mathematician and astronomer and, by implication, the capacity of any black person to do intellectual work equal in sophistication to that of whites. Banneker went on to remind Jefferson of his ringing endorsement of human equality in the Declaration of Independence and of the white man's espousal of the ideals of liberty for all mankind when he felt himself under the oppression of the British crown. How then, Banneker asked, could the Virginian continue to own slaves and ignore his own likeness to the once-detested tyrant George III? This challenge to Jefferson's intellectual and moral consistency became one of the central documents of antislavery activism, as well as early African American literature, for the next fifty years.

Writing across a full range of literary forms and activated by a widespread rhetoric of liberation from oppressive power, African Americans participated in the literature of revolution that swept through Europe and the Americas in the late eighteenth and early nineteenth centuries. While the twentieth century has often undervalued Wheatley and her fellow African American writers before Frederick *Douglass, the literature of early black America deserves to be read, studied, and appreciated with the dignity and interest accorded later periods.

[*See also* Periodicals, *article on* Black Periodical Press; Slavery.]

• Lorenzo J. Greene, *The Negro in Colonial New England*, 1942. William L. Andrews, *To Tell a Free Story: The First Century of Afro-American Autobiography, 1760–1865*, 1986. William D. Piersen, *Black Yankees: The Development of an Afro-American Subculture in Eighteenth-Century New England*, 1988. Blyden Jackson, *A History of Afro-American Literature: The Long Beginning, 1746–1895*, 1989. Sidney Kaplan and Emma N. Kaplan, *The Black Presence in the Era of the American Revolution*, rev. ed., 1989. Frances Smith Foster, *Written by Herself: Literary Production by African American Women, 1746–1892*, 1993. Sondra A. O'Neale, *Jupiter Hammon and the Biblical Beginnings of African-American Literature*, 1993. Frances Smith Foster, *Witnessing Slavery: The Development of Ante-bellum Slave Narratives*, 2d ed., 1994. Rose Zimbardo and Benilde Montgomery, guest eds., *African American Culture in the Eighteenth Century*, special issue of *Eighteenth-Century Studies* 27.4 (Summer 1994).

—John C. Shields

ANTISLAVERY ERA

From 1832 through the Civil War, African American writing grew in range, volume, and sophistication. No longer provincial, it took on a national, even international character.

In the earlier period, only one African American newspaper yet existed; by 1860 at least eighteen had been started. Earlier, no abolitionist groups had been active; by the mid-1850s thirty major organizations were at work, with fifty more satellite groups giving support—in New England, New York, across Pennsylvania, Ohio, Indiana, and Illinois, into Canada, the West, and California. Equally telling, they and their British allies usually had presses and *periodicals hungry for material. William Lloyd Garrison, driving force of the movement, said that abolitionists venerated the printed word. African American writing thus both entered and helped to extend a climactic phase of American romanticism, one in which the transcendentalist Theodore Parker could exalt the work of Frederick *Douglass and other slave narrators, holding that "all the original romance of America is in them, not in the white man's novel." Yet the spoken antislavery word often preceded the written. Hence it was an age of *oratory and *journalism, of memorable speeches eagerly recorded by the papers, then reproduced by every significant organ of the movement on two continents.

Much of the work distinctive to the age indeed radiates from the papers. Black and white, they sought to cultivate every possible contributor, every available argument, every possible occasion, and every available form. They printed news, *poetry, debate, *drama, *letters, speeches, *histories, *biographies, *autobiographies, and travel accounts. With less articulate sources, they took the stories by dictation. The gifted they cultivated as agents, writers, lecturers, and correspondents. The assumption that the word would make one not only free but strong had several consequences, important in a nation where one in seven was African American, but only one in seventy was a free black. Language could be assumed to be the nature and expression of self. If expression alone could do much to disprove proslavery arguments, how much more effective would be the personal history of a Harriet A. *Jacobs or the social analyses of a Martin R. *Delany or the eloquence of an Alexander *Crummell.

It was the first great age of autobiographies, the form many take to be the model for all later African American prose narratives. It was likewise the first great age of social and historical studies of black America by black Americans. Personal histories abound, but so too do histories of *churches, *families, leaders, soldiers, innovators. It was the initial age for the *novel, the *short story, the drama, and the travel book. It was the earliest age for the large-scale collection of songs and *spirituals, proverbs and folktales. The effects of such labor can be seen throughout the period, but in places uncommon for literary study. Opponents did not usually try to answer David *Walker or Henry Highland *Garnet or William Wells *Brown or Harriet Beecher *Stowe. Rather they tried to ban them. In the malevolence of the Fugitive Slave Act of 1850 some Southerners sought to expunge once and for all the entire talented class of free blacks in the North. No small tribute to the power of the pen.

Although not all have survived, African American newspapers were founded throughout the middle of the century, the earliest the work of the indefatigable Samuel *Cornish, who with John Browne *Russwurm established *Freedom's Journal in New York City in 1827. With its demise, Cornish returned with Rights of All in 1829, the Weekly Advocate in 1837, and, most influential of all, the Colored American 1837–1841, all in New York City. Businessman, skilled essayist, and leader of the Moral Reform Society, William *Whipper edited the National Reformer in Philadelphia 1838–1839. The Mirror of Liberty was the more radical effort of David *Ruggles from 1838 to 1840. In Pittsburgh the extremely talented Martin R. Delany published the Mystery 1843–1847, then assisted Douglass in Rochester with the North Star from 1847 to 1849. With an MD from Harvard, Delany was, in a full life, journalist, physician, lecturer, explorer, ethnologist, army officer, civil servant, trial judge, novelist, and organizer of *emigration projects. Only Douglass himself and his three papers (1847–1860) could approach such activity.

The scope of early magazines is suggested by the religious A.M.E. Magazine (1841–1842), the political Douglass's Monthly (1859–1860), and Thomas Hamilton's literary *Anglo-African Magazine (1859–1861). Growing in number, the religious magazines were an important outlet for the writing of women, both free and fugitive. On most matters black newspapers worked closely with their white counterparts, especially the Liberator, the Emancipator, and the National Anti-Slavery Standard.

While united against *slavery, abolitionists did offer differing strategies to combat it. Open rebellion was the most direct means, with the examples of Toussaint *L'Ouverture, Gabriel Prosser, and Denmark Vesey at hand. Yet no rebel had left a literary testament until The *Confessions of Nat Turner was published in 1831. Two years earlier, the most widely circulated work before the 1840s, David Walker's famous Appeal, had warned that peace and slavery could not coexist. In the 1830s David Ruggles continued the militant tradition in lectures and articles, as Henry Highland Garnet did into the succeeding decade. A former slave who ministered to a Presbyterian congregation in Troy, New York, Garnet delivered a fervent "Address to the Slaves of the United States of America" at a convention in 1843, published five years later in a volume with Walker's Appeal as a demand for political action. The convention movement, an innovation of the age, was a successful training ground for the *education and self-expression of many.

Few promoted rebellion. Many advocated escape. Because the rigors of bondage were growing as rapidly as the spirit of abolition, the rate of flight increased dramatically. So too did tales of flight, making the fugitive *slave narrative equally instrument and inscription of the age. Besides being exciting tales of adventure, the narratives were vivid description of the mechanisms of the peculiar institution from across the South, told from within, a point of view unfamiliar to most northern readers. The most popular literary form of the antebellum years, they became the springboards for professional careers. Some two dozen or so fugitives got their starts as agents, lecturers, or writers by recounting their personal histories. Douglass gained his reputation as orator and conscience of the nation by retailing his life story, later turning it into two masterpieces of the genre. The Narrative of 1845 is a small gem, surpassed only by *My Bondage and My Freedom ten years later. As Douglass was launching his independent literary career as editor and publisher (1847–1860), William Wells Brown was developing into a literary pioneer, striking out into fiction, drama, history, biography, and *travel writing. After publishing his narrative (1847) and a book of antislavery songs (1848) in Boston, he traveled to England, where, in a season of innovations, he produced Three Years in Europe, an important travel book, in 1852, and a year later the earliest African American novel, *Clotel, or The President's Daughter (later revised with different titles). He followed these with the earliest published play, The *Escape, or A Leap for Freedom (1858), a further memoir, more travel writing, and four histories. His method of historical chronicle was to become predominant later in the century. For instance, he contributed a long series of *essays on "Celebrated Colored Americans" to newspapers and then combined them into The Black Man, His Antecedents, His Genius, and His Achievements (1863). The example of Clotel following one year upon Uncle Tom's Cabin proved the effect of fiction. Douglass published the short novel "The *Heroic Slave" in the 1853 annual Autographs for Freedom. Frances Ellen Watkins *Harper's short story "The *Two Offers" appeared in the Anglo-African, which also serialized Delany's unfinished novel, *Blake, or The Huts of America (1859).

The same year saw publication of the initial novel by an African American woman, Harriet E. *Wilson's *Our Nig, or Sketches from the Life of a Free Black.

Fulfilling the narrative's ambition "to tell a free story," as William L. Andrews happily phrases it, is Harriet Jacobs's *Incidents in the Life of a Slave Girl, published in 1861 under the pen name Linda Brent. One of very few by a woman and one of the last to be published separately before the Civil War, it attempts the painstaking task of enfolding northern white women readers within the threads of its design as early as its opening sentence, "Reader, be assured this narrative is no fiction." Its subject is taboo, the sexual exploitation of slave women by their owners. Its style is crafted understatement. Its method of release is ingenious: While leaving clues that she has fled north, Jacobs retreats to the tiny garret of her grandmother's house, there for seven years to overlook the growth of her children.

Because of a low rate of escape, heavy responsibility for children once free, and a lack of encouragement from abolitionist sponsors, few fugitive women published their stories as books or pamphlets. Instead they joined free women in the growing *women's club movement; their writing is found more readily in the periodicals and antislavery annuals. Important free speakers and writers include Sojourner *Truth, Sarah P. Remond, Maria W. *Stewart, Frances Ellen Watkins Harper, Mary Ann *Shadd, and Margretta and Sarah Forten. Narratives by men, on the other hand, appeared with increasing frequency after 1840. Examples are Moses *Roper (1839), Lunsford Lane (1842), Moses Grandy (1844), Lewis and Milton Clarke (1845, 1846), Henry *Bibb (1849), James W. C. *Pennington (1849), Josiah *Henson (1849), Henry Box *Brown (1849), Solomon *Northup (1853), Samuel Ringgold Ward (1855), John Brown (1855), William and Ellen *Craft (1860), and J. D. *Green (1864).

While stirring ordinary northerners, the narratives also moved a sizable number of white authors. The gentle poet John Greenleaf Whittier, who had a hand in several, was compelled to tears. Richard Hildreth anonymously offered a novel in 1836 as The Slave, or Memoirs of Archy Moore. And the narratives both inspired and created the audience for the single most influential abolition volume of all, Uncle Tom's Cabin. Like so many others, it ran first as a serial for nine months in the antislavery press, then appeared in book form in spring 1852, selling three hundred thousand copies in America alone. Equally popular in Europe, it sold more than two million copies in the United States within a decade, making it in relation to population the best-seller of all time. While Harriet Beecher Stowe held that God had inspired the book, the narratives and the fugitive slave law were more immediate instruments. When Abraham *Lincoln was grappling with issues of slavery and emancipation in the summer of 1862, he asked the Library of Congress for a copy of A Key to Uncle Tom's Cabin, a later volume citing Stowe's sources in newspapers and narratives.

Included in that work are references to several studies of black American life. Going beyond the information of the periodicals and narratives, volumes were appearing that traced the social, cultural, and historical condition of African Americans. One of the most learned men of the day, James McCune Smith, from 1837 onward contributed dozens of essays to the black press containing what would soon be termed social and political analysis. Smith possessed an MD from the University of Glasgow and brought an international and evolutionary perspective to political questions. Presbyterian minister and holder of a doctorate from the University of Heidelberg, James W. C. Pennington wrote A Text Book on the Origin and History . . . of the Colored People (1841) and The Past and Present Condition, and the Destiny of the Colored Race (1848). Martin Delany produced in 1852 the most learned account of free blacks before the war, The Condition, Elevation, Emigration and Destiny of the Colored People of the United States, Politically Considered, followed by a pamphlet distilling his findings two years later. Within the decade he studied the practicability of various emigration schemes. Others writing political and historical commentary included William C. *Nell, William G. *Allen, Lewis H. Putnam, and John B. Meachum.

Quiescent as an issue for nearly a decade, colonization revived on the heels of the Fugitive Slave Act. Most thinkers of the period had rejected emigration, seeing it as at base a proslavery tactic. Theodore S. Wright's impassioned Address to Three Thousand Colored Citizens of New York (1846) is a summary of that view. Led by John Russwurm and Alexander Crummell, a small group of intellectuals nevertheless continued to press for colonization. Respected by all for his character and force of mind, Crummell labored for two of his most productive decades in Liberia and Sierra Leone, 1853 to 1873, with schooling and missionary ventures. Probably the most accomplished prose stylist of the century, he offered a nationalist vision of an Africa cleansed of her despoilers in The Relations and Duties of Free Colored Men in America to Africa (1861). Some of his finest writing is collected in The Future of Africa (1862).

Two poets, George Moses *Horton and James Monroe *Whitfield, were ardent proponents of colonization—a sign that verse had moved away from its nonpolitical position of the late 1820s and early 1830s, when Phillis *Wheatley was the favored figure. As with oratory, poetry too became absorbed in the antislavery cause. A slave at the university in Chapel Hill, Horton pressed his protest in The Hope of Liberty (1829, 1837, 1838). Whitfield dedicated his America, and Other Poems to Martin Delany. George B. *Vashon, an Oberlin graduate who taught in Port-au-Prince, wrote a long eulogy to a Haitian hero in "Vincent Ogé," (first published 1854). Frances Watkins Harper included "The Slave Mother" and "Bury Me in a Free Land" in Poems on Miscellaneous Subjects of 1854 (in its twentieth edition by 1874). Other abolitionist poets were Charles L. *Reason, Daniel A. *Payne, and James Madison *Bell.

By its very nature an age of crisis, the antebellum period was catalytic in its interests and intensity. Its accents echo whenever similar conditions recur: the 1890s or 1920s or 1960s. Once asked why the abolitionist press seemed to be thriving, Samuel Ringgold Ward replied, "Any Negro living well is an anti-slavery fighter." An explanation too for the richness and diversity of expression of the age.

[See also Antislavery Movement; Freedom; Periodicals, article on Black Periodical Press; Protest Literature.]

• Vernon Loggins, The Negro Author, 1931. Jean Fagin Yellin, The Intricate Knot: Black Figures in American Literature, 1776–1863, 1972. John Sekora and Darwin T. Turner, eds., The Art of Slave Narrative, 1982. William L. Andrews, To Tell a Free Story: The First Century of Afro-American Autobiography, 1760–1865, 1986. Shirley Yee, Black Women Abolitionists: A Study in Activism, 1828–1860, 1992. Frances Smith Foster, Written by Herself: Literary Production by African American Women, 1746–1892, 1993. Frankie Hutton, The Early Black Press in America, 1827 to 1860, 1993.   —John Sekora

RECONSTRUCTION ERA

The Reconstruction era (1866–1899) was marked by significant transitions in African American literature. Some of the writers whose careers began before emancipation remained active after. Frances Ellen Watkins *Harper continued to be productive, publishing new *poetry and four *novels, including her most noted, *Iola Leroy (1892). William Wells *Brown produced a post-Emancipation edition of *Clotel (1867), among other, additional works. Frederick *Douglass wrote the final versions of his *autobiography, Life and Times of Frederick Douglass (1881, 1892) during this time, as well.

But with the end of *slavery new forces emerged in African American writing. *Education progressed rapidly in African American communities after the Civil War, creating a growing African American middle class with strong literary interests. *Literary societies were among the more important community organizations, and literary efforts were encouraged by the explosive growth of an African American press. Newspapers appeared throughout the United States; several prominent journalists whose careers extended into the next century, including T. Thomas *Fortune of the New York Age and William Calvin Chase of the Washington Bee, began their careers during this period. Among periodicals, the African Methodist Episcopal Church Review (founded 1884), initially edited by the scholarly Benjamin T. *Tanner and, subsequently, by Levi J. Coppin, played a preeminent role in encouraging African American intellectual and literary activity.

Reconstruction era writing manifested its middle-class roots in its major characteristics. Through the 1890s, African American writers participated in a genteel, sentimental tradition that dominated American middle-class culture generally. Integrationist in orientation, they used literature to emphasize their similarities to other educated Americans and to protest their exclusion from the American mainstream.

Several important writers emerged within this genteel, Victorian framework. The most influential poet to begin his career during the era was Albery Allson* Whitman. Whitman published widely, but his fame rested on two book-length epic poems, Not a

Man, and Yet a Man (1877) and The Rape of Florida (1884; reissued as Twasinta's Seminoles, 1885, 1890). Drawing on Victorian models and on verse forms ranging from the strongly rhythmic patterns of Henry Wadsworth Longfellow's "Hiawatha" to Spenserian stanza, Whitman celebrated African American heroism in the face of white racial injustice, his heroes displaying dominant virtues of courage, self-control, and moral virtue.

Other poets, though not attempting the epic, worked within similarly conservative frameworks. Among the more prominent, such poets as Islay Walden, Henrietta Cordelia *Ray, and John Willis Menard created paeans to nature, love, and a sentimental piety. They broke with other Victorians only in persistently linking their writing to the demands of protesting prejudice and discrimination.

Writers of fiction also drew on Victorian themes and models. Dramatizing the genteel virtues of their heroes and heroines, they created, at the same time, a fiction of protest, putting their characters into settings of slavery, oppression, and white venality that strongly condemned the injustice of a racist world. Many writers, like James H. W. Howard in his novel Bond and Free (1886), also built on the tradition of the "tragic *mulatto," the cultured, virtuous young man or woman who grows up as white, and whose subsequent confrontation with racial barriers confirms the arbitrariness as well as the injustice of racial lines.

Their Victorian conservatism should not be taken to mean that writers from this period rejected an African American *identity. Encouraged by such figures as Alexander *Crummell, most made racial pride a dominant motif. They took special interest in African American *history, details of which they often incorporated into their works. This interest was supported by one of the more ambitious projects in African American letters from the period, that of George Washington *Williams, who published the first scholarly histories of African Americans. One was a two-volume History of the Negro Race in America from 1619 to 1880 (1883); the other, his History of the Negro Troops in the War of the Rebellion, 1861–1865 (1888). In Williams's histories and elsewhere, racial pride was central, if expressed less in terms of any distinctive African American characteristics than in terms of African American accomplishments measured within the framework of the larger society.

African American writers began the Reconstruction era on a note of high optimism. Emancipation had raised hopes, as had the relative flexibility of race relations prior to the end of Radical Reconstruction in 1877, including the effective participation of African Americans in the politics of the former slave states. Their writing was inspired by a sense that proof of equality and progress could overcome white prejudice. Williams's histories attempted to document such progress; other writers believed their literary accomplishments would help do so, too.

The last two decades of the century did much to dash that optimism. North and South saw a triumphant racism in Anglo-American thought, culture, and practice; the South was plagued by racial *violence, *lynching, and increasing segregation, as whites sought to confine African Americans to a subordinate place in social and economic life. The result among middle-class African Americans was, by the 1890s, cultural and ideological turmoil. Many followed Booker T. *Washington, who in his 1895 "*Atlanta Exposition Address" urged postponing integrationist efforts in favor of community building; more continued to hold to integrationist goals, but became increasingly pessimistic about their realization.

In literature, this turmoil was reflected in a reorientation of older motifs and the development of significant new directions. Toward the close of the century, one of the first genuinely nationalistic novels appeared, Sutton E. *Griggs's *Imperium in Imperio* (1899). A few writers began to use the theme of the "tragic mulatto" to say less about the arbitrariness of racial lines than about the virtue of choosing an identity centered in the African American community. Harper moved in this direction with *Iola Leroy*; so did Victoria Earle *Matthews in her *short story "Eugenie's Mistake," published in the *A.M.E. Church Review* (1892).

There was also a sense that changing conditions demanded an approach to literature that, in keeping with the increasing isolation of the African American community, would celebrate what was distinctive about African American life. Many people began to think about possibilities for using African American folk traditions to create a distinctively African American literature. Previously, writers had shown little interest in oral traditions. A few, including Harper, William Wells Brown, and Victoria Earle Matthews, sought to use "folk" characters in ways also consistent with their admiration for Victorian ideals, but folk culture as such was seen as part of the past, a legacy to be transcended. New moods, however, led to new orientations toward that legacy.

Outside the middle class, pre-Emancipation oral traditions, with roots in slave culture, had retained their vigor after *freedom. The popular *trickster tales, celebrating the power of wit in the face of oppression, remained current; so did the *spirituals, with their profound understanding of suffering and freedom. Reflecting the abiding force of racism and discrimination, as well as the growing independence of such institutions as the *church, these traditions had even come to play a more vital role in folk society in the Reconstruction era, helping to center identity and community ties.

They had also become more widely known. Popular entertainments including *minstrelsy, despite a reliance on *stereotypes, used genuine African American materials, and, though performed by whites in blackface as well as by African Americans, helped to diffuse those materials. The emergence of a white "*plantation tradition" literature, while equally dominated by stereotypes romanticizing the slave society of the Old South, did the same. White Georgia journalist Joel Chandler Harris, through his stories of the obsequious "Uncle Remus," gave traditional African American trickster tales a national audience. Hampton Institute's *Southern Workman*, though a white-edited *periodical, became a treasure trove of traditional materials contributed by members of the African American student body, particularly tales, folk beliefs, and songs. Richmond, Virginia, African American preacher John Jasper achieved celebrity status with his much-preached sermon, "De Sun Do Move," providing a popular view of traditional folk religion to white as well as African American audiences.

Interest in the spirituals was particularly strong. Known before the Civil War, they became widely appreciated in the Reconstruction era through their publication by such sympathetic white northern collectors as Thomas Wentworth Higginson and Lucy McKim Garrison. Even more influential were performances of the songs by the Jubilee Singers of Fisk University. The group was founded in 1871 and soon copied by similar organizations from other institutions. Using the songs to raise funds, the Fisk singers and others increased the spirituals' audience in performances given throughout the United States and Europe.

African American writers who hoped to explore the literary possibilities of oral traditions attempted to build on this interest, appealing to an audience that had already shown its receptiveness. Many also wanted to rescue folk society from the kinds of stereotypes that minstrel versions and such plantation writers as Harris employed in their renditions of African American tradition. Such efforts led directly to the success of the first African American writers to achieve a genuine national audience, Charles Waddell *Chesnutt and Paul Laurence *Dunbar.

Chesnutt's work with folk tradition appeared first. Written in a version of African American "dialect," his "*Uncle Julius" stories appeared in such popular journals as the *Atlantic* as early as 1889. Building on the trickster figure, Chesnutt recontextualized the white plantation tradition by deromanticizing the southern setting, dramatizing its violence and exploitation. He created a figure in Uncle Julius who, unlike Harris's Uncle Remus, left no doubt about the stories' aggressive possibilities.

Dunbar, however, had the greater impact, chiefly through his efforts at "*dialect poetry," written in the putative voice of the slaves and ex-slaves of the South. When his first major volume, *Lyrics of Lowly Life* (1896), appeared, endorsed by the dean of American letters, William Dean Howells, Dunbar attracted national attention, becoming, perhaps, the most popular poet, white or African American, in the United States. This attention inspired a vogue in dialect poetry, including work by such popular writers as James Edwin *Campbell and James D. *Corrothers. By the end of the century, virtually every African American writer had tried the form.

Neither Dunbar and Chesnutt nor their contemporaries broke entirely with the older plantation tradition. Most, with the possible exception of Campbell, used a dialect based as much on literary models as on folk speech. All used motifs with roots in popular writing as well as in oral tradition. But together, they helped define possibilities for a folk-based literature that few of their predecessors had thought possible.

At the same time, worsening conditions also brought a growing sense of the dilemma of being African American in a racist society, the dilemma of formulating an identity, as earlier writers had, in enthusiastically "American" terms. Here, too, Dunbar and Chesnutt were pioneers, departing from dialect to reorient genteel themes and traditional modes of protest to confront the changing times. Dunbar, who was never entirely comfortable with his success in dialect, expressed his frustration with all received formulations of identity in such works as his novel *The Uncalled* (1898). Chesnutt, in stories published as early as the late 1880s, and appearing most prominently in a collection entitled *The *Wife of His Youth* (1899), used the older motif of racial mixture and the "tragic mulatto" to delineate, pessimistically, relationships between racial structures and questions of identity and moral choice.

The dilemmas Dunbar and Chesnutt identified were to receive increasing attention among African American writers as the Reconstruction era drew to a close, especially as an understanding of those dilemmas was given theoretical shape by W. E. B. *Du Bois in "The Strivings of the Negro People" (1897). There, Du Bois described the *double consciousness" of the African American, a problem of being simultaneously "American" and "African," "American" and "not-American." Du Bois proposed to resolve the problem through the encouragement of distinctive African genius, pointing toward a distinctive African American culture and literature, as well. Although literary attempts to realize Du Bois's vision were not to appear until after 1900, the growing concern about identity he helped delineate was to be a profound legacy from the Reconstruction era to later African American writing.

[*See also* Folk Literature; Folklore; Periodicals, *article on* Black Periodical Press; Protest Literature.]

• J. Saunders Redding, *To Make a Poet Black*, 1939. Lawrence Levine, *Black Culture and Black Consciousness: Afro-American Folk Thought from Slavery to Freedom*, 1977. Arlene Elder, "The Hindered Hand": Cultural Implications of Early Afro-American Fiction, 1978. Joel Williamson, *The Crucible of Race: Black-White Relations in the American South since Emancipation*, 1984. Hazel Carby, *Reconstructing Womanhood: The Emergence of the Afro-American Woman Novelist*, 1987. Dickson D. Bruce, Jr., *Black American Writing from the Nadir: The Evolution of a Literary Tradition, 1877–1915*, 1989. Blyden Jackson, *A History of Afro-American Literature*, vol. 1, *The Long Beginning, 1746–1895*, 1989. Joan Sherman, *Invisible Poets: Afro-Americans of the Nineteenth Century*, 2d ed., 1989. Frances Smith Foster, *Written by Herself: Literary Production by African American Women, 1746–1892*, 1993.

—Dickson D. Bruce, Jr.

EARLY TWENTIETH CENTURY

Between the publication of W. E. B. *Du Bois's *The *Souls of Black Folk* (1903) and Gwendolyn *Brooks's Pulitzer Prize–winning *Annie Allen* (1949), African American culture underwent a series of radical transformations that freed black writers from the reactive postures of the segregation era and encouraged innovative articulations of modernist, American, and diasporic traditions. Sparked by the Great *Migration from the rural South to the industrial North, impres-

sive flowerings of cultural activity took place in Washington, Harlem, and Chicago, attracting writers from throughout the hemisphere with the promise of larger inter- and intraracial audiences. Supporting and critiquing the political activity surrounding Du Bois, Marcus *Garvey, and A. Philip Randolph, African American artists investigated the possibilities of nationalism, Marxism, modernist aesthetics, and woman-centered cultural activity that gave rise to a conscious tradition of African American *feminism. Like the folk and popular culture forms shaped by those James Weldon *Johnson called the "black and unknown bards," the literary works of Langston *Hughes, Zora Neale *Hurston, and Richard *Wright resound with the burdens and celebrations of individuals and communities adjusting to situations that had been almost unthinkable a generation before.

Toward the Harlem Renaissance. The most influential text of the early twentieth century, Du Bois's *The Souls of Black Folk*, defined crucial issues that have continued to elicit serious intellectual and artistic responses. Identifying the central concern of the new century as "the problem of the *color line," Du Bois defined the phenomenon of "*double consciousness": the awareness, enforced by oppressive institutions and *stereotypes, of one's self as both African and American. For Du Bois and those who responded to his call for the forging of a "better and truer" self, double consciousness required investigations of European, African, and specifically American traditions. Casting his assertive approach in stark relief against Booker T. *Washington's accommodationist philosophy, Du Bois emphasized the responsibility of the "*talented tenth" of black professionals to the less privileged members of their communities. Although Du Bois later repudiated the elitism of this position and embraced Marxist perspectives, the ideas of double consciousness and the talented tenth exerted a major influence on African American life prior to and during the *Harlem Renaissance.

Inspired by Anna Julia *Cooper, who insisted on the importance of women's contributions to "uplifting the race," and Ida B. *Wells-Barnett, who focused attention on *lynching while editing the Memphis *Free Speech*, women working in the club movement combined Du Bois's analytical sophistication with community-based activism. Writers affiliated with the clubs contributed frequently to church publications and journals including *Colored American Magazine* (founded 1900, edited by Pauline E. *Hopkins), the *Crisis* (founded 1910, edited by Du Bois until 1918), *Opportunity* (founded 1923, edited by Charles S. Johnson), and the *Messenger* (founded 1917). Complementing her editorial encouragement of young writers who would mature during the Harlem Renaissance, Hopkins provided a woman-centered perspective on double consciousness in her *novel *Contending Forces* (1900), which shares numerous thematic concerns with Paul Laurence *Dunbar's *The *Sport of the Gods* (1902), Charles Waddell *Chesnutt's *The *House Behind the Cedars* (1900), and James Weldon Johnson's *The *Autobiography of an Ex-Colored Man* (1912).

Like their white contemporaries, these novelists usually adhered to conventions of romantic, domestic, and realistic fiction. In addition, they were forced to confront the difficult rhetorical circumstances created by the power of *minstrelsy in American culture. In order to publish their work in influential mainstream periodicals, such as *Harper's, Century,* and the *Atlantic,* many African American writers wrote in a dialect derived from the *plantation tradition writings of Thomas Nelson Page and Joel Chandler Harris. The dialect poems of Dunbar and James D. *Corrothers often perpetuated stereotypes, thereby intensifying the burden of double consciousness, a situation Dunbar addressed directly in standard English lyrics in "The Poet" and "Sympathy." At times, however, African American writers drew on folk traditions of *masking to assert subversive ideas for black audiences while providing white audiences with seemingly innocuous surface meanings. Like the tradition of sacred music Du Bois labeled the "sorrow songs," Chesnutt's "*Uncle Julius" stories employ masking to express the sense of exile and potential for resistance present in the folk tradition.

The tension between minstrelsy, masking, and open expression haunted African American writers throughout the first half of the century. Nowhere was this more evident than in the *theater. Prior to the Federal Theatre Project in the 1930s, black playwrights were forced to choose between the lucrative Broadway revues that paid well but catered to white stereotypes and "little theaters" such as Cleveland's Karamu House, Washington's Krigwa Players, and Harlem's Lafayette Theatre. Although their audiences could not support playwrights financially, these theaters provided authors such as May *Miller, Willis *Richardson, and Georgia Douglas *Johnson with opportunities to focus on significant social problems and explore the theatrical possibilities of folk materials. The most vital forms of African American performance, however, developed on the Theatre Owners Booking Association (TOBA, also known as "tough on black asses") circuit, where comedians such as Pigmeat Markham and *blues singers such as Ma *Rainey manipulated minstrel conventions while tapping into the West African–based folk traditions explored at length in Hurston's *Mules and Men* (1935). The lyrics of Rainey, Ida Cox, and Bessie *Smith frequently addressed feminist and *lesbian themes with a frankness that would have been impossible for writers such as Nella *Larsen, Marita *Bonner, Jessie Redmon *Fauset, and the diarist Alice Moore *Dunbar-Nelson, who were forced to negotiate genteel literary conventions.

The Harlem Renaissance. The first cultural movement to attain widespread recognition both within and beyond black communities, the flowering that took place in Harlem between the mid-1910s and the mid-1930s occupies a central position in African American cultural history. Also called the "*New Negro Movement," the Harlem Renaissance attracted poets, dramatists, writers of fiction, painters, musicians, and intellectuals with its promise of a setting in which black artists could interact relatively freely with one another and with their white contemporaries. Defined by the "Harlem" issue of *Survey Graphic* magazine (Mar. 1925, edited by Alain *Locke and reprinted in expanded form as *The *New Negro*), the Renaissance drew energy from the Great Migration, the return of black World War I veterans willing to challenge the *Jim Crow system, and the new possibilities for dissenting voices created by the death of Booker T. Washington. Bringing together writers born in the North (Countee *Cullen, Du Bois), South (Hurston, James Weldon Johnson), Midwest (Langston Hughes), West (Wallace *Thurman), and Caribbean (Claude *McKay, Marcus Garvey), the Renaissance drew inspiration and energy from earlier literary scenes centered in Boston (around Hopkins), Washington (around Georgia Douglas Johnson's S Street Salon), and Philadelphia, where Fauset began her career before moving to New York to serve as literary editor of the *Crisis.*

Although Hughes, Hurston, McKay, Larsen, Cullen, and Jean *Toomer (who did not participate directly in the movement) dominate histories of the period, it derived its vitality from a diverse group, including Thurman, Richardson, Rudolph *Fisher, Eric *Walrond, Gwendolyn *Bennett, Eulalie Spence, and Richard Bruce *Nugent, who openly expressed the homosexuality he shared with several of the era's major figures. Most Renaissance writers had direct contact with white patrons and modernist artists (including Eugene O'Neill, William Carlos Williams, and H.D.), many of whom had been inspired by African and African American visual and musical traditions. While the financial support provided by Carl Van Vechten, author of the controversial novel *Nigger Heaven* (1926), and Charlotte Osgood Mason, who supported Hurston and Hughes, helped writers find time for their work, it remains a controversial topic. Many African American intellectuals of the period condemned most white participants for their stereotypical views of black character and the interracial politics of the period received a scathing denuciation in Thurman's *Infants of the Spring* (1932), the dystopian double to the romantic image advanced in McKay's *Home to Harlem* (1928).

In addition to meeting socially at events hosted by Van Vechten and black heiress A'Lelia Walker, Renaissance writers published their work in the *Crisis, Opportunity,* and the short-lived periodicals *Harlem* and *Fire!!* (both edited by Thurman); as well as in *anthologies such as Cullen's *Caroling Dust* (1927), Richardson's *Plays and Pageants of Negro Life* (1930), and James Weldon Johnson's *The Book of American Negro Poetry* (1922, expanded 1931). Although it has attracted less recognition, Garvey's *Negro World* newspaper played a unique role in African American literature. The most widely circulated black periodical of the time, *Negro World,* sponsored literary contests and published hundreds of poets and fiction writers from throughout the diaspora while advancing the pan-Africanist agenda of Garvey's Universal Negro Improvement Association.

Both thematically and aesthetically, the Harlem Renaissance introduced issues that dominated African American literary consciousness throughout the century. Locke's "The New Negro," Hughes's "The

Negro Artist and the Racial Mountain," and James Weldon Johnson's "Preface" to *The Book of American Negro Poetry* define concerns such as the relationship between African American expression and the American mainstream, the significance of oral and folk traditions, and the impact of modern urban society on literary forms. Similarly, Marita Bonner's *essay "On Being Young—A Woman—and Colored" (*Crisis*, 1925) and Elise Johnson McDougald's "The Task of Negro Womanhood" (*The New Negro*, 1925) connect the pioneering work of Wells-Barnett and Cooper with that of later womanists. Anticipating later debates over *Afrocentricity, Helene Johnson's "Bottled" and Cullen's "Heritage" raise the question Cullen phrased as, "What is Africa to me?" Like McKay, who expressed his militancy in sonnets such as "If We Must Die," Cullen used highly conventional formal structures to articulate his tormented double consciousness. Conversely, both Hughes and Hurston explored the literary possibilities of the blues, *jazz, *sermons, and folk tales in experimental forms paralleling those of their white modernist associates. Exploring the ambiguities of its author's position on the margins of both white and black worlds, Toomer's multi-genre epic *Cane* (1923) initiates an African American modernist tradition that includes Hurston's *Moses, Man of the Mountain* (1939), Hughes's *"Montage of a Dream Deferred" (1951), Ralph *Ellison's *Invisible Man* (1952), and Melvin B. *Tolson's *Harlem Gallery* (1965).

The Chicago Renaissance. In contrast to the consensus concerning the importance of Harlem in African American culture of the 1920s, the next two decades have been characterized in a variety of ways. While phrasings emphasizing "proletarian literature," "*protest literature," and the "School of Richard Wright" focus on the relationship between African American literature and leftist politics, each represses or distorts important aspects of the tradition. Placing greater emphasis on women's contributions and the lingering influence of the era's sociological premises, the idea of a "*Chicago Renaissance" has begun to attract widespread support among cultural historians of the period.

Prior to the 1980s, literary histories of the 1930s and 1940s focused almost obsessively on Richard Wright. By far the most popular novel published by a black writer until that time, *Native Son* (1940) reverberated with a power equivalent to that of John Steinbeck's *Grapes of Wrath* (1939). The first widely read African American novel to express an unequivocal anger over the growing *violence of ghetto life, *Native Son* was read—despite Wright's interest in modernist aesthetics—almost entirely as a political "protest" novel. The attention given *Native Son* and *Black Boy* (1945) created a context in which almost every black writer of the 1940s was automatically assigned membership in the "School of Wright." While such an approach seems apt for Willard *Motley's *Knock on Any Door* (1947) or some of the early stories of Frank *Yerby, it seriously distorted the reception of Ann *Petry, Arna *Bontemps, Chester *Himes, and especially Sterling A. *Brown, who was valued more for his protest poems than for his pioneering

literary histories or sophisticated modernist lyrics such as "Ma Rainey." Most crucially, Wright's dominance contributed to the invisibility of women writers such as Hurston and Dorothy *West, who did not share his leftist politics or his aggressively masculine perspective. Now recognized almost universally as a classic of African American literature, Hurston's *Their Eyes Were Watching God* (1937) was greeted by critical apathy or hostility and was allowed to fall out of print prior to its rediscovery sparked by literary descendants June *Jordan and Alice *Walker.

Somewhat broader than the "School of Wright," images of the 1930s as a period of proletarian writing acknowledge the links between black writers and white contemporaries such as Theodore Dreiser, Carl Sandburg, and Michael Gold, who, as literary editor of the communist newspaper the *Daily Worker*, played a major role in shaping leftist response to Wright, Hughes, McKay, and William *Attaway. Leftist publications such as *New Masses, Challenge*, and *Anvil* published black writers interested in Marxist approaches to the economic and political problems of the Great Depression. Wright, Ellison, Shirley *Graham (who later married Du Bois), Theodore *Ward, and Margaret *Walker were among the black writers who joined white contemporaries such as Nelson Algren and Saul Bellow in working for the Federal Theatre Project or the *Federal Writers' Project of the Works Progress Administration.

Recognizing the gradual shift of cultural activity away from New York, the idea of a black "Chicago Renaissance" (not to be confused with the earlier white-dominated Chicago Renaissance) provides what many critics find the most satisfactory approach to the diverse cultural production of the period and its impact on later developments. Coedited by Wright, Marian Minus, and Dorothy West, who had previously hailed the emergence of "a young Chicago group," *New Challenge* (1937) played a role similar in this new movement to that of the "New Negro" issue of *Survey Graphic* in the Harlem Renaissance. The touchstone of the issue was Wright's "Blueprint for Negro Writing," which highlights the tension between the period's leftist and folk-nationalist tendencies. Literary institutions of the period pursued various approaches to these tensions. Several black writers explored proletarian aesthetics in the communist-sponsored John Reed Clubs. An overlapping group including Wright, Ward, Bontemps, Frank Marshall *Davis, and Margaret *Walker, whose *For My People* (1942) was a touchstone for black *poetry of the period, participated in the South Side Writers group. Many South Side poets, including Walker, Davis, Margaret Esse *Danner, and the young Gwendolyn Brooks developed their poetry in workshops such as that sponsored by white socialite Inez Cunningham Stark at the South Side Community Center. Among the Chicago-based publishing outlets available to these writers were *Negro Digest, Negro Story*, published out of the South Side home of Alice Browning, and Harriet Monroe's *Poetry* magazine, where Hughes, Brooks, and other black poets published works alongside those of Ezra Pound, T. S. Eliot, and H.D.

Three other Chicago-based institutions—the *Chicago Defender* newspaper, the Julius Rosenwald Fund, and the sociology department of the University of Chicago—played important roles in shaping the national contours of black culture during the era. Like the *Pittsburgh Courier*, where George *Schuyler developed his black conservative perspective, the New York *Amsterdam News*, and the *Afro-American*, which published editions in several eastern cities, the *Defender* was carried throughout the nation by black railroad workers and porters. Painting a glowing picture of the economic opportunities available in Chicago as part of editor Robert Abbott's crusade to draw blacks away from the South, the *Defender* published literary work including many of Hughes's "*Simple" stories. Despite the disillusionment described in *Native Son*, migrants to the South Side played crucial roles in the transformation of southern folk and musical traditions. Drawing on sources such as the surrealistic blues lyrics of Robert Johnson, transplanted Southerners such as Muddy Waters and Howlin' Wolf established Chicago as a center of the electric blues that would play a crucial role in shaping rock and roll. Similarly, Mahalia Jackson, Sallie Martin, and Thomas A. Dorsey—whose religious songs paralleled blues composer W. C. Handy's polished re-creations of the blues—transformed southern sacred forms into the urban gospel music that formed the basis for the political poetry of the soul music created by Sam Cooke, Aretha *Franklin, and Curtis Mayfield.

If blues and gospel provided the cultural background for Chicago writing, the Rosenwald Foundation offered the patronage provided by individuals during the Harlem Renaissance. Providing an intellectual center for black cultural activity, the foundation funded the work of numerous writers and intellectuals, including Hughes, McKay, Hurston, Du Bois, James Weldon Johnson, Sterling Brown, Marian *Anderson, and Katherine *Dunham, whose research in the Caribbean established the foundation for later scholarship on diaspora culture.

Perhaps even more significant for the long-term development of African American literary culture, however, was the Department of Sociology at the University of Chicago, where black alumni such as Charles S. Johnson and E. Franklin Frazier developed extremely influential approaches to the developing problems of the urban ghetto. Grounded in the theories of Robert Park and articulated most powerfully in Horace Cayton and St. Clair Drake's *Black Metropolis* (1945), the Chicago school established perspectives that had a sometimes unfortunate impact on the understanding of African American culture well into the late twentieth century. Although the Chicago school made real contributions to the political activity culminating in the *Brown* v. *Board of Education* Supreme Court decision, its assimilationist premises and sociological vocabulary simplified understanding of black writing by focusing obsessively on texts as "representative" expressions of social unrest designed to increase white awareness of the "problems" of black life.

As the 1940s drew to a close, a younger generation of African American writers began to emerge, many of whom openly rejected the idea that political issues should play a central role in literary expression. Ralph Ellison and James *Baldwin published short fiction and essays during the 1940s in which they consciously distanced themselves from the School of Wright. Similarly, most poets who began their careers during the 1940s—Brooks, Melvin B. *Tolson, and Robert *Hayden—rejected the traditions of proletarian poetry and pursued the musical modernism of Langston Hughes. Echoing the intricate suites in which Duke Ellington transformed folk forms into sophisticated modernist compositions, Hughes's "Montage of a Dream Deferred" provided a touchstone both for these emerging major poets and for the poets of Washington's *Dasein* group, Cleveland's *Free Lance* group, and New York's *Umbra* group, whose black experimentalism provides a crucial but largely unrecognized link between the Chicago Renaissance, the universalist modernism of the 1950s, and the *Black Arts movement of the 1960s.

[See also Folklore; Music; Periodicals, *article on* Black Periodical Press.]

• Sterling Brown, *The Negro in American Fiction*, 1937. Sterling Brown, *Negro Poetry and Drama*, 1937. Robert Bone, *The Negro Novel in America*, 1965. Nathan Irvin Huggins, *Harlem Renaissance*, 1971. George Kent, *Blackness and the Adventure of Western Culture*, 1972. Wilson Jeremiah Moses, *The Golden Age of Black Nationalism, 1850–1925*, 1978. Abby Arthur Johnson and Ronald Maberry Johnson, *Propaganda and Aesthetics: The Literary Politics of Afro-American Magazines in the Twentieth Century*, 1979. David Levering Lewis, *When Harlem Was in Vogue*, 1981. Tony Martin, *Literary Garveyism: Garvey, Black Arts, and the Harlem Renaissance*, 1983. Robert Bone, "Richard Wright and the Chicago Renaissance," *Callaloo* 28 (Summer 1986): 446–468; Gloria T. Hull, *Color, Sex, and Poetry: Three Women Writers of the Harlem Renaissance*, 1987. Dickson D. Bruce, *Black American Writing from the Nadir: The Evolution of a Literary Tradition, 1877–1915*, 1989.

—Craig H. Werner

LATE TWENTIETH CENTURY

Writing a survey of post-1951 African American literature, one must take into account the significance of a proliferation of texts by both new and established authors, and even more important, the extraordinary changes in national and global economic, political, and intellectual culture during the second half of the twentieth century. These changes have raised crucial questions about what we mean when we talk about contexts, texts, traditions, and, indeed, what we mean when we talk about African Americans.

For instance, one might ask if contemporary African American literature ought to be read against the backdrop of domestic changes from segregation to affirmative action and threats of its demise, against that of the decolonization of third world countries, or, perhaps more appropriately, against some sense of the interconnections between the two. Moreover, at a time when new social movements have challenged the construction and maintenance of literary canons, one must consider that the category of "literature" includes not only traditional genres such as prose (fiction and nonfiction alike), *poetry, and *drama, but potentially *film and *music as well. With the rise of literary and cultural *feminism, familiar ideas of African American and other literary traditions have been reformulated in light of whom they include and whom they leave out. And in the context of ongoing debates about the meaning of *race as a category (Is it biologically determined or socially constructed? Is there such a thing as an authentic racial subject?), there is not even consensus about what we mean when we talk about African Americans.

The early 1950s ushered in a new, transitional era in U.S. racial politics. An emergent *civil rights movement sought to bring about an end to racial segregation of public facilities, modes of transportation, and educational institutions and publicly circulated a rhetoric of racial equality that has dominated ideas of citizenship until the present. At the same time, African American literary figures continued to capture the attention of an ever expanding reading public. It was a time when established writers such as Richard *Wright, Langston *Hughes, Ann *Petry, and Gwendolyn *Brooks developed their craft. Yet it was also a time when a generation of newer writers emerged on the literary scene.

Traditionally, studies of African American literary production identify Wright, Ralph *Ellison, and James *Baldwin as the dominant authors of the period from the early 1950s through the mid-1960s. But recent critiques of canon formation have made it impossible to ignore the significance of a wider range of influential writers of the period.

Wright's most famous work, *Native Son, was published in 1940, but he continued to loom large as a national and international literary figure throughout the 1950s, publishing three *novels—The Outsider (1953), Savage Holiday (1954), and The Long Dream (1958)—and four works of nonfiction—Black Power (1954), The Color Curtain (1956), Pagan Spain (1956), and White Man, Listen! (1957). (Eight Men, Lawd Today, and American Hunger appeared posthumously.) His mentorship of and subsequent breaks with Ellison and Baldwin are often described in critical histories of the period, for their disagreements about the relationship between art and ideology in African American writing prefigure debates that continue to shape ideas about the function of ethnic literatures.

Ellison first met Richard Wright in New York in the mid-1930s; Wright encouraged Ellison's literary aspirations and Ellison enthusiastically admired Wright's achievements. But by 1940 Wright began to feel that Ellison's prose style was derivative from his own and a rift sprang up between the two men. Indeed, by the mid-1960s, Ellison had substantially revised his early praise of Wright's work, considering *Bigger Thomas (the protagonist of Native Son) to be a one-dimensional, ideologically driven construction rather than a complex and fully realized character. Ellison published only one novel during his lifetime, *Invisible Man (1952, which won the 1953 National Book Award), but because of its stylistic and philosophical complexity, as well as its immersion in African American *history and *folklore, that book

was for many years considered to be the premier novel by an African American author. Recently, critics have become less likely to deploy such a formulation for several reasons: first, because it presupposes consensus around the idea of literary quality; second, because it underestimates the significance of other black writers; third, because it obviates the possibility of cross-cultural comparisons; and fourth, because it is complicit with reductive ideas of literary tokenism. These caveats notwithstanding, Invisible Man, *Shadow and Act (1964), and Going to the Territory (1987)—these last Ellison's two collections of *essays—have contributed substantially to the world of ideas and letters.

Baldwin met Wright for the first time in 1944 (also in New York) and, like Ellison, enjoyed Wright's support for a time. Wright read Baldwin's work and arranged for him to receive a fellowship and a promised reading of his novel. When two presses rejected the novel, Baldwin began to separate himself from Wright. Subsequently, he, like Ellison, published essays that criticized Wright's work on ideological grounds and consolidated the break with his former mentor. Baldwin felt that Wright sacrificed his characters' psychological complexity in order to make political points about racism and injustice. As a result, he argued, Wright's representations confirmed prevalent assumptions about African American inhumanity.

Baldwin was a versatile writer who frequently inspired controversy because of his own homosexuality, the place of homosexual relationships in some of his work, and his unwillingness to adopt easy political positions. The author of major works of fiction including *Go Tell It on the Mountain (1953), *Giovanni's Room (1956), *Another Country (1962), and several plays, including Blues for Mister Charlie (1964), he was an especially brilliant essayist. His reputation may rest ultimately on the achievement of collections such as *Notes of a Native Son (1955), Nobody Knows My Name: More Notes of a Native Son (1961), The *Fire Next Time (1963), and The Devil Finds Work (1976).

Although the significance of Wright, Ellison, and Baldwin to African American and U.S. literary history is indisputable, such a narrow construction of the early contemporary period overlooks many other important figures of the time. To mention but a few, Ann Petry, Chester *Himes, Gwendolyn *Brooks, and Lorraine *Hansberry all experimented with literary forms and explored how rapid demographic and political changes shaped the lives of African Americans.

Ann Petry ranks among the most versatile of African American writers. The *Street (1946) addresses the plight of a black mother struggling against race, *gender, and *class oppression in Harlem during the 1940s. Her second and third novels—Country Place (1947) and The Narrows (1953)—interrogate with extraordinary subtlety the notion of community in the context of small New England villages. Additionally, Petry has published many *short stories, and several books for children and adolescent readers based on black history and folklore.

With more than eighteen books to his credit, Chester Himes was an exceptionally prolific figure whose writing career spanned nearly forty years; he can be said to have expanded the terrain of black literature in at least two ways. First, he is one of the earliest African American writers to consider the impact of the *migration west on the lives and expectations of blacks at midcentury. Much fiction by African Americans is set in the urban Northeast or the rural South, but in his first two novels, *If He Hollers Let Him Go* (1945) and *Lonely Crusade* (1947), Himes explores the impact of changes in labor and urbanization in wartime Los Angeles upon the psyches of black men. Second, Himes published eight black detective novels featuring the team of *Coffin Ed Johnson and *Grave Digger Jones, making him (after Rudolph *Fisher) one of the first black writers to work successfully in this popular genre.

Gwendolyn Brooks published her first volume of poetry in 1945 and won the Pulitzer Prize for her second, *Annie Allen*, in 1949. *Maud Martha*, her only novel, appeared in 1953; although at the time it did not receive the attention it merited, it has inspired critical interest in recent decades because of the way in which it situates an exploration of urbanization and labor upon constructions of race, gender, and domesticity in resonant, poetic language. Indeed, her work registers the impact of profound social changes upon the lives and language of African Americans, for her poetry bears the traces of the struggles for civil rights as well as the impact of black nationalism and the *Black Arts movement that arose from it.

No history of early contemporary African American literature would be complete without acknowledging the significance of Lorraine Hansberry and especially her ever popular, award-winning play, *A *Raisin in the Sun*, first staged in 1959. (The film version was released in 1961.) The play, Hansberry's first, won her the New York Drama Critics Circle Award, making her the first black, fifth woman, and youngest person ever to receive it. Perhaps because the play is so familiar, it has not received much in the way of sustained critical attention. Nevertheless, it powerfully captures the spirit of the 1950s as it illuminates and brings into tension the changing aspirations of black people at midcentury.

From the mid-1950s through the mid-1960s, the antiracist struggle was defined largely in terms of nonviolent resistance; dominated by established integrated organizations such as Martin Luther *King, Jr.'s Southern Christian Leadership Conference, James Farmer's Congress of Racial Equality, and Whitney Young's Urban League; and inspired by faith in the possibilities of racial integration. In the face of white intransigence and elusive political change, African Americans grew increasingly impatient with the status quo; younger black people especially were compelled by the goals and strategies of nationalist organizations such as the Black Panther Party and the Nation of Islam.

Nationalist platforms presuppose a cultural, political, and spiritual unity among peoples of African descent throughout the African diaspora. For the most part they advocate black economic self-sufficiency, and they seek to separate black people from what they perceive as the destructive power of European culture and ideology. In response to the emergent nationalist movement of the mid- to late 1960s arose its cultural or aesthetic counterpart, the Black Arts movement.

In an effort to consolidate African American economic and cultural power, the Black Arts movement gave rise both to a range of journals such as *Negro Digest* (later known as *Black World*), *The Journal of Black Poetry*, and *Black Expression*, and to presses such as *Broadside Press, Jihad Press, Free Black Press, Black Dialogue Press, and *Third World Press. The Black Arts movement influenced cultural production in a variety of media: music, *theater, art, and *dance as well as literature. The leading literary figures were an eclectic mix of poets, fiction writers, playwrights, and essayists, and included LeRoi Jones (Amiri *Baraka), Mari *Evans, Ed *Bullins, Larry *Neal, Addison *Gayle, Jr., Gwendolyn Brooks, Nikki *Giovanni, Etheridge *Knight, Sonia *Sanchez, Ishmael *Reed, and Carolyn M. *Rodgers.

To the extent that the Black Arts movement sought to embrace the range of black cultural and artistic production and to connect aesthetics with the needs of "the black community," it was informed by a spirit of expansiveness. However, it also led to a kind of literary and ideological gatekeeping that judged African American writing on its conformity to a narrowly defined political and aesthetic agenda. By this light, only certain styles, topics, and positions were considered authentically black. Since the 1970s such nationalist policing has been criticized for its monolithic constructions of black art and community, its denial of the interplay between African and non-African cultural traditions, its misogyny, and its homophobia. As a result, the past twenty years have witnessed an expansion of the styles and subjects considered "acceptable" for black literature.

Indeed, the explosion of African American writing since the 1970s has made it increasingly difficult to generalize about the major themes and styles characteristic of the contemporary period. However, some of the most significant trajectories include the rise of African American women's writing, the reclamation of history, the resurgence of *autobiography, the rise of black *gay literature and *lesbian literature, incursions into popular literary forms, and postmodernist experimentations. As we shall see, these areas are not as discrete as they might initially appear; for example, postmodernist experiments often take the topic of *slavery as their subject.

The most visible of these newer movements is the rise of black feminist literature. Writers such as Toni *Morrison (Pulitzer and Nobel Prize winner), Alice *Walker (Pulitzer Prize winner), Paule *Marshall (MacArthur Prize winner), Octavia E. *Butler (MacArthur Prize winner), Rita *Dove (Pulitzer Prize winner), Gloria *Naylor, Ntozake *Shange, Toni Cade *Bambara, Gayl *Jones, and a host of others have achieved widespread attention for their powerful achievements in illuminating the interconnections of constructions of race, gender, and class in a range of literary forms.

As this partial list of accolades indicates, these writers have found an enthusiastic reception. However, because they have not shied away from topics that African American writers have often eschewed, such as domestic abuse and sexism, they have met with the disapprobation of some African American male (and indeed female) readers. The controversy surrounding their popularity reflects longstanding anxieties that African Americans often display about the revelation of cultural "dirty laundry."

The contemporary fascination with reclaiming history is nowhere more evident than in the sheer number and variety of novels written about slavery and its aftermath by African Americans since Margaret *Walker's *Jubilee (1966). Indeed, many of the major black writers of the past twenty years have felt the need to write at least one novel that takes slavery as its subject, although these novels take a variety of forms. From fairly straightforward realist historical accounts such as Alex *Haley's *Roots (1977), Barbara *Chase-Riboud's Sally Hemings (1979), and Louise *Meriwether's Fragments of the Ark (1994), to postmodernist experiments such as Gayl Jones's *Corregidora (1975), Ishmael Reed's *Flight to Canada (1976), Charles R. *Johnson's Oxherding Tale (1982) and *Middle Passage (1990), and Toni Morrison's *Beloved (1987), to a science fiction novel such as Octavia Butler's *Kindred (1979), to impressionist texts such as Sherley Anne *Williams's *Dessa Rose (1986) or Lorene Cary's The Price of a Child (1995), recent black writers have examined how historical distance as well as new literary, intellectual, and political movements have enabled reinterpretations of the meanings that attach to slavery, of inter- and intraracial relationships within the institution, and of the position both of masters and of slaves.

The contemporary authors' engagement with slavery illuminates the space between their reconstructions of a historically distant period and the accounts actually written during the period. Unrestrained by the conventions of an antislavery movement or the expectations of a Victorian reading public, they are free to address areas of experience to which the slave narrators could allude at best. They are freer, for example, to raise issues of sexual abuse and expression, to interrogate the limits of truth telling, indeed to explore the full range of emotions available to slaves. These later texts might be said, then, to reclaim the history of slavery and to liberate the literary *ancestors by representing what had previously been deemed unspeakable.

It is perhaps the self-consciousness of these retrospective fictions that made them especially attractive to some of the leading postmodernist writers of the period, such as Charles Johnson and Ishmael Reed. Other writers who have sought to push the boundaries of literary language and black vernacularity include Clarence *Major, Trey *Ellis, Edgar John *Wideman, and Xam Wilson *Cartiér. The more restrained prose of James Alan *McPherson, David *Bradley, and Ernest J. *Gaines, on the other hand, has produced resonant meditations upon the fragmentariness of *identity and community in the late twentieth century.

Long a mainstay of African American writing, autobiography continues to flourish in the contemporary period and dovetails with the impulse to reclaim history. Pivotal autobiographical texts of the period include Anne *Moody's Coming of Age in Mississippi (1968), Richard Wright's posthumously published American Hunger (1977), and the five volumes of Maya *Angelou's life story (especially her acclaimed 1970 book, *I Know Why the Caged Bird Sings). More recently, African American autobiographers have reflected upon what it meant to come of age before or during the civil rights movement, to be educated in integrated institutions of higher learning, and yet to continue to face veiled forms of racism. Works such as Jill Nelson's Volunteer Slavery (1993), Jake Lamar's Bourgeois Blues (1991), Itabari Njeri's Ev'ry Good-bye Ain't Gone (1990), Henry Louis *Gates, Jr.'s Colored People (1994), Gerald *Early's Daughters (1994), and Lorene Cary's Black Ice (1991) explore how the idea of "authentic" black experience becomes challenged in the context of changing ideas of class and its relation to constructions of race.

Just as black feminist and middle-class narratives challenge notions of the authentic black subject, so too does the growing body of black gay and lesbian literature. The late poet, essayist, activist, and autobiographer Audre *Lorde is, along with Baldwin, perhaps one of the most important figures to theorize the connections among race, gender, and *sexuality. However, important figures whose work has continued to explore these issues include Ann Allen *Shockley, the late Steve Corbin, the late Melvin *Dixon, and April Sinclair.

Increasingly, African American writers working in popular literary genres have discovered wide audiences. Terry *McMillan's Waiting to Exhale (1992) found an enthusiastic, diverse readership and made hers a household name. African American detective fiction writers such as Walter *Mosley, Gar Anthony Haywood, Barbara *Neely, Eleanor Taylor Bland, and Valerie Wilson Wesley have reached enthusiastic audiences both here and abroad. And *speculative fiction writers such as Octavia Butler and Samuel R. *Delany have achieved perhaps the greatest and most sustained notice.

[See also Canonization; Crime and Mystery Writing; Criticism.]

• Addison Gayle, Jr., ed. The Black Aesthetic, 1972. Mary Frances Berry and John W. Blassingame, Long Memory: The Black Experience in America, 1982. Bernard W. Bell, The Afro-American Novel and Its Tradition, 1987. Emory Elliott, ed., The Columbia History of the American Novel, 1991. Valerie Smith, ed., African American Writers, 1991. Angelyn Mitchell, ed., Within the Circle: An Anthology of African American Literary Criticism from the Harlem Renaissance to the Present, 1994.
—Valerie Smith

LITERARY SOCIETIES. African American literary societies were created between 1828 and 1846 primarily by northern blacks who were consciously trying to improve their mental and moral conditions. Among their expressed goals were the stimulation of reading and the spreading of useful knowledge by providing libraries and reading rooms, the encouragement of expressed literary efforts by providing audiences and channels of publication for their literary productions, and the training of future orators and leaders by means of debates.

Free African Americans in Philadelphia took the lead when on 20 March 1828 five men organized a society for the purpose of "the mental improvement of the people of color in the neighborhood of Philadelphia." In 1831, the Female Literary Association of Philadelphia and the Theban Literary Society of Pittsburgh were started. Having been invited to address the Female and Literary Society early in 1832, William Lloyd Garrison was so impressed that he collected several compositions written by its members to publish, not only for their merit but with the hope that women living in other cities would organize into similar groups. The Tyro Literary Association was organized in Newark, New Jersey, in 1832. The Phoenix Society, organized in New York City in 1833, exerted the widest influence and had the largest membership. It probably served as a model for other societies. By 1846, there were forty-five active groups in cities such as Albany, Buffalo, Poughkeepsie, Rochester, Schenectady, Troy, Boston, New Bedford, Hartford, Providence, Baltimore, Washington, Cincinnati, and Detroit.

These literary societies helped disseminate knowledge and teach advantageous ways to use leisure time. The lecturers who addressed these societies chose not only literary topics but also scientific and educational ones. Many of the addresses were printed and circulated widely. The societies' lecture platforms were workshops and preparatory schools for many of the African American antislavery lecturers who later won fame in America and England as public speakers.

As a result of these societies many African Americans started private libraries. Some, such as David *Ruggles, made their collections available as circulating libraries. Ruggles, a printer and abolitionist, not only made available his collection of antislavery and colonization publications but also sold books and frequently published in various newspapers book lists relating to African Americans and to *slavery.

While some were active for ten to twelve years, for the most part these societies were short-lived. The reasons were varied. The existence of several societies in one city caused competition for membership. The various antislavery organizations weakened the societies by calling constantly on them to furnish audiences for their lectures.

The story of the development of African American education in its broader implications would be incomplete without some reference to the endeavors of these societies. These societies indicate the influence of self-education activities among African Americans of their day. No doubt, these societies also influenced the shaping of *publishing opportunities available to African American writers in the nineteenth and twentieth centuries.

[See also Antislavery Movement; Education; Libraries and Research Centers; Literacy.]

• Joseph Wilson, Sketches of the Higher Classes of Colored Society in Philadelphia, 1841. Dorothy B. Porter, "The Organized Educational Activities of Negro Literary Society, 1828–1846," Journal of Negro Education 5 (Oct. 1936): 555–576; rpt. in The Making of Black America, ed. August Meier and Elliott Rudwick, 1969.

—Dorothy Burnett Porter Wesley

LITTLE, MALCOLM. See Malcolm X.

LOCKE, ALAIN (1885–1954), critic, educator, philosopher, and mentor of the Harlem Renaissance. Alain Locke's role as a general factotum of the *Harlem Renaissance has tended to overshadow the full dimensions of an active and productive life. John Edgar Tidwell and John Wright list more than three hundred items spanning the period from 1904 to 1953 in "Alain Locke: A Comprehensive Bibliography of His Published Writings" (Callaloo, Feb.–Oct., 1981). Born in (or near) Philadelphia to parents who were schoolteachers, Locke came to maturity in the self-conscious genteel ambiance of Philadelphia's black elite. After completing secondary and normal school studies in Philadelphia, he went to Harvard College, where he majored in philosophy. An appointment as a Rhodes scholar in 1907 followed his undergraduate Harvard experience and he spent time at both Oxford and the University of Berlin, returning to the United States in 1911. Shortly after, he began his long career as a teacher at Howard University. He received his PhD at Harvard in 1917.

Locke began to achieve wide attention as an advisor and contributor to *Opportunity, founded in 1923 by Charles S. Johnson under the auspices of the National Urban League. A by-product of this association was his editing The *New Negro, the signature anthology of the Harlem Renaissance. During the 1920s, Locke also edited in 1927 Four Negro Poets (Claude *McKay, Jean *Toomer, Countee *Cullen, and Langston *Hughes) and in the same year (with Montgomery Gregory) Plays of Negro Life. In 1929, Locke began a comprehensive yearly roundup of books relating to Africa and African Americans. These appeared in Opportunity until 1943, and thereafter in *Phylon until 1952. They constitute an important record of the discourse relating to African Americans in the period covered. During the 1930s he established the Associates in Negro Folk Education, which published critical works by Sterling A. *Brown and others. Locke's own contributions to the series were Negro Art: Past and Present and The Negro and His Music (both 1936). The crowning effort in this project was Locke's landmark illustrated book, The Negro in Art (1940).

From his college days, Locke had been interested in issues of *race and culture, leading to his embrace of the concepts of cultural pluralism and cultural relativism. Locke's concept of cultural pluralism had its origins in his interactions with a teacher at Harvard, Horace Kallen, then a graduate assistant to the philosopher George Santayana. Cultural pluralism offers a counter to the cultural amalgamation of the "melting pot" paradigm, since that paradigm would clearly exclude African Americans and other distinctive groups. Cultural relativism is the assertion of the parity of different cultures and the rejection of the social Darwinian hierarchy that supported nineteenth-century racial and political theories inimical to African Americans and other groups. Locke's cultural relativism is closely allied to that which became a tenet of American anthropology as it emerged under the aegis of Franz Boas. It is significant that both Kallen and Boas were Jewish. Locke's early interests in race were explored in a series of lectures offered in 1916, against opposition, at Howard University. These lectures were published only in 1992 in an edition by Jeffrey C. Stewart. Locke's more mature reflections on race and culture are perhaps best represented in his commentaries in the anthology (edited with Bernhard Stern) *When Peoples Meet* (1942).

By the late 1920s, however, Locke had also refined and propagated a theory of ancestral and folk tradition, particularly stressing its relevance for the visual and literary artist. At first, he was especially drawn to those young writers who seemed to exemplify the fulfillment of his expectations; of these, Langston Hughes, Zora Neale *Hurston, and Sterling Brown, only the latter retained his confidence in ensuing years.

Locke envisaged summarizing his views in a work to be entitled *The Negro in American Culture*. Ill health prevented his proceeding with it and the task was entrusted to a protégée, Margaret Just Butcher. The work that appeared under this title, although it mentions Locke's notes, owes little to Locke and must be regarded as an independent production.

Locke ranks with W. E. B. *Du Bois and Carter G. *Woodson as a seminal intellectual influence in African American culture; he shares with them political and social interests and a sense of mission in "uplifting the race"; he was unique, however, in the breadth and knowledge of artistic expression and achievement that he brought to their shared larger tasks.

[*See also* Talented Tenth, The.]

• Russell J. Linneman, ed., *Alain Locke: Reflections on a Modern Renaissance Man*, 1982. Jeffrey C. Stewart, ed., *The Critical Temper of Alain Locke*, 1983. Leonard Harris, ed., *The Philosophy of Alain Locke: Harlem Renaissance and Beyond*, 1989. Alain Leroy Locke, *Race Contacts and Interracial Relations*, ed. Jeffrey C. Stewart, 1992.

—Richard A. Long

LOMAX, PEARL CLEAGE. *See* Cleage, Pearl.

LORDE, AUDRE (1934–1992), poet, essayist, autobiographer, novelist, and nonfiction writer, also wrote under the pseudonym Rey Domini. American writer Audre Lorde names herself as "a black feminist lesbian mother poet" because her *identity is based on the relationship of many divergent perspectives once perceived as incompatible. Thematically, she expresses or explores pride, love, anger, fear, racial and sexual oppression, urban neglect, and personal survival. Moreover, she eschews a hope for a better humanity by revealing truth in her *poetry.

She states, "I feel I have a duty to speak the truth as I see it and to share not just my triumphs, not just the things that felt good, but the pain, the intense, often unmitigating pain." Lorde was a prolific writer who continually explored the marginalizations experienced by individuals in a society fearful of differences.

Audrey Geraldine Lorde was born in New York City to laborer Frederic Byron and Linda Belmar Lorde, immigrants from the West Indies who had hoped to return until the depression dashed their plans. The youngest of three daughters, she grew up in Manhattan where she attended Roman Catholic schools, retreating silently into reading and the discovery of writing poetry. She wrote her first poem when she was in the eighth grade. Rebelling at the isolation and strict rules of her parents, she befriended others at Hunter High School who were also viewed as outcasts. After graduating from high school, she attended Hunter College from 1954 to 1959, graduating with a bachelor's degree. While studying library science, Lorde supported herself working various odd jobs: factory worker, ghost writer, social worker, X-ray technician, medical clerk, and arts and crafts supervisor. In 1954, she spent a pivotal year as a student at the National University of Mexico, a period described by Lorde as a time of affirmation and renewal because she confirmed her identity on personal and artistic levels as a lesbian and poet. On her return to New York, Lorde went to college, worked as a librarian, continued writing, and became an active participant in the gay culture of Greenwich Village. Lorde furthered her education at Columbia University, earning a master's degree in library science in 1961. During this time she also worked as a librarian at Mount Vernon Public Library and married attorney Edward Ashley Rollins; they later divorced in 1970 after having two children, Elizabeth and Johnathan. In 1966, Lorde became head librarian at Town School Library in New York City where she remained until 1968.

A turning point for Lorde was the year 1968. She received a National Endowment for the Arts grant, and in spring of 1968 she became poet in residence at Tougaloo College, a small historically black institution in Mississippi. Her experiences as both teacher and writer of poetry virtually changed Lorde's life. Her first volume of poetry, *The First Cities* (1968), was published by the Poet's Press and edited by Diane di Prima, a former classmate and friend from Hunter High School. This volume was cited as an innovative and refreshing rhetorical departure from the confrontational tone prevalent in African American poetry at the time. Dudley *Randall, fellow poet and critic, asserted in his review of the book that "[Lorde] does not wave a black flag, but her blackness is there, implicit, in the bone." Lorde's second volume, *Cables to Rage* (1970), which was mainly written during her tenure at Tougaloo, addresses themes of love, betrayal, childbirth, and the complexities of raising children. It is particularly noteworthy for the poem "Martha" in which Lorde poetically confirms her homosexuality: "we shall love each other here if ever at all." This collection was published in London but distributed in America by Randall's *Broadside Press.

Her next volume of poetry, *From a Land Where Other People Live* (1973), was published by Broadside Press. There exists obvious personal and poetic growth in her expanding thematic scope and vision of worldwide injustice and oppression. Her subtle anger is fully developed yet she addresses other important concerns: the complexities surrounding her existence as an African American and as a woman, mother, lover, and friend. Anger, terror, loneliness, love, and impatience illuminate the pages of *From a Land Where Other People Live* as Lorde's personal experiences have now become universal. This volume was nominated for the National Book Award for poetry in 1973.

Lorde's *New York Head Shop and Museum* (1974) examines political and social issues and was often characterized as her most radical poetry yet. In this volume, Lorde takes the reader on a visual journey through her native New York City while presenting poetic images of urban decay, neglect, and poverty that confront its inhabitants every day. Lorde believed that political action was the necessary ingredient for change: "I have come to believe in death and renewal by fire." Occasionally, *New York Head Shop and Museum* resembles the rebellious yet proud tone of many black poets of the 1960s.

Coal (1976) introduced Lorde to a wider audience because it was her first volume to be released by a major publisher, W. W. Norton. This volume compiles poetry from her first two books, *The First Cities* and *Cables to Rage*, but is significant also because it began Lorde's association with Adrienne Rich, one of Norton's most acclaimed poets, who introduced her to a larger white audience. *Coal* contains many themes similar to those found in *New York Head Shop and Museum* and demonstrates her superb metaphorical craft. In the title poem "Coal" she asserts and celebrates her blackness. Lorde is painfully aware that many strangers overlook her blackness by "cancelling me out." Many of her poems in *Coal* are also an indictment of an unjust society that allows women to be treated unfairly, sometimes brutally, and this acknowledgment by Lorde intensifies her plea for cooperation and sisterhood among women.

Lorde's seventh book of poetry, *The Black Unicorn* (1978), also published by Norton, is widely considered the most complex yet brilliant masterpiece written during her prolific literary career. In this volume, Lorde spans three centuries of the black diaspora to reclaim African mythology as the basis for her themes about women, racial pride, motherhood, and spirituality. She also affirms her lesbianism and political concerns. Poet Adrienne Rich wrote: "Refusing to be circumscribed by any simple identity, Audre Lorde writes as a Black woman, a mother, a daughter, a Lesbian, a feminist, a visionary." In this remarkable work, Lorde opens up the myths of Africa to America readers and calls upon the female African gods to grant her wisdom, strength, and endurance.

Lorde's first work of nonfiction was *The *Cancer Journals* (1980), which chronicles introspectively a very frightening ordeal with breast cancer from September 1978 to March 1979. The brief introduction and three chapters based on Lorde's personal diary detail the intermittent despair, hopelessness, and fear for her life and art. When confronted with the possibility of death, Lorde writes candidly that she wants "to write a piece of meaning words on cancer as it affects my life and my consciousness as a woman, a black lesbian feminist mother lover poet all I am." After undergoing a radical mastectomy, Lorde's spirit still intact, she decides against wearing a prosthesis, rejecting the female physical ideal as presented by the male-dominated media. *A Burst of Light* (1988) is a continuation of this facet of Lorde's life as it recounts her second battle with the spreading cancer beginning in 1984. This brooding collection discusses Lorde's choice for a noninvasive treatment program utilizing meditation and homeopathy.

In 1982, Lorde cemented her reputation as a poet and expanded her prose writing with the publications of *Chosen Poems: Old and New*, a compilation of selections from her first five books and several new pieces, and *Zami: A New Spelling of My Name*, a fictionalized account of Lorde's life as a child to a young adult. This autobiographical narrative also exhibits the tenuous, difficult relationship between a daughter and her mother.

As a noted feminist, Lorde painstakingly struggled against the limitations of the label, insisting that *feminism is important to all factions of African American life. As a perceived outsider on many fronts, Lorde believed that bringing together divergent groups can only strengthen and heal a torn society: "When I say I am a Black feminist, I mean I recognize that my power as well as my primary oppressions come as a result of my Blackness as well as my womanness, and therefore my struggles on both these fronts are inseparable." These views are explored further in *Sister Outsider: Essays and Speeches* (1984), published by Crossing Press. This nonfiction collection explores the fear and hatred existing between African American men and women, feminists, or *lesbians and the challenge between African American women and white women to find common ground. Another crucial area of emphasis presented in *Sister Outsider* is the isolation found among African American women and their subsequent rejection of each other's trust, friendship, and gifts. Before her death in 1992, Lorde published *Our Dead behind Us* (1986), an influential volume of poetry that expresses many similar themes although more deeply and more expanded.

Audre Lorde, who wrote at a feverish pace throughout her literary career, remains an influential and serious talent. To Lorde, her writing was more than a choice or a vocation. It was a responsibility that was necessary for her survival and the survival of others. Her emotional precision blends rage, anger, and destruction with a luminous vision of hope, love, and renewal.

[See also Lesbian Literature.]

• Claudia Tate, ed., *Black Women Writers at Work*, 1983, pp. 100–116. Jerome Brooks, "In the Name of the Father: The Poetry of Audre Lorde," in *Black Women Writers (1950–*

1980): A Critical Evaluation, ed. Mari Evans, 1984, pp. 269–276. Joan Martin, "The Unicorn Is Black: Audre Lorde in Retrospect," in *Black Women Writers (1950–1980): A Critical Evaluation,* ed. Mari Evans, 1984, pp. 277–291. Irma Mc-Claurin-Allen, "Audre Lorde," in *DLB,* vol. 41, *Afro-American Poets since 1955,* eds. Trudier Harris and Thadious M. Davis, 1985, pp. 217–222. Margaret Homans, "Audre Lorde," in *African American Writers: Profiles of Their Lives and Works—from the 1700s to the Present,* eds. Valerie Smith et al., 1993, pp. 211–224.
                                        —Beverly Threatt Kulii

Lost Zoo, The. *See* Christopher Cat.

LOTUS PRESS was established in 1972 to make available a collection that other publishers had rejected because it did not follow the current trend in African American *poetry. Assuming sole ownership in 1974, Naomi Long *Madgett continued the policy of permitting African American poets to retain their independence in style and subject matter, insisting only on literary excellence. In 1980 the press was reorganized as a nonprofit corporation. Lotus Press has published 76 titles, most of them individual collections by some fifty-odd poets such as veterans Samuel W. *Allen, Robert Chrisman, James Emanuel, Lance *Jeffers, Dolores Kendrick, Pinkie Gordon *Lane, Haki R. *Madhubuti, May *Miller, E. Ethelbert *Miller, and Dudley *Randall, as well as first-time poets Houston A. *Baker, Jr., Toi *Derricotte, Gayl *Jones, Nubia Kai, and Paulette Childress *White. Three anthologies and two sets of poster-poems include many more.

In 1993 Michigan State University Press became distributor of Lotus Press books and appointed Madgett editor of its new Lotus Poetry series. Reading and selection of manuscripts and editing activities take place in Detroit at Lotus Press, which also serves as consultant to aspiring poets and small presses and continues a modified program of publication of poetry by African Americans.

[*See also* Periodicals; Publishing.]
                                        —Naomi Long Madgett

LOUIS, JOE (1914–1981), professional boxer. "We gon do our part, and we will win, because we are on God's side," Joe Louis intoned on 10 March 1942 at a dinner/show sponsored by the Navy Relief Society. In seven years, Louis had transformed himself in the eyes of white America from a sullen, unlettered, somewhat threatening black boy from the ghetto of Detroit to a transcendent symbol of patriotism and democratic nationalism, something more than a mere sports hero or champion boxer, although this transformation would not have been possible had he not become a champion athlete who dwarfed the competitors of his era. Born in Alabama on 13 May 1914, Joseph Louis Barrow migrated with his family to Detroit in 1926. He took to boxing as a teenager, had a successful amateur career, and turned professional in 1934. He won the heavyweight title in 1937 and successfully defended it twenty-five times before retiring for the first time in 1949. Louis became the most talked about black figure in American popular culture during the depression and World War II. He

was virtually a nationalist hero among blacks because his opponents were white. His fights with Primo Carnera, an Italian, in 1935, on the eve of Italy's invasion of Ethiopia, and his 1938 rematch against Max Schmeling, the German Nazi who defeated him two years earlier (Louis's only defeat until he returned to boxing after his 1949 retirement), were highly symbolic affairs politically, the latter being the most talked about and anticipated sporting event in American history at that time. Louis was viewed with considerable suspicion by white America when he emerged, largely because it was feared at first that he might be another Jack *Johnson, the first black heavyweight champion who broke a long-standing *color line when he defeated Tommy Burns for the title in 1908. Breaking a color barrier that had existed in heavyweight championship fights since Johnson's defeat, Louis deliberately and unerringly convinced the white public that he was not in any way like Jack Johnson and became, by the time of America's entry into World War II, one of the most beloved athletic figures ever produced in America. He did this by being generous to his white opponents, avoiding white women publicly, and demonstrably loyal to his country. He was a striking contrast to such black public figures as *Stepin Fetchit, Willie Best, and even Louis Armstrong in not seeming, in any way, to pander to whites as "the good, grinning darky." Louis has been written about or mentioned in works by Richard *Wright, James *Baldwin, *Malcolm X, Maya *Angelou, Chester *Himes, Ernest J. *Gaines, Amiri *Baraka, and many others, and has figured symbolically in numerous books and poems. He is largely seen as an icon of an ur-black nationalism and a heroic figure on the order of *John Henry. Louis died in Las Vegas in 1981. The most revealing and honest of Joe Louis's *autobiograhies is *Joe Louis: My Life,* coauthored with Edna and Art Rust, Jr., and published in 1981.

[*See also* Stereotypes; War Experience.]
                                        —Gerald Early

L'OUVERTURE, TOUSSAINT (c. 1743–1803), Haitian patriot and revolutionary leader. A self-educated former slave, François Dominique Toussaint-L'Ouverture joined the Haitian Revolution in 1791 and became its foremost general, defeating both French and British forces. In 1802, he was betrayed and captured, and he died imprisoned in France.

Toussaint figures importantly in the early-nineteenth-century writings of James McCune Smith, David *Walker, and Henry Highland *Garnet, among others, as a symbol and exemplar of resistance to *slavery, and as an example of the potential of the black race. William Wells *Brown, in his pamphlet *St. Domingo: Its Revolution and Its Patriots* (1854), compares Toussaint favorably to Napoleon and George Washington: "Toussaint liberated his countrymen; Washington enslaved a portion of his." George Clinton Rowe's seventy-stanza poem, *Toussaint L'Ouverture* (1890), lauds Toussaint as the "deliverer of his race." Later African American writers such as Carter G. *Woodson and W. E. B. *Du Bois argued for Toussaint's importance in inspiring slave rebellions, in the abolition of the slave trade (1807), and in Napoleon's decision to sell the Louisiana Territory (1803).

In the twentieth century, Toussaint has been the subject of several dramatic treatments. Leslie Pinckey *Hill's *Toussaint L'Ouverture: A Dramatic History* (1928), written in blank verse, aims "to help fill a long-continuing void": the presentation of black heroes. Hill draws explicit parallels between Toussaint and Christ, and sees Toussaint as exemplifying the best of "our universal human nature." Lorraine *Hansberry's unfinished play *Toussaint* (1958–1965), originally conceived as a *musical or an *opera, similarly aims at portraying Toussaint as a black hero and role model.

Toussaint has inspired several works by Afro-Caribbean writers, including Edouard Glissant's play *Monsieur Toussaint* (1961) and Aimé Césaire's historical work, *Toussaint Louverture* (1960). C. L. R. James's unpublished play *Toussaint L'Ouverture* (revised as *The Black Jacobins*, 1976), which featured Paul *Robeson in the title role in a 1936 London performance, and his historical study, also titled *The Black Jacobins* (1938), both portray Toussaint as a hero tragically flawed by a "neglect for his own people" and an exaggerated respect for the French.

Arna *Bontemps's *novel *Drums at Dusk* (1939) sees Toussaint as separated from common Haitians by his *literacy, heroic nature, and "god-like authority." Margaret *Walker, in her poem "The Ballad of the Free" (1970), groups Toussaint with other leaders of slave *insurrections as an African American hero. In two quite different works, Ralph *Ellison's *short story "Mister Toussan" (1941) and Ntozake *Shange's play *for colored girls who have considered suicide / when the rainbow is enuf* (1977), Toussaint becomes a kind of distant, fairytale hero for children.

[*See also* Afrocentricity; Drama; West Indian Literature.]

• J. Michael Dash, *Haiti and the United States: National Stereotypes and the Literary Imagination*, 1988. Alfred N. Hunt, *Haiti's Influence on Antebellum America*, 1988.

—Gary Ashwill

LUTIE JOHNSON. In Ann *Petry's *The *Street* (1946), Lutie Johnson, estranged from her husband and father, is a single mother, alone and struggling to make a better life for herself and her son, Bub. Lutie is one of the first African American urban heroines, breaking away from the tragic *mulatto and other southern woman characters.

From her experience as a suburban *domestic, she claims Benjamin Franklin as role model and strives to become a successful self-made American. Her obsession with upward mobility creates independence and self-reliance, yet also aloofness, which hinders her from forming coalitions with neighborhood women. Her independence also prevents her from believing that, as an African American woman, she cannot achieve the American dream. Lutie's constant struggle reveals how capitalism, racism, and sexism are intertwined; yet her hope for a better life reassures her struggle. Although she easily recognizes and confronts racism and attempts to overcome the economic oppression faced daily, as "a good-looking brown girl" she is stumped by the sexism and sexual advances of white and African American men who obstruct her upward mobility and offend her virtuous nature.

When Lutie is faced with attempted rape by an African American man, and forced concubinage to a white slumlord, she responds with *violence fueled by rage and frustration. Lutie may be the first African American female character to murder an African American male for participating in her oppression. Yet the violent act only makes Lutie lose self-respect, decide to abandon her son, and give up the struggle.

—Adenike Marie Davidson

LYNCH, JOHN R. (1847–1939), autobiographer, historian, lawyer, politician, and public official. A gifted and influential lawmaker in the postbellum era, John R. Lynch produced a significant body of historical and autobiographical writings that challenged dominant, racially biased versions of Reconstruction.

Born on a Louisiana plantation a few miles from Natchez, Mississippi, and freed when Union troops occupied Natchez, Lynch became at age twenty-one a justice of the peace. A year later he was elected to the Mississippi House of Representatives, where he served from 1870 to 1873, becoming a popular and respected speaker of the house. Elected to the U.S. House of Representatives in 1872, he served from 1873 to 1877, championing African American civil and voting rights. Defeated in the 1876 election, as Democratic opposition to Reconstruction gained force, he later returned to Congress in 1882–1883. At the 1884 Republican national convention, Lynch, the temporary chairman, delivered the keynote address. President Benjamin Harrison appointed him Fourth Auditor of the Treasury in 1889, and during the Spanish American War, President William McKinley made him a paymaster in the army, where he served as a major until 1911. The following year he moved to Chicago, where he practiced law, sold real estate, and wrote until his death in 1939.

Responding to factual errors in the prevailing accounts of Reconstruction, Lynch corrected their distortions by writing *The Facts of Reconstruction* (1913), *Some Historical Errors of James Ford Rhodes* (1922), and articles for the *Journal of Negro History*. In most respects his *autobiography, *Reminiscences of an Active Life: The Autobiography of John Roy Lynch* (published 1970, edited by John Hope Franklin), was a continuation of that project. By documenting the agency of African Americans in the making of Reconstruction, Lynch's work is the important forerunner of an antiracist historiographical tradition stretching from W. E. B. *Du Bois's *Black Reconstruction in America* (1935) through Eric Foner's *Reconstruction: America's Unfinished Revolution* (1988).

• John Hope Franklin, "John Roy Lynch: Republican Stalwart from Mississippi," in *Southern Black Leaders of the Reconstruction Era*, ed. Howard N. Rabinowitz, 1982, pp. 39–58.

—Gregory Eiselein

LYNCHING did not come out of nowhere. Its actual and symbolic grounding in history and literature goes back to *slavery and slavery's defining persons of African descent as property. During slavery there were numerous public punishments of slaves, none of which were preceded by trials or any other semblance of civil or judicial processes. Justice depended solely upon the slaveholder. Executions, whippings, brandings, and other forms of severe punishment, including sometimes the public separation of families, were meted out by authority or at the command of the master or his representative. Often, slaves from the plantation and, sometimes, nearby plantations were assembled and made to witness the punishment as an example of the master's absolute authority to wield the power of life and death over each and every slave. Underlying this action was the idea that black slaves were not truly human beings or, if human, certainly not equal or endowed with any right to life or liberty beyond what their owners saw fit to grant.

After emancipation, despite the efforts of the Thirteenth, Fourteenth, and Fifteenth amendments and federal Reconstruction legislation, white Southerners sought ways, legal and extralegal, to assert a white supremacy so extreme as to justify meting out ritual death to black persons without any formal legal process. The rise of lynching as a specific *race ritual of terror coincided with the systematic passage of state laws disenfranchising black voters and decreeing separate but equal civil and social facilities. This *Jim Crow way of life, law, and custom was given implicit national endorsement by the Supreme Court in its 1896 Plessy v. Ferguson "separate but equal" decision.

In its random quality, lynching was arguably as bad or worse than the murders committed against slaves. During slavery anyone doing violence to a slave had to answer to that slave's master; otherwise the full weight of the law could be brought down upon whoever presumed to raise a hand against another man's human property. With the rise of lynching after the Civil War and the cessation of Reconstruction there was no such restraint. In place of the master was the more vague standard of justice held by a particular "white community." Lynching derived its power from the participation of numerous white citizens in the ritual murder and the approval or acquiescence in the action by the remainder of the white community. Here it should be noted that through successful filibusters members of the U.S. Senate from the former Confederacy (and their occasional allies from other states) upheld the right of individual states to the custom of lynching.

Although abhorrent to many, even to some of its silent, acquiescent partners, lynching was not an aberration in American race relations. Rather, it served as an extreme reminder of the unreasoning power the basest passions, fears, and hatreds of white Americans could exercise over the lives and humanity of black Americans. For "the ultimate goal of lynchers," as Ralph *Ellison reflected in Going to the Territory (1986), "is that of achieving ritual purification through destroying the lynchers' identifica-tion with the basic humanity of their victims. Hence their deafness to cries of pain, their stoniness before the sight and stench of burning flesh. . . ." At issue, then, in historical terms and the imaginative terms of African American literature, is lynching's ritual capacity to define and annihilate the humanity of the black victim and that of every last member of his or her race, symbolically or, if necessary, literally.

According to John Hope Franklin (From Slavery to Freedom: A History of Negro Americans, 1967), "in the last sixteen years of the nineteenth century there had been more than 2,500 lynchings, the great majority of which were of Negroes." The early twentieth century did not see a significant decrease: "In the very first year of the new century more than 100 Negroes were lynched, and before the outbreak of World War I the number for the century had soared to more than 1,100." Lynchings declined in number but continued in ferocity during World War I. They were seized on so effectively by the Germans that, despite his Southern sympathies, President Wilson issued a statement against lynching and mob *violence. But after the war more than a few returning black soldiers were lynched, some in their uniforms. The "Red scare" of 1919 was eclipsed by the racial violence and lynching fever of what James Weldon *Johnson termed "the Red Summer." Riots and killings, some of them lynchings, occurred in Chicago, Texas, Washington, D.C., and with particular brutality that October in Arkansas. Although lynching was by no means an isolated, aberrant occurrence in the 1920s when the Klan was resurgent or in the 1930s when the depression fueled the hunt for racial as well as political scapegoats, the phenomenon was no longer virulent enough to claim one victim every two to three days. In its sporadic occurrences over the next decades, lynching continued to be a vehicle of terror and a last resort in opposition to the drive for political and civil rights through the 1950s, 1960s, and beyond.

There are convergences and divergences between lynching as a historical and a literary phenomenon. Though the sexual fears, guilt, and fantasies of white men and sometimes women (and to an almost negligible degree the actions of black men) played a role in lynching and became a central motif in literary representations by African American writers, the record is less sensational. "Although the impression was widely held that most of the Negroes lynched had been accused of committing rape on the bodies of white women," John Hope Franklin writes, "in the first fourteen years of the twentieth century only 315 lynch victims were accused of rape or attempted rape." Others were accused of homicide, robbery, insulting whites, and other "offenses." Not surprisingly, what literary expressions of lynching have in common with written and oral eyewitness accounts of mob violence are the ritual elements. Ralph Ellison calls lynching "a ritual drama that was usually enacted . . . in an atmosphere of high excitement and led by a masked celebrant dressed in a garish costume who manipulated the numinous objects (lynch ropes, the American flag, shotgun, gasoline and whiskey jugs) associated with the rite as he inspired and instructed the actors in their gory task."

Ellison's observations bridge the gap between history's documentary discourse and the imaginative, mythic rhetoric of literature. At times the mob has a leader, at times not; at times the leading participants are masked, at others not; at times the brutality, though appealing to and possessing ritual elements, is spontaneous and chaotic; at other times carefully planned in advance, even down to advertisements in local newspapers. What is striking, however, is that lynching as an American race-ritual has exerted a powerful pull upon the imaginations of African American writers. Paradoxically, lynching is an even stronger motif for writers after the period between 1880 and 1920 than for earlier writers. As African American literature became more abundant and more prominent in the latter half of the twentieth century, lynching, like slavery, came to seem a ritual actuality of race in American life that black writers felt bound to confront and perhaps imaginatively transform or transcend in asserting their African American *identity. For the writers who must somehow contain and create past, present, and future, lynching has been an unavoidable, inexorable consequence of race, slavery, and blackness in the United States. Furthermore, though lynching singled out its victims, its point was unmistakable: Any black person who enough white people suspected or considered guilty of any offense was subject to murderous, extralegal punishment almost certain not to call down any consequences upon the heads of the perpetrators. Whatever their different approaches to matters of form, technique, style, or subject matter, black writers have represented and confronted this condition and consequence of blackness in America.

Thoughout African American literature lynching tends to be a thread of the ancestors' common experience and a cautionary tale in the historical and imaginative present of American experience. In *Exorcising Blackness: Historical and Literary Lynching and Burning Rituals* (1984), Trudier Harris explores the connections between lynching as a historical and a literary phenomenon. Her study demonstrates the extent to which lynching has been and continues to be rooted in the imagination of black writers no matter what their generation, genre, or gender. Also noted is the great diversity with which the phenomenon of lynching is treated by African American writers even as these authors show, in Harris's words, that "black heritage, via black history, is a continuing and integral part of black existence in spite of its brutal and dehumanizing aspects."

In Jean *Toomer's "Blood-Burning Moon" and to a lesser extent in "Kabnis" and elsewhere in *Cane* (1923), for example, a surviving black character is utterly devastated as a consequence of lynching. In "Blood-Burning Moon," Louisa is moonstruck. She has no articulate sense that her involvement with a white man and then a black man would lead to the white man's ineffectual rage against his powerful black competitor. In the knife fight the white man starts he is quickly killed by the black man. Tom Burwell, who kills in self-defense, is then immediately burned alive in ritual fashion by a white mob. Toomer imagines Louisa alone in the street afterwards singing to the full "blood-burning moon," the other black folks huddled inside their shacks.

In a very different response the narrator of James Weldon Johnson's The *Autobiography of an Ex-Colored Man* (1927), a stranger *passing for white in a southern town, decides to continue passing after he witnesses a black man dragged into town and burned alive in a carefully planned lynching complete with the rebel yell and attended by men, women, and children. Few characters (or their creators) in African American literature enjoyed the ambivalent choice belonging to Johnson's narrator. In Richard *Wright's "Big Boy Leaves Home"(1938), when Big Boy and Bobo accidentally shoot and kill a white man, the black community swings into action knowing it will be subject to destruction by fire or worse. Its members realize all they can do is try to prevent the lynching of their sons, and they instantly put all of their ingenuity and resources behind the escape. Bobo is caught and lynched in a full carnival ritual of dismemberment and burning in front of the town's men, women, and children while Big Boy is an invisible witness from the bottom of a lime kiln in an adjacent field. In the morning Big Boy escapes hidden in the back of a truck bound for Chicago, driven by someone's brave relative.

The effects of lynching are diverse: paralysis, solidarity, and escape, often to ghettos in the North. One effect explored is the appalling sense of the absolute power, outside any process of law, justice, or rationality, that could be brought to bear to keep the idea and practice of white supremacy alive. Black writers from William Wells *Brown, whose *Clotel* (1853) depicts the burning of a black slave, to almost every African American writer of note, from Charles Waddell *Chesnutt and Paul Laurence *Dunbar at the turn of the century to Robert *Hayden and Ralph Ellison at midcentury, to Toni *Morrison, Michael S. *Harper, and Ernest J. *Gaines in the late twentieth century, have explored black Americans' response to lynching and its prevention through abundant use of what Ellison calls "shit, grit, and mother wit." In a reversal of the literary and historical pattern, John Edgar *Wideman had his novel, *The Lynchers* (1973), turn on the plot hatched by four black men to lynch a white policeman. Wideman's novel, like almost all other representations of actual or aborted lynchings in African American literature, shows such plans and deeds done at the cost of the humanity of victim and perpetrator alike.

A chilling exception is Robert Hayden's "Night Death Mississippi." Written in the 1950s, the poem is an arresting work of initiation in which Hayden presents the action from the point of view of the grandfather, father, and young son in a family of apparently ne'er-do-well white folks. (Subtly, Hayden gives voice to the victims of the lynching violence in the form of anonymous unspoken but perhaps sung lines like "O night, raw head and bloodybones night." Through such calls to folklore the victims' feelings—their pain and loss and grief—are heard and made visible.) Nonetheless, Hayden, without comment or explicit judgment, without putting his thumb on any moral scale, presents the lynching participants' views with such matter-of-factness as to be terribly believable. Worst and most convincing of all is the extent to which the element of initiation is realized. By focusing on the lynchers' point of view, Hayden gets near the core of how such ritual terror could not only be practiced but handed down to the next generation. All in the household are conditioned to treat the returning lynching father with the reverence due a hero whose words and actions protect the tribe.

Hayden's cri de coeur is not polemical but profoundly spiritual; the lynching alluded to is horrifyingly conventional and acceptable to the white family involved. And therefore Hayden's poem interprets lynching as a creation, however terrible, of the human heart. In so doing, he makes his poem a witness that is all at once a condemnation, an exorcism, a purification, and a timeless warning. For Hayden and African American literature in general, enactments of lynching are not mere obscene vestiges of the past but conscientious reminders of racial terrors dormant but not extinguished from the American heart.

[See also Crisis, The; Journal of Negro History; Literary History; Violence; Wells-Barnett, Ida B.]

• James E. Cutler, Lynch-Law: An Investigation into the History of Lynching in the United States, 1905. Walter F. White, The Fire in the Flint, 1924. Walter F. White, Rope and Faggot: A Biography of Judge Lynch, 1929. Ralph Ginsburg, 100 Years of Lynching, 1962. NAACP, Thirty Years of Lynching in the United States, 1889–1918, 1969. Ida B. Wells, On Lynchings: Southern Horrors; A Red Record; Mob Rule in New Orleans, 1969. James R. McGovern, Anatomy of a Lynching, 1982. Trudier Harris, Exorcising Blackness: Historical and Literary Lynching and Burning Rituals, 1984. Ralph Ellison, Going to the Territory, 1986.   —John F. Callahan

Lyrics of Lowly Life (1896) was Paul Laurence *Dunbar's first commercially published book and probably the best-selling volume of African American *poetry before the *Harlem Renaissance. Of the 105 poems in the volume, 97 had been previously published in Dunbar's Oak and Ivy (1893) and *Majors and Minors (1895), suggesting that Lyrics of Lowly Life was designed to serve as a showcase *anthology of what the poet and his supporters felt was an underrecognized literary achievement. The popular appeal and literary significance of Lyrics of Lowly Life was enhanced by the introduction that William Dean Howells, a well-established white literary critic, wrote for the volume. The major literary influences on the poems in Lyrics of Lowly Life are British Ro-

mantic poets such as John Keats and Percy Bysshe Shelley, and American regional poetry, particularly the work of the Indiana writer James Whitcomb Riley. What made Dunbar's poetry most notable to readers in his own time, however, were his evocations of the flavor of life and the folkways of "down home" black America through the *speech and dialect of rural African Americans.

The contents of Lyrics of Lowly Life may be conveniently divided between poems written in standard English and the *dialect poetry that gained Dunbar international fame. Among the poems in Lyrics of Lowly Life written in so-called Negro dialect are such favorites from previous Dunbar volumes as "When Malindy Sings," "A Negro Love Song," "An Ante-Bellum Sermon," "The Party," and "When de Co'n Pone's Hot." Dunbar's dialect verse displays his talent in rendering melodies associated with popular songs and ballads, such as "The Old Apple-Tree" and "A Banjo Song." In the introduction to Lyrics of Lowly Life, Howells reserved special praise for Dunbar's dialect poems, judging them a product of the poet's innate ability to "feel the negro life aesthetically and express it lyrically." Dunbar showed his appreciation of Howells's support by dedicating Lyrics of Lowly Life to the white critic as well as to Dunbar's mother, but the poet came to believe that Howells's praise of the dialect poems deflected attention away from his more serious verse in standard English.

Lyrics of Lowly Life contains a wealth of Dunbar's most thoughtful and ambitious verse. "Frederick Douglass" commemorates in a dignified style the life and example of the great freedom orator and abolitionist. Two odes, "Ode to Ethiopia" and "Columbian Ode," adapt a traditional Romantic poetic form to commemorate both racial and national patriotism. Many of Dunbar's poems about Nature, love, and death betray the poet's tendency to indulge in idealized and conventional responses to time-worn themes. But in such classic lyrics as "Not They Who Soar," which cautions that "flight is ever free and rare," and "We Wear the Mask," which warns of "the mask that grins and lies," Dunbar spoke eloquently and individually to the complexity of his struggle to articulate an African American poetic voice to a white American audience.

[See also Masking.]

• Jean Wagner, Black Poets of the United States, 1974. Joanne M. Braxton, ed., The Collected Poetry of Paul Laurence Dunbar, 1993.

—William L. Andrews and Patricia Robinson Williams

M

MACKEY, NATHANIEL (b. 1947), poet, novelist, essayist, music critic, editor, lecturer, and educator. Florida-born Nathaniel Mackey was raised in California, graduated from Princeton University with high honors, and earned a PhD in English and American literature in 1975. From 1976 to 1979 he was director of Black studies at the University of Southern California and assistant professor in both the English department and the ethnic studies program. He joined the faculty of the University of California, Santa Cruz in 1979, where he is a professor of American literature.

Evidence of the Black diaspora echoes throughout his writings. His *poetry, prose, and *essays situate African American poetry in diverse poetic and cultural traditions: North American, African, Caribbean, and, to some extent, Latin American. He argues that these poetic traditions reciprocally influence each other. The formal experimentation in his writing disrupts any notion that either African American poetry or poetry produced by either "white" or "non-white" Americans is created in an ahistorical vacuum, a disruption that in turn complicates the definition of the North American poetic tradition. To illustrate this, Mackey, in his critical meditation on American poetry entitled *Discrepant Engagement: Dissonance, Cross-Culturality, and Experimental Writing* (1993), describes his project as one that situates black writers from the United States and the Caribbean as well as from the so-called Black Mountain school under a common rubric.

He explains that "creative kinship and the lines of affinity it effects are much more complex, jagged, and indissociable than the totalizing pretensions of canon formation tend to acknowledge." Thus, by bringing their "writing into dialogue and juxtaposition with one another" he demonstrates that

> correspondences, counterpoint, and relevance to one another exist among authors otherwise separated by ethnic or regional boundaries. . . . This fact is especially relevant to the current institutionalization of an African-American canon and the frequent assumption that black writers are to be discussed only in relation to other black writers.

Mackey has written scholarly articles on and been influenced by the poetry of Robert Duncan, Edward Brathwaite, Robert Creely, Amiri *Baraka, and Ishmael *Reed. William Carlos Williams, Charles Olson, Denise Levertov, Federico García Lorca, Aimé Césaire, and Pablo Neruda also had an early influence on his work.

Difficult to categorize in academic terms, his writing questions boundaries between prose and poetry, and especially between writing *music; his writing particulary speaks out of and back to *jazz. He foregrounds the production of both poetry and jazz as an intellectual project.

His books of poetry include: *Four for Trane* (1978),

Septet for the End of Time (1983), *Eroding Witness* (1985), *Outlantish* (1992), and *School of Udhra* (1993). His prose texts include: *Bedouin Hornbook* (1986), an *epistolary novel, and its sequel, *Djbot Baghostus's Run* (1993), as well as a volume of collected essays, *Discrepant Engagement: Dissonance, Cross-Culturality and Experimental Writing* (1993). Edited volumes include *Hambone*, a literary magazine (1974–1992), and *Moment's Notice: Jazz in Poetry and Prose* (1993).

• Nathaniel Mackey, "An Interview with Nathaniel Mackey, "interview by Edward Foster, *Talisman: A Journal of Contemporary Poetry and Poetics* 9 (Fall 1992): pp. 48–61.

—Michelle Habell-Pallán

MADAM ALBERTA K. JOHNSON. Alberta K. Johnson, or Madam Alberta K. Johnson, as she insists on being called by all persons other than her family and friends, is the main character in a number of comic poems written by Langston *Hughes. The first piece to be published, "Madam and the Number Runner," appeared in *Contemporary Poetry* (Autumn 1943). At least seventeen more pieces appeared in various publications, including *Poetry, Common Ground,* and *Negro Story.*

Hughes began composing the pieces in the summer of 1943, soon after the major riot in Harlem early in August 1943 and immediately after the composition of a long poem, itself sardonic, "The Ballad of Margie Polite," about the woman whose altercation with a policeman in Harlem led directly to that riot.

The character of Madam may also be placed in the context of Hughes's Jesse B. Semple, or *Simple, who had emerged the previous February in Hughes's weekly column in the *Chicago Defender.* Like Simple, Alberta K. Johnson is an instantly recognizable Harlem type despite her memorable individuality. A middle-aged woman of uncertain means, she is resourceful, self-confident, sassy, and streetwise. Thus she faces down the world, including her lovers past and present, her landlord, her insurance man come to collect his premiums, other bill collectors, or her self-righteous minister anxious to save her independent, fun-loving soul.

[*See also* Bad Woman; Character Types.]

—Arnold Rampersad

MADGETT, NAOMI LONG (b. 1923), teacher, poet, publisher, and editor; born Naomi Cornelia Long. In "He Lives in Me," a poem in *Adam of Ifé* (1992) honoring her father, Clarence Marcellus Long, Sr., Naomi Long Madgett states the principles that underlie her own achievements: faith, integrity, and personal and social responsibility. As a child, she had free access to his book-lined study, discovering early her love of *poetry. When she was fifteen, her first collection, *Songs to a Phantom Nightingale* (1941), was accepted for publication, though two years had elapsed before it appeared. Two editions, containing additional early poems, have been issued: *Phantom Nightingale, Juvenilia* (1981) and *Remembrances of Spring: Early Collected Poems* (1993). The second of these also includes her second collection, *One and the Many* (1956).

Between her first two collections, Madgett completed a BA (Virginia State University, 1945), married, settled in Detroit, Michigan, worked briefly for the *Michigan Chronicle*, and gave birth to a daughter, Jill (who is also a publishing poet under the name Jill Witherspoon Boyer). The marriage ended in 1948, and Madgett worked for the Michigan Bell Telephone Company until 1954.

In 1955, she completed an MEd degree in English at Wayne State University and began her teaching career, first as a secondary-school teacher in the Detroit public schools (1955–1968), then at Eastern Michigan University (1968–1984). From the beginning of her teaching career, she has championed textbook reform to provide fairer representation to African American authors. She perceives her contribution to the teaching of this literature and of creative writing as her most influential work, her writing as her most personally satisfying.

In the early 1960s, encouraged by Rosey E. Pool, a Dutch scholar interested in African American poets, a group of poets began to meet for informal discussion and workshops. Dudley *Randall, Oliver La-Grone, James W. Thompson, Harold Lawrence, Edward Simpkins, Alma Parks, Betty Ford, Gloria Davis, and Madgett formed the nucleus of the group, which met at Boone House, the home of Margaret Esse *Danner, poet in residence at Wayne State University from 1962 to 1964. A later group included LaGrone, Randall, Davis, Madgett, Joyce Whitsitt, and several white poets. *Ten: Anthology of Detroit Poets* (1968) grew from this association.

Madgett's third collection, *Star By Star* (1965; rpt. 1970, 1972), includes poems from this period. In 1972, she, three friends, and her third husband, Leonard Patton Andrews, established the Lotus Press to publish her fourth book, *Pink Ladies in the Afternoon* (1972). The press, which Madgett and Andrews took over in 1974, has published well-received books for more than twenty years. Its major contribution has been to bring attention to African American poets. Although many of these have been young women, the press has also published established poets such as May *Miller, notably, her *Collected Poems* (1989). In 1993, having published seventy-six titles, Madgett turned over distribution to the Michigan State University Press, which established the Lotus Press Series and named Madgett its senior editor. In the same year, the Before Columbus Foundation presented her with its American Book Award as publisher-editor.

Her fifth collection of poems, *Exits and Entrances* (1978), appeared six years after the book that launched the Lotus Press, and it would be another ten years before her next new collection. While she did write a college-level textbook, *A Student's Guide to Creative Writing* (1980), her dedication to teaching

and the prodigious output of what was, with some volunteer help, a one-person publishing venture left little time for her own poems.

But the subject of her next collection, *Octavia and Other Poems* (1988), also demanded time. Madgett's poems are, in the broadest sense, personal, dealing even with major social concerns from an individual rather than a political viewpoint. This book, focused on family life as it reflects community, intensifies her customary lyric individuality. The sequence "Octavia" re-creates from family memorabilia the life of her father's sister, a schoolteacher who died before Madgett was born. As it does so, it re-creates African American life in Oklahoma and Kansas early in the twentieth century, emphasizing family and personal responsibility for the welfare of the community. The collection *Adam of Ifé: Black Women in Praise of Black Men* (1992), edited by Madgett, is similar in its emphasis on strong, positive African American manhood.

Pilgrim Journey, a collection of autobiographical *essays near completion, and a number of recent unpublished poems will testify, as have the past five decades of her poems, to Madgett's firm foundation in the faith, integrity, and sense of responsibility she sees as her patrimony.

Naomi Long Madgett's unpublished poems and papers are deposited in the Special Collections Library at Fisk University, Nashville, Tennessee.

• Robert P. Sedlack, "Naomi Long Madgett," in *DLB*, vol. 76, *Afro-American Writers, 1940–1955*, ed. Trudier Harris, 1988, pp. 104–112. Nagueyalti Warren, "Naomi Long Madgett," in *Notable Black Women in America*, vol. 1, ed. Jessie Carney Smith, 1992, pp. 716–719. Alice A. Deck, "Madgett, Naomi Long," in *Black Women in America*, vol. 2, ed. Darlene Clark Hine, 1994, pp. 741–743. Robert P. Sedlack, "Madgett, Naomi Long," in *The Oxford Companion to Women's Writing in the United States*, eds. Cathy N. Davidson and Linda Wagner-Martin, 1995, pp. 535–536. —George F. Wedge

MADHUBUTI, HAKI R. (b. 1942), poet, critic, essayist, teacher, editor, publisher, and businessperson. Given the name Don L. Lee, Haki R. Madhubuti changed his name in 1973 as a result of the ideological influences of the *Black Arts movement, of which he was a highly visible member. He was born 23 February 1942 in Little Rock, Arkansas. In 1943 he and his parents migrated to Detroit, Michigan, where his father deserted the family before the birth of Madhubuti's sister. In order to cope with poverty and feed her two children, his mother worked as a janitor and a barmaid, eventually becoming an alcoholic and a drug addict. When Madhubuti was sixteen, his mother died from a drug overdose.

This woman, Maxine Lee, was the prime mover behind the creative force that Haki R. Madhubuti has become. When Madhubuti was thirteen years old, his mother asked him to check out for her Richard *Wright's *Black Boy* from the Detroit Public Library. He became a reader with his discovery of Wright, who led him to other writers, such as Chester *Himes, Langston *Hughes, Claude *McKay, Melvin B. *Tolson, Jean *Toomer, Gwendolyn *Brooks, Margaret *Walker, and Arna *Bontemps.

After his mother's death, Madhubuti went to Chicago, where he attended Dunbar High School. Because he could not get a job after graduating, he traveled selling magazines, ending up penniless and sick in East St. Louis, Missouri, where he pawned everything he owned and joined the U.S. Army. When Madhubuti was eighteen, a white drill sergeant tore the pages of his copy of Paul Robeson's *Here I Stand*, stimulating in him a commitment to his Blackness, steepening his drive to study Black cultural and intellectual history, and instilling in him the desire to become a writer.

In 1963 Madhubuti left the army, and four years later Dudley *Randall's *Broadside Press published Madhubuti's first collection of *poetry, *Think Black* (1967), which had been previously published by the author himself. Six books, all published by Broadside Press, followed: five collections of poetry—*Black Pride* (1968), *Don't Cry, Scream* (1969), *We Walk the Way of the New World* (1970), *Directionscore: Selected and New Poems* (1971), *Book of Life* (1973)—and a collection of critical essays, *Dynamite Voices: Black Poets of the 1960s* (1971).

The titles of these early poetry collections demonstrate that he addressed his work to a Black audience and that he was intensely committed to illuminating for that audience the pitfalls of racism in all its psychological, economic, political, and historical guises. The themes and subjects found in these early collections appear in a more sophisticated form in his poetry collections of the 1980s and 1990s, among them the inner beauty and/or environmental difficulties of the Black woman; what it means to be a Black man in America; the importance of Black male–female relationships; political figures who fight racial problems; poets such as Conrad Kent *Rivers, Langston Hughes, Gwendolyn Brooks, Ted *Joans, and Sterling *Plumpp; the problems with Black assimilation into Western culture; how Blacks in the West have allowed themselves to be brainwashed by Christianity; Blacks who lack substance and commitment to their race; the contradiction of Blacks in the military; and the psychological and artistic contributions of Black musicians.

Madhubuti also involves himself in institution building. He took four hundred dollars he made from reading poetry, bought a mimeograph machine, and along with poets Carolyn M. *Rodgers and Johari *Amini as well as Roschell Rick founded *Third World Press in his basement apartment on Chicago's South Side on 12 December 1967. With Hoyt Fuller as their guide, Madhubuti and a number of his contemporaries founded the Organization of Black American Culture (OBAC), a city-wide group that tried to impact cultural activity in the arts. Around this time he and other members of OBAC met Gwendolyn Brooks in a *church. As is demonstrated by the poems Madhubuti dedicates to Brooks, by his editing and publishing a book that celebrates her seventieth birthday (*Say That the River Turns: The Impact of Gwendolyn Brooks*, 1987), and by his now consistent publication of her works, a special bond exists between the two poets.

When Madhubuti met Brooks, he was also a self-described "foot soldier" for the Student Nonviolent Coordinating Committee (SNCC), the Congress of Racial Equality (CORE), and the Southern Christian Leadership Conference (SCLC). He and other members of the Black Arts movement read and sold their poetry at Black Arts conferences and at SCLC gatherings. Like Sonia *Sanchez, Askia M. *Touré, Amiri *Baraka, and Larry *Neal, Madhubuti is as much political activist as he is poet. His role as writer–political activist emerges in *From Plan to Planet* (1973), *Earthquakes and Sunrise Missions: Poetry and Essays of Black Revival 1973–1983* (1984), *Black Men: Obsolete, Single, Dangerous?* (1990), and *Claiming Earth: Race, Rage, Redemption* (1994). While these publications illustrate Madhubuti's skill as essayist and poet, his 1978 collection of essays *Enemies: The Clash of Races* is the most political. In it he demonstrates that the psychological, the economic, and the sociological are all embodiments of the politics that affect Black lives. *Enemies*, which describes the poet's associations with SNCC, CORE, and SCLC, more than any publication that precedes it, illuminates Madhubuti's global interest, highlighting the Nationalist and Pan-Africanist thinking in his work.

Madhubuti's publication of *Black Books Bulletin* (*BBB*) also grew out of his political activity. He and Larry Neal cochaired a workshop on ideas for publishing at the 1970 meeting of the Congress of Afrikan People. Although *Black World, Soulbook,* and the *Liberator* were still being published, no book review journal existed, and in 1971 Madhubuti and Neal founded the *BBB*. It was published as a quarterly for eight years, after which the issues became very erratic because of a low subscriber base and a lack of a full-time staff. *The Challenge of the Twenty-first Century*, volume 8, and *Blacks, Jews and Henry Gates, Jr.: A Response*, volume 16, published in 1991 and 1994, respectively, both address intellectual and political issues controversial at the time among the Black and white intelligentsia.

Madhubuti's edition of *Why L.A. Happened: Implications of the '92 Los Angeles Rebellion*, published in 1993, also attests to his continued involvement in the politics that affect Black lives. This collection includes twenty-nine essays written by Black intellectuals from diverse academic disciplines. This array of writers and scholars underscores Madhubuti's varied interprofessional relationships and the different types of writers he brings to his press. An ability to clarify controversial issues in the Black community is also reflected in Madhubuti's 1990 edition of *Confusion by Any Other Name: Essays Exploring the Negative Impact of "The Blackman's Guide to Understanding the Blackwoman."*

His 1987 collection of poetry, *Killing Memory, Seeking Ancestors*, published by *Lotus Press, exemplifies the best of Madhubuti's poetic vision and shows his understanding that the same cultural, political, historical, economic, and educational issues that affected Black lives in the 1960s appear in new guises in the 1990s. "The Great Wait" in this collection beautifully exemplifies both the consistency in Madhubuti's style and the more than twenty years in which he has been honing that style, admonishing Blacks for waiting for others to improve the quality of their lives. In this critique of Blacks' failure to empower themselves, the poet carefully makes it clear that Blacks must overcome the psychological indoctrination that inhibits their taking charge of their lives. The poem progresses perfectly through the repetition of the words "waiting" and "waiters." The use of these words reflects a "jazzy rhythmic effect" that appears periodically throughout Madhubuti's collections of poetry. His love and knowledge of *music is a predominant aspect of his poetry; in various poems he merges diverse musical rhythms with narrative voice, aphorisms, and rhetorical devices such as asyndeton, hyperbole, synecdoche, anaphora, anastrophe, litotes, irony, and ellipsis. His heavy staccato rhythm, the dozens, and sharp humor come straight out of Black street language.

Understanding the need to focus on spiritual and physical health at the same time that one confronts political issues, Madhubuti, John Howell (a Black environmental engineer), and David Hall (a lawyer) founded the National Black Holistic Retreat Society in 1980 to address the multifaceted issues that impact Black men's lives. In addition to this work, Madhubuti reads his poetry and gives lectures on educational, political, literary, and historical issues throughout the United States. He has also spoken in Canada, Morocco, Liberia, Ghana, Tanzania, Senegal, Israel, Brazil, Paris, England, and Holland.

Madhubuti is director of the Gwendolyn Brooks Center at Chicago State University and a professor of English. Having received an MFA from the University of Iowa, he has taught as a writer in residence at Cornell, Howard, Morgan State, and Central State universities as well as the University of Illinois in Chicago. In addition to being named author of the year for 1991 by the Illinois Association of Teachers of English, he received an American Book Award for Publishing and Editing in 1991 and the African Heritage Studies Association's Community Service Award in 1994.

In mid-1996 Madhubuti lived in Country Club Hills, Illinois, with his wife Safisha, a published writer and a professor at Northwestern University in Evanston, Illinois, and their family. His collection of love poems entitled "Heart Love Essential Meditations of Commitment" and "Groundwork: Selected Poems 1966–1996," were both scheduled to be published in the summer of 1996. He was also working on a collection of critical essays entitled "Gifted Genius: Writings from the Frontline of the Black Arts Movement" and on a book that contains a page each on the hundred books that have most influenced his life.

• David Llorens, "Black Don Lee," *Ebony*, Mar. 1969, 72–80. Paula Giddings, "From a Black Perspective: The Poetry of Don L. Lee," in *Amistad 2*, eds. John A. Williams and Charles Harris, 1971, pp. 299–318. Annette Oliver Shands, "The Relevancy of Don L. Lee As a Contemporary Black Poet," *Black World* 21 (June 1972): 35–48. Catherine Daniels Hurst, "Haki R. Madhubuti (Don L. Lee)," in *DLB*, vol. 41, *Afro-American Poets since 1955*, eds. Trudier Harris and Thadious M. Davis, 1985, pp. 222–232. —Joyce A. Joyce

MAGAZINES. *See* Periodicals.

MAJOR, CLARENCE (b. 1936), poet, novelist, short fiction writer, visual artist, essayist, lexicographer, editor, and anthologist. Although known best for his metafictional *novels, Clarence Major has long demonstrated his versatility in both the artistic forms he uses and the subject matter he selects. He tests boundaries, asserting and enacting the *freedom of the artist to explore the full range of human experience. One source of his versatility is his early exposure to both the North and the South. Though born in Atlanta, he moved at the age of ten to Chicago with his mother after his parents were divorced. He maintained his southern connection through summer visits with his relatives. A key Chicago experience for him was exposure to modern art, especially the Impressionists. He studied briefly at the Chicago Art Institute when he was seventeen. Although he decided to focus his artistic efforts primarily on writing, he has made use of his painting and photography in his fiction, especially *Reflex and Bone Structure* (1975) and *Emergency Exit* (1979).

Much of his work, especially the fiction, has been experimental in that it has broken down conventional assumptions about character, plot, and narrative voice. The texts tend to be fragmentary rather than unified in structure; likewise, their principal theme is the impossibility of a coherent *identity in contemporary society. This pattern holds in the two novels mentioned above, as well as *All-Night Visitors* (1969), *No* (1973), *My Amputations* (1986), and some of the stories in *Fun and Games* (1988). In these works, he joins Donald Barthelme, Thomas Pynchon, and Ishmael *Reed in challenging the view that fiction either reflects or constructs a meaningful reality. Literature is, in effect, a set of verbal tricks and needs its artificiality to be acknowledged.

But like Reed, Major also sees cultural significance in metafictional storytelling. His fragmented characters exist in a world in which they are rootless and often paranoid, in quest of a meaning that forever eludes them. In two novels that are more "realistic," he examines the same issue. *Such Was the Season* (1987) uses a southern folklike narrative voice that echoes Ernest J. *Gaines's Jane Pittman and Gloria *Naylor's Mama Day in its down-home wisdom as well as its position as a moral center by which to judge others. But Major complicates the narrative by having Annie Eliza draw much of her knowledge not from traditional black experience but from *television talk shows and soap operas.

Similarly, *Painted Turtle: Woman with Guitar* (1988) tells the experiences of a Zuni woman who has been forced out of the tribe because she has worked as a *prostitute and because she questions the traditional ways. She makes her living as an itinerant folksinger whose songs become her means of trying to claim an identity for herself as a Zuni. The novel is narrated by a man who is himself Hopi-Navajo and thus outside of her experience as well as uncertain about his own identity.

The subject matter of *Painted Turtle* suggests the multicultural nature of Major's work. One of the early influences on his writing was the work of French artists such as Raymond Radiguet and Arthur Rimbaud, and his interest in white European and American literature is reflected in many allusions in both his fiction and poetry. The importance of the Western tradition is clear in a book of poetry, *Surfaces and Masks* (1988), which is entirely about the experiences of Americans in Venice, with literary references to Disraeli, Dickens, Shelley, and Thomas Mann. His exploration of Native American issues is continued in a collection of poems entitled *Some Observations of a Stranger at Zuni in the Latter Part of the Century* (1989).

The range of forms and subjects reflects Major's commitment to artistic freedom made explicit in his *essays and interviews, many of which are collected in *The Dark and Feeling* (1974). He insists that it is the quality of the work rather than its ideology that determines its importance. Even in his 1967 manifesto, "Black Criteria," which calls for greater use of African American materials and a rejection of much of Western tradition, he still concludes that the integrity of the artistic vision is the essential criterion. His work as editor and lexicographer has demonstrated his commitment to language and to literary freedom. His *Dictionary of Afro-American Slang* (1970), expanded and updated in *Juba to Jive* (1994), provides a major resource for discussions of African American language use. His two *anthologies, *The New Black Poetry* (1969) and *Calling the Wind: Twentieth-Century African-American Short Stories* (1993), offer a wide range of literary expression within the African American tradition. He is a professor of English at the University of California, Davis.

• *Black American Literature Forum*, special issue, 13 (Summer 1979). Larry D. Bradfield, "Beyond Mimetic Exhaustion: The *Reflex and Bone Structure* Experiment," in *Black American Literature Forum* 17 (Fall 1983): 120–123. Jerome Klinkowitz, "The Self-Apparent Word: Clarence Major's Innovative Fiction," in *Black American Prose Theory*, eds. Joe Weixlmann and Chester J. Fontenot, 1984, pp. 199–214. Keith Byerman, *Fingering the Jagged Grain: Tradition and Form in Recent Black Fiction*, 1986. Charles Johnson, *Being and Race: Black Writing Since 1970*, 1990. *African American Review*, special issue, 28 (Spring 1994).

—Keith E. Byerman

Majors and Minors (1895) was Paul Laurence *Dunbar's second collection of *poetry. Unlike the self-published *Oak and Ivy* (1893), *Majors and Minors* was underwritten by two of the poet's white benefactors and, after publication in Toledo, Ohio, achieved sufficiently wide circulation to be noticed by the prominent white literary critic William Dean Howells, who reviewed the volume in the 27 June 1896 issue of *Harper's Weekly*. Howells's admiring review, in which he praised Dunbar for displaying "white thinking and white feeling in a black man" (which Howells confessed never to have encountered before), gave the obscure twenty-four-year-old poet from Dayton,

Ohio, a national reputation. What Howells most enjoyed in Dunbar was his *dialect poetry, which was included under the rubric of "Humour and Dialect" in the second and shorter section of Dunbar's book. Most of the verse in *Majors and Minors* appears in the opening section, where Dunbar grouped sixty-nine poems in standard English.

Majors and Minors contains some of Dunbar's best-known poems in so-called Negro dialect. A few of these poems—"The Party" and "The Deserted Plantation," for example—elicit racial *stereotypes and nostalgia for preemancipation days that have earned Dunbar criticism for capitalizing on the popularity of the *plantation tradition. But other dialect poems, such as "An Ante-bellum Sermon" and "A Negro Love Song," richly evoke the communal lore and vernacular expression of the rural African American South. Although written in dialect, "When Malindy Sings," a paean to the genius of an untutored but magnificently talented black woman singer, scarcely hides the impatience of the black speaker with the uninspired conventionality of white musical idiom.

Among the poems in standard English, *Majors and Minors* reveals Dunbar experimenting early in his career with a variety of styles, forms, and subject matter. Although many of Dunbar's poems on love and Nature evidence his technical competence and his debt to the lyricism of the English Romantic poets, these works often culminate in familiar sentiments and conventional moralizing. On the other hand, among the "majors" of Dunbar's volume are an outspoken celebration of racial pride—"The Colored Soldiers," which memorializes the heroism and nobility of the black men who fought for the Union cause—and some provocative meditations on his situation as an African American poet struggling to negotiate a difficult passage between popularity and literary integrity. Among these brooding meditative verses are "Ere Sleep Comes Down to Soothe the Weary Eyes," which belies any impression of Dunbar as a simple comic poet, and "We Wear the Mask," which warns the reader of the masked character of the poet's expression and of the need to peer behind appearances in order to appreciate Dunbar's complex situation and his achievement.

[*See also* Masking.]

• Peter Revell, *Paul Laurence Dunbar*, 1979. Donald A. Petesch, *A Spy in the Enemy's Country: The Emergence of Modern Black Literature*, 1989.

—William L. Andrews *and* Patricia Robinson Williams

MALCOLM X (1925–1965), Nation of Islam minister, orator, and autobiographer. Born Malcolm Little (and later also known as el-Hajj Malik el-Shabazz) in Omaha, Nebraska, on 19 May 1925, Malcolm X was the fourth of eight children of the Reverend Earl Little and his wife, Louise. Soon after Malcolm's birth the Littles moved to the outskirts of East Lansing, Michigan. When Malcolm was six, his father died, presumably murdered by the Black Legion, a violent racist group similar to the Ku Klux Klan, and the Little home life became more and more difficult. Louise was eventually placed in the state mental hospital, and her children were declared wards of the state. In

1941 Malcom moved to Boston to live with his half sister, Ella. He became caught up in the nightlife of Boston and, later, New York. After a few years in the underworld of Harlem, selling drugs and working for call-girl services, Malcolm began a burglary ring in Boston. In 1946, at the age of twenty-one, he was arrested for armed robbery and sent to prison.

During his six years in Charlestown Prison, Concord Reformatory, and Norfolk Prison, Malcolm underwent a spiritual and intellectual transformation. While interred he corresponded with the Honorable Elijah Muhammad, the leader of the African American sect, the Nation of Islam. He converted to the Nation, attracted by its idea that whites are devils. In prison he also undertook a rigorous process of self-education, which included copying every page of the dictionary.

Upon his release he changed his name to Malcolm X, the X representing the unknown name of his African ancestors and their culture that had been lost during *slavery. After personal meetings with Elijah Muhammad, Malcolm became a minister for the Nation. From 1952 to 1963 Minister Malcolm X helped build the Nation of Islam from a tiny sect to a significant force in urban black America. His commanding stage presence, quick wit, and erudition, combined with the authenticity of his experience as a street hustler, made Malcolm a remarkable orator and a dynamic leader.

In 1963 jealousy in the Nation of Islam over Malcolm's increasing celebrity, and Malcolm's discovery of violations of the Muslim's strict moral code by the Honorable Elijah Muhammad precipitated a painful and bitter split. Once out from the strict teachings of the Nation of Islam, Malcolm drifted from the primarily spiritual philosophy of the Nation to a more political *black nationalism and, tentatively, to a more internationalist philosophy—*Pan-Africanism. Malcolm's position on race relations in the United States at the time of his assassination on 21 February 1965 at the Audubon Ballroom in Harlem has not been resolved. His major literary achievement, The *Autobiography of Malcolm X (1965), composed during the last two years of his life with the writer Alex *Haley, contains a montage of Malcolm's perspectives and only invites speculation as to which direction Malcolm's philosophy would have taken.

The Autobiography, published posthumously, stands as a major twentieth-century African American literary work. Its orality, its political intentions and ramifications, and its promise of unspoken truths about the African American experience all place it firmly in African American autobiographical traditions. The Autobiography, however, also resembles more general autobiographical models, most notably the spiritual narrative (his documentation of his conversion experience) and the success story of the self-made man. In fact, it is the text's remarkable meshing of so many modes, and so many "Malcolms," that may be its most significant achievement.

Malcolm X's speeches, found in such collections as Malcolm X Speaks (1965), edited by George Breitman, and Malcolm X: The Last Speeches (1989),

edited by Bruce Perry, are his other contribution to African American literature. His enduring speeches, such as "Message to the Grass Roots" (1963), were given in the last two years of his life and center on the political and social conditions of African Americans. In them, Malcolm blends set pieces and improvisation, and he is especially deft at using analogy to express the African American's plight in America.

Malcolm X also carries tremendous weight as a cultural icon, most notably in the *films of Spike *Lee. He has been used to symbolize an alternative, more militant vision of social protest than Martin Luther *King, Jr.'s nonviolence, and his name appears in rap and other African American *poetry as a symbol of black pride.

[See also Autobiography; Oratory.]

• C. Eric Lincoln, The Black Muslims in America, 1961. John Henrik Clarke, ed., Malcolm X: The Man and His Times, 1969. Peter Goldman, The Death and Life of Malcolm X, 2d ed., 1979. James H. Cone, Martin and Malcolm and America, 1991. David Gallen, Malcolm X As They Knew Him, 1992. Michael Eric Dyson, Making Malcolm: The Myth and Meaning of Malcolm X, 1995.
                                                 —J. D. Scrimgeour

Mama Day. Gloria *Naylor's third novel, Mama Day (1988) details the lives of the title character, also called Miranda Day, and her great-niece, Cocoa (Ophelia). With sections set in New York City and on Willow Springs—a barrier island that is due east of the border between South Carolina and Georgia and actually in neither state—Naylor creates a magical world set against a background of family history and unique geography.

Following an elaborate map of Willow Springs, a family tree of the Day lineage, and a bill of sale for the most important ancestor, Sapphira Wade, Mama Day begins with a prologue giving the pedigree of the island and its inhabitants, dating back to 1799. Naylor writes the prologue in the conversational, colloquial voice of Willow Springs itself, a narrator that returns later. From its current vantage point of August 1999, the prologue reaches back to 1823, the time that Sapphira Wade seized power from the white landowner, Bascombe Wade (whom she killed). Sapphira also convinced Bascombe Wade to deed all of Willow Springs to his former slaves and her descendants, who still own the land in 1999.

The first main section of Mama Day begins with Cocoa's frustrated job search in New York City just before she returns home to Willow Springs. While interviewing for a clerical position in an engineering firm, Cocoa meets and immediately dislikes George Andrews. However, apparently because of Mama Day's magical intervention, George and Cocoa begin to date. Their courtship starts gradually with George showing Cocoa New York City and also educating her about its ethnic richness. Even after their subsequent marriage, it is not until several years later that Cocoa and George return to Willow Springs together. In the interim Cocoa visits her grandmother Abigail and Mama Day alone each August, and George goes on annual solo vacations following professional football.

When George and Cocoa do go to Willow Springs together, the action that begins part 2 of the novel, the main characters converge, resulting in *Mama Day*'s climax during a violent storm. During this visit, rational George must confront the supernatural elements of the island's force, Mama Day's magical powers, and the idea that Cocoa's sudden desperately ill health comes from *conjuring by an enemy. Yet George's upbringing as an urban orphan does not prepare him for the demands of this mythical realm. While his attempts to suspend his disbelief ultimately fail, resulting in his own fatal heart attack, George's sincere efforts help heal Cocoa, and Naylor implies that his sacrifice is necessary for her recovery.

Throughout *Mama Day*, Naylor presents three different narrators. Much of the novel involves Cocoa and George speaking in passages that occur after his death and within their separate and shared consciousness. Naylor narrates other parts of the novel in the omniscient voice of the island—with special emphasis on Mama Day, whose musings involve her premonitions and attempts to "listen" to the messages of her heritage. At the very end of the work Naylor's all-knowing narrator looks forward to Cocoa assuming the matriarchal role after Mama Day passes on.

Mama Day has received substantial critical acclaim, with praise for its folkloric qualities, its use of magic, its poignant characterizations, its Shakespearean model (*The Tempest*), and its treatment of *gender, especially focused on generational sisterhood. Some critics have especially commended Naylor's positive depiction of men in the novel, particularly when compared to the more negative portrayals in her first work, *The *Women of Brewster Place* (1982).

[*See also* Folk Literature; Folklore.]

• G. Michelle Collins, "There Where We Are Not: The Magical Real in *Beloved* and *Mama Day*," *Southern Review* 24 (1988): 680–685. Henry Louis Gates, Jr., and K. A. Appiah, eds., *Gloria Naylor: Critical Perspectives Past and Present*, 1993.
—Kristine A. Yohe

MAMA LENA YOUNGER is a *domestic worker and *matriarch of the Younger family in *A *Raisin in the Sun* (1959) by Lorraine *Hansberry. Played in the original production by Claudia McNeil, a large dark-skinned actress, Lena conjured up the stereotypical image of the asexual, self-sacrificing *mammy. She dominates her adult children, all of whom live under her crowded roof, and decides, without consulting them, to purchase a house with the $10,000 insurance benefit paid on her husband's death.

However, Lena is not only the matriarch as immortalized in Langston *Hughes's poem, "The Negro Mother," but is also the revolutionary who sends her children to do battle in the *civil rights movement. Shattering the mammy *stereotype, Hansberry creates a Mama who dares to move her family into an all-white and hostile neighborhood in order to improve their living situation; who learns to appreciate, if not have faith in, her children's dreams; and who turns over the leadership of the family to her son,

*Walter Lee Younger, a transfer of power that implicitly endorses the growing militancy of the next generation. The Mrs. Johnson scene, cut from the original production but restored in the 1987 version, shows a Lena who rejects the accommodationist philosophy of Booker T. *Washington and implicitly aligns herself with W. E. B. *Du Bois. Her repositioning is further affirmed by Asagai, the young African intellectual and revolutionary who declares that Lena is the true visionary because she acts to bring about change.

[*See also* Beneatha Younger.]

• Lorraine Hansberry, "This Complex of Womanhood," *Ebony*, Aug. 1960, 40. Stephen R. Carter, *Hansberry's Drama: Commitment amid Complexity*, 1991.
—Margaret B. Wilkerson

MAMMY. Mammies exist as much as a concept in American culture as actual characters in American and African American literature. They may be defined as older black women who have been shaped by a heritage of *slavery; from working close to whites in their homes and taking care of their children, they believe that white people are intrinsically superior to black people and that blacks should therefore be subservient to whites. Their loyalties are to their white families, especially the children; many are guilty of neglecting their biological families. They believe that the whites for whom they and their ancestors have worked for generations will protect and defend them in difficult times. Although mammies historically are believed to have held significant roles in plantation households, particularly in the rearing and training of their young white charges, in reality they were relatively powerless black women whose nurturing skills were perhaps valued more than their humanity. Usually attired in bandannas and tight-collared, long-sleeved, ankle-length dresses, these frequently obese women became iconic images in American popular culture, particularly in photography and movies such as *Gone With the Wind*. Perceived as comforters without needs of their own, in the white American imagination these self-sacrificing women were almost as natural a part of the landscape as baseball and apple pie. Image and role were the important things, for seldom did depictors of these women pause to get to know the real women behind the image.

Charles Waddell *Chesnutt's depiction of Mammy Jane in *The *Marrow of Tradition* (1901) captures those traits in the mammy character that lead her to identify more with whites than with blacks. Mammy Jane goes so far as to denounce education for black people in order that they may not disrupt the master-servant relationships such as those that have characterized her family's interactions with several generations of the white Carteret family. Later literary works might not mention the word "mammy," but the concept is still apparent. The grandmother in Kristin *Hunter's *God Bless the Child* (1964) adopts the values and manners of the white family for whom she works. She never fully realizes the destructive consequences of this process upon her biological daughter and granddaughter. By giving their best energies to whites and encouraging their offspring to follow in their footsteps, mammies cultivated a pattern of interaction with whites that some black people are still feeling the consequences of today.

[See also Plantation Tradition; Stereotypes.]

• Jessie W. Parkhurst, "The Role of the Black Mammy in the Plantation Household," *Journal of Negro History* 23 (July 1938): 349–369. Trudier Harris, *From Mammies to Militants: Domestics in Black American Literature*, 1982.

—Trudier Harris

Manchild in the Promised Land.

"Where does one run to when he's already in the promised land?" Claude *Brown opens *Manchild in the Promised Land* (1965) with a political challenge framed as religious metaphor. His *autobiography explores this question, documenting his childhood in Harlem during the 1940s and 1950s, with a broader focus on an entire generation, the children of southern-born African Americans who had moved north after the depression. More specifically, Brown portrays the generational conflict that resulted when parents tried to impose rural ways of survival on their children, who struggled with the "new ways" of the urban street. As *Manchild* unfolds, Brown's sociological analysis becomes more apparent and his political consciousness emerges as he places his own life, and Harlem more generally, within the broader context of American racial and economic patterns.

Several story lines underlie the many specific and sometimes seemingly random episodes in the narrative. Brown charts his flight from *family conflict to the relative emotional security of life on the street with his friends. He finds relief from the street in juvenile detention, again accompanied by his closest friends. He escapes the perils of the drug scene and the real threat of longer incarceration by embracing the intellectual challenge of books, school, and *music; this embrace leads to a time of self-imposed exile from Harlem and a struggle with his *identity and sense of "home." Finally, he returns to Harlem with a redefined sense of self and community.

Brown's "sociological imagination" takes shape in the form of explicit and analytical social criticism. He documents the emerging "plague" of heroin in excruciating detail, an account remarkable for its harsh condemnation of the drug combined with profound (and intimate) compassion for the addicts, many of whom were his closest friends, including his beloved younger brother. In an autobiography framed by biblical and religious metaphor, Brown criticizes charismatic and "sanctified" Harlem *preachers at the same time that he lauds the activism of seminary-trained urban clergy. He gives a sometimes bemused and skeptical analysis of both the Coptic movement and the Black Muslims. Here Brown expresses an impatience with what he calls these "phases" of Harlem *Black Nationalism, but also, especially in regard to the Black Muslims, an appreciation for the social and political impact of their work in the community. *Manchild* also offers an interesting analysis of *class dynamics in Harlem. Brown is notably unapologetic and brutally honest in re-creating his early attitudes toward women and in showing his emerging per-

sonal (and political) maturity in relation to them as he grew older. He also offers revealing commentary on tensions between African American and Jewish communities in New York City.

Manchild in the Promised Land has not been the subject of extensive literary criticism; most book reviews contemporary with its publication focused on the sociological aspects of the book. These mid-1960s reviews varied depending on the political and racial frame of reference of the reviewer. James A. Emanuel and Theodore Gross, the editors of *Dark Symphony* (1968), placed *Manchild* in the long and complex tradition of African American autobiography, citing it as a "modern analogue" to Briton *Hammon's *slave narrative of 1760. The book's sociological emphasis crosses several genres: literary autobiography, sociology, and political analysis.

• Stephen Butterfield, *Black Autobiography in America*, 1974. David L. Dudley, *My Father's Shadow*, 1991.

—Sharon Carson

MANHOOD.

Describing the second of two crucial moments of transformation in *Narrative of the Life of Frederick Douglass* (1845)—the first being the young slave's recognition of an essential relationship between *literacy and *freedom—the former slave says of his subsequent refusal to capitulate to the will of his cruel overseer, Mr. Covey: "you have seen how a man was made a slave; you shall see how a slave was made a man." At least since Douglass's pointed rejection of the dehumanizing powers of America's peculiar institution, the subject of manhood has been a central concern of African American literature. It might even be argued that, before the African American women's literary renaissance and the emergence of black feminist criticism in the 1970s and 1980s, manhood was the tradition's dominant subject. The presentation of nearly all of the crucial issues that motivate the African American critical imagination, including racism, intraracial and interracial relations, *class, nationality, and *sexuality, relies upon notions of an assumed loss of, search for, and desired retrieval of, a sense of power, self-determination, and autonomy of which forms of white oppression like *slavery were believed to rob African American men.

While many key African American literary texts offer resounding critiques of aspects of extant power dynamics, particularly those that seek to naturalize racial oppression, such texts are often either silent about *gender inequity or promote the exercise of male power as a desirable state of affairs. *Novels like Richard *Wright's *Native Son* (1940) and Ernest J. *Gaines's *Of Love and Dust* (1968) seem to fully equate manhood with dominance and, while excoriating racist practices, bemoan the fact that these practices inhibit expression of a dominant black masculinity. In *Native Son*, during the course of his flight from policemen who seek to capture him for the murder of a young white heiress, *Bigger Thomas rapes and murders his girlfriend, Bessie Mears. In the context of the protagonist's gropings toward self-actualization, these acts serve primarily to confirm Bigger's capacity to act in a self-directed fashion, motivated by something other than fear. If

Bessie's victimized body is paraded around the courtroom to stir up more hate against him for killing *Mary Dalton, her victimization serves to stir readers' hatred for an American racism that contributes to such acts of intraracial *violence because it minimizes the possibilities of deep affection among black people. Unless one fails to connect Bessie's murder with Bigger's sexually mercantilistic relationship to her and to his manifest disdain for his mother and sister, one would be hard pressed to assert that Wright is centrally concerned in *Native Son* with condemning such acts of brutality against black women.

In response to the apparent failures of the literature and the unquestioned refusal of its scholars to pay significant analytical attention to the devastating consequences of such displays of power, black women writers and feminist critics began in the 1970s to explore some of the consequences of African American promotion of what we might call melodramas of beset black manhood. Because the inaccessibility of forms of dominant masculinity to African American men was believed to have more impact upon the race's health than the similarly remote possibilities for African American women to enact dominant notions of womanhood, the plight of men was privileged, and evidence of baleful behavior in pursuit of male power was often excused. Certainly one of the most poignant critiques of that view occurs in Toni *Morrison's *Song of Solomon* (1977). Just before *Milkman Dead departs on a journey where he discovers aspects of his impressive familial legacy, one of his sisters informs him that his assumption of masculine privilege and entitlement has negatively impacted the women in his immediate family. As is the case with *Janie Crawford's characterization of Joe Starks's aging private parts as looking like the change of life in Zora Neale *Hurston's *Their Eyes Were Watching God* (1937), Milkman is called upon to gaze figuratively under his trousers, to evaluate his assumptions about manhood that encourage his mistreatment of women. Unable to reconcile himself to the idea that he would be viewed as anything other than the personification of a powerful African American manhood, Joe Starks dies. Unlike Starks, however, Milkman appears to come to understand some of the devastating consequences of the practice of manhood that his familial legacy has bequeathed him, including his responsibility for his cousin and lover Hagar's demise and the pain caused by male desertion of females more generally. In texts like *Song of Solomon* and Alice *Walker's *The *Color Purple* (1982), self-centered enactments of masculine power are subject to critique and change.

This is not to suggest that until the 1970s, all African American texts manifested their authors' blind acceptance of masculine dominion. A careful reading of key texts discourages the view that critiquing unproblematized formulations of black manhood is solely the province of women or totally a post–civil rights phenomenon. Indeed, the seeds of a critique appear even in Douglass's aforementioned *Narrative*, which utilizes such pat masculinist devices as the downplaying of male intimacy with women and the extolling of the virtues of male homosocial

collectives. Despite his mother's herculean efforts to see her young enslaved son, Douglass admits to having been unmoved by the news of her death; despite her significant role in his escape from slavery and in his life generally, he barely discusses his first wife, Anna Murray. However, he waxes poetic about his mind-starved fellow male slaves with whom he plots to escape and who were willing to risk death in order to be taught to read by Douglass. According to Douglass,

> We were linked and interlinked with each other. I loved them with a love stronger than any thing I have experienced since. . . . I believed we would have died for each other. . . . We were one; and as much so by our tempers and dispositions, as by the mutual hardships to which we were necessarily subjected by our condition.

In describing slavery's capacity to blunt filial love and his unsurpassed affection for his compatriots, while failing to render his wife as a significant presence in his life, Douglass contributes to the promotion in African American circles of this masculine script. Largely because of this, Douglass's *Narrative* is viewed by many masculinist and feminist critics alike as helping to establish the contours, possibilities, and limitations of African American manhood. In Valerie Smith's view, Douglass "confirms the myth shared by generations of American men that inner resources alone can lead to success." But in his careful choice of words ("how a slave was made a man"), Douglass insists that rather than confirming myths of manly self-reliance, he is being acted upon, and that his transformation and his liberation are externally prompted.

What Douglass's *Narrative* offers its readers is a provocative formulation of concerns that persist in African American texts during the subsequent century and a half: specifically, the connections between black masculinity and freedom, obstacles to its achievement, and the contributions of others. Seminal texts in the tradition—*dramas such as LeRoi Jones's (Amiri *Baraka's) *Dutchman* (1964), Lorraine *Hansberry's A *Raisin in the Sun* (1958), and August *Wilson's *Fences* (1986); novels such as James Weldon *Johnson's The *Autobiography of an Ex-Colored Man* (1912), James *Baldwin's *Go Tell It on the Mountain* (1953), and Paule *Marshall's Praisesong for the Widow* (1983); *autobiographies such as Richard Wright's *Black Boy* (1945) and The *Autobiography of Malcolm X* (1965)—are concerned with the relationship between black manhood and freedom. For example, Gaines's *Of Love and Dust* focuses primarily upon African American males' efforts to exercise masculine power on a Louisiana plantation where the vestiges of slavery are prominent. Cognizant of the unmanliness of his capitulation to the demands of *Jim Crow, including going to "the nigger room" to be served in the town store, the narrator, Jim Kelly, writes, "I kept telling myself, 'one of these days I'm going to stop this, I'm going to stop this; I'm a man like any other man and one of these days I'm going to stop this.' But I never did. Either I was too thirsty to do it, or after I had been working in the field all day I was just too tired and just didn't care." While not all of these texts are as willing as Gaines's to promote unproblematized equations of manhood and power, all of them investigate manhood by exploring African American male capacity to negotiate circumstances dominated by whites.

After nearly two decades during which representations of and by African American women dominated the imaginative landscape, the 1990s have witnessed the reemergence of masculinity as a significant subject, as evidenced by the Whitney Museum's controversial exhibit, recorded for posterity in the form of *Black Male: Representations of Masculinity in Contemporary American Art* (1994). Perhaps we have reached a moment when African American womanhood and manhood will not compete for representational space and attention but will be seen as equally important to our understanding of art, literature, and subjectivity.

[*See also* Buck; Character Types; Double Consciousness; Feminism; Masking; Minstrelsy; Slave Narrative; Stereotypes; Womanism.]

• Richard Wright, *Eight Men*, 1961. Robert Stepto, *From behind the Veil: A Study of Afro-American Narrative*, 1979. Henry Louis Gates, Jr., ed., *The Classic Slave Narratives*, 1987. Valerie Smith, *Self-Discovery and Authority in Afro-American Narrative*, 1987. David Dudley, *My Father's Shadow: Intergenerational Conflict in African American Men's Autobiography*, 1991. Richard Majors and Janet Mancini Billson, *Cool Pose: The Dilemma of Black Manhood in America*, 1992. Michael Awkward, *Negotiating Difference: Race, Gender, and the Politics of Positionality*, 1995. Marcellus Blount and George Cunningham, eds., *Representing Black Men*, 1995.

—Michael Awkward

Man Who Cried I Am, The. A landmark work, John A. *Williams's *The Man Who Cried I Am* (1967; rpt. 1987) recounts journalist-novelist Max Reddick's struggles against an oppressive, murderous social structure. Terminally ill with colon cancer, Reddick inherits an enormous burden from his recently deceased friend and literary rival, Harry Ames: knowledge of the King Alfred Plan, an international agenda for annihilating all people of African origin. As he considers how to use the information, he reflects on his life and the events leading inevitably to this dilemma. Unaware of how closely he is being watched, Reddick transmits the information to an ally, Minister Q, over a tapped telephone, setting into motion events leading to his murder.

This synopsis risks oversimplification; part of the text's greatness lies in *Williams's stylistic innovations. A chronological *double consciousness controls the narrative, moving simultaneously through a single day in the present and the entire historical range of Reddick's literary and personal experience with racism in America, keying on events in his friendships with other African American writers to inform that movement. The flexibility of the chronological frame, and the subsequent breakdown of received linear preconceptions of history, is one of Williams's most significant contributions to contemporary African American literature. Similarly, his philosophical exploration of the interconnectedness of history and the states of being assigned to African Americans by the power structure sets a standard

upon which writers like Charles R. *Johnson, who acknowledges Williams's influence in *Being and Race: Black Writing since 1970* (1988), have built.

Another significant feature of the text that critics note is Williams's inclusion of thinly disguised portraits of actual events and real people. The 1962 *Prix de Rome* scandal, in which Williams was promised an award and then inexplicably denied it, appears, happening not to Reddick, who arguably represents Williams himself, but to Harry Ames. Ames is unmistakably modeled on Richard *Wright, just as Marion Dawes clearly represents James *Baldwin. Williams does not stop with literary figures, however; Minister Q seems to reflect the ideas and attitudes of *Malcolm X, and Paul Durrell appears to resemble Martin Luther *King, Jr. This revision of the actual historical record indicates Williams's stylistic sophistication; he takes the so-called truth of the era and presents an alternative perspective through the lens of literature, offering in the process an insightful commentary on national and international affairs. Williams's alteration of history and his fusion of "fact" and "fiction" mark *The Man* as a postmodernist work, reflecting the general upheaval regarding definitions of "truth" and "fiction" that characterized American culture in the late 1960s.

Critics generally agree that *The Man* is Williams's finest work, citing the richness of the characterization and the structural complexity of the narrative as reasons. Within the relatively small body of existing criticism, *The Man* has consistently received the most attention. Its postmodern innovations and frank challenging of preconceptions about American history establish it as a crucial work.

• William M. Burke, "The Resistance of John A. Williams: *The Man Who Cried I Am*," *Critique* 15.3 (1974): 5–14. Addison Gayle, Jr., *The Way of the New World: The Black Novel in America*, 1975. Gilbert H. Muller, *John A. Williams*, 1984.

—William R. Nash

MARRANT, JOHN (1755–1791), spiritual autobiographer and Native American captivity narrator. While training to become a Methodist minister in England, John Marrant related the story of his conversion experience and Native American captivity, published in London in 1785 as *A Narrative of the Lord's Wonderful Dealings with John Marrant, A Black*. It became an immediate success all over Europe and, in 1789, appeared in America, where it gained widespread popularity and achieved status as a celebrated captivity tale.

Born a freeman in New York, Marrant spent his youth in the South. In his *Narrative*, he describes the fateful day when he accidentally heard a sermon preached by George Whitefield, the English evangelical minister. Struck by the powerful words, Marrant journeys into the forest in search of spiritual guidance. He is captured by the Cherokees and encounters threatening incidents that he compares to similar events in the life of Jesus Christ. After winning their favor, Marrant attempts to convert the Cherokees as he takes on their dress and manners while expressing appreciation for their culture. Finally they release him, and he embarks upon a religious life.

However, during the Revolutionary War, the British capture him and force him to serve aboard their ships for more than six dangerous years. In England after the war, Marrant studies for the ministry. The final phase of his life is devoted to missionary work in Canada, which is described in Marrant's *Journal*, published in 1790.

[*See also* Autobiography.]

• Sidney Kaplan, *The Black Presence in the Era of the American Revolution, 1770–1800*, 1973. Angelo Costanzo, *Surprizing Narrative: Olaudah Equiano and the Beginnings of Black Autobiography*, 1987.   —Angelo Costanzo

MARRIAGE. African American literature depicts the married relationship as vulnerable to such forces in African American life as the racism in larger society and discrimination based on color within the African American community. African American writers may use the wedding ceremony and feast to satirize false community values and pretensions. And African American female writers, especially contemporary ones, may depict marriage from a feminist perspective. But since the period of *slavery, a happy marriage and *family life, whatever the difficulties of attainment, are ideals, as they have been in American culture in general.

Some of the earliest African American literature as well as later historical fiction depict the devastating effect of slavery on African American marriage. Such *slave narratives as the *Narrative of the Life of Moses Grundy, Late a Slave in the United States* (1844), *The Narrative of Lundsford Lane* (1842), and the *Narrative of the Life of Henry Bibb* (1849) illustrate how slaves valued their marriages and family ties, despite their lack of legal status. Frances Ellen Watkins *Harper's antislavery poem "The Fugitive's Wife" (1857) recounts the devastating pain the slave woman suffered in separation from her husband and children. In the abolitionist slave narrative *Incidents in the Life of a Slave Girl* (1861) by Harriet A. *Jacobs and the historical novel *Jubilee* (1966) by Margaret *Walker, the slave woman's desire to marry the man of her choice is thwarted by her master. In Alex *Haley's historical novel *Roots* (1976), Noah's failed escape attempt thwarts his and Kizzy's desire to spend the rest of their lives together.

Renderings of interracial liaisons and marriages, whether de facto or legal, have been common in African American literature. Early African American writers used often tragic liaisons between African American women, usually *mulattoes, and white men to protest against race prejudice and social discrimination. In *Clotel, or The President's Daughter* (1853), by William Wells *Brown, the first published novel by an African American, Clotel, the daughter of Thomas Jefferson and his former housekeeper, becomes the mistress of a young white aristocrat. *The Garies and Their Friends* (1857) by Frank J. *Webb, the second published novel by an African American, depicts an interracial marriage in that of the Garies. The long narrative poem *The Octoroon* (1901) by Albery Allson *Whitman depicts the doomed love of a beautiful octoroon and a young white man, who had planned a permanent liaison with her. In *The *House

Behind the Cedars (1900) by Charles Waddell *Chesnutt, the beautiful octoroon *Rena Walden becomes engaged to the blue blood George Tryon, who rejects her after learning of her mixed racial background. *Helga Crane, the heroine of Nella *Larsen's *Quicksand* (1928), rejects the marriage offer of a Danish painter because she cannot bring herself to marry a white man. In James Weldon *Johnson's *Autobiography of an Ex-Colored Man* (1927), the narrator's final step in *passing into the white world or becoming an "ex-colored man" is marrying a white woman. A marriage between a biracial man and a southern white woman in Frank *Hercules' "I Want a Black Doll" (1967) is unable to withstand the external pressures fostered by a racist society. In her historical novel *Sally Hemings* (1967), Barbara *Chase-Riboud returns to the liaison of Thomas Jefferson and the nearly white Sally Hemings. Their relationship persists for thirty-eight years because of her strong resemblance to his deceased wife (Hemings's half-sister).

African American literature also examines the internal color caste system in the African American community and its negative impact on marriage. Chesnutt's story "The Wife of His Youth" (1899) presents a leader of the *Blue Vein Society triumphing over his own class and color prejudices by acknowledging, after decades of separation, his illiterate, dark-skinned plantation wife. In *The *Blacker the Berry* (1929) by Wallace *Thurman, the heroine Emma Lou's mulatto mother and grandmother believe that selective marriage is a means of diminishing traces of their family's African ancestry in each generation. In Gwendolyn *Brooks's poem "the ballad of chocolate Mabbie," the dark-skinned heroine is jilted by her lover for a light-skinned girl. In her *Maud Martha* (1953), the heroine's awareness of her husband's preference for light-skinned women is a source of pain and insecurity. Bart Johnson in Dorothy *West's *The Living Is Easy* (1948), which negatively depicts African American middle-class values, chooses his wife Cleo on the basis of her good looks and light skin. As a result he finds himself trapped with a cold-hearted woman who calls him "nigger" and rarely allows him into her bed.

Novels such as *The *Bluest Eye* (1970) by Toni *Morrison, *Song of Solomon* (1977), also by Morrison, and *Linden Hills* (1985) by Gloria *Naylor similarly provide portraits of the sterile, often sexless marriages of the African American middle class. In *The Bluest Eye* Geraldine fakes orgasm in the marriage bed, yet receives a sensual pleasure from the feel of her pet cat in her lap. In *Song of Solomon* Ruth Foster Dead, whose husband refuses to touch her, compensates for the deadness of her marriage by overprotectiveness toward her son Milkman. Four generations of Needed wives in *Linden Hills* cope with psychologically abusive, sexless marriages through eating disorders, aphrodisiacs, and suicide.

In *Linden Hills*, *Brown Girl, Brownstones* (1959) by Paule *Marshall, and "Roselily" (1973) by Alice *Walker, wedding ceremonies and feasts are important. In the two novels lavish and costly wedding feasts are used to satirize the pretensions of the

African American middle-class community of Linden Hills and the upwardly mobile Barbadian immigrant community of Brooklyn. The wedding feast in *Brown Girl* becomes a community ritual for ostracizing Deighton Boyce for his flouting of its materialistic values. The dispirited bride, a young Barbadian woman in love with an African American, marries a Barbadian at the coercion of her mother. In *Linden Hills* a homosexual man, at the coercion of his father, marries to conform to the family-oriented values of his community. "Roselily" takes place during the wedding of the heroine and a man she does not love. The words of the marriage ceremony provide an ironic counterpoint to the heroine's musings on her past relationships and her present marriage of convenience.

Attitudes toward marriage and values surrounding marriage partners are crucial to the well-being of the heroine in works by African American female writers in particular. The nineteenth-century writer Frances Ellen Watkins *Harper anticipates some of the concerns of twentieth-century African American female writers. In her poem "Advice to Girls" (1854), she cautions her female readers against choosing a husband by his physical appearance. Her short story *"The Two Offers" (1859), generally considered the first published story by an African American, suggests that marriage is but one option open to an intelligent, socially conscious woman.

Angela Murray, the heroine of *Plum Bun* (1929) by Jessie Redmon *Fauset, exercises that option wisely. At the beginning of the novel she intends to pass for white and marry white and rich. Marriage to her white knight in shining armor, Roger Fielding, eludes her, however. Ironically at the point she puts skin color, money, and marriage in their proper perspective, Roger proposes, but he is no longer compatible with her new value system. Instead she marries Anthony Cross, a quaint but honorable African American.

Larsen's *Quicksand* reflects an enduring feminist perspective. Its heroine, the beautiful and cultured Helga Crane, impulsively marries a storefront preacher following a religious conversion. Subsequently finding herself trapped in a quicksand of childbearing and drudgery in the rural South, she questions the institution of marriage: "This sacred thing of which parsons and other Christian folk ranted so sanctimoniously, how immoral—according to their own standards—it could be."

In Dorothy West's short story "Hannah Bye" (1926), marriage becomes like a quagmire for the heroine. Hannah marries at twenty to escape social confinement. In due course marriage stifles her, but she sees no other possibility than passive acceptance of her fate, including an unwanted pregnancy.

Women in Terri *McMillan's novels, whether the lower-class heroine of *Mama* (1987) or the middle-class heroines of *Disappearing Acts* (1989) and *Waiting to Exhale* (1992), look for happiness (often unsuccessfully) in the conventional marriage relationship. But a realistic, mature outlook on life for McMillan's heroines may include accepting the idea of never finding Mr. Right. In *Waiting to Exhale*, Robin ad-

mits, "As much as I want to get married, I realize that just because I want to settle down doesn't mean I have to settle. I'm going to have to learn to stand on my own two feet. Learn to rely on Robin."

From its beginnings to the present, African American literature has depicted a successful marriage for African Americans as a worthy ideal but, for a variety of reasons, one extremely difficult to achieve and maintain. In addition to the ordinary strains found in any marriage, it is subject to the unique stresses borne by the individual of African descent in America.

• Trudier Harris and Thadious M. Davis, eds., *DLB*, vol. 33, *Afro-American Fiction Writers after 1955*, 1984. Trudier Harris and Thadious Davis, eds., *DLB*, vol. 50, *Afro-American Writers before the Harlem Renaissance*, 1986. Trudier Harris and Thadious M. Davis, eds., *DLB*, vol. 76, *Afro-American Writers, 1940–1955*, 1988. Blyden Jackson, *A History of Afro-American Literature*, 1989. Valerie Smith, *African American Writers*, 1991. Frank N. Magill, *Masterpieces of African-American Literature*, 1992. Ann duCille, *The Coupling Convention*, 1993.

—Phiefer L. Browne

Marrow of Tradition, The.

Marrow of Tradition, The. Published in 1901, at the nadir of American race relations and the zenith of fictional apologies for the *Jim Crow South, Charles Waddell *Chesnutt's second and most ambitious *novel offers a complex retelling of the 1898 Wilmington, North Carolina, "race riot." Though somewhat ambiguous in its messages to African Americans—and labeled too "bitter" by former Chesnutt booster William Dean Howells—*The Marrow of Tradition*'s incisive critique of white terrorism, national racial hysteria, and segregationist logic make it one of the most significant African American socioliterary statements of its day.

Chesnutt would have welcomed such a description, for he envisioned the book as his generation's successor to *Uncle Tom's Cabin*. His main plot traces the intersecting fortunes and genealogies of two southern families, the Carterets and Millers. Philip Carteret, the reactionary editor of "Wellington's" white newspaper, campaigns against the supposed domination of the post-Reconstruction South by African Americans. Enlisting the aid of an equally racist aristocrat (General Belmont) and a former overseer (Captain McBane), Carteret engineers a devastating race riot that purges Wellington of most of its African Americans and restores "rightful" power to the white supremacists. Carteret's wife Olivia, for her part, is determined to repudiate the legal and moral claims of her *mulatto half-sister—Janet Miller—on their father's estate. Janet's husband, William Miller, is a middle-class, mixed-blood physician whose considerable medical skills are spurned by Wellington whites. At the climax of the novel, after Carteret's rioters have burned Miller's hospital and a stray bullet has killed the Millers' child, the Carterets must plead with the African American doctor to save their own dying son. At first refusing, Miller agrees to see the child only at the direction of his wife. The novel ends with Miller poised at the foot of the Carterets' stairs, ready to try to save the boy's life.

To this principal story Chesnutt adds an array of subplots and secondary characters, including an African American *mammy and her obsequious grandson, whose loyalty to whites fails to save them during the riot; an honest aristocrat and his degenerate heir, for whose crimes an innocent African American is nearly lynched; a well-meaning but ineffectual white liberal; and a powerful African American laborer, who vows to kill McBane in revenge for the death of his father. While many of these subordinate characters are drawn stereotypically, the views of Josh Green, the laborer, represent a strong counterphilosophy to Miller's accommodationism and for many early reviewers offered proof that Chesnutt endorsed African American militancy. Later critics, however, generally align the text's (and Chesnutt's) sympathies with Miller, citing Josh's death as evidence that violent resistance—though potentially useful—must finally be sacrificed for more conciliatory methods. Yet even these readers acknowledge the irresolution of the novel's ending; the optimistic image of Miller climbing the Carterets' stairs provides no guarantee that reconciliation will prove an appropriate strategy. Indeed, the tensions implicit at the novel's close aptly represent the volatile historical and literary contexts within which Chesnutt wrote.

[*See also* Double Consciousness; Miscegenation; Plantation Tradition; Protest Literature; Violence.]

• William L. Andrews, *The Literary Career of Charles W. Chesnutt*, 1980. Eric J. Sundquist, *To Wake the Nations: Race in the Making of American Literature*, 1993.

—William A. Gleason

MARSHALL, PAULE (b. 1929), journalist, short fiction writer, novelist, essayist, lecturer, and educator. Paule Marshall (née Burke) is the daughter of second-generation Barbadian immigrant parents Samuel and Ada Burke. Although Marshall was born in Brooklyn, the influence of her West Indian ancestry has been profound in her writing. Even as a little girl, before her "formal" introduction to the world of African American literature, the sounds, the smells, the sights, the entire culture of the West Indies were a part of her future training as a world-renowned novelist, especially through the daily gatherings of her mother and her female West Indian friends around the kitchen table to discuss, in the language of a kind of folk poetry, personal, neighborhood, and world events. Paule Marshall has lovingly deemed her mother and her neighbor-friends kitchen poets. According to her, they are the foundation for all the beauty and skill with which she employs the often colorful and irreverent language of the "Bajan" (Barbadian) community in her novels.

As a young girl, Paule Marshall was a voracious reader. She grew up reading the sweeping English novels of Charles Dickens, William Makepeace Thackeray, and Henry Fielding. However, it was not until her discovery of the great African American poet Paul Laurence *Dunbar that she became aware of another type of literature, one that spoke to her like no other that she had read before and that expressed to her the possibility that she, too, might someday become a great writer.

The road to becoming the kind of writer who would inspire others to follow in her footsteps was long and hard. After graduating cum laude from Brooklyn College in 1953, she worked at various jobs to make ends meet. Even with her high degree of accomplishment, the prospects for a woman, especially an African American, for finding gainful employment were almost nonexistent. As would characterize the remainder of her career as a writer, Paule Marshall was the exception to the rule. She worked as a librarian for the New York Public Library and then, at first as a research assistant and later as a full-time journalist, for the once very influential African American magazine *Our World* (1955–1956). Her writing assignments would take her to parts of the Caribbean and South America, experiences she would later use to write her collection of short stories *Soul Clap Hands and Sing*.

Marshall ended up leaving *Our World* and married her first husband, Kenneth Marshall, in 1957. In 1958, she gave birth to her first and only child, Evan-Keith. Still, Marshall was not satisfied with the role deemed appropriate for her and most other women of the 1950s, that is, wife and mother exclusively; she needed more. A novel was slowly but surely forming in her consciousness, but because of her marriage and the birth of her child, she had very little free time for her writing. She needed, paraphrasing Virginia Woolf, a room of her own. Against the wishes of her husband, she enlisted someone to help with Evan-Keith and rented a small apartment in order to devote more time to her fledgling novel. Two years later, in 1959, her first novel, *Brown Girl, Brownstones*, was published.

At the time of its publication, few African American women were writing, had written, or had works still in print. There were, of course, Zora Neale *Hurston's seminal novel *Their Eyes Were Watching God* (1937), which would later serve as a model for Marshall's novel *Praisesong for the Widow*, Dorothy *West's novel *The Living Is Easy* (1948), and Gwendolyn *Brooks's singular novel *Maud Martha* (1953). According to Paule Marshall, Brooks's novel had the most influence upon her as a beginning writer.

Although critically acclaimed, *Maud Martha*, like many of the works by African American women writers during the 1940s and 1950s, was ignored commercially and quickly went out of print. Still, it had a profound influence upon Marshall and her work because for the first time since Hurston's *Their Eyes Were Watching God*, a novel focused on the interior life of an African American female protagonist. It went well beyond the stereotypes of African American women portrayed in the literature of the dominant culture. With the publication of *Brown Girl, Brownstones*, Paule Marshall took up the reigns passed down from Zora Neale Hurston to Dorothy West and Ann *Petry and finally to Gwendolyn Brooks.

Brown Girl, Brownstones is a milestone in African American fiction not only because it goes against stereotype in its portrayal of African Americans but also because for the first time since Claude *McKay, another West Indian immigrant writer, a connection had been made in literature between African American people and their West Indian counterparts. For both writers, the accurate depiction of language is vital for expressing the similarities and differences between the two cultures. The language of *Brown Girl, Brownstones* is exquisitely rendered. The feel and flavor of the West Indies is beautifully expressed through the language of protagonist *Selina Boyce's parents, especially her mother, Silla. Words like "c'dear" (dear), "lady-folks," and "wunna" (you) are sprinkled liberally and lovingly throughout the text. It is testimony to Paule Marshall's power as a writer to have been able to evoke such genuinely oral magic on paper.

Marshall's next literary project, published in 1961, is a collection of short fiction entitled *Soul Clap Hands and Sing*. The collection of four novellas, called "Barbados," "British Guiana," "Brooklyn," and "Brazil" concerns an overall theme heretofore unexplored in African American fiction, that is, the elderly in literature. The central characters in each of the four novellas are aged men who have consciously given up genuine human feeling for materialism and greed. The novellas explore the consequences of renouncing one's humanity for the seeming quiet and comfort of old age.

Because Marshall is an extremely meticulous writer and because of other demands upon her time, such as raising a family and teaching, eight years elapsed between the publication of *Soul Clap Hands and Sing* and Marshall's second novel, *The *Chosen Place, the Timeless People* (1969). The pressure of being both wife and mother as well as career woman proved to be too much for her marriage, and she was divorced during the writing of this second novel.

The Chosen Place, the Timeless People is a culmination of all the themes and concerns that Marshall had heretofore explored in her fiction. Through the characterization of its unforgettable protagonist, Merle Kimbona, the novel explores the search for and reconciliation of the self with an African diasporic historical past as well as the themes of ageism, sexism, Western hegemony, and nuclear proliferation. After the publication of this novel, Marshall married Nourry Menard in 1970.

The year 1983 was very important to Paule Marshall's career. It marked not only the publication of her third novel, *Praisesong for the Widow*, but also of another collection of short stories entitled *Reena and Other Stories*, which included her most anthologized short story, "To Da-duh, in Memoriam." In *Praisesong for the Widow*, Marshall returns to familiar themes. The story centers around Avatara "Avey" Johnson, a rather prim and proper middle-aged, middle-class, sixty-two-year-old African American woman who journeys on a Caribbean cruise only to find herself in a kind of psychic distress. Almost mystically forced to abandon her cruise, she finds herself drawn into a kind of reverse middle passage to the island of Carriacou, where she will undergo a reintegration of that part of her African heritage that she has allowed to lie dormant within her for so many years.

Marshall's *Daughters* (1991) is also about self-actualization. Marshall was inspired to write this particular novel by an epigraph on a program to an Alvin Ailey Dance Company recital that she attended in 1983. It read, "Little girl of all the daughters, / You ain't no more slave, / You's a woman now." The novel centers upon a young woman, Ursa Beatrice Mackenzie, the only child born to an American mother, Estell, and a West Indian politician father, Primus. She has been almost smothered by the sheer forcefulness of her father's personality, a pattern that continues well into her adult life. Through the course of the novel, Ursa must not only wrest herself from the controlling nature of her father, she must also bring him back to being the sort of decent man he was before he became involved in the corrupt politics of the island of Triunion.

Paule Marshall is without a doubt one of the major and most influential African American writers. She is a pioneer in the exploration of themes such as ageism, sexual harassment, and nuclear proliferation. With a career that spans almost half a century, she continues to garner both critical raves as well as literary success. In 1992 she was awarded the prestigious MacArthur Prize Fellowship for lifetime achievement. Paule Marshall continues to be a writer's writer, both steady and enduring.

[*See also* Diasporic Literature; West Indian Literature.]

• Paule Marshall, "Shaping the World of My Art," *New Letters* 40 (Autumn 1973): 97–112. Helen Ruth Houston, "Paule Marshall," in *The Afro-American Novel 1965–1975*, 1977, pp. 117–122. Paule Marshall, "The Making of a Writer: From the Poets in the Kitchen," *New York Times Book Review*, 9 Jan. 1983, 3, 34–35. Barbara Christian, "Paule Marshall," in *DLB*, vol. 33, *Afro-American Fiction Writers after 1955*, eds. Thadious M. Davis and Trudier Harris, 1984, pp. 103–117. Daryl Dance, "An Interview with Paule Marshall," in *Southern Review*, 28 Jan. 1992, pp. 1–20.

—Keith Bernard Mitchell

MARVIN X (b. 1944), poet, playwright, essayist, director, and lecturer. Marvin Ellis Jackmon was born on 29 May 1944 in Fowler, California. He attended high school in Fresno and received a BA and MA in English from San Francisco State College (now San Francisco State University). The mid-1960s were formative years for Jackmon. He became involved in theater, founded his own press, published several plays and volumes of poetry, and became increasingly alienated because of racism and the Vietnam War. Under the influence of Elijah Muhammad, he became a Black Muslim and has published since then under the names El Muhajir and Marvin X. He has also used the name Nazzam al Fitnah Muhajir.

Marvin X and Ed *Bullins founded the Black Arts/West Theatre in San Francisco in 1966, and several of his plays were staged during that period in San Francisco, Oakland, New York, and by local companies across the United States. His one-act play *Flowers for the Trashman* was staged in San Francisco in 1965 and was included in the anthology *Black Fire* (1968); a musical version, *Take Care of Business*, was produced in 1971. The play presents the confrontation between two cellmates in a jail—one a young African American college student, the other a middle-aged white man. Another one-act play, *The Black Bird*, a Black Muslim allegory in which a young man offers lessons in life awareness to two small girls, appeared in 1969 and was included in *New Plays from the Black Theatre* that year. Several other plays, including *The Trial, Resurrection of the Dead*, and *In the Name of Love*, have been successfully staged, and Marvin X has remained an important advocate of African American theater.

In 1967, Marvin X was convicted, during the Vietnam War, for refusing induction and fled to Canada; eventually he was arrested in Honduras, was returned to the United States, and was sentenced to five months in prison. In his statement on being sentenced—later reprinted in *Black Scholar* (1971) and also in Clyde Taylor's anthology, *Vietnam and Black America* (1973)—he argues that

> Any judge, any jury, is guilty of insanity that would have the nerve to judge and convict and imprison a black man because he did not appear in a courtroom on a charge of refusing to commit crimes against humanity, crimes against his own brothers and sisters, the peace-loving people of Vietnam.

Marvin X founded El Kitab Sudan publishing house in 1967; several of his books of poetry and proverbs have been published there. Much of Marvin X's poetry is militant in its anger at American racism and injustice. For example, in "Did You Vote Nigger?" he uses rough dialect and directs his irony at African Americans who believe in the government but are actually its pawns. Many of the proverbs in *The Son of Man* (1969) express alienation from white America. However, many of Marvin X's proverbs and poems express more concern with what African Americans can do positively for themselves, without being paralyzed by hatred. He insists that the answer is to concentrate on establishing a racial identity and to "understand that art is celebration of Allah." The poems in *Fly to Allah, Black Man Listen* (1969), and other volumes from his El Kitab Sudan press are characterized by their intensity and their message of racial unity under a religious banner.

Marvin X has remained active as a lecturer, teacher, theatrical producer, editor, and exponent of Islam. His work in advocating racial cohesion and religious dedication as an antidote to the legacy of racism he saw around him in the 1960s and 1970s made him an important voice of his generation.

• Lorenzo Thomas, "Marvin X," in *DLB*, vol. 38, *Afro-American Writers after 1955: Dramatists and Prose Writers*, eds. Thadious Davis and Trudier Harris, 1985, pp. 177–184. Bernard L. Peterson, Jr., "Marvin X," in *Contemporary Black American Playwrights and Their Plays*, 1988, pp. 332–333. "El Muhajir," in *CA*, vol. 26, eds. Hal May and James G. Lesniak, 1989, pp. 132–133.
                                    —Michael E. Greene

MARY DALTON. In Richard *Wright's *Native Son*, Mary Dalton is the daughter of the wealthy white Chicago realtor Mr. Dalton, who owns the rat-infested slum tenement in which *Bigger Thomas and his family live and who hires Bigger as his family chauffeur. Mary's chief interaction with Bigger occurs during and after the time she involves him, as

her chauffeur, in her clandestine love affair with the Communist Jan Erlone. She is oblivious to the discomfort she causes Bigger, who has always known whites only from a distance and who is frightened and intimidated by her socioeconomic class as well as her race. Mary and Jan force Bigger to accompany them to a restaurant in the ghetto for dinner. Later Bigger drives Mary and Jan around the city while they drink and make love in the backseat. Jan leaves the intoxicated Mary with Bigger to be driven home. Bigger half carries her to her room and becomes sexually aroused by this contact with her. The blind Mrs. Dalton enters the room, and Bigger, terrified, forces a pillow down over Mary's face in order to keep her quiet. By the time Mrs. Dalton leaves the room, Mary has suffocated, killed by Bigger's dread of the consequences of a black man being discovered in the bedroom of a white woman. Bigger, terror-stricken, carries Mary's body to the cellar in a trunk that was to accompany her on a trip to Detroit the next day. He forces her body into the blazing furnace, then leaves, imagining a version of the events of the preceding evening that will point to Jan as Mary's murderer. Later on, he feels a sense of exhilaration because in his violence against Mary he has dared to act outside the conventions governing interrelations between the races.

[*See also* Stereotypes.]
                                    —Donald B. Gibson

MARY RAMBO is both mother and spiritual guide for the narrator in Ralph *Ellison's *Invisible Man* (1952), who at this point in his life is trying to find a new identity. The narrator survived a paint-factory accident that hospitalized him and resulted in a symbolic rebirth after which his character is like a blank page. It is Mary Rambo who writes his new name and nurtures his new awareness of himself. Like Toni *Morrison's Circe in *Song of Solomon* (1977), Mary is the preserver of Black life who helps carry on a Black tradition. She becomes physical and spiritual provider/sustainer for the narrator.

When Mary first appears, her speech and physical characteristics (she is a "big dark woman") suggest the stereotypical southern *mammy. But Mary is no mammy; she typifies that down-home maternalism that is evident in the extended family of African Americans. And in her own way she is a race-conscious individual who believes strongly that if Blacks are to survive it will be through Black youths. When the narrator becomes unsure of his future it is Mary who encourages him: "It's you young folks what's going to make the changes. Y'all's the ones. You got to lead and . . . move us all on up a little higher."

Finding the narrator on the streets of Harlem, Mary nurses him back to health and then helps him to move from the sterile atmosphere of Men's House to a more fertile environment where he can recognize his African heritage. To this effect the narrator admits that Mary was "a force, a stable familiar force like something out of my past which kept me from whirling off into some unknown which I dared not face." Mary is no Beatrice, guiding the narrator through the underworld of Harlem, but she is a maternal figure and a moral gauge who helps the narrator on his way to self-determination.

—Ralph Reckley, Sr.

MASKING. A deceptive role-playing and a shrewd survival strategy, masking has historically been used by blacks in the presence of whites to maintain some semblance of empowerment in a racially prejudiced society. Masking, or role-playing a preconceived false image acceptable to whites, through expressive forms of deceptive behavior such as "laughing to keep from crying," "Tomming," or "Jumping Jim Crow," hides the true feelings, frustrations, cleverness, and sophisticated ambiguities of *identity held by the mask wearers when they are in racial conflict or competition. Masking one's true identity with an outer demeanor or perfected theatrics or showmanships is also called "playing the game." It is used to get ahead or to accomplish an intellectual feat that a black would not otherwise be able to achieve. Zora Neale *Hurston's poignant dramatics as a southern folk person in Harlem and as a conning autobiographer are examples of masking for self-advancement with philanthropists. Various manifestations of masking one's true identity in the guise of a second compromising racial image are evident in W. E. B. *Du Bois's *double consciousness or Black Veil theory of two black identities in America; Ralph *Ellison's grandfather character in *Invisible Man* (1952) who advises his grandson to "overcome 'em with yeses"; Paul Laurence *Dunbar's poem "We Wear the Mask," which states that it "grins, lies, hides our cheeks, and shades our eyes"; Charles Waddell *Chesnutt's *passing and conjure stories; Langston *Hughes's *Not without Laughter*; and Richard Wright's *Uncle Tom's Children*.

[*See also* Coon; Folklore; High John the Conqueror; Minstrelsy; Stepin Fetchit; Stereotypes; Trickster.]

—Pearlie Peters

MATHEUS, JOHN F. (1887–1983), short story writer, playwright, and book reviewer. John Frederick Matheus was born 10 September 1887, in Keyser, West Virginia, one of four sons, to Susan Brown Matheus (a housewife) and William Matheus (a bank messenger and tannery worker). He received his early schooling in Steubenville, Ohio, where his family moved when he was young. He graduated cum laude from Western Reserve University in 1910, received his AM degree from Columbia in 1921, pursued graduate studies at the Sorbonne in Paris (1925), and taught modern languages for more than a decade (1910–1922) at Florida A&M College in Tallahassee.

Author of more than twenty short stories, most of his writings in the 1920s serve as fictional counterparts to the urban literature of the *Harlem Renaissance writers. Themes of race pride, white hatred, and family conflict inform his early fiction. "Fog" (awarded first prize by *Opportunity, May 1925) exposes the cloud of race prejudice that envelops the minds of various races during a disastrous train ride one foggy night in a West Virginia coal-mining area.

"Clay" (*Opportunity*, Oct. 1926) describes a black tenant farmer's son who dares to knife a white man who accuses him of stealing a cow. In these stories and in several others, the dialect and folk sayings of illiterate southern blacks reveal the influence of Paul Laurence *Dunbar.

Matheus wrote six plays: *Black Damp, 'Cruiter, Guitar, Ouanga!, Tambour,* and *Ti Yette.* Most of these give glimpses of oppressive African American life. Set in West Georgia in 1918. 'Cruiter details the disintegration of a poor African American family when a northern recruiter separates an elderly grandmother from her grandson, who takes a better job in a munitions factory in Detroit. *Ti Yette,* set in New Orleans in 1855, reveals the tensions between two adult Creole siblings: Racine, the dark-hued nationalist brother who plans to exile himself to Haiti; and Ti Yette, his sister, declared white by a court order processed by her future husband, a white lawyer.

"Sallicoco," another of Matheus's short stories appearing in *Opportunity* (Sept. 1937), grew out of his visit to Liberia, where he served on the U.S. League of Nations Commission (1931) to investigate *slavery. To free her people, the Grebo maiden Sallicoco brings food laced with poison to northern Mendi soldiers who, with government sanction, have forced the warlike Grebos into slavelike labor to build a road leading to a rubber plantation. The nationalist theme is evident, but the story is marred by poor plot development.

After the 1930s, most of Matheus's work related to his teaching profession. He wrote numerous articles and book reviews during his lengthy professional career at West Virginia State College (1922–1953); Maryland State College (1953–1954); Dillard University, New Orleans (1954–1957); Morris Brown College, Atlanta (1958–1959); Texas Southern University, Houston (1959–1961); Hampton Institute, Hampton, Virginia (1961–1962); and Kentucky State College (1962). His reviews appearing in *CLA Journal* in the 1960s examined the usefulness of foreign language texts for the classroom. In 1974, Matheus privately issued a collection of his short stories, which Leonard A. Slade, Jr., edited. Finally, he served as treasurer of the College Language Association until 1975. Matheus's plays and short stories celebrate the indomitable will of his race in rural, sometimes southern, America at a time when much of African American literature concentrated on the urban North.

• Benjamin Brawley, *The Negro Genius: A New Appraisal of the Achievement of the American Negro in Literature and the Fine Arts,* 1966. Margaret Perry, "John F. Matheus," in *DLB,* vol. 51, *Afro-American Writers from the Harlem Renaissance to 1940,* ed. Trudier Harris, 1987, pp. 196–200.

—Rita B. Dandridge

MATHIS, SHARON BELL (b. 1937), children's and young adult author, columnist, librarian, and educator. Sharon Bell Mathis's concern for the welfare of young people is evident in her career as a teacher and librarian, but closest to her heart is her role as author. Mathis explains that "I write to salute the strength in Black children and to say to them,

'Stay strong, stay Black and stay alive'" (quoted in *Something about the Author*, vol. 3, 1987).

Born in Atlantic City, New Jersey, Mathis grew up in the Bedford-Stuyvesant area of Brooklyn, where she attended parochial schools. Her parents, John Willie and Alice Mary (Frazier) Bell, exposed her to a vast array of literary works and encouraged her to write poems, stories, and plays. Despite her affinity for this work, however, Mathis decided not to pursue a career as an author, believing that she would neither be able to make a living at it nor be as great a contributor as were Richard *Wright and other authors whom she admired. In 1960, after graduating from Morgan State College (now Morgan State University) in Baltimore with a BA in sociology, Mathis began teaching.

1969 marked the beginning of her literary career when "The Fire Escape" was published in *News Explorer* and she was named director of the children's literature division of the newly formed D.C. Black Writers Workshop. A year later, *Brooklyn Story* (1970) appeared and two of her poems, "Ladies Magazine" and "R.S.V.P.," were included in Nikki *Giovanni's *Night Comes Softly: An Anthology of Black Female Voices*.

Mathis's second book, *Sidewalk Story*, was chosen as one of the Child Study Association of America's Children's Books of the Year. Her third, *Teacup Full of Roses* (1972), was chosen as one of the Child Study Association of America's Children's Books of the Year, one of the *New York Times* Best Books of the Year, one of the American Library Association's Best Young Adult Books, and was a runner-up for the Coretta Scott King Award. During this period, Mathis was also serving as a writer in residence at Howard University while at work on a biography of Ray Charles. Starting in 1972, she became the author of "Ebony Juniors Speak!," a monthly column in *Ebony Jr!*, and "Society and Youth," a biweekly column in *Liteside: D.C. Buyers Guide*.

The juvenile biography *Ray Charles* (1973) won the Coretta Scott King Award in 1974 and was the inspiration for her next book, *Listen for the Fig Tree* (1974). *The Hundred Penny Box* (1975), in which the main character, like Mathis's own grandfather, keeps a collection of pennies, was chosen as a *Boston Globe-Horn Book* Honor Book and was the basis for a children's film. *Cartwheels* (1977) focuses on three girls' attempts to change their lives by winning a gymnastics competition. There was a long hiatus until 1991, when *Red Dog Blue Fly* was published.

Sharon Bell Mathis enables the young person to "stay strong, stay Black and stay alive" by infusing her works with references to other notable Black artists and art forms. Excerpts from Black gospel songs and Bible verses, plus quotes from African poet and political leader Léopold Sédar Senghor and African American poets Nikki Giovanni and June *Jordan, salute the heritage to which she attributes her achievements: "My success is due to the glorious African blood which flows throughout my body."

• Frances Smith Foster, "Sharon Bell Mathis," in *DLB*, vol. 33, *Afro-American Fiction Writers after 1955*, eds. Thadious M. Davis and Trudier Harris, 1984, pp. 170–173. *Something about the Author Autobiography Series*, ed. Adele Sarkissian, vol. 3, 1987, pp. 162–163. "Mathis Sharon Bell," in *Something about the Author*, vol. 58, ed. Anne Commire, 1990, pp. 124–132. *Who's Who in America*, vol. 2, 1994, p. 2252.
—Saundra Liggins

MATRIARCH. Matriachs have been maligned as well as praised in African American culture and literature. Strong black women who draw their moral force from Christianity and participation in a variety of fundamentalist churches, matriarchs are usually older if not elderly, have children and grandchildren, and are intimately involved in—if not downright controlling of—the affairs of their offspring. In African American literature, matriarchs and offspring often reside in the same space, thereby increasing the potential for strained relationships. The strength of the matriarch is thus her blessing as well as her curse. The strength certainly enables her to endure the indignity of manual labor, particularly *domestic work, in caring for her family, but it is also frequently the cause of conflict within the family.

Two of the most strikingly delineated matriarchs in American literature are Dilsey in William Faulkner's *The Sound and the Fury* (1929) and *Mama Lena Younger in Lorraine *Hansberry's *A *Raisin in the Sun* (1959). Dilsey bosses black folks and white folks; she controls her grandson Luster as effectively as she controls Benjie, the retarded Compson adult male. She knows the habits of the whites for whom she works and is able to exert her moral influence with them even as she exerts it with her own family. Her physical size is commensurate with her moral strength, and she is a force with whom even the arrogant Jason Compson has to deal. Mama Lena Younger shares size and moral strength with Dilsey as she orders her thirty-five-year-old son *Walter Lee Younger to act like a man and not allow his wife Ruth to have an abortion and as she beats Walter Lee when he loses the insurance money paid for the death of his father. Mama Lena's zeal for making sure that her family (Walter Lee, Ruth, her daughter *Beneatha Younger, and her grandson Travis) is morally upright carries the attendant risk of stunting the emotional growth of all of them. With God as her baton, Mama Lena wants to lead everyone into the promised land. Although she makes a slight effort to turn the reins of control over to Walter Lee, it is questionable at the end of the play whether that presumed transfer has been real or just another ploy Mama Lena uses to keep her family in line.

Frequently viewed as emasculators, matriarchal black women have earned criticism historically as well as in the literature. The charge that black women have been too vocal or too much in the forefront in matters in which black men and women were involved has surfaced and resurfaced throughout African American history. *The Moynihan Report* (1965) identified strong black women as the source of major problems in black communities; the report was used to shape public policy affecting blacks. During the *civil rights movement, black women were urged to curtail their strength in order to give black men an opportunity to have their day in the sun. Michele Wallace's *Black Macho and the Myth of the Superwoman* (1978) tried to shed new light on the problem. Matriarchs and the presumed effects they cause, therefore, continue to be a source of contentious debate in African American communities and a site for voyeuristic interest by the larger society.

[*See also* Churchwoman; Stereotypes.]

—Trudier Harris

MATTHEWS, VICTORIA EARLE (1861–1907), journalist, short story writer, social reformer, lecturer, and editor. Victoria Matthews was born Victoria Earle in Fort Valley, Georgia, to the slave Caroline Smith. Caroline fled to New York in order to escape a vicious master, probably Victoria's father. Saving her wages, the mother returned eight years later and won custody of Victoria and her sister and took them to New York around 1873. Though Victoria was an adept student, family crises prompted her to leave school for domestic service. Yet she soon harvested a rich education from her admiring employer's library. At eighteen, after marrying William Matthews and bearing a son, Lamartine, she applied her self-enlightenment to a thriving journalistic career, which commenced with work as a "sub"-reporter for publications like the *Times, Herald,* and *Sunday Mercury.* A prolific correspondent for African American newspapers, including the *Boston Advocate* and *New York Globe,* she became an authorial celebrity.

Matthews's career was driven by a belief in converting her people's internal devastations into brilliant external accomplishments, literary and civic. In her *essay "The Value of Race Literature" (1895), she advocated releasing the "suppressed inner lives" of African American women onto the printed page. An author of children's stories, she wrote a mininovel, *Aunt Lindy* (1893), which counseled against an ex-slavewoman's murder of an ailing former master: By healing him, she heals the diseased soul he fostered in her. Matthews thus repudiated the vengeful African persona of Maurice Thompson's poem "Voodoo Prophecy."

Matthews, too, espoused causes in her articles, causes that she galvanized into political reform. Noted for her lectures on "The Awakening of the Afro-American Woman," she founded the Woman's Loyal Union in 1892. In the same year she joined educator Maritcha Lyons in supporting the antilynching crusade of Ida B. *Wells-Barnett. And in 1893, she spoke eloquently at Chicago's World Columbian Exposition. Matthews helped found the National Federation of Afro-American Women in 1895: occupied the editorial board of its magazine, the *Woman's Era*; and was instrumental in the federation's merger with the National Colored Women's League into the National Association of Colored Women (1896). In 1898 she edited *Black Belt Diamonds,* selected speeches of Booker T. *Washington.

The death of Matthews's son at sixteen cast her into profound mourning. This time, she transformed her own grief into vigilant social welfare "for other people's boys and girls." Matthews investigated the so-called employment agencies that were really fronts for the internment of migrating rural "colored" girls into urban prostitution. Establishing the White Rose Industrial Association in 1897, Matthews deployed her own agents to deliver these adolescents to the foundation's home, which instructed them in domestic skills and, through a prodigious library, racial history. The subsidiary sections of the White Rose were eventually unified into the National League for the Protection of Colored Women, one of the founding organizations of the National Urban League. The White Rose thus provided an outlet for Matthews's own inner demons—a means by which her lost son could be reborn in the rescue of female children from sexual exploitation. The White Rose allowed her an active means of avenging both her mother Caroline's trauma as her master's abused object and the historical branding of African American women as sexual possessions.

[*See also* Women's Clubs.]

• *Afro-American Women Writers, 1746–1933,* ed. Ann Shockley, 1988, pp. 181–184 (the entry here is followed by Victoria Earle's *Aunt Lindy: A Story Founded on Real Life*). Frank W. Johnson, "Matthews, Victoria [Earle]," in *African-American Women: A Biographical Dictionary,* ed. Dorothy Salem, 1993, pp. 352–354.

—Deborah Garfield

Maud Martha. Maud Martha Brown is the protagonist of Gwendolyn *Brooks's first *novel, *Maud Martha* (1953). Set in the 1930s and 1940s, the novel treats the impact of the era on a group of people, but most especially on Maud Martha herself. Through a series of vignettes, the reader follows an impressionistic rendering of Maud's ordinary life from childhood through adolescence to womanhood. The novel runs counter to the historic black female character in fiction who is usually blessed or cursed (depending upon one's point of view) with a series of tragic incidents that render her life remarkable. Maud Martha is so ordinary, having ordinary problems, leading a life that is not beset by periods of great highs or impenetrable lows, that she is almost forgettable if one is accustomed either to the fictional black *mammy or the tragic *mulatto. Or, for those who are accustomed to some overpowering black woman in fiction or to one who is so pitiful as she suffers in silence or whimpers when no one is around to hear her, Maud Martha seems a fictional aberration. Certainly she seems different from many of the popular fictional female characters.

A dominant concern of the narrative is an examination of the effect of color upon characters. *Maud Martha* is from the days before the "black-is-beautiful" movement of the 1960s, and within the context of this brief, almost quiet, piece of fiction, Brooks comes to grips with issues of color. Through much of the story, the character thinks she is "ugly" because she does not fit a standard accepted by both black and white communities. Her dark skin becomes a defining characteristic for her. She realizes that Helen, her sister who "is beautiful," seems to get more attention. Maud feels inferior to Russell, her first boyfriend, and finally marries Paul Phillips who is as ordinary as Maud. When Paulette (their daughter) is born, Maud is determined to protect her from the hostile world; but even she cannot shield the child from a white Santa Claus who does not feel like petting a black child. Yet, in the midst of her struggles, she demonstrates an ability to hold on to her sense of dignity and exhibits her method of achieving self-esteem through what would be insignificant incidents to most people.

Like Brooks's *A *Street in Bronzeville* (1945), the setting is important in *Maud Martha* (1953). There are the inevitable kitchenette buildings, corner taverns, vacant lots, and crowded streets as well as beauty parlors that are the social centers of the daylight hours and pitiful nightclubs that attempt to provide a night of forgetfulness. Then there are quick glimpses of "white" Chicago. There is a downtown theater and the University of Chicago that abuts the Black Belt but that is as much foreign territory as downtown. Outside of the South Side, Chicago seems almost like a foreign land that one visits as a tourist but not as a resident of the city. By including these contrasts, Brooks gives a sense of the racial polarization in America's major cities, a separation that was very much a part of the era about which she writes. Yet, urban though this novel is, there is a general sense of quiet reflection that seems to prevail in this world. The cacophony of the city does not exist.

In the final analysis, *Maud Martha* accomplishes a number of things. First and foremost, it is a character study that gains its effectiveness from its terse intensity. At the same time it explores—once again—the changing roles of a woman as she moves through various stages from being primarily a daughter to being a wife and mother. And it presents succinctly the kinds of conflicts that prevail within the black community.

[*See also* Beautician; Family; Hair; Identity; Marriage.]

• Mary Helen Washington, "'Taming All That Anger Down': Rage and Silence in Gwendolyn Brooks's *Maud Martha*," *Massachusetts Review* 24 (Summer 1983): 453–466. Barbara Christian, "Nuance and the Novella: A Study of Gwendolyn Brooks's *Maud Martha*," in *A Life Distilled: Gwendolyn Brooks, Her Poetry and Fiction*, eds. Maria K. Mootry and Gary Smith, 1987, pp. 239–253.

—Kenny Jackson Williams

MAYFIELD, JULIAN (1928–1985), novelist, journalist, playwright, script-writer/producer, Broadway and Hollywood actor, critical essayist, university lecturer, freedom fighter, and advisor to world leaders. The son of Hudson and Annie Mae Prince Mayfield, Julian Mayfield was born on 6 June 1928 in Greer, South Carolina, but grew up in Washington, D.C., where his parents relocated when he was five. After graduation from high school in 1946 and army service in the Pacific, he attended Lincoln University in Pennsylvania. His choice of political science as a major was a logical outgrowth of his acknowledged fascination with words and the power of words, both written and spoken.

This fascination with words led him into another role, on the stage. Before graduating, he participated in several Off-Broadway productions, including his own one-act play *417*; he later made his Broadway debut playing the lead role in *Lost in the Stars*, a musical about apartheid.

In 1954, he married a physician, Ana Livia Cordero. Relocating to Mexico, his new role was that of cofounder/newscaster for Mexico's first English-language radio station and cofounder and editor/theater reviewer of the Puerto Rico *World Journal*. While in Mexico, Mayfield launched yet another career, this time in the field of creative writing, with the publication of his first novel, *The Hit* (1957). Based on his play *417*, like the novel, his subsequent publication *The Long Night*, is about lost or deferred dreams. Both novels also focus on the hopelessness and desolation of the African American family trapped in the quagmire of poverty, victimization, and oppression in the Harlem ghetto.

The Hit tells the story of the once prosperous Cooley family: Hubert, the father and successful-entrepreneur-turned-janitor; Gertrude, the abused mother; and James Lee, their son. The highlight of the story is the final desperate attempt by Hubert to ease his frustration by playing the "numbers" and his disillusionment when, by a strange twist of fate, he gets none of the money his magic number 417 hit.

The Long Night (1958) is a story of a broken family, the Browns: Paul, the father and law-school-dropout-turned-doorway-bum; Mae, the overworked mother; and ten-year-old Steeley, their eldest son. The story details the long night of adventures of the very courageous Steeley who is robbed by fellow gang members of the numbers hit that his mother sent him to collect. Reluctant to return home for fear of a beating, Steeley tries desperately to recoup the money by begging, stealing, and robbing. The last of these efforts results in his discovery of his long-absent but much loved, missed, and needed father, the drunk he rolls over with the intention of robbing. This discovery also serves as a catalyst for reuniting the Brown family.

The theme of Mayfield's third novel, *The Grand Parade* (1961), is very different from that of the first two. Set in the "nowhere" city of Gainsboro, the story covers a much broader spectrum of American society with a focus on political corruption, interracial conflicts, and public school segregation.

Between 1961 and 1966, Mayfield resided in Ghana serving as an aide/advisor to President Kwame Nkrumah and founder/editor of the *African Review*. He spent the following two years in Europe and Asia. Returning to the United States in 1968, Mayfield spent most of his remaining life in the milieu of academia, lecturing in universities both within the United States and abroad. His only break from academia was the period between 1971 and 1973, which he spent in Guyana where he served as advisor to Prime Minister Forbes Burnham.

Mayfield's many other post-1967 activities include playing the highly acclaimed leading role in the Paramount production *Uptight* (1968), a film about black militants; editing a collection of short stories, *Ten Times Black* (1972); and writing dozens of articles for newpapers, magazines, and periodicals.

The major significance of Mayfield to African American literature lies in his numerous critical essays, and also the important role his first two novels played in keeping the flame of protest alive at a time when few African Americans were published—the transition period between the end of the *Harlem Renaissance and the New Renaissance, which followed in the wake of the *civil rights movement.

Concluding her moving tribute to Mayfield and four other "great Afro-American souls" ("Ailey, Baldwin, Floyd, Killens, and Mayfield," 1990), Maya Angelou affirmed that we "can be" and are better off, "for they existed." The world is certainly a better place because Julian Mayfield existed.

• "Uptight," *Ebony*, Nov. 1968, 46–48. Holly I. West, "The Goal of Julian Mayfield: Fusing Art and Politics," *Washington Post*, 7 July 1975, B1, B3. Harriet J. Scarupa, "Eyewitness of Power," *New Directions*, Apr. 1979, 12–15. Arthur P. Davis, *From the Dark Tower: Afro-American Writers, 1990–1960*, 1981, pp. 198–203. William B. Branch, "Julian Mayfield," in *DLB Yearbook*, ed. Jean W. Ross, 1984. Estelle W. Taylor, "Julian Mayfield," in *DLB*, vol. 33, *Afro-American Fiction Writers after 1955*, eds. Thadious M. Davis and Trudier Harris, 1984, pp. 174–178.   —Ruby V. Rodney

MAYS, BENJAMIN E. (1895–1984), educator, scholar, literary critic, theologian, and civil rights activist. Born in South Carolina, Benjamin Elijah Mays completed his doctoral degree at the University of Chicago, then spent most of his life in the American South, working as a religious scholar, minister, president of Morehouse College (1940–1967), and political organizer. Mays was active in Atlanta and nationally in a wide range of civil rights projects, including the National Sharecroppers and Rural Advancement Fund, the NAACP, and the Urban League. In the 1970s, he served as political advisor to President Jimmy Carter. He is well known for his political and spiritual mentoring of Martin Luther *King, Jr., and other African American scholar-activists.

His classic study *The Negro Church* (1933, coauthored with Joseph W. Nicholson) remains a central text in the study of African American religious *history. Mays also wrote *The Negro's God as Reflected in His Literature* (1938), in which he examined the "idea of God" as it appears across a wide range of African American literary genres: sermon, *autobiography, *essay, *spiritual, prayer, *Sunday school literature, *poetry, and the *novel. *The Negro's God* is both a literary and sociological study. Mays critiques the presumption that *religion has played a predominantly "accommodationist" or "compensatory" role in African American culture. This book claims instead an evolving African American liberation theology.

Mays wrote his autobiography *Born to Rebel* (1971) as both a narrative of his own life and an "archetypal" story of twentieth-century African American experience. From the opening scene where, as a small child, he watches a white mob threaten his father in a frenzy of racist *violence, Mays sets his life story in the context of African American response to white racism. Mays challenges this racism all through *Born to Rebel* by composing an explicitly political autobiography that uses his personal life as the base for posing a more sweeping social critique.

Mays makes an important contribution to the genre of African American autobiography through his complex synthesis of literary technique, theology, and political analysis.

• Gayraud S. Wilmore, *Black Religion and Black Radicalism*, 2d ed., 1983. William L. Andrews, ed., *African American Autobiography*, 1993.   —Sharon Carson

MCADOO, JULIUS. *See* Uncle Julius McAdoo.

McCLUSKEY, JOHN A., JR. (b. 1944), novelist, short story writer, educator, and scholar. Born in Ohio, John A. McCluskey, Jr., earned his BA at Harvard (1966) and his MA at Stanford (1972). His first novel, *Look What They Done to My Song* (1974), is a highly episodic first-person narrative told by Mack, a twenty-six-year-old saxophone player. Set in the Boston area around 1970, the book depicts its narrator's search for direction and commitment following the assasinations of *Malcolm X and Martin Luther *King, Jr. In part a portrait of the artist, the novel also draws effectively upon the picaresque tradition. Its sprawling cast of characters voices the diversity of social-political opinions prevalent in the late 1960s. To the idealistic Mack, McCluskey juxtaposes the unprincipled Ubangi, hustler extraordinaire, whose strategems often misfire hilariously, as when the supposedly street-smart Ubangi decides to become a pimp—only to discover that his first whore, a female impersonator named Ova Easy, is already being pimped by the police. One of the novel's central concerns is change, both personal and social, and the function of art as an instrument of change. The closing chapter, set in a *church, presents Mack's vision of *music as "the spirit-healer." Through Mack, McCluskey expresses his own belief in the common purposes of art and *religion: their affirmation of spirit, hope, and love.

Mr. America's Last Season Blues (1983), McCluskey's second novel, is a third-person narrative centered on Roscoe Americus, Jr., an aging athlete. More complex in characterization and structure than its predecessor, the book subverts *stereotypes of the black athlete and engages the reader's emotions in the personal crises Roscoe confronts: his separation from his wife, his abortive comeback as player-coach for a semi-professional football team, and his inability to assist his lover's son, unjustly charged with mudering a white youth. Roscoe's efforts to gather evidence that would free Stone are stymied not only by the racism of the all-white jury but by the silence of those within the African American community whose testimony would lead to Stone's acquittal. The problems Roscoe faces enable McCluskey to movingly explore the legacy of racism, the issue of personal responsibility, and the importance of family ties and the past.

McCluskey's novels, like Ralph *Ellison's *Invisible Man*, incorporate social-political concerns without being dominated by them. His principal mode is literary realism, though his second novel invokes the magic realism of a Toni *Morrison work in its portrait of Roscoe's father's ghost. McCluskey draws extensively upon African American oral traditions and such musical forms as *jazz and the *blues. Some of his best writing can be found in his short stories, particularly "The Best Teacher in Georgia." McCluskey has also edited three volumes of *essays on African American historical figures, as well as the collected stories of Rudolph *Fisher (*City of Refuge*, 1987). Although he has produced few books of fiction, the artistry and moral force of *Mr. America's Last Season Blues* suggest that his work merits continuing attention.

• Frank E. Moorer, "John A. McCluskey, Jr.," in *DLB*, vol. 33, *Afro-American Fiction Writers after 1955*, eds. Thadious M. Davis and Trudier Harris, 1984, pp. 179–181.

—John Lang

McELROY, COLLEEN (b. 1935), poet, college professor, short story writer, and speech therapist. Although Colleen McElroy did not start composing *poetry until she was in her mid-thirties, she is a prolific writer: she has completed nine books of poetry (of which *Queen of the Ebony Islands*, 1984, and *What Madness Brought Me Here: New and Selected Poems, 1968–1988*, 1990, are probably the best known), two collections of *short stories (*Jesus and Fat Tuesday*, 1987, and *Driving under the Cardboard Pines*, 1991), two plays, and one work of nonfiction, in addition to working on a *novel. While heralded chiefly as a poet, McElroy's short stories have appeared in several *anthologies including Gloria *Naylor's *Children of the Night: The Best Short Stories by Black Writers, 1967 to the Present* (1996), Craig Lesley's *Dreamers and Desperadoes: Contemporary Short Fiction of the American West* (1993), and Terry *McMillan's *Breaking Ice: An Anthology of Contemporary African American Fiction* (1990).

Born Colleen Johnson in St. Louis, Missouri, she received both her BS (1958) and her MS (1963) from Kansas State University, and completed her PhD in 1973 at the University of Washington in Seattle, where she is a professor of English. She married David F. McElroy in 1968 and they had two children, Kevin and Vanessa, before divorcing. The daughter of an army officer, McElroy had to move often with her family when she was young; and being a child who spent a lot of time by herself, she began telling stories to make friends. Her poems are imbued with this storytelling quality—she has a keen sense of the cadence and lyricism of words, and the dialogue in her short fiction has been highly praised.

McElroy's poetry is varied and diverse. She often draws on the mundane—the cracked sidewalk of girlhood ("as veined as the backs of my Grandma's hands"), the runners outside a window loping past like wild deer in season, the flashing lights of an always illuminated and overly watched TV—to address more profound concerns: the lost sensual and hermetic world of childhood, the injustice of a social system prejudiced against black Americans, the loneliness of growing older. Alongside the mundane comes the sudden and the unexpected, the storyteller's twist that makes her poetry both brutal and beautiful.

The world inhabited by McElroy's fictional characters is one that defies easy categorization, one where the effects of racism are portrayed subtly, and one where sensuality and good humor reign (in the first lines of "The Dragon Lady Considers Dinner," the narrator cannot remember her date's name of the previous evening, but she has not forgotten the food: "there was that business with the flaming crepes"). Although McElroy is not as well known as other contemporary black women poets (indeed, she has been described by one critic as neglected), and her poetry has not received much scholarly attention, she has been the recipient of many honors, including two National Endowment for the Arts Fellowships, a Fulbright Creative Writing Fellowship, and a Rockefeller Fellowship.

• Irv Broughton, ed., *The Writer's Mind: Interviews with American Authors*, vol. 3, 1990. Colleen McElroy, "When the Shoe Never Fits: Myth in the Modern Mode," in *Poet's Perspectives: Reading, Writing, and Teaching Poetry*, eds., Charles R. Duke and Sally A. Jacobsen, 1992, pp. 37–46. J. J. Phillips, Ishmael Reed, Gundars Strads, and Shawn Wong, eds., *The Before Columbus Foundation Poetry Anthology*, 1992.

—Jennifer Margulis

McGIRT, JAMES EPHRAIM (1874–1930), poet, editor, short story writer, and publisher. James Ephraim McGirt was born in Robeson County, North Carolina, and brought up on a family farm. He attended public school in Greensboro, North Carolina, and in 1895 graduated from Bennett College, a Methodist institution just outside of Greensboro. In the preface to his first book, *Avenging the Maine, a Drunken A.B., and Other Poems* (1899), McGirt blames exhausting manual labor and a lack of leisure time for the slimness of the volume and the feebleness of the verse within it. In 1900, McGirt published an enlarged edition of his first collection of *poetry and brought out in Philadelphia the next year a new collection of lyrics entitled *Some Simple Songs and a Few More Ambitious Attempts*. Moving to Philadelphia gave McGirt a base on which to build a career as a magazine publisher, which he launched in September 1903 with the first issue of *McGirt's Magazine*, an illustrated monthly that dealt with African American art, literature, science, general culture, and politics. In addition to its editor's own poetry and fiction, *McGirt's Magazine* also featured the work of a wide range of skilled African American writers, including articles by Anna Julia *Cooper and W. E. B. *Du Bois, poems by Paul Laurence *Dunbar and Frances Ellen Watkins *Harper, and fiction by John E. *Bruce and Kelly *Miller. Politically, *McGirt's Magazine* maintained an unswerving faith in the ballot as the key to African American advancement.

In 1906, McGirt published a third volume of verse, *For Your Sweet Sake*. The following year *The Triumphs of Ephraim*, his only *short story collection, appeared. In 1909, declining sales compelled McGirt to change his magazine from a monthly to a quarterly. A year later *McGirt's* ceased publication, its editor having decided to return to Greensboro to go into business with his sister. During the last years of his life McGirt bought property in the Greensboro area and became a successful realtor.

As a writer McGirt's contribution to African American literature was small. His poetry, a few examples of which are reprinted in Joan Sherman's *African-American Poetry of the Nineteenth Century* (1992), is technically amateurish, often sentimental, and tritely didactic. His fiction, which usually deals with romantic problems faced by idealized African Americans, attempts to portray people of color to their advantage. But despite the reprinting of *The Triumphs of Ephraim* in 1972, McGirt's short stories have not attracted more than the passing attention of literary historians. Only as a magazine publisher who struggled for seven years to maintain a periodical of serious literary quality and self-respecting political outlook did McGirt leave a lasting mark on the history of African American literature.

[See also Periodicals, *article on* Black Periodical Press; Publishing.]

• Hugh M. Gloster, *Negro Voices in American Fiction,* 1948.

—William L. Andrews

M. C. Higgins, the Great. Virginia *Hamilton, wrote the first chapter of *M. C. Higgins, the Great* (1974) eleven times. Such meticulous revision reaped phenomenal awards, for this young adult novel was the first by an African American to win the Newbery Medal, and it also garnered the Boston-Hornbook Magazine Award, the National Book Award, the Lewis Carrol Shelf Award, and the International Board on Books for Young People Award.

M. C. Higgins, the Great centers on fifteen-year-old Mayo Cornelius (M. C.), who lives on Sarah's Mountain in southern Ohio. Steeped in stress because a spoil heap left from strip-mining threatens to crash down on his home, he spends most of his time sitting on a bicycle seat atop a 40-foot flag pole. The arrival of a folk song collector kindles his hope that the recording of his mother's singing will make her famous and enable the family to leave Sarah's Mountain. During the story M. C. has his first feelings of love, his first yearning for independence, his first questions about his belief and value system, and his first questions of his father's adamant desire to stay no matter what. In the end, M. C. and the neighborhood outcasts come together to build a wall around the heap, leaving the reader not knowing whether his first love would return, not knowing whether the recording artist would reconsider using his mother's voice, and ultimately not knowing whether the spoil heap of bulldozed trees and subsoil will indeed kill the whole family.

Praised by *children's and young adult literature critics Rudine Sims, Zena Sutherland, Betsy Hearne, Sheila Egoff, Virginia Haviland, and Violet Harris, Virginia Hamilton is renowned for her skillful use of nontraditional settings, poetic imagery, unique characterization, impactful dialogue, plot structures, and themes for African American children and young adults. She is also commended for being among the first in African American children's literature to insightfully use African American *folklore.

Perhaps the most provocative critical article on *M. C.* was written by Perry Nodelman, who explains the demanding structure of the novel and notes its binary oppositions, but fails to resolve or interpret them. On a higher level, since little is definitively resolved in Hamilton's works, the novel could reflect the indeterminacy of meaning in modern novels.

Critics praise the book for the linking of the ancestral past with the present and for being an African American young adult novel that has universal appeal, but few have discussed its pioneering ecological theme. No critic has psychoanalyzed M. C.'s character and interior dialogue even though the girl Louretta ironically represents his anima (yin side) and the recording artist and Jones, M. C.'s father, represents his animus side (yang). Few critics have yet tackled the psychological symbolism of the pole even though one critic simplistically reduced it to a phallic symbol. Critics have commended Hamilton for being so intriguingly unconventional, yet she is quite conventional in her use of mythology. No critic has ventured to give M. C. a Marxist interpretation even though the novel clearly hints at the negative effects of capitalism in the mountain exploitation.

As critic Nina Mikkelson has observed, Hamilton at her best is always puzzling and demanding, which sometimes makes her more favored by critics than by the average young reader. Indeed, M. C. has come a long way from the simplistic didacticism seen in early African American children's books such as Amelia E. *Johnson's *Clarence and Corinne, or God's Way* (1889).

Hamilton, the first American winner of the Hans Christian Andersen Medal (1992), is to be commended for not writing down to children, but up to them, showing them that like M. C., in the midst of multiple problems, they too can survive. She made this point in her acceptance speech for the Newbery Medal, which was printed in *Hornbook Magazine* (1975).

• Jessie Carney Smith, *Notable Black Women,* 1992. Nina Mikkelson, *Virginia Hamilton,* 1994.

—Margaret Bernice Smith Bristow

McKAY, CLAUDE (1890–1948), poet, novelist, journalist, and social and political radical, commonly associated with the Harlem Renaissance. Born Festus Claudius McKay, he was the son of relatively prosperous peasants living in upper Clarendon Parish, Jamaica. Around the age of seven McKay went to live with and be educated by his brother, Uriah Theodore, a schoolteacher. There McKay studied classical and British literary figures and philosophers as well as science and theology. He was also encouraged to write *poetry and, during his youth, favored conventional English forms. In 1907 McKay met Walter Jekyll, a white British expatriate and folklorist residing in Jamaica, who urged McKay to write *dialect poetry rooted in the island's folk culture. Jekyll remained McKay's close friend and patron for many years and was instrumental in the publication of McKay's first two volumes of poetry, *Songs of Jamaica* (1912) and *Constab Ballads* (1912). *Songs of

Jamaica attempts to capture peasant life and language; *Constab Ballads* is based on McKay's experiences during a brief period in 1911 as a policeman. Both are primarily in dialect and reveal McKay's efforts to define his literary voice in form and content.

In August 1912 under the pretext of studying agriculture, McKay migrated to the United States to advance his poetic career. He studied at Tuskegee Institute and Kansas State College, but by mid-1914, McKay abandoned the study of farming and moved to New York City. Between 1914 and 1919 McKay worked at various jobs, including as a dining-car waiter on the Pennsylvania Railroad, an experience later rendered in his first novel, *Home to Harlem* (1929). During this period McKay wrote poetry and became increasingly involved with political and literary radicals. For a short time in 1919 he was a member of the International Workers of the World; he was a close associate of several African Caribbean Socialists including Hubert H. Harrison, Richard B. Moore, and Cyril Briggs, and he was affiliated with the African Blood Brotherhood. He began a lifelong professional and personal relationship with Max and Crystal Eastman, editors of the *Liberator*. McKay's most widely anthologized poem, "If We Must Die," was published in the July 1919 issue of the *Liberator* and brought him immediate fame.

McKay's political associations led him to England, where he began writing for British Socialist Sylvia Pankhurst's *Workers' Dreadnought*. While there, his third volume of poetry, *Spring in New Hampshire* (1920), was published. Containing no dialect poetry, it was divided between poems commenting on race relations in the United States and others nostalgically recalling island life. Upon returning to the United States in 1921, McKay served as a coeditor of the *Liberator*, but due to disagreements about the aesthetic objectives of the magazine, McKay resigned his post in July 1922. In the spring of 1922 McKay's fourth volume of poetry, *Harlem Shadows*, was published and received favorable reviews. Income generated by this volume, combined with McKay's dissatisfaction with left-wing efforts to confront racism in both England and the United States, provoked him to travel to the Soviet Union. In November 1922 he attended the Third Communist International in an unofficial capacity. He was widely embraced by the Russian public and traveled throughout the country for six months, delivering lectures on both art and politics. While in Russia, McKay republished a series of articles he had written for the Soviet press under the title *Negroes in America* (1923); these essays offer a Marxist interpretation of the history of African Americans.

When McKay left the Soviet Union, he unknowingly embarked upon a decade of unsettled travel throughout Europe and Africa. Though he had been diagnosed with syphilis, an event that marks the beginning of health and financial problems that plagued him until his death, during 1923 McKay spent time in Paris and Berlin, meeting both white American *expatriates and African American artists including Alain *Locke, Jessie Redmon *Fauset, and Jean *Toomer. In January 1924, with the financial assistance of friends, he moved to southern France to recuperate from repeated illnesses and to complete a novel, "Color Scheme," which was rejected for publication and subsequently burned by McKay. In 1924 Alain Locke, despite significant political differences with McKay, selected some of McKay's poetry for the influential edition of *Survey Graphic* that served as the foundation for The *New Negro (1925). In 1928, while still in France, McKay published *Home to Harlem. Achieving widespread acclaim, *Home to Harlem* is McKay's most read novel and is often studied within the context of the *Harlem Renaissance. His second novel, *Banjo* (1929), is a commentary on colonialism that focuses on the lives of an international cast of drifters living on the Marseilles waterfront. In 1932, having moved to Morocco, McKay published *Gingertown*, a collection of short stories alternately set in Jamaica and the United States. In 1933 he published his final novel, *Banana Bottom*, a romantic tale set in Jamaica that explores both individual and cultural conflict between colonizing and folk forces. Neither book sold well, however.

In 1934, seriously ill and improverished, McKay returned to the United States, where he remained until his death in 1948. During these years McKay struggled to produce more literary works but had difficulty finding publishers; he did, however, write numerous articles for a variety of journals. In 1937 he published his autobiography, *A Long Way from Home*, and in 1940 he published *Harlem: Negro Metropolis*, an anti-Communist treatise calling for stronger, community-based African American leadership. In 1944 McKay converted to Catholicism. During the last years of his life he completed an autobiography of his youth titled *My Green Hills of Jamaica* (1979) and compiled a collection of his poetry for *Selected Poems of Claude McKay* (1953). Both books were published posthumously. McKay died in Chicago on 22 May 1948.

McKay's exploration of the relationship between art and politics, as conveyed in his complex and wide-ranging writings, establishes him as an important pioneer in African American and African Caribbean intellectual, cultural, and literary history. He is considered an influential predecessor of, as well as participant in, the *New Negro movement, an instrumental role model for the founders of the *Negritude movement and a resonant historical reference for *Black Nationalism during the civil rights era.

• Kenneth Ramchand, *The West Indian Novel and Its Background*, 1970. Wayne F. Cooper, ed., *The Passion of Claude McKay: Selected Poetry and Prose, 1912–1948*, 1973. Jean Wagner, *Black Poets of the United States: From Paul Laurence Dunbar to Langston Hughes*, 1973. James Giles, *Claude McKay*, 1976. Wayne F. Cooper, *Claude McKay: Rebel Sojourner in the Harlem Renaissance*, 1987. Tyrone Tillery, *Claude McKay: A Black Poet's Struggle for Identity*, 1992.

—Heather Hathaway

McKISSACK, PATRICIA C. (b. 1944), editor and consultant on minority literature, and writer of children's picture books, short stories, and nonfiction works primarily in the fields of African American history and biography.

Patricia C. McKissack incorporates distinctive African American cultural traits in her fictional works—the supernatural is a familiar companion, heroes are indefatigable in their opposition to oppression, African American communities are generously supportive, and the language of daily interchange is frequently playful and poetic. From this solid base, McKissack employs any genre that suits her purpose as an entertainer, educator, and strong civil rights advocate.

For pure entertainment, McKissack uses the picture book genre combined with African American folk traditions, as in *Mirandy and Brother Wind* (1988) and *Nettie Jo's Friends* (1989). In the former, a conjure woman links "Brother Wind" (a fanciful figure in a young girl's imagination) with a community frolic, a cake-walk contest, and hints of romance. In *Nettie Jo's Friends*, a resourceful black child outsmarts a harried rabbit, a "hip" fox, and a wisecracking panther. The author's use of a southern idiom adds regional charm.

Pleasure is joined with more serious intentions in *The Dark-Thirty: Southern Tales of the Supernatural* (1992). These original short stories are sometimes based on incidents from African American *history, and the tragic realities of *slavery shape plotlines and emotional tone. "The Legend of Pin Oak," for example, elaborates upon a system in which children in one family were frequently both African American and Euro-American. One brother (the slaveowner's white son) is in a position to sell the other and both perish in the end. The slaveocracy's wanton waste of human life is vividly conveyed. As a group of ghost stories and tales of transfiguration, this collection is provocatively mock-scary; as a compilation of historical vignettes it is vitally important to educators.

The civil rights advocacy of McKissack is indirectly apparent in *The Dark-Thirty* and openly central to her work as a biographer and nonfiction writer. She has chronicled the lives of such black leaders as Martin Luther *King, Jr., and Jesse Jackson, and in collaboration with her husband, Fredrick, has written biographies of Frederick *Douglass, W. E. B. *Du Bois, Sojourner *Truth, and others. The McKissacks' study of African American porters (*A Long Hard Journey: The Story of the Pullman Porter*, 1989) won both the Coretta Scott King Award and the Jane Addams Children's Book Award.

Patricia McKissack's historical placement is noticeably connected with the nature of her work. On the one hand, she directly experienced the world of *Jim Crow tyranny in her home state of Tennessee. On the other hand, she lived through the Kennedy era and being a "Kennedy product," she says, "made me very idealistic." That optimism would soon be tempered by the ensuing backlash to civil rights, but as a young eighth-grade teacher in Missouri, McKissack could aid her students in both opposing and understanding that hostility. Moreover, her dedication to countering racism on the larger world stage was born of these experiences, and her writings bear witness to that inestimable commitment.

• Diane Telgen, ed., *Something about the Author*, vol. 73, 1993, pp. 147–152. Patricia C. McKissack and Fredrick McKissack, "Sojourner Truth: Ain't I a Woman?" *Horn Book Magazine*, Jan./Feb. 1994, 53–57.

—Donnarae MacCann

McKNIGHT, REGINALD (b. 1956), short story writer, novelist, essayist, and educator. Because his father served in the air force, Reginald McKnight was born in Fuerstenteldbruck, Germany. His family relocated several times, staying briefly in New York, Texas, Alabama, Louisiana, and California, but McKnight considers Colorado, principally Colorado Springs and Denver, his home. He received an AA degree from Pikes Peak Community College (1978), his BA from Colorado College (1981), and an MA from the University of Denver (1987). McKnight taught English as a foreign language for the American Cultural Center in Dakar, Senegal, from 1981 to 1982. He is a former marine, honorably discharged in 1976; an English teacher, currently employed by the University of Maryland, College Park; and the author of the novel *I Get on the Bus* (1990) and two short story collections, *Moustapha's Eclipse* (1988) and *The Kind of Light that Shines on Texas* (1992).

Within the six-year span between 1985 and 1991, Reginald McKnight achieved distinction and earned praise as a crafter of excellent fiction, particularly in the short story. In 1985 he won a Thomas J. Watson Fellowship, which permitted him a year in Africa; there he gathered material that became strands in the semiautobiographical novel *I Get on the Bus*. Also in 1985, McKnight won the Bernice M. Slote Award for Fiction from the University of Nebraska for "Uncle Moustapha's Eclipse." In 1988 he received the Drue Heinz Literature Prize from the University of Pittsburgh Press for stories collected in *Moustapha's Eclipse*; this collection also earned him an Ernest Hemingway Foundation Award from PEN American Center in 1989. He was a Bread Loaf Fellow in 1988; in 1989, he was awarded the *Kenyon Review* New Fiction Prize and the O. Henry Award for "The Kind of Light that Shines on Texas." McKnight received a National Endowment for the Arts Grant for Literature in 1991.

Reviewers of McKnight's short fiction tend to focus first on his ability to create evocative, richly textured, and often humorous or comic narrative voices. "The Homunculus: A Novel in One Chapter," collected in *The Kind of Light that Shines in Texas*, was also anthologized in *The Year's Best Fantasy and Horror, Sixth Annual Collection* for 1992. McKnight's ability to manipulate a story's structural frame so that it functions as an active evocative dramatic element rather than a mere vehicle has also been noted, as has his use of the swiftly paced narrative and his ear for striking dialogue. An additional aural technique resonating in his fiction is his poetic prose, his skillful deployment of sound to ensnare a reader's immediate attention. It is through an unexpected blending of rhythm and syntax that his prose yields the remarkable or compelling image. Carolyn Megan, in a 1994 essay for the *Kenyon Review* titled "New Perceptions on Rhythm in Reginald McKnight's Fiction," argues that McKnight's writing relies upon a rhythmic sense, upon meter, sound, and rhythm as avenues into fiction.

If Megan's observations apply to McKnight's short stories, they are more applicable when the text examined is McKnight's novel *I Get on the Bus*, a surrealistic tale about black identity and its convoluted forms in the post–civil rights era. Readers sensitive to imagery are seduced by the effects of the staccato rhythms permeating the novel's highly intense opening passage. The novel reflects the peculiar experiences of a young African American male in Africa. Evan Norris, though serving in the Peace Corps in Senegal, must contend with an inner rootlessness and cultural ambivalence that echoes W. E. B. *Du Bois's concept of the divided self, the *double consciousness haunting many African Americans.

McKnight's skillful treatment of various narrative techniques, riffing off autobiographical elements, and his creation of the cultural *mulatto male protagonist show him to be an ultramodern African American novelist. Thematically, however, through the novel's emphasis on identity, ambiguity, responsibility, deracination, and the quest for self, McKnight shows an allegiance to James Weldon *Johnson's *The *Autobiography of an Ex-Colored Man* (1913) and Ralph *Ellison's *Invisible Man* (1952).

• Reginald McKnight, "Confessions of a Wannabe Negro," in *Lure and Loathing*, ed. Gerald Early, 1993. Carolyn E. Megan, "New Perceptions on Rhythm in Reginald McKnight's Fiction," *Kenyon Review* 16.2 (Spring 1994): 56–62. Reginald McKnight, "We Are in Fact a Civilization: An Interview with Reginald McKnight," interview by William Walsh, *Kenyon Review* 16.2 (Spring 1994): 27–42.

—Sandra Y. Govan

McMILLAN, TERRY (b. 1951), university professor, screenwriter, editor, and author. As a novelist, Terry L. McMillan has contributed to the body of literature that opens the doors of communication between African Americans and society at large. Family problems seem to permeate her texts, especially *Mama* and *Waiting to Exhale*, for which she assisted in creating a screenplay. McMillan was born 18 October 1951 in Port Huron, Michigan, the daughter of Madeline Washington Tillman and Edward Lewis McMillan, proletarians. Like Onika, the child of Bernadine in *Waiting to Exhale*, McMillan's parents divorced, and her mother raised her and her four siblings alone, working as a *domestic and an auto factory worker. McMillan graduated from the University of California at Berkeley with a BS degree in 1979 and attended the MFA film program at Columbia University in New York City that year.

McMillan's son, Solomon, who she raised as a single parent, was born in 1984. Dedicated to her writing and her son, McMillan was determined to make it in a man's world. In 1987, while serving as Visiting Writer at the University of Wyoming, Laramie, she published *Mama*, which she had written while working as a typist. She promoted her first novel by con-

tacting colleges and universities and organizing tours, and by publication date, *Mama* had sold out its first printing. *Mama* depicts the often troubled inter- and intrarelationships of a mother, Mildred Peacock, to her family and her community, but most of all to "self." McMillan places Mildred in the middle of social change in society: Feminists are still burning their "pretty bras" from the 1960s, and African Americans are faced with an *identity crisis. Society is dealing with civil rights, Black Power, student protests, and opposition to the Vietnam War. McMillan let all of this assist her in creating a text filled with social realism, and the book deals with much more than a woman's struggle in a sexist, antiwomanist society. The text emphasizes, through Mildred's life and her children's, that positive change is possible, and that a black woman and her people need not be limited by the roles society expects them to play, allows them to play, or prohibits them from playing by virtue of their status in their community.

McMillan's second book, *Disappearing Acts* (1989) is a novel that addresses the issues of urban love. The characters Zora Banks and Franklin Swift create a complex love that enables women who have loved and lost or walked away from love to understand Zora's dilemma. These star-crossed lovers tell their stories and create for the readers polarities that, to them, represent their individual struggles. Again, McMillan's use of language and dialogue gives her readers the needed flavor to continue wanting more and more of her characters.

In 1990, McMillan edited *Breaking Ice: An Anthology of Contemporary African American Fiction*, which consists of works by a wide range of post-1960 authors both established and emerging. In her introduction to the text, McMillan states her explanation for such a work: "I wish there hadn't been a need to separate our work from others, and perhaps, as Dr. Martin Luther King Jr. expressed, one day this dream may come true, where all of our work is considered equal, and measured not by its color content, but its literary merit."

In 1995, *Waiting to Exhale* (1992), the story of four intelligent and attractive but unattached middle-class black women, went to the big screen after selling three million copies. Terry McMillan, through dedication, determination, and her vernacular-based literary style, has created a novel that crosses *race and *gender. In a conversation with Oprah Winfrey, when asked about the surprise of *Waiting to Exhale*'s success, McMillan replied: "It's like having a baby and praying that people think that it's cute."

McMillan's most recent novel, *How Stella Got Her Groove Back* (1996), again chronicles the relationships of women to each other, their families, and the men in their lives. Stella, McMillan's protagonist, is a forty-two-year-old mother struggling in the male-dominated corporate world to find inner peace after her marriage has dissolved. Her two sisters represent polarized versions of womanhood: Angela, married and pregnant, "feels like nothing without a man" and a sense of family, and free-spirited, outspoken, and impulsive Vanessa, a single parent, wants Stella to live again and take risks. Stella finds her groove when she risks all and falls in love with a twenty-year-old Jamaican man she meets while vacationing. The novel is filled with explosive language and humor and portrayals of women's strength.

With her honesty and control of vernacular language, McMillan has paved the way for contemporary voices to emerge with their stories. Her "knotting up" of her characters will serve as icebreakers in conversations around the world. Readers can definitely view Terry McMillan as the Frank *Yerby of the 1990s.

• Robert G. O'Meally, "The Caged Bird Sings," *Newsday*, 13 Aug. 1986. Thulani Davis, "Don't Worry, Be Buppie: Black Novelists Head for the Mainstream," *Village Voice Literary Supplement* 85 (May 1990): 26–29. Jacqueline Trescott, "The Urban Author: Straight to the Point," *Washington Post*, 17 Nov. 1990. Daniel Max, "McMillan's Millions," *New York Times Magazine*, 9 Aug. 1992. Edward M. Jackson, "Images of Black Males in Terry McMillan's *Waiting to Exhale*," *MAWA Review* 8.1 (June 1993): 20–26.

—Wanda Macon

McPHERSON, JAMES ALAN (b. 1943), short story writer and essayist, and winner of the Pulitzer Prize in fiction for *Elbow Room* (1978). James Alan McPherson was born in Savannah, Georgia, son of James Allen and Mable (Smalls) McPherson. He attended Morgan State University (1963–1964), Morris Brown College (BA, 1965), Harvard University (LLB, 1968), and the University of Iowa (MFA, 1969). He has taught English at the University of Iowa Law School (1968–1969), the University of California, Santa Cruz (1969–1970), Morgan State University (1975–1976), the University of Virginia (1976–1981), and the University of Iowa Writer's Workshop (1981–).

McPherson published his first book of *short stories, *Hue and Cry* (1969), shortly after graduating from Harvard Law School, which may explain his lawyerly approach to storytelling. Like a good counsel, he knows how to make the strongest rhetorical case for each of his clients or characters—indirectly, through a balanced presentation of narrative detail, or directly, through the voices of the characters themselves. Like a good judge, he suspends authorial judgment, allowing readers to reach their own conclusions about guilt and innocence.

In his first collection of stories, McPherson dramatizes the themes of isolation, injustice, and self-definition in the dim light of contemporary America. While some reviewers found McPherson's language awkward, verbose, or inappropriately hip, the dust jacket included a statement from Ralph *Ellison commending McPherson for his commitment to craft. Many commentators praised the book as an eloquent study of the effects of racism on African Americans, despite the author's intention to keep race a secondary issue.

In *Elbow Room* (1977) McPherson deals with the theme of selfhood—how it is won, lost, or evaded—and offers a more affirmative vision of human possibility. In this case reviewers generally praised both McPherson's style and ability to see beyond color, yet others continued to insist that McPherson's strengths

and thematic concerns derive from his African American *identity.

Since 1977, McPherson has written only personal and political *essays, attempting through them to define his own background and outline his vision of an America where citizens would be, as he puts it in "On Becoming an American Writer," "a synthesis of high and low, black and white, city and country, provincial and universal." As the title of the essay and the quotation suggest, McPherson seems to be most comfortable thinking of himself as an American writer interested in how the distinctively American issues of identity and diversity might be defined and in how, as values, selfhood and diversity might be achieved and constructively preserved within a country beset by difference.

To be sure, McPherson is an African American and most of his characters are black, but both his fiction and his essays resist simple classification. Racism for him is a problem not only because it is cruel and unjust but also because it restricts humankind's imaginative *freedom and therefore its ability to discover better ways of being human.

In both his fiction and essays, McPherson challenges the reader to take the future as well as the past and present seriously.

• Patsy B. Perry, "James Alan McPherson," in *DLB*, vol. 38, *Afro-American Writers after 1955: Dramatists and Prose Writers*, eds. Thadious M. Davis and Trudier Harris, 1985, pp. 185–194. James Alan McPherson, "Chantpleure," in *Contemporary Authors Autobiography Series*, vol. 17, ed. Joyce Nakamura, 1993, pp. 121–136.

—Jon Wallace

MERIWETHER, LOUISE (b. 1923), short fiction writer, essayist, novelist, writer of children's literature, and black activist. Louise Meriwether holds an established place among literati whose writings reassess African Americans' past. Her fiction treats bygone times to revise American *history and to record African Americans' tremendous achievements despite overwhelming odds.

Born in Haverstraw, New York, to Marion Lloyd Jenkins (a bricklayer) and Julia Jenkins (a housewife), Meriwether grew up in Harlem during the depression. The only daughter of five children, she remembers her mother applying for welfare because her unemployed father could not sustain the family as a numbers runner. Despite her humble beginnings, she received her BA in English from New York University and her MA in *journalism from the University of Los Angeles in 1965. She has worked as a freelance reporter (1961–1964) for the *Los Angeles Sentinel*, a black story analyst (1965–1967) for Universal Studios, and a faculty member at Sarah Lawrence College in Bronxville, New York (1979–1988), and the University of Houston (1985–1988).

In the early 1960s, Meriwether published biosketches of important African American figures: Grace Bumbry, singer; Audrey Boswell, attorney; Vaino Spenser, Los Angeles judge; and Mathew Henson, explorer. Her short stories appeared later that same decade: "Daddy Was a Number Runner" (*Antioch Review*, 1967), "A Happening in Barbadoes" (*Antioch Review*, 1968), and "The Thick End Is for

Whipping" (*Negro Digest*, 1969). Three juvenile readers on historical black figures were published in the 1970s: *The Freedom Ship of Robert Smalls* (1971), *The Heart Man: Dr. Daniel Hale Williams* (1972), and *Don't Take the Bus on Monday: The Rosa Parks Story* (1973). Whether for adult or juvenile reading, each work includes some aspect of African American life not usually found in American history texts.

Meriwether's first novel, *Daddy Was a Number Runner* (1970), returns to the depression and captures the disintegration of a struggling African American family during difficult economic times. The novel is not autobiographical in the strictest sense, but parallels do exist between the author's family and that of Francie Coffin, the twelve-year-old protagonist. The depression took a toll on the physical, mental, and social health of both families; the first-person point of view makes plausible the Coffins' demise.

Fragments of the Ark (1994), Meriwether's second novel, recounts the daring escape of Peter Mango, a Charleston slave, to the Union army to achieve his freedom. Based on the real-life adventure of Robert Smalls, the novel changes the name of the historic figure to consider interpersonal relationships. This novel joins other historical fiction, such as Toni *Morrison's *Beloved* (1987) and Alex *Haley's *Roots* (1976), to retell the story of *slavery from an African American perspective.

Between the publication of *Fragments of the Ark* and *Daddy Was a Number Runner*, twenty-four years passed. Often Meriwether delayed her writings to engage in political activity. In 1965, Meriwether worked with the Congress of Racial Equality (CORE) in Bogalusa, Louisiana, and with the Deacons, a black coalition that armed itself to protect the community from Ku Klux Klan raids. Two years later, she and Vantile Whitfield, founder of the Performing Arts Society of Los Angeles, formed the Black Anti-Defamation Association to prevent Twentieth Century Fox's producer David L. Wolper from making a film of William Styron's controversial book *The Confessions of Nat Turner* (1967). Styron's book denigrated the Virginia insurrectionist and misinterpreted African American history. The outcome of Meriwether and Whitfield's efforts was that the film was not made.

Whether in her writings or in her militant tactics, Meriwether insists on revising American history to give African Americans a deserving, respectable place in it.

[*See also* Biography.]

• Rita B. Dandridge, "From Economic Insecurity to Disintegration: A Study of Character in Louise Meriwether's *Daddy Was a Number Runner*," *Negro American Literature Forum* 9 (Fall 1975): 82–85. Rita B. Dandridge, "Meriwether, Louise," in *Black Women in America*, vol. 2, ed. Darlene Clark Hine, 1993, pp. 783–784.
—Rita B. Dandridge

Messenger, The. The *Messenger*, a monthly journal (1917–1928), was remarkable for its editorials, occasional literature, and varied appeal. Variously subtitled, it was first a spartan *Journal of Scientific Radicalism* or the *Only Radical Negro Magazine in America*, describing itself as the "first publication to recognize the Negro problem as fundamentally a labor problem." Scintillating editorials by A. Philip Randolph and Chandler Owen rebuked President Warren G. Harding for endorsing California's exclusion of Japanese immigrants or lambasted W. E. B. *Du Bois for "demagogy" regarding socialist revolution, while sociopolitical poems by Claude *McKay and the memoirs of Bartolomeo Vanzetti appeared as occasional literature. Beginning in 1923, however, the *Messenger* as *New Opinion of the New Negro* or *World's Greatest Negro Monthly* began to feature what it called "pure literature"—poems by Langston *Hughes, Countee *Cullen, Georgia Douglas *Johnson, and Alice *Dunbar-Nelson. Fashion-plate covers and society photographs dominated until 1926, when muscular workers again appeared on the cover and the *Messenger* became the official organ of Randolph's Brotherhood of Sleeping Car Porters. Thanks however to Wallace *Thurman's brief managing editorship, in these last two years the *Messenger* also published Zora Neale *Hurston's "Eatonville Anthology" and Hughes's first *short stories.

[*See also* Crisis, The; Harlem Renaissance; Opportunity; Periodicals; Publishing.]

• Langston Hughes, *The Big Sea*, 1940. Chidi Ikonné, *From Du Bois to Van Vechten: The Early New Negro Literature, 1903–1926*, 1981.
—Craig Howard White

MEYER, JUNE. *See* Jordan, June.

MICHEAUX, OSCAR (1884–1951), director, producer, novelist, and leading director in early independent African American film. Oscar Micheaux was the first major African American director to produce feature *films with black characters for black audiences. Over a thirty-year period from 1919 to 1948 he wrote, directed, and produced thirty-four pictures. Among these are *Body and Soul* (1924), a silent film starring Paul *Robeson in his first American movie, and *The Exile* (1931), the first African American talkie made by a black film company. Micheaux was a legendary figure in early African American film, a field that began in earnest after the appearance of D. W. Griffith's controversial *Birth of a Nation* (1915). The great public outcry over the racism in Griffith's film created an underground movement of black filmmakers intent on presenting a more realistic appraisal of African American life.

Micheaux was born in Illinois and after a short period as a farmer and Pullman car porter turned his efforts to writing *novels for black audiences. Over a ten-year period Micheaux wrote and self-published ten novels. In 1918 he founded the Oscar Micheaux Corporation in Harlem, New York, and turned to producing and directing films. After a series of short films he made *The Homesteader* (1919), based on his own novel. In rapid succession during the 1920s and 1930s Micheaux made many films, among them: *Sons of Satan* (1922), *Birthright* (1924), *Wages of Sin* (1929), *Underworld* (1936), and *God's Stepchildren* (1937). Micheaux was also an indefatigable promoter of his creations, touring the country to publicize and finance his films. He convinced white theater owners to have special showings for black audiences; he also distributed his films to approximately one hundred black theaters. Filming on a shoestring budget, Micheaux used black actors and actresses anxious for work in films, among them Lorenzo Tucker, Ethel Moses, and Bee Freeman. Reputedly over six feet tall, Micheaux dressed in large black coats and wide-brimmed hats. As a maverick director he often chose his players on a whim and had them work without repeated takes. The films were shot in convenient locations such as friends' homes and hastily constructed sets. Although most films were shot in less than six weeks, Micheaux created films showing black life on realistic terms while also providing entertainment for the black masses. His films contained a range of types and attempted to show that blacks were often just as rich, educated, and cultured as whites.

Recently Micheaux has been criticized for presenting a *class system based on color in his movies. Often the most affluent or successful blacks in his films are the lightest-skinned with the straightest *hair. Although the nightclub and cabaret scenes in Micheaux's films provide valuable insight into black *music and *dance, some critics suggest they may have been added to entice white audiences to his films. Nevertheless Micheaux's strongest films confront the race problem head on while presenting the lifestyle and attitudes of the black middle class. His heroes and heroines suffer through conventional romantic and financial crises complicated by the issues of *passing and racial prejudice. In their own way Micheaux's films make a plea for black unity and black independence through *education and economic competition while presenting a positive image for black audiences.

Micheaux successfully fashioned almost single-handedly a popular black cinema and a black star system that provided a prototype for African American independent cinema in general. He created dynamic roles for aggressive black female actresses and many of his films featured females in the stronger roles. He gave black actors and actresses roles far different from the usual Hollywood *stereotype of servants, *Uncle Toms, and buffoons. Micheaux's extravagant personality, great creative flair, and independent vision made him a visionary filmmaker who could connect with the black audiences of the period. He examined and explored the shared, collective attitudes and outlooks of African Americans between the wars in a large body of films, many of which are now lost. Micheaux worked in both silent and sound film, one of the few black directors to bridge this important transitional era in American cinema. His final dream of widespread black and white audiences for his films was not to be. Micheaux's last film, Betrayal (1948), opened in New York at a white theater and received major attention from the press, but the public took little notice and the movie failed. Soon after, Micheaux died in relative obscurity, and his films remained neglected for over thirty years.

• Donald Bogle, Toms, Coons, Mulattoes, Mammies, and Bucks: An Interpretive History of Blacks in American Films, 1973. James P. Murray, To Find an Image: Black Films from Uncle Tom to Super Fly, 1973. Bernard L. Peterson, "Films of Oscar Micheaux: America's First Fabulous Black Filmmaker," Crisis 86.4 (Apr. 1979): 136–141. Kenneth Wiggins Portor, "Oscar Micheaux," in DANB, eds. Rayford W. Logan and Michael R. Winston, 1982, pp. 433–434. "Oscar Micheaux" in World Film Directors 1890–1945, vol. 1, ed. John Wakeman, 1987, pp. 765–770. Donald Bogle, Blacks in American Films and Television: An Encyclopedia, 1988. Marc A. Reid, "Pioneer Black Filmmaker: The Achievement of Oscar Micheaux," Black Film Review 4.2 (Spring 1988): 6–7.

—Stephen F. Soitos

MIDDLE PASSAGE. As part of their horrific experience of being kidnapped and transported across the Atlantic to the Americas, African slaves had to endure the inhumanities of the Middle Passage. The Middle Passage refers to the middle stage of the triangular "trading" route between England, Africa, and the Americas. While deaths occurred at each stage of the journey, mortality and suffering during the Middle Passage were exacerbated by many well-known factors including physical and psychological trauma; the length of the voyage; and diseases such as dysentery, "fever," measles, smallpox, scurvy, and intestinal disorders. Despite these debilitating and oppressive conditions, some African slaves revolted, and others committed or attempted suicide to release themselves from their bondage at sea.

The more than two-hundred-year history of African *slavery in the United States has had a profound impact on the literature of African American writers. For reasons not yet fully explored by scholars, however, there have been few extended autobiographical or fictional treatments of the Middle Passage until recently. Nineteenth-century *slave narratives often leave out or only briefly mention the experience, but Sterling Stuckey has identified two noteworthy tales of African origins and the Middle Passage in the folk memory of South Carolina blacks.

The Interesting Narrative of the Life of Olaudah Equiano, or Gustavus Vassa, the African (1789) is the most sustained autobiographical precedent to contemporary treatments of the Middle Passage. Written by a Beninese-born Ibo African who became a leader in the English *antislavery movement and an English citizen, The Interesting Narrative describes Olaudah *Equiano's experience of being kidnapped at age eleven and his suffering at the hands of white slavers during the ship's voyage to Barbados. Martin R. *Delany's *Blake, or The Huts of America (1859–1861) is another major precedent. In this radical *novel the protagonist, *Henry Blake, inveighs against the cruelties of the transatlantic slave trade while on board a slave ship en route to Cuba.

Using different genres, contemporary writers have experimented with ways to treat this traumatic historical event. Robert *Hayden's poem "Middle Passage" (1966) revisits the successful slave revolt on the Amistad in 1839. Hayden uses the voices of the crew ironically to reveal their own crimes and the Africans' heroism. Amiri *Baraka's play "Slave Ship. A Historical Pageant" (1967) re-creates the Middle Passage to emphasize a black nationalist message. While less explicitly political, Charles R. *Johnson's novel *Middle Passage (1990) dramatizes the horrors and hardships endured while suggesting in the journey a metaphor of the ways in which African and American cultures change and become interdependent after coming into contact with each other. Of the contemporary treatments, perhaps Alex *Haley's *Roots: The Saga of an American Family (1976) has had the greatest impact on the United States so far. Over 8 million copies of the novel were published and 130 million North Americans watched on *television African *Kunta Kinte's nightmarish voyage into slavery. Now that the silence has been broken, African American writers will no doubt continue to find new ways to speak about what has previously been mostly unspeakable.

[See also Migration; Neo–Slave Narrative.]

• James A. Rawley, The Transatlantic Slave Trade, 1981. Sterling Stuckey, Slave Culture, 1987. Mary Beth Norton, ed., A People and a Nation, 1991. Wolfgang Binder, "Uses of Memory: The Middle Passage in African American Literature," in Slavery in the Americas, 1993, pp. 539–564.

—Jonathan D. Little

Middle Passage, which won the 1990 National Book Award for Fiction marks the culmination of Charles R. *Johnson's philosophical exploration and formal innovation to date. Taking the form of ship's log entries, the *novel recounts the adventures of *Rutherford Calhoun, a freed slave from Illinois who relocates to New Orleans and leads a hedonistic life financed by petty thievery. While there, Rutherford becomes involved with two powerful figures: Isadora Duncan, the proper schoolmistress who treats Rutherford much like her adopted stray animals, and Philippe "Papa" Zeringue, a Creole gangster to whom Rutherford becomes indebted. Isadora learns of and buys Rutherford's debts; in return Zeringue helps her attempt to force Calhoun into marriage. Desperate to escape both oppressors, Rutherford stows away aboard the Republic, unwittingly choosing a slave ship in which Zeringue holds a partial interest.

Aboard the Republic, Rutherford is torn between the disparate influences of evil captain Ebenezer Falcon, a man literally and figuratively twisted and dissolute who seeks both to bed and subordinate him, and the example of the Allmuseri, the tribe of African wizards who, along with their god, make up the cargo of the Republic on her return voyage. Led by the wise and inscrutable Ngonyama, the Allmuseri present an entirely different picture of existence to Rutherford. Living a life characterized by complete harmony and speaking a language that cannot be subdivided into any discrete pieces, the Allmuseri contradict Falcon's rabid individualism. Convinced of the captain's insanity, the crew decides to mutiny and enlists Calhoun's aid, a plot that he reveals to Falcon under duress. His attempts to stop the mutineers are thwarted by the Allmuseri's rebellion, an event that forces Rutherford, one of the few crew members who understands Ngonyama's people, into the position of mediator between rebellious cargo and surviving crew. Enduring a number of painful adventures, Rutherford ultimately returns home in time to prevent Isadora's marriage to Zeringue. He reveals Zeringue's treachery, frees himself from debt,

and weds Isadora, settling down to a life he had not previously valued.

The linear plot masks philosophical twists that make the novel quite challenging. Drawing on sources including The Odyssey, Edgar Allan Poe's The Narrative of Arthur Gordon Pym, Herman Melville's Moby-Dick and "Benito Cereno," principles of phenomenology, and the Hegelian slave-master paradigm, Johnson creates a world in which conventional notions of time, language, *freedom, and loyalty are tested. Calhoun serves as mediator, both within the text and between audience and text, offering a model for the type of reading necessary to a full comprehension of the fictional landscape's significance.

This novel reinforces many points Johnson makes in Oxherding Tale (1982); however, where the philosophical substructure of the former novel is glaringly obvious, Middle Passage manages to submerge many of the same concerns in a narrative that easily entertains while offering challenging ideas. As a result, the work has attracted a variety of readers and exposed a large portion of the general public to Johnson's aesthetics, thereby firmly establishing him as an important contemporary author.

[See also Middle Passage (the term); Neo–Slave Narrative; Slavery.]

• Charles Johnson and Ron Chernow, In Search of a Voice, 1991, pp. 1–18. Ashraf H. A. Rushdy, "The Phenomenology of the Allmuseri: Charles Johnson and the Subject of the Narrative of Slavery," African American Review 26.3 (Winter 1992): 373–394. Charles Johnson, "An Interview with Charles Johnson," interview by Jonathan Little, Contemporary Literature 34.2 (Summer 1993): 159–181.   —William R. Nash

MIDWIFE. In their capacity as presiders over birth and assistants in the process, midwives hold a special place in African American culture and appear in several places in the literature. Reliance upon such figures in early African American history and through the first half of the twentieth century was as much a consequence of racism as of need and geography. White doctors were frequently not willing to treat black patients, and black doctors were few. Midwives thus filled the gap in rural communities as well as in more populated areas. Usually respected members of their communities, these women delivered babies in exchange for fresh meat from newly killed hogs, or for garden vegetables, or for the few dollars in cash that their clients could afford. Their "children" could number in the hundreds before their careers ended. With tightening medical regulations in the past two or three decades, and black people having more access to regular medical care, midwives have become almost a dying breed. Yet many of these women became legendary for their skills in black communities, particularly throughout the South.

Midwives appear as a part of whatever landscape is depicted in the literature. They can be ineffectual or impressively efficient, depending upon the dominant tone of the genre in which they are depicted. In Richard *Wright's "Down by the Riverside" (1938), for example, the midwife can only watch helplessly as Mann's pregnant wife, unable to give birth, is caught in the tragic naturalistic consequences that lead to her death as well as Mann's. The midwife is just as helpless as the other characters. The same is true of the midwives in Toni *Morrison's *Song of Solomon (1977) and Randall *Kenan's "Clarence and the Dead" (1992). Morrison's midwife can only watch helplessly as *Pilate Dead's mother dies giving birth to her. When the midwife arrives on the scene in Kenan's story, Clarence's mother has already given birth to him and has also died in the process. These works reflect the cultural recognition of the presence of the midwife more than the effectiveness of what she accomplishes.

On the other hand, the title character in Gloria *Naylor's 1988 *Mama Day is a tremendously effective and well-respected midwife, healer, and conjure woman. Her "children" repay her with a variety of made and purchased objects. In her mid-eighties, she has delivered countless babies. With her special gifts as a healer, she is also instrumental in enabling the infertile Bernice to conceive a child. Naylor depicts Mama Day as an essential part of a small-town island community where neighbors depend upon each other for everything from rides across the bridge to comfort in the time of sickness and death. While that should also be the case in Tina McElroy *Ansa's Baby of the Family (1989), that novel nonetheless depicts the consequences of modern medical practices upon the effectiveness of the nurse/midwife in a small community. Nurse Bloom would attend properly to Lena McPherson and the caul that covers her head at birth except for the upwardly mobile Mrs. McPherson, who circumvents what she views as interference and thus leads to unnatural consequences for her baby daughter.

—Trudier Harris

MIGRATION. From the forced migration of the *Middle Passage, the dangerous escape of the fugitive slave, the wanderings of the freed men and women following emancipation to the mass exodus of African Americans first to states like Kansas and Oklahoma and later to the urban centers of the North, the Midwest, and the West, much of the *history of black people in the United States is the history of a people in a constant state of motion. It is not surprising, therefore, that the theme of migration is a major one in African American history and culture. The *spirituals, *slave narratives, *blues, and the twentieth-century migration narratives all bear witness to the mobility, dispossession, and dispersal of black people in the United States.

The earliest forms of African American cultural production—oral folk tales and spirituals—are filled with references to migration. Interestingly, few, if any, document the horrors of the Middle Passage. Most references to mobility in these forms refer to Africa, Heaven, or the North. In many instances all three destinations are encoded within one reference to escape from the harshness of slave life. The event to which the spirituals often refer is the Exodus of the Jews out of Egypt. *Moses is as important a hero as Jesus in the spirituals.

The "Sometimes I feel like a feather in the air / And I spread my wings and fly" of the spiritual "Some-times I Feel Like a Motherless Child," is echoed in tales of flying Africans who lift up from the fields of the American South and take flight back to Africa. Literary critic and poet Melvin *Dixon argues that the language of the spirituals "called into being a place beyond the confines of the plantation" where the slaves underwent "a fundamental change in self-perception and moral status" (Ride out the Wilderness, 1987). Although this space was often symbolic, just as often it was a literal space of free territory. When the slave sang "Soon as you cease from your sins / Trains goin' to stop and take you in. / I'm goin' away to leave you / I'm goin' away to leave you / Sinner, I'm goin' away to leave you / And I can't stay here," she was just as likely singing of her imminent escape to the North as she was singing about her death and afterlife.

If the singers coded their escape in the language of religious transcendence, the slave narrators were more explicit in naming their earthly destination. The fugitives invariably document their escape from the oppressive South into a North that is ostensibly freer. However, unlike the spirituals, many of the slave narratives, like Harriet A. *Jacobs's *Incidents in the Life of a Slave Girl (1861), assert disappointment in discovering that the North is plagued by racial segregation and haunted by slave catchers who have been granted the right to hunt their human prey by the Fugitive Slave Act of 1850. This complicity of the North with the South's racial system of chattel *slavery foreshadows the similarities between the North and South documented by twentieth-century narrators of the migration narrative as well.

The slave narratives document their protagonists' trying to escape from slavery, often through the intricate system of the *Underground Railroad, a literal and figurative wilderness, and at times traveling on the ocean before finally arriving in the northern city, the place where he or she seeks anonymity. Eventually however the narrators come to realize that several markers make such anonymity almost impossible: the color of their skin, the downward cast of their eyes, the dialect in which they speak, their lack of familiarity with the urban landscape, and most significantly—some white person from back home. Toni *Morrison might have been speaking of the fugitive slaves in the slave narratives when in *Beloved (1987) she wrote, "Move. Walk. Run." Stay in a constant state of physical and psychic motion for no place is safe, no place is home.

Other nineteenth-century texts by African American authors stress migration as well. Although these fictional texts are not slave narratives, their protagonists traverse the same landscape and encounter the same conditions. Martin R. *Delany's *Blake, or The Huts of America (1859–1861) is the story of a Cuban-born black sailor who arrives in the United States enslaved. Later he escapes to Canada, but returns to the United States to free family members and incite slave rebellions. He travels to Africa and back to Cuba where he plans a major slave revolt. Blake's travels mirror the journeys of those Africans brought from Africa to the Caribbean and southern states before escaping and traveling north.

In the twentieth century, the theme of migration finds expression in the migration narrative—a form that documents the massive internal migration of African Americans from the South to the cities of the North, Midwest, and West, and in the *historical novels that revisit slavery, Reconstruction, and the turn-of-the-century segregation era. From Paul Laurence *Dunbar's The *Sport of the Gods (1902) to Toni Morrison's *Jazz (1992), the migration narrative emerges as one of the twentieth century's dominant forms of African American cultural production. Migration narratives—musical, visual, and literary—mark an attempt on behalf of African American artists and intellectuals to come to terms with the massive dislocation of black people following migration. The migration narrative shares with the slave narrative notions of ascent from the South into a "freer" North. However, the migration narrative departs from the slave narrative in its exploration of urbanism, explication of sophisticated modern power, and, in some instances, a return south. Some of the most significant migration narratives include: Jean *Toomer's *Cane (1923), Nella *Larsen's *Quicksand (1928), Richard *Wright's 12 Million Black Voices (1941), Ralph *Ellison's *Invisible Man (1952), James *Baldwin's *Go Tell It on the Mountain (1953), and Gloria *Naylor's The *Women of Brewster Place (1982).

Lawrence Rodgers identifies a form of migration narrative that he calls the Afro-American Great Migration Novel. According to Rodgers, these *novels, written during the Great Migration, "generally focus on how to come to terms with the spatial, communal, and psychological differences between South and North, rural and urban, industrial and rural, down home and downtown." Rodgers's canon includes Paul Laurence Dunbar's The Sport of the Gods, James Weldon *Johnson's The *Autobiography of an Ex-Colored Man (1912), Waters *Turpin's O Canaan! (1939), William *Attaway's Blood on the Forge (1941), Carl Ruthven *Offord's The White Face (1943), George Wylie *Henderson's Jule (1946), Alden Bland's Behold a Cry (1947), and Dorothy *West's The Living Is Easy (1948).

The twentieth-century migration narrative also finds form in *music, especially the blues and rhythm and blues. From the well-known "I'm Goin to Chicago baby / Sorry but I can't take you" to Stevie Wonder's classic "Livin' for the City," African American music retells and revises the story of black migration throughout this century.

As with their enslaved forbears, the protagonists and authors of contemporary migration narratives often find the North to be a hostile landscape. This sometimes leads to further migration—either to different cities, different countries, or back down south. This last choice is indicative of the actual return migration of many African Americans following the *civil rights movement. In fiction it takes on the qualities of what Robert Stepto defines as a journey of immersion:

A ritualized journey into a symbolic South, in which the protagonist seeks those aspects of tribal literacy that ameliorate, if not obliterate, the conditions imposed by solitude. The conventional immersion narrative ends almost paradoxically with the questing figure located in or near the narrative's most oppressive social structure, but free in the sense that he has gained sufficient tribal literacy to assume the mantle of an articulate kinsman.

This "journey of immersion" is traveled by a pantheon of African American protagonists in the works of W. E. B. *Du Bois, James Weldon Johnson, Zora Neale *Hurston, Amiri *Baraka, Paule *Marshall, and Speech of the rap group Arrested Development.

In addition to those narratives, poems, and songs documenting black migration from the South to the North, twentieth-century African American authors such as Marshall have also explored migration to and from the Caribbean: *Brown Girl, Brownstones (1959), The *Chosen Place, the Timeless People (1969), Praisesong for the Widow (1983), and Daughters (1991). Marita *Golden's Migrations of the Heart (1983) deals with Africa, Carlene Hatcher *Polite's The Flagellants (1967) with Europe.

Much black fiction of the second half of the twentieth century returns to slavery and concentrates on the forced migration of the Middle Passage, the escape of runaway slaves, and the mobility of newly freed slaves in search of *family, *work, and escape from the haunting past of slavery. Texts of this type include David *Bradley's The Chaneysville Incident (1981), Toni Morrison's Beloved, and Caryl Phillips's Crossing the River (1993). All of these texts revise the slave narratives from the standpoint of the present, attesting to the ongoing dispossession, displacement, and mobility that characterize black life in the Americas. To those early New World Africans who told fantastic tales of walking on water or flying back to Africa, the anonymous African narrator of Caryl Phillips's Crossing the River stands on the shores of Africa where he longs for the children he sold into slavery and tells them and us "There is no return."

[See also Bildungsroman; Diasporic Literature; Emigration; Expatriatism; Lynching; Neo–Slave Narrative; Places.]

• Robert Stepto, From Behind the Veil: A Study of Afro-American Narrative, 1979. Hazel Carby, Reconstructing Womanhood: The Emergence of the Black Woman Novelist, 1987. Melvin Dixon, Ride Out the Wilderness: Geography and Identity in Afro-American Literature, 1987. Susan Willis, Specifying: Black Women Writing the American Experience, 1987. Hazel Carby, "It Just Be Dat Way Sometimes: The Sexual Politics of Women's Blues" in Unequal Sisters: A Multicultural Reader in U.S. Women's History, eds. Ellen Carol DuBois and Vicki L. Ruiz, 1990, pp. 330–339. Lawrence R. Rodgers, "Dorothy West's The Living Is Easy and the Ideal of Southern Folk Community," African American Review, 26.1 (Spring 1992): 161–172. Lawrence R. Rodgers, "Paul Laurence Dunbar's The Sport of the Gods: The Doubly Conscious World of Plantation Fiction, Migration, and Ascent," American Literary Realism 24.3 (Spring 1992): 42–57. Charles Scruggs, Sweet Home: Invisible Cities in the Afro-American Novel, 1993. Farah Jasmine Griffin, Who Set You Flowin': The African American Migration Narrative, 1995.

—Farah Jasmine Griffin

MILDRED JOHNSON in Alice *Childress's *Like One of the Family . . . Conversations from a Domestic's Life (1956) is one of the most memorable characters ever created in African American literature. A day worker who goes from house to house across New York City, Mildred enlightens her white employers about their own foibles related to *race, *class, and *gender biases. She is motivated by her conscience to help her employers see their condescension and make changes. Mildred, a consummate storyteller, informs her best friend, Marge, about the daily confrontations with her white employers. Each of the sixty-two short conversations that Mildred has with Marge serves to comment on the social tensions of the 1950s while countering myths about African Americans and their place in society. Mildred is bold, witty, vivacious, and intellectually superior. Instead of quietly accepting abuses, she speaks out not only for herself but for all *domestics. She uses humor and cunning to insist upon better wages and working conditions. Mildred also serves as the voice of nationalistic pride, which places her in the context of other great African American spokespersons such as Olaudah *Equiano, Martin R. *Delany, Marcus *Garvey, and Langston *Hughes. Mildred, as mouthpiece for Childress, highlights the accomplishments of African Americans. Childress's Mildred, a supermaid, serves as heroine of the Black working class in the tradition of Langston Hughes's Jesse B. *Simple. Childress's Mildred voices with aplomb the frustrations and joys of the little people, the masses of poor, invisible people who have the power to disrupt life if they so choose.

[See also Black Nationalism; Class; Work.]

• Trudier Harris, introduction to Like One of the Family: Conversations from a Domestic's Life, 1956; rpt. 1986.

—Elizabeth Brown-Guillory

MILKMAN DEAD is the protagonist in Toni *Morrison's *Song of Solomon (1977). Named by the town gossip because his mother, Ruth, nursed him at her breast far longer than considered socially acceptable, Milkman's real name is Macon Dead III. The novel tells the story of his passage into manhood and the *identity crisis that comes from being the son of Macon Dead II, the most "propertied" African American man in their Michigan town. Macon not only intimidates his tenants, who regard him as a slum landlord, but also his wife and children. He forbids Milkman to associate with his aunt, *Pilate Dead, regarding her as the town pariah whose eccentric ways are a source of embarrassment to him and the middle-class identity he has struggled to secure for himself and his family. Milkman decides to give up his middle-class comforts to go south to look for the gold inheritance he has learned about from his father.

The second half of the novel traces Milkman's journey to the South, where he meets his father's people and learns the family history of Solomon, his paternal great-grandfather, who, according to the song he first heard Pilate sing when he was a child, flew back to Africa rather than remain in slavery. The novel also traces Milkman's journey into a new understanding of himself, the African American community, and his relationship to others. At the end of the novel he learns there is no gold, only a sack containing his grandfather's bones. He escorts Pilate to the South and helps her give her father a proper burial. As Pilate dies in his arms, he sings the song he learned from her, having learned that it was not only the song of his people, but also the song that had helped him reclaim a sense of self and his heritage.

• Marilyn Sanders Mobley, Folk Roots and Mythic Wings in Sarah Orne Jewett and Toni Morrison, 1992.

—Marilyn Sanders Mobley

MILLER, E. ETHELBERT (b. 1950), poet, essayist, critic, educator, and broadcast journalist. Eugene Ethelbert Miller was born in New York City to West Indian immigrant parents. He attended a predominantly Italian American and Jewish high school in the Bronx. These early cultural influences contribute to the thematic scheme of much of his *poetry. Before obtaining a BA in African American Studies from Howard University, Miller had intended to complete a degree in history and begin a career in law. It was during the time Miller reassessed his professional goals that the poetry and song of the 1960s and the *Black Arts movement were in full effect and would help him develop his voice.

Miller is a living cultural and literary resource. Since 1974, as director of the African American Studies Resource Center at Howard University, he has maintained an extensive, rare collection of African American literature and history of which he has an amazingly personal knowledge. Numerous young writers continue to benefit from Miller's commitment to cultivating the arts in the District of Columbia. He is founder and director of the Ascension Poetry Series, one of the oldest series in Washington, D.C. Through this series of readings and professional workshops, Miller has introduced the community to the undiscovered talents of many now renowned writers. Miller's insistence that the community respond to and provide encouragement for fresh and diverse new artists is evidenced in the volumes he has edited: Synergy D.C. Anthology (1975), Women Surviving Massacres and Men (1977), and In Search of Color Everywhere (1994).

Along with his informal interpersonal cultivation of advice, ideas, and information, Miller extends himself to academic and policy-making venues. As he expressed in a 1987 interview with the Washington Post, Miller is dedicated to involving himself in every aspect of writing. He is an associate faculty member at Bennington College, Bennington, Vermont; a visiting professor at the University of Nevada, Las Vegas; a member of the board of the National Writers Union, and Associated Writing Programs; and senior editor of African American Review and Washington Review.

Miller is essentially a cultural critic whose vision reaches beyond *race to examine the human condition. Miller's work captures the poetic struggle of day-to-day living: love, family, manhood, the liberation of women, the politics of protest and inclusion. The lines are quiet and succinct, much like the quickness and quietness that disguise the profundity of daily events. In "Only Language Can Hold Us Together," Miller identifies with the politics involved in a black woman's struggle for beauty, saying she did not understand why no one recognized the "beauty of her hair." In "The Kid," the poet unveils the hidden core beneath a comfortable mask, telling about how the subject talks candidly about his father "sometimes when we ain't talking about baseball."

Miller's collections attest to his twenty-year commitment to the continuing tradition of African American literature: *The Land of Smiles and the Land of No Smiles* (1974), *Andromeda* (1974), *The Migrant Worker* (1978), *Season of Hunger/Cry of Rain: Poems 1975–1980* (1982), *Where Are the Love Poems for Dictators?* (1986), *First Light: New and Selected Poems* (1993), and *How We Sleep on the Nights We Don't Make Love* (1996). In recognition of his talent, Miller has won the O. B. Hardison, Jr., Award for imaginative art and teaching (1995), the Columbia Merit Award (1993), the Public Humanities Award from the D.C. Community Council (1988), and the Mayor's Art Award for Literature (1982).

• Priscilla R. Ramsey, "E. Ethelbert Miller," in *DLB*, vol. 41, *Afro-American Poets since 1955*, eds. Trudier Harris and Thadious M. Davis, 1985, pp. 233–240.

—Elanna N. Haywood

MILLER, KELLY (1863–1939), educator, essayist, and sociologist. The son of Kelly Miller, a free African American cotton farmer, and Elizabeth (Roberts), a slave, Kelly Miller was reared on a backcountry farm near Winnsboro, South Carolina, and attended Howard University and Johns Hopkins, where he studied physics and mathematics. He held jobs in the United States Pension Office and in the Washington, D.C., public schools before joining Howard's faculty in 1890. While there he completed his AM (1901) and LLD (1903) degrees. He remained at his alma mater for forty-four years in a range of teaching and administrative positions, including professor of mathematics, chair of sociology, dean of the junior college, and dean of the College of Arts and Sciences. So closely identified with Howard that it was often known during his tenure as "Kelly Miller's University," he helped to modernize its curriculum, to institute the systematic study of Negro life, to promote the hiring of African American faculty and administrators, and by the 1930s, to champion segregated *education. Toward the end of his academic career, he came increasingly into conflict with his junior colleagues, who had been hired by Howard's first African American president, Mordecai Johnson. The scientific and theoretical methods of research pursued by these young professionals, who included Ralph Bunche, Sterling A. *Brown, and E. Franklin Frazier, were, in Miller's view, at odds with his more personal emphasis on self-help and character building.

Equally active outside the university, he wrote an influential column circulated in more than one hundred newspapers across the country, assisted W. E. B. *Du Bois as an editor of the *Crisis* magazine, and authored several important pamphlets, including "The Disgrace of Democracy: An Open Letter to President Woodrow Wilson" (1917), and a series of *essays, some of which were compiled and published as books. The best of these include *From Servitude to Service* (1905), *Race Adjustment* (1908), *Out of the*

House of Bondage (1917), and *The Everlasting Stain* (1924).

As a race leader, Miller was a philosophic moderate critical of both the militant agendas associated with the Niagara Movement (despite holding firm respect for the movement's leader, Du Bois) and the conservative views, especially on education, of Booker T. *Washington. Calling for a measured, middle-of-the-road response to the "oppressive conditions" of African Americans, he observed in *Race Adjustment* that "no thoughtful Negro is satisfied with the present status of his race." But as a pragmatist who sought progress through harmony, he held that African American advancement was a slow, if inevitable, process relying on black achievement and patience, middle-class virtue, economic development, and white goodwill. Later in his life, he was dismayed by the direction of American racial politics, which seemed to him to be driven by young radicals. In contrast to most African American intellectuals, he supported Roosevelt's New Deal, opposed organized labor, and spoke out strongly against African American migration to the urban industrial North, which challenged the roots of his agrarian values. Nonetheless, he will be remembered for typifying the African American intellectual elite of the early twentieth century.

[*See also* Literacy; Newspaper Columns; Talented Tenth, The.]

• August Meier, *Negro Thought in America, 1880–1915*, 1963, pp. 213–218. James Young, *Black Writers of the Thirties*, 1973, pp. 3–13. "Kelly Miller," in *Dictionary of American Negro Biography*, eds. Rayford W. Logan and Michael R. Winston, 1982, pp. 435–439.

—Lawrence R. Rodgers

MILLER, MAY (1899–1995), poet and playwright. May Miller was born on 26 January 1889 in Washington, D.C., to Annie May Butler and Kelly Miller, a distinguished professor of sociology at Howard University. At Paul Laurence *Dunbar High School, May Miller studied with prominent African American dramatist Mary Burrill and poet Angelina Weld *Grimké. As a drama major at Howard University, she directed, acted, and produced plays while collaborating with Alain *Locke and Montgomery Gregory in the founding of a black drama movement. Later, she taught speech, theater, and dance at Frederick *Douglass High School in Baltimore, Maryland, and was a lecturer and poet at Monmouth College, the University of Wisconsin–Milwaukee, and the Philips Exeter Academy.

Most of her plays were written between 1920 and 1945. A number won drama prizes, including *Within the Shadows*, *Bog Guide*, and *The Cuss'd Thing*. Four were published in the anthology she edited with Willis *Richardson in 1935: *Negro History in Thirteen Plays*, a collection that firmly established Miller's national reputation. Of these, *Sojourner *Truth* is notable for its inclusion of white characters who are changed by their contact with a black character, but this play seems somewhat wooden compared to the powerful *Harriet *Tubman*, about a spurned *mulatto suitor attempting to betray other slaves in pursuit of money with which to buy his own *freedom. The plays set in the African Sudan (*Samory*) and Haiti (*Christophe's Daughters*) lack the verisimilitude of her other work. Miller's *Ridin' the Goat* uses humor to challenge the values of the black middle class and to suggest the importance of community rituals and cultural practices. Other important plays include *Scratches* (1929) and the antilynching *Nails and Thorns* (1933).

By the mid-1940s, Miller devoted most of her attention to poetry. Fairly traditional in their form and language, Miller's volumes of poetry include *Into the Clearing* (1959); *Poems* (1962); *Lyrics of Three Women: Katie Lyle, Maude Rubin, and May Miller* (1964); *Not That Far* (1973); *The Clearing and Beyond* (1974); *Dust of Uncertain Journey* (1975); and *The Ransomed Wait* (1983). Editor of *Green Wind* (1978) and *My World* (1979), she also authored a book of children's poems, *Halfway to the Sun* (1981). Her poems frequently engage in significant spiritual and ethical questions. "Late Conjecture," for instance, questions the meaning of Christ's sacrifice, while Miller's "The Dream of Wheat" envisions "unnumbered rows of ripened wheat" that "March to greedy ovens." The poem ends by demanding starkly "Who will eat? / Who go hungry?" Her poems have been published in *Phylon, the Antioch Review,* the *Crisis,* the *Nation,* the *New York Times,* and *Poetry,* and have been praised by Gwendolyn *Brooks as "excellent and long-celebrated" and by Robert *Hayden, who has said of May Miller that she "writes with quiet strength, lyric intensity. She is perceptive and compassionate, a poet of humane vision." Miller read her poetry at the inauguration of President Jimmy Carter, and is included in a 1972 Library of Congress collection of poets reading their own works. May Miller, who died on 11 February 1995, lived to see the manifestation of her own prediction of the importance of the movement she encouraged, the "little one-act play groups that performed in churches and schools [and which were] a forerunner to what we're doing now" (quoted in *DLB,* vol. 41, 1985).

• Winifred L. Stoeling, "May Miller," *DLB,* vol. 41, *Afro-American Poets since 1955,* eds. Trudier Harris and Thadious Davis, 1985, pp. 241–247. James V. Hatch and Leo Hamalian, eds., *The Roots of African-American Theater,* 1991, pp. 307–327. Willis Richardson, *Plays and Pageants from the Life of the Negro,* 1993, pp. 109–177.   —Lynda Koolish

MILLICAN, ARTHENIA J. BATES (b. 1920), poet, educator, short fiction writer, lecturer, and humanist of the rural southern folk. Born Arthenia Bernetta Jackson on 1 June 1920, in Sumter, South Carolina, this African American woman of the South rose above her obscure place in letters in the 1980s. Her parents, Calvin Shepard Jackson and Susan Emma David, were both professionals who embraced education and *religion. The mother, however, was extremely class-conscious, a quality Arthenia Bates never adopted. In fact, a hallmark of her writing is her love of the folk, evident in her themes and the dialect and rhythms of her short stories. Her exposure, on an intimate level, to common people came through her two marriages to nonprofessional men,

Noah Bates on 11 June 1950, and Wilbert Millican on 14 August 1969. The marriage to Bates ended in divorce in 1956, and Millican's mother never forgave her for marrying the laborer Bates and the dockworker Millican, thus removing herself from the privileged African American middle *class.

Millican's early career was as a teacher and department head in South Carolina and Virginia public schools. She finished Morris College in Sumter, South Carolina, in 1941, earned a master's degree from Atlanta University in 1948, and earned a PhD from Louisiana State University in 1972, writing a dissertation on James Weldon *Johnson, "In Quest of an Afro-Centric Tradition for Black American Literature." This was a long-deferred dream. While in Atlanta, she studied the art of *poetry writing with Langston *Hughes, a major influence.

In 1969, after a lifetime of writing, Millican published her *Seeds Beneath the Snow: Vignettes from the South.* Much of her literary reputation is based on this work, a collection of short stories that has steadily gained a national reputation. Millican thought of the people of Virginia as late-blooming seeds that survived in spite of a blanket of snow.

Critical reception of *Seeds Beneath the Snow* was highly favorable, and Millican was compared to Paul Laurence *Dunbar, Charles Waddell *Chesnutt, Zora Neale *Hurston, and Thomas Hardy. The *Washington Post,* in a 1970 review, praised Millican for her "primitive themes." *CLA Journal,* in 1973, cited the writer for her unusual ability as a "local colorist." Millican's ability to sketch characters may be attributed to her immersion in Henry James and her direct involvement on the front porches with people of the community during her first marriage.

Millican's critical and scholarly articles have appeared in the *Southern University Bulletin, Negro American Literature Forum,* and *CLA Journal.* Harlo Press of Detroit published her *The Deity Nodded* in 1973, and Millican published *Such Things from the Valley* in 1977. Her fiction has appeared in *Black World* (July 1971), *Obsidian* (1975), and *Callaloo* (December 1975).

As an educator, Millican gave most of her career to Southern University in Baton Rouge, Louisiana, where she taught from 1956 until her retirement in 1980. In an unusual town-gown initiative, she and others at Southern University formed a group called the Academic Humanists in order to bridge the wide gap between college and community.

In July 1976, Millican received a $6,000 fellowship from the National Endowment for the Arts for her story "Where You Belong." Ignored by major anthologists until *Sturdy Black Bridges* (Bell et al., 1979), Millican is finally getting her due.

• Virginia Whatley Smith, "Arthenia J. Bates Millican," in *DLB,* vol. 38, *Afro-American Writers after 1955: Dramatists and Prose Writers,* eds. Thadious M. Davis and Trudier Harris, 1985, pp. 195–201.   —Glenda E. Gill

MILNER, RON (b. 1938), playwright, writer, editor, critic, and director. Born in Detroit, Michigan, Ron Milner graduated from Detroit's Northeastern High School. He attended Highland Park Junior College,

Detroit Institute of Technology, and Columbia University in New York. In the early 1960s, Milner received two prestigious literary grants, the John Hay Whitney Fellowship (1962) and a Rockefeller Fellowship (1965), to work on a novel, *The Life of the Brothers Brown.* Milner is one of the most significant figures to emerge from the *Black Arts movement. He is known affectionately as the "people's playwright" for his ongoing commitment to using Black theater for the advancement of Black people. Milner has taught widely and was writer in residence at Lincoln University (Pennsylvania) from 1966 to 1967, where his friendship with Langston *Hughes, who urged him to use a personal voice in his writing, matured.

A "born writer," Milner is a prolific playwright. His first major play, *Who's Got His Own,* premiered in Harlem in 1967. Milner went to New York with friend and producer-director Woodie *King, Jr., as part of a touring production of three plays by Malcolm Boyd in 1964. He and King joined the American Place Theatre, where *Who's Got His Own* and *The Warning: A Theme for Linda* (1969, published in *A Black Quartet: Four New Black Plays,* 1970) were conceived and performed. Other published plays include *The Monster* (Drama Review, 1968), *(M)Ego and the Green Ball of Freedom* (Black World, 1968), and *What the Wine-Sellers Buy* (Samuel French, 1974).

From 1979 to 1981 Milner lived in California, teaching creative writing at the University of Southern California and doing community work. Milner has since returned to Detroit, where he remains and where he feels he can better visualize the chronology of his stories. Milner feels his creative energy can feed on the unique experience of life in his hometown.

Milner's life and art reflect the driving force he calls for in his critical writing. In "Black Magic, Black Art" (*Negro Digest,* Apr. 1967; *Black Poets and Prophets,* 1972), Milner proclaimed that Black Art must affirm, inspire, and touch the souls of Black people. Milner's *Roads of the Mountaintops* (1986) deals with the internal struggle of Martin Luther *King, Jr., following his receipt of the Nobel Peace Prize in 1964. *What the Wine-Sellers Buy,* which earned over a million dollars in 1974, deals with a young Black man choosing between good and evil while simultaneously addressing the issue of Black male responsibility. *Checkmates* (1987), which starred Denzel Washington, portrays the potential strength of Black love. *Don't Get God Started* (1988) is a gospel-tinged musical play done for the family singing group the Winans.

A lesser-known work from Milner's career is his short story "Junkie Joe Had Some Money," which was anthologized in Langston Hughes's *Best Short Stories by Negro Writers* (1967). Perhaps Milner's most significant contribution to the field of African American letters is *Black Drama Anthology* (1972), coedited with Woodie King. One of the earliest and certainly one of the most respected *anthologies of black plays, it documented important works by Milner, Amiri *Baraka, Ed *Bullins, and Langston Hughes, among others.

Twice married and twice divorced, Milner is the father of four children. His son Raymarc is a filmmaker with whom Milner wishes to collaborate in the future. Milner currently writes *film and *television scripts in addition to teaching playwriting to younger Blacks.

Much of Milner's life revolves around working with children and using *theater to educate them. This "functional writing," as Milner calls it, brings young African Americans into a dialogue with his plays and raises critical concerns as a vehicle for their self-improvement. Milner currently persists in his endeavor to establish regional-level Black theater in Michigan.

• Jeanne E. Saddler, "Ron Milner: The People's Playwright," *Essence,* Nov. 1974, 20. Geneva Smitherman, "'We Are the Music': Ron Milner, People's Playwright," *Black World* 25.6 (Apr. 1976): 4–19.
—Derek A. Williams

MINNIE RANSOM. The "fabled healer" of Claybourne, Georgia, Minnie Ransom is the stimulus for *Velma Henry's *healing in Toni Cade *Bambara's *The *Salt Eaters* (1980). A multifaceted character, Minnie communes with her spirit guide, Old Wife; plays *jazz recordings; and has a "voluptuous eye" cast on a young doctor, all while guiding Velma in her healing journey.

Minnie's characterization is a departure from the usual representations of conjure women, healers, or *mammies in African American literature. Wearing a red dress, hot pink headwrap, kente cloth, a silk fringed shawl, and an armful of bangles, she is fully sexual, a celebration of African American womanhood. While deeply committed to her community and its collective as well as individual well-being, she refuses to take responsibility for the health of others, insisting, for example, that Velma be sure she is ready for the "weight" of being well.

Although Minnie's spirit guide, Old Wife, is a "good Christian," Minnie's spiritual system is more syncretic. She draws on the powers of the loa and astrology, as well as the "chapel" she visits with Old Wife. As able to read auras as she is to cure disease, Minnie came to her gift reluctantly, nearly going crazy as she realized what was happening to her. Seeing their "educated, well-groomed, well-raised" daughter eating dirt prompted her family to send Minnie off to a seminary. Like her patient Velma, however, Minnie grows and becomes wise, knowing that healing is not about being good or righteous, but being "available" to the powers and gifts within and around her.

[*See also* Conjuring; Folk Literature; Folklore.]
—Ann Folwell Stanford

MINSTRELSY. Known in nineteenth-century America as "Negro" or "Ethiopian" minstrelsy, the blackface minstrel show was an extremely popular form of commercial entertainment in which white men lampooned African Americans for sport and profit. Northern stage performers such as George Washington Dixon and T. D. Rice donned black makeup (usually greasepaint or burnt cork); parodied black dress, dance, speech, and song; and developed such enduring stereotypes as the wily but witless rustic slave *Jim Crow and the ridiculous urban dandy Zip Coon. In 1843, troupes such as Dan Emmett's Virginia Minstrels and E. P. Christy's Christy's Minstrels began to elaborate the minstrel show's classic tripartite structure: an opening section featuring a semicircle of performers who combined songs and dances with broad jokes and riddles, a middle or "olio" section offering comic or novelty set-pieces such as burlesque "sermons" or "stump speeches," and a final section usually consisting of an extended skit set in the South. After the Civil War, African American blackface performers developed competing versions of minstrelsy, reworking even as they adopted racist entertainment conventions. This led in the 1890s to the "*coon show," a reanimated form of minstrelsy featuring razor-toting hustlers and chicken-stealing loafers. Notwithstanding its renewed commitment to racist stereotypes, minstrelsy was nearly the only mainstream outlet for African American stage talent: the coon show provided a venue for the work of Will Marion Cook, Paul Laurence *Dunbar, Bert Williams, and others, while artists such as W. C. Handy and Ma *Rainey got their start in black minstrelsy.

African American writers have felt compelled to rebut and revise defamatory white images of blacks and to defend African American character. Rebuttals go back at least to Frederick *Douglass's 1840s editorial denunciations of minstrelsy in the *North Star, which were echoed in Martin *Delany's sardonic rewritings of minstrel lyrics in his novel *Blake (1859–1861) and later amplified in such works as Zora Neale *Hurston's "Characteristics of Negro Expression" (1934), Ralph *Ellison's "Change the Joke and Slip the Yoke" (1958), and LeRoi Jones/Amiri *Baraka's Blues People (1963). Even Jessie Redmon *Fauset's celebration of Bert Williams in a 1922 issue of the *Crisis contains an implicit rebuke of white minstrelsy. Other African American writers have made ironic or *signifying references to blackface in their work, from the blackface disguise of escaping slave Harriet A. *Jacobs (in *Incidents in the Life of a Slave Girl, 1861) to the racial transfigurations undergone by whites in Charles Waddell *Chesnutt's story "Mars Jeems's Nightmare" (1899) and Melvin Van Peebles's film Watermelon Man (1970). Booker T. *Washington's resort to coon-show stereotype in his *Atlanta Exposition Address's thinly veiled invocation of black chicken thieves (reprinted in his *Up from Slavery, 1901) is an exception in African American writing. Langston *Hughes's poem "Song for a Dark Girl" (1927) quotes the famous Dan Emmett minstrel song "Dixie" (1859) in the context of southern lynch law; satirical portrayals of black minstrelsy occur in novels by Paul Laurence Dunbar (The *Sport of the Gods, 1901) and Wallace *Thurman (The *Blacker the Berry, 1929); George C. Wolfe's play The Colored Museum (1986) reappropriates in order to explode images derived from the minstrel tradition; and Wesley Brown's historical novel Darktown Strut-

ters (1994) narrates the fate of an African American minstrel-show dancer.

[See also Theater.]

• Robert C. Toll, Blacking Up: The Minstrel Show in Nineteenth-Century America, 1974. Eric Lott, Love and Theft: Blackface Minstrelsy and the American Working Class, 1993.

—Eric Lott

MISCEGENATION. In his 1993 book of *essays, Race Matters, Cornel *West calls interracial sex between Anglo Americans and African Americans the last taboo that needs to be discussed before progress can be made in *race relations. African American writers have seldom shied away from the highly charged topic of mixing the races, or miscegenation. The earliest *novels and *slave narratives protest the practices of rape and concubinage of African American female slaves, while contemporary literature often depicts voluntary romantic interracial unions disintegrating because of the social and psychological pressures of breaking society's taboos. In whatever historical period, African American authors have used the drama of interracial sex to protest and explore racial attitudes and behavior in the United States.

From the perspective of an African American slave, Harriet A. *Jacobs, under the pseudonym of Linda Brent, dramatically recounts her efforts to avoid concubinage by one of her owners in *Incidents in the Life of a Slave Girl (1861). To exact revenge, protection, and possible *freedom for herself and her children, Brent has two children by another white man. After seven years of hiding in a tiny attic to be near her children, Brent escapes north with her family. While she is eventually able to triumph over her scheming owner, Jacobs's dramatic autobiographical narrative emphasizes the vulnerable condition of enslaved African American women, thought of merely as property.

One of the first African American novels, William Wells *Brown's *Clotel, or The President's Daughter (1853), offers an equally outraged portrait of miscegenation during *slavery. The protagonist of the novel, Clotel, is the daughter of a quadroon slave and the President of the United States, Thomas Jefferson. Brown elaborates on the rumor that Jefferson and one of his slaves, Sally *Hemings, had several children. As part of his antislavery efforts, Brown uses the theme of miscegenation to attack the hypocrisy of the founding fathers, who on the one hand proclaim self-evident truths about human equality and on the other hand were rumored to sell their own unackowledged children into slavery for profit. In showing the tragic suicide of Clotel at the end of the novel as she jumps into the Potomac to avoid the slave-catchers, Brown exposes the inequities of American democracy and the destructive effects of slavery on *families, children, and human rights.

While the central characters voluntarily cross the *color line for love in Frank J. *Webb's The Garies and Their Friends (1857), the results are similarly tragic. An interracial couple, the Garies move north to Philadelphia to avoid persecution, only to be murdered by an angry white mob. When their son is discovered *passing for white in order to marry a white woman, he is rejected by his fiancée and apparently dies of a broken heart. One of the first novels to deal with this topic extensively, *The Garies and Their Friends* urges African American solidarity and economic self-determination as a means of survival in such a harsh environment.

Similarly, Harriet E. *Wilson's *Our Nig, or Sketches from the Life of a Free Black* (1859) deals with interracial *marriages in the context of the allegedly free North. Like *The Garies and Their Friends*, Wilson's novel shows the ostracism that interracial couples have to endure. Once her first African American husband dies, the white woman, Mag Smith, takes up with her husband's business associate, also an African American. To increase their chances for financial survival the couple abandon their *mulatto daughter, Alfrado, and move out of the area. This family tragedy sets the stage for the rest of the novel as it documents the difficulties Alfrado experiences as an orphan and exploited servant to a bigoted white family.

Dealing with miscegenation in more middle-class contexts, turn-of-the-century novels, such as Charles Waddell *Chesnutt's *The *House behind the Cedars* (1900) and James Weldon *Johnson's *The *Autobiography of an Ex-Colored Man* (1912), explore, with great psychological complexity, the competing pressures of *class aspirations and racial loyalty among those light enough to pass for white. In *The Autobiography of an Ex-Colored Man*, the narrator marries a white woman and decides to pass permanently for white. At the end of the novel he remains divided about whether he has chosen the right path since the costs of abandoning his African American community and heritage have been so high. And in *The House behind the Cedars*, the racially mixed heroine of the novel collapses under the conflicts induced by her ambitious mother, a licentious African American suitor, and an ambivalent white lover whom she meets while passing for white. The novels of this period are insightful and complex psychological and social portraits, offering no easy solutions for their protagonists' internal and external dilemmas.

*Harlem Renaissance writers repeated these themes as their racially mixed characters struggle to reconcile their conflicts concerning racial loyalty and chances for wealth and status. In contrast to white-authored novels of passing for white, however, these novels, including Walter *White's *Flight* (1926), Nella *Larsen's *Passing* (1929), and Jessie Redmon *Fauset's *Plum Bun* (1929) and *Comedy: American Style* (1933), show the psychological dangers of passing and urge a return to a usually supportive African American community.

Although part of the group of African American writers associated with the Harlem Renaissance, Jean *Toomer's later writing offers an entirely different perspective on miscegenation and racial intermixture. Inspired by Eastern spirituality and philosophy, Toomer saw hope where others saw primarily exploitation and suffering. His poem "The Blue Meridian" (1936) sets forth his belief in creating a synthetic and superior blue or purple being, a being that transcends conventional and provincial racial categories.

Toomer's lead was not followed, however. The rise of the social protest novel, in fact, intensified the warnings against interracial mixture. Following the lead of Richard *Wright's influential *Native Son* (1940), African American literature after World War II warned more strongly against romantic interracial relationships, often showing the incompatibility of racial intermixture with the activist demands of a growing *civil rights movement.

Chester *Himes, for example, uses interracial sexual relations to document the perversity of race relations in the United States. In *If He Hollers Let Him Go* (1945), *Lonely Crusade* (1947), and *The Primitive* (1955), interracial romances and sexual liaisons are battlegrounds of racial strife and misunderstandings; as such, they parallel society's racial warfare. For example, in *The Primitive*, an African American male kills the white woman he is involved with to solve his love-hate feelings toward white women. Like *Bigger Thomas in *Native Son*, the protagonist of *The Primitive* rages against the deterministic forces that control and victimize him. Other novels that depict interracial relationships with graphic *violence include Frank *Hercules's *I Want a Black Doll* (1967) and Calvin C. *Hernton's *Scarecrow* (1974), in which the African American protagonist chops off his white lover's head and hides it in a suitcase in an obvious echo of Bigger Thomas's decision to dismember his white employer to hide her murder.

Also strongly influenced by Wright's powerful naturalistic precedent are the novels of William Gardner *Smith. Unlike Himes's novels, Smith's *Last of the Conquerors* (1948) and *South Street* (1954) depict interracial relationships succeeding quite well outside of the borders of the United States. There is a dreamlike atmosphere to the relationships in Smith's novels. Racial strife eventually intrudes upon the characters' romances, however, and compels the male protagonists back to the United States to fight against racial injustices. In *South Street*, the racially motivated murder of his brother spurs a character into a civil rights leadership role.

John O. *Killens's *'Sippi* (1967) documents the same tension between black activism and interracial romance found in Smith's novels. Chuck Othello Chaney comes of age when he realizes that marrying the white man's daughter and black activism do not mix. Chaney rejects his white lover, concluding that black solidarity is the only way to build black power and strength. He becomes a powerful activist leader at the novel's end, replacing a recently assassinated leader. In a subplot of Alice *Walker's *Meridian* (1977), two characters bitterly end their interracial relationship as the inclusive civil rights movement evolves into a more exclusive *Black Nationalism.

In more contemporary novels, the theme of miscegenation remains an especially vibrant topic for historical novelists re-creating slave narratives and slave experiences. Toni *Morrison's *Beloved* (1987) and Sherley Anne *Williams's *Dessa Rose* (1986) dramatically recount the threat and reality of sexual abuse for female slaves in a manner reminiscent of Linda Brent's autobiographical documentation in *Incidents*.

As somewhat of a counterpoint to established trends, in *Oxherding Tale* (1982), Charles R. *Johnson reverses nearly all of the conventions of violence, melodrama, and tensions associated with interracial relationships. In contrast to most of the precedents this novel depicts an antebellum interracial relationship that casually succeeds. The novel ends on a surprisingly upbeat note as the interracial couple look forward to rebuilding the world through their children.

These contemporary fictional slave narratives and *films such as Spike *Lee's *Jungle Fever* (1991) show that African American artists are continuing to use the provocative topic of miscegenation to examine race relations and to stimulate interest in their works.

[*See also* Double Consciousness; Hair; Identity; Neo–Slave Narrative; Plantation Tradition; Protest Literature.]

• Winthrop Jordan, *White over Black*, 1968. Janet Berzon, *Neither White nor Black*, 1978. John Mencke, *Mulattoes and Race Mixture: American Attitudes and Images, 1865–1918*, 1979. James Kinney, *Amalgamation!*, 1985. Mary Dearborn, *Pocahontas's Daughters: Gender and Ethnicity in American Culture*, 1986. Werner Sollors, "'Never Was Born': The Mulatto, An American Tragedy?" *Massachusetts Review* 27 (Summer 1986): 293–316.   —Jonathan D. Little

MITCHELL, LOFTEN (b. 1919), playwright, theater historian, and novelist. Loften Mitchell studied at Talledega College in Alabama (BA, 1943) and Columbia University (MA, 1951), and between degrees completed a navy tour during 1944 and 1945. Mitchell authored two historical works, one depicting the contributions of African Americans to American theater and culture, and the other presenting first-person narratives by noted actors of African descent. *Black Drama: The Story of the American Negro in the Theatre* (1967), a work receiving initial inspiration from Mitchell's freshman English professor at Talledega College—Maurice Lee—and *Voices of the Black Theatre* (1975) achieve the historical and artistic goal of articulating the vital role of African Americans in theater and the cultural benefits deriving from this genre.

Mitchell, a native of Harlem whose parents migrated from rural North Carolina, wrote sketches for the Progressive Dramatizers Groups at Salem Church while still at Dewitt Clinton High School and affiliated with the Rose McClendon Players of Harlem. His contributions in several public service appointments, theatrical performances, and demonstrations of artistic excellence earned him a Guggenheim Fellowship (1958–1959).

Mitchell's early plays include *Shattered Dreams* (1938), *The Bancroft Dynasty* (1948), *The Cellar* (1952), and *Land beyond the River* (1952). These encompass a wide range of themes from the pacifist philosophy of *Shattered Dreams* to the probing indictment in *Land beyond the River* of a republic that fails to accord, even to descendants of those who fought and died for America's freedoms, a just return on the sacrifice. Poignantly dramatizing the successful challenge to the separate but equal doctrine as national law and exploring the comparative effectiveness of violent and nonviolent philosophies, *Land beyond the River* retains some hope that the promise of America will ultimately be realized. *The Bancroft Dynasty*, exploring the conflict between tradition and change, and *Cellars*, dramatizing an African American's flight from the terrors of southern justice, were two of seven plays produced by Mitchell and the group that returned to Harlem's People's Theatre in 1947.

At least five of Mitchell's plays were produced during the 1960s: *Ballad for Bimshire* (1963), *Ballad of the Winter Soldiers* (1964), *Star of the Morning* (1965), *Tell Pharoah* (1967), and *The Phonograph* (1969). *Ballad for Bimshire* depicts the experiences of an African American stationed in occupied Germany, entertaining the somewhat ironic hope that after the war, the very land that once scolded him would think well of him. A similar theme runs through *Ballad of the Winter Soldiers*, that title deriving from Thomas Paine's description of the summer and sunshine patriots, those who sometimes retreat from service to their country. Mitchell and collaborator John O. *Killens conceived the notion of a winter soldier who would fight despite struggles and reversals.

In *Star of the Morning*, a tribute to actor Bert Williams, Mitchell acknowledges the debt owed to pioneer actors who often compromised pride to keep open opportunities for cultural expression in the theater. *Tell Pharoah* dramatizes the exploitation of African Americans who bought homes in Harlem at three times the fair price. The drama, capturing both the shame and the happiness of the Harlem era, is a powerful indictment of the greed driving the actions of real estate brokers who took advantage of the race's need to find safe homes. *Tell Pharoah* poignantly depicts the realities of a population finally acknowledging their disappointment in the environs once deemed as the promised land.

Mitchell's later plays include *Bubbling Brown Sugar* (1975) and *The Walls Came Tumbling Down* (1976), a one-act drama based on one of his earlier plays, *Sojourn to the South of the Wall* (1973). *Bubbling Brown Sugar* stands as the premier musical revue in African American theater, illustrating the evolution of African American *music on Broadway and in Harlem, and highlighting musical works popular from 1910 through the 1940s. The play, successful in both the United States and London, received a Tony Award nomination in 1976 and London's award for Best Musical of the Year in 1977.

Loften Mitchell, professor emeritus, held teaching appointments at the State University of New York at Binghamton from 1971 through 1985. His versatile writing career has yielded several critical works on race and the theater and a novel, *The Stubborn Old Lady Who Resisted Change* (1973). His shifts between purely dramatic concerns, music, and history did not result in artistic fragmentation. Rather, the versatility significantly enriched portrayals of culture and humanity. Overall, his contributions to art and history reflect a generous appreciation of his art, his heritage, and his country.

• Edward Mapp, *Directory of Blacks in the Performing Arts*, 1978. pp. 256–257. C. W. E. Bigsby, "Three Black Playwrights: Loften Mitchell, Ossie Davis, Douglas Turner Ward," in *The Theatre of Black Americans*, vol. 1, ed. Errol Hill, 1980, pp. 148–167. J. A. Jahannes, "Loften Mitchell," in *DLB*, vol. 38, *Afro-American Writers after 1955: Dramatists and Prose Writers*, eds. Thadious M. Davis and Trudier Harris, 1985, pp. 208–214. Bernard L. Peterson, Jr., ed., *Contemporary Black American Playwrights and Their Plays*, 1988, pp. 344–347. Bernard L. Peterson, Jr., *Early Black American Playwrights and Dramatic Writers*, 1990, pp. 210–211.

—Robbie Jean Walker

Montage of a Dream Deferred. In a prefatory note to *Montage of a Dream Deferred* (1951), Langston *Hughes wrote about his artistic influences, concerns, and aims in the book, which he saw as a single poem rather than as a collection of poems: In terms of current Afro-American popular *music and the sources from which it has progressed—*jazz, ragtime, swing, *blues, boogie-woogie, and bebop—this poem on contemporary Harlem, like bebop, is marked by conflicting changes, sudden nuances, sharp and impudent interjections, broken rhythms, and passages sometimes in the manner of the jam session, sometimes the popular song, punctuated by the riffs, runs, breaks, and disc-tortions of the music of a community in transition.

The volume appears to have sprung from a momentous occasion in his life: his moving into his own home in 1948 after a lifetime of rented or borrowed rooms and houses. (With the royalties from the 1947 musical play *Street Scene*, on which he had served as lyricist with Kurt Weill and Elmer Rice, he had purchased a rowhouse in Harlem.) In September 1948 he wrote to a friend: "I have completed a new book I wrote last week!" Hughes called it "a full book-length poem in five sections," and characterized it further as "a precedent shattering opus—also could be known as a *tour de force.*"

If the aggressive discordancies of bebop music as played by musicians such as Dizzy Gillespie and Charlie *Parker shaped the form of the book, its central idea is that of the "dream deferred." The dream had always been perhaps the central motif in Hughes's poetry, and especially the dream of political and social empowerment for blacks. But Hughes now faced the fact that the hopes that had drawn thousands of blacks to the northern cities had led many of them to disappointment, alienation, and bitterness. Some of these poems depict blacks still able to hope and dream, but the most powerful pieces raise the specter of poverty, violence, and death. In "Harlem," a dream deferred can "dry up," or "fester," or "crust and sugar over—*or does it explode?*"

At various times witty, sardonic, ironic, documentary, loving, or tragic, the volume touches on virtually every aspect of daily Harlem life, from the prosperous on Sugar Hill to the poorest folk living down below; it touches on the lives of Harlem mothers, daughters, students, ministers, junkies, pimps, police, shop owners, homosexuals, landlords, and tenants; its aim is to render in verse a detailed portrait of the community, which Hughes knew extremely well. Eventually he would take pride in the fact that of all major black writers, he alone still lived in the midst of a typical urban black community.

Despite Hughes's enthusiasm, his longtime publisher, Knopf, rejected the manuscript. The response when it appeared from Henry Holt in 1951 was lukewarm at best. To J. Saunders *Redding in the black *Pittsburgh Courier*, the book probed old emotions and experiences "but they reveal nothing new." In the *New York Times Book Review*, Babette Deutsch attacked Hughes's "facile sentimentality," his "cultivated naivete," and saw the work revealing the limitations of folk art." Nevertheless, the volume ranks among his finest works of art, a major product of his intimate, ongoing engagement with African American life and culture.

[*See also* Raisin in the Sun, A.]

—Arnold Rampersad

MOODY, ANNE (b. 1940), civil rights activist and writer. Anne Moody was born in 1940, the daughter of sharecroppers. In *Coming of Age in Mississippi* (1968), Moody describes growing up in rural Mississippi where racism, lack of opportunity, and economic failure devastated her family and others in the African American community. The *autobiography also chronicles the growth of the *civil rights movement in Mississippi in the 1950s and 1960s, thus making the work a record of personal and political importance.

Coming of Age in Mississippi emerges out of a long tradition in African American literature, dating back to the *slave narratives of the nineteenth century and continuing with autobiographies of the twentieth century. Moody's work has been compared to Harriet A. *Jacobs's *Incidents in the Life of a Slave Girl* (1861), Mary Church *Terrell's *A Black Woman in a White World* (1940), and Richard *Wright's *Black Boy* (1945).

Part 1 ("Childhood") concerns Moody's early years and her family's struggles and instability. While Jacobs and Terrell recalled Edenic periods in their early lives, Moody's did not contain such innocence. Even at a young age, Moody recognized the social and economic forces impacting on her family. Like Richard Wright, she questioned the position of superiority and privilege granted to whites, but met with fear and silence from the adults around her. Moody was angered by the apathy and seeming indifference that the black community had toward the inferior social and economic positions assigned to them. The eldest of six children, Moody was particularly aware of the plight of poor black women and their children. Her own mother's struggle to endure harsh field work, equally difficult domestic work, poverty, repeated childbearing, and desertion by her husband becomes an important subject in Moody's autobiography.

Parts 2 and 3 ("High School" and "College") describe the important role that school and *education had in Moody's life. In high school, Moody channeled her anger and confusion into academic achievement and playing basketball. However, high school brought a deepening awareness of the realities of black life in Mississippi. The murder of Emmet Till the week before high school began initiated Moody into these truths. It also brought her a new and devastating fear: "the fear of being killed just because I was black."

Moody continued her education at Natchez College for two years on a basketball scholarship. She then received a full academic scholarship to Tougaloo College. Here Moody became involved in the NAACP and the Student Nonviolent Coordinating Committee. Such involvement was fraught with danger for both Moody and her *family. However, this did not prevent her full immersion in civil rights activities during her senior year at Tougaloo, described in part 4, "The Movement."

Moody served as a canvasser and *church speaker for the NAACP, participated in boycotts of downtown Jackson, Mississippi, stores, led a sit-in team at a Woolworth's lunch counter, registered voters for the Committee on Racial Equality, and taught workshops on self-protection to potential demonstrators. With vivid detail Moody recounts these activities, as well as the demoralizing impact of the assassinations of Medgar Evers and John F. Kennedy. All told, *Coming of Age in Mississippi* bears poignant witness to the injustices and evils of segregation in the South and portrays the growth and development of individual social conscience.

• Lynn Z. Bloom, "Coming of Age in the Segregated South: Autobiographies of Twentieth-Century Childhoods, Black and White," in *Home Ground: Southern Autobiography*, ed. J. Bill Berry, 1991, pp. 110–122. Nellie Y. McKay, "The Girls Who Became Women: Childhood Memories in the Autobiographies of Harriet Jacobs, Mary Church Terrell, and Anne Moody," in *Tradition and the Talents of Women*, ed. Florence Howe, 1991, pp. 105–124.   —Paula Gallant Eckard

MOORE, OPAL (b. 1953), poet, short story writer, essayist, educator, and critic of children's literature. Born and raised in Chicago, Illinois, Opal Moore was influenced from childhood by the particular dynamics of the Pentecostal *church; echoes of that institution reverberate in her plots, themes, characters, tone, and language. When Moore entered Illinois Wesleyan University's School of Art in 1970, she was so shocked by her first real encounter with racism and her sense of powerlessness in the face of it that she sought some control over what was happening to her by writing, thus initiating her first journals. She also turned to writing *poetry. After receiving a BFA from Wesleyan in 1974, she enrolled in the graduate program at the University of Iowa, where she began writing fiction. She earned an MA from the University of Iowa's School of Art in 1981, and an MFA from the University of Iowa's Iowa Writers' Workshop in 1982. She has taught creative writing and African American literature at Virginia Commonwealth University, Virginia State University, Hollins College, Kassel University (Germany), Johannes Gutenberg-Universität Mainz (Germany), and Radford University.

Moore studied with Paule *Marshall and James Alan *McPherson, both of whom taught her much about the craft of writing. Long after she left Marshall's workshops, the novelist continued to critique Moore's drafts for her, persistently encouraging her to refine her sense of style and structure and to give thorough and legitimate handling to her male characters. Moore asserts that her first idol was Gwendolyn *Brooks. After reading Brooks and being captivated by her language, she concluded that the only *real* writing had to be poetic. Moore was also profoundly affected by her reading of Toni *Morrison's *Sula*, with its protagonist's rebellion against communal values and generally accepted assumptions.

In her 1989 short fiction, "A Happy Story" (published in *Callaloo*), Moore portrays a somewhat cynical female writer wrestling with questions such as, "How do we achieve happiness? How do we define it?" Presenting her story through sometimes humorous debates with her more optimistic husband, the narrator tries and rejects many different story lines, but from beginning to end there remains the same germ of a plan for her story: "It's about a woman, . . . Intelligent. Attractive. Educated." This story reflects some of Moore's major concerns in her poetry and short stories, which frequently focus on a black female child or adult who is unable to find happiness in a world with so many restrictions based on *religion, *race, and *gender. In this problematic world there is little happiness (the character in "A Happy Story" doesn't believe there is such a thing as a happy story and can't recall a truly happy moment in her life), little *humor, little *freedom, little real love, little true communication.

Communication (or the lack thereof) is a frequent concern in Moore's work. Often, she insists that silence is an effective, potentially revolutionary form of communication. This revolution through silence, through the unspoken word, is something that the author early learned: Ordered to sit at the Sunday dinner table until she asked to be excused, the six-year-old Opal silently faced her mother for hours, refusing to utter the phrase, "Excuse me"; she had, after all, done nothing to require her to ask to be excused. Similarly, her characters are constantly refusing in subtle and varying ways to comply with rules that do not make sense to them. And Moore, as a writer, is constantly wrestling with the possibility of writing honest stories that obviously go against the grains of someone's taboos.

Moore's work is very intense and often painful. There is little relief in the occasional humor, which tends to be caustic and sardonic, as in "Freeing Ourselves of History: The Slave Closet" (*Obsidian II*, 1988), in which a modern assimilationist, proud of his "freedom," is confronted by a slave. Satirical treatment of this individual who never reaches self-realization ends with him wondering what use a dead slave is to "a modern free man."

Though Moore claims to have given up poetry for short fiction, the poet is evident in everything she writes. Words on a page magically evoking felt life is the essence of her best work. Marked by a mesmerizing, rhythmic beauty, her work paints poetic word pictures (Moore is also an artist) in unexpected but tantalizing images and metaphors. A master stylist,

Moore, like Toni Morrison, grabs us with the opening phrase and has us pausing frequently to reflect, to relish some particularly apt description, some poignant picture, some surprising turn of phrase, some amazing use of language, some unusually melodic line.

Moore, whose fiction and poetry have appeared in a variety of journals and collections, is preparing a volume of short stories for publication. She has also published a number of critical and pedagogical *essays, in which she frequently focuses on literature for children.

• "Picture Books about Blacks: An Interview with Opal Moore," interview by Donnarae MacCann and Olga Richard, *Wilson Library Bulletin* 65 (June 1991): 24–28.

—Daryl Cumber Dance

MORRISON, TONI (b. 1931), novelist, essayist, editor, short fiction writer, lecturer, educator, and Nobel Prize laureate. From "Quiet as it's kept," the phrase that begins the narrative of *The Bluest Eye* (1970), her first novel, to "Look where your hands are. Now," the final phrase of *Jazz* (1992), her sixth novel, Toni Morrison has distinguished herself as an author, editor, and critic who has transformed the American literary landscape with her presence in the African American literary tradition. When she won the 1993 Nobel Prize in Literature, the Swedish Academy referred to her as one "who, in novels characterized by visionary force and poetic import, gives life to an essential aspect of American reality." Indeed, in her Nobel lecture, delivered on 7 December 1993 in Stockholm, she eloquently demonstrated that the visionary force and poetic import of her novels reflect her worldview and understanding of how language shapes human reality. Through her own use of the spoken and written word, she has created new spaces for readers to bring both their imaginations and their intellects to the complex cultural, political, social, and historical issues of our time. Moreover, through her work as an editor and novelist, she has made it possible for the texts of both African American and feminist writers to reshape the contours of what we call American literature.

Toni Morrison was born Chloe Anthony Wofford on 18 February 1931 in Lorain, Ohio, the second of four children of Ramah Willis Wofford and George Wofford. Having grown up in a family of storytellers and musicians, she developed an early appreciation for language, folk wisdom, and literature. Formative influences in her life not only include listening to family history through the stories of her relatives, but growing up in an ethnically and racially diverse community whose coherence seemed to come from its *identity as a poor steel town twenty-five miles west of Cleveland. Despite the sense of cooperation that *class consciousness created in Lorain neighborhoods, Morrison learned from her parents that racial politics were a reality with which African Americans had to contend. She tells of her father's blatant hostility toward white people and her mother's somewhat optimistic belief that over time race relations in America would improve. It is no surprise, therefore, that her novels reflect both the pessimism that racism produces and the optimism that has empowered African American people to survive and thrive in spite of racism.

After graduating from Lorain High School, Morrison attended Howard University, where she earned a BA degree in 1953. While at Howard, where she changed her name from Chloe to Toni, she appeared in campus productions as a member of the Howard University Players, a campus theater company, and she toured the South with a faculty-and-student repertory troupe. From Howard she went on to Cornell University, where she earned an MA in English in 1955, with a thesis on the theme of suicide in the works of William Faulkner and Virginia Woolf. After working for two years as an instructor at Texas Southern University in Houston, she joined the faculty of Howard University where she taught in the English department from 1957 to 1964. A year after going to Howard to teach, she married a Jamaican architect, Harold Morrison, with whom she had two sons, Harold Ford and Slade Kevin. Morrison regarded the marriage as part of the stifling situation that led her to turn to writing for solace during the early 1960s. She joined a writers' workshop and began work on a short story about a black girl who wanted blue eyes. This short story would later become her first novel, The *Bluest Eye. In 1964 she resigned from her teaching post at Howard, divorced her husband, and returned with her two sons to her parents' home in Lorain, where she stayed for eighteen months before moving to Syracuse, New York, to accept a position as a textbook editor for a subsidiary of Random House. Though she admits she began writing at night after her sons were asleep as a way to combat her own loneliness, it is clear that this activity was well on its way to reshaping her identity and her entire life. As she says, she realized, "Writing was . . . the most extraordinary way of thinking and feeling. It became the one thing I was doing that I had absolutely no intention of living without."

In 1968 Toni Morrison moved to New York City, where she became a senior editor at Random House. Her significance in this role cannot be overestimated because she was assigned to working, almost exclusively, on black writers. Authors who were published as a result of her work include Angela *Davis, Henry *Dumas, Toni Cade *Bambara, Muhammad *Ali, and Gayl *Jones. One of the most important books she edited during her time at Random House was The Black Book, published in 1974. An eclectic collection of more than three hundred years of history that attempts to record what it has been like to be of African descent on American soil, this book contains documents pertaining to *slavery (such as bills of sale and announcements of searches for runaway slaves), pictures of slave quilts, photographs from family albums, recipes, songs, newspaper clippings, advertisements, and other miscellaneous memorabilia. Viewing the book as a representation of "Black life as lived," Morrison considered The Black Book an antidote for the unhistorical sense of self she felt was emerging from the Black Power movement of the late 1960s and early 1970s. She integrates this same concern for the African American past, history, and cultural memory into each of her *novels.

During her early years as an editor at Random House, she developed the short story she began at Howard into her first novel, *The Bluest Eye*, and thus established her reputation as a writer with its publication in 1970. From 1970 to 1992, Morrison published five more novels, a play, a book of literary criticism, and an *anthology of social criticism. In the midst of her already demanding schedule of editing and writing, she also began teaching part-time at various places on the East Coast, taking positions at SUNY-Purchase in 1971, at Yale in 1976, at SUNY-Albany in 1984, and at Bard College in 1986. Since 1988 she has been the Robert F. Goheen Professor of the Humanities at Princeton University where she teaches in the Afro-American Studies and creative writing programs.

The rewards for deciding to devote her life to writing have been great. In 1975 Morrison received the National Book Award nomination for *Sula*, published in 1973. With *Song of Solomon*, published in 1977, she received even greater acclaim in the form of a Book-of-the-Month Club selection, the National Book Critics Circle Award, and the American Academy and Institute of Arts and Letters Award. Following the publication of *Tar Baby* in 1981, she wrote the play *Dreaming Emmett*, which was first produced in Albany, New York in 1986. In 1988 she won the Pulitzer Prize and the Robert F. Kennedy Award for *Beloved*, the novel she published in 1987. She received her most prestigious award, the Nobel Prize in literature, in 1993 after the publication of *Jazz* in 1992.

Toni Morrison has not only established herself in American and African American literature as a first-rate novelist but also as a popular lecturer and first-rate literary and cultural critic. On 7 October 1988 she delivered the Tanner Lecture on Human Values at the University of Michigan, a presentation entitled "Unspeakable Things Unspoken: The Afro-American Presence in American Literature." This often-quoted lecture is noteworthy for the ease with which she engages in the literary critical discourse about canon formation and curriculum revision at the precise moment that these were central issues on campuses throughout the nation; for its meticulous, close reading of the first line of each of her first five novels, which places her in company with other African American writers such as Ralph *Ellison, Richard *Wright, and Sterling A. *Brown, who were also critics and theorists of their own writing; and for the way it introduces the commentary that becomes the focus of *Playing in the Dark: Whiteness and the Literary Imagination* (1992), Morrison's first book of literary criticism. In this book, she argues that canonical texts in American literature are long overdue for an analysis of how they are structured in subtle and not so subtle ways by their antithesis to blackness. With the publication of *Race-ing Justice, En-Gendering Power: Essays on Anita Hill, Clarence Thomas, and the Construction of Social Reality*, a book she edited in 1992, Morrison offers insightful social commentary on the *race and *gender politics

of one of this nation's most significant moments in recent history.

More important than any of her literary and cultural criticism, however, are the six novels that have established her literary reputation as a writer whose work possesses tremendous aesthetic beauty and political power. We first bear witness to this power in *The Bluest Eye*, the novel about *Pecola Breedlove, the black girl whose insatiable desire to be loved is manifested in a desire for blue eyes that ultimately drives her into insanity. The novel's treatment of some tragic dimensions of black life, such as incest and poverty, and the larger racialized context from which some of this tragedy springs reflect Morrison's desire to invite her reader to examine the family values, gender politics, and community secrets that shape individual and collective identity. With her second novel, *Sula*, Morrison ventures into a treatment of female friendship, exploring the dynamics of the relationship between two women, *Sula Peace and Nel Wright, to examine what Deborah McDowell calls the representation of character as process, not essence. The novel not only narrates the story of how Sula and Nel become friends, but also the implications of the rift that separates them when one chooses a traditional life of marriage and family and the other chooses independence from traditional expectations for women. Moreover, through her meticulous treatment of *place in her depiction of the Bottom, the neighborhood where Sula and Nel grow up, Morrison illustrates how a black community's identity evolves and shapes itself with its own cultural resources and elaborate social structure.

In her third novel, *Song of Solomon*, Morrison narrates a complex tale of a black man, *Milkman Dead, and his search to understand himself in the context of family history and racial politics. Weaving memories of her own family stories of relatives who lost land during Reconstruction, *Song of Solomon* chronicles Milkman's journey from the North back to the South to the very places and people of his ancestry that his middle-class life had encouraged him to devalue. Morrison uses her fourth novel, *Tar Baby*, to synthesize an interest in racial politics and the African diaspora with gender relations. A love affair between a black upper middle-class model and art historian, *Jadine Childs, and *Son Green, the uneducated stowaway who intrudes in the Caribbean island mansion of her wealthy white benefactors, illustrates Morrison's interest in debates about how blackness and authenticity get defined in the African American community. In *Beloved*, Morrison connects her preoccupation with *history with an exploration of how personal and cultural memory operate in the formation of relationships. Using the story of *Sethe Suggs, a slave woman who took her child's life to protect it from slave catchers, Morrison takes the core of a real story recorded in *The Black Book* as the basis of this intricately narrated novel about two former slaves who work their way through remembering the pain of enslavement and dealing with the dead child's ghost, to healing, wholeness, and love. Finally, in *Jazz*, a novel inspired by her reading in *The Harlem Book of the Dead* about a young woman who, as she lay dying, refused to identify her lover as the person who shot her, Morrison combines the history and *music of the *Harlem Renaissance with a fascination with New York City, the story of a stale marriage, and a fatal love affair. What distinguishes the novel more than its plot is Morrison's innovative telling of it, a telling that is meant to emulate the improvisational techniques of *jazz.

In sum, Toni Morrison's novels reflect her desire to draw on the people, places, language, values, cultural traditions, and politics that have shaped her own life and that of African American people. In so doing, she offers no solutions to problems, nor does she simplify the complex realities of the past or present. Instead, out of respect for the cultural knowledge that black people bring to life and living, she uses the power and majesty of her imagination to address them and anyone interested in the stories that have created a permanent place for her among America's greatest writers.

[See also Baby Suggs; Eva Peace; Hannah Peace; Paul D; Pilate Dead; Shadrack.]

• Toni Morrison, "A Slow Walk of Trees (As Grandmother Would Say), Hopeless (As Grandfather Would Say)," New York Times Magazine, 4 July 1976, 104. Colette Dowling, "The Song of Toni Morrison," 1979. David L. Middleton, Toni Morrison: An Annotated Bibliography, 1987. Nellie Y. McKay, Critical Essays on Toni Morrison, 1988. Claudia Tate, Black Women Writers at Work, 1989. Trudier Harris, Fiction and Folklore in the Novels of Toni Morrison, 1991. Henry Louis Gates, Jr., and K. A. Appiah, eds., Toni Morrison: Critical Perspectives Past and Present, 1993. Denise Heinze, The Dilemma of "Double-Consciousness": Toni Morrison's Novels, 1993.
—Marilyn Sanders Mobley

MOSES. From the days of *slavery through the civil rights era, African Americans struggling for freedom from oppression have turned for inspiration to Moses, the biblical leader who guided the Israelites out of slavery in Egypt to the promised land. The slaves were so fascinated by Moses that they often called the South "Egyptland," the North "the promised land," and antislavery leaders like Harriet *Tubman "Moses"; also, slaves praised Moses' heroic deeds in sermons, folktales, and *spirituals (such as "Go Down Moses," "Oh, Mary Don't You Weep," and "Little Moses"). Literary works by modern and contemporary African American authors reflect the enduring importance of Moses to the African American community. Some works, such as Zora Neale *Hurston's Moses, Man of the Mountain (1939), straightforwardly retell and reinterpret the biblical account of Moses for twentieth-century African Americans. Other works, writes H. Nigel Thomas, employ Moses as a *character type: according to Thomas, such works as Paul Laurence *Dunbar's "The Strength of Gideon" (1900), Ralph *Ellison's *Invisible Man (1952), and William Melvin *Kelley's A Different Drummer (1959), present characters who attempt to help their fellow African Americans escape oppression as their prototype Moses had helped his people. Thomas also identifies a few works, like Toni *Morrison's *Sula (1973) and Leon *Forrest's The Bloodworth Orphans (1977), that present an ironic or

satiric interpretation of the Moses character type. In literary works like Ernest J. *Gaines's The *Autobiography of Miss Jane Pittman (1971) and Margaret *Walker's Jubilee (1966) that attempt to chronicle an individual's or a group's particular struggle for civil rights, fictional characters frequently discuss or refer to Moses, in part to provide an example of a people who have already successfully struggled for their civil rights. For similar reasons, twentieth-century African American civil rights leaders have frequently mentioned Moses in their speeches and writings.

[See also Biblical Tradition; Folklore; Religion; Sermons and Preaching.]

• H. Nigel Thomas, From Folklore to Fiction, 1988.
—Ted Olson

MOSLEY, WALTER (b. 1952), novelist. Born in 1952 to Leroy and Ella Mosley, Walter Ellis Mosley grew up in South Central Los Angeles, the setting for his first four novels. An intelligent and thoughtful young man but an indifferent student, Mosley eventually earned a degree in political science from Johnson State College in Vermont, then worked for several years as a computer programmer before enrolling in a creative writing program at City College New York. Lauded for his perfectly inflected dialogue, his simple but elegant prose, and his vivid characters, Golden Dagger prize-winner Walter Mosley's primary contributions to the detective genre are his hero, Ezekiel (Easy) Rawlins, and his expansion of the mystery novel to chronicle African American social history.

*Easy Rawlins is a working-class man, a reluctant private eye, prone to sleuthing mistakes and without the usual friends in the profession to ease his way. Easy succeeds because of his common sense, his integrity, and his community ties. Based upon Mosley's father and several acquaintances and created as a realistic black male hero, one who has "flaws that have to be overcome," Easy is divorced, has financial worries, and gets too involved with his clients. Easy has two adopted children: Jesus, a Mexican boy whose muteness testifies to his trauma as a child prostitute before Easy rescued him, and Feather, whose grandfather killed her mother because Feather's father was black. Easy wants what most men want: a house, a good income, a safe and happy family life; but he is also streetwise and capable of cruel vengeance. Easy's best friend, Raymond Alexander, better known as Mouse, is much less admirable and much more violent. Mouse does not hesitate to shoot a hogtied man first in the groin then the head in order to get a reluctant witness to provide information, and several times he almost shoots Easy over trifles. Mosley presents both as black male heroes. "Black male heroes are not sports stars or movies stars," Mosley asserts. Black male heroes are like Easy, "the guys who get up and go to work every day" and like Mouse who "demands and wins, at whatever cost, ultimate respect."

This unlikely duo dominates Walter Mosley's first four of a series recording experiences from post–World War II, when southern blacks optimistically arrived in southern California seeking and finding living wages and livable communities, to the present, which appears to offer less of both for most. Despite due attention to racism, discrimination, corruption, and other poisoners of dreams, Mosley's emphasis is upon resilience in the face of difficulties. As Malcolm Jones, Jr., says, "Easy Rawlins never whines."

Devil in a Blue Dress (1990) introduces Easy Rawlins, an intelligent and thoughtful veteran whose recent firing combined with an impending mortgage payment convinced him in 1948 to take the job of locating the missing Daphne Monet. *A Red Death* (1991) finds Easy in 1953 working as a janitor for and secretly buying the Magnolia Street Apartments when IRS troubles force him to spy on members of the First African Baptist Church, a decision that leads to his own investigation for murder. *White Butterfly* (1992) revolves around serial killings in 1956 that fail to interest law enforcement agents until Cyndi Starr, a stripper known as the "White Butterfly," who was also a white UCLA coed, is killed. In *Black Betty* (1994), it is 1961 and Easy, now forty-one years old, needs money to save his proposed neighborhood shopping mall from exploitative but politically powerful competitors. Easy discovers that the missing housekeeper a wealthy Beverly Hills family hires him to find is the same Elizabeth Eady he had a crush on when he was nine years old. Mosley plans to continue the saga until Easy is about seventy years old; but the protagonist of his current project is a jazz musician who travels back in time to study with bluesman Robert Johnson.

Mosley's popularity was not hurt by being named as President Bill Clinton's favorite writer. Readers also respond to his deliberate echoes of Raymond Chandler and Chester *Himes, and reviewers compare him to John D. MacDonald, Dashiell Hammett, Richard *Wright, and Ruldoph *Fisher. Both Valerie Wilson Wesley and Eleanor Brand have black single parent detectives, but they are female. Gar Anthony Haywood and Clifford Mason preceded Mosley with politically aware black private eyes. Playwright August *Wilson and novelist John Edgar *Wideman have created series that attempt to write ordinary black men into American social history. Walter Mosley stands alone, however, in his acclaimed combination of these and other elements as never before.

[*See also* Crime and Mystery Writing; Poinsettia Jackson.]

• Lynell George, "Cracking the L.A. Case," *Los Angeles Times Magazine*, 22 May 1994, 14–36. Guy Halverson, "Mystery Writer Walter Mosley Tackles the Mean Streets of L.A.," *Christian Science Monitor*, 12 Aug. 1994, 14. Malcolm Jones, Jr., "Kick Back with Crime," *Newsweek*, 14 July 1994, 66–67.
—Frances Smith Foster

MOSSELL, GERTRUDE (1855–1948), essayist, journalist, editor, and activist. Claudia Tate feels that Gertrude Bustill Mossell's life mirrored the lives of fictional heroines in black women's domestic *novels of the late-nineteenth century. Born into a prosperous Philadelphia family, Mossell's writing was a consistent thread through a seventy-five-year career that included the organization of several African American associations, fundraising for Frederick Douglass

Memorial Hospital (founded by husband Nathan F. Mossell in 1895), and activism for human rights and African American causes. After twenty-one years of teaching school and editing and writing for both African American and white publications, she published eight *essays and seventeen poems in *The Work of the Afro-American Woman* (1894). She also wrote *Little Dansie's One Day at Sabbath School* (1902), a children's book.

"The Opposite Point of View," a chapter title in *The Work*, could have served as the title for the volume itself. Mossell's book is a race-based, feminist corrective to many of the prevailing attitudes of post-Reconstruction America. She offers opposing viewpoints on the significance of African American literature and the education of African American women. While Mossell's *feminism is firmly within the discourse of the patriarchal family, it is feminism nonetheless. For example, while Mossell insists African American women should aspire to a "noble, pure womanhood," she also argues that "a woman who has a mind and will of her own will become monotonous to a less extent than one so continuously sweet and self-effacing." Mossell's chief concern, though, is the uplift of the race, most telling in her view of African American literature: While the works "vary in grade of excellence," she writes, all are "of invaluable interest; for in them is garnered that which must give inspiration to the youth of the race. Each had its effect of gaining the hearts of their enemy, winning respect and admiration, thus strengthening the bands of a common humanity."

• Joanne M. Braxton, introduction to *The Work of the Afro-American Woman*, 1988. Claudia Tate, *Domestic Allegories of Political Desire: The Black Heroine's Text at the Turn of the Century*, 1992.
—Bertram D. Ashe

MOTLEY, WILLARD (1909–1965), novelist, journalist, diarist, and essayist. The second son of a Pullman porter, Willard Francis Motley was raised in the only African American family in a predominantly white middle-class neighborhood on Chicago's South Side. At age thirteen his first short story appeared in the *Chicago Defender*. Unable to attend college during the Great Depression, as a young adult he trekked across the country accumulating real life experiences that informed much of his writing. He moved from his parents' home into a dingy apartment in a Chicago slum to better observe the lower-class whites he intended to portray. Simultaneously, he established contact with and was encouraged by the city's leading proletarian writers: Alexander Saxton, William Shenck, and Jack Conroy. They introduced him to the writings of numerous classic and modern authors.

Cofounding a literary journal, signing up with the WPA *Federal Writers' Project in 1940, and the assistance of two fellowships allowed Motley to focus more of his attention on creative writing. He was determined to humanize and place in social context the characters he researched and of which he had firsthand knowledge via his previous experiences as a hobo, day laborer, and even a jail inmate, among other things. By 1943 he had essentially completed the first of his massive novels, *Knock on Any Door* (1947), the story of the transformation of an Italian American altar boy into a streetwise tough destined for the electric chair, which indicts the criminal justice system while evincing compassion for the denizens of a big city ghetto. The novel received wide critical acclaim and Motley's harsh, unrelenting realism invited comparisons with Richard *Wright and the revered naturalists Theodore Dreiser and Frank Norris. A best-seller, the novel was made into a motion picture starring Humphrey Bogart, as was its sequel, *Let No Man Write My Epitaph* (1958), which featured Shelley Winters. His two other novels—*We Fished All Night* (1951), about societal forces impinging on the lives of three returning military veterans, and *Let Noon Be Fair* (1966), a sprawling tale of the exploitation of a Mexican village—were markedly less successful.

His emphasis on universality and the near absence of African Americans as major characters in his work placed him in the company of several gifted African American authors who flirted with "raceless" or "assimilationist fiction" in the 1940s and 1950s. Unlike the others in this group, though, Motley eschewed writing long fiction concerning those of his *race; his reputation and interest in his novels declined in succeeding decades partly as a result. Identifying himself as a member of no particular race save the human race, he publicly rebuked Chester *Himes and James *Baldwin (whom he called a "professional Negro") because he felt they portrayed virtually all whites as racist. Never married, Motley hoped to escape the cage of race, which he found increasingly discomforting, by immigrating to Mexico in 1951, where he adopted a son. At age fifty-five, surviving on meager royalty checks, he died of intestinal gangrene and was buried in Cuernavaca.

• Robert E. Fleming, *Willard Motley*, 1978. Willard Motley, *The Diaries of Willard Motley*, ed. Jerome Klinkowitz, 1979.

—Robert Fikes, Jr.

MOURNING CUSTOMS. *See* Funeral and Mourning Customs.

Mufaro's Beautiful Daughters. John *Steptoe's *Mufaro's Beautiful Daughters* (1987) was named a Caldecott Honor Book by the American Library Association and received the Coretta Scott King Award for Illustration. Dedicated to the children of South Africa, the book portrays the struggle for dignity in the face of sibling rivalry in the family and community life of a South African village. The illustrations delight and inform the reader just as the story does.

Mufaro ("Happy Man") lives with his two beautiful daughters, Manyara ("Ashamed") and Nyasha ("Mercy"). Nyasha endures her sister's unkindness patiently, singing and working out her hurt feelings as she cultivates her vegetable garden. One day she encounters a small garden snake resting under a yam vine, pats his head, treats him kindly, tells him he is welcome, and permits him to come and go as he wishes.

When the Great King from the nearby city, desiring to choose a Queen, sends for the Most Worthy and Beautiful Daughters in the Land, Mufaro plans to form a wedding party with other villagers to journey to the city and present his daughters to the king. Manyara disobeys her father, preferring to leave in the night and journey alone so she can avoid the competition of her sister. She treats all people and animals along her way in a most unkind manner.

The next day, noticing Manyara's footprints on the path to the city, the wedding party assembles, then leaves with Nyasha. Her conduct and consideration of all she meets, people and animals, wins her everyone's respect. By contrast, Manyara acts selfishly toward everyone, including the king, a great monster snake with five heads, who tells Manyara her faults displease him. Nyasha does not fear meeting the monster king but finds her little friend the garden snake instead. She greets him with pleasure and his form changes into that of Nyoka ("Snake"), the handsome young king, who asks her to marry him.

"The Story of Five Heads" in G. M. Theal's *Kaffir Folktales*, published in London in 1886 and reprinted in the United States in 1970, inspired John Steptoe to write and illustrate *Mufaro's Beautiful Daughters*. The tale was collected from the Kaffir people living near Zimbabwe ruins, which, along with the flora and fauna of the area, inspired Steptoe's illustrations. Nyasha follows the customary practice of the Kaffir women in cultivating millet and vegetables and permitting the snake to wander as it wishes. The Kaffirs also form a bridal party to travel to the groom's village. Steptoe's editor of seventeen years, Dorothy Briley, noted that he "wished to reach beyond his circumstances and share with children his vision of a better world. Through his books he wanted to share his conviction that African-Americans have reason to be proud. . . . All of John's books are about family and the struggle to maintain dignity in a world that he many times perceived as being hostile" (quoted in *Publisher's Weekly*, 29 Sept. 1989). Invoking an African myth that uses both a snake and a garden, Steptoe offers an African alternative to traditional Western symbols and thus a positive cultural model for African Americans.

• "John Steptoe 1950–1989," *Publishers Weekly*, 29 Sept. 1989, 38.

—Claire Taft

MUHAJIR, NAZZAM AL FITNAH. *See* Marvin X.

MULATTO. The nearly white, racially mixed character was an extremely popular figure in nineteenth-century American fiction and drama. The mulatto character, most often a beautiful young woman tragically victimized by *slavery, was first employed by antislavery writers to elicit sympathy, pity, and support from white readers. As critic Jules Zanger argues, it quickly evolved into the *stereotype of the tragic mulatto (one-half African American) and tragic quadroon or octoroon (one-fourth or one-eighth African American). This character's fate was predictable and melodramatic, similar to that of the female victim of sentimental romantic literature. The tragic mulatta's beauty, near-whiteness, vulnerability, and virtuousness made her inevitable suicide or death all the more emotional for white readers. Critics have long objected to the racism involved in writers' singling out the tragedy of the "white Negro," while neglecting the condition of the less exotic African American majority.

Recent critics have also raised questions about the presence of the stereotype of the tragic mulatto or mulatta in African American fiction. In William Wells *Brown's *Clotel, or The President's Daughter (1853), Brown emphasizes Clotel's whiteness and beauty as a traditional sentimental victim as she stands on the slave-auction block bought by men no whiter than herself. As William L. Andrews and Ann duCille point out, however, Brown also shows Clotel's independence and intelligence as she successfully outwits and outmaneuvers the slave catchers and struggles to reunite a *family fragmented by slavery. Even her suicide can be read less as victimization than as a powerful political statement since she jumps into the Potomac within sight of the Capitol, the center of a supposedly democratic nation.

While African American women novelists at the end of the nineteenth century continued using the mulatta character, they did not always portray her as a tragic victim. In Frances Ellen Watkins *Harper's *Iola Leroy (1892), the mulatta heroine marries an African American minister at the end of the *novel and devotes her life to the betterment of African Americans in a rural southern town. In this and other novels, such as Pauline E. *Hopkins's *Contending Forces (1900), mulatta heroines are used to celebrate African American *identity and to encourage racial solidarity, activism, and loyalty.

Like Harper and Hopkins, writers of the early twentieth century, including James Weldon *Johnson, Jessie Redmon *Fauset, Nella *Larsen, and Walter *White, all found in the racially mixed character a profound means of exploring the drama of North American race relations. Even though legally classified as African American or Negro, racially mixed characters were often caught between cultural and ethnic communities, and experimented with different racial identities by *passing for white. These passers, mostly women, quickly realize that their decision to pass is spiritually and psychologically destructive, despite their gains in wealth and status. These heroines are complex, multidimensional, and modernist explorations of the rigidity, arbitrariness, and oppressiveness of America's racial system. Characters like *Helga Crane in Nella Larsen's *Quicksand (1928) experience the existential angst of having no clear place in a society that recognizes no racial identity other than African American or white.

Fauset, Larsen, and Johnson, as well as Charles Waddell *Chesnutt, also use their mulatto characters to explore the intraracial prejudice that can occur once African Americans internalize white standards of beauty and develop self-hatred and colorism. One of the most dramatic examples of intraracial prejudice occurs in the ironically titled novel by Fauset, *Comedy: American Style (1933), in which a character is shunned by mother and sister alike because of his dark skin. Because of his despair he commits suicide, thus adding a new twist to the tragic mulatto character.

Contemporary African American writers no longer develop their characters solely in terms of their hereditary intermixture with whites, nor dwell on the whiteness of their characters' skin. While male characters have had a longer history of being fully black, it was not, as Alice *Walker reminds us, until the darker heroines of Zora Neale *Hurston that the nearly white female character went out of fashion. As if to emphasize the datedness of the mulatto and mulatta stereotypes, Charles R. *Johnson's fictional *slave narrative Oxherding Tale (1982) further reverses expectations. His narrator, the son of a white slave owner and his mistress, finds happiness in marrying a white woman and looks forward to rebuilding the world with their racially mixed children. Johnson stresses the possibilities of racial intermixture instead of its tragedies. For historical novelists like Johnson, the mulatto character still provides a powerful means of commenting on and examining race relations, both in today's world and in a world quickly fading from view.

[See also Character Types; Double Consciousness; Miscegenation; New Cultural Mulatto; Novel of Passing; Race.]

• Jules Zanger, "The Tragic Octoroon in Pre–Civil War Fiction," American Quarterly 18 (1966): 63–70. Werner Sollors, "'Never Was Born': The Mulatto, An American Tragedy?" Massachusetts Review 27 (Summer 1986): 293–316. Nancy Bentley, "White Slaves: The Mulatto Hero in Antebellum Fiction," American Literature 65 (Sept. 1993): 501–522. Ann duCille, The Coupling Convention, 1993.

—Jonathan D. Little

MULATTO, NEW CULTURAL. See New Cultural Mulatto.

Mule Bone. In 1931 Zora Neale *Hurston and Langston *Hughes began to collaborate on a comedy called Mule Bone. They worked in secret because their patron, Charlotte Mason, disapproved of theatrical ventures. Hughes and Hurston were exploring a new concept of *theater, free of the distortions of *minstrelsy, to be based on daily rituals of life in African American communities and performed with *music and *dance. The collaboration produced bitter recriminations and charges of plagiarism but no play. Hurston and Hughes never spoke again, and their dream of a "real Negro theatre" was stillborn.

Based on a folktale, "The Bone of Contention," which Hurston had collected and Hughes had adapted, Mule Bone was a series of oral and musical performances connected by the slenderest of plots. Guitar-playing Jim and dancing Dave are rivals for a woman, Daisy. When their musical and verbal dueling turns physical, Jim hits Dave with a mule bone. In the second act a trial divides the loyalties of the Eatonville townspeople: the Baptists versus the Methodists. The Baptist pastor demonstrates Jim's guilt by proving, according to scriptural citation, that a mule bone is a lethal weapon. Jim is expelled from Eatonville. In the final act Jim, Dave, and Daisy meet outside of town, and the two men reaffirm their friendship.

Mule Bone was finally produced by New York City's Lincoln Center in 1991, featuring veteran black performers and directed by Michael Schultz. A Hurston figure, dressed in the coat, hat, and fur skins familiar to many from an often reproduced photograph by Carl Van Vechten, provided a new prologue and coda. Crafted by editor George Bass, these monologues echo the introduction to Hurston's book of *folklore, *Mules and Men*. *Blues musician Taj Mahal composed the score, with most of the lyrics taken from Hughes's poetry. Reviews were mixed.

—Cheryl A. Wall

Mumbo Jumbo. Ishmael *Reed's third novel, *Mumbo Jumbo* (1972) is generally acknowledged to be his masterpiece. Complex, enigmatic, and ecstatic, it is impossible to summarize coherently with any brevity. Combining elements of collage, Marx Brothers movies, and film noir, illustrated histories, occult books, and the recombinant techniques of *jazz improvisation, the novel seems as resistant to complete interpretation, to the extraction of all its "flavors," as a gumbo, that cross-cultural culinary achievement constituting Reed's favorite metaphor for an aesthetic capable of unlimited possibilities and rewards.

The main action takes place in the 1920s, the Jazz Age and time of the *Harlem Renaissance when the Negro was "in vogue," but also, significantly, the age of Prohibition. Jes Grew, a "psychic plague" that threatens to free people from their inhibitions, is seeking its Text, the matrix that will give it legitimacy, while the Wallflower Order, agents of the forces of repression, strive to save "civilization as we know it"—that is, white, right, and uptight—from Jes Grew's positive vibrations. Working in this environment of clashing impulses, *Papa LaBas, a hoodoo detective, attempts to trace the missing Text and at the same time outwit the crusaders who are out to destroy it and thereby dissipate Jes Grew.

Reed adopts Nietzsche's vision of human history as a pendulum movement between opposing tendencies symbolized by the Greek gods Apollo (reason) and Dionysus (emotion), but Reed traces this polarity back to ancient Egypt—anterior to Greece—and the conflict between Osiris (the Egyptian Dionysus) and his brother/adversary Set, whom Reed sees as unnatural and obsessed with control. Jes Grew clearly is Osirian/Dionysian, while Set/Apollo are the progenitors of Jes Grew's eternal enemy, Atonism (named after the monotheism of the pharaoh Akhenaton), which in the novel represents rigid singularity of vision and belief, hostility to Nature, and a relentless drive to dominate. The struggle, as Reed portrays it, is one of puritanism versus paganism, knowledge versus "mumbo jumbo," the self-styled "universalism" of Western civilization versus the supposedly parochial cultures of the "underdeveloped" peoples of the world.

In an essay in *Obsidian* (Spring–Summer 1986), Lizabeth Paravisini discusses *Mumbo Jumbo* as a parody of the detective novel, in which crimes are solved by rational processes of investigation, whereas Papa LaBas employs "knockings" and astral procedures. But in a 1991 doctoral dissertation dealing with "detective undercurrents" in the work of several black novelists, Helen Mary Lock asserts that the story of Osiris provides the mythic framework for the African American detective tale, whose purpose is not to reveal "whodunit," but how to undo it. Mystery, moreover, is embraced, rather than dispelled. In this reading, *Mumbo Jumbo* fits into the tradition of the African American detective novel, which begins with Rudolph *Fisher's *The Conjure-Man Dies* (1932). In *Mumbo Jumbo*, the "conjure-man," Papa LaBas, lives and continues to fight the good fight against anti–Jes Grew forces, including the "crabs-in-a-barrel" syndrome found in Reed's next novel, *The *Last Days of Louisiana Red* (1974).

Darryl Pinckney (*New York Review of Books*, 12 Aug. 1989) calls *Mumbo Jumbo* Reed's "most ambitious" book, though Theodore O. Mason, Jr., in *Modern Fiction Studies* (Spring 1988), argues that Reed's elaborate intentions get the better of him. Acknowledging that it has flaws, Houston A. *Baker, Jr., nevertheless considers *Mumbo Jumbo* a work of genius (*Black World*, Dec. 1972). In fact, the book's appeal has been broad, as evidenced by the fact that it is on traditional scholar Harold Bloom's list of works that deserve inclusion in the Western literary canon, in addition to being one of the significant items in pop critic Nelson George's "Chronicle of Post-Soul Black Culture."

[*See also* Crime and Mystery Writing; Conjuring.]

• Henry Louis Gates, Jr., "On 'The Blackness of Blackness': Ishmael Reed and a Critique of the Sign," in *The Signifying Monkey: A Theory of Afro-American Literary Criticism*, 1988, pp. 217–238.

—Robert Elliot Fox

MURPHY, BEATRICE M. (1908–1992), poet, editor, columnist, and reviewer. Born in Monessen, Pennsylvania, Beatrice Murphy lived most of her life in Washington, D.C. In 1928 she graduated from Dunbar High School and published her first poem. From 1933 to 1935 she was a columnist and for the next two years an editor at the *Washington Tribune*. Converting to Catholicism in 1938, she also became book review editor that year for the *Afro-American* and published her first poetry anthology, *Negro Voices*. She was also a secretary at Catholic University and part owner of a circulating library and stenography shop. She became a regular columnist for the Associated Negro Press and contributed poetry and reviews to numerous serials and collections. In the 1940s and 1950s she worked for the Office of Price Administration and then the Veterans Administration. In 1954 she was suspended without pay from her job as procurement clerk for supposedly having joined a subversive organization. She disproved the allegations and was reinstated four months later. She reported great bitterness over the incident but succeeded in recovering her fundamental optimism.

Her most important accomplishment in the 1960s was founding the Negro Bibliographic and Research

Center and editing its journal, *Bibliographic Survey: The Negro in Print* (1965–1972). Active in charities and clubs, she continued her publishing career with a coauthored book of poems and an edited poetry anthology. She died of heart disease.

Murphy's major work of poetry, *Love Is a Terrible Thing* (1945), dramatizes the stages of love. Many of the poems are conventional in approach, but Murphy has some flair for vivid metaphor and asserts her freedom from her earlier stricter forms. Some of her strongest poems express desire, anger, or bitterness. Many of the later poems in the collection both vindicate youthful candor and lament its vulnerability. One of the most vivid extended images is of a scrapyard ("Salvage"), and one of the most poignant poems is "The Prostitute," in which the speaker welcomes Death into her bed for the price of peace. Murphy's later poems in *The Rocks Cry Out* (1969), while opposing the younger generation's violence, resemble the 1960s' "poetry-as-statement," as she called it, but show less vigor of imagery than her youthful poems.

As an editor of poetry *anthologies, Murphy sought above all to give voice to young unknown writers. *Negro Voices* (1938) and *Ebony Rhythm* (1948) are dominated by college students and working amateurs. Perhaps as the result of Nikki *Giovanni's exasperation (expressed in a 1969 *Negro Digest* review) with her conservatism in *The Rocks Cry Out*, she included several of Giovanni's and Carolyn M. *Rodgers's poems in her last anthology, *New Negro Voices* (1970), and showed respect for the new militancy and black pride (though once again omitting poems with foul language). Her prefaces, essays, and reviews frequently acknowledge the difficulty African Americans have getting published in the white publishing industry, criticize white liberal hypocrisy, and encourage African American education.

Although Murphy wrote some creditable poems on a variety of compelling subjects, her importance may have been more as publicist and midwife to others' work.

• Nikki Giovanni, review of *The Rocks Cry Out*, *Negro Digest* 19 (Aug. 1969): 97–98. Lorraine Roses and Ruth Randolph, eds., *Harlem Renaissance and Beyond*, 1990, pp. 247–249.

—Larry R. Andrews

MURRAY, ALBERT (b. 1916), essayist, novelist, and cultural critic. Albert Murray's contribution to African American literature has established the value and importance of the *blues idiom as the basis for approaching life as an African American. Whether writing fiction, social *essays, book reviews, memoirs, aesthetic theory, or *music criticism, Murray performs like the best-trained *jazz musician. In his essays, Murray turns the basic beliefs of "social science fiction" inside out, exposing and playing on their assumptions just as Billie *Holiday created soul-stirring art out of trite popular tunes. In his fiction, Murray draws from the modernism of Thomas Mann, James Joyce, and William Faulkner in order to interpret the basic raw materials of growing up

African American in the South, creating a style as innovative as the harmonically and rhythmically complex improvisations of Charlie *Parker. When his career is examined as a whole, Albert Murray seems similar to Duke Ellington, a modern composer for the entire orchestra of literary genres, capable of creating material suitable for the brassy tonalities of topical journalistic debate, the more somber muted timbres of philosophical reflection, and the soaring glissandos of the memoir and the *bildungsroman. Murray's work in each of these genres is motivated by the hard-driving assertive rhythm section of a single idea—that the blues idiom represents an entire set of cultural equipment for living, an expansive range of styles and attitudes and possibilities for creating meaningful art, and a strategy for survival and even victory over racism in American society.

Born in Nokomis, Alabama, on 12 May 1916, Murray received his BS from Tuskegee Institute in 1939. He joined the air force in 1943 and retired with the rank of major in 1962. During his period in the service, Murray earned his MA from New York University (1948) and taught literature and composition to civilians and soldiers both in the United States and abroad. *The Omni-Americans* (1970), Murray's first book, contains reviews, essays, and commentaries that engage and challenge the predominant frameworks within which matters of *race and culture were then being discussed. Critiquing what he called "the folklore of white supremacy and the fakelore of black pathology," the book argues that all Americans are multicolored and that social scientific attempts to explain black life in America are fundamentally mistaken. His next book, *South to a Very Old Place* (1971), extends that argument with a series of memoirs, interviews, and reports that document the positive nurturing aspects of the African American community in the South. In 1972, Albert Murray was invited to give the Paul Anthony Brick Lectures on Ethics at the University of Missouri. These lecturers were published as *The Hero and the Blues* (1973). Here Murray develops his concept of literature in the blues idiom, a theory he eloquently practiced in the *novel *Train Whistle Guitar* (1974), which won the Lillian Smith Award for Southern Fiction. The hero of this novel receives from his *family and neighbors in the segregated South the cultural equipment necessary for leading a successful life—a sense of fundamental individual worth combined with community responsibility akin to the relationship between the improvising jazz soloist and the supporting band. In 1976, Murray turned the concept of the blues idiom back on itself, writing perhaps the best book ever published on jazz aesthetics, *Stomping the Blues*. Murray collaborated with Count Basie on his *autobiography, *Good Morning, Blues* (1985), and in 1991 published *The Spyglass Tree*, the long-awaited sequel to his first novel. A catalog essay on the paintings of Romare Bearden (*Romare Bearden, Finding the Rhythm*, 1991), extends Murray's concepts of improvisation, rhythm, and synthesis even to the realm of the visual arts.

For Murray, the blues idiom functions like classical tragedy, as a means for making the best out of a very bad situation. Like tragedy, the blues idiom contains a stylistic code for representing the most difficult conditions, but it also provides a strategy for living with and triumphing over these conditions with dignity, grace, and elegance. As in any highly developed aesthetic form, the blues idiom enables the artist to transform stylistically the grit of raw experience into art of tremendous and subtle beauty. But the blues idiom is distinguished from tragedy in that it has grown out of the specific historical experiences of, and the cultural resources developed by, African Americans. Whether made manifest in literature, the visual arts, or music, the blues idiom challenges and affirms an individual's basic humanity and higher aspirations "in spite of the fact that human existence is so often mostly a low-down dirty shame."

[See also Blues Aesthetic.]

• James Alan McPherson, "The View from the Chinaberry Tree," *Atlantic* 234 (Dec. 1974): 11, 88, 120–123. John Wideman, "*Stomping the Blues*: Ritual in Black Music and Speech," *American Poetry Review* 7.4 (1978): 42–45. Elizabeth Schultz, "Albert L. Murray," in *DLB*, vol. 38, *Afro-American Writers after 1955: Dramatists and Prose Writers*, eds. Thadious M. Davis and Trudier Harris, 1985, pp. 214–224. John Gennari, "Jazz Criticism: Its Development and Ideologies," *Black American Literature Forum* 23.3 (Fall 1991): 449–523. Warren Carson, "Albert Murray: Literary Reconstruction of the Vernacular Community," *African American Review* 27.2 (1993): 287–295.   —Barry Shank

MURRAY, PAULI (1910–1985), poet, biographer, historian, lawyer, teacher, activist, and priest. Born in Baltimore, Pauli Murray was orphaned at age three and raised by her mother's sister in the home of her maternal grandparents (the Fitzgeralds) in Durham, North Carolina. The Fitzgerald family had a profound influence on Murray throughout her life. The aunt who raised her was a teacher, and Murray learned to read and write at a very early age. Her grandfather, wounded in the Civil War as a Union soldier, and among those who set up the first schools for free blacks in North Carolina and Virginia, and her grandmother, daughter of a prominent white North Carolinian and a slave woman, served as strong examples of fortitude. *Education, equal rights, and personal faith and courage are themes connecting the various spheres of Murray's work and life.

Murray received her BA from Hunter College in New York in 1933, with an English major and a minor in history. This was the time of the *Harlem Renaissance, and Murray had the opportunity to meet figures such as Dorothy *West, Countee *Cullen, Sterling A. *Brown, and Robert *Hayden, as well as Langston *Hughes, who helped her to publish her first poem, "The Song of the Highway," in Nancy Cunard's 1934 *anthology, *Color*. At Hunter she also encountered Stephen Vincent Benét—not in person, but through his poem "John Brown's Body," which strongly affected her. It was seven years, however, before she introduced herself to Benét, sending him an early version of what was to become the poem "Dark

Testament." When she did, he offered encouragement and served as her literary mentor until his death in 1943.

Murray's social and spiritual concerns took her beyond writing, however. She received her initial degree in law from Howard University in 1944. Denied entry to the graduate program at Harvard because she was a woman, Murray received her LLM (1945) from the University of California at Berkeley instead. She practiced law in California and New York and earned the JD from Yale (1965), eventually teaching at Yale and Brandeis, and in Ghana. During the 1940s Murray worked briefly for the National Urban League and was one of the original "freedom riders" protesting bus segregation. She worked to further education rights, bringing legal action against universities for denying women admission to their graduate schools. Murray also was one of the founders of NOW, the National Organization for Women, and in 1977 she was among the first ten women ordained in the Episcopal Church—the first African American woman ever to hold that office.

Years of historical research went into Murray's first major literary publication, *Proud Shoes: The Story of an American Family* (1956). Tracing the Fitzgerald family history from the time of *slavery, it looks unflinchingly at issues of racism, sexism, and *miscegenation. Critics have praised its willingness to address the full range of African American experience, in order to claim a past that is both honest and "usable," and it has been read as a microcosm of African American history as well.

Her second major work, *Dark Testament and Other Poems* (1970), is a collection written over four decades (although most were written in Harlem in the late 1930s). Murray began the long title poem in New York in the 1930s, finishing it during the Harlem riot of 1943. A history of American race relations, it emphasizes imagination as a tool to face and transform a painful past, and draws on religious language and imagery both to encourage the oppressed and to challenge the oppressor. The collection is diverse, and it connects different historical periods and various groups who share "the dream of *freedom." The book reflects, in fact, Murray's own breadth of experience and the range of her social and spiritual vision.

In both works Murray demonstrates her lifelong concern for social and spiritual integration, making various connections: between white and African American history; between African Americans and other cultural "outsiders" in America; between literature and activism; between *family and nation; and among the past, present, and future. Facing the tension between different perspectives and goals within herself and in her world was sometimes a difficult task. In the poem "Conflict," for example, Murray describes her anxiety over the poet and the warrior grappling in her brain. Consistently, however, she found the encouragement—in history and faith and among activists and poets—to apply her varied gifts to a common cause. When she died in 1985 Murray was preparing another personal history for publication, her memoir *Song in a Weary Throat* (1987;

reprinted as *Pauli Murray: The Autobiography of a Black Activist* in 1989), which traces the author's lifelong journey as both political pioneer and spiritual pilgrim. Although this deeply spiritual autobiography ends, rather than begins, with a call to ordained ministry, this conclusion to her final book testifies to the interwoven character of all Murray's previous struggles and vocations.

[*See also* Autobiography, *article on* Spiritual Autobiography.]

• Nellie McKay, "Pauli Murray," in *DLB*, vol. 41, *Afro-American Poets since 1955*, eds. Trudier Harris and Thadious M. Davis, 1985, pp. 248–251.   —Sheila Hassell Hughes

MUSIC. African Americans have exerted a bigger impact in music than in any other cultural expression in the United States. Not only have black Americans substantially shaped a great deal of American popular music, they have, through music, influenced other art forms. *Jazz, for instance, has influenced painters such as Romare Bearden and Jacob *Lawrence, poets from T. S. Eliot and Langston *Hughes to Amiri *Baraka and Allen Ginsberg, not to mention novelists like Jack Kerouac, Claude *McKay, and Ralph *Ellison. The *blues have influenced Hughes, Albert *Murray, Ellison, Zora Neale *Hurston, Frank Marshall *Davis, Dubose Heyward, and others. Black music in America has been shaped by sociological forces and has itself become a huge sociological force, having an extraordinary impact on race relations.

Although music was a seminal cultural and artistic force in African cultures, and despite the fact that American slaves not only developed field hollers, ring shouts, and *spirituals, but often became skilled fiddlers on many plantations, it was not until after the Civil War that blacks began to make their presence felt broadly in American popular music. Although black-face *minstrelsy, the most popular form of American *musical theater, was launched in the North at the time of the resurgence of the American *antislavery movement of the late 1820s and early 1830s, it was during its antebellum years almost exclusively a music performed by white men that had little, if any, genuine African or African American content.

After the Civil War, blacks began to move slowly but inexorably into this musical form, claiming themselves to be the authentic item as, after all, the music was supposed to be that of slaves on a plantation. In the 1880s and 1890s, blacks had more than modest success in minstrelsy, but not without considerable resistance on the part of white audiences to accept them on any terms and not without considerable pressure to perform as blacks in the same degrading manner that white performers portrayed blacks, even to being forced in many instances to use black-face makeup. It must be remembered that blacks had been received by white audiences as serious performers of their own music when the Fisk Jubilee Singers became a big hit both here and abroad in the early 1870s through the performance of slave spirituals. Nonetheless, by the 1890s, when Recon-struction ended, the bourbons having seized power again in the South, and amid rampant segregation and the terrorism of *lynching, blacks made considerable inroads on the American stage. James Weldon *Johnson, Rosamond Johnson, Will Marion Cook, and others were writing successful Broadway shows featuring blacks and Bert Williams and George Walker had become a successful comedy team. A good deal of this music was in the form of "coon songs," not surprising, as blacks, in a patronizing, often shockingly racist way, had become major advertising icons and there was in the United States at this time a great deal of romanticized nostalgia about the antebellum South. James Weldon Johnson provides a vivid account of this era in his *autobiography, *Along This Way*, published in 1933, as well as in his *history of blacks in New York, *Black Manhattan*, published in 1930.

By the early 1910s, ragtime music, largely performed on piano with considerable syncopation, drawing on the imaginative strength of its leading composer, Scott Joplin, had become the American rage. James Weldon Johnson's *novel, *The *Autobiography of an Ex-Colored Man*, published in 1912 during the height of the ragtime craze, dealt in part with the significance of this music. The novel also examined an important strand of African American musical ambition: transforming black popular music forms into a symphonic or classical music. If, with "coon songs" and the early Broadway stage, there was a strong vaudeville tradition in black American popular music, and if, with ragtime and later jazz, there was a "whorehouse" ambiance in the music, with the interest in symphonic music, there was, to be sure, a genteel tradition in African American music as well. Even ragtime had a certain genteel quality and was often associated with the African American parlor. Such noted African American musicians as James P. Johnson, Fats Waller, William Grant *Still, Duke Ellington, Harry T. Burleigh, and Will Marion Cook wrote symphonic or orchestral music at some time in their careers. Probably the most important African American musician playing in the North before 1920 was James Reese Europe, a trained musician reared in a genteel black musical family in Washington, D.C. Europe formed his own black musical union, the Clef Club, in New York around 1910, became the band leader for the famous dance couple, Vernon and Irene Castle, and played Carnegie Hall long before any other black musician or any musician associated with African American popular music or jazz. Europe's marching band became part of the all-black 369th Infantry that fought with distinction in World War I. He was killed by a deranged drummer in his band in 1919, shortly after returning from the war. But his musical influence was considerable.

After ragtime, the most influential African American music, by far, was jazz. It would be no overstatement to say that jazz revolutionized American culture. Although scholarly research has revealed that jazz was played in various parts of the country, its birthplace is rightly considered New Orleans. A highly rhythmic music, jazz made use of the blues song structure, regularized by W. C. Handy, and improvisational technique, influenced by the marching band. (John Philip Sousa, the most popular musician in America at the turn of the century, was as important in the development of jazz as anyone, although he never played this music. Most black jazz musicians in the early days played in marching bands, loved marching band music, and particularly admired Sousa.) Among the most important early black jazz musicians were Buddy Bolden, Kid Ory, King Oliver, Jelly Roll Morton, and Sidney Bechet, all either from New Orleans or eventual residents of that city.

After 1920, jazz, following the migratory patterns of southern blacks who were leaving the South in great numbers, and spread out all over the country, but particularly became focused in Chicago and New York. The greatest jazz musician of the 1920s, indeed, one of the finest musicians in the history of American music, was trumpeter Louis Armstrong, who by the late 1920s had become the most influential singer in popular music with the possible exception of Bing Crosby. Armstrong was mostly located in Chicago during this period, although he spent some time in New York. The two greatest jazz bandleaders of this period were Fletcher Henderson and Duke Ellington, both of whom played in New York. The blues was also popular at this time, largely dominated by black women singers such as Ida Cox, Mamie Smith, Ma *Rainey, and the great Bessie *Smith. One of the leading white supporters of the *Harlem Renaissance, Carl Van Vechten, was a fan of this music and wrote about it extensively.

The 1930s saw the development of swing music, a form of jazz built on highly rhythmic riffs that are passed around or harmonically played against each other by sections of a large band, usually consisting of at least sixteen players. Swing became the popular music of the 1930s and 1940s, and indeed was the most popular form of jazz. Jazz had become a highly professionalized music requiring virtuosic playing skills, many years of training, and highly developed reading ability. There were a number of black swing bands, among the most famous were Count Basie's, the Savoy Sultans, the Jay McShann band, the Chick Webb band, and Andy Kirk and His Clouds of Joy. But by and large, white swing bands earned most of the money, played the better venues, and received the press. Benny Goodman, Artie Shaw, Tommy Dorsey, Jimmy Dorsey, Glenn Miller, and other white bands dominated the 1930s. From its earliest days, jazz was a music played by whites, had a white audience, and was written about by whites. Of course, what many whites considered jazz would not have passed muster with many true jazz players, or "hot" players as they were called at this time. Nonetheless, despite the racism that seriously reduced the earning power of black bands, jazz broke down a number of racial barriers. Black musicians were often deeply respected and admired by their white counterparts. Jazz gave us the first integrated music in America, both on record and in live performance.

After the second world war, the expense of managing and maintaining a big band made them unfeasible and jazz became a small group music, usually of bands consisting of no more than five or six pieces. Moreover, after the war, blacks had become more militant and this was reflected in the music. Bebop, a more angular, complex, and less danceable music emerged, played by "cool" musicians who seemed aloof, even hostile to their audience, and who wanted to be considered artists and not *entertainers. The leading figures of bebop were saxophonist Charlie *Parker, trumpeter Dizzy Gillespie, and pianists Bud Powell and Thelonious Monk. The major musicians of the "cool" movement were trumpeter Miles *Davis and pianist John Lewis, as well as a number of white musicians. These forms of jazz were not as popular as swing, and much of jazz's black audience gravitated toward a new music called rhythm and blues, that combined the rhythmic punch and danceable beat of a kind of simplified swing with the structure of electric blues. The leading practitioner of this new form was saxophonist-singer Louis Jordan.

In the 1950s, the rhythm and blues (R&B) craze grew, fueled largely by the recording activities of a number of independent record companies that found serving the black market a lucrative enterprise. Many popular R&B records were "covered" or redone by white singers to appeal to white audiences, but the hunger among whites especially for this music led many to seek out the original black artists. By the mid-1950s a new popular music had mutated from R&B, combining in various ways country music, simplified aspects of harmony singing, the fervor of black gospel (enjoying a considerable revival in the 1950s), and the rhythm and danceable beat of R&B. This new music was called rock and roll. The most important black practitioners of this form in the 1950s were Chuck Berry, Jackie Wilson, Clyde McPhatter, James Brown, Ray Charles, Fats Domino, and Little Richard. The single most famous performer, however, was a white Southerner named Elvis Presley. The emergence of this form, along with the rise of a so-called youth culture or youth market, generated even more racial boundary crossing.

The 1960s saw the continued rise and development of this art form from its primitive beginnings to, by the end of the decade, the most dominant popular music in the world. Blacks continued to be an essential force in its advancement. Motown Records, formed in Detroit in 1959 by Berry Gordy, became the most successful independent record company in history, and a prime mover and shaker in rock and roll, producing a number of famous artists including Stevie Wonder, Marvin Gaye, Diana Ross, Smokey Robinson, and others. James Brown, a singer from Augusta, Georgia, produced a number of best-selling records, including the first million-selling "live" recording. He was a major innovator in this form. Other famous artists of this period were Jimi Hendrix, Sly and the Family Stone, Wilson Pickett, Otis Redding, Aretha *Franklin, and Curtis Mayfield. Many consider the 1960s the golden age of black popular music, or black dance music.

Today, black music continues to thrive with artists such as Michael Jackson, the artist formerly known as Prince, Boyz II Men, Jodeci, and others. The most significant new form of black music to emerge is rap, a highly stylized form of chanting, derivative of toasts and aspects of black sermonic recitation, that first developed in the late 1960s and early 1970s with politically conscious acts like the Last Poets and Gil *Scott-Heron, and by Kurtis Blow and Isaac Hayes. It re-emerged in the 1980s, spawning a variety of forms and styles, much of it with explicit political content that is meant to express the concerns and preoccupations of young blacks living in urban areas today. This music is not without its controversy, particularly over obscene lyrics about sex or *violence. There have been efforts underway by a strange coalition of groups including middle-class blacks, police officers, white feminists, and conservative politicians to have a subgenre called gangsta rap, known for its especially harsh, sometimes crude lyrics, banned from recording.

[See also Blues Aesthetic; Coltrane, John; Dance.]

• Amiri Baraka, *Blues People*, 1963. Eileen Southern, *The Music of Black Americans*, 1971. Albert Murray, *Stomping the Blues*, 1976. Daphne Duval Harrison, *Black Pearls: Blues Queens of the 1920s*, 1988. Kathy J. Ogren, *The Jazz Revolution: Twenties America and the Meaning of Jazz*, 1989. Burton Peretti, *The Creation of Jazz: Music, Race, and Culture in Urban America*, 1992. Tricia Rose, *Black Noise: Rap Music and Black Culture in Contemporary America*, 1994. Gerald Early, *One Nation under a Groove: Motown and American Culture*, 1995.   —Gerald Early

MUSICALS. The African American musical flows from a people who carry African seeds that are deeply planted in an earth of *music and words. The early musicals made it possible for African Americans to demonstrate the wealth of their music, dance traditions, and their artistic creativity. They created a stage for humor which allowed for self-laughter, ethos, and satire—three aspects often overshadowed in historical analyses of early musical history. Many of the early performers became important cultural heroes who paved the way for later generations of African American theater professionals, and some (e.g., Tom Fletcher) even hoped their humor would be an inroad to diminishing the ill feelings racially targeted at African Americans.

The major nineteenth-century breakthrough shows were *The Creole Show* (1890), *The Octoroons* (1895, also known as *The Royal Octoroons*), *Oriental America* (1896), Black Patti's *Troubadours* (1896), and Bob Cole's 1898 *A Trip to Coontown*. Cole's productions were owned, operated, and produced entirely by African Americans and opened the same year that composer Will Marion Cook and poet Paul Laurence *Dunbar presented their one-act musical comedy *Clorindy: The Origin of the Cakewalk*. Because Cook's production opened at the Casino Roof—a rooftop location patronized primarily by whites that was technically accepted as a Broadway house—*Clorindy* was the first African American musical ever to appear on Broadway.

It was not until 1903 that Cook made Broadway history again. This time the production was inspired by George Walker and Bert Williams, and named after one of the ancient West African countries where the last group of enslaved Africans had been brought to America, Dahomey (today known as Benin). *Dahomey*'s lyrics were by Alex Rogers, and J. A. Shipp wrote the libretto. They had also collaborated on two other Williams and Walker shows, *Abyssinia* (1906) and *Bandana Land* (1908), purported to be their best.

Except for Bob Cole and J. Rosmond Johnson's 1909 Broadway production of *The Red Moon*, a musical comedy based on the *folklore of American Indians and African Americans, the convention of earlier musical comedies did not make a major change until 1921 when the collaborative team of Flournoy Miller, Aubrey Lyles, Noble Sissle, and Eubie Blake presented *Shuffle Along*, the theatrical spark that ignited the *Harlem Renaissance. Its overwhelming popularity among African Americans proved that money could reshape segregation policies within New York's legitimate theaters; for example, seating restrictions gradually changed, and it became less of a shock to see African Americans seated in the orchestra instead of the balcony.

Shuffle Along was not a revue, but a complete story based on a book about a mayoral race where crime does not pay, that had its beginnings with Miller and Lyles when they were students at Fisk University. One of its alluring qualities—unlike previous African American presentations—was a sophisticated love story highlighted with memorable songs: "Love Will Find a Way" and "I'm Just Wild about Harry" (later used by Harry Truman as his campaign song). The show had a run of more than five hundred performances before it opened at the Sixty-Third Street Theater in New York where it remained for nearly a year and a half. Miller and Lyles also starred in the production along with Lottie Gee as the lead actress and Gertrude Saunders, the ingenue. The production appeared throughout several seasons during the 1920s on Broadway with a replacement cast that included Josephine *Baker (when she was sixteen years old), Adelaide Hall, and Paul *Robeson. The team of Miller and Lyles later went on to produce numerous musicals including their 1923 hit at the Colonial Theater, *Runnin' Wild*, which popularized the hit dance of the era, the Charleston. It was an immediate success, grossing nineteen thousand dollars during its first week.

The most popular African American musicals to close out the 1920s were Lew Leslie's *Blackbirds of 1928* at the Liberty Theater and *Hot Chocolates* (1929) at the Hudson Theater spotlighting the double-entendre scores of Thomas "Fats" Waller, Andy Razaf, and Harry Brooks with comedy sketches by Eddie Green. It was a memorable show that brought three heavyweights of the era together: Thomas "Fats" Waller, Edith Wilson, and Louis Armstrong. Edith sang, Fats played piano, Louis was on trumpet, and they were billed as the One Thousand Pounds of Harmony.

The depression forced musicals to be less elaborate. *Brown Buddies* starring Adelaide Hall and the tap dance maestro Bill "Bojangles" Robinson opened at the Liberty Theater in 1930 followed by *Rhapsody in Black*—a 1931 Lew Leslie production—popularizing the singing and acting talents of Ethel *Waters.

There was an unquestionable cultural influence from African Americans on American musicals. If African Americans were not creating the productions, the productions were created for them as in the case of the folk opera *Porgy and Bess* (1935); the 1939 New York productions of *Swing Mikado* and *Hot Mikado*; *Carmen Jones* (1943); *Memphis Bound!* (1945); and *Timbuktu!* (1978).

Staged musicals (whether written by or for African Americans) basically took a backseat to *film and *television from 1945 to 1960, and the consciousness movement of the 1960s was not fueled by the influence of earlier musicals. A major exception to this latter trend were works by Langston *Hughes: *Simply Heavenly* (1957), *Black Nativity* (1961), *Tambourines to Glory* (1963), *Jericho-Jim Crow* (1964), and the collaborative effort of a black and white writing team (C. Bernard Jackson and James Hatch): *Fly Blackbird* (1962). By the 1970s, the reappearance of African American musicals separated into five types: social, historical, personality, romantic, and sacred/gospel.

Social musicals relied on clarifying issues by telling balanced stories in their plots (albeit using humor and the seriousness of protagonists innocently combating with antagonists). Racism, social conditions, drug addiction, or television violence were some of the themes highlighted in musicals such as *Purlie* (based on Ossie *Davis's 1961 play *Purlie Victorious*), Melvin Van Peebles's *Ain't Supposed to Die a Natural Death* (1971), and *Don't Bother Me I Can't Cope*, a 1972 musical comedy by Micki Grant which ran for 1,065 performances and was directed by Vinnette Carroll.

The 1973 Broadway hit *Raisin* was a musical re-creation of Lorraine *Hansberry's social dramatic hit *A *Raisin in the Sun*. The musical, like the drama, is about the struggles of an urban African American family comprised of three generations. *Raisin* ran for 847 performances with Virginia Capers winning a Tony for the Best Performance of an Actress in a Musical. Two later social musicals that did not reach the Great White Way but found tremendous financial support and praise throughout African American communities were Runako Jahi's *Momma Don't* (1990) and Richard *Wesley's *The Dream Team* (1989), about two brothers who play baseball and are separated because of desegregation.

Romantic musicals are often struck by fate separating lovers in a milieu plagued by adverse social conditions. Lynn Ahren's *Once on This Island* (1990) and James M. Brown's *Count Your Blessings* (1990) depict lovers whose troubles stem from either class or race conditions. *Once on This Island* (adapted from a novel by Rosa *Guy) is set in the Caribbean and portrays an island peasant girl in love with a *mulatto landowner's son. *Count Your Blessings* features a young female lawyer who falls in love with her first client, an incarcerated rap artist. What is seemingly a traditional love story is also a call for social change.

The historical musical reflected a genre preserving important events and places. *Bubbling Brown Sugar* (1976) by Loften *Mitchell, concept by Rosetta LeNoire, was a landmark production portraying the era of the early musicals of Broadway and Harlem using veterans from the original shows: Joseph Attles, Avon Long, Josephine Premise. Honi Coles and Bobby Short's *Black Broadway* (1980) re-created the ambience of the 1920s and 1930s with the original stars—John Bubbles (Sportin' Life in *Porgy and Bess*, 1935), Adelaide Hall (in *Blackbirds*, 1928), Elisabeth Welch (*Runnin' Wild*, 1923), and Edith Wilson (*Plantation Revue*, 1922).

Scholar Samuel Hay assesses contemporary personality musicals as tributes celebrating the creations of individual musical geniuses that either lightly touched upon or avoided telling about hardships of the lives that the musicals heralded. There were memorable productions that highlighted the compositions of Thomas "Fats" Waller in the 1978 Tony Award–winner for Best Musical, *Sophisticated Ladies* (1981), a concept by Donald McKayle featuring the ingenious contributions of Duke Ellington with elaborate costuming and outstanding choreography; and Julian Swain's *Blue Indigo* (1981), hailing the contributions of Waller, Ma *Rainey, Bessie *Smith, Eubie Blake, Big Maybell, and Duke Ellington.

The sacred/gospel musical as a distinct musical form began in African American *churches before its appearance in public theaters. The sources of the plot are drawn from religious theology. Hughes's version of the Christmas story in his *Black Nativity* and his use of gospel music as an inherent part of the dramatic structure of *Tambourines to Glory* paved the way for other productions. For example, *Trumpets of the Lord* (1963) by Vinnette Carroll was an adaptation of James Weldon *Johnson's *God's Trombones* (1927), and Carroll's *Your Arms Too Short to Box with God* (1976) was adapted from the Book of Matthew. Throughout the 1960s to date, Jim Mapp's a cappella use of traditional African American *spirituals to segue the sermons of *God's Trombones* has been adapted in productions throughout the United States and Europe, while Ron *Milner's *Don't Get God Started* relies on dramatically re-creating a soul-stirring revival meeting. When *Mama I Want to Sing* (part 1, 1982; part 2, 1990) successfully ran for more than a decade throughout African American communities with record numbers, it proved, along with smart marketing, that gospel music and *theater have mass ministerial appeal.

The African American musical is evolving and transcending itself through music, words, and movements as a historical continuum. It may have a story line, as in *Dreamgirls* (1981), about the aspirations and struggles of a female singing group; or exist without a recognizable story line that can produce a "cultural earthquake" reminiscent of George C. Wolfe's *Jelly's Last Jam* (1990), which relies on an episodic structure to talk about the paradoxical life of jazz musician-composer Ferdinand "Jelly Roll" Morton. With the acclaim these and other productions have received, the African American musical in its varied arrangements will survive as a major American theater voice. The music, the words, the movements are means of sharing a story about the people;

their history; and their personalities, beliefs, and social conditions.

[*See also* Opera.]

• Allen Woll, *Black Musical Theatre*, 1989. Samuel Hay, *African American Theatre*, 1994.

—Beverly J. Robinson

My Bondage and My Freedom. Frederick *Douglass's second *autobiography, *My Bondage and My Freedom*, published by the New York commercial publishers Miller, Orton, and Mulligan in 1855, is larger, more self-consciously literary, and more self-analytical than the *Narrative of the Life of Frederick Douglass* (1845). From its opening pages, where the African American abolitionist James McCune Smith, known for his vehement criticism of William Lloyd Garrison, supplants Douglass's former mentor as prefacer of the memoir, *My Bondage and My Freedom* shows that it is more than a mere updated installment of the *Narrative*. The second autobiography offers a thoughtful revision of the meaning and goals of Douglass's life.

My Bondage and My Freedom introduces few incidents or figures from Douglass's past that do not appear in the *Narrative*. But the second autobiography says more about Douglass's complex relationship to his environment, particularly in the South, than emerges in the more famous fugitive *slave narrative. Douglass's grandmother, who appears in the *Narrative* only in the throes of a pathetic death, becomes the able and self-sufficient Betsey Bailey in the opening chapters of *My Bondage and My Freedom*, respectfully portrayed as the creator of the only real home young Frederick ever knew as a slave. Douglass's master, Aaron Anthony, tersely indicted in the *Narrative* as "a cruel man," is rehabilitated in *My Bondage and My Freedom* into "a wretched man" who could be "almost fatherly" toward Frederick when not tormented by his passions and bad temper. The slave youth engaged in a lonely struggle for direction and dignity in the *Narrative* finds much inspiration and support within the southern African American community as depicted in *My Bondage and My Freedom* and epitomized in Charles Lawson, unmentioned in the *Narrative* but dubbed by Douglass in 1855 his "spiritual father." The high seriousness of the *Narrative*'s rendition of Douglass's climactic hand-to-hand struggle with the satanic Maryland slave-breaker Edward Covey is tempered comically in *My Bondage and My Freedom* so as to emphasize Douglass's common humanity rather than his outsized heroism.

In 1845, Douglass brought his life story to a glorious culmination with an image of himself proclaiming the antislavery gospel from the lecture platform, a fugitive slave fully enlisted in the abolitionist crusade. Ten years later a chastened Douglass testified to the prejudice and paternalism among the Garrisonian abolitionists that caused him eventually to break from their ranks. Whereas the *Narrative* says almost nothing about northern racism, the better to draw a diametric opposition between the "free" North and the slave South, *My Bondage and My Freedom* catalogs the many forms of segregation that Douglass encountered after his escape from *slavery. Realizing the subtle bondage of racist paternalism in the North as well as the South, Douglass announces at the end of *My Bondage and My Freedom* his conviction that the best way to attack slavery in the South is to immerse himself in the cause of the quasi-free African Americans of the North. Thus Douglass moves away from the individualism of the *Narrative* and toward a greater communal identification in *My Bondage and My Freedom*.

[*See also* Antislavery Movement; Migration.]

• William L. Andrews, *To Tell a Free Story: The First Century of Afro-American Autobiography, 1760–1865*, 1986. Frederick Douglass, *My Bondage and My Freedom*, ed. William L. Andrews, 1987. Eric J. Sundquist, *To Wake the Nations: Race in the Making of American Literature*, 1993.

—William L. Andrews

MYERS, WALTER DEAN (b. 1937), poet, editor, and novelist. A versatile and prolific writer, Walter Dean Myers (also Walter M. Myers) has published short fiction, *essays, and *poetry in such disparate periodicals as the *Liberator*, *Negro Digest*, *McCall's*, *Essence*, *Espionage*, and Alfred Hitchcock's *Mystery Magazine*. He was a regular contributor to men's magazines until, as he says, "they gave themselves up to pornography." In 1968, he wrote his first children's book as an entry to a contest sponsored by the Council on Interracial Books for Children. He won, *Where Does the Day Go?* was published by *Parent's Magazine* Press, and thus began his career as a writer of *children's and young adult literature. To date, Myers has published more than forty books, many of which have earned awards and citations such as the American Library Association Best Book for Young Adults, the Newbery Honor Book, the *Boston Globe*/Horn Book Honor Book, and the Coretta Scott King Award.

Myers writes fantasy with black characters (*The Golden Serpent*, 1980, and *The Legend of Tarik*, 1981). He retells his father's and grandfather's ghost stories and legends (*The Black Pearl and the Ghost*, 1980, and *Mr. Monkey and the Gotcha Bird*, 1984). His adventure tales take black adolescents to Peruvian jungles and Hong Kong temples (*The Nicholas Factor*, 1983, and *The Hidden Shrine*, 1985). His nonfiction is often innovative in form and subject matter. In *Sweet Illusions* (1987), Myers examines pregnancy through the stories of fourteen teenage mothers, fathers, and their friends and relatives. Each chapter ends with blank pages for readers to complete the ending. His *biography of *Malcolm X (1994) uses actual photographs and inserts from newspapers, interviews, and magazines to create an inspirational and provocative book. Myers pairs poems and commentary to turn-of-the-century photographs of African American children in *Brown Angels* (1993) and Jacob *Lawrence's pictures in *The Great Migration* (1994).

Walter Dean Myers is best known, however, for his young adult novels about Harlem residents. Like many black writers, Myers loved to read but rarely encountered books about people like him or his friends and family. This desire to fill a void, to create for other youth that which had been lacking in his own adolescence, was further motivated by his displeasure with the prevalent images of African Americans as exotics, misfits, criminals, victims, and "unserious" people. Having grown up in Harlem, he was particularly upset by the negative and monolithic portrayals of that community. Myers's stories usually take place within a Harlem community of diverse people who love, laugh, work, and dream as much as any other people in the world. Though praised for his natural dialogues, his optimistic endings, and his eccentric but loveable characters, Myers does not romanticize. Drugs and violence, loneliness and indifference, sex, *religion, economics, and other oppressive and challenging agencies figure into his plots. In *It Ain't All for Nothin'* (1978), Tippy's grandmother is put into a nursing home and his ex-convict father involves him in a robbery. Steve's parents in *Won't Know Till I Get There* (1982) try to rehabilitate a troubled teen only to have their middle-class child and his friends end up in juvenile court. Lonnie Jackson escapes Harlem with an athletic scholarship but the predominantly white midwestern college presents a new set of problems in *The Outside Shot* (1984). Richie Perry's escape, on the other hand, moves him from the frying pan of Harlem to the fire of Vietnam in *Fallen Angels* (1989). Myers tends to focus upon male relationships but his female protagonists are neither stereotypical nor predictable. *Crystal* (1987) presents a sixteen-year-old fashion model and actress whose meteoric rise does not satisfy her. In *Motown and Didi: A Love Story* (1984), a disciplined and intelligent student's college career is jeopardized by her brother's drug addiction and her mother's mental instability. Each individual works out her or his own destiny, but each comes to recognize and value supportive relationships.

As a member of John O. *Killen's writers workshop, Walter Dean Myers practiced his craft with Wesley Brown, George Davis, and Askia M. *Touré. When he became an editor at Bobbs-Merrill in 1970, Myers learned not only the business of *publishing that helped his own career, but he published fellow writers Nikki *Giovanni, Ann Allen *Shockley, and Richard Perry. Among the African American writers who served as his literary models, Myers names Frank *Yerby and his Harlem neighbor and fellow children's book writer, Langston *Hughes. Today, Walter Dean Myers ranks with Virginia *Hamilton and Lucille *Clifton as the foremost writers in children's and young adult literature.

• Walter Dean Myers, *Something about the Author Autobiography Series*, vol. 2, ed. Adele Sarkissian, 1986, pp. 143–156. *Children's Literature Review*, vol. 16, ed. Gerald J. Senick, 1989, pp. 134–144. Rudine Sims Bishop, *Presenting Walter Dean Myers*, 1990. *Something about the Author*, vol. 71, ed. Diane Telgen, 1993, pp. 133–137.

—Frances Smith Foster

MYSTERY WRITING. *See* Crime and Mystery Writing.

N

NAMES AND NAMING. Herbert G. Gutman, one among many historians, affirms that name connections joined African American families with their forebears. Basing his findings upon plantation journals, family Bibles, court documents, and Freedmen's Bureau records, Gutman reports his conclusions in the *Black Family in Slavery and Freedom, 1750–1925.* Ties and allegiances, domestic structures, and kinship networks tied African American families to cultural norms. The literature reveals that names and naming practices used by African American parents (and significant others) continue today.

Africans James Albert Ukawsaw *Gronniosaw, Ottobah Cugoano, and Olaudah *Equiano wrote narratives about their ordeals in *slavery. Invaluable as one of the first depictions of an African society by an African and considered now as the text that commenced the *slave narrative tradition, Equiano's *The Interesting Narrative of the Life of Olaudah Equiano, or Gustavus Vassa the African, Written by Himself* (1789) details his life in a village east of the Niger River in what is now Nigeria. The title character's recapitulations offer readers direct insights into African (Ibo) customs and beliefs. The etymology of his name is an interesting study of name changing. Equiano scholar Paul Edwards and African novelist Chinua Achebe maintain that the Ibo terms Equiano uses are recognizable in modern Ibo. "Olaudah" means "having a loud voice, and well-spoken." When combined with the modern Ibo *ola* (ornament) with *ude* (fame), "Olaudah" signifies one favored. "Ekweano" means "if they agree I shall stay" and implies someone unhappy with his companions. "Ekwuano" means "when they speak others attend" and implies a member of a group of spokesmen. The latter term can still be found in south-central Nigeria (the region of the author's home). "Ekwuno" is a common name spoken by the Ika Ibo (western bank of the Niger River). In America, Equiano lost his African name, being called first Michael, then Jacob, and finally Gustavus Vassa, the latter being the name he used for the rest of his life.

Slave names with an African origin seemed strange or ridiculous to slaveowners. Africans would commonly name a child after the day or month of birth (day name), after some event, or after a particular personality trait (or fancied foreboding) discerned at the time of birth. Eugene D. Genovese's claim is that the slaves of South Carolina and Georgia low country never gave up the practice of giving their children African names. The preceding custom echoed across the South. It was common knowledge among West Africans that infants might fall prey to *tetanism* ("ninth-day fits"); thus, "superstitious" slaves would refuse to name their children until the ninth day after birth. Newborns who died before they were given a name were often listed as "unnamed," "no name," or "baby." Since they calculated time and foretold events, priests, magicians, and wise men in Africa were called *Ah-affoe-way-cah,* a term that signifies "calculators." Slaves were sometimes called Affy or Ah-affoe, meaning one year. The African *Quaco,* meaning "a male born on Wednesday," became Quack. *Quashee,* meaning "a female born on Sunday," became Squash. Commonly used, Cuffee suggests both a male born on Friday and the Ashanti name *Kofi.* Phoebe is a variation of *Phiba* or *Phibbi,* meaning "a female born on Friday." Other names with clear African origins are Cudjo and Juba. Later, slaves anglicized African names: Cudjo might become Monday in one generation and Joe in the next, Quaco might become Wednesday, or even Jacco, Jacky, or Jack, and Jeaceo became Jackson. In Toni *Morrison's *Beloved* (1987), *Sethe Suggs was conceived on a slave ship in an act of love. Her mother, according to Nan (the wet nurse), gave the baby a name commemorating that act. Sethe is a feminization of the African name of the father. Although they never wholly disappeared, African names steadily receded after the turn of the nineteenth century. Indeed, they have resurfaced within the past three decades in the *poetry, fiction, and *drama of Haki R. *Madhubuti, Alice *Walker, Toni Morrison, Toni Cade *Bambara, Amiri *Baraka, and Ntozake *Shange, among others.

Called Marse, Marster, Mars, Massa, Ole Massa, Ole Maussuh, Big Pappy, Young Massa, Missus, and Young Missus, owners identified slaves in journals, diaries, and plantation record books. Since slave women were not forced either to take husbands or even to name the fathers of their children, the fathers' names were rarely recorded in these books. Further, the social and business status of a slave child followed that of its mother. Contrary to legend, slave mothers (or both parents) named their own children although in numerous instances slaveowners took the liberty.

Many slaves had surnames, and these names often differed from the surnames of those who owned them. In other words, slaves had two names, and they usually identified themselves by the name of the first owner. Being English or French in its origin, the surname was infrequently used and rarely recorded. To cite one example, Nat *Turner belonged in 1831 (the year of his death) to Joseph Travis. Born Benjamin Turner's slave, he was later sold to Putnam Moore. Moore's widow married Travis, but Nat Turner retained his first owner's name. Sales or separation from slave family of origin encouraged slaves to retain different surnames. Slaves did not consider their surnames "family" names and refused to give these names to owners and other whites. In many places—especially South Carolina—it was against the law to use the surname.

Even though most slaves could not read, they often wanted to see their names written "down" in the master's family Bible. Besides Adam and Eve, many were given the names of Old Testament patriarchs, prophets, and kings, such as Abram, Isaac, Israel, *Moses, Joshua, Samuel, Elijah, Elisha, "Zekiel," Amos, Daniel, David, and Solomon. Other names were Cyrus, Titus, Jesse, Nathan, Abel, Jonas, Benjamin, Caleb, and Gabriel. New Testament male names were Matthew, Mark, Luke, Peter, Simon, Thomas, Andrew, John, Stephen, Paul, James, and Timothy. Some slave women were called Miriam, Sarah, Hagar, Esther, Ruth, Rebecca, Rachel, Leah, Hannah, Mary, Elizabeth, and Lydia. Between 1760 and 1865, many fugitives who became the subjects of slave narratives had biblical names. Some of these narrators were John *Marrant, Joseph Mountain, Benjamin Prentiss, John Jea, John Joyce, Solomon Bayley, Moses *Roper, Mary *Prince, Solomon *Northup, Joseph and Enoch (Louisiana female runaway slaves), Moses Grandy, Reverend Peter Randolph, Samuel Ringgold Ward, Peter Still, Josiah *Henson, Reverend Noah Davis, Israel Campbell, Jeremiah Asher, and Dinah. Biblical names have been and are still popular as first names. Satirist Ishmael *Reed is identifiable in this name category.

Farcical and having withered away as favored names before a host of English-sounding appellations, classical names, such as Caesar, Pompey, Cato, Hector, Hercules, Primus, Scipio, Bacchus, and Jupiter (as evident in the poet Jupiter *Hammon), were imposed on slave children by their owners. Rarely did slaves choose such pompous names. Classical names did not survive the Civil War. In *Roll, Jordan Roll* (1972), Eugene D. Genovese asserts, "Slaves often accepted a master's choice passively, especially if the name was unexceptionable, but sometimes they resisted." Slaves would sometimes Africanize Latin names. Hercules became a "fine idea," for *beke* in Mende means "large wild animal," and Cato suggests several perfectly good West African names. Condemning the system that denies the mother, who represents the family, the right to name her own child, Charles Waddell *Chesnutt in "A Deeper Sleeper" signifies on Latin slave naming practices. In the aforementioned tale, *Uncle Julius McAdoo explains that some of Tom's ancestors were named "Skundus," "Tushus," "Cottus," and "Squinchus," by ole Marse Dugal' McAdoo. In the tale, the names given the brothers are actually the Latin terms *secundus, tertius, quartus,* and *quintus,* meaning second, third, fourth, and fifth, spelled in such a way as to approximate Uncle Julius's pronunciation of them.

At mid-nineteenth century or earlier, the stereotyped *Sambo was given an Anglo name. About one in four slaves had such conventional names as William, George, John, Henry, Ann, Susannah, Nancy, Bridget, Malinda Jane, Laura, Phillis, or Amanda. The epitome of devotion, the Sambo was a synthesis of the clown, the contented slave, and the victim. As a dominant plantation type, he was a central character in the literature: the victim in antislavery propaganda and the wretched freedman in proslavery literature. Historian John Blassingame describes him as "indolent, faithful, humorous, loyal, dishonest, superstitious, improvident, and musical . . . inevitably a clown and congenitally docile." In light of the social perceptions of the enslaved, slave narrators attempted to make his portrayal more heroic by accentuating his positive traits while ignoring or refuting as misconceptions the negative ones. As a literary type, Sambo was presented as a martyr, a model, or a hero. Last, the Sambo type was a figure with whom sympathy was possible—never empathy.

Most slaves were known only by given names. Many names were given for the pleasure of the owner, such as King, Prince, Duke, General, Colonel, Major, and Captain—and on occasion Senator, Governor, Judge. In addition to literary characters (Richard and Claudia) and gemstones as names (Jasper and Sapphire), some children were given flower names (Rose and Violet). Besides day and month names, locales such as India, Scotland, Carolina, Georgia or Georgianna, Boston, Asbury, Charlotte, Harrison, and Bristol were names given on occasion to newborns. Such attributes and designations as "friendly," "patience," or "Santee River plantation slave" were given or identifiable names. Abolitionist, women's rights activist, freedom fighter, domestic servant, and evangelist Sojourner *Truth named herself. Isabella Baumfree was her given name, the surname being a Dutch nickname applied to her father. In *Narrative of the Life of Frederick Douglass, an American Slave, Written by Himself* (1845), the title character's mother named him Frederick Augustus Washington Bailey. He was called Frederick Bailey or simply Fred while he was growing up. Later he escaped from slavery under the name of Stanley, but when he reached New York, he took the name of Frederick Johnson and was married under that name. Finally, he found too many Johnsons in New Bedford and gave his host Nathan Johnson the privilege of choosing his surname. Douglass later writes, "Mr. Johnson had just been reading the 'Lady of the Lake,' and at once suggested that my name be 'Douglass.' From that time until now, I have been called Frederick *Douglass, and am more widely known by that name." Similarly, in *Up from Slavery* (1899), Booker T. *Washington was called Booker but adopted Washington (his stepfather's first name) when he entered school. William Wells *Brown lost his given name of Williams (for a time) when his master's nephew of that name arrived to live with them.

Many slaves were identified beyond their given name. The cook was called *Mammy, Ole Mammy, or Mammy ——. Being conscious of the individuality of their "treasures," as one female owner called her slaves, slaveowners addressed slave women by the name of their husbands, such as Tom's Sue or Joe's Mary. Similarly, mothers were sometimes called by their daughter's name, and children were frequently differentiated by reference to their mother. Common *identities were "bubbles" or "bubba" for brother, "titty" for sister, "nanna" for mother, "mother" for grandmother, and "father" for all the leaders in church and society. The common name for a relative was "parent." The latter word was used for the entire family, even cousins. Older slaves were called "aunt" or "uncle." Plantation etiquette decreed that the male slave be called "boy" or "uncle," but never "father." Slave men struggled to become and remain men, not the "boys" their owners called them. As Genovese reminds us, slaves resisted the appellations "boy" and "girl," referring to themselves and each other as "men" and "women," or "mens" and "womens." Prior to emancipation, white Southerners could not address any African American by the title Mr. or Mrs., and slaves were not permitted to say "sister" or "brother" to each other. In *I Know Why the Caged Bird Sings* (1969), Maya *Angelou paints Annie Henderson, her grandmother, as a realist who at one time was "the only Negro woman in Stamps referred to as 'Mrs.'" In Virginia and North and South Carolina, everyone was "aunt" or "cousin" to everyone else. For manner's sake in the African American community, the preceding practice continued well into the twentieth century. Maya Angelou reflects, "All adults had to be addressed as Mister, Missus, Miss, Auntie, Cousin, Uncle, Buhbah, Sister, Brother, and a thousand other appellations indicating familial relationships and the lowliness of the addresser."

Many persons were identified by adjectives. A "good nigger" was one who helped others (even if he had to play up to the owner) and was, in the estimation of the slaveholder, an asset in the slave community. However, a "bad nigger" had a strong tendency toward being a bully, and "ba-ad niggers" gave the slaveholders and the overseers much trouble. They were loners, outsiders, and defiant individuals who served as a source of strength to the other slaves, especially against the slaveholder. Slaves would refer to "others" from the same plantation (which included white individuals) as "same family as we." An "outsider" was one who resided outside the family, community, plantation, or neighborhood. Often slaves were identified by a reference to physical characteristics such as "Bill de Giant."

African Americans have always cared about their names. Genovese relates that a slave named "Sukey," for example, did not want to be called "Susannah," and that even a man named "John" would resist the slight modification to "Johnnie." Slaves themselves avoided diminutives, although some designations, such as Big Sally, Little Sally, or Yellow Joe, were used by owners to distinguish slaves with similar names from one another. It was a sign of disrespect to call other persons out of their name. In *Caged Bird*, Angelou remembers, "It was a dangerous practice to call a Negro anything that could be loosely construed as insulting because of the centuries of their being called niggers, jigs, dinges, blackbirds, crows, boots, and spooks." When Viola Cullinan calls Marguerite (Maya) Johnson a shortened version of her given name and her white friend replies, "'Margaret' is too long . . . I'd call her 'Mary' if I were you," Marguerite signifies, "Poor thing. No organs and couldn't even pronounce my name correctly." In Sherley Anne *Williams's *Dessa Rose* (1986), which is a contemporary adaptation of the slave narrative, Adam Nehemiah takes upon himself the writing of Dessa's history. He refers to her as "Odessa," a name used only by white characters. But she insists that her name is "Dessa, Dessa Rose. Ain't no O to it." Also, "Edana" in

Octavia E. *Butler's *Kindred* (1988) functions in approximately the same way. Upon her second return to the past, Rufus asks Dana her name, and she replies, "Edana. . . . Most people call me Dana." Neither Rufus nor any other white character in the text calls Dana out of her name.

Although they went unobserved among slaveowners, naming practices linked generations of blood kin. With their names, newly born babies shared allegiances with parents, grandparents, other adult kin, and adult nonkin. In the conventional two-parent slave family, a child was named more frequently from the paternal line—the father, grandfather, great grandfather, uncle, and others. Elizabeth *Keckley, the autobiographer of *Behind the Scenes* (1868), named her only son (George) for his grandfather. A firstborn son often had the father's name. Unlike nineteenth-century white Americans who regularly named daughters for their mothers, very seldomly would a slave mother give a daughter her name, but the mother would give the child the name of a close female relation, such as the child's grandmother, great-grandmother, or an aunt. The absence of infant slave girls named for their mothers was a distinctive slave practice. In a family from which the father was absent, a child was named from the maternal line. Babies were named in significant numbers for dead siblings and other immediate family members. Sometimes children were named for persons sold or separated from the family.

After the Civil War slaves took surnames or openly announced those they already had. They called these names "entitles." Seeking friendship and protection "in a dangerous world" as they called the period, many adopted their master's surname or that of a local notable. In such cases the desire was to capitalize on the close connection the name suggested. Newly freed men took particular surnames to establish a historical link with their own family. They went back in time to take the name of the first master they had ever had or the first whom they could remember as having been a decent man. A few found their master's name a burden. For instance, William Wells Brown hated the idea of keeping the surname of his white American father and took instead the name of the Quaker abolitionist who had helped him to escape. In some cases nationalistic names such as Washington, Lincoln, and Grant were borrowed, but, compared to an earlier era, these were relatively few. Many chose names that celebrated their new status, such as Freeman, Freeland, and Justice. Others, following an ancient European tradition, borrowed surnames from their crafts, trades, skills, surroundings, appearances, or personalities: Carter was a drayman, Mason a bricklayer, Green a gardener, Bishop a preacher, Cook a *domestic, Wheeler a wheelwright, and Taylor a tailor. Some identified themselves by their pigment and origin and took names like "Brown," "Coal," "Africa," and "Guinea," but never "Black." In sum, surnames reflected attempts for respectability.

Name changes and self-naming are revelatory. One's name is an assertion of identity—and in identity is *freedom. "Nobody knows my name," James

*Baldwin says. Yet the *spirituals remind us that slaves knew they had a "real name," known by God, and that a man's identity would emerge on Judgment Day: "O nobody knows who I am, who I am / Till the Judgment morning. / . . . My name is written in the book of life / Turn, sinner, turn O." Wendell Phillips once said, "In Massachusetts, it is dangerous for honest men to tell their real names." And yet in *Narrative of the Life*, Douglass had been saying his "real name" since escaping from slavery. For Douglass then and for many twentieth-century notables, such men and women as Elijah Muhammad, *Malcolm X, Toni Cade Bambara, Amiri Baraka, Haki Madhubuti, Ntozake Shange, and scores of others who moved away from sociohistorical sorts of bondage and complex forms of disempowerment, a new name signals both a new social identity and an act of political defiance. Ira Berlin says "a new name . . . reversed the enslavement process and confirmed newly won liberty." Because names and naming practices represent cultural ideas and values, personal experiences, and attitudes toward life, they symbolize, in their many variations, a striving toward personal identity and self-respect. As an aggregate, they represent a triumph of the spirit.

[*See also* Address, Forms of; Badman; Bad Woman; Buck; Character Types; Coon; Double Consciousness; Minstrelsy; Mulatto; Sapphire; Stepin Fetchit; Uncle Tom.]

• Ralph Ellison, *Shadow and Act*, 1964. Joel Williamson, *After Slavery: The Negro in South Carolina During Reconstruction, 1861–1877*, 1965. John Blassingame, *The Slave Community: Plantation Life in the Antebellum South*, 1972. Eugene Genovese, *Roll, Jordan Roll*, 1972. Ira Berlin, *Slaves without Masters: The Free Negro in the Antebellum South*, 1974. Herbert G. Gutman, *The Black Family in Slavery and Freedom, 1750–1925*, 1976. Frances Smith Foster, "Social and Literary Influences," in *Witnessing Slavery: The Development of Antebellum Slave Narrative*, 1979, pp. 62–81. Charles T. Davis and Henry Louis Gates, Jr., eds., *The Slave's Narrative*, 1985. Adam McKible, "'These are the facts of the darky's history': Thinking History and Reading Names in Four African American Texts," *African American Review* 28 (1994): pp. 223–235.

—Bettye J. Williams

Nanny. A character in Zora Neale *Hurston's *novel *Their Eyes Were Watching God* (1937), Nanny is protagonist *Janie Crawford's grandmother. A *domestic servant who was born a slave, Nanny has raised and sheltered her granddaughter. When sixteen-year-old Janie begins to consider her own dreams and desires, Nanny interposes a different vision. She compels Janie to marry an older man, Logan Killicks, whose sixty acres and a mule constitute his eligibility. For Nanny the marriage represents an opportunity for Janie to sit on the pedestal reserved for southern white women, far above the drudgery that has characterized Nanny's life and made the black woman "de mule uh de world." But by denying Janie the right to follow her dreams, Nanny inhibits her quest for selfhood.

Nanny's history explains her flawed vision. As a slave, Nanny was impregnated by her master. In freedom her best efforts fail to protect her daughter. Using the metaphor of the pulpit, the devoutly Christian

Nanny speaks of lost possibilities: "Ah wanted to preach a great sermon about colored women sittin' on high, but they wasn't no pulpit for me." She has saved the text for Janie, who, as long as Nanny lives, cannot resist her commands.

Physically ravaged by age, oppressed, and impoverished, Nanny derives her power from her ability to manipulate African American expressive codes. Even without a pulpit, Nanny is a powerful preacher whose metaphors fuse the biblical and the domestic in arresting ways. She is an accomplished storyteller and skilled slave narrator as well.

[*See also* Matriarch; Sermons and Preaching; Tea Cake.]

—Cheryl A. Wall

Narrative of the Life of Frederick Douglass.
The epitome of the antebellum fugitive *slave narrative, Frederick *Douglass's *Narrative* was published in May 1845 by the American Anti-Slavery Society of Boston. Priced at fifty cents a copy, the *Narrative's* first printing of five thousand sold out in four months. To satisfy demand, four additional reprintings of two thousand copies each were brought out within a year. By 1850 approximately thirty thousand copies of the *Narrative* had been sold in the United States and Great Britain. In 1846, a Dutch translation and in 1848, a French translation of the *Narrative* helped spread Douglass's fame on the European continent. Sales were helped greatly by positive reviews that compared Douglass's style to that of John Bunyan and Daniel Defoe. The fact that the *Narrative* bore the subtitle "Written by Himself" witnessed powerfully to the capacity of the African American, even when oppressed through years of *slavery, to speak eloquently on his own behalf against social and economic injustice.

The self-consciousness of the writing in the *Narrative* attests to Douglass's determination to make his story not merely an exposé of the evils of slavery but also an exploration of the mind of a slave aspiring to *freedom. The key to the originality and import of Douglass's rendition of his life, in contrast to that of most other fugitive slave narrators, is his emphasis on the psychological and intellectual struggle that he waged against slavery from his early childhood on Maryland's Eastern Shore. The *Narrative* recounts Douglass's boyhood as a series of challenges to white authorities intent on preventing him from achieving knowledge of himself and his relationship to the outside world. Resistance to slavery takes the form of an early clandestine pursuit of *literacy. Armed with the power to read and write, the young slave graduates to a culminating physical rebellion against a slave-breaker, Edward Covey. Douglass's reputation as a fighter gives him a leadership role in the slave community, which he uses to teach other slaves to read and then to engineer a runaway plot. The first attempt for freedom fails, but a second try, in early September 1838, successfully conveys Douglass to New York City. In the last chapter of the *Narrative*, Douglass recounts his *marriage, his integration into a new life of independence and self-sufficiency in the North, and, climactically, his discovery of a vocation as a speaker for the American Anti-Slavery Society.

In addition to what it did to open up the minds of whites in the North about the injustice of slavery, Douglass's *Narrative* also inspired a number of major early African American writers, including William Wells *Brown and Harriet A. *Jacobs, to undertake literary careers of their own. The *Narrative* is recognized today as a classic narrative of ascent from South to North in the African American literary canon, and a lasting contribution to the portrait of the romantic individualist in nineteenth-century American literature.

[*See also* Antislavery Movement.]

• William L. Andrews, *To Tell a Free Story: The First Century of Afro-American Autobiography, 1760–1865,* 1986. William L. Andrews, ed., *Critical Essays on Frederick Douglass,* 1991.

—William L. Andrews

NARRATIVES. *See* Autobiography; Neo–Slave Narrative; Novel; Short Story; Slave Narrative.

Native Son. Published in 1940, Richard *Wright's *Native Son* was the first novel by an African American writer to be a Book-of-the-Month Club selection. *Native Son* tells the story of *Bigger Thomas, an angry and vicious young black ghetto dweller who at first has little to recommend him beyond his membership in the human race.

The novel opens early one morning with Bigger killing a huge rat that has invaded the kitchenette in which he, his mother, sister, and brother live. After promising his mother he will keep an interview appointment for a job as a chauffeur, he meets his "gang" and starts a fight with one of them in order to conceal his fear of robbing a white grocer—his fear of whites leads him to believe he will be sought, captured, and severely punished. Later he goes to the interview and is hired as chauffeur to the Dalton family. His first assignment is to drive *Mary Dalton to a lecture at the university, but instead of going to a lecture, she meets her Communist boyfriend, Jan. At dinner in a ghetto restaurant, where Bigger is known, neither Mary nor Jan realizes the extent to which they at once condescend to Bigger and violate his sensitivities. The meal finished, Bigger drives Mary and Jan around the city while they drink and make love in the backseat. Jan leaves and Bigger takes Mary home, but she is too drunk to walk. Bigger carries her into her bedroom. Sexually aroused, he kisses her and fondles her breasts. The door opens and the blind Mrs. Dalton enters the room. Bigger, terrified, holds a pillow over Mary's face to keep her quiet. When Mrs. Dalton eventually leaves the room, Mary has suffocated. Bigger carries her body to the basement and stuffs it in the furnace. He later imagines that her death was intentional, that he is transformed by having stepped beyond the boundaries limiting him, and decides to assert his control by writing a note demanding ransom and signed "Red." When Mary's body is discovered, Bigger flees. Later, afraid of betrayal, he brutally murders his girlfriend Bessie. After a massive manhunt through the city, Bigger is captured and imprisoned.

The final section of the novel, "Fate" (following "Fear" and "Flight"), shows Bigger's trial and the racist outpouring of hatred and bigotry that it elicits. Whereas Bigger's fate is a foregone conclusion, the final disposition of his psyche is not. Through conversations with his lawyer, Max, Bigger mulls over his situation and finally comes to accept himself as the person who killed two people because of his irrational fear of whites. "What I killed for I am," he says at the end of the novel. Thus, prior to his execution he sees that his experience as a black person in his ghetto has created him.

[*See also* Badman; Character Types; Protest Literature.]

—Donald B. Gibson

NAYLOR, GLORIA (b. 1950), novelist, essayist, screenplay writer, columnist, and educator. Gloria Naylor was born in New York City on 25 January to Roosevelt and Alberta McAlpin Naylor, who had recently migrated northward from their native Robinsonville, Mississippi. Having worked as cotton sharecroppers in Mississippi, her father became a transit worker for the New York City subway system and her mother a telephone operator. Naylor, who was a very shy child, grew up in New York City, where she lived until she graduated from high school in 1968.

From shortly after her graduation until 1975, Naylor worked as a missionary for the Jehovah's Witnesses in New York, North Carolina, and Florida. Eventually deciding that missionary life and the Jehovah's Witnesses were not for her, Naylor returned to New York City and attended college while working as a telephone operator in several different hotels. Although she studied nursing for a short time at Medgar Evers College, she soon decided to pursue a BA in English at Brooklyn College, from which she graduated in 1981. Next Naylor entered Yale University on a fellowship and received an MA in Afro-American studies there in 1983. Having published her first novel, *The *Women of Brewster Place,* in 1982, she wrote for her master's thesis at Yale what would become her second novel, *Linden Hills* (published 1985).

In 1983 Naylor's literary career took off mainly because of the attention she received for her first book. *The Women of Brewster Place* was granted the American Book Award for Best First Novel that year, and Naylor received the annual Distinguished Writer Award from the Mid-Atlantic Writers Association. In 1983 she also served as writer in residence at Cummington Community of the Arts and as a visiting lecturer at George Washington University. During the 1980s Naylor had jobs at numerous other institutions, including working as a cultural exchange lecturer in India for the United States Information Agency, and teaching at Yale, the University of Pennsylvania, New York University, Princeton, Boston, Brandeis, and Cornell. Naylor also received several prestigious awards, such as a National Endowment for the Arts Fellowship in 1985, the 1986 Candace Award from the National Coalition of One Hundred Black Women, a Guggenheim Fellowship in 1988, and the 1989 Lillian Smith Award.

Since Naylor began publishing in the early 1980s, she has produced four *novels: *The Women of Brewster Place* (1982), *Linden Hills* (1985), *Mama Day* (1988), and *Bailey's Cafe* (1992). In addition to these primary works, she has also published *essays—including a column in the *New York Times* in 1986 and a scholarly piece, "Love and Sex in the Afro-American Novel," which was published in the *Yale Review* in 1988—and has written several unproduced screenplays. Another important publication is "A Conversation" between Naylor and Toni *Morrison, which appeared in the *Southern Review* in 1985.

Naylor's first novel, *The Women of Brewster Place*, consists of the interrelated tales of seven African American women who all end up on a dead-end street in a northern ghetto. Ranging in age from their twenties to their fifties, these characters have often suffered greatly because of the insensitive behavior of men. The protagonist of the novel, Mattie Michael, has found disaster in just about every interaction she has had with a man. Although her father in rural Tennessee is sternly caring during her childhood, his reaction to her later pregnancy is violent. And her son, Basil, who Mattie spoils, betrays his mother when she puts up her house as collateral for his bail: his pretrial flight instead of facing murder charges forces her to move to Brewster Place.

Most of the other women in the novel also suffer male exploitation. For instance, although Etta Mae Johnson, Mattie's childhood friend, sometimes has control in her relations with men, Etta's lifelong dependence on them for support and *identity leads to trouble. In addition, Lucielia Louise Turner (Ciel) reluctantly undergoes an abortion to try to hold onto her husband, who is threatening to leave. Indirectly resulting from the neglect created by this upheaval, their toddler daughter sticks a fork into an electrical outlet and dies. Ciel's horrified reaction almost kills her, but Mattie intervenes.

Other women exploited by men in *The Women of Brewster Place* include Cora Lee, whose addiction to having babies leads to her frequent and casual sexual encounters. But the most horrific incident of this sort in the novel occurs when Lorraine is raped by C. C. Baker and his gang of hoodlums. Because of the gang members' homophobia regarding Lorraine's lesbian relationship with Theresa, they feel compelled to teach her a lesson.

Ben, the one partially positive male character in the novel, is nevertheless flawed by his excessive drinking and by his earlier passive complicity when his daughter was repeatedly taken advantage of sexually. Ironically, this relatively likable man is bludgeoned to death beside the Brewster Place wall by Lorraine when she is deranged after being raped. The novel ends when all the women cathartically destroy the wall that has cut them off from the rest of the city—and from their chances for better lives.

Naylor's second novel, *Linden Hills* (1985), is loosely based on Dante's *Inferno*, but the hell she creates is in a middle-class neighborhood. Controlled by the Lucifer-like Luther Nedeed, who is an undertaker, Linden Hills consists of a sloping spiral of streets that become more elite as one nears the bottom of the hill, where Nedeed lives. In a fated pattern of reproduction, several generations of nearly identical Luther Nedeeds are born in Linden Hills, with their primary purposes in life being to continue their lineage and to reign over the growing neighborhood.

During the contemporary time of the novel, Luther Nedeed presides over an affluent, middle-class community where "successful" African Americans essentially sell their souls in order to live there. Luther's grand scheme, however, is thwarted by his wife, Willa, who bears him a son according to plan, but this son is too pale to fulfill his role as his father's replica. Wrongly accusing Willa of infidelity with a white man, Luther locks her up in the cellar, which was originally a morgue, with their son, who eventually dies there. While trapped, Willa explores relics left by her predecessors and eventually learns to assert her right to exist. The resultant action, however, causes the destruction of the Nedeed house by fire and Willa's and Luther's deaths—all on Christmas Eve.

Meanwhile, two young men, Willie and Lester, journey around Linden Hills seeking odd jobs. Their interaction with the neighborhood residents reveals the hollowness of the rich, as well as the comparable depth of those less wealthy. Willie and Lester serve as Naylor's equivalent of Vergil and Dante as they traverse the hellish terrain of Linden Hills. This Dantean parallel is effectively developed, including the two poets' escape over water (the moat around the Nedeed house) at the novel's end.

With her third novel, *Mama Day* (1988), Naylor has received the most praise. As the story of the title character and her great-niece, Ophelia (Cocoa) Day, this work fully develops Naylor's themes of magic, myth, and family. Naylor superimposes the two settings of Willow Springs—an island off the coast between (but not in) South Carolina and Georgia—and New York City, thereby contrasting the philosophical differences between Cocoa and her husband, George Andrews. In a 1989 interview with Nicholas Shakespeare, Naylor said that her purpose in *Mama Day* was to analyze the makeup of individual belief, as well as what constitutes individual definitions of reality. During the course of the novel, she compares her depictions of magic and personal faith with the willing suspension of disbelief that all readers of fiction undergo.

Following a prologue that explains the history of Willow Springs, and which is narrated by the collective consciousness of the island itself, part 1 of the novel primarily consists of exchanges between Cocoa and George. Although George is already dead during the time of these narrated memories, he and Cocoa continue to commune from beyond the grave. Focusing on New York City, where Cocoa and George meet and eventually marry, part 1 also introduces Miranda (Mama) Day, the *matriarch of Willow Springs, and her sister, Abigail, Cocoa's grandmother. Mama Day is a *midwife, healer, root doctor, herbalist, and, if the reader chooses to interpret Naylor's ambiguous signals this way, a conjure woman.

Part 2 of *Mama Day* depicts the events that occur after George and Cocoa travel to Willow Springs.

Following a tremendous storm, the bridge connecting the island to the mainland washes away. Cocoa then becomes dangerously ill, apparently as a result of poisoning and *conjuring by Ruby, an intensely jealous woman. In order to save his wife, George must suspend rational thought and fully accept the mystical ways of the island. Although his love for Cocoa almost makes him capable of this leap of faith, ultimately he cannot believe what the island and Mama Day demand of him. George's already weakened heart fails and he dies. Yet, partly because of George's sacrifice, Cocoa recovers. The novel's close in 1999, also the time of its beginning, shows Cocoa poised to succeed the 105-year-old Mama Day as the island's spiritual leader.

Naylor's novel *Bailey's Cafe* (1992) shows her continuing experimentation with patterns of narration, definitions of reality, and depiction of the supernatural. Centered on the New York City restaurant of its title and set in the late 1940s, the novel is orchestrated by the unnamed cafe owner, who is called Bailey. Bailey and his wife, Nadine, run the all-night eatery, which serves as a way station for lost souls of various backgrounds. Behind the cafe is the novel's most mystical realm: a dock on the water that is capable of transforming reality to match the expectations and needs of the wretched folks who come there.

One such character in need is Sadie, whose violent childhood at the hands of a drug-addicted *prostitute mother leads her to seek quiet and cleanliness. Yet after Sadie's dream of having a home of her own is hopelessly thwarted, she escapes into alcoholism and works as a whore, earning only enough to support her habit of cheap wine. When Iceman Jones, another cafe customer, offers to fulfill her dream of security, her fantasy back behind the restaurant wins out over reality.

Just down the street from the cafe is Eve's place, a brothel that only takes fresh flowers for payment. Presided over by Eve, who has suffered unspeakable abuse from her godfather in Louisiana, this establishment only accepts the particular women whose horrific backgrounds Eve can relate to. One of its residents, Peaches, is so haunted by her own beauty that she slashes her face in order to curb unwanted male attention. Another inhabitant, Jesse Bell, is a bisexual heroin addict whom Eve helps recover by means of brutal, hellish temptation. This unique boardinghouse is cleaned and protected by Miss Maple (Stanley), a heterosexual transvestite who wears women's clothes simply because he finds them more comfortable. While searching for a job after receiving his doctorate in mathematics from Stanford, Miss Maple discovers the impenetrable wall of racism in corporate America. Eventually giving up, Miss Maple seeks a gun in Gabe's pawnshop, but then stumbles into Bailey's Cafe, meets Eve, and finds his home.

The most startling section of *Bailey's Cafe* concerns Mariam, a fourteen-year-old Ethiopian Jew, who is expecting a baby and who is also a virgin. Having experienced genital mutilation in her homeland, Mariam inexplicably becomes pregnant and still insists on her innocence. After she is expelled from her village, she makes her way to Addis Ababa and then somehow ends up on the doorstep belonging to Gabe, who is a Russian Jew. Eve takes her in and then arranges for Mariam to give birth in a "proper" but fantastical setting behind the cafe, which transforms into the ceremonial hut of her native Ethiopian village. Although Mariam eventually dies, her son, George, survives and is placed in an orphanage. Interestingly, Naylor makes it clear that he is the same character as George Andrews, one of the protagonists of *Mama Day*.

Naylor's important contributions to African American literature include her expansion of narrative technique and privileging of the supernatural—both approaches similar to those used by Toni Morrison. Naylor's interrelated fictive terrain also resonates with the Yoknapatawpha County of William Faulkner, whose narrative style she has cited as an influence, especially on *Mama Day*. Gloria Naylor's most lasting contribution to literature may well be her vivid portraits of fascinating and fantastic characters.

• G. Michelle Collins, "There Where We Are Not: The Magical Real in *Beloved* and *Mama Day*," *Southern Review* 24 (1988): 680–685. Larry R. Andrews, "Black Sisterhood in Gloria Naylor's Novels," *CLA Journal* 33 (Sept. 1989): 1–25. Gloria Naylor, interview by Nicholas Shakespeare, *Institute of Contemporary Arts*—"*Guardian*" Conversations, directed by Fenella Greenfield, 1989. Barbara Christian, "Gloria Naylor's Geography: Community, Class, and Patriarchy in *The Women of Brewster Place* and *Linden Hills*," in *Reading Black, Reading Feminist*, ed. Henry Louis Gates, Jr., 1990, pp. 348–373. Henry Louis Gates, Jr., and K. A. Appiah, eds., *Gloria Naylor: Critical Perspectives Past and Present*, 1993.

—Kristine A. Yohe

NEAL, LARRY (1937–1981), poet, essayist, editor, playwright, critic, filmmaker, folklorist, and one of the Black Arts movement's spiritual journeymen. Born Lawrence Paul Neal to Woodie and Maggie Neal in Atlanta, Georgia, on 5 September 1937, Neal grew up in Philadelphia with his four brothers. Larry Neal graduated from Lincoln University and then completed a master's degree at the University of Pennsylvania. He spent most of his adult life in New York.

Although he was a prolific essayist, Neal is perhaps best known for editing *Black Fire: An Anthology of Afro-American Writing* with Amiri *Baraka. This collection, published in 1968, was among the early attempts to define the aesthetic of the new *Black Arts movement. Neal's essays included in *Black Fire* and elsewhere are recognized as some of the most cogent statements of that aesthetic. Neal was committed to politics in his life and writing; but he insisted on artistic rigor as well as revolutionary intent in literature.

Neal produced reviews of artists ranging from Lorraine *Hansberry to Ornette Coleman. His critical essays—on social issues, aesthetic theory, literary topics, and other subjects—appeared in such periodicals as *Liberator Magazine*, *Negro Digest*, *Essence*, and *Black World*. Neal wrote two plays, *The Glorious Monster in the Bell of the Horn* (1976) and *In An*

Upstate Motel: A Morality Play (1980). He published two collections of poetry: *Black Boogaloo: Notes on Black Liberation* in 1969 and *Hoodoo Hollerin' Bebop Ghosts* in 1974. Much of his poetry engages African American mythology, history, and language, but few poems simplify ideological issues. Instead Neal allowed for complexity and contradiction in his poems. His poems were frequently anthologized during the era but have received little critical attention since then. Some of Neal's work was collected and published posthumously in 1989 under the title *Visions of a Liberated Future: Black Arts Movement Writings*.

Larry Neal also edited several journals and magazines during his career. These include *Journal of Black Poetry*, the *Cricket*, and *Liberator Magazine*. Throughout his career Neal worked closely with Baraka; their collaboration began publicly in 1964 when both men helped to create the Black Arts Repertory Theater in Harlem. Neal's involvement with performance art expanded as he wrote films for television and private companies. Neal taught and lectured at several universities including City College of New York and Yale, Howard, and Wesleyan universities. He made television appearances, gave interviews, and profiled other main players in African American artistic life during his career. As a resident of New York's Sugar Hill section, Neal participated in and shaped the social climate of the city.

Larry Neal died of a heart attack at the age of forty-three on 6 January 1981. His significance in African American letters is primarily established by his influence on and engagement with the Black Arts movement.

• *Callaloo* 8.1 (Winter 1985), a special issue dedicated to Larry Neal.

—Elizabeth Sanders Delwiche Engelhardt

NEELY, BARBARA (b. 1941), short story writer, novelist, feminist, and community activist. While writing and a love for language had been deeply held interests since her childhood, Barbara Neely did not begin to take herself seriously as a writer nor consider earning a living as such until 1980 when the tensions between balancing a career and a stable emotional life lessened. The oldest child of parents Ann and Bernard, Neely grew up in the small Pennsylvania Dutch community of Lebanon. She attended the town's Catholic schools where she was the only African American through both elementary and high school. A nontraditional student who never acquired an undergraduate degree, Neely obtained her master's degree in urban and regional planning from the University of Pittsburgh in 1971. Until the publication of her first novel in 1992, Neely led the very demanding life of a community activist. Formerly the director of the Massachusetts-based Women for Economic Justice, she resigned in 1992, becoming cochair of the organization's board of directors to allow more time for her writing. Neely was also a founding member of Women of Color for Reproductive Freedom and is a member of the Jamaica Plain Neighborhood Arts Council. She lives in Boston.

Neely is the author of several short stories and two novels featuring Blanche White, a black maid who inadvertently becomes involved with murder or suspicious deaths. Yet despite the success of the two Blanche novels, the short story remains Neely's first love. In 1981 "Passing the Word," her first nationally published story, appeared in *Essence*; other tales have been anthologized in *Breaking Ice, Speaking for Ourselves, Things That Divide Us, Angels of Power, Street Talk, World of Fiction*, and *Test Tube Women*. The connecting link between Neely's professional life as an advocate for social issues and women's rights first surfaces in her short fiction. "Passing the Word" involves the dreams of two women about marriage, fulfillment, and taking control of and assuming responsibility for one's own life. A 1990 story, "Spilled Salt," illustrates a single mother's unmitigated pain when she must confront conflicting emotional duress because her son, whom she raised alone, has raped a young woman, gone to prison, and returned home. In both the short story and the novel, Neely's fiction reflects her clear intention of illustrating, often with a measure of humor, the issues of race, class, gender, and social values as these impact on her characters.

Blanche on the Lam (1992) is set in fictional Farleigh (Raleigh), North Carolina. Readers meet the very dark Blanche White, a very capable, articulate, proud, and perceptive African American woman whose very name is a pun. Fleeing from jail on a bad-check charge, Blanche finds work as a cook and maid for a wealthy white family. In the course of her service she uncovers a mystery and identifies a murderer. The true focus of the novel, however, is less about the murder and more about Blanche as distinctive character, as a social commentator and working woman with a very distinct view of her employers and firm ties to her own community. Neely's second novel, *Blanche among the Talented Tenth* (1994), takes Blanche from North Carolina to the Boston area and on to Amber Cove, Maine, an oceanside resort community for wealthy African Americans. Another mystery must be solved, and in the process, Blanche faces the twin barriers of class snobbery and intraracial color consciousness. Although the two novels developed in the mystery/detective mode have been well received, the tag "mystery writer," because it signals adherence to a defined genre format, makes Neely uncomfortable. Her aim was to write social novels, and creating the element of mystery was a means to that end. Indeed, in the second novel, the social commentary sometimes overshadows the mystery; and in her haste to critique lingering vestiges of an absurd class and color bias, the prose is somewhat strained.

Barbara Neely's fiction stems from a drive to write about those whom she believes the larger society shunts aside, those black women whose experiences have been scorned or unappreciated. Yet Neely's talents in the mystery/detective genre have been recognized by others. In 1992 she won the "Go on Girl!" Award for the best debut novel from the Black Women's Book Club; that same year, from three different organizations that support mystery fiction, she won the Agatha, the Anthony, and the McCavity awards for the best first mystery, the latter granted by Mystery Writers International. She also won the 1994 Women of Conviction Award for Arts and Literature from the Massachusetts section of the National Council of Negro Women.

Neely has read writers as diverse as Agatha Christie, P. D. James, Chester *Himes, and Walter *Mosley. It was Toni *Morrison, however, whose evocative fiction created the most lasting impression on her. Morrison served Neely as both model and inspiration, freeing her to use the experiences of black women, illustrating for her the evocative power good writing taps to tell the stories of ordinary people.

[See also Crime and Mystery Writing.]

• Barbara Neely, interview by Rebecca Carroll, in *I Know What the Red Clay Looks Like: The Voice and Vision of Black Women Writers*, 1994, pp. 174–184.   —Sandra Y. Govan

NEGRITUDE. The carving up of Africa by five of the most powerful western European nations (England, France, Germany, Portugal, and Spain) at the Conference of Berlin in 1884–1885 sent shock waves through African diaspora cultures in the United States, the Caribbean, and South America. The homeland had fallen in a symbolic defeat for black peoples of the world. Ironically, it was the best European-educated among the defeated who began almost immediately leading cultural counteroffensives intended to "take back" the African ideal and, eventually, the continent itself.

Related to several other political and cultural movements of the first half of the twentieth century—notably the *Harlem Renaissance and *Pan-Africanism—the Negritude movement was part of a growing trend of African-descended people to unify around a common sense of cultural *identity. The poetry of such African Americans as Langston *Hughes, Countee *Cullen, and Sterling A. *Brown had inspired its Caribbean and African founders. Negritude developed within the French language tradition but articulated many of the same ideals as the Pan-Africanist movement of English expression. Both were more well known than "Negrismo," a related cultural renaissance movement among Spanish-speaking people of African descent. Leaders in all of these movements, however, worked painstakingly to articulate models for understanding and neutralizing the cultural alienation experienced by those on the receiving end of European colonial expansion.

According to Léopold Sédar Senghor, former president of Senegal and himself a cofounder of the official movement in Paris in the 1930s, Edward Blyden was the primary precursor of Negritude. He was born in the Dutch West Indies in 1832, widely traveled, and an avid student of the "African dispersal." He lived through and commented broadly on a range of issues affecting African people globally, including the U.S. abolition of *slavery and the carving up of Africa. He died in 1912, somehow fittingly in Sierra Leone, West Africa, a state set up for the repatriation of former slaves from the "New World" and Europe.

Aimé Césaire of Martinique actually coined the term "Negritude" in 1934 when, working with Senghor, Léon Damas of French Guyana, and other black students, he published the first issue of the short-lived review *L'Etudiant noir*. Their goal was to combat the prevailing theory of "tabula rasa" with respect to Africans. These foreign black students studying in Paris sought to ignite a spiritual and intellectual revolution that would cause African-descended people to shed their borrowed cultural "clothing" and come into a full acceptance of their "Africanness." The tortuous nature of this undertaking is illustrated in the bench mark text of the Negritude movement, Aimé Césaire's *Cahier d'un retour au pays natal (Return to My Native Land)*, first published in 1939 in the review *Volontes*. This much quoted prose poem establishes a set of spiritual signposts for the journey toward self-acceptance—a personal journey of mythic proportions. In it, he calls for his own re-creation as "un homme d'ensemencement," a potent man capable of enlivening his people. Indeed, he strives to become "l'amant de cet unique peuple" (the lover of this unique people) (*Aimé Césaire, The Collected Poetry*, trans. Clayton Eshelman and Annette Smith, 1983).

The primer of Negritude poetics, *Pigments*, was published in 1937 by Léon Damas. The core themes of the movement echo throughout its poems: rejection of Europe; recollection of the weight of slavery through the generations; rejection of assimilation; nostalgia for a lost Africa; and an "antiracist racism," a theme that would be more and more actively debated as the movement evolved. With a stunning simplicity, Damas's poems cut to the core of the complex issues of exclusion and belonging.

Léopold Senghor was by far the most prolific Negritude poet of his generation, and was perceived by many as the most conciliatory. His *Chants d'ombre* (1945) and *Hosties noires* (1948) stand as his most representative poetic works in this regard. Often focusing on the global community, he reminded the world of the many unique and compelling aspects of African cultures. In particular, he stressed the qualities of emotion, sympathy, and the gift for imagery and rhythm he felt to be especially well developed in African people. His work from this period encourages society to move toward the inevitable cultural blending (*métissage culturel*) of each group's best traits.

Overall, however, the Negritude idea centered on a generalizing notion of "blackness" that was in many ways a reaction to the prevailing European cultural ethos that set African-descended peoples at the bottom of a cultural hierarchy. The impact of colonial policies was profoundly alienating. For example, the French as a matter of policy taught all of their subjects that their ancestors were the Gauls. "Nos ancêtres les gaulois" came to symbolize the identity crisis at the core of the Negritude challenge.

The Negritude reaction was to naturalize the idea of black identity in the face of the colonizer's conflicting and demeaning classifications. In so doing, it conflated the necessarily wide range of national, cultural, and *class differences among African-descended people into a "centrist" perspective that turned on the axis of the movement's core oppositions: exile and return; alienation and integration; loyalty and complicity; continuity and chaos; and past cultural purity and present cultural confusion.

Despite this, cultural differences among the proponents of Negritude were evident from the very beginning, as seen with the founding triumvirate. Césaire and Damas write from the African diaspora, as individuals dispossessed of a core historical culture. Senghor, on the other hand, whose people had remained culturally linked to their homeland, writes in a voice that draws upon living cultural memory.

Once released upon the world by its founders, the Negritude idea was left to respond, adapt, sink, or swim with the radically shifting political and cultural tides of the times. By the apogee of the movement in the early 1960s, there was an identifiable core of more than forty published writers that critics linked in some way with Negritude. Some of the best known were Hampate Ba, Bernard Dadie, David Diop, Tchicaya U Tamsi, Mongo Beti, Birago Diop, Camara Laye, Jean Malonga, and Ferdinand Oyono.

The fact that Negritude was the catalyst for an immense cultural resurgence around the African ideal did not protect the movement from critics—mostly African—who began chipping away at its core assumptions. An early criticism by Nigerian writer Wole Soyinka attacked the racial mysticism implicit in the movement's ideals. He found the expressions of the Negritude school to be overly sentimental and the romanticizing of Africa childish. A later assessment by a group of Nigerian critics also admits the rampant—albeit useful—romanticism of the Negritude school. In a very thorough reappraisal of African literatures, Pius Ngandu Nkashama aligns the growing popularity of the Negritude idea through the 1950s and 1960s with French academic and publishing priorities. He points to omissions of African authors in key French works (notably Lilyan Kesteloot's *Anthologie negro-africaine*) that, if included, would have completely changed the general way African literature was perceived in terms of its specificity, its "engagement," and its Negritude.

Today, it is generally agreed that the progression beyond the Negritude idea is the biggest testimony to its value as a developmental mechanism for identity formation. A rite of passage of sorts in the coming of age of contemporary African and African diaspora literatures, Negritude had a role to play in helping cultures look at themselves, and in creatively charting what they saw. In this way, the work of Negritude writers and of critics of the movement has helped bring the idea of cultural self-assessment into the mainstream canons of Western literature and critical thought.

[See also African Literature; Afrocentricity; Allen, Samuel W.; Black Nationalism; Diasporic Literature; Expatriatism; Literary History, *article on* Early Twentieth Century; West Indian Literature.]

• B. Fulchiron and C. Schlumberger, *Poetes et romanciers noirs*, 1980. Chinweizu et al., *Toward the Decolonization of African Literature*, vol. 1, 1983. Pius Ngandu Nkashama, *Litteratures africaines*, 1984.

—JoAnne Cornwell

Negro American Literature Forum. *See* African American Review.

Negro Digest. *See* First World.

"Negro National Anthem." *See* "Lift Every Voice and Sing."

"Negro Speaks of Rivers, The." "The Negro Speaks of Rivers" appeared in June 1921 in the **Crisis,* when *Langston Hughes was only nineteen years old. It was the first Langston Hughes poem published in a national magazine.

According to Hughes in The **Big Sea* (1940, 54–56), the poem was written in the summer of 1920, after his graduation from high school, while he was on a train going from Cleveland, Ohio, to Mexico. He was going to join his father, who lived there, and with whom the poet had a troubled relationship. "All day on the train," Hughes recalled, "I had been thinking about my father and his strange dislike of his own people. I didn't understand it, because I was a Negro, and I liked Negroes very much."

As the train crossed the Mississippi at sunset over a bridge near St. Louis, Hughes began to brood on the historical associations of that river with blacks, *slavery, and the myth that Abraham Lincoln had vowed to himself, on a journey in his youth, to free the slaves someday. "Then I began to think about other rivers in our past—the Congo, and the Niger, and the Nile in Africa—and the thought came to me: 'I've known rivers.'" The poem was finished within "ten or fifteen minutes."

The following year, it was accepted for publication by the literary editor of the *Crisis,* Jessie Redmon *Fauset, who had earlier discovered Hughes's talent. Later, when he included the poem in his first published volume, The **Weary Blues* (1926), he dedicated it to W. E. B. *Du Bois in response to Fauset's request that he honor the venerable editor.

Probably indebted in its basic structure—its long, irregular, unrhymed lines and its dignified but casual language—to the example of Walt Whitman, the poem sounded a note previously unheard in African American poetry. It invokes the subject of the violation of African people by slavery, but rage and the will to revenge are gently subsumed within lyric cadences that capture something of the noble spirit of the black *spirituals without ever appealing to traditional ideas about religion.

With its allusions to dusky rivers, soul, blood, the setting sun, and sleep, the poem is fairly suffused with images of death. However, it aims ultimately to affirm the ability of blacks to transcend their historic suffering and affirm their fundamental dignity and beauty. The words "I've seen its muddy bosom turn all golden in the sunset" capture the ability of the poetic vision and the poetic will, accessible to all sympathetic people through the communality of the first-person narrator of the poem, to turn the mud of black life, beset by racism and injustice, into gold.

"The Negro Speaks of Rivers" laid the foundation for the special bond between Hughes and African

Americans that led him at one time to be hailed as "the poet laureate of the Negro race."

• Langston Hughes, *Collected Poems*, 1994.

—Arnold Rampersad

Negro World. Published in Harlem between 1918 and 1933, *Negro World* was the literary journal of Marcus *Garvey's Universal Negro Improvement Association. With a top weekly circulation of two hundred thousand, *Negro World* was perhaps the most widely distributed and well-read black periodical of the early twentieth century. Its mission was to provide a forum for rank-and-file black writers, to promote art that espoused the causes of racial *freedom, justice, and equality, and to develop an Afrocentric, Garveyite aesthetic as defined by black critics and writers. Its editors included William H. Ferris, Hubert H. Harrison, Eric *Walrond, and T. Thomas *Fortune, and it counted among its contributors not only such well-known writers as Zora Neale *Hurston, Carter G. *Woodson, and Arthur A. *Schomburg, but an international cadre of writers from Central and South America, the Caribbean, and Africa. Had Garvey not been arrested, jailed, and eventually deported, *Negro World* no doubt would have provided an even stronger alternative to the currently better-known journals of the *Harlem Renaissance, the *Crisis, *Opportunity, and the *Messenger.

[See also Periodicals; Publishing.]

• Tony Martin, *Literary Garveyism: Garvey, Black Arts and the Harlem Renaissance*, 1983. Tony Martin, ed., *African Fundamentalism: A Literary and Cultural Anthology of Garvey's Harlem Renaissance*, 1991.

—Maggie Sale

NELL, WILLIAM C. (1816–1874), historian, journalist, orator, and abolitionist. Born into a Boston abolitionist family, William C. Nell attended an African American grammar school and graduated from an interracial school. As a student, he earned the right to an academic prize but, because of his race, was denied the award. The experience led him at an early age into battles against race discrimination and segregation in public schools. After studying law, Nell dedicated himself to *antislavery work, lecturing, organizing meetings, and assisting fugitive slaves. He helped establish in 1842 the Freedom Association, an organization of African Americans who provided escaped slaves with protection, food, clothing, and shelter. Inspired by white abolitionist William Lloyd Garrison, Nell joined the *Liberator* in the early 1840s. He managed the paper's Negro Employment Office and wrote articles, while continuing to lecture and organize antislavery meetings. Like Garrison, he consistently opposed separate African American antislavery conventions and organizations. In 1847, Nell moved to Rochester where he joined Frederick *Douglass in publishing Douglass's newspaper, the *North Star*. While busy with antislavery work in Rochester, he maintained close ties with abolitionists in Boston. In 1850, he made an unsuccessful Free Soil Party bid for the Massachusetts legislature. In response to the Fugitive Slave Act (1850), Nell and other abolitionists created a Committee of Vigilance to assist and protect escaped slaves.

During a temporary but serious illness in 1851, Nell finished his pamphlet, *Services of Colored Americans in the Wars of 1776 and 1812*, one of the first pieces of historical writing devoted to the experiences of African Americans. Following the breach between Garrison and Douglass, Nell resigned at the *North Star* and in 1852 returned to Boston. In April 1855, after years of struggle led largely by Nell, Massachusetts desegregated its public schools. Later that year, with an introduction by Harriet Beecher *Stowe, Nell published *The Colored Patriots of the American Revolution*, the first comprehensive work of African American *history. Less narrowly focused than the title suggested, *Colored Patriots* was a wide-ranging treatment of African American history, containing *biographies of "distinguished colored persons," a survey of "Conditions and Prospects of Colored Americans," and a variety of historically significant documents. In 1858, in protest of the Supreme Court's Dred Scott decision, Nell founded the Crispus Attucks celebration to honor the African American patriot killed in the Boston Massacre. During these years, Nell also assisted other African American writers. As early as 1854 he attempted to help Harriet A. *Jacobs find a publisher and in 1860, introduced her to Lydia Maria Child, who edited Jacobs's narrative and secured its publication. During the Civil War, Nell used speeches, meetings, and the pages of the *Liberator* to urge the inclusion of African Americans in the Union army. In 1862, he became a postal clerk, one of the first such federal appointments for an African American, and he held the position until his death in 1874.

Nell was a key figure in antebellum African American letters, in part because of his connections to more famous antislavery writers. More significantly, Nell's historical writings have remained the most important early texts in African American historiography.

• Benjamin Quarles, *Black Abolitionists*, 1969. Robert P. Smith, "William Cooper Nell: Crusading Black Abolitionist," *Journal of Negro History* 55 (July 1977): 182–199. James Oliver Horton and Lois E. Horton, *Black Bostonians: Family Life and Community Struggle in the Antebellum North*, 1979.

—Gregory Eiselein

NEO–SLAVE NARRATIVE. Neo–slave narratives are modern or contemporary fictional works substantially concerned with depicting the experience or the effects of New World *slavery. Having fictional slave characters as narrators, subjects, or ancestral presences, the neo–slave narratives' major unifying feature is that they represent slavery as a historical phenomenon that has lasting cultural meaning and enduring social consequences. They also assume the existence of a vital slave culture that prevented slaves from becoming the docile or absolutely servile automatons found in the *stereotypes of the plantation romance tradition. Another common feature in many of the neo–slave narratives is the use and celebration of "oral" modes of representation and a skepticism about the dangers and betrayals of "written" representations. There are two basic kinds of neo–slave narratives: (1) *historical novels set in the antebellum South and (2) social realist or magical realist *novels set in post-Reconstruction or twentieth-century America but dealing substantially with the demonstrable effects of slavery on contemporary African American subjects.

Primarily cultural productions of the twentieth century, neo–slave narratives are indebted to various forms of eighteenth- and nineteenth-century American writing. Among the network of literary forms within which neo–slave narratives situate themselves are antebellum *slave narratives, postbellum slave narratives, and abolitionist fiction, such as Harriet Beecher *Stowe's Uncle Tom's Cabin (1852) and William Wells *Brown's *Clotel (1853).

The history of neo–slave narratives can be divided into two periods, before and after 1966. Modern neo–slave narratives have appeared sporadically between the time Brown published the first version of Clotel and Margaret *Walker published *Jubilee (1966). During that time, neo–slave narratives that dealt with the legacy of slavery were much more common than historical novels about slavery. Aside from Clotel and Martin R. *Delany's *Blake (1861), Arna *Bontemps's *Black Thunder (1936), a fictional account of Gabriel Prosser's attempted slave revolt in 1800, appears to be the only example of a significant historical novel about slavery published before the 1960s. On the other hand, narratives about the social consequences of slavery have a more consistent history. Such novels appeared regularly in the 1890s and at the turn of the century from Frances Ellen Watkins *Harper, Charles Waddell *Chesnutt, Paul Laurence *Dunbar, and Pauline E. *Hopkins. Although the "New Negroes" of the *Harlem Renaissance felt themselves at a "more comfortable distance" from what Charles S. Johnson called that "generation in whom lingered memories of the painful degradation of slavery" and were therefore able to "find a new beauty" in their slave heritage, they did not produce any notable fiction about slavery.

The publication of Zora Neale *Hurston's *Their Eyes Were Watching God in 1937 marked a notable development in neo–slave narratives about the legacy of slavery. *Nanny, as the slave-born grandmother whose desires are at odds with and affect the development of her free-born granddaughter, is an early manifestation of the slave *ancestor as a figure representing the personal and familial legacy of slavery. In 1952, Ralph *Ellison would develop this theme in *Invisible Man as the narrator searches out the hidden, deeper meaning of his slave-born grandfather's dying words.

The publication of Margaret Walker's Jubilee in 1966 marks the transition between the modern and the contemporary history of the neo–slave narrative, standing as the final modern neo–slave narrative and the harbinger of a new and concentrated wave of contemporary neo–slave narratives. Walker began her novel in 1934 when she was a senior at Northwestern University, although she had planned to write the novel ever since her childhood, when she promised her maternal grandmother that she would write the story of their slave ancestor. Jubilee draws generously on the excavatory work and historical writing performed by the Old Left, and it is substantially based on the sort of folk material that the Works Project Administration collected during the thirties. Although it had its origins in the thirties, Jubilee appeared during the sixties in the era of the New Left, and it was published at precisely the moment when the *civil rights movement gave way to the Black Power movement.

The convergence of a series of events from this period inaugurated the new era in American fiction about slavery. First, the civil rights movement affected the production of knowledge about slavery by opening up previously denied academic positions to African American historians. The concomitant rise of New Left social *history, with its focus on history written "from the bottom up" allowed historians to reexamine forms of slave testimony that had hitherto been proscribed as valid historical evidence (a proscription formally issued by Ulrich B. Phillips in 1918). Using antebellum slave narratives and slave *folklore, these new studies emphasized the vitality of slave culture and focused on the function of the slave community in providing slaves with psychic survival resources. Second, the Black Power movement affected the production of neo–slave narratives by providing African Americans with an emergent sense of subjective empowerment that aided the novelists in creating new representations of slavery. As Sherley Anne *Williams stated, "The Civil Rights movement gave would-be writers of new African American histories and fictions the opportunity to earn financial security and thus the time to write, but it was the Black Power movement that provided the pride and perspective necessary to pierce the myths and lies that have grown up around the antebellum period as a result of southern propaganda and filled us also with the authority to tell it as we felt it" ("The Lion's History: The Ghetto Writes B[l]ack," Soundings, Summer–Fall 1993).

Since 1966, Black authors have written literally scores of novels about American chattel slavery, ranging from John O. *Killens's novelization of the *film Slaves in 1969 and Ernest J. *Gaines's The *Autobiography of Miss Jane Pittman in 1971 to the most recent spate of novels in 1994, including Caryl Phillips's Crossing the River (1994), J. California *Cooper's In Search of Satisfaction (1994), Louise *Meriwether's Fragments of the Ark (1994), Fred D'Aguiar's The Longest Memory (1994), and Barbara *Chase-Riboud's The President's Daughter (1994). This contemporary outpouring of fiction about slavery is not easily categorized, but for heuristic purposes we can discern at least four distinct forms of the contemporary neo–slave narrative in the post–civil rights era.

First, there are historical novels about slavery, some traditional in form, others with variations on the classic third-person narrator. These novels include Barbara Chase-Riboud's *Sally Hemings (1979), Alex *Haley's A Different Kind of Christmas (1988),

Chase-Riboud's *Echo of Lions* (1989), Haley's *Queen* (1993), and Louise Meriwether's *Fragments of the Ark* (1994). The most widely read and highly praised of these historical novels has been Toni *Morrison's *Beloved* (1987), a novel based on the historical incident of Margaret Garner's infanticide in Cincinnati in 1856.

Second, there are contemporary novels about the ongoing effects of slavery. What can be called "palimpsest narratives" are those first-person or third-person novels in which a contemporary African American subject describes modern social relations that are directly conditioned or affected by an incident, event, or narrative from the time of slavery. Sometimes these novels are premised on a contemporary subject's dealing with the discovery of an ancestor's narrative, while in other cases these novels deal with the destructive effects of an individual's or a community's attempts to forget a slave past. A partial list of novels about the archaeological imperative of modern African American subjects would include Gayl *Jones's *Corregidora* (1975), Octavia *Butler's *Kindred* (1979), David *Bradley's The *Chaneysville Incident* (1981), Gloria *Naylor's *Linden Hills* (1985) and *Mama Day* (1988), and J. California Cooper's *In Search of Satisfaction* (1994). Especially relevant among the writers of palimpsest narratives is Paule *Marshall, who inaugurated the contemporary use of the form in her The *Chosen Place, the Timeless People* (1969) and utilized it in new and important ways in her subsequent *Praisesong for the Widow* (1983) and *Daughters* (1991).

In addition to historical novels and palimpsest narratives, the post–civil rights era witnessed the development of two relatively original forms of writing about slavery, both of which are directly indebted to the rediscovery and new respect granted the oral and written testimony of former slaves. The first of these is what can be called the "genealogical narrative," consisting of novels that trace a *family line through the contours of a broadly defined African American experience, representing slavery as one of the determinant experiences of that familial passage. A very short list would include such novels as Alex Haley's *Roots* (1976) and J. California Cooper's *Family* (1991).

The final distinctive form of the neo–slave narrative includes writing that loosely imitates the original slave narrative form itself. Following the publication of William Styron's controversial *The Confessions of Nat Turner* in 1967, a novel told in Nat *Turner's unrelenting first-person narration, African American authors have produced a series of novels in which they experiment with the fugitive or manumitted slave as a first-person narrator. A list of those contemporary novels that assume the form and loosely adopt the conventions of the antebellum slave narrative would include Ernest Gaines's *The Autobiography of Miss Jane Pittman*, Ishmael *Reed's *Flight to Canada* (1976), Charles R. *Johnson's *Oxherding Tale* (1982) and *Middle Passage* (1990), Sherley Anne Williams's *Dessa Rose* (1986), and Chase-Riboud's *The President's Daughter*. A notable feature of the majority of these novels is that they all exhibit a great deal of play with discontinuous voices, self-referential moments, and parodic metafictional gestures.

These four lists could all be expanded by cataloging additional works within the given divisions, and the lists themselves could be further divided by including *short stories written about slavery—Charles Johnson's "The Education of Mingo" (in *Mother Jones*, Aug. 1977) and "The Sorcerer's Apprentice" (in *Callaloo*, Feb. 1983), John Edgar *Wideman's title story in *Damballah* (1981), and the title story in Randall *Kenan's *Let the Dead Bury Their Dead* (1992), for instance—or by including novels that offer us phantasms or ghosts of slaves in their representation of contemporary social life, such as Kenan's *A Visitation of Spirits* (1989) and Tina McElroy *Ansa's *Baby of the Family* (1989), or by also adding experimental fiction that partially deals with slavery, such as Jewelle *Gomez's *The Gilda Stories* (1991), which has its heroine live in seven different historical epochs and social systems, from slavery in 1850 to new familial formations in 2050. The list could likewise be lengthened if we included novels written by people of African descent living (but not born) in the United States, in which case we could include such works as Maryse Condé's *I, Tituba, Black Witch of Salem* (French publication 1986; English trans. 1992), Caryl Phillips's *Cambridge* (1991), Michelle Cliff's *Free Enterprise* (1993), and Fred D'Aguiar's *The Longest Memory* (1994).

• William L. Andrews, *To Tell a Free Story: The First Century of Afro-American Autobiography, 1760–1865*, 1986. Bernard W. Bell, *The Afro-American Novel and Its Traditions*, 1987. Deborah E. McDowell and Arnold Rampersad, eds., *Slavery and the Literary Imagination*, 1987. Ashraf H. A. Rushdy, "The Phenomenology of the Allmuseri: Charles Johnson and the Subject of the Narrative of Slavery," *African American Review* 26.3 (Fall 1992): 373–394. Ashraf H. A. Rushdy, "Reading Black, White, and Gray in 1968: The Origins of the Contemporary Narrativity of Slavery," in *Criticism and the Color Line: Desegregating American Literary Studies*, ed. Henry B. Wonham, 1995.

—Ashraf H. A. Rushdy

NEW CULTURAL MULATTO. A phrase in circulation since the mid-1980s, "new cultural mulattoes" encapsulates a reaction to "tragic mulattoes" while it offers a slant on W. E. B. *Du Bois's concept of "the *talented tenth." New cultural mulattoes are those characters in contemporary African American fiction who have all the advantages that money, middle-class status, and quality education can give them; they may have the lighter skin coloring inherent in the term "*mulatto," but that may also refer to the diminishing of cultural ties that such characters evince. These characters do not have roots in the South and frequently not even in a slave ancestry. They can separate themselves from the majority of black people in America by virtue of their "privilege" as well as by what they elect to identify with. Choice is important in how they are conceptualized, for they are frequently less attracted to the kinds of community-based actions that would have defined characters created against the backdrop of the *Harlem Renaissance or the *Black Arts movement of the 1960s; individualism and a desire to get ahead by the standards of the larger society drive these characters more than any sense of commitment to community.

While many scholars judge this trend in characterization to be problematic, others applaud it as diversity of representation. Consequently, characters such as *Jadine Childs in Toni *Morrison's *Tar Baby (1981); Sarah Phillips, her brother Matthew, and her friend Curry in Andrea *Lee's Sarah Phillips (1984); and William "Billy" Covington in Brent Wade's Company Man (1992) are examples of the type. They generally adhere to the values of the American dream, consider their blackness coincidental rather than essential, travel extensively (especially in Europe, particularly Paris), explore the ranges of sexual behavior (especially across racial lines), and reflect the era of their creation by being college age or slightly older (they usually attend Ivy League or other impressive schools).

[See also Class; Double Consciousness; Identity; Passing.]
                                              —Trudier Harris

NEW NEGRO. While the phrase "New Negro" has been used since at least 1895, the concept evolved over the years to become central to many aspects of the African American scene during the first three decades of the twentieth century, receiving the most attention during the peak years of the *Harlem Renaissance. From an 1895 editorial in the Cleveland Gazette through commentaries in other black newspapers to books such as A New Negro for a New Century (1900) edited by Booker T. *Washington, Fannie Barrier Williams, and N. B. Wood, and William *Pickens's The New Negro (1916), the New Negroes were seen invariably as men and women (mostly men) of middle-class orientation who often demanded their legal rights as citizens but almost always wanted to craft new images that would subvert and challenge old *stereotypes. In several *essays included in the *anthology The *New Negro (1925), which grew out of the 1924 special number of *Survey Graphic on Harlem, editor Alain *Locke contrasted the "Old Negro" with the "New Negro" by stressing black American assertiveness and self-confidence during the years following World War I and the Great *Migration. Race pride had been part of literary and political self-expression among African Americans in the nineteenth century—as reflected in the writings of Martin R. *Delany, Bishop Henry Turner, and Frederick *Douglass—but it found a new purpose and definition in the *journalism, fiction, poetry, and paintings of a host of figures associated with the Harlem Renaissance. A militant Negro editor indicated in 1920 how this "new line of thought, a new method of approach" included the possibility that "the intrinsic standard of Beauty and aesthetics does not rest in the white race" and that "a new racial love, respect, and consciousness may be created." It was felt that African Americans were poised to assert their own agency in culture and politics instead of just remaining a "problem" or "formula" for others to debate. The New Negroes of the 1920s, the "*talented tenth," included poets, novel-

ists, and *blues singers creating their art out of Negro folk heritage and *history; black political leaders fighting against corruption and for expanded opportunities for African Americans; businessmen working toward the possibility of a "black metropolis"; and Garveyites dreaming of a homeland in Africa. All of them shared in their desire to shed the image of servility and inferiority of the shuffling "Old Negro" and achieve a new image of pride and dignity. As W. E. B. *Du Bois himself recognized in his response to Locke's New Negro, the concept validated the rejection of the accommodationist politics and ideology represented by Booker T. Washington and his followers around the turn of the century when, despite Washington's access to the White House and mainstream politicians, *violence against African Americans continued unabated at a disturbing level with little progress in the area of civil rights and economic opportunities.

There are varied interpretations of the "New Negro" and its long-term significance. There is no doubt that despite the difficult challenges of *race and *class in the 1920s, black activity and expression in all areas was marked by a new spirit of hope and pride. Locke's view of New Negro potential in a pluralistic America, his view that political and economic benefits might flow to all African Americans from wider recognition of the literary and cultural expressions of Harlem Renaissance artists, was seen by many as politically naive or overly optimistic. As late as 1938, Locke was defending his views against attacks from John A. Davis and others that his emphasis was primarily on the "psychology of the masses" and not on offering any one solution to the "Negro problem." In dismissing the construction of the New Negro as a dubious venture in renaming, as merely a "bold and audacious act of language," Henry Louis *Gates, Jr., confirms Gilbert Osofsky's earlier criticism that the New Negroes of the 1920s helped to support new white stereotypes of black life, different from but no more valid or accurate than the old ones.

Maybe what is important for latter-day culture and literature is the New Negro's insistence in so many spheres on self-definition, self-expression, and self-determination, a striving after what Locke called "spiritual emancipation." The many debates during the Harlem Renaissance years regarding art and propaganda, representation and *identity, assimilation versus militancy, and parochialism versus globalism, have enriched the perspectives on issues of art, culture, politics, and ideology that have emerged on the African American scene since the 1930s, especially in the perspectives offered by Richard *Wright, Ralph *Ellison, and Toni *Morrison.

• Gilbert Osofsky, Harlem: The Making of a Ghetto, 1965. Nathan Irvin Huggins, Harlem Renaissance, 1971. Amritjit Singh, The Novels of the Harlem Renaissance, 1976. David Levering Lewis, When Harlem Was in Vogue, 1987. Henry Louis Gates, Jr., "The Trope of a New Negro and the Reconstruction of the Image of the Black," Representations 24 (Fall 1988): 129–155.
                                              —Amritjit Singh

New Negro, The. An *anthology edited by Alain *Locke, The New Negro was hailed immediately upon its publication in 1925 as a highly significant exemplar of the burgeoning creativity that came first to be known as the New Negro movement, then as the Negro Renaissance, and finally as the *Harlem Renaissance. Behind the publication of this work lay a number of events and activities of which *The New Negro* was the culmination.

In 1923, the monthly magazine *Opportunity* began publication as an organ of the National Urban League. Edited by Charles S. Johnson, *Opportunity* immediately took on the character of a literary and art review. Johnson called to his aid as advisor and mentor Alain Leroy Locke of Howard University, and Locke was to remain a principal collaborator of *Opportunity* throughout its history.

In 1924, Johnson organized a dinner at the Civic Club in New York City in order to celebrate the publication of Jessie Redmon *Fauset's first novel, *There Is Confusion* (1924), and simultaneously to bring some of the younger literary artists into contact with the New York literati. He invited Locke to be toastmaster. This led to a proposal by Paul Kellogg, editor of the influential magazine *Survey Graphic*, that Locke edit a special Harlem number of the magazine. As the Harlem number took shape, plans evolved to use it as the basis for a book. The Harlem number appeared in March 1925 and *The New Negro* in December of the same year.

The New Negro is divided into two sections—part 1, "The Negro Renaissance," and part 2, "The New Negro in a New World." Part 1 offered Locke's title essay "The New Negro" and articles on African art (by Albert C. Barnes) and literature (by William Stanley *Braithwaite). Fiction and *poetry are then presented. Authors of fiction included Rudolph *Fisher, Jean *Toomer, John F. *Matheus, Zora Neale *Hurston, Richard Bruce *Nugent, and Eric *Walrond. Poets were Countee *Cullen, Langston *Hughes, Claude *McKay, Anne *Spencer, Toomer, and Angelina Weld *Grimké. There are essays by Jessie Fauset and Montgomery Gregory on theater, as well as Arthur A. *Schomburg's "The Negro Digs up His Past."

In contrast to part 1, devoted primarily to creativity in the arts, part 2 offers social and political analysis. James Weldon *Johnson's essay on Harlem contains the kernel of his later *Black Manhattan* (1931). E. Franklin Frazier provides an early observation of the middle class in an article on Durham, North Carolina. Kelly *Miller and Robert R. Moton respectively portray education in the Howard and the Hampton-Tuskegee traditions. Walter White writes on the "Paradox of color," and W. E. B. *Du Bois provides an article on the international dimensions of color and imperialism.

Portraits of prominent individuals by the German-born artist Winold Reiss and the decorative motifs by Aaron Douglas are striking features of *The New Negro*. Bibliographies by Schomburg, Locke, and Arthur Huff *Fauset were appended.

The New Negro inspired other anthologies, including Charles S. Johnson's *Ebony and Topaz* (1927) and Countee Cullen's *Caroling Dusk* (1927). Other successor works were Nancy Cunard's *Negro* (1933) and *The Negro Caravan* (1941), edited by Sterling A. *Brown and others.

[See also Periodicals, *article on* Scholarly Journals and Literary Magazines; Publishing.]

• Arnold Rampersad, introduction to *The New Negro: Voices of the Harlem Renaissance*, 1992 (rpt.). David Levering Lewis, ed., *The Portable Harlem Renaissance Reader*, 1994.

—Richard A. Long

NEW NEGRO RENAISSANCE. *See* Harlem Renaissance.

NEWSOME, EFFIE LEE (1885–1979), children's poet, short fiction writer, and editor of a literary column for children in the *Crisis* from 1925 to 1929.

Effie Lee Newsome (born Mary Effie Lee) was an important link between the *Brownies' Book* (1920–1922) and works for children in the 1930s by such writers as Langston *Hughes and Arna *Bontemps. Under W. E. B. *Du Bois's editorship of the *Crisis*, Newsome was recruited to establish a regular column where she could delight children with nature *poetry, nonsense verse, and parables about the unique experience of being young and African American in the racially biased 1920s.

The poem in the *Crisis* (Oct. 1922) entitled "The Bronze Legacy" ("'Tis a noble gift to be brown, all brown") and the fable in the August 1928 issue, "On the Pelican's Back" (a comedy in which an arrogant white bird learns a humbling lesson), are significant examples of an early multicultural literature for the young.

On a personal plane, Newsome was an intellectual surrounded by prominent African Americans of her day. She had extensive university training at Wilberforce, Oberlin, and the University of Pennsylvania. She was the daughter of Dr. Benjamin Franklin Lee, a president of Wilberforce University and a bishop of the African Methodist Episcopal Church. She also married a minister: the Reverend Henry Nesby Newsome. Her poems for adult readers are included in Hughes's and Bontemps's *The Poetry of the Negro, 1746–1949* (1949), and she anthologized some of her poems for children in *Gladiola Garden* (1940).

Newsome decried the dearth of African and African American images in children's books and dedicated herself to giving youngsters two great gifts: a keen sense of their own inestimable value and an avid appreciation of the natural world.

• Effie Lee Newsome, "Child Literature and Negro Childhood," *Crisis* 34.8 (Oct. 1927): 260, 280, 282. Donnarae MacCann, "Effie Lee Newsome: African American Poet of the 1920s," *Children's Literature Association Quarterly*, (Summer 1988): 60–65.

—Donnarae MacCann

NEWSPAPER COLUMNS have provided an important voice for African American writers. The antebellum Negro press was a platform for expressing Negro sentiment on a range of human rights issues. Writers saw their literary talents as an extension of their commitment to uplifting the race. Accordingly, their contributions to newspapers reflected an interest in rescuing Negroes from stereotypes and social injustices. Due to economics and limited *literacy among

Negroes, the black press was a sporadic but important vehicle for creative and political expression. In its layout, frequency of distribution, and lack of affiliation with any united or associated presses, the early Negro press was fluid with its definition of "newspaper."

Authors Martin R. *Delany (1812–1884), William Wells *Brown (1813–1884), and Frederick *Douglass (1818–1895) forged a tradition of using the press to discuss the role and contribution of the Negro in all aspects of American life. Ida B. *Wells-Barnett (1862–1931) added her voice to this conversation through editorials, syndicated columns, and *essays on *lynching. It is from this tradition that poet and fiction writer Frances Ellen Watkins *Harper (1825–1911) emerged. It was in the press that Harper published poems and short stories. Gaining recognition, she began in the *Christian Recorder the column "Fancy Etchings," commenting upon sociopolitical events through fictional characters. Harper's *Aunt Chloe Fleet serialized the life of a folk character who narrates through poetry her experiences in *slavery and Reconstruction.

It was not until the *Harlem Renaissance era of the 1920s that African American novelists and poets would in large numbers continue the tradition popularized by Harper. Writers such as Langston *Hughes (1902–1967), George S. *Schuyler (1895–1977), Georgia Douglas *Johnson (1860–1966), Gwendolyn *Bennett (1902–1981), and Alice *Dunbar-Nelson (1875–1935) wrote columns directed toward a growing black readership. These columns provided a forum for discussing the social issues that had engaged their forerunners, but also the role of the "*New Negro" in creating a black literary aesthetic.

Langston Hughes owes much of his fame to his early work as a columnist for the *Chicago Defender. One of his columns, "Here to Yonder," was known for its discussions of local and global injustices, from the Klan to the Nazis. However, it was with the creation of his folk characters, *Madam Alberta K. Johnson and Jesse B. Semple (known as *Simple), that Hughes won enduring public acclaim. Full of spunk and folk wisdom, Madam Alberta K. Johnson and Simple were examples of resiliency in a hostile urban society. Begun in February 1943 in his column "Conversations after Midnight," the Simple stories eventually became Simple Speaks His Mind (1950), Simple Takes a Wife (1952), Simple Stakes a Claim (1957), and Simple's Uncle Sam (1965). The episodic structure of the Simple stories reflects their newspaper origins. Simple walks through Harlem with all the wit and wonderment of a modern-day black bard, aware of the politics of his life as a black man in America, but unwilling to let anyone, including his wife or mistress, destroy his love for life.

Hughes was also among several columnists using the press to foreground black critical theory. In "An Author with 21 Books Must Be Coming of Age" (Chicago Defender, 1955), Hughes voiced his concerns for his own writings and for the future of black literature, a future he helped to insure with hundreds of poems, many appearing in black literary magazines and newspapers.

Although Hughes was positive about the creation of a distinctive black literature, as evidenced in his "The Negro Artist and the Racial Mountain" (Nation, 23 June 1926), his contemporary George Schuyler was less optimistic, as expressed in "Negro-Art Hokum" (Nation, 16 June 1926). A journalist and fiction writer, Schuyler wrote several columns, including "Views and Reviews." More of a cynic and satirist than many of the other columnists, Schuyler criticized the black intelligentsia from college presidents to business persons and preachers. He commented upon the plight of racially mixed persons, the black beauty aesthetic, general health issues, and the military. Schuyler saw within his province any problem affecting him as an American. In addition to the black press, Schuyler wrote for the white press.

Particularly distinctive to this era were the number of African American women who were columnists. Georgia Douglas Johnson, Harlem Renaissance poet, playwright, and fiction writer, wrote a column, "Homely Philosophies." Like Hughes and Schuyler, Johnson was very interested in the era's debates on a black literary aesthetic. Johnson's home, the "S Street Salon," was a mecca for black writers and artists. In contrast to the lively discussions at her home, Johnson's column expressed conventional motivational sentiments. Syndicated in over twenty black newspapers from 1926 to 1932, the column gave advice on overcoming timidity, inferiority, negative criticism, and obstacles to success. Although the column was both short and predictable, its popularity confirmed its inspirational value for its audience.

Another poet, Gwendolyn Bennett, wrote a column, "Ebony Flute," consisting of tidbits on the social life of black writers and other professionals. Bennett's column provided general commentary on the literary and social world. In this respect, her column was very much like "Une Femme Dit: Crisp, Bright Opinions of Current Happenings from a Woman's Point of View," the weekly column of Alice Dunbar-Nelson. Dunbar-Nelson's column, however, covered a wider range of topics and was much more sophisticated in its analysis of events, films, and books. In fact, Dunbar-Nelson wrote several other columns, including "As in a Looking Glass" and "So It Seems." Dunbar-Nelson served several roles: political commentator, and literary and cultural critic.

The Harlem Renaissance was a time when African American intellectuals actively courted and shaped the black press. Along with writing newspaper columns, authors published their poems and fiction in black magazines, such as *Opportunity and the *Crisis. The press provided a forum for the promotion of the arts, and the development of the literary and creative talents of the writers. The writers, in turn, were creative journalists, moving easily among different genres and dismissing artificial boundaries between art and politics.

There are several reasons why fewer fiction writers and poets wrote columns for the black press in the decades after the Harlem Renaissance: a more economically sound white press courted occasional pieces from such writers as James *Baldwin, Ralph *Ellison, and Alex *Haley; *journalism became a more specialized field; major book publishing houses opened their doors; and other media, including television and *film, flourished. Nevertheless, in newspapers such as the *Pittsburgh Courier, Chicago Defender, *Baltimore Afro-American, Amsterdam News,* and others, black writers gave life to their poetry, prose, and politics.

[*See also* Periodicals; Publishing.]

• Irving Garland Penn, *The Afro-American Press and Its Editors,* 1891. Martin E. Dann, *The Black Press 1827–1890: The Quest for National Identity,* 1971. David Levering Lewis, *When Harlem Was in Vogue,* 1982. Gloria T. Hull, *Color, Sex and Poetry: Three Women Writers of the Harlem Renaissance,* 1987. Darlene Clark Hine, ed., *Black Women in America: An Historical Encyclopedia,* vols. 1 and 2, 1993.

—Valerie Lee

NIGGERATI MANOR. The rooming house(s) where *Harlem Renaissance writer Wallace *Thurman lived was (were) nicknamed Niggerati Manor. Scholarly sources identify at least three similar addresses: 314 West 138th Street (Arnold Rampersad, *The Life of Langston Hughes,* vol. 1, 1986); a "rent free" building at 136th Street, or the infamous "267 House" provided by Iolanthe Sydney, owner of a Harlem employment agency (David Levering Lewis, *When Harlem Was in Vogue,* 1979); and 137th Street where, in *The *Big Sea* (1940), Langston *Hughes says he and Harcout Tynes roomed with Thurman during the summer of 1926. The residence takes its name from a fusion of the words "Nigger" and "literati" made by folklorist, anthropologist, and novelist Zora Neale *Hurston, who also dubbed herself "Queen of the Niggerati." At Niggerati Manor, she, Hughes, Thurman, the outrageous Richard Bruce *Nugent, and other artists mocked themselves and the bourgeois pretensions that often alienated them from the African American community they sought to depict. They also met there to discuss artistic strategy and to throw what were rumored to be scandalous parties. Wallace Thurman's satiric novel, *Infants of the Spring* (1932), memorializes Niggerati Manor, as do several other renaissance writings and even later African American literature, such as Toni *Morrison's *Jazz* (1992).   —SallyAnn H. Ferguson

No Place to Be Somebody. Charles *Gordone's play *No Place to Be Somebody* (1969) recounts the happenings in a New York City bar and the past fifteen years in the life of its African American owner Johnny Williams. As part of the larger theme of the thwarted ambitions of motley bar patrons consisting of ex-convicts, hustlers, prostitutes, politicians, and artists, Johnny, rankled by a history of poor race relations, eagerly awaits the prison release of his mentor Sweets Crane to initiate a racketeering scheme and to claim a share of the organized crime market. However, after ten years of incarceration, Sweets is a reformed, old man whose recidivism and "Charlie fever" are tempered by poor health and *religion. Framed in all three acts by the multiple voices of Gab Gabriel, who simultaneously serves as writer, chorus, and aspiring actor in the play, *No Place to Be Somebody* examines the individual and communal struggle for identity and the potential destruction and regeneration this enterprise entails.

After numerous revisions and artistic and financial setbacks, *No Place* opened at Joseph Papp's New York Shakespeare Festival Public Theatre on 4 May 1969, moved to the ANTA Theatre on 30 December, and concluded a run of 903 performances Off-Broadway with a third opening at the Promenade Theatre on 20 January 1970. Distinguishing Gordone as the first African American playwright to receive the award, *No Place* was the first Off-Broadway play to win a Pulitzer Prize for drama (1970) and was in the same year the recipient of the Vernon Rice Award, the Drama Desk Award, and the New York and Los Angeles Critic's Circle awards. Directed by Gordone, the play made its Broadway debut on 9 September 1971 at the Morosco Theatre. Subsequently, the play has been revived by several schools and regional theaters and translated into French, German, Spanish, and Russian for productions throughout the world. Though some critics claimed that the play was too dense and that Gordone's artistic vision was unclear, *No Place to Be Somebody* was hailed widely as a critical success for its adept use of language, for its experimentation with varying dramatic forms, and for its candid commentary regarding racial tensions in America.

In the late 1960s and the early 1970s and at a time when there was an increased demand for racially conscious and constructive artistic production and the stage gained great significance as an arena for the exploration, negotiation, and assertion of African American identity, *No Place to Be Somebody* advanced the project of identity by positing what Gordone called an "American chemistry." In a 1988 interview with Susan Harris Smith in *Studies in American Drama,* Gordone suggests that the formulation of identity in American society emerges from a synthesis of cultural, racial, and religious experiences. This amalgam of cultures, races, and religions, according to Gordone, had profound implications not only in expanding the parameters of African American identity, but also offered a broader understanding of the American experience and ultimately of humanity.

• Jean W. Ross, "Charles Gordone," in *DLB,* vol. 7, *Twentieth-Century American Dramatists,* ed. John MacNicholas, 1981, pp. 227–231. Bernard L. Peterson, Jr., *Contemporary Black American Playwrights and Their Plays,* 1988.

—Charles Leonard

North Star, The. The *North Star* was founded on 3 December 1847 in Rochester, New York, by Frederick *Douglass, who obtained the startup costs for the weekly newspaper from friends in England. Named after the lodestar that guided runaway slaves to *freedom, the *North Star* was staunchly antislavery. However, the *North Star* also provided a forum for the discussion of civil rights, *temperance, peace, *education, and capital punishment. During its thirteen years of publication, the *North Star* faced several financial and editorial problems. During the first six months of publication, Douglass had to mortgage his home to finance his paper. Martin R. *Delany served as coeditor during the first year but left in 1848.

William C. *Nell, Douglass's copublisher and a follower of William Lloyd Garrison, resigned in 1851 because of political differences with Douglass. In 1851, the *North Star* merged with the *Liberty Party Paper,* and its name was changed to *Frederick Douglass's Paper.* Under this name, the newspaper continued publication until 1860.

[*See also* Antislavery Movement; Literacy; Periodicals, *article on* Black Periodical Press; Publishing.]

• Frederick Douglass, *The Life and Times of Frederick Douglass,* 1892. Nathan Huggins, *Slave and Citizen: The Life of Frederick Douglass,* 1980.   —Wendy Wagner

NORTHUP, SOLOMON (1808–1863), free-born resident of upstate New York, whose kidnapping, transport, and enslavement in the deep South are recounted in his 1853 *slave narrative, *Twelve Years a Slave.* Solomon Northup's early life took an ordinary course, from youth on the family farm to marriage at age twenty-one to Anne Hampton, followed by the birth of three children. A farmer, semiskilled laborer, but also a part-time fiddle player, Northup accepted an offer in March 1841 from two strangers in Saratoga, New York, to provide music for their traveling circus. But when the tour reached Washington, D.C., the men had him seized, delivered to slave traders, shipped to New Orleans aboard an American coastwise slaver, and sold to a succession of Louisiana slave owners, for whom he worked until returning to New York and freedom in January of 1853.

Though literate, Northup dictated his narrative of captivity to a ghostwriter, David Wilson, who proved less intrusive than many other white *amanuenses of slave narratives, allowing Northup to exercise final editorial decisions over the events narrated, but whose mannered style precludes the narrative from being as authentic as *autobiographies written by their own subjects. While abolitionist journals had previously warned of slavery's dangers to free African American citizens and published brief accounts of kidnappings, Northup's narrative was the first to document such a case in book-length detail. Dedicated to Harriet Beecher *Stowe, whose *Uncle Tom's Cabin* had appeared in 1852, Northup's narrative promised facts that would surpass Stowe's fiction. The narrative's immediate success (final sales exceeded thirty thousand copies) was boosted by such comparisons, especially that between the Red River region of Northup's enforced *slavery and the territory where Uncle Tom suffers the cruelty of Simon Legree. When Stowe published her *Key to Uncle Tom's Cabin* in 1853, she cited Northup's narrative to bolster her novel's credibility, and subsequent reprints of Northup's narrative in turn proclaimed it "Another Key to Uncle Tom's Cabin." Although capitalizing on the popularity of Stowe's fiction, Northup's narrative nevertheless asserts its unique value. In its insistence upon telling the whole ugly truth of slavery it not only departs from Stowe's self-proclaimed rhetorical restraint but also illustrates slave narratives' evolution during the 1850s and 1860s from earlier autobiographies whose authors had found it necessary to moderate their stories in order to win credibility from white audiences.

• William L. Andrews, *To Tell a Free Story,* 1988, pp. 181–183. Marion Wilson Starling, *The Slave Narrative: Its Place in American History,* 2d ed., 1988, pp. 171–174.

—Brad S. Born

NORTON, MR. Mr. Norton is a white man from the North who is a founder and financial supporter of the southern Negro college that the narrator attends in Ralph *Ellison's *Invisible Man* (1952). The narrator unwittingly drives the northern, white philanthropist through the backwash of the college community and, as a result, is expelled from the edenic campus environment. Structurally, Mr. Norton functions as a springboard for launching the Invisible Man on his quest for knowledge and self-identity. It should be understood though that Norton is not the philanthropist that he seems to be. He operates out of self-interest and guilt. If not physically (as *Trueblood did), he has psychologically and mentally raped his own daughter, and his philanthropy to Blacks becomes a monument to her memory. Then, too, Norton suffers from delusions of grandeur. He sees himself as a god directing the affairs of Black people for whom he has very little respect. He says of his association with the college: "That has been my real life's work, not my banking or my researchers, but my first-hand organization of human life." His philanthropy is nothing more than a guise for controlling the destiny of others.

Norton, in his self-righteousness, thinks of himself as a master builder. He says to the Invisible Man, "if you become a good farmer, a chef, a preacher, doctor, singer, mechanic—whatever you become, and even if you fail, you are my fate." Over and over again he reminds the Invisible Man that Blacks are associated with his "fate," his "destiny." But it must be remembered that it is the Mr. Nortons of America who are responsible for the Golden Day, the human zoo that is located in the hinterlands of the college community. Many of the patients (political prisoners) at the Golden Day are doctors, lawyers, teachers, civil service workers, preachers, politicians, and artists. The range of human endeavor is represented in the Black men who are detained in this mental facility. They, like the Invisible Man, were probably educated at this Black college or other Black colleges by other Nortons. But once the Blacks were educated and began to compete in the mainstream, the metaphorical Nortons herded them into institutions because they, the Nortons, were afraid of the talented, intellectually competent professionals they had created. In short, all the country's Mr. Nortons are nothing more than self-righteous hypocrites.

—Ralph Reckley, Sr.

Notes of a Native Son. James *Baldwin's first collection of *essays, *Notes of a Native Son* (1955) brought together pieces he had published in *Commentary, Harper's Magazine, Partisan Review,* and other journals. The essays solidified Baldwin's reputation as an essayist as well as his persistence in criticizing America for its racial shortcomings. An autobiographical section precedes the ten essays. Dominant in his own life and in the essays is a recurring theme: what it means to be a black man in America. His status as a writer gives a special twist to that problem and leads him to assert: "I want to be an honest man and a good writer."

Part 1, consisting of three essays, reflects Baldwin's early attempts at literary and cultural criticism. "Everybody's Protest Novel" revisits *Uncle Tom's Cabin* (1852), which Baldwin read so frequently as a child that his mother had to hide it from him. Now thirty-one and reexamining his childhood fascination, Baldwin concludes that the book "is a very bad novel," primarily because of its sentimentality and its protest theme. In "Many Thousands Gone," Baldwin comments on stereotyping and the dehumanization of the Negro, with a particular focus on the problems inherent in Richard *Wright's creation of *Bigger Thomas (*Native Son*, 1940). "Carmen Jones: The Dark Is Light Enough" focuses on the Hollywood production of *Carmen Jones*.

Part 2 contains some of Baldwin's most recognized and studied essays. As cultural historian and critic in "The Harlem Ghetto," Baldwin comments on familiar territory, giving particular attention to "the Negro press" and to the often tense relationships between blacks and Jews. "Journey to Atlanta" uses political commentary as the backdrop to discussing a disastrous trip Baldwin's brother David made to Atlanta as a member of a quartet. The title essay, "Notes of a Native Son," recounts the death of Baldwin's father, which was on the same day his last sibling was born and a few hours before a race riot in Harlem. For Baldwin, all of these events come together in trying to make sense of his tempestuous relationship with his father, of their *identity, of his place in his family, of his family's place in America. The challenge is to claim life and sanity in the midst of bitterness, poison, hatred, and fear, for these are the emotions that tie the disparate pieces of the essay together.

Baldwin moves from the United States to the international scene in part 3 of the volume as he explores his own reactions and those of others to his travels to Paris and other European cities; the concept of strangers underlies all the essays. "Encounter on the Seine: Black Meets Brown" highlights the difficulties of black Americans meeting Africans on French soil. "A Question of Identity" focuses on the American student colony in Paris, while "Equal in Paris" recounts a funny but nonetheless serious incident in which Baldwin was arrested for receiving stolen goods. The eight days he spent in jail were comparable to encountering the familiar institutional dehumanization in America. Finally, "Stranger in the Village," one of the most well-known of Baldwin's essays, relates his visit to a Swiss village in which, as a black man, he was an object of great curiosity among the villagers; that provided yet another opportunity for focusing on the situation of black people in America. Awareness of the central place black people have held in the world leads Baldwin to assert that "this world is white no longer, and it will never be white again."

[*See also* Afrocentricity; Double Consciousness; Emigration; Expatriatism; Pan-Africanism.]

• Keneth Kinnamon, *James Baldwin: A Collection of Critical Essays*, 1974. Fred L. Standley and Nancy V. Burt, eds., *Critical Essays on James Baldwin*, 1988.   —Trudier Harris

NOVEL. The African American novel emerged in the middle of the nineteenth century during the highly charged debates over *slavery and *freedom in America, but it was not until the 1920s that the novel became a fully recognized literary form according to standards set by mainstream scholarship. However, the unique development of the African American novel as a site where social, political, psychological, and philosophical conflicts are played out has made it a highly prized literary genre. Studies such as those by Barbara Christian and Bernard Bell, rediscoveries and revised bibliographies that reconstruct the African American novelistic tradition, the teaching of African American literature courses inside and outside of *black studies programs, and a host of bestsellers from Richard *Wright and Ralph *Ellison to Alice *Walker, Toni *Morrison, and Terry *McMillan have all led to the current prosperity enjoyed by the African American novel.

Tracing the history of the African American novel is not an easy task. Despite pathbreaking work by many, there remain huge gaps in our understanding of the processes of cultural production that have resulted in novels by African Americans being written, published, and read for nearly two hundred years. A history of this genre, therefore, that pays attention to the relationship among the novel as a written text, the forms of conveyance and production, and the politics of reading, both popular and critical, is still evolving, alongside the consistent and continuous disclosure of fugitive texts and authors. For our purposes here, we will consider: (1) the origin of the novel during slavery; (2) the growth of the African American novel during the late nineteenth century when rural life was the majority experience for African Americans; and (3) the transformation of the novel in modern, urban life focusing on the increased literary production in defining moments or periods, namely the 1920s, 1940s, and 1960s. The dividing line for the contemporary African American novel will be the *civil rights movement and its foregrounding of issues related to multiple forms of oppression, especially that among African American women.

The earliest-known African American novelists viewed their works as records of their own singular achievements as well as a way to carve out a social and cultural space that could accommodate a wider range of historical and ideological meanings. The four best-known novels written during slavery are *Clotel, or The President's Daughter. A Narrative of Slave Life in the United States* (1853) by William Wells *Brown; Frank J. *Webb's *The Garies and Their Friends* (1857); Martin R. *Delany's *Blake* (1859); and *Our Nig, or Sketches from the Life of a Free Black in a Two-Story White House, North. Showing That Slavery's Shadows Fall Even There* (1859) by Harriet

E. *Wilson. All four authors, though Webb perhaps least so, were compelled to "tell their own story" at the same time they appropriated the classic features of the popular fiction of the day. Brown dared to build his story around a tragic mulatta, thus inviting even more hostile readers to take action against the "great sin of slavery." Aside from the *slave narrative, the roots of these early novels and those that derive from them are *folklore and African American oral literature, abolitionist literature, the Bible, and popular fiction. This diverse heritage leads scholars such as Bernard Bell to designate the novel a "hybrid narrative." Both pedagogical and political functions made the early novel resilient and amenable to change, its forms somewhat fluid as ideological, social, and cultural boundaries were shifting.

The novels of slavery, though limited in number, set the canonical context and form for the African American novel as we know it today. First, it aligned itself with the tradition of *autobiography, or the naming of the self. African American novelists continue to seek out strategies for representing the individual and the group. Second, it made *history a priority, be it present, past, or future, although this did not always mean that what was real had to be comprehended in a particular way. Just as the *spirituals served to realign and transform the realities of slave oppression, African American novels became ways of engaging a certain set of issues through the formal act of literary creation.

If the first African American writers viewed the novel as a way of reshaping the discourse of slavery, those writing during emancipation and the days of Reconstruction expanded the novelistic paradigm to argue *race in a very definitive way. In these "race novels," writers were drawn to the alternating visions of antebellum romanticism and domestic realism as they shaped the contours of fiction to tell stories of racial conflict, color and caste discrimination, and the ultimate triumph over adversity. The novels written following emancipation absorbed an ideology of racial uplift and articulated the concerns of an emerging black middle class. The vast majority of freed slaves were illiterate, and the construction of fictional race heroes and heroines was intended to demonstrate the possibilities and prospects of racial progress. It is perhaps for this reason that many novels of this period foregrounded moralistic and sociopolitical concerns relevant for an African American community emerging from slavery. Codes of conduct and behavior were primary and a nascent nationalism took on greater and greater significance. But these novelists wanted to share the particularity of African American culture so that it might be understood in new and important ways. What most critics have observed, however, is an immersion within sentimental traditions of earlier nineteenth-century literature. However, the sentimentality, didacticism, and racial stereotyping in the novels by Frances Ellen Watkins *Harper, Sutton E. *Griggs, Paul Laurence *Dunbar, Charles Waddell *Chesnutt, and Pauline E. *Hopkins, as well as many of the lesser known writers of the period, may indicate the choices made by these authors to manipulate reader response. As Richard Yarborough suggests, "To dissemble, to overemphasize, even to misrepresent," could be a successful tactic, "elicting sympathy from the white reader" (qtd. in Eric Sunquist, ed., *New Essays on Uncle Tom's Cabin*, 1986). The frequent appearance of novels by educated African American women late in the century further suggests that there was, as Frances Smith Foster says, a specific "literature of conviction and conversion" designed to promote idealized models of racial progress and solidarity (*Written by Herself*, 1994).

Charles Chesnutt, more than any other writer of the period, pushed beyond the conventional boundaries of folk realism. A serious writer who kept his racial identity hidden in the formative years of his career, Chesnutt's three novels, *The *House behind the Cedars* (1900), *The *Marrow of Tradition* (1901), and *The Colonel's Dream* (1905), represent a solid achievement in novelistic technique, especially in character and plot development, language, and dialogue. Chesnutt's great achievement was in turning folktales and other stories of African American life into finely crafted short stories and folk novels.

Chesnutt, Harper, and others took moral positions against *passing by representing racial commitment, solidarity, and progress as more important than individual freedom. Harper's protagonist Iola Leroy (*Iola Leroy*, 1892), for example, makes a conscious choice not to pass and marry into the "good" life, preferring instead to open a school for African Americans in the South and marry "black." These "race" men and women abound in the fictions of the late nineteenth century as a means of promoting racial uplift and articulating the theory of the *talented tenth, a philosophy advocated by W. E. B. *Du Bois. Many of these novels demonstrate varying models of success based on nineteenth-century notions of a protestant work ethic.

Pauline E. Hopkins and Sutton E. Griggs both represent an important development in turn-of-the-century African American literary culture, the rise of an independent black press and periodical literature. Hopkins's idea of black book clubs sprang from a plan to give books as gifts for taking out subscriptions to the *Colored American Magazine* where she served as editor. Griggs turned entirely to the independent black press for his thirty-three published works, including five novels. In a climate of racial hatred and intense *violence that helped to spark the trend of outmigration from southern towns, Griggs offered a radical solution in *Imperium in Imperio* (1899), proposing a prototype of the NAACP. The most well-known writer of the period was poet Paul Laurence Dunbar, who also wrote four novels, the most important of which is *The *Sport of the Gods* (1902), an exploration of the impact of urban life on antebellum folk consciousness.

The urbanization of the African American population during the first decades of the twentieth century resulted from a number of factors: the *migration of African Americans from the rural areas of the South and of black people from the Caribbean; the economic pull of northern, urban jobs in industry and service occupations; and the commercialization of

African American cultural expression, especially *blues and *jazz music, vaudeville, and *minstrelsy. The subsequent impact on the literary culture was to broaden the novel's cultural base. African American writers felt greater freedom from overt racial hostility and the tyranny of southern segregation translated into numerous publications and at least fifty novels, many of them substantially experimental in form and technique. Appropriately called the Jazz Age for mainstream America, the 1920s epitomized a new type of Negro. Novelists characterized the "*New Negro" phenomenon and, along with the poets and other artists of the period, gave African American culture a more urban, assertive, and cosmopolitan voice. Alain *Locke and James Weldon *Johnson argued that this "New Negro" period also represented a highly stratified African American community with aggressive leadership, greater visibility, and increasing political sophistication. The 1920s saw African American writing embraced, encouraged, and produced like never before, and it is this outpouring that the New Negro Renaissance, also known as the *Harlem Renaissnace, came to symbolize.

There was no single type of novel during this period, according to Amritjit Singh's study The Novels of the Harlem Renaissance (1976). Writers broke new ground but continued to develop existing forms with texts such as Arna *Bontemps's *Black Thunder (1935), a *historical novel about the 1800 slave insurrection led by Gabriel Prosser; Jessie Redmon *Fauset's novel of middle-class color conflict, *There Is Confusion (1924); Nella *Larsen's highly problematic novels of passing, *Quicksand (1928) and *Passing (1929); and George S. *Schuyler's *Black No More (1931) and Wallace *Thurman's The *Blacker the Berry (1929), two social satires. The folk novel emerged to present realistic, if exaggerated, portraits of urban culture, often providing an exotic appeal for mainstream audiences. Claude *McKay (*Home to Harlem, 1928; and Banana Bottom, 1933), Countee *Cullen (One Way to Heaven, 1932), and Rudolph *Fisher (The *Walls of Jericho, 1928), are examples of folk novels. Fisher also produced a detective novel, The Conjure Man Dies: A Mystery Tale of Dark Harlem (1932).

Novelists who moved beyond the Harlem setting were perhaps more successful in their fictional representation of authentic aspects of African American experience. Langston *Hughes's Not without Laughter (1930), set in the Midwest, combines folk realism with a coming-of-age story, just as Zora Neale *Hurston's *Their Eyes Were Watching God (1937) employs the fullest measure of southern folk realism in her story of a young woman's journey toward self-actualization. Hurston based the novel on her own anthropological research. The quintessential folk novel, Their Eyes Were Watching God has an authenticity unlike its predecessors in the genre at the same time that it offers a reframing of the conventional *bildungsroman, the form that had been inherited from nineteenth-century success stories. James Weldon Johnson's fictionalized autobiography presented one approach for revising this paradigm in his 1912 novel The *Autobiography of an Ex-Colored Man.

The novel in which many aspects of renaissance fiction came together is Jean *Toomer's *Cane (1923). For Toomer, the novel was a self-conscious literary mode through which he could record his impressions of a rapidly changing cultural landscape, one he encountered on his brief sojourn to Sparta, Georgia. Toomer ultimately put two landscapes together—the South and the North—to provide the settings for this discontinuous narrative. Toomer searched for ways of representing the material world where *race, *class, and *gender distinctions were much harder to separate, and where meaning could be appropriated from mythical and metaphorical experience.

Although Richard Wright published his first collection of fiction only one year after Hurston's Their Eyes Were Watching God, his novels are significantly different in style and sensibility from those of the renaissance generation. Wright was himself the composite expression of the "folk" and one of the first African American writers to fully grasp the material implications of migration and urbanization. Wright's artistic innovation was to shift from sympathy to anger as a tool of manipulation. Adopting naturalistic techniques popularized by Upton Sinclair and Theodore Dreiser decades earlier, Wright presented a stark and hostile environment where racism was the most violent crime against African Americans. But Wright demonstrated through his fiction that one form of criminality only bred another; African Americans became both the victims of the crime of racism and, like *Bigger Thomas, the perpetrators of criminal behavior. By offering violence and criminality as the logical responses to a racist, neglectful society, Wright spoke for masses of African American men in a dehumanizing society that consistently denied them access and opportunity. *Native Son (1940) became a best-seller and a classic protest novel.

The brand of social realism popularized by Wright and the powerfully deterministic image of the African American male within the context of America was re-created variously by an entire generation of novelists during the 1940s. The popularity of Native Son gave other African American novelists entry into the world of protest fiction. Willard *Motley, Ann *Petry, Chester *Himes, Frank London *Brown, William Gardner *Smith, and William *Demby all followed Wright's example in their early novels. Later writers would expand the paradigm, but still found in Wright the compelling voice of social criticism.

By far the most significant development in the history of the African American novel after Richard Wright was the appearance of Ralph Ellison. Ellison openly attacked the protest tradition in his essays during the 1950s when overt protest could blacklist a writer. Although Ellison used the same South that Wright had used, *Invisible Man (1952) captured a different sensibility in the African American experience. Ellison's training as a musician attuned him to multiple levels of meaning and language, and he found in the novel a unique way to blend the forms of African American culture with those of Western culture as a whole. Drawing upon myths, dreams, and symbols, as well as upon the forms and structure of *blues and *jazz, Ellison tells a story of epic proportion. *Invisible Man*'s unnamed protagonist relives the history of black America during a personal journey that ends in his alienation. Like Toomer's *Cane*, a modernist impulse informs *Invisible Man*: it is highly stylized, multimodal, and multivocal.

Thus, the African American novel at midcentury was one whose boundaries for historical representation had been expanded. Historical time is exchanged for allegorical time, character development is exchanged for a complex array of symbols and rituals from African American folklore, and the external social environment is experienced in highly personal ways. One African American writer to take advantage of this new sensibility was James *Baldwin. While *Invisible Man* personifies the African American everyman as an alienated and disengaged intellectual searching for personal meaning, Baldwin's *Go Tell It on the Mountain* (1953) shows its male protagonist searching for personal meaning and understanding through suffering. Baldwin enlarges the cultural landscape of the African American novel even further through his exploration of religious and theological themes: suffering and salvation, sin and redemption. Both the sacred and the secular forms of African American culture find a place in Baldwin's novels; *sermons and preaching, blues, jazz, and *spirituals capture the spiritual and emotional texture of African American life.

The *civil rights movement permitted the coexistence of Wright's naturalistic vision where physical and psychological victimization left little that was human; Ellison's existential vision where the human quest was for individual meaning as it was extracted from historical encounters; and Baldwin's vision of human suffering that bound black and white together. Together, these writers set the literary stage for the contemporary African American novel, which could claim its inheritance from social realism, mythic symbolism, and humanism. This literary and cultural link has often been forgotten amid the social and political turbulence of the 1960s.

The cultural activity that accompanied the civil rights movement had a strong social base among the masses of African American people. The more politically radical wing of this movement, especially its youth, became identified as the "Black Power" generation, and their artistic and cultural expression the *Black Arts movement. As the 1960s gave way to the 1970s, and the *Black Aesthetic called for a cultural revolution, a search for more indigenous forms of cultural expression was underway. Black music, *theater, *poetry, and the visual arts witnessed a transformation in theme and style, focusing more on personal identification with Africa and radical political change.

Poetry and drama were the major forms of the period, but differences seen in the novel, though more subtle, were nevertheless critical. The African American novel began to transgress the boundaries between black and white readers and between male and female forms, between what was considered mainstream and southern, popular and literary, modern and postmodern. African American novelists took seriously their role of writing a new narrative for the nation that required a redefinition of consciousness and perception. Folk traditions, slavery, and the multiple forms of oppression, be they racial, sexual, or economic, were now understood in new ways.

For novelists like John A. *Williams, John O. *Killens, Paule *Marshall, Hal *Bennett, Ronald L. *Fair, Alice *Childress, John Edgar *Wideman, Ishmael *Reed, and Ernest J. *Gaines, the 1960s was a time of revelation. None of these novelists could escape the historical past. But they all began to realize that the relationship between historical conditions and internal realities was a complex dynamic that they, perhaps more than any other Americans, could explore. Primarily, the mindset of the period was to confront historical change and identity, and expose the social impact of racism. Increasingly for African American women novelists, there was also a need to confront the history of sexual oppression. Baldwin continued to be a major voice with his bold indictments of racism and explorations into the domain of sexual difference with *Giovanni's Room* (1956), *Another Country* (1962), and *Tell Me How Long the Train's Been Gone* (1968). There was considerable range in the styles and narrative techniques utilized by these writers, and some like Henry *Van Dyke, Charles S. *Wright, Carlene Hatcher *Polite, Clarence *Major, and William Melvin *Kelley brought to the African American novel stylistic innovations upon which writers of the 1970s would build.

The social and institutional structures that emerged were especially important in cultivating the new generation of novelists. One of the earliest was the Harlem Writers Guild in New York, founded by John O. Killens. For over thirty years, the guild served as a major training ground and attracted writers from all over, counting among its published novelists not only Killens himself, but also Marshall, Childress, Rosa *Guy, Julian *Mayfield, and Terry McMillan. The writers' workshop was not a new form, since one of the earliest had been organized by Richard Wright as a means of consolidating and collectivizing the artistic energy of a generation of writers during the depression period. Similarly, the Harlem Writers Guild had its parallels in the 1960s: the Organization of Black American Culture (OBAC) in Chicago; the Watts Writers Workshop on the West Coast; and the Free Southern Theater in the South. These became the contexts where writers came together to learn, to critique each others' work, and to get published. Writers' groups like these proliferated and the literature emerging from them flourished.

By the 1970s, the African American novel had become a complex discursive field where inventive language, innovative narrative structure, and historical meaning came together in texts with varying degrees of *literacy and literalness for a wide range of readers. *Class and *gender became two of the social issues long deserving of more attention, and it was African American women writers who took up this mantle.

What was not new was the tradition of writing represented by African American women writers historically. Frances Smith Foster argues, for example, that Harper's *Iola Leroy* was not the only novel exploring the concerns of her generation of African American women. Clarissa Minnie Thompson, Amelia E. *Johnson, Emma Dunham *Kelley, Katherine Davis Chapman *Tillman, and Pauline Hopkins all portrayed strong female protagonists in novels during the last decade of the nineteenth century. The conclusion that African American women's writing formed both a part of the mainstream tradition as well as a separate and distinct tradition, a "tradition within a tradition," recognition of which was long overdue, provided an important source of inspiration for African American women writers. These novelists looked to a variety of models, but especially to Zora Neale Hurston's *Their Eyes Were Watching God*, Gwendolyn *Brooks's *Maud Martha* (1953), Paule Marshall's *Brown Girl, Brownstones* (1959) and The *Chosen Place, the Timeless People* (1969), and Margaret *Walker's *Jubilee* (1966). Hurston gave to African American women's writing the canonical text, the journey of a young woman to maturity and self-actualization. Brooks and Walker, who had already established themselves as major poets, gave new meaning to the unacknowledged literary subject of the African American woman's experience. Walker in particular opened up the possibilities of the historical novel and the slave narrative for modern African American writing. Marshall, whose works were the best known, helped to make it clear that the world occupied by black women, whether in Bajan or African American culture per se, had its own rites of passage. These authors drew the connection between personal and societal change in ways that deepened the historical meaning of "America" and complicated American identity. Later women novelists would make more consistent use of personal growth, societal change, and historical meaning as subjects of their novels.

By the time the first novels by Toni Morrison and Alice Walker appeared, African American women writers were well prepared to provide leadership for a new era. The need to challenge the absence of women's stories in the recorded literary history, correct the distortions, and represent the complexity of women's lives was folded into the concept of "triple oppression." Thus a new feminist discourse enabled writers as part of the growing discipline of black women's studies to examine the lives of women, finding unique ways to focus on issues of black female identity and powerlessness, the circumscribed and restricted environments that characterized women's lives. The first generation of feminist novelists, which claimed Hurston as its foremother, included a range of writers, most notably Alice Walker, Toni Cade *Bambara, Gayl *Jones, Gloria *Naylor, and Toni Morrison. Their works focused on the quest for the female self and the historical conditions of racism and sexism. They were necessarily more oppositional in their approaches to male–female relationships, as they were eager to show the empowerment of African American women as they moved from silent object to speaking subject. Collective strength was found in communities that impel the reader to experience the pain of rage and oppression. In the novels of Alice Walker, for example, the restricted world of women becomes both context and metaphor. The *Third Life of Grange Copeland* (1970), *Meridian* (1976), and The *Color Purple* (1982) locate women in the isolated rural South where they are trapped within the conditions of their own existence. In Gayl Jones's highly innovative novels *Corregidora* (1975) and *Eva's Man* (1976), the characters live within the violently insane landscapes of the narratives they themselves create, whether on the conscious or subconscious level.

As the leading figure of the African American women's literary renaissance, Toni Morrison remembers a world in her novels that is shocking and outrageous, familiar and distant, terrifying and painful. The women who occupy her world take center stage, and their existence as exalted, nurturing, creative, transcendent beings imparts a transformative power to others. Morrison's role in the development of the novel is to bring multiple traditions together in the art novel. Drawing upon African American and Latin American forms, African myths, male and female myths, iconographies, and modern and postmodern techniques, Morrison makes the novel a narrative event in which one must confront the complexity of the novel's structure alongside that of its meaning. In all her novels, Morrison allows experiences to intersect with one another, whether it is gender, race, and self-identity; imagination and reality; or history and myth. For Morrison also, relationships between people are critical and the social is inscribed within personal, while the community is a focal point. Coherence comes in the form of an identifiable framework: The *Bluest Eye* (1970) and *Sula* (1974) present young women's coming-of-age stories: *Song of Solomon* (1977) is the picaresque or quest narrative; and *Beloved* (1987), *Tar Baby* (1981), and *Jazz* (1992) tell love stories.

For Morrison, like a number of other authors, postmodern techniques reframe narrative structures and invite a variety of experimental techniques, the very traditions that many contemporary African American authors see as already inscribed within the African American literary tradition. Thus marginality; unconventional and antirational patterns of behavior; the privileging of consciousness and memory; the blurring of distinctions among comedy, pathos, and tragedy; and discontinuity in narrative structure, all common to postmodern fiction, are present in varying degrees in works by some of the major writers of the contemporary African American novel. The novels of Ishmael Reed, Charles R. *Johnson, and John Edgar Wideman, and the *speculative fiction of Samuel R. *Delany and Octavia E. *Butler have all added richness and complexity to the contemporary African American novel that continues to make it a focus of critical debate and discussion. Each of these writers bridges the modern and postmodern traditions, where history is conjoined with myth and legend, the imaginary complements reality, and the material world exists alongside the metaphysical. As a way of deepening our understanding of the *Middle Passage and slavery, racism and oppression, themselves very conflicting modalities, these novelists comfortably operate within seemingly contradictory modes of literary representation. Familiar forms are ever present—the slave narrative, the detective novel, science fiction, the western romance, the biblical parable, the gothic tale—but there is ambiguity rather than certainty and an assertion that it is no longer possible to view the experiences of a people in mutually exclusive terms. The interrelated nature of cultural and ideological phenomena, of history and the memory of that history, of racial and gender cleavages, has opened up tremendous fictional possibilities regarding race and ethnicity, gender and sexuality, class and economic relations.

Ishmael Reed's achievements as a social satirist, who uses parody and burlesque in otherwise historical fictions of African American life, have earned him a considerable amount of good and bad praise. His sizeable canon, from *Free Lance Pallbearer* (1967) to *The Terrible Threes* (1989), has made him a foremost metafictionist. Other novelists have found Reed's boldness inspiring in their own efforts to reclaim the satirical and parodic traditions in rewriting mythologies of African American life. For example, Charles Johnson re-creates the Middle Passage in order to question our assumptions about the meaning it had for slave and slaver alike. Johnson uses a comic mode—the protagonist lands on a slave ship as an escape from his own rather immoral life—thus placing the novel squarely within the tradition of other mainstream postmodern fictions. Yet Johnson never gives up his connection to the "real" in what is otherwise a highly fantastic narrative, a strategy he observes in two earlier novels, *Faith and the Good Thing* (1974) and *Oxherding Tale* (1982). Similarly, John Edgar Wideman's novels *Hiding Place* (1981), *Sent for You Yesterday* (1983), and *Reuben* (1987) construct the fictional Homewood as a place where *family and personal history come together. The reader experiences these histories through a variety of narratives, *music, and conscious memory. In David *Bradley's The *Chaneysville Incident and Leon *Forrest's panoramic novels There Is a Tree More Ancient than Eden (1973) and Bloodworth Orphans (1977), the use and meaning of history receive their biggest challenge and must be filtered through the real and surreal.

Although one of the most derided of literary forms, the popular novel is one of the fastest growing contemporary genres. Science fiction, "ghetto novels," and popular romances by African American writers have widespread appeal. Samuel Delany is one of the best-known science fiction novelists, white or black, having won major awards for his work. His *Dhalgren* (1975) suggests that science fiction's importance as an experimental fiction genre should not be overlooked. Similarly, Octavia Butler's success as a novelist points to the range of strategies that popular writers have chosen to make their own social commentaries, and for creating a vision of a different and

better world or one that has reached its limits and is in need of transformation.

If Delany and Butler allow the reader to transcend reality, another group of contemporary popular novelists keeps the reader fully grounded in extreme reality. The world of the hustler, the pimp, the lumpen, and gang culture—the underclass—form the subject of novels by Donald *Goines, *Iceberg Slim, Joe Nazel, Odie Hawkins, Barry *Beckham, and Charlie Harris, who, along with others, form a sizeable group of Holloway House writers targeting a specifically black and mostly male audience. On the other hand, romance novels, like the black line put out by Harlequin, are aimed at a female market. Admittedly many of the popular works are formula fictions, but some are well-written, serious explorations into a modal experience within African American culture. Beckham's *My Main Mother* (1969), for example, introduces a young man confronting a world of psychological and physical abuse, and *Runner Mack* (1972) explores the political consciousness of a disaffected migrant and army defector who develops some revolutionary potential only to have his dreams thwarted by suicide. None of these novelists have matched Frank *Yerby's success with his thirty-three historical novels published over a forty-five-year period. Yerby pioneered in the popular novel genre but did not regularly use African American themes.

Young adult novels by African American writers have enjoyed an equal share of success as popular literature. Virginia *Hamilton, Kristin *Hunter, Rosa Guy, Sharon Bell *Mathis, Walter Dean *Myers, Gordon *Parks, and Mildred D. *Taylor have become household names among authors who recognize the pioneering work of Arna Bontemps in this area. Guy, Mathis, and Hunter acknowledge the impact of the 1960s on their development as best-selling children's authors. Primarily interested in giving black youth a way of responding to the tensions and developments of the 1960s, these authors allowed young people to tell their own stories and express their own concerns about the changing world they had inherited and the places they occupied within it.

Unique fictional subgenres have resulted from the linguistic experimentation and narrative inventiveness of many writers. Both "blues novels" and "jazz novels" were inspired by *Invisible Man* and Baldwin's play *Blues for Mr. Charlie*, but owe their origins to earlier sources: the blues texture of Hughes's *Not without Laughter*, for example, and the jazz or bebop texture of *Trumbull Park*, the 1959 novel by Frank London Brown. John A. *McCluskey, Jr. (*Look What They Done to My Song*, 1974, and *Mr. America's Last Season Blues*, 1983), Albert *Murray (*Train Whistle Guitar*, 1974, and *Spyglass Tree*, 1991), Al *Young (*Snakes*, 1971, and *Who Is Angelina*, 1978), A. R. *Flowers (*Another Good Loving Blues*, 1993), and others employ stylized language and dialogue that evoke the modalities of black musical forms like these earlier novels. Blues or jazz can refer to the texture of relationships, personal experience, or movement of the plot itself. When the characters in these stories are not bluespeople or jazz musicians, they are likely to experience some kind of disorientation or antagonism that is at the heart of their experience.

Explorations into *sexuality in gay and lesbian novels have expanded the boundaries of the African American novel even further. Melvin *Dixon (*Trouble de Water*, 1989, and *Vanishing Rooms*, 1991) and Ann Allen *Shockley (*Loving Her*, 1974) bring important issues of gender to the forefront of African American literature, something for which Baldwin had been criticized decades earlier. The more subtle treatment of female sexuality in the novels of Alice Walker (*The Color Purple*, 1982) and Gayl Jones (*Eva's Man*, 1976) introduced possibilities for fiction that led to more explicit sexual themes in E. Lynn *Harris's *Invisible Life* (1991) and Carolivia *Herron's *Thereafter Johnnie* (1991). These novels often link sexuality together with madness and violence and insist upon the right of difference—physical and sexual, spiritual and ideological—by challenging conventional notions of fixed identity.

The South has been reconfigured in important ways in the contemporary African American novel. In part because of the tragicomic relationship of African Americans to the South and the oppositional nature of southern politics and history, the South has appealed to every generation of American writers. The South of slavery and freedom, of moonlight and magnolias, has a complexity that southern African American novelists themselves are wont to explain. It is this complexity that Ernest Gaines presents in all his novels set in southwestern Louisiana. Gaines earned his reputation from his 1971 novel *The *Autobiography of Miss Jane Pittman*, which fictionalized the long walk to dismantle segregation in the South in the form of a mock-autobiography of a former slave. An explosion in southern African American literature has claimed many voices among the most recent African American novelists. Reginald *McKnight (*I Get on the Bus*, 1990), Lance *Jeffers (*Witherspoon*, 1983), Raymond *Andrews (*Apalachee Red*, 1978; *Rosiebelle Lee Wildcat Tennessee*, 1980; and *Baby Sweets*, 1983), and Lewis Edwards (*Ten Seconds*, 1991) demonstrate that the uniqueness in southern writing has as much to do with the story as it does the telling. These authors are as likely to create from the rawness of the Georgia backwoods as they are to extract visions from the supernatural or subconscious world.

A group of these southern writers—all African American women—have begun to depart somewhat from the definitive vision offered by the 1970s generation of black feminists. The objective of the novels by Dori *Sanders (*Clover*, 1990, and *Her Own Place*, 1993) Linda Beatrice *Brown (*Rainbow Roun Mah Shoulder*, 1984, and *Crossing over Jordan*, 1995), Marita *Golden (*Migrations of the Heart*, 1983; *Long Distance Life*, 1989; *And Do Remember Me*, 1992; and *A Woman's Place*, 1986), and Tina McElroy *Ansa (*Baby of the Family*, 1983, and *Ugly Ways*, 1993) is cultural affirmation. They construct a useable past that allows us to see ourselves in characters who are resilient, provocative, forgiving, and politically aware, while also asserting deeply felt psychological needs for human relationships. Although not based in the South, the novels by both Nettie Jones (*Mischief Makers*, 1989) and a long-awaited second novel by Dorothy *West (*The Wedding*, 1995) also examine the viability of human relationships within the context of color and class prejudices.

The useable past is exchanged for the useable present in the novels of Terry McMillan and J. California *Cooper, two of the most popular novelists of the 1990s. McMillan and Cooper have been able through their novels to reopen the dialogue between men and women. Rooted in the everyday lives of some African American women, *Disappearing Acts* (1989) and *Waiting to Exhale* (1992), for example, reveal what some critics have called the "girlfriend culture." The women in these novels are intelligent and work hard, but typically find themselves at odds with the residual elements of contemporary African American male culture. These novels are hard-hitting exposés of postfeminist culture, as the title of Connie Briscoe's 1994 novel *Sisters and Lovers* suggests.

The shift in African American women's novels may suggest the future direction of African American novels approaching the turn of the century. There is a continuing search for modes and styles derived from the cultural and historical experiences of African Americans. Postmodernist techniques are embraced by many; still other writers have a strong preference for conventional narrative forms. The boundaries between popular and literary, as well as other cultural forms, have grown less distinct, permitting novelists to shift more easily between modalities. The contemporary African American novel seems less disposed toward more explicit political commentary, but the political informs contemporary novels in a variety of ways. *Meridian* is for Alice Walker political in the sense that *Outsider* (1953) was political for Richard Wright or *The Lynchers* (1973) was for John Edgar Wideman. On the whole, the African American novel seems to be conscious of its position as a democratizing agent, ordering and shaping adversary roles, and accommodating rebellion, marginality, fragmentation, and stability as conditions of contemporary existence.

The autobiographical impulse remains strong and the quest for historical meaning central as today's African American novel continues to fill in the gaps of a cultural heritage by making known what is unknown or too little understood. There is, however, a continual process of breaking with the traditions that have bound together the master narratives of the modern world. A significant number of today's African American novelists are dedicated to creating their own master narratives; from the knowledge of African American history and culture they design and construct new meanings. Others have discerned a world so chaotic that they view their writing as a way of bringing order, reclaiming a past from which we all can learn. Regardless of their ideological orientation or literary affiliation, all these novelists are engaged in celebrating difference, naming the self that such difference implies, and viewing the impact of the collective presence of African American people on the nation and on the world.

[See also Literary History.]

• Vernon Loggins, The Negro Author: His Development in America to 1900, 1964. Robert Bone, The Negro Novel in America, 1965. Noel Schraufnagel, From Apology to Protest: The Black American Novel, 1973. Addison Gayle, Jr., The Way of the New World: The Black Novel in America, 1975. Amritjit Singh, The Novels of the Harlem Renaissance: Twelve Black Writers 1923–1933, 1976. Arlene Elder, "The Hindered Hand": Cultural Implications of Early African-American Fiction, 1978. Robert Stepto, From Behind the Veil: A Study of Afro-American Narrative, 1979. Barbara Christian, Black Woman Novelists: The Development of a Tradition, 1980. Houston A. Baker, Jr., Blues, Ideology, and Afro-American Literature: A Vernacular Theory, 1984. Marjorie Pryse and Hortense J. Spillers, eds. Conjuring: Black Women, Fiction, and Literary Tradition, 1985. Keith Byerman, Fingering the Jagged Grain, 1986. Bernard Bell, The Afro-American Novel and Its Tradition, 1987. Hazel Carby, Reconstructing Black Womanhood: The Emergence of the Afro-American Woman Novelist, 1987. Melvin Dixon, Ride out the Wilderness: Geography and Identity in Afro-American Literature, 1987. John F. Callahan, In the African American Grain: The Pursuit of Voice in Twentieth Century Black Fiction, 1988. Maryemma Graham, "The Origins of the Afro-American Novel," in Proceedings of the American Antiquarian Society 100, 1990, pp. 231–249. Eric Sundquist, To Wake the Nations: Race and the Making of American Literature, 1994.
—Maryemma Graham

NOVEL OF PASSING. African American writers have long used the novel of passing to explore and protest the *color line separating whites from African Americans. In repeating and revising this genre, authors show racially mixed characters choosing to pass for white for a variety of reasons, such as escaping from *slavery, avoiding racism, and improving their economic opportunity. Whether set in antebellum, postbellum, or early twentieth-century America, the novel of passing generally contains the taboo of interracial sex, and the built-in dramas of concealed *identity, tangled deceptions, fear of exposure, guilt, and the search for identity. Since most African American writers show passing characters eventually rejecting the decision to pass, this genre has largely been used to promote racial loyalty and solidarity.

In Williams Wells *Brown's *Clotel, or The President's Daughter: A Narrative of Slave Life in the United States (1853), several of the characters adopt white identities to escape from slavery. The novel's heroine, Clotel, crosses racial and sexual lines when she cleverly disguises herself as a white male traveling with a servant as she successfully returns to Richmond from Mississippi to be with her daughter. Her success is short-lived, however, and she commits suicide to avoid being caught again. Clotel's daughter fares better. She escapes to France and marries a former fellow slave who had also passed for white in his escape. While not a novel of passing, since its plot revolves around reuniting family members separated by slavery, Clotel is an unusual precedent. Where later novels often emphasize the problems associated with adopting a white identity, Clotel depicts the decision as a temporary strategy for survival and even empowerment.

*Passing is not viewed as positively in Frank J. *Webb's The Garies and Their Friends (1857). In this violent, tragic, and melodramatic novel, the passing characters all meet with unhappy ends. Mr. and Mrs. Garie move from a plantation in the South to Philadelphia in order to conceal the African ancestry of Mrs. Garie, one of Mr. Garie's former slaves. Her background is soon discovered and the Garies become the targets of self-interested whites who riot, burn, and vandalize their property in order to buy it more cheaply. In the riots Mr. Garie is shot and killed and Mrs. Garie dies of shock and exposure, also losing her prematurely born baby. The Garies' children's fates seem tied directly to their decisions about racial identification. Clarence Garie, who chooses to pass for white and attempts to marry a white woman, apparently dies of a broken heart after his racial identity is exposed and he is rejected by his fiancée. Before his death he regrets he had cast his lot with whites. In contrast, his sister chooses to marry within the middle-class African American community and her story ends on a hopeful note as she looks forward to a happy future.

In the novel *Iola Leroy, or Shadows Uplifted (1892), Frances Ellen Watkins *Harper extends Webb's antipassing sentiments. Harper creates a strong and self-reliant racially mixed female character who rejects the materialistic advantages and the psychological strain of adopting a white identity. Iola turns down an offer to marry a wealthy white suitor. Instead, she affirms her African ancestry, marries an African American, moves South, and dedicates herself to serving a rural African American community as a teacher. Her shadows are inspirationally "uplifted" by her race-affirming choices.

Charles Waddell *Chesnutt's first novel, The *House behind the Cedars (1900), offers a more ambivalent message about passing for white than its predecessors. Chesnutt's novel splits the passers into brother and sister. Both John and *Rena Walden are pushed into passing for white by their self-loathing and ambitious mother, who is one-fourth African American, yet longs to be fully white. Following the lead of her brother, Rena decides to leave home and conceal her African American heritage for economic and social gain. As whites they begin to flourish in a new southern city. Complications arise, however, when their mother's illness tests her children's loyalties and priorities. Rena, who feels a growing commitment to the African American community, returns to her mother and to a Negro identity, whereas John continues in his economically rewarding deception. Rena's decision to abandon her white identity results in a traumatic rejection by her white lover. The combined pressures of her white lover's tentative attempts to reunite, her mother's obsessive prejudice, and her desire to serve the African American community seem to affect Rena's health and she dies the sentimental and stereotypical death of the tragic *mulatto victimized by her circumstances. Chesnutt balances this tragic death with John's "success" as a passer.

Sustaining the theme of ambivalence, in The *Autobiography of an Ex-Colored Man (1912), James Weldon *Johnson shows a passer who ends his retrospective account reviewing the implications of his decision to cross the race line permanently. The well-educated and cultured narrator realizes that his decision has prevented him from becoming a race leader. Comparing himself to Booker T. *Washington and other contemporary race leaders, he feels selfish and materialistic, realizing he is only an ordinary white man who has had some business success. Yet he is not physically or psychologically destroyed by his decision to pass since he ends his retrospective account in a state of apparently mild regret about his decision, carefully considering its pros and cons. He realizes that his love for his children makes him happy with his decision, since he would not subject them to the second-class racial status of being categorized a Negro. At the same time, however, the narrator realizes that the costs have been great, and that he has sacrificed too much for financial gain and social status. While this novel is more understated and ambivalent in its depiction of the passer than some of its predecessors, it is not without aspects of social protest. The narrator, like Rena Walden or Mrs. Garie, seemingly has no choice in a society that recognizes only two categories of racial identity. Emphasizing this social critique, Johnson shows the narrator's internalized sense of shame at being labeled a second-class citizen because of his African heritage.

The passing for white genre reached its peak during the *Harlem Renaissance when four passing novels were written by major representatives of that period. With the Renaissance's concern for racial pride came an increased interest in this genre since it so dramatically allows scrutiny of issues of color, caste, community, and identity, and the possibilities for African American racial affirmation. Written closely together, these four novels are Flight (1926) by NAACP leader Walter *White; two novels by influential editor Jessie Redmon *Fauset, Plum Bun (1929) and *Comedy: American Style (1933); and *Passing (1929) by Nella *Larsen. Although offering different renditions of this genre, all of the authors agree on the importance of African American racial loyalty and solidarity for mixed-race characters light enough to pass for white.

Perhaps the most obvious example of this is Walter White's Flight, which shows its racially mixed heroine, Mimi Daquin, renouncing her white husband and her white identity at the end of the novel to return to the family and community she has avoided while passing for white. Her decision is an ecstatic and affirming one, with none of the ambivalence of the narrator of The Autobiography of an Ex-Colored Man. After a period of some vacillation between the two worlds, Mimi joyously leaves behind the mechanistic and conformist white world she has inhabited for mainly material gains and social status for the more spiritual and individualistic African American world she has so long denied. Daquin's racial loyalty is reawakened when she attends Carnegie Hall to hear African American *spirituals. During the performance she experiences a liberating epiphany that returns her to her son, whom she had abandoned, and her African American community.

Fauset's novels, Comedy: American Style and Plum Bun, similarly show the conflicting pressures of materialism and racial loyalty, although with more complexity than is seen in White's novel. In Plum Bun, Fauset's heroine, Angela Murray, ends her complicated and debilitating experience in passing and returns to the African American community and family with a strong sense of relief. In this community she will again experience the joys of true companionship and the stability of a tightly linked social world she has long missed. In the end she realizes that the romanticized aspirations for money and influence that motivated her decision are too costly. After her rejection of her white identity she looks forward to a financially difficult yet emotionally rewarding marriage to an African American artist.

Fauset's ironically titled second novel in this vein, Comedy: American Style, shows, as does Chesnutt's The House behind the Cedars, the destructiveness of intraracial prejudice. One of its main characters, Teresa Cary, is pushed into passing and *marriage with a white man by her obsessively status-seeking and prejudiced mother, who herself passes for white. Because of her capitulation, Teresa becomes a pathetically unhappy and suicidal character, and her refusal to harbor her brown-skinned brother in her home in France results in his suicide. Teresa's sister-in-law, however, marries into the African American community and ends the novel emotionally satisifed. Though often criticized for being an overly conservative and elitist writer, Fauset returned again and again to this genre for political purposes—to raise the consciousness of African and white Americans alike and to emphasize the psychological dangers involved in denying one's African American identity.

Nella Larsen's Passing repeats many of these same themes in her psychologically complex rendition of the passing genre. Larsen's subtle novel complicates the genre by denying the passer's (Clare Kendry) return to the African American community in Harlem. Whether pushed by her friend Irene Redfield, who suspects her of having an affair with her husband, or whether she commits suicide, or simply falls, Clare Kendry suffers a tragic death at the end of the novel after she announces her intention to leave her white husband and return to the African American community. In trying to decipher this mysterious death, readers are thrown back into the mind of the main character, Irene, who betrays conscious and unconscious motivations for murdering her friend, as she too struggles with the contradictions of materialist aspirations and racial loyalty. A novel often overlooked or simplified by critics, Passing offers a complex and angst-ridden portrayal of middle-class African Americans often forced to choose between lifestyles and racial loyalties in a persistently racist environment.

In the period since these Harlem Renaissance passing novels were published, the popularity and frequency of this genre has declined. African American writers have, by and large, turned to other genres that are not dependent on a secretive immersion into the white world. Among recent African American *historical novels, however, the passing-for-white theme is still used to interpret the past and to comment on the present.

One of the most sustained examples of contemporary treatments is found in Charles R. *Johnson's *Oxherding Tale* (1982), a novel set in the antebellum South. The main character, who is the offspring of a slave master and a slave, decides to pass for white to escape from slavery. Accompanying the *freedom that he finds is, unexpectedly, marriage to a white woman. There is nothing tragic about his fate. Unlike most of the previous novels in this genre, the passer, Andrew Hawkins, finds happiness in his marriage and in his new identity, and does not plan to return to his previous identity. Taking his cue from Buddhist thought, Johnson reverses the genre's conventional denouement of a return to the African American community to argue that his characters are capable of creating new identities not solely dependent on racial classification. Andrew Hawkins avoids the self-loathing and feelings of regret suffered by ambivalent passers such as the hero of James Weldon Johnson's *The Autobiography of an Ex-Colored Man*. Like Charles Johnson, African American historical novelists will continue to repeat and revise the passing-for-white genre to explore the intricately interlocking layers of race and community, class and money, and to promote their own ideological and philosophical perspectives.

[*See also* Afrocentricity; Class; Double Consciousness; Protest Literature; Talented Tenth, The.]

• Judith Berzon, *Neither White nor Black*, 1978. Barbara Christian, *Black Women Novelists: The Development of a Tradition, 1892–1977*, 1980. Michael G. Cooke, *Afro-American Literature in the Twentieth Century*, 1984. Bernard W. Bell, *The Afro-American Novel and Its Tradition*, 1987. Jonathan Little, "Nella Larsen's *Passing*: Irony and the Critics," *African American Review* 26 (Spring 1992): 173–182.

—Jonathan D. Little

NUGENT, RICHARD BRUCE (1906–1987), popular writer and artist of the Harlem Renaissance era, also known as Bruce Nugent and Richard Bruce. "Shadows," Richard Bruce Nugent's first published poem, on the subject of race, appeared in *Opportunity* and was reprinted in 1927 in Countee *Cullen's *Caroling Dusk*. "Sahdji," published in Alain *Locke's *The *New Negro* (1925), is a pseudo-African story characterized by the use of ellipses and contains the twin themes of homosexuality and biblical imagery that would often determine his later work. In collaboration with Locke this later became *Sahdji—An African Ballet* and appeared in Locke's anthology *Plays of Negro Life* (1927). Scored by William Grant *Still, it was performed at the Eastman School of Music in 1932.

In 1926, with Wallace *Thurman, Langston *Hughes, Zora Neale *Hurston, and Aaron Douglas, Nugent founded the controversial magazine *Fire!! Nugent's "Smoke, Lilies and Jade," apparently the first tale of explicit homosexuality published by an African American, features Alex, a young artist who resembles the author.

After the failure of *Fire!!*, Nugent coedited, with Wallace Thurman, *Harlem* (1928). His bold illustrations appear here as well as in *Fire!!*; other works are in *Opportunity* and the *Crisis; his ambitious *Drawing for Mulattoes* series appears in *Ebony* (1927).

Though never widely published, Nugent, as a fund of information and as an aid to other writers and artists, nevertheless had an important impact on art in Harlem. As cofounder in the 1960s with Romare Bearden of the Harlem Cultural Council, Nugent expressed his continuing commitment to African American life and culture.

[*See also* Harlem Renaissance.]

• David Levering Lewis, *When Harlem Was In Vogue*, 1981.

—Nathan L. Grant

O

Obsidian. The editorial policy of *Obsidian II: Black Literature in Review* encourages "the study and cultivation of creative works in English by Black writers worldwide, with scholarly critical studies by all writers on Black literature in English." *Obsidian II* is a continuation of *Obsidian: Black Literature in Review,* a periodical founded in 1975 by Alvin *Aubert at SUNY at Fredonia. The journal moved to Wayne State University in 1979, where it continued until 1982. Under the auspices of the Department of English at North Carolina State University, Gerald W. *Barrax revived the triannual journal and its original vision in 1986 and continues as editor.

A typical issue offers *essays, short fiction, *poetry, and reviews, and occasionally includes a dramatic work and a *bibliography on a specific author or subject. The important contribution of *Obsidian II* results from its balanced selection of creative works by and scholarship on English-speaking Africans worldwide, a presentation reflecting the rich diversity within the African diaspora. The journal receives a strong recommendation among professional bibliographers for academic collections supporting American, African American, and Third World literature programs and for all Black Studies libraries.

[*See also* Periodicals; Publishing.]

—Gregory S. Jackson

OCCOMY, MARITA BONNER. *See* Bonner, Marita.

OCTOROON. *See* Mulatto.

OFFORD, CARL RUTHVEN (b. 1910), novelist, short story writer, and journalist. Carl Ruthven Offord moved from his native Trinidad to New York City in 1929 and worked at a variety of jobs to support his acting career. He studied *drama, writing, and painting at the New School for Social Research. In 1943, his first book, *The White Face,* was published. Like the *novels of his contemporaries Richard *Wright, Chester *Himes, William *Attaway, and Ann *Petry, *The White Face* depicts the physical and psychological *violence spawned by racism and poverty. Chris Woods, like other African American protagonists from the *slave narratives to the present, flees the South to save his life but finds the North a hostile refuge. Unlike many literary fugitives, however, Chris flees with his wife and one of their children. In Harlem, Chris falls victim to fascist ideologies that fuel his rage but not his intellect, that persuade him to see his wife as another enemy, and that send him to prison for attacking a Jewish lawyer. While there is ample evidence that *The White Face* seriously explores the destructive effects of racism upon personal and public relationships, most critics followed the lead of Diana Trilling who praised the book as a "sociological report" about the influence of fascist agents in Harlem. After a two-year stint in the army, Offord tried several business ventures while continuing to write. His second novel, *The Naked Fear* (1954), explores the obverse side of *The White Face* when George and Amy Sutton, a white couple, flee to a black ghetto where George reverses his declining fortunes, a transformation that includes losing his phobia against blacks. Critics and scholars have generally ignored this book and Offord apparently turned his attention to other ventures such as founding the weekly newspaper *Black American* and creating the Black American Film Festival.

—Frances Smith Foster

OLIVER, DIANE (1943–1966), naturalist southern black feminist writer. Diane Alene Oliver lived only twenty-two years, but she left a legacy of *short stories to earn her recognition. Born 28 July 1943, Oliver grew up in Charlotte, North Carolina, where her passage into adolescence coincided with the racial upheavals in the Charlotte-Mecklenburg school system. The Supreme Court ruled on *Brown* v. *Board of Education* in 1954, mandating desegregation of public schools. Oliver never capitulated to notions of racial inferiority and went on to graduate from West Charlotte High School.

In 1960, she enrolled at the University of North Carolina at Greensboro; that marked the beginning of an auspicious writing career. Oliver served as managing editor of *The Carolinian,* the campus newspaper; studied under poet Randall Jarrell; and also began to write short stories. A career break occurred when Oliver won the guest editorship for the June 1964 edition of *Mademoiselle* magazine in its contest to honor outstanding college writers. A year later, she published her first short story in the fall 1965 issue of *Red Clay Reader.* "Key to the City" provided Oliver with a scholarship in 1965 to the University of Iowa, where she enrolled in the Writers' Workshop.

Oliver portrays strong-willed, black women caregivers of her era. As abandoned wives or nurturing daughters, the women struggle to maintain family unity while oppressive social forces work to disintegrate it. They are determined women but subtle in their warfare, as the ironic titles of the works illustrate. These stylistics are evident when Oliver's stories are examined thematically rather than chronologically.

Oliver's first and third stories, "Key to the City" and "Neighbors," published in the spring 1966 issue of *Sewanee Review,* invoke the *migration theme of South to North when blacks looked to Chicago as the promised land. Once Nora Murray completes high school in Still Creek, Georgia, she sets her goal to attend college in the North. "Key to the City" centers on Nora's domestic duties: settling the house and preparing her siblings and working mother for the bus trip to Chicago. They trade one dead-end situation for another, arriving in Chicago only to learn that their husband-father has abandoned them and that they must immediately go on welfare.

"Neighbors" continues the regional theme of Chicago to show reality as a racist enclave in the stead of Oliver's predecessors, Richard *Wright and Lorraine *Hansberry. Oliver's story differs, however, by her focus on racial tensions during the era of busing. Eloise Mitchell, a twenty-year-old working girl, resides with her family in a Chicago Housing Project that borders a white district that has been targeted for court-ordered school integration. The conflict concerns the family's responses to the bombing of their home and the welfare of the six-year-old son who is the test case. Eloise dissolves family tension in the most unobtrusive manner by redirecting their fears to the mundane issue of breakfast. Her clever ruse contrasts the disruptive force of the historical moment at hand.

In her second and fourth stories, "Health Service" and "Traffic Jam," published in the November 1965 and July 1966 issues of *Negro Digest*, respectively, Oliver invokes a Faulknerian device. She invents the fictional southern community of Fir Town where Libby, Hal, and their children struggle against the racial oppression of whites. Libby is the reticent, central consciousness of both works who endures derision from both the black and white communities because Hal has abandoned her and their children. The main conflict of "Health Care" concerns Libby's trek to Fir Town with five hungry children all under the age of six in order for Meetrie, the eldest, to get an immunization shot for day camp. The daylong plight ends with no health care and loss of a day's wages. "Traffic Jam" extends the theme of humiliation to Libby's job as a *domestic where she daily endures insults from her white female employer for Hal's desertion of them. He returns unexpectedly after a year, but with an automobile instead of money. Libby accepts Hal and his symbol of manhood since she knows that their socioeconomic condition will remain unchanged with or without Hal's car.

Oliver was the daughter of William Robert and Blanche Rann Oliver of Charlotte, North Carolina. She prefigured the black feminist writers of the 1970s. A motorcycle-automobile collision on 21 May 1966 in Iowa took her life just days before graduation. The University of Iowa conferred Oliver's Master of Fine Arts degree posthumously.

• "Remembering Young Talent," *Negro Digest* (Sept. 1966): 88–89. "Oliver, Diane," *Afro-American Encyclopedia*, vol. 7, 1974, p. 1944. "Oliver, Diane," in *Black American Writers Past and Present*, vol. 2, ed. Theresa Gunnels Rush, 1975, p. 573. Mary Pratt, *The Imaginative Spirit*, 1988, p. 77.

—Virginia Whatley Smith

OPERA. The origin of opera rests with Renaissance attention to Greek theater where, it was known, declamation was intoned. The few extant examples of Greek music available to seventeenth-century Florentines could not be deciphered. As an alternative to authenticity, composers were encouraged to create uncomplicated harmonies reinforcing the dramatic nuances of the plays. Thus, opera was invented. The first masterwork of the genre appeared in 1607, with Monteverdi's *Orfeo*, ending with a dance of African derivation. Topics for many operas during the first two hundred years of their history were fashioned on mythology or ancient history, with settings not infrequently African.

The first known operas by a Black composer were those of the *Chevalier de* Saint-Georges (1749–1799), a native of Guadeloupe who spent his adult life as a Parisian dilettante, active in *music, fencing, and politics. Although his operas do not reflect Black subjects, he was colonel of the first all-Black regiment of the French army, among whose members was the father of Alexandre Dumas *père*, whose son's *Camille* (1848) became the literary basis for Verdi's *La traviata* six years later.

Opera compositions by other non-American Black composers included several figures, particularly in Nigeria, none less important than Antônio Carlos Gomes (1836–1896) of Brazil. His works (many first admiringly received at Milan's Teatro alla Scala) were based on race relations. These often appeared in international repertoires and one, *Lo schiavo* ("The Slave"), encouraged Brazil to renounce *slavery.

National dialects of opera by 1750 gave rise to the British ballad opera wherein contemporary plots, currently popular musical styles, and spoken dialogue exhibit the roots of modern-day *musicals.

African American opera composers (who have not always distanced themselves significantly from the musical) began to appear in the nineteenth century, and included Edmond Dédé (1827–1903), Lucien Lambert (1828–1878), Gussie Davis (1864–1899), and Harry Freeman (1869–1954). The first opera composer to secure a degree of success was William Grant *Still (1895–1978), who routinely included racial themes in his work. His principal librettist was his wife, Verna Arvey (of Russian-Jewish extraction), although Langston *Hughes worked with Still, as well as some non-Black opera composers (e.g., Kurt Weill). The plots of the next generation came from the period of nondiscrimination, when even the music only rarely reflected the ethnic or folkloric, as in the operas of Ulysses Kay (1917–1995) and Julia Perry (1924–1979). That was not the case with Clarence White (1879–1960), whose *Ouanga* (1932) uses the Haitian setting of librettist John Frederick Matheus, or with Shirley *Graham (1907–1977), wife of W. E. B. *Du Bois. Few of these works secured more than an initial production.

The new wave of nationalism began in the 1970s and includes operas by T. J. Anderson (b. 1928) and Valerie Capers (b. 1937). Two works appear to have distinct promise for standard repertoires: *Frederick Douglass* by Dorothy Moore (completed in 1985 to her own libretto), and *X: The Life and Times of Malcolm X*, set by Anthony Davis to the libretto of his sister, Thulani, which premiered in 1986 in New York. The same potential is expected for *Blake* by Leslie Adams (libretto by Daniel Mayers), which had not yet been produced as of early 1996, and in-progress works by other major contemporaries.

• John Duncan, "Negro Composers of Opera," *The Negro History Bulletin* 29 (Jan. 1966): 79–80, 93. Dominique-René de

Lerma, *The Bibliography of Black Music*, 4 vols., 1981–1984. Eileen Southern, *Biographical Dictionary of Afro-American and African Musicians*, 1982. Eileen Southern, *The Music of Black Americans*, 1983. John Gray, *Blacks in Classical Music: A Bibliographical Guide to Composers, Performers, and Ensembles*, 1988. —Dominique-René de Lerma

Opportunity. *Opportunity*, subtitled "A Journal of Negro Life," was from 1923 to 1949 the monthly magazine of the National Urban League and a leading promoter and publisher of *Harlem Renaissance writing. "Not Alms, but Opportunity," the Urban League's slogan, exemplified both Chicago sociologist Charles S. Johnson's high editorial standards and the openings he created for *New Negro writers. Like the league, *Opportunity* originally studied and aided the "Great *Migration" of southern blacks to northern cities, but its cultural mission expanded to feature reviews of African American art and literature and works by writers Claude *McKay, Countee *Cullen, Eric *Walrond, Gwendolyn *Bennett, Georgia Douglas *Johnson, and Langston *Hughes. *Opportunity* under Charles Johnson also sponsored events: literary contests, awards dinners, and the 1924 "Writers Guild" dinner that convened two generations of African American writers with white publishers. The annual contest, begun in 1924, was announced in an editorial "confined to Negro contestants" and "designed to foster a market" for writing that "shakes itself free of deliberate propaganda and protest"; it counted among its judges well-known black and white editors and authors, and among the winners were Hughes, Cullen, Arna *Bontemps, and Zora Neale *Hurston, whose entries *Opportunity* published. With peak circulation of eleven thousand, *Opportunity* was never self-supporting like the *Crisis*; when Carnegie Corporation patronage discontinued, Johnson moved to Fisk University and was replaced by Elmer Carter, whose editorship stressed "sociological and economic aspects of the Negro's relation to American life." After becoming a quarterly in 1943, *Opportunity* ceased publication in 1949, but its glory years had, in Carter's words, brought together "a brilliant galaxy of men and women of both races."

[*See also* Newspaper Columns; Periodicals; Publishing.]

• Patrick J. Gilpin, "Charles S. Johnson: Entrepreneur of the Harlem Renaissance," in *The Harlem Renaissance Remembered*, ed. Arna Bontemps, 1972, pp. 215–246. Chidi Ikonné, *From Du Bois to Van Vechten: The Early New Negro Literature, 1903–1926*, 1981. —Craig Howard White

ORAL TRADITION. *See* Folklore; Literary History; Oratory.

ORATORY. One of the great paradoxes of American history is that the people who were violently severed from their African languages and forbidden to learn to read or write in English became the progenitors of the most fertile, distinctively American traditions of *music and oratory. Like the *blues and *jazz, African American oratory is rooted in the vernacular and develops stylistically through a call-response in-

teraction between the speaker and his/her audience. Although orators have ranged from agitators for violent revolution to advocates of moral suasion to practitioners of conciliatory "Uncle Tomism," African American oratory is fundamentally a rhetoric of revolt against *slavery and white supremacy. No understanding of African American literature is possible without recognition of the richness, vitality, and centrality of the oral tradition.

Documents dated before the Revolutionary War testify to slaves petitioning for freedom, and by the late eighteenth century numerous enslaved orators were denouncing slavery. Of the few extant texts written by these protesters, the most remarkable is Olaudah *Equiano's *The Interesting Narrative of the Life of Olaudah Equiano, or Gustavus Vassa, the African* (1789), which includes excerpts of speeches he delivered on multiple economic and political issues.

African American oratory came of age in the antebellum period (1830–1860), when American slaves developed the most comprehensive analyses of slavery ever recorded in the history of humanity from the perspective of the enslaved. In the early 1830s, antislavery societies (both black and white) upsurged in militancy and membership. By sponsoring conventions, *periodicals, and lecturers, African American abolitionists cultivated the conditions in which oratory could flourish. In 1831 William Lloyd Garrison began publishing the *Liberator*, a powerful white abolitionist journal, and his organization began hiring ex-slaves as lecturers to provide anecdotal, visual evidence in support of the speeches of white orators. In the same year, one of the most controversial orators in American history, Nat *Turner, led a violent slave revolt in Southampton County, Virginia.

Despite the editorial interventions that compromise "The Confessions of Nat Turner" (Thomas R. Gray interviewed Turner in prison and published his sensationalistic "Confessions" in November 1831) and despite signs of religious mania, Nat Turner's power as an orator and political analyst is evident in his narrative. While Turner terrified most whites, he inspired many blacks, including Frederick *Douglass, the greatest African American orator of the nineteenth century. Although Douglass changed history through the word rather than the sword and operated throughout his life as an agent of moral suasion, he often aligned himself rhetorically with revolutionaries such as Turner, Toussaint *L'Ouverture, and Patrick Henry. Even as a child, Douglass understood that the words and deeds that alarmed whites often advanced the position of blacks.

Douglass's formal career as an orator was launched by William Lloyd Garrison, who used Douglass on the abolitionist lecture circuit. Douglass's oratorical style pervades his first *autobiography, *Narrative of the Life of Frederick Douglass* (1845). After several years during which his rhetorical skills continued to surge, Douglass rebelled against the constraints of Garrison, who wanted his black orators solely to relate the "facts" of slavery, leaving the "philosophy" to whites. An advocate of women's rights as well as African American liberation, Douglass delivered countless speeches (many of which he published) dissecting American hypocrisy and calling for genuine democracy. Douglass sustained his verbal prowess as a public orator, writer, agitator, and diplomat until his death in 1895.

Among dozens of accomplished abolitionist orators, Sojourner *Truth is also particularly noteworthy. Although Truth could not write, her speech "Ain't I a Woman?" has become a classic of American literature through multiple transcriptions in prose and poetry. In the antebellum period, it was virtually impossible for a woman to earn a living as a public speaker. Far from sponsoring women as lecturers, male-run antislavery societies often forbade women to speak. At the same time, women-run antislavery societies and women's rights organizations often discriminated against black women. Not even an intellectual as verbally skilled as Harriet A. *Jacobs could find work as a public speaker; she had to support herself by working as a *domestic, even after publication of her extraordinary autobiography, *Incidents in the Life of a Slave Girl (1861). A few African American women managed to survive as itinerant preachers, and a handful received occasional public speaking invitations, some internationally (Mary *Prince, Ellen *Craft, Sarah Parker Remond). In this context, when Sojouner Truth rose amid a racist meeting, bared a breast, and dramatically repeated, "Ain't I a woman?!" she articulated both the rage at cultural exclusion and the pride in endurance, accomplishment, and physicality that have characterized African American women's oratory, music, and literature ever since.

In the late nineteenth century Booker T. *Washington assumed oratorical preeminence. He began lecturing in the 1870s and by the end of his career had delivered thousands of speeches throughout the United States and in Europe. While advocating manual labor for the masses of African Americans, Washington built his own power base through oratory. The speech that secured his fame, winning "hysterical enthusiasm" from audiences and newspapers but incurring challenge from African American intellectuals such as W. E. B. *Du Bois, was the *"Atlanta Exposition Address," delivered at the Cotton States Exposition in Atlanta in 1895. Washington argued that blacks and whites should work together like fingers in a hand: economically aligned but socially separate. Some critics argue that Washington's rhetoric bespoke soothing flattery toward whites and self-interested arrogance toward blacks. Others praise Washington as an effective rhetorical strategist who astutely judged how to overcome the post-Reconstruction racist backlash. Hundreds of his speeches survive in manuscript form at the Library of Congress and dozens have been published, but his influence endures primarily through his autobiography, *Up from Slavery (1901), written in his distinctive oratorical style (preaching the gospel of the toothbrush and salvation through brick-laying).

The renaissance of African American culture that occurred in Harlem, Chicago, Kansas City, and elsewhere in the 1920s is characterized more by achievements in music, visual arts, *theater, literature, and *journalism than in oratory, but the words of preachers, teachers, and political messiahs (most importantly, the West Indian Marcus *Garvey) electrified millions of African Americans. Artists continually paid tribute to the rich oral tradition that gave them birth. The musical texture of African American oratory is made tangible in the voices of such poets as Langston *Hughes and James Weldon *Johnson. Whether members of the *talented tenth speaking for racial uplife or advocates of marxist revolution, orators appear as pivotal agents of change in narratives such as Jessie Redmon *Fauset's Plum Bun (1928), Arna *Bontemps's *Black Thunder (1936), and Richard *Wright's *Uncle Tom's Children (1938). In contrast, Zora Neale *Hurston, the daughter of a Baptist preacher, cultivated a profound, humorous skepticism about oratory. In *Their Eyes Were Watching God (1937), Hurston shows that persuasive speakers like Joe Starks often use their rhetorical skills to gain unjust power—sexually, economically, and socially. Her heroine Janie must resist Joe's speechifying in order to claim her own power, voice, and selfhood.

In their most spectacular verbal feats, mid-twentieth-century African American writers roundly satirized religious and political orators. Cruelly injured by religious rhetoric as a child, Richard Wright as an adult also grew disillusioned with the rote oratory and intellectual repression of the Communist Party (see *Black Boy, 1945, and American Hunger, 1971). James *Baldwin exposed both the beauty and the sadism of church oratory in his autobiographical *novel, *Go Tell It on the Mountain (1953). And in what is arguably the most important post–World War II American novel, *Invisible Man (1952), Ralph *Ellison lambastes the self-serving ambitions of orators, from a Booker T. Washington facsimile to street preachers to communist agitators. For the well-intentioned invisible man, oratorical ambitions prove dangerous; public speaking always turns into a battle royal in which the young men who think they are players end up punching bags in reality.

Despite the disillusionment of literary figures, African American verbal achievement ascended unparalleled heights after World War II. The *civil rights movement of the 1950s and 1960s was fueled by a resurgence of oratory surpassing even the abolitionist period. Among hundreds of gifted orators, the most dynamic were Martin Luther *King, Jr., and *Malcolm X. Although both were assassinated at the peak of their intellectual and political powers, their rhetorical legacies continue to permeate American culture. Whether studied as literature (The *Autobiography of Malcolm X, 1965; *"I Have a Dream," 1963) or listened to on audio- and videotape, the voices of Martin and Malcolm continue to captivate and inspire.

The exhilarating explosion of African American culture since 1970 has produced far too many intellectual, musical, literary, and artistic testaments to the fertility of oratory to even begin listing the major figures, but Nobel-laureate Toni *Morrison must be mentioned. Like numerous predecessors (for example, James Weldon Johnson in "The Creation" and

God's Trombones, 1927), Morrison achieves poetic force by intertwining African American vernacular with biblical language. Her fiction often transposes biblical verses into African American history and jazz rhythms, but her most powerful use of oratory occurs in *Beloved* (1987) when *Baby Suggs, holy woman, preaches a sermon exhorting her community to love themselves and cherish their bodies in a world that would just as soon see them silenced, mutilated, and murdered. Resonating with Sojourner Truth's energy, Morrison's linguistic embrace of embodiment and affirmation of fleshly particularity is a pinnacle achievement of feminist, African Americanist oratory.

[*See also* Antislavery Movement; Sermons and Preaching; Woman's Era.]

• Carter G. Woodson, ed., *Negro Orators and Their Orations*, 1925. Arthur L. Smith, ed., *Language, Communication, and Rhetoric in Black America*, 1972. Eric J. Sundquist, *To Wake the Nations: Race in the Making of American Literature*, 1993.
—Kari J. Winter

OSBEY, BRENDA MARIE (b.1957), poet. Brenda Marie Osbey, born in New Orleans in 1957, has roots in Creole culture that run deep and give her work a haunting sense of place. No one since Walker Percy has made more memorable music out of the names of the city's streets and the people who throng them. Her poetry offers more than a slice of local color, however, for the metropolis she summons up quickly and magically becomes a backdrop for a display of the ambiance of the black feminine mind. Her women lead lives that often erupt in violence and sometimes end with madness. But alongside all this—and often because of it—we find a riveting poignance and searing beauty.

Osbey has said that her poetry forms a kind of cultural biography and geography of Louisiana, but one finds influences from her travels and sojourns elsewhere. She attended Dillard University, Université Paul Valéry at Montpéllièr, France, and received an MA from the University of Kentucky. She has taught at Dillard and the University of California at Los Angeles, and currently teaches at Loyola University in New Orleans. She has received several awards, including the Academy of American Poets' Loring-Williams Prize, an Associated Writing Program Award, and a National Endowment for the Arts Fellowship. Osbey has been a fellow of the Fine Arts Work Center at Provincetown, the Kentucky Foundation for Women, the MacDowell Colony, the Millay Colony, and the Bunting Institute, Harvard University. She has published three volumes of poetry, *Ceremony for Minneconjoux* (1983), *In These Houses* (1988), and *Desperate Circumstance, Dangerous Woman* (1991), and has just completed *All Saints*, a tribute to mythic New Orleaneans and a rich tapestry of the city's history.

Osbey's stunning first collection of poetry offered up the voices and visions of women through a series of vignettes, each framing and telling a story. One sees a fusion of incidents, remembrances, and details that uncoils in a disciplined way, yet somehow remains shrouded in mystery. Accordingly, these po-

ems possess a kind of uncanny tension, as she navigates between the rational and unexplainable. Her saturation in the Afro-Caribbean ambiance of New Orleans's Faubourgs (neighborhoods)—especially Marigny and Tremé—enables Osbey to plunge the reader into the eerie world of the Bahalia women, with their roots and tamborines, to introduce African Gods on the bankettes of the city. The central story of Lenazette of Bayou La Fouche and her Choctaw lover, as narrated to her daughter Minneconjoux, produces a murder; in another poem a woman writes letters to a man long dead; Ramona Veagis "falls off the world" and sits in a chair that erupts from a bathtub full of water. These tumbles into madness arrest and amaze, but also provoke a discomforting set of queries about the relation of madness and beauty, sanity and lies.

Osbey's next collection, *In These Houses*, continued her exploration of these women called "Madhouses," often merging them with swift "easy" women who Circe-like lure men into disaster, men like Diamond, who hangs himself out of desperate love for careless Reva. But there is also Thelma Picou, who runs out naked to eat dirt, crazed with the oppressive dominance of "Darling Henry"; Little Eugenia's Hispanic lover kills her when he mistakes her for lost diamond mines. Over and over again, characters end up in "infirmary," or Jackson, the state institution for the insane. Osbey appends a glossary of Louisiana ethnic expressions and place names, in part an indication of her growing awareness of herself as a kind of Virgil leading the Dante-like reader into "unknown realms." In many of these spectral poems the narration shifts without warning, from the man to the woman, the mother to the daughter, the sane to the insane. But if the reader sometimes loses his or her mooring, the author never does.

Osbey has been influenced by the work of Jean *Toomer in particular, but also by Robert *Hayden, the relatively unknown New Orleans poet Marcus Christian, and the music of Buddy Bolden, Dinah Washington, and Sarah Vaughan.

Her women reflect all ages: "Consuela" grows out of a girl's ring-game song, while "The Old Women on Burgundy Street" hymns an ode to learned resignation. "House of Bones," however, operates in the realm of abstractions, putting forth a recipe for a spiritual dwelling whose construction nevertheless proceeds, in Osbey's alchemy, visibly before you.

Desperate Circumstance, Dangerous Woman: A Narrative Poem was a new departure for Osbey, a single, long, richly evocative story. Ms. Regina, the hoodoo woman of the earlier collection, reappears here, ministering to the magnetically attractive narrator Marie Calcasieu ("Screaming Eagle"), who can "walk" in men's blood, especially Percy's. The Faubourg Marigny setting provides a tale for everything, as we gaze at the life of the quarter and see the bits of history in the debris of the daily. Every detail of life here is ritualistic, spiritual, and embued with meaning, even the empty rooms of Marie's house. The patterns of hoodoo assist here; Osbey sees them as a series of life principles. Generational influences interesect; Marie's life seems linked to the old story of her parents, to the old place out in Manchac swamp, and to the maroon people who live nearby.

Osbey's work in the mid-1990s, *All Saints*, continues her exploration of Louisiana's Creole–African American culture and features a number of meditations on historical and legendary figures.

• Violet Harrington Bryan, "Evocations of Place and Culture in the Works of Four Contemporary Black Louisiana Writers: Brenda Osbey, Sybil Kein, Elizabeth Brown Guillory, and Pinkie Gordon Lane," *Louisiana Literature Review* 4.2 (1987): 49–80. Brenda Marie Osbey, interview by John Lowe, in *The Future of Southern Letters*, 1995, pp. 93–118.

—John Lowe

OTTLEY, ROI (1906–1960), foreign correspondent, journalist, and author. Roi Ottley was born in New York City and educated at St. Bonaventure College, the University of Michigan, and St. John's School of Law. He studied playwriting at Columbia University, article writing at the City College of New York, and Negro folk literature under James Weldon *Johnson at New York University. However, at St. John's he decided writing would be his life's work. He began this career at the *Amsterdam Star-News* in Harlem, where he worked for seven years as, successively, a reporter, columnist, and editor. Following this period, he became a freelance writer for the following magazines: *New York Times, Liberty, Mercury, Ebony, Common Ground, Travel, Colliers, The Nation,* and *New Republic.* He became a foreign correspondent for *Liberty, PM* newspaper, the *Pittsburgh Courier,* and the Overseas News Agency. Ottley was the first African American to be employed as a working war correspondent for a nationally known magazine and a major white daily newspaper. He later became a reporter for the *Chicago Tribune* and broadcasted reports for both the Columbia Broadcasting System and the British Broadcasting System. In 1943, he served as publicity director for the National CIO War Relief Committee.

Ottley reported on such events as the Normandy Invasion, the hanging of Mussolini, and the Arab-French conflict in Syria. He interviewed important Allied political leaders and such personalities as Pope Pius XI, Governor Talmadge of Georgia, and Samuel Green, Grand Dragon of the Ku Klux Klan. At the *Chicago Tribune,* he wrote series on the migration of African Americans from the agricultural South to the industrial North and its impact, the voting trends among African Americans, and the war. Topics in the latter series included the plot to remove all African American soldiers from occupied Germany, the desire of the African American to fully participate in the war, the absence of race problems when African Americans were allowed full participation, and the stellar performance of the African American soldier. Additionally, he wrote articles on African American achievers in Chicago, such as Dr. Philip C. Williams, the first African American to be admitted to the Chicago Gynecological Society.

Based on his travels, observations, and interviews, Ottley wrote four books, contributed satirical short stories to *Negro Digest,* and at the time of his death was completing his first novel. His first book, *New World A-Coming: Inside Black America* (1944), presents the African American's history, problems, and hopes. It appeared a few weeks after a wave of race riots; this helped catapult it to best-seller status. According to Ottley, the way in which the African American is responded to will determine the way in which the world will heed America. It was published in Brazil and England as *Inside Black America.* He became the first African American to be published in the Houghton Mifflin Life-in-America series, was recognized for his contribution to interracial understanding by both the *Chicago Defender* and the Schomburg Library, and became the first African American journalist to receive a Rosenwald Fellowship. He won the Peabody Award for his radio dramatization *New World A-Coming,* a series designed to promote racial harmony. Following his overseas tour, he returned to the United States to work on his history of the African American's search for equality in America, *Black Odyssey: The Story of the Negro in America* (1948), which grew out of interviews and records in both America and Europe. This work, which details the origin of African American *slavery and other historical occurrences, is marked by its fusion of individuals and events, an emphasis upon the human aspect of history without the omission of facts. His third book, *No Green Pastures* (1951), which was published in England in 1952, cautions the reader not to believe that European racial tolerance and lack of color prejudice are realities, and the African American not to consider Ottley's European treatment as typical. His final book, *Lonely Warrior: The Life and Times of Robert S. Abbott* (1955), is the *biography of Robert Sengstacke Abbott, a multifaceted and often contradictory individual, the founder and editor of the *Chicago Defender.* Abbott created a channel through which individuals could speak out on the African American's behalf; lived and wrote history; called for the destruction of American race prejudice; established the Bud Billiken page in the *Defender,* devoted to issues of interest to young people; loved his race; and is considered by many to have initiated the modern African American press.

[*See also* Journalism.]

• "Roi Ottley Dies; Wrote on Negro," *New York Times,* 2 October 1960, 84.

—Helen R. Houston

Our Nig. The year 1859 was a year of important "firsts" for African American women's writing. Frances Ellen Watkins *Harper's short story "The *Two Offers" appeared, and Harriet E. *Wilson's *Our Nig* became the first *novel by an African American to be published in the United States. Wilson addressed race relations in the North. She extended the *slave narrative's attack on chattel relations below the Mason-Dixon line by offering a scathing revelation of northern racism and a forceful critique of the then-sacred realm of domesticity.

The hybrid form of *Our Nig* reflects the multi-pronged nature of Wilson's critiques. While a quiet debate has emerged about how to classify *Our Nig,* critics agree that Wilson blends aspects of sentimental fiction, *autobiography, and slave narratives. Wilson opens her tale with the seduction of "lonely Mag Smith . . . alone and inexperienced . . . as she merged into womanhood, unprotected, uncherished, uncared for." Her language mirrors, or perhaps parodies, the conventional seduction tale—the isolated young maiden, without a loving family to guide her, falls prey to "the voice" of her ravisher who then leaves her to her fate. Yet, rather than dying, Mag marries a black man in order to survive. While the child born in her seduction narrative dies, her second child, *Frado, lives; it is Frado's story that Wilson narrates.

Throughout the text Wilson makes it clear that Frado's life is based on her own. Indeed, Barbara White has corroborated almost all of the details concerning the Bellmonts, whose nonfictional name is Hayward. Wilson's title itself, *Our Nig, or Sketches of a Free Black in a Two Story White House, North, Showing that Slavery's Shadows Fall Even There; by "Our Nig,"* both modifies the common form of slave narrative titles (*Narrative of the Life of . . .*) and stresses its own autobiographical nature; *Our Nig* is written by "Our Nig." Likewise, in her closing pages, after referring to "my narrative," Wilson pleads for assistance from her readers, as she further establishes the autobiographical relation to the story she tells.

Wilson's ironic use of "our nig" ties the novel to the slave narrative form as well and shows that others call her this to claim her. In appended letters—themselves a standard convention of slave narratives—readers also find autobiographical confirmation. Margareta Thorn describes Wilson as "a slave, in every sense of the word." After Frado's father dies, her mother abandons the six year old at her wealthier and ill-reputed New Hampshire neighbors'; soon christened "nig," she is showed how her chores are *"always* to be done . . . any departure to be punished by a whipping."

In the Bellmont house, the principal source of abuse is "Mrs. B.," whose uncontrollable rage parallels depictions of the jealous southern mistress who beats and torments the master's illegitimate offspring. John Bellmont's ostensible affection for Frado, but virtual refusal to stand up to his (metaphorically wronged) wife, points to his symbolic status as a neglectfully benign slave father.

In the final chapters, Frado leaves the Bellmonts and then gets married. Frado's husband's actions echo Mr. Bellmont's—he is a poor protector and also abandons Frado, whose health is broken after years of overwork and beatings. Significantly, despite their legitimate marriage, like Frado herself, their boy is the son of an illegitimate partner. Thomas Wilson is a freeborn man who poses as a slave to lecture for the abolitionists; it is Wilson's need to provide for her son alone that drives her to write a metaphorical slave narrative.

Our Nig has been derided for its affiliations with sentimentality—a genre that asserts a woman's sphere is ruled by affection, love, and submissiveness. Yet arguably Wilson advances the most forceful critique of northern domesticity in nineteenth-century black women's fiction. As an indentured servant, Wilson reveals that when one considers *race and *class relations, abuse is perpetuated by women and that domesticity is violent. Moreover, in *Our Nig*, violence itself is domesticated. Whipping in *slavery is displayed publicly; Mrs. Bellmont tortures Frado privately, in the kitchen, near the hearth. The novel becomes markedly more violent while Frado is within the "two story white house, North," the symbol of true womanhood. In the first novel written by an African American woman, Wilson draws upon different generic conventions to create her own form and exposes multiple layers of northern hypocrisy.

• Elizabeth Ammons, "Stowe's Dream of the Mother Savior: *Uncle Tom's Cabin* and American Women Writers Before the 1920s," in *New Essays on Uncle Tom's Cabin*, ed. Eric Sundquist, 1986, pp. 155–195. Hazel Carby, *Reconstructing Womanhood: The Emergence of the Afro-American Woman Novelist*, 1987, pp. 40–61. Barbara Christian, "Somebody Forgot to Tell Somebody Something: African American Women's Historical Novels," in *Wild Women in the Whirlwind: Afra-American Culture and the Contemporary Literary Renaissance*, eds. Joanne Braxton and Andree McLaughlin, 1990, pp. 326–341. David Ames Curtis and Henry Louis Gates, Jr., "Establishing the Identity of the Author of *Our Nig*," in *Wild Women in the Whirlwind: Afra-American Culture and the Contemporary Literary Renaissance*, eds. Joanne Braxton and Andree McLaughlin, 1990, pp. 48–69. P. Gabrielle Foreman, "The Spoken and the Silenced in *Incidents in the Life of a Slave Girl* and *Our Nig*," *Callaloo* 13 (Spring 1990): 313–324. Barbara White, "Our Nig and the She-Devil: New Information about Harriet Wilson and the Bellmont Family," *American Literature* 65.1 (Mar. 1993): 19–52.   —P. Gabrielle Foreman

P

PAGEANTS. *See* Performances and Pageants.

PAN-AFRICANISM is generally viewed as a political ideology and social movement exemplified by Ghanaian president Kwame Nkrumah's post-independence government. Although primarily political in its thrust, Pan-Africanism has far-reaching implications—more as a current running through traditionally defined literary movements than as a movement in itself. The idea of one African people involved in a global struggle to reconnect with a core culture constitutes its grounding axis. The term originated within African diaspora cultures in the United States and the Caribbean during the early years of this century, but the concept is linked to the historical phenomenon of African enslavement and the resultant global dispersal of African peoples. These two factors have contributed significantly to the duration and the very broad cultural scope of the Pan-African ideal. They also account for differences in perspective with regard to the genesis, character, and evolution of that ideal.

One perspective places the beginning of Pan-Africanism with the minority of imperial African leaders opposed to the slave trade, and with the earliest known repatriation movements, dating from the eighteenth century, which worked to restore a disrupted sense of African *identity. Such inclusionist perspectives see Pan-Africanism as a quality or intentionality that can be found in every implicit or explicit connection with an African ideal.

In another view, Pan-Africanism in its modern form emerges from nineteenth-century evangelical movements in Africa and the series of five Pan-African conferences that spanned the first half of the twentieth century. St. Clair Drake distinguishes "traditional" Pan-Africanism from its contemporary expression by arguing that the traditional phase evolved into complex forms after the mid-1950s when African independence, subsequent military coups in the newly formed nations, and the militarization of the struggle in South Africa extinguished many people's hopes for an "uncomplicated united struggle."

The search for Pan-Africanist currents in African American literature reveals a fairly consistent flow of challenges to dominant aesthetic norms. Pan-Africanist currents are traceable in those works that withstand external pressure to segregate "art," social practice, and political praxis; works that, regardless of the explicit message of the text, have found ways to speak in the language of African dispersion and its consequences.

It is easy to connect Pan-Africanism in this way with the vast majority of literature produced by African-descended people from the earliest days of the global dispersion experience. One may find, for example, in aspects of Olaudah *Equiano's narrative and Phillis *Wheatley's *poetry those authors' self-conscious, albeit veiled, discourses of empowerment as African-descended people. Looking to social conditions and political events that serve as catalysts for creative response, one may find the work of individuals like W. E. B. *Du Bois of particular interest. His writing impacted and was affected by the decisive role he played in organizing the Second International Pan-African Congress in 1919. Du Bois's work stands for a period when African American and Caribbean writers were establishing models for creative response to the political and social realities of African peoples within the context of what might otherwise be viewed as purely political struggles.

The *Harlem Renaissance, a cultural arts movement centered in New York during the 1920s, also drew energy from the Pan-Africanist ideal. The "*New Negro" of that era was enriched by an awareness of deep cultural roots in Africa. During the 1930s in Paris, the *Negritude movement contributed its focus to the largely ignored cultural dimensions of the Pan-African ideal. Another *Black Arts movement emerged in several major American cities during the 1950s and 1960s, and was closely allied with the Black Power political movement. Poets such as LeRoi Jones (later Amiri *Baraka) revised prevailing aesthetic codes to ally them more closely with the lived political and social realities of African Americans involved in a global struggle.

During the post–civil rights era, the Pan-African current becomes more difficult to trace. In a society where concepts such as diversity and choice have become the hallmark, one finds that traditional Pan-African themes like African cultural identity connect in ever more complex ways to other themes that highlight difference as a mode of existence (i.e., *gender). As writers struggle with their creative representations, they do so in an intellectual climate of rapidly shifting theoretical paradigms, some of which directly challenge the core assumption of an African identity. These and other factors continue to complicate the evolution of Pan-Africanism since the 1950s. Nonetheless, the fact of dispersion continues to impact the lives of millions of people. Political and social struggles of the African diaspora go on, as writers find creative ways of relating this story to the world. In short, Pan-Africanism has not in any way outlived its usefulness, but it must find effective ways to keep pace with competing models if it is to continue to be perceived as an empowering response to both social and intellectual challenges facing Africa and its diaspora.

[*See also* Afrocentricity; Diasporic Literature.]

• St. Clair Drake, "Diaspora Studies and Pan-Africanism," in *Global Dimensions of the African Diaspora*, ed. Joseph E. Harris, 1982, p. 35. Michael Williams, "The Pan-African Movement," in *African Studies: A Survey of Africa and the African Diaspora*, ed. Mario Azevedo, 1993, pp. 169–181.

—JoAnne Cornwell

PAPA LaBAS is a major character in Ishmael *Reed's *novels *Mumbo Jumbo* (1972) and The *Last Days of Louisiana Red* (1974). Insofar as these books fit into the detective genre, Papa LaBas is a hoodoo investigator trying to solve crimes; but since these novels also are mysteries in the metaphysical sense, LaBas is, as Gerald Duff notes, a "cultural diagnostician and healer." Tracing his origins back to the plantation, W. E. B. *Du Bois in The *Souls of Black Folk* (1903) referred to such an individual as "interpreter of the Unknown," "supernatural avenger of wrong," and viewed him as the prototype of the preacher, the "most unique personality" developed by African Americans. On another level, Papa LaBas, like his Haitian counterpart Papa Legba, is descended from the West African deity known as Eshu/Elegbara, lord of transitions, conjoining the real with the unreal, a *trickster who is also a communicator. This last connection is especially important because, in *Mumbo Jumbo* and *Louisiana Red*, it is generally Papa LaBas who "runs the voodoo down" by providing crucial explanations and analyses.

If the Loop Garoo Kid (*Yellow Back Radio Broke-Down*, 1969) and *Raven Quickskill (*Flight to Canada*, 1976) are the alter egos of a youthful, combative Reed, Papa LaBas may be said to be Reed's imaginative counterpart of himself as spiritual elder statesman, wise but still acquiring wisdom, not impulsive in struggle but settled in for the long haul, resolutely rooted in the ancient traditions of his people.   —Robert Elliot Fox

PARKER, CHARLIE (1920–1955), also known as Bird or Yardbird, alto saxophonist and major figure in the development of bebop. The new *music known as "bebop" was based on experimentation with harmonic structures, but also possessed a strong political edge, which would make it the inspiration of numerous artists, black and white, who were looking for a means of confronting the sterility of Cold War culture. Charlie Parker's musicianship and skill as an improviser were unmatched, yet due to the exigencies of the jazz music business, he struggled to hold his life together. Parker was famous for his wit and thoughtfulness, but continued problems with drugs and failing physical and mental health led to his death in March 1955.

Parker's brilliance and irreverence made him as much of a legend as an important historical figure. His death led to the seemingly miraculous overnight appearance of the graffitti slogan "Bird Lives." For African American writers, and indeed for many American writers generally, Parker's life and death were resonant with the myth of the romantic artist who dies young, yet leaves an extraordinarily rich body of work behind. Some writers, like Bob *Kaufman, attempted to duplicate or imitate Parker's style in prose or *poetry, but more often than not it was the myth of Charlie Parker that captured the imagination of writers. Ralph *Ellison criticized this phenomenon in his essay "On Bird, Bird-Watching and Jazz," included in his *Shadow and Act* (1964). More positively, Parker's legend has led to his being memo-

rialized and celebrated in dozens of memoirs, poems, stories, and *novels.
[See also Jazz.]

• Robert Reisner, *Bird: The Legend of Charlie Parker,* 1972. Gary Giddins, *Celebrating Bird: The Triumph of Charlie Parker,* 1987.   —James C. Hall

PARKS, GORDON (b. 1912), photographer, journalist, essayist, autobiographer, biographer, novelist, poet, film director, screenwriter, and composer. Gordon Parks's first two publications—*Flash Photography* (1947) and *Camera Portraits: The Techniques and Principles of Documentary Portraiture* (1948)—while written primarily for the professional photographer, reveal an aesthetic and a social commitment that structures the astonishing diversity of his subsequent work. Embodying his conviction that the photographer must combine technical intelligence, especially in the use of light, with a sensitive response to people, both works are photographic portfolios representing a cross-section of American lives—rural and urban, wealthy and leisured, poor and laboring.

Frequently identified as a Renaissance man, given the range of his accomplishments and the variety of media he has used, Parks was also the first African American to work for *Life, Vogue,* the Office of War Information, and the Farm Security Administration and one of the first African Americans to write, direct, produce, and score a *film. While the commercial success of his work suggests he has fulfilled the American dream, a recognition of the demoralizing force of racism and poverty and the dignifying force of the struggle against these conditions underlies his entire creative output.

Parks grew up on a Kansas farm, where this defining dialectic was formed. As his autobiographical first *novel, The Learning Tree* (1963), and his subsequent *autobiographies demonstrate, here he learned to value his parents' hard work, compassion, integrity, and capacity for hope as well as to fear the brutality and perversity of personal and institutionalized racism. While the young hero of *The Learning Tree* is tormented by a series of deaths, from natural causes and from racist *violence, each of Parks's three autobiographies—*A Choice of Weapons* (1966), *To Smile in Autumn, A Memoir* (1979), *Voices in the Mirror, An Autobiography* (1990)—reviews these boyhood incidents, much as Frederick *Douglass returned to his experiences during *slavery in his three autobiographies. Parks's autobiographical works record his struggles first to survive and then to succeed in the white world; if he is able to record his relationships with well-known figures of this century, his *family relationships always remain paramount.

Set in New York City against a backdrop of labor unrest and an emerging socialism, World War I, and the depression, his nonautobiographical novel, *Shannon* (1981), is Dickensian in scope. Revealing America to be a racist and classist society, he describes the interdependent lives of Americans from differing racial and *class backgrounds. Although European immigrants in *Shannon* rise to attain enormous wealth, their wealth proves either corrupting or immaterial to their happiness, and although college-educated African American war heroes appear doomed by financial failure and injustice, they die with dignity.

Through the interrelation of words and photographs in several other works, Parks continues to reflect on dialectic differences in human life and to contemplate their resolution. Thus powerful black-and-white portraits illuminate *essays on African Americans prominent in the 1960s *civil rights movement and on a destitute Harlem family in *Born Black* (1971) as well as the story of Parks's personal involvement with a boy in a Brazilian slum in *Flavio* (1978). *Gordon Parks: A Poet and His Camera* (1968), *In Love* (1971), *Gordon Parks: Whispers of Intimate Things* (1971), and *Moments without Proper Names* (1975), however, experimentally juxtapose lyrical poems with impressionistic color photographs. Focusing on nature, romantic love, loneliness, beauty, childhood, aging, and death, both the photographic and poetic images suggest a view of life transcending economic and racial oppression. Given their various settings—Europe, Asia, North and South America—as well as their putative apolitical content, these images show Parks seeking a universal language. Yet, the explicit subject of the first section of *Moments without Proper Names* is the suffering of African Americans. His frequently reprinted poem "Kansas Land" concludes its catalog of pastoral images with an evocation of the violence and fear blacks have endured.

In his films—*The Learning Tree* (1968), *Shaft* (1971), *Shaft's Big Score* (1972), *The Super Cops* (1974), and *Leadbelly* (1976)—and in his ballet, *Martin* (1990), Parks integrates his multiple talents, writing the screenplay and/or the score for several of them. These works explore the African American male experience in addition to celebrating the African American ability to prevail—through violence and peaceful resistance, *music and love. In the mid-1990s Parks was at work on a *biography of the early-nineteenth-century British painter J. M. W. Turner, with whom he shares an interest in using light to reveal a complex world—one that includes slavery as well as multiple sources of beauty—more clearly.

• Martin H. Bush, *The Photographs of Gordon Parks*, 1983. Jane Ball, "Gordon Parks," in *DLB*, vol. 33, *Afro-American Fiction Writers after 1955*, eds. Thadious M. Davis and Trudier Harris, 1984, pp. 203–208. Deedee Moore, "Shooting Straight: The Many Worlds of Gordon Parks," *Smithsonian* 20.1 (Apr. 1989): 66–72, 74, 76–77. "Gordon Parks," in *Black Literature Criticism: Excerpts from Criticism of the Most Significant Works of Black Authors over the Past Two Hundred Years*, vol. 3, ed. James P. Draper, 1992, pp. 1551–1557. Elizabeth Schultz, "Dreams Deferred: The Personal Narratives of Four Black Kansans," *American Studies* 34.2 (Fall 1993): 25–52.
—Elizabeth Schultz

PASSING refers to the act of crossing the socially constructed "*color line" that separates white and black Americans, though the term has broad application for other ethnic or racial groups, as well as for categories of *gender, *sexuality, or *class. Racial passing has special importance for African American writers, who have used it as a theme that sheds light on the various meanings of *race, *identity, and color in the United States. While the depiction of passing in African American literature reflects the social reality of African Americans who have permanently or temporarily "crossed over" the color line, African American authors have also used passing as a narrative and ideological strategy in their work. Through the depiction of characters who pass, African American writers have satirized the values of white supremacy, explored the protective effects of "white" identity in an otherwise harsh or alienating world, expressed anxieties about social mobility predicated upon the "denial" of race, and voiced themes of pride or self-affirmation. While passing has usually been treated sentimentally in white American literature, African American writers have tended to treat the topic with greater psychological realism. Prominent African American fictional works about passing include Frank J. *Webb's *The Garies and Their Friends* (1857), Charles Waddell *Chesnutt's *The *House Behind the Cedars* (1900), James Weldon *Johnson's *The *Autobiography of an Ex-Colored Man* (1912), Walter *White's *Flight* (1926), Jessie Redmon *Fauset's *Plum Bun* (1928), Nella *Larsen's *Passing* (1929), and Charles R. *Johnson's *Oxherding Tale* (1982).

[See also Novel of Passing.]

• Hazel V. Carby, *Reconstructing Womanhood: The Emergence of the Afro-American Woman Novelist*, 1987.
—Gayle Wald

Passing. Nella *Larsen's second *novel, *Passing* appeared in 1929 at the peak of the *Harlem Renaissance. Many of its characters and occasions resemble other novels written during that era. Indeed, its working title, "Nig," alludes to *Nigger Heaven*, the novel by Larsen's friend and mentor Carl Van Vechten. *Passing* is more complex and ambitious than many of its predecessors, however, and this may account for the title change and for earning its author the distinction of being one of the first African American women to win a Guggenheim Fellowship for literature.

The central characters of *Passing* are Irene Redfield and Clare Kendry, two African Americans who look like Euro-Americans. These two women had been girlhood friends but separated for years before they accidentally meet when Clare is seated next to Irene in an expensive Chicago restaurant that only serves whites. Although both women are exploiting their appearance and *passing for white, for Irene this is an occasional indulgence. She has established an *identity as the doting mother of two sons, the wife of a prominent African American physician, and a supporter of appropriately conservative and uplifting community affairs. Clare on the other hand has married a successful white businessman, who not only believes she is white but deeply dislikes black people. From this accidental reunion, the two women's lives become entangled as Clare increasingly seeks opportunities to socialize with, and Irene reluctantly sponsors Clare's entrée into, the African American middle class. Clare's recklessness worries Irene because it threatens her carefully constructed white identity. But Irene also finds Clare's choices and the danger they entail both frightening and fascinating until she discovers that Clare is having an affair with her husband. Thus, when Clare's enraged husband rushes into one of these gatherings and in the confusion Irene reaches toward Clare and Clare suffers a fatal fall from the window, Irene's culpability is unclear.

Passing explores the relationships between appearance and reality, deception and unmasking, manipulation and imaginative management, aggression and self-defense. The novel's epigraph from Countee *Cullen's poem "Heritage" encourages one to read *Passing* as another in the genre that explores the ambiguity and contestations inherent in prevailing constructions of *race. When it was first published, many reviewers referred to the novel as a "tragedy," alluding to both its shocking ending and to its obvious similarities to the tragic *mulatto genre exemplified by works such as William Wells *Brown's *Clotel (1853). Larsen's examination of passing, however, is more in the tradition of Frances Ellen Watkins *Harper's Minnie's Sacrifice (1868) or James Weldon *Johnson's The *Autobiography of an Ex-Colored Man (1912) because it focuses more upon the psychological dimensions than upon the physical acts that the tragic mulatto novels portrayed. Most critics agree that Larsen's novel is also concerned with *class and *gender identities and the emotional and ethical consequences of their manipulation. Some such as Mary Helen Washington emphasize gender as well as race and argue that Larsen uses passing as a metaphor for "risktaking experiences," or lives lived without the communal support of other black women. Deborah E. McDowell and others have suggested that the text questions the safe and legitimate parameters of sex and flirts with the idea of lesbianism.

• Thadious M. Davis, *Nella Larsen, Novelist of the Harlem Renaissance,* 1994. Cheryl A. Wall, *Women of the Harlem Renaissance,* 1995.   —Frances Smith Foster

PATTERSON, LILLIE (b. 1920), biographer, fiction and nonfiction writer for young readers, teacher, library media services specialist, and Coretta Scott King Award winner. Lillie G. Patterson was raised on the island of Hilton Head, South Carolina, and earned a BS degree in education from Hampton Institute in Virginia and a second BS in library science from Catholic University in Washington, D.C. Since the publication of her first work, *Meet Miss Liberty* (1962), she has published twenty-four others. Patterson's output is unusually diverse, for her literary vision is to provide literature for young and intermediate readers on topics and within genres not readily available. She has been especially prolific with holiday theme-centered books. Her fictional works, including *The Grouchy Santa* (1979), *Haunted Houses on Halloween* (1979), *The Jack-o'Lantern Trick* (1979), *Janey, the Halloween Spy* (1979), and *Christmas Trick or Treat* (1979), are simple imaginative tales written in the *folklore tradition. Nonfiction works include *Halloween* (1963), *Birthdays* (1965), *Easter* (1966), *Lumberjacks of the North Woods* (1967), *Christmas*

Feasts and Festivals (1968), *Christmas in America* (1969), and *Christmas in Britain and Scandinavia* (1970). She has also edited a collection of *poetry entitled *Poetry for Spring* (1973).

With the exceptions of *Francis Scott Key* (1963), *Sequoyah: The Cherokee Who Captured Words* (1975), and *David, The Story of a King* (1985), Patterson's biographical contributions focus upon African American subjects. These include *Booker T. Washington* (1962), *Frederick Douglass: Freedom Fighter* (1965), *Martin Luther King, Jr.: Man of Peace* (1969), for which she won the 1970 Coretta Scott King Award, *Coretta Scott King* (1977), *Benjamin Banneker: Genius of Early America* (1978), *Sure Hands, Strong Heart: The Life of Daniel Hale Williams* (1981), *Martin Luther King, Jr. and the Freedom Movement* (1989), and *Oprah Winfrey: Talk Show Host and Actress* (1990).

In her African American works particularly, Patterson has made a genuine contribution to biography for young people in the intermediate (grades 4–6) range. With the exception of her most recent work on Martin Luther *King, Jr., she has chosen to highlight figures about whom relatively little has been written for the young at the time of publication. Her work is generally well researched, interesting to read, and in most cases includes bibliographies and indexes. Patterson takes a noncritical approach in that she does not delve into aspects of the lives of individual subjects that might evoke personal controversy. Yet, she avoids the pitfalls of early biographical tendencies to glorify the subject for the benefit of the young.

Patterson's overall literary presentation is contributory rather than pioneering in nature, but she should be regarded as an author whose informative and prolific output has made a clear contribution to informational literature, particularly for young people.

• Anne Commire, ed., "Patterson, Lillie G.," in *Something about the Author,* 1978, pp. 174–176. Helen E. Williams, *Books by African-American Authors and Illustrators for Children and Young Adults,* 1991. Barbara Rollock, "Patterson, Lillie G.," in *Black Authors and Illustrators of Children's Books,* 2d ed., 1992, p. 149.   —Karen Patricia Smith

PAUL D. In Toni *Morrison's *Beloved (1987), Paul D is one of six male slaves on Mr. Garner's Kentucky plantation ironically named Sweet Home. Paul D is described as a man with "peachstone skin; straight-backed. For a man with an immobile face it was amazing how ready it was to smile, or blaze or be sorry with you." Under Mr. Garner, a somewhat humane master, *slavery had been bearable; but when he dies, his brother and heir, schoolteacher, is brutal and inhumane. After Paul D's attempted escape is foiled, he is reduced to chattel, has his feet shackled, has a three-spoked collar placed on his neck and a bit placed in his mouth, and is tethered to a buckboard. Later sold, he spends eighty-six days on a chain gang after attempting to kill his new owner. He escapes during a torrential rain and eventually makes his way to Ohio.

When Paul D enters "124"—home of former Sweet Home slave *Sethe Suggs and her child Denver, and tormented by the ghost of baby Beloved, whom Sethe killed rather than see remanded to slavery—he immediately recognizes the ghost's presence and drives it out, only to have an older Beloved physically return and seduce him. Paul D falls in love with Sethe and becomes a support for her, but he abandons her and takes refuge in a church cellar when someone shows him the newspaper accounts of Sethe killing Beloved. He insults Sethe by implying she has acted as an animal—with four feet instead of two. Once the women of the community exorcise Beloved, he becomes sensitized to Sethe's plight and realizes that he had no right to judge her as he did, and he returns to 124 and once again becomes a comfort to her. The life of Paul D represents the continuing effort of African American men to overcome the malevolence of the slave past and a racist society.

• Wilfred D. Samuels and Clenora Hudson Weems, *Toni Morrison*, 1990. Trudier Harris, *Fiction and Folklore: The Novels of Toni Morrison*, 1991. Deborah Ayer Sitter, "The Making of a Man: Dialogic Meaning in *Beloved*," *African American Review* 26 (1992): 17–29. Trudier Harris, "Escaping Slavery but Not Its Images," in *Toni Morrison: Critical Perspectives Past and Present*, ed. Henry Louis Gates, Jr., and K. A. Appiah, 1993, pp. 330–341. Molly Abel Travis, "*Beloved* and Middle Passage: Race, Narrative and the Critic's Essentialism," *Narrative* 2.3 (Oct. 1994): 179–200.

—Betty Taylor-Thompson

PAYNE, DANIEL A. (1811–1893), minister, poet, historian, educator, and abolitionist. Long recognized as a leading nineteenth-century Christian activist and theologian, Daniel Payne's literary achievements are varied and equally important. From his childhood in Charleston, South Carolina, where he was born to free and deeply religious parents, through his long ministry with the African Methodist Episcopal (AME) Church and eventual presidency of Wilberforce University, Payne pursued a rigorous program of self-directed study. He began to write and teach at an early age, starting his first school in Charleston in 1829 when he was only nineteen years old, and teaching there until 1835, when the South Carolina legislature made it illegal to teach slaves to read or write. Forced to close his school, Payne moved to the North, where he published a collection of *poetry in 1850. In *The Pleasures and Other Miscellaneous Poems*, Payne included a poem heralding the emancipation of the West Indies in 1838, several poems concerning his family, and moving tributes to his wife and daughter after their deaths in the late 1840s. Much of Payne's poetry also expresses his concern for "moral purity" and "holy virtue." Payne was very active in the *temperance movement and other Christian efforts at social reform.

In 1888, the Publishing House of the AME Sunday School Union printed Payne's *autobiography, *Recollections of Seventy Years*. In this work Payne blends theology, personal experience, and political analysis. The autobiography provides a detailed account of important people and events in the antebellum African American abolitionist movement, the AME church, and African American activist communities nationwide through the extended Reconstruction years (1865–1888). Also a historian, Payne completed

his exhaustive two-volume *History of the African Methodist Episcopal Church* in 1891. A collection of his sermons was published posthumously in 1972 under the title *Sermons and Addresses, 1853–1891*.

In all of these works, readers can see the unique tensions present in Payne's dual commitments: first, to self-defined *freedom for African Americans, and second, to the spread of a form of "moral reform" that sometimes misapprehended the experience of non-Christians. For example, Payne supported missionary efforts to Africa by African American clergy but infused this support with the desire to convert "barbarous and savage men." At the same time, he helped found the Bethel Literary and Historical Association (1881), where he and other African American activists studied not only African American literature and *history but also celebrated the cultures of Africa in an effort described by some later scholars as Pan-Africanist and nationalist. Another interesting political tension is Payne's early involvement in the Philadelphia Vigilance Committee (1838–1844), where African Americans challenged the legal status quo of the country by assisting newly escaped fugitive slaves, tempered by his later apparently "assimilationist" claims for the legitimate authority of the U.S. government.

W. E. B. *Du Bois counted Payne among the most important African American leaders and also listed some of his literary work and sermons among the key documents of African American literary tradition. Payne's autobiography, especially, through its rhetorical blend of literary narrative, theology, and political observation, allows readers access to the challenging complexity of nineteenth-century African American culture.

[*See also* Literary Societies; Sermons and Preaching.]

• Benjamin Quarles, *Black Abolitionists*, 1969. Wilson Jeremiah Moses, *The Golden Age of Black Nationalism, 1850–1925*, 1978.

—Sharon Carson

PAYNTER, JOHN H. (1862–1947), memoirist and fiction writer. Graduating from Pennsylvania's Lincoln University in 1883, John H. Paynter judged his professional opportunities so limited by color that he chose to seek adventure in the navy. His first memoir, *Joining the Navy, or Abroad with Uncle Sam* (1895), includes a brief *autobiography and an unexceptional narrative of his two-year duty as a cabin boy aboard the USS *Ossippee* and the USS *Juniatu*. Although Paynter's impressions of maritime life and of the foreign places and peoples he encountered focus rarely on his status as an African American and often reproduce imperialist attitudes toward otherness, the 1911 edition of *Joining the Navy* features a one-page foreword by W. E. B. *Du Bois praising Paynter's "little contribution" for showing "a black man's experience in a great department of our American life." In contrast, Paynter's final memoir, *Horse and Buggy Days with Uncle Sam* (1943), bitterly protests the racial discrimination he suffered during his thirty-nine years as a messenger and clerk in the Treasury Department.

Fifty Years After (1940), another standard piece of *travel writing, describes Paynter's second journey abroad in 1934. The second part of *Fifty Years After* includes recollections of everyday life in Washington, D.C., especially in Old Georgetown.

Most of Paynter's maternal ancestors—the Edmonsons, one of the oldest African American families of Washington, D.C.—served as domestic servants for distinguished families of the district. Paynter's *historical novel, *Fugitives of the Pearl* (1930), offers a sentimental portrait of the widely acclaimed attempted escape aboard the schooner *Pearl* of seventy-seven slaves, several Edmonsons among them, from Washington, D.C., in 1848. The dramatic capture of the fugitives of the *Pearl* nearly caused a riot, and the affair won the attention of such abolitionists as Frederick *Douglass, William Lloyd Garrison, and Henry Ward Beecher. Before their freedom was secured, the middle-class Edmonsons had suffered the most harrowing experiences of chattel slaves, crowded and unprotected on slave ships, mistreated in slave pens, and humiliated on auction blocks.

Fugitives was noted in Hugh Gloster's *Negro Voices in American Fiction* (1948) as the first "genuine historical novel" by an African Americ n since World War I and part of a flowering of African American historical fiction in the 1930s. Reprinted in 1970, *Fugitives* has not been the subject of further commentary. *Fugitives* reflects Paynter's developing historical consciousness and the growing militance of African Americans of his time. It foregrounds the injustices done to African Americans, in spite of a national creed of democracy, and ennobles the spirit of revolt, suggesting that the arguments and sentiments underlying the *Pearl* incident in 1848 foreshadowed those that emerged with the Spanish-American War and World War I. In the end, Du Bois's foreword to *Joining the Navy* was justified, for Paynter's contribution proved more than little.

• WPA, *Washington: City and Capital*, 1937. Constance McLaughlin Green, *Washington*, 2 vols., 1962-1963.

—Cheryl Lester

PECOLA BREEDLOVE is the protagonist in Toni *Morrison's *The *Bluest Eye* (1970). An African American girl whose family life is in stark contrast to the image of perfection suggested in the epigraph from the primer that opens the *novel, Pecola's struggle is to be loved. She craves blue eyes, thinking that if she looked like the blue-eyed girls from storybooks, her parents, teachers, and boys would love her. Her tragedy is one that begins at home. Convinced of her ugliness, and finding no consolation from her parents—her mother works as a *domestic and seems to treasure her white employer's daughter more than her own, and her alcoholic father fights with her mother—Pecola is forced into isolation and fantasizes about escaping into whiteness. The narrator of the novel, Claudia McTeer, and her sister Frieda attempt to befriend Pecola when she comes to live with their family, after the Breedlove family has been put outdoors. Pecola's only real consolation comes from occasional visits to three *prostitutes who are the

only ones who give her any attention aside from Soaphead Church, the bootleg preacher, who out of compassion for her convinces her that he has given her blue eyes. Pecola's story ends with the premature death of her baby, her plunge into insanity, and the community's attempt to deny its role in her tragic demise. The narrator explains that the community is ultimately responsible for Pecola's fate because it has chosen to ignore its own warped values, distorted aesthetics, and obvious shortcomings and to scapegoat her instead.

[*See also* Double Consciousness; Identity; Mulatto; Passing.]

• Michael Awkward, *Inspiriting Influences: Tradition, Revision, and Afro-American Women's Novels*, 1989.

—Marilyn Sanders Mobley

PECULIAR INSTITUTION. *See* Slavery.

PEGGY. *See* Aun' Peggy.

PENNINGTON, JAMES W. C. (1807–1870), essayist and slave narrator. James William Charles Pennington was born into *slavery on the eastern shore of Maryland. At the age of four, he, his brother, and his mother were given to the son of his master, who moved to Washington County in the western part of the state. In his *slave narrative, *The Fugitive Blacksmith, or Events in the History of James W. C. Pennington* (1849), Pennington is particularly attentive to the effects of slavery on black children. Using the special abuses (lack of consistent parental attention, abusive white children, and brutal overseers) that slave children must endure as a gambit for his narrative, Pennington charted his development into an activist minister who witnessed, through word and deed, against slavery in the South and racism in the North.

Pennington escaped slavery in 1828. The next year he moved to Long Island, where he pursued an education in night school. Between 1829 and 1834 as a member of the "General Convention for the Improvement of the Free Colored People," Pennington was instrumental in efforts to improve the conditions of newly freed blacks of New York. His first book, *A Text Book of the Origin and History . . . of Colored People* (1841), was designed to meet the needs of teachers, such as himself, who were dedicated to the inspiration as well as instruction of African Americans.

From teaching Pennington's interests evolved into preaching. On 15 September 1838, Reverend Pennington officiated at the marriage of Anna Murray and Frederick *Douglass. During the 1840s and 1850s, Pennington held pastorates in African Congregational *churches in Newtown, Long Island; Hartford, Connecticut; and New York City. A few of his sermons and addresses were published as pamphlets. Pennington's fame as the author of *The Fugitive Blacksmith*, an international antislavery lecturer, and a New York City civil rights leader caused Harriet Beecher *Stowe to single him out in *Uncle Tom's Cabin* (1852) as an exemplary figure in the free African American community.

• William L. Andrews, *To Tell a Free Story: The First Century of Afro-American Autobiography, 1760–1865*, 1986.

—Charles E. Wilson, Jr.

PERFORMANCES AND PAGEANTS. African American literature's themes, metaphors, cadences, characters, plots, settings, and—in a few genres—structures are intimately intertwined with the many traditional forms of African American speech and *music. Consequently, Houston A. *Baker, Jr.'s *Black Literature in America* (1971) is just one of many *anthologies of African American literature that includes a sampling of folktales and folk songs in their chronicling of African American literature.

African American *poetry and prose often utilize such traditional conversational patterns as the dozens, a verbal contest in which the opponents swap family insults; *signifying, the agitating that often leads to dozens contests; and toasts, ritualized boasts of superhuman sexual and physical feats.

Examples of the dozens and signifying abound in African American literature. The title of Julius *Lester's *Look Out, Whitey! Black Power's Gon' Get Your Mama* (1968) is fashioned from a standard dozens insult. Muhammad *Ali recalled playing the dozens with Joe Frazier in his *autobiography, *The Greatest: My Own Story* (1975). Richard *Wright's *short story "Big Boy Leaves Home" opens with Big Boy and his friends playing the dozens. Langston *Hughes also used references to the dozens to inject *humor into the dialogue of *Simple Speaks His Mind* (1950). Maya *Angelou's poem "Thirteens" in *Just Give Me a Cool Drink of Water 'fore I Diiie* (1971) uses both the themes and form of the dozens.

The themes and characters of toasts also appear in African American literature. Sterling A. *Brown's "Slim in Hell" (1968) and H. Rap Brown's "Rap's Poem" (1968) are based on this oral poetry. Walter *Mosley's character Mouse and *Iceberg Slim in *Pimp: The Story of My Life* (1969) are literary versions of the toast hero.

Slave folktales have also been used by African American writers. Charles Waddell *Chesnutt's short story collection *The *Conjure Woman and Other Tales* (1899) is a literary adaptation of the ghost stories collected by Richard M. Dorson in *American Negro Folktales* (1956). Toni *Morrison's *novel *Tar Baby* (1981) is named after a traditional *Brer Rabbit *trickster folktale. And John and Efan slave trickster folktales are sprinkled throughout Cecil *Brown's novel *The Life and Loves of Mr. Jiveass Nigger* (1970).

Jokes satirizing *Jim Crow are popular with African American writers. Novelist John O. *Killens's *Youngblood* (1954) features some of the racial jokes collected by Daryl Cumber Dance in *Shuckin' and Jivin': Folklore from Contemporary Black America* (1978). Killens's novel *'Sippi* (1967) is a literary retelling of the civil rights joke that African Americans will no longer address Mississippi as Miss; it will just be 'Sippi from now on.

Family stories, such as those collected by Kathryn L. Morgan in *Children of Strangers: The Stories of a Black Family* (1980), give themes and structure to Alex *Haley's *Roots* (1976) and Albert *Murray's *Train Whistle Guitar* (1974). Haley's book was inspired by the family stories his grandmother told him when he was a boy in Hennings, Tennessee. Scooter, Murray's protagonist, was also culturally nourished by the stories he heard his elders tell in Gasoline Point, Alabama.

Racial rumors based on the theme of racial *identity have been used by African American writers. William Wells *Brown's *Clotel, or the President's Daughter* (1853), James Weldon *Johnson's *The *Autobiography of an Ex-Colored Man* (1912), Nella *Larsen's *Passing* (1929), and George S. *Schuyler's *Black No More* (1931) are four novels that explore the theme of *mulattoes *passing.

*Sermons and preaching, however, remain the most influential of all performed African American narrative genres on African American literature. James Weldon Johnson's *God's Trombones: Seven Negro Sermons in Verse* (1927) makes the greatest poetic use of this performed narrative. The Reverend Homer A. Barbee's eulogy of the Founder in Ralph *Ellison's novel *Invisible Man* (1952) is a masterful prose example of this traditional narrative performance. Novelist James *Baldwin's narrative style in *Go Tell It on the Mountain* (1953) is based on the fiery delivery of the African American folk preacher.

African American writers also draw upon the sacred and secular folk song traditions of their people. African American poets and playwrights have made great use of *spirituals such as "Go Down, Moses," analyzed in W. E. B. *Du Bois's *The *Souls of Black Folk* (1903). James Weldon Johnson's poem "O Black and Unknown Bards" (1917) praises these songs and their slave creators. Elements of *Heaven Bound*, the annually produced Atlanta folk drama whose plot, dialogue, settings, and action are drawn in large measure from the lyrics and music of the spirituals, are evident in Hall Johnson's *Run, Little Chillun* (1933).

Gospel songs, such as Thomas Dorsey's "Precious Lord," have had an even greater influence on African American drama. Themes, images, and dramatic techniques of *In the Rapture*, a popular gospel *drama in Indianapolis, are refined in James Baldwin's *The *Amen Corner* (1968), Vinnette Carroll and Micki Grant's *Don't Bother Me I Can't Cope* (1970), and Langston Hughes's *Tambourines to Glory* (1958). James Baldwin's novel *Just above My Head* (1978) is a fictional account of a gospel singer, Arthur Montana, who attempts to commercialize his gospel singing gifts.

Finally, *blues and work songs have had a deep impact upon African American literature. The secular folk songs published in John W. Work's *Folk Songs of the American Negro* (1915) have long been the inspiration for African American literature. Langston Hughes pioneered the use of the blues *aab* poetic structure to write several of his poems in *The *Weary Blues* (1926).

African American poets have written an impressive number of poems praising blues singers and *jazz musicians. Ma *Rainey is the subject of Sterling A. Brown's "Ma Rainey" in Stephen Henderson's *Understanding the New Black Poetry* (1972). Robert *Hayden praises Bessie *Smith in "Homage to the Empress of the Blues" (1968). Michael S. *Harper's "Dear John, Dear Coltrane" is one of four poems devoted to this legendary jazz musician in Henderson's anthology.

African American prose has also been greatly influenced by the blues. The title of Richard Wright's *autobiography, *Black Boy (1945), is taken from the traditional blues singer's signature: "If anybody ask you who sung this song / just tell 'em old black boy's been here and gone." The title of James Baldwin's novel Tell Me How Long the Train's Been Gone (1968) can be traced to Leroy Carr's "How Long Blues." John A. *McCluskey, Jr.'s Mr. America's Last Season Blues (1983) is a literary blues of Roscoe Americus, Jr., the novel's protagonist. And country blues singer Luzana Cholly is a romanticized hero in Murray's Train Whistle.

• Thomas Kochman, ed., Rappin' and Stylin' Out: Communication in Urban Black America, 1972. Geneva Smitherman, Talkin' and Testifyin': The Language of Black America, 1977. Houston A. Baker, Jr., Blues, Ideology, and Afro-American Literature: A Vernacular Theory, 1984. Gerald L. Davis, I Got the Word in Me and I Can Sing It, You Know: A Study of the Performed African-American Sermon, 1985. Henry Louis Gates, Jr., The Signifying Monkey: A Theory of Afro-American Literary Criticism, 1988. William H. Wiggins, Jr., "William Herbert Brewster: Pioneer of the Sacred Pagean' ' in We'll Understand It Better By and By: Pioneering African American Composers, ed. Bernice Johnson Reagon, 1992, pp. 245–251.

—William H. Wiggins, Jr.

PERIODICALS. *This entry consists of two articles that provide substantially detailed information about political and literary magazines that focus on black life in America, from the earliest magazines published in the nineteenth century to thriving contemporary journals. The separate essays are*

Black Periodical Press
Scholarly Journals and Literary Magazines

The articles illustrate the unwavering commitment of black activists, editors, and writers to providing outlets for expression of political and creative efforts relevant to black communities in the United States.

BLACK PERIODICAL PRESS

*Freedom's Journal, begun in 1827, claims the honor of being African America's first newspaper. Its companions-in-arms as the first black periodicals were the Mirror of Liberty, published in New York City in July 1838 under the rousing motto "Liberty Is the Word for Me—Above All, Liberty," and with David Ruggles, New England–born militant black abolitionist and friend of Frederick *Douglass, as editor, and the National Reformer (1838–1839), published in Philadelphia with William *Whipper as editor. Much as Freedom's Journal, a daily, and Mirror of Liberty and National Reformer, both quarterlies, understandably took up antislavery as their cause, they offered the occasional literary column of verse, *essay, *drama, and story.

In this they inaugurate a long tradition whereby both political *and* literary black voices have found working space in the periodicals—just as they had initially, in the early black newspapers like the daily

Colored American (1837–1841) or the weekly Zion's Wesleyan (1841–1843). For from *slavery time to the present, the press and its magazine counterparts have often and of necessity served as a first outlet and training ground, not to mention source of income, for the African American writer.

Frederick Douglass's weekly, the *North Star, begun in 1847 in Rochester, New York (and in 1851 changed to Frederick Douglass's Paper), and his Douglass' Monthly, begun in 1858, offer prime examples. Both, typically, editorialized against slavery, reported events like the Harpers Ferry raid, the Amistad case, and the *insurrections of Denmark Vesey and Nat *Turner, and readily included addresses by Abraham *Lincoln and a veteran white Boston abolitionist like Wendell Phillips. But black-written contributions, alongside Douglass's own speeches, came from the essayist James McCune Smith, Bishop Daniel A. *Payne of the African Methodist Episcopal Church, and, notably, the novelist, Civil War officer, and nationalist, Martin R. *Delany.

Delany's early *novel of black insurrection, *Blake, or The Huts of America was itself initially serialized in another early black periodical, Thomas Hamilton's monthly *Anglo-African Magazine (1859–1860) and continued over into his Weekly Anglo-African (1859–1865). Other founding African American literary names to appear in both include James W. C. *Pennington, whose The Fugitive Blacksmith (1849) would become a ranking *slave narrative, on "Slaveholding," Frances Ellen Watkins *Harper, whose *Iola Leroy, or Shadows Uplifted (1892) explores the workings of racial caste and color hierarchy, on "Haiti," the humorist William J. Wilson, and, reciprocally as it were, Douglass himself.

The Reconstruction years saw the black press and periodicals grow rapidly, whether Freedman's Torchlight (1866), Hampton Institute's Alumni Journal (1881–1895, 1904–), and Lincoln University's Alumni Journal (1884–1885), or the A.M.E. Church Review (1884–1909). But two magazines especially set the pace. The Boston-based *Colored American Magazine (1900–1909), edited initially by Walter W. Wallace and Pauline E. *Hopkins (whose own extracted novels like Hagar's Daughter, Winona, and Of One Blood make an important first appearance), would include in its contributions *poetry and *short stories by William Stanley *Braithwaite, verse by Paul Laurence *Dunbar, fiction by Angelina Weld *Grimké, memoirs from the vaudeville artist George Walker, and an essay on ragtime by Rosamond Johnson.

*Voice of the Negro (1904–1907), out of Atlanta, Georgia, though white-owned, was edited by the radical, politically savvy J. Max Barber, friend of W. E. B. *Du Bois. Barber was quick to take Du Bois's side against Booker T. *Washington in the divides over militancy even, paradoxically, as the journal was publishing early versions of Washington's Story of My Life and Work. Other Voice of the Negro contributions include an antilynching piece by Charles Waddell *Chesnutt, dialect and other poetry by Paul Laurence Dunbar, critiques by Du Bois, and Barber's own essays (most strikingly on the Atlanta race riot of

1906), together with an array of literary reviews and occasional writings.

These two, to be sure, were hardly the only outlets; the diversity of turn-of-the-century black magazines, both general and special interest, includes *Negro-American* (1887), *Monthly Review* (1894–1896), *Afro-American Review* (1899), *Small's Illustrated Monthly* (1905), *Paul Jones Monthly Magazine* (1907), and *Colored American Magazine* (1900–1909)—the latter especially notable as an outlet for the beginning essay-work of Alain *Locke as a new style of black voice for a new century.

Locke, Howard University professor, man-of-letters, animating spirit of the pioneer *anthology *The *New Negro: An Interpretation* (1925), provided a key link to the emergence of the *Harlem Renaissance. The 1920s witnessed not only a surge of black creativity—Countee *Cullen, Claude *McKay, Jean *Toomer, James Weldon *Johnson, Arna *Bontemps, Langston *Hughes, and Zora Neale *Hurston—but a flurry of magazine publication.

This path was anticipated in various periodicals, prime among them Du Bois's *Horizon* (1907–1910), which revealed his own literary-creative bent in poetry like "Song of the Smoke" and "The Burden of a Black Woman." The NAACP's *Crisis* (1910–), however, served as an even greater outlet, whether of the generation of Braithwaite, Benjamin *Brawley, Chesnutt, and Dunbar, or, especially when Jessie Redmon *Fauset became literary editor, of quite any and all of the stellar names of the Harlem Renaissance. No poem-anthem better caught the times than Hughes's "The *Negro Speaks of Rivers," which appeared in the *Crisis* for June 1921.

Slightly later appeared the Urban League's *Opportunity: Journal of Negro Life* (1923–1949), under the editorship of Charles Johnson. However "political," it was perfectly quick to publish poetry by Cullen and Gwendolyn *Bennett, stories by Eric *Walrond, and essay-work by Locke, Adam Clayton Powell, Sr., and Horace Mann Bond. It also opened itself to literary controversy as in the debate about Carl Van Vechten's *Nigger Heaven* (1926). Had Van Vechten given vent to racist patronage or not? Published under the auspices of the Brotherhood of Sleeping Car Porters, the *Messenger* (1917–1928) became a forum for leftist spirits like McKay, Rudolph *Fisher, and the eventual satirist-conservative George S. *Schuyler, with no shortage of ongoing contributions from Hughes, Wallace *Thurman, and Dorothy *West.

The smaller magazines came and went, replete with manifestos and often fierce exchanges of literary gunfire. Their ranks include Locke's *Stylus* (1916–1941), which launched the career of Hurston; *New Era* (1916), again under the editorship of Pauline Hopkins; *Survey Graphic* (1925), whose "Harlem" issue of March 1925 edited by Locke was the forerunner of *The New Negro*; the short-lived but important *Fire!!* (1925), with Thurman as editor and Hurston, Hughes, and Gwendolyn Bennett as boardmembers, and with poetry like Cullen's "From the Dark Tower" as a major contribution; *Harlem* (1928), another Thurman-inspired (and one-issue)

journal with reviews by Nella *Larsen and Fisher and an attack on Du Bois's style of literary conservatism; and "respectable," more belletristic magazines like the Philadelphia-based *Black Opals* and the Boston-based *Quill*.

"Our art is going proletarian," wrote Alain Locke, with mixed feelings, in *Opportunity* for June 1936. Depression America, 1930s America, had changed the rules: the call had gone up for a leftist turn, for socialism. Although *Opportunity*, like the *Crisis*, continued to publish black creative work, notably by Robert *Hayden, Chester *Himes, Langston Hughes, Ann *Petry, and Margaret *Walker, the best-known radical black periodical of the age was Dorothy West's *Challenge* (subsequently *New Challenge*), which ran from 1934 to 1937 and included Richard *Wright in its editorial lineup. It became a forum for black political debate, Marxism as against non-Marxism, *black nationalism as against cross-racial advance. In marked contrast were the "popular" magazines, *Bronzeman* (1929–1933), *Dawn* (1935), *Metropolitan* (1935), *Mirror* (1936), *Brown Magazine* (1936–1945), easy-read pieces whether in feature or story form. None, however, better signified than *Abbott's Monthly* (1930–1933), founded by Robert S. Abbott who had also created the *Chicago Defender*; it was the first magazine to publish Wright and Himes—and it served as a reminder that Harlem was not America's only black cultural center.

If any one ethos prevailed in the early post–World War II years, it lay in "integration," an invocation of the ideal of melting-pot America. So, at least, it was refracted in the better-known periodicals: *Negro Quarterly* (1942–1944) with Ralph *Ellison as managing editor; *Negro Story* (1944–1946), which Gwendolyn *Brooks supported and which published work by Owen *Dodson, Himes, Richard Bentley, and Ellison; *Negro Digest* (1942–1951, 1961–1970), which ran monthly installments of a number of key African American novels; *Phylon* (1940–1976), a journal at the heart of the ideological-racial wars, whose valedictory essay "Inventory at Mid-Century" by Alain Locke remains essential reading; and *Harlem Quarterly* (1949–1950), whose contributors included Hughes, Shirley *Graham, and John Lee Weldon.

When, in 1970, *Negro Digest*, having come under the editorship of Hoyt *Fuller, changed its name to *Black World* (1970–1976), it served as an epitaph for the age. "Black Power," "Black Is Beautiful," "Nation Time"—each marked a politics in which SNCC, the Black Panthers, and the Nation of Islam seemed to have taken over the black political reins. Fuller, along with Addison *Gayle, Jr., formulated the *Black Aesthetic, black art to be judged by black criteria, with behind it clenched-fist, black nationalist ideology. The magazines were quick to answer the call: the transitional *Umbra* (1963–1975), which published Ishmael *Reed, Clarence *Major, and Julian Bond; *Soulbook* (1964–1976), in which *The Toilet* by LeRoi Jones/Amiri *Baraka became a source of controversy with Langston Hughes; *Black Dialogue* (1964–1970), with further drama contributions from Jones/Baraka, Ed *Bullins, and Larry *Neal as well as poetry from Nikki *Giovanni; *Journal of Black Poetry*

(1966–1973), edited by Joe Goncalves and in which Reed launched some of his early satiric assaults on "the Black Aesthetic" as "a goon squad aesthetic"; *Nommo* (1969–1972), issued under the aegis of the Organization of Black American Culture (OBAC) and with Fuller as an influence and begetter; and *Black Creation* (1970–1975), edited by Fred Beauford, featuring creative work and *criticism that reflected the turn away from any one prescriptive "black" template.

This "Second Black Renaissance" of ideas and publication, nonetheless, would have overlapping impacts: a reference-standard for more recent black (and multicultural) literary debate and publication in post-1960s journals from *African American Review* to *Callaloo* to *Obsidian: Black Literature in Review*; a distant source of report for "glossies" like *Jet*, *Tan*, *Ebony*, or *Essence*; and a reminder of how the black periodical press, if now to an extent superceded by multicultural outlets, has been so vital to the emergence of African American writing at large.

[*See also* Journalism; Publishing.]

• Frederick G. Detweiler, *The Negro Press in the United States*, 1992. Charles S. Johnson, "The Rise of the Negro Magazine," *Journal of Negro History* 13 (Jan. 1928): 7–21. Ronald E. Wolseley, *The Black Press, U.S.A.*, 1972. Abby Arthur Johnson and Ronald Maberry Johnson, *Propaganda and Aesthetics: The Literary Politics of Afro-American Magazines in the Twentieth Century*, 1979. Penelope L. Bullock, *The Afro-American Periodical Press 1838–1909*, 1981.   —A. Robert Lee

SCHOLARLY JOURNALS AND LITERARY MAGAZINES

African American cultural and literary magazines have had a primary role in the shaping of African American literature. These publications, which include scholarly periodicals, organizational journals, and little magazines, have provided a platform, sometimes the only printed outlet available, for a succession of powerful writers, such as Pauline E. *Hopkins, W. E. B. *Du Bois, Alain *Locke, Zora Neale *Hurston, Richard *Wright, Amiri *Baraka, Alice *Walker, and Henry Louis *Gates, Jr. They have published scholarly and creative work important in framing the critical discourse, which has long focused on the proper function of black literature, on its role as propaganda advancing group interests, or as art expressing the individual writer. By so doing, the periodicals have met the goal articulated by J. Max Barber, dynamic editor of *Voice of the Negro* (1904–1907). He wanted his publication to be "more than a mere magazine," to record current historical and cultural events so accurately and vividly that "it will become a kind of documentation for the coming generations."

The initial generation of African American magazines, which emerged in New York during the early decades of the nineteenth century, were generally political in orientation. They existed to support the abolitionist movement, as underscored by a few representative titles: *Freedom's Journal* (1827), *National Reformer* (1833), and *Mirror of Liberty* (1837). In their campaigns against *slavery, the journals became an important part of the black protest tradition. Most of them had scant leisure for belles lettres, however.

The notable exception was the *Anglo-African Magazine* (1859–1862), which featured both protest pieces and nonpolitical writing, including scholarly articles, short fiction, and *poetry. In the decades that followed, the journal collected accolades from notable commentators on the reputation of its contributors, such as Frederick *Douglass, and on the quality of their writing. Poet Sterling A. *Brown, for example, claimed in *Negro Caravan* (1941) that Martin R. *Delany's *Blake, as published in the journal, presented "some pictures of slavery more convincing than anything in *Uncle Tom's Cabin* or *Clotel*."

The politics of African American magazines diverged in the postwar years with the failure of Radical Reconstruction and the emergence of racial segregation in the 1890s. Booker T. *Washington, educator, speaker, and writer, became a prominent spokesperson for a new generation of African Americans. Preaching accommodationism, he urged black Americans to work within the system of segregation. To spread his gospel, Washington engineered his ascendancy in a number of black periodicals, including *Alexander's Magazine* of Boston and the New York *Age*. Reacting against accommodationism and Washington's attempts to curb dissent, a small group of intellectuals reasserted the protest tradition in African American periodicals. Among them were Pauline E. Hopkins, who served briefly (1902–1904) as the outspoken editor of *Colored American Magazine* (1900–1909), J. Max Barber, who made *Voice of the Negro* a powerful advocate for black civil rights, and W. E. B. Du Bois, who founded and edited *Moon* (1905–1906) and *Horizon* (1907–1910) in support of his antiaccommodationist Niagara Movement. These editors used fiction and poetry, along with editorials and news articles, to encourage resistance against accommodationism.

In 1910 Du Bois established the *Crisis* (1910–) as the official journal of the NAACP and thereby inaugurated a new era in African American periodicals. While he covered politics and NAACP news, he also concentrated on literature, reminding writers that "the material about us in the strange, heart-rending race tangle is rich beyond dreams and only we can tell the tale. . . ." Functioning as both an organizational periodical and a literary magazine, *Crisis* established a formula for *Opportunity* (1923–1949), journal of the National Urban League, and to a lesser extent for the *Messenger* (1917–1928), journal of the Union of Sleeping Car Porters. These journals published the most prominent and promising contemporary writers, including James Weldon *Johnson, Claude *McKay, and Jean *Toomer. The *Crisis* and *Opportunity*, edited by Charles S. Johnson from 1923 to 1928, provided further incentives with their annual competitions for writers and artists in 1925, 1926, and 1927. The *Opportunity* contests were particularly successful. Contacts made at the dinners accompanying these events led to the publication of Langston *Hughes's The *Weary Blues*, Countee *Cullen's *Color, and Alain Locke's special Harlem issue of *Survey Graphic*.

By encouraging aspiring writers, the *Crisis* and *Opportunity* were instrumental in stimulating the renaissance of African American literature in the 1920s and in reinvigorating the critical discourse about this literature. The two editors, Du Bois and Johnson, developed contrasting opinions about the function of the arts. Du Bois stated that "all art is propaganda and ever must be," believing that the arts should be used to help African Americans gain full civil liberties. Johnson stressed aesthetics rather than politics: "What is most important is that these black artists should be free . . . to feel the pulsations and rhythms of their own life, philosophy be hanged."

Taking a lead from Johnson, the editors of little magazines and of special issues of African American literature concentrated more on art than on propaganda in the 1920s. In the special *Survey Graphic* number, published in March 1925, Locke announced the emergence of a *New Negro, "vibrant with a new psychology," and identified Harlem as "the sign and center of the renaissance of a people." This special issue formed the basis of Locke's influential edition of *The *New Negro, published by Boni in fall 1925. In addition, the issue encouraged other magazines to publish special numbers of African American literature, as did *Palms* (edited by Idella Purnell and Witter Bynner) in October 1926 and *Carolina Magazine* (a student publication at the University of North Carolina) in May 1927, May 1928, and April 1929. The *Survey Graphic* number also prepared a way for African American little magazines, which appeared shortly thereafter.

The earliest and most controversial of these magazines emerged in Harlem: *Fire!!* (Nov. 1926) and *Harlem* (Nov. 1928). Novelist Wallace *Thurman edited both publications, which were informed by his understanding that African American authors should focus on whatever phases of black life "seem most interesting." The magazines featured stories about *prostitutes, homosexual lovers, and other characters considered disreputable by the bourgeoisie. The larger black readership was more comfortable with periodicals appearing in other urban areas as outlets for young writers, such as *Black Opals* (1927–1928), established in Philadelphia by Arthur Huff *Fauset, and the *Saturday Evening Quill* (1928–1930), issued by the Boston Quill Club.

During the depression of the 1930s, African American writers focused increasingly on politics, particularly on the needs of the lower socioeconomic classes. They had limited outlets for their writing, however. The African American popular magazines, such as *Bronzeman* (1929–1933) and particularly *Abbott's Monthly* (1930–1933), published a sampling of established and new talent, including J. Max Barber, Langston Hughes, and Chester *Himes. The primary concentration of these magazines was, however, on entertainment. The two surviving organizational journals, the *Crisis* and *Opportunity*, were experiencing serious financial difficulties and had to attend to organizational needs. Roy Wilkins, who succeeded Du Bois to the editorship of the *Crisis* in 1934, remembered that "the big job was keeping alive." *Opportunity* managed, nevertheless, to publish Alain Locke's annual reviews of African American literature in 1929 and from 1931 to 1942. In his efforts to

chart "the march of ideas," Locke recognized a new mecca—Chicago—and a new spokesperson—Richard Wright—for young writers.

Chicago was home to the African American literary magazines emergent in the 1930s: *Challenge* (1934–1937), established by Dorothy *West, and the one issue of *New Challenge* (Fall 1937), edited by West, Marian Minus, and Richard Wright. In his "Blueprint for Negro Writing," published in *New Challenge*, Wright reaffirmed a social agenda for African American literature, urging his contemporaries to "stand shoulder to shoulder with Negro workers in mood and outlook."

Racial integration became the dominant motif in African American periodicals during World War II and in the postwar years. During the war, the *Crisis* and *Opportunity* published work that supported the effort overseas, denounced *Jim Crow at home, and articulated a new world built by blacks and whites together. Despite financial problems described as "desperate" by Elmer Carter, then editor of *Opportunity*, the two periodicals continued to function as literary magazines, as well as organizational and political journals. The *Crisis* was the more successful in its publication of quality creative work, including short fiction by Chester Himes and Ann *Petry. After the war, mounting financial pressures forced the *Crisis* and *Opportunity* to relinquish their historic role as literary periodicals.

Phylon (1940–), established by W. E. B. Du Bois at Atlanta University, fulfilled this function during the postwar years. Announced as "a scholarly journal of comment and research on world race problems," *Phylon* also became an important outlet for African American literary *criticism, including seven annual reviews of black literature contributed by Alain Locke from 1947 to 1953. After Locke's death in 1954, *Phylon* continued this feature for another decade, thereby compiling a detailed discussion of the aesthetics of integration.

Further illustrations of the aesthetics of integration come from African American little magazines of the 1940s—*Negro Quarterly* (1942–1944), edited by Angelo Herndon and Ralph *Ellison, *Negro Story* (1944–1946), edited by Alice Browning, *Harlem Quarterly* (1949–1950), edited by Benjamin Brown, *Free Lance* (1953–1976), edited by Russell *Atkins, and *Yugen* (1958–1963), edited by LeRoi Jones (later Amiri Baraka) and his first wife, Hettie Cohen. These magazines varied considerably in political and literary direction. *Negro Quarterly*, for example, advocated black and white unity on the political left, while *Yugen* was part of the Beat Generation. *Negro Story* occupied the political center. Editor Browning wanted "to publish creative writing which would reflect the struggle of the Negro for full integration into American life."

The most influential African American cultural and literary magazines of the 1960s advocated a different struggle, calling for separation from the larger society. The most prominent of these revolutionary publications was *Negro Digest* (1942–1951, 1961–1970), later *Black World* (1970–1976). Edited by Hoyt *Fuller, this periodical contributed to the rise of the

*Black Arts movement in the 1960s and then recorded its decline in the early 1970s. The other periodicals that took major roles in shaping the agenda of the Black Arts movement were all little magazines: *Liberator* (1961–1971), when influenced by Larry *Neal and LeRoi Jones in 1965–1966, and three journals originating in California, *Soulbook* (1964–1976), *Black Dialogue* (1964–1970), and *Journal of Black Poetry* (1966–1973).

These periodicals became the primary vehicle for defining and promoting the *Black Aesthetic. While key spokespersons did not always agree on the specifics of this term, they did share general ideas, beginning with the understanding that African American arts should be used to create a new black consciousness and hence a new black community. They talked about art-for-people's sake and promoted a literature exclusively by, about, and for black people. LeRoi Jones, the charismatic leader of the Black Arts movement, expressed tenets central to the Black Aesthetic in his poem "Black Art," published in the January 1966 *Liberator*. He called for "assassin poems" that would liberate African Americans from Western culture and reconnect them to their own heritage.

During the 1960s, a number of the established and new African American writers, including Ralph Ellison and Ishmael *Reed, rejected the literary politics of the Black Arts movement. They gained ascendancy in the mid-1970s with cultural and literary magazines that have remained open to a wide variety of critical approaches. One of the first and most successful of these magazines was *Black American Literature Forum* (founded 1967, retitled *African American Review* in 1992), which has been the official publication of the Modern Language Association's Division on Black American Literature and Culture since 1983. Joe Weixlmann, who became editor in 1976, recalled that his periodical "set out to help resituate the critical and theoretical planes of discourse about Afro-American literature and culture." The journal has been supported in this effort by a number of influential writers, including Houston A. *Baker, Jr., Henry Louis Gates, Jr., and Alice Walker, and by other magazines, particularly by *Hambone* (1974–), *Callaloo* (1976–), *Reconstruction* (1990–), and *Transition* (1991–). As guest editor for the winter 1981 and spring 1982 issues of *Black American Literature Forum*, Gates affirmed "a plurality of readings," including formalist, structuralist, and Marxist interpretations. Using the periodicals as a primary platform, he and others have continued this emphasis, encouraging debate that now incorporates multiculturalism, *feminism, and deconstructive interpretations.

In an *essay for *Negro Digest*, writer and critic Carolyn Gerald summarized the importance of African American magazines, saying that "the direction and developing quality of black literature can be but imperfectly seen if these journals are ignored." From the early nineteenth century to the present, African American cultural and literary magazines have provided a forum for wide-ranging discussions of art and politics, recorded historic battles over literary aesthetics, and stimulated the development of outstanding creative and critical work. In the process they have become a cultural legacy for current and future generations.

• Frederick J. Hoffman, Charles Allen, and Carolyn R. Ulrich, *The Little Magazine*, 1946. Penelope L. Bullock, *The Afro-American Periodical Press, 1838–1909*, 1981. Walter C. Daniel, *Afro-American Journals, 1827–1980: A Reference Book*, 1982. Abby Arthur Johnson and Ronald Maberry Johnson, *Propaganda and Aesthetics: The Literary Politics of African-American Magazines in the Twentieth Century*, 1979; rpt. with new introduction 1991. Abby Arthur Johnson and Ronald Johnson, "Charting a New Course: African American Literary Politics since 1976," in *The Black Columbiad: Defining Moments in African American Literature and Culture*, eds. Werner Sollors and Maria Diedrich, 1994, pp. 369–381.

—Abby Arthur Johnson *and* Ronald Maberry Johnson

PERKINS, EUGENE (b. 1932), poet, playwright, essayist, social worker, educator, and activist. Eugene Perkins was born in Chicago on 13 September 1932. His parents, Marion and Eva Perkins, created a family structure where Perkins was encouraged to pursue artistic endeavors and to be proud of his rich African American heritage. He recalls that when he was ten years old his father took him to see a performance of Shakespeare's *Othello* starring the celebrated actor, singer, and social activist Paul *Robeson. This was a turning point in his life and Perkins vowed he would become a writer. He published his first poem in the *Chicago Tribune* when he was eleven. While in high school, he wrote poems, *essays, and short plays for the school newspaper, of which he was editor. He graduated from George Williams College in 1961 with a bachelor's degree in group social work, and received his master's degree in group social work from the same school in 1964.

Most of Perkins's adult career has focused on helping inner-city children in Chicago. He has been involved with a number of social service organizations in Chicago and the Midwest. For almost twenty years he was executive director of the Better Boys Foundation Family Center. African American inner-city reality, which Perkins has dedicated a major part of his professional life to improving, informs his literary productions. Not only has he created a large body of work that responds to African American urban life (including his 1975 book, *The Social Oppression of Black Children*), but he has also encouraged young people and others to pursue their creative talents. Two volumes of *poetry that he edited attest to his dedication to providing forums where other inner-city voices might speak: *Black Expressions: An Anthology of New Black Poets* (1967) and *Poetry of Prison: Poems by Black Prisoners* (1972).

Perkins's first volume of poetry, *An Apology to My African Brother* (1965), was published during the dawning of the *Black Arts movement of the 1960s. Like a great deal of African American literature of this time, Perkins's poems pay special attention to African and African American heritage and the very real need for his readers to be proud of their blackness as a way to combat many of the oppressions they face in their daily lives. His 1968 volume of poetry, *Black Is Beautiful*, reflects his concern for creating affirmative images of black people. He has produced several other volumes of poetry, including

West Wall (1969), *Silhouette* (1970), *When You Grow Up: Poems for Children* (1982), and *Midnight Blues in the Afternoon and Other Poems* (1984). His recognition of his responsibility to create "homegrown" images of black people for black people, especially children, is reflected in his *The Black Fairy*, a musical play produced in 1976. He has written and staged several plays in Chicago and the Midwest. A few representative plays are *Nothing but a Nigger* (1969), *Cry of the Ghetto* (1970), *Black Is So Beautiful* (1970), *Fred Hampton* (1970), *Professor J. B.* (1974), and *Pride of Race* (1984). His tie to black communities is also noted by the fact that most of his plays were community produced. Eugene Perkins is a major player of the Black Arts movement whose work has yet to receive the scholarly and critical attention that it deserves.

• James V. Hatch and Omanii Abdullah, eds., *Black Playwrights, 1823–1977*, 1977, pp. 179–180.

—Charles P. Toombs

PETERSON, LOUIS (b. 1922), film and television screenwriter, and playwright. If one were to summarize the forty-year career of Louis Stamford Peterson, Jr., in one word, it would be "passages." Peterson's play of the 1950s, *Take a Giant Step*, earned him acclaim in American *theater. Since that time, he has released a play every decade. He strongly believes that people write out of what they do best, and that "best" means maintaining ethical standards learned from childhood.

Born 17 June 1922 in Hartford, Connecticut, Peterson grew up in a middle-class, multiethnic neighborhood. White immigrants were dominant but Peterson never felt deterred from aspiring for high ideals. He was trained by his parents to value education and the Protestant work ethic. Louis Stamford Peterson, Sr., worked as a bank guard and then as a money roller. His wife, Ruth Conover Peterson, accepted employment at a lunch counter in the same bank during the 1930s to insure that their two sons would acquire college educations. Peterson graduated from Bulkeley High School in 1940 and went south to attend Morehouse College (Atlanta, Georgia) from 1940 to 1944. He acted in collegiate productions, and upon graduation, Peterson spent a year at the Yale School of Drama and then enrolled in *drama at New York University, where he earned a master of arts degree in 1947.

Acting classes at New York University eventually led Peterson to playwriting. He performed in *A Young American* and *Our Lan'*, the latter taking Peterson to Broadway in 1947. However, he consistently found his character being lynched and became disturbed about these negative portraits of African Americans. He wrote two trial plays after *Our Lan'* and then studied playwrighting under Clifford Odets. While touring with *Members of the Wedding*, Peterson completed *Take a Giant Step*.

The play opened on 28 November 1953 on Broadway and ran for seventy-two performances that left an indelible mark on American theater. This adolescent play is set in New England in the 1950s and is reminiscent of Peterson's childhood of growing up

black in white suburbia. Critics of this period interpreted the painful rite-of-passage experience of seventeen-year-old Spencer "Spence" Scott as his sexual awakening and transition into *manhood. However, in the 1990s, critics recognize that the social factor of Spence's race is the subtext informing his feeling of ostracism by his white classmates and his precipitating subsequent sexual initiation into manhood. *Take a Giant Step* was listed in *Best Plays of 1953–1954*, ran Off Broadway for 264 performances in 1956, and was made into a *film in 1958, which Peterson cowrote with Julius Epstein.

The decades from 1960 to 1980 represent disparate passages during which Peterson attempted to reclaim the scintillating power of subject that he had attained with *Giant*. He became the first African American screenwriter in Hollywood, but he also found himself subject to its vicissitudes and left in the 1960s. Coupled with Hollywood's instability, Peterson found East Coast theatergoers expecting another *Giant*. One problem of his 1960s and 1970s plays was Peterson's adoption of intricate plots. *Entertain a Ghost*, a dual-plotted story about a self-absorbed young woman determined to become an actress, opened at the Actors Playhouse on 9 April 1962 to poor reviews. *Crazy Horse*, the story of an interracial marriage between a black journalist and white woman during the 1950s, enjoyed a brief stint at the New Federal Theater during November 1979.

In the 1980s, Peterson shifted his theatrical stage to the Theater Department at the State University of New York at Stony Brook. *Another Show* concerns another adolescent—this time a young male who commits suicide on campus—but the focus of the play involves the parent's reactions. This February 1983 student production enjoyed a two-week world premiere that caught the attention of Broadway critics.

The 1990s find Peterson, a widower, assiduously writing. While he retired from Stony Brook as a professor in 1993, he has been cowriting with Ken Lauber over the past several years. *Numbers* concerns a "black gangster and a Jewish boy" involved in the numbers racket in Harlem after World War II. Peterson anticipates a London production. Future projects include writing for *television once again.

• Seymour Peck, "The Man Who Took a Giant Step," *New York Times*, 20 Sept. 1953, 2:1. Howard Taubman, "Theatre and Peterson's Work," *New York Times*, 10 Apr. 1962, 1:48. Doris E. Abramson, *Negro Playwrights in the American Theatre, 1925–1959*, 1969, pp. 221–238. Donald T. Evans, "Bring It All Back Home: Playwrights of the Fifties," *Black World* 20 (Feb. 1971): 41–45. Mel Gussow, "Stage: 'Crazy Horse,' Drama by Louis Peterson at New Federal," *New York Times* 12 Nov. 1979, 3:13. Barbara Delatiner, "Playwright Eyes a New Giant Step," *New York Times*, 20 Feb. 1983, 21:19. Steven R. Carter, "Louis Peterson" in *DLB*, vol. 38, *Afro-American Writers after 1955: Dramatists and Prose Writers*, eds. Thadious M. Davis and Trudier Harris, 1985, pp. 134–139.

—Virginia Whatley Smith

PETRY, ANN (b. 1908), novelist, short story writer, author of books for children and juveniles, essayist, poet, and lecturer. Ann Petry was born above her father's drugstore on 12 October 1908 in Old Saybrook, Connecticut. She attended Old Saybrook's public schools, starting at the age of four. In 1931, she earned the PhG degree at the University of Connecticut, and, for more than nine years, worked as a pharmacist in the family-owned drugstores in Old Saybrook and Old Lyme. During these years, she also wrote *short stories. These stories remain unpublished.

Following her marriage to George D. Petry in 1938, Ann Petry moved to Harlem, abandoned the family profession, and, for the next eight years, actively pursued a career as a writer. From 1938 to 1941, she worked as a reporter for New York's *Amsterdam News*. From 1941 to 1944, she was a reporter and also the editor of the woman's page for *The People's Voice*, where from 1942 to 1943 she wrote about Harlem's upper middle class in the weekly column "The Lighter Side." During these years, she also enrolled in a writing workshop and a creative writing class at Columbia University. Petry's decision to change her profession to writer was a gamble that paid off. Her first short story, "Marie of the Cabin Club," a suspense-romance that is set in a Harlem night club, was published in 1939 in the Baltimore newspaper *Afro-American*. "On Saturday Night the Sirens Sound" (1943), which is also set in Harlem and focuses on children left home alone, was published in the *Crisis*. This story intrigued an editor at Houghton Mifflin who encouraged Petry to apply for Houghton's fellowship in fiction. Recipients of this fellowship received $2,400 and the publication of their winning work. In 1945, Petry won the fellowship, and in 1946, Houghton Mifflin published *The *Street*, a naturalistic/feminist *novel about a mother who tries to provide a better life for herself and her son in an urban environment that foreshadows failure.

Soon after its publication, *The Street* became a best-seller. Reprinted in 1985 as part of the Black Women Writers series at Beacon Press and reissued in 1992 by Houghton Mifflin, this novel has sold close to two million copies and is hailed universally as a "masterpiece" of African American fiction and a "classic" of urban American realism. Other widely acclaimed works by the writer that also continue to be reprinted or reissued are *The *Drugstore Cat* (1949), her only children's work; *The Narrows* (1953), a complex novel of psychological realism; *Miss Muriel and Other Stories* (1971), a collection that presents "well-founded" portrayals of characters in both urban and small town America; and *Harriet Tubman: Conductor on the Underground Railroad* (1955) and *Tituba of Salem Village* (1964), juvenile works with convincingly human depictions of well-known slaves Harriet *Tubman and Tituba Indian.

Outstanding works by Petry but with a smaller audience are *Country Place* (1947), a novel that examines class and gender within a white New England community; *Legends of the Saints* (1970), a juvenile work that includes in its documentation of saints an African American; and "The Moses Project" (1988), a short story about house arrest in modern times. Published in *anthologies but not bearing Petry's name

are five poems that are reminiscent of African American *poetry from the 1970s: "Noo York City 1," "Noo York City 2," and "Noo York City 3" (1976) and "A Purely Black Stone" and "A Real Boss Black Cat" (1981). Her *essays, which cover topics ranging from how to teach students to write creatively to the novel as social criticism, are mostly lectures revised for collections by other writers.

Critics call Petry's style versatile. Her novels, short stories, and poems evolve from her experiences in Harlem and Old Saybrook. History is the basis of her books for adolescents. When describing settings, Petry has an eye for details, and when creating characters, an ear for dialogue. Because of her sensitivity to landscapes and personalities, readers can almost see and feel with her narrators and characters.

Critics also call Petry a visionary and a humanist. In the 1940s and 1950s, long before feminism became ideological, she had created in *The Street* and *The Narrows* women who might be characterized as feminists. Long before interracial relationships between men of African descent and white women would become accepted in America, she described a love affair between an African American man and a white woman in *The Narrows*. Long before African American and white women in the 1960s would enter into dialogue to oppose patriarchy, she had provided in the 1940s such discourses in subtexts within *The Street* and *Country Place*.

Recognitions of Petry's aesthetics have also come in the form of honorariums, citations, lectureships at universities, library collections, and numerous translations of her novels, short stories, and juvenile works. In 1946, editor Martha Foley dedicated to Petry the collection *The Best American Short Stories, 1946*, which also included Petry's short story "Like a Winding Sheet." That same year, the New York Women's City Club honored her for her contributions to the city as a reporter and novelist; as an organizer of The Negro Women, Incorporated, a consumer watch-group for working-class women in Harlem; as a recreation specialist, particularly for her development of programs for parents and children in problem areas in Harlem; as a writer of skits and programs for children of laundry workers; and as a member of the American Negro Theatre, where during the year 1940 she performed at the Schomburg Center for Research in Black Culture as Tillie Petunia in *On Striver's Row*. Since the 1970s, Petry has appeared in *Who's Who of American Women*, *Who's Who among Black Americans*, and *Who's Who in Writers, Editors and Poets*. She has received citations from the Greater Women in Connecticut History, the United Nations Association, the city of Philadelphia, the Connecticut Commission on the Arts, and from literary groups such as the annual Celebration of Black Writing Conference in Philadelphia and the Middle Atlantic Writers Association. She has lectured at Miami University of Ohio and was a visiting professor at the University of Hawaii. She has received honorary degrees from Suffolk University (1983), the University of Connecticut (1988), and Mount Holyoke College (1989). All of her novels, several short stories, and one juvenile work have been translated, together, into at least twelve different languages. Collections of her manuscripts, letters, first editions, and translations have been compiled at Boston University, Yale University, and the Atlanta University Center.

Petry has said often that she wants to be remembered for not only *The Street*, her most celebrated work, but for everything she has written.

• Theodore L. Gross, "Ann Petry: The Novelist as Social Critic," in *Black Fiction: New Studies in the Afro-American Novel since 1945*, ed. A. Robert Lee, 1980, pp. 41–53. Trudier Harris, "On Southern and Northern Maids: Geography, Mammies and Militants," in *From Mammies to Militants: Domestics in Black American Literature*, 1982, pp. 88–100. Gloria Wade-Gayles, "Journeying from Can't to Can and Sometimes Back to 'Can't,'" in *No Crystal Stair: Visions of Race and Sex in Black Women's Fiction*, 1984, pp. 148–156. Marjorie Pryse, "'Patterns Against the Sky': Deism and Motherhood in Ann Petry's *The Street*," in *Conjuring: Black Women, Fiction and Literary Traditions*, eds. Majorie Pryse and Hortense J. Spillers, 1985, pp. 116–131. Suzanne Poirier, "From Pharmacist to Novelist," in *Pharmacy in History*, 1986, pp. 27–33. Gladys J. Washington, "A World Made Cunningly: A Closer Look at Ann Petry's Short Fiction," *CLA Journal* 30 (Sept. 1986): 14–29. Nellie McKay, introduction to *The Narrows*, 1988. Calvin Hernton, "The Significance of Ann Petry," in *The Sexual Mountain and Black Women Writers, Adventures in Sex, Literature and Real Life*, 1987; rpt. 1990, pp. 59–88. Hazel Arnett Ervin, introduction to *Ann Petry: A Bio-Bibliography*, 1993.   —Hazel Arnett Ervin

PHARR, ROBERT DEANE (1916–1992), novelist. Rediscovered in the late 1960s after an interrupted career, Robert Deane Pharr constructs a critique of the American dream and the African American community's ability to attain it. By handing his manuscript from one professor to another at the Columbia Faculty Club (where he worked as a waiter), he eventually saw the publication of his first *novel, The Book of Numbers*, in 1969. As Pharr's most widely respected and successful novel, this first major work relates the role crime and fate play in the African American attainment of the American dream.

Charting the rise and fall of a numbers runner named David Greene, Pharr suggests that in order to break into the restrictive confines of the American dream an African American must work outside the bounds of legitimacy. This novel, set in a small southern city during the depression, combines this critique with an overlay of biblical prophecy to paint a portrait of a community and a people caught between their hopes for success and the limited possibility that they might be realized. His characters (Blueboy Harris, Althea Goines, Delilah Mazique) defy the law and risk all for the illusion of certainty. Flawed by excessive length (a quality that would also plague his second novel, *S.R.O.*) and didacticism, *The Book of Numbers* nonetheless demonstrates Pharr's talent for relating dialect and dialogue. His evocative exploration of the ways in which chance bolsters human endurance established a framework for depicting the urban experience of African Americans that persists today. The book's success—eventually leading to an Avco film of the same title (1973)—buoyed Pharr's career and motivated the process of self-

reflection and imagination that his succeeding works described.

Pharr's second novel, *S.R.O.* (1971), moves his exploration of the dream to Harlem, where a picaresque parade of lesbians, drug addicts, and would-be artists explore the paths of fulfillment left open to them. This most autobiographical and self-reflexive of Pharr's works documents Sid Bailey's relationships with beautiful recovering addict Gloria Bascomb and with his writing (which he calls "his woman"). In particular, critics have praised the use of structural interchapters that alleviate and focus the first-person energies of the primary narrative. Once again, however, it is an extraordinarily long, didactic novel that harbors moments of exquisite dialogue and insight.

Pharr continued to write after *S.R.O.* (producing *The Welfare Bitch* in 1973 and *The Soul Murder Case: A Confession of a Victim* in 1975), but he never achieved the kind of success he tasted with *The Book of Numbers*. Relating its protagonist's unwilling protection of a relative's crime empire, *Giveadamn Brown* (1978), Pharr's final work, combines brevity of expression and the author's enduring skill with dialogue and quickly paced action. Of the late works, it comes closest to enacting the promise of his critical perspective on ambition and success in the United States.

The Book of Numbers is an important, groundbreaking analysis of the ironies that persist within the African American experience. As a social critic, literary realist, and pioneer in the exploration of the mechanics of writing, Robert Deane Pharr stands as an exemplar for authors who followed him.

• John O'Brien and Raman K. Singh, "Interview with Robert Deane Pharr," *Negro American Literature Forum* 8 (Fall 1974): 244–246. Garrett Epps, "To Know the Truth: The Novels of Robert Deane Pharr," *Hollins Critic* 13 (1976): 1–10.
                                     —Daniel M. Scott III

Philadelphia Fire (1990) is John Edgar *Wideman's seventh *novel and the second of his books to receive the prestigious PEN/Faulkner Award (*Sent for You Yesterday* won in 1984). A work that combines public events, personal *history, and the imagination, *Philadelphia Fire* has been referred to as "docufiction" (documentary fiction). It also could be called a metafiction because it deals in part with the circumstances of its own composition.

The book concerns the aftermath of the 13 May 1985 bombing by the city of Philadelphia of a house occupied by a militant African American organization known as MOVE, which had resisted an eviction order. Nearly everyone in the house died and an entire city block was consumed in the resulting conflagration. This event and Wideman's personal response to it are described in the middle section of the book, which also deals with the author's anguish over the conviction and imprisonment for murder of his youngest son, Jake.

In the main narrative, a writer named Cudjoe returns from self-imposed exile on a Greek island to attempt to trace the whereabouts of Simba Muntu, a child who is supposed to be the sole survivor of the fire. Precisely what motivates Cudjoe to return so precipitously to the United States is not clear, but it appears to have something to do with his growing sense of betrayal: of himself, his sons (from whom he has estranged himself since his divorce), his talent, and his former commitment to changing the world. Cudjoe's separation from his sons parallels Wideman's loss of his own son to prison, and Cudjoe's quest to find Simba Muntu counterpoints Wideman's quest to free his son. But Simba isn't found, and Wideman's son remains imprisoned, underscoring the tragedy of a lost generation of American youth, one of the book's principal themes.

Views of the book have been divergent. Celebrated African American writer Charles R. *Johnson, in a 1990 review in the *Washington Post*, calls Wideman "the most critically acclaimed black male writer of the last decade" and declares himself a fan, yet he finds *Philadelphia Fire* to be confusing and disappointing. For Darryl Pinckney, writing in 1991 in the *Times Literary Supplement*, the book is disorganized, a "parable" that "attempts too much." On the other hand, Mark Hummel, assessing the book in the same year for the *Bloomsbury Review*, finds it to be "difficult but immensely important and always eloquent." Ishmael *Reed in *Airing Dirty Laundry* (1993) blames the metafictional form for some of *Philadelphia Fire*'s problems—overdone details, uncertainty of plot—but he praises Wideman's courage as an artist and compares the novel to a Miles *Davis concert, finding the performance to be "terrific."

In an interview in *Callaloo* (Winter 1990), Wideman stated that in *Fever* and in *Philadelphia Fire*, he was forcing himself to stop and assess "what's happening to us." This "urgent desire to bear witness," as Darryl Pinckney calls it—also a principal motive in *Brothers and Keepers* (1985)—is one in which personal concerns converge with a concern for the state of the nation as a whole. Jan Clausen's description of *Philadelphia Fire* (in *The Kenyon Review*, Spring 1992) as "anguished, apocalyptic" underscores the unsettling nature of Wideman's testimony, the unsettled nature of our social being.

• Doreatha Drummond Mbalia, *John Edgar Wideman: Reclaiming the African Personality*, 1995, pp. 63–67, 107–112.

—Robert Elliot Fox

Phylon. Broadly conceived as a scholarly review for the study of *race and culture, *Phylon* has been for over fifty years an important outlet for the dissemination of ideas that are based on the notion of "race" as a social, cultural, and historical construction rather than a biological and psychological fact. Founded in 1940 by W. E. B. *Du Bois, who also served as the journal's editor in chief until 1944, *Phylon* was published under the auspices of Atlanta University to revive that institution's official publications issued between 1897 and 1914, documents which, according to *Phylon*'s first editorial statement, pioneered the application of sociology and anthropology to group problems. Du Bois, William Stanley *Braithwaite, Mercer Cook, and other prominent scholars who formed the journal's early editorial board considered the social sciences in need of transformation, a position reflected in the following excerpt from *Phylon*'s ambitious statement of purpose: "[We] foresee a re-interpretation of history, education, and sociology; a rewriting of history from the ideological and economic point of view."

While *Phylon* focused predominantly on issues within the social sciences, inclusions of literary criticism, book reviews, and original *poetry and fiction served to broaden the journal's appeal to a larger readership. *Phylon* thus emerged as a creative outlet for some of the most important figures in African American literary history, including Countee *Cullen, Langston *Hughes, James Weldon *Johnson, Ann *Petry, and Margaret *Walker, and the journal continues to make important contributions to African American cultural studies.

—Christopher C. De Santis

Piano Lesson, The. The winner of the 1990 Pulitzer Prize, *The Piano Lesson* is August *Wilson's second play to receive that award (*Fences* won in 1987). With this selection, Wilson became the first African American to receive the award twice and joined the select company of only seven American playwrights to be so honored. In addition, *The Piano Lesson* received the Drama Critics' Circle Award and the Tony Award for best play. Like Wilson's other plays, it was given a staged reading at the Eugene O'Neill National Playwrights Conference (1987) and directed by Lloyd Richards, the dean of the Yale Drama School, where it was first performed (1988) before, subsequently, touring other cities prior to its Broadway opening at the Walter Kerr Theatre on 16 April 1990. The cast included Charles S. Dutton in the role of Boy Willie and S. Epatha Merkerson as Berniece.

Set in 1936 in Pittsburgh, the play looks at the displacement of African Americans from Mississippi who have migrated north without coming to terms with their southern past. This struggle is objectified in the brother-sister conflict between Berniece and Boy Willie. They fight over a piano that their great-grandfather carved for a white man, which the brother and sister have now inherited.

Bringing along a truckload of watermelons to sell to finance his trip to see Berniece and reclaim his family legacy, Boy Willie wants to sell the piano and use the money to buy the farmland that his ancestors worked as slaves and sharecroppers. Berniece, however, does not want to part with this symbol of her family past; their father died stealing the piano—and its artistic legacy—from the white man who had exploited his family. The piano is a concrete representation of the still-existing conflicts and connections between the past and present; it works on several levels to suggest that white exploitation of blacks' artistic and manual accomplishment is an American tradition underlying the reality of the American dream. The play's resolution, which comes with the assistance of a ghost, suggests that claiming and transforming the suffering of the past into cultural artistry is necessary before Americans can begin to participate creatively in the present. As a result of their discussions and the activity of the ghost, the brother and sister achieve a family unity and closeness. Berniece's daughter and Boy Willie's niece, Maretha, will use the ancestral piano to produce *music and as a source of pride in her heritage.

Richard Hummler praised the play for its powerful and accurate rendering of black dialogue, and Frank Rich lauded Wilson for his ability to infuse the play with history lessons. While critics were also quick to point out that the success of this play helped cement Wilson's phenomenal rise to theatrical prominence, Robert Brustein, writing in the *New Republic*, questioned the play's commercialism and suggested that it lacked artistic merit. The drama critic for *Time*, however, argued that the play established Wilson as the "richest theatrical voice to emerge in the U.S. since . . . the flowering of Tennessee Williams and Arthur Miller."

—Marilyn Elkins

PICKANINNY. Pickaninnies were *stereotypes characteristic of the *plantation tradition that rendered through art and literature fond depictions and remembrances of the antebellum South and its way of life. The word "pickaninny" is believed to be derived from the Portuguese word "pequenino," meaning "very little," and was used to refer to African American slave children. Pickaninnies were usually portrayed as happy, playful, submissive, and animal-like. They were often referred to in the plural and appeared in the background of plantation scenes, frolicking and gambolling about like domesticated animals.

Pickaninnies were a staple of the plantation tradition. Slave owners and later apologists for the South used these stereotypes to justify many of the practices common on plantations, as well as their own racist views of African Americans as less than human. The portrayal of pickaninnies as playful and animal-like not only reinforced the belief that slaves were happy, contented, and carefree on the plantations, but also lent credence to practices such as separating children from their parents at a young age; if slaves were less than human, they could not be expected to have human emotional attachments to each other.

—Wendy Wagner

PICKENS, WILLIAM (1881–1954), orator, journalist, essayist, and autobiographer. William Pickens, one of the most popular African American speakers of his era, was born in Anderson County, South Carolina, on 15 January 1881, the son of former slaves who worked as tenant farmers. His parents moved their family to Arkansas in 1888 in search of better economic and educational opportunities. From the beginning a zealous student, Pickens's first systematic schooling came in 1890 in Argenta, across the river from Little Rock. With funds earned from a variety of manual labor jobs, Pickens paid his way to attend the Little Rock High School, from which he graduated at the top of his class in 1899. He then obtained admission to Talladega College in Alabama,

where he studied for three years before entering Yale University in 1902. At Yale Pickens won the Henry James Ten Eyck prize in *oratory for a speech on Haiti and was elected to Phi Beta Kappa. After completing his bachelor's degree in classics in 1904, Pickens rejected an offer to tour the country as a platform lecturer, choosing instead to return to the South to teach classics, literature, and sociology at Talladega (1904–1914), Wiley University in Texas (1914–1915), and Morgan College in Baltimore (1915–1920), where he served as dean and later vice-president.

Having been active as an organizer and recruiter for the NAACP since its founding in 1910, Pickens readily accepted an offer in 1919 to become assistant to James Weldon *Johnson, field secretary of the NAACP. When Johnson was elevated to executive director of the NAACP the following year, Pickens became associate field secretary. In this capacity and later as director of branches Pickens made a major contribution to the expansion of the NAACP, especially in the South, between 1920 and 1940. As a contributing editor of the Associated Negro Press for twenty-one years, Pickens helped publicize NAACP positions and activities in more than one hundred African American newspapers. After leaving the NAACP in 1942, Pickens went to work for the U.S. Treasury Department. During World War II, his efforts centered on selling war bonds in the African American community. After retirement from his government job in 1950, Pickens and his wife traveled internationally. He died aboard a ship off the coast of Jamaica on 6 April 1954 and was buried at sea.

Pickens first made a name for himself as a writer in 1904, when he began publishing increasingly blunt and controversial articles in the *Voice of the Negro*. "Choose!" (June 1906) demanded that every African American take an unequivocal stand against the philosophy and tactics of Booker T. *Washington and in favor of those of W. E. B. *Du Bois. Readers of Pickens's 1911 *autobiography, *The Heir of Slaves*, however, found only hints as to Pickens's public differences with Washington. Patterned after Washington's much celebrated *Up from Slavery* (1901), *The Heir of Slaves* emphasizes a young African American's devotion to *education and to the dedication of his learning and experience to the uplift of his people in the South. But with the 1916 publication of *The New Negro: His Political, Civil and Mental Status*, a collection of his *essays dedicated to the "essential humanity and justice" of "the white and the black men of tomorrow," Pickens made plain his uncompromising views on civil rights. The fundamental right Pickens demanded for African Americans in *The New Negro* was "full citizenship," by which he meant an end to all forms of segregation and a guarantee of the right to vote. In 1922, Pickens published *The Vengeance of the Gods and Three Other Stories of the Real American Color Line*, in which he denounces through highly didactic fiction the stereotyping of African American men and the illusory notions of superiority entertained by white Americans. A year later an expanded version of Pickens's autobiography appeared under the title *Bursting Bonds*. Retaining the nine chapters of *The*

Heir of Slaves, Pickens added five new ones to create *Bursting Bonds,* the title of which implied its author's determination to speak freely about matters on which he had previously been circumspect. *Bursting Bonds* exposes the mystique of white power and paternalism at Talladega, details the explosive intricacies of *Jim Crow in east Texas, and recalls Pickens's lonely, defiant ride in a forbidden Pullman car through Arkansas. By the end of the book, Pickens exemplifies in himself a model of what the *New Negro of the 1920s stood for and wrote about. In its candor about the contemporary *color line and sensitivity to its author's transition from conservative to militant, *Bursting Bonds* marks a turning point in the evolution of African American autobiography away from the deferential posture of *Up from Slavery* and toward the confrontational rhetoric of *Black Boy* (1945).

• Rebecca Chalmers Barton, *Witnesses for Freedom,* 1948. Sheldon Avery, *Up from Washington: William Pickens and the Negro Struggle for Equality,* 1989. William Pickens, *Bursting Bonds,* ed. William L. Andrews, 1991.

—William L. Andrews

PILATE DEAD is the aunt of *Milkman Dead, the protagonist in Toni *Morrison's *Song of Solomon* (1977). Represented in the *novel as the eccentric sister of Macon Dead II, who like her daughter Reba and her granddaughter Hagar has no navel, Pilate wears an earring made of a little box that contains her name and makes bootleg wine for a living. For these reasons and because he believes she tricked him out of the family inheritance of gold, Macon forbids Milkman to have any dealings with Pilate. Yet she is a part of his life from the beginning. The novel opens with her singing the song of her grandfather's flight back to Africa to escape from *slavery on the day before Milkman's birth. The fact that his mother even conceives him is supposedly attributed to a green potion Pilate, described as a "natural healer" and a "root worker," gives her. Described as her own person, Pilate is a woman who "threw away every assumption she had learned and began at zero." When Milkman starts to have questions about his *identity and where he fits in, he ignores his father's command and consults Pilate about his family history. As the family griot and *ancestor who knows the past, Pilate becomes the key to Milkman's quest to understand himself and his heritage. On his trip from Michigan to the South, he learns that the sack she keeps is really a sack of her father's bones. He escorts her back to the South to give her father a proper burial, and as she dies in his arms, he sings to her the song of his ancestors, the song he learned from her and that he had once regarded as a nonsense rhyme. Pilate is representative of the ancestor figure and griot in many of Morrison's novels, that member of the African American community who is both a link to the past and a key to the future.

[*See also* Conjuring; Folklore; Healing.]

• Marilyn Sanders Mobley, *Folk Roots and Mythic Wings in Sarah Orne Jewett and Toni Morrison,* 1992.

—Marilyn Sanders Mobley

PLACES. The names of spiritual and physical landscapes are sounded time and again in the language of African American folksongs, *spirituals, and *blues, and this cultural precedent is echoed in the figurative strategies of black writers. Like the broader culture of black Americans, their literature has tempered the historic experience of dislocation, *slavery, and discrimination by seeking terms with which to root their lives in the African diaspora. A characteristic vocabulary of place has become an imagery of belonging in America. The titles of a single writer—*Go Tell It on the Mountain* (1953), *The *Amen Corner* (1955), *Another Country* (1992), *If Beale Street Could Talk* (1974), and *Just above My Head* (1979), by James *Baldwin—exemplify a consistent literary strategy of allusion to a diversity of symbolic and spiritual spaces. Since the discourse of African American culture is disposed to transform literal spaces into topical spaces for rhetorical and figurative purposes, literary critics of African descent have addressed the ways in which landscapes become symbolic in order to study the cultural practice of evoking places of the spirit in critical and textual terms. In *From Behind the Veil: A Study of Afro-American Narrative* (1979), Robert B. Stepto examined how authors and texts have sought literary forms, including ritual and symbolic places, for what he calls the prefigurative or pregeneric myth of the quest for *freedom and *literacy. In *Ride out the Wilderness: Geography and Identity in Afro-American Literature* (1987), Melvin *Dixon demonstrated how writers have revealed a moral geography of social and political progress, turning figures of the landscape into settings that stake claims to "a physical and spiritual home in America."

The evolution of a discourse of spatial signing has produced a familiar lexicography of place that can be glossed usefully for an informed reading of African American texts, with one caveat: the usage and interpretation of these well-established signs of place and space always must be regarded as open-ended, provisional, and indeterminate, both inside and outside the circle of discourse. Take the ritual ground of Tuskegee Institute in Tuskegee, Alabama, for example. In *Up from Slavery* (1901) Booker T. *Washington aggregated the several historically black colleges founded in the aftermath of the Civil War into a single metonym standing for a national myth of racial uplift. Ralph *Ellison's *Invisible Man* (1952), however, placed a college resembling Tuskegee in close proximity to the incestuous family life of subsistence farmer *Trueblood in order to expose the tangle of unacknowledged motivations underwriting the college, and identified its educational mission with the repressive function of a nearby insane asylum in order to call into question the ritual of submission enacted in the myth of racial uplift. The significance of Tuskegee as a ritual ground was further complicated by its associations with the legendary Tuskegee Airmen who went on to play distinguished leadership roles in their communities across the nation, but also with the notorious syphilis experiments in which infected black patients were denied effective and available medical treatment so they could be exploited as experimental subjects in order to document the etiology of the degenerative disease.

The physical and spiritual geography of slavery invoked in the oral tradition and the narratives of former slaves constitute the original texts for the study of the places of the spirit of African American literature. The plantation with its big house and slave quarters, memorialized by generations of white authors in a popular tradition extending from John Pendleton Kennedy's *Swallow Barn, or A Sojourn in the Old Dominion* (1832) and Harriet Beecher *Stowe's *Uncle Tom's Cabin* (1852) to a twentieth-century blockbuster like Margaret Mitchell's *Gone with the Wind* (1936), was appropriated and reconfigured as a house of bondage in an array of literary texts of African American authors ranging from the antebellum fugitive slaves themselves to the postmodern feminists imagining slavery in the aftermath of the struggle for civil rights. The generic features of the plantation were first viewed from a former slave's perspective in the groundbreaking *Interesting Narrative of the Life of Gustavus Vassa, or Olaudah *Equiano, the African* (1789), and elaborated definitively by Frederick *Douglass in *My Bondage and My Freedom* (1855). Downriver, the all-encompassing term for the dreaded places in the lower South to which slaves were sold off, was the only alternative to the plantation allowed by the system of slavery, but various safe havens and sites of resistance to bondage were improvised within the domain of the plantation itself. The woods, the riverside, the swamp, and the wilderness—all locales of danger, discomfort, and disorder offering temporary refuge and relief in the House of Bondage—were put to use as settings for meditation, rebellion, and recuperation in texts, such as Nat *Turner's *Confessions* (1831) and Douglass's "The *Heroic Slave" (1853). In others such as Harriet A. *Jacobs's *Incidents in the Life of a Slave Girl* (1861), fearsome settings are inscribed as staging grounds for the proverbial flight North as when a terrified Linda Brent hides in the Dismal Swamp with poisonous snakes all around her until she can make her way to the vessel which is to ferry her to *freedom. A contemporary reinscription of the archetypal plantation occurs in feminist narratives, such as Octavia E. *Butler's *Kindred* (1979), Sherley Anne *Williams's *Dessa Rose* (1986), and Toni *Morrison's *Beloved* (1987).

A cryptic Old Testament geography of Egypt, Babylon, Gilead, River Jordan, Mount Pisgah, Canaan, and the promised land subsumed the North, Canada, and free land as the enslaved Africans identified themselves with the enslaved Israelites they heard or read about. This biblical vocabulary of place encoded the flight from slavery in the antebellum period and later provided significant new points of reference for the subsequent flights from the peonage, segregation, and socially sanctioned *violence of the South in the literature of the Great *Migration to the urban centers of the north. This terminology of place could still be evoked poignantly by Martin Luther *King, Jr., more than a century after emancipation, on the eve of his assassination on 4 April 1968 in Memphis, when he spoke of having gone to the mountain top (Mount Pisgah) and seen the promised land. The places of the religious vernacular received a secular inflection in the urban stories of Rudolph *Fisher, such as "City of Refuge" (1925), which identifies Harlem with the biblical cities of refuge in order to register the expansive psychology of possibility in the unprecedented setting of black Harlem of the 1920s, and was never more richly embellished than in the allusive language of the Harlem saints that James Baldwin turned to literary purposes in *Go Tell It on the Mountain*.

The northward trajectory of the Great Migration was reversed, at least symbolically and provisionally, by The *Souls of Black Folk* (1903) in which W. E. B. *Du Bois's narrator, a Northerner by birth and education, travels to the rejected ancestral landscape down South and immerses himself in the life of the region's Black Belt, the cluster of southern states—from North Carolina, South Carolina, and Georgia on the Atlantic coast, through Alabama and Louisiana, to Mississippi and Tennessee on the Mississippi River—associated with workers of African descent involved in the monoculture of cotton. Du Bois introduced the Black Belt in order to impart a new understanding of the spiritual strivings of the race in what he terms life "behind the veil." This cycle of return is recapitulated in a number of African American texts in which ritual immersion in southern folkways is envisioned as the point of departure for cultural reinvigoration and rebirth. The journey into blackness in the South is aborted in The *Autobiography of an Ex-Colored Man* (1912) when James Weldon *Johnson's narrator is confronted with the shame of belonging to a race that can be lynched with impunity on a public street, but in Jean *Toomer's *Cane* (1923), several male narrators of northern origins find the possibility of renewal in encounters with the blighted crops, twilight landscapes, and violated females of the South. Most notably in the final section of *Cane*, a group of African American southern males guide the title character of the piece through figurative rituals of passage into southern culture that finally bring him face to face with the enigmatic ancestral figure of a deaf, dumb, and blind emancipated slave entombed in a cellar dug out of the red clay of Georgia.

Nonetheless, the dominant vector of cultural movement continued to point north. In the first decades of the twentieth century, black New Yorkers seized a desired territory in Harlem and created a black city, which in the years following World War I promised to become the cultural capital of the race. Harlem became a singular symbolic figure and a primary ritual site as soon as this former community of gentlemen farmers, developed in the late nineteenth century as a comfortable suburb for a new class of white homeowners, was popularly perceived to have become black. The emergence of black Harlem, itself a product of the demographic dislocations of the Great Migration, overshadowed and supplanted the black and racially mixed areas of old New York City, such as Five Points, Little Africa, Chelsea, Hell's Kitchen, and San Juan Hill, and was identified with features of the bohemian lifestyle of the Tenderloin district first depicted in Paul Laurence *Dunbar's The *Sport of the

Gods (1902) and Johnson's *Autobiography of an Ex-Colored Man* (1912) as a subject for literature. The idea of black Harlem as the site for the twentieth-century repudiation of unacceptable inherited notions of racial *identity inspired a great many writers in a remarkably large number of works. Virtually every significant African American author identified with the *New Negro movement or the *Harlem Renaissance of the 1920s—Claude *McKay, Countee *Cullen, Langston *Hughes, Zora Neale *Hurston, Helene *Johnson, Walter *White, Jessie Redmon *Fauset, Nella *Larsen, Wallace *Thurman, Sterling A. *Brown, and Rudolph Fisher—published one or more poems, *novels, *short stories, and/or plays for which Harlem provides a literal and/or figurative setting. Many black writers outside of the United States celebrated black Harlem in their works, along with many authors who were not black, such as Federico García Lorca. Legendary addresses (409 Edgecombe Avenue), streets ("Strivers' Row" at 139th Street and "Bucket o' Blood" at 133rd Street), avenues (Lenox Avenue, Edgecombe Avenue, and St. Nicholas Avenue), *churches (Abyssinian Baptist Church and St. Philips Protestant Episcopal Church), neighborhoods (Sugar Hill), bars and cabarets (the Cotton Club, Small's Paradise, the Renaissance Casino, and the Savoy Ballroom), and cultural sites (the Tree of Hope, an aging elm in front of the Lafayette Theatre, which Harlemites, particularly artists and performers touched for good luck, and the Dark Tower, the townhouse heiress A'Lelia Walker organized as a literary salon in 1928) became part of a familiar lexicon of place for literary artists over the decades.

After each of the race riots (1943, 1964) in American cities with large black populations, new generations of black writers in the United States employed the Harlem motif as an icon of racial being, consolidating the status of the black enclave as a key location of the spirit. The emerging ghetto of Harlem was largely abandoned as a theme for *poetry by African Americans, but fiction writers found powerful significance in the deteriorating culture capital in the 1940s and 1950s in a large number of novels, among which Ralph Ellison's *Invisible Man* stands out as a unique accomplishment. No writer, however, evoked the spiritual setting of black Harlem more consistently over a long career than Langston Hughes. Like the other poets of his generation, Hughes first celebrated Harlem in the 1920s as a mythic landscape imbued with intimations of cultural possibility, but unlike his New Negro contemporaries, Hughes identified the daily life of Harlem with the sounds from the regional centers of *jazz and blues, like New Orleans, Memphis, St. Louis, Kansas City, and the Mississippi Delta, being heard everywhere on "race records" cut in Harlem for the Black Swan Phonograph Corporation founded in 1921. Hughes's jazz-and-blues Harlem offered the possibility of aesthetic as well as thematic revision when Harlem began to change for the worse, and for a time in the 1940s and 1950s only Hughes seemed able to respond to Harlem's disheartening alteration in poetry. His *Montage of a Dream Deferred* (1951) restored a credible sense of possibility and pointed the way for the coming literary generation. In the immediate aftermath of the ghetto riots of the 1960s, younger poets—Calvin C. *Hernton, Clarence *Major, Nikki *Giovanni, Audre *Lorde, Gayl *Jones, Gil *Scott-Heron, Conrad Kent *Rivers, David Henderson, James Emanuel, Raymond R. Patterson, Ted *Joans, Amiri *Baraka/LeRoi Jones, and many others—made Harlem a primary setting and symbol of the *Black Arts movement in a remarkable outpouring of new work. And along with several naturalistic fictions set in Harlem by new novelists, like Louise *Meriwether, John A. *Williams, George *Cain, Barry *Beckham, Rosa *Guy, Walter Dean *Myers, and Mary Elizabeth *Vroman, came strikingly original narratives in prose and verse, notably Melvin B. *Tolson's *Harlem Gallery, The Curator, Part I* (1964), Charles S. *Wright's *The Wig* (1966), and Ishmael *Reed's *Mumbo Jumbo* (1972).

Particular towns, regions, and terrains, whether historical or fictional, have been closely associated with the narratives of several African American writers because of the extent and significance of their treatment of the area or its recurrence in a number of works. Frederick Douglass, for example, recurred to the setting of the Chesapeake Bay and its environs in different ways in each of the three *autobiographies published over the course of his long and distinguished public life. *Narrative of the Life of Frederick Douglass, An American Slave* (1845) established the woods and waterways of the region as literal and symbolic alternative spaces to slavery, and as pathways to freedom. *My Bondage and My Freedom* exposed the topology of slavery as a total institution in an expansive portrayal of the Lloyd plantation. *Life and Times of Frederick Douglass* (1881; rev. 1892) put the Chesapeake Bay to use as the setting of a triumphant ritual return to the scenes of his former enslavement.

Some African American authors chose to mask their engagement with specific historical settings. Harriet Jacobs disguised the precision of her depiction of Edenton, North Carolina, to reinforce the pseudonymous character of *Incidents in the Life of a Slave Girl* (1861). Charles Waddell *Chesnutt imposed a degree of aesthetic distance from the North Carolina region in which many of his stories and novels are set around the turn of the century by assigning easily deciphered fictional names, such as Patesville for Fayetteville in *The *Conjure Woman* (1899) and Wellington for Wilmington in *The *Marrow of Tradition* (1901). Ernest J. *Gaines has set virtually all of his novels and short stories from *Catherine Carmier* (1964) to *A Lesson before Dying* (1993) in the same mythical landscape, the plantation country around the town of Bayonne in St. Raphael's Parish near Baton Rouge, Louisiana.

Many more, however, have chosen typically to turn literal and historical settings to figural and fictional purposes by embracing the verisimilitude of their chosen settings, such as the Mississippi of Alice *Walker and Richard *Wright, and the Chicago of Wright and Gwendolyn *Brooks. Two widely respected contemporary authors have undertaken formal literary cycles of works that make the depiction of authentic African American places over an extended historical period an important aspect of their literary mission. South Central, the minority area of Los Angeles, is the setting Walter *Mosley has chosen for a cycle of novels about his Houston-born private-investigator protagonist *Easy Rawlins and his sidekick Mouse. The time frame of the 1930s explored in *Devil in a Blue Dress* (1990), the first novel in the series, has been extended through the McCarthy period of the 1950s and into the 1960s in subsequent volumes. The Hill section of Pittsburgh is the locale August *Wilson has as the preferred setting for his grand design of writing a play about each of the decades of the twentieth century and the important questions confronted by African Americans in that decade.

Among the most celebrated instances of a writer's literary commitment to a place is Zora Neale Hurston's self-identification with Eatonville, Florida, the oldest incorporated black town in the United States. Many of the short narratives written by Hurston in the heyday of the Harlem Renaissance are set in Eatonville rather than in Harlem. The fictional lives of her characters are intertwined with the founding and evolution of this historic black township in the final years of the nineteenth century, and major characters are versions of dominant figures in the life of the town, such as John Pearson in *Jonah's Gourd Vine* (1934), based on her father, the Reverend John Hurston, and Joe Starks, *Janie Crawford's second husband in *Their Eyes Were Watching God* (1937), based on Joe Clark, Eatonville's principal storekeeper and first mayor.

The spiritual and moral geography of African American literature and culture has included places of the spirit from beyond the borders of the United States. Liberia was known to have been founded by American slaves who had returned to the homeland. Philip the Apostle had relayed Christianity to Ethiopia (or Abyssinia), according to the New Testament. African Americans often associated black nationhood with this ancient African kingdom and commonly alluded to it in their organizational and institutional names. The legendary figures of black heroism and independence in the slave uprising in Haiti were recognized as inspirational models for black Americans long before Claude McKay evoked a spiritual kinship between Jake, the uneducated protagonist of *Home to Harlem* (1928), and Ray, the young Haitian intellectual Jake meets while working for the Pullman Company, who reveals new landscapes of black myth and history to his racial compatriot in the figure of Haiti's Toussaint *L'Ouverture. African American contacts with the spiritual places of the diaspora were initiated on a different scale in the 1920s when Langston Hughes visited Port-au-Prince, Haiti, and Havana, Cuba, and established the first significant personal relationships with the young writers of African descent of the parallel racial awakenings occurring in the Greater Antilles, such as Jacques Roumain and Nicolás Guillén. His brief encounters with Haitian and Cuban intellectuals and artists anticipated

the wider reach of the mutual influences that would be shared among young writers from the different parts of the black world a few years later.

Paris, the capital city of novelist and dramatist Alexandre Dumas, enjoyed a reputation with the black elite as a setting of culture, hospitality, and tolerance lasting well into the twentieth century. Actor Ira Aldridge was one of the earliest *expatriate African American artists to work there; others were the painter Henry Ossawa Turner and the playwright Victor *Séjour, a French-speaking free man of color from New Orleans who established an important literary career for himself in Paris. In 1917 significant numbers of black men volunteered to fight for democracy in France, where they were generally well-received by the local populations. The black soldiers of World War I returned to America in triumph in the spring of 1919 with the recognition of the Croix de Guerre awarded collectively to the 369th Regiment by the French government and a new sense of *manhood and self-worth, which would be tested in the violent "Red Summer" of the same year. As Harlem was the crossroads of the black Americans in the 1920s, so Paris was the crossroads for black artists and intellectuals of African descent from the different parts of the diaspora in the early 1930s. Virtually all the writers of the Harlem Renaissance visited Paris, either briefly or for extended stays, and several of their works were published in French language translations. The Harlem writers and artists encountered students and writers from Haiti, French West Africa, and the Caribbean in Paris, and there a sense of the existence of a transnational, multilingual, cross-cultural, racial ethos across the breadth of the African diaspora, later to be termed *Negritude, began to bloom. After World War II Richard Wright, Chester *Himes, and James Baldwin became the most prominent African Americans in a growing colony of expatriate artists, which included cartoonist Ollie Harrington and painter Beauford Delaney, who moved to Paris in order to find a tolerant space in which to create. In recent decades, the expatriation to Paris and other French cities of new generations of African American writers has continued, including poets James Emanuel, Ted Joans, and Melvin Dixon, and novelists William Melvin *Kelley and Barbara *Chase-Riboud.

New places continue to be identified as legendary settings of the spirit for ritual and symbolic activities in African American literature and culture. Ibo Landing in the Sea Islands of South Carolina is one striking example. The slave ship *Wanderer* arrived in 1858 at Ibo Landing with a smuggled cargo of so-called salt-water, African-born slaves, imported half a century after the prohibition of the international slave trade. According to legend, the Ibo captives took one look at their new land, turned, and walked past the slave ship across the water in the direction of Africa. Immersion rituals of departure and return, corresponding to Toomer's male rituals but voiced in a different register with a new emphasis on African ancestral roots, have been set at Ibo Landing in Paule *Marshall's novel *Praisesong for* the Widow (1983) and also in Julie Dash's *film Daughters of the Dust (1992). Ibo Landing is a particular inflection of the *Middle Passage—the common term for the transatlantic crossing of African captives to the Americas in the holds of slave ships—which has emerged as a liminal space of increasing figurative significance in recent African American texts. For most of the nineteenth century, Africa was inscribed in the discourse of black Americans as an alien and inaccessible ancestral homeland. With the prohibition of the international slave trade in 1808, literary treatments of Africa and the Atlantic Middle Passage such as The Interesting Narrative of the Life of Gustavus Vassa, or Olaudah Equiano, the African (1789) gave way to the antebellum fugitive *slave narratives published by abolition societies in the effort to discredit and eliminate the internal slave trade of the United States. In the first decades of the twentieth century, however, Du Bois's Pan African Congresses, Marcus *Garvey's back to Africa movement, the enthusiasm of Picasso and the other modernist painters for African art, and their own increasing mobility, all provoked a fresh interest in the ancestral setting of Africa, and the spiritual journey back to southern roots acquired its African counterpart. "What Is Africa to Me?" was the provocative interrogative shaping Countee Cullen's long poem "Heritage" in The *New Negro (1925), the *anthology edited by Alain *Locke that introduced the young Harlem writers to a wider white readership. The poem was presented editorially in juxtaposition to Arthur A. *Schomburg's *essay, "The Negro Digs up His Past," and images of African artifacts offered a visual counterpart to the African American literary texts. Only with the appearance of Robert *Hayden's poem, "Middle Passage" (Selected Poems, 1966) decades later, however, was the transatlantic ordeal recognized and acknowledged as a transformative ritual connecting African Americans with the ancestral setting of Africa. In the last decade influential authors have consolidated the transatlantic passage as a primary imaginative and ritual plane of the diaspora transecting time and history, memory and space. In Toni Morrison's Beloved (1987) a ghost child is reincarnated in the form of a woman who steps fully grown out of a watery world beyond language that conflates features of the hold of a slave ship on a turbulent ocean with the burial ground of the dead child in Cincinnati. In Charles R. *Johnson's *Middle Passage (1990) a fugitive slave narrator reinscribes the log of the captain of the slave ship Republic with the Middle Passage of an extraordinary captured African tribe, as well as with his own voyage of self-discovery. And in Derek Walcott's Omeros (1990), the psychic divisions and the spiritual and moral wounds of history and exile are consummated, at least provisionally, in a richly figured Caribbean environment overlaid with the geography of Homer's transformative Mediterranean, when Walcott's visionary West Indian protagonist named Achilles is led in his fishing boat by a tutelary swift back to the ancestral slave coast of Africa in a restorative Middle Passage.

[See also Diasporic Literature; Folk Literature; West Indian Literature.]
—James de Jongh

PLANTATION TRADITION. The literature of the plantation tradition was penned in the decades following the Civil War primarily by white Southerners seeking, through romanticized images of plantation life, to recover for the nation the forms of power and racial order that the war and Reconstruction had dismantled. The literary climate established in the post–Civil War period favored the "local," that is, settings, plots, characters, and speech that stressed cultural difference at a time when a national communications system and economy were centralizing cultural norms. Fiction centered in plantation society, featuring the chivalrous master, the effervescent belle, and the childlike African American "servant," dominated southern literary production beginning in the 1830s, and these portraits intensified in antebellum responses to the rebuttals presented in the *slave narratives and Harriet Beecher *Stowe's Uncle Tom's Cabin (1852). By 1865 the outlines of a tradition were clearly marked: the white southern yeoman, the merchant class Southerner of the city, the freedom-loving or even self-willed slave had been expunged from the accepted literary vision of the culture, which became exclusively the domain of the noble master and his gracious, deferential mistress, presiding over a hierarchically arranged world of dependents on estates whose preservation was the theme, the plot, and the necessary conclusion of all action. In particular, novels like Caroline Gilman's Recollections of a Southern Matron (1836); John Pendleton Kennedy's Swallow Barn, or a Sojourn in the Old Dominion (1832; rev. ed. 1851); William Gilmore Simms's Woodcraft (1852); and Caroline Lee Hentz's The Planter's Northern Bride (1854) set the stage for the postwar rise of plantation mythology to full glory as a more potent force in national politics than it had been when actual plantations dotted the southern landscape.

In the years following the war, growing white concern over the free African American population provided the national market for a tradition that could, without much refinement, adapt the staples of antebellum plantation fictions to postwar demands. White post-Reconstruction America, instituting a legal system of segregation and disfranchisement, derived from the literature of the plantation tradition an ideological construct allowing the idealization of the past to combine with the subjugation of freedmen and -women in the present. To the already firmly fixed figures of the mythology, postbellum plantation literature added one powerful ingredient, the voice of the slaves themselves, freed only to wish that they were back in the idealized world of domestic *slavery that gave them the security of family protection in return for perpetual servitude. The remarkable effect of this strategy was its successful manipulation of northern public opinion. Northern magazines such as Scribner's, the Century, Harper's, and the Atlantic Monthly invited syrupy visions of the Old South delivered in dialect by its slave labor force recast as family retainers and hovering *mammies. Thus the reunion of North and South, and the effective establishment of a politics of white racial supremacy, were accomplished through a literary design in which pastoral nostalgia masked the *violence of the slave past and stereotyped African American characters became advocates for their own disempowerment.

Beginning with *dialect poetry in the 1870s, and reflecting the trappings and point of view of *minstrelsy, white plantation literature increasingly relied upon the convention of placing a philosophy of nostalgia for times "befo' deh wa'" in the mouths of comic, local color African American characters. Irwin Russell (1853–1879), credited by Joel Chandler Harris with discovering the potential of "negro character," created the best-known of these dialect poems in "Christmas-Night in the Quarters" (1878), a verse drama in which several slave darky types common to antebellum blackface minstrel shows are lovingly called upon to testify to a refurbishing of the old plantation as pastoral kingdom. The preacher, the fiddler, the mule driver, and the singer of *spirituals are Russell's African American spokespersons for an idyll of the lost cause. Russell was one of many early tillers of this myth; in fictional sketches Sherwood Bonner (1849–1883) published black dialect "Gran'-mammy tales" in northern magazines in the 1870s, and Uncle Remus had appeared in brief vignettes in the Atlanta *Constitution* in the 1870s before his tales were published in the first of several Remus collections, *Uncle Remus: His Songs and His Sayings*, in 1880. The accuracy of the dialect that these white writers employed is hardly as important in considering their impact as is the tremendous popular acceptance of the versions they offered up in the service of a white racist ideology. Applications of dialect could solidify the perception of the slave as ignorant, primitive, incapable of self-governance, and irretrievably "other," and so feed racist *stereotypes necessary to national policies of segregation. Yet the early white dialect works would also contribute by the end of the century to African American writers' much more complex strategies involving the use of dialect to mock and subvert present white social structures as well as to retain certain vital markers of slave culture.

The 1880s established the plantation tradition as a literary mode glorifying the Old South through nostalgia connected to the image of an aristocratic white society served by a contented slave force. The African American voice fashioned to sell this vision was perfected during this decade primarily through the fiction of Thomas Nelson Page (1853–1922) and Joel Chandler Harris (1848–1908). Page fashioned the most enchanted version of plantation mythology in his 1887 collection of stories, *In Ole Virginia*. Here antebellum Virginia is Eden, the master is gentleman, the mistress is lady, and yet the slave is the center around which the plantation revolves. The stories are set in the early 1870s, told by elderly African American family retainers who sustain, protect, and restore their white owners both in their stance as narrators and their acts of devotion as characters.

Sam in "Mars' Chan," Billy in "Meh Lady," and Edinburg in "Unc' Edinburg's Drowndin'" look back to the South of old as the time when the noble white cavalier and his damsels depended upon their slaves' heroics. The African American narrator, in his primitive language, exalts himself within the system of master-slave relations that makes *freedom seemingly unnecessary; slavery quite simply suits his temperament while allowing him to bask in the reflected glory of his master's position and even to secure that position for the master. The stories abound in duels, thwarted romances, the tragedies of "the war," and the intrigues of high society, all seen through the prism of the simple servant's wistful remembrance.

Dialect for Page in these very popular tales functions as an important part of both character portrayal and conveyor of mood; it is not only Sam who seems simple, but the world he conjures in "Mars' Chan'" is also deceptively simple because of the language in which it comes to life. Joel Chandler Harris's plantation world is vastly more complicated in the Uncle Remus stories because of the juxtapositions that set both the master's estate and the slave cabin against *Brer Rabbit's brier patch. Page may have given the definitive rendition of the Old South translated for a New South politics of white reclamation; however, out back of the big house, Harris provided, again through the voice of the slave storyteller, a full sense of the deceptions as well as the power of the illusions involved in the plantation tradition. The difference between the two men's productions might be explained in part in terms of class: Page was born to the aristocratic notions of generations of Virginia planters, the Nelsons and the Pages, both "first families," while Harris, born in Eatonton, middle Georgia, to an unwed Irish seamstress, had a decidedly different perspective and no doubt more divided loyalties from an early age.

Harris worked as a boy on Turnwold plantation, owned by literary entrepreneur–planter Joseph Addison Turner, and there he first heard the tales fashioned by slaves who detailed the exploits of Brer Rabbit and company as comfort and entertainment fairly exclusively for themselves. By the late 1870s, Harris, a columnist and then editor of the Atlanta *Constitution*, had finished the outlines of the character into whose mouth he would put the stories throughout the last two decades of the century. Harris's and the tradition's most durable creation was the old darky Uncle Remus, sometimes portrayed as a postwar Atlanta freedman longing for his old homeplace but increasingly set back into an imaginary reconstruction of that world, where he tells the stories of Brer Rabbit's precarious existence to a small boy over whose mind he exercises an affectionate but also devious control. When Harris returned to the plantation through Uncle Remus, Harris's own preference for a mythic African American world over the aristocratic world of the big house is clear. Harris escapes along with the white boy of the frame stories into the domain lit with the vigorous imaginative identification that Uncle Remus makes with Brer Rabbit. When the child questions him about some of the violence and injustice of the rabbit's adventures, Uncle Remus is coolly accepting, and his satisfaction in Brer Rabbit's triumphs over stronger animals, Harris makes clear, reflects the slave's satisfaction in outmaneuvering a master class whose power had no relation to any standard of morality.

In Harris's hands the plantation tradition becomes a complicated, multivoiced structure of negotiations between masters and slaves, the strong and the weak, the *trickster and the oppressor. Harris could be both liberal and reactionary, progressive and anti–New South, a bigot or at least a paternalist and an advocate of civil rights for African Americans. Brer Rabbit might be in a perpetual state of risk, yet he also courts danger, he makes power plays that are gratuitously cruel, and he takes tremendous pride in outwitting and outmastering others. In many stories he barely escapes, yet always makes his enemies feel his scorn as he lights out. Brer Rabbit, then, operates on both sides of American slave society's set of relations.

In the latter half of the twentieth century, most critical evaluations of Harris attempt to separate the important ethnographic contribution of the tales from the racism reflected in Uncle Remus as teller. It is important to point out, however, that on many occasions Uncle Remus gives clear hints as to the allegorical meaning of stories containing violence, subversion of power, and challenges to morality. Like Brer Rabbit, Uncle Remus can play both sides—he can be both pitiful and malicious, both simple and canny. Harris was quite consciously attuned to fitting his narrator to the folk materials, as he was careful in rendering both the dialect and the details of the folk stories he collected. Certainly Uncle Remus plays the minstrel type on occasion, for purposes that Harris seemed to recognize were contradictory. Yet Uncle Remus also reflects slyly on the tales' import and relishes the trickery; he is responsible, moreover, for establishing the mythic tone that lifts the tales out of antebellum sentimentalism. Harris called attention to his own divided consciousness not only in letters and essays, but in the substance of his most famous character as well. A wide cultural gulf separates Harris from Uncle Remus, yet a full accounting must allow that Harris developed the *masking and *signifying propensities of Uncle Remus in significant ways that affect the impact that the plantation tradition has had on later renderings of slavery and the South.

The relationship between Harris and Charles Waddell *Chesnutt (1858–1932), the most important African American writer to work in the plantation tradition, indicates how Harris complicated the uses of the slave voice and dialect within the tradition. While Chesnutt's aim, beginning with his first book, the collection of stories entitled The *Conjure Woman, was a thoroughgoing revision of plantation literature, he adapted rather than totally rejected the territory that Harris defined, which legitimizes an African American mythology and the figure of the trickster as necessarily subversive elements within the slave's portion of plantation culture. Harris attended to the marginal world of the slave and established its connections to the African dimension of the creatures of the tales. Chesnutt could take from Harris his complex crossings of the margins; what Chesnutt, as

an African American writer, could add, primarily through his understanding of "*conjuring" was a transformation of the plantation tradition from within into an antipastoral critique of its own devices and intentions.

Of Chesnutt's five works of fiction, only the first, The Conjure Woman (1899), relied upon elements that had attained the status of racist tropes. The stories in the collection had been written or published over a period of ten years beginning with the appearance of "The Goophered Grapevine" in the Atlantic Monthly in 1887. Yet long before Walter Hines Page helped to assemble The Conjure Woman in 1899, Chesnutt had resolved to work in a different mode, the mode of social realism portraying contemporary problems of *race. He recognized that, although he had been able to work a significant revision of plantation literature's accepted function, the genre's core was derogatory stereotypes admired by white audiences increasingly intolerant of African American demands for equality and freedom. Determined to present his case through characters and voices that reflected his own education and situation, Chesnutt largely abandoned the plantation setting after the 1890s. But in The Conjure Woman, Chesnutt fashioned a complex analogue to the Uncle Remus tales in his own storyteller *Uncle Julius McAdoo, yet Chesnutt worked several essential transformations on Harris's formula in order to effect an entirely different vision and the possibility of entirely different critical judgment. First, Julius is no petted former house servant but instead a local laborer who possesses firsthand knowledge of slavery's cruelties and the slave's range of responses. Second, Julius turns to a source of African lore very different from Remus's. The directly subversive properties of conjure, rooted in African custom, are central to Julius's stories of slavery times. Each story develops an inner plot in which a slave seeks a conjurer in order to gain control over his or her life, primarily to redress a power imbalance or to mitigate sufferings caused by a master's callous disregard of basic human needs. Third, the frame audience for these stories is not a credulous southern child but two transplanted northern adult listeners of differing sensibilities, a cynical white entrepreneur, John, and his more eagerly receptive, in other words more malleable, wife Annie.

Finally, and most importantly distinct from Harris's model, the black vernacular dialect of Uncle Julius never gains primacy but always exists in relation to the standard, educated dialect of his postwar employer, John, whose frame stories, explaining his relations with Julius, signal his tension with this not completely trustworthy former slave. Thus Julius has to negotiate for space with skeptical, demanding listeners and thus problematically embodies Chesnutt's own dilemmas as an African American and author. Julius's tales and his dialect operate more directly on the plane of late nineteenth-century values and crises than any other plantation literature and more ironically reflect upon the form's distortions of content and vice versa. Uncle Julius bargains with his employer as his characters bargain with the conjure woman, and as Chesnutt bargained with white racists and willfully naive readers in a post-Reconstruction environment that was shaping severe restraints against the African American's negotiating position. The layers of action and revelation within the joined worlds of Julius's and John's narratives trade motives and meanings through the juxtapositions of dialect and also the signifying metaphor of conjure. Conjure provided Chesnutt with his most powerful artistic motif for cutting through the stereotypes fixed within the plantation tradition, but just as his characters found conjure's limitations, so did Chesnutt have to acknowledge the limitations set on his ability to affirm African American culture and critique the powers against it within his subtle redirecting of the mode's conventions.

In white literature, the plantation tradition at the end of the century was ripe for the takeover that Thomas Dixon (1864–1946) was soon to unleash in his extremist fiction *The Leopard's Spots: A Romance of the White Man's Burden 1865-1900* (1902) and *The Clansman: An Historical Romance of the Ku Klux Klan* (1905). Catering to and encouraging white fears of African American advancement, Dixon twisted the implicit threat that the uncle figure suggested in his subversive stories into the nightmare image of the black beast, whose speech is no longer quaint and primitive vernacular but the animalistic snarling of a mongrel type incapable of improvement and bent on destruction of his keepers. In African American literature, Paul Laurence *Dunbar (1872–1906) signaled the deep split within his community of artists regarding the utility of African retentions and the slave past. What was the value of slavery, of Africa, of African American dialect in cultural expressions of an African American identity at the end of the nineteenth century is a question that Dunbar's work asks but does not answer. His third collection of *poetry, *Lyrics of Lowly Life* (1896), brought him celebrity primarily for dialect poems of the old plantation; an introduction by William Dean Howells praised his work in this genre primarily on sociological grounds reflecting white approval of what the dialect seemed to display: the good humor, simplicity, childishness, and ignorance of the black race generally. Often the slave voice of Dunbar's lyrics takes the reader back to a plantation evoked as a seemingly simpler, more romantic time. Yet much of his work in dialect within plantation settings, poems like "An Antebellum Sermon," "The Old Cabin," and "A Banjo Song," express the pride and pain within slave identity in messages that reiterate the point of Dunbar's most open statement on his strategies, "We Wear the Mask."

Dunbar's relegation to the place of a "*Sambo" in much African American criticism of the twentieth century indicates how difficult the plantation tradition's methods and trappings are to decipher. Both white and African American writers in the post-Reconstruction period found in its conventions a means for caricature and critique, for cover-ups and unmaskings. The grins and lies of the African American character voicing, in a cherished but limiting vernacular dialect, expressions of memory and desire, pride and degradation, are the tradition's final legacy.

[*See also* Literary History, *article on* Reconstruction Era; Speech and Dialect.]

• Paul Gaston, *The New South Creed: A Study in Southern Mythmaking*, 1970. Robert Bone, *Down Home: A History of Afro-American Short Fiction from Its Beginnings to the End of the Harlem Renaissance*, 1975. William L. Andrews, *The Literary Career of Charles W. Chesnutt*, 1980. Lucinda H. MacKethan, *The Dream of Arcady: Place and Time in Southern Literature*, 1980. Wayne Mixon, *Southern Writers and the New South Movement, 1865-1913*, 1980. R. Bruce Bickley, ed., *Critical Essays on Joel Chandler Harris*, 1981. Alan Dundes, ed., *Mother Wit from the Laughing Barrel: Readings in the Interpretation of Afro-American Folklore*, 1973; rpt. 1981. Lucinda H. MacKethan, "Plantation Fiction, 1865–1900," in *The History of Southern Literature*, eds., Louis D. Rubin et al., 1985, pp. 209–218. Houston Baker, *Modernism and the Harlem Renaissance*, 1987. Dickson D. Bruce, Jr., *Black Writing from the Nadir: The Evolution of a Literary Tradition, 1877–1915*, 1989. Eric Sundquist, *To Wake the Nations: Race in the Making of American Literature*, 1993.

—Lucinda H. MacKethan

PLATO, ANN (?–?), essayist and poet. Little is known about the life of Ann Plato. Apparently, she was a free black in Hartford, Connecticut, at a time when the city's free black residents outnumbered the town's slave population. She was also a member of Hartford's Colored Congregational Church. Knowledge about her is limited to the one book that she published. Entitled *Essays: Including Biographies and Miscellaneous Pieces of Prose and Poetry* (1841), it contains four biographical compositions, sixteen very short *essays, and twenty poems.

Her minister, the Reverend James W. C. *Pennington, wrote an introductory notice "To the Reader." After identifying Ann Plato as one of his parishioners, he repeatedly says she is young but does not make clear exactly how old she is. He says nothing about her family except to indicate that she is "of modest worth." Neither does he tell how long she had been a member of his church, but he does record she is "of pleasing piety."

If Pennington tells little about Ann Plato, she told even less about herself. There is some evidence that she was either a young teacher or preparing to be one. Her essays are conventional. Designed as didactic renderings of issues that she found important, they focus primarily on religious and educational matters. Her attitude toward Africa appears in an essay entitled "Education" in which she commends those Christian missionaries who were willing to forsake the comforts of home in order to take "a message of love to the burning clime of Africa." In keeping with an eighteenth-century tendency to eulogize one's friends, Plato mourns—in the four *biographies—the early deaths of some friends, one of whom was apparently a slave.

Although Plato's *poetry seldom deals with racial issues, she apparently was not totally oblivious to the concerns of her day. One of her poems, "To the First of August," celebrates the ending of *slavery in the British West Indies and may have been written shortly after that law went into effect on 1 August 1838. At the time there were a number of poems written by a variety of poets on the subject, and she presumably joined this contemporaneous group. "The Natives of America" is a dramatic poem which relates her consideration of the plight of Native Americans in the United States. But for the most part, her subjects seem to have little to do with the specific problems faced by African Americans in everyday life.

One might conclude her only value is as a link between Phillis *Wheatley, whose work she apparently knew, and later women writers. On the other hand, Plato does show in *Essays* some tendencies toward a lyricism not associated with Phillis Wheatley. For example, her elegaic "Reflections, Written on Visiting the Grave of a Venerated Friend" goes beyond the expected neoclassical tradition and shows real feeling about death. Her love poem "Forget Thee Not" is another example of a stylized lyric that conveys a sense of emotion. But in following neoclassical conventions, she did not write about herself. As a result, much about Ann Plato has—so far—been lost to history. Yet, one wonders how autobiographical are such poems as "On Examination for a Teacher," "I Have No Brother," or "The Residence of My Fathers."

• "Ann Plato" in *Afro-American Women Writers, 1746–1933,* 1988, ed. Ann Allen Shockley, pp. 26–28. Kenny J. Williams, introduction to *Essays,* by Ann Plato, 1988.

—Kenny Jackson Williams

PLUMPP, STERLING (b. 1940), poet, educator, editor, and critic. Writing "tales of who I am" (*Contemporary Authors Autobiography Series,* vol. 21, 1995), Sterling Plumpp struggles to create the homeland of the spirit that accidents of birth—racial and economic—and what might be called accidents of destiny—the deaths of loved ones, the historical changes that have swept the African American and world community since his birth—have denied him. Yet his poems have far more than autobiographical resonance, not only because of the allusive, lyrical language in which he writes his best work, but because his quest for *identity resonates with the surrounding struggle for *freedom of the African American community during the *civil rights movement and its aftermath, and, especially in poems chronicling his experiences in Africa, with the struggle during the same years of colonized peoples for national sovereignty.

Sterling Plumpp was born to unmarried parents on 30 January 1940 in Clinton, Mississippi. His maternal grandparents raised him on the cotton plantation where his grandfather, Victor Emmanuel Plumpp, labored as a sharecropper. At age seven, a year before he started school, he joined his grandfather, an older brother, and other relatives in the fields picking cotton, but no amount of work was sufficient to raise the family out of debt. Listening to his grandparents' nightly prayers, Plumpp learned that one "could use words to petition for a different reality."

The full power of *religion struck him in 1951 in a local evangelical *church, when the force of a singer's voice prompted him to march to the altar to signify a conversion that soon, however, had to compete with budding adolescent interests. One of the abrupt psychological blows the South could deliver came in 1954, when news of Emmett Till's murder for flirting with a white woman traumatized Plumpp and others of his generation. At sixteen, Plumpp converted to Catholicism, and, throughout high school, cast about for a way to escape the dangers of *Jim Crow. Success took the form of an academic scholarship to St. Benedict's College in Atchison, Kansas.

There he had a new kind of conversion experience when he discovered Greek literature and James *Baldwin, whose "Sonny's Blues" inspired Plumpp to become a writer. After two years, yearning to write and feeling cut off from black culture, Plumpp left St. Benedict's and traveled north to Chicago.

He found work there in the main post office, read and tried to write in his off hours, and eventually enrolled at Roosevelt University, where he majored in psychology. After completing his bachelor's degree, he enrolled in a graduate program in clinical psychology, but continued to read widely—everything from Amiri *Baraka to Jean-Paul Sartre, and, of course, Baldwin, whose *The *Fire Next Time* (1963) struck Plumpp like a thunderbolt—and immersed himself in *music. During a "nightmarish" 1964–1965 interlude in the U.S. army, such books were his window to the outside world.

He published his first book, *Portable Soul,* in 1969, offering poems that drew on the language of the Black Power movement, but also began to construct the vocabulary for Plumpp's tales of identity. Publication led to a job teaching African American studies at the Chicago campus of the University of Illinois, where Plumpp became a full professor teaching both literature and creative writing.

His second book, *Half Black, Half Blacker* (1970), continues his simultaneous grappling with late 1960s upheavals in African American identity, and with his ongoing self-creation. Every black man, he writes in "Daybreak," "is an epic." The fusion of personal and public struggles is expanded into an impressionistic psychological treatise in Plumpp's 1972 book, *Black Rituals.* Confronting what he calls the "dragons" of his existence—his sharecropping youth in the Jim Crow South, the saving power of black music as a conduit of the divine, and the centrality of the black church as a repository of African American culture and engine of change—Plumpp created in this book a rough theory of his own and his people's existence.

The theory continued to develop in two long poems, "Steps to Break the Circle" and "Clinton," published as pamphlets in 1974 and 1976, respectively, and later included in Plumpp's 1982 volume, *The Mojo Hands Call / I Must Go.* Plumpp's growing interest in international liberation movements also bore fruit in 1982 when he edited an *anthology of South African poetry, *Somehow We Survive.* With the anthology and the new collection, which won the 1983 Carl Sandburg Award, Plumpp established himself as a significant voice in American letters. The new collection's reference to irresistible "Mojo hands," furthermore, spotlights Plumpp's arrival at a new conceptual plateau in the collection. In "Steps to Break the Circle: An Introduction," for instance, Plumpp casts a critical, evaluative eye on 1960s *poetry and politics, and on his own evolution. He expresses doubts about whether the "answer" that will break the circle of African American pain is 1960s-style *black nationalism, and not something at once more "coldly programmatic" and more open to a poetics of individuality.

In *Blues: The Story Always Untold* (1989), Plumpp firmly attaches himself to the *blues as the root of African American poetics. An increasing faith in words as arbiters of reality is expressed in poems celebrating the power of blues singers and of the music that passes through them like a god: When the protagonist of his poem "Mississippi Griot" bent guitar strings, Plumpp writes that his grandfather's "fields were flooded."

The parallel between African American and South African experience is the force behind Plumpp's 1993 volume, *Johannesburg and Other Poems*, which grew out of a 1991 visit Plumpp made to South Africa. His observations there taught him, he says, the centrality of *class as well as *race in African and African American experience. Yet his spiritual repatriation is also a repatriation in suffering. In the title poem, the Johannesburg he experiences is both a song-rich African Harlem, and a dehumanizing "Cold Steel Mountain." Thus in his "homeland," Plumpp is cast back on his career-long sifting of memory and *history for the elements of identity: "I ask, Johannesburg, if your streets know my name." In his new volume, *Hornman* (1995), Plumpp returns to his abiding balm, music, seeking the link between his "blues roots" and *jazz improvisation. His importance lies in his ability to communicate the excitement of such quests, and to fix ready-made concepts such as race—inevitable broadcaster of racism that it is—in the way the late Richard Feynman was said to fix radios: by *thinking*. In his best work, Plumpp makes mind-dimming concepts transmit vision, not hate.

• James Cunningham, "Sterling Plumpp," in *DLB*, vol. 41, *Afro-American Poets since 1955*, eds. Trudier Harris and Thadious M. Davis, 1985, pp. 257–265. "Plumpp, Sterling D(ominic)," in *Contemporary Authors: New Revision Series*, vol. 24, ed. Deborah A. Straub, 1988, pp. 371–372. James Cunningham, "Baldwin Aesthetics in Sterling Plumpp's Mojo Poems," *Black American Literature Forum* 23 (Fall 1989): 505–518. Sterling Plumpp, "Sterling Plumpp," in *Contemporary Authors Autobiography Series*, ed. Joyce Nakamura, vol. 21, 1995, pp. 165–178.   —Michael Collins

Poems on Various Subjects, Religious and Moral, the first book published by an African American on the North American continent, first appeared early in September of 1773. Printed in London and backed by the British philanthropist Selina Hastings, Countess of Huntingdon, an earlier version of this book, which was to have been printed in Boston, was rejected for racist reasons. This projected volume of 1772 would have been quite different from that which actually did come out in September of the next year. Of the twenty-eight poems slated to appear in the planned 1772 volume, six are decidedly political

and patriotic in subject, while only two poems of the 1773 volume's thirty-eight pieces by Phillis *Wheatley (the thirty-eighth poem, by James Bowdoin, is a riddle that Wheatley "solves" in the thirty-ninth and final poem of the volume) specifically deal with patriotic topics.

While the 1772 proposals promise a volume that would probably have propelled Wheatley into the limelight as first poet for American Independence, eclipsing Philip Freneau's later claim to this distinction, the 1773 *Poems* is much less obviously political in nature. "To the King's Most Excellent Majesty. 1768" and "To the Right Honourable William, Earl of Dartmouth" both state Wheatley's preoccupation with *freedom, the central subject of her oeuvre. The former poem celebrates George III's repeal of the Stamp Act and concludes with the arresting line, "A monarch's smile can set his subjects free!" "To . . . the Earl of Dartmouth" opens with the enthusiastic couplet, "Hail, happy day, when smiling like the morn, / Fair *Freedom* rose *New-England* to adorn," but contains the affecting story of Wheatley's seizure by slavers from her father's embrace.

Such poems as "To Maecenas," "On Recollection," and "On Imagination" appear to take up aesthetic concerns. "To Maecenas," for example, ostensibly addresses the issue of literary patronage, paralleling Horace's dedication of his first *Book of Odes* to Maecenas. Yet Wheatley's structure is much more complex than that of her Latin predecessor. Expanding her poem from Horace's thirty-six lines of Latin to fifty-five of neoclassical American colonial verse, Wheatley introduces the classical pastoral mode ("myrtle shade" and shepherds piping in sunny meadows), which she exploits as a major part of her subversive style; declares she longs to emulate Homer and Virgil, which she later attempts in her two *epyllia* (short epics), "Goliath of Gath" and "Niobe in Distress"; specifies her personal struggle for freedom by calling Terence, the Latin comedic dramatist and former slave from North Africa, "happier" than she because his pen has effectually freed him; and states that she will sing the virtues of Maecenas and at the same time praise "him [God] from whom those virtues sprung," hence signaling the religious and moral subjects of her volume's title that she will explicate in her frequent use of myth and symbol adapted from the King James Bible. Wheatley also asserts her own poetic maturity, manifested by attainment of the poet's laurel (as does Horace, yet whereas what the Latin poet affirms comes to him by acknowledged right, the black woman poet must "snatch . . . While [others] indulgent smile upon the deed").

In a similar manner "On Recollection" and "On Imagination," seeming to address central issues of the aesthetic categories of the time, actually serve as vehicles for Wheatley's demonstration of power over words and permit her to break the "iron bands" of oppression and to move freely "through the unbounded regions of the mind."

The 1773 *Poems* is prefaced by several items, including a frontispiece or woodcut of Wheatley before a writing desk, a "Dedication to the Right Honourable the Countess of Huntington," a letter by

Wheatley's master, John Wheatley, and a second letter, "To the Publick," attesting to Wheatley's authenticity as author of the volume's poems and signed by the best-known dignitaries in Boston. Of these materials, the letter of attestation and the portrait are of particular interest.

The letter of attestation is a remarkable document. This testimony marks the first occasion that the *authentication procedure, to which so many African Americans subsequently found themselves subjected, was applied to verify either the *literacy of the African American author, as in this case, or the veracity of the African American who recited her or his "narrative" to an *amanuensis.

While the frontispiece of Wheatley may look innocuous to today's audience, it cannot have seemed so to Wheatley's. The presentation to the world of an obviously black woman, holding a quill pen resting on paper on which one can see writing, striking a meditative pose promising still more writing, definitely denies all notions that black people cannot participate in the creation of literate artifacts; in short, this portrait enacts rebellion. This rebellion against white oppression occurs at the beginning of the African American literary tradition, a moment whose significance cannot be exaggerated.

[See also Literary History, article on Colonial and Early National Eras; Poetry.]

• William H. Robinson, *Black New England Letters: The Uses of Writings in Black New England*, 1977. Houston A. Baker, Jr., *The Journey Back: Issues in Black Literature and Criticism*, 1980. Sondra A. O'Neale, "A Slave's Subtle War: Phillis Wheatley's Use of Biblical Myth and Symbol," *Early American Literature* 21.2 (Fall 1986): 144–165. John C. Shields, ed., *The Collected Works of Phillis Wheatley*, 1988. Philip M. Richards, "Phillis Wheatley and Literary Americanization," *American Quarterly* 44.2 (June 1992): 163–191. Frances Smith Foster, *Written by Herself: Literary Production by African American Women 1746–1892*, 1993.

—John C. Shields

POETRY. African American poetry is the aesthetic chronicle of a *race, as Gwendolyn *Brooks expresses it, struggling to lift "its face all unashamed" in an alien land. From the earliest attempts of African American poets in the eighteenth century to express lyrically their adjustment to existence in a society that debated their humanity to their intense exploration of their voice in the waning years of a racially charged twentieth century, they have built an aesthetic tradition that affirms them, using a language and literary models adapted to meet their cultural purposes. From the very beginning these poets had a challenging, often agonizing, set of problems: the selection of subject matter, themes, and forms to express their thoughts and feelings; the cultivation of a voice expressive of their racial consciousness; the reception of the desired audience; the support of a *publishing and critical infrastructure; the nature of their relationship with other literary traditions; and the identification of the anima and purpose of their literary efforts. In essence, African American poetry is metaphorically the "furious flower" of Gwendolyn Brooks's poem "Second Sermon on the Warpland" (1968), pointing to two significant intertwining developments: one radical and the other aesthetic.

When Lucy *Terry wrote "Bars Fight" (1746), the first poem written by an African in America, she set in motion a poetic tradition characterized by the furious pursuit of liberation in all of its dimensions as well as the cultivation of a cultural voice authenticated by its own distinctive oral forms and remembered, communal values. Speaking of this first development, Stephen Henderson in his seminal work *Understanding the New Black Poetry* (1972) writes that the idea of liberation permeated African American literary consciousness from *slavery to the tumultuous 1960s, when poets reflected widespread disenchantment with white middle-class values and embraced cultural values emanating from Africa and the African diaspora. From Jupiter *Hammon to Kevin Powell the idea of liberation has informed and energized African American poetry. African American poets have been creators and critics of social values as they envisioned a world of justice and equality. Nineteenth-century poets voiced the slaves' complaint in the abolitionist struggle and rallied the troops in the cause of emancipation and *freedom. African American poets in the twentieth century continued to rail against the status quo and protested attitudes and institutions that stood to impede the *civil rights movement that changed the nature of American society. As these poets reflected African American concerns in the context of a larger American culture, they created a body of poetry that grew out of folk roots; legitimized poetry as a performative, participatory activity; and succeeded in creating an aesthetic tradition defined by communal values, the primacy of musicality and improvisation, and inventive style.

Roots in Liberation. The fertile soil of American Wesleyanism and the revolutionary fervor for liberty that culminated in the American Revolution animated the poetic impulse in Jupiter Hammon and Phillis *Wheatley. Hammon, the first African American to publish a poem, "An Evening Thought" (1761), longed for salvation from this world and acquiesced to enslavement on earth. Phillis Wheatley, the precocious servant of the Wheatleys of Boston, wrote her earliest verse as a mere adolescent in the late 1760s. She chose subjects that reflected her comfortable and privileged position and her absorption of a New England education, which emphasized the reading of the Bible and the classics. Her first volume of poems, entitled *Poems on Various Subjects, Religious and Moral* (1773), contained occasional poems eulogizing notable figures and celebrating significant events such as George Washington's appointment as commander of the Continental Army. Phillis Wheatley, kidnapped at the age of seven, brought to America in a slave ship, and sold in 1761, noted as the "Sable Muse" of Boston whose fame spread to England, aware of her own fortunate status in contrast to the lot of impoverished blacks in Boston's ghetto, did not commit any of these subjects to poetry. Her own condemnation of slavery and censure of so-called Christian slaveholders as well as the joys and sorrows associated with her marriage and the birth of her children are preserved only in personal letters. Whether out of a sense of Christian humility or a preference for personal detachment taught by neoclassical conventions, she alluded to her own experience only on rare occasions. More pronounced, however, in her poems as well as in Hammon's, are the issues of religious devotedness, patriotism, and liberation, which were not generally clouded by the unsettling moral issues of slavery and universal equality.

It would be more than fifty years before George Moses *Horton made slavery the major subject of his poems. With *The Hope of Liberty* (1829), Horton staked his personal freedom on the fruits of his pen; however, the book failed to raise the money needed to buy his freedom. He would not realize his goal until 1865 when the Union Army freed him. Horton, who delighted the university students at Chapel Hill with his humorous and witty jingles and parlayed his art into a money-making enterprise, found liberty a less than lucrative subject matter. However, when Frances Ellen Watkins *Harper, the popular abolitionist orator and poet, published her *Poems on Miscellaneous Subjects* (1854), she found its reception enthusiastic. The volume, which included poems on the tragic circumstances of slavery, went through twenty editions by 1874.

Other nineteenth-century African American poets anticipated Paul Laurence *Dunbar's question concerning "why the caged bird sings." James Monroe *Whitfield appears to speak for several of his contemporaries when he has the speaker in "The Misanthropist" say, "In vain thou bid'st me strike the lyre, / and sing a song of mirth and glee." For Whitfield, James Madison *Bell, and Albery Allson *Whitman, the thoughts that troubled their minds—the evils of slavery, the hope of freedom, struggles with oppression and *violence—were frought "with gloom and darkness, woe and pain." These poets continued the tradition of protest begun by Horton. However, James Edwin *Campbell and Daniel Webster *Davis made mirth their dominant lyric and wrote dialect poems that mimicked the *stereotypes of the popular *plantation tradition. Other poets such as Ann *Plato and Henrietta Cordelia *Ray took the route of romantic escapism.

With the publication of *Oak and Ivy* in 1893, Paul Laurence Dunbar inaugurated a new era in African American literary expression, revealing himself as one of the finest lyricists America had produced. His second book, *Majors and Minors* (1895), attracted the favorable attention and endorsement of the literary critic William Dean Howells. Howells's now classic introduction to Dunbar's third volume of poems, *Lyrics of Lowly Life* (1896), became the quintessential literary piece of damning praise that elevated Dunbar's dialect poems above his poems written in standard English. It ensured his acceptance and popularity among an audience of white readers who were warmed by the good cheer of the hearthside and comforted by the aura of pastoral contentment, hallmarks of Dunbar's bucolic verse. His obligatory mimicking of the plantation tradition conventions popularized by Irwin Russell, Joel Chandler Harris, and Thomas Nelson Page resulted in a perpetuation of these conventions. However, there was no denying for many the immense popularity, freshness, *humor, and catchy rhythms of his memorable dialect poems. Nonetheless, Dunbar's meteoric rise to fame did not accommodate a thorough and broad appreciation of the other side of his genius displayed in his nondialect poems. Tragically, the young poet lived a scant ten years after the publication of *Lyrics of Lowly Life*, years that were filled with regret that the world had ignored his deeper notes "to praise a jingle in a broken tongue."

The turn of the century witnessed African American poets adopting popular literary traditions and with varied and eclectic approaches joining other poets as the "new" American poetry burst upon the scene. Poets such as Vachel Lindsay, Edgar Lee Masters, Carl Sandburg, Amy Lowell, Hilda Doolittle, and Robert Frost ushered in a respect for ordinary speech, freedom of choice in subject matter, concentration on vers libre and imagism, an unembarrassed celebration of American culture, and irreverent experimentation. African American poets were influenced by these experiments with local color, regionalism, realism, and naturalism and joined other American poets in a mutual rejection of sentimentality, didacticism, romantic escape, and poetic diction.

Several African American women nurtured their poetic talent in this atmosphere of literary freedom. Angelina Weld *Grimké wrote lush lyrics on nature and love. Using conventional forms, Alice Moore *Dunbar-Nelson explored a woman's heart in ways considered less than conventional by an audience gradually emerging from Victorianism. Anne *Spencer, never as celebrated as her prodigious talent warranted, achieved precision in her imagery and great depth of emotion. Unlike Spencer, who lived quietly in Lynchburg, Virginia, Georgia Douglas *Johnson was at the hub of Washington's literary circle and, with the encouragement of several literary luminaries, published three volumes of poems. However, as was the circumstance of African American women poets during the first three decades of the twentieth century, her limited exposure and promotion diminished her critical reception.

This was not, however, the case for Benjamin *Brawley and William Stanley *Braithwaite, nationally known scholars who also wrote poetry. Benjamin Brawley was a minor genteel poet but a major scholar who wrote several pioneering studies including *The Negro in Literature and Art* (1918) and *Early Negro American Writers* (1935), which remains an important study of writers who published from 1761 to 1900. William Stanley Braithwaite, like Brawley, wrote a genteel, nonracial poetry, reminiscent of British romantic poets. In 1913 he initiated his annual edition of the *Anthology of Magazine Verse*, which chronicled the outpouring of American poetry for several decades.

Two poets, however, hinted at the emergence of robust, militant racial poetry and tended seeds that were political and aesthetic. Fenton *Johnson struck a note of despair and pessimism much like Edgar Lee Masters's and Carl Sandburg's and prophetically envisioned what black urban life would become after its euphoric beginnings. W. E. B. *Du Bois, whose intellectual contribution to American political and historical thought, sociological and cultural inquiry, journalism and imaginative literature towers over those of the century's best minds, wrote little poetry. However, his most anthologized piece, "A Litany of Atlanta," written in response to the Atlanta riot of 1906, is representative and provides a bridge for the strains of protest prevalent in both the 1800s and the 1900s.

New Negro Renaissance. By the 1920s it was clear that an unprecedented flowering of literary expression was in full bloom. Called alternately the New Negro Renaissance and the *Harlem Renaissance, this literary movement, according to Alain *Locke, its major promoter and interpreter, was the first opportunity for group expression and self-determination. As Locke pointed out in The *New Negro (1925), the old attitudes of self-pity and apology were replaced by a frank acceptance of the position of African Americans in American society. A growing racial awareness among African American writers prompted self-discovery— discovery of the ancestral past in Africa, discovery of folk and cultural roots reaching back into colonial times, and discovery of a new kind of militancy, self-determination, and self-reliance. Langston *Hughes, in his famous manifesto "The Negro Artist and the Racial Mountain" (1926), captures the prevailing sentiment:

> We younger Negro artists who create now intend to express our individual dark-skinned selves without fear or shame. If white people are pleased we are glad. If they are not, it doesn't matter. We know we are beautiful. And ugly too. The tom-tom cries and the tom-tom laughs. If colored people are pleased we are glad. If they are not, their displeasure doesn't matter either. We build our temples for tomorrow, strong as we know how, and we stand on top of the mountain, free within ourselves.

Artistic freedom was the banner under which Jean *Toomer created *Cane (1923), one of the masterstrokes of the New Negro Renaissance. An unprecedented collection that combined poetry and prose with experimental verve, it was also Toomer's revelation piece, an unrestrained release of racial celebration. His poems in this volume are alive with the pine-scented landscape of Georgia and capture the mysterious and elusive beauty of folk spiritualism.

Unlike Toomer, Claude *McKay, the first and most radical voice to emerge in the 1920s, personified the tensions and contradictions lived by those too conflicted by racial anomalies to celebrate. With the publication of Harlem Shadows (1922), he became the poet that best expressed their rage and anger and newfound militancy. The popular "If We Must Die," "Baptism," and "To the White Fiends" expressed emotions chafing to be exposed. According to Alain Locke, McKay "pulled the psychological cloak off the Negro and revealed even to the Negro himself, those facts disguised till then by his shrewd protective mimicry or pressed down under the dramatic mask of living up to what was expected of him." Ironically, McKay was uncomfortable as a spokesman for the

black race, for he saw his poems speaking to the individual soul of all people.

In the midst of the New Negro Renaissance the issue of choice of subject matter was debated by the literary lights of the period: Langston Hughes, W. E. B. Du Bois, Claude McKay, James Weldon *Johnson, Arna *Bontemps, and Jessie Redmon *Fauset, among many others. However, Countee *Cullen, perhaps more than any of his contemporaries, agonized over the issue (freedom in choice of subject matter, delineation of character, decorum and representativeness of portrayal, and the bearing race should have on art). The most learned African American poet to emerge in this era, Countee Cullen demonstrated his enormous talent in his first book, entitled *Color (1925). At the young age of twenty-two, Cullen became the most famous and most quoted African American writer at the time.

Cullen became assistant editor of *Opportunity in 1926 and inaugurated his "A Dark Tower" columns; shortly thereafter he responded to the NAACP questionnaire feature entitled "The Negro in Art—How Shall He Be Portrayed—A Symposium," which ran in the *Crisis in 1926 and 1927. He made it clear that he would not "vote for any infringement of the author's right to tell a story, to delineate a character, or to transcribe an emotion in his own way and in light of the truth as he sees it." However, he was quick to add that African American artists have a duty "to create types that are truly representative." Just a year later, in what appears to be a critical reversal, he said that African American artists should not be bound by their race or restricted to race matters simply because they are a part of that racial group. Ironically, the poet who was recognized as best representing the emerging New Negro resented having his poetry judged on the basis of race: "If I am going to be a poet at all, I am going to be POET and not NEGRO POET." Langston Hughes was quick and relentless in his attack on Cullen's creed in "The Negro Artist and the Racial Mountain" (1926). Hughes's analysis and Cullen's own fierce battle with *double consciousness coalesce in the conundrum no better expressed than in Cullen's own lines in "Yet Do I Marvel" (1925): "Yet do I marvel at this curious thing: / To make a poet black, and bid him sing!" These lines capture the essence of Cullen's highest achievement and paradoxically the confluence of his most troubling dilemmas. It was his blackness that was at once his perceived handicap and his greatest asset.

Cullen was one of several poets who benefited from the numerous publishing opportunities and literary prizes available to promising writers. Under the editorship of Charles S. Johnson, Opportunity published works by Renaissance writers and offered the Alexander Pushkin Award. The Crisis, under the leadership of editor W. E. B. Du Bois and literary editor Jessie Redmon Fauset, was a showplace for literary artists and annually awarded poetry prizes for outstanding entries. For example, Arna Bontemps's early success at writing poetry won him recognition and prizes from both Opportunity and Crisis magazines in 1926 and 1927. Bontemps's poem "A Black Man Talks of Reaping," which won the Crisis prize, is representative of the note of bitterness that is a consistent tone in much Renaissance literature. It is also important to note that these magazines were instrumental in encouraging writers like Bontemps and in developing an audience for their work.

The development of the African American poetic tradition paralleled the development of an elaborate oral tradition that encompassed every aspect and attitude of black life, offering what Ralph *Ellison called "the first drawings of any group's character." Sterling A. *Brown, another critic who explored fully and consistently the inexhaustible possibilities of the folk tradition, found in its storehouse of songs, tales, sayings, and speech the originality, vitality, truthfulness, and complexity that would be his touchstones in the assessment of literature. The poetry of the nineteenth century, with its mimicry of popular stereotypes, sentimentalism, and escapism, would have been found wanting if held to these standards.

However, in the early twentieth century, especially during the period known as the Harlem Renaissance, African American poetry began to flower because of a greater exploration of the black voice as it consciously recognized and mined black *folklore. African American poets in varying degrees engaged in a kind of literary tropism by turning away from Western cosmology and mythology in preference for expressing their own cosmology and cultural myths. In their attempt to find a voice expressive of their racial consciousness, they turned to cultural tropes abounding in the universe of folk parlance. Among the African American poets who explored the unique vernacular resources of the *blues, *spirituals, proverbs, tales, and sayings were James Weldon Johnson, Langston Hughes, and Sterling Brown. James Weldon Johnson played a significant role as anthologist-critic in introducing African American poetry to the American public with The Book of American Negro Poetry (1922). In his preface, Johnson initiates the debate on the limitations of dialect by signaling African American writers' rejection of conventionalized dialect associated with *minstrelsy and by calling for a form of expression that would not limit the poet's emotional and intellectual response to black life. In some of his best poetry, collected in *God's Trombones (1927), he shows his skillful treatment of the black folk sermon and his use of racially authentic language.

Langston Hughes, indisputably the poet laureate of Harlem, was the most experimental and versatile poet of the New Negro Renaissance, launching his career as a poet at the age of nineteen with what has become his signature poem, "The *Negro Speaks of Rivers." Over the next forty-six years, Hughes had as his goal to discover the flow and rhythm of black life. Authoring more than 860 poems, he never tired of exploring the color, vibrancy, and texture of black culture and "his" beloved people who created it. In his first two volumes of poetry, The *Weary Blues (1926) and Fine Clothes to the Jew (1927), such poems as "Lenox Avenue Midnight," "Jazzonia," and "To a Black Dancer in the Little Savoy," re-create the jazzy, blues-tinged, frenzied, exotic world of Harlem nights.

Hughes called himself a folk poet, and he had faith in the inexhaustible resources to be mined in folk *music and speech. He sought to combine the musical forms of the blues, work songs, ballads, and jazz stylings with poetic expression in such a way as to preserve the originality of the former and achieve the complexity of the latter. As Hughes's biographer Arnold *Rampersad said, Hughes's fusion of African American music into his poetry was his "key technical commitment." Some of his critics will argue that he remained too close to the folk form to achieve much beyond weak imitation, and others considered his approach too simple and lacking in intellectual sophistication and rigor. But for Hughes it was enough that he became the voice of African American dreamers. In tones that ranged from poignantly conciliatory to acerbically radical, Hughes continued to point out the great distance between the premise and the promise of America in his last volumes, *Montage of a Dream Deferred (1951), Ask Your Mama (1961), and the posthumously published The Panther and the Lash (1967).

Like Langston Hughes, Sterling A. Brown (1901–1989) relished his title of folk poet. As such, Brown's most significant achievement is his subtle adaptation of folk forms to the literature. Experimenting with the blues, spirituals, work songs, and ballads, he invented combinations that at their best retain the ethos of folk forms and intensify the literary quality of the poetry. In his poem "Ma *Rainey," one of the finest in his first volume of poetry, Southern Road (1932), Brown skillfully brings together the ballad and blues forms and, demonstrating his inventive genius, creates the blues-ballad that is a portrait of the venerated blues singer and a chronicle of her transforming performance. With a remarkable ear for the idiom, cadence, and tones of folk speech, Brown absorbed its vibrant qualities in his poetry. Brown came as close as any poet had before to achieving James Weldon Johnson's ideal of original racial poetry, "capable of voicing the deepest and highest emotions and aspirations, and allowing the widest range of subjects and the widest scope of treatment."

The next three decades, 1930–1960, traced the continuing careers of Langston Hughes and Sterling A. Brown and marked the ascendancy of Melvin B. *Tolson, Robert *Hayden, Margaret *Walker, and Gwendolyn Brooks. These major voices joined a growing list of poets who brought African American poetic expression to new heights of competence and maturity. The list includes Samuel W. *Allen (Paul Vesey), Waring Cuney, Frank Marshall *Davis, Owen *Dodson, Ray Durem, Frank Horne, and Richard *Wright. These poets cultivated their individual voices by synthesizing elements from the Western literary tradition and their own vernacular tradition. They explored history as a riveting subject matter for their poetry, and they stretched the boundaries of language to have it hold the depth and complexity that the new poetry required. These poets, in keeping with the continuing development of the radical/political strain in African American poetry, also pursued a brand of social justice that emphasized integrationalism and a sensitivity to international connections and socialistic movements.

Melvin B. Tolson demonstrates all of these interests in his poetry. In brilliant strokes of irony and iconoclasm, he produced *Rendezvous with America* (1944), *Libretto for the Republic of Liberia* (1953), and *Harlem Gallery* (1965). Tolsonian style is a synthesis of classical imagery, racial symbolism, and extensive historical allusions. In "Psi," one of the sections of *Harlem Gallery*, Tolson describes the "Negro artist" as a "flower of the gods, whose growth is dwarfed at an early stage." Certainly, this was not Tolson's personal complaint, for, in truth, only his critical response was dwarfed, never his considerable gifts as a poet.

Equally gifted, Robert Hayden throughout his distinguished career as a poet held to his credo that poets "are the keepers of a nation's conscience, the partisans of freedom and justice, even when they eschew political involvement. By the very act of continuing to function as poets they are affirming what is human and eternal." Hayden, like Countee Cullen, insisted that poets should not be restricted to racial themes or any subject matter or polemic that would fetter their artistic expression. His consistent refusal to be limited by subject matter or to be relegated to a double standard of criticism ironically found him at odds with the white literary establishment as well as the 1960s proponents of the *Black Aesthetic and often exacted stiff penalties of critical neglect and racial ostracism. Though Hayden never retreated from his position, two of his most outstanding poems, "Middle Passage" (1945) and "Frederick *Douglass" (1947), show his lifelong commitment to exploring African American history and folklore. In *A Ballad of Remembrance* (1962), Hayden brought together revised versions of these poems and some of the best portraits of historical figures in American literature, including "The Ballad of Nat Turner," "*Runagate Runagate," and "Homage to the Empress of the Blues." Ironically, because of the excellence of his book, Robert Hayden, who had resisted racial categorization in judging his poetry, won the *Grand Prix de la Poesie*, a prize reserved to honor the best poet of *Negritude in the world.

Untroubled by a Hayden-like sensitivity to racial subject matter, Margaret Walker made the full absorption of racial material one of her highest goals. In her most famous poem, "For My People," she mirrors the collective soul of black folk. As W. E. B. Du Bois had succeeded in announcing the political, economic, and cultural strivings of African Americans in *The *Souls of Black Folk* (1903), Walker accomplished a stunning psychological portrait of "her people" during the unsettling years of the depression, and throughout the succeeding decades. As Eugenia Collier writes, the impact of the poem "melts away time and place and it unifies Black listeners," deriving its power from "the reservoir of beliefs, values, and archetypal characters yielded by our collective historical experience." With a verbal brilliance owing to an impressive absorption of the myths, rituals, music, and folklore of the African American tradition, Margaret Walker shares her cultural memories and creates new ones in *For My People* (1942),

Prophets for a New Day (1970), and *October Journey* (1972).

Another major voice, Gwendolyn Brooks, has produced some of the most outstanding poetry written in the twentieth century. With poetry that benefits from great compression, technical acumen, and emotional complexity, no poet lays better claim to heir of two hundred years of the maturation of African American poetry than Gwendolyn Brooks. In 1950 Brooks won the Pulitzer Prize for her volume of poetry *Annie Allen*, becoming the first African American to win this award. In 1968 she was named Poet Laureate of Illinois, succeeding the late Carl Sandburg. Author of more than twenty books, including *A *Street in Bronzeville* (1945), *The Bean Eaters* (1960), *In the Mecca* (1968), and *Riot* (1969), she is a master at manipulating language until it distills the pure essence of the life and character that she astutely observes in Chicago and the world. Brooks joined other poets who were writing in the 1950s—Owen Dodson, Sam Allen, Ray Durem, Margaret Esse *Danner, and Margaret Taylor Goss *Burroughs—in responding poetically to a nation carrying the anlage of social change in its mounting *civil rights movement. The year 1955 witnessed the Montgomery bus boycott, which brought Rosa Parks and Martin Luther *King, Jr., to national prominence; it also witnessed the senseless *lynching of Emmett Till, a fourteen-year-old black boy accused of whistling at a white woman in Mississippi. The latter event had a profound effect on Gwendolyn Brooks and is the subject of two of her poems, "A Bronzeville Mother Loiters in Mississippi, Meanwhile, a Mississippi Mother Burns Bacon" and "The Last Quatrain of the Ballad of Emmett Till."

Furious Flower. Ten years later another event, the assassination of *Malcolm X, would capture the imagination of a group of younger poets and be the catalyst for the *Black Arts movement and the furious flowering of African American poetry that it produced. Malcolm's ideas provided the radical, philosophical framework for the movement. According to Larry *Neal in *Visions of a Liberated Future* (1989), he "touched all aspects of contemporary black nationalism." Malcolm's voice sounded the tough urban street style, and his life became a symbol and inspiration. With his words resonating in their consciousness and his image inspiring a revolutionary world vision, poets such as David Henderson, James A. Emanuel, Robert Hayden, and Etheridge *Knight paid tribute to him after his death.

Three poets inspired by the example of Malcolm X emerged as the moving spirits and visionaries of the Black Arts movement in the late 1960s: Amiri *Baraka (LeRoi Jones), Larry Neal, and Askia M. *Touré (Rolland Snellings). Baraka saw the movement as a revolutionary force "to create an art, a literature that would fight for black people's liberation with as much intensity as Malcolm X our 'Fire Prophet' and the rest of the enraged masses who took to the streets in Birmingham after the four little girls had been murdered by the Klan and FBI, or the ones who were dancing in the street in Harlem, Watts, Newark, Detroit." Baraka captures in this statement the revolutionary fervor and commitment that led him, Larry Neal, and Askia Touré to create the Black Arts Repertory Theatre School in Harlem; that led to his collaboration with Neal in publishing *Black Fire* (1968), the seminal *anthology of the period; and that guided his constant spiritual striving toward building a black nation in America.

Out of this striving came a poetry that was emblazoned with the liberation struggle. Baraka, poet, activist, and playwright, gained a strong reputation as a poet among the avant-garde artists of Greenwich Village during the 1950s and collected his early poetry in *Preface to a Twenty-Volume Suicide Note* (1961). Since that time he has published eleven books of poetry, including *The Dead Lecturer* (1964), *Black Magic Poetry* (1969), *In Our Terribleness* (1970), *It's Nation Time* (1970), and *Spirit Reach* (1972). His poetry is experimental, explosive, improvisational, and allied to black music, especially *jazz.

Like Baraka, Larry Neal wrote poetry that had the sound and the pulsing, pumping rhythm of black music. His early death at forty-three curtailed a brilliant career as a poet, essayist, teacher, and community activist. However, his *essays, *drama, and poetry have been collected in *Visions of a Liberated Future: Black Arts Movement Writings* (1989). "Poppa Stoppa Speaks from His Grave" and "Don't Say Goodbye to the Porkpie Hat" are excellent examples of the hip, urbane, jazz-digging style that was his signature.

The music of John *Coltrane, Charlie *Parker, Theolonious Monk, and other jazz greats also suffuses the poetry of Askia M. Touré. To a rich lyricism he adds a cosmic vision that was first apparent in *JuJu: Magic Songs for the Black Nation* (with Ben *Caldwell, 1970) and *Songhai* (1973) and continues in *From the Pyramids to the Projects* (1990). His commitment to raising the national consciousness carried over to the 1990s, when his messages challenged the destructive forces wielding genocide both physical and mental. Reflecting on the Black Arts movement, Touré contends that it was "the largest cultural upsurge that our people have had in this century and that we were organically-linked writers, activists, musicians, playwrights and such."

Several forces converged to create the outpouring of African American poetry that has taken place since 1960. The political and social upheavals brought about by the civil rights movement of the 1950s and 1960s ushered in a dramatic change in the legal and social status of African Americans. With its nonviolent strategies of sit-ins, marches, freedom rides, boycotts, and voter registration drives, the movement united two generations of African American poets around the dream of freedom and equality and supplied them with a wealth of cultural heroes, including Martin Luther King, Jr., Rosa Parks, Emmett Till, Fannie Lou Hamer, and Medgar Evers, who became the subject matter of their poetry. The assassination of Martin Luther King inspired a groundswell of poems from such poets as Nikki *Giovanni, Haki R. *Madhubuti, Sam Allen, Quincy Thomas *Troupe, Jr., and Mari *Evans. In the wake of the urban riots and fires that were the people's response to King's

martyrdom came the Black Power movement with its bold language of racial confrontation, cultural separation, and insistence upon self-defense, self-reliance, and black pride. With their iconoclastic attacks on all aspects of white middle-class values, it is not surprising that the poets who shaped the Black Arts movement, the Black Power movement's cultural wing, rejected unequivocally Western poetic conventions. Their poetic technique emphasized free verse; typographical stylistics; irreverent, often scatological, diction; and linguistic experimentation. In addition to Baraka, Neal, and Touré, prominent among these poets were Sonia *Sanchez, Nikki Giovanni, Haki Madhubuti, Etheridge Knight, A. B. *Spellman, Calvin C. *Hernton, Mari Evans, David Henderson, June *Jordan, Clarence *Major, Jayne *Cortez, Henry *Dumas, Carolyn M. *Rodgers, and Quincy Troupe.

Following Maulana Ron Karenga's dictum that black art must be "functional, collective and committed," these poets addressed their messages primarily to African Americans and African people in the diaspora, and in their messages the artist and the political activist become one. Poets such as Sam Allen, Margaret Burroughs, and Margaret Danner set out to reclaim the lost African heritage, continuing the "literary Garveyism" that began in the 1920s. The strains of *Pan-Africanism nurtured by W. E. B. Du Bois appear in the poetry of W. Keorapetse Kgositsile, an exile from South Africa, and African and European cultures mesh in the poetry of West Indian poet Derek Walcott, continuing the tradition of the Negritude movement. Not only were these poets extending their boundaries, but they were also exploring the interior spaces of the African American *identity. Henry Dumas, "whose brief life held out the promise of brilliant and passionate writing," according to Eugene *Redmond in *Drumvoices* (1976), studded his poetry with raw and angry dimensions of the African American psyche. Conrad Kent *Rivers, who also died too young, was concerned with his inner world, where pain, violence, and destruction ended only with death. In the hands of Lucille *Clifton, Lance *Jeffers, Raymond Patterson, and Johari *Amini, among others, the concept of blackness is sculpted into a composite of courage, endurance, beauty, and stoicism—positive images for a nation reconstructing itself.

And more often than not, these poets created their own journals to disseminate their messages. Hoyt *Fuller, the influential editor of *Negro Digest* and *Black World*, edited *NOMMO*, the journal of the Organization of Black American Culture (OBAC) Writers Workshop and, like Gwendolyn Brooks, had a great impact on the younger poets as mentor and cultural guide. Tom *Dent and Kalamu ya *Salaam edited *Nkombo*, the journal of BLKARTSOUTH, a cultural organization that grew out of the Free Southern Theater in New Orleans. *Burning Spear* featured the poetry of the Howard poets such as Lance Jeffers. The collection was an outgrowth of the Dasein Literary Society at Howard University. As the *Crisis* and *Opportunity* magazines had stimulated artistic and intellectual activity during the New

Negro Renaissance, several journals founded during the late 1960s and 1970s increased readership for African American poetry over the next twenty years. Notable among them are the *Journal of Black Poetry*, founded by Joe Goncalves; the *Black Scholar*, founded by Robert Chrisman; *Black Dialogue*, founded by Abdul Karim and Edward S. Spriggs; *Callaloo*, founded in 1974 by Charles H. Rowell, Tom Dent, and Jerry Ward; and *Obsidian*, founded by Alvin *Aubert in 1975 with Gerald W. *Barrax assuming the editorship in 1985. Many poets were also responsible for establishing presses that encouraged emerging poets to publish. Haki Madhubuti's *Third World Press in Chicago, Dudley *Randall's *Broadside Press in Detroit, and Naomi Long *Madgett's *Lotus Press became invaluable outlets for African American poetic expression.

The proliferation of the ideas and the impact of the Black Arts movement were largely due to the formation of cultural organizations and writers' workshops committed to encouraging African American poets and increasing readership among an African American audience. The Umbra Workshop first gathered in Greenwich Village and the Lower East Side of New York in 1941 and listed among its members David Henderson, Calvin C. Hernton, Tom Dent, Ishmael *Reed, Askia M. Touré, Raymond Patterson, Charles Patterson, and Lorenzo *Thomas. It produced the first issue of *Umbra* in 1963. In Chicago, Haki Madhubuti and Walter Bradford were among the founding members of the Organization of Black American Culture (OBAC), which brought together Carolyn Rodgers, Gwendolyn Brooks, Johari Amini, Sterling *Plumpp, Eugene *Perkins, Ebon (Leo Thomas Hale), and Angela *Jackson, among others. Zealous in carrying out the ideals of black solidarity and empowerment, they read in schools, community centers, bars, parks, and on street corners.

Since the 1970s, these contemporary African American poets have developed a form of communal performance art that draws heavily on what Stephen Henderson called black music and black speech as poetic referents. The poets' work evidences a full absorption of musical forms such as blues and jazz, call-and-response features, and improvising lines, evoking the tones, rhythm, and structure of folk form and the entire range of spoken virtuosity seen in the sermon, the rap, the dozens, *signifying, toasts, and folktales. Poets such as Jayne Cortez, Sonia Sanchez, Haki Madhubuti, Amiri Baraka, Nikki Giovanni, Askia M. Touré, Victor Hernández *Cruz, Sun Ra, and Ted *Joans discovered how to transform the printed poem into a performance that unleashes the elegance and power of black speech and music. For example, Jane Cortez's ability to evoke the jazz sounds of Ornette Coleman, Bessie *Smith, and John Coltrane in her first volume of poetry, *Pisstained Stairs* (1969), suggested the power that she would develop as a performance poet. Sonia Sanchez significantly influenced the cultural landscape by the urgency of her sustained committed voice, often rendered in her deeply spiritual chanting-singing style. Eugene Redmond, Sarah Webster *Fabio, Gil *Scott-Heron, and Ted Joans are representative of those poets who incorporate rap, blues, jazz, and soul music into their poetry, making it move with the rhythm of contemporary beats. Nikki Giovanni achieved national popularity as she wedded her visionary, truth-telling poetry with the sounds of gospel music on her best-selling album *Truth Is on Its Way* in 1971. Haki Madhubuti, with his explosive, annunciatory, kinetic rap style, has been one of the most imitated poets among young artists seeking to develop a performance style. Though much of the poetry was involved with music, *oratory, and performance, for Alvin Aubert the poem has to "perform itself on the page." His poems in *If Winter Come: Collected Poems, 1967–1992* (1994), Pinkie Gordon *Lane's *I Never Scream: New and Selected Poems* (1985), and Naomi Long Madgett's *Octavia and Other Poems* (1988) illustrate a reliance upon quieter, muted strains to enhance their poetry.

The cultural movement of the 1960s and 1970s not only changed the way African Americans thought about their political and social status as American citizens, for the poets it also planted the seeds for a truly liberated exploration of literary possibilities. Poets such as Lucille Clifton, Audre *Lorde, Jay *Wright, and Michael S. *Harper cultivated their poetic imaginations in line with more personal and individualized goals. In *An Ordinary Woman* (1974), Lucille Clifton floods her private and public identities with light, illuminating family histories and relationships in epigrammatic flashes. Audre Lorde, during the course of a thirty-year career, struggled against the poet's death of being "choked into silence by icy distinction." In volumes such as *Coal* (1973) and *The Black Unicorn* (1978) she resisted categorization and definition by a narrow expectation of her humanity by boldly exploring all of the essences of womanhood. Jay Wright's eclecticism led him to create poetry that is a multicultural mosaic of his interests in history, anthropology, cosmology, *religion, and social thought as evident in *Death as History* (1967). As suggested by the title of Michael S. *Harper's second book of poems, *History Is Your Own Heartbeat* (1971), history is the heartbeat of his poetry as he chronicles personal and kinship relationships and cultural histories that link complex emotional and philosophical experiences shared by diverse ethnic groups.

Rita *Dove, acknowledging her own debt to the Black Arts movement, said that if it had not been for the movement, America would not be ready to accept a poet who explored a text other than blackness. Unencumbered by a necessarily political message, Dove in her Pulitzer Prize–winning book *Thomas and Beulah* (1987) brings wholeness and elegance to the histories of her grandparents. Dove, who held the post of Poet Laureate of the United States from 1993 until 1995, is representative of a large accomplished group of poets who published their first poems during the late 1970s and 1980s: Yusef *Komunyakaa, Cornelius Eady, Melvin *Dixon, Dolores Kendrick, Thylias Moss, Toi *Derricotte, Gloria Oden, and Sherley Anne *Williams.

Elizabeth Alexander is emblematic of the promise and wide range of variegated voices that have sprung forth during the first half of the 1990s. Her first collection, *The Venus Hottentot* (1990), reveals poems that explore the interior lives of historical figures, exposing emotions and experiences that strikingly illuminate public concerns. In a poem called "The Dark Room: An Invocation" she hails talented young poets who make up The Dark Room Collective: Thomas Sayers Ellis, Sharan Strange, Kevin Young, Carl Phillips, and Natasha Trethewey, to name a few. In highly individual styles, they shape metaphors and images in a fisted reading of contemporary life. Other young poets, such as Ras Baraka, Kevin Powell, Jabari Asim, and Esther Iverem, place themselves in the tradition of struggle that they see as artistic, political, spiritual, and psychological; they seek to revisit the ideals of the Black Arts movement in the language of a hip-hop nation.

In the closing decade of the twentieth century, African American poetry is again experiencing an expansive, renewing phase that some have termed the "Third Renaissance." This sense of renewal was dramatically evident at the Furious Flower Conference in 1994, when the largest gathering of poets and critics in more than two decades met at James Madison University in Virginia to read, discuss, and celebrate African American poetry. The conference, dedicated to Gwendolyn Brooks, brought together three generations of poets. In doing so it symbolized the continuity in the African American poetic expression and signaled the dimensions of its future development. Seasoned poets who began writing in the 1960s are continuing to write with skill and power. Sonia Sanchez's *Wounded in the House of a Friend* (1995) and Gerald Barrax's *Leaning Against the Sun* (1992) are prime examples. Derek Walcott's Nobel Prize for Literature in 1992, Rita Dove's appointment as Poet Laureate of the United States, and Gwendolyn Brooks's naming by the National Endowment for the Humanities as the Jefferson Lecturer for 1994 represent the unprecedented achievements of African American poets as recipients of the nation's highest honors. This newest renaissance is also marked by the emergence of a group of young poets who have been published in such anthologies as *In the Tradition: An Anthology of Young Black Writers* (1992), edited by Kevin Powell and Ras Baraka, and *On the Verge: Emerging Poets and Artists* (1993), edited by Thomas Sayers Ellis and Joseph Lease.

Just as Gwendolyn Brooks's poem "Second Sermon on the Warpland" suggests "furious flower" as a metaphor for the aesthetic chronicle of African American poetry, it also encourages the emerging generation to bloom "in the noise and whip of the whirlwind." After 250 years of African American poetry, these young poets are "the last of the loud," ferocious in their call for humanism and beautiful in their response to the magic and music of language.

• Countee Cullen, "The Negro in Art," *Crisis* 32.4 (Aug. 1926): 193. Langston Hughes, "The Negro Artist and the Racial Mountain," *Nation* 122.3181 (23 June 1926): 692. Sterling A. Brown, *Negro Poetry and Drama*, 1937. J. Saunders Redding, *To Make a Poet Black*, 1939. Rosey E. Pool, ed., *Beyond the Blues*, 1962. Arna Bontemps, ed., *American Negro Poetry*, 1963. Robert Hayden, ed., *Kaleidoscope*, 1967. Addison Gayle, Jr., ed., *Black Expression: Essays by and about Black Americans in the Creative Arts*, 1969. Houston A. Baker, Jr., *Long Black Song*, 1972. George E. Kent, *Blackness and the Adventure of Western Culture*, 1972. Richard A. Long and Eugenia W. Collier, eds., *Afro-American Writing: An Anthology of Prose and Poetry*, vols. 1 and 2, 1972. Eugene Redmond, *Drumvoices: The Mission of Afro-American Poetry*, 1976. Trudier Harris and Thadious M. Davis, eds., *DLB*, vol. 41, *Afro-American Poets since 1955*, 1985. Gwendolyn Brooks, *Blacks*, 1987. Henry Louis Gates, Jr., *Figures in Black: Words, Signs, and the "Racial" Self*, 1987. Gayl Jones, *Liberating Voices: Oral Tradition in African American Literature*, 1991. Michael S. Harper and Anthony Walton, eds., *Every Shut Eye Ain't Asleep: An Anthology of Poetry by African Americans since 1945*, 1994.
—Joanne V. Gabbin

POETRY, DIALECT. *See* Dialect Poetry.

POETRY, RELIGIOUS AND DIDACTIC. The inaugural moment of African American religious and didactic *poetry is also the founding moment of African American literature. The deep Christian faith that led Jupiter *Hammon and Phillis *Wheatley to voice their veiled protests against the slave system in terms of the Christian scriptures established a moral basis for literary protest and began a tradition of evoking the most strongly held moral standards of the time in order to force recognition of crimes against African Americans. The appeal to a higher authority gave weight to the words of these two slaves and other ignored voices. In using the language of the Bible and the teachings of Christ, for example, writers such as Wheatley and Hammon spoke to readers in familiar terms, thereby making it more likely that their white readers would accept their critiques. These two traditions of testifying about the presence of a higher power and teaching about moral rights and responsibilities and the consequences of oppression are important elements of African American literature up to the present day.

Jupiter Hammon's works include a broadside entitled "An Evening Thought: Salvation by Christ, with Penitential Cries" (1760), "An Address to Miss Phillis Wheatley," and "A Dialogue, Entitled, The Kind Master and Dutiful Servant." His poem to Phillis Wheatley establishes a tradition of dialogue and support among African American writers that has persisted up to the present day and makes it clear that Hammon felt solidarity with his black contemporaries. His *essays and a *sermon also show his concern with black uplift and community cohesion. For example, "A Dialogue" shows the servant's submission, not to his earthly master but to his heavenly one; the poem is thus subtly subversive of the creed of slaveholders.

In 1773, Phillis Wheatley published *Poems on Various Subjects, Religious and Moral.* Wheatley wrote in the elegiac, the lyric, and the epic modes, using classical and biblical imagery. The thirty-eight poems in her published volume address a range of topics, but Wheatley's overriding concerns are religious piety, *freedom, and death. Her poems "On Being Brought from Africa to America," "To the University of Cambridge, in New England," and "On the

Death of General Wooster" are typical of her style and subject matter. "On Being Brought" celebrates Wheatley's Christian conversion, yet it also calls attention to the fact that she is a kidnapped African and reminds her largely white readership that Africans are as eligible for salvation as they are. "To the University of Cambridge" highlights the moral authority with which Wheatley habitually addressed her audience; in it, one can see how empowering Christian discourse has been for some African American writers. "On the Death of General Wooster," constructed as a prayer spoken by the dying general, contains one of her clearest protests against *slavery.

In the nineteenth century, African Americans, like other writers of the time, viewed literature as a vehicle for moral suasion and firmly established the protest tradition in *oratory, essay-writing, and *slave narratives, as well as poetry. There emerged three broad categories of religious and didactic verse. In some poems, Christian imagery was deployed to convince white Americans that they were failing in their Christian duty to African Americans and to persuade those in power to change the prejudicial laws and practices of the land. Other poems were written for the moral instruction of African Americans and the general populace, urging *temperance and avoidance of sin. One can also see the didactic impulse beginning to operate without the Christian influence; a significant number of poems make their points without recourse to religion.

The many poets who wrote religious and didactic poetry in the nineteenth century include Elymas Payson *Rogers, author of "The Repeal of the Missouri Compromise Considered" and "On the Fugitive Slave Law"; Charles *Reason, author of "The Spirit Voice; or Liberty Call to the Disfranchised (State of New York)" and "Freedom"; and Ann *Plato, whose book *Essays: Including Biographies and Miscellaneous Pieces, in Prose and Poetry* (1841) includes poems offering moral guidance like "Advice to Young Ladies," as well as a poem commemorating the emancipation of slaves in the British West Indies, "To the First of August." In a book entitled *America and Other Poems* (1853), James Monroe *Whitfield (1822–1871) published a number of poems intended to enlighten his audience about the evils of slavery, including "How Long," and a long poem written in celebration of the fourth anniversary of the Emancipation Proclamation. Alfred Gibbs Campbell wrote poems almost exclusively on religious and abolitionist topics, some of which he published in his newsletter *The Alarm Bell*; he was also an advocate of women's rights. George Clinton Rowe, a minister and another writer who edited his own paper, composed sermons in verse and poems on African American heroes for the moral uplift of the race. "Vincent Ogé" by George B. *Vashon narrates the Haitian Revolution and glorifies the title character, who was put to death by the French for his part in the uprising. Well-known as an abolitionist, James Madison *Bell wrote and performed orations in verse that called for liberty and racial justice and reflected his piety and deep involvement with the AME Church.

Joshua McCarter Simpson and Albery Allson

*Whitman are notable for the forms in which their protest poems appear. Simpson pointed out the hypocrisy and moral bankruptcy of slave-holders and a slave-holding nation in his witty antislavery songs, set to the tunes of contemporary popular songs. These were collected and published under the title *The Emancipation Car* in 1874. Whitman's epic poem in Spenserian stanzas, *The Rape of Florida* (1884), protests the treatment of both Native Americans and African Americans.

George Moses *Horton was one of the few published slave poets. Many of Horton's poems, like "The Slave's Complaint," "Liberty and Slavery,"and "On Hearing of the Intention of a Gentleman to Purchase the Poet's Freedom," are protests against his own enslavement and against slavery in general. Despite his continuous efforts, his owner never manumitted him. Horton also wrote devotional poems, praising the beauties of nature and all of "Creation" and extolling the power of Christ. Because he did not learn to write until he was about thirty-five, his early poems were delivered orally, including those in his first book of poems, *Hope of Liberty* (1829).

The work of Frances Ellen Watkins *Harper most clearly exemplifies the religious and didactic impulses in nineteenth-century African American poetry. Harper's Christian moral conviction infuses virtually all of her poetry, especially the verse interpretations of biblical stories and the depictions of slavery written, like the slave narratives, with the express intent of creating moral opposition to that institution and to the continuing oppression of African Americans. She also draws attention to the social limitations placed on women in general and on black women in particular. "The Slave Mother" (1854), "Moses: A Story of the Nile" (1869), and "A Double Standard" (1895) are some of her best works in this mode. Her message in these poems is reinforced by her work in other genres, including fiction, speeches, and essays.

Although the majority of Paul Laurence *Dunbar's poems are neither religious nor didactic, some of his most influential poems seek to teach whites about the plight of African Americans and to preserve these insights about black life for the African American community. These poems, like "Sympathy" and "We Wear the Mask," have been widely anthologized and have served as points of reference for a number of later African American writers.

Dunbar's largely secular protests against the conditions of African American life prefigured the even greater secularization of didactic poetry and the near disappearance of religious poetry in the second half of the twentieth century. These changes are due in part to new aesthetic ideas about the mission of poetry and to the diminishing influence of the Christian church in African American communities and in the country at large. Throughout the century, religious meditations by African Americans became less Christian and more generally humanistic, often incorporating other spiritual traditions; and didactic poetry has generally come to mean protest poetry, which has lost its tone of supplication and become progressively more urgent.

The poetry of W. E. B. *Du Bois demonstrates these transitions. Du Bois wrote a series of poems in the form of prayers that were published in various magazines and then in book form as *Darkwater* (1920). In these poems, the fiery rhetoric against racial injustice and the urgent appeals to God to remember his children in their hour of need finally end on a note of hope and brotherhood that brings together Du Bois's socialist and Christian visions.

During the *Harlem Renaissance, African American religious and didactic poetry became clearly differentiated from that of the nineteenth century. In *The Black Christ and Other Poems* (1929), Countee *Cullen fuses concerns about racial issues like *lynching with a meditation on the figure of Christ. The poet explores the symbolic meaning of Christ and his Passion; as in Du Bois's prayer-poems, doubt in the power of God is introduced and later dispelled. This ambivalence in relationship to Christian faith is a feature of twentieth-century religious poetry that is almost entirely absent from the devotional poetry of the nineteenth centry.

James Weldon *Johnson, a self-proclaimed agnostic, recognized the importance of Christian faith within African American culture. His main religious poems constitute *God's Trombones* (1927), a cycle of sermons in the voice of a nineteenth-century African American folk preacher, beginning with "The Creation" and ending with "The Judgment Day."

Claude *McKay's passionate protest poetry is occasionally mixed with appeals to heaven. "If We Must Die," written during the widespread race riots of 1919, is a call to all African Americans to join with him in the dignity and honor of fighting back against oppression. "The White House" (also published as "White Houses") addresses white readers in a style reminiscent of Dunbar's "We Wear the Mask"; it seeks to alert those who discriminate to the effects of discrimination.

Other Harlem Renaissance poets who wrote didactic poetry include Georgia Douglas *Johnson whose book *Bronze* (1922) is a collection of "race" poetry that, in tone, harks back to the previous century. Langston *Hughes's communist-inspired social protest poetry and Sterling A. *Brown's *blues-infused laments about the exploitation of blacks illustrate the 1930s. Both began as Harlem Renaissance writers, but the less hopeful economic and social climate after the crash of 1929 influenced their later writings. Both writers critiqued the role of Christianity in helping African Americans to accept their oppression.

Jean *Toomer is one of the first African American writers whose spiritual explorations are not exclusively Christian. In the long poem "Blue Meridian" (1936), the poet envisions the unity of humankind through the transcendence of race, class, and gender differences. Toomer's theory of racial homogeneity had both material and spiritual aspects; his mysticism was influenced by the teachings of George Ivanovich Gurdjieff.

Robert *Hayden is another twentieth-century poet whose adherence to a non-Christian spiritual system finds its way into his poems. Hayden belonged to the Baha'i faith and a number of his poems, especially in *Words in the Mourning Time* (1970), contain references to the prophet Bahaullah. The Baha'i faith confirmed Hayden's belief in the unity of all people, regardless of race or religion.

In *For My People* (1942), Margaret *Walker protests the manipulation of African American spirituality for the purpose of continuing oppression and offers a healing vision for the future.

Both Melvin B. *Tolson and Gwendolyn *Brooks have written poems that teach those inside and outside the African American community about the toll of racism on African American lives and the creative responses that have sustained the community. One can see their influence, as well as that of Claude McKay and Margaret Walker, on the *Black Arts movement of the 1960s and early 1970s.

The *Black Arts movement sought to teach people of African descent about their history and culture, particularly *blues and *jazz, which were seen as the zenith of African American expressive forms. Amiri *Baraka (LeRoi Jones), the foremost poet of the Black Arts movement, forged his poetry as an instrument of revolution. Baraka's poetry, from the early "Black Art" (1969) to "In the Tradition" (1980), has urged black pride and action against oppression. Other leaders in the Black Arts movement include Haki R. *Madhubuti (Don L. Lee), Sonia *Sanchez, and Larry *Neal.

In the 1970s and 1980s, African American women poets came into their own, and many of these writers have addressed spirituality in their work. Alice *Walker has written numerous poems that urge awareness of and praise for the beauty of nature; this theme is emphasized in the title of her collected poems, *Her Blue Body Everything We Know*, which comes from the poem "We Have a Beautiful Mother" (1991). Lucille *Clifton, in *Good News about the Earth* (1972) and other books, has also spoken of a spiritual connection to the earth. Some of Audre *Lorde's work invokes pre-Christian godesses in woman-identified worship. The work of these writers and of other contemporary poets who address this theme bears little formal resemblance to the verses of Jupiter Hammon and Phillis Wheatley, but their words continue the African American tradition of teaching and testifying.

[See also Biblical Tradition; Churches; Religion.]

• J. Saunders Redding, *To Make a Poet Black*, 1939. Jean Wagner, *Black Poets of the United States: From Paul Laurence Dunbar to Langston Hughes*, trans. Kenneth Douglas, 1973. William P. French et al., *Afro-American Poetry and Drama, 1760–1975: A Guide to Information Sources*, 1979. John C. Shields, "Phillis Wheatley's Struggle for Freedom in Her Poetry and Prose," in *The Collected Works of Phillis Wheatley*, 1988, pp. 229–270. Joan R. Sherman, *Invisible Poets: Afro-Americans of the Nineteenth Century*, 1989. D. H. Melhem, *Heroism in the New Black Poetry: Introductions and Interviews*, 1990. Richard K. Barksdale, "Humanistic Protest in Recent Black Poetry," in *Praisesong of Survival*, 1992, pp. 41–47. Frances Smith Foster, "Doers of the Word: The Reconstruction Poetry of Frances Ellen Watkins Harper," in *Written by Herself: Literary Production by African American*

Women, 1746–1892, 1993, pp. 131–153. Sondra A. O'Neale, *Jupiter Hammon and the Biblical Beginnings of African-American Literature*, 1993.   —Arlene R. Keizer

POINSETTIA JACKSON, character in *A Red Death* (1991) by Walter *Mosley. Poor, sick, but still sexy as the *novel opens, and soon thereafter dead, Poinsettia Jackson is more catalyst than character in Walter Mosley's second *Easy Rawlins mystery, set in Los Angeles in Red-scared 1953. Her murder provides the key to subsequent murders, a window into other characters, and the novel's thematic center. In their reactions to Poinsettia's murder, unorthodox amateur investigator Easy Rawlins and uptight black police detective Quinten Naylor reveal what they have in common—a special sense of responsibility toward black people. When Easy finds Poinsettia hanging in her apartment in one of the buildings he pretends not to own, he thinks she has committed suicide for fear of eviction and blames himself. When Naylor's white partner, accepting too easily the evidence of suicide, asks, "Who's gonna care about this one girl, Quint?" Naylor replies, "I care." The process of solving the murder shifts the blame from Easy to another black man, his rental agent Mofass, to a racist Internal Revenue agent who has exploited bl. :ks' fear of the law in a racist society to extort money from them. As Easy is cleared of blame, however, he realizes he still bears responsibility, for Poinsettia is the victim not simply of murder but of a chain of victimization in which he, too, has participated. When targeted by the corrupt IRS agent, Easy had betrayed a more vulnerable friend of black people, Jewish labor organizer and alleged Communist Chaim Wenzler, just as Mofass had used Poinsettia, more vulnerable than he because of her sex and poverty, to save himself. Thus, though she plays little active role in the novel, Poinsettia is central to its unfolding of the process by which racism can make its victims participate in their own victimization.

[*See also* Crime and Mystery Writing.]

• Theodore O Mason, Jr., "Walter Mosley's Easy Rawlins: The Detective and Afro-American Fiction," *Kenyon Review* 14.4 (Fall 1992): 173–183.   —Susan L. Blake

POLITE, CARLENE HATCHER (b. 1932), novelist, essayist, dancer, activist, and educator. Carlene Hatcher Polite is among the important artists to emerge from the "second renaissance" of African American culture in the 1960s and 1970s. The author of two experimental *novels, *The Flagellants* (1966) and *Sister X and the Victims of Foul Play* (1975), Polite forged a unique prose style that helped establish innovative modes popularized by later writers. In addition to writing, her widespread career has included professional *dance training, performance, and instruction; political organizing; civil rights activism; and academic appointments. Born in Detroit to John and Lillian (Cook) Hatcher, international representatives of UAW-CIO, Polite attended Sarah Lawrence College and the Martha Graham School of Contemporary Dance. From 1955 to 1963, she pursued a career as a professional dancer. Polite performed with the Concert Dance Theater of New York City (1955–1959) and the Detroit Equity Theatre and Vanguard Playhouse (1960–1962), and taught modern dance in the Martha Graham technique as a guest instructor at the Detroit YWCA (1960–1962), the Detroit YMCA (1962–1963), and as a visiting instructor at Wayne State University.

In the early 1960s Polite turned from dance to political organizing and civil rights activism, joining in the cause with many African American artists and intellectuals. In 1962 she was elected to the Michigan State Central Committee of the Democratic Party. She was coordinator of the Detroit Council for Human Rights and participated in the historic June 1963 Walk for Freedom and the November 1963 Freedom Now Rally to protest the Birmingham church bombings. In 1963 Polite organized the Northern Negro Leadership Conference and was active in the NAACP throughout this time.

In 1964 Polite moved to Paris, where she lived until 1971. The influential French editor Dominique de Roux encouraged Polite's writing, and in 1966 *The Flagellants* was published in French by Christian Bourgois Editeur; Farrar, Straus and Giroux brought the novel out in English the following year. Polite received a National Foundation on the Arts and Humanities Fellowship in 1967 and a Rockefeller Foundation Fellowship in 1968. *Sister X and the Victims of Foul Play* was published in 1975, four years after Polite's return to the United States. As of the mid-1990s she is a full professor of English at the State University of New York at Buffalo, where she began as an associate professor in 1971. Polite continues to work on two other novels.

The Flagellants protests limited gender roles for African American women and men in a racially oppressive society and, by a series of interior monologues and exchanges, explores existential questions of identity that transcend yet must be part of racial cultural liberation. *Sister X* recounts the life of a dead black dancer in Paris who was a victim of foul play, racial stereotypes, and discrimination. Both novels have been underappreciated, though Polite's experimentation with form and attention to the rhythms and dialects of African American oral expression influenced the development of postmodern black fiction, especially the work of later innovators such as Gayl *Jones and Ishmael *Reed.

• Hammett Worthington-Smith, "Carlene Hatcher Polite," in *DLB*, vol. 33, *Afro-American Fiction Writers after 1955*, eds. Thadious M. Davis and Trudier Harris, 1984, pp. 215–218. Claudia Tate, introduction to *The Flagellants*, 1967; rpt. 1987.   —Ronna C. Johnson

Popo and Fifina. A juvenile *novel by Arna *Bontemps and Langston *Hughes with illustrations by E. Simms Campbell, *Popo and Fifina: Children of Haiti* was published in 1932. Papa Jean and Mamma Anna, peasant farmers grown tired of farming on the hillsides of Haiti, decide to pursue Papa Jean's dream to own a fishing boat, a decision that means moving the family from the interior to the coast. The story opens with a procession wending its way to the port village of Cape Haiti, parents leading the way with baby Pensia, followed by two burros laden with the family possessions, ten-year-old Fifina, and eight-year-old Popo.

Their new home is a single-room, windowless shack with a tin roof and a rickety door in a yard that includes fruit trees and fuel for cooking at their fingertips. Papa Jean secures work as a fisherman right away, and he is at sea over the succeeding days, but the reader-spectator is accorded a cultural excursion through home and village by accompanying Mamma Anna and the eager-eyed children through their daily routines.

Before the appeal of newness in Cape Haiti wears thin for the children, Mamma Anna is overtaken with homesickness for her birthplace, and the children join her for a holiday in the hills with Grandma Tercilia and other relatives, providing a brief view of the country Creole culture the family left behind. For Popo the high point of this visit occurs when he steals from his bed one evening, lured by the drums, to follow his young grownup cousin André to the dance of the Congo.

Back at Cape Haiti, Fifina and Popo are thrilled one afternoon by the sight of a sky full of kites with long tails and singing strings in the hands of children like themselves. Owning a kite becomes *their* dream, and Fifina suggests a plan to gain their parents' approval. The strategy succeeds, and for several days the children are solely preoccupied with the joy of flying. But just as Fifina predicts, their parents eventually determine that the children are neglecting their other responsibilities. They must set aside the kite so that Fifina can help Mama Anna at home and Popo can become an apprentice in Uncle Jacques's woodworking shop.

Besides Uncle Jacques, Papa Jean's older brother, the small wood shop employs old Durand, his helper, and cousin Marcel, his youngest son, who is near Popo's age. In no time, Popo focuses approval on a beautiful tray cousin Marcel is fashioning and, because he longs to craft one of his own, wonders if it is not modeled after an established pattern? The surprising knowledge that each tray is of a singular design provokes Popo's difficult question: How can anybody make a design without a pattern? His wonder about the sources of imagination prompts old Durand to observe the "riddle" that you have to put yourself into the design. Popo discovers both the pleasure and the pain of the act as he works his own tray, accompanied by the sad tale of the great King Christophe related by Uncle Jacques.

Later, when the two families picnic together along the coast, a more sober Popo climbs the steep cliffs to visit the lighthouse with Papa Jean, Uncle Jacques, Fifina, and Marcel. En route they pass several abandoned forts that remind Popo of the sad history of Christophe. The perspective from the lighthouse resonates in Popo's and Fifina's first approach to Cape Haiti, but now there are intimations that they are more grown up.

This juvenile narrative once represented a new genre in African American writing, and it was unani-mously praised for its simple charm, its attention to informative details, and its poetic style. It was trans-lated into many languages and remained in print for twenty years.

• Violet J. Harris, "From *Little Black Sambo* to *Popo and Fifina*: Arna Bontemps and the Creation of African-American Children's Literature," *The Lion and the Unicorn: A Critical Journal of Children's Literature* 14 (June 1990): 108–127.

—Charles L. James

PORTER, DOROTHY (1905–1995), bibliographer and curator. In the introduction to Richard Newman's *Black Access: A Bibliography of Afro-American Bibliographies* (1984), Dorothy Burnett Porter Wesley writes that her appointment in 1930 as "librarian in charge of the Negro Collection" at Howard University Library in Washington, D.C., was the turning point in her life. She had recently been one of the first two African Americans to receive the master's degree in library science from Columbia University. In accepting the Howard position, she brought the energy and intelligence necessary to make what would become the Moorland-Spingarn Research Center the renowned repository it is today. She has spent nearly six decades collecting, cataloging, and writing about the works of African Americans, Africans, Afro-Brazilians, Afro-Cubans, West Indians, and people of African descent living in the Spanish-speaking countries of South America. Moreover, her own scholarly publications about African American culture and people provide further evidence of her resourcefulness.

In 1914, Jesse E. Moorland gave Howard University most of his private collection about people of African descent, but it and many other items of Africana remained unavailable to readers until Dorothy Porter set about ripping open boxes and cataloging their contents. She determined that the Moorland donation amounted to about three thousand pieces, and eventually edited and annotated one segment of it in *A Catalogue of the African Collection in the Moorland Foundation Howard University Library* (1958). When she retired in 1973, the Moorland gift had grown to over one hundred and eighty thousand items, including those bequeathed to Howard University by bibliophile Arthur B. Spingarn. In fact, the Moorland-Spingarn Research Center has developed into the largest and most comprehensive repository on African Americans at an academic institution. Porter's collecting techniques ranged from buying and trading books, to encouraging donations, to actually picking up texts wherever they were available. She saved from the trash heap files from the Washington, D.C., chapter of the NAACP. Indeed, Porter was nicknamed "bag lady" because she made "salvage excursions" to basements and attics owned by the educator Mary Church *Terrell and other distinguished African Americans.

Perhaps Porter's greatest influences on African American literature have been her numerous published bibliographies and one *anthology. *North American Negro Poets: A Bibliographical Checklist of Their Writings 1760–1944* (1945) expands on the first notable bibliography of African American *poetry, *A*

Bibliographical Checklist of American Negro Poetry (1916), published by Arthur A. *Schomburg. Porter's volume includes annotated entries on books and pamphlets by individual poets, anthologies, as well as other annotated listings. Her anthology, *Early Negro Writing 1760–1837* (1971), reprints such items as books, pamphlets, broadsides, and parts of books that document the economic, social, and educational improvement societies founded by mostly northern African Americans. More specifically, the anthology includes constitutions and bylaws of beneficial societies, speeches, reports, debates about colonization outside America, and sermons. Porter has also published several scholarly articles in journals, such as "Early Manuscript Letters Written by Negroes" in *Journal of Negro History* (1939), "A Library on the Negro" in *American Scholar* (1938) and "Bibliography and Research in Afro-American Scholarship" in *Journal of Academic Librarianship* (1976).

• Esme E. Bhan, "Dorothy Porter," in *Notable Black American Women*, ed. Jessie Carney Smith, 1992, pp. 863–864. Arthur C. Gunn, "Dorothy Burnett Porter Wesley," in *Black Women in America: An Historical Encyclopedia*, 1993, pp. 1246–1248.

—SallyAnn H. Ferguson

Possessing the Secret of Joy. I ·dicated "With Tenderness and Respect to the Blameless Vulva," Alice *Walker's *Possessing the Secret of Joy* (1992) has raised the consciousness of the Western world concerning ritual clitoridectomy or female genital mutilation (also called circumcision or infibulation). The novel indites the centuries-old African tradition for its role in the torture, enslavement, and destruction of women. It announces with a vengeance that the secret of joy (that is, the secret of survival) is resistance.

Introduced first in The *Color Purple* (1982), female genital mutilation emerges in graphic detail in Walker's fifth *novel. Tashi, a minor character in both *The Color Purple* and The *Temple of My Familiar* (1989), is set at center stage. Saved from what the Olinka call "baths" by the presence of Christian missionaries, the adult Tashi (whose Americanized name is Evelyn Johnson) feels a need for a deeper bond with her African roots, her heritage. To achieve this bond she chooses to become a victim of her people's ceremonious rite of passage, a rite that years earlier left her sister dead in a pool of blood.

Again Walker breaks a taboo and speaks of the unspeakable and again some critics condemned her for doing so—claiming that she had no right to judge or condemn African culture and tradition. But, like one hundred million other women, Tashi's submission to the dominating power of the *tsunga*'s (the circumciser's) knife leaves her incapacitated both physically and psychologically (a confirmed reality that quieted Walker's most insistent opposing critics).

The novel details Tashi's battle with madness. Although she visits several therapists (among them Carl Jung and a student of Freud), she is unable to reconcile her loss. Tashi's act of resistance falls ironically within the guidelines of Olinka tradition: she murders the tsunga M'Lissa for her bloody betrayal of thousands of African girls and burns her body.

• Alice Walker and Pratibha Parmar, *Warrior Marks: Female Genital Mutilation and the Sexual Blinding of Women*, 1993.

—Debra Walker King

POSTON, TED (1906–1974), award-winning journalist, short fiction writer, and unionist. Born Theodore Roosevelt Augustus Major in Hopkinsville, Kentucky, Ted Poston was the youngest of eight children. His parents, Mollie and Ephraim Poston, were educators, a distinction that earned his family a leadership role within the African American community and some access to the white leadership of the town. It was the family's weekly paper that started Ted Poston on his journalistic career: as a teenager he wrote copy for the *Contender* until it became too radical and had to be moved out of town in 1921. After graduating from the Tennessee Agricultural and Industrial College in 1928, Poston became one of many to move north, settling in New York City.

Initially employed as a speech writer for presidential candidate Alfred E. Smith, by 1929 he was writing for one of the city's African American papers, the *New York Amsterdam News*, where he covered such explosive topics as the *Scottsboro boys trials. By 1932, when he went to Moscow to act in a never-completed Soviet film about American race relations, Poston had advanced to become the city editor for the *News*, a position he held until 1936, when he was fired after leading a successful effort to unionize the paper. Struggling to find work, in 1937 Poston interviewed for a position at the *New York Post*, only to be told that they would not hire him unless he could produce a front page story for the next day's edition. Rising to this seemingly impossible challenge, Poston got the job and worked at the *Post* for the next thirty-five years. As one of the first and only African American reporters employed by a white daily paper, Poston repeatedly traveled undercover to the South, where he risked his life reporting on several high-profile prosecutions of African Americans and providing early coverage of the *civil rights movement. He also pursued other stories and landed exclusive interviews with major public figures; he's credited with proving that African American reporters need not be restricted to "race issues."

In the early 1940s Poston began to write short fiction that was published in journals such as the *New Republic* and later anthologized in several collections of African American writing. Loosely autobiographical, Poston's stories explicitly addressed the contradictions of race in America, exploring with particular immediacy the inner costs exacted by racism upon its targets. In "You Go South" (1940), for example, he traces the psychological states "you" experience during a two-week return to the South: initially warily determined, arguing calmly with the train conductor as you are forced into the crowded Jim Crow car, you move quickly into rage and confusion, and it is only the last-minute realization that you will soon be back in Harlem that stops you from buying a pistol in helpless desperation. In one of his many childhood tales ("The Revolt of the Evil Fairies," 1942), Poston tackles the taboo issues of class and color-based divisions within the African American community.

• Ted Poston, *The Dark Side of Hopkinsville: Stories by Ted Poston*, ed. Kathleen A. Hauke, 1991.

—Melanie Boyd

POTTER, ELIZA (1820–?), autobiographer. Eliza Potter's anonymous *autobiography, *A Hairdresser's Experience in High Life* (1859), is the first of the genre of behind-the-scenes, tell-all autobiographies that African American women such as Elizabeth *Keckley and Lilian Rogers Parks wrote about their well-placed and famous employers, and one of the earliest examples of autobiographies that establish the African American woman as a social historian. Potter was an unblinking critic of such issues as *slavery (she reserves her harshest criticism for African American slave mistresses), female abolitionists, white standards of beauty, the slavery of fashion, and the "false class" of caste. True to her displacement of the "I" for the "eye," we learn nothing personal about Eliza Potter beyond a perfunctory factual introduction that recalls her previous occupations as maid and wet nurse, her trips to Europe as a governess, where she learned the art of hairdressing, and a short-lived marriage in Buffalo. More interesting is the revelation that she sheltered young African American women, many of them escaped slaves, in her home, trained them as hairdressers, and placed their children in the Cincinnati Colored Orphan's Asylum (where she is listed as a "lady manager").

Raised in New York, Potter moved to Philadelphia, where she gave birth to two *mulatto children, arriving in Cincinnati in 1840. Due perhaps to the scandalous nature of her revelations about the secret lives of the white women who vied for her services, by 1861 her name had disappeared from the city's directory. The literary significance of Potter's autobiography extends, however, beyond its insider/outsider perspective. It provides a crucial context for Harriet E. *Wilson's *Our Nig* (1859), published the same year, and for Toni *Morrison's *Beloved* (1987), which was based on the infamous Margaret Garner incident in Cincinnati in the 1850s.

• Susan P. Graber, *"A Hairdresser's Experience in High Life* by Mrs. Eliza Potter: Cincinnati in the Mid-Nineteenth Century," *Bulletin of the Historical and Philosophical Society of Ohio* 25.3 (1967): 215–224.

—Sharon G. Dean

PREACHERS AND DEACONS have always been topics of concern in African American folk literature and culture. Even though African American *churches, along with their preachers and deacons, have enjoyed the plateau of honorability and respectability, the folk could never resist hearing the "news behind the news" relative to church leaders. Just as Chaucer and Dante observed and wrote about the pronounced corruption in the medieval church, much folk literature has been passed down and recorded about the humorous misdeeds of African American deacons and preachers from the early days of *slavery to the present day.

While many African Americans revered and loved "the preacher," a love-hate relationship allowed them to poke fun at this man of the cloth. No aspect of the preacher's life, manner, or demeanor was immune from the folk. Even the "Godly call" into the ministry was translated by the people into an earthly avenue to rid one's self of the powerful craving of poverty or manual work. According to tradition, one preacher was called into the ministry after having developed a powerful craving for fried chicken and an aversion to work. Similarly, children often hated the Sunday that the preacher was visiting their home for Sunday dinner. As was customary, the preacher ate before the children and quite often, all of the chicken was eaten by "God's man." In one humorous legend, a child noticed that all of the chicken was gone but was comforted quickly by the preacher who told the boy to "sop gravy; gravy is good!"

The preacher and his deacon (if the two did not have an adversarial role grounded in competition) were also pictured in jokes as being greedy materialists who always wanted more money, bigger cars, and more expensive suits. To them it was unbecoming to parade in front of their congregation and throughout the community dressed in common fashion or driving an everyday car. Thus the finest suits of the earth could be seen on the preacher and his ace deacon on each Sunday morning. Likewise, pastors always drove Cadillacs that were pretty and almost too big "to turn the corner."

Oral literature quite often shows the preacher and deacons in "cahoots," attempting to exact more money from their congregation (money that will directly benefit these spiritual mentors). The formulaic timing of the expression "it is better to give than to receive" creates a sheeplike membership for the "money wolves." The deception is further pursued by deacons who flauntingly place large bills into the collection trays only to retrieve them when the money is counted in the backroom.

Another mark of the African American folk preacher/deacon is his unending sexual pursuit of the good sisters inside and outside church. According to one preacher tale, a man who was on his way to work gives specific instructions to his son about Greensboro's most notorious pastors. He tells the boy, "now if Rev. John comes over to the house, sit on the flour barrel. If Rev. James comes over, sit on your momma's purse. But if Rev. Carl comes over, sit on your momma's lap." Closely resembling Chaucer's Friar, the African American folk preacher is still pictured as one who performs numerous ceremonies, but is the primary cause for the need of *marriage.

The harshness of jokes and *humor about African American church leaders should not suggest that African Americans have lost their relationship with God. The literature, however, does show that there is a wealth of material in the oral tradition with powerful satiric qualities of correction.

[*See also* Oratory; Sermons and Preaching.]

• John Mason Brewer, *The Word on the Brazos: Negro Preacher Tales from the Brazos Bottoms of Texas*, 1953. Daryl Cumber Dance, *Shuckin' and Jivin': Folklore from Contemporary Black Americans*, 1978.

—Elon A. Kulii

PREACHING. *See* Sermons and Preaching.

Preface to a Twenty-Volume Suicide Note. Appearing in 1961, *Preface to a Twenty-Volume Suicide Note* is Amiri *Baraka's (LeRoi Jones) first published collection of verse. Published by Totem Press in association with Corinth Books, *Preface* contains a number of poems that had appeared earlier in such little magazines as the *Naked Ear, Swank, White Dove Review, Evergreen Review, Beat Coast East, Nomad, Provincetown Review,* and others. It is in this spare volume that Baraka first received the notice of serious critics, as evidenced in Denise Levertov's fairly typical review. Noting the "sensuous and incantatory" beauty of the poems, she says, "his special gift is an emotive music" (*Nation,* 14 October 1961). Critics of Baraka also took note of the extent to which various modern masters had influenced his early verse. Baraka himself acknowledges in a 1959 *essay entitled "How You Sound" (*New American Poetry 1945–1960,* ed. Donald M. Allen) and in a *Nomad/New York* interview (Autumn 1962) his debt to, among others, Charles Olson, William Carlos Williams, T. S. Eliot, Ezra Pound, and García Lorca.

Despite the acknowledgments, the young Baraka was even more pervasively influenced by the writers of the Beat Generation, a group characterized by its scorn for the forces of convention, pretense, and materialism, as well as its posture of cool disengagement. An index of the poet's attachment to the concerns of these writers is apparent in the dedication of several selections to such members of the Beat coterie as Allen Ginsberg, Gary Snyder, John Wieners, and Michael McClure. The poems uniformly reflect the angst of a thoroughly drained soul in search of meaning and commitment.

The title poem of the volume introduces the recurring themes of despair, alienation, and self-deprecation. "Preface to a Twenty-Volume Suicide Note" lays bare the weary psyche of the hipster, or Beatnik. Filled with images of the stultifying life of convention and respectability, the poem concludes on a profoundly pessimistic note that is intensified in the death-haunted lyrics of "The Bridge" and "Way out West."

The poems of *Preface* evidence yet another notable characteristic of Beat artistry in the frequency of reference to images from American popular culture. Allusions to *jazz and popular *music and references to characters from radio, *film, and comic strips are present in a good number of the works. The fascination with jazz music and musicians, evident in "The Bridge," is, in large part, a reflection of the Beat poet's reverence for an improvisational orientation to life as well as music. The attraction to the heroes of popular culture—most apparent in "In Memory of Radio," "Look for You Yesterday, Here You Come Today," "The Death of Nick Charles," and "Duke Mantee"—is evidence of the cynical, disengaged artist's hunger for commitment and positively directed action.

The remaining poems of *Preface* focus sharply on the related themes of racial identity and artistic engagement, matters that would receive ever growing attention in the later poems, plays, essays, and fiction of Baraka. Although minimally present in the previously cited poems, the question of the proper uses of *poetry receives its strongest evocation in works such as "Betancourt" and "One Night Stand." The racial *identity theme is addressed most directly in the long, sardonic "Hymn for Lanie Poo." In the final poem of *Preface,* "Notes for a Speech," the poet effects an uneasy marriage of these two themes.

• Lloyd Brown, *Amiri Baraka,* 1980. Henry C. Lacey, *To Raise, Destroy and Create: The Poetry, Drama and Fiction of Imamu Amiri Baraka,* 1981.   —Henry C. Lacey

PRESS, AFRICAN AMERICAN. *See* Journalism.

PRINCE, MARY (c. 1788–?), West Indian slave narrator, also known as Molly Wood, Mary James, or Mary, Princess of Wales. Mary Prince was born in Bermuda. She worked as a household slave there and in Antigua and in the salt mines of Turk Island under the most brutal of conditions. In 1828, she went to England with her owners hoping to secure manumission. Unable to purchase her *freedom and return to Antigua as a free woman, Prince dictated her story to Susanna Strickland, an abolitionist and poet. With Prince's approval, her narrative was pruned and edited for publication in accordance with the legal and social conventions governing the publication of such a controversial narrative. Little is known about Mary Prince beyond what is recorded in *The History of Mary Prince, a West Indian Slave, Related by Herself,* first published as an antislavery tract in England in 1831, with supporting documentation furnished by Thomas Pringle, Prince's employer, editor, publisher, and secretary of the Anti-Slavery Society. After testifying before the London Court of Common Pleas in a suit brought by Pringle against Thomas Cadell of *Blackwoods Magazine,* on 21 February 1833, Prince disappeared from public record.

The recovery and republication of Prince's *History* (1987) reconfigures assumptions about *race, *gender, and cultural production in modern Caribbean literature. It illuminates the oral beginnings of the literature, and anticipates its defining paradigms, such as the relationship between written and oral narrative, metropolis and colony, elite and subaltern, exile and return. This unique document elucidates the discourse of struggle versus memory in African American literary circuits in respect to the *autobiographies of those who do not write, and in respect to literature as a sanctioned space for the expression of social dissidence and marginality, especially among women.

[*See also* Slave Narrative; West Indian Literature.]

• Sandra Pouchet Paquet, "The Heartbeat of a West Indian Slave: The History of Mary Prince," *Black American Literature Forum* 26.1 (1992): 131–146. Moira Ferguson, introduction to *The History of Mary Prince, a West Indian Slave, Related by Herself,* 1993. Brenda F. Berrian, "Claiming an Identity: Caribbean Women Writers in English," *Journal of Black Studies* 25.2 (1994): 200–216.

—Sandra Pouchet Paquet

PRINCE, NANCY (1799–?), autobiographer, traveler, abolitionist, and humanitarian. *A Narrative of the Life and Travels of Mrs. Nancy Prince, Written by Herself* (1850) records an extraordinary nineteenth-century life and mind. Born into a nominally free family in Newburyport, Massachusetts, on 15 September 1799, Nancy Gardner Prince grew up enduring hunger, overwork, racism, and a stepfather's abuse, yet stories of her African and Indian ancestors' fights for *freedom infused her with a strong sense of self. She emphasizes that Africans were "stolen" from their homelands and exposes northern economic *slavery. Her oldest sister was "deluded" into a Boston brothel; Nancy walked from Salem to Boston in February to rescue her "lost sister," aided by a friend wielding a large cane.

In her mid-twenties Prince decided she had had enough of "anxiety and toil" in America. In 1824 she married Mr. Prince, an African American servant of a Russian princess, and traveled with him through Europe to the czar's court in St. Petersburg, where she remained for almost ten years, learning several languages, observing foreign customs, and witnessing major political events.

In the 1840s Prince worked with the Anti-Slavery Society in Boston and traveled in the Caribbean, risking life and liberty to help establish schools and orphanages. By 1850 Prince was growing infirm. She published her narrative (which incorporates an earlier fifteen-page pamphlet about the West Indies) in hopes of raising enough money to support herself without accepting charity. The narrative went through three editions (1850, 1853, 1856).

Prince's writing not only reveals her courage, intelligence, and dedication to helping other people, it also expands our understanding of antebellum life for "free" African Americans. Most critics have found Prince's description of her childhood to be the strongest section of her narrative because it provides an original analysis of a nineteenth-century woman's encounters with racism, domestic *violence, and sisterhood.

[*See also* Autobiography.]

• Anthony G. Barthelemy, introduction to *Collected Black Women's Narratives*, ed. Henry Louis Gates, Jr., 1988. Jo Dawn McEwan, "Nancy Gardner Prince," in *Notable Black American Women*, ed. Jessie Carney Smith, 1992, pp. 882–884.
—Kari J. Winter

PROSTITUTE. Prostitutes make rather surprising appearances on the landscape of African American literature. More often than not, instead of the traditional lost souls they may be considered to be, they appear as vibrant, healthy human beings whose chosen profession and way of earning money have not diminished their sense of self. While they certainly provide contrasts to the black women who adhere to more traditional roles and professions, they nonetheless manage to find a place in their communities, and though they may not earn acceptance from those around them, they at least enjoy tolerance. A striking example of this uneasy truce between prostitutes and women who are more inclined to church-going would be China, Poland, and Miss Marie in Toni

*Morrison's The *Bluest Eye* (1970). Morrison asserts that they are "whores in whores' clothing," content with themselves and refusing to alter their lives. While women like Mrs. MacTeer might shun them, children like *Pecola Breedlove are drawn to them. In a community where a little black girl seems to be rejected by family, schoolmates, teachers, and other adults, the three prostitutes serve nurturing roles for Pecola; they welcome her into their space, talk with her, and in turn listen to her. Few other people in the text exhibit such reactions to Pecola, which largely mitigates the potential negative judgment readers may wish to heap upon the heads of the prostitutes. The same casualness toward sex for sale exists in Ann *Petry's The *Street* (1946), where Mrs. Hedges identifies young girls to place in her whorehouse, which is an apartment in the front of the building in which most of the major characters live. Mrs. Hedges, like Morrison's three whores, therefore plays an integral role in the lives of people around her.

Not as grounded in their communities, but still a recognized part of them, prostitutes like Felice in Claude *McKay's *Home to Harlem* (1928) and Sweet in Toni Morrison's *Song of Solomon* (1977) become playing fields upon which the male characters establish a sense of self and a sense of community. Jake encounters Felice early in the novel and is so impressed by his evening with her (also, she secretly returns the fifty dollars he pays her) that he spends the remainder of the novel trying to find her. For *Milkman Dead, seeker after ancestors and male communitas, Sweet is the culmination of the process by which he bonds with other men. Once they have judged him to be okay, they send him to Sweet for her to tend his wounds after a night of hunting and to provide the sexual release they believe he has earned. Both women become objects that the men need in order to prove something to themselves.

"Whores in whores' clothing" are dramatically unlike Claude McKay's "timid" little prostitutes driven to the streets in "Harlem Shadows" (1922) and Charles R. *Johnson's Faith (*Faith and the Good Thing*, 1974), who is similarly driven to prostitution by economic necessity and a sense of loss upon her arrival in the foreboding city of Chicago. They are also unlike Jean *Toomer's Fern (*Cane*, 1923) who gives her body to many men, but who seems spiritually beyond the acts she commits. From easy acceptance to a forced burden—this is the range for treatment of prostitutes in the literature, a range suggesting that black writers view prostitution, like most other presumably illegal activities in black communities, as less than an absolute evil.
—Trudier Harris

PROTEST LITERATURE. Because of conditions created by racism in American history, protest has played a major role in African American literature from the earliest period. While not all African American writing has been directed toward protest, the need to challenge conditions confronting all African Americans has strongly influenced the African American literary tradition. It may even be argued that, by its very existence, African American literature, as a standing denial of white *stereotypes of African American inferiority, has historically represented a protest against American racism.

Several themes have dominated African American protest literature from its beginnings. Often drawing on dominant values and ideals, protest writers have stressed the equality of people of African descent with white people. They have exposed the brutality, psychological as well as physical, of white American racist practices and the absurdity of white American racist ideas. And they have taken an ironic stance toward American society as a whole, contrasting the Christian and democratic professions of white American rhetoric with the realities of *slavery and discrimination in white American life. With roots in African traditions of satire and mockery, and reinforced initially by trends in English and Anglo-American abolitionism—as well as by the obvious absurdities characterizing white racial ideas and practices—this ironic stance was to be a key element in African American protest literature through much of its history.

The pioneer of African American protest literature was Phillis *Wheatley, active in Boston around the time of the American Revolution, and the first African American writer to earn a wide audience. Working within conventions of genteel piety and classical verse, Wheatley nonetheless used *poetry to assert human equality and *freedom and to express her opposition to slavery. Ironically contrasting her own piety with the hypocrisy of her white contemporaries, Wheatley belittled white racial pretensions, even as she sought by her achievements to prove them wrong.

After Wheatley, the late eighteenth and early nineteenth centuries saw a proliferation of protest materials. The most widely publicized work from the period, scientist Benjamin *Banneker's open letter to Thomas Jefferson (1791), though couched in polite language, followed Wheatley in its firm assertion of human unity. Speeches and pamphlets of such influential figures as William Hamilton, Russell Parrott, and James Forten, leaders of the growing free black communities of the North, denounced slavery, inequality, and the racist hypocrisy of the young American nation.

In the antebellum period, encouraged by the growing movement against slavery, African American protest writing flowered. It achieved new levels of militance in the speeches and writings of such activists as Maria W. *Stewart and Henry Highland *Garnet, among the first to call for violent rebellion against slavery, and in David *Walker's controversial *Appeal to the Coloured Citizens of the World* (1829–1830), one of the first openly nationalist responses to racial injustice.

The late 1820s saw the development of a substantial body of protest poetry, much of it sentimental in character, contrasting slavery's brutality with the genteel ideals of American middle-class culture. Although many of the poets published anonymously, a few became well known. The North Carolina slave George Moses *Horton, hoping to use his poetry to earn his freedom, wrote stinging indictments of the system. Frances Ellen Watkins *Harper, from one of the leading free families of Baltimore, began publishing abolitionist pieces in the 1840s, becoming one of the most noted African American writers in the 1850s and after.

But the most influential protests of the antebellum period were conveyed in the *slave narratives. Contributions to the abolitionist movement, they graphically exposed the cruelty of slavery, commenting ironically on the inconsistencies of Christian slaveholding and of slaveholding in a so-called land of liberty. Although dating back to the late eighteenth century, they appeared most frequently in the quarter century prior to the Civil War, achieving a wide readership. Narratives by William Wells *Brown (1847), William and Ellen *Craft (1860), Josiah *Henson (1849), Henry "Box" *Brown (1849), and James W. C. *Pennington (1849) achieved great recognition. A few attained classic status, including Frederick *Douglass's two antebellum *autobiographies, *Narrative of the Life of Frederick Douglass* (1845) and *My Bondage and My Freedom* (1855), and Harriet A. *Jacobs's *Incidents in the Life of a Slave Girl* (1861).

Fiction by African American writers, appearing regularly only shortly before the Civil War, built on forms of protest developed in the autobiographies. William Wells Brown's *Clotel* (1853), perhaps the first African American *novel, used the "tragic mulatto" theme and motifs from slave narratives to expose the cruelty and brutality of the slave system. Frederick Douglass's novella, "The *Heroic Slave" (1853), dramatized events in the life of Madison Washington, a real fugitive who had led an 1841 mutiny aboard the slave ship *Creole*. Harriet E. *Wilson's *Our Nig* (1859), set in New England, used the autobiographical form to indict racial discrimination, and even servitude, in the North. Martin R. *Delany, an activist, nationalist, and advocate of emigration to Africa drew on traditional antislavery motifs in *Blake*, not only to expose the evils of slavery, but, in the tradition of Walker and Garnet, to advocate militant action to bring about its end.

Prior to the end of slavery in the United States, African American writers had not confined themselves to protest. Writers from Wheatley through Harper created sentimental and devotional works along with those protesting slavery and racism. Nevertheless, the bulk of writing was directed toward protest, an emphasis characterizing African American writing in the postemancipation era as well.

Through Reconstruction, and into the early 1890s, protest was underlain by optimism, the end of slavery giving hope for an end to discrimination. Much was aimed at challenging what were seen as vestiges of discrimination in a postslavery society. The middle-class men and women who did most of the writing knew that their own characters and accomplishments proved their ability to participate in the mainstream of American society, proved their moral and intellectual equality. Their writings were both properly Victorian and assertive at the same time, the failures of white Americans addressed in the same ironic voice that had conveyed African American literary protest since Wheatley. In such works as Frances Ellen Watkins Harper's novel *Iola Leroy* (1892) or Albery Allson *Whitman's epic poem *Not a Man, and Yet a Man* (1877), these writers exposed the absurdity of discrimination by portraying African American characters who met every criterion of middle-class propriety—indeed, who tended to outdo white characters in all respects—but who nonetheless faced insult and exclusion on account of color.

By the mid-1890s, however, a new element began to appear in African American protest, forced by changing conditions in American life. The optimism of Reconstruction was increasingly threatened by worsening developments in American race relations, increasing the urgency of protest in African American writing, giving it a militance and a bitterness greater than had been common before. Moving away from romantic conventions and gentility, writers from the last decade of the nineteenth century and the first two decades of the twentieth, leading up to World War I, detailed the barbarism of white southern practices, especially *lynching, and continued to expose white American hypocrisy, but as they had never before, protested injustice in a way that envisioned little expectation of triumph, and with a sense of despair.

These tendencies were visible in the works of two of the era's most notable novelists, Sutton E. *Griggs and Charles Waddell *Chesnutt. Griggs, a Baptist minister, wrote what has been considered the first African American nationalist novel—apart, perhaps, from Delany's *Blake*—in *Imperium in Imperio* (1899), the story of the birth and death of a black revolutionary movement. There, and in other novels, including *Overshadowed* (1901) and *The Hindered Hand* (1905), he focused on the absence of possibilities for African Americans, portraying a racism at the heart of American society that offered only tragic possibilities for men and women of color.

Chesnutt likewise made a pessimistic protest fiction the core of his literary work. In *The *House Behind the Cedars* (1900), *The *Marrow of Tradition* (1901), and *The Colonel's Dream* (1905), Chesnutt dramatized the power of racism to blind individuals to justice, honor, and human need, even as he portrayed the *violence underlying the American racial system. Although Chesnutt, like Griggs, did not depart completely from older conventions, both relying on genteel characters and conventions, the pessimism and desperation marking their works gave an edge to protest that was new.

The same may be said of two writers from the period who did more to break new formal ground, W. E. B. *Du Bois and James Weldon *Johnson. Du Bois's *The *Souls of Black Folk* (1903) combined fiction, poetry, and *essays to put the challenge to racism on a new foundation, one that spoke to the importance of cultural resistance even as it delineated the cruelty of racial injustice. In his novel *The *Quest of the Silver Fleece* (1911), at one level an attack on the oppressive, racist character of the southern economy, Du Bois also presented exotic images of African American characters, placing more hope in self-determination than in traditional integra-

tionist goals. In *The *Autobiography of an Ex-Colored Man* (1912), Johnson, though concerned primarily with protesting the arbitrariness of American racial distinctions, and their psychological danger, also brought Du Bois's cultural concerns to bear as he developed a deeper sense of the power of racism in American consciousness.

Johnson's novel looked forward to larger developments in African American literature generally, and protest writing in particular, over the next two decades. The events surrounding World War I, including a substantial *migration to northern urban centers and the experience of combat service in Europe, created a new vision and a new militance among African Americans, both of which informed protest literature.

That new vision was embodied in the *Harlem Renaissance. Built on Du Boisian notions of cultural distinctiveness and on high cultural ambitions, the Harlem Renaissance was also a literary movement with great self-consciousness about the role of protest in African American arts, about whether art could or should be "propaganda." Alain *Locke, the philosopher of the movement, was particularly hostile to literature whose chief purpose was protest, seeing it as an acknowledgment of the power of white oppression in African American consciousness, and thus contrary to the aims of the renaissance to build a distinctive literature. Du Bois, despite the key role of his ideas in the movement, believed that any African American art that was not propaganda was worthless.

In the literature itself, protest tended to be subordinate to the demands of cultural creation, but it was never entirely absent. The era produced significant works devoted to protest: NAACP official Walter *White's novel *Fire in the Flint* (1924) was one of the most influential antilynching novels in the African American tradition; George S. *Schuyler's fantasy *Black No More* (1931) returned to conventions of satire and irony to condemn the absurdity of "*race" as such. Countee *Cullen, in "Incident" (1925), a poem in which a young white boy gratuitously calls the narrator "nigger," protested the pervasiveness of prejudice in a way reminiscent of earlier genteel traditions; Claude *McKay's "If We Must Die" (1919) looked back to the ideas of Stewart, Walker, and Garnet to combine protest with a celebration of violent resistance.

Protest came to assume a more prominent role in the 1930s, even among writers who had done little such work during the Harlem Renaissance. This prominence was a product, in part, of the general radicalization of American literary life during the Great Depression and prior to World War II, a radicalization manifested by the widespread participation of many writers, including African Americans, in the Communist Party. Such writers from the Harlem Renaissance as Langston *Hughes turned increasingly to protest, as did Sterling A. *Brown, despite his general association with a poetry celebrating folk themes and traditions. Countee Cullen, joining other writers, used poetry to demand attention to racial oppression in "Scottsboro, Too, Is

Worth Its Song" (1934), focusing on the celebrated Alabama case. In addition, emerging poets including Frank Marshall *Davis and Robert *Hayden worked primarily in protest. It played a major role in the work of Margaret *Walker, whose "*For My People" (1937) documented the depressing conditions of the South, and Melvin B. *Tolson, whose "Dark Symphony" (1940), reviewed African American history not only to document oppression but to raise hopes for resistance.

No less important were adaptations of the radical "proletarian novel" to the purposes of African American protest, relating racial oppression to larger notions of *class struggle and to revolutionary ideals. Arna *Bontemps's *Black Thunder (1936), a fictional account of the 1800 Gabriel Prosser rebellion in Virginia, emphasized the revolutionary roots underlying that revolt, its connection to worldwide efforts to end oppression and exploitation. William *Attaway in Blood on the Forge (1941), focusing on the lives of African Americans pursuing improved conditions in northern industry, tied the protest against racial injustice to larger issues of class struggle.

But the most important protest work of the period was that of Richard *Wright in *Uncle Tom's Children (1938), a collection of stories; in the best-selling novel *Native Son (1940); and in an autobiography published in the last year of the war, *Black Boy (1945). Affiliated with the Communist Party part of his career, Wright wrote with a brutal realism informed by the era's sociological studies detailing the horrible effects of racial oppression on African American lives. The stories in Uncle Tom's Children, set in the South, graphically portrayed the violence of a racist region. Native Son showed how the racism that had created northern ghettoes had also brutalized its victims, embodied in his most important creation, *Bigger Thomas. Black Boy dramatized, in Wright's own Mississippi childhood and youth, the conclusions of social scientists who had explored the psychological cruelty of the Jim Crow South.

In postwar years, the tradition of protest continued, given added impetus by the *civil rights movement, a movement whose effects were evident before the end of the 1940s and which gathered momentum through the 1950s. Poet Gwendolyn *Brooks, though her work was hardly confined to protest, nonetheless did important protest pieces, including the "Ballad of Rudolph Reed," recounting the fatal harrassment of a black family moving into a "white neighborhood"; "A Bronzeville Mother Loiters in Mississippi. Meanwhile a Mississippi Mother Burns Bacon"; and "The Last Quatrain of the Ballad of Emmett Till," evoking the horrors of that infamous 1955 lynching. "The Chicago Defender Sends a Man to Little Rock" used one of the turning points of the civil rights movement to expose the hypocrisy and grotesqueness of white resistance to racial equality.

The most important novel of the civil rights era was Ralph *Ellison's *Invisible Man (1952). Although not primarily a protest novel, an exposé and indictment of racism was central to its significance. Featuring a nameless protagonist who was "visible" to white Americans only as a generic man of color, the novel looked back to the works of Chesnutt and James Weldon Johnson in its delineation of the dehumanizing force of racism in American life.

As in the 1920s, the civil rights era saw significant debate over the role of protest in literature, much of it sparked by James *Baldwin's important essay "Everybody's Protest Novel" (1949). Baldwin, challenging Wright's work, went beyond Locke to argue that a literature centered on protest entailed using the very categories of racial identity on which oppression had historically been based. Such a literature accepted racial categorization as a basis for self-definition, devaluing the fullness of the humanity that African Americans shared with all peoples. Baldwin's insights were given additional meaning by the French West Indian psychiatrist Frantz Fanon, who, in Black Skin, White Masks (1952, trans. 1967) and The Wretched of the Earth (1961, trans. 1963), explored the ultimate paradox of protest, its very dependence on the categories of the oppressor.

The caveats of Baldwin and, later, Fanon did not mean an end to protest literature. The 1960s saw the appearance of several major works, including Margaret Walker's *Jubilee (1966), a revival of antislavery traditions, and John A. *Williams's The *Man Who Cried I Am (1967), exposing the inescapability of "race," even in the world civil rights had begun to shape. Douglas Turner *Ward, especially in his play *Day of Absence (1965), revived traditions of irony and satire in attacking white racial ideas. Probably the two most influential works by African Americans from the 1960s were firmly within the protest tradition. These were Eldridge *Cleaver's *Soul on Ice (1968) and The *Autobiography of Malcolm X (written with Alex *Haley, 1965), autobiographical works that proposed militant action in the face of racism, drawing on ideas going back to militant abolitionism, but in a language informed by the era's urban realities.

However, beginning particularly in the mid-1960s, protest literature began to show the kind of self-consciousness that had been manifested during the Harlem Renaissance, and a linking of protest to the kinds of concerns for self-definition and self-determination that Baldwin and Fanon implied. Writers working under the aegis of the decade's *Black Arts movement, including Larry *Neal, Sonia *Sanchez, and Haki R. *Madhubuti, while well within the protest tradition—one of the leading figures, Amiri *Baraka, referred to them as "soldier poets"—began to use the language of the ghettoes to work toward a literature that sought to manifest cultural independence as well as to condemn the continuing racism of American life.

Late-twentieth-century African American writers have continued to expose and to decry American racism. Although the literature has been less characterized by protest, as such, the issue of racism has been an inevitable presence in African American writing, making most works, in a sense, works of protest, as has been the case since Wheatley. Moreover, protest represents a tradition that informs such major works as Toni *Morrison's *Beloved (1987), set during slavery and based on a story widely circulated by abolitionists to show the institution's cruelty, and

Charles R. *Johnson's *Middle Passage (1990), a work that reinvigorates the ironic tradition in which African American protest has so long been couched.

Protest has been endemic to the development of African American literary tradition. It is likely to remain important in African American literature so long as the conditions to which it is addressed remain a fact of American life.

• J. Saunders Redding, To Make a Poet Black, 1939. Robert A. Bone, The Negro Novel in America, 1965. Nathan I. Huggins, Harlem Renaissance, 1971. James O. Young, Black Writers of the Thirties, 1973. Addison Gayle, Jr., The Way of the New World: The Black Novel in America, 1975. Eugene B. Redmond, Drumvoices: The Mission of Afro-American Poetry, A Critical History, 1976. William L. Andrews, To Tell a Free Story: The First Century of Afro-American Autobiography, 1760–1865, 1986. Bernard W. Bell, The Afro-American Novel and Its Tradition, 1987. Henry Louis Gates, Jr., The Signifying Monkey: A Theory of Afro-American Literary Criticism, 1988. Dickson D. Bruce, Jr., Black American Writing from the Nadir: The Evolution of a Literary Tradition, 1877–1915, 1989. Blyden Jackson, A History of Afro-American Literature, vol. 1, The Long Beginning, 1746–1895, 1989.

—Dickson D. Bruce, Jr.

PUBLISHING. Historically, the objective of African American book publishing has been twofold: to correlate the response of African Americans to the larger society; and to record and preserve African American cultural heritage. In general African American book publishing consists of those activities managed and financed by African Americans for the purpose of manufacturing and distributing books. However, the African American book publishing sector of the American book publishing industry segments into six basic types: self-published authors; religious publishers; other organizational publishers; magazine and newspaper publishers; university presses; and trade book publishers.

Self-Published African American Authors. Although some African American authors financed the publication of their writings on broadsides or in pamphlets in the late eighteenth century, it was not until the early decades of the nineteenth century that African American authors self-published books of more than forty-eight pages or volumes of *poetry of any length. Prominent among the reasons that African American authors self-publish books have been the lack of opportunities to publish with established publishing firms and the unwillingness of some authors to subject their manuscripts to the editorial judgments of others. Nonetheless, these self-published African American authors have released significant additions to African American literature in such genres as sociopolitical commentaries, *autobiographies, *slave narratives, *novels, *poetry, and *histories.

One of the earliest books self-published by an African American author was *David Walker's Appeal, by David *Walker (1829). This scathing sociopolitical work, which was the most substantive treatise espousing *Black nationalism produced in the nineteenth century, was one of the most widely circulated books written by an African American in the United States prior to the Civil War. Walker's Appeal, which went through three editions, has become a classic sociopolitical commentary in African American literature. David Walker died mysteriously in Boston in 1830 shortly after he self-published the last edition of his Appeal.

Six years after Walker's death, The Life and Religious Experience of Jarena Lee (1836), telling the story of the first woman to be sanctioned to preach in the African Methodist Episcopal (AME) Church, was self-published as a pamphlet. In 1849 Jarena *Lee expanded the pamphlet into a book of sixty-nine pages and republished it as Religious Experience and Journal of Mrs. Jarena Lee, thus becoming one of the earliest self-published African American autobiographies to appear in booklength form. It was followed by other autobiographies, such as A Narrative of the Life and Travels of Mrs. Nancy Prince by Nancy *Prince (1850), and A Brand Plucked from the Fire: An Autobiographical Sketch by Julia A. J. *Foote (1879).

Many African American writers self-published books in a more specialized form of autobiographical writing: the slave narrative. Some of the more popular self-published slave narratives were William Hayden's The Narrative of William Hayden, Containing a Faithful Account of His Travels for a Number of Years Whilst a Slave in the South (1846); Henry *Bibb's Narrative of the Life and Adventures of Henry Bibb, An American Slave (1849); and *Incidents in the Life of a Slave Girl by Harriet A. *Jacobs (1861).

The development of the novel in African American literature includes some landmarks that were self-published by African American writers. In 1859 the first novel written and published in the United States by an African American, *Our Nig, or Sketches from the Life of a Free Black, in a Two-Story White House, North. Showing That Slavery's Shadows Fall Even There, by Our Nig (pseud.), was self-published by the author, Harriet E. *Wilson, according to Henry Louis *Gates, Jr., in his introduction to the reprint of the novel (1983). Forty years after Our Nig first appeared, Sutton E. *Griggs, a Baptist minister, self-published *Imperium in Imperio (1899), a fantastic account of an African American political organization, regarded by Hugh M. Gloster in his Negro Voices in American Fiction (1948) as the first political novel in African American literature. Two years later Griggs established Orion Publishing Company in Nashville, Tennessee, to publish his own books. Between 1901 and 1908 he wrote and published four militant novels depicting the oppression of African Americans by a white southern racist society: Overshadowed (1901); Unfettered (1902); The Hindered Hand (1905); and Pointing the Way (1908). The last book authored by Griggs, Wisdom's Call (1909), however, reflected a change in his race-relations philosophy. It was a collection of *essays advocating an accommodationist solution to the race problem in the South.

In 1913 Oscar *Micheaux, who later won fame as a pioneering African American filmmaker, self-published his first novel: The Conquest: The Story of a Negro Pioneer, the earliest novel in African American literature to portray as a lead character the African American in the role of a pioneer. Micheaux founded the first of his publishing firms in 1915, The Western Book Supply Company in Lincoln, Nebraska, to publish his second and third novels: *The Forged Note* (1915) and *The Homesteader* (1917). He made *The Homesteader* into his first motion picture, which premiered in Chicago in 1919, the first self-published African American novel to become the basis for a motion picture. Four other novels were written and published by Micheaux through his publishing firms before he died in 1951: *The Wind from Nowhere* (1941); *The Case of Mrs. Wingate* (1944); *Masquerade* (1947); and *The Story of Dorothy Stansfield* (1948).

Throughout the history of African American book publishing a host of aspiring African American poets, some of whom gained national recognition, initially self-published their early volumes of poetry to bring their work to the attention of the general public and critics. Notable among them was Paul Laurence *Dunbar, who financed the printing of and personally distributed his first two published volumes of poetry: *Oak and Ivy* (1893) and *Majors and Minors* (1895). Other African American poets who self-published their early volumes of poetry and later received national recognition were Frances Ellen Watkins *Harper, *Moses: A Story of the Nile* (1869) and *Southern Sketches* (1872); William Stanley *Braithwaite, *Lyrics of Life and Love* (1904); Benjamin *Brawley, *The Dawn and Other Poems* (1911); and Fenton *Johnson, *Visions of the Dusk* (1915).

One of the most widely read self-published African American authors during the first half of the twentieth century was Joel August Rogers. In 1917 this historian without a portfolio established J. A. Rogers Publications in Chicago, and later moved to New York, to publish his books. Between 1917 and 1959, Rogers published several groundbreaking historical works documenting the history of persons of African descent in Europe and the New World. Among these works, some of which have been issued in several editions, were *From Man to Superman* (1917); *As Nature Leads* (1919); *World's Greatest Men of African Descent* (1931); *World's Great Men of Color* (1946); and *Africa's Gift to America* (1951).

Chicago realtor Dempsey J. Travis has been one of the most successful self-published African American authors in recent years. In 1969 Travis established The Urban Research Institute to publish his works, including *An Autobiography of Black Chicago* (1981), winner of the Society of Midland Authors Award; *An Autobiography of Black Jazz* (1983), winner of the Art Deco Award; and *Harold: The People's Mayor* (1989).

The role of the self-published African American author has been, and continues to be, to make available to the public at his or her own personal expense books focusing on unique aspects of the African American experience that would not have received exposure through regular publishers. In some instances the books self-published by African American authors have had a profound influence on the growth and development of various facets of African American literature.

Religious Publishers. Since 1817, when the African American Methodist Episcopal Church established the *A.M.E. Book Concern in Philadelphia,

seven other African American religious denominational publishers have come into existence. They are The A.M.E. Zion Publishing House of the African American Episcopal Zion Church, Charlotte, North Carolina (1841); The CME Publishing House of the Christian Methodist Episcopal Church (formerly the Colored Methodist Episcopal Church), Memphis, Tennessee (1870); The A.M.E. Sunday School Union and Publishing House of the African Methodist Episcopal Church, Nashville, Tennessee (1881); The National Baptist Publishing Board, Nashville, Tennessee (1896); The Church of God and Christ Publishing House, Memphis, Tennessee (1907); The Sunday School Publishing Board of the National Baptist Convention, Nashville, Tennessee (1916); and Muhammad's Temple No. 2, Publications Department of the Nation of Islam, Chicago, Illinois (1966).

Each of these religious denominational publishers had stated or implied publishing objectives related to producing books to: instruct or assist clergy and laymen, adults and children, in their understanding and performance of denominational doctrines or practices; record the history of the denomination; and provide greater spiritual understanding of life through religion. *Historical Catechism of the A. M. E. Zion Church; for Use of Families and Sunday Schools* by Cicero Richardson Harris (A.M.E. Zion Publishing House, 1922) and *The Baptist Standard Hymnal* (Sunday School Publishing Board, 1974) are examples of books published to assist laymen and clergy in their understanding and performance of church doctrines and practices. C. H. Phillips's *History of the Colored Methodist Episcopal Church in America* (CME Publishing House, 1898) and *A Story of Christian Activism: The History of the National Baptist Convention, U. S. A., Inc.* by J. H. Jackson (Townsend Press [Sunday School Publishing Board], 1980) are illustrative of denominational histories. *Studies upon the Great Themes of Religion and of the Scriptures* by George Washington Henderson (A.M.E. Book Concern, 1917) and *Liberation and Unity: A Lenten Booklet for 1976* (CME Publishing House, 1976) were books published for the general spiritual and religious guidance of laymen.

Three religious publishers developed publishing programs that included the publication of books on secular subjects, specifically books documenting aspects of African American history or culture; commentaries, treatises, or essays upholding the civil rights of African Americans or defending African Americans against vicious attacks on their moral and mental sensibilities; and novels, short stories, poetry, and plays portraying aspects of African American life or thought.

The A.M.E. Book Concern was a prolific publisher of secular titles. In 1912 this religious publisher released Richard Robert Wright's *The Negro in Pennsylvania: A Study in Economic History*, a follow-up study of W. E. B. *Du Bois's classic *The Philadelphia Negro* (1899). *The Resentment: A Novel* by Mary Etta Spencer (1921) and *The Vengeance of the Gods, and Three Other Stories of Real American Color Line Life* by William *Pickens (1922) were two of its fiction titles. *Fifty Years of Freedom, or From Cabin to

Congress: A Drama in Five Acts by Katherine Davis Chapman *Tillman (1909) and *Daddy's Love and Other Poems* by Irvin Underhill (1930) were illustrative of plays and volumes of poetry published.

The National Baptist Publishing Board released a powerful civil rights treatise for the National Baptist Convention in 1909 entitled *The Separate or "Jim Crow" Car Laws, or Legislative Enactments of Fourteen Southern States: A Reply in Compliance with a Resolution of the National Baptist Convention*, compiled by Richard Henry Boyd. In the same year this firm released one of its first novels, J. W. Grant's *Out of Darkness, or Diabolism and Destiny*. And four years later The National Baptist Publishing Board began issuing volumes of poetry with the publication of *Sentimental and Comical Poems* by James Thomas (1913), which was followed by Maurice Corbett's *The Harp of Ethiopia* (1914). In 1993 *A Black Man's Dream: The First Hundred Years: Richard Henry Boyd and the National Baptist Publishing Board* by Bobby L. Lovett appeared.

In 1967 The Sunday School Publishing Board of the National Baptist Convention created the Townsend Press imprint to publish secular books. Two of the titles that have appeared are *Unholy Shadows and Freedom's Holy Light* by J. H. Jackson (1967), a commentary on the civil rights movement, and Kenny J. Williams's *They Also Spoke: An Essay on Negro Literature in America, 1787–1930* (1970). Religious and secular works continue to be released under the Townsend Press imprint.

African American religious publishers, the oldest and most stable segment of publishers in African American book publishing, have been and continue to be the largest producers and distributors of African American religious literature. Some of these religious publishers have published a significant body of secular African American literature in several genres.

Other Organizational Publishers. Several African American cultural, civil rights and political, and professional organizations have engaged in book publishing. The most active publishers have been the American Negro Academy (ANA), 1897–1928; the NAACP, founded in 1910; the National Urban League (NUL), founded in 1911; the Association for the Study of Afro-American Life and History (ASALH), founded in 1915; the Universal Negro Improvement Association (UNIA), 1918–1927; and the DuSable Museum of African American History, founded in 1961. These African American organizations published *children's and young adult literature; textbooks and handbooks; scholarly histories; sociological and political studies and treatises; and volumes of poetry.

Two of these produced young adult and children's books. The NAACP published *Hazel* by Mary Ovington White (1913), a novel for young adults, and *A Child's Story of Dunbar* by Julia L. Anderson (1913). Among the many books for young adults and children issued by Chicago's DuSable Museum have been *Whip Me, Whop Me, Pudding and Other Tales of Riley Rabbit and His Fabulous Friends* by Margaret Taylor Goss *Burroughs (1966); *My Name Is Arnold* by Essie

Branch (1968); and *Black Power in Old Alabama: The Life and Stirring Times of James T. Rapier* by Eugene Feldman (1986).

Books written as textbooks and handbooks were published by three organizational publishers. In 1915 one of the first textbooks in African American history for secondary schools was published by the American Negro Academy: *The Negro in American History* by John Wesley Crumwell. Carter G. *Woodson authored *The African Background, or Handbook for the Study of the Negro*, which was published by the ASALH in 1938. The NUL released *The Power of the Ballot: A Handbook for the Black Political Participation* in 1973.

Since 1918 the ASALH has published a host of scholarly histories in neglected areas of African Americana and Africana that have had a significant impact on American historiography. Among some of these classic historical studies have been *The Negro in South Carolina during the Reconstruction* by Alrutheus Ambush Taylor (1924); *Anti-Slavery Sentiment in American Literature Prior to 1865* by Lorenzo Dow Turner (1929); and *Extracts from the Records of the African Companies* by Ruth A. Fisher (1930).

*The Philosophy and Opinions of Marcus *Garvey*, volume 1 (1923) and volume 2 (1925), compiled and edited by Amy Jacques-Garvey, published by the UNIA, was one the most elaborate political treatises on *black nationalism produced by an African American publisher in the first decades of the twentieth century. It was during this same period that the NAACP and the NUL began publishing groundbreaking, booklength sociological and economic studies describing the plight of the African American as illustrated by such works as *Thirty Years of Lynching in the United States, 1889–1918* (NAACP, 1919) and *Negro Membership in American Labor Unions* (printed for the NUL by Alexander Press, 1930).

Under the editorship of Charles S. Johnson, the brilliant sociologist and promoter of the *Harlem Renaissance, the NUL published *Ebony and Topaz: A Collectanea* in 1927. This momentous *anthology, which included art, poetry, fiction, and essays by the major Harlem Renaissance artists and writers, has become a classic work in African American literature.

African American poets had their works published by two organizational publishers, the Freelance Press of Cleveland's Freelance Poetry Workshop and the DuSable Museum of African American History. Freelance Press's first published volume of poetry was Conrad Kent *Rivers's *Perchance to Dream, Othello* (1959), which was followed by such works as *Two by Atkins: The Abortionist and the Corpse, Two Poetic Dramas to Be Set to Music* by Russell *Atkins (1963), and *Dusk at Selma* by Conrad Kent Rivers (1965). Some of the early volumes of poetry released by the DuSable Museum of African American History were *What Shall I Tell My Children Who Are Black?* by Margaret Burroughs (1968); Helen Burleson Fredricks's *No Place Is Big Enough to House My Soul (1970);* and *House of My Soul* by Marion Black (1977).

Thus books published by African American organizational publishers have influenced the development of African American historical, sociological, children's, political, and belletristic literature.

Newspaper and Magazine Publishers. A small number of African American newspaper and magazine publishers issued books. While most of these firms did so only occasionally, one magazine publisher developed a book publishing division with substantial annual lists.

Newspaper firms that periodically issued books generally published books by local authors or on subjects of regional interests. The Fortune and Peterson Company of New York City, which published the *New York Age* from 1887 to 1905, released in 1905 a volume of poetry by T. Thomas *Fortune, the famed journalist and one of the owners of the firm, entitled *Dreams of Life*. In Cincinnati, Ohio, the Dabney Publishing Company, publishing the weekly *Union* from 1907 to 1952, issued three books authored by owner Wendell P. Dabney: *Cincinnati's Colored Citizens* (1926), a history of the city's African American community; *Chisum's Pilgrimage and Others* (1927), a collection of essays; and *Maggie L. Walker: The Woman and Her Work* (1927), the biography of the first African American woman banker. Des Moines's Iowa State Bystander Publishing Company, publisher of the *Iowa State Bystander* from 1897 to 1974, published two significant histories of local as well as national interest: *History and Views of Colored Officers Training Camp for 1917 at Des Moines* by John Lay Thompson (1917), one of the owners of the publishing company, and *The History of the Order of the Eastern Star among Colored People* by Sue M. Brown (1925). In Norfolk, Virginia, the Guide Publishing Company, publisher of the weekly *Journal and Guide*, issued two histories of local interest. They were *A History of the Virginia State Teachers Association* by Luther Porter Jackson, a prominent historian and professor at nearby Virginia State College, and *The African Society Becomes Immanuel African Methodist Church, Portsmouth, Virginia* by Charles E. Stewart (1944). The Afro-American Publishing Company in Baltimore, Maryland, publisher of the *Afro-American* since 1892, released several books, among them *This Is Our War Too* (1945), a collection of stories about African American soldiers in World War II written by the newspaper's war correspondents, and *Baltimore, America's Fifth Largest Negro Market* by the Afro-American staff (1946). In 1919 the *St. Louis Argus* Publishing Company, which publishes the weekly *St. Louis Argus*, released *Immediate Jewel of His Soul*, a militant novel by a local high school teacher, Herman Dreer, and a volume of poetry, *The Eagle* by Thomas Atkins (1936).

Magazine publishers who published books released books in many of the same genres as newspaper publishers. Thomas Hamilton, Sr., whose firm published the *Anglo-African Magazine* in New York City from 1859 to 1865, was the earliest African American magazine publisher to publish books. His firm published *A Pilgrimage to My Motherland: An Account of a Journey among the Egbas and Yorubas of Central Africa, 1859–1860* by Robert Campbell (1861), who had accompanied Martin R. *Delany on his exploratory trip to Africa from 1859 to 1860.

Three years after Hamilton's death his brother, Robert, published through the firm William Wells *Brown's collective biography *The Black Man, His Antecedents, His Genius and His Achievements* (1863). The Colored Cooperative Publishing Company in Boston, which issued the *Colored American Magazine* from 1900 to 1904, published one book: Pauline E. *Hopkins's classic *Contending Forces* (1900), a novel about African American life in Boston at the turn of the century. From early 1920 to late 1921, the Du Bois and Dill Publishing Company in New York City published the *Brownies' Book*, a pioneering magazine for African American children. In 1921 this firm, a partnership between W. E. B. Du Bois and August Granville Dill, published one book for young people: *Unsung Heroes* by Elizabeth Haynes, a collective biography of outstanding persons of African descent. In 1962 when the book division of Johnson Publishing Company of Chicago published Lerone Bennett, Jr.'s *Before the Mayflower* and the novel *Burn, Killer, Burn* by Paul Crump, the most ambitious book-publishing program launched by any African American magazine publisher came into existence. Titles in several literary genres have been issued by this publisher, notably Freda DeKnight's *The Ebony Cookbook* (1973); *What Manner of Man: A Biography of Martin Luther King, Jr.* by Lerone Bennett, Jr. (1964); *The Negro Handbook*, edited by Doris Saunders (1966); *To Gwen with Love*, edited by Patricia Brown, Don L. Lee, and Francis Ward (1971); *Names of Africa* by Oganna Chuks-Onji (1972); *Lil'l Tuffy and His ABC's* by Jean P. Smith (Ebony, Jr. Books, 1973); *I Wouldn't Take Nothin' for My Journey* by Leonidas Berry (1981); and *Bill Cosby in Words and Pictures* by Robert E. Johnson (1986).

University Presses. Although Howard University Press was the first formal university press established at an African American university when it commenced operations in 1972, a few African American colleges and universities had been publishing books under their imprints since the late 1890s.

Notable among the titles published by these institutions were significant studies that have made important contributions to the African American sociological literature. Published annually by the Atlanta University Press from 1896 to 1916, the Atlanta University Publications, under the initial direction of W. E. B. Du Bois, were some of the earliest studies in urban sociology conducted in the United States. This series included such monographs as *Mortality among Negroes in Cities* (Atlanta University Publications, no. 1, 1896); *The Negro Family* (Atlanta University Publications, no. 14, 1908); and *The Negro Common School and the Negro American* (Atlanta University Publications, no. 16, 1911). E. Franklin Frazier's *The Free Negro Family* (1932); *The Economic Status of Negroes* by Charles S. Johnson (1933); and *People Vs. Property: Race Restrictive Covenants in Housing* by Herman H. Long and Charles S. Johnson (1947) were landmark studies in sociology published by the Fisk University Press. During these years Howard University issued under the imprint of its name the Howard University Studies in Urban Sociology series, which included such titles as *Recreation and Amusement among Negroes in Washington, D. C.* (1927) and *The Housing of Negroes in Washington, D. C.* (1929), both by William H. Jones. At Tuskegee University, sociologist Monroe Work, one of the founders of the Negro Year Book Publishing Company, edited *The Negro Year Book* (1912–1952), the most comprehensive reference book on persons of African descent to appear in the first four decades of the twentieth century. Although *The Negro Year Book* was funded through private funds from 1912 to 1929, Tuskegee University assumed complete financial responsibility for its publication from 1929 to 1948 (10th ed.). The eleventh and last edition was copublished in 1952 by the William Wise Publishing Company and Tuskegee University.

With the debut of the Howard University Press in the American book-publishing market in 1974, annual lists of new books in several literary genres began emanating from this university press. Some of these titles have been: *Speaking for You: The Vision of Ralph Ellison,* edited by Kimberly W. Benston (1987); *Pillars in Ethiopian History: The William Leo Hansberry African History Notebook,* volume 1, edited by Joseph Harris (1974); *Black Engineers in the United States—A Directory,* edited by James Ho (1974); and *Jean Toomer: A Critical Evaluation,* edited by Therman B. O'Daniel (1988).

The number of books published by African American college and university presses before 1972 was relatively small when compared with other university presses, but the quality of these titles was high. Most of these works have been reprinted, which attests to their significance as genuine contributions to knowledge. Howard University Press, the only African American university press, is continuing the tradition of producing quality scholarly works in African Americana and Africana.

Trade Book Publishers. African American trade book publishers presently represent the largest segment of African American publishers in the American industry. Included here are all trade book publishing firms with the exception of those discussed earlier that were established to self-publish the books of their owners. Prior to the 1960s the number of African American trade book publishers was very small.

The Associated Publishers, founded by Carter G. Woodson in Washington, D.C., in 1921, was the most prolific African American trade book publisher during the first five decades of the twentieth century. The firm's founders sought to publish books that supplied all kinds of information for African Americans and persons interested in the uplift of African Americans. Titles were released in several literary genres. Two histories that were published were Carter G. Woodson's *The History of the Negro Church* (1921) and *The Negro in Tennessee, 1865–1880* by A. A. Taylor (1924). Among the several children's books released were *The Child's Story of the Negro* by Jane D. Shackelford (1938); *Negro Art, Music, and Rhyme for Young Folk* by Helen Whiting (1938); and *Word Pictures of the Great* by Elsie P. Derricotte (1941). Many works in *drama appeared such as *Plays and Pageants for the Life of the Negro* by Willis

**Richardson (1930); *The Negro in Drama* by Frederick W. Bond (1940); and *The Land of Cotton and Other Plays* by Randolph Edmonds (1942). Some of the biographical works published by this firm were *Women Builders* by Sadie Iola Daniel (1931); *Richard *Allen: Apostle of Freedom* by Charles Wesley (1935); and *Distinguished Negroes Abroad* by Beatrice J. Fleming (1945). Carter G. Woodson, the major shareholder in the firm, worked closely with authors until his death in 1950 to develop annual lists of titles that reflected market demands. Associated Publishers became the publishing arm of the Association for the Study of Afro-American Life and History in 1950, as stipulated in the will of Carter G. Woodson.

Less prolific was the Associates in Folk Education, a book-publishing enterprise established in Washington, D.C., by Howard University Professor Alain *Locke in 1935 with a grant from the American Adult Education Association. Serving as general editor, Locke decided on subject areas in African Americana, selected authors, and worked with each of them in developing manuscripts for publication as a series of books entitled the Bronze Booklets. Between 1935 and 1940 seven Bronze Booklets appeared under such titles as *A World View of Race* by Ralph J. Bunche (1936); *The Negro and Economic Reconstruction* by T. Arnold Hill (1937); and *Negro Poetry and Drama* and *The Negro in American Fiction* by Sterling A. *Brown (1937).

In New York City, trade book publisher A. Wendell Malliet and Company also flourished during this period. Notable among the books published by this firm were *Counter-Clockwise* by John M. Lee (1940); *The Negro Handbook,* edited by Florence Murray (1942); and *The Challenge of Negro Leadership* by Julius J. Adams (1949).

The growing self-consciousness among African Americans in the 1960s and 1970s catalyzed by the *civil rights movement increased demand for books about African American history and culture. To meet this growing demand many new African American trade book publishers sprang into existence. Some of these were specialty trade book firms publishing books that focused on one genre, advocated specific points of view, and were aimed at a specific market or age group. Other firms were general trade book publishers releasing books in a variety of genres, representative of many viewpoints and for several audiences.

In Detroit, poet-librarian Dudley *Randall, for example, established *Broadside Press in 1965 to publish African American poetry. Between 1965 and 1976, when Randall sold the firm, Broadside Press gave exposure to the poetry of a generation of new and eventually influential African American poets, espousing the *Black Aesthetic in their work. Some of these new poets and their works were Nikki *Giovanni, *Black Judgement* (1968); Etheridge *Knight, *Poems from Prison* (1968); Haki R. *Madhubuti (Don L. Lee), *Don't Cry, Scream* (1969); Sonia *Sanchez, *We A BaddDDD People* (1970); and Lance *Jeffers, *My Blackness Is the Beauty of this Land* (1970). Like Broadside Press, Chicago's *Third World Press has published many volumes of poetry by new African

American poets celebrating the Black Aesthetic. This publisher has also issued prose works addressing cultural, social, and psychological issues in the African American community. Some of the more popular works published by this firm have been Chancellor Williams's *The Destruction of Black Civilization* (1974); *Enemies: The Clash of the Races* by Haki R. Madhubuti (1978); *Explosion of Chicago's Black Street Gangs* by Useni Eugene Perkins (1986); *Black Women, Feminism, and Black Liberation: Which Way?* by Vivian Gordon (1987); *So Far, So Good* by Gil *Scott-Heron (1990); *Focusing: Black Male-Female Relationships* by Delores P. Aldridge (1991); and *Nightmare Overhanging Darkly: Essays on African Culture and Resistance* by Acklyn Lynch (1992).

Other African American trade book publishers focus on African American feminist literature. In the early 1970s San Francisco's Sapphire Publishing Company released *70 South Secrets of Sapphire* by Carolyn Jetter Green (1973), a humorous commentary on the state of African American womanhood. Novelist Alice *Walker's Wild Trees Press, established in 1984, published J. California *Cooper's collection of short stories entitled *A Piece of Mine* (1984) and Septima Clark's autobiography, *Ready from Within: Septima Clark and the Civil Rights Movement* (1986).

Some African American trade book publishers have specialized in producing materials for the educational market. These educational publishers have published books to assist in the teaching of African American history and culture in the classroom from elementary school through college, and to help solve some of the social and emotional problems facing African American students. *Pink Ladies in the Afternoon; New Poems, 1965–1971* by Naomi Long *Madgett (1972) and *Heartland: Selected Poems* by Ron Welburn (1981) are works published by Detroit's *Lotus Press for high school and college African American literature courses. Afro Am Publishing Company in Chicago released the popular *Great American Negroes: Past and Present* by Russell Adams (1969), which was adopted by several state boards of education, and *Colors Around Me* by Vivian Church (1972), a textbook used in many inner-city schools to instill positive image-building in African American children. Beryle Banfield's *Africa in the Curriculum: A Resource Bulletin and Guide for Teachers* (Blyden Press, 1968) was one of the many curriculum guides that have appeared. *Countering the Conspiracy to Destroy Black Boys* by Jawanza Kunjufu (1985) and *Rites of Passage* by Mary C. Lewis (1988) were among the books published by African American Images in Chicago to assist parents and high school counseling personnel in their advisement of African American teenaged boys and girls.

Since 1960 African American book publishers have actively expanded the number of titles available in African American children's literature. The leading African American publisher specializing in children's literature is Just Us Books in Orange, New Jersey. Working with African American authors and illustrators, Just Us Books has published such titles as *AFRO-BETS ABC BOOKS* by Cheryl Willis Hudson (1988); *When I Was Little* by Toyomi Igus, illustrated

by Higgins Bond (1992); and *From a Child's Heart* by Nikki Grimes, with pictures by Brenda Joysmith (1993).

Unrestricted by genre, intended audience, or philosophical viewpoint, African American general trade book publishers have released some noteworthy titles since 1960. Most of these have been significant additions to several areas of African American literature.

Emerson Hall Publishers, which went out of existence in the mid-1970s, produced such popular titles as *The Strengths of Black Families* by Robert B. Hill (1972); Dr. Alvin Poussaint's *Why Blacks Kill Blacks* (1972); *No, a Novel* by Clarence *Major (1973); and *New Days: Poems of Exile and Return* by June *Jordan (1974). Chicago's Path Press issued *American Diary, a Personal History of the Black Press* by former *Chicago Defender* editor Enoch P. Waters (1987); *Brown Sky* by David Covin (1989), a novel detailing the problems faced by an African American battalion stationed in Arkansas during World War II; *The Negotiations: A Novel of Tomorrow* by Herman Cromwell Gilbert (1983), a novel centering on negotiations by disillusioned African American leaders with the white power structure for a separate African American country within the United States; *To Benji with Love: A Biography and Tribute* by Mary Wilson, a children's book (1987); and *What Happens When Children Write* by Darlene Matthews Smith (1987). The formerly prosperous but defunct Third Press in New York published such important titles as *If They Come in the Morning: Voices of Resistance* by Angela *Davis (1971), a first-hand account of this charismatic African American woman activist's trial for conspiracy to murder; *American Negro Slavery and Abolition* by Wilbert E. Moore (1971); and *James Baldwin: A Critical Study* by Stanley Macebuh (1973). Black Classic Press in Baltimore, which publishes reprints and current books, has issued a reprint edition of Drusilla Dunjee Houston's 1926 masterwork *Wonderful Ethiopians of the Ancient Cushite Empire, Book 1* (1985), and such recent titles as *First Light: New and Selected Poems* by E. Ethelbert *Miller (1994); *African Americans in Pennsylvania: A History and Guide* by Charles L. Blockson (1994); and *A Time of Terror* by James Cameron (1974). And Winston-Derek Publishers in Nashville has published Mark Hyman's enlightening *Blacks Who Died for Jesus* (1983); *To Build the Bridge: A Commentary on Black/White Catholicism in America* by Sandra O. Smithson (1984); *SADCC: The Political Economy of Development in South Africa* by Margaret C. Lee (1989); and *Jamako and the Beanstalk* by Fred Crump (1989), an Africanized retelling of *Jack and the Beanstalk* for children.

African American trade book publishers, publishing the most diversified range of titles of any segment of African American book publishers, have contributed to the development of many areas of African American literature. The titles produced by these firms, owned and operated by African Americans, have been, in almost every instance, an authentic representation of African American life and thought.

Conclusion. Historically African American book publishers have produced annually only a small number of titles within the total title output of the American book publishing industry. These titles, representative of various areas of African American literature from sociopolitical treatises to belles lettres have largely been purposive. There are few romance novels or mysteries and no science fiction. Instead the genres that predominate are sociopolitical commentaries and treatises; autobiographies and biographies; religious treatises, songbooks, and handbooks; histories; sociological and political studies; *cookbooks; children's books; reference books; race-conscious novels; and poetry. By setting standards of aesthetics and scholarship in their publication of works in these genres, African American book publishers and self-published authors have made a multifaceted contribution to the growth and development of many areas of African American literature.

• Donald Franklin Joyce, *Gatekeepers of Black Culture: Black-Owned Book Publishing in the United States, 1817–1981*, 1983. Donald Franklin Joyce, *Black Book Publishers in the United States: A Historical Dictionary of the Presses, 1817–1990*, 1991.   —Donald Franklin Joyce

PULP FICTION has been traditionally defined as lurid, sensational, and escapist fiction that is printed on low-quality, wood-pulp paper and sold in paperback or magazine format. Such terminology, however, is often based on elitist notions of culture and literature that, by definition, exclude pulp fiction and other popular genres from serious literary study.

The genre of pulp fiction has been most closely associated with the 1920s and 1930s pulp magazines that specialized in *crime and mystery writing; however, the term also includes formulaic literature published in paperback format in the genres of the thriller or adventure story, the romance, and *speculative fiction—all of which can be subsumed under the more generic term the "black experience novel"— that are primarily aimed at a "mass" audience of urban and working-class African Americans.

Until recently African Americans have been more the subjects and readers of pulp fiction than its writers and publishers. There is little evidence that African Americans produced a significant amount of pulp fiction before the 1970s. Michael Denning's *Mechanic Accents* (1987), a study of the nineteenth century dime-novel, pulp fiction's precursor, concludes that the overwhelming majority of dime novels had been written by and for whites. Pauline E. *Hopkins's magazine fiction and John E. *Bruce's serialized detective story *The Black Sleuth* (1907–1909) both show the influence of late nineteenth-century dime novels and anticipate many of the concerns that will be raised by African American pulp fiction in the 1970s.

Black-owned *publishing companies, during both the nineteenth and twentieth centuries, rarely produced "cheap" and easily available literature whose primary function was to entertain. Low *literacy rates among African Americans limited the publishers' audience and explains their focus on middle-class African Americans whose literary tastes encompassed *poetry, *history, and "serious" literature

concerned with "racial uplift." In the twentieth century, though literacy was rapidly increasing, major publishing houses, including the pulp press, did not consider African Americans to be a viable audience with its own needs. "Cheap book" production continued to be aimed at a primarily white working-class readership. After the *civil rights movement, which, among other things, revealed the purchasing power of African Americans, publishers "discovered" the African American reader and African American interest books became a commodity for profit. Once this market was discovered, popular and pulp fiction publishers quickly followed suit.

The emergence of contemporary African American pulp fiction can be dated with the publication of *Pimp: The Story of My Life* (1967) and *Trick Baby* (1967) by Robert Beck, also known as *Iceberg Slim, by the Los Angeles publishing company Holloway House. Aware that they had tapped into a profitable market, the company, founded in 1961 with the intent to publish nonfiction books about contemporary events and personalities, immediately set out to recruit more African American authors who would write "lurid and sensational" fiction for African American audiences. Since the publication of Iceberg Slim's books, Holloway House has become the largest producer of fiction aimed at a "mass" African American audience; it has steadily expanded its list of imprints, boasts the largest number of books by African American authors in the United States, and calls itself "the World's largest publisher of black experience paperback books." Although some romance publishers have since added novels aimed at an African American audience, even a cursory glance at bibliographies of African American literature shows that Holloway House books constitute a major part of the African American popular fiction market and African American fiction as a whole.

Holloway House's list of imprints covers a wide range of popular fictions, ranging from "ghetto realism" to detective stories, thrillers, historical novels, romances, family sagas, confession stories, *autobiographies, and fictionalized autobiographies, as well as erotica and pornography. Holloway House also features a black American biography series on historical figures and celebrities such as *Malcolm X, Nat *Turner, Jesse Jackson, Ella Fitzgerald, Jackie *Robinson, the Supremes, and Eddie Murphy, as well as popular histories of African Americans, Hispanics, and American Indians.

Holloway House publications are predominantly aimed at a mass audience of urban African American males, indicated by the books' catchy titles, the gaudily illustrated covers, the brief and livid summaries of the book's content on the back, and prices as low as $1.95 for fiction and no more than $5.95 for nonfiction. Holloway House products can be bought at stores easily accessible to a popular audience: paperback and magazine bookstores in the inner city, newsstands, supermarkets, and the Stars-and-Stripes bookstores of the U.S. Army. Public libraries all over the country are also customers of Holloway House.

Though it constitutes a genre of its own, African American pulp fiction is squarely located within the

African American expressive tradition. As literary and cultural texts, pulp novels draw on the African American literary tradition—particularly the naturalist novels of the 1940s and 1950s and the *protest literature and autobiography of the late 1960s and early 1970s—and share similarities with commercial African American popular culture such as black action movies and rap *music. As popular fiction, on the other hand, pulp fiction is governed by the demands of the marketplace and adheres to formulaic conventions. In the hands of African American authors, however, its genres are far from the escapist and fantastic fictions they are often said to be. In bringing together the African American expressive tradition and popular genres, this pulp fiction plays out, scrutinizes, and contests popular conceptions of African American life.

For popular fiction to work, to be successful, and to attract a body of devoted readers, it has to embody elements of recognition and identification, "approaching a recreation and identification of recognizable experiences and attitudes to which people are responding," as Stuart Hall (1981) has pointed out. African American pulp fiction is written out of or makes meaning in the distinct material, and the social, historical, and cultural practices that inform the lives of many African Americans today; the texts are based on a collective memory that is repeated every day through actual social and material practices. Drawing on the everyday, African American pulp fiction represents the immediate condition of many urban African Americans in this country, offers perspectives on and solutions to the problems that plague many black communities, and provides examples of community, hope, and dignity.

Holloway House novels and other pulp fiction fall into three broad categories: (1) ghetto realism or cautionary tales modeled after formulaic gangster fiction; (2) standard pulp fiction such as political action thrillers, mysteries, and detective stories; and (3) romances, middle-class family sagas, and *historical novels, primarily aimed at female readers. These novels in many ways conform to standard conventions of pulp fiction. On first reading, the novels' contents are often lurid and sensational as much of the action revolves around *violence and sex. Written in an easily comprehensible style and language, the novels follow a simple formula and a linear plot line. The language is descriptive, denotative rather than connotative, and the dialogue often graphic. Characters are simple and one-dimensional and the plot leaves little room for ambiguity.

In the 1970s, "ghetto realism" was the predominant form. Beginning with Iceberg Slim's *Trick Baby*, the novels in this category follow the masterplot of the traditional hardboiled gangster story: A young man learns to be a hustler—either as a pimp, drug dealer, hitman, or gang-leader—succeeds as a member of the underworld, and dies violently at the end. Though the hustler's lifestyle seems to be celebrated, the novels always conclude with the protagonist's death. His endeavors at empire building—whether of a good "stable" of prostitutes or a powerful gang—are depicted as no more than an illusory way out of

poverty, a way of life that ultimately leads to the continued enslavement of African Americans. These novels can be read as "cautionary tales" designed to show that there is no hope in crime and in victimizing fellow African Americans. The purpose of this fiction is often didactic, as stated by Iceberg Slim: "If one intelligent valuable young man or woman can be saved from the destructive slime, then the displeasure I have given will have been outweighed by that individual's use of his potential in a socially constructive manner."

A large part of African American pulp fiction consists of "standard" genres whose plot lines, characters, and content have been modified to fit the "black experience" style. In these novels, we find action, suspense, political intrigue, conspiracies, mystery, and heroes who loom larger than life. Many of these novels are nationalist in character and explicitly focus on African American resistance to systemic and structural oppression. Their rhetoric is often Afrocentric, emphasizing black pride and self-determination. Astute in their political analyses, the texts use street-wise discourse to alert readers to the need for continued struggle against oppression. In these novels, African American neighborhoods become contested terrain and sites of conflict as plot lines revolve around threats to the African American community, political intrigues and conspiracies against the African American nation, mistreatments by the justice and legal system, and historical injustices against African American individuals and communities. These novels highlight the fragility of programs such as affirmative action and demonstrate that the fight for civil rights is not over, but has to be continued on a daily basis and on all levels. Historical novels, on the other hand, revise standard interpretations of American history and focus on African American success. Led by a cast of charismatic leaders, community activists, spiritual guides, and ordinary citizens, these texts vicariously depict African American history, recuperate the African American presence in American history, focus on the righting of injustices from the civil rights movement, and reclaim the southern roots of African Americans.

The third category encompasses romances and love stories for women, but also middle-class success narratives and family sagas. The romances marketed in Holloway House's Heartline Romance series and in the Pinnacle Books's Arabesque series closely follow the plot lines Janice Radway has outlined in her study *Reading the Romance* (1984). Most are set in a self-contained African American world that is free of racial prejudices, and focus solely on the romantic relationship between the heroine and the male protagonist. Middle-class success narratives and family sagas highlight African American success and individual achievement in the corporate world. Written in the tradition of Booker T. *Washington's *Up from Slavery*, these novels celebrate perseverance, dilligence, and the work ethic.

African American pulp fiction has produced numerous best-sellers and best-selling authors. Like most pulp fiction authors, Holloway House writers are extremely prolific and often write several books a year, many of them under a pseudonym. For example, Holloway House author Joe (Joseph) Nazel, with more than twenty-nine titles in print, rivals Frank *Yerby as the most prolific African American novelist. Nazel's novels run the gamut of pulp fiction, ranging from mystery to political action thriller to gangster story. Donald *Goines is undoubtedly the most famous Holloway House author; in fact, he is the only author, apart from Iceberg Slim, who has attracted any scholarly attention. In his short writing career of only four years, Goines published seventeen novels, all of which are still in print, and he is credited with having sold more than five million copies of his books.

Representative authors and texts include John E. Bruce's *The Black Sleuth, McGirt's Magazine* (1907–1909), Mark Allen Boone's *Reunion* (1989), Mickey Flemings's *About Courage* (1989), Omar Fletcher's *Miss Annie* (1978), Donald Goines's *Daddy Cool* (1974), Charles R. Goodman's *Bound by Blood* (1985), Odie Hawkins's *Menfriends* (1989) and *Secret Music* (1988), Pauline Hopkins's *The Magazine Novels of Pauline Hopkins* (rpt. 1988), Roland Jefferson's *The Secret below 103rd Street* (1976), Felicia Mason's *For the Love of You* (1994), Joe Nazel's *Wolves of Summer* and *Delta Crossing* (both 1984), Kent Smith's *Future X* (1990), and Rae Shawn Stuart's *Dying Is So Easy* (1984).

• Greg Goode, "Donald Goines," in *DLB*, vol. 33, *Afro-American Novelists since 1955*, eds. Thadious M. Davis and Trudier Harris, 1984, pp. 96–99. Greg Goode, "From *Dopefiend* to *Kenyatta's Last Hit*: The Angry Black Crime Novels of Donald Goines," *MELUS* 11 (Fall 1984): 41–48. Linda Cochlan, "Holloway House Publishing Company," in *American Literary Publishing Houses, 1900–1980: Trade and Paperback*, 1986, p. 189. Frankie Y. Bailey, *Out of the Woodpile: Black Characters in Crime and Detective Fiction*, 1991.

—Susanne B. Dietzel

PURVIS, ROBERT (1810–1898), lecturer, pamphleteer, and antislavery activist. Born in Charleston, South Carolina, to a wealthy English businessman and the free-born daughter of a slave, Robert Purvis was sent to Philadelphia at the age of nine for private schooling. When his father died in 1826, Purvis inherited $120,000, which gave him financial independence and allowed him to devote the rest of his life to reformist causes.

In 1830, Purvis met Benjamin Lundy and William Lloyd Garrison whose crusade against *slavery focused Purvis's sympathies for less-privileged African Americans and offered him a means of striking back at the racial discrimination he experienced firsthand. Purvis joined Garrison in the founding of the American Anti-Slavery Society in 1833. In the same year, he led in the organization of the Philadelphia Library Company of Colored Persons, dedicated to "promoting among our rising youth, a proper cultivation for literary pursuits." When the Pennsylvania legislature proposed to disfranchise the African American voters of the state, Purvis headed a convention of blacks in 1838 to protest the measure. As chair of a committee selected to speak for the convention, Purvis drafted an eighteen-page pamphlet entitled *Appeal of Forty Thousand Citizens, Threatened with Disfranchisement, to the People of Pennsylvania* (1838), which stressed the accomplishments and contributions of the African American citizenry to the economic, political, and cultural life of the state and invoked the "no taxation without representation" theme of the Declaration of Independence as a precedent for opposition to disfranchisement. Despite the vigor and logic of Purvis's argument, the *Appeal* did not succeed. But the *Appeal* was widely admired in antislavery circles and often reprinted and cited in the abolitionist press. Purvis's speeches denouncing the U.S. Supreme Court's *Dred Scott* decision in 1857 cemented his reputation as an important antislavery orator. In 1883, he coedited the *History of the Underground Railroad in Chester and the Neighboring Counties of Pennsylvania*, including a detailed autobiographical narrative.

[*See also* Antislavery Movement; Oratory.]

• Carter G. Woodson, ed., *The Mind of the Negro as Reflected in Letters Written During the Crisis 1800–1860*, 1926. Benjamin Quarles, *Black Abolitionists*, 1969.

—William L. Andrews

Q

QUADROON. *See* Mulatto.

Quest of the Silver Fleece, The. W. E. B. *Du Bois's first *novel, *The Quest of the Silver Fleece* (1911) shifts its action from rural Alabama to Washington, D.C., and back again, achieving its narrative unity through a carefully constructed framework of contrasting symbols and the maturation journeys of its young protagonists, Zora and Bles. Identified by Addison *Gayle, Jr., as "the first *Bildungsroman in African-American literature," *The Quest* traces the growth of the young, rural heroes from ignorance and exploitation (in Zora's case, sexual use by the wealthy landowners, the Cresswells); to their encounter in Washington, D.C., with political deception by urban, *talented tenth Africans, like the savvy, self-serving Carry Wynn; to the resulting appreciation of their own strengths and the potential of their people, and their return to Alabama to create a black-owned farming commune to develop the lucrative cotton crop, the "silver fleece."

Adding an African American voice to popular novels at the turn of the century such as Frank Norris's *The Octopus* (1901) and *The Pit* (1903) and Upton Sinclair's *The Jungle* (1906), which explored the consequences of unregulated, free market forces, Du Bois's primary concern is to demonstrate the physical and mental serfdom that trapped blacks in ignorance and poverty after emancipation, and to suggest effective courses of action to overcome this new kind of *slavery. To examine these economic issues and their personal results, he structures his work on the clash of two opposing world views, those of the Swamp and the Plantation.

The swamp represents all that is free, wild, joyful, and loving, but also the fear, jealousy, ignorance, and poverty fostered by racism, slavery, and the tenant farming system. The plantation, symbolic of a materialistic attitude clearly not confined to the southern locale, encourages all that is self-serving, cruel, and exploitative of humans and nature, but also thrives on knowledge, talent, and ambition, qualities Zora comes to recognize as essential for the self-reliance of rural workers, black or white. Throughout the first part of the narrative, the story of Jason and the Golden Fleece—with its correspondence of the valuable fleece with the special cotton Zora grows in the swamp and is cheated out of by Colonel Cresswell; Medea with the witch, Elsbeth, Zora's mother; and Jason with the thieving southern land owners and northern capitalists—appears as a mythic reference for Du Bois's complex plantation/swamp dichotomy.

The improvement of the situation of black farmers is intrinsically linked in *The Quest* to the development of Zora, who begins as the wild "elf-girl," her creativity inspired by the beauty of the swamp where she was born, but her early powerlessness also linked to its other side, the "gray and death-like wilderness"

symbolized by Elsbeth, in whose hut the local white men drink and sexually exploit black women. Nellie McKay believes "the 'black' heroine was born in this novel, marking a major breakthrough in the overthrow of the stereotypical use of near-white" heroines in earlier African American fiction. In *Dusk of Dawn* (1940), Du Bois referred to the novel simply as "an economic study of some merit."

• Addison Gayle, Jr., *The Way of the New World, The Black Novel in America*, 1976. Nellie McKay, "W. E. B. Du Bois: The Black Women in His Writings—Selected Fictional and Autobiographical Portraits," in *Critical Essays on W. E. B. Du Bois*, ed. William L. Andrews, 1985. David Levering Lewis, *W. E. B. Du Bois, Biography of a Race, 1868–1919*, 1993.
—Arlene A. Elder

Quicksand, Nella *Larsen's first published *novel, appeared in 1928 and won the Harmon Foundation's bronze medal. The *New York Times Book Review* proclaimed it had more "dignity" than most first novels and praised it for having a "wider outlook upon life" than writings by most African Americans. W. E. B. *Du Bois declared she had published "the best piece of fiction" by an African American since Charles Waddell *Chesnutt.

Quicksand is the story of *Helga Crane, whose mixed heritage (she is the daughter of a Danish American mother and an African American father) complicates her quest for security and self-realization. When the novel begins, Helga Crane has achieved high status as a teacher at Naxos (an African American college modeled after Tuskegee) and seems set for social success as the fiancée of James Vayle, a solid member of the Atlanta African American bourgeoisie. But she is dissatisfied. She quits her job, breaks off her engagement, and travels to Chicago hoping to be welcomed into the family of her Danish American uncle. Uncle Peter's new wife rebuffs Helga at the door. Alone and nearly broke, Helga finally obtains employment as a travel companion to Mrs. Hayes-Rore, an African American activist en route to New York. Hayes-Rore introduces Helga to Anne Gray, a wealthy Harlem widow who becomes her next benefactor. Though Helga lands a respectable job and is welcomed into Harlem middle-class society, she soon becomes dissatisfied again. Her quest this time takes her to Copenhagen, where her Danish relatives not only welcome but flaunt their dark family member, and for two years, Helga is feted. Alex Olsen, a socially prominent Danish artist, asks Helga to become his mistress, and when he rejects this proposition he proposes marriage; but Helga is now tired of being an exotic, rare specimen and returns to Harlem. Not long after her return, she discovers that Anne Gray is going to marry Dr. Robert Anderson, a man who has always provoked ambiguous but powerful passions in Helga. After an embarrassing incident with Robert, Helga despairs of ever finding happiness. Wandering about in a stormy night, she seeks refuge in a storefront church, where she has a conversion experience and meets the Reverend Mr. Pleasant Green. She marries this uneducated country preacher and returns with him to Alabama, where she has three children in twenty months.

Some critics find the novel's conclusion weak and ambiguous, but they generally praise its narrative unity and lush, evocative detail. They variously describe the tone of *Quicksand* as "wistful," "zestful," and "bitter" but generally agree that the book offers a pioneering psychological portrayal of a modern woman from a perspective that recognizes the inex-tricability of *race, *class, and *gender. Scholars recognize the book as revising the *stereotypes of the tragic mulatta and as providing one of the first serious considerations of both the limitations and the privileges of aspiring to the African American middle class. In her concern with gender and class, Larsen is often compared to Jessie Redmon *Fauset and Dorothy *West. Her interest in the particularities of race and sexuality also places her in conversation with Jean *Toomer and Claude *McKay.

• Deborah E. McDowell, introduction to *Quicksand and Passing,* ed. Deborah E. McDowell, 1986. Thadious M. Davis, *Nella Larsen, Novelist of the Harlem Renaissance,* 1994.

—Frances Smith Foster

R

RACE. In the introduction to *"Race," Writing, and Difference* (1986), Henry Louis *Gates, Jr., calls race "the ultimate trope of difference because it is so very arbitrary in its application," and because race masquerades as an objective, scientifically verifiable method of classifying humanity when, in fact, historically it has been a "dangerous trope." Moreover, "race has become a trope of ultimate, irreducible difference between cultures, linguistic groups, or adherents of specific belief systems, which—more often than not—also have fundamentally opposed economic interests." The resilient idea that race is a scientifically definable (and defensible) method of comprehending both physical differences and intrinsic "racial essences" or traits among human beings is a product of late-eighteenth- and nineteenth-century thinking that, despite sporadic resistance, has been repeatedly discredited by twentieth-century biological and anthropological study. However, in African American literary practice, the myth of race as an irreducible, biological "essence," on the one hand, and as a culturally constructed trope, or metaphor that challenges a diverse range of social institutions and practices, on the other, precariously coexists.

In the 1890s, for example, W. E. B. *Du Bois, in "The Conservation of the Races" (1897), argued forcefully for a construction of race that was predicated on a division of humanity into "eight distinctly different races," namely "the Slavs of Eastern Europe, the Teutons of middle Europe, the English of Great Britain and America, the Romance nations of Southern and Western Europe, the Negroes of Africa and America, the Semitic people of Western Asia and Northern Africa, the Hindoos [*sic*] of Central Asia and the Mongolians of Eastern Asia." Du Bois included American Indians among "other minor race groups."

Du Bois's schema is both an affirmation and a revision of prevailing late-nineteenth-century scientific views of race that were reflected in the writings of many white and black intellectuals. Aligning himself with T. H. Huxley and other social Darwinists, for example, Du Bois fundamentally agreed with the ways that the principle of natural selection was transferred to social systems. His essay "The *Talented Tenth" (1903) expresses the pervasive idea that powerful environmental forces—for example, centuries of de jure *slavery, and later, systemic racism—would permit only the most intellectually and morally resilient individuals within each racial group to succeed, while the masses would lag behind and, therefore, be dependent on the most "talented," if indeed collective progress were to be made. "The Negro race," Du Bois confidently asserted, "like all races, is going to be saved by its exceptional men. The problem of education, then, among Negroes must first of all deal with the Talented Tenth; it is the problem of developing the Best of this race that they may guide the Mass away from the contamination and death of the Worst, in their own and other races."

Throughout the nineteenth and early twentieth centuries, "the idea of natural selection," as Thomas F. Gossett stresses in *Race: The History of an Idea in America* (1963), "was translated to a struggle between individual members of a society, between members of classes of a society, between different nations, and between different races. This conflict, far from being an evil thing, was nature's indispensable method for producing superior men, superior nations, and superior races." The "evil," insofar as it was acknowledged at all, lay in the pernicious, quasi-scientific assertions of immutable hereditary racial differences—the environment was generally given little credit for evolutional development—that produced various "polygenic," hierarchical arrangements of humanity based on irreducible racial traits or "essences," such as temperament, character, and intelligence.

The significant revision that African American intellectuals—including Du Bois, Alexander *Crummell (1819–1898), Frances Ellen Watkins *Harper (1825–1911), Frederick *Douglass (1817–1895), Anna Julia *Copper (1859–1964), and William Stanley *Braithwaite (1878–1962)—make to the discourse about race at the turn-of-the-century is the unswerving insistence that the "Negro race" (in contradistinction to the prevailing "scientific wisdom") had enormously important contributions to make to civilization. And for those like Alexander Crummell, whose work intersected religion and social science, and Frances E. W. Harper, the advancement of black people was a matter less of science than of the undeniable acts of grace at work in all God's children. "Ethnologists may differ," Frances E. W. Harper asserted in "The Great Problem To Be Solved" (1875) "about the origin of the human race. [T. H.] Huxley may search for it in protoplasms, and Darwin send for the missing links, but there is one thing of which we may rest assured—that we all come from the living God and that He is the common Father."

For Du Bois, people of African descent were one of the "great races of today" that will be greater still when—through racial solidarity, for example, "a conscious striving together for certain ideals of life," resisting racial absorption, and moral and intellectual education—black people will be able to advance their already significant contributions to civilization. Collective "striving" depended on a level playing field of social and educational opportunity, which would not restrict black people, en masse, to manual or industrial education. At an early moment in his professional life, Alexander Crummell espoused "practical education" and disdained higher learning for black people, but unlike Booker T. *Washington (1856–1915), president and founder of Tuskegee Institute, who became the staunchest advocate for manual training, Crummell later recanted his position.

Representing a perspective that became an article of faith among the next generation of African American intellectual leaders, including Du Bois, Braithewaite, James Weldon *Johnson and William Monroe Trotter, Crummell rejected collective manual training as an "absurd notion which is stealing on the American mind." And, in words that implied agreement with the prevailing polygenic view of race, but words that rejected the putative superiority of any particular group, Crummell insisted in "The Attitude of the American Mind toward the Negro Intellect" that

> the [Negro] Race must declare that it is not to be put into a single groove; and for the simple reason (1) that *man* was made by his Maker to traverse the whole circle of existence, above as well as below; and that universality is the kernel of all true civilization, of all race elevation. And (2) that the Negro mind, imprisoned for nigh three hundred years, needs breadth and freedom, largeness, altitude, and elasticity; not stint nor rigidity, nor contractedness.

The familiar parlance that developed in the postbellum period for expressing race pride and the abiding belief in the collective capacity of the descendants of slaves to progress politically, educationally, socially, and morally included "racial uplift" and what Frances E. W. Harper called "the great work of upbuilding," which, for Harper and other black female champions of racial and *gender equality writing in the late nineteenth and early twentieth centuries, encompassed the enfranchisement of black women into increasingly wider spheres of public life. The politics of race, at this time, assumed the inveterate inferiority of women in general and was tacitly affirmed in most race theories and popular literature. The essays and speeches of Ida B. *Wells-Barnett, Anna Julia Cooper, then later the novels of Pauline E. *Hopkins, Jessie Redmon *Fauset, and finally the poetry of black women writing during the *Harlem Renaissance—especially Georgia Douglas *Johnson, Effie Lee *Newsome, and Alice Moore *Dunbar-Nelson—were passionately committed to fixing the marginalized "women's question" into the discourse about racial "upbuilding."

The "women's question" was inextricably tied to the "race problem" because the prevailing racist cultural and scientific constructions of black male *sexuality that depended on the intransigent myth of primitivism also consigned black female sexuality to a lower, only nominally human sphere outside the sacrosanct "cult of true womanhood" reserved for white women. Primitivism is, in several respects, an ironic inversion of the "cult of true womanhood" that bifurcates nature into two adversarial parts. One part corresponds to Jean-Jacques Rousseau's distinction between "the noble savage," that is man in the "state of nature," freed from the corruption of that paradisaical nature by the corrupting proliferation of social institutions. (Sigmund Freud's characterization of human nature as a perpetual battle between two instinctual drives, Eros and Thanatos, is influenced by this same eighteenth-century construction of Na-

ture.) The other part jettisons Rousseau's idea of nobility, leaving simply an unbridled, raw myth of bestiality. Using the central tropes that make up a "primitivist discourse" shaped, in part, by eminent ethnographers such as Bronislaw Malinowski (*The Sexual Life of Savages*, 1929), Marianna Torgovnick develops the presumptions underlying the popularization of racial theories in twentieth-century social life and literature: "Primitives are like children, the tropes say. Primitives are our untamed selves, our id forces—libidinous, irrational, violent, dangerous. Primitives are mystics, in tune with nature, part of its harmonies. Primitives are free. Primitives exist at the 'lowest cultural levels'; we occupy the 'highest.' . . ."

Primitivism, then, nurtured the widespread *stereotype that made black men rapists and, as Richard Yarborough notes, "black women, in turn, were presented as generally incapable of comprehending, much less embodying, the high moral propriety and sexual restraint that typified the white feminine bourgeois ideal." In response, black women wrote editorials, formed organizations like the National Federation of Afro-American Women (in 1895), and wrote and sometimes published poems, plays, and *novels that thematized the contemporary debate on race and gender. In the preface, for example, to *Contending Forces* (1900), Pauline Hopkins explains the higher political purpose her novel serves:

> In giving this little romance expression in print, I am not actuated by a desire for notoriety or for profit, but to do all that I can in an [sic] way to raise the stigma of degradation from my race. While I make no apology for my somewhat abrupt and daring venture within the wide field of romantic literature, I ask the kind indulgence of the generous public for the many crudities which I know appear in the work, and their approval of whatever may impress them as being of value to the Negro race and to the world at large.

Hopkins's unapologetically political agenda was the driving force behind a significant number of novels, short fiction, and *essays written during and after the publication of *Contending Forces*. Like Hopkins's political romances, the essays written on literature—including Alain *Locke's The *New Negro (1925), Du Bois's "Criteria of Negro Art" (1926), Richard *Wright's "Blueprint for Negro Writing" (1937), Ralph *Ellison's "Twentieth-Century Fiction and the Black Mask of Humanity" (1953), and Toni *Morrison's *Playing in the Dark* (1992)—have rejected the romantic ideal that art was, ipso facto, estranged from either moral or political matters, especially race.

The great debate about race that late-nineteenth-century natural and social science, early-twentieth-century social Darwinism, the "new psychology" of Freud, and the politics of progressivism had collectively etched into the American consciousness was transformed by African American fictionists during the Harlem Renaissance, and, later, the modern period into themes of racial uplift, racial pride, *passing, protest fiction, invisibility, existential angst, cultural nationalism, and Black Power. Charles Waddell *Chesnutt's short fiction and novels; the poetry of

Paul Laurence *Dunbar, Langston *Hughes, Countee *Cullen, and Georgia Douglas Johnson; and the fiction of James Weldon Johnson, Zora Neale *Hurston, Jessie Fauset, Nella *Larsen, Jean *Toomer, and Ralph Ellison—and later, Gwendolyn *Brooks, J. Saunders *Redding, Richard Wright, Gayl *Jones, Amiri *Baraka, Margaret *Walker and Toni Morrison—helped to shape a multivoiced dialogue about race in African American literary practice. These writers, and many others, approached race aesthetically and politically from diverse positions, but each writer, in her or his own unique way, has kept faith with the basic politics of racial uplift and cultural pride inscribed in the earliest stirrings of black creativity expressed in *autobiography, *poetry, and discursive prose that extends from the eighteenth century to the present.

In a statement that signifies on the ubiquitous and vexed presence of race in American culture, Toni Morrison, in *Playing in the Dark*, cautions that "for both black and white American writers, in a wholly racialized society, there is no escape from racially inflected language. . . ." At some level of construction—as "scientific fact," or as an irreducible archetype in the collective unconscious, or as a "trope" of insidious intent or racial pride—race informs American thought. The trope of race is thematically inflected in the fiction of both black and white writers and across a number of overlapping literary conventions, cultural myths, and issues including representations of the gothic and the grotesque, the tragic *mulatto, *miscegenation, slavery, primitivism, and passing. The fiction of nineteenth- and twentieth-century black and white writers that is complexly inscribed in these (and many other) racialized issues is far too numerous to list, but includes the work of Charles W. Chesnutt (*The *Wife of His Youth*, 1899); William Faulkner (*Light in August*, 1932; *Absalom, Absalom!*, 1936; and *Intruder in the Dust*, 1948); Nella Larsen (*Passing*, 1928; and *Quicksand*, 1929); Sherwood Anderson (*Dark Laughter*, 1925); Jean Toomer (*Cane*, 1923); Willa Cather (*Sapphira and the Slave Girl*, 1940); Richard Wright (*Native Son*, 1940); Jessie Fauset (*Plum Bun*, 1928); Herman Melville (*Moby Dick*, 1851; "Benito Cereno," 1856; and *The Confidence Man*, 1857); Ralph Ellison (*Invisible Man*, 1952); LeRoi Jones (*Dutchman* and *The Slave*, both 1964); Eudora Welty (*Collected Stories*, 1980); and Gayl Jones (*Corregidora*, 1975).

In African American literary practice during the 1920s and 1930s, both the trope and the politics of race were represented in short fiction and novels about passing. James Weldon Johnson's *The *Autobiography of an Ex-Colored Man* (1912), Jessie Fauset's *Plum Bun*, and Nella Larsen's *Quicksand* and *Passing* are profoundly shaped by the prevailing attitudes, myths, and politics of race at the time. The fiction of Fauset and Larsen, in particular, is inscribed in the rhetoric of racial uplift, pride, and solidarity that counterpointed the insidious racial theories of the era. Although there are meaningful differences in plot structure, point of view, and narrative technique, both Fauset's and Larsen's novels, in the end, emphatically reject the proposition advanced early in each novel's plot that racial passing is either a physically healthy way of living for the individual or beneficial to the "race" collectively.

Racial solidarity through intraracial relationships, liberal arts and "higher" education, and middle-class aspirations are, for example, the irrepressible implications of Fauset's *Plum Bun*—despite its odd subtitle, "a novel without a moral." In the second half, two situations occur that underscore the novel's racial politics. The two central figures are sisters, Virginia and Angela Murray, dark- and light-skinned heroines respectively. Both are proud and ambitious. One evening, they attend a standing-room-only lecture in Harlem by an eminent scholar named Van Meir, a thinly disguised characterization of W. E. B. Du Bois. Van Meir triumphantly concludes his speech by proclaiming:

> those of us who have forged forward, who have gained the front ranks in money and training, will not, are not able as yet to go our separate ways. . . . We must still look back and render service to our less fortunate, weaker brethren. And the first step toward making this a workable attitude is the acquisition not so much of a racial love as a racial pride. A pride that enables us to find our own beautiful and praiseworthy, an intense chauvinism that is content with its own types, that finds completeness within its own group. . . . Such a pride can accomplish the impossible.

Van Meir's text is a stinging indictment of Angela Murray's election to pass for white (which transforms her into Angéle) and of her doomed romance with Roger Fielding, a wealthy white opportunist interested less in marriage than in making Angela his mistress. Beyond the text, Van Meir's speech epitomizes both the rhetoric of the talented tenth and racial uplift espoused by a broad spectrum of black intellectuals and artists during this era. This scene also participates in the discourse on race in the modernist period by assailing the widespread cultural construction of the biracial body as a locus of perpetual contestation between white and black blood. This myth has its complement in the popular belief—politicized in the fiction of major twentieth-century white American writers as well, including Faulkner's *Light in August* and *Absalom, Absalom!*—that any evidence of achievement in a "mixed-blood," or biracial, individual is assignable to his or her white heritage. After Van Meir's speech, Roger Fielding "wonders" about "'what proportion of white blood he has in his veins. Of course that's where he gets his ability.'" The judgment on his blatant racism is swift and unequivocal: "'You make me tired,'" an acquaintance named Martha quips, "'Of course he doesn't get it from his white blood; he gets it from all his bloods. It's the mixture that makes him what he is.'"

Like so much of what Toni Morrison calls "the racially inflected language" of black and white American writers, Fauset's *Plum Bun*, on the one hand, signifies on the historical significance of race as a "fact," ratified by the vexed legacy of nineteenth-century natural and social science; and, on the other, like so much American literature, it exploits "race"—to appropriate Gates's qualifying punctuation—as an insidious trope that has subverted even as it affirms the unquestionable importance of race in American society. Despite the reductive, essentializing power that race has been assigned by natural and social scientists, intellectuals and artists alike, and precisely because it has been such a vexed question nibbling at the edges of our consciousness, the idea of race has, paradoxically, contributed enormously to ongoing national and global dialogues about the Other in ourselves.

[See also Miscegenation.]

• Thomas F. Gossett, Race: The History of an Idea in America, 1963. Judith R. Berzon, Neither White Nor Black: The Mulatto Character in American Fiction, 1978. Alexander Crummell, "The Attitude of the American Mind toward the Negro Intellect," in Afro-American Writing, eds. Richard A. Long and Eugenia W. Collier, 1985, pp. 125–128. Anthony Appiah, "The Uncompleted Argument: Du Bois and the Illusion of Race," in "Race," Writing, and Difference, ed. Henry Louis Gates, Jr., 1986, pp. 21–37. Henry Louis Gates, Jr., ed., "Race," Writing, and Difference, 1986. Nathan Huggins, ed,. Du Bois: Writings, 1986. Frances Smith Foster, A Brighter Coming Day: A Frances Ellen Watkins Harper Reader, 1990. Marianna Torgovnick, Gone Primitive: Savage Intellects, Modern Lives, 1990. Toni Morrison, Playing in the Dark: Whiteness and the Literary Imagination, 1992. David Levering Lewis, W. E. B. Du Bois: Biography of a Race, 1868–1919, 1993. Kwame Anthony Appiah, "Race," in Critical Terms for Literary Study, eds. Frank Lentricchia and Thomas McLaughlin, 1995, pp. 274–287. Henry Louis Gates, Jr., and Cornel West, The Future of the Race, 1996.

—Cedric Gael Bryant

RAHMAN, AISHAH (b. 1936), professor and avantgarde surrealistic playwright whose works are performed mostly at small theaters and on college campuses. A native of New York City, Aishah Rahman (born Virginia Hughes) has traveled and worked in Africa and Latin America. She graduated from Howard University with a BS in political science in 1968 and received an MA in playwriting and dramatic literature from Goddard College in 1985. Rahman, who started writing plays professionally in the 1970s, is an associate professor of English at Brown University, where she is also founder and editor in chief of NuMuse, an annual journal of new plays. Before joining the faculty at Brown, she spent ten years teaching at Nassau Community College on Long Island and was director of the Henry Street Settlement's Playwrights Workshop at the New Federal Theater for five years.

Rahman's plays are often rooted in the lives of historically important African American figures. Rahman's first play, Lady Day: A Musical Tragedy, originally produced in 1972, takes place on the stage of New York City's famed Apollo Theater and is based on the life and career of Billie *Holiday. Rahman's best-known work, Unfinished Women Cry in No Man's Land While a Bird Dies in a Gilded Cage, first produced by the New York Shakespeare Festival in June 1977, takes place on 12 March 1955 on the day of jazz saxophonist Charlie *Parker's death. While five teenage girls, confined to the Hide-A-Wee Home for unwed mothers, must decide whether to keep their babies or put them up for adoption, Charlie Parker, wasted by years of drug abuse and exploitation, dies in "Pasha's Boudoir," the lavish apartment of a

wealthy European baroness who was once his lover. The play juxtaposes the pain of these ordinary "unfinished women" with the suffering of a jazz musician of almost mythical status who has touched the girls' short lives.

Rahman's next play, The Tale of Madame Zora (1986), is a blues musical based on the life of author and folklorist Zora Neale *Hurston. Rahman then turned to another genre, opera, and wrote The Opera of Marie Laveau (1989) with composer Akua Dixon Turre, expanding on the traditional form and content of the European opera. A pastiche of *folklore and history about the nineteenth-century French, Native American, and African New Orleans voodoo queen, Rahman renamed the libretto Anybody Seen Marie Laveau?

Rahman's most recent plays are The Mojo and the Sayso (1987) and Only in America (1993). The Mojo and the Sayso, which has received excellent reviews, revolves around the lives of a working-class family devastated by the murder of the ten-year-old son, Linus, who was shot in the back by police. The paralyzing guilt that has gripped the Benjamin family since the boy's death is explored in this short (the running time is seventy minutes) play through surreal and often intentionally nonresponsive dialogue. Only in America is a farcical allegory in which the Greek prophetess Cassandra reappears as a contemporary victim of sexual harassment.

Rahman's plays are heavily symbolic and suggestive. While fictionalizing the lives of important historical figures, Rahman creates a surreal atmosphere by emphasizing the unexpected and the nonrational, and by exposing the fetishes and subconscious desires of her characters. She has been compared to award-winning playwrights August *Wilson and Eugene O'Neill, and she cites Adrienne *Kennedy, Amiri *Baraka, Sam Shephard, Federico García Lorca, and Bertolt Brecht as her literary influences. In 1996, Rahman was writing a novel, "Illegitimate Life," and an *anthology of her plays, Three Plays by Aishah Rahman, was scheduled to be published. Often described as underground classics, Rahman's work has yet to be accepted in commercial mainstream theater but has unquestionably enjoyed wide circulation, influence, and appeal.

• Aishah Rahman, "To Be Black, Female and a Playwright," Freedomways 19 (1979): 256–260. Bernard L. Peterson, Jr., ed., Contemporary Black American Playwrights and Their Plays, 1988. Alicia Kae Koger, "Jazz Form and Jazz Function: An Analysis of Unfinished Women Cry in No Man's Land While a Bird Dies in a Gilded Cage," MELUS 16.3 (Fall 1989–1990): 99–111.

—Jennifer Margulis

RAINEY, MA (1886–1939), blues singer, comedienne, songwriter, and theater owner. Born Gertrude Pridgett on 26 April 1886 in Columbus, Georgia, Ma Rainey began performing at the age of fourteen at the Springer Opera House in Columbus. In 1904 she married William "Pa" Rainey. Early in her career Rainey became leader of her own show and proved herself to be both an exciting *blues performer and a capable manager. In 1923 she began her recording career with Paramount Records; she stayed with the company until 1928. Rainey's performances and records incorporated rural as well as *jazz elements. She recorded with jug bands as well as with *jazz greats. One of her most well-known songs, "See See Rider," exemplifies her style. Her biographer, Sandra Lieb, characterized Rainey's style as a rich contralto filled with slurs and moans and "lisping diction" (*Ma Rainey*, 1959).

Throughout her career Rainey appealed most to southern audiences—both black and white. She returned south to Columbus in 1935, when she retired from active performing. At that time, Rainey purchased and operated the Lyric and Airdome theaters in Rome, Georgia.

Rainey's power as a performer and her success as a businesswoman have inspired African American writers. Sterling A. *Brown's poem "Ma Rainey" is a poetic portrayal of Rainey's impact upon her poor, southern black audience. Brown's Rainey is a charismatic spirit worker who is capable of articulating her audience's joy and sorrow. For the persona of Al *Young's poem "A Dance for Ma Rainey" (1969), Rainey continues to give voice to "that sick pain" he says he knows so well yet is forced to hide. In 1984 August *Wilson's Broadway play *Ma Rainey's Black Bottom* presented Rainey as a tough manipulator of the racist recording industry. Though the play focuses on the men in the band, Rainey emerges as the wise, powerful leader of the group. She also recognizes the limitations of her authority given the presence of racism, working what authority she does have to her advantage.

Like other classic blues singers, Ma Rainey has recently come to the attention of black feminist literary and cultural critics as the embodiment of black female independence, *sexuality, and creativity.

• Sandra Lieb, *Mother of the Blues: A Study of Ma Rainey*, 1981. Sandra Lieb, "Ma Rainey," in *Black Women in America: An Historical Encyclopedia*, 1992, pp. 958–960.

—Farah Jasmine Griffin

Raisin in the Sun, A.

Lorraine *Hansberry's *A Raisin in the Sun* won the 1959 New York Drama Critics Circle Award after opening on Broadway, 11 March 1959, at the Ethel Barrymore Theatre to instant critical and popular success. Hansberry's first produced play, realistic in style, dramatizes the struggles and frustrations of a multigenerational, African American, working-class family living in a cramped apartment on Chicago's South Side. An insurance benefit of ten thousand dollars paid on the death of Walter, Sr., becomes the source of conflict within the Younger family, as *Mama Lena Younger, his widow/beneficiary and matriarch, and her son, *Walter Lee Younger, argue over its use. Their debate reveals fundamental differences in values and ponders the relationship of material wealth to human dignity. An authentic portrayal of the economic dilemma and spiritual resilience of African Americans, the play captured the urgent voice of the *civil rights movement and catapulted its author into instant fame. The original cast, led by film star Sidney Poitier, was outstanding, and many of the cast members went on to highly successful theater careers: Claudia McNeil,

Ruby Dee, Lou Gossett, Jr., Glynn Turman, Diana Sands, and director Lloyd Richards. The play ran for 538 performances on Broadway and was made into a film, which won a special award at the Cannes Film Festival in 1961.

Now a classic of the American *theater, *A Raisin in the Sun* is one of the nation's most frequently produced plays, has been translated into over thirty languages on every continent, and has been produced in such diverse countries as the former Czechoslovakia, England, the former Soviet Union, and France. The play has been published in several editions since its inaugural production. The late Robert Nemiroff, Hansberry's former husband and literary executor, actively promoted this play and her other works after her death in 1965. In 1974, he produced *Raisin*, a *musical based on the play, which won a Tony Award. In 1987, he restored scenes and dialogue cut from the original script and promoted a production of the uncut version that ran at the Kennedy Center in Washington, D.C., and was subsequently produced on television's American Playhouse with actors Danny Glover and Esther Rolle in the lead roles.

The play is regarded as a model of stage realism whose authenticity, candor, and timeliness have made it one of the most popular plays ever produced on the American stage. Critics were nearly unanimous in praising the "honesty" and craft of the original production, although a few disparaged it as a "black soap opera." The play, whose strong affirmation of human potential opposed the drama of despair popular at the time, anticipated the *Pan-Africanism and growing militant mood of blacks soon to sweep the arts as well as the country in the 1960s. *A Raisin in the Sun* continues to have currency because of its evocation of the African American struggle and its poignant exploration of human values.

[*See also* Beneatha Younger.]

• Lorraine Hansberry, *A Raisin in the Sun and The Sign in Sidney Brustein's Window* (contains restored materials to both scripts), 1987. Margaret B. Wilkerson, "*A Raisin in the Sun*: Anniversary of an American Classic," in *Performing Feminisms: Feminist Critical Theory and Theatre*, ed. Sue-Ellen Case, 1990. Stephen R. Carter, *Hansberry's Drama: Commitment Amid Complexity*, 1991, pp. 119–130.

—Margaret B. Wilkerson

RAMPERSAD, ARNOLD (b. 1941), scholar, literary and cultural critic, educator, winner of the American Book Award, and MacArthur Fellow. Born in 1941 in Trinidad, Arnold Rampersad received a BA and MA from Bowling Green State University and an MA and PhD from Harvard. He has held teaching positions at Stanford, Rutgers, and Columbia. Rampersad has been Woodrow Wilson Professor of Literature at Princeton since 1990.

Although he began his career specializing in Herman Melville, Rampersad is best known for *biographies of W. E. B. *Du Bois and Langston *Hughes. In *The Art and Imagination of W. E. B. Du Bois* (1976), Rampersad sought to trace the intellectual development of one of this century's preeminent black political and social leaders. He achieved this by presenting the complete scope of Du Bois's complex and paradoxical beliefs and opinions. By bringing the conservative Du Bois into relation with the radical Du Bois, Rampersad made sense of what might appear to be a contradictory career.

In the two-volume *Life of Langston Hughes* (1986–1988), Rampersad again illuminated the life of a central figure in African American literary and cultural studies. As was the case with Du Bois, Hughes presented an instance of a writer whose complexities had been insufficiently revealed. Well known was Hughes's affection for "common everyday" African Americans. Less well known were the psychological and cultural groundings of this affection, subjects Rampersad sought to illuminate. Revealed, too, was the historical background against which Hughes so frequently reacted, such that *The Life of Langston Hughes* is not only concerned with the life of one person but also with the life of a culture and a nation. It is considered the authoritative biography of this central African American poet.

Rampersad is rightly credited with rehabilitating biography as a valued form of literary and cultural criticism in the face of the influence of literary theory in the late 1980s and the 1990s. While literary biography is not intended to replace literary or cultural criticism, per se, or literary theory, Rampersad's contribution is to restore a neglected mode of intellectual and scholarly discourse to its previous prominence. In *Days of Grace* (1993), tennis star Arthur Ashe's *autobiography, Rampersad's coauthorship brought the craft of the scholar to the enterprise of popular biography, illuminating the life of an instrumental figure in African American cultural life during the last quarter of the twentieth century. In dealing with all these subjects—Du Bois, Hughes, and Ashe—Rampersad sought to bring the individual life into relation with the life of the culture. The title of the second volume of *The Life of Langston Hughes*, *I Dream a World* powerfully indicates the extent to which Rampersad seeks to negotiate the connection between the visionary aspects of individual greatness and the demands of cultural representativeness by means of scholarly biography.

• Arnold Rampersad, *Melville's Israel Potter: A Pilgrimage and Progress*, 1969. Arnold Rampersad, *The Art and Imagination of W. E. B. Du Bois*, 2 vols., 1976. Arnold Rampersad, *The Life of Langston Hughes*, 2 vols., 1986–1988. Arthur Ashe and Arnold Rampersad, *Days of Grace*, 1993.

—Theodore O. Mason, Jr.

RANDALL, DUDLEY (b. 1914), poet, publisher, editor, and founder of Broadside Press. Dudley Randall was born 14 January 1914 in Washington, D.C., but moved to Detroit in 1920. His first published poem appeared in the *Detroit Free Press* when he was thirteen. His early reading included English poets from whom he learned form. He was later influenced by the work of Jean *Toomer and Countee *Cullen.

His employment in a foundry is recalled in "George" (*Poem Counterpoem*), written after encountering a once vigorous coworker in a hospital years later. His military service during World War II is reflected in such poems as "Coral Atoll" and "Pacific Epitaphs" (*More to Remember*).

Randall worked in the post office while earning degrees in English and library science (1949 and 1951). For the next five years he was librarian at Morgan State and Lincoln (Mo.) universities, returning to Detroit in 1956 to a position in the Wayne County Federated Library System. After a brief teaching assignment in 1969, he became librarian and poet in residence at the University of Detroit, retiring in 1974.

His interest in Russia, apparent in his translations of poems by Aleksander Pushkin ("I Loved You Once," *After the Killing*) and Konstantin Simonov ("My Native Land" and "Wait for Me" in *A Litany of Friends*), was heightened by a visit to the Soviet Union in 1966. His identification with Africa, enhanced by his association with poet Margaret Esse *Danner from 1962 to 1964 and study in Ghana in 1970, is evident in such poems as "African Suite" (*After the Killing*).

When "Ballad of Birmingham," written in response to the 1963 bombing of a church in which four girls were killed, was set to music and recorded, Randall established *Broadside Press in 1965, printing the poem on a single sheet to protect his rights. The first collection by the press was *Poem Counterpoem* (1966) in which he and Danner each thematically matched ten poems on facing pages. Broadside eventually published an anthology, broadsides by other poets, numerous chapbooks, and a series of critical essays. These publications established the reputations of an impressive number of African American poets now well known while providing a platform for many others whose writing was more political than literary.

Following the 1967 riot in Detroit, Randall published *Cities Burning* (1968), a group of thirteen poems, all but one previously uncollected. This pamphlet, like the first, contains poems selected on the basis of theme and does not follow a chronological development in the author's work. Fourteen love poems appeared in 1970 (*Love You*), followed by *More to Remember* (1971), fifty poems written over a thirty-year period on a variety of subjects, and *After the Killing* (1973), fifteen new poems that comment on such contemporary topics as contradictory attitudes during a period of racial pride and nationalism.

Publication of *A Litany of Friends* (1981; rpt. 1983) followed several years of suicidal depression that incapacitated Randall and put Broadside Press temporarily at risk. This period of recovery was his most productive, comprising some of his most original—though not necessarily his best—work. Included are eighty-four poems, thirty very recent ones and forty-six previously uncollected.

On the basis of "Detroit Renaissance," published in *Corridors* magazine in 1980, the mayor of Detroit named Randall poet laureate of that city in 1981.

A distinctive style is difficult to identify in Randall's poetry. In his early poems he was primarily concerned with construction. Many of those in *More to Remember* are written in such fixed forms as the haiku, triolet, dramatic monologue, and sonnet while others experiment with slant rhyme, indentation, and the blues form. He later concentrated on imagery and phrasing, yet some of his more recent work continues to suggest the styles of other poets. Although many of these move with more freedom, originality, and depth of feeling, and encompass a wider range of themes, others identifiable by printed date demonstrate a return to traditional form.

While Dudley Randall's reputation as a pioneer in independent African American book publishing is secure, he is sure to be remembered for his poems as well, including "Booker T. and W.E.B.," which succinctly summarizes philosophical differences between Booker T. *Washington and W. E. B. *Du Bois in a simple dialogue; "Ballad of Birmingham," "Southern Road," and "Souvenirs," all from *Poem Counterpoem*; "Roses and Revolutions," "Primitives," and "A Different Image" (*Cities Burning*); "Faces" and "Perspectives" (*More to Remember*); "The Profile on the Pillow" and "Black Magic" (*Love You*); "Frederick Douglass and the Slave Breaker" (*After the Killing*); and "A Poet Is Not a Jukebox" (*A Litany of Friends*).

• A. X. Nicholas, "A Conversation with Dudley Randall," in *Homage to Hoyt Fuller*, ed. Dudley Randall, 1984, pp. 266–274. R. Baxter Miller, "Dudley Randall," in *DLB*, vol. 41, *Afro-American Poets since 1955*, eds. Trudier Harris and Thadious M. Davis, 1985, pp. 265–273.

—Naomi Long Madgett

RAPE. *See* Violence.

RAS THE DESTROYER. In Ralph *Ellison's *Invisible Man* (1952) Ras the Exhorter (turned Ras the Destroyer) represents the nationalistic view of the African American. He is a foil to the narrator in that where the narrator seeks an integrated universe, Ras's major concern is nation-building for the Black American. As a result of his experiences the narrator has come to suspect any organization or group that is exclusive. He believes that the Blacks who do not become a part of the mainstream are "outside of history," and he therefore rejects Ras's nationalist rhetoric as nonsense. Ras has been linked to Marcus *Garvey. Certainly both the fictional character and the historical figure share a compelling view of *Black nationalism, and they both demanded social justice for Blacks. Also, like Garvey, Ras has strong ties with Africa.

Ras, patrolling the streets of a riot-torn Harlem in his ancestral attire, astride a great black horse, is "dressed in the costume of an Abyssinian Chieftan." Ras is also the short term for Rastafarian, originally a Jamaican religious group whose members trace their roots back to Ethiopia and to Haile Selassie. When Ras urges Blacks to unite, he, like Garvey, is not limiting his national movement to Harlem; he is pleading for nationalism throughout the Black diaspora. While Ellison (through the narrator) might reject Black nationalism as disruptive, Ras stands as a symbol of the malignant force that comes as a result of America's blindness (a blindness represented in the organization of the brotherhood and in the philanthropy of Mr. *Norton) to the needs of oppressed minorities.

While Ras is a powerful character in the novel, Ellison, through his use of the comic, undercuts Ras's dignity and makes him appear clownish at times. Even in the scene where he appears majestic, Ellison uses the comic to downplay his regality. Despite Ras's proud bearing on this occasion, Ellison says he had "a hauty, vulgar dignity." Instead of being robed in the skin of a lion or a leopard that is customary for African royalty, Ras is clad in a cape "made from the skin of some wild animal" that makes Ras himself look wild. And while Ras's appearance is "real, alive, [and] alarming," the narrator insists that it was "more out of a dream than out of Harlem." Ellison's depiction of Ras prefigures the negative images of the West Indian male that later appears in works by writers such as Toni *Morrison and Chester *Himes. One must add, however, that elements of the surreal and the comic pervade the novel, and Ras suffers no more from Ellison's pen than do other characters.

—Ralph Reckley, Sr.

RAVEN QUICKSKILL. A poet and runaway slave, Raven Quicksill is the principal protagonist of Ishmael *Reed's fifth novel, *Flight to Canada* (1976). He is an activist, aesthetician, and a master of the arts of resistance in the lineage of the *tricksters celebrated in African American oral tradition.

Raven is a synonym for black, but the raven also figures significantly in various Native American myths—especially those of the Tlingit people of Alaska—underscoring Reed's concern with multiculturalism. Quickskill resembles a Native American name (like many African Americans, Reed has Native American ancestry) but it functions here to highlight the creativity and resilience of all oppressed or "marginal" peoples. Quickskill suggests speed and dexterity, quick-wittedness, the ability to improvise on the spot. Quick also means living; thus, Quickskill possesses life-skill: he knows how to stay alive and he knows how to live. In connection with speech or writing, quick also means sharp or caustic. Like Ishmael Reed, Raven Quickskill is a satirist whose words are weapons.

Raven also brings to mind Edgar Allen Poe's famous poem "The Raven," especially since *Flight to Canada* contains many obvious allusions to Poe's work. While the "Nevermore!" of Poe's raven signals an end to being, Ishmael Reed's Raven says "nevermore" to slavery and all that is antilife; he is "free as a bird." The appropriateness of bird imagery is reinforced by the fact that Yardbird, or simply Bird, was the nickname of saxophonist Charlie *Parker, who is for Reed one of the prime exemplars of neohoodooism, his name for the aesthetic practices he champions and that Raven Quickskill personifies.

—Robert Elliot Fox

RAY, HENRIETTA CORDELIA (c. 1849–1916), poet and educator. Henrietta Cordelia Ray was one of five daughters born to Charles Ray and Charlotte Augusta Burrough. Ray's *poetry and prose are marked by tributes to her family and the heroes and heroines of her era. Ray's sonnets, ballads, and quatrains reflect a consummate understanding of traditional lyricism and meter. Despite exploring a full range of these forms, her themes of nature, platonic love, and Christian idealism are consistent and repetitious.

Ray attended the University of the City of New York, graduating with a master's degree in pedagogy in 1891. Her formal education resulted in proficiency in Greek, French, Latin, and German. Ray later taught at Colored Grammar School Number One before pursuing a career as a poet. *The A.M.E. Review* published her verses before they were collected in the volumes *Sonnets* (1893) and *Poems* (1910).

She was extremely close to her older sister Florence, her lifelong companion. Together they wrote a *biography of their father, *Sketches of the Life of Rev. Charles E. Ray* (1887), a short volume outlining his commitment to the abolitionist movement and his career as editor of the *Colored American Magazine*. In her best-known poem, "Verses to My Heart's-Sister," Ray writes with surprising passion about the depth of their affection and loyalty. Ray's strength as a writer lay in this kind of ornate tribute. *Poems* is heavily weighted by eulogies to Harriet Beecher *Stowe, Frederick *Douglass, Toussaint *L'Ouverture, and Paul Laurence *Dunbar.

Ray's diligence was rewarded when her eight-line verse "Commemoration Ode" or "Lincoln/Written for the Occasion of the Unveiling of the Freedman's Monument in Memory of Abraham Lincoln/April 14, 1876" (published in *Sonnets*, 1893) was read for the unveiling of the Freedman's Monument in Washington, D.C., during the commemoration of the eleventh anniversary of Lincoln's death.

• Hallie Q. Brown, *Homespun Heroines and Other Women of Distinction*, 1926. Ann Allen Shockley, *Afro-American Women Writers (1746–1933)*, 1988.

—Kimberly Wallace Sanders

REASON, CHARLES L.

REASON, CHARLES L. (1818–1893), essayist and poet. Charles Lewis Reason was born in New York City of West Indian parents, Elizabeth and Michiel Reason. He studied and taught at the African Free School in the city and graduated from McGrawville College (New York). From 1849 to 1850 Reason taught belles lettres, Greek, Latin, French, and mathematics at New York Central College; from 1852 to 1855 he was principal of the Institute for Colored Youth in Philadelphia, where he also worked with the General Vigilance Committee to aid fugitive slaves. For the next thirty-eight years Reason was a teacher and principal at several "colored" schools in New York City. All his life he fought for abolitionism, civil rights, suffrage, and *education as an officer, writer, and lecturer for many African American organizations alongside his friends Robert *Purvis, Charles Lenox Remond, Charles B. Ray, and Frederick *Douglass. He died in his New York City home of nephritis and heart disease.

Reason's *essays and *poetry which appeared in periodicals and remain uncollected, illustrate his devotion to reform, his vast learning, and his adroit literary techniques. "The Spirit Voice" (1841), an eighty-six line ode, stirringly summons the disenfranchised of New York "To vow, no more to sleep till raised and freed / From partial bondage, to a life indeed." His forty-eight stanza "Freedom" (1846) eloquently recounts freedom's victories in historical campaigns from ancient through modern times; the poem denounces state and church supporters of *slavery and pleads for freedom's return to America: "We lift imploring hands to Thee! / We cry for those in prison bound! / O! in thy strength, come! Liberty! / And 'stablish right the wide world round." Reason's contemporaries admired his brilliant intellect, so evident in his literary work, and the quiet perseverance with which he served his race for fifty years.

• Anthony R. Mayo, *Charles Lewis Reason, Pioneer New York Educator,* (n. d.), 12 pages. Joan R. Sherman, *Invisible Poets: Afro-Americans of the Nineteenth Century*, 2d ed., 1989.

—Joan R. Sherman

REBELLIONS.

REBELLIONS. *See* Insurrections.

REDDING, J. SAUNDERS

REDDING, J. SAUNDERS (1906–1988), literary critic and historian. Taught by Alice Moore *Dunbar-Nelson at his Wilmington, Delaware, high school, J. Saunders Redding earned an advanced degree in English at Brown University (1932) and was a professor at various colleges and universities, including Morehouse, Hampton, and Cornell. In 1949, his stint as a visiting professor at Brown made him the first African American to hold a faculty position at an Ivy League university. He wrote many books and articles on African American culture and other topics, including *To Make a Poet Black* (1939), a landmark history of African American literature; *No Day of Triumph* (1942), an autobiographical account of a journey through southern black communities; and *Stranger and Alone* (1950), a novel, as well as several more general historical and sociological works. He also edited with Arthur P. Davis an important anthology, *Cavalcade: Negro American Writing from 1760 to the Present* (1971).

Redding was an exponent of individual achievement as symbol and inspiration for all African Americans. He maintained the classical civil rights posture against segregation, thus opposing both black and white establishment interests in the 1930s and 1940s. Redding explicitly favored the "liberal" W. E. B. *Du Bois over the "conservative" Booker T. *Washington, and in fact lost his position at Morehouse (1931) because of his "radical" beliefs; yet he was later criticized by such 1960s black nationalists as Amiri *Baraka for his opposition to cultural separatism and racial essentialism.

Redding's best-known and most influential book is his first, *To Make a Poet Black*, one of the earliest important works of African American literary *criticism. In this book, Redding works to establish a canon of African American literature, from Jupiter *Hammon to Zora Neale *Hurston, pointedly excluding writers he regards as less central to the tradition. He rejects earlier, simplistic notions of racial identity, such as Benjamin *Brawley's theory of

"Negro genius," emphasizing instead what he calls "the pressure of the age," or social and historical forces, in shaping the racial consciousness and literary careers of the writers he treats in his study.

Redding's concern is with the historical development of a *Black Aesthetic, and he evaluates poets and novelists according to their contribution to this development. African American literature, in his view, has always been politically involved, "literature either of purpose or necessity." Necessity sometimes demands that the writer become a "propagandist," a development Redding applauds if, as in the case of Du Bois, it is "inspired" by "righteous wrath" and a selfless desire to further the interests of African Americans. Du Bois, in Redding's view, possessed "the rarest gift of all," the "power of setting forth the abstract concretely."

African American writers also contend with a split between black and white audiences: "Negro writers have been obliged to have two faces," he writes. Sometimes the "white" becomes dominant, with artistically unhealthy consequences: Redding, for example, deplores the "cheerful, prideless humility" of certain nineteenth-century dialect poets, such as Daniel Webster *Davis, who "wrote for a white audience in a way that he knew would please them." Redding's novel, *Stranger and Alone*, dramatizes the psychological and moral costs of denying one's racial identity and allowing one's "white face" to predominate. Striving for individual success through rejection of one's people, the novel implies, amounts to a betrayal of oneself, as well as a futile striving against history, "the time on the clock of the world." In *No Day of Triumph*, Redding begins with a chapter about his family, then records the results of a journey through African American communities in the South. He ultimately finds value in the lived experience of the community.

A similar concern with the language and experiences of the people is evident in *To Make a Poet Black*, which covers the evolution of literary uses of the black vernacular, from James Edwin *Campbell and Paul Lawrence *Dunbar to James Weldon *Johnson and Zora Neale Hurston. For Redding, the most important development in African American letters of the 1920s and 1930s was not necessarily the better-known, urban-centered writing of the *Harlem Renaissance but rather writing, such as Johnson's *God's Trombones* (1927), that acknowledged its debt to *folklore, *spirituals, and *sermons and preaching. The book concludes with a call for "a spiritual and physical return to the earth." Aside from his contributions to the development of the African American canon, the lasting importance of Redding's work for black theory and criticism lies here, in his recognition and celebration of the importance of the black vernacular in literary and social history, and in his view of African American literature as a self-contained tradition.

[See also Canonization.]

• Henry Louis Gates, Jr., introduction to *To Make a Poet Black*, 1988.   —Gary Ashwill

REDMOND, EUGENE (b. 1937), poet, playwright, critic, editor, educator, and important figure in the 1960s *Black Arts movement. Eugene Redmond was born 1 December 1937 in St. Louis, Missouri. Orphaned at age nine, he was raised by his grandmother and "neighborhood fathers," made up of members of the Seventh Day Adventist Church and friends of his older brother. During high school he worked on the newspaper and yearbook, performed in school and church plays, and composed for neighborhood singing groups.

From 1958 to 1961 Redmond served as a U.S. Marine in the Far East, acquiring a speaking knowledge of Japanese. He was an associate editor of the *East St. Louis Beacon* from 1961 to 1962. In 1963 Redmond cofounded a weekly paper in East St. Louis, the *Monitor*, working at different times as a contributing editor, executive editor, and editorial page editor.

At Southern Illinois University he was the first African American student editor of the university newspaper. After receiving his bachelor's degree in English literature in 1964, he earned a master's degree in English literature from Washington University in 1966.

In 1965, while still in graduate school, Redmond won first prize in the Washington University Annual Festival of the Arts for his poem "Eye in the Ceiling." In 1968 he published his first volume of *poetry, *A Tale of Two Toms, or Tom-Tom (Uncle Toms of East St. Louis and St. Louis)*. Subsequent volumes include *A Tale of Time & Toilet Tissue* (1969), *Sentry of the Four Golden Pillars* (1970), *River of Bones and Flesh and Blood* (1971), *Songs from an Afro/Phone* (1972), *Consider Loneliness as These Things* (1973), *In a Time of Rain & Desire* (1973), and *Eye on the Ceiling* (1991). Three of these collections were published by the Black Writers Press, which Redmond founded with Henry *Dumas and Sherman Fowler. He has been poet in residence at Oberlin College, California State University, University of Wisconsin, and Wayne State.

From 1967 to 1969 Redmond was a senior consultant to Katherine *Dunham at Southern University's Performing Arts Training Center, where he acted, directed, wrote plays, and supervised the drama and writing departments. Twelve of Redmond's plays, ballets, and choral dramas have been produced on university campuses and on California television. Redmond's one-act *Will I Still Be Here Tomorrow* was also produced Off-Broadway at the Martinique Theatre in New York in 1972. Redmond combined writing with performance with a 1973 recording of his poems, *Bloodlinks and Sacred Places*.

Redmond's poetic style displays his knowledge of the spoken word and performance. He sees basic rhythms and *music as a key to a style of African American writing. Many of his poems have a rap-like beat and contain direct references to *jazz, *blues, *spirituals, soul music, and black musicians.

Frequent allusions to African heritage also convey pride in African American culture and history and a black consciousness characteristic of the Black

Arts movement. Some of his other poems explore the bleakness of urban existence while some depart from the overtly political style of the period, lyrically exploring introspective or romantic themes.

Redmond's commitment to the concept of an "African continuum" is evident in his influential study, *Drumvoices: The Mission of Afro-American Poetry, A Critical History* (1976). A survey of poetry from 1746 to 1976 that took eight years to research, *Drumvoices* explores the "complex web of beliefs, customs, traditions and significant practices that tie diasporan black cultures to their African origins."

Redmond has also contributed significantly to African American letters by editing volumes of African American writing, establishing multi-cultural literary journals—including *Literati Internazionali* and *Drumvoices Revue*—and training young writers. He is Henry Dumas's literary executor and has edited seven volumes of Dumas's work, including *Goodbye Sweetwater* (1988) and *Knees of a Natural Man* (1989).

Redmond has been a professor at Southern Illinois University since 1990. He also works in the public schools and has established a feeder system, following some writers from elementary school through high school as a way of bringing "literacy to the many and the literary to the few." His other community activities include organizing the annual "Break Word with the World" event in East St. Louis, a month-long "mock trial of the media" culminating in a reading and publication.

Redmond has received wide recognition as a poet and teacher. In 1976 he became poet laureate of East St. Louis, the first poet laureate named by a municipality. He was awarded a National Endowment for the Arts creative writing fellowship in 1978. The Eugene B. Redmond Writers Club was founded in 1986, with writers such as Maya *Angelou and Amiri *Baraka on the board of directors. *Eye on the Ceiling* (1991) won an American Book Award. In 1993 Pan-African Movement USA awarded him a Pyramid Award for lifetime contributions to Pan-Africanism through poetry. He received a "Tribute to an Elder" award from African Poetry Theater in 1995.

• "Eugene B. Redmond," in *Contemporary Authors, New Revision Series*, vol. 25, eds. Hal May and Deborah A. Straub, 1985, pp. 375–377. Joyce Pettis, "Eugene B. Redmond," in *DLB*, vol. 41, *Afro-American Poets since 1955*, eds. Trudier Harris and Thadious M. Davis, 1985, pp. 274–281. Joyce Mercer, "A Contagious Enthusiasm for Life and Literature," *Chronicle of Higher Education* 40.29 (23 Mar. 1994): A5.

—Jennifer Burton

REED, ISHMAEL (b. 1938), poet, novelist, essayist, teacher, anthologist, publisher, and cultural activist. Ishmael Reed is one of the most original and controversial figures in the field of African American letters.

Reed was born in Chattanooga, Tennessee, on 22 February 1938, but he grew up in Buffalo, New York. After graduating from high school in 1956, he enrolled as a night student at Millard Fillmore College but transferred to the University of Buffalo as a day student with the assistance of an English teacher who was impressed with a story Reed had written. For financial reasons, however, Reed eventually withdrew without taking a degree. He remained in Buffalo for some time, working as a correspondent for the *Empire Star Weekly*, a black community newspaper, and serving as cohost of a local radio program that was canceled after Reed conducted an interview with *Malcolm X.

Moving to New York City in 1962, Reed served as editor of a Newark, New Jersey, weekly and helped establish the legendary *East Village Other*, one of the first and best-known of the so-called underground newspapers. Reed also was a member of the Umbra Writers Workshop, one of the organizations instrumental in the creation of the *Black Arts movement and its efforts to establish a *Black Aesthetic.

Reed's first novel, *The Freelance Pallbearers*, was published in 1967. That same year he moved to Berkeley, California, later relocating to the adjacent city of Oakland, where he currently resides with his wife, Carla Blank, a dancer and choreographer. They have a daughter, Tennessee. Reed also has a daughter, Timothy Brett, from a previous marriage.

Reed has taught at the University of California at Berkeley since the late 1960s, even though he was denied tenure in 1977 (a circumstance he wrote about in his first collection of essays, *Shrovetide in Old New Orleans*, 1978). He also has held visiting appointments at many other academic institutions, including Yale, Harvard, Dartmouth, Washington University in St. Louis, and SUNY Buffalo. In addition to winning several awards for his writing, Reed has been nominated for the Pulitzer Prize and was twice a finalist for the National Book Award (once in poetry and once in fiction).

As of 1995, Reed had published nine novels, five books of poems, and four collections of essays; he also had authored four plays, three television productions, and two librettos, and edited four anthologies. His publishing and editing enterprises have included Reed, Cannon and Johnson Publications, I. Reed Books, and the journals *Yardbird Reader*, *Y'Bird*, *Quilt*, and *Konch*.

In 1976, Reed cofounded what is—outside of his writing—perhaps his most significant venture, the Before Columbus Foundation, a multiethnic organization dedicated to promoting a pan-cultural view of America. One of Reed's outstanding attributes is his consistent advocacy of powerful, innovative, and neglected writing—not just by people of color but by white people as well. This might seem surprising to those who associate Reed with the combative, anti-white aesthetics and politics of the cultural nationalist program, but it is important to understand that Reed's involvement with the Black Arts movement, through his membership in the Umbra Workshop, was a complex one that can be described as both participatory and adversarial. True, Reed is a vigorous promoter of African-originated modes of being and performance, which he uses to challenge established canons of judgment and achievement, but a careful assessment of his work over three decades reveals that his problack position never was a dogmatic one. If much of Reed's work constitutes an intertext through which "the blackness of blackness" can be read, he nevertheless insists that this "blackness of blackness" cannot be categorized or prescribed. For Reed, as his masterpiece *Mumbo Jumbo* (1972) signifies, this indefinable but irresistible something "'jes grew." It may indeed be "mumbo jumbo"—an enigma to the ignorant, a function of "soul" to those who know—but it is not reducible to skin color alone or to a militant creed.

In Reed's view, the black element reveals the permeable nature of American experience and identity, but he also acknowledges the permeable nature of blackness; thus Reed actually belongs in the company of those for whom notions of "mainstream" and "margins" are falsely dichotomous. Reed insists, for example, that a black writer steeped in tradition is a "classical" writer. At the same time, Reed's postmodernism enables him to take in everything at once, so to speak, so that conventional ideas of form and genre are contested, as well as canonical considerations.

Neohoodooism is the name Reed gave to the philosophy and aesthetic processes he employs to take care of business on behalf of the maligned and the mishandled. Hoodoo—the African American version of voodoo, a misunderstood term that actually refers to traditional African religious practices as they have reasserted themselves in the diaspora—appeals to Reed because of its "mystery" and its eclectic nature, thus providing him with an appropriate metaphor for his understanding and realization of art. Reed's best statements concerning the workings of neohoodooism can be found in his first book of poetry, *Conjure* (1972)—especially "Neo-HooDoo Manifesto," "The Neo-HooDoo Aesthetic," and "catechism of d neoamerican hoodoo church"—while the most successful actualizations of neohoodooism as a practice are his novels *Yellow Back Radio Broke-Down* (1969), the aforementioned *Mumbo Jumbo*, and *Flight to Canada* (1976).

Neohoodooism is, in many ways, a truly "black" art, but at the same time, due to the undeniable mix of ingredients in the New World, it is also "something else." Unlike those who argue for a black essentialism, Reed sees this hybridity as a virtue, rather than a defect or betrayal. A deep immersion in blackness is simultaneously an immersion in Americanness, given the extent to which, as a result of *slavery and its aftermath, Africa helped to make America; and, considering the give-and-take of many other cultural influences, an immersion in Americanness is also an experience of the unfolding of multiculturalism.

Leaving aside for a moment his contributions as an author to American literature, it seems safe to say that when the history of multiculturalism in the late twentieth century is written, Ishmael Reed's entrepreneurial and promotional efforts will be seen to have played a meaningful role in demonstrating the degree to which we are—artistically as well as demographically—a nation of nations.

In his writing, Reed is a great improviser, a master of collage with an amazing ability to syncretize seemingly disparate and divergent materials into coherent "edutainments"—forms of surprise, revelation, and frequent hilarity. However, those who focus primarily on how funny or unfunny his works are miss the point of Reed's rollicking revisions, his apparently loony "'toons"—which is to employ humor as a weapon in the very serious enterprise of exposing human excesses and absurdities, and, at the same time, to remind us of the dangers of taking ourselves and our cherished opinions too seriously. (One of Reed's consistent gripes about militants of all perusasions is that they lack a sense of humor.)

From the start, Reed's iconoclasm has been aimed not only at the Western tradition, which has attempted to monopolize the world at the expense of other versions of experience, but at the black tradition as well. Reed's first novel, *The Freelance Pallbearers*, parodied Ralph Ellison's *Invisible Man*—for many critics, the masterwork of African American fiction and black autobiography in general—at a moment when *black studies was just being established and the principal critical approach was a documentary one that emphasized black art's sociopolitical aspects. For Reed to be seen as satirizing the black literary tradition in a period of Black Power and the long overdue recuperation and reassessment of that very tradition was not likely to endear him to either white liberals or black cultural nationalists.

The risk of censure and ridicule notwithstanding, Reed always has gone against the grain of the prevailing critical-polemical fashion—a sign of his fierce independence as an artist and thinker. He has insisted continually on his right to do things his own way, and possesses an uncanny skill at pinpointing the follies and inconsistencies of many aspects of our consensus reality. Although Reed prefers to ride ahead of the herd, he is viewed in certain quarters as conservative, even reactionary—a judgment of his own position that he satirized in "The Reactionary Poet" in his third collection of poems, *Secretary to the Spirits* (1978).

Using analogies from comedy and music, one could argue that Ishmael Reed is much closer to Richard Pryor and *In Living Color* than he is to Bill Cosby, more akin to George Clinton or Sun Ra than to Wynton Marsalis. Does this help us to place him within the black tradition? At the least, it forces us to relinquish any notion of "the" black tradition; there are, and always have been, several black traditions, sometimes conflicting, sometimes intersecting, but nonetheless coexistent. One of the reasons Reed's reputation has suffered over the years is that he has steadfastly refused to toe any party line with regard to African American authenticity, aspiration, and achievement. Moreover, as the title of his 1993 essay collection, *Airing Dirty Laundry*, indicates, Reed believes in "outing" what others wish to keep closeted. Rather than working toward closure, he vigorously engages in disclosure. Some critics have interpreted the openness (and occasional open-endedness) of Reed's works as indeterminacy. For example, Michael G. Cooke, in *Afro-American Literature in the Twentieth Century* (1984), while emphasizing Reed's importance based upon the distinctiveness of his vision, style, and scope, believes nonetheless that his work is "affected by an instinct of irresolution." Reed's target, however, is the overdetermined, which he combats by accentuating chance, spontaneity, and instinct, deliberately embracing what amounts to an uncertainty principle that acknowledges "other" positions, myriad possibilities.

Given Reed's chosen task of providing revelatory "readings" of, and putting operative "writings" on, both black and white mischief and miscreants, it would have been impossible for him to have received only praise for his efforts. Reed does, in fact, have his share of enemies and detractors, who, in a real sense, are as much of a defining presence for his career as the endorsements of his many admirers. Indeed, Reed made the negative pronouncements of some of his critics part of the "problem" to be solved by the proper decoding of *Mumbo Jumbo* when he included them on the back of the dust jacket of the original hardcover edition of the novel.

The impressive commercial success attained by some African American authors has eluded Reed; yet, over the course of a distinguished and turbulent career, he has received numerous, frequently potent, critical accolades. Musician Max Roach is said to have called Reed the Charlie *Parker of American fiction, while Fredric Jameson has judged him to be one of the principal postmodernists. Nick Aaron Ford, in *Studies in the Novel* (vol. 3, 1971), referred to him as the "most revolutionary" African American novelist to have appeared thus far, and Addison *Gayle, Jr., in *The Way of the New World* (1975), called Reed the best satirist in the black tradition since George S. *Schuyler. Acknowledging that his satire does derive in part from Schuyler, Wallace *Thurman, and Rudolph *Fisher, Henry Louis *Gates, Jr.'s essay on Reed in the *Dictionary of Literary Biography* (vol. 33), argues that he really has "no true predecessor or counterpart." For Gates, Reed's situation in the African American literary tradition is both "unique" and "ironic" because the conventions and canonical texts of the tradition itself are the principal targets of Reed's satire. It is crucial to insist, however, that Reed is in no way indulging in a gratuitous put-down of black writers and writings; rather, he is engaged in a project of emancipating an artistic heritage from predictable or predetermined forms and norms imposed by those who fail to fully comprehend the depth and complexity of that heritage, including its folkish inventiveness, hilarious undercurrents, and seasoned extravagances. Reed, in short, uses tradition to illuminate and reinvigorate tradition, combining continuity and improvisation in a cultural dynamic that Amiri *Baraka has astutely dubbed "the changing same."

[*See also* Last Days of Louisiana Red, The; Raven Quickskill; Terrible Twos, The.]

• Neil Schmitz, "Neo-Hoodoo: The Experimental Fiction of Ishmael Reed," *Twentieth Century Literature* 20.2 (Apr. 1974): 126–140. John O'Brien, ed., Juan Goytisolo/Ishmael Reed Issue, *The Review of Contemporary Fiction* 4.2 (Summer 1984): 176–244. Robert Elliot Fox, "Ishmael Reed: Gathering the Limbs of Osiris," in *Conscientious Sorcerers: The Black Postmodernist Fiction of LeRoi Jones/Amiri Baraka, Ishmael Reed, and Samuel R. Delany,* 1987, pp. 39–92. Reginald Martin, *Ishmael Reed and the New Black Aesthetic Critics,* 1988. Daryl Pinckney, "Trickster Tales," *New York Review of Books,* 12 Oct. 1989, 20–24. Kathryn Hume, "Ishmael Reed and the Problematics of Control," *PMLA* 108.3 (May 1993): 506–518. Bruce Dick and Amritjit Singh, eds., *Conversations With Ishmael Reed,* 1995. Robert Elliot Fox, "Blacking the Zero: Toward a Semiotics of Neo-Hoodoo," in *Masters of the Drum: Black Lit/oratures Across the Continuum,* 1995, pp. 49–62.

—Robert Elliot Fox

RELIGION. Informing the *spirituals, the Christian Bible is the Ur-text of African American literature. Religion's prevalence in the literature is largely due to the fact that millions of African Americans know spirituals and the biblical literature they echo. Whether with the high seriousness of Briton *Hammon, Jupiter *Hammon, George Moses *Horton, and Phillis *Wheatley in their respective works, or of Paul Laurence *Dunbar in "We Wear the Mask," or with the humor of Dunbar's "An Antebellum Sermon" and Sterling A. *Brown's "Slim [Greer] in Hell," or with the cynicism of Fenton *Johnson's "The Daily Grind," "The Scarlet Woman," and "Tired," or with the spiritual despair and then possible renewal of self-confidence of Amiri *Baraka's (LeRoi Jones's) *Preface to a Twenty-Volume Suicide Note (1961), or with other persuasions (e.g., skepticism, agnosticism, atheism, existentialism, and nihilism) in the works of many writers in all genres, religion has always abounded in African American literature. However, in the context of repudiating as inappropriate for African American writers all European-based aesthetics, late 1960s *Black Arts movement coleader Larry *Neal defined Judeo-Christian religious assumptions in almost all pre-1960s African American literature as the "Old Spirituality . . . generalized . . . to Universal Humanity," and said that African American art and real-world experience are in need of a "New Spirituality [that] is specific [and] see[s] the world from the" perspective of the oppressed ("The Black Arts Movement," *Drama Review,* Summer 1968). Playwrights whom Neal admires for exhibiting this new spirituality in their plays include Ed *Bullins (*Clara's Ole Man, 1965, and *In the Wine Time,* 1968), Ben *Caldwell (*The Militant Preacher,* 1968), Jimmy Garrett (*We Own the Night,* 1968), and Ron *Milner (*Who's Got His Own,* 1971). Nevertheless, each of these authors depicts characters—sometimes ironically, sometimes blasphemously, sometimes with seeming faithfulness—who use language specific to the Judeo-Christian legacy. The persistent reality is both that African American Christian practices and belief have kept religion significant in the lives of African Americans and that the perversions of Christianity evident in *slavery and racism have been indelibly stamped into the consciousness of African American writers. Therefore the literature contains evidence of the power of religion in the lives of its characters, as well as evidence of religion's absence by its failure to effect justice and love between God's white and black children—all supposedly "made in His image."

Besides distortions of religion in their lives related to white-black interaction, Christian African American literary characters also judge their own standards of appropriate behaviors as "true" children of God, who know that God is good, requires absolute obedience, rewards the faithful who do good, and punishes evil doers—the best exemplar of this type being Margaret *Walker's Vyry in *Jubilee (1966). However, from this point of view, though everyone can ask for and receive forgiveness—even for fornication—God does not excuse hypocrites, which is important for the characters Gabriel and Elizabeth in James *Baldwin's *Go Tell It on the Mountain (1953) and the reason for Maya *Angelou's fear after her courtroom lie in *I Know Why the Caged Bird Sings (1970). And as Christians must teach their children to be good, Momma Henderson must punish Maya in Caged Bird for taking the Lord's name in vain. Because scripture requires that children obey and respect adults, independent thinker Richard *Wright could not avoid conflict in his religiously fundamental home (*Black Boy, 1945). Jesus was once a homeless baby, so whether born in or out of wedlock, children are to be cared for and loved; not to love a child is an offense before both God and Jesus, whose personalities are recognized as very different, notwithstanding the oneness of the triune God. King David rejoiced in the Lord by singing, dancing naked, and playing music loudly; therefore, "feeling the spirit" during worship is normal and expected. In short, religious beliefs of African American Protestant Christian characters are rooted in scriptures understood quite fundamentally and literally, with strong emphases on justice, love, and forgiveness. Some religious characters violate their own religious standards by mistreating their families and others, as illustrated in Chester *Himes's The Third Generation (1954); Baldwin's Go Tell It on the Mountain; Lonne *Elder III's *Ceremonies in Dark Old Men (1969); and Alice *Walker's The *Third Life of Grange Copeland (1970)—among many other possible examples. Religion in African American literature is also manifested by spiritual emptiness and falling away from religious beliefs, as seen in *Beneatha Younger's nonbelief and *Walter Lee Younger's money-mania in Lorraine *Hansberry's A *Raisin in the Sun (1959). In African American literature there is a melding of religion per se with religious and/or spiritual values predicated on personal and collective African American belief that God and Jesus as the Christ actually know, care about, and enter into the everyday lives of believers—God's own chosen children, Christ's own brothers and sisters. Religion in African American literature regularly makes itself felt by scriptural allusions pertinent to its characters. As reflected by many African American literary characters, religion affirms God's permanence and shapes the characters' expectations of, and strides toward, temporal freedom and justice—realizable precisely because God wills such.

Religion in early and some contemporary African American literature is recognizable in authors' descriptions of characters ("Christian" or "God-fearing" or "religious," for example) and in dialogue among characters who claim religious faith, or who renounce religion and/or God, or denounce what they see as spiritual emptiness and the hypocrisy of institutionalized religion. Understandable, therefore, are invocations to God in works by early writers Jupiter Hammon, Olaudah *Equiano (Gustavus Vassa), Phillis Wheatley, Frederick *Douglass, and Harriet A. *Jacobs (Linda Brent). Personae in W. E. B. *Du Bois's poems "The Song of the Smoke" (1899) and "A Litany at Atlanta" (1906) assume the reality of God, God's oneness with black folk, and a powerful God capable of and willing to wreak vengeance upon evil white folk. The second poem suggests a too silent, noncaring God who is "blind . . . deaf . . . and dumb" to the agonies of black people. Persistent and renewed injustices inform the following plays, poems, and novel depicting African American characters questioning God, Jesus, and religious faith: The *Escape, or A Leap for Freedom (William Wells *Brown, 1858); Rachel (Angelina Weld *Grimké, 1916); "The Daily Grind" and "The Old Repair Man" (Fenton Johnson, 1915–1916); "Snapshots of the Cotton South" (Frank Marshall *Davis, 1935–1937); and The *Marrow of Tradition (Charles Waddell *Chesnutt, 1901). Nella *Larsen's *Quicksand (1928) also recognizes a possibly failed God, for it documents the degradation resulting from denial of the self in order to meet standards imposed by religious tradition. Other angry and despairing characters challenge God's existence and ask whether any God would care about black humans.

African American literary characters sometimes identify with Jesus-as-sufferer in order to endure until the ultimate triumph. Countee *Cullen and James Weldon *Johnson use Simon the Cyrenian within an African American tradition of making black the man who helped Jesus carry his heavy cross. In Cullen's poem "Simon the Cyrenian Speaks," Simon says that he had first thought not to carry the cross because his black skin prompted Jesus to try to "place it there." But Simon admired Jesus's "dream," recognized his meekness, pitied him, and thus decided to do for Christ what the power of Rome could not have forced him to do. In *God's Trombones (1927), the persona of Johnson's "The Crucifixion" narrates the life of Jesus, relating that "they laid hold on" Simon and made him bear the cross. "The Judgment Day" memorializes humankind's predilection for disobeying authority and law, and our expectation and fear of retribution. While specifying God's having noticed an ailing "Sister Caroline," whom God instructs Death to "bring to me," the preacher in "Go Down Death—A Funeral Sermon" speaks to all people, for there is "no hiding place," even in unheard-of "Yamacraw" in Savannah, Georgia, an idea projected symphonically in John Edgar *Wideman's 1981 novel Hiding Place.

African American writers concretize the negativity of religion within some of the faithful. Three poems by Cullen suggest the diversity of experienced pain: "Pagan Prayer" recognizes how small is the kinship of "Our Father God, Christ our Brother"; "For a Lady I Know" remarks on social, class, and racial division even in heaven; "The Shroud of Color" describes the relationship of black and white Christians. Two short stories—Langston Hughes's "On the Road" (1934) and Alice Walker's "The Welcome Table" (1966)—

portray each of two African Americans, respectively, after their ejection from white Christian churches; each proceeds to meet and walk home with Jesus—ubiquitous yet not to be found at these churches. Addressing Jesus as "Nigger" and "holy bastard," while silencing Mary as a southern mammy, Hughes's "Christ in Alabama" immortalizes the outrage of caste distinction within the Christian family, for despite becoming one with African American Christians, the atoning white Christ cannot make them acceptable to Anglo-American Christians.

Twentieth-century African American literature also reflects new belief systems, some of which have been inspired by charismatic leaders of movements or nationwide congregations such as Marcus *Garvey and Father Divine—new prophets able to provide racial pride, political and economic visibility, and renewed spiritual hope, as well as relief from material want. Garvey is referenced historically in *The *Autobiography of Malcolm X*, and alluded to in the character *Ras the Destroyer in Ralph *Ellison's *Invisible Man* (1952). In *The *Salt Eaters* (1980) Toni Cade *Bambara includes "Garveyites" as veterans in the 1970s of wars for racial justice. Paule *Marshall renders superbly characters most readers interpret as Father Divine and some followers in *Brown Girl, Brownstones* (1959). Other beliefs involve African American variations on non-Christian religions such as Islam—as seen in the U.S.–based Nation of Islam or Black Muslims, and as heard in such words as "Allah" and "jihad," as well as "Elijah" (for Elijah Muhammad, prophet of the Nation of Islam) and "Mecca," words used notably by poets Amiri Baraka, Sonia *Sanchez, and Jayne *Cortez. Alice Walker's "Roselily" (1973) relates the fearful thoughts of a young unwed Christian mother during her marriage ceremony in Mississippi to a Chicago-based member of the Nation of Islam.

Ras Tafari or Rastafarianism is the Jamaican-rooted belief that Ethiopian King Haile Selassie is God, whose chosen people are black peoples who will inherit the promised land of Ethiopia, defined as Africa. Rastas wear their hair in dreadlocks, as does the centuries-old, multiply incarnated Miss Lissie in Alice Walker's The *Temple of My Familiar* (1989). Also coifed like Rastafarians is Leroy McCullough in Ntozake *Shange's *Sassafrass, Cypress, and Indigo* (1982); a minor character, "the pan man"—possibly an advocate of *Pan-Africanism—in *The Salt Eaters* wears "dreadlocks and [a] knitted cap"; during treatment by a "fabled healer," Vilma imagines herself to be unkempt ("hair matted and dust") and recalls a dream in which she had to survive attack from the "woman with snakes in her hair." *Son Green in Toni *Morrison's *Tar Baby* (1981) seems not to wear dreadlocks but only not to have combed or cut his hair for a long time. Usually not shunning the Jesus of his own Protestant background, but as if seeking more than Christians have allowed that God to be, poet Robert *Hayden references Baha'i ideas and its prophet Bahaullah (whose religion teaches the oneness of all people) in several poems, naming the prophet variously as "The Glorious One," "Godlike imprisoned / One," "veiled / irradiant One,"

"irradiant veiled / terrible One," and "The Most Great Beauty."

Hoodoo (denoting belief and practice of magic expressed in, for example, *conjuring, sorcery, divination, relationships among spiritual forces, and the unusually effective use of herbs to cure, kill, control behavior, etc., also called root-worker or root-doctor skills) and the syncretic monotheistic religion Santeria sometimes seem to be conflated in African American literature in order to sustain African-based spiritual ties among all created things and beings, and to have access to powers and wisdom beyond that afforded by rationality. "Santeria" literally means the worship of saints, in particular, Catholic saints who have become identified as the pantheon of deities or orishas created by the Yoruba god Oloddumare as manifestations of his will, expressions of his essence in nature, and as humankind's guides and protectors. Hoodoo's full power and mysteries are evoked in "David, the Prophet," the root doctor whom Min beseeches in Ann *Petry's The *Street* (1946). Occurrences of Santeria itself in African American literary characters and atmosphere include many passages throughout *Sassafrass*. Several Cortez poems in *Poetic Magnetic* (1991) contain language associated with magic. Especially memorable in Arna *Bontemps's *Black Thunder* (1936), Alice Walker's "The Revenge of Hannah Kemhuff" (1973), Bambara's The *Salt Eaters*, and Gloria *Naylor's *Mama Day* (1988) is the powerful belief in root workers. Chapter 11 of Bambara's novel brings together several African-based—and now Caribbean- and South American–entrenched—religions understood by various characters to empower them. The real-world experience of a baby's being born with a caul over its face is accepted by some characters (who view the event as spiritual, not a hoodoo belief) as a sign that the baby is "link[ed] with . . . all kinds of powers that [others] don't have," and that the person will be able to see ghosts—all because "God has touched . . . [the baby] in the womb" (Tina McElroy *Ansa, *Baby of the Family*, 1989). "Good serpent of the sky" describes Damballah, Haitian voodoo god and name of John Edgar Wideman's 1981 novel that incorporates African-based beliefs and gods and African American Christian beliefs. Damballah glides throughout *Sassafrass*. In her poem "Kai Kai (For The Poets)," Cortez refers to Damballah as a god of fertility, and many of the poem's words suggest shaman's supplies for effecting life changes by unusual powers—here a "traditional medicinal recipe" against assassination. Frequently performed by Cortez to music with strong drumming, her poems contain quasi-religious language—"ancestral," "praise," "messiahs," "scriptures," and "conjuration"—that revivifies precolonial Africa to effect a closeness of old gods and the ancestors whom Cortez invokes as protection.

Toni Morrison also makes use of hoodoo in her work. *Pilate Dead's root-working in *Song of Solomon* (1977) helps make Ruth irresistible to Macon, who impregnates her with Milkman; Pilate's power also prevents Macon from causing Ruth to abort Milkman. The names "First Corinthians" and

"Magdalene" in *Song of Solomon* convey religion less powerfully than do intimations of pervasive and powerful spiritual forces in all of Morrison's novels, especially **Beloved* (1987), in which a human spirit persists in making itself felt even beyond the grave. Deeply religious Miranda of Naylor's *Mama Day* practices Christianity and understands the magic of roots, poisons, and their antidotes, as well as the spiritual powers of the natural world. Willing George to assume a less-than-rational role in her efforts to save Cocoa's life, Miranda prays, "Whatever Your name is, help him." Trying to keep Kaine alive, in Sherley Anne Williams's **Dessa Rose* (1986), *Dessa Rose calls "all the names I know . . . Lawd, Legba, Jesus, Conqueroo." ([E]legba is a divine trickster linguist of Nigeria, the spirit of communication between all spheres; Conqueroo is a powerful conjuring root named for Big John de Conquerer, a legendary African American folk hero, also called High John de Conquer.) Permeating much African American literature is an element of spirituality found in characters (such as Miss Lissie in *The Temple of My Familiar*) who can access spirits and ancestral and cultural powers rooted in a people's beginnings and connected through universally available creative forces. Some of these characters celebrate and are inspired by the spiritual power and physical survival of slave ancestors, for example—the feelings of the respective personae in Lance **Jeffers's poem "On Listening to the Spirituals" and James Weldon Johnson's "O Black and Unknown Bards."

In Ansa's novel *Ugly Ways* (1993), various tropes of religion in contemporary African American literature appear as if on a continuum of ignored distinctions, a flattening or conflation of all the acculturated verbal legacy. The oldest daughter rejects "New Age bullshit" but interprets as "higher power" the effects of the mother's helpful advice to her daughters. The three young daughters were once fearful enough to pray for protection from "God, the towering white-bearded God." They believe that their mother has "hexed" them with "bizarre voodoo rituals." One character refers to a "burnt offering to Yemaya, . . . Yoruba goddess of the womb." Emily scorns what she perceives as her mother's hypocritically intoning, "Well, Lord" as if the mother "and the Lord were . . . close." Her menses late, Annie Ruth had gone to chapel and "prayed so hard that her period had miraculously started." Ansa's projection exists in tension with Langston Hughes's deeply felt but at once reverent, fearful, penitent, humorous, humble, ironic, and blasphemous "Feet of Jesus" section of *Selected Poems* (1959) and Lucille **Clifton's "Some Jesus" poems (1972). Baldwin's characters feel profoundly, agonizingly, their kinship with, longing to know, or fear of God. (Trudier Harris's *Black Women in the Fiction of James Baldwin*, 1985, helps in understanding religion in his work.) Contrasting Baldwin's narrational and expository works epitomizing Christian religious content in African American literature, Ansa's novel seems to define religion in African American literature as allusional games.

Tropes of religion will continue to appear in African American literature. Writers born before the mid-1950s will probably appropriate newer as well as the oldest traditions. Such a writer is Quincy **Troupe, whose newer poems acknowledge several religious traditions: Baldwin is a "wordsaint"; a singer is a "root doctor" who knows how to "hoodoo down," and the poem assumes the source of spiritual power to be ancestral. Somewhat younger poet Paul Beatty also uses several traditions to denote religion. The four poems "Princess Cruises," "Malibu Yuletide," "New York Newsday: Truth, Justice, and Vomit," and "Twix. Caramel, Not Peanut Butter," for example, contain significant religious language. Additionally, Beatty uses "rastas [Rastafarians]," six of the opening seven words of the Lord's Prayer, and the often-heard greetings used by members of the Nation of Islam, "asalaam" and "alaikum" (*Big Bank Take Little Bank*, 1991). Octavia E. **Butler's narrator in *Parable of the Sower* (1993) acknowledges early that she thinks a lot about "the idea of God" but that hers has a name different from all three that denote "that God." These examples, just few among scores within contemporary African American works, proclaim that religion in African American literature is important and highly visible.

Religion permeates not the earliest written literature by an African American (slave Lucy **Terry's 25 August 1746 twenty-eight line "Bars Fight"), but the earliest African American oral literature—the spirituals, informed by the Old and New Testaments and often first in the syllabi of college teachers of African American literature. Since the end of their legal enslavement, African Americans have grown up hearing, singing, and having their psyches and consciences shaped by the spirituals, as well as by hymns and gospels in their religious services, although some later disavow Christianity as a "slave religion" and lapse into agnosticism or atheism or profess a new or different old religion. Few African American literary characters, therefore, would seem credible without being shown to have or to have had some experience with this music. A writer evoking this music also evokes religion. None does so more brilliantly than Richard Wright, whom Richard Yarborough accurately interprets as respectful of the cultural significance of African American religion and religious music but scornful of their efficacy to achieve political, economic, and other dimensions of equality for African Americans. For example, Big Boy and his buddies in "Big Boy Leaves Home" sing the spiritual "Dis Train Boun fer Glory" in response to hearing the whistle of a northbound train. But while this 1930s melding of the secular and the religious continues the slave-era code-song utility of some spirituals, Wright renders this cultural retention as poignancy—not the power of escape efforts via the **Underground Railroad to which selected slaves were called by, for example, "Swing Low, Sweet Chariot" and "Steal Away." Hence Sarah's agonized cry "'Naw, Gawd!'" at the end of "Long Black Song" might be understood as a religious wail metamorphosed into blues-idiom musical signature of the African American characters in **Uncle Tom's Children* (1938)—including the Reverend Taylor of "Fire and Cloud" and Sue of "Bright and Morning Star," together with the "twelve million" African Americans ("Negroes") of *Native Son* (1940), and *Bigger Thomas, who rejects a crucifix inspirited by a flaming Ku Klux Klan cross. But for most African American writers, the spirituals ameliorate this recurring nightmare.

The first African American belles lettres were composed by two unrelated slaves surnamed Hammon and published in 1760 in Boston, Massachusetts, and Long Island, New York, respectively. Briton Hammon's *Narrative* invokes God in a brief preface and in the last two paragraphs of the fourteen-page work, and ends with the persona's call upon all to "exalt" and "praise the Lord for His Goodness" and gifts to humankind. Composed on Christmas day, the eighty-eight lines of Jupiter Hammon's poem "An Evening Thought: Salvation by Christ with Penitential Cries" are filled with acknowledgment of, praise and honor to, trust in the power of, and certainty of redemption by Christ. Scholar-critic Sondra Ann O'Neale establishes Hammon's literary and historical significance among all African American writers who affirm both Christianity and freedom, saying that all his work resonates with biblical references and theological meaning brilliant in artistry and in their necessarily and creatively veiled slavery protests and demands for justice. O'Neale's landmark work is vital also to understanding the combined religious and political seriousness of other writers whom she discusses, including Phillis Wheatley, Olaudah Equiano (Gustavus Vassa), Harriet Jacobs (Linda Brent), George Moses Horton, and Frederick Douglass. This illuminating study should help future readers of these and other early African American writers (belletrists, as well as preachers, historians, journalists, and pamphleteers) to recognize, understand, and appreciate, first, those African American writers' literary expressions of religious fervor together with, and as contexts for, political protests for freedom and social justice; and, second, how ingrained in African American writers and their literature are the general ideas of a personal God of love who rewards acts of virtue, who "don't like ugly," and who will therefore eventually punish sinners.

Pre–Civil War African American literary texts with religious themes accommodate easily, naturally, and often with astonishing power the authors' widely diverse subjects addressed in many rhetorical forms: addresses and speeches, *oratory, *sermons and preaching, petitions and pamphlets; organizational laws, resolutions, and constitutions; letters, confessionals, and spiritual autobiographies. These literary pioneers pondered, explained, exhorted, and demonstrated that their sisters and brothers should seek education—intellectual, mechanical, moral, and spiritual—and improvement in all spheres of human development, help each other to survive materially and to advance socially and politically, think seriously about whether to emigrate (to Africa or Canada) or to remain in the United States, support abolition of the slave trade, repent criminal behavior, and cultivate their creative talent in "narratives, poems, and essays." Represented in Dorothy Porter's anthology (*Early Negro Writing*, 1971), Maria W. *Stewart, Benjamin *Banneker, Absalom Jones,

David *Ruggles, and Jarena *Lee are among many previously little-known African American writers who address religion in their work. Dozens more, including David Walker, William Wells Brown, Frances Ellen Watkins *Harper, and Sojourner *Truth (whose speeches were transcribed, as she never learned to write), all refer to God or Jesus or "Saviour" or heaven; all subscribe to religion and religious belief as sources of spiritual strength and morality. No writers question this despite their different social experiences and political persuasions. Moreover, "man's"—humankind's—potential, "his greater glory" as a "child of God," contextualizes most of whatever repentance and forgiveness appear in the literature: repentance by African Americans and by Anglo-Americans, forgiveness by African Americans of Anglo-American violations of "the brotherhood" of humankind, and (until the late 1960s) refusal by almost all African American characters to accept comfortably or rationalize any required killing of their white oppressors; to seek revenge for the oppressive acts of whites; or to descend in human relationships to the depths of Anglo-American depravity. Thus Frederick Douglass judges but does not hate slaveholder Auld or overseer Covey (*Narrative of the Life of Frederick Douglass, An American Slave*, 1845); Harriet E. *Wilson's *Frado does not hate even the worst Bellmont (*Our Nig*, 1859); Iola hates no one (Frances Ellen Watkins Harper's *Iola Leroy*, 1892), and neither does Belton Piedmont in *Imperium in Imperio* (Sutton E. *Griggs, 1899). Based on the writings of scores of early African American poets, narrators of autobiography and fiction, playwrights, essayists, and journalists, the axiom is established that strength is cultivated by, or exhibited in, Christian character. These early writers also reveal that some Christians practice racism and other forms of hypocrisy and oppression, as illustrated by three examples from the mid-1800s.

Notwithstanding their near absence from the Bellmont family, Wilson's Frado in *Our Nig* grows in the Christian virtues, including love, patience, hope, and perseverance. The adult son James Bellmont encourages Aunt Abby to teach Frado the ways of "the *Saviour*" so that she might have a glad, quiet heart, and be "sustained by *His* presence"; James attributes to Frado "elements in her heart" that "the gospel" would "transform . . . and purif[y]." In Frank J. *Webb's 1857 novel *The Garies and Their Friends*, a white "distinguished clergyman," Dr. Blackly, justifies his refusal to perform the marriage of Anglo-American Clarence Garie and the mulatto Emily by his belief in "the negro race['s]" having been "marked . . . by . . . God for servitude." James Monroe *Whitfield's persona in the 1853 poem "America" laments a slave's abduction from Africa, and his having been "stripped of . . . rights" given by "Nature's God" to all humans.

Eighty-five years after Whitfield's lament, the first two stories in *Uncle Tom's Children* memorialize suffering African American characters inclined not to kill or unable to kill the oppressor: Big Boy of "Big Boy Leaves Home" does not kill wantonly or even confidently; Wright denies to good, albeit conscripted, samaritan Mann of "Down by the Riverside" the fulfillment of his panic-inspired idea to kill a white child who has witnessed Mann's self-defense shooting of the boy's father. Instead Wright creates an epically heroic person—born "nigger" but a family and community protector now recognized as a Herculean black-male-become-a-"Mann" incapable of child-killing. The remaining three stories of *Uncle Tom's Children* establish this volume's pivotal role. Wright preserves the religious legacy of prayer, calling God's name in crises and singing religious songs, but the characters add revenge, social activism, and planned homicide to their respective self-understandings. On the horizon were cataclysmic characterological changes in African American literature: Bigger Thomas in Wright's own *Native Son* (1940) and Cross Damon in *The Outsider* (1953) for example; cannibalistic Boatwright in John A. *Williams's The *Man Who Cried I Am* (1967), as well as personae in novels, short stories, poems, and plays by some younger-generation writers also not willing for their characters—despite religious backgrounds —to achieve moral victories only.

One of religion's oldest questions—whether it can be right to kill another person for any reason—is pondered by Meridian in Alice Walker's 1976 novel of the same name. Meridian's reflections occur during a church service filled with traditional singing by African Americans seeking solace from the world's pain. She decides that she could kill if she had to. Criddle the stable boy in *Black Thunder* believes that his murdering a white farmer is necessary and justified by the freedom sought through Gabriel Prosser's planned slave rebellion. "Cause I can," replies Dessa in *Dessa Rose* when asked why she, together with other runaway slaves, kills white folks, although the novel convinces most readers that its depiction of a new humanity outweighs the homicides. The just God of religion ever-present in African American literature allows slaves to kill their enslavers.

Religion abounds in voluminous African American literature contextualized by all subjects relevant to all U.S. citizens, including racism, complicated by, for example, ecological destruction and nondiscriminatory, incurable lethal viruses. A fully commissioned study of religion in African American literature would require research into at least the belles lettres of all African American authors since 1760. Documented where found in each piece of African American literature would be every ideational, situational, geographical, descriptive, dialogical, characterological, and linguistic evidence deemed to be an attestation to religion or religious beliefs and assumptions, as well as to spiritual values.

[*See also* Autobiography, *article on* Spiritual Autobiography; Churches; Preachers and Deacons.]

• W. E. B. Du Bois, "Of the Sorrow Songs," *The Souls of Black Folk*, 1903. James Weldon Johnson and Rosamond Johnson, *The Books of American Negro Spirituals*, 1969. George Eaton Simpson, *Religious Cults of the Caribbean*, 1970. John Lovell, Jr., *Black Song*, 1972. Howard Thurman, *Deep River* (1945; rpt. 1955) and *The Negro Spiritual Speaks of Life and Death* (1947), bound together, 1975. Wyatt T. Walker, *Somebody's Calling My Name*, 1979. Luisah Teish, *Jambalaya: The Natural Woman's Book of Personal Charms and Practices*, 1985.

James H. Evans, *Spiritual Empowerment in Afro-American Literature: Frederick Douglass, Rebecca Jackson, Booker T. Washington, Richard Wright, Toni Morrison*, 1987. Sue E. Houchins, introduction to *Spiritual Narratives*, 1988. Migene Gonzalez-Wippler, *Santeria: The Religion*, 1989. James H. Cone, *The Spirituals and the Blues*, 1972; rpt. 1992. Sondra Ann O'Neale, *Jupiter Hammon and the Biblical Beginnings of African American Literature*, 1993.

—Agnes Moreland Jackson

REMOND, CHARLES LENOX (1810–1873), antislavery orator. One of the leading African American orators of the antebellum era, Charles Lenox Remond was born free in Salem, Massachusetts, where his comparatively prosperous parents were able to give him an education. In 1838, his talents earned him the distinction of being the first black man appointed a lecturer for the Massachusetts Anti-Slavery Society. Despite often hostile audiences and an unrelenting travel and speaking schedule, Remond faithfully fulfilled his duty, advocating immediate and unconditional emancipation for African Americans and serving as a public example of black intellectual achievement.

At the age of thirty, Remond sailed to London to represent the American abolitionist movement at the World's Anti-Slavery Convention. Discovering that the American female delegation was required to sit in the rear gallery of the convention auditorium, Remond joined William Lloyd Garrison and two other male American delegates who moved to the rear gallery in solidarity with the women. Hailed by enthusiastic listeners in England, Scotland, and Ireland, Remond remained abroad for nineteen months.

Remond also lent his support to civil rights activism in the northern United States. Invited in 1842 to address a legislative committee of the Massachusetts House of Representatives, Remond lectured the committee on the injustice of *Jim Crow in public conveyances. In the 1850s and 1860s he lent his support to efforts to abolish segregated public schools in Massachusetts. During the Civil War he served as an enlistment agent for the 54th Massachusetts Regiment. After the abolition of *slavery, Remond campaigned for universal suffrage, irrespective of color or sex.

Although Remond the speaker was highly respected in his own time, his reputation as an intellectual leader has been eclipsed by Frederick *Douglass, William Wells *Brown, and other contemporary African Americans who turned to writing as a means of articulating their individuality and extending their intellectual influence.

[*See also* Antislavery Movement; Oratory.]

• Vernon Loggins, *The Negro Author*, 1931.

—William L. Andrews

RENA WALDEN, the stately, beautiful, and light-complexioned mulatta heroine of Charles Waddell *Chesnutt's *The *House Behind the Cedars* (1900), attempts to pass for white in the Reconstruction South only to see her secret inadvertently revealed and her young life cut tragically short. In certain ways an alter ego for Chesnutt himself (who was light enough to pass but chose not to), Rena embodies the aspirations and frustrations of those African Americans barred by the *color line from the social, intellectual, and economic rewards available to "pure" whites. In comparison to her brother John, a *mulatto who has passed successfully for ten years, Rena also illustrates the special constraints on the mobility of African American women, as her prospects appear limited to those conferred by *marriage. Although Rena's own limitations—particularly her lack of imagination—may contribute to her downfall, she is in general more sympathetically portrayed as an innocent woman punished for the sins of her African American mother and white father. Yet Rena is no mere pathetic symbol of the supposed destructiveness of interracial sexuality. Despite her tragic end, at the close of the novel Rena is earnestly (if belatedly) sought by her former white fiancé, who has struggled to rid himself of his preconceptions about racial mixing. Rena's tale thus partially transcends the late-nineteenth-century conventions of the "tragic mulatto" formula and in so doing anticipates the powerful explorations of *passing and assimilation in the works of such later writers as James Weldon *Johnson, Jessie Redmon *Fauset, and Nella *Larsen.

• William L. Andrews, *The Literary Career of Charles W. Chesnutt*, 1980. SallyAnn H. Ferguson, "Rena Walden: Chesnutt's Failed 'Future American,'" *Southern Literary Journal* 15 (Fall 1982): 74–82.   —William A. Gleason

RESEARCH CENTERS. *See* Libraries and Research Centers.

RICHARDSON, WILLIS (1889–1977), playwright, director, teacher, magazine contributor, and government worker, began writing during the Harlem Renaissance. Willis Richardson's interest in the *theater was encouraged when he viewed a production of Angelina Weld *Grimké's *Rachel* and by his belief that African American life was richer in theme and character than was being portrayed on the stage in *musicals, comedies, and "serious" plays by whites. These were limited to stereotypical roles and one-dimensional representations. Added to this, theatrical groups were without plays by African American writers. With Richardson, all of this changed.

He began to write one-act plays; his early plays presented heroes such as Crispus Attacks, Antonio Maceo, and Simon the Cyrenian for children's edification and were published in *The *Brownie's Book*. In 1920, he published his first adult play, *The Deacon's Awakening*, in the *Crisis*. In 1923, he became the first African American playwright to have a nonmusical production on Broadway: *The Chip Woman's Fortune*; and in 1924 with *Mortgaged*, the first African American playwright produced by the Howard players. Richardson was the first to win the drama contest established by W. E. B. *Du Bois in the pages of the *Crisis* to encourage and extend African American theater; Richardson won with his *Broken Banjo, A Folk Tragedy* (1925) and again with *The Bootblack Lover* (1926). In these plays and others

(he wrote more than thirty), he presented the everyday African American and such concerns as *manhood, *family, middle-class behavior, and intraracial relations.

His recognition of the need for a national theater that would serve as a testing ground and an outlet for drama by and about African Americans and his belief that the theater should serve as a vehicle for education anticipated the *Black Aesthetic of the 1960s. His work increased the quantity and quality of African American drama. Even more, as playwright and director, he was influential in high school, college, and community African American theater groups. His plays provided production material for such groups as the Krigwa Players, the Ethiopian Art Players, and the Gilpin Players. Richardson also made plays accessible to theatrical groups and students by editing three anthologies over his lifetime: *Plays and Pageants from the Life of the Negro* (1930); *Negro History in Thirteen Plays* (1935), coedited by May Miller and including five of his history plays; and *The King's Dilemma and Other Plays for Children* (1956), containing six of his plays. These represent only a portion of his published works. He has unpublished plays at the Schomburg and Howard University libraries.

Richardson was the most prolific and recognized African American playwright of the 1920s; in addition to the prizes awarded by the *Crisis*, he won the Spingarn award, the Public School Prize in 1926, and the Edith Schwarb Cup from Yale University in 1928. He continues to be anthologized and recognized: Wilmington, North Carolina, his birthplace, established the Willis Richardson Players, a community group, in 1974, and his work is part of the Hatch-Billops Collection at City College, New York.

• Bernard L. Peterson, Jr., "An Evaluation—Willis Richardson: Pioneer Playwright," *Black World* 26 (Apr. 1975): 40–48, 86–88. Patsy B. Perry, "Willis Richardson," in *DLB*, vol. 51, *Afro-American Writers from the Harlem Renaissance to 1940*, ed. Trudier Harris, 1987, pp. 236–244.

—Helen R. Houston

RINEHART. Bliss Proteus Rinehart, a con artist in Ralph *Ellison's *Invisible Man* (1952), takes his middle name from the sea god Proteus, who had the power to assume many different shapes and disguises in order to elude those who would capture him and compel him to answer their questions. Like his namesake, Rinehart assumes many disguises: "Rine the [numbers] runner and Rine the gambler and Rine the briber and Rine the lover and Rinehart the Reverend." Ellison maintains that Rinehart's major function is to provide a mode of escape for the narrator. In truth, like Joseph Conrad's Lord Jim, everyone talks about Rinehart, but no one ever sees him. He is the *trickster par excellence.

Despite the fact that Rinehart never appears physically he is a powerful force in the novel because he represents a particular type of male. His first name, Bliss, his big hat, his dark shades, his Cadillac, his zoot suit, and his jive talk suggest a ghetto-specific culture that has always been associated with the Black males of America's inner cities. But in these stereotypical images of Black men Ellison sees the possibility of *freedom and growth. The narrator, through his education and his association with the Brotherhood, has been molded into a being still limited in his vision of himself and his universe, still limited in recognizing the potential of Blacks. Rinehart represents chaos, but he also represents freedom and growth. Through Rinehart, Ellison suggests that there are both negative and positive aspects of all cultural traditions and that instead of rejecting those traditions because we do not understand them or because they are outside of the traditional value system, we should embrace them and make them a part of the traditional culture. Through Rinehart, Ellison suggests that Blacks should not forget or deny their culture, their experience, their history.

—Ralph Reckley, Sr.

RITUALS. *See* Festivals; Performances and Pageants.

River Niger, The. Joseph A. *Walker's *The River Niger* (1973) is the dramatic emblem of an important era in African American theater and literary history. The renowned Negro Ensemble Company first produced the play, which was to become its biggest hit, Off-Broadway in 1972. The play then moved on to Broadway, continuing to draw large crowds and rave reviews. It won numerous awards, including the Drama Desk Award for best playwright, a Tony Award for best play, an Obie Award, a Burns Mantle Theatre Yearbook selection as best play, and an Audelco Black Theatre Recognition Award. In addition, Douglas Turner *Ward and Roxie Roker both won Obies for their performances. In 1976 the play was adapted as a full-length feature film.

Although white viewers and critics received the play warmly, finding a certain "universality" of characters and themes with which to identify, it was the response of African American theatergoers that truly marked and measured the play's significance. For the first time African Americans comprised the majority of the ticket-buying audience, lending unanimous praise and major financial support to the world-class production. What they found unique and satisfying in Walker's play were realistic portrayals of working-class characters struggling with what it meant to be African Americans in contemporary society. And, despite the violence of the plot, Walker's script incorporated a poetry representative of the *Black Aesthetic of the time, which inspired audiences with pride and hope.

Like Walker's previous work, *The River Niger* addressed the dilemma of "the black man," a figure struggling to assert his *manhood in the face of racism, violence, impending poverty, alcoholism, and the problematic women in his life. Although Walker has said that his own father's ghost haunted all of his work, this realistic play is especially autobiographical. The air force dropout son and the alcoholic poet father in *The River Niger* are modeled after Walker and his own father, and the stoic, cancer-stricken mother is taken from the playwright's family as well.

In the play, set in Harlem, the two heroic men, sur-

rounded by a predominantly supportive group of women relations and a divided male group, struggle with and against each other to determine the site and means of revolution. John, the father, finds meaning, joy, pride, and resistance primarily through his poetry. The son, Jeff, has tried integration, playing the "Super Culludguy," but now, turning instead to search for a racially identified integrity and self-possession, he walks the line between his father's artistry and his friends' militancy.

Although *The River Niger* continues to be viewed as a landmark of African American theater history, it is not without its historical limitations. It has drawn negative criticism more recently for its treatment of gender and sexuality, for instance. It seems that some of the very factors that contributed to its success in the 1970s—the valorization of "the [heterosexual] black man" at the expense of gay and female African Americans—are what might make it somewhat dated and troubling decades later. The play remains significant, however, as a theatrical and cultural icon of African American life in the 1970s.

• Maurice Peterson, "Taking Off With Joseph Walker," *Essence*, Apr. 1974, 55, 74, 78, 82. Clark Taylor, "In the Theater of Soul," *Essence*, Apr. 1975, 48–49. Anthony Barthelemy, "Mother, Sister, Wife: A Dramatic Perspective," *Southern Review* 21.3 (Summer 1985): 770–785.

—Sheila Hassell Hughes

RIVERS, CONRAD KENT (1933–1968), poet, fiction writer, and dramatist. In 1951, when he was in high school, Conrad Kent Rivers won the Savannah State Poetry Prize for his poem "Poor Peon." In 1959, when he was a senior at Wilberforce University, his first book of *poetry, *Perchance to Dream, Othello*, was published. The collection, which features a series of conversations with Othello, Harlem, and the United States, probes racism, alienation, and death—themes that would also dominate his later works. Rivers attended graduate school at Chicago Teacher's College and Indiana University, and taught high school in Chicago and in Gary, Indiana, all the while publishing poems in periodicals such as the *Antioch Review*, *Negro Digest*, *Ohio Poetry Review*, and *Kenyon Review*. Rivers is generally considered a poet of the *Black Aesthetic and his concern with issues such as racism and *violence, black history and black pride, self-love and self-respect are part and parcel of that movement. However, he was also fascinated with traditional poetic forms and techniques and his work evidences the influence of established writers such as his uncle Ray McIvers, James Weldon *Johnson, Langston *Hughes, Richard *Wright, and James *Baldwin. The title of his second book of poems, *These Black Bodies and This Sunburnt Face* (1962), alludes to William Blake and continues the intertextual conversations begun in his first. The poems in *Dusk at Selma* (1965) and *The Still Voice of Harlem* (1968) demonstrate increasing artistry; however, Rivers died a few weeks before the fourth volume appeared. According to Paul Breman, who published *The Wright Poems* (1972), a posthumous collection of poems Rivers wrote about or dedicated to Richard Wright, Rivers authored several *short stories and a play about Paul Laurence *Dunbar that still await "the sympathetic hand of a publisher or producer."

• Eugene B. Redmond, *Drumvoices: The Mission of Afro-American Poetry: A Critical History,* 1976. Edwin L. Coleman II, "Conrad Kent Rivers," in *DLB,* vol. 41, *Afro-American Poets since 1955,* eds. Trudier Harris and Thadious M. Davis, 1985, pp. 282–286.
—Frances Smith Foster

ROBESON, PAUL (1898–1976), influential African American singer, actor, and social activist. Paul Robeson was born in Princeton, New Jersey, and was the child of a clergyman who had been born a slave. After winning a scholarship competition, Robeson attended Rutgers University, distinguishing himself as both scholar and athlete. While at Rutgers he augmented his scholarship income by offering concerts and dramatic performances. After graduating from Columbia Law School in 1923, Robeson turned to dramatic and musical *theater where he became internationally celebrated. His roles in Eugene O'Neill's *All God's Chillun Got Wings* (1924) and *Emperor Jones* (1924 in New York and 1925 in London) catapulted him to prominence as a serious actor when opportunities for African Americans on stage were generally limited to the comic or to racist *stereotypes. Robeson's performances in productions of Shakespeare, particularly *Othello,* were enormously popular and won him enthusiastic critical acclaim.

Robeson was always acutely conscious of the complex racial politics of the American scene (even as early as his Rutgers years). From the mid-1930s on Robeson became increasingly interested in *Communism, particularly as it seemed to speak to the plight of African Americans. In this respect, the trajectory of Robeson's life mirrors that of many African American artists and intellectuals, such as Richard *Wright and Ralph *Ellison. Robeson's interest in radical politics deepened over the years, even as it limited his opportunities to perform. This limitation became especially pronounced in the early 1950s, given the advent of explicit conflict between the United States and the Soviet Union. Unlike Wright, who renounced Communism in favor of a more generalized anticolonialism, Robeson continued his interest in the politics of Communism, bringing him into conflict with the government of the United States, which revoked his passport (in 1950), though it was restored in 1958. Robeson spent the latter years of his life in ill health, living in Europe and later in the United States.

• Paul Robeson, *Here I Stand,* 1958. Martin Duberman, *Paul Robeson,* 1988.
—Theodore O. Mason, Jr.

ROBINSON, JACKIE (1919–1972), athlete and autobiographer. Jack Roosevelt Robinson was born in 1919 in Cairo, Georgia, and grew up in Pasadena, California. He was a star athlete in high school and junior college before becoming an athletic legend at the University of California at Los Angeles from 1939 to 1941, playing football, baseball, basketball, and competing in track and field. He joined the army in

1942 and was discharged as a lieutenant in 1945 after breaking a white bus driver's jaw in a disagreement about moving to the back of the bus.

Robinson was selected by Branch Rickey, general manager of the Brooklyn Dodgers, to become the first African American to play Major League baseball in the twentieth century. Entering the big leagues in 1947, Robinson had to abide by an agreement he made with Rickey not to be provoked to retaliation by taunts from white players and fans. Robinson endured racial epithets shouted by opposing players and patrons, segregated hotel and restaurant accommodations, balls thrown at his head by opposing pitchers, spiking incidents by opposing runners, volumes of hate mail, and a threatened strike by some white players including several on his own team. Nontheless, he performed brilliantly in the field and earned Rookie-of-the-Year honors in 1947. During his nine years with the Dodgers, Robinson also won a Most Valuable Player award and a batting title. He was elected to baseball's Hall of Fame in 1962.

Robinson's influence can be most easily seen in the film persona of Sidney Poitier in the 1950s and 1960s, who tended to play black characters who were forced to function under great pressure and stress in the white world, maintaining his dignity and poise while pacifistically revealing his contempt when he is mistreated. Robinson's behavior in his first few years in the big leagues became the model, along with Gandhi, for the nonviolent civil rights marchers in the 1950s and 1960s. Robinson died in 1972 at the age of fifty-three. Many believe that what he endured in his days as a player took a dramatic toll on his health. Robinson coauthored several *autobiographies including *Breakthrough to the Big Leagues* (with Alfred Duckett), published in 1965; *Jackie Robinson: My Own Story* (with black sportswriter Wendell Smith), published in 1948; and *I Never Had It Made* (with Alfred Duckett), published in 1974.
—Gerald Early

ROBINSON, SUGAR RAY (1921–1989), professional boxer. World welterweight champion and five times world middleweight champion, bon vivant, stylish dresser, night club owner, believed by many to be pound-for-pound the best boxer in the history of the sport, Sugar Ray Robinson, more than any other black public figure between World War II and the 1960s, epitomized black masculinity and the cool. He was unquestionably the most admired black male among African American males in the 1950s.

Born Walker Smith in Detroit on 3 May 1921, he borrowed the amateur card of a friend, Ray Robinson, and was known under that name for the rest of his life. "Sugar" was the signifying acknowledgment of the refulgence of his grace and overall athletic ability. With his processed hair, his smooth moves (he danced professionally for a time), his defiance of the Mob when he refused to "carry" Jake LaMotta in their sixth fight, his silk shirts, his apolitical aplomb, Robinson strikingly melded the personas of the street or underworld Negro, the working class black, and the gifted, aloof artist, representing a sense of the hip black male elegance and tough poise that was widely admired. Certainly, Norman Mailer had Robinson in mind for some portions of his 1957 essay, "The White Negro," just as Albert *Murray must have been thinking of him in certain parts of his 1970 book, *The Omni-Americans*. Ralph *Ellison surely had him in mind in describing the three cool-walking black boys with conked hair in his 1952 novel *Invisible Man*. It was not until the rise of Muhammad *Ali in the middle 1960s and the new era of Black Power and African American militancy that Robinson's influence as a major African American cultural icon began to fade, tarnished, in part, by his lack of political engagement. Robinson died on 12 April 1989 in Culver City, California, after a lengthy bout with Alzheimer's disease. With Dave Anderson, he coauthored *Sugar Ray*, an *autobiography published in 1970.

—Gerald Early

RODGERS, CAROLYN M. (b. 1945), poet, short-fiction writer, literary critic, and lecturer. A Chicago native, Carolyn Marie Rodgers was influenced artistically in young adulthood by Gwendolyn *Brooks and by the Organization of Black African Culture, a writers' group concerned with articulating the *Black Aesthetic. In the late 1960s, she emerged from the *Black Arts movement in Chicago as one of the "revolutionary poets" who created a profoundly black poetry in terms of language, technique, and theme.

Her early poems, collected in *Paper Soul* (1968), *2 Love Raps* (1969), and *Songs of a Black Bird* (1969), deal with her advocacy of African American cultural revolution and with the conflicts between militancy and the traditional African American life that nurtured her. Her identity as an African American female poet is also a prominent concern in these poems, particularly as she tries to reconcile complex relationships between mothers and daughters and men and women. Attempting to break away from the conventional forms, especially those considered appropriate for female poets, she uses a "hip" style that consists of free-verse form and street language, and that also features nonstandard structure, spelling, capitalization, and punctuation. There is some feeling that her work has been underappreciated because of criticism by the revolutionary male poets whose dominant positions in the Black Arts movement gave credence to their public devaluation of her uncommon poetic style.

Rodgers's mature and more accomplished poetry appears in two later volumes, *how i got ovah: New and Selected Poems* (1975) and *The Heart as Ever Green* (1978). These poems deal with feminist issues, especially the act of defining self. Many are autobiographical, portraying a militant woman who has begun to question the revolution and her relationship to it, and who now embraces her mother and the church as the solid foundations in her life. The issue guiding the latter collection, expressed metaphorically in the title, is that the freedom to grow and create, particularly for the woman and poet of African descent, is a feasible reality. Her latest volumes of poetry include *Translation* (1980) and *Eden and Other Poems* (1983).

The same insight and searching analysis that distinguish her poetry are integral to Rodgers's short fiction and her literary criticism. She portrays in her short fiction the ordinary and overlooked people in everyday African American life and emphasizes the theme of survival. Many consider her critical *essay "Black Poetry—Where It's At" (1969) to be the best essay on the work of the "new black poets." In it, she aesthetically evaluates contemporary African American poetry and sets up preliminary criteria of appraisal.

Although her reputation rests on her militant poetry of the late 1960s, Rodgers has continued to write, progressively moving from militant liberationist to religious believer. She holds a bachelor's degree from Roosevelt University and a master's degree in English from the University of Chicago. She has taught writing in colleges across the country, and has continued to publish *poetry in magazines and *anthologies.

• Bettye J. Parker-Smith, "Running Wild in Her Soul: The Poetry of Carolyn Rodgers," in *Black Women Writers (1950–1980): A Critical Evaluation*, ed. Mari Evans, 1984, pp. 393–410. Jean Davis, "Carolyn M. Rodgers," in *DLB*, vol. 41, *Afro-American Poets since 1955*, eds. Trudier Harris and Thadious M. Davis, 1985, pp. 287–295.
—Marsha C. Vick

ROGERS, ELYMAS PAYSON (1815–1861), clergyman, poet, and missionary. Rogers was a third-generation descendant of an African slave who had survived shipwreck off the coast of Connecticut in the early eighteenth century. Bought by Reverend Jonathan Tood, his great-grandmother and her descendants were employed on the Todd property as farmers. Determined to return to Africa as a missionary, Rogers left his parents in the early 1830s to work and pursue an education in Hartford. In 1835 he enrolled at Gerrit Smith's school in Peterboro, New York, and financed his education by teaching in a public school for Negro children in Rochester, New York. In 1837 he enrolled at Oneida Institute in Whitesboro, New York, and began studying for the ministry, teaching simultaneously in Rochester until his graduation from Oneida in 1841. During this time, Rogers's friendship with an illiterate fugitive slave, Jermain Wesley Loguen, resulted in Loguen's attendance at Oneida and his subsequent prominence as an abolitionist and AME bishop.

Rogers married Harriet Sherman of Rochester in 1841 and became principal of a public school in Trenton, New Jersey. In 1844 he was licensed by the New Brunswick Presbytery and pastored two churches in Princeton and Newark for a total of sixteen years.

Rogers wrote two satires expressing strong political views and publicly condemned the 1857 Dred Scott decision. "A Poem on the Fugitive Slave Law" (1855) advocates that a Higher Law should take precedence over man-made laws. "The Repeal of the Missouri Compromise Considered" (1856), a longer, 925-line poem, denounces the Compromise of 1820 and the Kansas-Nebraska Bill of 1854 as reflective of national greed and expedience. Rogers's satires are witty, well argued, and bold.

Rogers was a member of the African Civilization Society and died prematurely in Africa while fulfilling his lifelong dream of becoming a missionary.

[*See also* Protest Literature.]

• William Wells Brown, *The Black Man, His Antecedents, His Genius, and His Achievements*, 1863; rpt. 1968. Joan R. Sherman, *Invisible Poets: Afro-Americans of the Nineteenth Century*, 1974. —Marilyn D. Button

Roll of Thunder, Hear My Cry. In *Roll of Thunder, Hear My Cry*, a highly acclaimed novel that was a Newbery Medal winner and an American Library Association Notable Book, Mildred D. *Taylor created an African American saga for young people with her vivid portrayal of the Logan family.

The novel chronicles one traumatic year in the heroic lives of David Logan; his wife Mary; their children Cassie, Stacey, Little Man, and Christopher-John; and their extended family. Nine-year-old Cassie's narration enables Taylor to juxtapose childhood innocence and wonder with bigotry and racism. She creates a realistic world of rural Mississippi through the eyes of a child, without bitterness and polemics, but with surprise and growing disillusionment.

In 1933, the Great Depression grips the entire country, but what Cassie knows is that the price of cotton has dropped, forcing her father to leave home and find work on the railroad. Cassie learns what it means to be African American. She witnesses discrimination in her segregated school, feels terror when the Ku Klux Klan rides through the night, witnesses crimes against African Americans go unpunished, and is humiliated when she is forced to step off the sidewalk for Lillian Jean to pass, invoking white privilege.

The Logan family struggles to maintain its economic independence, symbolized by their ownership of four hundred acres of land. The land is their hope, representing, as it were, all of America's promises to its huddled masses longing to be free. The Logans, not sharecroppers, not illiterate, and not poverty-stricken, are educated, proud, and industrious. Their very presence threatens white supremacy, marking them for victimization. But the Logans are not victims—they are survivors. Their love for each other and for the land shelters them from the storm of aggression aimed to destroy them and take their land.

The author's angle of vision is unflinching. Taylor does not look away or soften the impact of racism for young readers. Instead, Cassie's movement from innocence to awareness to bitterness and disillusionment enables readers to experience vicariously these feelings and Taylor to show the influence events of the 1930s had on shaping the civil rights and Black Power movements of the 1950s and 1960s.

Most critics have praised Taylor's novel. However, Margery Fisher's review (*Growing Point*, Apr. 1978) claimed the book was altogether too natural and crowded with details and raw emotionalism. David Rees ("The Color of Skin: Mildred Taylor," *Horn Book*, 1980) complained that Taylor loses the excitement of direct action by forcing the children to overhear or eavesdrop on their parents' conversations. In her Newbery Award acceptance speech (18 June 1977), Taylor recalled her temptation to place Cassie at the heart of all the adult action, but explained that she felt compelled to maintain Cassie in a child's place. Whatever is lost to excitement is offset by the realistic portrayal of parental efforts to shelter children from danger and life's unpleasant realities.

• Emily R. Moore, review of *Roll of Thunder, Hear My Cry*, in *Interracial Books for Children*, vol. 7, 1976, p. 18. Gerard Senick, ed., *Children's Literature Review*, vol. 9, 1985, pp. 223–229. —Nagueyalti Warren

Roots. This 1976 Alex *Haley novel narrates a seven-generation story about his own family. It begins with the birth of West African *Kunta Kinte, Haley's maternal great-great-great-great-grandfather, and ends with Haley's own research and dramatic discoveries about his genealogy. Because it purports to be the first African American text to definitively locate an African ancestor and because of two widely watched *television miniseries—"Roots" (1977) and "Roots: The Next Generations" (1979)—loosely based on the novel, the book became an immensely popular cultural phenomenon. In 1977 *Roots* received a special citation Pulitzer Prize and the National Book Award.

Haley termed the narrative strategy in *Roots* "faction." While *Roots* is based on what he claims is factual material, Haley fictionalizes and enhances the story, adding imagined dialogue and incidents to flesh out the story and relay the horrific nature of American *slavery. The first half of the novel focuses on Kunta Kinte, his birth and often paradisical childhood in Juffure, his West African village, and his capture in 1767 and *Middle Passage journey to Maryland and then Virginia where he is enslaved. Eventually, after several unsuccessful escapes (he ultimately had his foot amputated to stop him), Kunta Kinte, now renamed Toby, settles down and marries Bell, a domestic slave, and they have one daughter, Kizzy.

Kunta Kinte's ultimate legacy is his own story and culture, parts of which he conveys to his daughter. In the novel's second part, when Kizzy is sold off to a North Carolina slaver, she is able to pass on her father's narrative to her son, Chicken George, an accomplished gamecock trainer, who does the same with his children. After the Civil War, George's fourth child, Tom, a blacksmith, moves the family to Henning, Tennessee. Tom's youngest daughter Cynthia marries Will Palmer, whose daughter Bertha George marries Alex Haley's father, Simon Alexander Haley.

Perhaps the most compelling part of *Roots* is Haley's chronicle of his own search for his family's genealogy. Starting with his recollections of his grandmother Cynthia's family stories about an African ancestor, Haley tells of his relentless, ten-year search through various American and British genealogical archives, discussions with Africanist scholars, and dramatic journeys back to Gambia, where he learns from a griot the history of the Kinte family, especially the late-eighteenth-century disappearance of Kunta Kinte.

Almost from the beginning, Haley and *Roots* have been criticized for historical inaccuracy and plagiarism. Mark Ottaway, Willie Lee Rose, and Gary B. and Elizabeth Shown Mills have challenged respectively Haley's Gambian story, his historical accuracy, and his genealogical research. More troubling are the accusations of plagiarism by Margaret *Walker and Harold Courlander. While Walker's suit was dismissed, Haley settled with Courlander for $500,000, admitting that parts of Courlander's *The African* (1967) inadvertently found their way into *Roots.*

Nevertheless, *Roots* provoked a renewed interest by many Americans in their own genealogy and instilled a new pride for African Americans about their African ancestry. It has also had a profound impact on the teaching of African American *history.

• Willie Lee Rose, "An American Family," *New York Review of Books*, 11 Nov. 1976, 3–4, 6. Mark Ottaway, "Doubts Raised over Story of the Big TV Slave Saga," *Sunday Times*, 10 Apr. 1977, 1, 17, 21. Harold Courlander, "'Roots,' 'The African,' and the Whiskey Jug Case," *Village Voice*, 9 Apr. 1979, 33–35, 84–86. Gary B. and Elizabeth Shown Mills, "'Roots' and the New 'Faction': A Legitimate Tool for Clio?" *Virginia Magazine of History and Biography* 89 (Jan. 1981): 1–26. Philip Nobile, "Uncovering Roots," *Village Voice*, 23 Feb. 1993, 31–38.

—Roger A. Berger

ROPER, MOSES (1816–?), slave narrator, orator, and missionary. Earning distinction as the first American slave to escape to England in search of *freedom, Moses Roper holds an important position in the *slave narrative tradition. Though not much is known about him beyond the scope of his *autobiography, *A Narrative of the Adventures and Escape of Moses Roper, from American Slavery* (1837), this text provides an insightful glimpse not only into the life of its author and *slavery, but also into the intellectual and emotional character of Roper.

Born on a plantation in Caswell County, North Carolina, Roper was sold often during his childhood and youth. As a result, he witnessed the horrors of slavery throughout much of the Southeast. He recounts with vivid detail the atrocities suffered by fellow slaves. After many unsuccessful attempts, he finally succeeded in escaping to Savannah, Georgia, in 1834, where he signed on as a steward on a merchant vessel bound for New York. After spending one year in New England, Roper set sail for England in 1835 with letters of recommendation from various American abolitionists who attested to his good character.

Roper was aided by English friends in earning an *education that would prepare him for missionary work. After the publication of his *Narrative*, he attended University College, London. The American edition of the *Narrative* was published in 1838. As late as 1839 Roper was still in England.

Though he is credited with no other publications, Roper's *Narrative* did undergo several printings. The original 1837 London edition was fifty-one pages. New editions were published in 1838, 1839, and 1840 in London and Philadelphia, the page numbers grad-

ually increasing to one hundred pages. Translated into Celtic in 1841, it appeared in a total of ten editions by 1856.

• William L. Andrews, *To Tell A Free Story: The First Century of Afro-American Autobiography, 1760–1865*, 1986. Marion Wilson Starling, *The Slave Narrative*, 1988.

—Charles E. Wilson, Jr.

RUFEL, MISS. In Sherley Anne *Williams's *Dessa Rose* (1986), Miss Rufel—a southern white lady and mistress of an unfinished plantation—serves as a revisioning of the abolitionist. In her home, which is an unfinished replica of a stop on the Underground Railroad, she is first antithesis, then coconspirator, and ultimately friend to the novel's protagonist, the runaway slave *Dessa Rose. Through Miss Rufel, Williams deconstructs the *stereotype of slave and mistress and suggests that the traditional roles that white and black women play cannot hold together when the economic structure of slavery falls apart.

Williams deconstructs Miss Rufel conceptually and spatially by divesting her of those agents that ensure her place as mistress, including her husband Bertie, who as master of their plantation represents the rigid constraints of southern society. When the terms by which slave relates to mistress are redrawn in this manner, what results is an equation of mistress with slave. Miss Rufel can see how she is a slave to the castes of economics, class, gender, and color. Yet hers is a precarious position: She cannot function as mistress without the runaways who run her farm, providing economic security in exchange for food and shelter from reenslavement. Therefore Miss Rufel as ex-mistress and revisioned abolitionist is a fitting metaphor for Williams's economic, spatial, and conceptual deconstruction and reconstruction of slavery, for it is primarily through the interactions between Rufel and the runaways that slaves and mistress become free.

• Marta E. Sanchez, "The Estrangement Effect in Sherley Anne Williams' *Dessa Rose*," *Genders* 15 (Winter 1992): 21–36.

—Mildred R. Mickle

RUFUS SCOTT. Arguably James *Baldwin's most tortured protagonist, Rufus Scott of *Another Country* (1962) reflects the author's view of the artist as prophet. Baldwin based him on Eugene Worth, a friend who committed suicide; like Worth, Rufus jumps from the George Washington Bridge. Ironically, Rufus's premature suicide catalyzes the other characters' physical and spiritual journeys.

A fledgling Greenwich Village jazz drummer, Rufus symbolizes American and existential loneliness; we first encounter him "peddling his ass." Psychologically and physically eviscerated, he is rescued temporarily by Vivaldo Moore, his Italian American best friend. Rufus also finds momentary solace with Leona, a white southerner. However, hegemonic oppression engenders an acute malaise in Rufus. Leona becomes the receptacle for his racial and self hatred and goes insane. We also learn of Rufus's former lover—another southerner, Eric Jones. Because of society's constricting definitions of manhood, Rufus repulsed Eric's affection. Ultimately, Rufus's multiple demons compel his suicide, which concludes the opening section.

Rufus's spiritual deformity is symptomatic of an American ethos that constructs racial and sexual barriers. Only when characters such as Vivaldo vitiate society's restrictions can they enter "another country," a metaphorical haven where love can exist. Rufus remains a groundbreaking figure in African American literature as one of the few suicides. Baldwin's characterization also signifies upon the discursive treatment of black men as archetypal victims, for Baldwin makes Rufus "partly responsible for his doom" (*Conversations with James Baldwin*, 1989).

• Therman B. O'Daniel, ed., *James Baldwin: A Critical Evaluation*, 1977. Trudier Harris, *Exorcising Blackness: Historical and Literary Lynching and Burning Rituals*, 1984. Fred L. Standley and Louis H. Pratt, eds., *Conversations with James Baldwin*, 1989.   —Keith Clark

RUGGLES, DAVID (1810–1849), abolitionist, New York bookseller, publisher, pamphleteer, and civic organizer. Born to free parents in Norwich, Connecticut, David Ruggles spent most of his adult life in New York City. He believed that a free press was the best weapon against *slavery. From 1820 to 1833, he ran a temperance grocery, a bookstore, a reading room, and a printing business. In 1834 he helped found the Garrison Literary and Benevolent Association, an African American cultural society. In 1835 he organized with other leaders the New York Committee of Vigilance, which, until its demise in 1842, aided fugitive slaves and thwarted the kidnapping of free African Americans into slavery. He edited and published the *Mirror of Liberty*, the Committee's official organ and one of the nation's first African American magazines. With the New York Manumission Society, he helped secure the right to a jury trial for African Americans accused of being runaway slaves. He personally aided the escapes of more than six hundred slaves, directing them to the underground. He was a frequent contributor to antislavery journals, especially the *Liberator* and the *Emancipator*. Ruggles tried to revive the African American convention movement in 1840 with his call for a National Reform Convention of Colored Citizens. After resigning from the New York Committee of Vigilance, he moved to Massachusetts and joined the Northhampton Association of Education and Industry. He then founded the nation's first hydropathic treatment center. Ruggles is remembered for his biting rhetorical style and his uncompromising promotion of full civil rights for all people, regardless of race or gender. He died in Northhampton, Massachusetts.

[*See also* Journalism.]

• Peter C. Ripley et al., eds., *The Black Abolitionist Papers: The United States, 1830–1846*, vol. 3, 1991, pp. 169–174.
                    —Mary C. Carruth

"Runagate Runagate." One of Robert *Hayden's most successful historical poems, "Runagate Runagate" (first published in 1962), employs a montage of voices to portray the tumultuous world of escaped slaves, and ultimately the fundamental human impulse toward freedom. "Runagate," a term for a runaway slave, refers specifically to Harriet *Tubman and by extension to a series of symbols suggesting freedom and emancipation. Divided into two sections, the poem's opening stanza strikes a particularly high level of dramatic tension, impressing upon the reader the visceral immediacy of escape. Entirely free of punctuation, the first stanza both describes and effects flight, rendering a sense of perpetual motion, tumult, and omnipresent threat. The ensuing stanzas reconfigure this sense of motion and confusion through the juxtaposition of voices. Employing multiple voices (and their implicit sense of contrast) in a manner reminiscent of T. S. Eliot and very similar to Hayden's "Middle Passage," Hayden echoes hymns, *spirituals, protest songs, wanted posters, slave voices, and ultimately Harriet Tubman. Though these voices appear in sequential fashion, the compression, typography, and absence of transitions suggest a simultaneity, a montage of personae and perspectives. Thus as multiple voices vie for visibility and ultimate control over the reader's attention, Hayden creates a complex signifying text whose multiple possibilities discourage unitary or rigid interpretations.

In order to hold these highly discursive voices in check, the poem relies upon the progression of its central symbols signifying freedom and possibility. In the first section the refrain "Runagate Runagate," strategically placed between disparate voices, reasserts the symbolic and thematic focus of the poem. The second section reconfigures the relatively abstract runagate as the historically concrete Harriet Tubman. Her voice dominates the first half of the second section, anticipating and effectively neutralizing oppositional voices that call for her incarceration or destruction. Tubman's final call to ride her train presents trains as the poem's final symbol. Sustaining her sense of defiance and affirmation, trains, here, reassert perpetual agitation through the historical specificity of the *Underground Railroad, and more broadly suggest the pan-historical struggle for freedom. The final line of the poem condenses and transforms the competing voices into a singular voice and impulse ultimately transcendent of its own immediate circumstances. One of Hayden's best uses of *history and montage, "Runagate Runagate" aptly illustrates one of his chief tenets expressed in his manifesto "Counterpoise," the unity of humanity and the crucial role the arts play in the struggle toward lasting peace. As the poem affirms physical, political, and psychic freedom, it suggests peace and resolution in the very act of resistance.

Hayden's focus on slavery and on the literal and symbolic act of escape revisits a theme important to a number of African American writers, particularly Octavia E. *Butler. Her novel *Kindred* (1979), perhaps her best-known work, also explores the physical and psychic perils of slavery, and the irrepressible impulse toward freedom.

• Wilburn Williams, Jr., "The Covenant of Timelessness and Time: Symbolism and History in Robert Hayden's *Angle of Ascent*," *Massachusetts Review* 18 (Winter 1977): 731–749. Howard Faulkner, "'Transformed by Steeps of Flight': The

Poetry of Robert Hayden," *CLA Journal* 21 (June 1978): 96–111.
                                                    —Mark A. Sanders

RUSSELL, CHARLIE L. (b. 1932), playwright, writer, educator, critic, actor, and director. Born in Monroe, Louisiana, Charlie Russell graduated from high school in Oakland, California. He received a BA in English from the University of San Francisco in 1959, an MSW from New York University in 1966, and an MFA from the University of California at San Diego in 1986. From 1969 until 1974 Russell was writer in residence with and chair of the Playwrights Workshop with the National Black Theatre. He is the father of two children.

Throughout his career Russell has written for television and film as well as for the stage, including "The Black Church" (ABC-TV) and "A Man Is Not Made of Steel" (for Boston's WGBH), both of which were 1950s productions. He was awarded an NAACP Image Award in 1975 for his 1973 screenplay *Five on the Black Hand Side*, based on his published play of the same name (1970). The 1984 screenplay *Five No-Trump* is also from a play. *Revival!* (1972), perhaps Russell's most important play, was cowritten with National Black Theatre director Barbara Ann Teer.

During the 1960s Russell became intimately associated with the *Black Arts movement. He worked as a cultural critic and fiction editor for *Liberator* magazine. While editor-in-chief of Onyx Publications, Russell produced *Report from the First Onyx Black Cultural Conference* (1970), proceedings from the 1968 conference, which was touted as the first occasion on which Black artists from all facets of the arts gathered to discuss their role in the use of art to liberate Black people.

In fiction, Russell published a 1970s novella, *A Birthday Present for Kathryn Kenyatta*. Russell's short story "Quietus" was anthologized both in Langston *Hughes's *Best Short Stories by Negro Writers* (1967) and the *Urban Reader* (1971). "Quietus" deals with its central character's difficulty in reconciling his role as the first Black salesman in a white corporation, Besso Oil, which uses him as a "token."
                                                    —Derek A. Williams

RUSSWURM, JOHN BROWNE (1799–1851), journalist and editor. Born a slave in Jamaica, John Browne Russwurm was sent by his white father to Quebec in 1807 to go to school. In his early teens Russwurm rejoined his father in Portland, Maine, where he was given an opportunity to continue his intellectual development. In 1824, Russwurm enrolled in Bowdoin College in Brunswick, Maine, from which he graduated in 1826 with one of the first bachelor's degrees earned by an African American in the United States.

Migrating to New York, Russwurm formed a partnership with Samuel *Cornish, a black Presbyterian minister, to found a newspaper. The result of their partnership was *Freedom's Journal*, the first African American newspaper in the United States, launched on 16 March 1827. *Freedom's Journal* was offered for sale in the United States, Canada, England, and Haiti. David *Walker, one of the newspaper's agents, first published his powerful *Appeal* in *Freedom's Journal*, lending support to the paper's editorial contention that the time had come for black Americans to plead their own cause in their own way.

In September 1827, Cornish resigned from his editorial duties to devote himself to the ministry. Russwurm continued as sole editor until March 1829, when he turned the newspaper over to Cornish, who renamed the paper the *Rights of All* and kept it financially afloat for another year. By the time the newspaper ceased publication in 1830, Russwurm had moved to Liberia, where he became editor of the *Liberia Herald* and superintendent of education in Monrovia, the capital of Liberia. Russwurm's decision to emigrate to Liberia angered some of his black compatriots in the American *antislavery movement, who felt he was deserting the cause. To Russwurm, however, Liberia offered a genuine opportunity for African Americans to put racial prejudice behind them and build a just and workable society. Russwurm remained a committed African colonizationist for the rest of his life.

[*See also* Emigration; Journalism.]

• Martin E. Dann, *The Black Press, 1827–1890*, 1971.
                                                    —William L. Andrews

RUTHERFORD CALHOUN. The protagonist of Charles R. *Johnson's novel *Middle Passage* (1990), Calhoun acts as interpreter for the Allmuseri, a tribe of African wizards Johnson created as a representation of his philosophical-aesthetic program. In the aftermath of a shipboard rebellion, Calhoun keeps the slave ship *Republic*'s logbook, simultaneously informing the reader of his history and tracing his further development. Presenting a people's alternative senses of time, history, language, and fidelity, Rutherford becomes like the Allmuseri as he grows to understand them. His is the sole perspective offered; as he grows through contact with the Allmuseri, the reader's consciousness evolves as well.

Calhoun's position in the text identifies him with a host of protagonists; three significant predecessors are Herman Melville's Ishmael, Ralph *Ellison's Invisible Man, and Johnson's own Andrew Hawkins of *Oxherding Tale* (1982). Like his forebears, Rutherford seeks self-knowledge through a series of adventures. Also like them, Rutherford must face a number of hostile forces that would limit his search and destroy him; furthermore, he must expand his definition of evil in the process. Drawing on the legacy of earlier writers and his own work, Johnson in Rutherford offers the fulfillment of his program, moving the reader from a look at an alternative mind-set to a chance to experience it. In *Oxherding Tale*, the reader learns a great deal from the solitary Allmuseri character; in *Middle Passage* Johnson expands his initiation and makes the reader part of the tribe. Johnson thereby achieves his goal of expanding people's consciousnesses through hermeneutical reading, a "real-life" process modeled in his fictional universe.
                                                    —William R. Nash

S

Sad-Faced Boy, a juvenile novel by Arna *Bontemps with illustrations by Virginia Lee Burton, was published in 1937. Three Dozier brothers steal away from their country home in Alabama aboard a freight train, retracing a similar journey to Harlem years earlier by their Uncle Jasper Tappin Dozier, their father's oldest brother. The wanderlusts eventually reach Harlem and wend their way to Sugar Hill where Uncle Jasper, the live-in janitor of an upscale apartment building, and his wife, Aunt Ludy, receive them with generous and sympathetic hospitality.

Slumber, the sad-faced boy, proves to be the guiding spirit of the brothers; both Rags, who is older, and Willie, younger, encounter experiences with caution and practicality and function as perfect foils for Slumber. All three are enthralled by the city, but with their first opportunity to explore up close, Slumber reveals his tendency to test the limits of experience by causing a free-for-all among the vendors on Eighth Avenue. No sooner do they catch their breaths from this incident than Slumber persuades them to invest their only nickels in a subway ride, a glamour that shortly fades when Slumber exits too soon and strands them far from home. Later, Slumber's curiosity leads them into the unfamiliar world of a free public library from which they are ejected for enjoying a book too audibly. Willie and Rags, meanwhile, wonder aloud how their impulsive brother could be so smart and yet so dumb.

The boys are befriended by Daisy Bee, a resident of the apartment building in which they are staying, who is city-wise but high-handed: she immediately acknowledges Slumber's musical talents but takes it upon herself to instruct Rags and Willie about rhythms even before she knows their names. When Daisy Bee later becomes their guide, she escorts them to a spectacular parade where all four join the procession as full-fledged participants, with a uniformed Slumber beating the bass drum and Daisy Bee the drum majorette.

Inspiration to organize the Dozier Brothers Band emerges from the thought that, unlike the country where—according to Slumber—pleasure can be gained by chewing on a stalk of sorghum, the city requires spending money. But Harlem offers no means to earn money for its pleasures; consequently, when little Willie finds a broken drum, Rags borrows Uncle Jasper's old guitar, and with Slumber playing the harmonica, they form a trio to earn spending money. Their sounds win over both Harlem and "Broadway" as appreciative New Yorkers shower the boys with coins, but little Willie suddenly falls ill and Slumber and Rags are unable to find a suitable replacement. This break in their successful run, however, reminds them of their nostalgia for Alabama where the persimmons are ripening anew and the cotton is high. In this mood, the adventurers bring their big city journey to a close with farewells to Aunt Ludy and Uncle Jasper and their intrepid friend Daisy Bee.

This story earned unanimous praise for its fresh humor, its sensitive portrayal of youth, and its faithful characterizations of youngsters. Typically critics noted Bontemps's poetic style and his capacity to effectively convey the flavor of black speech. Those familiar with *Popo and Fifina, Children of Haiti (1932), written jointly by Bontemps and Langston *Hughes, will recognize what is true about both works: style has as much to do with holding the reader's attention as the story line itself.

—Charles L. James

SALAAM, KALAMU YA (b. 1947), poet, playwright, essayist, literary and cultural critic, short story writer, editor, and activist. Kalamu ya Salaam was born Vallery Ferdinand III on 24 March 1947 in New Orleans. He attended Carleton College in Minnesota and Southern University in New Orleans in the 1960s but did not graduate from either school. He was expelled from Southern University for his student protests against the university administration in 1969. From 1965 until 1968 he served in the U.S. Army. He eventually received an associate degree from Delgado Junior College. After completing his formal education, Salaam moved into the next and most important phase of his life's work, social and political activism, and liberation of African Americans and Africans. His community-based work includes participation in such organizations as the World Black and African Festival of Arts and Culture, Free Southern Theater (which in 1969 changed its name to BLKARTSOUTH), and Ahidiana (a New Orleans Pan-African Nationalist Organization), and he was a founding member and editor of the *Black Collegian* and executive director of the New Orleans Jazz Heritage, among many other organizations.

His literary productions, whether as poet, playwright, *short story writer, or cultural critic, all address his fundamental position that art must be a vehicle to assist in the liberation of African people. To this end, a great deal of his work opposes Western cultural hegemony. His first plays, produced by the Free Southern Theater, reflect both in style and subject matter the nuances of the *Black Arts movement and the *Black Aesthetic of the 1960s and early 1970s. Salaam's The Picket (1968), Mama (1969), Happy Birthday Jesus (1969), Black Liberation Army (1969), Homecoming (1970), and Black Love Song (1971) were his attempts to capture the communality of black life in *drama. His first volumes of *poetry, The Blues Merchant (1969), Hofu Ni Kwenu (1973), and Pamoja Tutashinda (1974), not only created powerful and laudatory images of black people and their life in America but emphasized the need for art to serve a number of political and liberating functions for the black masses. His best-known volume of poetry is *Revolutionary Love* (1978), which connects the black liberation struggle to the notion of kinship in the black cultural heritage.

His literary and scholarly works since the mid-1970s include *Ibura* (1976), *Tearing the Roof off the Sucker* (1977), *South African Showdown* (1978), *Nuclear Power and the Black Liberation Struggle* (1978), *Who Will Speak for Us? New Afrikan Folktales* (1978, coauthored with his wife, Tayari kwa Salaam), *Herufi: An Alphabet Reader* (1978), *Iron Flowers: A Poetic Report on a Visit to Haiti* (1979), and *Our Women Keep Our Skies From Falling* (1980). His works are published in major African American literature *anthologies. These works continue earlier themes and subjects of empowering black people at the cultural and political levels. The communal thrust of Salaam's vision extends to his cultural criticism of literature, *music, and politics, as announced in his many *essays, reviews, and interviews, published in such forums as *Negro Digest, Black World, Black Collegian, First World, Black Scholar,* and *Black Theatre.* Salaam is one of the most prolific writers and creators of African American discourse in the late twentieth century. He continues to reside in New Orleans and to carry on his artistic and cultural work.

• Vincent Hardy, "The Seventies," *Black Collegian* 10 (Oct./Nov. 1979): 86–99. J. O. Lockhard, "An Ideology for Black Artists," *First World* 2 (1980): 20–22, 67.

—Charles P. Toombs

Salt Eaters, The. Toni Cade *Bambara's important multilayered novel *The Salt Eaters* (1980) is set in the community of Claybourne, Georgia, during the late 1970s. The novel centers on the attempted suicide and healing of the main character, *Velma Henry, as she comes to grips with the fragmentation, rage, and self-will that have driven her in the past. In the Southwest Community Infirmary, after her wounds are bandaged, Velma sits with the fabled healer, *Minnie Ransom, surrounded by a circle of twelve spiritual adepts (The Master's Mind); a group of nervous medical students; the clinic physician, Dr. Julius Meadows; and an assortment of casually interested clinic patients. Also surrounding Velma and Minnie, beyond the clinic itself, are a dazzling constellation of characters, institutions, and situations: Fred Holt, the bus driver nearing retirement and grieving the death of his friend, Porter; Velma's husband, Obie, who heads the also fragmented Academy of the Seven Arts; the Seven Sisters performing arts group who travel toward Claybourne for the annual Mardi Gras festival.

Boundaries of time and space, imagination and reality are frequently blurred, as when Minnie Ransom and her spirit guide, Old Wife, freely commune throughout Velma's healing and even "travel" to a chapel for prayer. *Jazz-inflected rhythms, lyrical language, flashbacks, digressions, and a panoply of characters and subplots create a novel that many reviewers initially found difficult—but ultimately worthwhile—to read. Gloria Hull, calling the novel "daringly brilliant," describes its structure as one of widening circles, and provides a diagram of how

those many circles and characters connect. While the novel was enthusiastically received, some felt that its strength—its panoramic sweeps and encompassing themes—eclipsed character development, leaving readers little connection with individual characters.

All of the main characters are related in some way to Velma, whose fractured psyche serves as a trope for the splinterings and fractures of the community, where fundamental values (like connections with the best of people's traditions and attention to spiritual well-being) have been left behind in the wake of the *civil rights movement. Like other African American women's novels of the 1970s and 1980s, *The Salt Eaters* deals with the gender oppression that African American women experienced before, during, and after civil rights. Minnie Ransom repeatedly asks Velma if she is ready for the "weight" of being well, a question the novel implicitly directs to the entire community.

The Salt Eaters integrates African and Afro-Caribbean spiritual and *healing traditions with those from Western religion and other spiritual practices. The novel includes references to prayer, tarot, cowrie shells, herbal and folk medicines, loa, rootwork, and obeah, among others. Under Minnie's guiding hand, Velma will move backward in time to relive her fear and rage, as well as to recover lost wisdom and rootedness. Illness, however, becomes a matter of community as well as individual healing; as Velma returns to health, she is also restored to a community badly in need of its own healing. The novel ends apocalyptically, with the culmination of preparations for a local Mardi Gras festival and a cataclysmic storm that signals changes in the characters who need them the most, including Velma, who rises from the stool as though from a "burst cocoon."

• Gloria Hull, "What It Is I Think She's Doing Anyhow: A Reading of Toni Cade Bambara's *The Salt Eaters*," in *Home Girls: A Black Feminist Anthology,* ed. Barbara Smith, 1983, pp. 124–141. Margot Anne Kelly, "'Damballah Is the First Law of Thermodynamics': Modes of Access to Toni Cade Bambara's *The Salt Eaters*," *African American Review* 27.3 (1993): 479–493.

—Ann Folwell Stanford

SAMBO. Variants of the name Sambo can be found in several African cultures, including Samba in Bantu; Samb and Samba in Wolof; Sambu in Mandingo; and Sambo in Hausa, Mende, and Vai. Throughout census materials and assorted other eighteenth-century documents, these names emerge as those of new world slaves. The name also has possible Hispanic antecedents: the sixteenth-century word "zambo" refers to a bowlegged or knock-kneed individual.

By the late eighteenth century, whites had begun to use the name in a generic fashion to refer to male slaves. Before long, comic associations were commonplace; childishness, sloppiness, and a propensity to mispronounce multisyllabic words were the key traits of a Sambo figure. Such characters emerged in late eighteenth-century plays and sheet music, and became mainstays of nineteenth-century minstrelsy. By the time Helen Bannerman's *The Story of Little Black Sambo* was published in 1898, the name was thoroughly linked with the image of an immature, fun-loving, inept, black male. The hero of her popular children's story was, in fact, from India and his cleverness is the cornerstone of the tale.

Throughout the twentieth century, African Americans have had to grapple with the tenacious Sambo image. The white public's love affair with Sambo-inspired characters undermined the efforts of African Americans to achieve equality. Black author Ralph *Ellison addressed the insidiousness of the Sambo image in his masterpiece *Invisible Man* (1952). Nonetheless, advertisers, filmmakers, and others continued to depict black characters in the familiar Sambo fashion. In the mid-1950s, white historian Stanley Elkins caused a furor by using the Sambo label to refer to an actual personality type he believed to be prevalent during the era of *slavery. But social critics continued to argue that Sambo was more representative of white wishful thinking than of any genuine personality profile evident within the African American population.

• Joseph Boskin, *Sambo: The Rise and Demise of an American Jester*, 1986. Clarence Major, ed., *Juba to Jive: A Dictionary of African-American Slang*, 1994.   —Patricia A. Turner

SANCHEZ, SONIA (b. 1934), poet, playwright, essayist, and educator. The life and work of Sonia Sanchez mark her progression toward enlightened understanding and expression of what it means to be Black and woman and connected to a larger world. At various periods she has been reborn: as child poet after her grandmother died, as militant revolutionary of the 1960s, as spiritual visionary of the 1970s—all were stages in becoming a self-possessed strong woman. Her writings have served as source and expression of her growth and commitment to harnessing political and spiritual energies to make a better world.

Born Wilsonia Benita Driver in Birmingham, Alabama, to Wilson L. Driver (musician and teacher) and Lena (Jones) Driver, who died when Sanchez was a baby, Sanchez had two siblings: Patricia and Wilson, who died in 1981. Her grandmother, whose strength and unconditional love provided the security Sanchez needed to withstand childhood traumas and adult pain, died when Sanchez was six. After this, possibly to compensate for a stutter she developed and that lasted throughout adolescence, Sanchez began to write *poetry. Moving to Harlem at age nine, she attended school, earned a BA in political science at Hunter College, and studied poetry under Louise Bogan at New York University. Sanchez became deeply embroiled with Amiri *Baraka and Larry *Neal in political activism and poetry. She taught at the Downtown Community School in San Francisco (1965–1967), then at San Francisco State University (1967–1969), where she helped found the first Black Studies program.

Sanchez's early work responds to political and personal upheavals of the 1960s with radical experiments in form, style, and theme. "Assassin poems" and "lyrical confessionals" dominate *Homecoming*

(1969) and *We a BaddDDD People* (1970). Sanchez targets the enemies—murdering "wite americans," cops, sanctimonious Black puritans, and revolutionary poseurs—and lauds the heroes: *Malcolm X, Bobby Hutton, John *Coltrane, and Billie *Holiday. Like e.e. cummings, whom she parodies, Sanchez disrupts normal typography, word shapes, and the use of space to convey both emotion and clues to performance. *Homecoming*'s title poem epitomizes her theme: the return to blackness—rejection of white values—represents a return to Black speech and rhythms, idioms (dozens, rap), and *music (*jazz, *blues) in a poetry as personal and confessional as it is insurgent. Loneliness and lyricism characterize the personal poems so infused by a blues sensibility and sound that some critics credit Sanchez with placing blues at the center of poetic discourse.

Sanchez's first plays display similar militant themes: *The Bronx Is Next* (1968), dramatizing a plot to burn down a Harlem ghetto, and *Sister Son/ja* (1969), portraying the journey of a sister who is "moving consciously black," despairs, and is reborn. Other plays focus on Malcolm X, Black male and female relationships, and political allegory.

The anger and confrontation of the 1960s were consolidated in the empowering 1970s, when African Americans sensed a new connectedness to the world outside of America. Travels in China, the Caribbean (1973), and Cuba (1979), and membership in the Nation of Islam (1972–1975) broadened Sanchez's vision. She held a succession of teaching positions in the Northeast (University of Pittsburgh, Rutgers University, Manhattan Community College, and Amherst College) before moving to Philadelphia, where she began teaching at Temple University in 1977 and is the Laura H. Cornell Professor of English.

The less strident, pastoral lyrics of *Love Poems* (1973) depict moving moments in Sanchez's life: estrangement from her Puerto Rican husband, indictment of her father for casting her adrift, memories of love's ecstasy and despair. Surrealistic imagery in "Old Words" gives way to anticipation of love in "Welcome home my Prince." An exquisite lyricism informs Sanchez's maturing vision and technique as she distills emotion into ever more restrictive forms: sonnets and ballads, tankas and haikus. Other poems express growing allegiance to Elijah Muhammad, heralding her conversion to Islam, which inspired *A Blues Book for Blue Black Magical Women* (1973), perhaps her strongest achievement before *Homegirls*. Sanchez experienced visions while writing this, her spiritual *autobiography in five parts. Exhorting the "Queens of the Universe" to forsake racist Western ways, she invokes the Earth Mother to guide her spiritual journey into the past, tracing her evolution from birth to rebirth; declares her devotion to the Nation of Islam; and returns to her ancestral home to be purified. The last section draws from the Bible and Koran to depict apocalyptic visions and ends with the repeated refrain "in the beginning / there was no end." Chanting rhythms and imagery of Egyptian myth and Swahili praise poem enact the symbolic death and rebirth of all

Black women. It is a "mountaintop poem" that transports African American rhythms to the pinnacle, then into deeper self-understanding.

During the 1970s Sanchez also wrote three children's books. *It's a New Day* (1971), *The Adventures of Fathead, Smallhead and Soaphead* (1973), and *A Sound Investment* (1980) address the need to instill in young people pride in their heritage and knowledge of their history and culture.

Throughout the 1980s and early 1990s Sanchez has been a dedicated teacher, mother, and prolific writer. Her work has appeared in numerous magazines, journals, and *anthologies, and six records exist of her readings. She has also received prestigious awards, among them a National Endowment for the Arts fellowship (1978–1979), the Lucretia Mott Award (1984), American Book Award (1985), Pennsylvania Governor's Award (1988), and Paul Robeson Social Justice Award (1989).

The 1980s witnessed the production of some of her finest work. In *I've Been a Woman: New and Selected Poems* (1981) earlier poems establish a context for new works. Four poems about her father trace her evolving feelings, from vengeful scorn to forgiveness and reconciliation. Love, "sweet as watermelon juice," pervades the "Haikus and Tankas and Other Love Syllables," which explode with sensual images of color, sound, taste, and touch. "Generations" honors Sterling A. *Brown, "griot of fire," Gerald Penny, a student who died in 1973, and Shirley *Graham. Haki R. *Madhubuti calls this book "a truly earth-cracking contribution," exuding a rage and "urgency" unmatched by most of her peers.

Sanchez's most acclaimed work, *Homegirls and Handgrenades* (1984), received the American Book Award in 1985. "Grenades" are words that explode people's deluding myths about themselves and the world. New poetry and prose poems, interspersed with selections from *Love Poems*, comprise the four sections documenting the lives and longings of people who have loved or betrayed, disappointed or inspired her. Affirmations of "The Power of Love" contrast with the bleak portraits of "Blues Is Bullets," exposing love's power to distort and destroy. Prevailing images of death in "Beyond the Fallout" contextualize tributes to Jesse Jackson, Margaret *Walker, and Ezekiel Mphehlele in "Grenades Are Not Free." Sanchez introduces a series of prose poems reminiscent of Jean *Toomer's *Cane* (1923), describing an encounter in a park between an old woman and an overburdened young mother, the ravages of drug addiction on a family, and meetings with former classmates whose youthful promise has been twisted into self-annihilation. The powerful climax—her letter to Martin Luther *King, Jr., announcing a new day, and "MIAs," commemorating those missing in action in Atlanta, Johannesburg, and El Salvador—exhorts all people to liberate the oppressed and alleviate suffering.

Under a Soprano Sky (1987) interweaves strands of earlier works with new themes and techniques to demonstrate Sanchez's political, spiritual, and artistic growth. The title poem's lyricism, sensuously mingling the body and the natural world, infuses elegies for her brother, for members of the back-to-nature movement MOVE slaughtered by Philadelphia police, and for the city itself. Chronicles of victims—a Hiroshima maiden, a Black man, Vietnam veteran James Thornwell, and Stephen Rinaldo, a murdered boy—inform tributes to heroes like Papa Joe, Paul *Robeson, John *Brown, and "Dear Mama," the grandmother who allowed her to grow. A melange of voices speak in haikus, tankas, and blues, alternating with more prosaic forms portraying a feisty "rough mama" and Mildred Scott Olmstead. The selections in "Endings" look ahead to the rise of a new earth, the work of tomorrow's poets, and the bright promise of her graduating sons.

For Sanchez poetry is a "subconscious conversation," a dialogue she has carried on for nearly three decades with the lost, lonely, and oppressed. She has been called a revolutionary, ritual singer, cultural worker, and people's poet—the roles intertwine, unified by an unshakable faith that the world can be changed and that one person can make a difference. She has certainly done her part. The revolutionary has ceaselessly agitated for radical reform, assaulting a morally bankrupt economic system, denouncing a racist agenda that incapacitates and kills, exhorting the "humanitarians" to join the struggle. The ritual singer has chanted the syllables of "ancestral" voices—Orisha, Oshun, Maat, Shirley Graham, Lizzie Driver—making past mysteries sound powerfully in the present. The cultural worker and people's poet has ministered to generations of writers, preaching the virtues of disciplined composition and living language, while celebrating African American sounds and sensibilities, boldness and beauty. Like Langston *Hughes, Sterling Brown, Jean Toomer, and Margaret Walker, with whom she is compared, Sonia Sanchez has opened a space in American letters where the racial self may be heard, affirmed, and strengthened. With her sense of fiery justice and her legacy of love, Sanchez stands as an inspiration, an example of what it means to survive whole and human in a troubled world.

• Claudia Tate, "Sonia Sanchez," in *Black Women Writers at Work*, 1983, pp. 132–148. Haki Madhubuti, "Sonia Sanchez: The Bringer of Memories," in *Black Women Writers (1950–1980)*, ed. Mari Evans, 1984, pp. 419–432. David Williams, "The Poetry of Sonia Sanchez," in *Black Women Writers (1950–1980)*, ed. Mari Evans, 1984, pp. 433–448. Houston A. Baker, Jr., "Our Lady: Sonia Sanchez and the Writing of a Black Renaissance," in *Black Feminist Criticism and Critical Theory*, eds. Joe Weixlmann and Houston Baker, 1988, pp. 169–202. Zala Chandler, "Voices beyond the Veil: An Interview with Toni Cade Bambara and Sonia Sanchez," in *Wild Women in the Whirlwind*, eds. Joanne Braxton and Andree Nicola McLaughlin, 1990, pp. 342–362. Joanne Veal Gabbin, "The Southern Imagination of Sonia Sanchez," in *Southern Women Writers: The New Generation*, ed. Tonette Bond Inge, 1990, pp. 180–203. D. H. Melhem, "Sonia Sanchez: The Will and Spirit," in *Heroism in the New Black Poetry*, ed. D. H. Melhem, 1990, pp. 132–179. Regina B. Jennings, "The Blue/Black Poetics of Sonia Sanchez," in *Language and Literature in the African-American Imagination*, ed. Carol Aisha Blackshire-Belay, 1992, pp. 119–132. William Cook, "The Black Arts Poets," in *The Columbia History of*

African-American Poetry, eds. Jay Parini and Brett C. Millier, 1993, pp. 674–706.

—Deborah Ayer Sitter

SANDERS, DORI (b. 1934), novelist. Dori Sanders, the popular storyteller and lifelong peach farmer in Filbert, South Carolina, made her literary debut with *Clover* (1990), a novel about a ten-year-old black farm girl whose widowed father dies only hours after marrying a white woman. Clover Hill and her stepmother, Sara Kate, build a life together in rural South Carolina while coming to terms with their grief, with Clover's extended family, and with their cultural differences. The child's perceptive and humorous first-person narrative depicts their experiences as they learn to live with and love each other.

Her Own Place (1993), Sanders's second novel, traces fifty years in the life of Mae Lee Barnes, a World War II bride who raises five children and runs her own farm in South Carolina after her husband abandons the family. She finds inner strength and meaning through her love of family, community, and the land. After her children are grown, she moves from the farm into town, where she becomes the first black volunteer at the local hospital. Her relationship with her white, upper-class colleagues is awkward, humorous, inspiring, and ultimately successful.

In 1995, Sanders published *Dori Sanders' Country Cooking: Recipes and Stories from the Family Farm Stand.* Throughout this autobiographical work, Sanders's spirited storytelling associates recipes with tales of farm traditions and memories of her family.

The tradition of African American women's writing has been enriched by Dori Sanders's particular insights into the southern rural African American community and its worldview. Her convincing folk vernacular, imaginative metaphor, humor, and keen observations of small details create drama and force in her commentary on the richness of family and community. Refusing to recognize limits to the possibilities of human relationships, Sanders develops in her novels a theme that is uncustomary in contemporary African American fiction: the celebration of everyday people, black and white, who live in the rural South and depend upon each other for personal and economic preservation during the years since the 1940s.

—Marsha C. Vick

SAPPHIRE. One of the most pervasive and persistent stereotypes of African American women, Sapphire is an overly aggressive, domineering, emasculating female. Her origins can be found in *Sam 'n' Henry,* a 1926 radio serial (renamed two years later as *Amos 'n' Andy*) in which two white actors, Freeman Gosden and Charles Correll, portrayed two southern African American men who had migrated to Chicago. Rooted in nineteenth-century minstrel shows and blackface vaudeville acts, in 1929 *Amos 'n' Andy* joined NBC and added the Kingfish and his wife, Sapphire, and became the most popular radio show in the United States.

Ernestine Wade's radio portrayal of the Kingfish's wife catapulted the character of Sapphire into fame as the most popular and most stereotypical female in the series. She was loud-talking, abrasive, overbearing, bossy, controlling, and emasculating. The most memorable scenes of the marriage were Sapphire scolding her husband about his dishonesty, laziness, and unreliability. Their relationship was consistent with the stereotypical matriarchal African American family that Black sociologist E. Franklin Frazier portrayed in his classic *The Negro Family in the United States* (1939). In 1951 *Amos 'n' Andy* premiered on *television and etched derogatory stereotypes of African Americans into the national consciousness for more than a decade.

"Sapphire" became, long after the name's association with the program had faded, an unquestioned characterization of the so-called emasculating African American woman. She also became a pervasive image in African American folk culture and one of the most damaging *stereotypes in the mass media, one that influences contemporary conceptions of Black womanhood.

• Melvin Patrick Kelley, *The Adventures of Amos 'n' Andy: A Social History of an American Phenomenon,* 1991.

—Beverly Guy-Sheftall

SCHOMBURG, ARTHUR A. (1874–1938), bibliophile, bibliographer, curator, historian, and Pan-Africanist; also wrote under the name Guarionex. Arthur Alfonso Schomburg's vast private collection, now housed in the Schomburg Center for Research in Black Culture (formerly the 135th Street branch of the New York Public Library), is one of the outstanding collections of materials concerning the *history and culture of people of African descent.

Schomburg was born on 24 January 1874 to an unwed freeborn mulatta, Maria Josepha, in Saint Thomas, U.S. Virgin Islands, and raised in Puerto Rico by his mother's family. Although he adopted his surname, there is no evidence that Schomburg's father, Carlos Federico Schomburg, a German-born merchant living in San Juan, acknowledged or supported his son. Little is known about Schomburg prior to his emigration to the United States. Upon arriving in New York in 1891, he settled into the Puerto Rican and Cuban community on Manhattan's east side. For most of his professional career, Schomburg worked for Bankers Trust Company in the bank's foreign mailing section. Schomburg became fully immersed in American Black culture in New York and focused his personal and scholarly attentions there.

The segue into African American culture was a natural consequence of Schomburg's personal life. He married three African American women—each named Elizabeth—who altogether bore him six sons and one daughter. Never much of a family man, Schomburg focused his energies on Freemasonry, research societies, community activities, and his passion for research and collecting.

Schomburg dedicated his life to collecting materials that would confirm and affirm the history and contributions of people of color. Thus he became widely known for his prodigious collection and respected for his bibliographic acumen—particularly his ability to find rare or lost materials. Schomburg sold his private collection to the New York Public

Library in 1926. While the original inventory has been lost, Schomburg's collection is estimated to have contained over ten thousand books, manuscripts, prints, and pieces of memorabilia. In 1930 Schomburg was asked to establish a collection of resources in Black history and culture for the Fisk University library and to map out a plan for the library's future acquisitions. He served as curator for the Negro Collection in Fisk's Cravath Memorial Library for two years. In January 1932 Schomburg returned to New York to become the curator for his former collection.

While he had no formal education, Schomburg became a respected lay authority on many subjects concerning Blacks around the world. He published a *bibliography, an exhibition catalogue, and various articles about Black subjects in the *Crisis, *Opportunity, *Survey Graphic, and *Negro World. He gave frequent public lectures at important cultural events. The *Harlem Renaissance—the political, social, and literary movement designed to celebrate the African American's talents and accomplishments—showcased Schomburg's extraordinary collection and his bibliographic genius.

[See also Libraries and Research Centers.]

• Arthur Schomburg, "The Negro Digs Up His Past," *Survey Graphic* 6 (Mar. 1925): 670–672; rpt. in *The New Negro*, ed. Alain Locke, 1968. Elinor DesVerney Sinnette, *Arthur Alfonso Schomburg*, 1989.   —Deborah H. Barnes

SCHUYLER, GEORGE S. (1895–1977), satirist, critic, and journalist. George Samuel Schuyler was born in Providence, Rhode Island, to Eliza Jane Fischer and George S. Schuyler. He grew up in a middle-class, racially mixed neighborhood in Syracuse, New York, where he attended public schools until he enlisted in the army at the age of seventeen. He spent seven years (1912–1919) with the black 25th U.S. Infantry and was discharged as a first lieutenant.

From early on, Schuyler possessed a high level of confidence and boasted of his family having been free as far back as the Revolutionary War. In 1921, Schuyler joined the Socialist Party of America, through which he connected with A. Philip Randolph, who hired him in 1923 as assistant editor for the *Messenger; in that position, from 1923 to 1928, Schuyler also wrote a column entitled "Shafts and Darts: A Page of Calumny and Satire." In 1924, Schuyler became the New York correspondent for the *Pittsburgh Courier*, contributing a weekly commentary, "Views and Reviews." Schuyler led several investigative series while with the *Courier*, including one entitled "Aframerican Today," reporting on race relations in Mississippi in 1925–1926. In 1926, his article "The Negro-Art Hokum," published in the *Nation*, propelled him into the middle of the literary debate of the *Harlem Renaissance. While Schuyler was concerned with race difference always being interpreted as inferiority and was trying to refute negative *stereotypes, his statement in that essay, "the Aframerican is merely a lampblacked Anglo-Saxon," caused him to be labeled as an assimilationist throughout his career. In 1927, "Our White Folks" was published in H. L. Mencken's *American Mercury*; from this, Schuyler's reputation grew and Mencken

published nine more of Schuyler's articles between 1927 and 1933.

By the end of the 1920s, Schuyler began to acquire a national reputation as an iconoclast; despite his constant attacks on white racism, his commitment to exposing fraud, regardless of race, caused some African Americans to doubt his racial loyalty. In 1928, Schuyler married Josephine Cogdell, a white Texan ex-model.

In 1931, Schuyler published his first satirical novel, *Black No More, Being an Account of the Strange and Wonderful Workings of Science in the Land of the Free. The bulk of Schuyler's reputation rests on the success of this novel, which attacks myths of racial purity and white supremacy and the ways in which the perpetuation of racism serves economic purposes. Also in 1931, Schuyler became the first African American writer to serve as a foreign correspondent for a metropolitan newspaper, when the *New York Evening Post* sent him to assess the controversy of Liberia's slave labor. The articles were condemned by Marcus Garvey supporters, but based on the experience he published *Slaves Today: A Story of Liberia* (1931).

Schuyler also had several literary alter egos. Between 1933 and 1939, he produced fifty-four short stories and twenty novels/novellas in serialized form under such pen names as Samuel I. Brooks and Rachel Call. Until recently, scholars paid no attention to this body of work and Schuyler's own attitude toward his serialized fiction ranged from amusement to disdain. The freedom of a pen name allowed him to explore melodrama, and in contrast to the audience for his satirical *essays and his novel, *Black No More*, Schuyler wrote his serialized fiction for an exclusively African American audience. To date, four of his serialized novels have been reprinted into two volumes: *Black Empire* (1991) and *Ethiopian Stories* (1995). *Black Empire* explores the success of the retaking of Africa from European colonial powers; *Ethiopian Stories* explores Ethiopia's wars against Italian occupation.

Schuyler continued his career as a journalist until 1966, when he published his *autobiography, *Black and Conservative*, which gives an inside track to the feuds among the leaders of the Harlem Renaissance, as well as a look at Schuyler's own anticommunist/ anticapitalist views. While Schuyler saw the major problem of the twentieth century to be the *color line, he felt that focusing on race conflict only would lead African Americans into second-class citizenship. George Schuyler is generally considered the most prominent African American journalist and essayist of the early twentieth century.

• Michael W. Peplow, *George S. Schuyler*, 1980.

—Adenike Marie Davidson

SCIENCE FICTION. *See* Speculative Fiction.

SCOTT-HERON, GIL (b. 1949), poet, composer, pianist, vocalist, and lyricist. Gil Scott-Heron's chosen form of creative production is a combination of oral *poetry and *jazz. Songs and poems offering commentary on the world's injustices have made him widely recognized as a voice for social change. During the late 1960s and the *Black Arts movement while Scott-Heron was a student at Lincoln University, a historically black college in rural Pennsylvania, he was influenced by the Last Poets, multimedia artists who disseminated revolutionary black and third world concepts in their jazz-influenced free verse poetry. He also encountered poet Gylan Kain and novelist Steve Cannon as sometime faculty, and visiting lecturers Ishmael *Reed and Larry *Neal. Scott-Heron has, in turn, become an inspiration for contemporary rap and hip-hop artists. While at Lincoln University he published the first of three books, *The Vulture* (1970), a novel concerned with the destructive impact of drugs and American corruption on black communities. He also began a musical collaboration with Brian Jackson and released his first album, *Small Talk at 125th and Lenox* (1970), accompanied by a book of poetry. Scott-Heron received an MA in creative writing from Johns Hopkins University and taught creative writing at Federal City College in Washington, D.C., between 1972 and 1976. Best known as a musician, he has used *music to address wide-ranging issues, including urban black experience (*Winter in America*, 1973), alcoholism (*The Bottle*, 1975), South African apartheid (*Johannesburg*, 1975), violent social change (*The Revolution Will Not Be Televised*, 1975), and spiritual sustenance and recovery (*Spirits*, 1994). Scott-Heron speaks with rage and hope about the difficulty of creating social change in a funky mixture of *blues, jazz, and poetry. Scott-Heron has produced seventeen recordings.

• Jon Woodson, "Gil Scott-Heron" in *DLB*, vol. 41, *Afro-American Poets since 1955*, eds. Thadious M. Davis and Trudier Harris, 1984, pp. 307–311. Dimitri Erlich, "Gil Scott-Heron," *Rolling Stone*, 25 Aug. 1994, 46.

—Tracy J. Patterson

SCOTTSBORO BOYS. Nearly lynched, quickly tried and sentenced to death for supposedly raping two white women in a railroad car near Scottsboro, Alabama, in 1931, the Scottsboro boys symbolized, in literature, law, and the minds of many, the desperate situation of southern African American men. Several writers, including Countee *Cullen and S. Ralph Harlow, wrote in response to this incident, but none more significantly than Langston *Hughes.

In his small volume, *Scottsboro Limited* (1932), Hughes presented this case as an exemplar of larger ethical, moral, and economic issues. In "Justice," Hughes gives infected eyes to the blind Justice of U.S. jurisprudence, reshaping a foundational figure of impartiality and reasoned judgment as an image of physical and ethical decay. In "Christ in Alabama," he casts violent and sexual overtones over the relation of a light-skinned God to a darker-skinned Mary, thereby asserting that the true sexual aggressor is not a martyred, African American Christ, but a powerful white man. In "Scottsboro," the imprisoned boys are joined by a series of other freedom fighters, including John *Brown, *Moses, Jeanne d'Arc, Nat *Turner,

and Lenin. In a more upbeat tone, Hughes's play, *Scottsboro Limited*, later staged by Amiri *Baraka in the 1960s, connects the plight of these nine men with that of white working people, using communist understandings of an oppressed underclass to call for solidarity across racial and along *class lines. Hughes symbolizes the communist activists who brought the Scottsboro case into the national spotlight with a chorus of Red voices that continually speak to the boys in their cell. The play ends hopefully with white and black workers pouring on stage, smashing the electric chair, and clasping hands while a red flag is rising. Hughes's volume eloquently illustrates the multiple and complex aspects of the African American experience that Scottsboro briefly brought to the fore.

[*See also* Communism.]

• Hugh T. Murray, Jr., "Changing America and the Changing Image of Scottsboro," *Phylon* 38 (1977): 82–92. Amiri Baraka, "Staging Langston Hughes's *Scottsboro Limited*: An Interview with Amiri Baraka," interview by Veve Clark, *Black Scholar* 10 (1979): pp. 62–69.   —Maggie Sale

SEACOLE, MARY (1805–1881), autobiographer and nurse. *The Wonderful Adventures of Mrs. Seacole in Many Lands* is an autobiography concerning the career of an African Caribbean nurse and hotelier among the military in the Caribbean and during the Crimean War (1854–1856). Published in 1857, this personal account of the "Crimean heroine" was a best-seller in England among other memoirs that focused only on the gruesome details of war.

Born in Kingston, Jamaica, in 1805, Mary Jane Grant was the daughter of a Scottish soldier and a free African American woman who owned a boardinghouse for military clientele. Following in her mother's footsteps, Mary became a successful hotelier as well as a nurse proficient in treating tropical diseases and performing minor surgery. A penchant for travel took Mary to England, the Bahamas, Haiti, and Cuba before her brief marriage to Edwin Horatio Seacole, godson of Viscount Horatio Nelson.

Following her husband's early death, Mary chose to move with her brother Edward to New Granada, a Spanish colony in Central America. Her success in treating cholera patients and performing surgery there prepared her for the 1853 yellow fever outbreak in Jamaica. Her wanderlust eventually took her to England in 1854 where she volunteered to serve initially as sutler to British soldiers fighting in the Crimean War. Her heroism in nursing the wounded garnered her commendations and medals of valor from the British government. Spending her last years in genteel comfort in Jamaica and England, Mary Seacole died of apoplexy and coma on 14 May 1881.

Like her counterparts in the United States, such as Charlotte *Forten and Elizabeth *Keckley, Mary Seacole illumines in *The Wonderful Adventures of Mrs. Seacole in Many Lands* the fortitude of the educated African American woman effectively dealing with the racism and sexism of her time.

• Ziggi Alexander and Audrey Dewjee, introduction to *The Wonderful Adventures of Mrs. Seacole in Many Lands*, 1984.

Sandra Pouchet Paquet, "The Enigma of Arrival: *The Wonderful Adventures of Mrs. Seacole in Many Lands*," *African American Review* 28 (1992): 651–663.

—Jacqueline Brice-Finch

SÉJOUR, VICTOR (1817–1874), dramatist, poet, novelist, and recipient of the French Legion of Honor. The most distinguished African American writer of nineteenth-century Louisiana, Victor Séjour's lengthy career as a successful dramatist in Paris makes him a unique figure, important to both the history of African American writing and the history of French *theater in the Second Empire (1851–1870).

Juan Victor Séjour Marcouet Ferrand was born a free Creole of color in New Orleans, son of prosperous merchant Juan François Louis Séjour Marcou, a free mulatto from Santo Domingo, and Eloisa Phillippe Ferrand, a free octoroon born in New Orleans. After secondary education under black writer and journalist Michel Séligny at New Orleans's Sainte-Barbe Academy, Séjour departed for Paris, like many other elite Creoles, to pursue further education and a career unencumbered by the racial constraints of American society.

In Paris Séjour entered literary circles where he associated with influential figures Emile Augier, Alexandre Dumas père, and abolitionist editor Cyrille Bisette (like Séjour, Dumas and Bisette were men of color). His first publication, a *short story entitled "Le mulâtre" ("The mulatto"), in which a slave murders his master only to discover he has killed his father, appeared in 1837 in Bisette's journal, *La revue des colonies*. References to *slavery and American racial dilemmas are overt in this first publication, one of the earliest African American fictionalizations of slavery, but thereafter occur only in allusions and metaphors such as the persecution of *Jews (*Diégarias*, 1844; *La tireuse de cartes*, 1860) and *class-based separatism in France (*Le martyre du coeur*, 1858). Literary success came in 1841 with *Le retour de Napoléon*, a heroic ode celebrating the return of Napoleon's remains to Paris. *Le retour de Napoléon* was reprinted in the United States in 1845 by editor Armand Lanusse as part of *Les *Cenelles*, the first *anthology of *poetry by African Americans.

Séjour's run of twenty-five years as a leading figure in Parisian theater, during which he brought over twenty plays to the stage, was extraordinary by any standards. His first plays, *Diégarias* (1844) and *La chute de Séjan* (*The Fall of Sejanus*, 1849), historical verse dramas in the romantic style of Victor Hugo, garnered critical praise. Wide popularity followed during the 1850s as he turned to prose melodramas, adventures, and comedies. During these years he lived well, brought his parents to France, and fathered three children with three mothers outside marriage. His success, however, was linked to precisely the kind of lavishly staged romantic melodrama that fell out of favor in the 1860s, and his personal fortunes declined with the genre's waning popularity.

Struggling in his last years with illness and a changing literary marketplace, further disrupted by the Franco-Prussian War and the Paris Commune (1870–1871), Séjour also produced a serialized *novel, *Le compte de Haag* (*The Count of Haag*, 1872), the story of a revolutionary in France, left unfinished because of declining health. Séjour was hospitalized for tuberculosis in 1873 and died in September 1874.

Overall, Séjour's career and significance are closely tied to the Second Empire's culture and values. The world of his writing is that of Bonapartism, emphasizing nationalism, liberalism, the *family, and religious life, attempting to steer a middle path between conservative monarchists and radical republicans. Nevertheless, as an African American his racially driven alienation from U.S. culture and career-long concern with ethnic and class conflict are noteworthy, and constitute a precedent for African American cultural *expatriates of later periods.

• T. A. Daley, "Victor Séjour," *Phylon*, First Quarter (1943): 5–16. Charles Edwards O'Neill, "Theatrical Censorship in France, 1844–1875: The Experience of Victor Séjour," *Harvard Library Bulletin*, 26.4 (Oct. 1978): 417–441. Charles Edwards O'Neill, "Victor Séjour," in *DANB*, eds. Rayford W. Logan and Michael R. Winston, 1982, pp. 551–552. J. John Perret, "Victor Séjour, Black French Playwright from Louisiana," *The French Review* 57.2 (Dec. 1983): 187–193. Thomas Bonner, Jr., "Victor Séjour," in *DLB*, vol. 50, *Afro-American Writers before the Harlem Renaissance*, ed. Trudier Harris, 1986, pp. 237–241.

—Philip Barnard

SELINA BOYCE, in Paule *Marshall's *Brown Girl, Brownstones* (1953), is one of the most psychologically complex female African American fictional characters since *Janie Crawford in Zora Neale *Hurston's *Their Eyes Were Watching God* (1937) and Gwendolyn *Brooks's Maud Martha (*Maud Martha*, 1953). Selina is a young woman of two worlds, two cultures. Born in the United States of Barbadian parentage, she must somehow bridge the gap between two identities that are often in conflict. Paule Marshall explores Selina's cultural identity crisis through the often ambivalent and volatile feelings she has toward members of the surrounding "Bajan" (Barbadian) community (and especially her mother), who exert strong pressure upon her to conform to their ideas concerning their position as immigrants in American society, as opposed to her father, who rejects the kinds of culturally and spiritually draining behavior that the pursuit of the American dream can inflict upon anyone not strong enough to withstand its pressures.

Selina, as a young woman, must carefully navigate herself between two worlds in order to utilize the best of both. By the end of the novel, she realizes that it was never a question of either/or in terms of her cultural identity. She learns that it is only the best of both her American and Barbadian cultures that has made her strong and that will continue to sustain her.

• Geta J. Leseure, "*Brown Girl, Brownstones* as a Novel of Development," *Obsidian II* 1 (1986): 119–129.

—Keith Bernard Mitchell

SEMPLE, JESSE B. *See* Simple.

SERMONS AND PREACHING. Stirred by the nimbus of imagination, the black preacher through his or her ritual form—the sermon—meditates on history in a world preoccupied with the vexing trinity of color, skin, and sin. Through the preached word, he or she displaces the discourse of a racist social order that maintains the exclusion of the black subject from history. One hears in the voice of the preacher the beat of the tom-tom. A synthesis of European and African cultures, the sermon is black people's first poetry in the United States.

Grounded in the *church and based to a large extent on improvisation, African American speech acts, keyed to the preacher's cadences and rhythms, provided the aesthetic underpinnings for black oral expression. Forced to creatively imagine their face, black people created a mythology to affirm their tradition as valid and meaningful for all people.

The black preacher is the transformational agent who walks the critical tightrope between the sacred and the secular; his speech act (sermon) is the agent for historical location. As the tap root of black American discourse, the sermon historicizes the experiences of blacks in America. The sermon as agent provides a link between generations of black families and makes it possible for the culture of black America to be transmitted over time and for members of the community to adapt to changing external circumstances. In the process, black America's first poet transformed a venerable Western genre and enriched American discourse.

During the largely unrecorded first century and a half of black life in the United States (1619–1770), the African gods were suppressed and forced to adjust to a new reality. In spite of the indifference and antipathy directed at blacks, many of them in the North followed the religious practices of the New Englanders. Led by their priests-turned-preachers, black people in the South began the process of transforming a largely Protestant Christianity that was daily profaned in their midst, and heavily influenced by a staid English tradition, into one that served African functions.

The first Great Awakening, that tumultuous series of outdoor revivals and camp meetings that swept the country around 1740, made the Christian religion reasonably accessible to the black masses. These revivals paved the way for unordained black lay workers to seize the moment in the late eighteenth and early nineteenth centuries for the emergence of the historic black church as "the foundation of Afro-American culture" (Albert J. Raboteau, *Slave Religion*, 1978). This independent black tradition was aptly termed "the Invisible Institution" by sociologist E. Franklin Frazier.

Two distinct but overlapping traditions emerged: the slave preachers or "exhorters" who brought color and drama to their imaginative retelling of the trials and triumphs of the Israelites in the Bible, and the learned tradition. The virtuoso style of the slave preacher has been variously described as "old-time Negro Preaching," "spiritual preaching," "whoopology," or "performed" preaching.

Representative figures of these traditions are Harry Hoosier ("Black Harry," d. 1810), who traveled throughout the United States with Bishop Francis Ashbury, and Richard *Allen (1760–1831). Hoosier, who some claimed to be the greatest orator in America, embodied the tradition of the slave exhorters. He represented the genius of "those black and unknown bards" who burst forth in all of their radiance in the wake of emancipation.

Allen represents those black preachers who preached from a manuscript or notes. Initially they were members of the Methodist Episcopal Church or Baptist Church, before founding their own black churches rather than remaining a segregated church within a church. These became the forerunners for the large urban congregations with a well-connected denominational church hierarchy. They took part in public policy debates at the state and national levels.

With several others in Philadelphia, Allen founded the Free Africa Society in 1787, the first organization for blacks in the United States. It was the institutional forerunner to the black church. Allen and Absalom Jones (1746–1818) founded the Bethel African Methodist Episcopal (AME) Church in 1816, which was the model for the Independent Black Church.

When George Washington (1732–1799) died, the Philadelphia *Gazette* published Richard Allen's Bethel AME Church sermon in which he stressed Washington's belated uneasiness about slavery as a sin. The first appearance of the summarized sermon in the historical record is an anonymous article entitled "Religious Intelligence: An Account of the Baptism of Nine Negroes in Boston, May 26, 1805." From its inception in the second decade of the nineteenth century, the Afro-Protestant press published sermons for distribution as well as news and literature for a community starved to know itself.

Among the early black preachers in America, there were such men as David George (c. 1742–1810), preacher of the First Baptist Church at Silver Bluff, South Carolina; George Liele (c. 1750–1820) of Burke County, Georgia, an eloquent preacher to blacks and whites; Andrew Bryan (1737–1812), founder of the First African Baptist Church of Savannah; the fearless Nat Turner (1800–1831), who served as a kind of exhorter, preaching on Sundays to slaves and some white people; John Chavis (c. 1763–1838) of North Carolina, who was commissioned as a missionary to slaves by the Presbyterians in 1801; and, most rare, Lemuel *Haynes (1753–1833), a man of learning and eloquence who through all of his life pastored only white Congregational churches in New England.

Haynes, who could have passed for white, did not flaunt his color; he seems to have spoken only once on race and in condemnation of slavery. In "The Nature and Importance of True Republicanism" (1801), he addressed the question of the "pitiful, abject state" of the "poor African among us." In his most famous sermon, "Mystery Developed," Haynes discussed religion, prison conditions, and errant justice. Haynes stood with Jonathan Edwards and George Whitefield with respect to the operations of the Holy Spirit.

Among the earliest black preachers in the Methodist Episcopal Church were Absalom Jones, Richard Allen, Daniel Coker, Abraham Thompson, Morris Brown, James Varick, Christopher Rush, and Henry Evans. Frederick *Douglass, who was licensed as a local AME Zion Church preacher, was fond of delivering his "Slaveholder's Sermon" to incite to action those who were fence straddlers in the cause of abolition.

The early black preachers shared a commonality of vision with generations of their pulpit brethren; they challenged the church to be relevant and asked the Lord to "give us this day our daily bread" as they created an African American aesthetic that the community recognized and endorsed.

Irrespective of their denominational affiliation, early black preachers were united in their call for freedom, justice, and human dignity. However, their solidarity with the patriarchal system blinded most of them to the injustices of their own practices, even when those practices were similar to what they were trying to escape from in the white church. For example, Richard Allen, the patron saint of the black church, had great difficulty in admitting women to the ministry.

Refusing to be silent in the face of black men taking advantage of their male privilege in relation to black women (which prefigures much of the post–civil rights literature by black women writers), black women preachers vigorously critiqued America's shortcomings and black theologies for the apparent lack of black women in a society that tends to devalue both blackness and womanhood. Feeling obliged to proclaim the word, Jarena *Lee, one of the most famous "daughters of thunder," issued the first official challenge to the restrictions on women preachers in a black denomination (c. 1811): "If the man may preach, because, the Savior died for him, why not the woman? seeing he died for her also. Is he not a whole Savior, instead of a half one? as those who hold it wrong for a woman to preach, would seem to make it appear" (Bert James Loewenberg and Ruth Bogin, eds., *Black Women in Nineteenth Century American Life*, 1976).

According to C. Eric *Lincoln and Lawrence H. Mamiya, in *The Black Church in the African American Experience* (1990), black women were not "officially recognized or ordained as preachers" until the late nineteenth or early twentieth century, though slave women undoubtedly "preached in clandestine services." Unlike their male counterparts, they were required to take "sublimated paths to the ministry" as exhorters, teachers, missionaries, evangelists, religious writers, and wives of clergymen. The AME Zion Church ordained Julia A. J. *Foote (1823–1900) as a deacon in 1884 and ordained Mary J. Small as a deacon in 1894. In 1976, Pauli *Murray (1910–1985) was consecrated and ordained as the first African American female priest of the Episcopal Church at the National Cathedral in Washington, D.C. In 1984 Leontine T. C. Kelly (b. 1930) became the first woman bishop of a major religious denomination in the United States when she was elected head of the United Methodists in the San Francisco area. On 12 February 1989, Barbara Harris (b. 1930), an African American, became the first female Anglican bishop in the world.

Among the earliest black women preachers were *Elizabeth, A Colored Preacher of the Gospel (1766–1867), Jarena Lee (1783–185?), Zilpha *Elaw (c. 1790–184?), Rebecca Cox *Jackson (1795–1871), and Amanda Berry *Smith (1837–1915). Those women who took sublimated paths to the ministry include Maria W. *Stewart (1830–1879), Harriet *Tubman (1823–1913), and Sojourner *Truth (1797–1883); they were associated with religious abolitionism. Other notable religiously motivated black women became teachers, for example, Fanny Jackson *Coppin (1836–1913), Lucy Craft Laney (1854–1933), Anna Julia *Cooper (1858–1964), Mary McCleod Bethune (1875–1955), and Nannie Helen Burroughs (1883–1961). Dr. Bethune often preached the required chapel service in the Daytona Normal School, the college she founded, which evolved into the Bethune-Cookman College. Until recently, black women were preachers sans portfolio in the large denominations.

Black religion with its Afro-Christian character surfaced in all of its glory in the wake of the Civil War. Simultaneously, divisions within the church became more pronounced as there was a push for an educated clergy. Preachers came to be defined as progressives as opposed to conservatives, spiritual rather than learned. The spiritual preachers placed a greater emphasis on the experiential dimension of religion, emotional and affective witnessing, and an ideology of blackness, as, for example, *Baby Suggs in Toni *Morrison's *Beloved* (1987).

The learned clergy included men such as Peter Williams, Jr. (c. 1780–1840), Episcopal; Daniel A. *Payne (1811–1893), AME; William H. Miles (1818–1892), Christian Methodist Episcopal; Henry Highland *Garnet (1850–1882), Presbyterian; Alexander *Crummell (1819–1898), Episcopal; James Augustine Healey (1830–1900), Catholic; Henry McNeal Turner (1834–1915), AME; William Paul Quinn (1788–1873), AME; and Francis J. *Grimké (1850–1937), Presbyterian, described as the last black Puritan. Payne was the arch-antagonist of anti-intellectual tradition within the black church (as was Booker T. *Washington, a deeply religious Baptist who often functioned as an unofficial preacher). He epitomized those blacks and whites who strove mightily to stamp out the resurgence of the "African cult," which they perceived as a threat to Western Christianity. Advocates of reparation, Crummell and Turner spent much time in West Africa. They left a diverse body of sermons.

The split in the black church that ensued in the wake of emancipation symbolizes the clash between African and European cultures. This division represents a cultural paradox in the black community: black vernacular tradition rooted in the church transformed American discourse, and its signature performance event was the performed sermon.

Nevertheless, the black bourgeoisie who set the social agenda tended to suppress the Afrocentric character of the community. Frances Ellen Watkins *Harper (1825–1911), an effective orator, ardent social reformer, active figure in the education of blacks, and widely published author, articulated these ideological tensions in her novel of uplift, *Iola Leroy (1892). The simmering tension provided a dynamic subtext for the *Harlem Renaissance debate on the authenticity of black culture in the 1920s, which flared anew with the cultural nationalism of the *Black Arts movement in the 1960s.

In spite of black America's move to assimilate, the end of the nineteenth century was dominated by the flamboyant John Jasper (1812–1901), who was steeped in the tradition of the "classic" folk preacher. This Richmond-based Baptist preacher's most famous sermon was "The Sun Do Move." In 1908 William E. Hatcher recorded some of Jasper's sermons and published them under the title From John Jasper. Perhaps the first widely available collection of black sermons may have been the book, Elder Cotney's Sermons, Gullah Negro Sermons, edited by John G. Williams (1895).

The self-consciousness of the sermon as art form marked the beginning of the twentieth century. W. E. B. Du Bois in The *Souls of Black Folk (1903) and James Weldon *Johnson in *God's Trombones: Seven Negro Sermons in Verse (1927) freed the depiction of the black folk preacher from the constraints of dialect under which Charles Waddell *Chesnutt (1858–1932) and Paul Laurence *Dunbar (1872–1906) chafed and made him palatable to a growing black middle class ambivalent about its place in American society. As sturdy black cultural bridges, Du Bois and Johnson showed a budding generation of black writers that the black sermon supplied the mythic frame through which the community viewed life in the United States from *spirituals, slave seculars, and *slave narratives to *blues, *jazz, *poetry, prose fiction, *drama, and, later, rap music. Their sage observations on black American religious life marked an important milestone in American cultural studies as they revealed the preacher as both a product and a producer of an aesthetic tradition.

Structurally, Souls, a mixture of theory, history, and sociology, soars with the rhetoric of the black preacher. Replete with words and imagery straight from the black pulpit, Du Bois's language took on the same biblical flavor black Americans used in the campaign to abolish slavery and to end the nightmare of Reconstruction—the South as Egypt, the promised land, and Canaan. Finally, Du Bois's incisive commentary in "Of the Faith of the Fathers" set the tone for American scholarship on the black church.

With the echo of Jasper's "whooped" sermon at his back, James Weldon Johnson in God's Trombones captured the essence of the classic black preacher. Johnson wrote these seven literary sermons "after the manner" of the preacher who is the master of metaphor, triumphant, transcendent, and moving in concert with the community. Johnson, as he notes in his preface, draws on a repertory of classic black sermons that includes the "Valley of the Dry Bones," the "Train Sermon," the "Heavenly March," and the "Creation."

The art and imagination of the black preacher informs the work of numerous Harlem Renaissance figures, such as Jean *Toomer, Langston *Hughes, Countee *Cullen, and Zora Neale *Hurston. The preacher as archetypal performer is the transitional figure in Toomer's modernist text *Cane (1923). Toomer structures much of his text around the dialogic call-and-response that is a staple of black religious discourse. Hughes devotes a section of his first poetry collection, The *Weary Blues (1926), as well as a section of his Selected Poems (1959), to poems shaped by the sermon. The textual richness of the symbolic universe of the black preacher informs Not Without Laughter (1930), "Thank You M'am" (1934), and Tambourines to Glory (1958).

Cullen was the adopted son of the Reverend Frederick A. Cullen of Harlem's fashionable Salem Methodist Episcopal Church; his poetic imagination was governed by an abiding Christian view of the world, as is evident in The Black Christ and Other Poems (1929). Much of his religious poetry is filtered through the lens of a vibrant black preaching tradition.

In her 1935 collection of folklore, Mules and Men, Hurston included an excerpt from a folk sermon. The sermon is the organizing principle in *Jonah's Gourd Vine (1934) and *Their Eyes Were Watching God (1937). Deeply influenced by the power of language and myth in and out of the homiletical mode, Their Eyes Were Watching God focuses on the emergence of a female self in a male-dominated world. Hurston also brought a theoretical bent to the Black Aesthetic tradition in her essays published as The Sanctified Church (1983).

In addition, Hurston, along with John and Alan Lomax, recorded authentic sermons in the 1930s for the Library of Congress's Archive of Folk Song. In 1941 the black folk sermon formally entered the academy with the publication of the landmark anthology The Negro Caravan, edited by Sterling A. *Brown, Arthur P. Davis, and Ulysses Lee. It now appears in most anthologies of American and African American literature.

Other archival work on the black sermon includes nine sermons recorded by sociologist Charles S. Johnson for Fisk University and John Henry Faulk's two-year study on black sermons in Texas, sponsored by the Julius Rosenwald Fund. They formed the core of his 1941 University of Texas MA thesis, "Quickened by de Spurit." Alice Jones's 1942 MA thesis for Fisk University was entitled "The Negro Folk Sermon: A Study in the Sociology of Folk Culture." Perceptive studies of African American sermonry include William H. Pipes, Say Amen Brother! (1951), J. Mason Brewer, The Word on the Brazos: Negro Preacher Tales from the Brazos Bottoms of Texas (1953), Bruce Rosenburg, Can Those Bones Live?: The Art of the American Folk Preacher (1970), Henry H. Mitchell, Black Preaching (1970), Hortense J. Spillers, "Fabrics of History: Essays on the Black Sermon" (PhD diss., Brandeis University, 1974), Gerald

L. Davis, *I Got the Word in Me and I Can Sing It, You Know: A Study of the Performed African-American Sermon* (1985), and Dolan Hubbard, *The Sermon and the African American Literary Imagination* (1994).

The archival collections of African Americana held in the libraries of Fisk, Howard University, the Atlanta University Center, other African American institutions, Boston University, the Library of Congress, and other municipal and university libraries around the nation include a number of significant and historically important sermons "published" by African American preachers or their congregations. For example, the Moorland-Spingarn Collection at Howard University is the repository for the sermons of Francis J. Grimké, Benjamin E. *Mays, and Howard Thurman.

The Great Migration coincided with the emerging cultural industry in the United States. "Race records" were located at the juncture between black transition from peasant culture to denizens of the city with its emergent jazz aesthetics. They presented black America with an alternative venue to the mainstream commercial recording firms. One of the foremost preaching stars of the "race records" was the Reverend J. M. Gates, whose sermon records in the 1920s were exceeded in the "race record" market only by Bessie *Smith's blues. Among those preachers that he influenced was Clarence LaVaughn Franklin (1915–1984), who shaped the religious imagination of the generation of preachers who came of age during the *civil rights movement.

The classic novels of the Great Migration introduce the notion of history as a sermon. In *Native Son* (1940) by Richard *Wright, in *Go Tell It on the Mountain* (1953) by James *Baldwin (as well as his play *The *Amen Corner*, 1968), and in *Invisible Man* (1952) by Ralph *Ellison, the storefront (sanctified) church is the site where blacks contest modernity and its implications for a people trapped in a perpetual present, acutely aware of their liminal status. Wright subverts the sermon, placing it in the mouth of attorney Boris Max and his passionate defense of Bigger Thomas as if to indict America for its failure to deal affirmatively with the problem of black suffering; Ellison uses sermonic rhetoric to enable his nameless narrator trapped outside of history to structure "the blackness of blackness"; and Baldwin, whose *Go Tell It* represents the apotheosis of the sermon in African American literature, reconstructs the corporate biography to tell how the community "looks back and wonders how we got ovah." This is the autobiographical impulse that drives black American religious discourse.

The civil rights movement presented black America as one nation under a sermon. Echoing the sentiments of anonymous black folk preachers, Martin Luther *King, Jr., invited the nation to step out on space and time and join his downtrodden community in making a more humane world. He called on Americans to adhere to the primary written cultural text (minus the discourse of racism) to which each American pledges allegiance. In his most famous sermon, *"I Have a Dream" (1963), King captures the national community's sense of metaphysical possibility when he says, as James Weldon Johnson's preacher does in *God's Trombones*, "I'll make me a world." At that moment he gave the nation a breathtaking vision of the Heavenly City. The essential writings of King are contained in *A Testament of Hope* (1987).

The hegemonic rhetoric of the sermon enabled people, regardless of their ideological orientation, to talk across socioeconomic lines as well as to demand full participation in the American dream. As a consciousness-raising activity, the civil rights movement spawned a call for a *black nationalism (SNCC, Black Panthers, *Malcolm X), a black theology (James A. Cone), and a womanist theology (Alice *Walker). These diverse voices disturbed the popular imagination when they suggested that we are not one nation under a sermon. Cultural nationalists whose work was influenced by the sermon include Amiri *Baraka, Haki R. *Madhubuti, Sonia *Sanchez, and Carolyn M. *Rodgers.

While King was calling on the republic to end its legacy of racism, black women, who were the backbone of the civil rights movement, were calling on the male-dominated pulpit fraternity to end its legacy of sexism. Alice Walker painted in broad brush strokes the outlines for *womanism in *In Search of Our Mothers' Gardens* (1983). It embraces the elements of tradition, community, self, and a critique of white feminist thought. The term was first used in print in Delores S. Williams's 1987 article "Womanist Theology: Black Women's Voices." Womanist theology signals black women's move from the pew to the pulpit. The essential challenge, however, remains to bring the word.

The cultural logic of the sermon infuses the fictive world of diverse African American women writers such as Alice Walker, Toni Morrison, Gloria *Naylor, and Ntozake *Shange. In *for colored girls who have considered suicide / when the rainbow is enuf* (1975), Shange captures the temper of a woman-centered discourse when the seven sisters in this choreopoem join hands at its conclusion and chant, "i found god in myself & i loved her." Using sermonic rhetoric as an entrée, black women writers interrogate the ideological, cultural, and sexual politics that take place under the cover of a male-dominated racial mountain. The self-voicing that emerges out of their work evinces a concern for nurturing and female independence.

Perhaps the most imitated preacher of his era, the incomparable C. L. Franklin (1915–1984), described as "the high priest of soul preaching," influenced a generation of black preachers who came of age during the civil rights movement. Franklin, pastor of Detroit's New Bethel Baptist Church, was a master of orality and technology. The recorded sermons of this Mississippian swept through a segregated black America like fire shut up in their bones. Among the preachers he influenced were Jasper Williams, Gardener Taylor, Martin Luther King, Jr., Clay Evans, C. L. Moore, Caesar Clark, Donald Parsons, and Jesse L. Jackson. Twenty of Franklin's best sermons have been published as *Give Me This Mountain* (1989). One of his best known sermons is "The Eagle Stirreth Her Nest."

Other outstanding black preachers of the second half of the twentieth century include: Howard Thurman, Benjamin E. Mays, Adam Clayton Powell, Jr., Manuel L. Scott, William Holmes Borders, Wyatt T. Walker, Malcolm X, Samuel D. Proctor, Ozro T. Jones, Jr., Calvin Butts, and Frank Madison Reid III. Notable sermon collections include William M. Philpot's *Best Black Sermons* (1972) and Samuel D. Proctor and William D. Watley's *Sermons from the Black Pulpit* (1984).

The triumph of the sermon in the black American literary imagination is the triumph of aesthetics. It issued directly out of the ethos of the slave community. African American writers transformed the responsive mythology of African American expressive culture, rooted in music and religion, into arresting artistic statements. Their resulting novels, poems, plays, autobiographies, and rap music, those polyvocal jeremiads, interact with each other in complex ways to constitute a specifically African American literary tradition. Their artistic statements speak to African Americans of history in their own words and rhythms and radiate the promise of the future. The preacher, as a sign of black people's subjugation and affirmation, represents the opaque community's historic struggle over language and, consequently, for self-definition. Through speech acts (sermons), the preacher provides the vehicle by which the entire community of faith may participate in shaping its own history and restructuring cultural memory.

Like preachers, black writers unite in their interrogation of what it means to be black in the United States, accenting the connections of their sermons with blacks' varied selves and with both historical and current social conditions. They transform historical consciousness into art, use it as a strategy for representation, and merge it with the political as they present the emergence of a self. The preachers preach beyond the ending of their earthly situation, while the writers write beyond the frame of their time-bound text. The preacher's voice and the writer's pen are the metonymically displaced voice of the community. The black sermon is the mother's milk of African American discourse.

[*See also* Churches; Oratory; Preachers and Deacons; Religion.]

• Henry H. Mitchell, *Black Preaching*, 1970. Charles V. Hamilton, *The Black Preacher in America*, 1972. Betty J. Overton, "Black Women Preachers: A Literary Overview," *Southern Quarterly* 23.3 (Spring 1985): 157–166. Eileen Southern and Josephine Wright, introduction to *African American Traditions in Song, Sermon, Tale, and Dance 1600s–1920*, 1990. Dolan Hubbard, *The Sermon and the African American Literary Imagination*, 1994. James Melvin Washington, *Conversations with God: Two Centuries of Prayers by African Americans*, 1994.

—Dolan Hubbard

SETHE SUGGS. In Toni *Morrison's *Beloved* (1987), Sethe Suggs is the epitome of the slave mother, even more tragic because she loved her children in a system that negated her humanity as well as her maternal instinct.

Purchased by Mr. Garner at age thirteen, Sethe marries Halle Suggs and he fathers every one of her four children—unusual in the slave system. With the death of Mr. Garner, whom the slaves considered humane, his heir schoolteacher takes over and subjects them to the full degradation and inhumanity of the system. Sethe feels she must escape to ensure the safety of her children (the fourth still unborn) and to feed her young daughter Beloved from her milk-laden breasts, but before she can leave, schoolteacher's three nephews hold her down in the barn, milk her like a cow, and beat her. This is the final blow to her sense of who and what she is, and she immediately sets out for the North, walking and crawling to *freedom when her feet become mutilated. When schoolteacher comes to reclaim his "property," Sethe kills Beloved with a handsaw rather than see her returned to *slavery. After Sethe serves a jail sentence for the murder, she and her children are free but Beloved's venomous and spiteful spirit begins to torment them, disappearing but then returning as a twenty-year-old. Moreover, Sethe is relentlessly haunted by guilt. Beloved's return is a horrible reminder of Sethe's history and, more significantly, of the horrific history of all African Americans.

[*See also* Paul D.]

• Wilfred D. Samuels and Clenora Hudson Weems, *Toni Morrison*, 1990. Trudier Harris, *Fiction and Folklore: The Novels of Toni Morrison*, 1991. Patrick Bryce Bjork, *The Novels of Toni Morrison: The Search for Self and Place within the Community*, 1994.

—Betty Taylor-Thompson

SEXUALITY. What is sexuality? An exhaustive catalog of physical acts, fantasies, positions, and identities might begin to suggest what various scholars look for when they are studying sexuality. But such a list would hardly begin to suggest the many assumptions or approaches possible in the exploration of that chosen subject. While some scholars may examine representations of desire, identity, or courtship, others may immerse themselves in theory, rarely looking at primary texts. The range of investigative opportunities is great, because sexuality not only means many things to many people, but it is also an essential component of patriarchal, racial, and class hegemonies.

In African American literature, theorists and nontheorists have made important contributions. African American women have been especially concerned with the political role of theory. Barbara Christian's "Race for Theory" (*Cultural Critique*, 1987), for example, provides a strong challenge to theorists who are unconcerned with reaching a general populace. Christian asks us to think beyond the boundaries of the academy in our search for language that does not exclude. These concerns are especially important to a study of sexuality and how it relates to reproductive rights, violence against women, and homophobia. Sexuality's intersection with race has been particularly important in texts such as *All the Women Are White, All the Blacks Are Men, But Some of Us Are Brave* (1982) and *This Bridge Called My Back* (1981), which relate to black women's studies.

Sexuality plays a provocative role within the African American literary tradition. Nineteenth- and twentieth-century African American writers have had to navigate between realistic depictions of sexual expression and stereotypical images of black sexuality. The stereotypes regarding black male and female sexuality that have existed since American slavery have tended to be contradictory. On one hand, in order to justify the institution of slavery, slave owners needed to foster an image of innocent and submissive Africans who required the benevolent dominion of a more civilized people. On the other hand, slave traders characterized Africans as primitive, savage beasts who possessed uncontrollable sexual appetites. Nevertheless, popular nineteenth-century figures such as *Uncle Tom, *Mammy, and *Sambo characterized black males and females as docile, loyal, dependent, and asexual folk who were unwilling to upset that "peculiar institution," American slavery. By containing black slaves within these defined categories, slave owners could preserve their ruling position within the hierarchy of slavery in the Americas and could manipulate the images of black sexuality in popular American culture.

Hazel Carby's *Reconstructing Womanhood: The Emergence of the Afro-American Woman Novelist* (1987) examines how the formation of black female sexuality in the nineteenth century relied in part on how slave women responded to white female sexuality. According to Barbara Welter's 1976 study on the "cult of true womanhood," white female sexuality reflects such virtues as "piety, purity, submissiveness and domesticity," virtues that nineteenth-century American women were expected to exemplify. Black female writers such as Harriet A. *Jacobs, Harriet E. *Wilson, Frances Ellen Watkins *Harper, and Pauline E. *Hopkins simultaneously contested and supported these sexual ideals as they combated the negative images of black female sexuality in their writing.

That American slave owners and writers perpetuated the myth of black women's primitive and promiscuous sexuality is evidenced in various slave narratives, historical accounts, and speeches written by Solomon *Northup, Mary *Prince, Frederick *Douglass, and Harriet Jacobs. Narratives written by male slaves rarely depicted female slaves in the roles of loving mothers, sisters, and daughters. For the most part, slave women in *Narrative of the Life of Frederick Douglass* (1945) become significant to Douglass only when they are victims of brutality and rape within the plantation system. Although there are significant absences of positive sexual images in early slave narratives, sexuality remains a fruitful area of exploration within this distinctly African American genre of literature, specifically because of these absences and silences.

Mary Prince's orally transcribed history of her experiences in the West Indies (1831) and Harriet Jacobs's *Incidents in the Life of a Slave Girl* (1861) recount the brutal physical and emotional treatment these women experienced at the hands of their slave owners. Jacobs, writing under the pseudonym Linda Brent about her life in North Carolina, vividly informs her readers that young female slaves between the ages of eleven and fifteen frequently became the subjects of their masters' unwarranted sexual advances. In *Black Looks: Race and Representations* (1992), bell *hooks argues that by defining black women as incapable of restraining their sexuality, white slave owners could view the black female body as an accessible, attractive commodity that would acquiesce to their desires. Jacobs challenges both her position as chattel property and as a sexual object within the slave system, because she asserts her ownership over her own body and proves that she is capable of expressing sentimental feelings toward black and white men.

Even though Jacobs willingly engages in a sexual liaison with a white man, Jacobs's narrative does not give in to the "tragic mulatto" scenario. The tragic mulatto figure, popularized in Harriet Beecher *Stowe's Uncle Tom's Cabin (1851) and William Wells *Brown's *Clotel (1853), is a biracial character who is betrayed by the white man she trusts and adores. The ambiguous racial status of the *mulatto allows for the projection of multiple fantasies based on color-coded stereotypes of virtue and wantonness, beauty and savagery, spirit and flesh. The mulatto figure almost always dies in these nineteenth-century narratives, for her body is nothing less than the site of racial and sexual conflict and impasse.

Although turn-of-the-century writers such as Charles Waddell *Chesnutt and Pauline E. Hopkins continue to reenact the tragic mulatto's sexual victimization in various literary works, it is Frances Ellen Watkins Harper, one of the most influential and prolific black writers of this era, who successfully avoids the tragic mulatto plot in her historical romance *Iola Leroy, or Shadows Uplifted* (1892). Iola Leroy, the progeny of a white Southern slave owner and a light-skinned ex-slave, is capable of *passing as white during Reconstruction, but she makes a conscious choice to assert her blackness even though some encourage her to pass as white.

The prevailing anxieties regarding *miscegenation at the turn of the century offered rich material for those writers interested in challenging stereotypes and racial myths. By constructing biracial characters who were socially mobile and intellectually equal or superior to whites, these writers worked against the racist arguments about blood mixing and black sexuality. Frances Smith Foster's *Written By Herself* (1993) has revived interest in Harper's work and that of other antebellum and postbellum black female writers who were addressing such concerns in America.

During Reconstruction, the *migration of freed slaves from the South to the North posed an economic threat to the white labor force. White anxiety over these massive changes resulted in a reversal of the stereotypes. Instead of the childlike Sambo figure, many white Americans viewed black men as menaces to society whose uncontrollable sexual desires endangered white women. This widespread fear of intermarriage and "intermixture" prompted stronger support of antimiscegenation laws, "one-drop" rules, and lynchings that would prevent or punish racial pollution. Although novels such as Thomas Dixon's The Clansman (1905) and The Leopard's Spots (1902) promoted racist notions about black male sexuality, African American writers like W. E. B. *Du Bois and Jessie Redmon *Fauset attempted to subvert these misconceptions.

In the early twentieth century, the *New Negro emerged as a quite fashionable and successful black woman or man who, with great optimism, was expected to safely negotiate the racism of America. The New Negro was an attempt by black leaders to counteract the racist perception of blacks as both promiscuous savages and innocent children. Du Bois's prim middle-class supporters and Claude *McKay's licentious Harlemites are representative of two extreme versions of black sexuality during the *Harlem Renaissance. In 1928 McKay's novel *Home to Harlem rose to the best-seller list within two weeks. McKay's narrative, filled with sex, *jazz, and drugs, contrasted with the elevated subject matter that Du Bois both wrote and encouraged others to write. In the *Crisis, Du Bois, the reigning dean of African American letters, confessed that after reading McKay's book, he felt "distinctly like taking a bath." Nevertheless, Carl Van Vechten, the most popular white patron of black artists in Harlem, would ask: "Are Negro writers going to write about this exotic material while it is still fresh?" Later writers such as Ralph *Ellison, Chester *Himes, Richard *Wright, Ed *Bullins, and Amiri *Baraka (LeRoi Jones) would contrast Du Bois's traditional, conservative representations of black males with more radical and sexually defiant black male characters.

The literature of the Harlem Renaissance is notable for its more explicit handling of sexuality. Although the music world had the more uninhibited voices of *blues singers like Bessie *Smith and Ma *Rainey, literary productions by women writers in the 1920s and 1930s more fully suggest the unique pressures African American women experienced with regard to sexual expression. Novels by Jessie Fauset, Nella *Larsen, and Zora Neale *Hurston suggest the complex ways that African American women wrote within and against prevailing stereotypes of women. There has been much recent criticism by Valerie Smith, Deborah MacDowell, and others that investigates the subversive qualities of female writers' texts.

According to such feminist critics as Cheryl Wall and Barbara Christian, works by Fauset and Larsen focused on a conservative black woman ensconced in a black bourgeois world. Promiscuity and seduction exist as threats and not as ways of life. Larsen's heroines, *Helga Crane in *Quicksand (1928) and both Clare Kendry and Irene Redfield in *Passing (1929), struggle to repress their sexual desires, which shape their identities and control their textual movements. The consequence of Helga's repressed sexuality affects her racial identity and her class ambitions, while Clare's racial passing affects her social acceptance in black Harlem.

The problem for Richard Wright was not so much whether to depict sexuality discreetly or explicitly, but how to unmake the myth of the black rapist. In *Native Son (1940), which became an instant bestseller, *Bigger Thomas does not rape Mary Dalton; but he knows the white world will believe he did. In a critique of Wright's novel, James *Baldwin reminds his readers that stereotypes about black males supersede their reality. Later, in Himes's *If He Hollers Let Him Go (1945), the protagonist, Bob Jones, makes the decison not to have sex with the white woman who corners him, and similarly Ellison's *Invisible Man (1952) resists the advance of a white woman who would make him into a rapist.

While these important male writers did much to challenge the stereotypes of black male sexuality, lesser-known female writers, such as Ann *Petry and Gwendolyn *Brooks, struggled to have their voices heard. Although there is a rising interest in these two writers, it should be pointed out that attention to the male writers of the 1940s and 1950s was then followed by a new controversy over the focus on black women writers in the 1970s and 1980s. It may be fruitful to ask what role sexuality has in determining these attentions. Alice *Walker's The *Color Purple (1982) has been described by critics as a sexual confessional. The confessional comes out of a Western tradition that links sexuality with sinfulness. In this confessional mode the characters are able to give voice to what could not be discussed publicly. Toni *Morrison's The *Bluest Eye (1970) also gives voice to the voiceless. *Pecola Breedlove, as her name ironically implies, is forced to breed without love, but she will no longer be silent about it.

This urge to give voice to the voiceless also may be seen in the rise of *gay literature and *lesbian literature written by African Americans. The surprising intersections of sexual and racial identities in James Baldwin's *Giovanni's Room (1956) and *Another Country (1962) did much to challenge notions of what black literature is or should be. Since Baldwin's homosexual and interracial subject matter had been critized, the resulting controversy probably did much to inspire African American writers and readers to explore new creative venues and representations of sexuality. But who could have anticipated the forcefulness of Sapphire and Wanda *Coleman's poetry, or Audre *Lorde's adamant call for "The Uses of the Erotic," which serves to reclaim black female sexuality as an empowering creative force? The legacy of this call is apparent also in the works of contemporary writers such as Melvin *Dixon and Carl Phillips, who investigate gay politics and an aesthetic of desire in their fiction, poetry, and criticism.

We might playfully say that African American writing has freed itself to enjoy its erotic potential. Anthologies such as Erotique Noire/Black Erotica (1992) and Wild Women Don't Wear No Blues (1993) give witness to this. In addition African American writers are creating and selling work in every genre. Octavia E. *Butler and Samuel R. *Delany have made a unique contribution in science fiction writing, creating racially marked characters who transform themselves from one sex to another, one identity modulating into another. Representations of black female and male sexuality will undoubtedly continue to change, always transgressive and always controversial.

[See also Gender.]

• Barbara Christian, *Black Women Novelists: The Development of a Tradition, 1892–1976,* 1980. Mary H. Washington, ed., *Invented Lives: Narratives of Black Women, 1860–1960,* 1988. Cheryl Wall, ed., *Changing Our Own Words: Essays on Criticism, Theory, and Writing by Black Women,* 1989. Henry Abelove et al., eds. *The Lesbian and Gay Studies Reader,* 1993. John Fout and Maura Tantillo, eds., *American Sexual Politics: Sex, Gender, and Race since the Civil War,* 1993. Emmanuel S. Nelson, ed., *Critical Essays: Gay and Lesbian Writers of Color,* 1993. Frances Smith Foster, *Witnessing Slavery: The Development of the Ante-bellum Slave Narrative,* 2d ed., 1994.   —Allison E. Francis *and* Juda Bennett

SHADD, MARY ANN (1823–1893), journalist, newspaper editor, educator, lawyer, and women's suffragist. At the age of ten Mary Ann Shadd moved with her family from her birthplace of Wilmington, Delaware, to West Chester, Pennsylvania, where she attended a Quaker school for six years before becoming a teacher herself, first in Wilmington, then in New York City and Morristown, Pennsylvania. Shortly after the passage of the 1850 Fugitive Slave Act, she emigrated to Windsor, Canada. First working there as a teacher, she soon embarked on her writing career, publishing in 1852 *Notes on Canada West,* a forty-page pamphlet promoting black immigration to that British colony. In 1853 she cofounded the abolitionist newspaper the *Provincial Freeman* with Samuel Ringgold Ward, and throughout its publication until 1858 she performed most of the editorial duties. Voicing through her *journalism recurring themes of African American pride, self-reliance, and integrationism, Shadd also used the paper to attack abolitionists whose philosophies she opposed, in particular Henry *Bibb and his Refugee Home Society, which in her view fostered fugitive slaves' dependence on funds gathered by "begging agents" and doomed them to second-class status in self-segregated communities. Having moved to Chatham, Canada, with the paper in 1855, she resumed teaching after its financial collapse. In 1860 her husband of four years, Thomas F. Cary, died. In 1863 she returned to the United States and recruited African American soldiers in Indiana for the U.S. Army. After the war Shadd settled in Washington, D.C., and became principal of a public school while contributing to various newspapers. Upon completing a law degree at Howard University in 1870, Shadd became one of the first African American women to practice law. An active member of the National Women's Suffrage Association, Shadd also organized the Colored Women's Progressive Franchise in 1880.

• Jim Bearden and Linda Jean Butler, *Shadd: The Life and Times of Mary Shadd Cary,* 1977.   —Brad S. Born

Shadow and Act. When it was first published in 1964, Ralph *Ellison's *Shadow and Act* was hailed as his *autobiography. Such critics as George P. Elliot and R. W. B. Lewis took their cue from Ellison himself, who in the volume's introduction wrote that the essays, "whatever their value," were autobiographical. While there are discussions of Ellison's early life in the text, the work is a statement of his literary credo as it had evolved over a twenty-two year period. As biography it is more concerned with the history of a *race rather than with the history of a person.

The text has an introduction and three divisions: "The Seer and the Seen," which deals with literature and Ellison's literary career; "Sound and the Mainstream," which deals with music and musicians; and "The Shadow and the Act," which concerns itself with racial issues. Each article has the original date of production at its end, allowing the reader to chart Ellison's development as a writer from 1942, the date of the earliest piece, to 1964.

In "The Seer and the Seen," Ellison uses literature as a vehicle for discussing the social consciousness of Blacks. He contends that whites assume that because Blacks have been brutalized in America they have become brutes and are unable to rise above this condition in life or in art. It is this vision that produces what Ellison calls "ideological" writing. But Blacks, according to Ellison, have been able to "deflect racial provocation and to master and control pain." In short, Blacks have been able through discipline to transcend the negative environment spiritually and artistically and to contribute to the national growth on all levels. The second section of the book is a variation of the first, but instead of using literature as a springboard for his discussion, Ellison uses *jazz. Originating in the Black community, jazz has been associated with poverty and low life, but the author contends that like the Black experience itself, the artists and the art form have transcended the limitations of the environment to triumph nationally. The third section is a bit more caustic. Here Ellison examines the effects of racism on Blacks and concludes that not only has it affected the population adversely, causing mental and emotional problems, but that during World War II it was responsible for the death of Blacks. The essays, coming as they did when America was experiencing a great deal of racial turbulence, must have had a sobering effect on the mainstream, for the book clearly indicates it is the Black experience in America that makes the American experience what it is: "It is practically impossible for the white American to think of sex, of economics, of children or women folk, or of sweeping sociopolitical changes without summoning into consciousness fear-flecked images of black men." For Ellison Blacks have become "the gauge of the human condition in America."

Shadow and Act is anchored in the African American literary canon between W. E. B. *Du Bois and Toni *Morrison. It shares a spiritual kinship with its "ancestor," Du Bois's The *Souls of Black Folk* (1903). *Shadow* differs in structure and style from *Souls,* but both works demonstrate that despite adversity Blacks have made great artistic contributions to America. Ellison's essays also share a kinship with Amiri *Baraka's *Blues People,* reviewed by Ellison in 1964, and James *Baldwin's *Notes of a Native Son* (1955) and *More Notes of a Native Son* (1961). *Shadow* anticipates such high-profile writers as Toni Morrison and Charles R. *Johnson. Morrison's *Playing in the Dark* (1992), like *Shadow,* inquires into the role Blacks play in the literature of whites. And Johnson's *Being* *and Race* (1988) questions, as *Shadow* does, the importance of experience in creating a work of art. *Shadow and Act* is an important literary and social document because it not only affirms Black humanity but also states emphatically that despite cultural deprivation Blacks have given much to America in the form of art.

—Ralph Reckley, Sr.

SHADRACK, the shell-shocked ex-soldier in Toni *Morrison's *Sula* (1974), is intimately connected with death. Having lost his sanity after his first battle in World War I, in which he saw a fellow private's face blown off, Shadrack believes that his hands have grown to monstrous proportions and he has no sense of self, "no past, no language, no tribe, no source, no address book, no comb, no pencil, no bed . . . and nothing nothing to do." Following his release from a veteran's hospital, he returns to his home neighborhood, in Medallion, where the *novel takes place. He institutes National Suicide Day, in which he walks down the street ringing a cow bell and holding a hangman's rope, thereby offering people a chance to kill themselves in a prescribed period so that death will not be a constant worry to them. The community eventually accepts Shadrack as an eccentric.

After *Sula Peace, the novel's protagonist, and her friend Nel participate in the drowning of a young boy, Sula goes to Shadrack's shack near the river to see if he witnessed anything. In the veteran's hospital he had dreamed of a river and a window, and to Sula he simply replies, "Always." This creates a bond between the two of them, both of whom are viewed as eccentrics by the community. Shadrack remains on the edges of the community physically but is very much a part of it. In an ironic twist, a group of black people follows him on one playful and fateful observance of National Suicide Day. They march out of Medallion and into the white section of town, into an unfinished tunnel on which the black men had been denied work. The tunnel breaks under their weight and they drown—without conscious intent to commit suicide—and Shadrack is one of few survivors. Shadrack, whose name comes from the biblical character who was saved from the fiery furnace by his faith in God, cannot be saved from the madness caused by the catastrophes and inhumanity of men and war.

• Wilfred D. Samuels and Clenora Hudson Weems, *Toni Morrison*, 1990. Trudier Harris, *Fiction and Folklore: The Novels of Toni Morrison*, 1991. Patricia Hunt, "War and Peace: Transfigured Categories and the Politics of *Sula*," *African American Review* 27 (1993): 443–459. Eileen Barrett, "Septimus and Shadrack: Woolf and Morrison Envision the Madness of War," in *Virginia Woolf: Emerging Perspectives*, 1994, pp. 26–32.

—Betty Taylor-Thompson

SHANGE, NTOZAKE (b. 1948), poet, playwright, novelist, and essayist. Ntozake Shange (En-to-za-kee Shong-gā) was propelled into the national literary and dramatic scene in 1974 with the dramatic debut of *for colored girls who have considered suicide / when the rainbow is enuf* and has since maintained a literary presence, garnering awards and honors for her achievements as a dramatist, poet, and novelist.

Her list of creative achievements has steadily increased through the writing of several *dramas such as *From Okra to Greens* (1978), *A Photograph: A Still Life with Shadows / A Photograph: A Study in Cruelty*, which was revised as *A Photograph: Lovers-In-Motion* and published with *Spell #7* (1979) and *Boogie Woogie Landscapes* (1979) in *Three Pieces* (1981). Other dramas include *Where the Mississippi Meets the Amazon*, (coauthored with Jessica Hegedorn and Thulani Nkabinda); *Mother Courage and Her Children* (1980); and *Daddy Says* (1989). Her *poetry collections include *Nappy Edges* (1978) and *Ridin' the Moon in Texas* (1989), and her books and *essays include *Sassafras: A Novella* (1977); *Some Men* (1981); *Sassafras, Cypress and Indigo* (1982); *A Daughter's Geography* (1983); *See No Evil: Prefaces Essays and Accounts, 1976–1983* (1984); and *Betsy Brown* (1985). Shange describes herself as a poet in the American theater, where she sees mostly shallow, stilted, and imitative action taking place on stages.

Shange was reared in a middle-class household in Trenton, New Jersey. Named Paulette Williams, she is the oldest of four children born to Eloise Owens Williams, a psychiatric social worker, and Paul T. Williams, a surgeon. The author seems to have enjoyed a childhood enhanced by material security and intelligent parents who exposed her to cultural influences, including *jazz, *blues, and soul, and literary artists such as Paul Laurence *Dunbar, Langston *Hughes, Shakespeare, and T. S. Eliot. She often mentions her family's Sunday afternoon variety shows, which sometimes consisted of her mother offering selections from Shakespeare, her father performing on the congas, and the children dancing or playing instruments. In the introduction to *Nappy Edges*, she indicates that her family members pursued whichever arts struck their fancy. These early artistic and cultural influences obviously affected Shange's life and art.

When she was eight, her family moved to St. Louis, Missouri. There she was among the first black children to integrate the public school system, and experiencing the cruelty and *violence of racist whites seems to have caused feelings of anger while strengthening her independence and her fighting spirit. When Shange was thirteen, the family moved back to New Jersey. She published poetry in the Morristown High School magazine, but after derogatory comments were made concerning her choice of African American subjects, she abandoned her poetry as she had once abandoned short story writing in elementary school because of racist comments. She feels that as a young black girl with an artistic bent she had no adequate role models in school.

Shange entered Barnard College in 1966 but became increasingly despondent over a recent separation from her husband and enraged at a society that she felt was unfair to intelligent women, and she attempted suicide four times. She managed, however, to graduate with honors in 1970 and pursued a master's degree in American Studies at the University of Southern California, living with other writers, dancers, and musicians. There she adopted a new name (Ntozake meaning "she who brings her own things," and Shange, "one who walks with lions"), after two South African friends baptized her in the Pacific Ocean. She earned a master's degree in 1973 and moved to the San Francisco Bay Area, teaching humanities and women's studies courses at Mills College in Oakland, the University of California Extension in San Francisco, and Sonoma State College. At Sonoma she worked with poets, dancers, and teachers who allowed her to study women's *history, write poetry, and theorize about the oppressive experiences of women.

In all her works, Shange suggests that black women should rely on themselves, and not on black men, for completeness and wholeness. She speaks for women of every race who see themselves as disinherited and dispossessed. The choreopoem (a descriptive name given by the author) *for colored girls* won the 1977 Obie, Outer Critics Circle, Audelco, and *Mademoiselle* awards, and received Tony, Grammy, and Emmy nominations. During 1994, for its twentieth anniversary, theaters around the country (including the Ensemble in Houston, Texas, where Shange once lived and worked), presented the drama, and Shange personally directed and served as consultant for the Houston production.

In an essay titled, "It is not so good to be born a girl" (in *Racism and Sexism*, ed. Paula S. Rothenberg, 1988), Shange discusses the disadvantages and restrictions that hinder a fulfilled life for African American women, noting that females all over the world and throughout history have been victimized and exploited sexually and emotionally from birth. Societies have thrown women away, sold them, and sewn up their vaginas, and in contemporary times, Shange avers, rape and violent crimes against women make even attending midnight mass dangerous. Nevertheless, the author asserts in this essay the same philosophy that she advances in *for colored girls*, namely, that only through finding "god inside themselves and finding meaning and self satisfaction in their own lives—that only by defining and living out their own destinies unsubjected to the whims of the oppressors, no matter their race or sex, can women become whole, self-sustaining humans."

Although *for colored girls* assured Shange's place in the African American dramatic canon and remains her most celebrated piece, the years from 1977 to 1982 were continually productive. *Mother Courage and Her Children* won Shange a second Obie in 1981; *Three Pieces* earned the *Los Angeles Times* Book Review Award in 1981, and that same year she was granted a Guggenheim Fellowship and Columbia University's Medal of Excellence. Shange was appointed to the New York State Council of the Arts and was an artist in residence at Houston's Equinox Theater.

Shange is known for her nonconventional use of English—unorthodox capitalization, punctuation, and spelling, and the use of African American idioms, dialect, slang, and rhythms. Her struggle to come to an articulate resolution in her work is acknowledged in articles such as the prefatory essay to *Three Pieces*, "unrecovered losses/black theater traditions." A preference for tension and complexity in

her themes and characters is also displayed in her fiction. She has a predilection to rework and expand her materials, as demonstrated by the expansion of her novella *Sassafras* into the novel *Sassafras, Cypress and Indigo*. Her love of *music is clear in the opening sentence of the novel: "Where there is a woman there is music." The novel tells about three sisters—Sassafras is a weaver, Cypress a dancer, and Indigo a midwife—all seeking to find themselves as creative people with a purpose. By the end of the novel they return home to their mother, but the reader doubts whether they can remain because of their need to pursue their own identities and *freedom. Shange's poetry also demonstrates her penchant for complexity and emphasizes her unconventional use of English. Much of her artistic philosophy and theories can be found in her prefaces, such as the preface to *Nappy Edges* where she states, "quite simple a poem shd fill you up with something / cd make you swoon, stop in yr tracks, change yr mind, or make it up."

Critic Mary Deshazer describes Shange as both writer and warrior. In the preface to *Three Pieces* Shange says her writing is fueled by "combat breath," a term borrowed from social observer Frantz Fanon. She tells the reader that the pieces were excruciating to write because they forced her to continually confront moments that had caused fury and homicidal desires. She says *Spell #7* and *Boogie Woogie Landscapes* contain "leaps of faith / in typical afro-american fashion." In her poetry, novels, and essays, Shange continues to engage readers with her unique literary warfare.

• Sandra L. Richards, "Conflicting Impulses in the Plays of Ntozake Shange," *Black American Literature Forum* 17 (Summer 1983): 73–78. Claudia Tate, *Black Women Writers at Work*, 1983. Elizabeth Brown-Guillory, "Ntozake Shange," in *DLB*, vol. 38, *Afro-American Writers after 1955: Dramatists and Prose Writers*, eds. Thadious M. Davis and Trudier Harris, 1985, pp. 240–250. Stella Dong, "Ntozake Shange," *Publishers Weekly*, 5 May 1985, 74–75. Elizabeth Brown-Guillory, *Their Place on the Stage: Black Women Playwrights in America*, 1988. Serena W. Anderlini, "Drama or Performance Art? An Interview with Ntozake Shange," *Journal of Dramatic Theory and Criticism* 6 (Fall 1991): 85–97. Betty Taylor-Thompson, "Female Support and Bonding in *for colored girls* . . . ," *Griot* 12.1 (Spring 1993): 46–51. Neal A. Lester, *Ntozake Shange: A Critical Study of the Plays*, 1995.

—Betty Taylor-Thompson

SHAW, NATE. *See* All God's Dangers; Cobb, Ned.

SHEARER, JOHN (b. 1947), photographer and author of fiction and nonfiction. Known for his books for children, John Shearer was born and raised in New York City and attended Rochester Institute of Technology and School of Visual Arts. In 1970, he became staff photographer for *Look* and *Life*, and contributed photographs to other national magazines, including *Popular Photography* and *Infinity*.

Shearer entered the field of *children's and young adult literature with *I Wish I Had an Afro* (1970), a nonfiction essay exploring the challenges of rearing an African American boy in poverty. Shearer's black-and-white photographs contribute to the intense depiction of an urban family's struggle against ignorance, gangs, and drugs. Shearer's talent for illustrating narratives of childhood experience is seen also in *Little Man in the Family* (1972), a double photographic essay exploring the lives of two boys from differing racial and class backgrounds. Louis Berrios is Puerto Rican and lives in a New York City ghetto with his mother and five sisters, while David Roth is white and the son of a suburban dentist. The essay explores the children's life ambitions through dialogue taken from interviews with the boys, their parents, teachers, and friends. The graphic candor of the photographs and the boys' revealing narratives communicate the sharp contrasts of their lives and the similarities of their dreams.

In 1976, John Shearer published *Billy Jo Jive Super Private Eye: The Case of the Missing Ten Speed Bike*, the first of five in the "Billy Jo Jive" fiction series for children. All illustrated by his father, Ted Shearer, *The Case of the Sneaker Snatcher* (1977), *Billy Jo Jive and the Case of the Missing Pigeons* (1978), *Billy Jo Jive and the Walkie Talkie Caper* (1981), and *Billy Jo Jive and the Case of the Midnight Voices* (1982) are mystery stories about a boy detective and his sidekick, Sunset Susie. Pairing up to solve small-time neighborhood crimes, the child "private eyes" recover stolen goods as well as locate the source of eerie noises. Targeted at primary grade readers, the series' fast-paced plots, first-person narration marked by urban vernacular, and vivid illustrations offer visually and textually entertaining yet educational stories. The series became so successful that short films based on the stories were shown regularly on the children's television program *Sesame Street*, produced by the author. In 1978, John Shearer received a Ceba award for the animated film adaptation of *Billy Jo Jive Super Private Eye: The Case of the Missing Ten Speed Bike*.

The recipient of over twenty national awards, John Shearer has had his work exhibited at the Metropolitan Museum of Art and in shows at Grand Central Terminal, the IBM Galleries, and Eastman Kodak. He has also taught photojournalism at the Columbia University School of Journalism. His essays and stories contribute to African American literature by offering young readers characters with whom they can identify, plots to which they can relate, and myriad images of African American children rarely seen in children's literature.

• "Shearer, John" in *Something about the Author*, vol. 43, ed. Anne Commire, 1986, pp. 192–196. "John Shearer" in *Children's Literature Review*, vol. 34, ed. Gerard J. Senick, 1995, pp. 165–168. —Kim Jenice Dillon

SHINE. Probably the most well-known twentieth-century *trickster, Shine is an epic figure in African American *folklore. His name could refer to the generic nickname given to black men who shined shoes or it could indicate that his skin was dark enough to literally "shine." In the toasts that celebrate him, the wiry-built Shine begins as the lowest-ranked employee on the ill-fated *Titanic*, the infamous luxury ship that hit an iceberg during its maiden voyage in 1912. Assigned to stoke coal in the ship's bowels, the fictional hero notices the encroaching water and repeatedly warns the captain. Unwilling to heed the lowly black man's advice, the captain waits too long before ordering the passengers and crew to evacuate. Shine's status has risen and many of the passengers seek his assistance in their quest for safety. Concerned only with his own well-being, Shine answers the pleas for help with his bawdy rhymes and emerges, in most versions of the toast, as the ship's only survivor. One version concludes, "When the word got to Washing'times the great *Titanic* was sunk / Shine was on Broadway, one-third drunk."

Tricksters such as Shine or even *Brer Rabbit appeal to African Americans for several reasons. Ostensibly, they are the least powerful characters in a given situation. But they use their cunning to undermine their larger, more powerful opponents. Their social world reflects that of many African Americans, accustomed to making their way in spite of handicaps. Also their verbal dexterity has considerable appeal.

• John Roberts, *From Trickster to Badman: The Black Folk Hero in Slavery and Freedom*, 1989.

—Patricia A. Turner

SHINE, TED (b. 1931), dramatist, television scriptwriter, educator, and contributor to the Black Arts movement and regional theater. Soon after Ted (Theodis) Shine's birth in Baton Rouge, he and his parents, Theodis and Bessie, moved to Dallas where he grew up. At Howard University he was encouraged to pursue satiric playwriting by Owen *Dodson, who tactfully indicated Shine's limits as a tragic writer. His play *Sho Is Hot in the Cotton Patch* was produced at Howard in 1951. Graduating in 1953, Shine studied at the Karamu Theatre in Cleveland on a Rockefeller grant through 1955 and then served two years in the army. Earning his MA at the University of Iowa in 1958, he began his career as a teacher of *drama at Dillard University in 1960, moving to Howard University from 1961 to 1967, and then settling at Prairie View A & M University where he became a professor and head of the drama department.

In 1964 Shine wrote *Morning, Noon and Night*, first produced at Howard University, which awarded it the Brooks-Hines Award for Playwriting in 1970 upon its publication in *The Black Teacher and the Dramatic Arts*. Combining humor and horror, Shine's play focuses on Gussie Black, who is manipulating her eleven-year-old grandson into becoming a traveling preacher and poisoning anyone who obstructs her project. Identifying himself as a Baptist, Shine often skewers those who cloak vicious ends in religiosity.

In 1970 Shine's 1969 plays, *Shoes* and *Contribution*, were produced and published together along with *Plantation* under the title *Contributions*. Strikingly different in theme, setting, and characterization, they collectively demonstrate Shine's skill in creating realistic, seemingly meandering, artfully constructed dialog, stunning, appropriate, meaningful plot twists, and thought-filled commentary on the black/human condition. *Shoes* points to the values that lead Smokey, a young waiter, to attempt shooting his benefactor, symbolically named Wisely, for withholding his summer earnings so he can reflect on his decision to blow them on fancy clothes. While warning about dehumanizing, community-undermining materialism, Shine remains sympathetic toward the poverty-striken childhood that drives Smokey to this extremity. *Contribution,* the most popular of Shine's many works, portrays Mrs. Grace Love, a spiritual-singing Christian who is chided by her activist grandson for loving the bigots she works for, but in reality she is contributing to the movement by poisoning them all. The farcical *Plantation* exposes a segregationist who discovers after his black son's birth that he is a mulatto. Following his suicide, a star rises in the east and three wise men appear in El Dorado, hilariously and hopefully hailing a new era.

From 1969 to 1973 Shine wrote over sixty scripts for the Maryland Center for Public Broadcasting's *Our Street* series while earning his doctorate from the University of California, Santa Barbara in 1971. The 1974 seminal anthology *Black Theater USA,* with Shine as consultant to editor James V. Hatch, includes his play *Herbert III,* a humorously insightful study of a couple with contrasting attitudes toward how to raise children amid racism. This play, like those preceding and following it, displays his shining contribution to contemporary black theater.

[*See also* Black Arts Movement.]

• Winona L. Fletcher, "Ted Shine," in *DLB,* vol. 38, *Afro-American Writers after 1955: Dramatists and Prose Writers,* eds. Thadious Davis and Trudier Harris, 1985, pp. 250–259. Bernard L. Peterson, Jr., "Ted Shine," in *Contemporary Black American Playwrights and Their Plays,* 1988, pp. 425–428.

—Steven R. Carter

SHOCKLEY, ANN ALLEN (b. 1927), librarian, newspaper columnist, teacher, lecturer, compiler, essayist, and fiction writer. A multitalented professional, Ann Allen Shockley has contributed to various fields, yet her contributions as writer remain invisible to much of America.

Born 21 June 1927, in Louisville, Kentucky, Shockley is the only daughter of Henry and Bessie Lucas Allen, both social workers. To her parents and a devoted eighth-grade teacher, she has attributed her insatiable desire to read and write. She edited her junior high school newspaper, wrote short pieces in the *Louisville Defender,* and penned *essays and short fiction for the *Fisk Herald* while an undergraduate at Fisk University (1944–1948)—all before her twenty-first birthday. These early pieces show Shockley's interest in social and cultural issues.

In 1949 Shockley began a weekly column called "Ebony Topics" for the *Federalsburg Times* (Md.). From 1950 to 1953 she penned a similar column for the *Bridgeville News,* in Bridgeville, Delaware, where she resided with her husband, William Shockley. Married in 1949 and later divorced, she had two children, William Leslie, Jr., and Tamara Ann. Political, cultural, and social events swelled Shockley's columns, which celebrated African American family unity, praised ebony heroes, and honored those who had excelled in their fields. Some of her pieces de-

fined Thanksgiving, Armistice Day, and Mother's Day; others championed women's issues, a position she would return to again in her later pieces. She also contributed articles to the *Baltimore Afro-American* and to the *Pittsburgh Courier.* During her years as freelancer for newspapers, she held jobs as public school teacher and librarian. In 1959 she received her master's degree in library science from Case Western Reserve University.

Shockley has written several reference books for the library. Her unpublished *History of Public Library Services to Negroes in the South, 1900–1955* gives an overview of the inadequate, segregated public library services that were available to African Americans in southern states during the first half of the twentieth century. *Living Black American Authors: A Biographical Directory* (1973) stands as a significant compilation of African American writers with entries ranging from Russell Adams to Andrew S. Young. *Handbook of Black Librarianship* (1977) identifies for librarians and archivists ways to collect and preserve materials that relate to the history of African Americans. *Afro-American Women Writers, 1746–1933: An Anthology and Critical Guide* (1988) documents the achievements of African American women writers and the effects their sociohistorical environments had on their works.

Most of Shockley's essays complement her books and pinpoint the neglected areas of librarianship related to African Americans. She examines African American librarians' attitudes toward their jobs ("Negro Librarians in Predominantly Negro Colleges"), assesses the need for special collections ("Does the Negro College Library Need a Special Negro Collection?"), and documents the library's role in encouraging students to read ("Reading Encouragement in the Maryland State College Library"). Shockley's essays and books on librarianship reflect her concerns as curator of African American collections at Delaware State College (1959–1960), University of Maryland, Eastern Shore (1960–1969), and at Fisk University (1969–).

Themes related to African American culture continue in Shockley's short stories, which mirror the social and political unrest of the 1960s and 1970s. She explores interracial dating ("End of an Affair"), de facto segregation in public schools ("Monday Will Be Better"), sexism ("To Be a Man"), the hypocrisy of some Black Power advocates ("Is She Relevant?"), the African American brain drain to white universities ("The Faculty Party"), student uprisings on African American campuses ("The President"), the plight of the Vietnam veteran ("The Saga of Private Julius Cole"), and homophobia ("Home to Meet the Folks"). These stories—growing out of the civil rights, Black Power, women's liberation, and lesbian and gay movements—entertain the experiences encountered and choices made by African Americans. Her literary influences—Richard *Wright, Ann *Petry, Lillian Smith, and Dorothy Parker—leave a noticeable tincture of naturalism.

Shockley's major contribution to African American literature is in *lesbian literature. *Loving Her* (1970) and *Say Jesus and Come to Me* (1982),

Shockley's two novels, and *The Black and White of It* (1980), her collection of ten short stories, focus on lesbian issues. *Loving Her* depicts the abusive marital relationship of Renay Davis, who finds romantic love with a wealthy white woman. *Say Jesus and Come to Me* profiles Myrtle Black, a charismatic lesbian minister whose presence highlights homophobia in the African American church. Influenced by the lesbian and gay movement, *The Black and White of It* explores infidelity ("The Play"), white lesbians ostracizing black lesbians ("A Meeting of the Sapphic Daughters"), the aging lesbian ("A Birthday Remembered"), self-denial ("Holly Craft Isn't Gay)," and homophobia in the African American community ("Home to Meet the Folks"). Reissued by Naiad Press and reviewed in fledgling women's magazines, these three volumes have not received adequate attention.

Shockley observes life as it is lived and considers nothing too insignificant or taboo to write about. A pioneer of lesbian themes and protagonists in African American literature, she waits for scholars to embrace fiction that reaches out to all subjects.

• Rita B. Dandridge, *Ann Allen Shockley: An Annotated Primary and Secondary Bibliography*, 1987. SDiane Adams Bogus, "Theme and Portraiture in the Fiction of Ann Allen Shockley," PhD diss., Miami University, 1988. Tracye A. Matthews, "Ann Allen Shockley," in *Black Women in America: An Historical Encyclopedia*, ed. Darlene Clark Hine, vol. 2, 1993, pp. 1029–1030.
—Rita B. Dandridge

SHORT STORY. Despite the apparently tenuous location of African American short fiction as a marginalized genre, this genre, when scrutinized closely, does not inhabit a realm of fragility. Quite the contrary, short fiction by African Americans, among whom number many of America's and the world's great authors, has been constructed upon what constitutes the most solid foundation of any genre within American literature—that of the African American oral tradition. Several scholars have pointed out that white culture in America cannot muster any such tradition of long duration, simply because white folks lack the homogeneity of African American culture. While white folks trace their origins to a multitude of distinctive European cultures and/or ethnicities, practically all African Americans have origins among the several peoples of West Africa. More to the point, however, is the fact that, as Charles Rowell's *Ancestral House: The Black Short Story in the Americas and Europe* (1995) makes clear, all African Americans, indeed all ancestors of the victims of the forced African diaspora, share the horrid experience of the *Middle Passage and its oppressive consequences. The memory of such an experience dynamically binds all progeny of this disastrous event.

The oral tradition that ineluctably evolved as a result of the Middle Passage amounts to a conscious and perhaps even an unconscious effort to make sense of this disaster and, subsequently, merely to survive. The tradition of *spirituals, homilies, and folktales, all manifestations of the African American oral tradition, map the dramatic struggle of displaced Africans to cope first with enslavement and

then with second-class citizenship. Indeed, as Gayl *Jones instructs us, the components of this oral tradition served first the Africans of the diaspora and later African Americans as voices of liberation. One does not need to pursue an investigation of African American literature in any great depth to grasp how vital to black culture storytelling has been, especially before the days of *television, to the *identity and even the survival of the *family. In *American Negro Folktales* (1967), Richard M. Dorson deemphasizes the solidity of the African American oral tradition, of folktales in particular, by observing that, "Only a few plots and incidents [among folktales] can be distinguished as West African," and by maintaining that the majority derive from the white European tradition. Whether African American folktales originated in Africa, their persistence established a tradition, and that tradition is *oral* as was the tradition in Africa *oral.*

As well, African American short fiction often displays an intimate familiarity with classical discourse. For that matter, this recurrent classicism appears with enough frequency to warrant occasional treatment in the ensuing attempt to give a survey of the genre's history. But of greater consequence are the incorporations by African American artists into their short fiction of the motifs of biblical stories and lore, of the recollection of a noble African and/or African American heritage, of call and response from black homiletics, and most significantly of black spirituals and *blues; each of these motifs may arguably be viewed as a modified component of the African American oral tradition. This oral tradition, evident in African American sermons, folktales, and spirituals and blues, has played an overwhelming role in the construction of African American short fiction, forming short fiction as practiced by African Americans into an identifiably African American art.

Biblical lore and tales are explicit in such titles as Jean *Toomer's "Calling Jesus" and Henry *Dumas's "Ark of Bones," while John Edgar *Wideman's "Damballah" (along with his collection *Damballah*, 1981) and Paule *Marshall's "To Da-Duh, in Memoriam" celebrate the African American cultural past. As early as 1860 Frances Ellen Watkins *Harper made good use of the call and response motif in her short story "The Triumph of Freedom—A Dream." The use of verses from spirituals and various motives from blues and *jazz (riff flourishes and low-down blues songs, for example) so pervade black short fiction and appear in so varying a set of patterns, these patterns having their origins in what has been called the "cante-fable" (a combination of folk narrative with song), that one may well identify this type of written, carefully crafted short story as a "cento" fiction, a medley of song and prose narrative, a term that will recur in this essay. Once again, while whites may indeed on occasion construct a cento fiction, this form does not reappear in white short fiction with anything like the regularity one discovers among short stories by African Americans.

Acknowledging black fiction's marginalized status, one must concede that such a body of art must be characterized as subversive by nature, at least in its beginnings. By circuitous traveling and subversive maneuvering, African American short stories before the 1960s can be surprisingly direct and bitter. During and after the era of the 1960s *civil rights movement and the *Black Arts movement, moreover, the double-voiced short fiction of African Americans becomes unabashedly aggressive, losing most of its subversive tones. In the following historical, largely chronological survey of the genre, certain short fiction collections by individual authors have played such significant roles in the development of the genre that they require special notice.

Nineteenth Century to 1887. While Henry Louis *Gates, Jr.'s Black Periodical Fiction Project may well recover specimens of short fiction dating from the late 1820s (the project's earliest source: John Browne *Russwurm and Samuel *Cornish's *Freedom's Journal, founded on 16 March 1827), perhaps the earliest attempt by an African American to write a short story dates from Victor *Séjour's 1837 "Le Mulatre" ("The Mulatto"), which first appeared in the French tongue in La Revue des colonies. This sentimental and at times gothic tale about the progressively hostile relationship between a white Haitian plantation master and his son by one of his slaves contains about two-thirds dialogue, predicting Séjour's future fame as a dramatist.

Frederick *Douglass's better-known "The *Heroic Slave," published in Douglass's the *North Star in 1853 and again in Julia Griffiths's Autographs for Freedom in the same year, marks the appearance of a short story much the superior of Séjour's. Based on the escape of Madison Washington from a life of *slavery in Virginia to *freedom in Canada and his return in 1841 to rescue his wife, the story presents its most diverting moments in its narration of Washington's capture and his subsequent role as leader of a successful rebellion aboard the domestic slaver Creole. Frances Ellen Watkins Harper's first short story, "The *Two Offers" (1859), mixes "a message of deliverance" with a somewhat sentimental tale of two middle-class, probably white female cousins. In a tale treating one cousin's decision to pursue a career while the other chooses an unhappy *marriage, Harper perhaps celebrates her own career, one that did not include marriage until November 1860 at age thirty-five. In any event, the unmarried cousin makes ample use of her *education by becoming "an earnest advocate" for "the down-trodden slave" to the extent that "the flying fugitive remembered her kindness . . . having broken the chains on which the rust of centuries had gathered." As well, Harper's career woman, perhaps the first in African American letters, promoted to those of her sex a theory of motherhood and self-education leading to "the full development and right culture of our whole natures." In later short fiction, Harper amply demonstrates her own educated, informed quest for knowledge. In "The Triumph of Freedom—A Dream," an allegory of the ravages of slavery, she remarks that "every drop" of the blood of the John *Brown–like martyr against slavery produces an armed man ready "to smite the terror-stricken power" of slavery, much like "the terrible teeth sown by Cadmus." Here she calls up an episode from classical myth, reshaping it for her own present needs.

Pre–Harlem Renaissance (1887–1919). In 1877 Charles Waddell *Chesnutt published his short story "The Goophered Grapevine," which, according to William L. Andrews, "marked Chesnutt's first appearance in a major American literary magazine." This and other "short stories in Negro dialect," using Chesnutt's own words, he collected into a book he called The *Conjure Woman in 1899, which after Paul Laurence *Dunbar's *Folks from Dixie (1898), is the second collection of short stories by an African American. The Conjure Woman includes seven stories, each deeply indebted to the oral African American folk tradition and each of which employs, as does "The Goophered Grapevine," *Uncle Julius McAdoo as narrator, a former slave steeped in work songs, ballads, *trickster and "hant" or haunt tales, tales of *Brer Rabbit and hoodoo conjure tales, all from the African American folktale tradition. As in "The Goophered Grapevine," Uncle Julius tells ironic, double-edged tales to unsuspecting would-be superior white males who are so certain that black folk lack the intellect for irony that they miss the putdowns engineered by Uncle Julius, though on occasion their wives have their suspicions. As an also marginalized, second-class group, the wives of these unsuspecting males function well as mediators between Uncle Julius's exaggerated, sometimes comic, sometimes tragic but always ironic narratives, better enabling the reader to perceive the real message. This collection is important not merely as the first of its kind but also because of its example to future writers of short fiction. Chesnutt went on to publish The *Wife of His Youth, a collection of nine short stories appearing during the Christmas season of the same year as The Conjure Woman. These two collections, along with those of Dunbar, served later African American writers as promises that their own work might see print.

Dunbar's Folks from Dixie is the first collection of short fiction published by an African American. Dunbar went on to publish three additional books of short stories before his death in 1906. Although comparatively few of his short stories examine the social problems of African Americans, the fact that he was the most prolific writer of short fiction among African Americans in his time recommends him to any treatment of the genre. In such tales as "The Ingrate" and "The Lynching of Jube Benson," Dunbar addresses serious sociopolitical issues central to African American welfare at the turn of the century.

Two other writers of this period who deserve at least a passing glance in this survey are Alice Moore *Dunbar-Nelson, at one time wife of Paul Laurence Dunbar, and Pauline E. *Hopkins, better known for her magazine *novels. With some forty-five stories to her credit, Alice Dunbar-Nelson achieved almost half the total output of her more famous husband. What is most remarkable about this indefatigable author and educator is the fact that her first of two published collections of short fiction, Violets and Other Tales (1895; published under her maiden name, Alice Ruth Moore), is interspersed with selections of her *poetry, these appearing between several, but not all, of the stories, a practice anticipating that of Jean Toomer's *Cane. This interspersal creates within the *anthology the effect of a medley presentation or of a cento fiction. Pauline Hopkins appears to have written only about eight short stories, never collected into a volume. Stories such as "The Mystery Within Us" (as well as Hopkins's longer fiction) are notable among the first attempts to deal with interracial marriage, in Hopkins's time a verboten subject. Hopkins sustained severe criticism for her courage.

Harlem Renaissance (1920–1935). Perhaps the richest period in the history of African Americans in the production of the literary and the visual arts, the *Harlem Renaissance saw the launching of the literary careers of such artists of short fiction as Claude *McKay, Jessie Redmon *Fauset (without whom some say there would have been no renaissance), Nella *Larsen, Rudolph *Fisher, Eric *Walrond, Richard Bruce *Nugent, Zora Neale *Hurston, Langston *Hughes, Wallace *Thurman, Arna *Bontemps (whose long-known, much-anthologized, and most affecting story, "A Summer Tragedy," was posthumously collected with other of Bontemps's stories in 1973 as *The Old South: "A Summer Tragedy" and Other Stories of the Thirties*), and not least among these, Jean Toomer. All these writers, with the exception of Nugent, have enjoyed considerable fame, while Hughes and Hurston are now recognized as major American authors.

This period in the development of the short story is especially rich in its affinity to *music. Jean Toomer in *Cane* (1923), for example, arranges lyrics between stories, these suggesting connections among the tales. He also incorporates lyrics within individual stories, thus creating a cento fiction wherein the organic mixture of poetry and prose becomes a medley. The lyric "Portrait in Georgia," which immediately precedes the fine story "Blood-Burning Moon," describes a chestnut-haired, slim-bodied temptress, a light-skinned *mulatto whose eyes burned like coals, through whose lips passed the breath of "the last sweet scent of cane," but whose body was "white as the ash / of black flesh after flame." This vivid, almost macabre description introduces Louisa of "Blood-Burning Moon" and presages the fates of her white and black lovers, Bob Stone and Tom Burwell. In Toomer's hands, the old folktale portrayal of competition between plantation master and male slave for the most attractive among the slave women transforms into a tale in which both men meet horrible deaths. The reader becomes tempted to view Louisa, figuratively covered by the blood of both lovers, as herself the "Red nigger moon" from the story's three-times repeated lyric: "Red nigger moon. Sinner! / Blood-burning moon. Sinner! / Come out that fact'ry door." The call and response here, evident in declaration followed by exclamation, owe something to the tendency in biblical Hebrew poetry toward repeating the content of one line in a rephrasing of the succeeding line. This single story from *Cane* resonates with a distinctly African American quality, one that the chant of the lyric "Red nigger moon" underscores in this brilliantly crafted cento fiction.

Both Rudolph Fisher's superb stories "Common Meter" and "Miss Cynthie" constitute cento fictions. "Common Meter" cannot be read without hearing the syncopated rhythm of "a low-down blues song," while "Miss Cynthie" invites one to join the successful young musician's grandmother as she forms the words of the song she had so completely internalized when she was a child and now hears her grandson deftly perform just for her, his inspiration.

Zora Neale Hurston's "Sweat," first published in the 1926 avant-garde journal *Fire!!*, may be called a cento fiction because its leading character, Delia Jones, sings repeatedly a variation of the old African American spiritual "Oh, Wasn't Dat a Wide Ribber" as she drives from her church's love feast to the house she has labored so devotedly to own. Whereas "Sweat" articulates the African American woman's predicament in rural Florida, Hurston's "The Gilded Six-Bits" tells of a similar predicament from the male point of view; here Joe Banks must deal with his wife's infidelity as Delia Jones must endure her husband's. Both tales give substantial attention to the Bible. Joe Banks, "like Samson awakening after his haircut," warns his wife not to "look back lak Lot's wife," while Delia Jones feels that, in her exertion to keep her home, she has "crawled over the earth in Gethsemane and up the rocks of Calvary many, many times." It is certainly no exaggeration to hold that, given Hurston's well-known contributions to the gathering of *folklore in her *Mules and Men* (1935) and *Tell My Horse* (1938), both her short fiction and her later long fiction are heavily indebted to her extensive knowledge of folk materials, especially those she gathered from her own past and from research in her native rural Florida.

Langston Hughes's *The Ways of White Folks* (1934) approaches its unmistakable use of music in two ways. Three of its stories, "Slave on the Block," "The Blues I'm Playing," and "Mother and Child," are each examples of cento fiction. Oceola Jones in "The Blues I'm Playing," for example, breaks into a blues song as she frees herself from the tyranny of her white patron by playing her piano to the throbbing rhythm of "tomtoms deep in the earth" rather than playing the demanded classical music. The other way by which Hughes expresses his deep ties to music in *Ways*, not really about white folks' ways but about the ways black folks cope with white attitudes toward them, is through a kind of prose blues or a syncopated alternation between happiness and sadness. Some of Hughes's characters enjoy a few moments of victory, for example, as in the case of Luther, the handsome young African American man in "Slave on the Block" who exploits the obsessive interest of a white couple in his physical prowess, or the consummate African American, but *passing, con artist Lesche in "Rejuvenation Through Joy." Sad times of defeat overtake the sensitive black violinist Roy Williams of "Home," who is lynched for talking to a white woman, and the "tall mulatto boy" of "Father and Son," as he takes his own life just moments after he has killed his white father.

The blues also play a determinative role in the construction of Richard Bruce Nugent's "Smoke, Lilies and Jade," a masterpiece of cento fiction that appeared first with Hurston's "Sweat" in *Fire!!* Here the substances named in the title and then repeated hypnotically many times act as melodies that interweave in counterpoint throughout the story, creating a blues fugue. The base melody, "the blue smoke" that causes the narrator Alex to muse, "was imagination blue [?]," is the first melody or motif to appear, and it is this melody against which the other voices, those of jade and lilies, move in counterpoint. Alex claims he wants "to do something . . . to write or draw" (sounding much like Nugent, who was a writer and artist, the major illustrator of *Fire!!*), but he resolves to be comfortable, "to lay there comfortably smoking" and remembering, blowing blue smoke.

The story concludes with Alex's half-dream, half-real notion that he and Melva, his "olive-ivory" African American sweetheart, and Adrian, his white male lover, all "walk music," apropos of the story's return to the initial voice's "blue smoke," once again in typical fugue fashion. Just so does Nugent stunningly accomplish completion of his prose blues fugue— but not before he signifies upon Langston Hughes's "Preface" to *Fire!!* by allowing the story's red calla lilies to provoke a vocalized version (which Nugent calls "Langston's spiritual") of "Fy-ah Lawd. / Fy-ah's gonna burn my soul," thus creating a spectacular variation for his grand cento fiction.

Post–Harlem Renaissance (1935–1964). The writers of this period greatly profited from such Harlem Renaissance experiments as Nugent's "Smoke, Lilies and Jade." At the same time, while the quality of long fiction soared during the post-Renaissance period, that of short fiction diminished somewhat, if only because of the period's greater attention to long fiction and because of a reduced number of contributors to the genre. Langston Hughes continued to write short stories, which formed part of a newspaper column he wrote for some twenty years, collecting them eventually into several volumes, the last of which was *The Best of *Simple* (1961); Hurston concentrated on novels; Bontemps turned to publishing anthologies (with Hughes) and to serving Fisk University as its head librarian; Thurman and Fisher died in 1934; and Nugent and Toomer all but ceased to publish.

Three major African American novelists and essayists did, nevertheless, emerge during this period. We are fortunate that each author, Richard *Wright, Ralph *Ellison, and James *Baldwin, made significant contributions to the genre of the short story. Wright's sagacious collection, *Uncle Tom's Children*, published in 1938 without "Bright and Morning Star" and again in 1940 (the year of *Native Son*) including this story, is assuredly a work of genius. Each of the five stories comprising this collection may be identified as a cento fiction. "Bright and Morning Star," whose title is taken from the old spiritual, makes constant reference to its title as the devoted mother, Sue, often lets "slip from her lips" the old songs "with their beguiling sweetness." To Sue her son Johnny-Boy was everything. As Wright phrases it, "Her love for him was for his happiness." Contrary to what one may suppose, Sue sacrifices her life not for the Communist Party of which her son is a member, but for her son's honor. Rather than constructing a fiction that serves as propaganda for the party (to which Wright himself at one time belonged), Wright has written a story of the heroism, courage, loyalty, love, and faith one human being can inspire in another, transcending political and/or racial boundaries. This sort of achievement characterizes all the stories of *Uncle Tom's Children*.

In such short stories as "Mister Toussan" (1941), "King of the Bingo Game" (1944), and "Flying Home" (1944), Ralph Ellison utilizes his own accomplished musicianship (Ellison was a studied player of the saxophone, among other instruments). "Toussan," signifying upon Toussaint *L'Ouverture, the Haitian revolutionary and statesman, contains verse from *slave narratives, spirituals, and a sort of rap chant, this last serving as the means by which the youth Buster tells his compatriot Riley the tale of how Toussan "whipped Napoleon!" "King of the Bingo Game" also may be called a cento fiction as it emphasizes the driving rhythm of the turning bingo wheel, the singing (chanting) crowd, and a tap-dancing vaudeville team, all to underscore the delirium of the protagonist.

In "Flying Home," Ellison creates a splendid conjunction of folktale, the Bible, classicism, and spiritual. Todd, the African American pilot of World War II, must learn in this tale to "measure himself" according to the dictates of his own soul, not by the standards of others. Like Icarus of Ovid's *Metamorphoses*, he has to learn that in flying too close to the sun, he exceeds the limits of moderation. Jefferson, the ostensibly crude country bumpkin, serves Todd as a Daedalus father figure, whose counsel Todd, unlike Icarus, finds compelling. Indeed, Todd concludes that the tale Jefferson tells in the strain of the African American folk tradition, evoking the spiritual "All God's Chillun Got Wings," is more relevant to his own predicament than he is willing to admit. But at first not accepting the old man's wisdom, Todd deludes himself into thinking his situation parallels that of "Jonah in the whale." At the story's conclusion, however, Todd has come to see himself and his high aspirations in terms of a dark bird gliding "into the sun" and glowing "like a bird of flaming gold"— the proverbial Phoenix who renews itself every five hundred years out of its own ashes.

While perhaps not as interested in ancient classical materials as Ellison, James Baldwin demonstrates a great fondness for African American rhythms and musical forms. Craig H. Werner has observed of Baldwin's "Sonny's Blues," probably his best-known piece of short fiction, that "As much as any Afro-American text" this story "acknowledges the grounding of the blues jazz process in the gospel impulse."

Other writers whose contributions to the short story have been noteworthy include Ann *Petry and John A. *Williams. Petry's "Has Anybody Seen Miss Dora Dean?" (1958) turns upon a lyric from the era of ragtime that is in fact the story's title. Petry is studious in this story to tell her readers some of the background of that older time, detailing, for example, how the cakewalk (called by the narrator's father "whorehouse music") was executed. Here and in Mrs. Forkes's giving the narrator her set of white cups and saucers that "belonged to my grandmother. Handed down," Petry displays a reverence for African American tradition. John A. Williams shows hostility in the later "Son in the Afternoon" (1962) toward another kind of tradition, too well-known to African Americans—that of white folks' pointed degradation of African Americans. In this story (which contains such vivid descriptions that it surely makes a good subject for film) about a young African American man who becomes outraged when his mother shows greater deference toward her white employer's child than toward him, Williams has Wendell, the young man, assert that, "if there is ever a Negro revolt, it will come during the summer and Negroes will descend upon the beaches around the nation and paralyze the country." This story marks a new, threatening attitude toward oppression that predicts the coming civil rights movement of the last period in the development of the African American short story.

Black Arts Movement and Later (1964–). Unlike the preceding period's relatively subdued interest in the production of the short story, the civil rights and Black Arts movements and their aftermath have seen an enthusiastic flourishing of African American contributions to this genre. Neither time (we need the lapse of a few more years in order to give these most recent contributions a judicious assessment) nor space permits a full treatment of this period's many fine short story authors. The names of several particularly outstanding practitioners of this genre do, nevertheless, rise to the surface. Ernest J. *Gaines's "The Sky is Gray," for example, has been made into a *film for the American Short Story Collection, and been gathered with four other short stories to comprise his only short story collection, *Bloodline* (1968). While this story and others of this volume deal with the maturation of young African American males into adulthood, Paule Marshall's anthology of her own short stories, *Reena and Other Stories* (1983), relates how an African American woman must struggle for her own identity by means of a conscious reclamation of her African and/or Barbadian (or Caribbean) past. In such stories as "To Da-Duh, in Memoriam" (1967), Marshall seeks to instill in her readers a reverence for tradition, and in African women in particular an eagerness to recapture the past and to pass it on to succeeding generations.

James Alan *McPherson is another recent artist of the short story who, in such short story collections as *Hue and Cry* (1969) and *Elbow Room* (1977; for which he was awarded the Pulitzer Prize), also celebrates the African American tradition, especially that of the folktale. In McPherson's own words, "The folktale is like a precedent . . . it points to some wisdom that was derived at a certain point and passed on." John Edgar Wideman has devoted much of his career to recovery of a noble African and African American heritage. In such stories as "Fever," which retells the abominable actions of whites against African Americans during the yellow fever epidemic in 1793 Philadelphia, Wideman restructures *history. In this case he presents the epidemic's consequences from the African American perspective of Richard *Allen, a founder of the African Methodist Episcopal Church who published an account of the disaster in 1794. While "Fever" becomes the title story for an anthology of Wideman's short stories published in 1989, the story "Damballah" ("good serpent of the sky") gives its name to an earlier collection (1981). In this affecting tale, the old African forced into slavery, named Orion but called Ryan by his white enslavers, delivers a summative observation when he pronounces, "This boy [a young man born into slavery, who reveres Orion] could learn the story and tell it again." Wideman himself appears to find learning "the story" and telling "it again" to be his chosen office and that of the African American writer in general.

One recent African American author who has entered the world of *speculative fiction and who sees her office as predicting future African American heroes and heroines is Octavia E. *Butler, winner of two Hugo awards (for "Bloodchild" in 1985 and for "Speech Sounds" in 1984) and one Nebula (for "Bloodchild" in 1984). Projecting in her fiction future multicultural worlds wherein some devastating disease often surges out of control, Butler creates protagonists whose roles serve *healing functions, bringing about possibilities for rapprochement among all peoples. Another innovative African American woman writer of short stories, better known for her novels and poetry, Alice *Walker constructs stories, according to Langston Hughes, that are simply "astounding." In his introduction to *The Best Short Stories by Negro Writers* (1967), Hughes remarks of Walker, "Neither you nor I have ever read a story like 'To Hell with Dying' before. At least, I do not think you have."

Old Mr. Sweet Little, the subject of Walker's first published short story, "To Hell with Dying," liked to play "Sweet Georgia Brown" on his guitar. The fact that Mr. Little leaves his guitar to Walker's narrator conjures up once again the importance to African American short fiction of a tradition of music. For as Opal *Moore puts it so well, "Maybe the truth will go better with a musical accompaniment." This wise sentiment, delivered in "A Happy Story," signifies upon the majority of short fiction by African Americans, identifying its heavy debt to music. In her observation that "nobody overcomes hardships: we merely survive them, like car wrecks, to haul the scars around with us until we die," she quite effectively signifies upon James Alan McPherson's "The Story of a Scar" (1973). Moore's emphasis in this story upon memory resembles the theoretical position of the Nobel Prize–winning novelist Toni *Morrison. Morrison's self-avowed single venture into the short story genre resulted in "Recitatif" (1983), which, according to Morrison, "was an experiment in the removal of all racial codes from a narrative about two characters of different races for whom racial identity is crucial." As a "recitatif" is a musical form that adapts itself to rapid changes of thought or emotion, this title comments effectively upon the two characters and upon Morrison's technique of revealing their tense relationship(s).

Clarence *Major in his "Scat" (1979) presents an earlier application of a musical form to prose narrative, this form distinctly African American. According to Major himself in his *Juba to Jive: A Dictionary of African-American Slang* (2d ed., 1994), "scat" is used in jazz and blues singing "to keep the rhythm going verbally, as a novelty, by using pure sounds without regard to their meaning." Knowing this definition does indeed assist one in reading Major's "Scat," which otherwise approaches jive. This final period, as one can easily see, is rich in innovation and experiment. But at the same time its authors display a great concern for an African American oral tradition of folktales, of blues and spirituals, and of cento or medley fictions—a tradition so distinctive that it continues to define the genre as identifiably African American. One discerns a palpable diminution during this last period in dependence upon the Bible and *biblical tradition. Opal Moore perhaps best distinguishes the whole of the African American short fiction tradition when she writes, "story can remind us that we have always been talking to each other across artificial divides of space, separation, death and loss."

[*See also* Literary History.]

• Richard M. Dorson, *American Negro Folktales*, 1967. Peter Bruck, ed., *The Black American Short Story: A Collection of Critical Essays*, 1977. William L. Andrews, *The Literary Career of Charles W. Chesnutt*, 1980. Cynthia Earl Kerman and Richard Eldridge, *The Lives of Jean Toomer*, 1987. Robert Bone, *Down Home: Origins of the Afro-American Short Story*, 1988. Gayle Jones, *Liberating Voices: Oral Tradition in African American Literature*, 1991. Toni Morrison, *Playing in the Dark: Whiteness and the Literary Imagination*, 1992. Frances Smith Foster, *Written by Herself: Literary Production by African American Women, 1746–1892*, 1993. Wolfgang Karrer and Barbara Puschlmann-Nolenz, eds., *The African American Short Story, 1970 to 1990: A Collection of Critical Essays*, 1993. Craig Hansen Werner, *Playing the Changes: From Afro-Modernism to the Jazz Impulse*, 1994.

—John C. Shields

SHUG AVERY. The symbol of self-determination and self-love in Alice *Walker's The *Color Purple (1982) is Lillie, better known as Shug Avery or the Queen Honeybee. Shug is a beautiful, vivacious, and flamboyant *blues singer who is considered a "loose woman" by some of the novel's characters. These opinions are of little concern to Shug, however. Unlike the novel's protagonist, *Celie, Shug does not accept imposed definitions of herself, nor does she allow anyone to control her. Instead, she is compassionate toward others and allows herself the freedom to enjoy love wherever she finds it—even in the arms of another woman. Her spirit of determination is the catalyst for Celie's transformation and the vehicle to freedom for Mary Agnes (a younger woman who wants to leave rural Georgia to become a blues singer).

Even though Shug is a positive influence on others, she is also a character in pain. True to her name, this Queen Honeybee moves from one garden of love to another as if trying to escape something she does not want to face. Her parents reject her because of her adulterous relationship with Albert, a man whose father forbids him to marry her. Although Shug does not want to marry Albert, she believes in their love. Knowing that he will always choose her over his wife, Shug remains his lover, gliding in and out of his life as she pleases. When she discovers Albert's true nature—his cowardliness—she rejects him and develops a relationship with his wife, Celie.

• Om P. Juneja, "The Purple Colour of Walker Women: Their Journey from Slavery to Liberation," *Literary Criterion* 25.3 (1990): 66–76.
—Debra Walker King

SIGNIFYING denotes a form of verbal play—centering primarily on the insult—common in African American communities. Roger Abrahams's early study *Deep Down in the Jungle: Negro Narrative Folklore from the Streets of Philadelphia* (1963, 1970) defines signifying as a verbal mechanism by which anger and aggression may be channeled into relatively harmless form. This form of play offers speakers the opportunity to demonstrate their improvisational mastery of rhyme and rhythm, as well as their capacity to improvise on the verbal play of others. Signifying implies the art of expressing ideas, opinions, feelings, and so forth, by indirection and is, therefore, a culturally specific form of irony. One who signifies says without explicitly saying, criticizes without actually criticizing, insults without really insulting. Abrahams interprets signifying as a fundamentally male ritual, whereby African American men reestablish their sense of *manhood so often diminished by the psychological weight of oppression. In its various forms ("riffing," "the dozens," "specifying"), signifying substitutes verbal power for political or economic power.

While Abrahams identifies signifying as a gender-specific practice, others (Mitchell-Kernan, Smitherman, et al.) see this display of verbal expertise within a broader social framework. Smitherman, for instance, identifies signifying's ritualistic quality (as does Abrahams) but further sees this verbal practice as using *humor in the service of a "nonmalicious and principled criticism." The rhetoric of signifying, therefore, aims at the formation of community rather than at the expression of dominance.

Recently signifying has developed as a prominent term of art in the realm of literary and cultural *criticism. As popularized by Henry Louis *Gates, Jr., in *The Signifying Monkey: A Theory of Afro-American Literature* (1988), signifying indicates a form of intertextual revision, by which texts establish their relation to other texts, and authors to other authors. The force of this revision is to establish a critical relation to previous discursive statements. In this sense, one signifies on a particular work, author, form, or tradition, by copying central elements or practices, even while revising those in some significant way. The repetition implicit in this form of signifying criticizes or extends the previous and frequently (though not exclusively) white literary or cultural source by setting it within the context of African American expressive culture. Frederick *Douglass signifies on the *autobiography in writing his *Narrative of the Life of Frederick Douglass* (1845); Charles Waddell *Chesnutt signifies on the *plantation tradition in *The *Conjure Woman* (1899); and Ralph *Ellison signifies on the *bildungsroman in *Invisible Man* (1952). Examples of intramural signifying include Harriet A. *Jacobs's revision of Douglass in her *Incidents in the Life of a Slave Girl* (1861), James Weldon *Johnson's troping of W. E. B. *Du Bois's *The *Souls of Black Folk* (1903) in *The *Autobiography of an Ex-Colored Man* (1912), or Toni *Morrison's reconstruction of the *slave narrative in *Beloved* (1987). In each of these examples, the antecedent text, author, and form are revisited and, hence, reworked. This version of signifying, consequently, offers a theory of how a literary or expressive cultural tradition is built, a theory based on a mode of verbal play deeply embedded in the African American vernacular.

[*See also* Speech and Dialect.]

• Claudia Mitchell-Kernan, *Language Behavior in a Black Urban Community*, 1971. Roger Abrahams, *Talking Black*, 1976. Houston Baker, *Modernism and the Harlem Renaissance*, 1987. Geneva Smitherman, *Black Talk: Words and Phrases from the Hood to the Amen Corner*, 1994. Clarence Majors, *Juba to Jive: A Dictionary of African-American Slang*, 1970; rpt. 1994.

—Theodore O. Mason, Jr.

SIMMONS, HERBERT ALFRED (b. 1930), novelist, playwright, and poet. Born in St. Louis, Missouri, Herbert Alfred Simmons spent two years in the U.S. Army and later received his BA from Washington University in St. Louis in 1958. After graduating from college, Simmons attended the University of Iowa Writers' Workshop on a fellowship. Simmons has been involved in various small-scale literary projects outside the mainstream. He was the onetime editor of *Spliv*, a literary experiment of the early 1960s, and was the producer of "Portraits in Rhythm," a jazz accompanied performance that combined *poetry and selected writings and was read in coffee houses.

The author of one play, *The Stranger* (1956; winner of the Sara B. Glasgow Award), and some poetry, Simmons is known chiefly for his two novels, *Corner Boy* (1957) and *Man Walking on Eggshells* (1962). The latter is a trumpet player's coming-of-age story. Raymond Douglas is born in a tornado and born into a family fraught with tension. Against his mother's explicit wishes, Raymond, whose talent is apparent even as a toddler, wants to follow in his grandfather's footsteps and become a musician. The novel is something of a pastiche; Simmons tells the story of this struggling African American family through many different voices, shifting in and out of the characters' consciousnesses and adding song lyrics and newspaper headlines to the body of the text. The novel, enriched with Simmons's musical and artistic sensibilities, has the desultory, improvised, and chaotic quality of a jazz performance but lacks the finesse of a carefully honed work.

Although his novels were reviewed in African American newspapers when they first appeared, Simmons's writing has not become part of the American literary canon and has gone largely without notice. None of his books are currently in print.

• "Simmons, Herbert A.," in *CA*, vols. 1–4, eds. James M. Ethridge and Barbara Kopala, 1962, p. 869. James A. Page, ed., *Selected Black American Authors*, 1977.

—Jennifer Margulis

SIMPLE, or Jesse B. Semple, first appeared in print on 13 February 1943 in the black-owned *Chicago Defender*. Langston *Hughes first intended Simple as a device to popularize the war effort among blacks, many of whom resented the disparity between racial injustice at home and the alleged democratic goals of the war, but Simple acquired a life beyond propaganda.

The classic setting for a Simple episode is a Harlem bar, with a conversation between the fun-loving, irreverent, but racially committed Simple, on the one hand, and the educated, poised, but dull narrator, on the other. However, Simple's world also includes memorable characters such as his girlfriend, Joyce, later his wife; a less respectable friend, Zarita; and his landlady, who calls him "Third Floor Rear."

Hughes claimed that Simple was based on a man he knew casually in Harlem, but both Simple and the narrator in reality are Hughes himself, who once pronounced Simple "really very simple. It is just myself talking to me. Or else me talking to myself" ("Simple and Me," *Phylon*, Oct.–Dec. 1945). The two voices form a sort of colloquium on Hughes's tensions of beliefs, as well as on his deeper fears and desires. The narrator may be seen as Hughes without love, laughter, and *poetry, the man he might have been without his writing in service to black America. Simple himself epitomizes the saving graces of black America, the gift of self-redemption in the face of historic adversity.

Over twenty years, Simple became one of Hughes's most successful artistic creations, admired and beloved by readers who followed his exploits in syndicated columns that eventually included the white *New York Post*. Edited, the columns led to five volumes in Hughes's lifetime: *Simple Speaks His Mind* (1950), *Simple Takes a Wife* (1953), *Simple Stakes a Claim* (1957), *The Best of Simple* (1961), and *Simple's Uncle Sam* (1965). A sixth volume, *The Return of Simple*, appeared in 1994, edited by Akiba Sullivan Harper. Simple is easily the most enduring and endearing creation of a comic character in African American journalism and literature.

—Arnold Rampersad

Sister Outsider (1984), a collection of fifteen *essays written between 1976 and 1984, gives clear voice to Audre *Lorde's literary and philosophical personae. These essays explore and illuminate the roots of Lorde's intellectual development and her deepseated and longstanding concerns about ways of increasing empowerment among minority women writers and the absolute necessity to explicate the concept of difference—difference according to sex, *race, and economic status. The title *Sister Outsider* finds its source in her *poetry collection *The Black Unicorn* (1978). These poems and the essays in *Sister Outsider* stress Lorde's oft-stated theme of continuity, particularly of the geographical and intellectual link between Dahomey, Africa, and her emerging self.

The subject matter of these essays is remarkably varied, yet homogeneous. The quality of these essays is consistently high and the unity is made possible by Lorde's emphasis on differences as a source of strength rather than divisiveness. In essay after essay, Lorde promotes the unity of difference. In lieu of remaining an isolato, she stresses the necessity of every individual, group, sect, cult, and movement to strive for unity in such diversity. Nowhere is this more clearly articulated than in "The Master's Tools Will Never Dismantle the Master's House," "Age, Race, Class, and Sex: Women Redefining Difference," and in "Scratching the Surface, Some Notes on Barriers to Women and Loving." In a powerful and persuasive manner, Lorde stresses the strengths of empowerment and acceptance as necessary acquisitions.

Perhaps the most well-known essay in *Sister Outsider* is "Uses of the Erotic: The Erotic as Power," an emotional and powerful study of the erotic explicated by Lorde's famous analogy between the World War II practice of mixing yellow food coloring with colorless margarine at home to give the margarine the "proper" popular appearance. Lorde makes this communal experience erotic and, by extension, makes other mundane tasks become erotic and, therefore, highly pleasurable. Moreover, differences are also homogenized.

Another major emphasis of *Sister Outsider* is poetic theory, explored primarily in "An Interview: Audre Lorde and Adrienne Rich" and "Poetry is not a Luxury." The interview with Rich becomes a proving ground for unity in diversity as both women explore their common ground as lesbian poets struggling with voicing their most private concerns while not yet being able to totally trust individuals of other color, political persuasion, or economic status. Conversely, "Poetry is not a Luxury," originally published in 1977, emphatically places poetry in the front ranks as "a vital necessity of an existence." Why? Because poetry gives us access to our dreams, which cause us to keep on keeping on.

One of the most moving essays here is also one of the shortest, namely "An Open Letter to Mary Daly," who is the author of *Gyn/Ecology: The Metaethics of Radical Feminism* (1978). In the letter Lorde challenges Daly to reexamine some of her statements regarding methods of achieving feminist unity. The last essay in *Sister Outsider* is "Grenada Revisited: An Interim Report," which brings full circle the theme of diversity complementing solidarity. Highly politicized, "Grenada Revisited" allows Lorde to make peace with her mother while simultaneously revealing her views concerning racism/colonialism, noting that the slogan of the Grenadian Revolution was "Forward Ever, Back Never," a spirit evoked by *Sister Outsider*.

Today *Sister Outsider* occupies a unique position in African American literature. The text presents a classic manifesto, one frequently referred to in women's/minority/alternative studies courses. *Sister Outsider* remains one of the few texts to explicate

brilliantly and forthrightly the paradigm of racism as it exists in the highest and most influential levels of American society, particularly in educational media. Here Audre Lorde asks her readers to undergo intense self-examination. This is particularly noteworthy since nine of these essays were written after Lorde discovered she had cancer, a mind-numbing discovery she explicates in "The Transformation of Silence into Language and Action."

Sister Outsider is not merely a collection of essays, interviews, and speeches. Every piece requires the reader to rethink bias and negative opinion. It compares quite favorably with Alice *Walker's *In Search of Our Mothers' Gardens* (1983) and Toni *Morrison's *Playing in the Dark* (1992).

• Charles H. Rowell, "Above the Winds: An Interview with Audre Lorde," *Callaloo*, 14 (1991): 83–95.

—Joseph Benson

SLAVE NARRATIVE. The autobiographical narratives of former slaves constitute one of the bedrock traditions of African American literature and culture. From Olaudah *Equiano's precedent-setting *Interesting Narrative of the Life of Olaudah Equiano, or Gustavus Vassa, the African* (1789) through the thousands of oral histories of former slaves gathered by the *Federal Writers' Project in the 1920s and 1930s, slave narratives have provided some of the most graphic and damning documentary evidence of the horrors of *slavery, America's "peculiar institution." The most widely read slave narratives, written by fugitives such as Frederick *Douglass, William Wells *Brown, and Harriet A. *Jacobs, became virtual testaments in the hands of abolitionists proclaiming the antislavery gospel during the antebellum era in the United States. These narratives not only exposed the inhumanity of the slave system; they also gave incontestable evidence of the humanity of the African American. After the Civil War, with slavery officially banned and the citizenship of African Americans legally guaranteed, former slaves continued to record their experiences under slavery, partly to ensure that the newly united nation did not forget what had threatened its existence, and partly to affirm the dedication of the ex-slave population to mutual progress for whites and blacks alike. In this conciliatory spirit, Booker T. *Washington wrote *Up from Slavery* (1901), which many critics and historians regard as the last great slave narrative authored in the United States. Whether born in slavery or not, most major writers of African American literature before World War I launched their literary careers via some form of the slave narrative.

During the shaping era of African American *autobiography, from 1760 to the end of the Civil War, the personal witness of hundreds of fugitive or former slaves appeared in brief narratives, reports, and interviews in the *periodical press in England and the United States. Approximately seventy narratives, either dictated or authored by fugitive or former slaves, were published as discrete entities. These separately published narratives were sometimes no longer than the New England broadside, *The Life and*

Confession of Johnson Green (1786). But a few former slaves, such as Samuel Ringgold Ward and Frederick Douglass, produced autobiographies that ran to more than four hundred pages; Equiano's narrative comprised two bulky volumes. Regardless of length, slave narratives dominated the literary landscape of antebellum black America, far outnumbering the comparatively rare autobiographies of free people of color, not to mention the handful of *novels published by American blacks during this time.

After slavery was abolished in North America, the ex-slave narrative remained the preponderant subgenre of African American autobiography. From 1865 to 1930, at least fifty former slaves wrote or dictated book-length accounts of their lives. During the 1930s the Federal Writers' Project gathered oral personal histories and testimony about slavery from 2,500 former slaves in 17 states, generating roughly 10,000 pages of interviews that were eventually published in the 1970s in a "composite autobiography" of 18 volumes. One of the slave narratives' most reliable historians has estimated conservatively that a grand total of all contributions to this genre, including separately published texts, materials that appeared in *periodicals, and oral histories and interviews, numbers approximately 6,000 accounts.

The earliest slave narratives have strong affinities with popular white American accounts of Indian captivity and Christian conversion in the New World. The first known American slave narrative, *A Narrative of the Uncommon Sufferings, and Surprizing Deliverance of Briton Hammon, a Negro Man* (1760), laments Briton *Hammon's sufferings at the hands of Florida Indians but says nothing untoward about his condition as a slave. Most narratives from the late eighteenth century decry the slavery of sin much more than the sin of slavery. But with the rise of the militant *antislavery movement in the early nineteenth century came a new demand for slave narratives that would highlight the harsh realities of slavery itself. Racial abolitionists like William Lloyd Garrison were convinced that the eyewitness testimony of former slaves against slavery would touch the hearts and change the minds of many in the northern population of the United States who were either ignorant of or indifferent to the plight of African Americans in the South. In the late 1830s and early 1840s the first of this new brand of outspokenly antislavery slave narratives found their way into print under such titles as *Slavery in the United States: A Narrative of the Life and Adventures of Charles Ball* (1836), *A Narrative of the Adventures and Escape of Moses *Roper, from American Slavery* (1838), and *The Narrative of Lunsford Lane, Formerly of Raleigh, N.C., Embracing an Account of His Early Life, the Redemption by Purchase of Himself and Family from Slavery, and His Banishment from the Place of His Birth for the Crime of Wearing a Colored Skin* (1842). These set the mold for what would become by midcentury a standardized form of autobiography in which personal memory and a rhetorical attack on slavery blend to produce a powerful expressive tool both as literature and as progaganda.

Typically the antebellum slave narrative carries a black message inside a white envelope. Prefatory (and sometimes appended) matter by whites attests to the reliability and good character of the narrator and calls attention to what the narrative will reveal about the moral abominations of slavery. The former slave's contribution to the text centers on his or her rite of passage from slavery in the South to *freedom in the North. Usually the antebellum slave narrator portrays slavery as a condition of extreme physical, intellectual, emotional, and spiritual deprivation, a kind of hell on earth. Precipitating the narrator's decision to escape is some sort of personal crisis, such as the sale of a loved one or a dark night of the soul in which hope contends with despair for the spirit of the slave. Impelled by faith in God and a commitment to liberty and human dignity comparable (the slave narrative often stresses) to that of America's founders, the slave undertakes an arduous quest for freedom that climaxes in his or her arrival in the North. In many antebellum narratives, the attainment of freedom is signaled not simply by reaching the free states but by renaming oneself and dedicating one's future to antislavery activism.

Advertised in the abolitionist press and sold at antislavery meetings throughout the English-speaking world, a significant number of antebellum slave narratives went through multiple editions, were translated into several European languages, and sold in the tens of thousands. Readers could see that, as one reviewer put it, "the slave who endeavours to recover his freedom is associating with himself no small part of the romance of the time." To the noted transcendentalist clergyman Theodore Parker, slave narratives qualified as America's only indigenous literary form, for "all the original romance of Americans is in them, not in the white man's novel." The most widely read and hotly debated American novel of the nineteenth century, Harriet Beecher *Stowe's *Uncle Tom's Cabin* (1852), was profoundly influenced by its author's reading of a number of slave narratives, in particular those of Josiah *Henson and Frederick Douglass, to which she owed many compelling incidents, not to mention the models for some of her most memorable characters. Centering on the attempt of a fugitive slave to gain his freedom, Mark Twain's *Huckleberry Finn* (1883) is another classic white American novel of the nineteenth century rooted in the slave narrative tradition.

The antebellum slave narrative reached its epitome with the publication in 1845 of the *Narrative of the Life of Frederick Douglass, an American Slave, Written by Himself.* Selling more than thirty thousand copies in the first five years of its existence, Douglass's *Narrative* became an international bestseller, its contemporary readership far outstripping that of such classic white autobiographies as Henry David Thoreau's *Walden* (1854). Garrison, Douglass's abolitionist mentor, introduced his *Narrative* by stressing how representative Douglass's experience of slavery had been. But Garrison could not help but note the extraordinary individuality of this black author's manner of rendering that experience. It is Douglass's style of self-presentation, through which he re-created the slave as an evolving self bound for mental as well as physical freedom, that has made his autobiography so memorable. After almost a century out of print Douglass's *Narrative* returned to modern literature in a number of reprints beginning in the late 1960s; since then it has been one of the most discussed American autobiographies of any era.

After Douglass's *Narrative*, the presence of the subtitle "Written by Himself" on a slave narrative bore increasing political and literary significance as an indicator of a narrator's self-determination independent of external expectations and conventions. In the late 1840s well-known fugitive slaves such as William Wells Brown, Henry *Bibb, and James W. C. *Pennington reinforced the rhetorical self-consciousness of the slave narrative by incorporating into their stories *trickster motifs from African American folk culture, extensive literary and Biblical allusions, and a picaresque perspective on the meaning of the slave's flight from bondage to freedom.

As the slave narrative evolved in the crisis years of the 1850s and early 1860s, it addressed the problem of slavery with unprecedented candor, unmasking as never before the moral and social complexities of the American caste and class system in the North as well as the South. In *My Bondage and My Freedom* (1855), Douglass revealed that his search for freedom had not reached its fulfillment among the abolitionists, although this had been the implication of his *Narrative*'s conclusion. Having discovered in Garrison and his cohorts some of the same paternalistic attitudes that had characterized his former masters in the South, Douglass could see in 1855 that the struggle for full liberation would be much more difficult and uncertain than he had previously imagined. He concluded his autobiography with a statement of personal dedication to civil rights activism in the North as well as agitation against slavery in the South. Harriet Jacobs, the first African American female slave to author her own narrative, challenged conventional ideas about slavery and freedom in her strikingly original *Incidents in the Life of a Slave Girl* (1861). Jacobs's autobiography shows how sexual exploitation made slavery especially oppressive for black women. But in demonstrating how she fought back and ultimately gained both her own freedom and that of her two children, Jacobs proved the inadequacy of the image of victim that had been pervasively applied to female slaves in the male-authored slave narrative.

Although the pre–Civil War slave narrative is primarily concerned with the individual's quest for personal power free from institutional control, the narratives of ex-slaves after the Civil War focus on the consolidation and institutionalization of communal power. After Reconstruction, most black autobiographers took as axiomatic the idea that in a racist America, individual black survival, not to mention fulfillment, depended largely on building institutional bulwarks against the divide-and-conquer strategy of American white supremacy. Slave narratives by women in the late nineteenth and early twentieth centuries stressed the importance of *marriage, the

home, and the traditional middle-class family as the institutions most essential to sustaining black communities in the increasingly polarized world of *Jim Crow. Most of the ex-slave narratives of this era are avowedly, even proudly, middle class in their values and purposes. The extent of this identification is suggested by the Algeresque titles of many ex-slave narratives published between 1865 and 1930: Peter Randolph, *From Slave Cabin to the Pulpit* (1893); Henry Clay Bruce, *The New Man* (1895); J. Vance Lewis, *Out of the Ditch: A True Story of an Ex-Slave* (1910); Thomas W. Burton, MD, *What Experience Has Taught Me* (1910); William H. Heard, *From Slavery to the Bishopric in the A. M. E. Church* (1924); and *From Slavery to Affluence: Memoirs of Robert Anderson, Ex-Slave* (1927).

In most post–Civil War slave narratives slavery is depicted as a kind of crucible in which the resilience, industry, and ingenuity of the slave were tested and ultimately validated. By emphasizing that slaves not only survived their bondage but were well-prepared by its rigors to take care of themselves both individually and communally, slave narrators after emancipation argued the readiness of the freedman and woman for full participation in the new social and economic order. While the large majority of slave narratives after the Civil War were privately printed, a few ex-slaves, such as Elizabeth *Keckley, dressmaker and confidante to Mary Todd Lincoln, and Henry O. Flipper, the first black graduate of the U.S. Military Academy, were able to find commercial publishers for their reminiscences. The biggest selling of the late-nineteenth- and early-twentieth-century slave narratives was Booker T. Washington's *Up from Slavery* (1901), a success story that enjoyed virtually universal approbation among blacks and whites alike because of its promotion of African American progress and interracial cooperation, as exemplified in the rise to national prominence of both Washington and the industrial school he founded in Tuskegee, Alabama. White enthusiasm for *Up from Slavery*'s brand of optimism and absence of bitterness was so great that few paid attention to the narratives of those former slaves whose autobiographies detailed the legacy of racial injustice burdening blacks in the South since the demise of Reconstruction.

Up from Slavery dictated the terms on which most African American autobiographers represented themselves during the first half of the twentieth century. But the depression helped spur the gradual return to autobiography of themes of resistance and struggle against oppression, particularly in the South, argued with an uncompromising candor that harked back to the antebellum slave narratives of Douglass and Jacobs. Angelo Herndon's *Let Me Live* (1937), J. Saunders *Redding's *No Day of Triumph* (1942), and Richard *Wright's *Black Boy* (1945) owe much, structurally and rhetorically, to the slave narrative tradition of a century before. The *civil rights movement of the 1950s and 1960s revived the long-standing ideals and urgent moral appeal of the antebellum freedom fighters, thereby creating a climate in which formidable new African American narratives of bondage and liberation could be conceived and appreciated. The *Autobiography of Malcolm X (1965), with its many affinities to the slave narrative tradition, made a lasting impression on a new generation of white readers and helped bring about the first serious scholarly study of the slave narrative. Novels such as Margaret *Walker's *Jubilee (1965), Ernest J. *Gaines's The *Autobiography of Miss Jane Pittman (1971), and Toni *Morrison's *Beloved (1987) testify to the continuing vitality of the slave narrative, as contemporary African-American writers probe the origins of psychological as well as social oppression and critique the meaning of freedom for twentieth-century blacks and whites alike.

[See also Amanuensis; Neo–Slave Narrative.]

• Vernon Loggins, The Negro Author: His Development in America to 1900, 1931. John Sekora and Darwin T. Turner, eds., The Art of Slave Narrative, 1982. Charles T. Davis and Henry Louis Gates, Jr., eds., The Slave's Narrative, 1985. William L. Andrews, To Tell a Free Story: The First Century of Afro-American Autobiography, 1760–1865, 1986. Angelo Costanzo, Surprizing Narrative: Olaudah Equiano and the Beginnings of Black Autobiography, 1987. Marion Wilson Starling, The Slave Narrative: Its Place in American History, 1988. William L. Andrews, "The Representation of Slavery and the Rise of Afro-American Literary Realism, 1865–1920," in Slavery and the Literary Imagination, eds. Deborah E. McDowell and Arnold Rampersad, 1989, pp. 62–80. Blyden Jackson, A History of Afro-American Literature, vol. 1, The Long Beginning, 1746–1895, 1989. Frances Smith Foster, Witnessing Slavery: The Development of Ante-bellum Slave Narratives, 2d ed., 1994.
—William L. Andrews

SLAVERY. "From the Narrative and the many other accounts of runaways published in Douglass's day, right down to Toni *Morrison's *Beloved in ours, there has been no escape from the slave in American letters," writes William S. McFeely, biographer of Frederick *Douglass. No escape. Using the language of the abolition movement, McFeely reminds us that slavery has remained close to the consciousness of Americans, white and black, ever since. Among popular writers since the mid-nineteenth century, it has been an uninterrupted fount of inspiration—Uncle Tom's Cabin, Gone with the Wind, and *Roots representing merely the most spectacular results. Among the learned, it has provided grand theories for social scientists and grand themes for creative writers, from Herman Melville and Mark Twain to two Nobel Prize winners of our century, William Faulkner and Toni Morrison. The lessons of Huckleberry Finn are translated in Absalom, Absalom! and deepened in *Song of Solomon and Beloved. As subject, slavery is far from exhausted, seemingly because it is more and worse than anything anyone can say about it.

For this preoccupation, at least four reasons can be suggested. From its earliest decades America has been engaged with tales of bondage—the African American *slave narratives being simply the major form of those tales for the earlier nineteenth century. During that half-century the literature of slavery was important to most of the writers of the nation. Following the war they remained absorbed in the issues raised by slavery, for many reasons, usually the better to understand the struggles of their own day. Finally,

looking back from the vantage of the present, several historians have seen a national literature mixed or creolized from its inception, with white writers borrowing freely from a large store of black images, themes, and language. The case is put by Shelley Fisher Fishkin: "A shift in paradigm is in order. Understanding African-American tradition is essential if one wants to understand mainstream American literary history. And understanding mainstream literary history is important if one wants to understand African-American writing in the twentieth century. We can no longer deny the mixed literary bloodlines on both sides" (Was Huck Black?, 1993).

In order to comprehend the national destiny, Americans have often turned to stories of confinement, challenge, and redemption. In 1697, Cotton Mather described such a pattern as Humiliations follow'd with Deliverances, in an instance of the most successful literary form in early America, the captivity narratives. These were stories of valiant white colonists morally tested during confinement by Indian tribes, then transmuting that harrowing experience into physical and spiritual salvation. With the Bible and Pilgrim's Progress, such tales were the best-selling literary publications of the nation's first century, establishing a pattern so familiar that, explaining the causes of the War of Independence, major writers reverted to it while defending the colonies' need to break their bondage to Great Britain. Like the Puritan settlers, the colonies as a group were held in thrall by a distant, uncaring foe. To withstand that foe, however, developed strength and nationhood—not simply a courageous people but a just one. Put to collective purposes, the captivity narratives thus pioneered the story of American exceptionalism.

Captives were not only as good as other Christians, they might have been even better. That lesson became especially poignant during the *antislavery movement, the period of nearly two generations when the most prominent captives in the nation were African American ex-slaves such as Douglass, William Wells *Brown, James W. C. *Pennington, and Sojourner *Truth. Not only were they internationally known for their efforts on behalf of abolition, they were also among the best-selling authors of the age. In the eyes of many whites, especially those who romanticized "the Negro" as a spiritually superior being, the heroic Douglass and the persevering Truth seemed paragons of resistance to bondage. If adversity tested one's virtue, then slavery was the supreme trial. Epitomized in Harriet Beecher *Stowe's Uncle Tom's Cabin (1852), the image of slavery promulgated by much antislavery literature by whites stressed the naked soul at its most besieged, the solitary journey at its most uncharted, the source of evil at its most blatant, the beauty of virtue at its most transparent.

For several decades the narratives of former slaves served as the Book of Job for the American consciousness, summarizing the nation's political sensibility as well as its literary sensitivity. Although unadorned, they were for contemporaries more eloquent in their authenticity than the measured cadences of senators. Dozens were published as book, pamphlet, or broadside, many more in *periodicals and as interviews with the Freedmen's Bureau. By emancipation slavery had replaced captivity as a central metaphor of American history, one that few writers could ignore.

But alter its meaning, its center of gravity—this they could do. The more than fifty autobiographies by former slaves published between the Civil War and the 1930s, as studied by William L. Andrews, reveal a different conception of the central experience of slavery from their antebellum predecessors. For Douglass, the first great slave narrator, writing in 1845, slavery is a tomb from which he must be resurrected. For Booker T. *Washington, who in many ways replaced Douglass as spokesperson and whose *Up from Slavery of 1901 has never been out of print, slavery is a school to be learned and graduated from. This more pragmatic postbellum view does not look so much at the facts of slavery as how the memory of slavery can change white attitudes in the present. What was being rehabilitated was not so much slavery as the contribution of black people to the South. It is no coincidence that white writers were also seeking to mitigate the harsher realities of slavery. So revised, slavery is capable, in Andrews's words, "of making a difference ultimately in what white people thought of black people as freedmen, not as slaves" ("The Representation of Slavery and the Rise of Afro-American Literary Realism 1865–1920," 1989).

Between Douglass and Washington more than a half-century passed. Yet the old and the new versions of the female slave narrative were compressed into a much shorter space of time—the seven years between Harriet A. *Jacobs's *Incidents in the Life of a Slave Girl (1861) and Elizabeth *Keckley's Behind the Scenes (1868). The two women had similar stories to tell. Light-skinned and of roughly the same age, both were bedeviled by insistent white men and both bore children by white men. Leaving slavery at about the same age, they may have known one another while working in Washington, D.C. Yet the books they chose to write were continents apart. Incidents is a powerful indictment of the institution of slavery, a culmination of antislavery *publishing, telling difficult truths plainly about sexual exploitation. Behind the Scenes in contrast is no indictment, and its main object of analysis is not slavery as an institution but success in the white world. Dressmaker to Mary Todd Lincoln, Keckley chose to relate stories of life in the White House. Rather than a frustrated maternal feeling, she emphasizes a satisfied commercial ambition. Rather than speedily escape slavery, she purchases her *freedom—for twelve hundred dollars, a large sum indeed. Rather than repudiate her own and all other slaveowners, she recounts a happy reunion with the Garlands, her former owners.

After the war former slaves found publication much more difficult—unless they had other stories, such as success in some area of white activity, to relate. For her account of achievement, Keckley was rewarded with a contract from a large commercial publisher, one of the first to an African American writer. The lesson was not lost upon Washington, Josiah *Henson, Elisha W. Green, and a half-dozen

or so postbellum narrators—to an extent even upon Douglass, whose third autobiography in 1881 chronicles at length his later successes. Many late nineteenth-century autobiographies were written by persons who were young at emancipation, who did not escape, who were not brutalized, and who express no grievance against the social system. They stress economic success over political rights, and social reconciliation overall, perhaps to the extent of including, like Keckley, a reunion scene with former owners. So strong a pattern was formed that it persisted well into the twentieth century—witness Sammy Davis's Yes, I Can (1965).

While Washington was perfecting his brand of pragmatism, several novelists were posing alternative uses for the memories and metaphors of slavery. Protest fiction like Frances Ellen Watkins *Harper's *Iola Leroy (1892), Pauline E. *Hopkins's *Contending Forces (1900), and W. E. B. *Du Bois's The *Quest of the Silver Fleece (1911) kept alive the passion ignited by the narrators. Two important works went further. Charles Waddell *Chesnutt's The *Conjure Woman (1899) presents itself as a series of slave stories transcribed by a white entrepreneur, offering thereby text and commentary that do not usually coincide. On one level, *Uncle Julius McAdoo retells the Uncle Remus stories without their *minstrelsy; on the other, the white businessman offers quaint redactions of southern folk culture. Since neither Chesnutt nor his publisher identified the author as African American, readers were faced with a modernist choice of two implied authors. Yet more demanding was James Weldon *Johnson's The *Autobiography of an Ex-Colored Man (1912), a *novel that, published anonymously, was convincingly presented as an autobiography, not a work of fiction. Among its many elements is a series of challenges to the certainties cherished by the Sage of Tuskegee.

Direct challenges to Washington's revisionism came in many forms, from Du Bois's reflections on slave life in The *Souls of Black Folk (1903) to William *Pickens's autobiography, Bursting Bonds (1923), with its title echoing Douglass as well as his earlier New Negro, published in 1916, a year after Washington's death. In their work and that of the *New Negroes of the *Harlem Renaissance, the abolitionist and modern views of slavery were melded. It was as though Chesnutt and Johnson had held on to the central *history of slavery long enough for contemporary visions of *folklore, narration, and psychology to catch up and absorb it.

The bridge-building of the 1920s was not only timely but substantial. It prepared the way for a decade when some Americans—and not only her creative thinkers—sought to recall the lessons of slavery. In spirit and specific goal, the depression provided such an occasion, spurring new histories, innovative fiction, and an extraordinary form of autobiography. Famous books by Charles S. Johnson, St. Clair Drake, Zora Neale *Hurston, Arna *Bontemps, and Richard *Wright illumine the era. Yet its signal achievement may well be the 2,194 narratives of slavery gathered from 1935 to 1939 by WPA and Fisk researchers. The New Deal agency most helpful to black writers was the *Federal Writers Project (FWP), established in 1935 as a subdivision of the WPA. It assisted several hundred African American writers of various degrees of talent, including masters such as Johnson, Drake, Hurston, Bontemps, Wright, Sterling A. *Brown, Claude *McKay, Chester *Himes, Ralph *Ellison, Frank *Yerby, William *Attaway, Willard *Motley, and Margaret *Walker. In addition to compiling 378 regional books and pamphlets, they took the opportunity to interview available survivors of slavery. Results were not fully published until the nineteen volumes brought together by George P. Rawick in 1972 (with later supplements). Yet statewide volumes were released earlier, and the most serious and talented writers were given occasion to continue their own creative projects. Echoing Douglass and Du Bois, many of these writers stressed slavery as the focal event of American history. For the very first time, a few made a related claim: The antebellum narratives supply the basic pattern for almost all later African American fiction and autobiography.

The generation of the depression cultivated a searching interest in unknown and relatively unreported history. Archivist and librarian at Fisk, Bontemps did important work preserving and editing slave materials. Two of his three novels deal with slave revolts, *Black Thunder (1936) with Gabriel Prosser's uprising in Virginia in 1800, Drums at Dusk (1939) with the Haitian Revolution of 1791–1803. All of Hurston's work of the time is imbued with folk culture, especially *Their Eyes Were Watching God (1937) and her autobiographical work, *Dust Tracks on a Road (1942), which has resemblances to those of Jacobs and Keckley. Looking equally backward and forward is the rich, complex work of Richard Wright. American Hunger, the autobiography he sent his editors in the early 1940s, was divided into southern and northern testaments, the earlier published as *Black Boy in 1945, the latter under its original title posthumously in 1977. Part of Black Boy reproduces the trajectory of Douglass and other male ex-slave narrators: radical individualism, freedom as *literacy and creation, a systematic analysis of white hegemony, Wright's attempt at the close to work himself into a community of like-minded souls. Yet other positions suggest an isolation so extreme as to belie any hope for community. American Hunger in its turn recalls the second of Douglass's narratives, as its description of Wright's break with the Communist Party recalls Douglass's estrangement from the Garrisonians. Stories such as "Big Boy Leaves Home" and "The Man Who Lived Underground" likewise combined with Wright's five novels to teach a younger generation the modern meaning of bondage and confinement.

As influential as Douglass, Wright brought to the slave narrative tradition a stark, naturalistic tunnel vision of the paradoxes that bind all Americans, yet victimize only some. It offered bondage as a metaphor for writers concerned with racism within the law, such as the *Scottsboro Boys, Chester Himes, Piri *Thomas, George Jackson, and Eldridge *Cleaver; for writers engrossed in the conflicts of *migration and urbanism, such as William Attaway, Ann *Petry, and John O. *Killens; and for those concerned with the prison house of *gender, such as Alice *Walker. Most significant are three works that fulfill the vision by transcending the technique. One of the supreme works of the century, Ellison's *Invisible Man (1952) blends an epic tale of myth, legend, and ritual with a fugitive's journey northward. The anonymous protagonist charts slavery past and present; like Douglass, he finds a home and sufficient light. If Ellison recreates Douglass's search for *identity, John A. *Williams rehearses his quest for meaning in the remarkable novel The *Man Who Cried I Am (1967). Williams reenacts a smaller portion of African American history—mainly the 1950s and 1960s—but tells the story with sardonic symbolism and a shifting frame of time and space. In it Max Reddick, a successful writer and advisor to presidents, discovers that he has been enslaved by ignorance and deceit. A fictionalized character in the novel, *Malcolm X relates a drama of mental enslavement and final redemption in The *Autobiography of Malcolm X (1965), written with Alex *Haley.

As these examples suggest, the 1960s carried with them a renewed sense of oppression and a flood of historical fiction about slavery. The most controversial example of the fiction was The Confessions of Nat Turner by William Styron (1967), whose prizewinning portrait of Turner was attacked for the liberties it took with Turner's character and with the record of his actions in the original Confessions of 1831. Margaret Walker's *Jubilee (1966) is the first such novel by an African American woman since Hopkins's *Contending Forces at the turn of the century and is notable for its scrupulous research and focus upon the lives of women under slavery. Equally distinctive is its attempt to reconcile domestic themes and political radicalism. A male novelist, Ernest J. *Gaines, faced a similar situation a few years later with the memorable heroine and narrator of The *Autobiography of Miss Jane Pittman (1971). He seeks to interweave several strands: the image of the female slave from the early narratives, a framing device akin to the WPA oral history, and changes in black consciousness since the *civil rights movement. Another instance of *neo-slave narrative—a term developed because so much was being written—is the novel *Dessa Rose (1986) by Sherley Anne *Williams, whose vibrant title character leads an elaborate revolt. Using slavery more as backdrop for character and incident than for historical reconstruction is Charles R. *Johnson in Oxherding Tale (1982) and *Middle Passage (1990). Ishmael *Reed uses it for his inimitable form of burlesque in *Flight to Canada (1976).

As Reed has dared to seek the absurd in places one normally finds only tragedy, so Toni Morrison has uncovered new dimensions of significance in her novel Beloved (1987). Retold from the 1856 story of Margaret Garner and her infant daughter, the novel is in several ways a culmination of the slave narrative. It can tell the truth as no nineteenth-century account ever could. Unlike the original narratives, which could bring retribution upon their authors, it has no need to deny, evade, or suppress anything. Its experimental format can elevate consciousness without evoking sentimentality. And it can do something neither Douglass nor Jacobs could do alone—namely, to tell the male and female tales together, in a carefully convergent way, to one another. This brings fruition to the tradition: a communal story, antiphonally, communally told.

• Orlando Patterson, *Slavery and Social Death*, 1982. William L. Andrews, *To Tell a Free Story: The First Century of Afro-American Autobiography, 1760–1865*, 1986. Bernard W. Bell, *The Afro-American Novel and Its Tradition*, 1987. John Sekora, "Black Message/White Envelope," *Callaloo* 10.3 (Fall 1987): 482–515. Deborah E. McDowell and Arnold Rampersad, eds., *Slavery and the Literary Imagination*, 1989. Albert E. Stone, *The Return of Nat Turner: History, Literature, and Cultural Politics in Sixties America*, 1992. Frank Shuffelton, ed., *A Mixed Race: Ethnicity in America*, 1993. Eric Sundquist, *To Wake the Nations: Race in the Making of American Literature*, 1993. Kenneth W. Warren, *Black and White Strangers: Race and American Literary Realism*, 1993.

—John Sekora

SLIM, ICEBERG. See Iceberg Slim.

SLIM GREER is both a literary character created by Sterling A. *Brown and the term designating his memorable series of satiric poems. In the cycle are five poems: "Slim Greer," "Slim Hears 'the Call,'" "Slim in Atlanta," "Slim in Hell," and "Slim Lands a Job?," all of which were published between 1930 and 1933. These poems reveal Brown's careful study of oral and written literatures, from Molière's satire to Mark Twain's *humor, and his absorption of less formal teaching from a gallery of African American raconteurs. After graduation from Harvard University (MA, 1923), he immersed himself in the cultural life and lore of Black folk by frequenting barbershops, "jook-joints," and isolated farms. In these places, "master liars" like "Preacher," Duke Diggs, and an actual Slim Greer transformed mundane, prosaic experiences into performances of high art. The results of their informal instruction are readily discerned in Brown's poems.

The Slim Greer poems represent the principal concern in nearly all of Brown's work: reclaiming the humanity of African Americans to insure the completion of selfhood. To accomplish this purpose, Brown adapts features of the American tall tale, including vernacular language, "deadpan" manner of narration, development from plausibility to frantic impossibility, and the snapper climax or exposure at the end. As in the best tall tales, these poems achieve their success by laughing the reader/listener into an awareness of practices that prevent the self from attaining wholeness, such as religious hypocrisy and the absurdity of racial segregation. In so doing, Brown makes his Slim Greer do in *poetry what Langston *Hughes's *Simple does in short fiction.

[*See also* Folklore.]

• Sterling A. Brown, "In the American Grain," *Vassar Alumnae Magazine* 36.1 (Feb. 1951): 5–9. John Edgar Tidwell, "The Art of Tall Tale in the Slim Greer Poems," *Cottonwood Magazine* 38/39 (Fall 1986): 170–176.

—John Edgar Tidwell

SMITH, AMANDA BERRY (1837–1915), international missionary and autobiographer. Amanda Berry Smith was born in Long Green, Maryland, to Samuel Berry, a slave who eventually bought his freedom and that of his wife and five children. Known for her charisma and power to convert, Smith was an international missionary, serving in the United States, England, Ireland, Scotland, India, and Africa from 1878 to 1890. She began as a member of the African Methodist Episcopal (AME) Church and was one of the growing numbers of female preachers pressing for the ordination of women. Perhaps disenchanted with the denomination, she became an independent evangelist, funded by both African American and white friends. She devoted eight years of missionary work to the people of the west coast of Africa and returned to the United States in 1890. To help raise funds for an orphanage for African American children, for what would become the Amanda Smith School in Harvey, Illinois, she began to publish a monthly newspaper, the *Helper*, and to write her life story. The latter was published in 1893 under the title *An Autobiography: The Story of the Lord's Dealings with Mrs. Amanda Smith, the Colored Evangelist*. Framed within the journey and adventure story motifs, this work interweaves two themes predominant in African American narratives: the quest for an *education, which is equated with *freedom, and the quest for spiritual purification. It also provides a history of women's struggles for authority in the AME Church. Smith died in Sebring, Florida.

• Hallie Q. Brown, *Homespun Heroines and Other Women of Distinction*, 1988. Joanne Braxton, *Black Women Writing Autobiography: A Tradition Within a Tradition*, 1989.

—Mary C. Carruth

SMITH, BESSIE (1894–1937), blues singer. Bessie Smith began her performance career as a dancer with a traveling minstrel troupe. Her vocal talents were quickly recognized, and by the age of nineteen she had begun to establish her reputation as one of the foremost *blues singers of her day. By the time she recorded her first record with Columbia Records in 1923, she was an established star on the southern vaudeville circuit.

Smith became known as Empress of the Blues because of her incredible voice, sexually aggressive lyrics, fierce independence, and glamour. These qualities have also endeared her to generations of African American poets, novelists, and critics, particularly black feminists. Literary interpretations of her life and work range from portrayals of a genius victim of American racism to portrayals of a protofeminist icon, an alternative to the fair upper-middle-class heroines of early black women novelists. For Amiri *Baraka's Clay (from *Dutchman*, 1964), Bessie Smith is the quintessential wearer of the mask, saying "Kiss my ass, kiss my black unruly ass." According to Clay, "If Bessie Smith had killed some white people she wouldn't have needed that music." In contrast, the Smith of Sherley Anne *Williams's "Someone Sweet Angel Chile" emerges as a woman who triumphs through her ability to make music and sing the song of her own personal life as well as the collective song of black people. Recently, Smith has been identified by African American feminist critics as an important foremother for black women writers, who celebrate her independence and forthright attitudes about *race and *sexuality.

• Chris Albertson, *Bessie*, 1972.

—Farah Jasmine Griffin

SMITH, EFFIE WALLER (1879–1960), poet and short story writer. Effie Waller Smith's work appeared over a thirteen-year period: in 1904 a volume of *poetry, *Songs of the Months*; in 1908 two poems, "Benignant Death" and "The Shepherd's Vision" and two short stories, "The Tempting of Peter Stiles" and "A Son of Sorrow"; in 1909 the *short story "The Judgement of Roxenie" and two volumes of poetry, *Rhymes from the Cumberland* and *Rosemary and Pansies*; in 1911 "The Faded Blossoms"; and in 1917 "Autumn Winds." These works' themes of nature, love, death, and religion primarily set in the Cumberland mountains received little critical attention.

The third of four children of Frank and Sibbie Waller, Effie was born 6 January 1879 near Pikeville, Kentucky. Educated in segregated public schools, she attended the Kentucky Normal School for Colored Persons and taught in Pikeville and eastern Tennessee. She married twice, in 1904 and 1908. Neither marriage lasted but the second produced a child who died in infancy. In 1916 Effie Smith moved with her mother to Waukesha, Wisconsin, to join the Metropolitan Church Association. They left the religious commune in 1924 but remained in Wisconsin. In 1935 Smith returned to Kentucky to adopt Ruth Ratliff, who provides details about Smith's later years. From the 1930s Smith led a relatively obscure life as she constructed a rock and flower garden that attracted visitors from near and far, kept track of these visitors, and continued to write poetry until her death on 2 January 1960. Smith belongs among the minor poets and regional writers of African American letters.

• Alice J. Kinder, "Effie Waller Smith: Singing Poet of the Cumberlands," *Appalachian News Express*, 18 June 1980, 3:1, 4. Effie Waller Smith, *The Collected Works of Effie Waller Smith*, introduction by David Deskins, 1991.

—Paula C. Barnes

SMITH, VENTURE (c. 1729–1805), autobiographer. Venture Smith, known as the black Bunyan because of his reputed feats of great strength, was born in Dukandarra, Guinea, West Africa. By Venture's own testimony his father named him Broteer. He was brought to America at the approximate age of eight, having already sold to an American slaver before he arrived on the shore of Rhode Island. His life for the next twenty-eight years was devoted almost exclusively to his quest for *freedom. He achieved what he called his "redemption" in his thirty-seventh year. Most of the remainder of his life was devoted to earning the money, through years of prodigious labor, to free his wife Meg, his sons Solomon and Cuff, his daughter Hannah, and three other black men.

Smith dictated his *A Narrative of the Life and Adventures of Venture, A Native of Africa: But resident above sixty years in the United States of America. Related by Himself* to an *amanuensis, who has been identified as the Connecticut schoolmaster Elisha Niles, in 1798. Calling Smith "destitute of all education but what he received in common with other domesticated animals" such that he could hardly "suppose himself superior to the beasts, his fellow servants," Smith's recorder refuses to refer to him as a freed African American but rather chooses to label him "an untutored African slave."

Yet no reader of Smith's narrative can escape this man's bitterness at having not realized "in a Christian land" the promise of reward available to white folks of industry. According to Smith's own testimony, no one could have worked harder to achieve the American dream, undeniable according to St. Jean de Crèvecoeur (in *Letters from an American Farmer*) to whoever would "be just, grateful and industrious."

Even though by his alleged sixty-ninth year Smith had acquired one hundred acres of land, some twenty "boats, canoes, and sail vessels," and three habitable dwelling houses, he found that in the American courts he was unable to exact justice for a white man's crime against him. In his native Africa, Smith protests, this crime would "have been branded ... highway robbery." But his adversary "was a *white gentleman*, and I a *poor African*, therefore it was *all right, and good enough for the black dog* [sic]." Despite all his bitterness, Smith still avows, "My freedom is a privilege which nothing else can equal."

Smith's *Narrative* is composed of three chapters: the first tracing what he chooses to remember for his largely white audience of his African homeland, the second accounting for his quest to free himself from *slavery, and the third revealing his herculean efforts to free his family and others, to participate in the American dream, and to realize for himself and his family a fair share of human dignity. In contrast to the Boston poet Phillis *Wheatley, who recalled little of her African homeland to her white captors, Smith presents substantial and fascinating details of his experiences in West Africa. Venture Smith died on 19 September 1805, and his grave is marked by this fitting inscription: "Sacred to the memory of Venture Smith, African though son of a king he was kidnapped and sold as a slave, but by his industry he acquired enough money to purchase his freedom."

[*See also* Slave Narrative.]

• Dorothy Porter, *Early Negro Writing: 1760–1837*, 1971. William L. Andrews, *To Tell a Free Story: The First Century of Afro-American Autobiography, 1760–1865*, 1986. Sidney Kaplan and Emma N. Kaplan, *The Black Presence in the Era of the American Revolution*, 2d ed., 1989.

—John C. Shields

SMITH, WILLIAM GARDNER (1927–1974), journalist, novelist, and English language editor. Born in 1927, William H. Gardner Smith produced a body of work reflective of the vast dilemmas he experienced as a pre–civil rights movement and post–World War II Black male. His views as a young man were largely shaped by his environment; however, his perceptions were altered by his travels abroad as reflected in his novels.

Smith's five novels: *Last of the Conquerors* (1948), *Anger of Innocence* (1950), *South Street* (1954), *The Stone Face* (1963), and *Return to Black America* (1970) all attempt to reconcile the "Negro" to his larger unaccepting community of white society. Smith contended that the Black writer has such a sensitivity and deeply felt empathy for suffering and ostracism that he has the potential to express truth unlike any other writer. However, Smith also charged the "Negro writer" with projecting Black victimization to the point of monotony, resulting in the writer's ineffectiveness. Smith wrote that "the chronicles of offenses constitute truth; however, they do not constitute art. And art is the concern of any novelist." Ironically, Smith's attempts to separate his art from himself were ultimately disappointing.

Robert Bone likens Smith's style in *Last of the Conquerors* to that of Richard *Wright. This novel details the life of a young Black soldier. Disillusioned and disenfranchised in American society, the youth is quickly seduced by the ideals of communism and a liaison with a young German woman. He becomes an expatriate only to encounter the bigotry of the German soldiers who go to great lengths to protect their women from eager young American Black soldiers. The actions in the novel echo Smith's own evolution as an artist and philosopher, for Smith soon realizes that pandering to white audiences would not eradicate racist perceptions and *stereotypes.

Indeed, Smith's late works reflect a marked shift in attitude. The protagonists in *South Street* and *The Stone Face* find consolation in returning to their original neighborhoods. Claude and Simeon find their sense of universality thwarted by their journeys abroad and liaisons with white women. Hence, in these novels acceptance takes a more introspective approach. Unlike Wright, James *Baldwin, or other African American male writers, whose characters grappled with similar personal and professional issues, Smith leaves his characters with a sense of resignation rather than triumph.

William Gardner Smith died in 1974 with his dilemmas about *race and artistry relatively unresolved. His collection of works enjoyed limited readership, though his conflicts were well documented in his own novels and those of his contemporaries. A predictor of his own fate, Smith stated about Black writers, "They write only about the here and now. Thus their novels come and they go: in ten years they are forgotten." More than twenty years after his death, Smith's prophetic statement holds true.

• Addison Gayle, Jr., comp., *Black Expression: Essays by and about Black Americans*, 1969. Jerry H. Bryant, "Individuality and Fraternity: The Novels of William Gardner Smith," *Studies in Black Literature* 3.2 (Summer 1972): 1–8.
—Emma Waters Dawson

SNELLINGS, RONALD. *See* Touré, Askia M. .

SOCIETIES AND CLUBS. African Americans have created and maintained societies and clubs in America since the eighteenth century. From mutual aid societies, to *literary societies, to secret and fraternal lodges, to *women's clubs, and even to political organizations, these groups flourished and increased as America tightened its racial segregation laws. While some substituted for the political and social activities that race forbade them to take part in, others promoted literary and educational opportunities. These latter clubs were important as a vent for literary expression, as an influence on the intellectual climate in which African Americans have worked, and as an important agent in shaping the publishing opportunities available to African Americans.

Mutual aid societies were small, beneficial organizations established by free African Americans during the eighteenth century to provide members and their families with sickness and death benefits. Hundreds existed and among the most popular ones (and their beginning dates) were The Free African Society (1778), The Brown Fellowship Society (1790), New York African Society for Mutual Relief (1808), The Female Benezet (1818), and The Female Lundy Society (1833). Some of these groups laid the groundwork for an intellectual climate by extending their philanthropic endeavors beyond the education of their members' children to others and by endorsing literary activities.

In 1803 seven members of the Brown Fellowship Society in Charleston, South Carolina, began the Minor's Moralist Society to support and educate colored orphans. Daniel A. *Payne, an orphan who later became a well-known African Methodist Episcopal (AME) Bishop, attended and benefitted from the Minor's Moralist Society school. At age eighteen Payne opened his own academy for free colored youth in Charleston and enrolled as many as sixty students. His school was closed in 1835 when South Carolina forbade teaching enslaved and free African Americans how to read or write. Also in the first three decades of the nineteenth century, the Woolman Benevolent Society maintained a school for African American children in New York; the Resolute Beneficial Society operated a school in Washington, D.C.; the Phoenix Society sponsored a school for African Americans in New York; and the African Dorcas Society encouraged school attendance among and distributed clothing to needy African American children in New York and Philadelphia.

A few mutual aid societies existed that encouraged literary aspirations. The Société des Artisans, which African American veterans organized in New Orleans for free colored mechanics and incorporated in 1834, afforded its members an outlet for business considerations and literary expression. Creole writer Victor *Séjour was a member who recited before this group his inflammatory poetry against the Société d'Economie, a snobbish rival Creole group in that city. It is believed that Hippolyte Castra, a free Creole soldier, recited his famous poem "Campaign of 1814–15" before members of the Société des Artisans. Whatever influence these early beneficial societies had on the intellectual life of African Americans will probably never be fully realized since many groups had short life spans, were not incorporated, and therefore kept no public records.

Literary societies also evolved in the nineteenth century, among which were debating societies, library assemblies, and groups emphasizing declamations, poetry, and prose. There are references to a small debating society in Boston in 1825, a book-collecting library group in Brooklyn in 1831, the Bonneau Library Society in Charleston, South Carolina, in 1830, and the New York Philomathean Society in 1831, which collected more than six hundred volumes for its circulating library.

The Phoenix Society, founded in New York in 1833 by African Americans and whites, seems to be the most prominent early literary society. It established a library, a discussion group, a lecture agenda, and small wards throughout the city charged with disseminating the benefits of educational and intellectual development to African Americans. Prominent officers in this group included intellectuals such as David *Ruggles, Samuel *Cornish, and Christopher Rush.

In Philadelphia in the mid-1830s, African American women established the Minerva Literary Society and the Edgewood Society, both of which promoted reading, writing, and recitation of poetry. In the same city men organized the Banneker Society, the Rush Library Company and Debating Society, and the Demosthenian Institute, the latter of which established a library and lecture series and started the *Demosthenian Shield*, a weekly newspaper. While it is difficult to ascertain the number of African American literary societies and African Americans' participation in them, their benefits are realized in the continued establishment of such societies throughout the latter half of the nineteenth century and into the twentieth century.

Literary societies that catered to a middle-class clientele in the late nineteenth century took the names of Phillis *Wheatley, Paul Laurance *Dunbar, John Mercer *Langston, or Frederick *Douglass—African Americans who had gained national and international prominence. These sponsored Sunday evening recitals and poetry readings. Upper-class literary societies had more flexible agendas. The smaller groups met in members' homes, studied the classics, read biographies of African American and Caucasian antislavery leaders, and discussed topics assigned to members. The intent of such clubs as the Pen and Pencil Club and the Mu-So-Lit Club of Washington, D.C., was to expand the intellectual outlook of their members. The larger upper-class literary societies, meeting in churches or segregated public halls, stressed literature and history and emphasized racial uplift themes. Well-known speakers such as Mary Church *Terrell, Booker T. *Washington, and Frederick Douglass were invited to talk before these literary associations, the best known of which was the American Negro Academy founded by Alexander *Crummell, minister of Saint Luke's Protestant Episcopal Church in Washington, D.C.

Founded in 1897, the American Negro Academy encouraged African American interest in literature, science, and art and published scholarly works by and about African Americans. From 1897 until 1916, it published and circulated *Occasional Papers* and established historical and literary archives. A forerunner of The Association for the Study of Negro Life

and History, founded in 1915 by Carter G. *Woodson, the American Negro Academy included classical scholar William S. Scarborough and literary figure W. E. B. *Du Bois among its members.

The largest and most prominent African American literary association in the twentieth century is the College Language Association (CLA). Formerly called the Association of Modern Language Teachers in Negro Colleges, it was founded in 1937 to promote scholarship among teachers of English and modern foreign languages in historically black colleges and universities. It presents the CLA Award for scholarly publications at its annual convention and sponsors a creative writing award for students. It publishes *CLA Journal*, a quarterly of scholarly articles and reviews and has imprinted books on James *Baldwin, Langston *Hughes, and Jean *Toomer.

Secret societies, so called because of their rituals and ceremonies, also influenced the intellectual climate of African Americans. The Masonic Order, the oldest secret fraternity among African Americans, has encouraged intellectual development since the eighteenth century. The African Lodge, the oldest organized body of African American Masons, was first established in Boston in 1784 under the leadership of Prince Hall as Worshipful Master. This lodge had significant cultural influence in the community. In 1787 Hall petitioned the Massachusetts state legislature to open schools for African Americans; in 1792 he urged African Americans to own their own schools; and in 1796 he appealed to white Boston officials to open a school for African Americans. Throughout the first quarter of the nineteenth century the African Lodge, which became the Prince Hall Grand Lodge in 1791, issued warrants for other lodges with similar intellectual and educational interests to be established in other cities.

Another secret lodge, the Philomanthean Lodge of New York, was established in 1843 by Peter Ogden. He applied for and received a charter from the English chapter of The Order of Odd Fellows after the New York chapter refused the admission of two African American literary societies—the Philomathean Society of New York and the Philadelphia Library Company of Colored Persons.

The Independent Order of St. Luke, founded in 1867 by Mary Prout and based in Richmond, Virginia, branched into several areas when Maggie Lena Walker succeeded the male leadership in 1899. In addition to acquiring a store and a bank, under Walker's financial guidance the organization founded the *St. Luke Herald*, the society's newspaper, in 1902. It was a forum for topics on lynching, women's issues, and occasional poems. Its subscribers helped to finance a profitable printing venture.

Other African American secret societies with varying degrees of influence on the intellectual life of African Americans include: the United Order of True Reformers, organized in Richmond, Virginia, in 1881; the National Order of Mosaic Templars of America, organized in Little Rock, Arkansas, in 1882; and the Improved Benevolent and Protective Order of the Elks of the World, organized in Cincinnati, Ohio, in 1899. In all instances the lodges encouraged its members to study to improve their status within the organization.

At the turn of the twentieth century, African American Greek-letter organizations were established, primarily on historically black college campuses. They functioned as social and cultural outlets in segregated educational enclaves, but they also promoted high moral and intellectual standards among their members. Their names and dates of origin are Alpha Phi Alpha (1906), Alpha Kappa Alpha (1908), Kappa Alpha Psi (1911), Omega Psi Phi (1911), Delta Sigma Theta (1913), Phi Beta Sigma (1914), and Zeta Phi Beta (1920). These contributed primarily to the intellectual development of the African American community by awarding partial and full-tuition scholarships to deserving high school graduates bound for college. Each has its own publication and a national membership exceeding twenty thousand.

Two fraternal organizations that support intellectual activities and in which African Americans are highly visible are Kiwanis International and Jack and Jill. Kiwanis International was founded in 1915 in Detroit and is a federation of civic organizations. Derived from the Native American word "kiwanis" which means to make oneself known, the term illuminates the organization's work in the community. Its intellectual endeavors include sponsoring educational programs for people of all ages: Primary One benefits children to age five; Key Club International, high school students; Circle K International, college students; and Builders Clubs, junior high school students.

Jack and Jill of America, founded in 1938, has as its aim to stimulate growth and development in children and to provide them with a well-rounded program including cultural, civic, recreational, and social activities. The organization also seeks equal opportunities for all children and aids parents in learning more about their children.

Women's clubs have contributed to the intellectual development of the African American community by raising the consciousness of women. They have existed since the antebellum days, but in the 1890s the National Club movement among black women developed in response to racism, to women's desires to make their achievements known, and to the need for club reform. With its strongest influence in three northeast urban areas—Washington, D.C., New York City, and Boston—the club movement boasted elite, educated colored women, the majority of whom were teachers and had experience in publishing, church work, beneficent endeavors, and small-scale literary associations. (Women's clubs in Chicago were also strong with Fannie Barrier Williams and Ida B. *Wells-Barnett as spokespersons.)

In Washington, D.C., club activities centered on Mary Ann *Shadd, cofounder and the first black female editor of *Provincial Freeman* (1853–1859), a protest newspaper inveighing against the treatment of runaway slaves in Canada; Hallie Q. *Brown, teacher, civil rights and women's rights activist, and organizer of colored women's clubs of Washington, D.C.; Anna Julia *Cooper, teacher, author of A *Voice from the South by a Black Woman of the South, and

the only female member in the American Negro Academy; and Mary Church Terrell, civil rights activist.

In New York City, the Woman's Loyal Union of New York City and Brooklyn was founded in 1892 by Victoria Earle *Matthews, freelancer, editor, and short story writer; and Maritcha Lyons, New York school teacher. Essentially the club performed as an information clearinghouse for New York City and Brooklyn and as a center for community affairs and race work.

In Boston in 1893, Josephine St. Pierre Ruffin with her daughter Florida Ridley and Agassiz School principal Maria Baldwin founded the Woman's Era Club, open to women of all races. Among various communal activities, this club supported a kindergarten in Atlanta, Georgia, and published antilynching leaflets in support of Ida Wells-Barnett's antilynching crusade. Each club group essentially worked in its individual environment raising the consciousness of the public about race matters, but efforts were already underway to form a nationwide collective for African American women.

A first step was taken in 1895 when Josephine St. Pierre Ruffin, president of the Woman's Era Club, called together a convention of colored women in protest of the slanderous remarks made by John W. Jacks, editor of the *Standard* in Montgomery City, Missouri, against African American women. Jacks had assailed the virtue of African American women in an open letter to English activist Florence Balgarnie, who forwarded the letter to Ruffin, founder of the *Woman's Era, the first American magazine owned and published by an African American woman. Little time was spent discussing the letter itself, but the meeting made clear the work in racial uplift that African American women still had to do in order to change public opinion about them. As a result of this meeting, the National Federation of Afro-American Women was formed. Fifty-four clubs came together with 101 delegates representing Washington, D.C., and fourteen states.

In 1896 the National Federation of Afro-American Women and the National League of Colored Women merged to form The National Association of Colored Women (NACW), with Mary Church Terrell as its first president. The largest organization of African American women in America, its essential purpose was to uplift the race by stimulating African American women to develop intellectual pursuits, encourage race pride, and promote racial solidarity. Mary McLeod Bethune, who became NACW's president in 1924, carried out the mission of the club while simultaneously serving as president of Bethune-Cookman College in Daytona, Florida, and transforming that school from a women's college to a coeducational institution. Elsewhere, the club's aims were disseminated through the published writings of members such as Anna Julia Cooper, Josephine St. Pierre Ruffin, and Josephine W. Turpin.

In the 1970s with the emergence of feminist groups, African American women organized a number of clubs to meet their various needs. The National Black Feminist Organization (1973), the

Combahee River Collective (1974), and other political groups provided African American women with a platform for voicing and publishing their concerns about welfare, reproductive freedom, and employment discrimination. At the academic level, the Black Women's Studies Faculty and Curriculum Development Project was organized in 1983 and convened at Spelman College. It assisted African American female faculty at historically black colleges in developing courses in African American women's studies at their respective schools.

In addition to women's groups, political organizations also contributed to the intellectual development of the African American community. Formed in 1910 in New York City as a protest organization against white racism, the National Association for the Advancement of Colored People (NAACP) published the *Crisis: A Record of the Darker Races* in the same year. This monthly journal contained literary works and articles on the history, culture, and social problems of the darker races worldwide.

The *Crisis* had several literary advantages. First, it afforded budding literary artists an opportunity to publish their works and contend for the journal's annual prizes for the best short story, poem, essay, or drama. Jessie Redmon *Fauset, Langston *Hughes, Walter *White, and Marita Bonner *Occomy were among literary figures who published their early works in the *Crisis*. Marita Occomy won the *Crisis* best play award for *Purple Flower* in 1927 and the best short story award for "Drab Rambles" the same year. Second, the tenor of literary reviews gauged the acceptance or rejection of African American novels. W. E. B. Du Bois's vitriolic review of Claude *McKay's *Home to Harlem* (1928), a rollicking novel about pimps, prostitutes, and cutthroats, registered middle-class African Americans' distaste for Harlem's low-life. Third, Jessie Fauset, literary editor of the *Crisis* and well-known novelist during the *Harlem Renaissance, sponsored literary teas and invited Harlem's literati. At these gatherings, W. E. B. Du Bois, NAACP's head, James Weldon *Johnson, executive secretary, and Walter *White, Johnson's assistant, met Harlem newcomers such as Arna *Bontemps, Richard Bruce *Nugent, and Zora Neale *Hurston. These teas offered those in attendance an opportunity to exchange notes and keep each other abreast of literary happenings. Finally, the *Crisis* included "A Selected List of Books" in which new works by fictionists such as Charles Waddell *Chesnutt, Paul Laurence Dunbar, and W. E. B. Du Bois were listed.

The National Urban League, established in 1911 when three interracial groups merged, focused on improving the industrial conditions of African Americans. In January 1923 it began publishing a general readers' monthly magazine called *Opportunity: A Journal of Negro Life*, whose purpose was to raise the standard of living among African Americans. *Opportunity* also offered young authors a publishing outlet and awarded annual prizes for the best literature. John F. *Matheus's "Fog" was *Opportunity's* prize-winning short story for 1925; the same year, Zora Neale Hurston's play *Color Struck* received second prize for drama. In 1926, Dorothy *West's first short story, "The Typewriter," won one of two second prizes that *Opportunity* awarded.

For more than two hundred years, African Americans have contributed to the intellectual development of their communities through various societies and clubs. While it is difficult to assess the total contributions of these organizations, they did provide unparalleled opportunities for African Americans to obtain an education, nurture their creative talents, and publish their works.

• Edward Nelson Palmer, "Negro Secret Societies," *Social Forces* 22 (Sept. 1944): 207–212. Allan H. Spear, *Black Chicago: The Making of a Negro Ghetto, 1890–1920*, 1967. Rodolphe Lucien Desdunes, *Our People and Our History*, 1973. Leonard P. Curry, *The Free Black in Urban America, 1800–1850*, 1981. Robert L. Harris, "Charleston's Free Afro-American Elite: The Brown Fellowship Society and the Humane Brotherhood," *South Carolina Historical Magazine* 82 (Jan. 1981): 289–310. W. Augustus Low and Virgil A. Clift, *Encyclopedia of Black America*, 1981. Alfred N. Moss, *The American Negro Academy: Voice of the Talented Tenth*, 1981. Paula Giddings, *When and Where I Enter*, 1984. Willard B. Gatewood, *Aristocrats of Color: The Black Elite, 1880–1920*, 1990. Patricia Hill Collins, "Feminism in the Twentieth Century," in *Black Women in America: An Historical Encyclopedia*, ed. Darlene Clark Hine, vol. 1, 1993, pp. 418–425.
—Rita B. Dandridge

Soldier's Play, A (1981). Charles H. *Fuller, Jr.'s presentation of institutional racism and self-hatred set in the 1940s explores the psychological effects of oppression on African Americans. The setting of *A Soldier's Play* is an army base in Fort Neal, Louisiana, in 1944. Fuller creates an ironic situation with an all-black company eager to fight for justice in World War II for a country that refuses to send the company overseas because of discrimination. The tragic hero, Sergeant Vernon C. Waters, has taken upon himself the role of savior of all African Americans in a racist society. This highly acclaimed commentary on the ills and trials of military life for the African American is built on a foundation of intricate characterizations and tone.

Fuller's use of the mystery plot provides the audience with Waters's identity as a tragic hero. The investigating officer, Captain Richard Davenport, through a series of interviews, discloses to the audience each of the enlisted men's stories. Fuller often allows one character to tell another's story. At a time when camaraderie among men is essential, Fuller creates dichotomies between them: Waters and his enlisted men form one, and later Davenport creates another in his leadership role.

Oftentimes the most powerful force in society is the role of its men. Whether the role is that of a father, follower, or leader, the status of men is closely scrutinized, and Fuller demonstrates how such expectations can become destructive. The African American male may often find himself trapped between the high expectations of his own society in comparison to the low esteem and extensive oppression exerted by his white counterparts. Waters appears to be a victim and worthy of pity when we see him groveling in drunkenness just before he is brutally shot in the head and heart, symbolic of the black man who fails to think for himself, hates himself, and has lost compassion for others.

Fuller does not allow the image of the downtrodden African American male to remain the only one projected. Private C. J. Memphis, a *blues-singing country boy, escapes the need to lead by creating lyrics and sounds that ring of following, whether it is a "woman to the dance floor" or Sergeant Waters to a detail. Through his *music and strength, C. J. Memphis sings his troubles away and believes in the initial good of man. He feels sorry for Sergeant Waters because "any man ain't sure where he belongs, must be in a whole lotta' pain." In C. J. there are indeed heroic qualities in spite of his eventual suicide.

Charles Fuller did not write *A Soldier's Play* just to offer another glimpse at the ugly face of racism, but to serve as a wake-up call for camaraderie among men; a call for men to accept, love, and support one another. He presents each character and asks the audience to examine each character through history. Because of his intense hatred for those African Americans he considered "inferior," Waters taught African Americans to love *Afrocentricity, to increase black sensibility, and to see institutional racism as a part of the whole society rather than individual targets of rage.

Frank Rich writing for the *New York Times* described Fuller as a playwright with a "compassion" for blacks who might be driven to murder their brothers because he sees them as victims of a world they haven't made. Rich views the play as a rock-solid piece of architecture with the right mixture of characters to create a historical literary movement. Walter Kerr saw the piece as tough but filled with honesty.

• Walter Kerr, "A Fine Work from a Forceful Playwright," 6 Dec. 1981, *New York Times*, 3:1. James Draper, *Black Literature Criticism*, vol. 2, 1992, pp. 824–825.

—Wanda Macon

Song of Solomon.

Toni *Morrison's third *novel, *Song of Solomon* (1977) was immediately acclaimed as one of beauty and power, mythical and magical in proportion and theme. Its protagonist, Macon Dead III, the first black baby born at Mercy Hospital (called No Mercy by the Michigan town's black population), is born on the day that the insurance man attempts to fly from its steeple. He and his family are portrayed in the novel's first section. Known as *Milkman Dead because of his mother's excessive and prolonged nursing, he grows up in a house with a passive mother, a greedy, abusive, and materialistic father, and silent, frustrated sisters. His grandfather, Macon Dead I, was murdered by whites for his property, leaving his son and daughter, Macon and Pilate. They are hunted by the white men who killed their father, and they, in turn, are later forced to kill a white man. This incident sets their values and life goals, for Macon believes the man was hiding money while Pilate rejects material goods. Macon Dead II later scorns his sister and becomes a wealthy property owner at the sacrifice of his family's happiness and psychological health. He abandons his wife spiritually and physically after the birth of Milkman,

who is only born through the intervention and magic of Pilate.

The novel's second part involves Milkman's search for gold that he believes was hidden in a cave in Virginia by his aunt and his father in their youth; however, this becomes a search for himself and his family history. Part 2 also focuses on Milkman's aunt, a character embracing mythology and magic, whom Milkman sees despite being forbidden to do so by his father. *Pilate Dead is a natural woman, "born wild" and without a navel, and she has values that directly oppose her brother's—she is moral, responsible, loving, generous, and unpretentious. Also a direct contrast to her sister-in-law Ruth, who is dominated first by her father and then by her husband, Pilate lives free of all materialistic conveniences (i.e., running water and electricity) and she is a bootlegger. She lives with her daughter and granddaughter, Hagar, who develops a destructive and obsessive love for Milkman.

At first Milkman is a selfish, pleasure-seeking young man; however, with Pilate and his childhood friend Guitar Bains as examples, he is guided to achieve self-knowledge and self-sufficiency. Arriving in the South in search of his father's treasure, Milkman is enthralled and overcome by the *folklore and myth surrounding his family's history, especially the legend of his paternal great-grandfather (Shalimar or Solomon), who, according to a song Pilate sang to Milkman when he was young, flew like a black eagle back to Africa to escape *slavery. When Milkman and Pilate later return to their ancestral home, they are tracked and hunted by Guitar Bains, who has become part of a group that takes revenge for the unjust murder of blacks by whites and who believes Milkman is going to retrieve gold and not share with him. Guitar shoots Pilate when aiming for Milkman, and Milkman notes that she can fly without leaving the ground. He then acknowledges Guitar's presence and leaps into the air, modeling the ability to fly.

Women are the main sources of knowledge in Milkman's world, with Pilate his primary guide and source of understanding. *Song of Solomon* has consistently been praised by critics for its inventiveness and variety of language and its handling of folklore, allegory, magic, fantasy, song, and legend. It won the prestigious National Book Critics Circle Award in 1977 and firmly established Morrison as a major American writer.

• Jacqueline de Weever, "Toni Morrison's Use of Fairy Tale, Folk Tale, and Myth in *Song of Solomon*," *Southern Folklore Quarterly* 44 (1980): 131–144. Charles Scruggs, "The Nature of Desire in Toni Morrison's *Song of Solomon*," *Arizona Quarterly* 38 (1982): 311–335. Susan Blake, "Toni Morrison," in *DLB*, vol. 33, *Afro-American Fiction Writers after 1955*, eds. Thadious M. Davis and Trudier Harris, 1984, pp. 187–199. Wilfred D. Samuels and Cleora Hudson Weems, *Toni Morrison*, 1990. Ja Mo Kang, "Toni Morrison's *Song of Solomon*: Milkman's Limited Moral Development," *Journal of English Language and Literature* (Seoul, Korea) 41.1 (1995): 125–147.

—Betty Taylor-Thompson

SON GREEN. In Toni *Morrison's *Tar Baby* (1981), William (Son) Green has been on the run for eight years (after killing his adulterous wife) when he becomes infatuated with *Jadine Childs, a Sorbonne-educated model who is visiting her benefactors in whose Caribbean-island house he's taken refuge. The affair that develops between them is emblematic of different cultural points of view: Son represents the humanistic African cultural heritage in contrast to the materialistic European culture Jadine has embraced.

They leave the island to continue their relationship in New York. When Son takes Jadine to see his hometown of Eloe, Florida, where buildings are sparse and shabby and tradition and human relationships valued, she feels threatened. In contrast, Jadine feels at home in New York, while Son confesses to feeling "out of place" in the Streets' home. Although Son is attracted to Jadine sexually, he is not completely intellectually or emotionally ensnared and refuses to succumb to her plans for a professional career for him. In fact, it is Son who narrates his version of the tar baby story to Jadine in an emotional tirade against her lifestyle. She leaves him shortly after their trip to Eloe. When he returns to the island to find her, he is diverted by Thérèse, an islander who does yard work. She directs him to the wild side of the island, supposedly inhabited by blind African horsemen, and Son goes to join them. In this clash between folk culture and commercialism, Son represents the black man who can be drawn to the very forces that could destroy him, whether those forces come in the shape of a mulatto woman or a law degree. Although Morrison portrays him sympathetically, it is finally ambiguous as to whether she prefers Jadine's education and mobility or Son's immersion in folk tradition and myth.

• Susan Blake, "Toni Morrison," in *DLB*, vol. 33, *Afro-American Fiction Writers after 1955*, eds. Thadious M. Davis and Trudier Harris, 1984, pp. 187–199. Wilfred D. Samuels and Clenora Hudson Weems, *Toni Morrison*, 1990. Judylyn S. Ryan, "Contested Visitions/Double Vision in Tar Baby," *Modern Fiction Studies* 39.3–4 (Fall/Winter 1993): 597–621. Trudier Harris, "Toni Morrison: Solo Flight through Literature into History," *World Literature Today* 68.1 (Winter 1994): 9–14.   —Betty Taylor-Thompson

SORORITIES. *See* Societies and Clubs.

SOUL. Originally an Afro-Christian concept of the essential or spirit self that need not be limited by the physical world, "soul" is one of many beliefs integral to the African American religious tradition that have influenced African American cultural production. Soul is a concept grounded in belief in the precedence of the spiritual over the material world and the rule of the soul over the body. This principle extends to a belief held by many that, in a test of wills, God would be on their side against oppressors who may be capable of chaining the body but not the soul. Soul has secular connotations in the same vein of the soul's ability to endure or overcome adversity, as exemplified in W. E. B. *Du Bois's The Souls of Black Folk* (1903).

In the twentieth century, soul has also come to represent African American identity, racial pride, and independence. In Eldridge *Cleaver's collection of essays *Soul on Ice* (1968), for example, it was used to signify the essence of blackness or an authentically black experience. Soul has been a popular vernacular term, especially in its association with the *blues and other music forms. In the 1960s and 1970s soul would identify a return to African American cultural heritage. Soul became synonymous with African American culture, truth, and validity and was applied to numerous icons, practices, and relationships, for example "Soul brother or sister," "Soul clap," and "Soul food."   —Tracy J. Patterson

Soul on Ice. Widely read and enormously influential, the collection of Eldridge *Cleaver's 1965–1966 prison *letters and *essays titled *Soul on Ice* (1968) remains one of the most important articulations of 1960s African American revolutionary nationalism. Published in 1968, *Soul on Ice* clearly captures the liberationist spirit of the moment through autobiographical accounts, personal letters, and sociopolitical essays. The volume generally outlines the devastating impact of American racism, especially on African American men, and suggests strategies for healing the profoundly wounded African American sense of *identity and for bridging the seemingly irreconcilable racial divide in America.

The opening section, "Letters from Prison," recounts Cleaver's early criminal and prison careers, details the everyday racial tension in the California penitentiary system, and provides vignettes of prison life and portraits of other prisoners, an influential teacher in San Quentin prison, and *Malcolm X. The second section, "Blood of the Beast," perhaps the most important part of the volume, offers sociocultural readings of the state of race relations in 1960s America. Cleaver acknowledges his admiration for the new generation of white youth who had jettisoned an unrealistic version of American history and thus their racist attitudes. He offers an allegorical interpretation of the Muhammad *Ali–Floyd Patterson fight as signifying the Lazarus-like awakening of the African American. Cleaver goes on to attack James *Baldwin for his supposed racial self-hatred and his homosexuality, elevating Richard *Wright as a masculine literary standard. Several essays linking the 1960s African American liberation movement with anticolonial struggles throughout the world, especially the war in Vietnam, conclude the second part of *Soul on Ice*. The last two sections, "Prelude to Love—Three Letters" and "White Woman, Black Man," focus more fully on *gender issues, particularly on the psychological emasculation of the African American male and on the pathological impact of racism on human *sexuality.

While Cleaver's discussion of sexual roles often seems masculinist and oversimplified, his description of the condition of the African American prisoner remains powerful and timely.

—Roger A. Berger

Souls of Black Folk, The. A collection of fourteen prose pieces by W. E. B. *Du Bois, *The Souls of Black Folk* had a powerful impact on African American intellectual life when it appeared in 1903. Thirty years later, James Weldon *Johnson declared that it "had a greater effect upon and within the Negro race in America" than any book since Harriet Beecher *Stowe's epochal *Uncle Tom's Cabin* (1852).

The collection included nine pieces previously published in some form in magazines, notably the prestigious *Atlantic Monthly*. Five new pieces rounded out this racial portrait, which reflects the remarkable breadth of Du Bois's interests, training, and temperament. Schooled in *history and sociology, he also had an abiding personal interest in fiction, *poetry, and the *essay.

One major concern of the book is the history of blacks from *slavery down to the present time of legal segregation. Another is a loosely sociological accounting of their lives, especially in the South, where the vast majority still lived in 1903. Closing the book are Du Bois's elegy for his son, an emblematic *short story, and essays on the *spirituals and on *religion. Here Du Bois concentrates on the psychological and expressive aspects of black culture, but the entire work attempts to probe the black American mind, in keeping with the title of the volume.

The meaning of the title is spelled out early. Blacks, who are prevented by the repressive white culture from ever possessing "true self-consciousness," can see themselves only as whites see them:

> It is a peculiar sensation, this *double-consciousness, this sense of always looking at one's self through the eyes of others, of measuring one's soul by the tape of a world that looks on in amused contempt and pity. One ever feels his twoness,—an American, a Negro; two souls, two thoughts, two unreconciled strivings; two warring ideals in one dark body, whose dogged strength alone keeps it from being torn asunder.

The book is also memorable for Du Bois's prophecy, first enunciated in the "Forethought," that "the problem of the Twentieth Century is the problem of the *color line."

In "Of Mr. Booker T. *Washington and Others," Du Bois challenged the leadership of the most powerful black American of the age. The head of Tuskegee Institute, Washington emphasized industrial training for blacks, rather than the liberal arts. He also urged blacks to surrender to southern whites on the issues of voting rights and racial integration in return for peace and prosperity. Attacking these positions, Du Bois's book split the black intelligentsia into two opposing camps.

Perhaps the most powerful single unifying element in this diverse collection, with its multiplicity of vignettes and approaches, is its portrait of Du Bois himself, so much so that the book is sometimes taken as an *autobiography. The record of his personal feelings, rendered in often brilliant language, is made central to his purpose—most notably in his elegy "Of the Passing of the First-Born." The final impression is of a highly intelligent, learned, generous, but deeply wounded individual, unusual and yet profoundly representative of African Americans in his inability, despite his gifts, to find peace in a nation hostile to its blacks.

• Herbert Aptheker, ed., *Annotated Bibliography of the Published Writings of W. E. B. Du Bois*, 1973. Arnold Rampersad, *The Art and Imagination of W. E. B. Du Bois*, 1976. David Levering Lewis, *W. E. B. Du Bois: Biography of a Race, 1868–1919*, 1993.
—Arnold Rampersad

Sounder. When *Sounder* was released in 1972, the *film received praise throughout the country as a landmark in its departure from the heretofore typical depiction of blacks on the screen. However, while *Sounder* was hailed by critics and moviegoers alike, that praise was also mixed with criticism of the movie as sentimental, superficial, and oversimplified.

The screenplay for *Sounder* was written by African American playwright Lonne *Elder III, based loosely on an award-winning children's book of the same title by white author William Armstrong. Elder's screen version tells the story of an African American sharecropping family in Louisiana during the Great Depression. Elder shifts the focus from the significance of the relationship between the eldest son and the family dog (for whom the story is named); in the film, the dog is an important "character" but not central. Instead, he provides companionship for the boy and serves a symbolic role as the plot develops around the family's major conflict. Set in 1933, the film stars Paul Winfield as the father, Nathan Lee Morgan; Cicely Tyson as his wife, Rebecca; and Kevin Hooks, in his first major role, as their eldest son, twelve-year-old David Lee. Two younger children (Earl and Josie Mae) are played by Hooks's younger brother, Eric, and a young girl (Yvonne Jarrell) from the Louisiana parish where the movie was filmed.

Nathan Lee shares a close and special father-son relationship with his eldest son, David Lee, which is often characterized by meaningful eye contact and smiles, spontaneous hugs, and solemn handshakes. David Lee has to quickly assume the role of adult when Nathan Lee, unable to feed his family, steals meat from a white neighbor's smokehouse. Following his arrest, Nathan Lee is tried, convicted, and sentenced to one year on a prison chain gang in a distant parish. While Nathan Lee is awaiting trial, Rebecca is rebuffed in her attempt to visit him after making a daylong trek to the jail in town. Following this failed attempt, the family suffers further humiliation and uncertainty as Rebecca is belittled by the plantation owner in his company store and is forced to plant and harvest the season's crop with the assistance of only her children. In an act of private rebellion and self-assertion, Rebecca buys supplies for a chocolate cake from the owner, which she promptly bakes and sends to her husband via David Lee, who, as a boy child, is allowed to visit. A sympathetic white woman for whom Rebecca does laundry, Mrs. Boatwright, promises David Lee that she will find out which prison camp his father has been sent to. Mrs. Boatwright steals an opportunity to rifle through the sheriff's files and finds the information. She is threatened by the sheriff and initially refuses to disclose the information to young David Lee. However, upon seeing his disappointment and utter loss of faith in her, Mrs. Boatwright tells David Lee what she has found. Armed with this information and advice from his mother and family friend, Ike (played by musician Taj Mahal), David Lee embarks on a journey to visit his father on the chain gang. He does not find him but is befriended by a black teacher, Camille Johnson (Janet MacLachlan), who invites him to come back and attend the school she runs for black children. Nathan Lee returns home limping from an injury he suffers in an accident while on the chain gang and attempts to pick up where he left off with his family, resuming the role of head of household. Things have changed, of course, and in a symbolic depiction of the end of one phase of the Morgans' lives and the beginning of another, the movie ends with Nathan Lee driving David Lee back to the parish to attend Miss Johnson's school the following term.

In a 1973 interview, Elder revealed that he hoped *Sounder* would be the first in a permanent movement toward honest, realistic portrayals of blacks on the screen. *Sounder* can be judged a classic in its ability to transcend time in its artful reflection of a particular experience through understatement and innuendo. The movie depicts the family's humanity in the face of pervasive racism rather than reinforcing or reiterating these ills from an outside or reactionary perspective. In his shift from the focus of Armstrong's book on the heroism of the dog to that of the family, Elder asserts his artistic vision and his desire to portray the humanity of African Americans and provides a film that opened the path for subsequent movies that sought and achieved the same end.

• "The Current Cinema—Soul Food," *New Yorker*, 30 Sept. 1972, 109–111. "Sounder," *Variety*, 16 Aug. 1972, 15. "The South: Movie *Sounder* is a Modern Rarity," *Ebony*, Oct. 1972, 82–84. Paul Warshow, "Sounder," *Film Quarterly* 26 (Spring 1973): 61–64.   —Karla Y. E. Frye

SOUTHERLAND, ELLEASE (b. 1943), poet, essayist, short story writer, and novelist. Ellease Southerland's works draw mainly from the folk tradition. Frank and deeply personal, she writes about childhood remembrances, the joys of family togetherness, and the sorrows of separation. *Folklore, *biblical tradition, Egyptology, African history and lore combine to inform her creative voice.

Southerland was born in Brooklyn, New York, to Ellease Dozier, a housewife, and Monroe Penrose Southerland, lay preacher, both migrants from the South. The third of fifteen children, Southerland received her BA from Queens College (1965) the same year her mother died from cancer. To help support twelve younger siblings, she worked in New York City as a social caseworker from 1966 to 1972. She received her MFA from Columbia University in 1974. She has traveled to Africa six times, has received the John Golden Award for Fiction (1964) for her novella *White Shadows*; and has won the Gwendolyn Brooks Poetry Award (1972) for her poem "Warlock."

The Magic Sun Spins (1975), Southerland's first collection of poetry, is an autobiographical celebration. "Black Is," the title poem, announces the beauty of her being. Another poem, "That Love Survives," af-

firms the love for her mother four years after her death, and "Ellease" lauds herself as a reservoir of knowledge and experience. The outpouring of her inner nature and the inspiration gathered from family love make Southerland's poems deeply spiritual.

Her short stories, "Soldiers" (*Black World*, June 1973) and "Beck-Junior and the Good Shepherd" (*Massachusetts Review*, Autumn 1975), contain personal ruminations. With a close friend in the Vietnam War and with nine brothers herself, Southerland wrote "Soldiers" to portray the hardships endured by family members and those physically and mentally maimed participants in the war. "Beck-Junior and the Good Shepherd" relates the story of Beck Torch, Southerland's sister, and her experiences at a Catholic school. Originally intended to be a part of a novel, the latter short story was noticed by an editor at Scribner's who published Southerland's novel, *Let the Lion Eat Straw* (1979).

A thinly disguised autobiographical novel, *Let the Lion Eat Straw* was named one of the best books of 1979 by the American Library Association. Based on her parents' relationship, it details the experiences of Abeba, the protagonist born out of wedlock in the South; her journey to Brooklyn, where she rejoins her mother and graduates from high school; her marriage to the mentally unstable Jackson, for whom she gives up a promising career as a concert pianist; and her struggles with their fifteen children. Infused with lilting dialect, haunting spirituals, and Southern lore, the novel gained immediate popularity, appearing in four editions within two years.

Southerland's autobiographical pieces extend beyond the geographical limits of America. Her essay "Seventeen Days in Nigeria" (*Black World*, Jan. 1972) recounts her first visit to Africa in search of her heritage. The country's ambience—its friendly roadside vendors, its different foods, unusual manners, and native innocence—add to Southerland's excitement about a place that she had longed to visit. "Ibo Man" and "Seconds," two poems appearing in *Présence Africaine*, 1974 and 1975 respectively, continue her impressions of Nigeria. So do "Blue Clay" and "Nigerian Rain," the latter of which expresses her fulfillment in and oneness with Nigeria, which she calls home.

An engaging writer, Southerland's fame is that she blends her family's history with the folk tradition to tell a rich story.

• Mary Hughes Brookhart, "Ellease Southerland," in *DLB*, vol. 33, *Afro-American Fiction Writers after 1955*, eds. Thadious M. Davis and Trudier Harris, 1984, pp. 239–244. Carolyn Mitchell, "Southerland, Ellease," in *Black Women in America*, ed. Darlene Clark Hine, 1993, vol. 2, pp. 1090–1091.
                                              —Rita B. Dandridge

Southern Workman, The. The *Southern Workman* was the official organ of the Hampton Normal and Agricultural Institute in Virginia, the first permanent school for freed slaves in the South. The journal was published from January 1872 to July 1939.

The *Southern Workman* served mainly as a promotional medium for the founder and first principal of

Hampton Institute, General Samuel C. Armstrong. Although he and subsequent editors of the journal usually avoided racial controversy, some criticism of internal race issues was not unusual. Benjamin *Brawley's article on the *Harlem Renaissance, published in April of 1927, attacked the superficiality he believed present in that movement.

Although the journal occasionally published some creative writing, it was more inclined, especially in its early years, to emphasize African American and Indian *folklore. Paul Laurence *Dunbar published his prose fiction "A Southern Silhouette" in the *Southern Workman*, and after 1900 the journal began to publish book reviews, editorials on race relations, and take note of the work of important African American leaders. In October of 1892 the *Southern Workman* eulogized John Greenleaf Whittier upon his death, and in 1906 Paul Laurence Dunbar. The *Southern Workman* remains an invaluable repository of over a half century of postbellum African American educational and cultural history.

[*See also* Periodicals.]

• Walter C. Daniel, *Black Journals of the United States*, 1982.
—Daniel J. Royer

SPECULATIVE FICTION. Since the late 1960s, the term speculative fiction has often been used by some literary scholars and critics as a synonym, or a more "respectable" designation, for the popular genre science fiction. Limiting the term to equate only with science fiction excludes a broader category of fantastic literature, that fiction which is not dependent upon the conventions of naturalism or realism. A more encompassing perspective sees speculative fiction as the umbrella genre that shelters the subgenres of fantasy, science fiction, utopian and dystopian fiction, supernatural fiction, and what has come to be called by some critics fabulative fiction or fabulation.

While each subgenre has its own specific matrix that shapes it, each also shares in the basic premise underlying speculative fiction—the presentation of a changed, distorted, alternative reality from the reality readers know. Fantasy, for instance, presents stories that could not happen in the real world of the past or the present; stories of this type rely upon the irrational, the magical or mythical, the occult or supernatural, the "quasi-scientific" explanation. Magicians or wizards exist and wield great power. By contrast, science fiction is often seen as the literature of change, the literature that deliberately evokes a sense of wonder, the literature that illustrates the responses of humanity to discoveries in the sciences and advances in technology. Science fiction extrapolates or projects from known data or experience and seeks to convince the reader that the alternate world presented, be it past, present, or future, is possible. This changed yet familiar world has as its base a rational scientific explanation for its imagined fantastic events. Thus, time travel or travel to the stars can be explained by noting human inventiveness in technology and science; aliens are possible because human beings cannot conceive of a universe where Earth is the only inhabited planet. This is the hold on the imagination and essential premise of series such as the popular *Star Trek*.

A broader conceptual framework of speculative fiction permits far more discussion of the contributions African American authors have made to the genre over time. While critics of African American literature have focused on mainstream traditional naturalistic and realistic fiction rather than speculative fiction, there have been, nonetheless, black writers who have either included elements of speculative fiction in their texts or, as have Octavia E. *Butler and Samuel R. *Delany, become major figures in the field.

Arguably the first African American authors to reflect a speculative sensibility were those whose speculative vision projected a transformed world, a social revolution, or a radical change in the depiction of an altered reality. In the nineteenth century, Martin R. *Delany's *Blake, or the Huts of America* (1859) adopts this strategy. Distorting his present reality, Delany presented a black male protagonist who organizes and leads a slave insurrection in several southern states and Cuba as well. The novel's incomplete ending suggests that a general uprising of slaves in all these areas is imminent. Forty years later, Sutton E. *Griggs's *Imperium in Imperio* (1899) adopted a similar premise. In this power fantasy, black men form a secret society and plan to take over Texas to create a separate black government in a separate black state. Charles Waddell *Chesnutt, for the stories he penned in The *Conjure Woman* (1899), relied upon *conjuring or magic, black folklore mixed with fantasy, to paint vivid stories of slave heartbreak and survival in the antebellum South. Chesnutt's shrewd black narrator, *Uncle Julius McAdoo, tells moving tales of slaves magically transformed through the power of hoodoo into trees or birds or animals.

In the early twentieth century, Pauline E. *Hopkins, a columnist, novelist, short story writer, and the literary editor of the *Colored American Magazine* (1900–1904) demonstrated her speculative bent in the short story "The Mystery within Us" and her 1900 novel, *Contending Forces*. Both works utilize the supernatural as either a formidable element in the story or a pivotal episode. While *Contending Forces* is largely a historical romance building upon the themes of the tragic mulatto, miscegenation, tangled race relations, and race pride, it nonetheless illustrates an early approach to a speculative sensibility. Her villain is shown a glimpse of his own terrible death through the agency of a fortune teller who can summon specifically identifiable images of the future. The speculative question for Hopkins was whether foreknowledge of the future would change or affect his evil behavior in the present. Another speculative thread woven into the novel derives from the thinly veiled supposition that "bad blood," inherited from an evil father, serves as a crude genetic marker and is thus responsible for the villain's evil traits.

Edward Johnson's *Light Ahead for the Negro* (1904) is another early twentieth-century speculative text. Johnson distorted his current reality to present a character who, while riding in a blimp, falls into suspended animation. When he awakens, he discovers that the United States has become a socialist state and that the South is leading a movement for social equality between the races. Curiously, however, at the dawn of the twentieth century, Johnson could not conceive of a future where interracial marriage could be accepted.

While he was best known perhaps as a news correspondent, a columnist for the *Pittsburgh Courier*, a social satirist, and one of the first African American political ultraconservatives, the 1930s novelist George S. *Schuyler must be recognized as a legitimate forerunner to the more polished and accomplished science fiction writers in the second half of the twentieth century. In 1931 Schuyler wrote the comic but caustic *Black No More, a highly speculative tale. Adapting a basic framing device found in popular pulp science fiction magazine tales—mad scientist with a secret formula changes the world—Schuyler presents his readers with a black doctor who has found that through the scientific application of "electrical nutrition and glandular control," he can turn black people white. The secret process of Dr. Junius Crookman becomes a panacea for solving the race question in America. Thousands of black Americans rush to purchase the formula, become white, and thereby escape the stigma of blackness. Forgotten is race pride, racial uplift, or pride in a distinctive African American culture. The pronounced satiric bite of Schuyler's instant utopia and his caustic wit is what captures most critical attention; overlooked are the speculative elements used to align the novel with developments in science fiction. Yet, though it was clearly not his main thrust and thus is somewhat labored, Schuyler sought to establish a plausible scientific rationale for his story through extrapolation from a present reality. Dr. Crookman had been studying vitiligo, an actual skin disease affecting the pigment in small areas. He subsequently develops the process to accelerate discoloration. Realizing the unexpected benefit of his discovery, he determines to capitalize on it.

Between 1936 and 1938 Schuyler wrote two additional novels, *The Black Internationale* and *Black Empire*, under the pen name Samuel I. Brooks. These novels were initially published as weekly serial installments in the *Pittsburgh Courier* (they were only published as complete texts in 1991 under the title *Black Empire*). Though highly melodramatic utopian black power fantasies, these two novels clearly build upon several classic speculative fiction themes. The subtitle of each tells the story: *The Black Internationale* is the "Story of Black Genius Against the World," while *Black Empire* was billed as "An Imaginative Story of a Great New Civilization in Modern Africa." Schuyler's protagonist, Dr. Henry Belsidus, is an exceptional and powerful African American in command of a legion of followers in every corner of black America, the Caribbean, and black Africa. More audacious and more ruthless than a Marcus *Garvey, Belsidus enacts a plan to sow bigotry and discord among America's white ethnic groups. With whites busily fighting each other, he can continue

unobserved and unmolested his secret organization and training of the best black engineering and scientific minds in America. The creation of a black utopia is almost a cliché of the genre; other plot devices clearly set the novel apart and establish its ties to actual science fiction, for Schuyler actually anticipates developments in contemporary science and technology. Farmers connected to Belsidus's enterprises grow their crops in water, anticipating modern day hydroponics or aquiculture techniques. His black elite build huge advanced underground technical facilities that power airplanes that can soar into the stratosphere.

In the sequel, *Black Empire*, Schuyler envisions a World War II where not only are the European countries battling each other, they are also fighting the scourge of deadly plague that Belsidus has reintroduced to further divert attention from his nation building in black Africa. While the Europeans fight each other, Belsidus removes the colonial foot from Africa and consolidates his territorial gains. When the white Western world unites to attack Belsidus, he employs defense systems made by black engineers. The cyclotrons are huge weapons of mass destruction; they use "proton rays" to annihilate entire naval fleets and squadrons of fighter planes by smothering the power sources of the enemy instantaneously. Intensely nationalistic and heroic, if short on narrative development, these stories create a near future with a radically altered political reality, show technology in the command of a black superpower, and paint a black utopia founded upon a dystopian beginning.

Works from the 1950s and 1960s that violate the strict social realist mode, evincing a more speculative mood, are William Melvin *Kelley's *A Different Drummer* (1959); Douglas Turner *Ward's play, *Day of Absence* (1966); Charles S. *Wright's *The Wig* (1966); and Sam *Greenlee's *The *Spook Who Sat by the Door* (1969). In the first two works, the local resident African American population suddenly, inexplicably, vanishes from the community en masse. The remaining white inhabitants are left to ponder the reasons for the disappearance of virtually all the African Americans. Neither satiric nor mythic, like Ward's play or Kelley's novel, and certainly not comic like Wright's *Wig*, Greenlee's *Spook* is an angry dystopian fantasy featuring an African American CIA agent who secretly foments a black revolution in the nation's urban areas. Where Greenlee depicted street revolution led by African Americans, John A. *Williams, in *The *Man Who Cried I Am* (1967), examined the potential for genocide against African Americans through a plot launched by the government. In his *Captain Blackman* (1972), he shows an even greater appreciation for speculative mood through the creation of a protagonist who travels through time from the Vietnam War to the Revolutionary War, and every war in between, as a participating soldier.

The late 1960s and early 1970s brought the novels of Ishmael *Reed with his neohoodoo aesthetic, vitriolic satire, and sharp speculative sensibility. *The Freelance Pallbearers* (1967) presents an encapsulated urban cityscape, HARRYSAM, ruled by the despotic

Harry Sam who issues edicts from the john, or toilet, for thirty years. Though his estate is surrounded by a polluted moat, Sam and his supernatural henchmen are dethroned by Reed's naive hero, the Nazarene apprentice, Bukka Doopeyduk. Expecting praise, Bukka is sacrificially crucified on meat hooks while a television audience watches. Reed combines elements of science fiction, the Western, satire, and popular media culture in *Yellow Back Radio Broke-Down* (1971), which features his black hoodoo cowboy, the Loop Garoo Kid, doing magic battle with an assortment of wretched villains. Loop is aided in his battle by Chief Showcase, an Indian flying a helicopter he made from spare parts. Later, the cavalry rides to the rescue in taxicabs, with rayguns to counter the six-shooters of the local villians, and the pope flies into town on a papal bull. Reed's speculative imagination leads him to juxtapose modern technological conveniences (television, shopping malls, used car lots, etc.) with an imaginatively reconstructed antebellum South in *Flight to Canada* (1976). This is his combined variation of the *slave narrative, the antislavery novel, and the seriocomic historical tale.

The antithesis of Reed's forceful and dynamic if eclectic style is seen in Virginia *Hamilton's direct, but careful and delicate, approach to speculative fiction. Although Hamilton is an oft overlooked writer because her domain is seen as juvenile literature, her Justice trilogy, *Justice and Her Brothers* (1978), *Dustland* (1980), and *The Gathering* (1981), is decidedly science fiction. Hamilton makes an eleven-year-old African American child, Justice, her protagonist. Justice becomes The Watcher, an enhanced sentient being; with her twin brothers, she can employ telepathic powers, maneuver time travel, journey to an alien dystopic future; she meets homo superior; she learns that even in the future, ecological concerns are central.

While the accomplishments of their predecessors seeking to shape speculative tales have been many and varied, with varying degrees of success dependent upon an author's other agenda for a story, in the last quarter of the twentieth century two obsidian pillars, one on the east coast, the other on the west, have risen to represent the presence of African Americans in authentic science fiction. Samuel R. Delany and Octavia E. Butler have not simply "contributed" to the field, they altered it; they made it acceptable and normal for black characters to be integral to any story; they took issues of race out of the guise of alien status; they explored the dynamics of race, sexuality, culture, and power; moreover, they opened up the genre to black audiences and the possibilities inherent in the genre to other African American authors.

Without question, Samuel R. Delany has been the most prolific African American writer irrespective of genre. Since the early 1960s he has written science fiction and fantasy novels, novellas, and short stories. In addition, he has composed poetry and music, scripted comic books, and been a filmmaker; he has served as an editor, critic, and teacher; and he has formulated literary theory, written literary criticism, and shaped two memoirs of his early life. The first,

called *Heavenly Breakfast* (1979), subtitled *An Essay in the Winter of Love*, concentrated on the winter and spring of 1967–1968. The second memoir, *The Motion of Light in Water* (1988), subtitled *Sex and Science Fiction Writing in the East Village, 1957–1965*, is a more extended autobiography that focuses on Delany's childhood and youth.

Delany emerged as a science fiction writer of extraordinary ability and imagination with the publication of *The Jewels of Aptor* (1962); he was nineteen when his first novel was published. He went on to publish in rapid succession eighteen science fiction or fantasy novels, three volumes of science fiction stories, five volumes of essays exploring the critical range of science fiction, two memoirs, and in 1994, *Silent Interviews*, the full written text comprising several interviews Delany has granted over the years. Once known as the "wunderkind of science fiction," Delany has accumulated numerous awards. He won the Science Fiction Writers of America Nebula Award several times. *Babel-17* was judged best novel in 1966, and in 1967 his *The Einstein Intersection* won best novel; Delany also took the Nebula for best short story, "Aye and Gomorrah," in 1967, and best novellette, "Time Considered as a Helix of Semi-Precious Stones" in 1969. "Time Considered as a Helix" also won a Hugo award in 1970. *His Tales of Neveryon* was nominated for the American Book Award in 1980. In 1985 Delany received the Pilgrim Award for Excellence in Science Fiction Criticism from the Science Fiction Research Association; and in 1993 he was honored with the Bill Whitehead Memorial Award for Lifetime Excellence in Gay and Lesbian Literature.

Delany's speculative fiction runs the gamut from the technologically based "hard science" science fiction to stories based on the "soft sciences" of anthropology and sociology, to the pure fantasy stories where science is absent. His 1993 novel, *They Fly at Ciron*, is the third reworking of a short story that was originally conceived in 1962. In 1969 James Sallis helped Delany revise the beginning of the story; their joint version appeared in *The Magazine of Fantasy and Science Fiction* in 1971. Then, in 1992, Delany reclaimed, revised, and further developed the tale he considers his second novel.

Fans and critics of Delany have noted that he is among the most polished, most "literary" writers in the science fiction field. His are not simple stories of aliens, space ships, or time warps. His fiction is far more likely to be a complex interweaving of differing mythologies, philosophies, psychological insights, ethics and moralities, social commentaries, and linguistic concerns. In addition, Delany introduced both metaphorically and overtly, issues of race into science fiction. He was a male feminist, and he was in the vanguard of those introducing authentic sexuality into science fiction. His characters are strong men and women. They are heterosexual, homosexual, and sometimes bisexual, and their sexuality is simply a fact of life. While he is at home in a number of art forms, everything from folksinging to comparative literature, Delany is decidedly the astute intellectual whose vision is most apparent in his fantasy fiction, his literary criticism, and his thoughtful and probing responses to interview questions. The parables, the mythological structures he creates in his stories of Neveryon, for instance, tend to be so elaborate that a deliberate artistic self-consciousness seemingly intrudes upon the text, leaving the reader to ponder which is more important to Delany, the exercise in narrative framing or the tale's plot, action, and characters.

Octavia Butler, a student of Delany's in the Clarion Science Fiction Writer's Workshop, made a stunning rise to success in the late 1970s. As a result of her continued hard work and dedication to her craft, she is a highly regarded science fiction author and an African American woman in a field dominated by white males. Winner of a 1995 MacArthur Prize Fellowship (often dubbed the "genius grant"), Butler earned her critical acclaim and her diverse audiences through diligent attention to theme, character, and plot. One result of her attention to these issues has been her unique ability to bring science fiction to a black audience and a feminist audience while simultaneously broadening and staying in touch with the traditional, largely white male, science fiction audience.

Butler has written ten novels and has one published collection of short stories, *Bloodchild and Other Stories* (1995). She won a Hugo Award in 1984 for her short story "Speech Sounds," and her "Bloodchild" won both a Nebula and a Hugo Award in 1984 and 1985 as best novella. Five novels comprise the rich and densely interwoven Patternist saga: *Patternmaster* (1976), *Mind of My Mind* (1977), *Survivor* (1978), *Wild Seed* (1980), and *Clay's Ark* (1984). *Dawn* (1987), *Adulthood Rites* (1988), and *Imago* (1989) shape the complex and brilliant Xenogenesis trilogy. *Kindred* (1979), the lone book outside of a series, is a historical fantasy based upon slavery. Its protagonist, Dana Franklin, inexplicably disappears from her home in 1975 California to reappear in antebellum Maryland. The first book of a new series called the Parable stories, *Parable of the Sower* appeared in 1993; a second book, *Parable of the Talents*, is scheduled for publication in early 1996.

Butler's diverse audience is the result of her global village constructs and the dynamics she sets in motion in a multicultural community. Her works feature black characters in prominent roles, people of color from varying ethnic backgrounds, and capable powerful heroines. Her themes are both racial and feminist. Regardless of her work's setting, Butler addresses issues such as isolation and alienation, adaptability and change, courage and the will to survive, lack of power and empowerment, parapsychology, environmental and ecological sensitivity, genetic permutations, the fear and the value of difference, the paradox of human intelligence and self destructiveness.

Following Delany and Butler, Steven *Barnes is the most visibly active African American writing science fiction. Like Butler, Barnes prefers the terms science fiction or fantasy to speculative fiction. And like both Delany and Butler, Barnes is certain that he has found his niche as a writer and has no interest in penning the "great American" mainstream realistic novel. His preferences are science fiction, action adventure/suspense, and fantasy. With a publishing start that began in 1981 with the coauthored *Dream Park*, Barnes has twelve novels to his credit. Of these, five are collaborations with veteran science fiction author Larry Niven whom Barnes considers a mentor as well. *Dream Park* and its sequels, *The Barsoom Project* (1989) and *California Voodoo Game* (1992), build upon a fascination with interactive video computer gaming, virtual reality, murder mystery, and superb technological wizardry in an extrapolation from a futuresque, highly advanced Disney-style theme park.

Having served an informal apprenticeship with Niven, Barnes branched out to work on his own projects. In 1983 came *Street Lethal*, the first of the Aubry Knight books about a larger than life African American hero, a superbly developed martial arts expert who must learn what it is to become human in a grim, violent, and dystopian near future. Other books in this series are *Gorgon Child* (1989) and *Fire Dance* (1993). The Aubry Knight books allow Barnes to work with several of his favorite themes, the centrality of family, the martial arts, human evolution or development, and the value of myth. Similarly, the semiautobiographical *Kundalini Equation* (1986) permits Barnes further exploration of some of these same issues; here, however, the mythological underpinning is vastly different, borrowing as it does from East Indian myth and legend, and the central protagonist is white, not black. This is a riveting novel that illustrates Barnes's skill in creating a richly textured multicultural landscape and blending into it an action-packed suspenseful science fiction tale about the nature of good and consummate evil, and the nature of humanity in the face of such evil. Like Butler, Barnes is primarily a novelist, although several of his short stories have appeared in various science fiction magazines and anthologies of science fiction.

Three less well-known voices that attest to the growing African American presence (creators, characters, themes, and subjects) and interest in speculative fiction are Jewelle *Gomez, Charles R. Saunders, and Stephen DeBrew. Gomez is the author of *The Gilda Stories: A Novel* (1991), in which she presents a culturally diverse and ethnically mixed group of vampires who are fighting for social justice. She explores the interconnection between power and responsibility, family creation, and heroism in the most inauspicious of people. Like Gomez, Charles R. Saunders, a freelance writer residing in Nova Scotia, writes fantasy fiction. His *Quest for Cush* (1984), *Quest for Cush: Imaro II* (1984), and the *Trail of Bohu: Imaro III* (1985) are African-based fantasy fiction clothed in authentic African historical and folkloric material. Debrew's *Death of a Native Alien* (1990) attempts to employ the framework of science fiction; sadly, it fails as an authentic representation of this genre. Though the novel is ostensibly set on the planet Terra, and despite its altered universe, the "aliens" of the country "Gringoa," and the efforts of the noble Tryon Blackmon, a "Zirconian" nonviolently fighting for his people, DeBrew's "speculative" novel is, unfortunately, little more than an extended allegorical comment on race relations in America circa the last quarter of the twentieth century.

African American authors of the nineteenth century were largely consumed with discharging an obligation to represent the race largely through biographical texts, historical fictions, or realistic novels that addressed slavery, the search for freedom, and the decades of oppression when Reconstruction died. Most could not take the time to dabble in an imaginative literary form so new it did not gain a name until christened "scientifiction" by Hugo Gernsback in 1926, becoming "science fiction" sometime in the 1930s. Since the late nineteenth century and the early twentieth century flirtations with elements borrowed from speculative fiction, African Americans have begun to dig deeper into the mine. Writers and diverse audiences have come to realize that speculative fiction is more than futuristically bound escapist fantasy. The best science fiction extrapolates from a plausible rational world to set a stirring tale about human responses to change or it creates a plausible fantastic realm wherein to enact its magic. But the magic, irrespective of either the science involved or the laws in a fantastic universe, must be the magic of a good story with characters readers care about and a message readers respond to. In the second half of the twentieth century Samuel R. Delany, Octavia E. Butler, and Steven Barnes followed childhood dreams of creating for themselves, and those they represent, a place in that fiction that most often consciously speculates about the future rather than a contemporary reality. Their continuing commitment to their craft means that others with a speculative sensibility will have more accessible models to follow.

• John Pfeiffer, "Black American Speculative Literature," *Extrapolation* 17 (Dec. 1975): 35–43. Charles R. Saunders "Blacks in Wonderland," *American Visions* 2.3 (June 1987): 50–53.   —Sandra Y. Govan

SPEECH AND DIALECT. How black people adapted and adopted American English after their forced arrival in the New World was marked by several nonlinguistic factors, beginning in the seventeenth century. Whether or not Africans could learn to speak English was directly tied to perceptions of their intelligence. Issues revolving around the shape of the African lips or otherwise centering upon the ability to form words in English were also central to the acquisition of language. When Africans acquired rudimentary English skills, questions then arose about their imitative abilities as opposed to true creative abilities with the language. And when enough Africans in America actually learned sufficient English to publish works in that language, questions were frequently raised about authenticity of composition. Language issues for African Americans, therefore, are clearly tied to questions of intelligence, creativity, literacy, culture, politics, race, and representation.

Throughout their history of representation in European American literary works, African Americans have been portrayed as questionable masters of the English language. European American writers such as John Pendleton Kennedy solidified the manner of representation in works such as *Swallow Barn* (1832), where black characters invariably sound like buffoons. The same trend is operative in works specifically identified with the *plantation tradition and with writers such as Thomas Nelson Page and Thomas Dixon. Page's *In Ole Virginia* (1887) portrays black people as loyal servants longing for the plantation days when they were protected and loved by their masters and where the illiterate sounds issuing from their mouths were considered an appropriate part of the plantation image. Dixon's more negative portrayal of African American speech coincided with his purpose of presenting newly freed blacks as dangerous intruders upon culture and particularly upon white women. Dixon's *The Clansman: An Historical Romance of the Ku Klux Klan* (1905), which was transformed into the movie *The Birth of a Nation*, depicts black males who are absurd in their efforts to make speeches in the legislative bodies in which insensitive northern overseers assured their presence. Their inadequate verbal abilities were barely covering for their menacing bodies, with which they animalistically pursued white women. Not even a veneer of culture, so Dixon posited, could change the basic need for such people to be caged in the benign plantation system.

While black people were being attacked through fiction by the likes of Dixon, black legislators duly elected to various congressional bodies were exemplars of the art of rhetoric. Robert Brown Elliott of South Carolina became well known in the 1870s for the speeches he delivered in the House of Representatives in his home state as well as in Washington, D.C. That was no less the case with Blanche K. Bruce, a Mississippi legislator who might have been one of the ancestors of *Harlem Renaissance writer Richard Bruce *Nugent. Elliott and Bruce were masters of *oratory, as were several other African Americans elected to state and national offices during Reconstruction.

Popular perceptions of black people's use of the English language, therefore, were at times dramatically at odds with historical truth, but the myth prevailed more often than not. Segments of minstrel shows in the nineteenth century frequently depended upon the inability of black characters to master English or the deliberate distortion and exaggerated concoction of words by characters who assumed that such creation made them masters of the language. These patterns are clearly portrayed in *Ethnic Notions*, a videotape that traces stereotypical portrayals of black people in American entertainment and advertising from the 1820s to the 1970s. One minstrel character, Zip Coon, was based on the created gibberish of a black man who thought he was being stylish and masterful in his speech.

African American writers were thus early confronted with a dilemma: how truthfully to represent black voices without intersecting overly much with the stereotypical perceptions of black literacy and intelligence. It was not an easy dilemma to resolve. William Wells *Brown, for example, in the novel *Clotel* (1853), could not reasonably present illiterate enslaved persons speaking in standard English, but that is precisely what he consciously or inadvertently does on occasion. At times Currer, Clotel's mother, speaks in the same dialect as other enslaved persons; on other occasions, Brown represents her as commanding the same skills in language as white plantation owners. When Currer is being sold along with her daughter Althesa, she says to the prospective buyer: "If you buy me, I hope you will buy my daughter too," yet when she is in the kitchen with the other enslaved house workers, she remarks: "Dat reminds me. . . dat Dorcas is gwine to git married." Of course it might be argued, and it seems highly probable, that Currer is aware of code-switching, for in a few sentences she is back to speaking in standard English. Perhaps, too, Brown is waging war with himself about representation, or trying to command so many things in the novel that he simply forgot to maintain consistency in Currer's speech. The problem nonetheless makes the issue of representation clear. If Currer is represented as the most highly educated of the enslaved persons, then she should probably speak differently from them, but she is nonetheless just as enslaved as they are, so Brown must run the risk of seeming to compromise her intelligence even as he tries to represent realistically what might have gone on in a conversation exclusively among enslaved persons.

Under these circumstances, speech in American culture is clearly perceived to be one of the definitive markers of race, culture, education, and civilization. It also serves to mark character, place, class, substance, and value. Standard English was looked upon as the purview of white American speakers, and blacks who attempted to master English were viewed as interlopers, usually humorous interlopers. The breeding, education, and culture that were to separate white Americans from those whom they enslaved were among the sites, therefore, on which language served as warrior. Standard English meant good breeding and class, which in turn meant whiteness; dialect meant second-class citizenship and the place of subservience designated for black people. It meant that they were of less substance and value, or, indeed, that their value and substance could be bartered.

One of the tasks for African American writers was to present speakers of African American origins in command of standard English, but not desiring to be white or to separate themselves from the black masses. Frances Ellen Watkins *Harper attempts such a project in *Iola Leroy* (1892). However, she, like Brown, nonetheless lapses into establishing educational and thus class levels among black characters by allowing some of them mastery and others not. Iola can certainly speak like a dictionary, but Aunt Linda and her husband are dialect speakers. Given the considerations of realistic representation and the emphasis upon local color during this period, however, sensitive readers might consider Harper's dialect more on the cutting edge of literary depictions, an effort to showcase both aesthetic and artistic skills, to portray character accurately. While wit and wisdom are centered in Aunt Linda, it is nonetheless

the case that representation of her speech serves as a marker indicating lesser social status and value. Notwithstanding this seeming inconsistency, Harper allows Iola's nationalistic perspective to overshadow to some extent the issues surrounding the representation of speech by blacks in the text. And indeed Harper herself could personally attest to these issues. She reports that people thought she was white or a man because she "spoke Standard English and spoke it well."

Some contemporaries of Harper directly confronted the proponents of the plantation tradition in their representation of black folk speech. Charles Waddell *Chesnutt and Paul Laurence *Dunbar tried to salvage the best possibilities inherent in dialect and to give agency and power to vernacular speakers. Chesnutt's *Uncle Julius McAdoo, the central reconteur in The *Conjure Woman (1899), uses his dialect to highlight values of harmonic interaction with nature, a preference for human beings over property, a sensitivity to the physical and mental conditions of others, and a general appreciation for African American folk culture and folk speakers. In "The Goophered Grapevine," for example, his description of *Aun' Peggy is designed to draw readers to the power of the conjure woman as well as to the power of African American folk culture, of which folk speech is an integral part. When Julius comments that Aun' Peggy "could wuk de mos' powerfulles' kin' er goopher,—could make people hab fits, er rheumatiz, er make 'em des dwinel away en die; en dey say she went out ridin' de niggers at night, fer she wuz a witch 'sides bein' a cunjuh 'oman," his respect for her reputation is contrasted with John's denigration of the culture of which Julius is a part. Chesnutt thus borrows from dialect and storytelling traditions that had been established by Joel Chandler Harris with his Uncle Remus tales to solicit reader engagement with Julius and his tales and thereby with African American culture. He essentially pours new wine into the old bottle of dialect by making Julius a cunning trickster figure who is intelligent enough not only to outsmart John, but to transform reader evaluation of black people.

While it is clear that Chesnutt uses dialect to the larger purpose of trying to "work roots" on his audience and win social acceptance for African Americans, Dunbar's motives are often less clear. He has been accused of buying into the plantation representation of black dialect simply because that was what sold. Readers more sensitive to Dunbar's positioning as a black writer trying to win readers from a primarily white audience are more forgiving of his dialect and indeed argue that, of all the writers who popularized dialect at the turn of the twentieth century, Dunbar was the master. These include the white Hoosier poet James Whitcomb Riley as well as fellow black poets James D. *Corrothers and James Edwin *Campbell.

One of the most famous Dunbar poems, "The Party" (1896), illustrates well the problem as well as the mastery: "Dey had a gread big pahty down to Tom's de othah; / Was I dah? You bet! I nevah in my lice see sich a sight." The light tone, together with the rhyme and meter, zip the poem through nearly a hundred lines, and characterization of black people during *slavery is just as problematic as the representation of their speech. They cut antics as if they were in a black folktale; they laugh, drink, eat, and have access to more food than any enslaved person perhaps saw in months; and they are stereotypically happy, singing, and good-timing. Even the visual representation of the dialect seems to highlight the good times. Thus Dunbar, struggling to become a writer at a time when that was difficult under any circumstances, was plagued by language issues that he could not resolve during his lifetime. He was aware that editors and publishers stereotyped him as a master of dialect poetry—even though he preferred his poems in standard English—but he could not escape their influence if he wanted to achieve recognition for his works.

A couple of decades later, James Weldon *Johnson would revisit the problematic issue of dialect in his preface to The Book of American Negro Poetry (1922, 1931). Having begun his own poetic career in the dialect tradition of Dunbar, and being aware of its limitations, he consciously encouraged younger poets to attempt what he considered greater achievement. Dialect itself was not the problem, Johnson maintained, but the mold of convention into which it had been set in the United States. Its identification with minstrelsy, as well as with happy-go-lucky black people, and its limitations to pathos and humor made it resistant to transformation. The black American poet, Johnson asserted, "needs to find a form that will express the racial spirit by symbols from within rather than by symbols from without—such as the mere mutilation of English spelling and pronunciation. He needs a form that is freer and larger than dialect, but which will still hold the racial flavor; a form expressing the imagery, the idioms, the peculiar turns of thought, and the distinctive humor and pathos, too, of the Negro, but which will also be capable of voicing the deepest and highest emotions and aspirations and allow the widest range of subjects and the widest scope of treatment." In explaining why he did not resort to dialect in representing his sermons in the folk manner in *God's Trombones (1927), Johnson simply reiterated the position he had taken in the earlier volume.

By 1932, however, when Sterling A. *Brown published Southern Road (1932) and exhibited all the skills in dialect that Johnson had assumed could only be exhibited elsewhere, Johnson recognized Brown's achievement by writing a brief introduction to that volume. Brown masterfully portrayed a variety of characters and situations based on working-class black people, and he showed the attendant range of emotions, philosophies, and beliefs—all in dialect. The 1930s also saw Richard *Wright and Zora Neale *Hurston taking on the challenges of the representation of black folk speech; critics generally assume that Hurston was more adept in doing so. In *Jonah's Gourd Vine (1934), *Their Eyes Were Watching God (1937), and a host of other fictional, folkloristic, dramatic, and essayistic works, Hurston captured the sounds and idioms of black folk simply being themselves. She is credited with some of the earliest realistic portrayals of African American women, from their speech to their beliefs and sentiments.

Wright, on the hand, was less concerned with accurate typographical representation of black folk speech than with attempting to imagine the nuances of the sound of that speech. The consequence is that his dialect on the page looks as if it is a mistake, and readers have difficulty "sounding it out" (that is not as consistently the case with Dunbar or with Hurston). Wright's dialect, in fact, looks on the page a lot like Jean *Toomer's in *Cane (1923). Both writers seemed to be more interested in other issues than accuracy of visual representation. In "Big Boy Leaves Home" (1938), for example, Wright could represent black folk speech in this manner: "Chile, will yuh c mere like Ah ast yuh?" It might also be noted that he was not appreciably different in his representation of white folk speech. Similarly, an example of black folk speech from Toomer's "Kabnis" is the following: "I'm only tryin t fool y. I used t love that girl. Yassur. An sometimes when th moon is thick an I hear dogs up th valley barkin an some old woman fetches out her song, an th winds seem like th Lord made them fer to fetch an carry th smell o pine an cane, an there aint no big job on foot, I sometimes get t thinkin that I still do." Wright uses dialect to capture the illiteracy of his southern sharecroppers whereas it is uncertain if Toomer is merely inept in trying to portray southern black rural folk speech. Certainly Toomer wants to indicate class distinctions at various points in his text, but numerous inconsistencies throughout the book would indicate as well that his skills in this area were somewhat limited.

The same could be said of the drama of this period. There was a group of women dramatists in the first three decades of the twentieth century who drew sharp lines of class and educational demarcation in their depictions of African Americans. One of the most striking examples is Angelina Weld *Grimké's Rachel (1916), in which Rachel is the counterpart to Iola Leroy without the strength of racial conviction that that comparison entails. Rachel speaks in the lofty standard English tones of a young girl lifted from the pages of poetry; her speech and education distance her from the lower-class black children with whom she interacts. Georgia Douglas *Johnson's A Sunday Morning in the South (1925) uses exaggerated dialect to represent illiterate southern blacks, as does Mary P. Burrill's Aftermath (1928). It is perhaps instructive to compare the use of dialect in these plays to Hurston's in Color Struck (1925), which is contemporary with these dramas.

Simultaneous with these representations, Langston *Hughes was experimenting in a different direction—trying to reflect the variety and range of African American lifestyles and speech. Whether in blues poems, the *Madam Alberta K. Johnson poems, the *Simple stories, or his poems in imitation of urban street speech, such as "Mother to Son" (1920), Hughes tried to look from the inside of black experience outward instead of imposing alien forms and patterns on the culture. He was able to achieve, in a more respectful way," what Dunbar attempted earlier

—accuracy without stereotyping or distortion. When the speaker in "Mother to Son" begins by telling her son that her life "ain't been no crystal stair," few readers are inclined to laugh at her or feel sorry for her. Hughes has managed effectively to match medium, voice, and sentiment. In this attempt, there is respect for the character as well as for her creator.

Speech and dialect were but two of the issues relevant to literary portrayal of black people in the 1920s. Indeed, the *Crisis had featured in 1926 the results of a forum in which black and white writers and critics, among others, responded to the question "The Negro in Art: How Shall He Be Portrayed?" Respondents included W. E. B. *Du Bois, Georgia Douglas *Johnson, Alfred A. Knopf, Vachel Lindsay, Langston Hughes, H. L. Mencken, Walter *White, and several others. Writers who believed in the "best foot forward," that is, portraying middle-class, well-educated blacks, would perhaps prefer Iola Leroy without her racial loyalty, and they would certainly prefer in all instances that characters like Chesnutt's Josh Green in The *Marrow of Tradition (1901) be obliterated from the African American literary imagination. On the other hand, for those writers who allowed for the working classes and how they spoke, Brown, Hughes, and Hurston were certainly to be applauded for their efforts.

In the mid-twentieth century, issues of speech were resolved with writers taking readers, without apology, where they wanted them to go. For Ralph *Ellison, this meant presenting a range of black voices in *Invisible Man (1952), from the naive but linguistically sophisticated narrator, to a lettered preacher, to a storytelling sharecropper, to a blues-singing folk rhymer, to a motherly savior, to two drunks appreciating the antics of a riot. Ellison wanted, he said, to capture the ranges of American speech, with the recognition that blacks were just as American as anyone else on U.S. soil. Margaret *Walker, it might be argued, makes a similar claim in *Jubilee (1966), which, while ostensibly called a folk novel, incorporates a range of narrative and verbal patterns.

A renewed interest in black folk speech was one of the features of the *Black Arts movement of the 1960s and thereafter, when some writers asserted that traditional music and the dialect of the people were the truest reflections of the culture. Poets especially went out of their way to represent a distinctively black typography and to coin letterings (black poet=blkpt; you=u) that would reclaim the troublesome English language for their own unique use. Sherley Anne *Williams's Peacock Poems (1975), which was nominated for a National Book Award, is in part defined by her experimentation with representing accurately the speech of black people in the 1970s. Prose writers like Toni Cade *Bambara were studied in their experimentation with narrative exclusively in black dialect or folk speech. In the stories in Gorilla, My Love (1972), Bambara allows the language of the folk all its flavor and range. During this period, therefore, resorting to the speech of the folk was a political act, one designed to show solidarity with the masses and to indicate that black writers

were not the chosen few. They were instead merely reflectors of sentiments for all black people.

This progression was also a statement that black writers had come of age. With many of their own publishing outlets, along with a seriously increased black readership, they did not have to depend exclusively upon the acceptance of white readers. They could therefore assert a renewed independence, declare a contemporary manifesto, in the very language they used. In the spirit of the revolutionary moment, language had a role to play in the same way that dashikis, Afros, and Swahili made statements. These writers embraced the full implications of language usage instead of writing against the grain; their characters were who they were—without apology.

The path to freer expression perhaps culminated in 1982 with Alice *Walker's publication of The *Color Purple. Written almost entirely in black folk speech and narrated by a character who could not be readily viewed as a "best foot forward" type, the novel captured in prose what Brown had achieved in poetry in Southern Road and other poems. Its language recognized the intrinsic value, intelligence, and life world of a character who was not of a privileged class, color, or social situation. When the novel was made into a movie in 1985, that transformation further signaled to viewers the value of seeing *Celie as she was, where she was, and respecting the life that she created under those circumstances.

In drama, the culmination perhaps began with Ntozake *Shange's *for colored girls (1977) and peaked with August *Wilson's plays. Shange's female characters celebrate their blackness, which includes their speech. They recount their adventures seducing and being seduced by men in language that garnered huge audiences for the play from California to Boston. In Wilson's plays, black male characters especially are given the opportunity to be themselves—in speech, action, and interactions. Boy Willie, in Wilson's Pulitzer Prize–winning The *Piano Lesson (1990), for example, comes north with all the rawness of his southern and prison backgrounds. While he may prove an embarrassment to his sister Berniece, he retains the unapologetic essence of himself. Wilson duplicates that feat many times over in the characters he has created in several plays, including the Pulitzer Prize–winning *Fences (1987).

A comparison of Shange's and Wilson's plays makes clear that gender is a factor in the representation of speech and dialect as well. The images that Shange's characters use to describe their experiences are peculiarly domestic and feminine, as are those that Celie and *Shug Avery use in The Color Purple; a quilting metaphor, for example, is especially relevant to Walker's novel. Women frequently must express themselves against the demands of the men in their lives, as Wilson's Rose does in Fences; the differences in what she hoped for in life and what Todd wanted finally estrange them beyond sexual reconciliation, although they continue to share the same physical space. How they speak of their desires (baseball versus domestic space; filling up versus emptying) emphasizes their gendered linguistic frames of reference.

Implicit in the works of most of these writers is also the issue of region and its influence upon the representation of black folk speech. The clearest regional division is North/South, with the North carrying healthy class overtones comparable to the black/white split in connotations of speech. Southern and rural usually carry negative values, and it is a tribute to writers like Sterling A. Brown, Zora Neale Hurston, and Richard Wright that southern black voices were embraced as readily as they were. In more contemporary times, the South still carries negative implications for speakers, but the use of that territory by writers as prominent as Toni *Morrison, Toni Cade Bambara, and Gloria *Naylor has gone a long way in transforming attitudes toward the South and its black speakers. Walter *Mosley has given us glimpses of western speech, though many of the characters in his novels are drawn from Texas, the near Southwest.

As Bambara, Walker, Shange, Wilson, and others suggested that black folk speech had intrinsic worth, however, there were trends in the literature away from such representation. This can be seen in works like Andrea *Lee's *Sarah Phillips* (1984) and Brent Wade's *Company Man* (1992), where middle-class African American characters consciously avoid the markers, such as dialect, that would identify them with the masses of un- or ill-educated blacks. This resorting to standard English as the primary medium of black speech has undertones of class and color that marked Harper's *Iola Leroy*, but the issues are not resolved as nationalistically as Harper resolved them. Highly educated young black writers are thus finding that issues surrounding the representation of language in their works are no less resolved in the 1990s than they were in the 1890s, for monitors of one kind or another are always looking over the writers' shoulders to their computer screens, trying to determine if what they are writing places them within or without the culture. Chances are that such issues will continue to inform the literature well into the twenty-first century.

[See also Black Aesthetic; Black Nationalism; Blue Vein Societies; Dialect Poetry; Federal Writers' Project; New Cultural Mulatto; New Negro; Novel of Passing; Passing.]

• James Weldon Johnson, preface to *The Book of American Negro Poetry*, 1922; rpts. 1931, 1969. Sterling A. Brown, "A Century of Negro Portraiture in American Literature," in *Black Insights: Significant Literature by Black Americans— 1760 to the Present*, ed. Nick Aaron Ford, 1971, pp. 66–78. Joseph Boskin, *Sambo: The Rise and Demise of an American Jester*, 1986. *Ethnic Notions*, KQED Television, California Newsreel, San Francisco, 1986. —Trudier Harris

SPELLMAN, A. B. (b. 1935), poet, music critic and historian, and arts administrator. Alfred B. Spellman has cut a wide swath in the world of the arts as a *music critic, poet, administrator, and educator. "It's a function of social consciousness," he said in a 1992 interview (*Dance/USA Journal*, Winter 1992), "to provide art, strong art." The creation, identification, and support of "strong art" have been the alternating currents of Spellman's career, whose highlights include

the publication of his book of poems, *The Beautiful Days*, in 1965, the appearance of his classic *Black Music: Four Lives* (as *Four Lives in the BeBop Business*) in 1966, and his two decades of service at the National Endowment for the Arts (NEA).

One of two sons of the schoolteachers Alfred and Rosa Bailey Spellman, Alfred B. Spellman was born 12 August 1935 in his grandmother's house in Nixonton, a hamlet outside Elizabeth City, North Carolina. Perhaps because of his parents' academic focus, Spellman was little challenged by the assignments at the public schools he attended. Some of his early memorable impressions of art and performance were provided by his father's paintings and, during his adolescence, by his success in sliding under the canvas tents of the traveling "Silas Green" blues troupe to see the half-dressed female dancers and ribald comics.

He became seriously interested in writing after entering Howard University in 1952. Classmates such as Amiri *Baraka (then LeRoi Jones) were his sounding boards and fellow cultural explorers. A famed instructor, Sterling A. *Brown, helped develop his interest in *jazz and in the relationship between literary and oral traditions in African American culture. In 1958, at Baraka's urging, Spellman left Howard to seek his fortune in New York City. He had earned a BA in political science and history and begun course work in law. He remained in New York until 1967—working in bookstores, writing *poetry, and, beginning in the early 1960s, hosting a WBAI radio morning show called "Where It's At."

The Beautiful Days appeared with an introductory note by Frank O'Hara praising Spellman for cutting "through a lot of contemporary nonsense to what is actually happening to him." What actually happens to Spellman in the best poems is extraordinary. In "'64 like a mirror in a darkroom. '63 like a mirror in a house afire," he measures his own vitality by his ability to continue caring about the "newly dead."

Four jazz musicians Spellman appears to have understood by their minds' "flutter" and their style of survival—Cecil Taylor, Ornette Coleman, Jackie McLean, and Herbie Nichols—are the subjects of *Black Music*, which enumerates, on the one hand, the tribulations of working in the jazz world, and, on the other hand, the ferocious will needed to avoid being silenced or destroyed. A reviewer for *Library Journal* found in the four interlocked portraits a "well reasoned statement of the position of the Negro in modern jazz and in modern America as well."

Spellman has said he wrote in defense of his subjects, who struggled variously against the failure of their peers, their reviewers, and existing funding organizations to acknowledge not only their brilliance, but even their competence. The urgency of his project is conveyed by his concluding remarks on Herbie Nichols: "It was typical of Herbie Nichols' life that *Metronome*, the magazine for which I was preparing the first article ever written on him, folded before the article could be published. By the time I placed it elsewhere, Herbie had died."

In 1976, after teaching jazz, literature, and writing at Emory, Harvard, and other universities, Spellman joined the NEA first as director of the Arts in Education Study Project and then as assistant director of the Expansion Arts Program. "We try to solidify and stabilize [arts] organizations, if we can, with the limited funds we have," he told *Dance/USA Journal.* He is currently the endowment's Acting Deputy Chair.

• Carmen Subryan, "A. B. Spellman," in *DLB*, vol. 41, *Afro-American Poets since 1955*, eds. Trudier Harris and Thadious Davis, 1985, pp. 311–315. A. B. Spellman, "Reflecting and Encouraging American Culture," interview by Bonnie Brooks, *Dance/USA Journal* 9.3 (Winter 1992): 16, 17, 26, 27.

—Michael Collins

SPENCER, ANNE (1882–1975), poet, librarian, community activist, and muse and confidante to Harlem Renaissance intellectuals and literati. Anne Spencer was born inauspiciously on a Virginia plantation. Yet the combination of loving, though irreconcilable, parents and an unorthodox, isolated youth formed her extraordinary independence, introspection, and conviction.

Her father, Joel Cephus Bannister, of African American, white, and Native American descent, and her mother, Sarah Louise Scales, the mulatta daughter of a slaveholder, separated when Spencer was six. While her mother worked as an itinerant cook, Spencer roomed with foster parents in Bramwell, West Virginia, where no other black children lived. In insular and parochial Bramwell, she was groomed for the African American bourgeoisie. Her mother dressed her in the finest frocks she could afford and withheld her from an outlying school that enrolled working-class children until she could attend Lynchburg's Virginia Seminary with socially suitable African American students. Spencer entered the seminary at age eleven. At seventeen, she graduated as valedictorian.

Two events there redirected her life. With a sonnet, "The Skeptic" (1896), she began writing poetry; and she met her husband, Edward. They settled in Lynchburg and raised three children. In 1918 Spencer was visited by James Weldon *Johnson (*The *Autobiography of an Ex-Colored Man,* 1912), then field secretary for the NAACP. Their meeting launched a lifetime friendship—and with "Before the Feast at Sushan," submitted to the the *Crisis* (1920), it inaugurated her publishing era.

Such poems as "At the Carnival" (1922), "Lines to a Nasturtium" (1926), "Substitution" (1927), and "Requiem" (1931) share the Romantics' affection for the ordinary and simple, retreat to nature's purity and peace, quest for love, disillusionment with earthly vanities, and passionate contemplation of eternity. Spencer flaunted tradition as much as she acknowledged it, laying claim to a modern poet's signature with sinister rhythms, slanted rhymes, blunt rejection of religious dogma, and enigmatic symbolism. During the 1920s, largely due to Johnson's mentorship, she published in such intellectual race magazines as the *Crisis* and *Opportunity,* in general anthologies of American poetry, in poet Countee *Cullen's *Caroling Dusk* (1927), in Johnson's *Book of American Negro Poetry* (1922), and in Alain *Locke's *The *New Negro* (1925), the official mission declaration of *Harlem Renaissance (New Negro movement) writers and artists.

She detested an editorial process that misread her meanings, misunderstood her motives, mercilessly alluded to her inconsistent output, and miscategorized her poems as either much too subtle or too subtly militant. For many poems, including "White Things" (1923) and "Grapes: Still-Life" (1929), Spencer stood at variance with editors and publishers who censored statements of racial and sexual equality and rejected whatever they judged too controversial and/or experimental for American audiences. Consequently, she confined her editorial submissions to a decade, and she never published a poetry collection. Of her thousands of unpublished writings, including a novel and cantos commemorating John *Brown, some fifty remain.

Her paradoxical lifestyle kindled her writing. During the depression and World War II, her salon at 1313 Pierce Street hosted notables from W. E. B. *Du Bois to Paul *Robeson. Yet she so enjoyed the solitude of her garden that Edward erected a cottage for her there, naming it Edankraal, and he hired housekeepers to liberate her from the average southern woman's sentence to domestic drudgery. "The Wife-Woman" (1922), "Lady, Lady" (1925), and "Letter to My Sister" (1927) confide Spencer's ambivalence about matrimony, motherhood, feminism, and the unattainability of gender equality for African American women. They identify the masculine prerogatives of seclusion, intellect, and leisure served by the madonnas found everywhere in productions of the Harlem Renaissance.

Spencer frequently abandoned her privacy to antagonize local racists and class snobs. She organized Lynchburg's NAACP chapter, opened a library at the African American Dunbar High School, and offered sanctuary to the pygmy Ota Benga, who had been exhibited in zoos as a specimen of African inferiority. She infuriated African Americans with her scandalous fondness for pants and stubborn opposition to integration of public schools. Lynchburg's whites, in turn, sniffed their noses at her interracial friendships and scathing editorial disclaimers against the alleged self-evidence of white superiority.

Spencer's overall contribution has been to refocus critical attention on the stake that southern African American writers, virtually dismissed, have held in the enduring legacy of the Harlem Renaissance. At once homespun and urbane, her writings complicate the arbitrary amputation of New Negroes into either the folk, epitomized by Langston *Hughes's *Simple stories, or the bourgeois *mulattoes of Jessie Redmon *Fauset's novels. Finally, Spencer's complexity advances our assessment of African American women writers in general, placing her at the center of a feminist renaissance midwifed by her forward vision.

• J. Lee Greene, *Time's Unfading Garden: Anne Spencer's Life and Poetry,* 1977. J. Lee Greene, "Anne Spencer of Lynchburg," *Virginia Cavalcade* 27 (1978): 178–185. Cheryl A. Wall, "Poets and Versifiers, Singers and Signifiers: Women of the Harlem Renaissance," in *Women, the Arts, and the 1920s in Paris and New York,* ed. Kenneth W. Wheeler and Virginia

Lee Lussier, 1982, pp. 74–99. William Drake, *The First Wave: Women Poets in America, 1915–1945*, 1987. Charita M. Ford, "Flowering a Feminist Garden: The Writings and Poetry of Anne Spencer," *Sage* 5 (Summer 1988): 7–14. Maureen Honey, *Shadowed Dreams: Women's Poetry of the Harlem Renaissance*, 1989.
—Barbara McCaskill

SPIRITUALS. Reflecting on the spirituals in "O Black and Unknown Bards" (1917), James Weldon *Johnson asked, "Heart of what slave poured out such melody?" Folklorists, musicologists, and historians have also pondered the origin of slave spirituals, but most accept Sterling A. *Brown's assertion that regardless of their birthplace, the spirituals are "the Negro's own." The spirituals constitute one of the earliest, largest, and best-known bodies of American folksong that have survived to the twentieth century. In *Slave Religion* (1978) Albert Raboteau identifies several kinds of antebellum spirituals, including shouts, anthems, and jubilees, each serving different occasions and reflecting different moods. Although the spirituals are principally associated with African American *church congregations of the antebellum South and the earlier, more informal and sometimes clandestine gatherings of enslaved people, most scholars now agree that a process of mutual influence and reciprocal borrowing credit the following as all contributing to the creation of the spirituals: evangelical sermons and hymns, biblical stories, traditional African chants and praise songs, and the combined experiences of enslaved people in the South. A debate over African and European musical contributions was once quite contentious and consumed the bulk of scholarly attention devoted to the spirituals, but in *Sinful Tunes and Spirituals* (1977) Dena Epstein has established that African influences account for many of the elements of spirituals. How they were subsequently acculturated can only be projected theoretically as a syncretic merging of African and Christian forms and beliefs.

At the beginning of the twentieth century, W. E. B. *Du Bois's examination of African American culture led him to the "sorrow songs" in which "the soul of the black slave spoke to men" as providing a model for survival and an interpretive framework for that culture. The *Souls of Black Folk* (1903) foregrounds the issue of African retentions and features the music and message of the spirituals as related to the history of black people striving for humanity in a society of oppression. As the "singular spiritual heritage of the nation and the greatest gift of the Negro people," the spirituals fascinated Du Bois because of their tension between polarities of joy and sorrow. He came to see them as reflections of the African American struggle to merge a double self into "a better and truer self" that held out "a faith in the ultimate justice of things . . . that sometime, somewhere, men will judge men by their souls and not by their skins." As the preeminent interpreter of spirituals, Du Bois's influence is borne out by the subsequent role the spirituals have played in providing a foundation for the development of a distinctive African American aesthetic articulated in many nonmusical genres. Key distinguishing terms by which we have come to

evaluate this tradition have derived from the spirituals, including the pattern of call and response and the act of *signifying. Reinforcing the importance of oral traditions, the spirituals give compelling testimony to the presence and influence of African retentions in the development of African American culture. The history of their reception and appreciation also reveals aspects of broader cultural currents, including the positions African Americans assumed in relation to their enslaved past, and the roles played by representatives of the dominant culture who either aided in the preservation and promotion of the spirituals or exploited and appropriated them.

Most important for interpreting the meaning of the spirituals is an appreciation of the context—social and religious—in which they were performed and the insight they lend into the extraordinary power of *music to shape the experience and conscious identity of a people. The spirituals created by enslaved people became a unique means to "keep on keeping on" under the physical and psychological pressures of daily life, testifying to the belief that the supernatural interacted with the natural and the whole world rested in the hands of God. As one contemporary reviewer described them, the spirituals were "God's image in Ebony." In creation as well as performance they exhibited the essential characteristics of spontaneity, variety, and communal interchange. The form of the spirituals was flexible and improvisational, thereby able to fit an individual slave's experience into the consciousness of the group, creating at once an intensely personal and vividly communal experience. Capable of communicating on more than one level, as noted by Booker T. *Washington and Frederick *Douglass in their *autobiographies, on occasion the spirituals functioned as coded songs to communicate information between enslaved people. Washington affirmed that the *freedom in their songs meant freedom in this world and Douglass insisted that references to Caanan implied the North. But formally and thematically spirituals were open to change and improvisation as a spiritual in one situation might mean something else in another. In nearly every instance, however, there is reflected an intertwining of theological and social messages, borne out in Douglass's description of how "every tone was a testimony against *slavery, and a prayer to God for deliverance from chains."

The first known reports of distinctive black religious singing date from the early nineteenth century, but many of these reports are vague and the musical notation practiced at the time was inadequate to capture distinctive features of music as performed. Before the Civil War descriptions of black music are scattered and intermittent. But when the war shattered the closed society to which enslaved Africans were confined and brought them into large-scale contact with the world outside the plantation, northerners, often agents of the federal government or missionaries, came to appreciate their distinctive music. As with ex-slave narratives, the African American authorship of the spirituals was challenged at first. But in an 1867 article published in the *Atlantic Monthly*, Thomas Wentworth Higginson, a militant

New England abolitionist who commanded the first freed slave regiment to fight against the Confederacy, was among the first to describe how he heard "the choked voice of a race at last unloosed." He diligently took down the songs sung by the First South Carolina Volunteers around evening campfires. Higginson failed to recognize the African musical components of the slave songs, but he did catch something of the communal process by which these songs evolved, describing them as a "stimulus to courage and a tie to heaven." Noting how at the outbreak of the Civil War, enslaved blacks sang, "We'll soon be free / When the Lord will call us home," Higginson confirms the layered meaning of many spirituals, citing a drummer boy who confided in him that "Lord" in the song was a code for the "Yankees."

But it was when the Port Royal Relief Committee was established as an experiment to show how formerly enslaved people could work and learn as free people that an opportunity arose for studying the spirituals, culminating in the landmark work *Slave Songs of the United States* (1867) by William Francis Allen, Charles Pickard Ware, and Lucy McKim Garrison. In their introduction the editors admit that they did "the best we can do with paper and types," but that even their efforts "will convey but a faint shadow of the original. . . . The intonation and delicate variations of even one singer cannot be reproduced upon paper." Since the people who composed and first sang the spirituals were not the people who wrote them down, there is considerable variety in the ways in which nineteenth-century African American dialect was rendered. Because of the difficulty in knowing precisely how many words would have been pronounced as they were originally sung, the lyrics will be reproduced in this article in standard English.

The distinguishing musical aesthetic of the spirituals derives from West African percussive forms, multiple meters, syncopation, a call-and-response structure, extensive melodic ornamentation, and an integration of song and movement, each involving improvisation. Call and response embodies the foundational principle behind the performance of the spirituals, denoting the ritual requirement of what is necessary for completion. The soloist in original performances of the spirituals was viewed as a mystic whose call inspired the participating group to respond. This full sense of process and communication reinforces the communal identity and its belief that art is an appropriate response to oppression. Very much a ritual act, when spirituals were sung by enslaved people they amplified their desire for liberation and created conditions of sacred space and time wherein the biblical stories of which they sang were transformed and the history of the ancient past became the history of the present.

Often linked in tradition with slave uprisings led by Denmark Vesey, Nat *Turner, and Gabriel Prosser, the spirituals were archetypes of protest for actual and spiritual liberation, embodying what Jon Spencer in *Protest and Praise* (1990) terms a theomusicology. Synthesizing sacred and secular meaning, creators of the spirituals drew images from the Bible to interpret their own experience, measuring it against a wider system of theological and historical meaning. Three themes dominate spirituals: the desire for freedom, the desire for justice, and strategies for survival. God is a liberator who is involved in history, and as "Wade in the Water" suggests, God will "trouble the waters" of oppression. Many spirituals like "Joshua Fit the Battle of Jericho" and "Didn't My Lord Deliver Daniel?" are drawn from biblical texts that stress God's involvement in the liberation of the oppressed. Although God's liberating work was not always concretely evident, enslaved people were confident that "You Got a Right" to "the tree of life." The songs also stress a need for enslaved people's own participation in God's liberation, to be "Singing With a Sword in My Hand." Enslaved people viewed their cry of "Let My People Go" as answered with the Emancipation Proclamation, when "Slavery Chain Done Broke at Last." God makes justice for the righteous and the unrighteous because "All God's Children Got Wings," but "everybody who's talking about heaven ain't going," and anyone who stands against liberation is called to account, "Were You There When They Crucified my Lord?" Jesus represents both a historical savior and whoever helps the oppressed. Jesus functions in a more personal way than God, as deliverer and comforter, because "you may have all the world," but "Give Me Jesus." He is affirmed both in his divinity and humanity, especially his identification with the oppressed who believe that "A Little Talk With Jesus Makes It Right." Hence his birth is an occasion to "Rise Up Shepherd and Follow," and "Go Tell It on the Mountain," and his life on earth a reminder to "Rise, Mourner, Rise."

Songs like "Steal Away" and "Let Us Praise God Together On Our Knees" may have served as a means to convene secret resistance meetings, while "Deep River, My Home Is Over Jordan" may imply a wish to cross over to Africa or the North. But getting to freedom is what occupies many of the lyrics that take as a theme a tired sojourner struggling through a hostile landscape while leaning and depending on God. Portraying a struggle against oppression in a variety of metaphors, many spirituals focus on the difficult movement through space and time but with the confidence to cheer the "Weary Traveler." Spatial and temporal metaphors of movement employing a variety of methods—sailing, walking, riding, rowing, climbing—all appear for a people "Bound to Go," urging them to "Travel On." The spirituals actually and symbolically moved a people toward liberation when they sang, "We Are Climbing Jacob's Ladder," even if they could only "Keep Inching Along." Noting the threat of adverse physical conditions, the creators appropriated symbols from their own situation and describe searching for God in the wilderness, rocks, darkness, storms, and valleys. Lyrics from songs such as "O Stand the Storm," "Sinner, Please Don't Let This Harvest Pass," or "Hold On!" gave inspiration to endure. Although an enslaved person often felt "Like a Motherless Child," lost where "I Couldn't Hear Nobody Pray," and for whom "Nobody Knows the Trouble I've Seen," faith is always affirmed because "All My Troubles Will Soon Be Over." Sometimes a lonely sojourner is aided by heavenly transportation, as in "Swing Low, Sweet Chariot," or the activity of the *Underground Railroad that invites "Get on Board, Little Children." But the destination is always freedom, sometimes construed as Africa, the North, or heaven, as in "Roll, Jordan, Roll." The role of the community—often expressed in concepts of home as in "I Got a Home in That Rock," or as a heavenly reunion with family as in "Band of Gideon," or as a place of safety in "There is a Balm in Gilead"—is also reinforced.

Significant contempoarary comments on the spirituals include James Cone's The Spirituals and the Blues (1972), which links the power of song in the struggle for black survival with liberation theology. Critical of the ways in which previous theologians (Howard Thurman and Benjamin Mays) had stressed a compensatory religious function of the spirituals, Cone examines the spirituals and their secular counterpart, the *blues, as cultural expressions of black people, delineating the functional techniques employed for cultural survival that the songs embody. John Lovell's comprehensive Black Song: The Forge and the Flame (1972) explores how the spirituals were "hammered out" in the forge of oppression and the subsequent social implications when, over time, their "flame" cast a liberative spirit far and wide. Emphasizing their African roots in the context of enslaved life, he demonstrates how the spirituals assisted in resistance to slavery, insisting that the songs project not just religious and otherworldly visions but were enslaved peoples' description and criticism of their environment and an index to their revolutionary sentiments and desire to be free. In Black Culture and Black Consciousness (1977) Lawrence Levine also argues persuasively for an appreciation of the profound connection between the other world and this world in slave consciousness that the spirituals describe. Like Cone and Lovell, Levine seeks to underscore the roots of resistance behind the spirituals and to rehistoricize the experience of enslaved people for whom *religion was wrought out of an encounter with the divine in the midst of social realities.

Essential to understanding the development of an African American literary tradition, the spirituals have functioned as the source, model, and inspiration for countless works, despite Mark Twain's observation that had the spirituals been a foreign product Americans would appreciate them more. *Slave narratives make abundant references to the spirituals, but they were not fully appreciated or celebrated until the *Harlem Renaissance. Along with Du Bois, Alain *Locke in The *New Negro (1925) affirmed the emotional power of the spirituals and drew attention to the originality and distinctive richness of black music, emphasizing how their function is not limited by race consciousness but affirms a universal ideal for the whole American nation. In his poetry and fiction, James Weldon Johnson alluded to spirituals directly and indirectly, making a case for how enslaved people who "sang a race from wood and stone to Christ" created a religion out of art and mediated the distinction between African religion and Christianity, thereby easing a painful transition from one culture

to another. With his brother, J. Rosamond, he also collected and edited spirituals in two volumes, Book of American Negro Spirituals (1925, 1926), offering in his preface an extensive argument for their African origins and developing a theory of the process of folk composition based on his own observations of songleaders that synthesizes the role of individuals and the community. It was by "sheer spiritual forces," Johnson asserted, that African chants metamorphosed into the "miracle" of the spirituals.

The biblical parallels with which the spirituals were imbued were exploited by fiction writers like Zora Neale *Hurston who in Moses, Man of the Mountain (1939) draws thematically and structurally on the identification of blacks with the enslaved Hebrews. Martin R. *Delany's *Blake (1859), J. Saunders *Redding's No Day of Triumph (1942), John O. *Killens's Youngblood (1954), and Margaret *Walker's *Jubilee (1966) also incorporate spirituals to structure their plots and advance their themes. Spirituals directly inform two works by James *Baldwin (The *Amen Corner, 1968, and *Go Tell It on the Mountain, 1953), and Ernest J. *Gaines claims that much of what he learned about writing came by way of listening to spirituals. Richard *Wright and Ralph *Ellison both pay homage to the spirituals in their creative and nonfiction work. Wright chose the spiritual "Sometimes I Wonder" as an epigraph for *Black Boy (1945) and appreciated "the bitter rebellion" simmering behind the spirituals. Wright's description of the spirituals as one of the "channels through which the racial wisdom flowed" is shared by Ellison who also cited the spirituals as central to the evolution of American music. *Invisible Man (1952) employs the spirituals and the folk forms they engendered as influences on the characters, plot, and figurative language in the novel. Toni *Morrison's *Song of Solomon (1978) and Paule *Marshall's Praisesong for the Widow (1983) both incorporate striking musical moments of call and response as essential to the unfolding of their plots. Poets associated with the spirituals include Paul Laurence *Dunbar (*Majors and Minors, 1895), James Weldon Johnson (*God's Trombones, 1927), Sterling Brown ("Strong Men," 1931), Melvin B. *Tolson ("Dark Symphony," 1944), and Langston *Hughes, whose two-act play, Tambourines to Glory (1949), carried the subtitle, "A Play with Spirituals, Jubilees, and Gospel Songs." White writers also turned to the spirituals for models and inspiration, including John Greenleaf Whittier ("At Port Royal. 1861," 1862), Vachel Lindsay ("The Congo: A Study of the Negro Race," 1929), Eugene O'Neill ("All God's Chillun Got Wings," 1924) and William Faulkner (Go Down Moses, 1942). What all writers understood was that in evoking the spirituals they were calling forth the spirit of a people struggling to be free, a people who asserted that "Before I'll be a slave / I'll be buried in my grave / And go home to my Lord and be free." For, as James Cone has observed, "Black history is a spiritual."

• Howard Thurman, Deep River: Reflections on the Religious Insight of Certain of the Negro Spirituals, 1955. Bernard Katz, ed., The Social Implications of Early Negro Music in the United States, 1969. Christa K. Dixon, Negro Spirituals: From

Bible to Folksong, 1976. John White, "Veiled Testimony: Negro Spirituals and the Slave Experience," *Journal of American Studies* 17.2 (1983): 251–263. Bernice Johnson Reagon and Bill Moyers, *The Songs Are Free*, videocassette, 1991. Arthur C. Jones, *Wade in the Water: The Wisdom of the Spirituals*, 1993. Eric J. Sundquist, *To Wake the Nations: Race in the Making of American Literature*, 1993.

—Kimberly Rae Connor

Spook Who Sat by the Door, The.

Sam *Greenlee's satirical *novel *The Spook Who Sat by the Door* (1969) criticizes the racist atmosphere of the United States by examining the life of a fictitious black CIA agent, Dan Freeman, who is recruited under the efforts of Senator Gilbert Hennington to integrate the Central Intelligence Agency. For five years Dan Freeman had been the best spook of all as he conned the entire CIA while "he sat by the door." After absorbing a sufficient amount of knowledge, Freeman resigned to "make a greater contribution to his people by returning to Chicago and working among them."

References to Freeman as a "spook" in both the title and the novel possess a sense of duality or *double consciousness: spook is used as a racial insult directed toward Blacks, in addition to being a slang term for spies. Greenlee uses this duality to establish a connection between Freeman's character and the African American experience during the turbulent 1960s. With this multifaceted character, Greenlee begins to examine the mask that has been worn by Blacks for generations to hide their true feelings. The author notes, as does Paul Laurence *Dunbar in "We Wear the Mask," that historically Blacks have veiled their emotions to meet white America's archetypes and expectations.

Freeman's persona escapes the boundaries of typical character definition as he openly supplies viewpoints and rationales on a wide range of topics—the Black man's pain, anger, fear, and frustrations. Freeman's multiple personalities leave him lonely: "his cover, his plans had forced him into himself and his loneliness ate at him like a cancer." He understands the paradoxical existence of the black middle class to be a collection of token Blacks who have been allowed to succeed to validate "whitey's integration movement." Greenlee's character represents the "*New Negro" mentality; his is assertive, self-respecting, and fed up with racism.

Freeman reaches great heights on the mountain of social analysis as he demarcates the life of a Black man. The novel, first published in Europe and later in the United States, is an explosive exposition that divulges the emotions of the Negro of the 1960s, and continues to demand reaction from the African American of the 1990s.

Freeman's underlying goal in *The Spook Who Sat by the Door* is to facilitate social criticism. Greenlee is masterful in his presentation of characters and community. His honest yet satirical examination of a system created on lies, perpetuated by lies, and often destroyed or brought to terms with the hypocrisy it advocates is still relevant in the struggle of the African American male. It is often by examining literature such as *The Spook Who Sat by the Door* that readers have an opportunity to analyze life's frustrations and fears.

• Catherine Starks, *Black Portraiture in American Fiction*, 1971.

—Wanda Macon

Sport of the Gods, The.

Paul Laurence *Dunbar's *The Sport of the Gods* appeared in the May issue of *Lippincott's* magazine and was published by Dodd, Mead in 1902. The *novel traces the dissolution and decline of the Hamiltons, a southern black *family prevented from shaping their own fate by forces beyond their control.

Berry Hamilton has been a butler and his wife, Fanny, a cook on Maurice Oakley's prosperous southern plantation, where they have raised two children, Joe and Kitty. Berry's thirty years of loyal service, since before emancipation, have brought the family financial comfort and made them the envy of their black neighbors. But their fortune changes drastically. When Maurice's dissipated brother, Francis, discovers money missing, Berry is wrongly accused of the theft. With no evidence against him, Berry is convicted and sentenced to ten years at hard labor. Evicted from the plantation and ostracized by both blacks and whites, the rest of the family migrates to New York City to make a fresh start.

The provincial Hamiltons are immediately attracted to the lure of the city and soon fall victim to its various temptations. Joe takes up with the lowly denizens of the "Banner Club," a "social cesspool" that feeds his thirst for alcohol and his hunger for urban nightlife. He meets Hattie Sterling, a rapidly aging chorus girl who tries to protect and educate him. In a jealous rage, Joe murders Hattie and goes to prison. Kitty becomes, in her mother's eyes, a fallen woman after being flattered into using her singing talent for a career on the vaudeville stage. Fanny mistakenly believes she is divorced from Berry and marries an abusive racetrack gambler. In a parallel plot Francis Oakley confesses to stealing the money, but in an effort to maintain the family's good name, his brother, Maurice, conceals Francis's guilt and allows Berry to remain in prison. Through a series of plot contrivances, a northern muckraker eventually exposes the cover-up and manages to get Berry freed. He travels to New York only to confront the tragic effect of the city on his family. The timely death of Fanny's second husband allows Berry and Fanny to remarry and return to the South where they take up a sad residence in their former cottage on the Oakley plantation.

The last of Dunbar's four novels, *The Sport of the Gods* is the author's most pessimistic examination of the powerlessness of African Americans. In contrast to his more famous *poetry, which positively portrays African American life in rural southern settings, *The Sport of the Gods* undercuts the *plantation tradition's assumption that African Americans have a benevolent relationship with white Southerners. As the first African American novel to show characters who participate in the Great *Migration from the rural South to the urban North, the novel also examines how ill-prepared unsophisticated Southerners are for the complexities of city life. By calling attention to the limitations of both the South and the North, *The Sport of the Gods* summarizes the deteriorating racial situation of turn-of-the-century America.

• Gregory Candela, "We Wear the Mask: Irony in Dunbar's *The Sport of the Gods*," *American Literature* 48 (1976): 60–72. Houston Baker, *Blues, Ideology, and Afro-American Literature: A Vernacular Theory*, 1984. Lawrence Rodgers, "Paul Laurence Dunbar's *Sport of the Gods*: The Doubly Conscious World of Plantation Fiction, Migration and Ascent," *American Literary Realism: 1870–1910* 24 (Spring 1992): 42–57.

—Lawrence R. Rodgers

STACKOLEE. Other spellings for Stackolee, the name of the notorious black folk bandit abound: Stagolee, Stackerlee, Stackalee, and Stagger Lee have all been collected. The first references to the outlaw emerged in the 1890s. It is important to note, however, that collections of *folklore from African Americans were virtually nonexistent before that time, so this tradition may be much older than the evidence suggests.

Stackolee is prominent in *folk literature, namely songs, toasts, and folktales. Many of these genres focus on the deeds of thoroughly "bad men." Stackolee is probably the most well-known of these characters. Because he has lost his beloved Stetson hat while gambling, Stackolee engages a hard-living black man Billy (or Bully) Lyons (or Lion) in a gun battle. Citing family considerations, Billy eventually begs for mercy, but Stackolee shows no sympathy. In most versions, Stackolee's reputation for evil is so powerful that law enforcement officials fear him; sheriffs and deputies refuse to pursue him. In some versions, the judge refuses to send Stackolee to jail because he fears the bandit will somehow seek retribution. In others, Stackolee responds to a ninety-nine year sentence by boasting, "Judge, ninety-nine ain't no goddamn time / My father's in Sing Sing doing two ninety-nine." In other versions, the hangman refuses to execute him, or his neck won't snap after the noose has been tightened. Folklorists have argued that Stackolee and other bad black men in folk tradition owe their appeal to the African American public's awe for men who disdain all conventions. So long victimized by the institution of *slavery and the second-class citizenship that followed, many African Americans developed a fondness for stories about men who disdain all conventions.

[*See also* Badman.]

• Lawrence Levine, *Black Culture and Black Consciousness: Afro-American Folk Thought from Slavery to Freedom*, 1977. Cecil Morris Brown, "Stagolee: From Shack Bully to Cultural Hero," PhD diss., University of California at Berkeley, 1993.

—Patricia A. Turner

STEINER, K. LESLIE. *See* Delany, Samuel R.

STEPIN FETCHIT (c. 1902–1985), actor. His name now nearly synonymous with slow-witted, shuffling servility, Stepin Fetchit was a talented comic actor and the first African American movie star. Born Lincoln Theodore Monroe Andrew Perry in Key West,

Florida, Fetchit was by 1914 performing in stage revues and vaudeville shows, largely for African American audiences. Fetchit's early work in Hollywood as a lazy, whining clown in films such as *In Old Kentucky* (1927) and *Salute* (1929) got him noticed, but it was *Hearts in Dixie* (1929), an all-black talking picture, that first highlighted his comic gifts. Bald, lanky, and shambling, Fetchit sometimes transcended his persona's stereotypical outlines through impeccable timing and projection of personality. Crafted in African American settings, Fetchit's character was not served well by the white contexts of the movies that made him an international star. He is little more than comic relief in films such as John Ford's *The World Moves On* (1934), the Shirley Temple vehicle *Stand Up and Cheer* (1934), and *Helldorado* (1935); he is whipping-boy and lackey to Will Rogers in *David Harum* (1934), *The County Chairman* (1935), and Ford's *Judge Priest* (1934) and *Steamboat 'Round the Bend* (1935); he is downright foolish in *Charlie Chan in Egypt* (1935). Yet even in the harshest surroundings Fetchit armors himself with a detachment that seems almost wise. His great success pointed the way toward more substantial African American film roles, and his legendary off-screen high life (including spending binges, car accidents, and brawls) only increased his allure. By the end of the 1930s, Fetchit's recklessness and the criticism of civil rights groups brought his stardom to an end; he appeared on *film only occasionally in the following decades. In the late 1960s Fetchit was a member of Muhammad *Ali's entourage and in 1968 filed a lawsuit against CBS for broadcasting a documentary that villainized him, the man who opened Hollywood's doors to African Americans.

• Donald Bogle, *Toms, Coons, Mulattoes, Mammies, and Bucks: An Interpretive History of Blacks in American Films*, 1973. Thomas Cripps, *Slow Fade to Black: The Negro in American Film, 1900–1942*, 1977.

—Eric Lott

STEPTOE, JOHN (1950–1989), artist, author, and illustrator of children's books. Born on 14 September 1950 and raised in the Bedford-Stuyvesant section of Brooklyn, New York, John Lewis Steptoe attended the New York School of Design and an afternoon art program sponsored by the Harlem Youth Opportunity Act from 1964 to 1967. In 1968, Steptoe was recruited as a senior in high school by John Torres to attend an eight-week summer program for minority artists at Vermont Academy. There Steptoe met Philip Dubois, who provided him with a place to work at the end of the summer session. While he was a student at Vermont Academy, Steptoe wrote and illustrated his first novel, *Stevie*. Published by Harper in 1969 and reprinted in *Life*, *Stevie* vaulted the nineteen-year-old Steptoe into the limelight. Written by an inner-city African American teenager and directed at inner-city African American youth, *Stevie* was lauded by the critics for its appeal to white as well as black audiences. Steptoe's use of inner-city dialect and his depiction of an urban setting targeted an audience previously ignored by children's book publishers: urban African American youth. What made *Stevie* so popular, however, was Steptoe's choice of subject matter. His tale of jealousy and reconciliation addressed a universal theme to which readers of all colors could relate.

Throughout his prolific career, Steptoe continued to write and illustrate books that dealt with experiences, issues, and concerns in the African American community. His works include *Uptown* (1970), *Train Ride* (1971), *Birthday* (1972), *My Special Best Words* (1974), *Marcia* (1976), *Daddy Is a Monster . . . Sometimes* (1980), *Jeffrey Bear Cleans Up His Act* (1983), *The Story of Jumping Mouse: A Native American Legend* (1984), **Mufaro's Beautiful Daughters: An African Tale* (1987), and *Baby Says* (1988).

Steptoe also used his considerable artistic talents to collaborate with other authors. His illustration credits include *All Us Come Cross the Water* (with Lucille *Clifton, 1972), *She Come Bringing Me that Little Baby Girl* (with Eloise *Greenfield, 1974), *OUTside/INside Poems* (with Arnold Adoff, 1981), *Mother Crocodile=Maman Caiman* (by Birago Diop, translated and adapted by Rosa *Guy, 1981), and *All the Colors of the Race: Poems* (with Arnold Adoff, 1982).

Steptoe won numerous awards for his work, including the Gold Medal from the Society of Illustrators (in 1970 for *Stevie*), the Irma Simonton Black Award from Bank Street College of Education in New York City (with Eloise Greenfield in 1975 for *She Come Bringing Me that Little Baby Girl*), the Lewis Carroll Shelf Award (in 1978 for *Stevie*), the Coretta Scott King Award for Illustration (in 1982 for *Mother Crocodile=Maman Caiman* and in 1988 for *Mufaro's Beautiful Daughters*), the Caldecott Honor Medal (in 1985 for *The Story of Jumping Mouse: A Native American Legend* and in 1988 for *Mufaro's Beautiful Daughters*), and the *Boston Globe-Horn Book* Award for Illustration (in 1987 for *Mufaro's Beautiful Daughters*).

In addition to *Stevie*, Steptoe's most well-known work is *Mufaro's Beautiful Daughters: An African Tale.* A retelling of the Cinderella story set in ancient Africa with vivid full-color paintings and fully realized characters, which Steptoe modeled on members of his family, *Mufaro's Beautiful Daughters* embodies Steptoe's conviction that ancient African culture bore no resemblance to the stereotypical view of Africa as a Dark Continent inhabited by savages. During the two and a half years it took him to write and illustrate the book, Steptoe consulted anthropological studies that detailed the technological sophistication of the ruins of Zimbabwe. In *Mufaro's Beautiful Daughters*, Steptoe captures the beauty of Africa and Africans while retelling a tale of sibling rivalry found in all cultures. His choice of such a universal theme echoed the approach he took with *Stevie* and with other works throughout his career.

Steptoe died on 28 August 1989 in New York City.

• Anne Commire, ed., *Something about the Author,* vol. 8, 1976, p. 198. Carolyn Riley, ed., *Children's Literature Review,* vol. 2, 1976, pp. 162–165. Gerard J. Senick, ed., *Children's Literature Review,* vol. 12, 1987, pp. 234–242. John Steptoe, "Mufaro's Beautiful Daughters," *Horn Book* 64.1 (Jan./Feb. 1988): 25–29. Anne Commire, ed., *Something about the Author,* vol. 63, 1991, pp. 157–167.   —Barbara Lowe

STEREOTYPES. *This entry consists of two essays that describe predominant racial stereotypes in African American literature and provide a context for their development:*

Black Stereotypes
White Stereotypes

The first essay discusses stereotypes of African Americans as they appear in literature by African American and Euro-American writers. The second focuses upon stereotypes of Euro-Americans in literature by African Americans. For further information, please refer to Character Types *in addition to the articles cross-referenced below.*

BLACK STEREOTYPES

The image of the African American in the American consciousness has been one based largely on stereotypes. In fact, until very recently in American history, expressions such as *"the* Negro" were most often used to represent the entire African American population. The construction and use of monolithic black figures to represent African American men and women during much of the nation's history have hindered generations of Americans in their ability truly to see and know the peoples of African descent who have lived in North America since the founding of the Jamestown colony in 1623.

As Seymour L. Gross explained in "Stereotype to Archetype: The Negro in American Literary Criticism" (in *Images of the Negro in American Literary Criticism,* 1966), representations of African Americans have been based more on contrived formulas than on accurate and specific representations of them as human beings. Although stereotypes of Africans, such as the "noble savages" of Aphra Behn (*Oroonoko, or The History of the Royal Slave,* c. 1678) and Daniel Defoe (*Captain Singleton,* 1720), originated in England and were imported to North America with the early settlers, it did not take long for American theories of the nature of the African to develop. Thomas Jefferson in his *Notes on the State of Virginia* (1785) speculated that blacks are sweaty and smelly, imaginatively dull, and lacking in reason but with a talent for *music and *religion, while being benevolent, grateful, and loyal. Winthrop Jordan contends that remarks like Jefferson's have had a significant and long-lasting influence in debates concerning African Americans' supposed inferiority to whites.

Sterling A. *Brown discussed the literary depiction of African Americans in "Negro Character as Seen by White Authors" (*Journal of Negro Education,* 1933), *The Negro in American Fiction* (1937), *The Negro in Poetry and Drama* (1937), the introduction to *The Negro Caravan* (with Arthur P. Davis and Ulysses Lee, 1941), and "A Century of Negro Portraiture" (*Massachusetts Review,* 1966). Brown offers numerous examples of how African Americans have been depicted as contented slaves, black brutes, bumbling minstrels, scarf-wearing *mammies with big bosoms, and exotic primitives. According to Brown, with the exception of writers such as Herman Melville, Mark Twain, and William Faulkner, the characterizations of African Americans in the works of white writers have almost always been exaggerated, when African Americans have been included at all. Typically, representations of African Americans were used to symbolize racial differences between whites and blacks in order to maintain the inferior status of African Americans.

Free and enslaved Africans appeared in the earliest works of American fiction but mostly in inconsequential roles. When the southern novel began to flourish, writers such as George Tucker (*The Valley of the Shenandoah*, 1824), John Pendleton Kennedy (*Swallow Barn*, 1832), and William Gilmore Simms (*The Yemassee*, 1835) not only included black characters but defended *slavery by constructing their black characters as creatures dependent on the slave system and their relationships with southern white owners and masters.

Although several of Harriet Beecher *Stowe's most important influences in writing *Uncle Tom's Cabin* (1852) were *slave narratives, like many other abolitionist works it failed to reject racist stereotypes of African Americans. According to Jean Fagan Yellin (*The Intricate Knot: Black Figures in American Literature, 1776–1863*, 1972), stereotyped black characters are more prominent in Stowe's novel than in those of Tucker or Kennedy. Despite the novel's success in galvanizing abolitionist supporters into action, *Uncle Tom's Cabin* added the figures of *Uncle Tom and Topsy to the ranks of popular black stereotypical representations, as the novel's characters became favorites among the audiences of minstrel shows. George and Eliza Harris are also symbolic of what developed into the dominant representation of African Americans in abolitionist writings, as antislavery forces turned the *mulatto, who generally possesses only small traces of "black" blood, into a character whites could idealize and sentimentalize.

Immediately after the publication of *Uncle Tom's Cabin*, proslavery forces countered with a barrage of works defending the South's use of slaves. The ensuing war of propaganda in the guise of literary works between pro- and antislavery writers further limited black representations in literature to stereotypes based on the images devised by the competing forces. After the Civil War, the *plantation tradition in the works of southern writers flourished. Writers such as Joel Chandler Harris (*Uncle Remus: His Songs and His Sayings*, 1881; *Gabriel Tolliver*, 1902), Thomas Nelson Page (*In Ole Virginia*, 1887), and Thomas Dixon (*The Leopard's Spots*, 1902; *The Clansman*, 1905) attempted to revise and reconstruct the South's slave past. In the tradition of earlier southern writers, they portrayed African American characters who were both loyal to and dependent on southern whites and who were truly content with their lives of bondage because they were depicted as unable to handle *freedom, especially in what was portrayed as a hostile North. With slavery no longer an issue, most northern writers lost interest in defending the plight of African Americans, which resulted in the near disappearance of black figures in the literary works produced in the North. This allowed the mostly southern reactionary writers of the Reconstruction period and

beyond to fix the image of the African American in the consciousness of the nation's majority population as minstrel figures, such as *pickaninnies, jigaboos, superstitious Jims, and bumbling chicken and watermelon thieves. Dixon, in his portrayal of African Americans, went far beyond humorous and comic portrayals in presenting blacks as discontented brutes and rapists of white women.

According to Joseph Boskin (*Sambo: The Rise and Fall of an American Jester*, 1986), minstrel images such as *Sambo and the black mammy greatly influenced white perceptions of African Americans until the late 1950s and 1960s. In order to be taken seriously, African American writers were forced to center their works on the kind of black figures that were acceptable to the mainstream reading public; therefore, early African American writers found themselves bound to many of the same formulas of African American representation that they also sought to overcome and subvert in their works. For example, because of the high degree of interest generated by mulatto characters, the majority of central characters in early African American *novels were of mixed racial heritage, with most coming from outstanding family stock, especially the white parent's family, which was almost always the father's side. Novelists such as William Wells *Brown (*Clotel*, 1853), Harriet E. *Wilson (*Our Nig*, 1859), and Frances Ellen Watkins *Harper (*Iola Leroy*, 1892), relied on sentimentality to persuade their largely white reading audience to sympathize with the social plight of their mixed-race characters and to identify with their human suffering. Although the publication of such works was important, James *Baldwin claims in "Everybody's Protest Novel" (*Notes of a Native Son*, 1955) that as literature they were not able to reveal the complexity and truth of human beings beneath the stereotype.

For much of the twentieth century, African American writers continued to be influenced by the conceptions of black people and black life produced in the popular culture, as well as by the images conceived by activists to promote various social and political causes. For example, several white and black writers during the *Harlem Renaissance, including Carl Van Vechten (*Nigger Heaven*, 1926) and Claude *McKay (*Home to Harlem*, 1928; *Banjo*, 1929), were taken to task by critics of that era for presenting updated versions of the exotic primitive stereotype. Although many of the writers of the period proclaimed themselves enemies of the stereotypes of African Americans that had developed throughout the nation's history, conservative critics complained that the more iconoclastic works of the renaissance were filled with images of pimps, whores, street hustlers, and other types that were as destructive as the old ones.

During the depression, characterizations of African Americans changed in response to the social protest that dominated the literature of the 1930s and much of the 1940s. Black life was depicted in terms of stark realism, and the representation of characters such as Richard *Wright's *Bigger

Thomas (*Native Son, 1940) was inscribed in *violence, hatred, and revolt. Irving Howe ("Black Boys and Native Sons," A World More Attractive, 1963) noted that Wright's portrayal of Thomas, which was based on the southern myth of the "bad nigger," helped change the way African Americans would be represented in future literary works. Instead of presenting a character whose very nature was restricted to either being irrationally comical or senselessly brutal, Wright created one that made the country realize its ignorance of the conditions faced by many African Americans in their daily lives. More important, he subverted one of the most injurious beliefs about the black male by transforming him into an archetypical African American literary figure. In creating such a figure, Wright paved the way for the creation of newer stereotypical representations of the black male, characters who seek self-affirmation through violence directed at whites, based on their belief that white people live in fear of those they oppress. Such characters are usually placed in conditions where they face urban and environmental oppression that they must attempt to overcome in order to realize some degree of *manhood and self-worth. Their representations, like Thomas's, are less concerned with their validity as realistic characters than with their effectiveness as symbols for articulating the social and political plight of African Americans.

The portrayal of African American life in Wright's novel prompted James Baldwin in "Everybody's Protest Novel" to claim Native Son as a direct descendant of Stowe's Uncle Tom's Cabin. With Ralph *Ellison ("The World and the Jug," *Shadow and Act, 1964), Baldwin argued that Wright's novel failed to portray the diversity and imaginative and cultural resources that sustain African American life. Works by Baldwin (*Go Tell It on the Mountain, 1953; *Another Country, 1963), Ellison (*Invisible Man, 1952), and other post–World War II African American writers such as Gwendolyn *Brooks (*Annie Allen, 1949; *Maud Martha, 1953) and Lorraine *Hansberry (A *Raisin in the Sun, 1957) sought out the human truth hidden behind stereotyped depictions of African Americans in order to present a more accurate portrayal of African American life. Zora Neale *Hurston, whose romantic novels, such as *Their Eyes Were Watching God (1937) and folktale collections (Mules and Men, 1935; Tell My Horse, 1938) were criticized by Wright, Brown, and other black critics for their failure to attack the racial problems in the South, later inspired what some have called a black women's literary and intellectual renaissance by revising stereotyped portrayals of southern black women.

In its zeal to promote positive images of "blackness" the *Black Arts movement of the 1960s and early 1970s often led to the production of new black-oriented stereotypes. The figure of the black musician and representations of heroes such as *Malcolm X, Nat *Turner, and Marcus *Garvey became popular symbols of militancy.

One of the dominant figures to emerge was the black male superhero, such as Sam *Greenlee's revolutionary agent Dan Freeman in The *Spook Who Sat By the Door (1969) and the popular black private eye

from the *film Shaft (1971). Black women were often portrayed as sex-crazed sluts and whores, although there were a few superwoman types, such as the protagonist from the Foxy Brown films (1974). In popular literature, film, and *television, African Americans appeared most often as slum dwellers, angry about their oppression but "super hip," as indicated by the so-called blackness of their speech, walk, and *dance. Characters who lacked tangible signs of blackness were almost always depicted as Uncle Tom figures who had "sold out" the race.

One factor that greatly influenced the production of black figures in the various media was the increasing tendency of African Americans to make fun of themselves and their circumstances. The emergence in the national spotlight of the 1960s and 1970s of comics such as Richard Pryor, whose jokes and monologues were designed to make light of the most intimate and sacred aspects of African American cultural life, served as an indication that African American representations in narrative expression were no longer limited to championing various causes of the race or promoting positive racial images. In literature, satirical representations of African Americans emerged in the poems and novels of Ishmael *Reed, whose characters are generally cartoons by design, created to present people boiled down to their essential elements.

Despite the formulaic depiction of characters in Reed's works, he is one of many recent African American writers who have dedicated themselves to offering depictions of African Americans that provide new insights into the current and historical experiences of blacks in this country from an African American cultural perspective. In recent years, works by African American women writers and black feminist approaches to the study of the literature have led to a reexamination of the earlier representations of black female figures in the African American literary tradition. This has helped elevate characters such as Brown's Clotel, Harper's protagonist in Iola Leroy (1892), Nella *Larsen's *Helga Crane (*Quicksand, 1928), and Hurston's *Janie Crawford from Their Eyes Were Watching God to levels of prominence in the study of African American letters previously occupied only by male characters such as Frederick *Douglass's autobiographical representation of himself, Wright's Bigger Thomas, and Ellison's protagonist in Invisible Man. Many of the most memorable characters in recent African American literary works, male and female, have been produced in works by black women, including Toni *Morrison's *Pecola Breedlove and Soaphead Church (The *Bluest Eye, 1970), *Sula Peace and *Shadrack (*Sula, 1973), *Milkman Dead and *Pilate Dead (*Song of Solomon, 1977), and *Sethe Suggs and the physical manifestation of her murdered daughter (*Beloved, 1987); several from Alice *Walker's The *Color Purple (1982), including *Celie and *Shug Avery; Paule *Marshall's Avey Johnson and Lebert Joseph (Praisesong for the Widow, 1983); and Gloria *Naylor's Miranda Day and George Andrew (*Mama Day, 1988). These characters are drawn from a variety of sources and are types that are usually familiar within African American cultural circles. Though some are products of various formulaic representations, most are unique individual representations; nevertheless, some characterizations in these works have resulted in controversy, as illustrated by the attacks on Walker's portrayal of Mr. —— in *The Color Purple*, which outraged many in the African American middle class, especially black males.

The struggle to overcome stereotypes in African American culture is a continuous one, as evidenced by Jess Mowry's attempt to provide intimate depictions of African American urban youth culture in novels such as *Way Past Cool* (1992), where he provides an account of the Friends, a "gang" of young teens and adolescents, in their attempt to rid their community of an oppressive drug dealer and corrupt cops. Although the text uses the idioms of today's contemporary urban youth culture, the novel subverts many of the common beliefs held about inner-city youths by showing the Friends to be motivated and sensitive young men who do not listen to boom boxes and whose lives are not defined by rap shows on cable television stations and schemes to "get over" by exploiting the people of their own communities. In his portrayal of black youths, Mowry subverts and refigures the commonly held stereotypes many Americans have toward black gangs by representing them as human beings who overcome the challenges of surviving the conditions of their marginalized urban existence.

• Ralph Ellison, "Twentieth-Century Fiction," in *Shadow and Act*, 1964, pp. 24–44. Lawrence W. Levine, *Black Culture and Black Consciousness: Afro-American Folk Thought from Slavery to Freedom*, 1977. Arlene A. Elder, *The "Hindered Hand": Cultural Implications of Early African-American Fiction*, 1978. Barbara Christian, *Black Women Novelists: The Development of a Tradition, 1892–1976*, 1980. Trudier Harris, *From Mammies to Militants: Domestics in Black American Literature*, 1982. Charles T. Davis and Henry Louis Gates, Jr., eds., *The Slave's Narrative*, 1985. Houston Baker, *Modernism and the Harlem Renaissance*, 1987. Bernard Bell, *The Afro-American Novel and Its Tradition*, 1987. Eric Lott, *Love and Theft: Blackface Minstrelsy and the American Working Class*, 1993. Dana D. Nelson, *The Word in Black and White: Reading "Race" in American Literature, 1638–1867*, 1993.

—Reggie Young

WHITE STEREOTYPES

Social psychologists have long debated the meaning of stereotypes. Are they always grounded in falsehood? Are they a function of social prejudice? Are they inevitable among cultural groups? Are they a rationalization of hostility or do they produce hostility? Are they always bad?

Hazel Carby has proposed that rather than attempting to investigate the relevance of stereotypes to some actual "reality" we should consider how the "objective of stereotypes is not to reflect or represent a reality but to function as a disguise or mystification of objective social relations" (*Reconstructing Womanhood*, 1987). Her framework is fundamental for decoding specific historical and material relations in stereotypes about African Americans. But Carby's reformulation is not as fully explanatory in its reverse application. African American literary stereotypes of

whites tend frequently toward a demystifying reversal, *signifying upon the miseducation offered by dominant cultural views about whites and white superiority. If one of the functions of stereotyping is "to bring pertinent features of past experience to bear upon a present . . . object" (W. Edgar Vinacke, "Stereotypes as Social Concepts," *Journal of Social Psychology*, 1957), we might read white stereotypes of minority cultures as an educational apparatus that warns the present generation based upon the record of the past. This is not to say that stereotypes about white people do *not* unfairly represent the group about which they generalize, but it is to suggest that stereotypes may function differently, depending upon the cultural and economic position of the group generating them.

"Cracker, your breed ain't exegetical." Sterling A. *Brown's response to Robert Penn Warren's line from "Pondy Woods" ("Nigger, your breed ain't metaphysical") provides a key insight into stereotypes about whites produced from within the African American community. These characterizations often function by indirection, to the extent that most Anglo-Americans frequently do not recognize negative stereotypes about themselves when they hear them. Labels like "The Man," "Charlie," and "Miss Ann" slip past the white auditor time and again, and the inability of the target to decode the label becomes part of their stereotype: "your breed ain't exegetical"—in other words, you can't interpret an insult. Brown's response signifies on the *literacy that middle- and upper-class Anglo-Americans historically prided themselves on, pointing out how, as Ben Sidran puts it in his study of African American oral literacy and musicality, *Black Talk*, "not only is it possible that oral man will be 'misunderstood' by the literate man . . . but that literate man will fail to recognize that an attempt at communication is even being made" (1971). Though black stereotypes mark and exclude African Americans explicitly, white stereotypes, thus coded, also function as a black register of exclusion around whites.

The frequent reliance of white stereotypes on indirection is an index to black-white power relations in the United States. As Thomas Webber has convincingly demonstrated, slave quarter *education inculcated a strong antipathy for white "education" and for whites themselves, but the reality of white power necessitated a careful disguising of quarter knowledge (*Deep Like the Rivers*, 1978), as we see in African American folktales such as the *Brer Rabbit and John and the Old Master cycles. Because *slavery provided a long context for black-white relations, it is the source of some of the earliest literary manifestations of white stereotypes. Frederick *Douglass's 1845 *Narrative of the Life of Frederick Douglass*, for instance, furnished a starkly drawn portrait of an overseer, Mr. Gore, that frames the mindless cruelty of The Man, whose authority is built upon racist oppression: "He spoke but to command, and commanded but to be obeyed . . . when he whipped, he seemed to do so from a sense of duty and feared no consequences." Writers such as Richard *Wright would later elaborate on the experiential validity of this stereotype. In "The Ethics of *Jim Crow" white male authority becomes an inhuman, perverted machinery, virtually impossible for one individual to defeat.

Slave experience gave rise to a generalization about white men as sexual predators of African American women. For instance, in his 1853 novel *Clotel, or The President's Daughter, William Wells *Brown fictionalizes the consequences of Thomas Jefferson's reputed relationship with Sally *Hemings. Clotel, the tragic heroine, having been sold into slavery and the clutches of lustful white men, escapes and drowns herself in the Potomac to avoid recapture. Harriet A. *Jacobs's pseudonymous 1861 narrative *Incidents in the Life of a Slave Girl expands on the type in her depiction of Dr. Flint, a lecherous, bullying, and ultimately cowardly master who spends his time, energy, and money trying to entrap Linda in a sexual relationship. Later writers, such as Louise *Meriwether in Daddy Was a Numbers Runner (1974), would deploy that stereotype to characterize the hazards white men posed to young African American girls like Francie Coffin, and others, such as Gayl *Jones in Corregidora (1974), would elaborate the stereotype into an intense story of sexual abuse and psychological damage.

White women also earned resonant characterizations in slavery, such as Douglass's depiction of Mrs. Auld, whose human compassion withers and is quickly replaced by punitive ferocity when she marries into a slaveholding family. Jacobs also offers an enduring depiction of the slaveholding mistress, portraying a paranoid, sexually jealous, and vicious woman. Such character types were not limited to slaveholding women, as Harriet E. *Wilson's 1859 novel, *Our Nig, makes clear. Mrs. Bellmont is a cruel, spiritually hollow woman, constantly abusing the heroine, *Frado, both physically and emotionally. As this stereotype would teach, white women's economic and psychological alliance with The Man and his institutions ultimately makes a mockery of their religious and social ideals. Literary explorations of this stereotype became important to both Anglo- and African American writers, ranging from William Faulkner's depiction of Rosa Coldfield's rejection of Clytie Sutpen in Absalom, Absalom! (1936), Willa Cather's memorable characterization of Sapphira Colbert's warped scapegoating of Nancy in Sapphira and the Slave Girl (1940), and Ellen Douglas's exploration of Cornelia in Can't Quit You Baby (1988) to Marita *Bonner's matron and relief workers in "The Whipping" (1939) and Alice *Childress's portrayals of white women employers in *Like One of the Family (1956).

The usefulness of (mis)education to the institutionalization of racism became a powerful motif in African American literature during and after slavery. White schoolteachers came to be depicted as dehumanizing enforcers of white power. Such characterizations culminate in recent works like Sherley Anne *Williams's portrayal of Nehemiah, the scholar of black slave uprisings in *Dessa Rose (1986), and Toni *Morrison's characterization of schoolteacher in *Beloved (1987).

Stereotypes of kindhearted, ineffectual whites also grew out of slavery, characterized alternatively by the minister in Incidents, who, though meaning well, could not combat the will of the slave owners, and the second Mrs. Bruce, who with good intentions ignored Linda's explicit wishes and purchased her freedom. This stereotype altered subtly during the *Harlem Renaissance to include liberal whites who considered themselves "friends of the race" and became freshly relevant again during the *civil rights movement. Such whites are often portrayed as being unconscious of their own exercise of superiority, as, for instance, in Nella *Larsen's portrayal of Hugh Wentworth in *Passing (1929), and Sam *Greenlee's Senator Gilbert Hennington in The *Spook Who Sat by the Door (1969).

Other stereotypes reversed accusations contained in black stereotypes. As Lawrence Levine observes in Black Culture and Black Consciousness (1977), a strong strand of African American *humor depends on stereotypical depictions of whites as dirty, ugly, conniving, thieving, selfish, and sexually and spiritually immoral, defining African Americans, by implicit contrast, as morally upright, family-centered, communalistic, and decent. Lorraine *Hansberry, for instance, chronicles these stereotypes as commonplace knowledge among ghetto residents in To Be Young, Gifted, and Black (1969). Langston *Hughes's story collection The Ways of White Folks (1934) riffs on relationships between caricatured whites and decent blacks, qualified loosely by the book's epigraph, "the ways of white folks, I mean, some white folks." Negative evaluations of Anglo-American cultural values and social behavior are implied in terms like ofay, honkie, cracker, white devil, the klan, and peckerwood. This conglomeration of stereotypes often crops up in portrayals of crowds, or mobs, of whites, as, for instance, in James *Baldwin's story "Going to Meet the Man" (1965), where Baldwin refracts the psychology of sexual perversion and racial dominance that drives the white *lynching mob through the perspective of the white deputy, Jesse, and his childhood memories, or, more recently, in Ishmael *Reed's portrayal of Minsk's murder by anti-Semitic white Southerners in Reckless Eyeballing (1986).

Another important literary stereotype is that of white women as sexual predators, as in the frequent motif that every white woman wants sex with and will claim rape by any black man who comes close to her. This is a stereotype that reacts to a real history of lynchings "justified" by the socioeconomically mystifying stereotype that black men are sexual predators of Anglo-American women. Variations on this theme include Richard Wright's "Big Boy Leaves Home" (1936), Ralph *Ellison's treatment of Sybil in *Invisible Man (1952), Ann *Petry's The Narrows (1953), and Gwendolyn *Brooks's "Ballad of Pearl Mae Lee" (1945). In an interesting recent usage, Alice *Walker's "Advancing Luna and Ida B. Wells" (1977) explores a friendship that starts between a white and black woman in the civil rights movement. Later, when the white character reveals that she was raped by a black man, the narrator ponders the historical realities that gave rise to the stereotype and its limiting consequences for interracial community.

As bell *hooks has observed, it is important to study white stereotypes not simply as a reaction to black stereotypes but "as a response to traumatic pain and anguish that remain a consequence of white racist domination, a psychic state that informs and shapes the way black folks 'see' whiteness" ("Representing Whiteness," in *Cultural Studies*, eds. Lawrence Grossberg, Cary Nelson, and Paula A. Treichler, 1992). If stereotypes record a distance between groups, they signal how far we need to go.

• John C. Brigham, "Ethnic Stereotypes," *Psychological Bulletin* 76.1 (1971): 15–38. Minrose Gwin, *Black and White Women of the Old South*, 1985. John Lowe, "Theories of Ethnic Humor," *American Quarterly* 38.3 (1986): 439–460. Geneva Smitherman, *Talkin and Testifyin*, 1986. Werner Sollors, *Beyond Ethnicity*, 1986. Anna Maria Chupa, *Anne, the White Woman in Contemporary African-American Fiction*, 1990. Clarence Major, *From Juba to Jive*, 1994.

—Dana D. Nelson

STEWARD, THEOPHILUS GOULD (1843–1924), minister, journalist, novelist, historian, and autobiographer. T. G. Steward was born in 1843 in Gouldtown, Pennsylvania, one of the oldest African American settlements in the state. Little is known of his early life. Ordained a minister in the African Methodist Episcopal (AME) *church in 1864, he moved to Charleston, South Carolina, immediately after the end of the Civil War to teach and preach among the freedpeople. His political activities in the late 1860s in Georgia, in particular his published call for federal troops to counteract the rise of the Ku Klux Klan, brought threats on his life. He moved back to the North in 1871, resuming his preaching career in Philadelphia and Wilmington, Delaware, and recording his controversial experience in the South in *My First Four Years in the Itinerancy of the African M. E. Church* (1876). In the 1870s, Steward helped lead protests against inadequate funding for African American Schools in Delaware and Philadelphia. Two of his early theological works, *Divine Attributes* (1884) and *Genesis Re-Read* (1885), reflect his conservative views on Biblical interpretation.

In 1886, Steward accepted the pastorate of the Metropolitan AME Church in Washington, D.C., where Federick *Douglass and Blanche K. Bruce were among his parishioners. Appointed chaplain of the 25th U.S. Infantry Division in 1891, Steward traveled considerably in connection with his official duties, which gave him the opportunity to comment on magazines such as the *Social Economist*, the *Colored American Magazine*, and *Frank Leslie's Popular Monthly* on domestic racial issues as well as conditions in Mexico, Haiti, the Philippines, and Europe. In 1899, Steward was assigned by the army to write a military *history, *The Colored Regulars in the United States Army*, which was published by the AME church in 1904. The year 1899 also saw the appearance of Steward's *A Charleston Love Story, or Hortense Vanross*, a *novel concerned with the deleterious social and moral effects of liberal *religion and "free love." Though the central characters of *A Charleston Love Story* are white and the questions at issue do not address *race explicitly, the novel's setting, Reconstruction South Carolina, allows for a quietly revisionist perspective on the slaveocracy. The novel also offers brief but respectful portrayals of African American soldiers in the occupying army and observes with confidence the rise of the freemen and -women to citizenship in the South. Although it was published commercially in London and in New York, this early African American novel was unknown until the 1980s.

In 1907, Steward retired from the army to become chair of the history department at Wilberforce University in Ohio. In 1913, J. B. Lippincott published *Gouldtown*, Steward's genealogical history of his home town. The following year Steward completed *The Haitian Revolution, 1791 to 1804*, which enjoyed enduring popularity as a work of African American history. In 1921, the *A.M.E. Book Concern published Steward's memoir, *From 1864 to 1914: Fifty Years in the Gospel Ministry*, a narrative that attests to Steward's multifaceted professional career and his dedication to social activism as well as preaching the gospel.

• Charles Spencer Smith, *A History of the African Methodist Episcopal Church*, 1922. William L. Andrews, "Liberal Religion and Free Love: An Undiscovered Afro-American Novel of the 1890s," *MELUS* 9 (Spring 1982): 23–36.

—William L. Andrews

STEWART, MARIA W. (1803–1879), essayist, lecturer, abolitionist, and women's rights activist. Maria Stewart was the earliest known American woman to lecture in public on political themes and leave extant copies of her texts. Her first publication, a twelve-page pamphlet entitled *Religion and the Pure Principles of Morality* (1831), revealed her distinctive style, a mix of political analysis and religious exhortation. Her message, highly controversial coming from the pen of a woman, called upon African Americans to organize against *slavery in the South and to resist racist restrictions in the North. She invoked both the Bible and the Constitution of the United States as documents proclaiming a universal birthright to *freedom and justice.

Influenced by the militant abolitionist David *Walker, Stewart raised the specter of armed rebellion by African Americans. In a lecture at Boston's African Masonic Hall in 1833 she declared, "[M]any powerful sons and daughters of Africa will shortly arise, . . . and declare by Him that sitteth upon the throne that they will have their rights; and if refused, I am afraid they will spread horror and devastation around."

She further advocated the establishment of strong, self-sufficient educational and economic institutions within African American communities. In particular, she called upon women to participate in all aspects of community life, from *religion and *education to politics and business. "How long," she asked in *Religion and the Pure Principles of Morality*, "shall the fair daughters of Africa be compelled to bury their minds and talents beneath a load of iron pots and kettles?"

Born in Hartford, Connecticut, orphaned at the age of five, Stewart grew up as a servant in the home of a white clergyman. As a young woman she went to Boston, where she married James W. Stewart, a successful ship's outfitter. Widowed after barely three years of marriage, Maria Stewart was left penniless through the legal machinations of unscrupulous white businessmen. An 1830 religious conversion led her to proclaim her distinctive social gospel.

During her public career in Boston, Stewart also published a collection of religious meditations (1832), delivered four public lectures (1832–1833), and saw her speeches printed in *The Liberator*. After moving to New York City, she published her collected works, *Productions of Mrs. Maria W. Stewart* (1835). During the Civil War, Stewart moved to Washington, D.C. There she established a school for children of families that had escaped from slavery during the war, and she later became head matron at Freedmen's Hospital. Her expanded 1879 edition of *Productions* includes an autobiographical sketch, "Sufferings During the War."

Writing to William Lloyd Garrison in March of 1852, historian William C. Nell remarked, "In the perilous years of '33–'35, Mrs. Maria W. Stewart [was] fired with a holy zeal to speak her sentiments on the improvement of colored Americans . . . [H]er public lectures awakened an interest acknowledged and felt to this day." Stewart's *essays and speeches presented original formulations of many ideas that were to become central to the struggles for African American freedom, human rights, and women's rights. In this she was a clear forerunner to Frederick *Douglass, Sojourner *Truth, and generations of the most influential African American activists and political thinkers.

• Marilyn Richardson, *Maria W. Stewart, America's First Black Woman Political Writer: Essays and Speeches*, 1987.

—Marilyn Richardson

STILL, WILLIAM (1821–1902), abolitionist and historian. Born of free black parents in New Jersey, William Still grew up on a farm, with little opportunity for formal schooling. He moved to Philadelphia in 1844, married in 1847, and in the same year went to work for the Pennsylvania Society for the Abolition of Slavery. In 1851 he became chairman of the society. Later in the decade he campaigned to end racial discrimination on Philadelphia railroad cars. Until the end of the Civil War, Still was involved in aiding fugitives from slavery, an activity that allowed him to meet and interview hundreds of runaways. The records he kept of these interviews, along with numerous other documents, such as biographical sketches of prominent activists and letters from abolitionists and escaped slaves, became the source material for his book, *The Underground Railroad*. Commissioned by the Pennsylvania Society for the Abolition of Slavery, this bulky volume was not published until 1872 because of Still's anxiety about reprisals that might await him because of his work on the *Underground Railroad. The book was sold through subscription. Well received, it was reprinted in 1879 and 1883.

The Underground Railroad paid tribute to the generous efforts of white abolitionists on the "liberty line" but also stressed the courage and self-determination of the fugitives themselves in their quest for freedom. Still's motive in writing his book was to encourage other African Americans to write of the heroic deeds of the race during the crisis years of the mid-nineteenth century and, in general, to promote African American literature.

• William Still, *The Underground Railroad*, 1872; rpt. 1968.

—Kenneth W. Goings

STILL, WILLIAM GRANT (1985–1978), composer of symphonic music and opera. William Grant Still's first major symphonic works, *Sahdji* and *First (Afro-American) Symphony*, both completed in 1930, combined a distinctly nationalistic and patriotic character with African American elements. By 1934 he had settled in Los Angeles, where he remained the rest of his life. His compositions received favorable reviews during the late 1930s and throughout the war years.

By the late 1950s, however, American *concert music was being composed by and supported by people who considered themselves modernists. Still refused to change his vision to accommodate the changing times. *Troubled Island*, his most important postwar *opera, which told the story of the overthrow of Dessalines in Haiti, premiered in 1949 to negative reviews because of his continued use of recurring melodic themes at a time the modernists wanted more experimental music. The fate of *Troubled Island* prefigured the general rejection of Still's work throughout the 1950s and 1960s.

William Grant Still has often been referred to as the dean of African American composers. He was the first African American to conduct a symphony in the South and to have a symphony and opera performed by a major company. Still, however, would have rejected that designation. His purpose in life was to be seen and heard as an American composer. He felt that his blackness was just one part of him and that he should be seen as a whole.

• Robert Bartlett Haas, ed., *William Grant Still and the Fusion of Cultures in American Music*, 1972. Jon Michael Spencer, ed., *The William Still Reader: Essays on American Music*, 1992.

—Kenneth W. Goings

STOWE, HARRIET BEECHER (1811–1896), novelist and abolitionist. Harriet Beecher Stowe wrote the widely popular antislavery novel *Uncle Tom's Cabin*, which was published in 1852 and went on to sell three hundred thousand copies the first year. Credited with mobilizing antislavery sentiment in the North, Stowe was praised, honored, and respected among African Americans both during her lifetime and in the years following.

Uncle Tom's Cabin was based on various *slave narratives, including those of Lewis Clarke, Frederick *Douglass, and Josiah *Henson. Legend has it that Henson was the model for *Uncle Tom, and Henson capitalized on this legend by writing two more narratives after *Uncle Tom's Cabin* was published.

The years following the publication of *Uncle Tom's Cabin* saw African American authors publish a number of narratives, novels, plays, and poems inspired by Stowe's work, including William Wells *Brown's *Clotel* (1853), Martin R. *Delany's *Blake* (1859), and Frances Ellen Watkins *Harper's *Iola Leroy* (1892). In addition, Harper published three known poems inspired by Stowe. "Eva's Farewell" and "Eliza Harris" are based on incidents in *Uncle Tom's Cabin*, and "Harriet Beecher Stowe" extols Stowe as a savior to African Americans. Other poets who paid tribute to Stowe in verse include Henrietta Cordelia *Ray and Paul Laurence *Dunbar, whose 1898 sonnet praises Stowe as a "prophet and priestess" whose voice "spoke to consciences that long had slept."

With a new century came a more critical look at Stowe. Sterling A. *Brown in his literary history *The Negro in American Fiction* (1937) suggested that Stowe's sentimentalized representations of African Americans paved the way for the more pernicious *stereotypes that characterized the works of racist writers such as Thomas Dixon. Richard *Wright indirectly referred to Stowe's most famous work in the names of both his short story collection, *Uncle Tom's Children* (1940), and the main character of *Native Son* (1940), *Bigger Thomas. For Wright, Stowe's novel signified the racist past that continued to influence the present aspirations of young African Americans. Similarly, in "Everybody's Protest Novel" (1955), James *Baldwin called *Uncle Tom's Cabin* a "bad novel" characterized by a "self-righteous, virtuous sentimentality" motivated less by sincere empathy for African Americans oppressed by *slavery and more by Stowe's desire for moral salvation and the assimilation of African Americans into her own moral and cultural purview.

Stowe's moral and theological views and domestic discourse were accepted as progressive, indeed radical, in the nineteenth century. It is ironic that in the twentieth century, she has come to exemplify both impotent white liberalism and the source of racist preconceptions about African Americans.

• Jean Ashton, *Harriet Beecher Stowe: A Reference Guide*, 1977. Joan D. Hedrick, *Harriet Beecher Stowe*, 1994.

—Wendy Wagner

STRAKER, DAVID AUGUSTUS (1842–1908), activist, essayist, jurist, and educator. Born on the island of Barbados, David Augustus Straker immigrated to the United States in 1868. He graduated from Howard Law School in 1871 and served in federal and state positions and was the first dean of the law school at Allen University. Straker opened law offices in Detroit in 1887. His most significant case was *Ferguson v. Gies* (1890), which challenged restrictions in African American access to public accommodations. The case was cited in civil rights suits well into the twentieth century. Straker was a founder and the first president of the National Federation of Colored Men of the United States (1895). The Federation convinced the Republican Party to include an antilynching plank in its 1896 platform. Straker was also one of the initial members of the Ni-

agara movement but died in 1908, two years before the founding of the NAACP.

Straker sought the full participation of African Americans in the body politic, and his writings outlined the components essential to this end. *Citizenship, Its Rights and Duties, Woman Suffrage* (1874) laid out the privileges and responsibilities of the citizen and supported women's suffrage. *Reflections on the Life and Times of Toussaint L'Ouverture* (1886), in addition to recounting the life of Toussaint *L'Ouverture, celebrated his achievement of black self-determination in Haiti as evidence of racial potential. *The New South Investigated* (1888) espoused a "ladder of success" for African Americans consisting of mutual confidence, unity, industry, *education, economy, and morality. *A Trip to the Windward Islands* (1896), though a travelogue, promoted democracy as the best means of progress. Several articles and speeches published between 1886 and 1896 in the *A.M.E. Church Review* exposed the political and racial roots of lynching, promoted an affiliation between Africans and African Americans, and delineated the role of received notions in devaluing the African American self-image.

[*See also* Travel Writing.]

• Dorothy Drinkard Hawkshawe, "David Augustus Straker, Black Lawyer and Reconstruction Politician, 1842–1908," PhD diss., Catholic University of America, 1974.

—Allen E. Johnson

Street, The. Ann Petry's first novel, published in 1946 by Houghton Mifflin and winner of the Houghton Mifflin Literary Fellowship, *The Street* follows the tradition of naturalism and protest fiction while rejecting the traditions of the tragic *mullato and the southern belle. Critics often compare the novel to Richard *Wright's *Native Son* (1942). At first publication, *The Street* received high acclaim, yet it went out of print for several decades. In 1985 Beacon Press reissued the novel as a part of the African American Women Writers series; and in 1991, forty-five years after the original, Houghton Mifflin reissued *The Street*, because its theme made the book seem pertinent enough to have been written today.

Petry's premise relies on environment being highly influential in determining one's life path. Harlem's 116th Street is the most foreboding character in the novel, and the book both begins and ends with its image, representing the evil in urban ghetto life. Portraying the interrelationships among racism, sexism, and economic oppression—revealed through the struggles of *Lutie Johnson, a beautiful brown woman, struggling as a single mother—*The Street* reveals the dreary despair of a black woman in the urban city whose plight can only end in crime and/or tragedy.

At the beginning of the novel, Lutie and her son, Bub, moves to 116th Street, intoxicated with the images of statesman Benjamin Franklin and the self-made individual. These American ideals replace her husband, father, and any sense of community; she isolates herself with this quest for wealth and a house with a white picket fence. This rosy-eyed outlook causes her to become the easy prey of many predators: The building superintendent sees her as the ultimate sexual conquest; Mrs. Hedges, the neighborhood madam, sees in her a great "business" opportunity; Boots Smith, smooth-talking band leader, wants Lutie as a means of easing his own struggles and pains; and Junto, white slumlord, wants Lutie as a personal concubine. The character of Junto is contrasted with her "role model," Ben Franklin; she thinks the latter will lead her to success, and the former only leads her to self-destruction.

Most of the novel's tension comes from Lutie's hopes for a promising future clashing against reality. Because of a lack of options and her unwillingness to face the grim truth, Lutie trusts those she should not—especially Franklin—and rejects building coalitions where she should. She insists on going against the tide in an attempt to break out of despair, but external forces combine to overpower her desires. By the end of the novel, the rosy-eyed outlook faded, Lutie finally understands that the ideals she believed in have always rejected black women and in the process she has lost that which she most valued: her son and her dignity.

—Adenike Marie Davidson

Street in Bronzeville, A. Gwendolyn *Brooks's first book of poetry, *A Street in Bronzeville* (1945), introduced a group of characters in a segregated urban area unknown to many in America's reading public but closely resembling Chicago's South Side.

Bronzeville was an enigma. There were enough examples of successful enterprises and hardworking people who could serve as true role models that "going to Chicago" made sense even when the rest of the country was facing severe economic and social problems. But, Bronzeville had many unlovely places and spaces: back alleys, street corners, vacant lots, and kitchenette buildings with all of the associated odors.

While they collectively represent an intensity unmatched in much urban poetry, the poems in *A Street in Bronzeville* are essentially realistic. In celebrating the life in urban streets, Brooks seems to work like others who create celebratory examinations of ordinary places and people. At the same time, she seems to be in the vanguard of those black writers intent upon looking at black city life. Not only does she present compassionate portraits drawn with skill, understanding, and great sensitivity, but she also does not idealize her characters. Despite the despair of most of them, they are not completely victimized by circumstances over which they have little or no control. They take life as it comes to them; and within these parameters, they exercise a degree of free will. This is not to suggest that there are no elements of protest within the collection. Brooks's protest, however, is often muted and ironic.

Her memorable characters range from workers in service-oriented jobs such as maids and beauty shop operators to the professional classes often represented by preachers. There are gamblers and "bad girls" and those who do not seem to have any visible means of support, but all of them are members of the very crowded urban ghetto. Despite their lack of heroism, there is a quiet dignity that comes to all of them predicated upon their humanity that is often unrecognized by the larger society. While many of the people who live in Brooks's Bronzeville are surrounded by failure, they refuse to succumb completely, and their lives frequently offer glimpses of a pitiful hope.

The irony of life in the ghetto is illustrated by "Gay Chaps at the Bar," consisting of a group of interrelated sonnets dealing with blacks in the military during World War II whose treatment often left much to be desired despite the announced nobility of the cause for which they fought. Like Claude *McKay, Brooks uses the sonnet form to prove that what had historically been a lyric form could also be used as a vehicle for protest.

Brooks's social concerns are etched against the universality of the nondemanding dreams of the young, the limited hopes for the future that mothers and fathers exhibit, and the general need shared by all people to seek and receive not only justice but also love. Sometimes—as in the case of Satin-Legs Smith—it is the hope to exist until the following Sunday when he can dress up and strut around the streets.

A Street in Bronzeville demonstrates social sensitivity while remaining free of the rhetoric of hate. Despite the setting, the problems, and the tragedies, there is an affirmation of life—not on some grand scale but simply in terms of small daily victories.

• Gary Smith, "Gwendolyn Brooks's *A Street in Bronzeville,* the Harlem Renaissance, and the Mythologies of Black Women," *MELUS* 10 (Fall 1983): 33–46.

—Kenny Jackson Williams

Sula (1974), the second *novel by Toni *Morrison, is set in an African American neighborhood known as the Bottom even though it is in the hills. This name comes from a "nigger joke" used to trick a slave who had been promised *freedom and a piece of bottom land. The narrative begins with the community's destruction to make way for the Medallion City Golf Course and then flashes backward to tell the story of *Sula Peace, who leaves the Bottom only to be perceived as an evil and suspicious force upon her return.

The novel is woven around the friendship between Sula and Nel Wright, two young girls who come from extremely different family environments yet become "two throats and one eye." Nel's mother runs an immaculate, orderly household while Sula's home is filled with disorder and casual or absent moral habits and values. Other characters include *Shadrack, the village madman; *Eva Peace, Sula's grandmother; *Hannah Peace, Sula's mother; the three Deweys, homeless boys taken in by Sula's grandmother; Ajax, Sula's friend and later boyfriend; and Plum, the drug-addicted son of Eva Peace who she burns rather than see degenerate and attempt figuratively to "return to her womb."

Evidence of Sula's detachment displays itself early on: When Nel and Sula are young, they accidentally let a young boy slip into a river and drown. Later Sula watches with curiosity as her mother burns to death. Sula and Nel learn early that in the Bottom they are restricted by *race, *gender, and economics, and Sula eventually leaves to seek her freedom. Nel stays within the community, subscribing to and being limited by its mores and conventions. When Sula returns to Medallion ten years later, her return is symbolically accompanied by a plague of robins. Seeing Sula perform a series of incomprehensible actions such as casually taking Nel's husband Jude as a lover and later just as casually discarding him, and putting her grandmother in a despicably kept old folks' home, the inhabitants of the Bottom treat her with contempt. Nel's chagrin and Jude's abandonment of his family cause a split in the women's friendship that is only somewhat mended when Sula becomes deathly ill. Sula dies a disinterested observer of her own death, remarking to herself that it does not hurt and that she must tell Nel. More than twenty years later, the elderly Eva Peace reminds Nel of her similarities to Sula, which leads Nel to conclude that all the time she thought she was missing Jude, she was really missing Sula.

Sula is an intriguing novel, not only because of its controversial and shocking protagonist, but because of her amoral actions and values, and the novel probes into the minds and lives of its characters. Sula seeks freedom and the ability to define herself, and her insistence on her own freedom helps others define themselves. The novel was selected as a Book-of-the-Month Club alternate and brought Morrison national recognition because of its distinctive view of African American life and the lives of black females coupled with the detached view of the novelist toward her characters, which some considered unsettling and original. The novel reflects Morrison's view of the importance and relevance of African American *history, and her ability to explain the underlying motives for the actions of her creations.

• Naana Banyiwa-Norne, "The Scary Face of the Self: An Analysis of the Character of Sula in Toni Morrison's *Sula*," *Sage* 2 (1985): 28–31. Barbara Christian, *Black Feminist Criticism*, 1985. Deborah E. McDowell, "'The Self and the Other': Reading Toni Morrison's *Sula* and the Black Female Text," in *Critical Essays on Toni Morrison*, ed. Nellie Y. McKay, 1988, pp. 77–89. Maurine T. Reddy, "The Tripled Plot and Center of Sula," *Black American Literature Forum* 22.1 (Spring 1988): 29–45. Wilfred D. Samuels and Clenora Hudson Weems, *Toni Morrison*, 1990.   —Betty Taylor-Thompson

SULA PEACE is the character who forms the center of action and controversy in *Sula* (1974), Toni *Morrison's second novel. The only child of *Hannah Peace and granddaughter of *Eva Peace, in whose home Hannah, Sula, and a host of other characters reside, Sula is a restless adolescent who forms a lifelong friendship with Nel Wright, an equally lonely child. Having discovered that they are neither "white nor male," the girls must find ways to grow and explore within the community of the Bottom. They share sexual awakening when Ajax, who will become Sula's lover twenty years later, calls them "pigmeat," his epithet for attractively developing female flesh. They share guilt and failed moral conscience when Sula accidentally lets Chicken Little, a neighbor child, slip to his death in a nearby river; though re-

morseful, neither girl fully accepts responsibility for the act.

Bored with life in the Bottom, Sula departs as a teenager and sojourns for ten years. Her return marks her as the witchlike personification of evil: she puts Eva in an old folks' home, sleeps with and discards her neighbors' husbands, sleeps with Nel's husband Jude, disrespects the church ladies' social functions, and generally disrupts the community's sense of propriety. More damning than any of her other actions, the belief that she sleeps with white men makes her a pariah. When she becomes ill, all the townspeople except Nel ignore her. Instead of using her brief encounter with Sula as a moment of reconciliation, Nel still blames Sula for Jude's desertion, which only gives way to true pain, the true expression of the loss of this special friend, twenty-five years after Sula's death. With Sula, Morrison explores the impact of an independent female spirit upon a town that can envision such a manifestation only in masculine guise. Members of the community therefore judge Sula harshly, but, true to her refusal to portray absolutes in her works, Morrison makes it difficult for readers to pass similar easy judgment.

—Trudier Harris

SUNDAY SCHOOL LITERATURE includes materials ranging from publications of hymnals and sermons, *church disciplines, Bible study lessons, and theological treatises, to cultural histories, *autobiographies, *novels, plays, and poems. Such diversity is a natural result of the historically symbiotic relationship between African American religion and literacy. From their conception, Sunday schools were rarely if ever devoted exclusively to religious instruction. In his narrative, Frederick *Douglass does not identify by title the books he used to teach the secretly gathered slaves in his Sabbath school but it is clear that any religious content was amply infused with radical secular applications, and later, Douglass actively opposed the Bibles for Slaves movements that distributed Bibles and other religious tracts and started schools to insure the material could be read.

As early as 1760 writers such as Jupiter *Hammon and Briton *Hammon were publishing didactic *poetry and spiritual narratives. Jupiter Hammon, a slave in Long Island, wrote several poems, including "An Evening Thought," which recites basic evangelical Protestant theology but with a strong emphasis upon its liberatory potential. In its eighty-eight lines, the poem uses the word "salvation" twenty-two times as it petitions Jesus to rescue the forsaken, judge the sinners, and change the hearts of "all the World." Briton Hammon published *A Narrative of the Uncommon Sufferings and Surprising Deliverance* to show "the great things the Lord has done for me" and to encourage others to expect similar deliverance. Among other early Sunday school literature were "Spiritual Song" (1801) by Richard *Allen, *A Narrative of the Lord's Wonderful Dealings with John Marrant* (1802), "New Year's Anthem" (1808) by Michael Fortune, William Hamilton's "An Address to the New York African Society" (1809), Lemuel *Haynes's *Universal Salvation . . . with Some Account of the Life and*

Character of Its Author (1810), "A Pastoral Letter, Addressed to the Colored Presbyterian Church" (1832) by Theodore S. Wright, and Maria W. *Stewart's *Productions*, which she presented to the First African Baptist Society in 1835.

One of the earliest known Sunday schools was founded in 1796 by Richard Allen and trustees of Bethel African Methodist Episcopal (AME) Church with the express purpose of teaching its members to read. The *A.M.E. Book Concern was established in 1817 in part to provide necessary educational materials. The Book Concern published hymnals, autobiographies, church histories, and other genres. It established periodicals such as the *Christian Recorder*, the *Repository of Religion and Literature and of Science and Art*, and the *A.M.E. Review*, which included poems, *essays, short fiction, and serialized novels among the conference minutes, theological dissertations, and reports of international events.

In his 1888 essay entitled "Sunday School Literature," R. Frank Taylor declared it to have the twofold purpose of providing "good, wholesome food for thought" that would build character and influence decisions while simultaneously presenting an alternative to "cheap, trashy reading matter." Such alternatives were poems such as Phillis *Wheatley's "Goliath of Gath" (1773) and Frances Ellen Watkins *Harper's "The Prodigal's Return" (1854) and "Ruth and Naomi" (1857), which retold biblical stories. There were also novels such as Amelia E. *Johnson's *Clarence and Corrine* (1890) and Sutton E. *Griggs's *Imperium in Imperio* (1899). Autobiographies such as Julia A. J. Foote's *A Brand Plucked from the Fire* (1879) and historical texts such as Octavia V. Rogers *Albert's *The House of Bondage* (1890) offered life stories deemed worthy of imitation.

Some Sunday school literature is published by denominational presses that offer texts such as Cicero Richardson Harris's *Historical Catechism of the A.M.E. Zion Church* (1922) and the *Baptist Standard Hymnal* (1974), as well as such academic works as Kenny J. Williams's *They Also Spoke: An Essay on Negro Literature in America, 1787–1930* (1970). Other Sunday school literature comes from nonsectarian and secular companies. Recent publications range from *The Original African Heritage Study Bible* (1993), edited by Cain Hope Felder, and Albert J. Raboteau's *A Fire in the Bones: Reflections on African-American Religious History* (1995) to Christian romances, meditations, and self-help books. One of the more noteworthy developments is the increase of womanist theological works such as Jacquelyn Grant's *White Women's Christ and Black Women's Jesus* (1989) and Emilie M. Townes's *In a Blaze of Glory* (1995). Sermons and meditations such as those by Martin Luther *King, Jr., and Howard Thurman provide inspiration and interpretation while James Weldon *Johnson's *God's Trombones* (1927), Langston *Hughes's *Black Nativity* (1961), and Maya *Angelou's poetry are perpetual favorites for Sunday school pageants and programs. But perhaps the most popular genre in Sunday school literature remains the autobiography as exemplified by Benjamin E. *Mays's *Lord, The People Have Driven Me On* (1981),

Pauli *Murray's *Song in a Weary Throat* (1987), and Andrew Young's *A Way Out of No Way* (1994).

[*See also* Autobiography, *article on* Spiritual Autobiography; Biblical Tradition; Literacy; Sermons and Preaching.] —Frances Smith Foster

Survey Graphic, social-work magazine (1910–1949). *Survey Graphic's "Harlem Number" of March 1925 helped to publicize the *Harlem Renaissance. Paul U. Kellogg, *Survey* editor, had devoted little attention to African American subjects until the March 1924 "Writers Guild" dinner (sponsored by *Opportunity's* Charles S. Johnson), which he and several other white editors attended. Alain *Locke subsequently contracted with Kellogg to edit a special issue of the monthly *Graphic* modeled after the "Mexico Number" of May 1924. The two generations of African American writers who met at the guild dinner were represented by Charles Johnson, W. E. B. *Du Bois, and James Weldon *Johnson, who assessed the status of Harlem and the African American, and by Langston *Hughes, Countee *Cullen, Jean *Toomer, and Anne *Spencer, who contributed poems, along with portraits by Winold Reiss and commentary by white sociologists. When later that year *The *New Negro: An Interpretation* appeared, Locke as editor made "especial acknowledgment" to "the *Survey Graphic* for the assignment of the material of the Harlem Number . . . , the bulk of which, with much additional new material, has been incorporated." —Craig Howard White

System of Dante's Hell, The. According to chapter headings and author Amiri *Baraka's (LeRoi Jones) assertions, *The System of Dante's Hell* (1965) is structured in a manner similar to *The Inferno*. However, the reader of *System* is hard-pressed to find readily apparent parallels between the two works. This difficulty lies primarily in the cryptic, fragmentary style of Baraka's only foray into the domain of the novelist. Like *Tales* (1967), the author's collection of short stories, *System* is a loosely structured, highly suggestive, and strongly autobiographical work of fiction. A vivid montage of scenes and characters from key phases of Baraka's life, this experimental *bildungsroman evidences that the author's debt to James Joyce is at least as compelling as that owed to Dante.

Critical reception of this work has reflected the continuing argument between those who favor Baraka's experimentation and the politicizing of his art and those who deem it detrimental. Bernard Bugonzi notes, for example, in a review of *System*, "This is ultimately a political act rather than an imaginative or creative one. And not, I think all that effective" (*New York Review of Books*, 20 Jan. 1966). On the other hand, William Harris, in praise of *System*, refers to Baraka as "the pioneer of black experimental fiction, probably the most important since Jean Toomer" (introduction to *The LeRoi Jones/Amiri Baraka Reader*, 1991).

The early sections of *System* are reminiscent of the lyrics of *Preface to a Twenty-Volume Suicide Note

(1961) in both tone and sentiment. The narrative voice of the "Heathen" sections, for example, expresses the same self-loathing and despair so powerfully felt in the earlier lyrics.

As in all of Baraka's writings, the most pervasive theme of *System* is that of racial identity. The protagonist's struggle is the same as that faced by Clay of *Dutchman* (1964). He is torn between the path of self-denial on the one hand and the path of authentic black identity on the other. The centrality of this theme is emphatically underscored in Baraka's characterization of those he calls "Heretics," individuals whom he places in "the deepest part of hell" because of their maniacal pursuit of assimilation. The narrator notes, "It is heresy, against one's own sources / running in terror, from one's deepest responses and insights . . . denial of / feeling . . . that I see as basest evil." The narrator's recollection of the Newark of his boyhood, adolescence, and young adult years deals with images of this "heretical" behavior and the sense of guilt thereby engendered. The book abounds with satirical snapshots of leaders and aspiring leaders of the black middle class, all twisted by cultural shame and motivated by the overwhelming desire to distance themselves as far as possible from their black roots.

This theme receives more compelling and direct treatment in the latter sections of the novel. In the section entitled "The Eight Ditch (Is Drama," Baraka dramatizes the split psyche of the assimilationist through the creation of two characters, "46" and "64," who represent the warring factions within. Toward the novel's conclusion, the experimental mode gives way to a markedly more accessible, or traditional, story line. Both "Circle 9: Bolgia 1— Treachery to Kindred" and "6. The Heretics" focus on the narrator's interaction with highly symbolic black women, each of whom represents, in almost allegorical fashion, racial authenticity and acceptance of self. Until he is able to embrace these women unconditionally, the narrator relegates himself to "the deepest part of hell," a psychological hell of self-contempt and guilt.

• Robert Eliot Fox, *Conscientious Sorcerers: The Black Postmodernist Fiction of LeRoi Jones/Baraka, Ishmael Reed, and Samuel R. Delany*, 1987.   —Henry C. Lacey

T

TALENTED TENTH, THE. The "talented tenth" was W. E. B. *Du Bois's label for a small group of African Americans charged with elevating the entire race. Articulating the principles of one of his best-known concepts, Du Bois published the *essay "The Talented Tenth" in the *anthology *The Negro Problem* in 1903, the same year *The *Souls of Black Folk* appeared. Du Bois contended that no nation was ever civilized by its uneducated masses and concluded that "the Negro race, like all other races, is going to be saved by its exceptional men." Including such contemporaries as Kelly *Miller, Archibald *Grimké, Francis J. *Grimké, Henry O. Tanner, Paul Laurence *Dunbar, and Charles Waddell *Chesnutt, the talented tenth profile encompassed mostly male college-educated urban northerners descended from relative privilege or affluence. Including artists, doctors, lawyers, undertakers, preachers, teachers, businessmen, and politicians, the talented tenth advocated a controversial *class-based dynamic of racial progress, which regarded the uplifting of the African American lower classes as its burden and duty. The theory behind Du Bois's recognition of the need to perform this service may in part be traced to his Harvard teacher William James's contention that a culture's greatness is measured in the way it takes care of its least empowered individuals. Du Bois's paternal system of racial elevation met strong resistance from Booker T. *Washington and the "Tuskegee Machine." The talented tenth's high regard for "classical" education and its lack of faith in the African American masses to help themselves opposed Washington's strategy of accommodation and economic self-determination through technical and industrial education.

• Arnold Rampersad, *The Art and Imagination of W. E. B. Du Bois*, 1976. David Levering Lewis, *W. E. B. Du Bois: Biography of a Race, 1868–1919*, 1993.

—Lawrence R. Rodgers

TANNER, BENJAMIN T. (1835–1923), author, editor, scholar, and eighteenth bishop of the African Methodist Episcopal (AME) Church. Born of free parents in Pittsburgh, Benjamin Tucker Tanner attended Avery College (1852–1857) and Western Theological Seminary (1857–1860). Licensed as an AME preacher in 1856, Tanner viewed the *church as God's instrument for improving conditions for African Americans. Inspired by biblical stories of persecution, struggle, and faith rewarded, he possessed a proclivity toward radicalism and assumed an activist posture as a progressive church leader. During the Civil War he served several pastorates and established schools for black soldiers and workers. But it was during Reconstruction, as editor of two of the nation's most enduring publications, that he established his reputation as a man of letters. Under his leadership (1868–1884), the *Christian Recorder*—the major AME organ—gained a reputation as a reliable national weekly and authority on race issues. He changed it to include not only church news but also information about events of general secular interest and opinions on social conditions. In editorials he advocated economic support of black-owned businesses as a means of combating racism and debated with Bishop Turner over his view that emigration to Africa was a positive solution to the "race problem." In 1884 he helped establish the *A.M.E. Church Review*, a quarterly he edited until 1888. A wide-ranging venue for high-quality literary, theological, and scientific expression for African Americans, the *A.M.E. Church Review* was popular among the AME population but also gained a significant secular readership.

Tanner wrote poetry, occasional journal articles, and scholarly books. He wrote texts specific to his denomination—believing "religion comes of faith but Methodism of reason"—yet reserved his greatest passion for ethnology, advancing the significant role people of color have played in history and refuting the New Hamite doctrine that removed blacks from the Bible. His books include: *Paul versus Pius Ninth* (1865); *An Apology for African Methodism* (1867); *The Negro's Origin, or Is He Cursed of God?* (1869); *An Outline of Our History and Government for African Methodist Churchmen* (1884); *Theological Lectures* (1894); *The Color of Solomon: What?* (1896); *The Negro in Holy Writ* (1898); and *A Hint to Ministers, Especially Those of the African Methodist Episcopal Church* (1900).

• Richard R. Wright, Jr., *The Bishops of the A.M.E. Church*, 1963.

—Kimberly Rae Connor

Tar Baby. The fourth *novel by Nobel Prize–winner Toni *Morrison, *Tar Baby* (1981) is the story of the ill-fated love affair between Jadine Childs and William (Son) Green. The title derives from an African American folktale about a farmer trying to capture a thieving rabbit in his cabbage patch by fashioning a sticky tar baby, enhancing the mythical quality of the work. In this case, *Jadine Childs is the tar baby fashioned by a rich white man, and she is subsequently alienated from her relatives, her history, and her culture.

In *Tar Baby*, Morrison brings together Valerian Street, a retired candy manufacturer who is Jadine's benefactor; his wife Margaret, once a beauty queen in Maine who physically abused their son; and Sydney and Ondine, Jadine's aunt and uncle and Valerian's faithful servants, in L'Arbe de la Croix, the Streets's Caribbean retirement home. Jadine, an orphan educated in Europe through the Streets's charity who has become a successful fashion model, comes to the island to contemplate her impending marriage to a white Parisian. *Son Green, a black man who jumped ship, takes secret refuge on the grounds and, at times, in the home. He and Jadine enter into an attraction/repulsion dance of sorts in which his "funkiness" contrasts sharply with her modeling and middle-class background. They eventually seduce each other and enter into a stormy relationship that takes them from the island to New York and to Son's hometown of Eloe, Florida. Uncomfortable in such a small town, increasingly critical of Son, and uncertain about the future of their troubled relationship, Jadine precedes Son to New York. When Son does not arrive on schedule, Jadine returns to the island, collects her belongings, pushes Son to the back of her mind, and returns to Paris. Shortly thereafter Son comes to the island looking for Jadine. He enlists the aid of Thérèse, the washerwoman with whom he had earlier formed a congenial relationship, but Thérèse purposely leads him to the "wrong side" of the island, where mythical blind African horsemen who escaped from slavery supposedly still reside. Son goes "lickety-split, lickety-split" to join them.

The focal point of the novel is Jadine's conflict with her African American culture, *history, and *identity, and this identity crisis is not resolved. The novel's overlapping narrative structure, mythological themes, and dependence on dialogue to advance the plot have been criticized by reviewers and readers, and *Tar Baby* is generally seen as Morrison's most difficult novel and a sharp departure from her earlier works. However, this criticism has been refuted as exaggeration since *Tar Baby* has as its themes identity, maternity, ancestral significance, and the sexuality of the African American woman, motifs that Morrison used in her earlier novels.

• Susan Blake, "Toni Morrison" in *DLB*, vol. 33, *Afro-American Fiction Writers after 1955*, eds. Thadious M. Davis and Trudier Harris, 1984, pp. 187–199. Craig Werner, "The Briar Patch as Modernist Myth: Morrison, Barthes and *Tar Baby* As-Is," in *Critical Essays on Toni Morrison*, ed. Nellie Y. McKay, 1988, pp. 150–167. Terry Otten, *The Crime of Innocence in the Fiction of Toni Morrison*, 1989. Wilfred D. Samuels and Clenora Hudson Weems, *Toni Morrison*, 1990. Margot Gayle Backus, "'Looking for That Dead Girl': Incest, Pornography, and the Capitalist Family Romance in *Nightwood, The Years*, and *Tar Baby*," *American Imago* 51.4 (Winter 1994): 521–545.

—Betty Taylor-Thompson

TARRY, ELLEN (b. 1906), journalist, autobiographer, and children's writer. Born on 26 September 1906 in Birmingham, Alabama, Ellen Tarry was raised in the Congregational church but converted to Catholicism (1922)—a motivating force throughout her life.

Tarry attended State Normal School (later Alabama State University), held teaching positions in the Birmingham schools, and wrote for the *Birmingham Truth* (1927–1929), combating racial injustice through her editorials and promoting an awareness of African American heritage in her column, "Negroes of Note."

After moving to New York (1929), Tarry joined the Negro Writers' Guild, through which she met Claude *McKay. He facilitated her introduction to the Bureau of Educational Experiments, where she ob-

tained a scholarship for learning to write children's literature.

After attending the Cooperative School for Student Teachers (1937–1939), Tarry wrote children's literature—*Janie Bell* (1940), *Herekiah Horton* (1942), *My Dog Rinty* (1946), and *The Runaway Elephant* (1950)—pioneering the production of children's texts that avoided stereotypes, depicting interracial friendship, and emphasizing hard work and ingenuity while portraying positive role models that reflected the experiences of inner-city African American children.

Guided by her mentor, Baroness Catherine de Hueck of Friendship House, a Harlem Catholic Center, Tarry increased her understanding of the complexities of racial injustice, which she expressed in articles written for *Catholic World* and *Commonweal* (1940).

Tarry's *The Third Door: The Autobiography of an American Woman* (1955) describes her personal development and details cultural issues, including segregation, discrimination, and the impact of the depression and World War II upon the African American community while also exploring the tensions of *class, *gender, color, and religious prejudice, which were manifested within the African American community.

Tarry's innovative children's literature, use of journalism to provide historical enlightenment and social protest, and description of African American life affirms her status as a significant figure in African American literature.

[*See also* Children's and Young Adult Literature.]

• Lorraine Elena Roses and Ruth Elizabeth Randolph, *Harlem Renaissance and Beyond: Literary Biographies of 100 Black Women Writers, 1900–1945*, 1990, pp. 304–309.

—Janet M. Roberts

TATE, ELEANORA (b. 1948), author of children's and young adult literature, poet, short fiction writer, journalist, storyteller, and media consultant. A former journalist in Iowa and Tennessee, a former president of the National Association of Black Storytellers, and a poet, Eleanora Tate has been most successful as a writer of *children's and young adult literature. The film version of her first book, *Just an Overnight Guest* (1980), was aired as a part of PBS's *Wonderworks* series. *The Secret of Gumbo Grove* (1987) is not only a mystery but a story with a strong message about the importance of history and heritage. *Thank You, Dr. Martin Luther King, Jr.!* (1990) chronicles young Raisin Stackhouse's journey toward self-appreciation. *Retold African Myths* (1993), illustrated by Tate's nephew, Don Tate, demonstrates her storytelling prowess. The same is true of *Front Porch Stories at the One-Room School* (1992) in which a father tells his daughter and niece the stories of his youth in their community.

The value of education is a recurring theme in Tate's work. The novel's front porch is modeled upon the Lincoln One-Room School in Canton, Ohio, that Tate attended as a girl. (She is a graduate of Roosevelt High School and Drake University, both in Des Moines, Iowa). More important, the father is a central figure in this book, as is also the case in *A Blessing in Disguise* (1995). Tate believes that the need for "father-daughter love" among blacks often goes unrecognized, but that it is connected to black girls' self-image and self-esteem. She is one of the first young people's writers to address openly the issue of self-esteem in the context of skin color and African heritage, accomplishing what Toni *Morrison's *The *Bluest Eye* does in adult literature.

• "Tate, Eleanora E(laine)," in *Something about the Author*, vol. 38, ed. Anne Commire, 1985, pp. 199–201.

—Dianne Johnson-Feelings

TAYLOR, MILDRED D. (b. 1943), writer of children's fiction, hailed for her realistic portrayal of the African American experience. Born in Jackson, Mississippi, at a time when African Americans were fighting overseas for liberties they did not possess at home, Mildred Delois Taylor and her family fled the South when she was scarcely three months old to prevent a violent confrontation between a white man and her father, Wilbert Lee Taylor.

The fleeing family settled in Toledo, Ohio, where Taylor grew up self-confident and loved in the large house her father purchased to shelter relatives and friends escaping the pre–civil rights South. In this house conversation was an art and storytelling a tradition. Taylor has stated that her father was the most influential person in her life. He was a master storyteller, keeping alive southern memories and traditions. Although Taylor visited the South many times with her parents, she never lived in her birthplace. She absorbed the rhythms and the nuances of African American southern speech and culture from her visits and her father's vivid rendering of the stories he told her.

An honor student, Taylor expressed an interest in writing during high school, becoming editor of the school newspaper. In 1960, she entered the University of Toledo and following her graduation, she joined the Peace Corps. After two years in Ethiopia, where she taught history and English, Taylor returned to the United States at the height of the Black Power movement of the late 1960s. She enrolled in a graduate program at the University of Colorado, where she earned an MA in journalism. Taylor, who had always been politically aware, became a student activist lobbying for the creation of a black studies program and helping to establish the Black Student Alliance.

Following her graduation from Colorado, Taylor worked as coordinator of the study skills center. The job was demanding and interfered with her growing urge to write. Taylor decided the time had come for her to inspire others as she had been by the stories of heroic men and women who overcame the obstacles of racial oppression. She resigned her position at the university and moved to Los Angeles, where she found a job that did not interfere with her writing.

Taylor completed her first work in 1973. *Song of the Trees* is a novella of scarcely fifty-two pages. She entered her manuscript in the Council on Interracial Books for Children competition, winning first place in the African American category. *Song of the Trees*, published in 1975, is dedicated "To the Family, who fought and survived," and introduces the Logans, consisting of several generations of grandparents and wise ones "who bridged the generations between slavery and freedom." Taylor patterns the story on her own family *history, setting a tone that rings clearly throughout her works, one of pride and perserverance.

Song of the Trees was hailed by critics for its simplicity, its finely rendered characters, and its *poetry. Taylor's second *novel continues the story of the Logans. Her second book, now considered a children's classic, *Roll of Thunder, Hear My Cry* (1976), was praised for its honest portrayal of racial prejudice and in 1977 won the Newbery Medal. She was the second African American to receive the medal. Taylor continued her chronicle of the Logans with *Let the Circle Be Unbroken* (1981), which won the Coretta Scott King Award in 1982 and was nominated for an American Book Award. The fourth book in the series, *The Friendship*, also won the Coretta Scott King Award, in 1984. Taylor's works compare favorably to such classics as *Huckleberry Finn* and *Little House on the Prairie*.

Other books by Taylor include *The Gold Cadillac* (1987), a humorous and ironic account of an African American family with the chutzpah to visit the South in a flashy, prestigious car. *Mississippi Bridge* and *The Road to Memphis*, both published in 1990, were named Notable Children's Books in the field of social studies.

Taylor's works appeared when Americans had etherized their memories of racial oppression with the promising results of the *civil rights movement. Holding the past at bay did not, however, insure a democratic future. Taylor urged understanding and acceptance of a history few would care to repeat. Children, having no painful psychic history to suppress, therefore were the perfect audience. Taylor reaches readers eager to learn about lives of people missing, even today, from history and literary textbooks. Her themes encompass real world problems and characters are lovable and brave. Taylor's future as a writer is assured because young readers embrace her books so wholeheartedly.

• Mildred Taylor, "Newbery Award Acceptance," *Horn Book Magazine*, Aug. 1977, 401–409. Violet Harris, "Taylor, Mildred," in *Black Women in America: An Historical Encyclopedia*, vol. 2, 1993, pp. 1144–1145.

—Nagueyalti Warren

TAYLOR, SUSIE KING (1848–1912), nurse, educator, domestic, and autobiographer. Susie Reed was born a slave on the Isle of Wight, off the coast of Georgia, in 1848. As a child, she was educated surreptitiously by white schoolchildren and slave neighbors. Once literate, she endorsed counterfeit passes for other slaves, early demonstrating both a defiance against bondage and injustice and a commitment to African American *education. During the Civil War, she attained *freedom when an uncle took her with his family to St. Catherine Island, South

Carolina, then under Union army administration. At age fourteen, she taught island children by day and conducted night classes for numerous adults. Later in 1862, she joined a troop of African American soldiers, under the command of Lieutenant Colonel C. T. Trowbridge, and served them as nurse, laundress, teacher, and cook. After the war, she and her first husband, Sergeant Edward King, returned to Savannah, where King died, leaving her to rear their infant son alone. From 1865 to 1868, she operated a private school, then performed domestic work in both southern and northern states. At age thirty-one, she married Russell Taylor. During Reconstruction, she organized the Women's Relief Corps, gaining national recognition for African American war heroes—men and women alike. In 1902 she published her *autobiography.

Reminiscences of My Life in Camp portrays Susie King Taylor as both altruistic and astute; in it, as a representative African American woman of the late nineteenth century, she analyzes race relations and *gender roles of her day. By reconstructing her army life, she tacitly demonstrates women's equality with men: while performing such traditional women's duties as sewing, women in the army revealed themselves to be as perceptive, valiant, and hardy as men. More overtly, Taylor condemns the post-Reconstruction racism manifest in *Jim Crow groups such as the ex–Confederate Daughters, and American-Cuban relations. Throughout her *Reminiscences*, Taylor emerges brave and benevolent.

• Anthony Barthelemy, ed., *Reminiscences of My Life in Camp: With the 33d United States Colored Troops Late 1st S.C. Volunteers*, 1988. Joanne Braxton, *Black Women Writing Autobiography: A Tradition Within a Tradition*, 1990.
—Joycelyn K. Moody

TEA CAKE. Vergible Woods, known as Tea Cake, is the third husband of *Janie Crawford, the protagonist of Zora Neale *Hurston's novel *Their Eyes Were Watching God* (1937). He is a troubadour, a traveling bluesman dedicated to aesthetic and joyful pursuits, and he presents a vivid contrast to Janie's second husband, Joe Starks, a politician and businessman. Tea Cake is, as his name implies, a veritable man of nature or natural man, who seems at ease being who and what he is. Unlike Joe, Tea Cake has no desire to be a "big voice." Tea Cake and Janie engage in small talk and invent variations of traditional courtship rituals. They play checkers, fish by moonlight, and display their affection freely. An unselfish lover, Tea Cake delights in Janie's pleasure. Janie soon concludes that Tea Cake "could be a bee to a blossom—a pear tree blossom in the spring." Despite the disapproval of her neighbors, she marries this man several years younger than she whose only worldly possession is a guitar. She travels with him to the "muck," where they both work in the field and share household chores.

Though their romance is idyllic, Tea Cake is not a completely idealized character. When he feels their relationship is threatened, he beats Janie. But at the novel's climax, he saves her life during a hurricane.

Later, having contracted rabies, he attacks his wife. Janie kills him in self-defense. In the epilogue, Janie cherishes Tea Cake's memory; not only her lover, he has been a cultural mentor and spiritual guide.
—Cheryl A. Wall

TELEVISION. The formation and development of commercial network television in the United States is intimately tied to the cultural representations of *race and the social relations in which they were embedded. Whether it was the search for a distictive voice and mode of representation that would define the medium and distinguish it from its more mature predecessors (*film and radio) or the development of a new genre within the medium (the miniseries), *race and family have been, perhaps, the key cultural and social spaces in which television has defined itself as a contemporary cultural and social medium of representation. The formation and maturation of American commercial network television are intimately tied to questions of race and the representation of African Americans in the twentieth century.

Seeing Television. Television might be viewed productively as both a representational medium and a key social institution. Even though it depends on formal strategies of representation (e.g., situation comedy) and organization (e.g., bureaucratic corporate structure), it is a dynamic social and cultural site of constant adjustment and readjustment. Because the predominant logic of television attempts to minimize risks and maximize profits, as a cultural form and social institution, commercial network television can ill afford to rest on its past success. Hence television is constantly faced with the challenge of presenting the new while building on the tried and true.

Because television is very much a social and cultural institution, it necessarily shapes and is in turn shaped by the historical, political, and cultural forces that organize the social world. Because of this quality, television remains one of the most vibrant social sites and cultural forums where some of our most salient and meaningful social experiences are expressed and represented. Since race remains at the center of contemporary life in the United States, television must be viewed with an eye toward the way in which issues of race are produced and represented there. Thus television is very much involved in the process of shaping, forming, and organizing the ways in which the significant issues and events of our time are expressed. Through its signifying practices, industrial organization, and economic imperatives, television plays a key role in the construction and representation of the world. This dimension of television's practice is political because it involves cultural struggles and negotiations over power (e.g., the power to represent).

From the very beginning of the medium, blacks have been involved in this struggle for representation. From a black perspective this struggle has taken many forms—critical viewer skepticism, industry boycotts, lobbying efforts, letter-writing campaigns, the creation of new programs, critical television scholarship, and so on. In the 1950s black engagement of the medium of television sought correctives to black *stereotypes and to black exclusion. In the 1960s and 1970s blacks struggled for more "authentic and realistic" portrayals of black life. Since the middle 1980s critical black engagements of television have shifted to a more explicit struggle for self-representation, resulting in significant attempts to produce less mediated constructions and representations of black lifeways and cultural sensibilities.

Social Context. As a medium, television is very much dependent on its own past as well as the broader social context in which it operates. Thus it is almost impossible to understand the political and cultural salience of television's role in the 1950s, 1960s, 1970s, 1980s, and 1990s without attending to the corresponding historical moments, social events, and cultural circumstances that shaped these periods.

Television representations of blacks in the 1950s were profoundly shaped by and engaged with racism, *minstrelsy, and segregation; the early 1960s might be described as the high moment of white liberalism, whose defining character was invisibility and colorblindness; the late 1960s and early 1970s saw a search for black authenticity and social relevance that was pressured by the social and cultural rebellions of the period; the 1980s and 1990s can be seen as an important era of black self-representation that has been enabled by the explosion of black cultural representations and debates in cinema, popular music, neonationalism, feminism, and gay studies.

Black Images and the Golden Age of Television. Contemporary images of blacks on commercial network television continue to be shaped by representations that began in television's early years. The 1950s—the golden age of television—is important in televisual representations of blacks for two major reasons: First, together with dominant representations of blacks in early film, radio, publishing, and vaudeville, the golden age of television helped shape the cultural and social terms in which images of blacks appeared in mass media and popular culture. Second, this formative period is a defining moment with which subsequent representations, including those in the 1980s and 1990s, remain in dialogue.

The early 1950s programs like *Amos 'n' Andy, Beulah, The Jack Benny Show,* and *Life With Father* portrayed blacks in stereotypic and subservient roles whose origins lay in eighteenth- and nineteenth-century popular forms. The representation of blacks as "servants" (e.g., Rochester in *The Jack Benny Show*), "toms," "con artists," "dead beats," (e.g., *Amos 'n' Andy*), "*mammies" (e.g., *Beulah*), and "*sapphires" (e.g., *Amos 'n' Andy*) was necessary for the legitimation of a social order built on racism and white supremacy. Media historians and scholars suggest that the networks, first with radio and later with television shows like *Beulah, Amos 'n' Andy,* and *The Jack Benny Show,* played a significant cultural role in the representation of blacks in the mass media. In television in the early 1950s, the cultural rules governing the social relations between blacks and whites were clearly on the side of white supremacy: black stereotypes were necessary for white supremacy; blacks and whites occupied separate and unequal worlds; black (*domestic) labor was always in the service of idealized white nuclear families; and black *humor was necessary for the amusement of whites.

Culturally, since stereotypic television images of blacks served white supremacy in these ways, the dominant social perspective of this world was always staged from a white point of view; and when television did venture inside the separate and unfamiliar world of blacks in a show like *Amos 'n' Andy,* viewers found comforting reminders of whiteness and the ideology of white supremacy that it served: here was the responsible, even sympathetic black domestic, Beulah, cleaning the home and taking care of the emotional needs of her white family; there were the responsible but naive members of the all-black world of *Amos 'n' Andy.* In these portrayals, however, seldom were there representations of the social competence and civic responsibilities that would place any of these black characters on equal footing with whites. Black characters who populated the television world of the early 1950s were happy-go-lucky social incompetents who knew their place and whose antics served to amuse and comfort culturally sanctioned assumptions of white superiority.

So pervasive and secure was this discourse of whiteness that in their amusement whites were incapable of seeing these shows and the images they presented as offensive. At the same time, of course, many middle-class blacks were so outraged by these shows, particularly *Amos 'n' Andy,* that in 1953 the NAACP successfully engineered a campaign to remove the show from the air. As stereotypically racist as these representations were, the cultural and racial politics they activated were far from simple; many black people still managed to respect the actors and find humor in the show. However, because of the charged racial politics between blacks and whites as well as the class and cultural politics in black America, the tastes, pleasures, and voices in support of the show were drowned out by the moral outrage of some middle-class blacks. While blacks and whites alike may have found the show entertaining and funny, the humor and the pleasures they produced meant different things. They were situated in very different material and cultural worlds. The social issues, political positions, and cultural alliances that programs like *Amos 'n' Andy* organized were powerful and far-reaching in their impact, so much so that contemporary representations only now have begun to transcend this formative period.

Colorblindness, Invisibility, and Containment. By the late 1950s and throughout the 1960s the few representations that did appear on network television offered more benign and less explicitly stereotypical images of blacks. Sanitized and limited representations of blacks in the late 1950s and throughout the 1960s developed in response to the stereotypic images that appeared in the golden age of television. Programs such as *The Nat "King" Cole Show* (1956–1957), *I Spy* (1965–1968), and *Julia* (1968–1971) attempted to make blacks acceptable to whites by containing them or rendering them, if not culturally white, virtually colorless. In these shows the social and cultural "fact of blackness" was treated as a minor if not coincidental theme—present but unimportant. In the racially tense and stratified America of the middle-1960s, Diahann Carroll and Bill Cosby lived and worked in mostly white worlds where white characters dared not notice and black characters dared not acknowledge their membership or participation in black social life and culture. Where the cultural and social "fact of blackness" was irrepressible, indeed, central to the aesthetics of a show, it was neutralized.

A strategy of containment, for instance, was used with Nat King Cole, the sophisticated star of *The Nat "King" Cole Show*. An accomplished pianist, Cole was packaged and presented by NBC to foreground his qualities as a universally appealing entertainer rather than the accomplished and respected black *jazz musician that he was as well. As the host of a television variety show that emphasized Cole's easy manner and polished vocal style, the containment of his social and cultural location within a black cultural tradition was clearly aimed to quell white fears and appeal to liberal white middle-class notions of responsibility and good taste. Despite this cautious strategy, the network's failure to secure a national sponsor for the show reaffirmed the power of whiteness and resulted in cancellation of *The Nat "King" Cole Show* after only one season.

The Turn Towards Relevance and Authenticity. Against this historical backdrop as well as the social rebellions of the 1960s, the representations of black Americans that appeared throughout the 1970s were a direct response to social protest and petitions in the late 1960s by blacks against American society in general and the media in particular for the general absence of black representations. Beginning in 1972, television program makers and the networks produced shows that reached for "authentic" representations of black life within poor urban communities. These programs were created as responses to angry and urgent calls by different sectors of the black community for "relevant" and "authentic" televisual images of black people.

Both the demand for relevant programs and the networks' responses were themselves profoundly influenced by the racial and cultural politics of the period. The new program offerings aimed to contain the anger and impatience of communities on the move politically and culturally; program makers, the networks, and "the community" never paused to critically examine the notions of relevance or authenticity. As a visible and polemical point of cultural access, television moved away from its treatment of blacks in the previous decades. The television programs involving blacks in the 1970s were largely representations of what white liberal middle-class television program makers assumed (or projected) were "authentic" accounts of poor black urban ghetto experiences. *Good Times* (1974–1979), *Sanford and Sons* (1972–1977), and *What's Happenin* (1976–1978), for example, were all set in poor urban communities and populated by blacks who were often unemployed or underemployed (e.g., the characters Lamont and Rollo from *Sanford and Son*). But more

importantly, for the times these black folks were united in racial solidarity regardless (or perhaps because) of their condition. Ironically, despite the humor and social circumstances of the characters, these shows continued to idealize and quietly reinforce a normative white middle-class construction of family, love, and happiness. These shows implicitly reaffirmed the common sense belief that the ideals and values they promoted are the rewards of individual sacrifice and hard work.

These themes appeared in perhaps the signal moment in commercial television representations of blacks—the hugely successful miniseries *Roots*. Building on the miniseries genre explored three years earlier in *The *Autobiography of Miss Jane Pittman*, Roots distinguished itself commercially and thematically as one of the most watched television programs in history. Based on Alex *Haley's book of the same name, *Roots* presented the epic story of the black American odyssey from Africa through *slavery to the twentieth century. For the first time television brought to millions of Americans the horrors of slavery and the noble struggles of black Americans. This television depiction of the historic black sojourn in America remained anchored by cultural commitments to economic mobility, family cohesion, private property, and the notion of America as a land of immigrants held together by shared struggles and ultimate triumph. For in the end the triumphant story of *Roots* is about the difficult and courageous struggle of a black family to enter the mainstream of American society—it is about the realization of the American dream.

There is little doubt that the success of *Roots* helped to recover and reposition television portrayal of blacks from its historic labors on behalf of white racism and myths of white superiority. And the miniseries also helped change, in commercial popular culture at least, how Americans think and talk about slavery as a historic part of America's past. This powerful television epic was so commercially compelling because it effectively presented the story of American slavery by appealing to conventional strategies of representation in television (and cinema)—emotional identifications and attachments to individual characters, a focus on family struggles, and the triumphant realization of the American dream. As a consequence, difficult and troubling social and political questions like the social organization of racial subordination, the cultural reliance on human degradation, and the economic exploitation of black labor receded almost completely from the story. And, of course, this quality is precisely what made this television miniseries such a huge commercial success.

In black-oriented situation comedies of the late 1970s and early 1980s, especially the long-running program *The Jeffersons*, as well as *Benson, Webster, Different Strokes,* and *Gimme a Break,* (black) upward social mobility and middle-class affluence replaced black urban poverty as both setting and theme. Even though these situation comedies were set in different kinds of "families"—single parent, multiracial, adoptive—that were supposed to represent an enlightened approach to racial difference, in the end they too were anchored by and in dialogue with conventional themes of whiteness, family stability, individualism, and middle-class affluence. Although black culture is explicity present in these shows, it is whiteness and its privileged status that remains invisible, beyond examination, and therefore culturally powerful as a symbol within television's (and society's) images of race and racial representation. As with their predecessors from the 1950s and 1960s, blacks in shows from the 1970s and early 1980s continued to serve as surrogate managers, nurturers, and objects of white middle-class fascination. Furthermore, as conventional staples of the genre, unusual and unfamiliar situations (e.g., black children in white families) were necessary for thematic structure and comedic payoff. In appearance this generation of shows seems more explicit, if not about the subject of race, at least about cultural difference. However, since these shows continued to construct and privilege white middle-class viewers and subject positions, in the end they were often as benign and contained as shows about blacks from earlier decades.

The Cosby Moment. In terms of the representation of blacks in television, *The Cosby Show* is significant because of the industrial space it created and the cultural images of black social life it enabled. Like the mini-series *Roots*, the critical and commercial success of *The Cosby Show* helped to reconfigure the aesthetic and commercial environment within which modern television images of blacks were presented.

Under the careful guidance of Bill Cosby, the program quite intentionally offered itself as a corrective to previous generations of television images of black life. The program's relationship to television's historical treatment of blacks as well as to contemporary social debates about race explains its insistent recuperation of black social equality, especially through the image of the stable and unified black middle-class family. In *The Cosby Show* black culture, while an element of the show's theme, character, and sensibility, was mediated and explicitly figured through the family's upper-middle-class status. The Huxtable family is universally appealing largely because it is a middle-class family that happens to be black. In black-oriented shows from the 1970s, the merger of race (blackness) and class (poverty) often left little room for whites and many middle-class blacks to identify with and construct meaning for the shows that was not troubling and derisive. *The Cosby Show* strategically used the Huxtables' upper-middle-class status to invite audience identifications across race, gender, and class lines. For poor working and middle-class audiences of all races and ethnicities it was impossible simply to laugh at the Huxtables and make their racial and cultural location objects of derision and fascination. Blackness coexisted in the show on the same plane as their upper-middle-class success.

In this respect, *The Cosby Show* is critical to the development of contemporary television representations of blacks. The program opened to some whites and affirmed for many (although by no means all)

blacks a vast and previously unexplored territory of diversity within the black experience. The program appropriated (some would argue rescued) the genre of situation comedy and in the process used the genre to present more complex portrayals of black life than shows from previous decades.

This ability to organize and bring together different audiences through television representations of upper-middle-class blacks accounts for *The Cosby Show*'s popularity as well as the criticism and suspicion it generated. To its credit, the program did not present a monolithic and one-dimensional view of black life since it often explored class, regional, and social differences among blacks; however, its major drawback was its unwillingness to build on the very diversity and complexity of black life that it showed. The show seemed unwilling to critique, even comment on, the economic disparities and social constraints facing millions of black Americans outside of the middle class. While effectively representing the black middle class as one expression of black diversity, the show in turn submerged other sites, tensions, and differences by consistently celebrating mobility, unlimited consumerism, and the patriarchal nuclear family.

Beyond the Cosby Moment. Many of the same contradictions and contributions found in the representation of blacks on *The Cosby Show* were also present in other black-oriented shows that appeared in the aftermath of the show's success. *Amen, Homeroom, 227, Family Matters, True Colors,* and *The Fresh Prince of Bel Air* all offered familiar (e.g., domestic settings and family dynamics) depictions of black middle-class family life in the United States. The cultural traditions, social experiences, and concerns of many blacks, although much more explicit, nevertheless functioned in these programs as comedic devices to stage the action or signal minor differences. While often staged from a black normative universe, these shows seldom presented black subjectivities and cultural traditions as alternative perspectives on everyday life. As a cultural and experiential referent, black experiences and perspectives were seldom privileged or framed as a vantage point for critical insights, guides to action, or explanations for what happens to black people in modern American society.

By contrast, *Frank's Place, A Man Called Hawk,* some of the programming on the Black Entertainment Television cable network, early episodes of *The Arsenio Hall Show, It's a Different World, Roc, South Central, Laurel Avenue, I'll Fly Away, In Living Color, Living Single,* (and some of the music television programming featuring rap music) often used race and social class in different ways. More often than not these shows presented perspectives in which black social locations and experiences were central to the show's structure, theme, and point of view. Of course, all of these shows operated squarely within the conventional aesthetic boundaries of their specific genre—situation comedy, variety, drama. In significant respects, however, these programs are both distinctive from and dependent on shows from the earlier periods, including *The Cosby Show.*

These post-*Cosby* programs are directly engaged in dialogues, debates, and forms of black cultural practice and politics outside of television, especially jazz and rap music, literature, and film. In many of these programs, questions of gender (*Living Single*, *Different World*), social class and violence (*Roc*, *South Central*), nationalism (*Fresh Prince of Bel Air*, *Roc*) sexuality (*Roc*, *In Living Color*), and race relations (*In Living Color*) are more explicit and more explicitly black. These shows are also significant, both commercially and aesthetically, because they utilized black producers, directors, writers, and technical crews to help shape their distinctive visions.

And this proliferation of black managerial, production, and on-air talent in the television industry was not limited to entertainment genres like situation comedy or variety. In the wake of the success of *The Cosby Show* blacks hosted or cohosted leading network news programs (e.g., Bryant Gumbal on NBC's *Today Show*; Charlene Hunter-Gault on PBS's *News Hour*) and afternoon talk shows (e.g., *Oprah Winfrey*; *Bertice*; *Roland*). Blacks also served as news anchors, color commentators, and play-by-play announcers on network broadcasts as well (e.g., Ahmad Rashaad for *NBA Jam!*; James Brown for Fox NFL broadcasts). These on-air talents were joined by a number of blacks—Debbie Allen, Susan Fales, Arsenio Hall, Kenan Ivory Wayans, Robert Townsend, Neema Barnett, Yvette Lee, Carl Franklin, Stan Robertson, Topper Carew, Quincy Jones, Marla Gibbs, and Tim Reid—in the industry who became central players in the management and production of successful television shows throughout the 1980s and 1990s.

The Cosby Show, *Frank's Place*, *Roc*, *South Central*, and *Living Single* as well as major black participation in news, sports, talk, and variety shows all form part of a continuing conversation with the history of television representations of blacks. How they all organize and present black subjects and experiences can be read only as part of an ongoing dialogue (adjustment, corrective, and critique) with prior shows. Building on the institutional and aesthetic space cleared by *The Cosby Show*, these post-*Cosby* programs continue to reposition and rewrite the representation of black life in commercial network television.

• Fred MacDonald, *Blacks and White TV: Afro Americans in Television Since 1948*, 1983. Janette Dates and William Barlow, eds., *Split Image: African Americans in the Mass Media*, 1990. Patrick Ely, *The Adventures of Amos 'n' Andy: A Social History of an American Phenomenon*, 1991. Marlon Riggs, *Color Adjustment*, 1991. Sut Jhally and Justin Lewis, *Enlightened Racism: The Cosby Show, Audiences, and the Myth of the American Dream*, 1992. Kristal Brent Zook, "How I Became the Prince of a Town Called Bel Air: Nationalist Desire in Black Television," PhD diss., University of California at Santa Cruz, 1994. Herman Gray, *Television and the Struggle for Blackness*, 1995.
—Herman Gray

TEMPERANCE. The temperance movement of the nineteenth century saw the abuse of alcohol as fundamentally involved in the abuse of women and children. African Americans and other abolitionists added further to this social critique by linking intemperance to the institution of *slavery. Abolitionists typically spoke of intemperance and slavery as similarly immoral and degrading in the way that each negated the highly esteemed republican values of rationality, self-discipline, *education, and hard work. Like other nineteenth-century U.S. citizens, African Americans were interested in laying claim to these values because they perceived them as effective strategies for self-determination. But in order to make this claim effectively, African Americans also had to challenge contemporary racialist discourses that represented them as innately and immutably inferior to Euro-Americans. Therefore the fights against slavery and addiction to alcohol, and for African Americans, against racialist discourses, were interconnected as progressive social movements.

Abolitionists and temperance advocates often represented drunkenness as a tool of slavery. In his autobiographies, Frederick *Douglass describes how slaveholders, as a strategy of control, encouraged enslaved people to drink excessively rather than be industrious during their brief period of rest between Christmas and New Year's Day. Drunkenness, Douglass argued, made *freedom seem like yet another kind of slavery.

Temperance was also fundamentally tied to women's rights. African American women activists, like their Euro-American counterparts, perceived alcohol abuse as especially destructive within an environment in which women were economically as well as emotionally dependent on men. In her short story "The *Two Offers" (1859), Frances Ellen Watkins *Harper represented men's abuse of alcohol as bringing about not only the destruction of the individual drunkard but the disintegration of his family. "More than once she had seen him come home from his midnight haunts," Harper writes of Laura Lagrange, "his manly gait changed to inebriate's stagger; and she was beginning to know the bitter agony that is compressed in the mournful words, a drunkard's wife." Harper portrays alcohol as an addicting substance capable of producing self-destructive behavior in an otherwise reasonable and responsible man.

African Americans remained committed to the temperance movement until the end of the nineteenth century, when the movement's agenda shifted dramatically. In the wake of the failure of Reconstruction, temperance societies, especially in the South, not only barred African Americans from membership but represented the supposed drunkenness of formerly enslaved men as the appropriate impetus for liquor reform. By supporting restrictive voting requirements, designed to exclude "drunken" black voters, the temperance movement became a means to impose state control on the formerly enslaved population.

After 1900 and in response to the migration of formerly enslaved people out of the "dry" rural South into the urban centers of the North, some African American writers developed a *folklore of pleasure seeking that celebrated alcohol as an important lubricant for an expressive and sensual lifestyle. While many African Americans still supported abstinence from alcohol, their expression of this belief moved from the political arena to the religious and social ones.

• Denise Herb, "The Paradox of Temperance: Blacks and the Alcohol Question in Nineteenth Century America," in *Drinking: Behavior and Belief in Modern History,* eds. Susanna Barrows and Robin Room, 1991.
—Maggie Sale

Temple of My Familiar, The. To experience the full flavor of Alice *Walker's fourth *novel, *The Temple of My Familiar,* a reader must allow him- or herself to expand and collapse within an intensely provocative expression of a womanist world view. In fact, calling *The Temple of My Familiar* a novel is a misnomer. The book, published in 1989, is anything but a novel. It is a collection of loosely related stories, a political platform, a sermon, and a stream of dreams and memories bound together by definitions of (and explanations for) the present state of human affairs.

The book explodes with imagination and presents a past (and a present) in which all things are possible through change, respect, and self-awareness. This optimistic view of the world is presented through the memories of Miss Lissie, a woman who has experienced several incarnations; Zedé and Carlotta, a mother and daughter who share the intimate affections and love of one man; Fanny Nzingha, granddaughter of *Celie from The *Color Purple (1982); Suwelo, an American history professor; and an array of other characters (including *Shug Avery from *The Color Purple*).

The Temple of My Familiar is the ultimate expression of *womanism. There is virtually no subject that escapes Walker's womanist commentary. The book speaks of homosexuality, AIDS, drug abuse, racism, religion, parenting, marriage, and death. A cascade of memories (ancient and contemporary) connect these issues to the various stories and messages of the book. Within all the stories dignity, honor, and grace are ruthlessly denied to those in spiritual, mental, or physical bondage, making it nearly impossible for them to achieve wholeness. Regardless of financial standing, throughout time the "enslaved" have endured an endless struggle for gracious living. The importance of this theme is summarized by the character Fanny Nzingha who comments that "all daily stories are in fact ancient and ancient ones current. . . . *There is nothing new under the sun.*"

Present in each story is the suppression of individuality by rules of morality and by the power one culture (usually white culture) wills over another. One clear message of this book is that although suffering is not new, it is inflamed by ignorance and freed by determination and change. Although *The Temple of My Familiar* demands respect for the instruments of change (self-awareness, freedom, equality, love, and respect), it does not insist that change is always positive. According to Zedé, the moment prehistoric man sought to emulate woman (and produce life through a physical opening that he did not possess) destruction, disorder, and death were conceived.

If this concept sounds somewhat mythic, that is only because it is. The entire book is a myth—a rewriting of *his*tory so that *her* story, or at least Walker's version of it, can surface and shine. In this book, an acknowledgment of the sacredness of woman, love for her essential nature, and respect of her power is the key to finding healing in a world that has gone wrong.

• Ikenna Dieke, "Toward a Monastic Idealism: The Thematics of Alice Walker's *The Temple of My Familiar,*" *African American Review* 26.3 (1992): 507–514. Clara Juncker, "Black Magic: Woman(ist) as Artist in Alice Walker's *The Temple of My Familiar,*" *American Studies in Scandinavia* 24.1 (1992): 37–49.
—Debra Walker King

TERRELL, MARY CHURCH (1863–1954), suffragist, humanitarian, and activist for racial equality and women's rights. An articulate lecturer and writer, Mary Church Terrell fought to end *lynching, disenfranchisement, employment discrimination, public segregation, and other injustices. Over her long career Terrell's activism evolved from *"Woman's Era" refinement to direct action, militant tactics involving picketing, sit-ins, and boycotts. In her late eighties she organized and led demonstrations against Washington, D.C., restaurants that refused to serve blacks. One such effort culminated in the famous Thompson Restaurant case and the 1953 Supreme Court ruling that opened Washington, D.C., eating establishments to all races.

The daughter of former slaves, Terrell was born in 1863 in Memphis, Tennessee. Her father, Robert Reed Church, was a prominent Memphis businessman and the first black millionaire in the South. Nicknamed Mollie, Mary Church Terrell graduated in 1884 from Oberlin College where she followed the "gentlemen's course," studying Latin and Greek and earning a BA degree rather than the two-year certificate women normally acquired. She taught at Wilberforce University and Washington, D.C.'s Colored High School before marrying Robert Terrell, a teacher, lawyer, and district court judge, in 1891. Terrell gave birth to four children, but only a daughter, Phyllis (named for Phillis *Wheatley), survived.

During the late nineteenth century, Terrell was one of the best educated black women in America. In 1895 she was appointed to the Washington, D.C., board of education, becoming the first African American woman in the country to hold such a position. Terrell was also a founder and first president of the National Association of Colored Women and an early organizer of the NAACP. In 1904 she addressed the International Council of Women in Berlin on the race problem in the United States, delivering speeches in both French and German.

Terrell fought tirelessly for the passage of the Nineteenth Amendment and later became involved in Republican politics. Although she admired Eleanor Roosevelt, Terrell never supported Franklin Roosevelt. In the 1940s, Terrell received doctor of letters degrees from Oberlin, Wilberforce, and Howard, but she was denied membership in the American Association of University Women (AAUW). She appealed to the AAUW's national board, and in 1949 the association admitted Terrell and voted to admit other minority women as well.

A prolific writer, Terrell published articles in over thirty newspapers, magazines, and journals. Her works focused on racial and social injustices, African American life and *history, and such notable personages as Frederick *Douglass, Phillis Wheatley, George Washington Carver, Samuel Taylor Coleridge, and Susan B. Anthony. In 1940 Terrell published *A Colored Woman in a White World*, an ambitious, full-length *autobiography chronicling her struggles against racial and sexual discrimination. While Terrell's writings have been criticized for failing to grasp the full complexity of the racial struggle in America, they served to boost the morale of African Americans, call attention to important social issues, and educate whites about black life.

• Dorothy Sterling, "Mary Church Terrell," in *Black Foremothers*, 1979, pp. 118–157. Beverly Washington Jones, *Quest for Equality: The Life and Writings of Mary Eliza Church Terrell, 1863–1954*, 1990.

—Paula Gallant Eckard

Terrible Twos, The. Ishmael *Reed's sixth novel, *The Terrible Twos* (1982) is the first of a proposed series, in which, as of 1996, only one other volume has appeared, *The Terrible Threes* (1989). The title *The Terrible Twos* refers to the temperamental, demanding nature of the two-year-old child, which Reed uses to characterize the contentious and immature "personality" of the two-centuries-old United States. It also suggests that troublesome condition of duality (white/black, rich/poor, the West/the rest) wherein opposites conflict, distracting us from possibilities for unity.

Like a gumbo, which, for Reed, symbolizes the diverse nature of his aesthetic practices, the recipe for a Reed novel typically combines many ingredients. *The Terrible Twos* is no exception, blending elements of Charles Dickens's *A Christmas Carol*, Dante's *Inferno*, and the films *Miracle on 34th Street* and *Mr. Smith Goes to Washington* with a hagiography of St. Nicholas, Rastafarianism, and a savage satire on the "season of greed" of the Reagan years in particular and the callousness of unrestrained capitalism in general.

Reed's first novel, *The Freelance Pallbearers* (1967), dealt in part with ecological and spiritual contamination, and this theme reasserts itself in *The Terrible Twos*. Nature appears to have had enough, unleashing volcanoes and bad weather, but the exploitation of people and resources continues unabated, exemplified by the image of Scrooge and the perversion of Christmas, a season of giving, into one of commodity fetishism and consumption. The economy is in a shambles, but a cabal of vested interests runs the government, insuring that the rich get richer; a single company has gained exclusive rights to Santa Claus; there is a plot afoot to reduce the "surplus" population of the United States and the Third World by nuking New York and Miami and blaming it on Nigeria, thus providing a pretext for war against that country; meanwhile, hell is full of former politicians, and an underground sect seeks to dispel this "cold famine of the spirit" by restoring the role of the original St. Nicholas as a populist miracle worker.

Henry Louis *Gates, Jr., has suggested that with the publication of *The Terrible Twos*, Reed overcame his "problematic" reception by reviewers; nevertheless, the novel came in for a variety of negative assessments. Stanley *Crouch, in *The Nation* (22 May 1982), considered *The Terrible Twos* to lack the invention of Reed's best work; Robert Towers, in *The New York Review of Books* (12 August 1982), found it to be an "odd contraption"; Michael Krasny, writing in the *San Francisco Review of Books* (January–February 1983), described the novel as "weak" and felt that, despite being championed by certain influential critics, Reed had never been a "heavyweight" author. On the other hand, Jerry H. Bryant, in *The Review of Contemporary Fiction* (Summer 1984), argues that despite the admitted unevenness of his critical reputation, Reed's contributions to American art make him impossible to ignore.

• David Mikics, "Postmodernism, Ethnicity and Underground Revisionism in Ishmael Reed," in *Essays in Postmodern Culture*, eds. Eyal Amiran and John Unsworth, 1993, pp. 295–324.

—Robert Elliot Fox

TERRY, LUCY (c. 1730–1821), poet. Lucy Terry was the creator of the earliest known work of literature by an African American. Her poem, "Bar's Fight," created when the poet was sixteen years old, records an Indian ambush of two white families on 25 August 1746 in a section of Deerfield, Massachusetts, known as "the Bars," a colonial word for meadows. Composed in rhymed tetrameter couplets and probably designed to be sung, Terry's ballad was preserved in the memories of local singers until it was published in Josiah Holland's *History of Western Massachusetts* in 1855. Although Terry had grown up a slave in Deerfield, "Bar's Fight" conveys genuine sympathy for the white men and women who died in the skirmish.

Lucy Terry was born in Africa, kidnapped as an infant, and sold into *slavery in Rhode Island. In 1735, when she was about five years old, she became the property of Ensign Ebenezer Wells of Deerfield, Massachusetts. After converting to Christianity she became a member of her master's church in 1744. She remained a slave until Obijah Prince, a wealthy free black, bought her *freedom and married her in 1756. In 1760, the Princes moved to Guilford, Vermont, where Lucy's reputation as a storyteller and a strong defender of African American civil rights grew. Committed to an education for her six children, Lucy Terry Prince encouraged her oldest son to apply for admission to Williams College. When he was refused, she traveled to Williamstown, Massachusetts, and delivered a three-hour argument to the college's trustees against Williams's policy of racial discrimination. Though unsuccessful, this effort augmented Lucy Terry Prince's regional reputation as a skilled orator. After her husband's death in 1794, she moved to Sunderland, Vermont, where she died in 1821. "Bar's Fight," though of slight significance from a purely literary point of view, testifies to African American participation, from early colonial times, in the inscription of the cultural memory of the United States.

[See also Poetry.]

• Josiah Holland, *History of Western Massachusetts*, vol. 2, 1855. Frances Smith Foster, *Written by Herself: Literary Production by African American Women, 1746–1892*, 1993.

—William L. Andrews

THEATER. When fifty Africans disembarked from a French ship near Jacksonville, Florida, in 1564, African music and dance had arrived in the New World. In their segregated worship African Americans passed along their styles of storytelling, call and response, the ring shout, and possession by the spirit. In the northern states, African Americans participated in a variety of celebrations—among them Pinkster, Election Day, and Governor's Day—where music, dance, and verbal wit earned skilled performers reputation and money. Their ritual and entertainment arts, originally created by and for themselves, would wed with European arts over the next four hundred years and evolve into juba dancing, the cakewalk, tap dancing, rhythm and blues, as well as the verbal play of toasting, dozens, storytelling, topping, and rap. Another cradle of creativity was the slave musicians and dancers who entertained at balls and weddings. They introduced the banjo, an African instrument, to America. Some of their folk amusements entered America's first mass popular entertainment—*minstrelsy.

Beginnings of a Literary Tradition. In 1821 William A. Brown established the African Grove Theatre in Lower Manhattan where he produced not only Shakespeare's plays but *The Drama of King Shotaway* (1823), the first play written by an African American. Here two classical actors appeared: James Hewlett and Ira Aldridge, the latter making an international reputation by performing Shakespeare in Europe. In 1858 William Wells *Brown published *The *Escape, or A Leap for Freedom* and during the nineteenth century various plays and pageants were written for local production; however, following the African Grove's demise in 1823, the literary tradition remained more or less dormant until the *Harlem Renaissance of the 1920s.

Minstrelsy. The popularity of blackface minstrelsy began in the 1820s and lasted until the turn of the century; however, the "darkie" *stereotypes it created remained firmly entrenched in American culture. Before the Civil War very few African Americans appeared in minstrelsy. William Henry Lane, known professionally as Juba, was one exception. His style of rapid and intricate dancing made him renowned in Europe and the United States. After the Civil War several companies (under white ownership) advertised themselves as "real *coons." By the 1890s, minstrelsy had become a caricature of itself. After seeing women mocked in performances by cross-dressing men, audiences welcomed the presence of real women dancing on stage to a new syncopated ragtime music.

Ragtime. African Americans in sawmill camps, in bars and brothels, on upright pianos, had syncopated European dance music—jigs, reels, and airs. By shifting the musical accent from first and third beats to the second and fourth, they transformed the old European rhythms to an upbeat expression of the nation's optimistic mood, that of Manifest Destiny.

Beginning in the 1890s, comic operettas with ragtime music and the high-stepping cakewalk swept on stage—*A Trip to Coontown* (1898), *Clorindy* (1898), *In Dahomey* (1903), *Abyssinia* (1906), and many others. Similar to European operettas of that time, except for their omission of serious romantic love scenes, improbable plots provided excuses for song and dance. Among the gifted writers, composers, and performers were Bob Cole, Will Marion Cook, Paul Laurence *Dunbar, Leubrie Hill, Ernest Hogan, Rosamond Johnson, James Weldon *Johnson, Abbie Mitchell, Alex Rogers, Jesse Shipp, Ada Overton Walker, George Walker, and the greatest comic of all, Bert Williams, who from 1911 to 1919 performed in the Ziegfeld Follies.

Women too took their place upon the stage in the nineteenth century. Pioneer concert artist Elizabeth Taylor-Greenfield, also known as the Black Swan (1809–1876), sang operatic selections at Metropolitan Hall in New York and before Queen Victoria at Buckingham Palace in London. The Hyers Sisters, Emma and Annie, mounted and toured a half a dozen shows including *Out of Bondage, the Underground Railroad* (1880). Matilda Sissieretta Jones, known as Black Patti because her style and talents were judged equal to the then popular Italian soprano, Adelina Patti, formed her own company, the Black Patti Troubadours (1896), and toured with *Oriental America*, whose kaleidoscopic finale flashed scenes from *Lucia*, *Martha*, and *Il Trovatore*. The commercial success of these women rested upon their exceptional talents (Greenfield had a range of twenty-seven notes) and upon the public's amazement that African Americans could sing *opera.

Stock Companies, Pageants, and Folk Plays. In 1904, on State Street in Chicago, Illinois, Robert Motts opened a vaudeville house, the Pekin Theatre. When fire destroyed the stage the next year, he renovated the Pekin for family entertainment, establishing the "first legitimate Black Theatre in the United States." The stock company presented a new bill every two weeks until it was disbanded in 1911 a few months before Mott's death. A number of actors, including Abbie Mitchell and Charles Gilpin, developed their talents there.

One of the great theater entrepreneurs, Anita Bush (1883–1974), founded an acting company in Harlem that became the Lafayette Players, the first theater group since the African Grove Theatre (1821) to perform serious *drama commercially. Between 1915 and 1932 nearly three hundred Lafayette Players practiced their profession, including Dooley Wilson, Inez Clough, Lottie Grady, Laura Bowman, and Ms. Bush, who also acted in early silent films.

To commemorate the fiftieth anniversary of the Emancipation Proclamation, W. E. B. *Du Bois conceived a pageant that would "put into dramatic form for the benefit of large masses of people, a history of the Negro race." On 22 October 1913 at the Twelfth Regiment Armory in New York City, *The Star of Ethiopia* began with: "Hear ye, hear ye! Men of all

Americans, and listen to the tale of the eldest and strongest of the races of mankind, whose faces be black."

The Star of Ethiopia, originally employing 350 participants, was repeated in Washington, D.C., with a cast of twelve hundred, and then in Philadelphia and Los Angeles. Later, Du Bois reflected, "It seemed to me that it might be possible with such a demonstration to get people interested in this development of Negro drama to teach, on the one hand, the colored people themselves the meaning of their history and their rich, emotional life through a new theatre, and on the other, to reveal the Negro to the white world as a human feeling thing."

On 17 April 1917 several of the Lafayette Players appeared in what James Weldon Johnson called "the most important single event in the entire history of the Negro in the American theatre"—*Three Plays for a Negro Theatre*. These folk dramas, opening at the Garden Theatre at Madison Square Garden, gave a white audience its first chance to see the Black actors in serious dramatic roles. Nearly universal praise greeted their debut, and only America's entry into World War I on the day following their debut obscured their triumph. Nonetheless, their success initiated a decade of new theater for African Americans, an era that would later be named the Harlem Renaissance.

The Harlem Renaissance. The 1920s, which philosopher Alain *Locke christened the era of the *New Negro, was a time of great creativity in all the arts. White America discovered Black *jazz, *novels, *poetry, *dance. To use Langston *Hughes's phrase, "the Negro was in vogue." This burst of African American arts stemmed from several sources. First, tens of thousands of southern Blacks had migrated north for freedom and for work in industries gearing up for war production. Second, because of northern segregation, these southern migrants were crowded into a few blocks of New York City—Harlem. Third, the passage of the Nineteenth Amendment in 1920 had empowered African American women to become social warriors on many fronts. Some became doctors, others nurses, and many taught school and went into social work. No play revealed women's concerns more clearly than Mary Burrill's *They That Sit in Darkness* (1919), a drama about birth control in which an impoverished mother literally dies after bearing too many children.

As the little theater movement spread across America, amateur drama groups produced plays in schools, ladies' clubs, men's lodges, churches, Ys, and settlement houses, one-acts that seldom required more than a single set, but these small plays addressed large and serious topics.

Some women playwrights addressed and questioned African American patriotism. Was military service an opportunity to prove *manhood, loyalty? Or was it a disgrace to fight for freedoms that African Americans did not have? Alice Moore *Dunbar-Nelson's *Mine Eyes Have Seen* (1918) posed the dilemma: Should the young man join the army or not? Joseph Seamon *Cotter, Jr.'s *On the Fields of France* (1920) dramatized two men, a white and a Black officer, dying together on the battlefield and wondering why they had not been friends.

One of America's painful tragedies, *lynching, became common after the Civil War. Between 1889 and 1921 southern mobs killed over 3,436 individuals. Nearly eighty were women, some pregnant. Causes varied from "insulting a white woman" to "wearing his soldier's uniform too long after discharge." Two of the best plays of this genre were Mary Burrill's *Aftermath* (1919) and Georgia Douglas *Johnson's *Sunday Morning in the South* (1925).

In 'Cruiter (1926), John F. *Matheus wrote about a poor family of migrants leaving the old southern homestead for war-time jobs in the North. Randolph Edmond's *Old Man Pete* (1934) presented a similar migrant family, perhaps a few years later, living a middle-class life in Harlem but at the expense of turning their backs upon their "down home" parents.

Not all Harlem Renaissance writers lived in New York. Willis *Richardson and May *Miller resided in Washington, D.C., where they published African American history plays for school children. Richardson is also remembered as the first African American to place a serious play in a Broadway theater; his one-act *The Chip Woman's Fortune* opened at the Frazee Theatre on 17 May 1923. The honor of being the first African American to have a full-length play on the Great White Way belongs to Garland Anderson whose *Appearances* opened in 1925. The only other nonmusical was a melodrama *Harlem* (1928) by Wallace *Thurman.

The theater of the Jazz Age is remembered for the splash of African American *musicals: *Shuffle Along* (1921); *Running Wild* (1923); *Rang Tang* (1927); *The Blackbirds of 1928*. These shows and others popularized the Charleston dance, as well as performers Josephine *Baker, Ethel *Waters, Johnny Hudgins, Flournoy Miller, Aubrey Lyles, and the music of Duke Ellington in *Chocolate Kiddies* (1925).

The Great Depression and the Federal Theatre Project. During the 1930s, white authors continued to write popular plays with all-Negro casts—for example, Marc Connelly's *The Green Pastures* (1930), which starred Richard Harrison as "de Lawd," and *Porgy and Bess* (1935) by Dubose and Dorothy Heyward with music by George Gershwin. In most commercial houses, audiences remained segregated; on stage Negroes played servants or slaves, and Negro playwrights were mostly relegated to community theater and college productions with the notable exception of Langston Hughes's drama *Mulatto* (1935), a tale of miscegenation that starred Rose McClendon on Broadway.

Ironically, the Great Depression gave African Americans an opportunity to earn a living while learning stage crafts. As part of the Roosevelt administration's WPA, Congress created the Federal Theatre Project (FTP, 1935–1939). FTP established sixteen segregated Negro units for the production of plays by or about African Americans. The most widely touted of these shows were Orson Welles's direction of the "Haitian voodoo" *Macbeth* (1936) and Shirley *Graham's *Swing Mikado* (1939) with Gilbert and Sullivan music arranged by Gentry Warden in jazz tempo. The best FTP plays by African Americans included Hughes Allison's *The Trial of Dr. Beck* (1937), a story about a doctor who proposed making Black people white, and Theodore *Ward's *Big White Fog* (1938), a family drama concerning the legacy of Marcus *Garvey. The Great Depression had transformed the art theater movement into one of social problems and leftist politics. By the time Congress closed the FTP, many Blacks had been trained in backstage technology and theater management, as well as in acting, writing, and directing.

African American College Theater. Southern segregated colleges for many years provided the major and nearly only training classes for actors. As early as the 1920s, Alain Locke and Montgomery Gregory had placed production classes in the curriculum of Howard University. In 1949, led by Anne Cooke, Owen *Dodson, and James Butcher, Howard became the first undergraduate theater department to tour Norway, Sweden, Denmark, and Germany. Other graduates from schools with seminal theater programs include Tom Pawley at Lincoln University; Baldwin W. Burroughs at Atlanta University; Fannin Belcher, Jr., at West Virginia State; Ted *Shine at Texas A & M; Lillian Vorhees at Talladega and Fisk University; and Randolph Edmonds at Dillard University and Morgan State College.

World War II and After. In 1940, in the basement of the public library on 135th Street in Harlem, Frederick O'Neal and Abram Hill founded the most renowned theater group of the 1940s—the American Negro Theater (ANT). Their successful productions included Theodore Browne's *Natural Man* (1941), Abram Hill's *Walk Hard* (1944), and Owen Dodson's *Garden of Time* (1945). An impressive list of distinguished actors trained and taught at ANT: Harry Belafonte, Sidney Poitier, Alice and Alvin Childress, Osceola Archer, Ruby Dee, Earle Hyman, Hilda Simms, and many others. ANT's greatest success contributed to the group's demise. *Anna Lucasta* (1944) was moved to Broadway and then to London. The result: the best actors left ANT for commercial work.

In 1941 the Japanese bombed Pearl Harbor. That same year, Richard *Wright's *Native Son* starring Canada Lee opened on Broadway. Many Black entertainers joined the USO (1941–1945) and toured military installations at home and overseas. Actor-director Dick Campbell organized over sixty-five all-Black USO camp shows. Seaman Owen Dodson at Great Lakes Training Station wrote and directed eleven spectacles (*Freedom, The Banner, The Ballad of Dorie Miller*, etc.), all designed to raise the morale of African American sailors.

On Broadway, Paul *Robeson's *Othello* (1943) set a record of 296 performances. Jane White in *Strange Fruit* (1945), Canada Lee in *On Whitman Avenue* (1946), and Ethel Waters in *The Member of the Wedding* (1949) received critical praise, as did Gordon Heath as the returning war veteran acting under Elia Kazan's direction in *Deep Are the Roots* (1945). Canada Lee, cast in *The Duchess of Malfi*, played in white face the same year that Ossie *Davis made his Broadway debut in *Jeb* (1946). Three musicals, *Fin-*

ian's Rainbow (1947), *Lost in the Stars* (1949), and *South Pacific* (1949), made gestures toward integration, but significant Black employment on Broadway happened only in shows with all-Black casts: *Carmen Jones* (1940), *St. Louis Woman* (1946), and *Anna Lucasta* (1944), which ran nearly a thousand performances. The only Black play on the Great White Way in the 1940s, other than *Native Son*, was *Our Lan'* (1947), a post–Civil War play by Theodore Ward, which lasted forty-one performances.

Two landmark dramas of family reflected the racial moods of the 1950s: Yale Drama School graduate Louis *Peterson's *Take A Giant Step* (1953), which presented a middle-class adolescent coming into racial awareness, and Lorraine *Hansberry's *A *Raisin in the Sun* (1959), which made her the first African American woman to be produced on Broadway. In the stellar cast of *A Raisin in the Sun* were Claudia McNeil, Glynn Turman, Sidney Poitier, Ruby Dee, Louis Gossett, Diana Sands, and Ivan Dixon, as well as Lloyd Richards, the first Black to direct on Broadway. Hansberry wrote several other dramas— an integrationist drama, *The Sign in Sidney Brustein's Window* (1964); an examination of neocolonialism in Africa, *Les Blancs* (1970); and an autobiographical play, *Young, Gifted, and Black* (1971). None achieved the success of her first effort, which was adapted by her husband, Robert Nemiroff, into the musical *Raisin* in 1973.

Civil Rights Drama. The United States Supreme Court had ruled in *Brown v. the Board of Education* (1954) that school segregation was inherently unequal and illegal. The Greenwich Mews then staged Loften *Mitchell's *Land Beyond the River* (1957), a dramatization of the court's decision. Other civil rights plays appeared: C. Bernard Jackson's and James V. Hatch's *Fly Blackbird* (1962), a musical about the sit-ins; Langston Hughes's *Jericho–Jim Crow* (1963); and James *Baldwin's *Blues for Mister Charlie* (1964). *Purlie Victorious* (1961) starred its author, Ossie *Davis, and his wife, Ruby Dee. This play became the basis of his musical *Purlie* (1970).

As the civil rights struggle continued, Obie Award–winning playwright LeRoi Jones (Amiri *Baraka) changed the struggle's mood from one of racial integration to one of separation. With his one-act *Dutchman* (1964), followed by *The Toilet, The Slave,* and *The Baptism,* he brought an increasing racial consciousness and political militancy to Black theater.

Charles *Gordone become the first African American dramatist to win the Pulitzer Prize. His play *No Place to Be Somebody* (1970) dramatized the protagonist's dilemma of having to choose between two ideologies: racial solidarity and separation, or the hope for an integrated society.

Between 1964 and 1974, over six hundred African American theater companies across the United States sprang into existence. The majority were supported by universities or as community theaters; most lasted only a year or two. When the government arts funding from President Lyndon Johnson's War on Poverty dried up, in most cases the theaters had not developed audiences loyal enough or large enough to sustain them, and few owned theater space.

A notable exception was the Inner City Cultural Center (ICCC) of Los Angeles, founded in 1965. With foresight, C. Bernard Jackson, Dr. J. A. Cannon, Josie Dodson, Jeanne Joe, and Elaine Kashiki purchased the Ivar Theatre in Hollywood where the organization has since pursued its original mission: to train minority youth in the theater arts and to present plays that have relevance to their lives. Their best known "graduate" is George *Wolfe, head of New York City's Public Theatre.

Black Is Beautiful and Militant. In 1965 Robert Hooks produced Douglas Turner *Ward's two plays *Day of Absence and Happy Ending as a double bill, which ran 504 performances. Two years later Ward as artistic director and Hooks as executive director founded the Negro Ensemble Company (NEC), the most widely known of the new producing groups. Using experienced actors, including Moses Gunn, Esther Rolle, and Ed Cambridge, they took over the St. Mark's Playhouse where they conducted actors' workshops, held readings of new scripts, and mounted four or five major shows a year.

Except for its first production, Song of the Lusitanian Bogey (1967), all of the scripts staged by NEC over the next twenty years would be by Blacks—American, Caribbean, and African. Phillip Hayes Dean's *Sty of the Blind Pig (1971) won the Drama Desk Award. Joseph A. *Walker's The *River Niger (1972) won a Tony Award for the best play on Broadway; Leslie Lee's The First Breeze of Summer (1975) won an Obie Award as the best Off-Broadway drama; and Charles H. *Fuller, Jr.'s A *Soldier's Play (1981) won the Pulitzer Prize. After a decade of building a faithful subscription audience, NEC failed to purchase a building, and in its second decade, as government and foundation support lessened, the cost of maintaining a producing company became impossible. By 1992 NEC was homeless.

Other important theaters of the 1960s and 1970s were The National Black Theater founded by Barbara Ann Teer on 125th Street in Harlem and the New Lafayette Theatre (1968–1972), which developed Ed *Bullins as a playwright. He wrote nearly fifty plays, winning an Obie Award for The Fabulous Miss Marie (1971) and a Critics Circle Award for The Taking of Miss Janie (1975). Other notable Harlem theaters included Ernie McClintock's Afro-American Studio and Mical Whitaker's East River Players, as well as theaters founded by two graduates of The American Negro Theater, Roger Furman of the New Heritage Repertory Theater and Gertrude Jeanette of the Hadley Players.

Woman Take the Stage. By the mid-1970s African American women determined to seize their equality in writing and directing. The play that set off the battle of the sexes was Ntozake *Shange's *for colored girls who have considered suicide / when the rainbow is enuf (1977), which presented males as violent and unfaithful, and Black men accused Shange of male bashing.

The militant 1960s and 1970s theater had been male-dominated. A "minority" within a minority, female playwrights and directors demanded attention. Shirley *Graham (I Gotta Home, It's Morning, and Tom, Tom,) and Alice *Childress (Florence, Trouble in Mind, Wedding Band, and Wine in the Wilderness), beginning in a series of plays in the 1940s and 1950s, had established themselves as superb craftswomen; however, few other Black women had been able to place their dramas on the stage. Then Adrienne *Kennedy won an Obie with Edward Albee's production of *Funnyhouse of a Negro (1963) and established herself as one of the very few poets in the theater. Sonia *Sanchez came to attention with two militant one-acts: The Bronx Is Next (1968) and Sister Son/ji (1969). In 1989 Aishah *Rahman's The Mojo and the Sayso won the Doris Abramson Award.

The Urban Arts Corps was directed by Vinnette Carroll, who nurtured performer-writer Micki Grant and took her revue Don't Bother Me, I Can't Cope (1970) to Broadway. Carroll with Grant and Alex Bradford then conceived Your Arms Too Short to Box with God (1975), a gospel musical. Two other important gospel plays were Lee Breuer and Bob Telson's The Gospel at Colonus (1983), an adaption of Sophocles' Oedipus at Colonus, which toured Europe and returned to play Broadway in 1988, and Vy Higginsen's Mama I Want to Sing (1980), which holds the record for the single longest-running gospel show—eight years.

Addressing race, gender, and class through deconstruction of incident and event, the playwrights of the 1980s utilized diverse styles. Suzan-Lori Parks seized upon the assassination of Lincoln for The American Play (1993), using a traditional music structure of theme and variation in lieu of plot development. In Fires in the Mirror (1992), Anna Devere Smith impersonated multiple characters based on her own interviews with Blacks and Jews after the Crown Heights riots in Brooklyn; after playing at the New York Shakespeare Festival, the play received an Obie and the Drama Desk Award. Her Twilight: Los Angeles, 1992 used the same format of quasi-documentary. Using a smaller story as a "personal" document, Robbie McCauley's Sally's Rape received an Obie Award in 1992.

Toward the Twenty-first Century. August *Wilson's plays—Ma Rainey's Black Bottom (1984), *Fences (1987), Joe Turner's Come and Gone (1988), The *Piano Lesson (1990), and Two Trains Running (1992)—all workshopped with director Lloyd Richards at the Eugene O'Neill National Playwrights Conference before traveling to Broadway where they won two Pulitzer Prizes and two Tony Awards. Wilson achieved his initial attention at Lou Bellamy's Penumbra Theatre in St. Paul, Minnesota, one of several vital, new regional African American theaters. Other play-developmental theaters of the 1990s included Jomandi Productions in Atlanta, Georgia; Black Repertory in St. Louis, Missouri; Freedom Theatre in Philadelphia, Pennsylvania; and the largest company with its nearly $3 million budget, Crossroads Theatre Company in New Brunswick, New Jersey. Founded in 1976 by two Rutgers University classmates, Richardo Khan and Lee Richardson, Crossroads premiered George Wolfe's The Colored Museum (1986).

Wolfe's career rose rapidly after the success of his Broadway musical *Jelly's Last Jam* (1992); subsequently, Wolfe directed Tony Kushner's Tony and Pulitzer Prize plays, *Angels in America* parts 1 and 2 (1992–1993), and then he was appointed director of the New York Public Theatre.

As African American theater moved into the 1990s, nonconventional casting, or casting roles for talent and not for color, became an issue for debate. Would cross-racial casting provide more roles or fewer? Would directors in the name of multiculturalism replace Black actors with other ethnics? The issue remained unresolved.

The twentieth century had brought momentous changes in racial imagery. Oprah Winfrey and Arsenio Hall had hosted programs on national television. In Hollywood Julie Dash and Spike *Lee had directed films. Whoopi Goldberg and Danny Glover had starred in major movies. Yet there are very few Black costume and set designers, talent and publicity agents, play producers, house managers, or theater owners. Nonetheless, over four hundred years African Americans had become a major source of art and pride in American theater.

[*See also* Performances and Pageants.]

- Bernard L. Peterson, Jr., comp., *Contemporary Black American Playwrights and Their Plays*, 2 vols., 1988. Leo Hamalian and James V. Hatch, eds., *The Roots of African American Drama, An Anthology of Early Plays: 1858–1938*, 1991. William B. Branch, ed., *Black Thunder, An Anthology of Contemporary African American Drama*, 1992. Bernard L. Peterson, Jr., comp., *A Century of Musicals in Black and White: An Encyclopedia of Musical Stage Works by, about, or Involving African Americans*, 1993. Willis Richardson, comp., *Plays and Pageants from the Life of the Negro*, 1993. Rena Fraden, *Blueprints for a Black Federal Theatre 1935–1939*, 1994. Samuel A. Hay, *African American Theatre, An Historical Critical Analysis*, 1994. Sydné Mahone, ed., *Moon Marked and Touched by Sun*, 1994. Darwin T. Turner, ed., *An Anthology: Black Drama in America*, 1994. Mel Watkins, *On the Real Side*, 1994. Woodie King, Jr., ed., *The National Black Drama Anthology*, 1995. Anna Bean, James V. Hatch, and Brooks McNamara, eds., *Behind the Minstrel Mask*, 1996. James V. Hatch and Leo Hamalian, eds., *Lost Plays of the Harlem Renaissance*, 1996. James V. Hatch and Ted Shine, eds., *Black Theatre USA, Plays 1847–Today*, 2 vols., 1996.

—James V. Hatch

Their Eyes Were Watching God. According to her autobiography, Zora Neale *Hurston wrote *Their Eyes Were Watching God* in seven weeks while she was conducting ethnographic fieldwork in Haiti and recovering from a failed romance. The circumstances were hardly promising, but the novel, published in September 1937, almost exactly a year after she arrived in Port-au-Prince, is her masterpiece. While it presents diverse oral performances—personal narratives, folktales, courtship rituals, speeches, and sermons—the folk material fuses seamlessly with a formal narrative that charts a woman's coming to voice and to selfhood. The protagonist, *Janie Crawford, begins a quest for romance but achieves spiritual fulfillment.

During a plot spanning twenty-odd years, Janie grows from a diffident teenager to a woman in possession of herself. She learns to resist the definitions of "what a woman should be" imposed on her by her grandmother, *Nanny, and by the three men she marries. Nanny chooses Janie's first husband, Logan Killicks, because he can provide protection and support. Janie dreams of love. Joe Starks becomes "a big ruler of things," who dominates his community and his wife. *Tea Cake (Vergible) Woods is a bluesman who guides Janie to a deeper understanding of African American culture even as he betrays its sexism. Through Janie's struggles with and against her husbands, the novel explores the relationship between voice and self-knowledge.

Janie is a master of metaphor. As a girl, she figures her life as a "tree in bloom." Dreaming of a man who will be "bee to her blossom," Janie rejects bourgeois marriage as an ideal. After Joe Starks's death frees her to dream again, she dreams of journeying to the horizon in search of people. She realizes both dreams through Tea Cake.

In the novel's frame tale, Janie returns to Eatonville after completing her quest. Townspeople sit on porches exchanging words full of drama and metaphor. For reasons of *gender and *class, Janie is excluded from this community; she is the object of its ridicule. Not only is storytelling mainly the province of men in Eatonville, but Mayor Starks has ordered Janie to remain aloof from other women and has forbidden her participation in their verbal rituals. With Tea Cake, Janie has learned the culture's expressive codes, however, and when she tells her story to her friend Pheoby it transforms teller and auditor.

Beginning with an early review by Richard *Wright, critics have faulted *Their Eyes* for its alleged lack of racial militancy. Some find the attacks on racism, present throughout the novel but especially in the scenes on the "muck," too indirect. Others contend that the novel's idealized representation of Tea Cake undercuts its critique of sexism. But Hurston's great accomplishment is the creation of a literary language equivalent to the oral performances she admired as a child and studied as an ethnographer. Vernacular voices speak in and through the novel, informing both its dialogue and narration. Like the oral performances it celebrates and critiques, the novel's words "[walk] without masters." *Their Eyes* is a singular achievement.

- Barbara Johnson, "Metaphor, Metonymy, and Voice in *Their Eyes Were Watching God*," in *A World of Difference*, 1987. Michael Awkward, ed., *New Essays on* Their Eyes Were Watching God, 1990. Henry Louis Gates, Jr., and Anthony Appiah, eds., *Zora Neale Hurston: Critical Perspectives Past and Present*, 1993.

—Cheryl A. Wall

THELWELL, MICHAEL (b. 1939), novelist, essayist, short fiction writer, educator, and activist. Michael Thelwell, born in Ulster Spring, Jamaica, came to the United States in 1959 to attend Howard University, where he earned his BA in 1964. While attending the university, Thelwell also acted as director of the Washington offices of the Student Nonviolent Coordinating Committee (1963–1964) and the Mississippi Freedom Democratic Party (1964–1965). After earning his MFA from the University of Massachusetts at Amherst in 1969, Thelwell founded and chaired

(1969–1975) the W. E. B. Du Bois Department of Afro-American Studies there. Thelwell also serves on the editorial boards of several scholarly journals, has written film scripts, including "Washington Incident" (1972) and "The Girl under the Lion" (1978), and has acted as an adviser for PBS/Blackside's "Eyes on the Prize II" and for PBS's "The American Experience."

Thelwell's writing, both fictional and nonfictional, is influenced both by his civil rights activism and by his youth in post-/neocolonial Jamaica. In his book prefaces, Thelwell identifies James *Baldwin, Richard *Wright, Sterling A. *Brown, Stokely *Carmichael, Lawrence Guyot, Chinua Achebe, and Andrew Salkey as being among those who have influenced him. His 1980 novel, *The Harder They Come*—inspired by Perry Henzel's film of the same title—is not a film novelization; it is more complexly layered and, as Thelwell states in the preface, it is the "novel from which the film might have been derived." Set in Jamaica during the 1940s and 1950s—a time of transition from colonial rule—the novel enables readers to view the culture from within: Thelwell writes in Jamaican dialect and uses local cultural narrative techniques and metaphors. He explores economic and racial oppression and the people's simultaneous resistance and survival, talent and promise gone awry, and the unraveling of personal and political ideals. Thelwell depicts Jamaican culture as distinct, not as a mimicry of colonial culture. He writes against those who portray the Caribbean and its people as subjected, not as subjects. Thelwell's narrative is not, however, romanticized, for he explores the interconnections among a colonial past and the racism, exploitation, and violence of the present.

His later book, *Duties, Pleasures, and Conflicts: Essays in Struggle* (1987)—a collection of short fiction and cultural criticism—is mostly about the American *civil rights movement. The essays and stories span the decades from the early 1960s to the late 1980s, both in terms of content and original publication dates. As in his novel, Thelwell's writing here is a form of social activism. Both books capture two different societies, American and Jamaican, in the process of transition and struggle. Thelwell places events in a historical continuum and reinforces the fact that not only does history influence people but that people also influence history. Thelwell shapes political and cultural perceptions through language. His writing is an act of black cultural nationalism: it underscores his belief that scholarship and activism are one and the same.   —Vivian M. May

There Is Confusion (1924), by Jessie Redmon *Fauset, was the author's first novel and was written in direct response to *Birthright* (1922), a novel by a white writer, T. S. Stribling. Fauset, along with renaissance writers Nella *Larsen and Walter *White, believed the *mulatto protagonist of Stribling's book to be unrealistic and felt that she was better "qualified" to write about the subject. Thus Fauset deliberately set about revising stereotypical representations of black life.

There Is Confusion centers on two families, the New York Marshalls and the Philadelphia Byes. In delineating their histories, Fauset stresses the significance of kinship and origins. She also shows the interconnectedness of the black and white races within these families in order to challenge the prevailing notion that black is evil and white is good. Making Peter Bye's "strain of white blood" responsible for all his faults reverses the conventional mulatto tales; however, her complicated genealogies sometimes confuse readers. Critics also agree that the book attempts to cover too much ground—too much time and space, too many characters, themes, and subplots.

A particular strength is its focus upon black women's psychological reactions to sexism and racism. Joanna Marshall—beautiful, ambitious, talented, confident, but snobbish—fights to overcome obstacles against her *race and *gender in her attempt to become a famous singer and dancer. Her attitude that with enough determination "colored" people can be anything they want helps her to achieve at least partial victories. Another woman, Maggie Ellersley, struggles against the same obstacles of race and gender but with the added struggle against classism. Maggie lives in a tenement with her laundress mother and slides further down the social scale when she marries a "common gambler," after her romance with Philip Marshall is thwarted by his sister Joanna. Eventually Maggie leaves her gambling husband, reunites with Philip, and marries him, but happiness is fleeting for Philip soon dies.

Many critics praise the novel for its revelation of middle-class attitudes; however, *There Is Confusion* is also important for its depiction of black women who question normative wife and mother roles by pursuing careers and self-reliance. Joanna believes women who give up everything for love are "poor silly sheep," and Maggie realizes she does not need anyone, not even a man. Maggie describes marriage as not very "interesting" or "picturesque"; and Joanna will not let it interfere with her other interests. By the end, however, Joanna marries Peter Bye and willingly forfeits her career for "pleasure" in "ordinary" things. Maggie, after Philip dies, still feels "bulwarked by the Marshall respectability." Some critics view the novel's conclusion as Fauset's capitulation to the very values she questions.

Rather than capitulating, however, Fauset seems to advocate men and women putting aside their individual desires and joining in love to fight racism. For Fauset, nothing was so difficult as the "problem of being colored in America." The didactic narrative voice that presses this thesis is a flaw in the novel, but the sentiment is a hallmark of the *Harlem Renaissance.

• Carolyn Wedin Sylvander, *Jessie Redmon Fauset, Black American Writer*, 1981. Ann duCille, *The Coupling Convention: Sex, Text, and Tradition in Black Women's Fiction*, 1993. Jacquelyn Y. McLendon, *The Politics of Color in the Fiction of Jessie Fauset and Nella Larsen*, 1995.
                    —Jacquelyn Y. McLendon

Third Life of Grange Copeland, The. Alice *Walker's first *novel, *The Third Life of Grange Copeland* (1970), is set in southern Georgia. A theme that dominates much of her writing (the survival whole of African Americans as individuals and as a race) is born within this epic story, setting the tone for Walker's entire body of work. This novel depicts the insurmountable difficulties that faced many uneducated and oppressed African Americans of the 1920s through the early 1960s—people whose hope faded and whose rage flared as each year's injustices fell upon them. Amidst the strife and struggle of life within a society dominated by racism, fear, and rage, three generations of an African American family struggle to survive.

The title character, Grange Copeland, is a sharecropper who beats his wife, Margaret, and has an extramarital affair with a prostitute named Josie. His son, *Brownfield Copeland, is a child whose father abandons him and whose mother commits suicide. At fifteen, Brownfield begins a search for his father that leads him into a world of lust and forbidden sex. At the Dew Drop Inn, he finds the beds of both Josie and her daughter, Lorene, are open to him. This sex triangle is broken, however, when Brownfield falls in love and marries Josie's niece, Mem.

Unfortunately, Brownfield follows his father's footsteps into the mire of the white man's sharecropping system. Feeling defeated and trapped, he turns his rage against his wife and children. Eventually, Mem grows tired of Brownfield's abuse and the unhealthy conditions in which they live. She forces Brownfield, at gun point, to get a factory job and returns to her profession as a school teacher. Mem succeeds in raising the family's standard of living until her health fails and Brownfield drags her back to the rat-infested shacks she despises. She takes a second step toward change but is defeated when Brownfield, jealous of her and fearful of any future she might be able to create, kills her.

Meanwhile, Grange returns from the North, marries Josie (for her money), and buys a farm. Together they raise Ruth, Mem's youngest daughter. Unlike his son, Grange has discovered that a cycle of hopelessness can only be broken if mistakes are faced with courage and life-building sacrifices for others are made. Based upon this belief, a bond of love develops between Grange and Ruth that distances Josie (who finds comfort in Brownfield's arms). Later, Brownfield gains legal custody of Ruth. Knowing that Brownfield's only objective is to destroy the possibility of wholeness within the child, Grange stops him. As the novel ends, Grange is hunted and killed for the murder of his only son.

This novel was not received with thunderous applause. Critics objected to the savage-like characterization of Brownfield. But like many African American women writers of the 1970s, Walker's purpose in telling this story is not to pick the sores of the African American male image. Her objective is to remove the blinders from the eyes of history so that the "real" stories of African American women's strengths and weaknesses can reveal themselves.

• Thomas Brooks, "The Third Life of Grange Copeland," in *Masterpieces of African-American Literature*, ed. Frank N. Magill, 1992, pp. 573–576. Robert James Butler, "Alice Walker's Vision of the South in *The Third Life of Grange Copeland*," *African American Review* 27.2 (Summer 1993): 195–204.

—Debra Walker King

THIRD WORLD PRESS. In 1967 Haki R. *Madhubuti (formerly Don L. Lee) invited fellow poets, Carolyn M. Rodgers and Johari *Amini, to help found a black *publishing company, Third World Press. The press's first books were collections of poetry by Rodgers and Amini.

Third World Press developed with the aid and encouragement of mentors such as Dudley *Randall (of *Broadside Press, Detroit), Margaret Taylor Goss *Burroughs and Charles Burroughs (of Chicago's DuSable Museum of African American History), and Hoyt *Fuller (of *Negro Digest* and *Black World Magazine*). The company continued to focus on poetry until the early 1970s, when it expanded to include prose and then children's literature.

African American literary history has been strengthened and enhanced by the contributions of Third World Press. In addition to publishing noted authors such as Sonia *Sanchez, Chancellor Williams, Ruby Dee, Gil *Scott-Heron, and Mari *Evans, the press has published several works by Pultizer Prize-winning author Gwendolyn *Brooks. Releases in the early 1990s cover a range of topics in various genres and include books by writer Pearl *Cleage and academic Joyce Ann Joyce.

As one of few independent black publishers, Third World Press remains committed to the publication of books that foster healthy development and sociopolitical activity among people of African descent.

• Donald Franklin Joyce, *Black Book Publishers in the United States*, 1991. *A Brief History of Third World Press*, 1994.

—Tiya Miles

This Child's Gonna Live (1969), the award-winning first novel by Sarah Elizabeth *Wright, was lauded as a prose poem–folk epic for its richness, texture, characterization, heroine of epic proportions, use of the regional vernacular, and graphic depictions of life in a small rural oyster farming community in the 1930s. This is the story of Mariah Upshur, a native of Tangierneck, Maryland, the wife of Jacob and the mother of Skeeter, Rabbit, and Gezee. It centers on her children—born, dead, and about-to-be-born—her husband, and her driving desire to move her children north to a better life to escape the land of death that engulfs them. This life on the eastern shore is rife with racism, *violence, brutality, dehumanizing incidents, interracial liaisons, hardships, illnesses (worms, tuberculosis), unrelenting poverty, oppression, calls on a gentle Jesus, dependence on a stern unyielding God, and the struggle of all to survive whole. Like Zora Neale *Hurston, Wright creates a detailed portrayal of a place, which leads to authenticity of language, culture, and community. Wright shows that both Black men and women are limited, measured, defined, and victimized by the same moral and sexual codes. Jacob, in an attempt to follow the code, becomes abusive and oppressive when his situation bars him from living up to the definition of what he should be and do. Mariah also suffers from the code and from an external definition of how she is to act, but she refuses to succumb. She takes hold of her life, defines herself, and with a passionate commitment strives for a better life without apologies or explanations—actions that in the 1990s label her a womanist. There is no evidence that things will change, but there is assurance that Mariah will continue to be her own person in spite of devotion to motherhood and family.

• Anne Z. Mickelson, "Winging Upward: Black Women: Sarah E. Wright, Toni Morrison, Alice Walker," in *Reaching Out: Sensitivity and Order in Recent American Fiction by Women*, 1979, pp. 112–124. Trudier Harris, "Three Black Women Writers and Humanism: A Folk Perspective," in *Black American Literature and Humanism*, ed. R. Baxter Miller, 1981, pp. 50–74. —Helen R. Houston

THOMAS, JOYCE CAROL (b. 1938), novelist, poet, playwright, and educator. Born in Ponca City, Oklahoma, Joyce Carol Thomas was the fifth child in a family of nine children. As an adult, Thomas moved to San Francisco, where she worked as a telephone operator during the day while raising four children and taking college courses at night. She received a bachelor's degree in Spanish from San Jose State University, and in 1967 she earned a master's degree in education from Stanford University. She has received several awards, including a Danforth Graduate Fellowship at the University of California at Berkeley, the Before Columbus American Book Award (for her first novel, *Marked by Fire*, 1982), and the Djerassi Fellowship for Creative Writing at Stanford University. She has taught creative writing, *black studies, and literature at California State University, Purdue University, and the University of Tennessee at Knoxville. In addition to lecturing at several universities and colleges in the United States, she has presented lectures, seminars, and workshops on creative writing and cultural studies in Nigeria and Haiti. Her work has appeared in a number of periodicals such as the as the *Black Scholar, American Poetry Review, Giant Talk, Yardbird Reader, Drum Voices*, and *Calafia*. She is a former editor of the West Coast black feminist magazine *Ambrosia*.

Before Thomas's first novel, *Marked by Fire*, was published she was known as a poet and playwright. As a poet, Thomas creates works that are commended for their serious themes, honest rendering of human experience, privileging of black people's customs, heritage, and language, and their believable personas. Her poems present vivid portraits of specific families and African American rituals. Her first forays into poetry are contained in three volumes, *Bittersweet* (1973), *Crystal Breezes* (1974), and *Blessing* (1975). In 1982, Thomas's earlier poems, along with new ones, were published in *Inside the Rainbow. Brown Honey in Broomwheat Tea* (1993) is Thomas's most recent volume of poetry. These lyrical poems continue to celebrate the beauty, heritage, and communality that make up a major part of the Thomas creative vision.

African American culture, heritage, and the need to pay homage to it also provide direction for Thomas's fictional canon, which to date includes six novels. Black children, their families, the black community, and the larger world's impingement on them is a key theme in the novels. Although Thomas's novels are accessible to juvenile audiences, and this is how they are usually classified, they offer much to adult readers. The award-winning *Marked by Fire*, the first novel of Thomas's Abyssinia series, signals its author's attention to the importance of community in black people's lives. Her other novels are *Bright Shadow* (1983), *Water Girl* (1986), *The Golden Pasture* (1986), *Journey* (1988), and *When the Nightingale Sings* (1992).

In her fiction and poetry, Joyce Carol Thomas is an important writer whose work is a significant contribution to the African American women's literary tradition.

• Charles P. Toombs, "Joyce Carol Thomas," in *DLB*, vol. 33, *Afro-American Fiction Writers after 1955*, eds. Thadious M. Davis and Trudier Harris, 1984, pp. 245–250. —Charles P. Toombs

THOMAS, LORENZO (b. 1944), poet, literary and music critic, and educator with roots in the Black Arts movement. Lorenzo Thomas emerged from the *Black Arts movement as one of the most prolific poets of the 1970s. Though best-known for his *poetry, he also actively promotes the understanding and appreciation of all African American cultural forms, particularly *music. Born in Panama to Herbert Hamilton Thomas and Luzmilda Gilling Thomas, Thomas immigrated to New York in 1948. As a native Spanish speaker, Thomas traces his interest in literature to his struggle to learn English in order to fit in with his schoolmates. While attending Queens College in the 1960s, Thomas joined the Umbra workshop, one of several experimental literary groups from which the Black Arts movement grew. Here, Thomas developed a poetic style marked by a wariness of the media and mass culture, pride in the African heritage and history, and a strong sense of political engagement. While Thomas also works powerfully in the lyric mode, such works as "Framing the Sunrise," "Historiography," and "The Bathers" typify his ability to combine heterogeneous source material into a comment on modern life. Underlying the often fragmented form of his poetry is Thomas's belief in the universal qualities of the experience of all people of African descent.

Thomas joined the United States Navy in 1968, serving as a military advisor in Vietnam in 1971. He reflects on the experience of war and the return to civilian life in such poems as "Wonders" and "Envoy." In 1973 he left New York to become writer in residence at Texas Southern University and has lived in the Southwest ever since. From his base in Texas, Thomas expanded his artistic range and increased his work with African American musical forms. He conducted writing workshops at Houston's Black Arts Center from 1974 to 1976 and was one of the first black authors to work in artists-in-the-schools programs in Texas, Oklahoma, and Arkansas. *Blues Music in Arkansas* (1982), cowritten with Louis Guida and Cheryl Cohen, is a product of his association with these programs. He was also an organizer for the Juneteenth Blues Festival. He remains active at both the grassroots and institutional levels, conducting readings, hosting music programs and writing for regional publications as well as working with the Texas Commission of Arts and Humanities and the Cultural Arts Council of Houston. He currently teaches at the University of Houston-Downtown.

Thomas's major collections of poetry are *Chances Are Few* (1979); *The Bathers* (1981), which contains uncollected early work as well as the text from three early publications; *Fit Music* (1972); *Dracula* (1973); and *Framing the Sunrise* (1975). His work also appears in *anthologies including *Black Fire* (1968), *New Black Voices* (1972), *The Poetry of Black America* (1973), *Jambalaya* (1974), *American Poetry Since 1970: Up Late* (1987) and *Erotique Noire* (1992). In prose, Thomas has published literary and music criticism for both academic and general audiences. As yet, little criticism has been published on Thomas's work.

• Charles H. Rowell, "'Between the Comedy of Matters and the Ritual Workings of Man': An Interview with Lorenzo Thomas," *Callaloo* 4.1–3 (Feb.–Oct. 1981): 19–35. Tom Dent, "Lorenzo Thomas," in *DLB*, vol. 41, *Afro-American Poets since 1955*, eds. Trudier Harris and Thadious M. Davis, 1985, pp. 315–326.
                                                —Jennifer H. Poulos

THOMAS, PIRI (b. 1928), autobiographer, essayist, playwright, poet, filmmaker, and lecturer. Piri Thomas was born Juan Pedro Tomás, in New York City's Spanish Harlem on 30 September 1928 of Puerto Rican and Cuban parentage. His early life was marked by involvement in *violence and drugs, culminating in his arrest and imprisonment for attempted armed robbery. Thomas served seven years (1950–1956) of a five-to-fifteen year sentence. Upon his release from prison, he began working in prison and drug rehabilitation programs in New York City and has subsequently written three volumes of *autobiography, a collection of *short stories for adolescent readers, and a play. Today Thomas travels, presenting a program entitled Unity Among Us, stressing human dignity and people's relationship to the earth.

In 1967 Thomas published *Down These Mean Streets*, a chronicle of his youth. In crude but forceful language, *Down These Mean Streets* recounts Thomas's life on the streets, his experiences with sex, drugs, and crime, and his groping toward empowerment and self-worth through the expression of machismo, an aggressive code of male behavior derived from Hispanic culture.

While noting the autobiography's stylistic flaws, critics praised *Down These Mean Streets* for its powerful depiction of the hellish conditions of inner-city life and hailed Thomas as a chronicler of a previously "silenced" group—the negritos, or black Puerto Ricans, of Spanish Harlem. Thomas was compared favorably with James *Baldwin and Claude *Brown as a writer documenting his successful struggle to achieve personhood despite the dehumanizing conditions of minorities in America.

Savior, Savior, Hold My Hand (1972) recounts how Piri Thomas, newly released from prison, strives to rebuild his life. He converts to Christianity, works with street youths, seeks employment, marries, and starts a family. Critics generally expressed disappointment with *Savior, Savior Hold My Hand* for lacking the emotional intensity of Thomas's first book. *Seven Long Times* (1974), Thomas's account of his prison years, was criticized by some as a tepid retelling of events more forcefully recorded in *Down These Mean Streets* but praised by others as a testament to the human will to survive and as a call for prison reform. Thomas's collection of stories for young adults, *Stories from El Barrio*, appeared in 1978, to mixed reviews.

Piri Thomas continues to write, work in *film production, and present his message of self-worth to varied audiences. He will probably be remembered, however, for *Down These Mean Streets*, the one volume of his autobiographical trilogy currently in print. The book provides readers with the satisfaction of seeing Thomas escape from the horror of his early life—a story often told in African American autobiography and fiction—but it speaks a note of warning, as well. More than twenty-five years after its publication, *Down These Mean Streets* reminds us that the conditions under which Thomas grew up are today the same or worse for thousands of young Americans. Tragically, many of them, unlike Piri Thomas, will not be able to leave the street and create new lives.

• "Thomas, Piri," in *CA*, vol. 73–76, ed. Frances C. Locher, 1978, pp. 604–605. "Piri Thomas," in *Contemporary Literary Criticism*, vol. 17, ed. Sharon C. Gunton, 1981, pp. 497–502.
                                                —David L. Dudley

Thomas and Beulah (1986), which won the Pulitzer Prize for poetry in 1987, is the most well-known work by U.S. poet laureate *Rita Dove. Loosely based on the lives of Dove's maternal grandparents, this volume of poems opens with instructions that "These poems tell two sides of a story and are meant to be read in sequence." This chronological order gives the poems a novelistic sense of narrative. Details from the chronology included at the end of the poems tell us that Thomas was born in Wartrace, Tennessee, in 1900, and Beulah was born four years later in Rockmart, Georgia. Beulah soon moved to Akron, Ohio, and Thomas met her there almost twenty years later. They marry, have four daughters over the next ten years, and live out their lives in this midwestern town with an African American population of fewer than five percent. The cover sports a photograph of Dove's grandparents, giving a sense of the ordinary people whose quotidian lives will be fleetingly sketched within.

Although they live together for decades, the poem sequences reveal lives that barely intersect, more often the two moving in their own worlds. For example, when Beulah is pregnant for the third time, Thomas plans what he would teach the child if the child were a male. Thomas's poems have revealed so little interest in his children, that his desire for a son whom he can teach to be a man leaps out. Beulah's life, on the other hand, is filled with her daughters.

In two linked poems, Dove continues to explore the disconnection among family. Dove illustrates

Thomas's main concern by naming the poem on his daughter's marriage "Variation on Gaining a Son." The poem begins with his focus on his daughter and the "shy angle" of her head, his ignorance of her life—and women's lives—revealed in his wonder: "where did they all learn it?" As he watches her with her bridegroom, Thomas forges a familiar relation from his empathetic response to the groom's fear, nervousness, and wonder. Dove skillfully connects this poem with one in Beulah's sequence, reversing father and daughter. In "Promises" Beulah recalls not her groom, but her father and the advice he whispered during the ceremony. Although her father, unlike Thomas with his daughter, may be focused on wishing her well, his words strike her as hypocrisy. Fathers and daughters, wives and husbands, all inhabit perspectives separated by lack of understanding and common interest. Yet the volume also mediates the sadness of disconnection with the richness of individual lives, imagined as well as lived.

• Helen Vendler, "In the Zoo of the New," *New York Review of Books*, 23 October 1986, 47–52. Ekaterini Georgoudaki, "Rita Dove: Crossing Boundaries," *Callaloo* 14.2 (Spring 1991): 419–433. Maxine Sample, "Dove's *Thomas and Beulah*," *Explicator* 52.4 (Summer 1994): 251–253.

—Maggie Sale

THOMPSON, ERA BELL (1906–1986), editor, journalist, and autobiographer. Born 10 August 1906 in Des Moines, Iowa, Era Bell Thompson grew up in Driscoll, North Dakota on her family's farm. Her contact with African Americans limited by regional population composition, she became fully aware of African American life, culture, and problems only after reaching adulthood.

Thompson attended North Dakota State University in Grand Forks, where she wrote for the university paper. Ill, Thompson left the university, and after recovering went to Chicago, working at a magazine, proofreading, writing advertising copy, and reviewing African Americans' books—exposing herself to the artistic outpourings of African Americans for the first time. She was particularly moved by W. E. B. *Du Bois's The Dark Princess* (1928), which exalted "Negroes" and "blackness." Thompson later moved to Minneapolis, where she wrote features, advertising copy, and straight news for the *Bugle*, a weekly.

Encouraged and subsidized by Dr. Riley, a white minister interested in educating African Americans, Thompson returned to North Dakota State and received her degree in 1933 from Dawn College in Iowa, where she had followed Dr. Riley, who had been elected college president, and his family.

Returning to Chicago, Thompson continued her studies in journalism at Northwestern University and worked as a senior typist at the Department of Public Works, where she produced the humorous newspaper *Giggle Sheet*. Thompson later worked for the Illinois and United States Employment Services, where she deplored interracial, *class, *gender, and religious prejudice, recognizing the fundamental similarities Americans shared and looking toward a time when the "chasm" would disappear.

Thompson obtained a fellowship from the New-berry Library and published her autobiography, *American Daughter* (1946), a humorous recollection of her past for which she received the Patron Saint's Award (1968). Launched in her literary career, Thompson worked for the *Negro Digest* as an editor (1947) and for *Ebony* as associate editor (1947–1951), co-managing editor (1951–1964), and international editor (1964–1986).

In 1954, Thompson published *Africa: Land of My Fathers*, recounting her attempt to comprehend and reconnect with the land of her "forefathers." In 1963 she coedited *White on Black*, a collection of articles written by whites reflecting their views of African Americans. Thompson's articles can be found in *Phylon*, "Negro Publications and the Writer" (1950), *Negro Digest*, "Girl Gangs of Harlem" (1951), and *Ebony*. These include; "Love Comes to Mahalia" (1964); "Instant Hair" (1965); "What Weaker Sex?" (1966), which denounces men's treatment of women, reflecting her feminist leanings; and "The Vaughan Family: A Tale of Two Continents" (1975), which recounts the maintenance of contact between African and American descendants of a former slave for over a century.

Thompson received honorary doctorates from Morningside College (1965) and the University of North Dakota (1969), was inducted into the North Dakota Hall of Fame, and received the State's Theodore Roosevelt Rough Rider Award (1976).

Thompson died 29 December 1986. Her literary career reflects her quest to understand her people and their heritage as well as to encourage an understanding and cooperation between all Americans as human beings.

• Lorraine Elena Roses and Ruth Elizabeth Randolph, *Harlem Renaissance and Beyond: Literary Biographies of 100 Black Women Writers, 1900–1945*, 1990, pp. 321–352.

—Janet M. Roberts

THURMAN, WALLACE (1902–1934), novelist, editor, poet, playwright, and literary critic. After leaving his native Salt Lake City, Utah, for the University of Southern California, Wallace Thurman established the *Outlet*, a magazine similar to those being published as part of the artistic renaissance then blossoming in Harlem, New York. When it failed after just six months, he himself headed for Harlem, arriving in September 1925. The younger Thurman became a scathing critic of the bourgeois attitudes that motivated the *Harlem Renaissance old guards like Alain *Locke and W. E. B. *Du Bois, charging that they professed their intellectual and artistic freedom while seeking white approval with slanted portrayals of African Americans. Eventually, he was able to articulate clearly, if not achieve completely, the aesthetic principles of the Harlem Renaissance from the late 1920s to the 1930s.

Thurman's *New Republic* essay, "Negro Artists and the Negro" (31 August 1927), decries the popular tendency to reduce African American *music, fiction, *poetry, and painting to the level of a fad presented in a "conventional manner about the 'best people.'" He claimed that many of the artists receiving praise from white and black critics alike were more interested in sociology and propaganda than art and, with few exceptions such as Langston *Hughes and Eric *Walrond, refused to create forms best suited for candid African American expression. Thurman published the experimental journal *Fire!!* (1926), which "was purely artistic in intent and conception," to address this problem. Contributors such as Langston Hughes, Zora Neale *Hurston, Arna *Bontemps, and Thurman himself were mainly interested in depicting African Americans "who still retained some individual race qualities and who were not totally white American in every respect save skin color." When the magazine folded after only one issue and left him with a thousand dollar debt (that took four years to discharge), he began the longer-running journal *Harlem, A Forum of Negro Life* (1928), which eventually suffered a similar financial fate. Undaunted, Thurman went on to write two novels. The *Blacker the Berry* (1929) addresses a variety of controversial themes including homosexuality, intraracial prejudice, abortion, and ethnic conflict between African Americans and Caribbean Americans. The satiric *Infants of the Spring* (1932) is the only renaissance novel that evaluates the renaissance itself and the judgment rendered is harsh and unsparing. A third novel, *The Interne* (1932), written in collaboration with white Abraham L. Furman, is an exposé of unethical behavior at City Hospital on Welfare Island (now Roosevelt Island), where Thurman ultimately died. In his short life, Thurman was a prolific author whose works include published *essays, screenplays, poetry, and short fiction.

While Thurman had an exceptional mind and was regarded as the spokesman for the younger generation of Harlem artists—especially by Langston Hughes who in The *Big Sea* (1940) marvels at his voracious reading ability—his bohemian behavior and personality tended to undermine his artistic ability. Many of his literary efforts failed not because they lacked merit but because they lacked funds, which he tended to dissipate in a decadent lifestyle imitative of literary counterparts from Greenwich Village. Even his greatest financial success, *Harlem* (1929), a play produced in collaboration with William Jourdan Rapp, editor of *True Story* magazine, left him in debt. Significantly, whenever Thurman became strapped for money, his high artistic standards quickly evaporated. For example, Thurman ghostwrote stories for the lowbrow *True Story* magazine under such pseudonyms as Ethel Belle Mandrake and Patrick Casey.

Thurman's greatest literary shortcoming was his inability to sustain serious criticism of white America. Indeed, in an essay in the *Independent* (24, September 1927) magazine, Thurman goes so far as to claim that whites could probably write the African American story better than African Americans because the whites could be more objective about it. Thus, even while he sharply castigates African Americans for assimilating into the American mainstream to the point of losing their unique identity, he cannot imagine that the fear of dark skin traditionally exhibited by whites might also render them unobjective in their portrayal of African Americans. Essentially, then, Thurman's works reflect the struggle during the

Harlem Renaissance to articulate an African American aesthetic while coping with the self-hatred that always hinders this endeavor. So far there is no biography or full-length critical study of his literary achievements.

• Dorothy West, "Elephant's Dance: A Memoir of Wallace Thurman," *Black World* 20 (Nov. 1970): 77–85. Mae Gwendolyn Henderson, "Portrait of Wallace Thurman," in *The Harlem Renaissance Remembered*, ed. Arna Bontemps, 1972, pp. 147–170. Arthur P. Davis, *From the Dark Tower: Afro-American Writers 1900 to 1960*, 1974. David Levering Lewis, *When Harlem Was in Vogue*, 1979. Daniel Walden, "The Canker Galls . . . , or, the Short Promising Life of Wallace Thurman," in *The Harlem Renaissance Re-Examined*, ed. Victor A. Kramer, 1988, pp. 201–211.

—SallyAnn H. Ferguson

TILLMAN, KATHERINE DAVIS CHAPMAN (1870–?), poet, novelist, playwright, and essayist of the post-Reconstruction era. Born on 19 February 1870 in Mound City, Illinois, Katherine Tillman began writing as a child. At the age of eighteen she published her first poem, "Memory," in the *Christian Recorder*. Tillman attended the State University of Louisville in Kentucky and Wilberforce University in Ohio. After her marriage to the Reverend G. M. Tillman, she continued writing for the publications of the AME Church, especially the *A.M.E. Church Review*, which serialized her two novellas—*Beryl Weston's Ambition: The Story of an Afro-American Girl's Life* (1893) and *Clancy Street* (1898–1899). The *Review* also published her *essays on famous African American women, poetry, Aleksandr Pushkin, and Alexandre Dumas. The *A.M.E. Book Concern published *Recitations* (1902), a collection of verse, and three *dramas—*Aunt Betsy's Thanksgiving* (n.d.), *Thirty Years of Freedom* (1902), and *Fifty Years of Freedom, or From Cabin to Congress* (1910).

Tillman's career demonstrates that African American women were very much a part of black literary culture during the post-Reconstruction era (1877–1915). Women writers like Frances Ellen Watkins *Harper, Amelia E. *Johnson, and Emma Dunham *Kelley defined roles for black women not only as wives and mothers but also as professionals and community leaders. In doing so these writers used literature to appropriate, critique, and revise the dominant conventions of *race, *gender, and *class. Even more important, African American women writers, like their male counterparts, employed literature to explore the possibilities of self-definition and U.S. citizenship at a time when such prerogatives invited racist violence.

• Claudia Tate, introduction to *The Works of Katherine Davis Chapman Tillman*, 1991. Claudia Tate, *Domestic Allegories of Political Desire: The Black Heroine's Text at the Turn of the Century*, 1992.

—Claudia Tate

Tituba of Salem Village (1964) is a novel for young adults by Ann *Petry. Before this novel, Arthur Miller's *The Crucible* (1953) was the only major work to explore the Salem witch trials and to include an analysis of Tituba Indian, an African Barbadian slave indicted of witchcraft and, in 1692, sentenced to hang. Miller's impressions of Tituba's personality and character, however, are familiar *stereotypes.

Unlike Miller, Petry examines Tituba's life history and arrives at more convincing interpretations of her character. In Petry's version, Tituba appears perceptive yet sometimes naive; courageous yet a victim; an outsider yet a survivor; a slave yet a heroine. The novel moves chronologically, emphasizing her servitude in Barbados, Boston, and Salem Village. Petry includes people whose words and actions affected Tituba's life—John Indian, her wise and devoted husband; Susanna Endicott, her uninhibited mistress in Barbados who sells her and John to raise cash to pay a gambling debt; Reverend Samuel Parris, her owner in Salem Village who prays and lectures about a loving God but votes to hang Tituba when people in the community accuse her of witchcraft; and Abigail, Parris's adolescent niece who first instigates the witch scare that ensnarls Tituba. The novel concludes with dramatizations of the arrests and trials of Tituba, Goody Good, and Goody Osborne, and the events that lead to the two women's deaths and Tituba's pardon.

Tituba emerges in this novel as a rounded character whose complexity derives from her words, thoughts, actions, and deeds within a dialogic context of circumstances surrounding her life as a slave and a foreigner. To paraphrase Petry, from her essay "The Common Ground" (*Horn Book Reflections*, 1969), which discusses the juvenile work, Tituba's history is retold across the centuries in her voice and the voices of her husband, owners, and accusers.

Following its publication, criticism of *Tituba* appeared mostly in library journals, newspapers, and popular magazines. Only after the 1970s did critics begin to analyze the work in scholarly journals and books. While critics praise the book for its absorbing story and convincingly human characters, their classifications differ. Throughout the 1960s critics applauded the book as biography for adolescents. In the 1970s critics noted the influence of history and called it a historical novel. In the 1990s critics began to reread *Tituba* as a novel that evolves from historical tidbit, similar to how Toni *Morrison created *Beloved* (1987).

• Lloyd W. Brown, "Tituba of Barbados and the American Conscience: Historical Perspectives in Arthur Miller and Ann Petry," *Carribean Studies* 13.4 (Jan. 1974): 118–126. Robert E. Morsberger, "The Further Transformation of Tituba," *New England Quarterly*, 48.3 (Sept. 1974): 456–458. Hazel Arnett Ervin, *Ann Petry: A Bio-Bibliography*, 1993. Trudier Harris, "Before the Stigma of Race: Authority and Witchcraft in Ann Petry's *Tituba of Salem Village*" in *Recovered Writers, Recovered Texts*, ed. Dolan Hubbard, forthcoming 1997.

—Hazel Arnett Ervin

TODD CLIFTON, moreso than any other black male in the Harlem episode of Ralph *Ellison's *Invisible Man* (1952), seems programmed for success in mainstream America. He is personable (*Ras the Destroyer sees in him an ancient prince), intelligent, handsome (the narrator tells us that he had that "velvet-over-stone, granite-over-bone" look), and charismatic (he leads the black youths of Harlem);

and he has managed to bridge the gap between his black world, Harlem, and the mainstream by working for the Brotherhood (an organization that represents the Communist Party in the novel). Yet this progressive Black male is shot down on the street like a common criminal—by a white officer who does not see Todd Clifton, the promising Black youth.

In the novel, Todd Clifton is a foil for the narrator to demonstrate the narrator's lack of vision and insight. From the structure of the novel it is obvious that long before the narrator realizes the duplicity of the Brotherhood, Clifton does, and, as a result, leaves the organization. In a brutal fight with the narrator, Ras is about to cut Clifton's throat, but he is afraid that in killing Clifton he might be killing a future king, so he pleads with Clifton to leave the Brotherhood and join his nationalistic group in its liberation struggle. Immediately after the altercation, Clifton thanks the narrator for saving his life, and the narrator responds: "you didn't have to worry. He [Ras] wouldn't have killed his king." The narrator then says Clifton "turned and looked at me as though he thought I meant it." Although the narrator does not realize it, Ras has affected Clifton profoundly, for Todd's response to the narrator is that they will have to watch Ras because "on the inside . . . [Ras] is strong." The narrator assumes that Todd is referring to Ras's infiltration of the Brotherhood. A more reasonable interpretation is that Clifton means that while outwardly Ras is disorganized and chaotic, internally he is a very strong individual who because of his inner resolve will be an extremely difficult opponent.

Both Clifton and the narrator see Ras as being "outside of history," outside the mainstream, but Clifton admits that in order for Blacks to maintain their sanity they have to "plunge outside of history." That Clifton has come to see the Brotherhood as a negative force is evident in his behavior. In the next brawl with Ras, instead of beating Ras's men he beats up the white boys in the Brotherhood, his own men, pretending it was accidental, and shortly thereafter leaves the party. Clifton's selling the *Sambo dolls is symbolic of his own behavior in particular and Blacks in general. In the same way that he becomes the puppeteer manipulating the doll, the Brotherhood has become the puppeteer and he has been the organization's puppet.

—Ralph Reckley, Sr.

TOLSON, MELVIN B. (1898–1966), poet, novelist, playwright, newspaper columnist, and educator. The son of a Methodist preacher and a seamstress, Melvin Beaunorus Tolson was born in Moberley, Missouri, and grew up in several small midwestern towns. His father had an eighth-grade education and was skeptical of the value of college, but he instilled in his son a strong desire for knowledge. Tolson attended Fisk University from 1918 to 1919 and then transferred as a freshman to Lincoln University in Pennsylvania, where he graduated, receiving a BA with honors in June of 1923.

While at Lincoln University he met Ruth Southall;

they married on 29 January 1922 and had four children. After graduating Tolson took a job as an instructor of English and speech at Wiley College in Marshall, Texas, where he remained for seventeen years. In addition to his teaching duties he coached the junior varsity football team, directed the theater club, cofounded the black intercollegiate Southern Association of Dramatic and Speech Arts, and organized the Wiley Forensic Society, a debating club that earned a national reputation by breaking the color barrier throughout the country and meeting with unprecedented success. Tolson also taught at Langston University in Oklahoma.

Working to support his family and becoming passionately involved in his projects, Tolson nevertheless reserved time for the arts. As a boy he enjoyed painting but was forced to give up that endeavor when his mother disapproved of a bohemian artist who expressed interest in taking the child to Paris. Turning to poetry, Tolson found an appropriate outlet for his creativity. In 1912 he published his first poem, "The Wreck of the *Titanic*," in the local newspaper of Oskaloosa, Iowa, where he was then living with his family. Several years later he was senior class poet at Lincoln High School in Kansas City, Missouri, and published two short stories and two poems in the school yearbook.

Tolson's first significant poem was published in 1939. "Dark Symphony" won the national poetry contest sponsored by the American Negro Exposition and was subsequently published in *Atlantic Monthly*, attracting the attention of an editor who would eventually publish Tolson's first collection of verse, *Rendezvous with America*, in 1944. This work was widely reviewed and generally well received.

During the academic year of 1931 to 1932 Tolson received a fellowship to pursue an MA in comparative literature at Columbia University, where he came into contact with the major figures of the *Harlem Renaissance. Taking as the subject of his master's thesis the Harlem writers, Tolson was inspired by the achievements of those around him and resolved to contribute to the legacy black writers were establishing. While at Columbia Tolson was working on another collection of poetry, published posthumously in 1979 as *A Gallery of Harlem Portraits*. Both works reflect the early influence of Walt Whitman, Edgar Lee Masters, and Langston *Hughes and highlight Tolson's proletarian convictions and optimistic spirit; his later interest in the theme of black dignity is already obvious, as is his celebration of multiracial diversity in America.

Between the years 1937 and 1944, Tolson also contributed a weekly *newspaper column to the *Washington Tribune*. Entitled "Caviar and Cabbage," the columns contain Tolson's views on race and class and have been collected in *Caviar and Cabbage: Selected Columns by Melvin B. Tolson* (1982), edited by Robert M. Farnsworth.

By the mid-1940s Tolson had written several novels and plays, all of which remain unpublished; several have been lost entirely. He was, however, gaining success as a poet. Named the poet laureate of

Liberia, he published *Libretto for the Republic of Liberia* in 1953. The work marks Tolson's increasing poetic ambition. The *Libretto* is long, complex, and allusive, in places a surreal dream-vision. Allen Tate, in the preface, commends Tolson not only for assimilating the modernist tradition but for contributing to it.

As Tolson began to adopt the tenets of modernism, he was compared stylistically with T. S. Eliot, Ezra Pound, and Hart Crane, though he shared little of the fame and popularity they enjoyed in his lifetime. Nor did he share their vision. Instead of looking backward to the decaying civilizations of the European past, Tolson embraced Africa and its rich, vital heritage. He maintained that artists must follow the direction of their imaginations to find freedom, and Tolson finally found poetic freedom in the people of Harlem.

While working on revisions of *Libretto*, Tolson returned to some of the poetry he had written in Harlem. Those poems became the inspiration for an epic of Harlem that Tolson intended to dramatize black life in America. He designed the project to have five books, each representing a stage of the African American diaspora, but he only lived to complete one book, a collection entitled *Harlem Gallery: Book I, The Curator* (1965), told from the point of view of the curator. He shares vignettes, conversations, and philosophy, commenting on daily occurrences in his art gallery and facilitating a discussion of the role of the black artist in white America.

This work demonstrates Tolson's poetic maturity as well as his unique ability to combine the high formality of modernism with the bluesy, oral quality of African American storytelling. The work is linguistically precise and stylistically complex, but the lyrical quality of the poem never suffers, and critics placed it in a category with *The Waste Land, The Bridge* and *Paterson*.

The first volume of *Harlem Gallery* was introduced by Karl Shapiro, whose remark that Tolson "writes and thinks in Negro" contributed to the controversy over Tolson's place in poetry. His work was not well received during the 1960s, largely because members of the *Black Aesthetic movement accused Tolson of posturing for a white audience and condemned his verse as too esoteric for the masses. Tolson's poetry indeed shares both the assimilationist tendencies Tate praised in his introduction to the *Libretto* and the distinctly African qualities Shapiro celebrated in his foreward to *Harlem Gallery*, making it difficult to classify him as either a modernist or a writer in the African American folk tradition. The publication of Robert Farnsworth's definitive biography in 1984, however, sparked renewed interest in Tolson; his work is now valued for the ethnic perspective it lends to modernism, and his poetry is now more frequently anthologized.

Melvin B. Tolson died in 1966, several months after being named to the Avalon Chair in humanities at Tuskegee Institute and receiving grants from the National Institute and American Academy of Arts and Letters and the Rockefeller Foundation. These honors indicate that *Harlem Gallery* had secured him public recognition in his lifetime and an established reputation that continues to grow.

• Joy Flasch, *Melvin B. Tolson*, 1972. Robert M. Farnsworth, *Melvin B. Tolson, 1898–1966: Plain Talk and Poetic Prophecy*, 1984. Michael Berube, "Masks, Margins, and African American Modernism: Melvin Tolson's *Harlem Gallery*," *PMLA* 105 (Jan. 1990): 57–69. Melvin B. Tolson, Jr., "The Poetry of Melvin B. Tolson," *World Literature Today* 64 (Summer 1990): 395–400. Aldon L. Nielsen, "Melvin B. Tolson and the Deterritorialization of Modernism," *African American Review* 26 (Summer 1992): 241–255.   —Elizabeth Ann Beaulieu

TOOMER, JEAN (1894–1967), poet, dramatist, novelist, essayist, and philosopher. Jean Toomer is the author of *Cane* (1923) and a bridge between two distinct but contemporaneous groups of American writers. The first group consists of authors such as Langston *Hughes and Zora Neale *Hurston whose writings define the scope of the *New Negro or *Harlem Renaissance. The second group consists of such writers as Waldo Frank and Gorham Munson who dominated the literary scene of Greenwich Village and whose writings are characterized by experimentalism and political liberalism. Toomer was a comrade-in-letters to Frank and Munson, and a distant but influential figure to Hughes and Hurston who admired the achievement of *Cane* (1923), the three-part collection of sketches, poetry, and drama that established a standard for the writers of the New Negro movement and that conveyed the profound search for meaning at the core of American modernism.

The only child of Nina Pinchback and Nathan Toomer, Nathan Pinchback Toomer was born on 29 March 1894 in Washington, D.C. Five years later Nina Pinchback divorced Nathan Toomer and returned to the home of her parents, Nina Hethorn Pinchback and P. B. S. Pinchback, former lieutenant governor of Louisiana during Reconstruction. After Nina Pinchback's death in 1909, the Pinchbacks assumed full responsibility for the rearing of their grandson. Toomer was encouraged in his literary pursuits by his grandmother, to whom *Cane* is dedicated, and by his uncle Bismarck Pinchback.

Educated in the public but segregated schools of Washington, Toomer graduated from Paul Laurence Dunbar High School in 1914. Between 1914 and 1919 he explored a spectrum of intellectual interests and attended such institutions as the University of Wisconsin, the American College of Physical Training in Chicago, the University of Chicago, and New York University. In 1919 Toomer returned to Washington with neither a college degree nor an income. However, in the previous year Toomer had completed "Bona and Paul," the first of several stories in *Cane*. Although without firm prospects, Toomer's career as a writer was slowly assuming significance. In 1920 during a sojourn in Greenwich Village where he established friendships with Frank and Munson, Nathan Pinchback Toomer assumed the name of Jean Toomer. In search of a means to solidify his emerging identity as a writer, Toomer adopted the new name shortly after his immersion in the literary life of Greenwich Village and after reading Romain Rolland's *Jean Christophe* (1904) in whose protagonist Toomer had glimpsed his own potentiality as an artist.

More than a change of names, Toomer's acceptance in the summer of 1921 of a two-month appointment as acting principal at the Sparta Agricultural and Industrial Institute in Sparta, Georgia, provided him with the experiences that forged a new identity in art. Visiting the South for the first time, Toomer was captivated by the landscape of Georgia, its complex history of *slavery and segregation, and the impact of African Americans upon southern culture. Enthralled by the beauty of African American vernacular culture, Toomer also detected its dissolution in the historic migration of African Americans from the South to the North and in the enlarging reach of industrialization.

Returning to Washington, Toomer began writing the masterpiece that he would later spurn but upon which his reputation as a writer remains secure. By December 1921 he had written "Kabnis," the drama that comprises the third section of *Cane*. One year later he had completed the experimental work that is a record of his discovery of his southern heritage, an homage to a folk culture that he believed was evanescent, and an exploration of the forces that he believed were the foundation for the spiritual fragmentation of his generation. With the assistance of Frank, who wrote the foreword to the first edition, Toomer's first and most important book was published in the spring of 1923 by Horace Liveright. Although it was praised by reviewers, *Cane* sold less than five hundred copies, casting a shadow on Toomer's triumphant literary debut.

After *Cane*, Toomer did not return to the setting that inspired the only book of fiction published during his lifetime. While the search for wholeness remains a central theme in Toomer's large but uneven canon, African American life is never again the subject. The later writings bear the influence of Georgei I. Gurdjieff, the Russian mystic and psychologist whose theories of human development Toomer accepted and promoted as gospel. Beginning in the year of *Cane*'s publication and continuing with few interruptions until his death on 30 March 1967, Toomer's commitment to Gurdjieff's theories had disastrous consequences for his writings. In his unpublished writings, Toomer creates situations that are little more than propaganda for Gurdjieff's theories. In these works one discovers protagonists who bear resemblances to Toomer himself and who function as teachers to characters who possess only a vague awareness of their spiritual potentiality. This regrettable mixture of cant and vanity explains Toomer's growing obscurity after 1923 for publishers foresaw only bankruptcy in such literary ventures. While Toomer continued to write until a few years before his death, he never again produced a work comparable to *Cane*.

Many African American writers claim Toomer as a literary ancestor. The nuanced portrayal of African

American women in *Cane* is clearly discernible in Alice *Walker's *Meridian* (1976) and Gloria *Naylor's *The *Women of Brewster Place* (1980). Toomer's philosophical treatment of identity and race in both *Cane* and *Essentials* (1931), a collection of aphorisms that express his philosophy of life, have influenced the approaches to hybridity in Michael S. *Harper's *Nightmare Begins Responsibility* (1975) and Charles R. *Johnson's *Oxherding Tale* (1982).

Physically white but racially mixed, Toomer did not define himself as an African American but as an American. Toomer's lifelong effort to transcend what he regarded as the narrow divisions of race is fully explored in *Essentials* (1931) and the epic *The Blue Meridian* (1936). Toomer's position on race is the principal reason for the absence of racial themes in the writings produced during and after his discovery of Gurdjieff, as well as for his conscious disassociation from *Cane*: the work that has earned him a central place in the African American literary tradition.

• Darwin T. Turner, *In A Minor Chord: Three Afro-American Writers and Their Search for Identity*, 1971. Nellie Y. McKay, *Jean Toomer, Artist*, 1984. Cynthia Earl Kerman and Richard Eldridge, *The Lives of Jean Toomer, A Hunger for Wholeness*, 1987. Therman B. O'Daniel, ed., *Jean Toomer: A Critical Evaluation*, 1988. Charles T. Davis, "Jean Toomer and the South: Region and Race as Elements Within a Literary Imagination," in *Black Is the Color of the Cosmos*, ed. Henry Louis Gates, Jr., 1989, pp. 83–119. Rudolph P. Byrd, *Jean Toomer's Years With Gurdjieff: Portrait of an Artist, 1923–1936*, 1990. Robert B. Jones, *Jean Toomer and the Prison-house of Thought: A Phenomenology of the Spirit*, 1993. Charles R. Larson, *Invisible Darkness: Jean Toomer and Nella Larsen*, 1993. Frederick L. Rusch, ed., *A Jean Toomer Reader: Selected Unpublished Writings*, 1993.   —Rudolph P. Byrd

TOURÉ, ASKIA M. (b. 1938), poet, community activist, lecturer, and educator. Askia M. Touré, in his multifaceted roles as poet, community activist, lecturer, and educator, is recognized as one of the original articulators of the *Black Arts movement, an artistic and political movement that exhorted black artists to slough off what Touré termed "the white plaster" of their "negroness" and ultimately bring about the cultural, political, and physical liberation of all black Americans. From the late 1960s through the mid-1970s, he served in various capacities: as a contributing editor for the magazine *Black Dialogue*, as an editor at large for the *Journal of Black Poetry*, and as a staff writer of *Liberator Magazine* and *Soulbook* with famed activist-playwright Amiri *Baraka and fellow poet-activist-critic Larry *Neal. Effecting a coalescence of poetic vision and social service, Touré has continued to combine his passion for *poetry and his zeal for a politics of black sociocultural empowerment in the tradition of Langston *Hughes and Gwendolyn *Brooks and in a way that few "community poets" (griots) have been able to realize as successfully.

Born Rolland Snellings in Raleigh, North Carolina, on 13 October 1938, Touré moved with his father, mother, and younger brother to Dayton, Ohio, in 1944. While a student at Dayton's Roosevelt High School from 1952 to 1956, he poetically expressed himself not as a writer, but as a singer. An accomplished crooner of 1950s doo-wop melodies, Touré, instead of cutting a record deal with King label, opted for a three-year stint in the air force. From 1956 to 1959, Touré, as an air force enlistee, served under what he called "apartheid basic training conditions, defending a country where [he] couldn't even eat in a restaurant."

In 1960 Touré came to New York to study painting at the Arts Students League. A frequenter of Louis Micheaux's Black Nationalist Bookstore on the corner of 125th Street and 7th Avenue, Touré was literally a stone's throw from and within earshot of Black Muslim activist *Malcolm X and his outdoor sermons. "Brother Malcolm" and then-fledgling writers of the pre–Black Arts magazine *Umbra* such as Calvin C. *Hernton, Ishmael *Reed, Lorenzo *Thomas, Tom *Dent, and David Henderson perhaps inspired Touré's pen more than his paintbrush, and in 1963 Touré coauthored with Tom Feelings and Matthew Meade *Samory Touré*, an illustrated biography of a nineteenth-century African freedom fighter.

In the late 1960s, with the Black Arts movement's political burgeoning into the Black Power movement, Touré continued actively writing and working in Harlem. In 1970, black-run *Third World Press published his long poem *Juju: Magic Songs for the Black Nation*, which pays homage to saxophonist John *Coltrane. Three years later, Touré published *Songhai!* A collection of poems and sketches that came out of novelist John O. *Killens's writers workshop at Columbia University, *Songhai!* reflects Touré's Afrocentric vision and his Islamic affiliation as a Sunni Muslim.

In 1974 Touré left a New York of personal, religious, and artistic turbulences for Philadelphia, carrying an intense commitment to community activism. Touré, along with the African People's Party, organized Philadelphia's black and poor communities against the alleged excesses of Mayor Frank Rizzo and the police department's attacks on the radical religious sect MOVE. Touré continued teaching, organizing, and writing into the 1980s, and his work culminated in *From the Pyramid to the Projects: Poems of Genocide and Resistance*, a collection of poems for which he won the American Book Award in 1989. The book, which recounts the horrors of white supremacy and the wonders of black resiliency, was the first American Book Award winner that has as its theme black genocide.

Touré lives and creates in Atlanta, has taught at Clark-Atlanta University, and since 1988 has been a dominant force in shaping and organizing the city's National Black Arts Festival. A tireless champion of his people, since 1985 Touré has spearheaded a campaign to introduce Africana studies in the Atlanta Public Schools System and is educating and organizing the black community against environmental racism throughout the South. Undaunted by such demanding work, Touré still finds time to write, having recently completed *Dawnsong*, which he calls an epic in lyric poetry.

• James A. Page, comp., *Selected Black American Authors*, 1977, pp. 267–268. Joanne V. Gabbin, "Askia Muhammad

Touré," in *DLB*, vol. 41, *Afro-American Poets since 1955*, eds. Trudier Harris and Thadious M. Davis, 1985, pp. 327–333.

—James.W. Richardson, Jr.

TRAGIC MULATTO. *See* Character Types; Mulatto.

TRAVEL WRITING. From *slave narratives describing either the *Middle Passage or the transition from bondage in the South to *freedom in the North, to fiction documenting the *migration, to twentieth-century *autobiographies portraying life as a journey, to recent novels depicting Africa by Charles R. *Johnson, Alice *Walker, John A. *Williams, and others, travel has always played a strategic thematic and metaphorical role in African American literature. Only since the turn of the century and after 1945 in particular, however, have African American authors more than sporadically engaged in travel writing, defined here as literary accounts of visits to or limited sojourns in foreign locations.

One of the oldest of literary genres, travel literature remains one of the most amorphous. In *The Witness and the Other World* (1988), Mary B. Campbell defines the travel book—as opposed to a work of autobiography, fiction, or ethnography—as "a kind of witness: it is generically aimed at the truth. Neither power nor talent gives a travel writer his or her authority, which comes only and crucially from experience." In other words, although literary travelers may exaggerate or even prevaricate, what matters is that they purport to be offering firsthand accounts of vistas actually beheld and events that really happened. Beyond this, travel writing requires that authors translate other places and people into language their readers can comprehend. As Mary Louise Pratt and other recent critics have noted, travel literature—the act of relating "them" and "theirs" to "us" and "ours"—implies a colonial situation; for this reason, the cultural yardstick has always been the most important piece of equipment in travel writers' suitcases or rucksacks. Moreover, far from guaranteeing objectivity and neutrality, the failure to reflect upon their political position vis-a-vis both their subjects and their readers often places literary travelers in the imperialist camp. Given African Americans' marginalized status in their own country and the dilemma of whether to write for a black, white, or mixed audience, the ambivalence that these writers have at times exhibited toward the whole project of travel writing is understandable.

As difficult to classify as its author, who has been claimed as an African, Anglo African, and African American writer, *The Interesting Narrative of the Life of Olaudah Equiano, or Gustavus Vassa, the African* (1789) may be the first example of African American travel writing. Part slave narrative, part spiritual autobiography, and part travel book, Olaudah *Equiano's *Narrative* concerns not only his kidnapping as a boy in Iboland, his experiences as a slave in the American colonies, the West Indies, and England, and his ultimately successful efforts to purchase his freedom but also his voyages to Latin American, Turkey, and the Arctic as a seaman. Although primarily autobiographical, Nancy *Prince's *Narrative*

(1850) details her experiences in Russia in the 1820s and 1830s and her missionary work in Jamaica in the 1840s. It may also represent the first book by an African American literary traveler written primarily for the purpose of making money; Prince explains in her preface that she decided to write the book out of a desire to avoid becoming a burden on the community. A year prior to publishing the first African American novel, *Clotel*, in 1853, William Wells *Brown wrote what might be considered the first conventional travel book by an African American, *Three Years in Europe, or Places I Have Seen and People I Have Met*, which consists of more than twenty *letters that describe the author's experiences in various European countries. Brown brought out a revised edition of *Three Years Abroad* in 1854, entitled *The American Fugitive in Europe. Sketches of Places and People Abroad*. Robert Campbell's *A Pilgrimage to My Motherland* (1861), describing his journey to what is now Nigeria with Martin R. *Delany and the Niger Valley Exploring Party, initiated a series of books about Africa that appeared in the second half of the nineteenth century, many of which were written by African American missionaries who had worked on the continent.

Although Africa has continued to dominate African American travel writing up until the present day, twentieth-century African American literary travelers, some of them major authors, have written about a wide variety of foreign lands. In 1912, Matthew Henson's account of reaching the North Pole in 1909 as part of Robert Peary's expedition appeared under the title *A Negro Explorer at the North Pole*. Zora Neale *Hurston's and Katherine *Dunham's anthropological work in the 1930s served as the basis for books they wrote about Haiti (Hurston's *Tell My Horse*, 1938) and Jamaica (Dunham's *Journey to Accompong*, 1946). During the 1920s and 1930s, Langston *Hughes published a number of brief descriptions of other countries. "People without Shoes: The Haytian Masses" (1933), for example, contains the following memorable Hughes sentence: "Hayti today: a fruit tree for Wall Street, a mango for the occupation, coffee for foreign cups, and poverty for its own black workers and peasants." As indicated by his books' titles, *The *Big Sea* (1940) and *I Wonder As I Wander* (1964), Hughes's travels to Africa, Cuba, Spain, Mexico, China, and Japan also figure prominently in his autobiographical works.

Reflecting the increased numbers of African American writers, journalists, field workers, and tourists visiting or temporarily settling in foreign countries, the postwar period has for the first time seen African American travel books produced on a consistent basis. The lands described range from Asia (J. Saunders *Redding's *An American in India*, 1954), to Russia (Homer Smith's *Black Man in Red Russia: A Memoir*, 1964), to Cuba (John Clytus's *Black Man in Red Cuba*, 1970). Starting with Eslanda Goode Robeson's *African Journey*, which appeared in 1945, Africa has continued to be a frequent subject for African American travel writers. Like Robeson's book, Era Bell *Thompson's *Africa: Land of My Fathers* (1954), Hoyt *Fuller's *Journey to Africa* (1971), and Eddy L. Harris's *Native Stranger* (1992) describe the authors' experiences in two or more nations. Other works concern individual countries, such as Richard *Wright's *Black Power* (1954), Ed Smith's *Where to, Black Man?* (1967), and Maya *Angelou's *All God's Children Need Traveling Shoes* (1986)—each of which is about Ghana.

The author of three travel books, Richard Wright stands as the single most important African American literary traveler. In addition to *Black Power*, Wright wrote *The Color Curtain* (1955), an account of the Bandung Conference in Indonesia in 1955 that brought together representatives from many African and Asian countries, and *Pagan Spain* (1957), based on three automobile trips he made throughout much of that country in 1954 and 1955. An expatriate for several years before he wrote his travel works, Wright believed that his experiences as an outsider first in the United States and later in France gave him special insight when he attempted to describe foreign countries; he also felt that his journeys to other lands helped him to maintain a certain detachment as a writer. As he explained to an interviewer in 1956, "I make many voyages to keep as close contact with contemporary man as possible. It is my way of avoiding the barrage of propaganda from all quarters and of exposing myself to reality at first hand. This is what an artist should do as much as possible in order that his sensibilities can carry a rich burden of concrete reference." Many critics, however, have argued that Wright failed to achieve the objectivity he was striving for, frequently revealing his Western biases in his discussions of African and Asian countries.

Rife with discourse tensions, *Black Power* illustrates some of the challenges facing African American literary travelers. Wright often announces his desire to escape his Western frames of reference and, like many other African American writers who have gone to Africa, he hopes to discover a level on which he can connect with Africans. However, Wright frequently finds himself baffled by the African customs, family relationships, and political organizations he encounters. In a remarkable passage, Wright discusses the distortions of Western thinking and writing about Africa:

> Africa is a vast dingy mirror and what modern man sees in that mirror he hates and wants to destroy. He thinks, when looking into that mirror, that he is looking at black people who are inferior, but, really he is looking at himself and, unless he possesses a superb knowledge of himself, his first impulse to vindicate himself is to smash this horrible image of himself which his own soul projects on Africa.

On the one hand, Wright powerfully describes the process of image projection prevalent in travel writing and fiction about Africa. On the other hand, he perpetuates this very cycle by coining a new image for the continent while declaring the bankruptcy of standard images. Wright's travel writing, in fact, is emblematic of a phenomenon experienced by many African American literary travelers. Although these writers go abroad to observe and participate in different approaches to life and often to escape grim realities that confront them at home, travel to other countries serves to remind many of them of the fact that they are indeed Americans.

• Langston Hughes, "People without Shoes: The Haytian Masses," in *Negro: An Anthology*, ed. Nancy Cunard, 1933; rpt. 1970, pp. 288–290. Russell Brignano, *Black Americans in Autobiography: An Annotated Bibliography of Autobiographies and Autobiographical Books Written since the Civil War*, 1974. John C. Gruesser, "Afro-American Travel Literature and Africanist Discourse," *Black American Literature Forum* 24.1 (Spring 1990): 5–20. Mary G. Mason, "Travel as Metaphor and Reality in Afro-American Woman's Autobiography, 1850–1972," *Black American Literature Forum* 24.2 (Summer 1990): 337–356. Mary Louise Pratt, *Imperial Eyes: Travel Writing and Transculturation*, 1992. Keneth Kinnamon and Michel Fabre, eds., *Conversations with Richard Wright*, 1993.
—John C. Gruesser

TREMAINE, PAUL. *See* Johnson, Georgia Douglas.

TRICKSTER. Crafty, wily, high-spirited and as old as human culture itself, tricksters are masters of disguise and consummate survivors, skillfully outmaneuvering their foes with guile, wit, and charm. African American trickster tales, derived largely from West African antecedents, flourished during *slavery and Reconstruction, and remain central to African American *folklore and literature. Best-known African American tricksters include *Brer Rabbit, John of the "John and the Old Master" tales, and the signifying monkey, all of whom outwit stronger, more powerful, and often dull-witted opponents.

African American trickster tales, while preserving the *humor and vitality of the African tales, were modified to meet the conditions of slavery and therefore emphasize the trickster's subversive *masking and *signifying skills. The trickster's reputation as a dissembling swindler has led to stereotyped views of him as a selfish, unprincipled fraud; yet the trickster's easy manipulation of appearances also ensures his survival. Maintaining any sort of cultural *identity under slavery demanded an overt acceptance of and covert resistance to the dehumanizing racial myths of slavery, tactics at which the trickster excels. In African American folktales, the trickster emerges not simply as a greedy, amoral clown but also as a folk hero whose subversive behavior helps to upset an unequal balance of power. When placed within the context of American slavery, the trickster's challenge to established order represents a revolutionary stance against oppression.

The trickster in the African American literary tradition has become a figure for cultural survival—and its costs. Charles Waddell *Chesnutt's *The *Conjure Woman* (1899) recasts early trickster tale collections within an elaborate narrative framework that questions the apparently simplistic motives behind the trickster's maneuvering and clarifies the trickster's subversive role in a slave society. Tricksters remain central figures in contemporary African American *novels; contemporary examples include the elusive *Rinehart of Ralph *Ellison's *Invisible Man* (1952) and Toni *Morrison's modern retelling of a well-known trickster tale, *Tar Baby* (1981).

Recent criticism has also associated the trickster with the development of an African American literary tradition. Henry Louis *Gates, Jr., locates the vernacular roots of the African American literary tradition in the African trickster Esu-Elegbara and his African American descendant, the signifying monkey. The trickster's power and identity lie in his skillful stories and mastery of verbal technique, and he therefore becomes both a figure of and a linguistic means for his culture's subversive strategies and creative expression.

The trickster's historical roots in social and political engagement, together with his fluidity of form and transgression of boundaries, make him a compelling figure not only for cultural resistance and survival, but also for blasting *stereotypes of African Americans. Because the trickster cannot be pinned down to any one form, shape, or position, and because he continually disrupts the status quo with laughter, outrage, and rebellion, he acts both as a figure of cultural strength and as a sign of diversity.

• John W. Roberts, *From Trickster to Badman: The Black Folk Hero in Slavery and Freedom*, 1989. Elizabeth Ammons and Annette White-Parks, eds., *Tricksterism in Turn-of-the-Century Multicultural United States Literature*, 1994.

—Jeanne R. Smith

TROUPE, QUINCY THOMAS, JR. (b. 1943), poet, journalist, editor, producer, and educator. Born 23 July 1943 in New York City, Quincy Troupe grew up in St. Louis and later graduated from Grambling College. While playing on the army basketball team from 1962 to 1964, Troupe traveled through Europe and began to write. He met Jean-Paul Sartre who encouraged him to write poetry. He later became influenced by such poets as Pablo Neruda, Aimé Césaire, Jean Joseph Rabearivello, Jean *Toomer, and Sterling A. *Brown.

Troupe's first poem "What Is A Black Man?" was published in *Paris Match* (1964) and examines what it is to be a black man in a racially charged society. In 1972 Troupe published his first collection of poems, *Embryo Poems 1967–1971*, which explores themes of the intense experiences of black people in America. The use of dialect and the influence of *jazz found in these poems become characteristic of Troupe's poetic style. *Snake-Back Solos: Selected Poems 1969–1977* (1979) won the American Book Award. Tom *Dent, reviewing Troupe's poetry in *Freedomways*, noted its roots in African oral traditions and found in his work the brilliance of African American *music. In the volume of poetry *Skulls Along the River* (1984), Troupe meditates on an array of subjects, including love, *family, and the importance of a folkloric past. *Weather Reports* (1991) is a collection of new and previously published poems. Wilfred D. Samuels writes in the introduction to the collection that the poems provide "insights into the hieroglyphics of Black culture deeply encoded in the matrix of its language and the *blues dues sounds of its songs." Ishmael *Reed has hailed Troupe as one of few American writers who can authentically embody the jazz aesthetic in poetry, while also noting the power and the strength of Troupe's imagery.

Troupe's poems are also published in various periodicals including *Mundus Artium, Black World, *Callaloo, Antioch Review, Umbra, Black Review*, the *Village Voice*, the *Black Scholar, American Music*, and others. His work also has been anthologized in *New Black Poetry, Poetry of Black America, A Rock Against the Wind, Celebrations: A New Anthology of Black American Poetry, The Before Columbus Foundation Anthology*, and *The New Cavalcade: African American Writing from 1760 to the Present*, among others. Troupe has also recorded his poetry with musicians George Lewis, Phil Upchurch, and Donal Fox, and in 1990 released an audio cassette entitled *Shaman Man*.

In 1968 Troupe edited *Watts Poets: A Book of New Poetry and Essays*, a project that arose from his participation in the Watts Writers' Movement. He was also associate editor of *Shrewd* magazine and the founding editor of *Confrontation: A Journal of Third World Literature and American Rag*. Troupe coedited with Rainer Schulte *Giant Talk: An Anthology of Third World Writing* (1972), which includes a large sampling of writings by American, African, Caribbean, and Latin American Authors. In 1989 he edited *James Baldwin: The Legacy*, a collection of what Malcolm Arthur Whyte, in a review for the *Black Scholar*, calls "touching and revealing." Troupe is currently a contributing editor for *Conjunctions* magazine and senior editor for *River Styx* magazine.

Troupe won the American Book Award for his coauthored book, *Miles: The Autobiography of Miles Davis with Quincy Troupe* (1990). Praised for the frankness, honesty, and sheer depth in which Davis's life and music are discussed, *Miles* is considered by many music critics as a crucial text about the legendary musician. Troupe coproduced the *Miles Davis Radio Project* for PBS (1991–1992), for which he received the Peabody Award and the Ohio State Award.

Troupe coauthored *The Inside Story of T.V.'s "Roots"* (1978) with David L. Wolper. In 1989 Troupe was featured on Bill Moyer's Emmy Award–winning series, *The Power of the Word*, and he was also a writer for the television documentary "Thelonius Monk: An American Composer" (1991).

Quincy Troupe has lectured at many universities and colleges including Richmond College, University of California at Berkeley, Columbia University, University of Ghana at Legon, Lagos University in Nigeria, and others. He is currently a professor of literature at the University of California at San Diego, where he teaches creative writing. Troupe is a member of the board of directors for the Frederick Douglass Creative Arts Center, curator of the reading series held every year at the Museum of Contemporary Art of San Diego, and he is a judge for awards, scholarships, and fellowships offered by organizations such as the National Endowment for the Arts, Poetry Society of America, and the New York Foundation for the Arts.

• Horace Coleman, "Quincy Thomas Troupe, Jr.," in *DLB*, vol. 41, *Afro-American Poets since 1955*, eds. Trudier Harris and Thadious Davis, 1985, pp. 334–338. "Troupe, Quincy (Thomas, Jr.)," in *Black Writers: A Selection of Sketches from Contemporary Authors*, ed. Linda Metzger, 1989, pp.

551–553. *Cavalcade: African American Writing from 1760 to the Present*, vol. 2, eds. Arthur P. Davis et al., 1992, pp. 702–703. Ishmael Reed, "Can Poetry's Big Daddy Deliver San Diego?: Quincy Troupe Goes West," *San Diego Weekly Reader*, 22.5 (16 Dec. 1993).   —Kim Jenice Dillon

TRUEBLOOD. Jim Trueblood has generally been depicted as a Black male who, unable to control his sexual appetites, breaks one of humanity's greatest taboos—incest. He further has the dubious distinction of impregnating both his daughter and his wife. Their swollen bellies attest to both his virility and his shame. In Ralph *Ellison's *Invisible Man* (1952), however, the Trueblood incident involves much more than one Black man's sexuality. First it sheds some light on Mr. *Norton, the founder of the college the narrator attends. In his heart, if not physically, Norton is just as guilty of incest as Trueblood is, but society does not see his behavior as deviant. Secondly, the incident sheds light on the poor living conditions of Blacks in the South. In *Cane* (1923), author Jean *Toomer explores the effects of housing on southern Blacks. In "Karintha," the titular character, while quite young, becomes sexually active; she "had seen or heard, perhaps she had felt her parents loving." Toomer blames the living conditions, the "two room" plan, which force children and adults to sleep in close proximity to one another. In like manner, Ellison attacks the living conditions of the Truebloods. Jim explains that his daughter, Mattie Lou, sleeps with him and his wife because there is no heat and all of them "had to sleep together." The conditions under which the Truebloods survive are evident from Jim's reflections as the family sleeps. He thinks about "how to get some grub [for them] for the next day," because "I tried to get help but wouldn't nobody help us and I couldn't find no work or nothin'." That Mattie Lou is in the bed with Jim or that Jim is awake thinking about providing for his family is more an indictment of the living conditions of southern Blacks than it is about a Black male's sexuality. Finally Trueblood is important in the novel because unlike the narrator who tries to define his selfhood in terms of Westernization, Trueblood identifies with the Black folk tradition and uses this tradition to realize his humanity. At the nadir of his existence, rejected by his *family, *church, and community, Trueblood turns to the *blues. "I sing me some blues that night ain't never been sung before, and while I'm singin' them blues I make up my mind that I ain't nobody but myself. . . ." The blues is cathartic, purging away both pain and guilt and allowing Trueblood to claim his humanity: "I ain't nobody but myself." This epiphany transforms Trueblood from a self-hating reprobate into a confident, self-affirming male, ready to brave family and community. "I'm a man," he affirms, "and a man don't leave his family."

—Ralph Reckley, Sr.

TRUTH, SOJOURNER (c. 1797–1883), itinerant preacher, abolitionist, and feminist. Sojourner Truth, born a slave in Ulster County, New York, a symbol of women's strength and black women's womanliness, is summed up in the phrase "ar'n't I a woman?" Known as Isabella VanWagener until 1843, she changed her name and became an itinerant preacher under the influence of Millerite Second Adventism.

In the 1840s Truth encountered feminist abolitionism during her stay in the Northampton (Mass.) Association of Education and Industry. There she met Olive Gilbert, who recorded *The Narrative of Sojourner Truth: A Bondswoman of Olden Time*, which Truth published in Boston in 1850. During the 1850s and 1860s sales to antislavery and feminist audiences of this narrative provided Truth's main source of income. Truth attended the 1851 Akron, Ohio, convention on women's rights in order to sell her book. The chair of that meeting, Frances Dana Gage, wrote the most popular version of Truth's speech and invented the "ar'n't I a woman?" refrain in 1863, which defined Truth's persona in the twentieth century.

The Narrative of Sojourner Truth went through seven editions, two of which—in 1875 (written) / 1878 (published) and 1884—entailed major additions. In the 1870s Truth's Battle Creek, Michigan, neighbor and manager, Frances Titus, added Truth's "Book of Life" (her scrapbook), which includes letters and clippings from periodicals; after Truth's death, Titus appended obituaries and eulogies. The most commonly reprinted version of Truth's *Narrative* is that of the 1870s, which includes the texts of Harriet Beecher Stowe's 1863 "Sojourner Truth, the Libyan Sibyl," which introduced Truth to a wide audience, and Gage's version of Truth's 1851 speech.

As the story of a religious woman who had been a northern slave, Truth's *Narrative* has not yet found its niche in the literature of former slaves, in which the South figures as the necessary context of *slavery. Truth is more widely acknowledged for her speech acts in the 1850s.

• Carleton Mabee, *Sojourner Truth: Slave, Prophet, Legend*, 1993. Nell Irvin Painter, "Representing Truth: Sojourner Truth's Ways of Knowing and Becoming Known," *Journal of American History* 81 (Sept. 1994): 461–492. Nell Irvin Painter, *Sojourner Truth, a Life, a Symbol*, 1996.

—Nell Irvin Painter

TUBMAN, HARRIET (c. 1820–1913), self-emancipated slave, conductor for the Underground Railroad, Union spy, army scout, and nurse. Originally called Araminta, Harriet Ross Tubman was born on the Brodas plantation, Dorchester County, Maryland. She was disabled by narcoleptic seizures throughout her life after sustaining a severe injury to her head during her youth. Despite this frailty, Tubman's considerable strength and endurance were legendary. As a field slave, she mastered the secrets of woodcraft and navigation—skills that ensured her success as a conductor for the *Underground Railroad. After her escape in 1849, Tubman returned to the South over fifteen times to rescue more than two hundred slaves. She successfully freed all of her family and never lost a single passenger during any of her escapes. More than forty thousand dollars was offered for her capture.

Tubman was a pivotal character in the war against slavery, first with the Underground Railroad, later with the Union army. She joined forces with the leading abolitionists of the day: William *Still, Thomas Garrett, Frederick *Douglass, Sojourner *Truth, and John *Brown. After emancipation Tubman served in the Union army as a spy, a scout, and a nurse. She was the only woman in American military history to plan and execute an armed expedition against enemy forces.

After the war Tubman recounted the story of her life to Sarah Elizabeth Bradford who wrote her *biography, *Scenes in the Life of Harriet Tubman* (1869). Using the small profits from her biography and her military pension, Tubman established a permanent home for aged ex-slaves in Auburn, New York.

Canonized in Robert *Hayden's *"Runagate Runagate," Tubman is a popular icon in African American literature. She has come to symbolize both the Black woman's role in Black liberation and the African American's determination to be free.

—Deborah H. Barnes

TURE, KWAME. *See* Carmichael, Stokely.

TURNER, NAT (1800–1831), slave revolutionary. The leader of the bloodiest and most celebrated slave rebellion in U.S. history, Nat Turner was born the slave of Benjamin Turner on 1 October 1800 in Southampton County, Virginia. In *The *Confessions of Nat Turner* (1831), a portion of which was reputedly taken down from Turner's dictation, the slave rebel portrays himself as a precocious child who was recognized by blacks and whites alike as "intended for some great purpose." He learned to read and write early on and displayed a strong interest in *religion. When not employed in field labor, Turner says he dabbled in experiments in making paper and gunpowder.

In 1821, Turner ran away from his master but returned voluntarily after about a month. In the next year he was sold to Thomas Moore, a Southampton farmer. In 1825, Turner received what he called his first heavenly vision, in which he was shown a war between "white spirits and black spirits" and warned of an approaching day of judgment. Communicating this knowledge to a local white man named Etheldred T. Brantley, Turner baptized himself and Brantley in anticipation of the great changes to come. On 12 May 1828, Turner witnessed a second vision, in which he learned of his messianic task: to "fight against the Serpent" in the approaching eschaton. In 1830, Turner was moved to the home of Joseph Travis, a local carriage maker who had married the widow of Thomas Moore. In February 1831, a solar eclipse convinced Turner that the time for an uprising of slaves was at hand. Planned to commence on 4 July 1831, the uprising was postponed until 21 August when Turner and his inner circle met at the home of Joseph Travis and killed Travis, his wife and child, and two apprentices. For the next forty hours, Turner and a varying number of followers (perhaps as many as eighty at the height of the rebellion) attacked a series of farms, executing at least fifty-seven white people, on their way to Jerusalem, the Southampton County seat. Repulsed by white militia on the afternoon of 22 August, Turner's forces became disorganized and scattered. After a final skirmish with whites on the morning of 23 August, Turner escaped, hiding in the general vicinity of the Travis farm until he was captured on 30 October. The next day he was taken to the county jail, where he was interviewed for three days by Thomas R. Gray. At his 5 November trial Turner pleaded not guilty to charges of conspiracy to rebel and making *insurrection; he was subsequently found guilty and was executed by hanging on 11 November 1831.

Turner's rebellion traumatized the white South and galvanized the radical *antislavery movement in the North. In spite of Gray's attempt in the *Confessions* to portray Turner as a demented religious fanatic, many African Americans in the South and the North regarded "Prophet Nat" as a political hero. Albert E. Stone's *The Return of Nat Turner* (1992) demonstrates that as a symbol of uncompromising militancy in the pursuit of *freedom, Turner's example remains as potent and as controversial in the late twentieth century as it was in the antebellum era.

• Henry Irving Tragle, *The Southampton Slave Revolt of 1831*, 1971. Eric J. Sundquist, *To Wake the Nations*, 1993.

—William L. Andrews

TURPIN, WATERS (1910–1968), educator, novelist, playwright, director, television lecturer, and drama critic. Waters Edward Turpin, the only child of Simon and Mary Rebecca (Waters) Turpin, was born 9 April 1910 on the eastern shore of Maryland in Oxford. At the time of his death, 19 November 1968, he had been married to Jean Fisher Turpin for thirty-two years. They had two children—Rosalie Rebecca Turpin Belcher and John Edward Turpin.

Although Turpin's career was multifaceted, he was primarily a teacher. He began his teaching career in 1935 at Storer College in Harpers Ferry, West Virginia, where he taught English and coached football. In June 1938, he left Storer to pursue a doctoral degree at Columbia University, where he had received his master's degree in 1932. (He received the EdD in 1960.) In 1940 Turpin joined the faculty at Lincoln University (Pa.) and stayed there until 1950, when he was invited by Nick Aaron Ford, chair of the English Department, to come to Morgan State College, where his wife Jean was already teaching. Returning to Morgan was returning to his roots. He had received his high school diploma from Morgan Academy and his BA from Morgan State College, where he was editor in chief of the *Morgan Newsletter*.

During his eighteen years at Morgan, Turpin was a teacher of composition and literature, assistant director of drama, chair of the Division of Humanities for two years, television lecturer, coauthor with Nick Aaron Ford of a textbook: *Basic Skills for Better Writing* (1959), and coeditor with Ford of *Extending Horizons: Selected Readings for Cultural Enrichment* (1969). As assistant director of drama, Turpin produced and directed two of his plays: *And Let the Day Perish* (1950) and *St. Michael's Dawn* (1956), a three-act drama of the life of Frederick *Douglass. There are other plays, short stories, and poetry in Turpin's unpublished collection.

However, Turpin's novels are what gained him recognition in African American literary history. Turpin's creative abilities were recognized early, and among those encouraging him to write was novelist Edna Ferber, who was the employer of Turpin's mother. Although Turpin worked on several novels, only three were published. The first, *These Low Grounds* (1937), set on the eastern shore of Maryland, tells the story of four generations of an African American family. The second novel, *O Canaan!* (1939), traces the progress of migratory farmers who left the South for Chicago during the depression. Turpin's third and final published novel, *The Rootless* (1957), is a historical novel that depicts slave practices in eighteenth-century Maryland.

Turpin's eloquent, dramatic, and imaginative writings are accurate portrayals of African American life during the first half of the twentieth century. The literary legacy of Waters Turpin to his students, colleagues, friends, and reading audience is most memorable.

• Nick Aaron Ford, "The Legacy of Waters E. Turpin, Part I and II," *Afro-American Newspaper,* Magazine Section, 14 and 21 Dec. 1968, 1.　　　　　　　　　—Margaret Ann Reid

"Two Offers, The." Frances Ellen Watkins *Harper's "The Two Offers" was first published in the *Anglo-African Magazine* in 1859 and is considered the first published *short story by an African American woman in the United States. Harper provides no racial dimension to the characters, and the thematic purpose of the story is to challenge contradictions inherent in social values regarding women's roles and to offer an alternative to those conventions and traditions. In this regard, the short story suggests strong similarities between black society and white society, as sexism dominates both social spheres. At the same time, it indicates the gender solidarity that existed in the radical abolitionist community and the feminist themes women activists, such as Harper, espoused in their literature.

The story concerns two cousins, Laura and Janette, who consider two offers of marriage extended to Laura. Though cousins, they represent two different classes, one of privilege and the other of poverty. By juxtaposing their class differences, Harper uses economic contrast to suggest that gender perspectives are related to class consciousness.

In particular, Laura feels she must marry or face the fate of becoming an old maid. Janette, on the other hand, is unmarried and has forsaken tradition to keep her independence and to pursue a writing career. In this regard, Janette parallels Harper, who was unmarried when she published the story. Even though Harper married in 1860, she continued to write and to lecture against *slavery. Janette, the feminist protagonist, completely rejects the role of woman as wife and mother, and her name, Janette Alston, alludes to Jane Austen, the nineteenth-century English writer.

Janette advises Laura to refuse both proposals because her indecision indicates a deficiency of affection for either of the two men. She also states that for Laura to marry for economic reasons relegates the bond to a business arrangement, which defiles the sanctity of the union. Janette's analysis is a provocative challenge to the economic bondage that many women faced during the nineteenth century, in which marriage offered security and class status, and, conversely, a kind of enslavement.

Ten years later when the cousins reunite, Laura is gazing into death's gaping mouth, having suffered a possessive, repressive marriage to a man who violated their vows and acted as if the marriage contract were a bill of sale. In response, the omniscient narrator reflects the feminist politics of Harper and the women's movement, criticizing society's denial of "the true woman," whose "conscience should be enlightened, her faith in the true and the right established and scope given to her Heaven-endowed and God-given faculties."

Harper's rejection of romantic illusions and her advocacy of women's independent spirit are not a wholesale rejection of marriage, as Janette does commit to an egalitarian union. Harper's intention is to dispel romantic attraction and emotional manipulation as determinants for marriage. Moreover, the theme illustrates how inequitable unions lead to spiritual demise and, in this case, to heartbreak and actual death. But the contrast between the two women represents the real two offers: independence, autonomy, and life, or oppression, depression, and death.

• Jean Fagan Yellin, *Women and Sisters,* 1989. Mary Helen Washington, *Invented Lives: Narratives of Black Women 1860–1960,* 1990.　　　　　　—Melba Joyce Boyd

U

UNCLE JULIUS McADOO. An aged former slave, Uncle Julius McAdoo serves as the folk narrator in the stories of Charles Waddell *Chesnutt's *The *Conjure Woman* (1889). He connects the frame stories told by his employer, a white midwestern businessman transplanted to the South, with the lives of slaves in eastern North Carolina and the conjuring activities of *Aun' Peggy. To a marked degree, Uncle Julius resembles the nineteenth-century *stereotype of the loyal family servant found in the nostalgic postbellum fiction of such white writers as Thomas Nelson Page and Joel Chandler Harris, the creator of Uncle Remus. Strongly superstitious, Uncle Julius seems naive and simple, but his remarkable narration reveals that he is imaginative, perceptive, and shrewd. He often uses storytelling as a means to advance his own interests, sometimes at the expense of the white businessman narrator. Julius's stories range widely in mood and effect, from the comic to the tragic. Unlike the "uncles" of Page and Harris, Julius never grows nostalgic for the "good ol' days" before emancipation. Instead his stories emphasize the threats *slavery presented to ordinary black people caught in its grip and their ingenuity in resisting slavery's dehumanization. Uncle Julius McAdoo represents one of the earliest adaptations of the slave *trickster to literary purposes in the African American tradition.

• Lucinda MacKethan, "Charles Chesnutt's Southern World: Portraits of a Bad Dream," in *The Dream of Arcady*, 1980, pp. 86–104. William L. Andrews, introduction to *The Collected Stories of Charles W. Chesnutt*, 1992.

—Paula Gallant Eckard

UNCLE TOM. Although Harriet Beecher *Stowe's extremely successful 1852 abolitionist novel *Uncle Tom's Cabin* was the original source for the Uncle Tom idiom, its meaning is best understood through an examination of the numerous stage shows loosely based on the best-selling book. Theatrical entrepreneurs who did not share Stowe's antislavery zeal took great liberties with the novel's protagonist. Uncle Toms of the stage were usually depicted as thoroughly subservient individuals who willingly betrayed their black brethren in order to please their white masters. As a result, the Uncle Tom label is assigned to individuals who sabotage other blacks in order to further their own advancement. Known popularly as Tom shows, stage productions of *Uncle Tom's Cabin* were a mainstay of American theater well into the twentieth century. Uncle Tom became a trope, a figure of speech used to refer to fawning, selfish black men. Thus Uncle Tom's ubiquitousness had a definitive impact on mainstream society's assumptions about actual black men.

By the turn of the century, a curious battle developed between the purveyors of popular culture, who continued to promote Uncle Tom, and African American writers and social critics eager to bury the demeaning image. Thus filmmakers made several *films similar to the stage shows. Even the Siam-based musical *The King and I* (1951) contains an ode to *Uncle Tom's Cabin*. For a collection of short stories on the black experience in the South, Richard *Wright used the title *Uncle Tom's Children* (1938). Ralph *Ellison noted that a Tom show was one of the original impetuses for his *novel *Invisible Man* (1952). Ishmael *Reed manipulated characters' names for his novel *Mumbo Jumbo* (1972), and Robert Alexander wrote a provocative play entitled *I Ain't Yo Uncle: The New Jack Revisionist Uncle Tom's Cabin* (performed in Hartford, 1995). Nonetheless, the negative associations of the name remain consistent. For example, the Uncle Tom label is often applied to staunchly conservative African American Supreme Court Justice Clarence Thomas. It seems likely that this pejorative label will remain in the American vernacular.

—Patricia A. Turner

Uncle Tom's Cabin. *See* Stowe, Harriet Beecher.

Uncle Tom's Children, a collection published in 1938 of four of Richard *Wright's short stories (two of which had appeared previously) and the earliest of Wright's major publications. The book we know as *Uncle Tom's Children* is a somewhat different book from the original because two extraordinarily important additions were made in 1940 in a new edition. These two additions, "The Ethics of Living Jim Crow," a preface to the collection, and "Bright and Morning Star," a new story, changed the shape of the book, giving it a different form and focus. "The Ethics of Living Jim Crow" is an extended essay describing events, largely from Wright's own life, outlining the unspoken rules and regulations governing interaction between blacks and whites in Richard Wright's Mississippi and in the South in general. All of the stories in *Uncle Tom's Children* are about some aspect of racial repression and black response to it.

The first, "Big Boy Leaves Home," is the story of a young, innocent adolescent boy who is forced by circumstances to shoot in self-defense a white man who threatens to take his life. Big Boy, while he hides waiting to escape with his friend on a truck headed north, sees that friend brutally lynched, burned alive, and his body mutilated.

"Down by the Riverside" takes its title from a *spiritual of that name. It tells of Mann, who in attempting to save his family during a flood steals a boat and must in self-defense kill the boat's white owner. It is discovered that he killed a white man, and rather than be lynched, he chooses to run for the river knowing he will be killed by soldiers armed with rifles.

"Long Black Song," the third story, tells of a farmer, Silas, and his wife, Sarah. It opens with Sarah tending her baby while Silas has gone to town. A young salesman appears who wants to sell Sarah a clock. Sarah, after a complicated series of events, has sexual relations with him. Silas discovers her infidelity and kills the salesman. A mob forms and Silas is burned to death defending himself with his rifle to the end.

"Fire and Cloud" recounts the experience of Reverend Taylor, a black minister who discovers the necessity of uniting political action with religion as he leads his congregation together with whites on a march to City Hall to obtain the promise of food. The story ends with the assertion, "Freedom belongs to the strong."

The final story in Uncle Tom's Children, "Bright and Morning Star," explores the possibility of union between black and white communists in order to achieve common political ends. The story reveals the heroism of an ordinary black Southerner, Johnny-Boy, who fights to organize across racial lines to bring about political and social change. Johnny-Boy's mother, Ant Sue, gives up her life to kill an informer before he is able to impart his information to the sheriff. The story ends with the deaths of both mother and son.

• Donald B. Gibson, The Politics of Literary Expression: Essays on Major Black Writers, 1981, pp. 25–35. Edward Margolies, "Wright's Craft: The Short Stories," in Critical Essays on Richard Wright, ed. Yoshinobu Hakutani, 1982, pp. 128–138.   —Donald B. Gibson

UNDERGROUND RAILROAD. After the Civil War the popular press promulgated melodramatic accounts of heroic abolitionists (notably Harriet *Tubman and various Quakers) who transported slaves through secret routes and hidden rooms from the Deep South to Canada. In legend the Underground Railroad was a highly organized network of people, *places, and vehicles. Historical evidence, however, suggests that most fugitive slaves had to rely primarily on their own courage, wit, luck, and acquaintances. Most branches of the *antislavery movement were focused on ending *slavery rather than helping individuals escape.

For two centuries African American writers have emphasized the roles that slaves played in freeing themselves. Assistance was sometimes organized but it was more often the result of coincidence, personal affection, or other individualized motives. While being careful not to give details that might endanger either the people who helped them escape or other slaves who were still trying to escape, antebellum writers such as Frederick *Douglass (1845, 1855), William Wells *Brown (1847), and Harriet A. *Jacobs (1861) credited many individuals, white and black, for assisting their escapes but gave no evidence of an organized underground railroad. Other slave narrators invented creative escapes such as cross-dressing and *passing (William and Ellen *Craft, 1860), bold con artistry (Henry *Bibb, 1849), and being mailed to *freedom in a large box (Henry "Box" *Brown, 1851). Twentieth-century writers such as Sherley Anne

*Williams (*Dessa Rose, 1986) and Toni *Morrison (*Beloved, 1987) have continued the tradition of representing the Underground Railroad as an important part of slave resistance and escape but not as a well-organized abolitionist scheme.

• Larry Gara, The Liberty Line: The Legend of the Underground Railroad, 1961.   —Kari J. Winter

Up from Slavery. As *autobiography, institutional history, and how-to book, Up from Slavery (1901) signals the beginnings of African American modernism. Though Booker T. *Washington was born a slave, it would be wrong to categorize Up from Slavery as a conventional *slave narrative. Indeed Washington makes a conscious effort to avoid an authorial fixation on the evils of *slavery. To live as a slave, Washington observes, was to live in "miserable, desolate, and discouraging surroundings," which was the case, he asserts, "not because my owners were especially cruel," but because life as a slave was a life of indigence and want.

Up from Slavery is a compelling literary event because Washington successfully weds his rags-to-riches story with narratives of racial conciliation and uplift. With antiblack sentiment in the South reaching a level where *lynching occurred "more than weekly," Washington's task was to assuage the fears of a white citizenry who viewed the relatively new African American labor force as a threat to their economic and political well-being. Washington needed to persuade his largely white readership that African Americans could, in spite of whites' post-Reconstruction enmity with them, make important contributions to the southern economy. Hence the message behind Washington's narrative, from the description of the squalid cabin in which he was born and raised to the triumphant moment when dusting and cleaning a classroom earns him an education at Hampton Institute, is that deprivation is not so much a source of disillusionment as it is an opportunity to prove one's merit. These moments provide signposts that point the reader to Washington's present station, Tuskegee Institute. The reader comes to understand that humility and industry provide entry to the American power elite, not for the purpose of individual gratification but for the improvement of an entire race and, eventually, an entire nation. Tuskegee stands as the physical symbol that blacks in the South have found their way to self-reliance: Washington relates difficulties overcome, remembers the school's humble beginnings in a stable and a hen house, and recounts the students' first attempt to make bricks with which to build the campus.

But it is Tuskegee as symbol that gives Washington space to preach his message of conciliation. The culminating moment of both the book and his life, then, is to be found in his *"Atlanta Exposition Address," delivered in 1895. The speech gave Washington a "reputation that in a sense might be called National." But if Washington allows himself a moment of self-aggrandizement, he quickly tempers it with self-depreciating irony when he states: "What were my feelings when this invitation came to me? I remembered that I had been a slave; that my early years had been spent in the lower depths of poverty and ignorance, and that I had had little opportunity to prepare me for such a responsibility as this."

The speech's startling success, with its claim that the social separation of the races need not impede economic progress in the South, underscores the main theme of *Up from Slavery,* that through cooperation and mutual respect whites and blacks, even in the slavery-scarred South, could move beyond the fears, animosities, and prejudices that had hampered regional development for decades. To accentuate this optimistic view of the South's potential, *Up from Slavery* avoids references to southern racial conflict, denies that racism is pervasive among southern whites, and attempts to inspire its white reader with a sense of moral, if not social obligation, to help lift the formerly enslaved and their children from their disadvantages.

Up from Slavery ends with Tuskegee Institute in a state of financial health and Washington in an exalted position as the confidant of U.S. presidents and the agent of business magnates intent on solving the race problem. The final scene of the autobiography finds Washington in Richmond, Virginia, the capital of the fallen Confederacy, lionized by whites and blacks alike after delivering a message of "hope and cheer" to a racially mixed audience. Reminded of the fact that as a penniless young man he had "slept night after night under a sidewalk" in Richmond, Washington savors his good fortune, not for himself alone but for the sake of "the state that gave me birth." Although the twentieth century saw many African Americans suffer the indignities of racial discrimination and poverty (both rural and urban), *Up from Slavery* accommodates, on its face, the notion that change was sweeping across the land.

• Booker T. Washington, *Up from Slavery,* ed. William L. Andrews, 1995.

—Herman Beavers

URSA CORREGIDORA. The protagonist and narrator of Gayl *Jones's 1975 novel, *Corregidora,* Ursa is a blues singer and songwriter who descends from a long line of *slavery and incest. Her earliest memories revolve around her being told the terrible history of her great-grandmother and grandmother who were enslaved, repeatedly raped, and forced into prostitution by the Brazilian plantation owner Old Corregidora; both Ursa's grandmother and her mother are his daughters. In order that Corregidora's atrocities are never forgotten, Ursa, like her mother, has been charged to "make generations" who will bear witness to this familial narrative of victimization and abuse. But she loses the baby she is carrying and is rendered sterile when Mutt Thomas, her jealous husband, pushes her down a flight of stairs.

Ursa's role as an artist is pivotal to her finding a way to bear witness and simultaneously break free of her foremothers' history; she must learn to identify herself through her voice and her creativity, rather than through her womb. Eventually, by recognizing her own (as well as her foremothers') potential for violence, Ursa also discovers her own capacity for pleasure and desire. Her uneasy acknowledgment of sexual desire alongside her history of racial and sexual abuse entails her understanding and working against the rigid self-identification imposed on her by her foremothers. Through Ursa, Gayl Jones grapples with pernicious stereotypes of black women's *sexuality as well as issues of speech, silence, art, history, and self-empowerment, all predominant themes in late-twentieth-century African American women's writing.

• Claudia C. Tate, *"Corregidora*: Ursa's Blues Medley," *Black American Literature Forum* 13 (Fall 1979): 139–141. Missy Dehn Kubitschek, *Claiming the Heritage: African-American Women Novelists and History,* 1991.

—Amy S. Gottfried

UTOPIAS. *See* Speculative Fiction.

V

VAN DYKE, HENRY (b. 1928), editor, journalist, and novelist. Born in Allegan, Michigan, Henry Van Dyke spent his childhood in Montgomery, Alabama, where his father taught at Alabama State Teachers College. He returned to Michigan for high school and remained to receive an MA in journalism from the University of Michigan in 1955. While at Michigan, Van Dyke received the Avery Hopwood Award for Fiction. After graduating he worked as a journalist and editor in Michigan, Pennsylvania, and New York. During his time on the editorial staff at Basic Books in New York he finished his first published novel, *Ladies of the Rachmaninoff Eyes* (1965). His short pieces have appeared in *Transatlantic Review, Generation, Antioch Review*, and *The O. Henry Prize Stories, 1979*.

Van Dyke's work addresses race relations issues prominent in the 1960s and 1970s. He writes about conflict among African Americans, between African Americans and white and Jewish Americans. He is influenced by modernist writers and ideas. The plot of *Ladies of the Rachmaninoff Eyes* revolves around the production of a Gertrude Stein play by self-proclaimed members of her circle. The production serves as the stage for exploring the relations between the young African American protagonist, Oliver, and the Jewish production team. His second novel, *Blood of Stawberries* (1968), is dedicated to the white chronicler of the *Harlem Renaissance, Carl Van Vechten. Issues of race relations again arise in *Dead Piano* (1971), his third novel, this time within the African American community. Drawing on current affairs at the time of publication, *Dead Piano* uses an outsider, a militant African American group, to upset the social structure of a light-skinned, middle-class African American family. In the microcosm of a few stressful hours in the family's apartment, the characters address large social issues of assimilation and separatism.

• Granville Hicks, "Literary Horizons," *Saturday Review,* 4 Jan. 1969, 93. Edward G. McGhee, "Henry Van Dyke," in *DLB*, vol. 33, *Afro-American Fiction Writers after 1955*, eds. Thadious M. Davis and Trudier Harris, 1984, pp. 250–255.

—Caroline Senter

VASHON, GEORGE B. (1824–1878), essayist and poet. George Boyer Vashon was the first African American to graduate from Oberlin College and the first to become a lawyer in New York State. Born in Carlisle, Pennsylvania, Vashon attended school in Pittsburgh and served there as secretary of the first Juvenile Anti-Slavery Society in the nation (1838). He earned a BA from Oberlin (1844) and studied law in Pittsburgh but was denied admittance to the bar because of his race. Embarking on a thirty-month exile in Haiti, Vashon stopped in New York, where he was admitted to the bar in 1848. He taught at College Faustin in Port-au-Prince; then from 1850 to 1854 he

practiced law in Syracuse, New York, and for the next three years was professor of belles lettres and mathematics at New York Central College in McGrawville. Returning to Pittsburgh, Vashon married Susan Paul Smith (1857), with whom he had seven children. He was a principal and teacher in Pittsburgh schools until 1867 and thereafter held government posts in Washington, D.C., worked for race advancement with the Colored Men of America, and published learned *essays, poems, and *letters in *periodicals. It is commonly thought that he died of yellow fever in Mississippi.

"Vincent Ogé" (1854), Vashon's 391-line epic on the Haitian *insurrection (1790–1791), is a signal imaginative achievement in African American *poetry of the nineteenth century. The slaves' revolt becomes not only a metaphor for universal racial conflict and mankind's resistance to tyranny, but also a symbol of a world in perpetual chaotic motion. Within a finely structured, dramatic whole Vashon sustains an ambience of instability with image patterns of flickering light, storms, blood, and warfare, and by shifts in diction, in metrical and stanzaic form, voices, and scenes. Measured by the artistry of "Vincent Ogé" and his essays, his labors for racial justice, and his academic achievements, Vashon was a man of extraordinary courage and talent.

• [George B. Vashon obituary notice], *Oberlin Review,* 20 Nov. 1878 (rpt. from *People's Advocate,* n.d.). Joan R. Sherman, *Invisible Poets: Afro-Americans of the Nineteenth Century,* 2d ed., 1989.

—Joan R. Sherman

VASSA, GUSTAVUS. *See* Equiano, Olaudah.

VELMA HENRY is the main character in Toni Cade *Bambara's *The *Salt Eaters* (1980), whose healing is the connecting thread for the many subplots in the novel. Velma is the kind of woman upon whom others depend and who appears to be perpetually strong. She has, with her husband Obie, founded and managed the now-fragmented and troubled Academy of Seven Arts. She actively participates in a women's political caucus and the Seven Sisters arts collective, as well as maintaining a marriage, raising a son, and working full-time as a computer programmer. The fragmentation and splintering that characterize the community exist also within Velma herself, and she attempts suicide as a means of finally sealing herself off from escalating rage and fear.

Velma's characterization mirrors many of the extraordinarily strong women in much of African American literature, but with a difference. She is one who, by virtue of her inability to remain self-sufficient, is given an alternative: the healing that comes from reconnecting with herself, her past, and the life-giving values she has forsaken in her unremitting struggle for justice. Velma's suicide attempt is the culmination of exhaustion and an alienation from her body and her legacy as an African American and a woman. As the healer *Minnie Ransom says, Velma must release the pain, but that release cannot come until she decides she wants the "weight of being well," and will return to the community a stronger, more able, but more deeply and spiritually connected human being.   —Ann Folwell Stanford

VERNACULAR. *See* Speech and Dialect.

VESEY, PAUL. *See* Allen, Samuel W.

VIOLENCE. From the eighteenth century onward, African American writers have addressed the subject of violence in an evolving American social arena, whether that violence manifests itself in the context of racial turmoil, within the small-scale setting of a local community, or within the privatized setting of the home. Black writers have also fully engaged in the politics of representing violence, especially the ways in which violence against men, women, or whole communities might be manifested differently against the backdrop of enduring social myths about *race, *gender, and aggression.

Early African American works such as Lucy *Terry's 1740s poem "Bars Fight," about a clash between Native Americans and New England settlers, and Briton *Hammon's Indian captivity narrative *A Narrative of the Uncommon Sufferings, and Surprising Deliverance of Briton Hammon* (1760) bear witness to the violence of early colonization that marked the European invasion of North America. However, in the late eighteenth and early nineteenth centuries most black writers came to public attention as slave narrators, novelists, and pamphleteers engaged in a struggle against *slavery. Writing under the auspices of various abolitionist groups, ex-slave writers such as Olaudah *Equiano in *The Interesting Narrative* (1789), Henry *Bibb in *Life and Adventures* (1845), Frederick *Douglass in *Narrative of the Life of Frederick Douglass* (1845), and William Wells *Brown in *Narrative of William Wells Brown, A Fugitive Slave* (1847) recounted scenes of slaughter, beatings, torture, and rape designed to shock audiences still unconverted to the abolition of slavery.

While many white abolitionists publicized the image of the helpless slave victimized by a brutal system, slave narrators and freeborn writers frequently highlighted the reality of black self-defense in light of the fact that from the black overthrow of Haiti's French colonists in 1791 through the Virginia revolt led by Nat *Turner in 1831, and beyond, the history of the New World had been one of bloody black rebellion. The most famous articulation of slave violence as self-defense, and consequently as transformative of the self, comes in Frederick Douglass's account of his fight with the brutal slavebreaker Covey. According to Douglass, "This battle with Mr. Covey was the turning-point in my career as a slave. It rekindled the few expiring embers of freedom, and revived within me a sense of my own manhood" (*Narrative of the Life*, 1845). Eventually Douglass would memorialize black slave defiance in his 1853 novella "The *Heroic Slave," about the real-life black rebel Madison Washington. The thematization of retaliatory violence as a necessary ingredient to the achievement of black *manhood, social equality, and community liberation was a primary issue for freeborn African American pamphleteer David *Walker. Walker's *Appeal, in Four Articles . . . to the Colored Citizens of the World* (1829) was written for the direct purpose of inciting southern slaves to revolt, and his militancy was echoed in Martin R. *Delany's serialized novel *Blake, or The Huts of America* (1859).

African American male writers such as Douglass, Walker, Delany, and especially ex-slave William Wells Brown in his novel *Clotel, or The President's Daughter* (1853), did stress that the rape of slave women was as much a violation of the slave's body as a beating might have been. However, heroic figures such as Madison Washington and the eponymous male hero of Delany's *Blake* were attempts to rescript notions of race, victimhood, and masculinity. Whether on the subject of slavery or indentured labor, discussions of female resistance to physical and sexual abuse necessitated different methods of description and necessarily evoked different modes of retaliation. This fact was exemplified by the domestic defiance advocated in Harriet E. *Wilson's *Our Nig, or Sketches from the Life of a Free Black* (1859), in the innuendo and sexual power play featured in Harriet A. *Jacobs's *Incidents in the Life of a Slave Girl, Written by Herself* (1861), and in the move to self-definition through mercantilism in Elizabeth *Keckley's *Behind the Scenes, or Thirty Years a Slave, and Four Years in the White House* (1868).

Despite the achievement of black emancipation after the Civil War, the tradition of black-white racial struggle begun under slavery continued into the years of Reconstruction and beyond. In the South freed blacks now had to deal with new systems of forced labor institutionalized under the guise of sharecropping and the convict lease system; at the same time they were subject to rape, torture, beatings, white race riots, and especially *lynching, this time at the hand of white supremacist groups such as the Ku Klux Klan. Though the organizational power of the Klan rose and fell throughout the post–Civil War years, lynching, race riots, and the general harassment of African Americas were the order of the day often—though not exclusively—in the South. There were complex reasons behind the specific rise in white violence in this period, but by the end of the century many Americans had come to believe that lynching in particular was a necessary response to the "threat" of the black male as rapist.

Sharpening the political purpose of their writing, black novelists, essayists, and journalists from Reconstruction onward worked to challenge the ideology behind lynching, representing the fact that entire communities of black men, women, and children were subject to white violence because of their desire to enter into the public sphere as economic and political equals and not because of the alleged criminality of black men. Undoubtedly, the African American journalist Ida B. *Wells-Barnett was the most famous antilynching advocate of these years. In countless speeches, editorials, and articles, and especially in three powerful pamphlets, *Southern Horrors: Lynch Law in All Its Phases* (1892), *A Red Record: Tabulated Statistics and Alleged Causes of Lynchings in the United States, 1892–1893–1894* (1895), and *Mob Rule in New Orleans: Robert Charles and His Fight to the Death* (1900), Wells indicted white violence with graphic accounts of lynching's brutality drawn from white newspaper reports, and she provided detailed statistics outlining the fact that lynching victims were often women and children and that the cause of execution was often simply petty crimes.

Among African American novelists, Frances Ellen Watkins *Harper represented the lynching of black women for their outspokenness in the early years of Reconstruction in her serialized novel *Minnie's Sacrifice* (1869), while in *Iola Leroy* (1892) she characterized lynching as a white terrorist method of control rather than as a weapon for white community protection. In particular *Iola Leroy* dramatized the history of sexual abuse suffered by African American women at the hands of white men, presenting the rarely publicized flip side to the allegation that the black rape of white women had reached epidemic proportions. Pauline E. *Hopkins echoed this argument in her novel *Contending Forces: A Romance of Negro Life North and South* (1900), in which she addressed the impact of both lynching and the white rape of black women on a turn-of-the-century African American Boston community. The effects of white violence on African American men, as well as women, were also taken up in David Bryant *Fulton's novel *Hanover, or The Persecution of the Lowly* (1900), written under the pseudonym "Jack Thorne." In particular, as did Ida B. Wells-Barnett in her public work, Fulton implicated white women in the perpetuation of violence, women in whose name many atrocities were committed and who, even if they did not partake in the slaughter of blacks, were nevertheless made guilty by their failure to protest such injustice.

As with earlier literature, the problem of how to constitute a strong image of black resistance was of increasing concern to African American writers responding to lynching. Some black leaders such as Booker T. *Washington enacted complex strategies of accommodation, while some black intellectuals such as Harper in *Iola Leroy* argued for a kind of moral persuasion coupled with a positive representation of emancipated blacks as capable citizens rather than marauding criminals. On the other hand more militant individuals such as Ida B. Wells-Barnett and fellow journalist Edward Bruce entertained and even celebrated the idea of violent black retaliation. Specifically in the case of black self-defensive violence, African American writers followed their predecessors in imagining militancy as primarily a male province, as was the case in novels such as Sutton E. *Griggs's *Imperium in Imperio* (1899) and *The Hindered Hand, or The Reign of the Repressionist* (1905) as well as in Charles Waddell *Chesnutt's *The *Marrow of Tradition* (1901). Neither Griggs nor Chesnutt finally saw black violence as the most viable response to white aggression; however, they did recognize the need to refigure black masculinity in a heroic and aggressive defense of African American communities under white supremacist attack.

With the advent of the twentieth century, as James Weldon *Johnson's *The *Autobiography of an Ex-Colored Man* (1912) amply demonstrated, racial discrimination, southern segregation, lynching, and race rioting were still the standard features of American life. Though black soldiers proved their devotion to the United States by fighting for their country in World War I, they and their communities had to endure the "Red Summer" of 1919, when race riots broke out in Chicago and Washington as well as in parts of Arkansas, South Carolina, and Texas. Thus the literature of *Harlem Renaissance writers in the 1920s and 1930s was necessarily produced within a context of almost unaltered racial violence generated by the smoldering resentment of past wrongs, the pressures of urban poverty, and renewed demands for the rights of citizenship. Texts as artistically diverse as Jean *Toomer's *Cane* (1923), Claude *McKay's poems "If We Must Die" (1919) and "The Lynching" (1919), and Arna *Bontemps's *Black Thunder* (1936) all bear to differing degrees a preoccupation with the horror of lynching and the pressure to formulate a strategy of black resistance.

Perhaps the most powerful meditation on black-white violence in the first half of the twentieth century came in Richard *Wright's *Native Son* (1940). A naturalistic novel that evokes America's fear of black criminality (the black protagonist *Bigger Thomas murders a white woman, then rapes and murders his own black girlfriend), Wright's work contextualizes black urban violence against the backdrop of institutionalized and overt white racism, segregation, and extreme urban poverty. While Wright does not absolve Bigger of his guilt as a murderer and rapist, America itself is made to bear great responsibility in the creation of such "native sons" as Bigger Thomas.

Since the publication of Wright's landmark novel, notable works include Ann *Petry's *The *Street* (1946); Ralph *Ellison's *Invisible Man* (1952); *The *Autobiography of Malcolm X* (1964); John Edgar *Wideman's *The Lynchers* (1973); Gayl *Jones's *Corregidora* (1975); Toni *Morrison's *The *Bluest Eye* (1970), *Song of Solomon* (1977), and *Beloved* (1987); Octavia E. *Butler's *Kindred* (1979); Alice *Walker's *The *Color Purple* (1982); Gloria *Naylor's *The *Women of Brewster Place* (1982); Ernest J. *Gaines's *A Gathering of Old Men* (1983); Jewelle *Gomez's *The Gilda Stories* (1991); and Albert French's *Billy* (1993). Against the backdrop of major events in the post–World War II United States—the turmoil of the civil rights era; the assassinations of Martin Luther *King, Jr.; *Malcolm X, and John and Robert Kennedy; the phenomenon of the Black Power movement; the advent of the Vietnam War; and horrific scenes of inner city violence, such as the 1992 multiracial riots in Los Angeles over the acquittal of police officers charged with beating black motorist Rodney King—these texts variously retell and reevaluate the complex history of racial violence and that history's impact on blacks and whites alike. As a body of African American autobiography and fiction, they document the brutality of rape and the problem of crushing urban poverty; they also address present-day realities of black anger and white discrimination, black incarceration and "legal" lynching within the American justice system, and the violence erupting among African Americans themselves when individuals are driven to the breaking point. But as they continue to imagine such gruesome realities, they also never fail to address the possibilities of communal resistance and communal healing, themes long advocated in the works of their predecessors.

[*See also* Insurrections.]

• George M. Fredrickson, *The Black Image in the White Mind: The Debate on Afro-American Character and Destiny, 1817–1914*, 1971. Ronald Takaki, *Violence in the Black Imagination: Essays and Documents*, 1972. Trudier Harris, *Exorcising Blackness: Historical and Literary Lynchings and Burning Rituals*, 1984. Joel Williamson, *The Crucible of Race: Black-White Relations in the South Since Emancipation*, 1984. Herbert Shapiro, *White Violence and Black Response: From Reconstruction to Montgomery*, 1988. Richard Yarborough, "Race, Violence, and Manhood: The Masculine Idea in Frederick Douglass's 'The Heroic Slave,'" in *Frederick Douglass: New Literary Essays*, ed. Eric J. Sundquist, 1990, pp. 166–188. Nellie Y. McKay, "Alice Walker's 'Advancing Luna—and Ida B. Wells' 'A Struggle Towards Sisterhood," in *Rape and Representation*, eds. Lynn A. Higgins and Brenda R. Silver, 1991, pp. 248–260. Robyn Wiegman, "The Anatomy of Lynching," *Journal of the History of Sexuality* 3 (1993): 445–467.   —Sandra Gunning

Voice from the South, A. Published during the period now known as the *Woman's Era, Anna Julia *Cooper's *A Voice from the South* (1892) is a landmark feminist text. In this volume of *essays and lectures, Cooper argues that just as white people cannot speak for African Americans, so African American men cannot "be wholly expected fully and adequately to reproduce the exact Voice of the Black Woman."

The volume consists of two parts, the first comprised of four essays focused directly on women's issues: "Womanhood, a Vital Element in the Regeneration and Progress of a Race," "The Higher Education of Woman," "Woman vs. the Indian," and "The Status of Woman in America." The second half, also made up of four essays, continues this attention to women's rights while broadening the focus to discuss U.S. history as multicultural from the beginning; representations of African Americans in contemporary American literature, especially fiction by William Dean Howells and Albion W. Tourgée; discrimination against African Americans in housing; and philosophical positivism and skepticism versus Cooper's own articulated belief in Christian optimism.

Cooper's *feminism in *A Voice from the South* springs from various sources. It combines Victorian ideologies of true womanhood (the belief that women are by divine design moral, intuitive, spiritual, and nurturing); a radical and uncompromising belief in women's intellectual equality with men; turn-of-the-century class-inflected theories of racial uplift; and Cooper's own deeply felt Christian egalitarianism and hatred of oppression. The result is an impassioned scholarly argument advocating fundamental change in the status and treatment of African American women. While Cooper's main target is white racism, she also criticizes African American men, of whom she observes, "While our men seem thoroughly abreast of the times on almost every other subject, when they strike the woman question they drop back into sixteenth century logic." Also singled out are the hypocrisy and racism of white feminists, including leaders such as Anna Shaw and Susan B. Anthony, whose pitting of white women's goals against the rights of people of color Cooper attacks in "'Woman vs. the Indian.'"

Cooper expresses her core belief in the inseparability of women's issues and the struggle for racial justice in her often-quoted statement, "Only the BLACK WOMAN can say 'when and where I enter, in the quiet, undisputed dignity of my womanhood, without violence and without suing or special patronage, then and there the whole *Negro race enters with me.*'" She names as basic civil rights issues: protecting African American women from sexual attacks; speaking out against racist female *stereotypes; making education available to all African American women; and addressing the economic oppression that consigns the majority of black women and their families to poverty. The African American woman's situation is the race's situation, in her view. Connecting issues of *gender and *race is mandatory.

Today scholars regard *A Voice from the South* as a pioneering African American feminist text. While it is limited by its *class bias, it is nevertheless highly valued for its intellectual and political arguments as well as its literary excellence, including Cooper's satiric wit.

• Hazel V. Carby, *Reconstructing Womanhood: The Emergence of the Afro-American Woman Novelist*, 1987. Claudia Tate, *Domestic Allegories of Political Desire: The Black Heroine's Text at the Turn of the Century*, 1992.
—Elizabeth Ammons

Voice of the Negro, The. The *Voice of the Negro* began publication in Atlanta, Georgia, in January 1904. This journal began by trying to steer a compromise between accommodationists and radicals. The first issues included writing by Booker T. *Washington; however, the magazine soon became the voice for a new generation of writers, including W. E. B. *Du Bois, John Hope, Kelly *Miller, Mary Church *Terrell, and William *Pickens. Confrontations with the city government in Atlanta after the race riots in September 1906 forced J. Max Barber, editor of the *Voice of the Negro*, to move the magazine to Chicago, where it ceased publication the next year.

The *Voice of the Negro* addressed many social issues, such as African American *education, the labor movement, and *religion. Although it became mainly associated with activist politics, it also kept the African American in the "New South" abreast of issues in art and culture. The *Voice of the Negro* published a number of respected African American poets, including James D. *Corrothers, Georgia Douglas *Johnson, and Paul Laurence *Dunbar.

[*See also* Periodicals.]

• Louis R. Harlan, "Booker T. Washington and the *Voice of the Negro*, 1904–1907," *Journal of Southern History* 45 (Feb. 1979): pp. 45–62. Walter C. Daniel, *Black Journals of the United States*, 1982.

—Daniel J. Royer

VROMAN, MARY ELIZABETH (192?–1967), short fiction writer, novelist, movie script writer, and first African American woman member of the Screen Writers Guild. Born in Buffalo, New York, sometime between 1924 and 1929, Mary Elizabeth Vroman grew up in the West Indies and graduated from Alabama State Teachers College, determined to make a difference in her students' lives. She taught for twenty years in Alabama, Chicago, and New York. Vroman's "See How They Run" focused upon the experiences of an idealistic African American first-year teacher in a third-grade rural Alabama school. Published in the June 1951 *Ladies' Home Journal*, the story elicited five hundred enthusiastic letters from readers.

Praised as the "finest story to come out of the South since *Green Pastures*," "See How They Run" won the Christopher Award for inspirational magazine writing because of its humanitarian quality. It also appeared in the July 1952 issue of *Ebony.

The protagonist, Jane Richards, describes her interactions with children in a school with a leaky roof and a potbellied stove. Many youngsters come to class without breakfast and share tattered, outdated textbooks. They help their overworked, underpaid teacher haul water from a well down the road, not far from a foul-smelling outhouse. The story serves as an excellent primary source showing the difficulties and joys of educating African American children in the segregated South.

In 1953, Vroman wrote a movie script of her story for a motion picture entitled *Bright Road*, featuring Harry Belafonte and Dorothy Dandridge. She became the first African American woman member of the Screen Writers Guild.

Vroman's first novel, *Esther* (1963), features a dignified grandmother, Lydia Jones, who saves her money as a midwife to purchase some land and uses her savings to encourage her granddaughter, Esther Kennedy, to pursue a nursing career. *Shaped to Its Purpose* (1965) told the history of the first fifty years of Delta Sigma Theta, a sorority of forty thousand college-trained professional African American women to which the author belonged. Vroman's third book, *Harlem Summer* (1967), was intended for young adult readers and features sixteen-year-old John, from Montgomery, Alabama, who spends the summer living with relatives and working in Harlem.

Mary Elizabeth Vroman honestly depicted African American lifestyles during the decades of the 1950s and 1960s without becoming cynical. In spite of adversities, her characters are proud and resilient. They retain their sense of humanity, finding joy in happy experiences with loving family members and understanding friends. Mary Elizabeth Vroman died in 1967 due to complications following surgery.

• Saul Bachner, "Writing School Marm: Alabama Teacher Finds Literary Movie Success with First Short Story," *Ebony*, July 1952, 23–28. Saul Bachner, "Black Literature: The Junior Novel in the Classroom—*Harlem Summer*," *Negro American Literature Forum* 7 (Spring 1973): 26–27. Edith Blicksilver, "See How They Run," in *The Ethnic American Woman: Problems, Protests, Lifestyle*, 1978, pp. 125–143.

—Edith Blicksilver

W

WALKER, ALICE (b. 1944), poet, novelist, essayist, biographer, short fiction writer, womanist, publisher, educator, and Pulitzer Prize laureate. Born the eighth child of a southern sharecropper and a part-time maid, Alice Walker has climbed the proverbial ladder of success to become one of America's most gifted and influential writers. She has received notoriety for her taboo-breaking and morally challenging depictions of African American passions and oppressions. Although her work is diverse in subject matter and varied in form, it is clearly centered around the struggles and spiritual development affecting the survival whole of women. Walker's writing exposes the complexities of the ordinary by presenting it within a context of duplicity and change. Within this context, Walker peels back the hard cast cover of African and African American women's lives to reveal the naked edge of truth and hope.

Walker was born in Eatonton, Georgia, where she learned early the value of looking within the hidden spaces of human experience and exploring them creatively. At the age of eight, a BB gun accident blinded and scarred her right eye. The experience of this disfigurement profoundly influenced Walker's life, leading her into a self-imposed isolation that was open only to her thirst for reading and her love of poetry. Her self-imposed alienation, coupled with her fear of becoming totally blind, encouraged the young girl to search people and relationships closely—to discover the inner truths masked by facades of acceptance and equality. Walker used her blinded eye as a filter through which to look beyond the surface of African American women's existence, and discovered that she cared about both the pain and spiritual decay she found hidden there.

Walker graduated from high school as valedictorian of her class and, in 1961, entered Spelman College on a Georgia rehabilitation scholarship. After a two-year stay at Spelman and while a student at Sarah Lawrence College (1963–1965), Walker visited Africa for a summer. There she fell in love and wrote several of the poems that were later included in her first book of poetry, *Once* (1968). Upon her return to Sarah Lawrence, Walker was pregnant and contemplating suicide. She felt trapped by her body and believed that only an abortion could free her. The poems of love, suicide, and civil rights published in *Once* were written during this, her second period of self-imposed isolation. After a serious contemplation of her options, Walker aborted her pregnancy and began her first published short story, "To Hell with Dying." First published in 1967, this story of an old man who is revived from death by the attentive love of two children was later published as a children's book (in 1988) with illustrations by Catherine Deeter.

Walker completed her studies at Sarah Lawrence College and received her bachelor of arts degree in 1965, moved to the lower east side of New York City, and began working for the Welfare Department. On 17 March 1967, she married Melvyn Roseman Leventhal, a Jewish civil rights lawyer, and, later that year, the couple moved to Jackson, Mississippi. While in Mississippi, Walker wrote and supported various civil rights activities. She worked as writer in residence at Jackson State College (1968–1969) and Tougaloo College (1970–1971) and was a black history consultant to the Friends of the Children of Mississippi Head Start program.

Although Walker gained some measure of success as a writer during her marriage to Leventhal, the pressures of racial prejudice prevented many readers from appreciating her creative genius. Her decision to marry outside of her race brought with it criticism and complaints. Existing Mississippi law made it a crime for her to live as Leventhal's legal wife and African American male critics insisted upon focusing on her interracial marriage instead of her writing. The marriage ended in 1977 when the couple divorced amicably. They had one child, Rebecca Grant, born on 17 November 1969.

The ten years of Walker's marriage were the most prolific in her creative career. In addition to the publication of her second book of poetry, titled *Five Poems* (1972), Walker published her first novel, *The *Third Life of Grange Copeland* (1970), joining Toni *Morrison in beginning what was to become known as a renaissance of African American women writers. *The Third Life of Grange Copeland* is a realistic novel that presents three generations of a family whose history is marred by race, class, and gender oppression. The main focus of this novel is not the social conflicts generated by race prejudice that were generally written about during the black nationalist movement. Instead, the novel challenges African Americans to take a scrutinizing look at themselves.

The Third Life of Grange Copeland exposes the abuses and maddening injustices of African American internal familial conflict and oppression. Because of this break with the norm, critics charged Walker with not presenting the "right image" of African American life. Walker refused to let negative criticism stifle her creative spirit, however. She continued to write, challenging the status quo of African American literary decorum at every turn. In 1973, she shared her vision of the victories and tribulations of African American women's lives in a collection of short stories titled *In Love and Trouble: Stories of Black Women*. The collection of thirteen stories won the American Academy and Institute of Arts and Letters Rosenthal Award in 1974. Her third book of poetry, *Revolutionary Petunias and Other Poems* (1973), won the Lillian Smith Award of the Southern Regional Council in 1974 and was nominated for the National Book Award. That same year Walker published two children's books: *Langston Hughes, American Poet* and *The Life of Thomas Hodge*.

Unlike *The Third Life of Grange Copeland*, Walker's second novel, *Meridian* (1976), focuses on the *civil rights movement and its fight for social change, However, *Meridian*'s social critique is woman-centered. In many ways, the novel's concern with women, specifically its commentary on African American motherhood, reflects Walker's own conflicts during her first pregnancy and abortion. *Meridian* redefines African American motherhood and reconstructs it as an inner spark that fuels a genuine sense of love and responsibility among people; it does not generate from within the womb, but from within the relationships developed by women that support and build their communities and their world.

In 1979, Walker edited *I Love Myself When I Am Laughing*. The stories this anthology contains were collected by Walker after working incessantly to restore the memory of Zora Neale *Hurston to the annals of history. Walker takes pride in the relationships and continuities developed from within a matrilineal tradition of writing. For Walker, women such as Gwendolyn *Brooks and Hurston are foremothers from whom she and other African American women writers can learn and grow. Although both of these writers are important to Walker and her creative vision, Hurston is an icon for her, representing superb literary achievement and courage. In 1973, Walker journeyed to Florida in search of the writer's past. There she found and marked Hurston's neglected gravesite with a headstone.

Walker is innovative in her attempts to save African American women writers from the dark recesses of oblivion. As co-owner of her own publishing house, Wild Tree Press, Walker promotes and mentors new writers such as J. California *Cooper. In 1977, while teaching at Wellesley College, she introduced academia to one of the first African American women's literature courses. Walker has also taught African American women's studies at Brandeis, the University of Massachusetts, Yale, and the University of California at Berkeley.

Walker's pattern of challenging the minds and morals of her readers continued into the 1980s. In 1982, she stepped across the line of a highly forbidden taboo with her portrayal of *Celie in The *Color Purple*. This novel examines not only "black-on-black" oppression but also incest, bisexual love, and lesbian love. Written in epistolary form, Walker's third novel exposes the internal turmoil parenting the spiritual decay of African American women who, like the novel's protagonist, silently endure abusive male-dominated relationships. In *The Color Purple*, Celie is raped by a man she believes is her father. Later, she is battered and mentally abused in a loveless marriage. Although this novel ignited controversy (especially from African American men who claimed Walker's novel was creative male-bashing), it was on the *New York Times* bestseller list for twenty-five weeks. Walker achieved the status of a major American writer when the novel won both the Pulitzer Prize for Fiction and the National Book Award in 1983. Two years later, it was adapted as a major motion picture directed by Steven Spielberg.

Walker published a collection of womanist prose entitled **In Search of Our Mothers' Gardens* in 1983. The book is a memoir of Walker's experiences and observations of African American women's culture and continues her exploration of the hidden truths defining female wholeness. In this collection of essays, reviews, and articles, Walker defines her feminist stance as *womanism. For her, a womanist is a black feminist who is "committed to survival and wholeness of entire people, male and female." The designation "womanist" and the ideologies it represents has extended Walker's influence beyond literary circles and into the domain of African American religious culture. The term has been adopted by prominent African American theologians such as Katie Cannon (*Black Womanist Ethics*, 1988) and Renita J. Weems (*Just a Sister Away*, 1988), as well as renowned ministers like Prathia Hall Wynn of Philadelphia and Ella Pearson Mitchell of the Inter-denominational Theological Center in Atlanta, Georgia.

Walker's concern for spiritual wholeness and cultural connectedness completely ascended the physical in her fourth novel, *The *Temple of My Familiar* (1989), a story that takes the reader into a time before the apparition of physical perfection and ownership began to dominate the mind of humanity. The reception of this novel was mixed and it did not receive the broad popularity of *The Color Purple*. The *Temple of My Familiar* solidly argues Walker's belief that the roots of African American women's hope for spiritual wholeness lies within the soil of their African origins. But for Walker, even these origins are not above reproach and evaluation.

In her fifth novel, **Possessing the Secret of Joy* (1992), Walker uncovers the mysteries of a ritualist past that has imposed its presence into a changing world—a world that defines clitoridectomy (female circumcision) as sexual blinding, domination, and abuse. *Possessing the Secret of Joy* brings the life and imagination of Tashi, a character who appeared in both *The Color Purple* and *The Temple of My Familiar*, into full view. The chilling reality of oppression and control mandated by the traditions of female circumcision is further explored by Walker in her documentary film (and accompanying book of 1993) *Warrior Marks* (1994), directed by the Indian-British filmmaker Pratibha Parmar.

Alice Walker is one of the first African American women writers to explore the paralyzing effects of being a woman in a world that virtually ignores issues like black-on-black oppression and female circumcision. Her efforts, however, have not always received favorable reception among blacks. In 1996, Walker published *The Same River Twice*, a book in which she addresses the pain of negative criticism. In her attempts to open the blinded eyes of those around her, Walker has written a total of five novels, four children's books, five volumes of poetry (the most recently published volume is *Her Blue Body Everything We Know*, 1991), two collections of short stories, three volumes of essays, one documentary film, and many uncollected articles. Today Walker continues to express creatively her wish for wholeness for those who have been erased from history, torn from their racial heritage, silenced, mutilated, and denied freedom. With incomparable vision and insight, she captures the folklore, language, pain, spirit, and memories of African Americans only to weave them into a quilt of compassion that she spreads before the world—full, rich, and flowing.

[See also Brownfield Copeland; Shug Avery.]

• "Alice Walker," in Black Women Writers at Work, ed. Claudia Tate, 1983, pp. 175–187. Barbara Christian, "Alice Walker," in DLB, vol. 33, Afro-American Fiction Writers after 1955, eds. Thadious M. Davis and Trudier Harris, 1984, pp. 258–271. Barbara Christian, "Alice Walker: The Black Woman Artist as Wayward," in Black Women Writers (1959–1980): A Critical Evaluation, ed. Mari Evans, 1984, pp. 457–477. Philip Royster, "In Search of Our Father's Arms: Alice Walker's Persona of the Alienated Darling," Black American Literature Forum 20.4 (1986): 347–370. Erma Banks and Keith Byerman, Alice Walker: An Annotated Bibliography, 1967–1986, 1989. Rudolph P. Byrd, "Spirituality in the Novels of Alice Walker: Models, Healing, and Transformation, or When the Spirit Moves So Do We," in Wild Women in the Whirlwind: Afra-American Culture and the Contemporary Literary Renaissance, eds. Joanne M. Braxton and Andrée Nicola McLaughlin, 1990, pp. 363–378. Grace E. Collins, "Alice Walker," in Notable Black American Women, ed. Jessie Carney Smith, 1992, pp. 1178–1182. Frank N. Magill, ed., Masterpieces of African American Literature, 1992, pp. 107–110, 301–304, 447–450, 573–576. Henry Louis Gates, Jr., and K. A. Appiah, eds., Alice Walker: Critical Perspectives Past and Present, 1993.
—Debra Walker King

WALKER, DAVID (1785–1830), abolitionist, orator, and author of David Walker's Appeal. Although David Walker's father, who died before his birth, was enslaved, his mother was a free woman; thus, when he was born in Wilmington, North Carolina, in September 1785, David Walker was also free, following the "condition" of his mother as prescribed by southern laws regulating *slavery. Little is known about Walker's early life. He traveled widely in the South and probably spent time in Philadelphia. He developed early on an intense and abiding hatred of slavery, the result apparently of his travels and his firsthand knowledge of slavery.

Relocating to Boston in the mid-1820s, he became a clothing retailer and in 1828 married a woman named Eliza. They had one son, Edward (or Edwin) Garrison Walker, born after David Walker's death in 1830. An active figure in Boston's African American community during the late 1820s, David Walker had a reputation as a generous, benevolent person who sheltered fugitives and frequently shared his income with the poor. He joined the Methodist Church and in 1827 became a general agent for *Freedom's Journal, a newly established African American newspaper. During the two years of the newspaper's existence, he regularly supported the New York City–based publication, finding subscribers, distributing copies, and contributing articles. He was also a notable member of the Massachusetts General Colored Association, an antislavery and civil rights organization founded in 1826. In lectures before the association, Walker spoke out against slavery and colonization, while urging African American solidarity.

In September 1829, he published *David Walker's Appeal. In this pamphlet, which quickly went through three editions, he fiercely denounced slavery, colonization, and the institutional exclusion, oppression, and degradation of African peoples. His Appeal was a militant call for united action against the sources of the "wretchedness" of African Americans, enslaved and free. Often reprinted, widely circulated, and highly regarded by a number of African American readers, Walker's Appeal generated a vehement response from white Americans, especially in the South. Several southern state legislatures passed laws banning such "seditious" literature and reinforced legislation forbidding the *education of slaves in reading and writing. The governors of Georgia and Virginia and the mayor of Savannah wrote letters to the mayor of Boston expressing outrage about the Appeal and demanding that Walker be arrested and punished. In Georgia, a bounty was offered on him, ten thousand dollars alive, one thousand dollars dead. In the North, newspapers attacked the pamphlet, as did white abolitionists (and pacifists) Benjamin Lundy and William Lloyd Garrison, who admired Walker's courage and intelligence but condemned the circulation of the Appeal as imprudent.

Walker died in the summer of 1830. Although the cause and circumstances of his death are mysterious, many have suspected that he was poisoned. After his death, the Appeal continued to circulate in various editions, including Henry Highland *Garnet's 1848 reprinting of the Appeal along with his own "Address to the Slaves" in a single volume. As one of the earliest and most compelling printed expressions of African American nationalism, militancy, and solidarity, the Appeal has remained a vital and influential text for successive generations of African American activists.

[See also Antislavery Movement.]

• Herbert Aptheker, "One Continual Cry": David Walker's Appeal to the Colored Citizens of the World (1829–30), 1965. Benjamin Quarles, Black Abolitionists, 1969. Donald M. Jacobs, "David Walker: Boston Race Leader, 1825–1830," Essex Institute Historical Collections 107 (Jan. 1971): 94–107. Jane H. Pease and William H. Pease, They Who Would Be Free: Blacks' Search for Freedom, 1830–1861, 1974. Wilson Jeremiah Moses, Black Messiahs and Uncle Toms: Social and Literary Manipulations of a Religious Myth, 1982. Sterling Stuckey, Slave Culture: Nationalist Theory and the Foundations of Black America, 1987.
—Gregory Eiselein

WALKER, JOSEPH A. (b. 1935), director, choreographer, actor, educator, Tony Award winner, and leading African American playwright of the 1970s. Born in Washington, D.C., in 1935, to working-class parents, Joseph A. Walker began his theatrical career in college with acting roles in several student productions at Howard University. He received his BA in 1956 and went on to begin graduate work in philosophy and serve a term in the U.S. Air Force before deciding to pursue a career in *theater.

Like the young protagonist, Jeff, in his most famous play, The *River Niger, Walker began military service as a navigation student but found himself too distracted by poetic impulses to continue. Rather than drop out altogether like his fictional creation, however, Walker persevered in the corps, becoming a first lieutenant and second-in-command of his squadron before his discharge in 1960. Evidently he emerged even more determined to write.

With an MFA from Catholic University (1963), Walker embarked on a teaching career—at secondary school in Washington, D.C., at the City College of New York, and finally at Howard University—which proved more amenable to his artistic pursuits. The young Walker had melded his poetic and theatrical abilities and began to show promise as a playwright, and from 1970 to 1971 he was playwright in residence at Yale University. He continued to appear on stage periodically as well during his most productive playwriting years—the late 1960s and early 1970s. He has also had roles in two motion pictures and has various television performances to his credit, including two in Emmy-nominated productions.

Walker's first Off-Broadway production, a coauthored musical, *The Believers*, was given a single performance at New York's Garrick Theatre in May 1968. Then, in 1969, Walker's first professional solo piece was mounted Off-Broadway by the Negro Ensemble Company (NEC), where Walker had been working as an understudy. The play—a series of four one-act works dealing with black men's anger and rebellion in the face of various oppressions—ran a full six weeks to generally positive reviews.

Dorothy Dinroe, who had provided musical collaboration on *The Harangues*, became Walker's second wife and professional partner in 1970 (he had divorced in 1965), when they founded their own musical-dance repertory company, the Demi-Gods. Walker was artistic director, writing and choreographing for the ensemble. The company struggled financially but served as an inspired and inspiring workshop and showcase for Walker's (and Dinroe-Walker's) creativity.

Ododo was the first play to come out of this new venture. Subtitled a "musical epic," the piece was a review of African American history, emphasizing the inevitability of "the black man's" emergence as a revolutionary. Not performed by the Demi-Gods until 1973 (at Howard University), NEC's production of *Ododo* opened to mixed reviews at St. Mark's Playhouse on 24 November 1970. Some critics considered the play too threatening, and others have since viewed it as lacking the sophistication of Walker's later work.

The Demi-Gods mounted the premiere production of Walker's most experimental play, *Yin-Yang*, at the Afro-American Studio in New York in June 1972. This theatrical collage reappeared around New York (including Off-Broadway) and at Howard University over the next two years. Dramatizing ancient and biblical conflicts between good and evil, the piece portrays God as "a hip swinging, fast talking Black mama . . . in conflict with Miss Satan, who is also a Black female swinger" (Walker, "Broadway's Vitality," *New York Times* 5 Aug. 1973). *Yin-Yang* too met with a mixed, if more heated, response from critics and theater-goers.

In 1972, with the smash success of the much more realistic *The River Niger*, Walker became a truly dominant figure in African American theater. First produced Off-Broadway by the NEC, the play was an instant hit and had the longest run on record at that company. Moving on to Broadway, it continued to draw crowds and receive rave reviews. Although critics praised the play partly for its "universality," they also stressed its careful representation of working-class African American life. In fact the play is highly autobiographical, with many of the characters and situations coming directly from the writer's family.

In addition to its popular and financial success, *The River Niger* garnered numerous awards, including a Tony Award for the best play of the 1973 to 1974 season and several Obies. Walker also received the Drama Desk Award for the most promising playwright of 1972 to 1973 and wrote the screenplay adaptation for the 1976 film production of his play. He has also received a Guggenheim Fellowship (1973) and a Rockefeller Foundation grant (1979).

Joseph A. Walker is a full professor of drama at Howard University and continues to be a significant figure in the development of African American theater.

• Maurice Peterson, "Taking Off With Joseph Walker," *Essence*, Apr. 1974, 55, 74, 78, 82. Clark Taylor, "In the Theater of Soul," *Essence*, Apr. 1975, 48–49.

—Sheila Hassell Hughes

WALKER, MARGARET (b. 1915), poet, novelist, essayist, and educator. Margaret Abigail Walker was born on 7 July 1915 in Birmingham, Alabama, the daughter of Sigismond Walker, a Methodist minister, and Marion Dozier Walker, a music teacher. Although she spent her childhood and youth in the racist, segregated South, Walker seems not to have been afflicted by the psychic wound of racism she poignantly describes in *Richard Wright: Daemonic Genius* (1988). The reason is not far to seek. Walker was protected to some extent by having been raised in an educated, middle-class family, surrounded by books and music and imbued with strong Christian values and belief in the innate dignity of humanity. She has drawn special attention to the inspiring character of her family and to the emphasis they placed on education and intellectual life. On the other hand, Walker's childhood was not devoid of exposure to oppression and injustice. The imprint of her formative years is reflected in her creative works, particularly in the poems in *For My People* (1942) that express an ambivalence about the South, and in *Jubilee* (1966), the culmination of her early exposure to stories of slave life from her maternal grandmother, Elvira Ware Dozier.

In 1925 the family moved to New Orleans, Louisiana. There she was educated at Gilbert Academy and finished high school at the age of fourteen. A precocious child, Walker completed two years of college at New Orleans University (Dillard University), where both of her parents taught. She was accustomed during her youth to meeting such famous people as James Weldon *Johnson, Roland Hayes, and W. E. B. *Du Bois.

In 1931 she was introduced to Langston *Hughes,

who would have great influence on her career. He read some of her poems and encouraged her to write and to get an education outside the South. The next year she transferred to Northwestern University, from which she received a BA in English in 1935, a few months before her twentieth birthday. Prior to graduation, she had published her first poems in the *Crisis* magazine (1934) and had begun a draft of a Civil War story.

The years Walker lived in Chicago during the Great Depression had a significant impact on her decision to be a writer. Shortly after graduating from Northwestern, she was hired by the Works Project Administration (WPA), first as a social worker and later as a member of the Federal Writers' Project. Assigned to work on the *Illinois Guidebook,* Walker learned much about the urban life of her people and about the craft of writing. In the years between 1936 and 1939, she benefited much from her friendships with the novelists Nelson Algren and Frank *Yerby, poets Arna *Bontemps and Frank Marshall *Davis, the artist Margaret Taylor Goss *Burroughs and the playwright Theodore *Ward. The most significant friendship was that with Richard *Wright, whom she met in February 1936 at a meeting of the South Side Writers Group. She was genuinely impressed with Wright's commitment to social change and his gift for writing. They shared their works, Walker providing technical assistance to Wright, Wright broadening her vision of how literature might be related to political action. It was under Wright's influence that Walker made the decision to be a writer for the people. She continued to help Wright after he moved to New York in 1937, sending him the newspaper clippings and other material pertinent to the Robert Nixon case he was using in writing *Native Son* (1940). During this period Walker also completed an urban novel, "Goose Island," which remains unpublished. Walker's obviously inspiring friendship with Wright ended abruptly in 1939, when she attended the League of American Writers Congress in New York, a rupture that she treats in detail in *Richard Wright: Daemonic Genius.*

Walker's tenure with the Federal Writers' Project ended in 1939, and she enrolled at the University of Iowa to complete studies for the master's degree in creative writing and prepared the poems that would appear in *For My People* as her thesis.

Walker began what would be a long and distinguished teaching career at Livingston College in North Carolina, taught for one year at West Virginia State College, and married Firnist James Alexander in June 1943. The fame she achieved with the publication of her first book was now complemented, and to some degree complicated, by the prospect of trying to write a novel as she handled the responsibilities of motherhood. A Rosenwald Fellowship in 1944 did enable her to resume research for the novel, but the freedom to write was brief. She returned to teaching, moving in 1949 with her husband and three children to Jackson, Mississippi, and a position at Jackson State College, where she taught until her retirement in 1979.

Jackson, Mississippi, became both harbor and site of frustration for Margaret Walker. Teaching duties and domestic responsibilities left little time for sustained writing. She was able to continue her historical research from 1953 to 1954 with the aid of a Ford Fellowship, but with four children to care for she would not be able to do substantial work on the manuscript until she returned to the University of Iowa in 1962 to work on her doctorate in English. She finished both the degree and the dissertation version of *Jubilee* in 1965. The long story of her struggle to bring this novel to life is the subject of her essay "How I Wrote *Jubilee*" (1972).

Walker's output increased dramatically in the years after *Jubilee. Prophets for a New Day* (1970) and *October Journey* (1973) created new audiences for her poetry as did *A Poetic Equation: Conversations between Nikki Giovanni and Margaret Walker.* She completed the long-awaited biography *Richard Wright: Daemonic Genuis* (1988), and published *This Is My Century: New and Collected Poems* (1989) and *How I Wrote* Jubilee *and Other Essays on Life and Literature* (1990). She is currently writing her *autobiography and preparing a second collection of her essays for publication.

Walker's public reception since the 1960s has been enthusiastic, partly because of her status as one of the few surviving members of a transitional generation of African American writers and partly because of her well-earned international reputation. Thus it is surprising that while her works are widely anthologized and taught in African American and women's studies courses, critical attention to her more than fifty years of writing has been less substantial than one might expect. Scholars of African American literature and culture are aware of her impact on such writers as Sonia *Sanchez and Nikki *Giovanni, her place in literary history with the landmark works *For My People* and *Jubilee,* and her special contribution to the academic world in founding the Institute for the Study of the History, Life, and Culture of Black People at Jackson State University (now the Margaret Walker Alexander National Research Center), and in organizing the legendary Phillis Wheatley Festival (1973). Perhaps one must conclude, as Maryemma Graham does in the preface to *How I Wrote* Jubilee *and Other Essays* (1990), that Walker's works have not been canonized because critics tend to be uncomfortable with her complex aesthetic vision. No such discomfort is evidenced by the audiences who respond warmly to Walker's public lectures and readings. It may be that Margaret Walker has the distinction of being canonized by her people.

• John Griffin Jones, "Margaret Walker Alexander," in *Mississippi Writers Talking,* vol. 2, 1983, pp. 1–65. Claudia Tate, "Margaret Walker," in *Black Women Writers at Work,* 1983, pp. 188–204. Joyce Pettis, "Margaret Walker: Black Woman Writer of the South," in *Southern Women Writers,* ed. Tonette Bond Inge, 1990, pp. 9–19. Mary Hughes Brookhart, "Margaret Walker," in *Contemporary Poets, Dramatists, Essayists, and Novelists of the South,* ed. Robert Bain and Joseph M. Flora, 1994, pp. 504–514.   —Jerry W. Ward, Jr.

Walls of Jericho, The. Published in 1928, Rudolph *Fisher's *The Walls of Jericho* presents a rich panorama of social classes in the late 1920s. The novel centers on the evolving relationship between Shine, a piano mover, and Linda, an ambitious maid. Shine's need for his tough-guy exterior, so important for his survival among the "rats," thwarts his feelings for Linda and the confrontation with his own past. An often bemused narrator deftly sketches the choreography of the couple's relationship, movements that summon forth themes of futile vengeance and self-delusion. Shine's conflict is made clear when a minister eloquently shapes the biblical story of Joshua and the walls of Jericho. With the words haunting him afterward, Shine can finally proclaim: "The guy that's really hard is the guy that's hard enough to be soft."

Fisher's comedy is genial here, his satire even-handed. As comic counterpoint throughout, Jinx and Bubber, coworkers with Shine, voice the irreverent views of the street crowd on a wide range of subjects. The African American bourgeoisie, no less than the white, liberal professional class, comes in for criticism, especially in the longest scene of the novel, the General Improvement Association costume ball. Fisher focuses his judicious satire on the deluded attempts at an easy racial harmony. Society woman Agatha Cramp bears much of the weight of this critique. Pomposity and aloofness are spoofed with quick and telling strokes.

At the novel's end, Shine and Linda have drawn much closer. Merrit, the black-and-blond lawyer who has briefly and mischievously passed for white at the costume ball, will help Shine start his own trucking company. Thus rifts within the African American community, rifts predicated on delusions generated by caste and *class, are healed for the moment.

Few other writers employed satire and comedy with much consistency during the *Harlem Renaissance. Fisher's shadings are more optimistic than those of Wallace *Thurman (*The Infants of the Spring*, 1932) and less caustic than those of George S. *Schuyler (*Black No More*, 1931). As with his second novel (*The Conjure Man Dies*, 1932) and his body of short fiction, Fisher's achievement was the affection, close criticism, and symmetry he brought to his portraits of the African American encounter with the modern city.

• Leonard J. Deutsch, "Rudolph Fisher's Unpublished Manuscripts: Description and Commentary," *Obsidian* 6 (Spring/Summer 1980): 82–97. John McCluskey, Jr., ed., introduction to *The City of Refuge: The Collected Stories of Rudolph Fisher*, 1987.

—John McCluskey, Jr.

WALROND, ERIC (1898–1966), short fiction writer, journalist, editor, and figure in the Harlem Renaissance. Although his residence in the United States was brief, Eric D. Walrond made lasting contributions to African American literature and culture. Born in Georgetown, British Guiana, in 1898, Walrond was educated at St. Stephen's Boys' School in Barbados and public schools in Colón, Panama. He left Panama for a ten-year residence in New York (1918–1928), where he continued his education at City College and Columbia University. His experiences with racism in the United States impelled his early fiction and sparked his interest in Marcus

*Garvey's Universal Negro Improvement Association (UNIA). After withdrawing his support of the UNIA, Walrond became a protégé of Urban League director Charles S. Johnson. It was during his affiliation with Johnson that Walrond's 1926 collection of short stories, *Tropic Death*, was published in New York by Boni and Liveright.

As the collection's title indicates, Walrond's ten stories set in British Guiana, Barbados, and Panama thematize death and the destruction wrought by natural disasters, colonialism, and modernization. Prominent figures such as W. E. B. *Du Bois and Langston *Hughes praised the collection's impressionistic form and historical content, as did anonymous reviewers from the *New York Times* and the *New York World*. Critics such as Robert Bone and David Levering Lewis note the Gothic strains in "The Yellow One," "The Wharf Rats," and "The White Snake." With the stories "Tropic Death" and "The Black Pin," Walrond explores coerced migration, cultural displacement, and xenophobia, three central concerns of his life as well as his writing.

While impressive thematically and stylistically, the short fiction from *Tropic Death* constituted neither the first nor the last of Walrond's contributions to the *Harlem Renaissance. In the early and mid-1920s, eight other stories thematizing race relations in New York and abroad were published in periodicals such as *Smart Set* and the *New Republic*. His fiction also appeared in *Opportunity*, including "Voodoo's Revenge," for which he was awarded third prize in the magazine's 1925 literary contest. He published one more piece in 1927, "City Love," before migrating to Europe, where he died in 1966.

Like Colombian novelist Gabriel García Márquez, Walrond began his writing career as a journalist, producing articles on Harlem and the Great Migration and nuanced critiques of contemporary African American leaders. From 1921 to 1923 he served as editor and co-owner of an African American weekly, the *Brooklyn and Long Island Informer*. His journalistic experience earned the respect of both Garvey and Johnson: Walrond was hired as associate editor of the UNIA's paper, *Negro World* (1923–1925), and business manager of the Urban League's *Opportunity* (1925–1927). An editor, journalist, and one of the first fiction writers to thematize migration and diaspora, Eric D. Walrond is an important, if overlooked, figure from the Harlem Renaissance. His manifold accomplishments during the 1920s ensure him a firm place in African American literary history.

• Jay A. Berry, "Eric Walrond," in *DLB*, vol. 51, *Afro-American Writers from the Harlem Renaissance to 1940*, eds. Trudier Harris and Thadious M. Davis, 1987, pp. 296–300. John E. Bassett, *Harlem in Review: Critical Reactions to Black American Writers, 1917–1939*, 1992.

—Margarita Barceló

WALTER, MILDRED PITTS (b. 1922), author of picture books, novels, and information books for children and young adult readers. Many songs, poems, novels, and plays extroll the virtues of home; others lament the heartaches that occur within the confines of home; and a few depict the search for a philosophical home that imparts a sense of meaning, belonging, and identity to an individual's life. Mildred Pitts Walter experienced and writes eloquently about these emotions in her books for youth.

Born in Sweetville, Louisiana, and raised in Gaytine, Louisiana, two small, segregated sawmill towns, Mildred Pitts Walter experienced and developed love of family and community, spiritual rootedness, duty to community uplift, ability to tell stories, and a powerful love of oral and written language. Starting at age seven with a job caring for a white child, she also acquired a strong work ethic.

Walter's teachers encouraged her intellectual growth and inspired her to dream about attending college. She attended Southern University in Louisiana (1940–1944) and graduated with a BA, majoring in English and minoring in social studies. Southern University provided access to intellectuals such as W. E. B. *Du Bois, Mordecai Johnson, and Benjamin E. *Mays, who engendered within her a sense of cultural heritage and intellectual curiosity. Walter completed certification requirements in elementary education at California State College; she received a master's degree several years later from Antioch College in Yellow Springs, Ohio.

Walter's sense of adventure took her to Los Angeles, where she worked as a school clerk, eventually earning the credentials to teach in elementary schools. She and her husband, Lloyd Walter, were active members of the Congress of Racial Equality (CORE) and engaged in actions to desegregate schools and public accommodations. Although Walter enjoyed teaching, political activism propelled her career as a writer. Walter wrote a letter to a critic at the Los Angeles Times who had disparaged comments made by author James *Baldwin at a CORE fundraiser. Subsequently, the critic invited Walter to write book reviews for the newspaper. She accepted and her literary career was launched.

Walter questioned an editor about the absence of literature featuring African Americans. The editor responded that she should write the stories because she lived the experience and possessed an insider's perspective. She considered the editor's comments and created Lillie of Watts (1969). Lillie is a spunky young girl growing up in gritty circumstances in the Watts section of Los Angeles who must overcome disappointments, make decisions, resolve conflicts, and retain a measure of happiness and hope. The sequel, Lillie of Watts Takes a Giant Step (1971), portrays Lillie's coming-of-age during a time of Black Power.

Initial success did not last. Walter submitted manuscripts that were rejected. Rather than becoming discouraged, she honed her creative writing skills through attendance at writer's workshops and discussions with editors and publishers. Soon, publishers' rejections of manuscripts turned into acceptances: in 1975 with The Liquid Trap, followed by Ty's One-Man Band (1980), The Girl on the Outside (1982), Because We Are (1983), My Mama Needs Me (1983), Brother to the Wind (1985), Trouble's Child (1985), Justin and the Best Biscuits in the World (1986), Mariah Loves Rock (1988), Have a Happy . . . (1984), Two and Two Much (1990), Mariah Keeps Cool (1990), and The Mississippi Challenge (1992).

Walter's growth as a writer is evident in such books as Ty's One-Man Band, Trouble's Child, and The Mississippi Challenge. Themes in these texts include achieving a sense of *identity, resolving problems, and understanding one's cultural heritage and *history. Walter creates male and female protagonists who usually face a challenge, sometimes as monumental as racism or desegregating a school, and other times less pressing, such as a summer of fun at the pool.

Critical response to Walter's books varies. Some praise her depiction of the cultural milieus in which her characters reside, her ability to capture the nuances of children and childhood, her facility with various dialects, and thematic issues. Other critics cite stock characterization, weak plots, and contrived endings. Nevertheless, Walter's books remain fairly popular and some have garnered children's book awards such as the Coretta Scott King Award for Justin and the Best Biscuits in the World and The Mississippi Challenge. Walter's lasting contribution to *children's and young adult literature is the creation of accessible characters who symbolize the range of experiences found among African Americans.

• "Mildred Pitts Walter," in Something about the Author Autobiography Series, vol. 12, ed. Adele Sarkissian, 1992, pp. 283–301.   —Violet J. Harris

WALTER LEE YOUNGER, the complex, fiercely independent, flawed, and angry protagonist of Lorraine *Hansberry's A *Raisin in the Sun (1959) is a first for the American stage. More articulate and moral than his 1940s Broadway predecessor, *Bigger Thomas of Richard *Wright's *Native Son (1940), Hansberry compared him to Willy Loman (Death of a Salesman) who is defeated not only by his own shortcomings but also by a social and economic system that has failed him.

Walter Lee represents the dilemma of African American males who inherited the pride and hopes of the *civil rights movement but who are thwarted in their achievement of full *manhood in the eyes of society. On the one hand, Walter Lee wants and needs for himself and his family the material comfort that will make their lives better; but on the other hand, he risks losing his sense of dignity to rank materialism. His defining moment comes when the white neighborhood offers to buy back his mother's house at a profit, a price that would allow the family to recover its financial loss and Walter Lee regain face. But in a dramatic reversal at the end of the play, Walter rejects the offer, recognizing its demeaning aspects, and moves the family into the new house. The familiarity of *Mama Lena Younger's strong, matriachal figure often competes with Walter Lee for focus, but Hansberry clearly intended A Raisin in the Sun to reflect the struggles, potential, and resilience of the working-class African American male in a racist, capitalistic society that devalues human life and aspiration. Walter Lee, a unique protagonist in the history of America's theatrical literature, is the father of more militant characters who strode the boards in the 1960s plays of LeRoi Jones/Amiri *Baraka, Ron *Milner, and others.

• Lorraine Hansberry, "Willy Loman, Walter Lee Younger and He Who Must Live," *Village Voice*, 12 Aug. 1959, 7–8. Douglas Turner Ward, "Lorraine Hansberry and the Passion of Walter Lee," *Freedomways* 19.4 (1979): 223–225.

—Margaret B. Wilkerson

WANIEK, MARILYN NELSON (b. 1946), poet, critic, and educator. A poet who has written for both children and adults, Marilyn Waniek (pronounced *Von*-yek) was born on 26 April 1946 in Cleveland, Ohio, daughter of Melvin M. (an air force serviceman) and Johnnie (Mitchell) Nelson (a teacher). Her family moved from one military base to another during her childhood. She started writing in elementary school. Waniek's higher education includes a BA from the University of California at Davis (1968), an MA from the University of Pennsylvania (1970), and a PhD from the University of Minnesota (1979). Her doctoral thesis was "The Schizoid Nature of the Implied Author in Twentieth-Century American Ethnic Novels." As a graduate student she argued in an article, "The Space Where Sex Should Be: Toward a Definition of the Black Literary Tradition" (*Studies in Black Literature*, 1975), that the relationships between "Black protagonists and their white friends" portrayed in African American writing substituted for male-female relationships: "[I]n the space where sex should be is instead the awful confrontation of Black self with white self, and the Black self with white society." A seminary-trained Lutheran, Waniek was lay associate in the National Lutheran Campus Ministry program from 1969 to 1970 in Ithaca, New York. She has taught English in Oregon, Denmark, and Minnesota. Her first marriage to Erdmann F. Waniek (1970–1979) ended in divorce; she has two children, Jacob and Dora, through her second marriage to Roger R. Wilkenfield. A 1976 Kent fellow and a 1982 National Endowment for the Arts fellow, Waniek has been a member of the English faculty at the University of Connecticut at Storrs since 1978, and a full professor since 1988.

Waniek's critical articles include "The Schizoid Implied Authors of Two Jewish-American Novels" (1980), "The Power of Language in N. Scott Momaday's *House Made of Dawn*" (1980), "Paltry Things: Immigrants and Marginal Men in Paule Marshall's Short Fiction" (1983), and "A Black Rainbow: Modern Afro-American Poetry" (with Rita *Dove, 1990). Competent in Danish, German, and Spanish, she translated from Danish Phil Dahlerup's *Literary Sex Roles* (1975).

Waniek has published six poetry collections, two for children. In 1982 Waniek and Pamela Espeland published their translation of Danish poet Halfdan Rasmussen's humorous poetry in *Hundreds of Hens and Other Poems for Children* (1982), work that sparked her interest in writing for children and led to *The Cat Walked Through the Casserole and Other Poems for Children* (with Espeland, 1984). In *For the Body* (1978), written predominantly in free verse,

Waniek explores childhood memories; in *Mama's Promises* (1985), she experiments with the ballad stanza. In *The Homeplace* (1990), a text interspersed with family trees and photos, Waniek uses dramatic dialogue and a range of ballad, villanelle, and sonnet forms to tell stories about her family, beginning with her great-great-grandmother Diverne and ending with her father and his fellow "Tuskegee Airmen." Her 1994 poetry collection, *Magnificat: Poems* received critical acclaim. Considered to be one of the major young African American poets, Waniek experiments with traditional and free-verse forms.

—Mary Anne Stewart Boelcskevy

WARD, DOUGLAS TURNER (b. 1930), dramatist, actor, director, and producer. Since the 1960s, the African American dramatic literature and aesthetic philosophy of Douglas Turner Ward have been highly influential. Guided by a burning desire to continue the legacy of W. E. B. *Du Bois, Ward was determined to create theater that was primarily written by, performed for, and representative of African American people. In his plays, Ward examines a mixed bag of attitudes and *stereotypes that permeate our environment both within and outside the African American community. He uses various comic conventions such as satire, farce, absurdism, and irony to attack widely divergent cultural philosophies, politics, and ethics as well as social, moral, and racial biases.

Douglas Turner Ward was born on 5 May 1930 in Burnside, Louisiana, to Roosevelt Ward and Dorothy Short. Ward spent his formative years on a plantation in this rural town. He was later sent to live with relations in New Orleans in order to attend public school, from which he graduated at the age of fifteen. Dissatisfaction with prevailing racist attitudes among many Southerners influenced Ward's decision to attend college in the North at Wilberforce University in Xenia, Ohio. In 1947 he transferred to the University of Michigan, where he played football on the junior varsity squad. A knee injury at the age of eighteen abruptly ended his career, so he headed for New York City at the end of the school year.

Ward had been involved in left-wing political activities during his undergraduate days, which he continued to practice as a writer for the *Daily Worker* in New York. Interestingly, his association with various political entities provided the desire to write satirical sketches. His newfound avocation was put on hold while he spent three months in jail for draft evasion before being released on appeal; he was then forced to spend two years in Louisiana until the U.S. Supreme Court overturned his conviction. Ward returned to New York City resolved to write plays solely. In order to understand the craft better, he enrolled in acting classes at the prestigious Paul Mann's Actor's Workshop.

Mel Gussow, reviewer for the *New York Times*, wrote that Ward ". . . as actor, playwright, journalist, director, artistic director of the Negro Ensemble Company—is a man of great force, dedication, and verbosity." Ward used these strong character traits to expound his sociocultural and political ideas, which he expressed in perhaps the most influential piece of writing of his career. In an article entitled "American Theatre: For Whites Only?" that appeared in the *New York Times* on 14 August 1966, Ward denounced the racist practices in professional theaters and called for the establishment of a permanent African American theater for playwrights, actors, technicians, and administrators. This article was instrumental in gaining the attention of the Ford Foundation, which ultimately funded the formation of the Negro Ensemble Company (NEC) in 1965 with a $434,000 grant. Ward was cofounder along with actor-director Robert Hooks and Off-Broadway producer Gerald A. Krone.

Throughout his theatrical career, and in the choice of plays and styles of production, Ward has created a repertory that presents world-class drama primarily focused on African American themes. Nonetheless he has never supported the concept of a separatist theater. The NEC has been criticized from the start by some African Americans for selecting plays by nonwhite playwrights, including Peter Weiss, Ray Lawler, and Jean Genet, and for the location of its first theater in lower Manhattan.

As a playwright, Ward is perhaps best known for his controversial one-act plays, *Happy Ending* and **Day of Absence*, both written in 1966. Both comedies examine black-white relations in dramatizing the interdependence between the races. White critics were generally in agreement that although the theme of racial interdependency was topical, the acting style and colloquial language were often exaggerated to the point of being difficult to understand. In spite of such occasional negative reactions and controversial dramatizations of topical subjects, the NEC continued to produce theatrical events of quality and substance with a list of Black artists that represented the elite of contemporary African American theater.

The right-wing shift in the American political climate during the 1980s severely curtailed the availability of government-sponsored arts program funds and private sector fellowships and grants. In order to address a deficit of $500,000, the NEC did not mount any productions during the 1991 and 1992 seasons. In April 1993, the NEC reopened its doors, this time at the La Guardia Performing Arts Center, with a production of Kenneth Franklin-Hoke Witherspoon's *Last Night at Ace High* directed by Ward, who is also president of the company. Although the NEC remains in debt, Susan Watson Turner, producing director, stated in a profile that appeared in *New York Newsday* on 11 May 1993, that it continues to be "a company run by and for African-American artists."

• Fred Beauford, "The Negro Ensemble Company: Five Years Against the Wall," *Black Creation* 3 (Winter 1972): 16–18. Mark Ribowsky, "'Father' of the Black Theatre Boom," *Sepia* 25 (Nov. 1976): 67–78. Trudier Harris, *From Mammies to Militants: Domestics in Black American Literature*, 1982, pp. 143–154. Cheryl McCourtie, "Whatever Happened to the Negro Ensemble?" *Crisis* 99.7 (Oct. 1992): 47–48.

—Floyd Gaffney

WARD, THEODORE (1902–1983), playwright. Although never a real force in American **theater,

Theodore Ward deserves more critical attention than he currently receives. His two most important plays, *Big White Fog* (1938) and *Our Lan'* (written in 1941) never enjoyed major commercial successes, although they did receive popular and critical notice and managed to generate some controversy. Tackling a myriad of contentious subjects such as Garveyism, anti-Semitism, color prejudice among blacks, the devastating effects of racism, the appeal of **Communism, and the failures of the United States Government to live up to its responsibilities to African Americans, Ward never eschews controversy, hoping always to educate and politicize his audience.

Born in Thibodaux, Louisiana, on 15 September 1902, Ward left Louisiana at the age of thirteen, shortly after his mother's death. Earning his living as a bootblack, porter, or bellhop, Ward wandered about the United States during his teens. He began formal literary study at the University of Utah in the late 1920s. In 1931 a scholarship allowed Ward to study creative writing at the University of Wisconsin where he remained until 1935. Moving to Chicago, Ward's ideological life took shape when he joined a John Reed Club and began working for the WPA. His one-act play *Sick and Tiahd* won second prize in a contest sponsored by the labor movement. This success prompted the playwright to join the Federal Theater Project. In 1938 *Big White Fog* was produced by the Theater Project in Chicago. In 1940 the playwright formed the Negro Playwrights Company to produce *Fog* in New York. Over the next thirty-five years other plays followed: *Deliver the Goods* (1942); *Our Lan'* (first produced in 1946); *John Brown* (1950); *Candle in the Wind* (1967); and *The Daubers* (1973). In 1976 Ward received a Rockefeller Foundation grant to produce *Our Lan'* with the Free Southern Theater in New Orleans. He assisted the company again when it produced his *Candle in the Wind* as its final production in 1978. Ward died in Chicago in May 1983.

Fog remains Ward's most significant work. Set in Chicago between 1922 and 1932, the play chronicles the struggles of the Mason family and its patriarch, Victor. Confronting a series of financial and racial crises, Victor tries to keep the family together and instill in its members race pride and a commitment to the struggle for social and economic justice. Before recognizing multiracial Communism as the solution to the economic and racial injustices of America, Victor places his faith and the family's savings in Marcus **Garvey's Black Star Line. With the depression the family's misery increases; finally Victor dies a victim of a gunshot wound inflicted by a sheriff evicting the family from their home. Before dying Victor looks upon his son's comrades who have arrived to aid the family in resisting the eviction. The son tells his father, "I just wanted to show you, they're [the comrades] black and white."

The optimistic conclusion of *Fog* may seem naive in the post-Marxist world, but in 1938 some feared the play's conclusion would prompt riots. Riots never occurred, but then neither did large audiences. Ward, however, never gave up in his attempt to reach large, especially black, audiences, a fact attested to by his commitment to the Free Southern Theater at the end of his career.

• Doris E. Abramson, *Negro Playwrights in the American Theatre, 1925–1959*, 1969.

—Anthony Gerard Barthelemy

WAR EXPERIENCE. Few literary texts offer a better dramatic conspectus of what war has meant in the lives of African Americans than John A. *Williams's novel *Captain Blackman* (1972). Under frontline fire in Vietnam and about to be cut down by a Viet Cong bullet, Captain Abraham Blackman fantasizes a serialized chronicle of black warriordom in historical spirals from the American Revolution to the nuclear age. Blackman even conducts his own "military history seminar" for the black soldiers, "the bloods," under his command. With a cast of characters (Woodcock and the aptly named Griot especially) who reincarnate through each war, he tells the one story in the many.

In Blackman's own words the story opens with independence-era black names such as "Prince Eastbrook, Peter Salem, Crispus Attucks and all the unnamed rest." It passes "from there to the War of 1812, the Civil War, the Plains Wars, the Spanish-American Wars—all the wars." The latter include black participation in World Wars I and II, Korea, and Vietnam, with a half-surreal closing episode in which Blackman's Aryan antagonist, General Ishmael Whittman, is finally out-finagled by a black takeover of America's entire nuclear facility. Tables are thus reversed in an imagining of American history as American war, which in its lattermost phase is put under quite racially alternative auspices. Williams provocatively leaves any or all speculative inference to the reader.

Another kind of departure point might be America's first published book by a black author, Phillis *Wheatley's *Poems on Various Subjects, Religious and Moral* (1773), in which a key biblical poem such as "Goliath of Gath" offers the silhouette, the muted allegory, of a possible war of slave liberation ahead. When, too, a Wheatley poem such as "America" speaks of "Great Brittania" as "Tyranny," an "Iron chain," is not the resonance as much of antislavery as anticolonialism? In this, she implies a role for blacks anything but the "putt'n on ol' massa" *stereotype of, say, Caesar, the black manservant in James Fenimore Cooper's Birth-of-a-Nation war novel *The Spy* (1821). The point is given even greater force in the accusing, angry *Walker's Appeal, in Four Articles* (1829) by the black abolitionist David *Walker, with its "I count my life not dear to me, but I am ready to be offered at any moment."

*Slave narratives, if not exactly dealing in "war," nonetheless offer their own analogous body of martial themes and images. As celebrated as any has to be the Covey fight in the *Narrative of the Life of Frederick Douglass* (1845) in which each thrust and counterthrust virtually takes body in Douglass's prose, a war-in-small as emblematic as the battle royal scenes in Ralph *Ellison's *Invisible Man* (1952). These belong, in fact, to a considerable lineage, whether *The Interesting Narrative of the Life of Olaudah *Equiano,*

or *Gustavus Vassa, the African* (1789), with its graphic scenes of slave seizure and transportation; Martin R. *Delany's *Blake* (1859), with its Deep South, insurrectionary fable of "a war upon the whites"; or Arna *Bontemps's *Black Thunder* (1936), with its portrait of the slave leader Gabriel Prosser and his insurrection in Richmond, Virginia, in 1800.

It was Edmund Wilson in *Patriotic Gore* (1962) who pointed out that the Civil War has oddly wanted for literary classics, notwithstanding Harriet Beecher *Stowe's abolitionist-prophetic *Uncle Tom's Cabin* (1852) or Stephen Crane's retrospective *The Red Badge of Courage* (1895). African American writing has been similarly mixed fare, from a literary-historical compendium as firsthand as Joseph T. Wilson's The *Black Phalanx: A History of the Negro Soldiers in the Wars of 1775–1812, 1861–'65* (1888) through to Margaret *Walker's *Jubilee* (1966), her highly popular Dixie melodrama and self-acknowledged riposte to Margaret Mitchell's *Gone with the Wind* (1936). Black Civil War reference has for sure been plentiful enough, be it the verse, say, of Charlotte *Forten (notably "The Grand Army of the Republic") and Paul Laurence *Dunbar ("The Colored Soldiers") or novels such as Frances Ellen Watkins *Harper's *Iola Leroy* (1892), whose mulatto theme does not obscure its celebration of black Civil War heroism; Sutton E. *Griggs's black nationalist *Imperium in Imperio* (1899); Charles Waddell *Chesnutt's The *Marrow of Tradition* (1901), with its post-Reconstruction story of a North Carolina "race riot" whose origins lie in the Civil War; or, again, Frederick Douglass's *Narrative* (and its two successor autobiographies); Booker T. *Washington's *Up from Slavery* (1901); and W. E. B. *Du Bois's The *Souls of Black Folk* (1903). But the more striking memorialization, in truth, has come from a quite later generation.

Ernest J. *Gaines's The *Autobiography of Miss Jane Pittman* (1971) offers a touchstone with its first-person scenes of secession, Yankee soldierdom, and would-be escaping slaves. In Alex *Haley's "fiction of fact," *Roots* (1976), the progeny of *Kunta Kinte are shown as caught up in a war intrinsic to their own identity and survival. Ishmael *Reed's *Flight to Canada* (1976) offers a daringly iconoclastic and postmodern pastiche of "The War," suitably backed up with an irreverent look at both Lincoln and southern chivalry. Leon *Forrest's The *Bloodworth Orphans* (1977) tells its own memory saga of a black (and black-white) dynasty unraveled by the Civil War and subsequent divided loyalties. And in Toni *Morrison's *Beloved* (1987) the impress, the madness, of *slavery into Civil War becomes the occasion of a uniquely poignant kind of haunting.

Despite the remembrance of scenes such as the all-black Fifteenth Regiment marching in deserved triumph up Fifth Avenue in February 1919, World War I was not a major reference point for the generation of *Harlem Renaissance writers. Nevertheless, however obliquely, it serves as a species of subtext in Alain *Locke's manifesto-anthology, The *New Negro* (1925) and in writings as various as Jean *Toomer's slavery-haunted *Cane* (1923), Claude

*McKay's "down-home," rambunctious *Home to Harlem* (1928)—Jake, the longshoreman hero, actually has gone AWOL—and Langston *Hughes's easeful first volume of autobiography, The *Big Sea* (1940).

World War II, due to the larger enlistment and draft, can look to a correspondingly larger gallery of voices. One landmark is Gwendolyn *Brooks's poem "Gay Chaps at the Bar," in A *Street in Bronzeville* (1945), with its fond but ominous premonitions of black soldierly death. John O. *Killens's And Then We Heard the Thunder* (1962) is a full-bodied, neorealist documentary novel involving platoon fighting and military racism, whether inside a Georgia basic-training camp or the South Pacific of Australia. Chester *Himes's *If He Hollers Let Him Go* (1945) and *Lonely Crusade* (1947), their backdrop wartime industry in California, equally make the *color line the centerpiece; Himes shows an especial concern with the role of the Communist Party in the politics of black redress. William Gardner *Smith's Last of the Conquerors* (1948) adds yet another kind of twist, the story of a black GI in the Allied Army of Occupation who finds a better racial destiny in Berlin than in the Philadelphia slum of his boyhood.

Honorable defeat, shame, trauma: no American war has left worse psychological scars than Vietnam, and especially for many African American veterans, given their disproportionate number of frontline soldiers. Two born-of-experience texts are indicative—George Davis's *Coming Home* (1971), which tells the lives of three fighter pilots flying bombing missions over Thailand and Vietnam, and Wallace Terry's *Bloods* (1984), a compilation of oral witness at once of rap, grief, and the memory of black military service played out in an Asian war more rife in contradiction than quite any other American war.

Black soldiers, nurses, and officers, not to say their families, have been intrinsic to America at war from the beginning, stretching from independence to the Clinton presidency's role in Haiti. Few, no doubt, have let, could let, pass unnoticed the paradox: service to country in a country so often hostile to their own well-being. Nor is that to overlook a number of unpredictable turns in the literature, be it latterly a "black" CIA novel like Sam *Greenlee's The *Spook Who Sat By the Door* (1969) or some of the science fiction racial-military parables of Samuel R. *Delany and Octavia E. *Butler. But whatever the literary form, and whether given over to war experience at home or abroad, the record has been singular, varied and long-standing—inextricably a part of both African American literary tradition and American literature at large.

• Edmund Wilson, *Patriotic Gore: Studies in the Literature of the American Civil War*, 1962. Ronald T. Takaki, *Violence in the Black Imagination: Essays and Documents*, 1972. Stephen Butterfield, *Black Autobiography in America*, 1974. Bernard W. Bell, *The Afro-American Novel and Its Tradition*, 1987. John F. Callahan, *In the African-American Grain: The Pursuit of Voice in Twentieth-Century Black Fiction*, 1988. Dana D. Nelson, *The Word in Black and White: Reading "Race" in American Literature 1638–1867*, 1992.   —A. Robert Lee

WASHINGTON, BOOKER T. (1856–1915), educator, autobiographer, biographer, and race leader. Few public figures in African American life excite as much passion and misunderstanding as Booker Taliaferro Washington. Born a slave on a Virginia plantation in 1856, Washington rose to become the founder and driving force behind Tuskegee Institute in Alabama. Washington is such a compelling subject because he focuses our attention on issues of leadership and public visibility, the nature of *work and how it impacts upon the quality of African American life, and the internecine struggles for power within the African American elite. In the late 1980s, many began to view Washington as a man of skewed racial allegiances, a figure for whom white approval was everything. This interpretation of his life, however, relies on Washington's public persona to substantiate its claims. What is very clear is that Booker T. Washington was a man of such complexity that his public guise fails to provide sufficient cause to dismiss his importance.

Though Washington was born a slave, the scope and influence of his public life in the twentieth century rival that of Frederick *Douglass in the nineteenth century. Though his career as racial spokesman was based on the idea that African Americans should eschew political agitation for civil rights in favor of industrial *education and agricultural expertise, Washington's secret activities, his attempt to exercise private influence on matters having to do with racial discrimination and segregation, suggest that his was a paradoxical life indeed. For how else are we to account for Washington's "*Atlanta Exposition Address" of 1895 and his attempts to challenge racial discrimination and segregated facilities by covert legal means?

To penetrate the mysteries swirling about the persona of Booker T. Washington, we must understand something of the times in which he lived and why the issues of African American leadership—who would lead and what kinds of political spoils they could garner for the African American community—played such an essential role in the African American's attempt to participate fully in American life. For Washington, participation meant identifying, and being identified with, the status quo, the dominant way of thinking in American life and culture. Thus, as Sheldon Avery has observed, Washington's positions on laissez-faire capitalism, Christian morality, and middle-class values allowed him to channel a large portion of white philanthropic dollars and black patronage through the Tuskegee machine.

If Washington's racial accommodationism is unpalatable, it needs to be understood in light of his beginnings in West Virginia. As the son of Jane Ferguson, a slave, and a white father whom he never knew (though he conjectures in his *autobiography that his father was his master), Washington sought to convey that his childhood had been one of poverty, not racial oppression. From working in the coal furnaces and salt mines of West Virginia to doing housework, Washington's insistence is that he achieved his position as racial spokesman through hard physical labor. He goes to great lengths, for example, to describe his admittance into Hampton Institute in Virginia in 1872 as the result of his ability to clean and dust a classroom. It is clear that Hampton would have a profound impact on Washington's views, for it was there he met General Samuel Chapman Armstrong, who would become his mentor and benefactor. Graduating from Hampton in 1875 with honors, Washington returned to Hampton briefly after two years of teaching back in his native West Virginia to implement a program for Native Americans. In 1881 Armstrong recommended Washington to the Alabama legislature, which was seeking to open a normal school for African American students in Tuskegee.

The Booker T. Washington who thus emerges in *Up from Slavery* (1901) is a humble, moral, disciplined man whose life is devoted to the improvement of the Negro. And it is Tuskegee Institute, where he served as principal from 1881 until his death in 1915, that best demonstrates these traits. Culminating with his speech at the Cotton States and International Exposition in Atlanta in 1895, and his honorary degree from Harvard in 1897, Washington's treatment of his life is characterized by his ability to hold the most unassuming exchange up as a shining example of his links to the working man. Though Washington would endear himself to industrialists like Andrew Carnegie and John D. Rockefeller (at least in part because of his antiunion stance), he nonetheless claimed to champion the cause of economic opportunity for all.

Washington's career in the public sphere seems to grow from his success at Tuskegee, but it is just as much a result of the profound link between his life as an educator and fundraiser and his writing, for it is Washington's ability to control his image by recycling the positive assessments of his work into his books that makes him a credible public figure. Between 1896 and 1913 Washington produced nearly twenty works ranging from his two autobiographies, *The Story of My Life and Work* (1900) and the aforementioned *Up from Slavery*, to a *biography of Frederick Douglass (1907). Moreover, it could be argued that Washington was one of the first African American writers to connect the "self-help" book to issues of African American citizenship, which explains titles like *Working with the Hands*, *Putting the Most into Life*, and *Sowing and Reaping*.

Though Washington depicts himself as the primary voice of the African American community, it is important to point out that there were alternatives to Washington's accommodationist philosophy. W. E. B. *Du Bois and newspaper editor Monroe Trotter insisted upon a much more radical and confrontational stance than that put forward by Washington. With his propensity to see himself as the power to whom all other African American leaders should bow, Washington was often highly intolerant of other points of view, especially those that threatened his ability to keep close counsel with white philanthropic and political interests. Indeed, when the Niagara movement began to gain momentum in 1905, Washington used his influence with black newspaper editors, none of whom wished to risk

openly repudiating Washington's policies, to get them to either ignore or belittle the movement. And yet, his heavy-handedness notwithstanding, Washington's quest for power was not without its success. He devoted a considerable amount of time, financial resources, and energy to defeating *Jim Crow in the courts of the United States. Indeed, he and Du Bois, publicly in disagreement, collaborated as late as 1904 in an attempt to challenge the public statutes upholding separate-but-equal arrangements. In 1907 they co-authored a study entitled *The Negro in the South*. Though the attempt to achieve a judicial remedy for Jim Crow failed, Washington originated a highly secret, well-maintained apparatus by which to affect the legal fortunes of southern blacks, one that other black leaders were forced to acknowledge. Though the Tuskegee machine was well known to whites as a smoothly running, innocuous vehicle, insufficient and, more importantly, ill-suited to mount a serious challenge to white hegemony, Washington's ability to dissemble, to make racial equality his ultimate concern, means he cannot be dismissed.

• August Meier, *Negro Thought in America, 1880–1915*, 1963. Louis R. Harlan, *Booker T. Washington: The Making of a Black Leader, 1856–1901*, 1972. Hugh Hawkins, ed., *Booker T. Washington and His Critics*, 1974. Louis R. Harlan, *Booker T. Washington: The Wizard of Tuskegee, 1901–1915*, 1983. Louis R. Harlan et al., eds., *The Booker T. Washington Papers*, 1972–1989. David L. Dudley, *My Father's Shadow: Intergenerational Conflict in African American Men's Autobiography*, 1991. Booker T. Washington, *Up from Slavery*, ed. William L. Andrews, 1995.
—Herman Beavers

WATERS, ETHEL (1896–1977), singer, actress, and author. Ethel Waters is credited with bringing an urbane sophistication to the classic *blues. She first became known for her clear and sweet articulation of song lyrics. Having already established herself as a very popular singer, she went on to star in several Broadway productions. She also became one of black America's first *film stars. During the second half of her life, Waters, a devoted Christian, gained exposure to an even broader audience through her appearances with the Reverend Billy Graham. In 1951 her first *autobiography, *His Eye Is on the Sparrow*, was published. Her second autobiography, *To Me It's Wonderful*, appeared in 1972.

Because of her tall, shapely figure and her sweet singing voice, Waters was dubbed Sweet Mama String Bean at the very beginning of her career. She recorded her first song in 1921 for Black Swan Records. Throughout the 1920s she broadened her repertoire to include *jazz and ballads. The latter became her trademark. By the end of the decade, Waters had embarked on her acting career. She appeared in several Broadway *musicals, and in 1939, she became the first black woman to star in a Broadway *drama, *Mamba's Daughters*. This was followed by her performance in the all-black musical *Cabin in the Sky*. In 1943 she also starred in the film version with Lena Horne. Her rendition of "Happiness Is Just a Thing Called Joe" is a highpoint of that film. Waters went on to star in several major motion pictures: *Pinky* (1949), *The Sound and the Fury* (1959), and

Member of the Wedding (1952). She received an Academy Award nomination for best supporting actress for her performance in *Pinky*.

—Farah Jasmine Griffin

WATKINS, GLORIA. *See* hooks, bell.

We a BaddDDD People. Sonia *Sanchez's second book of poems (Broadside Press, 1970), similar to *Homecoming* (1969) in experimental form and revolutionary spirit, is dedicated to "blk/wooomen: the only queens of this universe" and exemplifies the poetics of the *Black Arts movement and the principles of the *Black Aesthetic. It depicts the experiences of common black folk in courtrooms, slum bars, and on the streets, with pimps and jivers, boogalooing and loving *Malcolm X. It celebrates the majestic beauty of blackness and speaks of revolution in the language of the urban black vernacular. Rhythms deriving from the *jazz and *blues of John *Coltrane and Billie *Holiday create a *poetry of performance in which the audience participates vigorously in meaning-making. Experimental in style, it is antilyrical free verse, using spacing, slash marks, and typography as guides to performance.

Characterizing Sanchez as a genuine revolutionary whose "blackness" is not for sale, Dudley *Randall's introduction leads into the first of three sections, "Survival Poems," which approach survival from political and personal perspectives. Some show how "wite" practices imperil black people's survival, seducing by heroin, marijuana, and wine or by exploding dreams. Others show how blacks undermine their own survival: the "makeshift manhood" underlying sexual neediness in "for/my/ father," the willful blindness of black "puritans," and the hypocrisy of pseudorevolutionaries whose rhetoric masks self-indulgence. Personal poems recording moments of near-hysteria, depression, and longing lead to the revolutionary vision of "indianapolis/summer," proposing communal love as a necessary prelude to real change.

The second section, "Love/Songs/Chants," expresses a bluesy nostalgia for memories of past good times but recognizes that such fantasies are delusive and that we need to face the real world. Poems warn "brothas & sistuhs" to stay clear of "wite highs" spelling death and exhort black men to love "blk wooooomen." The more militant poems of the third section, "TCB-en poems," bristle with outrage, exposing the jive talk of slick black bloods. Taking care of business means taking care of self as well as tradition. Most of all, TCB involves a strident war cry for power, alternating fierce invective and a call to arms with amusement at how "real/bad" we "bees." Sanchez predicts a coming revolution and exhorts her readers to begin the "real work" of building nationhood. The book ends with her explosive "a coltrane/poem," which, to the jazzy rhythms of "Brother John" and "my favorite things," urges setting fire to capitalist millionaires and torturing promise-breaking liberals so that black people may rise and claim their place.

Critics agree that Sonia Sanchez is a revolutionary poet of undisputed integrity whose goal is to better the world, and they praise *We a BaddDDD People* for the originality of its forms and its singing and chanting voice. Some criticize the strident tone of the political poems, calling their message "tiresome," their rhetoric "facile," and find the personal poems, dealing with drug addiction and love relationships, more palatable, even more authentically revolutionary. All, however, seem to concur that Sanchez's most important contribution to African American literature and culture lies in legitimizing urban Black English, in making the language of the streets "sound" throughout the world.

• Haki Madhubuti, "Sonia Sanchez: Bringer of Memories," in *Black Women Writers (1950–1980)*, ed. Mari Evans, 1984, pp. 419–432. D. H. Melhem, "Sonia Sanchez: The Will and the Spirit," in *Heroism in the New Black Poetry*, 1990, pp. 132–179.

—Deborah Ayer Sitter

Weary Blues, The. Langston *Hughes's first volume of verse represents a selection of his poetry that had appeared mainly in magazines since the publication of "The *Negro Speaks of Rivers" in the *Crisis in 1921. The title poem, written in 1923 but held back from publication by Hughes, had won him the first prize in poetry in the 1925 *Opportunity magazine contest that helped to launch the major phase of the *Harlem Renaissance. Indeed, after the awards ceremony the sympathetic white writer Carl Van Vechten approached Hughes about putting together a volume of verse, and within a few days secured for him a contract with his own publisher, Alfred A. Knopf. The volume appeared in January 1926 with an essay, "Introducing Langston Hughes to the Reader," by Van Vechten.

The seven sections of the volume illustrate the variety of Hughes's poetic interests. The first section, also called "The Weary Blues," shows only indirect influence by the *blues on Hughes's verse, except in the title poem and a poem such as "Blues Fantasy." Instead the poems explore the urban, jazzy, race-inflected atmosphere of Harlem in the early 1920s, the world of cabarets, singers, dancers, and prostitutes, with an occasional throwback to an earlier age as in "Song for a Banjo Dance."

The second section, "Dream Variations," is touched lightly by race feeling, but dreaming generally takes the poet away from urban and racial themes toward nature, as in "Winter Moon." In the third section, "The Negro Speaks of Rivers," the poems protest against racism in one way or another, either by asserting the beauty and dignity of blacks or by exploring the tragedy of racism in America, as in "Cross," about *miscegenation, or "The South." The next section, "Black Pierrot," reflects Hughes's interest in the Pierrot figure, popularized among writers especially by the French symbolist poet Jules Laforgue. Hughes's Pierrot is often but not invariably race-inflected, but speaks mainly to the poet's bohemian desire for *freedom and the unconventional.

The poems in the section "Water-Front Streets" have even less to do with *race, but capture the sense of loneliness, lyrically expressed, that was a permanent feature of Hughes's psychology and art. "Shadows in the Sun" also emphasizes a fusion of colored exoticism and melancholy, as in "Soledad: A Cuban Portrait" and "To the Dark Mercedes of 'El Palacio de Amor'." The last section, "Our Land," reasserts the racial and political core of the book, with memorable poems such as "Mother to Son" and "Epilogue" ("I, too, sing America"), which powerfully closes the volume.

In general, reviewers praised the book, which established Hughes as the major rival to Countee *Cullen among the younger poets of the renaissance. The volume laid the foundation for Hughes's entire literary career; several poems remained extremely popular with his admirers. While his next volume, *Fine Clothes to the Jew* (1927), would represent a major step forward in his involvement in the blues and his development as a poet, *The Weary Blues* is richly representative of Hughes's sensibility as a poet.

• Langston Hughes, *Collected Poems*, 1994. Arnold Rampersad, *The Life of Langston Hughes*, vol. 1, *1902–1941: I Too Sing America*, 1986.   —Arnold Rampersad

WEATHERLY, TOM (b. 1942), poet, educator, and social activist. Born in Scottsboro, Alabama, on 3 November 1942, Tom Weatherly attended Morehouse College from 1958 to 1961 and Alabama A & M College during the 1961–1962 school year. During the mid-1960s, Weatherly became a minister of the African Methodist Episcopal (AME) Church and was named an assistant pastor of the AME *church in his hometown of Scottsboro. He found the demands of the church limiting and gave up his ministry to more actively pursue his *poetry. In the late 1960s, he left the South, moved to New York, and enrolled in an MFA program at Columbia University in 1974; he did not complete the program because he felt formal education was not quite as challenging as the world around him that he wanted to explore and include in his poetry. In New York, Weatherly lived in Harlem and in Greenwich Village. He was an active member of several burgeoning community-based art programs in Harlem and elsewhere in New York. While dedicating his life to art and the black community, Weatherly held a variety of largely low-paying jobs to support himself, including working as a dishwasher, bellhop, waiter, proofreader, and copy editor. He has devoted a significant amount of his time to teaching others the importance of the word. To this end he conducted a number of poetry writing and reading workshops, including the Afro-Hispanic Poets' Workshop in East Harlem, the Natural Process Workshop, the Saint Mark's Poetry Project, and the Brooklyn Poetry Project. In addition to these community-based and -informed poetry workshops, from 1970 to 1977 Weatherly conducted more institutionalized poetry writing and reading forums when he was poet in residence at Bishop College, Grand Valley State College, Morgan State College, poet-in-the-schools for the Richmond, Virginia, schools, and as poetry teacher at the Women's House of Detention of the New York Department of Corrections.

A part of his concern as teacher and as creator is to provide new images and myths of black people

and their reality that attest to their long tradition on Earth. His first volume of poetry, *Maumau Cantos* (1970), seeks to construct bridges between African American protest and demands for civil rights in the 1960s with the Kenyan uprisings against British colonial rule in the 1950s. In suggesting connections between Africans and African Americans, Weatherly's poems attempt to create a field of vision for African American cultural and political experience that is a part of a much larger playing field (mythmaking). His second volume of poetry, *Thumbprint* (1971), continues themes from *Maumau Cantos* but takes on new subject matter when the poems specifically pay homage to black women. His poems on black women are some of the few affirmative images of black women created by male poets belonging to the *Black Arts movement of the 1960s and early 1970s. In 1972 Weatherly coedited *Natural Process: An Anthology of New Black Poetry*, which contains poems that are in an Afrocentric tradition, where circularity and harmony are the guiding principles of black expression. Tom Weatherly's unique poetic voice makes him a significant figure of the Black Arts movement and an important minor writer in the African American literary tradition.

• Arnold Rampersad, "The Universal and the Particular in Afro-American Poetry," *CLA Journal* 25 (Sept. 1981): 1–17.
                                                    —Charles P. Toombs

WEBB, FRANK J. (?–?), author of *The Garies and Their Friends* (1857) and two novelettes, "Two Wolves and a Lamb," (1870) and "Marvin Hayle" (1870). The little that is known about Frank J. Webb's life comes from Harriet Beecher *Stowe's brief preface to *The Garies*. According to Stowe, he was born in Philadelphia, probably in the late 1820s or early 1830s. After growing up there, he likely resided in England sometime prior to the London publication of *The Garies* and may have moved in wealthy European social circles. Drawing on these experiences, Webb's novelettes focus on the leisure-time activities of upperclass society in London, Paris, and Cannes. *The Garies*'s prefaces by Stowe and Lord Brougham, both abolitionists, suggest he may have also played a role in the *antislavery movement.

Webb's contribution to African American literature is to be found in the number of pioneering themes and subjects addressed in *The Garies*. Published four years after William Wells *Brown's *Clotel*, *The Garies* is the second of four African American *novels published prior to the Civil War. Its contrived plot follows the fortunes of three *families with roots in the South: the dark-skinned Ellises, the interracial Garies, and the white Stevenses, headed by the villainous "slippery" George. Drawn together by circumstance in Philadelphia, these families allow Webb to explore the fortunes of the rising African American middle class and the virulence of northern racism, greed, and deceit found among both whites and blacks. The novel argues finally that wealth is the key to African American advancement. *The Garies and Their Friends* was the first novel to describe the lives of free African Americans in the North, to address interracial marriage and the problem of the *color line, and the first to make *passing a major theme.

• Gregory L. Candela, "Frank J. Webb," *DLB*, vol. 50, *Afro-American Writers before the Harlem Renaissance*, ed. Trudier Harris, 1986, pp. 242–244. Blyden Jackson, *A History of Afro-American Literature*, vol. 1, *The Long Beginning, 1746–1895*, 1989, pp. 323–348. —Lawrence R. Rodgers

WELLS-BARNETT, IDA B. (1862–1931), journalist, editor, diarist, autobiographer, lecturer, suffragist, antilynching crusader, and civil rights activist. The *essays, pamphlets, and newspaper articles of Ida B. Wells-Barnett shaped the post-Reconstruction discourse on *race, while her personal narratives, including two diaries, a travel journal, and an *autobiography, recorded the personal struggle of a professional woman to define African American womanhood in a pivotal era of American history. A complex woman of strong character and independent thought, Wells was shaped by firm moral convictions and profound religious beliefs. Her militant ideology of resistance, which found expression through the pen and at the podium, continued the tradition of resistance initiated by earlier African American writers and thinkers such as David *Walker, Maria W. *Stewart, Frederick *Douglass, and Frances Ellen Watkins *Harper.

The eldest of eight children, Ida B. Wells was born to Jim and Elizabeth Warrenton Wells in Holly Springs, Mississippi, on 16 July 1862. Wells attended Shaw University (later Rust College) until the deaths of her parents and youngest brother during the yellow fever epidemic of 1878. Only sixteen years old, she became a county schoolteacher, supporting her brothers and sisters on a salary of just twenty-five dollars a month. In 1882 or 1883 she began teaching in Woodstock, Tennessee, a rural community in Shelby County, but moved to Memphis when she obtained a position in the public schools in 1884.

That same year Wells sued the Chesapeake, Ohio and Southwestern Railroad after she was forcibly removed from the first-class ladies' coach. In December 1884 the circuit court ruled in her favor, but three years later the Tennessee Supreme Court reversed the decision. That experience prompted Wells to write letters to Memphis weeklies and, later, to African American newspapers like the *Detroit Plaindealer*, *Gate City Press*, and *New York Freeman*. Early articles, such as "Our Women" and "Race Pride," reveal the young journalist's increasing interest in issues of *gender and race. In 1886 Wells became "editress" of the *Evening Star* and began writing under the pen name Iola for a religious paper, the *Living Way*, earning the praise of newspapermen such as I. Garland Penn, who called her a militant journalist.

Between 1885 and 1887 Ida B. Wells kept a diary describing her struggle as a single professional woman to forge an independent life committed to work, self-improvement, and racial uplift. She recorded acts of mob *violence and the loss of her suit; she wrote about conferences in Kansas and Kentucky, where she was elected secretary of the Negro Press Association and was invited to speak on "Women in Journalism or How I Would Edit." Two years later, she bought an interest in the Memphis *Free Speech and Headlight* and became a full-time journalist in 1891, when she lost her teaching position because of editorials attacking inferior segregated schools.

After three African American grocers were brutally murdered by a white Memphis mob on 9 March 1892, Wells wrote fiery editorials urging citizens to flee the city. She maintained that *lynching was a racist strategy to eliminate independent and prosperous Negroes, while the charge of rape, she suggested, often masked consensual relations between white women and African American men. Whites were so incensed by these allegations that they destroyed her newspaper office while Wells was away and dared her to return to Memphis. Unintimidated by threats, Wells kept a gun in her house and advised that "a Winchester rifle should have a place of honor in every black home" (*Southern Horrors*, 1892).

Meanwhile she bought an interest in the *New York Age*, wrote two weekly columns entitled "Iola's Southern Field," and intensified her campaign against lynching through lectures, editorials, and carefully researched, well-documented pamphlets: *Southern Horrors: Lynch Law in All Its Phases* (1892); *A Red Record: Tabulated Statistics and Alleged Causes of Lynching in the United States, 1892, 1893, and 1894* (1895); and *Mob Rule in New Orleans* (1900). A forceful speaker and powerful writer, Wells uses strong, concrete language to examine the economic and political causes of racial oppression. In her writing she analyzes racist sexual ideology, exposes the collusion between terrorists and community leaders, and urges African Americans to resist oppression through boycotts and *emigration.

In 1893 Wells cowrote and printed *The Reason Why the Colored American Is Not in the Columbian Exposition—the Afro-American's Contribution to Columbia Literature* to protest the exclusion of African Americans from the World's Columbian Exposition in Chicago. That same year, convinced that international pressure might serve the antilynching cause, she undertook a lecture tour of Great Britain. On the voyage to England she began a short and spirited travel journal, which was later published in her autobiography. When she returned to England in 1894 for a six-month tour, Wells wrote a series of articles entitled "Ida B. Wells Abroad" for the Chicago *Inter-Ocean*.

After her 27 June 1895 marriage to Ferdinand L. Barnett, a Chicago lawyer, newspaperman, and widower with two sons, Wells-Barnett bought the *Chicago Conservator* from her husband. She continued to write following the births of her children, Charles Aked, Herman Kohlsaat, Ida B. Wells, Jr., and Alfreda M. Some of her published essays during this period include "Lynching and the Excuse for It" (1901), "Booker T. Washington and His Critics" (1904), and "Our Country's Lynching Record" (1913).

Wells-Barnett broadened her reformist activities and took up the suffragist cause. She had organized the Ida B. Wells Club in 1893; she later founded the Alpha Suffrage Club and cofounded the Cook County

League of Women's Clubs. She was elected secretary of the National Afro-American Council and called for a conference that led to the formation of the NAACP. In 1910 Wells-Barnett formed the Negro Fellowship League to employ southern migrants, using her salary as a probation officer to support the league. Her differences with race leaders became apparent when she challenged the accommodationism of Booker T. *Washington and the integrationist leanings of W. E. B. *Du Bois, while supporting Marcus *Garvey and his Universal Negro Improvement Association.

Wells-Barnett continued her crusade against violence into her fifties. In 1918 she covered the race riot in East St. Louis, Illinois, and wrote a series of articles on the riot for the *Chicago Defender.* Four years later she returned south to investigate the indictment for murder of twelve innocent Arkansas farmers. She then wrote *The Arkansas Race Riot* (1922) and raised money to publish and distribute one thousand copies of her report. Throughout her final years, she continued to write. In 1928 Wells-Barnett began an autobiography, which was edited and published posthumously by her daughter, Alfreda Duster, and she kept a diary in 1930 that depicts an active and vital woman attending meetings and lectures while campaigning for election to the Illinois State Senate. After a sudden illness, she died in Chicago on 25 March 1931.

Ida B. Wells-Barnett was one of the most outstanding women of the late nineteenth century. She was a militant thinker and writer whose essays, pamphlets, and books provide a theoretical analysis of lynching; she was a reformer whose insistence on economic and political resistance to oppression laid the foundation for the modern *civil rights movement; and she was an accomplished diarist and autobiographer whose personal narratives offer an insight into the formation of African American female identity in the late nineteenth century.

[See also Feminism; Journalism.]

• Alfreda M. Duster, ed., *Crusade for Justice: The Autobiography of Ida B. Wells*, 1970. Bettina Aptheker, ed., *Lynching and Rape*, 1977. Dorothy Sterling, *Black Foremothers*, 1979. Thomas C. Holt, "The Lonely Warrior: Ida B. Wells Barnett and the Struggle for Black Leadership," in *Black Leaders of the Twentieth Century*, eds. John Hope Franklin and August Meier, 1982, pp. 38–61. Paula Giddings, *When and Where I Enter: The Impact of Black Women on Race and Sex in America*, 1984. Hazel V. Carby, *Reconstructing Womanhood*, 1987. Mildred Thompson, *Ida B. Wells-Barnett*, 1990. Trudier Harris, ed., *Selected Works of Ida B. Wells-Barnett*, 1991. Miriam DeCosta-Willis, *The Memphis Diary of Ida B. Wells*, 1995.

—Miriam DeCosta-Willis

"We Shall Overcome." The most prominent freedom song of the *civil rights movement of the 1960s, "We Shall Overcome" has origins in African American *spirituals and has been used in a range of protest movements. The song emerged from multiple sources, including the old *spiritual "I Will Overcome" and the church hymn "I'll Overcome Someday" (published in 1901 by Reverend C. A. Tindley). Striking African American tobacco workers in Charleston, South Carolina, used an early version of the song on picket lines in 1945. It achieved wider use as a labor song after two of those union members brought the song to Highlander Folk School, a Tennessee training center for labor and civil rights organizers. In the 1960s student activists in the South used the song at sit-in demonstrations for desegregation. As its use spread, "We Shall Overcome" became the anthem of the civil rights movement, sung at demonstrations, police confrontations, mass meetings, and national events like the 1963 Freedom March in Washington, D.C. In addition to its continued use as a protest song in the United States, it is heard throughout the world in a variety of resistance movements. The adaptability and endurance of this song reveals the continuity of African American folk and spirituals, their ability to be reborn and to reappear in different forms and contexts. While drawing upon the tradition of African American congregational-style singing, various arrangements or styles have marked the song's appearance at different moments (in church, jail, or a mass demonstration; for desegregation, labor, or peace efforts), and new lyrics have been included to suit the occasion (during an armed police raid in Tennessee, for example, teenager Jamila Jones introduced the line "We are not afraid"). "We Shall Overcome" served as a powerful symbol of the civil rights movement and continues to function as a tool of solidarity and resistance.

• Guy Carawan and Candie Carawan, *We Shall Overcome: Songs of the Southern Freedom Movement*, 1963. Bernice Johnson Reagon, *Voices of the Civil Rights Movement: Black American Freedom Songs*, sound recording and accompanying text, Smithsonian Institution, 1980. Jim Brown et al., *We Shall Overcome: The Song that Moved a Nation*, video documentary, California Newsreel, 1989.

—Christina Accomando

WESLEY, DOROTHY PORTER. *See* Porter, Dorothy.

WESLEY, RICHARD (b. 1945), dramatist, screenwriter, and a major contributor to the Black Arts movement. Born in Newark, New Jersey, Richard Errol Wesley was the son of George Richard Wesley, a laborer, and Gertrude Thomas Wesley. While attending Howard University, Wesley studied playwriting under Owen *Dodson and Ted *Shine and wrote *Put My Dignity on 307*, for which he won an Outstanding Playwright Award from Samuel French Incorporated. After graduating in 1967 with a BFA from Howard, he continued to write while working as a passenger agent for United Airlines until September 1969. For his 1971 play *Gettin' It Together*, Wesley drew upon his airline experience to help shape the past of the protagonist, Nate. In this short, sensitive drama, Nate finds it hard to tell Coretta about his recent unfaithfulness, though she cares more about honesty than fidelity and urges him to help her break free from the self-destructive patterns of parents and friends. Uncertainty about their ability to get it together keeps the play crackling until the end. This play garnered a Drama Desk Award for Outstanding Playwriting.

Wesley's important 1971 drama, *Black Terror*, also examined self-destructive patterns, this time among revolutionaries. After proving himself by killing a white police commissioner, Keusi Kifo has to leave the Black Terrorists for refusing to assassinate a black reactionary because he believes fractricide will decimate the black struggle. The reactionary is executed by his daughter, after which she and the remaining terrorists die in a police shoot-out. Designed by a dramatist seeking radical social change, Wesley's play was meant to provoke debate among blacks about the desirability of suicidal tactics. Like *Hamlet*, it also pondered how to combat injustice without becoming unjust and whether righteousness should supersede kinship. Produced Off-Broadway and published in *The New Lafayette Presents* (1972), edited by Ed *Bullins, it earned Wesley a Drama Desk Award as most promising playwright of 1971–1972.

In 1972 Wesley married Valerie Wilson with whom he would later have two daughters.

At Sidney Poitier's request, Wesley wrote the filmscript for *Uptown Saturday Night*, a megahit in 1974. The film comically follows a factory worker (Poitier) and a cabdriver (Bill Cosby) striving to recover a lottery ticket from thieves. Having earned the NAACP Image Award for the original, Wesley scripted the 1975 sequel *Let's Do It Again*.

In 1974, Wesley also had several works produced and joined the board of directors of the writer's workshop formed by Frank Silvera, the well-known producer, director, and actor. One work, *The Past Is the Past*, was published in Stanley Richard's *The Best Short Plays 1975*. It portrays the unexpected meeting between a plant foreman and the twenty-year-old illegitimate son whom he abandoned and who is expecting an illegitimate child. The foreman, whose father had abandoned him, understands the mistake he made without being able to rectify it and warns the son to break free from the cycle of abandonment with his child. Another work, *The Sirens*, compassionately depicts three women, including two prostitutes, and the pain arising from illusions as well as the lack of them. One other 1974 production was a version of *The Mighty Gents*.

While lecturing at Manhattanville College in 1975, Wesley rewrote *The Mighty Gents* and in 1978 it opened at Broadway's Ambassador Theater. Despite a disappointing run of nine performances, Wesley's stunning, symbolic play, published by Dramatists Play Services (1979), was widely praised and won Morgan Freeman a Drama Desk Award for his role as Zeke, a derelict seeking dignity. Lauded for its universality, the play locates the illusions and economic degradation underlying the superman philosophy of a group of former youth gang members in the racist structure of American society. The gang members' disrespect toward fellow victim Zeke leads to their destruction at his hands, underscoring the message that we endanger ourselves in despising the seemingly weak.

After adapting Virginia *Hamilton's *The House of Dies Drear* for television in 1984 and Richard *Wright's *Native Son* for film in 1986, Wesley returned to the stage in 1989 with *The *Talented Tenth*, published in William Blackwell *Branch's *Crosswinds* (1993). A complex study of waning idealism among college-educated black professionals, the play focuses on Bernard Evan's rediscovery of W. E. B. *Du Bois's imperative for communally centered action by each generation's "talented tenth" until all have the opportunities meted out only to the self-advancing and guilt-laden few. Sensitive in its portrayals of Bernard's wife and mistress, it shines in the image of Habiba, Bernard's dead student love who simultaneously inspires youthful rebelliousness and adult dedication to community. Wesley's writing for stage and screen secure his place among the talented tenth of his time.

[*See also* Black Arts Movement.]

• "Richard Wesley," in *Contemporary Literary Criticism*, vol. 7, eds. Phyllis Carmen Mendelson and Dedria Bryfonski, 1977, pp. 518–519. Steven R. Carter, "Richard Wesley," in *DLB*, vol. 38, *Afro-American Writers after 1955: Dramatists and Prose Writers*, eds. Thadious Davis and Trudier Harris, 1985, pp. 271–278. Bernard L. Peterson, Jr., "Richard Wesley," in *Contemporary Black American Playwrights and Their Plays*, 1988, pp. 484–487. Sharon Malinowski, "Richard Errol Wesley," in *Contemporary Authors: New Revision Series*, vol. 27, eds. Hal May and James G. Lesniak, 1989, pp. 490–491.   —Steven R. Carter

WEST, CORNEL (b. 1953), essayist, public speaker, social activist, and major figure in African American academia. Cornel West was born in Tulsa, Oklahoma, on 2 June 1953. His mother was an elementary school teacher who later became principal; his father, a civilian administrator in the air force. Both of his parents attended Fisk University. The family, including West's brother, Clifton, moved often. They eventually settled in a middle-class African American neighborhood in Sacramento, California. West graduated with a degree in Near Eastern languages and literature from Harvard University. He received his doctorate in philosophy from Princeton University. As director of Princeton's Afro-American Studies Program from 1988 to 1994, and as a professor in Harvard's Department of Afro-American Studies since 1994, West is one of several high-profile scholars who have strengthend African American studies programs. He has taught at America's most presitigious universities and has lectured at many others. The blend of skills and styles employed by West inspires adjectives from his admirers and critics; unadorned nouns seem unable to capture his complexities.

West is a prolific essayist and author. His first book, *Prophesy Deliverance!: An Afro-American Revolutionary Christianity*, appeared in 1982 and attempts to synthesize elements of African American Christianity and thought, Western philosophy, and Marxist thinking. In 1988 West published *Prophetic Fragments*, a collection of *essays that discuss similarly disparate elements. *The American Evasion of Philosophy: A Genealogy of Pragmatism* (1989) engages populism and *race, *class, and *gender issues. *The Ethical Dimensions of Marxist Thought* (1991) and *Keeping Faith: Philosophy and Race in America* (1993) continue the discussion of those ideas in the context of modern America. *Prophetic Thought in Postmodern Times* and *Prophetic Reflections: Notes on Race* *and Power in America* also date from 1993. Throughout his career West has also produced collaborative work: *Post-Analytic Philosophy* (1985), edited with John Rajchman; *Breaking Bread: Insurgent Black Intellectual Life* (1991), cowritten with bell *hooks; *Jews and Blacks: Let the Healing Begin* (1995), authored with Michael Lerner; and *The Future of the Race* (1996), with Henry Louis *Gates, Jr. West's contributions to journals, popular magazines, and essay collections are myriad. His most influential book is *Race Matters* (1993), a short collection of essays that epitomizes West's careful attention to African American culture.

As a literary figure West is not easily categorized. His strength lies in his interdisciplinary focus. West synthesizes diverse topics in his writing leading to a careful control of language that is often poetic in its precision. He participates in African American oral and musical literary traditions with a spontaneous, performative element in his work that is as much a legacy from his grandfather, a Baptist preacher, as it is a language borrowed from *jazz and rap. In his writing he legitimizes all forms of African American speech and bends them to effective use, employing language as a polemical weapon for social activism. This crafting of language and blending of genres mark West's literary style.

Cornel West's contributions to African American literature and thought range across disciplines and worlds to comment upon African American life. His work exemplifies synthesis and innovation.

• Robert S. Boynton, "Princeton's Public Intellectual," *New York Times Magazine,* 15 September 1991, 39+.

—Elizabeth Sanders Delwiche Engelhardt

WEST, DOROTHY (b. 1907), novelist, short story writer, editor, and journalist. Through her various roles as writer, editor, and journalist, Dorothy West has influenced the direction and form of African American literary production. Prior to the publication of her first novel in 1948, West published frequently in the journals of the *Harlem Renaissance. As editor and founder of *Challenge* and *New Challenge,* she helped to oversee the transition from the Harlem Renaissance to the naturalistic realism of the 1930s. *The Living Is Easy* appeared about the same time as Ann *Petry's *The *Street* (1946), Gwendolyn *Brooks's *A *Street in Bronzeville* (1945) and *Annie Allen* (1949), and Zora Neale *Hurston's *Seraph on the Sewanee* (1948). It has become an important novel for newer generations of black women writers and critics.

Born into a middle-class black family in Boston, West displayed her literary talent early. As a schoolgirl, her first short story, "Promise and Fulfillment," was published by the *Boston Post.* Another story, "The Typewriter," won second place in an *Opportunity* literary contest. West shared the prize with Zora Neale Hurston. In 1926 West moved to New York to live with her cousin, the poet Helene *Johnson, and shortly thereafter her Harlem Renaissance career began. West became a beloved "little sister" of Harlem Renaissance writers like Zora Neale Hurston, Langston *Hughes, and Wallace *Thurman. Among her

many published stories during this period, two—"Funeral" (*Saturday Evening Quill,* Apr. 1928) and "Prologue to a Life" (*Saturday Evening Quill,* Apr. 1929)—rehearse themes that she would explore in greater depth in *The Living Is Easy.*

In addition to her writing, West pursued acting. In 1927 she had a small role in the original stage production of *Porgy* (based on Dubose Heyward's novel) and in 1932 she accompanied Langston Hughes and a group of black intellectuals and artists to the Soviet Union to make a film about race relations in the South. The film was never made and West returned to the United States.

In the 1930s West exerted her influence primarily as an editor and publisher, first of *Challenge* and then of *New Challenge.* She founded and financed both journals. *Challenge* sought to publish "quality" fiction by established writers and to avoid what James Weldon *Johnson called "propaganda." The first two numbers of the journal contained writings by known talents like Hughes, Hurston, and Countee *Cullen. West claimed that younger writers submitted bad fiction. *Challenge* was criticized by members of the Chicago group of writers, including Richard *Wright and Margaret *Walker, who felt it to be too aesthetic and nonpolitical. In 1937 *Challenge* became *New Challenge,* and at West's invitation Richard Wright became associate editor. The new journal leaned toward more political fiction and introduced new writers like Ralph *Ellison and Waters *Turpin. Richard Wright's classic manifesto on black literature, "Blueprint for Negro Writing" appeared in the journal as well. Because of financial difficulty and editorial conflicts between West and Wright, the journal folded after one issue.

Throughout this period West continued to write and publish *short stories. From 1926 to 1940 she published several stories in *Opportunity,* the *Messenger,* and *Saturday Evening Quill.* In 1945 she left New York for Martha's Vineyard to work on an autobiographical novel. *The Living Is Easy* was published by Random House in 1948. The story of the fiercely determined and independent Bostonian, Cleo Judson, the novel launches a satirical critique of the *class and color politics of the black bourgeoisie. Cleo seeks to acquire a balance between her loving southern upbringing and her aspirations toward material acquisitions and status. In the process she ruins her husband's financial empire and her sisters' marriages. The novel explores marital relations as well as the complex and at times painful relationships between mothers and daughters. West's influence is apparent in the mother-daughter relationship in Paule *Marshall's *Brown Girl, Brownstones* (1959).

When *The Living Is Easy* was republished in 1982, the novel was recognized as an important and influential text in the black woman's literary tradition. While Dorothy West continued to write articles and stories from her Martha's Vineyard home, it was not until 1995 that her second novel, *The Wedding,* appeared. *The Richer, the Poorer,* a collection of stories and reminiscences, was also published in 1995.

• SallyAnn H. Ferguson, "Dorothy West," in *DLB*, vol. 76, *Afro-American Writers, 1940–1955*, eds. Trudier Harris and Thadious M. Davis, 1987, pp. 187–195. Deborah MacDowell, "Conversations with Dorothy West," in *The Harlem Renaissance Re-Examined*, ed. Victor A. Kramer, 1987, pp. 265–282. Lawrence R. Rodgers, "Dorothy West's *The Living Is Easy* and the Ideal of Southern Folk Community," *African American Review* 26 (Spring 1992): 161–172.

—Farah Jasmine Griffin

WEST INDIAN LITERATURE begins logically with the arrival of Christopher Columbus in 1492. The islands and adjacent mainland first claimed by Spain were subsequently mythologized in the writings of sailors, adventurers, explorers, soldiers, merchants, traders, and priests as the New World of the Americas, a region of great wealth and beauty, innocence and barbarity. The region was fought over by the Spanish, the English, the French, and the Dutch, and the indigenous populations of Taino, Arawak, and Carib were decimated. When the mines and indigenous labor were exhausted, there were the sugar plantations and African slave labor to stimulate European expectations of wealth, privilege, and *freedom. After the abolition of *slavery in the British West Indies (1838), the importation of labor continued with indentured laborers from Africa, India, China, and Portugal. After the initial literature of discovery, exploration, conquest, and settlement, literary production in the British West Indies revolved around the agrosocial discourse of master and slave, and after emancipation around issues attendant on colonialism and nationalism.

West Indian literature during the period of slavery is not confined to the West Indian–born but includes visitors and those who, according to Kamau Brathwaite, had intimate knowledge of and were in some way committed by experience and/or attachment to the West Indies (*Roots*, 1993). These include the antislavery *novels *Hamel, the Obeah Man* (1827), *Marly, or The Life of a Planter in Jamaica* (1828), Michael Scott's *Tom Cringle's Log* (1836), and *Lady Nugent's Journal of Her Residence in Jamaica from 1801 to 1805* (1807). By the same token, one might include Olaudah *Equiano's *Interesting Narrative* (1789), and Captain John G. Stedman's *Narrative of Joanna: An Emancipated Slave of Surinam* (1838).

Gradually an indigenous literary culture emerged, producing a literature by West Indians about the West Indian reality at home and abroad. No other classification is possible when one reads the public and private writings of Elizabeth Hart Thwaites and Anne Hart Gilbert of Antigua ("History of Methodism," 1804), the pious, abolitionist daughters of a free black slaveholder (Moira Ferguson, *The Hart Sisters*, 1994), or J. B. Philippe's successful plea in *Free Mulatto* (1824) to the British government for the restoration of the civil rights free blacks and colored had enjoyed under Spanish rule. *The History of Mary Prince, a West Indian Slave, Related by Herself* (1831) calls attention to the undocumented literary culture of those who do not write. For Mary *Prince, dictating her story to Susanna Strickland and Thomas Pringle of the Anti-Slavery Society in England, Antigua is home. Her narrative, like the writings of the Harts and Phillipe, reveals a concrete geographical identity linked to the quest for civil rights in the colonies.

In the absence of a unifying cultural and political antiquity, West Indian literary culture in the nineteenth century reveals a cultural ambivalence that continues into the twentieth century. A deep cultural and political attachment to Britain coexists with nationalist thought and sentiment. In *Wonderful Adventures of Mrs. Seacole in Many Lands* (1857), Mary *Seacole is proud of her Jamaican womanhood, her Jamaican learned skills as a doctress and businesswoman, and her racial mixture; she is also the consummate Anglophile. Nationalist ideology finds strongest expression among the Creole intelligentsia in the nineteenth century, whether European, African, or *mulatto. For example, the racist diatribe of English historian J. A. Froude (*The English in the West Indies*, 1888) is vigorously resisted by J. J. Thomas, a black schoolmaster and later secretary to the Board of Education in Trinidad (*Froudacity: West Indian Fables Explained*, 1889). Thomas had already written a systematic study of French Creole, *The Theory and Practice of Creole Grammar* (1869), again indicative of a cultural nationalism that prepared the way for political nationalism in the twentieth century. Wilson Harris observes that Thomas's counterdiscourse, however admirable, is indebted to colonial discursive models (*History, Fable and Myth in the Caribbean and the Guianas*, 1976). The pattern persists into the twentieth century. Caribbean literary culture develops in tension with dominant colonial models, at once imitative and transformative, and in the process subverts the colonial and postcolonial discourses at their foundation.

In 1904, Thomas MacDermott and Herbert G. de Lisser, two white Jamaicans, established the All Jamaica Library with a view to publishing fiction, *poetry, *history, and *essays that dealt directly with Jamaica and Jamaicans. They published two of MacDermott's novels under the pseudonym Tom Redcam: *Becky's Buckra Baby* (1904) and *One Brown Girl and—, a Jamaican Story* (1909), before the All Jamaica Library folded. De Lisser published ten novels altogether, among them, the historical romance *White Witch of Rosehall* (1929) and two novels about the black Jamaican working *class, *Jane's Career* (1914) and *Susan Proudleigh* (1915). Despite the racist stereotyping of these novels, it is clear that indigenous literary production must accommodate the island's black majority and its Creole cultures. With the publication of Claude *McKay's *Songs of Jamaica* (1911) and *Constab Ballads* (1912), the folk poet is ensconced as the essence of the nativist enterprise in island consciousness. The romanticism that characterizes McKay's literary production, before and after his immigration to the United States, especially in the novels *Home to Harlem* (1928), *Banjo* (1929), and *Banana Bottom* (1933), and in the *autobiographies *A Long Way from Home* (1937), and *My Green Hills of Jamaica* (posthumously, 1979), is the signature of an anticolonial Jamaican nationalist. After McKay, Louise Bennett becomes Jamaica's premier folk poet (*Selected Poems*, 1982), and cultural nationalism takes a distinctly anticolonial, liberationist turn in the novels of a new generation of Jamaican writers, among them, Vic Reid's *New Day* (1949), Roger Mais's *The Hills Were Joyful Together* (1953) and *Brother Man* (1954), John Hearne's *Voices under the Window* (1955), Andrew Salkey's *A Quality of Violence* (1959), Sylvia Wynter's *The Hills of Hebron* (1962), and Orlando Patterson's *The Children of Sisyphus* (1964).

In Trinidad, two short-lived anticolonial nationalist reviews, *Trinidad* (1929–1930) and *The Beacon* (1931–1933, 1939), provided a forum for writers such as C. L. R. James, Alfred Mendes (*Pitch Lake*, 1934; and *Black Fauns*, 1935), and Ralph de Boissiere (*Crown Jewel*, 1952; and *Rum and Coca-Cola*, 1956). They promoted a fiction rooted in indigenous reality. James became the intellectual giant of his time, recovering a Caribbean culture of resistance for all the Anglophone Caribbean in a series of masterful works, among them, *The Case for West Indian Self-Government* (1933); *Minty Alley* (1936); *The Black Jacobins: Toussaint L'Ouverture and the San Domingo Revolution* (1938); *Mariners, Rengades and Castaways: The Story of Herman Melville and the World We Live In* (1953); and *Beyond a Boundary* (1963). With James, cultural, political, and geographic nationalism takes a Pan-Caribbean, Pan-Africanist turn. This reflects his wide-ranging literary and political interests and also his activism in the United States and Britain, agitating for civil rights in the United States as well as for independence in Africa and the Caribbean.

By mid-century the contrary impulses of West Indian literature are clearly defined. There is a new regional consciousness nurtured by a number of factors. Chief among these are literary magazines such as *Kyk-over-al* (Guyana, 1945–1961), *Focus* (Jamaica, occasional, 1943–1960), and *Bim* (Barbados, 1942–). Under the direction of Henry Swanzy, the British Broadcasting Service initiated the radio program *Caribbean Voices*, featuring writers from all over the Anglophone Caribbean. The University of the West Indies in Jamaica brought a heightened regional awareness to scholars and writers, as did the ill-fated Federation of the West Indies (1958–1962). Following World War II, London became the center of Caribbean literary production. This single site generated a sense of regional identity among writers who immigrated to England in search of publishers. The pulse of that critical place and moment in the genesis of Caribbean literary culture is analyzed comprehensively in George Lamming's *The Pleasures of Exile* (1960). That sense of London as literary capital of the West Indies is renewed and transformed with the advent of the Caribbean Arts movement (Anne Walmsley, *The Caribbean Arts Movement 1966–1972*, 1992), though today London competes with Canada, the United States, and the West Indies as sites of West Indian literary production.

In hindsight, the writers who dominated the literary scene in the 1950s are Sam Selvon and V. S. Naipaul from Trinidad, George Lamming from Barbados, and Derek Walcott from St. Lucia. Walcott goes to university in Jamaica, then to Trinidad, and the others go to England. They usher in a literary renaissance distinguished by its diversity. The thematics of Lamming's *In the Castle of My Skin* (1953) and *Season of Adventure* (1960); Selvon's *A Brighter Sun* (1952), *The Lonely Londoners* (1956), and *Turn Again Tiger* (1958); Naipaul's *Miguel Street* (1959) and *A House for Mr. Biswas* (1961); and Edgar Mittelholzer's *Morning at the Office* (1950) and his trilogy *Children of Kaywana* (1952), *The Harrowing of Hubertus* (1954), and *Kaywana Blood* (1958), generate images of an uneven colonial history, social instability, cultural and economic dependency, heterogeneous populations, a high degree of cultural interpenetration, different ethnic and national alignments, and major *migrations out of the region. By 1962, with the collapse of the Federation of the West Indies, any expectation of sociocultural homogeneity disappears and in its place is a free-floating interculturative model privileging a permanent, coexistent plurality that stimulates cultural production and leaves the region vulnerable to various forms of recolonization (Edward Kamau Brathwaite, "Caribbean Man in Space and Time," 1975).

In the 1960s, Naipaul's reputation grows with a series of masterful works of fiction and nonfiction that are severely critical of the Afrocentric anti-imperialist base of West Indian nationalism, among them: *The Middle Passage* (1962), *The Mimic Men* (1967), and *The Loss of El Dorado* (1969). A number of different writers establish their reputations with publications remarkable for their originality and diversity. Derek Walcott, 1993 Nobel Laureate, publishes *In a Green Night* (1962), *The Castaway and Other Poems* (1965), *The Gulf and Other Poems* (1969), and *Dream on Monkey Mountain and Other Plays* (1970). Wilson Harris of Guyana publishes ten books, each worthy of a place in the canon, among them, *The Palace of the Peacock* (1960), *The Whole Armour* (1962), *The Secret Ladder* (1963), *Heartland* (1964), *Ascent to Omai* (1970), and two key statements on West Indian aesthetics, *Tradition, the Writer and Society: Critical Essays* (1967) and *History, Fable and Myth in the Caribbean and Guyana* (1970). Harris rejects social realism for the marvelous real and staunchly resists the limited cultural horizons of nationalist anti-imperialism. This is also the decade of Edward Kamau Brathwaite, Barbadian poet, playwright, professor of history and literature, critic, and cultural historian. Brathwaite's trilogy *Rights of Passage* (1967), *Masks* (1968), and *Islands* (1969) galvanized Afrocentric thought and scholarship in the Caribbean. In this decade, Jean Rhys carves out a native space for herself with *Wide Sargasso Sea* (1966), and, among others, Merle Hodge (*Crick, Crack Monkey*, 1970), Michael Anthony (*The Games Were Coming*, 1963; *A Year in San Fernando*, 1965; *Green Days by the River*, 1967), Ismith Khan (*The Jumbie Bird*, 1961; *The Obeah Man*, 1964), Garth St. Omer (*A Room on the Hill*, 1968; *Shades of Grey*, 1968), and Earl Lovelace (*While Gods Are Falling*, 1965; *The School Master*, 1968) publish for the first time.

In the 1970s, the Caribbean enters a postcolonial phase politically and culturally. The new nations of the region are in a state of transition. Their diversity is unsettling to some in the absence of rigid colonial hierarchies of *race, class, and *gender. By custom and by need they are markedly dependent on each other and on metropolitan North America and Europe. Naipaul, Selvon, Lamming, Walcott, Harris, and Brathwaite dominate the literary scene with their diverse ideological positioning. Landmark publications include Walcott's autobiographical poem *Another Life* (1973); his poetry collections *Sea Grapes* (1976), *The Star-Apple Kingdom* (1979), *The Joker of Seville and O Babylon!* (1978), and the poem "The Muse of History" (in *Is Massa Day Dead?*, ed. Orde Coombs, 1974). Brathwaite publishes *The Development of Creole Society in Jamaica 1770–1820* (1971), *Contradictory Omens: Cultural Diversity and Integration in the Caribbean* (1974), and the first volume of an autobiographical trilogy, *Mother Poem* (1977). Selvon publishes the second volume of his *Moses trilogy, *Moses Ascending* (1975), and two Trinidad novels, *The Plains of Caroni* (1970) and *Those Who Eat the Cascadura* (1972). Lamming publishes *Water with Berries* (1971) and *Natives of My Person* (1972). The works of these major writers are complemented by many others, among them, Martin Carter's *Poems of Succession* (1977), Earl Lovelace's *The Dragon Can't Dance* (1979), Mervyn Morris's *The Pond* (1973) and *Shadowboxing* (1979), and Dennis Scott's *Uncle Time* (1973).

The nationalist project of reclamation and reconstruction, still a predominantly male enterprise, undergoes radical revision at this time, as West Indian women at home and abroad introduce a counterdiscourse of race, gender, and national identity and writers find new channels of opportunity in the United States and Canada. Among the women who distinguish themselves in the Caribbean and on both sides of the Atlantic are Jamaica *Kincaid (*At the Bottom of the River*, 1984; *Annie John*, 1985), Erna Brodber (*Jane and Louisa Will Soon Come Home*, 1980; *Myal*, 1988), Olive Senior (*Summer Lightning*, 1986; *Gardening in the Tropics*, 1994), Lorna Goodison (*Selected Poems*, 1992), Merle Collins (*Angel*, 1987), Dionne Brand (*Primitive Offensive*, 1982; *Chronicles of the Hostile Sun*, 1984), Michelle Cliff (*Abeng*, 1984; *No Telephone to Heaven*, 1987); and Zee Edgell (*Beka Lamb*, 1982). Literary production is still characterized by dependency on foreign presses and heavy out-migration, though many writers continue to live and work and publish in the Caribbean, accepting or chafing at the limited opportunities for the dissemination of their work. The pressure of an expanding diaspora continues to grow.

West Indian literary production today has never been keener. Brathwaite (*X-Self*, 1987; *Roots*, 1993; *Zea Mexican Diary*, 1993), Harris (*Explorations: A Selection of Talks and Articles 1966–1981*, 1981; *Carnival*, 1985; *The Infinite Rehearsal*, 1987), Naipaul (*The Enigma of Arrival*, 1987; *A Way in the World*, 1994), and Walcott (*Omeros*, 1990), continue to publish. Young writers of different ethnic and national alignments with a tradition of great West Indian writers behind them are publishing at an awesome rate. Robert Antoni, Lawrence Scott, Patricia Powell, Marlene Nourbese Philip, Sasenarine Persaud, David

and Cyril Dabydeen, Jane King, and Kwame Dawes are but a few who are scattered across the United States, Canada, Britain, and the Caribbean.

African American and African West Indian literary culture share a common history of slavery, ancestral reclamation and cultural reconstruction in a New World environment, often under the most hostile of circumstances. Even after slavery, the loss of their aboriginal base is exacerbated by the heterogenous populations of the Americas, mass migration, and exploitative social stratifications with respect to race, class, and culture. The narratives of J. J. Phillippe, Olaudah Equiano, and Nancy Prince establish some migratory patterns during slavery. In this century the cultures frequently penetrate each other's space. Jamaicans Marcus *Garvey and Claude McKay influence and are influenced by cultural and political developments in the United States. Eric *Walrond makes a brief contribution (*Tropic Death*, 1926), Zora Neale *Hurston publishes *folklore collected in Jamaica and Haiti (*Tell My Horse*, 1938). McKay's consciously wrought double identity as Jamaican and African American becomes an increasingly acceptable measure of cultural interpenetration in the works of Paule *Marshall and Michelle Cliff. In recent years major Caribbean writers such as Derek Walcott and Edward Kamau Brathwaite have taken up residence in the United States, and their Caribbean discourse has influenced and been influenced by African American literary discourse. Other writers who define themselves as West Indian are, for example, Jamaica *Kincaid and Michelle Cliff, who not only live and publish in the United States but actively contribute to value-shaping dialogues about literature and art.

Despite cross-cultural interpenetration, African American and West Indian literary discourses overlap and yet remain distinct. West Indian literary discourse tends to regional cultural inclusiveness rather than the rigid racial stratification that characterizes African American literary discourse. The "Black writing" model is one of several critical/theoretical approaches as is "Indo Caribbean writing" and the "Caribbean women writers." Recently, postcolonial and Pan-Caribbean models have gained favor among regional scholars, but none of these are rigidly adhered to. It may well be that *publishing houses in the United States, Canada, and Britain will continue to influence Caribbean discourse, but metropolitan dependency has been a feature of regional cultures since Columbus and they have so far maintained a distinctive course.

[*See also* Emigration; Literary History.]

• Bruce King ed., *West Indian Literature*, 1979. Edouard Glissant, *Caribbean Discourse: Selected Essays*, trans. J. Michael Dash, 1989. Patrick Taylor, *The Narrative of Liberation: Perspectives on Afro-Caribbean Literature, Popular Culture, and Politics*, 1989. Selwyn R. Cudjoe, ed., *Caribbean Women Writers: Essays from the First International Conference*, 1990. Antonio Benítez-Rojo, *The Repeating Island*, trans. James E. Maraniss, 1992. Simon Gikandi, *Writing in Limbo: Modernism and Caribbean Literature*, 1992. George Lamming, *Conversations: Essays, Addresses and Interviews 1953–1990*, eds. Richard Drayton and Andaiye, 1992. Gordon Rohlehr, *My Strangled City and Other Essays*, 1992.

Derek Walcott, *The Antilles: Fragments of Epic Memory*, 1992. Anne Walmsley, *The Caribbean Artists Movement 1966–1972: A Literary and Cultural History*, 1992. Evelyn O'Callaghan, *Woman Version: Theoretical Approaches to West Indian Fiction by Women*, 1993. Bruce King, ed., *West Indian Literature*, 2d rev. ed., 1995. —Sandra Pouchet Paquet

WHEATLEY, PHILLIS (c. 1753–1784), the first African American and the second woman to publish a book in the colonies on any subject. Phillis Wheatley was born, by her own testimony, in Gambia, West Africa, about the year 1753. Unlike her African American contemporary, Venture *Smith, who devoted over a third of his 1798 *Narrative* to a detailed recollection of his African homeland, Wheatley, who was seized and taken into *slavery when seven or eight years of age, recalled her homeland to her white captors in considerably less detail. While we may never know what memories this remarkable poet and cultivator of the epistolary style shared of her native Africa with her most frequent correspondent and black soulmate, Obour Tanner, we do know that her public memories were at least three.

She did recall the sight of her mother's daily ritual of pouring out water to the sun upon its rising, redolent of hierophantic solar worship, and then immediately prostrating herself in the direction of that rising sun, this practice probably describing the first of five daily prayers of Islam in which the believer kneels or prostrates her or himself toward Mecca, certainly the direction Wheatley's mother assumed. While the other two memories may not be as informative, they are more affecting. In her famous poem "To the Right Honourable William, Earl of Dartmouth," she holds that her "love of *Freedom* sprung" from the fact that she "Was snatch'd from *Afric's* fancy'd happy seat." "Steel'd was that soul," the poet continues, "and by no misery mov'd / That from a father seiz'd his babe belov'd." In several rhapsodic and descriptive lines from "Phillis's Reply to the Answer" in which the author to whom she is replying prompts her to respond that "pleasing Gambia on my soul returns," she extols Gambia's "soil spontaneous" which "yields exhaustless stores; / For phoebus revels on her verdant shores."

When the young girl of seven or eight found herself on the slave block in midsummer Boston on 11 July 1761, was she thinking of her fertile, verdant Gambia while she tried to conceal her nakedness in a public place with nothing more than a piece of dirty carpet? The Wheatleys bought her, nevertheless, for a trifle and with diseased imagination named her Phillis after the slave schooner that brought her from Africa to America.

Despite the lamentable disadvantage of her enslavement, only four years later Wheatley had acquired enough skill in the use of English that she could correspond with the Mohegan Indian minister and graduate of Dartmouth College, Samson Occom. As well, she must have begun to experiment with the writing of *poetry. Her first published writing, the poem "On Messrs. Hussey and Coffin" (about the remarkable survival of these gentlemen in a hurricane off Cape Cod), appeared on 21 December 1767 in the *Newport Mercury*. At the approximate age of fourteen, then, Wheatley became a published public poet, a capacity in which she continued to function throughout the remainder of her short life.

Probably during this same period Wheatley initiated her classical studies, perhaps being tutored by the Harvard graduate, minister of Old South Church, one-time prolific poet, and encourager of young poets, Mather Byles. Wheatley soon became an excellent student of Latin, as her superb version of Ovid's Niobe episode from Book VI of the *Metamorphoses* ably attests.

On 18 August 1771 Wheatley was baptized by Samuel Cooper, minister and future spiritual and literary advisor to the poet. By 29 February of the following year, Wheatley had composed enough poems to comprise a volume. This volume failed to appear because of a lack of subscribers and, according to William H. Robinson, because of racist reasons. By September 1773, however, Wheatley had found a London publisher with the help of Selina Hastings, philanthropist and Countess of Huntingdon. Prior to the appearance of her *Poems on Various Subjects, Religious and Moral*, Wheatley spent six weeks in London, from June 17 to July 26, during which time she prepared her *Poems* for the press and visited, or was visited by, several London dignitaries, such as Granville Sharp, who escorted the poet on tours of the Horse Armoury, the crown jewels, and the Tower of London; Thomas Gibbons, who Wheatley notes was a professor of rhetoric; the Earl of Dartmouth, who gave the poet five guineas, with which she purchased a set of Alexander Pope's complete *Works*; and Brook Watson, a wealthy merchant who gave Wheatley a folio edition of John Milton's *Paradise Lost*.

While in London Wheatley received Benjamin Franklin, who wrote to his American cousin, Jonathan Williams, that "Upon your recommendation I went to see the black poetess and offered her any services I could do her." Even no less an intellectual lion than Voltaire, who was living in England at the time, wrote in a letter to a French friend in 1774 that Wheatley was the composer of "*très-bons vers anglais*" (very good English verse). Certainly Wheatley earned for herself on this trip an international reputation, the first African American to do so. She had already enjoyed an international reputation of sorts for her elegy on the death of George Whitefield, privy chaplain to the Countess of Huntingdon; appearing first in 1770 in Boston, this elegy was widely reprinted on both sides of the Atlantic and perhaps first brought to the countess's attention the poetic talent of the sixteen- or seventeen-year-old poet.

Soon after the appearance of *Poems*, Wheatley achieved her manumission, as she remarked in a letter of 8 October 1773 to David Wooster, later a general in the Revolutionary War, "at the desire of my friends in England." Not until her pen brought her into the scrutiny of the British public did John Wheatley see fit to "give me my *freedom." Wheatley, therefore, is the first African American to free herself by means of her own writing ability. After Susanna Wheatley, the poet's former mistress, died on 3 March 1774, Wheatley continued to live at the

Wheatley mansion for a time and to write patriotic verse. She corresponded with George Washington, composing the famous poem "To His Excellency General Washington," on 26 October 1775, and received an invitation from the general to visit him. She did so at Washington's Cambridge headquarters, a few days before the departure of the British under General Howe from Boston, on 17 March 1776. Wheatley married John Peters, a free African American and jack-of-all-trades (grocery keeper, dandy, and advocate for black rights before the Massachusetts courts), on 1 April 1776.

After this time, given the ravages and uncertainties of the American Revolution, Wheatley's fortunes declined rapidly. She tried twice, but unsuccessfully, to solicit subscribers for a second volume of new poems, dedicated to Benjamin Franklin. On 30 October 1779 and in September 1784, just three months before her death, she published proposals for a collection that would have included an "Epithalamium" (perhaps showing the influence of Edmund Spenser), "Niagra," "Chloe to Calliope," "To Musidora or Florello," and several new elegies as well as thirteen *letters to such notables as Dartmouth, Benjamin Rush, and the Countess of Huntingdon. During this time, Wheatley served as part-time instructor in a petty school and as a domestic servant while trying to tend to three children. Wheatley died in abject poverty, preceded by her three children, on 5 December 1784, apparently from infection from having just given birth to her last child, unremembered and certainly unappreciated.

This internationally famous and accomplished artist nevertheless experienced an early career similar to that of most fine poets: an apprenticeship during which Wheatley produced a sizable body of juvenilia was followed by a period of maturity marked by poems of apparently aesthetic concerns. Wheatley's apprenticeship is characterized by statements of intense, Christian piety; such poems as "Atheism" and "An Address to the Deist," both from 1767, appear to be the sorts of declarations that a racist white catechist might have exacted from a catechumen of color during this time. "On Friendship" (1769) and "On the Nuptials of Mr. Spence to Miss Hooper" (1768) suggest the aesthetic interests of her mature period, while the poems "America," "On the Death of Mr. Snider Murder'd by Richardson," "On the Affray in King-Street, on the Evening of the 5th of March" (almost certainly written in celebration of Crispus Attucks), and "To the King's Most Excellent Majesty. 1768," predict Wheatley's preoccupation with American patriot politics.

Almost immediately after the publication in late February 1772 of her first proposal for a volume of poems, Wheatley's tone and subject matter shift away from pious testimony toward that of a zealous seeker for her own idea of God and for her own poetic idiom. In such works as "Thoughts on the Works of Providence," which (while naming Jehovah once) makes *no* mention of Jesus but syncretizes solar worship, animism, and classicism with a broad Judeo-Christianity, and "On Imagination," a complex poem that continues the religious syncretism

but which represents a concentrated expression of Wheatley's poetics, Wheatley displays a sophisticated handling of the poetic and intellectual materials available to her. For that matter, this poet suggests by her work that she has recognized full well white duplicity ("Some view our sable race with a scornful eye") and that she has constructed a poetics of subversion.

Several critics of Wheatley have recently recognized a subversive tone within her poetry. In a letter to Samson Occom dated 11 February 1774 and reprinted in colonial newspapers a dozen times during this year, Wheatley defines freedom in the following manner: "in every human Breast, God has implanted a Principle which we call Love of Freedom; it is impatient of Oppression, and pants for Deliverance." Surely any feeling, intelligent soul who can define freedom in these eloquent words can never be satisfied with servility. Lest any suspect Wheatley failed to recognize the implications for her and her black brothers and sisters of the American patriot cry for freedom from the British, observe what she says as she closes her letter to Occom: "How well the cry for Liberty, and the reverse Disposition for the Exercise of oppressive Power over others agree—I humbly think it does not require the Penetration of a Philosopher to determine."

Wheatley assumes her subversive voice in "To Maecenas," the opening poem of the 1773 *Poems*. Here she exploits the potential for subversion present in classical pastoral by donning the mask of an innocuous shepherd and by joining Maecenas, legendary Roman patron of Virgil and Horace, "beneath the myrtle shade," the classic site of pastoral, so that she can profess a burning ambition to achieve the height of expression in the epic mode, descant upon the subject of freedom, and "snatch a laurel," the symbol of poetic maturity, while her white patrons "indulgent smile upon the deed"—hardly the aspirations of an allegedly derivative imitator of the neoclassical manner of composition. This subversive voice is evident in all of her occasional poetry after February of 1772, including "On Being Brought from Africa to America" (written as early as 1768 but doubtless revised for the 1773 *Poems*).

As noted earlier, Wheatley's efforts to articulate her subversive objections to "oppressive Power" went largely unnoticed because of her declining fortunes after her marriage to Peters. This decline came about because of the Revolutionary War, the apparently desultory support of her husband, and the failures of the two proposal attempts to attract subscribers. Her bleak outlook is evident in what is probably one of her last poems, "An Elegy on Leaving _____," for what she is leaving behind is the world of poetry: "No more my hand shall wake the warbling lyre." Despite a despondent conclusion to a remarkably distinguished career, Phillis Wheatley represents a number of firsts in American culture. While she is author of the first book published by an African American, she is also the first woman who published her work largely through the efforts of a community of women: her mistress, Susanna, seems always to have encouraged her to write, and her daughter,

Mary, may have served as the poet's first tutor; Obour Tanner, her black soulmate, evidently gave Wheatley encouragement and spiritual counsel, but it was probably through the efforts of Selina Hastings, the Countess of Huntingdon, that she saw one of her volumes come into print. Wheatley also enjoys the distinction of being America's first woman writer who tried to make a living by the use of her pen, and she is certainly one of America's first authors, whether man or woman, to do so. In addition, Wheatley is one of America's first writers to cultivate for publication the epistolary style. According to Henry Louis *Gates, Jr., moreover, she is "the progenitor of the black literary tradition." For all these reasons and more Phillis Wheatley deserves to be recognized as a major American author.

[*See also* Literary History, *article on* Colonial and Early National Eras.]

• William H. Robinson, *Black New England Letters*, 1977. William H. Robinson, ed., *Critical Essays on Phillis Wheatley*, 1982. William H. Robinson, ed., *Phillis Wheatley and Her Writings*, 1984. Sondra A. O'Neale, "A Slave's Subtle War: Phillis Wheatley's Use of Biblical Myth and Symbol," *Early American Literature* 21.2 (Fall 1986): 144–165. Henry Louis Gates, Jr., *Figures in Black*, 1987. John C. Shields, ed., *The Collected Works of Phillis Wheatley*, 1988. John C. Shields, "Phillis Wheatley," in *African American Writers*, eds. Valerie Smith, Lea Baechler, and A. Walton Litz, 1991, pp. 473–491. Phillip M. Richards, "Phillis Wheatley and Literary Americanization," *American Quarterly* 44.2 (June 1992): 163–191. Frances Smith Foster, *Written by Herself: Literary Production by African American Women 1746–1892*, 1993. John C. Shields, guest ed., *Style: African-American Poetics* 26 (Fall 1993): 172–270.   —John C. Shields

WHIPPER, WILLIAM (c. 1804–1876), essayist and reformer. A respected civil rights theoretician and tactician, William Whipper played an active role in a variety of reform movements during the antebellum era. He was born in Little Britain township, Pennsylvania, the son of a white lumber merchant and his black domestic servant. He received an education from the same tutor whom his father employed for his white offspring. In 1835, Whipper formed a highly successful business partnership with Stephen Smith, a prosperous black lumber dealer in Columbia, Pennsylvania. Becoming one of the wealthiest African Americans of his time, Whipper used his considerable financial means to bankroll the *antislavery movement.

During the 1830s, Whipper played a leading role in the Philadelphia-based American Moral Reform Society, an organization made up primarily of African Americans dedicated to *education, temperance, and human liberation. During the abolitionist crusade, Whipper's *essays and *letters appeared in such notable periodicals as the *Liberator*, the *North Star*, and the *National Antislavery Standard*. He was editor of the *National Reformer* from 1830 to 1839. Whipper started his writing career attempting to stake out universal principles of justice that would appeal to all. By the outbreak of the Civil War he had abandoned his color-blind perspective in favor of an increasingly nationalistic posture that endorsed all-black institutions and *emigration to Canada.

Whipper's most famous essay, "An Address on Non-Resistance to Offensive Aggression," was published in the *Colored American Magazine* in September 1837. The essay makes a logical and learned argument against "the war principle" as a means of seeking justice. Instead Whipper recommends especially to "the colored population of this country, both free and enslaved" a course of "self-denial, patience and perseverance," rebuking "the spirit of *violence, both in sentiment and practice." Whipper's "Address" demonstrates some of the links between the moral suasion abolitionists of the early nineteenth century and the nonviolent civil rights activists of the mid-twentieth century.

• Vernon Loggins, *The Negro Author*, 1931.

—William L. Andrews

WHITE, PAULETTE CHILDRESS (b. 1948), short fiction writer, and poet. Paulette Childress White was born in Detroit, Michigan, on 1 December 1948, the third of thirteen children. After one year of art school, financial problems and the birth of the first of five sons interrupted her education. Her first published poem appeared in *Deep Rivers* in 1972, followed by a small collection, *Love Poem to a Black Junkie* (1975). Some of these poems reflect the *black nationalism and rediscovery of Africa apparent in current literature while others introduce more original themes that continue into her later work.

One such theme, the impotent anger of many African American men, is demonstrated in the *short story "Passing" and recurs in other short stories: in the street-corner argument overheard in "The Bird Cage" (*Redbook*, June 1978), and in the silent protagonist's daily distribution of old newspaper clippings in the neighborhood of a 1967 riot in "Paper Man" (*Michigan Quarterly Review*, Spring 1986).

White also writes of women who eventually bond through reluctant realization of their painful commonality that cuts across artificial lines. The poem "Humbled Rocks" (*Love Poem*) and the short stories "Alice" (*Essence*, Jan. 1977), "Dear Akua" (*Harbor Review*, 1986), and "Getting the Facts of Life" (*Rites of Passage*, ed. Tonya Bolden, 1994) all testify to the spiritual sustenance derived from sisterhood. The recurrence of this theme, encouraged by the rise of *feminism, is more directly related to personal experience.

White's writing is highly autobiographical with only minor details changed. "Getting the Facts of Life," in which a girl, sharing with her cohesive family the financial and emotional consequences of her father's employment layoff, makes her first humiliating trip with her mother to the "welfare office" through a racially divided neighborhood, creatively interprets actual events. *The Watermelon Dress: Portrait of a Woman* (1984), a narrative poem, traces the author's development as a closet artist and unfulfilled woman from adolescence through the conflicting demands and needs of a difficult first marriage and child-rearing and a period of emotional unconsciousness to the eventual awareness and challenge of selfhood.

The streets of Detroit are as essential to White's

writing as Chicago is to the work of Gwendolyn *Brooks. The memorable and superbly drawn characters who inhabit her world and the hungers that drive them are insightful and authentic. The occasional interplay between the narrator's reflections and the characters' actions and dialogue is effective and original. White's lyricism, sometimes reminiscent of Jean *Toomer's sentence fragments and poetic repetition, and her metaphorical and alliterative use of language make her fiction almost indistinguishable from her poetry.

Paulette White is now remarried, a PhD candidate at Wayne State University, and an instructor at Henry Ford Community College. When her schedule permits her more time for creativity, this unique voice may well encourage other writers to trust the validity of their own experiences as women emerging from the darkness of restriction and concealment into the sunlight of their own personhood and to express those realized selves with sensitivity, insight, and lyrical beauty.

• Mary Helen Washington, introduction to *Midnight Birds: Stories of Contemporary Black Women Writers,* ed. Mary Helen Washington, 1982, pp. 3–7.

—Naomi Long Madgett

WHITE, WALTER (1893–1955), novelist, essayist, civil rights leader, writer and patron of the Harlem Renaissance, and executive secretary of the NAACP. The son of a mail carrier and one of seven children, Walter Francis White grew up in Atlanta on the border between white and African American neighborhoods. During the Atlanta race riots of September 1906, a white mob nearly burned down his family's home. The event was formative for White, then thirteen, inaugurating his awareness of the meaning of racial identity and influencing his subsequent political and literary careers.

A 1916 graduate of Atlanta University, White worked for Atlanta's Standard Life Insurance Company until 1918, when James Weldon *Johnson, then NAACP field secretary, invited him to join the NAACP staff as assistant secretary at its New York City headquarters. Blond-haired and blue-eyed, White was easily able to pass for white and often risked his life to conduct undercover investigations of *lynchings. Twelve days into his NAACP job, White was sent to research the circumstances of a lynching in Estill Springs, Tennessee; he himself narrowly escaped being lynched on a trip to Arkansas in 1919. In 1922, the year White married NAACP staff member Leah Gladys Powell, he met writer H. L. Mencken, who encouraged White to try his hand at fiction. White completed the manuscript of *Fire in the Flint,* about a northern-trained African American physician who returns to his native small-town Georgia, in twelve days. Published by Knopf in 1924, the novel, which ends with the doctor's lynching, was praised for its realistic portrayal of southern life, went through several European editions, and became a modest bestseller. *Flight* (1926), White's second, less critically acclaimed novel, centers around a young New Orleans woman who crosses over the *color line, then later relinquishes racial *passing. White's literary

accomplishments earned him a 1926 Guggenheim Fellowship, and he moved to southern France intending to produce a third novel; instead, however, he wrote *Rope and Faggot: The Biography of Judge Lynch* (1929), an important study of the various political, economic, social, and sexual influences of lynching.

White's literary career and his NAACP work were closely intertwined, and throughout the 1920s and 1930s he continued to toil for federal anti-lynching legislation and civil rights while aiding and inspiring *Harlem Renaissance artists. Not only did White combine cultural and political leadership, but he also viewed cultural production in a political framework. An advocate of Alain *Locke's *New Negro metaphor, White helped start the Negro Fellowship Fund to support young writers and used his NAACP contacts to further their careers. In 1931, he replaced Johnson as the NAACP's second African American executive secretary and oversaw the organization through the crucial years following World War II and the landmark *Brown v. Board of Education* decision of May 1954. In addition to a column for the *Chicago Defender,* White's nonfiction includes *A Rising Wind* (1945), about African American soldiers during World War II, and his 1948 autobiography, *A Man Called White,* which details the history of the NAACP under his direction.

• Edward E. Waldron, "Walter White and the Harlem Renaissance: Letters from 1924–1927," *CLA Journal* 16 (June 1973): 438–457.

—Gayle Wald

WHITFIELD, JAMES MONROE (1822–1871), poet. James Monroe Whitfield worked as a barber all his life, and the bitter militancy of his writings reflects his abortive attempts to secure racial justice and become a man of letters. He was born in New Hampshire, and little is known about his youth or later private life. Whitfield was a barber in Buffalo, New York (1854–1859), and in California (1861–1871), with brief sojourns in his later years in Oregon, Idaho, and Nevada. His public support for colonization began in 1854 when he wrote the call for the National Emigration Convention (Cleveland) and a series of letters to the *North Star;* from 1859 to 1861 he probably traveled in Central America seeking land for an African American colony. From 1849 until his death, Whitfield's forceful protest *poetry and *letters appeared often in the *North Star, Frederick Douglass's Paper,* the San Francisco *Elevator,* and other African American *periodicals, and he read several of his commemorative odes in public. The majority of his writings remain uncollected; his only published volume is *America and Other Poems* (1853). Whitfield died of heart disease and was buried in the Masonic Cemetery of San Francisco.

Whitfield's verse is outstanding for its metrical control, breadth of classical imagery, commanding historical sense, and convincing anger. With biting cynicism, he denounces oppression worldwide and scourges America's morally corrupt church and state in two long antislavery jeremiads, "America" and "How Long?" "America" begins: "America, it is to thee / Thou boasted land of liberty, — / It is to thee I raise my song, / Thou land of blood, and crime, and wrong." "How Long?" moves from Europe's "princely pomp, and priestly pride" that tramples people's rights, hopes, and spirits to the insidious plague of moral corruption, *slavery, infecting America "with foul pestiferous breath." Whitfield's most compelling poems are dark imprecations against a world "disjoint and out of frame" where men, women, *religion, love, and nature are tainted and meaningless. With anguished pessimism, particularly in "Yes, Strike Again That Sounding String" and "The Misanthropist," the poet dramatizes the estrangement and defeat of an African American artist. In 1867 Whitfield delivered his robust four-hundred-line *Poem*, which surveys American history, the sowing of *freedom in New England and slavery in the South, the Civil War, and now, "Such fiendish murders as of late / Occur in every rebel State." Once again, the nation must be purged of poisonous bigotry; only "equal laws," the poet says, will re-create a "country of the free." No poet of his time combined anger and artistry as forcefully as Whitfield; he was a major propagandist for black separatism and racial retributive justice through his impassioned poetry and prose.

• Doris Lucas Larye, "James Monroe Whitfield" in *DLB*, vol. 50, *Afro-American Writers before the Harlem Renaissance*, ed. Trudier Harris, 1986, pp. 260–263. Joan R. Sherman, *Invisible Poets: Afro-Americans of the Nineteenth Century*, 2d ed., 1989.
—Joan R. Sherman

WHITMAN, ALBERY ALLSON, (1851–1901), poet and minister. The "Poet Laureate of the Negro Race" was born to slave parents in Hart County, Kentucky. Although he lived in bondage for twelve years and had only one year of schooling, Albery Allson Whitman published five volumes of *poetry, and both his art and his living gave substance to his motto: "Adversity is the school of heroism, endurance the majesty of man, and hope the torch of high aspirations." Orphaned at the age of twelve, Whitman labored on the farm of his birth; then, from 1864 to 1870, in Ohio and Kentucky, he worked in a plough shop, in railroad construction, and as a schoolteacher. He briefly studied under Bishop Daniel A. *Payne at Wilberforce University (1871) and later served as general financial agent of Wilberforce. Although never formally ordained, in 1877 Whitman was pastor of an AME church in Springfield, Ohio, and from 1879 to 1883 he established *churches and led congregations in Ohio, Kansas, Texas, and Georgia. During these years, critics and other poets highly praised Whitman's poetry. He died of pneumonia at his Atlanta home.

"Poetry," Whitman wrote, "is the language of universal sentiment.... Her voice is the voice of Eternity dwelling in all great souls. Her aims are the inducements of heaven, and her triumphs the survival of the Beautiful, the True, and the Good." Whitman's art is not utilitarian or polemical but rather art for art's sake and for the sake of showing the race's creative talent. He wrote full-blown Romantic poetry, looking back to legendary pastoral worlds (marred by race prejudice); seeing the present as a sphere of unlimited human potentiality; and looking forward to an ideal earth perfected by human love and poetic genius. Whitman tried to emulate the century's great Romantic poets but never had the opportunity to develop their disciplined craftsmanship. Much of his poetry is technically weak and diffuse, marred by careless versification, awkward shifts in diction, overblown rhetoric, and homiletic digressions. Nevertheless, Whitman did supremely well with what he had: a sure dramatic sense; talent for suspenseful narration, romantic description, communication of pathos, irony, and lovers' emotions; a catholic range of subjects; and the courage to employ varied and difficult meters and rhyme schemes in epic-length poems, suiting his music to shifting moods and meanings. To these poetic skills Whitman added a sense of honor, strong race pride, and sensitive perception of universal issues, poignantly personalized. His code of "manliness" challenges the African American man to fight for "place and power!": "The manly voice of freedom bids him rise, / And shake himself before Philistine eyes!" (*The Rape of Florida*, 1884).

The breadth of Whitman's interests are apparent in his long poems. *Leelah Misled* (1873), in 118 stanzas, is a tale of seduction and betrayal; but the poem dwells on man's distortion of nature's laws; the transience of human joy; virtue and sin; the state of Georgia; excellence in women; time; and comparative religions. *Not a Man, and Yet a Man* (1877), in 197 pages contrasts brave Indians, joined by a few rustics and the *mulatto hero, Rodney, with treacherous "civilized" white men, as Rodney journeys from *slavery to *freedom. *The Rape of Florida*, reprinted as *Twasinta's Seminoles* (1885), through 251 Spenserian stanzas rehearses events of the Seminole Wars (1816–1842); but the treacherous "rape" exemplifies the superiority of primeval nature over the world of "Mammon"; of fierce-spirited red and black braves over white men; and of love—of God and among natives —over the hatreds and hypocrisies of the church, state, and army. Whitman's finest lyrics lie within such long poems: "Come now, my love, the moon is on the lake; / Upon the waters is my light canoe;" (*The Rape of Florida*).

Whitman dared to be an innovator and a "fearless manly man" in his poetry. His considerable achievements place him in the first rank of contemporary African American and white poets.

[See also Manhood.]

• Albery A. Whitman, prefaces to *Leelah Misled*, 1873; *Not a Man, and Yet a Man*, 1877; *The Rape of Florida*, 1884; *Twasinta's Seminoles*; 1885. Carl L. Marshall, "Two Protest Poems by Albery A. Whitman," *CLA Journal* 19 (Sept. 1975): 50–56. Blydon Jackson, "Albery Allson Whitman in *DLB*, vol. 50; *American Writers before the Harlem Renaissance*, ed. Trudier Harris, 1986, pp. 263–267. Blyden Jackson, *A History of Afro-American Literature*, vol. 1, 1989. Joan R. Sherman, *Invisible Poets: Afro-Americans of the Nineteenth Century*, 2d ed., 1989.
—Joan R. Sherman

WIDEMAN, JOHN EDGAR (b. 1941), intellectual, educator, novelist, essayist, biographer, short fiction writer, social critic, and commentator. John Edgar Wideman was born on 14 June 1941 in Washington,

D.C., to Edgar and Betty (Lizabeth) French Wideman, but he grew up at the foot of Bruston Hill, in Pittsburgh, Pennsylvania's Homewood community. His maternal great-great-great-grandmother, Sybela Owens, a runaway slave, was among the original founders and settlers of this community. A Phi Beta Kappa graduate of the University of Pennsylvania, which he attended on a Benjamin Franklin Scholarship, he was captain of the university basketball team. Wideman holds the distinction of being the second African American Rhodes scholar. He graduated from Oxford University in 1966. Before doing so, however, he married Judy Ann Goldman of Virginia in 1965. They are the parents of three children.

Wideman began his teaching career in the English department of the University of Pennsylvania, where he also founded and chaired, for one year, its first African American studies program. He continued his career as a teacher at the University of Wyoming in Laramie, where he spent more than a decade. He is a full professor of creative writing and American studies at the University of Massachusetts at Amherst.

From the outset, Wideman, who spent a year as a Kent Fellow in the Creative Writing Workshop at the University of Iowa (1966–1967) and published his first *novel at the age of twenty-six, was placed among the most prominent and gifted contemporary African American (male) writers. He has continued to garner lofty accolades, being identified not solely as "our leading black male writer," and as "our most powerful and accomplished artist," but also as "one of this country's brightest literary lights." Critics hurry to compare him to James Joyce, T. S. Eliot, William Faulkner, Virginia Woolf, and even William Shakespeare. Wideman is a two-time recipient of the PEN/Faulkner Award and a finalist for both the National Book Critics Circle Award and the National Book Award; he joined the prestigious group of recipients of the MacArthur Prize Fellowship in 1994.

Wideman is the author of seven novels: A Glance Away (1967), Hurry Home (1970), The Lynchers (1973), Hiding Place (1981), Sent for You Yesterday (1983), Reuben (1987), and *Philadelphia Fire (1990); three collections of *short stories: Damballah (1981), Fever (1989), and All Stories Are True (1992). *Brothers and Keepers (1984), written with his brother Robert (Robby) Wideman, is a collection of autobiographical essays; he continues with more personal vignettes in Fatheralong; A Meditation on Fathers and Sons (1994).

Accurately identified as a writer-intellectual by critic James Coleman, Wideman has undergone a tremendous personal, ideological, and artistic transformation in the process of overcoming his feelings of alienation from the black community. When he published his first novel, A Glance Away, at the apex of the *civil rights movement, the African American literary communal voices to which he added his were, for the most part, vociferously championing the validation of a *Black Aesthetic through the *Black Arts movement. However, Wideman clearly wanted to distance himself from its most ardent proponents, such as LeRoi Jones (Amiri *Baraka), Larry *Neal, and Addison *Gayle, Jr., whose cardinal goal was to make African American art the "spiritual sister" of the Black Power concept.

The protagonists of A Glance Away, Eddie Lawson, a black rehabilitated drug addict, and Robert Thurley, a white English professor, are driven to seek wholeness and meaning by their sense that something is absent in their worlds. The clear existentialist thrust and modernist perspective of Wideman's innovative work do not ignore or totally circumvent issues of *race, but they subordinate them to the central theme of this novel. Wideman's second and third novels, Hurry Home and The Lynchers, confirmed his willingness to continue to glance away from any mandatory validation and fuller exploration of the unique qualities of the African American experience (particularly language and issues of race), which the prophets of the Black Arts movement saw as the serious and legitimate subject matter for art, although The Lynchers indicated a minor movement in that general direction.

Wideman peopled the fictional worlds of his first three novels with major white and black characters, establishing a more rudimentary hu(e)man and modernist experience as his principal concern. However, despite this more "universal" target, and despite the continued comparison to Eliot and Joyce made by critics, Wideman could not escape the "black writer" label; nor could he escape being placed in the vanguard of contemporary black literary production and contributions.

From 1975 to 1983 Wideman took an eight-year hiatus during which he tried to learn to use a different voice. He explains: "I was 'woodshedding,' as the musicians would say—catching up. . . . I was learning a new language to talk about my experience." With the publication of his "Homewood Trilogy" (Damballah, Hiding Place, and Sent for You Yesterday), Wideman emerged from his personal exile to (re)claim with pride his history and heritage as Sybela Owens's great-great-great-grandson. He concluded; "if you've read T. S. Eliot, James Joyce, or William Faulkner . . . those are not the only 'keys to the kingdom.' If you have grown up Black, you also have some 'keys.'" These "keys," Wideman seems to contend in Fatheralong, are inextricably intertwined with the "pervasive presence of the paradigm of race." He explains, "The paradigm of race wasn't an illness plaguing society, it was the engine creating and sustaining a particular way of life."

Thus the "Homewood Trilogy" and subsequent work represent a major turning point in the personal life and literary career of John Edgar Wideman. With them he intentionally embarks on a journey back to the historical self which in Damballah and Hiding Place is inscribed in the signifiers of his family tree, which he instrumentally positions with "beggat charts" at the beginning of these works. Each reconstructs the family history as well as (re)claims and (re)records the central role played by his maternal great-great-great-grandmother in the founding of yet another colonial city upon a hill, located in the space that to Wideman is more than the steel capital of the world. Wideman provides the genesis of yet another pivotal American tale.

For Wideman, Pittsburgh is a city of beginnings. There the Allegheny River, flowing southward from the northeast, converges with the Monongahela, flowing northward from the southeast, to form the beginning of the Ohio River, the line of demarcation between *slavery and *freedom. However, in his odyssey with his father to Promised Land, South Carolina, recorded in *Fatheralong*, Wideman discovers and claims an equally significant beginning. There, in the South, in the shadows of pine forests, meadows, arable fields, and rich pastures, his paternal grandparents embarked on their quest for freedom. Wideman concludes, "The South is a parent, an engenderer, part of the mind I think with, the mind thinking with me." Paradoxically, Promised Land does not appear on most maps of South Carolina, just as there is no mention of "Africans or slaves or slavery in the closely printed eight page outline of the 'Chronological History of South Carolina (1662–1825).'"

Wideman's inclusion of Africans is crucial, for saliently appurtenant to his remapping and reclamation is the recognition that neither Homewood nor Promised Land can be the sole genesis of his family. History is bound to cultural memory. Wideman writes in *Fatheralong*: "In our minds, our memories beats the pulse of history." Memory and history remain central to the economy of being.

Memory and history bridge the path from America to the African past which Orion, the protagonist of *Damballah*, refuses to relinquish. An African kidnapped and sold into slavery, Orion is lynched for killing the overseer on his plantation. His decapitated body is later found by a slave man/child, who knows that he must throw the murdered slave's head into the river to release his spirit, allowing it to return to Africa.

Since 1981 Wideman has become a "seer/writer" who uses his mediumistic powers as a vehicle through which African American history and culture are accessed, assessed, recorded, and restored. Through them he attempts to "break out, to knock down the walls" of the imprisoning cage(s) known by African Americans, a direct consequence of what he has come to call the "paradigm of race." His major protagonists struggle with memory against forgetting and assiduously work to create spaces to redeem and (re)create their past. Specificity is inscribed and particulars ("who we are and what we are about") are celebrated. Negating the superimposed "American Africanism," as Toni *Morrison calls the construction of African Americans in the literary and historical space assigned them by the Eurocentric mind, Wideman's characters and protagonists work from within the parameters of their marginalized spaces to create, validate, and celebrate alternative realities, such as the rhythm of their language and improvisation of their *jazz, providing meaningful insight into the complexity of the African American experience that makes it a unique and distinctive American experience.

• John O'Brien, ed., *Interviews with Black Writers*, 1973, pp. 213–223. Wilfred D. Samuels, "Going Home: An Interview with John Edgar Wideman," *Callaloo* 6.1 (1983): 40–59. Wilfred D. Samuels, "John Edgar Wideman," in *DLB*, vol. 33, *Afro-American Fiction Writers after 1955*, eds. Thadious M. Davis and Trudier Harris, 1984, pp. 271–278. John Bennion, "The Shape of Memory in John Edgar Wideman's *Sent for You Yesterday*," *Black American Literature Forum* 20.1–2 (Spring–Summer 1986): 143–160. James W. Coleman, *Blackness and Modernism: The Literary Career of John Edgar Wideman*, 1989. Ashraf Rushdy, "Fraternal Blues: John Edgar Wideman's Homewood Trilogy," *Contemporary Literature* 32 (Fall 1991): 312–345. Jan Clausen, "Native Fathers," *The Kenyon Review* 14.2 (Spring 1992): 44–55. Doreatha Drummond Mbalia, *John Edgar Wideman: Reclaiming the African Personality*, 1995.   —Wilfred D. Samuels

Wife of His Youth, The. *The Wife of His Youth and Other Stories of the Color Line*, a collection of nine *short stories published by Houghton Mifflin in the fall of 1899, was the second major work of fiction by Charles Waddell *Chesnutt. The fundamental social issue, as well as the unifying theme, in most of the stories of *The Wife of His Youth* is *miscegenation in the United States. The title story of the volume, as well as "A Matter of Principle" and to a lesser extent "Her Virginia Mammy," analyze with both irony and pathos the racial prejudices of light-skinned, middle-class African Americans in "Groveland" (patterned on Chesnutt's Cleveland), Ohio. Many of Chesnutt's fictional models in these stories were people he knew from his own membership in the Cleveland Social Circle, an exclusive society of upwardly mobile mixed-race African Americans who were reputed to discriminate against anyone with complexions darker than their own.

"The Wife of His Youth" tells how a leader of one of the *Blue Vein Societies triumphs over his *class and color prejudices by acknowledging after decades of separation his dark-skinned plantation wife. In a more satirical case, Chesnutt deflates the racial pretensions of Cicero Clayton, the protagonist of "A Matter of Principle," by showing how this *mulatto's "principle" of dissociation from dark-skinned Negroes spoils his daughter's chance to marry a congressman. In "Her Virginia Mammy," Chesnutt broke with American social mores and literary tradition in his unhysterical depiction of the betrothal of a Boston Brahmin to a Groveland woman unaware of her black ancestry.

Turning to the South, *The Wife of His Youth* examines social problems that resisted the kinds of individual ethical solutions on which Chesnutt's northern-based stories turn. Although "The Passing of Grandison" allows a tricky slave to hoodwink his complacent master and spirit his entire family off to freedom, in "The Web of Circumstance" a former slave who tries to pull himself up by his bootstraps is left broken and degraded by a combination of adverse circumstances, racism, and betrayal. In this story and in "The Sheriff's Children," the tragic tale of a white southern father's post–Civil War encounter with the mixed-race son he sold away during *slavery times, Chesnutt displayed his pessimistic reaction to the rise of white supremacist attitudes and the eclipse of black opportunity in the "New South" of the 1890s. From the sensationalism of "The Sheriff's Children" to the sentimentality of "The Bouquet," the burlesque energy of "The Passing of Grandison," and the urbane satire of "A Matter of Principle," Chesnutt adopted a variety of means in *The Wife of His Youth* to compel his readers to consider contemporary racial realities in the clarifying light of his brand of social realism.

Some critics, such as William Dean Howells, praised the author of *The Wife of His Youth* as a literary realist of the first order. Others were troubled by Chesnutt's concentration on such cheerless topics as segregation, mob *violence, and miscegenation. Late twentieth-century critics have proved more hospitable to Chesnutt's *color line fiction in general and more appreciative of the prototypical examples of it published in *The Wife of His Youth*.

• Helen M. Chesnutt, *Charles Waddell Chesnutt: Pioneer of the Color Line*, 1952. Sylvia Lyons Render, ed., *The Short Fiction of Charles W. Chesnutt*, 1974. Robert Bone, *Down Home: Pastoral Impulse in Afro-American Short Fiction*, 1975. William L. Andrews, *The Literary Career of Charles W. Chesnutt*, 1980.

—William L. Andrews

WILKINS, ROGER (b. 1932), journalist, government official, educator, historian, radio commentator, and documentary filmmaker. Roger Wilkins's *autobiography, A Man's Life* (1982), records his experiences as what he calls "the lead black in white institutions for sixteen years." "In a sense," he writes, "I have been an explorer and I sailed as far out into the white world as a black man of my generation could sail." Wilkins held prominent positions in the Kennedy and Johnson administrations, becoming in 1965 the first African American to reach the rank of assistant attorney general of the United States. After a stint at the Ford Foundation, Wilkins shared a 1973 Pulitzer Prize for his editorials on the Watergate scandal for the *Washington Post* and later in the decade became the first black member of the *New York Times* editorial board.

Laced with ambivalence over his position in the essentially white American power structure, Wilkins's autobiography combines an honest and somewhat confessional portrayal of his personal life with eyewitness accounts of important historical events, such as the *civil rights movement, the Vietnam War, the urban riots of the mid-1960s, and Watergate. The book is also filled with anecdotes about famous people: Lyndon Johnson, Stokely *Carmichael, McGeorge Bundy, Katherine Graham, and the author's uncle, Roy Wilkins.

The most searing parts of *A Man's Life* deal with Wilkins's confrontation with his own *identity as a middle-class African American, and his uncomfortable engagement with the radical black ideologies of the 1960s that increasingly identified true blackness with a ghetto upbringing. He ultimately recognizes the "psychological genocide" practiced so subtly upon blacks in a white-dominated society, through the identification of all good, desirable things as white, and the imposition of what he calls "black shame." Wilkins also depicts the racism prevalent in the powerful white circles he moved in and reaches a wryly pessimistic conclusion: "I don't believe in the perfectability of white people anymore."

—Gary Ashwill

WILKINSON, BRENDA (b. 1946), novelist for middle-school and young adult readers. Raised in Waycross, Georgia, Brenda Wilkinson migrated to New York City in the 1960s and attended Hunter College. She is the mother of two daughters and currently resides in New York City.

The *migration of African Americans to northern cities is not often depicted in children's literature. Wilkinson assigned herself the task of creating "factional" stories that chronicled this migration and the experiences of African Americans in the segregated South and North during the 1950s and 1960s. Although her stories portray hardship and racism, they also convey the sense of families and communities as nurturing of their members.

Wilkinson is a part of the renaissance in the late 1960s and 1970s in African American children's literature whose hallmarks were authenticity and excellence. Wilkinson contributed to this new literature with the publication of *Ludell* (1975), *Ludell and Willie* (1976), *Ludell's New York Time* (1980), *Not Separate, Not Equal* (1987), and *Definitely Cool* (1993). All of Wilkinson's novels, except *Definitely Cool*, which is contemporary fiction, are *historical novels.

Many would agree that Wilkinson handles language variations and dialects effectively. The southern dialects of the characters convey a sense of place as well as emotion through words and phases such as "dag," "shoot," and "chile, 'I 'on know" in the *Ludell* trilogy and *Not Separate, Not Equal*. Her characters speak in languages that reflect their ages, *gender, *race, and the setting of the novel.

Wilkinson's characters are complex. Ludell is sassy, spirited, annoying, kind, selfish, womanish, childish, and all the other conflicting traits teenagers embody. She experiences racism and gender discrimination; however, she is not defeated nor does she internalize the negative beliefs. The teens in *Not Separate, Not Equal* and *Definitely Cool* share these qualities as well. The adult characters in Wilkinson's novels are depicted as fully realized individuals.

Some recurring themes in Wilkinson's novels include the negative consequences of intragroup color discrimination among African Americans, the strengths and foibles of African American families and communities, the life-affirming strength an individual can acquire from being loved, *class and race conflicts, the search for racial identity, and the need to persevere in the face of adversity.

The quality of Wilkinson's writing, the strong characterization in her novels, and her ability to reproduce the milieu of a particular time period are some of the factors that account for the overwhelmingly favorable response from critics and readers.

• Rudine Sims, *Shadow and Substance*, 1982. "Brenda Wilkinson," in *Children's Literature Review*, ed. Gerald Senick, vol. 20, 1990, pp. 206–212.

—Violet J. Harris

WILLIAMS, FANNIE BARRIER. *See* Woman's Era.

WILLIAMS, GEORGE WASHINGTON (1849–1891), Civil War veteran, minister, politician, and historian. Born in Bedford Springs, Pennsylvania, to Thomas and Ellen Rouse Williams on 16 October 1849, George Williams was the oldest son of five siblings. Given the lack of educational opportunities for African Americans in western Pennsylvania, Williams received little formal schooling. In 1863, at the age of fourteen, he enlisted in the Union army. After leaving the army in 1868, Williams applied for admission and was accepted at Howard University in Washington, D.C., in 1869. He dropped out, however, and entered Wayland Seminary, also in Washington. In 1870 Williams entered Newton Theological Institution outside of Boston. Upon graduation from Newton, Williams was ordained and then offered the pastorate of a prominent African American congregation in Boston, the Twelfth Street Baptist Church, in 1875.

While pastor at Twelfth Street Baptist Church, Williams wrote a monograph, *History of the Twelfth Street Baptist Church*. He left the pastorate of Twelfth Street Baptist after a couple of months and returned to Washington to edit a journal, the *Commoner*. By December 1875 the journal was defunct. In 1876 Williams traveled to the Midwest to accept the pastorate of Union Baptist Church in Cincinnati, Ohio. In 1879 he was elected to the Ohio House of Representatives. At this juncture Williams embarked on the distinguishing task of his career—authorship of the first comprehensive history of African Americans, *History of the Negro Race in America from 1619 to 1880* (1883).

Originally published in two volumes by G.P. Putnam's Sons, Williams's *History of the Negro Race in America* offered an ably documented overview of African American *history from its inception in Africa to the postbellum years following the Civil War. Favorably reviewed in both the African American and white press, these volumes established Williams as the foremost historian of the race. In 1887 he produced a monograph on African American participation in the Civil War, *History of the Negro Troops in the War of the Rebellion*. Despite these accomplishments Williams was unable to exclusively pursue one career. In 1881 he was admitted to the Ohio bar and to the Boston bar in 1883. In 1885 President Chester Arthur appointed Williams minister to Haiti. However, he was never allowed to officially assume the post by the incoming Democratic administration. Williams devoted the latter portion of his career to influencing Belgian policies in the Congo. While writing a lengthy monograph on Belgian abuses in the Congo, Williams succumbed to tuberculosis and pleurisy and died in Blackpool, England, on 2 August 1891.

Despite his varied careers, Williams's contributions to the field of historical literature were inestimable. He utilized objectivity in constructing his historical narratives and consulted with historians such as Justin Winsor and George Bancroft. A pioneer in the writing of revisionist history and oral history, the utilization of newspapers, and the collection and interpretation of primary material, Williams's work laid the ground, in style, presentation, and methodology for the burgeoning field of historical literature in the late nineteenth century.

• John Hope Franklin, *George Washington Williams*, 1985.

—Stephen Gilroy Hall

WILLIAMS, JOHN A. (b. 1925), novelist, essayist, journalist, editor, and educator. Born in Hinds County, Mississippi, John Alfred Williams grew up in Syracuse, New York. After serving in the navy during World War II, Williams finished high school and enrolled at Syracuse University, graduating in 1950. He started graduate school but soon withdrew for economic reasons. Trying to establish his writing career, Williams contributed to *Ebony, Jet*, and *Holiday* while holding various jobs in the 1950s—foundry worker, grocery clerk, social worker, insurance company employee, and television publicity coordinator. This diversity of experience formed a foundation upon which he has often drawn for inspiration.

The American Academy of Arts and Letters' 1962 failure to deliver the promised *Prix de Rome* to Williams is also significant. The retraction came after an informal letter of congratulations promised Williams the prize, pending an interview (supposedly a mere formality), which apparently went badly. Williams remains the only candidate to have had the prize retracted; he fictionalized the events in *The *Man Who Cried I Am* (1967) and recounted them in "We Regret to Inform You That," an essay reprinted in his collection *Flashbacks* (1973). How much he has made from this incident indicates how heavily Williams draws on life for his art.

A prolific writer, Williams has produced eleven novels, six nonfiction books, three anthologies, one play, and numerous articles and essays. Throughout his career, Williams has articulated his artist's sense of African Americans' experiences, giving attention to societal power imbalances and exploring political and personal approaches to their resolution. His demands for social justice and frank articulation of its absence in modern society, coupled with his willingness to treat violent themes and suggest force as a means to achieve equality, cause some to label him "angry."

There is anger in his books; however, limiting Williams to that characterization overlooks the richness of his work. His insightful and confrontational nonfiction forces readers to see the realities of African American life in our culture; however, rather than just expressing anger, Williams explains how and why those conditions should be ameliorated. A notable example is *Beyond the Angry Black* (1966), an anthology of essays by black and white writers that describes and comments on American racial politics. In the introduction, Williams talks about reason, the next step beyond anger that he calls on Americans of all colors to make.

Williams also addresses social conditions, raising images of oppression and powerlessness before history in *This Is My Country Too* (1965), the product of an undertaking commissioned by *Holiday* magazine that chronicles Williams's travels across America in 1963. Providing portraits of many strong individuals, the work also reflects much of Williams's experience with the history of racial oppression, experience that he used in writing *The Man Who Cried I Am.*

Often viewed as Williams's major achievement, *The Man Who Cried I Am* marks a significant shift in his fiction. In works such as *One for New York* (1960) and *Sissie* (1963), Williams portrays the struggles of individual African Americans against an oppressive system and offers resolution. Gilbert H. Muller (*John A. Williams,* 1984) notes that the early novels find the characters succeeding within the oppressive system. In *The Man Who Cried I Am,* Williams creates a character who recognizes and fights historical oppression; however, he reaches no understanding with the dominant culture—violence is the only solution. Max Reddick, like Abraham Blackman in *Captain Blackman* (1972), sees himself as waging war on the forces of history that ultimately destroy him—Williams's major concern in the late 1960s and early 1970s.

In addition to sharing this dominant, historically aware, active consciousness, both *The Man* and *Captain Blackman* exhibit one of Williams's most significant stylistic innovations: a flexible chronological movement that starts from a relatively linear plot progression, weaving facts, dates, and experiences around that line and completely problematizing the question of history. For Williams, the concept of a monolithic, accurate, just history appears unacceptable. Many of his works, especially of this era, cite myriad forces shaping events and creating socio-economic-racial-intellectual tensions that characterize his conception of history. This vision, and his unique creation of a chronological structure to support it, marks Williams as forerunner to and significant influence on other African American writers, such as John Edgar *Wideman and Charles R. *Johnson, attempting to come to grips with and re-form American history.

In certain later works, Williams returns the question of historical, social, and intellectual power relationships to a more personal realm. As Muller notes, in some ways *!Click Song* (1982) is a summation of work begun in *The Man Who Cried I Am. !Click Song's* narrator, Cato Caldwell Douglass, is in many ways the spiritual descendent of Max Reddick; however, his quest is much more personal, abstracted from Reddick's political struggle by his focus on art. In *The Berhama Account* (1985), Williams fuses the personal approach of *!Click Song* with the more political elements of earlier works, intermingling an examination of love's healing power with a story of effective political struggle.

The Berhama Account treats a faked assassination plot in which the tossing of dummy hand grenades forces positive social action and paves the way for the rectification of a small Caribbean nation's racism. In the midst of this intrigue, a journalist recovering from cancer finds life-affirming love by rekindling an old affair. Several of these plot elements signal a reversal of Williams's earlier ideas. One thinks, for instance, of the King Alfred plot, the murderously real

violence, the failure of love, and Max Reddick's deterioration and death in *The Man Who Cried I Am.* Although Williams still has concerns about political and social questions, his later works suggest that his worldview is not so bleak as it once was.

Williams's importance to the development of the African American tradition should not be underestimated. His social, intellectual, and historical innovations mark his work as crucial to our understanding of the development of contemporary African American aesthetics.

• Earl A. Cash, *John A. Williams: The Evolution of a Black Writer,* 1975. Gilbert H. Muller, *John A. Williams,* 1984.

—William R. Nash

WILLIAMS, PAULETTE. *See* Shange, Ntozake.

WILLIAMS, SAMM-ART (b.1946), playwright and actor. Born 20 January 1946 in Burgaw, North Carolina, Samuel Arthur Williams, who from an early age wanted to become a writer, received encouragement from his mother, an English teacher and drama director. He graduated from Morgan State College in Baltimore, Maryland (1968), where he majored in political science in preparation for the legal career many members of his family wanted him to pursue.

One of Williams's plays, *Home,* was selected as a Burns Mantle Yearbook "Best Play of 1979–80"; it also received a Tony nomination and a John Gasner Playwriting Medallion. In addition to *Home,* Williams has written twelve or more representative works and acted in numerous productions with noted theatrical groups including the Freedom Theatre in Philadelphia, an organization he joined soon after arriving there in 1968, and the Negro Ensemble Company of New York. Williams traveled to New York in 1973 and found there the kind of artistic experiences to which he had long aspired. His talent as an actor initially paid greater dividends than did his writing talent.

Williams's range as a playwright encompasses numerous themes, among them crime, shame, pride, confused sexuality, and transcendence. The Negro Ensemble Company, an organization that Williams joined in 1974, produced five of his plays: *Welcome to Black River* (1975), *The Coming* (1976), *A Love Play* (1976), *The Frost of Renaissance* (1978, in workshop and showcase) and *Brass Birds Don't Sing* (1978). *Welcome to Black River* dramatizes the exploitation and racism experienced by a Black sharecropper in the 1950s in North Carolina. *The Coming* depicts the experiences of a New York skid row bum who has the delusion that he is talking to God, who in this *drama is an incarnation of several unsavory character types. Conflicting value systems of West Indian Blacks and African Americans receive attention in *Eyes of the American* (1980). The propensity toward capitalism, embodied in the American, becomes his nemesis as his worldview is adopted by his West Indian brother. Both men get what they deserve, learning that each should have been more suspicious of the other. The arrogant American now has a chance to experience the circumstances he once derided.

Another prominent theme in Williams's plays is sexuality. *A Love Play* (1976) dramatizes an exploration by four female characters into lesbianism, a pursuit motivated, in part, by their disappointing relationships with the men in their lives. *Kamilla* (1975) tells the story of a married woman whose dream consciousness forces her to admit to the realities of her sexual preference. *The Last Caravan* explores another dimension of sexuality as an aging protagonist seeks nontraditional cures to restore his fading virility.

Crime and corruption come to the forefront in several of Williams's plays. *Do Unto Others* (1976) dramatizes crime, revenge, and deception in the fury of a woman who escapes a death plot set by her husband, a Chicago numbers racketeer. *The Sixteenth Round* (1980) produced by the Negro Ensemble Company in 1980, tells the story of a desperate fighter who intentionally loses a fight, thereby inviting the wrath of an underworld figure out to kill him. *Eve of the Trial* tells the story of a Russian expatriate stranded in Louisiana. The drama, part of a series of dramas drawn from Chekhov's short fiction, reveals intolerance and the corruption of the legal system.

Home (1979), generally considered Williams's most successful work, returns to the site of *Welcome to Black River*, where both races, bound by circumstances and blood, unite to confront a common challenge. *Home* dramatizes the nostalgia of a young man from North Carolina who migrated north, bearing the heavy responsibility of returning home a winner. In addition to its antiwar emphasis, the play exposes for scrutiny the posturing of African Americans in the North who claim to have reached the promised land while inwardly longing for a return home. *Home* received the Audelco Award and the Outer Critics' Circle Award for Best Play 1980–1981.

Williams's career as a playwright is complemented by his work as an actor of stage, television, and *film. His contribution to the artistic opportunities of African Americans is underscored by his sense of history, vividly portrayed in *Cork* (1986), in which he pays due tribute to the precursors of the modern stage, the black minstrels. He expresses sensitivity for those forerunners who, through shame and humiliation, made possible opportunities for future generations of African American actors. This work and the entire corpus of Samuel Arthur Williams's activities in defining the moral and political contours of our diverse society will no doubt secure his place in American theater and culture.

• Trudier Harris, "Samm-Art Williams," in *DLB*, vol. 38, *Afro-American Writers after 1955: Dramatists and Prose Writers*, eds. Thadious M. Davis and Trudier Harris, 1985, pp. 283–290. Thomas Morgan, "Minstrels: The Myths and the Men," *New York Times*, 27 Dec. 1986, Sec. 1, 11.1. Hal Mays and Susan M. Trosky, eds., *CA*, 1988, pp. 467–469. Bernard L. Peterson, Jr., *Contemporary Black American Playwrights and Their Plays*, 1988, pp. 501–503. Edward Mapp, *Directory of Blacks in the Performing Arts*, 1990, pp. 551–552.

—Robbie Jean Walker

WILLIAMS, SHERLEY ANNE (b. 1944), poet, novelist, critic, professor, and social critic. The life and career of Sherley Anne Williams reveal why she is a major cultural and literary force in the African American and the larger multicultural American community. Williams, who teaches at the University of California at San Diego, La Jolla, was born in Bakersfield, California, on 25 August 1944. She earned a bachelor of arts in English in 1966 and a master's in 1972 from California State University at Fresno and Brown University respectively. She then went on to teach at several schools and to travel to Ghana under a 1984 Fulbright grant. As scholar, critic, writer, poet, and parent, her range extends from adult to child, and from academia to popular culture. Like Sterling A. *Brown, one of her mentors and role models, she manages to traverse several worlds, and this ability to extend her voice past the literary and into the ever-expanding field of African American cultural forms has been an invaluable contribution to African American literary studies.

As a scholar and critic Williams attributes great worth to exploring African American folk culture, and her literary criticism attests to this fact. The best and perhaps most well-known example is her first endeavor, *Give Birth to Brightness: A Thematic Study in Neo-Black Literature* (1972), a groundbreaking examination of the toast-and-boast traditions. Here she infuses the *Black Aesthetic *poetry of the 1960s (e.g., Mari *Evans, Michael S. *Harper, Amiri *Baraka, Etheridge *Knight, David Henderson, and Don L. Lee) into the beginning of each chapter to serve as an intertext and implicit statement that these poets are the next wave of heroes. She reviews how heroism manifests itself along class lines in African American poetry, *drama, and prose, in *music and performers, and from *folklore and history to the urban outlaw. In the process of recording her findings she ensures the position of heroism as a viable element of African American literary studies.

One element of folk culture that informs Williams's writing, both critical and creative, is "call and response." She writes as a response to other things that have been written or spoken and that affect the community, and this is an interesting example of the African American cultural phenomenon call and response *performing her.* Seen in this light, Williams's dedicating her first work to her son serves as a means of answering questions he may have about his history, and as a way of leaving him a legacy. This gesture represents the larger unspoken thesis of this work, for in investigating the boasts and toasts that come from the urban folk community, Williams affirms that there is an African American cultural legacy that has been passed down for years, that has mutated, and that will continue to mutate into many forms. Her recording and analyzing this work, as well as addressing it to her son, is a step in the process of passing the lore to the next generation. It seems that for Williams to have the scholarly analysis, the critic must converse with and receive affirmation from the folk community.

As a creative writer she invests great pride in African American musical forms and history. While *Give Birth to Brightness* explores primarily male authors and provides an overview of folk heroism,

Williams's creative endeavors focus primarily on women. *Dessa Rose* (1986), her critically acclaimed *historical novel, or *neo–slave narrative, is based on the *blues, for it tells of a solitary woman's experience of love thwarted, of bondage, revolt, *freedom, and of love regained. This follows the blues's *aaba* structure, because it repeats and varies a central theme: Dessa's story. Williams, as well, infuses *spirituals into *Dessa Rose* and shows how they worked as a means of coded communication, for they help Dessa to escape imprisonment. In keeping with Williams's methodology, this work is also a response to William Styron's flawed historical fiction *The Confessions of Nat Turner* (1967). Through musical form and the assertion of a female slave rebellion, Williams reclaims history, revises the racial memory of *slavery, and invests herself with the right to record an African American woman's silenced history.

Another way to record a silenced voice is through poetry, and Williams's first attempt at this is in *The Peacock Poems* (1975) and *Someone Sweet Angel Chile* (1982). She structures these works as well on the blues and spirituals. The poetry incorporates these musical modes in that they talk of an artist's alienation and heroic survival as she struggles to express her feelings and hopes for understanding. The blues also fit perfectly as a means of expressing the lyrical, for their subject matter articulates the historically isolated and silenced African American female voice. Underlying these blues poems is the theme of lost love and misunderstanding among men and women, and again this is Williams responding to a folk community that is at times split by miscommunication. In reaching out and embracing that communication, Williams exhorts the need for spiritual connection, mutual understanding, and respect, for these are the things that give men and women, the folk community, and the individual, life.

Working Cotton (1992) is Williams's latest creation, and it addresses perhaps the most important aspect that gives the folk community life and meaning: the children. It is a gesture that mirrors the dedication of her first work to her son, for this award-winning children's story is dedicated to her grandchildren and to the migrant laborers and their families, whose voices continue to be silenced. *Working Cotton* is a message of hope, pride, and regard for the sheer determination it takes to survive and still see beauty amongst so much harshness. It is written in the blues mode, and Williams, in recording a young girl's (Shelan's) experiences working in the fields with her family, praises the folk community for its endurance. This is her way of embracing one segment of the African American community, and in so doing she again affirms and documents a way of life and a worldview so that future generations will know a part of their history.

Williams's works reveal a bond to folk traditions and history, and a desire to generate, appreciate, and preserve them for future generations. For Williams, this is the role of the academician, and as teacher, writer, social critic, and parent, her efforts responding to the folk community mark her as an integral force in African American letters.

• Shirley M. Jordan, "Sherley Anne Williams," in *Black Women Writers At Work*, ed. Claudia Tate, 1983. pp. 205–213. Mary Kemp Davis, "Everybody Knows Her Name: The Recovery of the Past in Sherley Anne Williams's *Dessa Rose*," *Callaloo* 40.1 (1989): 544–558. Mae G. Henderson, "(W)riting *The Work* and Working the Rites," *Black American Literature Forum* 23.4 (Winter 1989): 631-660. Anne E. Goldman, "I Made the Ink": (Literary) Production and Reproduction in *Dessa Rose* and *Beloved*," *Feminist Studies* 16.2 (Summer 1990): 313–330. Marta E. Sanchez, "The Estrangement Effect in Sherley Anne Williams' *Dessa Rose*," *Genders* 15 (Winter 1992): 21–36. Sherley Anne Williams, interview by Shirley M. Jordan, in *Broken Silences: Interviews With Black and White Women Writers*, ed. Shirley M. Jordan, 1993, pp. 285–301.
—Mildred R. Mickle

WILSON, AUGUST (b. 1945), playwright, poet, essayist, and two-time recipient of the Pulitzer Prize. The winner of Bush, McKnight, Rockefeller, and Guggenheim Foundation fellowships in playwriting, August Wilson also had the distinction in 1988 of having two plays running simultaneously on Broadway: *Joe Turner's Come and Gone* and *Fences*. Clearly, he is one of America's most prominent playwrights, yet his origins offered few indications that he would achieve such dramatic accomplishment.

He was born as Frederick Kittel on "The Hill," a racially mixed area of Pittsburgh, Pensylvania, to Frederick Kittel, a German baker, and Daisy Wilson Kittel, a cleaning woman whose mother walked from North Carolina to Pittsburgh seeking greater opportunity. The fourth of six children, Wilson grew up in a a two-room apartment behind a grocery store. His white father was a distant figure whom Wilson seldom saw.

Following his parents' divorce and his mother's subsequent remarriage to David Bedford, Wilson and his family relocated to a white suburb where he encountered increased racism. In 1961—after being falsely accused of plagiarizing a paper he had written about Napoléon—Wilson dropped out of Gladstone High School. Unable to find satisfactory employment, he joined the army in 1963 and one year later was able to wrangle an early discharge.

On 1 April 1965, Wilson bought his first typewriter, having determined that he would become a writer. In the fall of that year, he moved into a rooming house and began a long and varied assortment of menial jobs to support his writing. That same year he helped form the Center Avenue Poets Theatre Workshop and heard Bessie *Smith's records for the first time. The latter had a profound effect upon his determination to capture black cultural and historical experience in his writing. It would also lead directly to one of Wilson's first publications: the poem "Bessie" eventually appeared in *Black Lines* in the summer of 1971.

Throughout the rest of the 1960s, Wilson continued to hone his writing skills and to be active in the community of African American writers, helping Rob Penny found the Black Horizons Theatre Company on the Hill. During this period Wilson was active in the Black Power movement and was also beginning to publish his *poetry: his first publication was "For Malcolm X and Others," which appeared in

Negro Digest in September 1969. He married Brenda Burton, a Muslim, in 1969 as well. Their daughter, Sakina Ansari, was born in 1970.

After the dissolution of this marriage in 1972, Wilson intensified his efforts as a writer. In 1973, he wrote "Morning Statement," a poem that he—borrowing a term from Robert Duncan—often cites as evidence of his achieving "surety" of his craft, and his poem "Theme One: The Variations" was included in the *anthology *The Poetry of Black America*. He had also begun writing plays, completing *Rite of Passage* during this period. In 1973, his unpublished play *Recycle* was produced by a community theater in Pittsburgh. In 1976, he saw a production of Athol Fugard's *Sizwe Bansi Is Dead*, which greatly encouraged him about his own ability to write *drama, and he wrote *The Homecoming*, which would not be produced until 1989 but whose subject matter foreshadows his first Broadway success, *Ma Rainey's Black Bottom*. A fictitious treatment of episodes in the life of *blues singer and guitarist Blind Lemon Jefferson, who froze to death in Chicago in 1930, *Homecoming* illustrates Wilson's growing concern for incorporating traditional black art forms and the lives of African American cultural icons into his work. In 1977, he wrote *Black Bart and the Sacred Hills*, a musical satire based on a group of poems about an outlaw of the Old West. Most critics consider this to be Wilson's serious theatrical debut; the play was produced in St. Paul, Minnesota, in 1981.

In 1978, Wilson moved to St. Paul to write plays for Claude Purdy and to work as a scriptwriter for the Science Museum of Minnesota. The following year he completed *Jitney*, a two-act play about jitney drivers in Pittsburgh, which would serve as his first rejection from the Eugene O'Neill Theatre Center National Playwrights Conference but which would be accepted by the Minneapolis Playwrights' Center in 1980 and produced at the Allegheny Repertory Theatre in Pittsburgh in 1982. In 1980, Wilson received a Jerome fellowship, became associate playwright with Playwrights' Center in Minneapolis, and wrote *Fullerton Street*—his play of the 1940s that looks at urban blacks who have migrated to the North and that remains unpublished and unproduced; this play was also rejected by the O'Neill Center.

In 1981, Wilson married Judy Oliver, a white social worker. The following year he wrote *Ma Rainey's Black Bottom*, which was accepted for workshop production at the O'Neill, and Wilson began the first of many collaborative efforts with Lloyd Richards, the director of the O'Neill and the dean of the Yale Drama School. When this play opened on Broadway at the Cort Theatre in 1984, it brought Wilson critical acclaim and launched his theatrical career. Set in 1920s Chicago, the play looks at the economic exploitation of black musicians by white record companies and at the ways in which victims of racism are forced to direct their rage at each other rather than at their oppressors. Although Clive Barnes criticized the play for its overemphasis on politics and its predictable ending, Frank Rich saw the play as a searing account of white racism's effect upon its victims and gave the play laudatory reviews. The play certainly treats the dangers of misplaced hatred. Because Levee cannot accept the salvation of his heritage, he slays the messenger who reminds him that such possibilities exist: Levee kills Toledo as a substitute for the white men who have raped his mother and those who are now rejecting his *music. The play won the New York Drama Critics' Circle Award (1985) and was nominated for a Tony.

Wilson joined New Dramatists in New York in 1983, and *Fences* was produced at the O'Neill. Unfortunately, Wilson's mother died in March before she could witness his Broadway success. Writing at least partly to show his critics that he could follow the traditional European American drama format of focusing on one major character, he gave the play a strong unity. It looks at the struggles of a 1950s working-class family to find economic security. A garbageman, ex-con, and former Negro Baseball League player, Troy Maxson is perhaps Wilson's best-known protagonist, a man who is unable to believe that his son will be allowed to benefit from the football scholarship he is being offered. White critics were quick to point out parallels between Troy and Willy Loman. *Fences* was produced at the Yale Repertory Theatre in 1986, and following its opening at the 46th Street Theatre in New York in 1987, it won the New York Drama Critics' Circle Award, the Drama Desk Award, the Tony, and the Pulitzer; the *Chicago Tribune* selected Wilson as Artist of the Year; and he received the John Gassner Outer Critics' Circle Award for Best American Playwright.

While *Fences* was still enjoying a successful run on Broadway in 1988, *Joe Turner's Come and Gone* opened at the Ethel Barrymore. Written in 1984 and workshopped at the O'Neill that same year, the play had been produced at Yale in 1986. Inspired by the Romare Bearden collage "Millhand's Lunch Bucket," it is Wilson's admitted favorite. It focuses on the personal and cultural aftermath of both *slavery and the black northern *migration as they are manifested in a Pittsburgh boarding house in 1911. Many critics consider this to be the most Afrocentric of Wilson's plays and his most successful literary effort. It was nominated for a Tony and won the New York Drama Critics' Award. This same year the New York Public Library added Wilson to its list of Literary Lions.

Wilson's fourth play to be produced on Broadway and his second to win a Pulitzer, *The *Piano Lesson*, was also inspired by a Bearden collage. It won the Drama Desk, New York Drama Critics' Circle, and the American Theatre Critics Outstanding Play awards. Written in 1986, it was presented at the O'Neill and the Yale Repertory in 1987 and opened after a long tour of regional theaters at the Walter Kerr in 1990. Focusing on the question of who has the right to own a family's heirloom piano, the play is set in 1936 and captures the conflict that arises between African American and mainstream cultural values. During this period, Wilson moved to Seattle.

Wilson was elected to the American Academy of Arts and Sciences in 1991. His play *Two Trains Running*, written in 1989, was produced by the Yale Repertory in 1990, and opened at the Walter Kerr on Broadway in 1992. It was nominated for a Tony and won the American Theatre Critics' Association Award. Returning to the Hill as a setting, Wilson places the action in a coffee shop where regulars converge to discuss their plight in 1960s America. The play stresses the necessity of coming to terms with the past before attempting to move forward.

At the outset of his career, Wilson envisioned *theater as a means to raise the collective community's consciousness about black life in twentieth-century America and committed himself to writing a cycle of ten plays that would rewrite the *history of each decade of this century so that black life becomes a more fully acknowledged part of America's theatrical history. His plays are not, however, agitprop. He avoids pat answers; instead, he effects a powerful experience that forces his audience to search for their own political conclusions as an extension of his characters' life situations. A playwright of startling imagination and depth, he is often considered a theatrical spokesperson for the African American experience, and his ability to infuse everyday language with the stuff of poetry is an essential, distinguishing factor of his work. Perhaps he no longer considers himself a poet, but it is his poetic gift that has helped him to become the preeminent playwright in contemporary American drama.

• Chip Brown, "The Light in August," *Esquire*, Apr. 1989, 116–125. Sandra Shannon, "The Good Christian's Come and Gone: The Shifting Role of Religion in August Wilson's Plays," *MELUS: The Journal of the Society for the Study of Multi-ethnic Literature of the United States* 16 (Fall 1989–1990): 127–142. Paul Carter Harrison, "August Wilson's Blues Poetics," in *August Wilson: Three Plays*, 1991, pp. 291–318. Yvonne Shafer, "August Wilson: A New Approach to Black Drama," *ZAA: Zeitschrift fur Anglistik und Amerikanistik*, vol. 39, 1991, pp. 17–27. Mark Rocha, "A Conversation with August Wilson," *Diversity: A Journal of Multicultural Issues* 1 (Fall 1992): 24–42. Alan Nadel, ed., *May All Your Fences Have Gates: Essays on the Drama of August Wilson*, 1993. Marilyn Elkins, ed., *August Wilson: A Casebook*, 1994.
—Marilyn Elkins

WILSON, HARRIET E. (c. 1827–?), first African American woman novelist. Rarely has an author's identity been so instrumental in the reclamation of her writing. Long thought to be white, Harriet E. Wilson and her one *novel, *Our Nig, had been mere footnotes to nineteenth-century American literary history, and obscure ones at that, until 1981. Henry Louis *Gates, Jr., and David Curtis's research came on the heels of the republication of rediscovered white women writers and the incipient attention paid to early African American women authors. When in 1984 Gates established that Wilson was indeed the first Black person to publish a novel in the United States, there was a developing historical and critical context into which to fit her work. *Our Nig's republication is both a reflection of and a key contribution to the vast resurrection of writings by what Toni *Morrison might call disremembered Black women.

Until the 1980s, Frances Ellen Watkins *Harper was widely accepted to be the first Black woman to publish a *short story (1859) and a novel (1892). Yet, since *Our Nig pushed back the conception of Black

women's novelistic writing thirty-three years, scores of newly rediscovered writers—Emma Dunham *Kelley and Amelia E. *Johnson, for example—and new novels by authors only established in the last fifteen years (such as Harper's and Pauline E. *Hopkins's) have been republished.

Biographical information on Harriet Adams Wilson remains sketchy, although information on the Bellmonts, whom Barbara White has discovered was the Hayward family of *Our Nig*, has emerged. Nehemiah Hayward, "Mr. Bellmont," married Rebecca Hutchinson, who belonged to a wealthy and established family of Milford, New Hampshire, Harriet Wilson's birthplace. Rebecca, the "she-devil" of *Our Nig*, was a direct descendent of Anne Hutchinson and cousin to the famous abolitionist Hutchinson family singers. Harriet Adams was born between 1825 and 1828 and was left at the Haywards' when she was six. She left when she was eighteen; in 1850, the year the Fugitive Slave Act endangered all Blacks living in the North, she resided with the Boyle family. One year later she married Thomas Wilson, an attractive lecturer who later proved to be a free man passing as a fugitive slave in order to earn his living by speaking of *slavery's horrors. Ironically, Thomas Wilson's abandonment of his wife and newborn son proved to be the catalyst for her to write a novel that closely reflected her own experiences; *Our Nig* rivals *slave narratives in its description of white violence directed toward the narrators themselves.

The "commands of God" and the demands of poverty were often accepted as proper justifications for a woman's entrance into the public realm of publishing. Harriet Beecher *Stowe claimed to have seen the final scenes of *Uncle Tom's Cabin* in a vision. Because of her confinement to bed, the result of the brutal treatment she received, Wilson was to write *Our Nig* in order to raise money to sustain herself and to reclaim her son; because of her physical and economic situation, he had been placed under others' care. Unfortunately, George Mason Wilson, then seven years old, died five months after the novel's publication; ironically, his death certificate established his mother's racial identity and facilitated her reintroduction to African American letters.

• David Ames Curtis and Henry Louis Gates, Jr., "Establishing the Identity of the Author of *Our Nig*," in *Wild Women in the Whirlwind: Afra-American Culture and the Contemporary Literary Renaissance*, eds. Joanne Braxton and Andree McLaughlin, 1990, pp. 48–69. Barbara White, "*Our Nig* and the She-Devil: New Information about Harriet Wilson and the Bellmont Family," *American Literature* 65.1 (Mar. 1993): pp. 19–52.
—P. Gabrielle Foreman

WOFFORD, CHLOE ANTHONY. *See* Morrison, Toni.

WOLFE, GEORGE (b. 1954), dramatist, librettist, and innovator in the satirical revue and the black musical. Born in Frankfort, Kentucky, George C. Wolfe took his BA in directing from California's Pomona College in 1976. While attending Pomona, he won the regional festival of the American College Theatre Festival in 1975 with a comedy-satire titled

Up for Grabs and in 1977 became his region's first repeat winner with *Block Party*, which centered on the difficulties facing a black male attempting to move beyond the block (literal and figurative) that shaped him. Receiving his MFA in playwriting and *musical theater from New York University in 1983, he wrote the libretto for Duke Ellington's music in *Queenie Pie*, produced at Washington's Kennedy Center in 1986.

While *Queenie Pie* had a moderate success, Wolfe's main claim to attention and acclaim that year was *The Colored Museum*, a collection of eleven exuberantly inventive exhibits, brief scenes highlighting African American oppression and the culture that evolved with and against it. In the first exhibit, an ever-smiling stewardess addresses the audience as passengers on "Celebrity Slaveship," a device implying the grip of the past and contuing racist exploitation amid apparent progress. Other exhibits, including the upwardly mobile black who temporarily "kills" the raging kid inside him and the Frenchified singer who rewrites her roots, expose the manifold ways in which blacks have striven to evade the pain shaping them. The most noted exhibit, "The Last Mama-on-the-Couch Play," satirizes major black theatrical responses to oppression, from Lorraine *Hansberry's emotive realism and Ntozake *Shange's poetic feminism to race-submerging classicism and the problem-denying black musical. The final exhibit, a party described by the character Topsy Washington, linking opposites like *Aunt Jemima and Angela *Davis, proclaims that all the past, pain, complexities, and contradictions are inescapable parts of black identity. While most critics applauded its production at New Brunswick's Crossroads Theatre and the New York Shakespeare Festival, Thulani Davis argued that the play was misogynistic and trivialized black struggle.

In 1989 Wolfe faithfully yet innovatively adapted three short stories by Zora Neale *Hurston for the stage in *Spunk*. Wolfe's device of having the tales introduced by Guitar Man and Blues Speak Woman while interacting with the Folk (a chorus representing black folk) was spiritually akin to Hurston's frame for *Mules and Men* (1935).

In 1990, Wolfe directed an adaptation of Bertolt Brecht's *The Caucasian Chalk Circle*. Apart from the quality and inventiveness of the production, which reset the play in François Duvalier's Haiti, this adaptation was notable for being written by Wolfe's critic Thulani Davis.

Jelly's Last Jam, Wolfe's exhilarating proof that musicals need not sidestep pain and problems to be successful, was produced to wide acclaim in 1991. A tribute to Jelly Roll Morton that shows him denying his black roots as the singer did in *The Colored Museum*, Wolfe's musical emphasizes the role of suffering and community in the creation of jazz. In 1993, he won a Tony as best director for *Angels in America: Millennium Approaches*, and in 1994 he was nominated for the same award for *Angels in America: Perestroika*. A multiple award-winning writer, adaptor, and director, Wolfe is among the most imaginative creators in American theater today.

• "George C. Wolfe," in *Contemporary Literary Criticism*, vol. 49, eds. Daniel G. Morowski et al., 1988, pp. 419–424. Bernard L. Peterson, Jr., "George C. Wolfe," in *Contemporary Black American Playwrights and Their Plays*, 1988, pp. 507–508.
—Steven R. Carter

Woman Called Fancy, A. Frank *Yerby's 1951 novel, *A Woman Called Fancy*, is his first to have a female protagonist. Set in Augusta, Georgia, the novel covers the period from 1880 to 1894 and races the rise of the heroine, a beautiful South Carolina woman, from poverty to prominence among Augusta's aristocrats. Seeking to escape marriage to an old man to whom her father is indebted, Fancy Williamson leaves South Carolina for Augusta. She begins as a dance girl on a show wagon and eventually marries into a bankrupt aristocratic family of Georgia. Her marriage to Courtland Brantley of the Hiberion Plantation, however, provokes the scorn of aristocrats and begins her downfall.

Three-fourths of *A Woman Called Fancy* chronicles Fancy's efforts to earn respectability in society. Although she cannot escape her sordid past, her background gives her a different set of values. She socializes with African Americans and poor whites, she ignores aristocratic conventions, and she befriends the town's most notorious prostitute. Yerby's characterization of Fancy is, therefore, ironic, emphasizing the ignoble origins of most Southerners. Not only does Fancy contradict southern ideals but in her saintlike manner, she possesses qualities nobler than those of the aristocrats with whom she seeks to identify.

Like all Yerby's novels, *A Woman Called Fancy* presents a protagonist who is an outcast but achieves success in an alien culture, it adheres to his proven formula for historical romance, and it continues his string of best-sellers. *A Woman Called Fancy* is significant, however, in at least one other way: It contains Yerby's most definitive statement about race relations in America before his expatriation. Employing a minor character as a mouthpiece, Yerby declares that African Americans and whites cannot live together in dignity in America. A year later, he quietly left America, and like African American *expatriates before him, sought refuge from American racism in Europe.

• Wilbur Watson, "Cloth of Purest Brass," *New York Times*, 6 May 1951, 16. Edward Fitzgerald, "A Woman Called Fancy," *Saturday Review of Literature*, 23 June 1951, 39.
—James L. Hill

WOMANISM. Introduced and explicated by Alice *Walker in *In Search of Our Mothers' Gardens: Womanist Prose* (1983), "womanism" refers to African American *feminism or the feminism of women of color. It is derived from "womanish," a folk term peculiar to the African American lexical tradition, which refers to a characteristic of boldness, premature adulthood, and a spirit of inquiry inappropriate to children, particularly female children, but which also suggests capability, responsibility, and leadership.

A womanist, according to Walker, loves women, womanhood, and women's culture. Sometimes a sexual and/or platonic lover of men, a womanist is committed to the welfare of an entire people and claims the universality and diversity of the black race. A womanist, moreover, values salient characteristics of the African American experience in general, of African American womanhood in particular, and loves herself. Finally, according to Walker, womanism is an empowered form of feminism just as purple is a bold and empowered version of lavender.

In its general usage, "womanism" is generally understood to address the triple impact of sex, *race, and *class on African American women and to compensate for the traditional shortcomings of feminist and African American liberation discourse that have routinely excluded the peculiar needs of African American women. While feminism has disregarded issues of race and class, African American liberation theory has ignored issues of *gender and class. Womanism, however, maintains a clear critical perspective on both feminist and African American modes of analysis. By its attention to gender and class, womanism furnishes a system of analysis and a world view hitherto unavailable to African American women and other women of color. The concept of womanism, therefore, removes African American women's discourse from subjugation to traditional white feminist and African American male discourse.

In its practical application, a dominant characteristic of womanism is sisterhood that decries the practice of certain women to exploit feminism in pursuit of their own opportunistic ambitions in a male-dominated society. The sisterhood inherent in womanism values the advancement of an entire group. This assumption of sisterhood is evident in a range of disciplines from imaginative literature to theology and can be found in the work of such persons as Toni Cade *Bambara, bell *hooks, Angela *Davis, Jacqueline Grant, and Renita Weems. This notion of sisterhood is evident even in nineteenth-century African American female writings where autobiography was frequently the form used to explore the evils of a patriarchal, slave-holding society in which even white women, while subjugated, were as oppressive as white men. Similarly, after emancipation other African American women's writings articulated the suffering of African American women and the entire African American community in a sexist, racist, classist society. In addition, sisterhood undergirded the tradition of the Colored Women's Clubs that developed as a psychological and social response to the evils of the larger society.

In twentieth-century African American women's literature, womanism has been a dominating ethos. The works not only explore gender issues but also raise questions of race as well as local and international culture in addition to national and global politics and economics. As a group, therefore, these texts are different from white feminist texts because African American women writers share a collective legacy of racist and sexist domination in addition to the residuum of Western cultural and political hegemony.

From the first half of the twentieth century, one of the most notable womanist writers was Zora Neale *Hurston. While Hurston did not achieve acclaim in her lifetime, she is now considered a literary foremother by African American women writers. Hurston's fiction, nonfiction, and drama clearly address questions of gender, race, and class. Moreover, her anthropological writings demonstrate a global vision and attention to the African presence in the Americas that resonates with the awareness of the universality of the black race that is essential to womanism.

Among contemporary women writers, we find several examples of womanist texts. Chief among these are the works of Alice Walker who is responsible for rescuing Hurston's literary reputation and whose Pulitzer Prize-winning The *Color Purple (1982) is one of the most widely read and studied pieces of contemporary womanist fiction. Also central are the novels of Nobel laureate Toni *Morrison and MacArthur Prize Fellow Paule *Marshall. In contemporary drama examples of womanist writing are found in the works of Lorraine *Hansberry, Alice *Childress, Adrienne *Kennedy, and Beah Richards. Similarly, in poetry, womanism is the axis of the work of Margaret *Walker, Gwendolyn *Brooks, Nikki *Giovanni, and Rita *Dove. All of these works express African American women's views of the world. They demonstrate an awareness of historical and global continuities. Most important, however, they posit a resistance to sexist dogma and racist oppression.

• Chikwenzi Okongo Ogunyemi, "Womanism: The Dynamics of the Black Female Novel in English," Signs 11.1 (Autumn 1985): 63–80. Sherley Anne Williams, "Some Implications of Womanist Theory," Callaloo 9.2 (Spring 1986): 303–308.

—Carol P. Marsh-Lockett

WOMAN'S ERA is the historical period, beginning in the 1890s, when activist black women assumed and asserted political authority by developing a national club movement. Under the leadership of Mary McLeod Bethune, the *women's club movement evolved into the National Council of Negro Women (NCNW). Established in January 1894 by the Boston's Woman's Era Club and edited by Josephine St. Pierre Ruffin, the *Woman's Era was the first monthly magazine published by African American women. When Ida B. *Wells-Barnett questioned Frances Willard, the head of the Women's Christian Temperance Union, about its position on *lynching, Willard was silent on mob violence but alleged that insofar as "the colored race" was concerned "the grogshop is its center of power. . . . The safety of women, of children, of the home is menaced in a thousand localities" (quoted in Paula Giddings's, When and Where I Enter, 1984). Wells-Barnett accused Willard of abetting lynching, which started a minor controversy. The July 1895 Woman's Era magazine supported Wells-Barnett.

At the World's Congress of Representative Women, which met during the Columbian Exposition in Chicago on 20 May 1893, Frances Ellen Watkins *Harper told the women in her audience, who were almost exclusively white, that they were on the threshold of the "woman's era." As Hazel Carby explains (Reconstructing Womanhood, 1987), Harper advised them to accept "the responsibility of political power," necessary for improving the moral and social conditions of all Americans. The six black women who spoke at this Congress—Hallie Q. *Brown, Anna Julia *Cooper, Fanny Jackson *Coppin, Sarah J. Early, Fannie Barrier Williams, and Harper—were well aware of the racist disposition of the Congress of Representative Women as well as other white women's organizations. While they spoke, Wells-Barnett stood outside the Haitian Pavilion and circulated her pamphlet, *The Reason Why: The Colored American Is Not in the World's Columbian Exposition.* These seven African American women were among the vanguard who realized that black women, as well as black men, must organize to fight for their civil rights.

Three early black women's organizations were instrumental in mobilizing the national club movement: The Woman's Era Club of Boston; The Colored Woman's League of Washington, D.C.; and The Woman's Loyal Union of New York City. The impetus for organizing was the demand that black women voice their collective outrage at repeated allegations that they were inherently promiscuous and that black people were by nature dishonest. Ruffin called for a national convention to address the habitual slanderous and ominous attacks on black womanhood and the race in general. The three-day convention was held in Boston and began on 29 July 1895 with one hundred black women in attendance from ten states. This convention resulted in the formation of the National Federation of Afro-American Women, which consisted of thirty-six clubs in twelve states. Margaret Murray Washington was elected president of the Federation. In Washington, D.C., the National League of Colored Women, under the leadership of Mary Church *Terrell, was similarly organizing the black women's organizations in its region. In 1896 the Federation and the League were united to form the National Association of Colored Women (NACW) with Terrell as its first president.

The African American women of the NACW knew that by redefining a woman's sphere they were defining themselves and an age. Harper proclaimed that "the nineteenth century is discovering woman herself." Williams declared the era to be "a woman's age." Anna Cooper announced that "to be alive at such an epoch is a privilege," and "to be a woman, sublime." These NACW women enlarged the sphere of influence for black women by insisting that black women be trained to uplift the race. The NACW understood racial uplift as the advancement of a collective of individual black families, and it measured social advancement according to bourgeois standards. Thus the patriarchal nuclear *family was the model to which the black clubwomen subscribed, even as they challenged male authority.

Training required resources: teachers, curricula, and institutions. Who would determine how the black masses were to be trained, and how they should protect their civil rights were two questions that dominated the age. Two prominent men arose to answer these questions—Booker T. *Washington and W. E. B. *Du Bois. Both men were products of the gender conventions of their age. Insofar as they were concerned, men were leaders and women were their helpmates.

Black women were not silent on these issues. They debated how best to uplift the black masses and what talents women possessed to assist the enterprise. Black women tended not to endorse industrial training at the expense of academic training; for as Anna Cooper insisted, "We can't all be professional people. We must have a backbone to the race." While Cooper (the first black woman to be awarded a doctoral degree) ran the famous college preparatory, Dunbar High School, Mary McLeod Bethune and Charlotte Hawkins Brown founded industrial schools.

The demand for *education among black people was not new. After emancipation, black people had increasingly endeavored to obtain education at all levels. However, during the 1880s and 1890s, African Americans realized that their survival was dependent on *education. This focus sharply raised black *literacy rates, encouraged black people to see themselves as subjects of their own fates, and gave rise to what Wilson Moses has called "the golden age of black nationalism." As a part of the agenda for promoting racial progress and protesting *Jim Crow, African Americans published scores of newspapers, journals, novels, short stories, and poems to disseminate their viewpoints. The decade of the 1890s witnessed an outpouring of literature by black women as well, much of which has been reproduced in the Schomburg Library of Nineteenth-Century Black Women Writers. For example, the novels include: Emma Dunham *Kelley's *Medga* (1891) and *Four Girls at Cottage City* (1898); Harper's *Iola Leroy* (1892); Amelia E. *Johnson's *Clarence and Corinne* (1890) and *The Hazeley Family* (1894); and Katherine Davis Chapman *Tillman's *Beryl Weston's Ambition* (1893) and *Clancy Street* (1898). The novels represented the currency of social issues at large in black communities at the turn of the century. In each work, an idealized female protagonist dramatizes the viewpoint that her engagement in social activism makes all types of happiness possible. Thus well-trained women, who are productive both in and out of the home, make good wives and foster happy marriages and prosperous communities. Activist fervor among African American women enlarged the audience for early black literature and inspired more black people, especially women, to write and to commit themselves to working for the progress of the race.

• Mary Church Terrell, *A Colored Woman in a White World*, 1968. Wilson Jeremiah Moses, *The Golden Age of Black Nationalism, 1850–1925*, 1978. Paula Giddings, *When and Where I Enter . . . The Impact of Black Women on Race and Sex in America*, 1984. Hazel V. Carby, *Reconstructing Womanhood: The Emergence of the Afro-American Woman Novelist*, 1987. Cynthia Neverdon-Morton, *Afro-American Women of the South and the Advancement of the Race, 1895–1925*, 1989. Claudia Tate, *Domestic Allegories of Political Desire: The Black Heroine's Text at the Turn of the Century*, 1992.

—Claudia Tate

Woman's Era, The. Published in Boston between 1894 and 1897, the *Woman's Era* was the first monthly journal completely owned and run by black women. Founded and edited by Josephine St. Pierre Ruffin (1842–1924) with the assistance of her daughter Florida Ruffin Ridley (1861–1943), the *Woman's Era* served initially as the organ of Boston's Woman's Era Club, an early black-led female civic organization. Ruffin envisioned a black, primarily middle-class, female audience for her journal, and she provided information on black women's activities nationwide, as well as published the minutes and proceedings of national women's club conventions. Ruffin also provided her readers with a host of articles and guest-edited opinion columns on any number of political and domestic issues, including *lynching, *education, and social reform. Contributing editors included Mary Church *Terrell (Washington, D.C.); Victoria Earle *Matthews (New York); Fannie Barrier Williams (Chicago); Josephine Silone Yates (Kansas City); and Alice Moore *Dunbar-Nelson (New Orleans). Later, as the club movement expanded among turn-of-the-century African American women, the well-established *Woman's Era* served as the journal for succeeding black *women's clubs, namely the National Federation of Afro-American Women (1895) and the National Association of Colored Women (1896).

[*See also* Journalism.]

• Penelope L. Bullock, *The Afro-American Periodical Press 1838–1909*, 1981. Darlene Clark Hine, ed., *Black Women in America: An Historical Encyclopedia*, 2 vols., 1993.

—Sandra Gunning

Women Of Brewster Place, The. The 1982 first *novel by Gloria *Naylor, *The Women of Brewster Place* tells the stories of seven African American women who live on a walled-off street in the ghetto of an anonymous northeastern city. While these characters come from varied backgrounds, they all have suffered great hardships, often caused by men.

After a prologue describes the history of the dead-end street, the first section of *The Women of Brewster Place* tells, primarily through flashback, the story of its aging title character, Mattie Michael. Mattie's one sexual experience results in her pregnancy, expulsion from her Tennessee home, and journey northward. As Basil, her son, grows up, Mattie overprotects him, and he becomes irresponsible. Following his accidental murder of another man, Basil skips his bail, causing Mattie to lose her house and sending her to Brewster Place.

The following sketch gives the story of Etta Mae Johnson, a strong-willed, flamboyant woman who stays with Mattie Michael on Brewster Place. After attending a church service, Etta pursues a widowed preacher with whom she dreams of a secure future but only finds a one-night stand. Returning to Mattie's home, Etta realizes that her friendship with Mattie is more valuable than fleeting male attention.

Next Naylor tells of Kiswana Browne, named Melanie by her middle-class mother. Kiswana has changed her name to reflect her new Afrocentrism and has rejected her privileged upbringing to live as an activist on Brewster Place. Yet after Kiswana and her mother undergo a painful interchange, the two women gain a new understanding of each other.

The following chapter relates the story of Lucielia (Ciel) Louise Turner, who has an abortion in order to try to keep her husband. Shortly thereafter, while the couple is arguing about his imminent departure, their toddler daughter is accidentally electrocuted. Ciel's numb response almost results in her own death until Mattie rescues her with loving attention.

Cora Lee is the subject of the next section, which tells of her fixation with having babies, subsequent neglect of them once they mature, and rapid production of seven children. After Kiswana persuades Cora and her children to attend an African American Shakespeare production, Cora begins to realize her irresponsibility, and the chapter ends optimistically.

Next, in "The Two," Naylor tells of a lesbian couple, Theresa and Lorraine, who move into Brewster Place. Disheartened by the community's rejection of them, Lorraine one evening seeks solace with the kind old handyman, Ben. Later that night, delinquent young men in an alley by the Brewster Place wall gang-rape Lorraine. When Ben discovers her, she is so traumatized that she kills him with a brick.

After these tragedies, "The Block Party" relates the grieving community's attempt to go on with life. When it begins to rain during the neighborhood fundraiser, the women perceive the raindrops on the Brewster Place wall as bloodstains, so they destroy the wall. Although these actions appear only to have been in Mattie's dream, the rain and ritual destruction purify the community.

When *The Women of Brewster Place* was first published, Naylor won the 1983 American Book Award for best first novel. The novel was adapted into a television production starring Oprah Winfrey in 1989. Critical interpretations of the novel emphasize its geography, naturalism, and mythical overtones. The novel's emphasis on women's bonding, *class, community, and motherhood are also common themes in its criticism, which often takes a feminist approach and compares Naylor to other African American authors, such as Toni *Morrison.

• Barbara Christian, "Gloria Naylor's Geography: Community, Class, and Patriarchy in *The Women of Brewster Place* and *Linden Hills*," in *Reading Black, Reading Feminist*, ed. Henry Louis Gates, Jr., 1990, pp. 348–373. Henry Louis Gates, Jr., and K. A. Appiah, eds., *Gloria Naylor: Critical Perspectives Past and Present*, 1993. —Kristine A. Yohe

WOMEN'S CLUBS. African American women's clubs and *literary societies appeared in the early nineteenth century and provided a forum for their writings that spanned into the next century. While enslaved and free African American women in the South were overwhelmingly denied access to *literacy and formal schooling prior to emancipation, free and literate African American women and men of the North organized clubs for intellectual stimulation and expression. One of the earliest such clubs for African American women was the Female Literary Association of Philadelphia, founded in 1831. Membership in this group was by election. Members submitted unsigned poems, *essays, and *short stories to be critiqued by the group. The abolitionist newspaper the *Liberator* frequently published samples of the women's literary works. After visiting a meeting of this organization and hearing their works read, William Lloyd Garrison wrote in the *Liberator* (17 Nov. 1832), "If the traducers of the colored race could be acquainted with the moral worth, just refinement, and large intelligence of this association, their mouths would hereafter be dumb."

One year after the founding of the Philadelphia literary club, African American women formed the Afri-American Female Intelligence Society in Boston. This organization also stressed the reading and discussing of literature and encouraged the literary pursuits of its members. Prominent lecturers spoke at the programs of the group. Maria W. *Stewart, who spoke before the group, was educated through membership in African American female literary societies. Her speeches and essays were published during her lifetime.

Literary societies were important educational vehicles for African Americans in the North prior to the Civil War. They significantly enhanced the intellectual development of their communities by providing lectures, libraries, reading rooms and instruction. They also fostered the literary talents of their members. The writings of African American women in these organizations can be found in the abolitionist newspapers as well as the African American newspapers of their period.

As African American women began to obtain formal *education in colleges and normal schools, many participated in the literary societies of these institutions. African American women who attended Oberlin College during the mid- and late nineteenth century participated in these groups. One such example is Fanny Jackson *Coppin. Coppin attended Oberlin from 1860 to 1865 and was a member of the Ladies Literary Association of Oberlin. After graduating from Oberlin, Coppin became a renowned educator in Philadelphia and an active women's club member and community activist. Coppin published a variety of literary works, including children's stories in the *Christian Recorder* under the pen name of Matilda.

Another Oberlin College graduate and active clubwoman whose literary talents flourished was Anna Julia *Cooper. Cooper graduated from Oberlin in 1884 and was active in the African American women's club movement, which was in full swing at the end of the nineteenth century. Her first volume of essays, *A *Voice from the South by a Black Woman from the South* was published in 1892. Cooper published many nonfiction works throughout her lengthy life. She wrote columns in various newspapers, including the *Washington Tribune* and the *Washington Evening Star,* and edited a journal, the *Southland,* in 1891. Cooper wrote a pageant entitled "From Servitude to Service: The contribution from the Negro peoples to American History" in 1940.

With the growth of the African American women's club movement at the end of the nineteenth century and the formation of the National Association of Colored Women, these organizations continued to play an essential role in giving exposure to the writings and voices of African American women. For example, the Woman's Era Club, founded in Boston in 1894, began a newspaper, the *Woman's Era.* The all-female-edited paper had Black women correspondents nationwide who provided news about the condition of African American women. In addition to the political content of the paper, the writers offered literary pieces as well.

Pauline E. *Hopkins of Boston, a member of the Woman's Era Club and a contributor to its newspaper, became a writer of great reputation in the late nineteenth century. Hopkins wrote essays, short stories, three *novels, and a musical *drama. She was a founder and editor of the literary *Colored American Magazine* in 1900. This magazine featured short stories and serialized articles.

The above women are but a few examples of outstanding African American women writers whose talents were nurtured and promoted within the Black women's clubs of the nineteenth century. These clubs provided audiences, encouragement, and appreciation for women such as Maria Stewart, the novelist and poet Frances Ellen Watkins *Harper (a founding member of the National Association of Colored Women), and many other lesser-known writers during an age when African American women's literary talents were overlooked.

[*See also* Societies and Clubs.]

• Linda M. Perkins, "Black Women and Racial 'Uplift' Prior to Emancipation," in *The Black Woman Cross-Culturally,* ed. Filomina Steady, 1981, pp. 314–317.

—Linda M. Perkins

WOODSON, CARTER G. (1875–1950), historian, educator, and editor. Born in Virginia to former slaves, Carter G. Woodson worked in coal mines until he entered high school at the age of nineteen, finishing in less than two years. Over the next several years, he taught high school and obtained a BL degree at the interracial Berea College (Kentucky). From 1903 to 1906 Woodson worked as supervisor of schools in the Philippines. In 1908 he received both BA and MA degrees from the University of Chicago and began teaching high school in Washington, D.C. He earned a PhD in history from Harvard University in 1912, becoming, after W. E. B. *Du Bois, the second African American to receive a doctorate in *history. From 1919 to 1922 he taught at Howard University and West Virginia Collegiate Institute, and served in high administrative posts at both institutions.

In 1915, Woodson, with several other scholars, founded the Association for the Study of Negro Life and History (ASNLH). ASNLH's *publishing subsidiary, Associated Publishers, was for many years the leading black-owned press in the United States. The following year he founded the *Journal of Negro History,* the premier professional journal of African American history. He retired from the academy in 1922 to concentrate on the journal and ASNLH, both of which he headed until his death, as well as his own historical writing. He also worked on stimulating popular interest in African American history, initiating Negro History Week (which later became Black History Month) in 1926, and founding the *Negro History Bulletin* (for use in primary and secondary education) in 1937.

Woodson's historical works include *The Education of the Negro Prior to 1861* (1915), *The History of the Negro Church* (1921), and *The African Background Outlined* (1936). He wrote several well-known textbooks, most notably *The Negro in Our History* (1922), popular in both high schools and universities. He was also greatly accomplished as an editor. He collected the speeches of Frederick *Douglass, Booker T. *Washington, and many others in *Negro Orators and Their Orations* (1925). He published a collection of *letters, *The Mind of the Negro as Reflected in Letters Written During the Crisis, 1800–1860* (1926), and edited the complete works of the minister and civil rights activist Francis J. *Grimké (1942).

Woodson was particularly concerned with social and economic history. His work built on a previous tradition of black historians such as William Wells *Brown and George Washington *Williams, who used history to illustrate the virtues and potential of African Americans, as individuals and as a race. In many cases he pioneered attention to the particular circumstances and contexts of African American history. In *Negro Orators and Their Orations*, for example, he emphasizes the importance of the spoken nature of speeches by black orators, arguing that their performance could never be entirely captured by the printed page. His signficance for the study of African American culture and history, however, derives less from his own work and more from the institutional foundations and personal leadership he provided to the emerging discipline of black history. He inspired (and mentored) an entire generation of historians of African American culture, including Rayford W. Logan, Luther Porter Jackson, James Hugo Johnston, and others. His work, the journal he founded, and the scholarly activity he inspired all contributed to the cultural flowering of the *Harlem Renaissance. The ongoing recovery of neglected aspects of African American history, literature, and culture owes much of its impetus to Woodson's founding efforts.

• Rayford W. Logan, "Carter G. Woodson," in *DANB*, eds. Rayford W. Logan and Michael R. Winston, 1982, pp. 665–667. August Meier and Elliott Rudwick, *Black History and the Historical Profession, 1915–1980*, 1986. Jacqueline Goggin, *Carter G. Woodson: A Life in Black History*, 1993.

—Gary Ashwill

WORK. Inasmuch as people of African descent were originally brought to the so-called New World as indentured servants and slave laborers, it is not surprising that work has played a pivotal role in both the lives and the literature of black Americans. Indeed, African American literature presents many variations on the American work ethic, the extremes of which are perhaps best represented in the respective positions held by two eminent historical figures: W. E. B. *Du Bois and Booker T. *Washington.

In one of his most famous essays, "The *Talented Tenth" (1903), Du Bois identified work, along with

*education, as the lever that would uplift the Negro race. It is important to note, however, that for Du Bois and like-minded African American intellectuals of his time, the truly significant, uplifting work was not the common drudgery of the black masses but the intellectual labor of the best and brightest—the "exceptional men"—who would "lead and elevate" the Negro *race. Du Bois's work ethic operated in direct contrast to that of Booker T. Washington—founder of the Tuskegee Institute—whose 1895 *"Atlanta Exposition Address" urged African Americans to cast down their work pails in such areas as agriculture, mechanics, commerce, and domestic service. Although Washington did not fail to include what he called "the professions" in his list of appropriate occupations for African Americans, his speeches, his autobiography *Up from Slavery* (1900–1901), and the curriculum of his school all promoted technical training for the masses of African Americans, who were destined to live by the product of their hands, rather than academic instruction for an elite black intelligentsia, whose superior intellects would save the race from itself. "No race can prosper," he argued in his Atlanta address, "till it learns that there is as much dignity in tilling a field as in writing a poem."

The great divide between Du Bois and Washington—between what they conceived of as the talented tenth, on the one hand, and the toiling masses, on the other—might not have been so wide were their respective positions less proscriptive and exclusive. In point of fact, many early African Americans combined the Du Bois and Washington work ethics. George Moses *Horton, for example, waxed poetic in finding a practical means by which to buy his way out of the drudgery and forced illiteracy of *slavery. Having taught himself to read and write, he reportedly earned his purchase price by composing and selling love lyrics to students at the state university of North Carolina. Phillis *Wheatley hoped, however futilely, to support herself with her pen; and like many of her white women contemporaries, Harriet E. *Wilson—author of *Our Nig, or Sketches from the Life of a Free Black* (1859)—turned to writing in order to support herself and her child. Harriet A. *Jacobs wrote *Incidents in the Life of a Slave Girl* (1861) during moments stolen from her official duties as a nursemaid. Her correspondence suggests, however, that she viewed writing as her true vocation, even as she earned her livelihood caring for her employers' children. As Jean Fagan Yellin notes in her introduction to the Harvard edition of *Incidents,* Jacobs used the limited fame and funds that came to her as an author to advance the cause of abolition and to assist freedmen and women in adjusting to life after emancipation. Writing was a somewhat more profitable and prestigious occupation for Jacobs's contemporary Frederick *Douglass. The publication of his *autobiography, *Narrative of the Life of Frederick Douglass,* in 1845, helped launch a lifelong career as a writer, orator, abolitionist, and civil rights activist.

Writing in these and other similar instances was not simply leisure activity but productive labor. Robert Bone begins his study *The Negro Novel in*

America (1958) by noting that the dawn-to-dusk work schedule of slaves was not conducive to the production of literature. Leisure and *literacy are the necessary requirements for literary activity, Bone maintains, and the "peculiar institution" by law and by custom denied slaves both the free time and the freedom to read and write. One might argue, however, that African American literature—broadly conceived—has its deepest, oldest roots not in leisure but in labor, not in higher education but in the very drudgery and technical skill that Du Bois feared would produce "artisans but not, in nature, men." For if we accept the popular notion that African American literature rises out of an oral tradition traceable back to Africa, we must then consider as part of that tradition the field hollers, work songs, and oral testimonies of anonymous, illiterate slaves, as well as the *poetry and prose of Lucy *Terry, Phillis Wheatley, Ann *Plato, Jupiter *Hammon, Olaudah *Equiano, and other early African Americans who put quill to paper. We must also consider the extent to which their cultural products—from field hollers to *slave narratives and other autobiographies to newspapers, magazines, and full-length *novels—were themselves consumable commodities. Consumers of such cultural products were not just the white audiences for whom many early African American authors are assumed to have written, but also the black communities on behalf of whom they wrote. As early as the 1830s, pockets of free blacks in urban areas such as Philadelphia, Boston, and Baltimore formed *literary societies whose members gathered together to read and discuss their own literary endeavors and those of both black and white writers.

Like George Moses Horton, who sold love lyrics to the lovelorn, some slaves with a special trade or skill were able to purchase their own freedom (or that of loved ones) by hiring themselves out for extra service. William Wells *Brown offers fictive renditions of this self-emancipating practice in *Clotel, or The President's Daughter* (1853). At one point in the novel, the title character escapes her master with the aid of an industrious slave named William, who finances their getaway with money he has earned hiring himself out as an expert mechanic. While she is not able to buy her freedom, Currer—whom Brown casts in the role of Thomas Jefferson's slave mistress—makes enough money as an expert laundress to outfit her two quadroon daughters in a manner befitting the progeny of a president. In fact as in fiction, the labor of industrious slaves gave members of the toiling masses entry into the community of free blacks, where they had greater access to literacy and to both the consumption and production of literature.

For African Americans, then, the production of literature, across genres and throughout history, has been a business finely concerned with business—with work roles, with both manual labor and "the professions," and with the difficulties the emerging black working and middle classes faced in finding and keeping jobs in a racist society. Like African American writers from Frank J. *Webb, writing in the 1850s, to Alice *Walker, writing in the 1970s and 1980s, Pauline E. *Hopkins used the literary text to address the issue of working conditions and job discrimination for both the unlearned masses and the educated elite. The black masses can do no better than the most arduous labor for the lowest wages, she wrote in *Contending Forces* (1900). The highly skilled and well-trained fared little better, because the prejudice of "the descendants of liberty-loving Puritans" kept the shop door closed to black workers. Although a well-trained, proficient stenographer, Hopkins's heroine Sappho Clark has to bring her work home because the white office workers refuse to have a colored woman in their midst. Skilled, industrious, and educated African Americans are similarly shut out of the market place in Frank Webb's 1857 novel *The Garies and Their Friends*, where black enterprise and entrepreneurship are constantly threatened and undermined by racial discrimination and mob violence.

But while it frequently attends to the problems of the poor and working classes—to, in Hopkins's works, "the poor Negro [who] finds himself banned in almost every kind of employment"—nineteenth- and early twentieth-century literature also gives "the professions" a place of honor and prominence. Novels such as Frances Ellen Watkins *Harper's *Iola Leroy* (1892), J. McHenry Jones's *Hearts of Gold* (1896), Sutton E. *Griggs's *Imperium in Imperio* (1899), Pauline Hopkins's *Contending Forces*, Nella *Larsen's *Quicksand* (1928) and *Passing* (1929), and Jessie Redmon *Fauset's *The Chinaberry Tree* (1931) and *Comedy: American Style* (1933) present a seemingly endless cast of black doctors, lawyers, teachers, ministers, artists, and businesspersons, who have put to good use the benefits of their education and training.

Education and professional opportunities turned toward the good of the people—toward uplifting the masses or seeking equality and justice for the race— are prized and praised, in early fiction in particular, while self-aggrandizement is often mocked. The professional preoccupations and bourgeois materialism of Fauset's and Larsen's success-minded, security-seeking doctors' wives is held up to scrutiny and perhaps ridicule in novels like *The Chinaberry Tree*, *Comedy: American Style*, *Quicksand*, and *Passing*. Both Zora Neale *Hurston and Dorothy *West show us shades of the work ethic gone monstrously amuck in the forms of Joe Starks of *Their Eyes Were Watching God* (1937) and Cleo Jericho Judson in *The Living Is Easy* (1948). This theme is further developed in contemporary novels like Toni *Morrison's *Song of Solomon* (1977), where Macon Dead's uncompromising pursuit of property and the almighty dollar leads one of his about-to-be evicted tenants to conclude that a "nigger in business is a terrible thing to see." In Paule *Marshall's 1959 novel *Brown Girl, Brownstones*, the hard-working Silla Boyce—anxious to make money and "get house"—is so disdainful of and hard on her less ambitious, dreamer husband that her daughter at one point likens her mother to Hitler.

Far more heroically drawn are characters such as Frances Harper's Iola Leroy and Pauline Hopkins's

Will Smith, who in keeping with the ideology of uplift put their fine educations (Smith is educated at Harvard and Heidelberg) to work teaching and aiding the less fortunate. Much the same can be said of Sutton Griggs's Harvard-educated Benton Piedmont, who becomes a "race patriot" using his material gains to plot political insurrection against the government that enslaved his ancestors. Although she lacks the formal education of which many other characters have the benefit, Morrison's heroine *Pilate Dead is endlessly giving and self-sacrificing, in direct contrast to her brother Macon, who—like Joe Starks in *Their Eyes Were Watching God*—is committed to owning things, property, and people.

Modern African American literature often returns to such sites as slavery, sharecropping, and urban migration, focusing on the struggles of African Americans throughout history to claim liberty, literacy, and the material benefits of their own labor. Classic twentieth-century texts—autobiographies such as Richard *Wright's *Black Boy* (1945); novels such as Wright's *Native Son* (1940), William *Attaway's *Blood on the Forge* (1941), Ann* Petry's The *Street* (1947), Ralph *Ellison's *Invisible Man* (1952), James *Baldwin's *Go Tell It on the Mountain* (1953) and *Another Country* (1962), Paule Marshall's *Brown Girl, Brownstones*, Margaret *Walker's *Jubilee* (1966), Ernest J. *Gaines's *Of Love and Dust* (1967), and Alice Walker's The *Third Life of Grange Copeland* (1970); and dramas such as Lorraine *Hansberry's A *Raisin in the Sun* (1958), Joseph A. *Walker's The *River Niger* (1973), and August *Wilson's *Fences* (1986)—all make literary use of the struggle of African Americans to eke out a living in an often hostile, discriminatory environment. In both *Native Son* and *Invisible Man*, for example, it is their search for work—their attempts to live up to their white employers' expectations of them as chauffeurs—that gets the main characters into such serious trouble.

In poetry as well as in prose, in drama as well as in fiction, work—both manual and intellectual, domestic and professional—has been one of the major forces around which texts have turned since the late eighteenth century. The works of contemporary writers such as Leon *Forrest, John Edgar *Wideman, Gayl *Jones, Gloria *Naylor, Charles R. *Johnson, Trey Ellis, Terry *McMillan, August Wilson, and Rita *Dove, as well as Toni Morrison and Alice Walker, suggest that this will continue to be true of African American literature well into the twenty-first century.

• E. Franklin Frazier, *Black Bourgeoisie: The Rise of a New Middle Class*, 1957. Nathan Hare, *The Black Anglo-Saxons*, 1965. J. H. Harman, Jr., Arnett G. Lindsay, and Carter G. Woodson, *The Negro as a Business Man*, 1929; rpt. 1969. Edward Jones, *Blacks in Business*, 1971. Jacqueline Jones, *Labor of Love, Labor of Sorrow: Black Women, Work, and the Family, from Slavery to the Present*, 1985. Benjamin Quarles, *The Negro in the Making of America*, 1964; rpt. 1987. Willard B. Gatewood, *Aristocrats of Color: The Black Elite, 1880–1920*, 1990. Shelley Green and Paul Pryde, *Black Entrepreneurship in America*, 1990. James Oliver Horton, *Free People of Color: Inside the African American Community*, 1993. Farah Jasmine Griffin, "Who Set You Flowin'?": The African-American Migration Narrative, 1995. —Ann duCille

WPA. *See* Federal Writers' Project.

WRIGHT, CHARLES S. (1932), novelist, columnist, short fiction writer, and black humorist. Charles Stevenson Wright was born and raised west of Columbia, Missouri, in the small town of New Franklin. Upon his release from the army in 1954, he wrote "No Regrets," an unpublished novel about an affair between a black beatnik from New York City's East Village and an upper-class white girl. Not until the 1960s would Wright begin publishing the blackly humorous, passionately idiosyncratic books that add tragic clarity to the nightmare of contemporary African American existence.

In *The Messenger* (1963), Wright draws so extensively upon his life that fact and fiction often blur. Realistically narrated in the first person by a fair-skinned black Manhattanite named Charles Stevenson, the novel dramatizes the isolation and alienation of persons who fall prey to America's social, economic, and racial caste systems. Stevenson, a New York City messenger, constantly finds himself on the edges of power, yet is utterly devoid of any. A man perceived as neither black nor white, "a minority within a minority," he is cast adrift in the naturalistic city of New York, where victory and defeat are accepted "with the same marvelous indifference."

The Messenger brought Wright recognition and modest commercial success, but initially his 1966 novel *The Wig* was not well-received. Today, however, many people would agree with Ishmael *Reed's 1973 assertion that *The Wig* is "one of the most underrated novels by a black person in this century" (John O'Brien, *Interviews with Black Writers*, 1973).

Wright's use of fantasy and hyperbole distinguishes *The Wig* from most African American fiction of the mid-1960s. Set "in an America of tomorrow," the novel depicts the desperately failed efforts of a twenty-one-year-old black Harlemite named Lester Jefferson to live the American dream. The book ends with his literal (and willed) emasculation, after Jefferson learns that the money he has earned parading around the streets in New York in an electrified chicken suit will prove useless to his successfully courting the black prostitute he has idealized as his "all-American girl."

The years between 1966 and 1973 found Wright in various foreign and domestic locales. But his literary psyche remained firmly planted in New York City, the setting of the nonfictional pieces he began writing for the *Village Voice*. Collected, amended, and supplemented, these columns came to comprise *Absolutely Nothing to Get Alarmed About* (1973), a book filled with the same drug users, male and female prostitutes, abusive policemen, and underinquisitive detectives one finds in his novels. These, plus America's unstinting racism, have rid Wright of his optimism as surely as Mr. Fishback rids Lester Jefferson of his masculinity at the end of *The Wig*.

Since the appearance of *Absolutely Nothing to Get Alarmed About*, Wright's literary profile has remained low. But even if he were to publish no significant new work, Wright, now living in Mexico, would be remembered as an innovator who in breaking with traditional fictional modes during the 1960s helped to negotiate space for Ishmael Reed, Clarence *Major, and other African American avant-gardists.

• Frances S. Foster, "Charles Wright: Black Black Humorist," *CLA Journal* 15 (1971): 44–53. John O'Brien, "Charles Wright," in *Interviews with Black Writers*, 1973, pp. 245–257. Eberhard Kreutzer, "Dark Ghetto Fantasy and the Great Society: Charles Wright's *The Wig*," in *The Afro-American Novel since 1960*, eds. Peter Bruck and Wolfgang Karrer, 1982, pp. 145–166.
—Joe Weixlmann

WRIGHT, JAY (b. c. 1935), poet, playwright, musician, educator, and MacArthur Fellow. Jay Wright's biography is a composite of uncertain and contradictory stories. He was born in either 1934 or 1935 in Albuquerque, New Mexico, to Leona Dailey, a Virginian of African and Native American descent, and George Murphy (also known as Mercer Murphy Wright), a construction worker, jitney driver, and handy man who claimed to be of African American, Cherokee, and Irish ancestry. Wright spent most of his childhood in the care of foster parents in Albuquerque. In his teens, he lived with his father in San Pedro, California. While in high school, Wright began to play minor league baseball and developed what would become a lifelong passion for the bass. From 1954 to 1957, he served in the U.S. Army medical corps. During most of his service, he was stationed in Germany, which gave him the opportunity to travel extensively throughout Europe. After he returned, Wright enrolled in the University of California at Berkeley under the G.I. Bill. He majored in comparative literature and graduated in only three years. Before continuing his literary studies at Rutgers in 1962, Wright spent a semester at Union Theological Seminary in New York. In 1964, Wright interrupted his graduate studies to spend a year teaching English and medieval history at the Butler Institute in Guadalajara, Mexico, one of many extended visits to that country. Back at Rutgers, he completed all but his dissertation in pursuit of a doctoral degree in comparative literature.

While at Rutgers in the 1960s, Wright lived and worked in Harlem, where he encountered several other young African American writers, among them Henry *Dumas, Larry *Neal, and LeRoi Jones/Amiri *Baraka. Unlike the work of these and other poets associated with the *Black Arts movement, Jay Wright's poems approach African American spiritual, intellectual, and social history from a cross-cultural perspective. Already in the 1960s and 1970s, Wright's was one of the most original voices in contemporary African American and American poetry, a voice that influenced younger poets such as Nathaniel *Mackey and Cyrus Cassells. But Wright's increasing distance from a budding Black Arts movement that rejected all European-derived literary forms and traditions did not attract a large readership.

Wright's self-declared "passion for what is hidden" (*Elaine's Book*, 1988) frequently takes the shape of a spiritual quest heavily infused with autobiographical elements. From the early collection *The Homecoming Singer* (1971) and the three book-length poems *Dimensions of History* (1976), *The Double Invention of Komo* (1980), and *Explications/Interpretations* (1984)—which, together with *Soothsayers and Omens* (1976), make up Wright's first poetic cycle—to *Elaine's Book* and *Boleros* (1991), Wright's poetic persona, which may be both male and female, traverses and connects far-flung geographies: New Hampshire, his home base since 1973; Mexico; the Southwest; California; and, more globally, Western Europe, Africa, the Caribbean, South America, and Asia. Wright's poetry insists on continuities across, as well as within, cultures. The scope and depth of Wright's vision derive from his extensive research in medieval and Renaissance literatures, *music, anthropology, the history of *religions, and the history of science. An admixture of Italian, German, and Spanish interspersed with Dogon, Bambara, and other African ideograms, Wright's literary English amounts at times almost to a foreign language. African American music, such as the *blues, *jazz, and a host of Caribbean and Latin American song and dance forms, plays an equally crucial role in his poetic projects.

Wright's poetry exemplifies what the Guyanese novelist Wilson Harris, whose work Wright has often cited as an inspiration, calls a poetics of the cross-cultural imagination (*The Womb of Space: The Cross Cultural Imagination*, 1983). Though his literary vision is firmly rooted in both African American history and African, particularly Akan and Dogon, religions, Wright's poetry seeks to restore to African American literature a sense of all the cultural resources available to it. For him, this very much includes Europe. Starting with his persona's acute consciousness of exile, Wright's poetic journeys retrace and reverse the *Middle Passage from Africa to the Americas. His poems offer rites of passage that both remember and try to heal the ruptures and dispersals of traditional cultures, African and Native American alike. Wright provides further insight into his intricate designs in "Desire's Design, Vision's Resonance: Black Poetry's Ritual and Historical Voice" (*Callaloo*, Winter 1987). This programmatic essay shows that his literary and cultural politics have far more in common with those of older poets such as Robert *Hayden and Melvin B. *Tolson than with the cultural nationalism many poets of his own generation espoused.

• Robert B. Stepto, "After Modernism, After Hibernation: Michael Harper, Robert Hayden, and Jay Wright," in *Chant of Saints: A Gathering of Afro-American Literature, Arts, and Scholarship*, eds. Michael S. Harper and Robert B. Stepto, 1979, pp. 470–486. "Jay Wright: A Special Issue," *Callaloo* 6 (Fall 1983). Wilson Harris, *The Womb of Space: The Cross-Cultural Imagination*, 1983. Kimberly W. Benston, "'I Yam What I Am': The Topos of (Un)naming in Afro-American Literature," in *Black Literature and Literary Theory*, ed. Henry Louis Gates, Jr., 1984, pp. 151–172. Vera M. Kutzinski, *Against the American Grain: Myth and History in William Carlos Williams, Jay Wright, and Nicolás Guillén*, 1987. Isidore Okpewho, "From a Goat Path in Africa: An Approach to the Poetry of Jay Wright," *Callaloo* 14 (Fall 1991): 692–726. Vera M. Kutzinski, review of *Boleros*, *Magill's Literary Annual*, 1992, 56–59.
—Vera M. Kutzinski

WRIGHT, RICHARD (1908–1960), novelist, short story writer, and political commentator. Richard Wright changed the landscape of possibility for African American writers. Wright's defiance, his refusal to give the reading public what it had hitherto demanded of the African American writer, his insistence on the expression of an African American voice, allowed later writers to do the same, allowed Toni *Morrison, for example, to write as she would—without concern for explaining her sometimes obscure meanings (e.g., her references to news events from long ago or words or phrases from African American vernacular speech) to a mainstream reading public. For other African American writers, positioning themselves against Wright allowed them to write about African American culture in a more positive way, to assume a posture not requiring that the subject of the fiction, the African American, be seen as victim.

Richard Wright's influence began primarily with the publication of *Native Son in 1940. The significance of the novel's publication lay in the new and daringly defiant character of its content and in its adoption by the Book-of-the-Month Club, which signaled for the first time since the nineteenth-century fugitive *slave narratives the willingness of a mainstream reading public to give ear to an African American writer, even one who appeared unapologetic in his bald and forthright representation of a large segment of African American culture.

Wright's understanding of African American life is rooted in his southern background. His first book, *Uncle Tom's Children (1938), a collection of short stories, comes out of his understanding and knowledge of the meaning of being a young black male growing up in the South. Its introduction, "The Ethics of Living Jim Crow" (added along with a fifth short story in 1940), forms the core for his later *autobiography, *Black Boy (1945). The ligature between the two is Native Son. It is no happenstance that *Bigger Thomas, the novel's hero, though living in Chicago at the time of the narrative, was born in Mississippi, the birthplace of Richard Wright. Bigger Thomas is conceived in Uncle Tom's Children as the character Big Boy, the titular hero of "Big Boy Leaves Home," who by the end of that story flees north to escape a lynch mob. In practically all of Wright's fiction, the hero faces capture and subsequent mutilation or death from some wrongfully avenging agency.

Richard Wright was born on 24 September on a farm near Natchez, Mississippi. His mother, Ella Wilson Wright, was a schoolteacher and his father, Nathan, a tenant farmer. Though Black Boy differs in important respects from his life, the general tenor of Wright's narrative is true. The desertion of his father when Wright was only six years old, the constant moves from one house, town, or state to another and back reflect the instability of his life. Poverty and illness were his family's lot; hunger, if we count the number of times the word appears in his autobiographical narrative, a more constant companion than any playmate.

As Wright matured and began to understand his circumstances as a black person in Mississippi in the early twentieth century, he came to know the fear and dread associated with racism and its narrow circumscription of black lives. He is frequently aware of the possibility of being killed or otherwise injured because of anything he might or might not say or do if that might inadvertently violate the "ethics of living Jim Crow." The most frequent mood in his early life is tension, if not the tension arising from direct contact with whites, then tension resulting from the pressures brought to bear on African Americans stemming from the racial climate. Wright makes abundantly clear that the most intimate interactions (involving friends, family members, lovers) among African Americans are largely influenced by the pervasive impact of *race. Wright keenly felt, as all his fiction reveals, that in interracial social relations, in both North and South ultimately, race is an omnipresent factor.

His autobiographies Black Boy and American Hunger give particular attention to his development as a writer. Black Boy claims that the author had something of dramatic significance to write about: the career of a black person, a male citizen within the American democratic commonwealth, growing up in the South. It points also to Wright's early sensitivity, to an awareness and predisposition to respond to the forces mediating the relation between self and social environment. It speaks of a youthful early interest in narrative, especially in the gothic children's story "Bluebeard," which prompted his earlier publication, the unrecovered "Voodoo of Hell's Half Acre."

Shortly before he "escapes" from the South (as he in part does because he is afraid to tell the whites who question his motives for moving north why he is leaving), Wright discovered a completely new perspective on American life provided by such national journals as Atlantic Monthly, Harper's, and the American Mercury. A northern white who managed an optical company where Wright was employed in Memphis, Tennessee, allowed him to use his library card to borrow books (a forbidden act), and he became acquainted with the writers who were most germane to the shaping of his literary career. These include Theodore Dreiser, Sherwood Anderson, Frank Harris, Alexandre Dumas, and O. Henry.

The two major events of Wright's life in Chicago are his employment at the post office and his involvement with the Communist Party. Though employed only intermittently by the post office, he had done extremely well on the competitive civil service examination. At the post office he met others, both black and white, also using the job as a steppingstone to higher status. It was at the post office that he first interacted with whites on a basis of equality, meeting, for example, Abraham Aaron, himself an aspiring writer, who eventually introduced him to the John Reed Club and thence to the Communist Party. In his relations with the Chicago Post Office, Wright finally had the last word. In 1937 he declined a job at $2,000 annually and went to New York to become a writer. The post office and figures he knew there supplied the characters, scenes, and action of his first written (though posthumously published) novel, Lawd Today (1963).

His relation to the Communist Party was the subject of most of Wright's fiction and the center around which his life turned even, seemingly, after his break with the party. Though a communist and a marxist, Wright's was never a doctrinaire commitment. He unfailingly challenged the party's interpretation and understanding of marxism, especially as these involved black people. *Uncle Tom's Children* and *Native Son* both instruct the party about its failures in addressing African Americans, thus implying its pathetic lack of knowledge and understanding of black *history, culture, and life. *Uncle Tom's Children* shows the depths of blacks' submersion in black history and culture, suggesting that African Americans cannot be politically addressed outside of that context. *Native Son* shows two significant levels of the failure of communication: on one level *Mary Dalton fails to understand her *class relation to Bigger Thomas, and Bigger's sense of his class and racial relation to Mary Dalton results in her death. The other more complicated level finds Max, the sophisticated marxist, as unable as Mary Dalton to see and communicate with Bigger Thomas on a totally human level. He understands Bigger's class situation but nothing about how that intersects with race, thus explaining the otherwise enigmatic line at the close of the novel, "Max groped for his hat like a blind man."

"The Man Who Lived Underground" reflects Wright's increasing disaffection with the Communist Party and with marxism. The loneliness and isolation of Fred Daniels, his discovery of the subjectivity of experience, shows Wright looking at the world in a far more psychological and existentially philosophical rather than dialectically materialistic way. Fred discovers the relativity of value, seeing that what he heretofore had seen as the truths and facts of the world are not truths and facts at all but merely arbitrarily assigned values. When the policeman at the conclusion of the novella says of Fred, "You've got to shoot his kind. They'd wreck things," his reference is not to race at all but to any who see behind appearances. With his 1944 article in *Atlantic Monthly*, "I Tried to Be a Communist," extracted from *American Hunger*, Wright made his final break with the party.

In 1947 Richard Wright left the United States for France with his wife, Ellen, and daughter, Julia, in order to further distance himself from Mississippi. Despite his success as the most famous black author ever to have published, Wright still felt beset by tensions arising out of racism. Even in New York it was not possible for him to live freely and easily wherever he chose. Still he was viewed not as a great author but as a great *black* author. He felt that in Europe, especially France, he could live unhampered by those feelings that harked back to the fear and misery he experienced growing up in the South. Paris had been home to other disillusioned American writers; perhaps it could become home for him, too.

Negative responses to him and to his work were not infrequent after his French exile. Was it because his creative powers did indeed diminish after he left the United States or was the American response to his work related to his politics? Did he indeed "lose touch" with his country when he remained away so long as was often asserted? His work was much better received in France than in the United States, so obviously the French did not see him as an author in decline. His income decreased considerably during the 1950s as the result of his loss of popularity in the United States. It is not clear whether his difficult relations with the State Department might have had something to do with that. (The FBI began a file on Wright in 1943 when an investigation was launched to determine whether his picture essay *12 Million Black Voices* was evidence of sedition. He had difficulty obtaining a passport because of his previous relations with the Communist Party. United States surveillance of his activities while he lived in France was maintained largely because of his political views.) The novels published while he lived in France are *The Outsider* (1953), *Savage Holiday* (1954), and *The Long Dream* (1958). In *The Outsider*, a tale much influenced by Fyodor Dostoyevsky's *Crime and Punishment*, Cross Damon tries to function outside the constraints of law and morality. Its existential orientation derives in part from the influence of European existentialists, especially Jean-Paul Sartre, Simone de Beauvoir, Albert Camus, Martin Heidegger, and Edmund Husserl, and in part from Wright's understanding of his own experiences in Mississippi. *Savage Holiday*, a novel whose major characters are not African Americans, was published in the United States but only in paperback by Avon. More than any other of his writings it was intended to entertain rather than to effect social change. *The Long Dream*, set in Mississippi, seems an attempt on Wright's part to return to his major theme, social protest against a punishing, unfair racist society.

Nonfiction works published during these years include *Black Power*, Wright's diary written when he visits the Gold Coast (1954); *The Color Curtain: A Report of the Bandung Conference*, an account of the Bandung Conference, in Bandung, Indonesia, in 1955, an international conference of people of color (1956); *Pagan Spain*, a wonderfully written and very readable travelogue (written following an extended motor tour) that reveals much of Wright's intelligence, knowledge, and sensitivity (1956); and *White Man, Listen*, a collection of four lectures delivered between 1950 and 1956 that contains in its author's introduction a sentiment that describes very accurately a sense one gets reading Wright: "I declare unabashedly that I like and even cherish the state of abandonment, of aloneness; . . . it seems the natural, inevitable condition of man, and I welcome it. . . . I've been shaped to this mental stance by the kind of experience I have fallen heir to" (1957).

When Wright died unexpectedly at the age of fifty-two, he was separated from his family, who were in London, where he wanted to live; he was in dire financial straits; and he was in conflict with the black expatriate community for a complex of reasons. The circumstances of his death excited questions of foul play. He was not known to suffer any heart malady; he seemed in better physical condition than he had been of late; he died in a hospital shortly after receiving an injection, his family was not notified of his death; and he was cremated almost immediately afterward without their consent, thus no autopsy was possible. Wright biographer Michel Fabre concludes that if Wright was killed, it was indirectly—through the pressures brought to bear on him at the time by his critics—and probably not by the CIA.

Richard Wright's influence on American literature is nearly inestimable. He demonstrated for the first time that an African American could indeed be a major writer of international fame and stature. He modeled possibilities hitherto not seen or known for African American writers. His influence extended well beyond the writing community, demonstrating that success was possible and that militancy in the face of racism constituted a valuable response. It was not Richard Wright alone who influenced the progressive social changes that occurred in the 1960s, whose effects are yet pervasive, but surely his was a great influence on the time. Because of his place in literary history and because of the widespread influence of his work, many see him as among the greatest writers of the century.

[See also Communism.]

• Richard Abcarian, *Richard Wright's "Native Son": A Critical Handbook*, 1970. Keneth Kinnamon, *The Emergence of Richard Wright: A Study in Literature and Society*, 1972. Michel Fabre, *The Unfinished Quest of Richard Wright*, 1973. Yoshinobu Hakutani, *Critical Essays on Richard Wright*, 1974. Richard Macksey and Frank Moorer, eds., *Richard Wright: A Collection of Critical Essays*, 1984. Joyce Ann Joyce, *Richard Wright's Art of Tragedy*, 1986. James C. Trotman, ed., *Richard Wright: Myths and Realities*, 1988. Margaret Walker, *Richard Wright, Daemonic Genius: A Portrait of the Man, A Critical Look at His Work*, 1988. Eugene Miller, *Voice of a Native Son: The Poetics of Richard Wright*, 1990. Robert J. Butler, *Native Son: The Emergence of a New Black Hero*, 1991. Henry Louis Gates, Jr., and K. A. Appiah, eds., *Richard Wright: Critical Perspectives Past and Present*, 1993.

—Donald B. Gibson

WRIGHT, SARAH ELIZABETH (b. 1928), poet, novelist, and lecturer. Sarah Elizabeth Wright was born in Wetipquin, Maryland, began writing in the third grade, and was encouraged to continue. While a student at Howard University, she was inspired by Sterling A. *Brown, Owen *Dodson, and Langston *Hughes. Throughout her career, she has demonstrated a thirst for knowledge and the need to share her craft. As a result, she is a Certified Poetry Therapist, has presented readings, lectured, and taught in a number of forums, including television and radio talk shows, high schools, community centers, libraries, and YMCAs, and spoken at the United Nations International Writers Day celebration of Martin Luther *King, Jr. (1993). Wright has participated in *poetry workshops and was a member of the Harlem Writer's Guild. She helped organize the First (1959) and the Second National Conference of Black Writers and the Congress of American Writers (1971). She was president of Pen & Brush, Inc. (1992–1993), the oldest professional organization of women in the United States. Her professional memberships include PEN, the Authors Guild, and the International Women's Writing Guild. Although she has not been a prolific writer, her work has been excellent, honest, and life-affirming. She has received numerous awards, including two MacDowell Colony fellowships for creative writing, the 1975 CAPS Award for Fiction, the 1976 Howard University Novelist-Poet Award, the Middle Atlantic Writers Association Award, and the Zora Neale Hurston Award. Her work has been included in *Freedomways;* the *Amsterdam News* (New York); the *Black Scholar*; the *African American Review*; *Confrontation*; *Southern Voices*, edited by John O. *Killens and Jerry Ward; *Court of Appeal*, edited by the staff of the *Black Scholar*; and *Fidel and Malcolm X*, edited by Rosemari Mealy.

Wright's first book, *Give Me a Child* (1955), was coauthored with Lucy Smith. It is a collection of poetry designed to make poetry accessible to the general public through its subject matter and presentation. Her first novel, *This Child's Gonna Live* (1969) was chosen by the *New York Times* as one of 1969's most important books and by the *Baltimore Sun* for the 1969 Readability Award. It is set in Tangierneck, Maryland, and is the story of Mariah Upshur, who struggles against oppressing forces during the depression and refuses to totally succumb to hopelessness. It emphasizes the need for women to be independent and define themselves regardless of *race, community, men, or society. Simultaneously, it presents an objective view of Jacob Upshur and points out that men, too, are victims of their definition and the forces that impact them. In 1994, the Feminist Press reissued the novel and Pen & Brush, Inc. celebrated both the novel's silver anniversary and the fact that it had been on sale constantly since 1969. Her third book, *A. Philip Randolph, Integration in the Workplace* (1990), was chosen by the New York Public Library as one of the Best Books for Young Adults published in 1990. In the mid-1990s, Wright was working on the sequel to her first novel, tentatively entitled "Twelve Gates to the City, Halleluh! Halleluh!"

• Virginia B. Guilford, "Sarah Elizabeth Wright," in *DLB*, vol. 33, *Afro-American Fiction Writers after 1955*, eds. Thadious M. Davis and Trudier Harris, 1984, pp. 293–300.

—Helen R. Houston

Y

YARBROUGH, CAMILLE (b. 1938), actress, composer, singer, teacher, and writer. Children tease and taunt each other wherever they gather. Some children's teasing is humorous. Occasionally, the taunting leads to hurt, anger, and confusion. Epithets such as "nappy headed," "ole black thing," and "African monkey" are a few of the insults that sting many African American children. Camille Yarbrough explores these taunts and the circumstances and feelings that engender them. Yarbrough's books illuminate intragroup disharmony and offer possible solutions for resolving this complex issue.

Yarbrough appeared on the children's book scene in 1979 with the publication of a picture book, *Cornrows* (1979). A multifaceted artist who danced with Katherine *Dunham and taught Dunham's technique, she has worked with children in various artistic programs performed in plays, and written and recorded music. During the 1980s she served as Professor of African Dance and Diaspora in the African Studies Department of New York's City College.

Children's literature depicting African Americans entered a new phase in the late 1960s and 1970s. A body of literature that reflected African American life and cultures in an authentic manner appeared and was labeled "culturally conscious" by scholar Rudine Sims Bishop. Camille Yarbrough's children's books, *Cornrows* and *The Shimmershine Queens* (1989), a novel, fit squarely within the culturally conscious category of *children's and young adult literature. Yarbrough attempts to inform readers about the African and African American pasts and their current connections to these ongoing histories.

Several themes recur throughout Yarbrough's two books. African American children are encouraged by adults to acquire knowledge about their histories so that they can survive psychologically unscathed. Typically, Yarbrough creates elderly characters—Great-Grammaw in *Cornrows* and Cousin Seatta in *The Shimmershine Queens*—who provide this knowledge in the manner of a griot. Respect for oneself and others is another central motif. Namecalling and fighting are discouraged among children because they represent the inculcation of racism. Negative self-images are reversed when the characters accomplish a goal and experience success through reconnecting with their root cultures, histories, and artistic performance. Yarbrough confronts the view that knowledge is not the domain of African American children. Angie, the protagonist in *The Shimmershine Queens*, demonstrates this in a confrontation with disruptive classmates. She tells them about how Cousin Seatta required that her students learn and achieve academically. She informs them that too many ancestors lost their lives or suffered in order to have the opportunities that they squander. They cannot dishonor the past by remaining ignorant.

Yarbrough's strongest characters are the children who appear in her works. They talk and act like children who are a bundle of conflicting traits. Another characteristic of her work is the realistic use of Black vernacular language.

Camille Yarbrough has written only two works for children, yet these books explore controversial and important ideas usually missing in children's literature.

- Rudine Sims, *Shadow and Substance*, 1982. "Camille Yarbrough", in *Children's Literature Review*, vol 29, ed. Gerald Senich, 1993, pp. 262–275. —Violet J. Harris

Yellow Back Radio Broke-Down (1969) is Ishmael *Reed's second novel and the first to embody the themes and principles of neohoodooism, Reed's rubric for his African-originated but ultimately pancultural aesthetic practice.

Yellow Back Radio is a Western in a double sense, dealing with Wild West themes of lurid yellow-covered dime novels (cowboys, Indians, outlaws) and with Western civilization and its dominational tendencies (us versus them). One of the characters calls it a "horse opera," a colloquial expression for the popular genre of the Western, but also alluding here to Reed's creation of a "hoodoo" Western—hoodoo being the black American derivative of African traditional religious practices in which a state of possession may occur, occasioned by a "spirit" mounting a devotee (its "horse"). In *Yellow Back Radio*, in short, Reed exposes the "other" character of the American West and of Western civilization by recasting their generic myths from a black, "magical" perspective.

Analyzing the title can assist us in understanding Reed's purposes. "Yellow Back Radio" represents the media and their broadcasts of "bad news"—messages of monotheism, monopoly capitalism, and control—that Reed sees as destructive of Nature and a perversion of our fuller human potential. "Broke-Down" indicates an explanation or deconstruction (what Reed would call a "reading") of Yellow Back Radio's functions and meaning, as well as referring to YBR's ultimate defeat by the book's hero, the Loop Garoo Kid—rebel angel, black cowboy, and writer of "circuses"—and the forces of imagination and spiritual pluralism (Reed's "neohoodooism").

The debate in the novel between "neo–social realist" Bo Shmo and the Loop Garoo Kid provides us with one of Reed's most succinct assertions of his aesthetic values (for which Loop is spokesperson and exemplar) and the manner in which these values differ from those of more restrictive "schools" of art. For Reed, a novel can be anything it wants to be, and *Yellow Back Radio Broke-Down* is an excellent demonstration that Reed's novels typically want to be many things at once.

Reed's characters are not intended to be realistic; they are archetypes or stereotypes, embodying aspects of myth that need revamping or exorcising. Thus Loop Garoo, whose name, one of Reed's poems explains, means "change into," represents art as a free, transformative process and the artist as improviser, impresario of the imagination, while his principal adversaries, Drag Gibson and the Pope, epitomize monopolistic practices and rigid orthodoxy.

Neil Schmitz, in an essay on Reed's fiction in *Twentieth Century Literature* (Apr. 1974), judged *Yellow Back Radio* to exhibit a "simplistic" focus and "diffused" energy, although many readers found it to be a comic tour de force. But in apparent reference to some of the harsher assessments of his critics, Reed, in a famous self-interview published in *Shrovetide in Old New Orleans* (1978), asked himself if he was drunk or on dope when he wrote *Yellow Back Radio*, then "defended" himself by stating that it was a "talking book" based on old radio scripts. In fact, much of his style and many of his themes are drawn from *folklore and American pop culture, and, to the degree that this has been misunderstood or unappreciated, Reed's fiction has been called cartoonish. But if a work like *Yellow Back Radio Broke-Down* is a cartoon, it is, in the tradition of Krazy Kat (creation of African American artist George Herriman), a cartoon with a brick in its hand, aimed at the head of the status quo.

• Michel Fabre, "Postmodern Rhetoric in Ishmael Reed's *Yellow Back Radio Broke-Down*," in *The Afro-American Novel Since 1960*, eds. Peter Bruck and Wolfgang Karrer, 1982, pp. 167–188. —Robert Elliot Fox

YERBY, FRANK (1916–1991), historical novelist, short story writer, poet, and successful popular writer. Frank Garvin Yerby, son of Rufus Garvin and Wilhelmina Yerby, was born 5 September 1916 in Augusta, Georgia. After graduation from Haines Institute, he attended Paine College and there began writing *poetry, *fiction, and *drama. While at Fisk University, Yerby's sister showed his poetry to James Weldon *Johnson who encouraged him, and in 1937, Yerby began graduate studies there.

Yerby's growing up in the South made an indelible impression on him and shaped his life in at least two distinct ways. Favorably, he gained a firsthand knowledge of southern mores and customs—eventually the subject of his fiction. Adversely, the harsh realities of racial segregation and discrimination weighed heavily on him, and like many African Americans before him, he migrated north to escape. After completing his master's degree in 1938, Yerby enrolled in the University of Chicago.

While in Chicago, he worked with the *Federal Writers Project of the WPA, through which he met other aspiring writers, including Arna *Bontemps, Richard *Wright, and Margaret *Walker. Yerby taught for brief stints at Florida A & M and Southern Universities (1939–1941), then migrated north again, working first as a technician at the Ford Motor Company at Dearborn, Michigan (1941–1944), and then at Ranger (Fairchild) Aircraft in Jamaica, New York (1944–1945).

During this period, Yerby wrote a protest novel about an African American steelworker who succeeded as a boxer but came to a tragic end. *Redbook* rejected Yerby's novel, but editor Muriel Fuller encouraged him to send her something else. The something else was "Health Card," which Fuller determined was unsuitable for *Redbook* and sent to *Harper's Magazine*. Published by *Harper's* in 1944, "Health Card" won the O. Henry Memorial Award Prize for best first short story. Other stories Yerby published included "White Magnolias," "Homecoming," and "My Brother Went to College."

Following unsuccessful attempts to publish his protest novel, Yerby turned to historical fiction, then in vogue. Believing that he could write more convincingly about African Americans than did Margaret Mitchell in *Gone with the Wind* (1936), he published *The *Foxes of Harrow* in 1946, catapulting himself to immediate financial and popular success unprecedented for an African American writer. In subsequent years, Yerby would publish thirty-two additional novels, which sold more than 55 million copies. Several—*The Foxes of Harrow* (1946), *The Golden Hawk* (1948), and *The Saracen Blade* (1952)—were turned into successful movies.

Yerby's career thrived in the midst of controversy. One of the most maligned of African American writers, Yerby was accused of imperfections in both his craft and his politics. Many reviewers recognized his talents but criticized his uninhibited use of popular fiction conventions. African American writers and intellectuals lauded his achievement as a pioneer in popular fiction but urged him to address racial concerns. Yerby, however, steadfastly refused to comment on contemporary social issues and continued to write best-sellers. By the mid-1950s, serious consideration of his fiction was waning, causing him to have misgivings about his limitations in popular fiction.

He attempted to publish another protest novel, *The Tents of Shem*, in 1963, and several of his novels—*The Serpent and the Staff* (1958), *The Garfield Honor* (1961), and *Griffin's Way* (1962)—focused increasingly on racial issues in the historical South. Another, *Speak Now* (1969), introduced his first black protagonist. Thus, while he continued to write popular fiction, he did explore serious themes, and among his best novels he counted *The Garfield Honor, An Odor of Sanctity* (1965), *Judas, My Brother* (1968), and *The Dahomean* (1971).

Yerby's chosen genre represented a compromise. Abandoning protest fiction in 1946, he proved that an African American could succeed in popular fiction. However, writing about white protagonists forced him outside the African American literary tradition and toward a primarily white audience. But contrary to prevailing critical opinion, he did not totally abandon racial protest. Yerby adapted protest fiction to suit the medium of popular fiction. Enlarging his protest motives and taking aim at inaccuracies in southern history, he became one of America's greatest debunkers of historical myths. Not surprisingly, too, Yerby's protest extended beyond his fiction; it was also personal. In 1952, he expatriated to

France because, he said, of racism; and in 1955, he moved to Madrid, Spain, where he spent the last thirty-six years of his life. Little is known about this period of Yerby's life. Except for occasional visits to the States for business or personal reasons, he remained an *expatriate. Yerby died on 29 November 1991. His death was as mysterious as his life, for before he died, he exacted a promise from his wife to keep his death a secret for five weeks.

In some ways, Frank Yerby was typical of the cadre of African American writers emerging in the post–World War II era; in other ways, he was their antithesis. Like many African American writers of the 1940s and 1950s, for example, he began his career writing *protest literature and served an apprenticeship with the WPA. Like Wright, Chester *Himes, and James *Baldwin, he expatriated early in search of a less racially hostile climate, and like Wright and Himes, he was profoundly influenced by his experiences of living in the South, causing him to make the South the primary focus of his fiction. Unlike his contemporaries, Yerby made a conscious decision to write the more profitable popular fiction. Unlike them, too, he chose to lend neither the prestige of his name nor the power of his pen to the cause of racial justice in America.

The significance of Yerby's novels lies not in the millions of copies he sold nor in his successful manipulation of the conventions of the historical romance novel. His novels present uncompromising criticisms of the romantic view of the South in southern fiction. His fictional recreations of the American South are intended to correct distorted myths and legends about such subjects as *slavery, aristocracy, the Civil War, Reconstruction, and the southern gentleman; and beyond America, he targets inaccuracies in the histories of other cultures. Thus, his novels teach more than one usually expects of the costume novelist. Too long discounted as an anomaly in African American literature, Yerby deserves more critical attention.

[*See also* Woman Called Fancy, A.]

• Nick Aaron Ford, "Four Popular Novelists," *Phylon* 15 (Mar. 1954): pp 29–39. Frank Yerby, "How and Why I Write the Costume Novel," *Harper's*, Oct. 1959, 145–50. William W. Hill "Behind the Magnolia Mask: Frank Yerby as Critic of the South," master's thesis, Auburn University, 1968. Darvin T. Turner, "Frank Yerby as Debunker," *Massachusetts Review* 20 (Summer 1968): 569–577. Maryemma Graham, "Frank Yerby, King of the Costume Novel," *Essence*, Oct. 1975, 70–71, 88–92. James L. Hill, "Anti-Heroic Perspectives: The Life and Works of Frank Yerby," PhD diss., University of Iowa, 1976. James L. Hill, "Between Philosophy and Race: Images of Blacks in the Fiction of Frank Yerby," *Umoja* (Summer 1981): 5–16. Frank Yerby, "An Interview with Frank Garvin Yerby," interview by James L. Hill, *Resources for American Literary Study* (Fall 1995): 206–239.

—James L. Hill

YOUNG, AL (b. 1939), poet, novelist, short story writer, screenwriter, editor, essayist, musician, and educator. Born Albert James Young in Ocean Springs, Mississippi, on 31 May 1939, Young later moved to Detroit, Michigan, with his parents. He resides in Palo Alto, California. His parents were Albert James, a professional musician and autoworker, and Mary Campbell Young Simmons. Young married Arline Belck, a freelance artist, on 8 October 1963. They have one son, Michael James. After attending the University of Michigan (1957–1961), Young was a Wallace E. Stegner Fellow in creative writing at Stanford University (1966–1967) and received his BA in Spanish from the University of California at Berkeley (1969). While at Berkeley, he worked as a writing instructor and language consultant for Berkeley Neighborhood Youth Corps and then took the position of as the Edward H. Jones Lecturer in Creative Writing at Stanford University (1969–1974). He wrote and collaborated on several screenplays including *Nigger, Sparkle* (1972), and *Bustin Loose* (1981) for Richard Pryor, and edited and founded several multicultural literary magazines such as *Loveletter* (1966–1968), *Quilt* (1981), and, with Ishmael *Reed, *Yardbird* (1972–1976). With Reed, he edited and contributed to *Yardbird Lives!* (1978) and *Calafia: The California Poetry* (1979). He began directing the Associated Writing Programs in 1979 and was writer in residence at the University of Washington, Seattle (1981–1982). In addition, he has been a Mellon Distinguished Professor of Humanities at Rice University. He is the recipient of the San Francisco Foundation's Joseph Henry Jackson Award (1969), National Arts Council awards for editing and poetry (1968–1970), several National Endowment for the Arts fellowships (1968, 1969, 1975), the Pushcart Prize (1980), a Guggenheim Memorial Foundation Fellowship (1974), the California Association of Teachers of English Special Award (1973), the New York Times Outstanding Book of the Year citation (1980), and the Before Columbus Foundation Award (1982).

Young's passion for *music permeates all of his writing. His belief in music as a central force in human lives appears in his early work *Snakes* (1970), where the main character MC grows up as he matures in his musical talent. Young's collections of "musical memoirs," *Bodies & Soul* (1966), *Kinds of Blue* (1984), *Things Ain't What They Used to Be* (1987), and *Drowning in the Sea of Love* (1995) all demonstrate the affinity between music and everyday life. As he discusses individual musicians, he illustrates how art intensifies human experiences and how music evokes powerful emotions and memories.

His *poetry imitates the improvisational style of *jazz music, especially in his first collection of poems, *Dancing* (1969), where Young uses flexible rhythms and juxtaposes long and short lines. His later works, *Geography of the Near Past* (1966) and *The Song Turning Back into Itself* (1971), are tighter and more controlled in both rhythm and structure. The poems in *Geography* narrate specific events such as his wife's pregnancy or a visit to a friend in jail. The rapid, stream-of-consciousness writing and the attention to cultural items show evidence of the Expressionist movement and the Beat poets. Later collections are *The Blues Don't Change: New and Selected Poems* (1982) and *Heaven: Collected Poems 1958–1988* (1989).

Young's novels are realistic and have been compared to those of John Updike because his stories glorify the middle class and focus on the everyday world. He compliments the musician Charles Mingus in the biography *Mingus/Mingus* (1989; cowritten with Janet Coleman) for his ability to incorporate musical traditions and still deliver the "soul and gut and night-and-dayness of being alive." Aware of the tendency on the part of black writers to fulfill popular expectations of African Americans in their writings, Young avoids polemical topics in his works. His much admired poem "Dance for Militant Dilettantes" critiques a white readership demanding a particular black "type" and indicting militant black rights advocates.

Young counteracts stereotypical conceptions of African Americans through his depiction of quirky, offbeat personalities. His characters are endearing not because they are marginal but because they portray those eccentricities that make Americans so fascinating. In *Snakes*, MC's friend Shakes speaks in Shakespearean phrases; the character of Sidney J. Prettymore in *Sitting Pretty* (1976), an aging philosopher of life, becomes a radio talk-show celebrity; and Mamie Franklin's husband in *Seduction by Light* (1988) returns to her as a ghost. Young's characters often search for self-definition and an understanding of how their past fits into their present. Angelina in *Who is Angelina?* (1975) wrestles with this question after a suicide attempt while Durwood Knight, the retired professional basketball player in *Ask Me Now* (1980), struggles to define his role as father and husband. Young's ear for language and music contributes to the success of his books and makes them especially enjoyable when he reads passages aloud in public. His characters' use of dialects grants them a great range of expression. In their mouths, the vernacular discourse provides a more versatile form of expression, much in the same way jazz music offers the musician a personal voice above and beyond the tradition.

• Sharon R. Gunton, ed., *Contemporary Literary Criticism*, 1981. Elizabeth Schultz, "Search for 'Soul Space': A Study of Al Young's 'Who is Angelina?' (1975) and the Dimensions of Freedom," in *The Afro-American Novel Since 1960*, eds. Peter Bruck and Wolfgang Karrer, 1982, pp. 263–287. Al Young, Larry Kart, and Michael S. Harper, "Jazz and Letters: A Colloquy," *Triquarterly* 68 (Winter 1987); 118–158. Irv Broughton, ed., *The Writer's Mind: Interviews with American Authors*, vol. 3, 1990. James P. Draper, ed., *Black Literature Criticism*, vol. 3, 1992. Don Lee, "About Al Young," *Ploughshares* 19.1 (Spring 1993): 219–224.

—Miriam M. Chirico

YOUNG ADULT LITERATURE. *See* Children's and Young Adult Literature

Z

Zeely, Virginia *Hamilton's first book for children, *Zeely* (1967) tells the story of the summer that a young African American girl, Elizabeth, spends with her brother John at their Uncle Ross's farm. The trip was special because Elizabeth and her brother went alone and because their father had hinted that something was going to happen that Elizabeth must take care of. Elizabeth's unexpected relationship with Zeely, the daughter of Nat Tayber, who rents a small part of Uncle Ross's farm, gives Elizabeth an opportunity to find out what he meant.

On the train, Elizabeth feels that the only way to celebrate the uniqueness of this trip with her brother is for them to change their names; Elizabeth becomes Geeder and John is to answer to Toeboy. This is only the first in a series of stories that Elizabeth creates. Upon arriving at her uncle's farm, Elizabeth renames the nearby town Crystal, and the road leading from the farm to the town Leadback Road. The most significant story that Elizabeth creates, however, surrounds the background of Zeely.

The unique and strikingly regal appearance of Zeely Tayber is enhanced when Elizabeth sees a picture of a Watutsi queen in a magazine and immediately equates Zeely with the woman in the picture. Elizabeth's storytelling increases, and she begins to imagine that she and Zeely are sisters, that she is Zeely's only confidant, and that Zeely eventually makes Elizabeth a queen. Elizabeth's feeling of importance builds as she tells these stories in town to her friends, who take them as the truth. It is only after Zeely meets with Elizabeth and talks about herself through real stories of her own that Elizabeth learns the significance of knowing herself, and of living for herself and not for the stories that she makes up about others.

Zeely originated from an eighteen-page short story that Hamilton had written in college. Only later, after being reminded of its existence by a college friend who was working at a publishing company, did she expand it into a children's book. That the publication of this book coincided with the civil rights and black consciousness movements of the late 1960s further highlights its cultural aspects. Not simply a coming-of-age book, *Zeely* chronicles the development of a young girl into a young women, and her increasing racial awareness as well. Hamilton's weaving of African American *folklore and *history into the stories of Zeely and other characters encourages readers to learn and to appreciate themselves and their histories.

• Nina Mikkelsen, *Virginia Hamilton,* 1994.

—Saundra Liggins

ZU-BOLTON, AHMOS, II (b. 1935), poet, editor, and journalist. Born 21 October 1935 in Poplarville, Mississippi, and raised in De Ridder, Louisiana, Ahmos Zu-Bolton II is one of the most influential figures in the development of the "new Black poetry" in the South during the 1970s. His career exemplifies the *Black Arts movement idea that African American artists should also be "cultural workers" responsive and responsible to their communities, affirming the belief—as Zu-Bolton expresses it in his 1976 poem "Struggle-Road Dance"—that "this place / must be a workshop" for Blacks. Zu-Bolton's role as poet is complemented by his work as a literary editor, small press publisher, teacher, and organizer of cultural events.

Zu-Bolton's free verse poems—collected in *A Niggered Amen* (1975)—employ African American vernacular speech and are sometimes cast in the form of dramatic monologues or modeled on the sermonic tradition. These works reflect the poet's many varied experiences, ranging from cutting sugarcane on Gulf Coast plantations to playing professional baseball for the Shreveport Twins of the American Negro Baseball League in the early 1950s. In 1965 he received a scholarship to Louisiana State University but military service as a medic in Vietnam interrupted his college career, and he eventually graduated from California State Polytechnic University in 1971.

Working at Howard University's Humanities Resource Center between 1973 and 1976 brought him into contact with Stephen E. Henderson, E. Ethelbert *Miller, and other writers who encouraged him to publish the literary magazine *HooDoo*. From 1977 to 1980 he also organized a series of HooDoo Festivals which presented poets and musicians in New Orleans, Galveston, Austin, Houston, and other cities. With Alan Austin and Etheridge *Knight, he coedited *Blackbox*, an innovative poetry magazine issued as tape-recorded cassettes. Throughout the same period Zu-Bolton was also one of the leading figures in the Southern Black Cultural Alliance (SBCA)—a network of writers, musicians, literary journals, and theater groups that promoted the ideas of the Black Arts movement.

For ten years (1982–1992) Zu-Bolton's Copasetic Bookstore and Gallery in New Orleans was one of that city's most active venues for literary events, presenting plays, poetry readings, children's programs, and workshops for young writers. While teaching at Tulane University and Xavier University for various periods, Zu-Bolton was also a journalist contributing articles to the New Orleans *Times-Picayune* and the *Louisiana Weekly*. His poems are included in *anthologies such as *Mississippi Writers: Reflections of Childhood and Youth* (1988), edited by Dorothy Abbott, and *Black Southern Voices* (1992), edited by John O. *Killens and Jerry W. Ward, Jr.

• Lorenzo Thomas, "Ahmos Zu-Bolton II," in *DLB*, vol. 41, *Afro-American Poets since 1955*, eds. Trudier Harris and Thadious M. Davis, 1985, pp. 360–364. "Ahmos Zu-Bolton II," in *Mississippi Writers*, vol. 3, ed. Dorothy Abbott, 1988, p. 423.

—Lorenzo Thomas

Editors

William L. Andrews is E. Maynard Adams Professor of English at the University of North Carolina at Chapel Hill. He is the author of *The Literary Career of Charles W. Chesnutt* (1980) and *To Tell a Free Story: The First Century of Afro-American Autobiography, 1760–1865* (1986) and the editor of numerous works on African American literature, including *Sisters of the Spirit* (1986), *Classic Fiction of the Harlem Renaissance* (1994), and *The Oxford Frederick Douglass Reader* (1996). He is a coeditor of the *Norton Anthology of African American Literature* (1997) and general editor of Wisconsin Studies in American Autobiography. His scholarship has received the Norman Foerster Prize from *American Literature* in 1976 and the William Riley Parker prize from *Publications of the Modern Language Association* in 1990.

Frances Smith Foster is Professor of English and Women's Studies at Emory University. She is the author of *Witnessing Slavery: The Development of the Ante-Bellum Slave Narrative* (1979, 2d ed. 1993) and *Written by Herself: Literary Production by African American Women, 1746–1892* (1993) and the editor of *A Brighter Coming Day: A Frances Ellen Watkins Harper Reader* (1990) and *Minnie's Sacrifice, Sowing and Reaping, Trial and Triumph: Three Rediscovered Novels by Frances Ellen Watkins Harper* (1994), for which she received the College Language Association Scholarly Discovery Award in 1995. She is a coeditor of the *Norton Anthology of African American Literature* (1997).

Trudier Harris is J. Carlyle Sitterson Professor of English at the University of North Carolina at Chapel Hill. She is the author of several volumes, including *Exorcising Blackness: Historical and Literary Lynching and Burning Rituals* (1984) and *Black Women in the Fiction of James Baldwin* (1985), for which she won the 1987 College Language Association Creative Scholarship Award. Among her numerous edited volumes are six in the Dictionary of Literary Biography series, one in the Oxford Schomburg Library of Nineteenth-Century Black Women Writers series, and *New Essays on Baldwin's Go Tell It on the Mountain* (1996). She is also one of the editors of *Call and Response: The Riverside Anthology of the African American Literary Tradition* (1997). Her most recent scholarly studies are *Fiction and Folklore: The Novels of Toni Morrison* (1991) and *The Power of the Porch: The Storyteller's Craft in Zora Neale Hurston, Gloria Naylor, and Randall Kenan* (1996).

Index